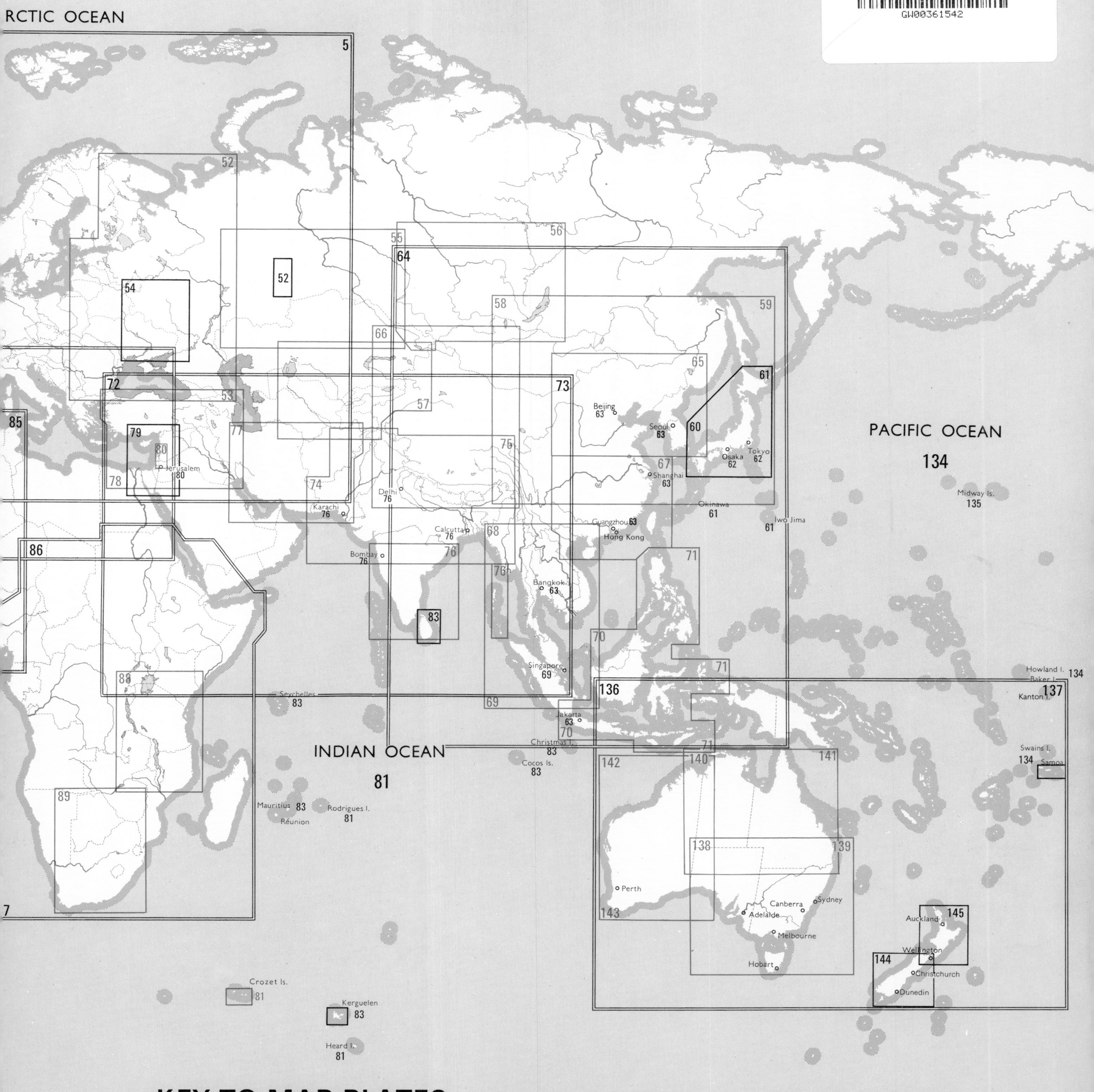

KEY TO MAP PLATES

excluding larger scales in North America and Europe *(see other end-paper)*

114 1:12 000 000 and smaller	83 1:3 000 000
116 1:6 000 000 and smaller	80 1:1 000 000 and larger

Inset maps of islands, cities, etc. are named

Introductory Section

4/31 States and Territories of the World
32/33 Geographical Comparisons
34/47 Physical Earth
48/49 Star Charts
50/51 Universe
52/53 Solar System
54/55 Space Flight
56/57 Earth Structure
58/59 Dynamic Earth
60/61 Climate
62/63 Vegetation and Minerals
64/65 Energy
66/67 Food and Population
68 Map Projections

General Maps

2/3 World - Political
50/51 Russian Federation
82 Africa
91 The Americas
146 Antarctica
147 Arctic Ocean

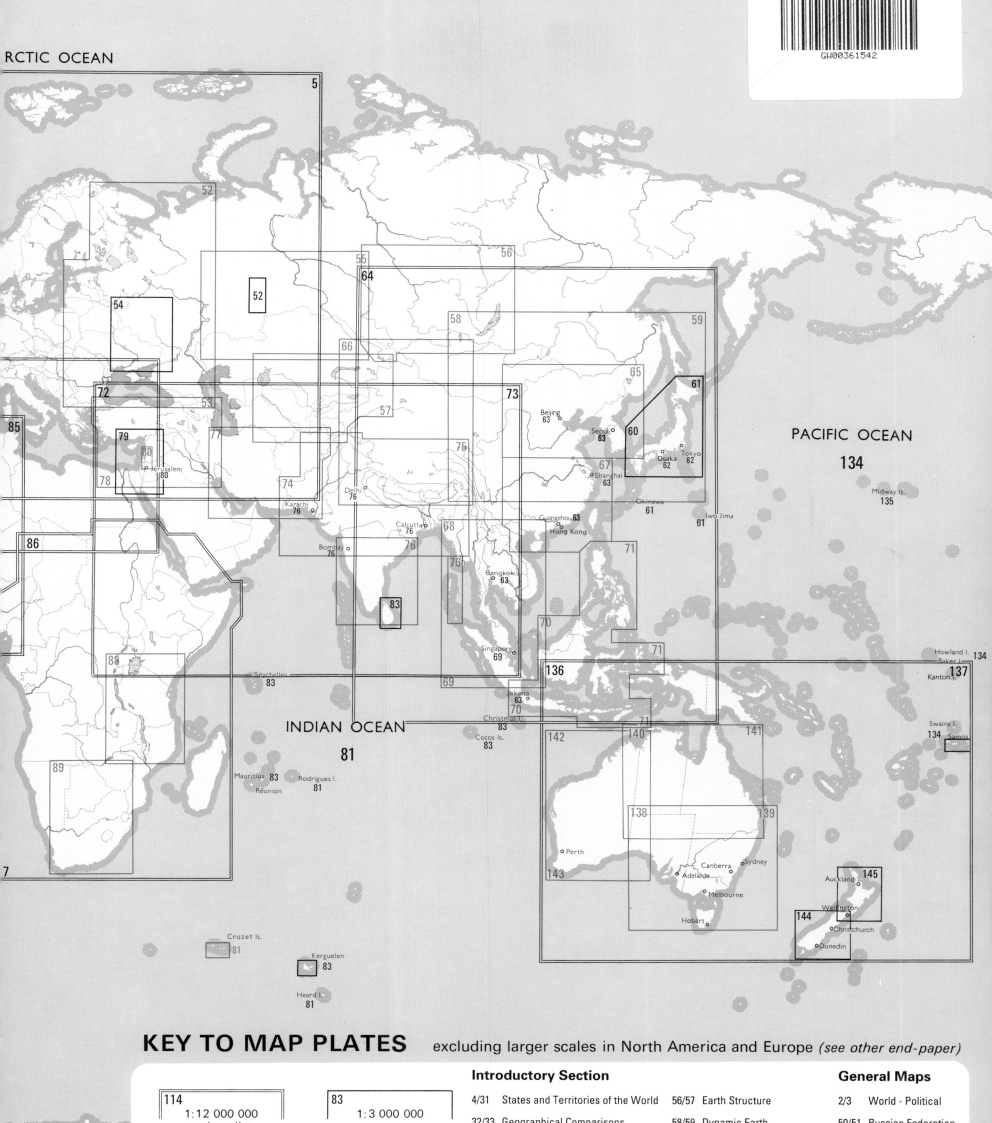

THE TIMES ATLAS OF THE WORLD

CONCISE EDITION

TIMES BOOKS
A Division of HarperCollins*Publishers*

Published in 1994 by
Times Books
A Division of* HarperCollins*Publishers
77–85 Fulham Palace Road
Hammersmith
London W6 8JB

First Edition 1972
Reprinted with revisions 1973, 1974
Second Edition 1975
Reprinted 1976, 1978
Third Edition 1978
Reprinted with revisions 1979
Fourth Edition 1980
Reprinted with revisions 1982
Reprinted 1984
Fifth Edition 1986
Reprinted with revisions 1987,1988, 1989, 1990, 1991
Sixth Edition 1992
Reprinted with revisions 1993
Reprinted with revisions and additions 1994
Reprinted 1995

Maps prepared by
Bartholomew, Edinburgh

Maps printed by
Bartholomew,
The Edinburgh Press Limited

Index processed and typeset by
Stibo Datagrafik, Århus,
Denmark

Index printed by
Scotprint, Musselburgh,
Scotland

Books bound by
Sigloch, Künzelsau,
Germany

Geographical Consultants
Mr H.A.G. Lewis OBE
Geographical Consultant to *The Times* and Chairman of The Permanent Committee of Geographical Place Names
Mr P.J.M. Geelan

Physical Earth Maps by
Duncan Mackay

British Library Cataloguing in Publication Data
"Times" atlas of the world. – ne.of.6.Rev.ed of Concise ed
912

ISBN 0 7230 0704 7

FOREWORD

This new edition of the *Times Concise Atlas of the World* will, it is hoped, find as much favour with those who acquire a copy for the first time as it has with those familiar with the earlier editions.

Every effort has been made to ensure that the maps are as up-to-date as possible. The index of names contains some 100,000 entries but it still does not contain all the names which appear on the maps. The reader may, however rest assured that the names of all important inhabited places and physical features are included together with the page number, country name and grid reference.

Great attention has been paid to the spelling of geographical names, a matter of great complexity due to the multiplicity of the World's languages, the diverse forms of writing or the absence of any writing system whatsoever. For want of a standard way of spelling names, the major languages of the world have evolved their own conventional way of spelling which differs greatly from the name found locally. In this atlas the name taken is always of the name used by the official administering body. Where necessary that name has been converted into the Roman alphabet by systems which follow English language usage. Those systems accord with the transcription and transliteration systems accepted for official use in the United States and the United Kingdom. For added reference the English language conventional names have been added parenthetically e.g. Roma (Rome), Moskva (Moscow).

Names, like maps, often invoke political protestations. The status of areas, the international boundaries and the names associated with them as shown in this edition are those which reflect the situation pertaining on the ground at the time of publication: where boundaries are the subject of international dispute this portrayal will not win the approval of the contending parties but, in the view of the publisher, the function of an atlas is to show facts and not to adjudicate between the rights and wrongs of political issues.

For the first time, the introductory section includes a gazetteer of the states and territories of the world illustrated with the flag of each nation and containing a summary of its current geographical status. It shows a world re-cast in a mould unforeseen and unforeseeable at the height of the Cold War. Yet the changes in the political scene are small in comparison with the way science has altered the pattern of life. No century in the world's history has witnessed changes so fundamental and widespread. Of more significance than the magnitude of the change is its rate, now such that any reliable prediction of the future beyond a decade or two cannot be made.

Unabated growth of this kind cannot continue indefinitely. The maps which make up the body of the atlas show the physical and political world of today. How the same maps will look in the future depends on the size of the world's population; the pattern of settlement; the spread of industry; the availability of food, minerals and sources of energy; the world's vegetation, atmosphere and climate all of which are in risk of catastrophic change.

To sustain ever increasing numbers of people requires constant stock-taking of natural resources. Remote-sensing, a product of the space age, is now beginning to reveal its eventual capacity for the kind of global monitoring required.

Our atlas, therefore, includes the Earth we live on, the solar system and the universe beyond. May it bring pleasure and interest to all who use it.

CONTENTS

INTRODUCTORY SECTION
States and Territories of the World pages 4-31
Geographical Comparisons 32-33
Physical Earth
North America and the Arctic 34-35
Central and South America, North 36-37
Antarctica and South America, South 38-39
Africa 40-41
Europe and the Near East 42-43
Asia 44-45
South-East Asia and Australasia 46-47
Star Charts 48-49
Universe 50-51
Solar System 52-53
Space Flight 54-55
Earth Structure 56-57
Dynamic Earth 58-59
Climate 60-61
Vegetation and Minerals 62-63
Energy 64-65
Food and Population 66-67
Map Projections 68

THE MAPS

PAGE 1
Symbols & Abbreviations
2-3
World, Political **1:66M**
4-5
Europe **1:15M**
6-7
The British Isles **1:3M**
8-9
Southern England & Wales **1:1M**
Channel Islands, Isles of Scilly **1:1M**
10
London **1:300 000**
11
South Lancashire, West Midlands **1:300 000**
12-13
N. England & S. Scotland **1:1M**
14
Ireland **1:1.5M**
15
Scotland **1:1.5M**
16-17
Spain: Portugal **1:3M**
Madrid **1:60 000**
18-19
France, *Corsica* **1:3M**
Rhône Valley **1:1M**
20-21
N.W. France: Normandy & Brittany **1:1.2M**
22
N.E. France: Belgium **1:1M**
23
Paris **1:300 000**
24
Amsterdam/The Hague **1:300 000**
Brussels **1:300 000**
25
Netherlands **1:1M**
26-27
Scandinavia **1:3M**
28-29
Denmark **1:1M**
Finland **1:3M**
Faeroes, Iceland **1:5M**
30-31
Central Europe **1:3M**
32-33
Northern Germany **1:1M**
34
Hamburg, Berlin **1:300 000**
PAGE 35
The Ruhr **1:300 000**
36-37
Southern Germany **1:1M**
38
Central Austria **1:1M**
39
Munich, Milan **1:300 000**
40-41
Switzerland: Italian Lakes **1:1M**
42-43
Italy: Slovenia: Croatia: Bosnia-Herzegovina **1:3M**
44-45
Italian Riviera & Po Valley **1:1M**
Rome, Naples regions **1:1M**
Ancient Rome **1:24 000**
46-47
S. Yugoslavia: Greece: Bulgaria: W. Turkey **1:3M**
Corfu, Rhodes **1:1.2M**
Bosporus **1:1.1M**
Athens-Piræus **1:150 000**
Istanbul **1:110 000**
Ancient Athens **1:12 000**
48
Hungary: Romania: N. Yugoslavia:**1:3M**
49
St. Petersburg, Moscow **1:300 000**
50-51
Russian Federation **1:18M**
52-53
E. Europe: Caucasus **1:6M**
Industrial Urals **1:3M**
54
S.W. Russia: E. Ukraine **1:3M**
55
S. Urals: N. Kazakhstan **1:6M**
56
Central Siberia **1:6M**
57
S. Kazakhstan: Central Asian Republics **1:6M**
Fergana Basin **1:3M**
58-59
North-East Asia **1:9M**
60-61
Japan **1:3M**
Okinawa **1:1.2M** *Iwo Jima* **1:300 000**
62
Tokyo, Osaka **1:300 000**
63
Bangkok, Beijing, Jakarta, Seoul, Shanghai **1:300 000**
Guangzhou **1:100 000**
64
China: S.E. Asia **1:24M**
65
N.E. China: Korea **1:6M**
66
Sinkiang & Tibet **1:9M**
67
South China **1:6M**
Hong Kong **1:300 000**
68-69
Indo-China: Burma: Malaya **1:6M**
Singapore **1:300 000**
70-71
Indonesia, Philippines **1:6M**
72-73
South Asia **1:15M**
74-75
N. India: Pakistan: Bangladesh **1:6M**
76
South India **1:6M**
Bombay, Calcutta, Delhi, Karachi **1:240 000**
77
Iran: Afghanistan **1:6M**
78
Turkey: Syria: Iraq: Jordan **1:6M**
79
Lebanon: Israel: Nile Delta **1:3M**
PAGE 80
Israel: Jordan **1:600 000**
Jerusalem **1:75 000**
81
Indian Ocean **1:48M**
Crozet Is **1:6M**
Heard I, Rodrigues I **1:1M**
82-83
Africa **1:24M**
Indian Ocean Islands
Kerguelen, Seychelles **1:3M**
Sri Lanka **1:2.4M**
Christmas I, Cocos Is, Mahé, Mauritius, Réunion **1:1M**
84
Mediterranean: N. Africa **1:12M**
85
West Africa, *Cape Verde, Azores* **1:12M**
86-87
Central & Southern Africa **1:12M**
Madagascar, Mauritius & Réunion **1:12M**
88
East Africa **1:6M**
89
South Africa **1:6M**
Witwatersrand **1:600 000**
90
Atlantic Ocean **1:48M**
Tristan da Cunha **1:1M**
Ascension, Bermuda, St. Helena **1:450 000**
91
The Americas **1:45M**
92-93
United States of America **1:12.5M**
94-95
North-East States **1:3M**
96
New York **1:500 000**
97
Baltimore, Boston, Philadelphia, Washington **1:500 000**
98-99
North Central States **1:3M**
100-101
North-West States **1:3M**
102-103
South-West States **1:3M**
Hawaiian Islands **1:9M** *Oahu* **1:1M**
104
Los Angeles, San Francisco **1:500 000**
105
Atlanta, Chicago, St. Louis **1:500 000**
106-107
South Central States **1:3M**
108-109
Texas **1:3M**
Fort Worth-Dallas **1:720 000**
Houston **1:600 000**
110-111
Southern States **1:3M**
New Orleans, St. Louis **1:300 000**
112-113
South-East States **1:3M**
Puerto Rico & Virgin Islands **1:3M**
Miami **1:1.2M**
New Providence **1:600 000**
114-115
Canada: Arctic America **1:12.5M**
116
Alaska **1:6M**
117
Western Canada **1:6M**
Vancouver **1:600 000**
118-119
Prairie Provinces **1:3M**
Winnipeg **1:300 000**
120-121
Central Canada **1:3M**
St. Lawrence Seaway **1:600 000**
Montreal, Toronto **1:300 000**
Ottawa **1:240 000**
PAGES 122-123
Maritime Provinces **1:3M**
Quebec **1:120 000**
124-125
Mexico: Central America **1:6M**
Panama Canal **1:900 000**
Mexico City **1:250 000**
126-127
West Indies **1:6M**
Antigua, Aruba, Barbados, Bonaire, Curaçao, Grenada, Guadeloupe, Jamaica, Martinique, St. Kitts – Nevis, Tobago, Trinidad **1:1.5M**
128-129
South America, North **1:12M**
Galapagos Is **1:12M**
130
South-East Brazil **1:6M**
131
Central Chile: Argentina: Uruguay **1:6 M**
Falkland Is, South Georgia, South Sandwich Is **1:6M**
132
Buenos Aires, Rio de Janeiro **1:300 000**
133
South America, South **1:12M**
Islas Juan Fernández, South Georgia **1:12M**
134-135
The Pacific Ocean **1:48M**
Tuamotu **1:12M**
Marquesas Is **1:6M**
American Samoa, Hawaiian Is, Western Samoa **1:3M**
Kiritimati **1:2.4M**
Robinson Crusoe, Tahiti **1:1.2M**
Tabuaeran **1:900 000**
Easter I, Gambier Is, Kanton I, Rarotonga **1:600 000**
Baker I, Howland I, Jarvis I, Midway Is, Palmyra I, Swains I **1:300 000**
Pitcairn I **1:210 000**
136-137
Australia: S.W. Pacific **1:15M**
138-139
South-East Australia **1:6M.**
Adelaide, Canberra, Hobart, Melbourne, Sydney **1:300 000**
140-141
North-East Australia **1:6M**
Brisbane **1:300 000**
142-143
Western Australia **1:6M**
Perth **1:300 000**
144-145
New Zealand **1:2.5M.**
Auckland, Christchurch, Dunedin, Wellington **1:300 000**
146
Antarctica **1:24M**
147
Arctic Ocean **1:15M**

THE INDEX

Metropolitan Areas 148
Glossary 149
Abbreviations used in the Index 150
Index to the maps 150
Acknowledgements 245

STATES AND TERRITORIES OF THE WORLD

AFGHANISTAN

STATUS: **Islamic State**
AREA: **652,225 sq km (251,773 sq miles)**
POPULATION: **19,062,000**
ANNUAL NATURAL INCREASE: **2.5%**
CAPITAL: **Kabul**
LANGUAGE: **Pushtu, Dari**
RELIGION: **90% Sunni, 9% Shi'a Muslim, Hindu, Sikh and Jewish minorities**
CURRENCY: **Afghani (AFA)**
ORGANIZATIONS: **Col. Plan, UN**

Afghanistan is predominantly mountainous with ranges bordered by fertile alluvial plains. In the south there is a desert plateau. The climate is of extremes – summers are hot and dry and the winters are cold, with heavy snowfalls. Annual rainfall varies between 101 and 406 mm (4 and 16 inches). The economy is based on agriculture. Main crops are wheat, fruit, cotton and vegetables. Sheep and goats are the main livestock. The fourteen-year civil war officially ended in 1992, but it will take many years for the country to recover fully from its effects.

ÅLAND

STATUS: **Self-governing Island Province of Finland**
AREA: **1,505 sq km (581 sq miles)**
POPULATION: **24,231**
CAPITAL: **Mariehamn**

ALBANIA

STATUS: **Republic**
AREA: **28,750 sq km (11,100 sq miles)**
POPULATION: **3,363,000**
ANNUAL NATURAL INCREASE: **1.7%**
CAPITAL: **Tirana (Tiranë)**
LANGUAGE: **Albanian (Gheg, Tosk)**
RELIGION: **70% Muslim, 20% Greek Orthodox, 10% Roman Catholic**
CURRENCY: **lek (ALL)**
ORGANIZATIONS: **UN**

Albania is situated on the eastern seaboard of the Adriatic. It is rugged and mountainous, with coastal plains. The climate has warm summers and cool winters, more severe in the mountains. Rain falls mainly between October and May, at around 1,353–1,425 mm (54–57 inches) per year. The country possesses considerable mineral resources, notably chrome, copper, iron ores and nickel, with rich deposits of coal, oil and natural gas. After decades of self-imposed political and economic isolation Albania shook off its own particular variant of communism in 1990.

ALEUTIAN ISLANDS

STATUS: **Territory of USA**
AREA: **17,665 sq km (6,820 sq miles)**
POPULATION: **11,942**

ALGERIA

STATUS: **Republic**
AREA: **2,381,745 sq km (919,355 sq miles)**
POPULATION: **26,346,000**
ANNUAL NATURAL INCREASE: **2.7%**
CAPITAL: **Algiers (Alger, El-Djezaïr)**
LANGUAGE: **83% Arabic, French, Berber**
RELIGION: **Muslim**
CURRENCY: **Algerian dinar (DZD)**
ORGANIZATIONS: **Arab League, OAU, OPEC, UN**

Most of Algeria lies within the Sahara desert where, in the south, the Hoggar massif approaches 3,000 m (9,800 ft) in height. In the north the coastal plain is fringed by the Atlas mountains. Algeria is hot, with negligible rainfall. Along the Mediterranean coast temperatures are more moderate, with most rain during the mild winters. Rainfall varies between 158 and 762 mm (6 and 30 inches), depending on altitude. The economy is built on agriculture, manufacturing and the exploitation of oil, gas and mineral resources. The main agricultural crops are cereals, vines, olives, citrus fruits, dates and tomatoes, produced in the small areas of the northern valleys and coastal strip. Minerals exploited are iron ore, lead, zinc and mercury. Oil production, centred in the southern deserts, has declined in recent years, but natural gas output has increased dramatically.

AMERICAN SAMOA

STATUS: **Unincorporated Territory of USA**
AREA: **197 sq km (76 sq miles)**
POPULATION: **46,773**
CAPITAL: **Pago Pago**

ABBREVIATIONS

The following abbreviations have been used. Codes given in brackets following the name of a currency are those issued by the International Standards Organization. Where capital city name forms are shown in brackets after the English name, these represent the local spelling of that name and are the forms that will be primarily found on both main maps and in index.

ANZUS	Australia, New Zealand, United States Security Treaty
ASEAN	Association of Southeast Asian Nations
Caricom	Caribbean Community and Common Market
CACM	Central American Common Market
CIS	Commonwealth of Independent States
Col. Plan	Colombo Plan
Comm.	Commonwealth
CSCE	Council for Security and Co-operation in Europe
ECOWAS	Economic Community of West African States
EEA	European Economic Area
EFTA	European Free Trade Association
EU	European Union
G7	Group of seven industrial nations (Canada, France, Germany, Italy, Japan, UK, USA)
Mercosur	Common Market of the Southern Cone
NAFTA	North American Free Trade Agreement
NATO	North Atlantic Treaty Organization
OAS	Organization of American States
OAU	Organization of African Unity
OECD	Organization for Economic Co-operation and Development
OIEC	Organization for International Economic Co-operation
OPEC	Organization of Petroleum Exporting Countries
UN	United Nations
WEU	Western European Union

ANDORRA

STATUS: **Principality**
AREA: **465 sq km (180 sq miles)**
POPULATION: **62,000**
CAPITAL: **Andorra la Vella**
LANGUAGE: **Catalan, Spanish, French**
RELIGION: **Roman Catholic majority**
CURRENCY: **French franc (FRF), Andorran peseta (ADP)**
ORGANIZATIONS: **UN**

Andorra is a small mountainous state located on the southern slopes of the Pyrenees. The climate is alpine with a long winter, which lasts for six months. Spring is mild and summer warm. Annual temperatures range between 2 and 19°C (36–37°F). Rainfall averages 808 mm (32 inches) over the year. Each year 12 million visitors are attracted to Andorra for duty-free shopping, where electronics and designer clothing are the main markets. In winter it is an important skiing centre.

ANGOLA

STATUS: **Republic**
AREA: **1,246,700 sq km (481,225 sq miles)**
POPULATION: **10,609,000**
ANNUAL NATURAL INCREASE: **2.9%**
CAPITAL: **Luanda**
LANGUAGE: **Portuguese, tribal dialects**
RELIGION: **mainly traditional beliefs, Roman Catholic and Protestant minorities**
CURRENCY: **new kwanza (AOK)**
ORGANIZATIONS: **OAU, UN**

Independent from Portugal since 1975, Angola is dominated by plateaux generally exceeding 1,000 m (3,300 ft). There is a pronounced central highland area around Huambo where the highest point reaches 2,610 m (8,563 ft). The climate shows great diversity and ranges from desert in the south to hot, humid equatorial conditions in the north. Rainfall varies from 254 mm (10 inches) in the north to 609 mm (24 inches) in the south. Angola is a fertile land and possesses considerable wealth in the form of diamonds, oil, iron ore and other minerals. Most of the population is engaged in agriculture producing cassava, coffee and maize.

ANGUILLA

STATUS: **UK Dependent Territory**
AREA: **115 sq km (60 sq miles)**
POPULATION: **8,960**
CAPITAL: **The Valley**

ANTIGUA AND BARBUDA

STATUS: **Commonwealth State**
AREA: **442 sq km (171 sq miles)**
POPULATION: **65,962**
CAPITAL: **St John's (on Antigua)**
LANGUAGE: **English**
ANNUAL NATURAL INCREASE: **1.0%**
RELIGION: **Anglican Christian majority**
CURRENCY: **E Caribbean dollar (XCD)**
ORGANIZATIONS: **Caricom, Comm., OAS, UN**

Antigua is low and undulating with a coast that is indented with many bays and fringed with coral reefs. Barbuda is a low, wooded coral island. The climate is tropical although modified by the trade winds and sea breezes. Rainfall is around 1,050 mm (42 inches) a year and temperatures average 27°C (81°F). Antigua and Barbuda became fully independent as a constitutional monarchy within the British Commonwealth in 1981. The main source of revenue is tourism but agriculture is encouraged to lighten the dependency on food imports. Oil refinery, the production of rum, clothing and household appliances, and electronics assembly are the main industries.

ARGENTINA

STATUS: **Republic**
AREA: **2,766,889 sq km (1,068,302 sq miles)**
POPULATION: **33,101,000**
ANNUAL NATURAL INCREASE: **1.3%**
CAPITAL: **Buenos Aires**
LANGUAGE: **Spanish**
RELIGION: **90% Roman Catholic, 2% Protestant, Jewish minority**
CURRENCY: **peso**
ORGANIZATIONS: **Mercosur, OAS, UN**

Relief is highest in the west in the Andes mountains, where altitudes exceed 6,000 m (19,500 ft). East of the Andes there are fertile plains known as the Pampas. In the northern rainforests of the Chaco hot tropical conditions exist. Central Argentina lies in temperate latitudes, but the southernmost regions are cold, wet and stormy. The economy of Argentina was long dominated by the produce of the rich soils of the Pampas, beef and grain. Agricultural products account for over 60 per cent of export revenue, with grain crops predominating, although the late 1980s saw a decline due to to competition and falling world grain prices. Beef exports also decreased by over 50 per cent between 1970 and 1983, due to strong competition from western Europe. Industry has suffered during the last decade. Shortages of raw materials and foreign aid debts have meant lower production, unemployment and a sharp decline in domestic demand.

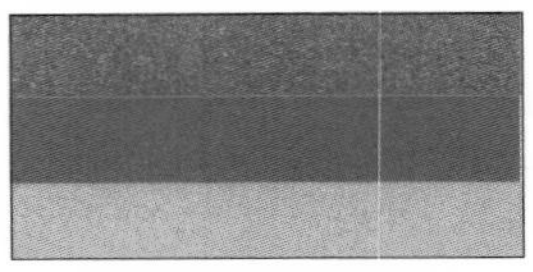

ARMENIA

STATUS: **Republic**
AREA: **30,000 sq km (11,580 sq miles)**
POPULATION: **3,677,000**
ANNUAL NATURAL INCREASE: **1.2%**
CAPITAL: **Yerevan**
LANGUAGE: **Armenian, Russian**
RELIGION: **Russian Orthodox, Armenian Catholic**
CURRENCY: **dram**
ORGANIZATIONS: **CIS, UN**

Armenia is a country of rugged terrain, with most of the land above 1,000 m (3,300 ft). The climate, much influenced by altitude, has warm summers and cold winters.

Rainfall, although occurring throughout the year, is heaviest in summer. Agriculture is dependent upon irrigation and the main crops are vegetables, fruit and tobacco. Industry is generally small-scale. Conflict over the disputed area of Nagornyy Karabakh, an enclave of Armenian Orthodox Christians within the territory of Azerbaijan, is casting a cloud over the immediate future of the country.

ARUBA

STATUS: **Self-governing Island of Netherlands Realm**
AREA: **193 sq km (75 sq miles)**
POPULATION: **68,897**
CAPITAL: **Oranjestad**

ASCENSION

STATUS: **Island Dependency of St Helena**
AREA: **88 sq km (34 sq miles)**
POPULATION: **1,007**
CAPITAL: **Georgetown**

ASHMORE AND CARTIER ISLANDS

STATUS: **External Territory of Australia**
AREA: **3 sq km (1.2 sq miles)**
POPULATION: **no permanent population**

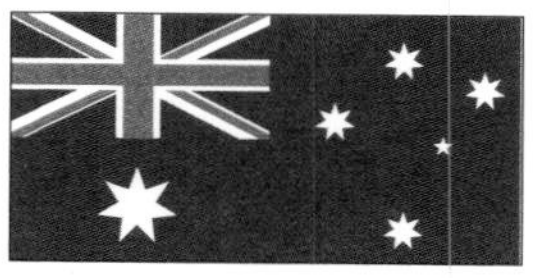

AUSTRALIA

STATUS: **Federal Nation**
AREA: **7,682,300 sq km (2,965,370 sq miles)**
POPULATION: **17,483,000**
ANNUAL NATURAL INCREASE: **1.6%**
CAPITAL: **Canberra**
LANGUAGE: **English**
RELIGION: **75% Christian, Aboriginal beliefs, Jewish minority**
CURRENCY: **Australian dollar (AUD)**
ORGANIZATIONS: **ANZUS, Col. Plan, Comm., OECD, UN**

The Commonwealth of Australia was founded in 1901. The British Monarch, as head of state, is represented by a governor-general. It is the sixth largest country in the world in terms of area. The western half of the country is primarily arid plateaux, ridges and vast deserts. The central-eastern area comprises lowlands of river systems draining into Lake Eyre, while to the east is the Great Dividing Range. Climate varies from cool temperate to tropical monsoon. Rainfall is high only in the northeast, where it exceeds 1,000 mm (39 inches) annually, and decreases markedly from the coast to the interior which is hot and dry. Over 50 per cent of the land area comprises desert and scrub with less than 250 mm (10 inches) of rain a year. The majority of the population live in cities concentrated along the southeast coast. Australia is rich in both agricultural and natural resources. It is the world's leading producer of wool, which together with wheat, meat, sugar and dairy products accounts for over 40 per cent of export revenue. There are vast reserves of coal, oil, natural gas, nickel, iron ore, bauxite and uranium ores. Gold, silver, lead, zinc and copper ores are also exploited. Minerals now account for over 30 per cent of Australia's export revenue. New areas of commerce have been created in eastern Asia, particularly in Japan, to counteract the sharp decline of the traditional European markets. Tourism is becoming a large revenue earner.

AUSTRALIAN CAPITAL TERRITORY

STATUS: **Federal Territory**
AREA: **2,432 sq km (939 sq miles)**
POPULATION: **294,000**
CAPITAL: **Canberra**

NEW SOUTH WALES

STATUS: **State**
AREA: **801,430 sq km (309,350 sq miles)**
POPULATION: **5,959,000**
CAPITAL: **Sydney**

NORTHERN TERRITORY

STATUS: **Territory**
AREA: **1,346,200 sq km (519,635 sq miles)**
POPULATION: **167,000**
CAPITAL: **Darwin**

QUEENSLAND

STATUS: **State**
AREA: **1,727,000 sq km (666,620 sq miles)**
POPULATION: **3,031,000**
CAPITAL: **Brisbane**

SOUTH AUSTRALIA

STATUS: **State**
AREA: **984,380 sq km (79,970 sq miles)**
POPULATION: **1,456,000**
CAPITAL: **Adelaide**

TASMANIA

STATUS: **State**
AREA **68,330 sq km (26,375 sq miles)**
POPULATION: **470,000**
CAPITAL: **Hobart**

VICTORIA

STATUS: **State**
AREA: **227,600 sq km (87,855 sq miles)**
POPULATION: **4,449,000**
CAPITAL: **Melbourne**

WESTERN AUSTRALIA

STATUS: **State**
AREA: **2,525,500 sq km (974,845 sq miles)**
POPULATION: **1,657,000**
CAPITAL: **Perth**

AUSTRALIAN ANTARCTIC TERRITORY

STATUS: **Territory**
AREA: **6,120,000 sq km (2,320,000 sq miles)**
POPULATION: **No permanent population**

AUSTRIA

STATUS: **Federal Republic**
AREA: **83,855 sq km (32,370 sq miles)**
POPULATION: **7,898,000**
ANNUAL NATURAL INCREASE: **0.6%**
CAPITAL: **Vienna (Wien)**
LANGUAGE: **German**
RELIGION: **89% Roman Catholic, 6% Protestant**
CURRENCY: **schilling (ATS)**
ORGANIZATIONS: **Council of Europe, EEA, EFTA, OECD, UN**

Austria is an alpine, land-locked country, characterized by mountains, valleys and lakes. To the east are low hills around the valley of the Danube, where most of the country's fertile farmland is to be found. Half is arable and the remainder mainly produces root or fodder crops. The climate is subject to variation according to altitude, but in general the summers are warm while average winter temperatures are around freezing. Rain falls throughout the year, often as snow in winter, but most occurs in the summer months between May and August. The economy is based on industry including iron and steel, chemicals and transport equipment, with Germany taking over a third of exports. Over 70 per cent of the country's power is hydroelectric. Tourism, in both summer and especially during winter with alpine sports, is an important foreign exchange earner.

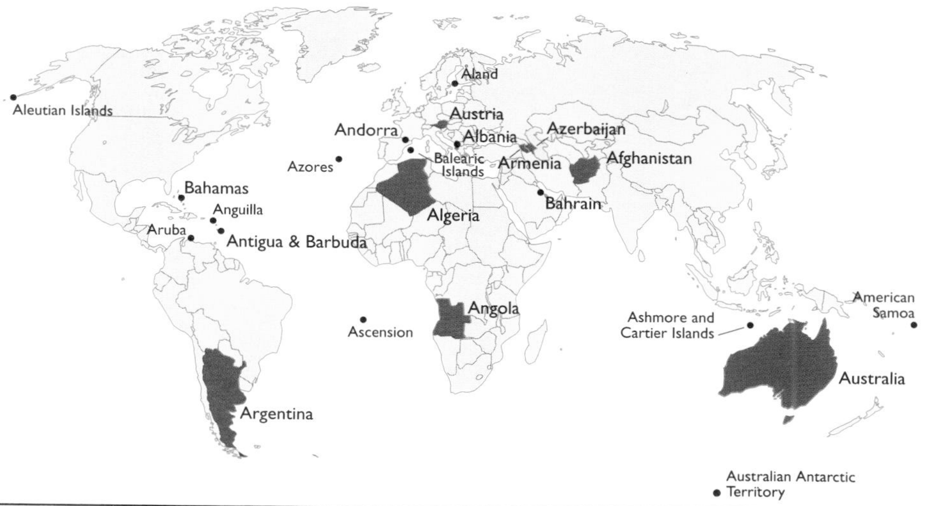

AZERBAIJAN

STATUS: **Republic**
AREA: **87,000 sq km (33,580 sq miles)**
POPULATION: **7,398,000**
ANNUAL NATURAL INCREASE: **1.0%**
CAPITAL: **Baku**
LANGUAGE: **83% Azeri, 6% Armenian, 6% Russian**
RELIGION: **83% Muslim, Armenian Apostolic, Orthodox**
CURRENCY: **manat**
ORGANIZATIONS: **CIS, UN**

The country is mountainous with the southern limits of the Caucasus mountain range extending into Azerbaijan in the northeast. Much of the land adjoining the Caspian Sea is flat and low-lying. The climate is continental. Rainfall is light overall with the heaviest falls in summer. The country includes two autonomous regions: Nakhichevan, which is cut off by a strip of intervening Armenian territory, and Nagornyy Karabakh. Long-standing tensions over the latter escalated into conflict in 1992. Originally based on oil extraction and refining, industrial development has been supplemented by manufacturing, engineering and chemicals.

AZORES

STATUS: **Self-governing Island Region of Portugal**
AREA: **2,335 sq km (901 sq miles)**
POPULATION: **257,100**

BAHAMAS

STATUS: **Commonwealth Nation**
AREA: **13,865 sq km (5,350 sq miles)**
POPULATION: **262,000**
ANNUAL NATURAL INCREASE: **1.9%**
CAPITAL: **Nassau**
LANGUAGE: **English**
RELIGION: **Anglican Christian majority, Baptist and Roman Catholic minorities**
CURRENCY: **Bahamian dollar (BSD)**
ORGANIZATIONS: **Caricom, Comm., OAS, UN**

The Bahamas is an archipelago of some 700 coral and limestone islands in an 805 km (500 mile) long chain south of Florida. Only 22 islands are inhabited, and over half the population live on New Providence. The climate is generally warm throughout the year although the proximity of the North American continent can lead to spells of cool weather in winter. Rainfall is plentiful; the summer months are wettest and the islands are occasionally struck by hurricanes. The Bahamian economy is heavily dependent on tourism, with around 90 per cent of visitors from the USA. Other revenue is earned from a large registered merchant fleet and from international financial services.

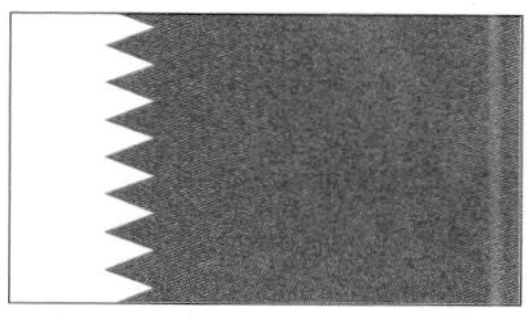

BAHRAIN

STATUS: **State**
AREA: **661 sq km (225 sq miles)**
POPULATION **539,000**
ANNUAL NATURAL INCREASE: **3.2%**
CAPITAL: **Manama (Al Manāmah)**
LANGUAGE: **Arabic, English**
RELIGION: **60% Shi'a and 40% Sunni Muslim, Christian minority**
CURRENCY: **Bahraini dinar (BHD)**
ORGANIZATIONS: **Arab League, UN**

The State of Bahrain is an archipelago of 33 islands, all low-lying. The summers are hot and humid, especially between April and October. The winters are mild. Annual rainfall is less than 76 mm (3 inches). Oil is still significant in the economy, providing 60 per cent of government revenue, but at the current rates of extraction the reserves are not expected to last for more than ten years. Gas is becoming increasingly important, and reserves are expected to last a further 50 years. Cheap gas supplies are the basis of Bahrain's aluminium smelting industry, which is the Gulf region's largest non-oil activity.

BALEARIC ISLANDS

STATUS: **Island Province of Spain**
AREA: **5,015 sq km (1,935 sq miles)**
POPULATION: **709,138**
CAPITAL: **Palma de Mallorca**

STATES AND TERRITORIES OF THE WORLD

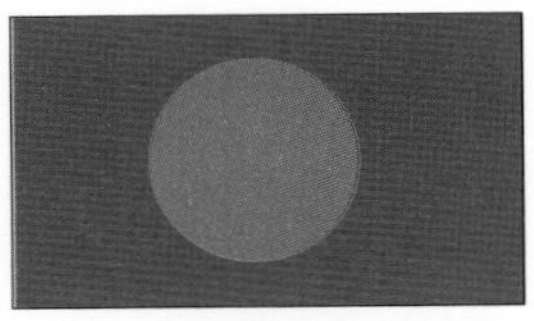

BANGLADESH

STATUS: **Republic**
AREA: **144,000 sq km (55,585 sq miles)**
POPULATION: **122,000,000**
ANNUAL NATURAL INCREASE: **2.2%**
CAPITAL: **Dhaka**
LANGUAGE: **Bengali (Bangla), Bihari, Hindi, English**
RELIGION: **85% Muslim, Hindu, Buddhist and Christian minorities**
CURRENCY: **taka (BDT)**
ORGANIZATIONS: **Col. Plan, Comm., UN**

The greater part of Bangladesh consists of alluvial plains and deltas of the Ganges and Brahmaputra rivers, which drain from the Himalayas into the Bay of Bengal. There are bamboo-forested hills in the southeast. The climate is hot, with heavy monsoon rainfall in the summer months. Severe cyclones and floods are common during the monsoon season. The Bangladeshi economy is heavily dependent upon agriculture, with the main cash crop being jute. There are no extensive mineral deposits, although large reserves of natural gas under the Bay of Bengal are beginning to be exploited. Bangladesh is one of the poorest and most densely populated countries in the world. It is heavily dependent on international aid, but there are now signs of economic improvement and the trade deficit is lessening.

BARBADOS

STATUS: **Commonwealth State**
AREA: **430 sq km (166 sq miles)**
POPULATION: **: 259,000**
ANNUAL NATURAL INCREASE: **0.3%**
CAPITAL: **Bridgetown**
LANGUAGE: **English**
RELIGION: **Anglican Christian majority, Methodist and Roman Catholic minorities**
CURRENCY: **Barbados dollar (BBD)**
ORGANIZATIONS: **Caricom, Comm., OAS, UN**

The former British colony of Barbados became fully independent in 1966. It is the most easterly of the Windward Islands, and is generally low-lying with some hilly country in the north. The climate is pleasant and warm throughout the year with temperatures ranging from 25° to 28°C (77° to 82°F). There is 1270–1900 mm (50–75 inches) of rainfall per year. December to June tend to be dry. The Barbadian economy was traditionally founded upon sugar production, but since the 1970s this has been overtaken in importance by tourism. About one third of the population is engaged in this industry. Barbados has one oilfield which supplies 30 per cent of domestic needs. There are also some natural gas reserves.

BEAR ISLAND (BJØRNØYA)

STATUS: **Island of Svalbard, Norway**
AREA: **176 sq km (68 sq miles)**
POPULATION: **no permanent population**

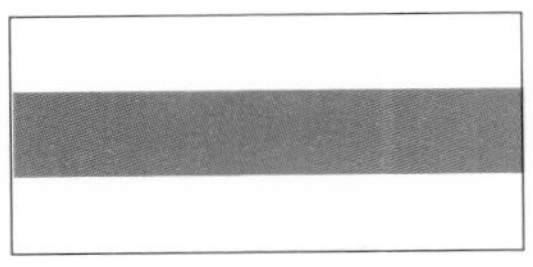

BELARUS

STATUS: **Republic**
AREA: **208,000 sq km (80,290 sq miles)**
POPULATION: **10,297,000**
ANNUAL NATURAL INCREASE: **0.5%**
CAPITAL: **Minsk**
LANGUAGE: **Belarussian, Russian**
RELIGION: **Roman Catholic, Uniate (Orthodox-rite Roman Catholic)**
CURRENCY: **rouble, zaichik**
ORGANIZATIONS: **CIS, UN**

Belarus is a land of plains and low hills covered with glacial soils. It is drained mainly by the Dnieper (Dnepr) river in the south and the headwaters of the Dvina river system in the north. About 30 per cent of the land area is forested. The climate is continental with warm summers and cold, fairly dry winters. Traditionally Belarus has had an agricultural economy based on beef cattle and crops such as hardy grains (rye, oats, buckwheat), sugarbeet, flax and potatoes. There are no oil, gas or coal reserves, although there are substantial peat deposits which are used in power stations and for domestic consumption. The republic's heavy industries, which include large petrochemical and engineering complexes, were dependent on Russian fuel, and independence has meant economic difficulties. In the future Belarus may be forced to concentrate on greater exploitation of the natural wealth of its timber reserves which have traditionally been an important source of economic wealth.

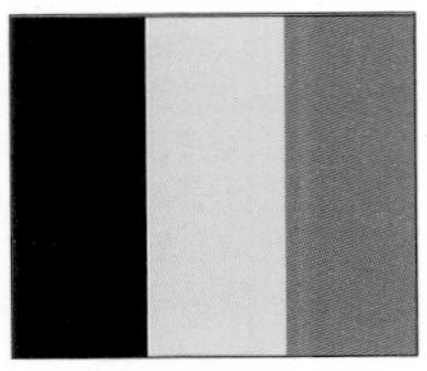

BELGIUM

STATUS: **Kingdom**
AREA: **30,520 sq km (11,780 sq miles)**
POPULATION: **9,998,000**
ANNUAL NATURAL INCREASE: **0.3%**
CAPITAL: **Brussels (Bruxelles/Brussel)**
LANGUAGE: **French, Dutch (Flemish), German**
RELIGION: **Roman Catholic majority, Protestant and Jewish minorities**
CURRENCY: **Belgium franc (BEF)**
ORGANIZATIONS: **Council of Europe, EEA, EU, NATO, OECD, UN, WEU**

Most of Belgium is fertile plain, covered by wind-blown loess. In the south are the forested mountains of the Ardennes. The climate is maritime and temperate, with mild winters and cool summers, although the country's proximity to the Atlantic means that low pressure fronts bring changeable weather and frequent rainfalls averaging 720–1200 mm (28–47 inches) a year. Over half the country is intensively farmed with extensive pastureland ensuring that Belgium is self-sufficient in food products. There are few mineral resources. However, the country is heavily industrialized, and produces textiles, diamonds, chemicals, machinery and metals. It is also one of the largest car exporters in the world. Belgium was a founder member of the Benelux Union and what is now the European Union and hosts the headquarters of the North Atlantic Treaty Organization. It is also the home base for over 800 other international organizations.

BELIZE

STATUS: **Commonwealth Nation**
AREA: **22,965 sq km (8,865 sq miles)**
POPULATION: **189,392**
ANNUAL NATURAL INCREASE: **2.6%**
CAPITAL: **Belmopan**
LANGUAGE: **English, Spanish, Maya**
RELIGION: **60% Roman Catholic, 40% Protestant**
CURRENCY: **Belizean dollar (BZD)**
ORGANIZATIONS: **CARICOM, Comm., OAS, UN**

Much of the country is jungle, with many rivers and lakes. The Maya mountain range in the southwest is heavily forested. Offshore there are cays and the world's second largest coral barrier reef. The climate is tropical with a heavy annual rainfall of 1,900 mm (75 inches). Temperatures vary only slightly with seasons, from 23 to 27°C (73–81°F). Principal crops for export are sugar cane, fruit, rice, maize and timber products. Tourism has grown steadily in recent years, with visitors drawn to the reef and the many historical ruins.

BENIN

STATUS: **Republic**
AREA: **112,620 sq km (43,470 sq miles)**
POPULATION: **5,047,000**
ANNUAL NATURAL INCREASE: **3.2%**
CAPITAL: **Porto Novo**
LANGUAGE: **French, Fon, Adja**
RELIGION: **majority traditional beliefs, 15% Roman Catholic, 13% Muslim**
CURRENCY: **CFA franc (W Africa) (XOF)**
ORGANIZATIONS: **ECOWAS, OAU, UN**

Beyond the coastal lowlands the land rises to plateaux culminating in the Atakora range (Chaine de l'Atakora). The climate throughout Benin is hot all year round, rainfall reaching its maximum in June. Benin is mainly an agricultural economy. Food crops include cash crops such as oil palms, cocoa and coffee. Cotton growing, though suffering from weak world prices, has expanded. Benin derives some income from limited offshore oil resources. The economy received a boost during the conflict in neighbouring Togo, causing much trade to be transferred from Lomé to Cotonou.

BERMUDA

STATUS: **Self-governing UK Crown Colony**
AREA: **54 sq km (21 sq miles)**
POPULATION: **74,837**
CAPITAL: **Hamilton**

BHUTAN

STATUS: **Kingdom**
AREA: **46,620 sq km (17,995 sq miles)**
POPULATION: **600,000**
ANNUAL NATURAL INCREASE: **2.2%**
CAPITAL: **Thimphu**
LANGUAGE: **Dzongkha, Nepali, English**
RELIGION: **Mahayana Buddhist, 30% Hindu**
CURRENCY: **ngultrum (BTN), Indian rupee (INR)**
ORGANIZATIONS: **Col. Plan, UN**

Bhutan, in the eastern Himalayas, is mountainous in the north, predominantly forested at its centre and has a tropical lowland to the south. The climate varies with altitude but the higher north remains perpetually cold. The southern lowlands are subtropical and the centre temperate. Monsoons occur between June and August. Subsistence agriculture predominates and cash crops are generally fruit and cardamom. Cement, talcum and timber are the main exports.

BIOKO (FERNANDO PÓO)

STATUS: **Island Province of Equatorial Guinea**
AREA: **2,034 sq km (785 sq miles)**
POPULATION: **57,190**

BOLIVIA

STATUS: **Republic**
AREA: **1,098,575 sq km (424,050 sq miles)**
POPULATION: **6,344,396**
ANNUAL NATURAL INCREASE: **2.5%**
CAPITAL: **La Paz**
LANGUAGE: **Spanish, Quechua, Aymara**
RELIGION: **Roman Catholic majority**
CURRENCY: **Boliviano (BOB)**
ORGANIZATIONS: **OAS, UN**

Most of Bolivia's development is in the high plateau, the Altiplano, within the ranges of the Andes. To the southeast there are semi-arid grasslands and to the north there are dense Amazon forests. High western regions experience wide diurnal variations in temperature but without much annual change. The western plains are arid in the south and subject to humid tropical conditions in the north. Subsistence agriculture occupies the majority of the population, and the economy relies on the exploitation of mineral resources. Military rule ended in 1978, since when power has been exercised by civilian governments.

BONAIRE

STATUS: **Self-governing Island of Netherlands Antilles**
AREA: **288 sq km (111 sq miles)**
POPULATION: **11,139**

BONIN ISLANDS (OGASAWARA-SHOTO)

STATUS: **Islands of Japan**
AREA: **104 sq km (40 sq miles)**
POPULATION: **1,879**

BOSNIA-HERZEGOVINA

STATUS: **Republic**
AREA: **51,130 sq km (19,736 sq miles)**

POPULATION: **2,900,000**
ANNUAL NATURAL INCREASE: **0.2%**
CAPITAL: **Sarajevo**
LANGUAGE: **Serbo–Croat**
RELIGION: **Muslim, Christian**
CURRENCY: **dinar**
ORGANIZATIONS: **UN**

Much of the country is mountainous, with limestone ridges oriented northwest to southeast traversing the country. The only lowlands of consequence are along the valley of the Sava in the north. Summer temperatures are warm but in winter, depending upon altitude and aspects, extremely cold conditions can occur. Before the civil war Bosnia's economy was based predominantly on agriculture, sheep rearing and the cultivation of vines, olives and citrus fruits. The civil war has ruined the economy. Large sections of the population face desperate hardship and are dependent for survival on UN relief. The currency is worthless; virtually all production has ceased and only the black economy operates.

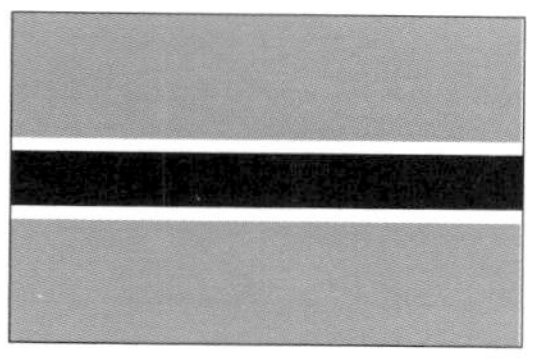

BOTSWANA

STATUS: **Republic**
AREA: **582,000 sq km (224,652 sq miles)**
POPULATION: **1,291,000**
ANNUAL NATURAL INCREASE: **3.4%**
CAPITAL: **Gaborone**
LANGUAGE: **Setswana, English**
RELIGION: **traditional beliefs majority, Christian minority**
CURRENCY: **pula (BWP)**
ORGANIZATIONS: **Comm., OAU, UN**

Over half of Botswana consists of the vast upland Kalahari Desert. Elsewhere there are salt pans and swamps, as in the Okavango Basin. The climate is drought-prone with unreliable rainfall of around 538 mm (21 inches) a year. The rain occurs in the hot summer months between October and April. Winters are warm with cold nights and occasional frosts. Botswana supports little arable agriculture, but over 2.3 million cattle graze the dry grasslands. Diamonds, copper, nickel and gold are mined in the east and are the main mineral exports. The growth of light industries around the capital has stimulated trade with neighbouring countries.

BOUGAINVILLE ISLAND

STATUS: **Part of Papua New Guinea**
AREA: **10,620 sq km (4,100 sq miles)**
POPULATION: **159,100**
CAPITAL: **Arawa**

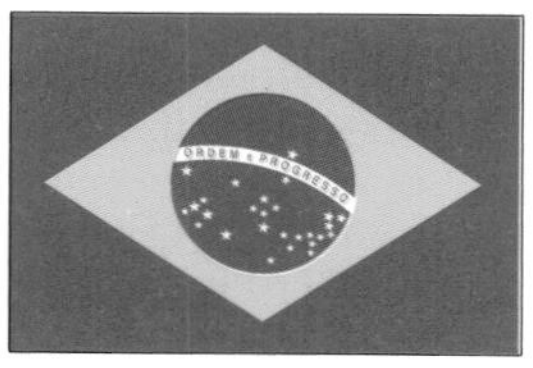

BRAZIL

STATUS: **Federal Republic**
AREA: **8,511,965 sq km (3,285,620 sq miles)**
POPULATION: **156,275,000**
ANNUAL NATURAL INCREASE: **2.2%**
CAPITAL: **Brasília**
LANGUAGE: **Portuguese**
RELIGION: **90% Roman Catholic, Protestant minority**
CURRENCY: **cruzeiro real (BRC),URV**
ORGANIZATIONS: **Mercosur, OAS, UN**

Brazil, covering nearly half of South America, is dominated by the Amazon basin which is bordered in the south by the vast dissected plateaux of the Brazilian highlands. Constant warm and humid conditions in Amazonia give way to seasonal variations towards southern latitudes; winters are cooler with rainfall in summer. The northeast region of Brazil is prone to drought. In agricultural production Brazil is one of the world's leading exporters with coffee, soya beans, sugar, bananas, cocoa, tobacco, rice and cattle. Brazil also has a vast variety and wealth of resources, including major reserves of iron ore and platinum. It has one of the fastest growing economies. Nevertheless, Brazil has severe economic problems with inflation running at a very high rate. Recent economic policies have concentrated on developing the industrial base, road and rail communications, light and heavy industry and the expansion of energy resources, particularly hydro-electric power harnessed from the great river systems.

BRITISH ANTARCTIC TERRITORY

STATUS: **U.K. Dependent Territory**
AREA: **1,554,000 sq km (599,845 sq miles)**
POPULATION: **no permanent population**

BRITISH INDIAN OCEAN TERRITORY

STATUS: **U.K. Dependency comprising the Chagos Archipelago**
AREA: **5,765 sq km (2,225 sq miles)**
POPULATION: **266,000**

BRUNEI

STATUS: **Sultanate**
AREA: **5,765 sq km (2,225 sq miles)**
POPULATION: **270,000**
ANNUAL NATURAL INCREASE: **3.2%**
CAPITAL: **Bandar Seri Begawan**
LANGUAGE: **Malay, English, Chinese**
RELIGION: **65% Sunni Muslim, Buddhist and Christian minorities**
CURRENCY: **Brunei dollar (BND)**
ORGANIZATIONS: **ASEAN, Comm, UN**

Brunei is a small forested state, mostly lowland but with mountains that reach 1,800 m (5,900 ft) in the southeast. The climate is tropical and humid with temperatures all year round in the range 26–28°C (79–82°F). There is heavy rainfall of 2,500–5,000 mm (100–200 inches) a year. Oil, both on shore and off shore, is the mainstay of the Brunei economy. Other exports include natural gas, which is transported to Japan, rubber and timber.

BULGARIA

STATUS: **Republic**
AREA: **110,910 sq km (42,810 sq miles)**

POPULATION: **8,467,000**
ANNUAL NATURAL INCREASE: **0.0%**
CAPITAL: **Sofia (Sofiya)**
LANGUAGE: **Bulgarian, Turkish**
RELIGION: **Eastern Orthodox majority, Muslim minority**
CURRENCY: **lev (BGL)**
ORGANIZATIONS: **Council of Europe, EFTA, OIEC, UN**

The Rhodope mountains dominate the west while the Balkan mountains (Stara Planina) form a chain running east–west through central Bulgaria. To the north lie the plains of the Danube, and to the south are the lowlands of Thrace and the Maritsa valley. Temperatures show significant seasonal variation, with summer averages exceeding 20°C (68°F) and winter averages around 0°C (32°F). Rainfall maxima are in summer. The basis of the Bulgarian economy is agriculture. Fertile lands allow the cultivation of a wide variety of crops including cereals, vines, cotton, tobacco and fruit. There are very few natural resources. However, the communist regime has left the country with a disastrous ecological legacy. The political institutions of post-communist Bulgaria are still in a state of flux, and it's society is undergoing a prolonged and painful crisis of transformation. Bulgaria's relationship with the International Monetary Fund is likely to be critical to the country's development.

BURKINA

STATUS: **Republic**
AREA: **274,122 sq km (105,811 sq miles)**
POPULATION: **9,490,000**
ANNUAL NATURAL INCREASE: **2.8%**
CAPITAL: **Ouagadougou**
LANGUAGE: **French, Moré (Mossi), Dyula**
RELIGION: **60% animist, 30% Muslim, 10% Roman Catholic**
CURRENCY: **CFA franc (W Africa) (OXF)**
ORGANIZATIONS: **ECOWAS, OAU, UN**

The north of Burkina lies in the Sahara and is thus very arid. The south is largely savannah. Burkina has a tropical climate with November to February experiencing dry, cool weather. Rainfall is erratic and the region is prone to severe droughts. Agriculture, despite its paucity, remains a major source of income. Together with livestock herding, agriculture varies with the amount and pattern of annual rainfall. Manganese is starting to be exported and zinc production is scheduled to begin at Perkoa.

BURMA (MYANMAR)

STATUS: **Union of states and divisions**
AREA: **678,030 sq km (261,720 sq miles)**
POPULATION: **41,550,000**
ANNUAL NATURAL INCREASE: **2.2%**
CAPITAL: **Rangoon (Yangon)**
LANGUAGE: **Burmese**
RELIGION: **85% Buddhist. Animist, Muslim, Hindu and Christian minorities**
CURRENCY: **kyat (BUK)**
ORGANIZATIONS: **Col. Plan, UN**

The heart of Burma is a great basin drained by the Irrawaddy system. To the west lie the Arakan mountains and to the east the Shan plateau. Much of the country is covered by tropical rainforest. Temperatures are very warm throughout the year. Most areas of the country have heavy monsoon rain in summer but are dry in winter. The economy is based on the export of rice and forestry products. Economic prospects are poor while the regime expends a high proportion of its resources on the armed forces. International aid is not forthcoming, inflation continues to rise, and the black economy flourishes.

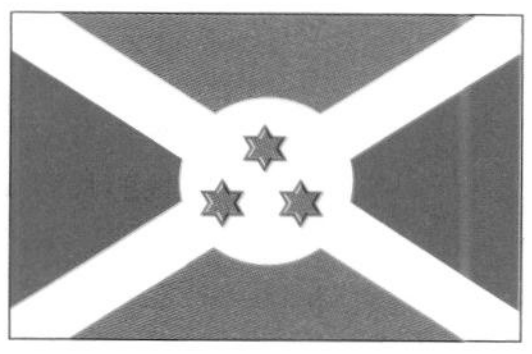

BURUNDI

STATUS: **Republic**
AREA: **27,835 sq km (10,745 sq miles)**
POPULATION: **5,786,000**
ANNUAL NATURAL INCREASE: **2.9%**
CAPITAL: **Bujumbura**
LANGUAGE: **French, Kirundi, Swahili**
RELIGION: **60% Roman Catholic, animist minority**
CURRENCY: **Burundi franc (BIF)**
ORGANIZATIONS: **OAU, UN**

Burundi is hilly, with high plateaux in the centre and savannah in the east. Temperatures are hot near Lake Tanganyika, and cooler elsewhere. Rainfall occurs between October and May. Coffee remains Burundi's chief export, although tea and cotton are also produced. Light manufactured products have recently become Burundi's second source of export earnings. The poverty of the country has two basic causes – repeated droughts and tribal violence.

STATES AND TERRITORIES OF THE WORLD

CAMBODIA

STATUS: **Kingdom**
AREA: **181,000 sq km (69,865 sq miles)**
POPULATION: **9,045,000**
ANNUAL NATURAL INCREASE: **2.7%**
CAPITAL: **Phnom Penh**
LANGUAGE: **Khmer**
RELIGION: **Buddhist majority, Roman Catholic and Muslim minorities**
CURRENCY: **reil (KHR)**
ORGANIZATIONS: **Col. Plan, UN**

Most of the country is a lowland basin drained by the Mekong river, with the Tonle Sap (Great Lake) at its heart. The climate is tropical, with average annual temperatures exceeding 25°C (77°F). Monsoon rainfall occurs from May to October. As a result of mass migration to the cities, much of the land is uncultivated. Manufacturing industry is almost non-existent, having suffered from power shortages and neglected transportation and telecommunications. The years of strife have left Cambodia bankrupt; its reconstruction will be dependent on massive aid, investment from overseas and a stable government.

CAMEROON

STATUS: **Republic**
AREA: **475,500 sq km (183,545 sq miles)**
POPULATION: **12,198,000**
ANNUAL NATURAL INCREASE: **3.0%**
CAPITAL: **Yaoundé**
LANGUAGE: **English, French**
RELIGION: **40% Christian, 39% traditional beliefs, 21% Muslim**
CURRENCY: **CRA franc (C Africa) (XAF)**
ORGANIZATIONS: **OAU, UN**

Cameroon is situated on the coast of West Africa just north of the equator. Coastal lowlands rise to densely forested plateaux. Rainfall varies from over 1,000 mm (40 inches) to only 50 mm (2 inches) per year. The majority of the population are farmers, with agricultural products accounting for over 80 per cent of export revenue. Coffee and cocoa are the main cash crops. Mineral resources are under-developed but Cameroon is already one of Africa's major producers of bauxite. Oil exploitation is playing an increasing role in the economy.

CANADA

STATUS: **Commonwealth Nation**
AREA: **9,922,385 sq km (3,830,840 sq miles)**
POPULATION: **27,743,000**
ANNUAL NATURAL INCREASE: **1.4%**
CAPITAL: **Ottawa**
LANGUAGE: **English, French**
RELIGION: **46% Roman Catholic, Protestant and Jewish minorities**
CURRENCY: **Canadian dollar (CAD)**
ORGANIZATIONS: **Col. Plan, Comm., G7, OAS, OECD, NATO, NAFTA, UN**

Canada is the world's second largest country. Arctic islands and tundra give way southwards to boreal forests, interspersed with lakes and mighty rivers, and then central prairies. In the east are the fertile lowlands of the St Lawrence basin. The Rocky Mountains rise to over 4,000 m (13,000 ft) in the west, beyond which are the coastal mountains, fjords and islands of British Columbia. Generally the climate is continental, with severe winters and hot summers, but considerable variations occur with latitude, altitude and maritime influence. The Great Lakes area provides fish, fruit, maize, root crops and dairy products; the prairies produce over 20 per cent of the world's wheat; and the grasslands of Alberta support a thriving beef industry. The Arctic tundra of the far north provides summer grazing for caribou. Further south coniferous forests grow on the thin soils of the ancient shield landscape and on the extensive foothills of the Rocky Mountains. In contrast, the rich soils of the central prairies support grasslands and grain crops. Most minerals are mined and exploited in Canada with oil and natural gas, iron ore, bauxite, nickel, zinc, copper, gold and silver the major exports. The country's vast rivers provide huge amounts of hydro-electric power, but most industry is confined to the Great Lakes and St Lawrence margins. The principal manufactured goods for export are steel products, motor vehicles, and paper for newsprint. Despite economic success, Canada still remains one of the world's most under-exploited countries, so vast are the potential mineral resources and areas of land for agricultural development. Canada is a great trading and industrialized nation and should receive a boost to trade with the implementation of the North American Free Trade Agreement.

ALBERTA

STATUS: **Province**
AREA: **661,190 sq km (225,220 sq miles)**
POPULATION: **2,577,000**
CAPITAL: **Edmonton**

BRITISH COLUMBIA

STATUS: **Province**
AREA: **948,565 sq km (366,160 sq miles)**
POPULATION: **3,342,000**
CAPITAL: **Victoria**

MANITOBA

STATUS: **Province**
AREA: **650,090 sq km (250,935 sq miles)**
POPULATION: **1,098,000**
CAPITAL: **Winnipeg**

NEW BRUNSWICK

STATUS: **Province**
AREA: **73,435 sq km (28,345 sq miles)**
POPULATION: **728,000**
CAPITAL: **Fredericton**

NEWFOUNDLAND AND LABRADOR

STATUS: **Province**
AREA: **404,520 sq km (156,145 sq miles)**
POPULATION: **576,000**
CAPITAL: **St John's**

NORTHWEST TERRITORIES

STATUS: **Territory**
AREA: **3,379,685 sq km (1,304,560 sq miles)**
POPULATION: **56,000**
CAPITAL: **Yellowknife**

NOVA SCOTIA

STATUS: **Province**
AREA: **55,490 sq km (21,420 sq miles)**
POPULATION: **897,000**
CAPITAL: **Halifax**

ONTARIO

STATUS: **Province**
AREA: **1,068,630 sq km (412,490 sq miles)**
POPULATION: **10,168,000**
CAPITAL: **Toronto**

PRINCE EDWARD ISLAND

STATUS: **Province**
AREA: **5,655 sq km (2,185 sq miles)**
POPULATION: **131,000**
CAPITAL: **Charlottetown**

QUEBEC

STATUS: **Province**
AREA: **1,540,680 sq km (594,705 sq miles)**
POPULATION: **6,954,000**
CAPITAL: **Quebec**

SASKATCHEWAN

STATUS: **Province**
AREA: **651,900 sq km (251,635 sq miles)**
POPULATION: **993,000**
CAPITAL: **Regina**

YUKON TERRITORY

STATUS: **Province**
AREA: **482,515 sq km (186,250 sq miles)**
POPULATION: **29,000**
CAPITAL: **Whitehorse**

CANARY ISLANDS

STATUS: **Island Provinces of Spain**
AREA: **7,275 sq km (2,810 sq miles)**
POPULATION: **1,493,784**
CAPITAL: **Las Palmas (Gran Canaria) and Santa Cruz (Tenerife)**

CAPE VERDE

STATUS: **Republic**
AREA: **4,035 sq km (1,560 sq miles)**
POPULATION: **384,000**
ANNUAL NATURAL INCREASE: **2.7%**
CAPITAL: **Praia**
LANGUAGE: **Portuguese, Creole**
RELIGION: **98% Roman Catholic**
CURRENCY: **Cape Verde escudo (CVE)**
ORGANIZATIONS: **ECOWAS, OAU, UN**

The country is an archipelago of ten main islands and several smaller ones. They lie some 600 km (375 miles) west of Africa and are of volcanic origin. Despite their maritime position the islands are arid. Temperatures are warm throughout the year. Irrigation encourages the growth of sugar cane, coconuts, fruit and maize. Fishing accounts for about 70 per cent of export revenue. All consumer goods are imported, and trade links continue to be maintained with Portugal.

CAYMAN ISLANDS

STATUS: **UK Dependent Territory**
AREA: **259 sq km (100 sq miles)**
POPULATION: **29,000**
CAPITAL: **George Town**

CENTRAL AFRICAN REPUBLIC

STATUS: **Republic**
AREA: **624,975 sq km (241,240 sq miles)**
POPULATION: **3,173,000**
ANNUAL NATURAL INCREASE: **2.7%**
CAPITAL: **Bangui**
LANGUAGE: **French, Sango (national)**
RELIGION: **Animist majority, 33% Christian, Muslim minority**
CURRENCY: **CFA franc (C Africa) (XAF)**
ORGANIZATIONS: **OAU, UN**

Most of the Central African Republic is plateaux covered by scrub or savannah. This is drained in the south by the Ubangi river system and in the north by the Chari, which flows into Lake Chad. To the north lies the Sahara desert. The climate is hot all the year round with moderately heavy rainfall for much of the year. Most farming is at subsistence level, although some cotton, coffee and groundnuts are produced for export. Diamonds and small quantities of gold and uranium are the principal sources of wealth and account for more than half of foreign earnings. Hardwood forests in the southwest provide timber, also for export. The Central African Republic is a poor country. The economy has declined since independence and the budget deficit has grown massively.

CEUTA

STATUS: **Spanish External Province**
AREA: **19.5 sq km (7.5 sq miles)**
POPULATION: **67,615**
CAPITAL: **Ceuta**

CHAD

STATUS: **Republic**
AREA: **1,284,000 sq km (495,625 sq miles)**
POPULATION: **6,288,000**
ANNUAL NATURAL INCREASE: **2.5%**
CAPITAL: **Ndjamena**
LANGUAGE: **French, Arabic, local languages**
RELIGION: **50% Muslim, 45% animist, 5% Christian**
CURRENCY: **CRA franc (C Africa) (XAF)**
ORGANIZATIONS: **OAU, UN**

Chad, one of the world's poorest countries, is a vast state stretching deep into the Sahara desert. Much of the country is plateaux sloping westwards to Lake Chad, (an area which is subject to seasonal fluctuations and is progressively drying up). Climatic conditions range from desert in the north, at the southern edge of the Sahara, through savannah to tropical forest in the southwest. Chad is heavily dependent on subsistence agriculture and cattle herding. The most important cash crop is cotton grown in the south and southwest, but output has been affected by severe droughts, increasing desertification and civil unrest. There are few other natural resources, except natron which is extracted north of Lake Chad. Some oil is also produced.

CHANNEL ISLANDS

STATUS: **British Crown Dependency**
AREA: **194 sq km (75 sq miles)**
POPULATION: **138,668**
CAPITAL: **St Hélier (Jersey). St Peter Port (Guernsey)**

CHILE

STATUS: **Republic**
AREA: **751,625 sq km (290,125 sq miles)**
POPULATION: **13,813,000**
ANNUAL NATURAL INCREASE: **1.7%**
CAPITAL: **Santiago**
LANGUAGE: **Spanish**
RELIGION: **85% Roman Catholic, Protestant minority**
CURRENCY: **Chilean peso (CLP)**
ORGANIZATIONS: **OAS, UN**

Chile is a long, narrow country on the west coast of South America. Its eastern border is the high Andes, whose peaks exceed 6,000 m (19,500 ft). The extreme latitudinal extent, combined with the range of altitude east–west, provides dramatic climatic variation. The Chilean economy is based on an abundance of mineral resources, especially mineral ores and timber products. Most energy is provided by hydro-electric power. Manufacturing is well developed and has compensated for the falling prices of copper, pulp and fishmeal. The past three years have seen a dramatic expansion in farm production, and food now accounts for 29 per cent of export earnings.

CHINA

STATUS: **People's Republic**
AREA: **9,597,000 sq km (3,704,440 sq miles)**
POPULATION: **1,154,887,381**
ANNUAL NATURAL INCREASE: **1.3%**
CAPITAL: **Beijing (Peking)**
LANGUAGE: **Mandarin Chinese, regional languages**
RELIGION: **Confucianist, Buddhist, Taoist. Christian and Muslim minorities**
CURRENCY: **yuan (CNY)**
ORGANIZATIONS: **UN**

China's vast territory is one of amazing physical diversity. In the west some of the world's greatest mountain chains, the Tien Shan and the Himalayas, flank the great Tibetan plateau, and to the north lies the arid Takla Makan basin (Taklimakan Shamo). Northeast and eastern China is a vast plain of fertile wind-blown glacial soils, while to the south lie the forested mountains of Yunnan. Climatic conditions of all kinds are found within China's borders. Extreme continental conditions occur in northern China where summers are hot with some rainfall and winters are bitingly cold and dry. By contrast the southwest enjoys a moist, warm subtropical climate. Between these two extremes much of the nation experiences temperate conditions. Seventy per cent of the population live in rural areas, the majority in the great drainage basin regions of the Yellow River (Huang He or Hwang Ho) and the Yangtze (Chang Jiang) where intensive irrigated agriculture produces one third of the world's rice as well as wheat, maize, sugar, soya beans and oilseeds. The country is self-sufficient in cereals, livestock and fish. The Yunnan plateau of the south is rich in tin, copper, and zinc; Manchuria possesses coal and iron ore; and oil is extracted from beneath the Yellow Sea. The natural mineral resources of China are considerable, varied and under-exploited. The main industrial centres are situated close to the natural resources and concentrate on the production of iron, steel, cement, light engineering and textile manufacturing. The economy is being built on this industrial base, with stable and adequate food production and increasing trade with the United States, Western Europe and Japan.

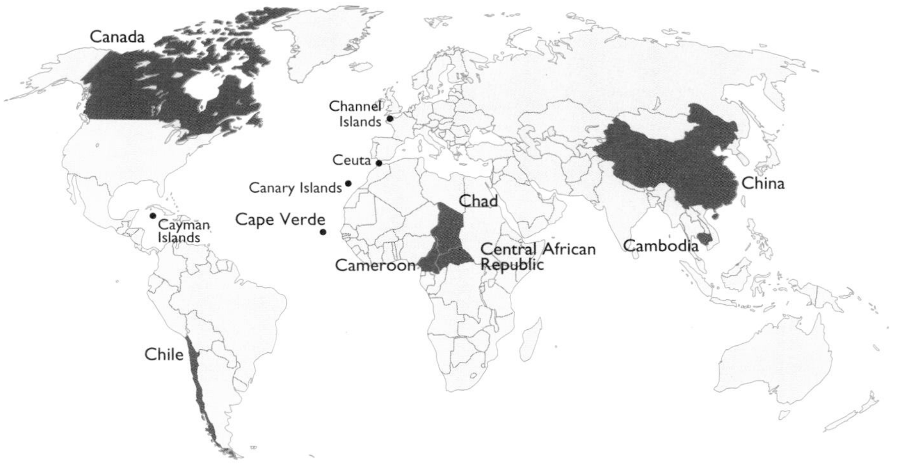

ANHUI (ANHWEI)

STATUS: **Province**
AREA: **139,900 sq km (54,000 sq miles)**
POPULATION: **52,290,000**
CAPITAL: **Hefei**

BEIJING (PEKING)

STATUS: **Municipality**
AREA: **17,800 sq km (6,870 sq miles)**
POPULATION: **10,870,000**

FUJIAN (FUKIEN)

STATUS: **Province**
AREA: **123,000 sq km (47,515 sq miles)**
POPULATION: **30,610,000**
CAPITAL: **Fuzhou**

GANSU (KANSU)

STATUS: **Province**
AREA: **530,000 sq km (204,580 sq miles)**
POPULATION: **22,930,000**
CAPITAL: **Lanzhou**

GUANGDONG (KWANGTUNG)

STATUS: **Province**
AREA: **231,400 sq km (89,320 sq miles)**
POPULATION: **59,280,000**
CAPITAL: **Guangzhou (Canton)**

GUANGXI (KWANGSI-CHUANG)

STATUS: **Autonomous Region**
AREA: **220,400 sq km (85,075 sq miles)**
POPULATION: **63,210,000**
CAPITAL: **Nanning**

GUIZHOU (KWEICHOW)

STATUS: **Province**
AREA: **174,000 sq km (67,165 sq miles)**
POPULATION: **42,530,000**
CAPITAL: **Guiyang**

HAINAN

STATUS: **Province**
AREA: **34,965 sq km (13,500 sq miles)**
POPULATION: **6,420,000**
CAPITAL: **Haikou**

HEBEI (HOPEI)

STATUS: **Province**
AREA: **202,700 sq km (78,240 sq miles)**
POPULATION: **60,280,000**
CAPITAL: **Schijiazhuang**

HEILONGJIANG (HEILUNGKIANG)

STATUS: **Province**
AREA: **710,000 sq km (274,060 sq miles)**
POPULATION: **34,770,000**
CAPITAL: **Harbin**

HENAN (HONAN)

STATUS: **Province**
AREA: **167,000 sq km (64,460 sq miles)**
POPULATION: **86,140,000**
CAPITAL: **Zhengzhou**

HUBEI (HUPEH)

STATUS: **Province**
AREA: **187,500 sq km (72,375 sq miles)**
POPULATION: **54,760,000**
CAPITAL: **Wuhan**

HUNAN

STATUS: **Province**
AREA: **210,500 sq km (81,255 sq miles)**
POPULATION: **60,600,000**
CAPITAL: **Changsha**

JIANGSU (KIANGSU)

STATUS: **Province**
AREA: **102,200 sq km (39,450 sq miles)**
POPULATION: **68,170,000**
CAPITAL: **Nanjing (Nanking)**

JIANGXI (KIANGSI)

STATUS: **Province**
AREA: **164,800 sq km (63,615 sq miles)**
POPULATION: **38,280,000**
CAPITAL: **Nanchang**

JILIN (KIRIN)

STATUS: **Province**
AREA: **290,000 sq km (111,940 sq miles)**
POPULATION: **25,150,000**
CAPITAL: **Changchun**

LIAONING

STATUS: **Province**
AREA: **230,000 sq km (88,780 sq miles)**
POPULATION: **39,980,000**
CAPITAL: **Shenyang**

NEI MONGOL (INNER MONGOLIA)

STATUS: **Autonomous Region**
AREA: **450,000 sq km (173,700 sq miles)**
POPULATION: **21,110,000**
CAPITAL: **Hohhot**

NINGXIA HUI (NINGHSIA HUI)

STATUS: **Autonomous Region**
AREA: **170,000 sq km (65,620 sq miles)**
POPULATION: **4,660,000**
CAPITAL: **Yinchuan**

QINGHAI (CHINGHAI)

STATUS: **Province**
AREA: **721,000 sq km (278.305 sq miles)**
POPULATION: **4,430,000**
CAPITAL: **Xining**

SHAANXI (SHENSI)

STATUS: **Province**
AREA: **195,800 sq km (75,580 sq miles)**
POPULATION: **32,470,000**
CAPITAL: **Xian (Xi'an)**

SHANDONG (SHANTUNG)

STATUS: **Province**
AREA: **153,300 sq km (59,175 sq miles)**
POPULATION: **83,430,000**
CAPITAL: **Jinan**

SHANGHAI

STATUS: **Municipality**
AREA: **5,800 sq km (2,240 sq miles)**
POPULATION: **13,510,896**

SHANXI (SHANSI)

STATUS: **Province**
AREA: **157,100 sq km (60,640 sq miles)**
POPULATION: **28,180,000**
CAPITAL: **Taiyuan**

SICHUAN (SZECHWAN)

STATUS: **Province**
AREA: **569,000 sq km (219,635 sq miles)**
POPULATION: **106,370,000**
CAPITAL: **Chengdu**

TIANJIN (TIENTSIN)

STATUS: **Municipality**
AREA: **4,000 sq km (1,545 sq miles)**
POPULATION: **8,830,402**

XINJIANG UYGUR (SINKIANG-UIGHUR)

STATUS: **Autonomous Region**
AREA: **1,646,800 sq km (635,665 sq miles)**
POPULATION: **15,370,000**
CAPITAL: **Urumchi (Ürümqi)**

XIZANG (TIBET)

STATUS: **Autonomous Region**
AREA: **1,221,600 sq km (471,540 sq miles)**
POPULATION: **2,220,000**
CAPITAL: **Lhasa**

YUNNAN

STATUS: **Province**
AREA: **436,200 sq km (168,375 sq miles)**
POPULATION: **36,750,000**
CAPITAL: **Kunming**

ZHEJIANG (CHEKIANG)

STATUS: **Province**
AREA: **101,800 sq km (39,295 sq miles)**
POPULATION: **40,840,000**
CAPITAL: **Hangzhou**

CHRISTMAS ISLAND

STATUS: **External Territory of Australia**
AREA: **135 sq km (52 sq miles)**
POPULATION: **1,275**

COCOS (KEELING) ISLAND

STATUS: **External Territory of Australia**
AREA: **14 sq km (5 sq miles)**
POPULATION: **647**

COLOMBIA

STATUS: **Republic**
AREA: **1,138,915 (439,620 sq miles)**
POPULATION: **33,391,000**
ANNUAL NATURAL INCREASE: **1.8%**
CAPITAL: **Bogotá**
LANGUAGE: **Spanish, Indian languages**
RELIGION: **95% Roman Catholic, Protestant and Jewish minorities**
CURRENCY: **Colombian peso (COP)**
ORGANIZATIONS: **OAS, UN**

Colombia is twice the size of France in geographical area. In the west are the northernmost peaks of the Andes. Beyond these extend the low plains, with many rivers. Bogotá, the capital, lies on the high plateau east of the Andes. Further east lie the prairies and southwards the jungle of the Amazon. Colombia has a tropical climate. Temperatures vary with altitude. The fertile river valleys in the uplands produce most of the famous Colombian coffee. Bananas, tobacco, cotton, sugar and rice are grown at lower altitudes. Manufacturing industries and the mining of coal, iron ore, copper and precious stones are becoming more dominant, along with British Petroleum's recent dramatic oil find at Cusiana. Immense quantities of cocaine are illegally exported to the USA and elsewhere.

COMOROS

STATUS: **Federal Islamic Republic**
AREA: **1,860 sq km (718 sq miles)**
POPULATION: **585,000**
ANNUAL NATURAL INCREASE: **3.7%**
CAPITAL: **Moroni**
LANGUAGE: **French, Arabic, Comoran**
RELIGION: **Muslim majority, Christian minority**
CURRENCY: **Comoro franc (KMF)**
ORGANIZATIONS: **OAU, UN**

The Comoros Islands, comprising Mwali, Njazidja and Nzwani, are situated between Madagascar and the east African coast. The climate is humid all the year round with a moderate rainfall, averaging 1,000–1,140 mm (40–45 inches) per year. Less than half of the land is cultivated, and the country is dependent on imports for food supplies. The main cash crops are vanilla, cloves and ylang-ylang, an essence extracted from trees and exported to France for the perfume industry. Timber and timber products are also important to local development. There is no manufacturing of any importance.

CONGO

STATUS: **Republic**
AREA: **342,000 sq km (132,010 sq miles)**
POPULATION: **2,368,000**
ANNUAL NATURAL INCREASE: **3.3%**
CAPITAL: **Brazzaville**
LANGUAGE: **French, Kongo, Teke, Sanga**
RELIGION: **50% traditional beliefs, 30% Roman Catholic, Protestant and Muslim minorities**
CURRENCY: **CFA franc (C Africa) (XAF)**
ORGANIZATIONS: **OAU, UN**

The country is for the most part forest or savannah-covered plateaux drained by the Oubangui and Zaire river systems. Its coast is lined with sand dunes and lagoons. Congo has a hot tropical climate. Over 60 per cent of the population are employed in subsistence farming, the main crops being plantains, maize and cassava, while coffee, groundnuts and cocoa are all exported. Timber and timber products account for 60 per cent of all Congo's exports. Its mineral resources are considerable and include industrial diamonds, gold, lead, zinc and extensive coastal oilfields. Manufacturing industry is concentrated in major towns and is primarily food processing and textiles.

COOK ISLANDS

STATUS: **Self-governing Territory Overseas in Free Association with New Zealand**
AREA: **233 sq km (90 sq miles)**
POPULATION: **19,000**
CAPITAL: **Avarua on Rarotonga**

CORAL SEA ISLANDS

STATUS: **External Territory of Australia**
AREA: **22 sq km (8.5 sq miles)**
POPULATION: **no permanent population**

COSTA RICA

STATUS: **Republic**
AREA: **50,900 sq km (19,650 sq miles)**
POPULATION: **3,099,000**
ANNUAL NATURAL INCREASE: **2.5%**
CAPITAL: **San José**
LANGUAGE: **Spanish**
RELIGION: **95% Roman Catholic**
CURRENCY: **Costa Rican colón (CRC)**
ORGANIZATIONS: **CACM, OAS, UN**

Costa Rica is comprised of coastal plains, narrow on the Pacific side but broader towards the Caribbean, rising to a central plateau which leads to a range of mountains running the length of the country. Volcanic peaks in this range exceed 3,500 m (11,500 ft). Coastal regions experience hot, humid tropical conditions, but the climate on the plateau is more equable. The mountain chains that run the length of the country form the fertile uplands where coffee (one of the main crops and exports) and cattle flourish. Bananas are grown on the Pacific coast. Although gold, silver, iron ore and bauxite are mined, the principal industries are the manufacture of textiles and chemicals, fertilizers and furniture.

CROATIA

STATUS: **Republic**
AREA: **56,540 sq km (21,825 sq miles)**
POPULATION: **4,726,000**
ANNUAL NATURAL INCREASE: **0.4%**
CAPITAL: **Zagreb**
LANGUAGE: **Serbo-Croat**
RELIGION: **Roman Catholic majority**
CURRENCY: **kuna**
ORGANIZATIONS: **UN**

Croatia is an oddly shaped country, which runs in a narrow strip along the Adriatic coast and extends inland in a broad curve. Along its coastal strip a series of limestone ridges run parallel to the sea. Central parts around Zagreb are hilly, while in the east, Slavonia is a lowland plain. There is a contrast in climatic conditions between the Adriatic coast and inland regions. Coastal areas experience Mediterranean conditions and mild winters. The fertile plains of central and eastern Croatia are intensively farmed and provide the country with surplus crops, meat and dairy products. Croatia used to be the most highly developed part of the former Yugoslavia, concentrating on electrical engineering, metal working and machine-building, chemicals and rubber. However, the military conflict in 1991 over the right to secession and for control of Serbian areas of settlement, caused a great deal of harm to the economy. In the future, political stability and an accommodation with the Serbs will be vital to the country's economic recovery.

CUBA

STATUS: **Republic**
AREA: **114,525 sq km (44,205 sq miles)**
POPULATION: **10,870,000**
ANNUAL NATURAL INCREASE: **1.0%**
CAPITAL: **Havana (Habana)**
LANGUAGE: **Spanish**
RELIGION: **Roman Catholic majority**
CURRENCY: **Cuban peso (CUP)**
ORGANIZATIONS: **OIEC, UN**

Cuba, the largest island in the Caribbean, consists mostly of plains interrupted by three mountain ranges. Forests of pine and mahogany cover 23 per cent of the land. The temperature is hot throughout the year. Hurricanes sometimes threaten the country in autumn. Sugar, tobacco and nickel are the main exports. Manganese, chrome, copper and oil are also exported. Cuba has enough cattle and coffee for domestic use but many other food products are imported. The break-up of the USSR and the collapse of Communism have led to a major disruption of Cuba's trade relations and an end to aid packages. Since then Cuba has suffered a decline in production, fuel shortages, serious power cuts and food rationing. This has forced thousands of Cubans to escape to Florida by boat.

CURAÇAO

STATUS: **Self-governing Island of the Netherlands Antilles**
AREA: **444 sq km (171 sq miles)**
POPULATION: **707,000**

CYPRUS

STATUS: **Republic (Turkish unilateral declaration of independence in northern area)**
AREA: **9,250 sq km (3,570 sq miles)**
POPULATION: **725,000**
ANNUAL NATURAL INCREASE: **1.1%**
CAPITAL: **Nicosia**
LANGUAGE: **Greek, Turkish, English**
RELIGION: **Greek Orthodox majority, Muslim minority**
CURRENCY: **Cyprus pound (CYP), Turkish Lira (TL)**
ORGANIZATIONS: **Comm., Council of Europe, UN**

The Troödos mountains dominate the centre-west of the island. To the east is the fertile plain of Messaoria, flanked by hills to the northeast. The Mediterranean climate gives Cyprus hot summers and mild winters. Rainfall generally occurs in the winter months. About two thirds of the island is under cultivation and produces citrus fruit, potatoes, barley, wheat and olives. Sheep, goats and pigs are the principal livestock. The main exports are minerals (including copper and asbestos), fruits, wine and vegetables. Most industry consists of local manufacturing (textiles, clothing, leather and shoes). Tourism is also an important source of foreign exchange, despite Turkish occupation of the north.

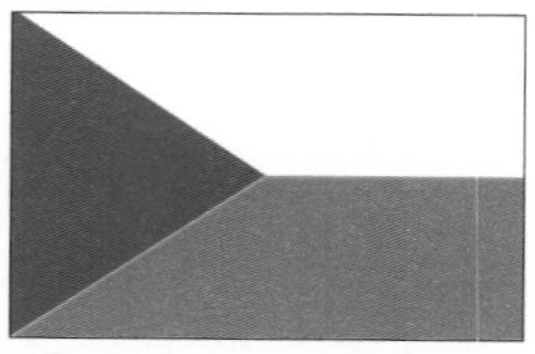

CZECH REPUBLIC

STATUS: **Federal Republic**
AREA: **127,870 sq km (49,360 sq miles)**
POPULATION: **10,330,000**
ANNUAL NATURAL INCREASE: **0.3%**
CAPITAL: **Prague (Praha)**
LANGUAGE: **Czech**
RELIGION: **40% Roman Catholic, 55% no stated religion**
CURRENCY: **Czech crown or koruna (CSK)**
ORGANIZATIONS: **Council of Europe, OIEC, UN**

The Czech Republic, in the heart of Europe, is a land of rolling countryside, wooded hills and fertile valleys. In Bohemia, to the west, the upper Elbe drainage basin, in the centre of which lies Prague, is surrounded by mountains. Moravia, separated from Bohemia by hills and mountains, is a lowland area centred on the town of Brno. The climate is temperate but with continental characteristics, featuring warm summers and relatively cold winters. The Czech Republic has long been one of the more advanced European economies, a position which it managed to retain through the communist period. It possesses valuable raw materials (coal, minerals and timber) and has a steel industry using cheap iron ore from the Ukraine. Although known for its production of cars, aircraft, tramways and locomotive diesel engines, traditionally the region has specialized in arms manufacture. The Czech economy faces difficulties exacerbated by separation from its neighbour, Slovakia, in 1993. Trade between the two, even though necessary to each, has declined.

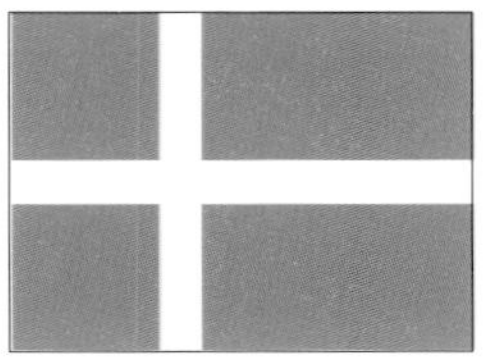

DENMARK

STATUS: **Kingdom**
AREA: **43,075 sq km (16,625 sq miles)**
POPULATION: **5,181,000**
ANNUAL NATURAL INCREASE: **0.1%**
CAPITAL: **Copenhagen (København)**
LANGUAGE: **Danish**
RELIGION: **94% Lutheran, Roman Catholic minority**
CURRENCY: **Danish krone (DKK)**
ORGANIZATIONS: **Council of Europe, EU, NATO, OECD, UN**

Denmark is the smallest of the Scandinavian countries. It consists of the Jutland peninsula and numerous small islands. The country is low-lying, with a mixture of fertile and sandy soils, generally of glacial origin. The climate is cool and temperate with rainfall spread fairly evenly throughout the year. Copenhagen has an average summer temperature of 20°C (68°F) with 0°C (32°F) in winter. The mainstay of the Danish economy is agriculture, in particular dairy products and bacon, much of which is exported to the UK and Germany. Oil and gas, beer and sugar are also exported. An extensive fishing industry is centred on the shallow lagoons of the indented western coastline. However, the fishing industry has recently had problems with over-fishing and disputes over quotas. Over 30 per cent of the total workforce are involved in industry, with manufactured goods being the main export. Manufacturing, developed in association with agriculture, includes machinery needed for the dairy industry and pharmaceutical products. Denmark has few mineral resources.

DJIBOUTI

STATUS: **Republic**
AREA: **23,000 sq km (8,800 sq miles)**
POPULATION: **467,000**
ANNUAL NATURAL INCREASE: **2.9%**
CAPITAL: **Djibouti**
LANGUAGE: **French, Somali, Dankali, Arabic**
RELIGION: **Muslim majority, Roman Catholic minority**
CURRENCY: **Djibouti franc (DJF)**
ORGANIZATIONS: **Arab League, OAU, UN**

Djibouti, a country about the size of Wales, consists almost entirely of low-lying desert, with some areas below sea level. To the north lies a mountainous area where the highest point, Musa Ālī Terara, reaches 2,063 m (6,768 ft). Temperatures are hot all year, between 25°and 35°C (78° and 96°F), although it is cooler between October and April. Cattle, hides and skins are the main exports. The port of Djibouti is an important transit point for Red Sea trade.

DOMINICA

STATUS: **Commonwealth State**
AREA: **751 sq km (290 sq miles)**
POPULATION: **72,000**
ANNUAL NATURAL INCREASE: **-0.3%**
CAPITAL: **Roseau**
LANGUAGE: **English, French patois**
RELIGION: **80% Roman Catholic**
CURRENCY: **East Caribbean dollar (XCD)**
ORGANIZATIONS: **Comm., OAS, UN**

Dominica, the largest of the Windward Islands, is mountainous and forested with a coastline of steep cliffs. Evidence of it s volcanic origin is provided by the presence of geysers and hot springs. The climate is tropical, with average temperatures exceeding 25°C (77°F) and abundant rainfall, especially in the summer months. Tropical rainforest covers the island, which obtains foreign revenue from sugarcane, bananas, coconuts, soap, vegetables and citrus fruits. Tourism is the most rapidly expanding industry.

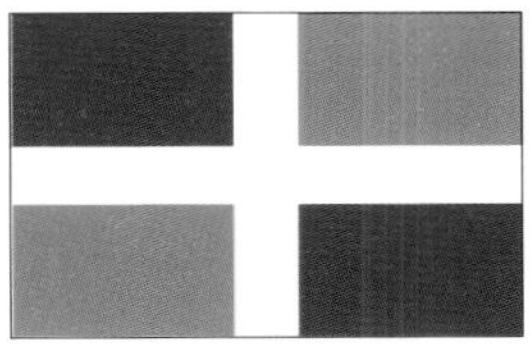

DOMINICAN REPUBLIC

STATUS: **Republic**
AREA: **48,440 sq km (18,700 sq miles)**
POPULATION: **7,471,000**
ANNUAL NATURAL INCREASE: **1.9%**
CAPITAL: **Santo Domingo**
LANGUAGE: **Spanish**
RELIGION: **90% Roman Catholic, Protestant and Jewish minorities**
CURRENCY: **Dominican peso (DOP)**
ORGANIZATIONS: **OAS, UN**

The country is one of relatively high mountains, fertile valleys and an extensive coastal plain in the east. The Dominican Republic has a hot tropical climate. Agriculture is the backbone of the economy; products include coffee, rice, tobacco, cocoa, fruit and vegetables. Gold, silver, nickel, bauxite and other minerals, but nickel in particular, account for over 40 per cent of the republic's merchandise exports.

ECUADOR

STATUS: **Republic**
AREA: **461,475 sq km (178,130 sq miles)**
POPULATION: **10,741,000**
ANNUAL NATURAL INCREASE: **2.5%**
CAPITAL: **Quito**
LANGUAGE: **Spanish, Quechua, other Indian languages**
RELIGION: **90% Roman Catholic**
CURRENCY: **sucre (ECS)**
ORGANIZATIONS: **OAS, UN**

Ecuador comprises three distinct physical zones: a broad coastal plain, the high ranges of the Andes, where peaks reach well over 6,000 m (20,000 ft), and the forested upper Amazon basin to the east. The territory also includes the Galapagos islands, nearly 1,000 km (620 miles) to the east. The climate is tropical. Ecuador's main agricultural exports are bananas, coffee and cocoa. The rapidly growing fishing industry, especially shrimps, is becoming more important. Large resources of crude oil have been found, and Ecuador is becoming South America's second largest oil producer. Mineral reserves include silver, gold, copper and zinc.

EGYPT

STATUS: **Republic**
AREA: **1,000,250 sq km (386,095 sq miles)**
POPULATION: **55,163,000**
ANNUAL NATURAL INCREASE: **2.4%**
CAPITAL: **Cairo (El Qâhira)**
LANGUAGE: **Arabic, Berber, Nubian, English, French**
RELIGION: **80% Muslim (mainly Sunni), Coptic Christian minority**
CURRENCY: **Egyptian pound (EGP)**
ORGANIZATIONS: **Arab league, OAU, UN**

Except for the Nile valley, Egypt is desert and semi-desert. The most rugged parts are in the Sinai peninsula, where Mt Katherine reaches 2,637 m (8,650 ft). The western desert, mostly plateau, falls to altitudes below sea level, as in the Qattara Depression. The climate is hot in summer and mild in winter. Rainfall is negligible everywhere, although a little occurs in winter along the Mediterranean coast. Cotton and Egyptian clover are the two most important crops, with agriculture being concentrated around the Nile floodplain and delta. In spite of this, however, Egypt has to import over half the food it needs. Buffalo, cattle, sheep, goats and camels are the principal livestock. Tolls from the Suez Canal are an important source of foreign revenue. Major manufactures include cement, cotton goods, iron and steel, and processed foods. The main mineral deposits are phosphates, iron ore, salt, manganese and chromium.

EL SALVADOR

STATUS: **Republic**
AREA: **21,395 sq km (8,260 sq miles)**
POPULATION: **5,048,000**
ANNUAL NATURAL INCREASE: **1.8%**
CAPITAL: **San Salvador**
LANGUAGE: **Spanish**
RELIGION: **80% Roman Catholic**
CURRENCY: **El Salvador colón (SVC)**
ORGANIZATIONS: **CACM, OAS, UN**

El Salvador features a Pacific coastal plain and inland mountain ranges of volcanic origin. The coastal plain is hot, with heavy summer rainfall, whereas the highlands enjoy a cooler, temperate climate. Coffee and cotton are important exports, and the country is the main producer of balsam. Industry has expanded considerably with the production of textiles, shoes, cosmetics, cement, processed foods, chemicals and furniture.

EQUATORIAL GUINEA

STATUS: **Republic**
AREA: **28,050 sq km (10,825 sq miles)**
POPULATION: **369,000**
ANNUAL NATURAL INCREASE: **2.3%**
CAPITAL: **Malabo**
LANGUAGE: **85% Fang, Spanish, Bubi, other tribal languages**
RELIGION: **96% Roman Catholic, 4% Animist**
CURRENCY: **CFA franc (C Africa) (XAF)**
ORGANIZATIONS: **OAU, UN**

Equatorial Guinea consists of the island of Bioko and the mainland region of Río Muni. The hot and humid climate has heavy rainfall all year round. Agriculture is the principal source of revenue. Cocoa and coffee from the island plantations are the main exports with wood products, fish and processed foods. An oil production and exploration industry, begun in 1992–3, could transform the economy, but the country still depends heavily on foreign aid.

ERITREA

STATUS: **Republic**
AREA: **91,600 sq km (35,370 sq miles)**
POPULATION: **2,853,000**
CAPITAL: **Asmara (Āsmera)**
LANGUAGE: **Arabic, native languages, English**
RELIGION: **50% Christian, 50% Muslim**
CURRENCY: **Ethiopian birr**
ORGANIZATIONS: **OAU, UN**

Eritrea gained its independence from Ethiopia in 1993. Its northern regions are an extension of the Ethiopian high plateau. Southwards the coastal plain widens and forms part of the great Rift Valley. The coast is hot but temperatures are much lower inland. Rainfall is unreliable. Agriculture remains a priority, but 80 per cent of the harvest was lost in 1993.

STATES AND TERRITORIES OF THE WORLD

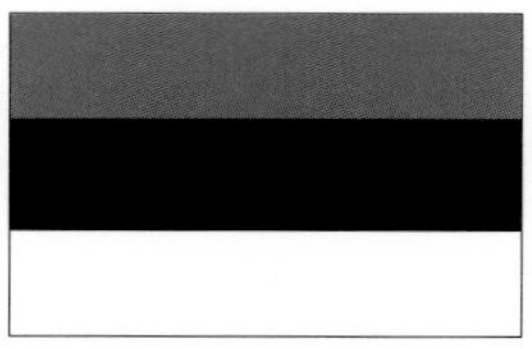

ESTONIA

STATUS: **Republic**
AREA: **45,100 sq km (17,413 sq miles)**
POPULATION: **1,181,000**
ANNUAL NATURAL INCREASE: **0.2%**
CAPITAL: **Tallinn**
LANGUAGE: **Estonian, Russian**
RELIGION: **Lutheran, Roman Catholic**
CURRENCY: **kroon**
ORGANIZATIONS: **Council of Europe, UN**

Estonia is situated on the southern coast of the Gulf of Finland. Its flat or undulating landscape, one third of which is forested, is generally low-lying with numerous lakes. There are about 800 islands. The climate is temperate with warm summers, cold winters and a heavy rainfall of 500–700 mm (20–28 inches) evenly distributed throughout the year. Apart from its forests and rich oil-shale deposits, there are few natural resources in Estonia. The land is difficult to farm, and agriculture, mainly livestock and dairying, accounts for less than 20 per cent of the gross national product. Industries include timber, furniture production, shipbuilding, leather, fur and food processing. The economy is currently undergoing a transformation from central planning and state ownership to a free market system based on private enterprise. Incorporated into the former Soviet Union in 1940, Estonia regained its independence in 1991.

ETHIOPIA

STATUS: **Republic**
AREA: **1,023,050 sq km (394,895 sq miles)**
POPULATION: **52,264,000**
ANNUAL NATURAL INCREASE: **3.4%**
CAPITAL: **Addis Ababa (Ādīs Ābeba)**
LANGUAGE: **Amharic, English, Arabic**
RELIGION: **Ethiopian Orthodox, Muslim and animist**
CURRENCY: **birr (ETB)**
ORGANIZATIONS: **OAU, UN**

Western Ethiopia, including the Tigray plateau and the Semien Mountains, is a mountainous region of mainly volcanic origin traversed from northeast to southwest by the great Rift Valley. Eastern Ethiopia is mostly arid plateaux. Highland regions have warm climates and, although droughts occur, in normal years rain falls in summer months in appreciable quantities. Eastern Ethiopia is hot and generally dry. Drought and starvation are perennial problems. Partly because of improved rainy seasons, agriculture has improved dramatically, but there are still areas of malnutrition and considerable food aid is necessary. The most important industries are cotton textiles, cement, canned foods, construction material and leather goods.

FAEROES

STATUS: **Self-governing Island Region of Denmark**
AREA: **1,399 sq km (540 sq miles)**
POPULATION: **47,000**
CAPITAL: **Tórshavn**

FALKLAND ISLANDS

STATUS: **UK Crown Colony**
AREA: **12,175 sq km (4,700 sq miles)**
POPULATION: **2,121**
CAPITAL: **Stanley**

FIJI

STATUS: **Republic**
AREA: **18,330 sq km (7,075 sq miles)**
POPULATION: **758,000**
ANNUAL NATURAL INCREASE: **1.8%**
CAPITAL: **Suva**
LANGUAGE: **Fijian, English, Hindi**
RELIGION: **51% Methodist Christian, 40% Hindu, 8% Muslim**
CURRENCY: **Fiji dollar (FJD)**
ORGANIZATIONS: **Col. Plan, UN**

Fiji comprises over 300 islands ranging from tiny atolls to the two largest, Vanua Levu and Viti Levu, which are of volcanic origin and mountainous. The smaller islands are mainly comprised of coral reefs. The climate is tropical, with a rainy season from December to April. Fiji's economy is geared to production of sugarcane, coconut oil, bananas and rice. Gold mining and tourism are other important industries, while timber and fish, especially tuna, are increasing rapidly in importance. Livestock include cattle, goats, pigs and poultry.

FINLAND

STATUS: **Republic**
AREA: **337,030 sq km (130,095 sq miles)**
POPULATION: **5,076,000**
ANNUAL NATURAL INCREASE: **0.4%**
CAPITAL: **Helsinki**
LANGUAGE: **Finnish, Swedish**
RELIGION: **87% Evangelical Lutheran, Eastern Orthodox minority**
CURRENCY: **markka (Finnmark) (FIM)**
ORGANIZATIONS: **Council of Europe, EEA, EFTA, OECD, UN**

In Finland forests cover 70 per cent of the land area and water another 10 per cent. The Saimaa lake area is Europe's largest inland water system. Summers are short but quite warm. Winters are long and severe and in the north the days are sunless. The sea freezes for several miles out from the coast during the severe winters. Because of the harsh northern climate most of the population live in towns in the far south. Forestry products (timber, wood pulp, paper and furniture), are Finland's main exports, although engineering, in particular shipbuilding and forest machinery, is increasing in importance. Manufacturing has been developing in recent years. Finland is virtually self-sufficient in basic foodstuffs such as dairy products, grain and root crops. The country depends heavily on energy imports, producing only 30 per cent of its total consumption (20 per cent by its four nuclear power stations). Independence was gained from Russia during the 1917 revolution. In that time it has had more than 60 governments. In international affairs Finland maintains a strict neutrality.

FRANCE

STATUS: **Republic**
AREA: **543,965 sq km (209,970 sq miles)**
POPULATION: **57,372,000**
ANNUAL NATURAL INCREASE: **0.6%**
CAPITAL: **Paris**
LANGUAGE: **French**
RELIGION: **90% Roman Catholic. Protestant, Muslim, Jewish minorities**
CURRENCY: **French franc (FRF)**
ORGANIZATIONS: **Council of Europe, EEA, EU, G7, NATO, OECD, UN, WEU**

The physiography of France encompasses a considerable variation in landscapes, ranging from the high peaks of the Alps and the Pyrenees to the flat plains of the north, the lowlands of the west coast, the granite moors of Brittany and the bleak massif of central France. The French climate is moderated by proximity to the Atlantic. The north is temperate but in the south the regime is Mediterranean with warm, dry summers and mild winters with some rainfall. Much of the French countryside is agricultural. It is estimated that one quarter of the workforce derives an income from agricultural pursuits, whether from the huge sugarbeet estates in the northeast, the small farms in Brittany or smallholdings in the Pyrenees. This tradition in agriculture has given rise to the world famous French cuisine. France is self-sufficient in cereals, dairy products, meat, fruit and vegetables, and a leading exporter of wheat, barley and sugarbeet. Wine is also a major export. Over the past years there has been a steady drift of labour, mainly young people, from the land to the urban, industrialized areas. France is the fourth industrial power in the world after the USA, Japan and Germany. It has reserves of coal, oil and natural gas, and its supplies of iron ore make France one of the world's leading producers. Its industries include iron and steel, chemicals, vehicles, aeronautics and armaments as well as food processing and electronics. Leading light industries include fashion, perfumes and luxury goods. Energy has been provided by reserves of coal, oil and natural gas but in recent years other sources of energy have increased in importance, such as tidal power at the Rrance estuary in Brittany, hydro-electric power in the mountains and nuclear energy using uranium from French mines. Most of its heavy industry is concentrated in the major industrial zone of the northeast. Tourism is important and will be encouraged further with the opening of the Channel Tunnel. In international politics France has traditionally adopted a fiercely independent role. It maintains its own nuclear deterrent as a cornerstone of that independence.

FRANZ JOSEF LAND

STATUS: **Islands of Russian Federation**
AREA: **16,575 sq km (6,400 sq miles)**
POPULATION: **unknown**

FRENCH GUIANA

STATUS: **Overseas Department of France**
AREA: **91,000 sq km (35,125 sq miles)**
POPULATION: **114,808**
CAPITAL: **Cayenne**

FRENCH POLYNESIA

STATUS: **Overseas Territory of France**
AREA: **3,940 sq km (1,520 sq miles)**
POPULATION: **188,814**
CAPITAL: **Papeete**

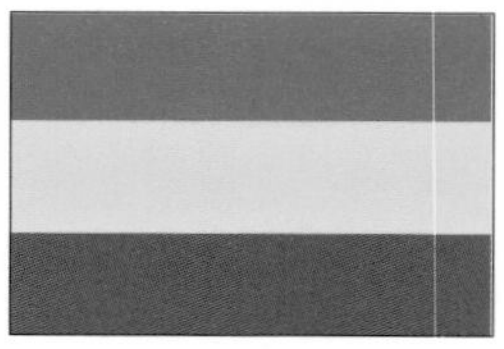

GABON

STATUS: **Republic**
AREA: **267,665 sq km (103,320 sq miles)**
POPULATION: **1,012,000**
ANNUAL NATURAL INCREASE: **2.7%**
CAPITAL: **Libreville**
LANGUAGE: **French, Bantu dialects, Fang**
RELIGION: **60% Roman Catholic.**
CURRENCY: **CFA franc (C Africa) (XAF)**
ORGANIZATIONS: **OAU, OPEC, UN**

Beyond the coastal strip, Gabon is a country of low plateaux of which approximately 75 per cent is forest covered. The climate is hot and tropical. Rainfall is heavy for most of the year but there is a pronounced dry season from June to August. Agriculture contributes little to the economy; most farming is subsistence. There are state-run plantations growing oil palms, bananas, sugarcane and rubber. Timber is an important export commodity. Gabon is one of the most prosperous states in Africa, largely due to its valuable mineral resources, oil, manganese and uranium. France supplies nearly half the country's total imports and French influence is evident everywhere.

GALAPAGOS ISLANDS

STATUS: **Archipelago Province of Ecuador**
AREA: **7,845 sq km (3,030 sq miles)**
POPULATION: **7,954**

GAMBIA, THE

STATUS: **Republic**
AREA: **10,690 sq km (4,125 sq miles)**
POPULATION: **1,026,000**
ANNUAL NATURAL INCREASE: **3.2%**
CAPITAL: **Banjul**
LANGUAGE: **English, Madinka, Fula, Wolof**
RELIGION: **90% Muslim, Christian and animist minorities**
CURRENCY: **dalasi (GMD)**
ORGANIZATIONS: **Comm., ECOWAS, OAU, UN**

The Gambia occupies a low-lying strip of territory, 470 km (292 miles) long, bordering the river of the same name. Nowhere is the territory wider than 50 km (30 miles). Long sandy beaches are backed by mangrove swamps along the river, beyond which is savannah and tropical woods. Two distinct seasons are evident: a warm dry season from November to mid-May and the rainy humid months from July to October. Groundnuts and subsidiary products are the mainstay of the economy but tourism is developing rapidly. The production of cotton, livestock, fish and rice is increasing to change the present economic reliance on groundnuts.

GEORGIA

STATUS: **Republic**
AREA: **69,700 sq km (26,905 sq miles)**
POPULATION: **5,471,000**
ANNUAL NATURAL INCREASE: **0.5%**
CAPITAL: **Tbilisi**
LANGUAGE: **70% Georgian, 8% Armenian, 6% Russian, 6% Azeri**
RELIGION: **Orthodox Christian**
CURRENCY: **coupon**
ORGANIZATIONS: **CIS**

Georgia is mountainous country, dominated by the Great Caucasus (Bol'shoy Kavkaz) and Little Caucasus (Malyy Kavkaz) mountain ranges, which are separated by the Kura valley. The main lowland area is along the Black Sea coast. The climate is generally warm, except where modified by altitude, with most rain falling in western regions. Agricultural land is in short supply. This is partly compensated by the cultivation of labour-intensive and profitable crops such as tea, grapes, tobacco and citrus fruit. Georgia lacks energy resources although it has reserves of coal so far unexploited. Many Georgians live in poverty and the numbers of impoverished people have increased with the thousands of refugees who fled Abkhazia during recent unrest. The potential for recovery is dependent upon political stability.

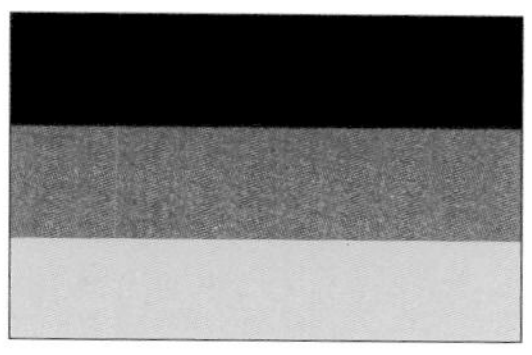

GERMANY

STATUS: **Federal Republic**
AREA: **356,840 sq km (137,740 sq miles)**
POPULATION: **81,980,000**
ANNUAL NATURAL INCREASE: **0.6%**
CAPITAL: **Berlin (seat of government Berlin/Bonn)**
LANGUAGE: **German**
RELIGION: **45% Protestant 40% Roman Catholic**
CURRENCY: **Deutsch mark (DM)**
ORGANIZATIONS: **Council of Europe, EEA, EU, G7, NATO, OECD, UN, WEU**

The northern plain of Germany, extending across the breadth of the country is a mixture of fertile farmland and sandy heaths. The uplands of the south include the Black Forest (Schwarzwald), the Swabian (Schwäbische Alb) and the Bavarian Alps (Bayerische Alpen). The climate is temperate, with continental tendencies in eastern parts where winters are colder. Rainfall is spread evenly throughout the year. Politically, the division of Germany, a product of the post-1945 Cold War between the victorious Allies against Hitler, was rapidly overcome after the collapse of communism in Eastern Europe, and the unification of the two German states was effected in 1990. In the west the Ruhr basin, historically the industrial heartland of Germany, with an emphasis on coal mining and iron and steel works, has long since been overtaken by more advanced industries elsewhere, notably in the Rhine-Main area and further south in the regions around Stuttgart and Munich. The rapidly expanding services sector apart, the German economy is now dominated by the chemical, pharmaceutical, mechanical engineering, motor and high-tech industries. To lessen the country's dependence on oil imports, an ambitious nuclear energy programme has been adopted. Although poor in minerals and other raw materials, with the exception of lignite and potash, Germany has managed to become one of the world's leading manufacturers and exporters of machine tools, electrical and electronic products and consumer goods of various descriptions, in particular textiles. But the massive balance of trade surplus West Germany used to enjoy has now disappeared due to the sucking in of imports by, and the redistribution of output to, the newly acquired territories in the east.

BADEN-WÜRTTEMBERG

STATUS: **State (land)**
AREA: **35,730 sq km (13,790 sq miles)**
POPULATION: **9,400,000**
CAPITAL: **Stuttgart**

BAYERN (BAVARIA)

STATUS: **State (land)**
AREA: **70,545 sq km (27,230 sq miles)**
POPULATION: **11,000,000**
CAPITAL: **Munich (München)**

BERLIN

STATUS: **State (land)**
AREA: **883 sq km (341 sq miles)**
POPULATION: **3,400,000**
CAPITAL: **Berlin**

BRANDENBURG

STATUS: **State (land)**
AREA: **29,059 sq km (11,220 sq miles)**
POPULATION: **2,700,000**
CAPITAL: **Potsdam**

BREMEN

STATUS: **State (land) City Territory**
AREA: **404 sq km (156 sq miles)**
POPULATION: **700,000**
CAPITAL: **Bremen**

HAMBURG

STATUS: **State (land) City Territory**
AREA: **755 sq km (291 sq miles)**
POPULATION: **1,600,000**
CAPITAL: **Hamburg**

HESSEN (HESSE)

STATUS: **State (land)**
AREA: **21,115 sq km (8,150 sq miles)**
POPULATION: **5,600,000**
CAPITAL: **Wiesbaden**

MECKLENBURG-VORPOMMERN

STATUS: **State (land)**
AREA: **23,838 sq km (9,204 sq miles)**
POPULATION: **2,100,000**
CAPITAL: **Schwerin**

NIEDERSACHSEN (LOWER SAXONY)

STATUS: **State (land)**
AREA: **47,425 sq km (18,305 sq miles)**
POPULATION: **7,200,000**
CAPITAL: **Hanover (Hannover)**

NORDRHEIN-WESTFALEN

STATUS: **State (land)**
AREA: **34,070 sq km (13,150 sq miles)**
POPULATION: **16,900,000**
CAPITAL: **Düsseldorf**

RHEINLAND-PFALZ

STATUS: **State (land)**
AREA: **19,840 sq km (7,660 sq miles)**
POPULATION: **3,700,000**
CAPITAL: **Mainz**

SAARLAND

STATUS: **State (land)**
AREA: **2,575 sq km (994 sq miles)**
POPULATION: **1,100,000**
CAPITAL: **Saarbrucken**

SACHSEN (SAXONY)

STATUS: **State (land)**
AREA: **18,337 sq km (7,080 sq miles)**
POPULATION: **4,900,000**
CAPITAL: **Dresden**

SACHSEN-ANHALT (SAXONY-ANHALT)

STATUS: **State (land)**
AREA: **20,445 sq km (7,894 sq miles)**
POPULATION: **3,000,000**
CAPITAL: **Halle**

SCHLESWIG-HOLSTEIN

STATUS: **State (land)**
AREA: **15,710 sq km (6,065 sq miles)**
POPULATION: **2,600,000**
CAPITAL: **Kiel**

THÜRINGEN (THURINGIA)

STATUS: **State (land)**
AREA: **16,251 sq km (6,275 sq miles)**
POPULATION: **2,500,000**
CAPITAL: **Erfurt**

GHANA

STATUS: **Republic**
AREA: **238,305 sq km (91,985 sq miles)**
POPULATION: **15,959,000**
ANNUAL NATURAL INCREASE: **3.3%**
CAPITAL: **Accra**
LANGUAGE: **English, tribal languages**
RELIGION: **42% Christian**
CURRENCY: **cedi (GHC)**
ORGANIZATIONS: **Comm., ECOWAS, OAU, UN**

Western Ghana is covered by dense rainforest. The terrain becomes hillier to the north, culminating in a plateau averaging some 500 m (1,600 ft). The climate is tropical with temperatures in the range 21–32°C (70–90°F). The average rainfall is 2,000 mm (80 inches) on the coast, less inland. The coastal climate has no real seasonal variation. Cocoa is the principal crop and chief export. There is also a thriving industrial base around Tema, the largest artificial harbour in Africa, where local bauxite is smelted into aluminium. Other exports include gold and diamonds, and principal imports are fuel and manufactured goods.

GIBRALTAR

STATUS: **UK Crown Colony**
AREA: **6.5 sq km (2.5 sq miles)**
POPULATION: **31,000**

GREECE

STATUS: **Republic**
AREA: **131,985 sq km (50,945 sq miles)**
POPULATION: **10,269,074**
ANNUAL NATURAL INCREASE: **0.4%**
CAPITAL: **Athens (Athínai)**
LANGUAGE: **Greek**
RELIGION: **97% Greek Orthodox**
CURRENCY: **drachma (GRD)**
ORGANIZATIONS: **Council of Europe, EC, NATO, OECD, UN**

Greece is mountainous and over one fifth of its area is comprised of numerous islands, 154 of which are inhabited. The climate is predominantly Mediterranean, with hot, dry summers and mild, wet winters. The mountains experience some heavy snowfalls. Poor irrigation and drainage mean that much of the agriculture is localized, but the main crop, olives, is exported and agricultural output generally is increasing. Products include fruit, vegetables, cotton, tobacco, olives, wine and cheese. The surrounding seas are important, providing two-thirds of Greece's fish and supporting an active merchant fleet. Athens is the manufacturing base and at least one quarter of the population lives there. Greece is a very popular tourist destination, which helps the craft industries in textiles, metals and ceramics and other local products. The war in neighbouring former Yugoslavia, together with the UN embargo on trade with Serbia, has lost Greece an important market. The closed frontier has also made it necessary to use new routes into Europe which are longer and costlier.

STATES AND TERRITORIES OF THE WORLD

GREENLAND
STATUS: **Self-governing Island Region of Denmark**
AREA: **2,175,600 sq km (836,780 sq miles)**
POPULATION: **55,558**
CAPITAL: **Godthåb (Nuuk)**

GRENADA
STATUS: **Commonwealth State**
AREA: **345 sq km (133 sq miles)**
POPULATION: **91,000**
ANNUAL NATURAL INCREASE: **-0.2%**
CAPITAL: **St George's**
LANGUAGE: **English, French patois**
RELIGION: **Roman Catholic majority**
CURRENCY: **E Caribbean dollar (XCD)**
ORGANIZATIONS: **Caricom, Comm., OAS, UN**

Grenada, whose territory includes the southern Grenadines, has a climate that is warm throughout the year. Rainfall is plentiful, mostly falling in summer. Agriculture is the main source of income, the most important crop being nutmeg. Other major crops are citrus fruits, bananas and cocoa. Tourism has increased generally and is now a potentially important revenue earner. Some light industries, such as furniture, garment and soft drinks production, have been developed.

GUADELOUPE
STATUS: **Overseas Department of France**
AREA: **1,780 sq km (687 sq miles)**
POPULATION: **400,000**
CAPITAL: **Basse-Terre**

GUAM
STATUS: **External Territory of USA**
AREA: **450 sq km (174 sq miles)**
POPULATION: **132,726**
CAPITAL: **Agaña**

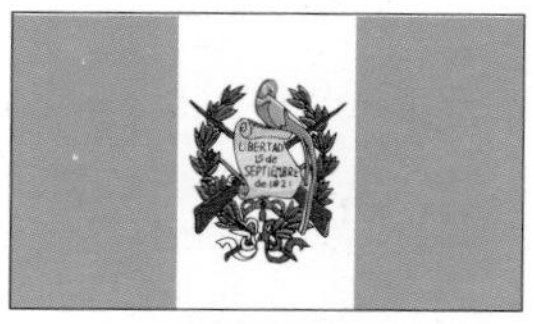

GUATEMALA
STATUS: **Republic**
AREA: **108,890 sq km (42,030 sq miles)**
POPULATION: **9,745,000**
ANNUAL NATURAL INCREASE: **2.9%**
CAPITAL: **Guatemala City (Guatemala)**
LANGUAGE: **Spanish, Indian languages**
RELIGION: **75% Roman Catholic, 25% Protestant**
CURRENCY: **quetzal (GTQ)**
ORGANIZATIONS: **CACM, OAS, UN**

Northern parts of Guatemala are lowland tropical forests. To the south lie high mountain ranges with volcanic peaks, some of which are active. A coastal plain borders the Pacific. The northern lowlands and the Pacific coastal strip have a hot tropical climate, but the central highlands are cooler. Rainfall is heaviest in summer. Agricultural products, notably sugarcane and bananas form the bulk of Guatemala's exports. Mineral resources including nickel, antimony, lead, silver and in the north crude oil, are only just beginning to be exploited. Manufacturing industry includes textiles, paper and pharmaceuticals.

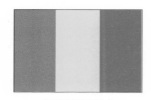

GUINEA
STATUS: **Republic**
AREA: **245,855 sq km (94,900 sq miles)**
POPULATION: **6,116,000**
ANNUAL NATURAL INCREASE: **2.8%**
CAPITAL: **Conakry**
LANGUAGE: **French, Susu, Manika**
RELIGION: **85% Muslim 10% animist, 5% Roman Catholic**
CURRENCY: **Guinea franc (GNF)**
ORGANIZATIONS: **ECOWAS, OAU, UN**

Guinea, a former French colony, is situated on the West African coast. Mangrove swamps are found along the coastal plains. Highlands dominate Guinea in the south, with further mountains and plateaux in the west. In the east savannah plains are drained by the upper Niger river system. The climate is tropical, the coastal zones experiencing heavy rainfall of around 4,369 mm (172 inches) annually, falling mainly between June and October. Agriculture occupies 80 per cent of the workforce, the main exports being coffee, bananas, pineapple and palm products. Guinea has some of the largest resources of bauxite (aluminium ore) in the world as well as gold and diamonds. Both bauxite and aluminium are exported.

GUINEA-BISSAU
STATUS: **Republic**
AREA: **36,125 sq km (13,945 sq miles)**
POPULATION: **1,006,000**
ANNUAL NATURAL INCREASE: **1.9%**
CAPITAL: **Bissau**
LANGUAGE: **Portuguese, Creole, Guinean dialects**
RELIGION: **Animist and Muslim majority, Roman Catholic minority**
CURRENCY: **Guinea-Bissau peso (GWP)**
ORGANIZATIONS: **ECOWS, OAU, UN**

Guinea-Bissau encompasses the Bijagos archipelago. The terrain is generally lowlying, with numerous estuaries and swamps. The plains inland are thickly forested, while to the east there are savannah plateaux. The climate is tropical. Eighty per cent of the country's exports consist of groundnuts, groundnut oil, palm kernels, palm oil and cashews. Fish, fish products, coconuts and tobacco also make an important contribution to trade. Many industries have yet to be developed; there are untapped reserves of phosphates and bauxite, and also offshore oil. However, Guinea-Bissau still relies heavily on foreign aid.

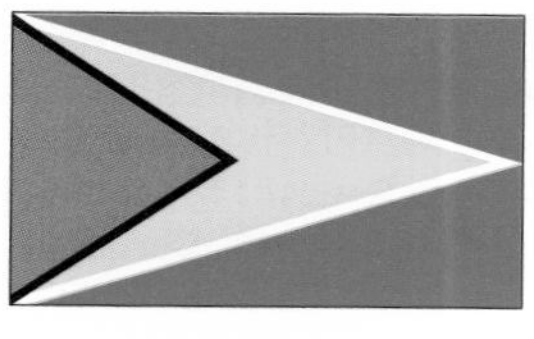

GUYANA
STATUS: **Co-operative Republic**
AREA: **214,970 sq km (82,980 sq miles)**
POPULATION: **808,000**
ANNUAL NATURAL INCREASE: **0.3%**
CAPITAL: **Georgetown**
LANGUAGE: **English, Hindi, Urdu, Amerindian dialects**
RELIGION: **Christian majority, Muslim and Hindu minorities**
CURRENCY: **Guyana dollar (GYD)**
ORGANIZATIONS: **Caricom, Comm., UN**

Guyana, formerly British Guiana, gained independence from Britain in 1966 and became a republic in 1970. Beyond its lowland coastal belt, the most densely populated area, the land rises inland to high savannah uplands and forested mountains. The climate is tropical with hot, wet and humid conditions, which are modified along the coast by sea breezes. Agriculture is dominated by the production of sugar and rice. Molasses and rum are also exported, but these have declined in importance in recent years. Guyana has considerable mineral wealth, and mining activities are beginning to be expanded. Bauxite and gold are the main mineral reserves.

HAITI
STATUS: **Republic**
AREA: **27,750 sq km (10,710 sq miles)**
POPULATION: **6,764,000**
ANNUAL NATURAL INCREASE: **2.0%**
CAPITAL: **Port-au-Prince**
LANGUAGE: **French, Creole**
RELIGION: **80% Roman Catholic, Voodoo folk religion minority**
CURRENCY: **gourde (HTG)**
ORGANIZATIONS: **OAS, UN**

Haiti, occupying western Hispaniola, is a mountainous and forested country. Temperatures are consistently high in coastal areas but become cooler with altitude. Agriculture is restricted to the plains which divide the ranges. Ninety per cent of the workforce are farmers, and coffee is the main export. There is little heavy industry, but some light manufacturing is concentrated around the capital. Violations of the human rights of the population and civil unrest have led to United Nations trade embargoes and the withholding of foreign aid. The economy has thus suffered severely. Vast numbers of Haitians have fled the country to seek refuge in the USA from starvation and persecution.

HEARD AND McDONALD ISLANDS
STATUS: **External Territory of Australia**
AREA: **412 sq km (159 sq miles)**
POPULATION: **no permanent population**
CAPITAL: **Edmonton**

HISPANIOLA
STATUS: **Island of the West Indies comprising Haiti and Dominican Republic**
AREA: **76,190 sq km (29,400 sq miles)**
POPULATION: **13,656,000**

HOKKAIDO
STATUS: **Island of Japan**
AREA: **78,460 sq km (30,285 sq miles)**
POPULATION: **5,671,000**

HONDURAS
STATUS: **Republic**
AREA: **112,085 sq km (43,265 sq miles)**
POPULATION: **5,462,000**
ANNUAL NATURAL INCREASE **3.1%**
CAPITAL: **Tegucigalpa**
LANGUAGE: **Spanish, Indian dialects**
RELIGION: **Roman Catholic majority**
CURRENCY: **lempira (HNL) or peso**
ORGANIZATIONS: **CACM, OAS, UN**

The terrain is rugged and mountainous. The lowland areas are along the Caribbean and Pacific coasts. Coastal regions are hot and humid, with the heaviest rainfall in the summer months. The interior enjoys a cooler, drier and more temperate climate. Agriculture is limited to the Caribbean coast. Coffee and bananas are the main exports along with sugar, rice, maize, beans and tobacco. Honduras has limited natural resources, although lead, silver and zinc are exported. The government is providing encouragement for a better-managed timber industry and diversification in agriculture with products such as tomatoes, shrimps and oil.

HONG KONG (INCLUDING KOWLOON AND THE NEW TERRITORIES)
STATUS: **UK Dependent Territory**
AREA: **1,067 sq km (412 sq miles)**
POPULATION: **5,812,000**

HONSHU
STATUS: **Island of Japan**
AREA: **230,455 sq km (88,955 sq miles)**
POPULATION: **98,352,000**

HUNGARY
STATUS: **Republic**
AREA: **93,030 sq km (35,910 sq miles)**
POPULATION: **10,289,000**
ANNUAL NATURAL INCREASE: **-0.6%**
CAPITAL: **Budapest**
LANGUAGE: **Hungarian (Magyar)**
RELIGION: **60% Roman Catholic, 20% Hungarian Reformed Church, Lutheran and Orthodox minorities**
CURRENCY: **forint (HUF)**
ORGANIZATIONS: **Council of Europe, OIEC, UN**

West of the Danube the country consists of rolling countryside. To the southeast lies a fertile great plain, while the highest terrain is in the northeast. The climate is continental, with warm summers and cold winters. Rainfall is fairly evenly distributed throughout the year. Bauxite is Hungary's only substantial mineral resource, and less than 15 per cent of the gross national product is now derived from agriculture. The massive drive for industrialization has transformed the structure of the economy in the period since 1945. Both capital and consumer goods industries were developed, and during the 1980s engineering accounted for more than half the total industrial output. After a series of more or less unsuccessful attempts to introduce market elements into what remained in essence a centrally planned and largely state-owned economy, the communist regime finally gave up in 1989/90. However, its democratically-elected successors have yet to prove that privatization and free competition will eventually bring general prosperity as well as political stability to what is now a profoundly troubled society.

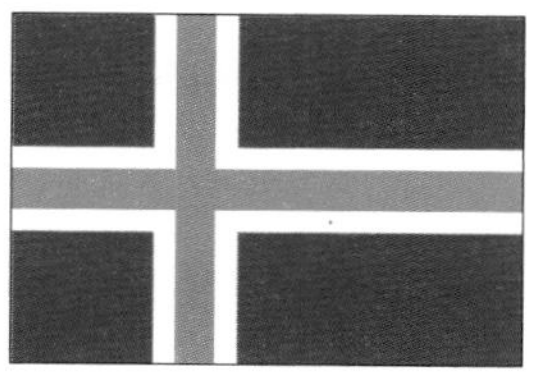

ICELAND

STATUS: **Republic**
AREA: **102,820 sq km (39,690 sq miles)**
POPULATION: **260,000**
ANNUAL NATURAL INCREASE: **1.2%**
CAPITAL: **Reykjavík**
LANGUAGE: **Icelandic**
RELIGION: **93% Evangelical Lutheran**
CURRENCY: **Icelandic krona (ISK)**
ORGANIZATIONS: **Council of Europe, EEA, EFTA, NATO, OECD, UN**

Iceland is one of the northernmost islands in Europe. One tenth of the country is covered by ice caps, but there is also active volcanicity in the form of volcanoes, geysers and hot springs. Over half the population lives in the Reykjavík area. The traditional mainstay of the Icelandic economy has been fishing, particularly cod. Less than 2 per cent of the land is suitable for cultivation; the rest is grazing for livestock. Wool and sheepskins are exported, and there has been a gradual increase in light industries such as the manufacture of blankets and knitwear. An aluminium smelting industry based on imported bauxite is run on hydroelectric power. Income is also derived from a growing tourist industry.

INDIA

STATUS: **Federal Republic**
AREA: **3,166,830 sq km (1,222,395 sq miles)**
POPULATION: **870,000,000**
ANNUAL NATURAL INCREASE: **2.1%**
CAPITAL: **New Delhi**
LANGUAGE: **Hindi, English, regional languages**
RELIGION: **83% Hindu, 11% Muslim**
CURRENCY: **Indian rupee (INR)**
ORGANIZATIONS: **Col. Plan, Comm., UN**

The heart of the Indian peninsula is the Deccan plateau, bordered on either side by the Eastern and Western Ghats. In the north India is bordered by the world's highest mountain range, the Himalayas, where many peaks reach over 6,000 m (19,685 ft). The Himalayan foothills are covered with lush vegetation and have an abundant water supply – rainfall in Assam reaches 10,070 mm (421 inches) a year. It is for these reasons that the cultivation of tea is centred here. Further south lies the Ganges river plain, one of the world's most fertile regions. Generally, the climate is tropical with monsoon rains in summer. In the pre-monsoon season the heat becomes intense, with average temperatures in New Delhi reaching 38°C (100°F). Rice, tea, wheat, cotton, jute, tobacco and sugar are the main crops. India's natural resources are immense – timber, coal, iron ore and nickel are mined, and oil has been discovered in the Indian Ocean. The main exports by value are precious stones and jewellery, engineering goods, clothing, leather goods, chemicals and cotton. There has been a rapid expansion of light industry and the manufacturing of consumer goods. Tourism is a valuable source of revenue. Nevertheless, 70 per cent of the population lives by subsistence farming.

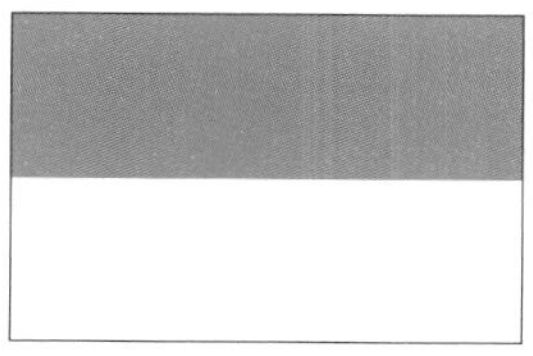

INDONESIA

STATUS: **Republic**
AREA: **1,919,445 sq km (740,905 sq miles)**
POPULATION: **191,170,000**
ANNUAL NATURAL INCREASE: **1.8%**
CAPITAL: **Jakarta**
LANGUAGE: **Bahasa Indonesian, Dutch**
RELIGION: **88% Muslim, 9% Christian, Hindu and Buddhist minorities**
CURRENCY: **rupiah (IDR)**
ORGANIZATIONS: **ASEAN, Col. Plan, OPEC, UN**

Indonesia consists of an archipelago of 13,677 islands along the Equator which includes Kalimantan (the central and southern parts of Borneo), Sumatra, Irian Jaya (the western part of New Guinea), Sulawesi and Java. It exhibits great physical diversity with tropical swamps, rainforest and over 300 volcanoes, many still active. The climate varies, but generally tropical monsoons produce a wet season from October to April with dry weather from June to September. It is a Muslim nation and has one of the largest populations in the world. Most people live on Java, leaving parts of the other islands virtually uninhabited. The majority of the people live in villages and are farmers. However, the crops produced are hardly enough to meet the needs of the population. Timber and oil production are important, and manufacturing has increased recently. Other exports include liquefied natural gas, coal, palm oil, rubber, spices, tobacco, tea, coffee and tin. Indonesia has rich mineral deposits, as yet not fully exploited.

IRAN

STATUS: **Republic**
AREA: **1,648,000 sq km (636,130 sq miles)**
POPULATION: **56,964,000**
ANNUAL NATURAL INCREASE: **3.7%**
CAPITAL: **Tehran**
LANGUAGE: **Farsi, Kurdish, Arabic, Baluchi, Turkic**
RELIGION: **Shi'a Muslim majority, Sunni Muslim and Armenian Christian minorities**
CURRENCY: **Iranian rial (IRR)**
ORGANIZATIONS: **Col. Plan, OPEC, UN**

Iran is a large, mountainous country situated between the Caspian Sea and the Persian Gulf. Eastern Iran is high plateaux country featuring large salt pans. In the west the Zagros mountains form a series of ridges, while to the north the Elburz mountains flank the southwestern shores of the Caspian Sea. The climate is one of extremes, with hot summers and bitterly cold winters. Temperatures range from –20–50°C (–4°–131°F). Most of the light rainfall is in winter. Iran is rich in oil and gas, and the revenues, from these have been used to improve communications and social conditions generally. The war with Iraq between 1980 and 1988 seriously restricted economic growth and particularly affected the Iranian oil industry in the Persian Gulf. Agricultural conditions are poor except around the Caspian Sea, and wheat is the main crop though fruit (especially dates) and nuts are grown and exported. The main livestock are sheep and goats. Iran has substantial mineral deposits that are relatively underdeveloped.

IRAQ

STATUS: **Republic**
AREA: **438,317 sq km (169,235 sq miles)**
POPULATION: **19,290,000**
ANNUAL NATURAL INCREASE: **3.3%**
CAPITAL: **Baghdad**
LANGUAGE: **Arabic, Kurdish, Turkoman**
RELIGION: **50% Shi'a, 45% Sunni Muslim**
CURRENCY: **Iraqi dinar (IQD)**
ORGANIZATIONS: **Arab League, OPEC, UN**

Iraq is mostly marsh and mountain with at its heart the lowland valley of the Tigris and Euphrates rivers. The two great rivers join and become the Shatt al Arab waterway which flows into the Persian Gulf. Northern Iraq is hilly, extending into the Zagros mountains, while western Iraq is desert. The climate is mainly arid. Summers are extremely hot. Winters are mild with unreliable rainfall; less than 500 mm (20 inches) per annum is normal. Basra is the principal port with oil the major export. Light industry is situated around Baghdad, the capital, and there are major petrochemical complexes around the Basra and Kirkuk oilfields. The war with Iran (1980–88), combined with the Gulf conflict (1991) and the US sanctions that followed, have placed great strains on the economy. The exports of oil and natural gas have been severely restricted. Price inflation is high and the black market has taken over. These pressures will mean that Iraq will take some time to recover from the damage caused to its infrastructure.

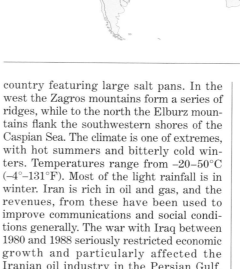

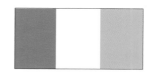

IRELAND (EIRE)

STATUS: **Republic**
AREA: **68,895 sq km (26,595 sq miles)**
POPULATION: **3,548,000**
ANNUAL NATURAL INCREASE: **-0.1%**
CAPITAL: **Dublin (Baile Átha Cliath)**
LANGUAGE: **Irish, English**
RELIGION: **95% Roman Catholic, 5% Protestant**
CURRENCY: **punt or Irish pound (IEP)**
ORGANIZATIONS: **Council of Europe, EEA, EU, OECD, UN**

The Irish Republic forms 80 per cent of the island of Ireland. It is a lowland country of wide valleys, lakes and marshes but with some hills of significance, especially in coastal regions, such as the Wicklow Mountains south of Dublin, the mountains of Connemara in the west and Macgillicuddy's Reeks in the southwest. The Irish climate is maritime and influenced by the Gulf Stream. Rainfall is plentiful throughout the year and temperatures are mild. The cool, damp climate makes for rich pastureland which is particularly suited to the farming of cattle, both for dairy produce and for meat, and sheep. Arable crops include barley, oats and potatoes. Large-scale manufacturing is centred around Dublin, the capital and main port. In this sector food processing, electronics and textiles have shown growth. Ireland also possesses reserves of oil, natural gas, peat and deposits of lead and zinc. Further encouraging discoveries of oil and gas deposits off the southern Irish coast may enhance economic prosperity. The tourist industry is an important revenue earner. The dominant trading partner is the UK, which is the destination for almost half of exports. A significant proportion of the remainder goes to other EU countries. There will be economic advantages for the Republic if the prize of peace in Northern Ireland can be secured. It would stimulate trade, reduce security costs and further benefit tourism.

IRIAN JAYA

STATUS: **Province of Indonesia**
AREA: **421,980 sq km (162,885 sq miles)**
POPULATION: **1,555,682**

ISRAEL

STATUS: **State**
AREA: **20,770 sq km (8,015 sq miles)**
POPULATION: **5,287,000**
ANNUAL NATURAL INCREASE: **2.7%**
CAPITAL: **Jerusalem**
LANGUAGE: **Hebrew, Arabic, Yiddish**
RELIGION: **85% Jewish, 13% Muslim**
CURRENCY: **shekel (ILS)**
ORGANIZATIONS: **UN**

This narrow country on the east Mediterranean littoral contains a varied landscape. The coastal plain of Sharon is bounded by a series of foothills and valleys in the south and by the Galilee highlands in the north. In the east of Israel is a deep trough extending from the Sea of Galilee, southwards through the Dead Sea to the Gulf of Aqaba. Southern Israel is part of the Negev desert. The climate is mostly Mediterranean with warm summers and mild winters. Southern Israel is hot and dry. Agriculture is based on the kibbutz system, providing citrus fruits, flowers and vegetables for export to Western Europe. Economic development in Israel is the most advanced in the Middle East. Manufacturing, particularly diamond finishing, electronics and mining are the most important industries. Some oil is extracted from the Negev desert. Ever since the creation of the state in 1948, Israel has been dominated by the struggle to maintain its existence, and by conflicts with its Arab neighbours. The issue of nationhood for the displaced Palestinian peoples has also been a major political issue, and recently greater autonomy was granted to the Palestinian enclaves of the Gaza Strip, on the Mediterranean coast, and Jericho, to the west of the river Jordan.

ITALY

STATUS: **Republic**
AREA: **301,245 sq km (116,280 sq miles)**
POPULATION: **56,767,000**
ANNUAL NATURAL INCREASE: **0.2%**
CAPITAL: **Rome (Roma)**
LANGUAGE: **Italian, German, French**
RELIGION: **90% Roman Catholic**
CURRENCY: **Italian lira (ITL)**
ORGANIZATIONS: **Council of Europe, EEA, EU, G7, NATO, OECD, UN, WEU**

Over 75 per cent of the landscape of Italy is either hill or mountain. The dominant physical feature of the north is the Alps, which slope southwards to form the plain of the river Po. The Apennines run along the country longitudinally, forming the 'spine' of Italy. Southern Italy is intermittently volcanically active. The Italian climate is typically Mediterranean, enjoying warm summers and mild winters with some rain. Agriculture flourishes, with cereals, vegetables, olives and vines the principal crops. Italy is the world's largest wine producer. Cheese is also an important commodity. In spite of the lack of mineral and power resources, textiles and manufacturing industry (cars, machine tools, textile machinery and engineering) are expanding rapidly and account for nearly 50 per cent of the workforce, mainly in the north. This is increasing the imbalance between the north and the south of the country, where average income is far less and investment is lacking. Tourism is also important, with visitors being drawn to the mountains and lakes of the Alps, the sunny southern coasts and the Italian cultural centres, such as Rome, Florence (Firenze) and Venice (Venezia).

IVORY COAST

STATUS: **Republic**
AREA: **322,465 sq km (124,470 sq miles)**
POPULATION: **12,910,000**
ANNUAL NATURAL INCREASE: **4.0%**
CAPITAL: **Yamoussoukro**
LANGUAGE: **French, tribal languages**
RELIGION: **65% traditional beliefs, 23% Muslim, 12% Roman Catholic**
CURRENCY: **CFA franc (W Africa) (XOF)**
ORGANIZATIONS: **ECOWAS, OAU, UN**

Independent from France since 1960, the Ivory Coast is divided into two main physical regions. In the south are low undulating plains and rainforest, while in the northern areas savannah and plateaux dominate. Temperatures are warm all year round. Annual rainfall occurs in two wet seasons near the coast, and a single wet season from June to October in the north. Much of the population is engaged in agriculture producing rice, cassava, maize, sorghum, plantains and yams. Exports are cotton, cocoa, coffee, tobacco and timber. Gold mining began in 1990, diamonds are extracted and there is some offshore oil production. Important industries are food processing, textiles and timber products.

JAMAICA

STATUS: **Commonwealth State**
AREA: **11,425 sq km (4,410 sq miles)**
POPULATION: **2,469,000**
ANNUAL NATURAL INCREASE: **0.8%**
CAPITAL: **Kingston**
LANGUAGE: **English, local patois**
RELIGION: **Anglican Christian majority. Rastafarian minority**
CURRENCY: **Jamaican dollar (JMD)**
ORGANIZATIONS: **Caricom, Comm., OAS, UN**

Jamaica is the third largest island in the Caribbean. It has a central mountain range, and low coastal plains interrupted by hills and plateaux. The climate is tropical, but temperate in the mountain regions. Jamaica is very prone to hurricanes. There is a plentiful supply of tropical fruits such as melons, bananas and guavas. Principal crops include sugarcane, bananas and coffee. Jamaica is rich in bauxite which provides over half of foreign exchange earnings. Main manufacturing industries are food processing, textiles, cement and agricultural machinery. Since 1988 tourism, mainly from the USA, has become a growing source of foreign earnings.

JAN MAYEN

STATUS: **Island Territory of Norway**
AREA: **380 sq kms (147 sq miles)**
POPULATION: **no permanent population**

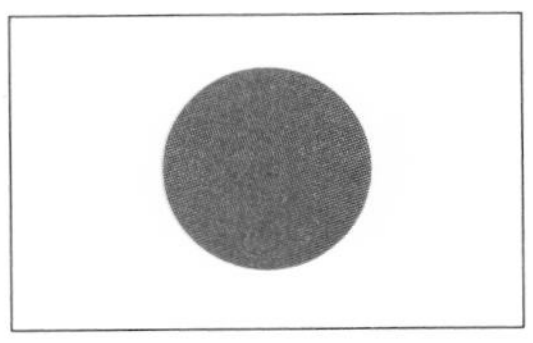

JAPAN

STATUS: **Constitutional monarchy**
AREA: **369,700 sq km (142,705 sq miles)**
POPULATION: **123,653,000**
ANNUAL NATURAL INCREASE: **0.4%**
CAPITAL: **Tokyo (Tōkyō)**
LANGUAGE: **Japanese**
RELIGION: **Shintoist, Buddhist, Christian minority**
CURRENCY: **yen (JPY)**
ORGANIZATIONS: **Col. Plan, G7, OECD, UN**

Japan consists of four major islands, Hokkaido, Honshu, Shikoku and Kyushu which stretch over 1,600 km (995 miles). Eighty per cent of the population lives on the central island of Honshu. There are more than 3,000 smaller volcanic mountainous islands and over 60 active volcanoes. Japan is also subject to frequent major earthquakes, monsoons, typhoons and tidal waves. Nearly three quarters of the land is mountainous and is generally heavily forested, with small, fertile areas. The highest point is Mt Fuji (Fuji-san) which reaches a height of 3,776 m (12,388 ft). The climate is generally temperate oceanic, with warm summers and mild winters, except in western Hokkaido and northwest Honshu, where the winters are very cold with heavy snowfall. Very little of the available land is cultivable and many of the farmers only work part-time. Most food has to be imported, but the Japanese catch and eat a lot of fish. The Japanese fishing fleet is the largest in the world. Almost all the population is concentrated on the coastal plains. The people exhibit a culture that blends both the traditions of ancient and present Japan with the modern commercial life styles of the west. The resurgence of the Japanese economy out of the disaster of World War II is truly astounding. Japan has the world's largest industrial base and employs most of its population within it. The country has become one of the world's largest manufacturers of cars and produces many consumer durables such as washing machines, electronic equipment, watches and calculators. Its chemical, plastics and iron and steel industries have become extremely profitable. Because of the importance of trade, the industrial sites have grown up round the major ports, especially those of Yokohama, Osaka and Tokyo. Japan has small reserves of natural resources and most raw materials have to be imported, including around 90 per cent of the country's energy requirements. To reduce this dependence, the country is developing nuclear power resources and increasing production from its limited coal, oil and natural gas fields.

JAVA (JAWA)

STATUS: **Island of Indonesia**
AREA: **134,045 sq kms (51,740 sq miles)**
POPULATION: **107,500,000**

JORDAN

STATUS: **Kingdom**
AREA: **90,650 sq km (35,000 sq miles)**
POPULATION: **4,291,000**
ANNUAL NATURAL INCREASE: **5.8%**
CAPITAL: **Amman ('Ammān)**
LANGUAGE: **Arabic**
RELIGION: **90% Sunni Muslim, Christian and Shi'ite Muslim minorities**
CURRENCY: **Jordanian dinar (JOD)**
ORGANIZATIONS: **Arab League, UN**

The Hashemite Kingdom of Jordan is predominately a desert country. Most of the land area of Jordan to the east and southeast is desolate plateaux with occasional salt pans. The lowest parts are along the eastern shores of the Dead Sea and the East Bank of the Jordan, behind which is a range of tree-covered hills. Most of Jordan is hot and dry. Temperatures rise to 49°C (120°F) in the eastern valleys. The west of the country is cooler and wetter, with rainfall of up to 290 mm (12 inches). Fruit and vegetables account for 20 per cent of Jordan's exports, and phosphate, the most valuable mineral, accounts for over 40 per cent of export revenue. Amman is the manufacturing centre, processing bromide and potash from the Dead Sea. Other important industries are food processing and textiles. However, the country still remains dependent on considerable injections of foreign aid.

KALIMANTAN

STATUS: **Province of Indonesia in Borneo**
AREA: **550,205 sq kms (212,380 sq miles)**
POPULATION: **9,100,000**

KAZAKHSTAN

STATUS: **Republic**
AREA: **2,717,300 sq km (1,048,880 sq miles)**
POPULATION: **17,035,000**
ANNUAL NATURAL INCREASE: **1.0%**
CAPITAL: **Alma-Ata**
LANGUAGE: **Kazakh, Russian**
RELIGION: **Muslim majority, Orthodox minority**
CURRENCY: **tenge**
ORGANIZATIONS: **CIS, UN**

Stretching across central Asia, Kazakhstan is the Russian Federation's southern neighbour. The republic covers a vast area of steppe lands, verging towards semi-desert in the south. The climate is essentially dry and with a marked seasonal variation in temperature. Summers are hot and winters are extremely cold. Although almost three quarters of the land is pastoral, the nomadic ways of the Kazakh people have all but disappeared. Across the steppes wheat is grown, and further south vegetables, cotton and tobacco are grown on irrigated land. Kazakhstan is exceptionally rich in raw materials, producing over 60 minerals. There are massive iron ore deposits, and important reserves of lead, zinc, titanium, chromium, vanadium, gold, silver and thallium. Close to the Caspian Sea large oil and natural gas reserves are being exploited.

During the Soviet period, there was a vast influx of foreign labour which swamped the indigenous population. The proportion of Kazakhs employed in the industrial sector has until recently been small, but with the move of the population to urban areas and with better training this imbalance is starting to be readjusted. Since independence in 1991, the country's economic prospects appear favourable, but the Soviet legacy includes environmental problems, such as the ruthless exploitation of the Aral Sea for irrigation, which will have to be faced.

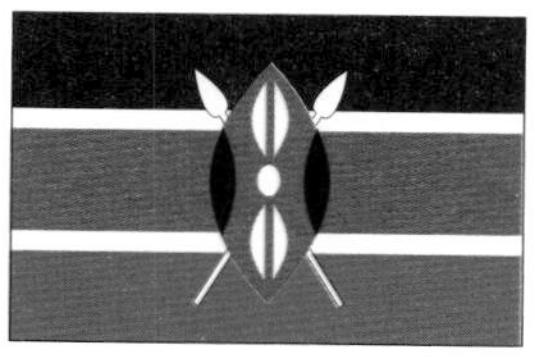

KENYA

STATUS: **Republic**
AREA: **582,645 sq km (224,900 sq miles)**
POPULATION: **25,700,000**
ANNUAL NATURAL INCREASE: **3.5%**
CAPITAL: **Nairobi**
LANGUAGE: **Kiswahili, English, Kikuyu, Luo**
RELIGION: **majority traditional beliefs, 25% Christian, 6% Muslim**
CURRENCY: **Kenya shilling (KES)**
ORGANIZATIONS: **Comm., OAU, UN**

The land rises from the coastal plains to plateaux of mainly volcanic material. Running northwest of Nairobi to Lake Turkana is the dramatic great Rift Valley. Although Kenya straddles the Equator, only the coastal fringes exhibit tropical characteristics because of the high average altitude. Much of the land north of the Equator is arid semi-desert, while to the south savannah conditions prevail. Kenya's economy is founded on agriculture and a growing tourist industry. Poor soil and a dry climate mean that little of the land is under cultivation but exports are nonetheless dominated by farm products – coffee, tea, sisal and meat. Nairobi and Mombasa are the manufacturing centres.

KERGUELEN ISLANDS

STATUS: **Part of French Southern and Antarctic Territories**
AREA: **7,215 sq kms (2,785 sq miles)**
POPULATION: **75**

KIRGHIZIA (KYRGYZSTAN)

STATUS: **Republic**
AREA: **198,500 sq km (76,620 sq miles)**
POPULATION: **4,502,000**
ANNUAL NATURAL INCREASE: **1.7%**
CAPITAL: **Bishkek**
LANGUAGE: **Kirghizian, Russian**
RELIGION: **Muslim**
CURRENCY: **som**
ORGANIZATIONS: **CIS, UN**

Kirghizia, occupying the western end of the Tien Shan range, is one of the world's most rugged and mountainous areas. It has a hostile climate, with hot summers and extremely cold winters. The Fergana basin in the west and the Chu valley in the north are the main areas of cultural and economic

development. The nation has valuable mineral deposits which include gold, silver, mercury, antimony and rare earth metals such as yttrium and lanthanum. Oil has been found in small quantities in the east of the country. However, the economy is agricultural, based on livestock farming, sericulture, beekeeping and tobacco growing. Independence came unexpectedly in 1991, and the country is now set firmly on the route of modernizing its economy.

KIRIBATI

STATUS: **Republic**
AREA: **717 sq km (277 sq miles)**
POPULATION: **66,000**
ANNUAL NATURAL INCREASE: **2.1%**
CAPITAL: **Bairiki (on Tarawa Atoll)**
LANGUAGE: **I-Kirbati, English**
RELIGION: **Christian majority**
CURRENCY: **Australian dollar (AUD)**
ORGANIZATIONS: **Comm., UN**

Kiribati, in the central and west Pacific, consists of sixteen Gilbert Islands, eight Phoenix Islands, several Line Islands and the volcanic island of Banaba (Ocean Island). The central islands have a maritime equatorial climate, whereas those to the north and south are tropical. The islanders grow coconuts, breadfruit, bananas and babai (a coarse vegetable). Now that reserves of phosphates have been exhausted, copra has become the major export, with fish (mainly tuna) accounting for a further third of exports. Kiribati has to import much, including machinery and manufactured goods.

KOREA, NORTH

STATUS: **Republic**
AREA: **122,310 sq km (47,210 sq miles)**
POPULATION: **22,618,000**
ANNUAL NATURAL INCREASE: **1%**
CAPITAL: **P'yŏngyang**
LANGUAGE: **Korean**
RELIGION: **Chundo Kyo, Buddhism, Confucianism, Daoism**
CURRENCY: **North Korean won (KPW)**
ORGANIZATIONS: **OIEC, UN**

Most of North Korea is rugged mountainous terrain, with the greatest extent of lowlying land being in the south and west of P'yŏngyang. Temperatures range widely from a summer maximum of above 30°C (86°F) to a winter minimum of – 10°C (14°F). Most rain falls in the summer months. Cultivation is limited to the river valley plains where rice, millet, maize and wheat are the principal crops. North Korea is rich in minerals including iron ore, coal and copper, and industrial development has been expanding. Further potential exists in the exploitation of the plentiful resources of hydro-electricity. Main exports are metal ores and metal products. Since its separation from South Korea at the end of World War II, North Korea has remained one of the few strongholds of Communism. Recently, the North Korean economy has suffered grievously after losing support from the Russian Federation as a trading partner.

KOREA, SOUTH

STATUS: **Republic**
AREA: **98,445 sq km (38,000 sq miles)**
POPULATION: **44,190,000**
ANNUAL NATURAL INCREASE: **1.9%**
CAPITAL: **Seoul (Sŏul)**
LANGUAGE: **Korean**
RELIGION: **26% Mahayana Buddhism, 22% Christian. Confucianism, Daoism, Chundo Kyo**
CURRENCY: **won (KPW)**
ORGANIZATIONS: **Col. Plan, UN**

South Korea is a product of the territory occupied by the USA at the end of World War II. Its terrain is less rugged than that of North Korea. The flattest parts lie along the west coast and in the extreme south of the peninsula. The majority of the population live in the arable river valleys and along the coastal plain. Agriculture is primitive, with rice the principal crop. South Korea has few natural resources apart from coal and tungsten. Oil and industrial materials have to be imported. Traditional industries include textiles, chemicals and vehicle manufacture, and South Korea builds more ships than any other country except Japan. In recent years the country has become known for specializing in electronics and computers.

KURIL ISLANDS (KURIL'SKIYE OSTROVA)

STATUS: **Islands of Russian Federation**
AREA: **15,540 sq kms (6,000 sq miles)**
POPULATION: **not known**

KUWAIT

STATUS: **State**
AREA: **24,280 sq km (9,370 sq miles)**
POPULATION: **1,500,000**
ANNUAL NATURAL INCREASE: **-2.3%**
CAPITAL: **Kuwait (Al Kuwayt)**
LANGUAGE: **Arabic, English**
RELIGION: **95% Muslim, 5% Christian and Hindu**
RELIGION: **Kuwaiti dinar (KWD)**
ORGANIZATIONS: **Arab League, UN**

Situated at the mouth of the Persian Gulf, Kuwait is essentially low-lying, undulating desert terrain. Cultivation is only possible along the coast. In winter temperatures are mild and little rain falls. By contrast summer months are very hot and dry, with temperatures being as high as 52°C (126°F). The Kuwaiti economy is dominated by its oil wealth. The oilfields have now largely recovered from the devastation of the 1991 Gulf War, and in 1992 revenue from oil and products amounted to nearly 90 per cent of exports. The natural gas fields have also been re-developed. Other industries include fishing (particularly shrimp), food processing, chemicals and building materials. In agriculture, the aim is to produce half the requirements of domestic vegetable consumption by expanding the irrigated area.

KYUSHU

STATUS: **Island of Japan**
AREA: **42,010 sq kms (16,215 sq miles)**
POPULATION: **296,000**

LAOS

STATUS: **Republic**
AREA: **236,725 sq km (91,375 sq miles)**
POPULATION: **4,469,000**
ANNUAL NATURAL INCREASE:: **2.9%**
CAPITAL: **Vientiane (Viangchan)**
LANGUAGE: **Lao, French, tribal languages**
RELIGION: **Buddhist majority, Christian and animist minorities**
RELIGION: **kip (LAK)**
ORGANIZATIONS: **Col. Plan, UN**

Much of Laos is rugged, forested mountain and plateaux terrain, but there are lowland areas along the Mekong valley and towards the south of the country. In general the climate is hot, with a rainy season between May and October. Most of the population are farmers growing small amounts of rice, maize, sweet potatoes and tobacco. Hydro-electric power is being developed, surpluses from which will be sold to Thailand. Laos has natural resources in the form of mineral ores, coal and timber, the major exports being tin and teak. Commercial exploitation is overshadowed by the trade in opium and illegal logging activities.

STATES AND TERRITORIES OF THE WORLD

LATVIA

STATUS: **Republic**
AREA: **63,700 sq km (24,590 sq miles)**
POPULATION: **2,577,000**
ANNUAL NATURAL INCREASE: **0.0%**
CAPITAL: **Riga**
LANGUAGE: **Latvian, Lithuanian, Russian**
RELIGION: **Lutheran, Roman Catholic and Orthodox minorities**
CURRENCY: **roublis (Latvian rouble), lats**
ORGANIZATIONS: **UN**

Latvia is situated on the shores of the Baltic Sea and the Gulf of Riga. The landscape is one of glaciated lowland, flat towards the Baltic coast but forested inland. The climate is one of distinct seasonal variation. Summers are warm but winters are cold with average temperatures well below freezing. Latvia is trying to make a successful transition from a republic within the Soviet Union to genuine independence (1991). Farmland supports livestock, mainly beef and dairy cattle and pigs. However, the farming community has seen it s standard of living fall as prices have decreased because no goods are now exported eastwards. Manufacturing industry is varied but specialized, concentrating on a few products such as radios, tape recorders, farm machinery and minibuses.

LEBANON

STATUS: **Republic**
AREA: **10,400 sq km (4,015 sq miles)**
POPULATION: **2,838,000**
ANNUAL NATURAL INCREASE: **2.3%**
CAPITAL: **Beirut (Beyrouth)**
LANGUAGE: **Arabic, French, English**
RELIGION: **62% Shi'a and Sunni Muslim, 38% Roman Catholic and Maronite Christian**
CURRENCY: **Lebanese pound (LBP)**
ORGANIZATIONS: **Arab League, UN**

Beyond the coastal strip the Lebanon (Jebel Liban) and Anti-Lebanon (Jebel esh Sharqi) mountains run parallel with the coast, separated by the Bekaa Valley (El Beqa'a). The climate in Beirut is hot in summer, and mild in winter. Agriculture accounts for nearly all the employment. Cement, fertilizers, jewellery, sugar and tobacco products are all manufactured on a small scale. Trade and tourism have been severely affected by civil war since 1975. The government is investing in reconstruction and infrastructure projects, important among which are the installation of reliable power distribution and telecommunication systems. Similarly, Beirut airport is to be reconstructed.

LESOTHO

STATUS: **Kingdom**
AREA: **30,345 sq km (11,715 sq miles)**
POPULATION: **1,836,000**
ANNUAL NATURAL INCREASE: **2.7%**
CAPITAL: **Maseru**
LANGUAGE: **Sesotho, English**
RELIGION: **80% Christian**
CURRENCY: **loti (LSL), S African rand (ZAR)**
ORGANIZATIONS: **Comm., OAU, UN**

Lesotho is completely encircled by South Africa. It is a mountainous country, and includes the Drakensberg mountains; from these peaks the land slopes westwards in the form of dissected plateaux. The climate is warm and pleasant with prolonged sunshine. Agriculture is restricted to the lowlands and foothills. The main crops are maize, barley, oats, legumes, sorghum and wheat, but experimental cultivation of sunflowers is showing promise. Cattle, sheep and goats graze on the highlands.

LIBERIA

STATUS: **Republic**
AREA: **11,370 sq km (42,990 sq miles)**
POPULATION: **2,580,000**
ANNUAL NATURAL INCREASE: **3.1%**
CAPITAL: **Monrovia**
LANGUAGE: **English, tribal languages**
RELIGION: **traditional beliefs, Christian, 5% Muslim**
CURRENCY: **Liberian dollar (LRD)**
ORGANIZATIONS: **ECOWAS, OAU, UN**

Beyond the coastal belt of sandy beaches and mangrove swamps the land rises to a forested plateau. The climate is hot, with average daily temperatures exceeding 25°C (77°F) throughout the year. Rainfall is plentiful and particularly heavy in June and July. Before the civil war of 1989–93 Liberia enjoyed a measure of prosperity. Iron ore deposits provided about 50 per cent of the nation's revenue, and rubber was also a major export. Liberia has the world's largest merchant fleet of over 2,500 ships due to its flag of convenience tax regime, which has been relatively unaffected by the war. A massive injection of foreign aid and investment will be necessary for recovery.

LIBYA

STATUS: **Republic**
AREA: **1,759,540 sq km (679,180 sq miles)**
POPULATION: **4,875,000**
ANNUAL NATURAL INCREASE: **3.6%**
CAPITAL: **Tripoli (Ṭarābulus)**
LANGUAGE: **Arabic, Italian, English**
RELIGION: **Sunni Muslim**
CURRENCY: **Libyan dinar (LYD)**
ORGANIZATIONS: **Arab League, OAU, OPEC, UN**

The desert plains and hills of the Sahara predominate. A coastal plain is interrupted by a mountain range east of Benghazi. The climate is hot and arid. Only the Mediterranean coast receives winter rainfall sufficient to sustain agriculture. In these areas, a wide range of crops are cultivated, including grapes, groundnuts, oranges, wheat and barley. Dates are grown in the desert oasis. Only 30 years ago Libya was classed as one of the world's poorest nations but the exploitation of oil has transformed the economy and now accounts for over 95 per cent of exports. Most imported goods come from Italy.

LIECHTENSTEIN

STATUS: **Principality**
AREA: **160 sq km (62 sq miles)**
POPULATION: **30,000**
ANNUAL NATURAL INCREASE: **1.1%**
CAPITAL: **Vaduz**
LANGUAGE: **Alemannish, German**
RELIGION: **87% Roman Catholic**
CURRENCY: **franken (Swiss franc)(CHF)**
ORGANIZATIONS **Council of Europe, EFTA, UN**

Two physical zones are evident, the fertile floodplains of the upper Rhine valley in the north and west and the mountains of the Austrian Alps in the east. The climate is temperate, with cool winters. Liechtenstein used to be primarily agricultural, but is now highly industrialized, with a variety of light industries and specialist manufacturing such as precision instruments, pharmaceuticals, ceramics and textiles. Other sources of revenue are postage stamps, food products, tourism and banking, the fastest-growing area.

LITHUANIA

STATUS: **Republic**
AREA: **65,200 sq km (25,165 sq miles)**
POPULATION: **3,742,000**
ANNUAL NATURAL INCREASE: **0.7%**
CAPITAL: **Vilnius**
LANGUAGE: **Lithuanian, Russian, Polish**
RELIGION: **80% Roman Catholic**
CURRENCY: **litas**
ORGANIZATIONS: **Council of Europe, UN**

Lithuania is a lowland country with many lakes and low ridges of glacial origin which are often pine covered. The climate is essentially temperate. After almost 50 years' involuntary incorporation into the Soviet Union, Lithuania led the renewed Baltic struggle for freedom, and in 1991 was able to win back its independence. The massive drive for industrialization during the Soviet period has done enormous damage to the environment but failed to create competitive enterprises that can survive under market conditions. This has led to a dramatic fall in production in the recent past and to rising unemployment. Lithuania's agriculture, with its emphasis on meat and dairy products, still awaits decollectivization.

LUXEMBOURG

STATUS: **Grand Duchy**
AREA: **2,585 sq km (998 sq miles)**
POPULATION: **390,000**
ANNUAL NATURAL INCREASE: **0.8%**
CAPITAL: **Luxembourg**
LANGUAGE: **Letzeburgish, French, German**
RELIGION: **95% Roman Catholic**
CURRENCY: **Luxembourg franc (LUF), Belgian franc (BEF)**
ORGANIZATIONS: **Council of Europe, EEA, EU, NATO, OECD, UN, WEU**

Luxembourg is situated between France, Belgium and Germany. The hills and forests of the Ardennes dominate the northern third of the country, with rolling pasture to the south. The climate is temperate. Winters are cold with heavy snowfall, particularly in the upland areas. Just over half the land is arable, mainly yielding cereals, dairy produce and potatoes, and wine is produced in the Moselle valley. Iron ore is found in the south and is the basis of the thriving steel industry. Other major industries are textiles, chemicals, metal goods and pharmaceutical products. Luxembourg has become a leading centre in Europe for banking and finance, encouraged by low tax rates and the government's strict secrecy laws.

MACAU (MACAO)

STATUS: **Chinese Territory under Portuguese Administration**
AREA: **16 sq km (6 sq miles)**
POPULATION: **374,000**
CAPITAL: **Macau**

MACEDONIA (Former Yugoslav Republic)

STATUS: **Republic**
AREA: **25,715 sq km (9,925 sq miles)**
POPULATION: **2,066,000**
ANNUAL NATURAL INCREASE: **1.1%**
CAPITAL: **Skopje**
LANGUAGE: **Macedonian, Albanian**
RELIGION: **Orthodox**
CURRENCY: **denar**
ORGANIZATIONS: **UN**

Macedonia is a rugged country, with the highest land in the Sar range in the northwest. The Vardar valley traverses the country from north to south, creating a major strategic route. The climate has fine hot summers but bitterly cold winters. Macedonia was a republic within Yugoslavia until 1992 when it declared its independence. Conflict over the republic's name has damaged trade with and through Greece, which is the natural link with the outside world. Economic prospects have been further worsened as a result of UN sanctions being imposed upon the former Yugoslavia.

MADAGASCAR

STATUS: **Republic**
AREA: **594,180 sq km (229,345 sq miles)**
POPULATION: **12,827**
ANNUAL NATURAL INCREASE: **3.1%**
CAPITAL: **Antananarivo**
LANGUAGE: **Malagasy, French, English**
RELIGION: **47% animist, 48% Christian, 2% Muslim**
CURRENCY: **Malagasy franc (MGF)**
ORGANIZATIONS: **OAU, UN**

Madagascar is essentially a high plateau with a narrow lowland strip along the east coast. The climate is tropical, with heavier rainfall in the north and monsoons affecting the east coast. Coffee, rice and cassava are the main products. The fishing industry has shown significant growth, and prawns are now a valuable commodity promising to rival vanilla and coffee. There are also prospects for other shellfish, such as lobsters, and tuna. Tourism, although undeveloped compared with Kenya, shows rapid growth and may provide the key to improve on the country's position as one of the world's poorest nations.

MADEIRA

STATUS: **Self-governing Island Region of Portugal**
AREA: **796 sq km (307 sq miles)**
POPULATION: **253,200**
CAPITAL: **Funchal**

MALAWI

STATUS: **Republic**
AREA: **94,080 sq km (35,315 sq miles)**
POPULATION: **8,823,000**
ANNUAL NATURAL INCREASE: **3.4%**
CAPITAL: **Lilongwe**
LANGUAGE: **Chichewa, English**
RELIGION: **traditional beliefs majority, 10% Roman Catholic, 10% Protestant**
CURRENCY: **kwacha (MWK)**
ORGANIZATIONS: **Comm., OAU, UN**

Malawi is a small hilly country at the southern end of the East African Rift Valley. A large area is covered by Lake Malawi which lies above sea level. The climate is mainly subtropical with varying rainfall. Malawi has an intensely rural economy and 96 per cent of the population work on the land. Maize is the main subsistence crop and the main exports are tobacco, tea, sugar and groundnuts. Manufacturing industry concentrates on consumer goods and construction materials. All energy is produced by hydro-electric power. Malawi has deposits of both coal and bauxite, but these are underexploited at present.

MALAYSIA

STATUS: **Federation**
AREA: **332,665 sq km (128,405 sq miles)**
POPULATION: **18,606,000**
ANNUAL NATURAL INCREASE: **2.5%**
CAPITAL: **Kuala Lumpur**
LANGUAGE: **58% Bahasa Malaysian, English, Chinese**
RELIGION: **53% Muslim, 25% Buddhist, Hindu, Christian and animist minorities**
CURRENCY: **Malaysian dollar or ringgit (MYR)**
ORGANIZATIONS: **ASEAN, Col. Plan, Comm., UN**

The Federation of Malaysia consists of two separate parts. Western Malaysia forms a peninsula with mountain ranges aligned along its axis. Eastern Malaysia, consisting of Sabah and Sarawak on the island of Borneo, is mainly jungle-covered hills and mountains with mangrove swamps along the coast. The climate everywhere is warm with heavy rainfall. Malaysia is one of the world's main tin producers, and produces over 40 per cent of the world's rubber. It is also a leading source of palm oil, bauxite and gold. Chief exports by value are manufactured goods, rubber, crude oil, palm oil, timber and timber products, and tin. Most industries are concerned with the production and processing of local products – palm oil, furniture, food processing and petroleum products. Most of the population is engaged in agriculture for local needs, but crops grown for export include pineapples, tobacco, cocoa and spices. Livestock is important to the home economy with pigs, cattle, goats, buffaloes and sheep.

PENINSULAR MALAYSIA

STATUS: **State**
AREA: **131,585 sq km (50,790 sq miles)**
POPULATION: **15,286,098**
CAPITAL: **Kuala Lumpur**

SABAH

STATUS: **State**
AREA: **76,115 sq km (29,380 sq miles)**
POPULATION: **1,736,902**
CAPITAL: **Kota Kinabalu**

SARAWAK

STATUS: **State**
AREA: **124,965 sq km (48,235 sq miles)**
POPULATION: **1,583,000**
CAPITAL: **Kuching**

MALDIVES

STATUS: **Republic**
AREA: **298 sq km (115 sq miles)**
POPULATION: **231,000**
ANNUAL NATURAL INCREASE: **3.3%**
CAPITAL: **Male**
LANGUAGE: **Dhivehi**
RELIGION: **Sunni Muslim majority**
CURRENCY: **rufiyaa (MVR)**
ORGANIZATIONS: **Comm., Col. Plan, UN**

The Maldive Islands are a string of well over 1,000 coral atolls, of which about 200 are inhabited. The climate is hot throughout the year. Humidity is high, while the heaviest monsoon rains fall between May and December. Fishing is the main activity, and fish and coconut fibre are both exported. Most staple foods have to be imported as there is little cultivable land, but bananas, coconuts, millet, cassava, yams and fruit are grown locally. Tourism is developing.

MALI

STATUS: **Republic**
AREA: **1,240,140 sq km (478,695 sq miles)**
POPULATION: **9,818,000**
ANNUAL NATURAL INCREASE: **2.8%**
CAPITAL: **Bamako**
LANGUAGE: **French, native languages**
RELIGION: **65% Muslim, 30% traditional beliefs, 1% Christian**
CURRENCY: **CFA franc (W Africa) (XOF)**
ORGANIZATIONS: **ECOWAS, OAU, UN**

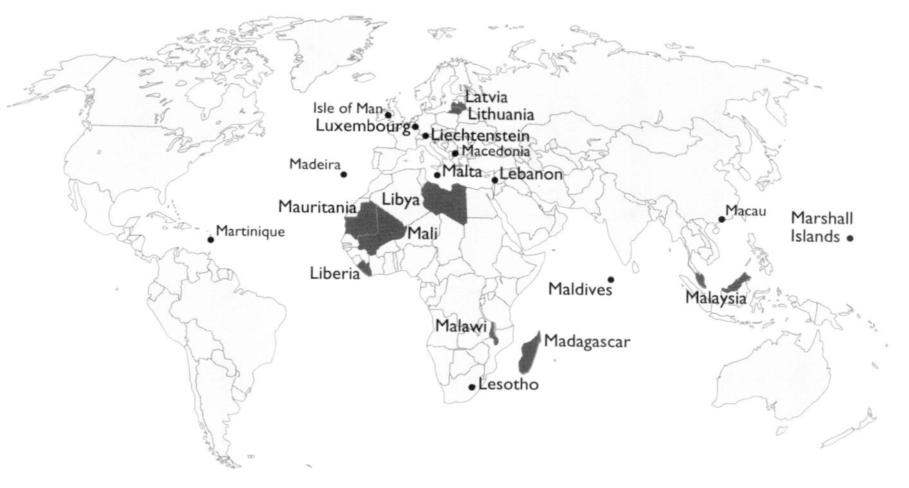

Over half the area is barren desert. To the south the land, through which the river Niger flows, is savannah. The climate is hot, with average temperatures for most of the year approaching 30°C (86°F). Rainfall, virtually absent in the north, usually occurs in appreciable quantities during summer in the south, but droughts are increasingly common. Most of the population lives in the Niger valley and grows cotton, seeds and groundnuts. Fishing is important. Mali has few mineral resources. Recent droughts have taken their toll of livestock and agriculture. Main exports are cotton and livestock. There is no industry.

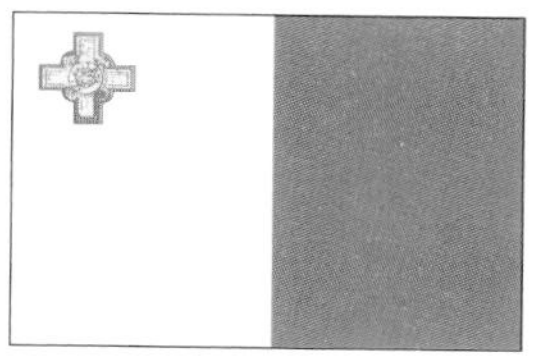

MALTA

STATUS: **Republic**
AREA: **316 sq km (122 sq miles)**
POPULATION: **359,000**
ANNUAL NATURAL INCREASE: **0.7%**
CAPITAL: **Valletta**
LANGUAGE: **Maltese, English, Italian**
RELIGION: **Roman Catholic majority**
CURRENCY: **Maltese lira (MTL)**
ORGANIZATIONS: **Comm., Council of Europe, UN**

The main island of Malta has a landscape of low hills and an indented coastline with numerous beaches and coves. Two thirds of the population live in the Valletta region. The climate is Mediterranean. About 40 per cent of the land is under cultivation, with wheat, potatoes, tomatoes and vines the main crops. The large natural harbour at Valletta has made it a major transit port. Tourism is also an important source of revenue. Principal exports are machinery, beverages, tobacco, flowers, wine, leather goods and potatoes.

MAN, ISLE OF

STATUS: **British Crown Dependency**
AREA: **588 sq km (227 sq miles)**
POPULATION: **71,000**
CAPITAL: **Douglas**

MARSHALL ISLANDS

STATUS: **Self-governing state in Compact of Free Association with USA**
AREA: **605 sq km (234sq miles)**
POPULATION: **45,563**
CAPITAL: **Majuro**
LANGUAGE: **English, local languages**
RELIGION: **Roman Catholic majority**
CURRENCY: **US dollar (USD)**
ORGANIZATIONS: **UN**

The Marshall Islands consist of over 1,000 atolls, islands and islets, generally within two chains, the Ratak (Sunrise) and Ralik (Sunset). The principal atolls are Majuro, Kwajalein, Jaluit, Enewetak and Bikini. The climate is tropical and hot. Rainfall is heavy, falling mainly between August and November. The majority of the population is employed in fishing and subsistence farming, although some products such as coconuts, melons and tomatoes are available for export. The islands are lacking in natural resources, apart from some phosphate deposits. There is a growing tourism trade.

MARTINIQUE

STATUS: **Overseas Department of France**
AREA: **1,079 sq km (417 sq miles)**
POPULATION: **373,000**
CAPITAL: **Fort-de-France**

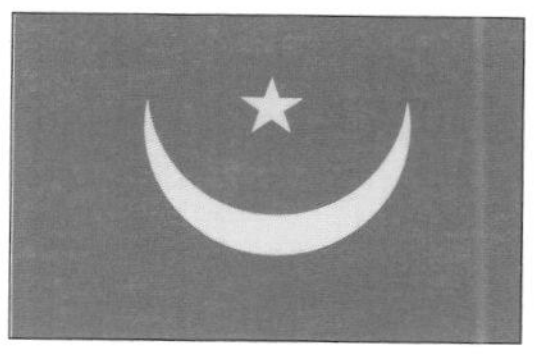

MAURITANIA

STATUS: **Islamic Republic**
AREA: **1,030,700 sq km (397,850 sq miles)**
POPULATION: **2,143,000**
ANNUAL NATURAL INCREASE: **2.7%**
CAPITAL: **Nouakchott**
LANGUAGE: **Arabic, French**
RELIGION: **Muslim**
CURRENCY: **ouguiya (MRO)**
ORGANIZATIONS: **Arab League, ECOWAS, OAU, UN**

Almost the entire area of Mauritania is desert, much of it completely uninhabitable. The only area of significant permanent vegetation is along the river Senegal at the country's southern border. Summers are extremely hot and winters are mild. Most of the population raises cattle, sheep, goats or camels. However, this has been seriously undermined by drought. Arable farming is practised in the south of the country where the waters of the Senegal are sufficient to allow irrigation. At present the typical cash crops are millet, rice and beans but eventually cash crops of cotton and sugarcane could be grown. The nation is dependent on it's mineral reserves, the most important being iron ore.

STATES AND TERRITORIES OF THE WORLD

MAURITIUS

STATUS: **Republic**
AREA: **1,865 sq km (720 sq miles)**
POPULATION: **1,098,000**
ANNUAL NATURAL INCREASE: **1.1%**
CAPITAL: **Port Louis**
LANGUAGE: **English, French Creole, Hindi, Bhojpuri**
RELIGION: **51% Hindu, 31% Christian, 17% Muslim**
CURRENCY: **Mauritian rupee (MUR)**
ORGANIZATIONS: **Comm., OAU, UN**

Mauritius comprises a main island and about 20 smaller ones, in the Indian Ocean. The climate is warm with tropical storms, mostly between December and March. The central plateau receives considerably more rain than experienced elsewhere. Sugarcane and its by-products are the mainstay of the economy, and tourism is developing rapidly. Other sources of income include clothing manufacture, molasses and tea.

MAYOTTE

STATUS: **'Territorial collectivity' of France**
AREA: **376 sq km (145 sq miles)**
POPULATION: **85,000**
CAPITAL: **Dzaoudzi**

MELILLA

STATUS: **Spanish External Province**
AREA: **13 sq km (5 sq miles)**
POPULATION: **56,600**

MEXICO

STATUS: **Federal Republic**
AREA: **1,972,545 sq km (761,400 sq miles)**
POPULATION: **89,538,000**
ANNUAL NATURAL INCREASE: **1.8%**
CAPITAL: **Mexico City**
LANGUAGE: **Spanish**
RELIGION: **96% Roman Catholic**
CURRENCY: **Mexican peso (MXP)**
ORGANIZATIONS: **NAFTA, OAS, UN**

The greater part of Mexico is high plateaux flanked by the western and eastern Sierra Madre mountain ranges. Altitudes increase towards the south. The greatest extent of lowland is the limestone Yucatán peninsula. The climate varies with latitude and altitude. The north is arid but heavy rainfall prevails in the tropical far south. The central plateaux are mild temperate, but with sharp diurnal variations, while the coastal plains are hot and humid. The land requires irrigation to support agriculture. Maize and beans are grown for local consumption. The population has outstripped food production, and many Mexicans have moved to the cities. Minerals, especially silver, uranium and gold are the main source of Mexico's wealth, but the mines are mostly foreign-owned. Oil, natural gas and coal all have considerable reserves and are gradually becoming more important. The main exports are crude oil and machinery, along with coffee and frozen shrimps. Tourism brings in important foreign revenue.

MICRONESIA

STATUS: **Self-governing Federation of States in Compact of Free Association with USA**
AREA: **702 sq km (271 sq miles)**
POPULATION: **109,000**
ANNUAL NATURAL INCOME: **2.4%**
CAPITAL: **Kolonia**
LANGUAGE: **English, eight indigenous languages**
RELIGION: **Christian majority**
CURRENCY: **US dollar (USD)**
ORGANIZATIONS: **UN**

Micronesia comprises 607 atolls and islands. The climate is hot with temperatures averaging 26°C (79°F) all year round. A third of the population live on Pohnpei. Most of the people throughout the islands derive a living from fishing or subsistence farming. Phosphates and copra are the major exports. Other income comes from a growing tourist industry and from Japanese, US and Korean fishing fleets which operate within the territorial waters.

MOLDOVA

STATUS: **Republic**
AREA: **33,700 sq km (13,010 sq miles)**
POPULATION: **4,356,000**
ANNUAL NATURAL INCREASE: **0.6%**
CAPITAL: **Kishinev**
LANGUAGE: **Moldovan, Russian, Romanian**
RELIGION: **Orthodox**
CURRENCY: **rouble**
ORGANIZATIONS: **CIS, UN**

Moldova consists of hilly plains drained by the Prut and Dniester (Dnestr) rivers. The climate is warm, with cold spells in winter. The mainstays of the economy are viticulture, fruit and vegetables which, together with industries such as food processing, account for over 50 per cent of national income. Moldova lacks any fuel reserves and is dependent on Russia for crude oil. It is also dependent on the Ukraine for access to the Black Sea.

MONACO

STATUS: **Principality**
AREA: **1.6 sq km (0.6 sq miles)**
POPULATION: **28,000**
ANNUAL NATURAL INCREASE: **1.4%**
CAPITAL: **Monaco-ville**
LANGUAGE: **French, Monegasque, Italian, English**
RELIGION: **90% Roman Catholic**
CURRENCY: **French franc (FRF)**

Monaco is situated on a rocky peninsula and occupies a narrow strip of coastline, backed by the foothills of the Alpes Maritimes. The climate is Mediterranean. Most revenue comes from tourism and casinos. The main products from light industry are chemicals, plastics and electronics. Land has been reclaimed from the sea to extend the area available for commercial development.

MONGOLIA

STATUS: **People's Republic**
AREA: **1,565,000 sq km (604,090 sq miles)**
POPULATION: **2,310,000**
ANNUAL NATURAL INCREASE: **2.8%**
CAPITAL: **Ulan Bator (Ulaanbaatar)**
LANGUAGE: **Khalkha Mongolian**
RELIGION: **some Buddhist Lamaism**
CURRENCY: **tugrik (MNT)**
ORGANIZATIONS: **OIEC, UN**

Mongolia is characterized by high steppe lands, becoming mountainous with many lakes and rivers in the north and west. In the south is the Gobi desert. The Mongolian climate is continental with mild summers and dry, long and very cold winters. Mongolia is predominantly a farming economy, its main exports being cattle, horses and wheat; barley, millet and oats are also grown. It is rich in natural resources including coal, copper, tin, gold, lead and tungsten. Half the country's exports come from the Erdenet copper mine.

MONTSERRAT

STATUS: **UK Crown Colony**
AREA: **106 sq km (41 sq miles)**
POPULATION: **13,000**
CAPITAL: **Plymouth**

MOROCCO

STATUS: **Kingdom**
AREA: **710,895 sq km (274,414 sq miles)**
POPULATION: **26,318,000**
ANNUAL NATURAL INCREASE: **2.5%**
CAPITAL: **Rabat**
LANGUAGE: **Arabic, French, Spanish, Berber**
RELIGION: **Muslim majority, Christian and Jewish minorities**
CURRENCY: **Moroccan dirham (MAD)**
ORGANIZATIONS: **Arab League, UN**

The coastal plain is interrupted in the east by the Rif mountains. To the south rise the Atlas mountains, beyond which lie the arid plains of the Saharan fringe. Most of Morocco is hot and arid, but the Mediterranean coast experiences more temperate conditions. Agriculture is important, but due to the continuing threat of drought it is heavily reliant upon irrigation. The major crops are wheat and barley. Morocco has the world's largest phosphate deposits. Tourism is a major industry.

MOZAMBIQUE

STATUS: **Republic**
AREA: **784,755 sq km (302,915 sq miles)**
POPULATION: **14,872,000**
ANNUAL NATURAL INCREASE: **2.7%**
CAPITAL: **Maputo**
LANGUAGE: **Portuguese, tribal languages**
RELIGION: **majority traditional beliefs, 15% Christian, 15% Muslim**
CURRENCY: **metical (MZM)**
ORGANIZATIONS: **OAU, UN**

The greater part of Mozambique is a plateau with savannah vegetation. The coast is fringed by coral reefs and lagoons. The climate, hottest along the coast, is tropical, with most rain falling in the period October to March. Over 90 per cent of the population are subsistence farmers cultivating coconuts, cashews, cotton, maize and rice. Mozambique also acts as an entrepôt, handling exports from South Africa and landlocked Zambia and Malawi. Coal is the main mineral deposit and there are large reserves. Other underexploited minerals are iron ore, bauxite and gold. However, Mozambique is a very poor country due to recent unrest, and the economy will require many years of reconstruction.

NAMIBIA

STATUS: **Republic**
AREA: **824,295 sq km (318,180 sq miles)**
POPULATION: **1,534,000**
ANNUAL NATURAL INCREASE: **3.1%**
CAPITAL: **Windhoek**
LANGUAGE: **Afrikaans, German, English, regional languages**
RELIGION: **90% Christian**
CURRENCY: **Namibian dollar (Namdollar)**
ORGANIZATIONS: **Comm., OAU, UN**

The Atlantic coast of Namibia is fringed by the Namib desert. Eastwards the land rises to a mountainous spine aligned north–south. The interior plateau, generally higher than 1,000m (3,300 ft), is part of the Kalahari desert region. Namibia has an arid climate, with any rain falling in summer months. Maize and sorghum are grown in the northern highlands and sheep are reared in the south. Namibia is, however, rich in mineral resources, with large deposits of diamonds, lead, tin and zinc, and the world's largest uranium mine. The rich coastal waters, fed by the Benguela Current, are the basis of a successful fishing industry.

NAURU

STATUS: **Republic**
AREA: **21.2 sq km (8 sq miles)**
POPULATION: **9,919**
ANNUAL NATURAL INCREASE: **-0.3%**
CAPITAL: **Yaren**
LANGUAGE: **Nauruan, English**
RELIGION: **Nauruan Protestant majority**
CURRENCY: **Australian dollar (AUD)**
ORGANIZATIONS: **Comm. (special member)**

Nauru is one of the world's smallest republics. Its relief is that of a coral atoll with a fertile strip surrounding a central barren plateau. Because of the lack of urban development, Nauru has no official capital; the largest settlement is Yaren. The climate is equatorial. Nauru is rich in phosphate, which is exported to Australia and Japan. However, deposits may soon be exhausted and Nauru will have to look elsewhere for its income.

NEPAL

STATUS: **Kingdom**
AREA: **141,415 sq km (54,585 sq miles)**
POPULATION: **20,577,000**
ANNUAL NATURAL INCREASE: **2.6%**
CAPITAL: **Katmandu (Kathmandu)**
LANGUAGE: **Nepali, Maithir, Bhojpuri**
RELIGION: **90% Hindu, 5% Buddhist, 3% Muslim**
CURRENCY: **Nepalese rupee (NPR)**
ORGANIZATIONS: **Col. Plan, UN**

The greater part of Nepal is in the Himalayas with access to some of the world's highest mountains, including Everest and Kangchenjunga. Southwards there is a hilly region dissected by valleys. A fertile plain lies along the southern border. The climate varies from subtropical on the plain to arctic on the peaks. Agriculture concentrates on rice, maize, cattle, buffaloes, sheep and goats. Industrial production has recently increased, in particular carpets and garments. Tourism is also very important to the economy.

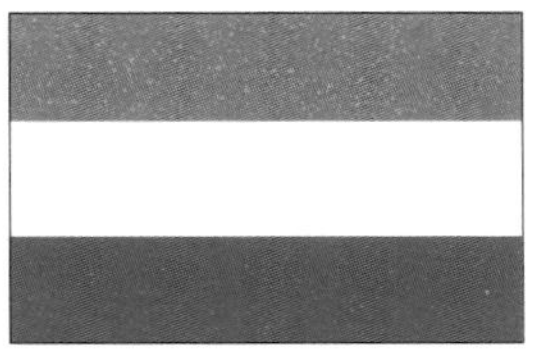

NETHERLANDS

STATUS: **Kingdom**
AREA: **41,160 sq km (15,890 sq miles)**
POPULATION: **15,269,000**
ANNUAL NATURAL INCREASE: **0.7%**
CAPITAL: **Amsterdam (seat of Government: The Hague)**
LANGUAGE: **Dutch**
RELIGION: **40% Roman Catholic, 30% Protestant, Jewish minority**
CURRENCY: **gulden (guilder or florin) (NLG)**
ORGANIZATIONS: **Council of Europe, EEA, EU, NATO, OECD, UN, WEU**

The Netherlands are the 'Low Countries' of Europe with much of the land below sea level and altitudes nowhere exceeding 330 m (1,080 ft). The coastline is often fringed by sand dunes, and inland large tracts of land reclaimed from the sea form the fertile polders. The Dutch climate is mild and maritime. The country is intensively farmed with livestock, diary farming and mixed crops, (including cereals, sugarbeet and vegetables) predominating. The Netherlands is a trading nation, with transport equipment and machinery, chemicals and plastics, and food, drink and tobacco accounting for well over half the export value in 1992. Lacking in mineral resources, much of the heavy industry of the Netherlands is dependent on natural gas. Most of the manufacturing industry has developed around Rotterdam. Here, oil refineries, steelworks, chemical and plastic industries and food processing plants have developed.

NETHERLANDS ANTILLES

STATUS: **Self-governing Part of Netherlands Realm**
AREA: **993 sq km (383 sq miles)**
POPULATION: **191,311**
CAPITAL: **Willemstad**

NEW CALEDONIA

STATUS: **Overseas Territory of France**
AREA: **19,105 sq km (7,375 sq miles)**
POPULATION: **164,173**
CAPITAL: **Nouméa**

NEW ZEALAND

STATUS: **Commonwealth Nation**
AREA: **265,150 sq km (102,350 sq miles)**
POPULATION: **3,470,000**
ANNUAL NATURAL INCREASE: **0.7%**
CAPITAL: **Wellington**
LANGUAGE: **English, Maori**
RELIGION: **35% Anglican Christian, 22% Presbyterian, 16% Roman Catholic**
CURRENCY: **New Zealand dollar (NZD)**
ORGANIZATIONS: **ANZUS, Col. Plan, Comm., OECD, UN**

The two main islands that make up New Zealand lie in the South Pacific Ocean. On the more heavily populated North Island, mountain ranges, broad fertile valleys and volcanic plateaux predominate. South Island is also mountainous, with the Southern Alps running its full length. The Canterbury Plains forms its only extensive lowland. North Island is temperate. South Island has cooler winters and upland snow. Rainfall is distributed throughout the year. Nearly 20 per cent of the land is forested and 50 per cent is pasture. Agriculture is the mainstay of the economy. The country is one of the world's leading exporters of beef, mutton and wool. Fish, timber and wood pulp have become increasingly important commodities, while coal, petroleum and recently natural gas have been successfully exported. Most exploited minerals are for industrial use – clay, iron sand, limestone and sand. For almost a decade New Zealand has undergone rigorous economic reform, with the abolition of subsidies and tariff barriers and extensive privatization. New trading links are developing with countries bordering the Pacific. Tourism is proving to be New Zealand's fastest-expanding industry.

NICARAGUA

STATUS: **Republic**
AREA: **148,000 sq km (57,130 sq miles)**
POPULATION: **4,130,000**
ANNUAL NATURAL INCREASE: **2.8%**
CAPITAL: **Managua**
LANGUAGE: **Spanish**
RELIGION: **Roman Catholic**
CURRENCY: **cordoba (NIC)**
ORGANIZATIONS: **CACM, OAS, UN**

Pine-clad hills separate the east, much of which remains covered with undisturbed forest, from the more developed western regions. The west is dominated by the large Lake Nicaragua. The highest land, the Cordillera Isabelia, is in the north. The climate is tropical. Agriculture is the main occupation, with cotton, coffee, sugarcane and fruit the main exports. However, some sugar plantations are idle because workers cannot afford to accept the meagre wages on offer, and cotton is not grown for lack of fertilizer and seeds. Around 60 per cent of the population is unemployed. Gold, silver and copper are mined.

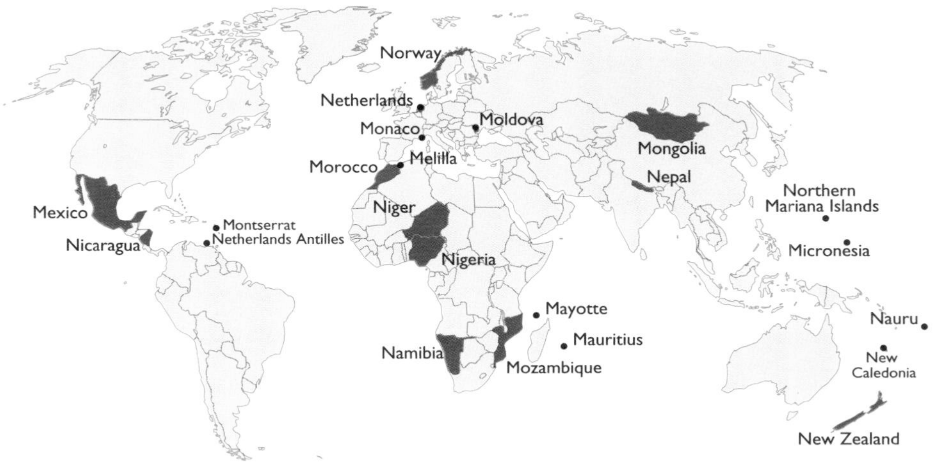

NIGER

STATUS: **Republic**
AREA: **1,186,410 sq km (457,955 sq miles)**
POPULATION: **8,252,000**
ANNUAL NATURAL INCREASE: **3.2%**
CAPITAL: **Niamey**
LANGUAGE: **French, Hausa and other native languages**
RELIGION: **85% Muslim, 15% traditional beliefs**
CURRENCY: **CFA franc (W Africa) (XOF)**
ORGANIZATIONS: **ECOWAS, OAU, UN**

Apart from savannah in the south and in the Niger valley, most of the vast country of Niger falls within the Sahara desert. The Aïr mountains in the central region rise from the plains to 2,000 m (6,562 ft). Rainfall is low. Temperatures are high for most of the year. More than 90 per cent of the population is engaged in agriculture, either in livestock rearing or in subsistence farming, with groundnuts and cotton as cash crops. Recent droughts have affected both cereals and livestock. Niger's only significant export is uranium. Phosphates, coal, tin and tungsten are also mined and other existing minerals are yet to be exploited.

NIGERIA

STATUS: **Federal Republic**
AREA: **923,850 sq km (356,605 sq miles)**
POPULATION: **115,664,000**
ANNUAL NATURAL INCREASE: **2.9%**
CAPITAL: **Abuja**
LANGUAGE: **English, Hausa, Yoruba, Ibo**
RELIGION: **Muslim majority, 35% Christian, animist minority**
CURRENCY: **naira (NGN)**
ORGANIZATIONS: **Comm., ECOWAS, OAU, OPEC, UN**

A coastal zone of sandy beaches, swamps and lagoons gives way to rainforest, grading into savannah on high plateaux. To the north is the semi-desert edge of the Sahara. The Niger delta, together with shallow offshore waters, holds vast underlying oil and gas reserves. The climate is tropical. The humid south has a heavy rainfall, falling mainly from April to October. Inland the rainfall is lower and the rainy season shorter. Virtually all Nigeria's foreign earnings come from its vast oil resources in the Niger delta. Gas reserves are relatively undeveloped. However, the Nigerian debt burden is heavy, inflation is 100 per cent a year, and poverty and unemployment have increased.

NORTHERN MARIANA ISLANDS

STATUS: **Self-governing Commonwealth of USA**
AREA: **471 sq km (182 sq miles)**
POPULATION: **43,345**
CAPITAL: **Saipan**
LANGUAGE: **English**
RELIGION: **Christian majority**
CURRENCY: **US dollar (USD)**

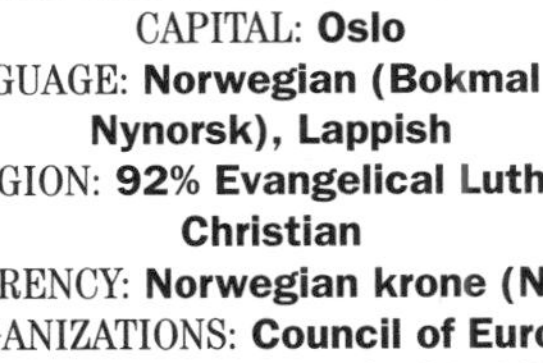

NORWAY

STATUS: **Kingdom**
AREA: **323,895 sq km (125,025 sq miles)**
POPULATION: **4,305,000**
ANNUAL NATURAL INCREASE: **0.4%**
CAPITAL: **Oslo**
LANGUAGE: **Norwegian (Bokmal and Nynorsk), Lappish**
RELIGION: **92% Evangelical Lutheran Christian**
CURRENCY: **Norwegian krone (NOK)**
ORGANIZATIONS: **Council of Europe, EEA, EFTA, NATO, OECD, UN**

The country is characterized by high mountainous terrain and a very long coastline which stretches from 58° to 72°N. To the north are long deep fjords and an offshore island belt, and in the south forests and many lakes. The climate is modified in coastal areas by the North Atlantic Drift. Summers become warmer and winters colder inland. Rainfall can reach up to 900 mm (36 inches) in the northern mountains. Norway is a fishing nation, with 90 per cent of its catch exported. Fish farming is an expanding sector, producing salmon. Two thirds of the population are engaged in service industries, often related to oil and shipping activities. Norway exploits the North Sea's vast oil and natural gas resources, making it Western Europe's largest oil producer. Other exports include timber, pulp and paper, based on widespread coniferous forests. Hydro-electric power supports industries such as electrical engineering and aluminium production.

STATES AND TERRITORIES OF THE WORLD

OMAN

STATUS: **Sultanate**
AREA: **271,950 sq km (104,970 sq miles)**
POPULATION: **1,637,000**
ANNUAL NATURAL INCREASE: **3.8%**
CAPITAL: **Muscat (Masqaṭ)**
LANGUAGE: **Arabic, English**
RELIGION: **75% Ibadi Muslim, 25% Sunni Muslim**
CURRENCY: **rial Omani (OMR)**
ORGANIZATIONS: **Arab League, UN**

The Sultanate occupies the northeast coast of Arabia with a detached portion, an enclave in the north of the Musandam peninsula, separated from the remainder of Oman by the territory of the United Arab Emirates. Oman is a land of deserts, with mountains in Dhofar (Ẓufār) in the south and in Jebel Akhdar (Jabal Akhḍar) in the north. There are some narrow coastal strips which are fertile. The climate is hot and mostly dry, although the coasts are more humid than the interior and the southern upland regions receive monsoon rains from June to September. The main crops are dates, alfalfa, tomatoes, aubergines, limes and in the south bananas. Mining has been developed in recent years, with copper ores from the Sohar region. However, oil provides over 95 per cent of export revenue.

PAKISTAN

STATUS: **Republic**
AREA: **803,940 sq km (310,320 sq miles)**
POPULATION: **119,107,000**
ANNUAL NATURAL INCREASE: **3.1%**
CAPITAL: **Islamabad**
LANGUAGE: **Urdu, Punjabi, Sindhi, Pushtu, English**
RELIGION: **90% Muslim**
CURRENCY: **Pakistan rupee (PKR)**
ORGANIZATIONS **Col. Plan, Comm., UN**

Dominated by the great lowland basin drained by the Indus river system, the land rises steeply northwards to the mountains of the Hindu Kush. The west is semi-desert plateaux and mountain ranges. Temperatures are generally warm except in the mountains, with temperatures averaging 27°C (80°F). Rainfall is monsoonal, reaching 900 mm (36 inches) in the northern mountains. Over 50 per cent of the population are engaged in agriculture, which is confined to the irrigated areas near the great rivers. The main crops are wheat, cotton, maize, rice and sugarcane. There are many types of low-grade mineral deposits, such as coal and copper, but these are little developed. The main industries are food processing and metals, but these contribute only 20 per cent to the economy.

PALAU

STATUS: **Self-governing state in Compact of Free Association with USA**
AREA: **497 sq km (192 sq miles)**
POPULATION: **15,450**
CAPITAL: **Babelthuap**

PANAMA

STATUS: **Republic**
AREA: **78,515 sq km (30,305 sq miles)**
POPULATION: **2,535,000**
ANNUAL NATURAL INCREASE: **2.1%**
CAPITAL: **Panama City (Panama)**
LANGUAGE: **Spanish, English**
RELIGION: **Roman Catholic majority**
CURRENCY: **balboa (PAB), US dollar (USD)**
ORGANIZATIONS: **OAS, UN**

Panama is situated at the narrowest part of Central America and has both Pacific and Caribbean coastlines. Mountain ranges reaching heights exceeding 3,000 m (9,800 ft) run the length of the country. Much of the tropical forest has been cleared, but some remains towards the border with Colombia in Darien. Panama has a hot, steamy climate with summer rainfall which is heaviest along the Pacific coast. The average temperature throughout the year is around 27°C (80°F). Panama has among the world's largest copper reserves, but these are hardly developed. Most foreign revenue is earned from the Panama Canal, and from the merchant fleet registered in the country's name. Petroleum products are also exported.

PAPUA NEW GUINEA

STATUS: **Commonwealth Nation**
AREA: **462,840 sq km (178,655 sq miles)**
POPULATION: **4,056,000**
ANNUAL NATURAL INCREASE: **2.3%**
CAPITAL: **Port Moresby**
LANGUAGE: **English, Pidgin English, native languages**
RELIGION: **Pantheist, Christian minority**
CURRENCY: **kina (PGK)**
ORGANIZATIONS: **Col. Plan, Comm., UN**

Papua New Guinea (the eastern half of New Guinea and neighbouring islands) is a mountainous country with the ranges of central New Guinea peaks reaching well over 4,000 m (13,100 ft). The forested mountains are bordered by plains, swamps and huge delta regions. The country includes some 600 other islands. It has an equatorial climate with temperatures of 21–32°C (70–90°F), and annual rainfall, averaging 2,000 mm (79 inches) annually, falls most heavily between December and March. Most of the population is engaged in agriculture, producing cash crops including coconuts, cocoa, coffee, rubber, tea and sugar. Tropical logs have become one of the mainstays of the economy. Papua New Guinea is rich in natural resources; copper, gold, silver are the three main minerals.

PARAGUAY

STATUS: **Republic**
AREA: **406,750 sq km (157,055 sq miles)**
POPULATION: **4,124,000**
ANNUAL NATURAL INCREASE: **2.9%**
CAPITAL: **Asunción**
LANGUAGE: **Spanish, Guarani**
RELIGION: **90% Roman Catholic**
CURRENCY: **guarani (PYG)**
ORGANIZATIONS: **OAS, UN**

Paraguay is a landlocked country in South America. The river Paraguay separates two distinct areas: a hilly, heavily forested region to the east and a western zone of marsh and flat alluvial plains. The climate is subtropical with hot, rainy summers from December to March and generally mild winters. Temperatures average 15°C (59°F) all year. Agriculture is the mainstay of the economy, with cash crops of cotton and soya beans, although livestock, forestry products and food processing are also important. The largest hydro-electric dam in the world is at Itaipú, on the Parana river. This was constructed as a joint project with Brazil, making Paraguay self-sufficient in energy.

PERU

STATUS: **Republic**
AREA: **1,285,215 sq km (496,095 sq miles)**
POPULATION: **22,454,000**
ANNUAL NATURAL INCREASE: **2.1%**
CAPITAL: **Lima**
LANGUAGE: **Spanish, Quechua, Aymara**
RELIGION: **Roman Catholic majority**
CURRENCY: **sol (PEN)**
ORGANIZATIONS: **OAS, UN**

A narrow plain along the Pacific coast rises sharply to the high cordilleras of the Andes chain. East of the Andes is high plateau country dissected by fertile valleys, which descends in the extreme east to the Amazon Basin and its tropical rainforests. Peru lies in tropical latitudes just south of the Equator but its climate is conditioned by its relief. The coastal plain is cooled by the Humboldt current. The Andes are snow covered and the interior plateau exhibits wide ranges of temperature. Only in the east of the country do the high rainfall and humidity associated with equatorial latitudes occur. The agricultural sector produces cotton and sugar for export. Fish and timber are also important. Peru is rich in natural resources; of copper, lead, zinc, silver and other minerals. There are also oil reserves in the interior. However, poor communications have hindered the development of Peru's economy.

PHILIPPINES

STATUS: **Republic**
AREA: **300,000 sq km (115,800 sq miles)**
POPULATION: **64,259,000**
ANNUAL NATURAL INCREASE: **2.3%**
CAPITAL: **Manila**
LANGUAGE: **Pilipino (Tagalog), English, Spanish, Cebuano**
RELIGION: **90% Christian, 7% Muslim**
CURRENCY: **Philippine peso (PHP)**
ORGANIZATIONS: **ASEAN, Col. Plan, UN**

Of the numerous islands that make up the nation, the larger ones are mountainous and forested. Volcanic activity is common, and the eruption of Mt Pinatubo in 1991 was one of the most violent this century. The climate is tropical, tempered by maritime influence. Rainfall, sometimes accompanied by typhoons, occurs mainly from June to October. Fishing is important, but small farms dominate the economy, producing rice and copra for domestic consumption and other coconut and sugar products for export. Forestry is becoming increasingly important. The main exports are textiles, fruit and electronic products. High unemployment and emigration are problems to be faced.

PITCAIRN ISLAND

STATUS: **UK Dependent Territory**
AREA: **45 sq km (17.25 sq miles)**
POPULATION: **71**
CAPITAL: **Adamstown**

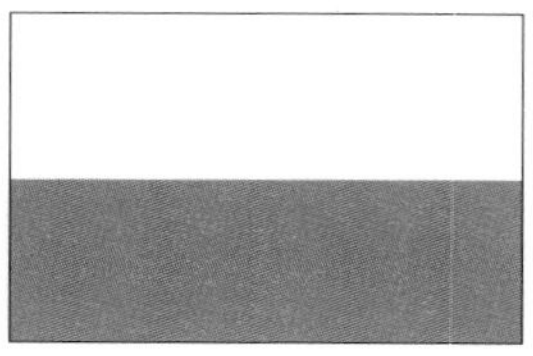

POLAND

STATUS: **Republic**
AREA: **312,685 sq km (120,695 sq miles)**
POPULATION: **38,365,000**
ANNUAL NATURAL INCREASE: **0.4%**
CAPITAL: **Warsaw (Warszawa)**
LANGUAGE: **Polish**
RELIGION: **90% Roman Catholic**
CURRENCY: **zloty (PLZ)**
ORGANIZATIONS: **Council of Europe, OIEC, UN**

Much of Poland lies in the North European plain and is a land of woods and lakes. The highest parts are in the south, where peaks in the Tatra (Tatry) mountains reach almost 2,500 m (8,200 ft). The climatic regime is continental, with warm summers and cold winters, when January temperatures fall well below freezing. Most rainfall occurs in the summer months, averaging 520–730 mm (21–29 inches). Both agriculture and natural resources play important roles in the economy. Agricultural output is increasing with improved yields of grain, potatoes and sugarbeet. There are large reserves of coal, copper, sulphur and natural gas. Manufacturing output has strengthened, and the private sector is expanding rapidly. Major industries are shipbuilding in the north and production of metals and chemicals in large mining centres in the south. The coalition government is committed to continuing the programme of reforms and privatization, and Poland may eventually apply for membership of the European Union.

PORTUGAL

STATUS: **Republic**
AREA: **91,630 sq km (35,370 sq miles)**
POPULATION: **9,846,000**
ANNUAL NATURAL INCREASE: **-0.7%**
CAPITAL: **Lisbon (Lisboa)**
LANGUAGE: **Portuguese**

RELIGION: **Roman Catholic majority**
CURRENCY: **escudo (PTE)**
ORGANIZATIONS: **Council of Europe, EEA, EU, NATO, OECD, UN, WEU**

Portugal occupies the western Atlantic coast of the Iberian Peninsula. North of the river Tagus most of the country is high ground with pine forests. Land to the south is generally less than 300 m (1,000 ft) above sea level. The north of the country is influenced by the Atlantic and is cool and moist. The south is warmer, with dry mild winters. Agriculture, although undeveloped, employs 12 per cent of the workforce; wines, olives, wheat, maize and beans are important exports. In industry the chief exports are textiles and clothing, footwear and wood products. The tendency in recent years has been for the closure of some older industries such as ship building, fertilizers and steel, whereas the rapid rise of new industry based on foreign investment is evident. Mineral deposits include coal, copper, kaolinite and uranium. Tourism is an important industry.

PUERTO RICO

STATUS: **Self-governing Commonwealth of USA**
AREA: **8,960 sq km (3,460 sq miles)**
POPULATION: **3,580,000**
CAPITAL: **San Juan**

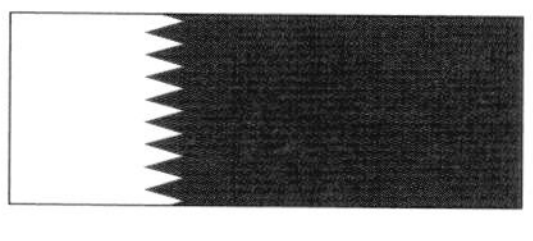

QATAR

STATUS: **State**
AREA: **11,435 sq km (4,415 sq miles)**
POPULATION: **453,000**
ANNUAL NATURAL INCREASE: **6%**
CAPITAL: **Doha (Ad Dawḩah)**
LANGUAGE: **Arabic, English**
RELIGION: **Muslim**
CURRENCY: **Qatari riyal (QAR)**
ORGANIZATIONS: **Arab League, OPEC, UN**

The country occupies all of the Qatar peninsula which reaches north from the north-east Arabian coast into the Persian Gulf. The peninsula is flat, never higher than 75 m (250 ft), and barren with sand dunes and salt pans. Vegetation is limited to small patches of scrub. The climate is typical of a desert region. Some very limited rainfall occurs in winter, averaging 63 mm (2.5 inches). Summer temperatures are hot and winters are warm. July temperatures average 37°C (98°F). Irrigation schemes are expanding production of fruit and vegetables for home consumption. The main source of revenue is from the exploitation of oil and gas reserves. The N.W. Dome oilfield contains 12 per cent of known world gas reserves. In 1992 phase 1 of the North Field gas project came on stream; this is to supply internal industrial needs. Phase 2, due for completion in 1997, is to provide liquefied natural gas for export, mainly to Japan.

RÉUNION

STATUS: **Overseas Department of France**
AREA: **2,510 sq km (969 sq miles)**
POPULATION: **624,000**
CAPITAL: **Saint-Denis**

RODRIGUES

STATUS: **Island of Mauritius**
AREA: **104 sq km (40 sq miles)**
POPULATION: **34,379**

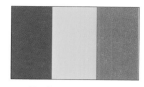

ROMANIA

STATUS: **Republic**
AREA: **237,500 sq km (91,699 sq miles)**
POPULATION: **22,767,000**
ANNUAL NATURAL INCREASE: **0.1%**
CAPITAL: **Bucharest (Bucureşti)**
LANGUAGE: **Romanian, Magyar**
RELIGION: **85% Romanian Orthodox,**
CURRENCY: **leu (ROL)**
ORGANIZATIONS: **OIEC, UN**

The dominant physical feature is the Carpathian mountains in the north and centre of the country which curve around the Transylvanian plateau. To the south lies the valley of the Danube which drains through a delta into the Black Sea. Lowlands to the west, east and south contain rich agricultural land. Romania enjoys fine warm summers tempered by breezes along the Black Sea coast. Winters are cold, especially in the mountains. The Romanian economy has not been successful in emerging from Communism. Forced industrialization has taken the economy from one based on agriculture to one dependent on heavy industry, notably chemicals, metal processing and machine-building. Political and economic prospects for the future look bleak.

ROSS DEPENDENCY

STATUS: **Antarctic Territory Overseas of New Zealand**
AREA: **425,000sq km (164,050 sq miles)**
POPULATION: **no permanent population**

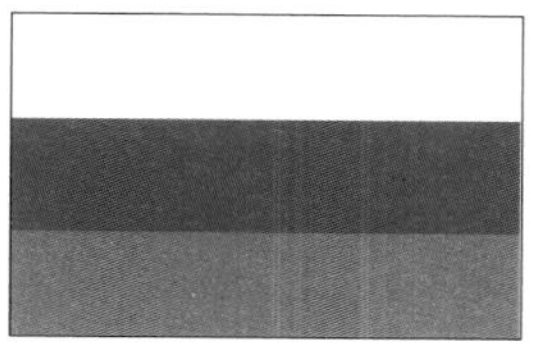

RUSSIAN FEDERATION

STATUS: **Federation**
AREA: **17,078,005 sq km (6,592,110 sq miles)**
POPULATION: **148,673,000**
ANNUAL NATURAL INCREASE: **0.5%**
CAPITAL: **Moscow (Moskva)**
LANGUAGE: **Russian**
RELIGION: **Russian Orthodox, Jewish and Muslim minorities**
CURRENCY: **rouble**
ORGANIZATIONS: **CIS, UN**

Covering much of eastern and northeastern Europe and all of northern Asia, the Russian Federation (Russia) displays an enormous variety of land forms and climates, which means that within its borders there is enormous physical diversity. The highest mountain ranges, such as the Caucasus and Altai, are found along its southern borders but much of the remainder is plain, steppe and plateaux, often forest covered. The great river systems of Siberia, such as the Ob, Yenisey and Lena, drain into the Arctic Ocean, but west of the Urals the major river, the Volga, runs southwards to the Caspian Sea. In general, Russia lies within temperate latitudes, though in its more northerly regions conditions are sub-arctic. The climate throughout most of the territory shows continental characteristics, with large sea-

sonal variations in temperature, and precipitation occurring mainly in the summer months. The majority of the population lives west of the north–south spine of the Urals but in recent decades there has been substantial migration eastwards to the Siberian basin in order to exploit its vast natural resources. Oil and gas pipelines link Siberia to refineries further west in Russia and elsewhere in Europe. Russia's extraordinary wealth of natural resources was a key factor in the Soviet period. Heavy industry still plays a decisive role in the economy, while light and consumer industries have remained relatively backward and underdeveloped. Agricultural land covers one sixth of Russia's territory, but there remains great potential for increase through drainage and clearance. By the mid-1980s the Soviet system was finally acknowledged to have reached an impasse, and the failure of the *perestroika* programme for reform precipitated the disintegration of the Soviet Union, which finally broke up in 1991. The challenge for Russia is to achieve transition from a state planned and run as a centralist economy to one which is market orientated. In 1993 a decree was signed which allowed Russians (but not foreigners) to buy and sell farm land, therefore creating a land market for the first time in decades. Future progress, however, may be slow due to political unrest.

RWANDA

STATUS: **Republic**
AREA: **26,330 sq km (10,165 sq miles)**
POPULATION: **7,526,000**
ANNUAL NATURAL INCREASE: **3%**
CAPITAL: **Kigali**
LANGUAGE: **French, Kinyarwanda (Bantu), tribal languages**
RELIGION: **50% animist, 50% Christian (mostly Roman Catholic)**
CURRENCY: **Rwanda franc (RWF)**
ORGANIZATIONS: **OAU, UN**

Formerly part of Runanda-Urundi, Rwanda gained independence in 1962. Small and isolated, Rwanda is comprised of mountains and moist plateaux to the east of the Rift Valley. A ridge of volcanic peaks, 3,000 m (9,800 ft) in height, traverses the country from north to south. The climate is warm with a dry season from June to August. Rwanda, one of the most densely populated countries in the world, survives by intense cultivation. Agriculture is basically subsistence, with coffee the major export. Few minerals have been discovered, and manufacturing is confined to food processing and construction materials. Rwanda is already dependent on foreign aid to supplement revenue from its only significant export crop, coffee. Civil war has left many thousands dead, created around 900,000 refugees and devastated the country, requiring massive international relief.

RYUKYU ISLANDS

STATUS: **Island of Japan**
AREA: **2,196 sq km (848 sq miles)**
POPULATION: **no permanent population**

ST HELENA

STATUS: **UK Dependent Territory**
AREA: **122 sq km (47 sq miles)**
POPULATION: **5,700**
CAPITAL: **Jamestown**

ST KITTS-NEVIS

STATUS: **Commonwealth State**
AREA: **262 sq km (101 sq miles)**
POPULATION: **44,000**
ANNUAL NATURAL INCREASE: **-0.4%**
CAPITAL: **Basseterre**
LANGUAGE: **English**
RELIGION: **Christian (mostly Protestant)**
CURRENCY: **E Caribbean dollar (XCD)**
ORGANIZATIONS: **CARICOM, Comm., OAS, UN**

St Kitts-Nevis gained full independence in 1983. The country, situated in the Leeward, Islands, comprises of two volcanic islands each which have peaks exceeding 1,000 m (3,300 ft). Their slopes are covered with tropical forest. The climate is warm but tempered with trade winds, with temperatures between 16°–33°C (61°–91°F). Rainfall is abundant throughout the year; the driest period is in spring. The economic mainstay of St Kitts is sugar, and most arable land is devoted to cane plantations. Other crops contributing to the economy are cotton, especially on Nevis, and a variety of tropical fruits. In recent years tourism has developed and there has been growth in light manufacturing and service industries, for example the production of electronic components and data processing.

STATES AND TERRITORIES OF THE WORLD

ST LUCIA

STATUS: **Commonwealth State**
AREA: **616 sq km (238 sq miles)**
POPULATION: **136,000**
ANNUAL NATURAL INCREASE: **1.9%**
CAPITAL: **Castries**
LANGUAGE: **English, French patois**
RELIGION: **82% Roman Catholic**
CURRENCY: **E. Caribbean dollar (XCD)**
ORGANIZATIONS: **Caricom, Comm., OAS, UN**

St Lucia is volcanic and features forested mountains, the highest of which approaches 1,000 m (3,300 ft). Temperatures are hot but tempered by trade winds. Rainfall, always abundant, is heaviest in summer and autumn. Most of the population is employed in farming, growing coconuts, citrus fruit, copra and bananas. Manufactured goods are varied, including electrical and electronic components for export. There are no commercial mineral deposits. Tourism is a rapidly developing industry.

ST PIERRE AND MIQUELON

STATUS: **Territorial Collectivity of France**
AREA: **241 sq km (93 sq miles)**
POPULATION: **6,392**
CAPITAL: **St Pierre**

ST VINCENT

STATUS: **Commonwealth State**
AREA: **389 sq km (150 sq miles)**
POPULATION: **107,598**
ANNUAL NATURAL INCREASE: **0.9%**
CAPITAL: **Kingstown**
LANGUAGE: **English**
RELIGION: **Christian**
CURRENCY: **E. Caribbean dollar (XCD)**
ORGANIZATIONS: **Caricom, Comm., OAS, UN**

St Vincent, in the Lesser Antilles, comprises a main island and a chain of smaller islands called the Grenadines. The climate is maritime tropical with warm temperatures throughout the year. The heaviest rainfalls are in summer and autumn. The economy is dependent on agriculture and tourism, the main crop being bananas. Arrowroot, used in medicines and the manufacture of computer paper, is also important. Tourism is well established.

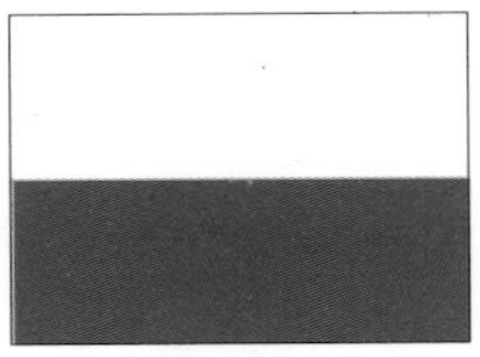

SAN MARINO

STATUS: **Republic**
AREA: **61 sq km (24 sq miles)**
POPULATION: **24,000**
ANNUAL NATURAL INCREASE: **1.2%**
CAPITAL: **San Marino**
LANGUAGE: **Italian**
RELIGION: **Roman Catholic**
CURRENCY: **Italian lira (ITL), San Marino coinage**
ORGANIZATIONS: **Council of Europe, UN**

An independent state within Italy, San Marino straddles a limestone peak in the Apennines south of Rimini. The hilly landscape culminates in the three peaks of Mt Titano at 739 m (2,425 ft). The climate is temperate, with snow in winter and showers in summer. Agriculture is based on livestock, wheat and grapes, and some sugarcane is grown for the production of rum and other drinks. The main export is wine, with others including building stone, ceramics, textiles and furniture. Sales of postage stamps contribute 10 per cent of the national income.

SÃO TOMÉ AND PRÍNCIPE

STATUS: **Republic**
AREA: **964 sq km (372 sq miles)**
POPULATION: **124,000**
ANNUAL NATURAL INCREASE: **2.3%**
CAPITAL: **São Tomé**
LANGUAGE: **Portuguese, Fang**
RELIGION: **Roman Catholic majority**
CURRENCY: **dobra (STD)**
ORGANIZATIONS: **OAU, UN**

Independent from Portugal since 1975, two large and several smaller islands make up this tiny state. Temperatures are consistent, with maxima approaching 30°C (86°F) throughout the year. Rainfall is plentiful, but July and August are dry. Cocoa, coconuts and palm oil are the main crops, grown on the rich volcanic soil. Industry is minimal and confined to factories producing beer, soap, textiles and processed food.

SARDINIA

STATUS: **Island Region of Italy**
AREA: **24,090 sq km (9,300 sq miles)**
POPULATION: **1,645,192**
CAPITAL: **Cagliari**

SAUDI ARABIA

STATUS: **Kingdom**
AREA: **2,400,900 sq km (926,745 sq miles)**
POPULATION: **16,900,000**
ANNUAL NATURAL INCREASE: **3.5%**
CAPITAL: **Riyadh (Ar Riyāḑ)**
LANGUAGE: **Arabic**
RELIGION: **90% Sunni Muslim, 5% Roman Catholic**
CURRENCY: **Saudi riyal (SAR)**
ORGANIZATIONS: **Arab League, OPEC, UN**

Most of Saudi Arabia's territory is desert or semi-desert plateaux. Towards the west ranges of mountains reaching heights over 3,000 m (9,800 ft) run parallel to the Red Sea and drop in a steep scarp to a coastal plain known as the Tihama (Tihāmat Âsīr). The temperature in summer is hot, with figures above 40°C (104°F) common. Winters are warm and rainfall is at best slight. The interior plateau slopes down gently eastwards to the Persian Gulf and supports little vegetation. The southeastern part of the country is well named as the 'Empty Quarter' (Ar Rub' al Khālī) as it is almost devoid of population. Only in the coastal strips and oases are cereals and date palms grown. Irrigation schemes and land reclamation projects are attempting to raise food production. Oil is the most important resource and export commodity, and economic development is dependent on its revenue.

SENEGAL

STATUS: **Republic**
AREA: **196,720 sq km (75,935 sq miles)**
POPULATION: **7,326,000**
ANNUAL NATURAL INCREASE: **3.0%**
CAPITAL: **Dakar**
LANGUAGE: **French, native languages**
RELIGION: **94% Sunni Muslim, animist minority**
CURRENCY: **CFA franc (W Africa) (XOF)**
ORGANIZATIONS: **ECOWAS, OAU, UN**

Arid semi-desert covers the north of Senegal, while the south is mainly fertile savannah bushland. In the southeast, plains rise up to the Fouta Djalon foothills. A tropical climate prevails, with humid rainy conditions between June and October and a drier season falling between December and May. The annual rainfall averages 560 mm (2 inches) and temperatures are in the range of 22–28°C (72–82°F). Over 70 per cent of the population is involved in agriculture. Groundnuts, the principal export crop, account for 40 per cent of all cultivated land, but frequent droughts have reduced their value as a cash crop. Ship-repairing and food processing are the major industries. Diversification into fish, phosphates, textiles and petroleum products is underway.

SEYCHELLES

STATUS: **Republic**
AREA: **404 sq km (156 sq miles)**
POPULATION: **72,000**
ANNUAL NATURAL INCREASE: **0.8%**
CAPITAL: **Victoria**
LANGUAGE: **English, French, Creole**
RELIGION: **92% Roman Catholic**
CURRENCY: **Seychelles rupee (SCR)**
ORGANIZATIONS: **Comm., OAU, UN**

The Seychelles is an archipelago of 115 islands in the Indian Ocean, the majority of which are mountainous granite. The remainder are low-lying uninhabited coral atolls. Eighty-eight per cent of the population lives on Mahé. The climate is hot and humid all year round. Rain, averaging 2,400 mm (95 inches) a year, falls mainly between December and May. Farming is restricted on the islands because of poor soil and uneven terrain; however copra, cinnamon, vanilla, coconuts, tobacco and tea are grown. Fishing is important, especially tuna which provides employment for many. Canned tuna has become a major export. Tourism has expanded greatly since the opening of the international airport in 1978.

SHIKOKU

STATUS: **Island Prefecture of Japan**
AREA: **18,755 sq km (7,240 sq miles)**
POPULATION: **4,195,000**

SICILY (SICILIA)

STATUS: **Island Region of Italy**
AREA: **25,710 sq km (9,925 sq miles)**
POPULATION: **4,989,871**
CAPITAL: **Palermo**

SIERRA LEONE

STATUS: **Republic**
AREA: **72,325 sq km (27,920 sq miles)**
POPULATION: **4,376,000**
ANNUAL NATURAL INCREASE: **2.4%**
CAPITAL: **Freetown**
LANGUAGE: **English, Krio Temne, Mende**
RELIGION: **52% animist, 39% Muslim and 8% Christian**
CURRENCY: **leone (SLL)**
ORGANIZATIONS: **Comm., ECOWAS, OAS, UN**

Sierra Leone comprises, a flat plain 113 km (70 miles) wide stretching the length of the coast, beyond which there is a forested area rising to a central highland. The climate is tropical, hot throughout the year, with a pronounced humid, rainy season between May and November. The land is not fertile due to the poor soils, with 75 per cent of the population involved in subsistence farming. The main cash crops are cocoa, coffee, ginger, nuts and palm kernels. Mining is the most important source of foreign exchange for the country. Diamonds, gold, bauxite and iron ore are mined and Sierra Leone is one of the few producers of rutile (titanium ore).

SINGAPORE

STATUS: **Republic**
AREA: **616 sq km (238 sq miles)**
POPULATION: **2,874,000**
ANNUAL NATURAL INCREASE: **1.2%**
CAPITAL: **Singapore**
LANGUAGE: **Malay, Chinese (Mandarin), Tamil, English**
RELIGION: **Daoist, Buddhist, Muslim, Christian and Hindu**
CURRENCY: **Singapore dollar (SGD)**
ORGANIZATIONS: **ASEAN, Col. Plan, Comm., UN**

Founded by Sir Stamford Raffles, Singapore has been transformed from an island of mangrove swamps into one of the world's major entrepreneurial centres. The Republic of Singapore comprises the main island, which is connected to Peninsular Malaysia by an artificial causeway, and 57 other islands. The climate is equatorial, with high temperatures, humidity and heavy rainfall throughout the year. With few natural resources, Singapore depends on the manufacture of precision goods and electronic products along with financial services. Singapore has full employment and the highest rate of home ownership and national savings anywhere in the world. However, there is one major problem for the economy: a chronic shortage of labour, exacerbated by the governments unwillingness to admit more than the absolute minimum of foreign nationals.

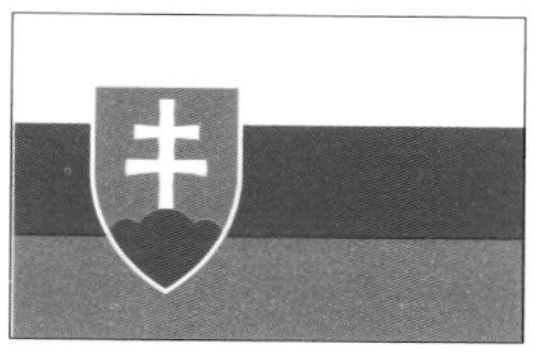

SLOVAKIA

STATUS: **Republic**
AREA: **49,035 sq km (18,932 sq miles)**
POPULATION: **5,320,000**
ANNUAL NATURAL INCREASE: **0.4%**
CAPITAL: **Bratislava**
LANGUAGE: **Slovak, Hungarian**
RELIGION: **Roman Catholic**
CURRENCY: **Slovak crown or koruna**
ORGANIZATIONS: **UN**

Slovakia is mountainous towards its border with Poland in the north, with peaks in the Tatra (Tatry) mountains exceeding 2,500 m (8,200 ft); from there the land slopes down to the lowland plains of the Danube. The climate is continental, with warm summers and cold winters. Slovakia's industrial inheritance was large manufacturing complexes devoted particularly to the armaments industry and specializing in tanks, armoured personnel carriers and artillery, but demand has declined dramatically due to the end of the Cold War. The economy has also suffered from separation from the Czech Republic. Slovakia lacks raw materials and minerals with the exception of coal. The results are harsh economic conditions which have been worsened by the influx of refugees from Romania and the former Yugoslavia.

SLOVENIA

STATUS: **Republic**
AREA: **20,250 sq km (7,815 sq miles)**
POPULATION: **1,990,000**
ANNUAL NATURAL INCREASE: **0.7%**
CAPITAL: **Ljubljana**
LANGUAGE: **Slovene**
RELIGION: **Roman Catholic**
CURRENCY: **Slovenian tolar (SLT)**
ORGANIZATIONS: **Council of Europe, UN**

Slovenia is a mountainous state in which the highest peaks of the Julian Alps (Julijske Alpe), in the northwest of the country, reach more than 2,500 m (8,200 ft). The Sava and Drava are the main river systems. The climate generally shows continental tendencies, with warm summers and cold winters, when snow is plentiful in the mountains. The small coastal strip has a Mediterranean regime. Extensive mountain pastures provide profitable dairyfarming, but the amount of cultivable land is restricted. There are large mercury mines in the northwest which, in recent decades, have supported the development of a broad range of light industries. Combined with tourism, this has given the country a well-balanced economy. After a brief military conflict Slovenia won its independence in 1991, which has since been internationally recognized. Slovenia has emerged from communist rule with a fair degree of success, even though it has lost the majority of its markets within the former Yugoslavia.

SOCOTRA

STATUS: **Island of Yemen**
AREA: **3,625 sq km (1,400 sq miles)**
POPULATION: **unknown**

SOLOMON ISLANDS

STATUS: **Commonwealth Nation**
AREA: **29,790 sq km (11,500 sq miles)**
POPULATION: **321,000**
ANNUAL NATURAL INCREASE: **2.9%**
CAPITAL: **Honiara**
LANGUAGE: **English, Pidgin English, native languages**
RELIGION: **95% Christian**
CURRENCY: **Solomon Islands dollar (SBD)**
ORGANIZATIONS: **Comm., UN**

The Solomon Islands archipelago contains several hundred islands of which six are large, volcanic, mountainous and forested. Guadalcanal, the dominant island, has the largest area of flat land. The climate in the northern islands of the group is hot and humid all year round, but a cool season develops further south. November to April is the wet season. Ninety per cent of the population is involved in subsistence agriculture, concentrated on the flat coastal zones. The main products are palm oil, cocoa, fish, timber and wood products. Mineral deposits include bauxite and phosphates mined on the island of Bellona, south of Guadalcanal. This former British protectorate became independent in 1978.

SOMALIA

STATUS: **Republic**
AREA: **630,000 sq km (243,180 sq miles)**
POPULATION: **9,204,000**
ANNUAL NATURAL INCREASE: **3.1%**
CAPITAL: **Mogadishu (Muqdisho)**
LANGUAGE: **Somali, Arabic, English, Italian**
RELIGION: **Muslim majority, Roman Catholic minority**
CURRENCY: **Somali shilling (SOS)**
ORGANIZATIONS: **Arab League, OAU, UN**

In the north an extension of the Ethiopian highlands provides the most rugged terrain. Southwards the flat landscape comprises scrub, although the coastal areas and valleys are more fertile. Inland and northern areas are relatively arid, but the Indian Ocean coasts receive moderate rains. Most of the population is nomadic, following herds of camels, sheep, goats and cattle. Little land is cultivated but cotton, maize, millet and sugarcane are grown. Bananas are a major export. Iron ore, gypsum and uranium deposits are found, but none is yet exploited. The lack of coherent government has meant the total collapse of the economy. The UN supplies aid to many famine-affected areas. However, following two years of reasonable rains, crops are starting to be harvested.

SOUTH AFRICA

STATUS: **Republic**
AREA: **1,220,845 sq km (471,369 sq miles)**

POPULATION: **37,600,000**
ANNUAL NATURAL INCREASE: **2.4%**
CAPITAL: **Pretoria (administrative) Cape Town (legislative)**
LANGUAGE: **Afrikaans, English, various African languages**
RELIGION: **mainly Christian, Hindu, Jewish and Muslim minorities**
CURRENCY: **rand (ZAR)**
ORGANIZATIONS: **Comm., UN**

The republic of South Africa is the most highly developed country in Africa. Much is an ancient plateau covered with grassland or bush, depending on the degree of aridity, and drained in the west by the Orange river system and in the east by the Limpopo and its tributaries. Mountain ridges running eastwards from the Cape culminate in the Drakensberg mountain range, overlooking the coastal lowlands of KwaZulu-Natal. There is a climatic contrast between the interior, which receives the majority of its rainfall in summer, and the coast around Cape Town, which experiences a Mediterranean style of climate with winter rains. Summers are warm and winters are mild everywhere. Rainfall in most areas is less than 500 mm (20 inches), becoming increasingly drier in the west. Agriculture is limited by poor soils, but sheep and cattle are extensively grazed. The main crops are maize, wheat, sugarcane, vegetables, cotton and vines. Wine is an important export commodity. South Africa abounds in minerals. Diamonds, gold, platinum, silver, uranium, copper, manganese and asbestos are mined and nearly 80 per cent of the African continent's coal reserves are in the country. Manufacturing and engineering are concentrated in Pretoria-Witwatersrand-Vereeniging and around the ports. Most foreign revenue is earned through exports of minerals, metals, precious stones, textiles, chemicals and tobacco. South Africa has the wealth and infrastructure to achieve prosperity for all its people, and could be a catalyst for progress in Africa generally. In 1994 the first ever multiracial elections were held in South Africa, with Nelson Mandela becoming the new president.

EASTERN CAPE

STATUS: **Province**
AREA: **174,405 sq km (67,338 sq miles)**
POPULATION: **5,900,000**
CAPITAL: **East London**

EASTERN TRANSVAAL

STATUS: **Province**
AREA: **73,377 sq km (28,311 sq miles)**
POPULATION: **2,600,000**
CAPITAL **Nelspruit**

KWAZULU-NATAL

STATUS: **Province**
AREA: **90,925 sq km (35,106 sq miles)**
POPULATION: **8,000,000**
CAPITAL: **Durban**

NORTHERN CAPE

STATUS: **Province**
AREA: **369,552 sq km (142,684 sq miles)**
POPULATION: **700,000**
CAPITAL: **Kimberley**

NORTHERN TRANSVAAL

STATUS: **Province**
AREA: **121,766 sq km (47,014 sq miles)**
POPULATION: **4,700,000**
CAPITAL: **Pietersburg**

NORTH WEST

STATUS: **Province**
AREA: **120,170 sq km (46,398 sq miles)**
POPULATION: **3,300,000**
CAPITAL: **Klerksdorp**

ORANGE FREE STATE

STATUS: **Province**
AREA: **123,893 sq km (47,835 sq miles)**
POPULATION: **2,500,000**
CAPITAL: **Bloemfontein**

PRETORIA-WITWATERSRAND-VEREENIGING (PWV)

STATUS: **Province**
AREA: **18,078 sq km(6,980 sq miles)**
POPULATION: **6,500,000**
CAPITAL: **Johannesburg**

WESTERN CAPE

STATUS: **Province**
AREA: **128,679 sq km (49,683 sq miles)**
POPULATION: **3,400,000**
CAPITAL: **Cape Town**

SOUTHERN AND ANTARCTIC TERRITORIES

STATUS: **Overseas Territory of France**
AREA: **439,580 sq km (169,680 sq miles)**
POPULATION: **180**

SOUTH GEORGIA AND THE SOUTH SANDWICH ISLANDS

STATUS: **UK Dependent Territory**
AREA: **3,755 sq km (1,450 sq miles)**
POPULATION: **no permanent population**

STATES AND TERRITORIES OF THE WORLD

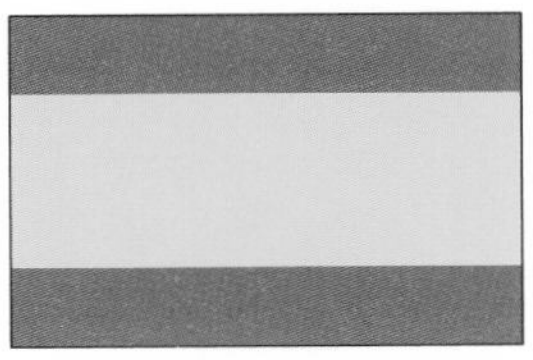

SPAIN

STATUS: **Kingdom**
AREA: **504,880 sq km (194,885 sq miles)**
POPULATION: **39,166,000**
ANNUAL NATURAL INCREASE: **0.5%**
CAPITAL: **Madrid**
LANGUAGE: **Spanish (Castilian), Catalan, Basque, Galician**
RELIGION: **Roman Catholic**
CURRENCY: **Spanish peseta**
ORGANIZATIONS: **Council of Europe, EEA, EU, NATO, OECD, UN, WEU**

Once a great colonial power, Spain occupies most of the Iberian Peninsula. Mainland Spain is mostly high plateaux, often forested in the north but more open in the south. The principal ranges are the Pyrenees and the central sierras northwest of Madrid, while the greatest extent of lowland is in the lower valley of the Guadalquivir. Climate is affected regionally by latitude and proximity to the Atlantic Ocean and Mediterranean Sea. Temperate maritime conditions in the north grade into hotter, drier regimes in the south. Winter can bring very cold weather to the central plateaux. Much of the land is covered by Mediterranean scrub, but wheat, barley, maize, grapes, olives, tobacco and citrus fruit are cultivated. Textile manufacturing in the northeast and steel, chemicals, consumer goods and vehicle manufacturing in the towns and cities have proved a magnet for great numbers of the rural population. Other major industries are cement, fishing and forestry. Main minerals are coal, iron ore, uranium and zinc. Tourism is of vital importance to the economy.

SPITSBERGEN

STATUS: **Main Island of Svalvard**
AREA: **39,045 sq km (15,070 sq miles)**
POPULATION: **3,477**

SRI LANKA

STATUS: **Republic**
AREA: **65,610 sq km (25,325 sq miles)**
POPULATION: **17,405,000**
ANNUAL NATURAL INCREASE: **1.5%**
CAPITAL: **Colombo**
LANGUAGE: **Sinhala, Tamil, English**
RELIGION: **70% Buddhist, 15% Hindu, Roman Catholic and Muslim minorities**
CURRENCY: **Sri Lanka rupee (LKR)**
ORGANIZATIONS: **Col. Plan, Comm., UN**

Situated only 19 km (12 miles) from the mainland of India and lying just above the Equator, Sri Lanka is an island that varies in character from tropical jungle to lush temperate hills. The highest point is Mt Pidurutalagala, which reaches 2,518 m (8,261 ft) above sea level. Its climate varies from exceptionally hot northern regions, where temperatures reach over 38°C (100°F), to a much cooler south. Annual rainfall averages only 1,000 mm (39 inches) in the north and east to 2,000 mm (79 inches) in the south and west. The two monsoon periods centre on May and November. Natural resources are limited but the rich agricultural land produces tea, rubber and coconuts. The manufacturing sector has overtaken tea and other crops as the main export earner and includes clothing, textiles, food processing, chemicals and rubber. Gemstones (sapphire, ruby, beryl, topaz), graphite and salt are mined. Tourism seriously affected by violent separatist activities during the 1980s, is re-emerging as an important industry.

SUDAN

STATUS: **Republic**
AREA: **2,505,815 sq km (967,245 sq miles)**
POPULATION: **24,941,000**
ANNUAL NATURAL INCREASE: **3.0%**
CAPITAL: **Khartoum**
LANGUAGE: **Arabic, tribal languages**
RELIGION: **60% Sunni Muslim, animist and Christian**
CURRENCY: **Sudanese pound (SDP)**
ORGANIZATIONS: **Arab League, OAU, UN**

Sudan, in the upper Nile basin, is Africa's largest country. Much of the country is an arid plain, although marshy conditions are found in the south. The only areas of high relief are along the Red Sea coast and at the southern boundary of the country. The Sudanese climate is hot and arid, with summer temperatures reaching 40°C (104°F) and light rains in summer. The White and Blue Niles are invaluable, serving not only to irrigate cultivated land but also as potential sources of hydro-electric power. Subsistence farming accounts for 80 per cent of the Sudan's total agricultural production. Major exports include cotton, groundnuts, sugarcane and sesame seed. The principal activity is nomadic herding, with over 40 million cattle and sheep and 14 million goats.

SURINAME

STATUS: **Republic**
AREA: **163,820 sq km (63,235 sq miles)**
POPULATION: **438,000**
ANNUAL NATURAL INCREASE: **2.5%**
CAPITAL: **Paramaribo**
LANGUAGE: **Dutch, English, Spanish, Surinamese (Sranang Tongo), Hindi**
RELIGION: **45% Christian, 28% Hindu, 20% Muslim**
CURRENCY: **Suriname guilder (SRG)**
ORGANIZATIONS: **OAS, UN**

Independent from the Dutch since 1976, Suriname is a small state lying on the northeast coast of South America, in the tropics. Most of Suriname is covered by tropical forests. There is a fertile coastal plain, central plateaux and southern uplands. The climate is tropical and hot, with high rainfall and humidity. Rice growing takes up 75 per cent of all cultivated land. The introduction of cattle-raising for meat and dairy products is not yet complete. The main exported products of Suriname are bauxite, alumina and aluminium, although exports of shrimp is growing. Agricultural exports include bananas, coconuts and citrus fruits. Timber resources are largely untapped and there is potential for future production.

SVALBARD

STATUS: **Archipelago Territory of Norway**
AREA: **62,000 sq km (23,930 sq miles)**
POPULATION: **3,942**

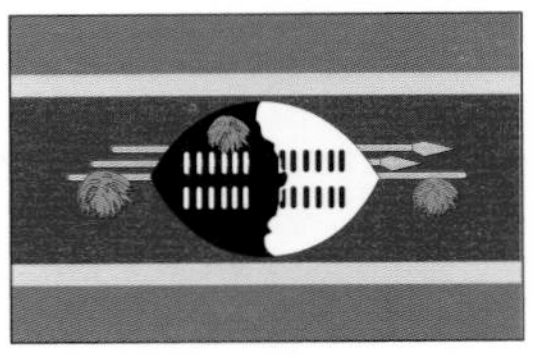

SWAZILAND

STATUS: **Kingdom**
AREA: **17,365 sq km (6,705 sq miles)**
POPULATION: **823,000**
ANNUAL NATURAL INCREASE: **3.4%**
CAPITAL: **Mbabane**
LANGUAGE: **English, Siswati**
RELIGION: **60% Christian, 40% traditional beliefs**
CURRENCY: **lilangeni (SZL), South African rand (ZAR)**
ORGANIZATIONS: **Comm., OAU, UN**

Landlocked Swaziland in southern Africa is a subtropical, savannah country. It is divided into four main regions: the high, middle and low velds and the Lebombo Mountains. The climate varies with altitude. A warm wet season lasts from October to March, while May to December are dry and cooler. Rainfall is abundant, promoting pasture for the many cattle and sheep. Agriculture involves over three quarters of the population, and is mostly subsistence farming. Cash crops include sugar, citrus fruits and pineapples. Industries include sugar refining and wood pulping. Other exports are asbestos and coal. The tourist trade is on the increase.

SWEDEN

STATUS: **Kingdom**
AREA: **449,790 sq km (173,620 sq miles)**
POPULATION: **8,721,000**
ANNUAL NATURAL INCREASE: **0.2%**
CAPITAL: **Stockholm**
LANGUAGE: **Swedish, Finnish, Lappish**
RELIGION: **95% Evangelical Lutheran**
CURRENCY: **Swedish krona (SED)**
ORGANIZATIONS: **Council of Europe, EEA, EFTA, OECD, UN**

Glacial debris, glacier-eroded valleys and thick glacial clay are all dominant features of the geomorphology of Sweden. Forested mountains cover the northern half of the country. Southwards there is a region characterized by thousands of lakes, then a central upland, and finally a fertile plain, in the far south. The climate varies with latitudinal extent: winters are long in the north, and heavy snow can persist for four to seven months. The rainfall, distributed all year round, is heavy but decreases eastwards. With over half the land area forested, a thriving timber industry has developed. Manufacturing industry, particularly cars and trucks, metal products and machine tools, are becoming increasingly dominant. Mineral resources are also rich and plentiful – iron ore production alone exceeds 17 million tons a year. There are also deposits of copper, lead and zinc.

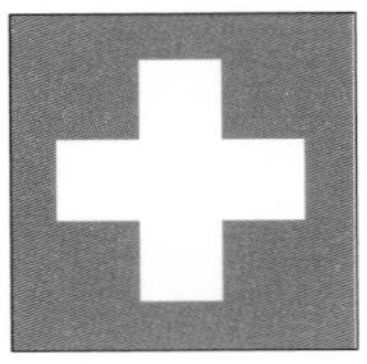

SWITZERLAND

STATUS: **Federation**
AREA: **41,285 sq km (15,935 sq miles)**
POPULATION: **6,908,000**
ANNUAL NATURAL INCREASE: **0.3%**
CAPITAL: **Bern (Berne)**
LANGUAGE: **German, French, Italian, Romansch**
RELIGION: **48% Roman Catholic, 44% Protestant, Jewish minority**
CURRENCY: **Swiss franc (CHF)**
ORGANIZATIONS: **Council of Europe, EFTA, OECD, UN**

Switzerland is the most mountainous nation in Europe. The southern half of the country lies within the Alps while its northwestern border with France coincides with the Jura range. The remainder of the country is high plateaux. Because of its altitude Switzerland experiences cold winters with heavy snowfalls. Summers are mild with an average July temperature of 18–19°C (64–66°F). Rainfall is normally restricted to the summer months. Agriculture is based mainly on dairy farming, but major crops include hay, wheat, barley and potatoes. Industry plays a major role in Switzerland's economy and is centred on metal engineering, food processing, textiles and chemicals. Tourism is an important source of income and employment, with alpine sports being particularly important during winter months. The financial services sector, especially banking, is also of great importance. Switzerland's history of neutrality has made it an attractive location for many international organizations.

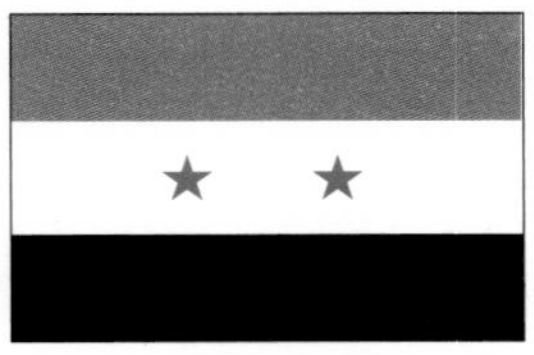

SYRIA

STATUS: **Republic**
AREA: **185,680 sq km (71,675 sq miles)**
POPULATION: **12,958,000**
ANNUAL NATURAL INCREASE: **3.6%**
CAPITAL: **Damascus, (Dimashq, Esh Sham)**
LANGUAGE: **Arabic**
RELIGION: **65% Sunni Muslim, Shi'a Muslim and Christian minorities**
CURRENCY: **Syrian pound (SYP)**
ORGANIZATIONS: **Arab League, UN**

Syria is situated at the heart of the Middle East bordered by Turkey, Iraq, Jordan, Israel and Lebanon. In the north of the country the coastal plain is backed by a low range of hills. The interior is a vast plateau through which the river Euphrates has cut its valley. In the south the Anti-Lebanon (Jebel esh Sharqi) range lies along the border with Lebanon, inland of which is the Syrian desert (Badiet esh Shām). The coastal regions have a Mediterranean climate, but further inland the climate becomes hotter and drier. Cotton is Syria's main export crop, and wheat and barley are also grown. Cattle, sheep and goats are the main livestock. Although a traditionally agriculturally based economy, the country is rapidly becoming industrialized as oil, natural gas and phosphate resources are exploited. Salt and gypsum are mined, and oil and oil products, food and textiles are also exported.

TAHITI

STATUS: **Main Island of French Polynesia**
AREA: **1,042 sq km (402 sq miles)**
POPULATION: **115,820**

TAIWAN

STATUS: **Island 'Republic of China'**
AREA: **35,990 sq km (13,890 sq miles)**
POPULATION: **20,600,000**
ANNUAL NATURAL INCREASE: **1.5%**
CAPITAL: **Taipei (T'ai-pei)**
LANGUAGE: **Mandarin Chinese, Taiwanese**
RELIGION: **Buddhist majority, Muslim, Daoist and Christian minorities**
CURRENCY: **Hew Taiwan dollar (TWD), yuan**
ORGANIZATIONS: **none**

Taiwan is separated from mainland China by the Taiwan Strait (the former Formosa Channel). Two thirds of Taiwan is mountainous, with peaks approaching heights of 4,000 m (13,100 ft). The flat to rolling coastal plains in the western part of the island are the focus for the bulk of the population, national commerce, industry and agriculture. Warm, humid climatic conditions prevail over much of the island. The monsoon rains fall in June to August, with an annual average rainfall of 2,600 mm (102 inches). Agriculture is highly productive, with rice, tea, fruit, sugarcane and seed potatoes as the leading crops. Industry varies from light to heavy, and principal exports include textiles, electrical goods and services. Natural resources are limestone, marble, asbestos, copper and sulphur. Natural gas is extracted from the Taiwan Strait.

TAJIKISTAN

STATUS: **Republic**
AREA: **143,100 sq km (55,235 sq miles)**
POPULATION: **5,465,000**
ANNUAL NATURAL INCREASE: **3.0%**
CAPITAL: **Dushanbe**
LANGUAGE: **Tajik, Uzbek, Russian**
RELIGION: **Sunni Muslim**
CURRENCY: **Russian rouble**
ORGANIZATIONS: **CIS, UN**

Tajikistan, with the western end of the Tien Shan and part of the Pamir range within its borders, is extremely rugged and mountainous. The only significant lowland lies within the Fergana valley. The climate varies from continental to subtropical. In the western areas of less severe altitude, summers are warm but winters are generally cold. Extensive irrigation, without which agriculture would be severely limited, has made it possible for cotton growing to develop into the leading branch of agriculture, and on that basis textiles have become the largest industry in the country. Tajikistan is rich in mineral and fuel deposits, the exploitation of which became a major feature of economic development during the Soviet era. Preceding full independence in 1991, there was an upsurge of sometimes violent Tajik nationalism, as a result of which many Russians and Uzbeks left the country. Civil war has brought the fragile economy near to collapse.

TANZANIA

STATUS: **Republic**
AREA: **939,760 sq km (362,750 sq miles)**
POPULATION: **27,829,000**
ANNUAL NATURAL INCREASE: **3.5%**
CAPITAL: **Dodoma**
LANGUAGE: **Swahili, English**
RELIGION: **40% Christian, 35% Muslim**
CURRENCY: **Tanzanian shilling**
ORGANIZATIONS: **Comm., OAU, UN**

Apart from a forested coastal plain, most of mainland Tanzania is a plateau at a height above 1,000 m (3,300 ft) covered with savannah vegetation, lying to the east of the great Rift Valley. In the north Mt Kilimanjaro dominates the landscape. The climate is tropical; the central lowlands and Zanzibar are particularly hot and humid. Temperatures inland average 25°C (77°F) throughout the year and the heaviest rains fall from March to May. Subsistence farming is the main way of life, although coffee, cotton, sisal, cashew nuts and tea are exported. Industry is limited, but gradually growing in importance, and involves textiles, food processing and tobacco. Tourism could be a future growth industry.

THAILAND

STATUS: **Kingdom**
AREA: **514,000 sq km (198,405 sq miles)**
POPULATION: **57,760,000**
ANNUAL NATURAL INCREASE: **1.9%**
CAPITAL: **Bangkok (Krung Thep)**
LANGUAGE: **Thai**
RELIGION: **Buddhist, 4% Muslim**
CURRENCY: **baht (THB)**
ORGANIZATIONS: **ASEAN, Col. Plan, UN**

The most populated centre of Thailand is an undulating plain through which the Chao Phraya flows. One third of the country is occupied by a plateau in the northeast, drained by tributaries of the Mekong river. The climate is tropical, with temperatures reaching 36°C (97°F). There are three seasons: November to February is cooler, March to May is hot and the monsoon rains arrive between May and October, with an annual average rainfall of 1500 mm (59 inches). Thailand is the world's biggest exporter of rice, rubber and tin. Other agricultural products include maize, beans, coconuts and groundnuts. Since 1984 manufacturing has overtaken agriculture as the dominant economic sector. The most rapidly developing area is around Chieng-Mai in the north, the new centre for industry. Textiles and clothing are the main industries, and the petrochemical industry has also been developed. Tourism is a growing industry.

TIMOR

STATUS: **Island of Indonesia (E. Timor annexed by Indonesia)**
AREA: **33,915 sq km (13,090 sq miles)**
POPULATION: **714,847**

TOGO

STATUS: **Kingdom**
AREA: **699 sq km (270 sq miles)**
POPULATION: **130,000**
ANNUAL NATURAL INCREASE: **3.5%**
CAPITAL: **Lomé**
LANGUAGE: **French, Kabre, Ewe**
RELIGION: **Christian**
CURRENCY: **pa'anga (TOP)**
ORGANIZATIONS: **Comm.**

Togo, formerly a German protectorate and French colony, is situated between Ghana and Benin in West Africa. A long, narrow country, it has only 65 km (40 miles) of coast. The interior consists of plateaux rising to mountainous areas. The climate is tropical, with average temperatures of 27°C (81°F) and rainfall of 890 mm (35 inches). The country is almost self-sufficient in food, and farming is the livelihood of most of the population; maize, cassava, yams, groundnuts and plantains are grown. Industry is minimal, although oil is refined at Lomé and there is food processing and consumer goods manufacturing for the domestic market. High-grade phosphates contribute half of the export revenue.

TOKELAU ISLANDS

STATUS: **Overseas Territory of New Zealand**
AREA: **10 sq km (4 sq miles)**
POPULATION: **1,690**
CAPITAL: **none, each island has its own administration centre**

TONGA

STATUS: **Kingdom**
AREA: **699 sq km (270 sq miles)**
POPULATION: **103,000**
ANNUAL NATURAL INCREASE: **0.4%**
CAPITAL: **Nuku'alofa**
LANGUAGE: **Tongan, English**
RELIGION: **Christian**
CURRENCY: **pa'anga (TOP)**
ORGANIZATIONS: **Comm.**

Tonga is composed of some 170 islands in the Pacific, 180 km (112 miles) north of New Zealand. There are seven groups of islands, but the most important are Tongatapu, Ha'apai and Vava'u; the remainder are mostly uninhabited and are covered with dense tropical vegetation. About 60 per cent of the population lives on Tongatapu. Temperatures are warm all year. Rainfall is plentiful, heaviest in February and March. Agriculture is self-sufficient; land is rented from the government and is used to grow crops such as yams and manioc. The main export crops are bananas and products of the cocoa palm. Fishing is also important in sustaining the population. The government has agreed with Intelsat to provide facilities for satellite communications and earns revenue by leasing these facilities to foreign operators. Tourism has increased in recent years.

TRINIDAD & TOBAGO

STATUS: **Republic**
AREA: **5,130 sq km (1,980 sq miles)**
POPULATION: **1,265,000**
ANNUAL NATURAL INCREASE: **1.7%**
CAPITAL: **Port of Spain**
LANGUAGE: **English, Hindi, French, Spanish**
RELIGION: **60% Christian, 25% Hindu, 6% Muslim**
CURRENCY: **Trinidad and Tobago dollar (TTD)**
ORGANIZATIONS: **Caricom, Comm., OAS, UN**

These Caribbean islands lie only 11 and 30 km (7 and 19 miles) respectively from the Venezuelan coast. The mountains in the north of Trinidad overlook undulating land and a flat central area, while swamps border Cocos Bay in the east. Tobago is mostly mountainous. High temperatures throughout the year vary little from 26°C (79°F). The annual rainfall is 1,631 mm (65 inches), falling most frequently in July to December. Sugar was once the mainstay of the economy but oil is now the leading source of revenue, coming chiefly from offshore fields. A petrochemical industry is based on significant gas reserves. Oil and petrochemical products account for over 70 per cent of exports. Asphalt is also important. In the agricultural sector sugar, coffee, cocoa, citrus fruits and rubber are produced.

TRISTAN DA CUNHA

STATUS: **Dependency of St Helena**
AREA: **98 sq km (38 sq miles)**
POPULATION: **306**

STATES AND TERRITORIES OF THE WORLD

TUNISIA

STATUS: **Republic**
AREA: **164,150 sq km (63,360 sq miles)**
POPULATION: **8,401,000**
ANNUAL NATURAL INCREASE: **2.0%**
CAPITAL: **Tunis**
LANGUAGE: **Arabic, French**
RELIGION: **Muslim**
CURRENCY: **Tunisian dinar (TND)**
ORGANIZATIONS: **Arab League, OAU, UN**

The northern half of the country has rugged mountains, often tree-covered. These are separated from Saharan plains by the Chott El Jerid, a low-lying area of salt pans. Northern parts experience winter rainfall, but arid conditions prevail in the south. Wheat, barley, olives and citrus fruit are the main crops. Olives occupy one third of the arable land, and the nation is the world's fifth largest producer. In the south, using water from hot springs, the growing of tomatoes and melons has developed. Oil, natural gas and sugar refining are the main industries. The tourist industry is expanding.

TURKEY

STATUS: **Republic**
AREA: **779,450 sq km (300,870 sq miles)**
POPULATION: **58,775,000**
ANNUAL NATURAL INCREASE: **2.2%**
CAPITAL: **Ankara**
LANGUAGE: **Turkish, Kurdish**
RELIGION: **98% Sunni Muslim, Christian minority**
CURRENCY: **Turkish lira (TRL)**
ORGANIZATIONS: **Council of Europe, NATO, OECD, UN**

Turkey, occupying the peninsula of Asia Minor, is dominated by two major mountain ranges, the Pontine (Anadolu Dağlari) in the north and the Taurus (Toros Dağlari) in the south; and between the two is the high plateau of Anatolia. The coast has a Mediterranean climate. The interior experiences great extremes, with hot, dry summers, and cold, snowy winters. The main crops are wheat and barley, but tobacco, olives, sugarbeet, tea and fruit are also grown, and sheep, goats and cattle are raised. Textiles account for over a third of the total exports, and the car industry is also important. Turkey is becoming increasingly industrialized and now leads the Middle East in the production of iron, steel, chrome, coal and lignite. Minerals exploited include copper, borax and chromium.

TURKMENISTAN

STATUS: **Republic**
AREA: **488,100 sq km (188,405 sq miles)**
POPULATION: **3,714,000**
ANNUAL NATURAL INCREASE: **2.5%**
CAPITAL: **Ashkhabad**
LANGUAGE: **Turkmen, Russian, Uzbek**
RELIGION: **Muslim**
CURRENCY: **manat**
ORGANIZATIONS: **CIS, UN**

Most of Turkmenistan is a lowland desert known as the Kara Kum (Karakumy); the only areas not so classified are the shores of the Caspian Sea, the mountains along the border with Iran and the valley of the Amudar'ya along the northern boundary. Summers are hot, with maximum temperatures exceeding 30°C (86°F), while winter temperatures approach freezing point. Turk-menistan has substantial oil and natural gas reserves and is rich in potassium, sulphur and salt. Cotton is the principal crop, but cereals, fruit and melons are also grown, made possible by extensive irrigation. Cotton cleaning is important, and food industries are developing on a modern basis. Turkmenistan is also famous for its carpet making.

TURKS & CAICOS ISLANDS

STATUS: **UK Dependent Territory**
AREA: **430 sq km (166 sq miles)**
POPULATION: **11,696**
CAPITAL: **Cockburn Town**

TUVALU

STATUS: **Special membership of the Commonwealth**
AREA: **24.6 sq km (9.5 sq miles)**
POPULATION: **10,000**
ANNUAL NATURAL INCREASE: **1.5%**
CAPITAL: **Funafuti**
LANGUAGE: **Tuvaluan, English**
RELIGION: **98% Protestant**
CURRENCY: **Australian dollar (AUD), Tuvaluan coinage**
ORGANIZATIONS: **Comm. (special member)**

Tuvalu, one of the world's smallest nations, consists of nine coral atolls. The climate is hot all the year round. The traditional occupations of the islanders are fishing and subsistence farming, but agriculture is restricted by poor soils and the only significant cash crop is coconuts for copra export. Other sources of income are from postage stamps and handicrafts. Revenue is also raised from fishing licences.

UGANDA

STATUS: **Republic**
AREA: **236,580 sq km (91,320 sq miles)**
POPULATION: **18,674,000**
ANNUAL NATURAL INCREASE: **3.1%**
CAPITAL: **Kampala**
LANGUAGE: **English, tribal languages**
RELIGION: **62% Christian, 6% Muslim**
CURRENCY: **Uganda shilling (UGX)**
ORGANIZATIONS: **Comm., OAU, UN**

Most of Uganda is a plateau with savannah vegetation, bordered in the west by the Ruwenzori Range and the great Rift Valley. Southeast Uganda includes Lake Victoria, from which the Nile flows northwards through Lake Kyoga. The climate is tropical; temperatures, though warm throughout the year, are modified by altitude. Rainfall occurs in all months. Agriculture dominates the economy. Lake Victoria is a source of wealth, the surrounding area has been cleared for cultivation, and the lake itself provides a valuable supply of freshwater fish. The main crops are coffee, cotton and tea.

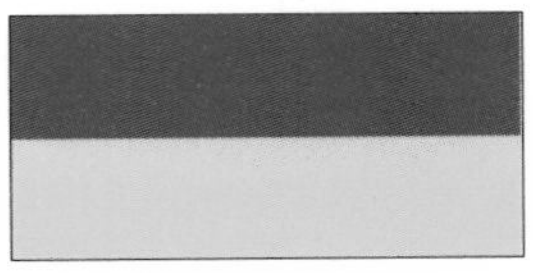

UKRAINE

STATUS: **Republic**
AREA: **603,700 sq km (233,030 sq miles)**
POPULATION: **52,194,000**
ANNUAL NATURAL INCREASE: **0.3%**
CAPITAL: **Kiev (Kiyev)**
LANGUAGE: **Ukrainian, Russian**
RELIGION: **Russian Orthodox, Roman Catholic (Uniate)**
CURRENCY: **karbovanets (coupon)**
ORGANIZATIONS: **CIS, UN**

Much of the country is steppe, relatively flat and often forested. Ukraine has warm summers and cold winters, with milder conditions in the Crimea (Krym). Deposits of 'black earth', among the most fertile soils, cover about 65 per cent of Ukraine. Grain, potatoes, vegetables and fruits, industrial crops (notably sugarbeet and sunflower seeds) and fodder crops are grown. Food processing is important to the economy, and the southern regions are renowned for wines. Ukraine is rich in mineral resources, but historically imported all its oil from Russia and is now short of energy. Extensive mining, metal production, machine-building, engineering and chemicals dominate industry, most of which is located in the Dontesk (Donets) basin and the Dneiper (Dnepr) lowland. Only percentage of state enterprises have been privatized and the government maintains centralized control.

UNITED ARAB EMIRATES (UAE)

STATUS: **Federation of seven Emirates**
AREA: **75,150 sq km (29,010 sq miles)**
POPULATION: **1,629,000**
ANNUAL NATURAL INCREASE: **3.1%**
CAPITAL: **Abu Dhabi (Abū Ẓabī)**
LANGUAGE: **Arabic, English**
RELIGION: **Sunni Muslim**
CURRENCY: **UAE dirham (AED)**
ORGANIZATIONS: **Arab League, OPEC, UN**

Most of the United Arab Emirates is flat desert with sand dunes and salt pans. The only hilly area is in the northeast adjacent to the Gulf of Oman. Summers are hot and winters are mild. Coastal areas may receive a little rainfall in winter. Only the desert oases are fertile, producing fruit and vegetables. Dubai is a thriving entrepôt trade centre, and desalination and irrigation have brought many acres into cultivation, allowing self-sufficiency in some vegetables and the export of strawberries and flowers to Europe. The economic wealth of the United Arab Emirates is founded on its reserves of hydrocarbons, mainly within the largest Emirate, Abu Dhabi, with smaller supplies in three others – Dubai, Sharjah and Ras al Khaimah. Natural gas and oil are the major exports.

ABU DHABI

STATUS: **Emirate**
AREA: **64,750 sq km (24,995 sq miles)**
POPULATION: **670,175**

AJMAN

STATUS: **Emirate**
AREA: **260 sq km (100 sq miles)**
POPULATION: **64,318**

DUBAI

STATUS: **Emirate**
AREA: **3,900 sq km (1,505 sq miles)**
POPULATION: **419,104**

FUJAIRAH

STATUS: **Emirate**
AREA: **1,170 sq km (452 sq miles)**
POPULATION: **54,425**

RAS AL KHAIMAH

STATUS: **Emirate**
AREA: **1,690 sq km (625 sq miles)**
POPULATION: **116,470**

SHARJAH

STATUS: **Emirate**
AREA: **2,600 sq km (1,005 sq miles)**
POPULATION: **268,722**

UMM AL QAIWAIN

STATUS: **Emirate**
AREA: **780 sq km (300 sq miles)**
POPULATION: **29,229**

UNITED KINGDOM OF GREAT BRITAIN & NORTHERN IRELAND (UK)

STATUS: **Kingdom**
AREA: **244,755 sq km (94,475 sq miles)**
POPULATION: **57,998,400**
ANNUAL NATURAL INCREASE: **0.3%**
CAPITAL: **London**
LANGUAGE: **English, Welsh, Gaelic**
RELIGION: **Protestant majority, Roman Catholic, Jewish, Muslim, Hindu minorities**
CURRENCY: **pound sterling (GBP)**
ORGANIZATIONS: **Col. Plan, Comm., Council of Europe, EEA, EU, G7, NATO, OECD, UN, WEU**

The Highland zone of Britain consists of ancient uplifted rocks which now form the mountainous dissected and glaciated areas of the Lake District, in the northwest of England, Wales, the Southern Uplands and the Grampians of Scotland which rise to the highest point in the UK – 1,344 m (4,409 ft) at Ben Nevis. The latter are divided by the wide Central Lowland. Central England is dominated by the Pennine mountain chain which stretches southwards from the Southern Uplands down the centre of England to the river Trent. The landscape of the southwest consists of the ancient uplifted granite domes of Dartmoor and Bodmin Moor. Lowland Britain is a very contrasting landscape. Limestone and sandstone hills are separated by flat clay vales, east of a line joining the rivers Humber and Exe. Both the richest agricultural land and the densest population are found here. Northern Ireland is generally hilly and has the UK's largest lake, Lough Neagh, at its centre. The climate of the UK is mild, wet and variable. Although a small percentage of the nation's workforce are employed in agriculture, farm produce is important to both home and export markets. Seventy-six per cent of the total UK land area is farmland. The main cereal crops are wheat, barley and oats. Potatoes, sugar beet and green vegetable crops are widespread. About 20 per cent of the land is permanent pasture for the raising of dairy and beef stock; and 28 per cent of the land, mainly hill and mountain areas, is used for rough grazing of sheep. Pigs and poultry are widespread in both England and lowland Scotland. The best fruit-growing areas are the southeast, especially Kent and East Anglia and the central Vale of Evesham, for apples, pears and soft fruit. Both the forestry and fishing industries contribute to the economy. The major mineral resources of the UK are coal, oil and natural gas. Coal output goes towards the generation of electricity, but oil and natural gas from the North Sea, and to a lesser extent nuclear power, are divided between the needs of industry and the consumer. Iron ore, once mined sufficiently to satisfy industry, is now imported to support the iron and steel manufacturing sector. The UK produces a great range of industrial goods for home consumption and export. General and consumer goods manufacturing is located in all heavy industrial areas, but London, the West Midlands, Lancashire and Merseyside predominate. Main products are food and drinks, chemicals, light engineering products, cotton and woollen textiles, electrical and electronic goods.

ENGLAND
STATUS: **Constituent Country**
AREA: **130,360 sq km (50,320 sq miles)**
POPULATION: **48,378,300**
CAPITAL: **London**

NORTHERN IRELAND
STATUS: **Constituent Region**
AREA: **14,150 sq km (5,460 sq miles)**
POPULATION: **1,589,000**
CAPITAL: **Belfast**

SCOTLAND
STATUS: **Constituent Country**
AREA: **78,750 sq km (30,400 sq miles)**
POPULATION: **4,957,000**
CAPITAL: **Edinburgh**

WALES
STATUS: **Principality**
AREA: **20,760 sq km (8,015 sq miles)**
POPULATION: **2,898,500**
CAPITAL: **Cardiff**

UNITED STATES OF AMERICA (USA)
STATUS: **Federal Republic**
AREA: **9,363,130 sq km (3,614,170 sq miles)**
POPULATION: **255,020,000**
ANNUAL NATURAL INCREASE: **0.9%**
CAPITAL: **Washington D.C.**
LANGUAGE: **English, Spanish**
RELIGION: **Christian majority, Jewish minority**
CURRENCY: **US dollar (USD)**
ORGANIZATIONS: **ANZUS, Col. Plan, G7, NAFTA, NATO, OAS, OECD, UN**

The eastern states, originally forested and still largely tree covered, include the Atlantic coastal plain, which widens southwards, and the Appalachian mountains running from the northeastern extremity to Georgia. The central states form the Great Plains, with prairie vegetation drained by the Mississippi–Missouri river system. To the west lie the Rocky Mountains, separated from the Pacific coastal ranges by a great intermontane basin. The coastal ranges extend northwards and are a feature of the state of Alaska. The 50th state, Hawaii, is an archipelago of some 20 volcanic islands. Climatic conditions are tropical in the south and southeast, often hot and dry in the southwest and more temperate elsewhere. The northwest coast is rich in coniferous forest, especially Douglas fir, while the Appalachian mountain region is well endowed with hardwoods, notably maple and oak. In the arid southwest, vegetation is limited to desert scrub whereas the Gulf and south Atlantic coast are fringed with swampy wetlands. The central lowlands are endowed with rich 'black earth' soils (the agricultural heartland), gradually supplanted, by tall-grass prairie, towards the Rockies. The northern states of Illinois, Iowa, Indiana and Nebraska form the so-called 'corn belt', whereas further west wheat supplements corn as the main crop. Spring wheat is grown in the northern states of North and South Dakota and Minnesota. The northeastern corner of the USA is predominantly dairy country, and the states of the deep south are famous for their cotton, though cotton cultivation is declining. The USA consumes 25 per cent of all the world's energy resources but is well endowed with energy reserves. There are substantial coal reserves in Pennsylvania, the Appalachian region, the Dakotas and Wyoming, and oil and natural gas reserves in Texas, Louisiana, Alaska, and off shore, in the Gulf of Mexico. The vast resources of America's great rivers have been harnessed extensively for hydro-electric power. In the west, mineral deposits include copper, lead, zinc and silver, and there is iron ore around Lake Superior. Most specialist industrial minerals are imported. Diamonds, tin, chromite, nickel, asbestos, platinum, manganese, mercury, tungsten, cobalt, antimony and cadmium are not found in sufficient quantities for home demand. Main non-metallic minerals extracted within the USA are cement, clays, gypsum, lime, phosphate, salt, sand, gravel and sulphur. Atlantic and Pacific fishing, particularly around Alaska, is mainly carried out within the 200-mile fishery zone. Chicago is the main steel-producing town, while Pennsylvania and Pittsburgh are famous for their steel and chemical industries. Manufacturing industries are more predominant towards the east of this zone. Most of the fast growing industrial areas are along the west coast. These stretch from Seattle and Portland in the north to San Francisco, Oakland and San Jose in central California and to Los Angeles, Anaheim, Santa Ana and San Diego in the south. The industries are vehicle manufacture, armaments, machinery, electrical goods, electronics, textiles and clothing and entertainment.

ALABAMA
STATUS: **State**
AREA: **131,485 sq km (50,755 sq miles)**
POPULATION: **4,089,000**
CAPITAL: **Montgomery**

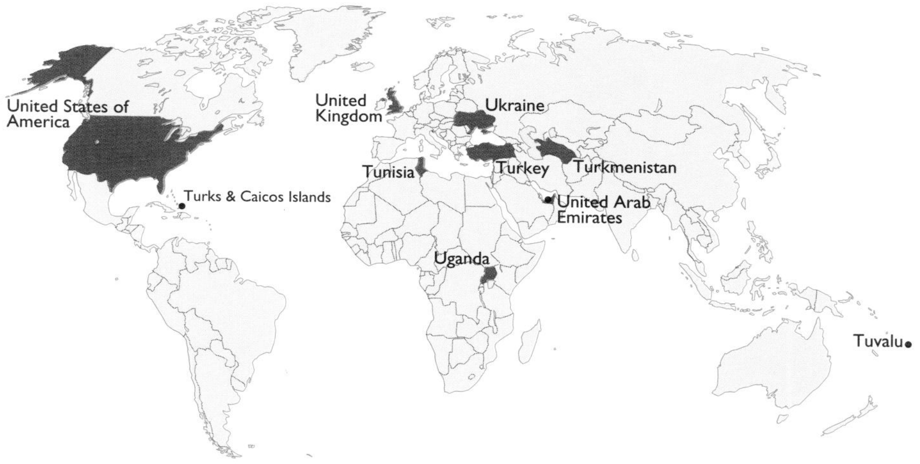

ALASKA
STATUS: **State**
AREA: **1,478,450 sq km (113,480 sq miles)**
POPULATION: **570,000**
CAPITAL: **Juneau**

ARIZONA
STATUS: **State**
AREA: **293,985 sq km (113,480 sq miles)**
POPULATION: **3,750,000**
CAPITAL: **Phoenix**

ARKANSAS
STATUS: **State**
AREA: **134,880 sq km (52,065 sq miles)**
POPULATION: **2,372,000**
CAPITAL: **Little Rock**

CALIFORNIA
STATUS: **State**
AREA: **404,815 sq km (156,260 sq miles)**
POPULATION: **30,380,000**
CAPITAL: **Sacramento**

COLORADO
STATUS: **State**
AREA: **268,310 sq km (103,570 sq miles)**
POPULATION: **3,377,000**
CAPITAL: **Denver**

CONNECTICUT
STATUS: **State**
AREA: **12,620 sq km (4,870 sq miles)**
POPULATION: **3,291,000**
CAPITAL: **Hartford**

DELAWARE
STATUS: **State**
AREA: **5,005 sq km (1,930 sq miles)**
POPULATION: **680,000**
CAPITAL: **Dover**

DISTRICT OF COLUMBIA
STATUS: **Federal District**
AREA: **163 sq km (63 sq miles)**
POPULATION: **589,000**
CAPITAL: **Washington D.C.**

FLORIDA
STATUS: **State**
AREA: **140,255 sq km (54,1405 sq miles)**
POPULATION: **13,277,000**
CAPITAL: **Tallahassee**

GEORGIA
STATUS: **State**
AREA: **150,365 sq km (58,040 sq miles)**
POPULATION: **6,623,000**
CAPITAL: **Atlanta**

HAWAII
STATUS: **State**
AREA: **16,640 sq km (6,425 sq miles)**
POPULATION: **1,135,000**
CAPITAL: **Honolulu**

IDAHO
STATUS: **State**
AREA: **213,445 sq km (82,390 sq miles)**
POPULATION: **1,039,000**
CAPITAL: **Boise**

ILLINOIS
STATUS: **State**
AREA: **144,120 sq km (55,630 sq miles)**
POPULATION: **11,543,000**
CAPITAL: **Springfield**

INDIANA
STATUS: **State**
AREA: **93,065 sq km (35,925 sq miles)**
POPULATION: **5,610,000**
CAPITAL: **Indianapolis**

IOWA
STATUS: **State**
AREA: **144,950 sq km (55,950 sq miles)**
POPULATION: **2,795,000**
CAPITAL: **Des Moines**

KANSAS
STATUS: **State**
AREA: **211,805 sq km (81,755 sq miles)**
POPULATION: **2,495,000**
CAPITAL: **Topeka**

KENTUCKY
STATUS: **State**
AREA: **102,740 sq km (39,660 sq miles)**
POPULATION: **3,713,000**
CAPITAL: **Frankfort**

LOUISIANA
STATUS: **State**
AREA: **115,310 sq km (44,510 sq miles)**
POPULATION: **4,252,000**
CAPITAL: **Baton Rouge**

MAINE
STATUS: **State**
AREA: **80,275 sq km (30,985 sq miles)**
POPULATION: **1,235,000**
CAPITAL: **Augusta**

MARYLAND
STATUS: **State**
AREA: **25,480 sq km (9,835 sq miles)**
POPULATION: **4,860,000**
CAPITAL: **Annapolis**

MASSACHUSETTS
STATUS: **State**
AREA: **20,265 sq km (7,820 sq miles)**
POPULATION: **5,996,000**
CAPITAL: **Boston**

MICHIGAN
STATUS: **State**
AREA: **147,510 sq km (56,940 sq miles)**
POPULATION: **9,368,000**
CAPITAL: **Lansing**

MINNESOTA
STATUS: **State**
AREA: **206,030 sq km (79,530 sq miles)**
POPULATION: **4,432,000**
CAPITAL: **St Paul**

MISSISSIPPI
STATUS: **State**
AREA: **122,335 sq km (47,220 sq miles)**
POPULATION: **2,592,000**
CAPITAL: **Jackson**

MISSOURI
STATUS: **State**
AREA: **178,565 sq km (68,925 sq miles)**
POPULATION: **5,158,000**
CAPITAL: **Jefferson City**

MONTANA
STATUS: **State**
AREA: **376,555 sq km (145,350 sq miles)**
POPULATION: **808,000**
CAPITAL: **Helena**

NEBRASKA
STATUS: **State**
AREA: **198,505 sq km (76,625 sq miles)**
POPULATION: **1,593,000**
CAPITAL: **Lincoln**

NEVADA
STATUS: **State**
AREA: **284,625 sq km (109,865 sq miles)**
POPULATION: **1,284,000**
CAPITAL: **Carson City**

NEW HAMPSHIRE
STATUS: **State**
AREA: **23,290 sq km (8,990 sq miles)**
POPULATION: **1,105,000**
CAPITAL: **Concord**

NEW JERSEY
STATUS: **State**
AREA: **19,340 sq km (7,465 sq miles)**
POPULATION: **7,760,000**
CAPITAL: **Trenton**

NEW MEXICO
STATUS: **State**
AREA: **314,255 sq km (121,300 sq miles)**
POPULATION: **1,548,000**
CAPITAL: **Sante Fe**

NEW YORK
STATUS: **State**
AREA: **122,705 sq km (47,365 sq miles)**
POPULATION: **18,058,000**
CAPITAL: **Albany**

NORTH CAROLINA
STATUS: **State**
AREA: **126,505 sq km (48,830 sq miles)**
POPULATION: **6,737,000**
CAPITAL: **Raleigh**

NORTH DAKOTA
STATUS: **State**
AREA: **179,485 sq km (69,280 sq miles)**
POPULATION: **635,000**
CAPITAL: **Bismarck**

OHIO
STATUS: **State**
AREA: **106,200 sq km (40,995 sq miles)**
POPULATION: **10,939,000**
CAPITAL: **Columbus**

OKLAHOMA
STATUS: **State**
AREA: **177,815 sq km (68,635 sq miles)**
POPULATION: **3,175,00**
CAPITAL: **Oklahoma City**

OREGON
STATUS: **State**
AREA: **249,115 sq km (96,160 sq miles)**
POPULATION: **2,922,000**
CAPITAL: **Salem**

PENNSYLVANIA
STATUS: **State**
AREA: **116,260 sq km (44,875 sq miles)**
POPULATION: **11,961,000**
CAPITAL: **Harrisburg**

RHODE ISLAND
STATUS: **State**
AREA: **2,730 sq km (1,055 sq miles)**
POPULATION: **1,004,000**
CAPITAL: **Providence**

SOUTH CAROLINA
STATUS: **State**
AREA: **78,225 sq km (30,195 sq miles)**
POPULATION: **3,560,000**
CAPITAL: **Columbia**

SOUTH DAKOTA
STATUS: **State**
AREA: **196,715 sq km (75,930 sq miles)**
POPULATION: **703,000**
CAPITAL: **Pierre**

TENNESSEE
STATUS: **State**
AREA: **106,590 sq km (41,145 sq miles)**
POPULATION: **4,953,000**
CAPITAL: **Nashville**

TEXAS
STATUS: **State**
AREA: **678,620 sq km (261,950 sq miles)**
POPULATION: **17,349,000**
CAPITAL: **Austin**

UTAH
STATUS: **State**
AREA: **212,570 sq km (82,050 sq miles)**
POPULATION: **1,770,000**
CAPITAL: **Salt Lake City**

VERMONT
STATUS: **State**
AREA: **24,015 sq km (9,270 sq miles)**
POPULATION: **567,000**
CAPITAL: **Montpelier**

VIRGINIA
STATUS: **State**
AREA: **102,835 sq km (39,695 sq miles)**
POPULATION: **6,286,000**
CAPITAL: **Richmond**

WASHINGTON
STATUS: **State**
AREA: **172,265 sq km (66,495 sq miles)**
POPULATION: **5,018,000**
CAPITAL: **Olympia**

WEST VIRGINIA
STATUS: **State**
AREA: **62,470 sq km (24,115 sq miles)**
POPULATION: **1,801,000**
CAPITAL: **Charleston**

WISCONSIN
STATUS: **State**
AREA: **140,965 sq km (54,415 sq miles)**
POPULATION: **4,955,000**
CAPITAL: **Madison**

WYOMING
STATUS: **State**
AREA: **251,200 sq km (96,965 sq miles)**
POPULATION: **460,000**
CAPITAL: **Cheyenne**

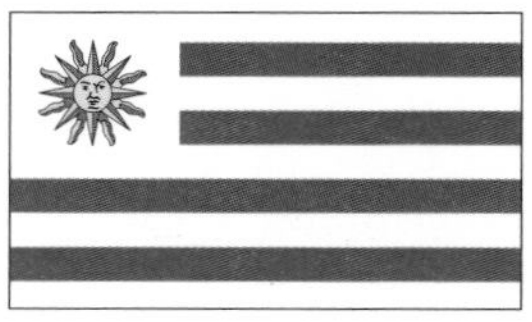

URUGUAY
STATUS: **Republic**
AREA: **186,925 sq km (72,155 sq miles)**
POPULATION: **3,131,000**
ANNUAL NATURAL INCREASE: **0.6%**
CAPITAL: **Montevideo**
LANGUAGE: **Spanish**
RELIGION: **Roman Catholic**
CURRENCY: **Uruguayan peso (UYP)**
ORGANIZATIONS: **Mercosur, OAS, UN**

Uruguay is a low-lying land of prairies, reaching only 500 m (1,600 ft) above sea level at its highest point. The Atlantic coast and the estuary of the river Plate in the south are fringed with lagoons and sand dunes. The climate is one of equable warm summers and mild winters. Moderate rainfall is spread evenly at about 100 mm (4 inches) through each month of the year. Eighty-five per cent of the land is given over to the grazing of sheep and cattle. Meat and wool are the most important exports and source of revenue.

UZBEKISTAN
STATUS: **Republic**
AREA: **447,400 sq km (172,695 sq miles)**
POPULATION: **20,708,000**
ANNUAL NATURAL INCREASE: **2.4%**
CAPITAL: **Tashkent**
LANGUAGE: **Uzbek, Russian, Turkish**
RELIGION: **Muslim**
CURRENCY: **sum**
ORGANIZATIONS: **CIS, UN**

Established in 1924 as a constituent republic of the Soviet Union, Uzbekistan became an independent state in 1991. Most of the country comprises the flat desert of the Kyzyl Kum, which rises eastwards towards the mountains of the western Pamirs. The Aral Sea in the north has shrunk by one third over the past 20 years, due to demand for irrigation water. The climate is dry and arid. The fertile soils (when irrigated) and good pastures support the raising of cattle and production of cotton; the country is the world's third largest cotton producer. Uzbekistan is the largest producer of machines and heavy equipment in central Asia, and has been specializing mainly in machinery for cotton cultivation and harvesting, machines for road-building and textile processing. The southern mountains are of great economic importance, providing ample supplies of water for hydro-electric plants and irrigation schemes. The mountain regions contain substantial reserves of natural gas, oil, coal, iron and other metals. However, the country's future development will be severely hampered by the damage done to the natural environment under communism.

VANUATU
STATUS: **Republic**
AREA: **14,765 sq km (5,700 sq miles)**
POPULATION: **154,000**
ANNUAL NATURAL INCREASE: **2.4%**
CAPITAL: **Port-Vila**
LANGUAGE: **Bislama (national), English, French, Melanesian languages**
RELIGION: **Christian**
CURRENCY: **vatu (VUV)**
ORGANIZATIONS: **Comm., UN**

Vanuatu is an archipelago of some 80 islands, many of which are densely forested and mountainous. The climate is tropical with high rainfall and a continual threat of cyclones. Copra accounts for 75 per cent of Vanuatu's export earnings, and cocoa and coffee are also important products. Fish, pigs and sheep are important for home consumption as well as yam, taro, manioc and bananas. Manganese is the only mineral. Tourism is becoming an important industry.

VATICAN CITY
STATUS: **Ecclesiastical State**
AREA: **0.44 sq km (0.17 sq miles)**
POPULATION: **1,000**
LANGUAGE: **Italian, Latin**
RELIGION: **Roman Catholic**
CURRENCY: **Italian lira (ITL), Papal coinage**
ORGANIZATIONS: **none**

Vatican City, occupying a hill to the west of the river Tiber, is located entirely within Rome. It is the headquarters of the Roman Catholic church and the world's smallest independent state. Income is derived from the Vatican's investments and from voluntary contributions (Peter's Pence). Tourism is important, with attractions including Michelangelo's works in the Sistine Chapel.

VENEZUELA
STATUS: **Republic**
AREA: **912,045 sq km (352,050 sq miles)**
POPULATION: **20,249,000**
ANNUAL NATURAL INCREASE: **2.5%**
CAPITAL: **Caracas**
LANGUAGE: **Spanish**
RELIGION: **Roman Catholic**
CURRENCY: **bolivar (VEB)**
ORGANIZATIONS: **OAS, OPEC, UN**

Mountain ranges, initially running parallel to the Caribbean coast and then turning southwestwards, form the most northerly extension of the Andes chain and traverse the country. To the south and east of these mountains there are lowland grasslands drained by the Orinoco river system; north-west are the lowlands around Lake Maracaibo. Temperatures are warm throughout the year. The wettest months are in summer. The economy is built around oil production in the Maracaibo region; over three quarters of export revenue comes from oil. Bauxite and iron ore are also important.

VIETNAM

STATUS: **Republic**
AREA: **329,566 sq km (127,246 sq miles)**
POPULATION: **69,306,000**
ANNUAL NATURAL INCREASE: **2.3%**
CAPITAL: **Hanoi**
LANGUAGE: **Vietnamese, French, Chinese**
RELIGION: **Buddhist**
CURRENCY: **dong (VND)**
ORGANIZATIONS: **OIEC, UN**

The Red river delta lowlands are separated from the Mekong delta in the south by generally rough mountainous terrain. The climate is tropical. Summer monsoon rains fall from May to October; winters are relatively dry. Rice is grown extensively throughout the north along with coffee and rubber in other parts of the country. Vietnam possesses a wide range of minerals including coal, lignite, anthracite, iron ore and tin. Industry is expanding rapidly, but decades of warfare and internal strife have impeded development.

VIRGIN ISLANDS (UK)

STATUS: **UK Dependent Territory**
AREA: **153 sq km (59 sq miles)**
POPULATION: **16,749**
CAPITAL: **Road Town**

VIRGIN ISLANDS (USA)

STATUS: **External Territory of USA**
AREA: **345 sq km (133 sq miles)**
POPULATION: **101,809**
CAPITAL: **Charlotte Amalie**

WALLIS & FUTUNA ISLANDS

STATUS: **Self-governing Overseas Territory of France**
AREA: **274 sq km (106 sq miles)**
POPULATION: **14,100**
CAPITAL: **Mata-Uta**

WESTERN SAHARA

STATUS: **Territory in dispute, administered by Morocco**
AREA: **266,000 sq km (102,675 sq miles)**
POPULATION: **250,000**
CAPITAL: **Laayoune**

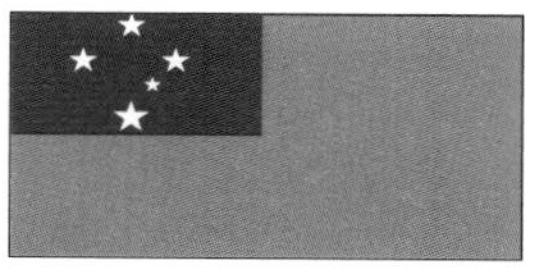

WESTERN SAMOA

STATUS: **Commonwealth State**
AREA: **2,840 sq km (1,095 sq miles)**
POPULATION: **170,000**
ANNUAL NATURAL INCREASE: **0.5%**
CAPITAL: **Apia**
LANGUAGE: **English, Samoan**
RELIGION: **Christian**
CURRENCY: **tala (dollar) (WST)**
ORGANIZATIONS: **Comm., UN**

Western Samoa is a group of seven small islands and two larger mountainous islands. Three quarters of the population lives on Upolu. The climate is tropical and very humid, but cooler between May and November. Main exports are copra, timber, taro, cocoa and fruit. The only industries are food processing and timber products. Main imports are food products, consumer goods, machinery and animals.

YEMEN

STATUS: **Republic**
AREA: **527,970 sq km (328,065 sq miles)**
POPULATION: **11,092,084**
ANNUAL NATURAL INCREASE: **4.4%**
CAPITAL: **San'a (Şan'ā')**
LANGUAGE: **Arabic**
RELIGION: **Sunni and Shi'a Muslim**
CURRENCY: **Yemeni dinar and rial**
ORGANIZATIONS: **Arab League, UN**

Yemen is a land of mountains and desert. From the Red Sea, beyond the coastal plain, rises a rugged mountain range. Eastwards the land descends to the deserts of the Empty Quarter (Ar Rub' al Khālī). In general Yemen has a hot and arid climate, although rainfall in the western mountains supports agriculture. A large proportion of the population are farmers and nomadic herders; the main livestock are sheep, goats, cattle and poultry. The only commercial mineral being exploited is salt, and there is a certain amount of oil production from the Mar'ib area. The Yemen Arab Republic and the People's Democratic Republic of Yemen were unified in 1990. However, conflict within the country may see a return to independence for these former states.

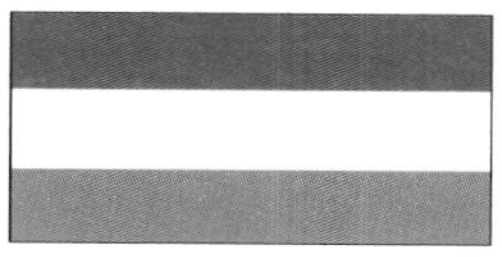

YUGOSLAVIA

STATUS: **Federation of former Yugoslav Republics of Serbia and Montenegro**
AREA: **102,170 sq km (39,435 sq miles)**
POPULATION: **10,474,000**
ANNUAL NATURAL INCREASE: **0.8%**
CAPITAL: **Belgrade (Beograd)**
LANGUAGE: **Serbo-Croat, Albanian and Hungarian**
RELIGION: **Orthodox Christian, 10% Muslim**
CURRENCY: **new dinar (YUD)**
ORGANIZATIONS: **UN (suspended)**

Serbia and Montenegro, following the secession of Slovenia, Croatia, and Bosnia-Herzegovina and the declaration of independence by Macedonia, are all that is now left of the former Yugoslavia. Armed conflict followed secession as Serbs, Croats and Muslims fought to support their kinfolk in the ethnically complex former republics. Yugoslavia's physical geography is varied. Montenegro, Kosovo and southern Serbia have rugged, mountainous, forested landscapes. Northern Serbia and Vojvodina are mainly low-lying, drained by the Danube river system. Generally speaking, the climate is continental with warm summers and cold winters, but the extremes vary with altitude and from north to south. Rainfall is spread fairly evenly throughout the year, though snow is common in winter.

Agriculture is largely in private hands. The fertile plains of Vojvodina and Kosovo provide cereals and cotton, central Serbia provides livestock products and Kosovo grows fruits and tobacco. Industry, which accounts for over 80 per cent of the economy, has suffered from socialist planning and over-centralization. Further damage resulted from the civil war and economic sanctions, which have ruined Serbia's economy and caused severe damage to Montenegro's. The future depends on restructuring of industry, on the restoration of links with Slovenia and Croatia, the most prosperous of the six former republics, and on external relations.

MONTENEGRO

STATUS: **Constituent Republic**
AREA: **13,810 sq km (5,330 sq miles)**
POPULATION: **664,000**
CAPITAL: **Podgorica**

SERBIA

STATUS: **Constituent Republic**
AREA: **88,360 sq km (34,105 sq miles)**
POPULATION: **9,815,000**
CAPITAL: **Belgrade (Beograd)**

ZAIRE

STATUS: **Republic**
AREA: **2,345,410 sq km (905,330 sq miles)**
POPULATION: **39,882,000**
ANNUAL NATURAL INCREASE: **3.3%**
CAPITAL: **Kinshasa**
LANGUAGE: **French, Lingala, Kiswahili, Tshiluba, Kikongo**
RELIGION: **46% Roman Catholic, 28% Protestant, traditional beliefs**
CURRENCY: **zaire (ZRZ)**
ORGANIZATIONS: **OAU, UN**

Most of the country consists of the basin of the Zaire river flanked by plateaux, with high mountain ranges to the north and east. The climate is tropical with rainforest close to the Equator and savannah in the northern and southern parts. The majority of the population is engaged in shifting agriculture. Cassava, cocoa, coffee, millet, rubber and sugarcane are grown. Zaire is rich in minerals, and exports copper, cobalt, diamonds, gold, manganese, uranium and zinc, with copper being the most important. However, the copper mines are closing and the only commodity providing income is diamonds. Zaire has abundant wildlife, and tourism is becoming important.

ZAMBIA

STATUS: **Republic**
AREA: **752,615 sq km (290,510 sq miles)**
POPULATION: **8,638,000**
ANNUAL NATURAL INCREASE: **3.5%**
CAPITAL: **Lusaka**
LANGUAGE: **English, African languages**
RELIGION: **75% Christian, animist minority**
CURRENCY: **kwacha (ZMK)**
ORGANIZATIONS: **Comm., OAU, UN**

The country is dominated by high savannah plateaux. Its southern boundary is the Zambezi river. The climate is tropical with three seasons: cool and dry, hot and dry, then rainy from November until May. Farming is at subsistence level, the main crop being maize. Copper is still the mainstay of the country's economy although reserves are declining rapidly and may be exhausted by the end of the century. Lead, zinc, cobalt and tobacco are also exported. Wildlife is diverse and abundant and contributes to expanding tourism.

ZIMBABWE

STATUS: **Republic**
AREA: **390,310 sq km (150,660 sq miles)**
POPULATION: **10,402,000**
ANNUAL NATURAL INCREASE: **3.0%**
CAPITAL: **Harare**
LANGUAGE: **English, native languages**
RELIGION: **58% Christian, traditional beliefs**
CURRENCY: **Zimbabwe dollar (ZWD)**
ORGANIZATIONS: **Comm., OAU, UN**

Extensive high plateaux in central Zimbabwe are bordered by the Zambezi river valley and Lake Kariba in the north and the Limpopo in the south. Although the climate is tropical, temperatures are moderate because of the altitude of the high plateaux. Average rainfall is 740 mm (29 inches) a year, occurring mainly from November to March. Maize is the most important crop as it is the staple food of a large proportion of the population. Tobacco, tea, sugarcane and fruit are also grown. Manufacturing industry is slowly developing and now provides a wide range of consumer products. Mineral deposits include chrome, nickel, platinum and coal, with gold and asbestos especially important.

GEOGRAPHICAL COMPARISONS

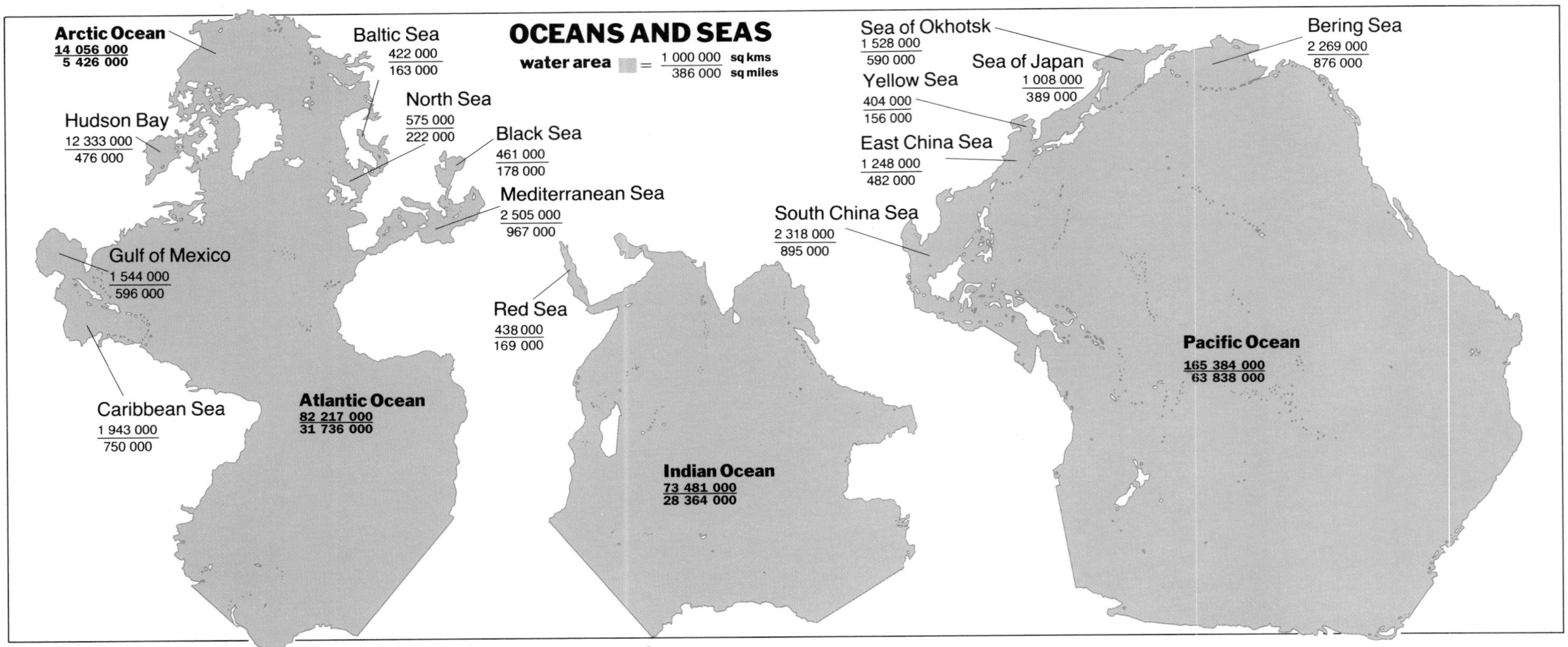

INLAND WATERS

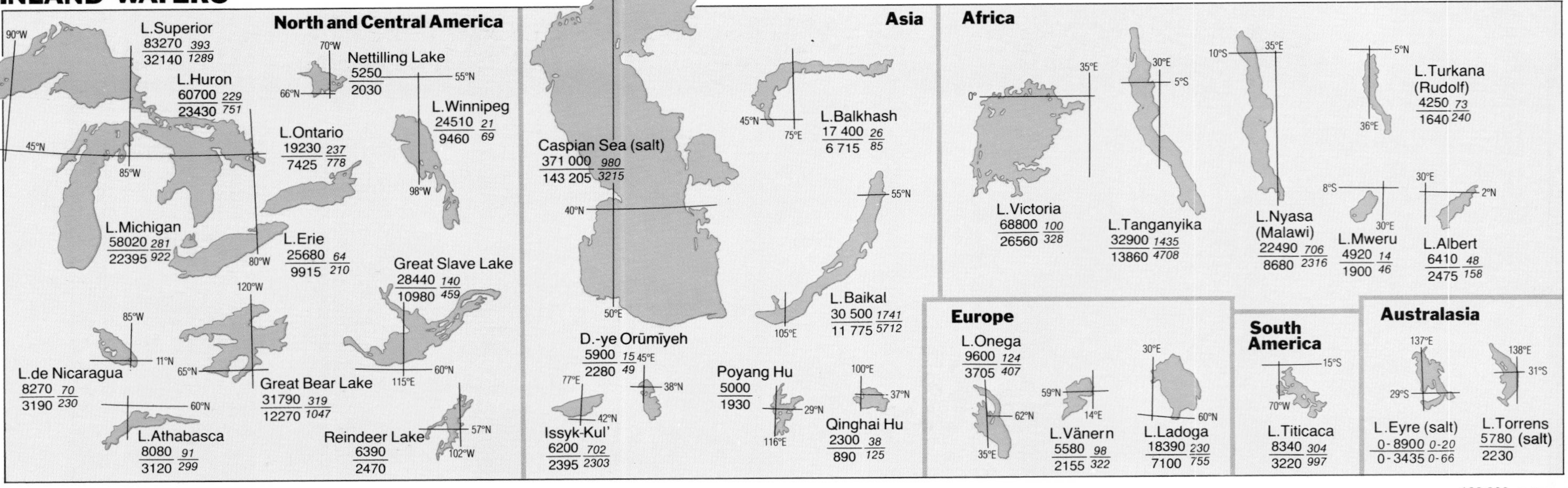

DRAINAGE BASINS

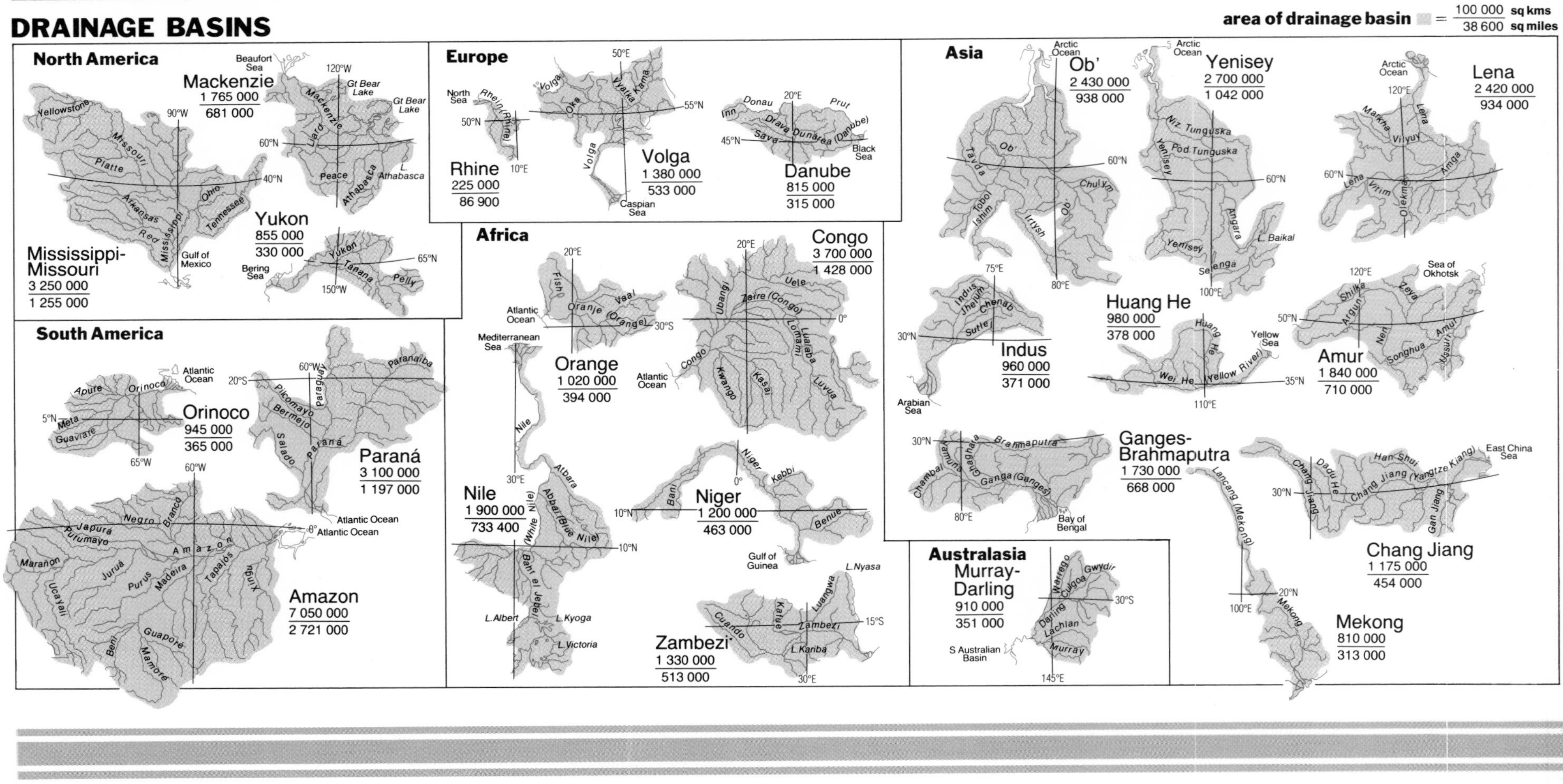

MOUNTAIN HEIGHTS

Mountain	Metres	Feet	Location
Everest (Qomolangma)	8,848	29,028	China-Nepal
K2(Godwin Austen)(Qogir Feng)	8,611	28,250	Kashmir-China
Kangchenjunga	8,586	28,170	India-Nepal
Makalu	8,463	27,766	China-Nepal
Cho Oyu	8,201	26,906	China-Nepal
Dhaulagiri	8,167	26,795	Nepal
Manaslu	8,163	26,781	Nepal
Nanga Parbat	8,125	26,657	Kashmir
Annapurna	8,091	26,545	Nepal
Gasherbrum	8,068	26,470	Kashmir
Xixabangma Feng (Gosainthan)	8,012	26,286	Tibet, China
Distaghil Sar	7,885	25,869	Kashmir
Masherbrum	7,821	25,659	Kashmir
Nanda Devi	7,816	25,643	India
Kamet	7,756	25,446	India
Namjagbarwa Feng (Namcha Barwa)	7,756	25,446	Tibet, China
Gurla Mandhata	7,728	25,354	Tibet, China
Muztag	7,723	25,338	East Sinkiang, Tibet
Kongur Shan (Kungur)	7,719	25,325	China
Tirich Mir	7,690	25,230	Pakistan
Gongga Shan	7,556	24,790	Sichuan, China
Pik Kommunizma	7,495	24,590	Tajikistan
Pik Pobedy (Tomur Feng)	7,439	24,406	Kirghizia-China
Aconcagua	6,960	22,834	Argentina
Ojos del Salado	6,880	22,572	Argentina-Chile
Bonete	6,872	22,546	Argentina
Huascarán	6,768	22,205	Peru
Sajama	6,542	21,463	Bolivia
Illampu	6,485	21,276	Bolivia
Chimborazo	6,310	20,702	Ecuador
McKinley	6,194	20,320	Alaska, U.S.A.
Logan	5,959	19,551	Yukon, Canada
Cotopaxi	5,896	19,344	Ecuador
Kilimanjaro	5,895	19,340	Tanzania
Citlaltépetl (Orizaba)	5,699	18,697	Mexico
Damāvand	5,671	18,605	Iran
El'brus	5,642	18,510	Caucasus, Russian Federation
Kenya (Kirinyaga)	5,199	17,057	Kenya
Ararat (Büyük Ağri Daği)	5,123	16,808	Turkey
Jaya (Carstensz)	5,030	16,503	New Guinea, Indonesia
Vinson Massif	4,897	16,066	Antarctica
Mont Blanc	4,808	15,774	France-Italy
Meru	4,565	14,979	Tanzania
Dom (Mischabel group)	4,545	14,910	Switzerland
Ras Dashen	4,533	14,872	Ethiopia
Kirkpatrick	4,528	14,855	Antarctica
Karisimbi	4,507	14,786	Rwanda-Zaire
Matterhorn	4,478	14,690	Italy-Switzerland
Whitney	4,418	14,495	U.S.A.
Elbert	4,398	14,431	U.S.A.
Rainier	4,392	14,410	U.S.A.
Elgon	4,321	14,178	Kenya-Uganda
Mauna Kea	4,205	13,796	Hawaii, U.S.A.
Toubkal	4,165	13,664	Morocco
Cameroon (Caméroun)	4,095	13,435	Cameroon
Kinabalu	4,094	13,431	Sabah, Malaysia
Eiger	3,975	13,041	Switzerland
Erebus	3,794	12,447	Antarctica
Fuji	3,776	12,388	Japan
Cook (Aoraki)	3,754	12,316	New Zealand
Teide	3,718	12,198	Canary Is.
Mulhacén	3,482	11,424	Spain
Etna	3,323	10,902	Sicily, Italy
Kosciusko	2,230	7,316	Australia

The mountains listed here are a selection from every continent rather than a strict numerical ordering.

RIVER LENGTHS

River	Kms	Miles	Location
Nile	6,695	4,160	Africa
Amazon	6,515	4,050	South America
Yangtze (Chang Jiang)	6,380	3,965	Asia
Mississippi-Missouri	6,019	3,740	U.S.A.
Ob'-Irtysh	5,570	3,460	Russian Federation-Kazakhstan
Yenisei	5,550	3,450	Russian Federation
Yellow River (Huang He)	5,464	3,395	China
Congo (Zaire)	4,667	2,900	Africa
Paraná	4,500	2,800	South America
Mekong	4,425	2,750	Asia
Amur	4,416	2,744	Russian Federation-China
Lena	4,400	2,730	Russian Federation
Mackenzie	4,250	2,640	Canada
Niger	4,030	2,505	Africa
Missouri	3,969	2,266	U.S.A.
Mississippi	3,779	2,348	U.S.A.
Murray-Darling	3,750	2,330	Australia
Volga	3,688	2,290	Russian Federation
Madeira	3,200	1,990	Brazil
Yukon	3,185	1,980	Canada-Alaska
Indus	3,180	1,975	Pakistan
Syrdar'ya	3,078	1,913	Kazakhstan
Salween	3,060	1,901	Asia
St Lawrence	3,058	1,900	Canada
São Francisco	2,900	1,800	Brazil
Rio Grande	2,870	1,785	U.S.A.-Mexico
Danube	2,850	1,770	Europe
Brahmaputra	2,840	1,765	India-Tibet
Euphrates	2,815	1,750	Iraq-Syria-Turkey
Pará-Tocantins	2,750	1,710	Brazil
Zambezi	2,650	1,650	Africa
Amudar'ya	2,620	1,630	Uzbekistan-Turkmenistan
Paraguay	2,600	1,615	South America
Nelson-Saskatchewan	2,570	1,600	Canada
Ural	2,534	1,575	Russian Federation-Kazakhstan
Ganges (Ganga)	2,510	1,560	India
Orinoco	2,500	1,555	Venezuela
Shabeelle	2,490	1,550	Somalia-Ethiopia
Arkansas	2,348	1,459	U.S.A.
Colorado	2,333	1,450	U.S.A.
Dnieper (Dnepr)	2,285	1,420	Ukraine-Belarus
Irrawaddy	2,150	1,335	Burma
Don	1,870	1,162	Russian Federation
Orange	1,860	1,155	Africa
Rhine	1,320	820	Europe
Elbe	1,159	720	Germany-Czech Republic
Vistula (Wisła)	1,014	630	Poland
Loire	1,012	629	France
Tagus (Tejo)	1,006	625	Portugal-Spain

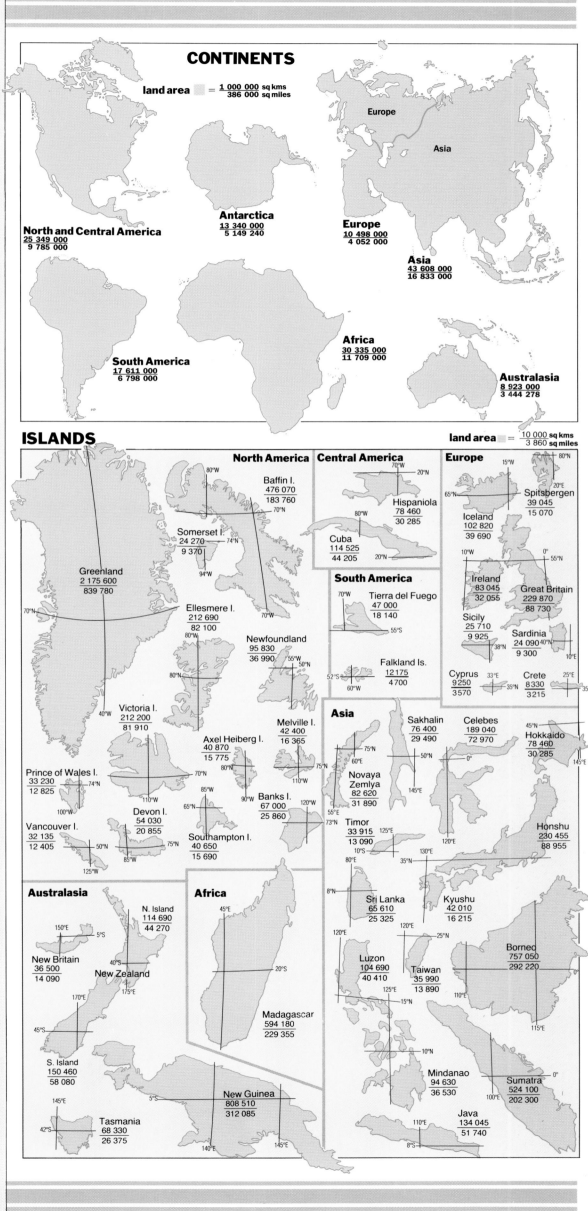

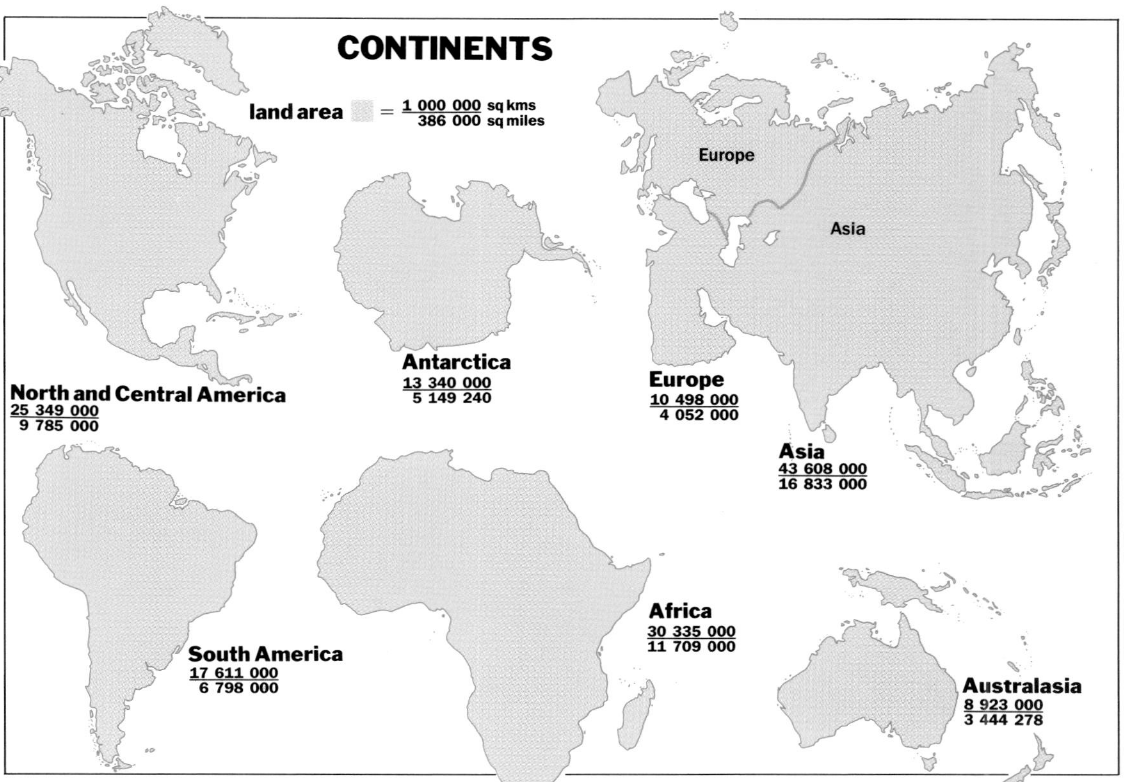

ISLANDS

land area = 10 000 sq kms / 3 860 sq miles

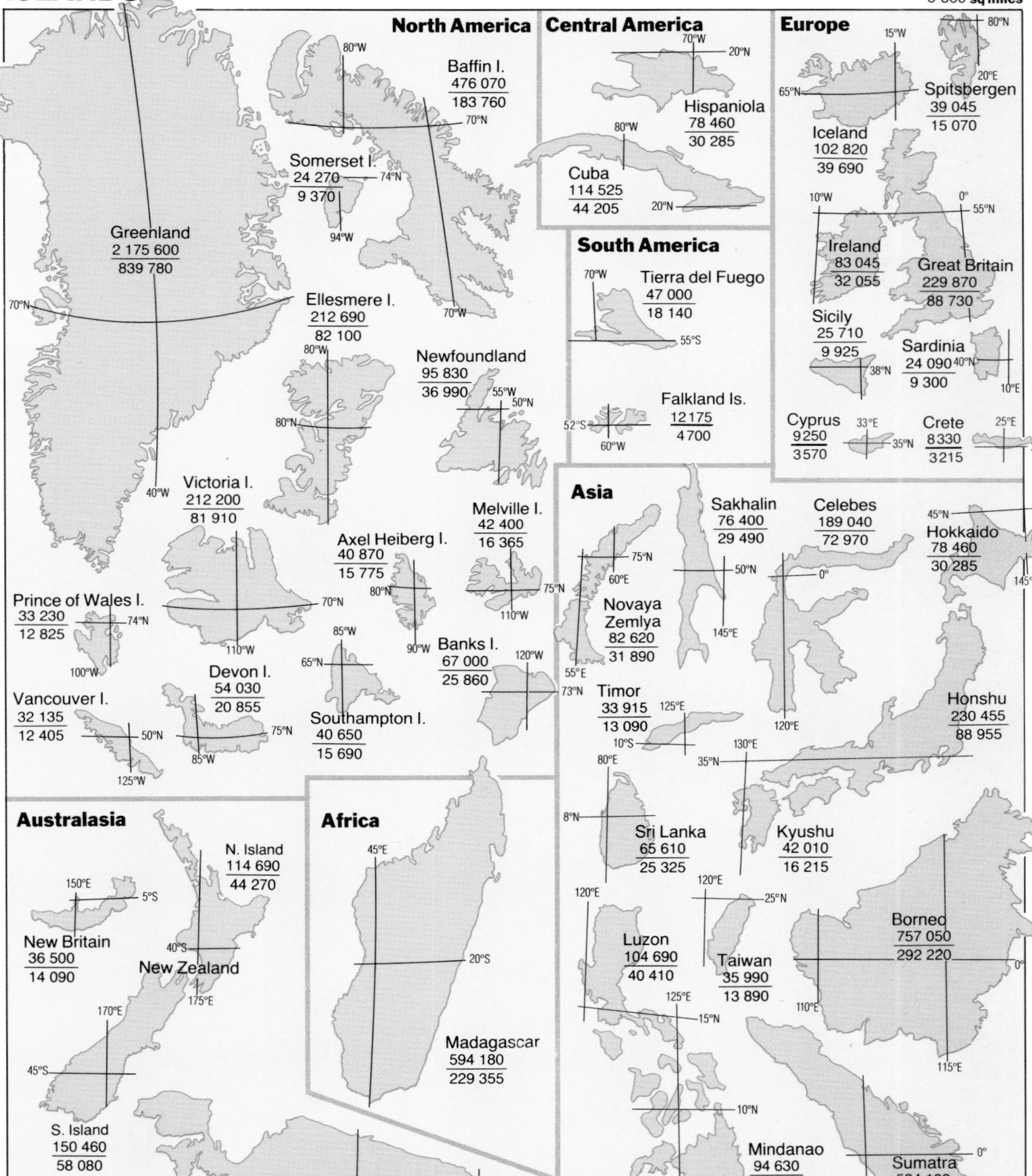

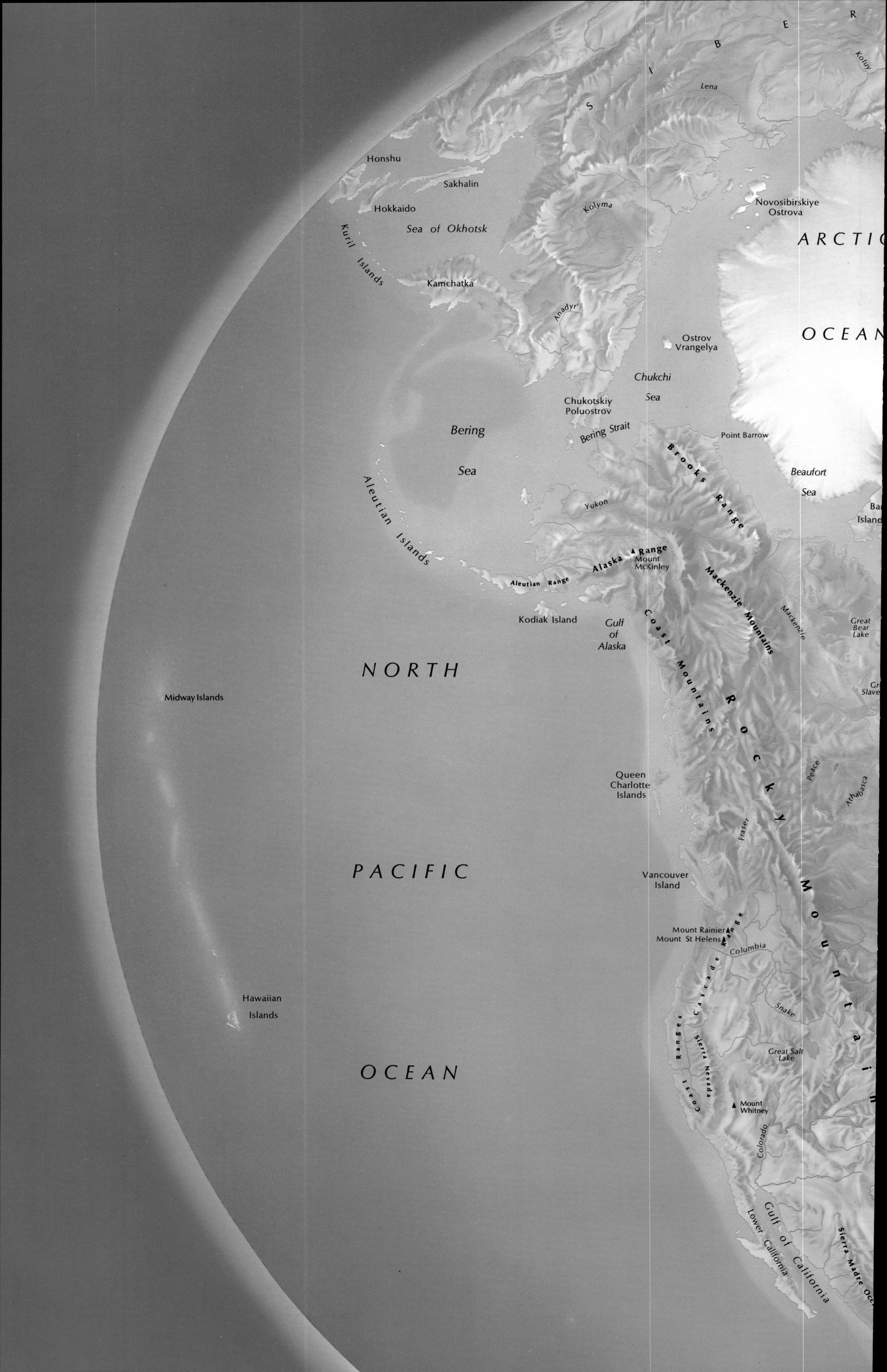
S I B E R
Lena
Kolyma
Honshu
Sakhalin
Hokkaido
Sea of Okhotsk
Kuril Islands
Kamchatka
Anadyr'
Novosibirskiye Ostrova
ARCTIC
OCEAN
Ostrov Vrangelya
Chukchi Sea
Chukotskiy Poluostrov
Bering Strait
Bering Sea
Point Barrow
Brooks Range
Beaufort Sea
Aleutian Islands
Yukon
Alaska Range
Mount McKinley
Aleutian Range
Mackenzie Mountains
Mackenzie
Great Bear Lake
Kodiak Island
Gulf of Alaska
Coast Mountains
NORTH
Midway Islands
ROCKY MOUNTAINS
Queen Charlotte Islands
Peace
Athabasca
Fraser
PACIFIC
Vancouver Island
Mount Rainier
Mount St Helens
Cascade Range
Columbia
Snake
Hawaiian Islands
Coast Ranges
Sierra Nevada
Great Salt Lake
OCEAN
Mount Whitney
Colorado
Lower California
Gulf of California
Sierra Madre Occ

Yenisey
Ob'
Urals
Black Sea
Novaya Zemlya
Severnaya Zemlya
North Cape
SCANDINAVIA
Limit of permanent pack ice
Svalbard
Norwegian Sea
NORTH POLE
North Sea
Mediterranean Sea
Jan Mayen
Denmark Strait
BRITISH ISLES
Bay of Biscay
Iceland
Greenland
Ellesmere Island
Queen Elizabeth Islands
NORTH AFRICA
Parry Islands
Baffin Bay
Davis Strait
Cape Farewell
Victoria Island
Baffin Island
Madeira
NORTH
Canary Islands
Foxe Basin
Southampton Island
Hudson Strait
Cape Chidley
Labrador Sea
Azores
Hudson Bay
Labrador
Lake Athabasca
Churchill
Churchill
Reindeer Lake
Southern Indian Lake
La Grande Rivière
Laurentian Highlands
Newfoundland
Cape Race
ATLANTIC
James Bay
Rupert
Saskatchewan
Lake Winnipeg
Nova Scotia
Lake Manitoba
St Lawrence
Lake of the Woods
Lake Superior
Lake Huron
Cape Cod
Lake Ontario
Lake Michigan
Missouri
Mississippi
Lake Erie
Appalachian Mountains
Great Plains
Platte
Ohio
Bermuda
OCEAN
Cape Hatteras
Ozark Plateaus
Tennessee
Savannah
Arkansas
Mississippi
Red River
Florida
Bahamas
West Indies
Rio Grande
Sierra Madre Oriental
Gulf of Mexico
Caribbean Sea
Orinoco
Yucatan

CENTRAL AND SOUTH AMERICA, NORTH

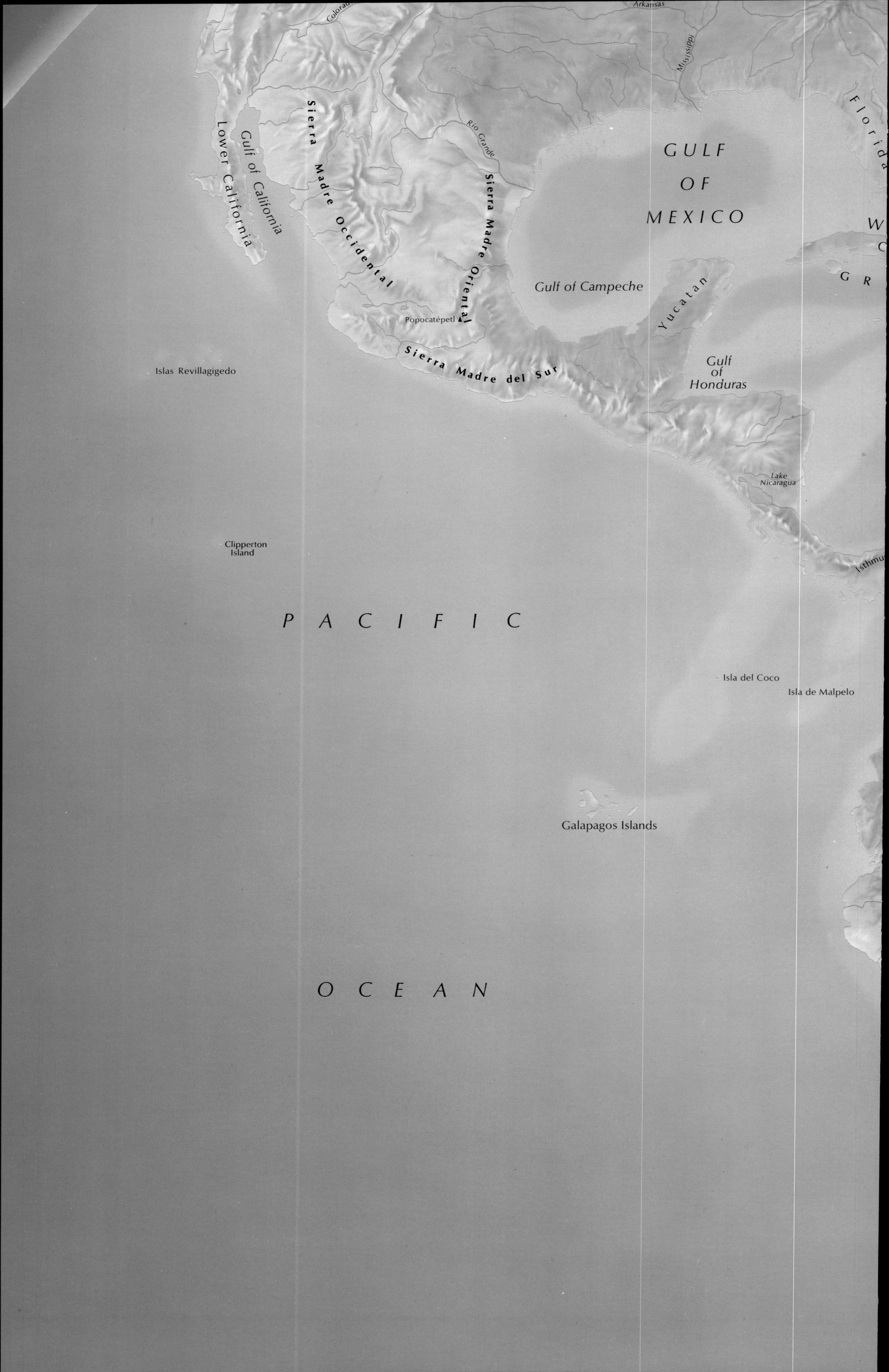

Bermuda
BAHAMAS
WEST INDIES
Cuba
GREATER ANTILLES
Hispaniola
Jamaica
Puerto Rico
CARIBBEAN SEA
LESSER ANTILLES
NORTH ATLANTIC OCEAN
Trinidad
Lake Maracaibo
Gulf of Darien
Panama
LLANOS
Orinoco
Cauca
Magdalena
Cordillera Occidental
Cordillera Oriental
Roraima
Guiana Highlands
Branco
Mouths of the Amazon
Cotopaxi
Negro
Japurá
Putumayo
Amazon
Marañon
Juruá
Purus
Madeira
Tapajós
Xingu
Tocantins
Ucayali
Parnaíba
São Francisco
Huascarán
Araguaia
ANDES
Madre de Dios
MATO GROSSO
Brazilian Highlands
Lake Titicaca
Ancohuma
Lake Poopó
Salar de Uyuni
Atacama Desert
GRAN CHACO
Paraguay
Paraná
Pilcomayo

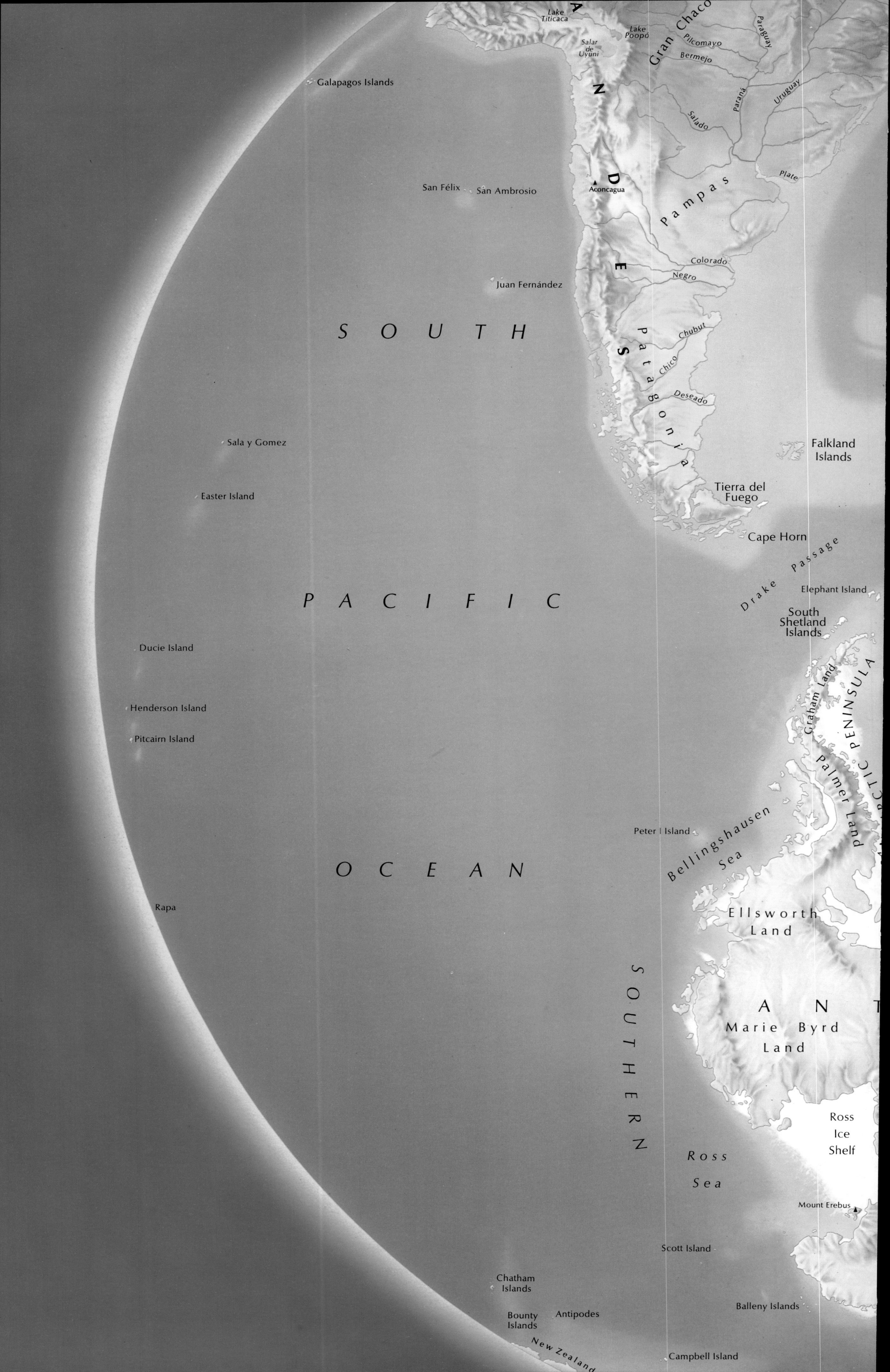
Lake Titicaca
Lake Poopó
Salar de Uyuni
Gran Chaco
Pilcomayo
Bermejo
Paraguay
Paraná
Uruguay
Salado
Plate
Galapagos Islands
San Félix
San Ambrosio
Aconcagua
A N D E S
Pampas
Colorado
Negro
Juan Fernández
S O U T H
Patagonia
Chubut
Chico
Deseado
Sala y Gomez
Falkland Islands
Easter Island
Tierra del Fuego
Cape Horn
Drake Passage
Elephant Island
P A C I F I C
South Shetland Islands
Ducie Island
Graham Land
PENINSULA
Henderson Island
Pitcairn Island
Palmer Land
Peter I Island
Bellingshausen Sea
O C E A N
Rapa
Ellsworth Land
S O U T H E R N
A N T
Marie Byrd Land
Ross Ice Shelf
Ross Sea
Mount Erebus
Scott Island
Chatham Islands
Balleny Islands
Bounty Islands
Antipodes
New Zealand
Campbell Island

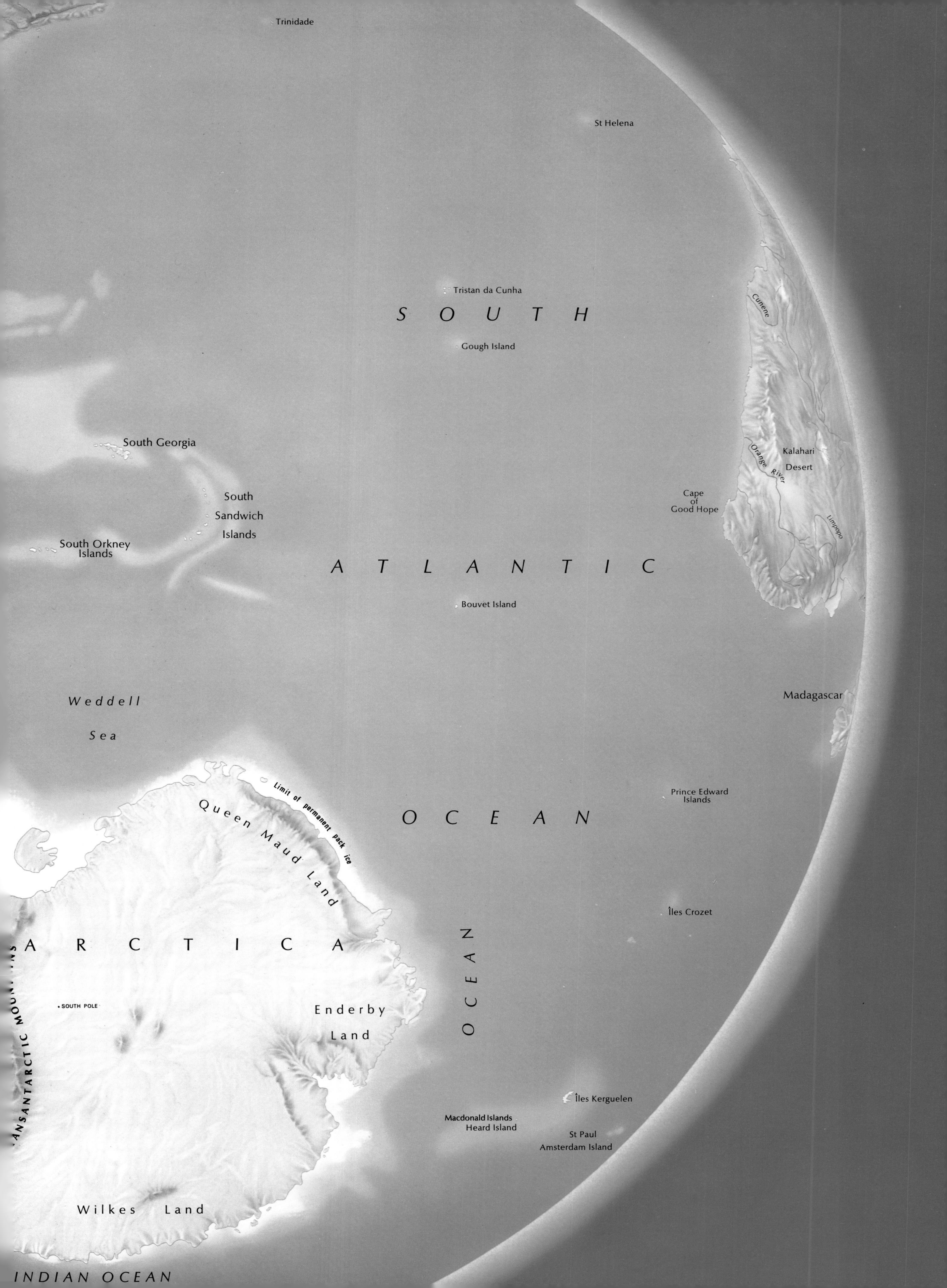

Trinidade
St Helena
Tristan da Cunha
S O U T H
Gough Island
Cunene
Kalahari
Desert
Orange
River
South Georgia
South
Sandwich
Islands
Cape
of
Good Hope
Limpopo
South Orkney
Islands
A T L A N T I C
Bouvet Island
Weddell
Sea
Madagascar
Limit of permanent pack ice
Queen Maud Land
Prince Edward
Islands
O C E A N
Îles Crozet
A R C T I C A
O C E A N
SOUTH POLE
Enderby
Land
Îles Kerguelen
Macdonald Islands
Heard Island
St Paul
Amsterdam Island
Wilkes Land
INDIAN OCEAN

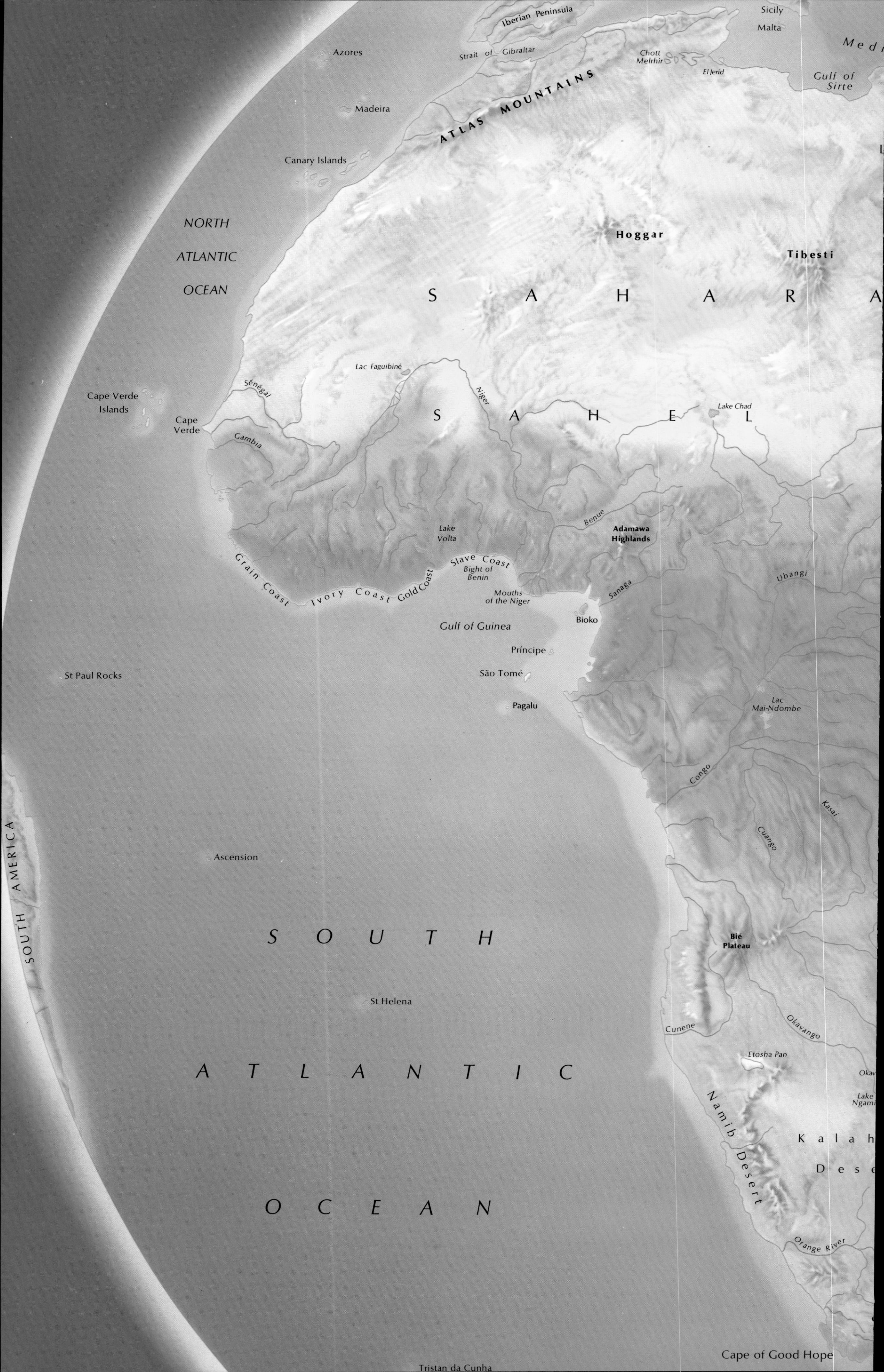
Iberian Peninsula
Sicily
Malta
Azores
Strait of Gibraltar
Chott Melrhir
El Jerid
Gulf of Sirte
Madeira
ATLAS MOUNTAINS
Canary Islands
NORTH ATLANTIC OCEAN
Hoggar
Tibesti
S A H A R A
Lac Faguibine
Sénégal
Niger
Cape Verde Islands
Cape Verde
S A H E L
Lake Chad
Gambia
Benue
Adamawa Highlands
Lake Volta
Slave Coast
Bight of Benin
Grain Coast
Ivory Coast
Gold Coast
Mouths of the Niger
Sanaga
Ubangi
Gulf of Guinea
Bioko
Príncipe
São Tomé
St Paul Rocks
Pagalu
Lac Mai-Ndombe
Congo
Kasai
Cuango
Ascension
SOUTH AMERICA
S O U T H
A T L A N T I C
O C E A N
Bié Plateau
St Helena
Cunene
Okavango
Etosha Pan
Namib Desert
Orange River
Cape of Good Hope
Tristan da Cunha

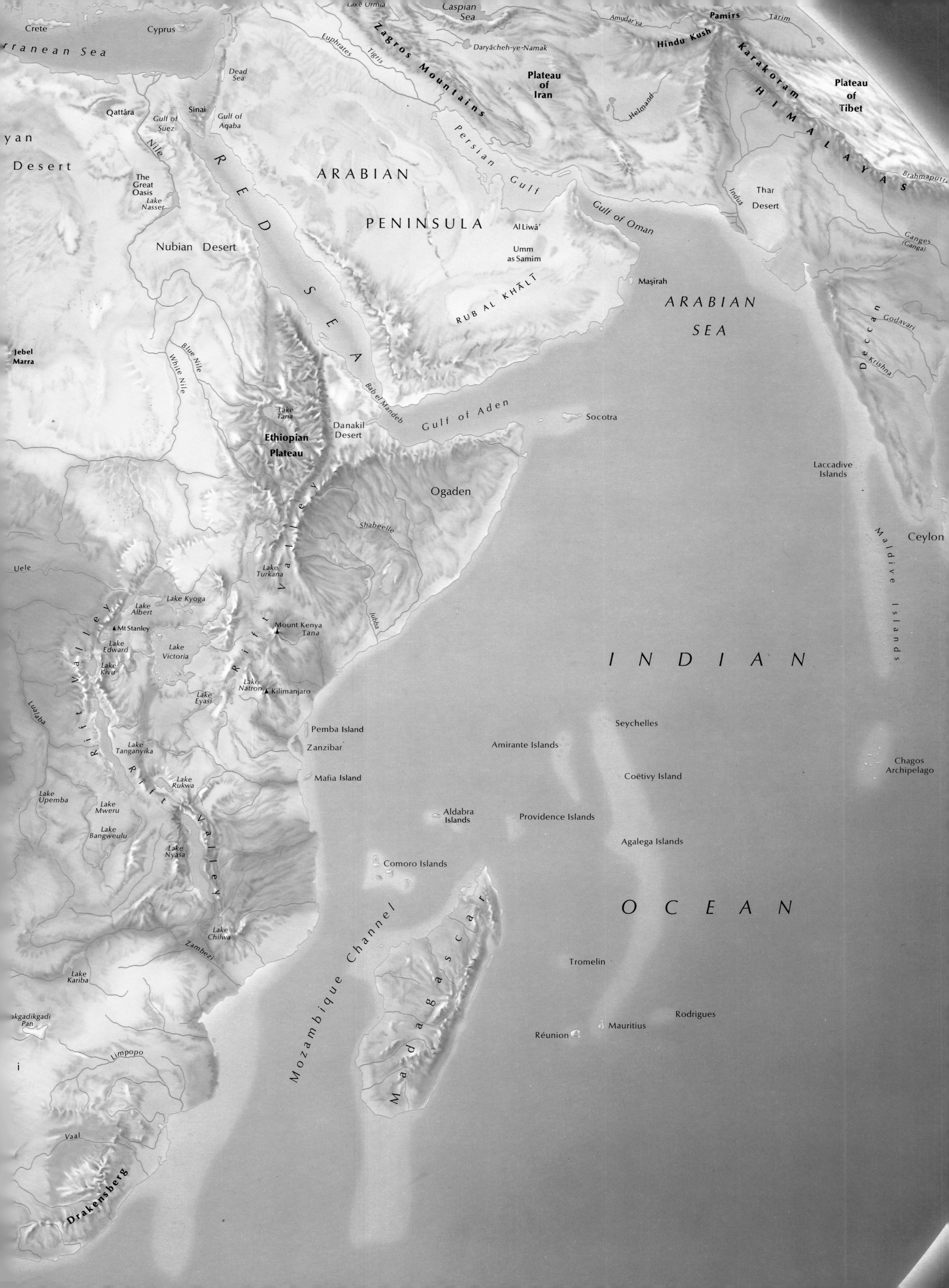
Lake Urmia
Caspian Sea
Crete
Cyprus
rranean Sea
Euphrates
Tigris
Zagros Mountains
Daryācheh-ye-Namak
Amudar'ya
Pamirs
Tarim
Hindu Kush
Karakoram
Plateau of Iran
Plateau of Tibet
HIMALAYAS
Dead Sea
Qattâra
Sinai
Gulf of Suez
Gulf of Aqaba
yan
Desert
Nile
RED SEA
Persian Gulf
Helmand
ARABIAN
PENINSULA
Brahmaputra
The Great Oasis
Lake Nasser
Thar Desert
Indus
Gulf of Oman
Al Liwā'
Nubian Desert
Umm as Samim
Ganges (Ganga)
Maṣirah
RUB AL KHĀLĪ
ARABIAN SEA
Godavari
Deccan
Krishna
Jebel Marra
Blue Nile
White Nile
Bab el Mandeb
Gulf of Aden
Socotra
Lake Tana
Danakil Desert
Ethiopian Plateau
Laccadive Islands
Ogaden
Rift Valley
Shabeelle
Ceylon
Maldive Islands
Uele
Lake Turkana
Lake Kyoga
Lake Albert
Mt Stanley
Mount Kenya
Tana
Jubba
Lake Edward
Lake Victoria
Lake Kivu
INDIAN
Lake Natron
Kilimanjaro
Lake Eyasi
Lualaba
Seychelles
Pemba Island
Zanzibar
Amirante Islands
Lake Tanganyika
Chagos Archipelago
Mafia Island
Coëtivy Island
Lake Rukwa
Lake Upemba
Lake Mweru
Aldabra Islands
Providence Islands
Lake Bangweulu
Agalega Islands
Lake Nyasa
Comoro Islands
OCEAN
Mozambique Channel
Madagascar
Lake Chilwa
Zambezi
Tromelin
Lake Kariba
akgadikgadi Pan
Rodrigues
Mauritius
Réunion
Limpopo
Vaal
Drakensberg

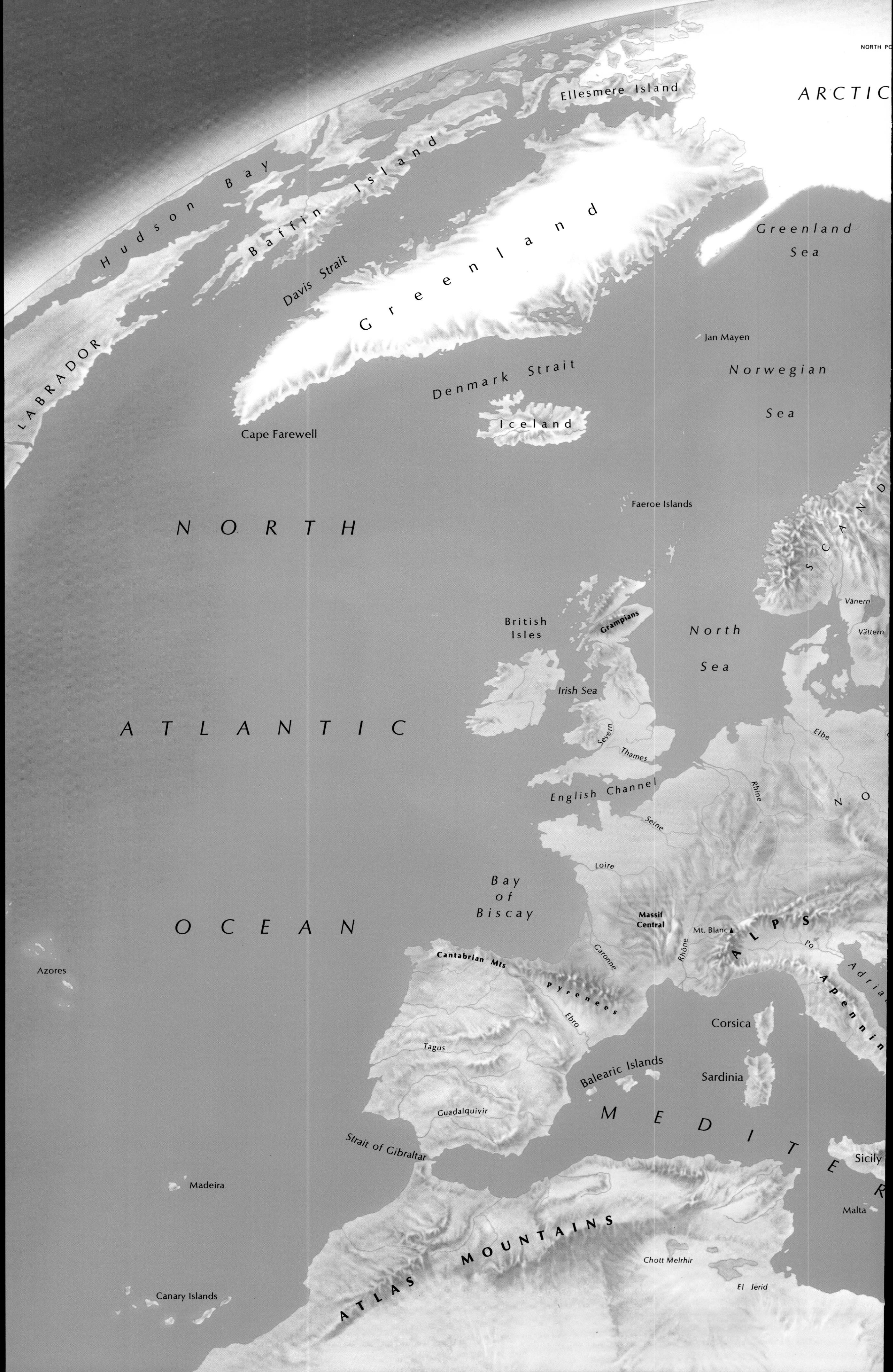
NORTH PO
ARCTIC
Ellesmere Island
Hudson Bay
Baffin Island
Davis Strait
Greenland
LABRADOR
Greenland Sea
Jan Mayen
Norwegian Sea
Denmark Strait
Iceland
Cape Farewell
Faeroe Islands
NORTH ATLANTIC OCEAN
British Isles
Grampians
North Sea
Vänern
Vättern
Irish Sea
Severn
Thames
Elbe
English Channel
Rhine
Seine
Loire
Bay of Biscay
Massif Central
Mt. Blanc
ALPS
Po
Adria
Apennin
Rhône
Garonne
Cantabrian Mts
Pyrenees
Ebro
Azores
Corsica
Tagus
Balearic Islands
Sardinia
Guadalquivir
MEDITER
Strait of Gibraltar
Sicily
Madeira
Malta
ATLAS MOUNTAINS
Chott Melrhir
El Jerid
Canary Islands

Novosibirskiye Ostrova
OCEAN
Severnaya Zemlya
Limit of permanent pack ice
Franz Josef Land
Kara Sea
Svalbard
Novaya Zemlya
Barents Sea
North Cape
Lena
CENTRAL SIBERIAN PLATEAU
Nizhnyaya Tunguska
Lena
Yenisey
WEST SIBERIAN PLAIN
SIBERIA
Angara
Lake Baikal
Pechora
URAL MOUNTAINS
Ob
Ob
White Sea
Severnaya Dvina
Irtysh
Gulf of Bothnia
Onega
Ladoga
Gulf of Finland
Baltic Sea
Volga
Dvina
Central Russian Uplands
EUROPEAN PLAIN
KIRGHIZ STEPPE
Lake Balkhash
Vistula
Ural
Neisse
Aral Sea
Volga
Syrdar'ya
Dnieper
CARPATHIANS
Dniester
Don
Kyzylkum
Caspian Sea
Danube
Hungarian Plain
Tisza
Sea of Azov
Amudar'ya
Caucasus
Karakumy
Danube
Black Sea
Balkan Mountains
Dinaric Alps
Rhodope
Thrace
Bosporus
Araxes
Lake Van
Lake Urmia
Sea of Marmara
Kizil Irmak
Dardanelles
ASIA MINOR
Tuz Gölü
Daryācheh-ye-Namak
Pindus
Aegean Sea
Zagros Mountains
Taurus
Helmand
Plateau of Iran
Mesopotamia
Cyprus
Tigris
Crete
Euphrates
MEDITERRANEAN SEA
Jordan
Syrian Desert
Dead Sea
Persian Gulf
Gulf of Sirte
Gulf of Oman
Nile
Gulf of Suez
Gulf of Aqaba
ARABIAN PENINSULA
Libyan Desert

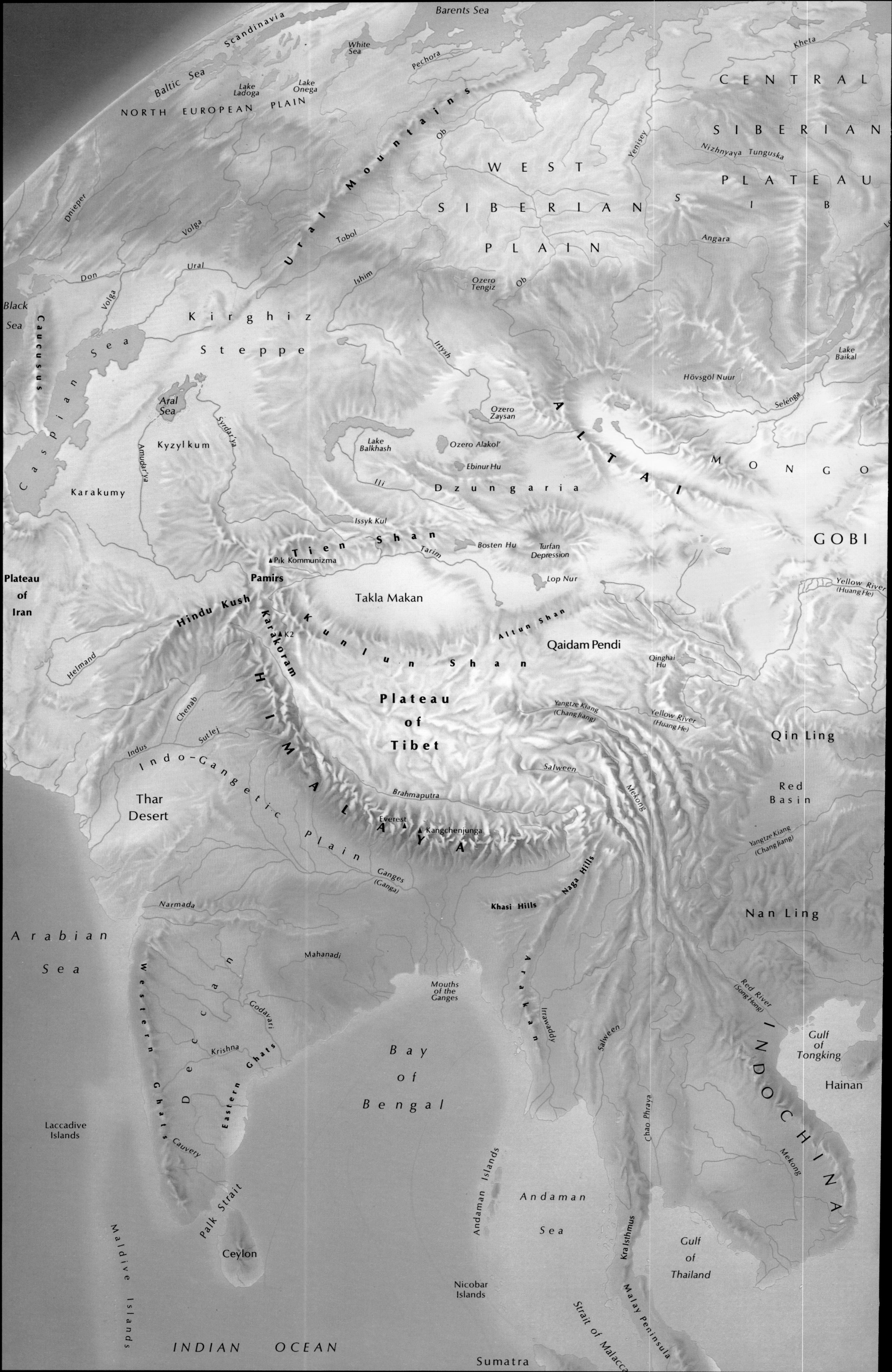
Barents Sea
Scandinavia
White Sea
Pechora
Kheta
CENTRAL SIBERIAN PLATEAU
Baltic Sea
Lake Ladoga
Lake Onega
NORTH EUROPEAN PLAIN
Ural Mountains
Ob
Yenisey
Nizhnyaya Tunguska
WEST SIBERIAN PLAIN
Dnieper
Volga
Tobol
Angara
Don
Ural
Ishim
Ozero Tengiz
Black Sea
Caucusus
Kirghiz Steppe
Caspian Sea
Irtysh
Lake Baikal
Hövsgöl Nuur
Selenga
Aral Sea
Syrdar'ya
Amudar'ya
Kyzylkum
Ozero Zaysan
ALTAI
Lake Balkhash
Ozero Alakol'
Ebinur Hu
MONGO
Karakumy
Ili
Dzungaria
Issyk Kul
GOBI
Tien Shan
Tarim
Bosten Hu
Turfan Depression
Pik Kommunizma
Plateau of Iran
Pamirs
Lop Nur
Yellow River (Huang He)
Takla Makan
Hindu Kush
Karakoram
K2
Kunlun Shan
Altun Shan
Qaidam Pendi
Helmand
Qinghai Hu
HIMALAYA
Plateau of Tibet
Yangtze Kiang (Chang Jiang)
Yellow River (Huang He)
Chenab
Qin Ling
Sutlej
Indus
Indo-Gangetic Plain
Salween
Red Basin
Mekong
Brahmaputra
Thar Desert
Everest
Kangchenjunga
Yangtze Kiang (Chang Jiang)
Ganges (Ganga)
Narmada
Khasi Hills
Naga Hills
Nan Ling
Arabian Sea
Mahanadi
Arakan
Western Ghats
Deccan
Mouths of the Ganges
Godavari
Irrawaddy
Red River (Song Hong)
Salween
Gulf of Tongking
Krishna
Eastern Ghats
Bay of Bengal
INDOCHINA
Hainan
Laccadive Islands
Cauvery
Chao Phraya
Mekong
Andaman Islands
Andaman Sea
Palk Strait
Maldive Islands
Kra Isthmus
Gulf of Thailand
Ceylon
Nicobar Islands
Strait of Malacca
Malay Peninsula
INDIAN OCEAN
Sumatra

Laptev Sea
Novosibirskiye Ostrova
Alaska
Bering Strait
Anadyr
Nunivak Island
Yana
Indigirka
Kolyma
Verkhoyanskiy Khrebet
Lena
Vilyuy
Bering Sea
Aleutian Islands
Kamchatka
Komandorskiye Ostrova
Aldan
Khr. Dzhungdzhur
Sea of Okhotsk
Yablonovyy Khrebet
Shilka
Sakhalin
Tatarskiy Proliv
Kuril Islands
Greater Khingan Range
Amur
Hulun Nur
Manchuria
Ussuri
Sikhote Alin
Songhua
Oz Khanka
Hokkaido
NORTH PACIFIC OCEAN
Midway Islands
Sea of Japan
Changbai Shan
Honshu
Bo Hai
Korea
Yellow River (Huang He)
Yellow Sea
Great Plain of China
Korea Strait
Shikoku
Kyushu
Yangtze Kiang (Chang Jiang)
East China Sea
Bonin Islands
Dongting Hu
Poyang Hu
Ryukyu Islands
Volcano Islands
Taiwan Strait
Taiwan
Marianas
Marshall Islands
South China Sea
PHILIPPINES
Guam
Kiribati
Paracel Islands
Luzon
Caroline Islands
Mindoro
Samar
Panay
Palawan
Negros
Sulu Sea
Mindanao
Spratly Islands
Celebes Sea
Borneo
Admiralty Islands
New Ireland

South China Sea
Malay Peninsula
Strait of Malacca
Sumatra
Borneo
Celebes Sea
Makassar Strait
Celebes
Moluccas
Java Sea
Banda Sea
Java
Bali
Timor
Arafura Sea
EAST INDIES
Timor Sea
Christmas Island
Cocos (Keeling) Islands
Arnhem Land
Victoria
Barkly
Kimberley Plateau
Fitzroy
Tanami Desert
INDIAN
Great Sandy Desert
Ashburton
Macdonnell Ranges
Gibson Desert
Gascoyne
Lake Amadeus
Finke
Great Victoria Desert
Lake Barlee
Lake Moore
Nullarbor Plain
Lake Gardner
Great Australian Bight
OCEAN
SOUTHERN
St Paul
Kerguelen
Heard Island
Macdonald Islands
ANTARCTICA

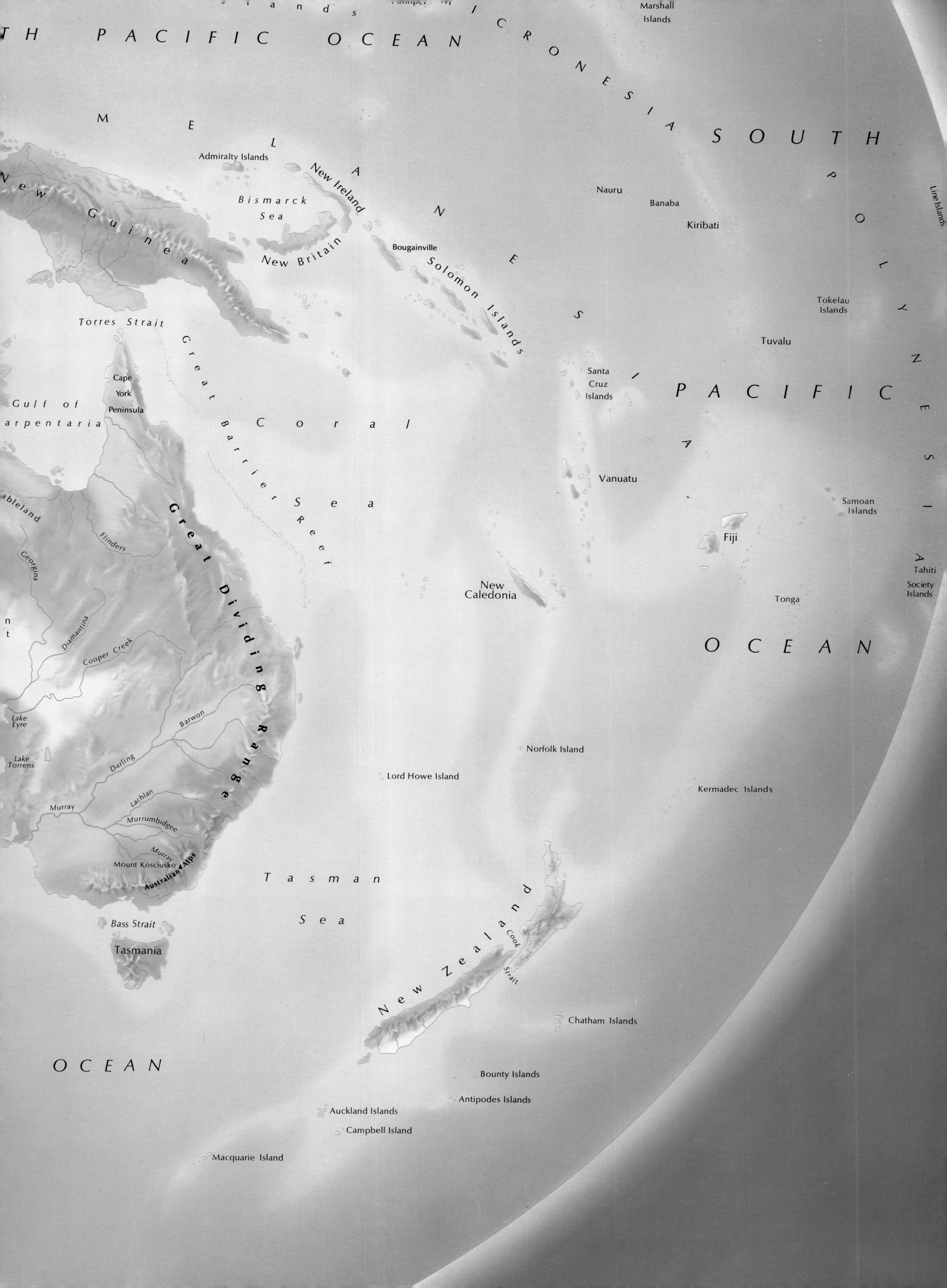

Marshall Islands
PACIFIC OCEAN
MICRONESIA
SOUTH PACIFIC OCEAN
MELANESIA
POLYNESIA
Admiralty Islands
New Ireland
Bismarck Sea
New Guinea
New Britain
Bougainville
Solomon Islands
Nauru
Banaba
Kiribati
Line Islands
Tokelau Islands
Tuvalu
Torres Strait
Great Barrier Reef
Cape York Peninsula
Gulf of Carpentaria
Coral Sea
Santa Cruz Islands
Vanuatu
Samoan Islands
Fiji
Tahiti
Society Islands
Tonga
New Caledonia
Great Dividing Range
Flinders
Georgina
Diamantina
Cooper Creek
Lake Eyre
Lake Torrens
Barwon
Darling
Lachlan
Murray
Murrumbidgee
Mount Kosciusko
Australian Alps
Norfolk Island
Lord Howe Island
Kermadec Islands
Tasman Sea
Bass Strait
Tasmania
New Zealand
Cook Strait
Chatham Islands
OCEAN
Bounty Islands
Antipodes Islands
Auckland Islands
Campbell Island
Macquarie Island

STAR CHARTS

NORTHERN SKY

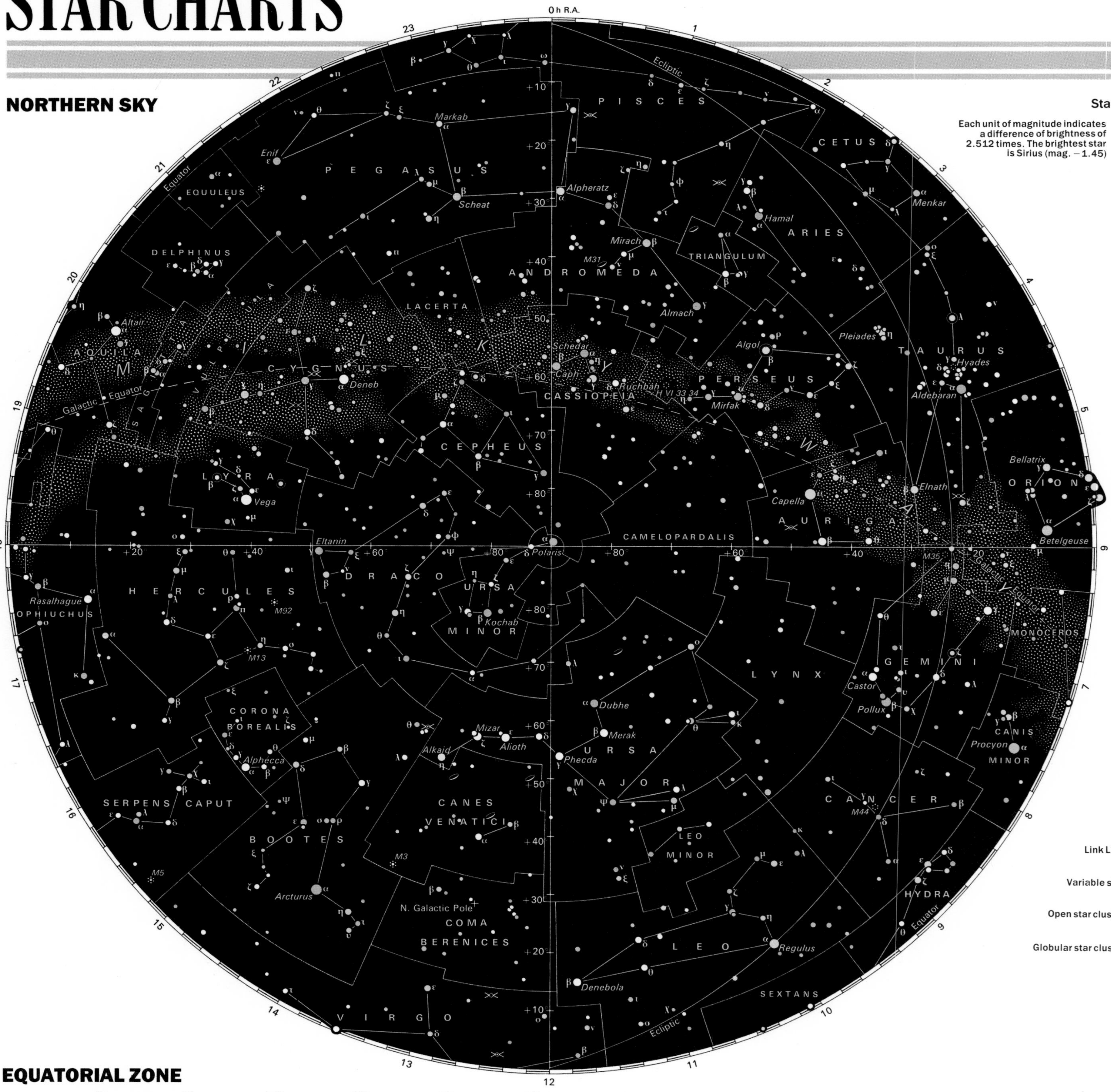

Star Magnitude

Each unit of magnitude indicates a difference of brightness of 2.512 times. The brightest star is Sirius (mag. −1.45)

0
1
2
3
4
5

Link Line

Variable star

Open star cluster

Globular star cluster

EQUATORIAL ZONE

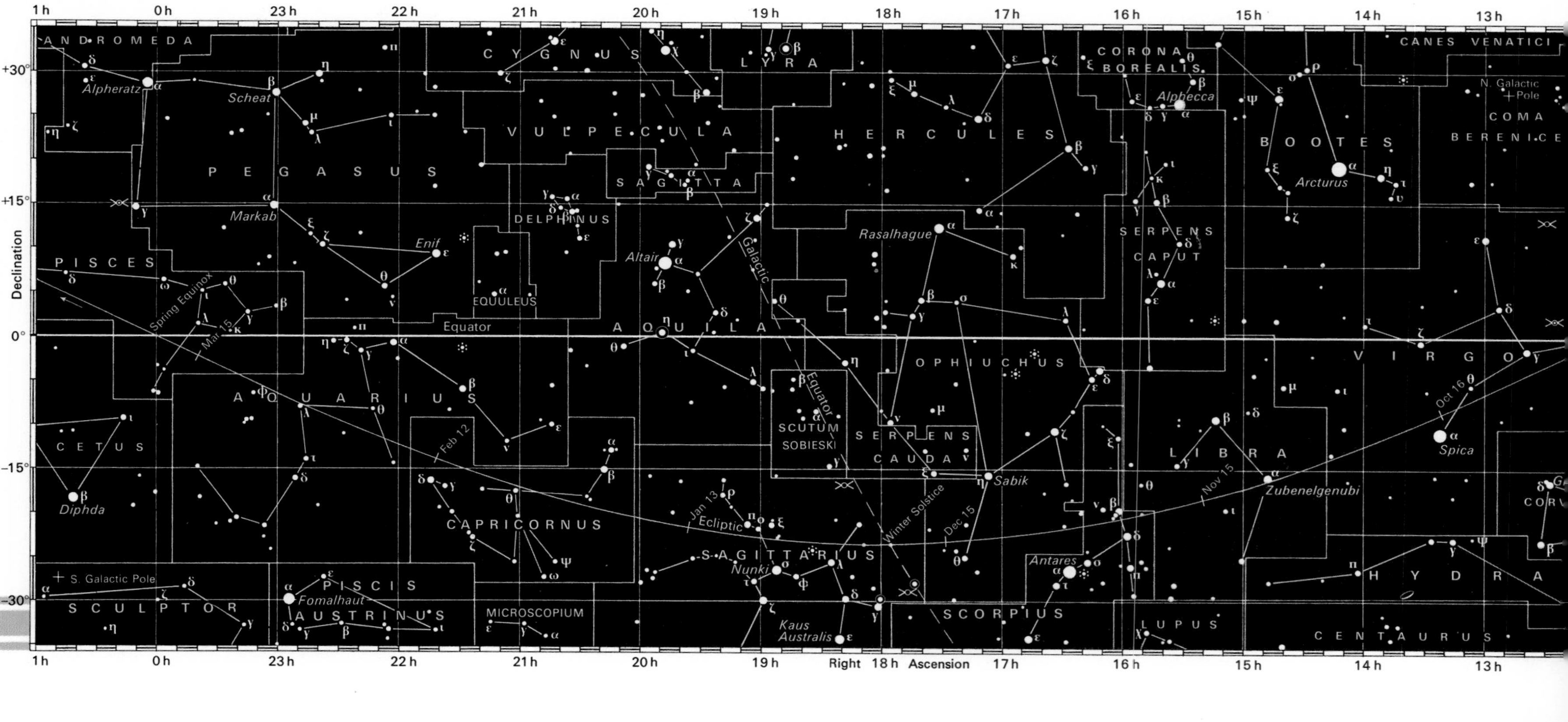

Star Colours and Spectral Types

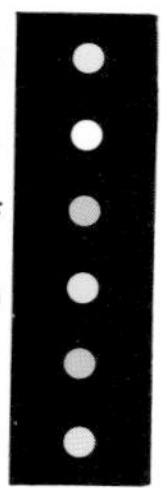

O-B	*Temp in 000°C 50.0–25.0
A	11.0
F	7.5
G	6.0
K	5.0
M	3.5

The surface temperature of a star is indicated both by its colour and its spectrum

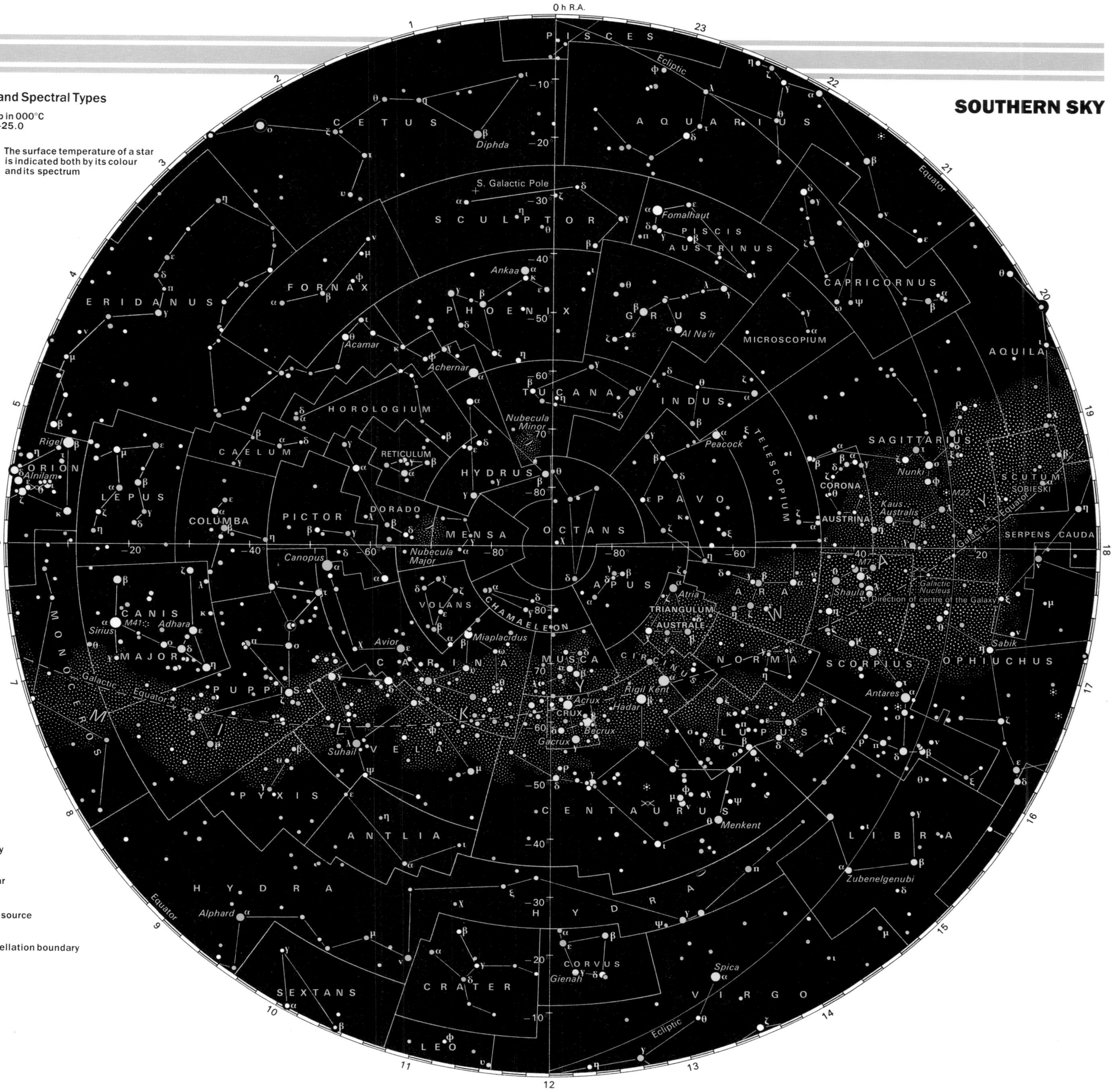

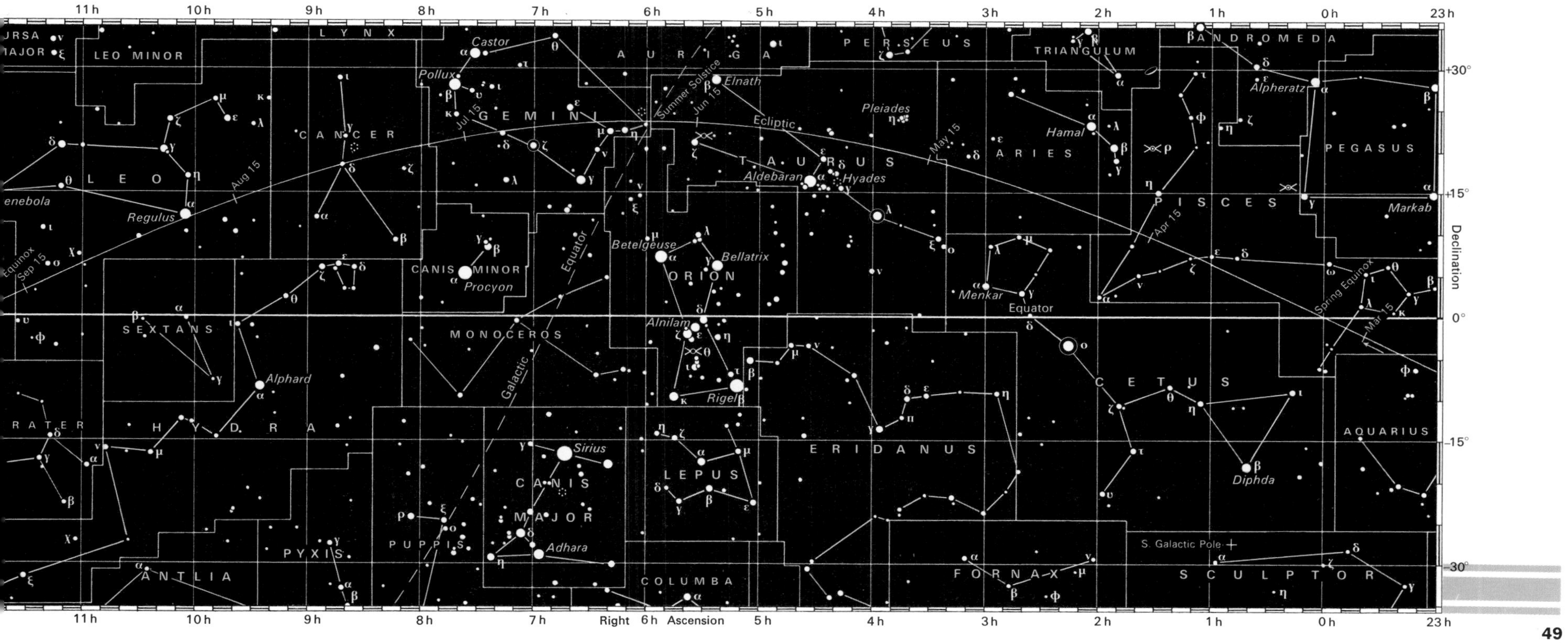

UNIVERSE

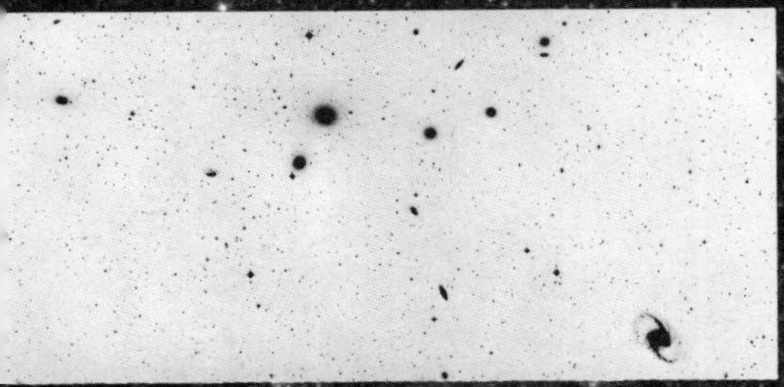

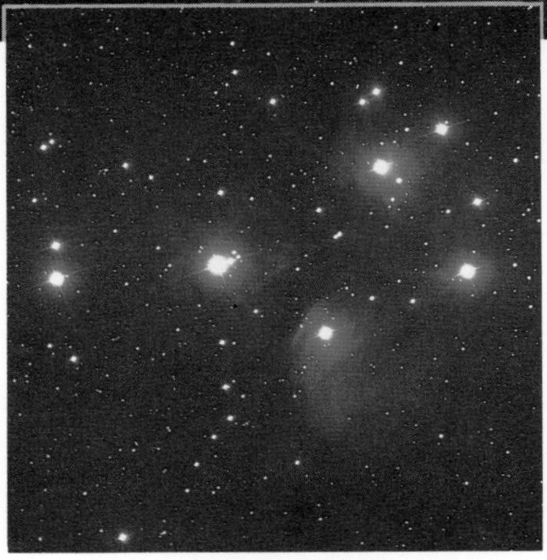

ORIGIN AND STRUCTURE OF THE UNIVERSE

Most astronomers believe that the Universe was created some ten to twenty thousand million years ago in an event often called the big bang or primordial fireball. The subsequent evolution of the universe can be described mathematically but the very early stages in particular are difficult to imagine.

The very high temperature mix of particles and radiation, the products of the big bang, expanded and cooled quickly allowing hydrogen and helium atoms to form and gravitate together to form huge clouds of gas. Turbulence within these contracting clouds caused them to fragment into rotating galaxy-sized clouds. Within these primitive galaxies smaller gas clouds condensed into clusters of stars, populating the galaxies much as we see them today. Most of these galaxies still belong to clusters, some containing thousands of members. There are probably several thousand million galaxies within the universe to the farthest distance so far observed.

Due to light travelling through space at a finite speed we see distant objects as they were when the light left them and in looking deep into space we also look far back in time. Over the past 40 years, larger optical telescopes, radio telescopes, space-borne instruments and computers have allowed astronomers to study the universe over a much wider range of the electromagnetic spectrum, much of it inaccessible from the Earth's surface.

Some galaxies are powerful emitters of radio waves and quasars, probably the nuclei of early galaxies, were first discovered by radio methods and later identified with optical objects: they appear so compact that they were mistaken for stars in our own galaxy. Many show very large 'red shifts' interpreted as velocities of recession which would make them amongst the most distant objects known. If all quasars are distant objects, it means that either our part of the universe is different from the rest or that they only occurred early on in the history of the universe. However, a few very experienced astronomers still believe they are nearer objects and that their red shifts have another origin. Perhaps the most difficult problem to be faced is that of finding reliable confirmation of estimates for the distances of the more distant galaxies and quasars.

In intergalactic space the more distant the object, the faster it seems to be receding from us. This is the expanding universe and the Hubble constant relates speed and distance. Already we believe we see objects receding at speeds approaching that of light or more then four-fifths of the way back to the big bang. However, the study of the universe even closer to its origin will be increasingly difficult and the moment of the big bang itself will be forever inaccessible to observation but the predicted isotropic background radiation from soon after this event has been observed.

Astronomy moves forward by theories to account for observations and further observations to test these theories. Two generally accepted simplifying principles were that our part of the universe is typical of the whole and that the same physical laws we apply to the present can also be applied to the past. The second principle is difficult to test back beyond the age of the Earth.

It is becoming more difficult to say what is a typical part of the universe now that surveys have confirmed a picture of the clustering of clusters of galaxies, which seem to be concentrated on a very large scale into 'walls' or surfaces with large intervening voids, likened to the surfaces of bubbles. Did these galaxies condense from this early distribution of gas or have these structures formed from existing galaxies? The formation of galaxies was probably largely completed within the first five billion years after the big bang when the universe was smaller, so the more distant galaxies or clusters of galaxies should be more closely packed as we look back into the past. This would be easier to test if galaxies were randomly distributed in space as was once thought and not concentrated in superclusters.

The average density of matter in the universe is thought to determine its future evolution, whether it will continue to grow larger, slow to a halt or eventually begin to contract. A current problem is that all the matter so far discovered in the universe in galaxies, interstellar dust and gas, stars and other forms appears to be insufficient to account for the behaviour of the universe as we find it. Some astronomers believe that as much as nine-tenths of the total matter in the universe remains to be discovered. It could be in the form of intergalactic matter, faint or dead stars or black holes, or hard to detect atomic particles such as neutrinos.

Black holes have been postulated to explain the origin of intense but small energy sources. If they exist they are so dense that not even light can escape from them so they can only be studied from the effects they have on nearby matter and radiation. Their strong gravitational fields draw in dust, gas, stars and perhaps even galaxies and the enormous amounts of energy released as this matter falls together and heats up produces light, heat and radio waves. As they become more massive their sphere of influence grows larger. Quasars may be the observable effects of the largest of black holes of the early universe, producing more light than a whole galaxy and very strong radiation at radio wavelengths. At the other end of the scale uncountable small or even microscopic black holes have been proposed to account for some extra mass. Knowledge of the nature, form and whereabouts of this 'missing mass' is of urgent importance.

Main picture The Large Magellanic Cloud (Nebecula Major), at 160,000 light years, is our nearest neighbour galaxy. The bright object (left centre) is the 30 Doradus or 'Tarantula' nebula near which SN1987A appeared.

Top Some of the thousands of elliptical and spiral galaxies in the Virgo cluster.

Top centre The Fornax cluster forms a small part of the Southern Supercluster of galaxies.

Bottom centre The spiral galaxy NGC 6744. Our galaxy is similar but being in a spiral arm ourselves, we see our stars concentrated into a bright band, the Milky Way.

Bottom The Pleiades (the 'seven sisters' of mythology) is a conspicuous star cluster in Taurus. Formed 80 million years ago, this cluster is 400 light years away.

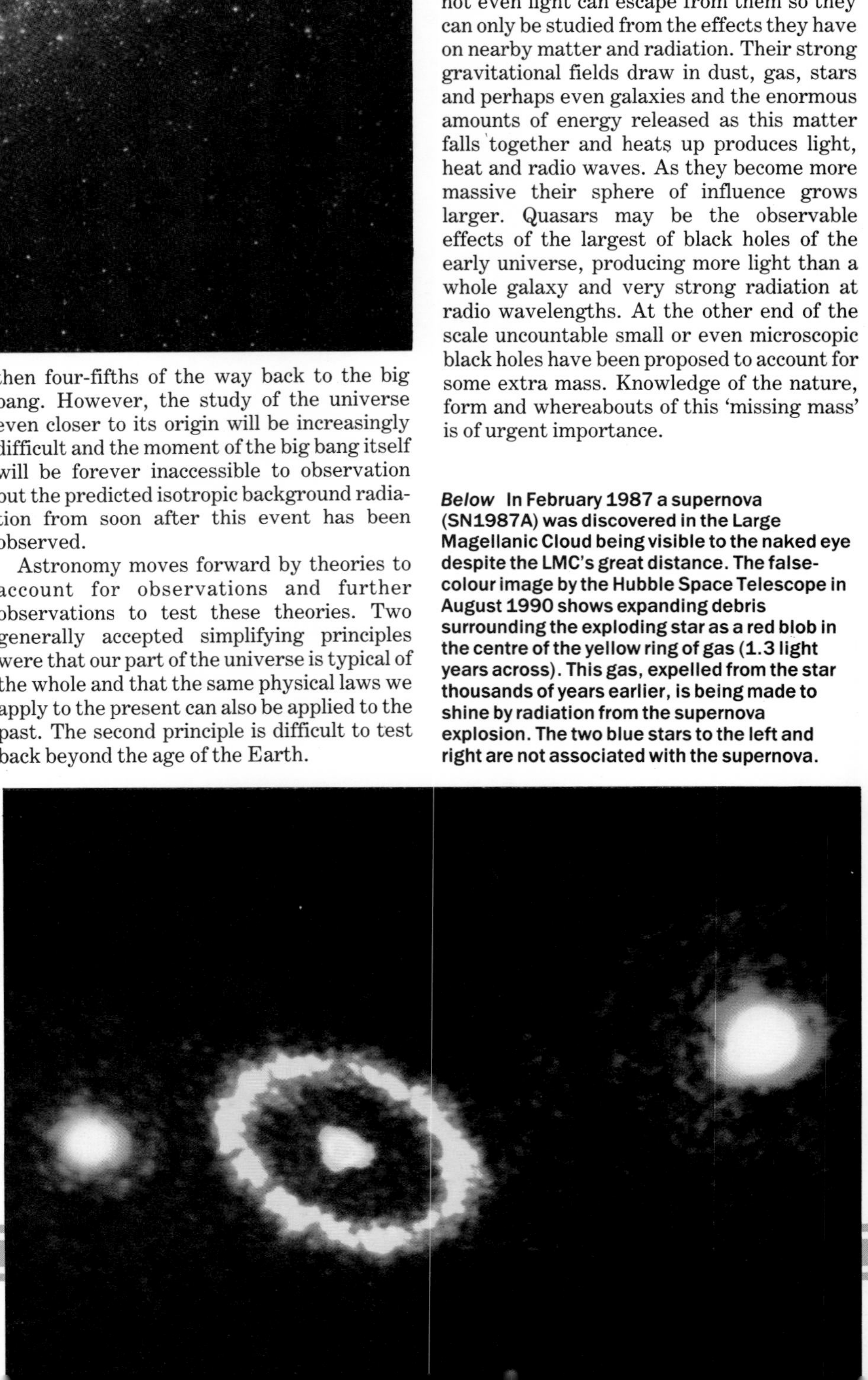

Below In February 1987 a supernova (SN1987A) was discovered in the Large Magellanic Cloud being visible to the naked eye despite the LMC's great distance. The false-colour image by the Hubble Space Telescope in August 1990 shows expanding debris surrounding the exploding star as a red blob in the centre of the yellow ring of gas (1.3 light years across). This gas, expelled from the star thousands of years earlier, is being made to shine by radiation from the supernova explosion. The two blue stars to the left and right are not associated with the supernova.

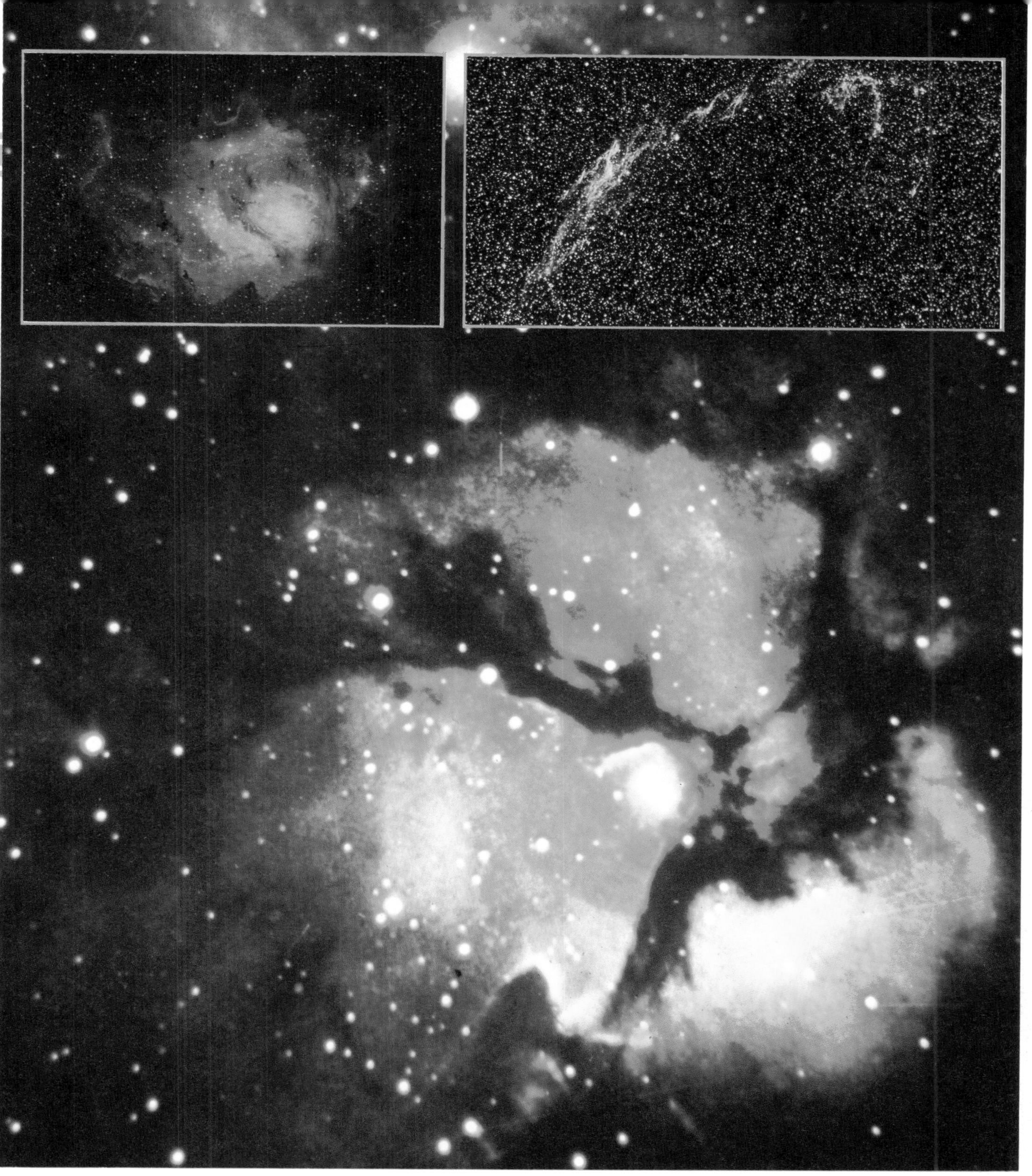

GALAXIES AND STARS

Galaxies take many forms from the giant globular galaxies, through ellipticals, spirals, barred spirals to irregular forms. This was once thought to be an evolutionary sequence but is now believed to reflect the speed with which star formation proceeded, the ellipticals turning their gas into stars before there was time for some of it to flatten into a disc where star formation could continue to form spiral arms.

The Virgo cluster is 75 million light years away and contains thousands of galaxies. On its fringes is the Local Group which contains our Milky Way system (the Galaxy), two other large spiral galaxies, the Magellanic Clouds and about twenty-five other smaller galaxies. These all lie within a distance of 5 million light years and form a gravitationally-bound group. In these galaxies astronomers can recognise many individual bright stars and nebulae while only exceptionally bright objects such as supernovae are visible in more distant galaxies.

Our Galaxy is a spiral, some hundred thousand light years across containing one or two hundred thousand million stars. At its centre in the direction of the great star clouds in Sagittarius is a massive core which may be like a supercluster of stars, almost a small galaxy in itself, and some astronomers believe, a black hole. The centre of the Galaxy is hidden by dust clouds from optical telescopes but these are largely transparent to some infrared and radio waves.

Like other similar galaxies it has two populations of stars. Population II stars form a more globular distribution and were formed first from hydrogen and helium. Population I stars lie mostly in the plane of the spiral arms and formed later from the flattened gas clouds and contain some heavier elements produced inside the first generation stars which were later expelled into space by exploding stars called supernovae. The Sun condensed from this contaminated gas and dust, and some of the matter left over from the birth of the Sun became the solar system. Without these heavier elements created inside stars there could be no Earth and no life as we know it. Elliptical galaxies contain mainly Population II stars.

Stars are still forming inside clouds of dust and gas such as the Horsehead Nebula in Orion. As the globules of gas contract they heat up until nuclear reactions start in their cores, turning hydrogen into helium. The outflow of radiation blows away remaining dust and gas to reveal a new star cluster. The stars are moving round the galactic centre, along with everything else in the Galaxy, and in time the stars in the cluster will disperse. The spiral arms are the areas of a galaxy where star formation is continuing and are mainly defined by a relatively small number of very bright hot stars. The bulk of the faint stars which greatly predominate are more uniformly spread throughout the galaxy.

The most massive stars use up their main source of energy quickly and fade within a few million years while a star such as the Sun, a yellow dwarf star, has been in much the same state for five thousand million years and will continue for as long again before major changes take place. When it can no longer convert hydrogen into helium it will start to convert helium to heavier elements swelling to become a red giant, enveloping the Earth and inner planets. However, these reactions can only proceed so far and as less heat is produced the Sun will shrink to become a very dense hot white dwarf about the size of the Earth, later cooling and fading to obscurity. Stars more than 1.4 times the mass of the Sun are unstable in the white-dwarf stage and collapse into even smaller bodies only a few kilometres across called neutron stars.

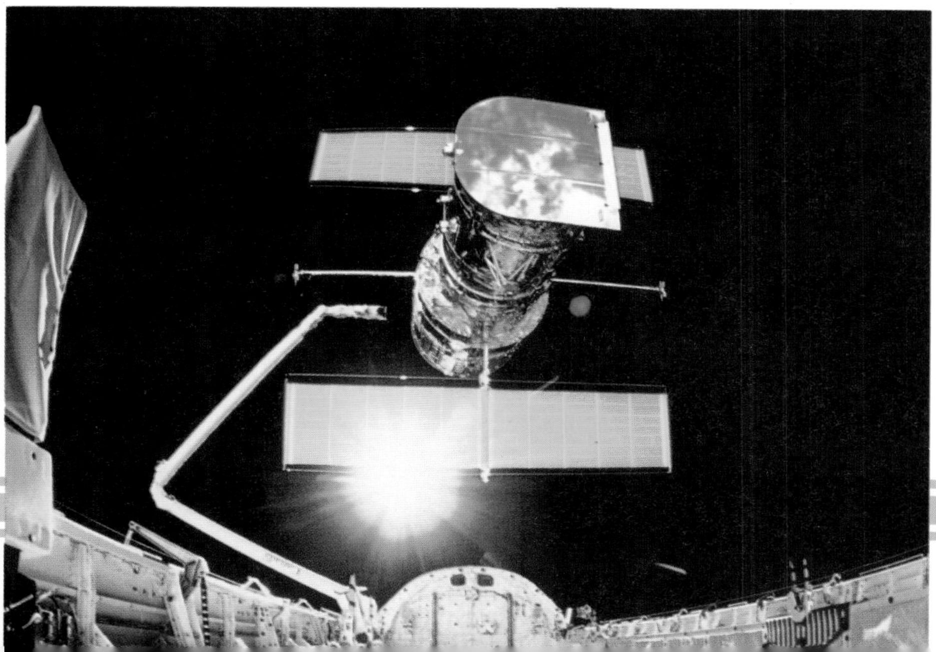

Above **The Trifid Nebula is an example of a vast cloud of gas and dust. Globules of cold gas develop and condense and form new stars.**
Below left **The Hubble Space Telescope was released from the Shuttle Discovery in 1991. At 540 km above the Earth, objects can now be observed unhindered by the atmosphere.**

Top left **The Lagoon Nebula in the constellation of Sagittarius consists of a cloud of hydrogen and dust. The brightest region includes the new star Herschel 36, less than 10 000 years old.**
Top right **The Veil Nebula in Cygnus is the remnant of a supernova. The dust will eventually break up into small cold clouds.**

Some collapse towards this stage so rapidly that the sudden generation of radiation blows off the outer layers of the star in a supernova explosion, for a few weeks giving off as much light as a whole galaxy of stars. Indeed supernovae are regularly observed in distant galaxies and can outshine the combined light of billions of more ordinary stars.

Early sky surveys revealed that many stars have companions; they appear double. Some were just chance alignments, but in many cases the stars are revolving around each other. The spectrograph reveals binary stars too close together to be seen directly. Stars show a wide variation in their colour, which is a measure of surface temperature, ranging from hot blue stars like Rigel through cooler yellow stars like Capella and the Sun to cool red stars like Betelgeuse. The spectrograph also tells astronomers about stars' composition.

Double stars give us stars' masses which range from about 50 times to one tenth that of the Sun while their diameters range from 2000 times the Sun to a hundredth or less. Stars differ in intrinsic brightness from 50,000 times (Deneb, Rigel) to only one-thousandth that of the Sun. Many stars vary in brightness, the more violent changes occurring in novae and in supernovae where the collapse in seconds of a complete star can make it appear as bright as a whole galaxy.

Astronomers' means of studying the universe have widened dramatically over the past fifty years. Parts of the energy spectrum inaccessible from the ground can be studied from artificial satellites, from gamma rays, X-rays, ultra violet to some infrared wavelengths while infrared telescopes and radio telescopes are operated on the ground. New detectors, much more sensitive than photographic film, are now commonplace, and computer-controlled optics are making it possible to build eight- and ten-metre aperture optical telescopes. Radio telescopes on different continents can be linked together to give an equivalent aperture of thousands of kilometres, allowing very fine structure to be studied that even the best optical telescopes are unable to resolve. The Hubble Space Telescope, despite its problems, shows much finer detail than telescopes on the surface of the Earth. New facilities to detect neutrinos and gravity waves are planned.

SOLAR SYSTEM

Current theory suggests that the solar system condensed from a primitive solar nebula of gas and dust during an interval of a few tens of millions of years about 4600 million years ago. Gravity caused this nebula to contract, drawing most of its mass into the proto-sun at the centre. Turbulence gave the original cloud a tendency to rotate, and as it contracted conservation of angular momentum caused the proto-sun to spin faster and faster, forcing the remainder of the cloud into a disc shape.

The centre of the cloud heated up as it compressed, and so eventually became hot enough for the Sun to begin to shine, through nuclear energy released at its core. Meanwhile the surrounding disc cooled, allowing material to condense into solid form. Particles stuck together as they collided and progressively larger bodies were built up. These swept up most of the debris to form the planets, which orbit the Sun close to the plane of the now vanished disc. The first materials to condense were the least volatile refractory compounds such as oxides of iron, nickel and aluminium. Decreasing temperature allowed rocky silicate material to appear followed by more volatile compounds such as water and methane. Thus composition of the planets progressed from less refractory cores to more volatile outer layers.

The planets nearest to the Sun are dense with metallic cores mantled by rocky silicate materials; planets further from the Sun accreted and retained large volumes of volatiles and are thus much more massive. They may have cores of rock and ice, surrounded by solid or liquid hydrogen enveloped in thick gassy atmospheres. These Gas Giants are accompanied by captured rocky and icy satellites which are mostly too small to have accreted and held atmospheres.

The subsequent evolution of the solar system was dominated by continuing chemical segregation within the planets and surface bombardment by waning numbers of smaller bodies. This bombardment was over by 3–4000 million years ago, although minor impacts still occur. Traces of these events remain on the surfaces of those bodies which have insufficient internal heat to drive any kind of resurfacing process.

Right An ultra-violet image of the Sun from Skylab in 1973. A spectacular eruption of gas rises for half a million kilometres, channelled by the Sun's magnetic field.

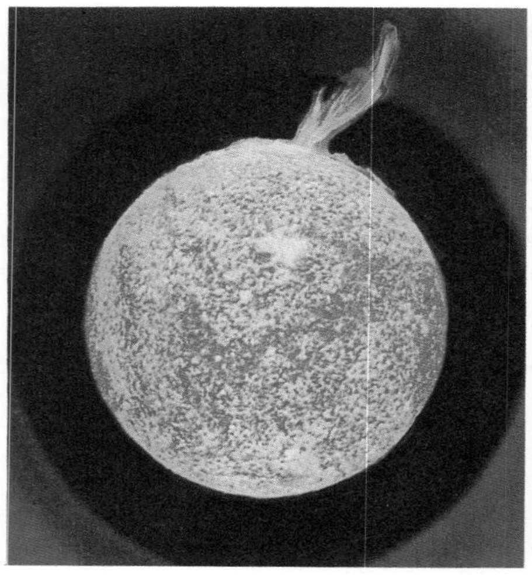

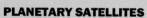

	SUN	MERCURY	VENUS	EARTH	(MOON)	MARS	JUPITER	SATURN	URANUS	NEPTUNE	PLUTO
Mass (Earth=1)	333 400	0.055	0.815	1 (5.97 10^{24}kg)	0.012	0.107	317.8	95.2	14.5	17.2	0.003
Volume (Earth=1)	1 306 000	0.06	0.88	1	0.020	0.150	1 323	752	64	54	0.007
Density (water=1)	1.41	5.43	5.24	5.52	3.34	3.94	1.33	0.70	1.30	1.64	2.0
Equatorial diameter (km)	1 392 000	4 878	12 104	12 756	3 476	6 794	142 800	120 000	52 000	48 400	2 302
Polar flattening	0	0	0	0.003	0	0.005	0.065	0.108	0.060	0.021	0
'Surface' gravity (Earth=1)	27.9	0.37	0.88	1	0.16	0.38	2.69	1.19	0.93	1.22	0.05
Number of satellites greater than 100 km diameter	—	0	0	1	—	0	7	13	7	6	1
Total number of satellites	—	0	0	1	—	2	16	17	15	8	1
Period of rotation (in Earth days)	25.38	58.65	−243 (retrograde)	23hr 56m 4 secs	27.32	1.03	0.414	0.426	−0.74 (retrograde)	0.67	−6.39 (retrograde)
Length of year (in Earth days and years)	—	88 days	224.7 days	365.26 days	—	687 days	11.86 years	29.46 years	84.01 years	164.8 years	247.7 years
Distance from Sun (max) Mkm	—	69.7	109	152.1	—	249.1	815.7	1 507	3 004	4 537	7 375
Distance from Sun (min) Mkm	—	45.9	107.4	147.1	—	206.7	740.9	1 347	2 735	4 456	4 425
Distance from Sun (mean) Mkm	—	57.9	108.9	149.6	—	227.9	778.3	1 427	2 870	4 497	5 900
Mean orbital velocity km/sec	—	47.9	35.0	29.8	—	24.1	13.1	9.6	6.8	5.4	4.7
Inclination of equator to orbit plane	7.25°	0.0°	177.3°	23.45°	6.68°	25.19°	3.12°	26.73°	97.86°	29.56°	122°
Inclination of orbit to ecliptic	—	7.01°	3.39°	0°	5.15°	1.85°	1.30°	2.48°	0.77°	1.77°	17.13°

	Mean Distance from Planet (1 000km)	Orbital Period (days) R=retrograde	Diameter (km)*
Mars			
Phobos	9.38	0.319	28x22x18
Deimos	23.46	1.262	16x12x12
Jupiter			
Metis	128.00	0.295	(40)
Adrastrea	129.00	0.297	(24x16)
Amalthea	181.30	0.498	(270x150)
Thebe	221.90	0.675	(100)
Io	421.60	1.769	3 630
Europa	670.90	3.551	3 138
Ganymede	1 070.00	7.155	5 262
Callisto	1 880.00	16.689	4 800
Leda	11 094.00	238.700	(15)
Himalia	11 480.00	250.600	(180)
Lysithea	11 720.00	259.200	(40)
Elara	11 737.00	259.700	(80)
Ananke	21 200.00	631R	(30)
Carme	22 600.00	692R	(45)
Pasiphae	23 500.00	735R	(70)
Sinope	23 700.00	758R	(40)
Saturn			
Atlas	137.70	0.602	40x30
Prometheus	139.50	0.613	140x80
Pandora	141.70	0.629	110x70
Epimetheus	151.40	0.694	140x100
Janus	151.50	0.695	220x160
Mimas	185.50	0.942	392
Enceladus	238.00	1.370	500
Tethys	294.70	1.888	1 060
Telesto	294.70	1.888	(24)
Calypso	294.70	1.888	30x20
Dione	377.40	2.737	1 120
Helene	377.40	2.737	36x30
Rhea	527.00	4.518	1 530
Titan	1 221.80	15.945	5 150
Hyperion	1 481.10	21.277	350x200
Iapetus	3 561.30	79.331	1 440
Phoebe	12 952.00	550.480R	220
Uranus			
Cordelia	49.75	0.335	(30)
Ophelia	53.76	0.376	(30)
Bianca	59.16	0.435	(50)
Cressida	61.77	0.464	(70)
Desdemona	62.66	0.475	(60)
Juliet	64.36	0.493	(80)
Portia	66.09	0.513	(110)
Rosalind	69.92	0.588	(60)
Belinda	75.26	0.624	(70)
Puck	85.89	0.762	150
Miranda	129.40	1.414	470
Ariel	191.20	2.520	1 160
Umbriel	266.00	4.144	1 170
Titania	435.90	8.706	1 580
Oberon	582.60	13.463	1 520
Neptune			
Naiad	48.20	0.296	(50)
Thalassa	50.00	0.312	(80)
Despina	52.50	0.333	(180)
Galatea	62.00	0.429	(150)
Larissa	73.60	0.554	(190)
Proteus	117.60	1.121	(400)
Triton	354.80	5.877	2 700
Nereid	5 513.40	360.160	(340)
Pluto			
Charon	19.64	6.387	1 190

*Many satellites are not spherical in shape, in which case two or three axes are quoted. Dimensions given in brackets are uncertain by at least ten per cent.

1

5
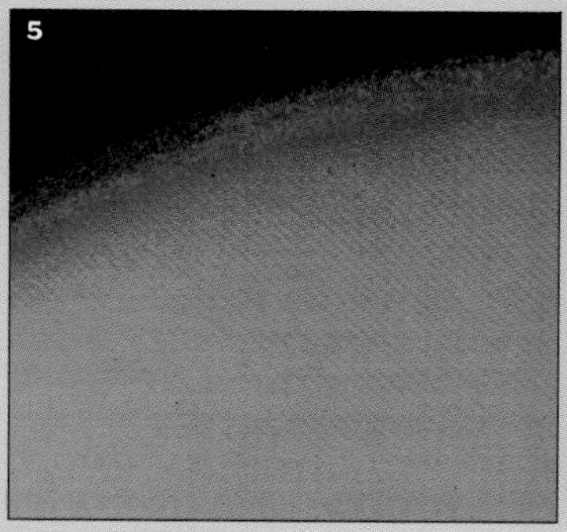

6
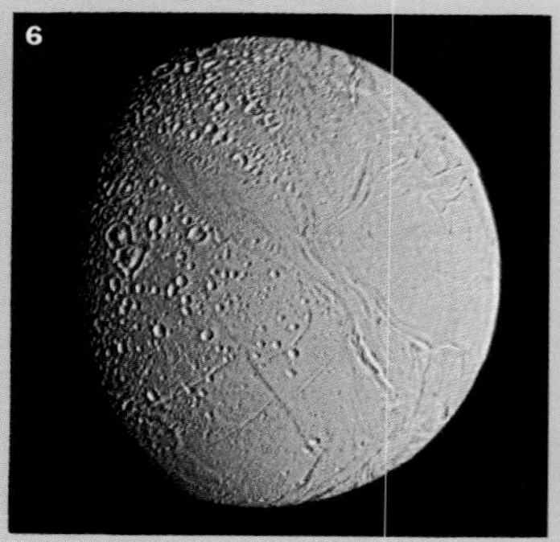

7

2

3
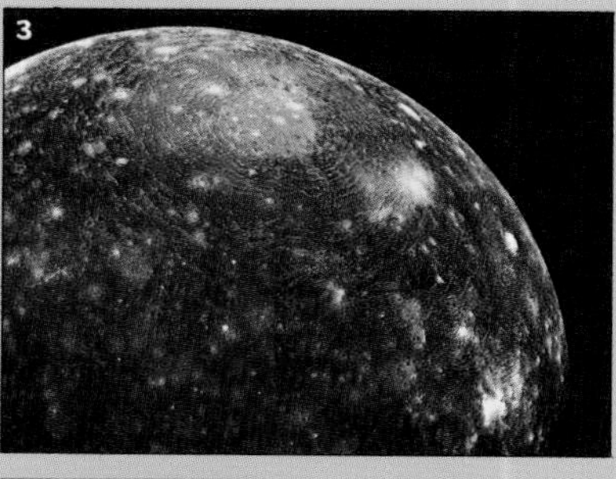

4
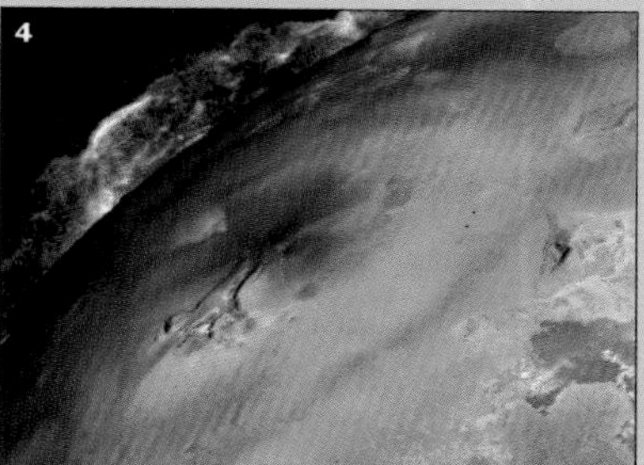

PLANETARY SATELLITES

All the planets except Mercury and Venus have bodies in orbit around them. The Earth-Moon system can be described as a double planet, whereas Mars' two satellites appear to be captured asteroids. The Gas Giants have a greater number of satellites ranging from bodies of less than 100km across to larger moons of around 1000km in diameter with rocky cores and usually icy crusts. Some of the more interesting bodies are illustrated here: the table on the left gives the full list.

1 Deimos is the smaller, outer irregular-shaped moon of Mars. The surface is covered by about 10 metres of loose rock.
2 The dark background material of **Ganymede** shows a high density of impact craters. The lighter network of grooves may have been formed by movements of the ice crust.
3 Callisto is among the most cratered in the Solar System with a surface at least 4 billion years old.
4 This Voyager 1 image of **Io** shows a plume of vaporized sulphur rising for 300km above the first known active extraterrestrial volcano, Pele.
5 Titan is Saturn's largest moon and holds an extremely dense atmosphere of nitrogen and methane above a surface of rock and ice.
6 Enceladus has experienced recent geological activity which has modified the cratered landscape.
7 The surface of **Mimas** is heavily cratered and shows no sign of geological activity.
8 This Voyager 2 mosaic of **Miranda** shows a variety of geological features.
9 Much of **Ariel**'s surface is pitted with craters 5 to 10kms across and criss-crossed by valleys.
10 Titania displays many impact scars and also evidence of geological activity.

8
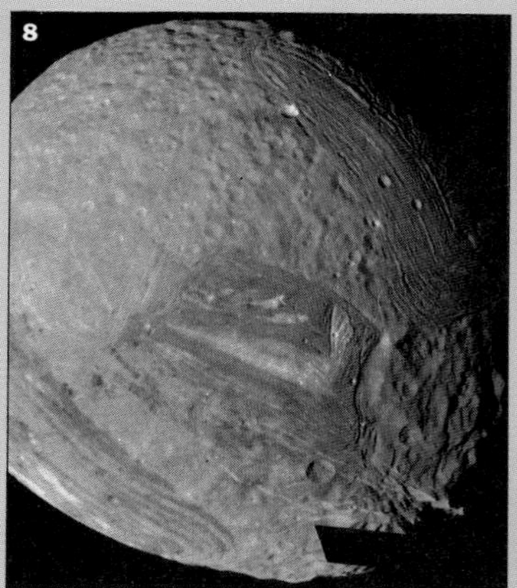

9

10
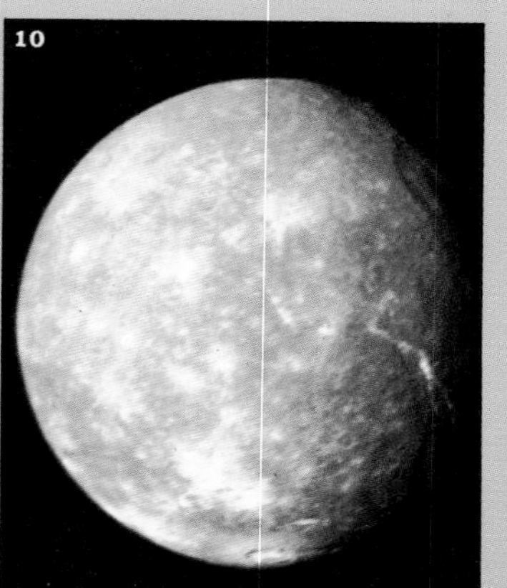

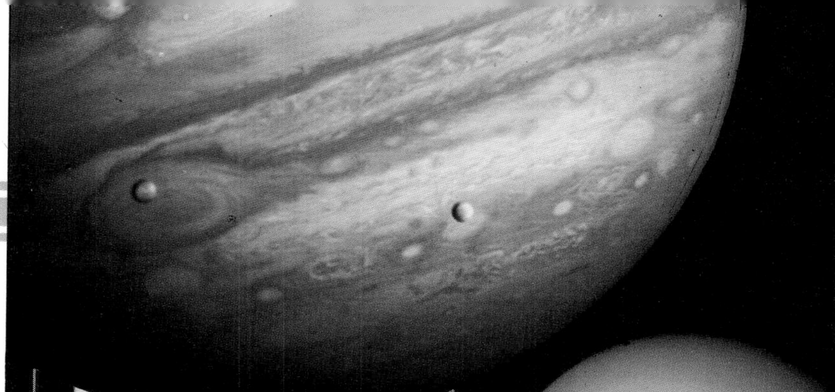

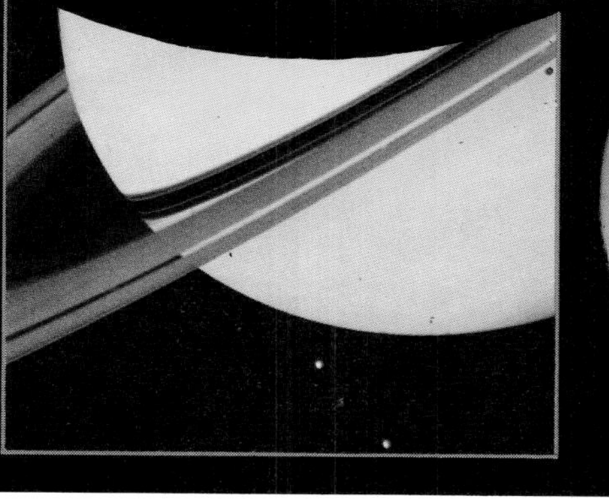

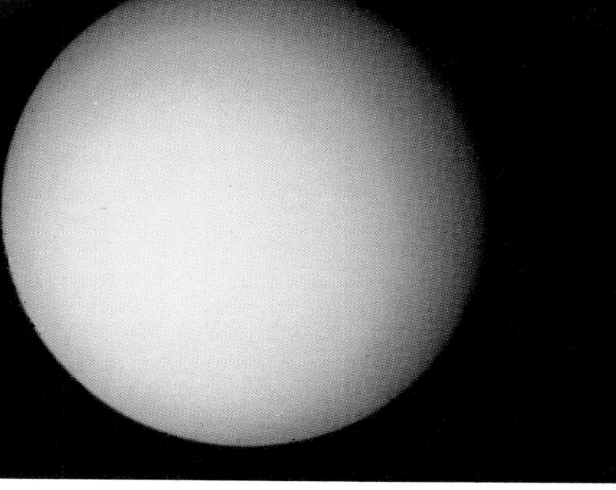

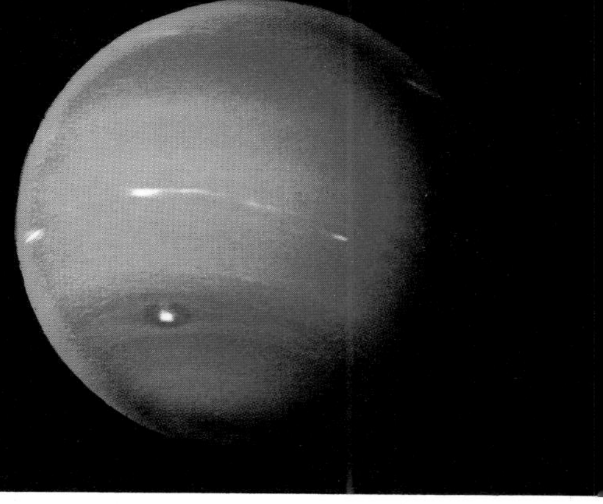

Left Io and Europa are clearly visible as they transit the face of Jupiter. The Great Red Spot of Jupiter has been observed for 300 years but the white ovals nearby did not appear until the 1930s. They are all centres of high pressure in this turbulent atmosphere.

Lower left The rings of Saturn lie in the equatorial plane and consist of countless small ice-covered particles. Tethys and Dione orbit Saturn at less than 400000km.

Below left The true-colour photograph of Uranus was taken from 9.1 million km by Voyager 2.

Below right Voyager 2 produced this composite false-colour image of Neptune in August 1989. The red edge around the planet is where the surrounding haze scatters sunlight.

GAS GIANTS

Jupiter has at least 16 satellites and a debris ring system about 50000km above the cloud tops. The outer atmosphere is all that can be directly observed of the planet itself. It is mostly hydrogen with lesser amounts of helium, ammonia, methane, water vapour and more exotic compounds. Jupiter's rapid rotation causes it to be flattened towards the poles. This rotation and heat flow convection from the interior cause complex weather patterns. Liquid droplets and solid particles of ammonia and other compounds, cause the clouds to be opaque. Where cloud systems interact vast storms can occur in the form of vortices. Some last only a few days, but the most persistent of these, the Great Red Spot, has been present since it was first detected in the 17th century.

The internal structure of Jupiter can be deduced. At about 1000km below the cloud tops hydrogen and helium may liquify to form a 10000km layer. Convection currents in this region generate the planet's intense magnetic field. The denser core, about 4% of the planet's mass, is mostly of rock and ice, with a little iron near the centre.

Saturn is the least dense of the planets. It has a stormy atmosphere situated above a 30000km layer of liquid molecular hydrogen and helium distorted by the planet's rotation. Below is a thin shell of liquid metallic hydrogen wrapped around a rock and ice core containing 25% of Saturn's mass.

The rings of Saturn are thought to be mostly made of icy debris, from 10m down to a few microns in size, derived from the break-up of a satellite. The rings are less than 1km thick but extend from above the cloud layer out to about 170000km from the centre. The rings are divided by gaps swept clear by complex gravitational interaction.

Uranus was little known until Voyager 2 flew by it in January 1986. It has a cloud cover even more featureless than either Jupiter or Saturn, and consists mostly of hydrogen. Unique among the planets, its axis is tilted almost into the plane of its orbit, with the south pole presently facing towards the Sun. Voyager 2 discovered ten more satellites and provided detailed images of the planet's eleven rings of icy debris.

Neptune provided a number of surprises when Voyager 2 flew by, on 24 August 1989, passing within 5,000km of the planet's north pole. The planet rotates in 16 hours 3 minutes, one hour faster than was believed to be the rate. Six new satellites were discovered, all irregular in shape and with impact craters, little changed since soon after their formation. Neptune has four rings. The magnetic axis is inclined 50° to the axis of rotation and displaced 10,000km from the centre. Neptune's atmosphere, a mixture of hydrogen, helium and methane, exhibits great turbulence. There is a great dark spot at 22°S latitude and a smaller dark spot nearer the south pole. Triton was found to be smaller than previous estimates.

Pluto, usually the most distant planet, is temporarily within the orbit of Neptune. The atmosphere is thought to be composed mostly of methane.

LUNAR DATA

Earth/Moon Mass Ratio	M_e/M_m 81.3015
Density (mean)	3.34g/cm^3
Synodic Month (new Moon to new Moon)	29.530 588d
Sidereal Month (fixed star to fixed star)	27.321661 days
Inclination of Lunar orbit to ecliptic	5°8′43″
Inclination of equator to ecliptic	1°40′32″
Distance from Moon to Earth (mean)	384 400km (238 860 mi)
Optical libration	longitude ± 7.6° latitude ± 6.7°
Magnitude (mean of full Moon)	−12.7
Temperature	−153°C to + 134°C (−244°F to +273°F)
Escape velocity	2.38km/sec (1.48 mi/sec)
Diameter of Moon	3 476km (2 160mi)
Surface gravity	162.2 cm/sec^2

PHASES OF THE MOON

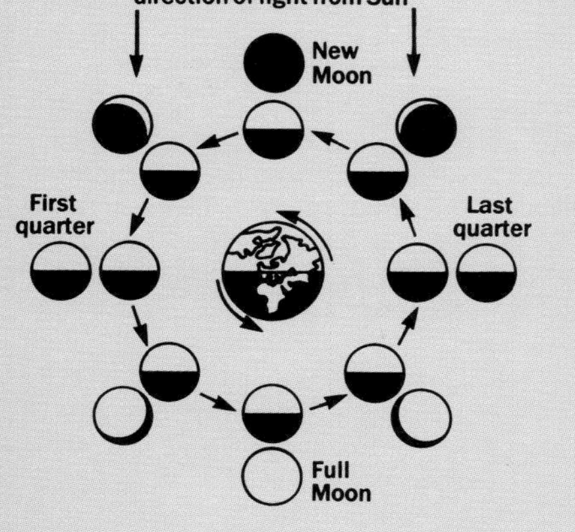

Above The Moon passes through a cycle of passes from New Moon to Full Moon.
Below An Apollo 16 photograph of the Moon.

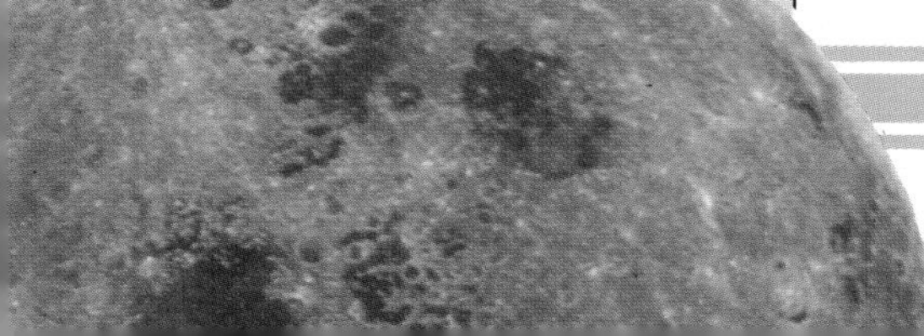

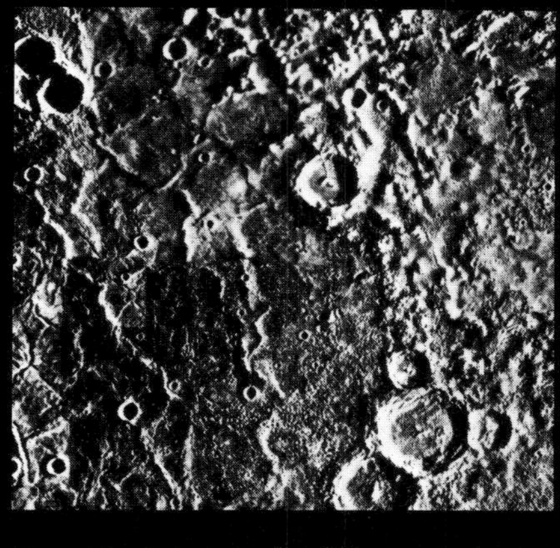

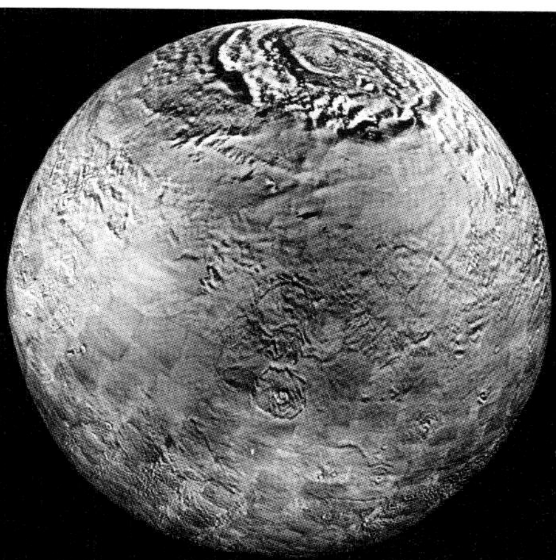

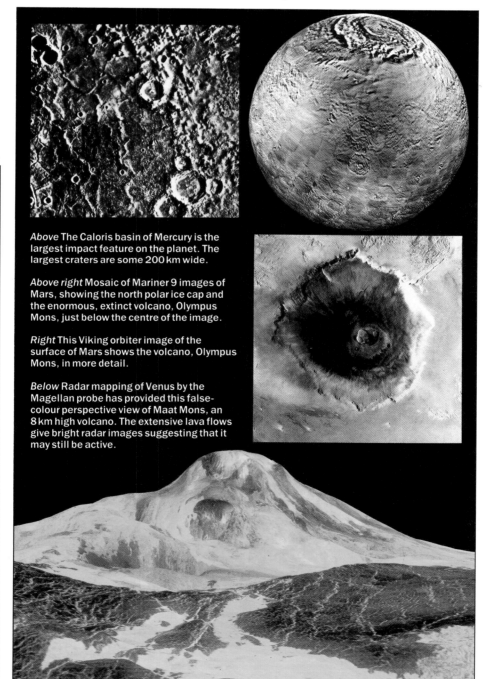

Above The Caloris basin of Mercury is the largest impact feature on the planet. The largest craters are some 200km wide.

Above right Mosaic of Mariner 9 images of Mars, showing the north polar ice cap and the enormous, extinct volcano, Olympus Mons, just below the centre of the image.

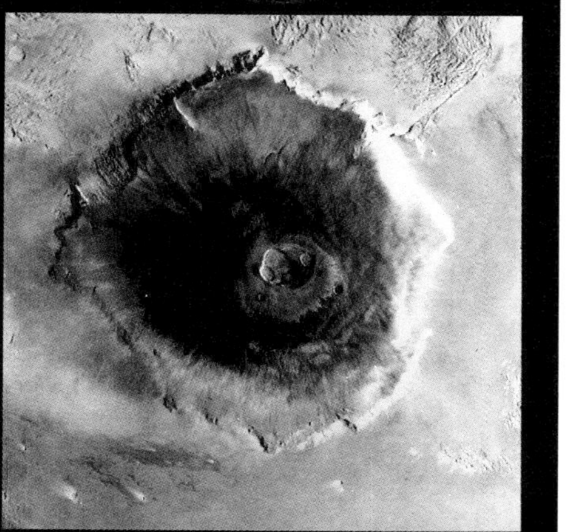

Right This Viking orbiter image of the surface of Mars shows the volcano, Olympus Mons, in more detail.

Below Radar mapping of Venus by the Magellan probe has provided this false-colour perspective view of Maat Mons, an 8km high volcano. The extensive lava flows give bright radar images suggesting that it may still be active.

EARTHLIKE PLANETS

Mercury is the nearest planet to the Sun, spinning three times for every two orbits around the Sun. It has an exceptionally large metallic core which may be responsible for Mercury's weak magnetic field. Mercury is an airless world subject to vast extremes of temperature, from −180°C at night to 430°C near the middle of its long day.

The Mariner 10 spacecraft probe during the mid-1970s, revealed the surface to be dominated by heavily cratered areas dating from the early meteorite bombardment of the inner solar system. As the bombardment was tailing off Mercury's radius contracted by between 1 and 2km, forming compressional features (lobate scarps) which may have been caused by a change in the core from liquid to solid.

Venus has a dense atmosphere of 96% carbon dioxide mixed with nitrogen, oxygen, sulphur dioxide and water vapour which hides the surface under permanent cloud and maintains a mean surface temperature of about 480°C. The planet's slow rotation means that weather systems are driven mostly by solar heat, rather than by spin. As a result, beyond 10 kilometres above the surface, westerly winds of up to 100 m/sec cause a bulk rotation of the atmosphere in about four days.

Russian spacecraft have landed and sent back pictures of the surface. Imaging radar has been used to map most of the planet from orbiting spacecraft. The most recent survey by the Magellan probe began in 1990 and resolves features as small as 150m across. Mountains, valleys, impact craters and many other features have been mapped and 3-dimensional simulations generated by computer from the Magellan data.

Mars has a thin atmosphere of about 95% carbon dioxide mixed with other minor constituents. The polar caps consist of semi-permanent water ice and ephemeral solid carbon dioxide. Day and night surface temperatures vary between about −120°C and −20°C. Mars has two small satellites, each less than about 25km across, probably captured asteroids.

A variety of landscapes has been identified, including ancient heavily cratered terrains and plains which may consist of lava flows. There are several large volcanoes; the best preserved of these, Olympus Mons, rises 26km above the surface and is 550km across at its base.

Mars shows evidence of erosional processes. The effect of winds is seen in the degraded form of the older craters and the deposition of sand dunes. Dust storms frequently obscure the surface. The large channels, such as the 5000km long Valles Marineris, may have been cut by flowing water. Water is abundant in the polar caps and may be widespread held in as permafrost below the surface.

SPACE FLIGHT

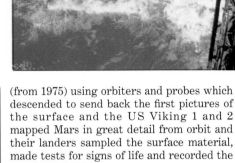

Possibly no other field of human endeavour has excited the imaginations of so many people over the past thirty-seven years as the exploration of space. There are many difficulties involved in leaving the Earth. A large amount of energy is needed to lift a worthwhile payload 200 km or more but it will fall back to the Earth's surface unless it is also given a velocity parallel to the ground of 29,000 km per hour. To put a satellite into a higher orbit, or accelerate a spacecraft away from the Earth to the Moon or another planet, requires even greater energy and larger rockets for the same payload. Expendable rocket boosters are used which are jetisoned in stages as their fuel becomes exhausted.

On 4 October 1957 the USSR launched the first artificial satellite, Sputnik 1. The first American satellite, Explorer 1, followed within four months and discovered the Van Allen radiation belt about the Earth. The Russian lead in what developed into a space race was maintained by the first pictures of the far side of the Moon (Luna 3, 1959) and the first manned spaceflight (Yuri Gagarin, 1961), whereas the Americans at the same time were developing specialist satellites such as TIROS 1 (the first weather satellite), Transit 1B (the first navigation satellite) and Echo 1 (the first communications satellite), all launched in 1960.

During the 1960s and 1970s the nearby planets began to be investigated by flybys, orbiting probes and hard (crash) and soft landings, the Russians being more successful with Venus and the Americans with Mars. The surface of the Moon was studied by the US Ranger craft (1964/65) which resolved detail to a metre or so just before impact, the seven soft-landing Surveyors (1966/68) which surveyed potential manned landing sites and five Lunar Orbiters (1966/67). Meanwhile the one-man Mercury and two-man Gemini flights of up to 11 days continued during which the techniques required for travel to the Moon were developed. On 20 July 1969 the first manned landing was made using the Saturn V rocket (US astronauts Armstrong, Aldrin and Collins, Apollo XI).

The Russian manned programme continued with longer flights in Earth orbit and the launch of their first Salyut space stations (from 1971) while their lunar program continued with robot exploration and the return of small samples to Earth. The American probe Pioneer 10 (1972 was the first to cross the asteroid belt: both Pioneer 10 and 11 were, by 1994, well beyond the farthest planets and still being tracked. Skylab provided a useful working area in orbit (1973/74). A large part of Mercury was mapped by Mariner 10 (1973/74), a survey that has not yet been repeated. The USSR started its long series of Venera to Venus (from 1975) using orbiters and probes which descended to send back the first pictures of the surface and the US Viking 1 and 2 mapped Mars in great detail from orbit and their landers sampled the surface material, made tests for signs of life and recorded the weather (1976/77).

The US Voyagers 1 and 2 were launched in 1977 with Voyager 2 visiting Jupiter (1979), Saturn (1981), Uranus (1986) and Neptune (1989), sending back detailed images of all these planets and many of their satellites and discovering many new satellites and rings around Neptune. IRAS (1983) mapped the whole sky in the infrared discovering many new objects: so much data was sent back in its few months operation that much is still not analysed. Other satellites observed gamma-rays, x-rays and the ultra-violet region of the spectrum while another large group of satellites looked towards the Earth to study the weather, the sea, land utilisation and many other aspects of the Earth's environment, many of which have commercial and military applications while both the USA and USSR have made much use of reconnaissance or spy satellites. The Soviet Mir space station which was launched in 1986 has been inhabited continuously by relays of cosmonauts, some of whom were in orbit for a year, some new modules having been added.

The UK launched only one small satellite before abandoning its own launch programme to join what is now the European Space Agency (ESA) which has used the Ariane rocket (developed and built in France from 1965) to launch both commercial satellites and space probes. China, Japan, Israel and India now also have their own launch capability.

The American ICE probe passed through the tail of comet Giacobini-Zinner in 1985 and two Japanese, two Soviet and the ESA Giotto observed Halley's comet in 1986, Giotto sending back close up views of the nucleus. Giotto was re-activated in 1992 to flyby comet Grigg-Skjellerup. Hipparcos made accurate measurements of star positions (1989-93), COBE of cosmic background radiation (1989-93), and in 1989 Magellan began detailed radar mapping of Venus. The Hubble Space Telescope was launched into Earth orbit in 1990 and refurbished by the Space Shuttle in 1993: it is sending back images of a quality impossible from the ground. Japan put a small probe in orbit round the Moon and the Compton Gamma-Ray Observatory was launched, both in 1991.

Meanwhile, Galileo (1989) sent back the first close-up pictures of asteroids Gaspra (1991) and Ida (1993) en route to Jupiter (1995). Ulysses (1990) will pass over both the Sun's poles (1994/95). Contact was lost with Mars Observer as it prepared to enter orbit around Mars in August 1993. Clementine, designed for Star Wars' tests, mapped the Moon before making a fly-by with asteroid Geographos (August 1994): it may have detected water in lunar polar regions.

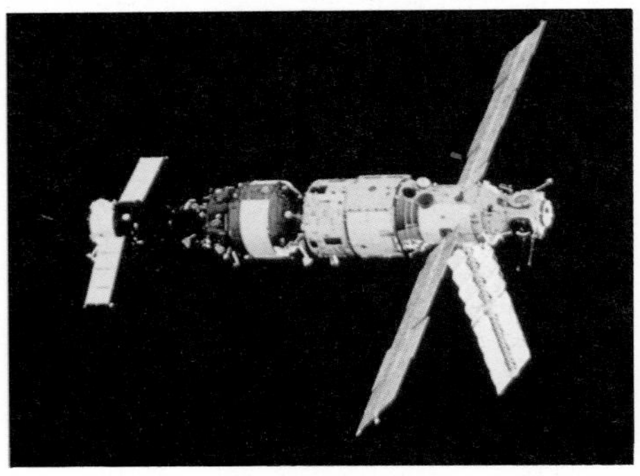

Top Right **The Hubble Space Telescope still attached to the Remote Manipulator Arm (lower right) of the Space Shuttle Discovery during deployment in 1990.**

Above **ESA's Ariane launch vehicle, developed and built in France, being prepared for flight at Kourou, French Guiana.**

Left **The First modules of the Mir space-station were launched into Earth orbit by the former USSR in 1986. It has been inhabited continuously by relays of cosmonauts.**

WEATHER SATELLITES

The impact of space flight on meteorology is becoming more obvious now that satellite pictures are routinely used as illustrations on TV weather forecasts. However, weather monitoring was among the major military and civil aims of the early space programme. Weather satellites can operate on a global basis, observing phenomena distant from meteorological observatories, such as over the ocean or unfriendly territory.

The most famous series of weather satellites, TIROS (Television and Infra-Red Observation Satellite), began with TIROS 1 in 1960 and continues, in advanced form, today. TIROS satellites are placed in non-synchronous orbits inclined to the equator to give close-up repeat coverage of middle and lower latitudes. Other satellites in higher, geosynchronous orbits provide effectively continuous low resolution coverage of almost complete hemispheres. A good example is the European Space Agency's Meteosats situated above 0°N, 0°W which have produced half-hourly images in the visible, water vapour infra-red and thermal infra-red bands since late 1977. The higher latitudes and polar regions, foreshortened by Meteosats, are best covered by weather satellites in lower, high inclination orbits.

Such satellites can detect and monitor hurricane formation and movement, allowing advance warning which has saved many countless lives and minimised damage to property. More routinely, cloud patterns, water vapour content and vertical temperature profiles within the atmosphere and ground surface temperature are determined, which permit accurate forecasts a week in advance. Satellite observations are also essential for global investigation of the radiative properties of the Earth's surface and atmosphere so that we understand the dynamics of our climate much more fully than before the space age.

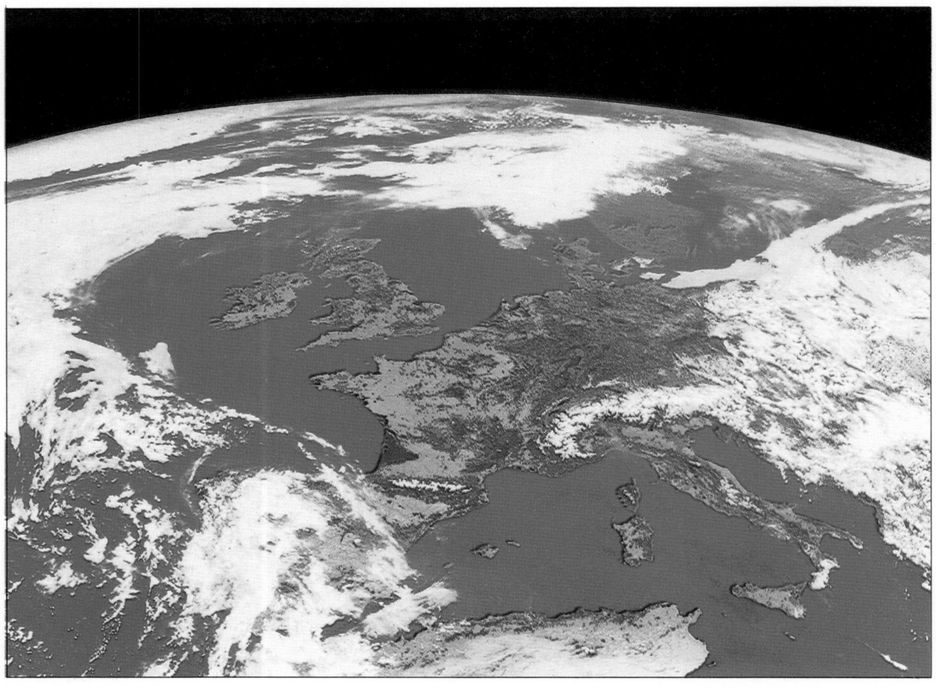

Right **Weather satellites placed in geostationary orbits provide coverage over much of a hemisphere. However, to remain stationary relative to the ground they must be located over the equator, leading to severe foreshortening near the polar regions, as this Meteosat image shows.**

EARTH RESOURCES

Spacecraft either leave the Earth on missions to other parts of the solar system or remain in orbit where they may look outwards to the stars or inwards to the Earth. The Earth orientated satellites are mainly concerned with communications, navigation, military surveillance, short-term weather forecasting and climate, Earth resources and agriculture, the Earth's environment, geology and the science of the Earth itself. Much of the information obtained has military, commercial or social implications, as well as being of scientific interest.

Apart from the aspects of remote sensing mentioned under Weather Satellites, satellites can now record sea temperatures, wind speeds, wave heights, current strengths and ice movements over the oceans which play such a large part in determining weather and climate. They can use radar to map in three dimensions mountainous and inaccessible areas, even through cloud, and can detect gravity anomalies under the oceans from radar altimeter measurements of sea heights. Small changes in satellites' orbits reveal the more dense areas below the continents.

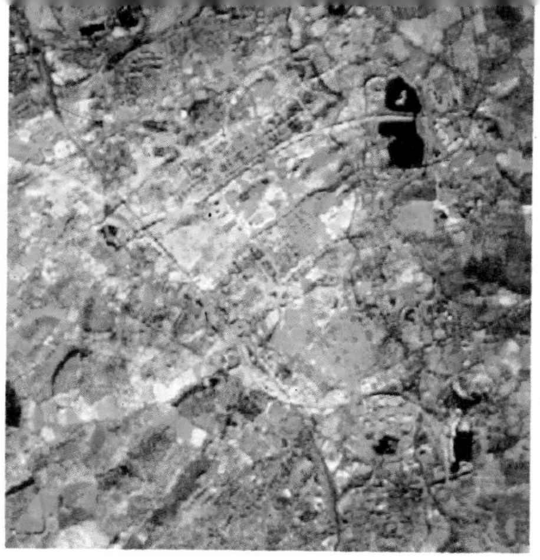

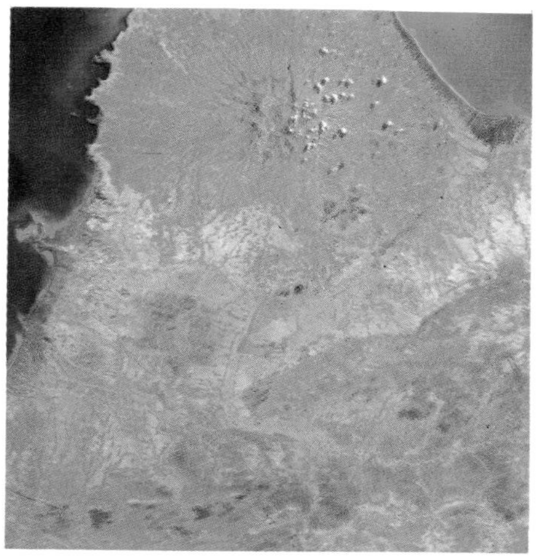

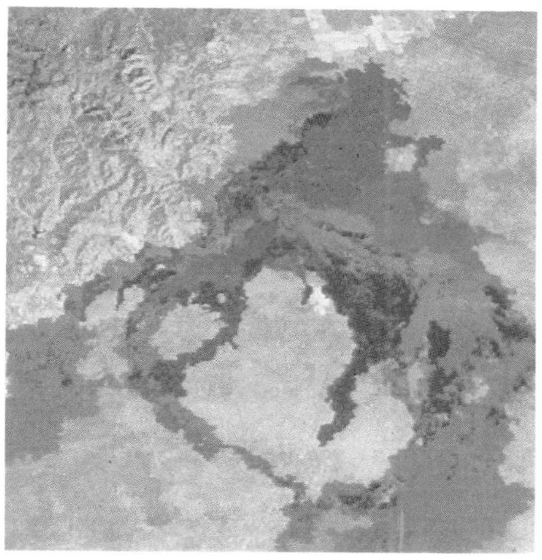

Above left **The false colour Landsat Thematic Mapper image of Milton Keynes, England, depicts built-up areas as blue, water black and vegetation red. The same image *above centre* has been computer enhanced to reveal recent landscape changes. Colour has been used to show areas of the same spectral characteristics.**
Above right **Landsat Multispectral Scanner false colour image of the south coast of Portugal near Faro. The airport runway shows as a bright line by the lagoon in the lower left-hand corner.**
Left **Another multi-spectral Landsat image showing Gunung Muryo (1602m) and Tanjung (Cape) Bugel on the island of Java.** **This area is shown on page 70–N9.**
Right **Landsat Multispectral Scanner false colour image of Craters of the Moon in Idaho, U.S.A. There is little vegetation except in and near the mountainous area in the north-west.**

From orbit a camera or other imaging system is ideally placed to record and monitor large areas of the Earth on a regular basis. Photography may be useful for very high resolution work such as military surveillance but is restricted to the visible and near infrared wavelengths and requires the return of the film to Earth. Images recorded by electronic means and converted to digital form are not restricted to the photographic part of the spectrum and can be transmitted to a ground receiving station while the satellite continues in orbit. Such data can be directly computer processed in various ways or made available by satellite link to any number of users. In order to cover most of the globe, remote sensing satellites are usually placed in near-polar orbits which are highly inclined to the equator. Many are in Sun-synchronus orbits arranged so that the Earth rotates beneath them at sufficient rate to keep the satellites over each strip of the Earth's surface at approximately the same local time throughout their north-south passage, so that the angle of the Sun above the horizon is fairly constant for some weeks at a time.

In this way using several satellites frequent and regular floods can be monitored forest fires and sea pollution spotted, volcanic dust clouds tracked and the movement of polar ice followed. Land usage can be checked, field by field if necessary, for types of crops and crop and timber diseases. Communications satellites even allow individual birds and animals to be tracked by means of tiny transmitters they carry and with satellite navigation equipment travellers can know their position to within a few metres anywhere on the Earth. Satellites can be used to monitor air pollution and ozone levels in the vital but less accessible polar regions. New applications are continually arising.

The Landsat programme originally known as ERTS began in 1972 with satellites placed in near-polar Sun synchronous orbits. Complete global coverage in visible and near-infrared bands was achieved every 18 days. New satellites too numerous to mention have followed on. For example, the ESA ERS-l and ERS-2 (1994) will be followed by a new space platform, the Polar Platform, that can be loaded with up to four interchangeable payloads. The first mission will be Envisat-l (1998) which will test instruments and Metop-1 (2000) will begin regular routine land, sea and atmospheric observations and climate monitoring.

A current proposal is Geowarn a global disaster warning system using aircraft and satellites to monitor areas at risk and provide a relief control system.

Not all objects in space;are so useful. Nearly forty years of space flight has left thousands of items in Earth orbit, from spent boosters to flecks of paint. Items larger than a few centimetres are tracked by radar but smaller objects are effectively lost and can damage spacecraft and spacesuits.

THE FUTURE

From a purely scientific point of view spaceflight could have a very bright future, extensions of known technology being sufficient for manned exploration of the Moon and even Mars and further unmanned exploration of the universe. However, there has been a decline in public interest in space and with future projects requiring ever more resources, a difficulty in raising the necessary funds. In the USA projects such as the Freedom space station have undergone several redesigns in the interest of economy. With the present uncertainties concerning the former USSR states, their future space programme is also under review.

A more hopeful sign arising at least partly from these problems is the new spirit of international co-operation. It makes sense for several nations to share the design, cost and construction of major projects and to share their use. To gain practical experience, two Space Shuttles are being fitted with docking facilities compatible with the Russian Mir space station, in orbit since 1986. A Shuttle-Mir rendezvous should take place in 1994 with the first docking in 1995: cosmonauts will fly in the Shuttle and astronauts spend months aboard Mir. ESA is also providing astronauts for Russian space flights.

The Russians have designed a Mir-2 to replace the aging Mir-l but current talks may lead to Mir-2 and Freedom becoming a single project probably also involving ESA who are already developing Columbus, a space laboratory for launch in 2002, and other nations. ESA have modified their Hermes winged mini-shuttle project to a normal re-entry vehicle that could become the Assured Crew Return Vehicle or space lifeboat. If progress could be made on a joint spacestation then joint expeditions to the Moon and Mars could follow, but there seems little prospect of a single nation carrying out either until well into the next century.

The cost of launching payloads into space is still too high: the largely re-usable Shuttle was to bring these down but has proved too expensive to put conventional launchers out of business. While the Shuttle will be flying for a decade or two yet, the search is on for cheaper reusable launchers that would require only airline type servicing and simpler launch facilities involving far fewer personnel. While there are proposals for aircraft launched rockets and boosters with deployable wings for landing, a 13m tall test vehicle using the "one stage to orbit" principle called Delta Clipper or DC-X is actually under hovering tests in the USA. Made of lightweight materials and using advanced engines, the full-scale DC-X would take off from simply prepared airports, reach orbit and return to land by rocket power on extendable legs.

ESA plan to launch ISO, the Infrared Space Observatory and successor to IRAS, in 1995 while a larger 1.7m infrared telescope called Edison is under discussion.

Specific interplanetary missions that are scheduled for the next decade; include Japanese probes to Mars (1996) and the Moon (1997), and if approved, NASA Mars Observer orbiters (1996, 1998, 2001) with Mars Environmental Pathfinder (MESUR) landing on Mars (1996-). ESA also have a proposal for a network of small weather stations on Mars called MARSNET. Due to be launched in 1997 is the NASA/ESA Cassini-Huygens Saturn orbiter and Titan lander, which will fly by way of Venus, the Earth and Jupiter to arrive in 2004. The US Johns Hopkins University will send a small probe to the asteroid Eros in 1996 and a mission to Pluto and Charon taking up to 10 years to arrive is being discussed by NASA for 1999 launch. Rosetta would be an ESA series of probes designed to rendezvous with asteroids and comets with landers carrying equipment for analysing surface material in situ and relaying the results to Earth but not returning samples as originally proposed (from 2002).

Right **The Jupiter probe Galileo is taking a gravity-assisted route to Jupiter with close approaches to Venus (1990) and Earth (1990 and 1992). In 1995 a probe will be released to descend through Jupiter's atmosphere while the main spacecraft orbits the planet. In October 1991 Galileo passed only 1600km from asteroid Gaspra.**

EARTH STRUCTURE

Internally the earth may be divided broadly into crust, mantle and core.

The crust is a thin shell constituting only 0.2% of the mass of the Earth. The continental crust varies in thickness from 20 to 90km and is less dense than ocean crust. Two-thirds of the continents are overlain by sedimentary rocks of average thickness less than 2km but attaining 20km. Ocean crust is on average 7km thick. It is composed of igneous rocks, basalts and gabbros.

Crust and mantle are separated by the Mohorovičić Discontinuity (Moho). The mantle differs from the crust. It is largely igneous. The upper mantle extends to 350km. There is a low velocity zone between 50km and 150km indicating a partial melting. The lower mantle has a more uniform composition. A sharp discontinuity defines the meeting of mantle and core. The inability of the outer core to transmit seismic waves suggests it is liquid. It is probably of metallic iron with other elements – sulphur, silicon, oxygen, potassium and hydrogen have all been suggested. The inner core is solid and probably of nickel-iron.

Temperature at the core-mantle boundary is about 3700°C and 4000°–4500°C in the inner core.

Evolution of the lithosphere, hydrosphere and atmosphere has been strongly influenced by the biosphere – the sphere of living things. The ancestral atmosphere lacked free oxygen. Plant life added oxygen to the atmosphere and transferred carbon dioxide to the crustal rocks and the hydrosphere. The composition of air at 79% nitrogen and 20% oxygen remains stable by the same mechanism.

Solar energy is distributed around the Earth by the atmosphere. Most of the weather and climate processes occur in the troposphere. The atmosphere also shields the Earth. Ozone which exists to the extent of 2 parts per million is at its maximum at 30km. It is the only gas which absorbs ultra-violet radiation. Water-vapour and CO_2 keep out infra-red radiation.

Above 80km nitrogen and oxygen cannot retain their molecular form. They tend to separate into atoms which become ionized (an ion is an atom lacking one or more of its electrons).

The ionosphere is a zone of ionized belts which reflect radio waves back to earth. These electrification belts change their position dependent on light and darkness and external factors.

Beyond the ionosphere, the magnetosphere extends to outer space. Ionized particles form a plasma (a fourth state of matter i.e. other than solid, liquid, gas) constrained by the Earth's magnetic field.

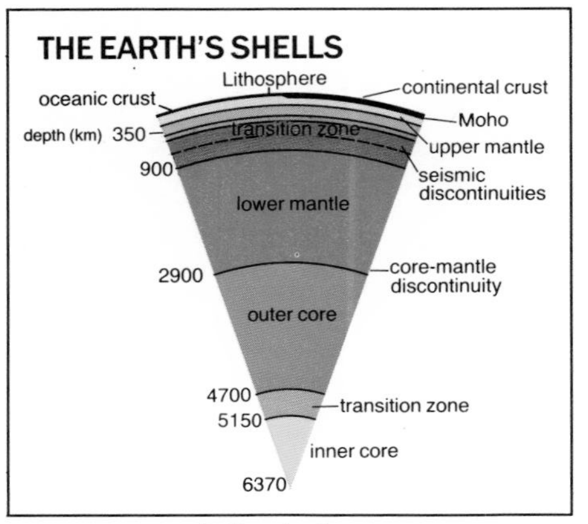

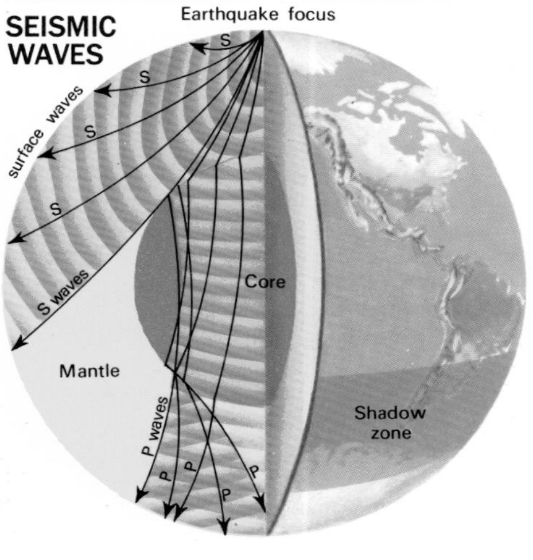

Above In an earthquake the shock generates vibrations, or seismic waves, which radiate in all directions from the focus. Surface waves travel close to the surface of the Earth. They cause most motion in the ground and, therefore, most damage to structures.

Other waves known as body waves pass through the body of the Earth. They are of two kinds. Primary (P) waves are compressional waves. They are able to travel through solids and fluids and cause the particles of the Earth to vibrate in the direction of travel of the wave. Secondary (S) waves are transverse, or shear, waves. They can only pass through solids. They travel at about half the velocity of 'P' waves and they vibrate at right angles to the path travelled by the wave.

Both types of wave obey normal rules of reflection and refraction. Their velocities depend on the nature of the medium through which they pass. Where the physical or chemical properties of the Earth change, the velocity and path of the waves are changed too. From the way the waves travel the nature of the internal layers of the Earth is revealed. By the same means the fluid nature of the outer core is confirmed. Because of the different paths followed by the two types of waves, there is a 'shadow zone' at 105° to 142° from the earthquake focus where waves of both kinds fail to reach the surface.

EARTH'S GRAVITY AND MAGNETIC FIELDS

The Earth is spheroidal in form because it is a rotating body. Were it not so it would take the form of a sphere. The shape is determined by the mass of the Earth and its rate of rotation. Centrifugal force acting outwards reduces the pull of gravity acting inwards so that gravity at the equator is less than at the poles. In theory gravity would be expected to vary progressively from the equator to the poles. In fact, it does not. Uneven distribution of matter within the Earth distorts the shape taken up by the mean sea-level surface (the geoid). In consequence a plumb-line or spirit-level may depart from the assumed vertical or horizontal. Moreover, the orbits of artificial satellites are perturbed by the irregularity of the Earth's gravity.

MAGNETISM

Like gravity, magnetism is strongest at the poles and weakest at the equator. The magnetic field of the Earth resembles that of a bar magnet displaced slightly from the geographical poles. It was long believed that the core being made of iron acted as a magnet but the temperatures prevailing there would destroy such magnetism. Today the belief is that electric currents generated in the semi-molten outer core are responsible for the magnetic field. The magnetic poles are not coincident with the geographical poles. Were a bar magnet substituted for the Earth's field it would not pass through the centre of the Earth but through a point in the plane of the equator about 1200km from the centre in the direction of Indonesia. The bar itself would be inclined at about 12° to the Earth's axis. The magnetic poles change their position from year to year so maps of magnetic declination used for navigation need to be updated annually.

Magnetism is expressed scientifically in three components, intensity, declination (departure from true north), and dip (the inclination in the vertical plane).

When molten rocks cool and solidify materials which are magnetic acquire the alignment of the Earth's local magnetic field at the time they solidified. The magnetism becomes frozen in the rocks. From this historic record the geographical position of the rocks at the time can be estimated from the magnetic alignments within the rocks. From such rock it was discovered that the Earth's magnetic poles had experienced a number of reversals the north pole becoming the south and vice-versa. A system of classification of the field allowed the ages of the various parts of the ocean floor to be deduced thus providing the evidence for sea-floor spreading and plate tectonics.

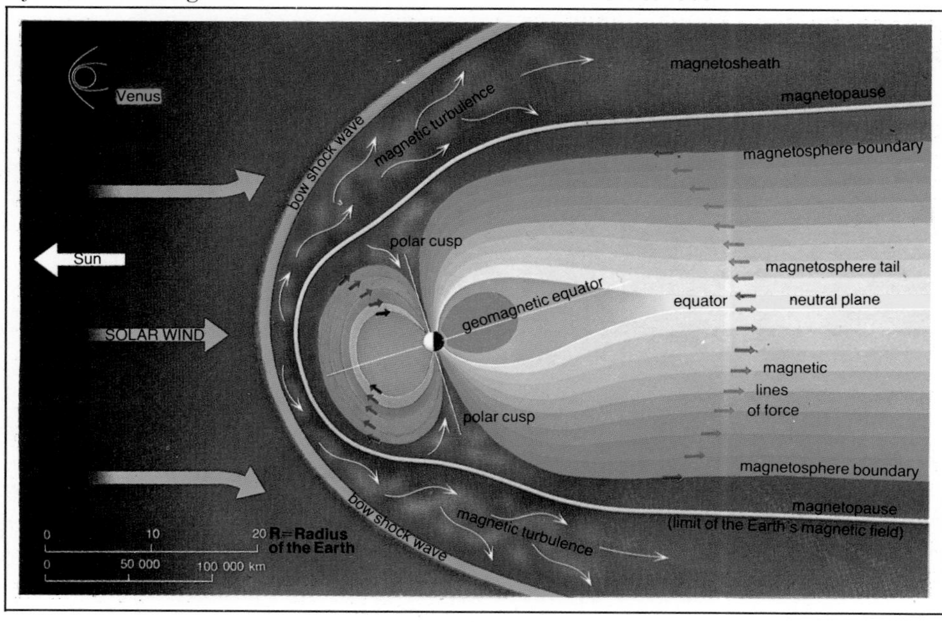

THE MAGNETOSPHERE

A stream of ionized gas, or plasma, the solar wind pours out from the Sun. Travelling at 1000km/sec its encounter with the Earth's magnetic field creates a bow shock wave. The magnetopause, the effective limit of the magnetic field, is pushed back to within 10 Earth radii measured in the direction of the Sun. It is stretched out in a long tail on the opposite side of the Earth. Between the bow-wave and magnetopause is the magnetosheath a region of charged particles producing fluctuations in the magnetic field. On the inner side of the magnetopause is a transition zone where charged particles react with the magnetic field and the magnetosheath. From this zone particles enter the internal magnetic field by the magnetic poles to produce aurorae. Particles trapped by the Earth's magnetism are deflected at the polar cusps and become trapped to form the Van Allen belts at about 5 Earth radii measured from the magnetic equator.

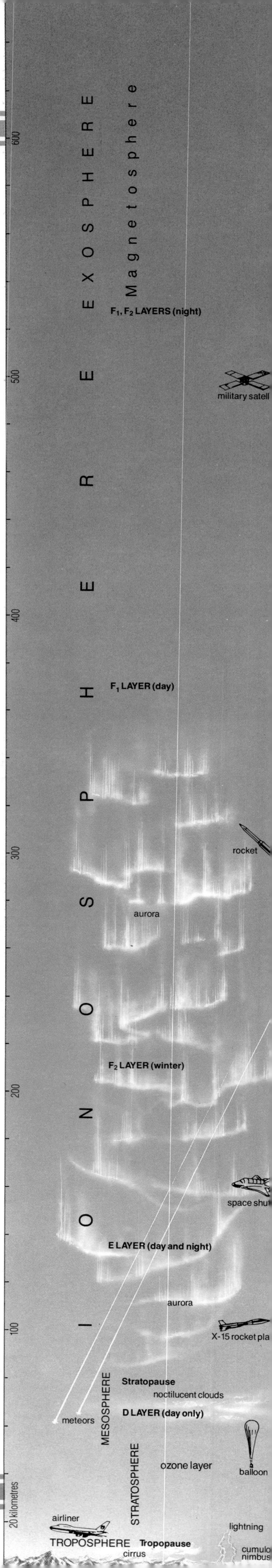

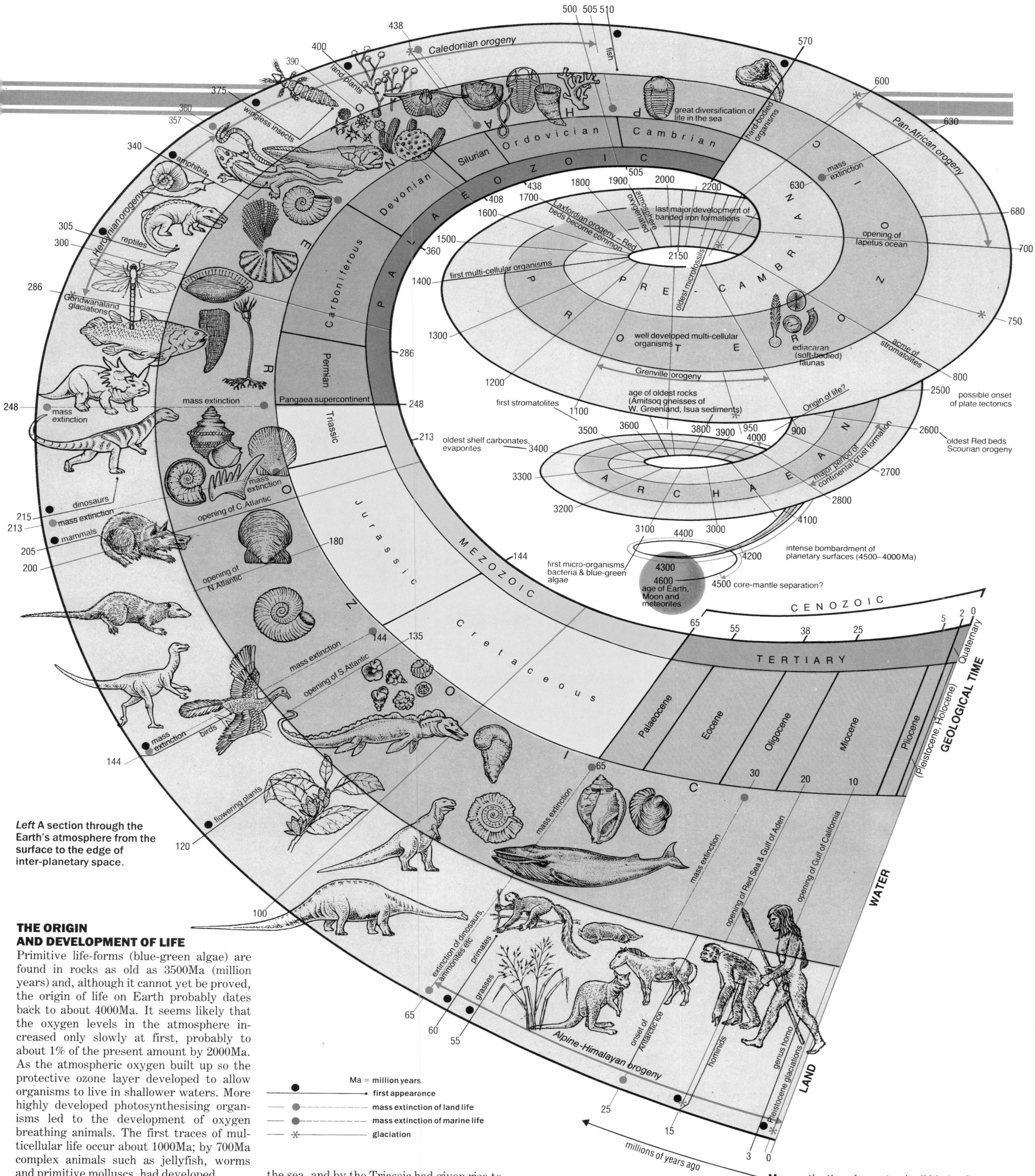

Left **A section through the Earth's atmosphere from the surface to the edge of inter-planetary space.**

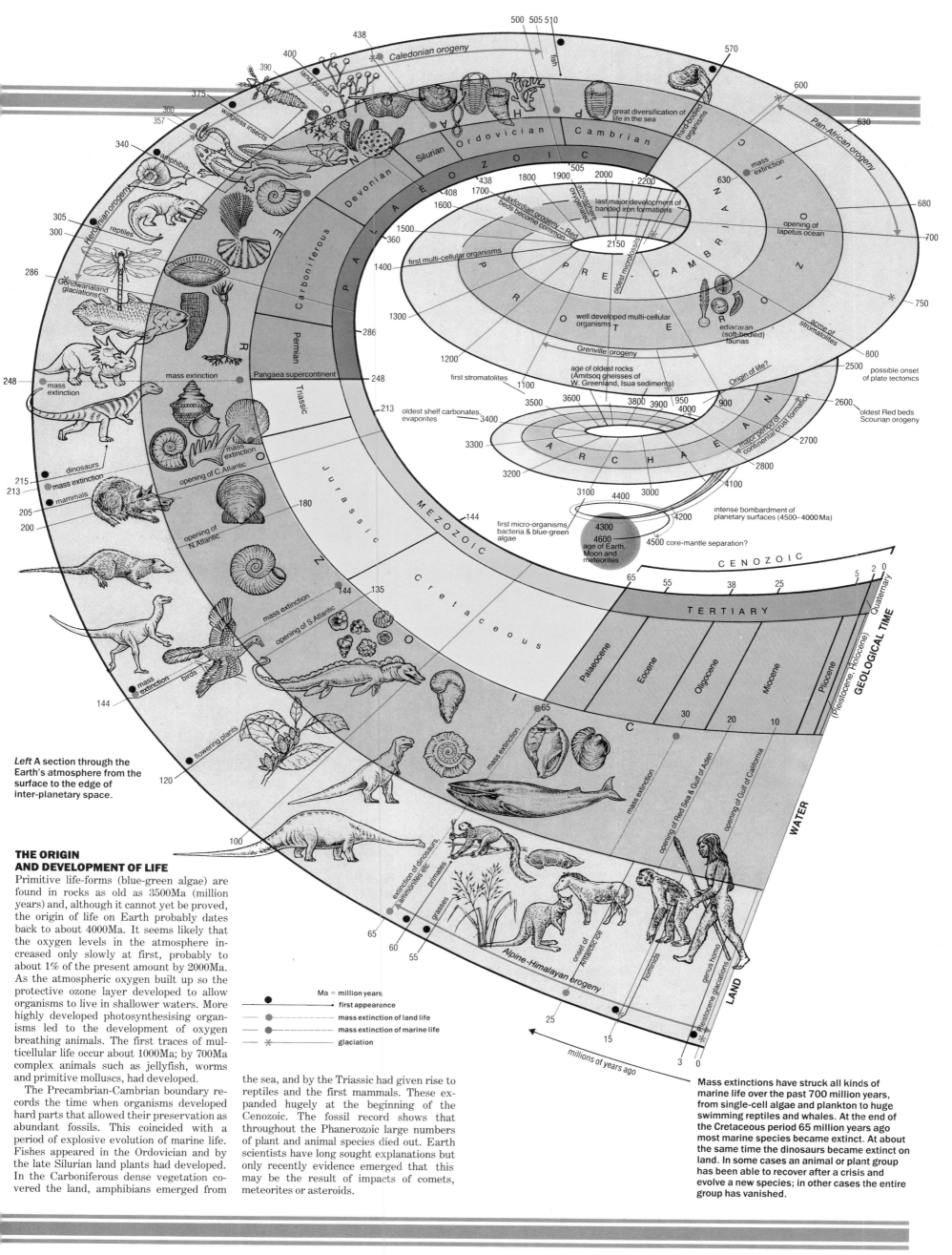

THE ORIGIN AND DEVELOPMENT OF LIFE

Primitive life-forms (blue-green algae) are found in rocks as old as 3500Ma (million years) and, although it cannot yet be proved, the origin of life on Earth probably dates back to about 4000Ma. It seems likely that the oxygen levels in the atmosphere increased only slowly at first, probably to about 1% of the present amount by 2000Ma. As the atmospheric oxygen built up so the protective ozone layer developed to allow organisms to live in shallower waters. More highly developed photosynthesising organisms led to the development of oxygen breathing animals. The first traces of multicellular life occur about 1000Ma; by 700Ma complex animals such as jellyfish, worms and primitive molluscs, had developed.

The Precambrian-Cambrian boundary records the time when organisms developed hard parts that allowed their preservation as abundant fossils. This coincided with a period of explosive evolution of marine life. Fishes appeared in the Ordovician and by the late Silurian land plants had developed. In the Carboniferous dense vegetation covered the land, amphibians emerged from the sea, and by the Triassic had given rise to reptiles and the first mammals. These expanded hugely at the beginning of the Cenozoic. The fossil record shows that throughout the Phanerozoic large numbers of plant and animal species died out. Earth scientists have long sought explanations but only recently evidence emerged that this may be the result of impacts of comets, meteorites or asteroids.

Mass extinctions have struck all kinds of marine life over the past 700 million years, from single-cell algae and plankton to huge swimming reptiles and whales. At the end of the Cretaceous period 65 million years ago most marine species became extinct. At about the same time the dinosaurs became extinct on land. In some cases an animal or plant group has been able to recover after a crisis and evolve a new species; in other cases the entire group has vanished.

DYNAMIC EARTH

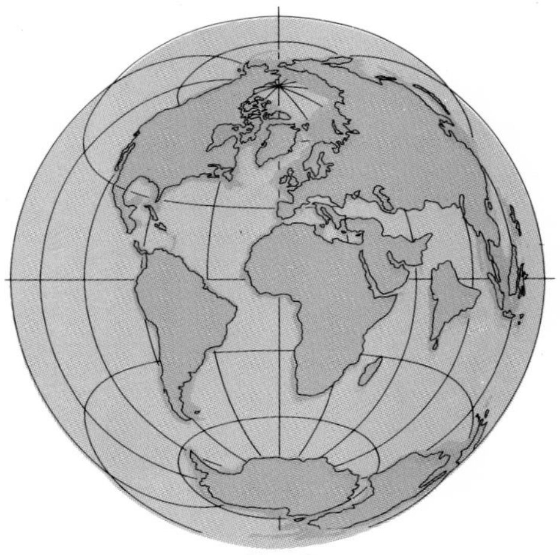

Map 1
50 million years ago

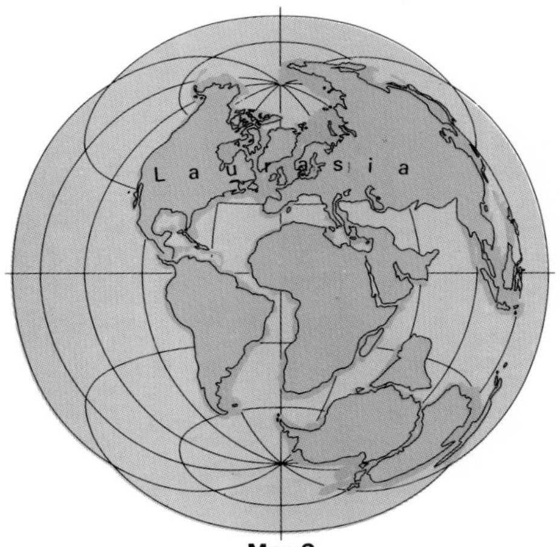

Map 2
100 million years ago

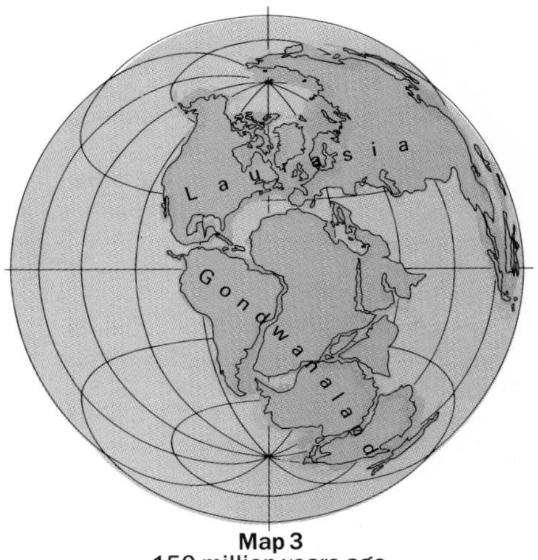

Map 3
150 million years ago

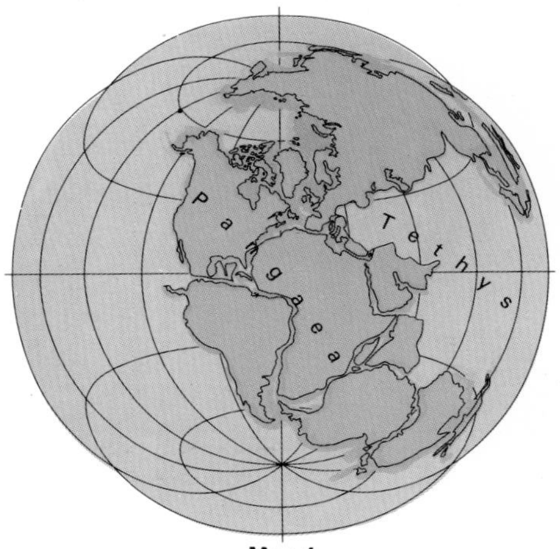

Map 4
200 million years ago

PLATE TECTONICS

Tectonics means the act of building. As applied to geology, the word, which comes from Greek, refers to study of the processes which produce faults, joints, folds and cleavage or cause magma to rise to the surface as the Earth's crust reacts to forces from below. Plate tectonics attribute such tectonic effects to the movement of the parts of the lithosphere. The lithosphere is defined as the rigid outer layer of the Earth consisting of the crust and the part of the upper mantle immediately below. Together they form a rigid layer which is split into a number of plates all in motion, like rafts, carrying the continents and the oceans with them to drift apart, to collide, to unite or sub-divide in a process of destruction and renewal. There are six major plates and a number of minor ones diverging, converging or sliding past each other at varying rates.

The plates are able to move because the rigid lithosphere rests on a less rigid asthenosphere a zone where the mantle is hotter and less resistant. Temperature increases at the rate of 20°C to 40°C with each km of depth in the outer parts of the Earth.

At mid-ocean ridges, a continuous chain some 40 000km in length running through all the oceans, new crust is created. Magma (hot molten rock) rises to flow out of the rift and solidify as pillow lavas or gabbros without reaching the crustal surface. The intrusion of new material forces the rift sides to move outwards and they are pushed further apart as still more magma injects itself into the rift. The rifts are regions of low seismic activity with a high heat flow.

Evidence of sea-floor spreading is provided by the magnetism locked into the rocks at the time they solidified. Evidence is also provided by the ocean sediments which become increasingly thicker outwards from the rift indicating a longer period of time for their deposition and consequently a greater age of the ocean floor on which they lie.

At mid-ocean ridges the plate margins are divergent (or extensional), new crust is formed and the boundary is said to be constructive. Where two plates meet the margins are convergent (or compressional) and are destructive. One plate slides under the other the plate margin descending at a steep angle, sometimes to a depth of 700km, into the asthenosphere, until melting occurs. Lighter material rises to attach itself to the underside of the continents. Continental plates containing much lighter material float over the ocean plates. Where the ocean plate is subducted, the subduction zone is marked by an ocean trench. Island areas are also formed in the oceans and young folded mountain ranges at the edge of a continent.

At some plate boundaries crust is neither created nor destroyed: the plates slide past each other at transform faults. The margins are translational and by type, conservative.

From study of all the oceans it can be said that the ocean floors are less than 200M years old. The Pacific plate contains only ocean crust. The other major plates consist of both continental and ocean crust. A fairly authoritative account can be given of the way the continents have drifted, divided and collided over the past 200M years. A very incomplete picture can be drawn of the course of events in the preceding 400M years and only a sketchy picture before that.

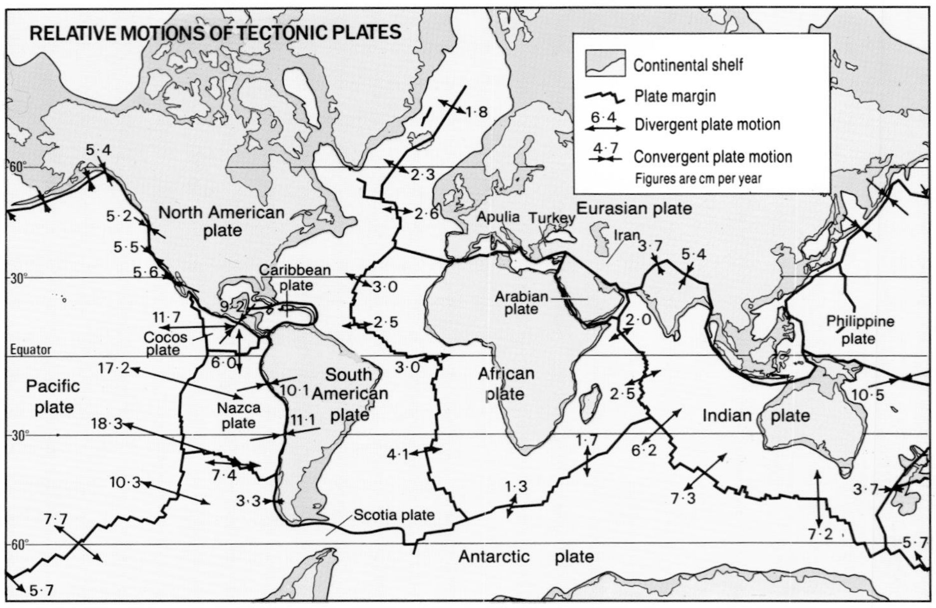

PLATE TECTONIC CYCLE

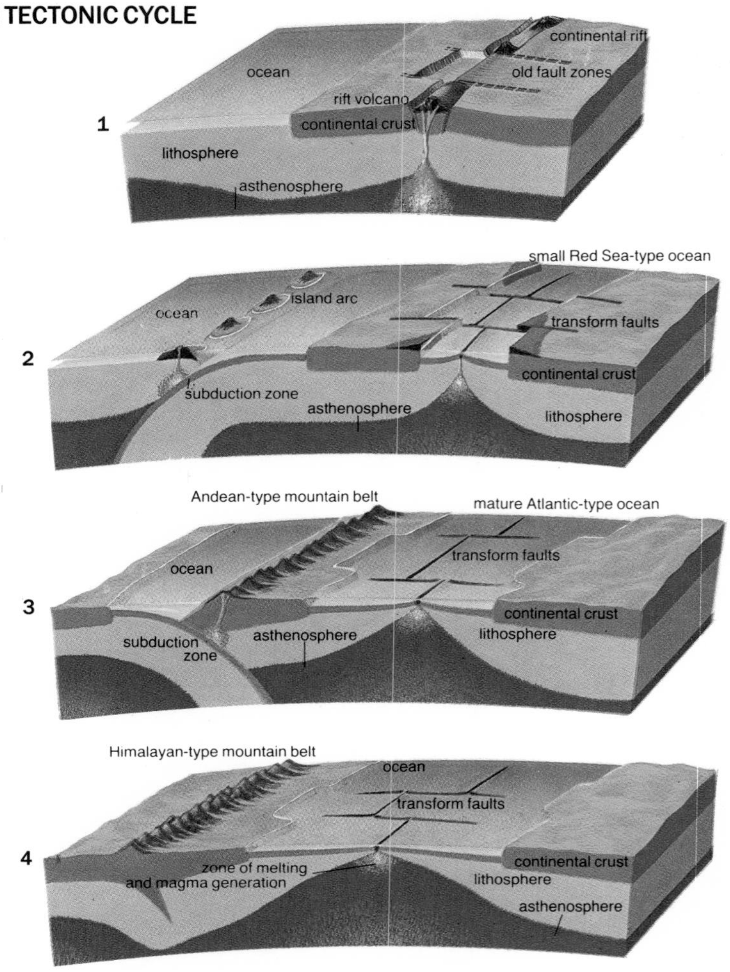

Above When continental lithosphere is subjected to tensional forces, it can become so attenuated that fault zones develop and crustal rocks subside. Hot magma rises from the asthenosphere to fill the space and that increases the heat flow through the lithosphere. Partial melting of mantle material ensues in the process of basaltic volcanism at a mid-ocean ridge. A rift develops in the continent and the two sides of the rift are forced further apart. Separation may be arrested after a while as in the case of the Rio Grande of south-west USA and the rift valley of East Africa. Should the process not be arrested, the rift will lengthen until the continent is split into two diverging plates.

1 Continental rifting in part following old faults in the continental basement.
2 Continental break-up with the formation of new oceanic crust in a small Red Sea-type ocean basin. Transform faults follow continental fractures.
3 A large mature Atlantic-type ocean basin has now formed on the site of the former continent. The subduction zone changes in direction (flips) to dip beneath the continent, forming a cordillera-type mountain belt.
4 Where continental collision occurs one continent partly underthrusts the other producing a Himalayan-type mountain belt underlain by thick continental crust (75-90km).

MAJOR TECTONIC FEATURES

Right Particular features are associated with different types of mineral deposits: continental rifts with tin and fluorine, mid-ocean ridges with marine metallic sulphides, island arcs and cordilleran-type mountains with a variety of metallic deposits.

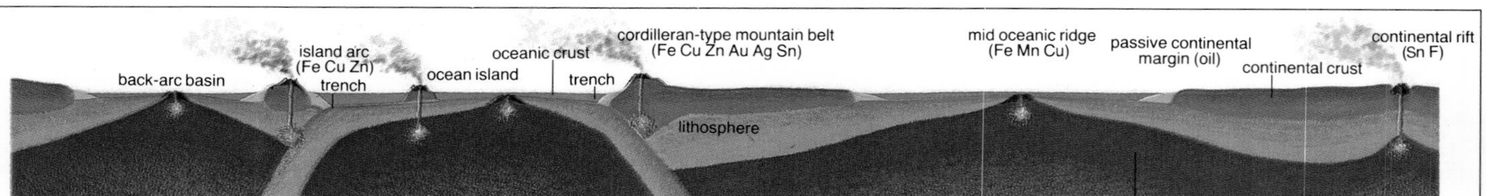

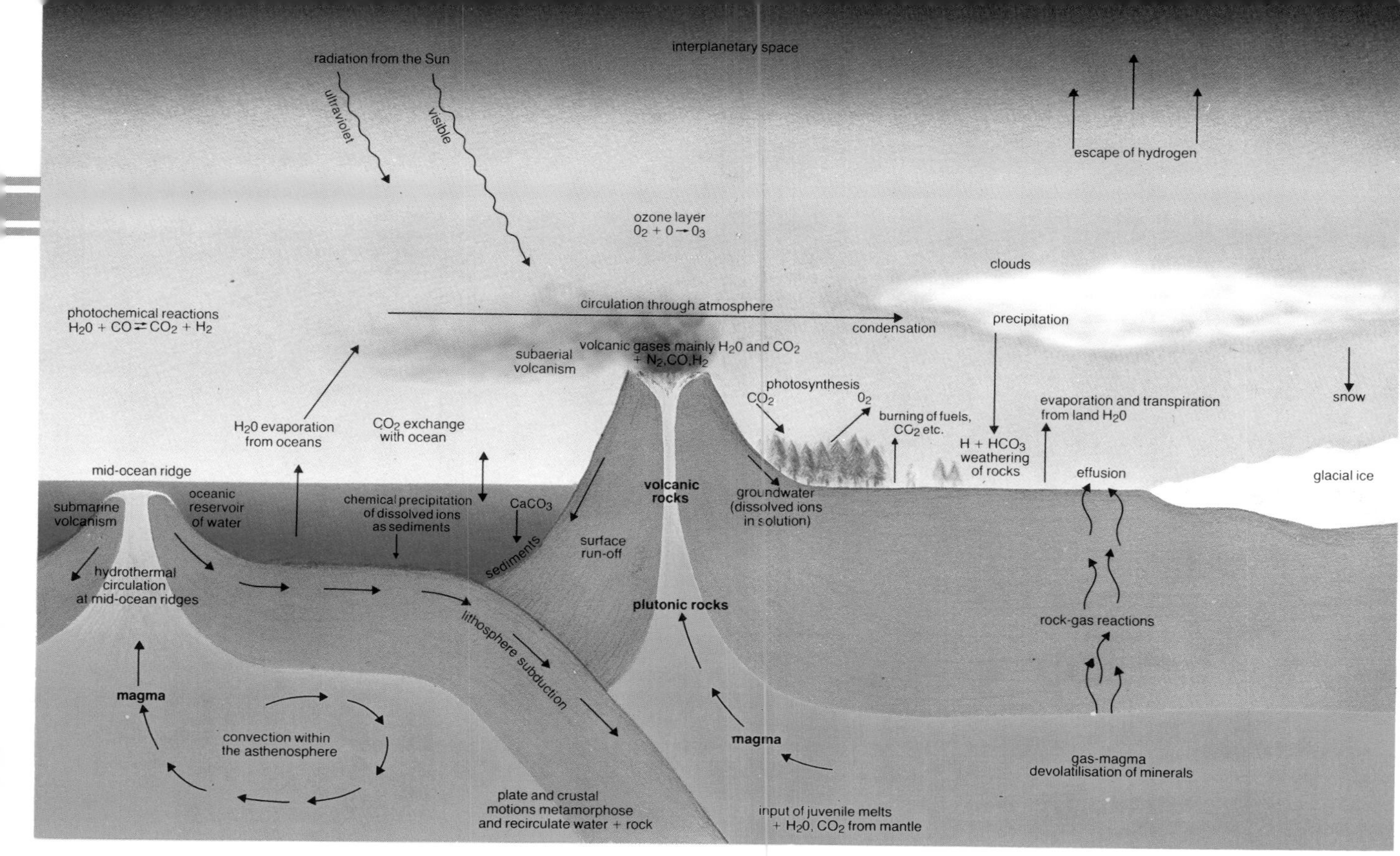

ROCK AND HYDROLOGICAL CYCLES

Left **In the most familiar cycle rain falls onto the land, drains to the sea, evaporates, condenses into cloud and is precipitated onto the land again. Water is also released and recirculated as a result of plate movements and volcanic activity. In the rock cycle rocks are weathered and eroded, forming sediments which are in turn compacted into rocks that are eventually exposed and then weathered again. Man's industrial activity has modified the atmosphere by increasing the amount of CO_2 and adding other gases that may affect the vital ozone layer that shields the Earth from the Sun's ultra-violet rays. In the oceans, CO_2 and calcium are converted into calcium carbonate which forms sedimentary rocks which are re-cycled by the action of plate tectonics. In the atmosphere, CO_2, dust and water-vapour absorb infra-red energy and re-radiate it both to space and the atmosphere. If the level of CO_2 is increased, less of the Earth's own heat escapes to space, more is returned to the atmosphere and the Earth becomes warmer.**

SURFACE PROCESSES

The lithosphere, the outermost layer of the Earth; the hydrosphere of salt and fresh water and the atmosphere composed of gases are all closely connected. There is a constant transfer of material from one to the other. The air in the atmosphere does not remain motionless. Convection and other influences impart complex patterns of motion in which matter is conveyed from one area to another. Atmospheric water vapour deposited on the lithosphere as water containing dissolved gases, reacts physically and chemically with surface rocks.

Variation in temperature, particularly frost, precipitation and winds cause a gradual fragmentation of surface rocks and physical decay in the process called weathering. Vegetation also plays its part in the alteration of surface rocks, by adding organic matter to weathered rocks to create soils and by resisting erosion. Water, however, is the major factor since it also acts as a transport medium.

Rivers transport enormous quantities of material varying from large boulders to particles of sand or clay carried in suspension. Where rivers overflow their banks, sand, gravel and clays are deposited in the flood plains to produce fertile valleys. On reaching the ocean or a lake the carrying capacity of the current is dissipated and material carried in suspension is deposited to form a delta.

Slumping of ocean floor material or earthquakes can put large quantities of fine sediments into suspension as a turbid layer which erodes the continental slope, thereby gathering more material all of which is deposited on the continental rise or the floor of the abyssal plain as "turbidites".

VOLCANOES

Almost all the world's active volcanoes, numbering 500–600 are located at convergent plate boundaries. Those are the volcanoes which give spectacular demonstrations of volcanic activity. Yet far greater volcanic activity continues unnoticed and without cessation at mid-ocean ridges where magma from the upper mantle is quietly being extruded on to the ocean floor to create new crustal material. The basalts erupted there are derived more or less directly from material of the mantle. Similar lavas are seen in the Columbia plateau, U.S.A. and the Deccan, India.

Chemical composition of magmas and the amount of gas they contain are important factors in determining the nature of a volcanic eruption. Gas-charged basalts produce cinder cones. Mount Etna in Italy has numerous such cinder cones. Violent eruptions usually occur when large clouds of lava come into contact with water to produce fine-grained ash. The name Surtseyan is given to this type after the volcanic island which appeared off Iceland in 1963. Andesites are more viscous. When charged with gas they erupt with explosive violence. Volcanoes like Fujiyama, Vesuvius and most of the other renowned volcanoes with steep sides are of this type.

Nuées ardentes (burning clouds) are extremely destructive. They are produced by rhyolitic magmas which erupt explosively sending molten lava fragments and gas at great speed down the mountain sides.

In spite of the destructiveness of many volcanoes people still live in their vicinity because of the fertile volcanic soils. Geothermal energy in regions of volcanic activity is another source of attraction.

EARTHQUAKES

Earthquakes are the manifestation of a slippage at a geological fault. The majority occur at tectonic plate boundaries. The interior of a plate tends to be stable and less subject to earthquakes. When plates slide past each other strain energy is suddenly released. Even though the amount of movement is very small the energy released is colossal. It is transferred in shock waves.

Most earthquakes originate at not very great depths – 5km or so. At the San Andreas fault earthquakes originate at about 20km depth. Over 70% of all foci are at depths of less than 70km. Some, however, may be as deep as 700km. The precise cause of those very deep earthquakes is not known. The point from which the earthquake is generated is the focus and the point on the surface immediately above the focus is the epicentre. Plotting the foci of deep earthquakes at convergent plate boundaries allows the path of the subducted plate to be traced.

Two types of scale are used to define the magnitude of earthquakes. In the logarithmic Richter Scale each unit is thirty times the intensity of the next lower on the scale. The intensity is recorded by seismographs. There is no upper limit but the greatest magnitude yet recorded is 8.9.

The Modified Mercalli Earthquake Intensity Scale is in common use. It is based on the observed effects of an earthquake. At the lowest end the numeral I means the shock is felt by only a few people under special circumstances. A shock felt generally, with minor breakages indoors is classed as V. General alarm is equivalent to VIII and 'Panic' with varying categories of total destruction are graded IX to XII.

EXTERNAL INFLUENCES

Every day over a million tons of extraterrestrial material falls on the Earth. Most of this material is ultra-fine cosmic dust. Only a small proportion of the incoming material actually reaches the surface of the Earth. Most is burned up by friction with the atmosphere where it vaporises after being heated to incandescence when it may be seen as so-called shooting stars.

Meteors come both sporadically and in showers. They are part of the solar system and rotate round the Sun. When the Earth comes in contact with them a meteor display occurs.

Occasionally a larger body survives passage through the atmosphere and strikes the ground. One very large meteorite fell in Arizona about 25,000 years ago. Meteor Crater is the result. Another devastating impact occurred in 1908 when an object struck the Tunguska area of Siberia, devastating an area of several kilometres radius in which all the trees were felled.

Tektites are curious objects. They are small and glassy and are found lying on the surface of several places - Australia, South-East Asia, Ivory Coast, Czech Republic and Slovakia. Terrestrial and extra-terrestrial origins have been ascribed to them. They have the appearance of melted rocks formed as the result of meteorite impact but no local evidence of such impact has been detected at any of the sites.

It seems inevitable that a comet or an asteroid will, in the course of time, collide with the Earth. Both comets and asteroids pass within the Earth's orbit. A collision will occur if the Earth happens to be located in that part of its orbit when one or the other crosses it.

FOLDING AND FAULTING

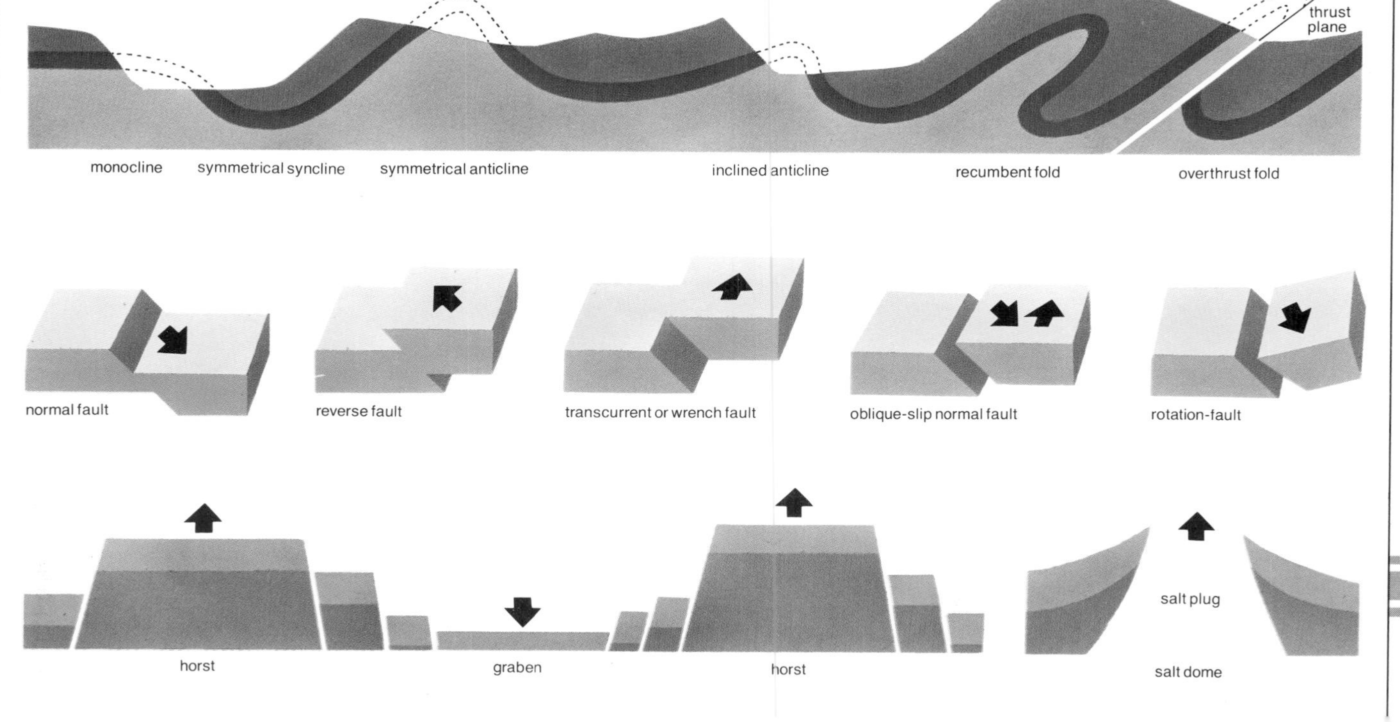

Left **When the Earth's crust bends under compression, folds develop. The simplest of these is a monocline, a one-sided fold, although downfolds (synclines) and upfolds (anticlines) are more usual. Increasing pressure steepens the side facing the pressure until one side is pushed under the other, to form a recumbent fold. Finally it may break along its axis, one limb being thrust over the other. Mountain chains often demonstrate intense folding between converging plates.**

Faults occur when the Earth's crust breaks, often causing earthquakes. When tension stretches the crust normal faulting occurs and the rocks on one side of the fault-plane override those on the other.

A horst is a block of the crust thrust up between faults; the reverse is a graben or rift valley. Repeated horst and graben forms give basin and range topography as in Nevada, USA.

The upward movement of a plug of salt, some thousands of feet in depth, may force up strata and the surface layers to form a salt dome, often associated with oil and gas.

CLIMATE

Climate is generally said to be the average weather conditions observed over a long period. The factors which determine climate are temperature and rainfall.

Although heated slightly by the passage of the Sun's rays the atmosphere is warmed by the re-radiation of solar heat energy stored in the oceans and continents. Air which contains as much water vapour as possible (i.e. the air is saturated) is said to have a relative humidity of 100 and half-saturated air, 50. Air at a temperature of 32°C (90°F) can hold more than nine times as much water vapour as air at 0°C (32°F). For this reason polar regions have low precipitation.

Near the equator where the north-east and south-east trade winds meet is a zone known as the Inter-tropical Convergence Zone. Here warm, water-laden air rises to some 12-15km in altitude, its high content of water-vapour visible as cumulonimbus clouds. On cooling with altitude rain falls. This low-pressure doldrum zone of light winds has daily afternoon rains.

The two tropics are zones of descending air and, therefore, high atmospheric pressure and low rainfall. On the other hand, the arctic and antarctic circles are low pressure zones and between them and the tropics the winds are 'anti-trade' i.e. blowing from the SW and NW respectively in the northern and southern hemispheres. This is the zone of the 'westerlies' in which weather is determined by depressions (low-pressure centres) and anti-cyclones (high pressure centres), the first rain-bearing, the second dry. In the polar regions the winds tend to be easterly. The poles themselves are high-pressure areas.

But for the rotation of the Earth, winds would blow south or north from high-pressure zones at the poles and tropics towards the polar circles and equator. Rotation and centrifugal force impart a west or east motion. The system of pressure belts moves from 6° to 10° north or south following the seasonal movements of the Sun.

Continents and oceans also influence the global pattern especially in the northern hemisphere where most land lies. The interiors of N. America and Eurasia become very hot in summer and very cold in winter causing air to flow respectively from and to the oceans. Monsoons are an expression of this seasonal reversal of direction.

Tropical cyclones (typhoons and hurricanes and many local names) are highly destructive systems. They occur in a belt between 5° and 30° latitude, the majority in the northern hemisphere. They can be 800km in diameter, rotating clockwise in the southern hemisphere and counter-clockwise in the northern. Wind speeds above Force

BEAUFORT SCALE OF WIND FORCE

†wind velocity	0	4	9	16	23	31	40	50	60	72
*maximum waveheight	0	0.1	0.2	0.3	1.0	1.0–1.7	2.5	3.5	6.0	10.0
Beaufort scale no.	**0**	**1**	**2**	**3**	**4**	**5**	**6**	**7**	**8**	**9**
	Smoke rises vertically. Leaves on trees still.	Smoke rises straight but not vertically. Leaves rustle.	Smoke blown out of vertical still more.	Flags flutter. Leaves and small twigs in motion. Ripple on ponds.	Small flags flying fully. Small branches in motion even when leafless. Paper and dust blown about.	Large flags stretched. Tops of large trees shake. Small waves on ponds. Wind whistles.	Large bare branches in motion. Wind whistles around buildings. Humming of telephone wires.	Trunks of small (leafless) trees in motion. White tops on waves in ponds.	Large trees in motion; twigs and branches break off. Wind impedes walking.	Large boug break off. I objects lift ground. Ro tiles blown.

† km/hr
* trough to crest in metres

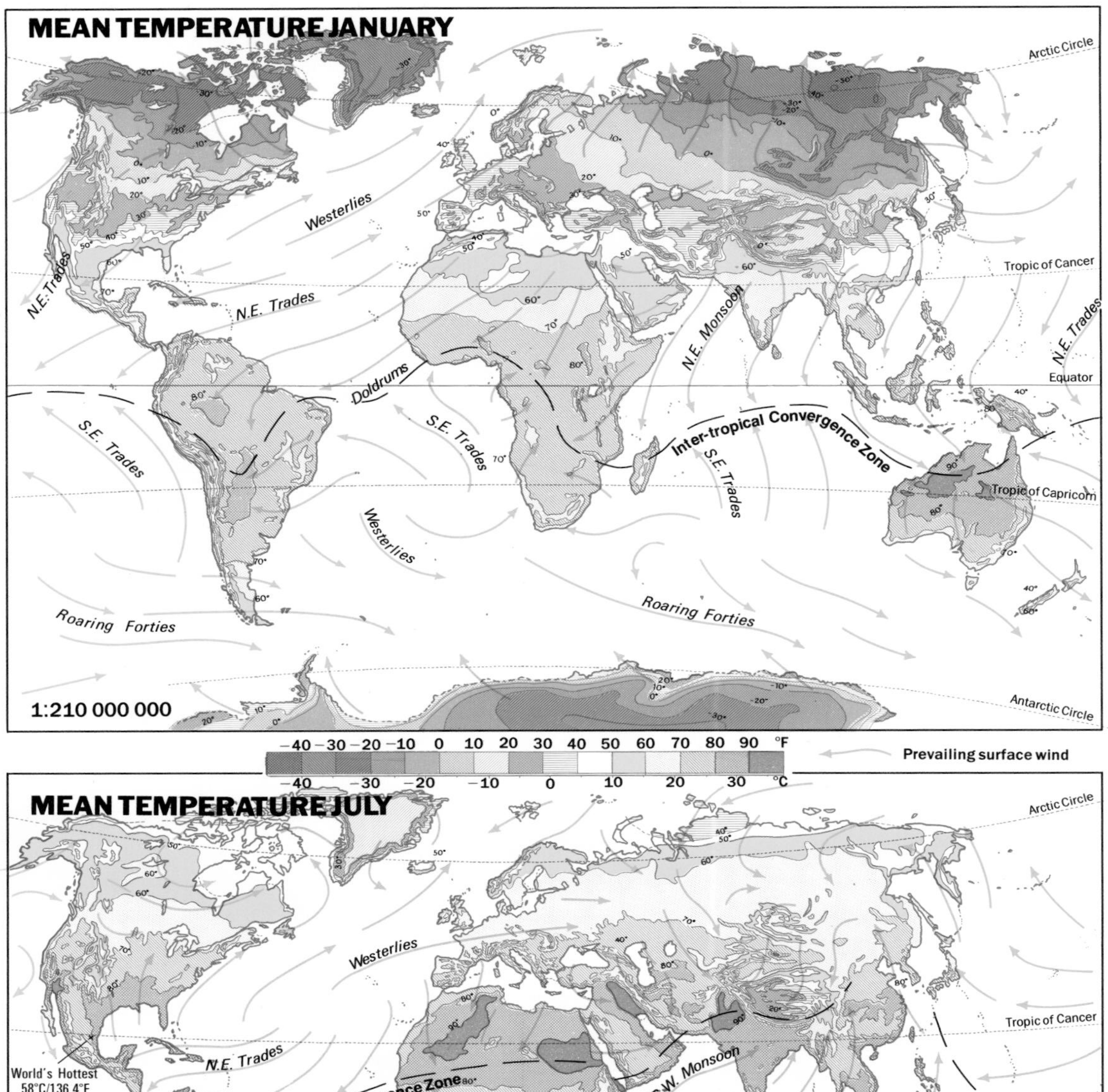

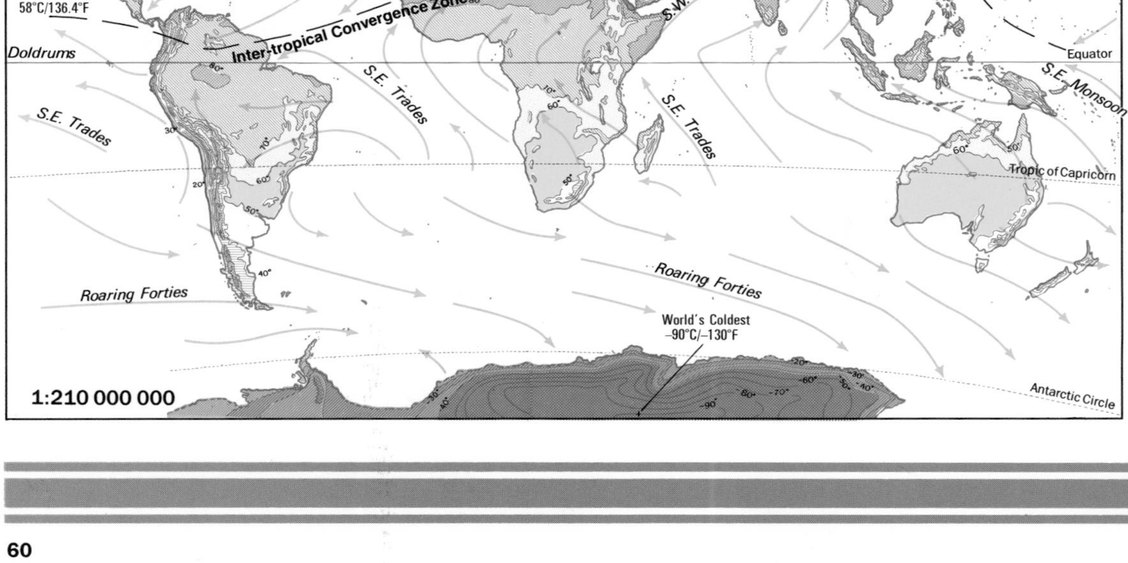

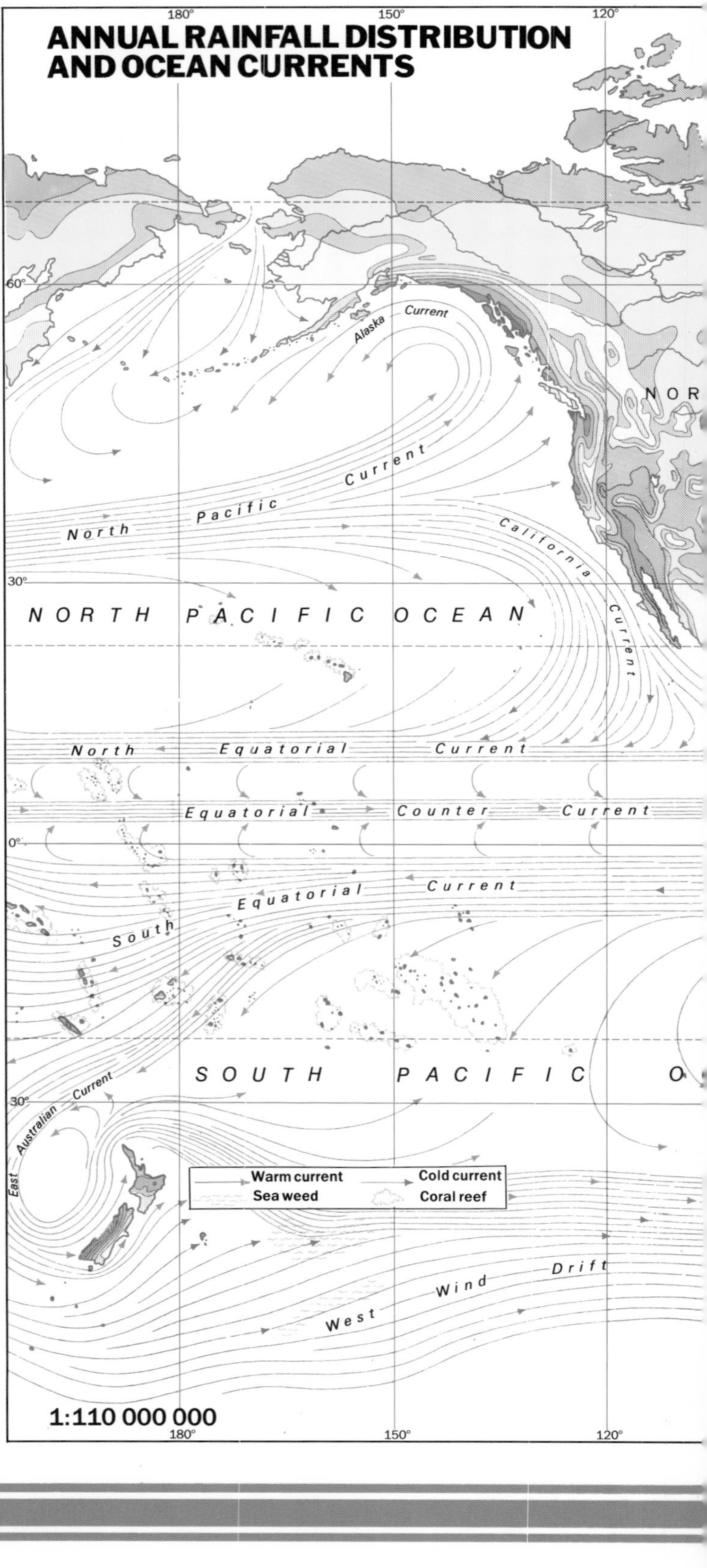

84	97	104
12.0	over 16.0	over 16.0
10	**11**	**12**
Trees uprooted considerable damage.	Major destruction.	Disastrous destruction

12, seas rising to 16–17m and torrential rain cause the destruction.

Far from destructive are the Chinook of N. America and the Föhn winds of the Alps. Air, depleted of moisture, is warmed in its descent of the rain-shadow side of high mountain ranges.

Tsunamis, destructive ocean waves, are not the result of weather but of submarine seismic activity. A wave of no more than 1m but travelling at 650km/hr can rise to 16m or more on impact with the shore.

Left In 1805, the British admiral, Francis Beaufort, devised a sequence of numbers to indicate the force of winds at sea. Associated effects at sea and on land were added later to show that 'white horses' occasional at Force 3 became widespread at Force 6, that waves became higher and longer, that spray and foam increased with turbulence until visibility was affected. Wind speeds were added later still. More scientific methods exist but the scale is easily assimilable and the Beaufort number with temperature; pressure; precipitation; visibility and outlook together provide a concise weather summary.

Right Waterspouts are sea tornadoes, short-lived phenomena lasting from one minute to half-an-hour. A rapidly gyrating vortex descends from a cumulus or cumulonimbus cloud whipping the sea and sucking up a column of water from 1m to 300m diameter which travels with the cloud but with the base moving at a different speed. High velocity peripheral winds, the disturbed sea-surface and descent of water inflict the damage. It should be noted that the African tornado, also highly destructive, is actually a violent squall.

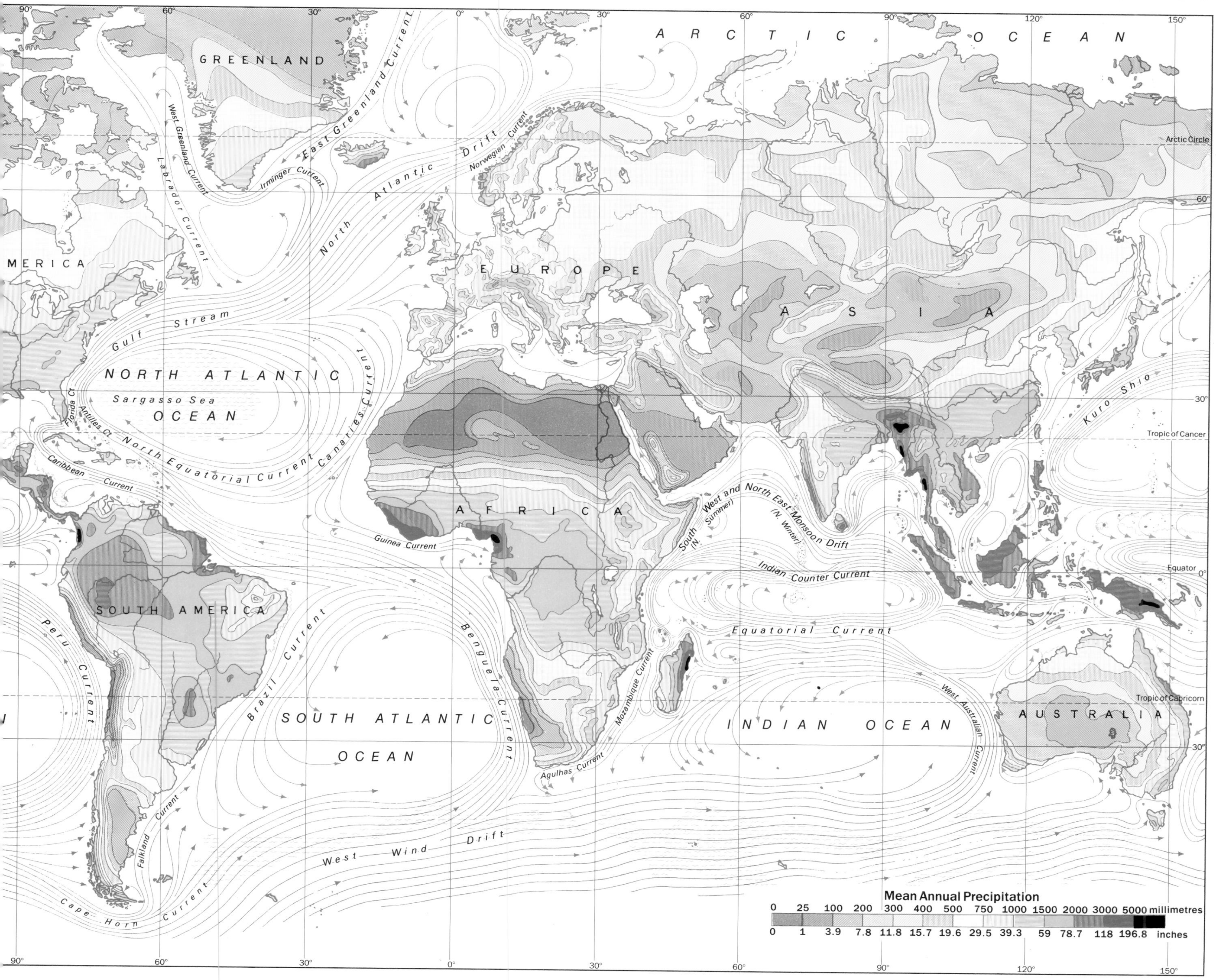

VEGETATION

In a world so subordinated to human beings, it is salutory to be reminded that the atmosphere itself and fertile soils which support agriculture are the creations of plant life. Yet there is far less general concern for the preservation of plants threatened with extinction than there is over endangered animal species.

Perhaps the most remarkable feature of plant life is its almost complete ubiquity. Unless inhibited by ice, plants establish themselves wherever conditions allow and once established encourage the formation or collection of soil and the means to generate their species. The type of plant is determined primarily by climate and soil. Soil is composed of solid, liquid and gas, the solid part being the primary parent rock with secondary rock material changed through moisture and chemical reaction. Humus, decayed vegetable matter, is both solid and liquid. The gas is air.

Russian research first linked soil type to climate, so Russian terms are used for soils. Vegetation zones broadly match soil classes. Thus in the tundra, low temperature and a permanently frozen sub-soil retard organic decay. Thaw in the peaty surface produces swamps. Trees and shrubs are sparse and stunted. South of the tundra is the boreal forest (taiga) of coniferous trees, largely evergreen with some deciduous trees. Their resinous leaves protect against extreme cold and limit transpiration. Soils are podzols, a name applied to whitish-grey sandy soils in which leaching has taken place, a process by which water percolates downwards carrying organic and other matter in solution. These soils are acid. The coniferous vegetation does not produce a rich humus when it decays. Because Siberian rivers flow north the lower reaches are still frozen when the upper reaches thaw. Floods then ensue. Trees of the taiga are, therefore, less healthy than those of N. America.

South of the taiga the mixed coniferous and deciduous temperate forests merge into a zone of deciduous forests where trees have a resting period in winter and summers are dry enough and warm enough to allow humus to form. Further south again are the chernozems, fine-grained loams rich in humus hence their name 'black-earth'. This is the zone of the naturally occurring wooded grassy steppes. The soils are of various kinds but they are very like the loess of northern China where the cohesive properties of the soil allow it to form vertical faces. These fertile soils which are found in Europe, Asia and N. & S. America have all been given over to agriculture.

South again are the rather less fertile chestnut soils of the true steppes. Next follow red and grey soils of the semi-desert and desert steppes.

Beyond the hot deserts are the tropical grasslands and finally at the equator the rain forests (selva) where very tall evergreen trees form a dense forest, denser in S. America than in Africa or Asia. The resting period in which the trees shed their leaves occurs at various times throughout the year.

More than two fifths of all living things on earth are found in the rain forests and there is a tremendous variety of trees and other forms of life in even a small area of forest.

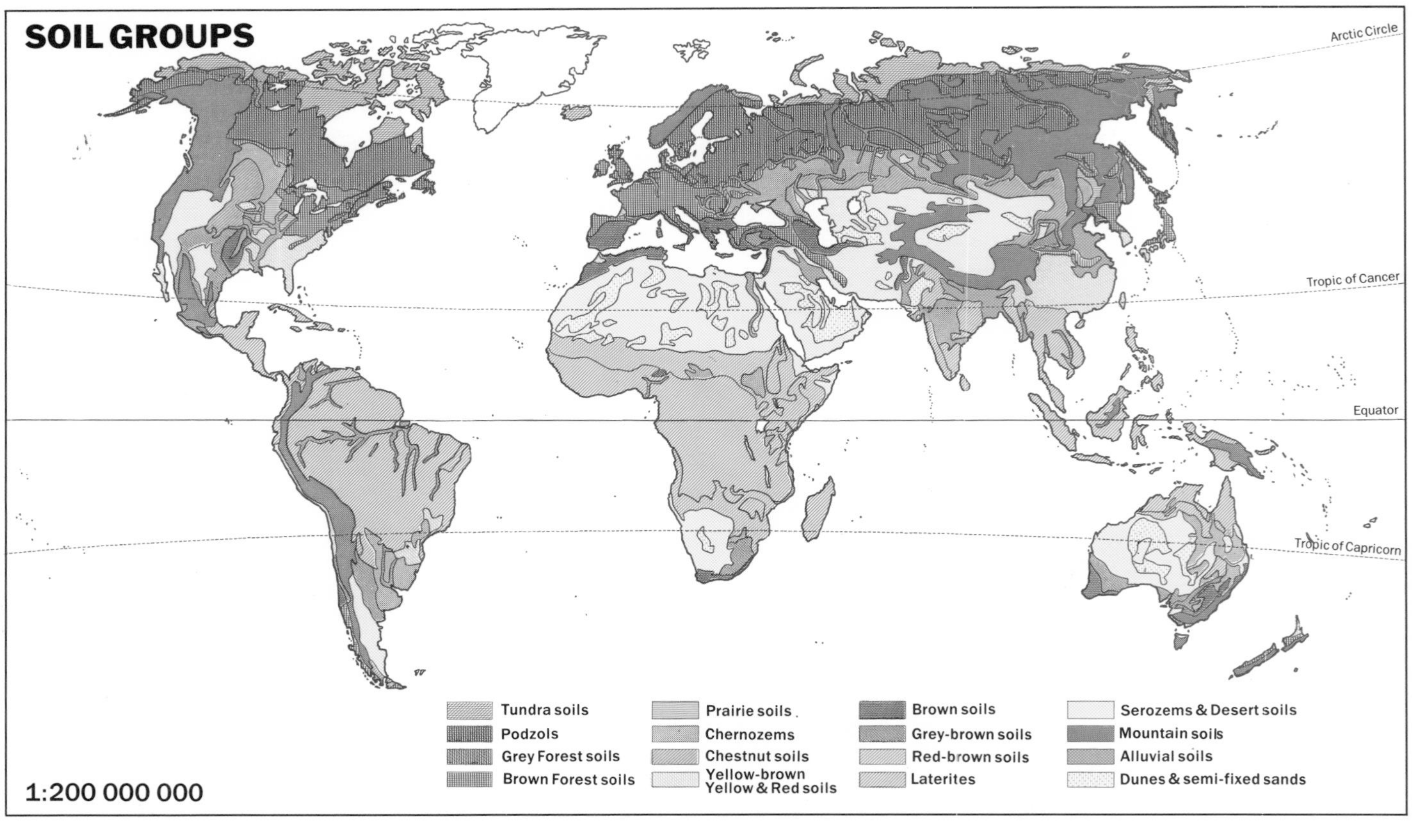

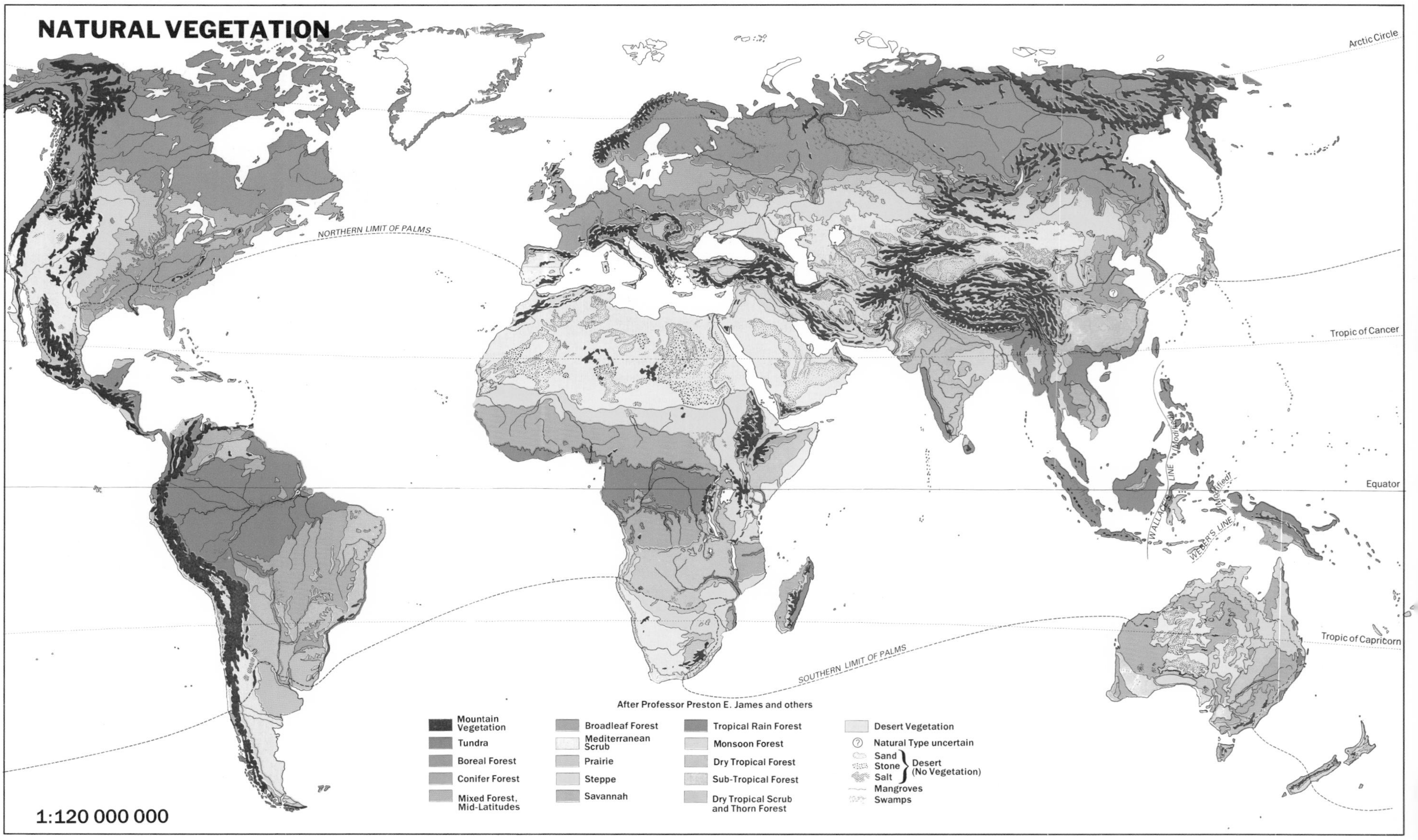

MINERALS

Rare metals

Uranium, the best known and most important of the rare metals owes the expansion of its production to the development of nuclear power and related industries. North America is the largest producer but there are significant deposits in Australia, South Africa, Niger and France. **Niobium**, a metal used in alloys and toolmaking is mined mainly in Brazil, Canada and Russian Federation, while **Tantalum**, a corrosion resistant metal valuable to the electronic and chemical industries is found in N. America and Nigeria.

Precious metals

Over and above their more glamorous associations, gold, platinum and silver have a wide range of applications within industry including electronics, chemicals and photography. South Africa dominates the western world's production of **gold** and **platinum**, accounting for over 30% of total output (the major platinum mines are located in Bophuthatswana). Russian Federation, also a substantial producer of platinum is the other major gold producing country while smaller amounts are found in North America and several other localities worldwide. **Silver** production is less dominated by any one country and is mined throughout the Americas, Central Asia and Australia.

Above Manganese nodules form gradually over millions of years around a foreign body. Although they occur over 20% of the ocean floor, only in limited areas are they of economic importance.

Chemical and Fertilizer minerals

This grouping embraces a variety of minerals occurring in a range of forms and requiring very different recovery techniques. Their usage is widespread in chemical processes throughout industry, **apatite, potash** and **phosphate rock** being especially important in the manufacture of fertilizers. Phosphate rock is exploited widely, though the main volume of production is from U.S.A., Russian Federation and Morocco. The former U.S.S.R., North America, Germany and France are the leading suppliers of potash. Sources of **borax, fluorite** and **sulphur** occur throughout N. America, Europe and western Asia, with U.S.A. a leading producer of all three.

Other Industrial minerals

Asbestos, well-known as a fibrous insulating material; it is produced in Central Asia, North America, Canada, Southern Africa, China and Italy. **China clay**, a fine white clay used in the paper, ceramic and cosmetic industries is found in China, Europe and U.S.A.

Magnesite, a magnesium ore comes particularly from Central Asia, Europe and China for use in the production of refractories and chemicals.

Mica, used as an electrical insulator, is principally produced in U.S.A. and in smaller quantities throughout Europe and Asia.

Talc, a soft greasy mineral is used as a lubricant and in paper manufacture, paint and cosmetics. Production is mainly from U.S.A., Russian Federation and Europe.

Light metals

Aluminium is extracted from bauxite, an ore occurring in feldspars and other silicates which readily breaks down in tropical conditions. It is therefore often found as a surface crust in tropical areas. Principal producers are Australia, Guinea and Jamaica with smaller but substantial amounts from S.E. Europe, Central Asia and the northern regions of South America. **Titanium** is a heat resistant metal used in high grade steel alloys largely in the aircraft and aerospace industries. The two main ores, rutile and ilmenite, are widespread and plentiful; the main sources include Brazil, Canada and Norway.

Iron

Iron is the second most abundant metallic element in the Earth's crust after aluminium. Rarely found as a free metal it exists in ores of varying constitutions which are smelted to produce metallic iron. Further processing produces steel and combination with other metals makes special steels and alloys. Iron ore is mined in many locations but the principal producing areas are Ukraine, Russian Federation, Australia, Brazil and U.S.A. followed by Canada, China and India. Many other countries produce smaller but nonetheless substantial tonnages.

Ferro-alloy metals

These metals are variously mined in many locations throughout the world but, taken collectively, the most important producing areas are the former U.S.S.R., South Africa and Canada followed by U.S.A. and China. All of these metals offer specific qualities and properties for the manufacture of a variety of special steels and alloys. **Nickel** and **chromium**, for example, are necessary for the production of high quality stainless steel whilst **vanadium** and **tungsten** help produce very hard steels.

Base metals

Generally mined as ores and compounds the free metal is released after smelting. **Antimony, copper, tin** and **zinc** are important in the making of alloys but each has individual uses related to its specific properties. Copper, **lead**, tin and zinc for example, are corrosion resistant under certain conditions, and the liquidity of **mercury** has obvious uses. Often found together or in combination with other metals, they are distributed widely over the earth's surface and there are many significant producing countries.

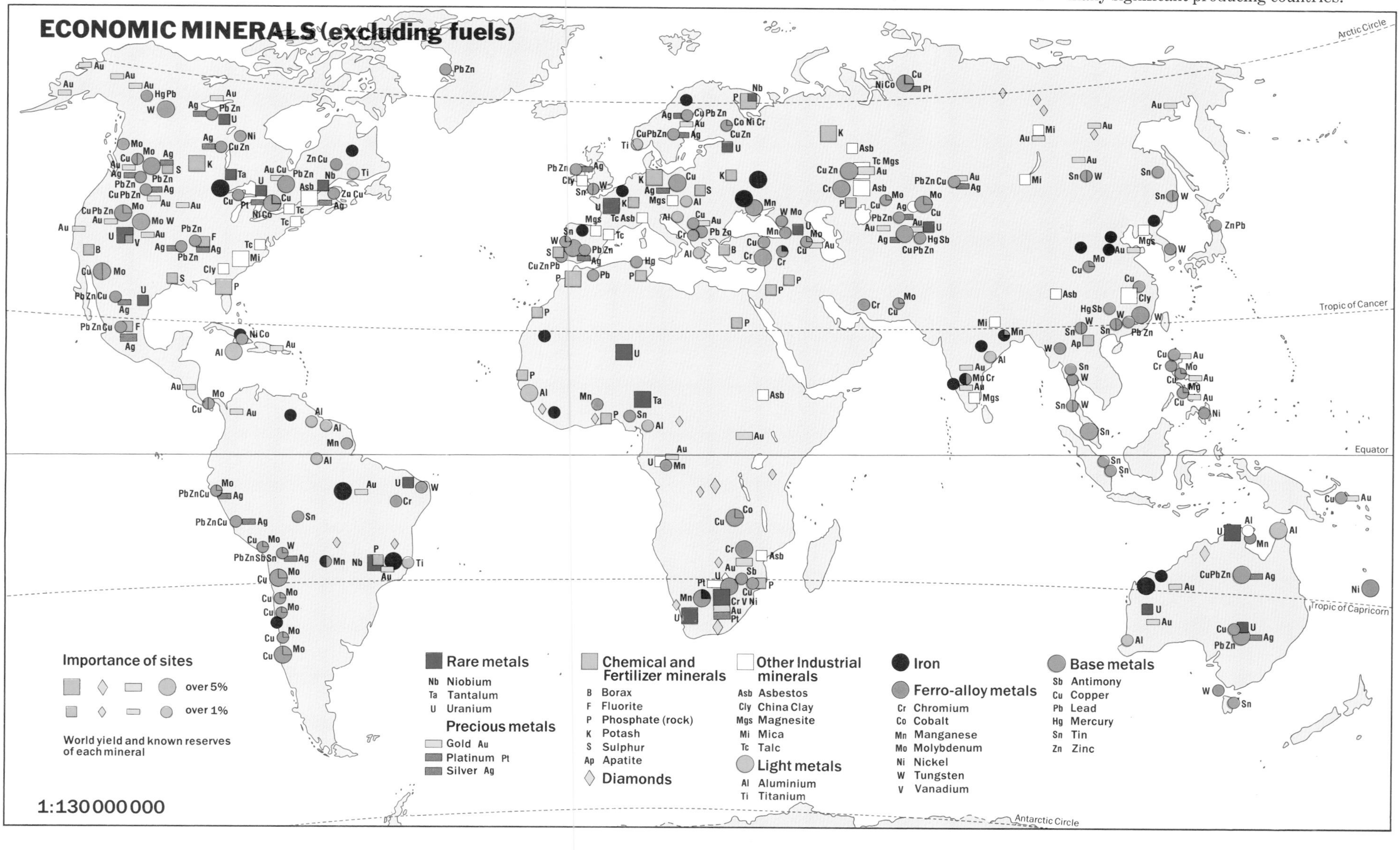

ENERGY

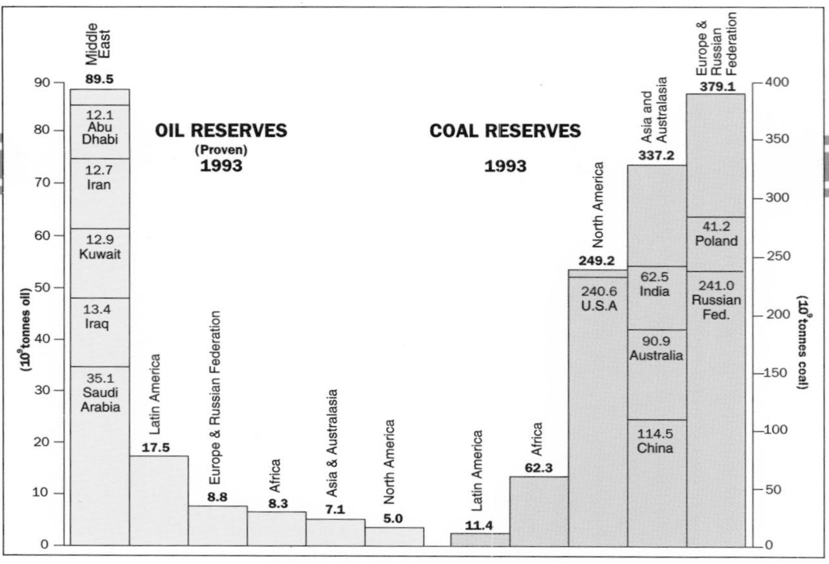

Taken together, the maps and diagrams though concerned with energy, give in graphic form, a summary of two centuries of economic growth.

Coal powered the industrial revolution and replaced wood as the primary source for industrial and domestic heat.

From the end of World War I another economic transformation began. Oil which had been used since remotest times to provide light and heat began to achieve major industrial importance. The last coal-fired ships vanished from the seas and with them the coal-bunkering stations disposed around the world. On land the internal-combustion engine replaced the horse; oil-fired electricity generation began to challenge coal-fired plants.

The end of World War II marked the start of unparalleled economic growth. Between 1950 and 1990 world energy demand increased four-fold, the steepest rise occurring between 1960 and 1970. In this period coal lost its pre-eminence as a source of energy. An oil industry developed to produce a variety of fuels and lubricants. It contained a large petro-chemical element.

Eighty per cent of this stupendous industrial expansion was based in North America (particularly the U.S.A.), Europe, the former U.S.S.R. and Japan. Oil and gas were the sources of the additional energy required for the expansion and the Middle East was the source of half the oil consumed.

The oil producing and exporting nations (OPEC) decided to raise the price of oil in 1973 thus bringing to an end the era of low-price energy. Revolution in Iran and the outbreak of war between Iraq and Iran caused a further escalation in price in 1979. Oil was then 17 times dearer than in 1972. Demand fell. The continued search for alternative sources was intensified. Rate of production fell below rate of discovery once more. Middle East share of world oil production fell from 50% to 27% by 1990. However, the Middle East still possesses over 50% of proved reserves.

Off-shore technology in exploration and exploitation have created a new oil technology. Operations in Alaska and Siberia have taxed the ingenuity of the oil-industry in combating severe climatic conditions.

Oil and gas reserves are constantly reviewed as new discoveries are made but the life of both is relatively short. Coal reserves are probably adequate for the next 250 years. In the coming decades the use of oil will increasingly be restricted to areas like transport where no alternative exists. Coal will once more be in the ascendancy. Coal gas which has been virtually replaced by natural gas may once more be used. Extraction of oil from coal may also be practised. Other sources of oil and gas are bituminous shales and tar sands.

Among the possible alternative energy sources are those in which the energy expended is renewed. Wind-generation and tidal power are two such examples. Although they may well be economically operated the installation costs are prodigious.

Nuclear energy alone promises to be capable of meeting future demands. Early promises of this form of generation providing abundant and cheap energy were not fulfilled. Fears that the supply of uranium would run out have been dispelled by enrichment techniques which yield 50 to 60 times the output. Strong opposition from those concerned for the environment has been the principle reason why the nuclear industry has been retarded. The accident at Three-Mile Island in the United States in 1979 had a profound effect on public opinion which was reinforced by the Chernobyl' disaster in the Ukraine in April 1986.

Still further options remain. All nuclear energy at the moment is based on nuclear fission. If nuclear fusion can be harnessed then an unlimited supply of energy could be provided by the oceans. The process would be the same as that by which the Sun creates its energy. Geothermal power is practical and feasible. Another source is the transformation of the Sun's light into electricity by photovoltaique techniques. Alternatively, solar energy can be converted into micro-waves by satellite. Such methods are for the next century, not this.

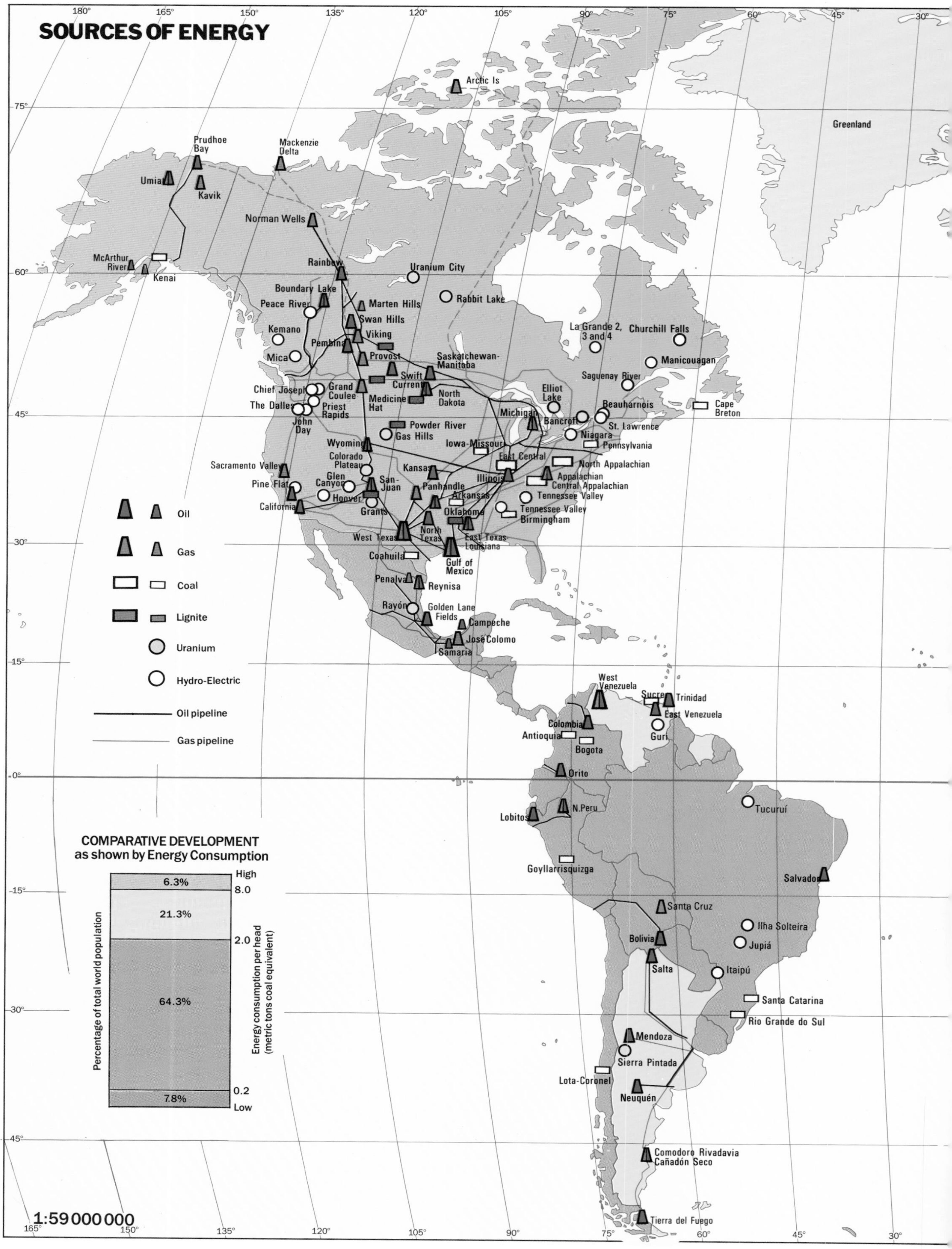

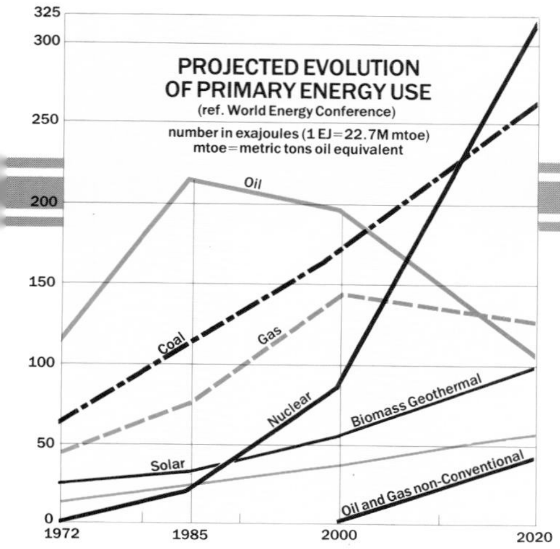

Far left The Middle East accounts for more than 50% of the world reserves of oil. Oil consumption in South East Asia has risen by more than 40% over the past decade which reflects the growing importance of this region as a market.

Below the rate of growth in energy demand for the years 1960-70 could not continue. World recession and the oil crisis of 1973 and 1979 reduced the rate of growth. Coal will again become an important source of future energy.

Near left Environmental considerations have been an obstacle to the building of nuclear power stations. Yet only coal and nuclear power have the potential for replacing oil and gas as reserves of each become depleted.

Map below Although the geographical distribution of coal reserves is more evenly spread than that of oil and gas; the USA, Russian Federation and China have by far the greatest reserves.

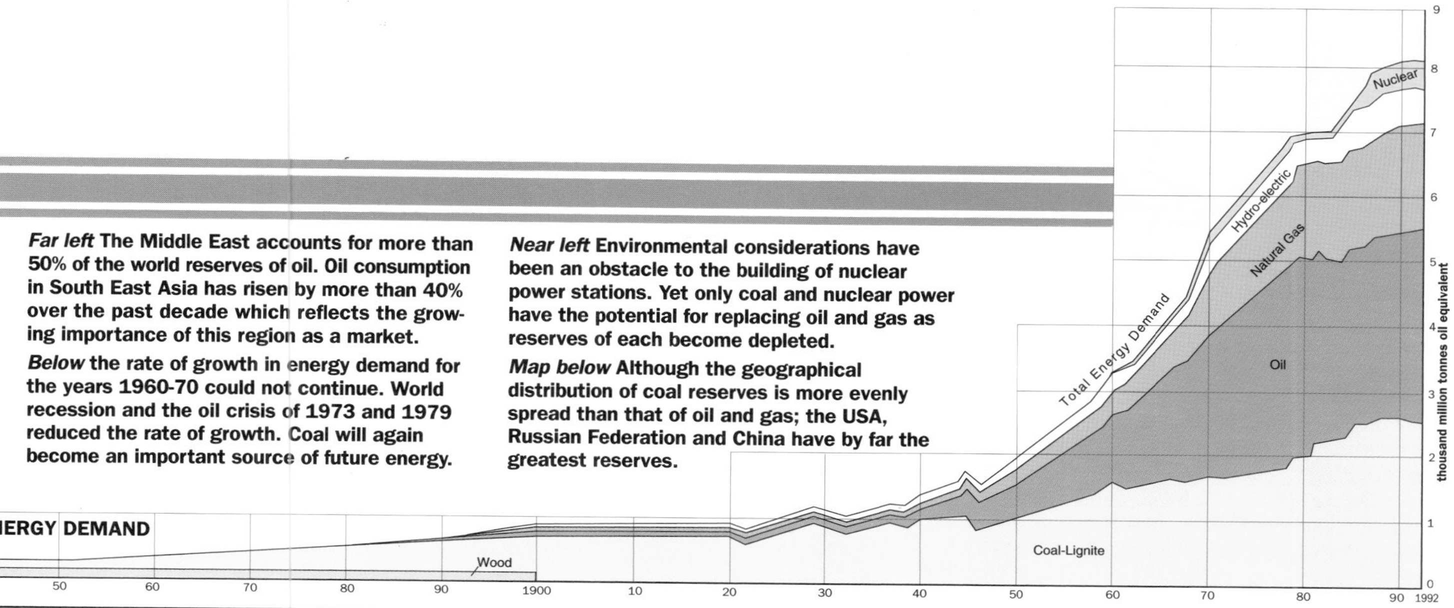

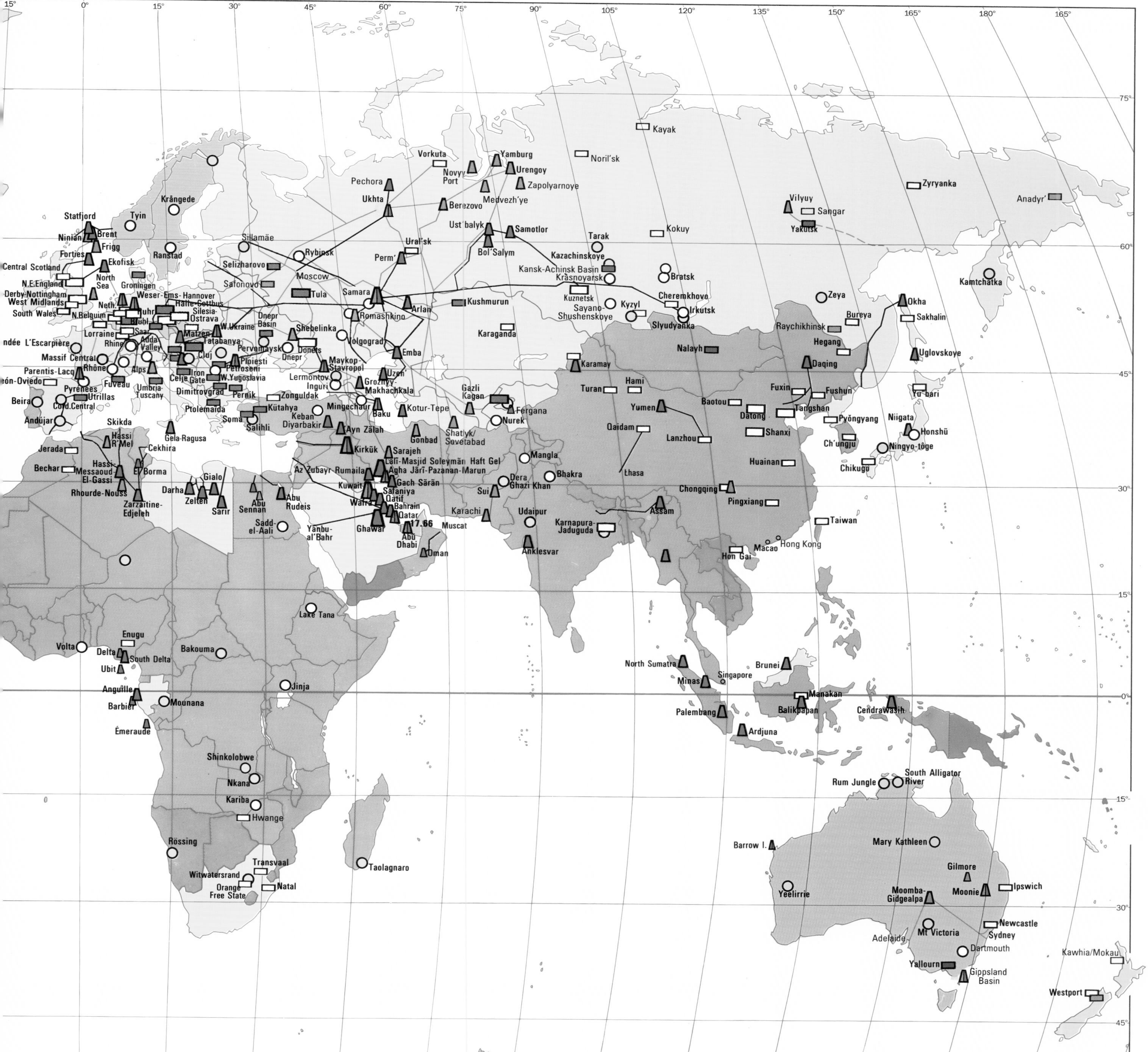

FOOD

With a world population which has doubled in the half-century between 1925 and 1975, it is a source of wonderment that more people are not starving. Especially since a further increase of 25% in the number of mouths to feed occurred in the decade up to 1985. It is still more remarkable when it is remembered that only about 11% of the Earth's land surface is under cultivation and that includes areas of non-food products like rubber. The credit for this achievement must be given to the development of artificial fertilizers; the conditioning of plants to alien climates; the development of high-yield seeds and new strains and generally improved agricultural technology. There is no great reserve of land ready to be brought into crop production. The outlook for the future is of a world in which the poorest areas have the highest population growth and the greatest difficulty in producing sufficient food. Matters of immediate concern are the current rate of soil erosion through the felling of trees, over-cropping, and the loss of fertility of world soils through unwise use of artificial fertilizers. Animal manure and vegetable waste are frequently used as fuel. Cash crops are planted where food crops are needed. Even if organic matter were returned to the soil and all the land were devoted to food crops, the required yields would not necessarily be achieved. In many of the poorest areas improved seeds and fertilizers would still be required. Food provision is not therefore, simply a matter of agricultural technology and distribution. Political and social factors are also involved.

From the land now under cultivation 98% of all food is produced. The other 2% comes from the sea. Unless, through some miracle of laboratory science, protein can be artificially created in sufficient quantities, the sea is the only major source available in the immediate future for supplementing the food potential of the land. Fish-farming, practised in East Asia for four thousand years, has been taken up in several parts of the world but it has been restricted to certain types of fish and shell-fish. The land, however, remains the main source of food and future yields depend on soil conservation and recovery; the development of new strains; conservation of food plants now under threat of extinction; elimination of pests and diseases; improved animal husbandry; investigating new sources of vegetable protein and synthetic food production.

Nutritional standards vary from nation to nation as do diets. North America, Western Europe, Australia and New Zealand are the great meat-eaters; East Asia consumes more fish and less meat but much of the world is dependent on cereal crops, beans and pulses. In overall calorie terms the best-fed nations take in on average, daily, almost three times the average of the worst-fed. Comparing the daily calorie intake of average low-calorie groups of countries with Canada, the United States, Argentina, Western Europe, Australia, and New Zealand there is a gap of more than 1300 calories. Reducing this disparity must depend on improved local food production provided at the same time the present high rate of population growth can be abated.

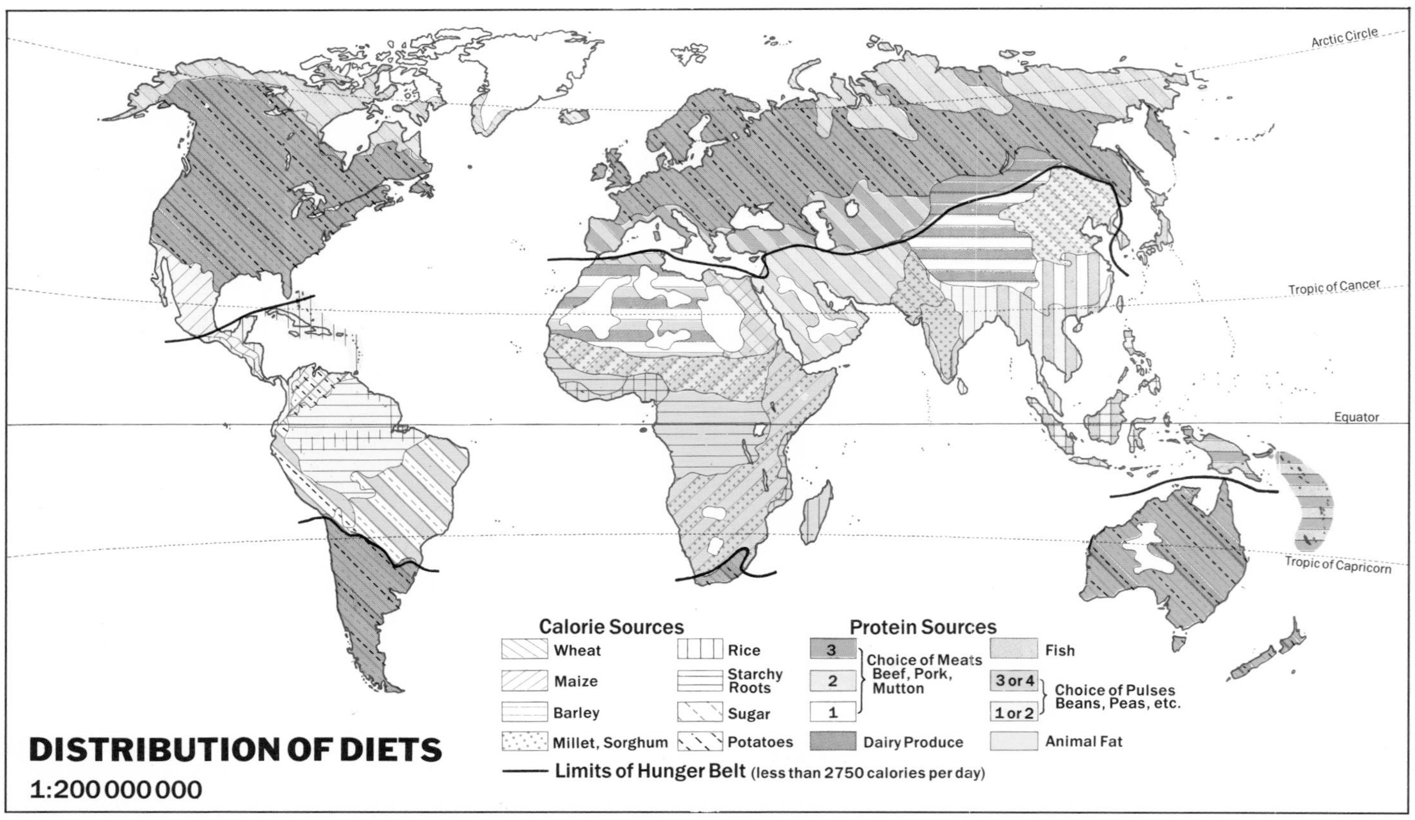

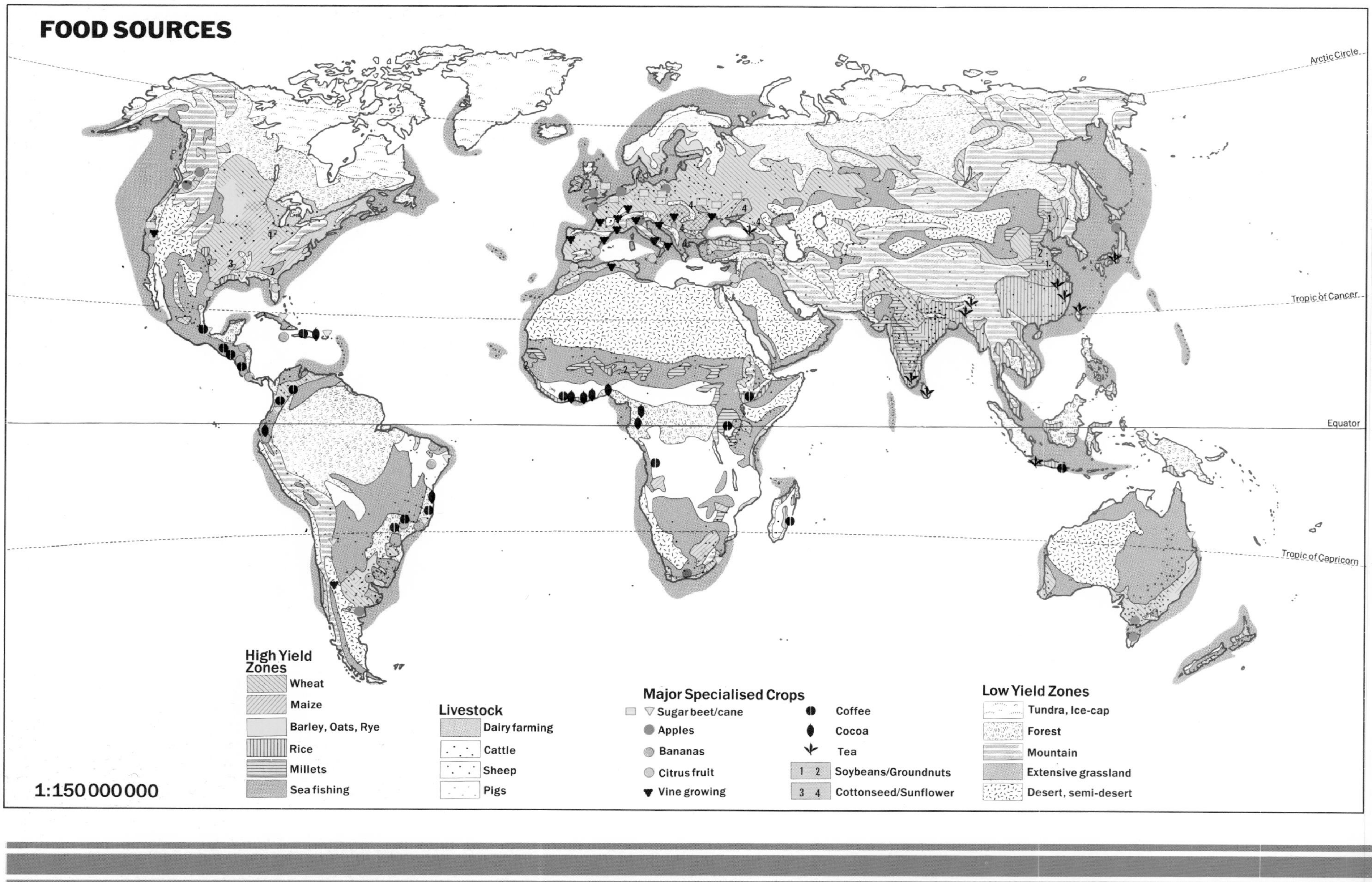

In the view of many people, proliferation of the human race is, in itself and its environmental consequences, a threat to the future of all life on this planet. The twentieth century promises to close with 3.6 times as many people as there were at the beginning. Fortunately, the high rate of annual increase (1.99%) of the period up to 1975 has been reduced, and consequently, there will be almost 1.5 billion fewer people at the end of the century than was at one time anticipated. Assuming that the present growth (1.7%) continues, there will be 6.2 billion people by AD2000.

For any country a growth rate in excess of 2% can spell disaster: 2% means a doubling of population in 35 years, 2.5% gives a doubling in 28 years and a growth of 3.5% doubles in only 20 years. Rate of growth is dependent on the number of live births, infant mortality and the death rate. The increase in numbers has been largely the result of reduction in infant mortality and the death rate in adults. People are living longer and a reduction in the number of live births may well be counterbalanced by prolonged life.

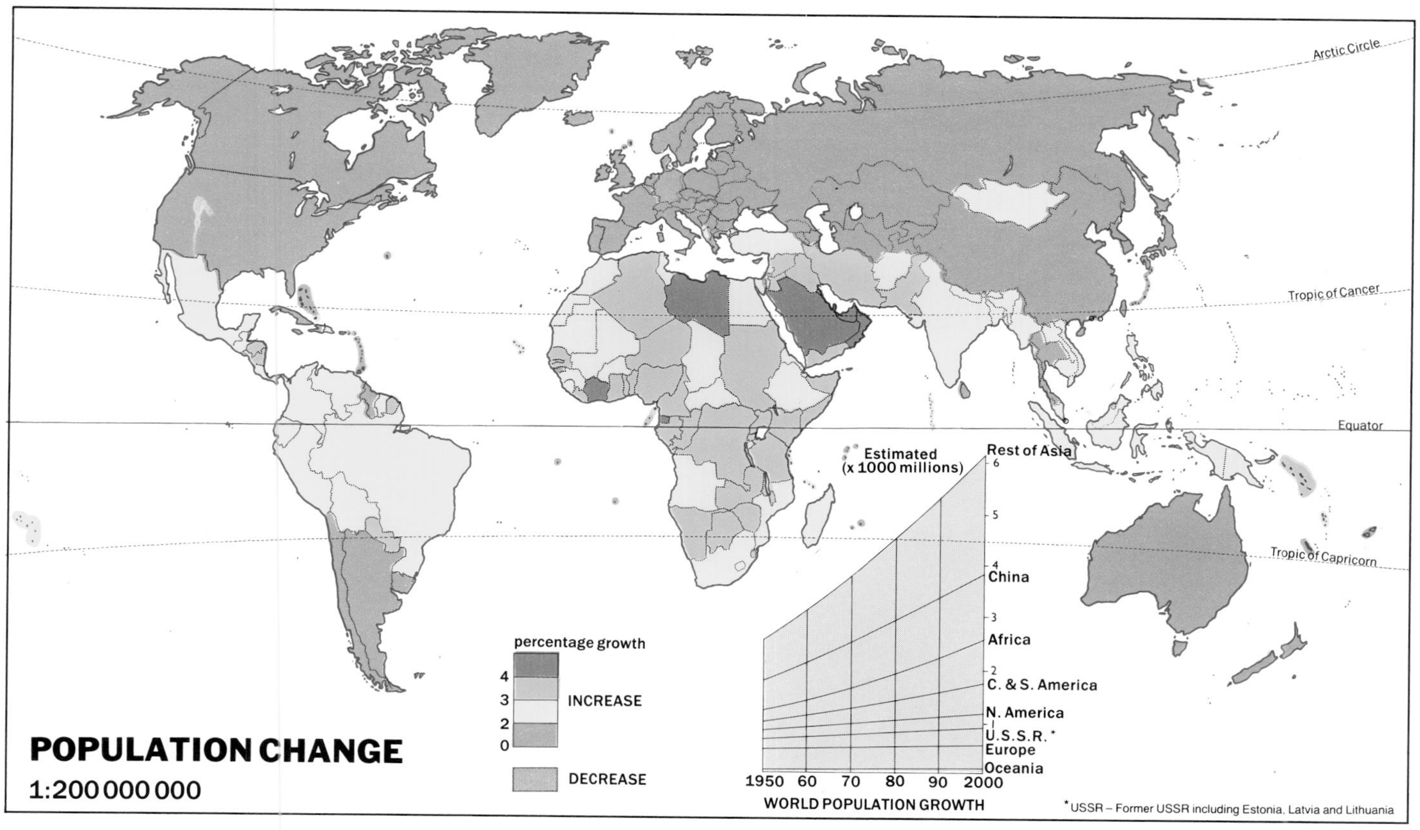

There is a kind of north-south divide, if one excludes Australia and New Zealand, with the technologically developed world approaching zero growth while the rest of the world continues to increase, in some areas at an alarming rate. In Africa, many countries have a growth rate of more than 3% in spite of shorter life expectancy and higher infant mortality (114 per 1000 compared with 16 for Europe and 12 for North America). The Middle Eastern countries although sparsely populated are now seeing increases of well over 4%.

Today, Albania alone in Europe has a rate of growth in excess of 1.5%. Bulgaria, Denmark, Ireland and Spain have achieved a growth rate of less than 0.2%, with Portugal and Hungary now experiencing negative growth. Japan and Russian Federation have achieved a rate below 1%.

China's policy of population control has brought the growth rate down to 1.5% not far removed from U.S.A. and Canada the highest of the northern nations. India, likewise has, by its birth control policy, slowed its rate of growth yet at present rates the combined populations of China and India will exceed 2.5 billion by the end of the century at which time the population of Asia will have equalled or surpassed the total world population of 1975.

In Central and South America a high average birth-rate by country is accompanied by a general lowering of the death-rate which for most of the area is about the same as that of Canada and U.S.A., Europe, Russian Federation, Japan, China, Australia and New Zealand all of which are either 10 or less per 1000 compared with 10 to 20 for Africa and Southern Asia (except Malaysia, Thailand and Philippines). Life expectancy is lowest in parts of Africa and Asia - below 40 years compared with over 70 for almost all the developed world.

Increased longevity, reduced infant mortality and a high birth rate will inevitably change the numbers of young and old who live as dependents. Providing for them is a great challenge for the next few generations.

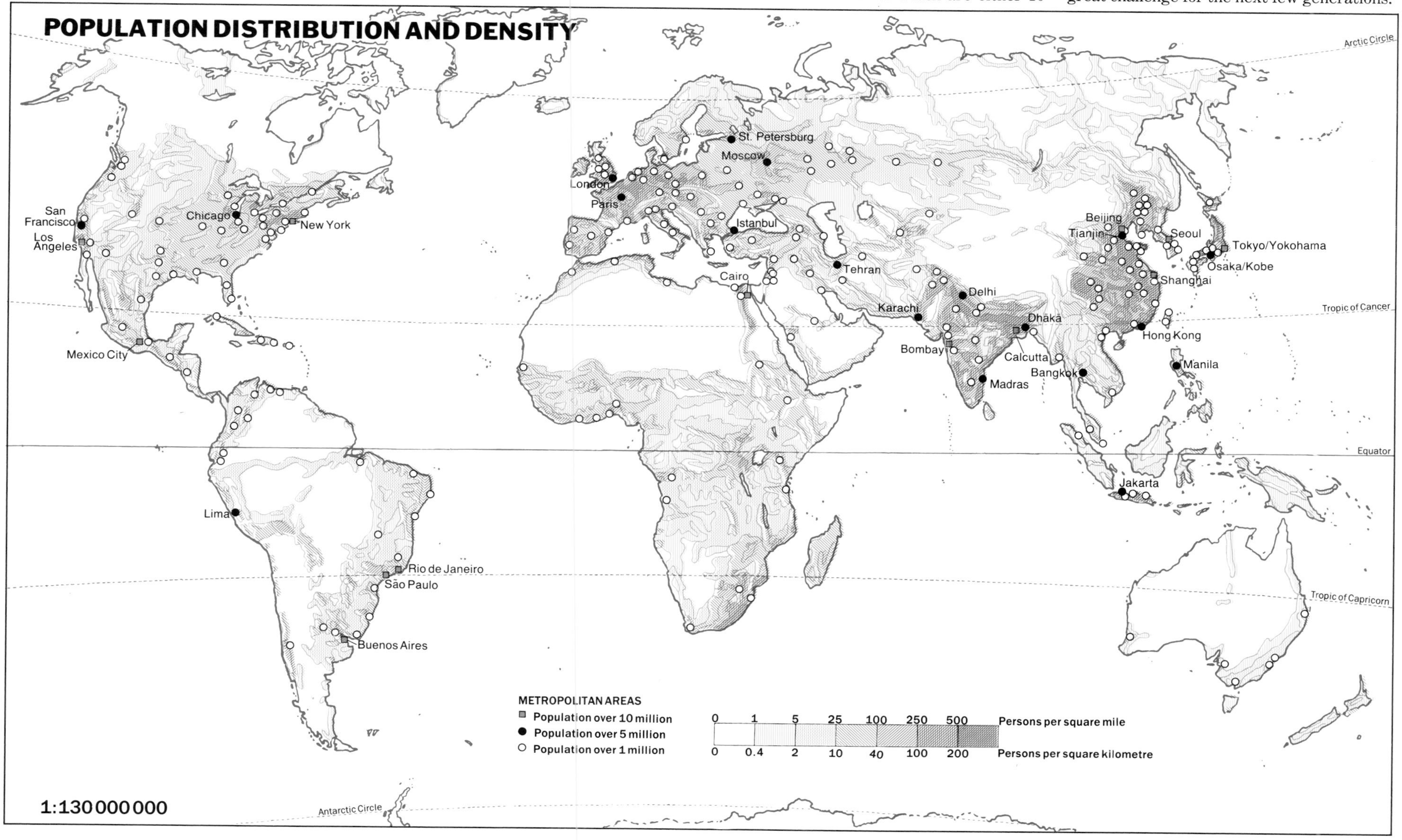

MAP PROJECTIONS

Map projection is the means by which the imaginary lines of latitude and longitude (the graticule) on a three-dimensional globe are transferred to two-dimensional paper. This transfer cannot be made without error of some kind. Most map projections are no more than a mathematical arrangement of the lines of latitude and longitude to try to achieve a specified result but their underlying principles are firmly based on the concept of perspective projection from a view-point, or light-source onto a plane, a cone or a cylinder tangent to (touching) the globe or secant to (cutting) it.

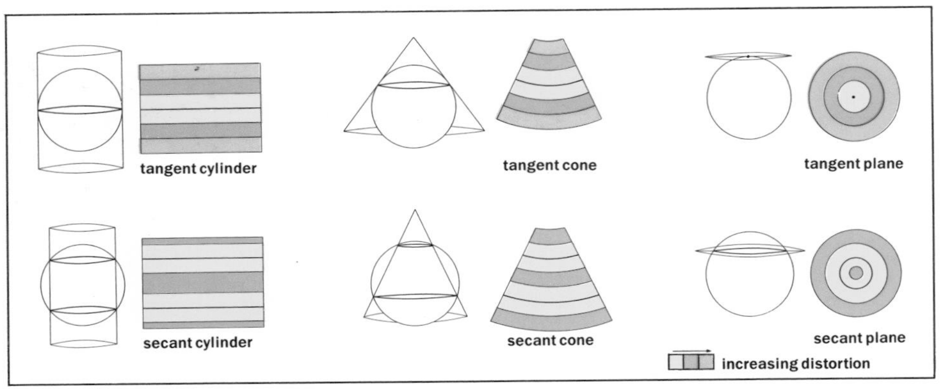

The cylinder and the cone can be opened to form a plane and, therefore, serve for projection of the graticule. Either may be tangent, with one standard parallel, or be secant, with two in order to reduce scale-errors overall. Projections may preserve shape (be *conformal*) or area (when they are called *equal-area*) or preserve distance from a central point (be *equidistant*). No two of those properties can exist in a single projection. A projection may dispense with all three in favour of another property e.g. minimum scale-error. It may just aim at good general shape for land, ocean or a region.

MAPS OF THE HEMISPHERE

Orthographic projection gives the view as seen from an infinite distance. It is most used for the visible face of the Moon. Other azimuthal projections are best explained by their polar case. In the *stereographic* the projection is from one pole on to a plane tangent at the other. Meridians and parallels plot as circles, arcs of circles or straight lines. In the *equidistant*, the straight, radiating meridians are true to scale. The parallels are equally-spaced concentric circles. Distances are correct along a meridian (but not in other directions). In *Lambert's Equal-Area*, the parallels are so spaced that the area enclosed by two meridians and any two parallels is in true proportion to the corresponding area on the globe.

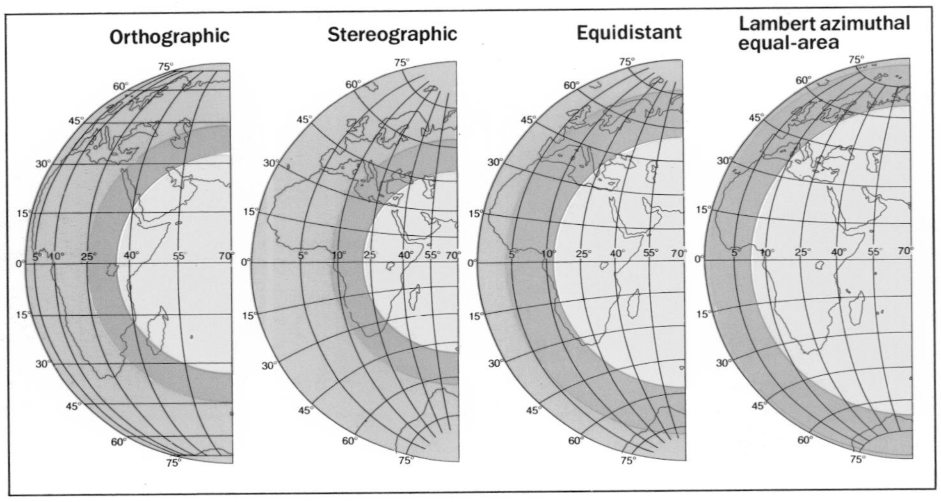

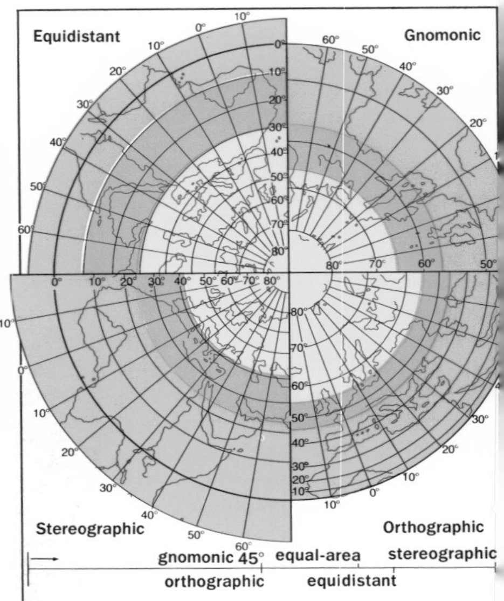

The bar scale shows the comparative lengths of half-meridians (90°) in four projections. To these, Lambert's Equal-Area has been added.

POLAR PROJECTIONS

The *gnomonic* is the projection (view) from the centre of the Earth. The limit plotted here is 45° from the tangent point (the pole). This gives a circle equal in radius to 90° (the equator) on the *orthographic* projection. The other two projections are plotted on this same equator. They are, therefore, not to scale but they show the way the parallels are equally spaced in the *equidistant*; are increasingly spaced in the *stereographic* and become very crowded near the equator in the *orthographic* projection.

REGIONAL MAPS

In the *conic with one standard parallel*, the parallel of tangency is made true to scale. Others are concentric circles drawn from the apex of the cone, usually at their correct spacing. Scale errors are reduced with *two standard parallels* of true length and spacing. Neither projection is conformal or equal-area but they can be made so. The conformal version of both has been widely used in topographic maps and aeronautical charts. *Bonne*, a modified conic with one standard parallel is equal-area. The central meridian and all parallels are correctly subdivided. The standard parallel is true to scale. Other parallels are arcs of circles concentric with it. Meridians are curved lines where they are straight in the other two.

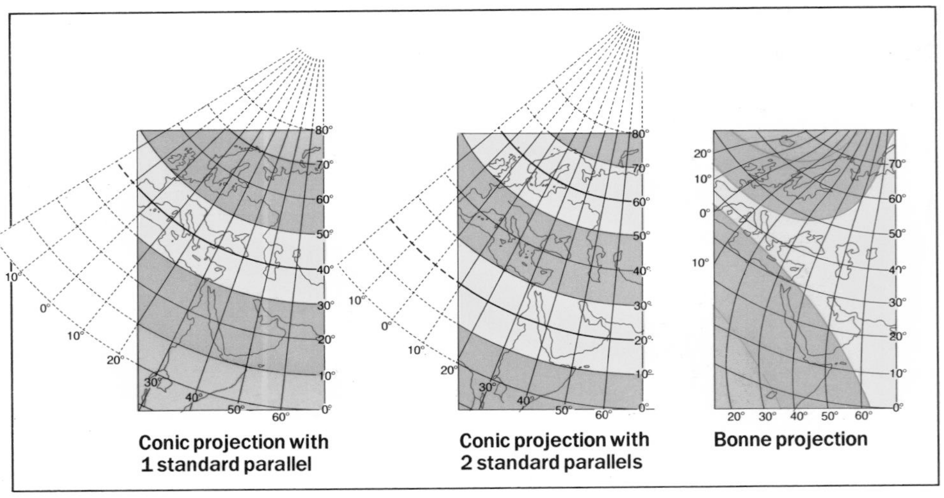

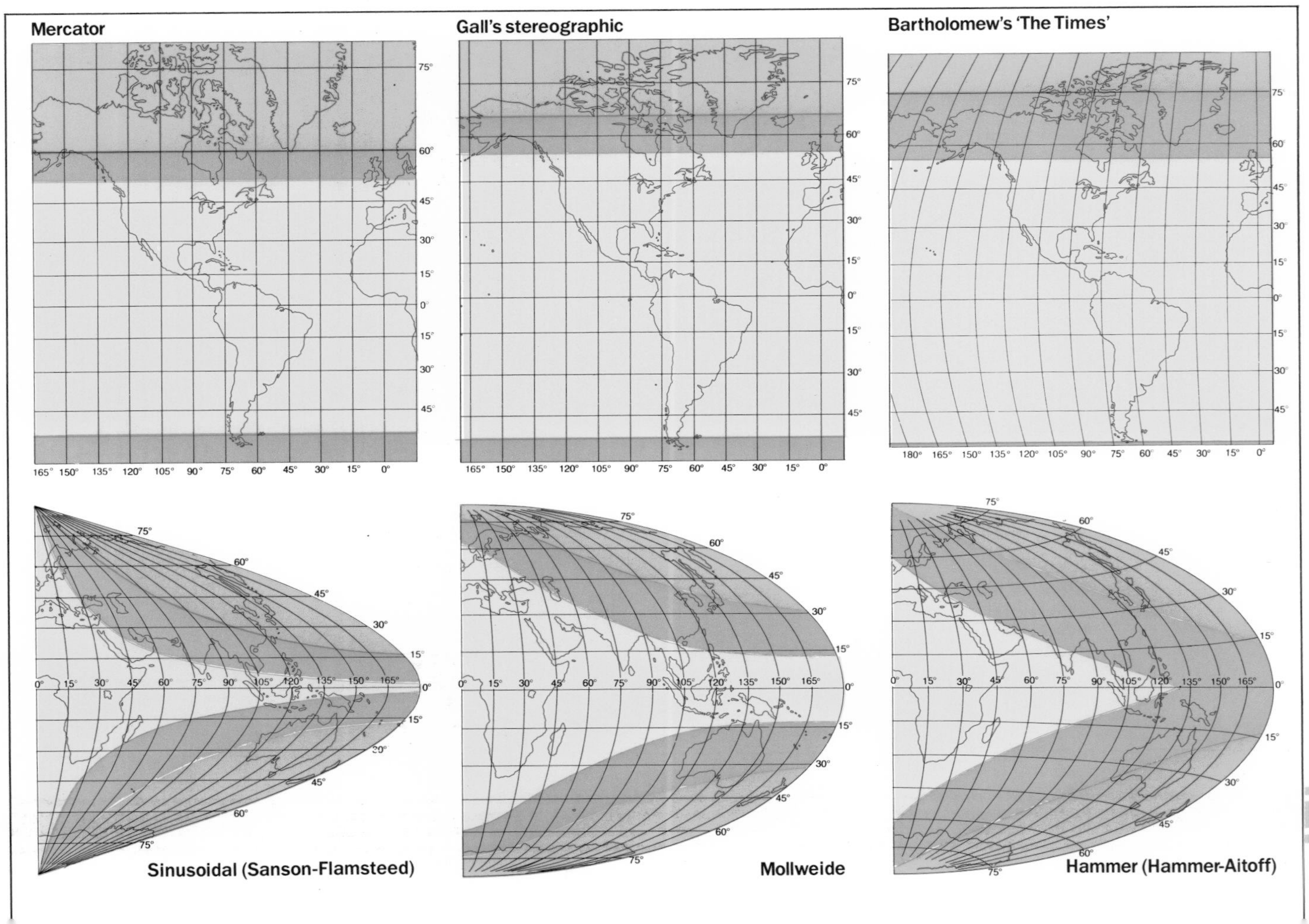

WORLD MAPS

Mercator is conformal (scale at any point i the same in all directions). Lines of constan bearing (loxodromes or rhumb lines) plot a straight lines, hence its importance to navigators. *Gall's* projection, a kind of stereographic is neither conformal nor equal-area. cylinder is secant at 45°N and S. Projectio is from a point on the equator diametricall opposite. *"The Times"* projection has Gall' parallels but the meridians are modifie from the sinusoidal and considerably les curved. In the *sinusoidal* projection, th central meridian is perpendicular to th equator and half its length. Parallels ar straight, equally spaced and equally subdivided. Meridians drawn through the subdivisions are sine curves. In *Mollweide*, th central meridian cuts the equator and a parallels at right angles. All are subdivide equally. Meridians 90° east and west o centre form a circle equal in area to hemisphere. From that equation the spacin of the parallels can be calculated. *Hammer'* projection, derived from Lambert's equa area, has the equator doubled in length. A three projections are equal-area. *Wink Tripel* is the mean of Hammer and Plat Carrée. It is not equal-area. *Plate Carrée* the simplest projection (not shown here) is system of squares based on the equator.

BOUNDARIES

- International
- International, Undefined or Alignment Uncertain
- Limits of Sovereignty across Water Areas
- Autonomous, Federal State
- Main Administrative
- Other Administrative
- Offshore Administrative
- Armistice, Cease-Fire Line
- Demilitarised Zone
- National Park
- Reserve, Reservation

COMMUNICATIONS

- Main Railways
- Other Railway
- Light Railway
- Projected Railways
- Railway Tunnels
- Road Tunnel
- Special Highway (Projected)
- Main Road (Projected)
- Other Road (Projected)
- Tracks
- Car Ferries
- Rail Ferries
- Navigable Canals (Locks)
- Projected or Disused Canal
- Drainage or Irrigation Canal
- Canal Tunnel
- Tunnel Aqueduct

LAKE TYPES

- Fresh-water
- Reservoir (Dam)
- Seasonal Fresh
- Seasonal Brackish
- Salt-lake, Lagoon
- Perennial Salt-lake
- Seasonal Salt-lake
- Saline Mud-flat
- Salt-flat

LANDSCAPE FEATURES

- Ice-field and Glaciers
- Ice-cap, Ice-sheet
- Lava-fields
- Lava-fields
- Sand Desert, Dunes
- Saline Marsh, Salt Desert
- Marsh, Swamp
- Swamp, Flood-area
- Mangrove Swamp
- Tidal Area
- Atoll

OTHER FEATURES

- River, Stream
- Seasonal Watercourses
- Seasonal Flood-plain
- Undefined Course of River
- Pass; Gorges
- Waterfalls, Rapids
- Dam, Barrage
- Escarpments
- Flood Dyke
- Limits of Ice-shelf
- Reefs
- Rocks
- Spot Depth (9650)
- Lighthouse
- Lightship; Beacon
- Waterhole, Well
- Active Volcano
- Summit, Peak
- Oil Wells
- Oil or Natural Gas Pipeline
- Mine
- Site of Battle
- Historic Site
- Historic Ruin
- Ancient Walls
- Mosque, Sheikh's Tomb
- Cathedral, Monastery, Church
- International or Main Airport
- Airport, Airfield

CITY MAPS

- State Boundary
- County, Department Boundary
- City Limits
- Borough, District Boundary
- Main Railways (Station)
- Other Railways (Bridge)
- Projected Railways
- Underground Railway (Station)
- Special Highway (Projected)
- Main Road
- Secondary Road
- Other Road, Street
- Track
- Road Tunnel
- Bridge; Flyover
- Seaway (Locks)
- Canals
- Drainage Canal
- Waterfalls, Rapids
- Historic Walls
- Airports
- Racecourses
- Stadium
- Cemetery; Churches
- Woodland, Park
- Built-up Area

STYLES OF LETTERING

TOGO	Country Name
ALBERTA	Major Administrative Divisions
KENT CHER	Other Administrative Divisions
PARIS Bern	National Capitals
Omsk, Denver, Kraków	Administrative Centres
GANDER Gatwick	Airports
MOAB	Historic Region
DECCAN, *SINAI*, *Mato Grosso*	Physical Regions
ATLAS *Nile*, *Mt Blanc* *Thames*	Physical Features
BASIN *Ridge*	Ocean Bottom Features
MASAI	Tribal Name

PRINCIPAL MAP ABBREVIATIONS

A.	1. Alp, Alpen, Alpi. 2. Alt
Abb^{e}	Abbaye
A.C.T.	Australian Capital Territory
Aig.	Aiguille
Akr.	Ákra, Akrotírion
Anch.	Anchorage
A.O.	Avtonomnaya Oblast'
App^{no}	Appennino
Aqued.	Aqueduct
Ar.	Arroyo
Arch.	Archipel, Archipelago, Archipiélago
Arr.	Arrecife
Ay.	Ayía, Áyioi, Áyion, Áyios
B.	1. Baai, Bahía, Baía, Baie, Baja, Bay, Bucht, Bukhta, Bukt. 2. Bad. 3. Ban. 4. Barazh, Barrage, Barragem. 5. Bayou. 6. Bir. 7. Bonto. 8. Bulu
B^{c}	Banc
B^{ca}	Boca
Bel.	Belgium, Belgian
Bg.	Berg
Bge	Barrage
Bgt.	Bight, Bugt
B^{i}	Bani, Beni
B^{j}	Burj
B^{k}	Bank
Bk.	Buku
B^{n}	Basin
Bol.	Bol'shoy, -oye, -aya, -iye
Bos.	Bosanski
Br.	1. Branch. 2. Bredning. 3. Bridge, Brücke. 4. Britain, British. 5. Burun
Bt.	Bukit
Bü.	Büyük
Bukh.	Bukhta
C.	1. Çabo, Cap, Cape. 2. Česká, -é, -ý. 3. Col.
Ç	Çay
Cab^{o}	Cabeço
Cach.	Cachoeira, -o
Can.	1. Canal. 2. Canale. 3. Canavese. 4. Cañon, Canyon
Cas.	Castle
Cat.	1. Cataract. 2. Catena
Cath.	Cathedral
C^{d}	Ciudad
Červ.	Červená, -é
Ch.	1. Chapel, Chapelle, Church. 2. Chaung. 3. Chott.
Chan.	Channel
Ch^{au}	Château
Ch^{e}	Chaine
Ch^{lle}	Chapelle
C^{ma}	Cima
C^{no}	Corno
C^{o}	Cerro
$Const^{n}$	Construction
Cord.	Cordillera
Cr.	Creek
Cuch.	Cuchilla
Cuc^{ru}	Cuccuru
Cy.	City
Czo.	Cozzo
D.	1. Da, Dag, Dagh, Dağı, Dağları. 2. Danau. 3. Darreh. 4. Daryācheh
-d.	-dake
D.C.	District of Columbia
Den.	Denmark
Dists.	Districts
Div.	Division
Dj.	Djebel
Dns.	Downs
Dz.	Dzong
E.	East
Eil.	Eiland, Eilanden
Escarp.	Escarpment
Est.	Estación
E^{tg}	Étang
F.	Firth
F.D.	Federal District
Fj.	1. Fjell. 2. Fjord, Fjörður
F^{k}	Fork
Fl.	Fleuve
Fr.	France, French
Ft.	Fort
F^{te}	Fonte
Fy.	Ferry
-g	-gawa
G.	1. Gebel. 2. Ghedir. 3. Göl, Gölü, Gōl. 4. Golfe, Golfo, Gulf. 5. Gompa. 6. Gora, Gory. 7. Guba, 8. Gunung
G^{a}	Gara
G^{d}	Grand
G^{de}	Grande
Geb.	Gebergte, Gebirge
$Geog^{l}$	Geographical
Gez.	Gezira
Ghub.	Ghubba
Gl.	1. Gamle, Gammel. 2.Glacier
Gp.	Group
Gr.	1. Graben. 2. Gross, -e, Grande
G^{r}	Gasr
Gr^{tes}	Grottes
Gt.	Great, Groot, -e
H.	1. Hawr. 2. Hill. 3. Hoch. 4. Hora, Hory
Halv.	Halvøy
Har.	Harbour
H^{d}	Head
H.E.P.	Hydro-Electric Power
H^{g}	Hegység
H^{gts}	Heights
H^{i}	Hasi, Hasy
Hist.	Historic
H^{n}	Horn
Hosp.	1. Hospice, Hospiz. 2. Hospital
Ht.	Haut
Hte.	Haute
H^{ter}	Hinter
H^{y}	Highway
I.	Île, Ilha, Insel, Isla, Island, Isle, Isola, Isole
IJ.	IJssel
im.	imeni
In.	1. Inder, Indre, Inner, Inre. 2. Inlet
IND.	India
Inf.	Inferior, -e, Inférieure
Int.	International
I^{s}	Îles, Ilhas, Islands, Islas, Isles
ISR.	Israel
Isth.	Isthmus
J.	1. Jabal, Jebel, Jibāl. 2. Järvi, Jaure, Jazira, Jezero, Jezioro. 3. Jökull
Jap.	Japan, Japanese
Jct.	Junction
K.	1. Kaap, Kap, Kapp. 2. Kaikyō. 3. Kato. 4. Kerang, Kering. 5. Kiang. 6. Kirke. 7. Ko. 8. Koh, Kūh, Kūhha. 9. Kólpos. 10. Kopf. 11. Kuala. 12. Kyst
Kan.	Kanal, Kanaal
Kap.	Kapelle
Kep.	Kepulauan
Kg.	Kampong, Kompong, Kong
Kh.	1. Khawr. 2. Khirbet, Khīābān, -e. 3. Khowr
Khr.	Khrebet
Kl.	1. Kechil. 2. Klein, -e
Kör.	Körfez, -i
Kr.	Kangar
Kü.	Küçük
L.	1. Lac, Lago, Lagôa, Lake, Liman, Limni, Liqen, Loch, Lough. 2. Lam
Lag.	Lagoon, Laguna, -e
L^{d}	Land
Ldg.	Landing
Lit.	Little
Ll.	Lille
M.	1. Mae, Me. 2. Meer. 3. Muang. 4. Muntil. 5. Muong. 6. Mys. 7. Monte
m	metre/s
Mal.	Malyy, -aya, -oye
Mem.	Memorial
Mex.	Mexico, Mexican
M^{f}	Massif
M^{gna}	Montagna
M^{gne}	Montagne
Mkt.	Markt
Mon.	Monasterio, Monastery
Mont.	Monument
Mt.	Mont, Mount, Mountain
Mte.	Monte
M^{tes}	Montes
Mti.	Monti, Munţi
Mts.	Monts, Mountains
N.	1. Nam. 2. Neu, Ny. 3. Nevado, Nudo. 4. Noord, Nord, Nörre, Nørre, North. 5. Nos
N^{a}	Nuestra
Nat.	National
N.D.	Notre Dame
N^{dr}	Neder, Nieder
N.E.	North East
Neth.	Netherlands
Nizh.	Nizhne, -neye, -niy, -nyaya
Nizm.	Nizmennost
N.O.	Noord Oost, Nord Ost
Nor.	Norway, Norwegian
N^{os}	Nudos
Nov.	Novyy, -aya, -iye, -oye
N^{r}	Nether
N.W.	North West
N.Z.	New Zealand
O.	1. Old. 2. Oost, Ost. 3. Ostrov
Ö.	1. Östre. 2. Öy
Ø.	1. Østre. 2. Øy
Ob.	Ober
O^{de}	Oude
O^{et}	Oguilet
Ogl.	Oglat
O.L.V.	Onze Lieve Vrouw
Or.	Óri, Óros
Orm.	Ormos
Os(t)	Ostrova
Ot.	Olet
Öv.	Över, Övre
O^{va}	Ostrov, -a
Oz.	Ozero
P.	1. Pass. 2. Pic, Pico, Piz. 3. Pulau. 4. Pou
Pal.	Palace, Palacio, Palais
Pass.	Passage
Peg.	Pegunungan
Pen.	Peninsula, Penisola
Per.	Pereval
Ph.	Phum
Phn.	Phnom
P^{gio}	Poggio
Pk.	1. Park. 2. Peak, Pik
Pkwy.	Parkway
Pl.	1. Planina, Planinski. 2. Plei
P^{la}	Playa
Plat.	Plateau
Plosk.	Ploskogor'ye
P^{no}	Pantano
P^{nte}	Pointe
Pol.	Poluostrov
Por.	Porog
Port.	Portugal, Portuguese
P^{ov}	Poluostrov
P.P.	Pulau-pulau
Pr.	1. Proliv. 2. Przylądek. 3. Prince
$Prom^{y}$	Promontory
Prop.	Proposed
PROT.	Protectorate
PROV.	Provincial
Psa	Presa
P^{so}	Passo
Pt.	1. Point. 2. Pont
P^{t}	1. Petit. 2. Point. 3. Pont
P^{ta}	1. Ponta, Punta. 2. Puerta
P^{te}	1. Pointe. 2. Ponte, Puente
P^{to}	1. Porto, Puerto. 2. Ponto, Punto
P^{zo}	Pizzo
Q.	Qala, Qara, Qarn
R.	1. Reka, Río, River, Rivière, Rud, Rzeka. 2. Ria
Ra.	Range
Rap.	Rapids
R^{ca}	Rocca
R^{d}	Road
REC.	Recreation
Res.	Reservoir
Resp.	Respublika
R^{f}	Reef
R^{ge}	Ridge
Rib^{a}	Ribeira
Rly.	Railway
Rom.	Romania, Romanian
R^{te}	Route
Rus. Fed.	Russian Federation
S.	1. Salar, Salina. 2. San. 3. Saw. 4. See. 5. Seto. 6. Sjö. 7. Sör, South, Syd. 8. Sung. 9. sur. 10. Sebjet
S^{a}	Serra, Sierra
Sab.	Sabkhat
Sc.	Scoglio
S^{d}	Sound, Sund
S.E.	South East
Seb.	Sebjet, Sebkhat, Sebkra
Sev.	Sever, -naya, -nyy
S^{gno}	Stagno
Sh.	1. Sh'aīb. 2. Sharif. 3. Shatt. 4. Shima. 5. Shankou
S^{i}	Sidi
S^{knoll}	Seaknoll
S^{kt}	Sankt
Sl.	Slieve
S^{mt}	Seamount
Snr^{a}	Senhora
Snr^{o}	Senhoro
Sp.	1. Spain, Spanish. 2. Spitze
S^{pk}	Seapeak
Spr.	Spring
S^{r}	Sönder, Sønder
Sr.	Sredniy, -nyaya
S^{t}	Saint, Sint, Staryy
St.	1. State. 2. Stor, Store. 3. Stung
Sta	Santa
Sta.	Station
Stby.	Staby, Statsjonsby
S^{te}	Sainte
Ste.	Store
Sten.	Stenón, Stenós
S^{to}	Santo
Str.	Strait
S^{tu}	Stuvina
Sv.	Svaty, Sveti
S.W.	South West
T.	1. Tal. 2. Tal, Tall, Tell. 3. Tepe, Tepesi
Talsp.	Talsperre
Tel.	Teluk
Terr.	Terrace
$Terr^{y}$	Territory
Tg.	Tanjung
Thwy.	Throughway, Thruway
Tk.	Teluk
T^{mt}	Tablemount
T^{o}	Tando
Tpk.	Turnpike
Tr.	Trench, Trough
T^{re}	Torre
Tun.	Tunnel
U	Uad
U.A.E.	United Arab Emirates
Ug.	Udjung
U.K.	United Kingdom
Unt.	Unter
Up^{r}	Upper
U.S.A.	United States of America
V.	1. Val, Valle. 2. Väster, Vest, Vester. 3. Vatn. 4. Ville. 5. Vorder. 6. Volcán
V^{a}	Vila
Vdkhr.	Vodokhranilishche
Vel.	Velikiy, -aya, -iye
Ven.	Venezuela, Venezuelan
Verkh.	Verkhniy, -neye, -ne, -nyaya
Vn.	Volcán
Vol.	Volcán, Volcano, Vulkán
Vost.	Vostochnyy
Vozv.	Vozvyshennost'
W.	1. Wadi. 2. Wald. 3. Wan. 4. Water. 5. Well. 6. West
W^{r}	Wester
-y	-yama
Y^{t}	Ytre, Ytter, Ytri
Yuzh.	Yuzhnaya, -no, -nyy
Z.	Zaliv
Zal.	Zaliv
Zap.	Zapadnyy, -aya, -o, -oye
Zem.	Zemlya

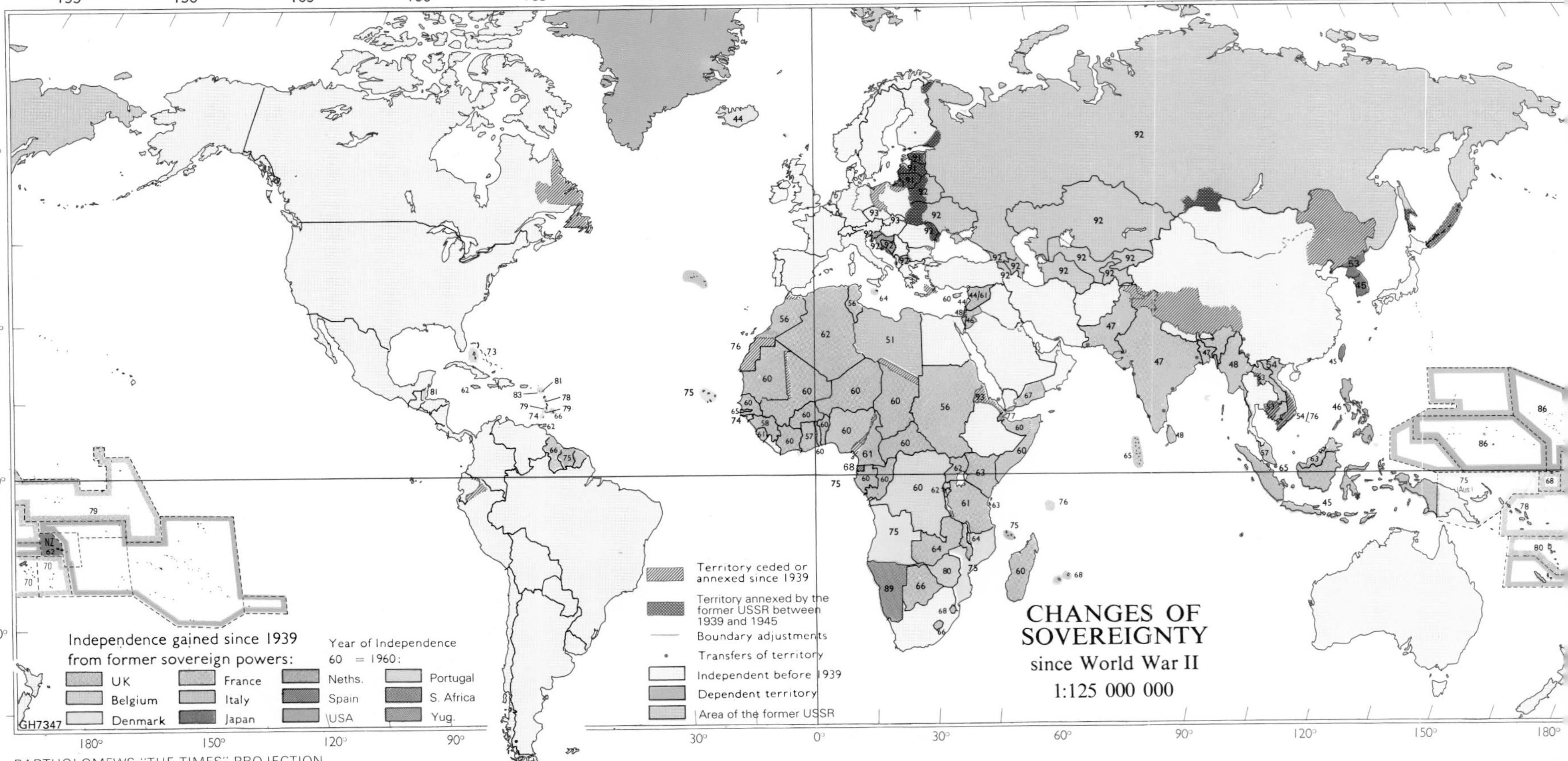

CHANGES OF SOVEREIGNTY

since World War II

1:125 000 000

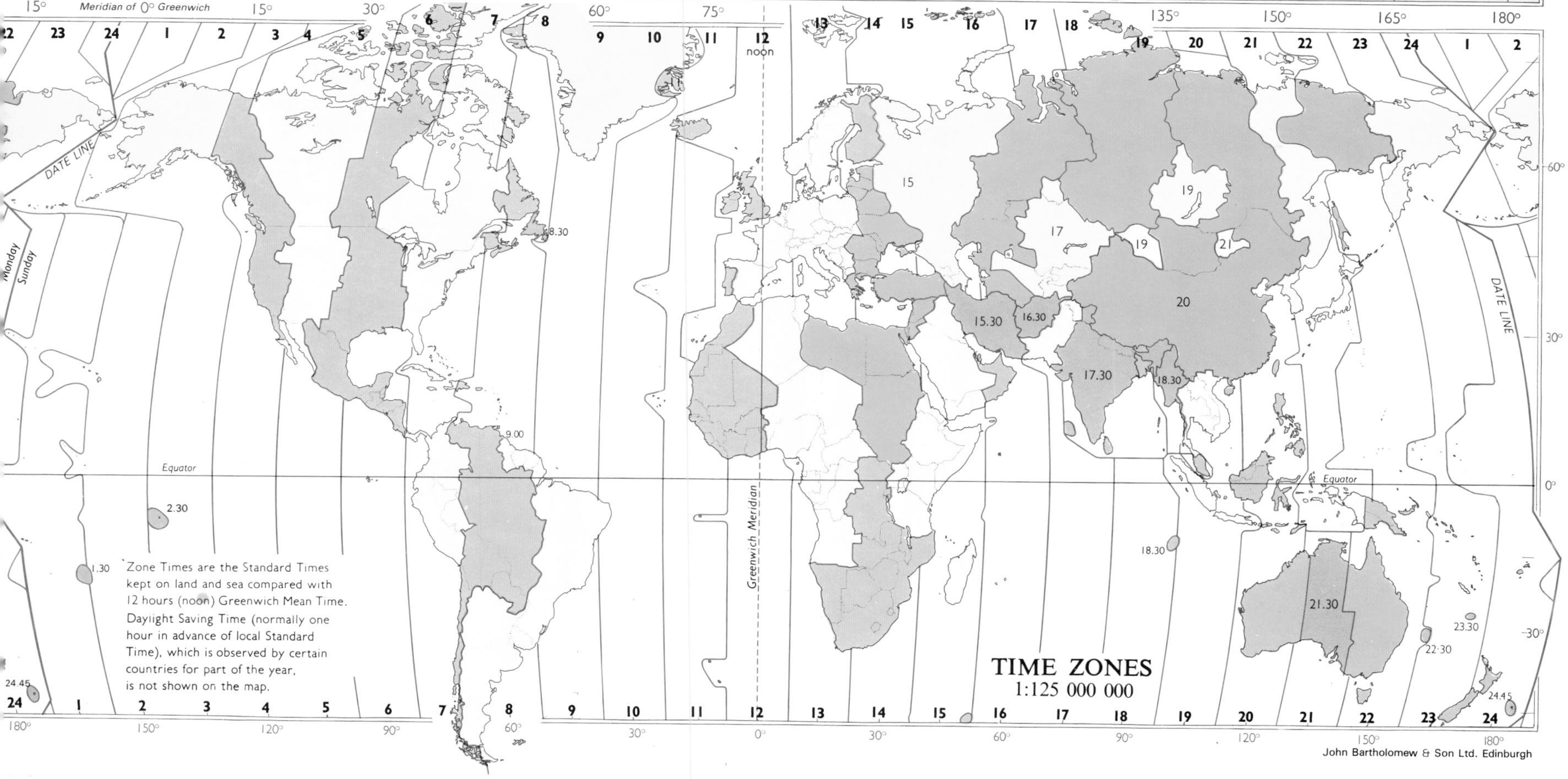

John Bartholomew & Son Ltd. Edinburgh

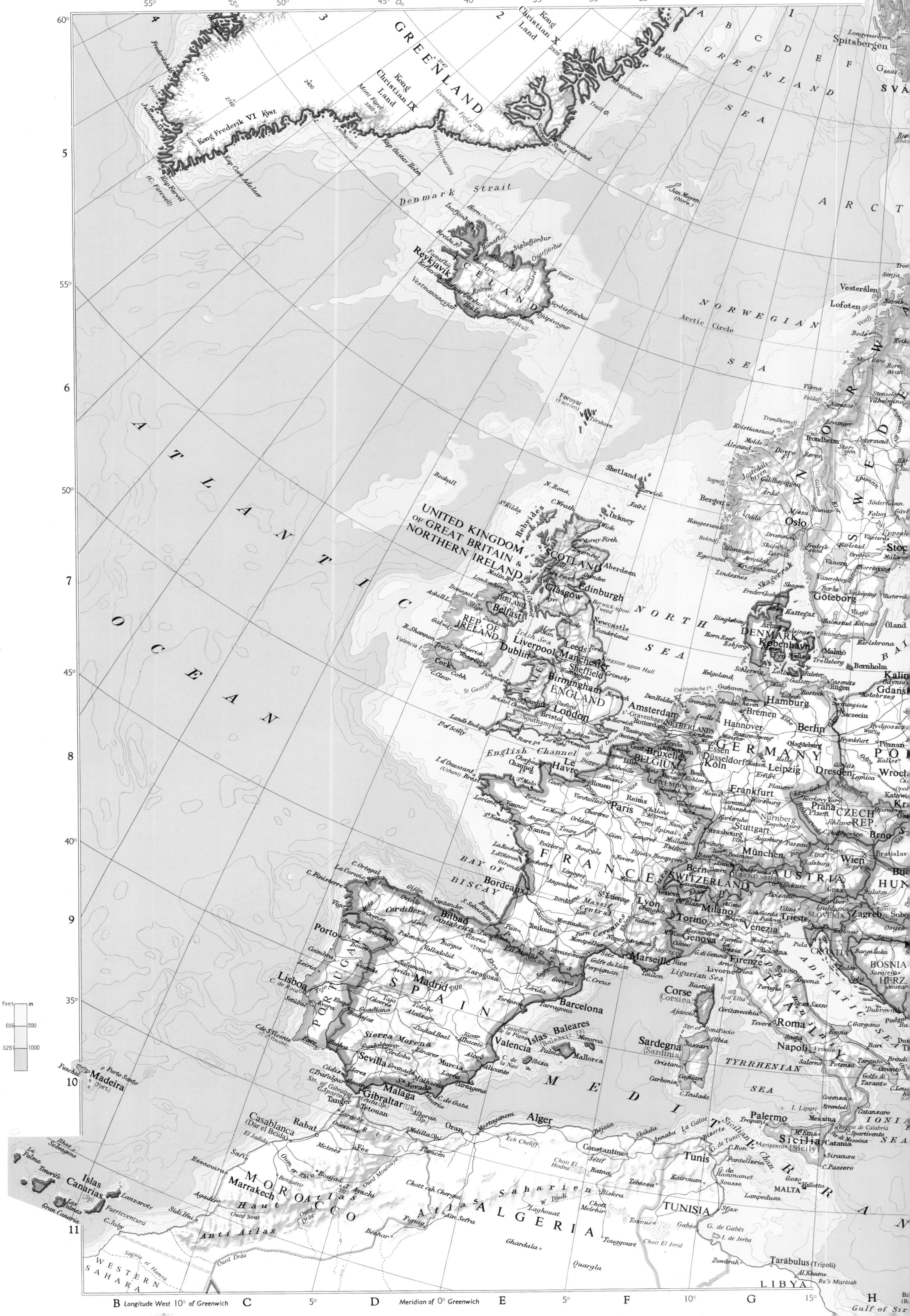
GREENLAND
Kong Christian X Land
Kong Christian IX Land
Kong Frederik VI Kyst
GREENLAND SEA
Denmark Strait
ICELAND
Reykjavík
Jan Mayen (Norw.)
NORWEGIAN SEA
Arctic Circle
Spitsbergen
Føroyar (Faeroes)
Tórshavn
Shetland
Rockall
ATLANTIC OCEAN
UNITED KINGDOM OF GREAT BRITAIN & NORTHERN IRELAND
SCOTLAND
Aberdeen
Edinburgh
Glasgow
Belfast
REP. OF IRELAND
Dublin
Liverpool
Manchester
Leeds
Newcastle
Sheffield
Birmingham
ENGLAND
WALES
London
Bristol
Southampton
NORTH SEA
English Channel
Oslo
Göteborg
DENMARK
København
Amsterdam
NETHERLANDS
Bruxelles
BELGIUM
GERMANY
Hamburg
Bremen
Hannover
Berlin
Köln
Düsseldorf
Leipzig
Dresden
Frankfurt
München
Praha
CZECH REP.
Wien
AUSTRIA
SWITZERLAND
Paris
Le Havre
Rouen
Nantes
FRANCE
Bordeaux
Lyon
Marseille
BAY OF BISCAY
SPAIN
Madrid
Barcelona
Valencia
Bilbao
Sevilla
Málaga
Gibraltar (UK)
PORTUGAL
Lisboa
Porto
Islas Baleares
Mallorca
Corse (Corsica)
Sardegna (Sardinia)
Milano
Torino
Genova
Venezia
Firenze
Roma
Napoli
ITALY
Palermo
Sicilia (Sicily)
TYRRHENIAN SEA
ADRIATIC SEA
Zagreb
CROATIA
BOSNIA HERZ.
MALTA
Tunis
TUNISIA
Alger
ALGERIA
MOROCCO
Rabat
Casablanca (Dar el Beida)
Marrakech
Tanger
Madeira
Islas Canarias (Sp)
WESTERN SAHARA
LIBYA
Tarābulus (Tripoli)
MEDITERRANEAN
Longitude West 10° of Greenwich
Meridian of 0° Greenwich

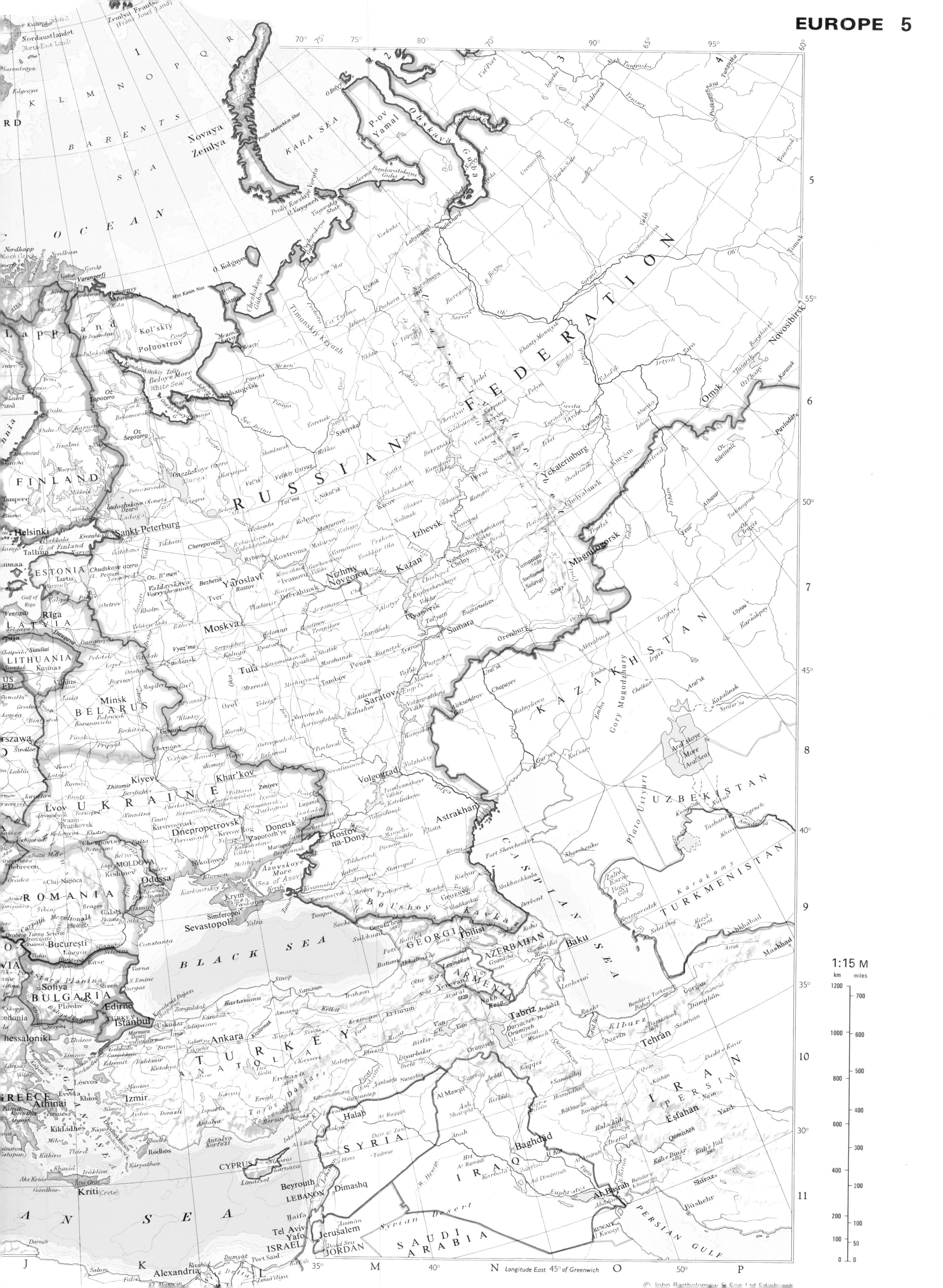
RUSSIAN FEDERATION
KAZAKHSTAN
UZBEKISTAN
TURKMENISTAN
IRAN
(PERSIA)
IRAQ
SYRIA
TURKEY
SAUDI ARABIA
JORDAN
ISRAEL
LEBANON
CYPRUS
GEORGIA
ARMENIA
AZERBAIJAN
UKRAINE
BELARUS
MOLDOVA
ROMANIA
BULGARIA
GREECE
FINLAND
ESTONIA
LATVIA
LITHUANIA
BARENTS SEA
KARA SEA
WHITE SEA
BLACK SEA
CASPIAN SEA
PERSIAN GULF
Aral'skoye More
Aral Sea
Azovskoye More
(Sea of Azov)
Novaya Zemlya
Moskva
Sankt-Peterburg
Helsinki
Tallinn
Riga
Minsk
Kiyev
Khar'kov
Odessa
Dnepropetrovsk
Donetsk
Rostov na-Donu
Volgograd
Astrakhan
Samara
Kazan
Nizhniy Novgorod
Yaroslavl'
Izhevsk
Perm'
Yekaterinburg
Chelyabinsk
Magnitogorsk
Orenburg
Saratov
Ufa
Omsk
Novosibirsk
Tbilisi
Baku
Ankara
Istanbul
Izmir
Tehran
Tabriz
Baghdad
Dimashq
Halab
Beyrouth
Jerusalem
Al Basrah
Al Kuwayt
Esfahan
Sofiya
Bucureşti
Chişinău
Athinai
Alexandria
Sevastopol
Simferopol
Arkhangel'sk
Murmansk
Kol'skiy Poluostrov
Bol'shoy Kavkaz
Elburz
Mashhad
1:15 M
km
miles
Longitude East 45° of Greenwich
© John Bartholomew & Son Ltd Edinburgh

NORWAY
Bergen
SHETLAND
ORKNEY
FØROYAR (FAEROES) (To Denmark)
SCOTLAND
HIGHLAND
GRAMPIAN
WESTERN ISLES
Aberdeen
Inverness
Dundee
Lewis
Harris
Skye
Rum
Mull
Tiree
Coll
St Kilda
North Rona
Sula Sgeir
Sule Skerry
Stack Skerry
Fair Isle
Foula
Unst
Yell
Hoy
Pentland Firth
Moray Firth
Little Minch
North Minch
Outer Hebrides
Great Fisher Bank
Long Forties
Buchan Deep
Little Halibut Bank
Bergen or Old Viking Bank
Viking Bank
Devil's Hole
Faeroe Bank
Bill Baileys Bank
Rosemary Bank
Outer Bailey or Lousy Bank
Stanton Banks
Rockall (U.K.)
Rockall Bank
ATLANTIC
NORTH SEA
MEDIAN LINE
Natural Gas
Ekofisk
Forties
Brent
Piper
Frigg
Montrose
Auk
Argyll
Josephine
Lomond
Beryl
Heather
Cormorant
Ninian
Thistle
Murchison
Statfjord
Gullfaks
Balder
Heimdal
Sleipner
Crawford
Buchan
Brae
Claymore
Tartan
Balmoral
Maureen
Andrew
Gannet
200 m
100 m
500 m
1000 m
2000 m
1° 30'
3°
4° 30'
9°
10° 30'
12°
13° 30'
56°
57°
58°
59°
60°
61°

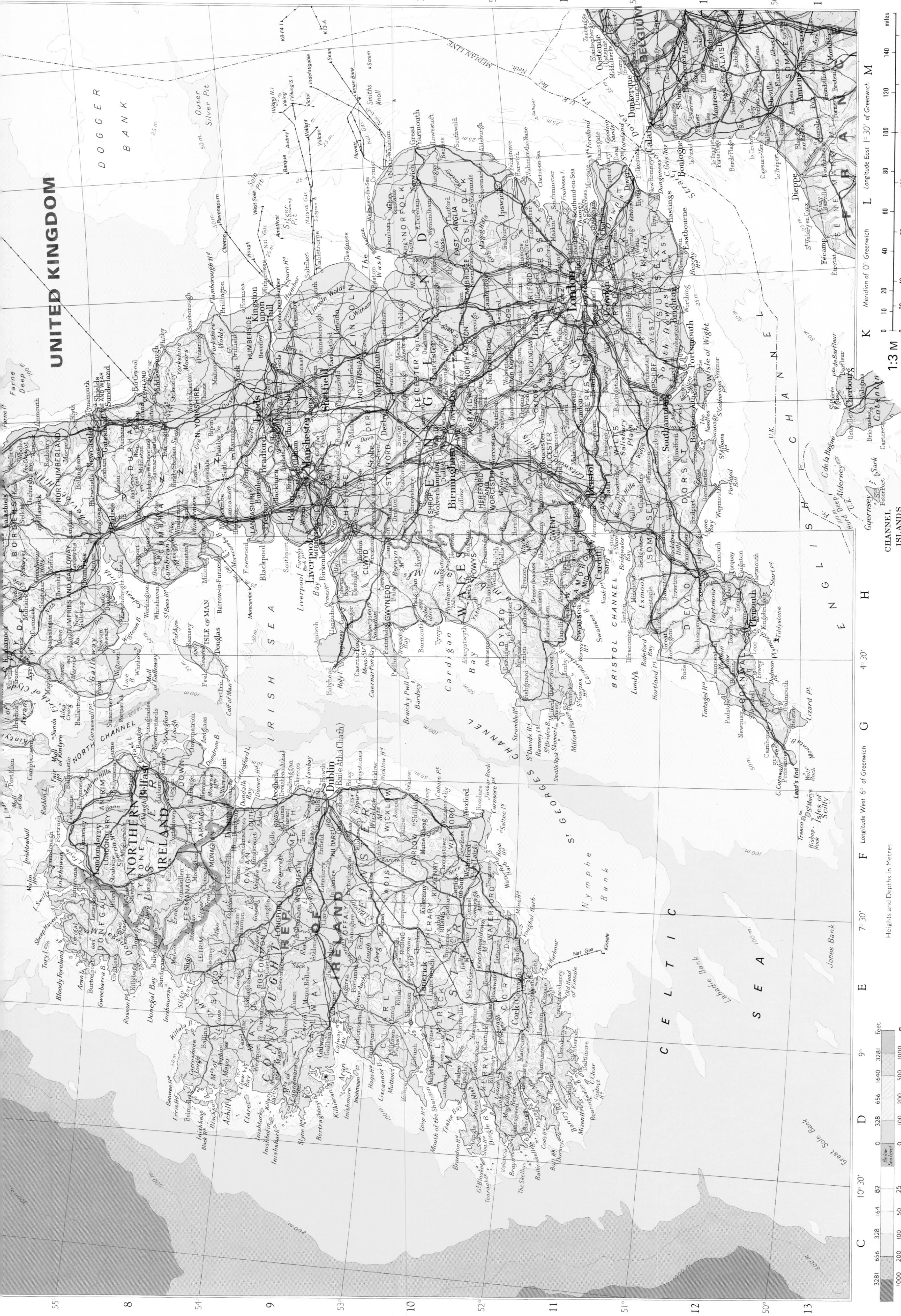
UNITED KINGDOM
REP. OF IRELAND
NORTHERN IRELAND
ENGLAND
WALES
FRANCE
BELGIUM
CHANNEL ISLANDS
ISLE OF MAN
IRISH SEA
NORTH CHANNEL
ST GEORGES CHANNEL
BRISTOL CHANNEL
CELTIC SEA
ENGLISH CHANNEL
DOGGER BANK
Cardigan Bay
Nymphe Bank
Labadie Bank
Jones Bank
Great Sole Bank
London
Dublin
Belfast
Birmingham
Manchester
Liverpool
Bristol
Cardiff
Plymouth
Southampton
Cork
Galway
Limerick
Brest
Calais
Dunkerque
Amiens
Cherbourg
1:3 M
Longitude West 6° of Greenwich
Meridian of 0° Greenwich
Longitude East 1° 30' of Greenwich
Heights and Depths in Metres
feet
m
Below Sea level
miles
km

A
B
C
D
E
5°
4°
53°
52°
51°
1
2
3
4
5
6
7
CARDIGAN BAY
BRISTOL CHANNEL
ANGLESEY
GWYNEDD
CLWYD
WALES
POWYS
DYFED
WEST GLAMORGAN
MID GLAMORGAN
SOUTH GLAMORGAN
GWENT
SHROPSHIRE
HEREFORD AND WORCESTER
CHESHIRE
MERSEYSIDE
AVON
SOMERSET
DEVON
CORNWALL
DORSET
Manchester
Liverpool
Birkenhead
Chester
Wrexham
Shrewsbury
Telford
Wolverhampton
Holyhead
Bangor
Caernarfon
Llandudno
Aberystwyth
Cardigan
Fishguard (Abergwaun)
Haverfordwest
Pembroke
Carmarthen (Caerfyrddin)
Llanelli
Swansea (Abertawe)
Neath
Port Talbot
Bridgend
Merthyr Tydfil
Pontypridd
Caerphilly
CARDIFF (Caerdydd)
Newport (Casnewydd)
Brecon (Aberhonddu)
Hereford
Bristol
Bath
Weston super-mare
Taunton
Bridgwater
Minehead
Lynmouth
Ilfracombe
Barnstaple
Bideford
Exeter
Torquay
Plymouth
Bodmin
Truro
Penzance
St Ives
Newquay
Dorchester
Weymouth
Lundy
To Dublin & Dun Laoghaire
To Rosslare
To Cork
Lyme Bay
Longitude West 3° of Greenwich
CONIC PROJECTION
m
feet
609
2000
304
1000
152
500
76
250
0
0
Below Sea Level

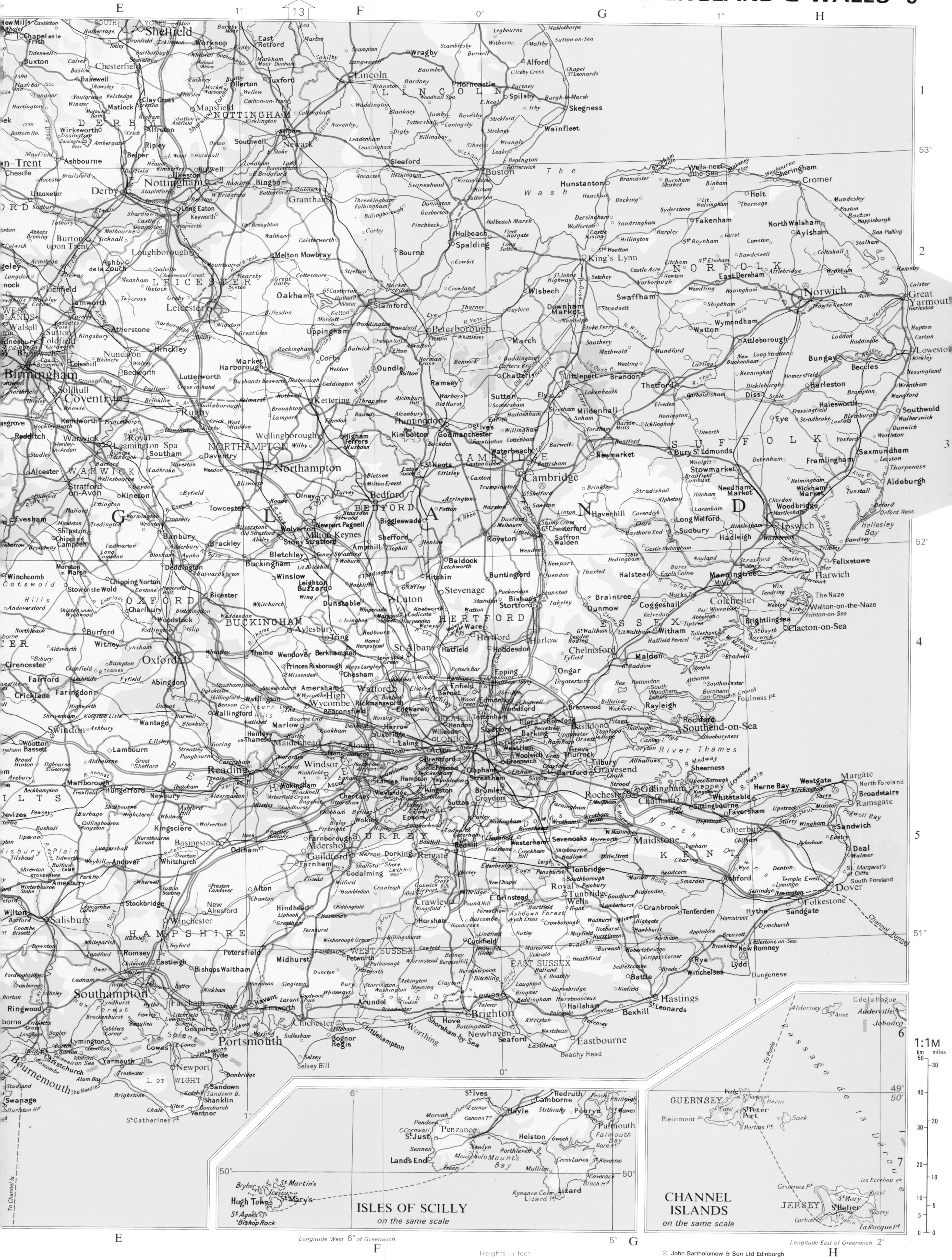
13
LINCOLN
NOTTINGHAM
DERBY
LEICESTER
NORTHAMPTON
WARWICK
BEDFORD
CAMBRIDGE
NORFOLK
SUFFOLK
ESSEX
HERTFORD
BUCKINGHAM
OXFORD
BERKSHIRE
SURREY
KENT
HAMPSHIRE
WEST SUSSEX
EAST SUSSEX
I. OF WIGHT
ENGLAND
GREATER LONDON
The Wash
River Thames
Sheffield
Nottingham
Derby
Leicester
Birmingham
Coventry
Northampton
Peterborough
Norwich
Great Yarmouth
Lowestoft
King's Lynn
Cambridge
Ipswich
Colchester
Chelmsford
Southend-on-Sea
Luton
Oxford
Reading
Swindon
Salisbury
Southampton
Portsmouth
Brighton
Hastings
Eastbourne
Canterbury
Dover
Maidstone
Bournemouth
ISLES OF SCILLY
on the same scale
CHANNEL ISLANDS
on the same scale
GUERNSEY
JERSEY
1:1M
km
miles
Longitude West 6° of Greenwich
Heights in feet
Longitude East of Greenwich 2°

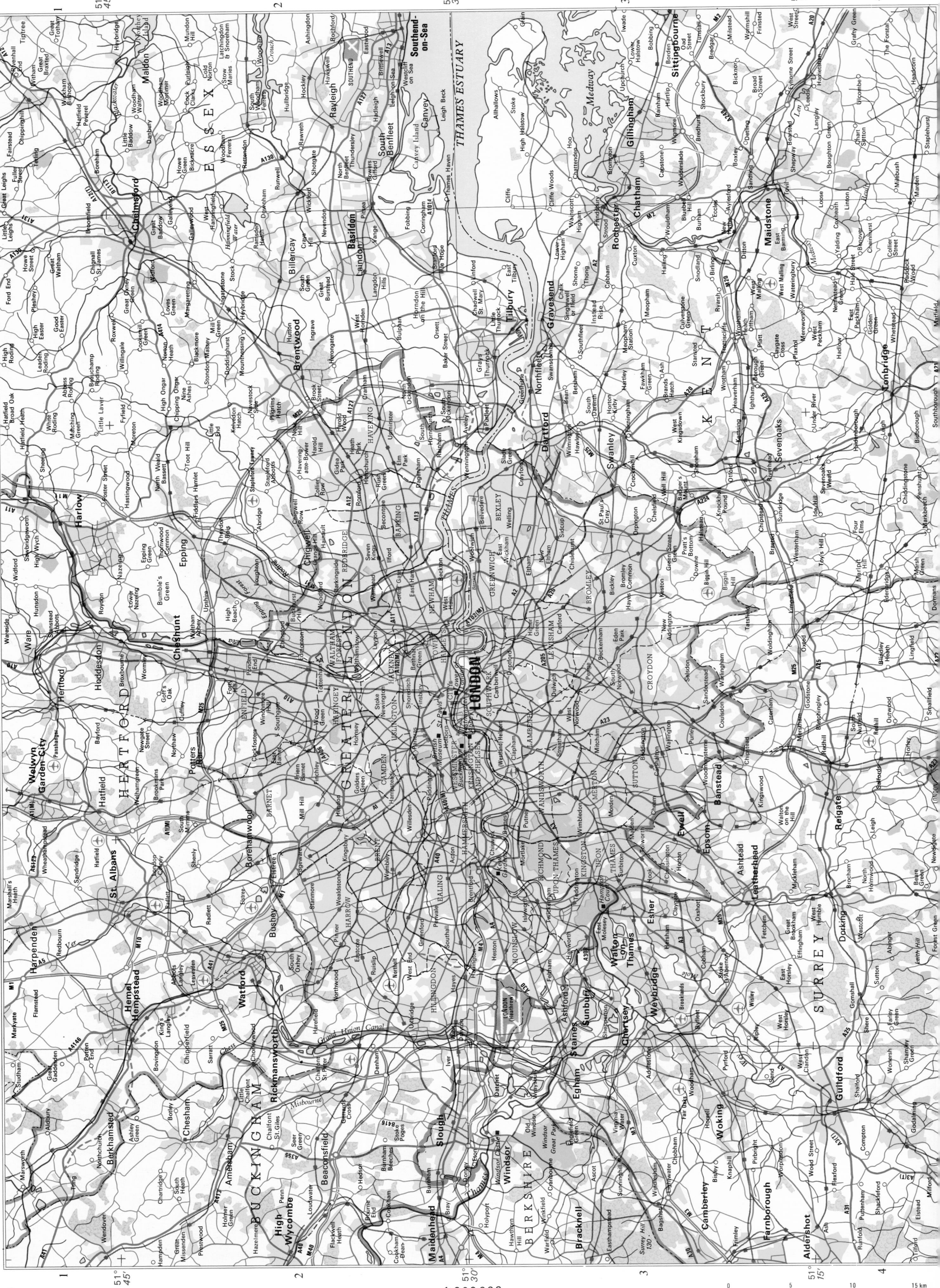

1:300 000

0 5 10 15 km

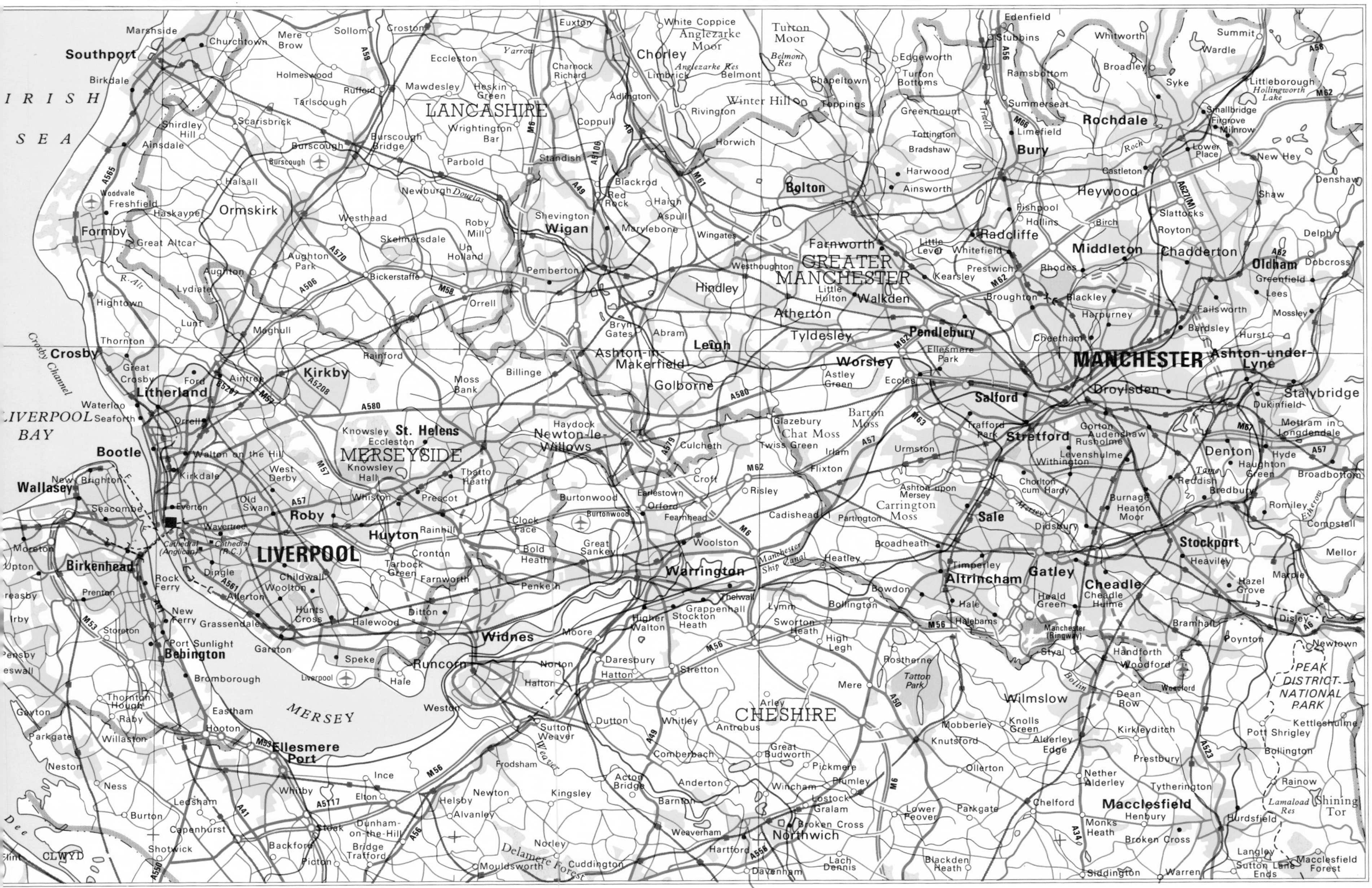

IRISH SEA
LIVERPOOL BAY
LANCASHIRE
MERSEYSIDE
GREATER MANCHESTER
CHESHIRE
CLWYD
PEAK DISTRICT NATIONAL PARK
Southport
Formby
Ormskirk
Crosby
Litherland
Bootle
Wallasey
Birkenhead
Bebington
Ellesmere Port
LIVERPOOL
Kirkby
St. Helens
Huyton
Roby
Widnes
Runcorn
Warrington
Wigan
Chorley
Bolton
Bury
Rochdale
Heywood
Radcliffe
Middleton
Chadderton
Oldham
Farnworth
Walkden
Atherton
Tyldesley
Leigh
Hindley
Worsley
Pendlebury
Salford
MANCHESTER
Ashton-under-Lyne
Stalybridge
Droylsden
Stretford
Sale
Altrincham
Gatley
Cheadle
Stockport
Denton
Wilmslow
Macclesfield
Northwich
Golborne
Newton-le-Willows
Ashton-in-Makerfield
Manchester Ship Canal
MERSEY

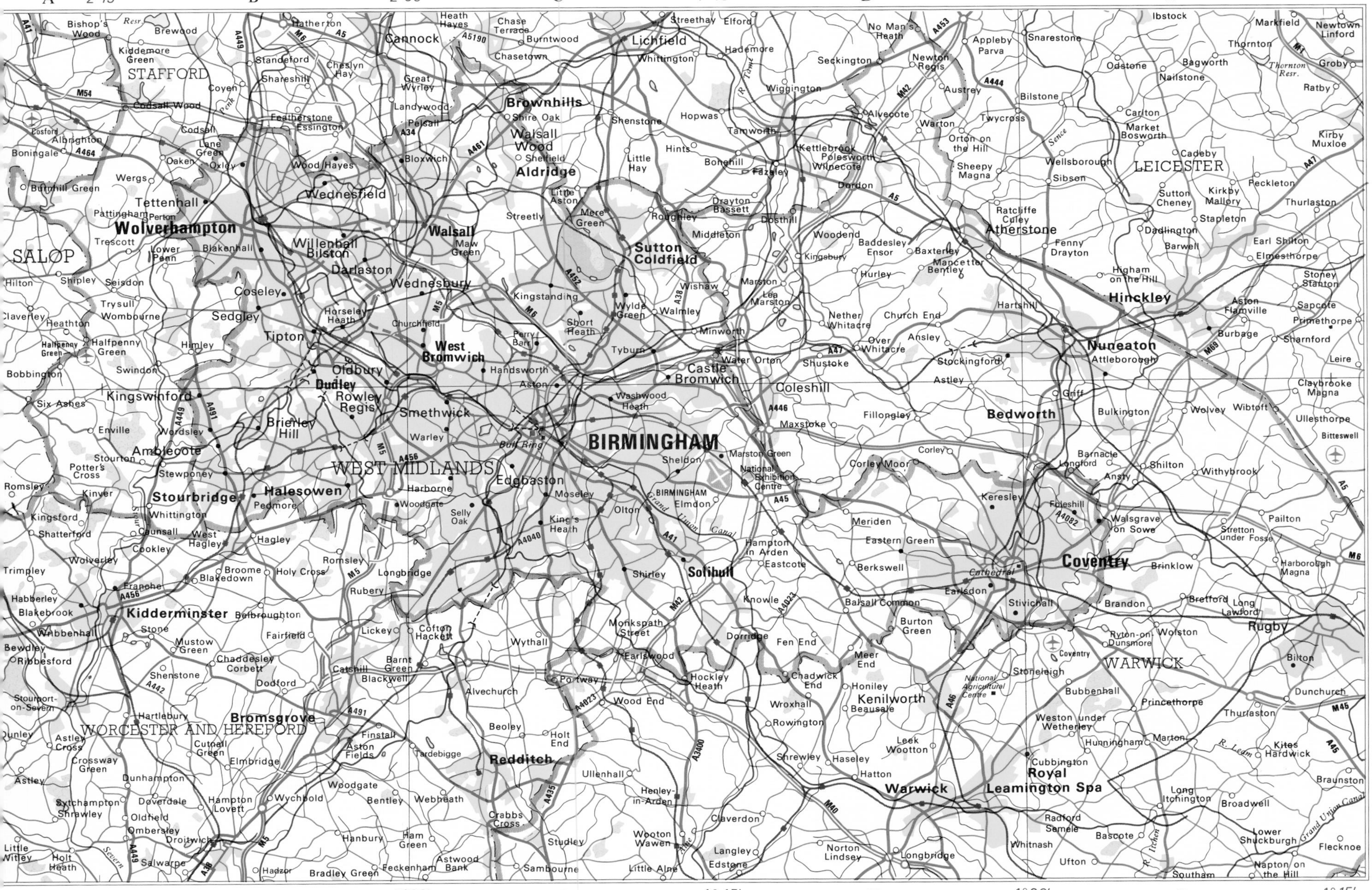

STAFFORD
SALOP
WEST MIDLANDS
WORCESTER AND HEREFORD
LEICESTER
WARWICK
Cannock
Lichfield
Brownhills
Aldridge
Walsall
Wolverhampton
Wednesfield
Willenhall
Bilston
Darlaston
Wednesbury
Tettenhall
Sedgley
Coseley
Tipton
West Bromwich
Oldbury
Dudley
Rowley Regis
Smethwick
Brierley Hill
Kingswinford
Amblecote
Stourbridge
Halesowen
BIRMINGHAM
Sutton Coldfield
Castle Bromwich
Edgbaston
Solihull
Kidderminster
Bromsgrove
Redditch
Atherstone
Hinckley
Nuneaton
Bedworth
Coventry
Rugby
Kenilworth
Warwick
Royal Leamington Spa

1:300 000

CONIC PROJECTION

Heights in feet

9

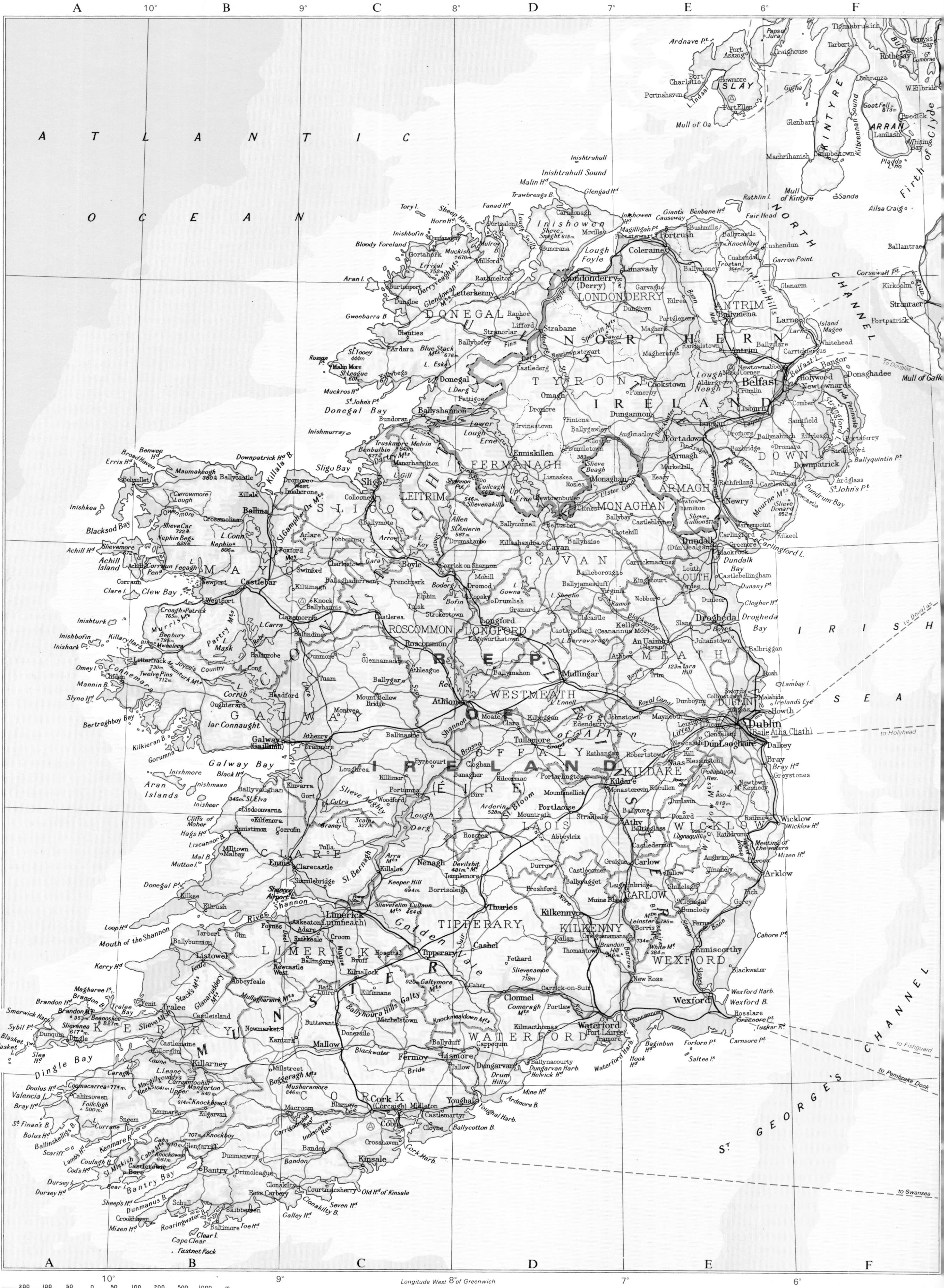

Heights and Depths in metres

200 100 50 0 50 100 200 500 1000 m

660 330 160 0 160 330 660 1640 3280 feet

Longitude West 8° of Greenwich

CONIC PROJECTION

1:1.5 M

0 10 20 40 60 80 km

0 5 10 20 30 40 50 miles

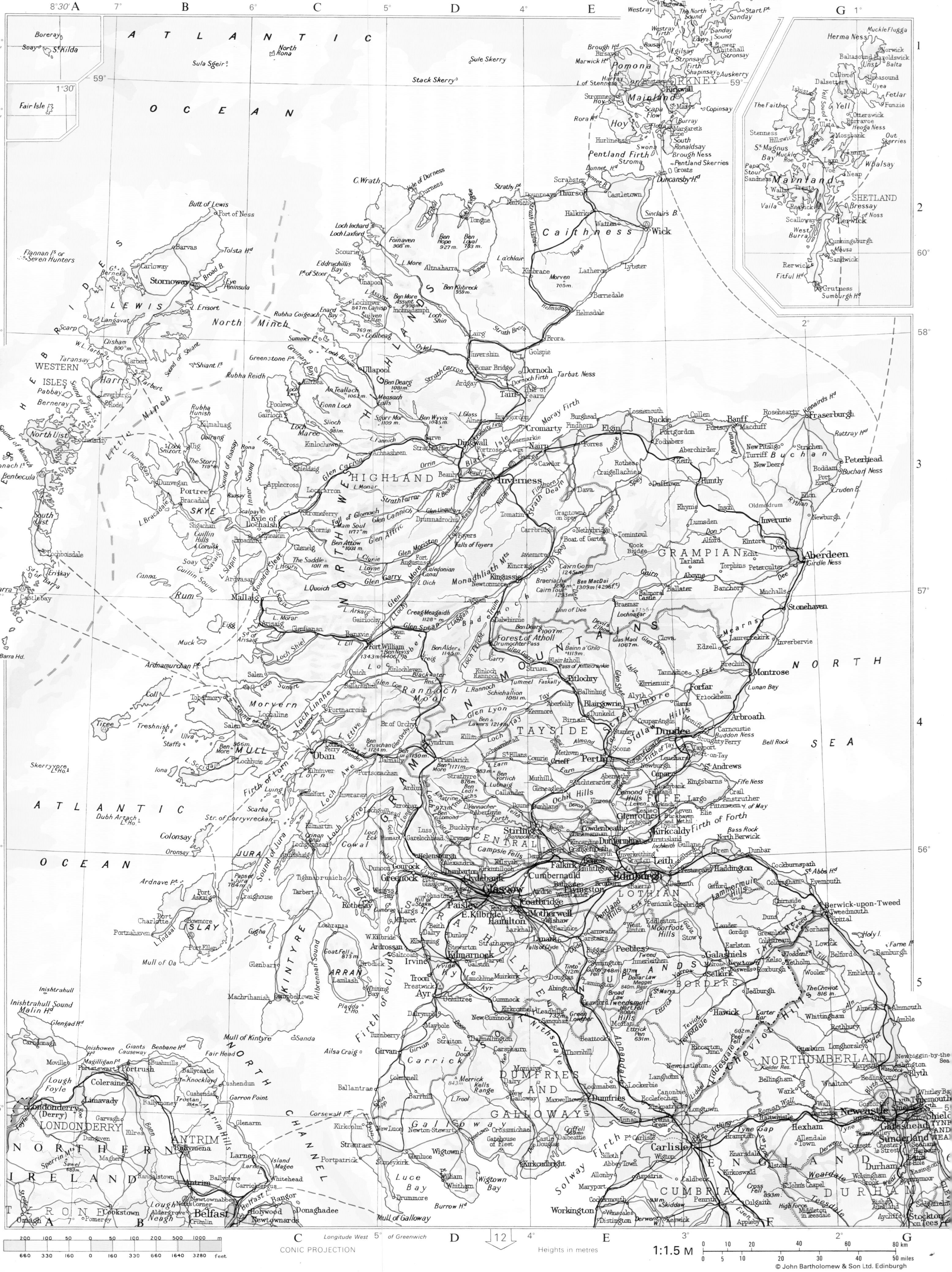
ATLANTIC OCEAN
NORTH SEA
ORKNEY
SHETLAND
WESTERN ISLES
HEBRIDES
LEWIS
North Minch
Little Minch
SKYE
Rum
MULL
JURA
ISLAY
ARRAN
KINTYRE
HIGHLAND
NORTH WEST HIGHLANDS
GRAMPIAN MOUNTAINS
GRAMPIAN
TAYSIDE
CENTRAL
FIFE
LOTHIAN
STRATHCLYDE
BORDERS
DUMFRIES AND GALLOWAY
SOUTHERN UPLANDS
Caithness
Buchan
Moray Firth
Firth of Forth
Firth of Clyde
Firth of Lorn
Solway Firth
NORTH CHANNEL
NORTHERN IRELAND
ANTRIM
LONDONDERRY
CUMBRIA
NORTHUMBERLAND
DURHAM
ENGLAND
Cheviot Hills
Wick
Thurso
Stornoway
Ullapool
Inverness
Aberdeen
Fraserburgh
Peterhead
Elgin
Fort William
Oban
Mallaig
Perth
Dundee
Stirling
Glasgow
Edinburgh
Leith
Greenock
Paisley
Kilmarnock
Ayr
Dumfries
Carlisle
Newcastle
Sunderland
Berwick-upon-Tweed
Belfast
Londonderry (Derry)
Coleraine
Larne
CONIC PROJECTION
Heights in metres
Longitude West of Greenwich
1:1.5 M
© John Bartholomew & Son Ltd. Edinburgh

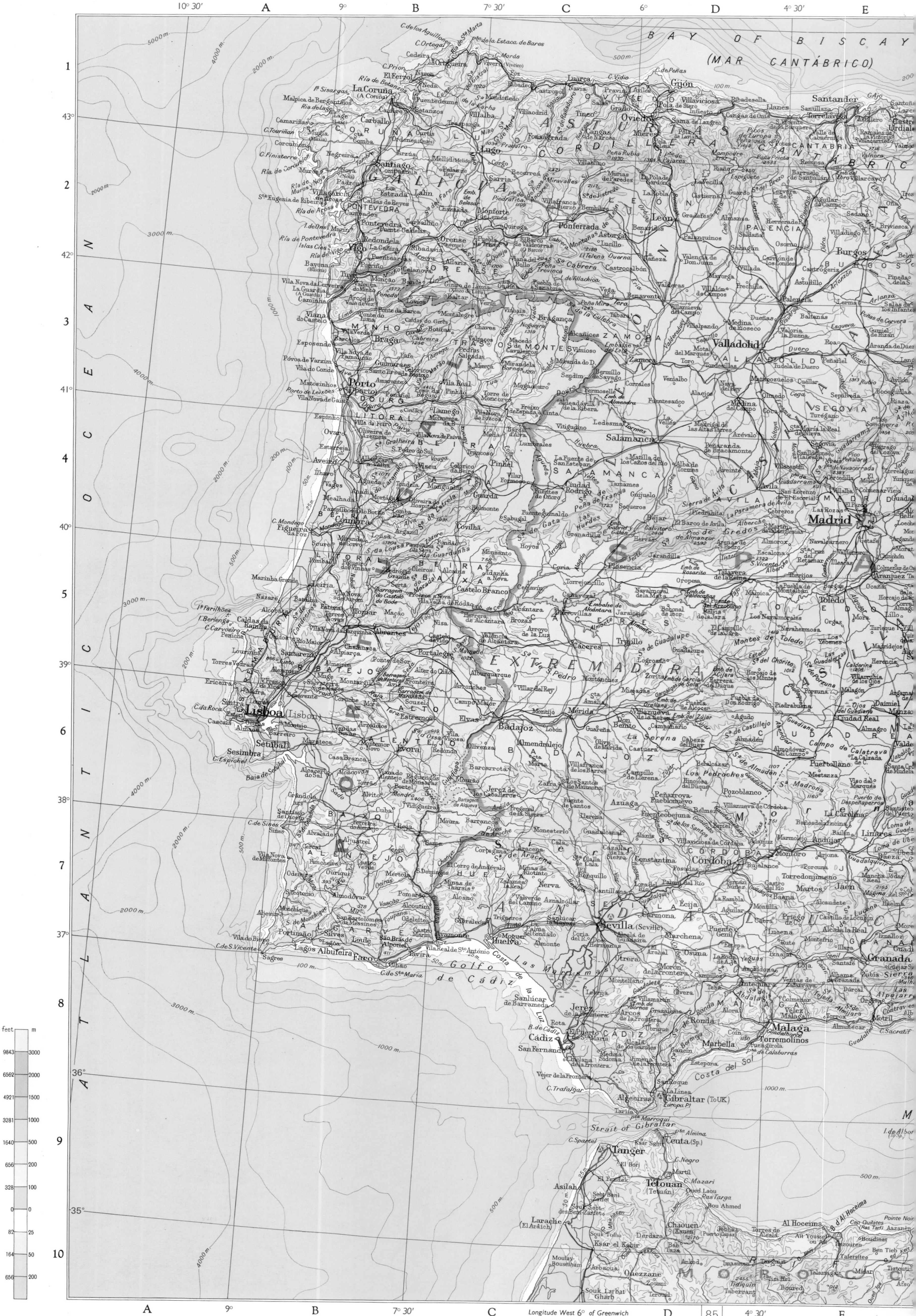

CONIC PROJECTION

FRANCE
GOLFE DE GASCOGNE (GOLFO DE GASCUÑA)
GOLFE DU LION
Toulouse
Montpellier
Marseille
Perpignan
Narbonne
Carcassonne
Béziers
Pamplona
Logroño
Zaragoza
Huesca
Lérida
Barcelona
Tarragona
Gerona
ANDORRA
Valencia
Golfo de Valencia
Castellón de la Plana
Alicante
Murcia
Cartagena
Albacete
Teruel
Cuenca
ISLAS BALEARES (BALEARIC ISLANDS) (To Spain)
MALLORCA (MAJORCA)
MENORCA (MINORCA)
IBIZA (IVIZA)
Palma
Ciudadela
Mahón
Formentera
MEDITERRANEAN SEA
ALGERIA
Oran
Mostaganem
Tlemcen
Sidi Bel Abbès
Mascara
Longitude East 3° of Greenwich
Meridian of 0° Greenwich
MADRID 1:60 000
CIUDAD UNIVERSITARIA
CHAMARTIN
TETUAN
CHAMBERÍ
SALAMANCA
RETIRO
MONCLOA
Casa de Campo
LATINA
ARGANZUELA
CARABANCHEL
VALLECAS
Parque del Retiro
Parque del Oeste
1:3 M

Heights and Depths in metres

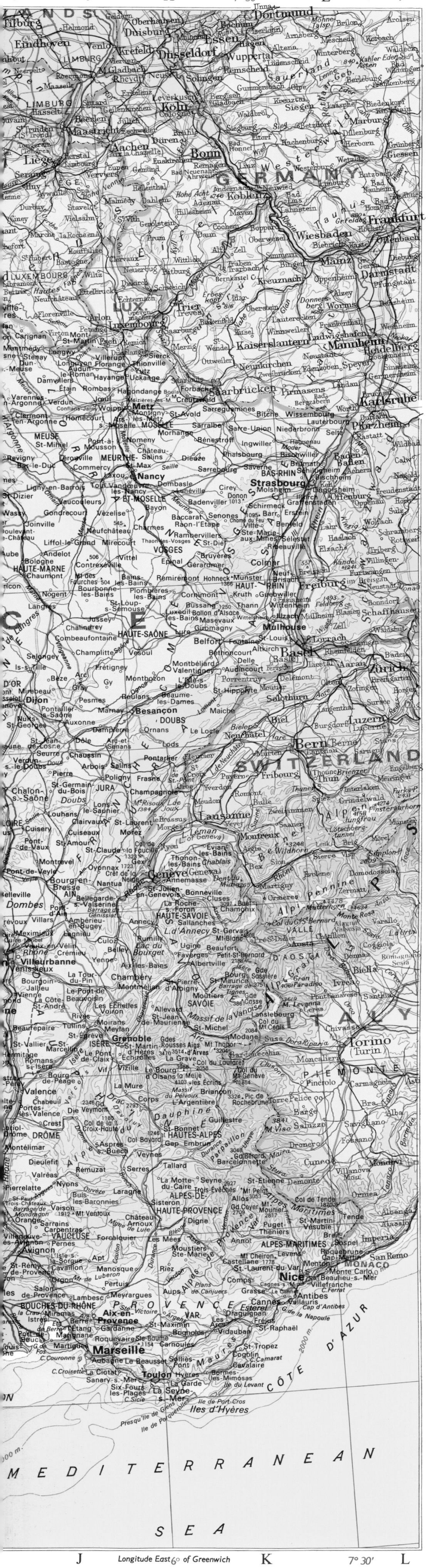
GERMANY
LUX.
SWITZERLAND
ITALY
MEDITERRANEAN
SEA
CÔTE D'AZUR
Longitude East 6° of Greenwich

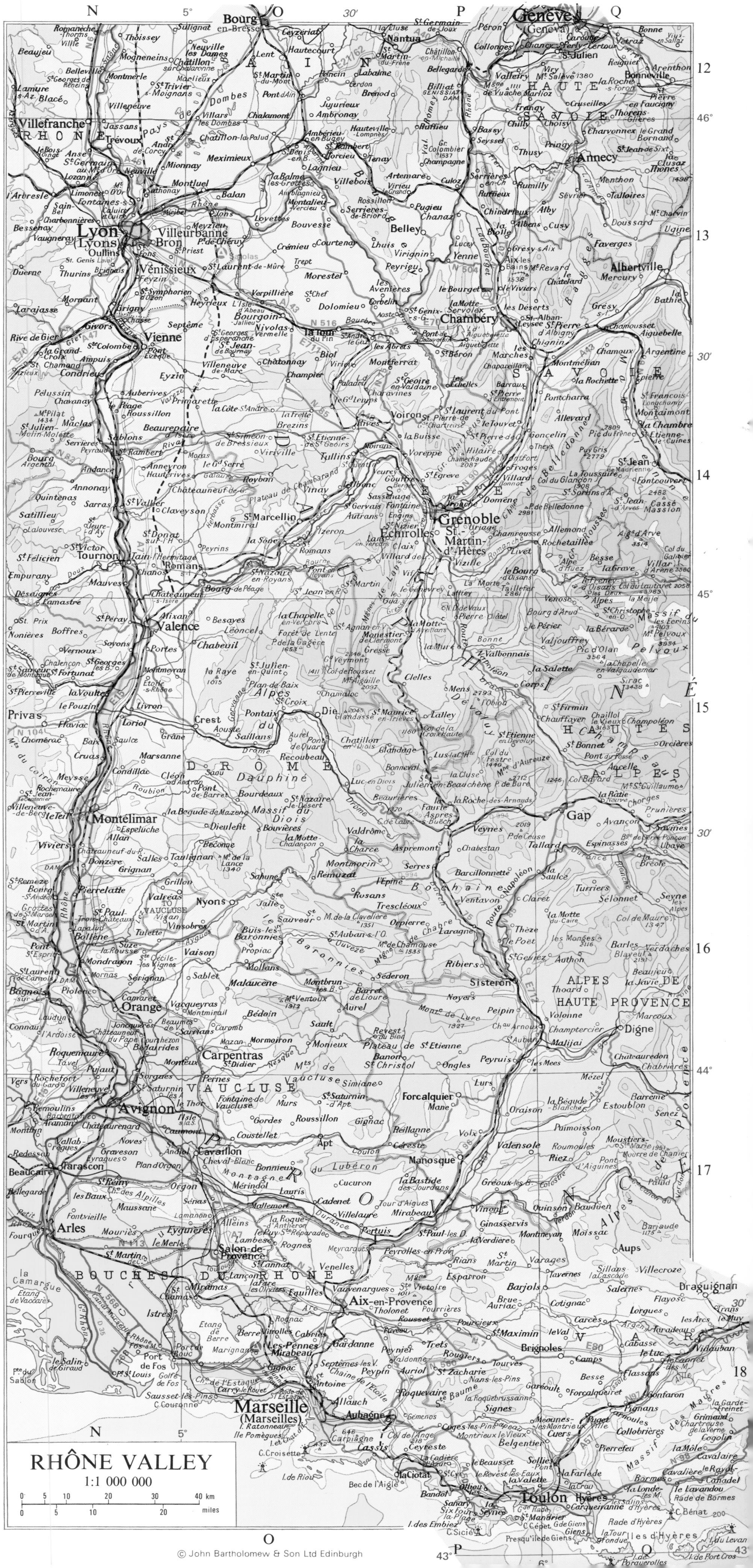
RHÔNE VALLEY
1:1 000 000
Lyon
Genève
Grenoble
Valence
Avignon
Marseille
Toulon
AIN
SAVOIE
DRÔME
VAUCLUSE
BOUCHES-DU-RHÔNE

CONIC PROJECTION

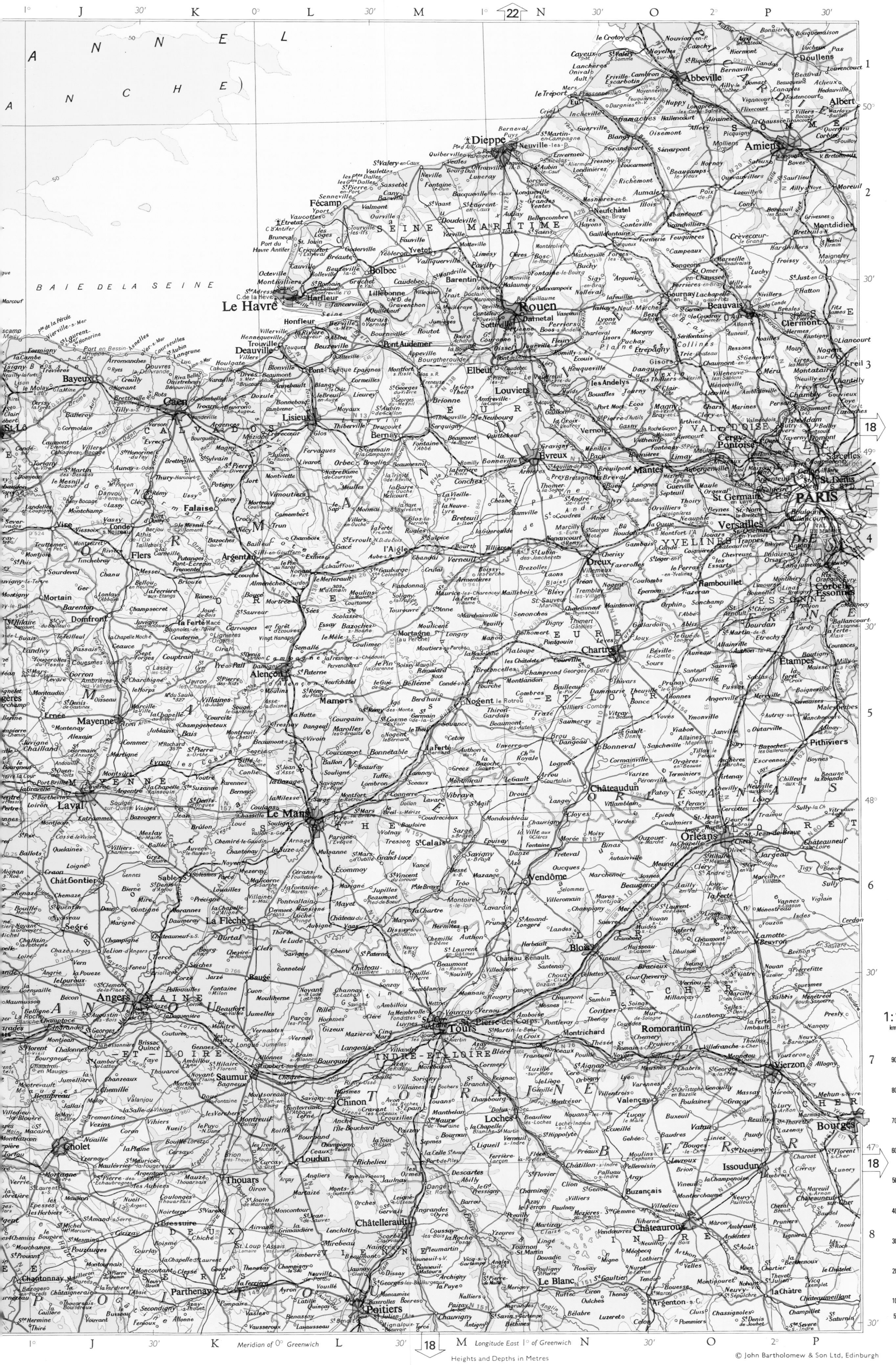

Heights and Depths in Metres

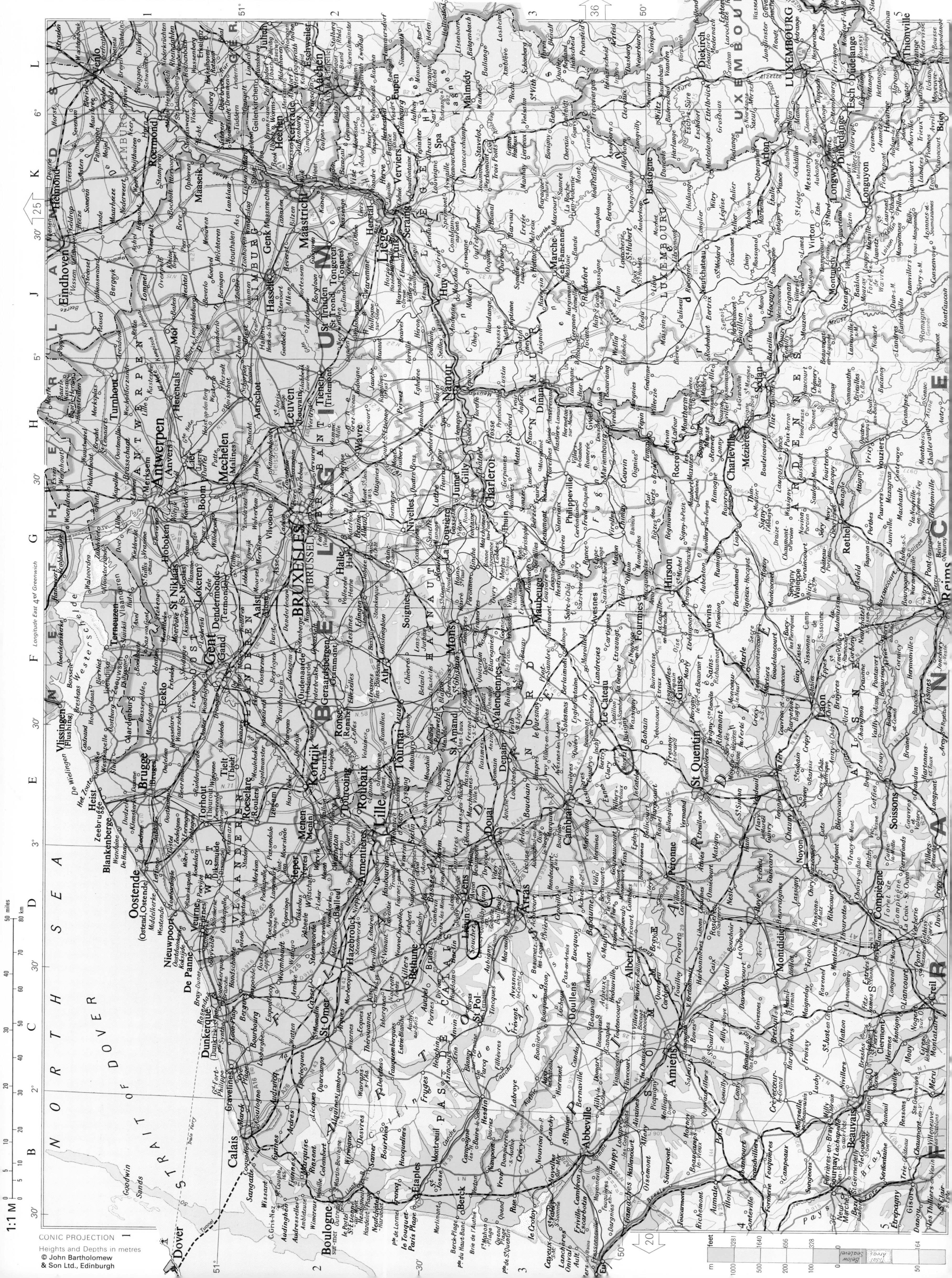
NORTH SEA
STRAIT OF DOVER
BELGIUM
FRANCE
LUXEMBOURG
LIMBURG
ANTWERPEN
BRABANT
HAINAUT
LIÈGE
LUXEMBOURG
NAMUR
OOST VLAANDEREN
WEST VLAANDEREN
NORD
PAS-DE-CALAIS
SOMME
AISNE
ARDENNES
OISE
BRUXELLES (BRUSSEL)
Antwerpen (Anvers)
Gent (Gand)
Brugge (Bruges)
Oostende (Ostend, Ostende)
Liège
Namur
Charleroi
Mons
Lille
Roubaix
Tourcoing
Dunkerque
Calais
Boulogne
Amiens
Reims
Laon
Saint Quentin
Arras
Douai
Cambrai
Valenciennes
Maastricht
Aachen
Eindhoven
Mechelen (Malines)
Leuven (Louvain)
Hasselt
Genk
Kortrijk (Courtrai)
Ieper
Abbeville
Soissons
Compiègne
Beauvais
Creil
Charleville-Mézières
Sedan
Dinant
Verviers
Bastogne
Arlon
LUXEMBOURG
Thionville
Dover
Vlissingen (Flushing)
Venlo
Roermond
Heerlen
Turnhout
Herentals
Aalst
Sint Niklaas (St Nicolas)
Tournai
Lens
Béthune
Saint Omer
Hazebrouck
Armentières
Albert
Montdidier
Longwy
Malmédy
Spa
Huy
Rethel
Hirson
Maubeuge
Dendermonde (Termonde)
Roeselare (Roulers)
Nieuwpoort
De Panne
Knokke
Zeebrugge
Blankenberge
Heist
Gravelines
Étaples
Berck
Le Crotoy
Saint Valéry
Cayeux
Mers
Eu
Gisors
Chaumont-en-Vexin
Clermont
Noyon
Péronne
Guise
Vervins
Fourmies
Avesnes
Le Cateau
Denain
Saint Amand
Diksmuide
Tielt (Thielt)
Menen (Menin)
Doullens
Saint Pol
Hesdin
Montreuil
Fruges
Longitude East of Greenwich
CONIC PROJECTION
Heights and Depths in metres
1:1 M
miles
km
feet
m

0 5 10 15 km
0 5 10 miles

1:300 000

AMSTERDAM / THE HAGUE

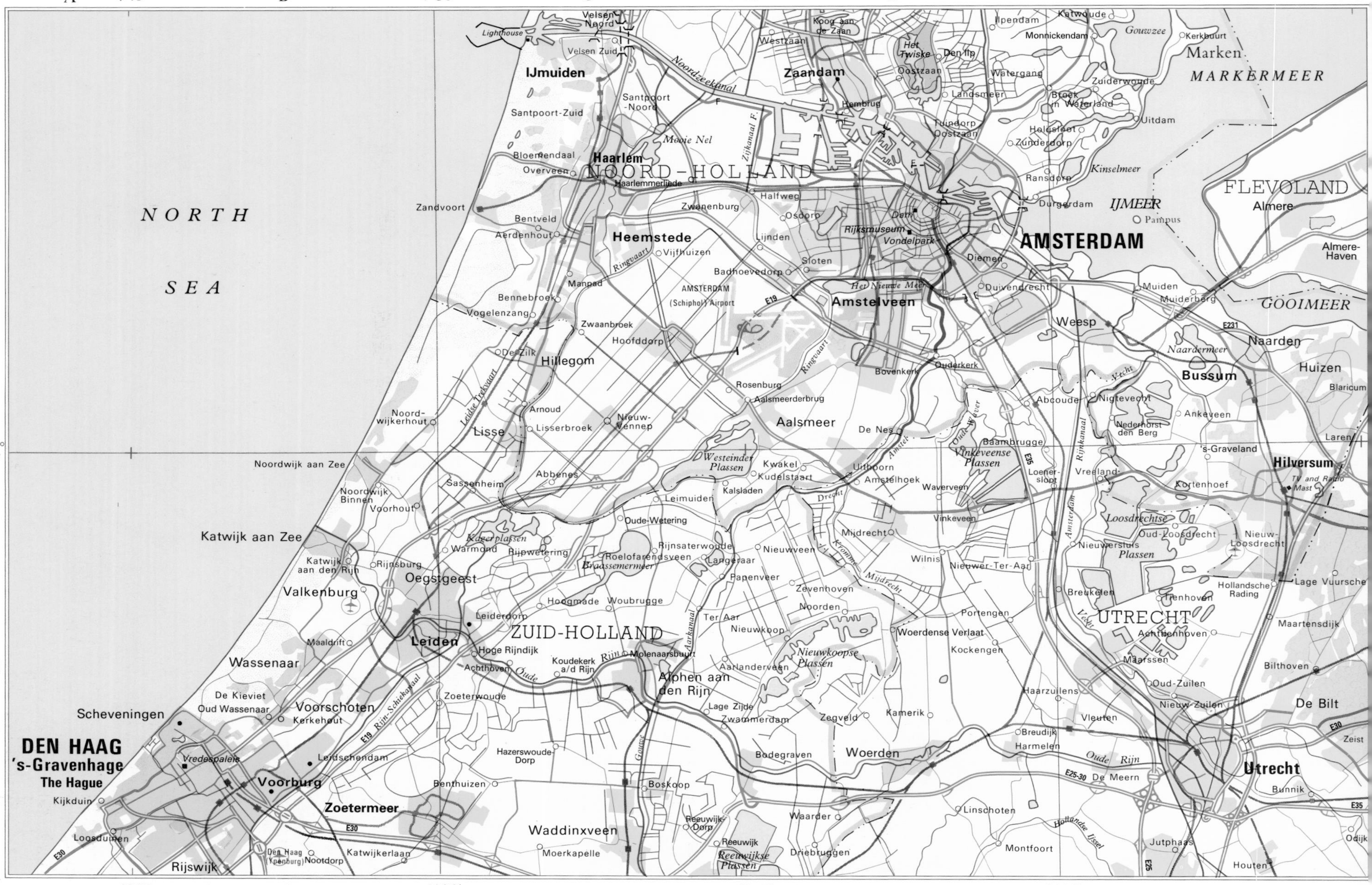

BRUSSELS

1:300 000

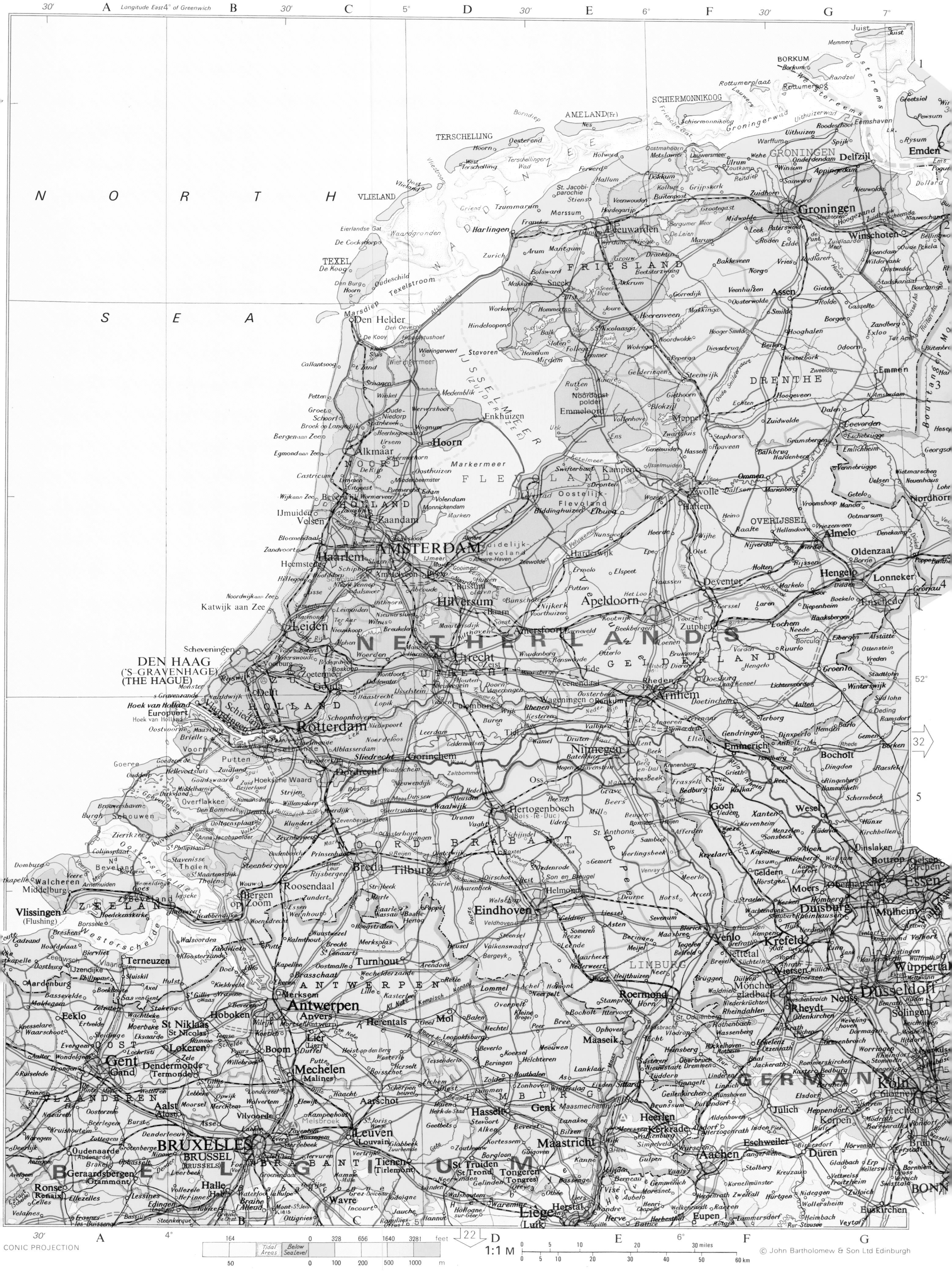
Longitude East 4° of Greenwich
N O R T H
S E A
NETHERLANDS
BELGIUM
GERMANY
AMSTERDAM
Rotterdam
DEN HAAG
('S-GRAVENHAGE)
(THE HAGUE)
Utrecht
Groningen
Leeuwarden
Eindhoven
Antwerpen
BRUXELLES
BRUSSEL
(BRUSSELS)
Gent
Köln
Düsseldorf
Essen
Aachen
Maastricht
Liège
Nijmegen
Arnhem
Apeldoorn
Zwolle
Haarlem
Hilversum
Amersfoort
Tilburg
Breda
Middelburg
Vlissingen
(Flushing)
FRIESLAND
DRENTHE
OVERIJSSEL
GELDERLAND
FLEVOLAND
NOORD-HOLLAND
ZUID-HOLLAND
ZEELAND
NOORD-BRABANT
LIMBURG
UTRECHT
ANTWERPEN
VLAANDEREN
IJSSELMEER
Markermeer
WADDENZEE
TEXEL
VLIELAND
TERSCHELLING
AMELAND
SCHIERMONNIKOOG
BORKUM
Westerschelde
Oosterschelde
CONIC PROJECTION
1:1 M
feet
m
Tidal Areas
Below Sea Level
30 miles
60 km
© John Bartholomew & Son Ltd Edinburgh

NORWEGIAN SEA
FINLAND
Trondheim
Östersund
Kristiansund
Ålesund
Molde
Bodø
Narvik
Luleå
Umeå
Skellefteå
Piteå
Kemi
Tornio
Oulu
Vaasa
Hammerfest
Lofoten
Vestfjorden
Arctic Circle

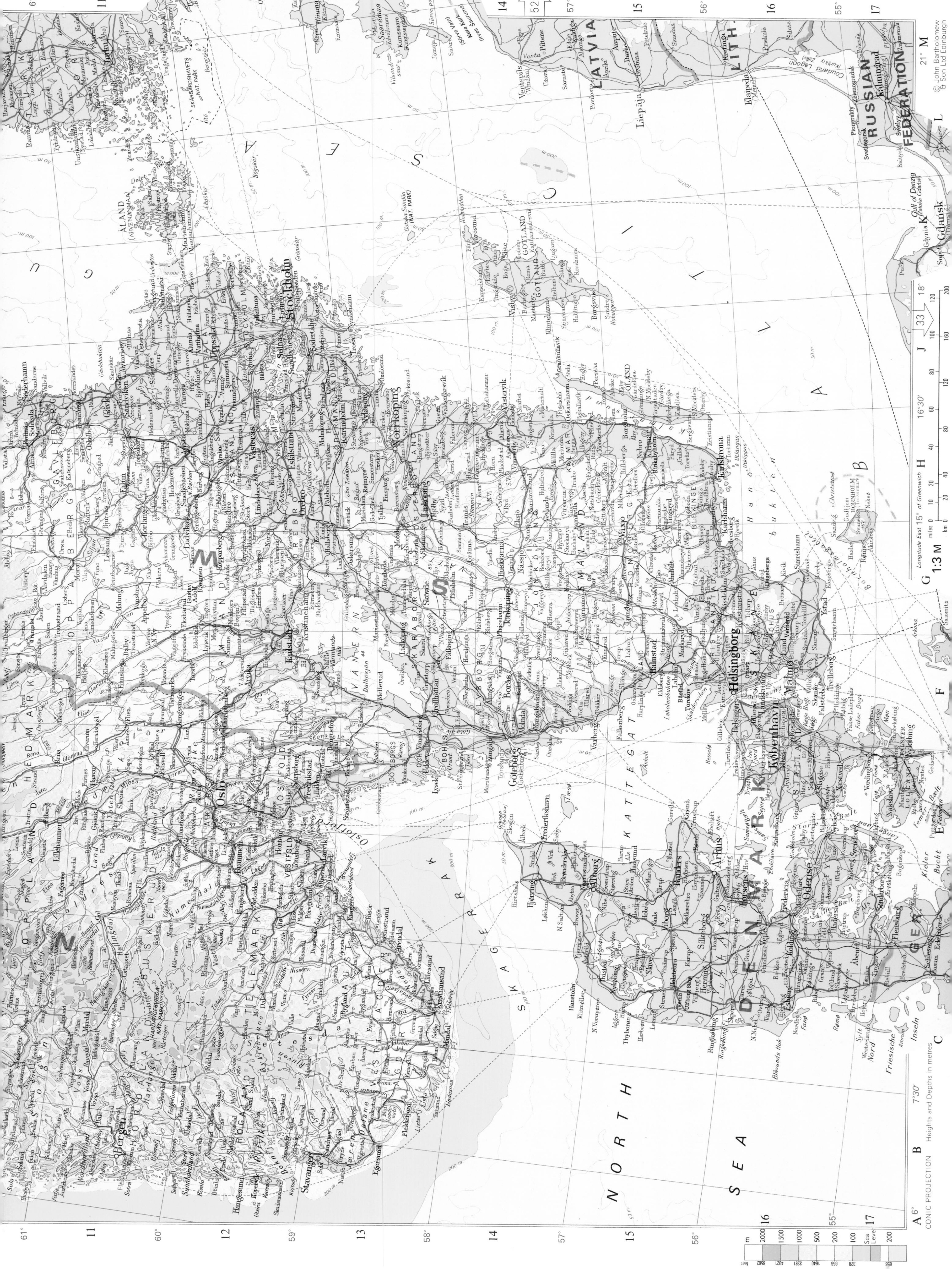
NORTH SEA
SKAGERRAK
KATTEGAT
BALTIC SEA
DENMARK
LATVIA
LITH.
RUSSIAN FEDERATION
Oslo
Stockholm
København
Göteborg
Malmö
Helsingborg
Norrköping
Linköping
Jönköping
Örebro
Västerås
Uppsala
Gävle
Karlstad
Kalmar
Karlskrona
Halmstad
Borås
Stavanger
Bergen
Kristiansand
Århus
Ålborg
Odense
Esbjerg
Gdańsk
Kaliningrad
Liepāja
Klaipėda
Ventspils
Visby
GOTLAND
ÖLAND
BORNHOLM
ÅLAND
Vänern
Vättern
Mälaren
1:3M
CONIC PROJECTION
Heights and Depths in metres
Longitude East 15° of Greenwich
© John Bartholomew & Son Ltd Edinburgh

SKAGERRAK
KATTEGAT
DENMARK
ICELA
GERMANY
Skagen
Hirtshals
Hjørring
Frederikshavn
Læsø
Jammerbugt
Ålborg
Limfjorden
Thisted
MORS
Nykøbing
Skive
Viborg
Randers
Hobro
Ålborg Bugt
Anholt
Holstebro
Lemvig
Struer
Herning
Silkeborg
Århus
Ringkøbing
Skjern
Horsens
Vejle
Fredericia
Kolding
Esbjerg
Fanø
Ribe
Haderslev
Åbenrå
Tønder
Sønderborg
Flensburg
Sylt
Westerland
FRIESISCHE INSELN
Föhr
Amrum
ALS
Odense
FYN
Nyborg
Svendborg
Fåborg
Assens
Middelfart
LANGELAND
Ærø
Samsø
Kalundborg
Holbæk
Roskilde
Helsingør
Slagelse
Korsør
Ringsted
Næstved
Vordingborg
Nakskov
LOLLAND
Maribo
FALSTER
Nykøbing
Gedser
Store Bælt
Lille Bælt
Femer Bælt
Smålandsfarvandet
Reykjavík
Akureyri
Longitude East 10° of Greenwich
1:1 M

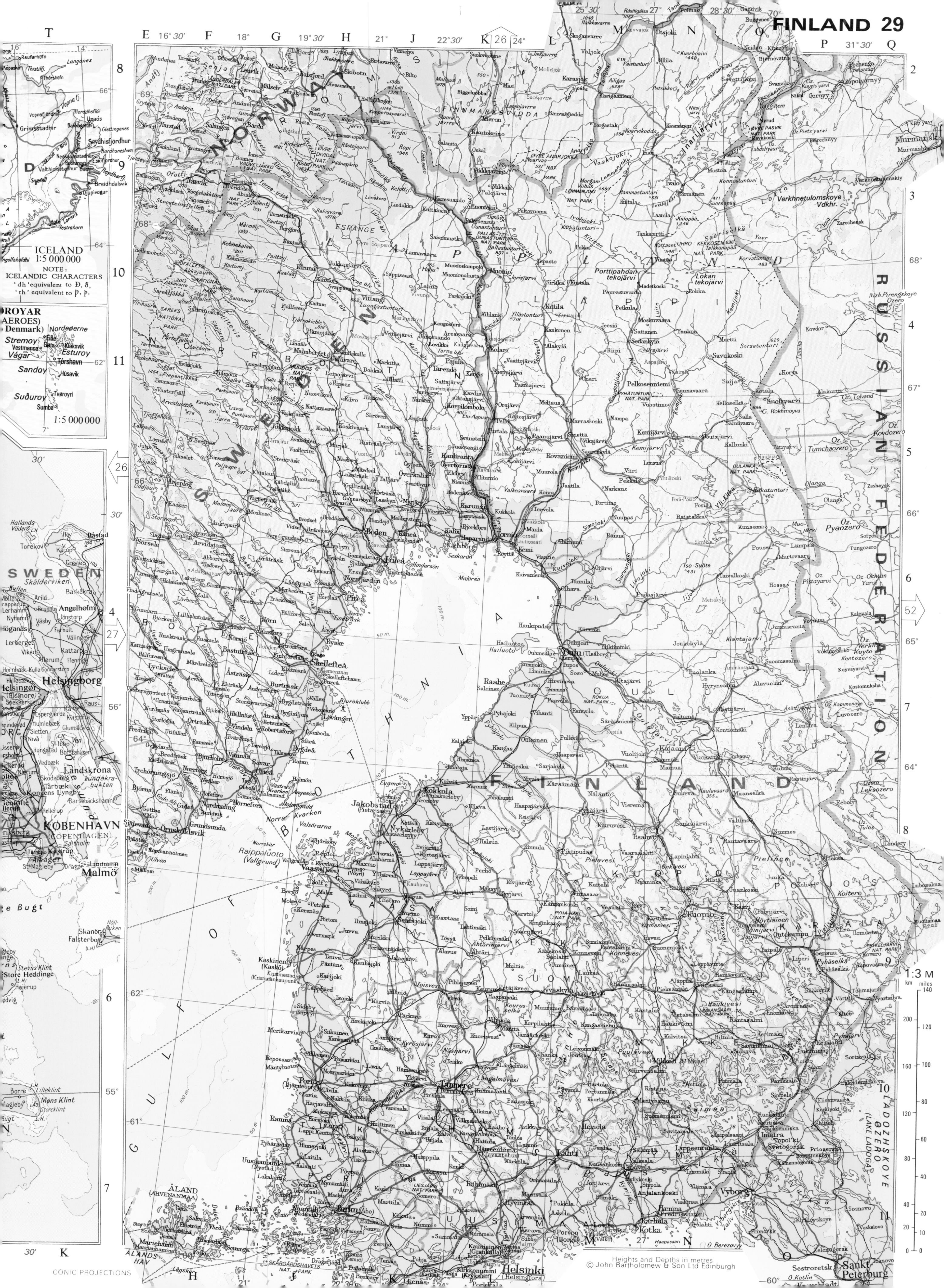
NORWAY
SWEDEN
FINLAND
RUSSIAN FEDERATION
GULF OF BOTHNIA
LAPPI
OULU
VAASA
KESKI SUOMI
KUOPIO
POHJOIS KARJALA
MIKKELI
TURKU-PORI
HÄME
KYMI
UUSIMAA
ÅLAND (AHVENANMAA)
ICELAND 1:5 000 000
NOTE: ICELANDIC CHARACTERS 'dh' equivalent to Ð, ð, 'th' equivalent to Þ, þ.
FØROYAR (FAEROES) (to Denmark)
1:5 000 000
Helsinki (Helsingfors)
Turku (Åbo)
Tampere
Oulu (Uleåborg)
Vaasa (Vasa)
Kuopio
Jyväskylä
Lahti
Pori (Björneborg)
Kokkola (Gamlakarleby)
Jakobstad (Pietarsaari)
Rovaniemi
Kemi
Tornio
Luleå
Umeå
Skellefteå
Piteå
Kiruna
Murmansk
Vyborg
Sankt-Peterburg
København (Copenhagen)
Malmö
Helsingborg
Mariehamn
Ladozhskoye Ozero (Lake Ladoga)
1:3 M
km miles
Heights and Depths in metres
© John Bartholomew & Son Ltd Edinburgh
CONIC PROJECTIONS

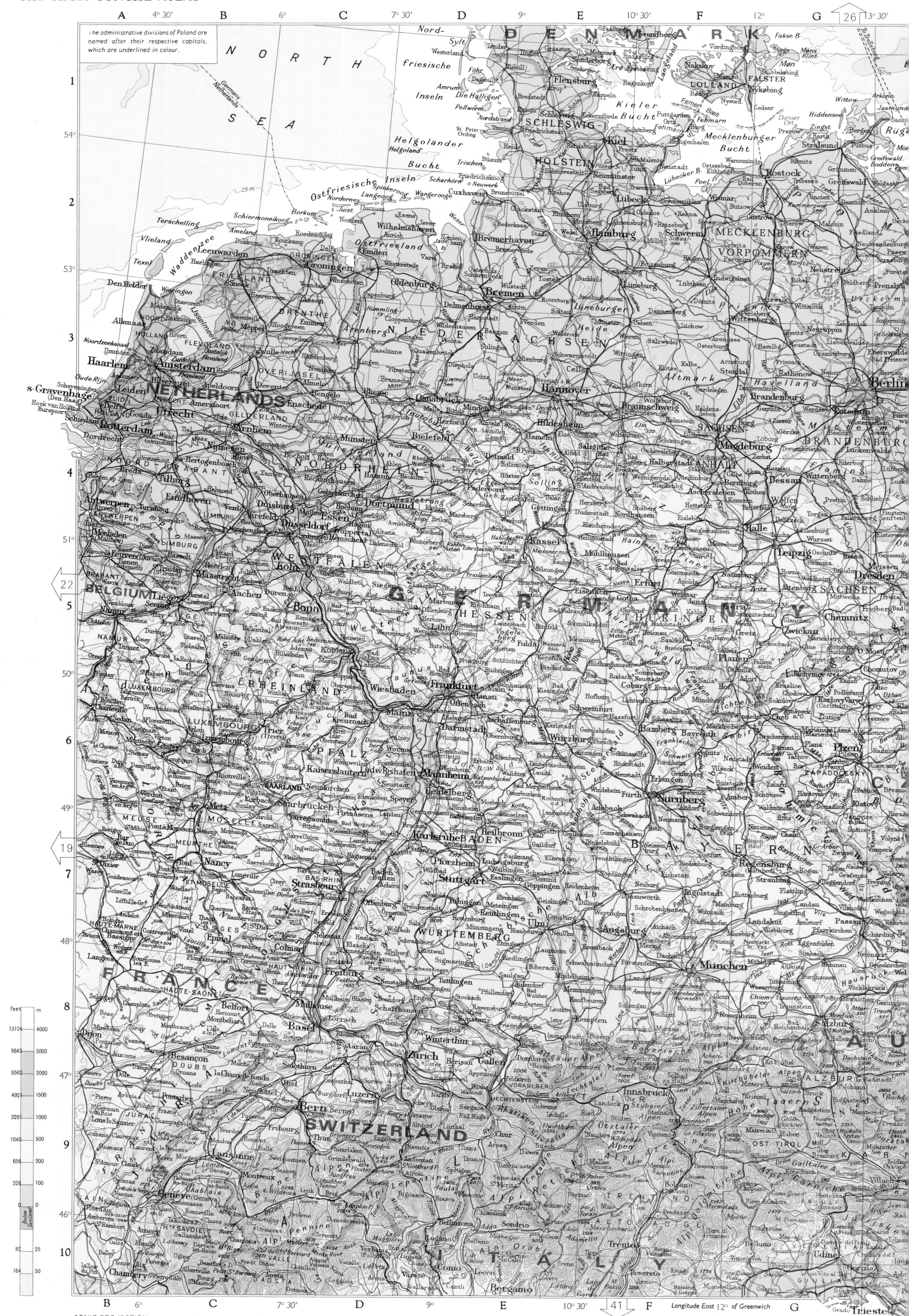

CONIC PROJECTION

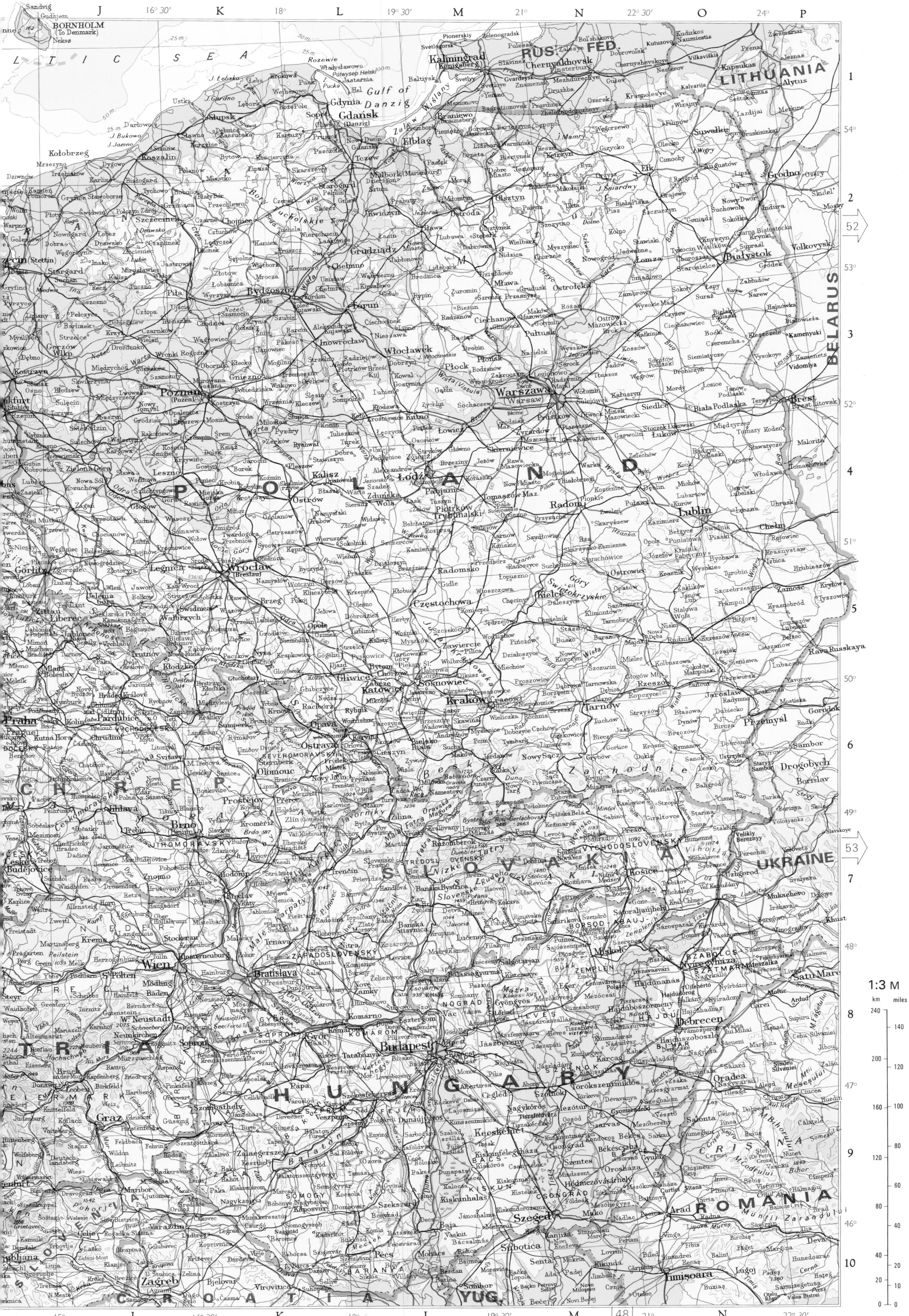
BORNHOLM
(To Denmark)
Gulf of Danzig
RUS. FED.
LITHUANIA
BELARUS
POLAND
Gdańsk
(Danzig)
Kaliningrad
(Königsberg)
Warszawa
(Warsaw)
Poznań
(Poznan)
Wrocław
(Breslau)
Łódź
Kraków
Białystok
Lublin
Brest
Bratislava
(Pressburg)
Wien
Budapest
Debrecen
Szeged
Košice
Zagreb
(Agram)
Timişoara
Oradea
SLOVAKIA
HUNGARY
UKRAINE
ROMANIA
CROATIA
YUG.
52
53
48
1:3 M
km
miles

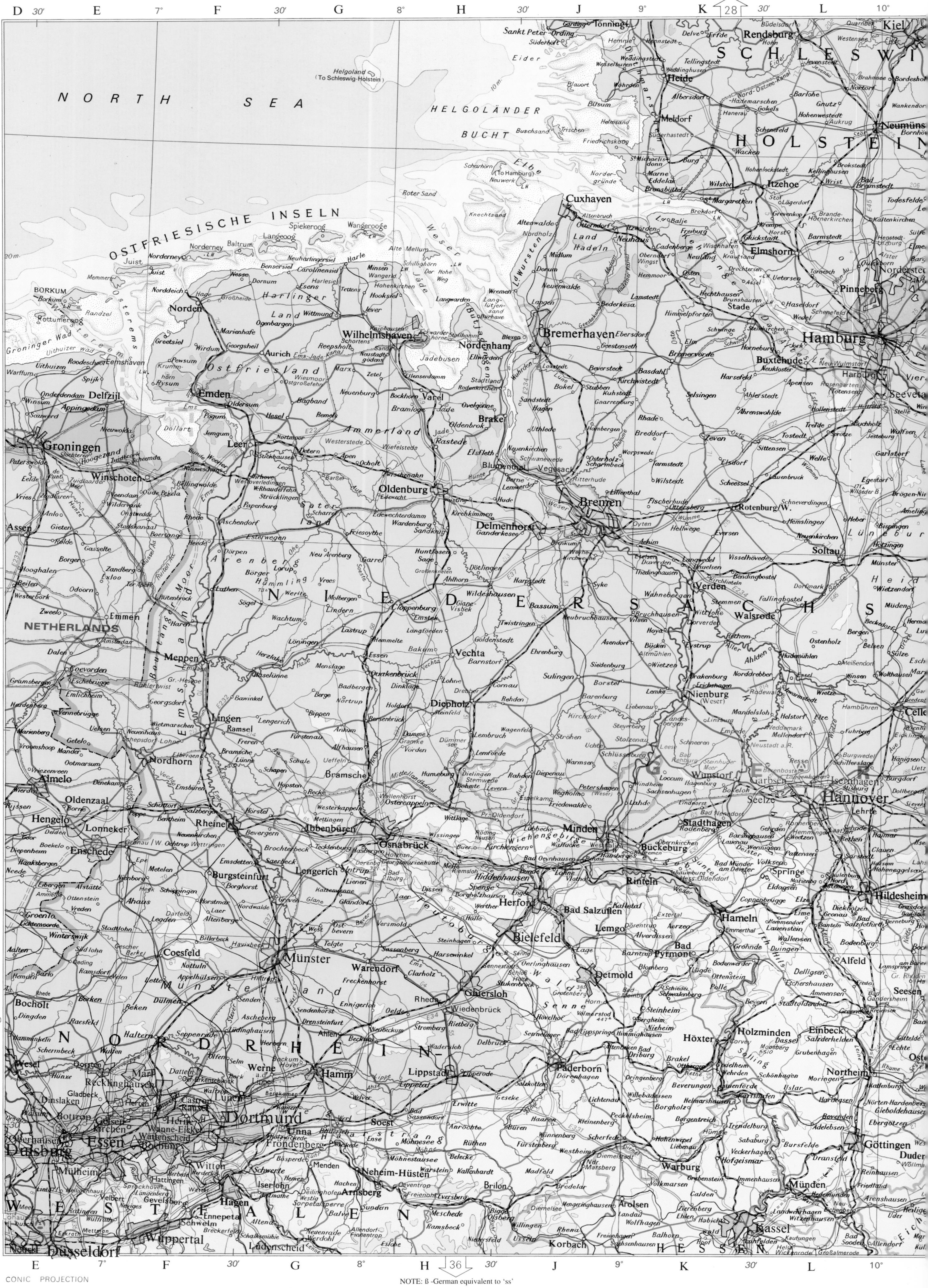

CONIC PROJECTION

NOTE: ß -German equivalent to 'ss'

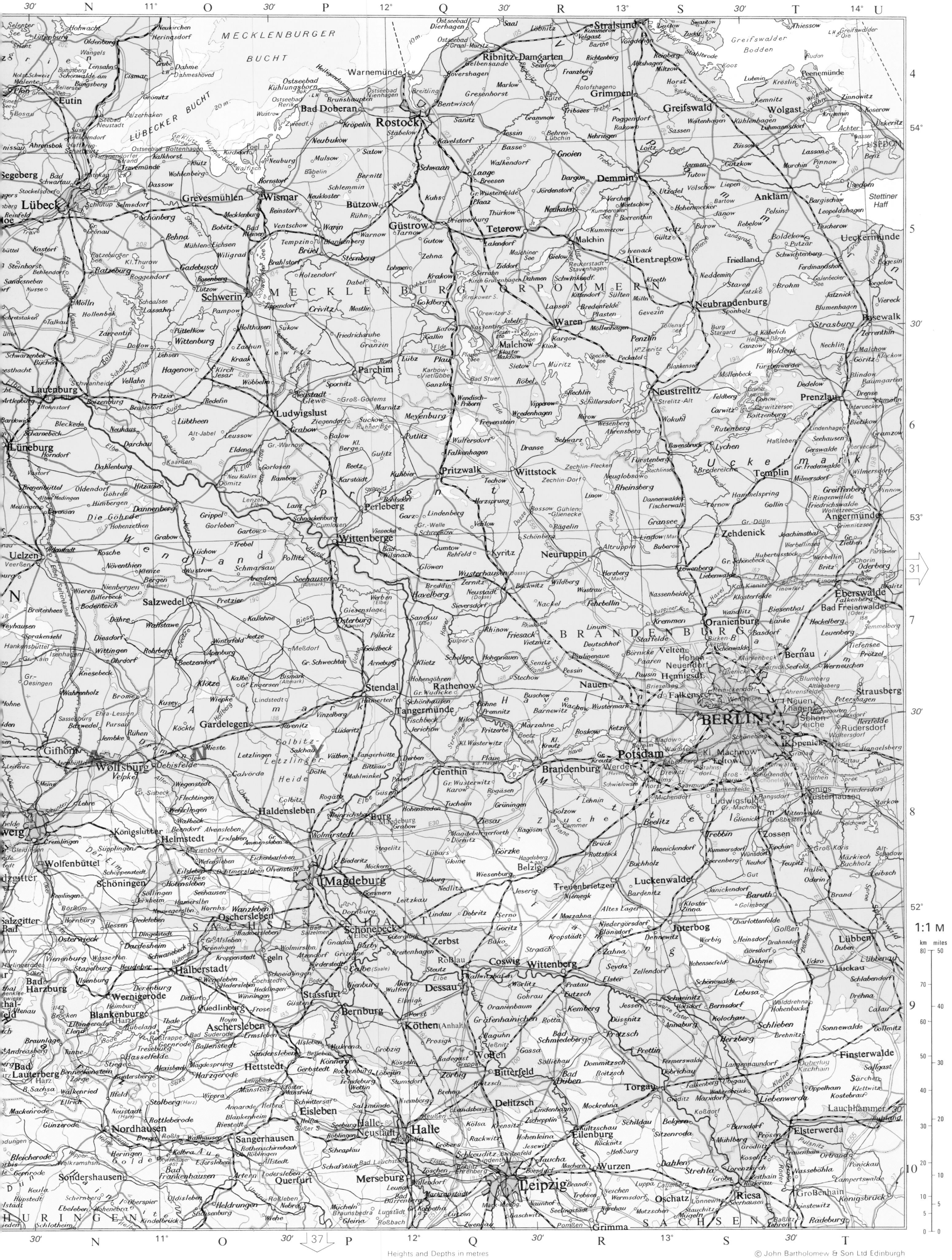

Heights and Depths in metres

HAMBURG

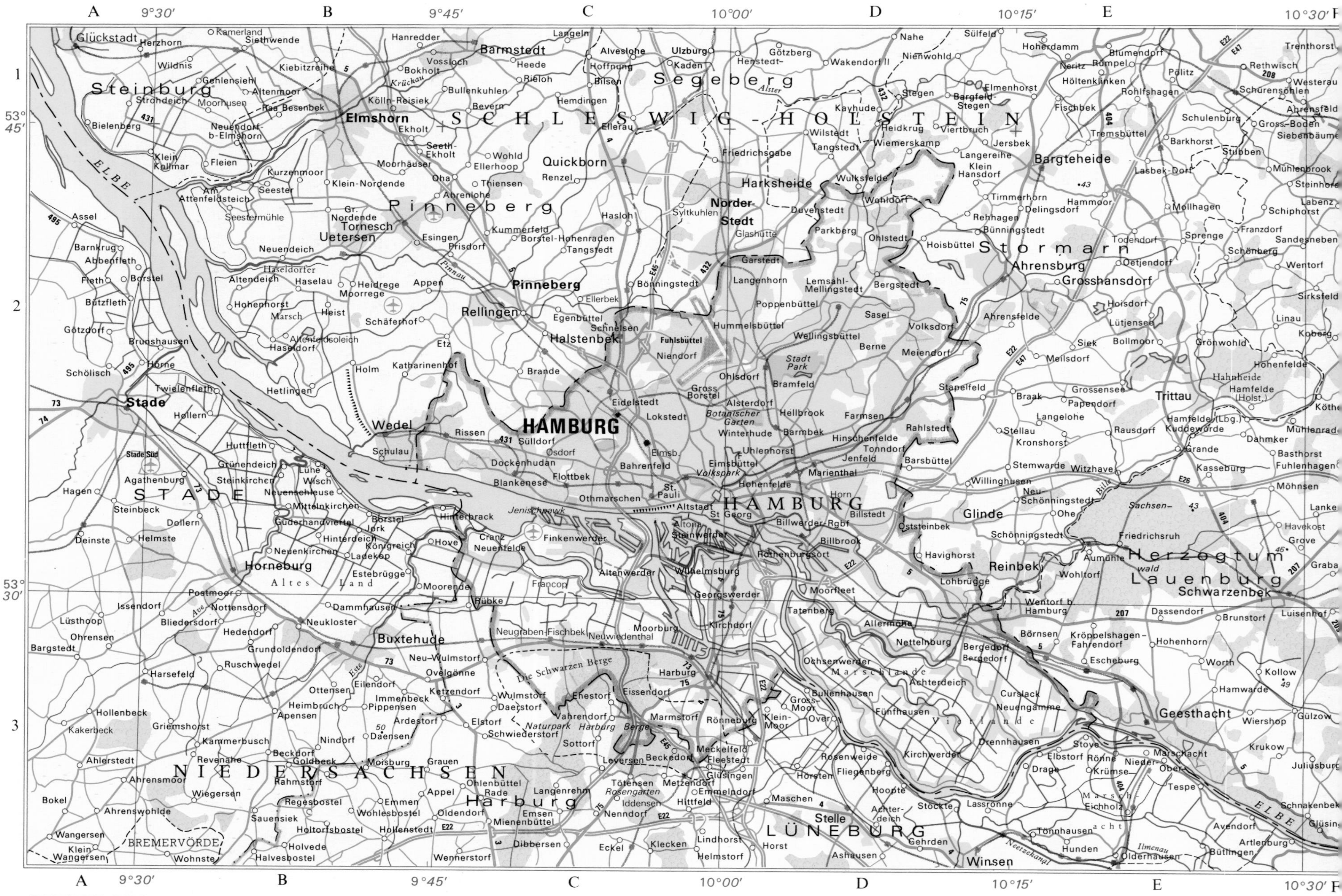

BERLIN

1:300 000

0 5 10 15 km
0 5 10 mi

0 5 10 15 km

0 5 10 miles

1:300 000

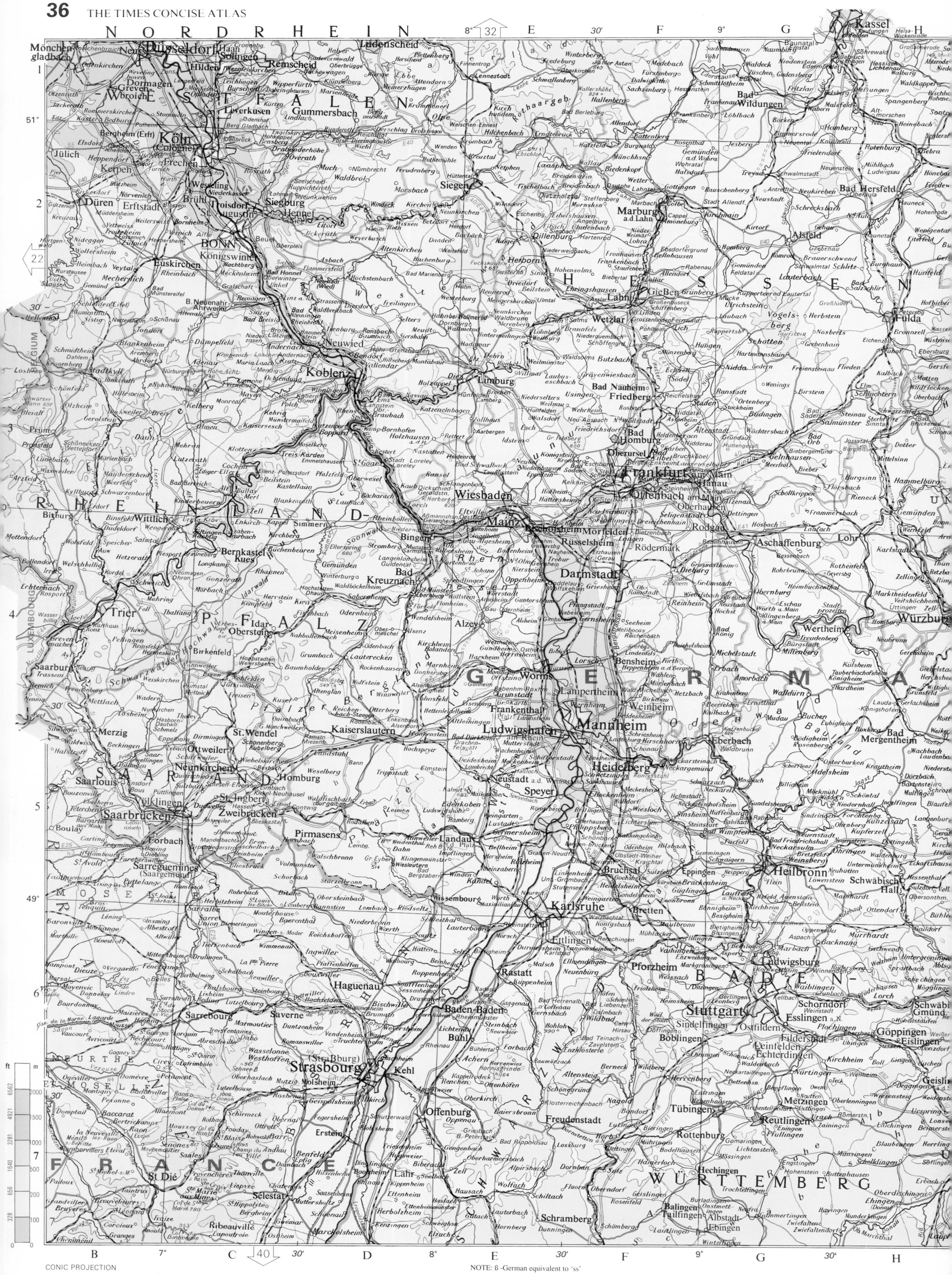

NOTE: ß -German equivalent to 'ss'

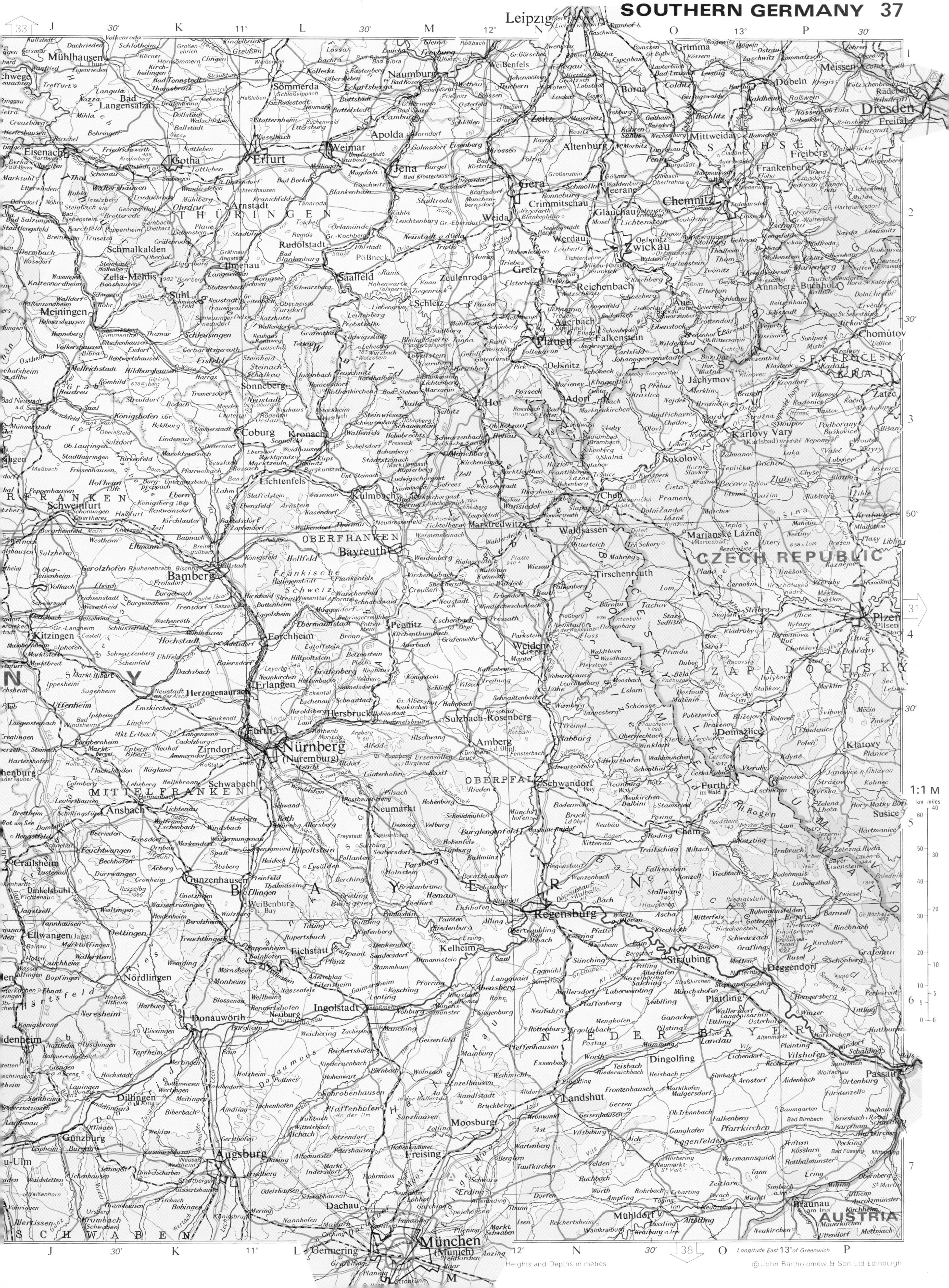

Heights and Depths in metres

Longitude East 13° of Greenwich

CENTRAL AUSTRIA

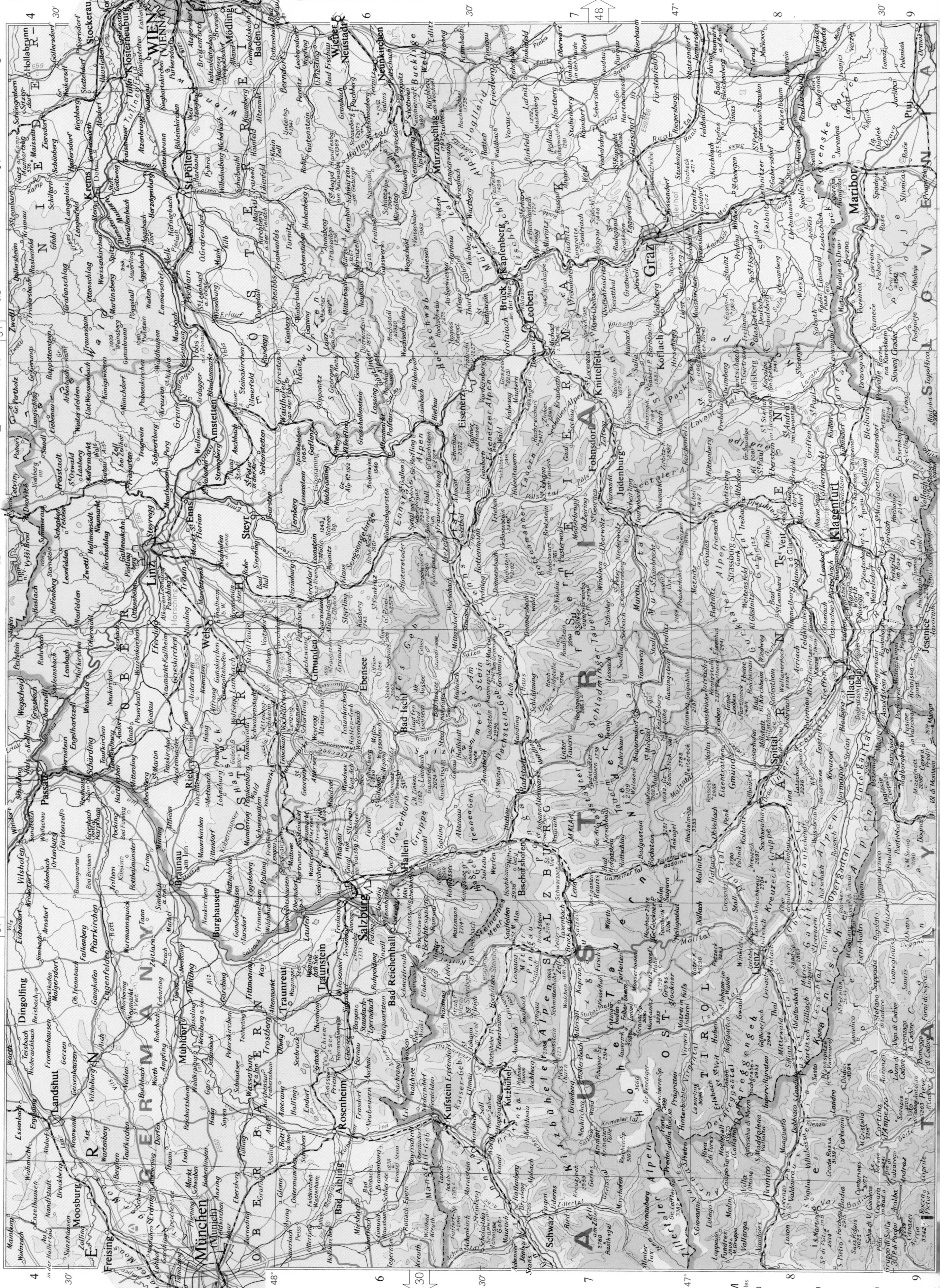

CONIC PROJECTION

Heights in metres

1:1 M

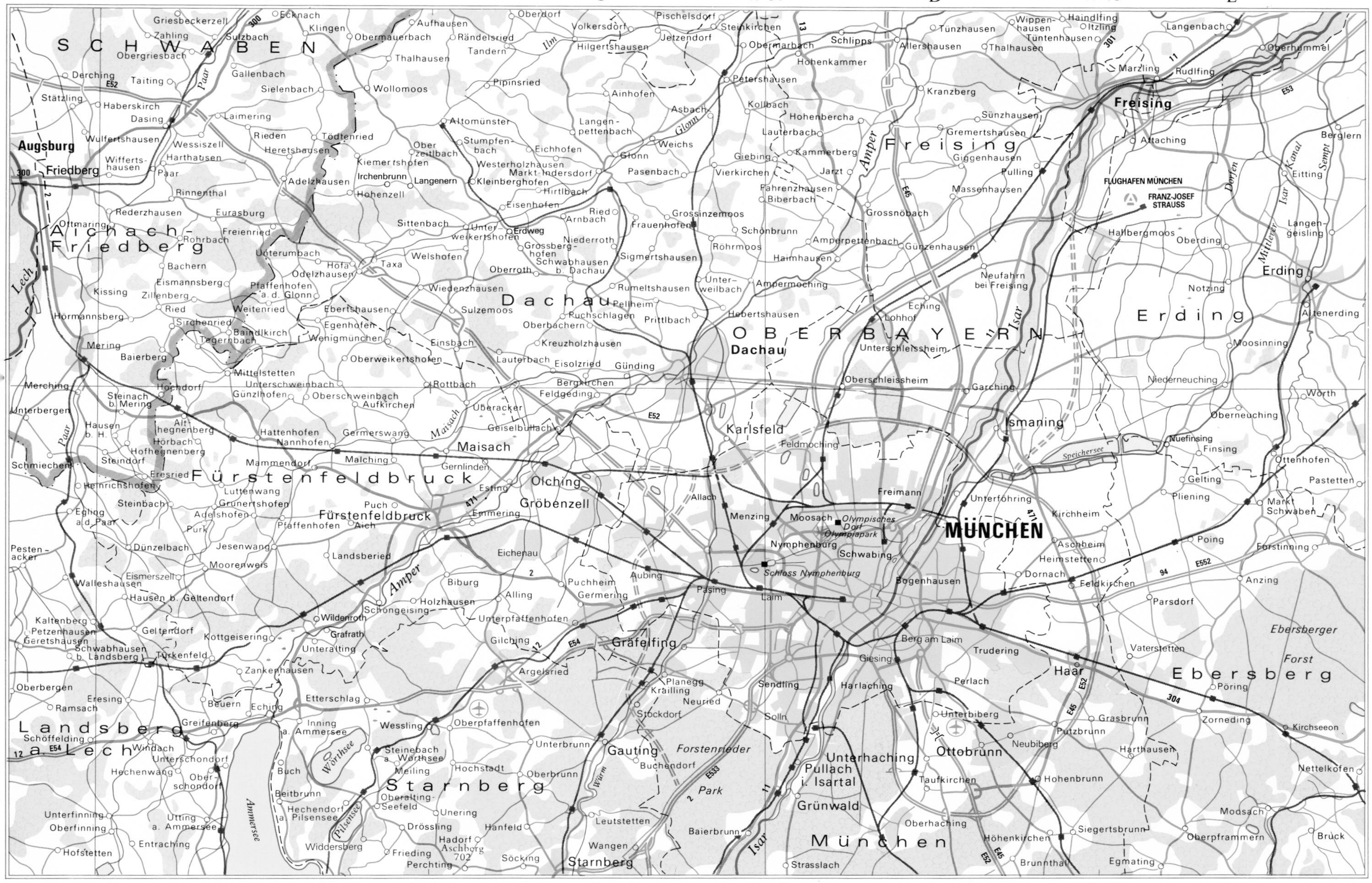

A 11°00′ B 11°15′ C 11°30′ D 11°45′ E

MILAN

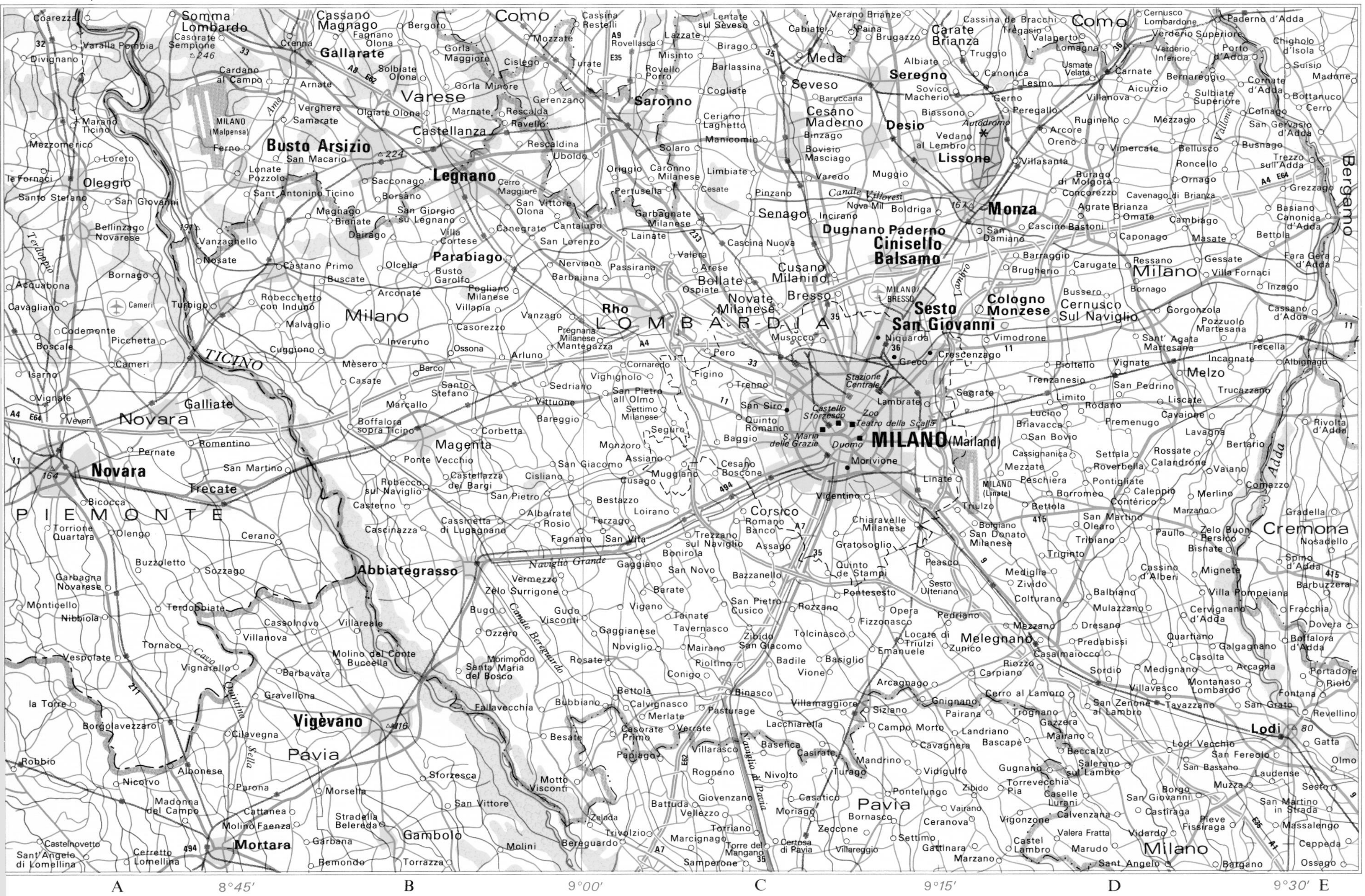

A 8°45′ B 9°00′ C 9°15′ D 9°30′ E

0 5 10 15 km
0 5 10 miles

1:300 000

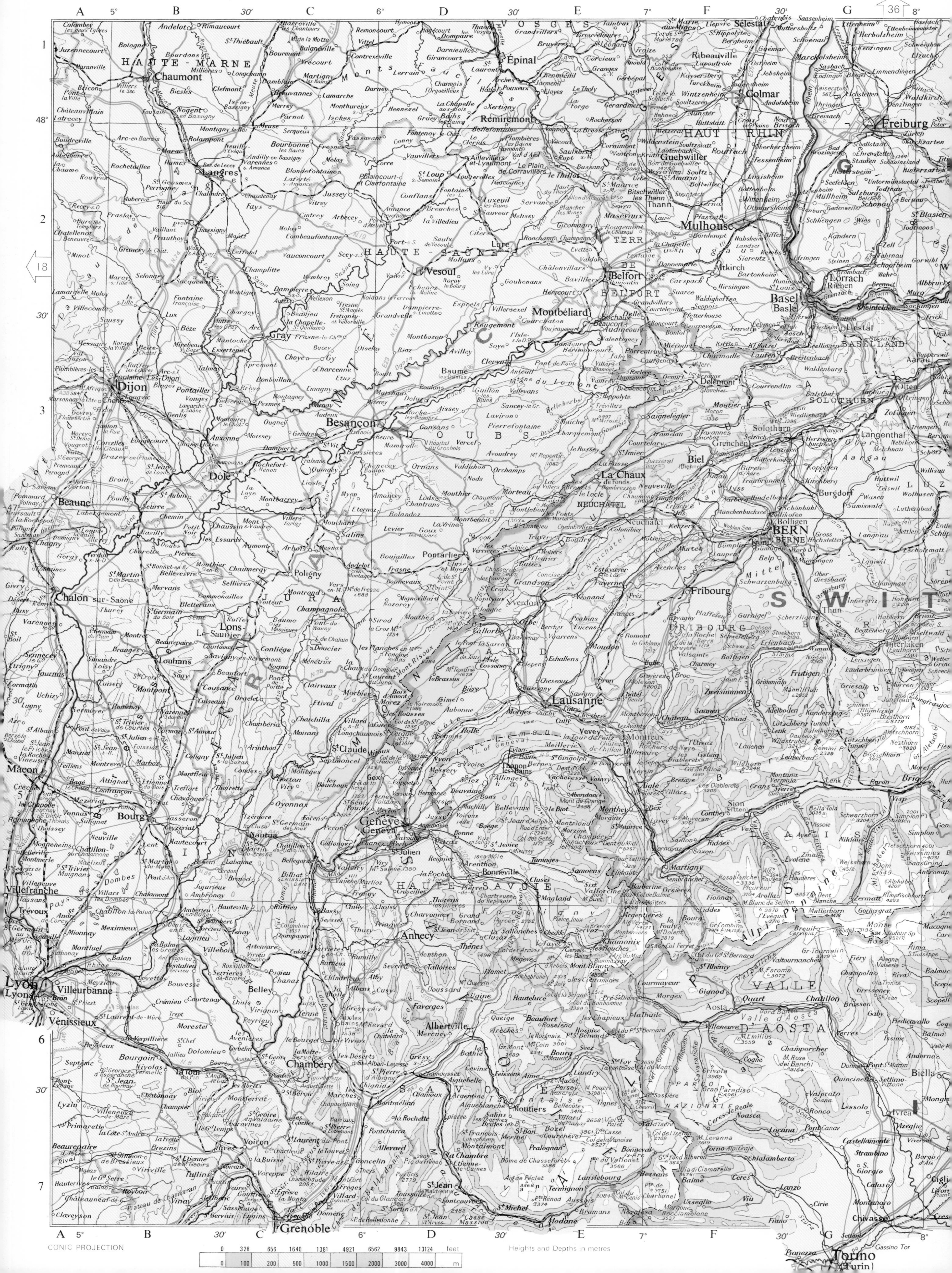

HAUTE-MARNE
HAUTE-SAÔNE
HAUT-RHIN
VOSGES
DOUBS
JURA
AIN
HAUTE-SAVOIE
SAVOIE
BELFORT
NEUCHÂTEL
SOLOTHURN
BASELLAND
FRIBOURG
BERN
VALLE D'AOSTA
SWIT
Chaumont
Langres
Dijon
Beaune
Dôle
Besançon
Vesoul
Épinal
Remiremont
Colmar
Mulhouse
Belfort
Montbéliard
Basel (Basle)
Freiburg
Lörrach
Chalon sur-Saône
Lons-Le-Saunier
Bourg
Mâcon
Lyon
Lyons
Villeurbanne
Vénissieux
Pontarlier
Neuchâtel
La Chaux de Fonds
Biel
Solothurn
BERN BERNE
Fribourg
Lausanne
Genève Geneva
Annecy
Chambéry
Grenoble
Albertville
Aosta
Torino (Turin)
Thun
Sion
Martigny
Chamonix
CONIC PROJECTION
Heights and Depths in metres
0 328 656 1640 3281 4921 6562 9843 13124 feet
0 100 200 500 1000 1500 2000 3000 4000 m

36
18

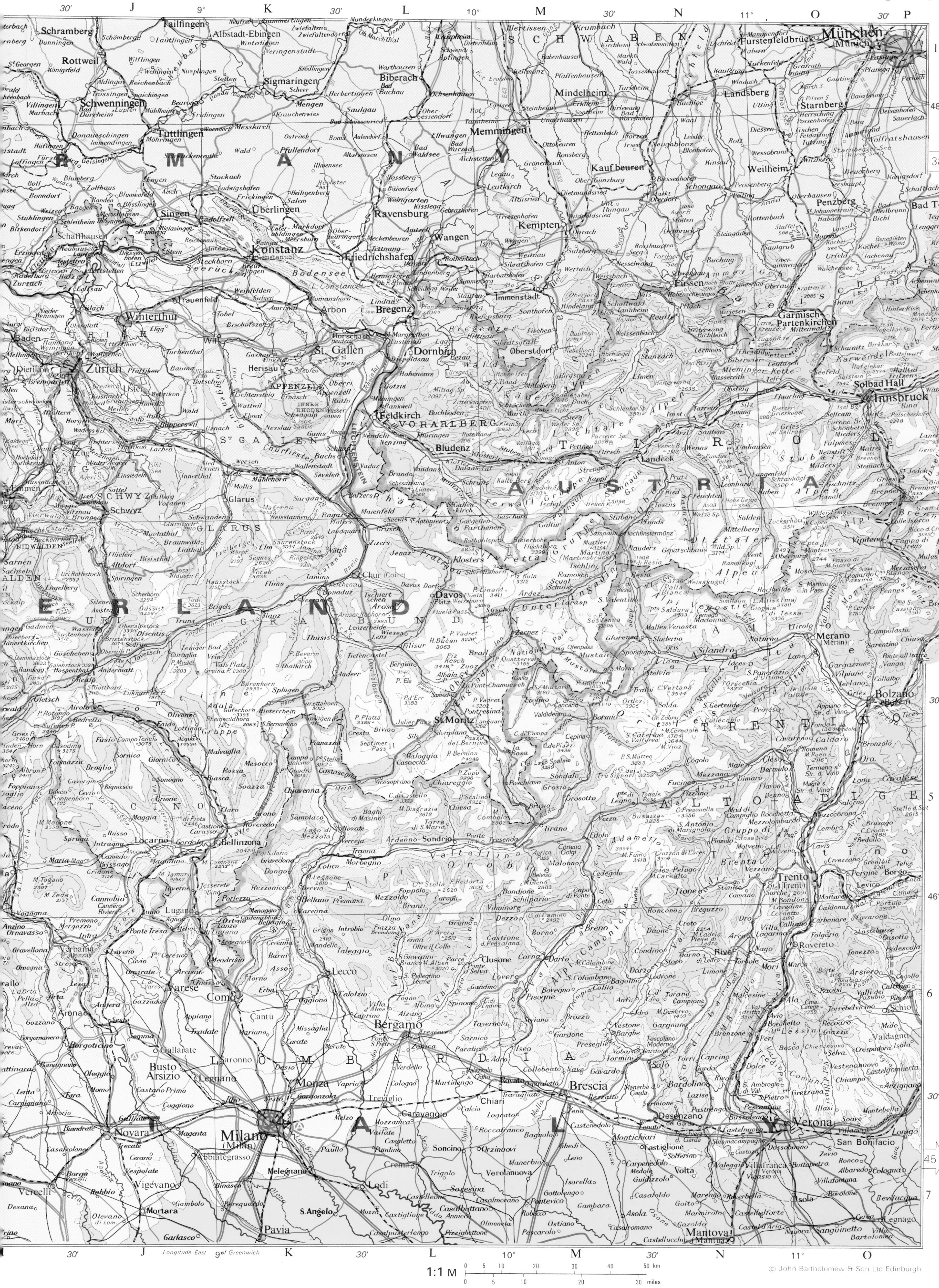
München
Innsbruck
Zürich
St. Gallen
Konstanz
Friedrichshafen
Bregenz
Kempten
Memmingen
Ravensburg
Sigmaringen
Schwenningen
Tuttlingen
Schaffhausen
Winterthur
Feldkirch
Bludenz
Chur
Davos
St. Moritz
Landeck
Merano
Bolzano
Trento
Bellinzona
Locarno
Lugano
Como
Lecco
Bergamo
Brescia
Verona
Milano
Novara
Monza
Pavia
Mantova
Sondrio
Garmisch-Partenkirchen
Bodensee
SCHWABEN
VORARLBERG
LIECHTENSTEIN
AUSTRIA
TIROL
TRENTINO
ALTO ADIGE
LOMBARDIA
TICINO
GRAUBÜNDEN
GLARUS
SCHWYZ
APPENZELL
ST GALLEN
Longitude East of Greenwich
1:1 M
km
miles
38
45

48
38
19

CONIC PROJECTION

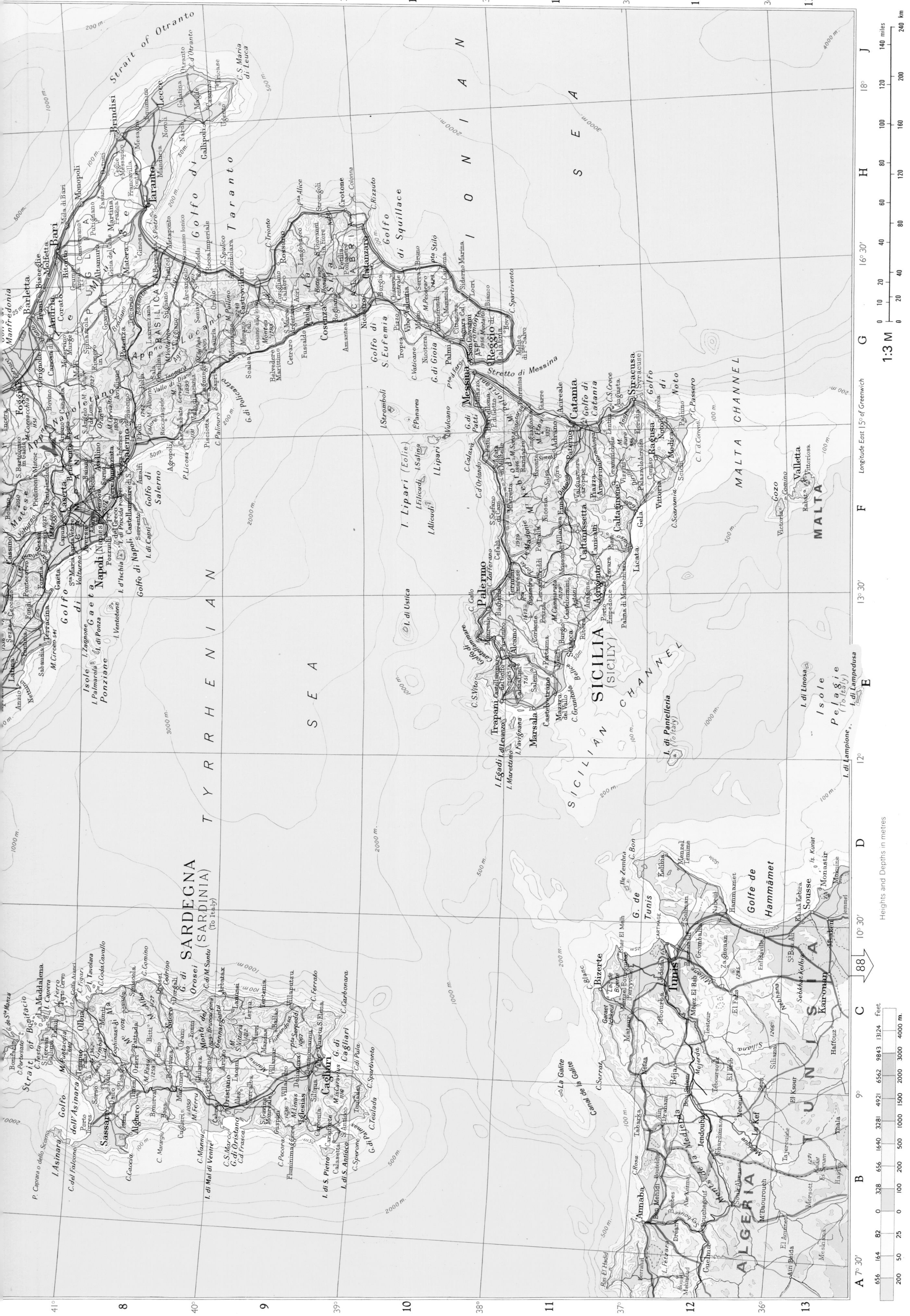
TYRRHENIAN SEA
IONIAN SEA
SARDEGNA (SARDINIA) (To Italy)
SICILIA (SICILY)
SICILIAN CHANNEL
MALTA CHANNEL
MALTA
TUNISIA
ALGERIA
Strait of Otranto
Golfo di Taranto
Golfo di Squillace
Stretto di Messina
Golfo de Hammāmet
G. de Tunis
Strait of Bonifacio
Golfo dell'Asinara
Isole Ponziane
I. Lipari (Eolie)
Isole Pelagie (To Italy)
I. di Pantelleria (To Italy)
I. di Ustica
Napoli
Palermo
Catania
Messina
Siracusa
Cagliari
Sassari
Tunis
Bari
Taranto
Brindisi
Lecce
Reggio di Calabria
Catanzaro
Cosenza
Salerno
Valletta
Bizerte
Sousse
Annaba
1:3 M
Longitude East 15° of Greenwich
Heights and Depths in metres
88

B
30'
C
40
8°
D
30'
E
9°
F
30'
G
10°
1
2
3
4
45°
44°
19
Milano
Novara
Vercelli
Torino (Turin)
Chivasso
Casale Monferrato
Vigevano
Pavia
Lodi
Crema
Cremona
Piacenza
Alessandria
Asti
Voghera
Tortona
Novi Ligure
Acqui Terme
Ovada
Alba
Bra
Cuneo
Mondovì
Pinerolo
Saluzzo
Savigliano
Fossano
Carmagnola
Moncalieri
Chieri
Genova (Genoa)
Savona
Varazze
Rapallo
Chiavari
Sestri Levante
La Spezia
Sarzana
Carrara
Marina di Carrara
Pietrasanta
Viareggio
Livorno
Finale Ligure
Albenga
Alassio
Imperia
San Remo
Bordighera
Ventimiglia
Menton
Monte-Carlo
MONACO
Nice
Antibes
Cannes
Grasse
FRANCE
GOLFO DI GENOVA
LIGURIAN SEA
RIVIERA DI PONENTE
RIVIERA DI LEVANTE
Fidenza
Salsomaggiore Terme
Pontremoli
Stradella
Codogno
Busseto
B
30'
C
8°
D
30'
E
9°
F
30'
G
10°

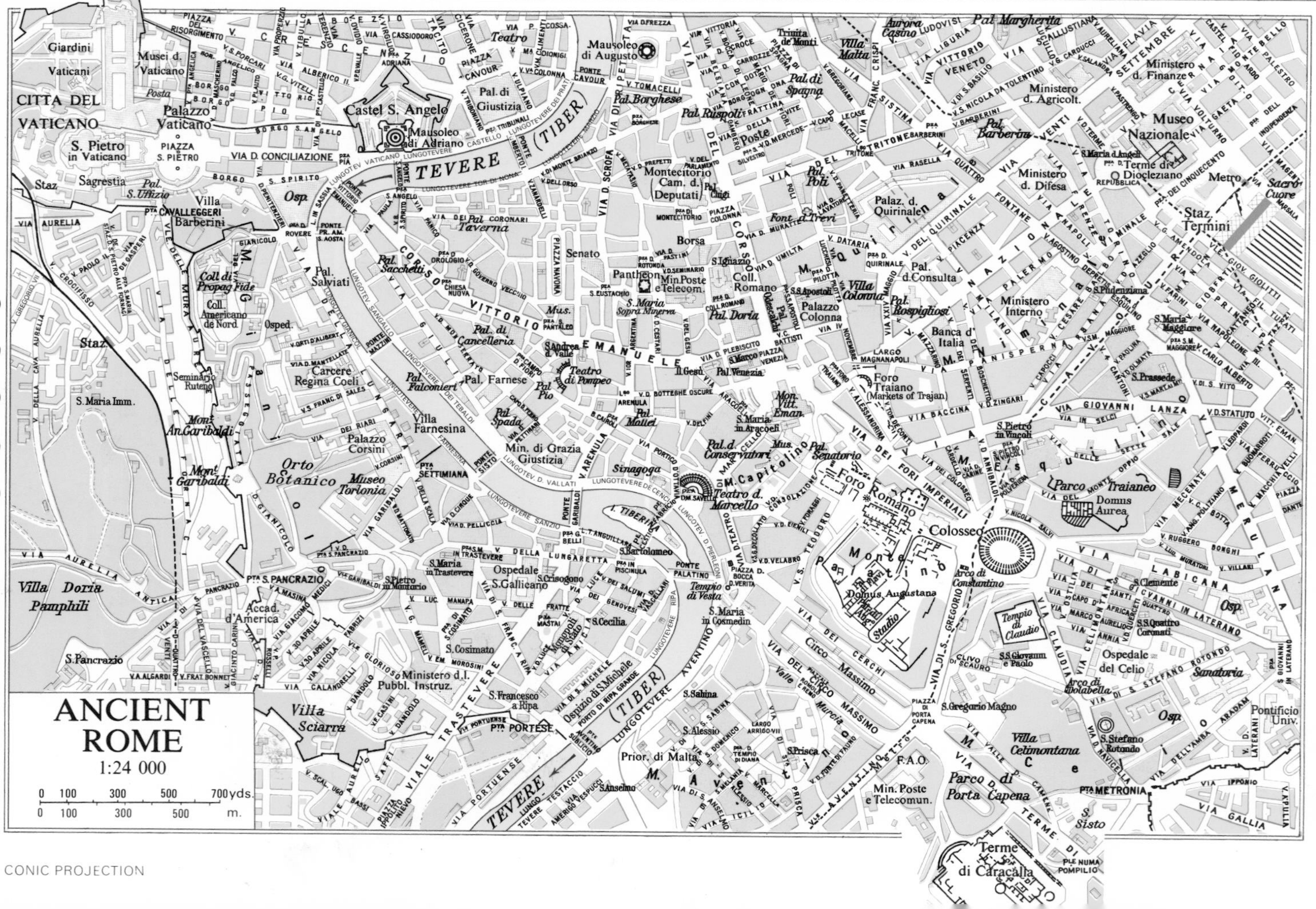
CITTA DEL VATICANO
S. Pietro in Vaticano
Castel S. Angelo
TEVERE (TIBER)
Mausoleo di Augusto
Pal. di Giustizia
Montecitorio
Pantheon
Fontana di Trevi
Pal. Barberini
Terme di Diocleziano
Staz. Termini
S. Maria Maggiore
Foro Romano
Colosseo
Foro Traiano
Palatino
Circo Massimo
Terme di Caracalla
Villa Doria Pamphili
Orto Botanico
Villa Sciarra
Teatro di Marcello
Tempio di Vesta
Pal. Venezia
Pal. Farnese
ANCIENT ROME
1:24 000
0 100 300 500 700 yds.
0 100 300 500 m.

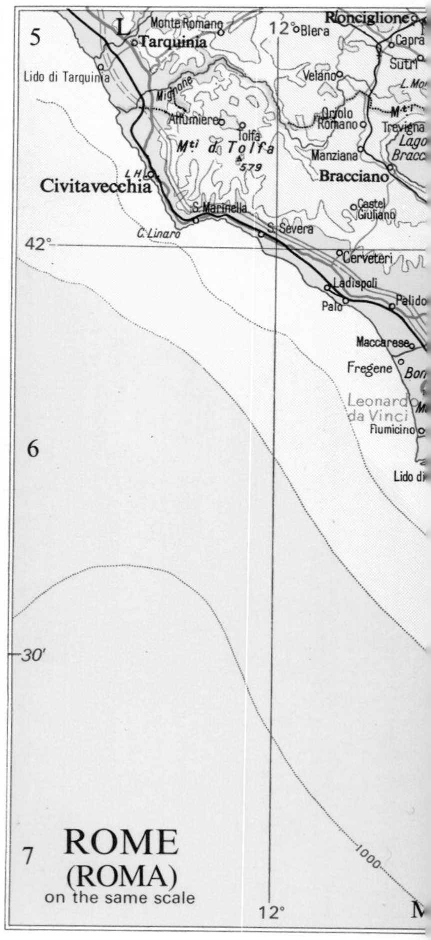
5
6
7
Tarquinia
Civitavecchia
Bracciano
Cerveteri
Ladispoli
Fregene
Fiumicino
42°
30'
12°
ROME
(ROMA)
on the same scale

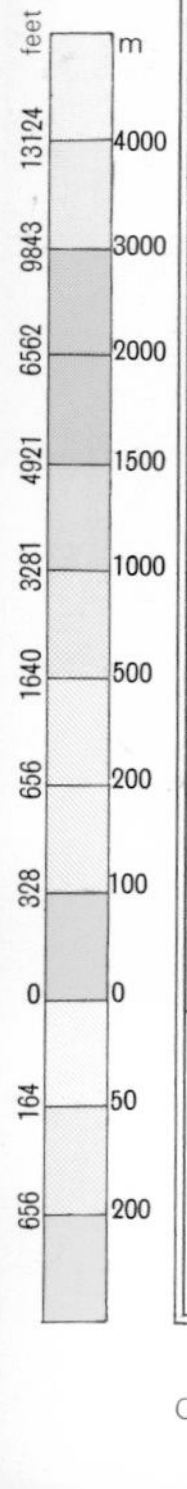
feet
m
13124 4000
9843 3000
6562 2000
4921 1500
3281 1000
1640 500
656 200
328 100
0 0
164 50
656 200

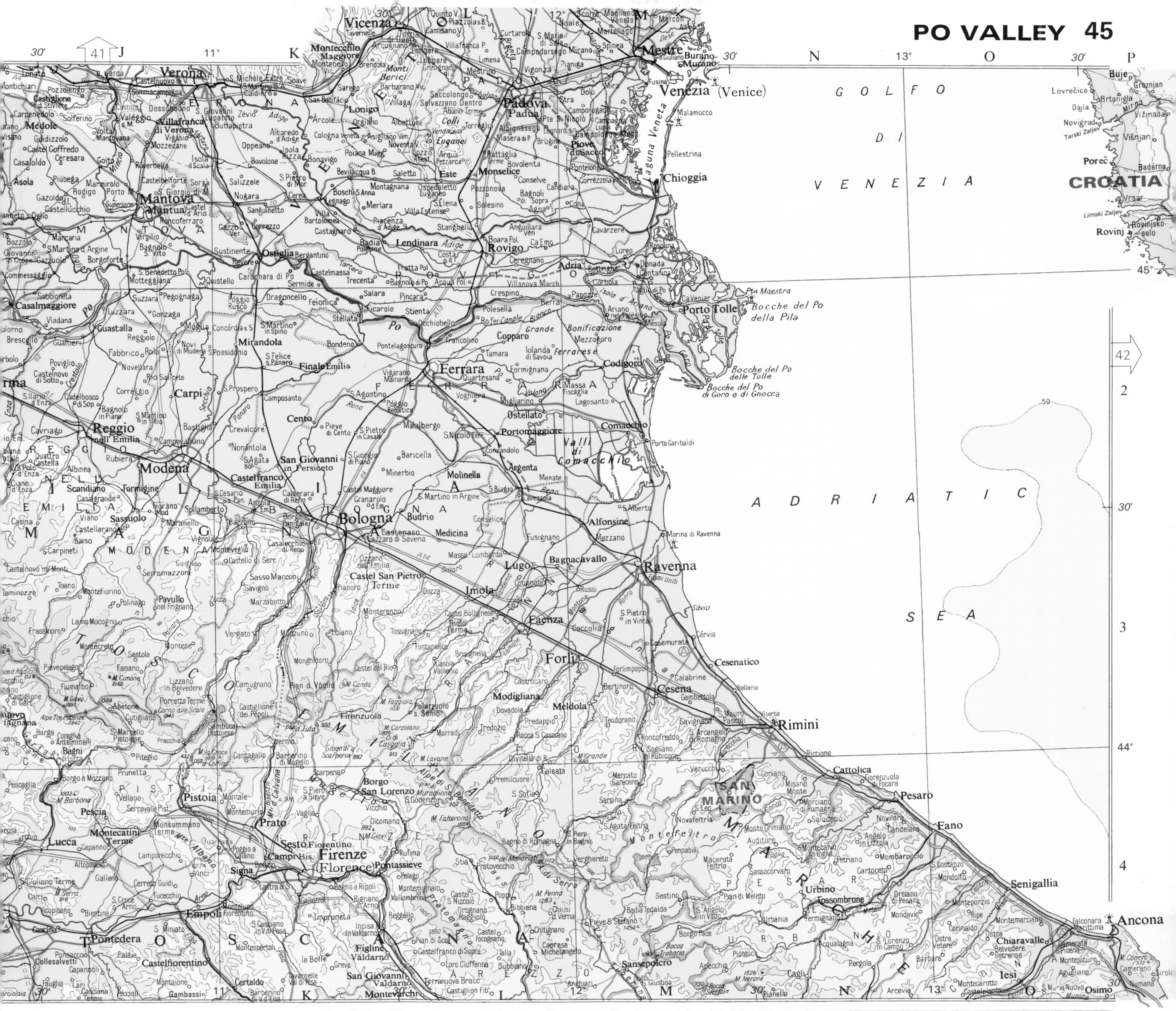
Verona
Vicenza
Padova
Padua
Mestre
Venezia (Venice)
Chioggia
Mantova
Mantua
Rovigo
Ferrara
Reggio nell'Emilia
Modena
Bologna
Ravenna
Forlì
Cesena
Rimini
SAN MARINO
Pesaro
Fano
Senigallia
Ancona
Pistoia
Prato
Firenze
Florence
Lucca
Pontedera
GOLFO DI VENEZIA
ADRIATIC SEA
CROATIA
Poreč
Rovinj
Comacchio
Imola
Faenza
Urbino

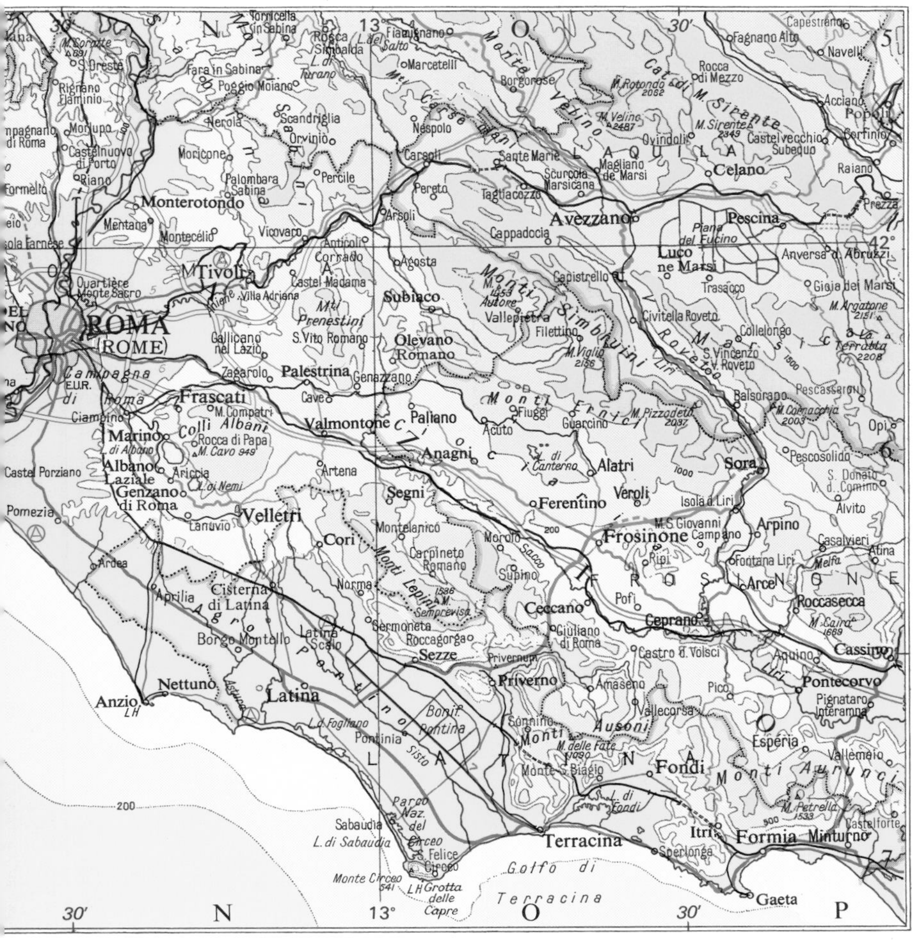
ROMA
(ROME)
Tivoli
Avezzano
Frosinone
Latina
Anzio
Terracina
Gaeta
Velletri
Frascati
Sora
Fondi

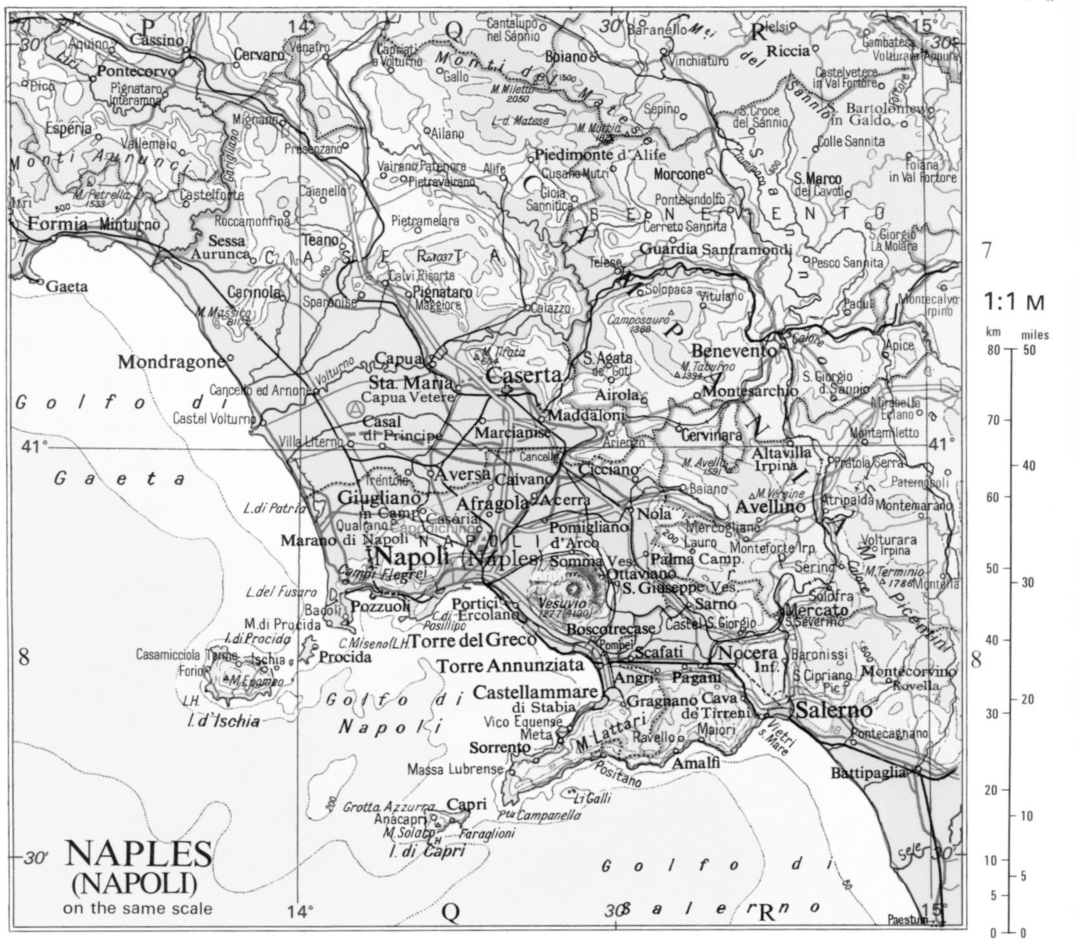
NAPLES
(NAPOLI)
on the same scale
Napoli (Naples)
Caserta
Benevento
Avellino
Salerno
Pozzuoli
Torre del Greco
Torre Annunziata
Castellammare di Stabia
Sorrento
Capri
Ischia
Gaeta
Formia
Golfo di Napoli
Golfo di Salerno
1:1 M
km
miles

48
42
BOSNIA-HERZEGOVINA
CROATIA
YUGOSLAVIA
MONTENEGRO
KOSOVO
ALBANIA
MACEDONIA
BULGARIA
ROMANIA
GREECE
ITALY
PUGLIA
ADRIATIC SEA
IONIAN SEA
MEDITERRANEAN SEA
AEGEAN SEA
MIRTOAN SEA
SEA OF CRETE
Strait of Otranto
Golfo di Taranto
Golfo di Squillace
IÓNIOI NÍSOI (IONIAN ISLANDS)
DHYTIKÍ MAKEDHONÍA
KEDRIKÍ MAKEDHONÍA
ANATOLIKÍ MAKEDHONÍA KAI THRÁKI
THESSALÍA
ÍPIROS
STEREÁ ELLÁS
DHYTIKÍ ELLÁS
ATTIKÍ
PELOPÓNNISOS
KRÍTI
VORÍAI SPORÁDHES (NORTHERN SPORADES)
ÉVVOIA (EUBOEA)
KIKLÁDHES (CYCLADES)
Sarajevo
Split
Dubrovnik (Ragusa)
Podgorica
Beograd
Niš
Priština
Skopje
Sofiya
Plovdiv
Tiranë (Tirana)
Durrës
Shkodër
Vlorë
Bari
Brindisi
Taranto
Lecce
Thessaloníki
Lárisa
Vólos
Ioánnina
Kérkira (Corfu)
Pátrai
Athínai (Athens)
Piraiévs
Kalamái
Khaniá
Iráklion
Ólimbos
Áyion Óros
1:3 M
km
miles
feet
m
ANCIENT ATHENS
1:12 000
AKROPOLIS
PARTHENON
ERECHTHEION
AGORA
Plaka
THESEION
PNYX
CONIC PROJECTION
Longitude East 21° of Greenwich

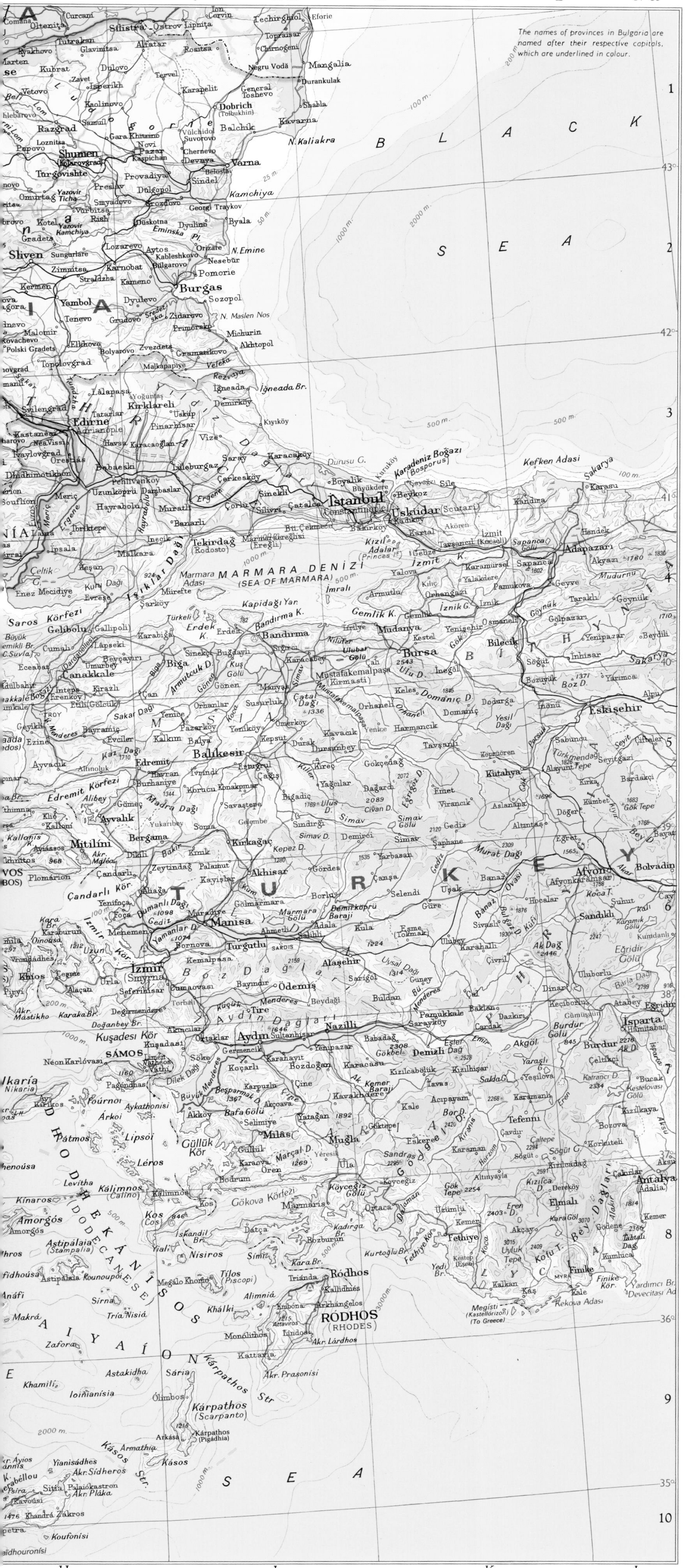
The names of provinces in Bulgaria are named after their respective capitals, which are underlined in colour.
BLACK SEA
MARMARA DENİZİ (SEA OF MARMARA)
TURKEY
AIYAÍON SEA
DHODHEKÁNISOS (DODECANESE)
Heights and Depths in metres

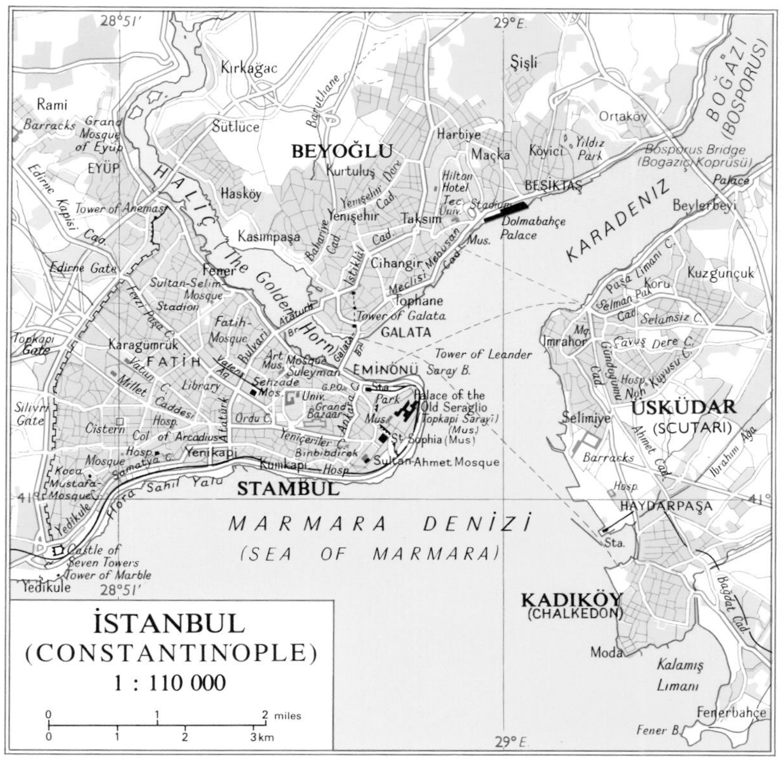
İSTANBUL (CONSTANTINOPLE)
1 : 110 000
MARMARA DENİZİ (SEA OF MARMARA)
BEYOĞLU
STAMBUL
ÜSKÜDAR (SCUTARI)
KADIKÖY (CHALKEDON)

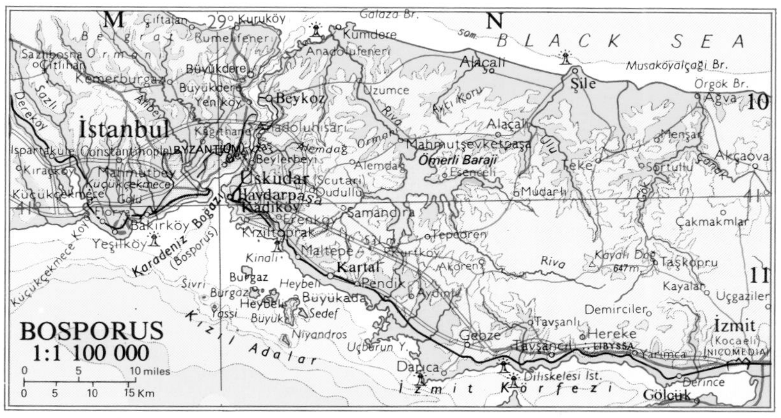
BOSPORUS
1:1 100 000
BLACK SEA

CORFU (KÉRKIRA)
(To Greece)
1:1 200 000
ALBANIA
Kérkira

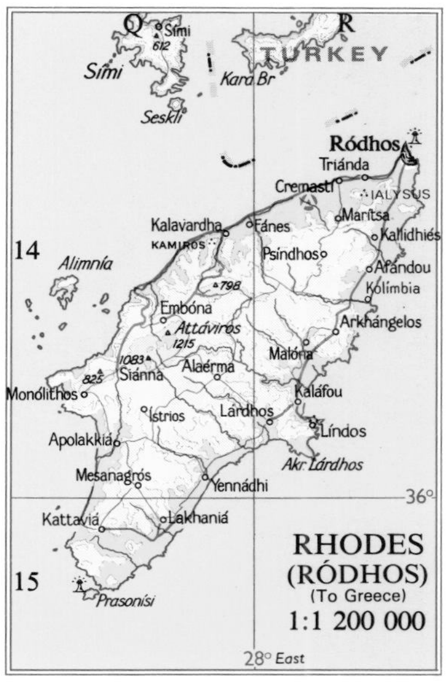
RHODES (RÓDHOS)
(To Greece)
1:1 200 000
TURKEY
Ródhos

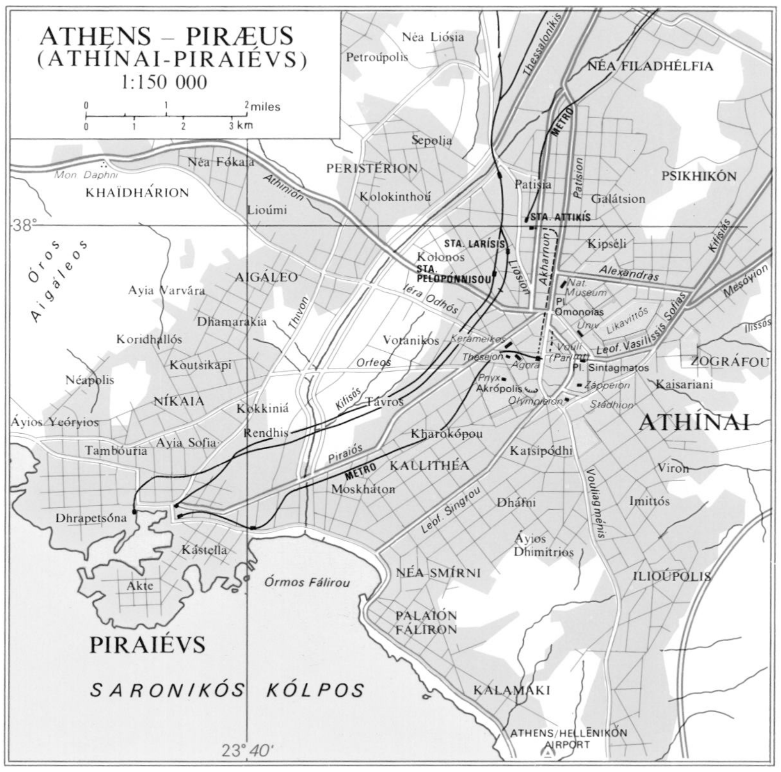
ATHENS – PIRÆUS (ATHÍNAI-PIRAIÉVS)
1:150 000
ATHÍNAI
PIRAIÉVS
SARONIKÓS KÓLPOS

1:3 M
miles
km
BLACK SEA
The names of regions in Romania are shown only where they differ from their respective capitals, which are underlined in black
MOLDOVA
MOLDAVIA
Kishinev
Odessa
Budapest
Bucureşti
Beograd
Sarajevo
Bratislava
Wien
Debrecen
Cluj-Napoca
Constanţa
Galaţi
Brăila
Iaşi
Timişoara
Szeged
Oradea
Ploieşti
Braşov
Sibiu
Craiova
Novi Sad
Ruse
Pleven
Lvov
Ternopol'
Chernovtsy
Przemyśl
Košice
Miskolc
Olomouc
Brno
Osijek
Subotica
Kecskemét
Pécs
Győr
Szolnok
54
31
42

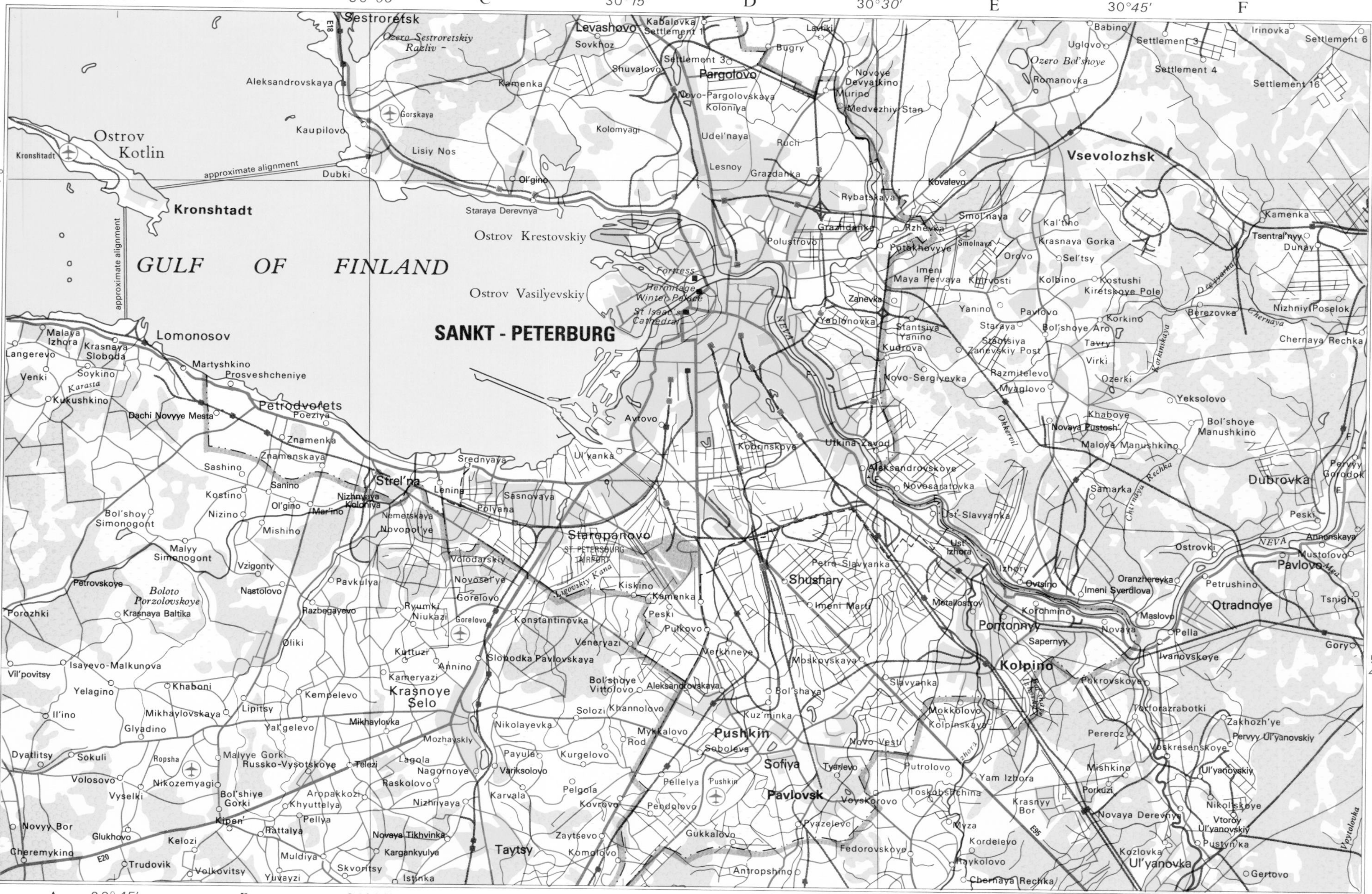

MOSCOW

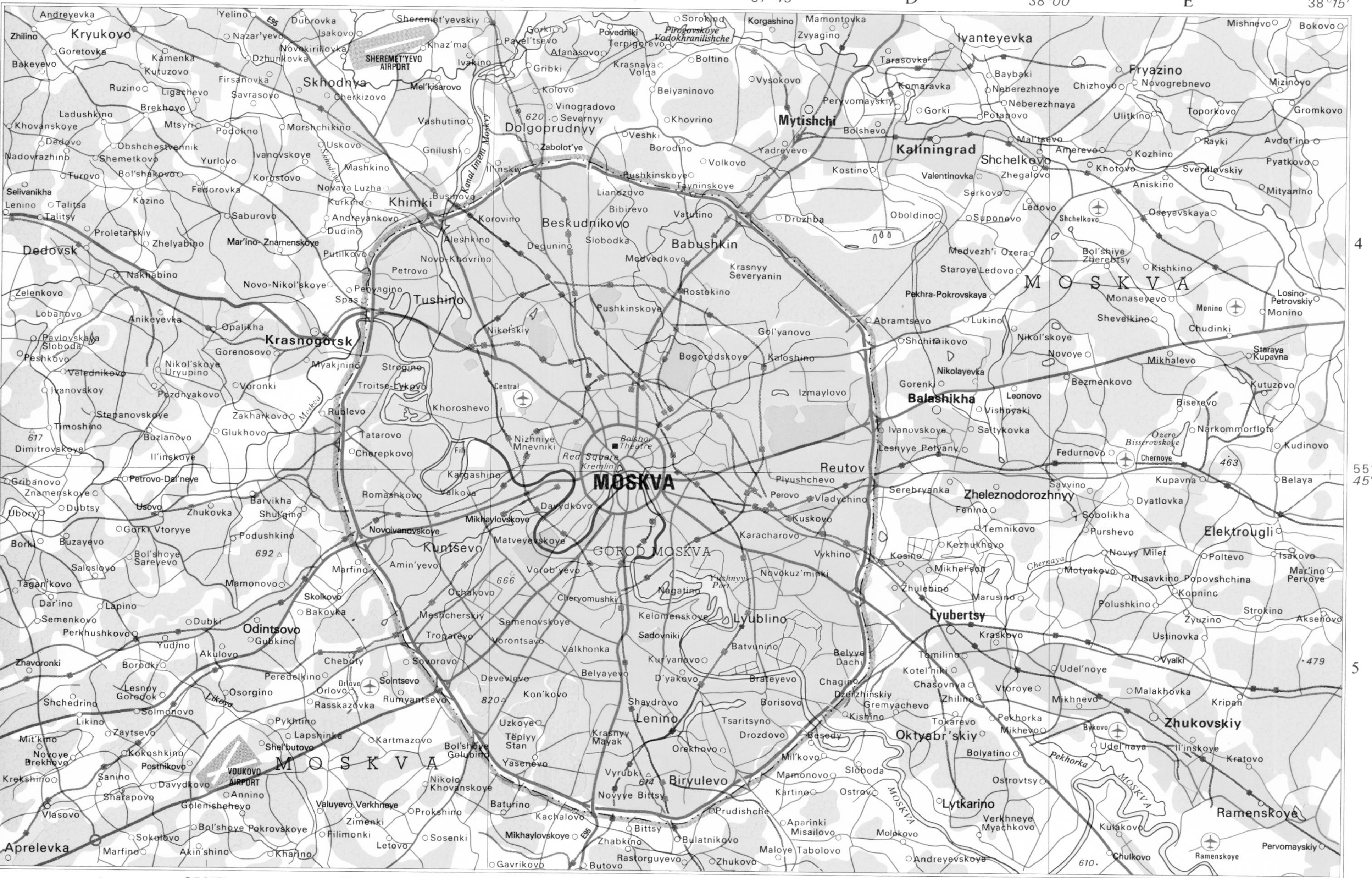

A 37°15′ B 37°30′ C 37°45′ D 38°00′ E 38°15′

5 10 15 km
5 10 miles

1:300 000

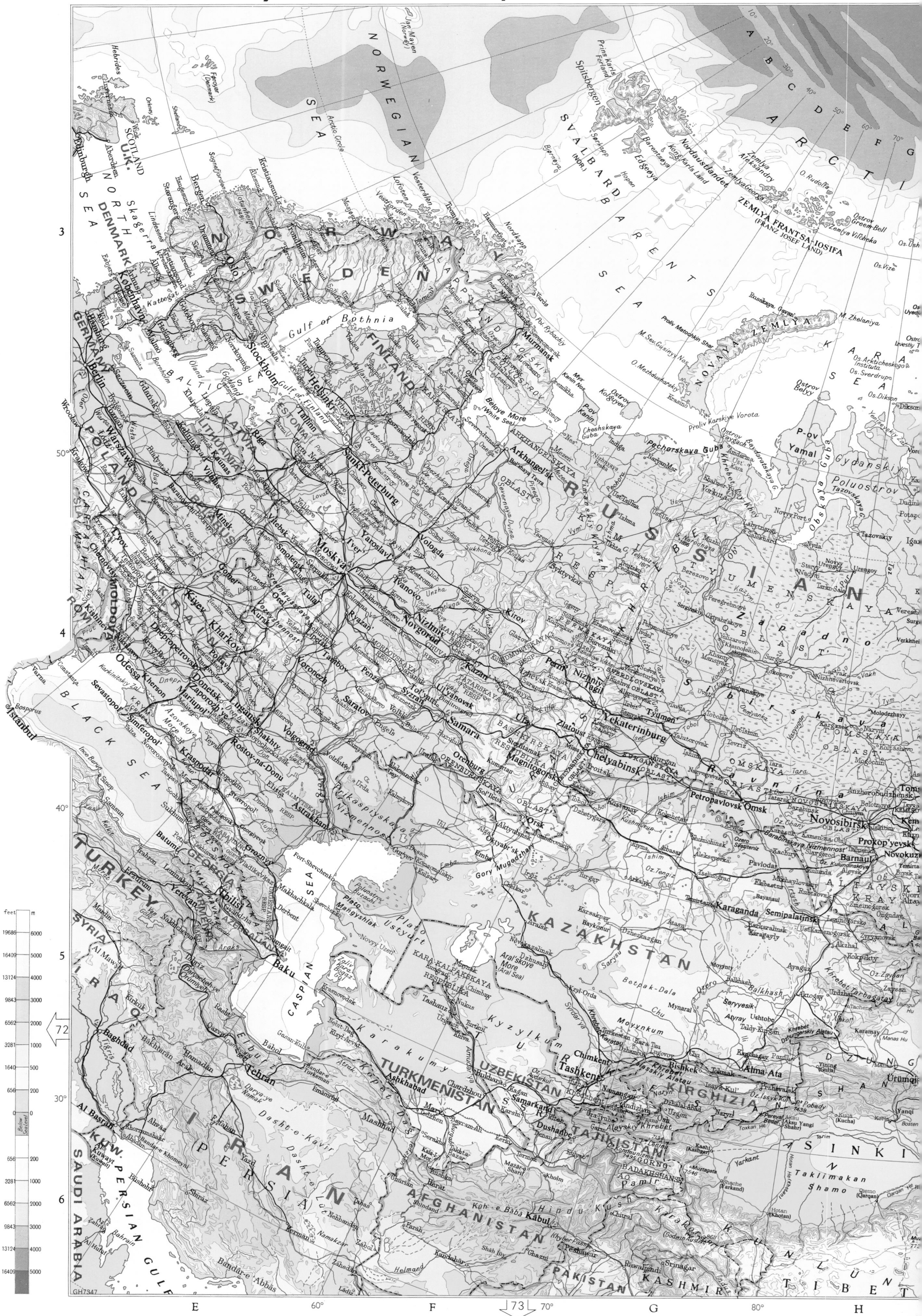

72
73

CONIC PROJECTION

RUSSIAN FEDERATION
ARCTIC OCEAN
EAST SIBERIAN SEA
LAPTEV SEA
CHUKCHI SEA
BERING SEA
SEA OF OKHOTSK
SEA OF JAPAN
YELLOW SEA
EAST CHINA SEA
ALASKA (USA)
Bering Str.
SEVERNAYA ZEMLYA (NORTH LAND)
NOVOSIBIRSKIYE OSTROVA (NEW SIBERIAN ISLANDS)
MONGOLIA
INNER MONGOLIA
MANCHURIA
CHINA
NORTH KOREA
SOUTH KOREA
JAPAN
HONSHU
HOKKAIDO
Shikoku
Kyūshū
SAKHALIN
KAMCHATSKAYA OBLAST'
SAKHALINSKAYA OBLAST'
PRIMORSKIY KRAY
CHITINSKAYA OBLAST'
BURYATSKAYA
Yakutsk
Magadan
Petropavlovsk Kamchatskiy
Khabarovsk
Vladivostok
Irkutsk
Ulan Ude
Chita
Krasnoyarsk
Ulaanbaatar (Ulan Bator)
Harbin
Changchun
Shenyang (Mukden)
Beijing (Peking)
Tianjin (Tientsin)
Dalian
Qingdao
Jinan
Taiyuan
Shijiazhuang
Zhengzhou
Xi'an
Lanzhou
Nanjing (Nanking)
Shanghai
Hangzhou
Wuhan
Hefei
Ningbo
Wenzhou
Seoul
Pusan
Tokyo
Yokohama
Nagoya
Osaka
Kyoto
Hiroshima
Sapporo
Sendai
Nagasaki
Kagoshima
Fukuoka
Hakodate
1:18 M
km miles
Longitude East 100° of Greenwich
64
Heights and Depths in metres

INDUSTRIAL URALS
Central Area
1:3 000 000
RUSSIAN FEDERATION
FINLAND
ESTONIA
BELOYE MORE
(WHITE SEA)
MURMANSKAYA OBLAST'
Arkhangel'sk
Sankt-Peterburg
Yekaterinburg
Chelyabinsk
Nizhniy Novgorod
Helsinki
(Helsingfors)
Tallinn
Riga
Murmansk
Petrozavodsk
Vologda
Yaroslavl'
Kazan'

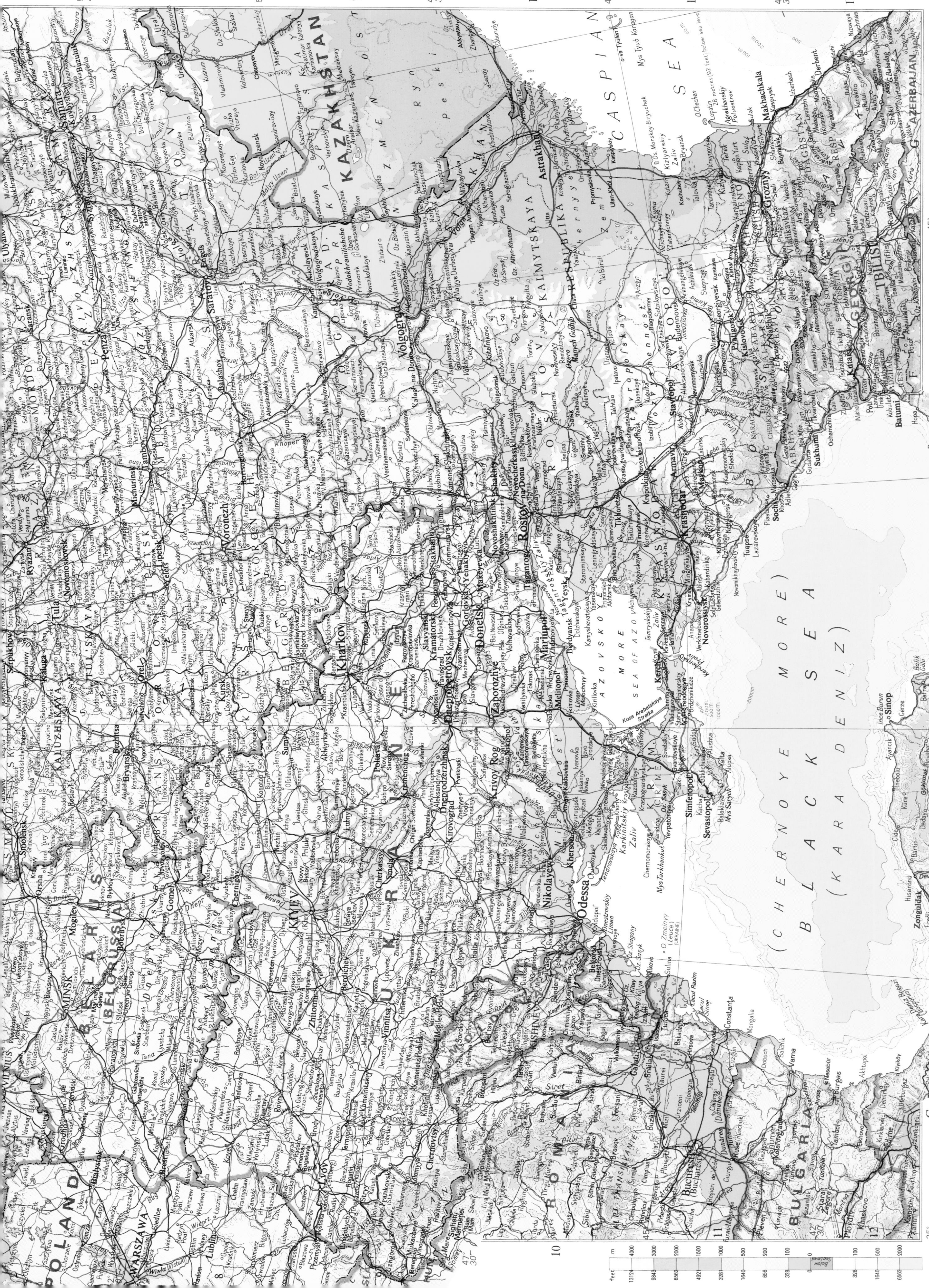
BLACK SEA
(CHERNOYE MORE)
(KARA DENIZ)
CASPIAN SEA
KAZAKHSTAN
AZOVSKOYE MORE
SEA OF AZOV
1:6 M
CONIC PROJECTION

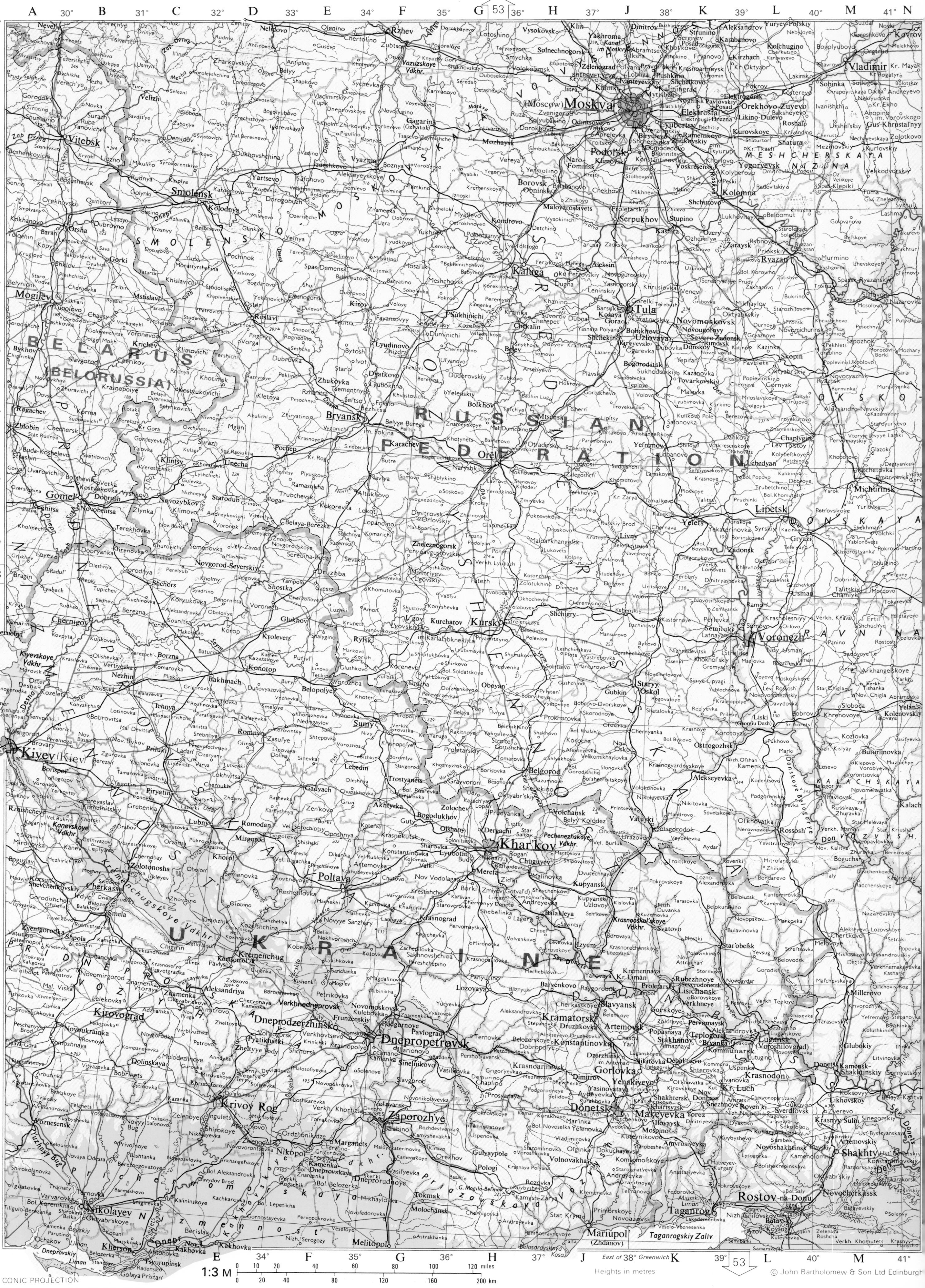
RUSSIAN FEDERATION
UKRAINE
BELARUS
(BELORUSSIA)
Moskva
(Moscow)
Smolensk
Vitebsk
Orsha
Mogilev
Gomel'
Bryansk
Orel
Kaluga
Tula
Ryazan'
Vladimir
Lipetsk
Voronezh
Kursk
Belgorod
Khar'kov
Sumy
Poltava
Kiyev (Kiev)
Chernigov
Cherkassy
Kremenchug
Kirovograd
Dnepropetrovsk
Zaporozh'ye
Krivoy Rog
Nikolayev
Kherson
Melitopol'
Donetsk
Lugansk
Mariupol'
(Zhdanov)
Taganrog
Rostov-na-Donu
Shakhty
Taganrogskiy Zaliv
SMOLENSKO-MOSKOVSKAYA VOZVYSHENNOST'
SREDNE-RUSSKAYA VOZVYSHENNOST'
PRIDNEPROVSKAYA VOZVYSHENNOST'
MESHCHERSKAYA NIZINA
OKSKO-DONSKAYA RAVNINA
PRICHERNOMORSKAYA NIZMENNOST'
Kremenchugskoye Vdkhr.
Kiyevskoye Vdkhr.
Kanevskoye Vdkhr.
Kakhovskoye Vdkhr.
CONIC PROJECTION
1:3 M
East of 38° Greenwich
Heights in metres
© John Bartholomew & Son Ltd Edinburgh
53

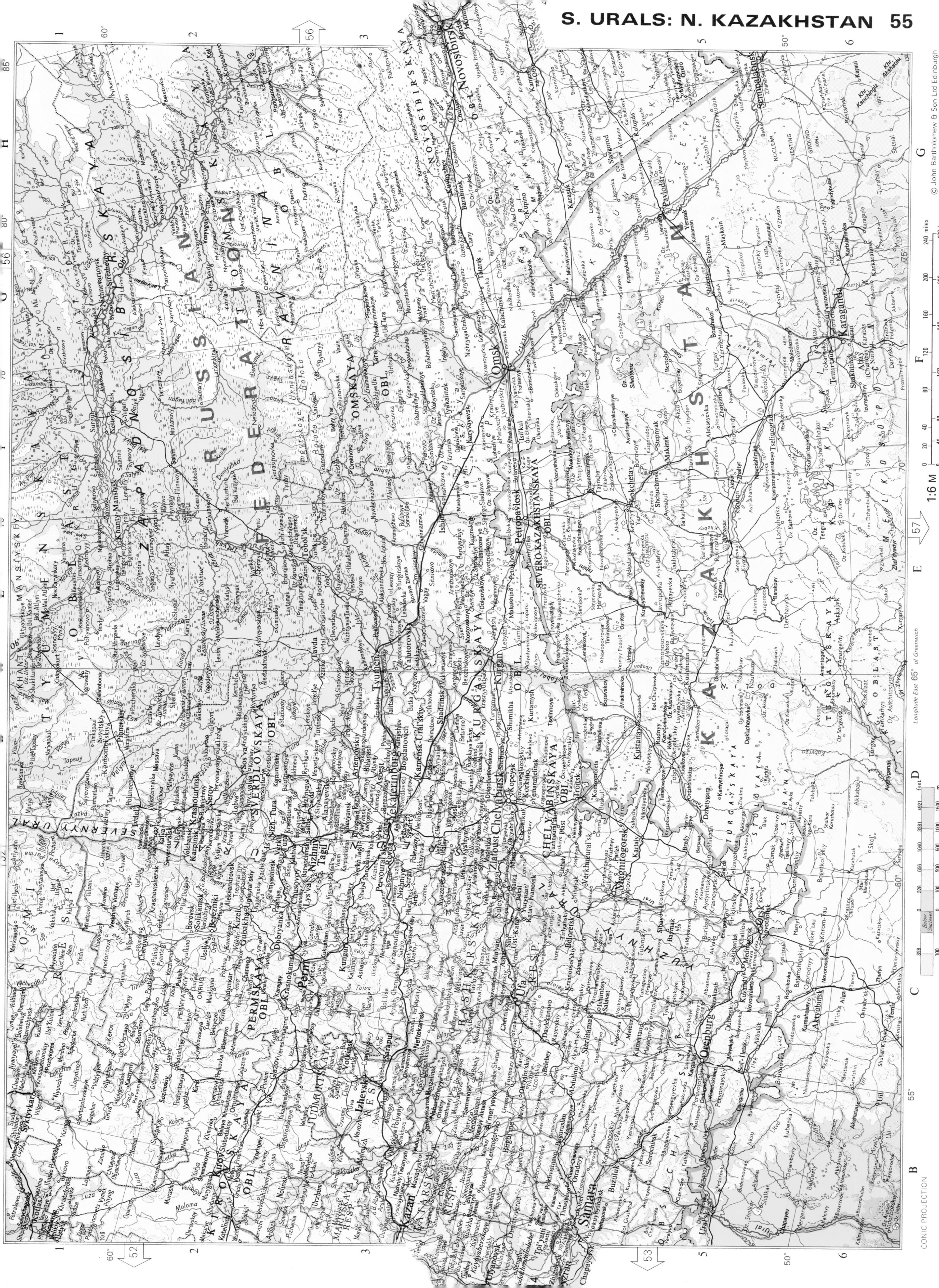
RUSSIAN FEDERATION
KAZAKHSTAN
ZAPADNO-SIBIRSKAYA RAVNINA
SEVERO-KAZAKHSTANSKAYA OBL.
KUSTANAYSKAYA
TURGAYSKAYA
CHELYABINSKAYA OBL.
KURGANSKAYA
SVERDLOVSKAYA OBL.
PERMSKAYA OBL.
BASHKIRSKAYA RESP.
UDMURTSKAYA RESP.
OMSKAYA
NOVOSIBIRSKAYA OBL.
Novosibirsk
Omsk
Tyumen'
Kurgan
Petropavlovsk
Kokchetav
Tselinograd
Karaganda
Pavlodar
Semipalatinsk
Chelyabinsk
Yekaterinburg
Perm'
Ufa
Orenburg
Samara
Kazan'
Izhevsk
Kirov
Syktyvkar
Kustanay
Magnitogorsk
Aktyubinsk
Orsk
Zlatoust
Nizhniy Tagil
Kamensk-Ural'skiy
Khanty-Mansiysk
Surgut
Nizhnevartovsk
Tobol'sk
NUCLEAR TESTING GROUND
Longitude East 65° of Greenwich
CONIC PROJECTION
1:6 M
miles
km
feet
m
Below Sea Level
52
53
56
57

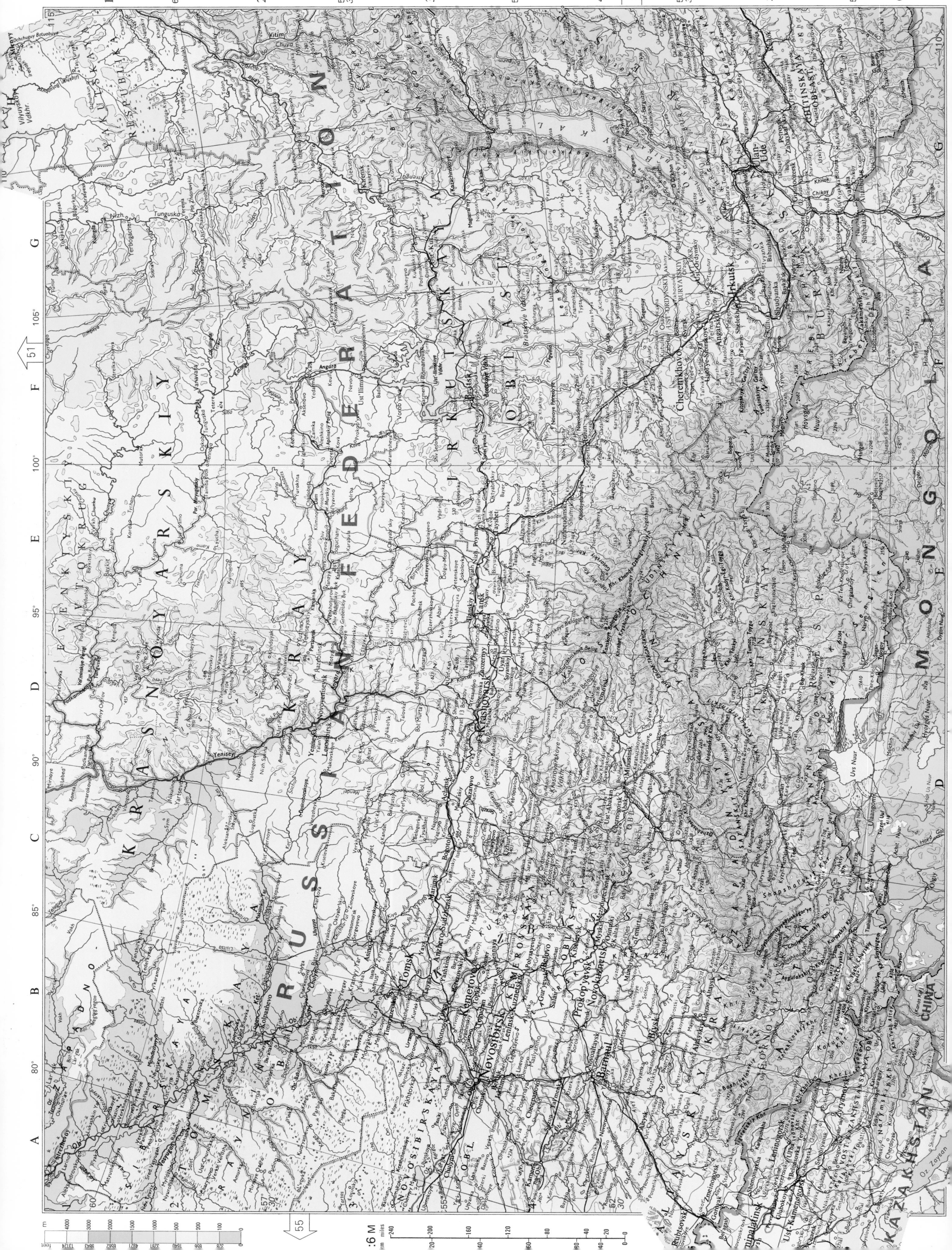
RUSSIAN FEDERATION
MONGOLIA
KAZAKHSTAN
CHINA
Novosibirsk
Krasnoyarsk
Irkutsk
Ulan-Ude
Tomsk
Kemerovo
Barnaul
Bratsk
Yenisey
Angara
Uvs Nuur
Hövsgöl Nuur

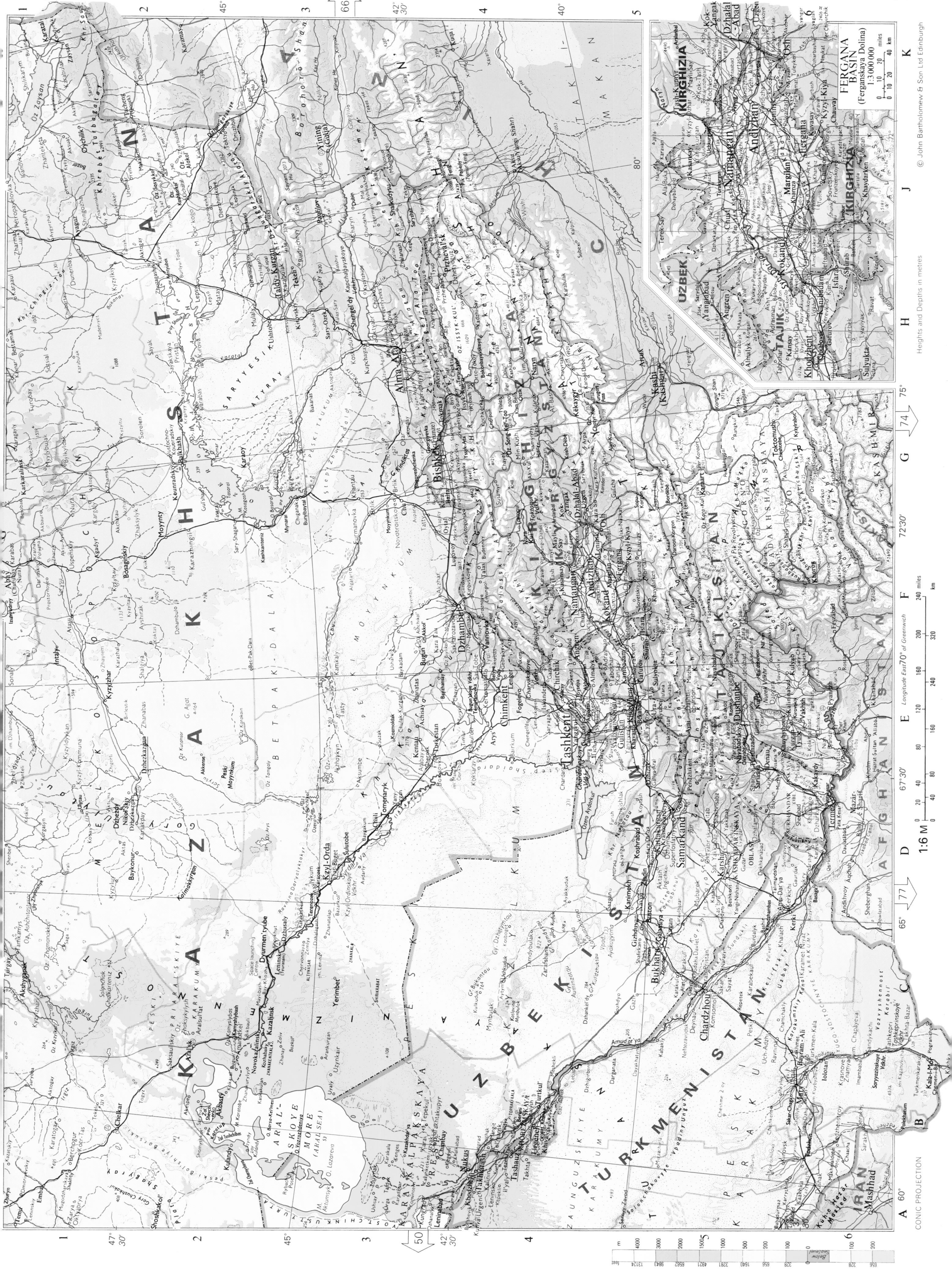
KAZAKHSTAN
UZBEKISTAN
TURKMENISTAN
KIRGHIZIA
TAJIKISTAN
AFGHANISTAN
IRAN
ARAL'SKOYE MORE (ARAL SEA)
FERGANA BASIN (Ferganskaya Dolina) 1:3 000 000
Tashkent
Alma-Ata
Bishkek
Samarkand
Dushanbe
Chimkent
Dzhambul
Kzyl-Orda
Bukhara
Chardzhou
Nukus
Mashhad
Kashi (Kashgar)
Yining (Gulja)
Andizhan
Namangan
Fergana
Kokand
Osh
1:6 M
CONIC PROJECTION
Heights and Depths in metres
© John Bartholomew & Son Ltd Edinburgh
Longitude East 70° of Greenwich

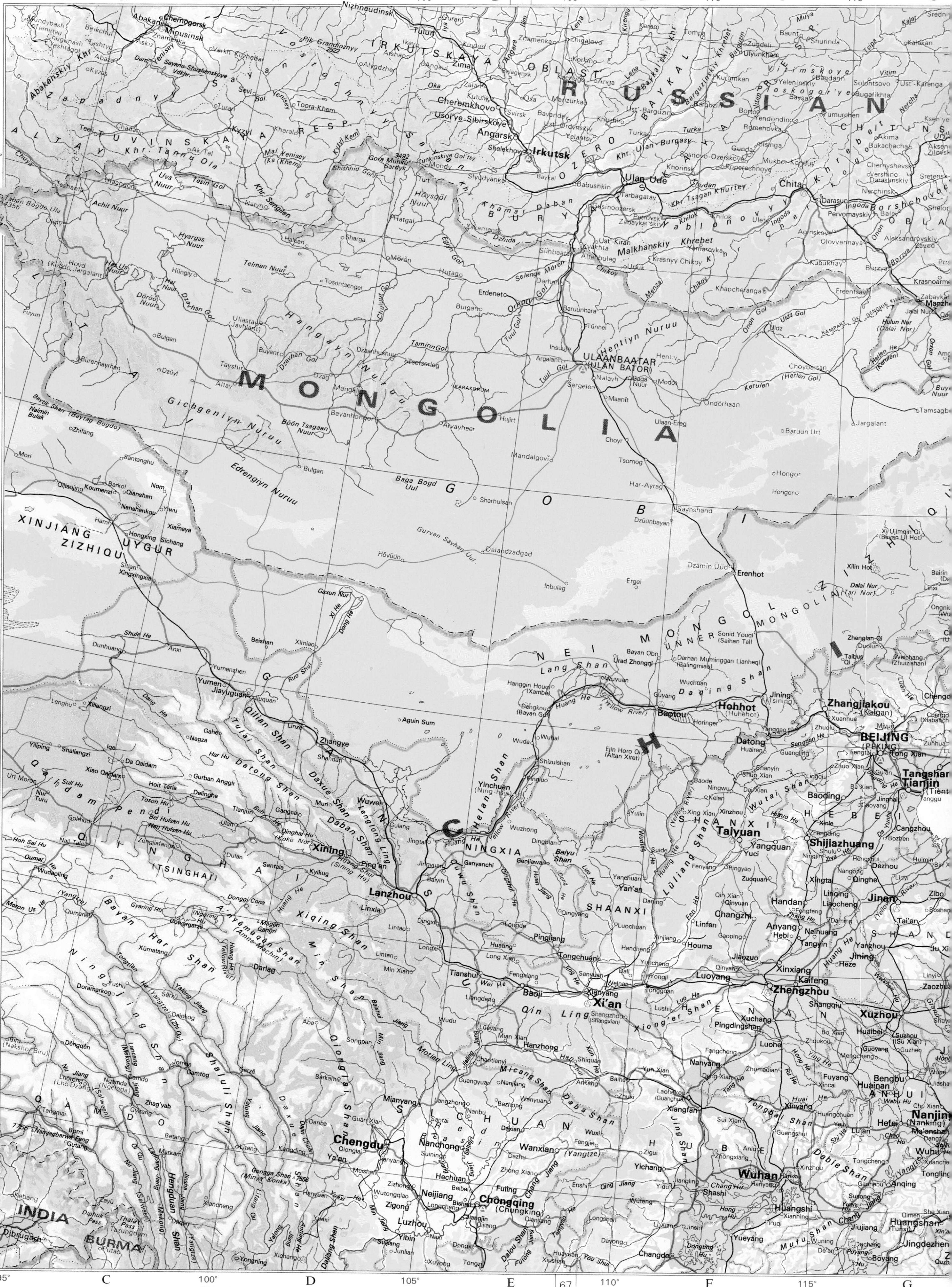

ALBERS CONIC PROJECTION

m	1000	200	0	200	500	1000	2000	3000	4000	5000	6000
feet	3281	656	0	656	1640	3281	6562	9843	13124	16409	19686

Heights and Depths in metres

1:9 M

Continuation on the same scale
SEA OF OKHOTSK
SEA OF JAPAN
HOKKAIDŌ
Sapporo
Asahikawa
Hakodate
Muroran
Otaru
Kushiro
Obihiro
Abashiri
Wakkanai
Rumoi
Tsugaru kaikyō
Aomori
Nemuro
Rishiri-tō
Rebun-tō
Okushiri-tō
Shiretoko misaki
Rus. Fed. admin. claimed by Japan
Kunashir (Kunashiri-tō)
Sernovodsk (Tōfutsu)
Golovnino (Tomari)
Erimo-misaki
Sōya-misaki
Uchiura-wan (Volcano Bay)
SOUTH KOREA
Taegu
Pusan
Masan
Chinju
Kōje-do
KOREA STRAIT
Nishi-suidō (Chōsen-kaikyō)
Higashi-suidō
Tsushima
Iki
Oki
Dōgo
Dōzen
Matsue
Tottori
Okayama
Hiroshima
Yamaguchi
Shimonoseki
Kita-Kyūshū
Fukuoka
Saga
Sasebo
Nagasaki
Kumamoto
Ōita
Beppu
Miyazaki
Kagoshima
Nobeoka
Sendai
Kanoya
Kōchi
Matsuyama
Tokushima
Takamatsu
Himeji
Kōbe
Akashi
Uwajima
Niihama
Kurashiki
Fukuyama
Suō-nada
Iyo-nada
Harima-nada
Tosa-wan
Bungo-suidō
Ashizuri-misaki
Muroto-zaki
Sata-misaki
Gotō-rettō
Koshiki-rettō
Kyūshū
Shikoku
Amakusa-shimo-shima
CONIC PROJECTION
feet
m

Aomori
Hirosaki
Hachinohe
Noshiro
Oga-hantō
Akita
Morioka
Miyako
Kamaishi
Sakata
Tsuruoka
Yamagata
Sendai
Shiogama
Sado
Niigata
Fukushima
Kōriyama
Iwaki
Nagaoka
Jōetsu
Toyama
Kanazawa
Fukui
Noto hantō
Nagano
Matsumoto
Takayama
Maebashi
Utsunomiya
Mito
Hitachi
Takasaki
Kōfu
TOKYO
Chiba
Yokohama
Kawasaki
Gifu
Nagoya
Shizuoka
Hamamatsu
Toyohashi
Yokkaichi
Tsu
Izu-shotō
Miyake-jima
Hachijō-jima
SEA OF JAPAN
PACIFIC OCEAN
1:3 M
IWO JIMA
1:300 000
OKINAWA
1:1 200 000
Naha
East 136° of Greenwich
Heights and Depths in metres

TOKYO

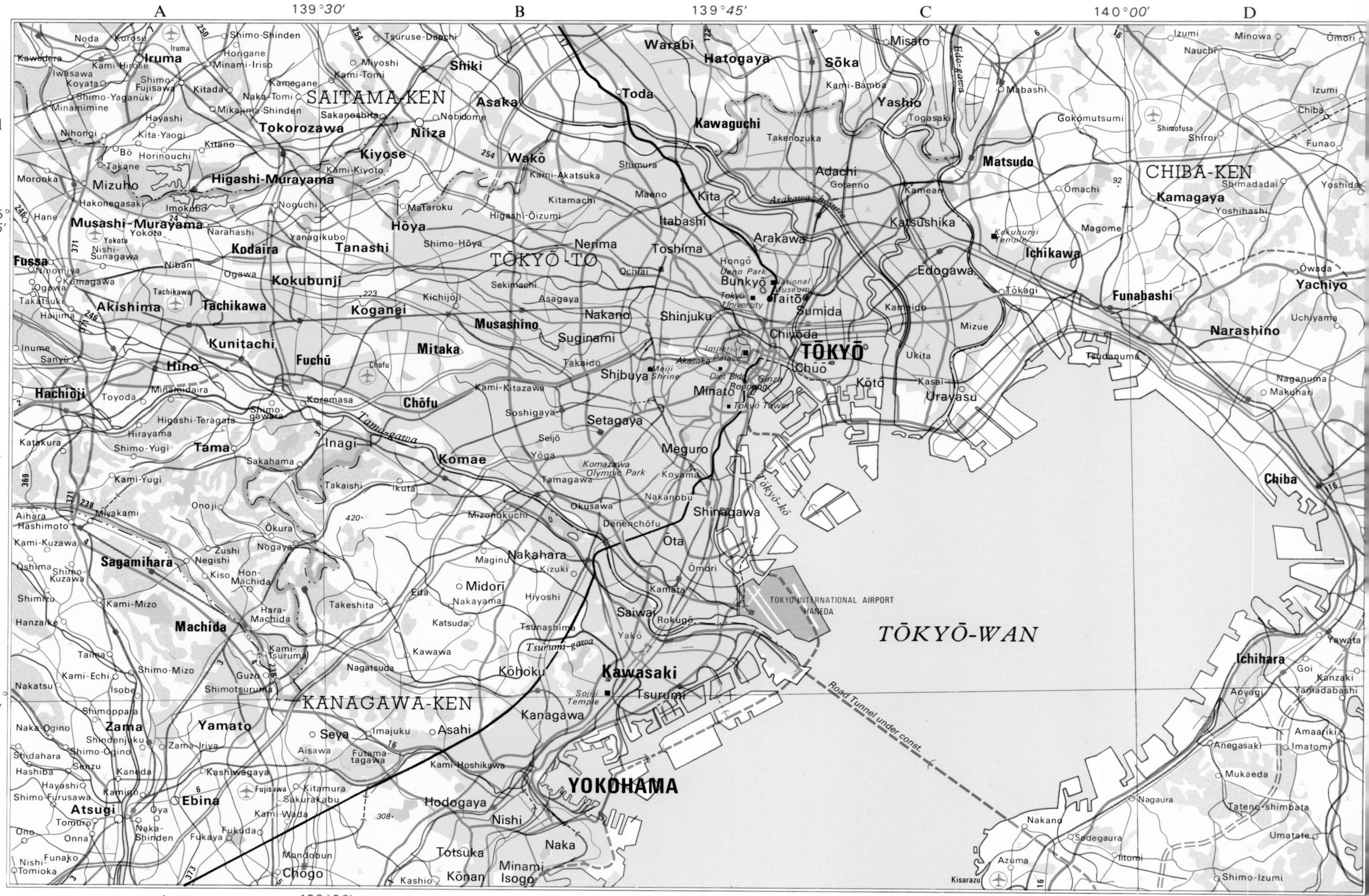

OSAKA

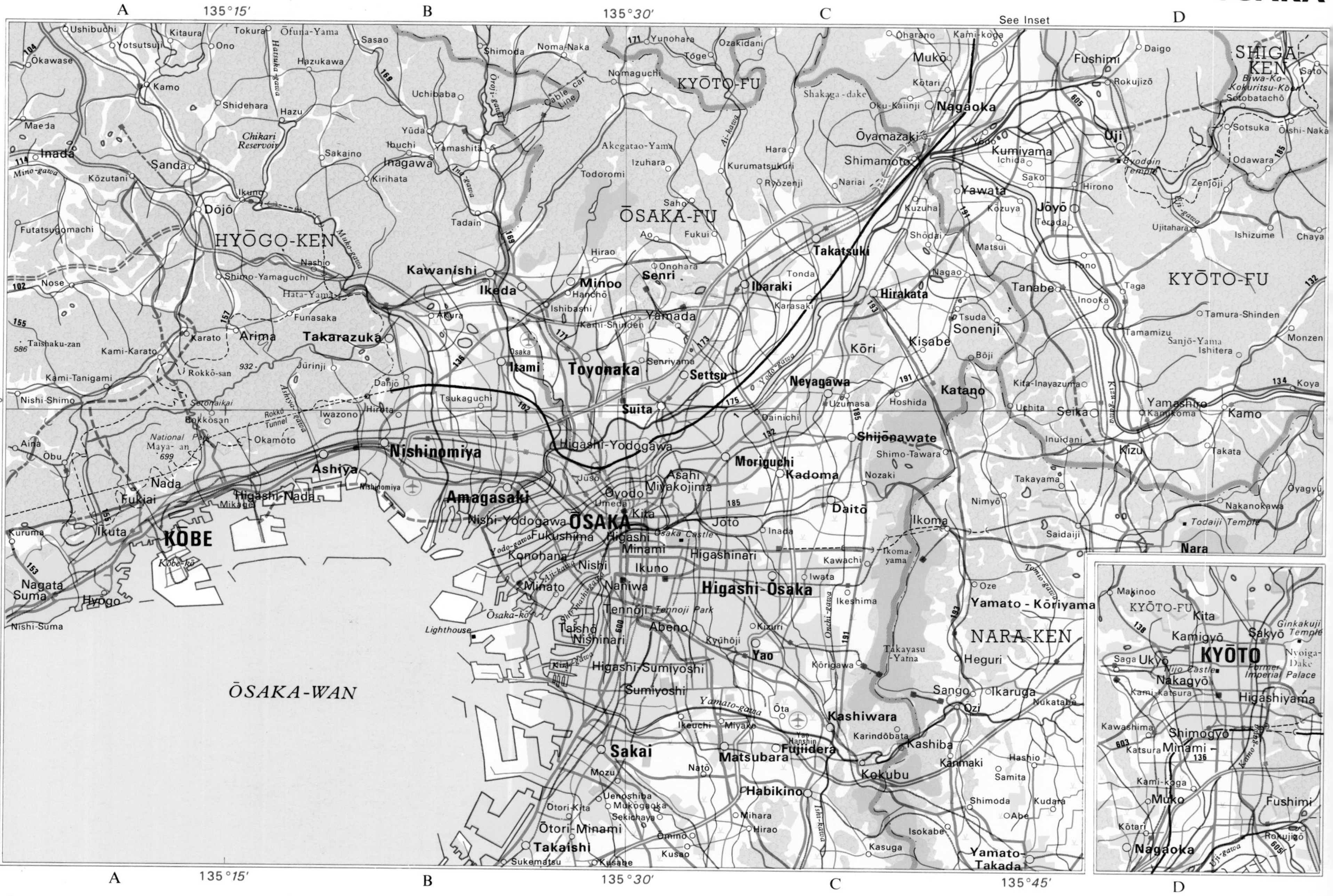

1:300 000

0 5 10 15 km

SEOUL

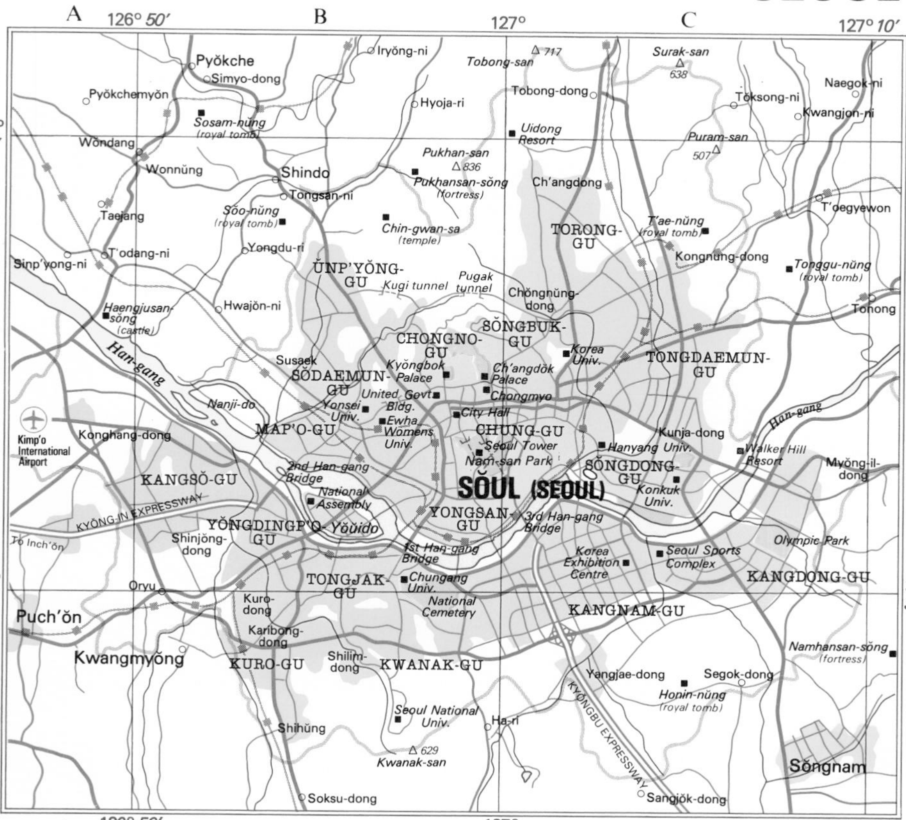

1:300000

BEIJING

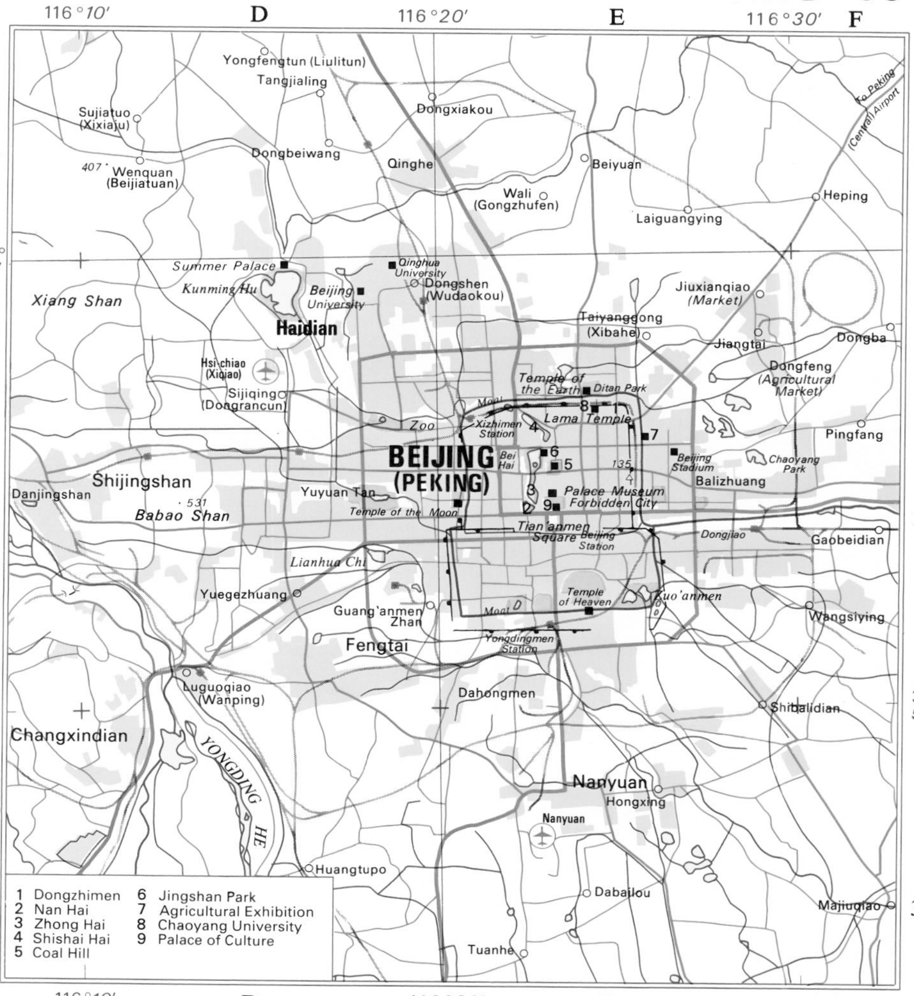

1:300000

SHANGHAI

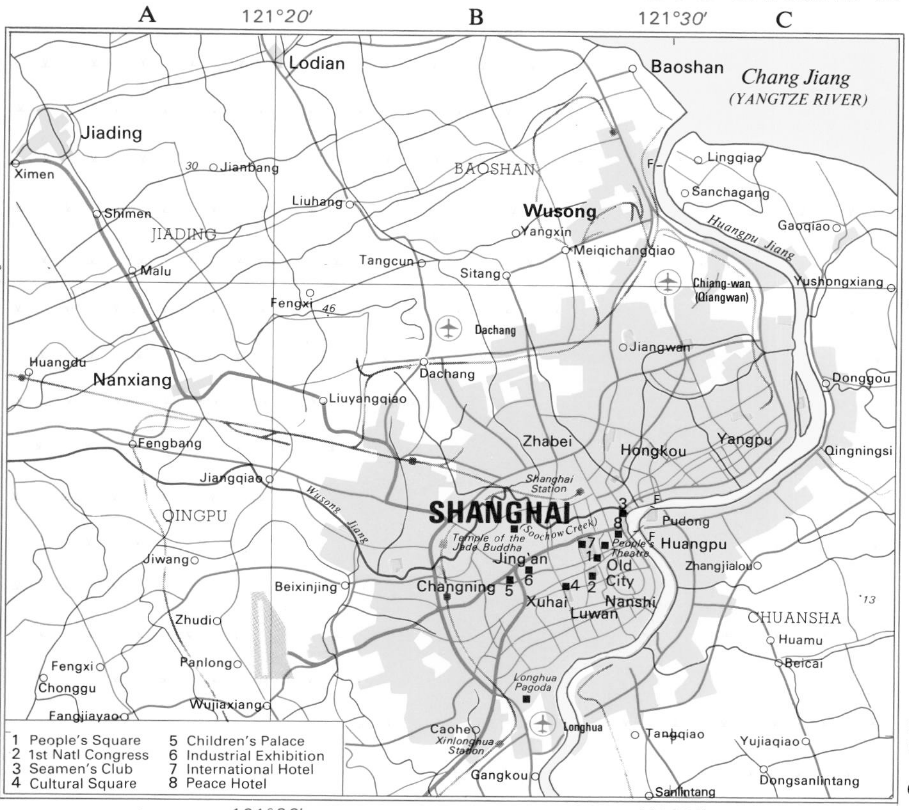

1:300000

GUANGZHOU

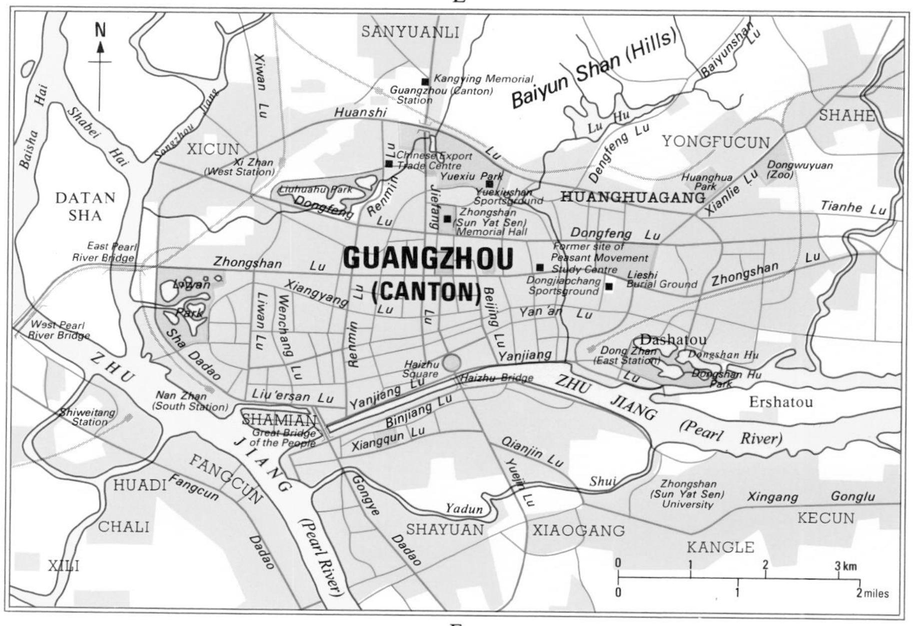

1:100 000

BANGKOK

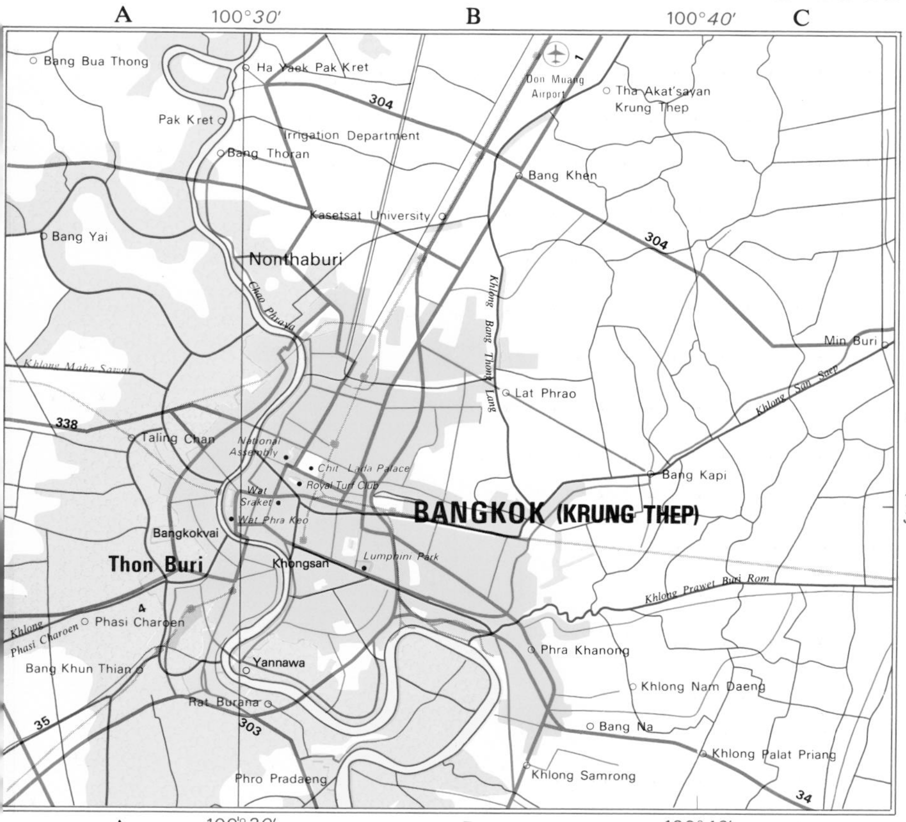

0 5 10 15 km
0 5 10 miles

1:300000

JAKARTA

1:300000

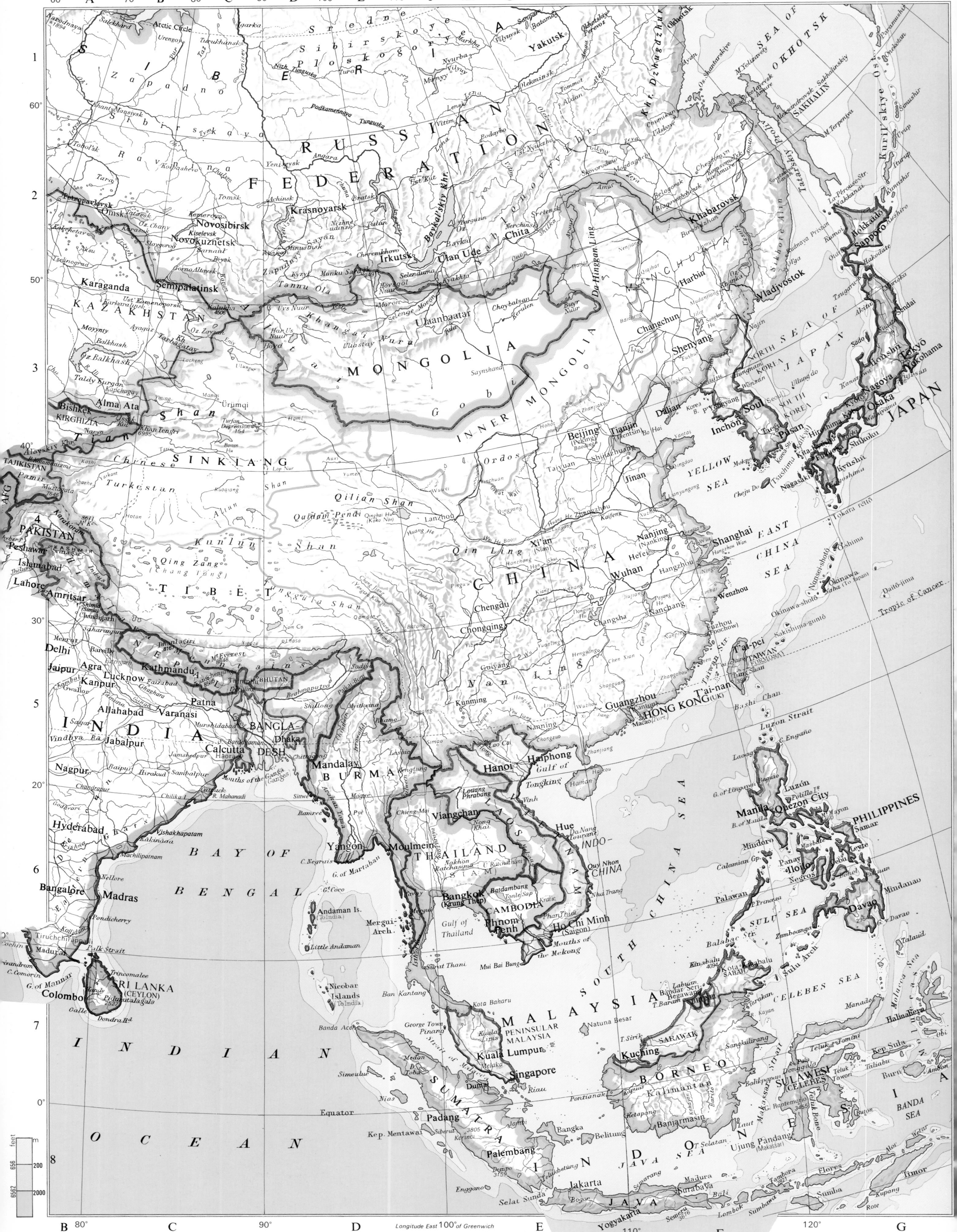

LAMBERT AZIMUTHAL EQUAL-AREA PROJECTION

1:24 M — 80 160 320 480 640 800 960 miles; 160 320 640 960 1280 1600 km

Longitude East 100° of Greenwich

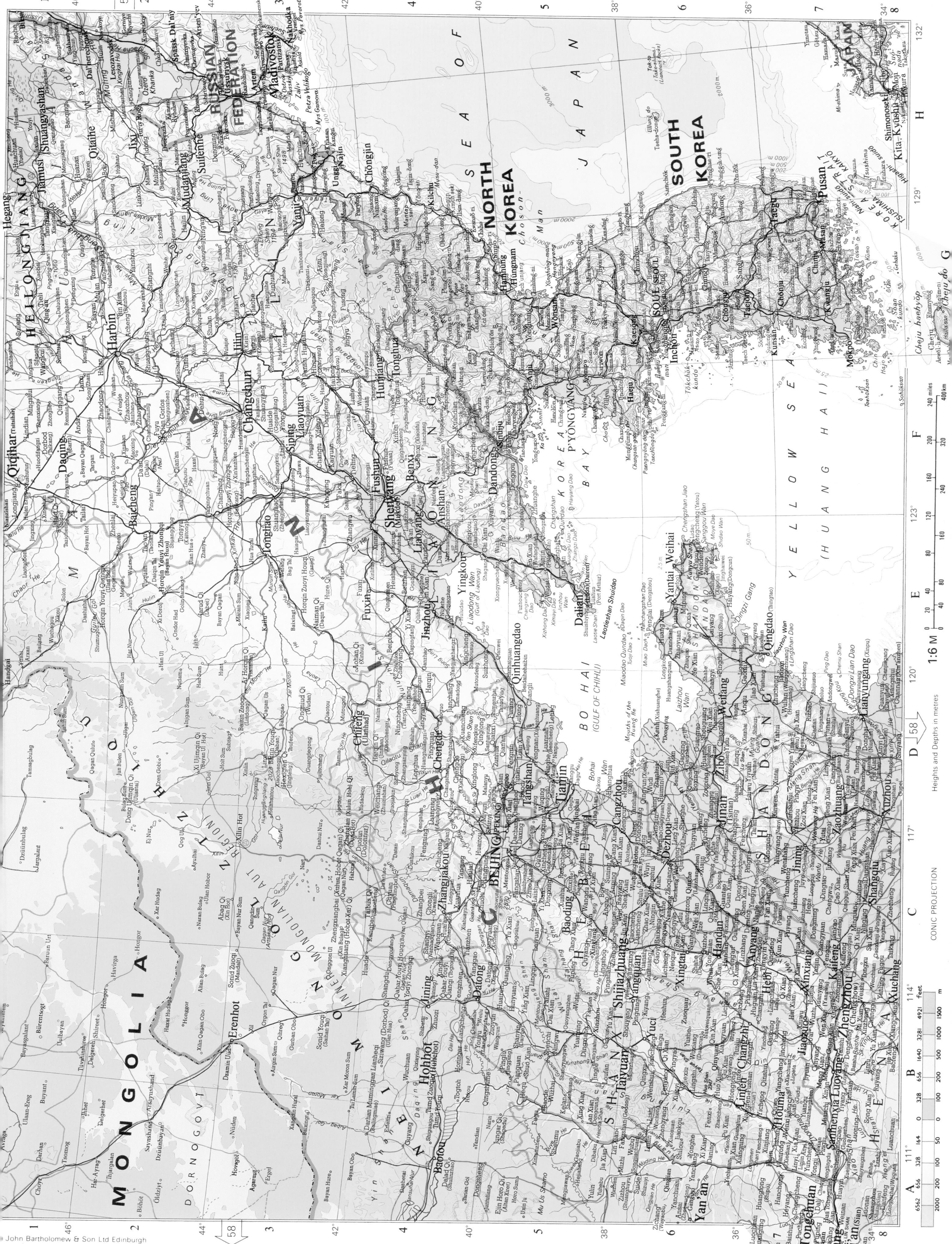
MONGOLIA
SOUTH KOREA
NORTH KOREA
RUSSIAN FEDERATION
JAPAN
SEA OF JAPAN
YELLOW SEA
(HUANG HAI)
KOREA BAY
BO HAI
(GULF OF CHIHLI)
HEILONGJIANG
JILIN
LIAONING
HEBEI
SHANXI
SHANDONG
HENAN
SHAANXI
NEI MONGOL ZIZHIQU
INNER MONGOLIAN AUT. REGION
BEIJING
Tianjin
Harbin
Changchun
Shenyang
Dalian
P'YONGYANG
SEOUL
Pusan
Vladivostok
Qiqihar
Hohhot
Baotou
Taiyuan
Shijiazhuang
Jinan
Qingdao
Zhengzhou
Xi'an
Heights and Depths in metres
CONIC PROJECTION
1:6 M
miles
km

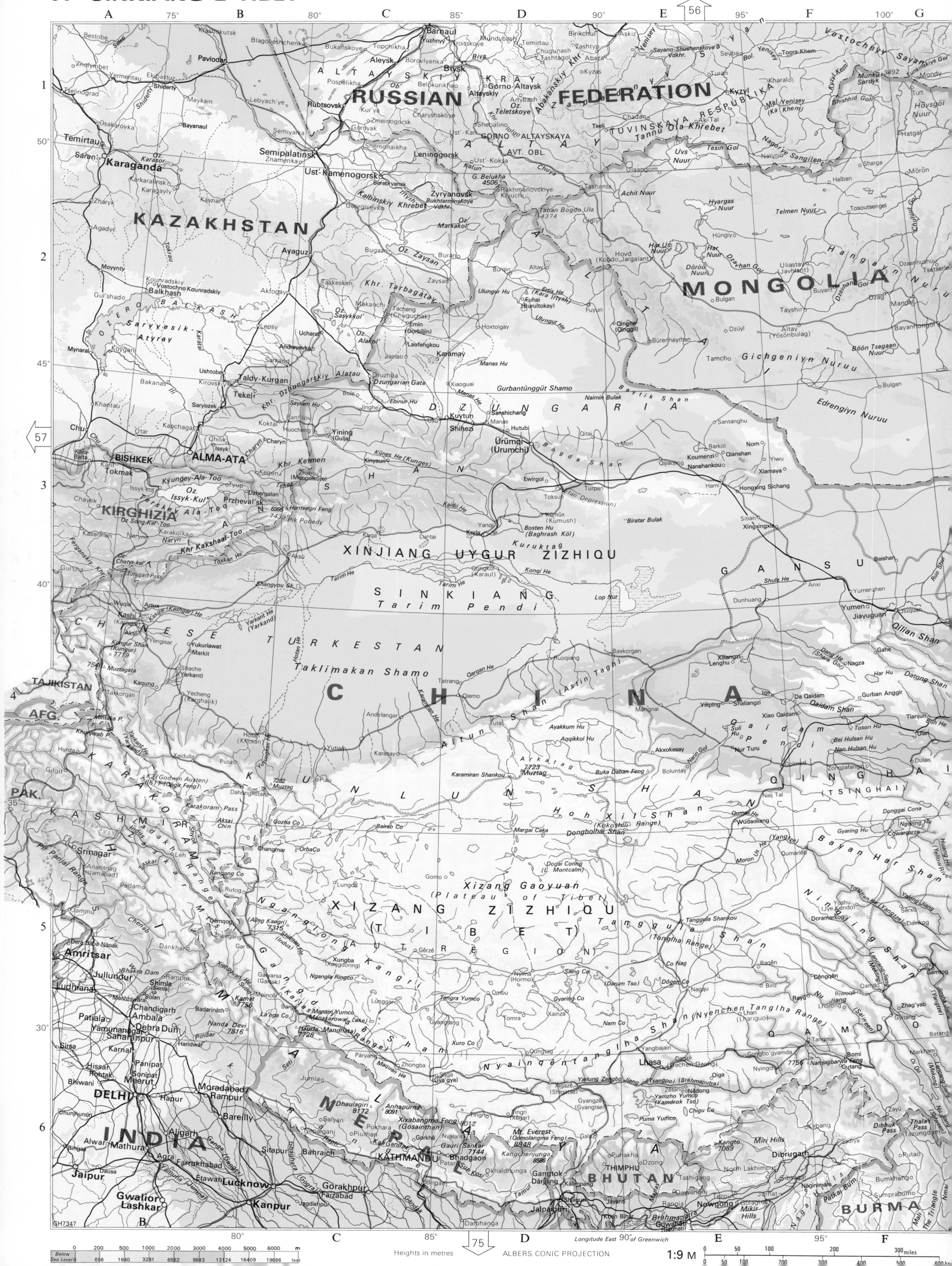
RUSSIAN FEDERATION
KAZAKHSTAN
MONGOLIA
KIRGHIZIA
TAJIKISTAN
AFG
PAK.
KASHMIR
CHINA
XINJIANG UYGUR ZIZHIQU
SINKIANG
Tarim Pendi
TURKESTAN
Taklimakan Shamo
DZUNGARIA
TIAN SHAN
KUNLUN SHAN
Altun Shan
QINGHAI (TSINGHAI)
GANSU
Qaidam Pendi
Xizang Gaoyuan (Plateau of Tibet)
XIZANG ZIZHIQU (TIBET AUT. REGION)
Tanggula Shan (Tangha Range)
Nyainqêntanglha Shan (Nyenchen Tanglha Range)
QAMDO
Gangdisê Shan
KARAKORAM
NEPAL
BHUTAN
INDIA
BURMA
DELHI
KATHMANDU
Lhasa
Mt. Everest (Qomolangma Feng) 8848
ALMA-ATA
BISHKEK
Karaganda
Semipalatinsk
Ust'-Kamenogorsk
Barnaul
Ürümqi (Urumchi)
Kashi (Kashgar)
Yining (Gulja)
Lop Nur
Dunhuang
Amritsar
Lucknow
Kanpur
Jaipur
Gwalior Lashkar
THIMPHU
Longitude East 90° of Greenwich
Heights in metres
ALBERS CONIC PROJECTION
1:9 M
miles
GH7347

CHINA
SOUTH CHINA SEA
GULF OF TONGKING
TAIWAN (FORMOSA)
TAIWAN STRAIT
HAINAN
VIETNAM
LAOS
HONG KONG 1:300 000
HONG KONG (To U.K.)
MACAO
Heights and Depths in metres
Longitude East 114° of Greenwich
CONIC PROJECTION
1:6 M
km miles

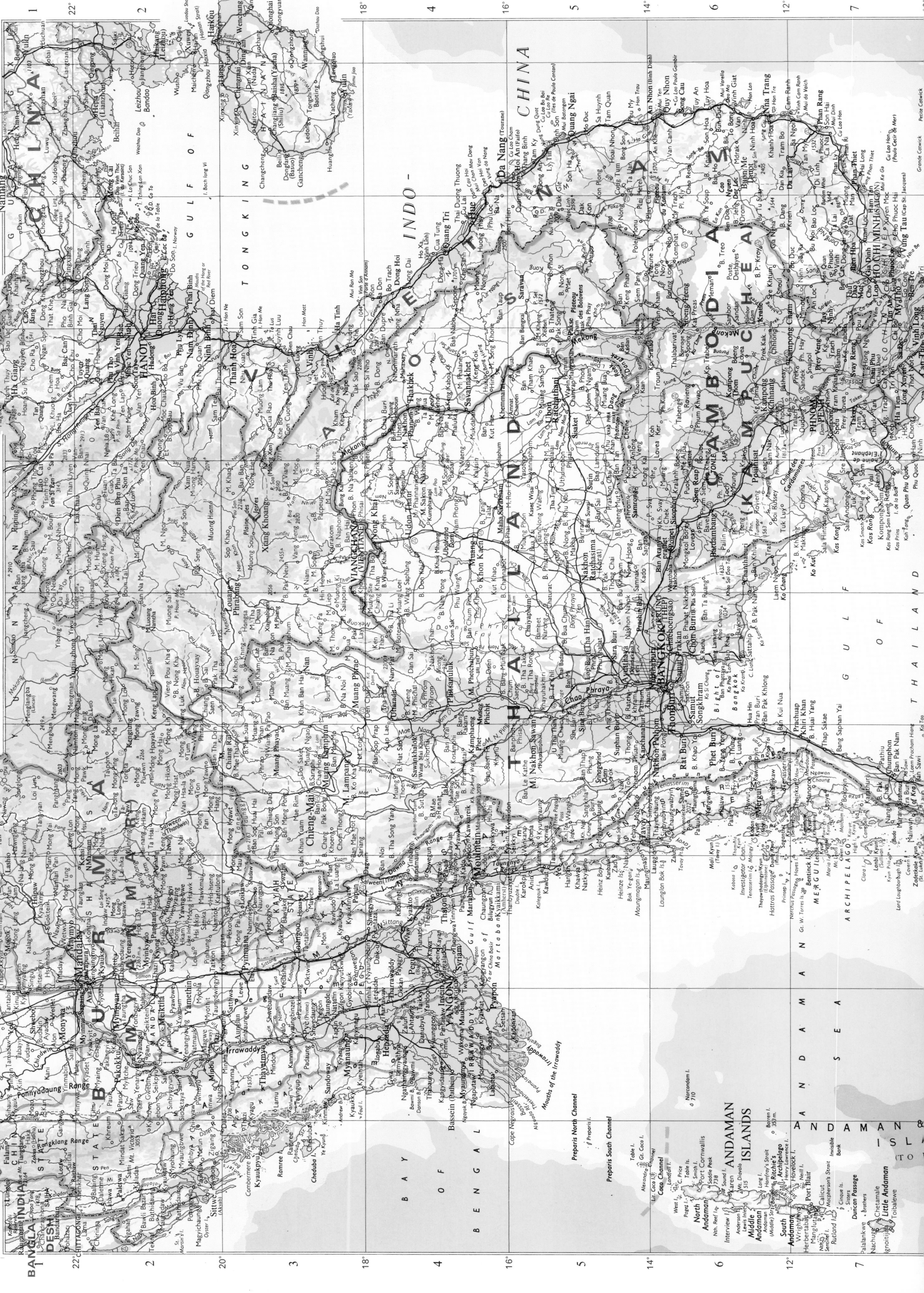
CHINA
BURMA
THAILAND
CAMBODIA
KAMPUCHEA
VIETNAM
LAOS
INDO-CHINA
GULF OF TONKING
GULF OF THAILAND
BAY OF BENGAL
ANDAMAN SEA
ANDAMAN ISLANDS
MERGUI ARCHIPELAGO
Gulf of Martaban
BANGKOK
HANOI
VIANGCHAN (VIENTIANE)
PHNOM PENH
RANGOON (YANGON)
Mandalay
Chieng-Mai
Da Nang
Haiphong
Moulmein
Nanning
Hai Kou
Luang Phrabang
Mekong
Irrawaddy
Salween (Thanlwin)
Chao Phraya
Mouths of the Irrawaddy
Preparis North Channel
Preparis South Channel
Coco Channel
North Andaman
Middle Andaman
South Andaman
Little Andaman
Port Blair
Duncan Passage

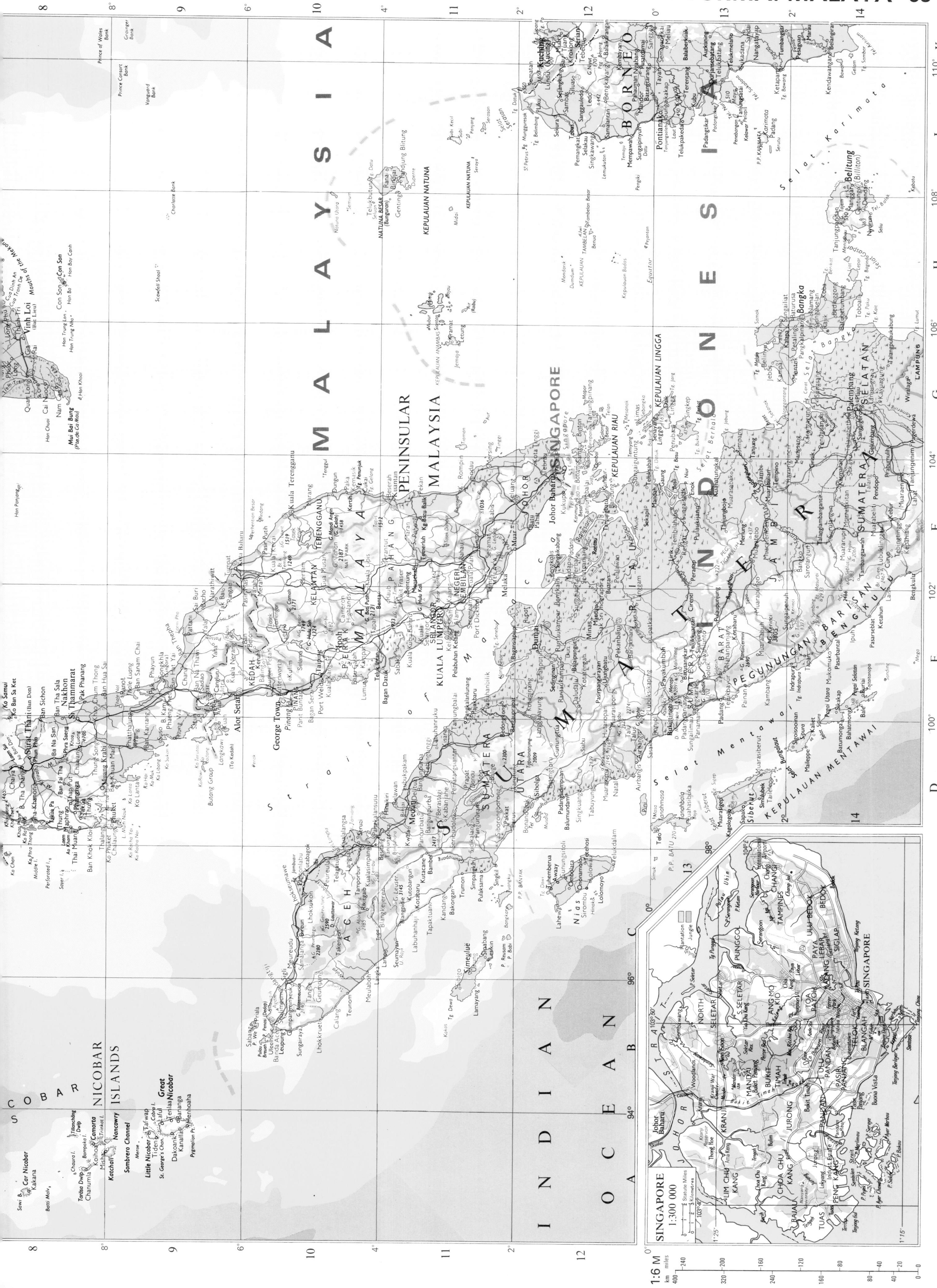
MALAYSIA
INDONESIA
PENINSULAR MALAYSIA
SUMATERA
BORNEO
SINGAPORE
INDIAN OCEAN
NICOBAR ISLANDS
KEPULAUAN NATUNA
KEPULAUAN RIAU
KEPULAUAN LINGGA
KEPULAUAN MENTAWAI
Selat Mentawai
Selat Karimata
Belitung
Bangka
Nias
Simeulue
Siberut
KUALA LUMPUR
George Town
Johor Baharu
Melaka
Pontianak
Kuching
Palembang
Medan
Padang
Pekanbaru
Jambi
Bengkulu
Alor Setar
Kota Baharu
Kuala Terengganu
Kuantan
Ipoh
Port Dickson
Surat Thani
Nakhon Si Thammarat
Car Nicobar
Great Nicobar
Little Nicobar
Katchall
Nancowry
Camorta
Sombrero Channel
Con Son
Vinh Loi
Mui Bai Bung
SINGAPORE 1:300 000
MERCATOR PROJECTION
Heights and Depths in metres
1:6 M

BORNEO & CELEBES
PHILIPPINES
M A L A Y S I A
BRUNEI
BANDAR SERI BEGAWAN
SABAH
SARAWAK
KALIMANTAN TIMUR
KALIMANTAN BARAT
KALIMANTAN TENGAH
KALIMANTAN SELATAN
B O R N E O
SULAWESI (CELEBES)
C E L E B E S   S E A
SULU SEA
J A V A   S E A
I N D O N E S I A
Makassar Strait
Selat Karimata
KEPULAUAN NATUNA
NATUNA BESAR (Bunguran)
Kota Kinabalu (Jesselton)
Sandakan
Tawau
Tarakan
Kuching
Sibu
Miri
Pontianak
Samarinda
Balikpapan
Banjarmasin
Palangkaraya
Ujung Pandang (Makassar)
Palu
Poso
Teluk Tomini
KEPULAUAN LAUT KECIL
Longitude East 116° of Greenwich
JAVA (JAWA)
(To Indonesia)
SUMATERA SELATAN
LAMPUNG
Palembang
Tanjungkarang Telukbetung
JAKARTA (BATAVIA)
JAWA BARAT
JAWA TENGAH
JAWA TIMUR
Bandung
Semarang
Surabaya
Surakarta
Madura
BALI
Denpasar
Lombok
J A V A   S E A
B A L I   S E A
Longitude East 110° of Greenwich
22967 16404 9843 3281 656 0 328 656 1640 3281 6562 feet
7000 5000 3000 1000 200 0 100 200 500 1000 2000 m
Heights and Depths in metres
MERCATOR PROJECTION

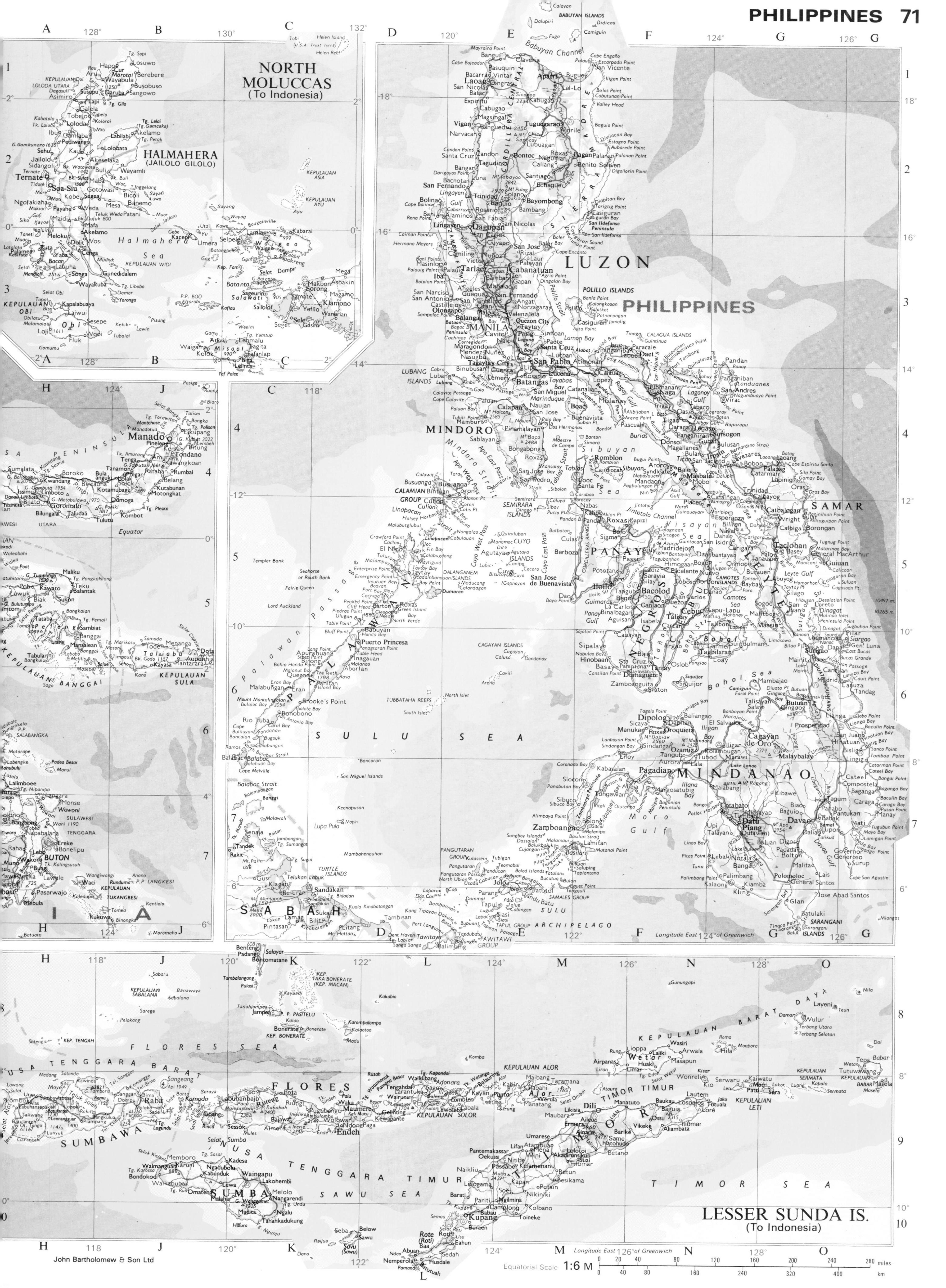
NORTH MOLUCCAS
(To Indonesia)
HALMAHERA
(JAILOLO GILOLO)
Halmahera Sea
LUZON
PHILIPPINES
MINDORO
PANAY
NEGROS
CEBU
BOHOL
LEYTE
SAMAR
PALAWAN
MINDANAO
SULU SEA
SULU ARCHIPELAGO
Moro Gulf
Bohol Sea
Sibuyan Sea
Visayan Sea
Palawan Passage
SABAH
Manila
Quezon City
Davao
Zamboanga
Cebu
Puerto Princesa
Manado
KEPULAUAN SULA
KEPULAUAN BANGGAI
BUTON
FLORES
FLORES SEA
SUMBAWA
SUMBA
NUSA TENGGARA BARAT
NUSA TENGGARA TIMUR
TIMOR
TIMOR TIMUR
TIMOR SEA
SAWU SEA
KEPULAUAN ALOR
KEPULAUAN BARAT DAYA
LESSER SUNDA IS.
(To Indonesia)
Longitude East 124° of Greenwich
Longitude East 126° of Greenwich
Equatorial Scale 1:6 M
miles
km
John Bartholomew & Son Ltd

BONNE PROJECTION

KAZAKHSTAN
KIRGHIZIA
TAJIKISTAN
SINKIANG
(XINJIANG)
Taklimakan Shamo
KUNLUN SHAN
Qing Zang
(Chang Tang)
TIBET
(XIZANG)
CHINA
Red Basin
Qaidam Pendi
Bayan Har Shan
Tanggula Shan
HIMALAYA
NEPAL
BHUTAN
BANGLADESH
BURMA
THAILAND
VIETNAM
CAMBODIA
INDIA
Deccan
Thar
KASHMIR
BAY OF BENGAL
GULF OF THAILAND
ANDAMAN ISLANDS
(To India)
NICOBAR ISLANDS
(To India)
LACCADIVE ISLANDS
(To India)
MALDIVES
SRI LANKA
(CEYLON)
PENINSULAR MALAYSIA
INDIAN OCEAN
Carpenter Ridge
Mentawai Trench
Mouths of the Ganga (Ganges)
Alma-Ata
Bishkek
Tashkent
Dushanbe
Ürümqi
Lanzhou
Xi'an
Chengdu
Chongqing
(Chungking)
Kunming
Hanoi
Kābul
Peshawar
Islamabad
Rawalpindi
Lahore
Amritsar
Delhi
Agra
Jaipur
Lucknow
Kānpur
Varanasi
Allahabad
Patna
Kathmandu
Lhasa
Mt. Everest
8848
Dhaka
Calcutta
Chittagong
Mandalay
Yangon
Pegu
Moulmein
Bangkok
(Krung Thep)
Ahmadabad
Vadodara
Surat
Bombay
Pune
Hyderabad
Nagpur
Jabalpur
Indore
Madras
Bangalore
Mysore
Madurai
Cochin
Trivandrum
Colombo
Kandy
Jaffna
Trincomalee
Karachi
Kuala Lumpur
Medan
Padang
1:15 M
Heights and Depths in metres

ALBERS CONIC PROJECTION

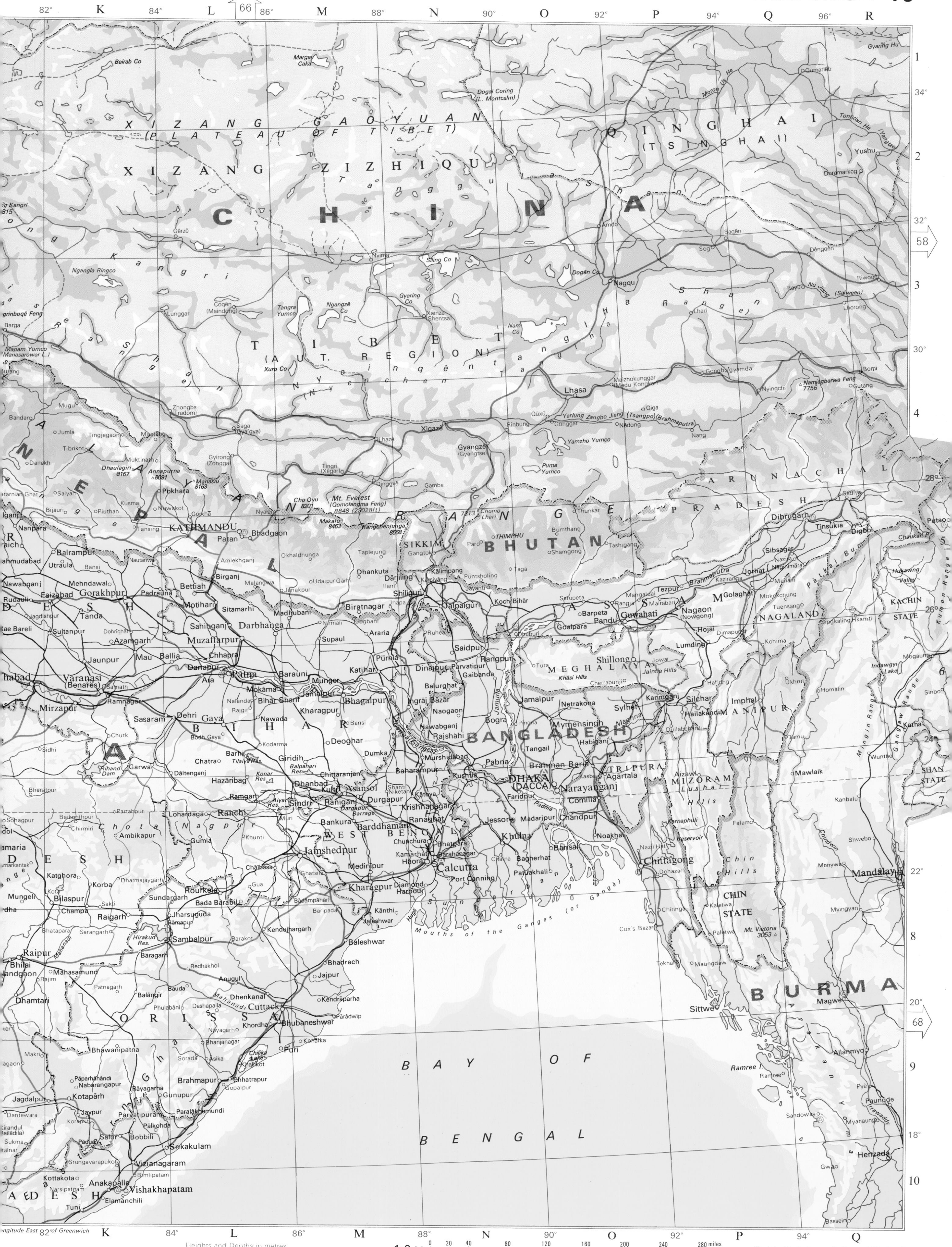

Heights and Depths in metres

1:6 M

0 20 40 80 120 160 200 240 280 miles

0 40 80 160 240 320 400 km

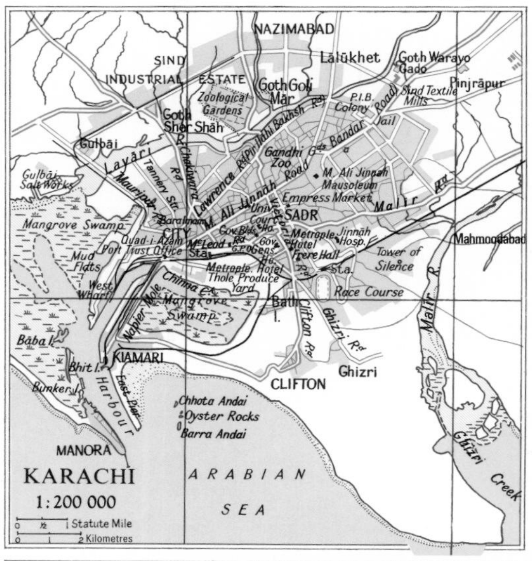
KARACHI
1:200 000
Statute Mile
Kilometres
ARABIAN SEA
NAZIMABAD
SIND INDUSTRIAL ESTATE
CLIFTON
KIAMARI
MANORA
SADR
Oyster Rocks

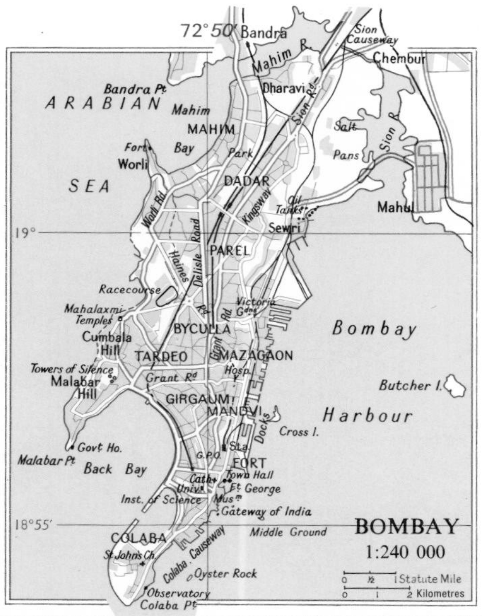
BOMBAY
1:240 000
Statute Mile
Kilometres
ARABIAN SEA
Bombay Harbour
Bandra
Mahim
Dharavi
Worli
DADAR
PAREL
BYCULLA
TARDEO
MAZAGAON
GIRGAUM
MANDVI
FORT
Back Bay
Malabar Pt
COLABA
Butcher I.
Cross I.

DELHI
1:240 000
Statute Mile
Kilometres
Wazirabad
Azadpur
Shakurpur
Wazirpur
Civil Lines
Shastrinagar
SADAR BAZAR
OLD CITY
Karol Bagh
PAHAR GANJ
NEW DELHI
Rajouri Gdn
Kirtinagar
Madipur
Naraina
New Cantonment
Palam International Airport
Ring Road
Lodi Tombs
Safdar Jang's Tomb
Aliganj
Lajpat Nagar
Keth Wara

CALCUTTA
1:240 000
COSSIPORE
CHITPUR
Ramrajatala
HAORA
SIMLA
BELIAGHATA
GARDEN REACH
KIDDERPORE
ALIPUR
BHAWANIPORE
BALLYGUNGE
TOLLYGUNGE
BEHALA
Hugli

MAHARASHTRA
MADHYA PRADESH
ORISSA
ANDHRA PRADESH
KARNATAKA
TAMIL NADU
KERALA
GOA
DAMAN
DIU
Bombay
Pune
Nasik
Aurangabad
Solapur
Kolhapur
Hyderabad
Secunderabad
Warangal
Vijayawada
Guntur
Rajahmundry
Kakinada
Vishakhapatnam
Vizianagaram
Cuttack
Bhubaneshwar
Brahmapur
Nellore
Madras
Bangalore
Mysore
Mangalore
Hubli
Dharwad
Belgaum
Bellary
Kurnool
Anantapur
Cuddapah
Vellore
Pondicherry
Salem
Coimbatore
Calicut
Cochin
Ernakulam
Madurai
Tiruchchirappalli
Thanjavur
Tuticorin
Trivandrum
Nagercoil
Cape Comorin
Quilon
Alleppey
LAKSHADWEEP (Laccadive Islands)
Laccadive, Minicoy and Amindivi Islands (India)
Nine Degree Channel
Eight Degree Channel
MALDIVES
SRI LANKA (CEYLON)
COLOMBO
Jaffna
Trincomalee
Kandy
Galle
Matara
Batticaloa
Gulf of Manaar
Palk Strait
Malabar Coast
Coromandel Coast
Mouths of The Godavari
ANDAMAN ISLANDS
North Andaman
Middle Andaman
South Andaman
Port Blair
Little Andaman
Duncan Passage
Coco Channel
Ten Degree Channel
Car Nicobar
NICOBAR ISLANDS
Great Nicobar
Little Nicobar
on the same scale
1:6M
miles km
Heights and Depths in metres
feet

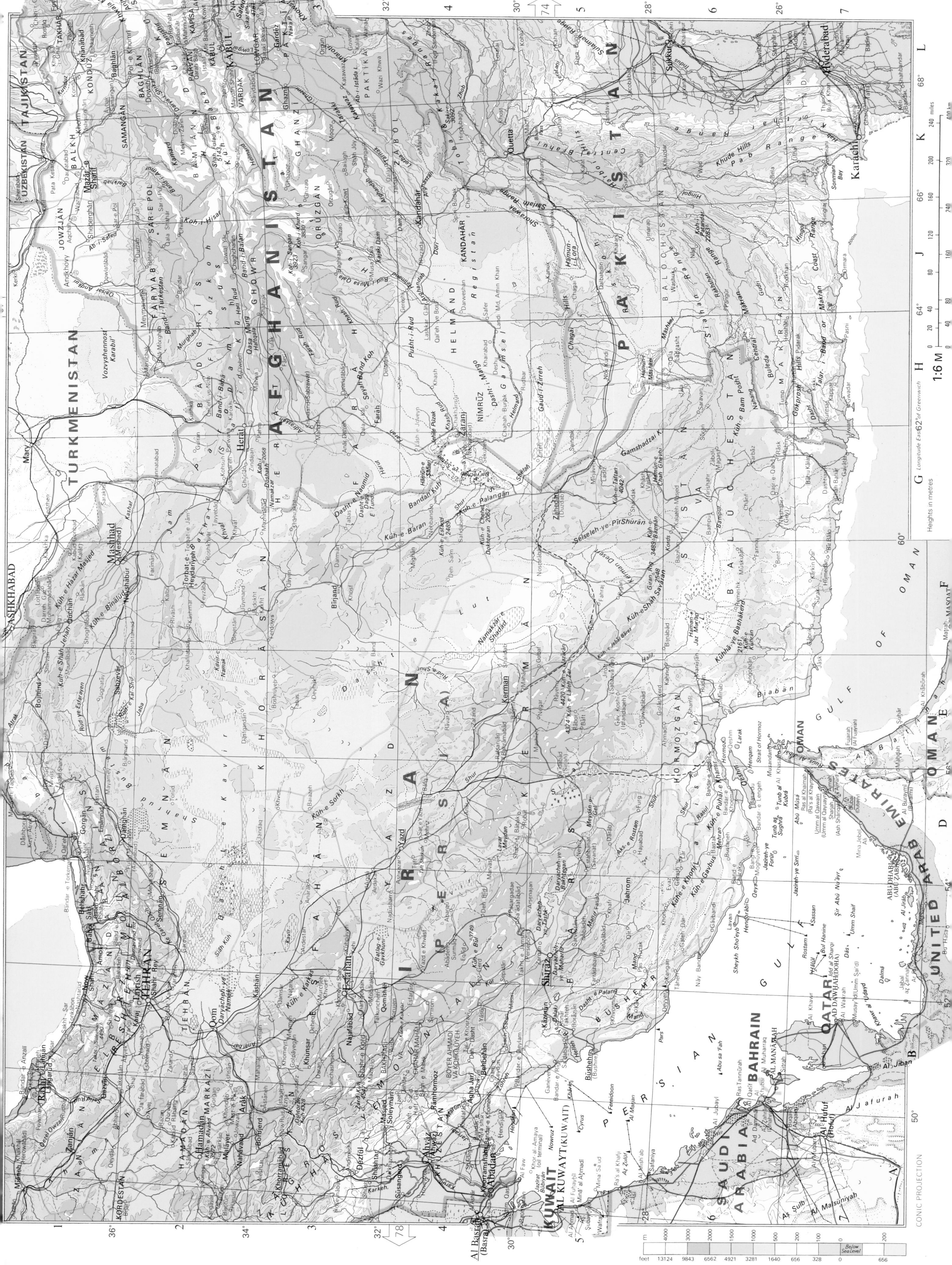
AFGHANISTAN
IRAN
PAKISTAN
TURKMENISTAN
TAJIKISTAN
UZBEKISTAN
KUWAIT
BAHRAIN
QATAR
SAUDI ARABIA
UNITED ARAB EMIRATES
OMAN
PERSIAN GULF
GULF OF OMAN
TEHRAN
KABUL
Herat
Mashhad
Kandahar
Quetta
Karachi
Hyderabad
Shiraz
Esfahan
Yazd
Kerman
Zahedan
Qom
Ahvaz
Abadan
Mary
ASHKHABAD
1:6 M
Heights in metres
Longitude East of Greenwich
CONIC PROJECTION
Below Sea Level

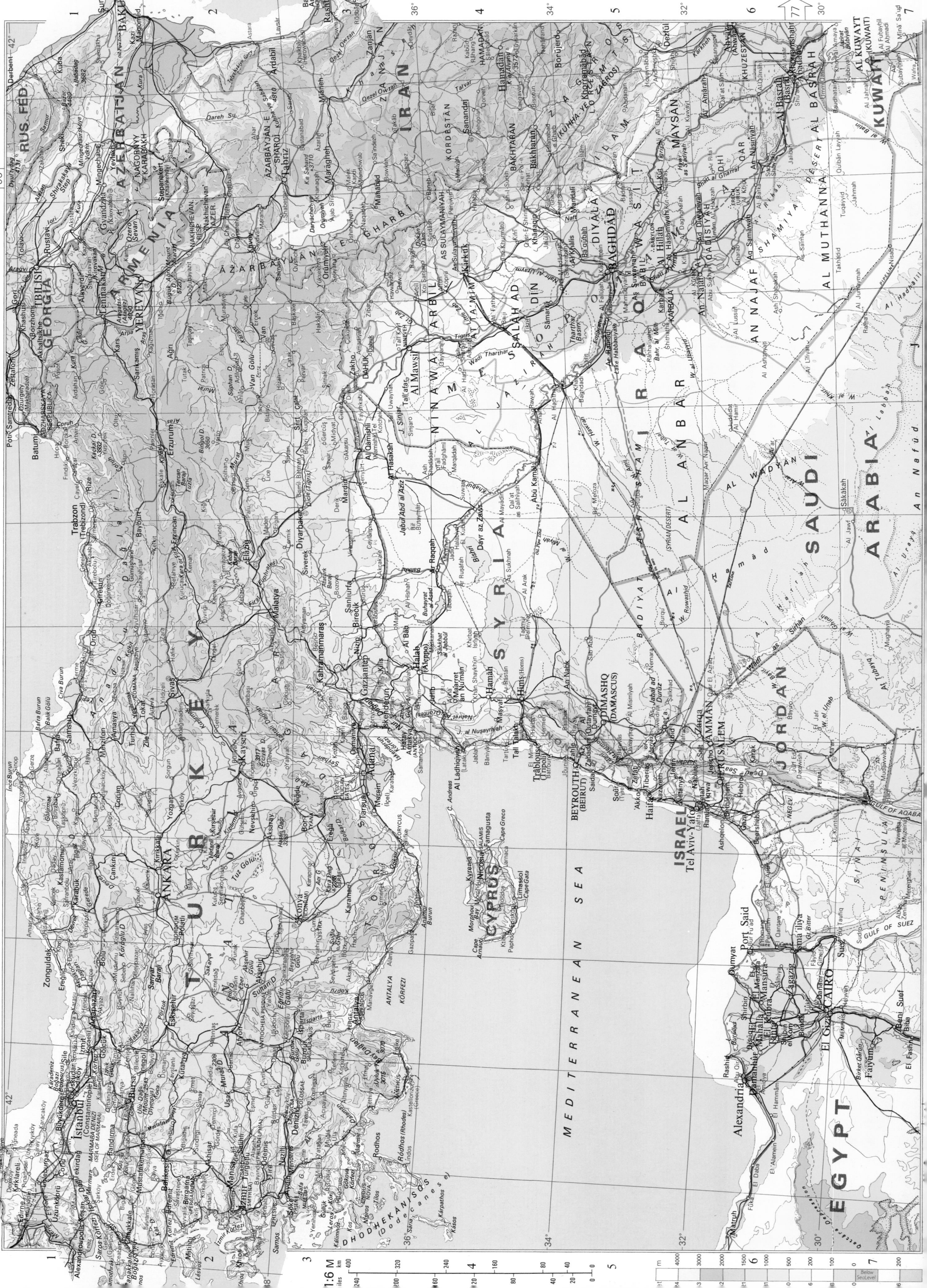
TURKEY
SYRIA
IRAQ
JORDAN
ISRAEL
CYPRUS
EGYPT
SAUDI ARABIA
IRAN
KUWAYT
GEORGIA
ARMENIA
AZERBAIJAN
RUS. FED.
MEDITERRANEAN SEA
ANKARA
İstanbul
BAGHDAD
DIMASHQ (DAMASCUS)
'AMMAN
JERUSALEM
BEYROUTH (BEIRUT)
CAIRO
TBILISI
YEREVAN
BAKU
Nicosia
Tel Aviv-Yafo
Alexandria
Port Said
Halab (Aleppo)
Al Mawşil
Al Başrah
Tabriz
Adana
Konya
Izmir
Trabzon (Trebizond)
Erzurum
Diyarbakır
Malatya
Gaziantep
Kayseri
Sivas
Samsun
Eskişehir
Bursa
Antalya
Hamāh
Hims (Homs)
Tripoli
Al Hillah
Karbalā'
An Najaf
Kirkuk
Al Jawf
Sakakah
Hamadān
Sanandaj
Rodhos (Rhodes)
Zonguldak
Dayr az Zawr
Ar Raqqah
Al Fallūjah
1:6 M

TURKEY
CYPRUS
LEBANON
SYRIA
ISRAEL
JORDAN
EGYPT
SAUDI ARABIA
MEDITERRANEAN SEA
Antalya Körfezi
Adana
Mersin
Tarsus
Ceyhan
İskenderun
Gaziantep
Halab (Aleppo)
Al Ladhiqiyah (Latakia)
Hamah
Hims (Homs)
Nicosia
Famagusta
Larnaca
Limassol
Trâblous (Tripoli)
BEYROUTH (BEIRUT)
Saida (Sidon)
Soûr (Tyre)
DIMASHQ (DAMASCUS, ESH SHEM, DAMAS)
Haifa
Tel Aviv Yafo
JERUSALEM
AMMAN
Gaza
Beersheba
Port Said
CAIRO (EL QÂHIRA)
Suez
Alexandria (Iskandariya)
Sinai
Elat
Aqaba
Gulf of Suez
Gulf of Aqaba
Ma'ān
Karak
Irbid
Zarqa
Dar'a
Alexandria
Ismâ'iliya
Tanta
Zagazig
El Mansûra
Dumyât (Damietta)
El Faiyûm
Beni Suef
El Minya
1:3 M
CONIC PROJECTION
Longitude East 36° of Greenwich
Heights and Depths in metres
© John Bartholomew & Son Ltd. Edinburgh

JERUSALEM
1 : 75 000
WHOLE AREA OF INSET
UNDER ISRAEL CONTROL,
JUNE 1967.
Bethlehem
Beit Jala
Beit Sahur
LEBANON
SYRIA
ISRAEL
JORDAN
LAKE TIBERIAS
(YAM KINNERET)
(SEA OF GALILEE)
DEAD SEA
(YAM HAMELAH)
(BAHRET LUT)
BAY OF HAIFA
Haifa
Nahariyya
'Akko
Nazareth
Tiberias
Zefat
(Safad)
Qiryat Shemona
Afula
Hadera
Netanya
Tulkarm
Nablus
Herzliyya
Tel Aviv
-Yafo
(Jaffa)(JOPPA)
Ramallah
JERUSALEM
(EL QUDS ESH SHERIF)
(YERUSHALAYIM)
Jericho
Bethlehem
Hebron
(El Khalil)
Ashdod
Ashqelon
GAZA
STRIP
Gaza
Beersheba
Rishon LeZiyyon
Rehovot
Lod
Ramla
Jenin
Irbid
Jarash
Ajlun
Salt
AMMAN
(RABBAH)
Madaba
Karama
Allenby Bridge
Abdallah Bridge
Dhiban
En Gedi
1:0.6M
1:600 000
CONIC PROJECTION
Longitude East of Greenwich
79

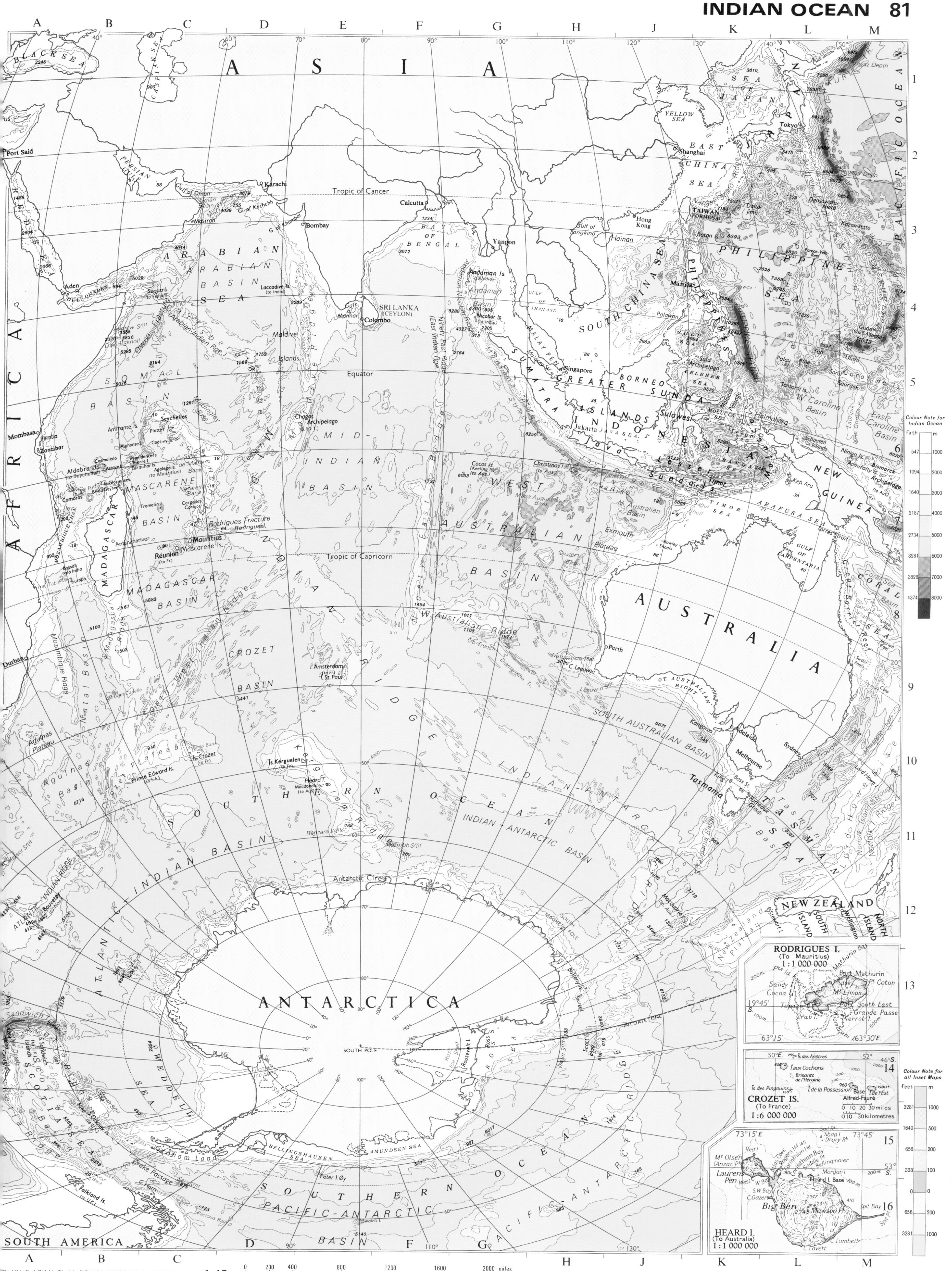

OBLIQUE AZIMUTHAL EQUAL AREA PROJECTION 1:48 M 0 200 400 800 1200 1600 2000 miles 0 400 800 1600 2400 3200 km

Heights and Depths in metres

MILLER'S PROLATED STEREOGRAPHIC PROJECTION

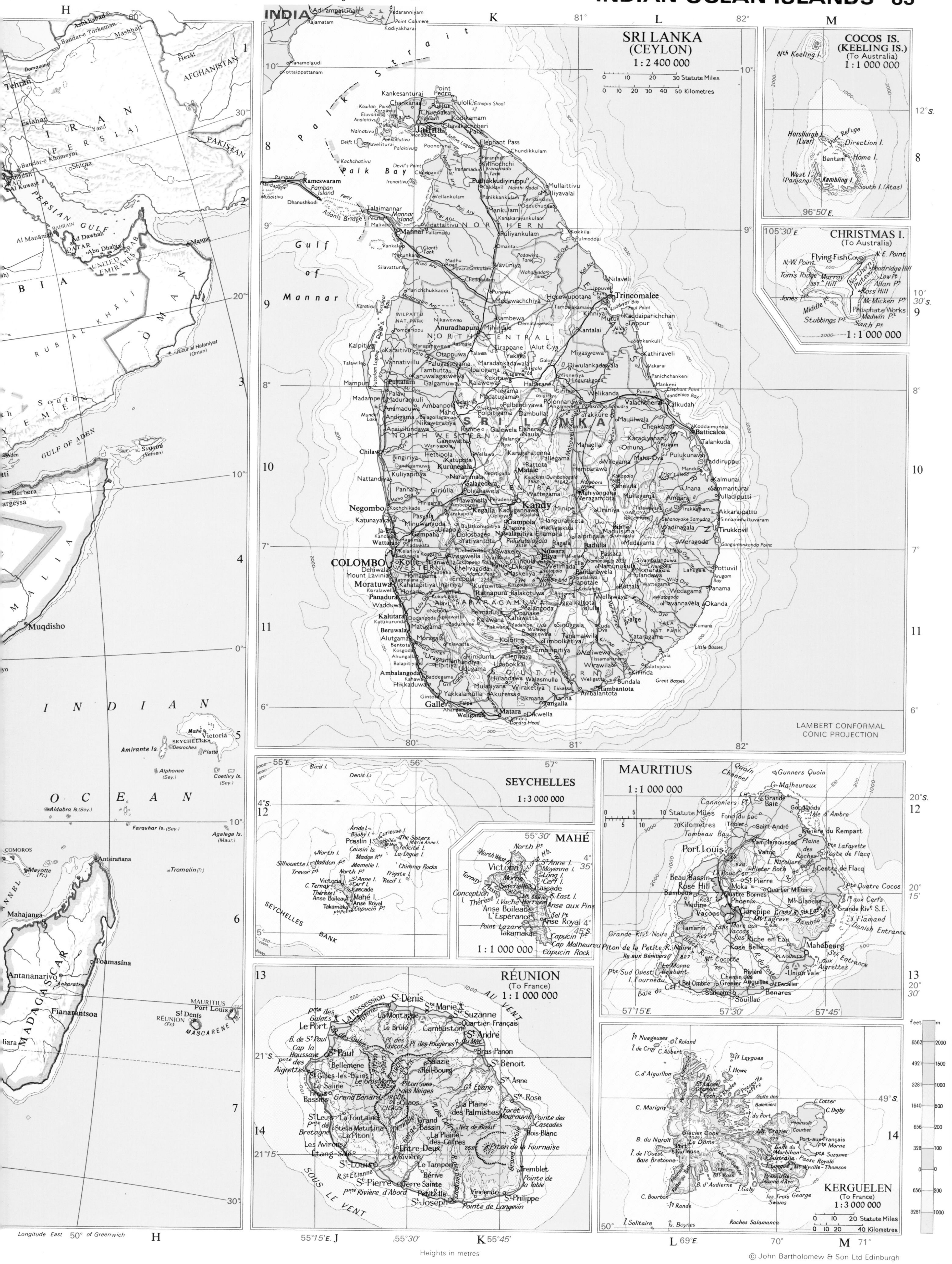
SRI LANKA (CEYLON)
1 : 2 400 000
Statute Miles
Kilometres
LAMBERT CONFORMAL CONIC PROJECTION
INDIA
Palk Strait
Palk Bay
Gulf of Mannar
Adam's Bridge
Jaffna
Trincomalee
Anuradhapura
Puttalam
Kurunegala
Negombo
Kandy
COLOMBO
Kotte
Moratuwa
Kalutara
Ratnapura
Badulla
Batticaloa
Galle
Matara
Hambantota
NORTHERN
NORTH CENTRAL
NORTH WESTERN
CENTRAL
WESTERN
SABARAGAMUWA
SOUTHERN
SRI LANKA
COCOS IS. (KEELING IS.)
(To Australia)
1 : 1 000 000
CHRISTMAS I.
(To Australia)
1 : 1 000 000
SEYCHELLES
1 : 3 000 000
MAHÉ
1 : 1 000 000
Victoria
MAURITIUS
1 : 1 000 000
Port Louis
Curepipe
Mahebourg
RÉUNION
(To France)
1 : 1 000 000
St Denis
St Pierre
Piton de la Fournaise
KERGUELEN
(To France)
1 : 3 000 000
IRAN (PERSIA)
AFGHANISTAN
PAKISTAN
OMAN
UNITED ARAB EMIRATES
GULF OF ADEN
INDIAN OCEAN
MADAGASCAR
Antananarivo
Toamasina
Mahajanga
Fianarantsoa
Muqdisho
Tehran
Masqat
Longitude East 50° of Greenwich
Heights in metres

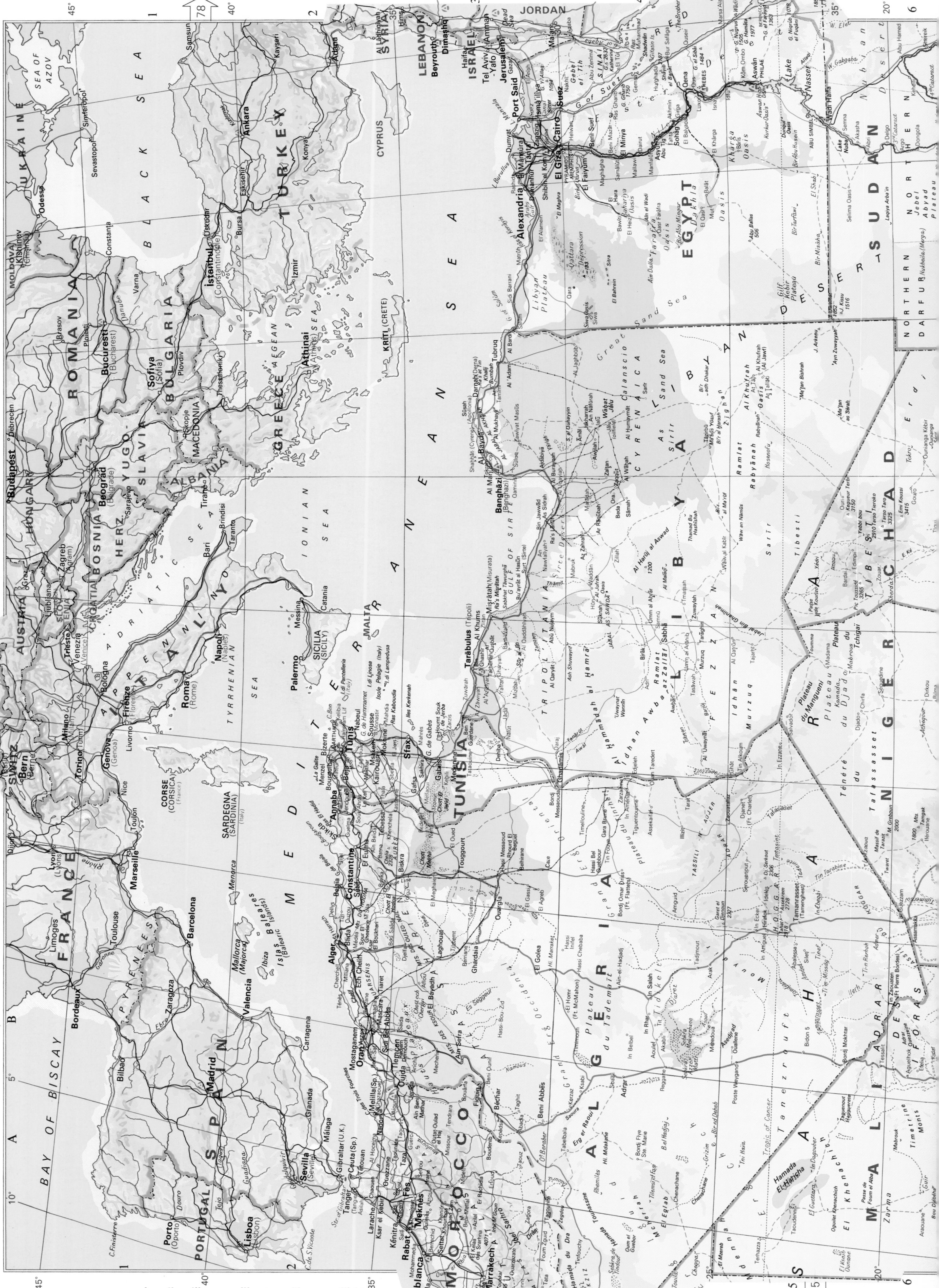

MEDITERRANEAN SEA
BLACK SEA
SEA OF AZOV
ADRIATIC SEA
TYRRHENIAN SEA
IONIAN SEA
AEGEAN SEA
BAY OF BISCAY
RED SEA
FRANCE
SPAIN
PORTUGAL
ITALY
SWITZ.
AUSTRIA
HUNGARY
ROMANIA
BULGARIA
YUGOSLAVIA
ALBANIA
GREECE
TURKEY
UKRAINE
MOLDOVA
CYPRUS
SYRIA
LEBANON
ISRAEL
JORDAN
EGYPT
LIBYA
TUNISIA
ALGERIA
MOROCCO
MALI
NIGER
CHAD
SUDAN
SAHARA
LIBYAN DESERT
NUBIAN DESERT
Great Sand Sea
Madrid
Lisboa (Lisbon)
Barcelona
Marseille
Roma (Rome)
Napoli (Naples)
Athinai (Athens)
Istanbul (Constantinople)
Ankara
Bucuresti (Bucharest)
Sofiya (Sofia)
Beograd (Belgrade)
Budapest
Tunis
Alger
Tarabulus (Tripoli)
Banghazi (Benghazi)
Alexandria
Cairo
Casablanca
Rabat
Heights in metres
1:12 M
km
miles

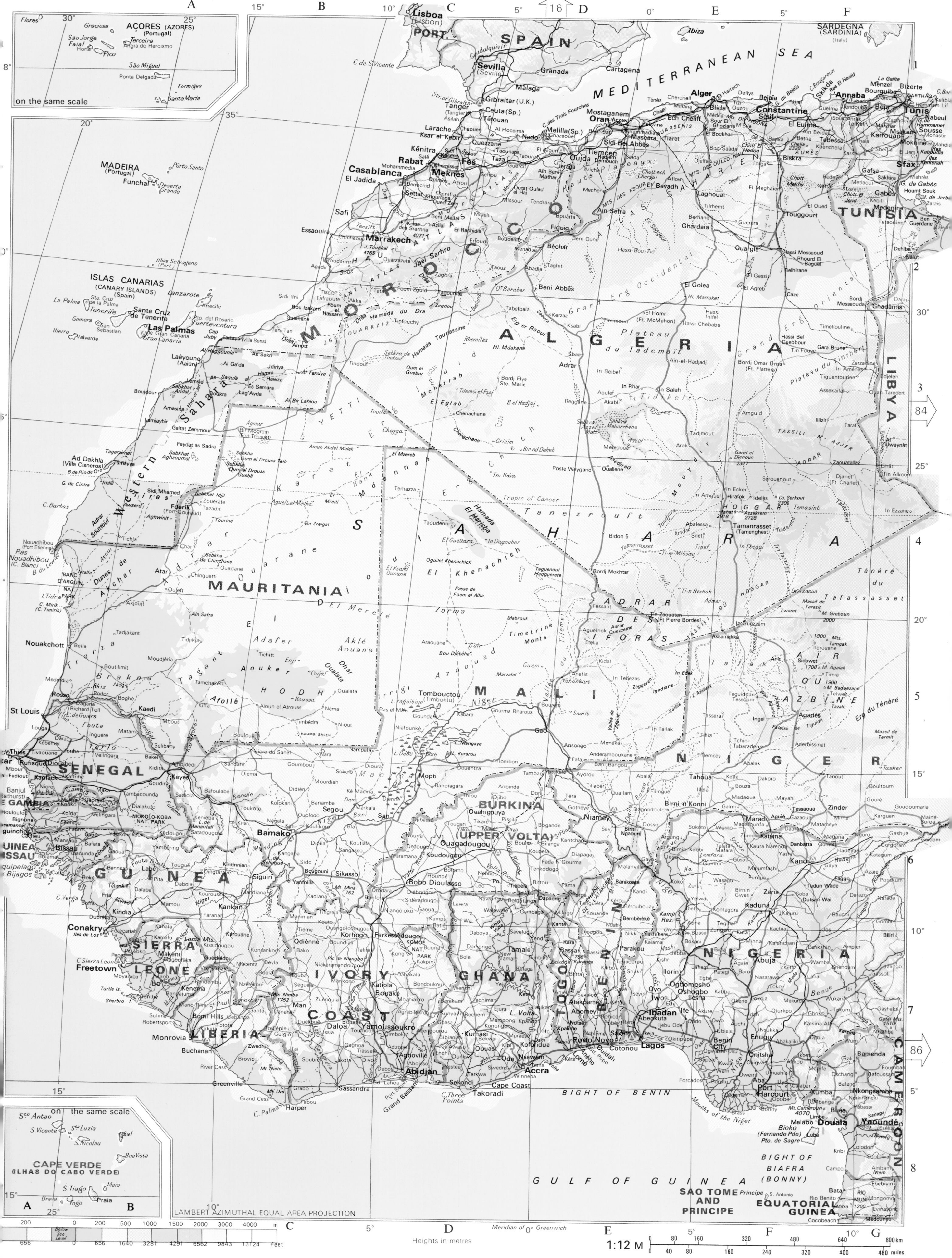
AÇORES (AZORES) (Portugal)
on the same scale
MADEIRA (Portugal)
ISLAS CANARIAS (CANARY ISLANDS) (Spain)
SPAIN
PORT.
MEDITERRANEAN SEA
MOROCCO
ALGERIA
TUNISIA
LIBYA
Western Sahara
MAURITANIA
SAHARA
MALI
NIGER
SENEGAL
GAMBIA
GUINEA
SIERRA LEONE
LIBERIA
IVORY COAST
GHANA
TOGO
BENIN
BURKINA (UPPER VOLTA)
NIGERIA
CAMEROON
BIGHT OF BENIN
BIGHT OF BIAFRA (BONNY)
GULF OF GUINEA
SAO TOME AND PRINCIPE
EQUATORIAL GUINEA
CAPE VERDE (ILHAS DO CABO VERDE)
on the same scale
Tropic of Cancer
Meridian of 0° Greenwich
LAMBERT AZIMUTHAL EQUAL AREA PROJECTION
Heights in metres
1:12 M
84
86
16

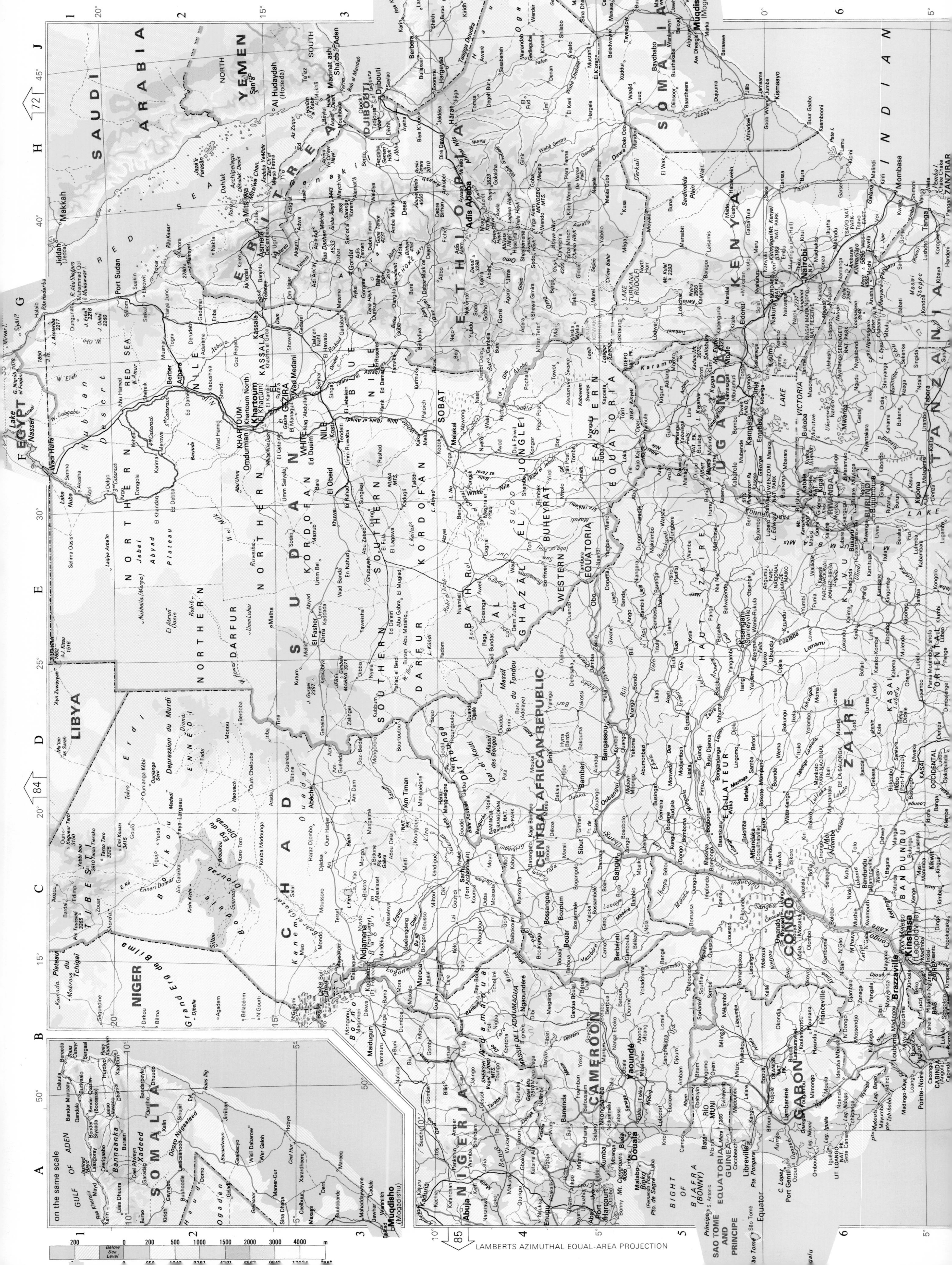
SAUDI ARABIA
NORTH YEMEN
SOUTH YEMEN
Makkah
Jiddah
Şan'ā'
Aden
RED SEA
ERITREA
Mits'iwa
Asmera
DJIBOUTI
Djibouti
ETHIOPIA
Adis Abeba
SOMALIA
Muqdisho (Mogadishu)
Kismaayo
KENYA
Nairobi
Mombasa
INDIAN
UGANDA
Kampala
Lake Victoria
TANZANIA
Tanga
RWANDA
Kigali
BURUNDI
Bujumbura
ZAIRE
Kisangani (Stanleyville)
Kinshasa (Léopoldville)
CONGO
Brazzaville
GABON
Libreville
CAMEROON
Yaoundé
Douala
EQUATORIAL GUINEA
RIO MUNI
SAO TOME AND PRINCIPE
BIGHT OF BIAFRA (BONNY)
NIGERIA
Abuja
Kaduna
CENTRAL AFRICAN REPUBLIC
Bangui
CHAD
Ndjamena
Abéché
Lake Chad
SUDAN
Khartoum
Omdurman
El Obeid
Wad Medani
Kassala
Port Sudan
LIBYA
EGYPT
Lake Nasser
Wadi Halfa
NIGER
TIBESTI
Nubian Desert
on the same scale
GULF OF ADEN
SOMALIA
72
84
85
LAMBERTS AZIMUTHAL EQUAL-AREA PROJECTION
Below Sea Level
200 0 200 500 1000 1500 2000 3000 4000 m

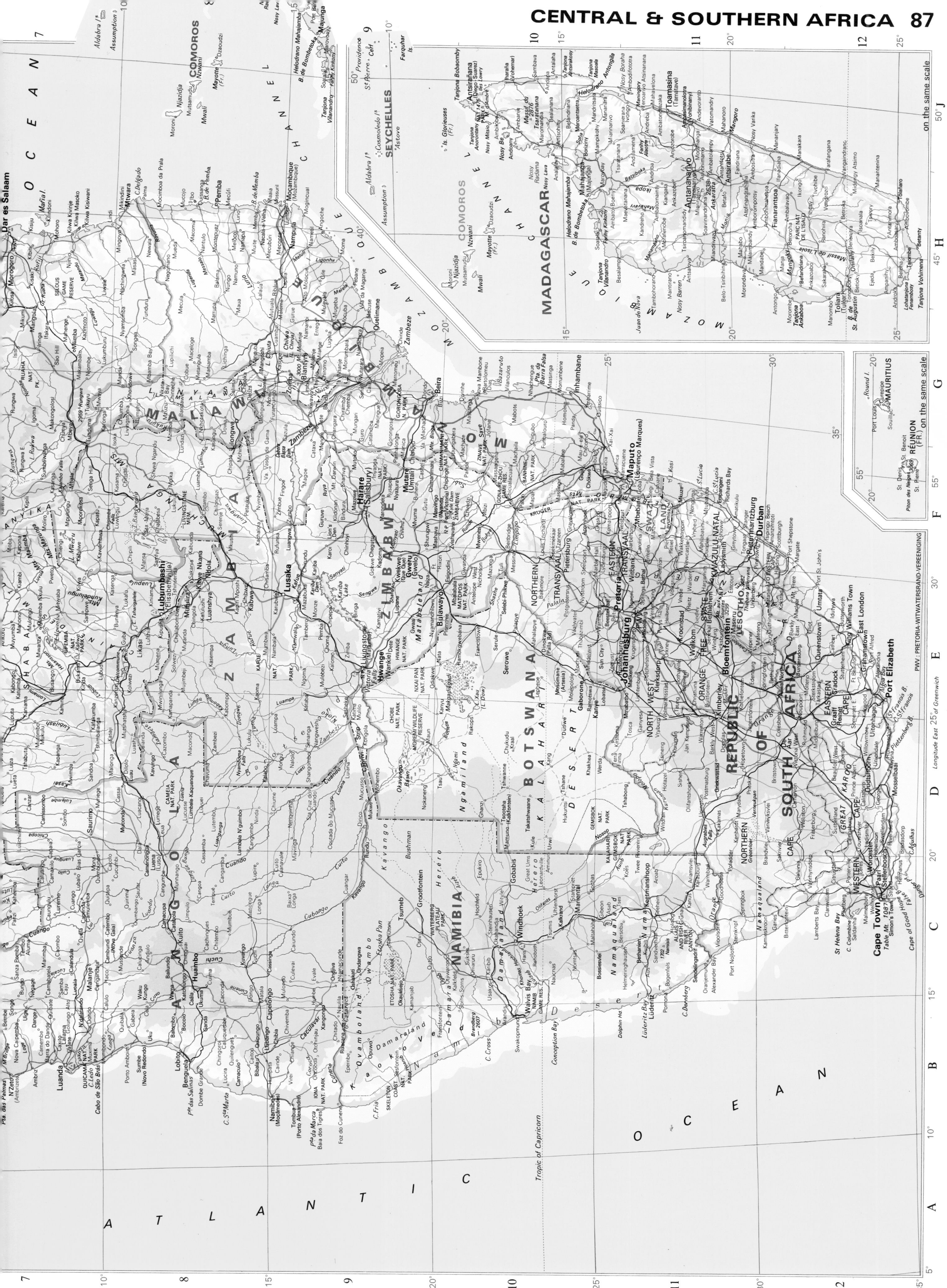

Heights in metres

1:12 M 0 80 160 320 480 640 800 960 km
0 40 80 160 240 320 400 480 560 miles

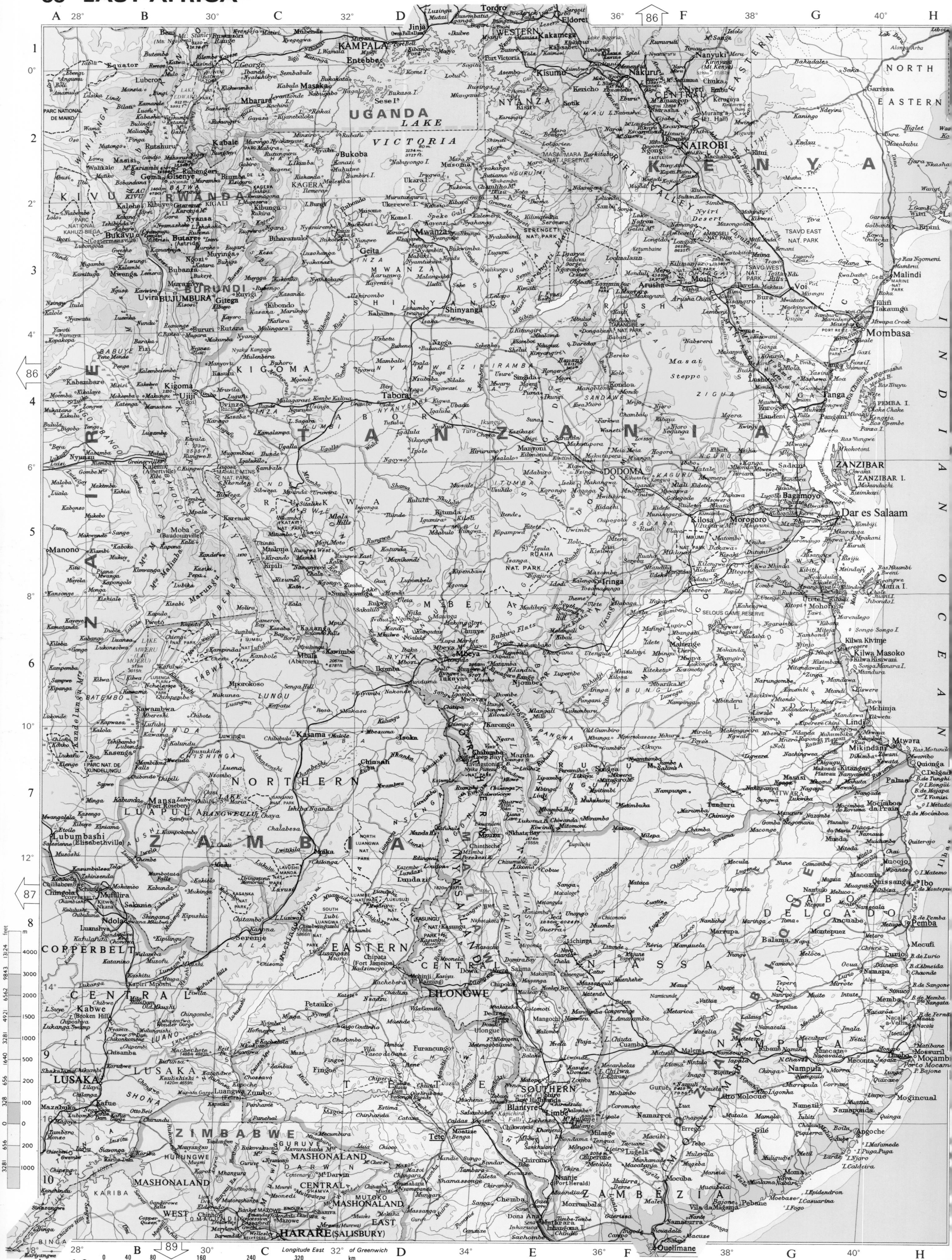
UGANDA
KENYA
TANZANIA
ZAMBIA
ZAIRE
RWANDA
BURUNDI
ZIMBABWE
MOZAMBIQUE
INDIAN OCEAN
LAKE VICTORIA
KAMPALA
NAIROBI
DODOMA
LILONGWE
LUSAKA
HARARE (SALISBURY)
Dar es Salaam
Mombasa
Zanzibar
Tabora
Kigoma
Mwanza
Arusha
Tanga
Mbeya
Iringa
Morogoro
Blantyre
Ndola
Kabwe
Quelimane
Nampula
Mtwara
Lindi
Entebbe
Jinja
Eldoret
Nakuru
Kisumu
Kigali
Bujumbura
Lubumbashi
NORTH EASTERN
WESTERN
NYANZA
CENTRAL
COPPERBELT
NORTHERN
EASTERN
SOUTHERN
LUAPULA
MASHONALAND
ZAMBEZIA
NIASSA
CABO DELGADO
1:6 M
km
miles
Longitude East of Greenwich
Heights in metres and feet
LAMBERT AZIMUTHAL EQUAL-AREA PROJECTION
© John Bartholomew & Son Ltd Edinburgh

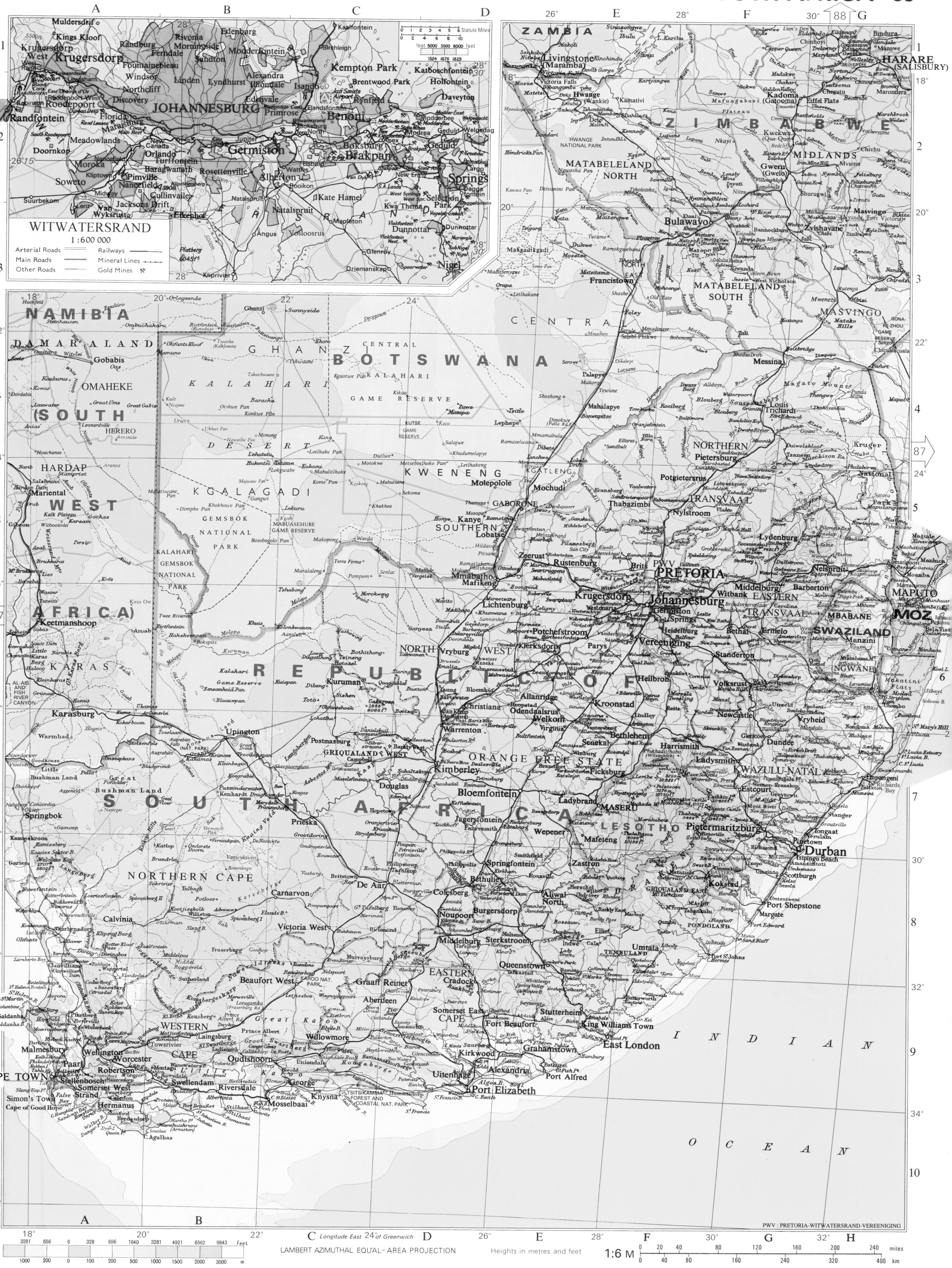
WITWATERSRAND
1 : 600 000
Arterial Roads
Main Roads
Other Roads
Railways
Mineral Lines
Gold Mines
JOHANNESBURG
Krugersdorp
Germiston
Benoni
Brakpan
Springs
Soweto
NAMIBIA
BOTSWANA
ZIMBABWE
ZAMBIA
REPUBLIC OF SOUTH AFRICA
LESOTHO
SWAZILAND
MOZ
INDIAN OCEAN
PRETORIA
Johannesburg
Bloemfontein
Kimberley
Durban
Pietermaritzburg
Port Elizabeth
East London
Bulawayo
Gaborone
HARARE (SALISBURY)
MAPUTO
MASERU
MBABANE
NORTHERN CAPE
WESTERN CAPE
EASTERN CAPE
ORANGE FREE STATE
KWAZULU-NATAL
NORTHERN TRANSVAAL
EASTERN TRANSVAAL
PWV
NORTH WEST
PWV : PRETORIA-WITWATERSRAND-VEREENIGING
Longitude East of Greenwich
LAMBERT AZIMUTHAL EQUAL-AREA PROJECTION
Heights in metres and feet
1:6 M
miles
km

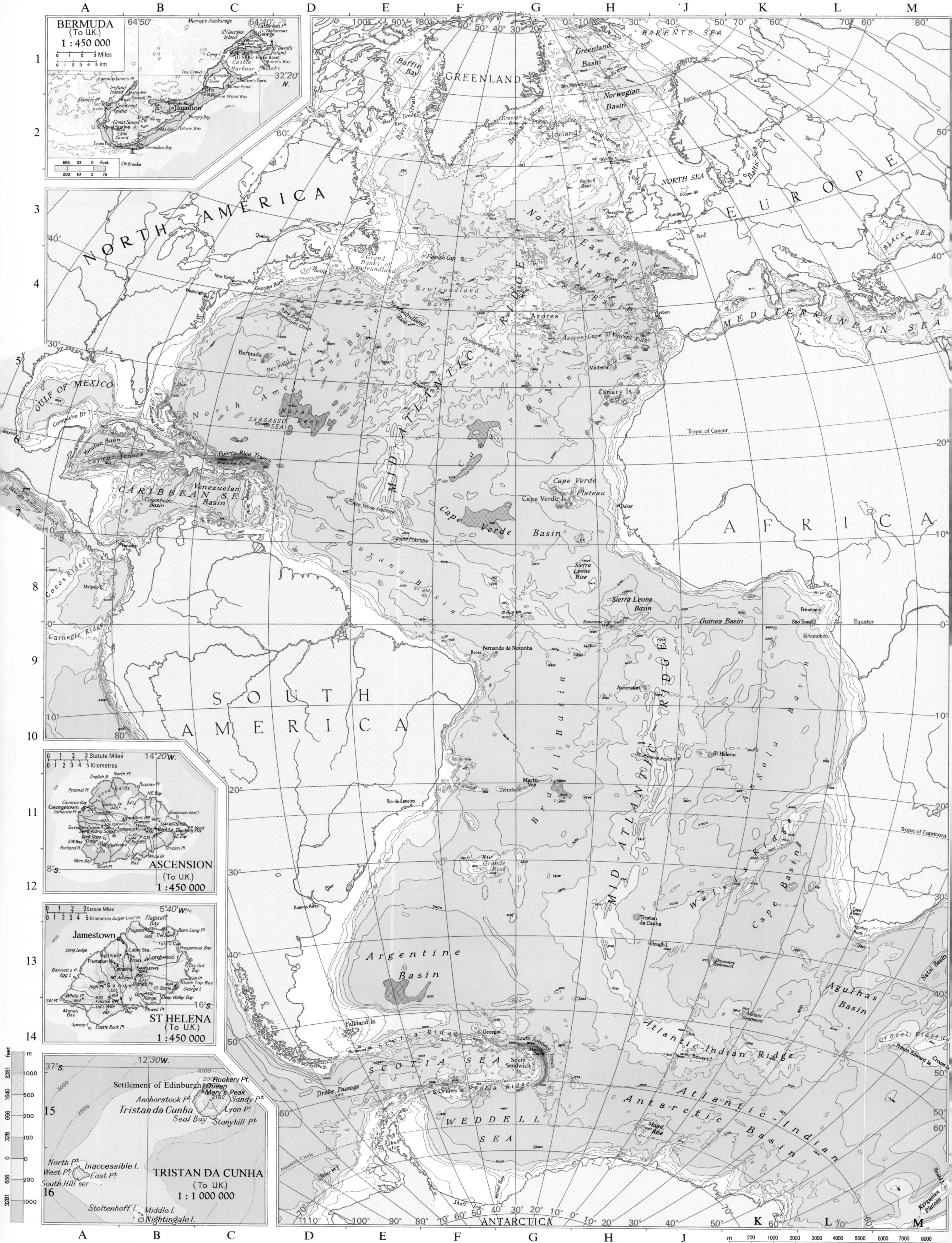

LAMBERT AZIMUTHAL EQUAL-AREA PROJECTION

Heights and Depths in metres

1: 48 000 000

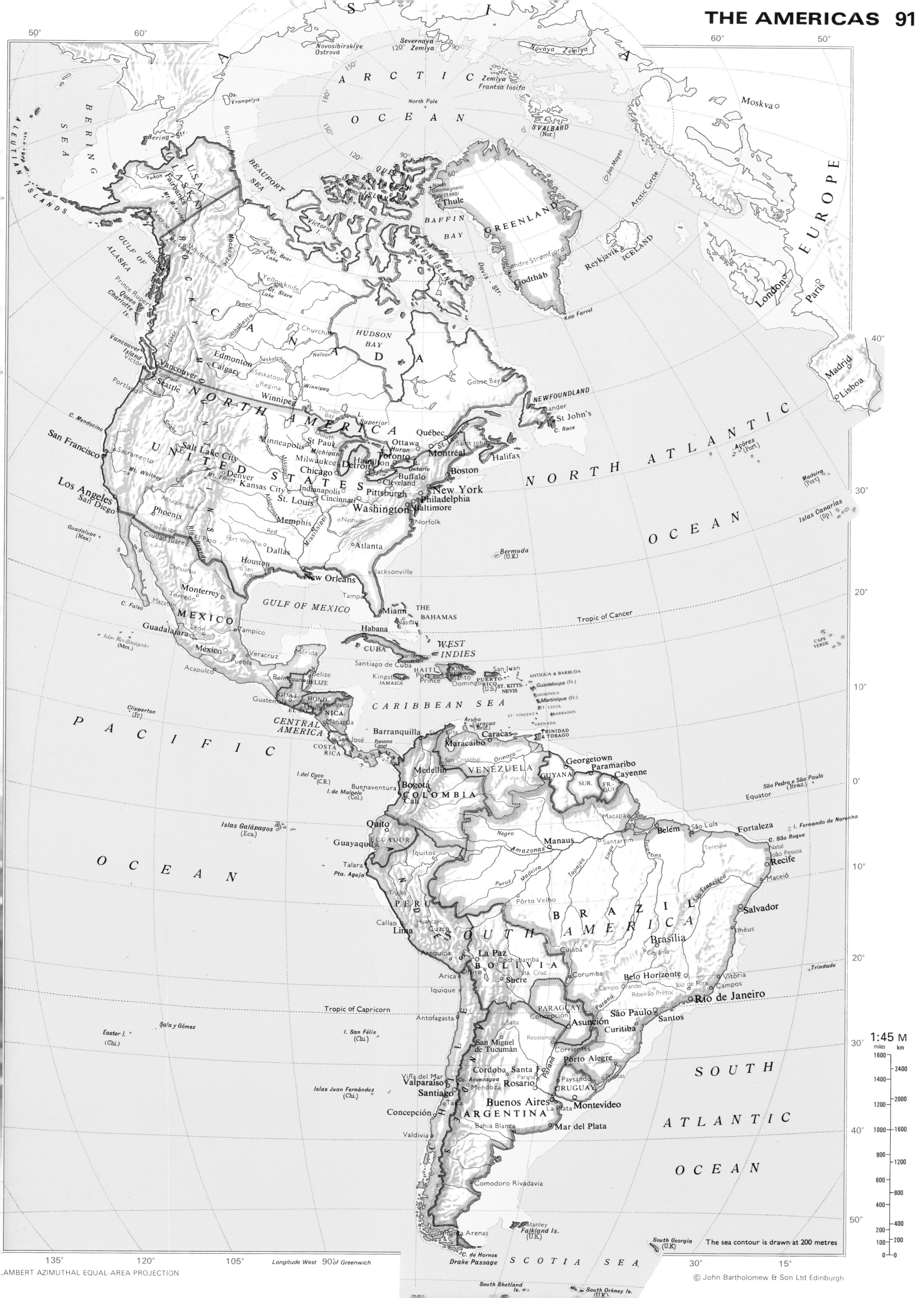
ARCTIC OCEAN
North Pole
Novosibirskiye Ostrova
Severnaya Zemlya
Novaya Zemlya
Zemlya Frantsa Iosifa
Os. Vrangelya
SVALBARD (Nor.)
Jan Mayen
BERING SEA
Bering Str.
ALEUTIAN ISLANDS
U.S.A.
ALASKA
Yukon
Fairbanks
Mt. McKinley
Anchorage
GULF OF ALASKA
Juneau
Prince Rupert
Queen Charlotte Is.
BEAUFORT SEA
North Geomagnetic Pole (1990)
Thule
BAFFIN BAY
BAFFIN ISLAND
Davis Str.
GREENLAND
Søndre Strømfjord
Godthåb
Kap Farvel
Reykjavík
ICELAND
Arctic Circle
Moskva
EUROPE
London
Paris
Madrid
Lisboa
Whitehorse
Mackenzie
Gt. Bear Lake
Yellowknife
Gt. Slave Lake
Peace
Athabasca
CANADA
Churchill
HUDSON BAY
Nelson
Saskatchewan
Edmonton
Calgary
Saskatoon
Regina
Winnipeg
L. Winnipeg
Vancouver Island
Vancouver
Victoria
Seattle
Portland
Columbia
Goose Bay
NEWFOUNDLAND
Gander
St John's
C. Race
NORTH AMERICA
Thunder Bay
L. Superior
Duluth
St. Paul
Minneapolis
Québec
Ottawa
Montréal
St. Lawrence
Saint John
Halifax
L. Huron
L. Michigan
Milwaukee
Chicago
Detroit
Hamilton
Toronto
L. Ontario
L. Erie
Buffalo
Cleveland
Boston
New York
Philadelphia
Pittsburgh
Baltimore
Washington
Norfolk
Indianapolis
Cincinnati
St. Louis
Kansas City
Missouri
UNITED STATES
C. Mendocino
San Francisco
Sacramento
Salt Lake City
Mt. Whitney
Denver
Mt. Elbert
Colorado
Snake
ROCKY MOUNTAINS
Los Angeles
San Diego
Albuquerque
Phoenix
Tucson
Ciudad Juárez
El Paso
Rio Grande
Fort Worth
Dallas
Red
Arkansas
Memphis
Mississippi
Nashville
Atlanta
Houston
San Antonio
New Orleans
Jacksonville
Tampa
Miami
Guadalupe (Mex.)
Chihuahua
Monterrey
Torreón
C. Falso
Mazatlán
MEXICO
León
Tampico
Guadalajara
México
Veracruz
Puebla
Acapulco
Mérida
Islas Revillagigedo (Mex.)
GULF OF MEXICO
THE BAHAMAS
Nassau
Habana
CUBA
Santiago de Cuba
WEST INDIES
HAITI
Port au Prince
DOM. REP.
Santo Domingo
Kingston
JAMAICA
San Juan
PUERTO RICO (U.S.)
ST. KITTS-NEVIS
ANTIGUA & BARBUDA
Guadeloupe (Fr.)
DOMINICA
Martinique (Fr.)
ST. LUCIA
BARBADOS
ST. VINCENT
GRENADA
TRINIDAD & TOBAGO
Aruba
Curaçao (Neth.)
CARIBBEAN SEA
Belize
BELIZE
Belmopan
GUAT.
Guatemala
HOND.
Tegucigalpa
EL SAL.
NICA.
Managua
CENTRAL AMERICA
San José
COSTA RICA
Panama Canal
PANAMA
Clipperton (Fr.)
Bermuda (U.K.)
NORTH ATLANTIC OCEAN
Açôres (Port.)
Madeira (Port.)
Islas Canarias (Sp.)
Tropic of Cancer
CAPE VERDE
Barranquilla
Maracaibo
Caracas
Orinoco
San Cristóbal
VENEZUELA
Georgetown
Paramaribo
Cayenne
GUYANA
SUR.
FR. GUI.
Medellín
Bogotá
COLOMBIA
Cali
Buenaventura
I. del Coco (C.R.)
I. de Malpelo (Col.)
São Pedro e São Paulo (Braz.)
Equator
Quito
ECUADOR
Guayaquil
Islas Galápagos (Ecu.)
Macapá
Belém
São Luís
Fortaleza
I. Fernando de Noronha
C. São Roque
Natal
João Pessoa
Recife
Maceió
Teresina
Negro
Manaus
Amazonas
Santarém
Tocantins
Xingu
Tapajós
Madeira
Purus
Iquitos
Talara
Pta. Aguja
Trujillo
PERU
Callao
Lima
Huancayo
Cuzco
Pôrto Velho
SOUTH AMERICA
BRAZIL
São Francisco
Salvador
Ilhéus
Brasília
Goiânia
Cuiabá
Arequipa
La Paz
Cochabamba
BOLIVIA
Sucre
Sta. Cruz
Corumbá
Arica
Iquique
Belo Horizonte
Vitória
Campos
Juiz de Fora
Campo Grande
Ribeirão Prêto
Rio de Janeiro
Trindade
Tropic of Capricorn
Antofagasta
PARAGUAY
Concepción
Asunción
São Paulo
Santos
Curitiba
Easter I. (Chi.)
Sala y Gómez
I. San Félix (Chi.)
Salta
Resistencia
San Miguel de Tucumán
Corrientes
Pôrto Alegre
Paraná
Córdoba
Santa Fé
Rosario
Paysandú
URUGUAY
Pelotas
Viña del Mar
Valparaíso
Co. Aconcagua
Mendoza
Santiago
Islas Juan Fernández (Chi.)
Buenos Aires
ARGENTINA
La Plata
Montevideo
Talca
Concepción
Bahía Blanca
Mar del Plata
Valdivia
CHILE
Comodoro Rivadavia
Punta Arenas
Stanley
Falkland Is. (U.K.)
C. de Hornos
Drake Passage
SCOTIA SEA
South Georgia (U.K.)
South Shetland Is.
South Orkney Is. (U.K.)
PACIFIC OCEAN
SOUTH ATLANTIC OCEAN
The sea contour is drawn at 200 metres
1:45 M
miles
km
1600
1400
1200
1000
800
600
400
200
100
0
2400
2000
1600
1200
800
400
200
0
50°
60°
40°
30°
20°
10°
0°
135°
120°
105°
Longitude West 90° of Greenwich
30°
15°
LAMBERT AZIMUTHAL EQUAL-AREA PROJECTION

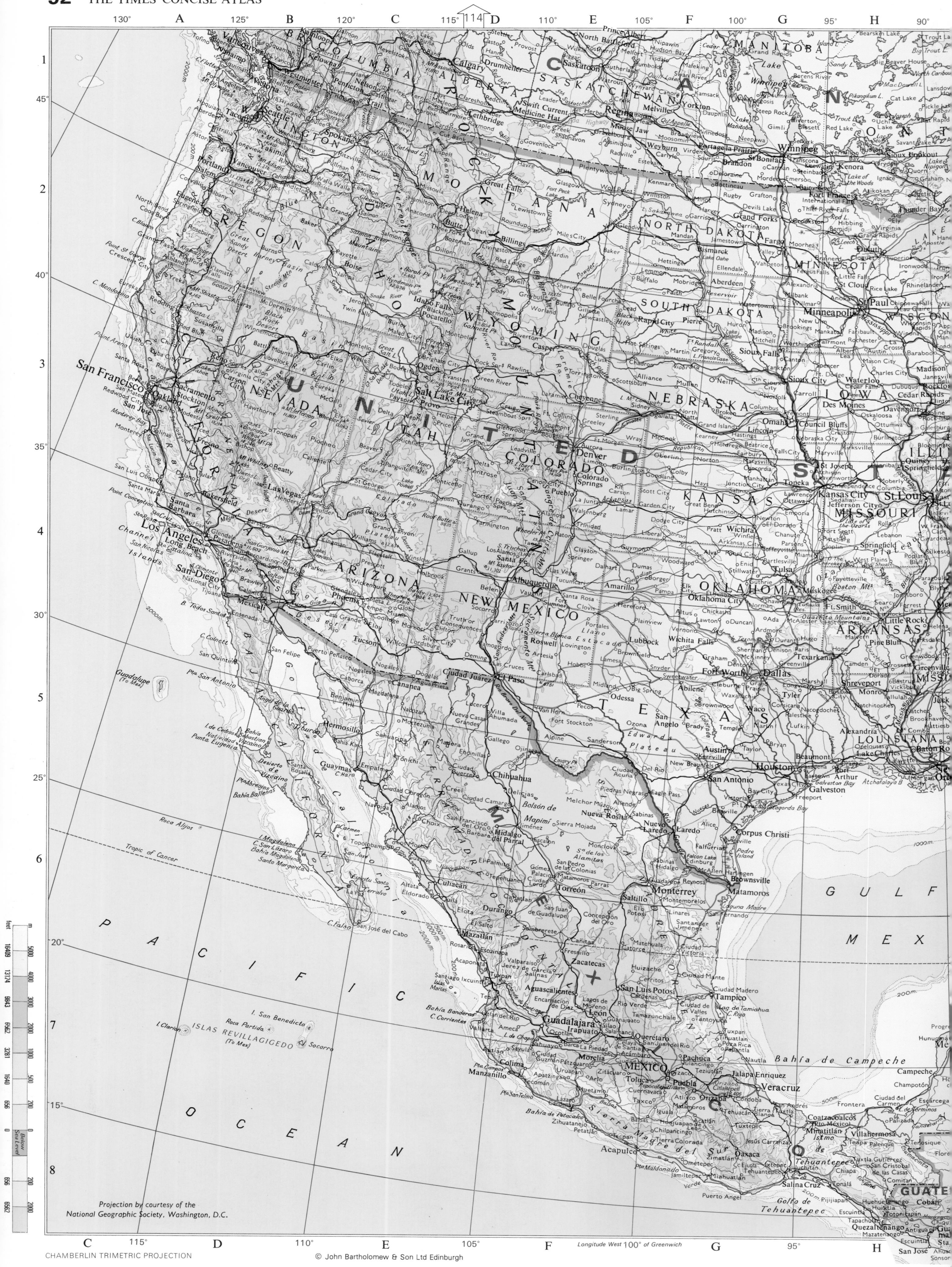
CANADA
BRITISH COLUMBIA
ALBERTA
SASKATCHEWAN
MANITOBA
ONTARIO
UNITED STATES
WASHINGTON
OREGON
CALIFORNIA
NEVADA
IDAHO
MONTANA
WYOMING
UTAH
COLORADO
ARIZONA
NEW MEXICO
NORTH DAKOTA
SOUTH DAKOTA
NEBRASKA
KANSAS
OKLAHOMA
TEXAS
MINNESOTA
IOWA
MISSOURI
ARKANSAS
LOUISIANA
MEXICO
PACIFIC OCEAN
GULF OF MEXICO
Tropic of Cancer
ISLAS REVILLAGIGEDO
Bahía de Campeche
Golfo de Tehuantepec
Projection by courtesy of the National Geographic Society, Washington, D.C.
Longitude West 100° of Greenwich
feet
m
Below Sea Level

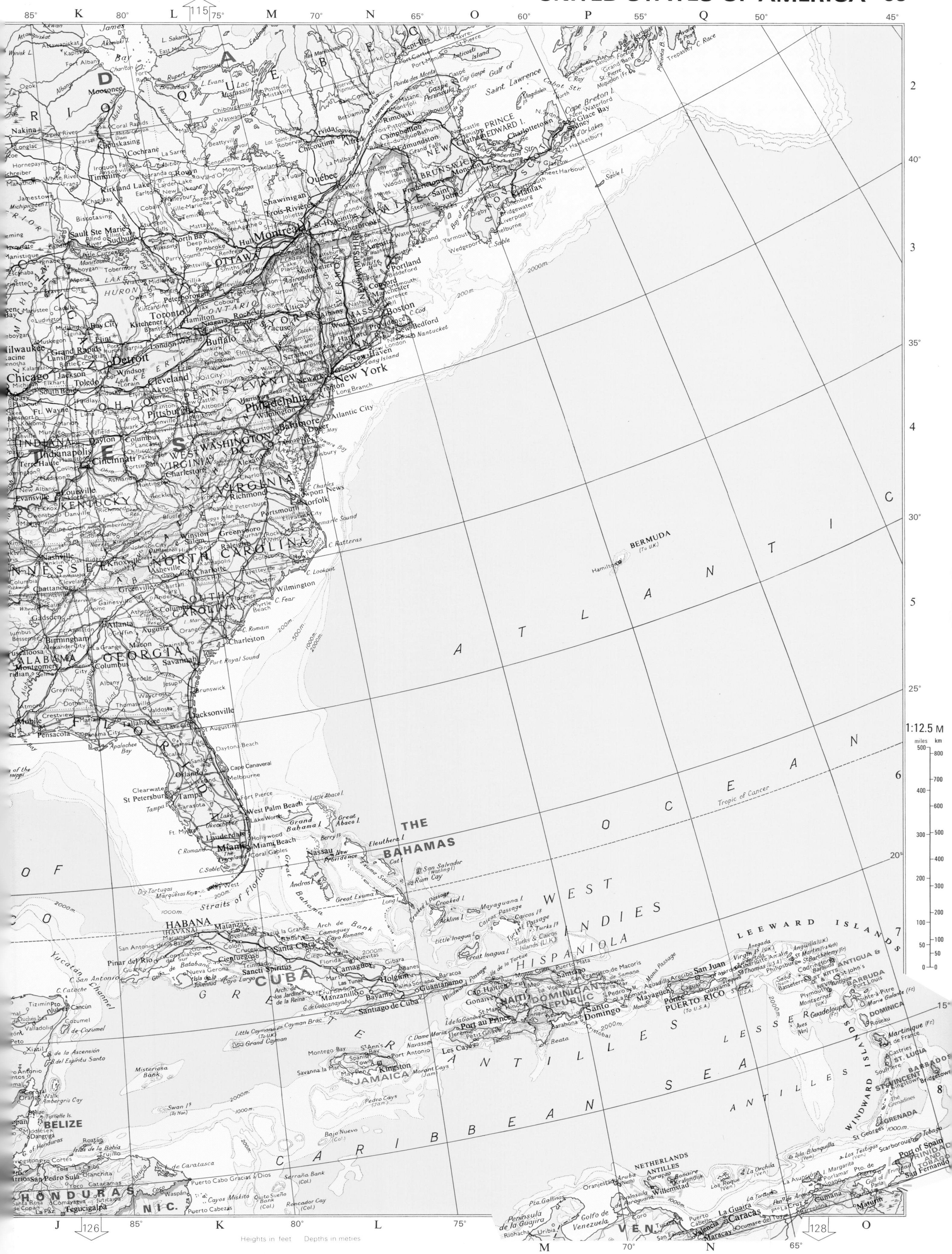

QUEBEC
ONTARIO
PRINCE EDWARD I.
NEW BRUNSWICK
NOVA SCOTIA
MAINE
NEW HAMPSHIRE
VERMONT
MASS.
NEW YORK
PENNSYLVANIA
OHIO
INDIANA
KENTUCKY
WEST VIRGINIA
VIRGINIA
NORTH CAROLINA
SOUTH CAROLINA
GEORGIA
ALABAMA
FLORIDA
WASHINGTON D.C.
New York
Boston
Philadelphia
Baltimore
Montreal
Ottawa
Toronto
Québec
Detroit
Chicago
Cleveland
Pittsburgh
Cincinnati
Atlanta
Charleston
Savannah
Jacksonville
Miami
Tampa
BERMUDA (To U.K.)
Hamilton
A T L A N T I C O C E A N
Tropic of Cancer
THE BAHAMAS
Nassau
WEST INDIES
GREATER ANTILLES
LESSER ANTILLES
CUBA
HABANA (HAVANA)
HAITI
DOMINICAN REPUBLIC
Port au Prince
Santo Domingo
PUERTO RICO (To U.S.A.)
San Juan
JAMAICA
Kingston
LEEWARD ISLANDS
WINDWARD ISLANDS
C A R I B B E A N S E A
NETHERLANDS ANTILLES
BELIZE
HONDURAS
NIC.
Tegucigalpa
Caracas
TRINIDAD AND TOBAGO
Port of Spain
Straits of Florida
Yucatan Channel
1:12.5 M
miles
km
Heights in feet
Depths in metres
115
126
128

LAMBERT CONFORMAL CONIC PROJECTION

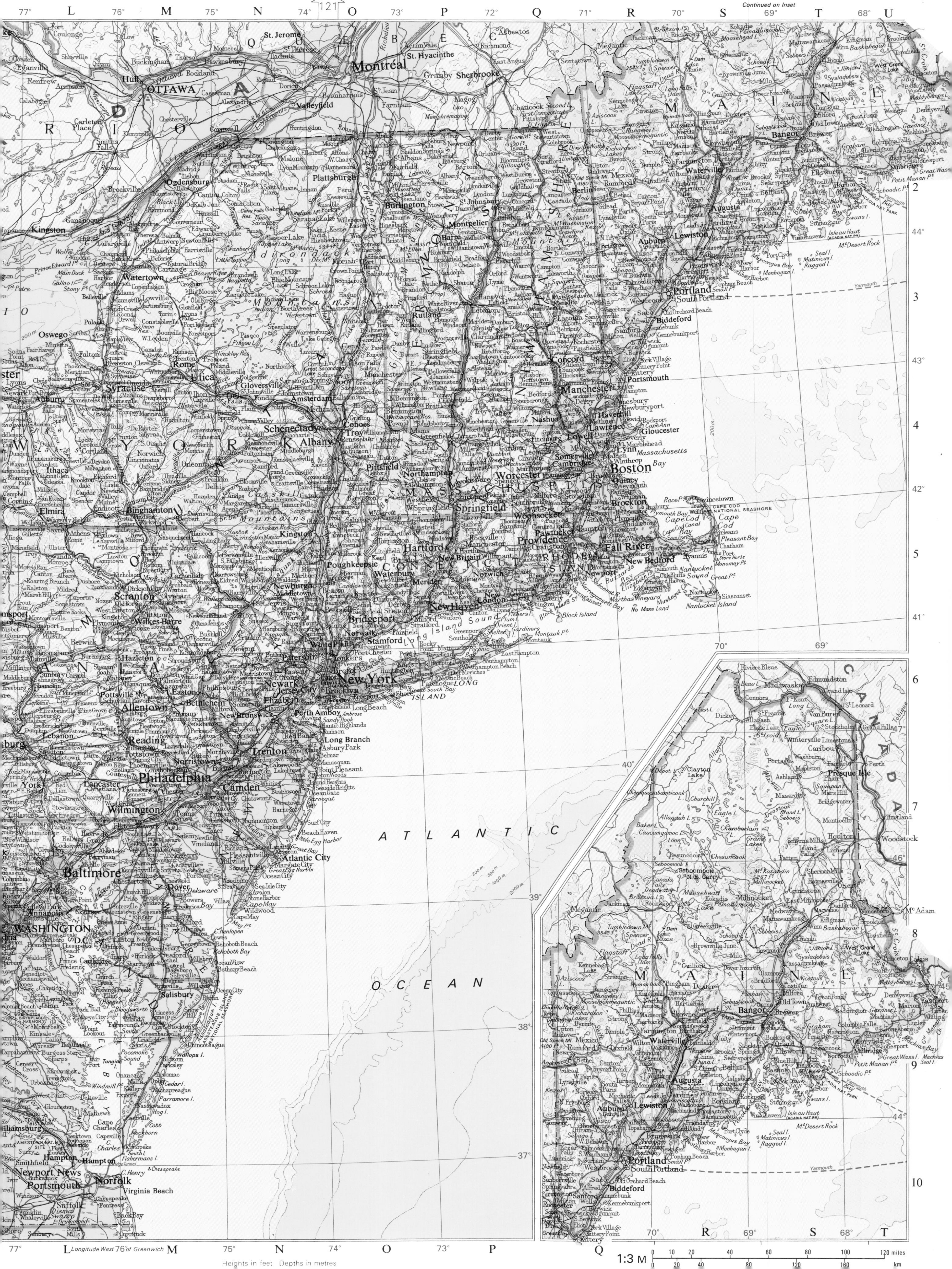
Continued on Inset
121
ATLANTIC
OCEAN
NEW YORK
MAINE
Montréal
OTTAWA
Boston
New York
Philadelphia
Baltimore
WASHINGTON D.C.
Albany
Portland
Providence
Hartford
Springfield
Worcester
Manchester
Concord
Bangor
Augusta
Lewiston
Burlington
Montpelier
Syracuse
Utica
Schenectady
Binghamton
Scranton
Wilkes-Barre
Allentown
Reading
Trenton
Camden
Wilmington
Atlantic City
Newark
Jersey City
Paterson
Bridgeport
New Haven
Stamford
Waterbury
New Bedford
Fall River
Norfolk
Newport News
Portsmouth
Long Island Sound
Massachusetts Bay
Cape Cod Bay
Nantucket Sound
Nantucket Island
Block Island
Longitude West 76° of Greenwich
Heights in feet Depths in metres
1:3 M
miles
km

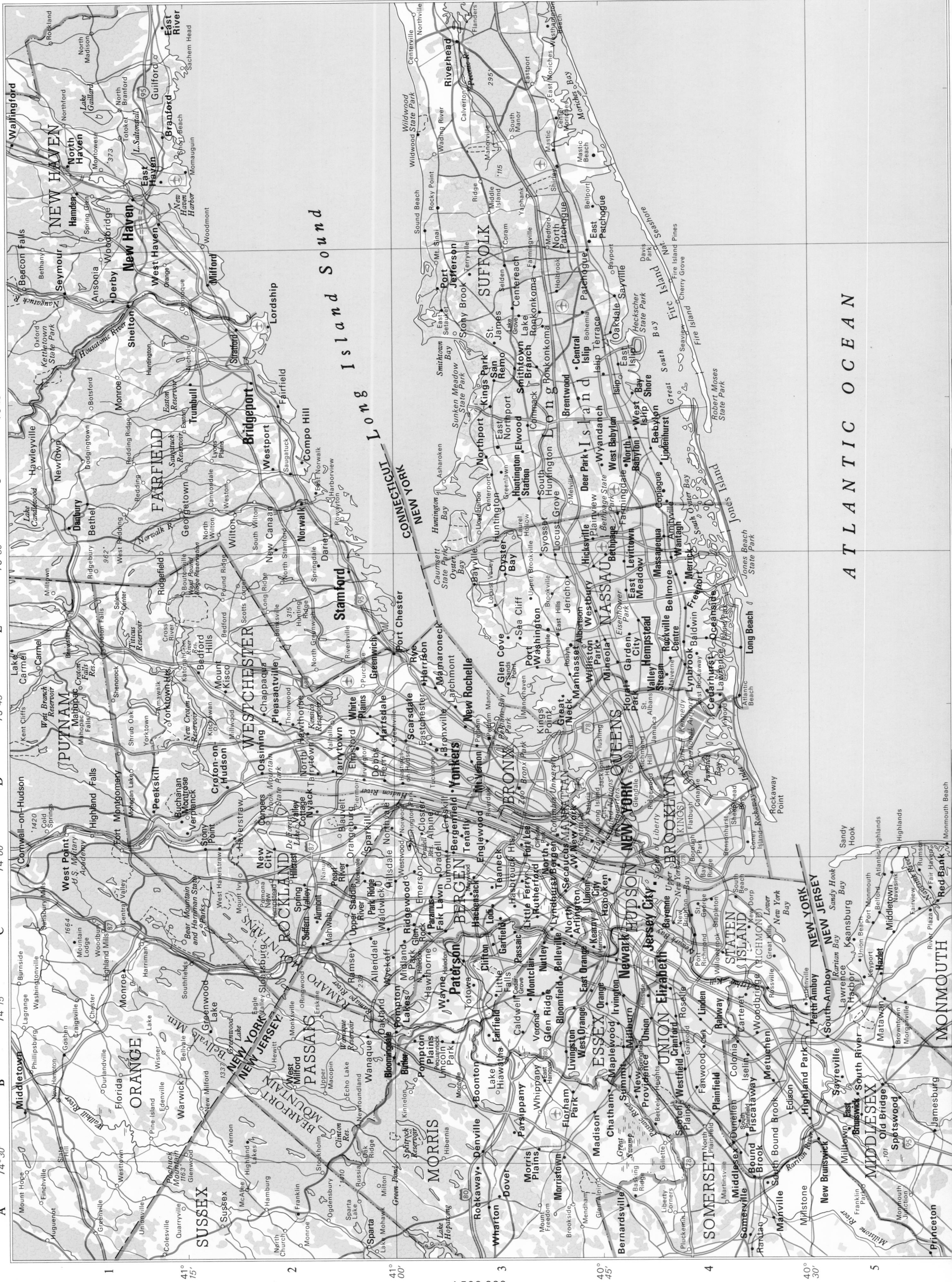
ATLANTIC OCEAN
Long Island Sound
Long Island
NEW HAVEN
FAIRFIELD
PUTNAM
WESTCHESTER
ROCKLAND
ORANGE
SUSSEX
PASSAIC
MORRIS
BERGEN
ESSEX
HUDSON
UNION
SOMERSET
MIDDLESEX
MONMOUTH
STATEN ISLAND
BRONX
QUEENS
NASSAU
SUFFOLK
NEW YORK
BROOKLYN
CONNECTICUT
NEW YORK
NEW JERSEY
New Haven
Bridgeport
Stamford
Yonkers
Newark
Jersey City
Paterson
Elizabeth
Fire Island
Jones Beach State Park

1:500 000

PHILADELPHIA

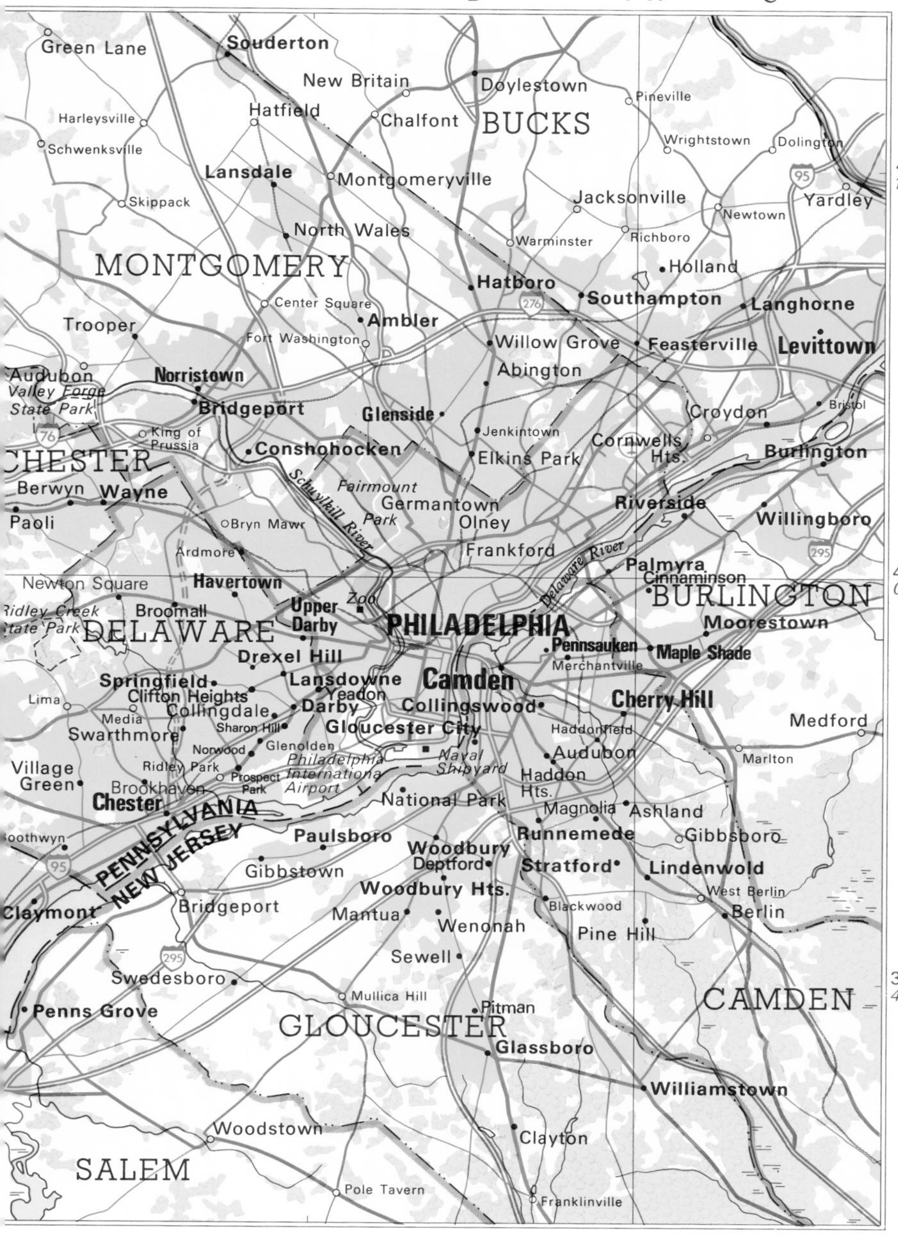

BOSTON

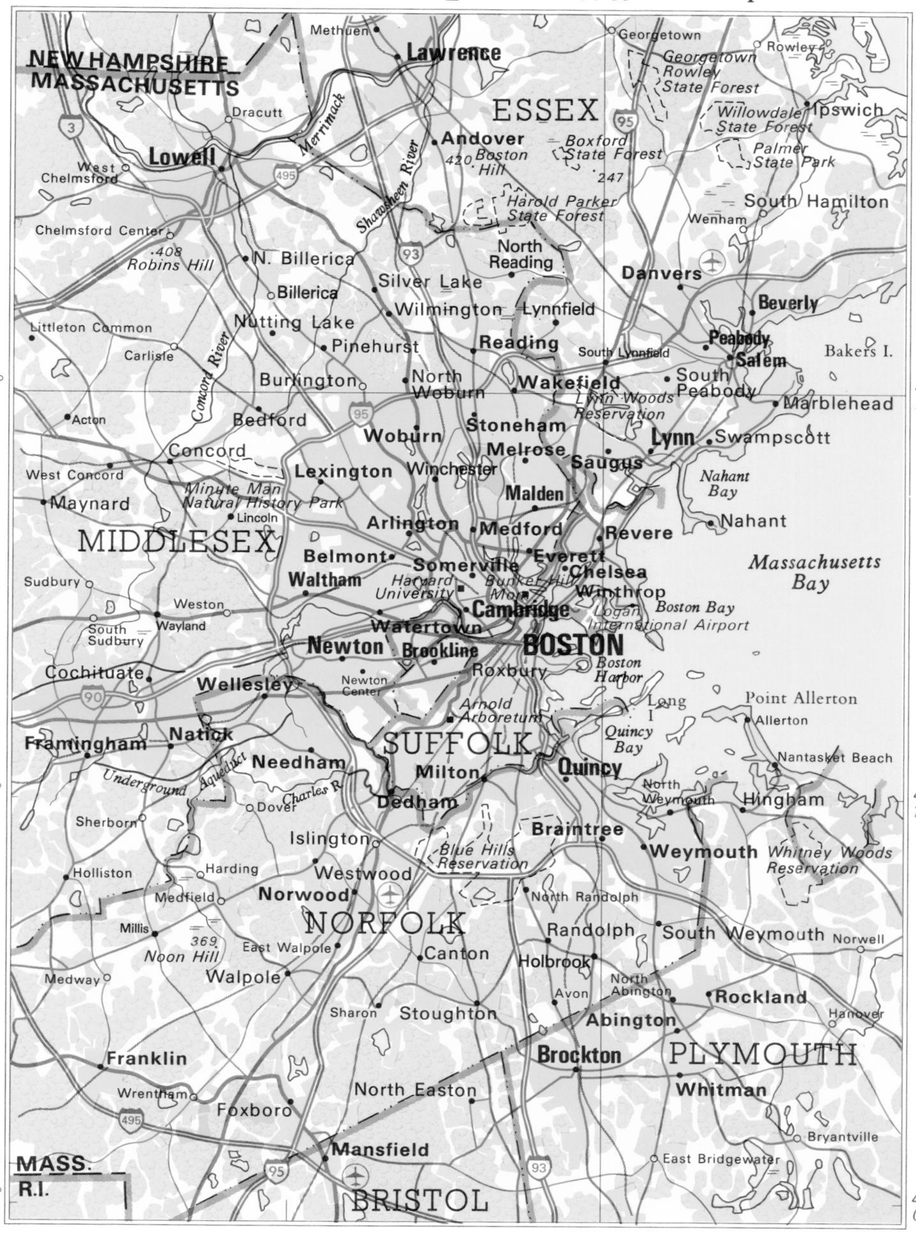

WASHINGTON

BALTIMORE

1:500 000

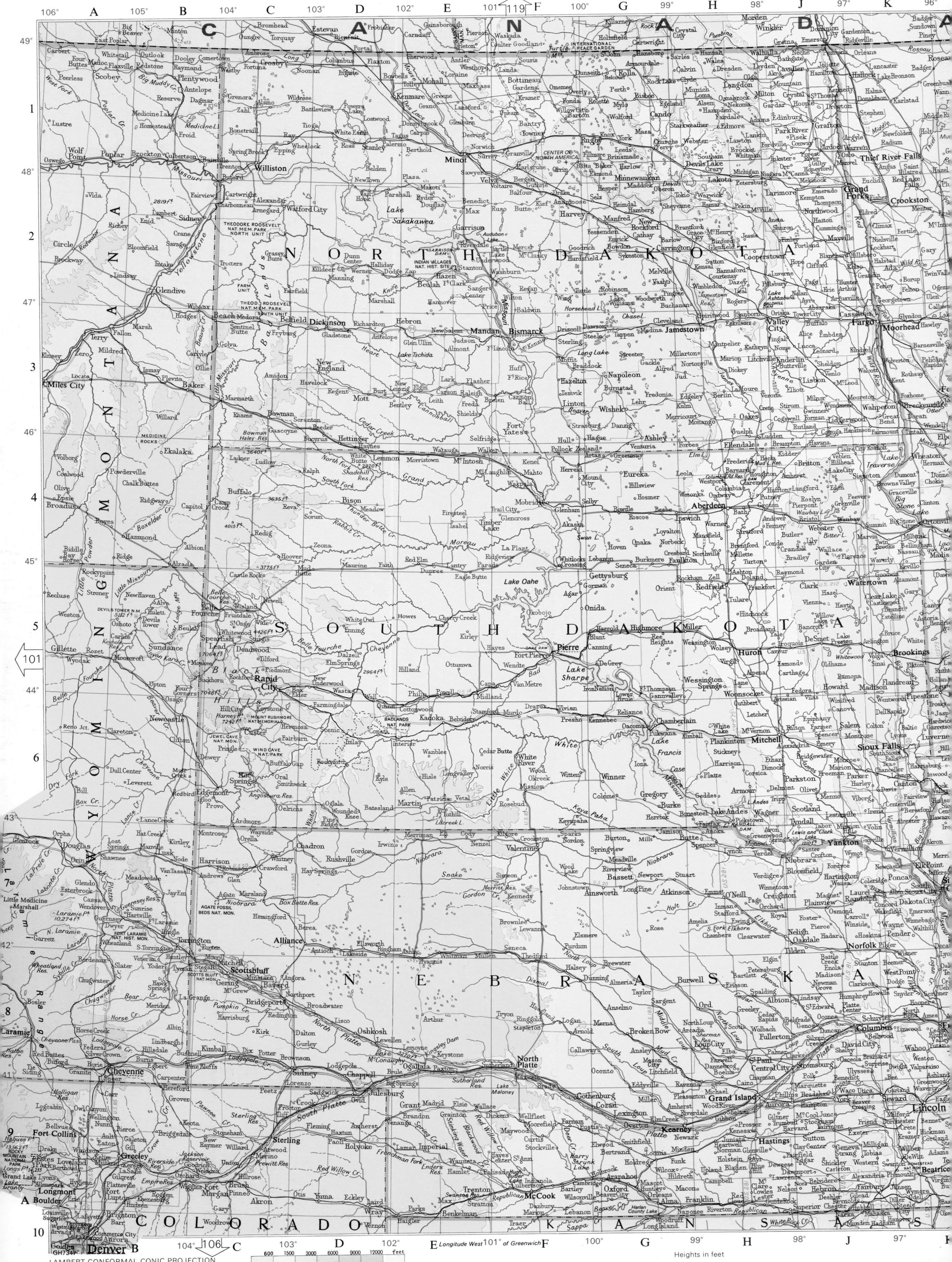

LAMBERT CONFORMAL CONIC PROJECTION

LAKE SUPERIOR
LAKE MICHIGAN
ONTARIO
MINNESOTA
WISCONSIN
MICHIGAN
IOWA
ILLINOIS
MISSOURI
Lake of the Woods
Upper Red Lake
Lower Red Lake
Mille Lacs
Thunder Bay
Duluth
Superior
Minneapolis
St. Paul
St. Cloud
Rochester
Eau Claire
La Crosse
Green Bay
Milwaukee
Madison
Racine
Kenosha
Waukegan
Chicago
Gary
Rockford
Dubuque
Cedar Rapids
Waterloo
Des Moines
Davenport
Moline
Rock Island
Iowa City
Peoria
Springfield
Bloomington
Champaign
Danville
Decatur
Quincy
Hannibal
Council Bluffs
St. Joseph
Burlington
Galesburg
Sault Ste Marie
Marquette
Escanaba
Oshkosh
Appleton
Wausau
Sheboygan
Manitowoc
Mankato
Fort Dodge
Mason City
Ottumwa
Kankakee
Joliet
Aurora
Elgin
Grand Marais
Brainerd
Bemidji
Hibbing
Virginia
Grand Rapids
International Falls
Isle Royale
Apostle Islands (NAT. LAKESHORE)
North Manitou I.
South Manitou I.
Muskegon
Terre Haute
on the same scale
118
110
94
1:3 M
0 10 20 40 60 80 100 miles
© John Bartholomew & Son Ltd Edinburgh

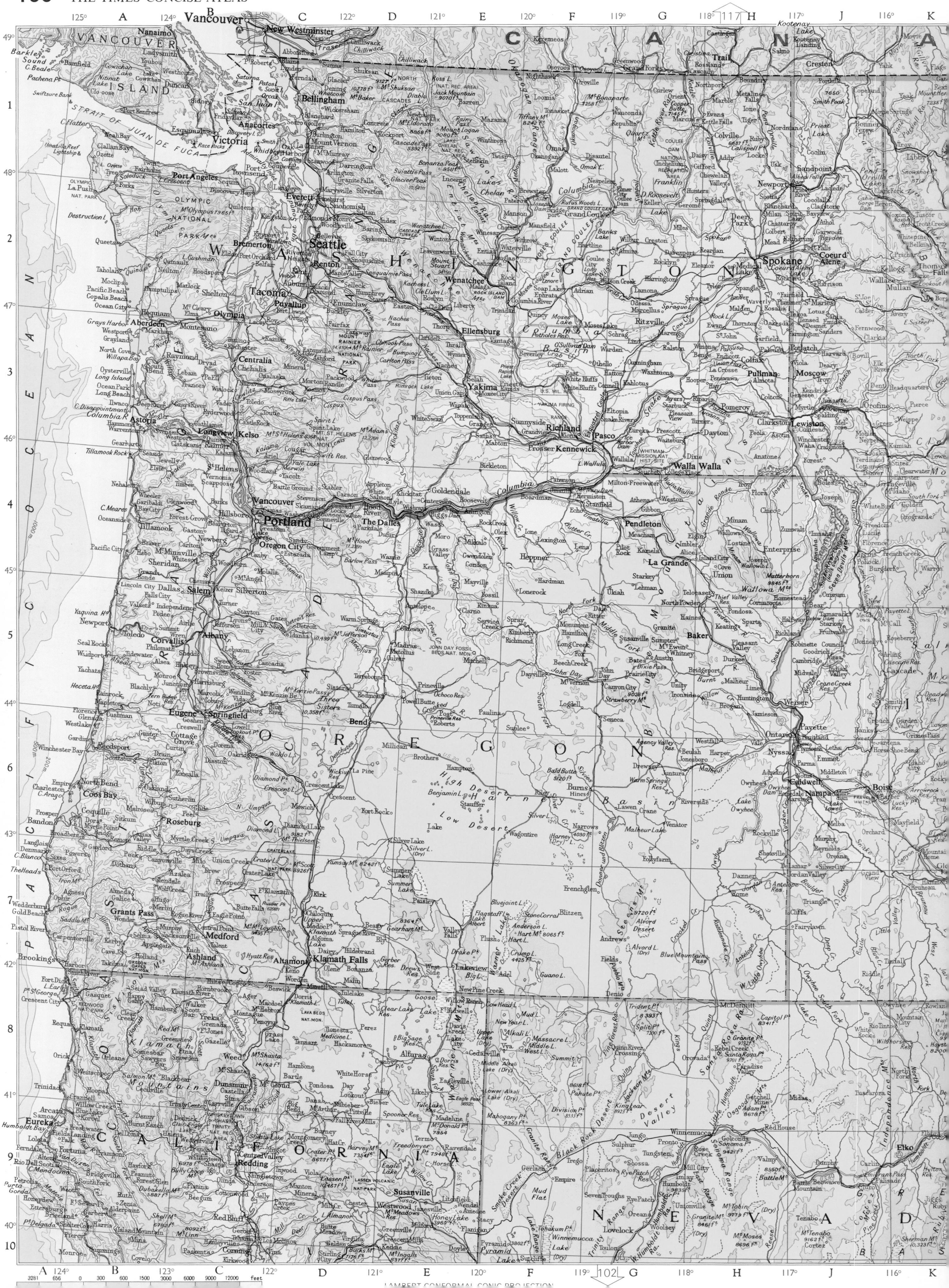
117
CANADA
VANCOUVER ISLAND
Vancouver
New Westminster
Victoria
STRAIT OF JUAN DE FUCA
WASHINGTON
Seattle
Tacoma
Olympia
Everett
Bellingham
Spokane
Yakima
Ellensburg
Wenatchee
Richland
Kennewick
Pasco
Walla Walla
Vancouver
Portland
The Dalles
Pendleton
La Grande
Baker
Salem
Eugene
Corvallis
Albany
Bend
Medford
Klamath Falls
Grants Pass
Roseburg
Coos Bay
OREGON
PACIFIC OCEAN
Columbia Basin
Harney Basin
High Desert
Low Desert
Wallowa Mts
Blue Mountains
CASCADE RANGE
Lewiston
Moscow
Boise
Nampa
Caldwell
Ontario
Eureka
Redding
Susanville
Alturas
Winnemucca
Elko
CALIFORNIA
NEVADA
Klamath Mountains
Black Rock Desert
Desert Valley
102
LAMBERT CONFORMAL CONIC PROJECTION

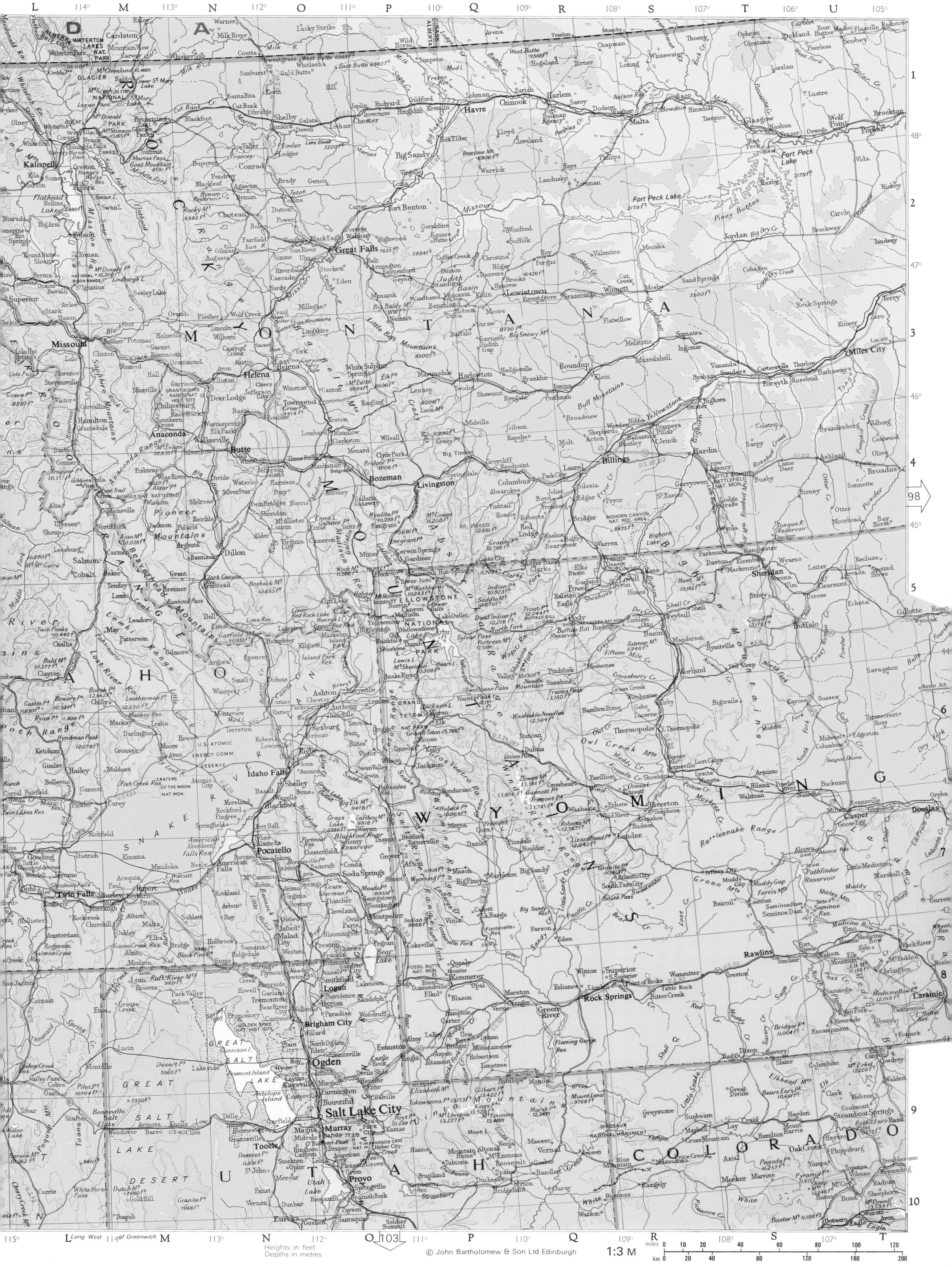
MONTANA
IDAHO
WYOMING
UTAH
COLORADO
DAKOTA
Kalispell
Missoula
Helena
Butte
Anaconda
Great Falls
Havre
Lewistown
Bozeman
Livingston
Billings
Miles City
Glasgow
Sheridan
Casper
Rawlins
Rock Springs
Laramie
Pocatello
Idaho Falls
Twin Falls
Blackfoot
Logan
Ogden
Brigham City
Salt Lake City
Murray
Provo
Tooele
GREAT SALT LAKE
GREAT SALT LAKE DESERT
YELLOWSTONE NATIONAL PARK
GLACIER NATIONAL PARK
Fort Peck Lake
Bear Lake
Utah Lake
Flathead Lake
98
103
Long West of Greenwich
Heights in feet
Depths in metres
© John Bartholomew & Son Ltd Edinburgh
1:3 M
miles 0 10 20 40 60 80 100 120
km 0 20 40 80 120 160 200

LAMBERT CONFORMAL CONIC PROJECTION

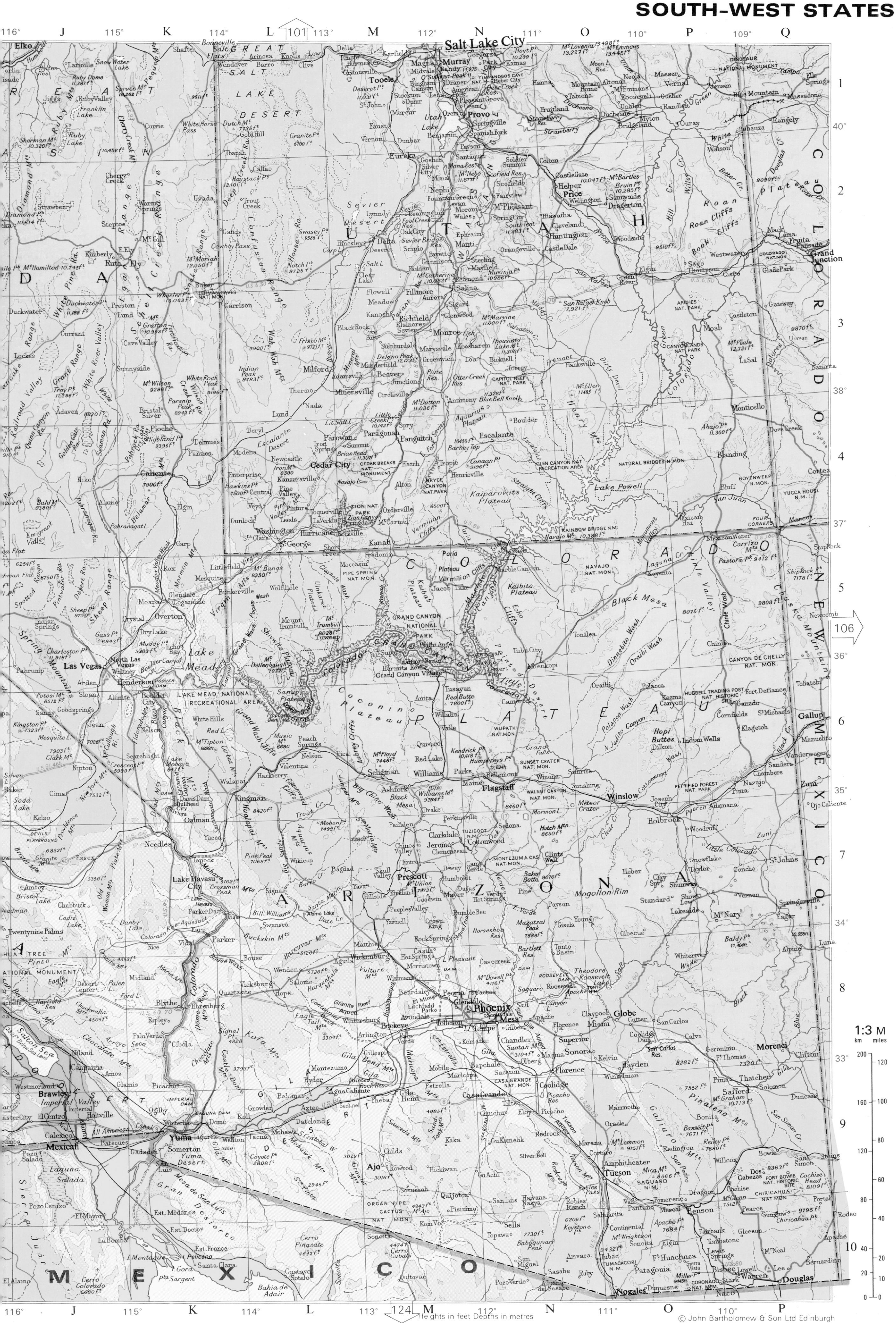

Heights in feet Depths in metres

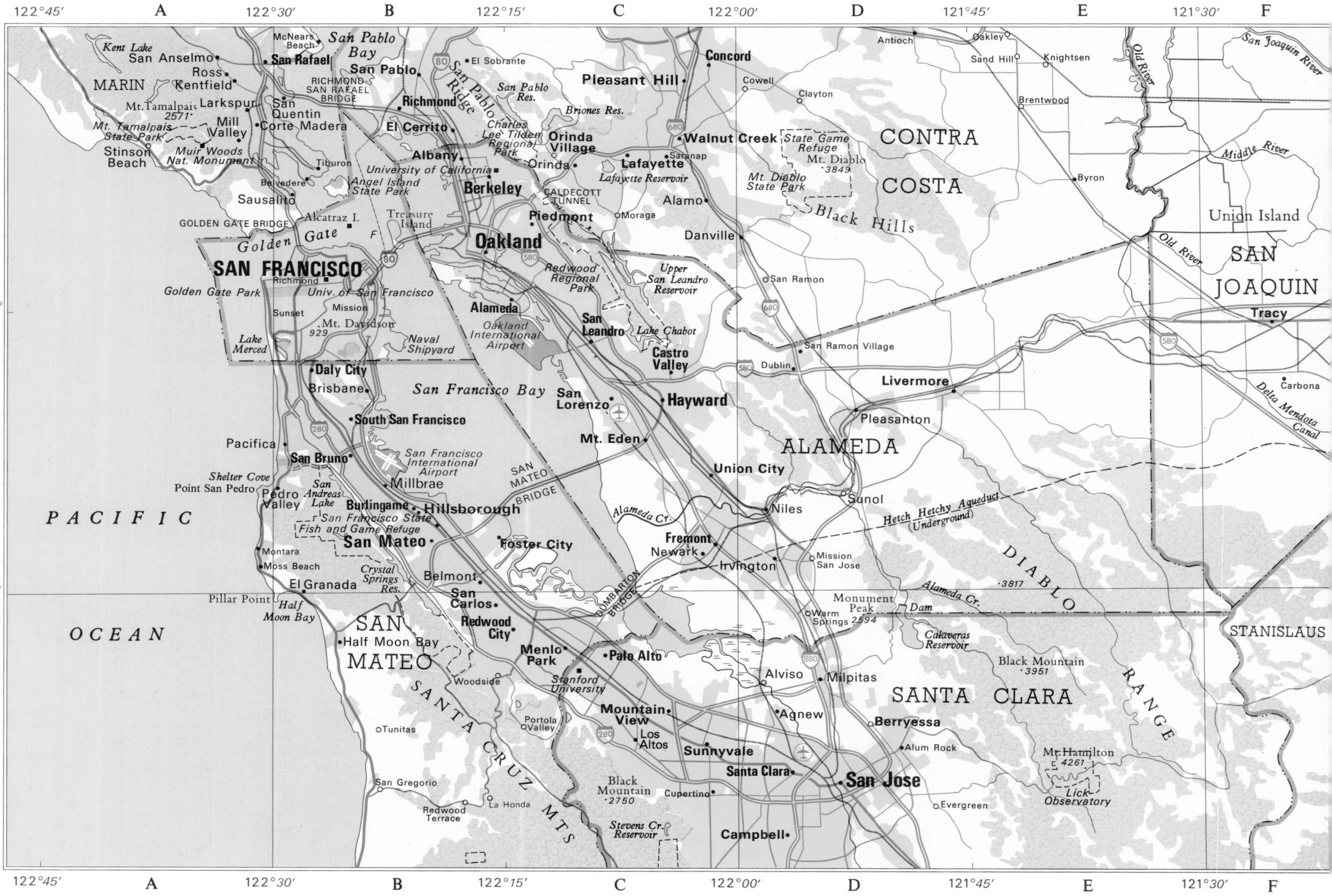
122°45′
A
122°30′
B
122°15′
C
122°00′
D
121°45′
E
121°30′
F
1
2
3
37° 45′
37° 30′
MARIN
Kent Lake
San Anselmo
San Rafael
Ross
Kentfield
Larkspur
San Quentin
Corte Madera
Mill Valley
Mt. Tamalpais 2571
Mt. Tamalpais State Park
Muir Woods Nat. Monument
Stinson Beach
Tiburon
Belvedere
Sausalito
Angel Island State Park
Alcatraz I.
GOLDEN GATE BRIDGE
Golden Gate
Treasure Island
McNears Beach
San Pablo Bay
San Pablo
RICHMOND SAN RAFAEL BRIDGE
Richmond
El Sobrante
San Pablo Ridge
San Pablo Res.
Briones Res.
El Cerrito
Charles Lee Tilden Regional Park
Albany
University of California
Berkeley
Orinda Village
Orinda
CALDECOTT TUNNEL
Piedmont
Moraga
Oakland
Lafayette
Lafayette Reservoir
Saranap
Pleasant Hill
Concord
Walnut Creek
Cowell
Clayton
State Game Refuge
Mt. Diablo 3849
Mt. Diablo State Park
CONTRA COSTA
Black Hills
Alamo
Danville
San Ramon
Antioch
Oakley
Sand Hill
Knightsen
Brentwood
Old River
San Joaquin River
Middle River
Byron
Union Island
Old River
SAN JOAQUIN
Tracy
Carbona
Delta Mendota Canal
SAN FRANCISCO
Richmond
Golden Gate Park
Univ. of San Francisco
Mission
Sunset
Mt. Davidson 929
Lake Merced
Naval Shipyard
Alameda
Oakland International Airport
Redwood Regional Park
Upper San Leandro Reservoir
San Leandro
Lake Chabot
Castro Valley
San Ramon Village
Dublin
Livermore
Pleasanton
Daly City
Brisbane
San Francisco Bay
San Lorenzo
Hayward
South San Francisco
Mt. Eden
ALAMEDA
Pacifica
San Bruno
San Francisco International Airport
Union City
Shelter Cove
Point San Pedro
Pedro Valley
San Andreas Lake
Millbrae
SAN MATEO BRIDGE
Burlingame
Hillsborough
San Francisco State Fish and Game Refuge
Alameda Cr.
Niles
Sunol
Hetch Hetchy Aqueduct (Underground)
San Mateo
Foster City
Fremont
Newark
Irvington
Mission San Jose
DIABLO
PACIFIC
Montara
Moss Beach
El Granada
Crystal Springs Res.
Belmont
San Carlos
DUMBARTON BRIDGE
3817
Alameda Cr.
Dam
Monument Peak 2594
Warm Springs
Pillar Point
Half Moon Bay
OCEAN
SAN MATEO
Half Moon Bay
Redwood City
Menlo Park
Palo Alto
Stanford University
Calaveras Reservoir
Alviso
Milpitas
Black Mountain 3951
RANGE
STANISLAUS
Woodside
SANTA CLARA
Tunitas
SANTA CRUZ MTS
Portola Valley
Mountain View
Los Altos
Agnew
Berryessa
Alum Rock
Sunnyvale
Santa Clara
San Jose
Mt. Hamilton 4261
Lick Observatory
San Gregorio
La Honda
Redwood Terrace
Black Mountain 2750
Cupertino
Evergreen
Stevens Cr. Reservoir
Campbell

LOS ANGELES

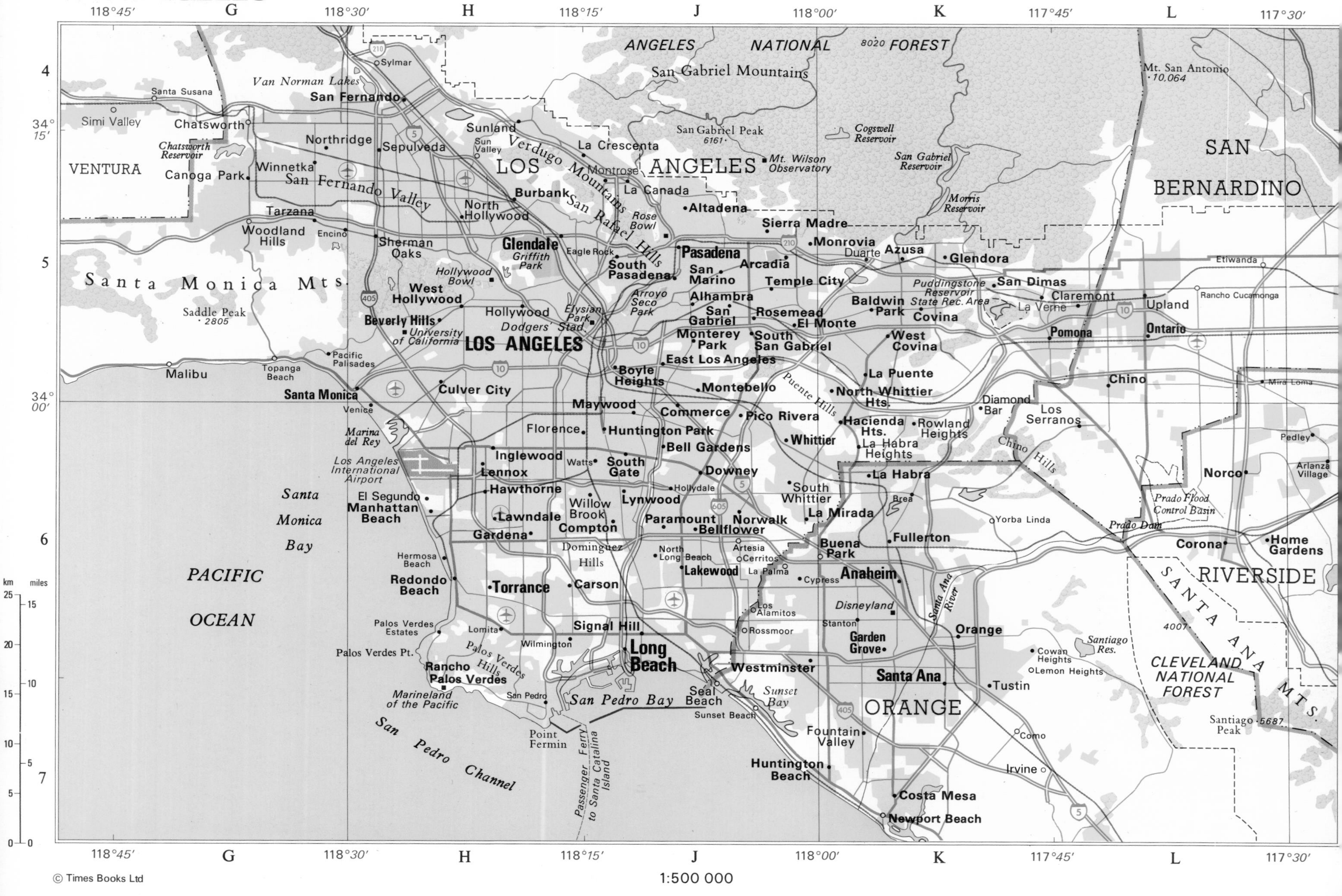
118°45′
G
118°30′
H
118°15′
J
118°00′
K
117°45′
L
117°30′
4
5
6
7
34° 15′
34° 00′
km
miles
ANGELES NATIONAL FOREST
8020
San Gabriel Mountains
Mt. San Antonio 10,064
Sylmar
Van Norman Lakes
San Fernando
Santa Susana
Simi Valley
Chatsworth
Chatsworth Reservoir
Northridge
Sepulveda
Sunland
Sun Valley
La Crescenta
San Gabriel Peak 6161
Cogswell Reservoir
San Gabriel Reservoir
Mt. Wilson Observatory
SAN BERNARDINO
VENTURA
Canoga Park
Winnetka
San Fernando Valley
LOS ANGELES
Verdugo Mountains
Montrose
La Canada
Burbank
San Rafael Hills
Altadena
Morris Reservoir
Tarzana
North Hollywood
Rose Bowl
Woodland Hills
Encino
Sherman Oaks
Glendale
Griffith Park
Eagle Rock
Sierra Madre
Monrovia
Duarte
Azusa
Glendora
Etiwanda
Pasadena
Arcadia
South Pasadena
San Marino
Temple City
Santa Monica Mts
Hollywood Bowl
West Hollywood
Arroyo Seco Park
Alhambra
Puddingstone Reservoir
San Dimas
Claremont
Rancho Cucamonga
Saddle Peak 2805
Beverly Hills
Hollywood
Elysian Park
Dodgers' Stad.
San Gabriel
Rosemead
Baldwin Park
State Rec. Area
La Verne
Upland
Covina
University of California
LOS ANGELES
Monterey Park
South San Gabriel
El Monte
West Covina
Pomona
Ontario
Topanga Beach
Pacific Palisades
Malibu
East Los Angeles
Boyle Heights
La Puente
Santa Monica
Culver City
Montebello
Puente Hills
North Whittier Hts.
Diamond Bar
Chino
Mira Loma
Venice
Maywood
Commerce
Pico Rivera
Los Serranos
Marina del Rey
Florence
Huntington Park
Hacienda Hts.
Rowland Heights
Whittier
La Habra Heights
Chino Hills
Pedley
Los Angeles International Airport
Inglewood
Bell Gardens
Lennox
Watts
South Gate
Downey
La Habra
Norco
Arlanza Village
Santa Monica Bay
El Segundo
Hawthorne
Hollydale
South Whittier
Brea
Prado Flood Control Basin
Manhattan Beach
Willow Brook
Lynwood
Lawndale
Compton
Paramount
Norwalk
La Mirada
Yorba Linda
Prado Dam
Gardena
Bellflower
Fullerton
Corona
Home Gardens
Dominguez Hills
North Long Beach
Artesia
Buena Park
Hermosa Beach
Lakewood
La Palma
Cerritos
Anaheim
RIVERSIDE
PACIFIC OCEAN
Redondo Beach
Torrance
Carson
Cypress
Santa Ana River
SANTA ANA MTS.
Los Alamitos
Disneyland
Palos Verdes Estates
Lomita
Signal Hill
Rossmoor
Stanton
Garden Grove
Orange
4007
Wilmington
Long Beach
Santiago Res.
Palos Verdes Pt.
Palos Verdes Hills
Cowan Heights
Lemon Heights
CLEVELAND NATIONAL FOREST
Rancho Palos Verdes
Westminster
Santa Ana
Tustin
Marineland of the Pacific
San Pedro
San Pedro Bay
Seal Beach
Sunset Bay
Sunset Beach
ORANGE
Santiago Peak 5687
Point Fermin
Fountain Valley
Como
San Pedro Channel
Passenger Ferry to Santa Catalina Island
Huntington Beach
Irvine
Costa Mesa
Newport Beach

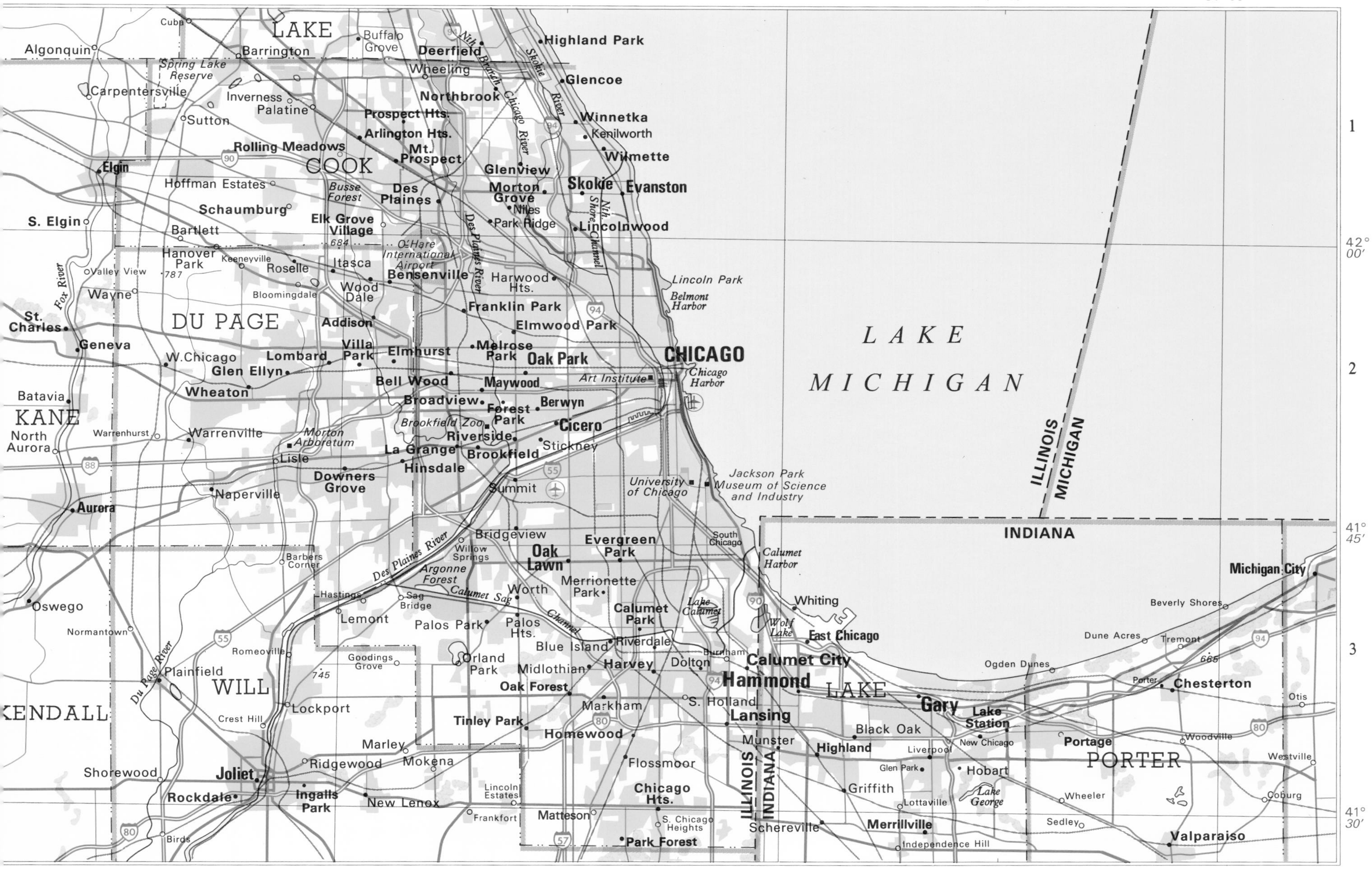

ST. LOUIS

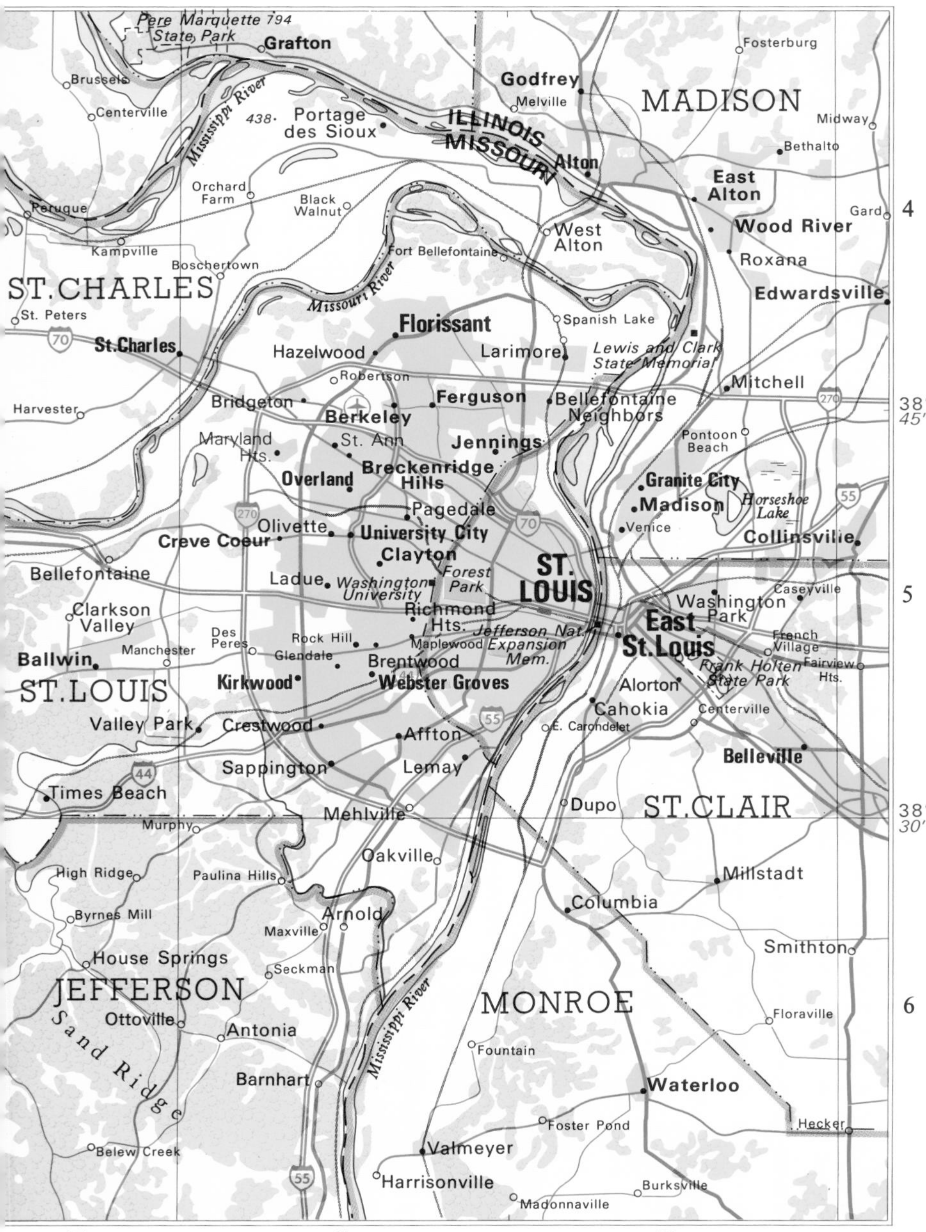

ATLANTA

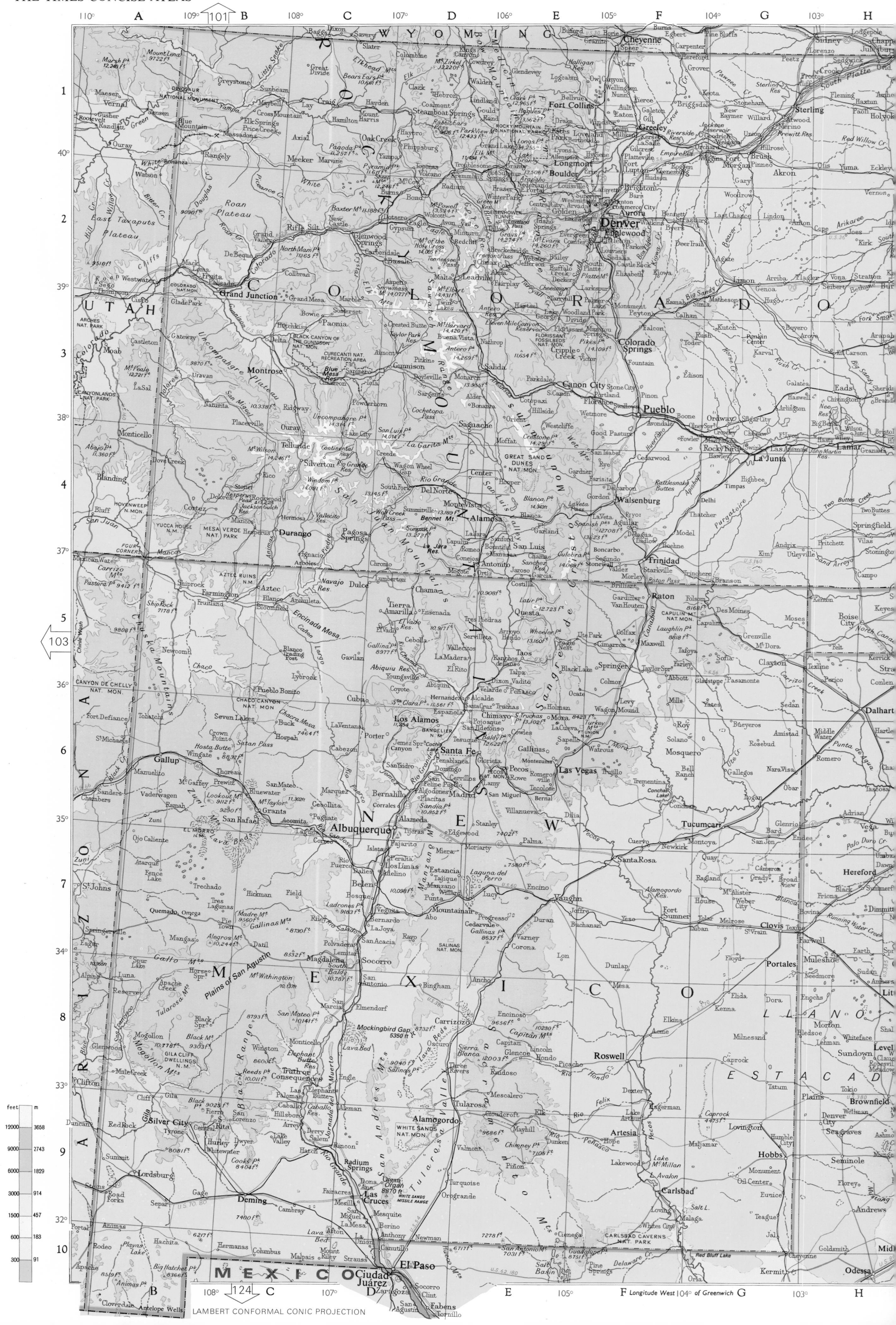
101
103
124
WYOMING
COLORADO
UTAH
ARIZONA
NEW MEXICO
MEXICO
ROCKY MOUNTAINS
LLANO ESTACADO
Cheyenne
Fort Collins
Greeley
Boulder
Denver
Aurora
Englewood
Grand Junction
Colorado Springs
Pueblo
Canon City
Trinidad
Durango
Alamosa
Montrose
Gunnison
Leadville
La Junta
Lamar
Sterling
Raton
Taos
Los Alamos
Santa Fe
Las Vegas
Albuquerque
Gallup
Farmington
Tucumcari
Clovis
Roswell
Carlsbad
Hobbs
Alamogordo
Las Cruces
Deming
Lordsburg
Silver City
Socorro
El Paso
Ciudad Juárez
Odessa
feet
m
12000
3658
9000
2743
6000
1829
3000
914
1500
457
600
183
300
91
Longitude West 104° of Greenwich
LAMBERT CONFORMAL CONIC PROJECTION

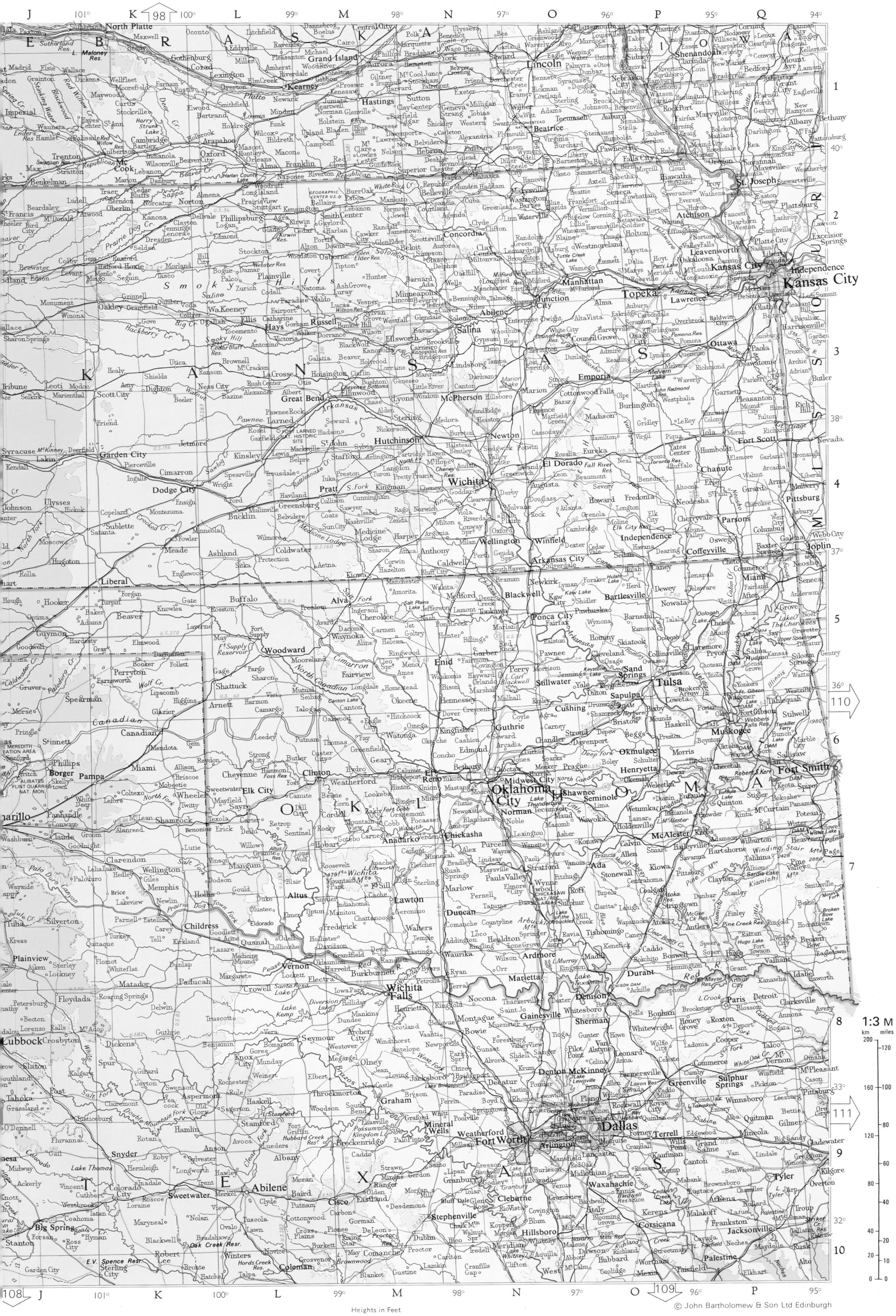

Heights in Feet

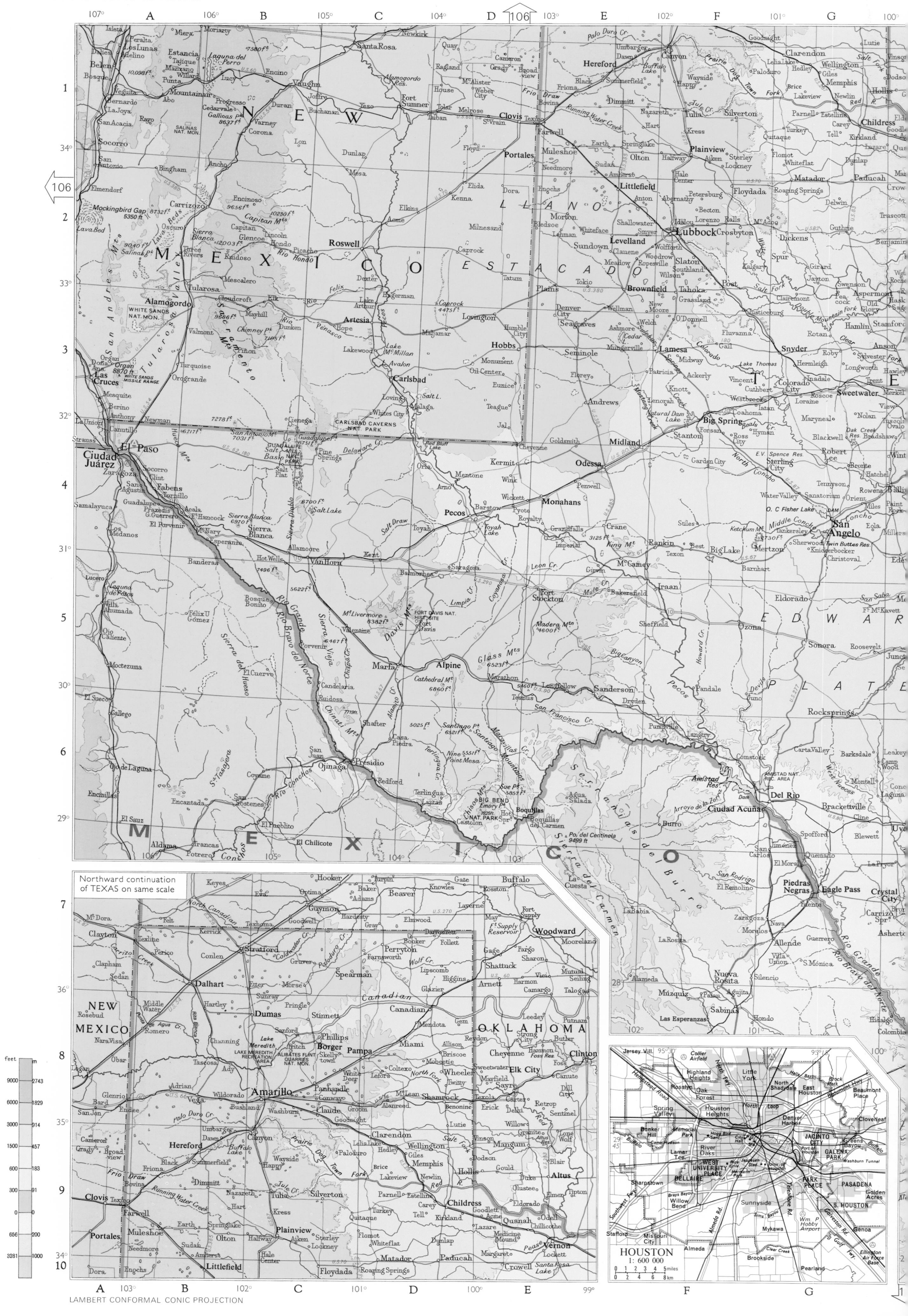

LAMBERT CONFORMAL CONIC PROJECTION

Heights in feet
Depths in metres

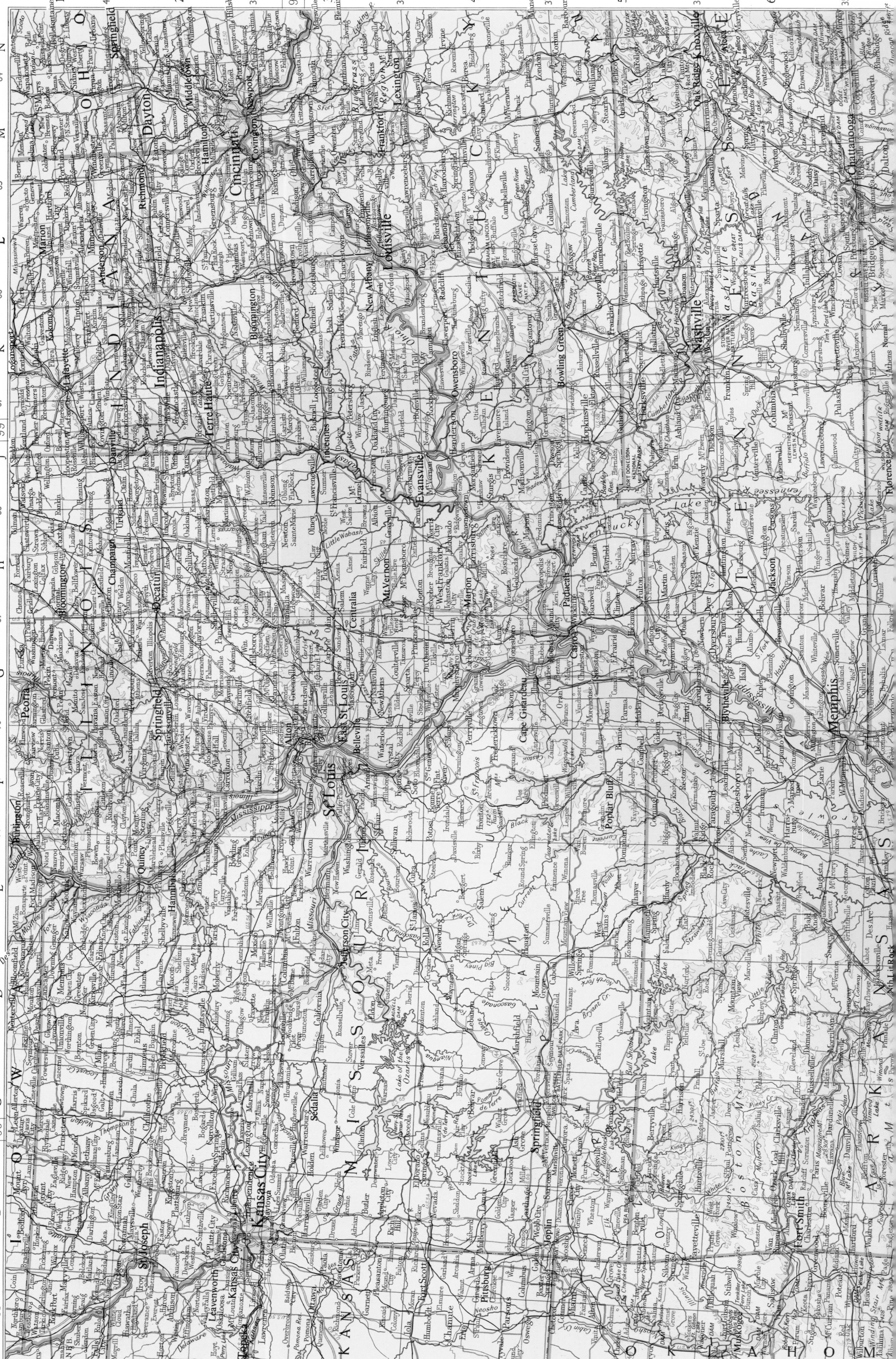

LAMBERT CONFORMAL CONIC PROJECTION

Heights in feet Depths in metres

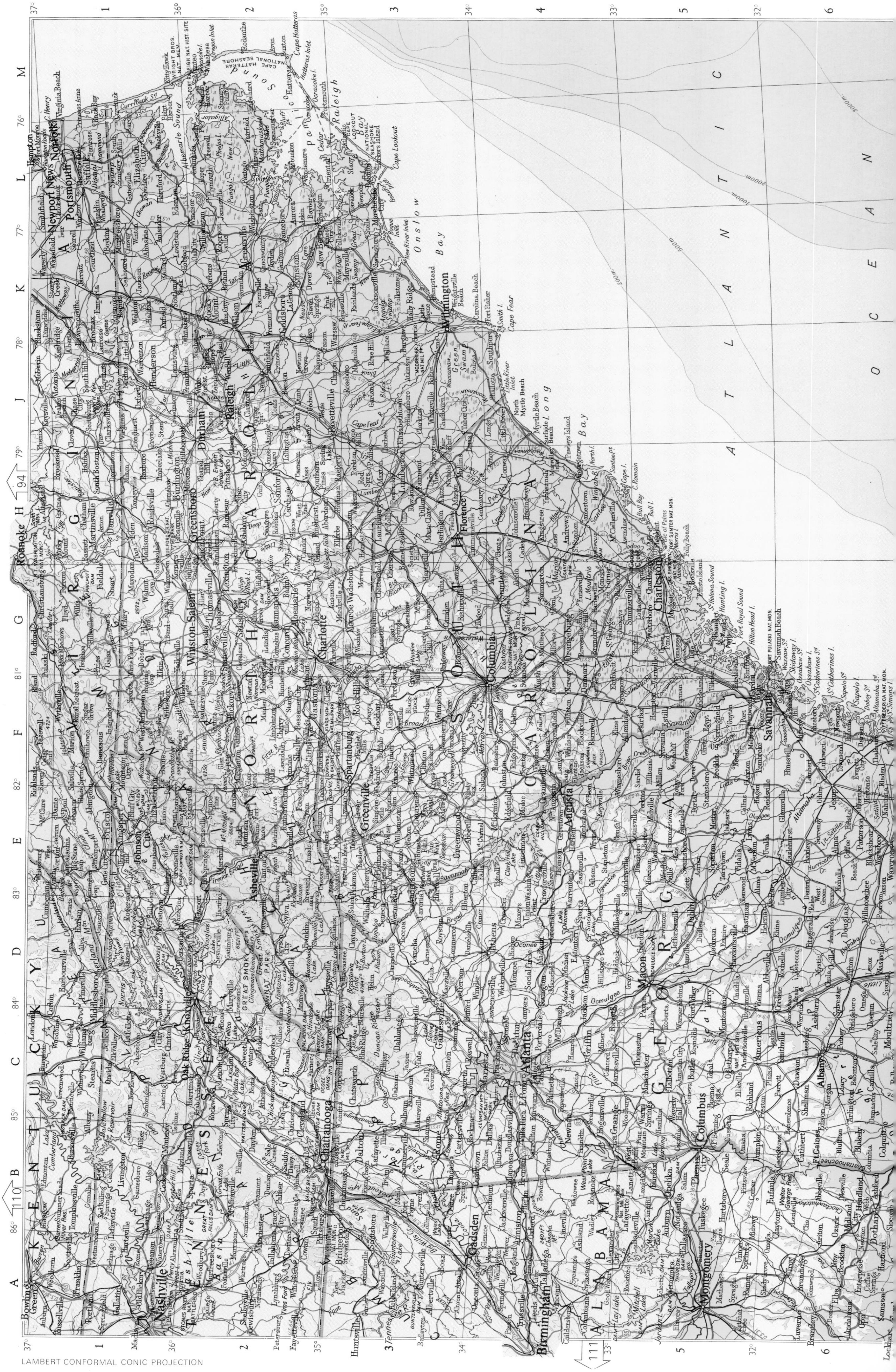

LAMBERT CONFORMAL CONIC PROJECTION

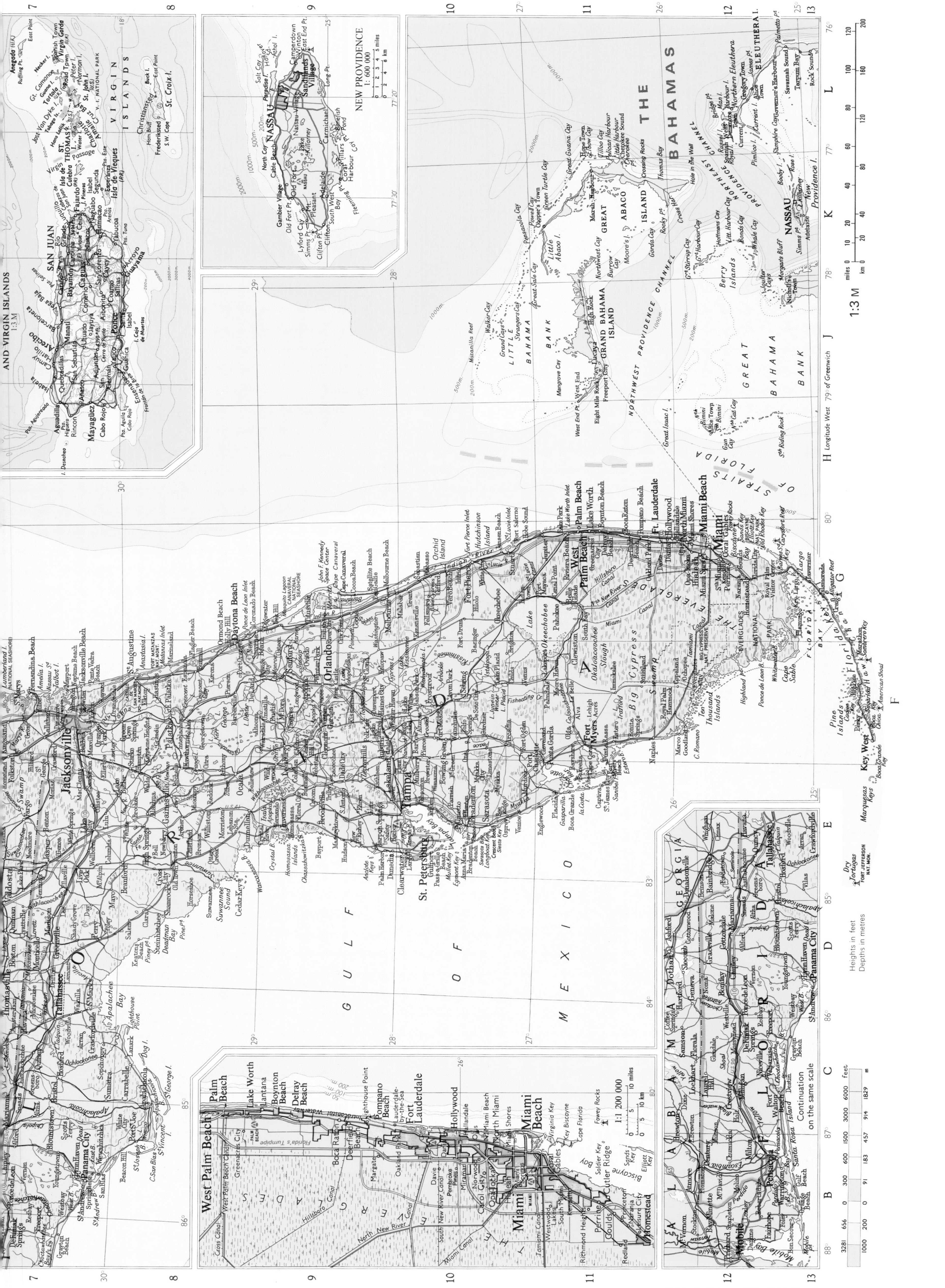
PUERTO RICO AND VIRGIN ISLANDS
1:3 M
SAN JUAN
VIRGIN ISLANDS
NEW PROVIDENCE
1:600 000
NASSAU
THE BAHAMAS
GREAT ABACO ISLAND
GRAND BAHAMA ISLAND
LITTLE BAHAMA BANK
GREAT BAHAMA BANK
NORTHWEST PROVIDENCE CHANNEL
NORTHEAST PROVIDENCE CHANNEL
STRAITS OF FLORIDA
GULF OF MEXICO
FLORIDA
Jacksonville
Tallahassee
Orlando
Tampa
St. Petersburg
Daytona Beach
West Palm Beach
Fort Myers
Miami
Miami Beach
Ft. Lauderdale
Key West
Lake Okeechobee
EVERGLADES NATIONAL PARK
Big Cypress Swamp
ALABAMA
GEORGIA
Pensacola
Mobile
Panama City
1:1 200 000
Continuation on the same scale
Heights in feet
Depths in metres
Longitude West 79 of Greenwich

51
92
On the same scale
East of 170° Greenwich
West of 170° Greenwich
BERING SEA
ALEUTIAN ISLANDS
(To U.S.A.)
Near Islands
Rat Is
Andreanof Islands
Fox Islands
Dutch Harbor
Unalaska
Attu
Adak
Atka
Komandorskiye Ostrova (To Rus. Fed.)
RUS. FED.
Chukchi Sea
BERING SEA
Bering Str.
St. Lawrence I.
BEAUFORT SEA
Permanent Polar Ice
Brooks Range
De Long Mts.
Barrow
Point Barrow
Wainwright
Kotzebue
Nome
Seward Peninsula
U.S.A.
ALASKA
Yukon
Holy Cross
Bethel
Kuskokwim Mountains
McGrath
Fairbanks
Fort Yukon
Tanana
Galena
Anchorage
Kenai
Homer
Seward
Valdez
Cordova
Kodiak Island
Kodiak
Bristol Bay
Dillingham
Alaska Pen.
Aleutian Ra.
Gulf of Alaska
Yakutat
Juneau
Sitka
Skagway
Alexander Archipelago
Petersburg
Wrangell
Ketchikan
YUKON TERRITORY
Dawson
Whitehorse
Watson Lake
Mackenzie Mountains
Selwyn Mountains
Ogilvie Mts
Old Crow
Fort McPherson
Inuvik
Tuktoyaktuk
Aklavik
INUVIK
Banks Island
Victoria Island
Melville Island
Prince Patrick I.
Viscount Melville Sound
Amundsen Gulf
Coronation Gulf
Coppermine
Norman Wells
Great Bear Lake
Fort Norman
Great Slave Lake
Yellowknife
Fort Providence
Fort Simpson
Hay River
Fort Smith
Uranium City
Lake Athabasca
FORT SMITH
NORTHWEST TERRITORIES
CANADA
BRITISH COLUMBIA
Queen Charlotte Islands
Prince Rupert
Kitimat
Hazelton
Fort Nelson
Dawson Creek
Prince George
Williams Lake
Kamloops
Kelowna
Penticton
Vancouver
Vancouver Island
Victoria
Nanaimo
ROCKY MOUNTAINS
ALBERTA
Peace River
Grande Prairie
Fort Vermilion
Edmonton
Jasper
Red Deer
Calgary
Lethbridge
Medicine Hat
SASKATCHEWAN
La Ronge
Prince Albert
Saskatoon
Regina
Moose Jaw
Swift Current
Lloydminster
North Battleford
WASHINGTON
Seattle
Tacoma
Spokane
Yakima
IDAHO
MONTANA
Great Falls
Helena
Butte
Billings
Missoula
OREGON
Portland
Salem
Eugene
NORTH
PACIFIC OCEAN
Projection by courtesy of the National Geographic Society, Washington, D.C.
GH7347
Heights in feet
Depths in metres
feet
m
19686
16409
13124
9843
6562
3281
1640
656
0
656
6562
6000
5000
4000
3000
2000
1000
500
200
0
200
2000

GREENLAND
(KALAALLIT NUNAAT)
ICELAND
BAFFIN BAY
Baffin Island
DAVIS STRAIT
DENMARK STRAIT
LABRADOR SEA
ATLANTIC OCEAN
NEWFOUNDLAND
HUDSON BAY
HUDSON STRAIT
FOXE BASIN
Ungava Bay
James Bay
LABRADOR
QUEBEC
ONTARIO
MANITOBA
KEEWATIN
FRANKLIN
NORTHWEST TERRITORIES
NEW BRUNSWICK
NOVA SCOTIA
PRINCE EDWARD I.
Island of Newfoundland
Gulf of Saint Lawrence
LAKE SUPERIOR
LAKE HURON
L. ERIE
LAKE ONTARIO
MINNESOTA
WISCONSIN
MICHIGAN
MAINE
NEW YORK
VERMONT
NEW HAMPSHIRE
MASS.
Arctic Circle
Reykjavík
Godthåb (Nuuk)
Thule
Frobisher Bay
Goose Bay
Schefferville
Churchill
Winnipeg
Québec
Montréal
OTTAWA
Toronto
Detroit
Boston
New York
Halifax
St John's
1:12·5 M
km
miles
800
700
600
500
400
300
200
100
0
93
Greenwich

ARCTIC OCEAN
CHUKCHI SEA
BERING STRAIT
NORTON SOUND
BRISTOL BAY
KUSKOKWIM BAY
GULF OF ALASKA
ALEUTIAN ISLANDS
U.S.A.
ALASKA
CANADA
RUS. FED.
Barrow
Wainwright
Point Hope
Kotzebue
Nome
Unalakleet
Fairbanks
Anchorage
Tanana
McGrath
Bethel
Dillingham
Kodiak
Seward
Homer
Cordova
Palmer
Wasilla
Valdez
Whittier
Kenai
Dutch Harbor
Brooks Range
Seward Peninsula
Alaska Range
Kenai Peninsula
Fox Islands
Andreanof Islands
Rat Islands
Near Islands
Pribilof Is
St Matthew I.
Nunivak I.
St Lawrence I.
Kodiak Island
Unimak I.
Unalaska I.
Umnak I.
on the same scale
CONIC PROJECTION
Heights in feet
Depths in metres
1:6 M

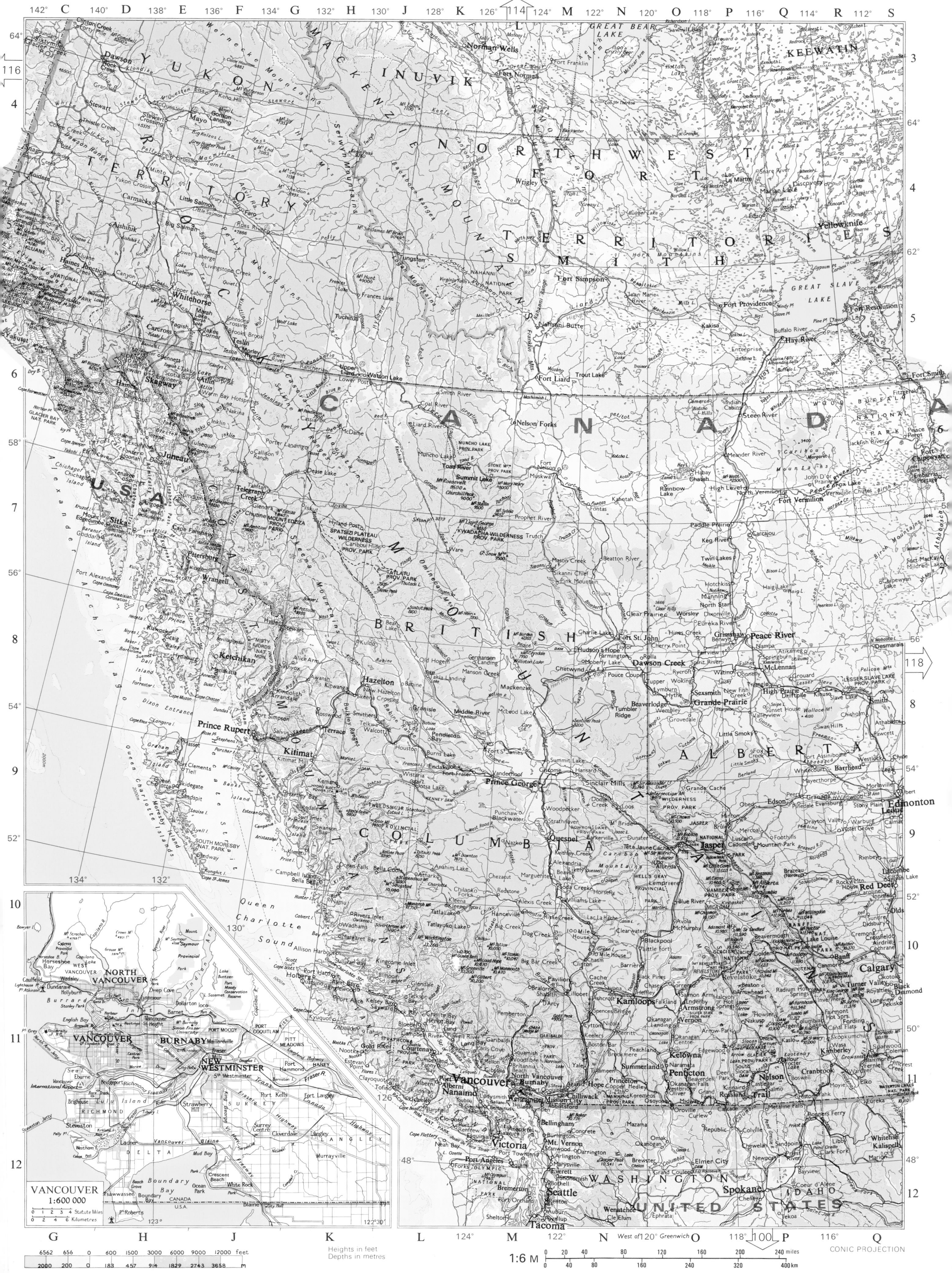
YUKON TERRITORY
NORTHWEST TERRITORIES
FORT SMITH
INUVIK
KEEWATIN
MACKENZIE MOUNTAINS
CANADA
BRITISH COLUMBIA
ALBERTA
U.S.A.
WASHINGTON
IDAHO
UNITED STATES
Dawson
Whitehorse
Yellowknife
Great Slave Lake
Great Bear Lake
Norman Wells
Fort Simpson
Fort Nelson
Fort St. John
Dawson Creek
Grande Prairie
Peace River
Prince Rupert
Prince George
Edmonton
Red Deer
Calgary
Kamloops
Vancouver
Victoria
Seattle
Spokane
Juneau
Sitka
Ketchikan
Queen Charlotte Islands
Jasper
Banff
Kelowna
Penticton
VANCOUVER
1:600 000
NORTH VANCOUVER
BURNABY
NEW WESTMINSTER
RICHMOND
SURREY
DELTA
LANGLEY
Heights in feet
Depths in metres
1:6 M
West of 120° Greenwich
CONIC PROJECTION

CONIC PROJECTION

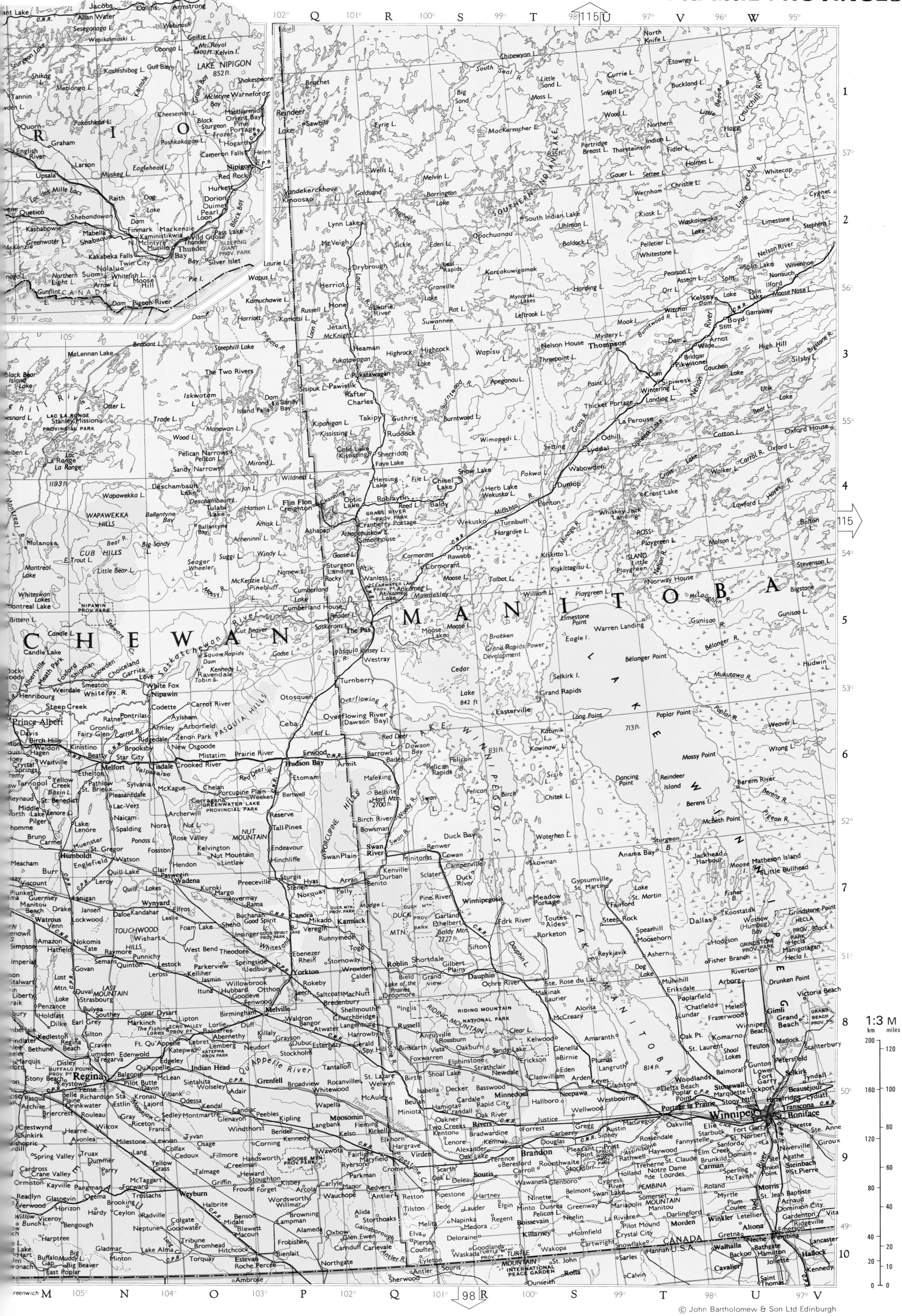
MANITOBA
SASKATCHEWAN
LAKE NIPIGON
LAKE WINNIPEG
LAKE WINNIPEGOSIS
LAKE MANITOBA
SOUTHERN INDIAN LAKE
Winnipeg
Regina
Brandon
Prince Albert
Thompson
The Pas
Flin Flon
Dauphin
Portage la Prairie
Yorkton
Thunder Bay
CANADA
U.S.A.
1:3 M
km
miles
115
98

ONTARIO
LAKE SUPERIOR
LAKE MICHIGAN
LAKE HURON
GEORGIAN BAY
LAKE ERIE
LAKE NIPIGON
MICHIGAN
CANADA
U.S.A.
115
99
94
Longitude West 81° of Greenwich
OTTAWA
1:240 000
TORONTO
1:300 000
Statute Miles
Kilometres
Feet
m
3000 914
1500 457
600 183
300 91
0 0

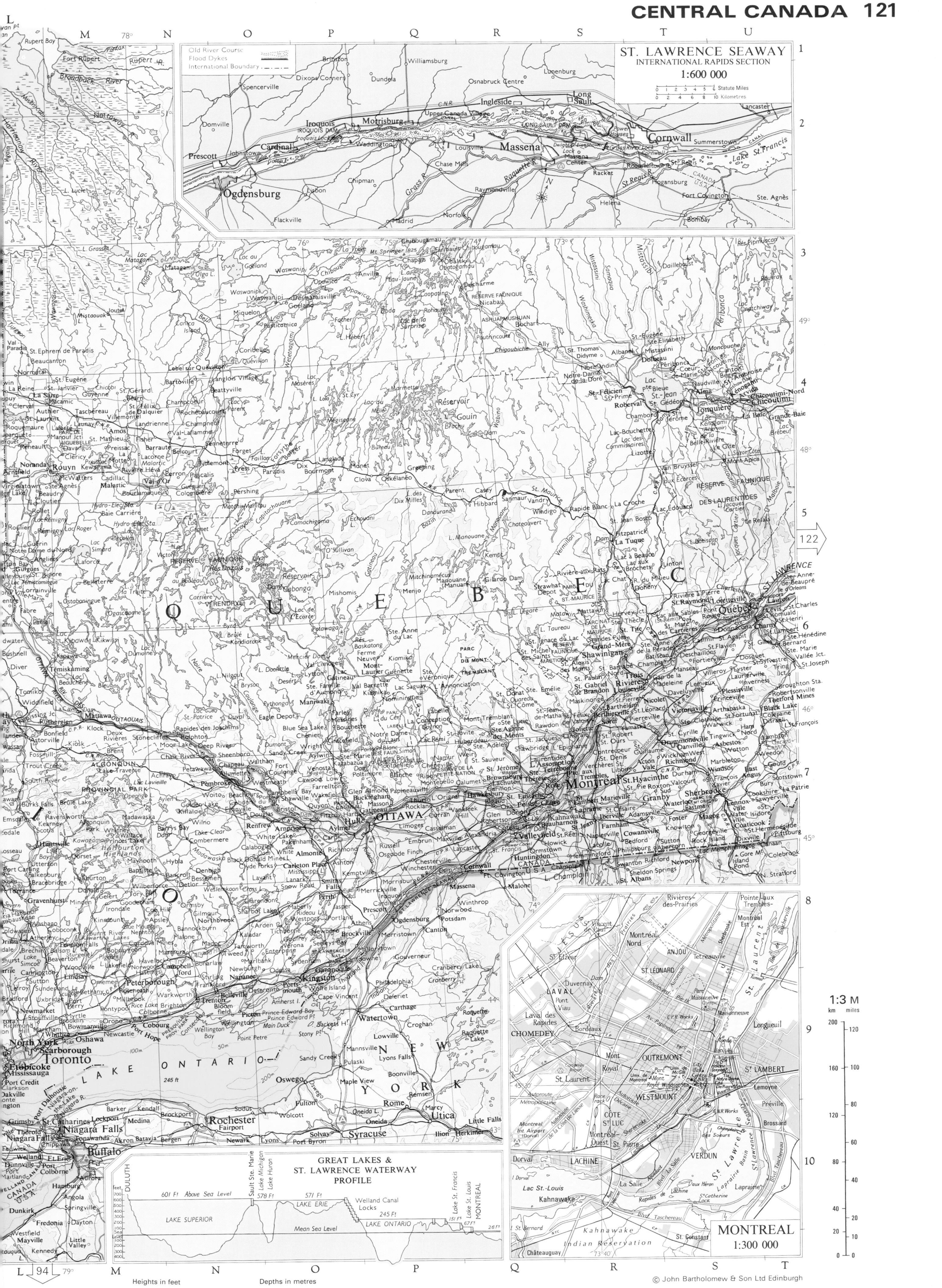
ST. LAWRENCE SEAWAY
INTERNATIONAL RAPIDS SECTION
1:600 000
Old River Course
Flood Dykes
International Boundary
Statute Miles
Kilometres
Ogdensburg
Prescott
Cardinal
Iroquois
Morrisburg
Ingleside
Long Sault
Massena
Cornwall
Lake St. Francis
QUEBEC
ONTARIO
NEW YORK
LAKE ONTARIO
Montreal
OTTAWA
Québec
Trois Rivières
Sherbrooke
Toronto
Niagara Falls
Buffalo
Rochester
Syracuse
Kingston
122
GREAT LAKES &
ST. LAWRENCE WATERWAY
PROFILE
DULUTH
Sault Ste. Marie
Lake Michigan
Lake Huron
601 Ft Above Sea Level
578 Ft
571 Ft
LAKE SUPERIOR
LAKE ERIE
Welland Canal Locks
245 Ft
LAKE ONTARIO
Lake St. Francis
Lake St. Louis
MONTREAL
151 Ft
67 Ft
26 Ft
Mean Sea Level
Heights in feet
Depths in metres
MONTREAL
1:300 000
1:3 M
km
miles
94

QUÉBEC
NEW BRUNSWICK
MAINE
U.S.A.
NOVA SCOTIA
PRINCE EDWARD ISLAND
ST. LAWRENCE
GASPÉ PENINSULA
BAY OF FUNDY
JACQUES-CARTIER PASSAGE
HONGUEDO PASSAGE
ANTICOSTI
Shickshock Mountains
Notre Dame Mountains
Québec
Lévis
Chicoutimi
Jonquière
Alma
Rimouski
Matane
Baie Comeau
Sept Îles
Port-Cartier-Ouest
Gaspé
Campbellton
Dalhousie
Bathurst
Chatham
Newcastle
Moncton
Fredericton
Saint John
Edmundston
Charlottetown
Summerside
Amherst
Truro
New Glasgow
Halifax
Dartmouth
Yarmouth
Digby
Annapolis Royal
Kentville
Windsor
Bangor
Augusta
Waterville
Lewiston
Auburn
Portland
Biddeford
Houlton
Presque Isle
Caribou
Bar Harbor
Ellsworth
Rivière-du-Loup
Trois Pistoles
La Malbaie
Thetford Mines
Mégantic
Manicouagan
Réservoir Manicouagan
Gagnon
Mingan
Havre St. Pierre
Chandler
Caraquet
Sackville
Liverpool
Lunenburg
Shelburne
Eastport
Calais
St. Stephen
Machias
Millinocket
Cape Sable Island

LABRADOR
NEWFOUNDLAND
ATLANTIC OCEAN
GULF OF ST. LAWRENCE
CABOT STRAIT
CAPE BRETON ISLAND
SAINT-PIERRE & MIQUELON
(To France)
ÎLES DE LA MADELEINE
(Magdalen Islands)
(To Quebec)
STRAIT OF BELLE ISLE
LONG RANGE MOUNTAINS
SABLE ISLAND BANK
Port Hope Simpson
Battle Harbour
Cape Charles
Belle Isle
St. Anthony
Roddickton
Harbour Deep
Daniel's Harbour
Sally Cove
Deer Lake
Corner Brook
Humbermouth
Stephenville
Stephenville Crossing
Springdale
Twillingate
Fogo
Lewisporte
Botwood
Bishop's Falls
Grand Falls
Windsor
Gander
Wesleyville
Bonavista
Catalina
Trinity
Clarenville
Carbonear
Harbour Grace
St. John's
Holyrood
Bay Bulls
Ferryland
Trepassey
Cape Race
Placentia
Argentia
Marystown
Burin
Grand Bank
Fortune
St. Lawrence
Harbour Breton
Burgeo
Channel-Port aux Basques
Cape Ray
Miquelon
St.-Pierre
Havre Aubert
Cape St. Lawrence
Chéticamp
Inverness
Baddeck
North Sydney
Sydney
Sydney Mines
Glace Bay
Louisbourg
St. Peters
Port Hawkesbury
Canso
Antigonish
Guysborough
Sherbrooke
Sable Island
QUEBEC
1:120 000
Statute Miles
Kilometres
Québec
Lévis
Lauzon
Charlesbourg
Beauport
Giffard
Vanier
Duberger
Ste.-Foy
Sillery
St. Romuald
Chaudière Bassin
New Liverpool
Pont Etchemin
St. David
St. Télesphore
Ste.-Pétronille
Ile d'Orléans
St. Lawrence
St.-Laurent
Trans Canada Highway
1:3 M
km
miles
West 62 of Greenwich

San Diego
Tijuana
Mexicali
El Centro
Yuma
Ensenada
Tucson
Nogales
Douglas
Agua Prieta
Cananea
El Paso
Ciudad Juárez
Las Cruces
Lordsburg
Deming
Carlsbad
Hobbs
Midland
Odessa
Big Spring
Pecos
ARIZONA
NEW MEXICO
TEXAS
SONORA
CHIHUAHUA
COAHUILA
DURANGO
ZACATECAS
JALISCO
MICHOACÁN
BAJA CALIFORNIA
BAJA CALIFORNIA SUR
Golfo de California
Hermosillo
Guaymas
Empalme
Ciudad Obregón
Navojoa
Los Mochis
Culiacán
Mazatlán
Chihuahua
Delicias
Ciudad Camargo
Hidalgo del Parral
Torreón
Gómez Palacio
Ciudad Lerdo
Durango
Tepic
Pto. Vallarta
Guadalajara
Aguascalientes
Zacatecas
Manzanillo
Colima
La Paz
Santa Rosalía
Tropic of Cancer
PACIFIC OCEAN
MEXICO
MEXICO CITY
1:250 000
PANAMA CANAL
1: 900 000
CARIBBEAN SEA
Colón
Cristóbal
Balboa
PANAMÁ
PACIFIC OCEAN

Continuation on the same scale
CARIBBEAN SEA
HONDURAS
NICARAGUA
COSTA RICA
PANAMA
GULF OF MEXICO
Bahía de Campeche
Golfo de Tehuantepec
GUATEMALA
BELIZE
OCEAN
MEXICO
TEGUCIGALPA
MANAGUA
S. JOSÉ
Golfo de Honduras
Golfo de Panamá
Golfo de Chiriquí
Golfo de los Mosquitos
YUCATAN
CAMPECHE
QUINTANA ROO
CHIAPAS
OAXACA
San Antonio
Monterrey
Tampico
Veracruz
Puebla
Mérida
Acapulco
1:6 M
Continued on Inset
Heights and Depths in metres
© John Bartholomew & Son Ltd Edinburgh
Longitude West 100° of Greenwich

CURAÇAO
1:1 500 000
Willemstad
ARUBA
1:1 500 000
Oranjestad
1:1.5m
BONAIRE
Kralendijk
FLORIDA
U.S.A.
Miami
Miami Beach
Ft. Lauderdale
West Palm Beach
Key West
Straits of Florida
Tropic of Cancer
GRAND BAHAMA
GREAT ABACO
ELEUTHERA
NEW PROVIDENCE
Nassau
ANDROS
GREAT EXUMA
THE BAHAMAS
SAN SALVADOR
CAT I.
LONG I.
ACKLINS I.
Great Bahama Bank
(HAVANA)
HABANA
Matanzas
Pinar del Río
Cienfuegos
Trinidad
Santa Clara
Camagüey
Holguín
Bayamo
Santiago de Cuba
Guantánamo
CUBA
Isla de la Juventud
(Isla de Pinos)
Yucatan Channel
MEXICO
Cancún
I. de Cozumel
Grand Cayman
Little Cayman
Cayman Brac
CAYMAN TRENCH
Montego Bay
Spanish Town
KINGSTON
JAMAICA
Jamaica Channel
Windward Passage
GREATER ANTILLES
CARIBBEAN SEA
Pedro Bank
Rosalind Bank
Serranilla Bank
Alice Shoal
HONDURAS
La Ceiba
Islas de la Bahía
Mosquitia
NICARAGUA
MANAGUA
León
Granada
Matagalpa
Bluefields
Lago de Nicaragua
COSTA RICA
SAN JOSÉ
Limón
Puntarenas
PANAMÁ
Colón
Golfo de Panamá
Golfo de los Mosquitos
PACIFIC OCEAN
COLOMBIA
Barranquilla
Cartagena
Santa Marta
Golfo del Darién
feet
m
13124
9843
6562
3281
1640
656
0
Below Sea Level
22966
4000
3000
2000
1000
500
200
6000
113
125
128
CONIC PROJECTION
Longitude West 74° of Greenwich

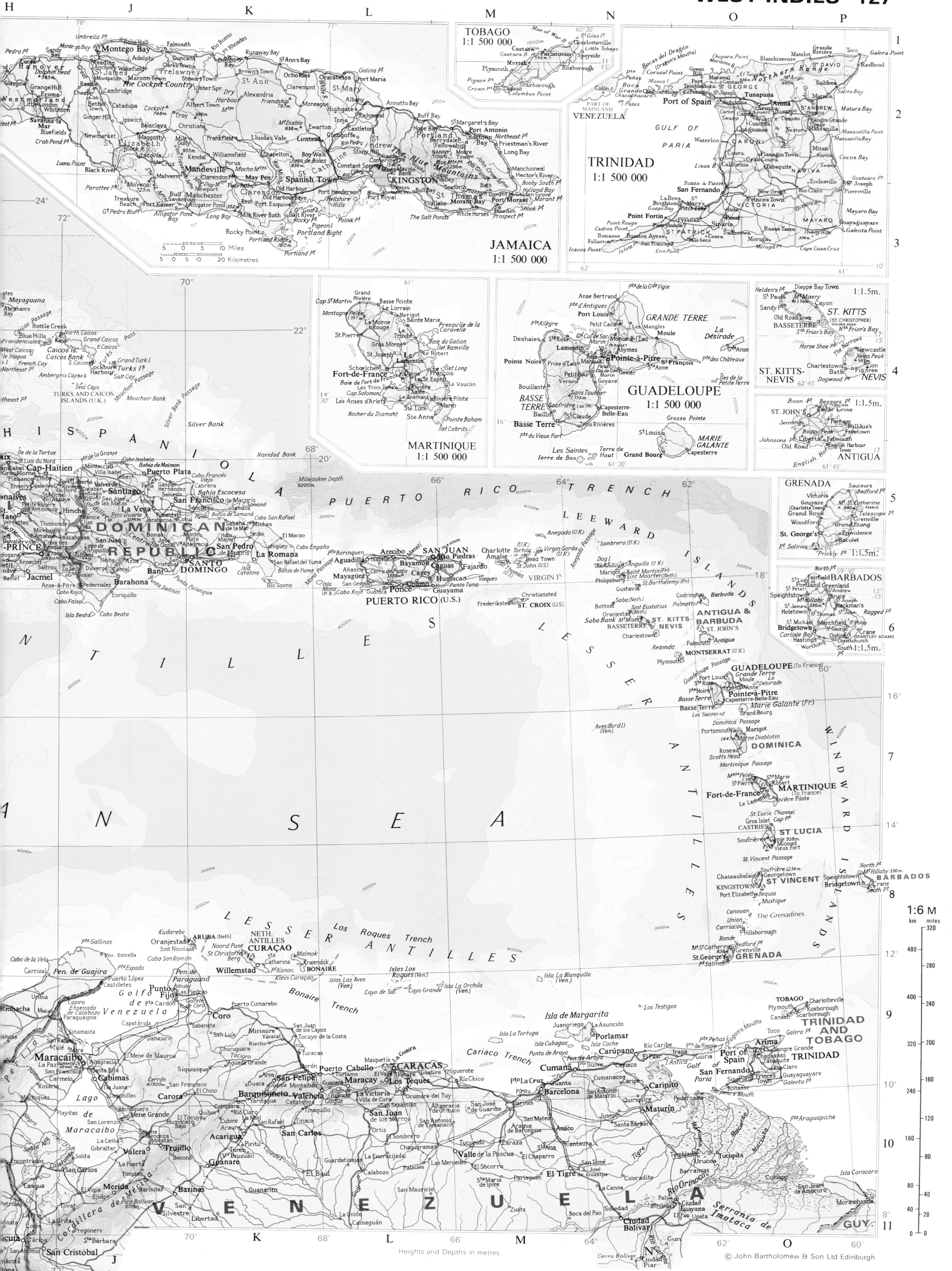
TOBAGO
1:1 500 000
Scarborough
Charlotteville
TRINIDAD
1:1 500 000
Port of Spain
San Fernando
GULF OF PARIA
Northern Range
PART OF MAINLAND VENEZUELA
JAMAICA
1:1 500 000
Montego Bay
Spanish Town
KINGSTON
May Pen
Mandeville
Port Antonio
The Blue Mountains
5 0 5 10 Miles
5 0 5 10 20 Kilometres
MARTINIQUE
1:1 500 000
Fort-de-France
GUADELOUPE
1:1 500 000
GRANDE TERRE
BASSE TERRE
Pointe-à-Pitre
MARIE GALANTE
ST. KITTS
1:1.5m.
ST. KITTS-NEVIS
NEVIS
BASSETERRE
ANTIGUA
1:1.5m.
ST. JOHN'S
GRENADA
1:1.5m.
St. George's
BARBADOS
1:1.5m.
Bridgetown
HISPANIOLA
DOMINICAN REPUBLIC
SANTO DOMINGO
Cap-Haïtien
Santiago
Puerto Plata
La Romana
PUERTO RICO TRENCH
SAN JUAN
PUERTO RICO (U.S.)
Ponce
Mayagüez
VIRGIN Is
ST. CROIX (U.S.)
LEEWARD ISLANDS
LESSER ANTILLES
ANTIGUA & BARBUDA
MONTSERRAT (U.K.)
GUADELOUPE (To France)
DOMINICA
MARTINIQUE (To France)
ST LUCIA
CASTRIES
ST VINCENT
KINGSTOWN
The Grenadines
GRENADA
BARBADOS
WINDWARD ISLANDS
TURKS AND CAICOS ISLANDS (U.K.)
Silver Bank
Navidad Bank
Milwaukee Depth 9200m.
ANTILLES
SEA
ARUBA (Neth)
NETH. ANTILLES
CURAÇAO
BONAIRE
Willemstad
Oranjestad
Los Roques Trench
Bonaire Trench
Isla de Margarita
Cariaco Trench
TOBAGO
TRINIDAD AND TOBAGO
TRINIDAD
VENEZUELA
CARACAS
Maracaibo
Lago de Maracaibo
Golfo de Venezuela
Barquisimeto
Valencia
Maracay
Barcelona
Cumaná
Maturín
Ciudad Bolívar
Ciudad Guayana
Rio Orinoco
Serrania de Imataca
Cordillera de Mérida
Mérida
San Cristóbal
GUY.
1:6 M
km miles
Heights and Depths in metres

LAMBERT AZIMUTHAL EQUAL AREA PROJECTION

Longitude West 50° of Greenwich
NORTH ATLANTIC OCEAN
Equator
SURINAME
FRENCH GUIANA
Paramaribo
Cayenne
Macapá
Belém
São Luís
Teresina
Fortaleza (Ceará)
Natal
João Pessoa
Recife (Pernambuco)
Maceió
Aracaju
Salvador (Bahia)
Brasília
Goiânia
Belo Horizonte
Vitória
Rio de Janeiro
São Paulo
Santos
Campo Grande
Cuiabá
Corumbá
MARANHÃO
PIAUÍ
CEARÁ
RIO GRANDE DO NORTE
PARAÍBA
ALAGOAS
SERGIPE
BAHIA
TOCANTINS
GOIÁS
MATO GROSSO
MATO GROSSO DO SUL
MINAS GERAIS
ESPÍRITO SANTO
SÃO PAULO
PARANÁ
AMAPÁ
PARÁ
Ilha de Marajó
Mouths of the Amazon
Amazonas
Planalto de Mato Grosso
Fernando de Noronha (To Brazil)
Rocas
I. Martin Vaz
I. Trindade (To Brazil)
1:12 M
km miles
GUAY
G H J K L M
55° 50° 45° 40° 35° 30°
1 2 3 4 5 6 7 8
10° 5° 0° 5° 10° 15° 20°

BRAZIL
MINAS GERAIS
GOIÁS
SÃO PAULO
MATO GROSSO DO SUL
PARANÁ
SANTA CATARINA
ESPÍRITO SANTO
RIO DE JANEIRO
PARAGUAY
ATLANTIC OCEAN
Rio de Janeiro
São Paulo
Belo Horizonte
Brasília
Curitiba
Florianópolis
Vitória
Campo Grande
Asunción
RECIFE on the same scale
LAMBERT AZIMUTHAL EQUAL-AREA PROJECTION
Heights and Depths in metres
Longitude West 51° of Greenwich
1:6 M
GH7347
129
133

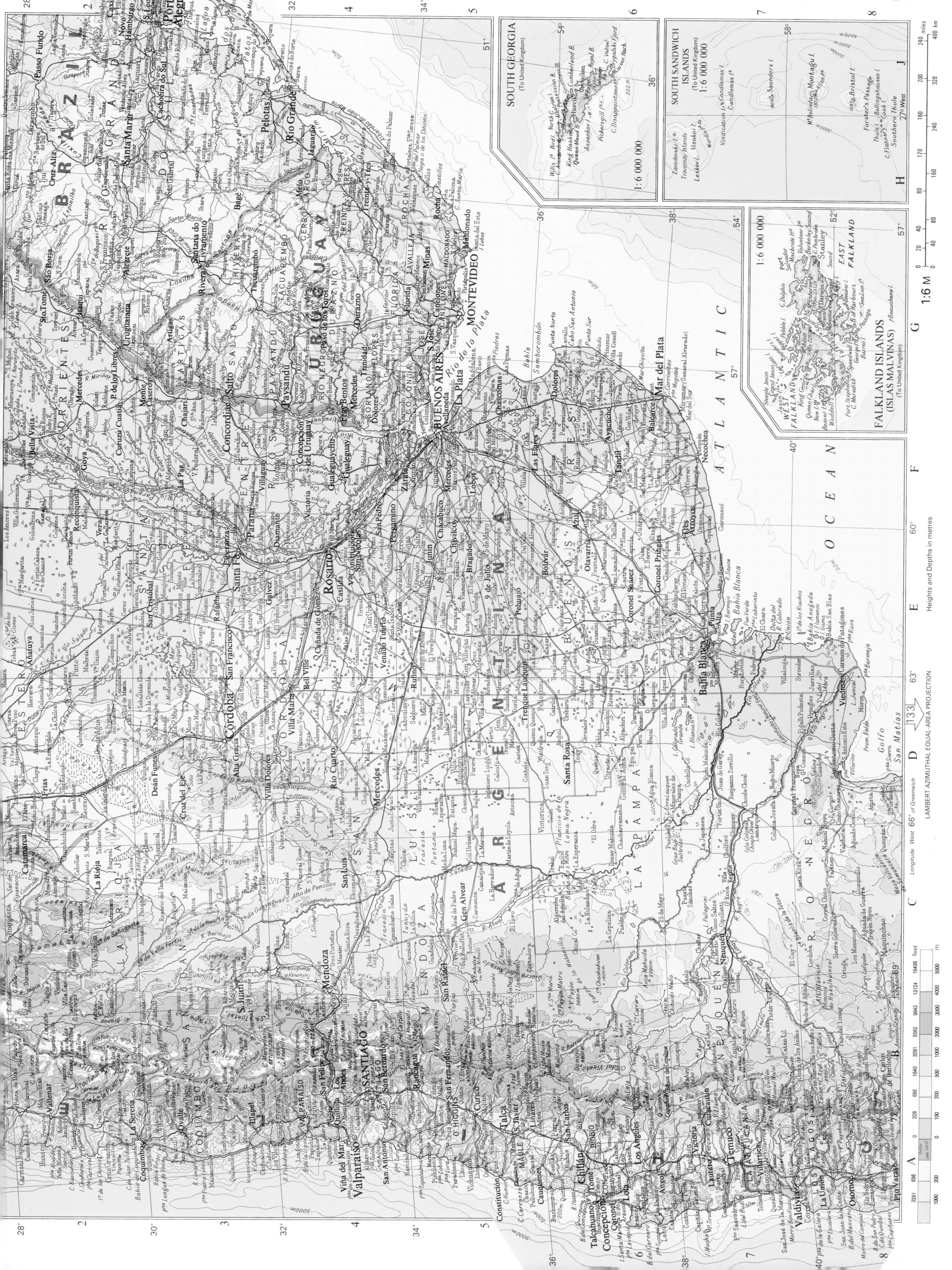
SOUTH GEORGIA
(To United Kingdom)
1:6 000 000
SOUTH SANDWICH ISLANDS
(To United Kingdom)
1:6 000 000
FALKLAND ISLANDS
(ISLAS MALVINAS)
(To United Kingdom)
1:6 000 000
WEST FALKLAND
EAST FALKLAND
Stanley
ATLANTIC OCEAN
BRAZIL
URUGUAY
ARGENTINA
BUENOS AIRES
MONTEVIDEO
SANTIAGO
VALPARAISO
Mendoza
Córdoba
Rosario
Mar del Plata
Bahía Blanca
Concepción
Río de la Plata
1:6 M
LAMBERT AZIMUTHAL EQUAL AREA PROJECTION
Heights and Depths in metres
Longitude West 66° of Greenwich
133

RIO DE JANEIRO

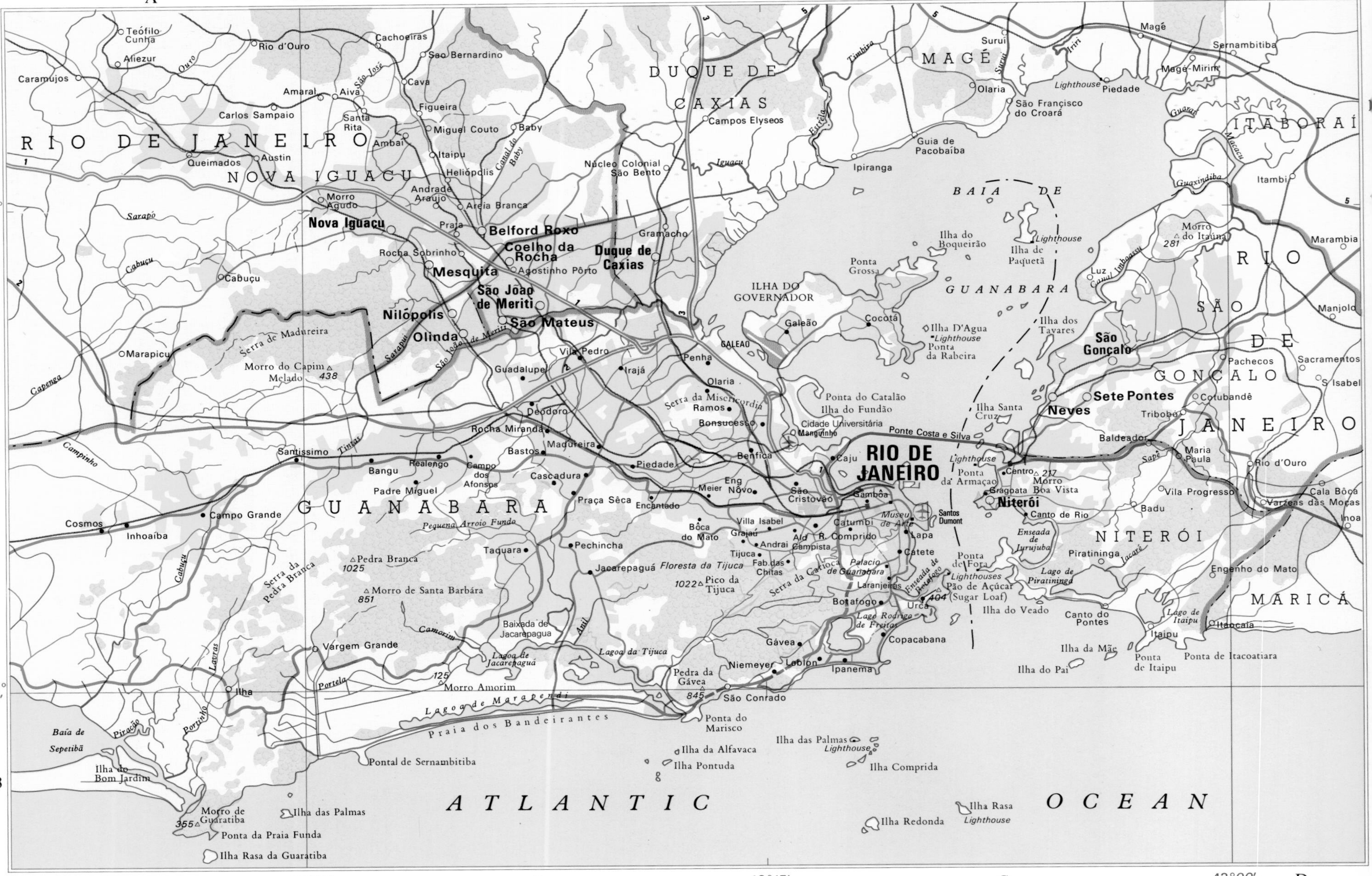

BUENOS AIRES

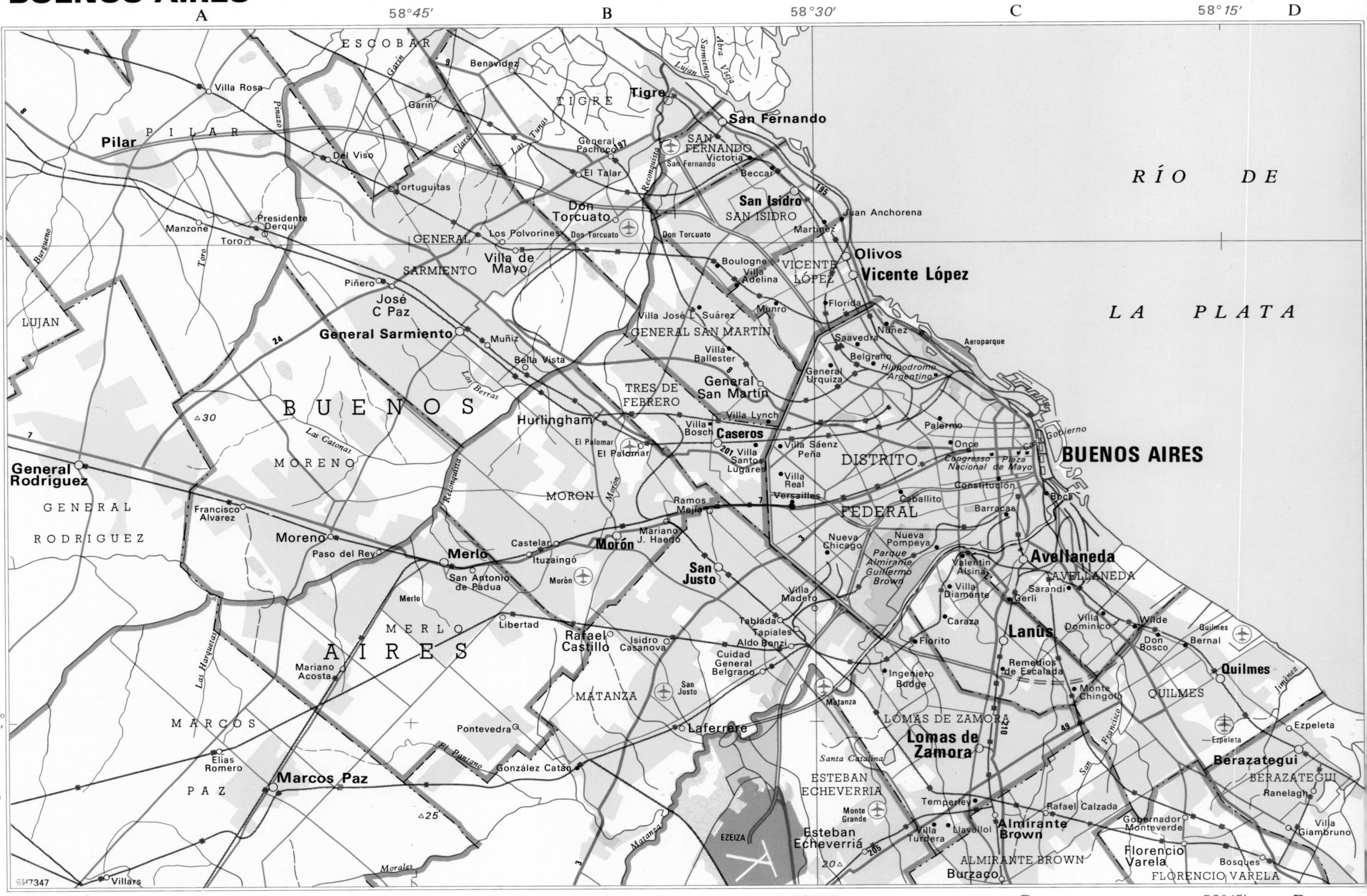

1:300 000

0 5 10 15 km
0 5 10 miles

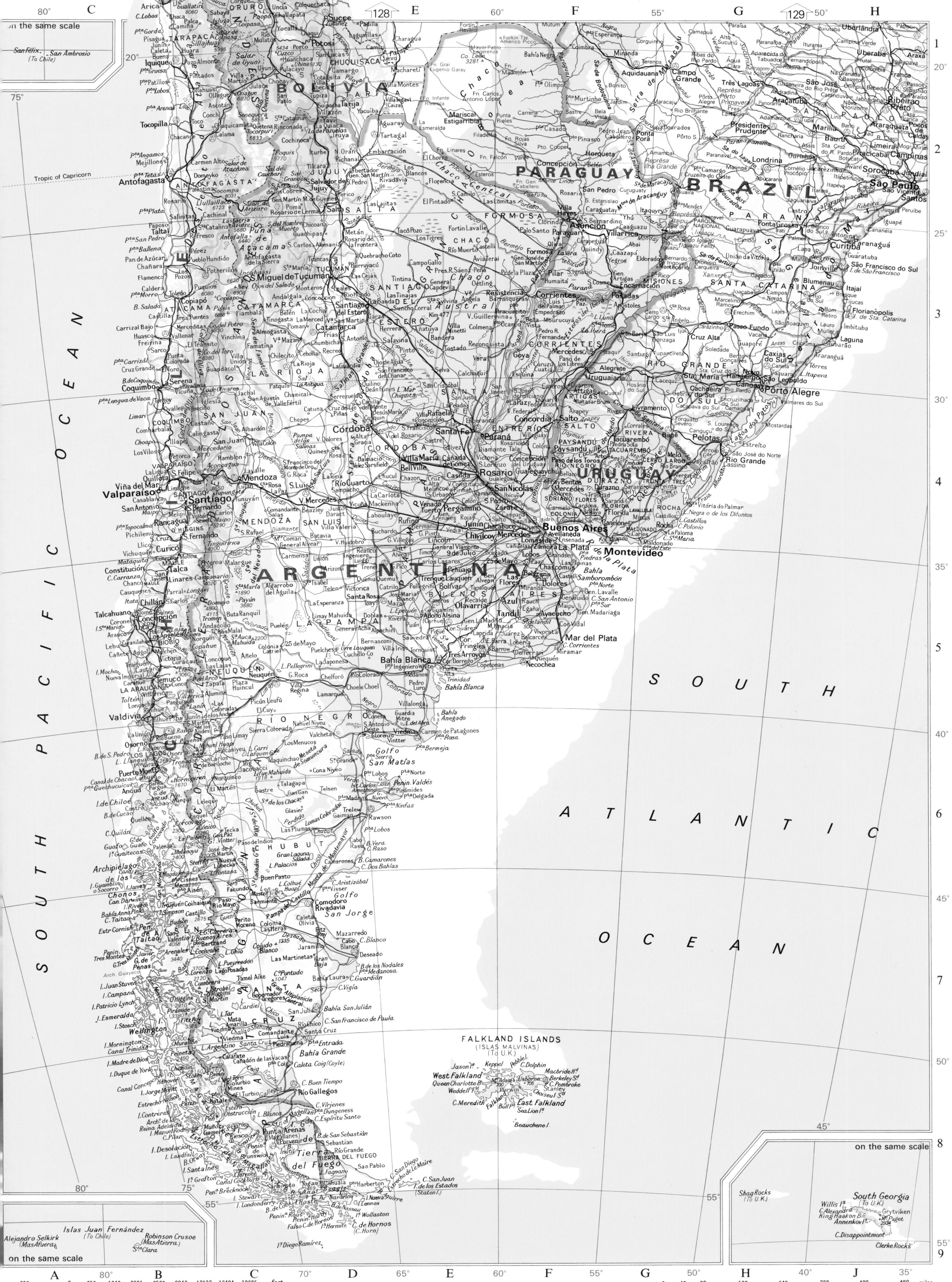

LAMBERT AZIMUTHAL EQUAL AREA PROJECTION

Heights in metres

1:12 M

feet	656	0	656	1640	3281	6562	9843	13123	16404	19685
m	200	0	200	500	1000	2000	3000	4000	5000	6000

Below Sea Level

miles	0	40	80	160	240	320	400	480
km	0	80	160	320	480	640	800	

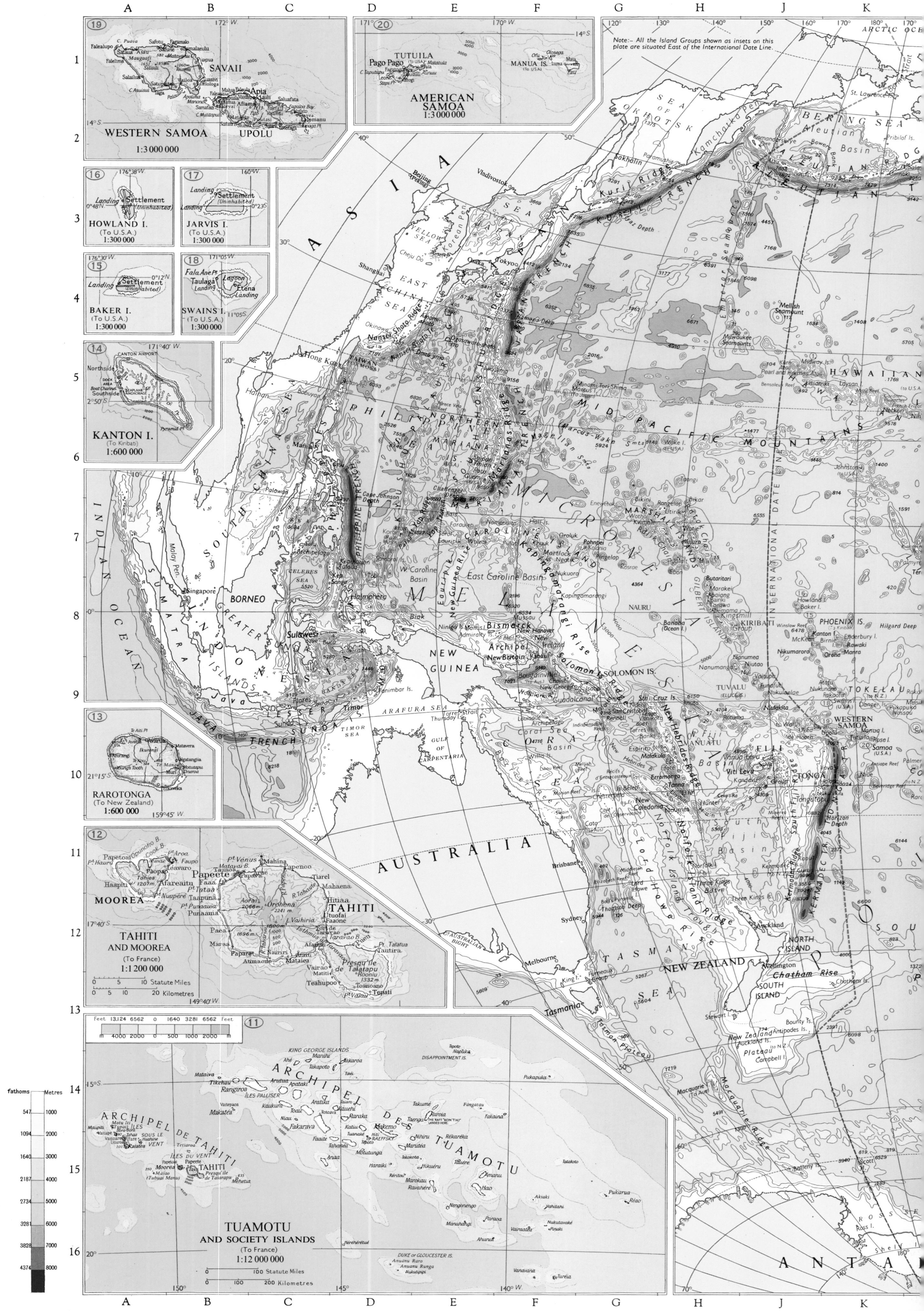
WESTERN SAMOA
1:3 000 000
SAVAII
UPOLU
Apia
TUTUILA
Pago Pago
MANUA IS.
AMERICAN SAMOA
1:3 000 000
Note:– All the Island Groups shown as insets on this plate are situated East of the International Date Line.
HOWLAND I.
(To U.S.A.)
1:300 000
JARVIS I.
(To U.S.A.)
1:300 000
BAKER I.
(To U.S.A.)
1:300 000
SWAINS I.
(To U.S.A.)
1:300 000
KANTON I.
(To Kiribati)
1:600 000
RAROTONGA
(To New Zealand)
1:600 000
TAHITI AND MOOREA
(To France)
1:1 200 000
Statute Miles
Kilometres
MOOREA
TAHITI
Papeete
TUAMOTU AND SOCIETY ISLANDS
(To France)
1:12 000 000
ARCHIPEL DES TUAMOTU
ARCHIPEL DE TAHITI
fathoms
Metres
ASIA
INDIAN OCEAN
SOUTH CHINA SEA
EAST CHINA SEA
YELLOW SEA
SEA OF OKHOTSK
BERING SEA
Beijing
Shanghai
Vladivostok
Hong Kong
Manila
Singapore
BORNEO
SUMATRA
Java
Sulawesi
INDONESIA
NEW GUINEA
Bismarck Archipel
SOLOMON IS.
MICRONESIA
MELANESIA
MARSHALL ISLANDS
KIRIBATI
NAURU
TUVALU
TOKELAU
PHOENIX IS.
HAWAIIAN
MID PACIFIC MOUNTAINS
PHILIPPINE TRENCH
ARAFURA SEA
TIMOR SEA
JAVA TRENCH
Coral Sea Basin
CORAL SEA
AUSTRALIA
Brisbane
Sydney
Melbourne
Tasmania
TASMAN SEA
NEW ZEALAND
NORTH ISLAND
SOUTH ISLAND
Wellington
Auckland
Chatham Rise
KERMADEC TRENCH
TONGA
FIJI
VANUATU
New Caledonia
WESTERN SAMOA
ANTA

NORTH AMERICA
CENTRAL AMERICA
SOUTH AMERICA
MIDWAY IS.
(To U.S.A.)
1:300 000
HAWAIIAN IS.
(To U.S.A.)
1:3 000 000
OAHU
HONOLULU
MOLOKAI
MAUI
LANAI
KAHOOLAWE
KAUAI
NIIHAU
HAWAII
PALMYRA I.
(To U.S.A.)
1:300 000
TABUAERAN
(FANNING I.)
(to Kiribati)
1:900 000
KIRITIMATI
(CHRISTMAS I.)
(to Kiribati)
1:2 400 000
PITCAIRN I.
(To U.K.)
1:210 000
ROBINSON CRUSOE
(JUAN FERNANDEZ)
(To Chile)
1:1 200 000
MARQUESAS IS.
(ÎS. MARQUISES)
(To France)
1:6 000 000
GAMBIER IS.
(ÎLES GAMBIER)
(To France)
1:600 000
EASTER I.
(I. DE PASCUA)
(RAPA NUI)
(To Chile)
1:600 000
SOUTH EAST PACIFIC BASIN
PACIFIC-ANTARCTIC RIDGE
EAST PACIFIC RIDGE
Peru Basin
Chile Basin
Tropic of Cancer
Tropic of Capricorn
Equator
Clarion Fracture Zone
Clipperton Fracture Zone
Molokai Fracture Zone
Easter Island Fracture Zone
Challenger Fracture Zone
PERU-CHILE TRENCH
Middle America Trench
San Francisco
Los Angeles
Mexico
Panama
Lima
Santiago
Islas Galápagos
MARQUESAS
TUAMOTU
SOCIETY IS.
TUBUAI IS.
Heights and Depths in metres
1:48 M

64
INDONESIA
MOLUCCAS
SULAWESI (Celebes)
BANDA SEA
FLORES SEA
TIMOR
IRIAN JAYA
NEW GUINEA
PAPUA NEW GUINEA
BISMARCK SEA
ARAFURA SEA
TIMOR SEA
Timor Trough
Sahul Shelf
Java Trench
INDIAN OCEAN
Gulf of Carpentaria
Gulf of Papua
Torres Strait
Coral Sea
CORAL SEA ISLANDS
Coral Sea Plateau
Great Barrier Reef
Cape York Peninsula
Arnhem Land
Joseph Bonaparte Gulf
Kimberley Plateau
Great Sandy Desert
Gibson Desert
Great Victoria Desert
Simpson Desert
Nullarbor Plain
Great Australian Bight
Barkly Tableland
Macdonnell Ranges
GREAT DIVIDING RANGE
AUSTRALIA
WESTERN AUSTRALIA
NORTHERN TERRITORY
QUEENSLAND
SOUTH AUSTRALIA
NEW SOUTH WALES
VICTORIA
TASMANIA
CANBERRA A.C.T.
Bass Strait
Leeuwin Sill
SOUTH AUSTRALIAN BASIN
Darwin
Alice Springs
Ayers Rock (Uluru) 867
Perth
Fremantle
Kalgoorlie
Geraldton
Carnarvon
Broome
Port Hedland
Dampier
Adelaide
Port Augusta
Port Pirie
Whyalla
Port Lincoln
Melbourne
Geelong
Ballarat
Bendigo
Sydney
Newcastle
Wollongong
Brisbane
Rockhampton
Mackay
Townsville
Cairns
Mount Isa
Broken Hill
Hobart
Launceston
Port Moresby
Jayapura
Ujung Pandang (Makassar)
Ambon
Kupang
L. Eyre North
Eyre South
L. Torrens
L. Gairdner
L. Frome
L. Mackay
L. Amadeus
Kangaroo I.
Melville I.
Bathurst I.
Groote Eylandt
Kosciusko
BONNE PROJECTION
East of Greenwich

PACIFIC OCEAN
NAURU
GILBERT ISLANDS (To Kiribati)
KIRIBATI
SOLOMON ISLANDS
Bougainville
Guadalcanal
Honiara
San Cristobal
Santa Cruz Is.
TUVALU (ELLICE IS.)
Melanesian Border Plateau
VANUATU (NEW HEBRIDES)
Espiritu Santo
Port-Vila
NTH FIJI (PANDORA) BASIN
FIJI
Vanua Levu
Viti Levu
Suva
Nadi
WESTERN SAMOA
Savaii
Upolu
Apia
NEW CALEDONIA (NOUVELLE CALÉDONIE) (To France)
Nouméa
Is. Loyauté
Bellona Plateau
Chesterfield (To Fr.)
Coral Sea Basin
Rennell Ridge
Louisiade Rise
New Hebrides Basin
Mellish Rise
Lau Ridge
Lau Basin
Tonga Ridge
TONGA
Nuku'alofa
Tongatapu Group
Vava'u Group
Ha'apai Group
TONGA TRENCH
Niue (To N.Z.)
Vityaz Depth III 10882
10633m.
Tropic of Capricorn
SOUTH FIJI BASIN
South Fiji (Lau) Ridge
Hunter Ridge
Norfolk (To Aust.)
Norfolk Ridge
Norfolk Island Trough
Lord Howe I. (To Aust.)
Ball's Pyramid
Lord Howe Smts.
LORD HOWE RISE
Three Kings Basin
North Cape Rise
Kermadec Is. (To N.Z.)
Raoul
Kermadec Ridge
KERMADEC TRENCH
INTERNATIONAL DATE LINE
Brisbane
Ipswich
Maryborough
Fraser I.
Lismore
Grafton
Port Macquarie
TASMAN SEA
NEW ZEALAND
NORTH ISLAND
Auckland
Hamilton
Whangarei
Great Barrier I.
Bay of Plenty
East Cape
New Plymouth
Wanganui
Napier
Gisborne
Palmerston North
WELLINGTON
SOUTH ISLAND
Nelson
Westport
Greymouth
Hokitika
Blenheim
Kaikoura
Christchurch
Lyttelton
Timaru
Oamaru
Dunedin
Invercargill
Stewart I.
Chatham Is. (To N.Z.)
Chatham Rise
1:15 M
km miles
Heights and Depths in metres

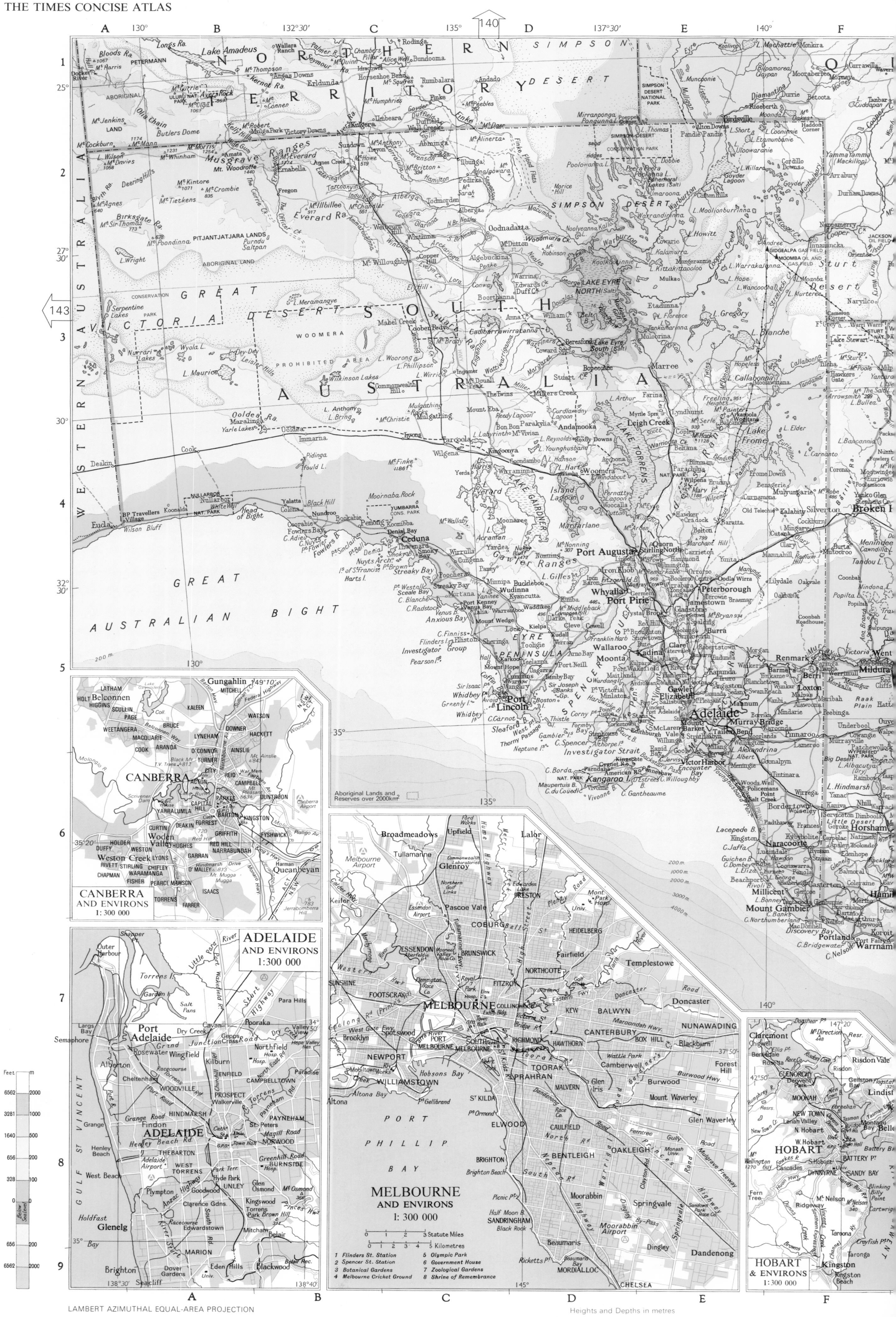

LAMBERT AZIMUTHAL EQUAL-AREA PROJECTION

Heights and Depths in metres

NEW SOUTH WALES
TASMANIA
SOUTH PACIFIC OCEAN
BASS STRAIT
Brisbane
Sydney
Newcastle
Wollongong
Canberra
Melbourne
Geelong
Ballarat
Bendigo
Hobart
Launceston
Toowoomba
Bundaberg
Maryborough
Gympie
Ipswich
Gold Coast
Lismore
Grafton
Coffs Harbour
Port Macquarie
Tamworth
Armidale
Dubbo
Orange
Bathurst
Goulburn
Wagga Wagga
Albury
Charleville
Cunnamulla
Bourke
Parramatta
SYDNEY AND ENVIRONS
1:300 000
1 Government House
2 Public Offices
3 Observatory
4 General Post Office
5 Town Hall
6 Opera House
7 Anzac Mem. (Hyde Pk.)
8 Central Railway Sta.
9 Sydney University
10 Cricket Ground
11 Macquarie University
12 University of N.S. Wales
1:6 M
Longitude East 145° of Greenwich

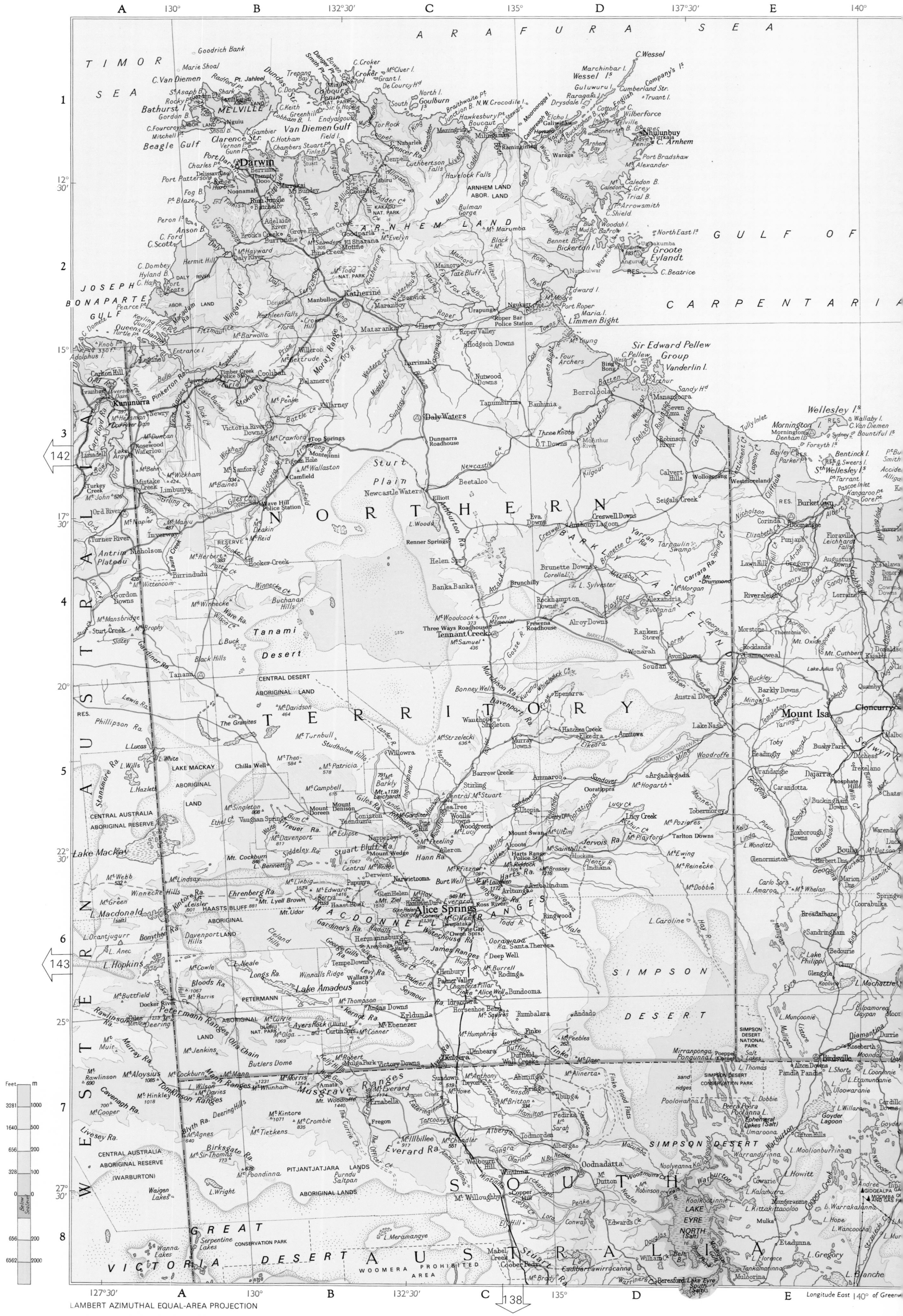

LAMBERT AZIMUTHAL EQUAL-AREA PROJECTION

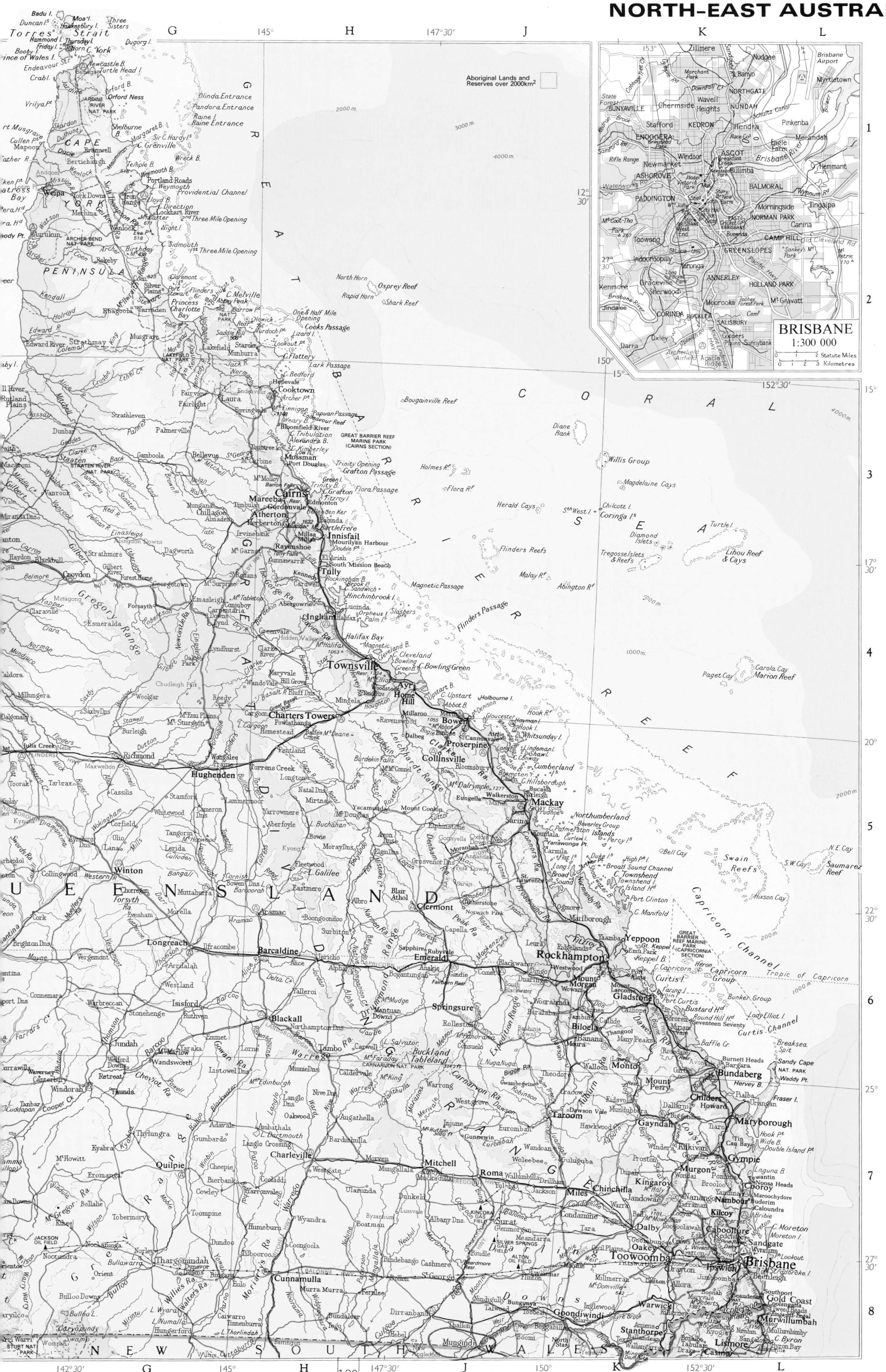

139

Heights and Depths in metres

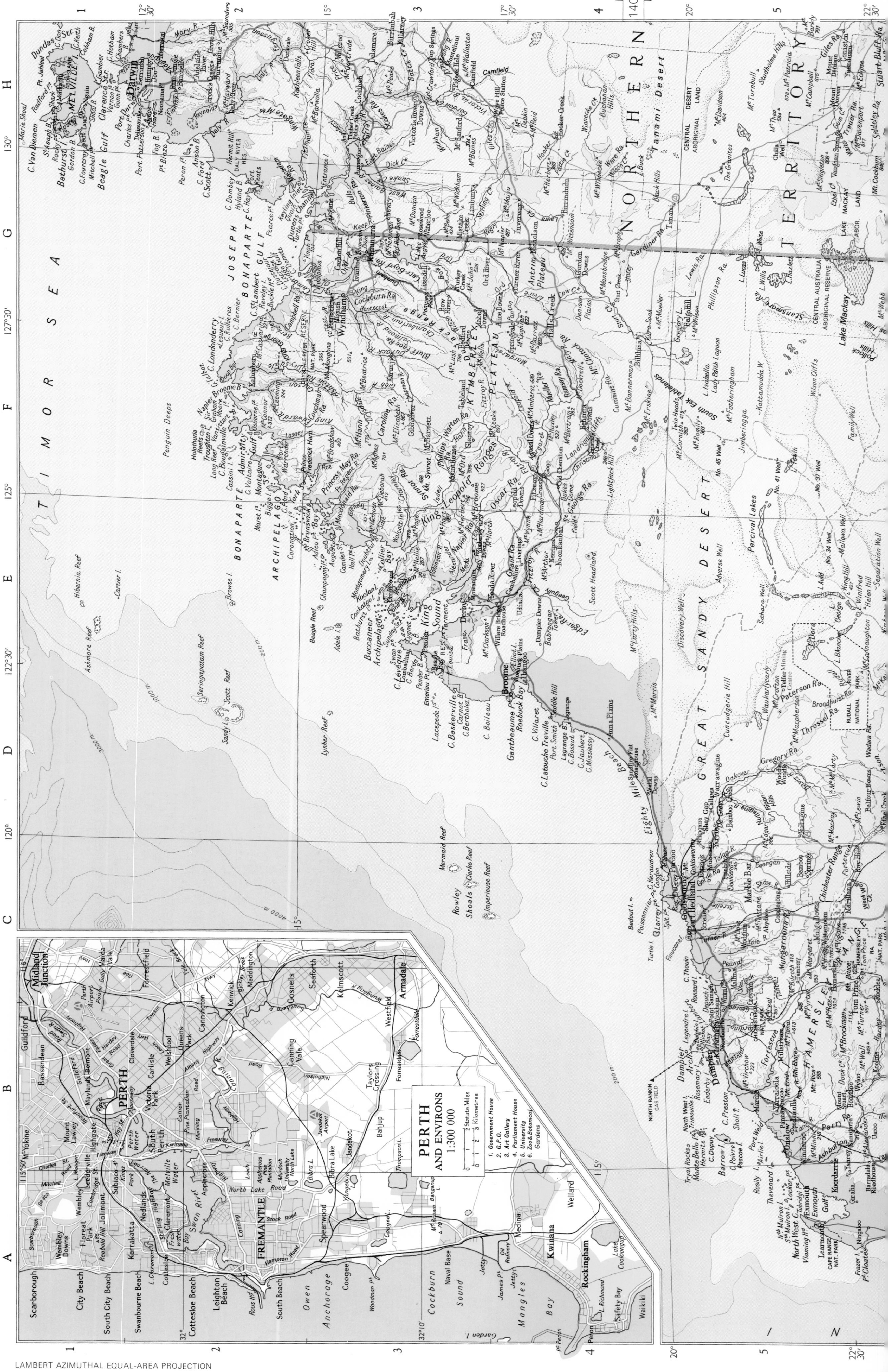
TIMOR SEA
JOSEPH BONAPARTE GULF
BONAPARTE ARCHIPELAGO
KIMBERLEY PLATEAU
NORTHERN TERRITORY
GREAT SANDY DESERT
Tanami Desert
HAMERSLEY RANGE
Darwin
Wyndham
Kununurra
Derby
Broome
Port Hedland
Dampier
Karratha
Onslow
Exmouth
King Sound
Roebuck Bay
Eighty Mile Beach
Lake Mackay
Beagle Gulf
Melville I.
Bathurst I.
Admiralty Gulf
Buccaneer Archipelago
Collier Bay
Leopold Ranges
Oscar Ra.
Penguin Deeps
Scott Reef
Seringapatam Reef
Ashmore Reef
Cartier I.
Hibernia Reef
Browse I.
Rowley Shoals
Mermaid Reef
Clerke Reef
Imperieuse Reef
Lynher Reef
Beagle Reef
PERTH AND ENVIRONS 1:300 000
1. Government House
2. G.P.O.
3. Art Gallery
4. Parliament House
5. University
6. Zoo & Botanical Gardens
PERTH
FREMANTLE
Midland Junction
Guildford
Bassendean
Armadale
Kwinana
Rockingham
Scarborough
City Beach
Cottesloe
Cockburn Sound
Owen Anchorage
Mangles Bay
Safety Bay
Garden I.
Swan River
Jandakot Airport
Perth Airport

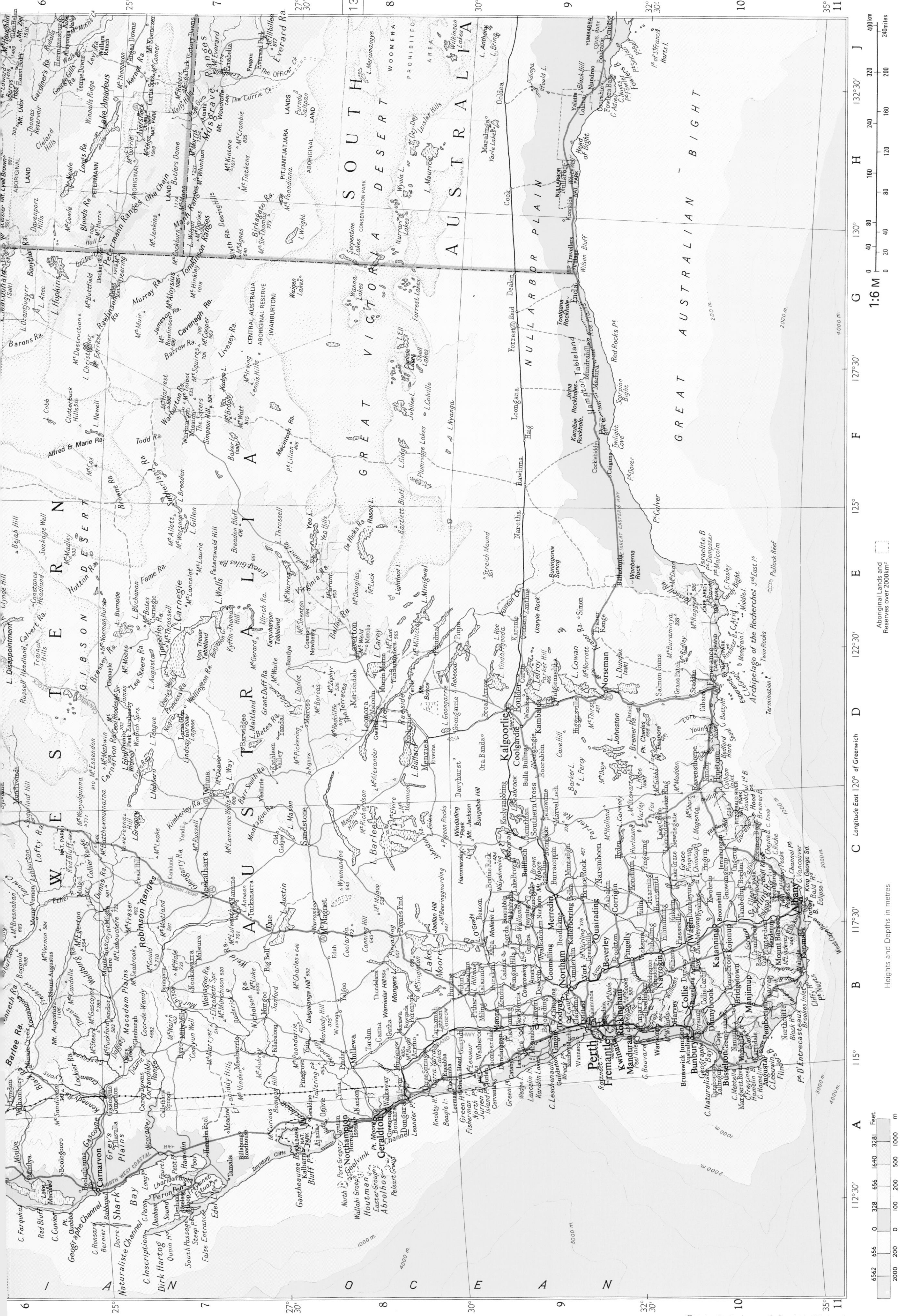

W E S T E R N
A U S T R A L I A
S O U T H
A U S T R A L I A
GIBSON DESERT
GREAT VICTORIA DESERT
NULLARBOR PLAIN
GREAT AUSTRALIAN BIGHT
I N D I A N
O C E A N
Perth
Fremantle
Kalgoorlie
Coolgardie
Geraldton
Carnarvon
Albany
Bunbury
Esperance
Norseman
Northam
Meekatharra
Mount Magnet
Leonora
Laverton
Menzies
Wiluna
Lake Amadeus
Shark Bay
Abrolhos
Nullarbor Plain
Longitude East 120° of Greenwich
Heights and Depths in metres
Aboriginal Lands and Reserves over 2000km²
1:6 M
138

CHRISTCHURCH
AND ENVIRONS
1:300 000
Statute Miles
Kilometres
PEGASUS BAY
CHRISTCHURCH
Riccarton
Lyttelton
LYTTELTON HARBOUR
New Brighton
Sumner
SOUTH ISLAND
TASMAN SEA
PACIFIC OCEAN
CANTERBURY BIGHT
PEGASUS BAY
TASMAN BAY
FOVEAUX STRAIT
NELSON BAYS
MARLBOROUGH
CANTERBURY
AORANGI
COASTAL/NORTH OTAGO
CLUTHA/CENTRAL OTAGO
SOUTHLAND
WEST COAST
FIORDLAND NATIONAL PARK
Nelson
Blenheim
Picton
Westport
Greymouth
Hokitika
Kaikoura
Christchurch
Ashburton
Timaru
Oamaru
Dunedin
Queenstown
Invercargill
Bluff
Gore
Balclutha
STEWART ISLAND
DUNEDIN
AND ENVIRONS
1:300 000
OTAGO HARBOUR
OTAGO PENINSULA
Port Chalmers
Longitude East 170° of Greenwich
CONIC PROJECTION
Feet
m

AUCKLAND AND ENVIRONS 1:300 000
WELLINGTON AND ENVIRONS 1:300 000
PACIFIC
OCEAN
TASMAN
SEA
NORTH ISLAND
NORTHLAND
AUCKLAND
WAIKATO
BAY OF PLENTY
THAMES VALLEY
EAST CAPE
TARANAKI
TONGARIRO
HAWKE'S BAY
WANGANUI
HOROWHENUA
MANAWATU
WAIRARAPA
WELLINGTON
NELSON
MARLBOROUGH
COOK STRAIT
HAURAKI GULF
Auckland
Whangarei
Kaitaia
Kaikohe
Dargaville
Manukau
Papakura
Pukekohe
Thames
Paeroa
Waihi
Te Aroha
Huntly
Morrinsville
Hamilton
Cambridge
Te Awamutu
Te Kuiti
Tauranga
Te Puke
Mount Maunganui
Matamata
Putaruru
Rotorua
Tokoroa
Whakatane
Opotiki
Kawerau
Taupo
Taumarunui
Gisborne
Wairoa
Napier
Hastings
Havelock North
New Plymouth
Waitara
Inglewood
Stratford
Hawera
Patea
Wanganui
Marton
Feilding
Palmerston North
Dannevirke
Waipukurau
Levin
Otaki
Paraparaumu
Masterton
Porirua
Upper Hutt
Lower Hutt
Petone
Eastbourne
Wellington
Nelson
Richmond
Motueka
Picton
Blenheim
Heights in feet
Depths in metres
Longitude East 174° of Greenwich
1:2·5 M
100 miles
160 km

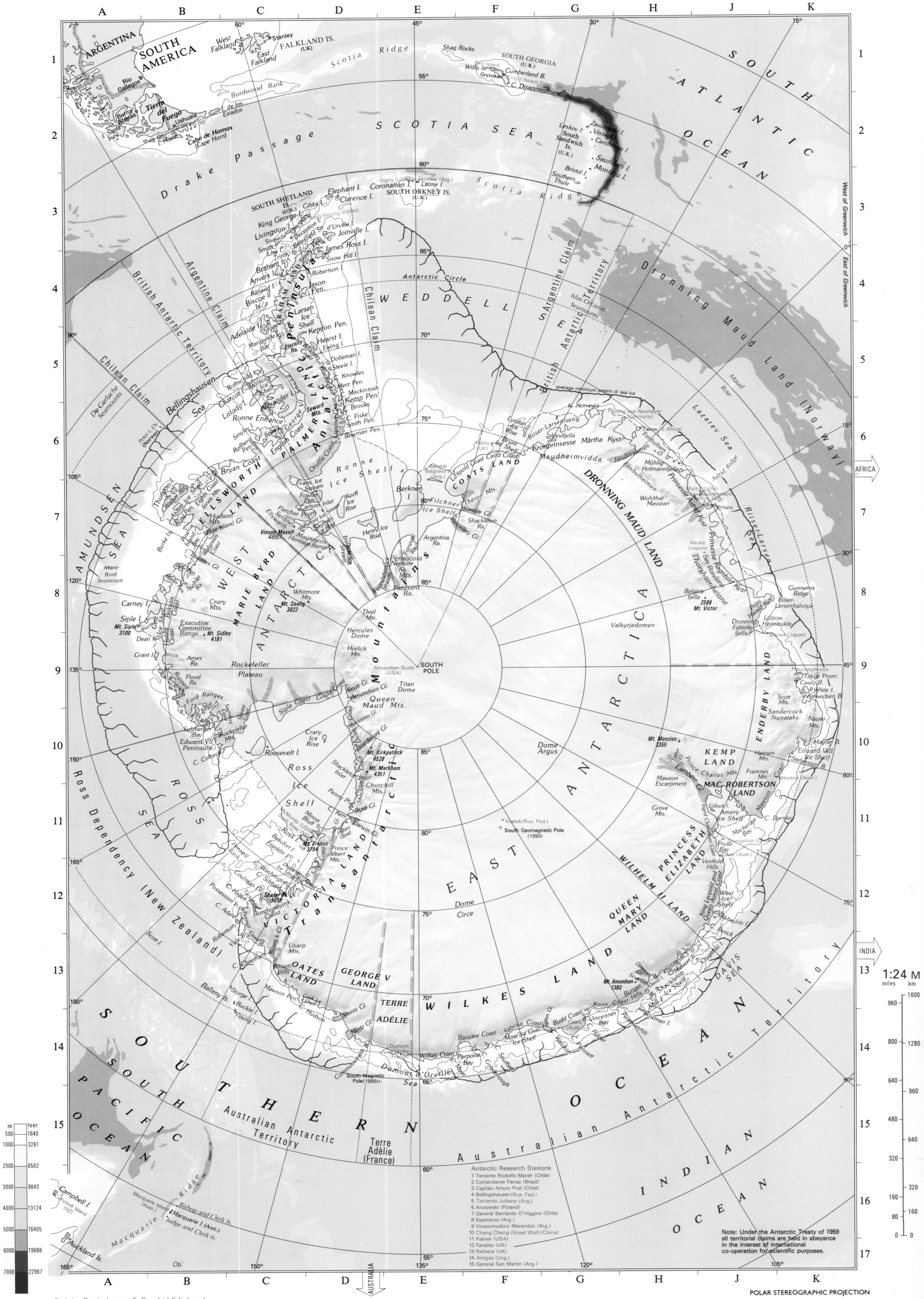
SOUTH AMERICA
ARGENTINA
FALKLAND IS. (UK)
West Falkland
East Falkland
Stanley
Rio Gallegos
Punta Arenas
Tierra del Fuego
Ushuaia
Cabo de Hornos (Cape Horn)
Burdwood Bank
Drake Passage
SCOTIA SEA
Scotia Ridge
Shag Rocks
SOUTH GEORGIA (U.K.)
Grytviken
Cumberland B.
C. Disappointment
South Sandwich Is. (U.K.)
Zavodovski I.
Visokoi I.
Candlemas I.
Saunders I.
Montagu I.
Bristol I.
Southern Thule
SOUTH ATLANTIC OCEAN
SOUTH ORKNEY IS. (U.K.)
Coronation I.
Laurie I.
SOUTH SHETLAND IS. (U.K.)
Elephant I.
Clarence I.
King George I.
Livingston I.
Joinville I.
James Ross I.
Snow Hill I.
Anvers I.
Adelaide I.
Alexander I.
Charcot I.
Graham Land
Antarctic Peninsula
Palmer Land
Larsen Ice Shelf
Antarctic Circle
WEDDELL SEA
British Antarctic Territory
Argentine Claim
Chilean Claim
Bellingshausen Sea
Ronne Entrance
Ronne Ice Shelf
Berkner I.
Filchner Ice Shelf
COATS LAND
Vinson Massif 4897
ELLSWORTH LAND
Ellsworth Mountains
Pensacola Mts.
Transantarctic Mountains
DRONNING MAUD LAND
Dronning Maud Land (Norway)
Lazarev Sea
Riiser-Larsen Sea
AFRICA
AMUNDSEN SEA
Marie Byrd Seamount
MARIE BYRD LAND
WEST ANTARCTICA
Siple I.
Mt. Siple 3100
Executive Committee Range
Mt. Sidley 4181
Rockefeller Plateau
Edward VII Peninsula
Roosevelt I.
Ross Ice Shelf
ROSS SEA
Ross Dependency (New Zealand)
SOUTH POLE
Amundsen-Scott (USA)
Queen Maud Mts.
Mt. Kirkpatrick 4528
Mt. Markham 4351
Ross I.
Mt. Erebus 3794
VICTORIA LAND
Vostok (Rus. Fed.)
South Geomagnetic Pole (1990)
EAST ANTARCTICA
Dome Argus
Dome Circe
Valkyrjedomen
ENDERBY LAND
KEMP LAND
MAC.ROBERTSON LAND
Prince Charles Mts.
Amery Ice Shelf
PRINCESS ELIZABETH LAND
WILHELM II LAND
QUEEN MARY LAND
WILKES LAND
TERRE ADÉLIE
GEORGE V LAND
OATES LAND
South Magnetic Pole (1990)
Dumont d'Urville Sea
DAVIS SEA
INDIA
Australian Antarctic Territory
Terre Adélie (France)
SOUTHERN OCEAN
SOUTH PACIFIC OCEAN
INDIAN OCEAN
Balleny Is.
Campbell I.
Macquarie I. (Aust.)
Macquarie Ridge
Auckland Is.
AUSTRALIA
Antarctic Research Stations
1 Teniente Rodolfo Marsh (Chile)
2 Comandante Ferraz (Brazil)
3 Capitán Arturo Prat (Chile)
4 Bellingshausen (Rus. Fed.)
5 Teniente Jubany (Arg.)
6 Arctowski (Poland)
7 General Bernardo O'Higgins (Chile)
8 Esperanza (Arg.)
9 Vicecomodoro Marambio (Arg.)
10 Chang Cheng (Great Wall) (China)
11 Palmer (USA)
12 Faraday (UK)
13 Rothera (UK)
14 Artigas (Urg.)
15 General San Martín (Arg.)
Note: Under the Antarctic Treaty of 1959 all territorial claims are held in abeyance in the interest of international co-operation for scientific purposes.
1:24 M
miles km
POLAR STEREOGRAPHIC PROJECTION

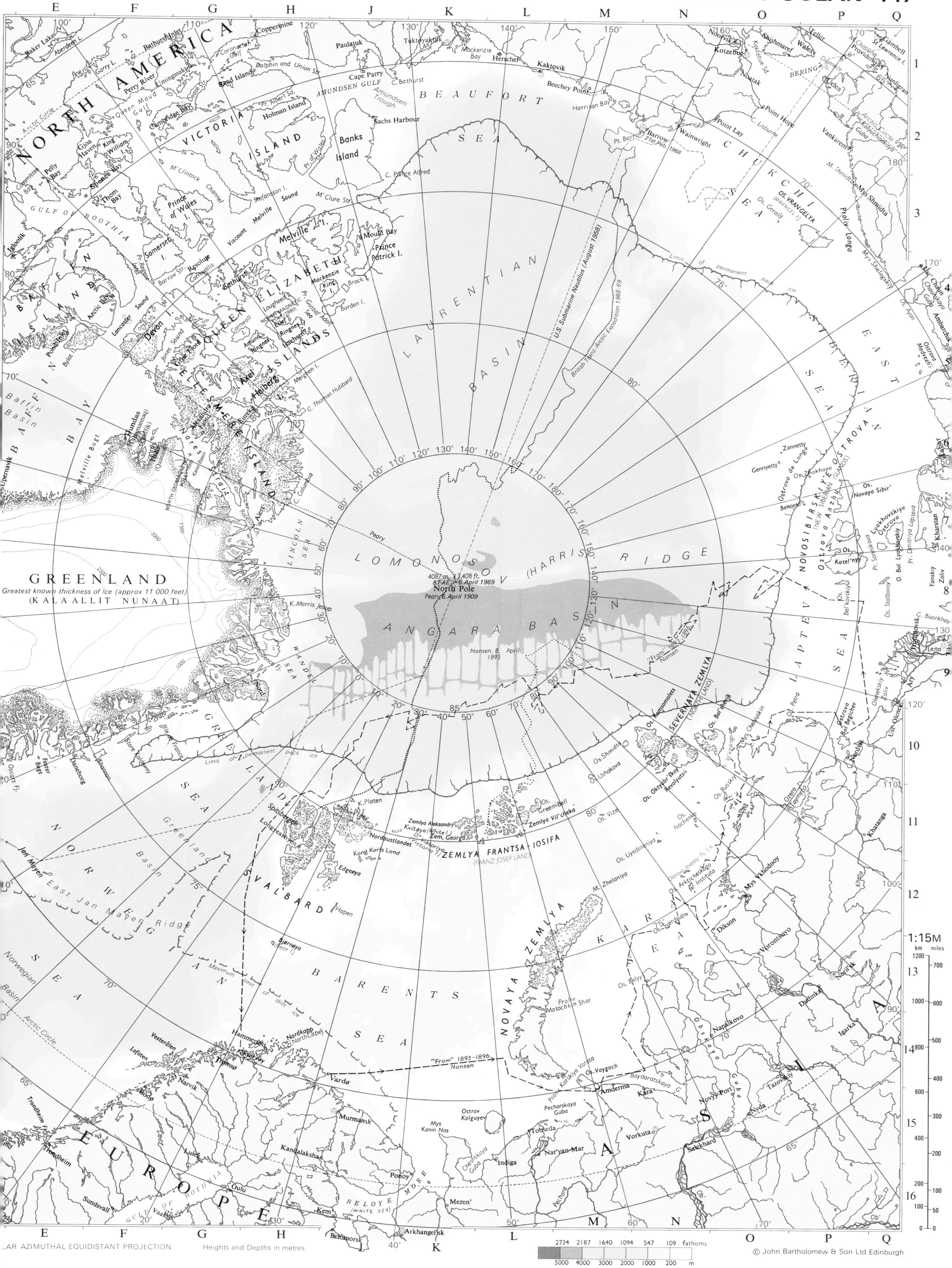

LAR AZIMUTHAL EQUIDISTANT PROJECTION Heights and Depths in metres

2734	2187	1640	1094	547	109	fathoms
5000	4000	3000	2000	1000	200	m

METROPOLITAN AREAS

A metropolitan area is a continuous built-up area containing a number of cities and towns. The total combined population is given either as an estimate or from census returns.

Metropolitan areas with populations greater than 7 million.

Country	***Metropolitan area***	*Population*
Mexico	MEXICO CITY	18,748,000
Brazil	SÃO PAULO	17,112,712
USA	NEW YORK	16,198,000
Egypt	CAIRO	15,000,000
China	SHANGHAI	13,341,896
Argentina	BUENOS AIRES	12,604,018
India	BOMBAY	12,571,720
Japan	TOKYO	11,935,700
Brazil	RIO DE JANEIRO	11,205,567
South Korea	SEOUL	10,979,000
India	CALCUTTA	10,916,272
USA	LOS ANGELES	10,845,000
China	BEIJING	10,819,407
Indonesia	JAKARTA	9,253,000
France	PARIS	9,060,000
Russian Fed.	MOSCOW	9,000,000
China	TIANJIN	8,785,402
UK	LONDON	8,620,333
Japan	OSAKA-KOBE	8,520,000
India	DELHI	8,375,188
Philippines	MANILA - QUEZON CITY	7,832,000
Pakistan	KARACHI	7,702,000

Country	***Metropolitan area***	*Population*
Afghanistan	**Kabul**	2,000,000
Algeria	**Algiers**	3,033,000
Angola	**Luanda**	1,717,000
Argentina	**Buenos Aires**	12,604,018
	Córdoba	1,136,000
	Rosario	1,084,000
Armenia	**Yerevan**	1,300,000
Australia	**Adelaide**	1,050,000
	Brisbane	1,302,000
	Canberra	310,000
	Melbourne	3,081,000
	Perth	1,193,000
	Sydney	3,657,000
Austria	**Vienna**	1,531,000
Azerbaijan	**Baku**	1,780,000
Bangladesh	**Chittagong**	2,289,000
	Dhaka	6,646,000
Belarus	**Minsk**	1,637,000
Belgium	**Antwerp**	473,082
	Brussels	970,501
Brazil	**Belem**	1,418,061
	Belo Horizonte	3,615,234
	Brasília	1,803,478
	Curitiba	1,966,426
	Pôrto Alegre	2,906,472
	Recife	2,814,795
	Rio de Janeiro	11,205,567
	Salvador	2,424,878
	São Paulo	17,112,712
Bulgaria	**Sofia**	1,190,000
Burma	**Rangoon**	3,295,000
Canada	**Montreal**	3,084,100
	Ottawa	885,300
	Quebec	622,000
	Toronto	3,822,400
	Vancouver	1,586,600
	Winnipeg	648,500
Chile	**Santiago**	4,734,000
China	**Anshan**	2,517,080
	Baotou	1,257,000
	Beijing (Peking)	10,819,407
	Changchun	2,214,000
	Changsha	1,362,000
	Chengdu	3,004,000
	Chongqing	3,151,000
	Dalian	2,543,000
	Fushun	1,420,000
	Fuzhou	1,361,000
	Guangzhou (Canton)	3,671,000
	Guiyang	1,587,000
	Hangzhou	1,412,000
	Harbin	2,966,000
	Huainan	1,519,420
	Jilin	1,327,000
	Jinan	2,415,000
	Kunming	1,718,000
	Lanzhou	1,566,000
	Luoyang	1,227,000
	Nanchang	1,415,000
	Nanjing	2,265,000
	Qingdao	2,010,000
	Qiqihar	1,460,000
	Shanghai	13,341,896
	Shenyang	4,763,000
	Shijiazhuang	1,352,000
	Taiyuan	2,199,000
	Tangshan	1,590,000
	Tianjin	8,785,402
	Wuhan	3,921,000
	Xian	2,859,000
	Zhengzhou	1,759,000
	Zibo	2,400,000
Colombia	**Barranquilla**	1,019,000
	Bogotá	4,851,000
	Cali	1,555,000
	Medellín	1,585,000
Croatia	**Zagreb**	1,174,512
Cuba	**Havana**	2,099,000
Czech Republic	**Prague**	1,294,000
Denmark	**Copenhagen**	1,337,114
Dominican Republic	**Santo Domingo**	2,203,000
Ecuador	**Guayaquil**	1,764,170
	Quito	1,281,849
Egypt	**Alexandria**	3,684,000
	Cairo	15,000,000
	El Giza	1,670,800
Estonia	**Tallinn**	482,000
Ethiopia	**Addis Ababa**	1,891,000
France	**Marseilles**	1,087,000
	Paris	9,060,000
Finland	**Helsinki**	4,986,000
Georgia	**Tbilisi**	1,264,000
Germany	**Berlin**	3,400,000
	Bonn	280,000
	Bremen	700,000
	Cologne	934,000
	Dresden	501,000
	Duisburg	525,000
	Düsseldorf	567,000
	Essen-Dortmund	2,745,700
	Frankfurt	624,000
	Hamburg	1,600,000
	Hanover	497,000
	Leipzig	530,000
	Munich	1,631,000
	Nuremberg	477,000
	Stuttgart	560,000
Greece	**Athens**	3,097,000
Guatemala	**Guatemala City**	2,000,000
Haiti	**Port-au-Prince**	1,031,000
Hong Kong	**Hong Kong**	5,448,000
Hungary	**Budapest**	2,115,000
India	**Ahmadabad**	3,279,655
	Bangalore	4,086,548
	Bombay	12,571,720
	Calcutta	10,916,272
	Delhi	8,375,188
	Hyderabad	4,280,261
	Jaipur	1,514,425
	Kanpur	2,111,284
	Lucknow	1,642,134
	Madras	5,361,468
	Nagpur	1,661,409
	Pune	2,485,014
Indonesia	**Bandung**	2,535,000
	Jakarta	9,253,000
	Medan	1,850,000
	Semarang	1,224,000
	Surabaya	2,383,000
Iran	**Isfahan**	1,484,000
	Mashhad	1,882,000
	Tehran	6,773,000
Iraq	**Baghdad**	4,044,000
Ireland (Rep of)	**Dublin**	926,000
Israel	**Jerusalem**	508,000
	Tel Aviv	1,029,700
Italy	**Milan**	1,449,403
	Naples	1,204,149
	Rome	3,051,000
	Turin	1,002,863
Ivory Coast	**Abidjan**	2,168,000
Japan	**Fukuoka**	1,169,000
	Hiroshima	1,049,000
	Kawasaki	1,128,000
	Kitakyushu	1,030,000
	Kyoto	1,460,000
	Nagoya	2,160,000
	Osaka-Kobe	8,520,000
	Sapporo	1,370,000
	Tokyo	11,935,700
	Yokohama	3,220,000
Jordan	**Amman**	1,025,000
Kazakhstan	**Alma-Ata**	1,151,300
Kenya	**Nairobi**	1,503,000
Korea, North	**P'yŏngyang**	2,230,000
Korea, South	**Inchon**	1,739,000
	Pusan	3,875,000
	Seoul	10,979,000
	Taegu	2,518,000
Kuwait	**Kuwait**	200,000
Latvia	**Riga**	915,000
Lebanon	**Beirut**	1,500,000
Libya	**Tripoli**	2,062,000
Lithuania	**Vilnius**	582,000
Malaysia	**Kuala Lumpur**	1,711,000
Mexico	**Guadalajara**	2,846,720
	Mexico City	18,748,000
	Monterrey	2,521,697
	Puebla de Zaragoza	1,267,000
Morocco	**Casablanca**	3,213,000
	Rabat	1,068,000
Netherlands	**Amsterdam**	1,062,000
	The Hague	683,631
	Rotterdam	1,037,000
New Zealand	**Auckland**	864,700
	Christchurch	303,400
	Wellington	325,700
Nicaragua	**Managua**	1,012,000
Nigeria	**Abuja**	523,900
	Lagos	4,100,000
Norway	**Oslo**	458,364
Pakistan	**Faisalabad**	1,507,000
	Islamabad	537,000
	Karachi	7,702,000
	Lahore	4,092,000
	Rawalpindi	1,099,000
Peru	**Lima**	6,404,500
Philippines	**Manila - Quezon City**	7,832,000
Poland	**Warsaw**	1,655,100
Portugal	**Lisbon**	1,603,000
	Oporto	1,314,794
Puerto Rico	**San Juan**	1,390,000
Romania	**Bucharest**	2,194,000
Russian Federation	**Chelyabinsk**	1,367,000
	Kazan	1,094,000
	Moscow	9,000,000
	Nizhniy Novgorod	1,438,000
	Novosibirsk	1,436,000
	Omsk	1,148,000
	Perm	1,091,000
	Rostov-on-Don	1,020,000
	Samara	1,257,000
	St Petersburg	5,035,000
	Ufa	1,083,000
	Volgograd	999,000
	Yekaterinburg	1,367,000
Saudi Arabia	**Jeddah**	1,800,000
	Riyadh	1,500,000
Senegal	**Dakar**	1,492,000
Singapore	**Singapore**	2,723,000
South Africa	**Cape Town**	2,310,000
	Durban	1,057,000
	Johannesburg	1,714,000
Spain	**Barcelona**	1,677,699
	Madrid	2,991,223
Sri Lanka	**Colombo**	616,000
Sudan	**Khartoum**	1,947,000
Sweden	**Stockholm**	1,662,000
Switzerland	**Geneva**	373,000
Syria	**Aleppo**	2,501,000
	Damascus	2,651,000
Taiwan	**Kaohsiung**	1,512,000
	Taipei	2,961,000
Tanzania	**Dar-es-Salaam**	1,657,000
Thailand	**Bangkok**	5,832,843
Tunisia	**Tunis**	1,636,000
Turkey	**Ankara**	3,022,236
	Istanbul	6,665,000
	Izmir	2,665,105
UK	**Birmingham**	2,310,900
	Glasgow	872,900
	Leeds	1,461,000
	Liverpool	1,227,700
	London	8,620,333
	Manchester	2,445,000
Ukraine	**Dnepropetrovsk**	1,179,000
	Donetsk	1,110,000
	Kharkov	1,611,000
	Kiev	2,624,000
	Odessa	1,115,000
Uruguay	**Montevideo**	1,197,000
USA	**Atlanta**	2,737,000
	Baltimore	2,342,000
	Boston	2,845,000
	Buffalo	959,000
	Chicago	6,216,000
	Cincinnati	1,449,000
	Cleveland	1,845,000
	Columbus	1,344,000
	Dallas - Fort Worth	3,766,000
	Denver	1,640,000
	Detroit	4,352,000
	Houston	3,247,000
	Indianapolis	1,237,000
	Kansas City	1,575,000
	Los Angeles	10,845,000
	Miami	1,814,000
	Milwaukee	1,398,000
	Minneapolis - St Paul	2,388,000
	New Orleans	1,307,000
	New York	16,198,000
	Oklahoma City	964,000
	Philadelphia	4,920,000
	Phoenix	2,030,000
	Pittsburg	2,094,000
	Portland	1,188,000
	Rochester	980,000
	Sacramento	1,385,000
	San Antonio	1,323,000
	San Diego	2,370,000
	San Francisco	5,028,000
	Seattle	1,862,000
	St Louis	2,467,000
	Tampa-St Petersburg	1,995,000
	Washington D.C.	3,734,000
Uzbekistan	**Tashkent**	2,100,000
Venezuela	**Caracas**	4,092,000
	Maracaibo	1,365,308
	Valencia	1,227,472
Vietnam	**Haiphong**	1,397,000
	Hanoi	1,088,862
	Ho Chi Minh	3,237,000
Yugoslavia	**Belgrade**	1,575,000
Zaire	**Kinshasa**	3,505,000

GLOSSARY

Language Abbreviations

The entries in this short glossary have been restricted to the less widely-known geographical terms. It also omits terms which are visually similar eg. banc, banco, bank.

Afr	Afrikaans	*Kor*	Korean
Alb	Albanian	*Lao*	Laotian
Ar	Arabic	*Lap*	Lappish
Ben	Bengali	*Lat*	Latvian
Ber	Berber	*Mal*	Malay
Bul	Bulgarian	*Mlg*	Malagasy
Bur	Burmese	*Mon*	Mongolian
Cam	Cambodian	*Nor*	Norwegian
Ch	Chinese	*Per*	Persian
Cz	Czech	*Pol*	Polish
Dan	Danish	*Por*	Portuguese
Dut	Dutch	*Rom*	Romanian
Est	Estonian	*Rus*	Russian
Fae	Faeroese	*Sca*	Scandinavian
Fin	Finnish	*S-C*	Serbo-Croat
Fr	French	*Sla*	Slavonic
Gae	Gaelic	*Som*	Somali
Ger	German	*Sp*	Spanish
Gr	Greek	*Swe*	Swedish
Heb	Hebrew	*Th*	Thai (Siamese)
Hin	Hindi	*Tib*	Tibetan
Hun	Hungarian	*Tu*	Turkish
Ice	Icelandic	*Ur*	Urdu
Ind	Indonesian	*Vt*	Vietnamese
It	Italian	*Wel*	Welsh
Jpn	Japanese		

Name	Language	Meaning
A, –å, –á	*Sca, Ice*	stream
Adasi	*Tu*	island
Adrar	*Ber*	mountains
Aiguille	*Fr*	peak, needle
Ain, 'Aīn, 'Ayn	*Ar*	spring, well
Akrotírion	*Gr*	cape, point
Ala–	*Fin*	lower
Alt–a, –o	*It, Por, Sp*	upper
Ao	*Ch, Th*	bay
Arro-io, yo	*Por, Sp*	watercourse
Au	*Cam*	river
Aust–	*Nor*	east(ern)
Ayía, Ayios	*Gr*	saint
Ba	*Vt*	mountain
Bāb	*Ar*	strait
Bādiyah, Badiet	*Ar*	desert
Baelt	*Dan*	strait
Bahía	*Sp*	bay
Baḥr, Baḥrah	*Ar*	sea, channel
Baixo	*Por*	lower
Baj–a, –o	*Sp*	lower
Ban	*Cam, Lao, Th*	village
–bana	*Jpn*	point, cape
Bandao	*Ch*	peninsula
Bandar	*Ar, Mal, Per,*	port, harbour
Bas, –se	*Fr*	lower
Batin, Batn	*Ar*	depression
Be'er(ot)	*Heb*	well(s)
Bei	*Ch*	north(ern)
Bereg	*Rus*	bank, shore
–berg, Berg(e)	*Sca, Ger*	mountain(s)
Bid	*Ar*	waterhole
Bir, Bir, B'ir	*Ar*	well
Birk–at, –et	*Ar*	well, pool
–bjerg	*Dan*	hill
Boca	*Por, Sp*	mouth
Bocche	*It*	mouths, estuary
Boğazi	*Tu*	strait
Bol'sh–e, –aya, –oy	*Rus*	big
Bonom	*Vt*	mountain
–botn, –botten	*Nor, Swe*	valley floor
Bouche	*Fr*	mouth, estuary
–bre(en)	*Nor*	glacier
Bredning	*Dan*	bay
Bucht	*Ger*	bay
Bugt	*Dan*	bay
Bukhta	*Rus*	bay
Bukt(en)	*Nor, Swe*	bay
Bur–un, –nu	*Tu*	point, cape
Cabo	*Por, Sp*	cape, highland
Caka	*Tib*	salt lake
cañad–a, –ón	*Sp*	ravine, gorge
Canon	*Sp*	canyon
Cap, Capo	*Fr, It*	cape, headland
Cerro	*Sp*	hill, peak
Chaco	*Sp*	jungle region
Chaine, Chaîne	*Fr*	mountain chain
Chiang	*Th*	town
Chott	*Ar*	salt lake, marsh
Cima, Cime	*It, Sp, Fr*	summit
Citta	*It*	town, city
Ciudad	*Sp*	town, city
Co	*Tib*	lake
Col	*Fr*	high pass
Cordillera	*Sp*	mountain chain
Corn–e, –o	*Fr, It*	peak
Côte	*Fr*	coast, slope
Cu Lao	*Vt*	island
Cua	*Vt*	estuary inlet
Cun	*Ch*	village
Da	*Vt*	river
Da	*Ch*	big
Dag–i	*Tu*	mountain
Dagh	*Per*	mountain
Daglar–i	*Tu*	mountains
–dal, –ur	*Sca, Ice,Afr*	valley
–dalur	*Ice*	valley
Dao	*Ch*	island
Darreh	*Per*	valley
Daryachech	*Per*	lake
Dasht	*Per, Ur*	desert
Denizi	*Tu*	sea
–diep	*Dut*	channel
Djebel, Djibal	*Ar*	mountain
–djup	*Ice*	fjord
Do, –do	*Vt, Kor*	island
Dolina	*Rus*	valley
Dong	*Ch*	east(ern)
Dorf, –dorf	*Ger, Afr*	village
–dwip	*Hin*	island
Eiland(en)	*Afr, Dut*	island(s)
–elv(a)	*Nor*	river
Embalse	*Sp*	reservoir
Embouchure	*Fr*	estuary
'Emeq	*Heb*	plain
Erg	*Ar*	desert with dunes
Eski	*Tu*	old
Espigao	*Por*	upland
Estero	*Sp*	inlet, estuary; swamp
Estrecho	*Sp*	strait
Estreito	*Por*	strait
Etang	*Fr*	lake, lagoon
–ye(jar)	*Ice*	island(s)
Ezers	*Lat*	lake
Fels	*Ger*	rock
Feng	*Ch*	peak
Fiume	*It*	river
–fjall, fjell	*Swe, Nor*	mountain
–fjord(en)	*Dan, Nor*	fjord; lagoon
–fjordhur	*Ice*	fjord
–floi	*Ice*	bay
Foce, Foci	*It*	river-mouth
–fonn	*Nor*	glacier
Fuente	*Sp*	source, well
Gang	*Ch*	harbour
–gata	*Jpn*	inlet, lagoon
–gawa	*Jpn*	river
Gebel	*Ar*	mountain
Gebirge	*Ger*	mountains
Geziret	*Ar*	island
Gipfel	*Ger*	peak
Gji	*Alb*	inlet, bay
Gletscher	*Ger*	glacier
Gobi	*Mon*	desert
Gol	*Mon*	river
Göl(u)	*Tu*	lake
Gonglu	*Ch*	highway
Gor–a, –y	*Rus, (Sla)*	mountain(s)
–got	*Kor*	point, cape
Greben'	*Rus*	ridge
Gryada	*Rus*	ridge
Guan	*Ch*	pass
Guba	*Rus*	bay
–gunto	*Jpn*	island, group
Gunung	*Ind, Mal*	mountain
–haehyop	*Kor*	strait
Haff	*Ger*	bay
Hai	*Ch*	sea
Halbinsel	*Ger*	peninsula
halvoya	*Nor*	peninsula
Ham(m)ad–a	*Ar*	plateau
Hamakhtesh	*Heb*	depression
Hassi	*Ar*	well
–haug	*Nor*	hill
–havn	*Dan, Fae, Nor*	harbour
He	*Ch*	river
–hede, hei	*Dan, Nor*	heath
–hegyseg	*Hun*	mountains
Heide	*Ger*	heath, moor
Hka	*Bur*	river
–ho	*Nor*	peak
Hon	*Vt*	island
Hory	*Cz*	mountains
Hot	*Mon*	town
Hu	*Ch*	lake
Ia	*Vt*	stream, river
imeni	*Rus*	in the name of
Ipsoma	*Gr*	high ground
Irhzer	*Ber*	watercourse
Irmak	*Tu*	large river
'Irq	*Ar*	sand dunes
Iso–	*Fin*	big
Jabal	*Ar*	mountain
–jarv, –i	*Est, Fin*	lake
–jaure, javrre	*Lap*	lake
Jazīrah	*Ar*	island
Jezioro	*Pol*	lake
Jiang	*Ch*	river
–jima	*Jpn*	island
–jok–i, –ka	*Fin, Lap*	river
–jokull	*Ice*	glacier
–kai	*Jpn*	bay, inlet, sea
–kaikyo	*Jpn*	strait
Kamen'	*Rus*	stone
–kawa	*Jpn*	river
Kefar	*Heb*	village
Kenet	*Alb*	inlet
Kep	*Alb*	point, cape
Kepulauan	*Ind*	archipelago, islands
Khalig, Khalij	*Ar*	bay, gulf
Khawr	*Ar*	inlet
Khersonisos	*Gr*	peninsula
Khrebet	*Rus*	mountain range
Klit	*Dan*	dunes
Klong	*Th*	canal, creek
–ko	*Jpn*	lake, inlet
Ko	*Th*	island
Kofel, Koge(e)l	*Ger*	dome-shaped hill
Kolpos	*Gr*	gulf
Kopf	*Ger*	hill
Körfezi(i)	*Tu*	bay, gulf
Kosa	*Rus*	spit of land
Kray	*Rus*	region
Kryazh	*Rus*	ridge
Kuh(ha)	*Per*	mountains(s)
Kum	*Rus*	sandy desert
–kundo	*Kor*	island group
Laem	*Th*	point
Lago	*It, Por, Sp*	lake
laht	*Est*	bay
Lam	*Th*	stream
Lande	*Ger*	sandy moor, heath
Laut	*Ind*	sea
Lednik	*Rus*	glacier
Les	*Cz, Rus*	woods, forest
les, lez	*Fr*	near, beside
Lieh-tao	*Ch*	group of islands
Liman	*Rus*	bay, gulf
Liman–i	*Tu*	harbour, port
Limni	*Gr*	lake, lagoon
Ling	*Ch*	mountain range
Llano	*Sp*	plain, prairie
Llyn	*Wel*	lake
Lohatanjona	*Mlg*	point
Loma	*Sp*	hill
Lu	*Ch*	street, road
Madinat	*Ar*	town, city
Mae Nam	*Th*	river
Mal	*Alb*	mountain(s)
Mal–a, –o, –yy	*Sla*	small
Male	*Cz*	small
Marsa, Mersa	*Ar*	anchorage, inlet
Masabb	*Ar*	canal, estuary
Mega, Magal–a, –o	*Gr*	big
Mesto	*Sla*	place, town
Mikr–i, on	*Gr*	small
Mina'	*Ar*	port, harbour
Moni	*Gr*	monastery
More	*Rus*	sea
Muntii	*Rom*	mountains
Mynydd	*Wel*	mountain
–myr	*Nor, Swe*	moor, swamp
Mys	*Rus*	cape
na	*Sla*	on
nad	*Sla*	above, over
Nafud	*Ar*	desert, dune
Nagor'ye	*Rus*	highland, uplands
Nagy–	*Hun*	big, great
Nahr	*Ar*	river
Nakhon	*Th*	town
Nam	*Bur, Th, Vt*	river
Nan	*Ch*	south(ern)
Ne–a, –on, –os	*Gr*	new
Nei	*Ch*	inner
–nes	*Ice, Nor*	point, cape
Ngoc	*Vt*	mountain, peak
–ni	*Kor*	village
Nizhn–eye, –iy	*Rus*	lower
Nizina	*Cz, Rus*	lowland
Nizmennost'	*Rus*	lowlands
Nos	*Bul, Rus*	ness, point
Nosy	*Mlg*	island
Nov–a, –o	*Sla*	new
Nuur	*Mon*	lake
Ny–	*Sca*	new
ø, øy	*Sca*	island
Okrug	*Rus*	district
–oog	*Ger*	island
Ormos	*Gr*	bay
Oros (Ori)	*Ger*	mountain(s)
Ostrov(a)	*Rus*	island(s)
Otok(i)	*S–C*	island(s)
Oued	*Ar*	dry river-bed
Ozero (Ozera)	*Rus*	lake(s)
pää	*Fin*	hill
Pal–a, –ai, –o, –io	*Gr*	old
Parbat	*Ur*	mountain
Pegunungan	*Ind*	mountain range
Pelabohan	*Mal*	harbour
Pellg	*Alb*	bay
Pendi	*Ch*	basin
Pereval	*Rus*	pass
Pertuis	*Fr*	opening, strait
Perv–o, –yy	*Rus*	first
Peski	*Rus*	sands, desert
Pingyuan	*Ch*	plain
Ploskogor'ye	*Rus*	plateau
Pod	*Sla*	under, sub–
Poluostrov	*Rus*	peninsula
Polwysep	*Pol*	peninsula
Porogi	*Rus*	rapids
Poselok	*Rus*	settlement
Pradesh	*Hin*	state
presqu'ile	*Fr*	peninsula
Pri	*Rus*	near, cis–
Proliv	*Rus*	strait
Protok–a	*Rus*	channel
pulau	*Ind, Mal*	island(s)
Puy	*Fr*	peak
Qi	*Ch*	admin. div.
Qiao	*Ch*	bridge
Qiryat	*Heb*	town
Qu	*Tib*	stream
Quan	*Ch*	spring
Qundao	*Ch*	archipelago
Rade	*Fr*	roadstead
rags	*Lat*	point, cape
Ramlat	*Ar*	sands
–rani	*Ice*	spur
Ra's	*Ar, Per*	point, cape
Ravnina	*Rus*	plain
Rayon	*Rus*	district
Represa	*Por*	dam
Reshteh	*Per*	mountain range
–retsugan	*Jpn*	chain of rocks
–retto	*Jpn*	chain of islands
–rev	*Nor*	reef, cliff
Ri	*Tib*	mountain
–ri	*Kor*	village
Rosh	*Heb*	point, cape
Rt	*S–C*	point, cape
Rubha	*Gae*	point, cape
Rud (khaneh)	*Per*	river
Rudohorie	*Cz*	mountains
–saar(i)	*Est, Fin*	island
Sabkhat	*Ar*	salt-flat
Saghir	*Ar*	small
sahra	*Ar*	plain
saḥrž, saḥārā	*Ar*	desert(s)
–saki, –misaki	*Jpn*	point, cape
San, –san	*Lao, Jpn, Kor*	mountain
Sebkra	*Ar*	salt-flat
Selat	*Ind*	strait, channel
Selatan	*Ind, Mal*	south(ern)
selka	*Fin*	ridge; open water
Selo	*Rus, S–C*	village
Selva	*Sp*	forest
–sen	*Jpn*	mountain
–seto	*Jpn*	strait, channel
Sever–o, –naya	*Rus*	north(ern)
Shamo	*Ch*	desert
Shan	*Ch*	mountain(s)
Shandi	*Ch*	mountainous area
Shang	*Ch*	upper
Shankou	*Ch*	pass
Shanmai	*Ch*	mountain range
Shatt	*Ar*	river (–mouth)
–shima	*Jpn*	island
–shoto	*Jpn*	group of islands
Shuiku	*Ch*	reservoir
–sjo	*Nor*	lake
So	*Dan, Nor*	lake
Song	*Vt*	river
Spitze	*Ger*	peak
Sredn–a, –e, –ayz	*Sla*	middle
Sredn–e, –eye, –iy, –yaya	*Rus*	middle
Star–a, –e	*Cz*	old
Star–a, –i	*S–C*	old
Star–aya, –oye, –yy, –yye	*Rus*	old
Step'	*Rus*	steppe
Stor–, Stora	*Swe*	big
–suido	*Jpn*	strait, channel
Sungai	*Ind, Mal*	river
–suo	*Fin*	swamp, marsh
Sveti	*S–C*	saint
Szenti–	*Hun*	saint
–take	*Jpn*	peak
Tanjong	*Ind, Mal*	cape, point
Tao	*Ch*	island
Tasek	*Mal*	lake
Tassili	*Ber*	plateau
Tau	*Rus*	mountain(s)
Tekojarvi	*Fin*	reservoir
Teluk	*Ind*	bay
Tengah	*Ind*	middle
Tepe–si	*Tu*	hill, peak
Thale	*Th*	lake
Timur	*Ind*	east(ern)
–tjakka	*Lap*	mountain
–to	*Jpn*	island
–tong	*Kor*	village
Tonle	*Cam*	lake
–udden	*Swe*	point, cape
Uj–	*Hun*	new
Ujung	*Ind*	point, cape
Urzyq	*Ar*	area of dunes
Ust'ye	*Rus*	estuary
Utara, Uttar	*Ind, Hin*	north(ern)
v	*Sla*	in
–vaara(t)	*Fin*	hill(s)
–vag	*Nor*	bay
–vann, Vatn	*Nor*	lake
–varos	*Hun*	town
–varre	*Nor*	mountain
Vast–er, –ra	*Swe*	western
Vaux	*Fr*	valleys
Velik–a, –o, –aya	*Sla*	big
Verkhn–e, –aya, –iy	*Rus*	upper
–vesi	*Fin*	water, lake
Vig–ik	*Dan, Nor*	bay
Vinh	*Vt*	bay
Vodokhranil-ishche	*Rus*	reservoir
Vorota	*Rus*	gate, strait
Vostochn –aya, –yy	*Rus*	eastern
Vozvyshennost'	*Rus*	uplands
Vpadina	*Rus*	depression
Vrch(y)	*Cz*	mountain(s)
Vung	*Vt*	bay, gulf
Vysok–aya, –o, –iy	*Rus*	high
Vyssh–aya, –e, –iy	*Rus*	higher
Wad	*Dut*	sand–flat
Wadi	*Ar*	watercourse
Wai	*Ch*	outer
Wan	*Ch*	bay
–wan	*Jpn*	bay
Wielk–a, –i, –o	*Pol*	big
Wysok–a, –i, –o	*Pol*	high
Xi	*Ch*	west; stream
Xia	*Ch*	lower; gorge
Xian	*Ch*	country
Xiao	*Ch*	small
Xu	*Ch*	islet
Yam	*Heb*	lake, sea
–yama	*Jpn*	mountain(s)
Ye	*Bur*	island
Yli–	*Fin*	upper
Yoma	*Bur*	mountain range
You	*Ch*	right
Yuzhn–o, –yy	*Rus*	southern
Za	*Rus*	behind, beyond
–zaki	*Jpn*	point, cape
Zalew, Zaliv	*Pol, Rus*	bay
–zan	*Jpn*	mountain
Zapadn–aya, –o	*Rus*	western
Zapovednik	*Rus*	reserve
Zemlya	*Rus*	land
–zhen	*Ch*	town
Zhong	*Ch*	middle
Zhou	*Ch*	islet
Zui	*Ch*	point, spit
Zuid	*Dut*	south
Zuidelijk	*Dut*	southern

INDEX

Abbreviations used in the Index

Afghan	Afghanistan
Afr	Africa, African
Ala	Alabama
Amer	America, American
Anc mon	Ancient monument
Anc site	Ancient site
Arch	Archipel, archipelago, archipiélago
Arg	Argentina
Ariz	Arizona
Ark	Arkansas
Aust	Australia
Aut	Autonomous
B	Bay
Berks	Berkshire
Br	British
Br Col	British Columbia
Bucks	Buckinghamshire
C	Cape
Cal, Calif	California
Can	Canal
Cat(s)	Cataract(s)
Cent	Central
Chan	Channel
Co	County, Coast
Colo	Colorado
Conn	Connecticut
Den	Denmark
Dept	Department Département
Des	Desert
Dist	District
Div	Division
Dom Rep	Dominican Republic
E	East, Eastern
Eng	England, English
Eq, Equat	Equatorial
Est	Estuary
Fed	Federation
Fj	Fjord
Fr	French
G	Gulf
Ger	Germany
Gla	Glacier
Gloucs	Gloucestershire
Grp	Group
Gt	Great
Hants	Hampshire
Hbr	Harbour
Hd	Head
H.E.	Hydro Electric
Herts	Hertfordshire
Hist reg	Historic region
Hist site	Historic site
I, isld	Island
Ind	Indian
Is, islds	Islands
Isld king	Island kingdom
Isth	Isthmus
Jct, junc, junct	Junction
L	Lake
Lancs	Lancashire
Lincs	Lincolnshire
Lt Ho	Lighthouse
Madhya Prad	Madhya Pradesh
Man	Manitoba
Mass	Massachusetts
Med	Mediterranean
Mich	Michigan
Minn	Minnesota
Miss	Mississippi
Mon	Monument
Mont	Montana
Moz	Mozambique
Mt, Mte	Mountain
Mth(s)	Mouth(s)
Mt ra	Mountain range
Mts	Mountains
N	North, Northern, New
Nat Park	National Park
Neth, Nether, Neths	Netherlands
Nev	Nevada
New Bruns	New Brunswick
New Hamps	New Hampshire
New Mex	New Mexico
Nfld	Newfoundland
Notts	Nottinghamshire
N Scotia	Nova Scotia
N S W	New South Wales
N W Terr	Northwest Territories
N Y	New York
Oc	Ocean
Okla	Oklahoma
Old prov	Old province
Oxon	Oxford, Oxfordshire
Pac	Pacific
Pass	Passage
Pen	Peninsula
Penn	Pennsylvania
People's Rep	People's Republic
Physical reg	Physical region
Pk	Peak
Plat	Plateau
Port	Portugal, Portuguese
Pr	Prince
Prefect	Prefecture
Princ	Principality
Prom	Promontory
Prot	Protectorate
Prov	Province
Pt, Pta, Pto	Point
Qnsld	Queensland
R	Rio, river
Ra	Range
Rdg	Ridge
Reg	Region
Rep	Republic
Res	Reservoir
Rus Fed	Russian Federation
S	South, Southern
Sa	Serra, Sierra
Sask	Saskatchewan
Sd	Sound
Sk	Shuiku (reservoir)
Span	Spanish
Spr	Spring
St, Ste	Saint, Sainte
Sta	Station
Staffs	Staffordshire
Stat Area	Statistical Area
Str	Strait
Switz	Switzerland
Tenn	Tennessee
Terr	Territory
Tex	Texas
Tribal dist	Tribal district
U.A.E.	United Arab Emirates
U.K.	United Kingdom
Union Terr	Union Territory
U.S.A.	United States of America
V	Valley
Ven	Venezuela
Vict	Victoria
Virg	Virginia
Vol	Volcano
W	West, Western
Wash	Washington
W I	West Indies
Wilts	Wiltshire
Wyo	Wyoming
Yorks	Yorkshire

Aa — Aguisan

A

22 C2 **Aa** *R* France
32 E9 **Aa** *R* Germany
41 J2 **Aach** Germany
25 F7 **Aachen** Germany
37 J6 **Aalen** Germany
80 D1 **Aalma edh Chaab** Lebanon
25 C4 **Aalsmeer** Netherlands
22 G2 **Aalst** Belgium
25 G5 **Aalten** Netherlands
22 E1 **Aalter** Belgium
29 M9 **Äänekoski** Finland
29 M4 **Aapajärvi** Finland
115 O3 **Aappilattoq** Greenland
40 H3 **Aarau** Switzerland
36 E3 **Aarbergen** Germany
25 A6 **Aardenburg** Netherlands
40 H3 **Aargau** *canton* Switzerland
22 H2 **Aarschot** Belgium
Aasiaat *see* **Egedesminde**
16 E9 **Aazanèn** Morocco
58 D5 **Aba** China
85 F7 **Aba** Nigeria
86 F5 **Aba** Zaire
128 G5 **Abacaxis** *R* Brazil
113 K11 **Abaco, Great** *isld* Bahamas
113 K11 **Abaco, Little** *isld* Bahamas
77 A4 **Abadan** Iran
77 C5 **Ābādeh** Iran
130 F6 **Abadia dos Dourados** Brazil
85 D2 **Abadla** Algeria
130 F6 **Abaeté** Brazil
129 J4 **Abaetetuba** Brazil
65 C2 **Abag Qi** China
133 F3 **Abai** Paraguay
103 P4 **Abajo Pk** Utah U.S.A.
86 A4 **Abakaliki** Nigeria
56 D4 **Abakan** Russian Federation
56 C5 **Abakanskiy Khrebet** *mts* Russian Federation
85 E6 **Abala** Niger
85 F5 **Abalak** Niger
85 E4 **Abalessa** Algeria
137 P1 **Abamama** *isld* Kiribati
128 D6 **Abancay** Peru
21 O2 **Abancourt** France
45 L1 **Abano Terme** Italy
77 C4 **Abarqū** Iran
60 S1 **Abashiri** Hokkaido Japan
125 K5 **Abasolo** Mexico
55 F3 **Abatskoye** Russian Federation
136 K4 **Abau** Papua New Guinea
86 G3 **Ābay** *R* Ethiopia
57 G1 **Abay** Kazakhstan
86 G4 **Ābaya Hāyt'** *L* Ethiopia
20 G6 **Abbaretz** France
99 S3 **Abbaye, Pt** Michigan U.S.A.
86 H3 **Abbe, L** Ethiopia
21 O4 **Abbé,l'** France
9 G4 **Abberton** England
21 O1 **Abbeville** France
111 L10 **Abbeville** Alabama U.S.A.
112 D6 **Abbeville** Georgia U.S.A.
111 D12 **Abbeville** Louisiana U.S.A.
112 E3 **Abbeville** South Carolina U.S.A.
118 J8 **Abbey** Saskatchewan Canada
14 B4 **Abbeyfeale** Ireland
12 E4 **Abbey Head** Scotland
14 D4 **Abbeyleix** Ireland
141 G2 **Abbey Pk** Queensland Australia
13 F6 **Abbeystead** England
41 J7 **Abbiategrasso** Italy
26 K6 **Abborrträsk** Sweden
141 J4 **Abbot B** Queensland Australia
146 B7 **Abbot Ice Shelf** Antarctica
141 J5 **Abbot,Mt** Queensland Australia
8 D6 **Abbotsbury** England
117 M11 **Abbotsford** British Columbia Canada
13 F2 **Abbotsford** Scotland
99 Q5 **Abbotsford** Wisconsin U.S.A.
106 F5 **Abbott** New Mexico U.S.A.
109 K4 **Abbott** Texas U.S.A.
74 E1 **Abbottabad** Pakistan
25 C4 **Abcoude** Netherlands
16 D8 **Abdalagís, Sa. de** *mts* Spain
78 H3 **'Abd al Azīz** *mts* Turkey
80 F6 **Abdallah Br** Jordan
52 H6 **Abdi** Russian Federation
53 H7 **Abdulino** Russian Federation
86 D3 **Abéché** Chad
17 F3 **Abejar** Spain
22 D2 **Abele** Belgium
86 G4 **Ābeltī** Ethiopia
26 E7 **Abelvaer** Norway
26 G6 **Abelvattnet** *L* Sweden
37 K5 **Abenberg** Germany
16 E6 **Abenjar** *R* Spain
16 E6 **Abenojar** Spain
28 C6 **Åbenrå** Denmark
Åbenrå-Sønderborg *co see* **Sønderjylland** *co*
37 M6 **Abens** *R* Germany
37 M6 **Abensberg** Germany
85 E7 **Abeokuta** Nigeria
8 B1 **Aber** Wales
86 G4 **Ābera** Ethiopia
8 B3 **Aberaeron** Wales
13 E1 **Aberargie** Scotland
8 C4 **Aberavon** Wales
20 A4 **Aber-Benoit** *R* France
15 F3 **Aberchirder** Scotland
121 S7 **Abercorn** Quebec Canada
Abercorn Zambia *see* **Mbala**
139 J5 **Abercrombie** *R* New South Wales Australia
8 C4 **Aberdare** Wales
88 F2 **Aberdare Mts** *ra* Kenya
8 B2 **Aberdaron** Wales
139 K4 **Aberdeen** New South Wales Australia
118 L6 **Aberdeen** Saskatchewan Canada
89 D9 **Aberdeen** S Africa
15 F3 **Aberdeen** Scotland
101 N7 **Aberdeen** Idaho U.S.A.
95 L7 **Aberdeen** Maryland U.S.A.
111 H8 **Aberdeen** Mississippi U.S.A.
112 H2 **Aberdeen** North Carolina U.S.A.
98 H4 **Aberdeen** South Dakota U.S.A.
100 B3 **Aberdeen** Washington U.S.A.
147 E1 **Aberdeen L** Northwest Territories Canada
13 E1 **Aberdour** Scotland
8 B2 **Aberdyfi** Wales
15 E4 **Aberfeldy** Scotland
8 B1 **Aberffraw** Wales
8 B1 **Aberffraw B** Wales
13 G6 **Aberford** England
141 H5 **Aberfoyle** Queensland Australia
12 D1 **Aberfoyle** Scotland
8 C4 **Abergavenny** Wales
8 C1 **Abergele** Wales
85 D7 **Abergourou** Ivory Coast
141 H4 **Abergowrie** Queensland Australia
8 C3 **Abergwesyn** Wales
8 B4 **Abergwili** Wales
13 F1 **Aberlady** Scotland
119 O8 **Abernethy** Saskatchewan Canada
13 E1 **Abernethy** Scotland
8 B3 **Aberporth** Wales
8 B2 **Abersoch** Wales
8 C4 **Abertillery** Wales
12 E1 **Aberuthven** Scotland
20 A4 **Aber Wrach,L'** France
8 B3 **Aberystwyth** Wales
45 J3 **Abetone** Italy
52 K2 **Abez'** Russian Federation
38 G8 **Abfaltersbach** Austria
53 F9 **Abganerovo** Russian Federation
72 E5 **Abhā** Saudi Arabia
85 D7 **Abidjan** Ivory Coast
28 B7 **Abild** Denmark
28 B4 **Abild Å** *R* Denmark
118 F4 **Abilene** Alberta Canada
107 N3 **Abilene** Kansas U.S.A.
108 H3 **Abilene** Texas U.S.A.
94 J9 **Abilene** Virginia U.S.A.
21 M8 **Abilly** France
9 E4 **Abingdon** England
99 Q9 **Abingdon** Illinois U.S.A.
94 E10 **Abingdon** Virginia U.S.A.
141 G4 **Abingdon Downs** Queensland Australia
141 J4 **Abingdon Reef** Gt Barrier Reef Australia
12 E3 **Abington** Scotland
53 E11 **Abinsk** Russian Federation
106 D5 **Abiquiu** New Mexico U.S.A.
26 K3 **Abisko** Sweden
120 J2 **Abitibi** *R* Ontario Canada
120 J3 **Abitibi Canyon** Ontario Canada
120 K4 **Abitibi,L** Ontario Canada
86 G3 **Abīy Ādī** Ethiopia
86 G4 **Abiyata Hāyk'** *L* Ethiopia
53 F11 **Abkhazskaya Respublika** Georgia
21 O4 **Ablis** France
21 L3 **Ablon** France
138 C2 **Abminga** South Australia Australia
Åbo *see* **Turku**
106 D7 **Abo** New Mexico U.S.A.
74 F3 **Abohar** India
85 D7 **Aboisso** Ivory Coast
85 E7 **Abomey** Benin
69 C10 **Abongabong, Gunung** *mt* Sumatra
86 B5 **Abong Mbang** Cameroon
48 F3 **Abony** Hungary
71 D6 **Aborlan** Philippines
26 J8 **Åbosjo** Sweden
86 C3 **Abou Deïa** Chad
15 F3 **Aboyne** Scotland
Abqaiq *see* **Buqayq**
110 L4 **Abraham Lincoln Nat. Hist. Site** Kentucky U.S.A.
133 E6 **Abra, L. del** Argentina
99 S5 **Abrams** Wisconsin U.S.A.
54 J1 **Abramtsevo** Russian Federation
16 B5 **Abrantes** Portugal
124 C4 **Abreojos, Pta** *C* Mexico
36 C6 **Abreschwiller** France
84 J5 **Abri** Sudan
9 G4 **Abridge** England
129 L7 **Abrolhos, Arquipélago dos** *islds* Brazil
48 H4 **Abrud** Romania
118 B8 **Abruzzi,Mt** British Columbia Canada
42 F6 **Abruzzo** *prov* Italy
98 J2 **Absaraka** North Dakota U.S.A.
101 P5 **Absaroka Ra** Mont/Wyoming U.S.A.
101 Q4 **Absarokee** Montana U.S.A.
37 K5 **Absberg** Germany
21 J8 **Absie,l'** France
38 H6 **Abtenau** Austria
36 H1 **Abterode** Germany
36 H6 **Abtsgmünd** Germany
33 S4 **Abtshagen** Germany
79 H3 **Abū aḍ Ḍuhūr** Syria
80 G6 **Abu 'Alanda** Jordan
71 L10 **Abuan** Indonesia
84 H5 **Abu Ballas** *mt* Egypt
80 D5 **'Abud** Jordan
77 D7 **Abu Dhabi** U.A.E.
79 D10 **Abu Durba** Egypt
79 F8 **Ābū el Jurdhān** Jordan
128 F5 **Abufari** Brazil
86 E3 **Abu Gabra** Sudan
84 J6 **Abu Hamed** Sudan
79 A7 **Abu Hummus** Egypt
85 F7 **Abuja** Nigeria
78 H4 **Abū Kamāl** Syria
79 B8 **Abu Kebîr** Egypt
61 O8 **Abukuma** *R* Japan
61 O9 **Abukuma-kōchi** *hills* Japan
86 E3 **Abu Matariq** Sudan
86 D5 **Abumonbazi** Zaire
77 D7 **Abū Mūsá** *isld* U.A.E.
128 E5 **Abuná** Brazil
84 E3 **Abū Nujaym** Libya
80 G3 **Abu Qanṭarah** Syria
79 A10 **Abu Qurqâs** Egypt
60 E14 **Aburatsu** Japan
74 E6 **Abu Road** India
79 D10 **Abu Rudeis** Egypt
77 B6 **Abu Sa'fah** *oil well* Persian Gulf
86 G1 **Abu Shagara, Ras** *C* Sudan
80 F5 **Abu Sidra** Israel
84 J5 **Abu Simbel** *hist site* Egypt
60 O3 **Abuta** Japan
84 J4 **Abu Tig** Egypt
86 F2 **Abu 'Uruq** Sudan
124 F5 **Abuya** Mexico
86 G3 **Ābuye Mēda** *mt* Ethiopia
71 G5 **Abuyog** Philippines
86 E3 **Abu Zabad** Sudan
Abū Ẓabi *see* **Abu Dhabi**
84 J4 **Abu Zenîma** Egypt
86 F4 **Abwong** Sudan
28 D2 **Åby** Denmark
27 H15 **Åby** Kalmar Sweden
27 H13 **Åby** Östergotland Sweden
86 E3 **Abyad** Sudan
26 L6 **Åby älv** *R* Sweden
28 D2 **Åbybro** Denmark
142 C5 **Abydos** W Australia Australia
86 E4 **Abyei** Sudan
77 B2 **Ābyek** Iran
127 N4 **Abymes** Guadeloupe W Indies
26 M6 **Åbyn** Sweden
72 D6 **Abyssinian Highlands** Ethiopia
55 C4 **Abzakovo** Russian Federation
55 C5 **Abzanovo** Russian Federation
141 K2 **Acacia Ridge** *dist* Brisbane, Qnsld Australia
118 G7 **Acadia Valley** Alberta Canada
130 E8 **Acaí** Brazil
108 B4 **Acala** Texas U.S.A.
125 J7 **Acámbaro** Mexico
126 F10 **Acandí** Colombia
124 G6 **Acaponeta** Mexico
125 K9 **Acapulco de Juárez** Mexico
129 J4 **Acará** *R* Brazil
129 K4 **Acarau** Brazil
130 C9 **Acaray, R** Paraguay
130 H9 **Acarí** Brazil
128 D7 **Acari** *R* Peru
127 K10 **Acarigua** Venezuela
125 K8 **Acatlán** Mexico
125 M9 **Acayucan** Mexico
45 P5 **Acciano** Italy
140 F3 **Accident Inlet** Queensland Australia
97 G6 **Accotink** *R* Virginia U.S.A.
94 F9 **Accoville** West Virginia U.S.A.
85 D7 **Accra** Ghana
13 F6 **Accrington** England
69 C10 **Aceh** *prov* Sumatra
101 M7 **Acequia** Idaho U.S.A.
43 F8 **Acerra** Italy
41 K2 **Ach** *R* Germany
128 E2 **Achaguas** Venezuela
74 G8 **Achalpur** India
38 E7 **Ache** *R* Austria
84 E6 **Achegour** Niger
22 J1 **Achel** Belgium
38 F6 **Achen** *R* Germany
59 J2 **Acheng** China
119 P4 **Acheninni L** Saskatchewan Canada
38 E6 **Achenkirch** Austria
41 P2 **Achen Pass** Germany
38 E6 **Achen-Tal** *R* Austria
41 P2 **Achenwald** Austria
36 E6 **Achern** Germany
144 D5 **Acheron** *R* New Zealand
21 P1 **Acheux-en-Amienois** France
22 D3 **Achicourt** France
22 D3 **Achiet-le-Grand** France
53 F11 **Achikulak** Russian Federation
14 B3 **Achill** Ireland
109 L2 **Achille** Oklahoma U.S.A.
32 K6 **Achim** Germany
55 G1 **Achimovy 2-ye** Russian Federation
56 D3 **Achinsk** Russian Federation
55 E2 **Achiry** Russian Federation
57 E3 **Achisay** Kazakhstan
58 B2 **Achit Nuur** *L* Mongolia
15 C3 **Achnasheen** Scotland
33 T4 **Achter-Wasser** *L* Germany
53 E10 **Achuyevo** Russian Federation
86 F5 **Achwa** *R* Uganda
20 G5 **Acigne** France
78 D3 **Acı Gölü** *L* Turkey
47 K7 **Acıpayam** Turkey
43 G11 **Acireale** Sicily
108 F3 **Ackerly** Texas U.S.A.
111 G8 **Ackerman** Mississippi U.S.A.
99 N7 **Ackley** Iowa U.S.A.
126 G3 **Acklins I** Bahamas
111 M7 **Ackworth** Georgia U.S.A.
71 F5 **Aclan Pt** Philippines
14 C2 **Aclare** Ireland
9 H2 **Acle** England
118 D7 **Acme** Alberta Canada
106 F8 **Acme** New Mexico U.S.A.
112 J3 **Acme** North Carolina U.S.A.
108 H1 **Acme** Texas U.S.A.
106 C6 **Acomita** New Mexico U.S.A.
133 D4 **Aconcagua** *mt* Argentina
131 B4 **Aconcagua** *R* Chile
85 A1 **Açores** *islds* Atlantic Oc
87 F10 **Acornhoek** S Africa
45 N4 **Acqualagna** Italy
42 D6 **Acquapendente** Italy
21 N3 **Acquigny** France
44 D2 **Acqui Terme** Italy
138 D4 **Acraman, L** South Australia Australia
128 D5 **Acre** *state* Brazil
128 E5 **Acre** *R* Brazil
80 D2 **Acre** Israel
43 G9 **Acri** Italy
44 D3 **Acroscia** *R* Italy
48 D3 **Acs** Hungary
48 E3 **Acsa** Hungary
135 N10 **Actaeon Grp** *islds* Pacific Oc
9 F5 **Acton** England
102 F7 **Acton** California U.S.A.
101 R4 **Acton** Montana U.S.A.
8 D4 **Acton Turville** England
121 S7 **Acton Vale** Quebec Canada
130 H8 **Açu** Brazil
129 K4 **Açude Areras** *L* Brazil
130 E9 **Acunguí** Brazil
130 C4 **Açurizal** Brazil
45 O6 **Acuto** Italy
112 C3 **Acworth** Georgia U.S.A.
61 Q12 **Ada** Okinawa
107 N2 **Ada** Kansas U.S.A.
94 B4 **Ada** Michigan U.S.A.
98 K2 **Ada** Minnesota U.S.A.
94 D6 **Ada** Ohio U.S.A.
107 O7 **Ada** Oklahoma U.S.A.
48 F5 **Ada** Serbia Yugoslavia
85 C5 **Adafer** *reg* Mauritania
119 O8 **Adair** Saskatchewan Canada
99 M8 **Adair** Iowa U.S.A.
110 A5 **Adair** Oklahoma U.S.A.
103 L10 **Adair, B. de** Mexico
112 C3 **Adairsville** Georgia U.S.A.
16 D4 **Adaja** *R* Spain
144 A6 **Ada, L** New Zealand
47 J6 **Adala** Turkey
27 D11 **Adals-elv** *R* Norway
26 J8 **Ådalshøen** Sweden
Adama *see* **Nazrēt**
80 F5 **Adamah** Jordan
84 G3 **Adam, Al'** Libya
103 P7 **Adamana** Arizona U.S.A.
130 D7 **Adamantina** Brazil
117 O10 **Adamant Mt** British Columbia Canada
86 B4 **Adamaoua** *reg* Cameroon
42 D2 **Adamello** *mt* Italy
80 D1 **Adamit** Israel
133 F8 **Adam,Mt** Falkland Is
55 C5 **Adamovka** Russian Federation
100 H8 **Adam Peak** *mt* Nevada U.S.A.
102 B3 **Adams** California U.S.A.
95 O4 **Adams** Massachusetts U.S.A.
99 O6 **Adams** Minnesota U.S.A.
98 K9 **Adams** Nebraska U.S.A.
98 H1 **Adams** North Dakota U.S.A.
107 J5 **Adams** Oklahoma U.S.A.
110 J5 **Adams** Tennessee U.S.A.
99 R6 **Adams** Wisconsin U.S.A.
83 J8 **Adam's Bridge** Sri Lanka/India
117 O10 **Adams L** British Columbia Canada
145 E4 **Adams, Mt** New Zealand
100 D3 **Adams,Mt** Washington U.S.A.
107 P7 **Adamson** Oklahoma U.S.A.
83 K11 **Adam's Peak** Sri Lanka
102 D2 **Adams Pk** California U.S.A.
135 U11 **Adamstown** Pitcairn I Pacific Oc
95 L6 **Adamstown** Pennsylvania U.S.A.
121 S7 **Adamsville** Quebec Canada
111 K8 **Adamsville** Alabama U.S.A.
94 F6 **Adamsville** Ohio U.S.A.
110 H6 **Adamsville** Tennessee U.S.A.
109 J4 **Adamsville** Texas U.S.A.
103 M3 **Adamsville** Utah U.S.A.
16 D6 **Adamuz** Spain
78 E3 **Adana** Turkey
118 H6 **Adanac** Saskatchewan Canada
70 E5 **Adang,Teluk** *B* Kalimantan
78 C1 **Adapazari** Turkey
86 G2 **Adarama** Sudan
146 C12 **Adare, C** Antarctica
70 D5 **Adas** Kalimantan
80 D8 **Adasha** *R* Israel
141 G7 **Adavale** Queensland Australia
103 J3 **Adaven** Nevada U.S.A.
99 M7 **Adaza** Iowa U.S.A.
41 M5 **Adda** *R* Italy
9 E3 **Adderbury** England
109 M6 **Addicks** Texas U.S.A.
13 G6 **Addingham** England
107 N7 **Addington** Oklahoma U.S.A.
80 E3 **Addirim** Israel
111 E11 **Addis** Louisiana U.S.A.
Addis Ababa *see* **Ādīs Abeba**
111 J7 **Addison** Alabama U.S.A.
95 U2 **Addison** Maine U.S.A.
95 K4 **Addison** New York U.S.A.
109 O8 **Addison** Texas U.S.A.
95 O2 **Addison** Vermont U.S.A.
94 G8 **Addison** West Virginia U.S.A.
73 L9 **Addu Atoll** Maldives
79 G4 **Ad Duraykish** Syria
100 H1 **Addy** Washington U.S.A.
112 D6 **Adel** Georgia U.S.A.
99 M8 **Adel** Iowa U.S.A.
100 F7 **Adel** Oregon U.S.A.
138 B8 **Adelaide** South Australia Australia
126 F2 **Adelaide** New Providence I Bahamas
146 C5 **Adelaide I** Antarctica
115 K4 **Adelaide Pen** Northwest Territories Canada
140 B2 **Adelaide River** N Terr Australia
102 G7 **Adelanto** California U.S.A.
Adelaye *see* **Bani**
40 G5 **Adelboden** Switzerland
32 L9 **Adelebsen** Germany
142 E3 **Adele I** W Australia Australia
145 D4 **Adele I** New Zealand
106 D7 **Adelino** New Mexico U.S.A.
37 J6 **Adelmannsfelden** Germany
127 J2 **Adelphi** Jamaica
37 L6 **Adelschlag** Germany
37 K4 **Adelsdorf** Germany
36 G5 **Adelsheim** Germany
17 G4 **Ademuz** Spain
72 F6 **Aden** Yemen
36 B3 **Adenau** Germany
85 F5 **Aderbissinat** Niger
71 G6 **Adgaoan** *R* Mindanao Philippines
79 G5 **'Adhrā'** Syria
80 D2 **'Adi** Israel
136 G2 **Adi** *isld* W Irian
86 G3 **Ādī Ārk'ey** Ethiopia
138 B4 **Adieu, Cape** South Australia Australia
45 K1 **Adige** *R* Italy
86 G3 **Ādīgrat** Ethiopia
74 H9 **Adilabad** India
86 F5 **Adilang** Uganda
78 J2 **Adilcevaz** Turkey
59 L2 **Adimi** Russian Federation
100 E8 **Adin** California U.S.A.
22 D1 **Adinkerke** Belgium
95 N2 **Adirondack Mts** New York U.S.A.
86 G4 **Ādīs Abeba** Ethiopia
86 G4 **Ādīs Alem** Ethiopia
86 G3 **Ādīs Zemen** Ethiopia
86 G3 **Ādī Ugrī** Eritrea
78 G3 **Adiyaman** Turkey
48 L4 **Adjud** Romania
53 E11 **Adler** Russian Federation
8 D1 **Adlington** England
118 J9 **Admiral** Saskatchewan Canada
145 D4 **Admiralty B** New Zealand
116 K1 **Admiralty Bay** Alaska U.S.A.
142 F2 **Admiralty G** W Australia Australia
117 F7 **Admiralty I** Alaska U.S.A.
117 F7 **Admiralty I Nat Mon** Alaska U.S.A.
115 L3 **Admiralty Inlet** Northwest Territories Canada
100 C1 **Admiralty Inlet** Washington U.S.A.
136 K2 **Admiralty Is** Bismarck Arch
107 O3 **Admire** Kansas U.S.A.
38 K6 **Admont** Austria
133 E5 **Adolfo Alsina** Argentina
26 J5 **Adolfsström** Sweden
142 G3 **Adolphus I** W Australia Australia
71 L9 **Adonara** *isld* Indonesia
76 C3 **Adoni** India
48 E3 **Adony** Hungary
80 C7 **Adora** Jordan
80 C8 **Adorayim** *R* Israel
32 J10 **Adorf** Germany
37 N3 **Adorf** Germany
86 B4 **Adoumaoua, Massif de l'** *mts* Cameroon
18 E9 **Adour** *R* France
16 E8 **Adra** Spain
43 F11 **Adrano** Sicily
85 D3 **Adrar** Algeria
85 B4 **Adrar** *reg* Mauritania
85 E4 **Adrar des Iforas** *mt reg* Algeria/Mali
85 E5 **Adrar Quezzeine** *mts* Mali
85 A4 **Adrar Souttouf** *reg* Mauritania
77 H3 **Adraskand** *R* Afghanistan
57 F4 **Adrasman** Tajikistan
86 D3 **Adré** Chad
84 E4 **Adri** Libya
42 E3 **Adria** Italy
112 E5 **Adrian** Georgia U.S.A.
99 L6 **Adrian** Minnesota U.S.A.
110 B3 **Adrian** Missouri U.S.A.
100 H6 **Adrian** Oregon U.S.A.
100 F2 **Adrian** Washington U.S.A.
94 G8 **Adrian** West Virginia U.S.A.
Adrianople *see* **Edirne**
45 N2 **Adriatic Sea**
28 D7 **Adsbøl** Denmark
103 N10 **Aduana del Sasabe** Mexico
41 K4 **Adula Gruppe** *mt* Switzerland
80 C7 **'Adullam** *dist* Israel
110 G4 **Advance** Missouri U.S.A.
142 E5 **Adverse Well** W Australia Australia
122 H8 **Advocate Harbour** Nova Scotia Canada
86 G3 **Ādwa** Ethiopia
80 G2 **'Adwān** Syria
108 B8 **Ady** Texas U.S.A.
51 N2 **Adycha** *R* Russian Federation
53 E10 **Adygeyskaya Avtonomnyy Oblast'** Russian Federation
78 H1 **Adzharskaya Respublika** Georgia
85 D7 **Adzope** Ivory Coast
28 E5 **Æbelø** *isld* Denmark
46 G6 **Aegean Sea** Greece
28 E7 **Ærø** *isld* Denmark
8 B3 **Aeron,R** Wales
28 E7 **Ærøskøbing** Denmark
40 G3 **Aesch** Switzerland
118 D9 **Aetna** Alberta Canada
107 M4 **Aetna** Kansas U.S.A.
52 H5 **Afanas'yevo** Russian Federation
47 R14 **Afándou** Rhodes Greece
80 D2 **Afeq** Israel
20 F6 **Aff** *R* France
85 B5 **Affollé** *reg* Mauritania
77 H3 **Afghanistan** *rep* Asia
86 H5 **Afgooye** Somalia
86 A4 **Afikpo** Nigeria
53 E11 **Afips** *R* Russian Federation
80 F2 **Afiq** Syria
26 D8 **Åfjord** Norway
85 E2 **Aflou** Algeria
86 H5 **Afmadow** Somalia
129 L5 **Afogados da Ingázeira** Brazil
116 L7 **Afognak I** Alaska U.S.A.
85 B5 **Afollé** *reg* Mauritania
8 C2 **Afon Dyfi** *R* Wales
130 C4 **Afonso** Brazil
45 Q8 **Afragola** Italy
86 H3 **Āfrēra YeCh'ew Hāyk'** *L* Ethiopia
82 **Africa**
52 D1 **Afrikanda** Russian Federation
79 G2 **'Afrīn** Syria
40 A3 **Afrique,Mt** France
38 J8 **Afritz** Austria
16 E10 **Afso** Morocco
99 M8 **Afton** Iowa U.S.A.
99 O5 **Afton** Minnesota U.S.A.
106 D9 **Afton** New Mexico U.S.A.
95 M4 **Afton** New York U.S.A.
107 Q5 **Afton** Oklahoma U.S.A.
99 R7 **Afton** Wisconsin U.S.A.
101 P7 **Afton** Wyoming U.S.A.
129 H4 **Afua** Brazil
80 E3 **'Afula** Israel
80 E3 **'Afula 'Illit** Israel
78 C2 **Afyon** Turkey
86 B2 **Agadem** Niger
85 F5 **Agadès** Niger
85 C2 **Agadir** Morocco
57 G1 **Agadyr'** Kazakhstan
85 F7 **Agaie** Nigeria
121 L2 **Again** *R* Quebec Canada
85 F5 **Agalak, Mt** Niger
83 H6 **Agalega Is** Mauritius Indian Oc
125 M2 **Agalta,Sa.de** *ra* Honduras
55 F1 **Agan** *R* Russian Federation
134 E6 **Agaña** Guam Pacific Oc
61 N8 **Agano** Japan
55 C4 **Agapovka** Russian Federation
74 G7 **Agar** India
98 F5 **Agar** South Dakota U.S.A.
28 C5 **Ågård** Denmark
86 G4 **Āgaro** Ethiopia
117 N11 **Agassiz** British Columbia Canada
106 G2 **Agate** Colorado U.S.A.
98 C7 **Agate** Nebraska U.S.A.
98 C7 **Agate Fossil Beds Nat. Mon.** Nebraska U.S.A.
73 L6 **Agatti** *isld* Lakshadweep Indian Oc
120 F5 **Agawa** Ontario Canada
101 N2 **Agawam** Montana U.S.A.
85 D7 **Agboville** Ivory Coast
18 H9 **Agde** France
18 H9 **Agde,Cap d'** France
28 E6 **Ågedrup** Denmark
61 L10 **Agematsu** Japan
18 F8 **Agen** France
100 G6 **Agency Valley Res** Oregon U.S.A.
107 N2 **Agenda** Kansas U.S.A.
100 C8 **Ager** California U.S.A.
28 E5 **Agernæs** Denmark
28 B3 **Agerø** *isld* Denmark
28 C6 **Agerskov** Denmark
28 G6 **Agersø** Denmark
28 E2 **Agersted** Denmark
28 H5 **Agerup** Denmark
89 A7 **Aggeneys** S Africa
28 A3 **Agger** Denmark
36 C2 **Agger** *R* Germany
28 C3 **Aggersborg** Denmark
28 A3 **Agger Tange** *pen* Denmark
38 M5 **Aggsbach** Austria
77 K3 **Aghangai** Afghanistan
116 J8 **Aghiyuk I** Alaska U.S.A.
85 B4 **Aghwinit** Mauritania
85 B4 **Aghzoumal, Sabkhat** *salt lake* Western Sahara
124 E4 **Agiabampo** Mexico
58 F1 **Aginskoye** Russian Federation
43 F11 **Agira** Sicily
18 G10 **Agly** *R* France
85 B3 **Agmar** Mauritania
45 L1 **Agna** Italy
118 L2 **Agnes Lake** Ontario Canada
142 F3 **Agnes, Mt** W Australia Australia
143 G7 **Agnes, Mt** W Australia Australia
100 A7 **Agness** Oregon U.S.A.
143 D8 **Agnew** W Australia Australia
85 D7 **Agnibilekrou** Ivory Coast
48 J5 **Agnita** Romania
42 D3 **Agno** *R* Italy
42 F7 **Agnone** Italy
44 E1 **Agogna** *R* Italy
20 G3 **Agon** France
67 B3 **Agong** China
38 K6 **Agonitz** Austria
42 E2 **Agordo** Italy
45 O6 **Agosta** Italy
18 G9 **Agout** *R* France
74 H5 **Agra** India
107 L2 **Agra** Kansas U.S.A.
107 O6 **Agra** Oklahoma U.S.A.
53 G11 **Agrakhanskiy Poluostrov** *pen* Russian Federation
Agram *see* **Zagreb**
17 H3 **Agramunt** Spain
17 F3 **Agreda** Spain
43 G8 **Agri** *R* Italy
78 J2 **Ağrı** Turkey
71 E3 **Agria Pt** Luzon Philippines
111 H11 **Agricola** Mississippi U.S.A.
43 F11 **Agrigento** Sicily
131 B7 **Agrio,R** Argentina
43 F8 **Agropoli** Italy
45 N6 **Agro Pontino** *plain* Italy
47 O12 **Agrós** Greece
71 E3 **Agta Pt** Philippines
124 G6 **Agua Brava, L** Mexico
103 L9 **Agua Caliente** Arizona U.S.A.
129 H8 **Água Clara** Brazil
127 K9 **Aguada Grande** Venezuela
128 C2 **Aguadas** Colombia
127 L5 **Aguadilla** Puerto Rico
109 K8 **Agua Dulce** Texas U.S.A.
103 M7 **Agua Fria** *R* Arizona U.S.A.
109 H9 **Agualeguas** Mexico
102 H8 **Aguanga** California U.S.A.
123 K3 **Aguanish** Quebec Canada
124 F3 **Agua Nueva** Mexico
109 J9 **Agua Nueva** Texas U.S.A.
123 K3 **Aguanus R** Quebec Canada
130 E7 **Aguapeí** *R* Brazil
128 G7 **Aguape,Sa** *mts* Brazil
131 G2 **Aguapey** *R* Argentina
124 E2 **Agua Prieta** Mexico
128 F8 **Aguaray** Argentina
130 C8 **Aguaray Guazú,R** Paraguay
128 C4 **Aguarico** *R* Ecuador
17 G3 **Aguas** *R* Spain
120 C4 **Aguasabon Dam** Ontario Canada
108 E6 **Agua Salada** Mexico
130 H10 **Águas Belas** Brazil
124 H7 **Aguascalientes** Mexico
130 H5 **Aguas Formosas** Brazil
128 C5 **Aguaytia** Peru
16 D6 **Agudo** Spain
130 E8 **Agudos** Brazil
16 B4 **Agueda** Portugal
16 C4 **Agueda** *R* Spain
85 E5 **Aguelhok** Mali
85 C4 **Aguelt el Melha** Mauritania
45 O4 **Agugliano** Italy
85 F6 **Aguié** Niger
103 L8 **Aguila** Arizona U.S.A.
106 F4 **Aguilar** Colorado U.S.A.
16 E2 **Aguilar de Campoo** Spain
109 H8 **Aguilares** Texas U.S.A.
17 F7 **Águilas** Spain
124 H8 **Aguililla de Iturbide** Mexico
58 D4 **Aguin Sum** China
133 D8 **Aguirre,B** Argentina
71 F5 **Aguisan** Philippines

128 D1 **Aguja, C. de la** *C* Colombia
128 B5 **Aguja, Pta** *pt* Peru
56 E3 **Agul** *R* Russian Federation
90 L13 **Agulhas Bank** Atlantic Oc
90 L13 **Agulhas Basin** Indian Oc
89 B10 **Agulhas,C** S Africa
130 G8 **Agulhas Negras** *pk* Brazil
81 A10 **Agulhas Plateau** Indian Oc
70 P10 **Agung, G** *mt* Bali Indonesia
80 C7 **'Agur** Israel
71 G6 **Agusan** *R* Mindanao Philippines
71 E5 **Agutaya** *isld* Philippines
47 N10 **Ağva** Turkey
61 Q12 **Aha** Okinawa
78 L2 **Ahar** Iran
79 H3 **Ahaş, Jebel** *mts* Syria
144 C5 **Ahaura** New Zealand
32 F8 **Ahaus** Germany
145 F3 **Ahimanawa Range** New Zealand
145 D1 **Ahipara** New Zealand
76 E1 **Ahiri** India
79 C1 **Ahırlı** Turkey
145 E3 **Ahititi** New Zealand
116 G7 **Ahklun Mts** Alaska U.S.A.
29 J10 **Ahlainen** Finland
32 L7 **Ahlden** Germany
32 G9 **Ahlen** Germany
32 K6 **Ahlerstedt** Germany
32 H7 **Ahlhorn** Germany
74 E7 **Ahmadabad** India
77 E6 **Ahmadī** Iran
77 A5 **Aḩmadi, Al** Kuwait
80 G1 **Ahmadīyah** Syria
74 F9 **Ahmadnagar** India
74 G9 **Ahmadpur** India
74 D3 **Ahmadpur** Pakistan
74 D4 **Ahmadpur** Pakistan
86 H4 **Ahmar Mts** Ethiopia
47 J6 **Ahmetli** Turkey
124 E5 **Ahome** Mexico
37 L4 **Ahorntal** Germany
112 K1 **Ahoskie** North Carolina U.S.A.
Ah-pa *see* **Aba**
36 B3 **Ahr** *R* Germany
36 B3 **Ahrdorf** Germany
33 S6 **Ahrensberg** Germany
33 N4 **Ahrensbök** Germany
32 M5 **Ahrensburg** Germany
33 T7 **Ahrensfelde** Germany
32 K6 **Ahrenswohlde** Germany
Ahrweiler *see* **Bad Neuenahr-Ahrweiler**
32 H9 **Ahse** *R* Germany
29 L9 **Ähtäri** Finland
29 L9 **Ähtärinjärvi** *L* Finland
68 B4 **Ahtaung** Burma
29 K8 **Ähtävä** Finland
124 G7 **Ahuacatlán** Mexico
125 P11 **Ahuachapán** El Salvador
124 H7 **Ahualulco de Mercado** Mexico
145 F3 **Ahuriri Pt** New Zealand
144 B6 **Ahuriri R** New Zealand
27 G16 **Åhus** Sweden
77 A4 **Ahvāz** Iran
116 K8 **Aiaktalik I** Alaska U.S.A.
128 F4 **Aiapua,L** Brazil
128 E3 **Aiari** *R* Brazil
65 A3 **Aibag Gol** *R* China
60 Q2 **Aibetsu** Japan
38 J7 **Aich** *R* Austria
37 N7 **Aich** Germany
37 L7 **Aichach** Germany
61 L10 **Aichi** *prefect* Japan
116 Q2 **Aichilik** *R* Alaska U.S.A.
26 N3 **Aiddejavrre** Norway
37 P6 **Aidenbach** Germany
46 F6 **Aidhipsoú** Greece
80 G3 **Aidun** Jordan
102 S12 **Aiea** Hawaiian Is
40 E5 **Aigle** Switzerland
21 M4 **Aigle, l'** France
122 G2 **Aigle, L. à l'** Quebec Canada
18 H8 **Aigoual,Mt** France
18 E7 **Aigre** France
18 E6 **Aigrefeuille d'Aunis** France
20 H7 **Aigrefeuille-sur-Maine** France
19 Q14 **Aigu** France
19 Q13 **Aiguebelle** France
121 M4 **Aiguebelle, Parc de** Quebec Canada
18 H9 **Aigues-Mortes** France
40 E6 **Aiguille du Midi** *mt* France
19 Q14 **Aiguilles d'Arves** *mts* France
40 E6 **Aiguille Verte** *mt* France
18 F8 **Aiguillon** France
83 L13 **Aiguillon,C d'** Kerguelen Indian Oc
18 G6 **Aigurande** France
Aihui *see* **Heihe**
47 O12 **Aikateríni, Akra Ayios** *C* Greece
61 M7 **Aikawa** Japan
112 F4 **Aiken** South Carolina U.S.A.
45 Q7 **Ailano** Italy
140 C6 **Aileron** N Terr Australia
22 E5 **Ailette** *R* France
71 M9 **Aileu** Timor
29 M2 **Ailigas** *mt* Finland
19 Q18 **Aille** *R* France
40 D2 **Aillevillers-et-Lyaumont** France
21 P1 **Ailly-le-Haut-Clocher** France
21 M2 **Ailly, Pte, d'** France
21 P2 **Ailly-sur-Noye** France
120 J9 **Ailsa Craig** Ontario Canada
12 C3 **Ailsa Craig** *isld* Scotland
51 N3 **Aim** Russian Federation
71 L9 **Aimaro** Indonesia
71 K9 **Aimere** Indonesia
129 K7 **Aimores** Brazil
129 K7 **Aimores,Serra dos** *mts* Brazil
40 B5 **Ain** *dept* France
40 B6 **Ain** *R* France
52 B5 **Ainaži** Latvia
43 A13 **Aïn Beïda** Algeria
85 D2 **Aïn Beni Mathar** Morocco
21 O3 **Aincourt** France
84 H4 **'Ain Dalla** Egypt
37 K7 **Aindling** Germany
43 B12 **Aïn Draham** Tunisia
80 E1 **Aïn Ebel** Lebanon
80 G3 **Ain el Ghazal** Jordan
80 E7 **'Ain el Ghuweir** Jordan
85 E3 **Aïn-el-Hadjadj** Algeria
17 H10 **Ain el Hadjar** Algeria
84 H4 **Aîn el Wadi** Egypt
80 G3 **Ain esh Shilaq** Jordan
86 C2 **Aïn Galakka** Chad
68 B2 **Ainggyi** Burma
80 G4 **Ain Janna** Jordan
43 B12 **Aïn Kerma** Algeria
80 E6 **Ain Qilt** Jordan
17 H2 **Ainsa** Spain
85 B5 **Ain Safra** Mauritania
Ain Salah *see* **In Salah**
13 E6 **Ainsdale** England
85 D2 **Aïn Sefra** Algeria
123 L7 **Ainslie,L** C Breton I, Nova Scotia
79 C9 **'Ain Sukhna** Egypt
98 G7 **Ainsworth** Nebraska U.S.A.
17 H9 **Aïn Tédèles** Algeria
17 G9 **Aïn Témouchent** Algeria
Aïn Touta *see* **El Homr**
60 R2 **Aioi** Japan
60 H11 **Aioi** Japan
85 C4 **Aïoun Abdel Malek** Mauritania
85 C5 **Aïoun el Atrouss** Mauritania
128 E7 **Aiquile** Bolivia
69 H11 **Air** *isld* Indonesia
21 O2 **Airaines** France
128 F4 **Airao** Brazil
69 D12 **Airbangis** Sumatra
118 C7 **Airdrie** Alberta Canada
12 D2 **Airdrie** Scotland
22 C2 **Aire** France
17 K5 **Aire,I.del** Balearic Is
21 H3 **Airel** France
13 G6 **Aire,R** England
18 E9 **Airè sur L'Adour** France
115 M4 **Air Force I** Northwest Territories Canada
65 B3 **Airgin Sum** China
141 J5 **Airlie** Queensland Australia
100 B5 **Airlie** Oregon U.S.A.
142 B5 **Airlie I** W Australia Australia
45 R7 **Airola** Italy
85 F5 **Aïr ou Azbine** *mt reg* Niger
71 M8 **Airpanas** Indonesia
8 C1 **Air,Pt of** Wales
12 E1 **Airth** Scotland
21 K8 **Airvault** France
37 K4 **Aisch** *R* Germany
133 C7 **Aisén** *prov* Chile
117 E5 **Aishihik** Yukon Territory Canada
22 F5 **Aisne** *dept* France
22 H5 **Aisne** *R* France
40 D3 **Aissey** France
80 E1 **Aïta ech Chaab** Lebanon
136 J2 **Aitape** Papua New Guinea
80 E1 **Aitaroun** Lebanon
37 O6 **Aiterhofen** Germany
144 A7 **Aitken, Mt** New Zealand
99 N3 **Aitkin** Minnesota U.S.A.
46 E6 **Aitolikón** Greece
55 B4 **Aitova** Russian Federation
16 E9 **Aït Youssef ou Ali** Morocco
48 H4 **Aiud** Romania
18 E6 **Aix** *isld* France
18 G5 **Aix d'Angillon,les** France
19 O18 **Aix-en-Provence** France
18 F7 **Aixe-sur-Vienne** France
Aix-la-Chapelle *see* **Aachen**
117 J8 **Aiyansh** British Columbia Canada
79 B9 **'Aiyat,El** Egypt
46 F7 **Aíyina** *isld* Greece
46 F4 **Aiyínion** Greece
46 E6 **Aíyion** Greece
46 F7 **Áiyos Andréas** Greece
47 H9 **Áiyos Ioánnis, Akr** *C* Crete Greece
75 P7 **Aizawl** India
87 C10 **Aizeb** *R* Namibia
20 G8 **Aizenay** France
27 M15 **Aizpute** Latvia
61 N8 **Aizu-Takada** Japan
61 N8 **Aizu-Wakamatsu** Japan
78 L3 **Ajab Shir** Iran
18 L11 **Ajaccio** Corsica
74 J6 **Ajaigarh** India
128 D3 **Ajaju** *R* Colombia
80 G3 **'Ajamī** Syria
143 A8 **Ajana** W Australia Australia
121 M9 **Ajax** Ontario Canada
144 D5 **Ajax, Mt** New Zealand
101 M4 **Ajax Mt** Idaho/Montana U.S.A.
84 G3 **Ajdābiyā** Libya
42 F3 **Ajdovščina** Slovenia
61 O5 **Ajigasawa** Japan
61 N10 **Ajiro** Japan
61 P7 **Aji-shima** *isld* Japan
48 D3 **Ajka** Hungary
80 G4 **Ajlun** Jordan
77 D7 **'Ajmān** U.A.E.
74 F5 **Ajmer** India
103 M9 **Ajo** Arizona U.S.A.
16 E1 **Ajo,C** Spain
129 G3 **Ajoewa** Suriname
103 M9 **Ajo,Mt** Arizona U.S.A.
71 C2 **Aju** *isld* W Irian
128 E4 **Ajuana** *R* Brazil
125 J8 **Ajuchitlán** Mexico
71 F5 **Ajuy** Philippines
60 Q2 **Akabira** Japan
85 E3 **Akabli** Algeria
59 L1 **Akademii, Zaliv** *B* Russian Federation
71 M9 **Akadirunsikun** Indonesia
61 M8 **Akadomari** Japan
61 M10 **Akaishi-dake** *pk* Japan
74 G10 **Akalkot** India
60 S2 **Akan** Japan
79 D3 **Akanthou** Cyprus
60 G12 **Akaoka** Japan
47 L6 **Akar** *R* Turkey
61 P12 **Akarie-Ue** Okinawa
144 D5 **Akaroa** New Zealand
27 G15 **Åkarp, N** Sweden
78 H3 **Akarsu** Turkey
60 G10 **Akasaki** Japan
86 F1 **Akasha** Sudan
60 H11 **Akashi** Japan
29 K4 **Äkäsjoki** *R* Finland
29 K4 **Äkäsjokisuu** Finland
98 F4 **Akaska** South Dakota U.S.A.
61 N8 **Akatani** Japan
26 J4 **Akavare** *mt* Sweden
80 F2 **'Akbara** Israel
57 B2 **Akbasty** Kazakhstan
57 G1 **Akbaur** Kazakhstan
55 F5 **Akbeit** Kazakhstan
55 C5 **Akbulak** Russian Federation
78 F2 **Akçadağ** Turkey
78 G3 **Akçakale** Turkey
78 C1 **Akçakoca Dağları** *mts* Turkey
47 N10 **Akçaova** Turkey
47 K8 **Akçay** Turkey
85 A4 **Akchar,Dunes de l'** Mauritania
57 G1 **Akchatau** Kazakhstan
57 H3 **Akchi** Kazakhstan
47 J7 **Akçoava** Turkey
47 K6 **Ak Dağ** *mt* Turkey
78 E2 **Akdağmadeni** Turkey
56 D5 **Ak Dovurak** Russian Federation
61 L10 **Akechi** Japan
71 B2 **Akelamo** Halmahera Indonesia
9 F3 **Akeley** England
99 M2 **Akeley** Minnesota U.S.A.
27 B13 **Åkernes** Norway
27 K12 **Akersberga** Sweden
27 E12 **Akershus** *county* Norway
26 G8 **Åkersjön** Sweden
27 J12 **Akers-styckebruk** Sweden
71 B2 **Akeselaka** Halmahera Indonesia
57 B2 **Akespe** Kazakhstan
47 K7 **Akgöl** *L* Turkey
53 F12 **Akhalkalaki** Georgia
53 F12 **Akhaltsikhe** Georgia
57 E4 **Akhangaran** Uzbekistan
46 F6 **Akharnaí** Greece
80 F2 **'Akhbera** Israel
84 G3 **Akhḑar, Al Jabal al** *mts* Libya
79 G10 **Akhḑar, Wādī al** *watercourse* Saudi Arabia
46 E5 **Akhelóös** *R* Greece
116 K8 **Akhiok** Alaska U.S.A.
78 A2 **Akhisar** Turkey
84 J4 **Akhmim** Egypt
Akhna *see* **Athna**
79 H2 **Akhterīn** Syria
53 C12 **Akhtopol** Bulgaria
53 G9 **Akhtubinsk** Russian Federation
53 G12 **Akhty** Russian Federation
53 D8 **Akhtyrka** Ukraine
57 K6 **Akhunbabayev** Uzbekistan
60 G12 **Aki** Japan
116 G6 **Akiak** Alaska U.S.A.
52 H3 **Akim** Russian Federation
58 G1 **Akima** Russian Federation
115 L7 **Akimiski I** Northwest Territories Canada
53 E10 **Akimovka** Ukraine
60 F11 **Aki-nada** *sea* Japan
79 F2 **Akıncı Burun** *C* Turkey
47 J7 **Akıncılar** Turkey
27 G16 **Åkirkeby** Denmark
61 O6 **Akita** Japan
145 F4 **Akitio** New Zealand
56 G3 **Akitkan, Khrebet** *mts* Russian Federation
85 B5 **Akjoujt** Mauritania
80 G4 **'Akka** Jordan
85 C3 **Akka** Morocco
55 D6 **Akkabak** Kazakhstan
26 J4 **Akkajaure** *L* Sweden
116 B4 **Akkani** Russian Federation
55 D5 **Akkarga** Kazakhstan
57 E2 **Akkense** Kazakhstan
60 S2 **Akkeshi** Japan
80 D2 **'Akko** Israel
57 H2 **Akkol'** Kazakhstan
57 F3 **Akkol'** Kazakhstan
47 J7 **Akköy** Turkey
55 B6 **Akkozinskiy** Kazakhstan
25 E2 **Akkrum** Netherlands
53 G10 **Akkystau** Kazakhstan
46 F7 **Akladhókambos** Greece
114 F4 **Aklavik** Northwest Territories Canada
85 C5 **Aklé Aouana** *reg* Mauritania
52 B6 **Akmene** Lithuania
52 C6 **Akniste** Latvia
86 F4 **Akobo** *R* Ethiopia/Sudan
74 G8 **Akola** India
116 F6 **Akolmiut** Alaska U.S.A.
86 G2 **Āk'ordat** Eritrea
47 N11 **Akören** Turkey
74 G8 **Akot** India
56 C5 **Ak-Oyuk, Gora** *mt* Russian Federation
115 N5 **Akpatok I** Northwest Territories Canada
79 D1 **Akpınar** Turkey
57 J4 **Akqi** China
98 J1 **Akra** North Dakota U.S.A.
79 G2 **Akrād, Jabal al** *mt* Syria
27 B12 **Åkrafjorden** *inlet* Norway
28 R9 **Akranes** Iceland
46 E6 **Akráta** Greece
46 E8 **Akrítas, Akra** *C* Greece
28 D6 **Åkrog Bugt** *B* Denmark
120 F4 **Akron** Ontario Canada
111 J9 **Akron** Alabama U.S.A.
98 C9 **Akron** Colorado U.S.A.
94 A5 **Akron** Indiana U.S.A.
98 K7 **Akron** Iowa U.S.A.
94 D3 **Akron** Michigan U.S.A.
94 J3 **Akron** New York U.S.A.
94 F5 **Akron** Ohio U.S.A.
95 L6 **Akron** Pennsylvania U.S.A.
46 G9 **Akrotíri** Crete Greece
79 D4 **Akrotiri B** Cyprus
74 H1 **Aksai Chin** *L* Kashmir
55 B4 **Aksakovo** Russian Federation
78 E2 **Aksaray** Turkey
57 H4 **Aksay** *R* Kirghizia
78 C2 **Akşehir** Turkey
78 C2 **Akşehir Gölü** *L* Turkey
55 B4 **Aksenovo** Russian Federation
58 G1 **Aksenovo-Zilovskoye** Russian Federation
77 D5 **Aks-e Rostam** *R* Iran
51 L3 **Aksha** Russian Federation
55 B6 **Akshatau** Kazakhstan
57 J1 **Akshatau, Khrebet** Kazakhstan
57 C1 **Akshyganak** Kazakhstan
53 G12 **Akstata** Azerbaijan
66 C3 **Aksu** China
57 J2 **Aksu** *R* Kazakhstan
47 L7 **Aksu** *R* Turkey
47 L8 **Aksu** Turkey
55 D5 **Aksuat** Kazakhstan
52 H7 **Aksubayevo** Russian Federation
57 J4 **Aksu He** *R* China
86 G3 **Aksum** Ethiopia
57 E3 **Aksumbe** Kazakhstan
Aksu Yangi Shahr *see* **Aksu** China
52 H6 **Aktanysh** Russian Federation
57 D1 **Aktas** Kazakhstan
56 C5 **Aktash** Russian Federation
57 D5 **Aktash** Uzbekistan
55 D5 **Aktasty** Kazakhstan
55 F5 **Aktau** Kazakhstan
46 G4 **Akti** Greece
66 B4 **Akto** China
57 B1 **Aktogay** Kazakhstan
57 J2 **Aktogay** Kazakhstan
57 H5 **Aktu** China
57 A3 **Aktumsyk, Mys** *C* Uzbekistan
55 C5 **Aktyubinsk** Kazakhstan
53 D7 **Akulichi** Russian Federation
60 D13 **Akune** Japan
116 E9 **Akun I** Aleutian Is
85 F7 **Akure** Nigeria
28 S9 **Akureyri** Iceland
116 D9 **Akutan I** Aleutian Is
116 D9 **Akutan Pass** Aleutian Is
56 B5 **Akutikha** Russian Federation
Akyab *see* **Sittwe**
55 C5 **Ak'yar** Russian Federation
79 F2 **Akyatan Göl** *L* Turkey
47 L4 **Akyazı** Turkey
56 B6 **Akzhal** Kazakhstan
57 L1 **Akzhar** Kazakhstan
57 E3 **Akzhaykin, Ozero** *L* Kazakhstan
27 C11 **Ål** Norway
41 O6 **Ala** Italy
111 K8 **Alabama** *state* U.S.A.
111 J10 **Alabama R** Alabama U.S.A.
111 K8 **Alabaster** Alabama U.S.A.
94 D2 **Alabaster** Michigan U.S.A.
144 B6 **Alabaster, L** New Zealand
71 F3 **Alabat** *isld* Luzon Philippines
55 E4 **Alabota, Oz** *L* Kazakhstan
78 E1 **Alaca** Turkey
47 N10 **Alaçah** Turkey
47 N10 **Alaçali** Turkey
47 H6 **Alaçatı** Turkey
113 E8 **Alachua** Florida U.S.A.
16 D3 **Alaejos** Spain
47 Q14 **Alaérma** Rhodes Greece
86 G3 **Ālagē** *mt* Ethiopia
53 F11 **Alagir** Russian Federation
40 G6 **Alagna Valsesia** Italy
18 H7 **Alagnon** *R* France
130 J9 **Alagoa Grande** Brazil
130 H10 **Alagoas** *state* Brazil
129 L6 **Alagoinhas** Brazil
16 C4 **Alagón** *R* Spain
17 G3 **Alagón** Spain
71 G7 **Alah** Mindanao Philippines
69 E13 **Alahanpanjang** Sumatra
29 K8 **Alahärmä** Finland
87 C11 **Al-Ais and Fish River Canyon** *nat park* Namibia
79 F3 **Ālāja** Syria
29 K8 **Alajärvi** Finland
79 G3 **'Alā,Jebel al** *mts* Syria
125 M4 **Alajuela** Costa Rica
47 L8 **Alakır** *R* Turkey
57 K2 **Alakol', Ozero** *L* Kazakhstan
29 P5 **Alakurtti** Russian Federation
29 L4 **Alakylä** Finland
80 G3 **'Al'al** Jordan
135 T3 **Alalakeiki Channel** Hawaiian Is
128 F4 **Alalaú** *R* Brazil
119 P9 **Alameda** Saskatchewan Canada
124 H3 **Alameda** Mexico
102 B4 **Alameda** California U.S.A.
101 N7 **Alameda** Idaho U.S.A.
106 D6 **Alameda** New Mexico U.S.A.
71 D2 **Alaminos** Luzon Philippines
124 D3 **Alamito** Mexico
108 C6 **Alamito Creek** Texas U.S.A.
124 H4 **Alamítos, Sa. de los** *ra* Mexico
103 J9 **Alamo** *R* California U.S.A.
112 E5 **Alamo** Georgia U.S.A.
103 J4 **Alamo** Nevada U.S.A.
98 C1 **Alamo** North Dakota U.S.A.
110 G6 **Alamo** Tennessee U.S.A.
109 J9 **Alamo** Texas U.S.A.
106 E9 **Alamogordo** New Mexico U.S.A.
106 F7 **Alamogordo Res** New Mexico U.S.A.
103 L7 **Alamo Lake** *res* Arizona U.S.A.
43 C8 **Ala, Monti di** Sardinia
124 E4 **Alamos** Mexico
106 E4 **Alamosa** Colorado U.S.A.
124 F2 **Alamos de Peña** Mexico
76 D3 **Ālampur** India
26 H7 **Alanäs** Sweden
29 H11 **Åland** *isld* Finland
33 P7 **Aland** *R* Germany
74 G10 **Aland** India
27 J12 **Åland** Sweden
26 J9 **Ålandsbro** Sweden
29 H11 **Ålands Hav** Finland/Sweden
70 E2 **Alang** Kalimantan
88 H1 **Alanga Bay** Kenya
70 E6 **Alangalang Tg** Kalimantan
69 G13 **Alangangtang** *isld* Sumatra
29 L6 **Alaniemi** Finland
108 D8 **Alanreed** Texas U.S.A.
87 H11 **Alaotra, Farihy** *L* Madagascar
112 D6 **Alapaha** *R* Georgia U.S.A.
55 D2 **Alapayevsk** Russian Federation
Alappuzha *see* **Aleppey**
80 G2 **'Alaq** *R* Syria
79 F9 **'Alāqān** Saudi Arabia
17 F5 **Alarcón, Embalse de** Spain
71 H9 **Alas** Indonesia
78 B2 **Alaşehir** Turkey
56 C5 **Alash** *R* Russian Federation
77 A4 **Al Ashār** Iran
116 **Alaska** *state* U.S.A.
116 O7 **Alaska,G.of** Alaska U.S.A.
135 L2 **Alaska Pen** Alaska U.S.A.
70 Q10 **Alas,Selat** Indonesia
44 D3 **Alassio** Italy
29 K11 **Alastaro** Finland
57 C5 **Alat** Uzbekistan
116 L3 **Alatna** Alaska U.S.A.
45 O6 **Alatri** Italy
52 G7 **Alatyr'** Russian Federation
17 F2 **Alava** *prov* Spain
78 K1 **Alaverdi** Armenia
29 O7 **Alavuokki** Finland
29 K9 **Alavus** Finland
138 F5 **Alawoona** South Australia Australia
8 B1 **Alaw Res** Wales
57 G4 **Alay-Ku** Kirghizia
17 K5 **Alayor** Menorca
57 F5 **Alayskiy Khrebet** *mts* Tajikistan/Kirghizia
47 L5 **Alayunt** Turkey
78 L1 **Alazan** *R* Azerbaijan/Georgia
109 K8 **Alazan Bay** Texas U.S.A.
53 G12 **Alazani** *R* Georgia
51 P2 **Alazeya** *R* Russian Federation
40 H2 **Alb** *R* Germany
44 D2 **Alba** Italy
48 H4 **Alba** *reg* Romania
94 C2 **Alba** Michigan U.S.A.
109 M3 **Alba** Texas U.S.A.
17 F5 **Albacete** Spain
17 F6 **Albacete** *prov* Spain
138 F6 **Albacutya,L** Victoria Australia
16 D4 **Alba de Tormes** Spain
28 E1 **Albæk** Denmark
28 E1 **Albæk Bugt** *B* Denmark
56 C5 **Albagan, Gora** *mt* Russian Federation
79 F3 **Al Bahlūlīyeh** Syria
17 G6 **Albaida** Spain
48 H4 **Alba Iulia** Romania
144 B6 **Alba, Mt** New Zealand
121 S4 **Albanel** Quebec Canada
46 D2 **Albania** *rep* S Europe
42 E7 **Albani,Colli** *hills* Italy
45 N6 **Albano** *L* Italy
45 N6 **Albano Laziale** Italy
45 J4 **Albano, Mte** Italy
143 C10 **Albany** W Australia Australia
127 L2 **Albany** Jamaica
111 M10 **Albany** Georgia U.S.A.
99 Q8 **Albany** Illinois U.S.A.
110 L1 **Albany** Indiana U.S.A.
110 L5 **Albany** Kentucky U.S.A.
111 F11 **Albany** Louisiana U.S.A.
110 B1 **Albany** Missouri U.S.A.
95 O4 **Albany** New York U.S.A.
94 E7 **Albany** Ohio U.S.A.
100 B5 **Albany** Oregon U.S.A.
109 H3 **Albany** Texas U.S.A.
95 P2 **Albany** Vermont U.S.A.
101 T8 **Albany** Wyoming U.S.A.
141 J7 **Albany Downs** Queensland Australia
133 D4 **Albardón** Argentina
45 K1 **Albaredo d'Adige** Italy
40 B6 **Albarine** *R* France
17 F4 **Albarracín, Sa. de** *mt* Spain
141 F2 **Albatross B** Queensland Australia
126 G6 **Albatross Bank** Caribbean
32 K9 **Albaxen** Germany
71 F4 **Albay Gulf** Luzon Philippines
40 H2 **Albbruck** Germany
112 G2 **Albemarle** North Carolina U.S.A.
112 L1 **Albemarle Sound** North Carolina U.S.A.
44 D3 **Albenga** Italy
100 J1 **Albeni Falls Dam** Idaho U.S.A.
16 E4 **Alberche** *R* Spain
130 B10 **Alberdi** Paraguay
18 G10 **Albéres** *mts* France
138 D2 **Alberga** South Australia Australia
16 B4 **Albergaria a Valha** Portugal
17 G5 **Alberique** Spain
117 L11 **Alberni** British Columbia Canada
32 K4 **Albersdorf** Germany
140 E4 **Albert** *R* Queensland Australia
122 H8 **Albert** New Brunswick Canada
22 D3 **Albert** France
107 L3 **Albert** Kansas U.S.A.
114 H7 **Alberta** *prov* Canada
118 D5 **Alberta** Canada
111 J9 **Alberta** Alabama U.S.A.
94 K10 **Alberta** Virginia U.S.A.
117 P9 **Alberta,Mt** Alberta Canada
48 F3 **Albertirsa** Hungary
22 J1 **Albert Kanaal** Belgium
138 E6 **Albert, L** South Australia Australia
86 F5 **Albert, L** Uganda/Zaire
100 E7 **Albert, L** Oregon U.S.A.
86 F5 **Albert Nile** *R* Uganda
122 H7 **Alberton** Prince Edward I Canada
126 G3 **Albert Town** Long Cay Bahamas
127 K2 **Albert Town** Jamaica
144 B6 **Albert Town** New Zealand
Albertville *see* **Kalémié**
119 M5 **Albertville** Saskatchewan Canada
40 D6 **Albertville** France
48 L6 **Albeşti** Romania
36 B6 **Albestroff** France
45 L1 **Albettone** Italy
18 G9 **Albi** France
99 O8 **Albia** Iowa U.S.A.
45 L1 **Albignásego** Italy
98 B8 **Albin** Wyoming U.S.A.
129 H2 **Albina** Suriname
45 J2 **Albinea** Italy
102 A2 **Albion** California U.S.A.
101 M7 **Albion** Idaho U.S.A.
110 H3 **Albion** Illinois U.S.A.
94 B5 **Albion** Indiana U.S.A.
99 O7 **Albion** Iowa U.S.A.
94 C4 **Albion** Michigan U.S.A.
98 B4 **Albion** Montana U.S.A.
98 H8 **Albion** Nebraska U.S.A.
94 J3 **Albion** New York U.S.A.
110 A7 **Albion** Oklahoma U.S.A.
94 G5 **Albion** Pennsylvania U.S.A.
44 E3 **Albisola Marina** Italy
44 D3 **Albisola Superior** Italy
44 D3 **Albissola-Marina** Italy
25 C5 **Alblasserdam** Netherlands
17 H4 **Albocácer** Spain
27 J15 **Alböke** Sweden
43 C8 **Albo,M** Sardinia
17 G5 **Alboraya** Spain
Ålborg *co see* **Nordjylland** *co*
28 D2 **Ålborg** Denmark
99 O3 **Alborn** Minnesota U.S.A.
17 F7 **Albox** Spain
117 O9 **Albreda** British Columbia Canada
8 D2 **Albrighton** England
141 H6 **Albro** Queensland Australia
36 G7 **Albstadt-Ebingen** Germany
16 B7 **Albufeira** Portugal
17 G5 **Albufera** *L* Spain
41 L4 **Albula Pass** Switzerland
37 J1 **Albungen** Germany
16 E8 **Albuñol** Spain
130 B6 **Albuquerque** Brazil
106 D6 **Albuquerque** New Mexico U.S.A.
84 F3 **Al Burayqah** Libya
95 O2 **Alburg** Vermont U.S.A.
43 G8 **Alburno, Monte** Italy
16 C5 **Alburquerque** Spain
139 H6 **Albury** Victoria Australia
144 C6 **Albury** New Zealand
6 M6 **Albuskjell** *oil rig* North Sea
19 Q13 **Alby** France
26 H9 **Alby** Sweden
16 B6 **Alcacer do Sal** Portugal
17 H4 **Alcalá de Chisvert** Spain
16 D7 **Alcalá de Guadaira** Spain
17 G5 **Alcalá del Júcar** Spain
16 D8 **Alcalá de los Gazules** Spain
16 E7 **Alcala la Real** Spain
131 B2 **Alcalde, Pta** *C* Chile
43 E11 **Alcamo** Sicily
17 G3 **Alcanadre** *R* Spain
17 H4 **Alcanar** Spain
16 C3 **Alcañices** Spain
17 G3 **Alcañiz** Spain
16 C5 **Alcántara** Spain
16 C5 **Alcántara, Embalse de** *res* Spain
17 G7 **Alcantarilla** Spain
130 D5 **Alcantilado** Brazil
17 F6 **Alcaraz** Spain
17 F6 **Alcaraz, Sa. de** *mts* Spain
16 E7 **Alcaudete** Spain
16 E5 **Alcázar de San Juan** Spain
9 E3 **Alcester** England
98 K6 **Alcester** South Dakota U.S.A.
17 G5 **Alcira** Spain
111 C10 **Alco** Louisiana U.S.A.
112 D2 **Alcoa** Tennessee U.S.A.
129 L7 **Alcobaça** Brazil
16 B5 **Alcobaca** Portugal
17 F3 **Alcolea del Pinar** Spain
112 G4 **Alcolu** South Carolina U.S.A.
118 D5 **Alcomdale** Alberta Canada
118 L1 **Alcona** Ontario Canada
9 F3 **Alconbury Hill** England
140 C6 **Alcoota** N Terr Australia
17 G4 **Alcora** Spain
17 G4 **Alcorisa** Spain
101 T7 **Alcova** Wyoming U.S.A.
17 G6 **Alcoy** Spain
17 G3 **Alcubbiere, Sa. de** *mt* Spain
83 G5 **Aldabra Is** Seychelles Indian Oc
124 G3 **Aldama** Mexico
51 M3 **Aldan** Russian Federation
51 M3 **Aldanskoye Nagorye** Russian Federation
9 E5 **Aldbourne** England
13 H6 **Aldbrough** England
16 C3 **Aldeadávila de la Ribera** Spain
9 H3 **Aldeburgh** England
107 M3 **Alden** Kansas U.S.A.
94 B2 **Alden** Michigan U.S.A.
94 J4 **Alden** New York U.S.A.
25 F7 **Aldenhoven** Germany
9 H3 **Alde,R** England
106 D3 **Alder** Colorado U.S.A.
101 N4 **Alder** Montana U.S.A.
14 E2 **Aldergrove** N Ireland
100 C3 **Alder L** Washington U.S.A.
9 E5 **Aldermaston** England
145 F2 **Aldermen Is, The** New Zealand
20 F2 **Alderney** *isld* Channel Is
102 C6 **Alder Pk** California U.S.A.
101 M4 **Alder Pk** Montana U.S.A.
102 A1 **Alderpoint** California U.S.A.
9 F5 **Aldershot** England
28 D4 **Alderslyst** Denmark
118 F8 **Alderson** Alberta Canada
94 G9 **Alderson** West Virginia U.S.A.
118 D8 **Aldersyde** Alberta Canada
8 D1 **Aldford** England
9 E4 **Aldsworth** England
28 D5 **Åle** Denmark
99 Q8 **Aledo** Illinois U.S.A.
85 B5 **Aleg** Mauritania
130 B5 **Alegra** *R* Brazil
130 F6 **Alegre** Brazil
133 F3 **Alegrete** Brazil
106 B7 **Alegros Mt** New Mexico U.S.A.
133 A9 **Alejandro Selkirk** *isld* Juan Fernández Is Pacific Oc
116 H7 **Aleknagik** Alaska U.S.A.
54 E8 **Aleksandriya** Ukraine
54 M3 **Aleksandro-Nevskiy** Russian Federation
52 E6 **Aleksandrov** Russian Federation
48 G6 **Aleksandrovac** Serbia Yugoslavia
53 G8 **Aleksandrov Gay** Russian Federation
52 J5 **Aleksandrovsk** Russian Federation
58 G1 **Aleksandrovskiy Zavod** Russian Federation
53 F11 **Aleksandrovskoye** Russian Federation
59 M1 **Aleksandrovsk Sakhalinskiy** Russian Federation
31 L4 **Aleksandrów** Poland
31 L3 **Aleksandrów Kujawski** Poland
147 K11 **Aleksandry, Zemlya** Russian Federation
55 E4 **Alekseyevka** Kazakhstan
56 G2 **Alekseyevsk** Russian Federation
53 F8 **Alekseyevskaya** Russian Federation
54 F1 **Alekseyevskoye** Russian Federation
53 F8 **Aleksikovskiy** Russian Federation
54 J2 **Aleksin** Russian Federation
46 E1 **Aleksinac** Serbia Yugoslavia
27 F14 **Älekulla** Sweden
27 H15 **Ålem** Sweden
106 C9 **Aleman** New Mexico U.S.A.
133 D3 **Alemania** Argentina
47 N10 **Alemdağ** Turkey
47 N10 **Alemdağ Ormanı** *forest* Turkey
129 K8 **Alem Paraíba** Brazil
21 L5 **Alençon** France
21 L5 **Alençon, Campagne d'** *plain* France
129 H4 **Alenquer** Brazil
16 A5 **Alenquer** Portugal
102 V13 **Alenuihaha Chan** Hawaiian Is
76 C6 **Aleppey** India
Aleppo *see* **Halab**
115 N1 **Alert** Northwest Territories Canada
128 D6 **Alerta** Peru
117 K10 **Alert Bay** British Columbia Canada
18 H8 **Alès** France
43 B9 **Ales** Sardinia
48 G3 **Aleşd** Romania
52 G2 **Alëshki** Russian Federation
26 K3 **Alesjaure** *L* Sweden
44 D1 **Alessandria** *prov* Italy
44 E2 **Alessándria** Italy
Alessio *see* **Lezhë**
28 C3 **Ålestrup** Denmark
26 B9 **Ålesund** Norway
18 G10 **Alet** France
116 L10 **Aleutian Is** Alaska U.S.A.
116 H8 **Aleutian Ra** Alaska U.S.A.
107 N7 **Alex** Oklahoma U.S.A.
137 Q4 **Alexa Bank** Pacific Oc
21 J5 **Alexain** France
119 R9 **Alexander** Manitoba Canada
80 C4 **Alexander** Israel
107 L3 **Alexander** Kansas U.S.A.
98 C2 **Alexander** North Dakota U.S.A.
117 E7 **Alexander Archipelago** Alaska U.S.A.
87 C11 **Alexander B** S Africa
111 L9 **Alexander City** Alabama U.S.A.
146 C5 **Alexander Island** Antarctica
140 D2 **Alexander, Mt** N Terr Australia
142 B6 **Alexander, Mt** W Australia Australia
143 D8 **Alexander, Mt** W Australia Australia
140 F4 **Alexandra** *R* Queensland Australia
144 B6 **Alexandra** New Zealand
131 H6 **Alexandra,C** S Georgia
117 P5 **Alexandra Falls** Northwest Territories Canada
147 G6 **Alexandra Fiord** Northwest Territories Canada
140 D4 **Alexandria** N Terr Australia
117 M9 **Alexandria** British Columbia Canada
121 Q7 **Alexandria** Ontario Canada
79 A7 **Alexandria** Egypt
84 H3 **Alexandria** Egypt
127 K2 **Alexandria** Jamaica
46 G1 **Alexandria** Romania
89 E9 **Alexandria** S Africa
12 D2 **Alexandria** Scotland
110 L1 **Alexandria** Indiana U.S.A.
110 M3 **Alexandria** Kentucky U.S.A.
111 D10 **Alexandria** Louisiana U.S.A.
99 L4 **Alexandria** Minnesota U.S.A.
110 E1 **Alexandria** Missouri U.S.A.
98 J9 **Alexandria** Nebraska U.S.A.
98 J6 **Alexandria** South Dakota U.S.A.
110 K5 **Alexandria** Tennessee U.S.A.
95 K8 **Alexandria** Virginia U.S.A.
95 M2 **Alexandria Bay** New York U.S.A.
138 E6 **Alexandrina, L** South Australia Australia
144 C5 **Alexandrina, L** New Zealand
80 E5 **Alexandrium** Jordan
78 A1 **Alexandroúpolis** Greece
99 Q8 **Alexis** Illinois U.S.A.
115 O7 **Alexis B** Labrador, Nfld Canada
33 O9 **Alexisbad** Germany
117 M9 **Alexis Creek** British Columbia Canada
123 P1 **Alexis R** Labrador, Nfld Canada
118 B6 **Alexo** Alberta Canada
79 F5 **'Aley** Lebanon
56 B4 **Aley** *R* Russian Federation
56 B5 **Aleysk** Russian Federation
36 B3 **Alf** *R* Germany
36 C3 **Alf** Germany
17 G4 **Alfambra** *R* Spain
128 C4 **Alfaro** Ecuador
17 F2 **Alfaro** Spain
47 J1 **Alfatar** Bulgaria
32 L9 **Alfeld** Germany
37 M5 **Alfeld** Germany
130 F7 **Alfenas** Brazil
55 G4 **Alferovka** Russian Federation
32 G8 **Alfhausen** Germany
45 M3 **Alfonsine** Italy
9 G1 **Alford** England
15 F3 **Alford** Scotland
111 L11 **Alford** Florida U.S.A.
26 A10 **Ålfotbreen** *gla* Norway
95 R3 **Alfred** Maine U.S.A.
98 G3 **Alfred** North Dakota U.S.A.
143 F6 **Alfred and Marie Ra** W Australia Australia
81 M14 **Alfred-Fauré, Base** *France Base* Crozet Is Indian Oc
130 H7 **Alfredo Chaves** Brazil
145 E4 **Alfredton** New Zealand
9 E1 **Alfreton** England
9 G6 **Alfriston** England
27 H10 **Alfta** Sweden
36 C2 **Alfter** Germany
55 C6 **Alga** Kazakhstan
27 A13 **Ålgård** Norway
133 D5 **Algarrobo del Aguila** Argentina
16 B7 **Algarve** *prov* Portugal
53 F7 **Algasovo** Russian Federation
57 F3 **Algatart** Kazakhstan
16 D8 **Algeciras** Spain
85 E1 **Alger** Algeria
94 C2 **Alger** Michigan U.S.A.
94 D6 **Alger** Ohio U.S.A.
84 B4 **Algeria** *rep* N Africa
43 B8 **Alghero** Sardinia
27 H14 **Älghult** Sweden
Algiers *see* **Alger**
111 J12 **Algiers** New Orleans, Louisiana U.S.A.
17 G5 **Alginet** Spain
89 D9 **Algoa B** S Africa
130 H10 **Algodões** Brazil
106 D6 **Algodones** New Mexico U.S.A.
16 E5 **Algodor** *R* Spain
120 H6 **Algoma** Ontario Canada
100 D7 **Algoma** Oregon U.S.A.
99 T5 **Algoma** Wisconsin U.S.A.
99 M6 **Algona** Iowa U.S.A.
121 M7 **Algonquin Park** Ontario Canada
110 L5 **Algood** Tennessee U.S.A.
22 L5 **Algrange** France
26 J7 **Älgsjön** Sweden
68 B5 **Alguada Reef** Burma
17 F2 **Alhama** *R* Spain
78 G5 **Al Ḩamād** *reg* Jordan/Saudi Arabia
17 F3 **Alhama de Aragón** Spain
16 E7 **Alhama de Granada** Spain
17 F7 **Alhama de Murcia** Spain
17 F8 **Alhamilla, Sa** *mt* Spain
84 E4 **Al Ḩammādah al Ḩamrā'** *plateau* Libya
78 G3 **Al Hishah** Syria
16 E9 **Al Hoceima** Morocco
16 E9 **Al Hoceima, B d'** Morocco
79 E9 **Al Ḩumayḑah** Egypt
84 G4 **Al Ḩumaymāt** Libya
26 B10 **Ålhus** Norway
57 E6 **'Alīābād** Afghanistan
17 G4 **Aliaga** Spain
47 H6 **Aliağa** Turkey
46 E4 **Aliákmon** *R* Greece
71 N9 **Aliambata** Indonesia
74 F9 **Alībāg** India
74 E9 **Alibagh** India
47 M10 **Alibey** *R* Turkey
48 M5 **Alibey,Oz** *L* Ukraine
71 F4 **Alibijaban** Luzon Philippines
86 G4 **Ālībo** Ethiopia
48 F5 **Alibunar** Serbia Yugoslavia
46 F3 **Ali Butús** *mt* Greece
124 F5 **Alicama** Mexico
17 G6 **Alicante** *prov* Spain
17 G6 **Alicante** Spain
141 F3 **Alice** *R* Queensland Australia
141 H6 **Alice** Queensland Australia
98 J3 **Alice** North Dakota U.S.A.
109 J8 **Alice** Texas U.S.A.
117 J8 **Alice Arm** British Columbia Canada
142 G4 **Alice Downs** W Australia Australia
100 H4 **Alicel** Oregon U.S.A.
43 H9 **Alice,Pta** Italy
126 E6 **Alice Shoal** Caribbean
140 C6 **Alice Springs** N Terr Australia
113 H12 **Alice Town** Bahamas
126 E2 **Alice Town** Bimini Is Bahamas
111 H8 **Aliceville** Alabama U.S.A.
140 C6 **Alice Well** N Terr Australia
71 F7 **Alicia** Mindanao Philippines
110 E6 **Alicia** Arkansas U.S.A.
141 F5 **Alick** *R* Queensland Australia
43 F10 **Alicudi, I** Italy
119 Q9 **Alida** Saskatchewan Canada
45 Q7 **Alife** Italy
74 H5 **Aligarh** India
77 A3 **Alīgudarz** Iran
Alihe *see* **Oroqen Zizhiqi**
59 H1 **A-li-ho** China
77 L3 **Alī Kheyl** Afghanistan
52 G6 **Alikovo** Russian Federation
86 B6 **Alima** *R* Congo
125 M3 **Alimicamba** Nicaragua
47 U17 **Alimniá** *isld* Greece
71 F5 **Alimodian** Philippines
71 E7 **Alimpaya Pt** Mindanao Philippines
86 D4 **Alindao** Cent Afr Republic
70 F5 **Alindau** Sulawesi Indonesia
107 M5 **Aline** Oklahoma U.S.A.
138 D2 **Alinerta,Mt** South Australia Australia
77 L2 **Alingar** *R* Afghanistan
66 C5 **Aling Kangri** *mt* China
27 F14 **Alingsås** Sweden
94 G6 **Aliquippa** Pennsylvania U.S.A.
124 D2 **Alisos** *R* Mexico
46 F3 **Alistáti** Greece
116 K8 **Alitak B** Alaska U.S.A.
46 G6 **Alivérion** Greece
89 E8 **Aliwal North** S Africa
118 D6 **Alix** Alberta Canada
80 G7 **Aliyan** Jordan
Al Jawf *see* **Al Khufrah**
16 B7 **Aljezur** Portugal
80 G2 **Al Jukhadar** Syria
16 B7 **Aljustrel** Portugal
100 F8 **Alkali L** Nevada U.S.A.
22 J2 **Alken** Belgium
84 G5 **Al Khufrah** Libya
25 C3 **Alkmaar** Netherlands
95 R6 **Allagash** Maine U.S.A.
95 R7 **Allagash L** Maine U.S.A.
75 J6 **Allahabad** India
21 O5 **Allaines-Mervilliers** France
21 O5 **Allainville** France
20 F6 **Allaire** France
83 L9 **Allai Tank** *L* Sri Lanka
103 J9 **All American Can** California U.S.A.
108 C4 **Allamoore** Texas U.S.A.
118 L7 **Allan** Saskatchewan Canada
19 N16 **Allan** France
80 G2 **'Allan** *R* Syria
83 M9 **Allan Pt** Christmas I Indian Oc
89 E6 **Allanridge** S Africa
84 J5 **Allaqi,Radi** Egypt
121 N3 **Allard** *R* Quebec Canada
122 G6 **Allardville** New Brunswick Canada
16 B2 **Allariz** Spain
36 C7 **Allarmont** France
112 C3 **Allatoona Res** Georgia U.S.A.
22 H4 **Alle** Belgium
94 B4 **Allegan** Michigan U.S.A.
94 J4 **Allegany** New York U.S.A.
94 H5 **Allegheny** *R* Pennsylvania U.S.A.
94 E10 **Allegheny Mts** U.S.A.
94 H5 **Allegheny Res** Pennsylvania U.S.A.
127 M4 **Allègre, Pte** Guadeloupe W Indies
19 O17 **Alleins** France
111 F12 **Allemands** Louisiana U.S.A.
89 E7 **Allemanskraal Dam** *res* S Africa
19 Q14 **Allemont** France
71 G4 **Allen** Philippines
94 E9 **Allen** Kentucky U.S.A.
98 K7 **Allen** Nebraska U.S.A.
109 L1 **Allen** Oklahoma U.S.A.
98 E6 **Allen** South Dakota U.S.A.
109 L2 **Allen** Texas U.S.A.
14 D3 **Allen, Bog of** Ireland
112 F4 **Allendale** South Carolina U.S.A.
13 F4 **Allendale Town** England
125 J3 **Allende** Mexico
32 G10 **Allendorf** Germany
32 L10 **Allendorf** Germany
36 F1 **Allendorf** Germany
36 F2 **Allendorf** Germany
120 J8 **Allenford** Ontario Canada
13 F4 **Allenheads** England
119 M7 **Allen Hills** Saskatchewan Canada
14 C2 **Allen,L** Ireland
144 A7 **Allen, Mt** New Zealand
116 Q5 **Allen,Mt** Alaska U.S.A.
106 E1 **Allenspark** Colorado U.S.A.
31 J7 **Allensteig** Austria
95 Q3 **Allenstown** New Hampshire U.S.A.
110 J5 **Allensville** Kentucky U.S.A.
95 M6 **Allentown** Pennsylvania U.S.A.
33 M7 **Aller** *R* Germany
22 K3 **Allerborn** Luxembourg
36 E6 **Allerheiligen** Germany
37 L5 **Allersberg** Germany
28 J6 **Allerslev** Denmark
110 C1 **Allerton** Iowa U.S.A.
29 K4 **Allerum** Sweden
21 O2 **Allery** France
40 D7 **Allevard** France
127 K3 **Alley,The** Jamaica
109 L6 **Alleyton** Texas U.S.A.
41 M3 **Allgäuer Alpen** *mts* Austria/Germany
8 D1 **Allgreave** England
9 G5 **Allhallows** England
118 F6 **Alliance** Alberta Canada
98 D7 **Alliance** Nebraska U.S.A.
94 F6 **Alliance** Ohio U.S.A.
18 H6 **Allier** *R* France
18 H6 **Allier** *dept* France
145 E4 **Alligator Headland** New Zealand
127 J3 **Alligator Pond** Jamaica
112 L2 **Alligator R** North Carolina U.S.A.
140 C2 **Alligator R., E** N Terr Australia
113 G13 **Alligator Reef** Florida U.S.A.
28 D4 **Alling** Denmark
37 M6 **Alling** Germany
28 E4 **Alling Å** *R* Denmark
28 E4 **Allingåbro** Denmark
99 O7 **Allison** Iowa U.S.A.
117 K10 **Allison Harbour** British Columbia Canada
12 E1 **Alloa** Scotland
21 P7 **Allogny** France
13 E4 **Allonby** England
80 G1 **Alloné HaBashan** Syria
80 D2 **Allon HaGalil** Israel
80 D3 **Allonim** Israel
21 K8 **Allonne** Deux Sèvres France
21 P3 **Allonne** Oise France
21 O5 **Allonnes** Eure-et-Loir France
21 L7 **Allonnes** Maine-et-Loire France
80 D7 **Allon Shevut** Jordan
141 K8 **Allora** Queensland Australia
143 E7 **Allott, Mt** W Australia Australia
99 S2 **Allouez** Michigan U.S.A.
12 D3 **Alloway** Scotland
33 O10 **Allstedt** Germany
70 F7 **Allu** Sulawesi Indonesia
Alluitsup Paa *see* **Sydprøven**
121 N7 **Allumette I** Quebec Canada
121 R4 **Ally** Quebec Canada
38 J6 **Alm** *R* Austria
38 G7 **Alm** Austria
122 H8 **Alma** New Brunswick Canada

121 T4 Alma Quebec Canada
110 B6 Alma Arkansas U.S.A.
106 D2 Alma Colorado U.S.A.
112 E6 Alma Georgia U.S.A.
107 O2 Alma Kansas U.S.A.
94 C3 Alma Michigan U.S.A.
110 C2 Alma Missouri U.S.A.
98 G9 Alma Nebraska U.S.A.
99 P5 Alma Wisconsin U.S.A.
57 H3 Alma-Ata Kazakhstan
16 A6 Almada Portugal
141 G3 Almaden Queensland Australia
16 D6 Almadén Spain
16 D6 Almadén, Sa. de mts Spain
80 F2 Almagor Israel
71 G5 Almagro isld Philippines
48 G6 Almăjului Muntii mts Romania
84 F4 Al Malāqī well Libya
57 E4 Almalyk Uzbekistan
102 C1 Almanor, L California U.S.A.
17 G6 Almansa Spain
16 D2 Almanza Spain
117 K7 Alma Peak British Columbia Canada
17 F3 Almarza Spain
48 H3 Almaş R Romania
130 E4 Almas, R das Brazil
17 F3 Almazán Spain
57 E4 Almazar Uzbekistan
54 K8 Almaznaya Ukraine
56 H1 Almaznyy Russian Federation
27 H12 Almby Sweden
32 J9 Alme R Germany
27 H15 Älmeboda Sweden
100 B7 Almeda Oregon U.S.A.
129 H4 Almeirim Brazil
16 B5 Almeirim Portugal
25 G4 Almelo Netherlands
107 L2 Almena Kansas U.S.A.
129 K7 Almenara Brazil
17 F7 Almenara, Sa. de mt Spain
17 F3 Almenar de Soria Spain
16 C3 Almendra, Embalse de res Spain
16 C6 Almendralejo Spain
21 L4 Alménêches France
55 D4 Al'menevo Russian Federation
8 D6 Almer England
25 D4 Almere Netherlands
25 D4 Almere-Haven Netherlands
17 F7 Almería prov Spain
17 F8 Almería Spain
98 G8 Almeria Nebraska U.S.A.
17 F8 Almería,G.de Spain
52 H7 Al'met'yevsk Russian Federation
27 G15 Älmhult Sweden
16 E8 Almijara, Sierra de mts Spain
28 C5 Almind Vejle Denmark
28 C4 Almind Viborg Denmark
100 G2 Almira Washington U.S.A.
130 E9 Almirante Tamandaré Brazil
46 G6 Almiropótamos Greece
46 F5 Almirós Greece
46 G9 Almiroú Kólpos G Crete Greece
101 M7 Almo Idaho U.S.A.
16 B7 Almodôvar Portugal
16 E6 Almodóvar del Campo Spain
17 F5 Almodóvar del Pinar Spain
133 D3 Almogasta Argentina
94 K4 Almond New York U.S.A.
99 R5 Almond Wisconsin U.S.A.
15 E4 Almond,R Scotland
8 D4 Almondsbury England
106 D3 Almont Colorado U.S.A.
94 D4 Almont Michigan U.S.A.
98 E3 Almont North Dakota U.S.A.
121 O7 Almonte Ontario Canada
16 C5 Almonte R Spain
74 H4 Almora India
16 E4 Almorox Spain
100 H3 Almota Washington U.S.A.
27 G15 Almundsryd Sweden
16 E8 Almuñécar Spain
27 H14 Almvik Sweden
101 P8 Almy Wyoming U.S.A.
111 E7 Almyra Arkansas U.S.A.
13 G3 Aln Br England
15 D3 Alness Scotland
13 G3 Alnmouth England
26 J9 Alnö Sweden
13 G3 Alnwick England
137 R4 Alofi isld Îles de Horn Pacific Oc
137 T5 Alofi Niue Pacific Oc
94 C1 Aloha Michigan U.S.A.
68 B1 Alon Burma
139 H9 Alonnah Tasmania Australia
71 E5 Alonon Pt Philippines
119 T8 Alonsa Manitoba Canada
71 M9 Alor isld Indonesia
16 D8 Alora Spain
71 M8 Alor,Kep isld Indonesia
71 L9 Alor,Selat Indonesia
69 E9 Alor Setar Malaysia
16 C7 Alosno Spain
Alost see Aalst
143 G7 Aloysius, Mt W Australia Australia
52 D2 Alozero Russian Federation
133 E5 Alpachiri Argentina
38 E7 Alpbach Austria
19 Q14 Alpe d'Huez mt France
110 C5 Alpena Arkansas U.S.A.
94 D1 Alpena Michigan U.S.A.
98 H5 Alpena South Dakota U.S.A.
94 H8 Alpena West Virginia U.S.A.
17 G6 Alpera Spain
129 J5 Alpercatas, Serra das mts Brazil
19 K8 Alpes-de-Haute-Provence dept France
19 O15 Alpes du Dauphiné mts France
19 K9 Alpes-Maritime dept France
46 D2 Alpet mt Albania
44 C3 Alpet mt Italy
141 H6 Alpha Queensland Australia
99 Q8 Alpha Illinois U.S.A.
95 M6 Alpha New Jersey U.S.A.
94 J9 Alpha Virginia U.S.A.
25 C4 Alphen Netherlands
83 H5 Alphonse I Seychelles Indian Oc
16 B5 Alpiarça Portugal
44 B1 Alpignano Italy
103 P8 Alpine Arizona U.S.A.
108 D5 Alpine Texas U.S.A.
36 E7 Alpirsbach Germany
16 B7 Alportel,S Braz de Portugal
4 F7 Alps, The mt ra Europe
47 L5 Alpu Turkey
79 G3 Al Qadmūs Syria
22 B2 Alquines France
79 G4 Al Quşayr Syria
84 E3 Al Quşbāt Libya
79 G5 Al Quţayfah Syria
123 L6 Alright I Madeleine Is, Quebec Canada
28 E5 Alrø isld Denmark
140 D4 Alroy Downs N Terr Australia
28 E3 Als Denmark
28 D7 Als isld Denmark
19 K4 Alsace prov France
118 H7 Alsask Saskatchewan Canada
17 F2 Alsasua Spain
25 F7 Alsdorf Germany
100 B5 Alsea Oregon U.S.A.
117 E6 Alsek R British Columbia Canada
98 H1 Alsen North Dakota U.S.A.
36 D4 Alsenz Germany
110 F2 Alsey Illinois U.S.A.
36 G2 Alsfeld Germany
28 D6 Als Fjord inlet Denmark
36 E4 Alsheim Germany
26 J5 Alsjaur L Sweden
33 P9 Alsleben Germany
28 A5 Alslev Denmark
28 C6 Alslev Kro Denmark
28 F4 Ålsø Denmark
26 F6 Alstahaug Norway
32 E8 Alstätte Germany
95 P3 Alstead New Hampshire U.S.A.
26 F6 Alsten isld Norway
32 M5 Alster R Germany
13 F4 Alston England
27 M15 Alsunga Latvia
26 N2 Alta Norway
101 L4 Alta Montana U.S.A.
26 N2 Altaelv R Norway
26 N1 Altafjord inlet Norway
131 D3 Alta Gracia Argentina
127 J9 Altagracía Venezuela
128 E2 Altagracia de Orituco Venezuela
109 L6 Altair Texas U.S.A.
128 E7 Altamachí Bolivia
112 E6 Altamaha R Georgia U.S.A.
133 E4 Alta Melincué Argentina
129 H4 Altamira Brazil
125 N9 Altamirano Mexico
102 C4 Altamont California U.S.A.
110 H2 Altamont Illinois U.S.A.
100 D7 Altamont Oregon U.S.A.
98 K5 Altamont South Dakota U.S.A.
110 L6 Altamont Tennessee U.S.A.
101 P8 Altamont Wyoming U.S.A.
144 B6 Alta, Mt New Zealand
43 H8 Altamura Italy
65 B2 Altan Bulag China
56 E6 Altanbulag Mongolia
124 D2 Altar Mexico
118 G7 Altario Alberta Canada
124 F5 Altata Mexico
45 R7 Altavilla Irpina Italy
99 O6 Alta Vista Iowa U.S.A.
107 O3 Alta Vista Kansas U.S.A.
94 H9 Altavista Virginia U.S.A.
66 D2 Altay China
58 C2 Altay Mongolia
56 C5 Altay mts Russian Federation
56 C5 Altayskiy Russian Federation
56 B5 Altayskiy Kray terr Russian Federation
37 L5 Altdorf Germany
37 N6 Altdorf Niederbayern Germany
41 J4 Altdorf Switzerland
17 G6 Altea Spain
33 O6 Alte Elde R Germany
32 H5 Alte Mellum Germany
36 B3 Altenahr Germany
33 M9 Altenau Germany
32 J9 Altenbeken Germany
32 F8 Altenberge Germany
32 J5 Altenbruch Germany
37 N2 Altenburg Germany
37 M7 Altenerding Germany
36 C4 Altenglan Germany
36 E1 Altenhundem Germany
36 D2 Altenkirchen Germany
38 L6 Altenmarkt Ober Österreich Austria
38 H7 Altenmarkt Salzburg Austria
37 P6 Altenmarkt Germany
33 N6 Alten Medingen Germany
36 H6 Altenstadt Baden-Württemberg Germany
36 F3 Altenstadt Hessen Germany
36 F6 Altensteig Germany
33 S5 Altentreptow Germany
32 J5 Altenwalde Germany
16 B5 Alter do Chão Portugal
33 R8 Altes Lager Germany
26 K3 Altevatn L Norway
111 L11 Altha Florida U.S.A.
37 J6 Altheim Germany
111 E7 Altheimer Arkansas U.S.A.
38 K8 Althofen Austria
9 G4 Althorne England
13 H6 Althorpe England
138 D6 Althorpe Is South Australia Australia
139 G3 Altiboullin, L New South Wales Australia
45 M1 Altino Italy
47 H5 Altınoluk Turkey
47 L5 Altıntaş Turkey
47 K8 Altınyala Turkey
33 O6 Alt-Jabel Germany
19 K5 Altkirch France
33 T7 Altlandsberg Germany
36 E5 Altleiningen Germany
37 M6 Altmannstein Germany
95 L3 Altmar New York U.S.A.
33 O7 Altmark reg Germany
36 H1 Altmorschen Germany
37 K5 Altmühl R Germany
32 K7 Altmühlen Germany
15 D2 Altnaharra Scotland
111 A10 Alto Texas U.S.A.
16 B6 Alto Alentejo prov Portugal
130 D5 Alto Araguaia Brazil
126 G4 Alto Cedro Cuba
130 C4 Alto Coité Brazil
130 D5 Alto Garças Brazil
87 G9 Alto Molocue Mozambique
44 D3 Alto,Monte Italy
37 L7 Altomünster Germany
9 F5 Alton England
102 A1 Alton California U.S.A.
110 F3 Alton Illinois U.S.A.
95 L3 Alton New York U.S.A.
103 M4 Alton Utah U.S.A.
118 D1 Altona Manitoba Canada
99 Q8 Altona Illinois U.S.A.
101 P9 Altonah Utah U.S.A.
138 E2 Alton Downs South Australia Australia
141 J8 Alton Oilfield Queensland Australia
111 K7 Altoona Alabama U.S.A.
113 F9 Altoona Florida U.S.A.
107 P4 Altoona Kansas U.S.A.
94 J6 Altoona Pennsylvania U.S.A.
128 G8 Alto Paraguay dept Paraguay
130 C9 Alto Paraná dept Paraguay
129 J5 Alto Parnaiba Brazil
45 J4 Altopascio Italy
129 H7 Alto Sucuriú Brazil
38 G5 Altötting Germany
129 J4 Alto Turi Brazil
130 C10 Alto Uruguai Brazil
126 A1 Alto Vista hill Aruba W Indies
13 F6 Altrincham England
33 R7 Altruppin Germany
33 T8 Alt-Schadow Germany
54 F4 Altukhovo Russian Federation
78 K4 Altun Köprü Iraq
66 C4 Altun Shan mts China
99 O5 Altura Minnesota U.S.A.
100 E8 Alturas California U.S.A.
113 F10 Alturas Florida U.S.A.
107 L7 Altus Oklahoma U.S.A.
107 L6 Altus Res Oklahoma U.S.A.
41 M2 Altusried Germany
36 B6 Altwiller France
57 C2 Altynasar Kazakhstan
55 D3 Altynay Russian Federation
53 G10 Altyn-Khutsan, Ozero Russian Federation
52 C6 Alūksne Latvia
28 D4 Alum Denmark
9 E6 Alum Bay England
133 C5 Aluminé Argentina
26 M6 Ålund Sweden
27 K11 Alunda Sweden
103 K6 Alunite Nevada U.S.A.
76 C3 Alur India
53 D11 Alushta Ukraine
17 F4 Alustante Spain
83 J11 Alutgama Sri Lanka
83 K9 Alut Oya Sri Lanka
Aluva see Alwaye
84 E4 Al 'Uwaynāt Libya
16 B4 Alva R Portugal
12 E1 Alva Scotland
113 F11 Alva Florida U.S.A.
94 D10 Alva Kentucky U.S.A.
107 M5 Alva Oklahoma U.S.A.
98 B5 Alva Wyoming U.S.A.
16 B7 Alvalade Portugal
125 M8 Alvarado Mexico
109 K3 Alvarado Texas U.S.A.
128 F4 Alvaraes Brazil
26 E9 Alvdal Norway
118 L6 Alvena Saskatchewan Canada
33 O8 Alvensleben Germany
32 K8 Alverdissen Germany
117 D5 Alverstone Mt Alaska/Yukon Terr U.S.A./Canada
27 A11 Alversund Norway
27 G15 Alvesta Sweden
8 D4 Alveston England
27 G10 Älvho Sweden
110 J1 Alvin Illinois U.S.A.
109 M6 Alvin Texas U.S.A.
99 S4 Alvin Wisconsin U.S.A.
45 P6 Alvito Italy
16 B6 Alvito Portugal
27 J11 Älvkarleby Sweden
98 K9 Alvo Nebraska U.S.A.
109 K2 Alvord Texas U.S.A.
100 G7 Alvord L Oregon U.S.A.
26 F10 Älvros Sweden
27 F14 Älvsborg reg Sweden
26 M6 Älvsbyn Sweden
27 F14 Älvsered Sweden
99 M2 Alvwood Minnesota U.S.A.
78 H6 Al Wadyān reg Iraq/Saudi Arabia
84 G4 Al Wāḩah Libya
87 E12 Alwal Nth S Africa
74 G5 Alwar India
76 C5 Alwaye India
13 F3 Alwinton England
6 M2 Alwyn oil rig North Sea
110 C7 Aly Arkansas U.S.A.
140 D2 Alyangula N Terr Australia
51 N2 Alyaskitovyy Russian Federation
55 E2 Alymka R Russian Federation
15 E4 Alyth Scotland
31 P1 Alytus Lithuania
38 G5 Alz R Germany
98 B4 Alzada Montana U.S.A.
36 G3 Alzenau Germany
22 L4 Alzette R Luxembourg
36 E4 Alzey Germany
128 F2 Amacuro Delta Venezuela
140 B6 Amadeus,L N Terr Australia
86 F4 Amadi Sudan
115 M4 Amadjuak L Northwest Territories Canada
60 J11 Amagasaki Japan
29 K5 Amager isld Denmark
60 D12 Amagi Japan
61 N11 Amagi-san mt Japan
22 G5 Amagne France
21 L4 Amain, Mt. d' France
116 F9 Amak I Alaska U.S.A.
60 C13 Amakusa-nada sea Japan
60 D13 Amakusa-Shimo-shima isld Japan
60 D13 Amakusa-shotō islds Japan
84 G4 Āmāl Libya
27 F12 Åmål Sweden
76 F2 Amalapuram India
43 F8 Amalfi Italy
46 E7 Amaliás Greece
16 C5 Amalia,Sta Spain
74 F8 Amalner India
129 G8 Amambai Brazil
130 C8 Amambaí, Serra de mts Brazil/Paraguay
130 C8 Amambay dept Paraguay
133 F2 Amambay, Sa. de mts Brazil/Paraguay
128 F4 Amaná,L Brazil
40 D2 Amance France
40 D3 Amancey France
94 E7 Amanda Ohio U.S.A.
42 E6 Amandola Italy
55 E6 Amangel'dy Kazakhstan
55 D4 Amankaragay Kazakhstan
60 J10 Amano-hashidate inlet Japan
43 G9 Amantea Italy
55 E5 Amantogay Kazakhstan
87 F12 Amanzimtoti S Africa
129 H3 Amapa Brazil
78 L6 Amārah, Al Iraq
88 F9 Amaramba,L Mozambique
129 K5 Amarante Brazil
119 T8 Amaranth Manitoba Canada
68 C2 Amarapura Burma
102 H5 Amargosa Ra California U.S.A.
106 D5 Amarilla New Mexico U.S.A.
108 C8 Amarillo Texas U.S.A.
131 B4 Amarillo,Cerro pk Argentina
75 J7 Amarkantak India
129 J6 Amaro Leite Brazil
140 E6 Amaroo,L Queensland Australia
61 N7 Amarume Japan
80 D8 'Amasa Jordan
99 S3 Amasa Michigan U.S.A.
45 O7 Amaseno Italy
85 B3 Amasine Western Sahara
78 D1 Amasra Turkey
78 F1 Amasya Turkey
138 B2 Amata South Australia Australia
128 E4 Amataura Brazil
125 N9 Amatenango Mexico
87 F11 Amatikulu S Africa
124 H7 Amatitán Mexico
125 L8 Amatlan Mexico
124 G7 Amatlán de Cañas Mexico
61 O10 Amatsu-Kominato Japan
22 J2 Amay Belgium
Amazon R see Amazonas R
119 M7 Amazon Saskatchewan Canada
128 E4 Amazonas state Brazil
128 D4 Amazonas div Colombia
128 C5 Amazonas dept Peru
129 H4 Amazonas R S America
128 E3 Amazonas state Venezuela
110 B2 Amazonia Missouri U.S.A.
129 J3 Amazon,Mouths of the Brazil
80 C7 Amazya Israel
74 E1 Amb Pakistan
74 G9 Ambajogai India
74 G3 Ambala India
83 J11 Ambalangodo Sri Lanka
87 H12 Ambalavao Madagascar
140 C6 Ambalindum N Terr Australia
85 G8 Ambam Cameroon
86 G3 Āmba Maryam Ethiopia
83 K10 Amban Ganga R Sri Lanka
87 H10 Ambanje Madagascar
70 N9 Ambarawa Java
51 Q2 Ambarchik Russian Federation
18 E8 Ambarès et Lagrave France
52 D2 Ambarnyy Russian Federation
141 H7 Ambathala Queensland Australia
128 C4 Ambato Ecuador
87 H11 Ambato-Boeny Madagascar
87 H11 Ambatolampy Madagascar
131 C2 Ambato,Sa ra Argentina
18 F7 Ambazac France
107 N6 Amber Oklahoma U.S.A.
100 H2 Amber Washington U.S.A.
116 J8 Amber B Alaska U.S.A.
37 M5 Amberg Germany
99 T4 Amberg Wisconsin U.S.A.
9 E1 Ambergate England
127 H4 Ambergris Cays islds Turks & Caicos Is
19 O13 Ambérieu-en-Bugey France
120 J8 Amberley Ontario Canada
144 D5 Amberley New Zealand
22 K3 Amberloup Belgium
21 L8 Amberre France
18 H7 Ambert France
18 G9 Ambialet France
85 B6 Ambidédi Mali
75 K7 Ambikapur India
71 E4 Ambil isld Philippines
21 L7 Ambillou France
21 K7 Ambillou-Château France
87 H10 Ambilobe Madagascar
117 H7 Ambition,Mt British Columbia Canada
21 P3 Amblainville France
13 G3 Amble England
116 J3 Ambler R Alaska U.S.A.
13 F5 Ambleside England
22 B2 Ambleteuse France
22 L3 Amblève Belgium
87 H12 Amboasary Madagascar
87 H11 Ambodifototra Madagascar
87 H12 Ambohimahasoa Madagascar
21 N7 Amboise France
20 E6 Ambon France
136 F2 Ambon Moluccas Indonesia
87 H12 Amborompotsy Madagascar
86 G6 Amboseli, L Kenya
87 H12 Ambositra Madagascar
87 H13 Ambovombe Madagascar
103 J7 Amboy California U.S.A.
99 R8 Amboy Illinois U.S.A.
95 N6 Amboy,S New Jersey U.S.A.
21 O8 Ambrault France
94 G6 Ambridge Pennsylvania U.S.A.
21 J5 Ambrières-les-Vallées France
87 B7 Ambriz Angola
19 O12 Ambronay France
112 D6 Ambrose Georgia U.S.A.
98 C1 Ambrose North Dakota U.S.A.
137 O5 Ambrym isld Vanuatu
71 E2 Ambuklao Dam Luzon Philippines
71 K9 Ambulombo Vol Indonesia
70 O10 Ambulu Java
70 O9 Ambunten Java
76 D4 Ambur India
141 J7 Amby Queensland Australia
27 C12 Åmdal Norway
86 D3 Am Dam Chad
85 E4 Amded watercourse Algeria
50 F2 Amderma Russian Federation
75 O2 Amdo China
86 G3 Amedamit mt Ethiopia
102 D1 Amedee California U.S.A.
25 E2 Ameland isld Netherlands
42 E6 Amelia Italy
98 H7 Amelia Nebraska U.S.A.
94 K9 Amelia Virginia U.S.A.
113 F7 Amelia I Florida U.S.A.
32 M6 Amelinghausen Germany
43 H9 Amendolara Italy
67 A5 Ameng China
17 J2 Amer Spain
102 D2 American R California U.S.A.
130 F8 Americana Brazil
101 N7 American Falls Idaho U.S.A.
103 N1 American Fork Utah U.S.A.
138 E6 American River South Australia Australia
134 E1 American Samoa islds Pacific Oc
113 F13 American Shoal lighthouse Florida U.S.A.
112 C5 Americus Georgia U.S.A.
25 D4 Amerongen Netherlands
25 D4 Amersfoort Netherlands
9 F4 Amersham England
143 B9 Amery W Australia Australia
99 O4 Amery Wisconsin U.S.A.
146 J11 Amery Ice Shelf Antarctica
99 N7 Ames Iowa U.S.A.
98 K8 Ames Nebraska U.S.A.
107 M5 Ames Oklahoma U.S.A.
118 E3 Amesbury Alberta Canada
9 E5 Amesbury England
95 R4 Amesbury Massachusetts U.S.A.
118 J1 Amesdale Ontario Canada
120 F3 Ameson Ontario Canada
146 B9 Ames Range mts Antarctica
94 F7 Amesville Ohio U.S.A.
7 L9 Amethyst oil rig North Sea
122 J8 Amet Sound Nova Scotia Canada
46 F6 Amfíklia Greece
46 E6 Amfilokhía Greece
46 F4 Amfípolis Greece
46 E6 Ámfissa Greece
20 H3 Amfreville France
21 M3 Amfreville-la-Campagne France
51 N2 Amga Russian Federation
51 M3 Amga R Russian Federation
58 G2 Amgalang Bulag China
51 N4 Amgu Russian Federation
59 L2 Amgu Russian Federation
86 D3 Am Guéréda Chad
85 F3 Amguid Algeria
59 K1 Amgun' R Russian Federation
86 G3 Amhara reg Ethiopia
Amherst see Kyaikkami
122 H8 Amherst Nova Scotia Canada
106 H1 Amherst Colorado U.S.A.
95 T2 Amherst Maine U.S.A.
95 P4 Amherst Massachusetts U.S.A.
98 G9 Amherst Nebraska U.S.A.
95 Q4 Amherst New Hampshire U.S.A.
94 E5 Amherst Ohio U.S.A.
98 J4 Amherst South Dakota U.S.A.
94 H9 Amherst Virginia U.S.A.
120 G10 Amherstburg Ontario Canada
94 F9 Amherstdale West Virginia U.S.A.
123 K6 Amherst I Madeleine Is, Quebec Canada
121 O8 Amherst I Ontario Canada
99 R5 Amherst Junction Wisconsin U.S.A.
142 F4 Amherst, Mt W Australia Australia
42 D6 Amiata,Monte Italy
98 C3 Amidon North Dakota U.S.A.
141 K8 Amiens Queensland Australia
21 P2 Amiens France
78 H5 Amij,Wadi Iraq
46 E4 Amíndaion Greece
73 L6 Amindivi Is Lakshadweep Indian Oc
60 H10 Amino Japan
87 C10 Aminuis Namibia
79 F4 Amioun Lebanon
80 F1 'Amir Israel
83 H5 Amirante Is Indian Oc
118 F6 Amisk Alberta Canada
119 P4 Amisk L Saskatchewan Canada
106 G6 Amistad New Mexico U.S.A.
108 G106 Amistad Nat. Recreation Area Texas U.S.A.
108 F6 Amistad Res Mexico
111 F11 Amite Louisiana U.S.A.
111 C7 Amity Arkansas U.S.A.
95 O6 Amityville Long I, New York U.S.A.
75 L5 Amlekhganj Nepal
27 C13 Amli Norway
8 B1 Amlwch Wales
80 G6 'Ammān Jordan
8 C4 Ammanford Wales
26 H5 Ammarfjallet mt Sweden
26 H6 Ammarnäs Sweden
140 D5 Ammaroo N Terr Australia
115 Q4 Ammassalik Greenland
28 E4 Ammelhede Denmark
33 P10 Ammendorf Germany
32 L9 Ammensen Germany
41 O2 Ammer R Germany
41 N2 Ammer Gebirge mt Germany
32 G6 Ammerland reg Germany
41 O2 Ammerland Germany
116 R2 Ammerman Mt Yukon Territory Canada
37 K5 Ammerndorf Germany
41 O1 Ammer See L Germany
80 F2 'Ammi 'ad Israel
101 O6 Ammon Idaho U.S.A.
68 G5 Amnat Charoen Thailand
Amne Machin see A'nyêmaqên Shan
80 F2 Amnun Israel
77 C1 Āmol Iran
130 B6 Amolar Brazil
36 F2 Amöneburg Germany
36 G4 Amorbach Germany
131 F2 Amores R Argentina
47 H8 Amorgós isld Greece
107 M5 Amorita Oklahoma U.S.A.
111 H8 Amory Mississippi U.S.A.
121 M4 Amos Quebec Canada
103 J8 Amos California U.S.A.
28 G5 Åmose Å R Denmark
27 H11 Åmot Sweden
27 D12 Åmot Akershus Norway
27 C12 Åmotsdal Norway
85 B3 Amott Morocco
Amoy see Xiamen
70 D5 Ampah Kalimantan
70 G5 Ampana Sulawesi Indonesia
87 G12 Ampanihy Madagascar
130 F8 Amparo Brazil
87 H11 Ampasimanolotra Madagascar
128 D7 Ampato, Cord. de mts Peru
70 Q10 Ampenan Indonesia
37 M7 Amper R Germany
37 N7 Ampfing Germany
103 O9 Amphitheater Arizona U.S.A.
70 G5 Ampibaku Sulawesi
85 F7 Ampier Nigeria
13 G5 Ampleforth England
70 G5 Ampoa Sulawesi Indonesia
17 H4 Amposta Spain
9 F3 Ampthill England
19 N14 Ampuis France
17 J2 Ampurdán dist Spain
80 D2 'Amqa Israel
122 E5 Amqui Quebec Canada
74 G8 Amravati India
74 D8 Amreli India
74 F3 Amritsar India
30 D1 Amrum isld Germany
26 K7 Åmsele Sweden
38 J7 Am Stein mt Austria
25 C4 Amstelveen Netherlands
24 Amsterdam conurbation Netherlands
25 C4 Amsterdam Netherlands
113 C7 Amsterdam Georgia U.S.A.
101 L7 Amsterdam Idaho U.S.A.
95 N4 Amsterdam New York U.S.A.
94 G6 Amsterdam Ohio U.S.A.
81 E9 Amsterdam, I Indian Oc
38 L5 Amstetten Austria
27 F12 Åmtervik, V Sweden
86 D3 Am Timan Chad
28 B2 Amtoft Denmark
41 L2 Amtzell Germany
127 J9 Amuay Venezuela
57 D5 Amu-Dar'ya Turkmenistan
57 B4 Amudar'ya R Turkmenistan/Uzbekistan
147 H5 Amund Ringness I Northwest Territories Canada
146 K9 Amundsen B Antarctica
146 D9 Amundsen Glacier Antarctica
147 J1 Amundsen Gulf Northwest Territories Canada
146 H13 Amundsen, Mt Antarctica
146 E9 Amundsen-Scott U.S.A. Base Antarctica
146 A8 Amundsen Sea Antarctica
147 J2 Amundsen Trough Arctic Oc
27 H10 Amungen L Sweden
70 D6 Amuntai Kalimantan
59 L1 Amur R Russian Federation
71 J4 Amurang Sulawesi Indonesia
71 J4 Amurang Teluk B Sulawesi Indonesia
144 D5 Amuri Pass New Zealand
17 F1 Amurrio Spain
59 L1 Amursk Russian Federation
59 J1 Amurskaya Oblast' prov Russian Federation
55 C4 Amurskiy Russian Federation
46 E6 Amvrakía, L Greece
46 D6 Amvrakikós Kólpos G Greece
54 K9 Amvrosiyevka Ukraine
107 K3 Amy Kansas U.S.A.
56 D4 Amyl R Russian Federation
120 F4 Amyot Ontario Canada
68 B3 An Burma
70 G6 Anabanua Sulawesi
138 F5 Ana Branch R New South Wales Australia
80 D4 Anabta Jordan
102 E7 Anacapa Is California U.S.A.
45 Q8 Anacapri Italy
127 M10 Anaco Venezuela
111 C10 Anacoco Louisiana U.S.A.
101 N3 Anaconda Montana U.S.A.
101 M4 Anaconda Range Montana U.S.A.
100 C1 Anacortes Washington U.S.A.
107 M6 Anadarko Oklahoma U.S.A.
130 H10 Anadia Brazil
16 B4 Anadia Portugal
78 F1 Anadolu Dağlari mt Turkey
47 N10 Anadolufeneri Turkey
47 N10 Anadoluhisarı Turkey
51 R2 Anadyr Russian Federation
51 R2 Anadyrskoye Ploskogor'ye tableland Russian Federation
47 H8 Anáfi isld Greece
26 F9 Anafjället mt Sweden
47 H8 Anafópoulo isld Greece
130 H4 Anagé Brazil
45 O6 Anagni Italy
102 F8 Anaheim California U.S.A.
117 L9 Anahim Lake British Columbia Canada
135 O1 Anahola Hawaiian Is
125 J4 Anáhuac Mexico
111 B12 Anahuac Texas U.S.A.
102 R11 Anahulu R Hawaiian Is
76 C5 Anaimalai Hills India
75 K10 Anakapalle India
141 J6 Anakie Queensland Australia
116 M2 Anaktuvuk Pass Alaska U.S.A.
87 H10 Analalava Madagascar
128 F4 Anama Brazil
119 T7 Anama Bay Manitoba Canada
126 E4 Ana Maria, Cayos de islds Cuba
69 G11 Anambas, Kepulauan isld Indonesia
61 L8 Anamizu Japan
98 F2 Anamoose North Dakota U.S.A.
129 G3 Anamu R Brazil
78 D3 Anamur Turkey
60 H12 Anan Japan
46 G8 Anánes isld Greece
71 J7 Anano isld Indonesia
76 C3 Anantapur India
74 F2 Anantnag Kashmir
48 M3 Anan'yev Ukraine
53 E11 Anapa Russian Federation
43 G11 Anapo R Sicily
129 J7 Anápolis Brazil
129 H4 Anapú R Brazil
77 D4 Anār Iran
77 C3 Anārak Iran
77 G3 Anār Darrah Afghanistan
26 F8 Anaris Fjällen mt Sweden
26 O3 Anarjokka R Norway/Finland
127 L5 Añasco Puerto Rico
26 M7 Ånåset Sweden
113 F8 Anastasia I Florida U.S.A.
78 D2 Anatolia reg Turkey
46 E3 Anatolikí Makedhonía Kaí Thráki admin region Greece
137 O6 Anatom isld Vanuatu
100 H3 Anatone Washington U.S.A.
80 E6 'Anatot Jordan
29 O7 Änättijärvi L Finland
131 E2 Añatuya Argentina
128 F3 Anauá R Brazil
78 H5 Anbār, Al prov Iraq
69 G8 An Bien Vietnam
128 C5 Ancash dept Peru
9 F2 Ancaster England
101 O4 Anceney Montana U.S.A.
21 H7 Ancenis France
21 L7 Anché France
130 H7 Anchieta Brazil
106 E8 Ancho New Mexico U.S.A.
116 N6 Anchorage Alaska U.S.A.
94 B8 Anchorage Kentucky U.S.A.
94 E4 Anchor Bay Michigan U.S.A.
144 A6 Anchor I New Zealand
116 M7 Anchor Point Alaska U.S.A.
127 J2 Anchovy Jamaica
65 C5 Anci China
121 T6 Ancienne Lorette airport Quebec Canada
113 E9 Anclote Keys islds Florida U.S.A.
128 E7 Ancohuma mt Bolivia
128 C6 Ancón Peru
45 O4 Ancona Italy
128 C3 Ancon de Sardinas B.de Ecuador
95 O4 Ancram New York U.S.A.
22 D4 Ancre R France
13 F2 Ancroft England
13 F3 Ancrum Scotland
88 G8 Ancuabe Mozambique
133 C6 Ancud Chile
133 C5 Andacollo Argentina
140 D7 Andado N Terr Australia
128 D6 Andahuaylas Peru
107 N4 Andale Kansas U.S.A.
133 D3 Andalgala Argentina
26 C9 Åndalsnes Norway
16 D7 Andalucía reg Spain
111 K10 Andalusia Alabama U.S.A.
68 A6 Andaman Islands Bay of Bengal
138 D4 Andamooka South Australia Australia
52 G5 Andanga Russian Federation
77 L2 Andarāb Afghanistan
129 K6 Andaria Brazil
79 H3 Andarīn, Al Syria
67 B5 Ande China
86 H2 Āndeba Ye Midir Zerf Ch'af C Eritrea
41 K4 Andeer Switzerland
52 H1 Andeg Russian Federation
21 N3 Andelle R France
19 J4 Andelot France
21 N3 Andelys,les France
22 J3 Andenne Belgium
85 E5 Anderamboukane Mali
26 J2 Ånderdalen Nat. Park Norway
41 J4 Andermatt Switzerland
36 C3 Andernach Germany
36 C3 Andernach-Land Germany
57 F6 Anderov Tajikistan
26 L7 Andersfors Sweden
114 G4 Anderson R Northwest Territories Canada
100 C9 Anderson California U.S.A.
94 B6 Anderson Indiana U.S.A.
110 B5 Anderson Missouri U.S.A.
112 E3 Anderson South Carolina U.S.A.
139 H8 Anderson Bay Tasmania Australia
68 A6 Anderson I Andaman Is
100 F7 Anderson L Oregon U.S.A.
101 K6 Anderson Ranch Res Idaho U.S.A.
112 C5 Andersonville Georgia U.S.A.
110 L2 Andersonville Indiana U.S.A.
27 G14 Anderstorp Sweden
95 N4 Andes New York U.S.A.
133 D3 Andes, Cordillera de los mts S America
98 H6 Andes,L South Dakota U.S.A.
87 H11 Andevoranto Madagascar
26 H2 Andfjord inlet Norway
76 D2 Andhra Pradesh prov India
17 F2 Andía,Sierra de mt Spain
83 J10 Andigama Sri Lanka
46 F9 Andikíthira isld Greece
87 H11 Andilamena Madagascar
46 G8 Andímilos isld Greece
46 G7 Andipáros isld Greece
47 P13 Andípaxoi isld Greece
47 H6 Andípsara isld Greece
78 F3 Andırın Turkey
66 C4 Andirlangar China
47 H5 Ándissa Greece
53 G12 Andiyskoye Koysu R Russian Federation
57 F4 Andizhan Uzbekistan
77 J1 Andkhvoy Afghanistan
36 C7 Andlau France
87 H10 Andoany Madagascar
40 F1 Andolsheim France
52 E4 Andomskiy Pogost Russian Federation
65 G6 Andong S Korea
65 D7 Andongwei China
141 F1 Andoom Queensland Australia
44 D4 Andora Italy
26 J3 Andörja isld Norway
17 J2 Andorra princ Pyrenees
17 H2 Andorra la Vella Andorra
21 J5 Andouille France
9 E5 Andover England
95 R2 Andover Maine U.S.A.
95 Q3 Andover New Hampshire U.S.A.
95 N6 Andover New Jersey U.S.A.
94 K4 Andover New York U.S.A.
94 G5 Andover Ohio U.S.A.
98 J4 Andover South Dakota U.S.A.
9 E4 Andoversford England
26 H2 Andöya isld Norway
130 D7 Andradina Brazil
17 J5 Andraix Majorca
116 O10 Andreanof Is Aleutian Is
52 D6 Andreapol' Russian Federation
12 D5 Andreas I of Man U.K.
79 E3 Andreas,C Cyprus
87 H11 Andreba Madagascar
138 F2 Andree,L South Australia Australia
115 R3 Andrée Land Greenland
130 G7 Andrel lândia Brazil
31 M4 Andrespol Poland
118 E5 Andrew Alberta Canada
6 L4 Andrew oil rig North Sea
99 Q7 Andrew Iowa U.S.A.
68 B3 Andrew B Burma
143 E10 Andrew, Mt W Australia Australia
94 B6 Andrews Indiana U.S.A.
98 C7 Andrews Nebraska U.S.A.
112 D2 Andrews North Carolina U.S.A.
100 G7 Andrews Oregon U.S.A.
112 H4 Andrews South Carolina U.S.A.
108 E3 Andrews Texas U.S.A.
53 H8 Andreyevka Russian Federation
54 N1 Andreyevo Russian Federation
53 D9 Andreyevo-Ivanovka Ukraine
55 E2 Andreyevskoye, Oz L Russian Federation
53 D8 Andreykovichi Russian Federation
43 G7 Andria Italy
46 D2 Andrijevica Montenegro Yugoslavia
46 E7 Andrítsaina Greece
106 G4 Andrix Colorado U.S.A.
87 G12 Androka Madagascar
116 G9 Andronica I Alaska U.S.A.
Andropov see Rybinsk
126 E2 Andros isld Bahamas
46 G7 Ándros isld Greece
95 R2 Androscogg R New Hamps/Maine U.S.A.
53 G7 Androsovka Russian Federation
126 F2 Andros Town Andros Bahamas
73 L6 Androth I Lakshadweep Indian Oc
76 A5 Āndrott isld Indian Oc
53 C8 Andrushevka Ukraine
31 L6 Andrychów Poland
55 D2 Andryushino Russian Federation
26 K2 Andselv Norway
16 E6 Andújar Spain
87 C8 Andulo Angola
18 H8 Anduze France
27 G14 Aneby Sweden
143 G6 Anec, L W Australia Australia
131 B8 Anecón Grande pk Argentina
85 E5 Anefis Mali
113 L7 Anegada isld Virgin Is
133 E6 Anegado, B Argentina
85 E7 Aného Togo
118 K7 Anerley Saskatchewan Canada
118 K9 Aneroid Saskatchewan Canada
21 N4 Anet France
98 J2 Aneta North Dakota U.S.A.
67 E3 Anfu China
140 B3 Angalarri R N Terr Australia
133 C2 Angamos, Pta C Chile
125 J8 Angangue Mexico
59 H2 Ang'angxi China
56 D2 Angara R Russian Federation
147 K8 Angara Basin Arctic Oc
56 F4 Angarsk Russian Federation
140 B7 Angas Downs N Terr Australia
142 G6 Angas Ra W Australia Australia
138 E5 Angaston South Australia Australia
71 E3 Angat Luzon Philippines
130 E8 Angatuba Brazil
26 H9 Ånge Sweden
26 H10 Ångebo Sweden
124 C3 Angel de la Guarda isld Mexico
71 E3 Angeles Luzon Philippines
128 F2 Angel Falls waterfall Venezuela
27 F15 Ängelholm Sweden
94 J4 Angelica New York U.S.A.
111 B10 Angelina R Texas U.S.A.
28 D7 Angeln reg Germany
43 G8 Angelo de Lom,S Italy
27 H12 Ängelsberg Sweden
102 D3 Angels Camp California U.S.A.
38 N7 Anger Austria
41 J6 Angera Italy
26 J8 Ångermanälven R Sweden
26 K9 Ångermanälven isld Sweden
32 E10 Angermund Germany
21 J7 Angers France
26 G10 Ängersjö Sweden
21 O5 Angerville France
26 M5 Ängeså Sweden
26 N5 Ängesan R Sweden
26 L8 Ängesön isld Sweden
70 E5 Anggana Kalimantan
70 G7 Anggowala, Bk mt Sulawesi Indonesia
45 M4 Anghiari Italy
112 J2 Angier North Carolina U.S.A.
115 K5 Angikuni L Northwest Territories Canada
8 A4 Angle Wales
144 A7 Anglem, Mt New Zealand
120 D4 Angler Ontario Canada
139 G7 Anglesea Victoria Australia
8 B1 Anglesey isld Wales
21 M8 Angles sur-l'Anglin France
18 D9 Anglet France
109 M6 Angleton Texas U.S.A.
118 J7 Anglia Saskatchewan Canada
21 L8 Angliers France
21 N8 Anglin R France
Angmagssalik see Ammassalik
88 G10 Angoche Mozambique
77 E6 Angohrān Iran
131 A6 Angol Chile
87 C8 Angola rep Africa
94 B5 Angola Indiana U.S.A.
94 H4 Angola New York U.S.A.
90 K11 Angola Basin Atlantic Oc
112 K3 Angola Swamp North Carolina U.S.A.
117 F7 Angoon Alaska U.S.A.
98 C8 Angora Nebraska U.S.A.
124 E5 Angostura Mexico
125 J6 Angostura Mexico
128 D3 Angostura I, Salto cataract Colombia
124 E2 Angostura, Presa de la res Mexico
125 N9 Angostura, Psa. de la res Mexico
98 C6 Angostura Reserve South Dakota U.S.A.
18 F7 Angoulême France
18 F7 Angoumois prov France
129 K8 Angra dos Reis Brazil
45 R8 Angri Italy
21 J6 Angrie France
37 L2 Angstedt-Gräfinau Germany
68 E5 Ang Thong Thailand
17 G2 Angués Spain
126 E3 Anguila Isles Bahamas
127 N5 Anguilla isld Lesser Antilles
45 L1 Anguillara Ven Italy
123 N6 Anguille, C Newfoundland Canada
86 E6 Angumu Zaire
65 C5 Anguo China
140 D2 Angurugu Northern Territory Australia
98 K1 Angus Minnesota U.S.A.
119 Q8 Angusville Manitoba Canada
88 C10 Angwa R Zimbabwe
129 H8 Anhandui R Brazil
28 H3 Anholt isld Denmark
28 H3 Anholt Denmark
67 D2 Anhua China
58 G5 Anhui prov China
130 C5 Anhumas Brazil
Anhwei prov see Anhui prov
61 O5 Aniai Japan
116 H6 Aniak Alaska U.S.A.
116 H8 Aniakchak Nat Mon and Preserve Alaska U.S.A.
116 H8 Aniakchak Vol. Crater Alaska U.S.A.
80 F2 Ani'am Syria
22 E3 Aniche France
130 E5 Anicuns Brazil
47 H8 Ánidhros isld Greece
85 E7 Anié Togo
45 N6 Aniene R Italy
18 E10 Anie, Pic d' mt Spain/France
55 D5 Anikhovka Russian Federation
52 F5 Anikovo Russian Federation
106 C4 Animas R Colorado U.S.A.
106 B10 Animas New Mexico U.S.A.
124 C3 Animas,Pta Las C Mexico
68 C5 Anin Burma
48 G5 Anina Romania
103 M6 Anita Arizona U.S.A.
99 M8 Anita Iowa U.S.A.
71 G5 Anitaguipan Pt Philippines
130 E10 Anitápolis Brazil
116 J2 Aniuk R Alaska U.S.A.
59 M2 Aniva, Zaliv B Russian Federation
99 R4 Aniwa Wisconsin U.S.A.
22 E4 Anizy-le-Chât France
29 M11 Anjalankoski Finland
74 D7 Anjar India
80 G4 'Anjara Jordan

67 F1 **Anji** China
65 G2 **Anjia** China
Anjiang *see* **Qianyang**
Anjiangying *see* **Luanping**
61 L11 **Anjō** Japan
21 H7 **Anjou** *reg* France
87 H11 **Anjozorobe** Madagascar
59 J4 **Anjŭ** N Korea
77 L2 **Anjuman** *reg* Afghanistan
87 G12 **Ankaboa, Tanjona** *C* Madagascar
58 E5 **Ankang** China
78 D2 **Ankara** Turkey
87 H11 **Ankaratra** *mt* Madagascar
27 H14 **Ankarsrum** Sweden
26 J6 **Ankarsund** Sweden
87 G12 **Ankazoabo** Madagascar
99 N8 **Ankeny** Iowa U.S.A.
68 J6 **An Khe** Vietnam
33 T5 **Anklam** Germany
74 E8 **Ankleshwar** India
86 G4 **Ānkober** Ethiopia
16 D10 **Ankod** Morocco
38 H7 **Ankogel** *mt* Austria
87 E7 **Ankoro** Zaire
52 E6 **An'kovo** Russian Federation
32 G7 **Ankum** Germany
13 H6 **Anlaby** England
67 E3 **Anle** China
22 K4 **Anlier** Belgium
68 H7 **An Loc** Vietnam
67 B4 **Anlong** China
68 G5 **Anlong Veng** Cambodia
58 F5 **Anlu** China
26 F8 **Ånn** Sweden
25 C3 **Anna** Netherlands
53 F8 **Anna** Russian Federation
110 G4 **Anna** Illinois U.S.A.
94 C6 **Anna** Ohio U.S.A.
109 L2 **Anna** Texas U.S.A.
85 F1 **Annaba** Algeria
38 H7 **Annaberg** Austria
37 P2 **Annaberg-Buchholz** Germany
79 G4 **An Nabk** Syria
33 S9 **Annaburg** Germany
84 G4 **An Nāfūrah** Libya
128 G3 **Annai** Guyana
25 B5 **Anna Jacobapolder** Netherlands
61 M9 **Annaka** Japan
94 K8 **Anna, L** Virginia U.S.A.
68 G3 **Annam** *reg* Vietnam
113 E10 **Anna Maria** Florida U.S.A.
13 E4 **Annan** Scotland
141 J5 **Annandale** Queensland Australia
15 E5 **Annandale** Scotland
99 M4 **Annandale** Minnesota U.S.A.
13 E3 **Annan Water** Scotland
133 C7 **Anna Pink, B** Chile
142 D4 **Anna Plains** W Australia Australia
95 L8 **Annapolis** Maryland U.S.A.
122 G9 **Annapolis R** Nova Scotia Canada
75 K4 **Annapurna** *mt* Nepal
94 D4 **Ann Arbor** Michigan U.S.A.
33 O9 **Annarode** Germany
78 L7 **An Nāsirīyah** Iraq
99 R8 **Annawan** Illinois U.S.A.
143 C7 **Annean, L** W Australia Australia
21 L3 **Annebault** France
19 Q13 **Annecy** France
40 D6 **Annecy,L.d'** France
131 H6 **Annenkov Is** S Georgia
141 K2 **Annerley** *dist* Brisbane, Qnsld Australia
117 H8 **Annette I** Alaska U.S.A.
20 G3 **Anneville-sur-Mer** France
19 N14 **Anneyron** France
68 J6 **An Nhon** Vietnam
141 G2 **Annie** *R* Queensland Australia
123 P5 **Annieopsquotch Mts** Newfoundland Canada
58 D6 **Anning He** *R* China
28 J5 **Annisse** Denmark
111 L8 **Anniston** Alabama U.S.A.
140 D5 **Annitowa** N Terr Australia
40 G5 **Anniviers Val d'** Switzerland
Annobón *isld see* **Pagalu** *isld*
90 L9 **Annobón** *isld* Equat Guinea
109 N2 **Annona** Texas U.S.A.
19 N14 **Annonay** France
127 L2 **Annotto Bay** Jamaica
22 D2 **Annœulin** France
36 D5 **Annweiler** Germany
46 G9 **Áno Arkhánai** Crete Greece
99 N4 **Anoka** Minnesota U.S.A.
98 H7 **Anoka** Nebraska U.S.A.
47 P13 **Ano Lefkímmi** Greece
54 M1 **Anopino** Russian Federation
22 G4 **Anor** France
87 H10 **Anorontany, Tanjona** *C* Madagascar
36 B7 **Anould** France
46 G9 **Áno Viánnos** Crete Greece
47 O12 **Ano Virón** Greece
68 J7 **An Phuoc** Vietnam
65 C5 **Anping** China
67 C6 **Anpu** China
67 C6 **Anpu Gang** *B* China
58 G5 **Anqing** China
65 D6 **Anqiu** China
25 F6 **Anrath** Germany
67 D3 **Anren** China
32 H9 **Anröchte** Germany
22 K2 **Ans** Belgium
28 B5 **Ansager** Denmark
65 A6 **Ansai** China
37 K5 **Ansbach** Germany
40 A6 **Anse** France
127 H5 **Anse-à-Galets** Haiti
127 J5 **Anse-à-Pitre** Haiti
122 H5 **Anse-au-Griffon** Quebec Canada
126 H5 **Anse-à-Veau** Haiti
127 N4 **Anse Bertrand** Guadeloupe W Indies
126 G5 **Anse d'Hainault** Haiti
98 G8 **Anselmo** Nebraska U.S.A.
22 H3 **Anseremme** Belgium
139 H7 **Anser Gr** *islds* Tasmania Australia
122 B5 **Anse St.Jean,L'** Quebec Canada
127 L4 **Anses d'Arlets, Les** Martinique W Indies
59 H3 **Anshan** China
67 B3 **Anshun** China
131 B3 **Ansilta** *pk* Argentina
131 B3 **Ansilta, Cord. de** *ra* Argentina
109 P3 **Ansley** Louisiana U.S.A.
98 G8 **Ansley** Nebraska U.S.A.
140 B2 **Anson B** N Terr Australia
85 E5 **Ansongo** Mali
94 C6 **Ansonia** Ohio U.S.A.
120 K4 **Ansonville** Ontario Canada
112 G2 **Ansonville** North Carolina U.S.A.
28 C6 **Anst** Denmark
94 F8 **Ansted** West Virginia U.S.A.
15 F4 **Anstruther** Scotland
128 D6 **Anta** Peru
Antakya *see* **Hatay**
78 C3 **Antalya** Turkey
87 H11 **Antananarivo** Madagascar
87 H11 **Antanifotsy** Madagascar
87 H12 **Antanimora** Madagascar
146 **Antarctica**
90 D16 **Antarctic Circle**
146 D6 **Antarctic Pen** Antarctica
81 C10 **Antares Bank** Indian Oc
130 H11 **Antas** Brazil
130 D10 **Antas,R das** Brazil
15 C3 **An Teallach** *mt* Scotland
118 J8 **Antelope** Saskatchewan Canada
98 B1 **Antelope** Montana U.S.A.
98 D3 **Antelope** North Dakota U.S.A.
109 J2 **Antelope** Texas U.S.A.
101 Q9 **Antelope** Utah U.S.A.
87 E10 **Antelope** Zimbabwe
100 H7 **Antelope Cr** Oregon U.S.A.
130 H9 **Antenor Navarro** Brazil
16 D7 **Antequera** Spain
130 B9 **Antequera,Pto** Paraguay
106 D3 **Antero Pk** Colorado U.S.A.
106 E3 **Antero Res** Colorado U.S.A.
38 F8 **Anterselva di Mezzo** Italy
107 N4 **Anthony** Kansas U.S.A.
106 D9 **Anthony** New Mexico U.S.A.
108 A3 **Anthony** New Mex/Tex U.S.A.
138 C4 **Anthony, L** South Australia Australia
140 D4 **Anthony Lagoon** N Terr Australia
138 C2 **Anthony,Mt** South Australia Australia
85 C3 **Anti Atlas** *mts* Morocco
44 B4 **Antibes** France
44 B4 **Antibes,C.d'** France
127 N9 **Antica, I** Venezuela
45 N5 **Anticoli Corrado** Italy
122 J4 **Anticosti I** Quebec Canada
21 L2 **Antifer,C.d'** France
21 M8 **Antigny** France
123 K8 **Antigonish** Nova Scotia Canada
125 O10 **Antigua** Guatemala
127 P4 **Antigua** *isld* Lesser Antilles
127 O6 **Antigua and Barbuda** *islds* West Indies
127 N4 **Antigues Pte. d'** Guadeloupe W Indies
118 B3 **Antikameg** Alberta Canada
133 C5 **Antilhue** Chile
126 G4 **Antilla** Cuba
103 N3 **Antimony** Utah U.S.A.
Antioch *see* **Hatay**
102 C3 **Antioch** California U.S.A.
99 S7 **Antioch** Illinois U.S.A.
98 D7 **Antioch** Nebraska U.S.A.
18 E6 **Antioche, Pertuis d'** *B* France
128 C2 **Antioquia** *div* Colombia
80 C5 **Antipatris** Israel
52 D6 **Antipovo** Russian Federation
128 C4 **Antisana** *mt* Ecuador
119 Q9 **Antler** Saskatchewan Canada
98 E1 **Antler** North Dakota U.S.A.
107 P7 **Antlers** Oklahoma U.S.A.
133 C2 **Antofagasta** Chile
133 D3 **Antofagasta de la Sierra** Argentina
133 D3 **Antofalla** *vol* Argentina
109 O1 **Antoine** Arkansas U.S.A.
22 E2 **Antoing** Belgium
44 F2 **Antola,Monte** Italy
106 G2 **Anton** Colorado U.S.A.
108 E2 **Anton** Texas U.S.A.
87 J11 **Antongila, Helodrano** *B* Madagascar
87 G12 **Antongo** Madagascar
130 E9 **Antonina** Brazil
107 L3 **Antonino** Kansas U.S.A.
48 K1 **Antoniny** Ukraine
129 K7 **Antônio** *R* Brazil
130 G7 **Antônio Carlos** Brazil
130 G6 **Antônio Dias** Brazil
Antonio Enes *see* **Angoche**
130 C8 **Antônio Joâo** Brazil
106 D4 **Antonito** Colorado U.S.A.
54 D10 **Antonovka** Ukraine
47 H1 **Antonovo** Bulgaria
126 D3 **Antón Recio** Cuba
21 P4 **Antony** France
140 D4 **Antony Lagoon** N Terr Australia
20 H5 **Antrain** France
52 C4 **Antrea** Russian Federation
36 G5 **Antrefftal** Germany
14 E2 **Antrim** *co* N Ireland
14 E2 **Antrim** N Ireland
95 P3 **Antrim** New Hampshire U.S.A.
95 K5 **Antrim** Pennsylvania U.S.A.
14 E2 **Antrim Hills** N Ireland
142 G4 **Antrim Plat** W Australia Australia
87 G11 **Antsalova** Madagascar
52 D5 **Antsiferovo** Russian Federation
87 H11 **Antsirabe** Madagascar
87 J11 **Antsirakosy, Tanjona** *C* Madagascar
87 H10 **Antsirañana** Madagascar
52 C5 **Antsla** Estonia
87 H10 **Antsohihy** Madagascar
29 N10 **Anttola** Finland
65 G3 **Antu** China
Antwerp *see* **Antwerpen**
95 M2 **Antwerp** New York U.S.A.
94 C5 **Antwerp** Ohio U.S.A.
22 H1 **Antwerpen** Belgium
14 E3 **An Uaimh** Ireland
75 L8 **Anugul** India
116 F6 **Anukslak L** Alaska U.S.A.
26 K8 **Anundsjö** Sweden
74 E4 **Anupgarh** India
83 K9 **Anuradhapura** Sri Lanka
Anvers *see* **Antwerpen**
45 P6 **Anversa degli Abruzzi** Italy
146 C4 **Anvers Island** Antarctica
116 G5 **Anvik** Alaska U.S.A.
121 P3 **Anvilla** Quebec Canada
117 G4 **Anvil Range** Yukon Territory Canada
22 C3 **Anvin** France
58 C3 **Anxi** China
67 F4 **Anxi** China
67 A1 **An Xian** China
67 D2 **Anxiang** China
65 C5 **Anxin** China
138 C5 **Anxious B** South Australia Australia
58 F4 **Anyang** China
70 K9 **Anyar** Java
58 C5 **A'nyêmaqên Shan** *mts* China
65 B7 **Anyi** China
67 E2 **Anyi** China
67 D7 **Anyou** China
117 J8 **Anyox** British Columbia Canada
67 E4 **Anyuan** China
52 J3 **An'yudin** Russian Federation
67 B1 **Anyue** China
51 Q2 **Anyuy** *R* Russian Federation
42 B3 **Anza** *R* Italy
118 F2 **Anzac** Alberta Canada
17 G2 **Anzánigo** Spain
40 H6 **Anzasca, Valle** Italy
18 F10 **Anzat** France
65 B6 **Anze** China
22 E2 **Anzegem** Belgium
56 C3 **Anzhero-Sudzhensk** Russian Federation
147 P7 **Anzhu Os** *isld* Russian Federation
22 E3 **Anzin** France
38 E5 **Anzing** Germany
45 N7 **Anzio** Italy
128 F2 **Anzoátegui** *state* Venezuela
45 K2 **Anzola dell'Emilia** Italy
137 O5 **Aoba** *isld* Vanuatu
59 L5 **Aoga-shima** *isld* Japan
65 D3 **Aohan Qi** China
18 E10 **Aoiz** Spain
61 O5 **Aomori** Japan
60 N3 **Aonae** Japan
Aoraki *mt see* **Cook, Mt**
144 C6 **Aorangi** *admin region* New Zealand
145 E4 **Aorangi Mts** New Zealand
145 D4 **Aorere R** New Zealand
68 D7 **Ao Sawi** *B* Thailand
40 F6 **Aosta** Italy
145 E3 **Aotea Harbour** New Zealand
85 C5 **Aouker** *reg* Mauritania
85 E3 **Aoulef** Algeria
67 B3 **Aoxi** China
60 G10 **Aoya** Japan
86 C1 **Aozou** Chad
103 P10 **Apache** Arizona U.S.A.
109 J1 **Apache** Oklahoma U.S.A.
106 B8 **Apache Creek** New Mexico U.S.A.
103 N8 **Apache Junct** Arizona U.S.A.
103 O10 **Apache Pk** Arizona U.S.A.
113 C7 **Apalachee B** Florida U.S.A.
112 C2 **Apalachia Dam** North Carolina U.S.A.
113 C8 **Apalachicola** Florida U.S.A.
128 D3 **Apaporis** *R* Colombia
130 B8 **Apa.R** Brazil/Paraguay
130 D7 **Áparecida do Tabuado** Brazil
144 B7 **Aparima R** New Zealand
71 E1 **Aparri** Luzon Philippines
70 E6 **Apar, Teluk** *B* Kalimantan
145 D2 **Apata** New Zealand
48 E5 **Apatin** Serbia Yugoslavia
52 D1 **Apatity** Russian Federation
124 H8 **Apatzingán** Mexico
116 C5 **Apavawook C** St Lawrence I, Alaska U.S.A.
52 C5 **Ape** Latvia
45 M4 **Apecchio** Italy
119 S3 **Apeganau L** Manitoba Canada
25 E4 **Apeldoorn** Netherlands
32 G6 **Apen** Germany
33 O7 **Apenburg** Germany
32 L6 **Apensen** Germany
128 E6 **Apere** *R* Bolivia
112 J2 **Apex** North Carolina U.S.A.
41 L1 **Apfingen** Germany
101 L1 **Apgar** Montana U.S.A.
80 C5 **Aphek** Israel
116 E6 **Aphrewn** *R* Alaska U.S.A.
86 E5 **Api** Zaire
134 C1 **Apia** Western Samoa
129 G5 **Apiacás,Serra dos** *mts* Brazil
130 E9 **Apiaí** Brazil
45 R7 **Apice** Italy
71 J9 **Api,Gunung** *vol* Indonesia
70 E2 **Apin-Apin** Sabah
130 B10 **Apipe Grande** *isld* Argentina
106 F4 **Apishapa** *R* Colorado U.S.A.
70 G5 **Api,Tg** *C* Sulawesi Indonesia
145 E3 **Apiti** New Zealand
125 K8 **Apizaco** Mexico
124 H5 **Apizolaya** Mexico
56 F2 **Aplinskiy Porog** *falls* Russian Federation
129 L5 **Apodi** *R* Brazil
71 E4 **Apo East Pass** Philippines
47 Q14 **Apolakkiá** Rhodes Greece
37 M1 **Apolda** Germany
Apollonia *see* **Sūsah**
46 G8 **Apollonía** Greece
128 E6 **Apolo** Bolivia
113 F9 **Apopka** Florida U.S.A.
113 F9 **Apopka,L** Florida U.S.A.
133 G1 **Aporé** *R* Brazil
129 H3 **Aporema** Brazil
99 Q2 **Apostle Is** Michigan U.S.A.
133 F3 **Apostoles** Argentina
54 E9 **Apostolovo** Ukraine
128 G3 **Apoteri** Guyana
71 E4 **Apo West Pass** Philippines
94 E10 **Appalachia** Virginia U.S.A.
94 F10 **Appalachian Mts** U.S.A.
27 G11 **Äppelbo** Sweden
32 F9 **Appelhülsen** Germany
44 D3 **Appennino Ligure** *mt* Italy
42 C4 **Appennino Tosco-Emiliano** *mts* Italy
42 E5 **Appennino Umbro-Marchigiano** *mts* Italy
36 D6 **Appenweier** Germany
41 K3 **Appenzell** *canton* Switzerland
13 G6 **Apperley Br** England
21 M3 **Appeville** France
41 O5 **Appiano sulla Strada del Vino** Italy
25 G2 **Appingedam** Netherlands
109 N4 **Appleby** Texas U.S.A.
13 F4 **Appleby-in-Westmorland** England
142 A2 **Applecross** *dist* Perth, W Aust Australia
8 B5 **Appledore** Devon England
9 G5 **Appledore** Kent England
102 D3 **Applegate** California U.S.A.
100 B7 **Applegate** Oregon U.S.A.
122 H8 **Apple River** Nova Scotia Canada
109 N4 **Apple Springs** Texas U.S.A.
95 S2 **Appleton** Maine U.S.A.
100 D4 **Appleton** Washington U.S.A.
99 S5 **Appleton** Wisconsin U.S.A.
110 B3 **Appleton City** Missouri U.S.A.
94 J9 **Appomattox** Virginia U.S.A.
54 J1 **Aprelevka** Russian Federation
22 J5 **Apremont** France
20 G8 **Apremont** Vendée France
27 M15 **Apriki** Latvia
43 E7 **Aprilia** Italy
46 G2 **Apriltsi** Bulgaria
53 E11 **Apsheronsk** Russian Federation
138 F6 **Apsley** Victoria Australia
121 M8 **Apsley** Ontario Canada
140 B1 **Apsley Str** N Terr Australia
19 O17 **Apt** France
45 H3 **Apuane** Italy
135 V6 **Apua Pt** Hawaiian Is
130 D8 **Apucarana** Brazil
130 D8 **Apucarana, Serra Da** *mts* Brazil
71 D6 **Apurauan** Philippines
128 E2 **Apure** *state* Venezuela
128 D6 **Apurímac** *dept* Peru
48 H4 **Apuseni Muntii** *mt* Romania
88 D6 **Apwa** Tanzania
79 F9 **'Aqaba** Jordan
84 J4 **Aqaba,G.of** Red Sea
77 J1 **Aqchah** Afghanistan
78 K2 **Āq Chai** Iran
77 D1 **Āq Qal'eh** Iran
66 D4 **Aqqikkol Hu** *L* China
80 G3 **'Aqraba** Jordan
103 L7 **Aquarius Mts** Arizona U.S.A.
103 N4 **Aquarius Plat** Utah U.S.A.
130 B8 **Aquidabán,R** Paraguay
130 C7 **Aquidauana** Brazil
130 C6 **Aquidauana,R** Brazil
124 G3 **Aquiles Serdán** Mexico
109 K4 **Aquilla** Texas U.S.A.
126 H5 **Aquin** Haiti
45 P7 **Aquino** Italy
75 L6 **Ara** India
17 G2 **Ara** *R* Spain
80 F3 **Arab** *R* Jordan
79 F3 **'Arab al Mulk** Syria
38 E8 **Arabba** Italy
112 D6 **Arabi** Georgia U.S.A.
111 K12 **Arabi** New Orleans, Louisiana U.S.A.
Arabian Gulf *see* **Persian Gulf**
123 N3 **Arabian L** Quebec Canada
84 H3 **Arabs Gulf** Egypt
78 D1 **Araç** Turkey
128 F3 **Araçá** *R* Brazil
129 L6 **Aracaju** Brazil
130 C9 **Aracanguy, Mt de** Paraguay
126 G9 **Aracataca** Colombia
129 L4 **Aracati** Brazil
130 E7 **Araçatuba** Brazil
16 C7 **Aracena** Spain
16 C7 **Aracena, Sa. de** *mts* Spain
130 G5 **Araçuaí** Brazil
48 G4 **Arad** Romania
86 D2 **Arada** Chad
56 D5 **Aradanskiy Khrebet** *mts* Russian Federation
81 L7 **Arafura Sea** Aust/New Guinea
129 H7 **Aragarças** Brazil
78 J1 **Aragats** *mt* Armenia
61 M9 **Ara-gawa** *R* Japan
100 A6 **Arago,Cape** Oregon U.S.A.
17 G2 **Aragón** *R* Spain
17 G4 **Aragon** *reg* Spain
43 F11 **Aragona** Sicily
17 F4 **Aragoncillo** *mt* Spain
128 E2 **Aragua** *state* Venezuela
129 J6 **Araguaçu** Brazil
128 F2 **Aragua de Barcelona** Venezuela
129 H3 **Araguari** *R* Brazil
129 J7 **Araguari** Brazil
133 H1 **Araguari** *R* Brazil
129 J5 **Araguatins** Brazil
53 F12 **Aragvi** *R* Georgia
144 C5 **Arahura** New Zealand
61 M8 **Arai** Japan
79 E8 **Araif el Naqa** *mt* Egypt
80 G8 **Ara'ir** Jordan
85 E3 **Arak** Algeria
77 A2 **Arāk** Iran
61 N8 **Arakai-yama** *mt* Japan
128 G2 **Arakaka** Guyana
78 G4 **Arak, Al** Syria
116 A4 **Arakamchechen, Ostrov** *isld* Russian Federation
68 A2 **Arakan** *prov* Burma
68 B2 **Arakan Yoma** *ra* Burma
46 F6 **Arákhova** Greece
46 D5 **Árakhthos** *R* Greece
76 D4 **Arakkonam** India
120 C2 **Ara L** Ontario Canada
57 B2 **Aral'sk** Kazakhstan
57 A3 **Aral'skoye More** *sea* Kazakhstan/Uzbekistan
55 B6 **Aralsor, Oz** *L* Kazakhstan
26 A9 **Åram** Norway
141 G6 **Aramac** *R* Queensland Australia
141 H6 **Aramac** Queensland Australia
125 K5 **Aramberri** Mexico
19 N17 **Aramon** France
43 C7 **Aranci, G** Sardinia
16 E3 **Aranda de Duero** Spain
17 F3 **Aranda de Moncayo** Spain
87 B10 **Arandis** Namibia
145 D1 **Aranga** New Zealand
128 E7 **Arani** Bolivia
76 D4 **Arani** India
14 C1 **Aran I** Ireland
16 E4 **Aranjuez** Spain
8 C2 **Aran Mawddwy** *mt* Wales
89 A5 **Aranos** Namibia
109 L7 **Aransas B** Texas U.S.A.
109 K8 **Aransas Pass** Texas U.S.A.
130 E6 **Arantes,R** Brazil
137 P1 **Aranuka** *isld* Kiribati
85 D5 **Araouane** Mali
106 E1 **Arapaho** *mt* Colorado U.S.A.
106 H3 **Arapahoe** Colorado U.S.A.
98 G9 **Arapahoe** Nebraska U.S.A.
101 R7 **Arapahoe** Wyoming U.S.A.
128 E7 **Arapa,L** Peru
145 E4 **Arapawa I** New Zealand
133 F4 **Arapey** Uruguay
131 G3 **Arapey Grande** *R* Uruguay
130 H10 **Arapiraca** Brazil
78 G2 **Arapkir** Turkey
130 D8 **Arapongas** Brazil
145 E3 **Arapuni** New Zealand
130 E10 **Araquari** Brazil
78 H6 **'Ar'ar** Saudi Arabia
80 D4 **'Ar'Ara** Israel
133 H3 **Araranguá** Brazil
129 J8 **Araraquara** Brazil
130 F8 **Araras** São Paulo Brazil
130 D6 **Araras,Serra das** Mato Grosso Brazil
130 D9 **Araras, Serra das** *mts* Paraná Brazil
139 G6 **Ararat** Victoria Australia
Ararat,Mt *see* **Bügük Ağri**
129 K4 **Arari** Brazil
75 M5 **Araria** India
130 G8 **Araruama L.de** Brazil
78 H6 **Arar,Wadi** Saudi Arabia
80 D5 **A-ras** Jordan
78 J1 **Aras** *R* Turkey
17 G5 **Aras de Alpuente** Spain
126 A1 **Arasji** Aruba W Indies
145 D2 **Aratapu** New Zealand
145 F3 **Aratiatia** New Zealand
61 O7 **Arato** Japan
128 F5 **Araua** *R* Brazil
128 D2 **Arauca** Colombia
128 D2 **Arauca** *div* Colombia
133 C5 **Arauco** Chile
127 K10 **Araure** Venezuela
80 E2 **'Arav** Israel
74 E6 **Aravalli Range** India
137 M3 **Arawa** Bougainville I Papua New Guinea
144 B6 **Arawata R** New Zealand
129 J7 **Araxá** Brazil
128 F1 **Araya,P.de** Venezuela
61 P14 **Ara-zaki** *C* Okinawa
17 G3 **Arba** *R* Spain
86 G4 **Ārba Minch'** Ethiopia
43 C9 **Arbatax** Sardinia
52 G5 **Arbazh** Russian Federation
40 C2 **Arbecey** France
37 K5 **Arberg** Germany
78 J4 **Arbīl** *prov* Iraq
27 H12 **Arboga** Sweden
27 H12 **Arbogaån** *R* Sweden
40 C4 **Arbois** France
41 K2 **Arbon** Switzerland
101 N7 **Arbon** Idaho U.S.A.
119 O5 **Arborfield** Saskatchewan Canada
9 F5 **Arborfield Cross** England
119 U8 **Arborg** Manitoba Canada
99 R4 **Arbor Vitae** Wisconsin U.S.A.
27 H10 **Arbrå** Sweden
13 F1 **Arbroath** Scotland
102 B2 **Arbuckle** California U.S.A.
113 F10 **Arbuckle,L** Florida U.S.A.
109 K1 **Arbuckle Mts** Oklahoma U.S.A.
107 O7 **Arbuckles, Lake of the** Oklahoma U.S.A.
110 F5 **Arbyrd** Missouri U.S.A.
19 J5 **Arc** France
19 O18 **Arc** *R* France
18 E8 **Arcachon** France
94 J4 **Arcade** New York U.S.A.
118 A3 **Arcadia** Alberta Canada
113 F10 **Arcadia** Florida U.S.A.
94 A6 **Arcadia** Indiana U.S.A.
107 Q4 **Arcadia** Kansas U.S.A.
111 D9 **Arcadia** Louisiana U.S.A.
99 U5 **Arcadia** Michigan U.S.A.
110 F4 **Arcadia** Missouri U.S.A.
98 G8 **Arcadia** Nebraska U.S.A.
94 D5 **Arcadia** Ohio U.S.A.
107 N6 **Arcadia** Oklahoma U.S.A.
99 P5 **Arcadia** Wisconsin U.S.A.
95 T2 **Arcadia Nat. Park** Maine U.S.A.
43 G8 **Arcangelo,S** Italy
94 C7 **Arcanum** Ohio U.S.A.
21 L8 **Arçay** France
102 G3 **Arc Dome** *mt* Nevada U.S.A.
45 P6 **Arce** Italy
125 J8 **Arcelia** Mexico
25 F6 **Arcen** Netherlands
45 N4 **Arcévia** Italy
46 F1 **Archar** Bulgaria
95 M5 **Archbald** Pennsylvania U.S.A.
94 C5 **Archbold** Ohio U.S.A.
112 H2 **Archdale** North Carolina U.S.A.
141 F2 **Archer** *R* Queensland Australia
113 E8 **Archer** Florida U.S.A.
141 F2 **Archer Bend Nat. Park** Queensland Australia
109 J2 **Archer City** Texas U.S.A.
141 K2 **Archerfield Airfield** Brisbane, Qnsld Australia
141 H3 **Archer Pt** Queensland Australia
119 O6 **Archerwill** Saskatchewan Canada
40 E1 **Arches** France
103 P3 **Arches Nat. Park** Utah U.S.A.
110 B3 **Archie** Missouri U.S.A.
21 M8 **Archigny** France
119 M8 **Archive** Saskatchewan Canada
106 C5 **Archuleta** New Mexico U.S.A.
18 H4 **Arcis sur Aube** France
138 C2 **Arckaringa** *R* South Australia Australia
101 M6 **Arco** Idaho U.S.A.
98 K5 **Arco** Minnesota U.S.A.
119 P9 **Arcola** Saskatchewan Canada
99 S10 **Arcola** Illinois U.S.A.
111 F8 **Arcola** Mississippi U.S.A.
45 K1 **Árcole** Italy
18 H6 **Arconce** *R* France
138 D4 **Arcoona** South Australia Australia
131 B7 **Arco, Paso de** Arg/Chile
130 F7 **Arcos** Brazil
16 D8 **Arcos de la Frontera** Spain
16 B3 **Arcos de Vale de Vez** Portugal
17 G3 **Arcos,Sierra de** *mt* Spain
76 D4 **Arcot** India
20 D4 **Arcouest,l'** France
130 H10 **Arcoverde** Brazil
19 J5 **Arc-Senans** France
147 F4 **Arctic Bay** Northwest Territories Canada
90 J2 **Arctic Circle**
116 D4 **Arctic Lagoon** Alaska U.S.A.
147 **Arctic Ocean**
114 F4 **Arctic Red River** Northwest Territories Canada
116 P2 **Arctic Village** Alaska U.S.A.
146 D3 **Arctowski, Henryk** *Poland Base* Antarctica
45 L1 **Arcugnano** Italy
22 E5 **Arcy-Ste. Restitue** France
44 G2 **Arda** *R* Italy
78 M2 **Ardabīl** Iran
38 L5 **Ardagger** Austria
78 J1 **Ardahan** Turkey
77 C3 **Ardakan** Esfahān Iran
77 B4 **Ardal** Iran
27 C10 **Årdal** Opland Norway
27 B12 **Årdal** Rogaland Norway
14 C2 **Ardara** Ireland
118 K7 **Ardath** Saskatchewan Canada
52 F6 **Ardatov** Russian Federation
120 K7 **Ardbeg** Ontario Canada
12 B2 **Ardbeg** Scotland
45 N6 **Ardea** Italy
18 H8 **Ardèche** *dept* France
14 E3 **Ardee** Ireland
119 S8 **Arden** Manitoba Canada
121 O8 **Arden** Ontario Canada
103 J5 **Arden** Nevada U.S.A.
138 E4 **Arden Mt** South Australia Australia
18 H3 **Ardennes** *dept* France
22 H4 **Ardennes** France
21 O8 **Ardentes** France
12 D1 **Ardentinny** Scotland
77 C3 **Ardestān** Iran
15 D3 **Ardgay** Scotland
14 F2 **Ardglass** N Ireland
46 E4 **Ardhéa** Greece
16 C6 **Ardila,R** Spain
119 M9 **Ardill** Saskatchewan Canada
124 H6 **Ardilla, Cerro La** *pk* Mexico
46 G3 **Ardino** Bulgaria
18 E10 **Ardisa** Spain
70 P9 **Ardjasa** Java
70 O9 **Ardjuna,G** *mt* Java
145 F3 **Ardkeen** New Zealand
118 D6 **Ardley** Alberta Canada
15 D4 **Ardlui** Scotland
12 C2 **Ardminish** Scotland
139 H6 **Ardmona** Victoria Australia
118 G4 **Ardmore** Alberta Canada
107 N7 **Ardmore** Oklahoma U.S.A.
98 C6 **Ardmore** South Dakota U.S.A.
110 K6 **Ardmore** Tennessee U.S.A.
14 D5 **Ardmore B** Ireland
15 B4 **Ardnamurchan Pt** Scotland
15 B5 **Ardnave Pt** Scotland
98 J1 **Ardoch** North Dakota U.S.A.
22 B2 **Ardres** France
12 C1 **Ardrishaig** Scotland
138 E5 **Ardrossan** South Australia Australia
118 D5 **Ardrossan** Alberta Canada
15 D5 **Ardrossan** Scotland
14 F2 **Ards Pen** N Ireland
12 B2 **Ardtalla** Scotland
48 H3 **Ardud** Romania
15 C3 **Ardvasar** Scotland
53 F7 **Ardym** Russian Federation
26 F8 **Åre** Sweden
26 N4 **Areavaara** Sweden
127 L5 **Arecibo** Puerto Rico
131 F5 **Areco** *R* Argentina
48 J5 **Areful** Romania
129 L4 **Areia Branca** Brazil
45 Q7 **Areinzo** Italy
118 K6 **Arelee** Saskatchewan Canada
27 E12 **Aremark** Norway
36 B3 **Aremberg** Germany
118 H9 **Arena** Saskatchewan Canada
71 E6 **Arena** Philippines
95 N4 **Arena** New York U.S.A.
133 C7 **Arenales** *mt* Chile
130 C4 **Arenápolis** Brazil
71 F4 **Arena Pt** Luzon Philippines
124 E6 **Arena, Pta** *C* Mexico
16 D4 **Arenas de S.Pedro** Spain
128 D8 **Arenas,Pta** *C* Chile
32 F7 **Arenberg** *reg* Germany
27 C13 **Arendal** Norway
22 J1 **Arendonk** Belgium
33 O7 **Arendsee** Germany
32 L10 **Arenshausen** Germany
19 Q12 **Arenthon** France
28 D2 **Arentsminde** Denmark
17 J3 **Arenys de Mar** Spain
46 E8 **Areópolis** Greece
128 D7 **Arequipa** Peru
129 H4 **Arere** Brazil
18 E8 **Arés** France
16 D3 **Arévalo** Spain
140 B6 **Areyonga** N Terr Australia
42 D5 **Arezzo** Italy
46 E7 **Arfará** Greece
17 F2 **Arga** *R* Spain
140 D5 **Argadargada** N Terr Australia
58 E2 **Argalant** Mongolia
16 E5 **Argamasilla de Alba** Spain
16 E4 **Arganda** Spain
16 B4 **Arganil** Portugal
71 F6 **Argao** Philippines
45 P6 **Argatone, M** *mt* Italy
55 D3 **Argayash** Russian Federation
55 D3 **Argazi, Oz** Russian Federation
18 H10 **Argelès sur Mer** France
41 L2 **Argen** *R* Germany
21 K3 **Argences** France
19 Q18 **Argens** *R* France
117 P10 **Argenta** British Columbia Canada
45 L2 **Argenta** Italy
101 N4 **Argenta** Montana U.S.A.
21 K4 **Argentan** France
42 D6 **Argentario,Monte** Italy
18 G7 **Argentat** France
44 B3 **Argentera Mt** Italy
21 P4 **Argenteuil** Seine-et-Oise France
123 S6 **Argentia** Newfoundland Canada
40 E6 **Argentières** France
44 C4 **Argentina** *R* Italy
131 D5 **Argentina** *rep* S America
146 E7 **Argentina Range** *mts* Antarctica
90 E13 **Argentine Basin** Atlantic Oc
133 C8 **Argentino,L** Argentina
20 A4 **Argenton** France
21 K7 **Argenton** *R* France
21 K8 **Argenton-Château** France
21 O8 **Argenton-sur-Creuse** France
122 C3 **Argent,R à l'** Quebec Canada
21 J5 **Argentre** France
21 H5 **Argentré-du-Plessis** France
18 G5 **Argent sur Sauldre** France
48 J5 **Argeș** *R* Romania
48 J5 **Argeș** *reg* Romania
48 J6 **Argeșel** *R* Romania
77 J4 **Arghandab** *R* Afghanistan
77 K4 **Arghastan** *R* Afghanistan
84 J6 **Argo** Sudan
20 B5 **Argol** France
46 F7 **Argolikós Kólpos** *B* Greece
107 N4 **Argonia** Kansas U.S.A.
22 J5 **Argonne** *reg* France
99 S4 **Argonne** Wisconsin U.S.A.
70 O9 **Argopura G** *mt* Java
101 N5 **Argora** Idaho U.S.A.
46 F7 **Argos** Greece
94 A5 **Argos** Indiana U.S.A.
46 E4 **Árgos Orestikón** Greece
20 H4 **Argouges** France
18 D10 **Arguedas** Spain
21 O2 **Argueil** France
20 F5 **Arguenon** *R* France
59 H1 **Argun** *R* China/Rus Fed
85 E6 **Argungu** Nigeria
146 G10 **Argus, Dome** *ice dome* Antarctica
102 G6 **Argus Ra** California U.S.A.
98 J2 **Argusville** North Dakota U.S.A.
21 N8 **Argy** France
122 G10 **Argyle** Nova Scotia Canada
112 E6 **Argyle** Georgia U.S.A.
94 E3 **Argyle** Michigan U.S.A.
98 K1 **Argyle** Minnesota U.S.A.
99 R7 **Argyle** Wisconsin U.S.A.
142 G3 **Argyle, L** W Australia Australia
6 M6 **Argyll** *oil rig* North Sea
Argyrokastron *see* **Gjirokastër**
65 E3 **Ar Horquin Qi** China
28 E4 **Århus** Denmark
28 E4 **Århus** *co* Denmark
145 E3 **Aria** New Zealand
139 H5 **Ariah Pk** New South Wales Australia
60 D13 **Ariake-kai** *G* Japan
87 C11 **Ariamsvlei** Namibia
43 G7 **Ariano Irpino** Italy
45 M2 **Ariano Nel Polésine** Italy
128 D3 **Ariari** *R* Colombia
73 L8 **Ari Atoll** Maldives
85 D6 **Aribinda** Burkina
128 D7 **Arica** Chile
128 D4 **Arica** Colombia
45 N6 **Ariccia** Italy
123 M8 **Arichat** C Breton I, Nova Scotia
60 J11 **Arida** Japan
60 J11 **Arida-gawa** *R* Japan
85 B3 **Aridal, Sabkhat** *salt lake* Western Sahara
143 E10 **Arid, C** W Australia Australia
83 J12 **Aride I** Seychelles
Arid I *see* **Rakitu I**
18 G9 **Ariège** *dept* France
18 G10 **Ariège** *R* France
80 D5 **Ari'el** Jordan
100 C4 **Ariel** Washington U.S.A.
48 H4 **Arieș** *R* Romania
80 G8 **Ariha** Jordan
79 G3 **Arīḩā** Syria
106 H2 **Arikaree** *R* Colorado U.S.A.
60 C13 **Arikawa** Japan
29 K4 **Arild** Sweden
48 F7 **Arilje** Serbia Yugoslavia
128 F5 **Arima** Brazil
60 J11 **Arima** Japan
127 O2 **Arima** Trinidad
101 N7 **Arimo** Idaho U.S.A.
128 G3 **Arinda** Guyana
129 G6 **Arinos** *R* Brazil
129 J7 **Arinos** Brazil
101 M9 **Arinosa** Utah U.S.A.
99 L8 **Arion** Iowa U.S.A.
127 P1 **Aripo, Mt** Trinidad
128 D2 **Ariporo** *R* Colombia
128 F5 **Aripuana** *R* Brazil
128 F5 **Ariquemes** Brazil
130 D5 **Ariranha** *R* Brazil
15 C4 **Arisaig** Scotland
79 D7 **'Arîsh, El** Egypt
117 J9 **Aristazabal I** British Columbia Canada
133 D7 **Aristizábal, C** Argentina
111 L10 **Ariton** Alabama U.S.A.
43 C9 **Aritzo** Sardinia
103 N10 **Arivaca** Arizona U.S.A.
87 H11 **Arivonimamo** Madagascar
17 F3 **Ariza** Spain
18 F9 **Arize** *R* France
133 D5 **Arizona** Argentina
103 L7 **Arizona** *state* U.S.A.
124 D2 **Arizpe** Mexico
27 F12 **Årjäng** Sweden
26 J5 **Arjeplog** Sweden
128 D1 **Arjona** Colombia
16 E7 **Arjona** Spain
51 O2 **Arka** Russian Federation
110 F7 **Arkabutla Res** Mississippi U.S.A.
53 F8 **Arkadak** Russian Federation
109 O1 **Arkadelphia** Arkansas U.S.A.
55 E5 **Arkalyk** Kazakhstan
109 O1 **Arkansas** *state* U.S.A.
110 C6 **Arkansas** *R* Arkansas U.S.A.
111 E8 **Arkansas City** Arkansas U.S.A.
107 O4 **Arkansas City** Kansas U.S.A.
111 E7 **Arkansas Post Nat. Mem** Arkansas U.S.A.
84 G5 **Arkanu Jebel** *mt* Libya
138 E4 **Arkaroola** South Australia Australia
47 J9 **Arkása** Kárpathos I Greece
66 D4 **Arkatag** *mts* China
117 F5 **Arkell,Mt** Yukon Territory Canada
27 G15 **Arkelstorp** Sweden
47 V14 **Arkhángelos** Rhodes Greece
52 F3 **Arkhangel'sk** Russian Federation
53 F11 **Arkhangel'skoye** Russian Federation
59 K2 **Arkhara** Russian Federation
53 D7 **Arkhipovka** Russian Federation
53 D8 **Arkino** Russian Federation
14 E4 **Arklow** Ireland
47 H7 **Árkoi** *isld* Greece
120 J9 **Arkona** Ontario Canada
30 H1 **Arkona** Germany
27 J13 **Arkösund** Sweden
94 K4 **Arkport** New York U.S.A.
52 H6 **Arkul'** Russian Federation
95 N4 **Arkville** New York U.S.A.
27 J12 **Ärla** Sweden
18 H7 **Arlanc** France
16 E2 **Arlanza** *R* Spain
41 M3 **Arlberg** *pass* Austria
101 L2 **Arlee** Montana U.S.A.
19 N17 **Arles** Bouches du Rhône France
18 G10 **Arles** Pyrénées-Orientales France
22 E3 **Arleux** France
100 J5 **Arling** Idaho U.S.A.
8 D4 **Arlingham** England
103 M8 **Arlington** Arizona U.S.A.
102 G8 **Arlington** California U.S.A.
106 G3 **Arlington** Colorado U.S.A.
113 F7 **Arlington** Florida U.S.A.
112 C6 **Arlington** Georgia U.S.A.
99 P7 **Arlington** Iowa U.S.A.
107 M4 **Arlington** Kansas U.S.A.
110 G5 **Arlington** Kentucky U.S.A.
99 M5 **Arlington** Minnesota U.S.A.
98 K8 **Arlington** Nebraska U.S.A.
94 D6 **Arlington** Ohio U.S.A.
100 E4 **Arlington** Oregon U.S.A.
98 J5 **Arlington** South Dakota U.S.A.
110 G6 **Arlington** Tennessee U.S.A.
109 N9 **Arlington** Texas U.S.A.
95 O3 **Arlington** Vermont U.S.A.
95 K8 **Arlington** Virginia U.S.A.
117 M11 **Arlington** Washington U.S.A.
101 T8 **Arlington** Wyoming U.S.A.
99 S7 **Arlington Heights** Illinois U.S.A.
110 E4 **Arlington Res** Missouri U.S.A.
85 F5 **Arlit** Niger
22 K4 **Arlon** Belgium
140 C6 **Arltunga** N Terr Australia
107 Q4 **Arma** Kansas U.S.A.
118 E8 **Armada** Alberta Canada
143 B9 **Armadale** W Australia Australia
12 E2 **Armadale** Scotland
122 B7 **Armagh** Quebec Canada
14 E2 **Armagh** *co* N Ireland
14 E2 **Armagh** N Ireland
18 F9 **Armagnac** *reg* France
18 H5 **Armançon** *R* France
47 H9 **Armathia** *isld* Greece
13 F4 **Armathwaite** England
53 F10 **Armavir** Russian Federation
128 C3 **Armenia** Colombia
78 K1 **Armenia** *rep* W Asia
48 G5 **Armeniș** Romania
22 D2 **Armentières** France
21 M4 **Armentières** Eure France
101 P2 **Armington** Montana U.S.A.
101 S6 **Arminto** Wyoming U.S.A.
119 Q6 **Armit** Saskatchewan Canada
9 E2 **Armitage** England
55 E3 **Armizonskoye** Russian Federation
119 N5 **Armley** Saskatchewan Canada
98 H6 **Armour** South Dakota U.S.A.
98 G1 **Armourdale** North Dakota U.S.A.
120 D3 **Arms** Ontario Canada
36 E4 **Armsheim** Germany
101 N5 **Armstead** Montana U.S.A.
140 B3 **Armstrong** *R* N Terr Australia
117 O10 **Armstrong** British Columbia Canada
99 T9 **Armstrong** Illinois U.S.A.
99 M6 **Armstrong** Iowa U.S.A.
110 D2 **Armstrong** Missouri U.S.A.
109 K9 **Armstrong** Texas U.S.A.
59 L2 **Armu** *R* Russian Federation
74 H9 **Armur** India
47 J4 **Armutcuk Dağ** *mt* Turkey
47 K4 **Armutlu** Turkey
53 D10 **Armyansk** Ukraine
28 B7 **Arnå** *R* Denmark
21 L6 **Arnage** France
46 F4 **Arnaía** Greece
28 R9 **Arnarstapi** Iceland
118 D1 **Arnaud** Manitoba Canada
115 M6 **Arnaud,R** Quebec Canada
79 C3 **Arnauti, C** Cyprus
18 J5 **Arnay le Duc** France
28 B4 **Arnborg** Denmark
37 P5 **Arnbruck** Germany
33 Q7 **Arneburg** Germany
18 D10 **Arnedo** Spain
98 C2 **Arnegard** North Dakota U.S.A.
22 C2 **Arneke** France
26 M6 **Arnemark** Sweden
25 A6 **Arnemuiden** Netherlands
27 E11 **Årnes** Norway
107 L5 **Arnett** Oklahoma U.S.A.
94 F9 **Arnett** West Virginia U.S.A.
28 R9 **Arngerdhareyri** Iceland
25 E5 **Arnhem** Netherlands
140 D1 **Arnhem,C** N Terr Australia
140 C2 **Arnhem Land** *reg* N Terr Australia
140 C2 **Arnhem Land Aboriginal Land** N Terr Australia
21 N4 **Arnières** France
45 H4 **Arno** *R* Italy
138 D5 **Arno Bay** South Australia Australia
102 D3 **Arnold** California U.S.A.
110 F3 **Arnold** Missouri U.S.A.
98 F8 **Arnold** Nebraska U.S.A.
94 H6 **Arnold** Pennsylvania U.S.A.
99 L6 **Arnolds Park** Iowa U.S.A.
38 J8 **Arnoldstein** Austria
21 P7 **Arnon** *R* France
119 V3 **Arnot** Manitoba Canada
26 L1 **Arnöy** Norway
16 B2 **Arnoya** *R* Spain
12 D1 **Arnprior** Scotland
32 G10 **Arnsberg** Germany
13 F5 **Arnside** England
37 K2 **Arnstadt** Germany
37 L3 **Arnstein** Germany
37 O6 **Arnstorf** Germany
121 L4 **Arntfield** Quebec Canada
28 B6 **Arnum** Denmark
128 F2 **Aro** *R* Venezuela
127 K9 **Aroa** Venezuela
87 C11 **Aroab** Namibia
46 E7 **Aroánia** *mt* Greece
124 H4 **Arocha** Mexico
130 C7 **Aroeira** Brazil
32 K10 **Arolsen** Germany
55 E3 **Aromashevo** Russian Federation
21 J5 **Aron** France
21 J5 **Aron** *R* Mayenne France
42 B3 **Arona** Italy
122 E7 **Aroostook** New Brunswick Canada
95 S7 **Aroostook** *R* Maine U.S.A.
116 E6 **Aropuk L** Alaska U.S.A.
137 Q2 **Arorae** *isld* Kiribati
71 F4 **Aroroy** Philippines
28 D6 **Arøsund** Denmark
127 O2 **Arouca** Trinidad
17 F9 **Aroui, Mt** Morocco
145 F3 **Arowhana** *mt* New Zealand
106 G3 **Aroya** Colorado U.S.A.
109 M3 **Arp** Texas U.S.A.
57 G4 **Arpa** Kirghizia
18 G8 **Arpajon** France
21 P4 **Arpajon** France
48 J5 **Arpasu de Jos** Romania
55 D1 **Arpavla** Russian Federation
120 K4 **Arpin** Ontario Canada
45 P6 **Arpino** Italy
45 L1 **Arquà Petrarca** Italy
45 L1 **Arquà Polesine** Italy
21 N2 **Arques** *R* France
22 C2 **Arques** Pas-de-Calais France
21 N2 **Arques-la-Bataille** France
80 E2 **'Arraba** Israel
141 F7 **Arrabury** Queensland Australia
36 B6 **Arracourt** France
20 E6 **Arradon** France
131 D2 **Arraga** Argentina
16 C4 **Arrago** *R* Spain
129 J6 **Arraias** Brazil
16 B6 **Arraiolos** Portugal
14 C4 **Arra Mts** Ireland
119 Q7 **Arran** Saskatchewan Canada
15 C5 **Arran** *isld* Scotland
111 M11 **Arran** Florida U.S.A.
80 E4 **'Arrana** Jordan
117 H8 **Arrandale** British Columbia Canada
78 G4 **Ar Raqqah** Syria
84 F4 **Ar Rāqūbah** Libya
22 D3 **Arras** Pas-de-Calais France
79 G4 **Ar Rastan** Syria
18 F9 **Arrats** *R* France
28 B5 **Arre** Denmark
18 F10 **Arreau** France
128 E3 **Arrecifal** Colombia
85 B3 **Arrecife** Canary Is
20 C5 **Arrée,Mtgne.d'** France
28 J5 **Arresø** *L* Denmark
106 C9 **Arrey** New Mexico U.S.A.
45 L4 **Arrezzo** *reg* Italy
38 J8 **Arriach** Austria
125 N9 **Arriaga** Mexico
106 G2 **Arriba** Colorado U.S.A.
141 G6 **Arrilalah** Queensland Australia
28 B6 **Arrild** Denmark
9 F3 **Arrington** England
143 B8 **Arrino** W Australia Australia
12 D1 **Arrochar** Scotland
133 G4 **Arroio Grande** Brazil

21 J3 **Arromanches** France
16 C5 **Arronches** Portugal
44 M6 **Arrone** *R* Italy
18 F9 **Arros** *R* France
21 N5 **Arrou** France
18 H6 **Arroux** *R* France
101 Q2 **Arrow Cr** Montana U.S.A.
117 P10 **Arrowhead** British Columbia Canada
119 O2 **Arrow L** Ontario Canada
14 C2 **Arrow,L** Ireland
117 O10 **Arrow Park** British Columbia Canada
110 D2 **Arrow Rock** Missouri U.S.A.
100 K6 **Arrowrock Res** Idaho U.S.A.
138 F4 **Arrowsmith Mt** New South Wales Australia
144 C5 **Arrowsmith, Mt** New Zealand
140 D2 **Arrowsmith Pt** N Terr Australia
144 B6 **Arrowtown** New Zealand
118 D8 **Arrow Wood** Alberta Canada
16 C5 **Arroyo de la Luz** Spain
108 F6 **Arroyo de la Zorra** *R* Mexico
131 F6 **Arroyo Grande** *R* Argentina
102 D6 **Arroyo Grande** California U.S.A.
106 E5 **Arroyo Hondo** New Mexico U.S.A.
131 F4 **Arroyo Negro** *R* Uruguay
103 J8 **Arroyo Seco** *R* California U.S.A.
128 F6 **Arroyos,L de Los** Bolivia
130 B9 **Arroyos-y-Esteros** Paraguay
130 C4 **Arruda** Brazil
78 G4 **Ar Ruşāfah** Syria
79 H3 **Ar Ruwayḑah** Syria
28 D3 **Års** Denmark
77 C5 **Arsenajan** Iran
118 J3 **Arsenault L** Saskatchewan Canada
117 Q3 **Arseno L** Northwest Territories Canada
59 K3 **Arsen'yev** Russian Federation
55 C3 **Arshinka** Russian Federation
41 O6 **Arsiero** Italy
76 C4 **Arsikere** India
52 G6 **Arsk** Russian Federation
26 J9 **Årskogen** Sweden
57 G4 **Arslanbal** Kirghizia
45 O5 **Arsoli** Italy
19 K3 **Ars-sur-Moselle** France
27 J11 **Årsunda** Sweden
79 F2 **Arsuz** Turkey
22 D5 **Arsy** France
46 D5 **Árta** Greece
17 K5 **Artá** Majorca
80 D7 **Artas** Jordan
98 G4 **Artas** South Dakota U.S.A.
17 K5 **Artá,Sierra de,Mt** Majorca
124 H8 **Arteaga** Mexico
59 K3 **Artem** Russian Federation
19 P13 **Artemare** France
126 C3 **Artemisa** Cuba
51 J3 **Artemovak** Russian Federation
54 G7 **Artemovka** Ukraine
56 D4 **Artemovsk** Russian Federation
53 F9 **Artemovskiy** Russian Federation
45 N6 **Artena** Italy
21 O5 **Artenay** France
33 O10 **Artern** Germany
17 H3 **Artesa de Segre** Spain
Artesia *see* **Mosomane**
111 H8 **Artesia** Mississippi U.S.A.
98 J5 **Artesian** South Dakota U.S.A.
109 H7 **Artesia Wells** Texas U.S.A.
26 G6 **Artfjallet** *mt* Sweden
121 T6 **Arthabaska** Quebec Canada
18 E9 **Arthez** France
21 O3 **Arthies** France
21 O8 **Arthon** France
20 G7 **Arthon-en-Retz** France
139 H8 **Arthur** *R* Tasmania Australia
110 H2 **Arthur** Illinois U.S.A.
98 E8 **Arthur** Nebraska U.S.A.
98 J2 **Arthur** North Dakota U.S.A.
109 M2 **Arthur City** Texas U.S.A.
138 E4 **Arthur,L** South Australia Australia
139 H8 **Arthur,L** Tasmania Australia
142 E4 **Arthur, Mt** W Australia Australia
145 D4 **Arthur, Mt** New Zealand
141 K5 **Arthur Pt** Queensland Australia
143 B10 **Arthur River** W Australia Australia
144 C5 **Arthur's Pass** New Zealand
126 G2 **Arthur's Town** Cat I Bahamas
55 C3 **Arti** Russian Federation
146 C3 **Artigas** *Uruguay Base* Antarctica
133 F4 **Artigas** Uruguay
114 J5 **Artillery L** Northwest Territories Canada
29 M11 **Artjärvi** Finland
118 H6 **Artland** Saskatchewan Canada
33 M6 **Artlenburg** Germany
22 C3 **Artois** *prov* France
102 B2 **Artois** California U.S.A.
22 D3 **Artois Collines d'** France
46 E6 **Artotína** Greece
78 F1 **Artova** Turkey
Artsakan Nor *see* **Qagan Nur** *L*
48 M5 **Artsiz** Ukraine
66 B4 **Artux** China
71 B1 **Aru** Halmahera Indonesia
86 F5 **Aru** Zaire
129 H6 **Aruanã** Brazil
126 A2 **Aruba** *isld* W Indies
18 E9 **Arudy** France
80 E8 **Arugot** *R* Jordan
136 G3 **Aru,Kep** *islds* Moluccas Indonesia
25 D2 **Arum** Netherlands
128 F4 **Arumá** Brazil
61 Q12 **Arume** *B* Okinawa
75 Q4 **Arunachal Pradesh** *prov* India
9 F6 **Arundel** England
144 C5 **Arundel** New Zealand
9 F5 **Arun,R** England
28 E6 **Årup** Denmark
76 D6 **Aruppukkottai** India
80 D5 **'Arūra** Jordan
88 F3 **Arusha** Tanzania
70 G4 **Arus,Tg** *C* Sulawesi Indonesia
70 B5 **Arut** *R* Kalimantan
70 E6 **Aru,Tg** *C* Kalimantan
83 K9 **Aruvi Aru** *R* Sri Lanka
86 D5 **Aruwimi** *R* Zaire
106 E2 **Arvada** Colorado U.S.A.
101 T5 **Arvada** Wyoming U.S.A.
26 K7 **Arvån** Sweden
58 D2 **Arvayheer** Mongolia
40 D5 **Arve** *R* France
26 K5 **Arvestuottar** *mt* Sweden
74 H8 **Arvi** India
121 T4 **Arvida** Quebec Canada
26 K6 **Arvidsjaur** Sweden
27 F12 **Arvika** Sweden
102 F6 **Arvin** California U.S.A.
94 J9 **Arvonia** Virginia U.S.A.
65 E1 **Arxan** China
147 Q9 **Ary** Russian Federation
55 C3 **Aryazh** Russian Federation
47 O13 **Aryirádhes** Greece
46 G9 **Aryiroúpolis** Crete Greece
55 E4 **Aryk-Balyk** Kazakhstan
57 E4 **Arys'** *R* Kazakhstan
57 E4 **Arys'** Kazakhstan
57 D2 **Arys,Ozero** *L* Kazakhstan
20 E6 **Arz** *R* France
20 F6 **Arzal, Barrage d'** *dam* France
52 F6 **Arzamas** Russian Federation
20 D6 **Arzano** France
37 N3 **Arzberg** Germany
37 L5 **Arzberg** *mt* Germany
32 K8 **Ärzen** Germany
85 D1 **Arzew** Algeria
36 B3 **Arzfeld** Germany
53 F10 **Arzgir** Russian Federation
41 O6 **Arzignano** Italy
41 N3 **Arzl** Austria
20 E6 **Arzon** France
16 B2 **Arzúa** Spain
22 K1 **As** Belgium
37 N3 **Aš** Czech Rep
26 E8 **Ås** Norway
28 E2 **Aså** Denmark
27 F14 **Åsa** Sweden
87 C11 **Asab** Namibia
74 D1 **Asadābād** Afghanistan
69 D11 **Asahan** *R* Sumatra
60 G10 **Asahi** *R* Japan
61 O10 **Asahi** Chiba Japan
60 Q2 **Asahi-dake** *mt* Japan
61 N7 **Asahi-dake** *mt* Japan
60 Q2 **Asahikawa** Japan
86 H3 **Āsalē** *L* Ethiopia
61 M9 **Asama yama** *vol* Japan
65 G6 **Asan Man** *B* S Korea
75 M7 **Asansol** India
26 G9 **Åsarna** Sweden
84 F5 **Asawanwah** Libya
36 C2 **Asbach** Germany
71 C3 **Asbakin** W Irian
55 D3 **Asbest** Russian Federation
121 T7 **Asbestos** Quebec Canada
89 C7 **Asbestos Mts** S Africa
107 Q4 **Asbury** Kansas U.S.A.
110 B4 **Asbury** Missouri U.S.A.
Ascalon *see* **Tel Ashqelon**
90 B12 **Ascension** *isld* Atlantic Oc
128 F7 **Ascensión** Bolivia
124 E2 **Ascensión** Chihuahua Mexico
126 A1 **Ascension** Curaçao Neth Antilles
37 O6 **Ascha** Germany
38 L5 **Aschbach** Austria
33 M4 **Ascheberg** Germany
32 G9 **Ascheberg** Nordrhein-Westfalen Germany
32 F6 **Aschendorf** Germany
21 O5 **Aschères-le-Marché** France
33 O9 **Aschersleben** Germany
17 H3 **Asco** Spain
12 C2 **Ascog** Scotland
42 F6 **Ascoli Piceno** Italy
141 K1 **Ascot** *dist* Brisbane, Qnsld Australia
9 F5 **Ascot** England
133 D2 **Ascotán** Chile
86 H3 **Āseb** Eritrea
27 H14 **Åseda** Sweden
85 E4 **Asedjrad** *hills* Algeria
53 H7 **Asekeyevoye** Russian Federation
86 G4 **Āsela** Ethiopia
26 J7 **Åsele** Sweden
26 E8 **Åsen** Norway
27 G10 **Åsen** Sweden
32 K7 **Asendorf** Germany
46 G3 **Asenovgrad** Bulgaria
27 B13 **Åseral** Norway
79 G5 **Aşfar, Tall al** *mt* Syria
22 G5 **Asfeld-la-ville** France
27 D12 **Asgårdstr** Norway
55 C3 **Asha** Russian Federation
80 C8 **Ashan** *R* Israel
52 J5 **Ashan** Russian Federation
55 C3 **Ashap** Russian Federation
9 E1 **Ashbourne** England
112 D6 **Ashburn** Georgia U.S.A.
142 B6 **Ashburton** *R* W Australia Australia
8 C6 **Ashburton** England
144 C5 **Ashburton** New Zealand
140 C4 **Ashburton Ra** N Terr Australia
9 E4 **Ashbury** England
95 N6 **Ashbury Park** New Jersey U.S.A.
99 L3 **Ashby** Minnesota U.S.A.
9 E2 **Ashby de la Zouch** England
57 D2 **Ashchikol', Ozero** *L* Kazakhstan
57 C1 **Ashchitastysor, Ozero** *L* Kazakhstan
117 N10 **Ashcroft** British Columbia Canada
80 B6 **Ashdod** Israel
109 N2 **Ash Down** Arkansas U.S.A.
9 G5 **Ashdown Forest** England
112 H2 **Asheboro** North Carolina U.S.A.
107 O7 **Asher** Oklahoma U.S.A.
119 T7 **Ashern** Manitoba Canada
108 H7 **Asherton** Texas U.S.A.
112 E2 **Asheville** North Carolina U.S.A.
110 E5 **Ash Flat** Arkansas U.S.A.
9 G5 **Ashford** England
113 D11 **Ashford** Alabama U.S.A.
100 C3 **Ashford** Washington U.S.A.
9 E5 **Ashford Hill** England
103 M6 **Ashfork** Arizona U.S.A.
141 K1 **Ashgrove** *dist* Brisbane, Qnsld Australia
107 M2 **Ash Grove** Kansas U.S.A.
110 C4 **Ash Grove** Missouri U.S.A.
145 E4 **Ashhurst** New Zealand
60 Q2 **Ashibetsu** Japan
61 N9 **Ashikaga** Japan
9 F6 **Ashington** England
61 N9 **Ashio** Japan
52 G6 **Ashit** *R* Russian Federation
60 J11 **Ashiya** Japan
60 G13 **Ashizuri-misaki** *C* Japan
77 D4 **Ashkazar** Iran
77 F1 **Ashkhabad** Iran
77 F1 **Ashkhabad** Turkmenistan
13 F3 **Ashkirk** Scotland
99 T9 **Ashkum** Illinois U.S.A.
111 L8 **Ashland** Alabama U.S.A.
110 F2 **Ashland** Illinois U.S.A.
107 L4 **Ashland** Kansas U.S.A.
94 E8 **Ashland** Kentucky U.S.A.
95 S7 **Ashland** Maine U.S.A.
101 T4 **Ashland** Montana U.S.A.
98 K8 **Ashland** Nebraska U.S.A.
95 Q3 **Ashland** New Hampshire U.S.A.
94 E6 **Ashland** Ohio U.S.A.
100 C7 **Ashland** Oregon U.S.A.
95 L6 **Ashland** Pennsylvania U.S.A.
94 K9 **Ashland** Virginia U.S.A.
99 Q3 **Ashland** Wisconsin U.S.A.
110 J5 **Ashland City** Tennessee U.S.A.
144 D5 **Ashley** New Zealand
110 G3 **Ashley** Illinois U.S.A.
94 C3 **Ashley** Michigan U.S.A.
98 G3 **Ashley** North Dakota U.S.A.
120 K4 **Ashley Mine** Ontario Canada
55 E3 **Ashlyk** *R* Russian Federation
118 F4 **Ashmont** Alberta Canada
108 E3 **Ashmore** Texas U.S.A.
142 E1 **Ashmore Reef** Timor Sea
79 A8 **Ashmûn** Egypt
80 F1 **Ashmura** Syria
95 N5 **Ashokan Res** New York U.S.A.
60 R2 **Ashoro** Japan
80 B7 **Ashqelon** Israel
78 J4 **Ash Sharqat** Iraq
72 F6 **Ash Shaykh' Uthmān** Yemen
72 F6 **Ash Shihr** Yemen
84 E4 **Ash Shuwayrif** Libya
94 G5 **Ashtabula** Ohio U.S.A.
98 J2 **Ashtabula,L** North Dakota U.S.A.
74 F9 **Ashti** India
77 A2 **Āshtiān** Iran
121 O7 **Ashton** Ontario Canada
101 O5 **Ashton** Idaho U.S.A.
99 R8 **Ashton** Illinois U.S.A.
94 B3 **Ashton** Michigan U.S.A.
98 H5 **Ashton** South Dakota U.S.A.
13 F6 **Ashton-in-Makerfield** England
142 F3 **Ashton Ra** W Australia Australia
13 F6 **Ashton-under-Lyne** England
115 N7 **Ashuanipi,L** Labrador, Nfld Canada
121 R3 **Ashuapmushuan** *R* Quebec Canada
121 R3 **Ashuapmushuan, Réserve Faunique** Quebec Canada
78 J4 **Ashur** Iraq
78 J6 **Ashuriyah, Al** Iraq
111 K8 **Ashville** Alabama U.S.A.
79 G3 **'Āsī** *R* Syria/Lebanon
42 D3 **Asiago** Italy
71 C2 **Asia Pulau Pulau** *islds* Indonesia
71 F4 **Asid Gulf** Philippines
124 H6 **Asientos** Mexico
45 K1 **Asigliano Ven** Italy
75 L9 **Āsika** India
85 C1 **Asilah** Morocco
71 A1 **Asimiro** Halmahera Indonesia
43 B7 **Asinara, Golfo dell'** Sardinia
43 B7 **Asinara, I** Sardinia
56 C3 **Asino** Russian Federation
78 H2 **Aşkale** Turkey
53 D10 **Askaniya Nova** Ukraine
55 C4 **Askarovo** Russian Federation
14 C4 **Askeaton Adare** Ireland
27 D12 **Asker** Norway
13 G6 **Askern** England
27 G13 **Askersund** Sweden
72 H1 **Askhabad** Turkmenistan
26 J7 **Åskilje** Sweden
27 E12 **Askim** Norway
112 K2 **Askin** North Carolina U.S.A.
55 C3 **Askino** Russian Federation
28 G7 **Askø** Denmark
29 M11 **Askola** Finland
65 J3 **Askol'd, O** *isld* Russian Federation
28 C6 **Askov** Denmark
99 O3 **Askov** Minnesota U.S.A.
13 F5 **Askrigg** England
27 A10 **Askvoll** Norway
79 C9 **Asl** Egypt
47 K5 **Aslanapa** Turkey
79 E2 **Aslanköy Dere** *str* Turkey
74 D1 **Asmar** Afghanistan
Asmara *see* **Āsmera**
86 G2 **Āsmera** Eritrea
29 K5 **Asminderød** Denmark
28 F5 **Asnæs** *pen* Denmark
28 G5 **Asnæs** Denmark
21 J3 **Asnelles** France
27 G15 **Åsnen** Sweden
27 E11 **Åsnes** Norway
129 G3 **Asoenangka** Brazil
45 J1 **Asola** Italy
28 S9 **Asólfsstadhir** Iceland
60 E13 **Aso Nat. Park** Japan
86 F3 **Āsosa** Ethiopia
86 G1 **Asoteriba, Jebel** *mt* Sudan
100 H3 **Asotin** Washington U.S.A.
85 E3 **Asouf** *watercourse* Algeria
60 C11 **Asō-wan** *B* Japan
60 E13 **Aso zan** *vol* Japan
36 G6 **Aspach** Germany
48 C3 **Aspang** Austria
26 G8 **Aspås** Sweden
13 E4 **Aspatria** England
17 G6 **Aspe** Spain
26 J8 **Aspeå** Sweden
106 D2 **Aspen** Colorado U.S.A.
101 P8 **Aspen** Wyoming U.S.A.
118 D6 **Aspen Beach Prov. Park** Alberta Canada
36 G6 **Asperg** Germany
28 D6 **Asperup** Denmark
19 P16 **Aspremont** France
46 D5 **Asprókavos, Akr** *C* Greece
47 P13 **Asprókavos, Akra** *C* Greece
43 G10 **Aspromonte** *mts* Italy
123 M7 **Aspy B** C Breton I, Nova Scotia
118 K6 **Asquith** Saskatchewan Canada
79 H3 **Aş Şā'ān** Syria
74 D1 **Assad-Abad** Afghanistan
79 H2 **As Safirah** Syria
21 K8 **Assais-les-Jumeaux** France
75 O5 **Assam** *prov* India
85 F5 **Assamakka** Niger
95 M8 **Assateague I** Maryland U.S.A.
22 G2 **Asse** Belgium
19 Q17 **Asse** *R* France
119 V2 **Assean L** Manitoba Canada
89 G6 **Assegai** *R* Swaziland
85 F3 **Assekaifaf** Algeria
85 F4 **Assekreme** *mt* Algeria
32 K5 **Assel** Germany
21 K5 **Asse la Boisne** France
22 K3 **Asselborn** Luxembourg
25 G3 **Assen** Netherlands
36 F3 **Assenheim** Germany
28 E3 **Assens** Århus Denmark
28 D6 **Assens** Fyn Denmark
20 F7 **Asserac** France
22 J3 **Assesse** Belgium
122 G2 **Assigny,L** Quebec Canada
118 L9 **Assinboia** Saskatchewan Canada
28 B4 **Assing** Denmark
118 L9 **Assiniboia** Saskatchewan Canada
117 Q10 **Assiniboine,Mt** Br Col/Alberta Canada
119 Q8 **Assiniboine R** Manitoba/Sask Canada
84 G4 **As Sirīr** *sands* Libya
46 F4 **Ássiros** Greece
129 H8 **Assis** Brazil
42 E5 **Assisi** Italy
36 D3 **Assmannshausen** Germany
41 K6 **Asso** Italy
78 G4 **As Sukhnah** Syria
87 H9 **Assumption** *isld* Seychelles
110 G2 **Assumption** Illinois U.S.A.
78 K5 **Aş Şuwayrah** Iraq
36 C5 **Assweiler** Germany
37 N7 **Ast** Germany
27 E10 **Asta** *R* Norway
18 F8 **Astaffort** France
47 H9 **Astakidha** *isld* Greece
46 E6 **Astakós** Greece
77 A1 **Astaneh** Iran
28 E2 **Åsted** Nordjylland Denmark
28 B3 **Åsted** Viborg Denmark
25 E6 **Asten** Netherlands
77 C1 **Asterabad** Iran
44 D2 **Asti** Italy
16 E1 **Astillero** Spain
Astin Tagh *mt ra see* **Altun Shan**
47 H8 **Astipálaia** *isld* Greece
9 E1 **Aston** England
8 D3 **Aston Cross** England
74 F1 **Astor** Kashmir
16 C2 **Astorga** Spain
99 Q9 **Astoria** Illinois U.S.A.
100 B3 **Astoria** Oregon U.S.A.
98 K5 **Astoria** South Dakota U.S.A.
27 F15 **Åstorp** Sweden
121 L6 **Astorville** Ontario Canada
87 H10 **Astove** *isld* Br Indian Oc Terr
53 G10 **Astrakhan'** Russian Federation
55 E5 **Astrakhanka** Kazakhstan
26 L7 **Åsträsk** Sweden
146 J6 **Astrid Ridge** *ridge* Antarctica
46 F7 **Astros** Greece
28 E6 **Astrup** Fyn Denmark
28 B5 **Åstrup** Ribe Denmark
28 D6 **Åstrup** Sønderjylland Denmark
28 J7 **Åstrup** *isld* Storstrøm Denmark
28 D5 **Åstrup** Vejle Denmark
16 E2 **Astudillo** Spain
45 N7 **Astura** *R* Italy
16 C1 **Asturias** *reg* Spain
9 F3 **Astwood** England
146 J8 **Asuka** *Japan Base* Antarctica
28 E6 **Åsum** Denmark
133 F3 **Asunción** Paraguay
27 H14 **Åsunden** *L* Sweden
28 E5 **As Vig** *B* Denmark
84 J5 **Aswân** Egypt
84 J5 **Aswan High Dam** Egypt
84 J4 **Asyût** Egypt
48 E3 **Aszód** Hungary
137 R6 **Ata** *isld* Pacific Oc
57 E3 **Atabay** Kazakhstan
47 L7 **Atabey** Turkey
133 C3 **Atacama** *reg* Chile
128 E8 **Atacama, Des de** Chile
133 D3 **Atacama, Puna de** *plateau* Argentina
48 L2 **Ataki** Moldova
85 E7 **Atakpamé** Togo
130 J10 **Atalaia** Brazil
46 F6 **Atalándi** Greece
128 D6 **Atalaya** Peru
130 H6 **Ataléia** Brazil
71 M9 **Atambua** Timor Indonesia
61 N10 **Atami** Japan
115 O5 **Atammik** Greenland
55 F4 **Atansor, Oz** *L* Kazakhstan
79 C9 **'Ataqa, G** *mt* Egypt
85 B4 **Atar** Mauritania
80 D5 **'Atara** Jordan
80 F7 **Ataroth** Jordan
106 B7 **Atarque** New Mexico U.S.A.
80 F7 **Ataruz** Jordan
Atas *isld see* **South I** Cocos Is
102 D6 **Atascadero** California U.S.A.
109 J6 **Atascosa** *R* Texas U.S.A.
57 F1 **Atasu** Kazakhstan
68 C4 **Atatano** *R* Burma
78 G3 **Ataturk Baraji** *res* Turkey
17 F2 **Atauri** Spain
71 M9 **Atauro** *isld* Indonesia
86 F2 **Atbara** Sudan
86 G2 **Atbara** *R* Sudan
55 E5 **Atbasar** Kazakhstan
57 H4 **At-Bash** Kirghizia
111 E12 **Atchafalaya Bay** Louisiana U.S.A.
107 P2 **Atchison** Kansas U.S.A.
116 G5 **Atchueelinguk** *R* Alaska U.S.A.
112 C3 **Atco** Georgia U.S.A.
95 N7 **Atco** New Jersey U.S.A.
17 F3 **Ateca** Spain
58 E4 **A-t'eng-hsi-lien** China
124 G7 **Atenguillo** Mexico
61 O7 **Aterazawa** Japan
42 F6 **Aterno** *R* Italy
42 D2 **Atesine,Alpi** Italy
42 F6 **Atessa** Italy
22 F2 **Ath** Belgium
117 D4 **Athabasca** Alberta Canada
114 J6 **Athabasca, L** Alberta/Sask Canada
119 Q4 **Athapap** Manitoba Canada
119 Q4 **Athapapuskow L** Manitoba Canada
28 C4 **Atheden** *reg* Denmark
110 B1 **Athelstan** Iowa U.S.A.
100 G4 **Athena** Oregon U.S.A.
14 C3 **Athenry** Ireland
121 P8 **Athens** Ontario Canada
Athens Greece *see* **Athínai**
110 K7 **Athens** Alabama U.S.A.
112 D4 **Athens** Georgia U.S.A.
99 R10 **Athens** Illinois U.S.A.
109 O3 **Athens** Louisiana U.S.A.
95 S2 **Athens** Maine U.S.A.
94 B4 **Athens** Michigan U.S.A.
94 E7 **Athens** Ohio U.S.A.
95 L5 **Athens** Pennsylvania U.S.A.
112 C2 **Athens** Tennessee U.S.A.
109 M3 **Athens** Texas U.S.A.
99 Q4 **Athens** Wisconsin U.S.A.
121 L8 **Atherley** Ontario Canada
9 E2 **Atherstone** England
141 H3 **Atherton** Queensland Australia
13 F6 **Atherton** England
85 E7 **Athiémé** Benin
22 F4 **Athies** Aisne France
22 D4 **Athies** Somme France
46 F7 **Athínai** Greece
21 K4 **Athis-de-l'Orne** France
14 C3 **Athleague** Ireland
14 D3 **Athlone** Ireland
79 D3 **Athna** Cyprus
76 B2 **Athni** India
144 B6 **Athol** New Zealand
100 J2 **Athol** Idaho U.S.A.
95 P4 **Athol** Massachusetts U.S.A.
113 L9 **Athol I** New Providence I Bahamas
122 F6 **Atholville** New Brunswick Canada
46 G4 **Áthos** *mt* Greece
Athos, Mt *reg see* **Áyion Óros**
79 G9 **Ath Thāyat** *mt* Saudi Arabia
22 K4 **Athus** Belgium
14 E4 **Athy** Ireland
86 C3 **Ati** Chad
145 F3 **Atiamuri** New Zealand
130 F8 **Atibaia** Brazil
128 D7 **Atico** Peru
123 N2 **Aticonipi L** Quebec Canada
17 F3 **Atienza** Spain
119 Q4 **Atik** Manitoba Canada
117 Q8 **Atikameg** Alberta Canada
119 R4 **Atikameg Lake** Manitoba Canada
99 P1 **Atikokan** Ontario Canada
115 N7 **Atikonak, L** Labrador, Nfld Canada
122 H1 **Atikonal L** Labrador, Nfld Canada
118 J1 **Atikwa L** Ontario Canada
71 E3 **Atimonan** Philippines
45 P6 **Atina** Italy
76 D5 **Atirampattinam** India
116 P9 **Atka** Aleutian Is
51 P2 **Atka** Russian Federation
53 F8 **Atkarsk** Russian Federation
116 J1 **Atkasuk** Alaska U.S.A.
110 D6 **Atkins** Arkansas U.S.A.
99 Q8 **Atkinson** Illinois U.S.A.
98 G7 **Atkinson** Nebraska U.S.A.
112 J3 **Atkinson** North Carolina U.S.A.
71 B3 **Atkri** W Irian
105 **Atlanta** *conurbation* Georgia U.S.A.
111 M8 **Atlanta** Georgia U.S.A.
101 K6 **Atlanta** Idaho U.S.A.
110 G1 **Atlanta** Illinois U.S.A.
94 A6 **Atlanta** Indiana U.S.A.
107 O4 **Atlanta** Kansas U.S.A.
110 D2 **Atlanta** Missouri U.S.A.
95 K4 **Atlanta** New York U.S.A.
109 N2 **Atlanta** Texas U.S.A.
99 L8 **Atlantic** Iowa U.S.A.
112 L2 **Atlantic** North Carolina U.S.A.
95 N7 **Atlantic City** New Jersey U.S.A.
101 R7 **Atlantic City** Wyoming U.S.A.
95 N6 **Atlantic Highlands** New Jersey U.S.A.
90 J15 **Atlantic-Indian Basin** Southern Oc
90 J14 **Atlantic-Indian Ridge** S Atlantic Oc
128 D1 **Atlántico** *div* Colombia
90 **Atlantic Oc**
90 E5 **Atlantis Fracture** Atlantic Oc
94 D4 **Atlas** Michigan U.S.A.
85 C2 **Atlas, Haut** *mts* Morocco
85 C2 **Atlas, Moyen** *mts* Morocco
85 E2 **Atlas Saharien** *mts* Algeria
118 G8 **Atlee** Alberta Canada
117 G6 **Atlin** British Columbia Canada
80 C3 **'Atlit** Israel
125 K8 **Atlixco** Mexico
26 A10 **Atlöy** *isld* Norway
76 D3 **Atmakur** India
113 B11 **Atmore** Alabama U.S.A.
117 L9 **Atnarko** British Columbia Canada
26 D10 **Atnasjö** *L* Norway
55 E2 **Atnis** Russian Federation
60 E11 **Atō** Japan
87 H12 **Atofinandrahana** Madagascar
107 O7 **Atoka** Oklahoma U.S.A.
101 N6 **Atomic City** Idaho U.S.A.
124 H7 **Atotonilco el Alto** Mexico
77 E1 **Atrak** *R* Iran
27 F14 **Atran** Sweden
26 L7 **Åträsk** Sweden
128 C2 **Atrato** *R* Colombia
42 F6 **Atri** Italy
45 R8 **Atripalda** Italy
56 G4 **Atsikyak** Russian Federation
61 N10 **Atsugi** Japan
61 N7 **Atsumi** Japan
61 L11 **Atsumi-hantō** *pen* Japan
140 C4 **Attack Cr** N Terr Australia
111 K7 **Attalla** Alabama U.S.A.
68 H5 **Attapu** Laos
47 U14 **Attaviros** *mt* Rhodes Greece
115 L7 **Attawapiskat** Ontario Canada
80 G1 **Aţ Ţayḩah** Syria
36 D1 **Attendorn** Germany
38 J6 **Attersee** Austria
110 J1 **Attica** Indiana U.S.A.
107 M4 **Attica** Kansas U.S.A.
94 D3 **Attica** Michigan U.S.A.
94 J4 **Attica** New York U.S.A.
94 E5 **Attica** Ohio U.S.A.
22 E5 **Attichy** France
40 B5 **Attignat** France
22 H5 **Attigny** France
46 F6 **Attikí** *admin region* Greece
95 Q5 **Attleboro** Massachusetts U.S.A.
9 H2 **Attleborough** England
9 H2 **Attlebridge** England
26 J9 **Attmar** Sweden
109 N4 **Attoyac Bayou** *R* Texas U.S.A.
116 J9 **Attu** Aleutian Is
115 O4 **Attu** Greenland
76 D5 **Attur** India
133 D5 **Atuel** *R* Argentina
131 C6 **Atuel, Banados del** *swamps* Argentina
27 H13 **Åtvid** Sweden
27 H13 **Åtvidaberg** Sweden
119 P8 **Atwater** Saskatchewan Canada
102 D4 **Atwater** California U.S.A.
99 M4 **Atwater** Minnesota U.S.A.
13 H6 **Atwick** England
106 G1 **Atwood** Colorado U.S.A.
110 H2 **Atwood** Illinois U.S.A.
107 J2 **Atwood** Kansas U.S.A.
94 F6 **Atwood Res** Ohio U.S.A.
53 G7 **Atyashevo** Russian Federation
38 N5 **Atzenbrugg** Austria
33 P9 **Atzendorf** Germany
36 D2 **Au** Rheinland-Pfalz Germany
128 E4 **Auati-Paraná** *R* Brazil
135 S3 **Auau Chan** Hawaiian Is
37 J4 **Aub** Germany
19 P18 **Aubagne** France
22 K4 **Aubange** Belgium
71 F2 **Aubarede Pt** Luzon Philippines
18 H4 **Aube** *R* France
18 H4 **Aube** *dept* France
22 K2 **Aubel** Belgium
22 E3 **Aubencheul-Au-Bac** France
22 G4 **Aubenton** France
21 O4 **Aubergenville** France
83 L13 **Aubert,C** Kerguelen Indian Oc
21 M4 **Aube-sur-Rille** France
18 F7 **Aubeterre** France
21 J8 **Aubiers, les** France
21 L6 **Aubigné** Sarthe France
22 D3 **Aubigny** Pas-de-Calais France
20 H8 **Aubigny** Vendée France
18 G5 **Aubigny sur Nère** France
18 G8 **Aubin** France
18 H8 **Aubrac, Mts d'** France
103 M6 **Aubrey Cliffs** Arizona U.S.A.
143 B7 **Aubrey, Mt** W Australia Australia
114 G4 **Aubry L** Northwest Territories Canada
141 K7 **Auburn** *R* Queensland Australia
111 L9 **Auburn** Alabama U.S.A.
102 C3 **Auburn** California U.S.A.
110 G2 **Auburn** Illinois U.S.A.
94 B5 **Auburn** Indiana U.S.A.
107 P3 **Auburn** Kansas U.S.A.
110 K5 **Auburn** Kentucky U.S.A.
95 R2 **Auburn** Maine U.S.A.
94 C3 **Auburn** Michigan U.S.A.
99 L9 **Auburn** Nebraska U.S.A.
95 L4 **Auburn** New York U.S.A.
117 M12 **Auburn** Washington U.S.A.
113 F9 **Auburndale** Florida U.S.A.
99 R5 **Auburndale** Wisconsin U.S.A.
141 K7 **Auburn Ra** Queensland Australia
18 G7 **Aubusson** France
133 D5 **Auca Mahuida,Sa** *mt* Argentina
52 B6 **Auce** Latvia
18 F9 **Auch** France
22 C3 **Auchel** France
12 E4 **Auchencairn** Scotland
12 D4 **Auchenmalg** Scotland
85 F7 **Auchi** Nigeria
12 D3 **Auchinleck** Scotland
12 E1 **Auchterarder** Scotland
13 E1 **Auchterderran** Scotland
13 E1 **Auchtermuchty** Scotland
22 C2 **Auchy-au-Bois** France
113 D7 **Aucilla** *R* Florida U.S.A.
145 F1 **Auckland** New Zealand
145 E2 **Auckland** *admin region* New Zealand
68 D6 **Auckland B** Burma
18 G9 **Aude** *R* France
18 G9 **Aude** *dept* France
120 C2 **Auden** Ontario Canada
Audenarde *see* **Oudenaarde**
18 E8 **Audenge** France
20 G2 **Auderville** France
20 A5 **Audierne** France
20 B6 **Audierne, B. d'** France
83 L14 **Audierne, Bd'** Kerguelen Indian Oc
40 E3 **Audincourt** France
22 B2 **Audinghen** France
45 N4 **Auditore** Italy
8 D2 **Audlem** England
22 B2 **Audresselles** France
7 M9 **Audrey** *oil rig* North Sea
22 C2 **Audruicq** France
99 M8 **Audubon** Iowa U.S.A.
98 E2 **Audubon Lake** *res* North Dakota U.S.A.
19 J3 **Audun le Roman** France
32 G6 **Aue** *R* Germany
37 O2 **Aue** Germany
84 E4 **Auenat Uennin** Libya
36 G5 **Auenstein** Germany
37 N2 **Auerbach** Germany
36 F4 **Auerbach** Hessen Germany
41 N2 **Auer Berg** *mt* Germany
37 O2 **Auerswalde** Germany
111 E12 **Au Far, Point** Louisiana U.S.A.
21 N2 **Auffay** France
20 F6 **Augan** France
141 H7 **Augathella** Queensland Australia
14 E2 **Aughnacloy** N Ireland
14 E4 **Aughrim** Ireland
89 B7 **Augrabies** S Africa
89 B7 **Augrabies Falls** Orange R S Africa
94 D2 **Au Gres** Michigan U.S.A.
37 K7 **Augsburg** Germany
143 B10 **Augusta** W Australia Australia
43 G11 **Augusta** Sicily
110 E6 **Augusta** Arkansas U.S.A.
112 E4 **Augusta** Georgia U.S.A.
110 F1 **Augusta** Illinois U.S.A.
107 O4 **Augusta** Kansas U.S.A.
94 C8 **Augusta** Kentucky U.S.A.
95 S2 **Augusta** Maine U.S.A.
94 B4 **Augusta** Michigan U.S.A.
101 N2 **Augusta** Montana U.S.A.
99 P5 **Augusta** Wisconsin U.S.A.
143 E7 **Augusta, L** W Australia Australia
116 R6 **Augusta,Mt** Yukon Territory Canada
94 H8 **Augusta Springs** Virginia U.S.A.
116 L7 **Augustine I** Alaska U.S.A.
130 G6 **Augusto de Lima** Brazil
130 H8 **Augusto Severo** Brazil
31 O2 **Augustów** Poland
140 E4 **Augustus Downs** Queensland Australia
142 E3 **Augustus Island** W Australia Australia
143 B6 **Augustus, Mt** W Australia Australia
37 M6 **Au in der Hallertau** Germany
40 B2 **Aujon** *R* France
6 M6 **Auk** *oil rig* North Sea
32 L4 **Aukrug** Germany
26 K6 **Auktsjaur** Sweden
112 K1 **Aulander** North Carolina U.S.A.
142 E5 **Auld, L** W Australia Australia
18 E6 **Aulnay de Saintonge** France
21 P5 **Aulnay-la-Rivière** France
20 B5 **Aulne** *R* France
118 H1 **Aulneau Pen** Ontario Canada
22 F3 **Aulnoye** France
106 F1 **Ault** Colorado U.S.A.
15 C3 **Aultbea** Scotland
54 F8 **Auly** Ukraine
37 M2 **Auma** *R* Germany
37 M2 **Auma** Germany
21 O2 **Aumale** France
18 G6 **Aumance** *R* France
22 K5 **Aumetz** France
57 C4 **Auminzatau,Gory** *mt* Uzbekistan
40 C4 **Aumont** France
18 H8 **Aumont** Lozère France
33 M5 **Aumühle** Germany
21 J3 **Aunay-sur-Odon** France
74 F10 **Aundh** India
21 L6 **Aune** *R* France
21 O5 **Auneau** France
21 P3 **Auneuil** France
68 B3 **Aunglan** Burma
28 E4 **Auning** Denmark
18 E6 **Aunis** *prov* France
87 C11 **Auob** *R* Namibia
71 J5 **Auponhia** Moluccas Indonesia
19 Q17 **Aups** France
69 G11 **Aur** *isld* Malaysia
29 K11 **Aura** Finland
26 C9 **Aura** *R* Norway
37 K4 **Aurach** *R* Germany
74 H5 **Auraiya** India
29 K11 **Aurajoki** *R* Finland
74 F9 **Aurangabad** India
20 E6 **Auray** France
21 J3 **Aure** *R* France
26 C8 **Aure** Norway
19 O16 **Aurel** France
99 L7 **Aurelia** Iowa U.S.A.
85 F1 **Aurès** *mts* Algeria
32 F6 **Aurich** Germany
130 E5 **Aurilândia** Brazil
18 G8 **Aurillac** France
19 P18 **Auriol** France
70 B5 **Aurkuning** Kalimantan
27 B11 **Aurland** Norway
130 H9 **Aurora** Brazil
121 L9 **Aurora** Ontario Canada
106 F2 **Aurora** Colorado U.S.A.
99 S8 **Aurora** Illinois U.S.A.
94 C7 **Aurora** Indiana U.S.A.
107 N2 **Aurora** Kansas U.S.A.
110 C5 **Aurora** Missouri U.S.A.
98 H9 **Aurora** Nebraska U.S.A.
112 L2 **Aurora** North Carolina U.S.A.
103 N3 **Aurora** Utah U.S.A.
19 P15 **Aurouze, Mt d'** France
76 D4 **Auroville** India
26 C9 **Aursjöen** *L* Norway
27 E12 **Aurskog** Norway
26 E9 **Aursunden** *L* Norway
141 F2 **Aurukun** Queensland Australia
45 P7 **Aurunci Monti** Italy
87 C11 **Aus** Namibia
94 C2 **Au Sable** *R* Michigan U.S.A.
95 O2 **Ausable Forks** New York U.S.A.
94 D2 **Au Sable Pt** Michigan U.S.A.
128 D6 **Ausangate** *mt* Peru
80 F4 **Ausara** Jordan
88 B7 **Aushi** Zambia
15 F1 **Auskerry** Scotland
45 O7 **Ausoni, Monti** *mt* Italy
41 K3 **Ausser-Rhoden** *dist* Switzerland
8 D4 **Aust** England
27 C13 **Austad** Norway
27 C13 **Aust Agder Fylker** Norway
112 C4 **Austell** Georgia U.S.A.
Austerlitz *see* **Slavkov**
119 T9 **Austin** Manitoba Canada
99 O6 **Austin** Minnesota U.S.A.
101 N3 **Austin** Montana U.S.A.
100 G5 **Austin** Oregon U.S.A.
94 J5 **Austin** Pennsylvania U.S.A.
109 K5 **Austin** Texas U.S.A.
143 C8 **Austin, L** W Australia Australia
109 M4 **Austonio** Texas U.S.A.
140 E5 **Austral Downs** N Terr Australia
136 **Australia** *dominion* Australia
146 F15 **Australian Antarctic Territory** Antarctica
143 B10 **Australind** W Australia Australia
135 M11 **Austral Ridge** Pacific Oc
26 D8 **Austråt** Norway
27 A11 **Austrheim** Norway
38 E7 **Austria** *rep* Cent Europe
26 G3 **Austvågöy** *isld* Norway
109 L7 **Austwell** Texas U.S.A.
21 N6 **Autainville** France
128 G4 **Autazes** Brazil
22 K4 **Autelbas** Belgium
18 G9 **Auterive** France
123 L3 **Auteuil, L. d'** Quebec Canada
22 C3 **Authie** *R* France
121 M4 **Authier** Quebec Canada
21 K7 **Authion** *R* France
21 M6 **Authon** Loir-et-Cher France
21 M5 **Authon-du-Perche** France
21 O5 **Authon-la-Plaine** France
124 G8 **Autlán de Navarro** Mexico
45 O6 **Autore, M** *mt* Italy
99 U3 **Au Train** Michigan U.S.A.
19 P14 **Autrans** France
21 P5 **Autruy-sur-Juine** France
22 H5 **Autry** France
18 H6 **Autun** France
140 B3 **Auvergne** N Terr Australia
18 H7 **Auvergne** *prov* France
21 K6 **Auvers-le-Hamon** France
21 P3 **Auvers-sur-Oise** France
18 F7 **Auvezère** *R* France
22 G4 **Auvillers-les-Forges** France
21 L8 **Auxances** *R* France
94 E2 **Aux Barques, Pt** Michigan U.S.A.
18 H5 **Auxerre** France
21 P1 **Auxi-le-Château** France
40 B3 **Auxonne** France
110 E2 **Auxvasse** Missouri U.S.A.
128 F2 **Auyán Tepui** *mt* Venezuela
115 M4 **Auyuittuq Nat Park** Northwest Territories
20 G8 **Auzance** *R* France
18 G6 **Auzances** France
68 B2 **Ava** Burma
110 G4 **Ava** Illinois U.S.A.
110 D5 **Ava** Missouri U.S.A.
26 M5 **Avafors** Sweden
18 F6 **Availles-Limouzine** France
116 H1 **Avalik** *R* Alaska U.S.A.
18 H5 **Avallon** France
102 F8 **Avalon** California U.S.A.
111 F8 **Avalon** Mississippi U.S.A.
95 N7 **Avalon** New Jersey U.S.A.
108 C3 **Avalon, L** New Mexico U.S.A.
123 T6 **Avalon Pen** Newfoundland Canada
131 F2 **Avalos** *R* Argentina
124 J5 **Avalos** Mexico
19 Q15 **Avançon** France
107 M5 **Avard** Oklahoma U.S.A.
129 J8 **Avaré** Brazil
53 G12 **Avarskoye Koysu** *R* Russian Federation
134 A10 **Avarua** Rarotonga Pacific Oc
47 H4 **Ávas** Greece
116 E9 **Avatanak I** Aleutian Is
26 H7 **Avaträsk** Sweden
26 L5 **Avaudden** Sweden
26 K6 **Avaviken** Sweden
102 H6 **Avawatz Mts** California U.S.A.
47 N10 **Avci Koru** *forest* Turkey
54 J8 **Avdeyevka** Ukraine
9 E5 **Avebury** England
16 D4 **Aveinte** Spain
129 G4 **Aveiro** Brazil
16 B4 **Aveiro** Portugal
77 A2 **Avej** Iran
22 E2 **Avelgem** Belgium
94 G6 **Avella** Pennsylvania U.S.A.
133 F4 **Avellaneda** Argentina
45 R8 **Avellino** Italy
102 D6 **Avenal** California U.S.A.
40 F4 **Avenches** Switzerland
95 Q4 **Aver** Massachusetts U.S.A.
28 E6 **Avernak By** *B* Denmark
26 B8 **Averöy** *isld* Norway
45 Q8 **Aversa** Italy
100 K2 **Avery** Idaho U.S.A.
99 O8 **Avery** Iowa U.S.A.
109 N2 **Avery** Texas U.S.A.
111 E12 **Avery Island** Louisiana U.S.A.
22 F3 **Avesnes** France
22 D3 **Avesnes le Comte** France
22 E3 **Avesnes-les-Aubert** France
90 C7 **Aves Ridge** Atlantic Oc
20 G6 **Avessac** France
27 H11 **Avesta** Sweden
18 F8 **Aveyron** *R* France
18 G8 **Aveyron** *dept* France
45 O5 **Avezzano** Italy
46 E5 **Avgó** *mt* Greece
46 F8 **Avgó** *isld* Greece
47 H9 **Avgó** *isld* Greece
133 E3 **Aviá Terai** Argentina
15 E3 **Aviemore** Scotland
144 C6 **Aviemore, L** New Zealand
115 P5 **Avigaat** Greenland
80 B7 **Avigedor** Israel
43 G8 **Avigliano** Italy
19 N17 **Avignon** France
16 D4 **Avila** *prov* Spain
16 D4 **Ávila, Sa. de** *mts* Spain
16 D1 **Avilés** Spain
40 D3 **Avilley** France
109 N3 **Avinger** Texas U.S.A.
22 D3 **Avion** France
47 O12 **Aviótes** Greece
95 K5 **Avis** Pennsylvania U.S.A.
41 O5 **Avisio** *R* Italy
80 E1 **Avivim** Israel
16 B5 **Aviz** Portugal
46 F6 **Avlón** Greece
28 B4 **Avlum** Denmark
80 G2 **Avné Etan** Syria
80 G2 **Avne Etan** Syria
28 H6 **Avnø Fjord** *inlet* Denmark
28 F6 **Avnslev** Denmark
139 G6 **Avoca** Victoria Australia
14 E4 **Avoca** Ireland
144 C5 **Avoca** New Zealand
94 E3 **Avoca** Michigan U.S.A.
95 K4 **Avoca** New York U.S.A.
108 H3 **Avoca** Texas U.S.A.
14 E4 **Avoca,Vale of** Ireland
138 D5 **Avoid B** South Australia Australia
117 O10 **Avola** British Columbia Canada
43 G12 **Avola** Sicily
8 D5 **Avon** *co* England
15 E3 **Avon** *R* Scotland
106 D2 **Avon** Colorado U.S.A.
95 P5 **Avon** Connecticut U.S.A.
110 F1 **Avon** Illinois U.S.A.
99 M4 **Avon** Minnesota U.S.A.
101 N3 **Avon** Montana U.S.A.
94 K4 **Avon** New York U.S.A.
112 M2 **Avon** North Carolina U.S.A.
94 E5 **Avon** Ohio U.S.A.
98 H6 **Avon** South Dakota U.S.A.
141 K6 **Avondale** Queensland Australia
103 M8 **Avondale** Arizona U.S.A.
106 F3 **Avondale** Colorado U.S.A.
110 B2 **Avondale** Missouri U.S.A.
109 L8 **Avondale** Texas U.S.A.
140 D4 **Avon Downs** N Terr Australia
141 H5 **Avon Downs** Queensland Australia
94 E5 **Avon Lake** Ohio U.S.A.
119 M8 **Avonlea** Saskatchewan Canada
21 L7 **Avon-les-Roches** France
94 H6 **Avonmore** Pennsylvania U.S.A.
8 D4 **Avonmouth** England
113 F10 **Avon Park** Florida U.S.A.
143 B9 **Avon, R** W Australia Australia
9 E3 **Avon, R** England
9 E5 **Avon, R** England
130 E10 **Avoredo** *lighthouse* Brazil
40 D3 **Avoudrey** France
65 A1 **Avraga** Mongolia
20 H4 **Avranches** France
22 D4 **Avre** *R* France
21 N4 **Avre** *R* Eure France
36 B6 **Avricourt** France
48 J5 **Avrig** Romania
22 K5 **Avril** France
48 E7 **Avtovac** Bosnia-Herzegovina
61 P12 **Awa** Okinawa
69 C12 **Awaay** Indonesia
60 H11 **Awaji-shima** *isld* Japan
145 E3 **Awakino** New Zealand
84 E4 **Awāl** *watercourse* Libya
70 Q10 **Awang** Indonesia
145 D1 **Awanui** New Zealand
86 H4 **Āwarē** Ethiopia
144 B7 **Awarua** New Zealand
86 G4 **Āwasa Hāyk'** *L* Ethiopia
86 H4 **Āwash** Ethiopia
61 N7 **Awa-shima** *isld* Japan
85 D7 **Awaso** Ghana
57 K4 **Awat** China
86 G4 **Āwat'a** *R* Ethiopia
145 E4 **Awatere R** New Zealand
84 E4 **Awbārī** Libya
86 H5 **Aw Dheegle** Somalia
12 C1 **Awe,L** Scotland
112 H4 **Awendaw** South Carolina U.S.A.
84 G4 **Awjilah** Libya
70 G6 **Awo** *R* Sulawesi Indonesia
117 Q4 **Awry L** Northwest Territories Canada
85 B4 **Awserd** Mauritania
116 J2 **Awuna** *R* Alaska U.S.A.
8 D5 **Axbridge** England
25 A6 **Axel** Netherlands
27 F14 **Axelfors** Sweden
147 H5 **Axel Heiberg I** Northwest Territories Canada
106 C1 **Axial** Colorado U.S.A.
128 G4 **Axinim** Brazil
18 G10 **Ax-les-Thermes** France
8 D6 **Axminster** England
112 E6 **Axson** Georgia U.S.A.

107 O2 Axtell Kansas U.S.A.
27 G13 Axvall Sweden
18 H3 Ay France
20 H3 Ay R France
128 C4 Ayabaca Peru
60 J10 Ayabe Japan
78 D1 Ayaç Turkey
133 F5 Ayacucho Argentina
128 D6 Ayacucho Peru
68 B1 Ayadaw Burma
57 K1 Ayaguz Kazakhstan
57 D4 Ayakkuduk Uzbekistan
66 D4 Ayakkum Hu L China
16 C7 Ayamonte Spain
78 E1 Ayancık Turkey
80 C6 Ayanot Israel
126 G10 Ayapel Colombia
128 D6 Ayaviri Peru
77 L1 Āybak Afghanistan
13 G4 Aycliffe England
55 E4 Aydabul' Kazakhstan
54 L8 Aydar R Ukraine
57 D4 Aydarkul', Ozero L Uzbekistan
112 K2 Ayden North Carolina U.S.A.
47 J7 Aydın Turkey
78 A3 Aydın Turkey
Aydıncık see Gılındire
47 J7 Aydin Dağlar mts Turkey
79 B1 Aydınkent Turkey
47 N11 Aydınlı Turkey
55 C5 Aydrlinskiy Russian Federation
86 H3 Ayelu Terara mt Ethiopia
40 G5 Ayer Switzerland
17 G2 Ayerbe Spain
100 G3 Ayers Washington U.S.A.
140 C7 Ayers Ra N Terr Australia
140 B7 Ayers Rock mt N Terr Australia
55 F3 Ayev R Russian Federation
19 O16 Aygues R France
56 C5 Aygulaskiy Khrebet mts Russian Federation
46 F5 Ayiá Greece
46 F6 Ayía Ánna Greece
46 G5 Ayía Iríni Akra C Greece
47 H5 Ayiássos Greece
46 G4 Áyion Óros reg Greece
46 F7 Áyios isld Greece
46 G5 Áyios Evstrátios isld Greece
47 O12 Ayios Matthaíos Greece
46 G9 Áyios Míron Crete Greece
47 H9 Ayios Nikólaos Crete Greece
46 D6 Ayios Pétros Greece
79 D3 Ayios Seryios Cyprus
79 E3 Ayios Theodhoros Cyprus
116 L2 Ayiyak R Alaska U.S.A.
47 H7 Aykathonisi isld Greece
86 G3 Āykel Ethiopia
47 H7 Ay Kírikos Greece
36 B4 Ayl Germany
121 N7 Aylen,L Ontario Canada
119 M8 Aylesbury Saskatchewan Canada
9 F4 Aylesbury England
144 D5 Aylesbury New Zealand
122 H8 Aylesford Nova Scotia Canada
9 H5 Aylesham England
117 D6 Aylesworth, Mt Br Col/Alaska Canada/U.S.A.
16 E3 Ayllón Spain
16 E3 Ayllón, Sa. de mts Spain
121 P7 Aylmer Quebec Canada
114 J5 Aylmer L Northwest Territories Canada
118 B7 Aylmer,Mt Alberta Canada
119 O5 Aylsham Saskatchewan Canada
9 H2 Aylsham England
121 O7 Aylwin Quebec Canada
17 F6 Ayna Spain
79 H4 'Ayn al Bayḍā' Syria
78 J3 Ayn Diwār Syria
9 E3 Aynho England
112 H4 Aynor South Carolina U.S.A.
80 G1 Ayn Ziwān Syria
84 G5 'Ayn Zuwayyah well Libya
147 Q4 Ayon,Ostrov isld Russian Federation
17 G5 Ayora Spain
85 E6 Ayorou Niger
55 G2 Aypolovo Russian Federation
141 H4 Ayr Queensland Australia
12 D3 Ayr Scotland
98 H9 Ayr Nebraska U.S.A.
98 J2 Ayr North Dakota U.S.A.
21 L8 Ayron France
99 M6 Ayrshire Iowa U.S.A.
141 G5 Ayrshire Downs Queensland Australia
55 F4 Aysarinskoye Kazakhstan
13 G5 Aysgarth England
86 H3 Āysha Ethiopia
57 F1 Ayshirak Kazakhstan
57 G3 Aytau mts Kazakhstan
13 H5 Ayton N Yorks England
13 F2 Ayton Scotland
47 J2 Aytos Bulgaria
57 C4 Aytym Uzbekistan
61 P7 Ayukawahama Japan
65 C2 Ayulhai China
124 G7 Ayutla Mexico
68 E5 Ayutthaya Thailand
78 A2 Ayvacik Turkey
47 H5 Ayvalık Turkey
22 K3 Aywaille Belgium
80 E1 Ayyelet Ha Shaḥar Israel
77 D1 Āzād Shahr Iran
100 B7 Azalea Oregon U.S.A.
61 P13 Azama Okinawa
79 G7 Azamān, Qā' depression Saudi Arabia
75 K5 Azamgarh India
55 C3 Azangulovo Russian Federation
55 D2 Azanka Russian Federation
22 J5 Azannes-et-Soumazannes France
77 A1 Āzarān Iran
78 K2 Āzārbāyjān-e Gharbī Iran
78 L2 Āzārbāyjān-e Sharqī Iran
85 G6 Azare Nigeria
52 E5 Azatskoye, Oz L Russian Federation
21 N8 Azay-le-Ferron France
21 L7 Azay-le-Rideau France
21 M7 Azay-sur-Cher France
21 K8 Azay-sur-Thouet France
79 H2 A'zāz Syria
Azbine reg Niger see Aïr ou Azbine
21 N6 Azé Loire France
40 G7 Azeglio Italy
78 L1 Azerbaijan rep W Asia
19 N13 Azergues R France
53 F7 Azeyevo Russian Federation
55 G4 Azhbulat, Oz L Kazakhstan
56 C5 Azho-Tayga, Gora mt Russian Federation
85 C2 Azilal Morocco
22 C3 Azincourt France
86 A6 Azingo, L Gabon
95 R1 Aziscoos L Maine U.S.A.
84 E3 'Azīzīyan, Al Libya
16 C7 Aznàlcóllar Spain
128 C4 Azogues Ecuador
52 G2 Azopol'ye Russian Federation
Azores islds see Açores
90 G5 Azores-Cape St Vincent Ridge Atlantic Oc
86 D3 Azoum R Chad
54 L9 Azov Russian Federation
Azov, Sea of see Azovskoye More
54 L9 Azovskiy Kanal Russian Federation
53 E10 Azovskoye More Rus Fed/Ukraine
17 F1 Azpeitia Spain
85 C2 Azrou Morocco
103 L9 Aztec Arizona U.S.A.
106 C5 Aztec New Mexico U.S.A.
106 B5 Aztec Ruins Nat.Mon New Mexico U.S.A.
127 J5 Azua Dominican Rep
16 D6 Azuaga Spain
17 G3 Azuara Spain
128 C4 Azuay prov Ecuador
60 C12 Azuch-Ō-shima isld Japan
17 F6 Azuer R Spain
125 O6 Azuero,Pen.de Panama
131 B3 Azufre, P. del Chile
48 K5 Azuga Romania
133 F5 Azul Argentina
131 B5 Azul pk Chile
125 P9 Azul R Mexico
131 B8 Azul, Cerro pk Neuquén Argentina
130 E7 Azul Paulista, Mte Brazil
130 C4 Azul,Serra mts Mato Grosso Brazil
61 O8 Azuma-yama mt Japan
80 B8 Azza Israel
79 G5 Az Zabadānī Syria
84 F4 Aẕ Zahrah Libya

B

71 L10 Baa Indonesia
41 M3 Baad Austria
70 E4 Baai R Kalimantan
25 F6 Baal Germany
79 G4 Baalbek Lebanon
86 H5 Baardheere Somalia
25 C6 Baarle-Hertog Belgium
25 C6 Baarle Nassau Netherlands
25 D4 Baarn Netherlands
60 D14 Baba Japan
46 E4 Baba mt Macedonia
47 H5 Baba Burun C Turkey
78 M1 Babadag mt Azerbaijan
48 M6 Babadag Romania
47 J3 Babaeski Turkey
128 C4 Babahoyo Ecuador
71 G7 Babak Philippines
143 C9 Babakin W Australia Australia
77 K2 Bābā, Koh-i- mts Afghanistan
79 H2 Bāb, Al Syria
72 E6 Bab al Mandab str Arabia/Djibouti
79 G3 Bābannā Syria
67 B5 Babao China
71 O8 Babar isld Indonesia
71 O9 Babar,Kep islds Indonesia
70 O9 Babat Java
57 E5 Babatag, Khr mts Tajikistan/Uzbekistan
88 E4 Babati Tanzania
71 L10 Babau Timor Indonesia
80 G7 Babayir et Tiwal Jordan
101 M1 Babb Montana U.S.A.
116 S2 Babbage R Yukon Territory Canada
143 A6 Babbage I W Australia Australia
99 P2 Babbitt Minnesota U.S.A.
99 Q5 Babcock Wisconsin U.S.A.
33 P5 Bābelin Germany
88 C5 Babemba tribe Zaire
88 C7 Babemba tribe Zambia
36 F4 Babenhausen Hessen Germany
31 M6 Babia Góra mts Poland/Slovakia
124 E3 Babícora Mexico
124 F3 Babícora, L. de Mexico
78 K5 Bābil prov Iraq
141 H3 Babinda Queensland Australia
117 L8 Babine L British Columbia Canada
117 K8 Babine Ra British Columbia Canada
69 C11 Babi, Pulau isld Indonesia
136 G2 Babo W Irian
48 D4 Babócsa Hungary
77 C1 Bābol Iran
103 N10 Baboquivari Pk Arizona U.S.A.
142 E4 Babrongan Tower mt W Australia Australia
113 F10 Babson Park Florida U.S.A.
36 G5 Babstadt Germany
16 D9 Bab Taza Morocco
67 B3 Babu China
46 E3 Babuna mt Macedonia
56 G5 Babushkin Russian Federation
71 E1 Babuyan islds Philippines
71 D6 Babuyan Philippines
71 E1 Babuyan Ch Philippines
124 E4 Baca Mexico
86 A2 Bacaadweyn Somalia
124 E4 Bacabáche Mexico
129 G5 Bacabal Brazil
129 H4 Bacaja R Brazil
71 A3 Bacan isld Indonesia
124 E3 Bacanora Mexico
71 E1 Bacarra Philippines
48 K4 Bacău Romania
68 G1 Bac Can Vietnam
19 K4 Baccarat France
122 G10 Baccaro Pt Nova Scotia Canada
45 L1 Bacchiglione R Italy
41 H5 Baceno Italy
48 L4 Băceşti Romania
68 H2 Bac Giang Vietnam
37 N5 Bach Germany
94 D3 Bach Michigan U.S.A.
127 J10 Bachaquero Venezuela
36 D3 Bacharach Germany
115 M2 Bache Pen Northwest Territories Canada
124 F3 Bachiniva Mexico
68 J2 Bach Long Vi isld Vietnam
69 E9 Bacho Thailand
37 L1 Bachra Germany
57 J5 Bachu China
115 K4 Back R Northwest Territories Canada
48 E5 Backa reg Serbia Yugoslavia
27 G14 Bäckaby Sweden
48 E5 Bačka Palanka Serbia Yugoslavia
48 F5 Bačka Topola Serbia Yugoslavia
95 L10 Back Bay Virginia U.S.A.
117 J4 Backbone Ranges Northwest Territories Canada
26 H8 Backe Sweden
27 F13 Bäckefors Sweden
27 G12 Bäckhammar Sweden
36 G6 Backnang Germany
119 U10 Backoo North Dakota U.S.A.
48 F5 Bačko Petrovo Selo Serbia Yugoslavia
138 E6 Backstaiys Pass South Australia Australia
26 H6 Bäckstrand Sweden
99 M3 Backus Minnesota U.S.A.
8 D5 Backwell England
Bac Lieu see Vinh Loi
71 E2 Bacnotan Luzon Philippines
127 P5 Bacolet Grenada
45 Q8 Bacoli Italy
71 F5 Bacolod Philippines
71 E4 Baco, Mt Philippines
112 C6 Baconton Georgia U.S.A.
21 N2 Bacqueville-en-Caux France
48 E4 Bácsalmás Hungary
48 E4 Bács-Kiskun co Hungary
9 H2 Bacton England
124 F5 Bacubirito Mexico
71 G7 Baculin Bay Mindanao Philippines
13 F6 Bacup England
129 J4 Bacuri,I de Brazil
98 F5 Bad R South Dakota U.S.A.
Bada see Xilin
75 L7 Bada Barabil India
37 N6 Bad Abbach Germany
76 B5 Badagara India
38 E6 Bad Aibling Germany
129 J4 Badajós Brazil
16 C6 Badajoz prov Spain
16 C6 Badajoz Spain
128 F4 Badajoz, L Brazil
77 L1 Badakhshān prov Afghanistan
17 J3 Badalona Spain
76 B3 Badami India
75 M7 Bādāmpāhārh India
56 E3 Badan, Khrebet mts Russian Federation
65 H3 Badaohe China
Badaojiang see Hunjiang
124 F5 Badariguato Mexico
74 H3 Badarīnaāth India
70 D2 Badas Brunei
69 H12 Badas,Kep isld Indonesia
38 J6 Bad Aussee Austria
94 E3 Bad Axe Michigan U.S.A.
32 G7 Badbergen Germany
36 D5 Bad Bergzabern Germany
37 L2 Bad Berka Germany
36 E1 Bad Berleburg Germany
37 M3 Bad Berneck Germany
36 B3 Bad Bertrich Germany
37 M1 Bad Bibra Sachsen-Anhalt Germany
37 P7 Bad Birnbach Germany
37 L2 Bad Blankenburg Germany
37 J3 Bad Bocklet Germany
32 L5 Bad Bramstedt Germany
123 M7 Baddeck C Breton I, Nova Scotia
32 M8 Baddeckenstedt Germany
26 M2 Badderen Norway
33 P4 Bad Doberan Germany
32 K9 Bad Driburg Germany
33 R9 Bad Düben Germany
36 E5 Bad Dürkheim Germany
33 Q10 Bad Dürrenberg Germany
37 N3 Bad Elster Germany
36 D3 Bad Ems Germany
48 C2 Baden Austria
119 Q6 Baden Manitoba Canada
20 E6 Baden France
41 H3 Baden Switzerland
94 G6 Baden Pennsylvania U.S.A.
36 E6 Baden-Baden Germany
15 D4 Badenoch Scotland
19 K4 Badenviller France
36 G6 Baden-Württemberg Germany
45 P1 Baderna Croatia
33 U7 Bad Freienwalde Germany
36 G5 Bad Friedrichshall Germany
37 P7 Bad Füssing Germany
32 M9 Bad Gandersheim Germany
118 F1 Badger Manitoba Canada
123 Q5 Badger Newfoundland Canada
102 E5 Badger California U.S.A.
98 K1 Badger Minnesota U.S.A.
101 Q5 Badger Basin Wyoming U.S.A.
77 H2 Bādghīs prov Afghanistan
38 N8 Bad Gleichenberg Austria
36 C2 Bad Godesberg Germany
30 H5 Bad Gottleuba Germany
32 M9 Bad Grund Germany
38 K5 Bad Hall Austria
33 N9 Bad Harzburg Germany
36 E6 Bad Herrenalb Germany
36 H2 Bad Hersfeld Germany
38 H7 Bad Hofgastein Austria
36 F3 Bad Homburg Germany
36 C2 Bad Honnef Germany
45 K1 Badia Polesine Italy
45 M4 Badia Tedalda Italy
32 H8 Bad Iburg Germany
79 H6 Badiet esh Sham desert Jordan/Syria
74 C6 Badin Pakistan
112 G2 Badin North Carolina U.S.A.
112 G2 Badin L North Carolina U.S.A.
38 J6 Bad Ischl Austria
37 J3 Bad Kissingen Germany
33 O5 Bad Kleinen Germany
37 M2 Bad Klosterlausnitz Germany
37 M1 Bad Kösen Germany
36 D4 Bad Kreuznach Germany
98 C2 Bad Lands reg North Dakota U.S.A.
98 E6 Badlands Nat.Park South Dakota U.S.A.
37 K1 Bad Langensalza Germany
33 P10 Bad Lauchstädt Germany
37 O1 Bad Lausik Germany
33 M9 Bad Lauterberg Germany
38 K8 Bad Leonhard Austria
37 K2 Bad Liebenstein Germany
36 F6 Bad Liebenzell Germany
32 J9 Bad Lippspringe Germany
32 J9 Bad Meinberg Germany
36 H5 Bad Mergentheim Germany
32 K8 Bad Münder am Deister Germany
36 D4 Bad Münster Germany
36 B2 Bad Münstereifel Germany
31 H4 Bad Muskau Germany
36 F3 Bad Nauheim Germany
32 K8 Bad Nenndorf Germany
36 C2 Bad Neuenahr Germany
36 C2 Bad Neuenahr-Ahrweiler Germany
37 J3 Bad Neustadt Germany
32 J8 Bad Oeynhausen Germany
33 M5 Bad Oldersloe Germany
68 H4 Ba Don Vietnam
67 C1 Badong China
69 H8 Ba Dong Vietnam
36 B6 Badonviller France
36 G3 Bad Orb Germany
65 D6 Badou China
36 E7 Bad Peterstal Germany
32 K9 Bad Pyrmont Germany
36 G5 Bad Rappenau Germany
38 G6 Bad Reichenhall Germany
36 E7 Bad Rippoldsau Germany
32 M8 Bad Salzdetfurth Germany
33 P8 Bad Salzelmen Germany
36 H2 Bad Salzschlirf Germany
32 J8 Bad Salzuflen Germany
37 J2 Bad Salzungen Germany
32 H9 Bad Sassendorf Germany
33 R9 Bad Schmiedeberg Germany
36 F5 Bad Schönborn Germany
36 E3 Bad Schwalbach Germany
33 N5 Bad Schwartau Germany
33 M5 Bad Segeberg Germany
36 E3 Bad Soden Germany
32 L10 Bad Sooden Germany
37 M3 Bad Steben Germany
33 Q6 Bad Stuer Germany
33 O9 Bad Suderode Germany
37 M1 Bad Sulza Germany
33 R4 Bad Sülze Germany
36 F6 Bad Teinach-Zavelstein Germany
37 K1 Bad Tennstedt Germany
41 P2 Bad Tölz Germany
141 F1 Badu I Queensland Australia
83 L10 Badulla Sri Lanka
36 F3 Bad Vilbel Germany
38 O6 Bad Voslau Austria
102 H5 Badwater L California U.S.A.
36 G1 Bad Wildungen Germany
33 P7 Bad Wilsnack Germany
36 G5 Bad Wimpfen Germany
37 J5 Bad Windsheim Germany
59 K1 Badzhal'skiy Khrebet mt Russian Federation
26 O2 Baeivašgiedde Norway
28 C5 Bække Denmark
28 A4 Bækmarksbro Denmark
28 E3 Bælum Denmark
16 E7 Baena Spain
36 D6 Baerenthal France
128 C4 Baeza Ecuador
16 E7 Baeza Spain
47 J7 Bafa Gölü L Turkey
86 B4 Bafang Cameroon
85 B6 Bafata Guinea-Bissau
115 K3 Baffin dist Northwest Territories Canada
109 K8 Baffin B Texas U.S.A.
147 E6 Baffin Basin Arctic Oc
115 N3 Baffin Bay Greenland/Canada
90 E2 Baffin-Greenland Rise Atlantic Oc
115 M3 Baffin I Northwest Territories Canada
141 K6 Baffle Creek Queensland Australia
86 B5 Bafia Cameroon
85 B6 Bafing R Guinea/Mali
79 H2 Bafliyun Syria
85 B6 Bafoulabé Mali
86 B4 Bafoussam Cameroon
77 D4 Bāfq Iran
78 E1 Bafra Turkey
86 E5 Bafwasende Zaire
58 D3 Baga Bogd Uul mt Mongolia
71 E3 Bagac Bay Luzon Philippines
76 B2 Bagalkot India
88 G5 Bagamoyo Tanzania
69 E11 Bagan Datuk Malaysia
71 G7 Baganga Mindanao Philippines
71 F7 Baganian Peninsula Mindanao Philippines
69 E10 Bagan Serai Malaysia
69 E11 Bagansiapiapi Sumatra
142 A3 Baganup L W Australia Australia
58 E2 Baga Nuur Mongolia
44 H2 Baganza R Italy
55 D3 Bagaryak Russian Federation
32 G6 Bagband Germany
109 K10 Bagdad Mexico
103 L7 Bagdad Arizona U.S.A.
110 L3 Bagdad Kentucky U.S.A.
58 F1 Bagdarin Russian Federation
131 G3 Bagé Brazil
28 F7 Bagenkop Denmark
101 S8 Baggs Wyoming U.S.A.
78 K5 Baghdād Iraq
78 K5 Baghdād prov Iraq
77 A4 Bāgh-e Malek Iran
75 N7 Bagherhat Bangladesh
43 F10 Bagheria Sicily
77 E4 Baghīn Iran
77 L1 Baghlān Afghanistan
77 L2 Baghlān prov Afghanistan
77 J3 Baghran Afghanistan
Baghrash Köl L see Bosten Hu L
14 E4 Baginbun Hd Ireland
69 H14 Baginda, Tanjong C Indonesia
99 L2 Bagley Minnesota U.S.A.
99 P7 Bagley Wisconsin U.S.A.
116 Q6 Bagley Icefield Alaska U.S.A.
45 L3 Bagnacavallo Italy
43 G10 Bagnara Cálabra Italy
110 D3 Bagnell Dam Missouri U.S.A.
18 F9 Bagnères de Bigorre France
18 F10 Bagnères de Luchon France
40 F6 Bagnes,Val De Switzerland
21 K7 Bagneux Maine-et-Loire France
45 J3 Bagni di Lucca Italy
41 L5 Bagni di Masino Italy
44 B3 Bagni di Vinádio Italy
45 K4 Bagno A Ripoli Italy
45 L4 Bagno di Romagna Italy
21 K4 Bagnoles-de-l'Orne France
45 L1 Bagnoli di Sopra Italy
45 L1 Bagnolo di Po Italy
45 J2 Bagnolo in Piano Italy
44 H1 Bagnolo Mella Italy
45 J1 Bagnolo San Vito Italy
19 N16 Bagnols-sur-Cèze France
Bago see Pegu
28 D6 Bågø isld Denmark
85 C6 Bagoe R Ivory Co/Mali
Bagong see Sansui
77 L2 Bagrāmī Afghanistan
31 M1 Bagrationovsk Russian Federation
9 F5 Bagshot England
65 E3 Bag Tal China
128 C5 Bagua Peru
85 F5 Baguezane, Mt Niger
71 N9 Baguia Timor Indonesia
71 E2 Baguio Luzon Philippines
71 G7 Baguio Mindanao Philippines
71 F2 Baguio Pt Luzon Philippines
86 C3 Baguirmi dist Chad
126 E2 Bahama Bank,Great Bahamas
126 F1 Bahama Bank, Little Bahamas
126 F2 Bahamas, The W Indies
127 M4 Baham, Pte Martinique W Indies
75 N6 Baharampur India
84 H4 Baharîya Oasis Egypt
69 E14 Bahatmonga Indonesia
70 D3 Bahau R Sarawak
70 D6 Bahaur Kalimantan
74 E4 Bahawalnagar Pakistan
74 D4 Bahawalpur Pakistan
79 G1 Bahçe Turkey
88 E4 Bahi Tanzania
129 K6 Bahia state Brazil
131 E7 Bahia Blanca Argentina
125 L1 Bahía, Islas de la Honduras
124 C3 Bahia Kino Mexico
133 D7 Bahía Laura Argentina
133 C6 Bahia Pargua Chile
124 B4 Bahía Tortugas Mexico
86 G3 Bahir Dar Ethiopia
48 L3 Bahluiul R Romania
48 J4 Bahnea Romania
88 B5 Baholoholo tribe Zaire
70 G6 Bahombelu Sulawesi Indonesia
70 G6 Bahomonte Sulawesi
69 H8 Ba,Hon isld Vietnam
79 A7 Baḥra el Burullus lagoon Egypt
79 B7 Baḥra el Manzala lagoon Egypt
75 J5 Bahraich India
77 B6 Bahrain sheikhdom Persian Gulf
86 D3 Bahr Aouk R Chad
86 C4 Bahr Aoukale R Cent Afr Republic
86 F3 Bahr el Abiad R Sudan
86 E4 Bahr el Arab watercourse Sudan
86 F3 Bahr el Azraq R Sudan
86 E4 Bahr el Ghazal R Sudan
86 E4 Bahr el Ghazal prov Sudan
86 F4 Bahr ez Zeraf R Sudan
79 H5 Baḥr Şaygal Sab 'Ābār L Syria
71 H6 Bahubulu isld Sulawesi Indonesia
77 G7 Bāhu Kālat Iran
129 J4 Baiā Brazil
48 H6 Baia de Aramă Romania
48 H4 Baia de Cris Romania
16 B6 Baia de Setúbal Portugal
87 B9 Baia doz Tigres Angola
128 F7 Baia Grande,L Brazil
48 H3 Baia Mare Romania
45 R8 Baiano Italy
48 H3 Baia Sprie Romania
77 D3 Baiazeh Iran
86 C4 Baïbokoum Chad
65 H3 Baicaogou China
57 K4 Baicheng China
65 F2 Baicheng China
48 K5 Băicoi Romania
121 N5 Baie Carrière Quebec Canada
122 D4 Baie-Comeau Quebec Canada
126 H5 Baie de Henne Haiti
122 E5 Baie de Sables Quebec Canada
123 P2 Baie-du-Milieu Quebec Canada
115 M7 Baie-du-Poste Quebec Canada
122 G6 Baie du Vin New Brunswick Canada
68 F7 Baie,I.de la Cambodia
122 K3 Baie Johan Beetz Quebec Canada
127 N4 Baie Mahault Guadeloupe W Indies
36 E7 Baiersbronn Germany
122 C5 Baie Ste.Catherine Quebec Canada
122 H4 Baie Ste.Clair Quebec Canada
122 B6 Baie St.Paul Quebec Canada
122 E4 Baie Trinité Quebec Canada
122 J7 Baie Verte New Brunswick Canada
123 Q4 Baie Verte Newfoundland Canada
67 D3 Baifang China
Baiguan see Shangyu
74 J7 Baihar India
58 F5 Baihe China
65 B6 Baijiazhuang China
Baikal L see Baykal,Ozero L
75 K7 Baikunthpur India
Bailādila see Kirandul
Bailādila see Kirandul
65 E1 Bailang China
48 J6 Băile Govora Romania
48 G6 Băile Herculane Romania
16 E6 Bailén Spain
48 J5 Baile Olăneşti Romania
48 H6 Băileşti Romania
48 K4 Băile Tuşnad Romania
22 G3 Baileux Belgium
106 E2 Bailey Colorado U.S.A.
112 J2 Bailey North Carolina U.S.A.
143 D8 Bailey Ra W Australia Australia
111 K7 Baileyton Alabama U.S.A.
95 U1 Baileyville Maine U.S.A.
14 D3 Bailieborough Ireland
67 D3 Bailin China
129 H3 Bailique, I Brazil
21 N5 Bailleau-le-Pin France
22 D2 Bailleul France
21 K4 Bailleul Orne France
22 D3 Bailleul-Sire-Berthoult France
115 K2 Baillie Hamilton I Northwest Territories Canada
114 G3 Baillie Is Northwest Territories Canada
127 M4 Baillif Guadeloupe W Indies
77 K3 Bailugh Afghanistan
87 C8 Bailundo Angola
111 M11 Bainbridge Georgia U.S.A.
95 M4 Bainbridge New York U.S.A.
94 D7 Bainbridge Ohio U.S.A.
20 G6 Bain-de-Bretagne France
140 B3 Baines, Mt N Terr Australia
127 H5 Bainet Haiti
Baini see Yuqing
19 K4 Bains-les-Bains France
13 H6 Bainton England
98 B1 Bainville Montana U.S.A.
59 J2 Baiquan China
66 C4 Bairab Co L China
109 H3 Baird Texas U.S.A.
116 E6 Baird Inlet Alaska U.S.A.
116 G3 Baird Mts Alaska U.S.A.
134 H8 Bairiki Tarawa Kiribati
65 D3 Bairin Youqi China
58 G3 Bairin Zuoqi China
139 J7 Bairnsdale Victoria Australia
101 S7 Bairoil Wyoming U.S.A.
79 H7 Bā'ir, Wādī watercourse Jordan
20 H6 Bais Ille-et-Vilaine France
21 K5 Bais Mayenne France
18 F8 Baïse R France
Baisha see Jiande
65 B7 Baisha China
67 B2 Baisha China
67 C7 Baisha China
65 B7 Baisha Shuiku res China
67 E3 Baishi Feng mt China
65 A7 Baishui China
58 D5 Baishui Jiang R China
22 E2 Baisieux France
45 J3 Baiso Italy
52 B6 Baisogala Lithuania
74 J4 Baitadi Nepal
68 G3 Bai Thoung Vietnam
19 N15 Baix France
65 C6 Baixiang China
65 A3 Baixingt China
65 E3 Baixingt China
16 B6 Baixo Alentejo prov Portugal
130 H6 Baixo Guandu Brazil
87 C9 Baixo Longa Angola
65 C5 Baiyang Dian L China
67 C1 Baiyangping China
Baiyashi see Dong'an
58 D4 Baiyin China
86 F2 Baiyuda Sudan
67 E3 Baiyun Shan mt China
58 E4 Baiyu Shan mts China
67 B1 Baizi China
48 E4 Baja Hungary
124 B3 Baja California state Mexico
70 Q10 Bajan Indonesia
124 J4 Baján Mexico
124 B3 Baja, Pta C Mexico
69 H11 Bajau isld Indonesia
71 K9 Bajawa Flores Indonesia
48 F7 Bajina Bašta Serbia Yugoslavia
48 E5 Bajmok Serbia Yugoslavia
128 C2 Bajo Baudo Colombia
70 N9 Bajonegoro Java
126 E7 Bajo Nuevo Caribbean
141 K6 Bajool Queensland Australia
28 C7 Bajstrup Denmark
48 D4 Bak Hungary
70 E3 Bakajan, G mt Kalimantan
55 C4 Bakal Russian Federation
86 D4 Bakala Cent Afr Republic
57 J2 Bakanas R Kazakhstan
57 H3 Bakanas Kazakhstan
70 E6 Bakaucengal Kalimantan
56 B3 Bakchar R Russian Federation
85 B6 Bakel Senegal
133 C7 Baker R Chile
103 H6 Baker California U.S.A.
101 M4 Baker Idaho U.S.A.
98 B3 Baker Montana U.S.A.
103 K2 Baker Nevada U.S.A.
98 G1 Baker North Dakota U.S.A.
100 H5 Baker Oregon U.S.A.
94 J7 Baker West Virginia U.S.A.
103 N7 Baker Butte mt Arizona U.S.A.
137 R1 Baker I Pacific Oc
117 G8 Baker I Alaska U.S.A.
95 R7 Baker L Maine U.S.A.
143 F7 Baker Lake W Australia Australia
115 K5 Baker Lake Northwest Territories Canada
100 D1 Baker,Mt Washington U.S.A.
125 P9 Bakers Belize
102 F6 Bakersfield California U.S.A.
112 E1 Bakersfield North Carolina U.S.A.
108 E5 Bakersfield Texas U.S.A.
95 P2 Bakersfield Vermont U.S.A.
9 E1 Bakewell England
77 G2 Bakharz reg Iran
53 D11 Bakhchisaray Ukraine
54 D5 Bakhmach Ukraine
78 L4 Bākhtarān Iran
77 B3 Bakhtiarī va Chahār Mahāll prov Iran
77 B4 Bakhtiyāri Iran
47 J5 Bakır R Turkey
47 M11 Bakırköy Turkey
29 T9 Bakkagerdhi Iceland
25 F2 Bakkeveen Netherlands
47 K7 Baklan Turkey
86 G4 Bako Ethiopia
85 C7 Bako Ivory Coast
69 C11 Bakongan Sumatra
48 D4 Bakony mts Hungary
86 D4 Bakouma Cent Afr Republic
85 C6 Bakoye R Guinea/Mali
54 L1 Baksheyevo Russian Federation
26 K6 Baktsjaure Sweden
78 M1 Baku Azerbaijan
71 G6 Bakulin Pt Mindanao Philippines
32 H7 Bakum Germany
69 G12 Bakung isld Indonesia
146 B8 Bakutis Coast Antarctica
121 L7 Bala Ontario Canada
80 D4 Bal'a Jordan
78 D2 Bâlâ Turkey
8 C2 Bala Wales
71 C7 Balabac Str Borneo/Philippines
70 E6 Balabalangan, Kep islds Indonesia
71 H8 Balabalangan Pulau Pulau islds Indonesia
54 H1 Balabanovo Russian Federation
71 C7 Balabec isld Palawan Philippines
54 G9 Balabino Ukraine
128 E6 Bala,Cerros de mts Bolivia
48 H6 Bălăciţa Romania
127 J2 Balaclava Jamaica
77 B1 Baladeh Iran
80 F3 Balad el Basha Jordan
80 F3 Balad el Mansura Jordan
56 F4 Balagansk Russian Federation
74 J8 Balaghat India
17 H3 Balaguer Spain
70 B5 Balaiberkuak Kalimantan
70 B4 Balaikarangan Kalimantan
68 A2 Balaing Burma
69 D12 Balaipungut Sumatra
70 B6 Balairiam Kalimantan
70 B4 Balaisepuac Kalimantan
70 K8 Balak, Gunung Sumatra
138 E5 Balaklava South Australia Australia
54 H7 Balakleya Ukraine
8 C2 Bala L Wales
87 G8 Balama Mozambique
70 E1 Balambangan isld Indonesia
77 H2 Balā Morghāb Afghanistan
40 B6 Balan France
48 K4 Bălan Romania
125 O9 Balancán Mexico
71 E3 Balanga Luzon Philippines
75 K8 Balāngīr India
71 H5 Balantak Sulawesi
70 M9 Balapulang Java
71 F5 Balaring Negros Philippines
70 G6 Balase R Sulawesi
48 E2 Balassagyarmat Hungary
84 H4 Balât Egypt
48 D4 Balaton L Hungary
99 L5 Balaton Minnesota U.S.A.
48 D4 Balatonfüred Hungary
48 D4 Balatonszentgyörgy Hungary
71 L9 Balauring Flores Indonesia
128 G4 Balbina Brazil
128 F4 Balbina, Reprêsa de res Brazil
124 F10 Balboa Panama
14 E3 Balbriggan Ireland
141 H8 Balbuna Queensland Australia
13 G6 Balby England
86 J5 Balcad Somalia
144 D5 Balcairn New Zealand
138 E4 Balcanoona South Australia Australia
131 F6 Balcarce Argentina
119 O8 Balcarres Saskatchewan Canada
48 H6 Bălceşti Romania
47 J1 Balchik Bulgaria
109 O9 Balch Springs Texas U.S.A.
144 B7 Balclutha New Zealand
9 F5 Balcombe England
100 F6 Bald Butte mt Oregon U.S.A.
94 K6 Bald Eagle Mt Pennsylvania U.S.A.
41 H3 Baldegg See L Switzerland
6 M3 Balder oil rig North Sea
143 C11 Bald Hd W Australia Australia
44 D2 Baldichieri d'Asti Italy
110 E6 Bald Knob Arkansas U.S.A.
94 F9 Bald Knob West Virginia U.S.A.
101 L5 Bald Mt Idaho U.S.A.
103 J4 Bald Mt Nevada U.S.A.
9 F4 Baldock England
119 T2 Baldock L Manitoba Canada
42 D3 Baldo,Monte Italy
113 F7 Baldwin Florida U.S.A.
110 A3 Baldwin Kansas U.S.A.
94 B3 Baldwin Michigan U.S.A.
98 F2 Baldwin North Dakota U.S.A.
99 O5 Baldwin Wisconsin U.S.A.
102 H7 Baldwin L California U.S.A.
116 F3 Baldwin Pen Alaska U.S.A.
118 H6 Baldwinton Saskatchewan Canada
95 P4 Baldwinville Massachusetts U.S.A.
95 R3 Baldwin, W Maine U.S.A.
111 H7 Baldwyn Mississippi U.S.A.
119 R7 Baldy Mt Manitoba Canada
103 P8 Baldy Pk Arizona U.S.A.
106 E6 Baldy Pk New Mexico U.S.A.
57 E5 Bal'dzhuvon Tajikistan
69 E14 Bale Indonesia
17 J5 Baleares, Islas arch Spain
Balearic Is see Baleares, Islas arch
70 C4 Baleh R Sarawak
130 H5 Baleia, Pta da C Brazil
115 N6 Baleine,à la R Quebec Canada
83 L14 Baleiniers, Golfe des Kerguelen Indian Oc
71 C7 Balembangan isld Sabah
22 J1 Balen Belgium
48 K6 Băleni Romania
71 E3 Baler Luzon Philippines
71 E3 Baler Bay Luzon Philippines
15 E5 Balerno Scotland
75 M8 Bāleshwar India
58 G1 Baley Russian Federation
141 H5 Balfe's Creek Queensland Australia
48 D4 Bal Földvár Hungary
26 K7 Bålforsen Sweden
117 P11 Balfour British Columbia Canada
144 B6 Balfour New Zealand
98 F2 Balfour North Dakota U.S.A.
142 D6 Balfour Downs W Australia Australia
12 D1 Balfron Scotland
77 F1 Bālgirān Iran
142 G5 Balgo Hill W Australia Australia
119 N8 Balgonie Saskatchewan Canada
32 K10 Balhorn Germany
86 B4 Bali Cameroon
70 P10 Bali isld Indonesia
71 F6 Baliangao Mindanao Philippines
69 D11 Balige Sumatra
31 N6 Baligród Poland
65 D4 Balihan China
47 J5 Balıkesir Turkey
78 G4 Balīkh R Syria
86 C3 Bal Illi R Chad
70 G2 Balimbing Tawitaw isld Philippines
69 E10 Baling Malaysia
70 C3 Balingian R Sarawak
70 C3 Balingian Sarawak
65 D3 Balinqiao China
48 G5 Balint Romania
70 P9 Bali Sea Indonesia
70 P10 Bali,Selat Bali/Java
70 G2 Baliungan Tawitawi Philippines
130 D5 Baliza Brazil
32 K5 Balje Germany
118 K6 Baljennie Saskatchewan Canada
25 E3 Balk Netherlands
48 G3 Balkány Hungary
55 C4 Balkany Russian Federation
55 E4 Balkashino Kazakhstan
25 F3 Balkbrug Netherlands
77 K1 Balkh prov Afghanistan
77 K1 Balkhab R Afghanistan
57 G2 Balkhash Kazakhstan
57 G2 Balkhash, Ozero L Kazakhstan
74 H9 Balkonda India
15 C4 Ballachulish Scotland
143 E9 Balladonia W Australia Australia
14 C3 Ballaghaderreen Ireland
21 P4 Ballancourt-sur-Essonne France
141 K8 Ballandean Queensland Australia
26 J3 Ballangen Norway
101 R4 Ballantine Montana U.S.A.
15 C5 Ballantrae Scotland
119 O4 Ballantyne Bay Saskatchewan Canada
114 H2 Ballantyne Str Northwest Territories Canada
43 C9 Ballao Sardinia
139 G6 Ballarat Victoria Australia
102 G5 Ballarat California U.S.A.
143 D8 Ballard, L W Australia Australia
80 F4 Ballas Jordan
15 E3 Ballater Scotland
12 D5 Ballaugh I of Man U.K.
28 F4 Balle Denmark
21 K6 Ballée France
28 F5 Ballen Denmark
133 C3 Ballena,Pta C Chile
33 O9 Ballenstedt Germany
146 C13 Balleny Islands Antarctica
21 J3 Balleroy France
29 K5 Ballerup Denmark
112 C3 Ball Ground Georgia U.S.A.
75 L6 Ballia India
14 B2 Ballina Ireland
14 C3 Ballinasloe Ireland
14 C3 Ballindine Ireland
28 B3 Balling Denmark
14 C4 Ballingarry Ireland
108 H4 Ballinger Texas U.S.A.
15 E4 Ballinluig Scotland
14 B3 Ballinrobe Ireland
14 A5 Ballinskelligs B Ireland
37 J6 Ballmertshofen Germany
118 B7 Ball,Mt Alberta Canada
12 D1 Balloch Scotland
21 L5 Ballon France
19 K5 Ballon d'Alsace mt France
21 H6 Ballots France
46 D4 Ballsh Albania
137 M8 Ball's Pyramid isld Pacific Oc
37 K1 Ballstädt Germany
95 O4 Ballston Spa New York U.S.A.
28 B6 Ballum Denmark
14 E2 Ballybay Ireland
14 D2 Ballybofey Ireland
14 B4 Ballybunnion Ireland
14 B2 Ballycastle Ireland
14 E1 Ballycastle N Ireland
14 E2 Ballyclare N Ireland
14 D2 Ballyconnell Ireland
14 D5 Ballycotton B Ireland
14 C4 Ballyduff Ireland
14 C3 Ballygar Ireland
14 D2 Ballygawley N Ireland
12 B2 Ballygrant Scotland
14 D2 Ballyhaise Ireland
14 C3 Ballyhaunis Ireland
14 C4 Ballyhoura Hills Ireland
14 D3 Ballyjamesduff Ireland
14 D3 Ballymahon Ireland
14 E2 Ballymena N Ireland
14 E1 Ballymoney N Ireland
14 C2 Ballymote Ireland
14 D4 Ballynacourty Ireland
14 F2 Ballynahinch N Ireland
14 F2 Ballyquintin Pt N Ireland
14 D4 Ballyragget Ireland
14 C2 Ballyshannon Ireland
14 E3 Ballytore Ireland
14 B3 Ballyvaughan Ireland
12 D3 Balmaclellan Scotland
12 D1 Balmaha Scotland
95 M2 Balmat New York U.S.A.
48 G3 Balmazújváros Hungary
40 F7 Balme Italy
40 G5 Balmhorn mt Switzerland
141 K1 Balmoral dist Brisbane, Qnsld Australia
138 F6 Balmoral Victoria Australia
119 U8 Balmoral Manitoba Canada
144 D5 Balmoral New Zealand
6 L4 Balmoral oil rig North Sea
15 E3 Balmoral Castle Scotland
108 D5 Balmorhea Texas U.S.A.
13 F1 Balmullo Scotland
74 A4 Balochistān prov Pakistan
87 B8 Balombo Angola
141 J7 Balonne R Queensland Australia
141 J8 Balonne R Queensland Australia
55 D2 Balotovskoye Russian Federation
74 E6 Balotra India
33 P6 Balow Germany
12 D1 Balquhidder Scotland
75 K5 Balrampur India
48 J6 Balş Romania
99 O4 Balsam L Wisconsin U.S.A.
121 M8 Balsam Lake Ontario Canada
129 J5 Balsas Brazil
124 H8 Balsas R Mexico
26 K2 Balsfjord inlet Norway
26 K2 Balsfjord Norway
45 P6 Balsorano Italy
27 J12 Bålsta Sweden
26 G3 Balstad Norway
48 M3 Balta Ukraine
98 F1 Balta North Dakota U.S.A.
16 E3 Baltanás Spain
16 B3 Baltar Spain
133 F4 Baltasar Brum Uruguay
98 K6 Baltic South Dakota U.S.A.
27 H16 Baltic Sea N Europe
79 B7 Balṭîm Egypt
14 B5 Baltimore Ireland
87 E10 Baltimore S Africa
95 L7 Baltimore Maryland U.S.A.
97 Baltimore conurbation Maryland U.S.A.
14 E4 Baltinglass Ireland
Baltit see Hunza
31 M1 Baltiysk Russian Federation
32 F5 Baltrum Germany
80 G8 Balu R Jordan
80 G8 Balu Jordan
77 G6 Balūchestān va Sīstān Iran
Balūchistān prov see Balochistān
72 J3 Balūchistān reg Pakistan/Iran
70 C3 Balui R Sarawak
71 E7 Balukbaluk isld Philippines
69 D12 Balumundan Sumatra
70 C5 Baluran, Gunung mt Kalimantan
75 N6 Balurghat India
71 G8 Balut isld Philippines
32 G10 Balve Germany
52 C6 Balvi Latvia
47 J5 Balya Turkey
84 J4 Balyana,El Egypt
56 H4 Bal Yeravnoye, Oz L Russian Federation
56 C4 Balyksa Russian Federation
56 E5 Balyktyg Khem R Russian Federation

118 C7 **Balzac** Alberta Canada
77 F5 **Bam** Iran
67 B4 **Bama** China
86 B3 **Bama** Nigeria
141 F1 **Bamaga** Queensland Australia
85 C6 **Bamako** Mali
128 C5 **Bambamarca** Peru
71 E3 **Bamban** Luzon Philippines
71 E2 **Bambang** Luzon Philippines
71 E8 **Bambannan** *isld* Philippines
86 D4 **Bambari** Cent Afr Republic
141 H4 **Bambaroo** Queensland Australia
13 F6 **Bamber Br** England
37 K4 **Bamberg** Germany
112 F4 **Bamberg** South Carolina U.S.A.
86 E5 **Bambesa** Zaire
86 E5 **Bambili** Zaire
86 C5 **Bambio** Cent Afr Republic
27 D13 **Bamble** Norway
142 D5 **Bamboo Creek** W Australia Australia
142 C5 **Bamboo Springs** W Australia Australia
83 M13 **Bambou Mts** Mauritius
130 F7 **Bambui** Brazil
70 D5 **Bambulung** Kalimantan
13 G2 **Bamburgh** England
86 B4 **Bamenda** Cameroon
117 L11 **Bamfield** British Columbia Canada
77 K2 **Bāmīān** Afghanistan
77 K2 **Bāmīan** *prov* Afghanistan
67 C4 **Bamian** China
65 F3 **Bamiancheng** China
Bamiantong *see* **Muling**
86 C4 **Bamingui** *R* Cent Afr Republic
86 C4 **Bamingui-Bangoran Nat. Park** Cent Afr Republic
68 G6 **Bam Nak** Cambodia
68 E5 **Bamnet Narong** Thailand
124 E5 **Bamoa** Mexico
69 A8 **Bampoka I** Nicobar Is
77 H6 **Bam Posht, Kūh-e** *mts* Iran
8 C6 **Bampton** England
9 E4 **Bampton** England
77 G6 **Bampūr** Iran
77 G6 **Bampur** *R* Iran
74 J9 **Bāmrāgad** India
68 H4 **Ba Na** Vietnam
137 O1 **Banaba** *isld* Pacific Oc
129 L5 **Banabuiu Açude** *res* Brazil
14 D3 **Banagher** Ireland
71 E4 **Banahao, Mt** Luzon Philippines
86 E5 **Banalia** Zaire
68 G7 **Banam** Cambodia
85 C6 **Banamba** Mali
124 D2 **Banámichi** Mexico
141 K6 **Banana** Queensland Australia
129 H6 **Bananal, Ilha do** Brazil
113 G9 **Banana R** Florida U.S.A.
130 J9 **Bananeiras** Brazil
76 G7 **Bananga** Nicobar Is
68 F6 **Ban Aranyaprathet** Thailand
47 J3 **Banarlı** Turkey
69 D8 **Ba Na San** Thailand
48 F6 **Banatsko Novo Selo** Serbia Yugoslavia
15 C4 **Banavie** Scotland
71 J8 **Banawaja** *isld* Indonesia
78 B2 **Banaz** Turkey
68 E4 **Ban Bang Mun Nak** Thailand
68 E4 **Ban Bang Rakam** Thailand
71 G6 **Banbayan Pt** Mindanao Philippines
69 E10 **Ban Betong** Thailand
68 J6 **Ban Bik** Vietnam
14 E2 **Banbridge** N Ireland
68 E5 **Ban Bua Chum** Thailand
68 F5 **Ban Bua Yai** Thailand
68 E5 **Ban Bu Khanum** Thailand
68 G5 **Ban Bungxai** Laos
68 H5 **Ban Bungxai** Laos
9 E3 **Banbury** England
71 C6 **Bancalan** Palawan Philippines
138 F4 **Bancannia, L** New South Wales Australia
85 A4 **Banc d'Arguin Nat. Park** Mauritania
68 D3 **Ban Chang Khoeng** Thailand
68 F4 **Ban Channabot** Thailand
68 D3 **Ban Chiang Dao** Thailand
15 F3 **Banchory** Scotland
68 E4 **Ban Chum Phae** Thailand
125 Q8 **Banco Chinchorro** *isld* Mexico
71 D7 **Bancoron** *isld* Philippines
121 N7 **Bancroft** Ontario Canada
101 O7 **Bancroft** Idaho U.S.A.
99 M6 **Bancroft** Iowa U.S.A.
98 J5 **Bancroft** South Dakota U.S.A.
48 J4 **Band** Romania
74 J6 **Banda** India
69 B10 **Banda Aceh** Sumatra
69 C11 **Bandahara, Gunung** *mt* Sumatra
61 N7 **Bandai-Asahi Nat.Pk** Japan
61 O8 **Bandai-san** *mt* Japan
85 B7 **Bandajuma** Sierra Leone
27 C12 **Bandak** *L* Norway
85 C7 **Bandama** *R* Ivory Coast
68 G5 **Ban Dan** Thailand
77 G4 **Bandan Kuh** *mt* Iran
Bandar *see* **Machilipatnam**
77 J2 **Bandar** Afghanistan
87 F9 **Bandar** Mozambique
75 J4 **Bandar** Nepal
70 K8 **Bandaragung** Sumatra
86 B2 **Bandarbeyla** Somalia
77 E6 **Bandar-e 'Abbās** Iran
77 A1 **Bandar-e Anzalī** Iran
77 B4 **Bandar-e Deylam** Iran
77 D6 **Bandar-e Khoemir** Iran
77 A4 **Bandar-e Khomeynī** Iran
77 D6 **Bandar-e Lengeh** Iran
77 A4 **Bandar-e Ma'shūr** Iran
77 B5 **Bandar-e Rīg** Iran
77 D1 **Bandar-e Torkeman** Iran
86 B1 **Bandar Murcaay** Somalia
70 D2 **Bandar Seri Begawan** Brunei
136 F3 **Banda Sea** Indonesia
88 E7 **Bandawe** Malawi
22 J3 **Bande** Belgium
16 B2 **Bande** Spain
129 K8 **Bandeira** *mt* Brazil
130 H7 **Bandeira** *mt* Brazil
130 E8 **Bandeirantes** Brazil
130 D8 **Bandeirantes, I. dos** Brazil
106 D6 **Bandelier Nat.Mon** New Mexico U.S.A.
77 D6 **Band-e Moghūyeh** Iran
109 H6 **Bandera** Texas U.S.A.
108 B4 **Banderas** Mexico
124 G7 **Banderas,B de** Mexico
28 G7 **Bandholm** Denmark
85 D6 **Bandiagara** Mali
77 K2 **Band-i-Amur** *R* Afghanistan
77 J2 **Band-i-Balan** *mts* Afghanistan
78 B1 **Bandırma** Turkey
47 J4 **Bandırma Körfezi** *G* Turkey
77 J2 **Band-i-Turkestan** *mts* Afghanistan
70 M9 **Bandjar** Java
70 D6 **Bandjarmasin** Kalimantan
70 M9 **Bandjarnegara** Java
19 P18 **Bandol** France
Ban Don *see* **Surat Thani**
14 C5 **Bandon** *R* Ireland
14 C5 **Bandon** Ireland
100 A6 **Bandon** Oregon U.S.A.
68 G4 **Ban Dong** Laos
68 F4 **Ban Don Khi** Thailand
74 E9 **Bandra** India
86 C6 **Bandundu** Zaire
70 L9 **Bandung** Java
69 F12 **Bandung** Sumatra
68 G4 **Ban Dupre** Laos
94 F9 **Bandy** Virginia U.S.A.
143 D7 **Bandya** W Australia Australia
48 L5 **Băneasa** Romania
78 K4 **Baneh** Iran
71 B2 **Banema** Halmahera Indonesia
17 G6 **Bañeras** Spain
126 G4 **Banes** Cuba
69 D8 **Ban Fai Tha** Thailand
118 B7 **Banff** Alberta Canada
15 F3 **Banff** Scotland
85 D6 **Banfora** Burkina
86 D7 **Banga** Zaire
71 F7 **Bangaan** Mindanao Philippines
71 G7 **Bangai Pt** Mindanao Philippines
71 E7 **Bangalao** *isld* Philippines
76 C4 **Bangalore** India
71 E2 **Bangar** Luzon Philippines
70 D2 **Bangar** Sarawak
70 E3 **Bangatan** Kalimantan
71 H7 **Bangbong** Sulawesi
27 H12 **Bångbro** Sweden
86 C5 **Bangé** Cameroon
110 E4 **Bangert** Missouri U.S.A.
70 C4 **Bang,G** *mt* Kalimantan
71 H6 **Banggai, Kep** *islds* Indonesia
71 C7 **Banggi** *isld* Sabah
84 F3 **Banghāzī** Libya
68 G4 **Bang Hieng** *R* Laos
70 O9 **Bangil** Java
69 G14 **Bangka** *isld* Indonesia
71 J4 **Bangka** Sulawesi Indonesia
70 C8 **Bangkal** Kalimantan
70 O9 **Bangkalan** Java
70 F7 **Bangkala, Teluk** *B* Sulawesi
69 C11 **Bangkaru** *isld* Sumatra
69 G14 **Bangka,Selat** *str* Sumatra
69 D12 **Bangkinang** Sumatra
70 G4 **Bangkir** Sulawesi Indonesia
69 F14 **Bangko** Sumatra
63 **Bangkok** *conurbation* Thailand
68 E6 **Bangkok,Bight of** Thailand
70 D6 **Bangkuang** Kalimantan
71 H5 **Bangkulu** Sulawesi Indonesia
71 H9 **Bangkulua** Sumbawa Indonesia
75 N6 **Bangladesh** *rep* S Asia
68 E6 **Bang Lamung** Thailand
68 J7 **Ba Ngoi** Vietnam
66 B5 **Bangong Co** *L* China
119 P8 **Bangor** Saskatchewan Canada
20 B7 **Bangor** France
14 F2 **Bangor** N Ireland
95 T2 **Bangor** Maine U.S.A.
94 A4 **Bangor** Michigan U.S.A.
95 M6 **Bangor** Pennsylvania U.S.A.
8 B1 **Bangor** Wales
86 C4 **Bangoran** *R* Cent Afr Republic
109 H4 **Bangs** Texas U.S.A.
70 E5 **Bangsalsepulun** Kalimantan
68 D7 **Bang Saphan Yai** Thailand
28 F2 **Bangsbostrand** Denmark
103 L5 **Bangs,Mt** Arizona U.S.A.
26 E7 **Bangsund** Norway
71 E2 **Bangued** Luzon Philippines
86 C5 **Bangui** Cent Afr Republic
71 E1 **Bangui** Luzon Philippines
69 D11 **Bangunpurba** Sumatra
88 B7 **Bangweulu, L** Zambia
68 F3 **Ban Hai** Laos
68 D4 **Ban Hat Sao** Thailand
69 E9 **Ban Hat Yai** Thailand
87 F10 **Banhine Nat. Park** Mozambique
68 F3 **Ban Hin Heup** Laos
68 J6 **Ban Ho** Vietnam
68 E2 **Ban Houayxay** Laos
68 F3 **Ban Huai Kho** Thailand
68 D7 **Ban Huai Yang** Thailand
86 D4 **Bani** Cent Afr Republic
127 J5 **Baní** Dominican Rep
85 C6 **Bani** *R* Mali
71 D2 **Bani** Luzon Philippines
116 L7 **Ban I** Alaska U.S.A.
85 E5 **Bani Bangou** Niger
127 J5 **Bánica** Dominican Rep
31 H2 **Banie** Poland
85 E6 **Banikoara** Benin
86 B6 **Banio, Lagune** *lagoon* Gabon
71 D3 **Bani Pt** Luzon Philippines
94 H10 **Banister** *R* Virginia U.S.A.
84 E3 **Banī Walīd** Libya
79 F3 **Baniyās** Syria
80 F1 **Bāniyās** Syria
48 E6 **Banja Koviljača** Bosnia-Herzegovina
42 H4 **Banja Luka** Bosnia-Herzegovina
70 D6 **Banjarbaru** Kalimantan
68 H6 **Ban Jeng Drom** Vietnam
85 A6 **Banjul** The Gambia
70 M9 **Banjumas** Java
142 B3 **Banjup** *dist* Perth, W Aust Australia
140 C4 **Banka Banka** N Terr Australia
68 G5 **Ban Kadian** Laos
68 E4 **Ban Kaeng** Thailand
69 E9 **Ban Kam Phaeng Phet** Thailand
69 D9 **Ban Kantang** Thailand
89 D9 **Bankberg** *mts* S Africa
12 E3 **Bankend** Scotland
68 H5 **Ban Keng Phao** Cambodia
68 F2 **Ban Keo Lom** Vietnam
68 E6 **Ban Khai** Thailand
68 F1 **Ban Khang Kha** Vietnam
68 D6 **Ban Khao Yoi** Thailand
111 J8 **Bankhead L** Alabama U.S.A.
68 E3 **Ban Khing** Laos
68 F6 **Ban Khlung** Thailand
69 D8 **Ban Khok Kloi** Thailand
69 D9 **Ban Khuan Mao** Thailand
68 F4 **Ban Khuk Muang** Thailand
68 E3 **Ban Khun Ban Hai** Thailand
68 F5 **Ban Khu Noi** Thailand
68 C3 **Ban Khun Yuam** Thailand
68 J6 **Ban Kniet** Vietnam
70 E7 **Bankobankoang** *isld* Indonesia
68 D4 **Ban Krai** Thailand
100 J5 **Banks** Idaho U.S.A.
110 F7 **Banks** Mississippi U.S.A.
100 B4 **Banks** Oregon U.S.A.
138 F7 **Banks,C** South Australia Australia
117 H9 **Banks I** British Columbia Canada
147 J2 **Banks I** Northwest Territories Canada
100 F2 **Banks L** Washington U.S.A.
144 D5 **Banks Peninsula** New Zealand
139 K7 **Bankstown Airfield** Sydney, New S Wales Australia
68 D6 **Ban Kui Nua** Thailand
75 M7 **Bankura** India
68 G4 **Ban Kut Hae** Thailand
46 F2 **Bankya** Bulgaria
68 F5 **Ban Lamduan** Thailand
71 F3 **Banla Pt** Philippines
68 D5 **Ban Le Kathe** Thailand
68 E5 **Ban Len** Thailand
68 C3 **Ban Mae La Luang** Thailand
68 D3 **Ban Mae Mo** Thailand
68 D4 **Ban Mae Ramat** Thailand
68 C3 **Ban Mae Sariang** Thailand
68 D4 **Ban Mae Sot** Thailand
68 D3 **Ban Mae Suai** Thailand
68 D3 **Ban Mae Thalop** Thailand
68 E5 **Ban Mi** Thailand
68 D3 **Ban Mong Pong** Thailand
68 E3 **Ban Muang** Thailand
68 F5 **Ban Muang Phon** Thailand
14 E4 **Bann** *R* Ireland
14 E2 **Bann** *R* N Ireland
71 E1 **Banna** Luzon Philippines
69 D8 **Ban Na** Thailand
68 F4 **Ban Na Baek** Thailand
68 H4 **Ban Nabo** Laos
101 N4 **Bannack** Montana U.S.A.
68 G4 **Ban Na Kae** Thailand
68 E3 **Ban Na Kon** Thailand
20 C6 **Bannalec** France
68 E2 **Ban Na Mo** Laos
68 E4 **Ban Nam Pong** Thailand
68 F1 **Ban Nam Sau** Vietnam
68 E3 **Ban Na Noi** Thailand
68 F3 **Ban Naphong** Laos
68 F3 **Ban Na Sabaeng** Thailand
69 E9 **Ban Na Thawi** Thailand
142 F4 **Bannerman, Mt** W Australia Australia
126 F2 **Bannerman Town** Eleuthera Bahamas
102 H8 **Banning** California U.S.A.
Banningville *see* **Bandundu**
40 H6 **Bannio** Italy
41 H6 **Bannio-Anzino** Italy
121 N8 **Bannockburn** Ontario Canada
144 B6 **Bannockburn** New Zealand
12 E1 **Bannockburn** Scotland
101 M5 **Bannock Pass** Idaho/ Montana U.S.A.
101 N7 **Bannock Ra** Idaho U.S.A.
68 C4 **Ban Noi** Thailand
68 E2 **Ban Nong Kha** Laos
68 F5 **Ban Nong Makha** Thailand
68 H5 **Ban Nong Met** Laos
68 F5 **Ban Nong Waeng** Thailand
74 D2 **Bannu** Pakistan
17 J2 **Bañolas** Spain
19 P16 **Banon** France
124 H6 **Bañón** Mexico
31 L7 **Bánovce** Slovakia
Banow *see* **Andarāb**
68 F3 **Ban Pacpeup** Laos
68 D3 **Ban Pak Bong** Thailand
68 D7 **Ban Pak Chan** Thailand
68 D6 **Ban Pak Khlong** Thailand
68 E6 **Ban Pak Nam** Thailand
68 D7 **Ban Pak Nam** Thailand
68 E3 **Ban Pak Neun** Laos
68 F5 **Ban Pak Thong Chai** Thailand
68 E5 **Ban Phachi** Thailand
68 G4 **Ban Phaeng** Thailand
68 F5 **Ban Phai** Thailand
68 E6 **Ban Phanat Nikhom** Thailand
68 D6 **Ban Phattaya** Thailand
68 H5 **Ban Phon** Laos
68 G5 **Ban Phon Ngam** Thailand
68 D5 **Banphot Phisai** Thailand
68 D4 **Ban Phran Katai** Thailand
68 E4 **Ban Phrom Phirom** Thailand
68 F5 **Ban Phutthaisong** Thailand
Ban Pla Soi *see* **Chon Buri**
68 D6 **Ban Pong** Thailand
67 A3 **Banqiao** China
65 D7 **Banquan** China
68 D4 **Ban Saen To** Thailand
68 E2 **Ban Sai** Laos
68 F5 **Ban Sai** Thailand
68 D5 **Ban Sai Yok** Thailand
69 E9 **Ban Sanam Chai** Thailand
68 F5 **Ban Sangae** Thailand
68 D3 **Ban Saraphi Chae Hom** Thailand
68 E6 **Ban Sattahip** Thailand
68 D7 **Ban Sawi** Thailand
75 K5 **Bansi** India
69 E8 **Ban Sichon** Thailand
31 L7 **Banská Bystrica** Slovakia
31 L7 **Banská Stiavnica** Slovakia
46 F3 **Bansko** Bulgaria
68 D3 **Ban Sop Huai Hai** Thailand
68 D4 **Ban Sop Prap** Thailand
68 G3 **Ban Sot** Laos
68 D4 **Ban Sut Ta** Thailand
68 F5 **Ban Suwai** Thailand
74 F7 **Banswara** India
71 J9 **Banta** *isld* Sumbawa Indonesia
70 F7 **Bantaeng** Sulawesi Indonesia
68 E5 **Ban Ta Khli** Thailand
69 E13 **Bantal** Sumatra
83 M8 **Bantam** Cocos Is Indian Oc
68 F5 **Ban Tan** Thailand
68 F6 **Ban Ta Ruang** Thailand
68 H4 **Ban Taup** Laos
68 F3 **Ban Ta Viang** Laos
71 F5 **Bantayan** *isld* Philippines
32 L8 **Banteln** Germany
70 L9 **Banten** Java
69 D8 **Ban Tha Chang** Thailand
68 G5 **Ban Tham Khae** Thailand
68 D5 **Ban Thap Phung** Thailand
69 E8 **Ban Tha Sala** Thailand
68 D4 **Ban Tha Song Yang** Thailand
68 E5 **Ban Tha Tako** Thailand
68 H5 **Ban Thateng** Laos
68 G4 **Ban Tha Uthen** Thailand
69 E9 **Ban Thepha** Thailand
22 J5 **Bantheville** France
68 D6 **Ban Thung Luang** Thailand
71 F4 **Banton** *isld* Philippines
68 H6 **Ban Treo** Cambodia
14 B5 **Bantry** Ireland
98 F1 **Bantry** North Dakota U.S.A.
14 B5 **Bantry B** Ireland
70 N9 **Bantul** Java
74 D8 **Bantva** India
76 B4 **Bantval** India
68 F4 **Ban Waeng Noi** Thailand
68 E4 **Ban Wang Saphong** Thailand
68 G4 **Ban Wang Ta Mua** Thailand
8 D5 **Banwell** England
68 F4 **Ban Wiang Khuk** Thailand
46 G2 **Banya** Bulgaria
69 C11 **Banyak, Kep.** *isld* Indonesia
68 F4 **Ban Yang Talat** Thailand
68 D6 **Ban Yang Yong** Thailand
68 H6 **Ban Ya Soup** Vietnam
141 K1 **Banyo** *dist* Brisbane, Qnsld Australia
86 B4 **Banyo** Cameroon
Bañyoles *see* **Bañolas**
69 G14 **Banyuasin** *R* Sumatra
70 P10 **Banyuwangi** Java
37 L3 **Banz** Germany
146 E14 **Banzare Coast** Antarctica
81 E11 **Banzare Seamount** Southern Oc
67 B4 **Bao'an** China
67 E5 **Bao'an** China
Baocheng *see* **Taibus Qi**
58 F4 **Baode** China
65 D5 **Baodi** China
58 G4 **Baoding** China
65 B7 **Baofeng** China
67 A5 **Bao Ha** Vietnam
65 D4 **Bao He** *R* China
58 E5 **Baoji** China
67 C2 **Baojing** China
Baokang *see* **Horqin Zouyi Zhongqi**
67 D1 **Baokang** China
68 G1 **Bao Lac** Vietnam
65 F3 **Baolizhen** China
68 H7 **Bao Loc** Vietnam
65 J1 **Baoqing** China
67 G1 **Baoshan** China
68 J3 **Baoting** China
58 E3 **Baotou** China
85 C6 **Baoulé** *R* Mali
59 G5 **Baoying** China
Baoyou *see* **Ledong**
76 E3 **Bapatla** India
22 D3 **Bapaume** France
103 N8 **Bapchule** Arizona U.S.A.
121 M7 **Baptiste** Ontario Canada
80 D4 **Bāqa el Gharbiya** Israel
66 E5 **Baqên** China
79 F9 **Bāqir, J** *mt* Jordan
78 K5 **Ba'Qūbah** Iraq
80 F3 **Baqura** Jordan
22 H4 **Bar** *R* France
48 L1 **Bar** Ukraine
42 J6 **Bar** Montenegro Yugoslavia
86 F3 **Bara** Sudan
68 H7 **Ba Ra** Vietnam
86 H5 **Baraawe** Somalia
70 D6 **Barabai** Kalimantan
55 G3 **Barabinsk** Russian Federation
55 G4 **Barabinskaya Nizmennost'** *lowland* Russian Federation
99 R6 **Baraboo** Wisconsin U.S.A.
122 H5 **Barachois** Quebec Canada
126 G4 **Baracoa** Cuba
79 H3 **Baradah** Syria
99 S3 **Baraga** Michigan U.S.A.
48 L6 **Bărăganul** Romania
75 K8 **Baragarh** India
86 G5 **Baragoi** Kenya
75 N7 **Barahanager** India
127 J5 **Barahona** Dominican Rep
Barak *see* **Karkamiş**
57 F6 **Barak** Afghanistan
79 H2 **Barak** Turkey
88 B4 **Baraka** Zaire
77 L3 **Baraki Barak** Afghanistan
75 L8 **Barakot** India
55 E5 **Barakpay** Kazakhstan
141 K7 **Barakula** Queensland Australia
141 J6 **Baralaba** Queensland Australia
80 E1 **Bar'am** Israel
70 D3 **Baram** *R* Sarawak
128 G2 **Barama** *R* Guyana
74 F9 **Baramati** India
141 K7 **Barambah** *R* Queensland Australia
70 C2 **Baram,Tg** *C* Sarawak
54 B2 **Baran'** Belarus
74 G6 **Baran** India
55 C2 **Baranchinskiy** Russian Federation
45 R6 **Baranello** Italy
86 E5 **Baranga** Zaire
21 P7 **Barangeon** *R* France
77 G4 **Baran, Kūh-e-** *mts* Iran
126 G9 **Baranoa** Colombia
117 F7 **Baranof I** Alaska U.S.A.
31 N5 **Baranów** Poland
48 E5 **Baranya** *co* Hungary
129 G6 **Barao de Capenema** Brazil
130 C5 **Barão de Melgaço** Mato Grosso Brazil
48 K4 **Baraolt** Romania
48 K4 **Baraoltului Munti** *mt* Romania
22 K3 **Baraque-le Fraiture** Belgium
22 L2 **Baraque Michel** Belgium
70 L9 **Barat** Java
70 B5 **Barat** Kalimantan
111 F12 **Barataria** Louisiana U.S.A.
111 G12 **Barataria B** Louisiana U.S.A.
71 N8 **Barat Daya, Kep** *islds* Philippines
71 L9 **Barati** Indonesia
138 E4 **Baratta** South Australia Australia
70 E5 **Baratus, Gunung** *mt* Kalimantan
75 M6 **Barauni** India
130 G7 **Barbacena** Minas Gerais Brazil
128 C3 **Barbacoas** Colombia
127 P6 **Barbados** Lesser Antilles
130 G9 **Barbalha** Brazil
45 O4 **Bárbara** Italy
120 C3 **Barbara L** Ontario Canada
45 L1 **Barbarano Vicentino** Italy
85 A4 **Barbas,C** Western Sahara
20 F8 **Barbâtre** France
122 D2 **Barbel,L** Quebec Canada
100 J6 **Barber** Idaho U.S.A.
45 K3 **Barberino di Mugello** Italy
45 K4 **Barberino di Val d'Elsa** Italy
102 R12 **Barbers Pt** Hawaiian Is
89 G5 **Barberton** S Africa
94 F5 **Barberton** Ohio U.S.A.
113 F8 **Barberville** Florida U.S.A.
18 E7 **Barbezieux** France
45 J4 **Barbona, M** *mt* Italy
128 D2 **Barbosa** Colombia
48 L5 **Barbosi** Romania
94 J8 **Barboursville** Virginia U.S.A.
110 N5 **Barbourville** Kentucky U.S.A.
127 O6 **Barbuda** *isld* Lesser Antilles
33 P9 **Barby** Germany
16 C4 **Barca d'Alva** Portugal
126 A2 **Barcadera** Bonaire Neth Antilles
126 A2 **Barcadera** Aruba W Indies
141 H6 **Barcaldine** Queensland Australia
16 C6 **Barcarrota** Spain
17 J3 **Barcelona** *prov* Spain
17 J3 **Barcelona** Spain
127 M9 **Barcelona** Venezuela
128 F4 **Barcelos** Brazil
16 B3 **Barcelos** Portugal
37 J2 **Barchfeld** Germany
19 P16 **Barcillonnette** France
31 K3 **Barcin** Poland
112 L1 **Barco** North Carolina U.S.A.
141 G6 **Barcoo** *R* Queensland Australia
141 G6 **Barcoo Cr** Qnsld/S Aust Australia
141 H6 **Barcoorah, L** Queensland Australia
48 D5 **Barcs** Hungary
106 G6 **Bard** New Mexico U.S.A.
84 F5 **Bardaï** Chad
47 L5 **Bardakçi** Turkey
75 M7 **Barddhamān** India
31 N6 **Bardejov** Slovakia
33 R8 **Bardenitz** Germany
84 G3 **Bardī, Al** Libya
139 J4 **Bardine** New South Wales Australia
9 F1 **Bardney** England
41 N6 **Bardolino** Italy
122 E2 **Bardoux,L** Quebec Canada
33 M6 **Bardowick** Germany
13 E5 **Bardsea** England
8 B2 **Bardsey** *isld* Wales
8 B2 **Bardsey Sd.** Wales
110 L4 **Bardstown** Kentucky U.S.A.
26 K3 **Bardu** Norway
26 K3 **Barduelv** *R* Norway
141 H7 **Barduthulla** Queensland Australia
110 G5 **Bardwell** Kentucky U.S.A.
109 L3 **Bardwell** Texas U.S.A.
145 F3 **Bare I** New Zealand
74 H4 **Bareilly** India
32 J7 **Barenburg** Germany
37 O3 **Bärenstein** Germany
21 M2 **Barentin** France
21 J4 **Barenton** France
22 F4 **Barenton-Bugny** France
50 B1 **Barentsöya** *isld* Spitzbergen
147 J13 **Barents Sea** Arctic Oc
86 G2 **Barentu** Eritrea
70 D3 **Bareo** Sarawak
20 H2 **Barfleur** France
20 H2 **Barfleur, Pte. de** France
9 E3 **Barford** England
9 E5 **Barford** England
66 C5 **Barga** China
45 H3 **Barga** Italy
86 B1 **Bargaal** Somalia
141 K6 **Bargara** Queensland Australia
16 E5 **Bargas** Spain
86 G4 **Bargē** Ethiopia
44 B2 **Barge** Italy
123 Q2 **Barge B** Labrador, Nfld Canada
33 T5 **Bargischow** Germany
32 M5 **Bargteheide** Germany
56 H3 **Barguzin** *R* Russian Federation
56 G4 **Barguzinskiy Khrebet** *mts* Russian Federation
56 G4 **Barguzinskiy Zaliv** *G* Russian Federation
139 G6 **Barham** New South Wales Australia
95 T2 **Bar Harbor** Maine U.S.A.
75 L6 **Barhi** India
86 D4 **Bari** *R* Cent Afr Republic
74 G5 **Bari** India
43 H7 **Bari** Italy
128 E3 **Baria** *R* Venezuela
45 L2 **Baricella** Italy
44 G2 **Barigazzo Monte** Italy
85 F1 **Barika** Algeria
71 M9 **Barike** Indonesia
128 F2 **Barima,Pta** *C* Venezuela
127 J10 **Barinas** Venezuela
128 D2 **Barinas** Venezuela
110 D1 **Baring** Missouri U.S.A.
100 D2 **Baring** Washington U.S.A.
143 E10 **Baring, Mt** W Australia Australia
28 D5 **Båring Vig** *B* Denmark
127 J10 **Barinitas** Venezuela
75 M8 **Baripada** India
130 E8 **Bariri** Brazil
84 J5 **Bârîs** Egypt
22 E4 **Barisis** France
70 D5 **Barito** *R* Kalimantan
19 Q17 **Barjaude** *mt* France
19 P17 **Barjols** France
84 E4 **Barjūj** *watercourse* Libya
29 K4 **Barkåkra** Sweden
58 D5 **Barkam** China
27 H11 **Barken,N** *L* Sweden
94 J3 **Barker** New York U.S.A.
143 D9 **Barker L** W Australia Australia
117 N9 **Barkerville** British Columbia Canada
94 H5 **Barkeyville** Pennsylvania U.S.A.
9 G4 **Barking** England
120 H6 **Bark L** Ontario Canada
110 J5 **Barkley Res** Kentucky U.S.A.
100 A1 **Barkley Sound** British Columbia Canada
140 E5 **Barkly Downs** Queensland Australia
140 D4 **Barkly Highway** N Terr Australia
140 B5 **Barkly, Mt** N Terr Australia
140 D4 **Barkly Tableland** Qnsld/N Terr Australia
89 D7 **Barkly West** S Africa
66 E3 **Barkol** China
99 T4 **Bark River** Michigan U.S.A.
108 G6 **Barksdale** Texas U.S.A.
47 L6 **Barla Dağı** *mt* Turkey
9 E1 **Barlborough** England
19 J4 **Bar le Duc** France
143 C8 **Barlee** *L* W Australia Australia
143 B6 **Barlee Ra** W Australia Australia
8 C5 **Barle, R** England
19 Q16 **Barles** France
43 G7 **Barletta** Italy
22 D3 **Barlin** France
31 J3 **Barlinek** Poland
27 K14 **Barlingbo** *isld* Gotland Sweden
32 E9 **Barlo** Germany
32 L4 **Barlohe** Germany
98 G2 **Barlow** North Dakota U.S.A.
100 D4 **Barlow Pass** Oregon U.S.A.
13 H6 **Barmby Moor** England
139 H5 **Barmedman** New South Wales Australia
74 D6 **Barmer** India
138 F5 **Barmera** South Australia Australia
8 B2 **Barmouth** Wales
32 L5 **Barmstedt** Germany
122 G7 **Barnaby River** New Brunswick Canada
74 F7 **Barnagar** India
107 N2 **Barnard** Kansas U.S.A.
98 H4 **Barnard** South Dakota U.S.A.
13 G4 **Barnard Castle** England
117 E6 **Barnard,Mt** Br Col/Alaska Canada/U.S.A.
37 N4 **Bärnau** Germany
56 B4 **Barnaul** Russian Federation
56 B4 **Barnaulka** *R* Russian Federation
9 E1 **Barnby Moor** England
95 N7 **Barnegat** New Jersey U.S.A.
107 O2 **Barnes** Kansas U.S.A.
94 J6 **Barnesboro** Pennsylvania U.S.A.
115 M3 **Barnes Icecap** Northwest Territories Canada
113 G12 **Barnes Sd** Florida U.S.A.
98 K9 **Barneston** Nebraska U.S.A.
112 C4 **Barnesville** Georgia U.S.A.
98 K3 **Barnesville** Minnesota U.S.A.
9 F4 **Barnet** England
25 E4 **Barneveld** Netherlands
20 G3 **Barneville** France
33 R7 **Barnewitz** Germany
99 M8 **Barney** Iowa U.S.A.
103 N4 **Barney Top** *mt* Utah U.S.A.
108 F4 **Barnhart** Texas U.S.A.
33 T7 **Barnim** *reg* Germany
122 F5 **Barn Mtn** Quebec Canada
20 E3 **Barnouic** *isld* France
107 O5 **Barnsdall** Oklahoma U.S.A.
13 G6 **Barnsley** England
95 R5 **Barnstable** Massachusetts U.S.A.
8 B5 **Barnstaple** England
8 C6 **Barnstaple Cross** England
95 Q3 **Barnstead** New Hampshire U.S.A.
32 H7 **Barnstorf** Germany
32 K9 **Barntrup** Germany
99 O3 **Barnum** Minnesota U.S.A.
118 E9 **Barnwell** Alberta Canada
112 F4 **Barnwell** South Carolina U.S.A.
37 P6 **Bärnzell** Germany
86 F4 **Baro** *R* Ethiopia
85 F7 **Baro** Nigeria
Baroda *see* **Vadodara**
22 K5 **Baroncourt** France
45 R8 **Baronissi** Italy
19 O16 **Baronnies, Les** *reg* France
118 D9 **Barons** Alberta Canada
143 F6 **Baron's Ra** W Australia Australia
36 B6 **Baronville** France
87 D8 **Barotseland** *reg* Zambia
75 O5 **Barpeta** India
80 D4 **Barqay** Israel
7 L9 **Barque** *gas field* North Sea
99 U4 **Barques, Pt. Aux** Michigan U.S.A.
127 K9 **Barquisimeto** Venezuela
19 K4 **Barr** France
12 D3 **Barr** Scotland
98 B10 **Barr** Colorado U.S.A.
129 K6 **Barra** Brazil
15 A3 **Barra** *isld* Scotland
130 E8 **Barra Bonita** Brazil
130 G5 **Barracão** Brazil
128 G5 **Barracão do Barreto** Brazil
89 B10 **Barracouta,C** S Africa
129 K6 **Barra da Estiva** Brazil
142 A6 **Barradale Roadhouse** W Australia Australia
124 G8 **Barra de Navidad** Mexico
130 H8 **Barra de sã João** Brazil
130 B4 **Barra do Bugres** Brazil
129 J5 **Barra do Corda** Brazil
130 H6 **Barra do Cuieté** Brazil
87 B7 **Barra do Dande** Angola
130 D4 **Barra do Garças** Brazil
130 F6 **Barra do Paraopeba** Brazil
130 G8 **Barra do Pirai** Brazil
129 G5 **Barra do São Manuel** Brazil
87 G10 **Barra Falsa,Pta.da** Mozambique
16 B5 **Barragem de Maranhão** *res* Portugal
16 B5 **Barragem de Montargil Res** Portugal
16 B5 **Barragem do Castello do Bode** Portugal
138 E6 **Barrages** South Australia Australia
15 A4 **Barra Head** Scotland
129 K8 **Barra Mansa** Brazil
128 C4 **Barranca** Peru
128 D2 **Barrancabermeja** Colombia
131 F2 **Barrancas** *R* Corrientes Argentina
127 H9 **Barrancas** Colombia
127 N10 **Barrancas** Venezuela
131 B6 **Barrancas,R** Mendoza Argentina
130 B7 **Barranco Branco** Brazil
16 C6 **Barrancos** Portugal
133 F3 **Barranqueras** Argentina
126 G9 **Barranquilla** Colombia
13 F3 **Barrasford** England
121 N4 **Barraute** Quebec Canada
19 P14 **Barraux** France
17 F5 **Barrax** Spain
95 P4 **Barre** Massachusetts U.S.A.
95 P2 **Barre** Vermont U.S.A.
20 F8 **Barre-de-Monts, la** France
21 M4 **Barre-en-Ouche, la** France
129 K6 **Barreiras** Brazil
129 G4 **Barreirinha** Brazil
129 K4 **Barreirinhas** Brazil
130 D4 **Barreiro** *R* Brazil
16 A6 **Barreiro** Portugal
130 J10 **Barreiros** Brazil
110 K5 **Barren** *R* Kentucky U.S.A.
68 A6 **Barren I** Andaman Is
116 L7 **Barren Is** Alaska U.S.A.
110 K5 **Barren River Res** Kentucky U.S.A.
19 P16 **Barret de Lioure** France
129 J8 **Barretos** Brazil
102 H9 **Barrett L** California U.S.A.
142 F4 **Barrett, Mt** W Australia Australia
118 C4 **Barrhead** Alberta Canada
12 D2 **Barrhead** Scotland
15 D5 **Barrhill** Scotland
121 L8 **Barrie** Ontario Canada
120 H7 **Barrie I** Ontario Canada
145 E2 **Barrier, C** New Zealand
117 N10 **Barrière** British Columbia Canada
138 F4 **Barrier Range** New South Wales Australia
141 H8 **Barrington** New South Wales Australia
122 G10 **Barrington** Nova Scotia Canada
99 S7 **Barrington** Illinois U.S.A.
119 R1 **Barrington L** Manitoba Canada
139 K4 **Barrington Tops** New South Wales Australia
141 H8 **Barringun** New South Wales Australia
129 L6 **Barris** *R* Brazil
28 D5 **Barrit** Denmark
101 M9 **Barro** Utah U.S.A.
130 E4 **Barro Alto** Brazil
100 E1 **Barron** Washington U.S.A.
99 P4 **Barron** Wisconsin U.S.A.
99 P4 **Barronett** Wisconsin U.S.A.
141 H3 **Barron Falls** Queensland Australia
109 J8 **Barroso** Texas U.S.A.
124 J4 **Barroterán** Mexico
21 M8 **Barrou** France
133 E5 **Barrow** Argentina
14 E4 **Barrow** *R* Ireland
116 J1 **Barrow** Alaska U.S.A.
140 D2 **Barrow, C** N Terr Australia
140 C5 **Barrow Creek** N Terr Australia
142 B5 **Barrow I** W Australia Australia
13 E5 **Barrow-in-Furness** England
141 G2 **Barrow Pt** Queensland Australia
147 M2 **Barrow,Pt** Alaska U.S.A.
143 F7 **Barrow Ra** W Australia Australia
119 Q6 **Barrows** Manitoba Canada
115 K3 **Barrow Str** Northwest Territories Canada
143 D7 **Barr Smith Ra** W Australia Australia
70 F7 **Barru** Sulawesi
16 E2 **Barruelo de Santullán** Spain
13 F1 **Barry** Scotland
110 E2 **Barry** Illinois U.S.A.
8 C5 **Barry** Wales
121 N7 **Barrys Bay** Ontario Canada
94 B3 **Barryton** Michigan U.S.A.
144 C5 **Barrytown** New Zealand
95 N5 **Barryville** New York U.S.A.
28 H6 **Bårse** Denmark
29 K5 **Barsebäckshamn** Sweden
76 B1 **Barsi** India
32 K8 **Barsinghausen** Germany
28 D6 **Barsø** *isld* Denmark
32 G6 **Barssel** Germany
102 G7 **Barstow** California U.S.A.
108 D4 **Barstow** Texas U.S.A.
54 J2 **Barsuki** Russian Federation
19 J4 **Bar-sur-Aube** France
18 H4 **Bar-sur-Seine** France
80 D4 **Barta'a** Jordan
36 H5 **Bartenstein** Germany
116 Q1 **Barter I** Alaska U.S.A.
30 G1 **Barth** Germany
33 R4 **Barthe** *R* Germany
122 G6 **Bartibog** New Brunswick Canada
128 G2 **Bartica** Guyana
78 D1 **Bartin** Turkey
100 D8 **Bartle** California U.S.A.
141 H3 **Bartle Frere,Mt** Queensland Australia
103 O2 **Bartles,Mt** Utah U.S.A.
107 P5 **Bartlesville** Oklahoma U.S.A.
98 H8 **Bartlett** Nebraska U.S.A.
95 Q2 **Bartlett** New Hampshire U.S.A.
109 K5 **Bartlett** Texas U.S.A.
117 O4 **Bartlett L** Northwest Territories Canada
103 N8 **Bartlett Res** Arizona U.S.A.
145 F3 **Bartletts** New Zealand
123 P3 **Bartlett's Harbour** Newfoundland Canada
143 E8 **Bartlett Soak** *L* W Australia Australia
98 F9 **Bartley** Nebraska U.S.A.
117 G8 **Bartolome, C** Alaska U.S.A.
87 G10 **Bartolomeu Dias** Mozambique
13 F6 **Barton** England
71 D5 **Barton** Palawan Philippines
98 F1 **Barton** North Dakota U.S.A.
95 P2 **Barton** Vermont U.S.A.
94 D2 **Barton City** Michigan U.S.A.
9 G3 **Barton Mills** England
13 H6 **Barton-upon-Humber** England
31 M1 **Bartoszyce** Poland
121 N4 **Bartoville** Quebec Canada
33 S5 **Bartow** Germany
113 F10 **Bartow** Florida U.S.A.
112 E5 **Bartow** Georgia U.S.A.
126 G9 **Barú, I. de** Colombia
69 E12 **Barumun** *R* Sumatra
70 O10 **Barung** *isld* Java
56 G6 **Barun-Shabartuy, Gora** *mt* Russian Federation
69 D11 **Barus** Sumatra
33 S8 **Baruth** Germany
58 E2 **Baruunharaa** Mongolia
58 F2 **Baruun Urt** Mongolia
125 N5 **Barú, Volcán** Panama
15 B2 **Barvas** Scotland
22 J3 **Barvaux** Belgium
54 J8 **Barvenkovo** Ukraine
74 G7 **Barwah** India
74 F7 **Barwani** India
33 N7 **Barwedel** Germany
99 N1 **Barwick** Ontario Canada
113 D7 **Barwick** Georgia U.S.A.
143 D7 **Barwidgee** W Australia Australia
140 B2 **Barwolla, Mt** N Terr Australia
80 F7 **Barza** Jordan
57 D5 **Basaga** Turkmenistan
77 D6 **Basaidu** Iran
106 D2 **Basalt** Colorado U.S.A.
101 N6 **Basalt** Idaho U.S.A.
102 F3 **Basalt** Nevada U.S.A.
141 H4 **Basalt R** Queensland Australia
86 C5 **Basankusu** Zaire
48 L6 **Basarabi** Romania
57 G2 **Basaral, Ozero** *L* Kazakhstan
71 F6 **Basay** Negros Philippines
71 E8 **Basbas** Philippines
131 B2 **Bascuñán,C** Chile
32 K6 **Basdahl** Germany
33 S7 **Basdorf** Germany
22 F2 **Basècles** Belgium
40 G2 **Basel** Switzerland
40 G3 **Baselland** *canton* Switzerland
43 G8 **Basento** *R* Italy
48 K2 **Başeu** *R* Romania
71 G5 **Basey** Samar Philippines
77 F6 **Bashākerd, Kūhhā-ye** *mts* Iran
118 E6 **Bashaw** Alberta Canada
56 B5 **Bashchelakskiy Khrebet** *mts* Russian Federation
57 C5 **Bashir** Turkmenistan
56 C5 **Bashkaus** *R* Russian Federation
55 C3 **Bashkirskaya Respublika** Russian Federation
Bashkortostan *see* **Bashkirskaya Respublika**
71 F3 **Basiad Bay** Luzon Philippines
71 F7 **Basilan** *isld* Mindanao Philippines
71 F7 **Basilan Str** Mindanao Philippines
9 G4 **Basildon** England
111 D11 **Basile** Louisiana U.S.A.
43 G8 **Basilicata** *prov* Italy
Basim *see* **Wāshīm**
101 N3 **Basin** Montana U.S.A.
101 R5 **Basin** Wyoming U.S.A.
113 F10 **Basinger** Florida U.S.A.
9 E5 **Basingstoke** England
119 M6 **Basin L** Saskatchewan Canada
95 U1 **Baskahegan L** Maine U.S.A.
78 K2 **Başkale** Turkey
121 P6 **Baskatong, Rés** Quebec Canada
142 D3 **Baskerville, C** W Australia Australia
79 C2 **Başköy** Turkey
Basle *see* **Basel**
9 E1 **Baslow** England
26 G5 **Båsmoen** Norway
69 F13 **Baso** *isld* Sumatra
41 H5 **Basodino** *mt* Switzerland
86 D5 **Basoko** Zaire
86 D6 **Basongo** Zaire
126 A2 **Basora,Pt** Aruba W Indies
78 L6 **Başrah, Al** *prov* Iraq
78 L6 **Basrah, Al** Iraq
36 D6 **Bas Rhin** *dept* France
118 E8 **Bassano** Alberta Canada
42 D3 **Bassano del Grappa** Italy
85 E7 **Bassar** Togo
81 A8 **Bassas da India** *isld* Mozambique Chan
33 R5 **Basse** Germany
22 D3 **Bassée, la** France
68 B4 **Bassein** Burma
142 B1 **Bassendean** *dist* Perth, W Aust Australia
22 K2 **Bassenge** Belgium
13 E4 **Bassenthwaite** *L* England
127 L4 **Basse Pointe** Martinique W Indies
127 O3 **Basse Terre** Trinidad
127 M4 **Basse Terre** Guadeloupe W Indies
127 P4 **Basseterre** St Kitts W Indies
98 G7 **Bassett** Nebraska U.S.A.
103 O9 **Bassett Pk** Arizona U.S.A.
22 F1 **Bassevelde** Belgium
111 G10 **Bassfield** Mississippi U.S.A.
85 E7 **Bassila** Benin
22 F2 **Bassilly** Belgium
102 E4 **Bass Lake** California U.S.A.
33 T10 **Basslitz** Germany
122 J8 **Bass River** Nova Scotia Canada
15 F4 **Bass Rock** Scotland
139 H7 **Bass Strait** Tasmania Australia
32 J7 **Bassum** Germany
119 R8 **Basswood** Manitoba Canada
99 P1 **Basswood L** Ontario Canada
19 P13 **Bassy** France
27 F15 **Båstad** Sweden
77 D6 **Bastak** Iran
77 D1 **Bastam** Iran
18 M10 **Bastia** Corsica
45 J2 **Bastiglia** Italy
123 M2 **Bastille,L** Quebec Canada
22 K3 **Bastogne** Belgium
112 E4 **Bastonville** Georgia U.S.A.
111 E9 **Bastrop** Louisiana U.S.A.
109 K5 **Bastrop** Texas U.S.A.
26 L7 **Bastuträsk** Sweden
Basuo *see* **Dongfang**
69 F13 **Basu, Tanjong** *C* Sumatra
Basutoland *see* **Lesotho**
55 D2 **Bas'yanovskiy** Russian Federation
86 B7 **Bas Zaïre** *prov* Zaire
86 A5 **Bata** Equat Guinea
85 F8 **Bata** Mbini Equat Guinea
71 E3 **Bataan Penin** Luzon Philippines
126 C3 **Batabanó, G. de** Cuba
71 E1 **Batac** Luzon Philippines
71 G4 **Batag** *isld* Philippines
130 D7 **Bataguaçu** Brazil
46 G3 **Batak** Bulgaria
74 F3 **Batala** India
16 B5 **Batalha** Portugal
51 M2 **Batamay** Russian Federation
71 G4 **Batan** *isld* Philippines
58 C5 **Batang** China
70 M9 **Batang** Java
86 C4 **Batangafo** Cent Afr Republic
71 E4 **Batangas** Luzon Philippines
69 F13 **Batanghari** *R* Sumatra
71 C3 **Batangpele** Waigeo Indonesia
69 J12 **Batangtarang** Indonesia
69 D12 **Batangtoru** Sumatra
71 C3 **Batanta** *isld* W Irian
48 E4 **Bataszék** Hungary
130 F7 **Batatais** Brazil
Batavia *see* **Jakarta**
133 D4 **Batavia** Argentina
99 S8 **Batavia** Illinois U.S.A.
94 J3 **Batavia** New York U.S.A.
110 M2 **Batavia** Ohio U.S.A.
54 L9 **Bataysk** Russian Federation
71 E5 **Batbatan** Panay Philippines
120 F6 **Batchawana** Ontario Canada
140 B2 **Batchelor** N Terr Australia
68 F6 **Batdambang** Cambodia
69 B10 **Bateemeucica, Gunung** *mt* Sumatra
88 B6 **Batembo** Zaire
61 P13 **Baten** Okinawa
25 E5 **Batenburg** Netherlands
56 D4 **Batenevskiy Kryazh** *ridge* Russian Federation
103 J9 **Bateques** Mexico
101 O6 **Bates** Idaho U.S.A.
100 G5 **Bates** Oregon U.S.A.
112 F4 **Batesburg** South Carolina U.S.A.
98 D6 **Batesland** South Dakota U.S.A.
143 E7 **Bates,Mt** W Australia Australia
143 D7 **Bates Ra** W Australia Australia
110 E6 **Batesville** Arkansas U.S.A.
110 L2 **Batesville** Indiana U.S.A.
111 G7 **Batesville** Mississippi U.S.A.
109 H7 **Batesville** Texas U.S.A.
52 D5 **Batetskiy** Russian Federation
122 E7 **Bath** New Brunswick Canada
8 D5 **Bath** England

127 M3 Bath Jamaica
110 F1 Bath Illinois U.S.A.
95 S3 Bath Maine U.S.A.
95 K4 Bath New York U.S.A.
112 L2 Bath North Carolina U.S.A.
112 F4 Bath South Carolina U.S.A.
98 H4 Bath South Dakota U.S.A.
127 P4 Bath Nevis W Indies
86 C3 Batha R Chad
68 G6 Batheay Cambodia
12 E2 Bathgate Scotland
98 J1 Bathgate North Dakota U.S.A.
139 J5 Bathurst New South Wales Australia
122 G6 Bathurst New Brunswick Canada
Bathurst The Gambia see Banjul
141 G2 Bathurst Bay Queensland Australia
114 G3 Bathurst,C Northwest Territories Canada
140 B1 Bathurst I N Terr Australia
115 K2 Bathurst I Northwest Territories Canada
114 J4 Bathurst Inlet Northwest Territories Canada
142 E3 Bathurst Is W Australia Australia
85 D7 Batié Burkina
70 G6 Batikala,Tg B Sulawesi Indonesia
48 E5 Batina Croatia
78 L7 Batin, Wadi al Iraq
69 E10 Bati Putih, Gunung mt Malaysia
121 S6 Batiscan Quebec Canada
121 T5 Batiscan,L Quebec Canada
77 C3 Batlag-e-Gavkhuni Iran
13 G6 Batley England
78 H3 Batman Turkey
85 F1 Batna Algeria
71 F4 Bato,L Luzon Philippines
111 E11 Baton Rouge Louisiana U.S.A.
86 B5 Batouri Cameroon
130 D4 Batovi Brazil
68 H7 Ba Tri Vietnam
42 H3 Batrina Croatia
79 F4 Batroûn Lebanon
26 R1 Båtsfjord Norway
80 D3 Bat Shelomo Israel
45 L1 Battáglia Terme Italy
140 D3 Batten R N Terr Australia
36 F1 Battenberg Germany
143 C6 Batthewmurnarna mt W Australia Australia
83 L10 Batticaloa Sri Lanka
22 K2 Battice Belgium
69 A8 Batti Malv isld Nicobar Is
45 R8 Battipaglia Italy
9 G6 Battle England
140 B3 Battle Cr N Terr Australia
100 J7 Battle Cr Idaho U.S.A.
101 Q1 Battle Cr Montana U.S.A.
98 J8 Battle Cr Nebraska U.S.A.
118 H9 Battle Creek Saskatchewan Canada
94 B4 Battle Creek Michigan U.S.A.
8 D2 Battlefield England
118 J6 Battleford Saskatchewan Canada
118 J5 Battlefords Prov.Park,The Saskatchewan Canada
100 C4 Battle Ground Washington U.S.A.
123 R1 Battle Harbour Labrador, Nfld Canada
102 G1 Battle Mt Nevada U.S.A.
118 F6 Battle R Alberta Canada
118 H6 Battle R Saskatchewan Canada
98 D1 Battleview North Dakota U.S.A.
48 G4 Battonya Hungary
118 J8 Battrum Saskatchewan Canada
70 D4 Batuajau, Bt mt Kalimantan
71 H8 Batuata isld Indonesia
69 F11 Batu Balik, Kampung Malaysia
69 H14 Batubetumbang Indonesia
70 D3 Batu Bora mt Sarawak
70 D4 Batubrok, Bt mt Kalimantan
70 G5 Batudaka Indonesia
70 C4 Batuesambang, Bukit mt Kalimantan
69 E10 Batu Gajah Malaysia
71 H5 Batuhitam,Tg C Sulawesi Indonesia
70 D4 Batuilangmebang, G mt Kalimantan
70 P10 Batukau, Bt mt Bali Indonesia
71 H9 Batulanteh Indonesia
71 H9 Batulanteh mt Indonesia
70 D6 Batulicin Kalimantan
70 D3 Batu Mabun mt Sarawak
78 H1 Batumi Georgia
69 D14 Batumonga Indonesia
69 F12 Batu Pahat Malaysia
69 C13 Batu,Pulaupulau isld Indonesia
70 F4 Batuputih Kalimantan
70 K8 Baturaja Sumatra Indonesia
70 N9 Baturetno Java
70 P10 Batur, Gunung mt Java
52 D6 Baturino Russian Federation
129 L4 Baturité Brazil
69 H14 Baturusa Indonesia
69 E13 Batusangkar Sumatra
70 G6 Batusitanduk Sulawesi
70 F3 Batu Tg B Kalimantan
71 L10 Batutuah Indonesia
80 B5 Bat Yam Israel
20 F7 Batz France
20 B4 Batz,I. de France
71 H7 Baubau Sulawesi Indonesia
86 A3 Bauchi Nigeria
20 D6 Baud France
75 L8 Bauda India
128 C2 Baudo, Sa. de mts Colombia
21 O7 Baudres France
19 Q17 Bauduen France
21 K6 Baugé France
19 Q13 Bauges dist France
140 D3 Bauhinia N Terr Australia
141 J6 Bauhinia Downs Queensland Australia
71 N9 Baukau Timor
70 G7 Baula Sulawesi Indonesia
123 R2 Bauld,C Newfoundland Canada
20 F7 Baule,la France
20 G6 Baulon France
41 J3 Bauma Switzerland
9 F1 Baumber England
19 K5 Baume-les-Dames France
33 T6 Baumgarten Germany
37 O7 Baumgarten Germany
36 C4 Baumholder Germany
70 G6 Bauna Sulawesi
37 K3 Baunach R Germany
37 K4 Baunach Germany
70 C6 Baung Kalimantan
58 F1 Baunt Russian Federation
128 F6 Baures Bolivia
130 E8 Bauru Brazil
130 D6 Baús Brazil
52 B6 Bauska Latvia
31 H4 Bautzen Germany
109 P1 Bauxite Arkansas U.S.A.
Bavaria see Bayern
107 N3 Bavaria Kansas U.S.A.
22 F3 Bavay France
89 C9 Baviaanskloofberge mts S Africa
124 E2 Bavispe Mexico
70 C5 Bawan Kalimantan
139 H7 Baw Baw, Mt Victoria Australia
9 H2 Bawdeswell England
9 H3 Bawdsey England
70 O8 Bawean isld Java
32 F7 Bawinkel Germany
84 H4 Bawîti Egypt
120 D3 Bawk Ontario Canada
85 D6 Bawku Ghana
68 C3 Bawlake Burma
118 E6 Bawlf Alberta Canada
68 A2 Bawli Bazar Burma
68 B4 Bawmi Burma
13 G6 Bawtry England
68 F1 Ba Xat Vietnam
58 G4 Ba Xian China
67 B2 Ba Xian China
66 D4 Baxkorgan China
112 E6 Baxley Georgia U.S.A.
99 N8 Baxter Iowa U.S.A.
99 M3 Baxter Minnesota U.S.A.
101 S10 Baxter Mt Colorado U.S.A.
110 B4 Baxter Springs Kansas U.S.A.
122 C7 Baxter State Park Maine U.S.A.
80 D3 Bayada Israel
126 F4 Bayamo Cuba
127 L5 Bayamón Puerto Rico
59 J2 Bayan China
55 G5 Bayanaul Kazakhstan
56 G4 Bayanday Russian Federation
Bayan Gol see Dengkou
58 C5 Bayan Har Shan China
58 D2 Bayanhongor Mongolia
65 E1 Bayan Hot China
65 A3 Bayan Hure China
Bayan Huxu see Horqin Youyi Zhongqi
65 C3 Bayan Nur Sum China
58 E3 Bayan Obo China
126 E10 Bayano L. Panama
Bayan Qagan see Qahar Youyi Houqi
65 F1 Bayan Qagan China
65 E2 Bayan Qagan China
113 F7 Bayard Florida U.S.A.
99 M8 Bayard Iowa U.S.A.
98 C8 Bayard Nebraska U.S.A.
94 H7 Bayard West Virginia U.S.A.
19 Q15 Bayard, Col pass France
65 B1 Bayasgalant Mongolia
47 L6 Bayat Turkey
71 F6 Bayawan Negros Philippines
71 G5 Baybay Leyte Philippines
112 L2 Bayboro North Carolina U.S.A.
123 U6 Bay Bulls Newfoundland Canada
78 H1 Bayburt Turkey
69 H8 Bay Canh, Hon isld Vietnam
94 D3 Bay City Michigan U.S.A.
100 B4 Bay City Oregon U.S.A.
109 M7 Bay City Texas U.S.A.
99 O5 Bay City Wisconsin U.S.A.
84 G3 Baydā,Al Libya
50 F2 Baydaratskaya Guba G Russian Federation
123 U5 Bay de Verde Newfoundland Canada
86 H5 Baydhabo Somalia
123 R6 Bay du Nord Newfoundland Canada
37 P5 Bayer-Eisenstein Germany
41 O2 Bayerische Alpen mt Germany
37 N5 Bayerischer Wald mts Germany
37 K5 Bayern land Germany
21 J3 Bayeux France
120 J9 Bayfield Ontario Canada
99 Q3 Bayfield Wisconsin U.S.A.
123 O2 Bayfield I Quebec Canada
122 E5 Bayfield Mtn Quebec Canada
57 D3 Baygakum Kazakhstan
55 D4 Baygara Kazakhstan
98 A4 Bay Horse Montana U.S.A.
47 J6 Bayındır Turkey
55 D3 Baykalovo Russian Federation
56 G4 Baykal,Ozero L Russian Federation
56 F5 Baykal'sk Russian Federation
56 G4 Baykal'skiy Khrebet mts Russian Federation
56 D5 Bay-Khaak Russian Federation
57 C2 Bay-Khozha Kazakhstan
55 C3 Baykibashevo Russian Federation
56 E1 Baykit Russian Federation
57 D1 Baykonur Kazakhstan
71 E3 Bay, Laguna de Luzon Philippines
123 R6 Bay l'Argent Newfoundland Canada
140 E3 Bayley Pt Queensland Australia
55 C4 Baymak Russian Federation
48 L4 Baymakliya Moldova
111 J11 Bay Minette Alabama U.S.A.
9 E4 Baynard's Green England
71 E2 Bayombong Luzon Philippines
19 K4 Bayon France
16 B2 Bayona Spain
18 E9 Bayonne France
71 E5 Bayo Pt Panay Philippines
111 E7 Bayou Bartholomew R Arkansas U.S.A.
111 D9 Bayou D'Arbonne Louisiana U.S.A.
111 D9 Bayou D'Arbonne L Louisiana U.S.A.
110 E6 Bayou de View R Arkansas U.S.A.
111 H11 Bayou La Batre Alabama U.S.A.
111 F12 Bayou Lafourche R Louisiana U.S.A.
111 E9 Bayou Macon R Louisiana U.S.A.
111 E7 Bayou Meto R Arkansas U.S.A.
111 F9 Bayou Pierre R Mississippi U.S.A.
111 E12 Bayou Vista Louisiana U.S.A.
128 B5 Bayovar Peru
113 E9 Bayport Florida U.S.A.
94 D3 Bay Port Michigan U.S.A.
99 O5 Bayport Minnesota U.S.A.
117 K10 Bay Pt British Columbia Canada
71 D5 Bay Pt Philippines
47 H5 Bayramiç Turkey
37 M4 Bayreuth Germany
123 T6 Bay Roberts Newfoundland Canada
58 F1 Baysa Russian Federation
111 G11 Bay St.Louis Mississippi U.S.A.
113 F11 Bayshore Florida U.S.A.
95 O6 Bay Shore Long I, New York U.S.A.
112 E1 Bays Mt Tennessee U.S.A.
56 E5 Bay-Soot Russian Federation
111 G10 Bay Springs Mississippi U.S.A.
Baytag Bogdo see Baytik Shan
9 G3 Baythorn End England
66 E2 Baytik Shan mt ra China/ Mongolia
109 N6 Baytown Texas U.S.A.
145 F3 Bay View New Zealand
117 P12 Bayview Idaho U.S.A.
57 E3 Bayzhansay Kazakhstan
17 F7 Baza Spain
48 K1 Bazaliya Ukraine
22 G5 Bazancourt France
57 K1 Bazar R Kazakhstan
107 O3 Bazar Kansas U.S.A.
53 G12 Bazardyuzyu, Gora mt Azerbaijan/Rus Fed
52 G6 Bazarnyye Mataki Russian Federation
87 G10 Bazaruto, I Mozambique
18 E8 Bazas France
17 F7 Baza,Sierra de Spain
22 J4 Bazeilles France
67 B1 Bazhong China
48 G6 Baziaş Romania
18 G9 Baziége France
121 Q5 Bazin R Quebec Canada
107 L3 Bazine Kansas U.S.A.
77 G5 Bazmān, Kūh-e mt Iran
77 F6 Bazman Iran
21 M5 Bazoche-Gouet,la France
22 F5 Bazoches France
21 K4 Bazoches-au-Houlme France
21 P5 Bazoches-les Gallerandes France
21 L4 Bazoches-sur-Hoëne France
21 L5 Bazoge,la France
21 H8 Bazoges-en Paillers France
21 J8 Bazoges-en-Pareds France
21 J5 Bazougers France
20 G5 Bazouges-la-Perouse France
45 K3 Bazzano Italy
79 F4 Bcharre Lebanon
112 E6 Beach Georgia U.S.A.
98 C3 Beach North Dakota U.S.A.
95 N7 Beach Haven New Jersey U.S.A.
138 E6 Beachport South Australia Australia
95 N7 Beachwood New Jersey U.S.A.
9 G6 Beachy Head England
143 C9 Beacon W Australia Australia
95 O5 Beacon New York U.S.A.
118 H4 Beacon Hill Saskatchewan Canada
113 B8 Beacon Hill Florida U.S.A.
139 H8 Beaconsfield Tasmania Australia
9 F4 Beaconsfield England
13 G2 Beadnell England
142 E3 Beagle Bay W Australia Australia
133 D8 Beagle, Canal str Chile/Arg
140 A1 Beagle G N Terr Australia
143 A8 Beagle I W Australia Australia
142 E3 Beagle Reef W Australia Australia
87 H10 Bealanana Madagascar
117 L11 Beale,C British Columbia Canada
94 K8 Bealeton Virginia U.S.A.
108 F3 Beals Cr Texas U.S.A.
118 C1 Beaman Manitoba Canada
8 D6 Beaminster England
100 J4 Bear Idaho U.S.A.
101 O7 Bear R Idaho U.S.A.
111 J7 Bear Cr Alabama U.S.A.
107 J4 Bear Cr Kansas U.S.A.
99 S5 Bear Cr Wisconsin U.S.A.
98 B8 Bear Cr Wyoming U.S.A.
101 Q4 Bearcreek Montana U.S.A.
95 M5 Bear Cr.Res Pennsylvania U.S.A.
111 D8 Bearden Arkansas U.S.A.
120 C3 Beardmore Ontario Canada
146 D10 Beardmore Glacier Antarctica
141 J8 Beardmore Res Queensland Australia
103 M8 Beardsley Arizona U.S.A.
107 J2 Beardsley Kansas U.S.A.
110 F1 Beardstown Illinois U.S.A.
123 K4 Bear Head Anticosti I, Quebec
118 J7 Bear Hills,The Saskatchewan Canada
115 L7 Bear I Northwest Territories Canada
14 B5 Bear I Ireland
120 K6 Bear Island Ontario Canada
119 V3 Bear L Manitoba Canada
101 O7 Bear L Idaho/Utah U.S.A.
117 K7 Bear Lake British Columbia Canada
94 A2 Bear Lake Michigan U.S.A.
98 B5 Bear Lodge Mts Wyoming U.S.A.
101 M3 Bearmouth Montana U.S.A.
121 M4 Béarn Quebec Canada
18 E9 Béarn prov France
101 Q1 Bearpaw Mt Montana U.S.A.
146 B8 Bear Pen Antarctica
119 N4 Bear R Saskatchewan Canada
101 N8 Bear R.City Utah U.S.A.
12 D2 Bearsden Scotland
101 S9 Bears Ears Pk Colorado U.S.A.
115 K7 Bearskin L Ontario Canada
74 F3 Beas R India
18 D9 Beasain Spain
17 F6 Beas de Segura Spain
127 J6 Beata, I Dominican Rep
40 G4 Beatenberg Switzerland
117 P10 Beaton British Columbia Canada
6 J4 Beatrice oil rig North Sea
111 J10 Beatrice Alabama U.S.A.
98 K9 Beatrice Nebraska U.S.A.
140 D2 Beatrice,C Aust
142 F3 Beatrice,Mt W Australia Australia
107 O2 Beattie Kansas U.S.A.
15 E5 Beattock Scotland
117 N7 Beatton River British Columbia Canada
119 N6 Beatty Saskatchewan Canada
102 H5 Beatty Nevada U.S.A.
100 D7 Beatty Oregon U.S.A.
121 N4 Beattyville Quebec Canada
94 D9 Beattyville Kentucky U.S.A.
19 N17 Beaucaire France
21 O2 Beaucamps-le-Vieux France
121 L3 Beaucanton Quebec Canada
21 M6 Beauce plain France
122 B7 Beauceville Quebec Canada
20 H4 Beauchamps France
131 G8 Beauchene I Falkland Is
121 M6 Beauchêne, Lac Quebec Canada
40 E2 Beaucourt France
141 L8 Beaudesert Queensland Australia
121 L4 Beaudry Quebec Canada
21 L5 Beaufay France
40 E6 Beaufort France
22 L4 Beaufort Luxembourg
70 D2 Beaufort Sabah
112 L3 Beaufort North Carolina U.S.A.
112 G5 Beaufort South Carolina U.S.A.
79 F5 Beaufort Castle hist site Lebanon
21 K7 Beaufort-en-Vallée France
146 C11 Beaufort I Antarctica
112 L3 Beaufort Inlet North Carolina U.S.A.
116 R2 Beaufort Lag Alaska U.S.A.
147 K2 Beaufort Sea Arctic Oc
89 B9 Beaufort West S Africa
21 O6 Beaugency France
121 R7 Beauharnois Quebec Canada
121 Q7 Beauharnois Power Canal Quebec Canada
19 N12 Beaujeu France
19 Q16 Beaujeu France
18 H6 Beaujolais, Mts du France
95 S6 Beau L Maine/New Brunswick U.S.A./Canada
9 E6 Beaulieu England
21 N7 Beaulieu-lès-Loches France
15 D3 Beauly Scotland
15 D3 Beauly, R Scotland
8 B1 Beaumaris Wales
21 M3 Beaumesnil France
22 D3 Beaumetz-les-Loges France
22 G3 Beaumont Belgium
123 R4 Beaumont Newfoundland Canada
21 L8 Beaumont Vienne France
144 B6 Beaumont New Zealand
102 H8 Beaumont California U.S.A.
107 O4 Beaumont Kansas U.S.A.
111 H10 Beaumont Mississippi U.S.A.
111 B11 Beaumont Texas U.S.A.
18 F9 Beaumont de Lomogne France
18 F8 Beaumont de Périgord France
22 J4 Beaumont-en-Argonne France
21 L3 Beaumont-en-Auge France
22 E3 Beaumont-en-Cambrésis France
20 G2 Beaumont-Hague France
21 M6 Beaumont-la-Ronce France
21 M3 Beaumont-le-Roger France
21 M5 Beaumont-les-Autels France
21 L6 Beaumont-Pied-de-Bœuf France
21 P3 Beaumont-sur-Oise France
21 L5 Beaumont-sur-Sarthe France
19 J5 Beaune France
21 P5 Beaune-la Rolande France
121 T6 Beauport Quebec Canada
21 J7 Beaupréau France
21 P1 Beauquesne France
22 H3 Beauraing Belgium
40 B7 Beaurepaire d'Isère France
19 P15 Beaurières France
22 F5 Beaurieux France
118 E1 Beausejour Manitoba Canada
139 H6 Beauty,Mt Victoria Australia
21 P3 Beauvais France
118 C9 Beauvais Lake Prov. Park Alberta Canada
118 K3 Beauval Saskatchewan Canada
21 P1 Beauval France
118 F5 Beauvallon Alberta Canada
20 F8 Beauvoir-sur-Mer France
118 F4 Beaver R Alberta Canada
117 L5 Beaver R Yukon Terr/Br Col Canada
116 O3 Beaver Alaska U.S.A.
107 M3 Beaver Kansas U.S.A.
98 F3 Beaver R North Dakota U.S.A.
108 D7 Beaver Oklahoma U.S.A.
100 B4 Beaver Oregon U.S.A.
94 G6 Beaver Pennsylvania U.S.A.
103 L3 Beaver R Utah U.S.A.
103 M3 Beaver Utah U.S.A.
122 J9 Beaverbank Nova Scotia Canada
122 G6 Beaver Brook New Brunswick Canada
98 G9 Beaver City Nebraska U.S.A.
116 O4 Beaver Cr Alaska U.S.A.
106 G2 Beaver Cr Colorado U.S.A.
101 N5 Beaver Cr Idaho U.S.A.
107 J2 Beaver Cr Kansas U.S.A.
110 D5 Beaver Cr Missouri U.S.A.
98 B3 Beaver Cr Montana U.S.A.
98 F9 Beaver Cr Nebraska U.S.A.
98 B6 Beaver Cr Wyoming U.S.A.
117 C4 Beaver Creek Yukon Territory Canada
98 J9 Beaver Crossing Nebraska U.S.A.
110 K4 Beaver Dam Kentucky U.S.A.
99 S6 Beaver Dam Wisconsin U.S.A.
117 O11 Beaverdell Falls British Columbia Canada
94 G6 Beaver Falls Pennsylvania U.S.A.
101 N4 Beaverhead R Montana U.S.A.
101 M4 Beaverhead Mts Idaho/ Montana U.S.A.
118 E5 Beaverhill L Alberta Canada
99 V4 Beaver I Michigan U.S.A.
123 N2 Beaver Island L Quebec Canada
99 U3 Beaver L Michigan U.S.A.
117 N9 Beaver Lake British Columbia Canada
117 O8 Beaverlodge Alberta Canada
117 P10 Beavermouth British Columbia Canada
116 J5 Beaver Mts Alaska U.S.A.
118 F4 Beaver R Alberta Canada
118 H4 Beaver R Saskatchewan Canada
118 K4 Beaver R Saskatchewan Canada
110 C5 Beaver Res Arkansas U.S.A.
95 M3 Beaver R.Flow New York U.S.A.
121 L8 Beaverton Ontario Canada
94 C3 Beaverton Michigan U.S.A.
100 C4 Beaverton Oregon U.S.A.
95 K6 Beavertown Pennsylvania U.S.A.
99 T9 Beaverville Illinois U.S.A.
74 F5 Beawar India
133 D4 Beazley Argentina
131 C4 Bebedero, Salina Argentina
129 J8 Bebedouro Brazil
36 G6 Bebenhausen Germany
129 L4 Beberibe Brazil
36 H2 Bebra Germany
47 H2 Bebrovo Bulgaria
9 H3 Beccles England
48 F5 Bečej Serbia Yugoslavia
48 K5 Beceni Romania
16 C2 Becerreá Spain
126 C7 Becerro,Cayos reefs Caribbean
85 D2 Béchar Algeria
116 J7 Becharaf National Monument Alaska U.S.A.
116 J8 Becharof L Alaska U.S.A.
85 D7 Bechem Ghana
144 C5 Beche, Mt de la New Zealand
20 G5 Bécherel France
46 G1 Bechet Romania
116 F9 Bechevin B Alaska U.S.A.
37 K5 Bechhofen Germany
Bechuanaland Prot see Botswana
31 H6 Bechyně Czech Rep
32 M7 Beckedorf Germany
13 E4 Beckfoot England
9 E5 Beckhampton England
36 B5 Beckingen Germany
8 D5 Beckington England
94 F9 Beckley West Virginia U.S.A.
144 B6 Becks New Zealand
32 H9 Beckum Germany
109 N3 Beckville Texas U.S.A.
102 D2 Beckwourth California U.S.A.
48 J3 Beclean Romania
21 J6 Bécon France
19 O16 Béconne France
9 G4 Becontree England
37 O3 Bečov nad Teplou Czech Rep
108 F2 Becton Texas U.S.A.
31 K6 Bečva R Czech Rep
84 F4 Beda Libya
70 O10 Bedadung R Java
13 G5 Bedale England
18 H9 Bédarieux France
19 N16 Bedarrides France
36 B1 Bedburg Germany
8 B1 Beddgelert Wales
9 G6 Beddingham England
119 R9 Bede Manitoba Canada
20 G5 Bédée France
28 E4 Beder Denmark
32 J5 Bederkesa Germany
55 C3 Bedeyeva Polyana Russian Federation
122 J9 Bedford Nova Scotia Canada
121 S7 Bedford Quebec Canada
9 F3 Bedford England
110 K3 Bedford Indiana U.S.A.
99 M9 Bedford Iowa U.S.A.
94 B8 Bedford Kentucky U.S.A.
95 Q4 Bedford New Hampshire U.S.A.
94 J6 Bedford Pennsylvania U.S.A.
94 H9 Bedford Virginia U.S.A.
101 P7 Bedford Wyoming U.S.A.
141 H3 Bedford C Queensland Australia
142 F3 Bedford Downs W Australia Australia
143 D10 Bedford Harb W Australia Australia
127 P5 Bedford Pt Grenada
9 F3 Bedfordshire co England
74 D7 Bedi India
69 H14 Bedinggong Indonesia
13 G3 Bedlington England
19 O16 Bédoin France
41 O5 Bedollo Italy
69 E11 Bedongkong Sumatra
140 E6 Bedourie Queensland Australia
142 A4 Bedout I W Australia Australia
8 A7 Bedruthan Steps England
28 C6 Bedsted Denmark
9 E3 Bedworth England
98 J8 Bee Nebraska U.S.A.
110 E6 Beebe Arkansas U.S.A.
98 G4 Beebe South Dakota U.S.A.
141 H7 Beechal R Queensland Australia
94 K5 Beech Cr Pennsylvania U.S.A.
110 J4 Beech Creek Kentucky U.S.A.
100 F5 Beech Creek Oregon U.S.A.
99 T8 Beecher Illinois U.S.A.
110 H2 Beecher City Illinois U.S.A.
116 N1 Beechey Point Alaska U.S.A.
110 L4 Beech Fork R Kentucky U.S.A.
110 K2 Beech Grove Indiana U.S.A.
99 S3 Beechwood Michigan U.S.A.
139 H6 Beechworth Victoria Australia
118 K8 Beechy Saskatchewan Canada
32 M7 Beedenbostel Germany
100 C9 Beegum California U.S.A.
25 E5 Beek Gelderland Netherlands
25 E4 Beekbergen Netherlands
111 E9 Beekman Louisiana U.S.A.
107 K3 Beeler Kansas U.S.A.
33 R8 Beelitz Germany
98 K8 Beemer Nebraska U.S.A.
33 O8 Beendorf Germany
141 L8 Beenleigh Queensland Australia
37 K2 Beerberg mt Germany
33 S8 Beeren Germany
36 F4 Beerfelden Germany
113 E10 Bee Ridge Florida U.S.A.
143 C8 Beeringgnurding, Mt W Australia Australia
22 F2 Beerlegem Belgium
79 F8 Beer Menuha Israel
22 E1 Beernem Belgium
79 E9 Beer Ora Israel
80 C8 Be'er Pehar Israel
25 E5 Beers Netherlands
80 C8 Beersheba Israel
Be'er Sheva see Beersheba
25 D6 Beerze R Netherlands
31 H3 Beeskow Germany
87 E11 Beestekraal S Africa
9 E2 Beeston England
140 C3 Beetaloo N Terr Australia
25 F2 Beetsterzwaag Netherlands
33 O7 Beetzendorf Germany
33 R8 Beetz-see L Germany
109 K7 Beeville Texas U.S.A.
86 D5 Befale Zaire
87 H11 Befandriana Madagascar
86 D5 Befori Zaire
20 D4 Bégard France
8 B4 Begelly Wales
127 P4 Beggars Pt Antigua W Indies
107 O6 Beggs Oklahoma U.S.A.
86 F4 Bēgī Ethiopia
51 L1 Begicheva, Ostrov isld Russian Federation
20 C6 Beg-Meil France
27 D11 Begna R Norway
28 E4 Begtrup Vig B Denmark
19 N15 Begude-de-Mazenc, la France
77 B4 Behbehān Iran
33 N5 Behlendorf Germany
117 H8 Behm Can Alaska U.S.A.
140 A3 Behn, Mt N Terr Australia
22 L3 Beho Belgium
33 R4 Behren-Lübchin Germany
37 L4 Behringersmühle Germany
77 C1 Behshahr Iran
59 J2 Bei'an China
26 G4 Beiarn Norway
67 B2 Beibei China
67 A1 Beichuan China
65 A6 Beichuan He R China
65 D5 Beidaihehaibin China
32 M10 Beienrode Germany
37 O2 Beierfeld Germany
68 J2 Beihai China
36 G6 Beihingen Germany
66 F4 Bei Hulsan Hu L China
67 D4 Bei Jiang R China
63 Beijing conurbation China
85 A5 Beila Mauritania
25 G3 Beilen Netherlands
68 J3 Beili China
68 K1 Beiliu China
37 L5 Beilngries Germany
36 G5 Beilstein Baden-Württemberg Germany
36 E2 Beilstein Hessen Germany
36 C3 Beilstein Rheinland-Pfalz Germany
67 B6 Beilun Ai pass China
36 H7 Beimerstetten Germany
44 C1 Beinasco Italy
22 G5 Beine France
36 E6 Beinheim France
15 E4 Beinn a' Ghlo mt Scotland
40 H3 Beinwil Switzerland
67 B4 Beipan Jiang R China
65 E4 Beipiao China
87 F9 Beira Mozambique
16 B4 Beira Alta prov Portugal
16 B5 Beira Baixa prov Portugal
16 B4 Beira Litoral prov Portugal
Beirut see Beyrouth
118 D7 Beiseker Alberta Canada
58 C3 Beishan China
65 F2 Beitaolaizhao China
87 E10 Beitbridge Zimbabwe
15 D5 Beith Scotland
80 D6 Beit Haninā Jordan
80 F4 Beit Idis Jordan
80 D7 Beit Jala Jordan
80 D7 Beit Kahil Jordan
80 A7 Beit Lahiya Israel
80 D7 Beit Lahm Jordan
80 E1 Beit Lif Lebanon
80 G3 Beit Ras Jordan
80 D7 Beit Sahur Jordan
26 E7 Beitstad Norway
26 E8 Beitstadfjord inlet Norway
48 G4 Beius Romania
67 G2 Beiyandang Shan mt China
65 E4 Beizhen China
65 D6 Beizhen China
16 B6 Beja Portugal
43 C12 Béja Tunisia
143 E6 Bejah Hill W Australia Australia
85 E1 Bejaïa Algeria
85 F1 Bejaïa, Golfe de G Algeria
16 D4 Béjar Spain
77 F2 Bejestān Iran
143 B9 Bejoording W Australia Australia
57 E4 Bekabad Tajikistan
70 L9 Bekasi Java
48 F4 Békés co Hungary
48 G4 Békés Hungary
48 G4 Békéscsaba Hungary
85 D7 Bekwai Ghana
Bela see Villach
74 B5 Bela Pakistan
86 B2 Bélabérim Niger
86 B4 Bélabo Cameroon
21 N8 Bélâbre France
48 G6 Bela Crkva Serbia Yugoslavia
56 B5 Bel'agash Kazakhstan
20 E5 Bel Air mt France
20 F6 Bel-Air France
95 L7 Bel Air Maryland U.S.A.
70 D4 Belajan R Kalimantan
70 D4 Belajan, G mt Kalimantan
16 D6 Belalcázar Spain
74 H9 Belampalli India
37 O4 Bělá nad Radbuzou Czech Rep
71 J4 Belang Sulawesi Indonesia
119 U5 Bélanger Pt Manitoba Canada
119 U5 Bélanger R Manitoba Canada
70 B6 Belangiran Kalimantan
46 E1 Bela Palanka Serbia Yugoslavia
139 H4 Belaraboon New South Wales Australia
54 B3 Belarus rep E Europe
129 G8 Bela Vista Brazil
87 F11 Bela Vista Mozambique
130 C8 Bela Vista Paraguay
130 E5 Bela Vista de Goiás Brazil
69 D11 Belawan Sumatra
54 G5 Belaya Russian Federation
54 E4 Belaya-Berezka Russian Federation
54 M8 Belaya-Kalitva Russian Federation
55 B2 Belaya Kholunitsa Russian Federation
48 N1 Belaya Tserkov' Ukraine
44 D2 Belbo R Italy
48 L3 Belceşti Romania
115 K2 Belcher Chan Northwest Territories Canada
115 M6 Belcher, Les Iles Northwest Territories Canada
17 G3 Belchite Spain
14 D2 Belcoo N Ireland
121 N4 Belcourt Quebec Canada
98 G1 Belcourt North Dakota U.S.A.
102 C1 Belden California U.S.A.
98 D1 Belden North Dakota U.S.A.
94 B3 Belding Michigan U.S.A.
52 D5 Belebelka Russian Federation
55 B4 Belebey Russian Federation
86 J5 Beledweyne Somalia
129 J4 Belém Brazil
129 L5 Belém de São Francisco Brazil
128 C3 Belén Colombia
129 G8 Belén Paraguay
108 A1 Belen New Mexico U.S.A.
131 G3 Belén,Cuchilla de mt Uruguay
124 H7 Belén del Refugio Mexico
46 G1 Belene Bulgaria
137 N5 Belep,Îles New Caledonia
86 G3 Beles R Ethiopia
16 B2 Belesar, Embalse de res Spain
54 H3 Belev Russian Federation
86 C5 Bélézé Cent Afr Republic
100 C2 Belfair Washington U.S.A.
122 K7 Belfast Prince Edward I Canada
144 B4 Belfast New Zealand
14 F2 Belfast N Ireland
95 S2 Belfast Maine U.S.A.
25 F6 Belfeld Netherlands
98 C3 Belfield North Dakota U.S.A.
86 F3 Bēlfodiya Ethiopia
13 G2 Belford England
19 K5 Belfort France
40 E2 Belfort, Terr De France
101 Q4 Belfry Montana U.S.A.
76 B3 Belgaum India
19 P18 Belgentier France
33 S10 Belgern Germany
146 H8 Belgicafjella ra Antarctica
99 T6 Belgium Wisconsin U.S.A.
22 E2 Belgium kingdom W Europe
54 H6 Belgorod Russian Federation
48 N4 Belgorod Dnestrovskiy Ukraine
53 E8 Belgorodkaya Oblast' prov Russian Federation
Belgrade see Beograd
101 O4 Belgrade Montana U.S.A.
98 H8 Belgrade Nebraska U.S.A.
133 F5 Belgrano Argentina
131 E7 Belgrano,Pto Argentina
47 M10 Belgrat Ormani forest Turkey
145 D4 Belgrove New Zealand
85 F3 Bel Guebbour, Hassi Algeria
112 L2 Belhaven North Carolina U.S.A.
85 F2 Belhirane Algeria
21 N4 Belhomert France
43 E11 Belice R Sicily
53 G12 Belidzhi Russian Federation
47 H1 Beli Lom R Bulgaria
48 E5 Beli Manastir Croatia
70 K8 Belimbing Indonesia
69 J12 Belimbing, Tanjong C Indonesia
18 E8 Belin France
86 B5 Bélinga Gabon
94 H7 Belington West Virginia U.S.A.
69 G13 Belinyu Indonesia
46 F3 Belitsa Bulgaria
69 J14 Belitung isld Indonesia
125 P9 Belize Belize
125 P9 Belize Central America
48 G6 Beljanića mt Serbia Yugoslavia
143 C9 Belka W Australia Australia
99 O9 Belknap Iowa U.S.A.
100 K2 Belknap Montana U.S.A.
147 P8 Bel'kovskiy Os isld Russian Federation
141 K7 Bell Queensland Australia
121 N3 Bell R Quebec Canada
113 E8 Bell Florida U.S.A.
117 J9 Bella Bella British Columbia Canada
18 F6 Bellac France
133 F4 Bellaco Uruguay
117 K9 Bella Coola British Columbia Canada
107 M2 Bellaire Kansas U.S.A.
94 B2 Bellaire Michigan U.S.A.
94 G6 Bellaire Ohio U.S.A.
109 M6 Bellaire Texas U.S.A.
141 G7 Bellalie Queensland Australia
42 C2 Bellano Italy
76 C3 Bellary India
40 G5 Bella Tola mt Switzerland
131 F2 Bella Vista Argentina
128 C4 Bellavista Loreto Peru
128 C5 Bellavista San Martin Peru
139 J8 Bell B Tasmania Australia
145 E3 Bell Block New Zealand
141 K5 Bell Cay isld Gt Barrier Reef Aust
110 E3 Belle Missouri U.S.A.
123 R6 Belle B Newfoundland Canada
33 P9 Belleben Germany
94 D6 Belle Center Ohio U.S.A.
40 E7 Bellecôte mt France
19 P14 Belledonne, Pic de mt France
94 D6 Bellefontaine Ohio U.S.A.
94 K6 Bellefonte Pennsylvania U.S.A.
98 C5 Belle Fourche South Dakota U.S.A.
98 A5 Belle Fourche R Wyoming U.S.A.
18 G5 Bellegarde France
19 P12 Bellegarde France
18 G7 Bellegarde-en-Marche France
113 G11 Belle Glade Florida U.S.A.
40 E3 Belleherbe France
20 D7 Belle Ile France
123 R2 Belle Isle Newfoundland Canada
20 D4 Belle-Isle-en-Terre France
123 R2 Belle Isle Landing Belle Isle, Nfld
123 Q2 Belle Isle,Strait of Newfoundland Canada
21 M5 Bellême France
110 K5 Belle Meade Tennessee U.S.A.
103 N6 Bellemont Arizona U.S.A.
21 N2 Bellencombre France
141 H3 Bellenden Ker ra Queensland Australia
22 E4 Bellenglise France
123 R6 Belleoram Newfoundland Canada
119 M8 Belle Plaine Saskatchewan Canada
99 O8 Belle Plaine Iowa U.S.A.
107 N4 Belle Plaine Kansas U.S.A.
99 N5 Belle Plaine Minnesota U.S.A.
110 H3 Belle Rive Illinois U.S.A.
121 T4 Belle-Rivière,Lac de la Quebec Canada
121 M5 Belleterre Quebec Canada
94 F7 Belle Valley Ohio U.S.A.
40 E5 Bellevaux France
40 B4 Bellevesvre France
113 E8 Belleview Florida U.S.A.
121 N8 Belleville Ontario Canada
19 N12 Belleville France
110 G3 Belleville Illinois U.S.A.
107 N2 Belleville Kansas U.S.A.
95 L3 Belleville New York U.S.A.
94 K6 Belleville Pennsylvania U.S.A.
94 F7 Belleville West Virginia U.S.A.
99 R7 Belleville Wisconsin U.S.A.
20 H8 Belleville sur Vie France
141 G3 Bellevue Queensland Australia
118 C9 Bellevue Alberta Canada
101 L6 Bellevue Idaho U.S.A.
99 Q7 Bellevue Iowa U.S.A.
94 B4 Bellevue Michigan U.S.A.
94 E5 Bellevue Ohio U.S.A.
109 J2 Bellevue Texas U.S.A.
100 C2 Bellevue Washington U.S.A.
19 P13 Belley France
110 H1 Bellflower Illinois U.S.A.
110 E2 Bellflower Missouri U.S.A.
36 E5 Bellheim Germany
123 R3 Bell I. Newfoundland Canada
123 T6 Bell I Newfoundland Canada
22 E4 Bellicourt France
21 H7 Belligne France
13 F3 Bellingham England
98 K4 Bellingham Minnesota U.S.A.
100 C1 Bellingham Washington U.S.A.
146 D3 Bellingshausen Rus Fed Base Antarctica
146 B6 Bellingshausen Sea Antarctica
25 H2 Bellingwolde Netherlands
41 K5 Bellinzona Switzerland
118 E4 Bellis Alberta Canada
36 F2 Bellnhausen Germany
12 C2 Bellochantuy Scotland
137 M6 Bellona Plateau Coral Sea
102 C3 Bellota California U.S.A.
21 K4 Bellou-en-Houlme France
95 P3 Bellows Falls Vermont U.S.A.
21 P3 Belloy-en-France France
115 L5 Bell Pen Northwest Territories Canada
138 C4 Bell,Pt South Australia Australia
106 F6 Bell Ranch New Mexico U.S.A.
13 F1 Bell Rock Scotland
110 G6 Bells Tennessee U.S.A.
109 L2 Bells Texas U.S.A.
119 Q6 Bellsite Manitoba Canada
42 E2 Belluno Italy
131 D4 Bell Ville Argentina
94 E6 Bellville Ohio U.S.A.
109 L6 Bellville Texas U.S.A.
106 E1 Bellvue Colorado U.S.A.
111 C10 Bellwood Louisiana U.S.A.
98 J8 Bellwood Nebraska U.S.A.
94 J6 Bellwood Pennsylvania U.S.A.
118 D9 Belly R Alberta Canada
95 N6 Belmar New Jersey U.S.A.
16 D6 Bélmez Spain
99 N7 Belmond Iowa U.S.A.
142 B1 Belmont dist Perth, W Aust Australia
119 S9 Belmont Manitoba Canada
122 J8 Belmont Nova Scotia Canada
120 J10 Belmont Ontario Canada
102 H3 Belmont Nevada U.S.A.
95 Q3 Belmont New Hampshire U.S.A.
94 K4 Belmont New York U.S.A.
112 F2 Belmont North Carolina U.S.A.
109 K6 Belmont Texas U.S.A.
94 K8 Belmont Virginia U.S.A.
99 Q7 Belmont Wisconsin U.S.A.
129 L7 Belmonte Brazil
16 C4 Belmonte Portugal
17 F5 Belmonte Spain
125 P9 Belmopan Belize
141 F4 Belmore R Queensland Australia
14 A2 Belmullet Ireland
130 H4 Belo Campo Brazil
56 C3 Belogorsk Russian Federation
59 J1 Belogorsk Russian Federation
55 E1 Belogorye Russian Federation
54 M6 Belogor'ye Voronezhskaya obl Russian Federation
46 F1 Belogradchik Bulgaria
87 G13 Beloha Madagascar
129 K7 Belo Horizonte Brazil
107 M2 Beloit Kansas U.S.A.
99 R7 Beloit Wisconsin U.S.A.
130 H10 Belo Jardim Brazil
48 M5 Beloles'ye Ukraine
129 H4 Belo Monte Brazil
52 D3 Belomorsk Russian Federation
147 J16 Belomorsk Russian Federation
52 D3 Belomorsko-Baltiyskiy Russian Federation
54 L2 Beloomut Russian Federation
70 G6 Belopa Sulawesi
54 F5 Belopol'ye Ukraine
16 E2 Belorado Spain
79 C1 Belören Turkey
55 C4 Beloretsk Russian Federation
Belorussia see Belarus
47 J1 Beloslav Bulgaria
114 G4 Belot,L Northwest Territories Canada
87 G11 Belo-Tsiribihina Madagascar
56 B5 Belousovka Kazakhstan
46 F2 Belovo Bulgaria
56 C4 Belovo Russian Federation
71 L10 Below Indonesia
52 E2 Beloye More Russian Federation
52 E3 Beloye Ozero L Russian Federation
46 G2 Belozem Bulgaria
55 C4 Belozerka Russian Federation
55 E3 Belozerskoye Russian Federation
54 J8 Belozerskoye Donetskaya obl Ukraine

9 E1 **Belper** England
107 L4 **Belpre** Kansas U.S.A.
13 G3 **Belsay** England
32 L7 **Belsen** Germany
101 P2 **Belt** Montana U.S.A.
138 E4 **Beltana** South Australia Australia
138 D3 **Belt B** South Australia Australia
103 H4 **Belted Ra** Nevada U.S.A.
129 G4 **Belterre** Brazil
110 B3 **Belton** Missouri U.S.A.
101 M1 **Belton** Montana U.S.A.
112 E3 **Belton** South Carolina U.S.A.
109 K4 **Belton** Texas U.S.A.
109 K4 **Belton Res** Texas U.S.A.
131 E2 **Beltrán,L** Argentina
48 L3 **Bel'tsy** Moldova
14 D2 **Belturbet** Ireland
116 M6 **Beluga L** Alaska U.S.A.
56 C6 **Belukha,Gora** *mt* Kazakhstan/Rus Fed
71 C8 **Beluran** Sabah
31 L6 **Beluša** Slovakia
43 G9 **Belvedere Marittimo** Italy
45 O4 **Belvedere Ostrense** Italy
18 F8 **Belvès** France
99 S7 **Belvidere** Illinois U.S.A.
107 L4 **Belvidere** Kansas U.S.A.
98 J9 **Belvidere** Nebraska U.S.A.
95 M6 **Belvidere** New Jersey U.S.A.
112 L1 **Belvidere** North Carolina U.S.A.
98 E6 **Belvidere** South Dakota U.S.A.
16 D5 **Belvis de la Jara** Spain
80 F3 **Belvoir** Israel
141 H5 **Belyando** *R* Queensland Australia
48 N4 **Belyayevka** Ukraine
54 A3 **Belynichi** Belarus
52 D6 **Belyy** Russian Federation
48 J2 **Belyy Cheremosh** *R* Ukraine
54 F3 **Belyye Berega** Russian Federation
57 E4 **Belyye Vody** Kazakhstan
54 J6 **Belyy Kolodez'** Ukraine
50 F1 **Belyy, Ostrov** *isld* Russian Federation
55 F2 **Belyy Yar** Russian Federation
20 D6 **Belz** France
31 O5 **Bełżec** Poland
33 R8 **Belzig** Germany
111 F8 **Belzoni** Mississippi U.S.A.
31 N4 **Bełżyce** Poland
87 B7 **Bembe** Angola
85 E6 **Bembéréké** Benin
16 D6 **Bembézar** *R* Spain
89 F2 **Bembezi** *R* Zimbabwe
16 C2 **Bembibre** Spain
9 E6 **Bembridge** England
99 M2 **Bemidji** Minnesota U.S.A.
110 H6 **Bemis** Tennessee U.S.A.
36 G6 **Bempflingen** Germany
13 H5 **Bempton** England
94 H4 **Bemus Point** New York U.S.A.
88 E6 **Bena** Tanzania
17 H2 **Benabarre** Spain
86 D6 **Bena Dibele** Zaire
138 F4 **Benagerie** South Australia Australia
70 D5 **Benagin** Kalimantan
17 G5 **Benaguacil** Spain
15 D4 **Ben Alder** *mt* Scotland
118 C6 **Benalto** Alberta Canada
Benares *see* **Varanasi**
16 D2 **Benarides** Spain
21 L8 **Benassay** France
19 Q18 **Bénat,C** France
15 C3 **Ben Attow** *mt* Scotland
16 B6 **Benavente** Portugal
16 D2 **Benavides** Spain
109 J8 **Benavides** Texas U.S.A.
14 E1 **Benbane Hd** N Ireland
15 A3 **Benbecula** *isld* Scotland
109 L9 **Benbrook** Texas U.S.A.
109 K3 **Benbrook L** Texas U.S.A.
14 C2 **Benbulbin** *mt* Ireland
14 B3 **Benbury** *mt* Ireland
68 H7 **Ben Cat** Vietnam
Bencheng *see* **Luannan**
144 B7 **Bench I** New Zealand
101 P2 **Benchland** Montana U.S.A.
109 L5 **Benchley** Texas U.S.A.
15 C4 **Ben Cruachan** *mt* Scotland
143 C9 **Bencubbin** W Australia Australia
100 D5 **Bend** Oregon U.S.A.
109 J4 **Bend** Texas U.S.A.
15 D3 **Ben Dearg** *mt* Scotland
116 F4 **Bendeleben Mts** Alaska U.S.A.
88 C5 **Bende Pimbwe** Tanzania
119 P8 **Bender** Saskatchewan Canada
86 A1 **Bender Qaasim** Somalia
86 A1 **Bender Siyaada** Somalia
48 M4 **Bendery** Moldova
138 E4 **Bendieuta** *R* South Australia Australia
139 G6 **Bendigo** Victoria Australia
32 K7 **Bendingbostel** Germany
68 H6 **Ben Don** Vietnam
36 D3 **Bendorf** Germany
44 C2 **Bene** Italy
80 C5 **Bene'Atarot** Israel
80 C5 **Bene Beraq** Israel
80 G1 **Bené Betira** Syria
45 L4 **Benedetto Alpe di S** *mt* Italy
107 P4 **Benedict** Kansas U.S.A.
95 L8 **Benedict** Maryland U.S.A.
98 J8 **Benedict** Nebraska U.S.A.
98 E2 **Benedict** North Dakota U.S.A.
41 O2 **Benediktenwand** *mt* Germany
129 K5 **Beneditinos** Brazil
87 H12 **Benenitra** Madagascar
31 H6 **Benešov** Czech Rep
19 K4 **Bénéstroff** France
18 G6 **Bénévent L'Abbaye** France
43 F7 **Benevento** Italy
112 C6 **Benevolence** Georgia U.S.A.
94 J5 **Benezett** Pennsylvania U.S.A.
80 C5 **Bene Ziyyon** Israel
19 L4 **Benfeld** France
75 N9 **Bengal, Bay of** S Asia
58 G5 **Bengbu** China
Benghazi *see* **Banghāzī**
65 D7 **Beng He** *R* China
69 F12 **Bengkalis** Sumatra
69 J12 **Bengkayang** Indonesia
70 E6 **Bengkung** Kalimantan
119 M9 **Bengough** Saskatchewan Canada
27 F12 **Bengtsfors** Sweden
27 M12 **Bengtskär** *lighthouse* Finland
87 B8 **Benguela** Angola
85 G2 **Ben Guerdane** Tunisia
84 J3 **Benha** Egypt
68 H5 **Ben Hien** Vietnam
15 D2 **Ben Hope** *mt* Scotland
128 E6 **Beni** *dept* Bolivia
88 B1 **Beni** Zaire
85 D2 **Beni Abbès** Algeria
117 R4 **Beniah L** Northwest Territories Canada
17 H4 **Benicarló** Spain
17 G6 **Benidorm** Spain
17 F10 **Beni Iznassèn** *mts* Morocco
79 A10 **Beni Mazâr** Egypt
85 C2 **Beni Mellal** Morocco
85 E8 **Benin,Bight of** W Africa
85 F7 **Benin City** Nigeria
36 B5 **Bening** France
9 G1 **Benington** England
85 E7 **Benin, Rep. of** W Africa
85 D2 **Beni Ounif** Algeria
17 G9 **Beni Saf** Algeria
79 B9 **Beni Suef** Egypt
47 O12 **Benitses** Greece
103 N1 **Benjamin** Utah U.S.A.
128 D4 **Benjamin Constant** Brazil
124 D2 **Benjamín Hill** Mexico
100 E6 **Benjamin L** Oregon U.S.A.
60 O3 **Benkei Misaki** *C* Japan
98 E9 **Benkelman** Nebraska U.S.A.
15 D2 **Ben Klibreck** *mt* Scotland
42 G4 **Benkovac** Croatia
15 D4 **Ben Lawers** *mt* Scotland
15 D4 **Ben Ledi** *mt* Scotland
15 D4 **Ben Lomond** *mt* Scotland
15 D2 **Ben Loyal** *mt* Scotland
15 D4 **Ben Lui** *mt* Scotland
15 E3 **Ben Macdhui** *mt* Scotland
43 B12 **Ben Mehidi** Algeria
15 D4 **Ben More** *mt* Central Scotland
15 B4 **Ben More** *mt* Highland Scotland
15 D2 **Ben More Assynt** *mt* Scotland
144 C6 **Benmore, L** New Zealand
144 C6 **Benmore Pk** *mt* New Zealand
33 N9 **Benneckenstein** Germany
98 K9 **Bennet** Nebraska U.S.A.
140 D2 **Bennet B** N Terr Australia
117 F6 **Bennett** British Columbia Canada
99 P8 **Bennett** Iowa U.S.A.
99 P3 **Bennett** Wisconsin U.S.A.
51 P1 **Bennetta, Ostrov** *isld* Russian Federation
140 B6 **Bennett, L** N Terr Australia
117 F6 **Bennett L** British Columbia Canada
112 H3 **Bennettsville** South Carolina U.S.A.
15 D4 **Ben Nevis** *mt* Scotland
145 E3 **Benneydale** New Zealand
101 O7 **Bennington** Idaho U.S.A.
107 N2 **Bennington** Kansas U.S.A.
95 Q3 **Bennington** New Hampshire U.S.A.
107 O7 **Bennington** Oklahoma U.S.A.
95 O4 **Bennington** Vermont U.S.A.
85 B6 **Bénnsané** Guinea
120 J6 **Benny** Ontario Canada
20 B6 **Bénodet** France
20 B6 **Benodet,Anse de** *B* France
144 C6 **Ben Ohau Range** New Zealand
99 P3 **Benoit** Wisconsin U.S.A.
87 E11 **Benoni** S Africa
107 K6 **Benonine** Oklahoma U.S.A.
86 B4 **Bénoué** *R* Cameroon
21 K3 **Bénouville** France
36 B1 **Benrath** Germany
36 C2 **Bensberg** Germany
32 G5 **Bensersiel** Germany
37 K2 **Benshausen** Germany
36 F4 **Bensheim** Germany
119 O9 **Benson** Saskatchewan Canada
9 E4 **Benson** England
103 O10 **Benson** Arizona U.S.A.
99 R9 **Benson** Illinois U.S.A.
111 C10 **Benson** Louisiana U.S.A.
99 L4 **Benson** Minnesota U.S.A.
112 J2 **Benson** North Carolina U.S.A.
68 H7 **Ben Suc** Vietnam
77 F6 **Bent** Iran
69 E10 **Benta** Malaysia
71 K8 **Benteng** Indonesia
32 F8 **Bentheim** Germany
68 G3 **Ben Thuy** Vietnam
16 E9 **Ben Tieb** Morocco
140 E3 **Bentinck I** Queensland Australia
68 C7 **Bentinck I** Burma
86 E4 **Bentiu** Sudan
80 E1 **Bent Jbail** Lebanon
118 C6 **Bentley** Alberta Canada
13 G6 **Bentley** S Yorks England
107 N4 **Bentley** Kansas U.S.A.
98 D3 **Bentley** North Dakota U.S.A.
94 G6 **Bentleyville** Pennsylvania U.S.A.
130 B5 **Bento Gomes,R** Brazil
133 G3 **Bento Gonçalves** Brazil
118 G7 **Benton** Alberta Canada
122 E8 **Benton** New Brunswick Canada
111 K9 **Benton** Alabama U.S.A.
111 D7 **Benton** Arkansas U.S.A.
102 F4 **Benton** California U.S.A.
113 E7 **Benton** Florida U.S.A.
110 H3 **Benton** Illinois U.S.A.
110 H5 **Benton** Kentucky U.S.A.
109 O3 **Benton** Louisiana U.S.A.
110 G4 **Benton** Missouri U.S.A.
95 L5 **Benton** Pennsylvania U.S.A.
99 Q7 **Benton** Wisconsin U.S.A.
99 U7 **Benton Harbor** Michigan U.S.A.
111 F9 **Bentonia** Mississippi U.S.A.
110 B5 **Bentonville** Arkansas U.S.A.
68 H7 **Ben Tre** Vietnam
69 E11 **Bentung** Malaysia
33 Q4 **Bentwisch** Germany
69 H12 **Benua** *isld* Indonesia
70 P10 **Benua** Bali Indonesia
70 C4 **Benuamartinus** Kalimantan
86 A4 **Benue** *R* Nigeria
12 D1 **Ben Venue** *mt* Scotland
15 D4 **Ben Vorlich** *mt* Scotland
14 B2 **Benwee Hd** Ireland
109 M3 **Ben Wheeler** Texas U.S.A.
15 D3 **Ben Wyvis** *mt* Scotland
65 F4 **Benxi** China
21 J4 **Bény Bocage,le** France
33 U5 **Benz** Germany
80 B6 **Ben Zakkay** Israel
99 U5 **Benzonia** Michigan U.S.A.
48 F5 **Beočin** Serbia Yugoslavia
48 F6 **Beograd** Serbia Yugoslavia
70 K8 **Bepagut, G** *mt* Sumatra Indonesia
60 E12 **Beppu** Japan
80 E5 **Beqaot** Jordan
80 C6 **Beqoa' Latrun** Israel
80 E5 **Berakha** Jordan
70 E6 **Berangas** Kalimantan
37 M5 **Beratzhausen** Germany
70 E3 **Berau** *R* Kalimantan
86 F2 **Berber** Sudan
86 J3 **Berbera** Somalia
86 C5 **Berbérati** Cent Afr Republic
17 H6 **Berbería, C** Balearic Is
37 L5 **Berching** Germany
57 A1 **Berchogur** Kazakhstan
38 G6 **Berchtesgaden** Germany
22 B3 **Berck** France
22 B3 **Berck Plage** France
109 K7 **Berclair** Texas U.S.A.
56 B4 **Berd'** *R* Russian Federation
21 M5 **Berd'huis** France
48 M1 **Berdichev** Ukraine
51 M2 **Berdigestyakh** Russian Federation
86 D2 **Berdoba** Chad
56 B4 **Berdsk** Russian Federation
55 C3 **Berdyaush** Russian Federation
55 E3 **Berdyuzh'ye** Russian Federation
98 D7 **Berea** Nebraska U.S.A.
94 F5 **Berea** Ohio U.S.A.
71 B1 **Berebere** Halmahera Indonesia
86 B1 **Bereeda** Somalia
48 J2 **Beregomet** Ukraine
48 H2 **Beregovo** Ukraine
85 D7 **Berekum** Ghana
32 L8 **Berenbostel** Germany
102 D4 **Berenda** California U.S.A.
84 J5 **Berenice** Egypt
119 U6 **Berens I** Manitoba Canada
119 V6 **Berens River** Manitoba Canada
8 D6 **Bere Regis** England
138 D3 **Beresford** South Australia Australia
119 R9 **Beresford** Manitoba Canada
122 G6 **Beresford** New Brunswick Canada
98 K6 **Beresford** South Dakota U.S.A.
48 L4 **Beresti** Romania
48 G3 **Berettyo** *R* Hungary
48 G3 **Berettyóújfalu** Hungary
48 J1 **Berezhany** Ukraine
54 C5 **Berezna** Ukraine
52 J5 **Berezniki** Russian Federation
55 C2 **Berezovka** Russian Federation
50 F2 **Berezovo** Russian Federation
56 C3 **Berezovskiy** Russian Federation
29 N11 **Berezovyy,Ostrov** *isld* Russian Federation
26 J2 **Berg** Norway
26 G9 **Berg** Sweden
37 N2 **Berga** Germany
17 J2 **Berga** Spain
27 H14 **Berga** Sweden
27 G15 **Berga** Sweden
78 A2 **Bergama** Turkey
42 C3 **Bergamo** Italy
45 K1 **Bergantino** Italy
32 G7 **Berge** Germany
32 M6 **Bergedorf** Germany
32 L7 **Bergen** Germany
27 A11 **Bergen** Norway
121 N9 **Bergen** New York U.S.A.
98 F1 **Bergen** North Dakota U.S.A.
25 C3 **Bergen aan Zee** Netherlands
6 M2 **Bergen Bank** North Sea
25 E5 **Berg-en-Dal** Netherlands
25 B6 **Bergen op Zoom** Netherlands
18 F8 **Bergerac** France
25 D6 **Bergeyk** Netherlands
26 L3 **Bergfors** Sweden
36 C1 **Berg. Gladbach** Germany
145 D1 **Berghan Pt** New Zealand
36 C7 **Bergheim** France
36 B2 **Bergheim** Germany
94 G6 **Bergholz** Ohio U.S.A.
32 G9 **Bergkamen** Germany
27 H15 **Bergkvara** Sweden
99 M1 **Bergland** Ontario Canada
99 R3 **Bergland** Michigan U.S.A.
37 M7 **Berglern** Germany
26 K5 **Bergnäs, N** Sweden
36 D1 **Bergneustadt** Germany
29 J9 **Bergö** Finland
94 G8 **Bergoo** West Virginia U.S.A.
37 J3 **Bergrheinfeld** Germany
25 C5 **Bergse Maas** *R* Netherlands
27 K12 **Bergshamra** Sweden
26 J10 **Bergsjö** Sweden
37 N6 **Bergstorf** Germany
37 J4 **Bergtheim** Germany
22 C2 **Bergues** France
25 F2 **Bergumer Meer** *L* Netherlands
41 L4 **Bergün** Switzerland
45 L1 **Berici,Monti** Italy
143 B7 **Beringarra** W Australia Australia
22 J1 **Beringen** Belgium
25 E6 **Beringen** Netherlands
116 Q6 **Bering Glacier** Alaska U.S.A.
116 P6 **Bering L** Alaska U.S.A.
116 E3 **Bering Land Bridge Nat Preserve** Alaska U.S.A.
114 B5 **Bering Sea**
116 C4 **Bering Strait** Rus Fed/U.S.A.
106 D9 **Berino** New Mexico U.S.A.
54 E10 **Berislav** Ukraine
17 F8 **Berja** Spain
21 K4 **Berjou** France
26 D9 **Berkåk** Norway
32 F9 **Berkel** *R* Germany
25 F4 **Berkel** *R* Netherlands
8 D4 **Berkeley** England
102 B4 **Berkeley** California U.S.A.
114 J3 **Berkeley,C** Northwest Territories Canada
142 G2 **Berkeley, R** W Australia Australia
133 F8 **Berkeley Sd** Falkland Is
9 F4 **Berkhamsted** England
146 E7 **Berkner I** Antarctica
46 F1 **Berkovitsa** Bulgaria
9 E5 **Berkshire** *co* England
95 O4 **Berkshire Hills** Massachusetts U.S.A.
22 F3 **Berlaimont** France
117 P8 **Berland** *R* Alberta Canada
110 K6 **Berland Plateau** Tennessee U.S.A.
17 F3 **Berlanga de Duero** Spain
16 A5 **Berlenga** *isld* Portugal
26 R1 **Berlevåg** Norway
33 S8 **Berlin** *land* Germany
34 **Berlin** *conurbation* Germany
89 E9 **Berlin** S Africa
95 M8 **Berlin** Maryland U.S.A.
95 Q2 **Berlin** New Hampshire U.S.A.
98 H3 **Berlin** North Dakota U.S.A.
94 J7 **Berlin** Pennsylvania U.S.A.
99 S6 **Berlin** Wisconsin U.S.A.
115 L3 **Berlinguet Inlet** Northwest Territories Canada
94 G6 **Berlin Res** Ohio U.S.A.
144 C4 **Berlins** New Zealand
133 E6 **Bermeja,Pta** Argentina
16 D8 **Bermeja, Sa** *mt* Spain
124 H5 **Bermejillo** Mexico
128 F8 **Bermejo** *R* Argentina
133 D4 **Bermejo** *R* Argentina
131 E7 **Bermejo, I** Argentina
17 F1 **Bermeo** Spain
16 C3 **Bermillo de Sayago** Spain
20 G8 **Berm-sur-Mer** France
90 A1 **Bermuda** *isld* Atlantic Oc
90 D5 **Bermuda Rise** Atlantic Oc
40 G4 **Bern** Switzerland
99 L10 **Bern** Kansas U.S.A.
43 H8 **Bernalda** Italy
106 D6 **Bernalillo** New Mexico U.S.A.
118 K8 **Bernard** Saskatchewan Canada
99 Q7 **Bernard** Iowa U.S.A.
103 P10 **Bernardino** Arizona U.S.A.
130 E8 **Bernardino de Campos** Brazil
114 G3 **Bernard Is** Northwest Territories Canada
122 J3 **Bernard,L** Quebec Canada
119 M3 **Bernard L** Saskatchewan Canada
130 D10 **Bernardo de Irigoyen** Argentina
133 E5 **Bernasconi** Argentina
33 T7 **Bernau** Germany
21 P1 **Bernaville** France
21 M3 **Bernay** Eure France
21 K5 **Bernay** Sarthe France
33 P9 **Bernburg** Germany
38 O6 **Berndorf** Austria
Berne *see* **Bern**
32 H6 **Berne** Germany
110 M1 **Berne** Indiana U.S.A.
22 K2 **Berneau** Belgium
36 F6 **Berneck** Germany
15 A3 **Berneray** *isld* Scotland
20 F7 **Bernerie la** France
40 G4 **Berner Oberland** *reg* Switzerland
16 D2 **Bernesga** *R* Spain
21 N2 **Berneval** France
111 D9 **Bernice** Louisiana U.S.A.
110 G5 **Bernie** Missouri U.S.A.
115 L3 **Bernier B** Northwest Territories Canada
143 A6 **Bernier I** W Australia Australia
41 L5 **Bernina, Passo del** Switzerland
22 F3 **Bernissart** Belgium
33 P5 **Bernitt** Germany
36 C4 **Bernkastel-Kues** Germany
33 S9 **Bernsdorf** Germany
95 L6 **Bernville** Pennsylvania U.S.A.
37 K5 **Berolzheim** Germany
80 B7 **Beror Hayil** Israel
87 H12 **Beroroha** Madagascar
80 B8 **Berosh** Israel
85 E6 **Béroubouay** Benin
30 H6 **Beroun** Czech Rep
30 H6 **Berounka** *R* Czech Rep
46 F3 **Berovo** Macedonia
45 L2 **Berra** Italy
40 F4 **Berra** *mt* Switzerland
43 A12 **Berrahal** Algeria
19 O18 **Berre** France
85 C2 **Berrechid** Morocco
19 O18 **Berre, Etang de** France
36 B2 **Berrenrath** Germany
138 F5 **Berri** South Australia Australia
85 E2 **Berriane** Algeria
15 E2 **Berriedale** Scotland
20 C5 **Berrien** France
99 U8 **Berrien Springs** Michigan U.S.A.
139 H6 **Berrigan** New South Wales Australia
140 B1 **Berrimah** N Terr Australia
22 G5 **Berru** France
21 N7 **Berry** *reg* France
111 J8 **Berry** Alabama U.S.A.
110 M3 **Berry** Kentucky U.S.A.
22 F5 **Berry-au-Bac** France
127 M2 **Berrydale** Jamaica
102 B3 **Berryessa,L** California U.S.A.
8 C7 **Berry Head** England
113 K12 **Berry Is** Bahamas
140 B6 **Berrys Pass** N Terr Australia
110 C5 **Berryville** Arkansas U.S.A.
94 K7 **Berryville** Virginia U.S.A.
87 C11 **Berseba** Namibia
22 E3 **Bersée** France
32 G7 **Bersenbrück** Germany
48 M2 **Bershad'** Ukraine
22 G3 **Bersillies** Belgium
122 B5 **Bersimis, Les Lacs** Quebec Canada
55 D4 **Bersuat** Kazakhstan
69 F10 **Bertam** Malaysia
122 D3 **Berté,L** Quebec Canada
21 P8 **Berthenoux,la** France
121 R6 **Berthierville** Quebec Canada
98 E1 **Berthold** North Dakota U.S.A.
98 A9 **Berthoud** Colorado U.S.A.
141 F1 **Bertiehaugh** Queensland Australia
22 D3 **Bertincourt** France
45 M3 **Bertinoro** Italy
22 K3 **Bertogne** Belgium
86 B5 **Bertoua** Cameroon
14 B3 **Bertraghboy B** Ireland
120 F3 **Bertram** Ontario Canada
109 J5 **Bertram** Texas U.S.A.
142 F4 **Bertram,Mt** W Australia Australia
98 G9 **Bertrand** Nebraska U.S.A.
36 B7 **Bertrichamps** France
22 H4 **Bertrix** Belgium
22 E3 **Bertry** France
119 P6 **Bertwell** Saskatchewan Canada
57 B4 **Beruni** Uzbekistan
128 F4 **Beruri** Brazil
83 J11 **Beruwala** Sri Lanka
137 Q2 **Berv** *isld* Kiribati
21 L3 **Berville-sur-Mer** France
139 H6 **Berwick** Victoria Australia
122 H8 **Berwick** Nova Scotia Canada
95 R3 **Berwick** Maine U.S.A.
95 L5 **Berwick** Pennsylvania U.S.A.
13 G2 **Berwick-upon-Tweed** England
117 P7 **Berwyn** Alberta Canada
7 H10 **Berwyn Mts** Wales
6 M3 **Beryl** *oil rig* North Sea
103 L4 **Beryl** Utah U.S.A.
22 G3 **Berzee** Belgium
48 D4 **Berzence** Hungary
70 E3 **Besah** Kalimantan
87 G11 **Besalampy** Madagascar
19 K5 **Besançon** France
71 L9 **Besar** Flores Indonesia
70 O8 **Besar, G** *mt* Java
70 D6 **Besar, G** *mt* Kalimantan
69 E10 **Besar,Gunung** Malaysia
69 E11 **Besar Hantu** *mt* Malaysia
19 O15 **Besayes** France
43 B12 **Besbes** Algeria
116 G4 **Besboro I** Alaska U.S.A.
18 H6 **Besbre** *R* France
69 F11 **Beserah** Malaysia
57 H6 **Besharyk** Uzbekistan
54 A1 **Beshenkovichi** Belarus
36 G5 **Besigheim** Germany
71 M9 **Besikama** Timor Indonesia
47 N10 **Beşiktas** Turkey
78 H3 **Beşiri** Turkey
69 C11 **Besitang** Sumatra
31 L6 **Beskidy Zachodnie** *reg* Poland
53 F11 **Beslan** Russian Federation
46 E2 **Besna Kobila** *mt* Serbia Yugoslavia
57 G1 **Besoba** Kazakhstan
47 J7 **Beşparmak Dağ** *mt* Turkey
26 D7 **Bessaker** Norway
48 L2 **Bessarabia** *old prov* Moldova
48 M4 **Bessarabka** Moldova
19 Q14 **Besse** Isère France
19 Q18 **Besse** Var France
18 H8 **Bessèges** France
121 N7 **Bessemer** Ontario Canada
111 K8 **Bessemer** Alabama U.S.A.
99 Q3 **Bessemer** Michigan U.S.A.
94 G6 **Bessemer** Pennsylvania U.S.A.
112 F2 **Bessemer City** North Carolina U.S.A.
19 N13 **Bessenay** France
36 G4 **Bessenbach** Germany
28 F5 **Besser** Denmark
21 M6 **Bessé-sur-Braye** France
107 M6 **Bessie** Oklahoma U.S.A.
21 J3 **Bessin** *reg* France
18 F6 **Bessines sur Gartempe** France
25 D5 **Best** Netherlands
57 J1 **Bestamak** Kazakhstan
28 A3 **Bested** Denmark
55 F4 **Bestobe** Kazakhstan
140 C2 **Beswick** N Terr Australia
100 C8 **Beswick** California U.S.A.
87 H11 **Betafo** Madagascar
71 M9 **Betano** Timor
87 H13 **Betanty** Madagascar
16 B1 **Betanzos** Spain
16 B1 **Betanzos, Ría de** Spain
17 G5 **Bétara** Spain
86 B4 **Bétaré Oya** Cameroon
80 C6 **Bet 'Arif** Israel
122 C4 **Betchie L** Quebec Canada
99 T2 **Bete Grise Bay** Michigan U.S.A.
80 D6 **Bet Él** Jordan
80 D6 **Bet Él B** Jordan
69 G13 **Betet** *isld* Sumatra
80 C7 **Bet Guvrin** Israel
80 E6 **Bet Ha'Arava** Jordan
80 D2 **Bet Ha'Emeq** Israel
80 B8 **Bet Ha Gaddi** Israel
87 E11 **Bethal** S Africa
89 F6 **Bethal** S Africa
80 C3 **Bet Hananya** Israel
87 C11 **Bethanien** Namibia
110 B1 **Bethany** Missouri U.S.A.
107 N6 **Bethany** Oklahoma U.S.A.
95 M8 **Bethany Beach** Delaware U.S.A.
116 G6 **Bethel** Alaska U.S.A.
95 O5 **Bethel** Connecticut U.S.A.
95 M8 **Bethel** Delaware U.S.A.
95 R2 **Bethel** Maine U.S.A.
99 N4 **Bethel** Minnesota U.S.A.
99 O10 **Bethel** Missouri U.S.A.
112 K2 **Bethel** North Carolina U.S.A.
110 M3 **Bethel** Ohio U.S.A.
95 P3 **Bethel** Vermont U.S.A.
94 G6 **Bethel Park** Pennsylvania U.S.A.
127 J2 **Bethel Town** Jamaica
22 G5 **Bétheniville** France
95 K7 **Bethesda** Maryland U.S.A.
94 F6 **Bethesda** Ohio U.S.A.
8 B1 **Bethesda** Wales
80 F1 **Bet Hillel** Israel
21 M8 **Béthines** France
22 D5 **Béthisy-St.Pierre** France
80 D7 **Bethlehem** Jordan
89 F7 **Bethlehem** S Africa
95 Q2 **Bethlehem** New Hampshire U.S.A.
95 M6 **Bethlehem** Pennsylvania U.S.A.
122 A2 **Béthoulet, L** Quebec Canada
110 K5 **Bethpage** Tennessee U.S.A.
89 D8 **Bethulie** S Africa
119 M8 **Bethune** Saskatchewan Canada
21 N2 **Béthune** *R* France
22 D2 **Béthune** France
106 H2 **Bethune** Colorado U.S.A.
112 G3 **Bethune** South Carolina U.S.A.
130 G6 **Betim** Brazil
87 G12 **Betioky** Madagascar
70 O10 **Betiri, G** Java
80 D2 **Bet Ke'rem** Israel
80 D3 **Bet Lehem** Israel
8 D1 **Betley** England
80 C7 **Bet Nir** Israel
70 B4 **Betong** Sarawak
140 F7 **Betoota** Queensland Australia
80 D3 **Bet Oren** Israel
86 C5 **Bétou** Congo
57 E2 **Betpak-Dala** *reg* Kazakhstan
80 C8 **Bet Qama** Israel
87 H12 **Betroka** Madagascar
80 E3 **Bet She'an** Israel
80 B7 **Bet Shiqma** Israel
122 D5 **Betsiamites** Quebec Canada
122 C4 **Betsiamites, R** Quebec Canada
87 H11 **Betsiboka** *R* Madagascar
99 U5 **Betsie, Pt** Michigan U.S.A.
99 V3 **Betsy L** Michigan U.S.A.
22 K4 **Bettembourg** Luxembourg
75 L5 **Bettiah** India
109 N3 **Bettie** Texas U.S.A.
116 M3 **Bettles** Alaska U.S.A.
27 J13 **Bettna** Sweden
20 G5 **Betton** France
74 G8 **Betul** India
71 M9 **Betun** Timor Indonesia
70 C4 **Betung, G** *mt* Kalimantan
73 M3 **Betwa** *R* India
8 C1 **Betws-y-Coed** Wales
80 C4 **Bet Yannay** Israel
80 C4 **Bet Yizhaq** Israel
80 F3 **Bet Yosef** Israel
36 D2 **Betzdorf** Germany
37 L4 **Betzenstein** Germany
41 O2 **Beuerberg** Germany
25 E5 **Beugen** Netherlands
119 Q8 **Beulah** Manitoba Canada
99 V5 **Beulah** Michigan U.S.A.
98 E2 **Beulah** North Dakota U.S.A.
100 G6 **Beulah** Oregon U.S.A.
98 B5 **Beulah** Wyoming U.S.A.
8 C3 **Beulah** Wales
112 K3 **Beulaville** North Carolina U.S.A.
9 G5 **Beult,R** England
36 B4 **Beurig** Germany
22 D4 **Beuvraignes** France
21 O6 **Beuvron** *R* France
21 K3 **Beuvron-en-Auge** France
20 A5 **Beuzec-Cap-Sizun** France
21 L3 **Beuzeville** France
21 L2 **Beuzeville-la-Grenier** France
33 N6 **Bevensen** Germany
32 G8 **Bever** *R* Germany
22 G1 **Beveren** Oost Vlanderen Belgium
112 H2 **B. Everett Jordan Lake** North Carolina U.S.A.
32 G8 **Bevergern** Germany
41 K4 **Beverin,Piz** *mt* Switzerland
143 B9 **Beverley** W Australia Australia
118 K8 **Beverley** Saskatchewan Canada
13 H6 **Beverley** England
100 F3 **Beverley** Washington U.S.A.
141 J5 **Beverley Grp** *islds* Queensland Australia
116 H7 **Beverley,L** Alaska U.S.A.
22 J1 **Beverlo** Belgium
118 D5 **Beverly** Alberta Canada
107 N2 **Beverly** Kansas U.S.A.
95 R4 **Beverly** Massachusetts U.S.A.
94 F7 **Beverly** Ohio U.S.A.
94 H8 **Beverly** West Virginia U.S.A.
102 F7 **Beverly Hills** California U.S.A.
114 J5 **Beverly L** Northwest Territories Canada
100 C2 **Beverly Park** Washington U.S.A.
32 L9 **Bevern** Germany
22 J2 **Beverst** Belgium
32 J6 **Beverstedt** Germany
32 K9 **Beverungen** Germany
25 C4 **Beverwijk** Netherlands
99 O10 **Bevier** Missouri U.S.A.
45 K1 **Bevilacqua Boschi** Italy
21 O5 **Béville-le-Comte** France
28 C6 **Bevtoft** Denmark
128 C7 **Beware,Pta** *C* Peru
8 D3 **Bewdley** England
40 F5 **Bex** Switzerland
9 G6 **Bexhill** England
144 D5 **Bexley** New Zealand
47 H4 **Beyçayırı** Turkey
78 C3 **Bey Dağlari** Turkey
47 L4 **Beydili** Turkey
47 N10 **Beykoz** Turkey
85 C7 **Beyla** Guinea
47 N10 **Beylerbeyi** Turkey
86 H3 **Bēylul** Eritrea
21 O4 **Beynes** France
78 B1 **Beyoglu** Turkey
78 C1 **Beypazari** Turkey
76 B5 **Beypore** India
79 F5 **Beyrouth** Lebanon
78 C3 **Beyşehir** Turkey
80 C7 **Beyt 'Awwa** Jordan
48 E5 **Bezdan** Serbia Yugoslavia
37 O4 **Bezdružice** Czech Rep
19 J5 **Bèze** France
80 F4 **Bezeq** *R* Israel
52 C6 **Bezhanitsy** Russian Federation
46 G1 **Bezhanovo** Bulgaria
18 H9 **Béziers** France
46 F3 **Bezlet** *mt* Bulgaria
21 O3 **Bezu-la-Forêt** France
75 L5 **Bhadgaon** Nepal
75 M8 **Bhadrach** India
76 E2 **Bhadrachalam** India
76 B4 **Bhadravati** India
74 B4 **Bhag** Pakistan
75 M6 **Bhagalpur** India
74 G9 **Bhainsa** India
76 E1 **Bhairamgarh** India
74 D3 **Bhakkar** Pakistan
74 G9 **Bhalki** India
76 E1 **Bhamragarh** India
74 H8 **Bhandara** India
75 L9 **Bhanjanagar** India
75 J7 **Bharatpur** India
74 E8 **Bharuch** India
74 F3 **Bhatinda** India
76 B4 **Bhatkal** India
75 N7 **Bhatpara** India
74 E2 **Bhaun** Pakistan
76 C5 **Bhavani** India
74 E8 **Bhavnagar** India
75 K9 **Bhawanipatna** India
74 E2 **Bhera** Pakistan
75 J8 **Bhilai** India
74 F6 **Bhilwara** India
73 M5 **Bhima** *R* India
76 E2 **Bhimavaram** India
74 H5 **Bhind** India
74 G4 **Bhiwani** India
74 H10 **Bhongir** India
74 G7 **Bhopal** India
76 E1 **Bhopalpatnam** India
74 E9 **Bhor** India
75 L8 **Bhubaneshwar** India
74 C7 **Bhuj** India
68 D4 **Bhumiphol Dam** Thailand
74 F8 **Bhusawal** India
75 N5 **Bhutan** *kingdom* S Asia
77 E6 **Bīabān** *coastal reg* Iran
85 F8 **Biafra,Bight of** W Africa
71 H5 **Biak** Sulawesi Indonesia
136 H2 **Biak** *isld* W Irian
31 N2 **Biała Piska** Poland
31 O3 **Biała Podlaska** Poland
31 M4 **Białobrzegi** Poland
31 J1 **Białogard** Poland
31 K2 **Biały Bór** Poland
31 O2 **Białystok** Poland
44 G3 **Bianca,P** *C* Italy
43 G10 **Bianco** Italy
45 L2 **Bianco, Canale** Italy
65 F4 **Bianmen** China
Bianzhuang *see* **Cangshan**
71 G7 **Biao** Mindanao Philippines
68 F3 **Bia,Pou** *mt* Laos
77 D1 **Biārjmand** Iran
71 J4 **Biaro** *isld* Indonesia
18 D9 **Biarritz** France
55 G3 **Biaza** Russian Federation
79 A10 **Biba** Egypt
87 B8 **Bibala** Angola
42 D5 **Bibbiena** Italy
41 L1 **Biberach** Germany
37 K5 **Bibert** *R* Germany
16 C2 **Bibey,R** Spain
85 D7 **Bibiania** Ghana
36 E4 **Biblis** Germany
Biblos *see* **Jbail**
37 J3 **Bibra** Thüringen Germany
142 A3 **Bibra Lake** *dist* Perth, W Aust Australia
9 E4 **Bibury** England
122 D5 **Bic** Quebec Canada
46 D3 **Bicaj** Albania
130 G7 **Bicas** Brazil
48 K4 **Bicaz** Romania
9 E4 **Bicester** England
41 O2 **Bichl** Germany
41 N3 **Bichlbach** Austria
122 D5 **Bic, I. du** Quebec Canada
140 D2 **Bickerton I** N Terr Australia
8 C6 **Bickington** England
8 C6 **Bickleigh** England
100 E3 **Bickleton** Washington U.S.A.
142 B2 **Bickley Brook** Perth, W Aust Australia
94 F8 **Bickmore** West Virginia U.S.A.
110 J3 **Bicknell** Indiana U.S.A.
103 N3 **Bicknell** Utah U.S.A.
48 E3 **Bicske** Hungary
85 F7 **Bida** Nigeria
70 F2 **Bidadari, Tanjong** *C* Sabah
76 C2 **Bidar** India
95 R3 **Biddeford** Maine U.S.A.
80 D6 **Biddu** Jordan
8 D1 **Biddulph** England
8 B5 **Bideford** England
85 E4 **Bidon 5** Algeria
94 E8 **Bidwell** Ohio U.S.A.
36 G3 **Bieber** Germany
100 D8 **Bieber** California U.S.A.
36 G3 **Biebergemünd** Germany
36 D5 **Biebermühle** Germany
36 F2 **Biebertal** Germany
36 E3 **Biebrich** Germany
31 O2 **Biebrza** *R* Poland
31 N6 **Biecz** Poland
36 F2 **Biedenkopf** Germany
33 P8 **Biederitz** Germany
70 O9 **Biega** Java
40 G1 **Biegel** Germany
60 Q2 **Biei** Japan
40 F3 **Biel** Switzerland
31 K5 **Bielawa** Poland
119 Q7 **Bield** Manitoba Canada
32 J8 **Bielefeld** Germany
41 M4 **Bielerhöhe** *pass* Austria
40 F3 **Bieler See** *L* Switzerland
42 B3 **Biella** Italy
17 H2 **Bielsa** Spain
31 L6 **Bielsko-Biała** Poland
31 O3 **Bielsk Podlaski** Poland
36 C2 **Bielstein** Germany
33 M6 **Bienenbüttel** Germany
119 P9 **Bienfait** Saskatchewan Canada
68 H7 **Bien Hoa** Vietnam
Bienne *see* **Biel**
45 J4 **Bientina** Italy
67 C2 **Bi'er** China
141 H7 **Bierbank** Queensland Australia
36 F7 **Bieringen** Germany
21 J6 **Bierne** France
28 D2 **Biersted** Denmark
25 A6 **Biervliet** Netherlands
33 P7 **Biese** *R* Germany
33 T7 **Biesenthal** Germany
40 B1 **Biesles** France
36 E6 **Bietigheim** Germany
36 G6 **Bietigheim** Germany
33 T6 **Bietikow** Germany
22 J4 **Bièvre** Belgium
21 P4 **Bièvres** France
31 M3 **Bieżun** Poland
43 F7 **Biferno** *R* Italy
86 B6 **Bifoun** Gabon
116 K5 **Big** *R* Alaska U.S.A.
47 J4 **Biga** *R* Turkey
78 A1 **Biga** Turkey
47 J5 **Bigadiç** Turkey
101 L2 **Big Arm** Montana U.S.A.
Big B *see* **Big B**
101 P2 **Big Baldy Mt** Montana U.S.A.
117 M10 **Big Bar Creek** British Columbia Canada
144 B6 **Big Bay** New Zealand
99 T3 **Big Bay** Michigan U.S.A.
102 H7 **Big Bear City** California U.S.A.
109 N8 **Big Bear Cr** Texas U.S.A.
102 G7 **Big Bear L** California U.S.A.
119 M9 **Big Beaver** Saskatchewan Canada
120 H3 **Big Beaver Falls** Ontario Canada
115 L7 **Big Beaver House** Ontario Canada
143 C7 **Big Bell** W Australia Australia
101 O3 **Big Belt Mts** Montana U.S.A.
100 D8 **Big Bend** California U.S.A.
106 H3 **Big Bend** Colorado U.S.A.
108 D6 **Big Bend Nat.Pk** Texas U.S.A.
111 G8 **Big Black** *R* Mississippi U.S.A.
112 G3 **Big Black Cr** South Carolina U.S.A.
94 E10 **Big Black Mt** Kentucky/Virg U.S.A.
8 C7 **Bigbury B** England
8 C7 **Bigbury-on-Sea** England
108 E5 **Big Canyon** *R* Texas U.S.A.
122 E3 **Big Caotibi L** Quebec Canada
103 M6 **Big Chino Wash** Arizona U.S.A.
110 K4 **Big Clifty** Kentucky U.S.A.
107 K3 **Big Cr** Kansas U.S.A.
117 M10 **Big Creek** British Columbia Canada
94 F8 **Big Creek** West Virginia U.S.A.
113 F12 **Big Cypress Nat Preserve** Florida U.S.A.
113 F11 **Big Cypress Swamp** Florida U.S.A.
116 O4 **Big Delta** Alaska U.S.A.
138 F6 **Big Desert** Victoria Australia
101 T2 **Big Dry Cr** Montana U.S.A.
99 Q5 **Big Eau Pleine Res** Wisconsin U.S.A.
101 O6 **Big Elk Mt** Idaho U.S.A.
107 O2 **Bigelow** Kansas U.S.A.
99 N1 **Big Falls** Minnesota U.S.A.
99 N2 **Bigfork** Minnesota U.S.A.
101 L1 **Bigfork** Montana U.S.A.
109 M9 **Big Fossil Cr** Texas U.S.A.
118 K6 **Biggar** Saskatchewan Canada
12 E2 **Biggar** Scotland
36 D1 **Bigge** *R* Germany
142 F2 **Bigge I** W Australia
26 N2 **Biggeluobbal** Norway
141 K7 **Biggenden** Queensland Australia
32 H10 **Bigge-Olsberg** Germany
141 J7 **Bigge Range** *mts* Queensland Australia
117 E6 **Bigger,Mt** British Columbia Canada
110 F5 **Biggers** Arkansas U.S.A.
9 F3 **Biggleswade** England
102 C2 **Biggs** California U.S.A.
100 E4 **Biggs** Oregon U.S.A.
99 Q9 **Biggsville** Illinois U.S.A.
106 B10 **Big Hatchet Pk** New Mexico U.S.A.
118 C7 **Big Hill Sp.Prov.Pk** Alberta Canada
101 N4 **Big Hole** *R* Montana U.S.A.
101 M4 **Bighole Nat. Battlefield** Montana U.S.A.
101 S4 **Bighorn** *R* Montana U.S.A.
101 S4 **Bighorn** *R* Wyo/Mont U.S.A.
101 R4 **Bighorn Canyon Nat. Recreation Area** Montana U.S.A.
101 S5 **Bighorn Mts** Wyo/Mont U.S.A.
126 G3 **Bight of Acklins** Bahamas
126 G2 **Bight,The** Cat I Bahamas
115 M5 **Big I** Northwest Territories Canada
118 H1 **Big I** Ontario Canada
111 E8 **Big I** Arkansas U.S.A.
94 H9 **Big Island** Virginia U.S.A.
117 F4 **Big Kalzas L** Yukon Territory Canada
116 H9 **Big Koniuji I** Alaska U.S.A.
117 R3 **Big L** Northwest Territories Canada
95 U1 **Big L** Maine U.S.A.
100 E7 **Big L** Oregon U.S.A.
116 N3 **Big Lake** Alaska U.S.A.
108 F4 **Big Lake** Texas U.S.A.
95 K7 **Biglerville** Pennsylvania U.S.A.
144 A7 **Big Moggy I** New Zealand
95 N3 **Big Moose** New York U.S.A.
110 G4 **Big Muddy** *R* Illinois U.S.A.
98 B1 **Big Muddy Cr** Montana U.S.A.
119 N9 **Big Muddy L** Saskatchewan Canada
20 E6 **Bignan** France
44 C4 **Bignone,Monte** Italy
20 G7 **Bignon,le** France
94 H9 **Big Otter** *R* Virginia U.S.A.
102 F4 **Big Pine** California U.S.A.
99 L3 **Big Pine L** Minnesota U.S.A.
102 E7 **Big Pine Peak** California U.S.A.
110 D4 **Big Piney** *R* Missouri U.S.A.
101 P7 **Big Piney** Wyoming U.S.A.
123 M8 **Big Pond** C Breton I, Nova Scotia
94 B3 **Big Rapids** Michigan U.S.A.
99 Q4 **Big Rib** *R* Wisconsin U.S.A.
118 K5 **Big River** Saskatchewan Canada
99 U5 **Big Sable Pt** Michigan U.S.A.
100 E8 **Big Sage Res** California U.S.A.
117 F5 **Big Salmon** *R* Yukon Territory Canada
119 S1 **Big Sand L** Manitoba Canada
103 L7 **Big Sandy** *R* Arizona U.S.A.
101 P1 **Big Sandy** Montana U.S.A.
109 M3 **Big Sandy** Texas U.S.A.
101 Q7 **Big Sandy** Wyoming U.S.A.
106 H3 **Big Sandy Cr** Colorado U.S.A.
119 N4 **Big Sandy L** Saskatchewan Canada
99 N3 **Big Sandy L** Minnesota U.S.A.
118 H1 **Bigsby I** Ontario Canada
98 K5 **Big Sioux** *R* South Dakota U.S.A.
102 G3 **Big Smoky Valley** Nevada U.S.A.
101 Q3 **Big Snowy Mt** Montana U.S.A.
144 A7 **Big South Cape I** New Zealand
108 F3 **Big Spring** Texas U.S.A.
101 O5 **Big Springs** Idaho U.S.A.
98 D8 **Big Springs** Nebraska U.S.A.
118 H8 **Bigstick L** Saskatchewan Canada
98 K4 **Big Stone City** South Dakota U.S.A.
94 E10 **Big Stone Gap** Virginia U.S.A.
119 W5 **Bigstone L** Manitoba Canada
98 K4 **Big Stone L** Minnesota U.S.A.
119 W3 **Bigstone R** Manitoba Canada
102 C5 **Big Sur** California U.S.A.
109 M5 **Big Thicket L** Texas U.S.A.
109 N5 **Big Thicket Nat. Preserve** Texas U.S.A.
101 Q4 **Bigtimber** Montana U.S.A.
101 S6 **Bigtrails** Wyoming U.S.A.
115 L7 **Big Trout Lake** Ontario Canada
130 E10 **Biguaçú** Brazil
118 E6 **Big Valley** Alberta Canada
109 H7 **Big Wells** Texas U.S.A.
111 L7 **Big Wills Cr** Alabama U.S.A.
120 K6 **Bigwood** Ontario Canada
101 L6 **Big Wood** *R* Idaho U.S.A.
42 G4 **Bihac** Bosnia-Herzegovina
75 L6 **Bihar** *prov* India
75 L6 **Bihār Sharīf** India
48 G4 **Bihor** *reg* Romania
48 G4 **Bihorului Muntii** *mts* Romania
67 F2 **Bihu** China
85 A6 **Bijagós, Arquipélago dos** Guinea-Bissau
74 G5 **Bijaipur** India
76 B2 **Bijapur** India
77 A2 **Bijar** Iran
75 K4 **Bijauri** Nepal
48 E6 **Bijeljina** Bosnia-Herzegovina
46 D1 **Bijelo Polje** Montenegro Yugoslavia
67 B3 **Bijie** China
76 E1 **Bijji** India
77 F6 **Bijnābād** Iran
74 H4 **Bijnor** India
74 E4 **Bikaner** India
79 F5 **Bikfaiya** Lebanon
59 K2 **Bikin** Russian Federation
59 L2 **Bikin** *R* Russian Federation
134 G7 **Bikini** *atoll* Marshall Is
31 L6 **Bílá** Czech Rep
71 G6 **Bilaa Pt** Mindanao Philippines
85 E6 **Bilanga** Burkina
70 F3 **Bilangbilangen** Kalimantan
74 E5 **Bilara** India
79 H4 **Bil'as, Jabal** *mt* Syria
74 G3 **Bilaspur** India
70 F2 **Bilatan** *isld* Philippines
71 H4 **Bilato** Sulawesi Indonesia
68 D5 **Bilauktaung Range** Burma/Thailand
17 F1 **Bilbao** Spain
79 B8 **Bilbeis** Egypt
42 J6 **Bileća** Bosnia-Herzegovina
78 B1 **Bilecik** Turkey
48 F5 **Biled** Romania
48 D2 **Bilé Karpaty** Czech Rep/Slovakia
31 O5 **Biłgoraj** Poland

86 E5 **Bili** Zaire
55 A3 **Bilimbay** Russian Federation
68 C4 **Bilin** Burma
30 H5 **Bílina** *R* Czech Rep
85 G7 **Biliri** Nigeria
71 D8 **Bilit** Sabah
65 E5 **Biliu He** *R* China
98 A6 **Bill** Wyoming U.S.A.
143 B7 **Billabalong** W Australia Australia
143 A7 **Billabong Roadhouse** W Australia Australia
6 D2 **Bill Baileys Bank** N Atlantic Oc
20 H5 **Billé** France
33 M5 **Bille** *R* Germany
32 F9 **Billerbeck** Germany
9 G4 **Billericay** England
9 F2 **Billesdon** England
19 P12 **Billiat** France
36 G5 **Billigheim** Germany
142 G4 **Billiluna** W Australia Australia
9 F2 **Billingborough** England
27 F16 **Billinge** Sweden
9 F1 **Billinghay** England
101 R4 **Billings** Montana U.S.A.
107 N5 **Billings** Oklahoma U.S.A.
9 F5 **Billingshurst** England
8 D3 **Billingsley** England
Billiton *see* **Belitung** *isld*
18 H7 **Billom** France
28 A5 **Billum** Denmark
28 C5 **Billund** Denmark
103 M6 **Bill Williams Mt** Arizona U.S.A.
56 G1 **Billyakh Porog** *falls* Russian Federation
22 K5 **Billy-sous-Mangiennes** France
86 B2 **Bilma** Niger
141 K6 **Biloela** Queensland Australia
42 H3 **Bilogora** *dist* Croatia
111 H11 **Biloxi** Mississippi U.S.A.
140 E7 **Bilpamorea Claypan** Queensland Australia
142 C5 **Bilroth,Mt** W Australia Australia
25 D4 **Bilthoven** Netherlands
86 D3 **Biltine** Chad
26 M2 **Bilto** Norway
68 C4 **Bilugyun** *isld* Burma
71 H4 **Bilungala** Sulawesi Indonesia
125 N2 **Bilwascarma** Nicaragua
22 K2 **Bilzen** Belgium
71 J9 **Bima,Teluk** *B* Sumbawa Indonesia
126 E2 **Bimini Is** Bahamas
75 K10 **Bimlipatam** India
71 F5 **Binalbagan** Negros Philippines
77 F1 **Bīnālūd, Kūh-e-** *mts* Iran
21 N6 **Binas** France
70 B3 **Binatang** Sarawak
141 J5 **Binbee** Queensland Australia
13 H6 **Binbrook** England
22 G3 **Binche** Belgium
28 C5 **Bindeballe** Denmark
141 H8 **Bindebango** Queensland Australia
28 D3 **Binderup** Denmark
69 J11 **Bindjai** Indonesia
141 J8 **Bindle** Queensland Australia
118 G8 **Bindloss** Alberta Canada
89 G1 **Bindura** Zimbabwe
17 H3 **Binéfar** Spain
98 H2 **Binford** North Dakota U.S.A.
87 E9 **Binga** Zimbabwe
87 F9 **Binga,Mt** Mozambique/Zimbabwe
141 G8 **Bingara** Queensland Australia
140 B3 **Bing Bong** N Terr Australia
36 D4 **Bingen** Germany
107 M6 **Binger** Oklahoma U.S.A.
9 F2 **Bingham** England
95 S1 **Bingham** Maine U.S.A.
99 V5 **Bingham** Michigan U.S.A.
108 A2 **Bingham** New Mexico U.S.A.
101 N9 **Bingham Canyon** Utah U.S.A.
95 M4 **Binghamton** New York U.S.A.
84 E3 **Bin Ghashīr** Libya
120 K4 **Bingle** Ontario Canada
13 G6 **Bingley** England
Bingmei *see* **Congjiang**
78 H2 **Bingöl** Turkey
78 H2 **Bingol D** Turkey
9 G2 **Binham** England
Binh Dinh *see* **An Nhon**
68 G7 **Binh Minh** Vietnam
68 J5 **Binh Son** Vietnam
20 E4 **Binic** France
69 J11 **Binjai** Indonesia
69 D11 **Binjai** Sumatra
84 F3 **Bin Jawwād** Libya
71 J7 **Binongka** *isld* Indonesia
119 Q8 **Binscarth** Manitoba Canada
144 C5 **Binser, Mt** New Zealand
36 B4 **Binsfeld** Germany
69 G12 **Bintan** *isld* Indonesia
71 H4 **Bintauna** Sulawesi Indonesia
71 E4 **Bintuan** Philippines
70 C3 **Bintulu** Sarawak
71 E4 **Binubusan** Philippines
58 G4 **Bin Xian** China
65 G2 **Bin Xian** China
80 C3 **Binyamina** Israel
67 C5 **Binyang** China
Binzhou *see* **Bin Xian**
131 A6 **Bíobío** *prov* Chile
46 D2 **Bioča** Montenegro Yugoslavia
42 G5 **Biograd** Croatia
85 F8 **Bioko** *isld* Equat Guinea
42 H5 **Biokovo** *mts* Yugoslavia
19 O14 **Biol** France
40 E5 **Biot, le** France
32 G7 **Bippen** Germany
94 B6 **Bippus** Indiana U.S.A.
80 E2 **Biq'at Bet Netofa** Israel
74 F9 **Bir** India
80 D6 **Bira** Jordan
48 L3 **Bîra** Romania
59 K2 **Bira** Russian Federation
84 J5 **Bir Abu Husein** Egypt
84 H4 **Bir Abu Minqar** Egypt
71 E2 **Birac** Philippines
84 G4 **Bi'r adh Dhakar** *well* Libya
84 E4 **Birāk** Libya
59 K2 **Birakan** Russian Federation
80 G1 **Bi'r al 'Ajam** Syria
84 G4 **Bi'r al Ḩarash** *well* Libya
86 D3 **Birao** Cent Afr Republic
66 E3 **Biratar Bulak** *spring* China
75 M5 **Biratnagar** Nepal
77 F7 **Bīr Bālo** Iran
78 G3 **Bi'r Butaymān** Syria
46 F1 **Birca Gingiova** Romania
116 P3 **Birch Cr** Alaska U.S.A.
116 L4 **Birches** Alaska U.S.A.
145 D4 **Birch Hill** New Zealand
119 M5 **Birch Hills** Saskatchewan Canada
119 S6 **Birch I** Manitoba Canada
9 H5 **Birchington** England
48 G5 **Birchiş** Romania
118 F5 **Birch L** Alberta Canada
117 P4 **Birch L** Northwest Territories Canada
118 J5 **Birch L** Saskatchewan Canada
99 P2 **Birch L** Minnesota U.S.A.
117 R7 **Birch Mts** Alberta Canada
117 R6 **Birch R** Alberta Canada
119 Q6 **Birch River** Manitoba Canada
110 E5 **Birch Tree** Missouri U.S.A.
144 A6 **Birchwood** New Zealand
116 N6 **Birchwood** Alaska U.S.A.
99 P4 **Birchwood** Wisconsin U.S.A.
31 N6 **Bircza** Poland
115 K6 **Bird** Manitoba Canada
107 J2 **Bird City** Kansas U.S.A.
89 E9 **Bird I** *lighthouse* S Africa
83 J12 **Bird I** Seychelles
116 H9 **Bird I** Alaska U.S.A.
146 F1 **Bird Island** *U.K. Base* S Georgia S Atlantic Oc
8 D4 **Birdlip** England
123 L6 **Bird Rocks** *lighthouse* Madeleine Is, Quebec Canada
110 K3 **Birdseye** Indiana U.S.A.
140 E7 **Birdsville** Queensland Australia
140 C3 **Birdum** *R* N Terr Australia
85 D3 **Bir ed Deheb** Algeria
85 D3 **Bir el Hadjaj** Algeria
69 C10 **Bireun** Sumatra
79 H10 **Bi'r Fajr** Saudi Arabia
75 L5 **Birganj** Nepal
37 M5 **Birgland** Germany
27 E11 **Biri** Norway
71 G4 **Biri** *isld* Philippines
89 G1 **Biri** *R* Zimbabwe
130 E7 **Birigüi** Brazil
56 D4 **Birikchul'** Russian Federation
79 G3 **Bīrīn** Syria
86 D4 **Birini** Cent Afr Republic
77 F3 **Bīrjand** Iran
28 B6 **Birkelev** Denmark
28 D2 **Birkelse** Denmark
36 F4 **Birkenau** Germany
41 H2 **Birkendorf** Germany
27 C13 **Birkenes** Norway
36 C4 **Birkenfeld** Germany
13 E6 **Birkenhead** England
33 S7 **Birkenwerder** Germany
29 K5 **Birkerød** Denmark
36 B2 **Birkesdorf** Germany
28 G7 **Birket** Denmark
79 A9 **Birket Qârûn** *L* Egypt
38 N7 **Birkfeld** Austria
41 O3 **Birkkar Sp** Austria
28 D7 **Birknack** *C* Germany
138 A2 **Birksgate Ra** South Australia Australia
48 L4 **Bîrlad** *R* Romania
48 L4 **Bîrlad** Romania
79 D7 **Bîr Lahfân** Egypt
85 C3 **Bir Lahlú, Al** Morocco
78 H5 **Bir Meloza** Iraq
119 P8 **Birmingham** Saskatchewan Canada
9 E3 **Birmingham** England
11 C5 **Birmingham** *conurbation* England
111 K8 **Birmingham** Alabama U.S.A.
99 P9 **Birmingham** Iowa U.S.A.
94 D4 **Birmingham** Michigan U.S.A.
84 H5 **Bir Misâha** Egypt
85 B3 **Bir Mogreïn** Mauritania
15 E4 **Birnam** Scotland
101 T4 **Birney** Montana U.S.A.
134 K8 **Birnie I** Phoenix Is Pacific Oc
85 E6 **Birni Ngaouré** Niger
85 F6 **Birnin Gwari** Nigeria
85 E6 **Birnin-Kebbi** Nigeria
85 F6 **Birni n'Konni** Niger
71 D6 **Birong** Palawan Philippines
79 H3 **Bi'r Qutnah** *well* Syria
14 D3 **Birr** Ireland
140 A4 **Birrindudu** N Terr Australia
118 K7 **Birsay** Saskatchewan Canada
55 C3 **Birsk** Russian Federation
13 G6 **Birstal** W Yorks England
36 G3 **Birstein** Germany
55 D5 **Birsuat** Kazakhstan
26 L2 **Birtavarre** Norway
141 G2 **Birthday Mt** Queensland Australia
116 J2 **Birthday Pass** Alaska U.S.A.
13 G4 **Birtley** England
66 E5 **Biru** China
56 E3 **Biryusa** *R* Russian Federation
56 E3 **Biryusinsk** Russian Federation
52 B6 **Biržai** Lithuania
85 C4 **Bir Zreigat** Mauritania
88 C8 **Bisa** Zambia
61 K10 **Bisai** Japan
74 H4 **Bisalpur** India
103 P10 **Bisbee** Arizona U.S.A.
18 C7 **Biscay,B of** France/Spain
113 G12 **Biscayne Nat. Park** Florida U.S.A.
43 G7 **Bisceglie** Italy
37 K4 **Bischberg** Germany
36 H1 **Bischhausen** Germany
36 D6 **Bischheim** France
37 M3 **Bischofsgrün** Germany
37 J3 **Bischofsheim** Germany
38 H7 **Bischofshofen** Austria
31 H4 **Bischofswerda** Germany
19 L4 **Bischwiller** France
112 H2 **Biscoe** North Carolina U.S.A.
146 C4 **Biscoe Is** Antarctica
120 H5 **Biscotasing** Ontario Canada
61 P12 **Bise** Okinawa
45 K4 **Bisenzio** *R* Italy
47 H3 **Biser** Bulgaria
55 C2 **Biser** Russian Federation
52 H5 **Biserovo** Russian Federation
55 C3 **Bisert'** Russian Federation
42 G6 **Biševo** *isld* Croatia
61 P12 **Bise-zaki** *C* Okinawa
67 A5 **Bisezhai** China
67 B2 **Bishan** China
57 G3 **Bishkek** Kirghizia
89 E9 **Bisho** S Africa
102 F4 **Bishop** California U.S.A.
112 D4 **Bishop** Georgia U.S.A.
95 M8 **Bishop** Maryland U.S.A.
109 K8 **Bishop** Texas U.S.A.
146 B16 **Bishop and Clerk Is** *islds* S Pacific Oc
144 A7 **Bishop and Clerks Is** New Zealand
13 G4 **Bishop Auckland** England
12 D2 **Bishopbriggs** Scotland
101 L8 **Bishop Creek Res** Nevada U.S.A.
117 P3 **Bishop L** Northwest Territories Canada
119 M8 **Bishopric** Saskatchewan Canada
9 E7 **Bishop Rock** Isles of Scilly England
8 C3 **Bishops Castle** England
123 R4 **Bishop's Falls** Newfoundland Canada
8 C5 **Bishop's Lydeard** England
9 G4 **Bishop's Stortford** England
9 E3 **Bishops Tachbrook** England
9 E6 **Bishops Waltham** England
112 G3 **Bishopville** South Carolina U.S.A.
80 G3 **Bishra** Jordan
78 G4 **Bishrī, Jabal** *mts* Syria
85 F2 **Biskra** Algeria
31 M2 **Biskupiec** Poland
28 D3 **Bislev** Denmark
9 F5 **Bisley** England
71 G6 **Bislig** Mindanao Philippines
71 G6 **Bislig Bay** Mindanao Philippines
111 C7 **Bismarck** Arkansas U.S.A.
99 T9 **Bismarck** Illinois U.S.A.
110 F4 **Bismarck** Missouri U.S.A.
98 F3 **Bismarck** North Dakota U.S.A.
136 K2 **Bismarck Archipelago** Papua New Guinea
136 J3 **Bismarck Range** Papua New Guinea
136 K2 **Bismarck Sea** Papua New Guinea
33 P7 **Bismark** Germany
78 H3 **Bismil** Turkey
107 N5 **Bison** Oklahoma U.S.A.
98 D4 **Bison** South Dakota U.S.A.
117 P7 **Bison L** Alberta Canada
77 A2 **Bīsotūn** Iran
36 B6 **Bisping** France
32 L6 **Bispingen** Germany
85 A6 **Bissau** Guinea-Bissau
115 K7 **Bissett** Manitoba Canada
37 K6 **Bissingen** Germany
117 O6 **Bistcho L** Alberta Canada
46 F1 **Bistretu** Romania
48 J3 **Bistriţa** Romania
48 K4 **Bistriţa** *R* Romania
48 J3 **Bistriţa Năsăud** *reg* Romania
48 K3 **Bistriţei, Muntii** *mt* Romania
71 E5 **Bisucay** *isld* Philippines
31 M1 **Bisztynek** Poland
86 B5 **Bitam** Gabon
36 B4 **Bitburg** Germany
19 K3 **Bitche** France
80 B8 **Bit'ha** Israel
47 L4 **Bithynia** Turkey
71 B2 **Bitjoli** Halmahera Indonesia
86 C3 **Bitkine** Chad
78 H2 **Bitlis** Turkey
46 E3 **Bitola** Macedonia
43 H7 **Bitonto** Italy
42 H5 **Bitovnja** *mt* Bosnia-Herzegovina
40 F2 **Bitschwiller les Thann** France
8 B5 **Bittadon** England
103 P2 **Bitter Cr** Utah U.S.A.
101 R8 **Bitter Creek** Wyoming U.S.A.
33 Q9 **Bitterfeld** Germany
87 C12 **Bitterfontein** S Africa
84 J3 **Bitter L** Egypt
98 J4 **Bitter L** South Dakota U.S.A.
9 E6 **Bitterne** England
144 C6 **Bitterness, Mt** New Zealand
119 M5 **Bittern L** Saskatchewan Canada
118 D5 **Bittern Lake** Alberta Canada
101 L3 **Bitterroot** *R* Montana U.S.A.
100 K2 **Bitterroot Ra** Mont/Idaho U.S.A.
43 C8 **Bitti** Sardinia
33 P8 **Bittkau** Germany
85 D6 **Bittou** Burkina
71 J4 **Bitung** Sulawesi Indonesia
86 B3 **Biu** Nigeria
48 L3 **Bivolari** Romania
48 K3 **Bivolu** *mt* Romania
59 L4 **Biwa Ko** *L* Japan
110 E4 **Bixby** Missouri U.S.A.
107 P6 **Bixby** Oklahoma U.S.A.
56 C5 **Biya** *R* Russian Federation
86 H3 **Bīye K'obē** Ethiopia
56 C4 **Biysk** Russian Federation
18 G9 **Bize** France
60 H11 **Bizen** Japan
85 G1 **Bizerte** Tunisia
43 C11 **Bizerte, Lac de** Tunisia
80 B6 **Bizzaron** Israel
28 J6 **Bjæverskov** Denmark
27 H13 **BJärka-Säby** Sweden
26 J3 **Bjarköy** Norway
26 K8 **Bjästa** Sweden
48 E7 **Bjelašnica** *mt* Bosnia-Herzegovina
27 C13 **Bjelland** Norway
42 F3 **Bjelo-lasica** *mt* Croatia
42 H3 **Bjelovar** Croatia
28 E1 **Bjergby** Denmark
28 G6 **Bjergby** Denmark
28 G5 **Bjerge** Denmark
28 G5 **Bjergsted** Denmark
27 G11 **Björbo** Sweden
27 A10 **Bjordal** Norway
27 B11 **Bjoreia** *R* Norway
26 D9 **Björgan** Norway
27 E12 **Björkelangen** Norway
26 H5 **Björkfjall** *mt* Sweden
26 N6 **Björkfors** Sweden
26 K3 **Björkliden** Sweden
27 J11 **Björklinge** Sweden
27 K12 **Björkö** Sweden
29 J8 **Björköby** Finland
26 K7 **Björksele** Sweden
26 J8 **Björksele** Sweden
26 K8 **Björna** Sweden
27 M10 **Björneborg** Finland
27 G12 **Björneborg** Sweden
115 L2 **Bjorne Pen** Northwest Territories Canada
27 C11 **Bjornesford** *L* Norway
27 J12 **Björnlunda** Sweden
28 E6 **Bjørnø** *isld* Denmark
147 H13 **Bjørnøya** *isld* Arctic Oc
28 C3 **Bjornsholm Å** *R* Denmark
26 H3 **Björnskinn** Norway
28 E5 **Bjørnsknude** *C* Denmark
27 H13 **Björsäter** Sweden
26 J10 **Bjuråker** Sweden
26 K8 **Bjurholm** Sweden
27 H11 **Bjursås** Sweden
27 G12 **Bjurtjärn** Sweden
26 K7 **Bjurträsk** Sweden
85 C6 **Bla** Mali
28 A5 **Blåbjerg** *hill* Denmark
9 E2 **Blaby** England
42 H5 **Blace** Croatia
19 N12 **Blace** France
122 C3 **Blache,L.de la** Quebec Canada
100 B5 **Blachly** Oregon U.S.A.
111 J8 **Black** *R* Alabama U.S.A.
103 P8 **Black** *R* Arizona U.S.A.
110 F5 **Black** *R* Arkansas U.S.A.
111 E10 **Black** *R* Louisiana U.S.A.
94 E3 **Black** *R* Michigan U.S.A.
111 H11 **Black** *R* Mississippi U.S.A.
110 F4 **Black** *R* Missouri U.S.A.
112 J3 **Black** *R* North Carolina U.S.A.
112 H4 **Black** *R* South Carolina U.S.A.
99 Q5 **Black** *R* Wisconsin U.S.A.
116 R3 **Black** *R* Alaska/Yukon Terr U.S.A./Canada
141 H6 **Blackall** Queensland Australia
144 C5 **Blackball** New Zealand
119 P2 **Black Bay** Ontario Canada
100 B8 **Blackbear** California U.S.A.
119 M3 **Black Bear Island L** Saskatchewan Canada
111 H8 **Black Belt** Miss/Ala U.S.A.
8 D2 **Blackbrook** England
141 F4 **Blackbull** Queensland Australia
13 F6 **Blackburn** England
12 E2 **Blackburn** Scotland
116 Q6 **Blackburn,Mt** Alaska U.S.A.
103 K6 **Black Canyon** Nevada U.S.A.
106 C3 **Black Canyon of the Gunnison Nat.Mon** Colorado U.S.A.
146 D5 **Black Coast** Antarctica
103 P6 **Black Creek** Arizona U.S.A.
99 S5 **Black Creek** Wisconsin U.S.A.
118 C8 **Black Diamond** Alberta Canada
100 C2 **Black Diamond** Washington U.S.A.
117 K9 **Black Dome** *mt* British Columbia Canada
121 O7 **Black Donald Mines** Ontario Canada
141 G3 **Blackdown** Queensland Australia
8 C6 **Blackdown Hills** England
99 M2 **Blackduck** Minnesota U.S.A.
101 O2 **Black Eagle** Montana U.S.A.
94 E9 **Blackey** Kentucky U.S.A.
13 F4 **Black Fell** England
118 G5 **Blackfoot** Alberta Canada
101 N6 **Blackfoot** Idaho U.S.A.
101 O6 **Blackfoot** *R* Idaho U.S.A.
101 N1 **Blackfoot** Montana U.S.A.
12 E1 **Blackford** Scotland
118 J2 **Black Hawk** Ontario Canada
14 B3 **Black Head** Ireland
145 F4 **Black Head** New Zealand
123 T5 **Blackhead B** Newfoundland Canada
139 K5 **Blackheath** New South Wales Australia
138 B4 **Black Hill** South Australia Australia
140 A4 **Black Hills** N Terr Australia
98 C5 **Black Hills** South Dakota U.S.A.
119 V7 **Black I** Manitoba Canada
15 D3 **Black I** Scotland
118 D8 **Blackie** Alberta Canada
116 H8 **Black L** Alaska U.S.A.
111 C9 **Black L** Louisiana U.S.A.
94 C1 **Black L** Michigan U.S.A.
95 M2 **Black L** New York U.S.A.
112 J3 **Black L** North Carolina U.S.A.
121 T6 **Black Lake** Quebec Canada
106 E5 **Black Lake** New Mexico U.S.A.
101 N1 **Blackleaf** Montana U.S.A.
127 P6 **Blackman's** Barbados
103 M6 **Black Mesa** *plateau* Arizona U.S.A.
112 E2 **Black Mountain** North Carolina U.S.A.
140 C2 **Black Mt** N Terr Australia
102 G6 **Black Mt** California U.S.A.
106 B8 **Black Mt** New Mexico U.S.A.
122 E6 **Black Mts** Quebec Canada
103 K6 **Black Mts** Arizona U.S.A.
8 C3 **Black Mts** Wales/England
89 A4 **Black Nossob** *R* Namibia
101 M7 **Black Pine Pk** Idaho U.S.A.
117 N10 **Black Pines** British Columbia Canada
106 B9 **Black Pk** New Mexico U.S.A.
117 N10 **Black Pool** British Columbia Canada
13 E6 **Blackpool** England
83 L13 **Black R** Mauritius
143 B6 **Black Ra** W Australia Australia
106 C8 **Black Range** New Mexico U.S.A.
94 D2 **Black River** Michigan U.S.A.
99 Q5 **Black River Falls** Wisconsin U.S.A.
14 E3 **Blackrock** Ireland
110 E5 **Black Rock** Arkansas U.S.A.
103 M3 **Black Rock** Utah U.S.A.
100 F9 **Black Rock Desert** Nevada U.S.A.
112 F2 **Blacksburg** South Carolina U.S.A.
94 G9 **Blacksburg** Virginia U.S.A.
53 D11 **Black Sea** S E Europe
101 P8 **Blacks Fork** *R* Utah/Wyoming U.S.A.
122 F8 **Blacks Hbr** New Brunswick Canada
112 E6 **Blackshear** Georgia U.S.A.
112 D6 **Blackshear, L** Georgia U.S.A.
14 A2 **Blacksod B** Ireland
106 B8 **Black Springs** New Mexico U.S.A.
27 H14 **Blackstad** Sweden
14 E4 **Blackstairs Mts** Ireland
112 F3 **Blackstock** South Carolina U.S.A.
94 J9 **Blackstone** Virginia U.S.A.
120 B3 **Black Sturgeon L** Ontario Canada
94 G7 **Blacksville** West Virginia U.S.A.
94 H6 **Blackuck** Pennsylvania U.S.A.
122 G7 **Blackville** New Brunswick Canada
112 F4 **Blackville** South Carolina U.S.A.
141 J6 **Blackwater** Queensland Australia
141 G7 **Blackwater** *R* Queensland Australia
14 E3 **Blackwater** *R* Ireland
14 E4 **Blackwater** Ireland
113 C12 **Blackwater** *R* Florida U.S.A.
110 C3 **Blackwater** *R* Missouri U.S.A.
110 D3 **Blackwater** Missouri U.S.A.
12 C3 **Blackwaterfoot** Scotland
117 M3 **Blackwater L** Northwest Territories Canada
9 G4 **Blackwater,R** England
15 D4 **Blackwater Reservoir** Scotland
107 N5 **Blackwell** Oklahoma U.S.A.
108 G3 **Blackwell** Texas U.S.A.
107 M3 **Black Wolf** Kansas U.S.A.
98 E9 **Blackwood Cr** Nebraska U.S.A.
143 B10 **Blackwood, R** W Australia Australia
112 F6 **Bladen** Georgia U.S.A.
98 H9 **Bladen** Nebraska U.S.A.
112 J3 **Bladenboro** North Carolina U.S.A.
118 L7 **Bladworth** Saskatchewan Canada
8 C2 **Blaenau-Ffestiniog** Wales
8 C4 **Blaenavon** Wales
8 B3 **Blaenporth** Wales
8 C4 **Blaen Rhondda** Wales
28 C3 **Blære** Denmark
8 C6 **Blagdon** England
18 F9 **Blagnac** France
53 F10 **Blagodarnyy** Russian Federation
46 F2 **Blagoevgrad** Bulgaria
57 G3 **Blagoveshchenka** Kazakhstan
59 J1 **Blagoveshchensk** Russian Federation
55 C3 **Blagoveshchensk** Bashkirskaya Respublika Russian Federation
52 G3 **Blagoyevo** Russian Federation
28 B5 **Blåhøj** Denmark
20 G7 **Blain** France
94 K6 **Blain** Pennsylvania U.S.A.
107 O2 **Blaine** Kansas U.S.A.
117 M11 **Blaine** Washington U.S.A.
94 H7 **Blaine** West Virginia U.S.A.
118 L6 **Blaine Lake** Saskatchewan Canada
20 G3 **Blainville** France
98 K8 **Blair** Nebraska U.S.A.
107 L7 **Blair** Oklahoma U.S.A.
94 F9 **Blair** West Virginia U.S.A.
99 P5 **Blair** Wisconsin U.S.A.
141 H6 **Blair Athol** Queensland Australia
15 E4 **Blair Atholl** Scotland
15 E4 **Blairgowrie** Scotland
102 G3 **Blair Junction** Nevada U.S.A.
12 D1 **Blairmore** Scotland
102 D2 **Blairsden** California U.S.A.
112 D3 **Blairsville** Georgia U.S.A.
94 H6 **Blairsville** Pennsylvania U.S.A.
21 N4 **Blaise** *R* Eure France
48 H4 **Blaj** Romania
112 C6 **Blakely** Georgia U.S.A.
9 H2 **Blakeney** England
99 S1 **Blake Pt** Michigan U.S.A.
99 O9 **Blakesburg** Iowa U.S.A.
26 K2 **Blåmannen** *mt* Norway
26 H4 **Blåmannsisen** *mt* Norway
36 B6 **Blâmont** France
43 C11 **Blanc** *C* Tunisia
131 E7 **Blanca,B** Argentina
106 G7 **Blanca Cr** New Mex/Tex U.S.A.
131 D7 **Blanca Grande,L** Argentina
133 C8 **Blanca,L** Chile
106 E4 **Blanca Pk** Colorado U.S.A.
106 E8 **Blanca, Sa** *mt* New Mexico U.S.A.
100 J1 **Blanchard** Idaho U.S.A.
94 B3 **Blanchard** Michigan U.S.A.
98 J2 **Blanchard** North Dakota U.S.A.
107 N6 **Blanchard** Oklahoma U.S.A.
120 E2 **Blanche** Ontario Canada
121 P7 **Blanche** Quebec Canada
138 C5 **Blanche,C** South Australia Australia
138 F3 **Blanche,L** South Australia Australia
142 E5 **Blanche, L** W Australia Australia
94 D7 **Blanchester** Ohio U.S.A.
138 E5 **Blanchetown** South Australia Australia
127 O1 **Blanchisseuse** Trinidad
13 F4 **Blanchland** England
21 N8 **Blanc,Le** France
128 F7 **Blanco** *R* Bolivia
128 D5 **Blanco** *R* Peru
106 C5 **Blanco** New Mexico U.S.A.
109 J5 **Blanco** Texas U.S.A.
128 B4 **Blanco,C** Peru
100 A7 **Blanco,C** Oregon U.S.A.
123 P2 **Blanc-Sablon** Quebec Canada
94 F9 **Bland** Virginia U.S.A.
28 S9 **Blanda** *R* Iceland
8 D6 **Blandford** England
103 P4 **Blanding** Utah U.S.A.
99 Q9 **Blandinsville** Illinois U.S.A.
17 J3 **Blanes** Spain
112 G3 **Blaney** South Carolina U.S.A.
99 V3 **Blaney Park** Michigan U.S.A.
69 C11 **Blangkejeren** Sumatra
69 C11 **Blangpidie** Sumatra
21 L3 **Blangy-le-Château** France
21 O2 **Blangy-sur-Bresle** France
22 C3 **Blangy-sur-Ternoise** France
30 H6 **Blanice** *R* Czech Rep
33 P5 **Blankenberg** Germany
22 E1 **Blankenberge** Belgium
33 N9 **Blankenburg** Germany
37 N2 **Blankenhain** Sachsen Germany
37 L2 **Blankenhain** Thüringen Germany
33 O9 **Blankenheim** Germany
36 B3 **Blankenheim** Germany
36 C3 **Blankenrath** Germany
33 S6 **Blankensee** Germany
109 J4 **Blanket** Texas U.S.A.
9 F1 **Blankney** England
31 K6 **Blansko** Czech Rep
87 G9 **Blantyre** Malawi
12 D2 **Blantyre** Scotland
22 F3 **Blaregnies** Belgium
94 J4 **Blasdell** New York U.S.A.
26 G7 **Blåsjön** *L* Sweden
31 L4 **Błaszki** Poland
37 P3 **Blatno** Czech Rep
22 F3 **Blaton** Belgium
26 J6 **Blattnicksele** Sweden
71 H4 **Blau** Sulawesi Indonesia
36 H7 **Blaubeuren** Germany
36 H5 **Blaufelden** Germany
32 J4 **Blauort** *isld* Germany
20 D5 **Blavet** *R* France
13 H6 **Blaxton** England
13 G4 **Blaydon** England
18 E7 **Blaye** France
142 C5 **Blaze,Mt** W Australia Australia
140 B2 **Blaze Pt** N Terr Australia
31 N6 **Błazowa** Poland
33 N6 **Bleckede** Germany
42 F2 **Bled** Slovenia
8 C3 **Bleddfa** Wales
31 J3 **Bledzew** Poland
27 D12 **Blefjell** *mt* Norway
22 E3 **Bleharies** Belgium
36 B3 **Bleialf** Germany
38 L8 **Bleiburg** Austria
33 N10 **Bleicherode** Germany
37 M3 **Bleilochsperre** *res* Germany
27 H15 **Blekinge** *reg* Sweden
99 L8 **Blencoe** Iowa U.S.A.
120 J10 **Blenheim** Ontario Canada
145 D4 **Blenheim** New Zealand
21 M7 **Bléré** France
25 F6 **Blerick** Netherlands
19 J4 **Blesmes** France
109 L7 **Blessing** Texas U.S.A.
14 E3 **Blessington** Ireland
9 E4 **Bletchingdon** England
9 F3 **Bletchley** England
40 B4 **Bletterans** France
121 M6 **Bleu,L** Quebec Canada
111 C8 **Blevins** Arkansas U.S.A.
21 N4 **Blévy** France
119 O9 **Blewett** Saskatchewan Canada
108 G6 **Blewett** Texas U.S.A.
112 H2 **Blewett Falls L** North Carolina U.S.A.
32 J5 **Blexen** Germany
85 E1 **Blida** Algeria
80 F1 **Blida** Lebanon
27 K12 **Blidö** Sweden
27 F14 **Blidsberg** Sweden
36 C5 **Blies** *R* Germany
36 C5 **Blieskastel** Germany
116 O6 **Bligh I** Alaska U.S.A.
38 L5 **Blindenmarkt** Austria
33 T6 **Blindow** Germany
120 G6 **Blind River** Ontario Canada
46 D3 **Blinisht** Albania
138 E4 **Blinman** South Australia Australia
101 L7 **Bliss** Idaho U.S.A.
94 D5 **Blissfield** Michigan U.S.A.
9 F3 **Blisworth** England
70 O10 **Blitar** Java
85 E7 **Blitta** Togo
100 F7 **Blitzen** Oregon U.S.A.
37 O5 **Blížejov** Czech Rep
54 H8 **Bliznyuki** Ukraine
95 Q5 **Block I** Rhode I U.S.A.
117 L10 **Bloedel** British Columbia Canada
25 C4 **Bloemehdaal** Netherlands
89 E7 **Bloemfontein** S Africa
87 E11 **Bloemhof** S Africa
21 N6 **Blois** France
28 D2 **Blokhus** Denmark
25 E3 **Blokzijl** Netherlands
32 K9 **Blomberg** Germany
99 L5 **Blomkest** Minnesota U.S.A.
70 Q10 **Blongas** Indonesia
31 M3 **Błonie** Poland
33 R9 **Blönsdorf** Germany
21 L3 **Blonville** France
140 A6 **Bloods Ra** N Terr Australia
95 L8 **Bloodsworth I** Maryland U.S.A.
14 C1 **Bloody Foreland** Ireland
106 G4 **Bloom** Colorado U.S.A.
99 P4 **Bloomer** Wisconsin U.S.A.
121 N9 **Bloomfield** Ontario Canada
110 K2 **Bloomfield** Indiana U.S.A.
110 D1 **Bloomfield** Iowa U.S.A.
94 B9 **Bloomfield** Kentucky U.S.A.
110 G5 **Bloomfield** Missouri U.S.A.
98 B2 **Bloomfield** Montana U.S.A.
98 J7 **Bloomfield** Nebraska U.S.A.
106 C5 **Bloomfield** New Mexico U.S.A.
95 Q2 **Bloomfield** Vermont U.S.A.
141 H3 **Bloomfield River** Queensland Australia
109 L3 **Blooming Grove** Texas U.S.A.
99 N6 **Blooming Prairie** Minnesota U.S.A.
101 O7 **Bloomington** Idaho U.S.A.
99 S9 **Bloomington** Illinois U.S.A.
110 K2 **Bloomington** Indiana U.S.A.
99 N5 **Bloomington** Minnesota U.S.A.
109 L7 **Bloomington** Texas U.S.A.
99 Q7 **Bloomington** Wisconsin U.S.A.
95 L5 **Bloomsburg** Pennsylvania U.S.A.
141 J5 **Bloomsbury** Queensland Australia
110 F3 **Bloomsdale** Missouri U.S.A.
95 N4 **Bloomville** New York U.S.A.
94 D5 **Bloomville** Ohio U.S.A.
70 N9 **Blora** Java
37 K6 **Blosenau** Germany
95 K5 **Blossburg** Pennsylvania U.S.A.
115 R4 **Blosseville Kyst** *coast* Greenland
109 M2 **Blossom** Texas U.S.A.
51 R2 **Blossom, Mys** *C* Russian Federation
111 L11 **Blountstown** Florida U.S.A.
126 F6 **Blower Rock** Caribbean
112 F1 **Blowing Rock** North Carolina U.S.A.
9 E3 **Bloxham** England
95 M9 **Bloxom** Virginia U.S.A.
13 G6 **Blubberhouses** England
41 L3 **Bludenz** Austria
103 P8 **Blue** *R* Arizona U.S.A.
106 D2 **Blue** *R* Colorado U.S.A.
107 O7 **Blue** *R* Oklahoma U.S.A.
103 N3 **Blue Bell Knoll** *pk* Utah U.S.A.
117 N7 **Blueberry** *R* British Columbia Canada
144 C6 **Blue Cliffs** New Zealand
101 N8 **Blue Creek** Utah U.S.A.
113 G10 **Blue Cypress L** Florida U.S.A.
94 D9 **Blue Diamond** Kentucky U.S.A.
99 M6 **Blue Earth** *R* Minnesota U.S.A.
99 M6 **Blue Earth** Minnesota U.S.A.
110 C5 **Blue Eye** Missouri U.S.A.
94 F9 **Bluefield** W Virginia/Virginia U.S.A.
125 N3 **Bluefields** Nicaragua
110 M3 **Bluegrass Reg** Kentucky U.S.A.
95 T2 **Blue Hill** Maine U.S.A.
98 H9 **Blue Hill** Nebraska U.S.A.
127 H4 **Blue Hills** Turks & Caicos Is
123 O6 **Blue Hills of Couteau** Newfoundland Canada
100 F7 **Bluejoint L** Oregon U.S.A.
94 J6 **Blue Knob** *mt* Pennsylvania U.S.A.
100 B9 **Blue Lake** California U.S.A.
94 K7 **Bluemont** Virginia U.S.A.
110 G2 **Blue Mound** Illinois U.S.A.
121 N8 **Blue Mountain** Ontario Canada
106 B1 **Blue Mountain** Colorado U.S.A.
110 G7 **Blue Mountain** Mississippi U.S.A.
110 B7 **Blue Mt** Arkansas U.S.A.
94 K6 **Blue Mt** Pennsylvania U.S.A.
95 L6 **Blue Mt** Pennsylvania U.S.A.
110 C6 **Blue Mt,L** Arkansas U.S.A.
95 N3 **Blue Mt. Lake** New York U.S.A.
100 H7 **Blue Mt. Pass** Oregon U.S.A.
127 M2 **Blue Mt.Pk** Jamaica
144 B6 **Blue Mts** New Zealand
100 G5 **Blue Mts** Oregon/Wash U.S.A.
139 J5 **Blue Mts Nat Park** New South Wales Australia
127 L2 **Blue Mts, The** Jamaica
140 D2 **Blue Mud B** N Terr Australia
Blue Nile *R see* **Bahr el Azraq**
86 F3 **Blue Nile** *prov* Sudan
114 H4 **Bluenose L** Northwest Territories Canada
117 J6 **Blue R** British Columbia Canada
107 O2 **Blue Rapids** Kansas U.S.A.
118 B4 **Blue Ridge** Alberta Canada
112 C3 **Blue Ridge** Georgia U.S.A.
94 G10 **Blue Ridge** *mts* Virginia U.S.A.
112 C3 **Blue Ridge L** Georgia U.S.A.
117 O9 **Blue River** British Columbia Canada
100 C5 **Blue River** Oregon U.S.A.
121 O6 **Blue Sea Lake** Quebec Canada
14 C2 **Blue Stack Mt** Ireland
106 C6 **Bluewater** New Mexico U.S.A.
144 B7 **Bluff** New Zealand
103 P4 **Bluff** Utah U.S.A.
107 N4 **Bluff City** Kansas U.S.A.
112 E1 **Bluff City** Tennessee U.S.A.
109 J3 **Bluffdale** Texas U.S.A.
141 H4 **Bluff Downs** Queensland Australia
142 F3 **Bluff Face Ra** W Australia Australia
143 C10 **Bluff Knoll** *mt* W Australia Australia
143 A8 **Bluff Pt** W Australia Australia
71 D6 **Bluff Pt** Palawan Philippines
110 F2 **Bluffs** Illinois U.S.A.
126 F2 **Bluff, The** Eleuthera Bahamas
118 C6 **Bluffton** Alberta Canada
110 C7 **Bluffton** Arkansas U.S.A.
112 C6 **Bluffton** Georgia U.S.A.
94 B6 **Bluffton** Indiana U.S.A.
99 L3 **Bluffton** Minnesota U.S.A.
94 D6 **Bluffton** Ohio U.S.A.
112 G5 **Bluffton** South Carolina U.S.A.
109 K3 **Blum** Texas U.S.A.
130 E10 **Blumenau** Brazil
33 O8 **Blumenberg** Germany
33 T5 **Blumenhagen** Germany
118 K8 **Blumenhof** Saskatchewan Canada
32 J6 **Blumenthal** Germany
36 B3 **Blumenthal** Germany
40 G4 **Blümlisalp** *mt* Switzerland
98 G5 **Blunt** South Dakota U.S.A.
100 D7 **Bly** Oregon U.S.A.
89 C9 **Blyde Berg** *mt* S Africa
116 N7 **Blying Sound** Alaska U.S.A.
140 C1 **Blyth** *R* N Terr Australia
120 J9 **Blyth** Ontario Canada
13 G3 **Blyth** England
13 E2 **Blyth Br** Scotland
9 H3 **Blythburgh** England
110 C1 **Blythedale** Missouri U.S.A.
138 A2 **Blythe Ra** W Australia Australia
110 G6 **Blytheville** Arkansas U.S.A.
138 A2 **Blyth Ra** South Australia Australia
13 H6 **Blyton** England
55 G3 **Blyudtsy** Russian Federation
26 G3 **Bø** Norway
27 D12 **Bø** Norway
85 B7 **Bo** Sierra Leone
27 H13 **Bo** Sweden
71 E4 **Boac** *isld* Philippines
125 M3 **Boaco** Nicaragua
130 F7 **Bóa Esperança** Brazil
65 B7 **Bo'ai** China
67 B5 **Bo'ai** China
120 K7 **Boakview** Ontario Canada
86 C4 **Boali** Cent Afr Republic
67 D7 **Bo'ao** China
79 F5 **Boaqline** Lebanon
45 L1 **Boara Polesine** Italy
94 B2 **Boardman** *R* Michigan U.S.A.
141 H7 **Boatman** Queensland Australia
15 E3 **Boat of Garten** Scotland
128 F3 **Boa Vista** Brazil
71 D5 **Boayan** *isld* Palawan Philippines
111 K7 **Boaz** Alabama U.S.A.
68 J1 **Bobai** China
87 H10 **Bobaomby, Tanjona** *C* Madagascar
75 K9 **Bobbili** India
44 F2 **Bobbio** Italy
121 M8 **Bobcaygeon** Ontario Canada
36 E4 **Bobenheim-Roxheim** Germany
37 K7 **Bobingen** Germany
33 O5 **Bobitz** Germany
36 F6 **Böblingen** Germany
85 D6 **Bobo Dioulasso** Burkina
31 K2 **Bobolice** Poland
71 G4 **Bobon** Philippines
128 C4 **Bobonaza** Ecuador
46 F2 **Boboshevo** Bulgaria
46 F2 **Bobov Dol** Bulgaria
31 J4 **Bóbr** *R* Poland
54 D8 **Bobrinets** Ukraine
48 J1 **Bobrka** Ukraine
54 M5 **Bobrov** Russian Federation
54 C6 **Bobrovitsa** Ukraine
31 H4 **Bobrowice** Poland
94 H7 **Bobtown** Pennsylvania U.S.A.
113 F13 **Boca Chica** *isld* Florida U.S.A.
109 K10 **Boca Chica** Texas U.S.A.
127 M10 **Boca del Pao** Venezuela
128 E5 **Bôca do Acre** Brazil
128 E5 **Bôca do Curuquetê** Brazil
129 H4 **Bôca do Jari** Brazil
128 E5 **Bôca do Moaca** Brazil
21 J6 **Bocages** *reg* France
127 N1 **Boca Grande** *chan* Trinidad/Ven
113 E11 **Boca Grande** Florida U.S.A.
113 F13 **Boca Grande Key** *isld* Florida U.S.A.
130 F6 **Bocaina, Parque Nacional de Serra de** Brazil
129 K7 **Bocaiúva** Brazil
130 E9 **Bocaiúva do Sul** Brazil
130 C8 **Bocajá** Brazil
113 G11 **Boca Raton** Florida U.S.A.
127 N1 **Bocas del Dragon** *chan* Trinidad
125 M2 **Bocay** Nicaragua
45 M2 **Bocche del Po Della Pila** Italy
45 M2 **Bocche del Po Delle Tolle** Italy
45 M2 **Bocche del Po di Goro e di Gnocca** Italy
16 E3 **Boceguillas** Spain
19 P16 **Bochaine** *reg* France
121 R3 **Bochart** Quebec Canada
31 M6 **Bochnia** Poland
22 K1 **Bocholt** Belgium
32 E9 **Bocholt** Germany
37 P3 **Bochov** Czech Rep
32 F10 **Bochum** Germany
37 O3 **Bockau** Germany
32 M8 **Bockenem** Germany
32 H6 **Bockhorn** Germany
31 O3 **Boćki** Poland
38 H7 **Böckstein** Austria
33 T10 **Bockwitz** Germany
87 B8 **Bocoio** Angola
127 J10 **Boconó** Venezuela
124 F4 **Bocoyna** Mexico
48 G5 **Bocşa** Romania
86 C5 **Boda** Cent Afr Republic
27 H10 **Boda** Sweden
27 J14 **Böda** Sweden
27 G14 **Bodafors** Sweden
143 C9 **Bodallin** W Australia Australia
51 L3 **Bodaybo** Russian Federation
15 G3 **Boddam** Scotland
99 M7 **Bode** Iowa U.S.A.
102 A3 **Bodega Head** California U.S.A.
86 C2 **Bodele** *dist* Chad
36 F7 **Bodelhausen** Germany
26 M6 **Boden** Sweden
32 L8 **Bodenburg** Germany
36 E4 **Bodenheim** Germany
37 J3 **Bodenlaube** Germany
37 P5 **Bodenmais** Germany
41 K2 **Bodensee** *L* Switzerland
33 N7 **Bodenteich** Germany
32 L9 **Bodenwerder** Germany
38 L6 **Bodenwies** *mt* Austria
37 N5 **Bodenwöhr** Germany
14 C3 **Boderg,L** Ireland
102 F6 **Bodfish** California U.S.A.
74 G9 **Bodhan** India
75 L6 **Bodh Gaya** India
36 G5 **Bödigheim** Germany
20 B4 **Bodilis** France
76 C5 **Bodinayakkanur** India
8 B7 **Bodinnick** England
70 O9 **Bodjonegoro** Java
8 B7 **Bodmin** England
8 B6 **Bodmin Moor** England
118 G6 **Bodo** Alberta Canada
26 G4 **Bodö** Norway
25 C4 **Bodograven** Netherlands
130 C6 **Bodoquena** Brazil
78 A3 **Bodrum** Turkey
26 G9 **Bodsjö** Sweden
68 H7 **Bo Duc** Vietnam
48 F2 **Bodva** *R* Hungary
31 M3 **Bodzanów** Poland
40 D5 **Boëge** France
25 G4 **Boekelo** Netherlands
22 F1 **Boekhoute** Belgium
98 H8 **Boelus** Nebraska U.S.A.
18 H7 **Boën** France
86 D6 **Boende** Zaire
68 G6 **Boeng Lovea** Cambodia
68 G6 **Boeng Me Alpa** Cambodia
70 G7 **Bo Epinang** Sulawesi Indonesia
109 J6 **Boerne** Texas U.S.A.
25 H2 **Boertange** Netherlands
28 G6 **Boeslunde** Denmark
111 E8 **Boeuf** *R* Arkansas U.S.A.
85 B6 **Boffa** Guinea
14 D3 **Bofin,L** Ireland
68 B4 **Bogale** Burma
68 B5 **Bogale** *R* Burma
111 F11 **Bogalusa** Louisiana U.S.A.
85 D6 **Bogande** Burkina
86 C4 **Bogangolo** Cent Afr Republic
141 H6 **Bogantungan** Queensland Australia
17 F6 **Bogarra** Spain
118 B8 **Bogart,Mt** Alberta Canada
109 M2 **Bogata** Texas U.S.A.
53 H7 **Bogatoye** Russian Federation
31 H5 **Bogatynia** Poland
86 C5 **Bogbonga** Zaire
55 D3 **Bogdanovich** Russian Federation
66 D3 **Bogda Shan** *mts* China
27 K14 **Boge** *isld* Gotland Sweden
55 F4 **Bogembay** Kazakhstan
37 O6 **Bogen** Germany
87 C11 **Bogenfels** Namibia
28 E5 **Bogense** Denmark
14 C4 **Boggeragh Mts** Ireland
143 C6 **Boggola** *mt* W Australia Australia
26 H8 **Boggsjö** Sweden
85 B5 **Boghé** Mauritania
141 J5 **Bogie** *R* Queensland Australia
9 F6 **Bognor Regis** England
22 H4 **Bogny-sur-Meuse** France
28 J7 **Bogø** Denmark
71 F5 **Bogo** Cebu Philippines
54 G6 **Bogodukhov** Ukraine
70 L9 **Bogor** Java
48 J2 **Bogorodchany** Ukraine
59 M1 **Bogorodskoy** Russian Federation
128 D3 **Bogotá** Colombia
111 A8 **Bogota** Texas U.S.A.
56 C3 **Bogotol** Russian Federation
56 F5 **Bogotol** Russian Federation
75 N6 **Bogra** Bangladesh
27 L12 **Bogskär** *lighthouse* Finland
56 E2 **Boguchany** Russian Federation
54 M7 **Boguchar** Russian Federation
107 L2 **Bogue** Kansas U.S.A.
111 F10 **Bogue Chitto** Mississippi U.S.A.
112 K3 **Bogue Inlet** North Carolina U.S.A.
54 B2 **Bogushevsk** Belarus
54 B7 **Boguslav** Ukraine
31 J5 **Boguszów** Poland
127 L2 **Bog Walk** Jamaica
70 D4 **Boh** *R* Kalimantan
65 D5 **Bo Hai** *G* China
22 E4 **Bohain** France
65 D5 **Bohai Wan** *B* China
119 M8 **Boharm** Saskatchewan Canada
38 N5 **Böheimkirchen** Austria
30 H6 **Bohemia** *old region* Czech Rep
142 F4 **Bohemia Downs** W Australia Australia

85 E7 **Bohicon** Benin
42 F2 **Bohiniska Bistrica** Slovenia
37 N1 **Böhlen** Germany
32 K7 **Böhme** Germany
37 N4 **Böhmer Wald** *mts* Germany
32 H8 **Bohmte** Germany
33 Q7 **Böhne** Germany
71 G6 **Bohol** *isld* Philippines
71 F6 **Bohol Str** Philippines
16 D5 **Bohonal de Ibor** Spain
48 D4 **Böhönye** Hungary
65 A2 **Böhöt** Mongolia
80 B8 **Bohu** Israel
128 F4 **Boiaçu** Brazil
43 F7 **Boiano** Italy
122 F7 **Boiestown** New Brunswick Canada
21 P5 **Boigneville** France
122 B5 **Boileau** Quebec Canada
130 C9 **Boi Preto,Serra de** *mts* Brazil
130 F8 **Boi, Pta. do** *C* Brazil
129 J7 **Bois** *R* Brazil
94 C1 **Bois Blanc I** Michigan U.S.A.
123 M7 **Boisdale** C Breton I, Nova Scotia
40 D4 **Bois d' Amont** France
20 G8 **Bois-de-Cené** France
18 H5 **Bois du Roi** *mt* France
100 J6 **Boise** Idaho U.S.A.
106 H5 **Boise City** Oklahoma U.S.A.
20 F5 **Boisgervilly** France
21 N3 **Bois Guillaume** France
114 G4 **Bois, Lac Des** *L* Northwest Territories Canada
Bois-le-Duc *see* **'s-Hertogenbosch**
21 K8 **Boismé** France
18 H7 **Bois Noirs** *hills* France
22 H1 **Boisschot** Belgium
119 R9 **Boissevain** Manitoba Canada
21 M4 **Boissy-les-Perche** France
21 M5 **Boissy-Maugis** France
38 F9 **Boite** *R* Italy
130 F8 **Boituva** Brazil
33 T6 **Boitzenburg** Germany
33 N6 **Boize** *R* Germany
33 N6 **Boizenburg** Germany
46 C3 **Bojana** *R* Albania
28 E6 **Bøjden** Denmark
71 E1 **Bojeador,C** Luzon Philippines
77 E1 **Bojnūrd** Iran
69 D13 **Bojo** *isld* Indonesia
70 K9 **Bojong** Java
48 F5 **Boka** Serbia Yugoslavia
42 J6 **Boka Kotorska** *B* Montenegro Yugoslavia
85 F7 **Bokani** Nigeria
70 G4 **Bokat** Sulawesi
85 B6 **Boké** Guinea
113 E11 **Bokeelia** Florida U.S.A.
32 J6 **Bokel** Germany
32 K8 **Bokeloh** Germany
56 F4 **Bokhan** Russian Federation
68 H6 **Bo Kheo** Cambodia
89 A8 **Bokkeveld Berg** *mt* S Africa
27 A12 **Boknfjorden** *inlet* Norway
56 B6 **Boko** Kazakhstan
57 H4 **Bokonbayevskoye** Kirghizia
86 C3 **Bokoro** Chad
107 Q6 **Bokoshe** Oklahoma U.S.A.
86 D6 **Bokote** Zaire
59 H2 **Bo-ko-tu** China
68 D7 **Bokpyin** Burma
86 D6 **Bokungu** Zaire
68 C5 **Bok Ye-gan** *isld* Burma
70 G5 **Bolaäng** Sulawesi Indonesia
86 D6 **Bolaiti** Zaire
85 A6 **Bolama** Guinea-Bissau
124 H7 **Bolaños** Mexico
67 C5 **Bolao** China
21 L2 **Bolbec** France
55 E2 **Bolchary** Russian Federation
99 M9 **Bolckow** Missouri U.S.A.
48 E4 **Bölcske** Hungary
33 T5 **Boldekow** Germany
28 C6 **Bolderslev** Denmark
48 K5 **Boldeşti-Scăeni** Romania
66 C3 **Bole** China
85 D7 **Bole** Ghana
101 N2 **Bole** Montana U.S.A.
48 H1 **Bolekhov** Ukraine
86 D6 **Boleko** Zaire
100 J4 **Boles** Idaho U.S.A.
31 J4 **Bolesławiec** Poland
107 O6 **Boley** Oklahoma U.S.A.
85 D6 **Bolgatanga** Ghana
121 O4 **Bolger** Quebec Canada
48 M5 **Bolgrad** Ukraine
59 K2 **Boli** China
86 C6 **Bolia** Zaire
26 L7 **Boliden** Sweden
111 H9 **Boligee** Alabama U.S.A.
71 D2 **Bolinao,C** Luzon Philippines
48 K6 **Bolintin Vale** Romania
71 H4 **Boliohutu,Gunung** *mt* Sulawesi Indonesia
131 E6 **Bolivár** Argentina
128 D2 **Bolívar** *div* Colombia
128 C3 **Bolivar** Colombia
128 C4 **Bolivar** *prov* Ecuador
110 C4 **Bolivar** Missouri U.S.A.
94 J4 **Bolivar** New York U.S.A.
110 H6 **Bolivar** Tennessee U.S.A.
128 E2 **Bolivar** *state* Venezuela
128 F2 **Bolivar,Cerro** *mt* Venezuela
109 N6 **Bolivar Pen** Texas U.S.A.
127 J10 **Bolivar, Pico** *mt* Venezuela
128 E7 **Bolivia** *rep* S America
112 J3 **Bolivia** North Carolina U.S.A.
46 E1 **Boljevac** Serbia Yugoslavia
78 E3 **Bolkar Dağları** *mts* Turkey
27 D12 **Bolkesjö** Norway
120 G4 **Bolkow** Ontario Canada
31 J5 **Bolków** Poland
36 H6 **Boll** Germany
41 H2 **Boll** Germany
27 F14 **Bollebygd** Sweden
45 K4 **Bolle,Le** Italy
36 B4 **Bollendorf** Germany
19 N16 **Bollène** France
40 G4 **Bolligen** Switzerland
28 B5 **Bølling** Denmark
8 D1 **Bollington** England
27 H10 **Bollnäs** Sweden
141 H8 **Bollon** Queensland Australia
27 G15 **Bolmen** *L* Sweden
9 F6 **Bolney** England
71 F5 **Bolo** Panay Philippines
86 C6 **Bolobo** Zaire
71 E7 **Bolod Islands** Philippines
42 D4 **Bologna** Italy
19 J4 **Bologne** France
52 D6 **Bologovo** Russian Federation
54 J2 **Bolokhovo** Russian Federation
86 C5 **Bolomba** Zaire
86 D6 **Bolombo** Zaire
59 L2 **Bolon'** Russian Federation
125 P7 **Bolonchén de Rejón** Mexico
71 F7 **Bolong** Mindanao Philippines
59 L2 **Bolon,Oz** *L* Russian Federation
71 F1 **Bolos Pt** Luzon Philippines
43 B8 **Bolotana** Sardinia
56 B3 **Bolotnoye** Russian Federation
68 H5 **Bolovens, Plateau des** Laos
131 C2 **Bolsa,Cerro** *pk* Argentina
42 D6 **Bolsena,L.di** Italy
31 N1 **Bol'shakovo** Russian Federation
54 F9 **Bolshaya Belozerka** Ukraine
55 F3 **Bol'shaya Tava** *R* Russian Federation
52 F3 **Bol'shaya Tavra** Russian Federation
56 G1 **Bol'shaya Yerema** *R* Russian Federation
55 F3 **Bol'sherech'ye** Russian Federation
51 P3 **Bol'sheretsk** Russian Federation
55 C3 **Bolshe-ustikinskoye** Russian Federation
54 B4 **Bol'shevik** Belarus
51 K1 **Bol'shevik, Ostrov** *isld* Russian Federation
55 F3 **Bolshiye Uki** Russian Federation
56 B1 **Bolshoi Megtyg'yegan** *R* Russian Federation
48 J1 **Bol'shovtsy** Ukraine
55 E1 **Bol'shoy Atlym** Russian Federation
55 F1 **Bol'shoy Balyk** *R* Russian Federation
147 P10 **Bol'shoy Begichev,Os** *isld* Russian Federation
56 H2 **Bol'shoy Chuya** *R* Russian Federation
55 E3 **Bol'shoye Sorokino** Russian Federation
55 G4 **Bol'shoye Topol'noye, Oz** *L* Russian Federation
55 G4 **Bol'shoye Yaravoye, Oz** *L* Russian Federation
55 E1 **Bol'shoy Kamen'** Russian Federation
55 F2 **Bol'shoy Kun'yak** Russian Federation
55 D3 **Bol'shoy Kuyash** Russian Federation
51 O1 **Bolshoy Lyakhovskiy,Ostrov** *isld* Russian Federation
56 D2 **Bol'shoy Pit** *R* Russian Federation
55 F1 **Bolshoy Salym** *R* Russian Federation
59 L1 **Bol'shoy Shantar,Oz** *isld* Russian Federation
55 E1 **Bol'shoy Tap** *R* Russian Federation
52 C5 **Bol'shoy Tyuters, Os.** *isld* Estonia
55 F3 **Bol'shoy Uvat, Oz** *L* Russian Federation
56 D5 **Bolshoy Yenisey** *R* Russian Federation
55 F2 **Bol'shoy Yugan** *R* Russian Federation
124 G4 **Bolsón de Mapimí** *desert* Mexico
25 E2 **Bolsward** Netherlands
17 H2 **Boltaña** Spain
8 C7 **Bolt Head** England
121 L9 **Bolton** Ontario Canada
13 F6 **Bolton** England
112 J3 **Bolton** North Carolina U.S.A.
13 G6 **Bolton Br** England
119 W4 **Bolton L** Manitoba Canada
13 F5 **Bolton le-Sands** England
78 C1 **Bolu** Turkey
66 E4 **Boluntay** China
14 A5 **Bolus Hd** Ireland
54 F3 **Bolva** *R* Russian Federation
47 L6 **Bolvadin** Turkey
78 C2 **Bolvadin** Turkey
8 B6 **Bolventor** England
48 E5 **Bóly** Hungary
47 H2 **Bolyarovo** Bulgaria
42 D2 **Bolzano** Italy
86 B7 **Boma** Zaire
22 K3 **Bomal** Luxembourg/Belgium
86 B5 **Bomandjokou** Congo
109 H2 **Bomarton** Texas U.S.A.
86 C5 **Bomassa** Congo
74 E9 **Bombay** India
145 E2 **Bombay** New Zealand
87 H11 **Bombetoka,B.de** Madagascar
86 F5 **Bombo** Uganda
86 C5 **Bomboma** Zaire
130 H10 **Bom Conselho** Brazil
129 J7 **Bom Despacho** Brazil
66 E6 **Bomi** China
85 B7 **Bomi Hills** Liberia
130 J9 **Bom Jardim** Brazil
130 D5 **Bom Jardim de Goiás** Brazil
128 E5 **Bom Jardin** Brazil
129 K5 **Bom Jesus** Brazil
129 K5 **Bom Jesus da Gurgueia, Serra** *mts* Brazil
129 K6 **Bom Jesus da Lapa** Brazil
130 H7 **Bom Jesus do Itabapoana** Brazil
130 H7 **Bom Jesus do Norte** Brazil
27 A12 **Bömlafjorden** *inlet* Norway
27 A12 **Bömlo** Norway
86 E5 **Bomokandi** *R* Zaire
86 C5 **Bomongo** Zaire
143 B7 **Bompas Hill** W Australia Australia
130 E10 **Bom Retiro** Brazil
130 G7 **Bom Sucesso** Brazil
118 D5 **Bon Accord** Alberta Canada
94 K9 **Bon Air** Virginia U.S.A.
126 A3 **Bonaire** *isld* Neth Antilles
127 K9 **Bonaire Trench** Caribbean
116 R6 **Bona,Mt** Alaska U.S.A.
69 D12 **Bonandolok** Sumatra
139 J6 **Bonang** Victoria Australia
125 M3 **Bonanza** Nicaragua
106 D3 **Bonanza** Colorado U.S.A.
100 D7 **Bonanza** Oregon U.S.A.
106 A1 **Bonanza** Utah U.S.A.
127 J5 **Bonao** Dominican Rep
99 P9 **Bonaparte** Iowa U.S.A.
142 E2 **Bonaparte Arch** W Australia Australia
100 F1 **Bonaparte,Mt** Washington U.S.A.
15 D3 **Bonar Bridge** Scotland
121 N8 **Bonarlaw** Ontario Canada
116 G5 **Bonasila Dome** *mt* Alaska U.S.A.
127 N3 **Bonasse** Trinidad
44 G3 **Bonassola** Italy
122 G5 **Bonaventure** Quebec Canada
122 H5 **Bonaventure I** Quebec Canada
123 T5 **Bonavista** Newfoundland Canada
40 C3 **Bonboillon** France
138 D4 **Bon Bon** South Australia Australia
85 G1 **Bon,C** Tunisia
106 F4 **Boncarbo** Colorado U.S.A.
21 O5 **Bonce** France
13 F3 **Bonchester Br** Scotland
9 E6 **Bonchurch** England
101 T10 **Bond** Colorado U.S.A.
86 B6 **Bonda** Gabon
28 C7 **Bonden Au** *R* Germany
45 K2 **Bondeno** Italy
86 D5 **Bondo** Zaire
71 F4 **Bondoc Penin** Luzon Philippines
71 F4 **Bondoc Pt** Luzon Philippines
71 H9 **Bondokodi** Sumbawa Indonesia
36 F6 **Bondorf** Germany
85 D7 **Bondoukou** Ivory Coast
70 O9 **Bondowoso** Java
126 F2 **Bonds Cay** *isld* Bahamas
144 C5 **Bonds Peak** *mt* New Zealand
99 S5 **Bonduel** Wisconsin U.S.A.
101 P6 **Bondurant** Wyoming U.S.A.
101 O6 **Bone** Idaho U.S.A.
70 G6 **Bonebone** Sulawesi
113 L9 **Bonefish Pond** New Providence I Bahamas
71 H7 **Bonelipu** Indonesia
70 G7 **Bonelowe** Indonesia
68 G4 **Boneng** Laos
71 K8 **Boneogeh** Indonesia
71 K8 **Bonerate** *isld* Indonesia
71 K8 **Bonerate** Indonesia
26 K3 **Bones** Norway
15 E5 **Boness** Scotland
98 H6 **Bonesteel** South Dakota U.S.A.
131 C2 **Bonete,Cerro** *pk* Argentina
70 G7 **Bone, Teluk** *B* Sulawesi Indonesia
98 C1 **Bonetraill** North Dakota U.S.A.
121 L6 **Bonfield** Ontario Canada
71 E4 **Bongabong** Philippines
86 D5 **Bongandanga** Zaire
70 F2 **Bongao** Philippines
70 M9 **Bongkok** *mt* Java
71 G7 **Bongo** *isld* Mindanao Philippines
86 C3 **Bongor** Chad
68 J5 **Bong Son** Vietnam
109 L2 **Bonham** Texas U.S.A.
118 L1 **Bonheur** Ontario Canada
12 D2 **Bonhill** Scotland
36 C7 **Bonhomme, Col du** *pass* France
43 B7 **Bonifacio,Str.of** Corsica/Sardinia
111 L11 **Bonifay** Florida U.S.A.
Bonin Is *see* **Ogasawara-shoto**
103 P9 **Bonita** Arizona U.S.A.
111 E9 **Bonita** Louisiana U.S.A.
113 F11 **Bonita Springs** Florida U.S.A.
130 C7 **Bonito** Brazil
69 E13 **Bonjol** Sumatra
36 C2 **Bonn** Germany
18 G6 **Bonnat** France
19 Q12 **Bonne** France
19 P15 **Bonne** *R* France
123 P4 **Bonne Bay** Newfoundland Canada
21 L3 **Bonnebosq** France
22 G3 **Bonne Esperance** Belgium
123 P2 **Bonne Espérance** Quebec Canada
21 P4 **Bonnelles** France
20 G5 **Bonnemain** France
101 M3 **Bonner** Montana U.S.A.
140 D1 **Bonner Mt** N Terr Australia
100 J1 **Bonners Ferry** Idaho U.S.A.
110 B2 **Bonner Springs** Kansas U.S.A.
28 A3 **Bonnet** Denmark
21 L5 **Bonnétable** France
110 F4 **Bonne Terre** Missouri U.S.A.
21 P2 **Bonneuil-les-Eaux** France
21 M8 **Bonneuil-Matours** France
21 N5 **Bonneval** Eure-et-Loir France
40 F7 **Bonneval-sur-Arc** France
40 D4 **Bonnevaux** France
19 Q12 **Bonneville** France
100 D4 **Bonneville** Oregon U.S.A.
101 R6 **Bonneville** Wyoming U.S.A.
21 N3 **Bonneville,la** France
101 N7 **Bonneville Pk** Idaho U.S.A.
101 L9 **Bonneville Salt Flats** Utah/Nev U.S.A.
138 F6 **Bonney,L** South Australia Australia
140 C5 **Bonney Well** N Terr Australia
21 P1 **Bonnières** Pas-de-Calais France
21 O3 **Bonnières** Seine-et-Oise France
143 C9 **Bonnie Rock** W Australia Australia
19 O17 **Bonnieux** France
36 G5 **Bönnigheim** Germany
36 H3 **Bonnland** Germany
18 G5 **Bonny** France
85 F8 **Bonny** Nigeria
Bonny, Bight of *see* **Biafra, Bight of**
106 H2 **Bonny Res** Colorado U.S.A.
122 F8 **Bonny River** New Brunswick Canada
118 G4 **Bonnyville** Alberta Canada
20 E6 **Bono** France
43 C8 **Bono** Sardinia
110 F6 **Bono** Arkansas U.S.A.
71 C6 **Bonobond** Palawan Philippines
60 D14 **Bōno-misaki** *C* Japan
68 H7 **Bonom Mhai** *mt* Vietnam
43 B8 **Bonorva** Sardinia
21 M8 **Bonres** France
111 J11 **Bon Secour** Alabama U.S.A.
70 E4 **Bontang** Kalimantan
89 A9 **Bonteberg** *mts* S Africa
85 B7 **Bonthe** Sierra Leone
71 E2 **Bontoc** Luzon Philippines
71 K8 **Bontomatane** Indonesia
70 G7 **Bontosunggu** Sulawesi
109 O5 **Bon Wier** Texas U.S.A.
48 E4 **Bonyhád** Hungary
143 G6 **Bonython Ra** N Terr/W Aust Australia
141 F1 **Booby I** Queensland Australia
113 K12 **Booby I** Bahamas
127 M3 **Booby South Pt** Jamaica
36 D7 **Boofzheim** France
138 C4 **Bookabie** South Australia Australia
143 A8 **Bookara** W Australia Australia
103 P2 **Book Cliffs** Utah U.S.A.
108 D7 **Booker** Texas U.S.A.
94 H9 **Booker T. Washington Nat Mon** Virginia U.S.A.
85 C7 **Boola** Guinea
142 B6 **Boolaloo** W Australia Australia
143 A6 **Boolathanna** W Australia Australia
138 E5 **Booleroo Centre** South Australia Australia
143 A6 **Boologooro** W Australia Australia
22 G1 **Boom** Belgium
94 B2 **Boon** Michigan U.S.A.
141 L8 **Boonah** Queensland Australia
106 F3 **Boone** Colorado U.S.A.
99 N7 **Boone** Iowa U.S.A.
112 F1 **Boone** North Carolina U.S.A.
94 H9 **Boones Mill** Virginia U.S.A.
110 C6 **Booneville** Arkansas U.S.A.
110 N4 **Booneville** Kentucky U.S.A.
110 H7 **Booneville** Mississippi U.S.A.
94 D9 **Booneville Res** Kentucky U.S.A.
141 H6 **Boongoondoo** Queensland Australia
127 P4 **Boon Pt** Antigua W Indies
94 K7 **Boonsboro** Maryland U.S.A.
58 C2 **Bööntsagaan Nuur** *L* Mongolia
102 A2 **Boonville** California U.S.A.
110 J3 **Boonville** Indiana U.S.A.
110 D3 **Boonville** Missouri U.S.A.
95 M3 **Boonville** New York U.S.A.
71 B3 **Boo,Pulau Pulau** *islds* W Irian
143 D9 **Boorabbin** W Australia Australia
86 H4 **Boorama** Somalia
21 N3 **Boos** France
Boosaaso *see* **Bender Qaasim**
13 E5 **Boot** England
147 E3 **Boothia, Gulf of** Northwest Territories Canada
115 K3 **Boothia Pen** Northwest Territories Canada
111 J8 **Boothton** Alabama U.S.A.
13 E5 **Bootle** England
13 F6 **Bootle** England
37 J6 **Bopfingen** Germany
65 C6 **Boping** China
36 D3 **Boppard** Germany
Boputhatswana *see* **North West, Orange Free State**
20 E5 **Boqueho** France
129 K6 **Boqueirão, Serra do** *mts* Brazil
128 F8 **Boquerón** *dept* Paraguay
108 E6 **Boquillas** Texas U.S.A.
108 E6 **Boquillas del Carmen** Mexico
37 O4 **Bor** Czech Rep
86 E4 **Bo R** Sudan
27 G14 **Bor** Sweden
78 E3 **Bor** Turkey
48 G6 **Bor** Serbia Yugoslavia
135 M10 **Bora-Bora** *isld* Society Is Pacific Oc
101 M5 **Borah Pk** Idaho U.S.A.
27 F14 **Borås** Sweden
77 B5 **Borāzjān** Iran
128 G4 **Borba** Brazil
28 B4 **Borbjerg** Denmark
71 G5 **Borbon** Cebu Philippines
130 H9 **Borborema, Planalto da** *plateau* Brazil
48 K3 **Borca** Romania
48 L6 **Borcea** *R* Romania
146 C12 **Borchgrevink Coast** *coast* Antarctica
78 H1 **Borçka** Turkey
25 G4 **Borculo** Netherlands
138 D6 **Borda,C** South Australia Australia
47 K7 **Bor Dağı** *mt* Turkey
18 E8 **Bordeaux** France
98 B8 **Bordeaux** Wyoming U.S.A.
57 G5 **Bordëbë** Kirghizia
143 C10 **Borden** W Australia Australia
122 J7 **Borden** Prince Edward I Canada
118 K6 **Borden** Saskatchewan Canada
114 H2 **Borden I** Northwest Territories Canada
115 L3 **Borden Pen** Northwest Territories Canada
95 N6 **Bordentown** New Jersey U.S.A.
15 F5 **Borders** *reg* Scotland
138 F6 **Bordertown** South Australia Australia
32 M4 **Bordesholm** Germany
28 S9 **Bordheyri** Iceland
44 C4 **Bordighera** Italy
85 D3 **Bordj Flye Ste Marie** Algeria
85 F2 **Bordj Messaouda** Algeria
85 E4 **Bordj Mokhtar** Algeria
85 F3 **Bordj Omar Driss** Algeria
6 F1 **Borðoy** *isld* Faeroes
57 H4 **Bordunskiy** Kirghizia
85 D5 **Boré** Mali
143 D8 **Boreas,Mt** W Australia Australia
31 K4 **Borek** Poland
Borgå *see* **Porvoo**
28 S9 **Borgarnes** Iceland
44 C1 **Bórgaro Torinese** Italy
26 G3 **Borge** Norway
26 G6 **Börgefjell** *mt* Norway
32 K9 **Borgentreich** Germany
32 G7 **Börger** Germany
25 G3 **Borger** Netherlands
108 C8 **Borger** Texas U.S.A.
32 K9 **Borgholz** Germany
32 H8 **Borgholzhausen** Germany
32 F8 **Borghorst** Germany
43 H10 **Borgia** Italy
22 J2 **Borgloon** Belgium
28 D2 **Børglum** Denmark
40 G5 **Borgne** *R* Switzerland
41 O5 **Borgo** Italy
45 J4 **Borgo a Mozzano** Italy
45 J1 **Borgoforte** Italy
44 E1 **Borgolavezzaro** Italy
45 N6 **Borgo Montello** Italy
44 F1 **Borgonovo Val Tidone** Italy
45 M4 **Borgo Pace** Italy
45 K2 **Borgo Panigale** Italy
45 O5 **Borgorose** Italy
42 D5 **Borgo S. Lorenzo** Italy
41 J6 **Borgoticino** Italy
44 G3 **Borgo Val di Taro** Italy
42 D2 **Borgo Valsugana** Italy
41 H7 **Borgo Vercelli** Italy
26 H9 **Borgsjö** Sweden
27 F14 **Borgstena** Sweden
12 D4 **Borgue** Scotland
26 B9 **Borgund** Norway
27 C10 **Borgund** Norway
26 H8 **Borgvattnet** Sweden
98 B8 **Borie** Wyoming U.S.A.
68 F3 **Borikhane** Laos
31 O6 **Borinya** Ukraine
26 S2 **Boris Gleb** Russian Federation
31 O6 **Borislav** Ukraine
57 E3 **Borisovka** Kazakhstan
55 F4 **Borisovskoye** Russian Federation
54 B6 **Borispol** Ukraine
87 H11 **Boriziny** Madagascar
130 C9 **Borja** Paraguay
17 F3 **Borja** Spain
42 H4 **Borja Planina** Bosnia-Herzegovina
17 H3 **Borjas Blancas** Spain
26 M6 **Börjelslandet** Sweden
32 F9 **Bork** Germany
32 E9 **Borken** Germany
36 G1 **Borken** Germany
54 H7 **Borki** Ukraine
28 D5 **Børkop** Denmark
86 C2 **Borkou** *dist* Chad
52 C6 **Borkovichi** Belarus
32 E5 **Borkum** Germany
27 H11 **Borlänge** Sweden
47 J6 **Borlu** Turkey
44 D3 **Bormida di Millésimo** *R* Italy
44 D3 **Bormida di Spigno** *R* Italy
42 C2 **Bormio** Italy
37 O1 **Borna** Germany
25 E2 **Borndiep** Netherlands
25 G4 **Borne** Netherlands
70 B4 **Borneo** *isld* E Indies
16 C3 **Bornes** *mt* Portugal
36 B2 **Bornheim** Germany
27 H16 **Bornholm** *isld* Denmark
27 G16 **Bornholmsgattet** *str* Sweden/Denmark
32 M4 **Bornhöved** Germany
33 R7 **Börnicke** Germany
33 R8 **Bornim** Germany
86 B3 **Borno** *prov* Nigeria
16 D8 **Bornos, Embalse de** *res* Spain
86 E4 **Boro** *R* Sudan
48 K3 **Boroaia** Romania
70 M9 **Borobudur** *ruins* Java
71 E5 **Borocay** *isld* Panay Philippines
51 N2 **Borogontsy** Russian Federation
57 L3 **Borohoro Shan** *mt ra* China
71 H4 **Boroko** Sulawesi Indonesia
85 D6 **Boromo** Burkina
102 G6 **Boron** California U.S.A.
141 K6 **Bororen** Queensland Australia
13 G5 **Boroughbridge** England
56 B5 **Borovlyanka** Russian Federation
55 F4 **Borovoye** Kazakhstan
54 H1 **Borovsk** Russian Federation
55 E3 **Borovskiy** Russian Federation
55 D4 **Borovskoy** Kazakhstan
27 G16 **Borrby** Sweden
29 K6 **Borre** Denmark
33 R5 **Borrenthin** Germany
138 E5 **Borrika** South Australia Australia
28 B5 **Borris** Denmark
14 E4 **Borris** Ireland
14 D4 **Borrisoleigh** Ireland
140 D3 **Borroloola** N Terr Australia
27 J13 **Börrum** Sweden
48 J3 **Borşa** Romania
58 G1 **Borsch Chovochnyy Khrebet** *mt* Russian Federation
33 R10 **Borsdorf** Germany
48 K4 **Borsec** Romania
26 P1 **Börselv** Norway
48 H2 **Borshava** *R* Ukraine
48 K2 **Borshchev** Ukraine
48 F2 **Borsod-Abaúj Zemplén** Hungary
25 A6 **Borssele** Netherlands
33 N8 **Börssum** Germany
29 K5 **Borstahusen** Sweden
32 J7 **Borstel** Germany
57 K3 **Bortala He** *R* China
8 B3 **Borth** Wales
18 G7 **Bort-les-Orgues** France
26 G9 **Börtnan** Sweden
58 F1 **Borto** Russian Federation
77 B4 **Borūjen** Iran
77 A3 **Borūjerd** Iran
28 E4 **Borum** Denmark
28 H5 **Borup** Denmark
98 K2 **Borup** Minnesota U.S.A.
56 D4 **Borus,Khrebet** *mts* Russian Federation
31 K2 **Bory Tucholskie** *forest* Poland
31 M5 **Borzęcin** Poland
78 J1 **Borzhomi** Georgia
54 D5 **Borzna** Ukraine
58 G1 **Borzya** *R* Russian Federation
58 G1 **Borzya** Russian Federation
57 G1 **Bosaginskiy** Kazakhstan
48 E5 **Bosanski Brod** Croatia
42 G4 **Bosanski Petrovac** Bosnia-Herzegovina
33 M4 **Bosau** Germany
8 B6 **Boscastle** England
95 Q3 **Boscawen** New Hampshire U.S.A.
45 K1 **Boschi Santa Anna** Italy
21 N2 **Bosc-le-Hard** France
99 Q6 **Boscobel** Wisconsin U.S.A.
9 E6 **Boscombe** England
45 Q8 **Boscotrecase** Italy
67 B5 **Bose** China
38 K7 **Bosenstein,Gross** *mt* Austria
65 D6 **Boshan** China
89 D7 **Boshof** S Africa
77 E3 **Boshruyeh** Iran
46 E2 **Bosilegrad** Serbia Yugoslavia
27 G12 **Bosjön** Sweden
25 C4 **Boskoop** Netherlands
98 A8 **Bosler** Wyoming U.S.A.
8 D1 **Bosley** England
42 H4 **Bosna** *R* Bosnia-Herzegovina
Bosna i Hercegovina *see* **Bosnia-Herzegovina**
42 H4 **Bosnia-Herzegovina** *rep* S Europe
86 C5 **Bosobolo** Zaire
61 O10 **Bōsō-hantō** *pen* Japan
32 G10 **Bösperde** Germany
Bosporus *str see* **Karadeniz Boğazı** *str*
106 D7 **Bosque** New Mexico U.S.A.
124 G2 **Bosque Bonito** Mexico
86 C4 **Bossambélé** Cent Afr Republic
86 C4 **Bossangoa** Cent Afr Republic
86 C4 **Bossemtele** Cent Afr Republic
111 C9 **Bossier City** Louisiana U.S.A.
87 C9 **Bossiesvlei** Namibia
86 B3 **Bosso** Niger
66 D3 **Bosten Hu** *L* China
9 F2 **Boston** England
113 D7 **Boston** Georgia U.S.A.
95 Q4 **Boston** Massachusetts U.S.A.
97 **Boston** *conurbation* Massachusetts U.S.A.
117 N11 **Boston Bar** British Columbia Canada
127 M2 **Boston Bay** Jamaica
138 D5 **Boston I** South Australia Australia
110 C6 **Boston Mts** Arkansas U.S.A.
13 G6 **Boston Spa** England
28 F6 **Bøstrup** Fyn Denmark
28 D4 **Bøstrup** Viborg Denmark
48 E5 **Bosut** *R* Croatia
123 O5 **Boswarlos** Newfoundland Canada
117 P11 **Boswell** British Columbia Canada
99 T9 **Boswell** Indiana U.S.A.
107 P7 **Boswell** Oklahoma U.S.A.
94 H6 **Boswell** Pennsylvania U.S.A.
110 C2 **Bosworth** Missouri U.S.A.
74 D7 **Botad** India
139 K5 **Botany B** New South Wales Australia
26 J8 **Boteå** Sweden
46 G2 **Botev** *mt* Bulgaria
46 F2 **Botevgrad** Bulgaria
118 E6 **Botha** Alberta Canada
9 F1 **Bothamsall** England
87 E11 **Bothaville** S Africa
13 E4 **Bothel** England
117 M12 **Bothell** Washington U.S.A.
26 L8 **Bothnia,Gulf of** Sweden/Finland
139 H8 **Bothwell** Tasmania Australia
120 J10 **Bothwell** Ontario Canada
12 D2 **Bothwell** Scotland
16 B3 **Boticas** Portugal
87 D10 **Botlete** *R* Botswana
9 E6 **Botley** England
48 M4 **Botna** *R* Moldova
28 H7 **Bøtø** Denmark
71 D3 **Botolan Pt** Luzon Philippines
48 K3 **Botoşani** Romania
65 C5 **Botou** China
68 H4 **Bo Trach** Vietnam
22 L3 **Botrange** *mt* Belgium
26 L7 **Botsmark** Sweden
89 C4 **Botswana** *rep* Africa
43 G9 **Botte Donato** *mt* Italy
89 A8 **Botter Kloof Pass** S Africa
89 B8 **Bottersleegte** S Africa
9 F2 **Bottesford** England
98 F1 **Bottineau** North Dakota U.S.A.
9 G3 **Bottisham** England
127 N6 **Bottom** Saba W Indies
9 E1 **Bottom House** England
45 M1 **Bottrighe** Italy
32 E9 **Bottrop** Germany
46 F1 **Botunya** *R* Bulgaria
123 R4 **Botwood** Newfoundland Canada
85 C7 **Bouaflé** Ivory Coast
21 N3 **Bouafles** France
16 D9 **Bou Ahmed** Morocco
85 D7 **Bouaké** Ivory Coast
86 C4 **Bouala** Cent Afr Republic
86 C4 **Bouar** Cent Afr Republic
85 D2 **Bouârfa** Morocco
43 A12 **Bouati Mahmoud** Algeria
20 G7 **Bouaye** France
30 H6 **Boubín** *mt* Czech Rep
86 C4 **Bouca** Cent Afr Republic
18 D9 **Boucau** France
140 C1 **Boucaut B** N Terr Australia
21 K4 **Boucé** Orne France
22 E3 **Bouchain** France
21 L7 **Bouchard, l'Île** France
22 D4 **Bouchavesnes** France
43 B12 **Bouchegouf** Algeria
123 N2 **Boucher,L** Quebec Canada
19 N17 **Bouches-du-Rhône** *dept* France
121 P6 **Bouchette** Quebec Canada
22 D4 **Bouchoir** France
85 D2 **Boudenib** Morocco
16 E9 **Boudinar** Morocco
85 D5 **Bou Djébéha** Mali
40 A2 **Boudreville** France
40 E4 **Boudry** Switzerland
20 G7 **Bouée** France
21 O8 **Bouesse** France
20 H5 **Bouexière, la** France
122 E3 **Bouffard,L** Quebec Canada
83 K14 **Bœuf, Nez de** *pk* Réunion
137 M3 **Bougainville** *isld* Papua New Guinea
142 F2 **Bougainville, C** W Australia Australia
141 H3 **Bougainville Reef** Gt Barrier Reef Aust
71 C2 **Bougainville,Selat** W Irian
85 F1 **Bougaroun,C** Algeria
21 O7 **Bouges le-Château** France
Bougie *see* **Bejaïa**
85 C6 **Bougouni** Mali
43 C11 **Bouhairet Benzart** *G* Tunisia
17 G9 **Bou Hanifa** Algeria
17 G9 **Bou Hanifa, Barrage de** Algeria
127 M4 **Bouillante** Guadeloupe W Indies
21 M3 **Bouille,la** France
21 K7 **Bouillé Loretz** France
21 J6 **Bouillé-Ménard** France
22 J4 **Bouillon** Belgium
20 G8 **Bouin** France
85 C3 **Bou Izakam** Morocco
85 B3 **Boujdour** Western Sahara
85 B3 **Boukra** Western Sahara
123 L3 **Boulain,L** Quebec Canada
19 K3 **Boulay** France
143 D9 **Boulder** W Australia Australia
98 A9 **Boulder** Colorado U.S.A.
101 N3 **Boulder** Montana U.S.A.
103 N4 **Boulder** Utah U.S.A.
101 Q7 **Boulder** Wyoming U.S.A.
103 K5 **Boulder Can** Nevada U.S.A.
103 K6 **Boulder City** Nevada U.S.A.
102 B4 **Boulder Cr** California U.S.A.
100 J7 **Boulder Cr** Idaho U.S.A.
121 N5 **Bouleau, L. au** Quebec Canada
102 H9 **Boulevard** California U.S.A.
140 E6 **Boulia** Queensland Australia
20 H8 **Boulogne** *R* France
22 B2 **Boulogne** France
21 P4 **Boulogne-Billancourt** France
21 M6 **Bouloire** France
85 C5 **Boulouli** Mali
85 D6 **Boulsa** Burkina
22 H5 **Boult-aux-Bois** France
85 G6 **Boultoum** Niger
22 H4 **Boulzicourt** France
86 C5 **Boumba** *R* Cameroon
85 D7 **Bouna** Ivory Coast
117 C3 **Boundary** Alaska U.S.A.
102 F4 **Boundary Pk** Nevada U.S.A.
118 J9 **Boundary Plateau** Mont/Sask U.S.A./Canada
85 C7 **Boundiali** Ivory Coast
68 H6 **Boung Long** Cambodia
68 E2 **Boun Neua** Laos
106 E4 **Bountiful** Colorado U.S.A.
140 E3 **Bountiful Is** Queensland Australia
118 K7 **Bounty** Saskatchewan Canada
21 J8 **Boupère, le** France
21 P1 **Bouquemaison** France
110 E3 **Bourbeuse** *R* Missouri U.S.A.
94 A5 **Bourbon** Indiana U.S.A.
110 E3 **Bourbon** Missouri U.S.A.
83 L14 **Bourbon,C** Kerguelen Indian Oc
18 H6 **Bourbon-Lancy** France
18 H6 **Bourbon l'Archambault** France
18 H6 **Bourbonnais** *prov* France
40 C2 **Bourbonne les Bains** France
18 G7 **Bourboule,la** France
19 J5 **Bourboune les Bassigny** France
22 C2 **Bourbourg** France
19 O13 **Bourbre** *R* France
20 D5 **Bourbriac** France
19 O15 **Bourdeaux** France
36 B6 **Bourdonnay** France
16 E10 **Boured** Morocco
85 D5 **Bourem** Mali
18 E7 **Bourg** Gironde France
18 G7 **Bourganeuf** France
21 M3 **Bourg-Archard** France
18 H7 **Bourg Argental** France
19 Q15 **Bourg d'Arud** France
19 O14 **Bourg-de-Péage** France
20 G6 **Bourg-des-Comptes** France
21 M2 **Bourg Dun** France
19 O12 **Bourg-en-Bresse** France
21 P7 **Bourges** France
22 F5 **Bourg et Comin** France
40 C6 **Bourget,L.du** France
21 P4 **Bourget,le** Paris France
18 G10 **Bourg-Madame** France
21 K6 **Bourg-Neuf** France
20 F7 **Bourgneuf,B.de** France
21 J7 **Bourgneuf-en-Mauges** France
20 G7 **Bourgneuf-en-Retz** France
21 J5 **Bourgneuf,le** France
22 G5 **Bourgogne** France
19 O13 **Bourgoin** France
40 E6 **Bourg-St-Maurice** France
21 M3 **Bourgtheroulde-Infreville** France
21 K3 **Bourguébus** France
21 L7 **Bourgueil** France
120 K4 **Bourkes** Ontario Canada
121 N4 **Bourlamaque** Quebec Canada
22 E3 **Bourlon** France
121 P4 **Bourmont** Quebec Canada
40 C1 **Bourmont** France
21 M7 **Bournan** France
21 L7 **Bournand** France
9 F2 **Bourne** England
115 K1 **Bourne,C** Northwest Territories Canada
9 F4 **Bourne End** England
9 E6 **Bournemouth** England
21 M3 **Bourneville** France
21 H8 **Bournezeau** France
18 E8 **Bourriot Bergonce** France
32 F7 **Bourtanger Moor** Germany
21 M4 **Bourth** France
22 B2 **Bourthes** France
86 D3 **Bourtoutou** Chad
22 L4 **Bous** Luxembourg
85 E1 **Bou Saâda** Algeria
43 B12 **Bou Salem** Tunisia
103 K8 **Bouse** Arizona U.S.A.
103 K8 **Bouse Wash** *R* Arizona U.S.A.
36 B5 **Bous/Saar** Germany
18 G6 **Boussac** France
20 G4 **Boussac,la** France
21 H7 **Boussay** France
22 L5 **Bousse** France
86 C3 **Bousso** Chad
43 B12 **Bouteldja** Algeria
21 P5 **Boutigny** France
85 B5 **Boutilimit** Mauritania
18 E6 **Boutonne** *R* France
143 B10 **Bouvard,C** W Australia Australia
19 O13 **Bouvesse** France
90 J14 **Bouvet I** S Atlantic Oc
81 A12 **Bouvetøy** *isld* S Atlantic Oc
20 G7 **Bouvron** France
36 C6 **Bouxwiller** France
85 F6 **Bouza** Niger
21 O8 **Bouzanne** *R* France
36 B5 **Bouzonville** France
28 C7 **Bov** Denmark
43 G11 **Bova** Italy
32 L9 **Bovenden** Germany
70 C4 **Boven Kapuas** *mts* Sarawak
28 F6 **Bovense** Denmark
26 C10 **Böverdal** Norway
21 P2 **Boves** France
44 C3 **Boves** Italy
8 C6 **Bovey Tracey** England
22 K3 **Bovigny** Belgium
100 J3 **Bovill** Idaho U.S.A.
43 G7 **Bovino** Italy
28 A4 **Bøvlingbjerg** Denmark
45 L1 **Bovolenta** Italy
45 K1 **Bovolone** Italy
8 C6 **Bow** England
98 D1 **Bowbells** North Dakota U.S.A.
127 M3 **Bowden** Jamaica
113 F7 **Bowden** Florida U.S.A.
98 G4 **Bowdle** South Dakota U.S.A.
101 S1 **Bowdoin,L** Montana U.S.A.
112 B4 **Bowdon** Georgia U.S.A.
98 G2 **Bowdon** North Dakota U.S.A.
143 B10 **Bowelling** W Australia Australia
141 J5 **Bowen** *R* Queensland Australia
141 J5 **Bowen** Queensland Australia
110 E1 **Bowen** Illinois U.S.A.
141 H5 **Bowen Downs** Queensland Australia
117 M11 **Bowen I** British Columbia Canada
140 B1 **Bowen Str** N Terr Australia
95 M7 **Bowers** Delaware U.S.A.
94 D7 **Bowersville** Ohio U.S.A.
101 L5 **Bowery Pk** Idaho U.S.A.
13 F5 **Bowes** England
143 B8 **Bowgada** W Australia Australia
141 H5 **Bowie** Queensland Australia
103 P9 **Bowie** Arizona U.S.A.
106 C3 **Bowie** Colorado U.S.A.
109 K2 **Bowie** Texas U.S.A.
118 F9 **Bow Island** Alberta Canada
78 L3 **Bowkan** Iran
12 D2 **Bowling** Scotland
113 F10 **Bowling Green** Florida U.S.A.
110 J2 **Bowling Green** Indiana U.S.A.
110 K4 **Bowling Green** Kentucky U.S.A.
110 E2 **Bowling Green** Missouri U.S.A.
94 D5 **Bowling Green** Ohio U.S.A.
95 K8 **Bowling Green** Virginia U.S.A.
141 H4 **Bowling Green,C** Queensland Australia
112 D3 **Bowman** Georgia U.S.A.
98 C3 **Bowman** North Dakota U.S.A.
146 H14 **Bowman I** Antarctica
146 D6 **Bowman Peninsula** *pen* Antarctica
121 M9 **Bowmanville** Ontario Canada
15 B5 **Bowmore** Scotland
118 C7 **Bowness** Alberta Canada
13 F5 **Bowness** England
118 C7 **Bow R** Alberta Canada
142 G3 **Bow River** W Australia Australia
117 N9 **Bowron Lake Prov. Park** British Columbia Canada
117 J7 **Bowser L** British Columbia Canada
119 Q6 **Bowsman** Manitoba Canada
118 B7 **Bow Valley Prov. Park** Alberta Canada
36 H5 **Boxberg** Germany
98 C7 **Box Butte Res** Nebraska U.S.A.
98 A6 **Box Cr** Wyoming U.S.A.
101 P1 **Box Elder** Montana U.S.A.
98 C5 **Box Elder** South Dakota U.S.A.
106 F2 **Box Elder Cr** Colorado U.S.A.
98 B4 **Boxelder Cr** Montana U.S.A.
101 R2 **Boxelder Cr** Montana U.S.A.
9 F5 **Box Hill** England
27 H13 **Boxholm** Sweden
58 G5 **Bo Xian** China
65 D6 **Boxing** China
25 E5 **Boxmeer** Netherlands
25 D5 **Boxtel** Netherlands
78 E1 **Boyabat** Turkey
128 D2 **Boyacá** *div* Colombia
47 K3 **Boyalık** Turkey
58 G6 **Boyang** China
143 B10 **Boyanup** W Australia Australia
111 D10 **Boyce** Louisiana U.S.A.
94 J7 **Boyce** Virginia U.S.A.
143 D8 **Boyce,Mt** W Australia Australia
46 F1 **Boychinovtsi** Bulgaria
119 V3 **Boyd** Manitoba Canada
101 Q4 **Boyd** Montana U.S.A.
109 K2 **Boyd** Texas U.S.A.
123 S4 **Boyd's Cove** Newfoundland Canada
94 J10 **Boydton** Virginia U.S.A.
65 C5 **Boye** China
99 L7 **Boyer** *R* Iowa U.S.A.
99 L7 **Boyer** Iowa U.S.A.
77 B4 **Boyer Ahmadī va Kohkīlūyeh** *prov* Iran
106 G3 **Boyero** Colorado U.S.A.
95 M6 **Boyertown** Pennsylvania U.S.A.
98 A4 **Boyes** Montana U.S.A.
95 K10 **Boykins** Virginia U.S.A.
118 E4 **Boyle** Alberta Canada
14 C3 **Boyle** Ireland
111 F8 **Boyle** Mississippi U.S.A.
123 L8 **Boylston** Nova Scotia Canada
141 K6 **Boyne** *R* Queensland Australia
14 E3 **Boyne** *R* Ireland
94 C1 **Boyne City** Michigan U.S.A.
94 C1 **Boyne Falls** Michigan U.S.A.
21 P5 **Boynes** France
110 C1 **Boynton** Missouri U.S.A.
107 P6 **Boynton** Oklahoma U.S.A.
113 G11 **Boynton Beach** Florida U.S.A.
86 E5 **Boyoma Falls** Zaire
101 R6 **Boysen Res** Wyoming U.S.A.
143 B10 **Boyup Brook** W Australia Australia
47 J8 **Bozburun** Turkey
47 H5 **Bozcaada** *isld* Turkey
47 L5 **Boz Dağ** *mt* Turkey
79 G2 **Bozdağ** *mt* Turkey
47 J6 **Boz Dağları** *mts* Turkey
47 J7 **Bozdoğan** Turkey
101 P4 **Bozeman** Montana U.S.A.
Bozen *see* **Bolzano**
86 C5 **Bozene** Zaire
31 K1 **Boże Pole** Poland
65 C5 **Bozhen** China
37 O3 **Boží Dar** Czech Rep
78 D3 **Bozkır** Turkey
54 F1 **Boznya** Russian Federation
78 G3 **Bozova** Turkey
48 G6 **Bozovici** Romania
55 F5 **Bozshakol'** Kazakhstan
45 J1 **Bozzolo** Italy
138 A4 **BP Travellers Village** South Australia Australia
44 C2 **Bra** Italy
22 G2 **Brabançonne** *prov* Belgium
22 G2 **Brabant** *prov* Belgium
146 C4 **Brabant I** Antarctica
119 O2 **Brabant L** Saskatchewan Canada
28 E4 **Brabrand** Denmark
28 H6 **Bråby** Denmark
42 H5 **Brač** *isld* Croatia
15 B3 **Bracadale** Scotland
129 H6 **Braça Menor** *R* Brazil
44 M5 **Bracciano** Italy
42 E6 **Bracciano,Lago di** Italy
44 M5 **Bracciano, Lago di** Italy
121 L7 **Bracebridge** Ontario Canada
21 O6 **Bracieux** France
26 H9 **Bräcke** Sweden
118 J9 **Bracken** Saskatchewan Canada
109 J6 **Bracken** Texas U.S.A.
36 G5 **Brackenheim** Germany
13 G6 **Brackenhill** England
119 S5 **Bracken L** Manitoba Canada
108 G6 **Brackettville** Texas U.S.A.
9 E3 **Brackley** England
9 F5 **Bracknell** England
32 J9 **Brackwede** Germany
12 E1 **Braco** Scotland
43 G8 **Bradano** *R* Italy
98 F3 **Braddock** North Dakota U.S.A.
94 H6 **Braddock** Pennsylvania U.S.A.
99 L9 **Braddyville** Iowa U.S.A.
113 E10 **Bradenton** Florida U.S.A.
113 E10 **Bradenton Beach** Florida U.S.A.
28 B7 **Braderup** Germany
121 L8 **Bradford** Ontario Canada
8 D5 **Bradford** England
13 G6 **Bradford** England
110 E6 **Bradford** Arkansas U.S.A.

99 R8 **Bradford** Illinois U.S.A.
99 N7 **Bradford** Iowa U.S.A.
95 T1 **Bradford** Maine U.S.A.
95 P3 **Bradford** New Hampshire U.S.A.
94 C6 **Bradford** Ohio U.S.A.
94 J5 **Bradford** Pennsylvania U.S.A.
95 Q5 **Bradford** Rhode I U.S.A.
94 B9 **Bradfordsville** Kentucky U.S.A.
111 C8 **Bradley** Arkansas U.S.A.
102 D6 **Bradley** California U.S.A.
99 T8 **Bradley** Illinois U.S.A.
107 N7 **Bradley** Oklahoma U.S.A.
110 D5 **Bradleyville** Missouri U.S.A.
94 D5 **Bradner** Ohio U.S.A.
123 P2 **Bradore Bay** Quebec Canada
123 P2 **Bradore Hills** Quebec Canada
140 B3 **Bradshaw** N Terr Australia
98 J9 **Bradshaw** Nebraska U.S.A.
142 F3 **Bradshaw,Mt** W Australia Australia
119 R9 **Bradwardine** Manitoba Canada
118 L7 **Bradwell** Saskatchewan Canada
9 G4 **Bradwell** England
98 F8 **Brady** Nebraska U.S.A.
109 H4 **Brady** Texas U.S.A.
117 E6 **Brady Glacier** Alaska U.S.A.
138 C3 **Brady,Mt** South Australia Australia
28 D5 **Brædstrup** Denmark
138 E5 **Braemar** South Australia Australia
15 E3 **Braemar** Scotland
15 E3 **Braeriach** mt Scotland
16 B3 **Braga** Portugal
131 E5 **Bragado** Argentina
129 J4 **Bragança** Brazil
16 C3 **Bragança** Portugal
130 F8 **Bragança Paulista** Brazil
112 E6 **Braganza** Georgia U.S.A.
110 G5 **Bragg City** Missouri U.S.A.
118 C7 **Bragg Creek Prov. Park** Alberta Canada
54 B5 **Bragin** Belarus
99 N4 **Braham** Minnesota U.S.A.
33 N6 **Brahlstorf** Mecklenburg-Vorpommern Germany
75 O7 **Brahmanbaria** Bangladesh
75 L9 **Brahmapur** India
75 P5 **Brahmaputra** R S Asia
32 L4 **Brahmsee** L Germany
77 K5 **Brahui,Cen** reg Pakistan
99 S8 **Braidwood** Illinois U.S.A.
48 L5 **Brăila** Romania
9 E2 **Brailsford** England
98 J8 **Brainard** Nebraska U.S.A.
22 F5 **Braine** France
22 G2 **Braine L'Alleud** Belgium
22 G2 **Braine-le Château** Belgium
22 G2 **Braine-le Comte** Belgium
99 M3 **Brainerd** Minnesota U.S.A.
21 L7 **Brain-sur-Allonnes** France
9 G4 **Braintree** England
13 E4 **Braithwaite** England
111 G12 **Braithwaite** Louisiana U.S.A.
140 C1 **Braithwaite Pt** N Terr Australia
22 J2 **Braives** Belgium
89 F4 **Brak** R S Africa
32 H6 **Brake** Germany
22 F2 **Brakel** Belgium
32 K9 **Brakel** Germany
85 B5 **Brakna** reg Mauritania
57 D1 **Brali** Kazakhstan
117 M10 **Bralorne** British Columbia Canada
107 N5 **Braman** Oklahoma U.S.A.
Brambach see **Radiumbad-Brambach**
38 F7 **Bramberg** Austria
13 G6 **Bramham** England
32 H6 **Bramloge** Germany
28 B6 **Bramming** Denmark
44 B3 **Bram,Monte** Italy
26 J9 **Brämö** isld Sweden
9 H3 **Brampton** England
98 J3 **Brampton** North Dakota U.S.A.
141 J5 **Brampton I** Queensland Australia
32 G8 **Bramsche** Germany
141 G1 **Bramwell** Queensland Australia
94 F9 **Bramwell** West Virginia U.S.A.
9 G2 **Brancaster** England
13 G4 **Brancepeth** England
123 T7 **Branch** Newfoundland Canada
99 U6 **Branch** Michigan U.S.A.
95 K4 **Branchport** New York U.S.A.
112 G4 **Branchville** South Carolina U.S.A.
130 B7 **Branco** R Mato Grosso Brazil
128 F3 **Branco** R Roraima Brazil
130 J9 **Branco,Cabo** Brazil
131 B2 **Branco,R** Argentina
41 L3 **Brand** Austria
37 O3 **Brand** Czech Rep
87 B10 **Brandberg** mt Namibia
26 H9 **Brändbo** Sweden
28 C5 **Brande** Denmark
32 L5 **Brande-Hörnerkirchen** Germany
101 T4 **Brandenberg** Montana U.S.A.
33 R7 **Brandenburg** land Germany
33 R8 **Brandenburg** Germany
110 K4 **Brandenburg** Kentucky U.S.A.
37 P2 **Brand-Erbisdorf** Germany
28 C6 **Branderup** Denmark
13 H6 **Brandesburton** England
89 E7 **Brandfort** S Africa
33 R10 **Brandis** Germany
29 J11 **Brändö** Finland
119 S9 **Brandon** Manitoba Canada
9 G3 **Brandon** England
106 H3 **Brandon** Colorado U.S.A.
98 E9 **Brandon** Nebraska U.S.A.
95 O3 **Brandon** Vermont U.S.A.
99 S6 **Brandon** Wisconsin U.S.A.
14 A4 **Brandon B** Ireland
14 A4 **Brandon Hd** Ireland
14 E4 **Brandon Hill** mt Ireland
14 A4 **Brandon Mt** Ireland
95 N3 **Brandreth** New York U.S.A.
13 G5 **Brandsby** England
133 F5 **Brandsen** Argentina
28 D6 **Brandsø** isld Denmark
110 E5 **Brandsville** Missouri U.S.A.
98 K5 **Brandt** South Dakota U.S.A.
27 F11 **Brandval** Norway
87 D12 **Brandvlei** S Africa
94 K8 **Brandy** Virginia U.S.A.
95 L8 **Brandywine** Maryland U.S.A.
48 K6 **Brăneşti** Romania
95 P5 **Branford** Connecticut U.S.A.
113 E8 **Branford** Florida U.S.A.
27 L17 **Braniewo** Poland
31 M1 **Braniewo** Poland
31 M6 **Branisko** mts Slovakia
18 E8 **Branne** France
102 A2 **Branscomb** California U.S.A.
146 C3 **Bransfield Str** Antarctica
106 G4 **Branson** Colorado U.S.A.
110 C5 **Branson** Missouri U.S.A.
9 F1 **Branston** England
118 D8 **Brant** Alberta Canada
70 O9 **Brantas** Java
70 O10 **Brantas** R Java
120 K9 **Brantford** Ontario Canada
98 H2 **Brantford** North Dakota U.S.A.
111 K10 **Brantley** Alabama U.S.A.
18 F7 **Brantôme** France
138 F7 **Branxholme** Victoria Australia
123 M8 **Bras d'or L** Nova Scotia Canada
99 O9 **Brashear** Missouri U.S.A.
128 E6 **Brasiléia** Brazil
129 J7 **Brasília** Brazil
129 G4 **Brasilia Legal** Brazil
52 C6 **Braslav** Belarus
48 K5 **Brasov** Romania
20 C5 **Brasparts** France
85 F8 **Brass** Nigeria
22 G1 **Brasschaat** Belgium
140 C6 **Brassey Mt** N Terr Australia
143 D6 **Brassey Ra** W Australia Australia
70 E2 **Brassey Ra** mts Sabah
139 G5 **Brassi** New South Wales Australia
28 D4 **Brassø** L Denmark
95 R1 **Brassua L** Maine U.S.A.
48 H4 **Bratca** Romania
48 L5 **Brates, L** Romania
46 G1 **Brateş, Lacul** L Romania
31 K7 **Bratislava** Slovakia
46 G3 **Bratsigovo** Bulgaria
56 F3 **Bratsk** Russian Federation
56 F3 **Bratskoye Vodokhranilishche** res Russian Federation
48 M2 **Bratslav** Ukraine
26 K7 **Bratten** Sweden
95 P4 **Brattleboro** Vermont U.S.A.
32 M8 **Brau** Germany
36 D3 **Braubach** Germany
36 G2 **Brauerschwend** Germany
38 H5 **Braunau** Austria
36 E3 **Braunfels** Germany
33 N9 **Braunlage** Germany
33 P10 **Braunsbedra** Germany
Braunsberg see **Braniewo** Poland
33 N8 **Braunschweig** Germany
8 B5 **Braunton** England
36 B2 **Brauweiler** Germany
131 D4 **Brava, L. la** Argentina
94 G7 **Brave** Pennsylvania U.S.A.
27 H13 **Bråviken** L Sweden
131 D2 **Bravo,Sa** mt Argentina
14 E3 **Bray** Ireland
22 D1 **Bray-Dunes** France
22 E5 **Braye** France
21 M6 **Braye,R** France
21 O3 **Bray-et-Lû** France
8 C5 **Brayford** England
14 A5 **Bray Hd** Ireland
115 M4 **Bray I** Northwest Territories Canada
110 C2 **Braymer** Missouri U.S.A.
18 H4 **Bray sur Seine** France
22 D4 **Bray-sur-Somme** France
118 A6 **Brazeau** Alberta Canada
118 B6 **Brazeau Dam** Alberta Canada
128 F6 **Brazil** rep S America
110 J2 **Brazil** Indiana U.S.A.
90 G11 **Brazil Basin** Atlantic Oc
109 M6 **Brazoria** Texas U.S.A.
109 L4 **Brazos** R Texas U.S.A.
86 C6 **Brazzaville** Congo
48 E6 **Brčko** Bosnia-Herzegovina
31 K2 **Brda** R Poland
48 D1 **Brdo** mt Czech Rep
140 E6 **Breadalbane** Queensland Australia
143 E7 **Breaden Bluff** hill W Australia Australia
143 F7 **Breaden,L** W Australia Australia
141 K1 **Breakfast Creek** dist Brisbane, Qnsld Australia
144 A6 **Breaksea I** New Zealand
144 B7 **Breaksea Is** New Zealand
141 L6 **Breaksea Spit** Queensland Australia
20 G5 **Bréal-sous-Montfort** France
8 D4 **Bream** England
6 N4 **Bream** oil rig North Sea
145 E1 **Bream Bay** New Zealand
27 F15 **Breared** Sweden
21 L2 **Bréaute** France
111 E11 **Breaux Bridge** Louisiana U.S.A.
48 K5 **Breaza** Romania
70 M9 **Brebes** Java
70 M9 **Brebes,Tg** C Java
121 U4 **Brébeuf, L** Quebec Canada
122 B5 **Brébeuf,L** Quebec Canada
21 H4 **Brécey** France
20 E6 **Brech** France
36 E3 **Brechen** Germany
121 L8 **Brechin** Ontario Canada
15 F4 **Brechin** Scotland
20 F3 **Brechou** isld Channel Is English Chan
22 H1 **Brecht** Belgium
106 D2 **Breckenridge** Colorado U.S.A.
98 K3 **Breckenridge** Minnesota U.S.A.
110 C2 **Breckenridge** Missouri U.S.A.
109 J3 **Breckenridge** Texas U.S.A.
133 C8 **Brecknock, Pen** Chile
31 K7 **Břeclav** Czech Rep
8 C4 **Brecon** Wales
8 C4 **Brecon Beacons** mts Wales
25 C5 **Breda** Netherlands
99 M7 **Breda** Iowa U.S.A.
26 M6 **Bredåker** Sweden
27 H15 **Bredåkra** Sweden
27 G14 **Bredaryd** Sweden
87 D12 **Bredasdorp** S Africa
33 Q7 **Breddin** Germany
32 K6 **Breddorf** Germany
28 B6 **Brede** Denmark
9 G6 **Brede** England
28 B6 **Brede Å** R Denmark
28 B6 **Bredebro** Denmark
32 J10 **Bredelar** Germany
22 E1 **Bredene** Belgium
33 R5 **Bredenfelde** Germany
119 P8 **Bredenyur** Saskatchewan Canada
33 S6 **Bredereiche** Germany
28 C7 **Bredevad** Denmark
26 L6 **Bredsel** Sweden
27 G12 **Bredsjö** Sweden
30 E1 **Bredstedt** Germany
28 C5 **Bredsten** Denmark
26 K8 **Bredträsk** Sweden
55 D4 **Bredy** Russian Federation
22 K1 **Bree** Belgium
89 A9 **Breede** R S Africa
110 G3 **Breese** Illinois U.S.A.
33 Q5 **Breesen** Germany
46 E3 **Bregalnica** R Macedonia
41 H2 **Brege** R Germany
41 L2 **Bregenz** Austria
41 L3 **Bregenzer Ache** R Austria
41 L3 **Bregenzer Wald** mt Austria
28 G5 **Bregninge** Denmark
48 H6 **Bregovo** Bulgaria
20 G4 **Bréhal** France
20 E4 **Bréhat** isld France
122 B1 **Bréhat, L** Quebec Canada
33 Q9 **Brehna** Germany
33 T9 **Brehnitz** Germany
36 E2 **Breidenbach** Germany
28 R9 **Breidhafjördhur** B Iceland
29 T9 **Breidhdalsvik** Iceland
98 E3 **Breien** North Dakota U.S.A.
21 L5 **Breil-sur-Mérize,le** France
26 B10 **Breim** Norway
40 G1 **Breisach** Germany
37 M5 **Breitenbrunn** Germany
33 Q10 **Breitenfeld** Germany
37 K4 **Breitengüssbach** Germany
33 P9 **Breitenhagen** Germany
33 M7 **Breitenhees** Germany
37 O3 **Breitenhof** Germany
33 S6 **Breiter Luzinsee** L Germany
40 G5 **Breithorn** mt Switzerland
33 Q4 **Breitling** Germany
37 J2 **Breitungen** Germany
26 M1 **Breivikbotn** Norway
28 A4 **Brejning** Denmark
129 K4 **Brejo** Brazil
94 C3 **Brekenridge** Michigan U.S.A.
26 E9 **Brekken** Norway
26 D8 **Brekstad** Norway
26 A10 **Bremangerland** isld Norway
41 L6 **Brembana, Val** Italy
41 L6 **Brembo** R Italy
32 J6 **Bremen** Germany
112 B4 **Bremen** Georgia U.S.A.
94 A5 **Bremen** Indiana U.S.A.
94 E7 **Bremen** Ohio U.S.A.
140 D1 **Bremer** isld N Terr Australia
143 C10 **Bremer Bay** W Australia Australia
32 J5 **Bremerhaven** Germany
143 D10 **Bremer Ra** W Australia Australia
117 M12 **Bremerton** Washington U.S.A.
32 K6 **Bremervörde** Germany
41 H3 **Bremgarten** Switzerland
116 Q6 **Bremner** R Alaska U.S.A.
109 L4 **Bremond** Texas U.S.A.
26 E6 **Bremsteinen** lighthouse Norway
139 H3 **Brenda** New South Wales Australia
28 D6 **Brenderup** Denmark
45 K1 **Brendola** Italy
8 C5 **Brendon Hills** England
109 L5 **Brenham** Texas U.S.A.
21 N8 **Brenne** reg France
21 M6 **Brenne** R Indre-et-Loire France
41 O3 **Brenner** Austria
101 M5 **Brenner** Montana U.S.A.
41 O4 **Brennero** Italy
41 O3 **Brenner Pass** Austria/Italy
41 M6 **Breno** Italy
42 C3 **Breno** Italy
19 P12 **Brénod** France
36 C5 **Brenschelbach** Germany
121 M6 **Brent** Ontario Canada
6 M1 **Brent** oil rig North Sea
111 J9 **Brent** Alabama U.S.A.
42 D3 **Brenta** R Italy
41 N5 **Brenta, Gruppa di** mt Italy
9 F5 **Brentford** England
98 H4 **Brentford** South Dakota U.S.A.
123 T4 **Brenton Rock** Newfoundland Canada
9 G4 **Brentwood** England
102 C4 **Brentwood** California U.S.A.
37 J6 **Brenz** R Germany
9 G5 **Brenzett** England
89 G6 **Brereton Park** S Africa
45 J2 **Brescello** Italy
41 M6 **Brescia** Italy
25 A6 **Breskens** Netherlands
Breslau see **Wrocław**
21 O2 **Bresle** R France
21 P3 **Bresles** France
143 C6 **Bresnahan,Mt** W Australia Australia
41 P4 **Bressanone** Italy
40 B5 **Bresse** reg France
21 K8 **Bressuire** France
31 O3 **Brest** Belarus
20 B5 **Brest** France
20 D5 **Brest à Nantes, Canal de** France
46 E1 **Brestovac** Serbia Yugoslavia
20 A5 **Brest,Rade de** B France
83 J14 **Bretagne, Pnte de** Réunion Indian Oc
21 N4 **Bretagnolles** France
48 K4 **Breţcu** Romania
18 G8 **Bretenoux** France
21 M4 **Breteuil-sur-Iton** France
21 P2 **Breteuil-sur-Noye** France
20 G8 **Brétignolles-sur-Mer** France
21 P4 **Brétigny** France
118 C5 **Breton** Alberta Canada
21 M5 **Bretoncelles** France
111 G12 **Breton I** Louisiana U.S.A.
18 E6 **Breton, Pertuis d'** B France
95 N6 **Breton Woods** New Jersey U.S.A.
38 K7 **Bretstein** Austria
145 E1 **Brett, C** New Zealand
36 F5 **Bretten** Germany
21 K3 **Bretteville** France
21 K3 **Bretteville-l'Orgueilleuse** France
37 J5 **Brettheim** Germany
36 G5 **Bretzfeld** Germany
36 G4 **Breuberg** Germany
69 B10 **Breueh, Pulau** isld Sumatra
21 L3 **Breuil-en-Auge,le** France
21 N4 **Breuilpont** France
25 D4 **Breukelen** Netherlands
40 C1 **Breuvannes** France
21 O4 **Bréval** France
112 E2 **Brevard** North Carolina U.S.A.
129 H4 **Breves** Brazil
27 D12 **Brevik** Norway
95 T2 **Brewer** Maine U.S.A.
95 L3 **Brewerton** New York U.S.A.
113 E10 **Brewster** Florida U.S.A.
107 J2 **Brewster** Kansas U.S.A.
98 G8 **Brewster** Nebraska U.S.A.
95 O5 **Brewster** New York U.S.A.
94 F6 **Brewster** Ohio U.S.A.
117 O11 **Brewster** Washington U.S.A.
115 R3 **Brewster, Kap** C Greenland
144 B6 **Brewster, Mt** New Zealand
111 J10 **Brewton** Alabama U.S.A.
25 F6 **Breyell** Germany
Brezhnev see **Naberezhnyye Chelny**
19 O14 **Brezins** France
46 F2 **Breznik** Bulgaria
48 F2 **Brezno** Slovakia
38 M8 **Brezno** Slovenia
48 J5 **Brezoi** Romania
21 N4 **Brezolles** France
16 D2 **Brezo, Sa. del** mts Spain
46 G2 **Brezovo** Bulgaria
42 H3 **Brezovo Polje** mt Croatia
86 D4 **Bria** Cent Afr Republic
103 M4 **Brian Head** Utah U.S.A.
18 G5 **Briare** France
141 L7 **Bribie I** Queensland Australia
108 G1 **Brice** Texas U.S.A.
99 N6 **Bricelyn** Minnesota U.S.A.
48 L2 **Brichany** Moldova
110 F7 **Brickeys** Arkansas U.S.A.
19 J4 **Bricon** France
123 M2 **Briconnet,L** Quebec Canada
20 G3 **Bricquebec** France
20 G4 **Bricqueville-sur-Mer** France
14 C4 **Bride** R Ireland
12 D5 **Bride** I of Man U.K.
8 B3 **Bridell** Wales
8 B6 **Bridestowe** England
119 U3 **Bridgar** Manitoba Canada
117 M10 **Bridge** R British Columbia Canada
101 M7 **Bridge** Idaho U.S.A.
112 D6 **Bridgeboro** Georgia U.S.A.
12 B2 **Bridgend** Islay Scotland
13 E1 **Bridgend** Tayside Scotland
8 C5 **Bridgend** Wales
12 E1 **Bridge of Allan** Scotland
12 D3 **Bridge of Doon** Scotland
12 D2 **Bridge of Weir** Scotland
110 L7 **Bridgeport** Alabama U.S.A.
102 E3 **Bridgeport** California U.S.A.
95 O5 **Bridgeport** Connecticut U.S.A.
107 N3 **Bridgeport** Kansas U.S.A.
98 C8 **Bridgeport** Nebraska U.S.A.
100 H5 **Bridgeport** Oregon U.S.A.
100 F2 **Bridgeport** Washington U.S.A.
109 K2 **Bridgeport, L** Texas U.S.A.
102 E3 **Bridgeport Res** California U.S.A.
113 L12 **Bridge Pt** Bahamas
101 R4 **Bridger** Montana U.S.A.
101 P4 **Bridger Pk** Montana U.S.A.
101 S8 **Bridger Pk** Wyoming U.S.A.
95 M7 **Bridgeton** New Jersey U.S.A.
112 K2 **Bridgeton** North Carolina U.S.A.
143 B10 **Bridgetown** W Australia Australia
127 P6 **Bridgetown** Barbados
122 G9 **Bridgetown** Nova Scotia Canada
122 K8 **Bridgeville** Nova Scotia Canada
100 B9 **Bridgeville** California U.S.A.
122 H9 **Bridgewater** Nova Scotia Canada
95 S7 **Bridgewater** Maine U.S.A.
95 R5 **Bridgewater** Massachusetts U.S.A.
98 J6 **Bridgewater** South Dakota U.S.A.
94 J8 **Bridgewater** Virginia U.S.A.
138 F7 **Bridgewater,C** Victoria Australia
94 A5 **Bridgman** Michigan U.S.A.
8 D2 **Bridgnorth** England
95 R2 **Bridgton** Maine U.S.A.
8 C5 **Bridgwater** England
13 H5 **Bridlington** England
139 H8 **Bridport** Tasmania Australia
8 D6 **Bridport** England
18 G4 **Brie** reg France
20 B5 **Briec** France
25 B5 **Brielle** Netherlands
112 F4 **Brier Creek** Georgia U.S.A.
119 M8 **Briercrest** Saskatchewan Canada
118 F4 **Briereville** Alberta Canada
122 F9 **Brier I** Nova Scotia Canada
22 H5 **Brieulles-sur-Bar** France
21 O4 **Brieval** France
22 K5 **Briey** France
40 G5 **Brig** Switzerland
41 H1 **Brigarh** R Germany
120 H10 **Brigden** Ontario Canada
13 H6 **Brigg** England
109 K5 **Briggs** Texas U.S.A.
98 B9 **Briggsdale** Colorado U.S.A.
101 N8 **Brigham City** Utah U.S.A.
13 G6 **Brighouse** England
9 E6 **Brighstone** England
103 M5 **Bright Angel Pt** Arizona U.S.A.
9 H4 **Brightlingsea** England
138 E6 **Brighton** South Australia Australia
121 N8 **Brighton** Ontario Canada
9 F6 **Brighton** England
98 B10 **Brighton** Colorado U.S.A.
113 F10 **Brighton** Florida U.S.A.
110 F2 **Brighton** Illinois U.S.A.
99 P8 **Brighton** Iowa U.S.A.
94 D4 **Brighton** Michigan U.S.A.
141 F6 **Brighton Downs** Queensland Australia
145 D4 **Brightwater** New Zealand
20 B4 **Brignogan-Plage** France
123 T6 **Brigus** Newfoundland Canada
17 F4 **Brihuega** Spain
42 F4 **Brijuni** isld Croatia
26 G4 **Briksvoer** isld Norway
130 C7 **Brilhante,R** Brazil
106 F5 **Brilliant** New Mexico U.S.A.
99 S5 **Brillion** Wisconsin U.S.A.
32 J10 **Brilon** Germany
99 R9 **Brimfield** Illinois U.S.A.
43 H8 **Brindisi** Italy
138 C4 **Bring,L** South Australia Australia
94 E6 **Brinkhaven** Ohio U.S.A.
9 G3 **Brinkley** England
110 E7 **Brinkley** Arkansas U.S.A.
9 E3 **Brinklow** England
53 E10 **Brin'kovskaya** Russian Federation
32 J6 **Brinkum** Germany
138 E5 **Brinkworth** South Australia Australia
21 P6 **Brinon-sur-Sauldre** France
98 G1 **Brinsmade** North Dakota U.S.A.
113 C7 **Brinson** Georgia U.S.A.
21 J6 **Briollay** France
21 O8 **Brion** Indre France
123 L6 **Brion, I** Madeleine Is, Quebec Canada
21 M3 **Brionne** France
21 K7 **Brion-près-Thouet** France
18 H7 **Brioude** France
21 K4 **Briouze** France
141 L8 **Brisbane** Queensland Australia
141 L7 **Brisbane R** Queensland Australia
108 D8 **Briscoe** Texas U.S.A.
45 L3 **Brisighella** Italy
6 N4 **Brisling** oil rig North Sea
21 K7 **Brissac-Quincé** France
41 J4 **Bristenstock** mt Switzerland
122 E7 **Bristol** New Brunswick Canada
121 O7 **Bristol** Quebec Canada
8 D5 **Bristol** England
106 H3 **Bristol** Colorado U.S.A.
95 P5 **Bristol** Connecticut U.S.A.
113 C7 **Bristol** Florida U.S.A.
112 E6 **Bristol** Georgia U.S.A.
94 B5 **Bristol** Indiana U.S.A.
95 Q3 **Bristol** New Hampshire U.S.A.
95 M6 **Bristol** Pennsylvania U.S.A.
95 Q5 **Bristol** Rhode I U.S.A.
98 J4 **Bristol** South Dakota U.S.A.
95 O2 **Bristol** Vermont U.S.A.
94 E10 **Bristol** Virginia/Tenn U.S.A.
116 G8 **Bristol B** Alaska U.S.A.
8 C5 **Bristol Chan** England/Wales
146 G3 **Bristol I** S Sandwich Is Atlantic Oc
103 J7 **Bristol L** California U.S.A.
103 J7 **Bristol Mts** California U.S.A.
103 K3 **Bristol Silver** Nevada U.S.A.
107 O6 **Bristow** Oklahoma U.S.A.
117 M11 **Britannia Beach** British Columbia Canada
146 A3 **British Antarctic Terr** Antarctica
117 K7 **British Columbia** prov Canada
115 L1 **British Empire Ra** Northwest Territories Canada
British Guiana see **Guyana**
British Honduras see **Belize**
81 E6 **British Ind.Oc.Terr** colony Indian Oc
116 Q2 **British Mts** Alaska/Yukon Terr U.S.A./Canada
British N. Borneo see **Sabah**
British Solomon Is see **Solomon Is.**
123 M7 **Briton Cove** C Breton I, Nova Scotia
8 C4 **Briton Ferry** Wales
87 E11 **Brits** S Africa
87 D12 **Britstown** S Africa
120 K7 **Britt** Ontario Canada
99 N6 **Britt** Iowa U.S.A.
27 G14 **Brittatorp** Sweden
107 N6 **Britton** Oklahoma U.S.A.
98 J4 **Britton** South Dakota U.S.A.
138 C2 **Britton,Mt** South Australia Australia
33 T7 **Britz** Germany
18 G7 **Brive-la-Gaillarde** France
16 E2 **Briviesca** Spain
20 G2 **Brix** France
38 F7 **Brixental** V Austria
8 C7 **Brixham** England
48 D1 **Brno** Czech Rep
27 F12 **Bro** Sweden
112 D3 **Broad** R Georgia U.S.A.
112 F3 **Broad** R South Carolina U.S.A.
118 J6 **Broadacres** Saskatchewan Canada
95 N3 **Broadalbin** New York U.S.A.
143 D9 **Broad Arrow** W Australia Australia
121 M1 **Broadback** R Quebec Canada
15 B2 **Broad Bay** Scotland
100 A6 **Broadbent** Oregon U.S.A.
109 N4 **Broaddus** Texas U.S.A.
15 C3 **Broadford** Scotland
14 B2 **Broad Haven** Ireland
8 A4 **Broad Haven** Wales
9 E5 **Broad Hinton** England
142 D5 **Broadhurst Ra** W Australia Australia
98 H5 **Broadland** South Dakota U.S.A.
15 E5 **Broad Law** Scotland
116 N5 **Broad Pass** Alaska U.S.A.
141 J5 **Broad Sound** Queensland Australia
141 K5 **Broad Sound Chan** Queensland Australia
141 J6 **Broadsound Ra** Queensland Australia
9 H5 **Broadstairs** England
98 A4 **Broadus** Montana U.S.A.
119 P8 **Broadview** Saskatchewan Canada
101 R3 **Broadview** Montana U.S.A.
108 A9 **Broadview** New Mexico U.S.A.
9 F6 **Broadwater** England
98 D8 **Broadwater** Nebraska U.S.A.
9 E3 **Broadway** England
8 D6 **Broadwey** England
8 D6 **Broadwindsor** England
145 D1 **Broadwood** New Zealand
126 C3 **Broa, Ensenada de la** B Cuba
28 D7 **Broager** Denmark
28 E6 **Broby** Denmark
27 G15 **Broby** Sweden
119 Q1 **Brochet** Manitoba Canada
122 C4 **Brochet,L.au** Quebec Canada
32 G8 **Brochterbeck** Germany
121 Q4 **Brochu,L** Quebec Canada
118 J7 **Brock** Saskatchewan Canada
99 L9 **Brock** Nebraska U.S.A.
32 L6 **Brockel** Germany
33 N9 **Brocken** mt Germany
9 E6 **Brockenhurst** England
118 D9 **Brocket** Alberta Canada
98 H1 **Brocket** North Dakota U.S.A.
114 H2 **Brock I** Northwest Territories Canada
13 H6 **Brocklesby** England
142 B5 **Brockman,Mt** W Australia Australia
94 K3 **Brockport** New York U.S.A.
98 G7 **Brocksburg** Nebraska U.S.A.
140 B2 **Brock's Creek** N Terr Australia
95 Q4 **Brockton** Massachusetts U.S.A.
98 B1 **Brockton** Montana U.S.A.
121 P8 **Brockville** Ontario Canada
98 A2 **Brockway** Montana U.S.A.
94 J5 **Brockway** Pennsylvania U.S.A.
110 J2 **Brocton** Illinois U.S.A.
94 H4 **Brocton** New York U.S.A.
46 E3 **Brod** Macedonia
48 F7 **Brodarevo** Serbia Yugoslavia
118 L7 **Broderick** Saskatchewan Canada
115 L3 **Brodeur Pen** Northwest Territories Canada
99 R7 **Brodhead** Wisconsin U.S.A.
48 G6 **Brodica** Serbia Yugoslavia
12 C2 **Brodick** Scotland
94 K10 **Brodnax** Virginia U.S.A.
31 L2 **Brodnica** Poland
55 D3 **Brodokalmak** Russian Federation
25 C3 **Broek op Langedijk** Netherlands
100 H5 **Brogan** Oregon U.S.A.
21 M3 **Broglie** France
20 F5 **Brohinière,la** France
36 C3 **Brohl-Lützing** Germany
33 T5 **Brohm-Cosa** Germany
33 M8 **Broistedt** Germany
31 N3 **Brok** Poland
99 R4 **Brokaw** Wisconsin U.S.A.
32 K5 **Brokdorf** Germany
107 P5 **Broken Arrow** Oklahoma U.S.A.
139 K5 **Broken Bay** New South Wales Australia
98 G8 **Broken Bow** Nebraska U.S.A.
107 Q7 **Broken Bow** Oklahoma U.S.A.
107 Q7 **Broken Bow L** Oklahoma U.S.A.
138 F4 **Broken Hill** New South Wales Australia
Broken Hill Zambia see **Kabwe**
129 G3 **Brokopondomeer** L Suriname
29 K12 **Bromarv** Finland
33 N7 **Brome** Germany
8 D3 **Bromfield** England
98 C1 **Bromhead** Saskatchewan Canada
9 G5 **Bromley** England
27 D11 **Bromma** Norway
28 G5 **Bromme** Denmark
70 O9 **Bromo** mt Java
13 H5 **Brompton** England
99 O9 **Brompton** Iowa U.S.A.
8 D3 **Bromsgrove** England
8 D3 **Bromyard** England
19 N13 **Bron** France
40 A6 **Bron** France
110 B4 **Bronaugh** Missouri U.S.A.
28 D2 **Brønderslev** Denmark
28 A5 **Brøndum** Denmark
8 C3 **Bronllys** Wales
37 L4 **Bronn** Germany
27 G15 **Brönnestad** Sweden
55 E2 **Bronnikovo** Russian Federation
26 F6 **Brönnöysund** Norway
36 H2 **Bronnzell** Germany
28 B6 **Brøns** Denmark
113 E8 **Bronson** Florida U.S.A.
94 B5 **Bronson** Michigan U.S.A.
109 N4 **Bronson** Texas U.S.A.
121 L9 **Bronte** Ontario Canada
43 F11 **Bronte** Sicily
108 G4 **Bronte** Texas U.S.A.
139 H8 **Bronte Park** Tasmania Australia
95 O6 **Bronx** New York U.S.A.
41 O5 **Bronzolo** Italy
122 E3 **Brooch L** Quebec Canada
99 T9 **Brook** Indiana U.S.A.
94 K8 **Brooke** Virginia U.S.A.
109 O4 **Brookeland** Texas U.S.A.
113 E8 **Brooker** Florida U.S.A.
71 C6 **Brooke's Pt** Palawan Philippines
122 J8 **Brookfield** Nova Scotia Canada
110 C2 **Brookfield** Missouri U.S.A.
111 F10 **Brookhaven** Mississippi U.S.A.
119 N9 **Brooking** Saskatchewan Canada
100 A7 **Brookings** Oregon U.S.A.
98 K5 **Brookings** South Dakota U.S.A.
141 H4 **Brook Is.Lt.Ho** Queensland Australia
9 G6 **Brookland** England
94 K5 **Brookland** Pennsylvania U.S.A.
112 F5 **Brooklet** Georgia U.S.A.
121 M9 **Brooklin** Ontario Canada
95 Q4 **Brookline** Massachusetts U.S.A.
110 K2 **Brooklyn** Indiana U.S.A.
99 O8 **Brooklyn** Iowa U.S.A.
94 C4 **Brooklyn** Michigan U.S.A.
111 G10 **Brooklyn** Mississippi U.S.A.
95 O6 **Brooklyn** New York U.S.A.
95 M5 **Brooklyn** Pennsylvania U.S.A.
117 N11 **Brookmere** British Columbia Canada
94 H10 **Brookneal** Virginia U.S.A.
99 N4 **Brook Park** Minnesota U.S.A.
110 H4 **Brookport** Illinois U.S.A.
118 F8 **Brooks** Alberta Canada
95 S2 **Brooks** Maine U.S.A.
101 Q2 **Brooks** Montana U.S.A.
117 G5 **Brooks Brook** Yukon Territory Canada
119 N5 **Brooksby** Saskatchewan Canada
146 D6 **Brooks, Cape** C Antarctica
109 M6 **Brookshire** Texas U.S.A.
116 D4 **Brooks Mt** Alaska U.S.A.
116 M5 **Brooks,Mt** Alaska U.S.A.
116 H2 **Brooks Range** Alaska U.S.A.
99 O3 **Brookston** Minnesota U.S.A.
109 M2 **Brookston** Texas U.S.A.
113 E9 **Brooksville** Florida U.S.A.
111 H8 **Brooksville** Mississippi U.S.A.
143 B9 **Brookton** W Australia Australia
95 U1 **Brookton** Maine U.S.A.
95 L4 **Brooktondale** New York U.S.A.
110 M2 **Brookville** Indiana U.S.A.
107 N3 **Brookville** Kansas U.S.A.
94 H5 **Brookville** Pennsylvania U.S.A.
111 J8 **Brookwood** Alabama U.S.A.
141 L7 **Brooloo** Queensland Australia
123 K4 **Broom B** Anticosti I, Quebec
142 D4 **Broome** W Australia Australia
143 C10 **Broomehill** W Australia Australia
142 F3 **Broome, Mt** W Australia Australia
20 F5 **Broons** France
99 L4 **Brooten** Minnesota U.S.A.
142 G4 **Brophy,Mt** W Australia Australia
143 F7 **Brophy,Mt** W Australia Australia
15 E2 **Brora** Scotland
28 B5 **Brørup** Denmark
27 G16 **Brösarp** Sweden
14 D3 **Brosna** R Ireland
48 K3 **Brosteni** Romania
68 A7 **Brothers** islds Andaman Is
100 E6 **Brothers** Oregon U.S.A.
145 E4 **Brothers, The** New Zealand
84 K4 **Brothers,The** islds Red Sea
37 J2 **Brotterode** Germany
21 N5 **Brou** France
13 F4 **Brough** England
15 E1 **Brough Hd** Orkney Scotland
15 F2 **Brough Ness** Scotland
9 F3 **Broughton** England
13 E5 **Broughton** Cumbria England
13 E2 **Broughton** Scotland
110 H4 **Broughton** Illinois U.S.A.
107 N2 **Broughton** Kansas U.S.A.
121 T6 **Broughton Station** Quebec Canada
15 F4 **Broughty Ferry** Scotland
86 C2 **Broulkou** Chad
36 B7 **Brouvelieures** France
25 A5 **Brouwershaven** Netherlands
20 H8 **Brouzils,les** France
40 E4 **Brove** R Switzerland
85 C7 **Brovio** Liberia
28 D2 **Brovst** Denmark
99 L3 **Browerville** Minnesota U.S.A.
71 C5 **Brown Bank** Palawan Philippines
94 E3 **Brown City** Michigan U.S.A.
107 L3 **Brownell** Kansas U.S.A.
143 E7 **Browne Ra** W Australia Australia
108 E2 **Brownfield** Texas U.S.A.
119 P9 **Browning** Saskatchewan Canada
110 C1 **Browning** Missouri U.S.A.
101 M1 **Browning** Montana U.S.A.
144 C5 **Browning Pass** New Zealand
143 C9 **Brown,L** W Australia Australia
119 M8 **Brownlee** Saskatchewan Canada
98 F7 **Brownlee** Nebraska U.S.A.
138 F3 **Brown,Mt** South Australia Australia
138 E4 **Brown,Mt** South Australia Australia
142 A3 **Brown,Mt** W Australia Australia
138 C4 **Brown Pt** South Australia Australia
141 G3 **Brown R** Queensland Australia
120 J3 **Brownrigg** Ontario Canada
144 B7 **Browns** New Zealand
110 J3 **Browns** Illinois U.S.A.
109 M3 **Brownsboro** Texas U.S.A.
121 Q7 **Brownsburg** Quebec Canada
110 K2 **Brownsburg** Indiana U.S.A.
126 E2 **Browns Cay** isld Bahamas
145 G1 **Browns I** New Zealand
98 C8 **Brownson** Nebraska U.S.A.
127 K2 **Brown's Town** Jamaica
94 A8 **Brownstown** Indiana U.S.A.
98 K4 **Browns Valley** Minnesota U.S.A.
110 L2 **Brownsville** Indiana U.S.A.
110 K4 **Brownsville** Kentucky U.S.A.
100 C5 **Brownsville** Oregon U.S.A.
94 H6 **Brownsville** Pennsylvania U.S.A.
110 G6 **Brownsville** Tennessee U.S.A.
109 K10 **Brownsville** Texas U.S.A.
99 M5 **Brownton** Minnesota U.S.A.
99 R7 **Browntown** Wisconsin U.S.A.
111 J8 **Brownville** Alabama U.S.A.
99 L9 **Brownville** Nebraska U.S.A.
95 M2 **Brownville** New York U.S.A.
95 S1 **Brownville Junc** Maine U.S.A.
109 J4 **Brownwood, L** Texas U.S.A.
142 E2 **Browse I** Australia
142 E2 **Browse I** Indian Oc
15 E5 **Broxburn** Scotland
112 E6 **Broxton** Georgia U.S.A.
16 C5 **Brozas** Spain
45 K4 **Brozzi** Italy
45 P1 **Brtonigla** Croatia
22 D3 **Bruay** France
22 F3 **Bruay-sur-l'Escaut** France
127 P6 **Bruce** Barbados
118 E5 **Bruce** Alberta Canada
145 E4 **Bruce** New Zealand
6 L3 **Bruce** oil rig North Sea
111 G7 **Bruce** Mississippi U.S.A.
99 P4 **Bruce** Wisconsin U.S.A.
144 B5 **Bruce Bay** New Zealand
99 R3 **Bruce Crossing** Michigan U.S.A.
120 J9 **Brucefield** Ontario Canada
142 C5 **Bruce,Mt** W Australia Australia
120 J7 **Bruce Pen** Ontario Canada
120 J7 **Bruce Peninsula National Park** nat park Ontario Canada
143 C9 **Bruce Rock** W Australia Australia
110 H5 **Bruceton** Tennessee U.S.A.
109 K4 **Bruceville** Texas U.S.A.
19 K4 **Bruche** R France
32 K7 **Bruchhausen-Vilsen** Germany
36 F3 **Bruchköbel** Germany
36 F5 **Bruchsal** Germany
31 K7 **Bruck** Austria
33 R8 **Brück** Germany
37 L4 **Bruck** Bayern Germany
38 M7 **Bruck-an-der-Mur** Austria
37 M6 **Bruckberg** Germany
38 L8 **Brückl** Austria
21 K3 **Brucourt** France
19 P18 **Brue-Auriac** France
118 E5 **Bruederheim** Alberta Canada
33 P5 **Brüel** Germany
14 C4 **Bruff** Ireland
20 H7 **Bruffière,la** France
Bruges see **Brugge**
40 H3 **Brugg** Switzerland
22 E1 **Brugge** Belgium
36 D1 **Brügge** Germany
25 F6 **Brüggen** Germany
45 L1 **Brùgine** Italy
44 F2 **Brugneto, L. di** Italy
36 B2 **Brühl** Germany
94 H5 **Bruin** Pennsylvania U.S.A.
103 O2 **Bruin Pt** Utah U.S.A.
117 P9 **Brûlé** Alberta Canada
98 E8 **Brule** Nebraska U.S.A.
99 P3 **Brule** Wisconsin U.S.A.
121 N6 **Brûlé, L** Quebec Canada
121 M7 **Brûlé Lake** Ontario Canada
21 K6 **Brûlon** France
22 J4 **Brûly** Belgium
129 K6 **Brumado** Brazil
25 F4 **Brummen** Netherlands
140 C4 **Brunchilly** N Terr Australia
43 C8 **Bruncu Spina** mt Sardinia
108 H7 **Brundage** Texas U.S.A.
111 L10 **Brundidge** Alabama U.S.A.
100 K7 **Bruneau** Idaho U.S.A.
22 G4 **Brunehamel** France
70 D2 **Brunei** state Borneo
70 D2 **Brunei B** Brunei
Brunei Town see **Bandar Seri Begawan**
140 D4 **Brunette Downs** N Terr Australia
123 Q6 **Brunette I** Newfoundland Canada
21 L2 **Bruneval** France
26 G8 **Brunflo** Sweden
109 J8 **Bruni** Texas U.S.A.
42 D2 **Brunico** Italy
118 D1 **Brunkild** Manitoba Canada
Brünn see **Brno**
37 N2 **Brunn** Germany
29 K4 **Brunnby** Sweden
41 J3 **Brunnen** Switzerland
119 M6 **Bruno** Saskatchewan Canada
99 O3 **Bruno** Minnesota U.S.A.
32 K5 **Brunsbüttelkoog** Germany
32 L5 **Brunshausen** Germany
25 E7 **Brunssum** Netherlands
Brunswick see **Braunschweig**
112 F6 **Brunswick** Georgia U.S.A.
95 S3 **Brunswick** Maine U.S.A.
94 K7 **Brunswick** Maryland U.S.A.
94 F5 **Brunswick** Ohio U.S.A.
142 E3 **Brunswick B** W Australia Australia
143 B10 **Brunswick Junction** W Australia Australia
120 G3 **Brunswick L** Ontario Canada
133 C8 **Brunswick, Pen. de** Chile
31 K6 **Bruntál** Czech Rep
146 F6 **Brunt Ice Shelf** ice shelf Antarctica
139 H9 **Bruny I** Tasmania Australia
46 F1 **Brusartsi** Bulgaria
106 G1 **Brush** Colorado U.S.A.
95 N2 **Brushton** New York U.S.A.
112 F1 **Brushy Mts** North Carolina U.S.A.
130 E10 **Brusque** Brazil
Brussels see **Bruxelles**
120 J9 **Brussels** Ontario Canada
99 T5 **Brussels** Wisconsin U.S.A.
8 D5 **Bruton** England
22 G2 **Bruxelles** Belgium
24 **Bruxelles** conurbation Belgium
19 K4 **Bruyères** France
20 G5 **Bruz** France
128 E2 **Bruzual** Venezuela
22 F3 **Bry** France
94 C5 **Bryan** Ohio U.S.A.
109 L5 **Bryan** Texas U.S.A.
146 C6 **Bryan Coast** Antarctica
54 K8 **Bryanka** Ukraine
138 E5 **Bryan,Mt** South Australia Australia
53 G11 **Bryansk** Russian Federation
54 F3 **Bryansk** Russian Federation
53 D8 **Bryanskaya Oblast'** prov Russian Federation
109 P1 **Bryant** Arkansas U.S.A.
110 M1 **Bryant** Indiana U.S.A.
110 D5 **Bryant Cr** Missouri U.S.A.
95 R2 **Bryant Pond** Maine U.S.A.
22 C3 **Bryas** France
103 M4 **Bryce Canyon Nat. Park** Utah U.S.A.
144 B7 **Brydone** New Zealand
9 F7 **Bryher** isld Isles of Scilly England
8 C4 **Bryn-amman** Wales
8 B2 **Bryn-crug** Wales
8 C1 **Bryneglwys** Wales
26 M1 **Brynilen** Norway
8 C4 **Bryn Mawr** Wales
48 L2 **Brynzeny** Moldova
28 C4 **Bryrup** Denmark
112 D2 **Bryson City** North Carolina U.S.A.
121 N6 **Bryson,L** Quebec Canada
48 G6 **Brza Palanka** Serbia Yugoslavia
31 K5 **Brzeg** Poland
31 L3 **Brześć Kuj** Poland
31 M6 **Brzesko** Poland
31 L6 **Brzeszcze** Poland
31 M4 **Brzeziny** Poland
31 L4 **Brzeźnica** Poland
31 N6 **Brzozów** Poland
21 O4 **Bû** France
88 E8 **Bua** R Malawi
71 H5 **Buabuang** Sulawesi
71 H7 **Buagi** Indonesia
21 J4 **Buais** France
69 D12 **Buatan** Sumatra
84 F3 **Bu'ayrāt al Hasūn** Libya
33 S7 **Buberow** Germany
89 F2 **Bubi** R Zimbabwe
77 A5 **Būbiyān, Jazīrat** isld Kuwait
20 D6 **Bubry** France
71 F7 **Bubuan** isld Mindanao Philippines
13 H6 **Bubwith** England
87 F10 **Bubye** R Zimbabwe
47 L7 **Bucak** Turkey
128 D2 **Bucaramanga** Colombia
71 G6 **Bucas Grande** Philippines
141 J5 **Bucasia** Queensland Australia
111 H10 **Bucatunda** Mississippi U.S.A.
142 E3 **Buccaneer Arch** W Australia Australia
43 G8 **Buccino** Italy
48 K3 **Bucecea** Romania
47 K3 **Bü Çekmece** Turkey
48 J1 **Buchach** Ukraine
6 L5 **Buchan** oil rig North Sea
15 F3 **Buchan** dist Scotland
140 D4 **Buchanan** R N Terr Australia
119 P7 **Buchanan** Saskatchewan Canada
85 B7 **Buchanan** Liberia
112 B4 **Buchanan** Georgia U.S.A.
99 U8 **Buchanan** Michigan U.S.A.
106 F7 **Buchanan** New Mexico U.S.A.
98 G2 **Buchanan** North Dakota U.S.A.
94 H9 **Buchanan** Virginia U.S.A.
109 J5 **Buchanan Dam** Texas U.S.A.
140 B4 **Buchanan Hills** N Terr Australia
141 H5 **Buchanan,L** Queensland Australia
143 E7 **Buchanan,L** W Australia Australia
109 J5 **Buchanan, L** Texas U.S.A.
115 M3 **Buchan Gulf** Northwest Territories Canada
15 G3 **Buchan Ness** Scotland
123 Q5 **Buchans** Newfoundland Canada
123 Q5 **Buchans Jnct** Newfoundland Canada
133 E4 **Buchardo** Argentina
Bucharest see **Bucureşti**
37 N7 **Buchbach** Germany
36 G4 **Buchen** Germany

36 C4 Büchenbeuren Germany
37 L1 Buchenwald Germany
32 L6 Buchholz Germany
33 R8 Buchholz Germany
41 N2 Buching Germany
41 N1 Buchloe Germany
15 D4 Buchlyvie Scotland
41 K3 Buchs Switzerland
21 N2 Buchy France
106 C6 Buck New Mexico U.S.A.
9 F3 Buckden England
32 K8 Bückeburg Germany
32 K7 Bücken Germany
103 M8 Buckeye Arizona U.S.A.
94 E7 Buckeye Lake Ohio U.S.A.
95 K7 Buckeystown Maryland U.S.A.
8 C7 Buckfastleigh England
94 G8 Buckhannon West Virginia U.S.A.
15 E4 Buckhaven & Methil Scotland
98 C5 Buckhorn Wyoming U.S.A.
15 E3 Buckie Scotland
121 P7 Buckingham Quebec Canada
9 E3 Buckingham England
94 J9 Buckingham Virginia U.S.A.
140 D1 Buckingham B N Terr Australia
140 E5 Buckingham Downs Queensland Australia
140 B4 Buck,L N Terr Australia
118 C5 Buck L Alberta Canada
116 G4 Buckland Alaska U.S.A.
119 V1 Buckland L Manitoba Canada
145 G1 Bucklands Beach New Zealand
141 J6 Buckland Tableland Queensland Australia
146 C13 Buckle I Antarctica
140 E5 Buckley R Queensland Australia
110 H1 Buckley Illinois U.S.A.
94 B2 Buckley Michigan U.S.A.
100 C2 Buckley Washington U.S.A.
38 O6 Bucklige Welt reg Austria
107 L4 Bucklin Kansas U.S.A.
110 D2 Bucklin Missouri U.S.A.
Buckner Bay see Nakagusuku-wan
102 C2 Bucks California U.S.A.
103 L7 Buckskin Mts Arizona U.S.A.
102 C2 Bucks Mt California U.S.A.
95 T2 Bucksport Maine U.S.A.
33 Q7 Bückwitz Germany
31 K6 Bučovice Czech Rep
86 B6 Buco Zau Angola
22 D3 Bucquoy France
122 H7 Buctouche New Brunswick Canada
48 K6 București Romania
71 E7 Bucutua isld Philippines
22 F4 Bucy-les-Pierrepont France
98 D3 Bucyrus North Dakota U.S.A.
26 B9 Bud Norway
68 D7 Buda isld Burma
109 K5 Buda Texas U.S.A.
48 E3 Budafok Hungary
54 B4 Buda-Koshelevo Belarus
68 B1 Budalin Burma
48 E3 Budapest Hungary
74 H4 Budaun India
9 E1 Budby England
146 G14 Budd Coast Antarctica
53 F10 Buddenovsk Russian Federation
143 B8 Budd,Mt W Australia Australia
15 F4 Buddon Ness Scotland
8 B6 Bude England
32 L4 Büdelsdorf Germany
32 G9 Büderich Germany
141 L7 Buderim Queensland Australia
22 K4 Buderscheid Luxembourg
48 K6 Budești Romania
139 K5 Budgewoi New South Wales Australia
28 S9 Budhardalur Iceland
29 T9 Budhareyri Iceland
28 R9 Budhir Iceland
29 T9 Búdhir Iceland
131 A7 Budi,L.del Chile
36 G3 Büdingen Germany
86 C5 Budjala Zaire
8 C6 Budleigh Salterton England
45 L2 Budrio Italy
70 F6 Budungbudung Sulawesi
42 J6 Budva Montenegro Yugoslavia
54 H7 Budy Ukraine
86 A5 Buéa Cameroon
19 P16 Buech R France
21 N4 Buéil France
102 D7 Buellton California U.S.A.
128 C3 Buenaventura Colombia
71 E4 Buenavista Philippines
71 G6 Buenavista Mindanao Philippines
106 D3 Buena Vista Colorado U.S.A.
112 C5 Buena Vista Georgia U.S.A.
94 H9 Buena Vista Virginia U.S.A.
126 E3 Buenavista, B. de Cuba
17 F4 Buendía, Embalse de Spain
Buene R see Bojana
131 A8 Bueno R Chile
130 E4 Buenolândia Brazil
129 K7 Buenópolis Brazil
131 E6 Buenos Aires prov Argentina
132 Buenos Aires conurbation Argentina
128 D4 Buenos Aires Colombia
133 C7 Buenos Aires,L Chile/Arg
127 N3 Buenos Ayres Trinidad
133 D7 Buen Pasto Argentina
133 D8 Buen Tiempo,C Argentina
130 H4 Buerarema Brazil
40 E5 Buet,Mt France
117 Q6 Buffalo R Alberta/N W Terr Canada
89 G6 Buffalo R S Africa
110 C5 Buffalo R Arkansas U.S.A.
107 P4 Buffalo Kansas U.S.A.
110 L4 Buffalo Kentucky U.S.A.
98 K3 Buffalo R Minnesota U.S.A.
99 N4 Buffalo Minnesota U.S.A.
110 C4 Buffalo Missouri U.S.A.
101 Q3 Buffalo Montana U.S.A.
94 J4 Buffalo New York U.S.A.
107 L5 Buffalo Oklahoma U.S.A.
112 F3 Buffalo South Carolina U.S.A.
98 C4 Buffalo South Dakota U.S.A.
110 J6 Buffalo R Tennessee U.S.A.
99 P5 Buffalo R Wisconsin U.S.A.
101 T5 Buffalo Wyoming U.S.A.
101 Q5 Buffalo Bill Dam Wyoming U.S.A.
101 Q5 Buffalo Bill Res Wyoming U.S.A.
99 N6 Buffalo Center Iowa U.S.A.
106 E2 Buffalo Creek Colorado U.S.A.
119 M9 Buffalo Gap Saskatchewan Canada
98 C6 Buffalo Gap South Dakota U.S.A.
118 E6 Buffalo, L Alberta Canada
117 Q5 Buffalo L Northwest Territories Canada
108 E1 Buffalo L Texas U.S.A.
139 H6 Buffalo,Mt Victoria Australia
118 J3 Buffalo Narrows Saskatchewan Canada
119 M8 Buffalo Pound Prov Park Saskatchewan Canada
127 L2 Buff Bay Jamaica
112 C3 Buford Georgia U.S.A.
98 C1 Buford North Dakota U.S.A.
98 A8 Buford Wyoming U.S.A.
48 K6 Buftea Romania
31 O4 Bug R Belarus/Poland etc
128 C3 Buga Colombia
18 G10 Bugarach, Pic de mt France
58 G1 Bugarikhta Russian Federation
47 J4 Buğdaylı Turkey
70 N9 Bugel,Tg Java
40 B6 Bugey dist France
Buggs Island Lake see John H. Kerr Res. N Carolina/Virginia
88 D1 Bugiri Uganda
26 R2 Bugöynes Norway
54 C10 Bugskiy Liman lagoon Ukraine
71 C6 Bugsuk isld Palawan Philippines
59 H2 Bugt China
18 F8 Bugue,Le France
71 E1 Buguey Luzon Philippines
78 K2 Bügük Ağri mt Turkey
57 F3 Bugun' Kazakhstan
57 E3 Bugun'skoye Vodokhranilishche res Kazakhstan
78 G4 Buhayrat al Asad L Syria
87 F9 Buhera Zimbabwe
58 C4 Buh He R China
71 F4 Buhi Luzon Philippines
36 E6 Bühl Germany
101 L7 Buhl Idaho U.S.A.
99 O2 Buhl Minnesota U.S.A.
36 E6 Bühlerhöhe Germany
36 E6 Bühlertal Germany
36 H5 Bühlertann Germany
88 E6 Buhoro Flats Tanzania
48 K4 Buhuși Romania
117 N7 Buick British Columbia Canada
25 C4 Buiksloot Netherlands
8 C3 Builth Wells Wales
137 M3 Buin Bougainville I Papua New Guinea
41 M4 Buin,Piz mt Switz/Austria
130 H10 Buíque Brazil
36 B2 Buir Germany
22 B3 Buire-le-Sec France
22 F4 Buironfosse France
19 O16 Buis-les-Baronnies France
25 F2 Buitenpost Netherlands
67 B7 Bui Thon Vietnam
122 J2 Buit,L Quebec Canada
16 E7 Bujalance Spain
46 E2 Bujanovac Serbia Yugoslavia
17 G3 Bujaraloz Spain
42 F3 Buje Croatia
88 B3 Bujumbura Burundi
48 D3 Bük Hungary
137 L3 Buka isld Papua New Guinea
66 E4 Buka Daban Feng mt China
88 D2 Bukakata Uganda
87 E7 Bukama Zaire
88 D2 Bukasa I Uganda
88 B3 Bukavu Zaire
88 C2 Bukene Tanzania
88 B3 Bukeye Burundi
57 C5 Bukhara Uzbekistan
46 F2 Bukhovo Bulgaria
56 B6 Bukhtarminskoye Vodokhranilishche res Kazakhstan
70 C6 Bukitlidi Kalimantan
69 E13 Bukittinggi Sumatra
48 F2 Bükk mt Hungary
79 F8 Bukka, J. el mt Jordan
48 D4 Bükkösd Hungary
33 Q9 Buko Germany
88 C2 Bukoba Tanzania
48 J2 Bukovina old prov Romania/Ukraine
31 J1 Bukowo,Jezioro L Poland
136 G2 Bula Moluccas Indonesia
71 H4 Bula anguki Sulawesi
41 J2 Bülach Switzerland
56 H5 Bulagansk Russian Federation
65 D2 Bulag Sum China
139 K4 Bulahdelah New South Wales Australia
71 E4 Bulalacao Philippines
71 E5 Bulalacao Calamian Group Philippines
71 F4 Bulan Philippines
71 E7 Bulan isld Philippines
55 D3 Bulanash Russian Federation
55 C4 Bulanavo Russian Federation
89 F3 Bulawayo Zimbabwe
55 F3 Bulayevo Kazakhstan
28 C2 Bulbjerg hill Denmark
47 K6 Buldan Turkey
74 G8 Buldana India
77 H6 Buleda reg Pakistan
70 P10 Buleleng Bali Indonesia
89 G5 Bulembu Swaziland
9 E5 Bulford England
56 F5 Bulgan Mongolia
58 B2 Bulgan Mongolia
58 D2 Bulgan Mongolia
58 C3 Bulgan Mongolia
46 F2 Bulgaria rep E Europe
47 J2 Bŭlgarovo Bulgaria
47 K6 Bulgaz Dağ mt Turkey
40 C1 Bulgnéville France
77 C7 Bul Hanine oil well Persian Gulf
71 B2 Buli Halmahera Indonesia
71 C6 Buliluyan,C Palawan Philippines
141 K1 Bulimba dist Brisbane, Qnsld Australia
141 L2 Bulimba Cr Brisbane, Qnsld Australia
67 B4 Buliu He R China
117 K8 Bulkley R British Columbia Canada
143 D9 Bulla Bulling W Australia Australia
22 L3 Bullange Belgium
16 E5 Bullaque R Spain
109 M3 Bullard Texas U.S.A.
27 E13 Bullaren S L Sweden
17 F6 Bullas Spain
141 G8 Bullawarra,L Queensland Australia
86 H3 Bullaxaar Somalia
36 C3 Bullay Germany
127 L3 Bull Bay Jamaica
112 H5 Bull Bay South Carolina U.S.A.
40 F4 Bulle Switzerland
138 F4 Bullea,L New South Wales Australia
116 O1 Bullen Alaska U.S.A.
126 A1 Bullen Baai B Curaçao Neth Antilles
139 H6 Buller, Mt Victoria Australia
145 D4 Buller R New Zealand
143 C9 Bullfinch W Australia Australia
103 K6 Bullhead City Nevada U.S.A.
112 H5 Bull I South Carolina U.S.A.
102 H7 Bullion Mts California U.S.A.
101 R3 Bull Mts Montana U.S.A.
141 G5 Bullock R Queensland Australia
141 G8 Bulloo R Queensland Australia
141 G8 Bulloo Downs Queensland Australia
141 F8 Bulloo, L Queensland Australia
133 F8 Bull Pt Falkland Is
118 B9 Bull R British Columbia Canada
145 E4 Bulls New Zealand
127 J3 Bull Savannah Jamaica
110 D5 Bull Shoals Lake Missouri U.S.A.
22 D3 Bully France
100 C9 Bully Choop Mt California U.S.A.
140 C2 Bulman Gorge N Terr Australia
139 G6 Buloke,L Victoria Australia
77 L2 Bulola Afghanistan
136 K3 Bulolo Papua New Guinea
138 F5 Bulpunga New South Wales Australia
87 E11 Bultfontein S Africa
71 G7 Buluan Mindanao Philippines
70 G7 Bulubulu Sulawesi
70 E3 Bulu, G mt Kalimantan
70 G7 Bulukumba Sulawesi
51 M1 Bulun Russian Federation
86 D7 Bulungu Zaire
71 G4 Bulusan Luzon Philippines
118 F6 Bulwark Alberta Canada
9 E2 Bulwell England
141 L1 Bulwer I Brisbane, Qnsld Australia
9 F2 Bulwick England
119 N8 Bulyea Saskatchewan Canada
86 D5 Bumba Zaire
84 G3 Bumbah, Khalīj Libya
48 H5 Bumbești-Jiu Romania
103 M7 Bumble Bee Arizona U.S.A.
70 G4 Bumbulan Sulawesi Indonesia
70 F2 Bum-Bum Sabah
70 M9 Bumiaju Java
66 F6 Bumkhang Burma
100 D3 Bumping L Washington U.S.A.
40 F4 Bümpliz Switzerland
75 O5 Bumthang Bhutan
109 O5 Buna Texas U.S.A.
71 G7 Bunawan Mindanao Philippines
143 B10 Bunbury W Australia Australia
110 B6 Bunch Oklahoma U.S.A.
14 E4 Bunclody Ireland
14 D1 Buncrana Ireland
141 K6 Bundaberg Queensland Australia
141 H8 Bundaleer Queensland Australia
32 F6 Bunde Germany
32 J8 Bünde Germany
140 D5 Bundey R N Terr Australia
74 F6 Bundi India
111 C11 Bundick L Louisiana U.S.A.
111 C11 Bundicks Cr Louisiana U.S.A.
140 C6 Bundooma N Terr Australia
14 C2 Bundoran Ireland
68 J6 Bun Duc Vietnam
12 B1 Bunessan Scotland
71 G7 Bunga R Mindanao Philippines
143 C9 Bungalbin Hill W Australia Australia
9 H3 Bungay England
68 E5 Bung Boraphet L Thailand
146 H13 Bunger Hills Antarctica
141 J7 Bungil R Queensland Australia
71 H6 Bunginkela isld Sulawesi Indonesia
68 F3 Bung Kan Thailand
70 G6 Bungku Sulawesi Indonesia
87 C7 Bungo Angola
60 G2 Bungo-suidō str Japan
141 J8 Bungunya Queensland Australia
Bunguran see Natuna Besar
Bunguran Utara, Kepulauan see Natuna Besar
86 B3 Buni Nigeria
86 F5 Bunia Zaire
143 E9 Buningonia Spring spring W Australia Australia
70 E3 Bunju isld Kalimantan
110 E4 Bunker Missouri U.S.A.
141 K6 Bunker Grp islds Gt Barrier Reef Aust
116 E4 Bunker Hill Alaska U.S.A.
110 G2 Bunker Hill Illinois U.S.A.
110 K1 Bunker Hill Indiana U.S.A.
107 M3 Bunker Hill Kansas U.S.A.
103 K5 Bunkerville Nevada U.S.A.
87 E8 Bunkeya Zaire
111 D11 Bunkie Louisiana U.S.A.
113 F8 Bunnell Florida U.S.A.
145 E4 Bunnythorpe New Zealand
70 G4 Bunobagu Sulawesi
68 H7 Bu Noi Vietnam
17 G5 Buñol Spain
25 D4 Bunschoten Netherlands
143 B8 Buntine W Australia Australia
9 F4 Buntingford England
70 D5 Buntok Kalimantan
70 D5 Buntokecil Kalimantan
141 K1 Bunyaville dist Brisbane, Qnsld Australia
68 E3 Bun Yun Thailand
51 L1 Buolkalakh Russian Federation
68 J6 Buon Me Thuot Vietnam
51 N1 Buor-khaya, Guba G Russian Federation
80 G1 Buq'ātā Syria
77 A7 Buqayq Saudi Arabia
28 A4 Bur Denmark
88 G3 Bura Kenya
86 A1 Buraan Somalia
71 L10 Buraen Timor Indonesia
Buraimi see Buraymī, Al
143 B9 Burakin W Australia Australia
86 E3 Buram Sudan
143 E10 Buraminya,Mt W Australia Australia
141 K2 Buranda dist Brisbane, Qnsld Australia
75 J3 Burang China
130 H5 Buranhaém Brazil
45 M1 Burano Italy
86 J4 Burao Somalia
111 G12 Buras Louisiana U.S.A.
71 G5 Burauen Leyte Philippines
72 E3 Buraydah Saudi Arabia
55 C3 Burayevo Russian Federation
79 G4 Burayj, Al Syria
77 D7 Buraymī, Al U.A.E.
80 G1 Burayqah Syria
36 E2 Burbach Germany
9 E5 Burbage England
102 F7 Burbank California U.S.A.
98 K9 Burchard Nebraska U.S.A.
139 H5 Burcher New South Wales Australia
99 N6 Burchinal Iowa U.S.A.
57 C5 Burdalyk Turkmenistan
141 H5 Burdekin R Queensland Australia
141 H5 Burdekin Falls Queensland Australia
117 M7 Burden,Mt British Columbia Canada
118 F9 Burdett Alberta Canada
95 L4 Burdett New York U.S.A.
48 K3 Burdujeni Romania
78 C3 Burdur Turkey
47 L7 Burdur Gölü L Turkey
90 E14 Burdwood Bank Atlantic Oc
86 G3 Burē Ethiopia
86 G4 Burē Ethiopia
26 M7 Bureå Sweden
121 P4 Bureau, L Quebec Canada
59 K1 Bureinskiy, Khrebet mts Russian Federation
32 J9 Büren Germany
25 D5 Buren Netherlands
58 B2 Bürenhayrhan Mongolia
65 B1 Bürentsogt Mongolia
59 K1 Bureya R Russian Federation
59 J2 Bureya Russian Federation
9 E4 Burford England
32 K5 Burg Germany
33 P8 Burg Germany
36 D5 Burgalben Germany
47 J2 Burgas Bulgaria
38 O7 Burgau Austria
37 J7 Burgau Germany
112 J3 Burgaw North Carolina U.S.A.
47 N11 Burgaz Turkey
47 N11 Burgaz isld Turkey
37 J5 Burgbernheim Germany
32 M8 Burgdorf Germany
40 G3 Burgdorf Switzerland
100 K4 Burgdorf Idaho U.S.A.
37 K4 Burgebrach Germany
37 M2 Bürgel Germany
48 C3 Burgenland prov Austria
123 P6 Burgeo Newfoundland Canada
87 E12 Burgersdorp S Africa
9 F6 Burgess Hill England
95 L9 Burgess Store Virginia U.S.A.
13 E4 Burgh England
25 A5 Burgh Netherlands
36 H2 Burghaun Germany
38 G5 Burghausen Germany
37 L6 Burgheim Germany
9 G1 Burgh-le-Marsh England
43 E11 Burgio Sicily
36 H3 Burgjoss Germany
37 L3 Burgkunstadt Germany
37 N5 Burglengenfeld Germany
16 E2 Burgos prov Spain
16 E2 Burgos Spain
37 K3 Burgpreppach Germany
36 H3 Burgsinn Germany
36 G4 Bürgstadt Germany
37 O2 Burgstädt Germany
33 S6 Burg Stargard Germany
32 F8 Burgsteinfurt Germany
27 K14 Burgsvik Sweden
17 G2 Burguete Spain
36 F2 Burgwald Germany
32 L7 Burgwedel Germany
37 K4 Burgwindheim Germany
47 H5 Burhaniye Turkey
32 H5 Burhave Germany
130 E8 Buri Brazil
69 E14 Buriai Indonesia
71 F4 Burias isld Philippines
71 F4 Burias Pass Luzon Philippines
123 R6 Burin Newfoundland Canada
68 F5 Buriram Thailand
130 E7 Buritama Brazil
128 G6 Buriti R Brazil
130 E6 Buriti Alegre Brazil
129 K5 Buriti Bravo Brazil
130 F4 Buritis Brazil
80 C8 Burj el Baiyara Jordan
79 G4 Burj Sāfita Syria
28 C7 Burkal Denmark
109 J1 Burkburnett Texas U.S.A.
140 F5 Burke R Queensland Australia
140 E6 Burke R Queensland Australia
100 K2 Burke Idaho U.S.A.
98 G6 Burke South Dakota U.S.A.
109 N4 Burke Texas U.S.A.
117 K9 Burke Chan British Columbia Canada
146 B7 Burke I Antarctica
144 C6 Burke Pass New Zealand
110 L5 Burkesville Kentucky U.S.A.
140 E4 Burketown Queensland Australia
109 H4 Burkett Texas U.S.A.
94 J9 Burkeville Virginia U.S.A.
37 O2 Burkhardtsdorf Germany
85 D6 Burkina rep W Africa
98 G4 Burkmere South Dakota U.S.A.
121 L7 Burk's Falls Ontario Canada
55 G4 Burla Russian Federation
36 G7 Burladingen Germany
141 G5 Burleigh Queensland Australia
109 K3 Burleson Texas U.S.A.
13 G6 Burley England
101 M7 Burley Idaho U.S.A.
8 D3 Burley Gate England
55 D4 Burli Kazakhstan
55 B5 Burlin Kazakhstan
107 P3 Burlingame Kansas U.S.A.
123 Q4 Burlington Newfoundland Canada
121 L9 Burlington Ontario Canada
106 H2 Burlington Colorado U.S.A.
99 P9 Burlington Iowa U.S.A.
107 P3 Burlington Kansas U.S.A.
95 N6 Burlington New Jersey U.S.A.
112 H1 Burlington North Carolina U.S.A.
95 O2 Burlington Vermont U.S.A.
117 M11 Burlington Washington U.S.A.
101 R5 Burlington Wyoming U.S.A.
110 A1 Burlington Junction Missouri U.S.A.
8 D2 Burlton England
57 J2 Burlyu-Tobe Kazakhstan
80 G5 Burma Jordan
68 B2 Burma rep S E Asia
139 H6 Burmah Forest Victoria Australia
55 D1 Burmantovo Russian Federation
101 N9 Burmester Utah U.S.A.
118 C9 Burmis Alberta Canada
144 D5 Burnbrae New Zealand
109 J5 Burnet Texas U.S.A.
141 K7 Burnett R Queensland Australia
141 K6 Burnett Heads Queensland Australia
100 D9 Burney California U.S.A.
8 C5 Burnham England
144 D5 Burnham New Zealand
95 S2 Burnham Maine U.S.A.
94 K6 Burnham Pennsylvania U.S.A.
9 G2 Burnham Deepdale England
9 G2 Burnham Market England
9 G4 Burnham-on-Crouch Essex England
40 F2 Burnhaupt France
139 H8 Burnie Tasmania Australia
13 H5 Burniston England
13 F6 Burnley England
13 G4 Burnopfield England
57 F3 Burnoye Kazakhstan
101 T10 Burns Colorado U.S.A.
100 F6 Burns Oregon U.S.A.
98 B8 Burns Wyoming U.S.A.
13 G5 Burnsall England
110 M5 Burnside Kentucky U.S.A.
94 J6 Burnside Pennsylvania U.S.A.
143 E7 Burnside,L W Australia Australia
117 L8 Burns Lake British Columbia Canada
98 G3 Burnstad North Dakota U.S.A.
122 G6 Burnsville New Brunswick Canada
110 H7 Burnsville Mississippi U.S.A.
112 E2 Burnsville North Carolina U.S.A.
94 G8 Burnsville West Virginia U.S.A.
101 P8 Burntfork Wyoming U.S.A.
126 G3 Burnt Ground Long I Bahamas
13 E1 Burntisland Scotland
122 J1 Burnt L Labrador, Nfld Canada
116 Q3 Burnt Paw Alaska U.S.A.
100 H5 Burnt R Oregon U.S.A.
100 B9 Burnt Ranch California U.S.A.
121 M8 Burnt River Ontario Canada
119 R3 Burntwood L Manitoba Canada
33 S5 Burow Germany
66 D2 Burqin China
119 M6 Burr Saskatchewan Canada
138 E5 Burra South Australia Australia
143 C9 Burracoppin W Australia Australia
139 K5 Burragorang L New South Wales Australia
15 F2 Burray Scotland
46 D3 Burrel Albania
140 C6 Burrell,Mt N Terr Australia
13 E1 Burrelton Scotland
139 J5 Burrendong Res. New South Wales Australia
17 G5 Burriana Spain
13 H6 Burringham England
108 F6 Burro Mexico
124 J3 Burro Mexico
99 P6 Burr Oak Iowa U.S.A.
107 M2 Burr Oak Kansas U.S.A.
94 B5 Burr Oak Michigan U.S.A.
94 E7 Burr Oak Res Ohio U.S.A.
103 L7 Burro Cr Arizona U.S.A.
108 E6 Burro, Serranias del mts Mexico
113 K11 Burrow Cay Bahamas
140 F3 Burrowes, Pt Queensland Australia
15 D6 Burrow Head Scotland
107 N3 Burrton Kansas U.S.A.
140 B2 Burrundie N Terr Australia
133 E3 Burruyacú Argentina
111 G13 Burrwood Louisiana U.S.A.
8 B4 Burry Port Wales
78 B1 Bursa Turkey
84 J4 Bur Safâga Egypt
36 C1 Burscheid Germany
13 F6 Burscough England
32 L9 Bursfelde Germany
8 D1 Burslem England
28 G7 Bursø Denmark
22 F2 Burst Belgium
118 H8 Burstall Saskatchewan Canada
99 M6 Burt Iowa U.S.A.
98 D3 Burt North Dakota U.S.A.
138 F4 Burta New South Wales Australia
94 C1 Burt L Michigan U.S.A.
9 E6 Burton England
98 G7 Burton Nebraska U.S.A.
109 L5 Burton Texas U.S.A.
8 B4 Burton Wales
13 H5 Burton Agnes England
13 F5 Burton-in-Kendal England
112 D3 Burton L Georgia U.S.A.
14 C2 Burtonport Ireland
9 E2 Burton upon Trent England
26 L7 Burträsk Sweden
122 F7 Burtts Corner New Brunswick Canada
138 F5 Burtundy New South Wales Australia
140 C6 Burt Well N Terr Australia
136 F2 Buru isld Moluccas Indonesia
84 J3 Burullus L Egypt
Burultokay see Fuhai
88 B3 Burundi rep Cent Africa
88 B3 Bururi Burundi
85 F7 Burutu Nigeria
8 D3 Burwarton England
9 G6 Burwash England
9 G1 Burwell England
98 G8 Burwell Nebraska U.S.A.
33 S10 Burxdorf Germany
121 T7 Bury Quebec Canada
9 F6 Bury England
13 F6 Bury Greater Manchester England
56 F5 Buryatskaya Respublika Russian Federation
9 G3 Bury St.Edmunds England
43 E11 Busambra, Rca mt Sicily
71 F7 Busan B Mindanao Philippines
87 D7 Busango Zaire
118 D5 Busby Alberta Canada
101 T4 Busby Montana U.S.A.
44 B2 Busca Italy
33 R7 Buschow Germany
32 J4 Buschsand isld Germany
46 E3 Buševa Planina mt Macedonia
46 D3 Bushat Albania
77 B5 Būshehr Iran
88 C2 Bushenyi Uganda
95 M5 Bushkill Pennsylvania U.S.A.
87 C9 Bushland homeland Namibia
108 B8 Bushland Texas U.S.A.
121 L6 Bushnell Ontario Canada
113 E9 Bushnell Florida U.S.A.
110 F1 Bushnell Illinois U.S.A.
98 C8 Bushnell Nebraska U.S.A.
107 M3 Bushton Kansas U.S.A.
140 E5 Bushy Park Queensland Australia
89 F1 Busi R Zimbabwe
88 E1 Busia Uganda
22 E3 Busigny France
86 D5 Businga Zaire
86 C6 Busira R Zaire
48 J1 Busk Ukraine
27 C11 Buskerud reg Norway
31 M5 Busko Poland
37 P3 Buškovice Czech Rep
55 D4 Buskul' Kazakhstan
71 B1 Busobuso Halmahera Indonesia
79 G6 Buşrá ash Shām Syria
19 K5 Bussang France
40 E2 Bussang,Col.de pass France
21 J8 Busseau,le France
143 B10 Busselton W Australia Australia
44 H2 Busseto Italy
99 O8 Bussey Iowa U.S.A.
41 N7 Bussolengo Italy
25 D4 Bussum Netherlands
77 D6 Bustaneh Iran
80 D2 Bustan Ha Galil Israel
141 K6 Bustard Hd Queensland Australia
48 K5 Buşteni Romania
42 B3 Busto Arsizio Italy
57 C4 Buston Uzbekistan
71 D4 Busuanga Philippines
86 D5 Busu Djanoa Zaire
32 J4 Büsum Germany
86 D5 Buta Zaire
131 G2 Butai R Brazil
70 O9 Butak, G mt Java
69 D9 Butang Group isld Thailand
133 D5 Buta Ranquil Argentina
88 B3 Butare Rwanda
71 F3 Butaunan isld Philippines
138 E5 Bute South Australia Australia
15 C5 Bute isld Scotland
117 J9 Butedale British Columbia Canada
117 L10 Bute Inlet British Columbia Canada
88 B1 Butembo Zaire
22 L3 Bütgenbach Belgium
Butha Qi see Zalantun
68 A2 Buthidaung Burma
47 P12 Buthrotum hist site Albania
86 F5 Butiaba Uganda
86 B1 Butiyaalo Somalia
32 H5 Butjadingen reg Germany
55 D3 Butka Russian Federation
68 B3 Butle R Burma
111 H9 Butler Alabama U.S.A.
112 C5 Butler Georgia U.S.A.
94 C5 Butler Indiana U.S.A.
110 M3 Butler Kentucky U.S.A.
110 B3 Butler Missouri U.S.A.
95 N6 Butler New Jersey U.S.A.
94 E6 Butler Ohio U.S.A.
107 L6 Butler Oklahoma U.S.A.
94 H6 Butler Pennsylvania U.S.A.
98 J4 Butler South Dakota U.S.A.
138 B2 Butlers Dome mt N Terr Australia
80 G2 Butmiye Syria
71 H7 Buton isld Sulawesi Indonesia
71 H7 Buton, Selat str Indonesia
46 D5 Butrintit, Liqen i L Albania
41 K3 Bütschwil Switzerland
45 K1 Buttapietra Italy
101 N4 Butte Montana U.S.A.
98 H7 Butte Nebraska U.S.A.
98 F2 Butte North Dakota U.S.A.
100 C7 Butte Falls Oregon U.S.A.
37 L1 Buttelstedt Germany
102 C1 Butte Meadows California U.S.A.
36 G7 Buttenhausen Germany
37 L4 Buttenheim Germany
37 K6 Buttenwiesen Germany
100 F4 Butter Cr Oregon U.S.A.
99 M6 Butterfield Minnesota U.S.A.
13 E5 Buttermere England
9 G2 Butterwick England
87 E12 Butterworth S Africa
14 C4 Buttevant Ireland
143 G6 Buttfield, Mt W Australia Australia
27 K14 Buttle Sweden
117 L11 Buttle L British Columbia Canada
15 B2 Butt of Lewis Scotland
115 K6 Button B Manitoba Canada
115 N5 Button Is Northwest Territories Canada
102 E6 Buttonwillow California U.S.A.
37 L1 Buttstädt Germany
98 J3 Buttzville North Dakota U.S.A.
71 G6 Butuan Mindanao Philippines
71 G6 Butuan B Mindanao Philippines
Butung isld see Buton
54 M6 Buturlinovka Russian Federation
68 H6 Bu Tu Suay Vietnam
36 F3 Butzbach Germany
33 P5 Bützow Germany
86 J4 Buuhoodle Somalia
86 J5 Buulobarde Somalia
86 H6 Buur Gaabo Somalia
84 H5 Buurhakaba Somalia
26 E9 Buvika Norway
79 E10 Buwārah, J mt Saudi Arabia
21 L8 Buxerolles France
21 O7 Buxeuil France
32 L6 Buxtehude Germany
9 E1 Buxton England
112 M2 Buxton North Carolina U.S.A.
19 J6 Buxy France
55 C3 Buy R Russian Federation
58 C2 Buyant Mongolia
65 A1 Buyant Mongolia
58 G2 Buyr Nuur L Mongolia
47 N11 Büyük isld Turkey
47 N11 Büyükada Turkey
47 N10 Büyükdere Turkey
47 H4 Büyük Kemikli Br C Turkey
47 J7 Büyük Menderes R Turkey
21 N8 Buzançais France
22 H5 Buzancy France
48 K5 Buzău R Romania
48 K5 Buzău Romania
48 K5 Buzăului Muntii mt Romania
55 B4 Buzdyak Russian Federation
60 E12 Buzen Japan
87 F9 Buzi Mozambique
48 G5 Buziaș Romania
55 C4 Buzov'yazy Russian Federation
95 R5 Buzzards B Massachusetts U.S.A.
8 C4 Bwlch Wales
27 H11 By Sweden
47 H1 Byala Bulgaria
46 F1 Byala Slatina Bulgaria
114 J2 Byam Martin I Northwest Territories Canada
109 K1 Byars Oklahoma U.S.A.
31 O4 Bychawa Poland
31 L4 Byczyna Poland
31 K2 Bydgoszcz Poland
Byelorussia see Belarus
106 F2 Byers Colorado U.S.A.
109 J1 Byers Texas U.S.A.
94 F7 Byesville Ohio U.S.A.
9 E3 Byfield England
9 F5 Byfleet England
26 L7 Bygdeå Sweden
26 L7 Bygdeträsk Sweden
27 C10 Bygdin L Norway
26 L7 Bygdsiljum Sweden
28 D5 Bygholm Å R Denmark
27 C13 Bygland Norway
27 C13 Byglandsfj Norway
110 G7 Byhalia Mississippi U.S.A.
54 B3 Bykhov Belarus
27 B12 Bykle Norway
27 B12 Bykleheiane Norway
59 M2 Bykov Russian Federation
28 C7 Bylderup Denmark
57 H1 Bylkyldak Kazakhstan
115 M3 Bylot I Northwest Territories Canada
140 F4 Bynoe R Queensland Australia
140 B2 Bynoe Harbour N Terr Australia
101 N2 Bynum Res Montana U.S.A.
111 F9 Byram Mississippi U.S.A.
146 D11 Byrd Glacier Antarctica
121 O5 Byrd,L Quebec Canada
13 F3 Byrness England
143 B7 Byro W Australia Australia
112 D5 Byromville Georgia U.S.A.
102 C4 Byron California U.S.A.
99 R7 Byron Illinois U.S.A.
95 R2 Byron Maine U.S.A.
101 R5 Byron Wyoming U.S.A.
139 L3 Byron Bay New South Wales Australia
51 J1 Byrranga,Gory mt Russian Federation
109 J2 Byrson Texas U.S.A.
28 F2 Byrum Denmark
26 M7 Byske Sweden
26 L6 Byske älv R Sweden
48 F1 Bystra mt Slovakia
55 F2 Bystryy Russian Federation
31 K5 Bystrzyca Kłodzka Poland
51 N2 Bytantay R Russian Federation
31 L6 Bytča Slovakia
31 L5 Bytom Poland
54 F3 Bytosh Russian Federation
31 K1 Bytów Poland
Byzantium see İstanbul
141 J7 Byzantium Queensland Australia
31 M3 Bzura R Poland

C

130 B9 Caacupé Paraguay
130 C9 Caaguazú dept Paraguay
133 F3 Caaguazu Paraguay
130 C9 Caaguazú, Cord de mts Paraguay
87 C8 Caála Angola
130 B10 Caapucú Paraguay
130 C8 Caarapó Brazil
130 F5 Caatinga Brazil
130 C10 Caazapá Paraguay
129 G7 Cabacal R Brazil
130 H9 Cabaceiras Brazil
126 E3 Cabaiguán Cuba
71 E3 Cabalantian Luzon Philippines
71 G5 Cabalian Leyte Philippines
106 C9 Caballo New Mexico U.S.A.
128 D4 Caballococha Peru
106 C9 Caballo Res New Mexico U.S.A.
124 G3 Caballos Mesteños, Llano de los Mexico
71 E3 Cabanatuan Luzon Philippines
122 D6 Cabano Quebec Canada
71 E2 Cabarruyan isld Luzon Philippines
19 Q18 Cabasse France
141 K1 Cabbage Tree Cr Brisbane, Qnsld Australia
16 B2 Cabe R Spain
130 F4 Cabeceiras Brazil
130 J9 Cabedelo Brazil
99 S8 Cabery Illinois U.S.A.
16 D6 Cabeza del Buey Spain
128 F7 Cabezas Bolivia
106 C6 Cabezon New Mexico U.S.A.
71 F6 Cabilao isld Philippines
127 J9 Cabimas Venezuela
107 P5 Cabin Creek Oklahoma U.S.A.
86 B7 Cabinda Angola
100 J1 Cabinet Gorge Dam Idaho U.S.A.
100 J1 Cabinet Mts Idaho U.S.A.
71 E8 Cabingan isld Philippines
99 P3 Cable Wisconsin U.S.A.
113 L9 Cable Beach New Providence I Bahamas
133 D7 Cabo Blanco Argentina
17 F8 Cabo de Gata,Sierra del Spain
88 G8 Cabo Delgado dist Mozambique
130 G8 Cabo Frio Brazil
121 O5 Cabonga, Rés Quebec Canada
110 D4 Cabool Missouri U.S.A.
141 L7 Caboolture Queensland Australia
88 D9 Cabora Bassa Dam Mozambique
133 D6 Cabo Raso Argentina
113 H7 Cabo Rojo Puerto Rico
110 E6 Cabot Arkansas U.S.A.
120 J7 Cabot Head C Ontario Canada
123 M6 Cabot Str Nfld/Nova Scotia Canada
21 K3 Cabourg France
85 A8 Cabo Verde, Ilhas do islds Atlantic Oc
71 E4 Cabra isld Philippines
16 E7 Cabra del Santo Cristo Spain
69 A9 Cabra I Nicobar Is
127 J5 Cabral Dominican Rep
130 G5 Cabral,Serra do mts Brazil
43 B9 Cabras Sardinia
19 P15 Cabre, Col de pass France
16 B3 Cabreira mt Portugal
17 J5 Cabrera isld Balearic Is
127 K5 Cabrera Dominican Rep
16 C2 Cabrera R Spain
126 F4 Cabreras R Cuba
16 C2 Cabrera,Sierra mt Spain
118 J8 Cabri Saskatchewan Canada
17 F5 Cabriel R Spain
19 O18 Cabriès France
102 G9 Cabrillo Nat Mon California U.S.A.
127 M4 Cabrits, I Martinique W Indies
130 G10 Cabrobó Brazil
128 E2 Cabruta Venezuela
71 E7 Cabucan isld Philippines
71 E2 Cabugao Luzon Philippines
71 E5 Cabulauan isld Philippines
124 E2 Cabullona Mexico
71 G8 Caburan Mindanao Philippines
128 E1 Cabure Venezuela
71 F1 Cabutunan Pt Luzon Philippines
133 G3 Caçador Brazil
46 D1 Čačak Serbia Yugoslavia
122 F3 Cacaoui L Quebec Canada
130 F8 Cacapava Brazil
133 G4 Caçapava do Sul Brazil
94 J7 Cacapon R West Virginia U.S.A.
68 H2 Cac Ba isld Vietnam
43 B8 Caccia,C Sardinia
133 G3 Cacequi Brazil
129 G7 Cáceres Brazil
130 B5 Cáceres Brazil
16 C5 Cáceres prov Spain
16 C5 Cáceres Spain
110 E6 Cache R Arkansas U.S.A.
110 G4 Cache R Illinois U.S.A.
107 M7 Cache Oklahoma U.S.A.
120 K6 Cache Bay Ontario Canada
102 B3 Cache Cr California U.S.A.
85 A6 Cacheu Guinea-Bissau
129 G5 Cachimbo, Serra do mts Brazil
133 D2 Cachinal Chile
87 C8 Cachingues Angola
129 L6 Cachoeira Brazil
130 E6 Cachoeira Alta Brazil
130 E5 Cachoeira de Goiás Brazil
131 H3 Cachoeira do Sul Brazil
130 F8 Cachoeira Paulista Brazil
130 H7 Cachoeiro de Itapemirim Brazil
102 E7 Cachuma, L California U.S.A.
16 E7 Cacín R Spain
42 H3 Čačinci Croatia
71 D5 Cacnipa isld Philippines
87 C8 Cacolo Angola
87 C8 Caconda Angola
86 B7 Cacongo Angola
122 C6 Cacouna Quebec Canada
103 M8 Cactus Arizona U.S.A.
109 H8 Cactus Texas U.S.A.
118 H6 Cactus Lake Saskatchewan Canada
102 H4 Cactus Ra Nevada U.S.A.
130 D6 Caçu Brazil
87 B9 Caculavar R Angola
129 K6 Caculé Brazil
130 D5 Caçununga Brazil
86 J5 Cadale Somalia
31 L6 Čadca Slovakia
111 C7 Caddo R Arkansas U.S.A.
107 O7 Caddo Oklahoma U.S.A.
109 J3 Caddo Texas U.S.A.
111 B9 Caddo L Texas U.S.A.
109 L2 Caddo Mills Texas U.S.A.
45 J2 Cadelbosco di Sopra Italy
111 F12 Cade,L.de Louisiana U.S.A.
140 C1 Cadell R N Terr Australia
141 F5 Cadell R Queensland Australia
128 D6 Cadena del Pantiacolla Peru
32 K5 Cadenberge Germany
19 O17 Cadenet France
125 K5 Cadereyta Mexico
8 C2 Cader Idris mt Wales
112 H4 Cades South Carolina U.S.A.
138 D3 Cadibarrawirracanna,L South Australia Australia
19 P18 Cadière-d'Azur France
71 F3 Cadig Mts Philippines
121 M4 Cadillac Quebec Canada
118 K9 Cadillac Saskatchewan Canada
18 E8 Cadillac France
94 B2 Cadillac Michigan U.S.A.
18 G10 Cadi, Sierra del mts Spain
71 F5 Cadiz Negros Philippines
16 C8 Cádiz Spain
16 D8 Cádiz prov Spain
110 J5 Cadiz Kentucky U.S.A.
94 G6 Cadiz Ohio U.S.A.
16 C8 Cádiz, B. de Spain
103 J7 Cadiz L California U.S.A.
118 G6 Cadogan Alberta Canada
117 P9 Cadomin Alberta Canada
38 F9 Cadore reg Italy
99 P5 Cadott Wisconsin U.S.A.
117 P7 Cadotte R Alberta Canada
143 B9 Cadoux W Australia Australia
8 C5 Cadoxton Wales
41 N6 Cadria,Monte Italy
45 L1 Ca Emo Italy
21 K3 Caen France
13 H6 Caenby Corner England
8 C1 Caergwrle Wales
8 D4 Caerleon Wales
8 B1 Caernarfon Wales
8 B1 Caernarfon B Wales
8 C4 Caerphilly Wales
8 C3 Caersws Wales
8 D4 Caerwent Wales
80 C3 Caesarea Israel
80 F1 Caesarea Philippi Syria
112 E2 Caesars Head South Carolina U.S.A.

130 G6 **Caete** Brazil
129 K6 **Caetite** Brazil
130 E7 **Cafelândia** Brazil
83 K14 **Cafres,Pl.des** Réunion Indian Oc
129 G3 **Cafuini** *R* Brazil
71 E1 **Cagayan** *R* Luzon Philippines
71 G6 **Cagayan de Oro** Mindanao Philippines
71 E6 **Cagayan Is** Philippines
47 J5 **Çağiş** Turkey
42 E5 **Cagli** Italy
43 C9 **Cagliari** Sardinia
43 C9 **Cagliari,G.di** Sardinia
44 B4 **Cagnes** France
71 F4 **Cagraray** *isld* Philippines
127 L5 **Caguas** Puerto Rico
111 J9 **Cahaba** *R* Alabama U.S.A.
21 J3 **Cahagnes** France
14 B5 **Caha Mts** Ireland
14 D4 **Caher** Ireland
14 A5 **Cahirsiveen** Ireland
14 E4 **Cahore Pt** Ireland
18 G8 **Cahors** France
87 G9 **Caia** Mozambique
129 G6 **Caiabis, Serra dos** Brazil
87 D8 **Caianda** Angola
45 Q7 **Caianello** Italy
129 H7 **Caiapó** *R* Brazil
130 D5 **Caiapónia** Brazil
130 D5 **Caiapo, Serra do** *mts* Brazil
45 Q7 **Caiazzo** Italy
126 E3 **Caibarién** Cuba
68 H7 **Cai Be** Vietnam
130 J9 **Caicará** Brazil
128 E2 **Caicara** Bolívar Venezuela
128 F2 **Caicara** Monagas Venezuela
129 L5 **Caico** Brazil
127 H4 **Caicos Is** W Indies
Caidian *see* **Hanyang**
143 F9 **Caiguna** W Australia Australia
21 J8 **Caillère, la** France
122 E1 **Cailleteau,L** Quebec Canada
128 D7 **Cailloma** Peru
111 E12 **Caillou B** Louisiana U.S.A.
126 G5 **Caimanera** Cuba
71 D3 **Caiman Pt** Luzon Philippines
109 J5 **Cain City** Texas U.S.A.
87 B9 **Cainde** Angola
133 D1 **Caine** *R* Bolivia
122 G7 **Cains R** New Brunswick Canada
99 N9 **Cainsville** Missouri U.S.A.
69 G8 **Cai Nuoc** Vietnam
45 P6 **Caira, M** *mt* Italy
146 F6 **Caird Coast** Antarctica
12 C1 **Cairnbaan** Scotland
94 J6 **Cairnbrook** Pennsylvania U.S.A.
139 G6 **Cairn Curran Dam** Victoria Australia
15 E3 **Cairn Gorm** *mt* Scotland
116 K6 **Cairn Mt** Alaska U.S.A.
12 C4 **Cairnryan** Scotland
141 H3 **Cairns** Queensland Australia
15 E3 **Cairn Toul** *mt* Scotland
79 B8 **Cairo** Egypt
44 D3 **Cairo** Italy
113 C7 **Cairo** Georgia U.S.A.
110 G4 **Cairo** Illinois U.S.A.
110 D2 **Cairo** Missouri U.S.A.
98 H8 **Cairo** Nebraska U.S.A.
95 N4 **Cairo** New York U.S.A.
94 C6 **Cairo** Ohio U.S.A.
94 F7 **Cairo** West Virginia U.S.A.
67 A3 **Caishentang** China
67 F1 **Caishi** China
9 H2 **Caister** England
13 H6 **Caistor** England
15 E2 **Caithness** *dist* Scotland
87 B8 **Caitou** Angola
87 C9 **Caiundo** Angola
48 K4 **Căiuţi** Romania
45 Q8 **Caivano** Italy
141 G8 **Caiwarro** Queensland Australia
22 D4 **Caix** France
Caiyuanzhen *see* **Shengsi**
67 F1 **Caizi Hu** China
128 C5 **Cajamarca** *dept* Peru
128 C5 **Cajamarca** Peru
18 G8 **Cajarc** France
130 H9 **Cajàzeiras** Brazil
48 F7 **Čajetina** Serbia Yugoslavia
71 F4 **Cajidiocan** Philippines
48 E7 **Čajniče** Bosnia-Herzegovina
130 F7 **Cajuru** Brazil
47 L8 **Çakırlar** Turkey
47 N11 **Çakmakmlar** Turkey
47 K6 **Çal** Turkey
16 C7 **Cala** Spain
85 F7 **Calabar** Nigeria
121 O7 **Calabogie** Ontario Canada
127 L10 **Calabozo** Venezuela
43 G9 **Calabria** *prov* Italy
71 D5 **Calabugdong** Philippines
16 D8 **Calaburras, Pta. de** Spain
128 E7 **Calacoto** Bolivia
46 F1 **Calafat** Romania
133 C8 **Calafate** Argentina
71 F5 **Calagnaan** *isld* Philippines
71 F3 **Calagua** *islds* Philippines
17 F2 **Calahorra** Spain
122 E8 **Calais** New Brunswick Canada
22 B2 **Calais** France
95 T8 **Calais** Maine U.S.A.
Calais, Pas de *see* **Dover, Str. of**
128 F5 **Calama** Brazil
133 D2 **Calama** Chile
126 G9 **Calamar** Colombia
71 D4 **Calamian Group** *islds* Philippines
99 Q7 **Calamine** Wisconsin U.S.A.
22 L2 **Calamine,la** Belgium
48 H5 **Călan** Romania
128 F4 **Calanaque** Brazil
17 G4 **Calanda** Spain
41 K4 **Calanda** *mt* Switzerland
71 E5 **Calandagan** *isld* Philippines
87 C7 **Calandula** Angola
69 B10 **Calang** Sumatra
20 D5 **Calanhel** France
84 G4 **Calanscio Sand Sea** Libya
71 E4 **Calapan** Philippines
100 C5 **Calapooia** *R* Oregon U.S.A.
48 K6 **Călăraşi** *reg* Romania
48 L6 **Călăraşi** Romania
20 D5 **Calarhel** France
43 B9 **Calasetta** Sardinia
17 F6 **Calasparra** Spain
43 E11 **Calatafimi** Sicily
17 F3 **Calatayud** Spain
48 H4 **Călăţele** Romania
33 T9 **Calau** Germany
71 F4 **Calauag** Philippines
43 F10 **Calavà, C** Sicily
102 C4 **Calaveras Res** California U.S.A.
71 E4 **Calavite,Cape** Philippines
71 E1 **Calayan** *isld* Luzon Philippines
71 G4 **Calbayog** Philippines
33 P9 **Calbe** Germany
71 G5 **Calbiga** Samar Philippines
131 A8 **Calbuco** *pk* Chile
129 L5 **Calcanhar, Pta. do** *C* Brazil
111 C12 **Calcasieu L** Louisiana U.S.A.
128 B4 **Calceta** Ecuador
133 E3 **Calchaqui** Argentina
45 J4 **Calci** Italy
45 J1 **Calcinato** Italy
129 H3 **Calcoene** Brazil
75 N7 **Calcutta** India
48 J6 **Căldăraru** Romania
128 C2 **Caldas** *div* Colombia
16 A5 **Caldas da Rainha** Portugal
17 J3 **Caldas de Montbuy** Spain
16 B2 **Caldas de Reyes** Spain
16 B3 **Caldas do Gerês** Portugal
130 E5 **Caldas Novas** Brazil
13 E4 **Caldbeck** England
88 G10 **Caldeira** *isld* Mozambique
32 K10 **Calden** Germany
117 G7 **Calder** Alaska U.S.A.
100 J2 **Calder** Idaho U.S.A.
133 C3 **Caldera** Chile
125 M5 **Caldera** Costa Rica
45 K2 **Calderara di Reno** Italy
12 E2 **Caldercruix** Scotland
16 E5 **Calderina** *mt* Spain
141 H7 **Caldervale** Queensland Australia
8 D4 **Caldicot** Wales
100 J6 **Caldwell** Idaho U.S.A.
107 N4 **Caldwell** Kansas U.S.A.
94 F7 **Caldwell** Ohio U.S.A.
109 L5 **Caldwell** Texas U.S.A.
8 B4 **Caldy I** Wales
89 E8 **Caledon** *R* S Africa
89 A10 **Caledon** S Africa
122 G9 **Caledonia** Nova Scotia Canada
94 B4 **Caledonia** Michigan U.S.A.
99 P6 **Caledonia** Minnesota U.S.A.
94 K4 **Caledonia** New York U.S.A.
94 E6 **Caledonia** Ohio U.S.A.
15 D3 **Caledonian Canal** Scotland
140 D2 **Caledon,Mt** N Terr Australia
17 J3 **Calella** Spain
141 J5 **Calen** Queensland Australia
124 G3 **Calera** Mexico
111 K8 **Calera** Alabama U.S.A.
124 H6 **Calera Victor Rosales** Mexico
128 D7 **Caleta Buena** Chile
133 D8 **Caleta Coig** *est* Argentina
133 D7 **Caleta Olivia** Argentina
131 B8 **Caleufu** *R* Argentina
103 J9 **Calexico** California U.S.A.
12 D5 **Calf of Man** *isld* I of Man U.K.
118 C7 **Calgary** Alberta Canada
106 F2 **Calhan** Colorado U.S.A.
111 M7 **Calhoun** Georgia U.S.A.
110 J4 **Calhoun** Kentucky U.S.A.
111 G8 **Calhoun City** Mississippi U.S.A.
112 E3 **Calhoun Falls** South Carolina U.S.A.
128 C3 **Cali** Colombia
47 K4 **Çalı** Turkey
71 G5 **Calicoan** *isld* Samar Philippines
110 D5 **Calico Rock** Arkansas U.S.A.
68 A7 **Calicut** Andaman Is
76 B5 **Calicut** India
102 F6 **Caliente** California U.S.A.
103 K4 **Caliente** Nevada U.S.A.
127 O2 **California** Trinidad
102 C1 **California** *state* U.S.A.
110 D3 **California** Missouri U.S.A.
94 H6 **California** Pennsylvania U.S.A.
102 F7 **California Aqueduct** California U.S.A.
102 G6 **California City** California U.S.A.
124 D4 **California,G.de** Mexico
102 F6 **California Hot Springs** California U.S.A.
48 J5 **Călimăneşti** Romania
48 J3 **Călimani, Muntii** *mts* Romania
76 D5 **Calimere,Pt** India
133 D4 **Calingasta** Argentina
143 B9 **Calingiri** W Australia Australia
Calino *isld see* **Kálimnos** *isld*
111 D8 **Calion** Arkansas U.S.A.
103 J8 **Calipatria** California U.S.A.
100 H1 **Calispell Peak** Washington U.S.A.
71 E5 **Calis Pt** Philippines
102 B3 **Calistoga** California U.S.A.
87 D12 **Calitzdorp** S Africa
71 E4 **Calivite Passage** Philippines
109 O5 **Call** Texas U.S.A.
138 F3 **Callabonna** *R* South Australia Australia
113 F7 **Callahan** Florida U.S.A.
14 D4 **Callan** Ireland
121 L6 **Callander** Ontario Canada
12 D1 **Callander** Scotland
71 E2 **Callang** Luzon Philippines
25 C3 **Callantsoog** Netherlands
128 C6 **Callao** Peru
99 O10 **Callao** Missouri U.S.A.
103 L2 **Callao** Utah U.S.A.
95 L9 **Callao** Virginia U.S.A.
142 D5 **Callawa** W Australia Australia
98 G8 **Callaway** Nebraska U.S.A.
43 B12 **Calle, la** Algeria
125 K6 **Calles** Mexico
141 K6 **Callide** Queensland Australia
109 J7 **Calliham** Texas U.S.A.
118 D3 **Calling L** Alberta Canada
118 E3 **Calling River** Alberta Canada
8 B7 **Callington** England
141 K6 **Calliope** Queensland Australia
117 H6 **Callison Ranch** British Columbia Canada
17 G6 **Callosa de Ensarriá** Spain
143 B7 **Callytharra Springs** W Australia Australia
118 D5 **Calmar** Alberta Canada
99 P6 **Calmar** Iowa U.S.A.
36 F6 **Calmbach** Germany
118 L2 **Calm L** Ontario Canada
9 E5 **Calne** England
71 G4 **Calolbon** Philippines
71 F6 **Calolot** Mindanao Philippines
113 F11 **Caloosahatchee** *R* Florida U.S.A.
43 G8 **Calore** *R* Italy
141 L7 **Caloundra** Queensland Australia
17 H6 **Calpe** Spain
101 P7 **Calpet** Wyoming U.S.A.
79 A2 **Çalpınar** Turkey
102 D2 **Calpine** California U.S.A.
125 K8 **Calpulálpam** Mexico
120 F3 **Calstock** Ontario Canada
43 F11 **Caltagirone** Sicily
43 F11 **Caltanissetta** Sicily
47 K7 **Çaltepe** *mt* Turkey
87 C7 **Caluango** Angola
87 C8 **Calucinga** Angola
87 B8 **Calulo** Angola
121 Q7 **Calumet** Quebec Canada
99 S2 **Calumet** Michigan U.S.A.
107 M6 **Calumet** Oklahoma U.S.A.
87 B8 **Caluquembe** Angola
71 E6 **Calusa** *isld* Philippines
40 G7 **Caluso** Italy
86 B1 **Caluula** Somalia
71 E5 **Caluya** *isld* Philippines
103 O8 **Calva** Arizona U.S.A.
18 E3 **Calvados** *dept* France
45 K4 **Calvana,Monte Della** Italy
9 E1 **Calver** England
140 D3 **Calvert** *R* N Terr Australia
111 H10 **Calvert** Alabama U.S.A.
109 L5 **Calvert** Texas U.S.A.
110 H4 **Calvert City** Kentucky U.S.A.
140 D3 **Calvert Hills** N Terr Australia
117 J10 **Calvert I** British Columbia Canada
94 K8 **Calverton** Virginia U.S.A.
143 E6 **Calvert Ra** W Australia Australia
124 H7 **Calvillo** Mexico
119 T10 **Calvin** North Dakota U.S.A.
107 O7 **Calvin** Oklahoma U.S.A.
89 A8 **Calvinia** S Africa
45 Q7 **Calvi Risorta** Italy
45 J1 **Calvisano** Italy
16 D4 **Calvitero** *mt* Spain
33 O8 **Calvörde** Germany
36 F6 **Calw-Hirsau** Germany
112 J2 **Calypso** North Carolina U.S.A.
87 C7 **Camabatela** Angola
129 L7 **Camacá** Brazil
87 B8 **Camacaio** Angola
124 H5 **Camache** Mexico
121 O5 **Camachigama,L** Quebec Canada
87 C8 **Camacupa** Angola
127 L10 **Camaguán** Venezuela
126 F4 **Camagüey** Cuba
126 E3 **Camagüey, Arch. de** *islds* Cuba
69 E10 **Camah, Gunung** Malaysia
128 G5 **Camaitu** *R* Brazil
126 E3 **Camajuaní** Cuba
128 D7 **Camaña** Peru
71 G5 **Camandag** Samar Philippines
100 C1 **Camano I** Washington U.S.A.
87 D8 **Camanongue** Angola
130 C6 **Camapuã** Mato Grosso Brazil
133 G4 **Camaquã** Rio Grande do Sul Brazil
131 H3 **Camaquã,R** Brazil
128 F4 **Camara** Brazil
128 G6 **Camarare** *R* Brazil
17 H3 **Camarasa,Embalse de** Spain
18 G9 **Camarès** France
19 N16 **Camaret** France
20 A5 **Camaret** Finistère France
107 L5 **Camargo** Oklahoma U.S.A.
19 N17 **Camargue, La** *reg* France
102 E7 **Camarillo** California U.S.A.
16 A1 **Camariñas** Spain
124 F6 **Camaronero, L. del** Mexico
133 D6 **Camarones** Argentina
101 N5 **Camas** Idaho U.S.A.
100 C4 **Camas** Washington U.S.A.
101 L6 **Camas Cr** Idaho U.S.A.
100 B6 **Camas Valley** Oregon U.S.A.
Ca Mau, Pte De *see* **Mui Bai Bung**
87 C7 **Camaxilo** Angola
16 B2 **Cambados** Spain
142 E4 **Camballin** W Australia Australia
130 B5 **Cambara** Brazil
Cambay, G. of *see* **Khambhat, G. of**
8 B6 **Cambeak** England
21 H3 **Cambe, la** France
36 E3 **Camberg** Germany
20 H3 **Cambernon** France
68 F6 **Cambodia** *rep* S E Asia
13 G3 **Cambois** England
18 E9 **Cambo les B** France
130 E10 **Camboriú** Brazil
8 A7 **Camborne** England
22 E3 **Cambrai** France
16 B1 **Cambre** Spain
21 L3 **Cambremer** France
102 C6 **Cambria** California U.S.A.
99 R6 **Cambria** Wisconsin U.S.A.
7 H10 **Cambrian Mts** Wales
144 B6 **Cambrians** New Zealand
120 K9 **Cambridge** Ontario Canada
9 G3 **Cambridge** England
127 J2 **Cambridge** Jamaica
145 E2 **Cambridge** New Zealand
100 J5 **Cambridge** Idaho U.S.A.
99 Q8 **Cambridge** Illinois U.S.A.
99 N8 **Cambridge** Iowa U.S.A.
107 O4 **Cambridge** Kansas U.S.A.
95 L8 **Cambridge** Maryland U.S.A.
95 Q4 **Cambridge** Massachusetts U.S.A.
99 N4 **Cambridge** Minnesota U.S.A.
98 F9 **Cambridge** Nebraska U.S.A.
95 O3 **Cambridge** New York U.S.A.
94 F6 **Cambridge** Ohio U.S.A.
114 J4 **Cambridge Bay** Northwest Territories Canada
142 G2 **Cambridge G** W Australia Australia
9 F3 **Cambridgeshire** *co* England
94 G5 **Cambridge Springs** Pennsylvania U.S.A.
17 H3 **Cambrils** Spain
22 D3 **Cambrin** France
21 O1 **Cambron** France
87 C8 **Cambundi-Catembo** Angola
130 F7 **Cambuquira** Brazil
37 M1 **Camburg** Germany
12 D2 **Cambuslang** Scotland
139 K5 **Camden** New South Wales Australia
111 J10 **Camden** Alabama U.S.A.
111 D8 **Camden** Arkansas U.S.A.
95 M7 **Camden** Delaware U.S.A.
95 S2 **Camden** Maine U.S.A.
94 C5 **Camden** Michigan U.S.A.
95 N7 **Camden** New Jersey U.S.A.
95 M3 **Camden** New York U.S.A.
112 G3 **Camden** South Carolina U.S.A.
110 H5 **Camden** Tennessee U.S.A.
111 B11 **Camden** Texas U.S.A.
116 P1 **Camden B** Alaska U.S.A.
94 G8 **Camden on Gauley** West Virginia U.S.A.
142 E3 **Camden Sd** W Australia Australia
110 D3 **Camdenton** Missouri U.S.A.
87 D8 **Cameia,Parque Nacional da** Angola
8 B6 **Camelford** England
8 B7 **Camel,R** England
87 B7 **Camembe** Angola
21 L4 **Camembert** France
45 O4 **Camerano** Italy
45 O4 **Camerata Picena** Italy
42 E5 **Camerino** Italy
103 N6 **Cameron** Arizona U.S.A.
99 Q9 **Cameron** Illinois U.S.A.
111 C12 **Cameron** Louisiana U.S.A.
110 B2 **Cameron** Missouri U.S.A.
101 O4 **Cameron** Montana U.S.A.
106 G7 **Cameron** New Mexico U.S.A.
95 K4 **Cameron** New York U.S.A.
112 H2 **Cameron** North Carolina U.S.A.
94 J5 **Cameron** Pennsylvania U.S.A.
109 L5 **Cameron** Texas U.S.A.
94 G7 **Cameron** West Virginia U.S.A.
99 P4 **Cameron** Wisconsin U.S.A.
88 C6 **Cameron B** Zambia
141 F8 **Cameron Corner** Queensland Australia
141 G5 **Cameron Downs** Queensland Australia
120 B3 **Cameron Falls** Ontario Canada
69 E10 **Cameron Highlands** Malaysia
117 O6 **Cameron Hills** Alberta Canada
114 J2 **Cameron I** Northwest Territories Canada
144 A7 **Cameron Mts** New Zealand
86 B4 **Cameroon** *rep* Africa
85 F8 **Cameroun, Mt** Cameroon
129 J4 **Cameta** Brazil
140 B3 **Camfield** N Terr Australia
140 B3 **Camfield** *R* N Terr Australia
71 G6 **Camiguin** *isld* Philippines
71 E1 **Camiguin** *isld* Luzon Philippines
71 E3 **Camiling** Luzon Philippines
111 M10 **Camilla** Georgia U.S.A.
133 D1 **Camiña** Chile
16 B3 **Caminha** Portugal
102 D3 **Camino** California U.S.A.
129 J4 **Camiranga** Brazil
133 E2 **Camiri** Bolivia
128 D6 **Camisea** *R* Peru
87 D7 **Camissombo** Angola
117 R4 **Camlaren** Northwest Territories Canada
79 E1 **Camlıyayla** Turkey
95 K5 **Cammal** Pennsylvania U.S.A.
43 F11 **Cammarata, Monte** *mt* Sicily
33 R8 **Cammer** Germany
124 E4 **Camoa** Mexico
125 M3 **Camoapa** Nicaragua
129 K4 **Camocim** Brazil
41 K5 **Camoghe** *mt* Switzerland
44 F3 **Camogli** Italy
41 M6 **Camonica,Val** Italy
140 E4 **Camooweal** Queensland Australia
129 H3 **Camopi** Fr Guiana
20 E6 **Camors** France
69 A8 **Camorta** Nicobar Is
71 G5 **Camotes Islands** Philippines
71 G5 **Camotes Sea** Philippines
124 G8 **Camotlán de Miraflores** Mexico
41 M6 **Camowiche,Alpi** *mt* Italy
42 E7 **Campagna** *reg* Italy
45 M1 **Campagna Lupia** Italy
45 M5 **Campagnano di Roma** Italy
22 B3 **Campagne-lès-Hesdin** France
125 L2 **Campamento** Honduras
133 F4 **Campana** Argentina
124 H4 **Campana** Mexico
133 B7 **Campana, I** Chile
130 C8 **Campanario** Mato Grosso Brazil
130 H6 **Campanário** Minas Gerais Brazil
133 C5 **Campanario** *mt* Chile/Arg
16 D6 **Campanario** Spain
45 Q8 **Campanella, Pta** *C* Italy
130 F7 **Campanha** Brazil
45 R7 **Campania** *reg* Italy
117 J9 **Campania I** British Columbia Canada
141 H5 **Campaspe** *R* Queensland Australia
102 C2 **Camp Beale** California U.S.A.
141 J6 **Campbell** *R* Queensland Australia
102 C4 **Campbell** California U.S.A.
110 F5 **Campbell** Missouri U.S.A.
98 H9 **Campbell** Nebraska U.S.A.
95 K4 **Campbell** New York U.S.A.
94 G5 **Campbell** Ohio U.S.A.
145 E4 **Campbell, C** New Zealand
121 N8 **Campbellford** Ontario Canada
68 D7 **Campbell I** Burma
102 R12 **Campbell Industrial Pk** Hawaiian Is
146 A16 **Campbell Island** *N Z Base* Antarctica
117 J9 **Campbell Island** British Columbia Canada
140 B5 **Campbell, Mt** N Terr Australia
117 D3 **Campbell, Mt** Yukon Territory Canada
74 E2 **Campbellpore** Pakistan
142 G2 **Campbell Ra** W Australia Australia
117 L10 **Campbell River** British Columbia Canada
121 O7 **Campbell's Bay** Quebec Canada
99 S6 **Campbellsport** Wisconsin U.S.A.
110 L4 **Campbellsville** Kentucky U.S.A.
122 F6 **Campbellton** New Brunswick Canada
123 S4 **Campbellton** Newfoundland Canada
109 J7 **Campbellton** Texas U.S.A.
139 K5 **Campbelltown** New South Wales Australia
139 J8 **Campbell Town** Tasmania Australia
12 C3 **Campbeltown** Scotland
20 G7 **Campbon** France
98 C4 **Camp Crook** South Dakota U.S.A.
99 Q6 **Camp Douglas** Wisconsin U.S.A.
21 O2 **Campeaux** France
125 O8 **Campeche** Mexico
90 A6 **Campeche Bank** Atlantic Oc
125 N8 **Campeche, B.de** Mexico
126 F4 **Campechuela** Cuba
20 F6 **Campénéac** France
139 G7 **Camperdown** Victoria Australia
113 L9 **Camperdown** New Providence I Bahamas
119 R7 **Camperville** Manitoba Canada
141 K2 **Camphill** *dist* Brisbane, Qnsld Australia
111 L9 **Camp Hill** Alabama U.S.A.
45 K4 **Campi Bisenzio** Italy
45 Q8 **Campi Flegrei** Italy
16 D6 **Campillo de Llerena** Spain
16 D7 **Campillos** Spain
130 H9 **Campina Grande** Brazil
130 F8 **Campinas** Brazil
130 E6 **Campina Verde** Brazil
102 F5 **Camp Nelson** California U.S.A.
86 A5 **Campo** Cameroon
18 F10 **Campo** Spain
106 H4 **Campo** Colorado U.S.A.
43 F7 **Campobasso** Italy
122 F9 **Campobello I** New Brunswick Canada
130 F7 **Campo Belo** Brazil
130 E10 **Campo Belo do Sul** Brazil
45 L1 **Campodarsego** Italy
16 E6 **Campo de Calatrava** *physical reg* Spain
16 E5 **Campo de Criptana** Spain
129 H6 **Campo de Diauarum** Brazil
126 G9 **Campo de la Cruz** Colombia
130 D10 **Campo Erê** Brazil
130 E6 **Campo Florido** Brazil
129 K6 **Campo Formoso** Brazil
45 J2 **Campogalliano** Italy
133 E3 **Campo Gallo** Argentina
133 G2 **Campo Grande** Brazil
130 C7 **Campo Grande** Mato Grosso Brazil
130 B9 **Campo Grande** *airport* Paraguay
130 E9 **Campo Largo** Brazil
45 L1 **Campolongo Maggiore** Italy
129 K4 **Campo Maior** Brazil
130 D9 **Campo Mourão** Brazil
130 D10 **Campo Novo** Brazil
45 H3 **Camporgiano** Italy
130 H7 **Campos** Brazil
130 F6 **Campos Altos** Brazil
45 K2 **Camposanto** Italy
45 R7 **Camposauro** *mt* Italy
130 D10 **Campos de Palmas** *plains* Brazil
130 F8 **Campos do Jordão** Brazil
130 D9 **Campos Eré** Brazil
133 G3 **Campos Novos** Brazil
41 J5 **Campo Tencia** *mt* Switzerland
128 E3 **Campo Troco** Colombia
42 D2 **Campo Tures** Italy
99 P9 **Camp Point** Illinois U.S.A.
102 D6 **Camp Roberts** California U.S.A.
109 H5 **Camp San Saba** Texas U.S.A.
12 D1 **Campsie Fells** Scotland
111 C10 **Campti** Louisiana U.S.A.
94 D9 **Campton** Kentucky U.S.A.
95 Q3 **Campton** New Hampshire U.S.A.
102 C2 **Camptonville** California U.S.A.
103 N7 **Camp Verde** Arizona U.S.A.
68 J7 **Cam Ranh** Vietnam
118 E5 **Camrose** Alberta Canada
45 L1 **Camsano Vicentino** Italy
117 M4 **Camsell Range** Northwest Territories Canada
45 K3 **Camugnano** Italy
47 J4 **Çan** Turkey
122 G7 **Canaan** New Brunswick Canada
127 M2 **Canaan** Tobago
95 O4 **Canaan** Connecticut U.S.A.
121 T8 **Canaan** Vermont U.S.A.
103 N4 **Canaan Pk** Utah U.S.A.
122 G8 **Canaan R** New Brunswick Canada
129 J6 **Cana Brava** *R* Brazil
130 F5 **Canabrava** Brazil
71 C6 **Canabungan** *isld* Philippines
114 **Canada** *dominion* N America
123 Q3 **Canada B** Newfoundland Canada
131 E4 **Canãda de Gómez** Argentina
95 R8 **Canada Falls** Maine U.S.A.
95 M5 **Canadensis** Pennsylvania U.S.A.
106 F5 **Canadian** *R* New Mexico U.S.A.
108 D8 **Canadian** *R* Texas U.S.A.
108 D8 **Canadian** Texas U.S.A.
133 D8 **Cañadón de las Vacas** Argentina
133 D6 **Cañadón Grande, Sa** *ra* Argentina
112 G4 **Canadys** South Carolina U.S.A.
42 G4 **Čanak** Croatia
47 N10 **Çanak** *R* Turkey
47 H4 **Çanakkale** Turkey
47 H4 **Çanakkale Boğazi** *str* Turkey
43 B11 **Canal de la Galite** *str* Tunisia
127 H5 **Canal de St. Marc** Haiti
129 H3 **Canal do Norte** Brazil
129 J4 **Canal do Sul** Brazil
117 Q10 **Canal Flats** British Columbia Canada
110 G5 **Canalou** Missouri U.S.A.
113 G11 **Canal Point** Florida U.S.A.
94 E7 **Canal Winchester** Ohio U.S.A.
128 D5 **Canama** Brazil
95 K4 **Canandaigua L** New York U.S.A.
124 D2 **Cananea** Mexico
130 F9 **Cananéia** Brazil
128 E3 **Canapiari,Co** *mt* Colombia
21 P1 **Canaples** France
130 E6 **Canápolis** Brazil
128 C4 **Cañar** *prov* Ecuador
126 C4 **Canarreos,Arch.de los** Cuba
90 F6 **Canary Basin** Atlantic Oc
85 A3 **Canary Is** Atlantic Oc
94 K4 **Canaseraga** New York U.S.A.
130 F7 **Canastra, Parque Nacional da Serrada** Brazil
130 E4 **Canastra, Serra da** *mts* Goiás Brazil
130 F7 **Canastra, Serra da** *mts* Minas Gerais Brazil
124 G5 **Canatlán** Mexico
44 B1 **Canave** Italy
16 C5 **Cañaveral** Spain
113 G9 **Canaveral, C** Florida U.S.A.
113 G9 **Canaveral National Seashore** Florida U.S.A.
17 F4 **Cañaveras** Spain
129 L7 **Canavieiras** Brazil
38 E9 **Canazei** Italy
139 H4 **Canbelego** New South Wales Australia
139 J6 **Canberra** Aust Capital Terr Australia
138 A6 **Canberra & Environs** Australia
100 E8 **Canby** California U.S.A.
98 K5 **Canby** Minnesota U.S.A.
100 C4 **Canby** Oregon U.S.A.
20 G4 **Cancale** France
41 M4 **Cancano, Lago di** Italy
45 Q8 **Cancello** Italy
45 Q7 **Cancello ed Arnone** Italy
22 B3 **Canche** *R* France
21 O1 **Canchy** France
18 F8 **Cancon** France
125 Q7 **Cancún** Mexico
45 K3 **Canda, M** *mt* Italy
47 H6 **Çandarlı** Turkey
47 H6 **Çandarlı Körfezi** *G* Turkey
21 P1 **Candas** France
21 H6 **Candé** France
16 B5 **Candeeiros,Sa.de** Portugal
128 F5 **Candeias** *R* Brazil
130 F7 **Candeias** Brazil
43 G7 **Candela** Italy
45 N4 **Candelara** Italy
130 C10 **Candelaria** Argentina
124 F2 **Candelaria** Mexico
108 C5 **Candelaria** Texas U.S.A.
139 J6 **Candelo** New South Wales Australia
Candia *see* **Iráklion**
119 O8 **Candiac** Saskatchewan Canada
45 L1 **Candiana** Italy
130 D9 **Cãndido de Abreu** Brazil
130 E8 **Cândido Mota** Brazil
116 F4 **Candle** Alaska U.S.A.
119 M5 **Candle L** Saskatchewan Canada
146 G2 **Candlemas I** S Sandwich Is S Atlantic Oc
95 O5 **Candlewood,L** Connecticut U.S.A.
118 J6 **Cando** Saskatchewan Canada
98 G1 **Cando** North Dakota U.S.A.
133 G3 **Candói** Brazil
143 B6 **Candolle, Mt** W Australia Australia
71 E2 **Candon** Luzon Philippines
95 L4 **Candor** New York U.S.A.
112 H2 **Candor** North Carolina U.S.A.
120 K5 **Cane** Ontario Canada
Canea *see* **Khaniá**
94 J4 **Caneadea** New York U.S.A.
129 J6 **Canéia** Brazil
133 G3 **Canela** Brazil
133 F4 **Canelones** Uruguay
130 C9 **Canendiyu** *dept* Paraguay
133 C5 **Cañete** Chile
128 C6 **Cañete** *R* Peru
17 F4 **Cañete** Spain
107 P4 **Caney** Kansas U.S.A.
107 O7 **Caney** Oklahoma U.S.A.
110 L6 **Caney Fork** *R* Tennessee U.S.A.
110 K4 **Caneyville** Kentucky U.S.A.
111 C8 **Canfield** Arkansas U.S.A.
94 G5 **Canfield** Ohio U.S.A.
18 E10 **Canfranc** Spain
87 C8 **Cangamba** Angola
87 C7 **Cangandala** Angola
16 C1 **Cangas de Narcea** Spain
16 D1 **Cangas de Onís** Spain
21 N7 **Cangey** France
69 E9 **Canglun** Malaysia
87 C8 **Cangoa** Angola
89 B9 **Cango Caves** S Africa
87 D8 **Cangombe** Angola
59 H1 **Cangshan** China
65 D7 **Cangshan** China
130 J9 **Canguaretama** Brazil
133 G4 **Canguçu** Brazil
131 H3 **Canguçu,Sa.do** *mt* Brazil
87 C8 **Cangumbe** Angola
67 D5 **Cangwu** China
67 B1 **Cangxi** China
65 C5 **Cang Xian** China
68 D1 **Cangyuan** China
65 C5 **Cangzhou** China
130 H10 **Canhotinho** Brazil
115 N6 **Caniapiscau** *R* Quebec Canada
115 N7 **Caniapiscau,Lac** Quebec Canada
121 N3 **Canica I** Quebec Canada
43 F11 **Canicatti** Sicily
71 G5 **Canigao Ch** Philippines
18 G10 **Canigou** *mt* France
17 F7 **Caniles** Spain
117 N10 **Canim L** British Columbia Canada
129 K5 **Caninde** *R* Brazil
71 E5 **Canipo** *isld* Philippines
15 C2 **Canisp Mt** Scotland
94 K4 **Canisteo** New York U.S.A.
95 K4 **Canisteo** *R* New York U.S.A.
21 H3 **Canisy** France
124 H6 **Cañitas** Mexico
17 F7 **Canjáyar** Spain
78 D1 **Çankırı** Turkey
71 E3 **Canlubang** Luzon Philippines
118 B7 **Canmore** Alberta Canada
143 B8 **Canna** W Australia Australia
15 B3 **Canna** *isld* Scotland
76 B5 **Cannanore** India
110 K4 **Cannelton** Indiana U.S.A.
41 J5 **Cannero Riviera** Italy
44 B4 **Cannes** France
45 J1 **Canneto s. Oglio** Italy
122 H8 **Canning** Nova Scotia Canada
116 O2 **Canning** *R* Alaska U.S.A.
98 G5 **Canning** South Dakota U.S.A.
143 C8 **Canning Hill** W Australia Australia
142 B2 **Canning River** W Australia Australia
142 B2 **Cannington** *dist* Perth, W Aust Australia
121 L8 **Cannington** Ontario Canada
142 B2 **Canning Vale** W Australia Australia
41 J5 **Cannobio** Italy
99 O5 **Cannon** *R* Minnesota U.S.A.
98 E3 **Cannonball** *R* North Dakota U.S.A.
98 F3 **Cannon Ball** North Dakota U.S.A.
99 O5 **Cannon Falls** Minnesota U.S.A.
139 J7 **Cann R** Victoria Australia
133 G3 **Canoas** Brazil
130 D10 **Canõas, R. das** Brazil
140 F4 **Canobie** Queensland Australia
130 F6 **Canoeiros** Brazil
118 J3 **Canoe L** Saskatchewan Canada
117 O9 **Canoe R** British Columbia Canada
130 E10 **Canoinhas** Brazil
15 F5 **Canonbie** Scotland
106 E3 **Canon City** Colorado U.S.A.
106 C5 **Cañon Largo** *R* New Mexico U.S.A.
94 G6 **Canonsburg** Pennsylvania U.S.A.
112 F6 **Canoochia** *R* Georgia U.S.A.
138 F5 **Canopus** South Australia Australia
119 P7 **Canora** Saskatchewan Canada
43 G7 **Canosa di Puglia** Italy
127 O8 **Canouan** *isld* Lesser Antilles
98 J6 **Canova** South Dakota U.S.A.
139 J5 **Canowindra** New South Wales Australia
47 K6 **Çanşa** Turkey
71 F6 **Cansilan Pt** Negros Philippines
123 M8 **Canso** Nova Scotia Canada
123 L8 **Canso,Str.of** Nova Scotia Canada
16 E1 **Cantabria** *prov* Spain
18 D10 **Cantabria,Sierra de** *mts* Spain
Cantábrica, Mar *see* **Biscay, Bay of**
45 K3 **Cantagallo** Italy
18 G7 **Cantal** *dept* France
45 Q6 **Cantalupo nel Sánnio** Italy
127 O2 **Cantaro** Trinidad
127 M10 **Cantaura** Venezuela
21 N3 **Canteleu** France
122 E8 **Canterbury** New Brunswick Canada
9 H5 **Canterbury** England
144 D5 **Canterbury** *admin region* New Zealand
144 D6 **Canterbury Bight** New Zealand
144 C6 **Canterbury Plains** New Zealand
45 O6 **Canterna, L. di** Italy
68 G7 **Can Tho** Vietnam
102 G6 **Cantil** California U.S.A.
71 G6 **Cantilan** Mindanao Philippines
16 D7 **Cantiliana** Spain
129 K5 **Canto do Buriti** Brazil
63 **Canton** *conurbation* China
Canton China *see* **Guangzhou**
112 C3 **Canton** Georgia U.S.A.
110 F1 **Canton** Illinois U.S.A.
107 N3 **Canton** Kansas U.S.A.
95 R2 **Canton** Maine U.S.A.
111 F9 **Canton** Mississippi U.S.A.
110 E1 **Canton** Missouri U.S.A.
101 O3 **Canton** Montana U.S.A.
121 P8 **Canton** New York U.S.A.
112 E2 **Canton** North Carolina U.S.A.
94 F6 **Canton** Ohio U.S.A.
107 M5 **Canton** Oklahoma U.S.A.
95 L5 **Canton** Pennsylvania U.S.A.
98 K6 **Canton** South Dakota U.S.A.
109 M3 **Canton** Texas U.S.A.
121 T4 **Canton-Bégin** Quebec Canada
134 A5 **Canton I** Pacific Oc
107 M5 **Canton L** Oklahoma U.S.A.
110 D1 **Cantril** Iowa U.S.A.
41 K6 **Cantù** Italy
118 J8 **Cantuar** Saskatchewan Canada
130 D9 **Cantú,R** Brazil
130 D9 **Cantú, Serra do** *mt* Brazil
130 G10 **Canudos** Brazil
133 F5 **Cañuelas** Argentina
128 G4 **Canuma** Brazil
128 F5 **Canutama** Brazil
107 L6 **Canute** Oklahoma U.S.A.
124 G4 **Canutillo** Mexico
108 A4 **Canutillo** Texas U.S.A.
145 D4 **Canvastown** New Zealand
9 G5 **Canvey I** England
118 L5 **Canwood** Saskatchewan Canada
21 M2 **Cany-Barville** France
120 F5 **Canyon** Ontario Canada
117 E5 **Canyon** Yukon Territory Canada
108 F1 **Canyon** Texas U.S.A.
101 P5 **Canyon** Wyoming U.S.A.
100 G5 **Canyon City** Oregon U.S.A.
100 K6 **Canyon Cr** Idaho U.S.A.
118 C3 **Canyon Creek** Alberta Canada
101 N3 **Canyon Creek** Montana U.S.A.
103 P5 **Canyon de Chelly Nat.Mon** Arizona U.S.A.
101 O3 **Canyon Ferry Dam** Montana U.S.A.
103 N8 **Canyon L** Arizona U.S.A.
109 J6 **Canyon L** Texas U.S.A.
103 P3 **Canyonlands Nat. Park** Utah U.S.A.
117 K4 **Canyon Ranges** Northwest Territories Canada
100 B7 **Canyonville** Oregon U.S.A.
87 D7 **Canzar** Angola
33 T6 **Canzow** Germany
67 B5 **Cao Bang** Vietnam
65 C5 **Caogoubu** China
67 A3 **Cao Hai** *L* China
65 F4 **Cao He** *R* China
65 F4 **Caohekou** China
Caojiahe *see* **Qichun**
12 C2 **Caolisport, L** Scotland
87 C7 **Caombo** Angola
68 J6 **Cao Nguen Dar Lac** *plateau* Vietnam
122 F1 **Caopacho L** Quebec Canada
122 F2 **Caopacho R** Quebec Canada
121 Q3 **Caopatina, L** Quebec Canada
65 F3 **Caoshi** China
67 D3 **Caoshi** China
65 C7 **Cao Xian** China
98 F5 **Capa** South Dakota U.S.A.
87 D7 **Capaia** Angola
128 E2 **Capanaparo** *R* Venezuela
129 J4 **Capanema** Brazil
130 D9 **Capanema, R** Brazil
45 J4 **Capannoli** Italy
45 J4 **Capannori** Italy
130 F5 **Capão Redondo** Brazil
130 H7 **Caparaó,Sa do** *mts* Brazil
128 E3 **Caparro, Co** *mt* Colombia
71 E3 **Capas** Luzon Philippines
127 J9 **Capatárida** Venezuela
48 H5 **Căpăţînei, Muntii** *mt* Romania
71 D7 **Capayan Sulu** *isld* Philippines
18 D9 **Capbreton** France
122 F4 **Cap Chat** Quebec Canada
121 S6 **Cap de la Madeleine** Quebec Canada
18 G8 **Capdenac** France
122 H4 **Cap de Rabast** Quebec Canada
122 H5 **Cap-d'Espoir** Quebec Canada
95 R4 **Cape Ann** Massachusetts U.S.A.
143 E10 **Cape Arid Nat Park** W Australia Australia
139 J8 **Cape Barren I** Tasmania Australia
90 K12 **Cape Basin** Atlantic Oc
Cape Bastion *see* **Jinmu Jido**
123 M7 **Cape Breton Highlands Nat Pk** C Breton I, Nova Scotia
123 N7 **Cape Breton I** Nova Scotia Canada
123 U6 **Cape Broyle** Newfoundland Canada
113 G9 **Cape Canaveral** Florida U.S.A.
123 R1 **Cape Charles** Labrador, Nfld Canada
95 L9 **Cape Charles** Virginia U.S.A.
85 D7 **Cape Coast** Ghana
95 S5 **Cape Cod** Massachusetts U.S.A.
95 R5 **Cape Cod B** Massachusetts U.S.A.
95 R5 **Cape Cod Canal** Massachusetts U.S.A.
95 R5 **Cape Cod Nat.Seashore** Massachusetts U.S.A.
113 F11 **Cape Coral** Florida U.S.A.
115 M5 **Cape Dorset** Northwest Territories Canada
115 N4 **Cape Dyer** Northwest Territories Canada
112 K4 **Cape Fear** North Carolina U.S.A.
110 G4 **Cape Girardeau** Missouri U.S.A.
112 M2 **Cape Hatteras** North Carolina U.S.A.
115 N5 **Cape Hopes Advance** Quebec Canada
Cape Horn *see* **Hornos, C. de**
112 H4 **Cape I** South Carolina U.S.A.
116 F3 **Cape Krusenstern Nat Mon** Alaska U.S.A.
143 B10 **Capel** W Australia Australia
129 L6 **Capela** Brazil
123 P6 **Cape la Hune** Newfoundland Canada
8 C1 **Capel Curig** Wales
143 D10 **Cape Le Grand Nat Park** W Australia Australia
130 G5 **Capelinha** Brazil
116 E2 **Cape Lisburne** Alaska U.S.A.
141 J6 **Capella** Queensland Australia
22 F4 **Capelle-en-Thierache, la** France
22 K4 **Capellen** Luxembourg
87 C9 **Capelongo** Angola
95 N8 **Cape May** New Jersey U.S.A.
87 C7 **Capenda-Camulemba** Angola
89 A10 **Cape of Good Hope** S Africa
114 G3 **Cape Parry** Northwest Territories Canada
Cape Province *see* **Eastern Cape, Northern Cape, North West, Western Cape**
89 A10 **Cape Pt** S Africa
141 H5 **Cape R** Queensland Australia
123 T7 **Cape Race** Newfoundland Canada
142 A5 **Cape Range Nat Park** W Australia Australia
123 N6 **Cape Ray** Newfoundland Canada
80 F2 **Capernaum** Israel
112 H5 **Cape Romain** South Carolina U.S.A.
103 N5 **Cape Royal** Arizona U.S.A.
113 F12 **Cape Sable** *pen* Florida U.S.A.
122 G10 **Cape Sable I** Nova Scotia Canada
122 F9 **Cape St.Mary** Nova Scotia Canada
123 S7 **Cape St. Mary's** *lighthouse* Newfoundland Canada
127 O5 **Capesterre** Marie Galante W Indies
127 N4 **Capesterre-Belle-Eau** Guadeloupe W Indies
45 P5 **Capestrallo** Italy
89 A9 **Cape Town** S Africa
90 E7 **Cape Verde Fracture** Atlantic Oc
90 G7 **Cape Verde Is** *rep* Atlantic Oc
90 G7 **Cape Verde Plateau** Atlantic Oc
95 M9 **Capeville** Virginia U.S.A.
95 L2 **Cape Vincent** New York U.S.A.
15 C2 **Cape Wrath** Scotland
141 F1 **Cape York Pen** Queensland Australia
127 H5 **Cap-Haïtien** Haiti
130 B9 **Capiatá** Paraguay
128 E3 **Capibara** Venezuela
130 J9 **Capibéribe** *R* Brazil
133 F4 **Capilla** Argentina
133 E4 **Capilla del Monte** Argentina
129 J4 **Capim** *R* Brazil
128 E7 **Capinota** Bolivia
41 H6 **Capio, Monte** Italy
45 O6 **Capistrello** Italy
121 O5 **Capitachouane** *R* Quebec Canada
106 E8 **Capitan** New Mexico U.S.A.
146 C3 **Capitan Arturo Prat** *Chile Base* Antarctica
130 C8 **Capitán Bado** Paraguay
131 A8 **Capitanes, Pta** *C* Chile
106 E8 **Capitan Mts** New Mexico U.S.A.
42 E6 **Capitignano** Italy
98 B4 **Capitol** Montana U.S.A.
100 H8 **Capitol Peak** *mt* Nevada U.S.A.
103 N3 **Capitol Reef Nat. Park** Utah U.S.A.
129 K5 **Capivara, Parque Nacional da Serra da** Brazil
122 G5 **Caplan** Quebec Canada
20 A5 **Cap, Le** *pen* France
71 E5 **Capnoyan** *isld* Philippines
88 D9 **Capoche** *R* Mozambique
129 G5 **Capoeiras, Cachoeira das** *waterfall* Brazil
44 D4 **Capo Mele** Italy
139 K3 **Capoompeta** *mt* New South Wales Australia
45 O5 **Cappadocia** Italy
36 F2 **Cappel** Germany
14 D4 **Cappoquin** Ireland
127 O7 **Cap Pt** St Lucia
42 C5 **Capraia, I.di** Italy
43 B7 **Caprara o dello Scorno, Pta** *pt* Sardinia

120 K6 **Capreol** Ontario Canada
43 C7 **Caprera, I** Sardinia
45 L4 **Caprese Michelangelo** Italy
45 Q8 **Capri** Italy
45 Q7 **Capriati a Volturno** Italy
141 K5 **Capricorn Chan** Gt Barrier Reef Aust
141 K6 **Capricorn Grp** *islds* Gt Barrier Reef Aust
143 B6 **Capricorn Ra** W Australia Australia
42 D3 **Caprino Veronese** Italy
87 D9 **Caprivi Strip** Namibia
108 D2 **Caprock** New Mexico U.S.A.
123 M7 **Capstick** C Breton I, Nova Scotia
135 U5 **Captain Cook** Hawaiian Is
139 J6 **Captain's Flat** New South Wales Australia
18 E8 **Captieux** France
113 E11 **Captiva** Florida U.S.A.
45 Q7 **Capua** Italy
71 E7 **Capual** *isld* Philippines
83 K12 **Capucin Pt** Mahé I Indian Oc
71 G4 **Capul** Philippines
106 D4 **Capulin** Colorado U.S.A.
106 G5 **Capulin** New Mexico U.S.A.
128 D3 **Caqueta** *div* Colombia
128 D4 **Caquetá** *R* Colombia
71 E4 **Carabao** *isld* Philippines
128 D6 **Carabaya, Cord.de** *mts* Peru
128 F4 **Carabinani** *R* Brazil
128 E1 **Carabobo** *state* Venezuela
48 J6 **Caracal** Romania
127 L9 **Caracas** Venezuela
129 K5 **Caracol** Brazil
130 C7 **Caracol** Brazil
125 J8 **Caracuaro** Mexico
71 G7 **Caraga** Mindanao Philippines
14 B4 **Caragh,L** Ireland
131 G4 **Caraguatá** *R* Uruguay
130 F8 **Caraguata-tuba** Brazil
130 C9 **Caraguatay** Paraguay
133 C5 **Carahue** Chile
130 H5 **Caraí** Brazil
12 C2 **Cara I** Scotland
129 H5 **Carajás, Serra dos** *mts* Brazil
18 G9 **Caraman** France
120 D3 **Caramat** Ontario Canada
71 F4 **Caramoan Pen** Philippines
128 F5 **Caranapatuba** Brazil
130 G7 **Carandaí** Brazil
130 B6 **Carandazal** Brazil
140 E5 **Carandotta** Queensland Australia
129 K8 **Carangola** Brazil
128 F3 **Caransaca,Co** *mt* Venezuela
48 G5 **Caransebeș** Romania
20 C4 **Carantec** France
130 B9 **Carapeguá** Paraguay
138 D5 **Carappee Hill** South Australia Australia
122 H6 **Caraquet** New Brunswick Canada
122 H6 **Caraquet Bay** New Brunswick Canada
128 B4 **Caráquez,B.de** Ecuador
48 G5 **Carașova** Romania
48 G5 **Caraș-Severin** *reg* Romania
125 N2 **Caratasca** Honduras
130 G6 **Caratinga** Brazil
69 G14 **Carat, Tanjung** *C* Indonesia
128 E4 **Carauari** Brazil
130 H8 **Caraúbas** Brazil
17 F6 **Caravaca de la Cruz** Spain
41 L7 **Caravaggio** Italy
130 J5 **Caravelas** Brazil
128 D7 **Caraveli** Peru
43 B9 **Caravius, M. is** *mt* Sardinia
128 C5 **Caraz** Peru
131 H2 **Carazinho** Brazil
16 B2 **Carballiño** Spain
16 B1 **Carballo** Spain
16 B1 **Carba, Sa. de la** *mts* Spain
119 S9 **Carberry** Manitoba Canada
101 U1 **Carbert** Montana U.S.A.
118 D7 **Carbon** Alberta Canada
43 C9 **Carbonara,C** Sardinia
45 K1 **Carbonara di Po** Italy
118 D5 **Carbondale** Alberta Canada
106 C2 **Carbondale** Colorado U.S.A.
107 P3 **Carbondale** Kansas U.S.A.
95 M5 **Carbondale** Pennsylvania U.S.A.
123 T6 **Carbonear** Newfoundland Canada
17 F8 **Carboneras** Spain
111 J8 **Carbon Hill** Alabama U.S.A.
43 B9 **Carbonia** Sardinia
43 B8 **Carbonin** Italy
130 G5 **Carbonita** Brazil
18 F9 **Carbonne** France
17 G5 **Carcagente** Spain
117 P7 **Carcajou** Alberta Canada
18 E7 **Carcans, Etang de** *L* France
71 F5 **Carcar** Cebu Philippines
131 E4 **Carcaraña** *R* Argentina
18 G9 **Carcassonne** France
128 C3 **Carchi** *prov* Ecuador
139 J5 **Carcoar** New South Wales Australia
117 F5 **Carcross** Yukon Territory Canada
142 A6 **Cardabia** W Australia Australia
47 K7 **Çardak** Turkey
119 R8 **Cardale** Manitoba Canada
68 F7 **Cardamones,Chaîne des** *mts* Cambodia
125 K6 **Cárdenas** Mexico
139 G3 **Cardenyabba** *R* New South Wales Australia
133 C7 **Cardiel,L** Argentina
8 C6 **Cardiff** Wales
8 B3 **Cardigan** Wales
123 K7 **Cardigan B** Prince Edward I Canada
8 B2 **Cardigan B** Wales
121 P8 **Cardinal** Ontario Canada
94 E6 **Cardington** Ohio U.S.A.
17 J3 **Cardona** Spain
17 J3 **Cardoner,R** Spain
127 J9 **Cardón,Pta** Venezuela
130 E7 **Cardoso** Brazil
130 F9 **Cardoso,I.do** Brazil
144 B5 **Cardrona** New Zealand
144 B6 **Cardrona, Mt** New Zealand
119 M9 **Cardross** Saskatchewan Canada
12 D2 **Cardross** Scotland
118 D9 **Cardston** Alberta Canada
141 H4 **Cardwell** Queensland Australia
41 O6 **Carega, Cima** *mt* Italy
48 G3 **Carei** Romania
120 D2 **Carenage** Trinidad
22 D3 **Carency** France
20 H3 **Carentan** France
18 F5 **Carentoir** France
8 B4 **Carew** Wales
101 M6 **Carey** Idaho U.S.A.
94 D6 **Carey** Ohio U.S.A.
108 G1 **Carey** Texas U.S.A.
143 B7 **Carey Downs** W Australia Australia
143 D8 **Carey, L** W Australia Australia
81 C7 **Cargados Carajos** *islds* Indian Oc
18 L10 **Cargèse** Corsica
120 J8 **Cargill** Ontario Canada
13 E1 **Cargill** Scotland
141 G5 **Cargoon** Queensland Australia
20 C5 **Carhaix-Plouguer** France
122 E1 **Carheil,L** Quebec Canada
47 J7 **Caria** *hist reg* Turkey
130 H7 **Cariacica** Brazil
127 N9 **Cariaco** Venezuela
126 F10 **Caribana,Pta** Colombia
126 C5 **Caribbean Sea** Central America
117 N9 **Cariboo Mts** British Columbia Canada
117 K5 **Caribou** *R* Northwest Territories Canada
122 K8 **Caribou** Nova Scotia Canada
116 G9 **Caribou** *R* Alaska U.S.A.
95 S7 **Caribou** Maine U.S.A.
117 K7 **Caribou Hide** British Columbia Canada
122 K8 **Caribou I** Nova Scotia Canada
120 E5 **Caribou I** Ontario Canada
117 R5 **Caribou Is** Northwest Territories Canada
101 O6 **Caribou Mt** Idaho U.S.A.
117 Q6 **Caribou Mts** Alberta Canada
124 F4 **Carichic** Mexico
119 Q9 **Carievale** Saskatchewan Canada
71 G5 **Carigara** Leyte Philippines
22 J4 **Carignan** France
44 C2 **Carignano** Italy
121 Q7 **Carillon** Quebec Canada
139 J4 **Carinda** New South Wales Australia
17 G3 **Cariñena** Spain
129 K6 **Carinhanha** Brazil
45 P7 **Carinola** Italy
129 J6 **Caripare** Brazil
127 N9 **Caripe** Venezuela
127 N9 **Caripito** Venezuela
130 G9 **Caririaçu** Brazil
128 F5 **Caritianas** Brazil
130 G9 **Cariús** Brazil
107 N5 **Carl Blackwell, L** Oklahoma U.S.A.
22 E4 **Carlepont** France
17 G5 **Carlet** Spain
122 F5 **Carleton** Quebec Canada
94 D4 **Carleton** Michigan U.S.A.
98 J9 **Carleton** Nebraska U.S.A.
122 F6 **Carleton,Mt** New Brunswick Canada
121 O7 **Carleton Place** Ontario Canada
122 K4 **Carleton Pt** Quebec Canada
98 B5 **Carlile** Wyoming U.S.A.
103 H1 **Carlin** Nevada U.S.A.
36 B5 **Carling** France
14 E2 **Carlingford** Ireland
110 G2 **Carlinville** Illinois U.S.A.
142 B2 **Carlisle** *dist* Perth, W Aust Australia
13 F4 **Carlisle** England
110 E7 **Carlisle** Arkansas U.S.A.
110 J3 **Carlisle** Indiana U.S.A.
94 C8 **Carlisle** Kentucky U.S.A.
95 K6 **Carlisle** Pennsylvania U.S.A.
112 F3 **Carlisle** South Carolina U.S.A.
127 P6 **Carlisle B** Barbados
143 F8 **Carlisle Lakes** W Australia Australia
18 G10 **Carlitte** *mt* France
43 B9 **Carloforte** Sardinia
13 E2 **Carlops** Scotland
133 E6 **Carlos Ameghino, Istmo** Argentina
133 E5 **Carlos Casares** Argentina
130 H5 **Carlos Chagas** Brazil
131 G4 **Carlos Reyles** Uruguay
14 E4 **Carlow** *co* Ireland
14 E4 **Carlow** Ireland
15 B2 **Carloway** Scotland
Carlsbad Czech Rep *see* **Karlovy Vary**
102 G8 **Carlsbad** California U.S.A.
108 C3 **Carlsbad** New Mexico U.S.A.
108 C3 **Carlsbad Caverns Nat. Park** New Mexico U.S.A.
72 H7 **Carlsberg Ridge** Indian Oc
37 O3 **Carlsfeld** Germany
99 T3 **Carlshend** Michigan U.S.A.
118 L6 **Carlton** Saskatchewan Canada
99 O3 **Carlton** Minnesota U.S.A.
100 B4 **Carlton** Oregon U.S.A.
109 J4 **Carlton** Texas U.S.A.
142 G3 **Carlton Hill** W Australia Australia
9 F1 **Carlton-on-Trent** England
100 D3 **Carlton Pass** Washington U.S.A.
12 E2 **Carluke** Scotland
119 P9 **Carlyle** Saskatchewan Canada
110 G3 **Carlyle** Illinois U.S.A.
98 B3 **Carlyle** Montana U.S.A.
118 D1 **Carman** Manitoba Canada
118 D8 **Carmangay** Alberta Canada
123 S4 **Carmanville** Newfoundland Canada
8 B4 **Carmarthen** Wales
8 C4 **Carmarthen Van** *mt* Wales
18 G8 **Carmaux** France
119 M6 **Carmel** Saskatchewan Canada
102 C5 **Carmel** California U.S.A.
94 A7 **Carmel** Indiana U.S.A.
110 K2 **Carmel** Indiana U.S.A.
95 O5 **Carmel** New York U.S.A.
95 S2 **Carmel** Maine U.S.A.
80 D3 **Carmel,Mt** Israel
112 E3 **Carmel, Mt** South Carolina U.S.A.
80 D3 **Carmel National Park, Mt** Israel
133 F4 **Carmelo** Uruguay
127 J9 **Carmelo** Venezuela
102 C5 **Carmel Valley** California U.S.A.
126 G10 **Carmen** Colombia
125 M8 **Carmen** *R* Mexico
124 D5 **Carmen** *isld* Mexico
71 G6 **Carmen** Philippines
101 M4 **Carmen** Idaho U.S.A.
107 M5 **Carmen** Oklahoma U.S.A.
133 D8 **Carmen Alto** Chile
130 C10 **Carmen del Paraná** Paraguay
133 E6 **Carmen de Patagones** Argentina
131 B2 **Carmen,R.del** Chile
133 D5 **Carmensa** Argentina
108 E7 **Carmen, Sa del** *mts* Mexico
110 H3 **Carmi** Illinois U.S.A.
113 L9 **Carmichael** New Providence I Bahamas
118 J8 **Carmichael** Saskatchewan Canada
141 J5 **Carmila** Queensland Australia
109 L5 **Carmine** Texas U.S.A.
130 G7 **Carmo** Brazil
44 D3 **Carmo** *mt* Italy
130 F6 **Carmo da Cachoeira** Brazil
130 E5 **Carmo do Paranaiba** Brazil
143 C9 **Carmody, L** W Australia Australia
16 D7 **Carmona** Spain
13 H5 **Carnaby** England
20 D6 **Carnac** France
143 B8 **Carnamah** W Australia Australia
138 F4 **Carnanto,L** South Australia Australia
143 A6 **Carnarvon** W Australia Australia
89 C8 **Carnarvon** S Africa
141 H7 **Carnarvon Nat. Park** Queensland Australia
141 J7 **Carnarvon Ra** Queensland Australia
143 D7 **Carnarvon Ra** W Australia Australia
71 C5 **Carnatic Shoal** S China Sea
14 D2 **Carndonagh** Ireland
119 Q9 **Carnduff** Saskatchewan Canada
8 C1 **Carnedd Llewelyn** *mt* Wales
143 E7 **Carnegie** W Australia Australia
107 M6 **Carnegie** Oklahoma U.S.A.
94 G6 **Carnegie** Pennsylvania U.S.A.
143 E7 **Carnegie, L** W Australia Australia
90 A9 **Carnegie Ridge** Pacific Oc
21 K4 **Carneille, la** France
107 N3 **Carneiro** Kansas U.S.A.
131 A6 **Carnero,B.del** Chile
112 D3 **Carnesville** Georgia U.S.A.
146 B8 **Carney** *isld* Antarctica
99 T4 **Carney** Michigan U.S.A.
107 O6 **Carney** Oklahoma U.S.A.
13 F5 **Carnforth** England
42 E2 **Carniche, Alpi** *mts* Italy
69 A8 **Car Nicobar** *isld* Nicobar Is
22 E3 **Carnières** France
20 C5 **Carnoët** France
86 C5 **Carnot** Cent Afr Republic
138 D5 **Carnot,C** South Australia Australia
19 Q18 **Carnoules** France
13 F1 **Carnoustie** Scotland
14 E4 **Carnsore Pt** Ireland
12 E2 **Carnwath** Scotland
116 N3 **Caro** Alaska U.S.A.
94 D3 **Caro** Michigan U.S.A.
141 K4 **Carola Cay** *isld* Gt Barrier Reef Australia
112 F2 **Caroleen** North Carolina U.S.A.
129 J5 **Carolina** Brazil
128 C3 **Carolina** Ecuador
87 F11 **Carolina** S Africa
112 K3 **Carolina Beach** North Carolina U.S.A.
118 C6 **Caroline** Alberta Canada
144 B6 **Caroline** New Zealand
135 M9 **Caroline I** Pacific Oc
134 E7 **Caroline Is** Pacific Oc
140 D6 **Caroline, L** N Terr Australia
32 G5 **Carolinensiel** Germany
144 A6 **Caroline Pk** New Zealand
142 F3 **Caroline Ra** W Australia Australia
20 G4 **Carolles** France
119 M8 **Caron** Saskatchewan Canada
137 S3 **Carondelet Reef** Phoenix Is Pacific Oc
127 O2 **Caroni** Trinidad
128 F2 **Caroni** *R* Venezuela
127 O2 **Caroni Swamp** Trinidad
127 J9 **Carora** Venezuela
127 O2 **Carp** Ontario Canada
103 K4 **Carp** Nevada U.S.A.
53 B9 **Carpathian Mts** E Europe
48 H5 **Carpaţii Meridionali** *mts* Romania
41 M7 **Carpenèdolo** Italy
141 G4 **Carpentaria Downs** Queensland Australia
140 E2 **Carpentaria,Gulf of** Australia
98 B8 **Carpenter** Wyoming U.S.A.
99 S7 **Carpentersville** Illinois U.S.A.
100 A7 **Carpenterville** Oregon U.S.A.
19 O16 **Carpentras** France
45 J2 **Carpi** Italy
19 P18 **Carpiagne** *mt* France
130 J9 **Carpina** Brazil
45 J2 **Carpineti** Italy
45 O6 **Carpineto Romano** Italy
48 F5 **Cărpiniș** Romania
102 E7 **Carpinteria** California U.S.A.
98 E1 **Carpio** North Dakota U.S.A.
117 M8 **Carp L** British Columbia Canada
103 M2 **Carp L** Utah U.S.A.
94 C1 **Carp Lake** Michigan U.S.A.
138 F6 **Carpolac** Victoria Australia
20 H7 **Carquefou** France
19 Q18 **Carqueiranne** France
106 F1 **Carr** Colorado U.S.A.
113 C8 **Carrabelle** Florida U.S.A.
119 O6 **Carragana** Saskatchewan Canada
14 B3 **Carra,L** Ireland
16 B4 **Carramulo, Sa. do** *mts* Portugal
131 A5 **Carranza,C** Chile
125 J4 **Carranza, Presa V.** *res* Mexico
128 F2 **Carrao** *R* Venezuela
44 H3 **Carrara** Italy
102 H5 **Carrara** Nevada U.S.A.
140 D4 **Carrara Range** N Terr Australia
17 F4 **Carrascosa del Campo** Spain
17 G7 **Carrascoy,Sierra de** *mts* Spain
139 H5 **Carrathool** New South Wales Australia
14 B5 **Carrauntoohil** *mt* Ireland
142 G3 **Carr Boyd Ra** W Australia Australia
15 E3 **Carrbridge** Scotland
133 F2 **Carreria** Paraguay
131 B6 **Carrero,Cerro** *pk* Argentina
127 O8 **Carriacou** *isld* Lesser Antilles
15 D5 **Carrick** Scotland
14 F2 **Carrickfergus** N Ireland
14 E3 **Carrickmacross** Ireland
14 C3 **Carrick on Shannon** Ireland
14 D4 **Carrick-on-Suir** Ireland
111 G11 **Carriere** Mississippi U.S.A.
121 N5 **Carrière,L** Quebec Canada
110 H4 **Carriers Mills** Illinois U.S.A.
138 E4 **Carrieton** South Australia Australia
131 B8 **Carri Lafquén, L** Argentina
98 G2 **Carrington** North Dakota U.S.A.
16 D2 **Carrion** *R* Spain
16 D2 **Carrión de los Condes** Spain
127 H8 **Carrizal** Colombia
124 F2 **Carrizal** Mexico
133 C3 **Carrizal Bajo** Chile
131 B2 **Carrizal, Pta** *C* Chile
103 H9 **Carrizo Cr** California U.S.A.
106 G5 **Carrizo Cr** New Mex/Tex U.S.A.
103 P5 **Carrizo Mts** Arizona U.S.A.
108 H7 **Carrizo Springs** Texas U.S.A.
106 E8 **Carrizozo** New Mexico U.S.A.
119 R9 **Carroll** Manitoba Canada
99 M7 **Carroll** Iowa U.S.A.
98 J7 **Carroll** Nebraska U.S.A.
111 H8 **Carrollton** Alabama U.S.A.
112 B4 **Carrollton** Georgia U.S.A.
110 F2 **Carrollton** Illinois U.S.A.
94 B8 **Carrollton** Kentucky U.S.A.
111 G8 **Carrollton** Mississippi U.S.A.
110 C2 **Carrollton** Missouri U.S.A.
94 F6 **Carrollton** Ohio U.S.A.
109 O8 **Carrollton** Texas U.S.A.
94 J6 **Carrolltown** Pennsylvania U.S.A.
99 T7 **Carrollville** Wisconsin U.S.A.
141 F4 **Carron** *R* Queensland Australia
12 E3 **Carronbridge** Scotland
119 V4 **Carrot R** Manitoba Canada
119 O5 **Carrot River** Saskatchewan Canada
21 K4 **Carrouges** France
14 B2 **Carrowmore L** Ireland
118 H6 **Carruthers** Saskatchewan Canada
100 C8 **Carrville** California U.S.A.
95 N2 **Carry Falls Res** New York U.S.A.
19 O18 **Carry-le-Rouet** France
78 F1 **Çarşamba** Turkey
118 D8 **Carseland** Alberta Canada
13 E1 **Carse of Gowrie** *dist* Scotland
45 O5 **Carseolani, Mti** Italy
9 E1 **Carsington Resr.** England
45 O5 **Carsoli** Italy
99 L8 **Carson** Iowa U.S.A.
102 E2 **Carson** *R* Nevada U.S.A.
98 E3 **Carson** North Dakota U.S.A.
100 D4 **Carson** Washington U.S.A.
94 C3 **Carson City** Michigan U.S.A.
102 E2 **Carson City** Nevada U.S.A.
146 D7 **Carson Inlet** *inlet* Antarctica
102 F2 **Carson L** Nevada U.S.A.
142 F3 **Carson, R** W Australia Australia
102 F2 **Carson Sink** *dry lake* Nevada U.S.A.
94 E3 **Carsonville** Michigan U.S.A.
12 D3 **Carsphairn** Scotland
118 C7 **Carstairs** Alberta Canada
12 E2 **Carstairs** Scotland
Carstensz, G *see* **Jaya Pk**
128 C1 **Cartagena** Colombia
17 G7 **Cartagena** Spain
128 C3 **Cartago** Colombia
125 N5 **Cartago** Costa Rica
102 F5 **Cartago** California U.S.A.
108 G6 **Carta Valley** Texas U.S.A.
101 P2 **Carter** Montana U.S.A.
107 L6 **Carter** Oklahoma U.S.A.
101 P8 **Carter** Wyoming U.S.A.
13 F3 **Carter Bar** England
20 G3 **Carteret** France
141 G2 **Carter, Mt** Queensland Australia
9 G3 **Carters Bridge** England
111 M7 **Cartersville** Georgia U.S.A.
101 O3 **Cartersville** Montana U.S.A.
145 E4 **Carterton** New Zealand
43 C12 **Carthage** Tunisia
85 G1 **Carthage** *ruins* Tunisia
109 P1 **Carthage** Arkansas U.S.A.
99 P9 **Carthage** Illinois U.S.A.
94 B7 **Carthage** Indiana U.S.A.
111 G9 **Carthage** Mississippi U.S.A.
110 B4 **Carthage** Missouri U.S.A.
95 M3 **Carthage** New York U.S.A.
112 H2 **Carthage** North Carolina U.S.A.
98 J5 **Carthage** South Dakota U.S.A.
94 B10 **Carthage** Tennessee U.S.A.
109 N3 **Carthage** Texas U.S.A.
120 J6 **Cartier** Ontario Canada
142 E1 **Cartier I** Timor Sea
22 F3 **Cartignies** France
13 F5 **Cartmel** England
45 N4 **Cartoceto** Italy
48 J6 **Cartojani** Romania
115 O7 **Cartwright** Labrador, Nfld Canada
119 S9 **Cartwright** Manitoba Canada
98 C2 **Cartwright** North Dakota U.S.A.
129 L5 **Caruaru** Brazil
130 H10 **Caruarú** Brazil
127 N9 **Carúpano** Venezuela
129 J4 **Carutapera** Brazil
110 G5 **Caruthersville** Missouri U.S.A.
94 D9 **Carver** Kentucky U.S.A.
22 D3 **Carvin** France
16 A5 **Carvoeira,C** Portugal
128 F4 **Carvoeiro** Brazil
101 M1 **Carway** Alberta Canada
141 H6 **Carwell** Queensland Australia
33 S6 **Carwitz** Germany
111 F9 **Cary** Mississippi U.S.A.
112 J2 **Cary** North Carolina U.S.A.
139 G3 **Caryapundy Swamp** New S Wales/Queensland
113 G12 **Carysfort Reef** Florida U.S.A.
45 K3 **Carzolano,Mt** Italy
133 C4 **Casablanca** Chile
85 C2 **Casablanca** Morocco
130 F7 **Casa Branca** Brazil
16 B6 **Casa Branca** Portugal
42 F7 **Casacalenda** Italy
41 L5 **Casaccia** Switzerland
127 P3 **Casa Cruz, C** Trinidad
124 E2 **Casa de János** Mexico
129 G8 **Casado** Paraguay
103 N9 **Casa Grande** Arizona U.S.A.
103 N9 **Casa Grande Nat. Mon** Arizona U.S.A.
17 G5 **Casa Ibáñez** Spain
41 L7 **Casalbuttano** Italy
45 Q7 **Casal di Principe** Italy
44 D1 **Casale** Italy
45 K3 **Casalecchio di Reno** Italy
45 J2 **Casalgrande** Italy
42 D3 **Casalmaggiore** Italy
45 J1 **Casaloldo** Italy
44 G1 **Casalpusterlengo** Italy
45 P6 **Casalvieri** Italy
45 R8 **Casamicciola Terme** Italy
128 D2 **Casanare** *div* Colombia
116 E4 **Casapedaga** Alaska U.S.A.
108 C6 **Casa Piedra** Texas U.S.A.
43 J8 **Casarano** Italy
124 F2 **Casas Grandes** Mexico
109 G9 **Casa View** Texas U.S.A.
100 J5 **Cascade** Idaho U.S.A.
101 O2 **Cascade** Montana U.S.A.
95 Q2 **Cascade** New Hampshire U.S.A.
100 D4 **Cascade Locks** Oregon U.S.A.
117 N11 **Cascade Mts** Br Col/Wash Canada
100 D1 **Cascade Pass** Washington U.S.A.
100 C7 **Cascade Ra** U.S.A.
100 K5 **Cascade Res** Idaho U.S.A.
100 D2 **Cascade Tunnel** Washington U.S.A.
100 C5 **Cascadia** Oregon U.S.A.
16 A6 **Cascais** Portugal
122 G5 **Cascapedia** Quebec Canada
122 F5 **Cascapedia** *R* Quebec Canada
130 D9 **Cascavel** Brazil
42 E6 **Cascia** Italy
95 R2 **Casco** Maine U.S.A.
99 T5 **Casco** Wisconsin U.S.A.
95 R3 **Casco B** Maine U.S.A.
45 M3 **Casemurate** Italy
15 J4 **Casentina** Italy
133 E5 **Caseros** Argentina
45 Q7 **Caserta** Italy
94 D3 **Caseville** Michigan U.S.A.
146 K7 **Casey** *Australia Base* Antarctica
121 Q5 **Casey** Quebec Canada
99 T10 **Casey** Illinois U.S.A.
146 K9 **Casey B** Antarctica
86 B1 **Caseyr, Raas** *C* Somalia
14 D4 **Cashel** Ireland
87 E9 **Cashel** Zimbabwe
107 N6 **Cashion** Oklahoma U.S.A.
141 J8 **Cashmere** Queensland Australia
100 E2 **Cashmere** Washington U.S.A.
99 Q6 **Cashton** Wisconsin U.S.A.
71 E2 **Casiguran** Luzon Philippines
71 F2 **Casiguran B** Luzon Philippines
71 E3 **Casiguran Sound** Luzon Philippines
133 E4 **Casilda** Argentina
48 L6 **Casimcea** Romania
130 J8 **Casimiro de Abreu** Brazil
45 H2 **Casina** Italy
139 L3 **Casino** New South Wales Australia
128 E3 **Casiquiare** *R* Venezuela
124 D2 **Casita** Mexico
31 J6 **Čáslav** Czech Rep
128 C5 **Casma** Peru
71 G5 **Casogoran B** Philippines
42 E6 **Casola Valsenio** Italy
109 N2 **Cason** Texas U.S.A.
45 Q8 **Casória** Italy
42 B2 **Caspar** California U.S.A.
17 G3 **Caspe** Spain
101 T7 **Casper** Wyoming U.S.A.
111 C9 **Caspiana** Louisiana U.S.A.
53 G10 **Caspian Sea**
20 F2 **Casquets Lt.Ho** English Chan
144 C5 **Cass** *R* New Zealand
144 C5 **Cass** New Zealand
110 D6 **Cass** Arkansas U.S.A.
94 H8 **Cass** West Virginia U.S.A.
98 B7 **Cassa** Wyoming U.S.A.
18 G8 **Cassagnes-Bégonhès** France
87 D8 **Cassai** Angola
130 F7 **Cássai** Brazil
Cassaigne *see* **Sidi Ali**
87 D8 **Cassamba** Angola
43 G9 **Cassano allo Ionio** Italy
94 D3 **Cass City** Michigan U.S.A.
121 P7 **Casselman** Ontario Canada
98 J3 **Casselton** North Dakota U.S.A.
19 Q14 **Casse Massion** *mt* France
117 J6 **Cassiar** British Columbia Canada
117 H6 **Cassiar Mts** British Columbia Canada
130 D6 **Cassilândia** Brazil
139 J4 **Cassilis** New South Wales Australia
141 G5 **Cassilis** Queensland Australia
87 C9 **Cassinga** Angola
142 F2 **Cassini I** W Australia Australia
133 G4 **Cassino** Brazil
43 F7 **Cassino** Italy
129 H3 **Cassiporé** *R* Brazil
19 P18 **Cassis** France
99 M2 **Cass L** Minnesota U.S.A.
107 O3 **Cassoday** Kansas U.S.A.
94 B5 **Cassopolis** Michigan U.S.A.
110 C5 **Cassville** Missouri U.S.A.
99 Q7 **Cassville** Wisconsin U.S.A.
20 B5 **Cast** France
45 K1 **Castagnaro** Italy
102 F7 **Castaic** California U.S.A.
129 J4 **Castanhal** Brazil
131 B3 **Castaño** *R* Argentina
133 D4 **Castaño** Argentina
124 J4 **Castaños** Mexico
127 M1 **Castara** Tobago
17 G3 **Castejón,Mt.de** Spain
45 J1 **Castelbelforte** Italy
45 L3 **Castel Bolognese** Italy
45 J1 **Castel d'Ario** Italy
42 D4 **Castel del Rio** Italy
42 F7 **Castel di Sangro** Italy
45 L4 **Castel Focognano** Italy
45 P7 **Castelforte** Italy
45 L4 **Castelfranco di Sopra** Italy
45 K2 **Castelfranco Emilia** Italy
42 D3 **Castelfranco Veneto** Veneto Italy
45 J1 **Castel Goffredo** Italy
18 F8 **Casteljaloux** France
37 J4 **Castell** Germany
109 J5 **Castell** Texas U.S.A.
100 C8 **Castella** California U.S.A.
43 F8 **Castellabate** Italy
43 E10 **Castellammare del Golfo** Sicily
45 Q8 **Castellammare di Stabia** Italy
40 G7 **Castellamònte** Italy
45 J2 **Castellarano** Italy
133 F5 **Castelli** Argentina
45 K3 **Castello di Serravalle** Italy
17 G4 **Castellón** *prov* Spain
17 G5 **Castellón de la Plana** Spain
17 G4 **Castellote** Spain
45 J1 **Castellucchio** Italy
45 N6 **Castel Madama** Italy
45 K2 **Castel Maggiore** Italy
45 K1 **Castelmassa** Italy
18 G9 **Castelnaudary** France
18 E7 **Castelnau de Médoc** France
18 F8 **Castelnau de Montratier** France
18 F9 **Castelnau-Magnoac** France
45 J2 **Castelnovo di Sotto** Italy
45 H3 **Castel novo ne'Monti** Italy
45 H3 **Castelnuovo di Garfagnana** Italy
45 N5 **Castelnuovo di Porto** Italy
45 J1 **Castelnuovo di Verona** Italy
130 H7 **Castelo** Brazil
16 C5 **Castelo de Vide** Portugal
45 O4 **Castelplanio** Italy
45 M6 **Castel Porziano** Italy
45 R8 **Castel San Giorgio** Italy
45 L4 **Castel San Niccolo** Italy
45 L3 **Castel San Pietro Terme** Italy
18 F8 **Castelsarrasin** France
44 F1 **Castel S.Giov** Italy
43 F11 **Casteltermini** Sicily
45 P5 **Castelvecchio Subequo** Italy
43 E11 **Castelvetrano** Sicily
45 P7 **Castel Volturno** Italy
45 K3 **Castenaso** Italy
41 M7 **Castenedolo** Italy
138 F6 **Casterton** Victoria Australia
18 E9 **Castets** France
122 F7 **Castigan Mts** New Brunswick Canada
45 K3 **Castiglione dei Pepoli** Italy
45 J1 **Castiglione delle Stiviere** Italy
45 H3 **Castiglione di Garfagnana** Italy
45 L4 **Castiglion Fibocchi** Italy
42 D5 **Castiglion Fiorentino** Italy
94 K4 **Castile** New York U.S.A.
133 C3 **Castilla** Chile
16 D4 **Castilla La Vieja** *reg* Spain
71 E3 **Castillejos** Luzon Philippines
16 D6 **Castillejo, Sa. de** *mts* Spain
127 J9 **Castilletes** Venezuela
133 C7 **Castillo** *mt* Chile
131 B4 **Castillo,Cerro del** *pk* Argentina
113 F8 **Castillo de San Marcos Nat. Mon** Florida U.S.A.
124 H3 **Castillón** Mexico
18 F8 **Castillon et Capitourlan** France
18 F8 **Castillonnés** France
133 D7 **Castillo,Pampa del** *plain* Argentina
133 G4 **Castillos** Uruguay
95 T2 **Castine** Maine U.S.A.
9 G2 **Castle Acre** England
14 B3 **Castlebar** Ireland
15 A4 **Castlebay** Scotland
14 E3 **Castlebellingham** Ireland
111 J10 **Castleberry** Alabama U.S.A.
14 E2 **Castleblayney** Ireland
9 E3 **Castle Bromwich** England
13 F4 **Castle Carrock** England
8 D5 **Castle Cary** England
14 D4 **Castlecomer** Ireland
100 J7 **Castle Cr** Idaho U.S.A.
103 N2 **Castle Dale** Utah U.S.A.
14 D2 **Castlederg** N Ireland
14 E4 **Castledermot** Ireland
103 K8 **Castle Dome Mts** Arizona U.S.A.
9 E2 **Castle Donington** England
12 E4 **Castle Douglas** Scotland
12 E3 **Castlefern** Scotland
13 G6 **Castleford** England
101 L7 **Castleford** Idaho U.S.A.
100 H1 **Castlegar** British Columbia Canada
103 O2 **Castle Gate** Utah U.S.A.
90 C1 **Castle Harbour** Bermuda
112 K3 **Castle Hayne** North Carolina U.S.A.
103 M8 **Castle Hot Sp** Arizona U.S.A.
126 G3 **Castle I** Bahamas
14 B4 **Castleisland** Ireland
139 G6 **Castlemaine** Victoria Australia
14 B4 **Castlemaine** Ireland
14 C5 **Castlemartyr** Ireland
118 B7 **Castle, Mt** Alberta Canada
117 F3 **Castle Mt** Yukon Territory Canada
102 D6 **Castle Mt** California U.S.A.
101 L5 **Castle Peak** Idaho U.S.A.
145 F4 **Castlepoint** New Zealand
14 D3 **Castlepollard** Ireland
14 C3 **Castlerea** Ireland
139 J4 **Castlereagh** *R* New South Wales Australia
140 D1 **Castlereagh B** N Terr Australia
9 G2 **Castle Rising** England
106 F2 **Castle Rock** Colorado U.S.A.
98 C5 **Castle Rock** South Dakota U.S.A.
101 O8 **Castle Rock** Utah U.S.A.
100 C3 **Castle Rock** Washington U.S.A.
99 R6 **Castle Rock Res** Wisconsin U.S.A.
13 G4 **Castleside** England
9 E1 **Castleton** England
127 L2 **Castleton** Jamaica
103 P3 **Castleton** Utah U.S.A.
95 O3 **Castleton** Vermont U.S.A.
95 O4 **Castleton on Hudson** New York U.S.A.
12 D5 **Castletown** I of Man U.K.
14 B5 **Castletown Bere** Ireland
14 F2 **Castlewellan** N Ireland
98 J5 **Castlewood** South Dakota U.S.A.
108 D6 **Castolon** Texas U.S.A.
118 F6 **Castor** Alberta Canada
111 C9 **Castor** Louisiana U.S.A.
111 D9 **Castor** *R* Louisiana U.S.A.
95 M3 **Castorland** New York U.S.A.
20 H3 **Castre, Mt** France
18 G9 **Castres** France
25 C3 **Castricum** Netherlands
127 O7 **Castries** St Lucia
133 C6 **Castro** Chile
16 D2 **Castrocalbón** Spain
45 L3 **Castrocaro** Italy
45 O6 **Castro dei Volsci** Italy
16 E2 **Castrogeriz** Spain
16 C1 **Castropol** Spain
32 F9 **Castrop-Rauxel** Germany
16 E1 **Castro Urdiales** Spain
16 B7 **Castro Verde** Portugal
43 G9 **Castrovillari** Italy
102 C5 **Castroville** California U.S.A.
109 J6 **Castroville** Texas U.S.A.
16 D6 **Castuera** Spain
88 G10 **Casuarina** *isld* Mozambique
142 G2 **Casuarina, Mt** W Australia Australia
116 N6 **Caswell** Alaska U.S.A.
144 A6 **Caswell Sd** New Zealand
48 E3 **Čata** Slovakia
87 C8 **Catabola** Angola
143 B9 **Cataby** W Australia Australia
127 J2 **Catadupa** Jamaica
130 G7 **Cataguases** Brazil
111 D10 **Catahoula L** Louisiana U.S.A.
71 F4 **Cataiñgan** Philippines
78 J2 **Çatak** Turkey
78 J3 **Çatak** *R* Turkey
130 F6 **Catalão** Brazil
47 J3 **Çatalca** Turkey
47 J5 **Çatal Dağı** *mt* Turkey
127 K5 **Catalina, I** Dominican Rep
139 H9 **Catamaran** Tasmania Australia
131 D2 **Catamarca** Argentina
133 D3 **Catamarca** *prov* Argentina
71 F4 **Catanauan** Philippines
87 F9 **Catandica** Mozambique
71 G4 **Catanduanes** *isld* Philippines
130 E7 **Catanduva** Brazil
130 D9 **Catanduvas** Brazil
43 G11 **Catania** Sicily
43 G11 **Catania,Golfo di** Sicily
43 H10 **Catanzaro** Italy
113 K7 **Cataõ** Puerto Rico
111 F12 **Cataouatche,L** Louisiana U.S.A.
110 K2 **Cataract L** Indiana U.S.A.
130 C9 **Cataratas del Iguazú** *waterfalls* Arg/Brazil
71 G4 **Catarman** Philippines
71 G7 **Catarman Pt** Mindanao Philippines
123 Q3 **Cat Arm Reservoir** *res* Newfoundland Canada
17 G5 **Catarroja** Spain
95 M6 **Catasauqua** Pennsylvania U.S.A.
128 D2 **Catatumbo** *R* Venezuela/Colombia
111 M9 **Cataula** Georgia U.S.A.
129 G4 **Catavara** Brazil
99 Q4 **Catawba** Wisconsin U.S.A.
112 F2 **Catawba L** South Carolina U.S.A.
95 L6 **Catawissa** Pennsylvania U.S.A.
87 F9 **Cataxa** Mozambique
71 G5 **Catbalogan** Samar Philippines
126 E2 **Cat Cays** *islds* Bahamas
101 R2 **Cat Creek** Montana U.S.A.
22 F3 **Cateau,Le** France
71 G7 **Cateel** Mindanao Philippines
20 E3 **Catel** Channel Is
22 E3 **Catelet, le** France
125 M8 **Catemaco** Mexico
45 P5 **Catena di Monte Sirente** Italy
130 J10 **Catende** Brazil
118 J5 **Cater** Saskatchewan Canada
9 F5 **Caterham** England
87 B7 **Catete** Angola
107 L3 **Catharine** Kansas U.S.A.
98 G2 **Cathay** North Dakota U.S.A.
139 J6 **Cathcart** New South Wales Australia
87 E12 **Cathcart** S Africa
108 D5 **Cathedral Mt** Texas U.S.A.
109 P1 **Catherine,L** Arkansas U.S.A.
103 M2 **Catherine, Mt** Utah U.S.A.
127 L2 **Catherine's Peak** Jamaica
89 F7 **Cathkin Pk** *mt* Lesotho
100 B3 **Cathlamet** Washington U.S.A.
94 D1 **Cathro** Michigan U.S.A.
126 G2 **Cat I** Bahamas
111 G11 **Cat I** Mississippi U.S.A.
22 F3 **Catillon-sur-Sambre** France
85 A6 **Catio** Guinea-Bissau
128 F3 **Catisimiña** Venezuela
79 F1 **Çatkıt Suyu** *R* Turkey
115 K7 **Cat Lake** Ontario Canada
94 E8 **Catlettsburg** Kentucky U.S.A.
99 T9 **Catlin** Illinois U.S.A.
144 B7 **Catlins** *R* New Zealand
137 M6 **Cato** *isld* Coral Sea
95 L3 **Cato** New York U.S.A.
94 K7 **Catoctin Mt** Maryland/Virg U.S.A.
130 H9 **Catolé do Rocha** Brazil
42 E5 **Catria,Monte** Italy
133 E5 **Catrilo** Argentina
128 F3 **Catrimani** Brazil
95 O4 **Catskill** New York U.S.A.
95 N4 **Catskill Mts** New York U.S.A.
94 J4 **Cattaraugus** New York U.S.A.
22 L5 **Cattenom** France
13 F6 **Catterall** England
13 G5 **Catterick** England
45 N4 **Cattolica** Italy
87 F11 **Catuane** Mozambique
133 D4 **Catuna** Argentina
128 E3 **Cauaburi** *R* Brazil
45 M1 **Cauárzera** Italy
129 J4 **Cauaxi** *R* Brazil
71 F6 **Cauayan** Negros Philippines
128 C3 **Cauca** *div* Colombia
126 G10 **Cauca,R** Colombia
72 E1 **Caucasus** *mt ra* Georgia/Rus Fed etc
119 V3 **Cauchon L** Manitoba Canada
95 R7 **Caucomgomoc L** Maine U.S.A.
21 M2 **Caudebec** France
21 N3 **Caudebec-les-Elbeuf** France
17 G6 **Caudete** Spain
22 E3 **Caudry** France
88 C9 **Cauese Mts** Mozambique
71 G6 **Cauit Pt** Philippines
20 F5 **Caulnes** France
43 G10 **Caulonia** Italy
19 N17 **Caumont** France
21 J3 **Caumont-l'Eventé** France
126 E4 **Caunao** *R* Cuba
18 G9 **Caunes** France
87 C7 **Caungulu** Angola
131 A5 **Cauquenes** Chile
133 C5 **Cauquenes** Chile
128 F2 **Caura** *R* Venezuela
20 D5 **Caurel** France
122 E5 **Causapscal** Quebec Canada
18 G8 **Caussade** France
128 F6 **Cautário** *R* Brazil
18 E10 **Cauterets** France
131 A7 **Cautin** *prov* Chile
126 F4 **Cauto** Cuba
21 L2 **Cauville** France
21 L2 **Caux** *reg* France
45 R8 **Cava** Italy
16 B3 **Cavado** *R* Portugal
40 H7 **Cavaglia** Italy
19 O17 **Cavaillon** France
19 Q18 **Cavalaire** France
129 J6 **Cavalcante** Brazil
41 O5 **Cavalese** Italy
98 J1 **Cavalier** North Dakota U.S.A.
119 U10 **Cavalier** North Dakota U.S.A.
145 D1 **Cavalli Is** New Zealand
109 L7 **Cavallo, Pass** Texas U.S.A.
85 C7 **Cavally** *R* Ivory Co/Liberia
14 D3 **Cavan** *co* Ireland
14 D3 **Cavan** Ireland
47 K7 **Çavdır** Turkey
45 N6 **Cave** Italy
144 C6 **Cave** New Zealand
110 E6 **Cave City** Arkansas U.S.A.
94 B9 **Cave City** Kentucky U.S.A.
103 N8 **Cavecreek** Arizona U.S.A.
143 D9 **Cave Hill** W Australia Australia
110 H4 **Cave in Rock** Illinois U.S.A.
130 E10 **Caveiras,R** Brazil
100 B7 **Cave Junction** Oregon U.S.A.
120 C2 **Cavell** Ontario Canada
118 J6 **Cavell** Saskatchewan Canada
143 G7 **Cavenagh Ra** W Australia Australia
138 F6 **Cavendish** Victoria Australia
118 G8 **Cavendish** Alberta Canada
9 G3 **Cavendish** England
45 M2 **Ca Venier** Italy
131 G3 **Cavera** *R* Brazil
131 G3 **Cavera, Serra do** *mts* Brazil
68 C7 **Cavern I** Burma
130 D9 **Cavernoso, Serra do** *mts* Brazil
120 C4 **Cavers** Ontario Canada
9 F5 **Caversham** England
111 L7 **Cave Spring** Georgia U.S.A.
103 K3 **Cave Valley** Nevada U.S.A.
129 H3 **Caviana** *isld* Brazil
18 E7 **Cavignac** France
71 E6 **Cavili** Philippines
71 E3 **Cavite** Luzon Philippines
48 H3 **Cavnic** Romania
45 N6 **Cavo, M** *mt* Italy
44 B2 **Cavour** Italy
98 H5 **Cavour** South Dakota U.S.A.
45 J2 **Cavriago** Italy
42 J6 **Cavtat** Croatia
15 E3 **Cawdor** Scotland
107 M2 **Cawker City** Kansas U.S.A.
138 F4 **Cawndilla L** New South Wales Australia
Cawnpore *see* **Kanpur**
13 G6 **Cawood** England
121 P7 **Cawood Low** Quebec Canada
9 H2 **Cawston** England
130 G7 **Caxambu** Brazil
129 K4 **Caxias** Brazil
128 D4 **Caxias** Amazonas Brazil
131 H2 **Caxias do Sul** Brazil
87 B7 **Caxito** Angola
9 F3 **Caxton** England
9 F3 **Caxton Gibbet** England
47 L6 **Çay** Turkey
47 K3 **Çayağzı** Turkey
128 C3 **Cayambe** *vol* Ecuador
112 F4 **Cayce** South Carolina U.S.A.
68 F8 **Cay Dua** *B* Vietnam
78 H1 **Çayeli** Turkey
129 H3 **Cayenne** Fr Guiana
21 O1 **Cayeux-sur-Mer** France
127 L5 **Cayey** Puerto Rico
18 H9 **Caylar, le** France
118 D8 **Cayley** Alberta Canada
18 G8 **Caylus** France
126 E5 **Cayman Brac** *isld* W Indies
126 D5 **Cayman, Grand** *isld* W Indies
126 D5 **Cayman, Little** *isld* W Indies
90 A6 **Cayman Trench** Caribbean
68 G7 **Cay Mit** Vietnam
86 A2 **Caynabo** Somalia
125 P9 **Cayo** Belize
127 P4 **Cayon** St Kitts W Indies
126 D3 **Cay Sal Bank** Bahamas
102 D6 **Cayucos** California U.S.A.
99 T10 **Cayuga** Indiana U.S.A.
98 J3 **Cayuga** North Dakota U.S.A.
109 M4 **Cayuga** Texas U.S.A.
95 L4 **Cayuga L** New York U.S.A.
16 D7 **Cazalla de la Sierra** Spain
48 L6 **Căzănești** Romania
18 E9 **Cazaubon** France
18 E8 **Cazaux, Etang de** *L* France
85 F2 **Caze** Algeria
95 M4 **Cazenovia** New York U.S.A.
18 F9 **Cazères** France
42 G4 **Cazin** Bosnia-Herzegovina
42 H3 **Čazma** Croatia
87 D8 **Cazombo** Angola
16 E7 **Cazorla** Spain
87 F9 **Cazula** Mozambique
16 D2 **Cea** *R* Spain
48 K3 **Ceahlău** Romania
48 K4 **Ceahlău** *mt* Romania
130 J8 **Ceará Mirim** Brazil
21 J5 **Ceauce** France
48 H6 **Ceauru, Lacu** *L* Romania
21 L7 **Ceaux-en-Loudun** France
119 P5 **Ceba** Saskatchewan Canada
125 O6 **Cebaco,I** Panama
124 G4 **Ceballos** Mexico
106 D5 **Cebolla** New Mexico U.S.A.
133 D3 **Cebollar** Argentina
133 G4 **Cebollati** *R* Uruguay
17 F3 **Cebollera** *mt* Spain
106 C6 **Cebollita** New Mexico U.S.A.
16 E4 **Cebreros** Spain
71 F5 **Cebu** Philippines
71 F7 **Cebuano Barracks** Mindanao Philippines
43 E7 **Ceccano** Italy
48 E4 **Cece** Hungary
94 C5 **Cecil** Ohio U.S.A.
99 S5 **Cecil** Wisconsin U.S.A.
141 K8 **Cecil Plains** Queensland Australia
143 D7 **Cecil Rhodes, Mt** *mt* W Australia Australia
95 M7 **Cecilton** Maryland U.S.A.
100 B8 **Cecilville** California U.S.A.
42 D5 **Cecina** Italy
16 C5 **Ceclavín** Spain
99 O7 **Cedar** *R* Iowa U.S.A.
107 M2 **Cedar** Kansas U.S.A.
94 C2 **Cedar** *R* Michigan U.S.A.
98 H8 **Cedar** *R* Nebraska U.S.A.
111 H8 **Cedarbluff** Mississippi U.S.A.
94 F9 **Cedar Bluff** Virginia U.S.A.
107 L3 **Cedar Bluff Res** Kansas U.S.A.
107 K2 **Cedar Bluffs** Kansas U.S.A.
98 K8 **Cedar Bluffs** Nebraska U.S.A.
103 M4 **Cedar Breaks Nat.Mon** Utah U.S.A.
99 T6 **Cedarburg** Wisconsin U.S.A.
98 E6 **Cedar Butte** South Dakota U.S.A.
110 D3 **Cedar City** Missouri U.S.A.
103 L4 **Cedar City** Utah U.S.A.

98 D3 Cedar Cr North Dakota U.S.A.
109 K5 Cedar Creek Texas U.S.A.
109 O9 Cedar Crest Texas U.S.A.
109 L3 Cedar Cr. L Texas U.S.A.
101 L7 Cedar Cr.Res Idaho U.S.A.
99 O7 Cedar Falls Iowa U.S.A.
94 F8 Cedar Grove West Virginia U.S.A.
99 T6 Cedar Grove Wisconsin U.S.A.
127 P4 Cedar Grove Antigua W Indies
112 L2 Cedar I North Carolina U.S.A.
95 M9 Cedar I Virginia U.S.A.
113 D8 Cedar Key Florida U.S.A.
119 R5 Cedar L Manitoba Canada
108 E3 Cedar L Texas U.S.A.
99 T8 Cedar Lake Indiana U.S.A.
109 M7 Cedar Lane Texas U.S.A.
102 G3 Cedar Mts Nevada U.S.A.
94 D5 Cedar Pt Ohio U.S.A.
99 P8 Cedar Rapids Iowa U.S.A.
98 H8 Cedar Rapids Nebraska U.S.A.
95 K5 Cedar Run Pennsylvania U.S.A.
120 H10 Cedar Springs Ontario Canada
94 B3 Cedar Springs Michigan U.S.A.
111 L7 Cedartown Georgia U.S.A.
107 O4 Cedar Vale Kansas U.S.A.
106 E7 Cedarvale New Mexico U.S.A.
127 L2 Cedar Valley Jamaica
100 E8 Cedarville California U.S.A.
95 M7 Cedarville New Jersey U.S.A.
110 N2 Cedarville Ohio U.S.A.
106 F4 Cedarwood Colorado U.S.A.
94 K8 Cedon Virginia U.S.A.
119 O9 Cedoux Saskatchewan Canada
43 C8 Cedrino R Sardinia
130 G9 Cedro Brazil
124 B3 Cedros isld Mexico
124 E4 Cedros Mexico
127 N3 Cedros Pt Trinidad
138 C4 Ceduna South Australia Australia
86 J4 Ceel Afweyn Somalia
86 A3 Ceelbuur Somalia
86 A2 Ceel Hur Somalia
86 A1 Ceerigaabo Somalia
43 F10 Cefalù Sicily
16 E3 Cega R Spain
48 F3 Cegléd Hungary
43 H8 Ceglie Messapico Italy
17 F6 Cehegin Spain
67 B4 Ceheng China
48 H3 Cehu Silvaniei Romania
48 G4 Ceica Romania
128 E3 Cejal Colombia
87 C8 Cela Angola
Celah, Gunung see Mandi Angin, Gunung
45 P5 Celano Italy
16 B2 Celanova Spain
125 J7 Celaya Mexico
Celebes isld see Sulawesi
70 G3 Celebes Sea Indonesia
109 L2 Celeste Texas U.S.A.
94 C6 Celina Ohio U.S.A.
94 B10 Celina Tennessee U.S.A.
109 L2 Celina Texas U.S.A.
17 G4 Cella Spain
48 D3 Celldömölk Hungary
32 M7 Celle Germany
22 E2 Celles Belgium
21 M7 Celle-St.Avant,la France
21 N6 Cellettes France
21 N8 Celon France
16 B3 Celorico de Basto Portugal
7 E12 Celtic Sea British Isles/France
47 L7 Çeltikçi Turkey
47 L4 Çeltik Gölü L Turkey
41 O5 Cembra Italy
107 M7 Cement Oklahoma U.S.A.
94 C4 Cement City Michigan U.S.A.
46 D1 Čemerna Planina mt Serbia Yugoslavia
42 H4 Čemernica mt Bosnia-Herzegovina
48 E7 Čemerno Bosnia-Herzegovina
8 B1 Cemlyn B Wales
8 B1 Cemmaes Wales
17 F6 Cenajo, Embalse del res Spain
8 B3 Cenarth Wales
136 H2 Cenderawasih, Teluk B W Irian
71 A3 Cenga Indonesia
43 G4 Ceno R Italy
133 C6 Cenoa R Argentina
86 C4 Cent.Afr.Rep Equat Africa
130 D8 Centenario do Sul Brazil
112 H3 Centenary South Carolina U.S.A.
101 T8 Centennial Wyoming U.S.A.
103 L8 Centennial Wash R Arizona U.S.A.
106 D4 Center Colorado U.S.A.
110 E2 Center Missouri U.S.A.
98 E2 Center North Dakota U.S.A.
111 B10 Center Texas U.S.A.
94 E6 Centerburg Ohio U.S.A.
99 O4 Center City Minnesota U.S.A.
95 L9 Center Cross Virginia U.S.A.
113 F9 Center Hill Florida U.S.A.
110 L5 Center Hill L Tennessee U.S.A.
95 P6 Center Moriches Long I, New York U.S.A.
95 Q3 Center Ossipee New Hampshire U.S.A.
109 H6 Center Point Texas U.S.A.
110 D1 Centerville Iowa U.S.A.
111 E12 Centerville Louisiana U.S.A.
94 H6 Centerville Pennsylvania U.S.A.
98 K6 Centerville South Dakota U.S.A.
110 J6 Centerville Tennessee U.S.A.
109 M4 Centerville Texas U.S.A.
101 O9 Centerville Utah U.S.A.
100 E4 Centerville Washington U.S.A.
108 E6 Centinela, Picacho del pk Mexico
124 H3 Centinela, Pico del mt Mexico
42 D4 Cento Italy
44 G3 Cento Croci, Passo di Italy
107 O7 Centrahoma Oklahoma U.S.A.
89 D3 Central dist Botswana
130 B9 Central dept Paraguay
15 D4 Central reg Scotland
116 P4 Central Alaska U.S.A.
106 B9 Central New Mexico U.S.A.
112 E3 Central South Carolina U.S.A.
103 L4 Central Utah U.S.A.
86 C4 Central African Republic Africa
118 L8 Central Butt Saskatchewan Canada
106 E2 Central City Colorado U.S.A.
99 P7 Central City Iowa U.S.A.
110 J4 Central City Kentucky U.S.A.
98 H8 Central City Nebraska U.S.A.
94 J6 Central City Pennsylvania U.S.A.
140 B5 Central Desert Aboriginal Land N Terr Australia
95 Q5 Central Falls Rhode I U.S.A.
110 G3 Centralia Illinois U.S.A.
107 O2 Centralia Kansas U.S.A.
110 E3 Centralia Missouri U.S.A.
100 C3 Centralia Washington U.S.A.
94 G8 Centralia West Virginia U.S.A.
94 B1 Central Lake Michigan U.S.A.
140 C5 Central Mt. Stewart N Terr Australia
100 C7 Central Point Oregon U.S.A.
136 J2 Central Ra Papua New Guinea
56 Central Siberia
95 L3 Central Square New York U.S.A.
102 B1 Central Valley California U.S.A.
111 L7 Centre Alabama U.S.A.
144 A7 Centre I New Zealand
122 E7 Centreville New Brunswick Canada
122 F9 Centreville Nova Scotia Canada
111 J9 Centreville Alabama U.S.A.
95 L7 Centreville Maryland U.S.A.
94 B5 Centreville Michigan U.S.A.
111 E10 Centreville Mississippi U.S.A.
111 J11 Century Florida U.S.A.
94 G7 Century West Virginia U.S.A.
67 B4 Cenwanglao Shan mt China
67 C5 Cenxi China
48 E7 Čeotina R Bosnia-Herzegovina/Yugoslavia
19 P18 Cépet,C France
Cephalonia isld Greece see Kefallinia
41 M5 Cepina Italy
44 C4 Ceppo Monte mt Italy
45 O6 Ceprano Italy
21 L6 Cerans-Foulletourte France
128 E2 Cerbatana, Sa. de la mts Venezuela
103 K6 Cerbat Mts Arizona U.S.A.
18 H10 Cerbère, C France
16 B7 Cercal Portugal
16 E4 Cercedilla Spain
37 O5 Čerchov mt Czech Rep
21 O6 Cercottes France
18 H6 Cercy la Tour France
18 G10 Cerdaña dist Spain
21 P8 Cerdon France
18 G8 Cère R France
45 K1 Cerea Italy
118 G7 Cereal Alberta Canada
45 L1 Ceregnano Italy
21 N7 Céré-la-Ronde France
20 H4 Cérences France
130 E4 Ceres Brazil
40 F7 Ceres Italy
87 C12 Ceres S Africa
13 F1 Ceres Scotland
102 C4 Ceres California U.S.A.
45 J1 Ceresara Italy
40 F7 Ceresole Reale Italy
18 G10 Céret France
126 G10 Cereté Colombia
19 J3 Cerf isld Br Indian Oc Terr
83 J12 Cerf I Mahé I Indian Oc
121 P6 Cerf. L du Quebec Canada
22 G3 Cerfontaine Belgium
21 P3 Cergy-Pontoise France
44 D3 Ceriale Italy
43 G7 Cerignola Italy
Cerigo isld Greece see Kíthira
18 G6 Cerilly France
21 P3 Cerisy-la-Forêt France
20 H3 Cerisy-la-Salle France
21 J8 Cérizay France
47 J3 Çerkeşköy Turkey
42 F3 Cerknica Slovenia
48 G4 Cermei Romania
48 H5 Cerna R Romania
48 L5 Cerna Romania
48 L6 Cernavodă Romania
19 K5 Cernay France
8 D6 Cerne Abbas England
42 H3 Cernik Croatia
37 O4 Černošín Czech Rep
109 H9 Cerralvo Mexico
124 E5 Cerralvo isld Mexico
45 J4 Cerreto Guidi Italy
44 H3 Cerreto, Passo di Italy
45 R7 Cerreto Sannita Italy
8 C1 Cerrigydrudion Wales
46 D3 Cerrik Albania
106 D6 Cerrillos New Mexico U.S.A.
125 J6 Cerritos Mexico
130 E9 Cerro Azul Brazil
128 C6 Cerro de Pasco Peru
127 L5 Cerro de Punta pk Puerto Rico
110 H2 Cerro Gordo Illinois U.S.A.
131 G4 Cerro Largo dept Uruguay
127 J10 Cerrón mt Venezuela
124 F4 Cerro Prieto Mexico
21 K7 Cersay France
45 K4 Certaldo Italy
143 B9 Cervantes W Australia Australia
42 F5 Cervaro R Italy
45 P7 Cervaro Italy
45 G8 Cervati, M mt Italy
44 H2 Cervellino mt Italy
17 H3 Cervera Spain
17 F2 Cervera del Rio Alhama Spain
16 D2 Cervera de P Spain
42 E4 Cervia Italy
43 G8 Cervialto, M mt Italy
45 R7 Cervinara Italy
41 H7 Cervo R Italy
44 D4 Cervo Italy
128 D2 César div Colombia
126 H10 César,R Colombia
42 E4 Cesena Italy
45 M3 Cesenatico Italy
52 C6 Cēsis Latvia
37 P5 Česká Kubice Czech Rep
37 O5 Česká Lípa Czech Rep
31 H5 České Budějovice Czech Rep
31 J6 Českomoravská Vysočina mts Czech Rep
31 H5 Český Brod Czech Rep
31 H7 Český Krumlov Czech Rep
37 O4 Český les Sumava mts Czech Rep
48 E1 Český Těšín Czech Rep
78 A2 Çeşme Turkey
47 H6 Çeşme Turkey
139 K5 Cessnock New South Wales Australia
48 K5 Cetate Romania
42 H5 Cetina R Croatia
42 J6 Cetinje Montenegro Yugoslavia
21 M5 Ceton France
43 G9 Cetraro Italy
19 P15 Ceuse, Pic de mt France
85 C1 Ceuta Spanish exclave Morocco
16 D9 Ceuta Spain
137 P6 Ceva-i-Ra reef Pacific Oc
18 H8 Cevennes mts France
78 G3 Ceylânpınar Turkey
Ceylon rep see Sri Lanka
119 N9 Ceylon Saskatchewan Canada
99 M6 Ceylon Minnesota U.S.A.
19 P18 Ceyreste France
57 B6 Chacha Turkmenistan
19 P16 Chabestan France
19 O15 Chabeuil France
142 A6 Chabjuwardoo B W Australia Australia
18 H5 Chablis France
19 P16 Chabre, Mt de France
19 Q16 Chabrières France
21 O7 Chabris France
133 C1 Chaca Chile
131 E5 Chacabuco Argentina
127 N1 Chacachacare I Trinidad
133 D2 Chacance Chile
133 C6 Chacao, Canal de Chile
133 D6 Chacays, Sa. de los mts Argentina
131 C6 Chachahuen,Sa mt Argentina
128 D7 Chachani mt Peru
128 C5 Chachapoyas Peru
68 E6 Chachoengsao Thailand
74 D6 Chachro Pakistan
133 E3 Chaco prov Argentina
128 F8 Chaco dept Paraguay
133 E3 Chaco Austral reg Argentina
133 E2 Chaco Boreal reg Paraguay
106 B5 Chaco Canyon Nat. Mon New Mexico U.S.A.
133 E2 Chaco Central reg Argentina
117 H8 Chacon,C Prince of Wales I, Alaska
129 G5 Chacorão, Cachoeira do waterfall Brazil
106 C6 Chacra Mesa mt New Mexico U.S.A.
86 C3 Chad rep Equat Africa
56 D5 Chadan Russian Federation
112 J3 Chadbourn North Carolina U.S.A.
131 C6 Chadileo,R Argentina
133 D5 Chadileuvú R Argentina
86 B3 Chad,L Equat Africa
56 F2 Chadobets R Russian Federation
98 D7 Chadron Nebraska U.S.A.
99 R7 Chadwick Illinois U.S.A.
48 M4 Chadyr Lunga Moldova
110 G4 Chaffee Missouri U.S.A.
94 J4 Chaffee New York U.S.A.
74 A4 Chagai Pakistan
77 H5 Chagai Hills Pakistan
53 H8 Chagan R Kazakhstan/Rus Fed
51 N3 Chagda Russian Federation
8 C6 Chagford England
77 J2 Chaghcharān Afghanistan
55 E4 Chaglinka R Kazakhstan
40 A4 Chagny France
52 E5 Chagoda Russian Federation
52 E5 Chagodoshcha R Russian Federation
81 E6 Chagos Arch Indian Oc
94 F5 Chagrin Falls Ohio U.S.A.
127 O2 Chaguanas Trinidad
127 N1 Chaguaramas Trinidad
127 L10 Chaguaramas Venezuela
77 H4 Chahah Burjak Afghanistan
77 G7 Chāh Bahār Iran
77 G5 Chah Ghevhī, Hamún-e L Iran
77 L1 Chāh-i-Ghab Afghanistan
78 K4 Chah-i-Surkh Iraq
68 E5 Chai Badan Thailand
75 L7 Chāībāssa India
Chaigoubu see Huai'an
21 J5 Chailland France
19 P14 Chaîne de Belledonne mts France
85 E6 Chaîne de l'Atakora mts Benin
19 N17 Chaîne des Alpilles mts France
18 H7 Chaise Dieu, la France
69 D8 Chaiya Thailand
68 E5 Chaiyaphum Thailand
20 H8 Chaize-le-Vicomte,la France
131 F3 Chajari Argentina
116 L6 Chakachamna L Alaska U.S.A.
74 F2 Chak Amru Pakistan
88 G4 Chake Chake Tanzania
77 H4 Chakhānsūr Afghanistan
74 E2 Chakwal Pakistan
128 D7 Chala Peru
87 F8 Chalabesa Zambia
40 C4 Chalain,L.de France
18 F7 Chalais France
59 H2 Cha-lan-t'un China
128 D7 Chala,Pta Peru
125 P10 Chalatenango Honduras
69 D9 Chalaung Thailand
124 H6 Chalchihuites Mexico
125 P11 Chalchuapa El Salvador
Chalcis see Khalkís
9 E6 Chale England
122 G6 Chaleurs, Baie des Quebec/New Bruns Canada
128 D6 Chalhuanca Peru
133 C7 Chalía R Argentina
88 B7 Chali,L Zambia
19 J5 Chalindrey France
67 D3 Chaling China
74 F8 Chalisgaon India
9 G5 Chalk England
98 B4 Chalk Buttes Montana U.S.A.
109 K3 Chalk Mountain Texas U.S.A.
121 N6 Chalk River Ontario Canada
144 A7 Chalky Inlet New Zealand
116 Q3 Chalkyitsik Alaska U.S.A.
21 H6 Challain-la-Potherie France
20 G8 Challans France
133 D1 Challapata Bolivia
115 M1 Challenger Mts Northwest Territories Canada
22 H5 Challerange France
101 L5 Challis Idaho U.S.A.
52 E2 Chal'mny Varre Russian Federation
75 N7 Chalna Bangladesh
52 D4 Chalna Russian Federation
21 J7 Chalonnes France
18 H4 Chalons-sur-Marne France
19 J6 Chalon-sur-Saône France
65 J3 Chaluhe China
18 F7 Châlus France
57 B4 Chalysh Uzbekistan
37 O5 Cham R Germany
37 O5 Cham Germany
106 E4 Chama Colorado U.S.A.
106 D5 Chama New Mexico U.S.A.
74 B3 Chaman Pakistan
68 E6 Chamao,Khao mt Thailand
106 D5 Chama, R New Mexico U.S.A.
128 C5 Chamaya R Peru
74 G2 Chamba India
73 M3 Chambal R Madhya Prad/Rajasthan India
40 B7 Chambaran, Plat. de France
126 E3 Chambas Cuba
119 M8 Chamberlain Saskatchewan Canada
98 G6 Chamberlain South Dakota U.S.A.
95 R7 Chamberlain L Maine U.S.A.
142 G3 Chamberlain R W Australia Australia
116 P2 Chamberlin,Mt Alaska U.S.A.
103 P6 Chambers Arizona U.S.A.
98 H7 Chambers Nebraska U.S.A.
140 B1 Chambers B N Terr Australia
94 K7 Chambersburg Pennsylvania U.S.A.
99 T4 Chambers I Wisconsin U.S.A.
138 C1 Chambers Pillar pk N Terr Australia
19 P13 Chambéry France
88 C7 Chambeshi R Zambia
128 C4 Chambira R Peru
21 P3 Chambly France
21 L4 Chambois France
18 H7 Chambon, le Loire France
121 S4 Chambord Quebec Canada
21 O6 Chambord France
21 M7 Chambourg-sur-Indre France
66 E5 Chamdo prov China
124 G8 Chamela Mexico
77 B4 Cham-e Zeydun Iran
77 B3 Chamgordan Iran
133 D4 Chamical Argentina
106 D5 Chamita New Mexico U.S.A.
86 G4 Chamo Hāyk' L Ethiopia
110 E3 Chamois Missouri U.S.A.
74 H3 Chamoli India
40 E6 Chamonix France
19 P16 Chamouse,Mt.de France
75 K7 Champa India
89 F7 Champagne Castle mt Lesotho
40 C4 Champagnole France
142 E3 Champagny Is W Australia Australia
99 S9 Champaign Illinois U.S.A.
131 D3 Champaqui pk Argentina
68 G5 Cham Pasak Laos
121 N4 Champcoeur Quebec Canada
36 C7 Champ du Feu mt France
21 O8 Champenoise,la France
21 K5 Champgeneteux France
19 O14 Champier France
21 J6 Champigné France
21 N6 Champigny France
21 L8 Champigny le Sec France
21 L7 Champigny-sur-Veude France
21 P8 Champillet France
22 J3 Champion Belgium
118 D8 Champion Alberta Canada
99 T3 Champion Michigan U.S.A.
94 G5 Champion Heights Ohio U.S.A.
121 S6 Champlain Quebec Canada
95 O2 Champlain New York U.S.A.
121 R8 Champlain New York U.S.A.
95 O3 Champlain Canal New York U.S.A.
19 J5 Champlitte France
40 B2 Champlitte France
121 N4 Champneuf Quebec Canada
19 Q15 Champoléon France
40 G6 Champorcher Italy
21 N5 Champrond France
21 J4 Champsecret France
21 J7 Champtocé France
20 H7 Champtoceaux France
76 C5 Chamrajnagar India
19 P14 Chamrousse France
16 B5 Chamusca Portugal
69 E9 Chana Thailand
18 H8 Chanac France
131 B2 Chañaral R Chile
133 C3 Chañaral Chile
131 B2 Chañaral, I Chile
98 K6 Chancellor South Dakota U.S.A.
133 C5 Chanco Chile
21 M4 Chandai France
116 P2 Chandalar R Alaska U.S.A.
116 N3 Chandalar Alaska U.S.A.
111 G11 Chandeleur Sound Louisiana U.S.A.
122 H5 Chandler Quebec Canada
116 M2 Chandler R Alaska U.S.A.
103 N8 Chandler Arizona U.S.A.
107 O6 Chandler Oklahoma U.S.A.
109 M3 Chandler Texas U.S.A.
116 L2 Chandler L Alaska U.S.A.
138 C2 Chandler,Mt South Australia Australia
99 Q9 Chandlerville Illinois U.S.A.
128 D6 Chandless R Peru/Brazil
75 O7 Chandpur Bangladesh
74 H9 Chandrapur India
77 G6 Chānf Iran
Chang'an see Rong'an
65 A7 Chang'an China
87 F9 Changara Mozambique
65 G4 Changbai China
65 G4 Changbai Shan mt ra China
146 D3 Chang Cheng China Base Antarctica
68 J3 Changcheng China
67 B1 Changchi China
65 F3 Changchun China
65 F2 Changchunling China
67 F1 Changdang Hu L China
67 D2 Changde China
123 S4 Change I Newfoundland Canada
65 B7 Changge China
65 E5 Changhai China
58 F5 Chang Hu L China
67 F1 Changhua China
67 G4 Chang-hua Taiwan
67 C7 Changhua Jiang R China
67 C1 Chang Jiang R China
67 C7 Changjiang China
67 E2 Chang Jiang R Jiangxi China
65 G4 Changjin Res N Korea
68 F6 Chang,Ko isld Thailand
65 D6 Changle China
67 G2 Changle China
67 F4 Changle China
65 D5 Changli China
59 H3 Changling China
66 B5 Changmar China
67 A2 Changning China
67 D3 Changning China
65 C4 Changping China
Changpuzhen see Suining
65 C6 Changqing China
65 F5 Changsan-got C N Korea
67 D2 Changsha China
67 F2 Changshan China
65 E5 Changshan Qundao islds China
65 D4 Changshanyu China
67 B2 Changshou China
67 G1 Changshu China
67 B3 Changshun China
67 F4 Changtai China
65 G2 Changting China
67 E4 Changting China
65 F3 Changtu China
65 G2 Changwu China
67 F1 Changxing China
65 E5 Changxing Dao isld China
67 D1 Changyang China
65 D6 Changyi China
59 H4 Changyon N Korea
65 C7 Changyuan China
Changzhai see Changshun
65 B6 Changzhi China
67 G1 Changzhou Jiangsu China
67 E1 Changzhuyuan China
83 J8 Chankanai Sri Lanka
116 H8 Chankluit I Alaska U.S.A.
69 C8 Chan,Ko isld Thailand
21 L7 Channay-sur-Lathan France
145 E2 Channel I New Zealand
102 E8 Channel Is California U.S.A.
20 E3 Channel Islands English Chan
123 N6 Channel-Port aux Basques Newfoundland Canada
143 C10 Channel Pt W Australia Australia
126 F3 Channel Rock Bahamas
76 C4 Channiapatna India
119 P4 Channing airfield Manitoba Canada
99 S3 Channing Michigan U.S.A.
108 B8 Channing Texas U.S.A.
16 B2 Chantada Spain
21 K6 Chantenay Sarthe France
68 F6 Chanthaburi Thailand
21 P3 Chantilly France
21 H8 Chantonnay France
115 K4 Chantrey Inlet Northwest Territories Canada
21 J4 Chanu France
69 A8 Chanumla Nicobar Is
107 P4 Chanute Kansas U.S.A.
110 A4 Chanute Kansas U.S.A.
55 G3 Chany Russian Federation
21 J7 Chanzeaux France
17 G10 Chanzy Algeria
Chao'an see Chaozhou
65 C6 Chaocheng China
16 D9 Chaoen Morocco
58 G5 Chao Hu L China
128 C5 Chao, I Peru
68 E5 Chao Phraya Ra Thailand
65 E1 Chaor He R China
58 E5 Chaotianyi China
67 F1 Chao Xian China
Chaoyang see Huinan
59 K2 Ch'ao-Yang China
67 E5 Chaoyang Guangdong China
65 E4 Chaoyang Liaoning China
65 A7 Chaoyi China
67 E5 Chaozhou China
129 J5 Chapada das Mangabeiras mts Brazil
129 K6 Chapada Diamantina mts Brazil
129 K5 Chapada do Araripe mts Brazil
130 C4 Chapada dos Guimarães Brazil
129 K4 Chapadinha Brazil
121 Q3 Chapais Quebec Canada
124 H7 Chapala,L.de Mexico
129 K8 Chaparao,Serra do mts Brazil
53 H8 Chapayev Kazakhstan
57 C6 Chapayeva, Imeni Turkmenistan
53 G7 Chapayevsk Russian Federation
121 N7 Chapeau Quebec Canada
130 D10 Chapecó Brazil
130 D10 Chapecózinho R Brazil
9 E1 Chapel en le Frith England
112 H2 Chapel Hill North Carolina U.S.A.
110 K6 Chapel Hill Tennessee U.S.A.
21 K5 Chapelle-au-Riboul,la France
40 D1 Chapelle-aux-Bois, La France
20 H7 Chapelle Basse Mer, la France
21 M7 Chapelle, Blanche-St. Martin, la France
20 G6 Chapelle-Bouexic,la France
21 K6 Chapelle d'Aligné, la France
18 G5 Chapelle d' Angillon,la France
20 F7 Chapelle-des-Marais,la France
21 H6 Chapelle-Glain,la France
20 H7 Chapelle-Heulin,la France
22 J4 Chapelle, la France
20 F6 Chapelle,La Morbihan France
123 L3 Chapelle,L. de la Quebec Canada
21 K4 Chapelle-Moche,la France
21 J5 Chapelle-Rainsouin,la France
21 N5 Chapelle Royale France
21 K8 Chapelle St. Laurent, la France
21 O6 Chapelle-st.Mesmin,la France
20 G7 Chapelle-sur-Erdre, La France
9 G1 Chapel St Leonards England
127 K2 Chapelton Jamaica
13 G6 Chapeltown England
99 Q10 Chapin Illinois U.S.A.
110 F2 Chapin Illinois U.S.A.
120 G4 Chapleau R Ontario Canada
120 G5 Chapleau Ontario Canada
120 H4 Chapleau-Nemecosenda Wild R. Prov. Pk Ontario Canada
118 L8 Chaplin Saskatchewan Canada
147 P1 Chaplina,Mys C Russian Federation
54 H8 Chaplino Ukraine
54 L3 Chaplygin Russian Federation
111 K10 Chapman Alabama U.S.A.
107 N3 Chapman Kansas U.S.A.
101 R1 Chapman Montana U.S.A.
98 H8 Chapman Nebraska U.S.A.
117 O10 Chapman,Mt British Columbia Canada
142 F3 Chapman R W Australia Australia
109 K8 Chapman Ranch Texas U.S.A.
94 E9 Chapmanville West Virginia U.S.A.
52 E2 Chapoma Russian Federation
98 D8 Chappell Nebraska U.S.A.
109 L5 Chappell Hill Texas U.S.A.
139 J8 Chappell Is Tasmania Australia
95 L8 Chaptico Maryland U.S.A.
18 E7 Chapus, le France
120 K4 Chaput Ontario Canada
128 E7 Chaqui Bolivia
133 D1 Chaqui Bolivia
74 G2 Char Kashmir
85 B4 Char Mauritania
51 L3 Chara Russian Federation
133 E1 Charagua Bolivia
124 E4 Charay Mexico
98 C2 Charbonneau North Dakota U.S.A.
40 C3 Charcenne France
21 K5 Charchigné France
109 K7 Charco Texas U.S.A.
146 C5 Charcot I Antarctica
118 G3 Chard Alberta Canada
8 D6 Chard England
57 E4 Chardara Kazakhstan
57 E4 Chardarinskoye Vdkhr res Kazakhstan/Uzbekistan
94 F5 Chardon Ohio U.S.A.
126 G5 Chardonnière Haiti
57 C5 Chardzhou Turkmenistan
18 E7 Charente R France
18 E7 Charente dept France
18 E7 Charente-Maritime dept France
21 M3 Charentonne R France
18 G6 Charenton-sur-Cher France
86 C3 Chari R Chad
77 L2 Chārīkār Afghanistan
9 G5 Charing England
116 D2 Chariot Alaska U.S.A.
18 H5 Charité, la France
99 N8 Chariton Iowa U.S.A.
99 N9 Chariton R Iowa U.S.A.
110 D2 Chariton R Missouri U.S.A.
128 G2 Charity Guyana
52 H2 Charkayuvom Russian Federation
74 H6 Charkhari India
9 E4 Charlbury England
22 H3 Charleroi Belgium
94 H6 Charleroi Pennsylvania U.S.A.
119 Q3 Charles Manitoba Canada
121 T6 Charlesbourg Quebec Canada
95 M9 Charles,C Virginia U.S.A.
99 O6 Charles City Iowa U.S.A.
115 M5 Charles I Northwest Territories Canada
143 B8 Charles,Mt W Australia Australia
143 D10 Charles Pk W Australia Australia
140 B1 Charles Pt N Terr Australia
144 A6 Charles Sd New Zealand
144 C4 Charleston New Zealand
110 B6 Charleston Arkansas U.S.A.
99 S10 Charleston Illinois U.S.A.
111 F7 Charleston Mississippi U.S.A.
110 G5 Charleston Missouri U.S.A.
100 A6 Charleston Oregon U.S.A.
112 H5 Charleston South Carolina U.S.A.
112 C2 Charleston Tennessee U.S.A.
94 F8 Charleston West Virginia U.S.A.
103 J5 Charleston Pk Nevada U.S.A.
14 C3 Charlestown Ireland
94 B8 Charlestown Indiana U.S.A.
95 P3 Charlestown New Hampshire U.S.A.
94 K7 Charles Town West Virginia U.S.A.
127 P4 Charlestown Nevis W Indies
118 A1 Charles Wood Manitoba Canada
Charlet,Ft see Djanet
21 N3 Charleval France
141 H7 Charleville Queensland Australia
22 H4 Charleville-Mézières France
94 B1 Charlevoix Michigan U.S.A.
94 B1 Charlevoix,L Michigan U.S.A.
116 Q4 Charley R Alaska U.S.A.
117 N7 Charlie Lake British Columbia Canada
18 H6 Charlieu France
94 C4 Charlotte Michigan U.S.A.
112 G2 Charlotte North Carolina U.S.A.
109 J7 Charlotte Texas U.S.A.
127 M5 Charlotte Amalie Virgin Is
117 L9 Charlotte L British Columbia Canada
27 F12 Charlottenberg Sweden
33 S7 Charlottenburg Berlin
33 S9 Charlottenfelde Germany
94 J8 Charlottesville Virginia U.S.A.
122 J7 Charlottetown Prince Edward I Canada
Charlotte Town Grenada see Gouyave
127 N1 Charlotteville Tobago
139 G6 Charlton Victoria Australia
120 K5 Charlton Ontario Canada
115 M7 Charlton I Northwest Territories Canada
19 K4 Charmes France
40 F4 Charmey Switzerland
40 F3 Charmoille Switzerland
8 D6 Charmouth England
21 M8 Charnizay France
142 F3 Charnley,R W Australia Australia
121 T6 Charny Quebec Canada
60 R2 Charo-gawa R Japan
18 H6 Charolles France
21 P8 Charost France
52 E4 Charozero Russian Federation
122 J2 Charpeney,L Quebec Canada
21 O3 Chars France
74 D1 Charsadda Pakistan
57 D5 Charshanga Turkmenistan
56 B6 Charsk Kazakhstan
99 L7 Charter Oak Iowa U.S.A.
141 H5 Charters Towers Queensland Australia
122 A8 Chartierville Quebec Canada
21 M6 Chartre,la France
21 N5 Chartres France
57 F4 Charvakskoye Vdkhr. Uzbekistan
19 Q13 Charvin, Mt France
19 Q13 Charvonnex France
56 B5 Charysh R Russian Federation
131 F5 Chascomas Argentina
117 O10 Chase British Columbia Canada
107 M3 Chase Kansas U.S.A.
99 P6 Chaseburg Wisconsin U.S.A.
94 J10 Chase City Virginia U.S.A.
98 G3 Chase L North Dakota U.S.A.
55 D3 Chashi Russian Federation
57 B5 Chashkent Turkmenistan
99 N5 Chaska Minnesota U.S.A.
144 B7 Chaslands Mistake New Zealand
117 N10 Chasm British Columbia Canada
52 D1 Chasnachorr, Gora mt Russian Federation
52 E3 Chasovenskaya Russian Federation
52 H4 Chasovo Russian Federation
54 J8 Chasov Yar Ukraine
113 E9 Chassahowitzka B Florida U.S.A.
99 S2 Chassell Michigan U.S.A.
18 F7 Chasseneuil France
18 H8 Chassezac R France
21 O8 Chassignoles France
21 K5 Chassille France
55 E3 Chastoozer'ye Russian Federation
52 H6 Chastyye Russian Federation
21 J8 Châtaigneraie,la France
116 O4 Chatanika Alaska U.S.A.
121 L10 Chatauqua L New York U.S.A.
127 O8 Chateaubelair St Vincent
20 G7 Chateau Bougon airport France
20 H5 Châteaubourg France
20 H6 Châteaubriant France
18 H5 Château Chinon France
19 O18 Château d'If isld France
18 E7 Château d'Oléron, le France
21 L6 Château-du-Loir France
21 N5 Châteaudun France
21 P4 Châteaufort France
95 N2 Chateaugay New York U.S.A.
20 H5 Châteaugiron France
21 J6 Château-Gontier France
21 L6 Château-la-Vallière France
20 B5 Châteaulin France
21 P8 Châteaumeillant France
19 N14 Châteauneuf-de-Galaure France
20 G4 Châteauneuf-d'Ille-et-Vilaine France
20 C5 Châteauneuf-du-Faou France
21 N4 Châteauneuf-en-Thymerais France
18 E7 Châteauneuf-sur-Charente France
21 P8 Châteauneuf-sur-Cher France
21 P6 Châteauneuf-sur-Loire France
21 J6 Châteauneuf-sur-Sarthe France
22 G4 Château-Porcien France
20 D4 Château,Pte.du France
19 Q16 Châteauredon France
19 N17 Châteaurenard France
21 M6 Château-Renault France
122 A7 Chateau Richer Quebec Canada
21 O8 Châteauroux Indre France
19 K4 Château Salins France
18 H3 Château-Thierry France
121 R5 Chateauvert, L Quebec Canada
127 O4 Châteaux, Pte. des Guadeloupe W Indies
117 O6 Chateh Alberta Canada
20 E4 Châtelaudren France
22 H3 Châtelet Belgium
21 P8 Châtelet,le France
21 N5 Châtelets,les France
18 H7 Chatelguyon France
40 A2 Chatellenot France
21 M8 Châtellerault France
36 C7 Chatenois France
99 O6 Chatfield Minnesota U.S.A.
122 G6 Chatham New Brunswick Canada
120 H10 Chatham Ontario Canada
9 G5 Chatham England
117 F7 Chatham Alaska U.S.A.
99 R10 Chatham Illinois U.S.A.
110 G2 Chatham Illinois U.S.A.
111 D9 Chatham Louisiana U.S.A.
95 S5 Chatham Massachusetts U.S.A.
95 O4 Chatham New York U.S.A.
94 H10 Chatham Virginia U.S.A.
137 R10 Chatham Is Pacific Oc
117 H8 Chatham Sd British Columbia Canada
133 C8 Chatham Stokes mt Chile
22 K4 Châtillon Belgium
40 G6 Châtillon Italy
18 G5 Châtillon-Coligny France
19 P12 Châtillon de Michaille France
21 H5 Châtillon-en-Vendelais France
19 O13 Chatillon-la-Palud France
21 N8 Châtillon-sur-Indre France
18 G5 Châtillon-sur-Loire France
57 F4 Chatkal R Kirghizia
57 F4 Chatkal'skiy Khr mts Kirghizia/Uzbekistan
111 H10 Chatom Alabama U.S.A.
75 L6 Chatra India
21 O8 Châtre, la France
140 F5 Chatsworth Queensland Australia
120 K8 Chatsworth Ontario Canada
112 C3 Chatsworth Georgia U.S.A.
110 H1 Chatsworth Illinois U.S.A.
95 N7 Chatsworth New Jersey U.S.A.
89 G2 Chatsworth Zimbabwe
111 L8 Chattahoochee R Alabama/Georgia
111 M11 Chattahoochee Florida U.S.A.
112 B2 Chattanooga Tennessee U.S.A.
100 H2 Chattaroy Washington U.S.A.
94 E9 Chattaroy West Virginia U.S.A.
9 G3 Chatteris England
144 B6 Chatto Cr New Zealand
13 G2 Chatton England
111 L7 Chattooga R Georgia/Alabama U.S.A.
112 D3 Chattooga R S Carolina/Georgia U.S.A.
112 D2 Chatuge L North Carolina U.S.A.
68 E5 Chaturat Thailand
57 H4 Chatyr-Kël' Ozero L Kirghizia
20 H8 Chauché France
18 H8 Chaudes-Aigues France
22 K2 Chaudfontaine Belgium
Chau Doc see Chau Phu
21 J7 Chaudron-en-Mauges France
22 E5 Chaudun France
116 H6 Chauekuktuli L Alaska U.S.A.
19 Q15 Chauffayer France
68 B2 Chauk Burma
75 R5 Chaukan Pass Burma/India
22 D4 Chaulnes France
40 B4 Chaumergy France
40 D3 Chaumont mt France
19 J4 Chaumont Haute-Marne France
21 O3 Chaumont-en-Vexin France
22 G4 Chaumont-Porcien France
21 N7 Chaumont-sur-Loire France
21 O6 Chaumont-sur-Tharonne France
94 E7 Chauncey Ohio U.S.A.
68 D6 Chaungwabyin Burma
68 C4 Chaungzon Burma
51 Q2 Chaunskaya Guba G Russian Federation
22 E4 Chauny France
68 G7 Chau Phu Vietnam
69 A8 Chaura I Nicobar Is
20 G4 Chausey Is France
21 P2 Chaussée-Tirancourt,la France
19 J6 Chaussin France
54 B3 Chausy Belarus
94 H4 Chautauqua New York U.S.A.
94 H4 Chautauqua L New York U.S.A.
57 F4 Chauvay Kirghizia
20 G7 Chauvé France
21 N6 Chauvigny Loir-et-Cher France
21 M8 Chauvigny Vienne France
118 G6 Chauvin Alberta Canada
19 K5 Chaux de Fonds, la France
40 E3 Chaux de Fonds, La Switzerland
20 H8 Chavagnes-en-Paillers France
19 N14 Chavanay France
52 E2 Chavan'ga Russian Federation
130 D4 Chavantina Brazil
130 D7 Chavantina Brazil
16 C3 Chaves Portugal
94 D9 Chavies Kentucky U.S.A.
22 F5 Chavignon France
87 D8 Chavuma Zambia
69 D8 Chawang Thailand
9 F5 Chawton England
56 G2 Chaya R Russian Federation
88 C7 Chaya, L Zambia
57 E3 Chayan Kazakhstan
57 G4 Chayek Kirghizia
52 H6 Chaykovskiy Russian Federation
78 K2 Chāypareh Iran
66 F6 Ch'a-yü China
21 J6 Chazé-sur-Argos France
52 H4 Chazhegovo Russian Federation
133 E4 Chazon Argentina
95 O2 Chazy New York U.S.A.
118 D7 Cheadle Alberta Canada
9 E2 Cheadle England
111 L8 Cheaha Mt Alabama U.S.A.
94 H7 Cheat R West Virginia U.S.A.
110 J5 Cheatham L Tennessee U.S.A.
37 N3 Cheb Czech Rep
55 D4 Chebarkul' Russian Federation
52 G6 Cheboksary Russian Federation
94 C1 Cheboygan Michigan U.S.A.
52 E5 Chebsara Russian Federation
53 G11 Checheno-Ingushskaya Respublika Russian Federation
54 B4 Chechersk Belarus
31 M5 Chęciny Poland
107 P6 Checotah Oklahoma U.S.A.
21 P6 Chécy France
123 L8 Chedabucto B Nova Scotia Canada
8 D5 Cheddar England
83 K9 Cheddikulam Sri Lanka
68 A3 Cheduba isld Burma
68 A3 Cheduba Burma
68 A3 Cheduba Str Burma
118 G2 Cheecham Alberta Canada
120 J2 Cheepash R Ontario Canada
120 G1 Cheepay R Ontario Canada
141 G7 Cheepie Queensland Australia
119 O1 Cheeseman L Ontario Canada
106 E2 Cheesman,L Colorado U.S.A.
146 C13 Cheetham, C Antarctica
18 E6 Chef-Boutonne France
111 G11 Chef Menteur Louisiana U.S.A.
Chefoo see Yantai
116 E6 Chefornak Alaska U.S.A.
121 R3 Chef,R.du Quebec Canada
59 K1 Chegdomyn Russian Federation
85 C3 Chegga Mauritania
116 A3 Chegitun R Russian Federation
89 G2 Chegutu Zimbabwe
100 B3 Chehalis R Washington U.S.A.
100 C3 Chehalis Washington U.S.A.
67 B4 Chehe China
87 F8 Cheif Serenje Zambia
21 L7 Cheillé France
59 J5 Cheju S Korea
65 G8 Cheju do isld S Korea
65 G8 Cheju haehyŏp str S Korea
54 H2 Chekalin Russian Federation
52 H7 Chekan Russian Federation
54 J1 Chekhov Russian Federation
Chekiang prov see Zhejiang
55 G2 Chekino Russian Federation
51 N3 Chekunda Russian Federation

52 E3 **Chekuyevo** Russian Federation
119 O6 **Chelan** Saskatchewan Canada
100 F2 **Chelan** Washington U.S.A.
100 E1 **Chelan,L** Washington U.S.A.
100 E1 **Chelan Range** Washington U.S.A.
116 M5 **Chelatna L** Alaska U.S.A.
133 D5 **Chelforó** Argentina
85 F1 **Chelia** *mt* Algeria
85 E1 **Chélif** *R* Algeria
55 C3 **Chelkakovo** Russian Federation
57 A1 **Chelkar** Kazakhstan
31 O4 **Chelm** Poland
31 L2 **Chelmno** Poland
120 J6 **Chelmsford** Ontario Canada
9 G4 **Chelmsford** England
52 E3 **Chelmuzhi** Russian Federation
31 L2 **Chelmża** Poland
99 O8 **Chelsea** Iowa U.S.A.
94 C4 **Chelsea** Michigan U.S.A.
107 P5 **Chelsea** Oklahoma U.S.A.
95 P3 **Chelsea** Vermont U.S.A.
8 D4 **Cheltenham** England
20 H6 **Chelun** France
17 G5 **Chelva** Spain
55 D3 **Chelyabinsk** Russian Federation
55 D4 **Chelyabinskaya Oblast'** *prov* Russian Federation
94 F8 **Chelyan** West Virginia U.S.A.
56 C5 **Chelyush** Russian Federation
51 K1 **Chelyuskin,Mys** *C* Russian Federation
117 M11 **Chemainus** British Columbia Canada
100 C4 **Chemawa** Oregon U.S.A.
21 J6 **Chemaze** France
87 F9 **Chemba** Mozambique
57 B6 **Chemen-i-Bit** Turkmenistan
21 N7 **Chemery** France
22 H4 **Chémery-sur-Bar** France
21 J7 **Chemillé** France
21 M6 **Chemillé-sur-Dême** France
40 B4 **Chemin** France
21 K6 **Cheminé-le-Gaudin** France
37 O2 **Chemnitz** Germany
95 R7 **Chemquasabamticook L** Maine U.S.A.
56 B4 **Chemskiy** Russian Federation
95 K4 **Chemung** *R* New York U.S.A.
116 O4 **Chena** *R* Alaska U.S.A.
74 D3 **Chenab** *R* Pakistan
85 D3 **Chenachane** *watercourse* Algeria
85 D3 **Chenachane** Algeria
116 O4 **Chena Hot Springs** Alaska U.S.A.
95 M4 **Chenango** *R* New York U.S.A.
86 G4 **Ch'ench'a** Ethiopia
22 K2 **Chênée** Belgium
18 G6 **Chénérailles** France
121 P7 **Chénéville** Quebec Canada
99 N8 **Cheney** Kansas U.S.A.
100 H2 **Cheney** Washington U.S.A.
111 D10 **Cheneyville** Louisiana U.S.A.
76 E4 **Chengalpattu** India
65 C6 **Cheng'an** China
67 B4 **Chengbihe Shuiku** *res* China
67 B3 **Chengbu** China
65 A7 **Chengcheng** China
Chengchow *see* **Zhengzhou**
65 D4 **Chengde** China
67 E1 **Chengdong Hu** *L* China
67 A1 **Chengdu** China
67 A4 **Chenggong** China
67 E5 **Chenghai** China
67 A4 **Chengjiang** China
65 D5 **Chengkou** China
67 B1 **Chengkou** China
67 C7 **Chengmai** China
65 E6 **Chengshan Jiao** *pen* China
Chengtu *see* **Chengdu**
65 C7 **Chengwu** China
65 E6 **Chengyang** China
67 F2 **Chengyang** China
65 E5 **Chengzitan** China
121 O6 **Chenier** Quebec Canada
123 N2 **Chenil,L** Quebec Canada
36 B7 **Cheniménil** France
65 D7 **Cheniu Shan** *isld* China
65 D7 **Chenjiagang** China
65 C7 **Chenliu** China
110 H1 **Chenoa** Illinois U.S.A.
21 N7 **Chenonceaux** France
40 B3 **Chenôve** France
67 G1 **Chenqian Shan** *isld* China
21 L6 **Chenu** France
67 C1 **Chenxi** China
67 D4 **Chen Xian** China
Chenying *see* **Wannian**
68 J6 **Cheo Reo** Vietnam
67 F3 **Chepan** China
46 G3 **Chepelare** Bulgaria
128 C5 **Chepén** Peru
133 D4 **Chepes** Argentina
8 D4 **Chepstow** Wales
99 Q3 **Chequamegon B** Wisconsin U.S.A.
21 M7 **Cher** *R* France
22 K3 **Cherain** Belgium
44 C2 **Cherasco** Italy
106 G3 **Cheraw** Colorado U.S.A.
111 G10 **Cheraw** Mississippi U.S.A.
112 H3 **Cheraw** South Carolina U.S.A.
20 G2 **Cherbourg** France
85 E1 **Cherchell** Algeria
52 J4 **Cherdyn'** Russian Federation
20 G6 **Chère** *R* France
52 B2 **Cheremisskoye** Russian Federation
56 F4 **Cheremkhovo** Russian Federation
55 D3 **Cheremshanka** Russian Federation
55 D1 **Cheremukhovo** Russian Federation
56 E4 **Cheremushki** Russian Federation
56 B4 **Cherepanovo** Russian Federation
54 H2 **Cherepet'** Russian Federation
52 E5 **Cherepovets** Russian Federation
52 D5 **Chereptsovo** Russian Federation
118 C5 **Cherhill** Alberta Canada
54 C3 **Cherikov** Belarus
21 N4 **Cherisy** France
54 J8 **Cherkasskoye** Ukraine
53 F11 **Cherkessk** Russian Federation
46 G1 **Cherkovitsa** Bulgaria
55 F4 **Cherlak** Russian Federation
55 F4 **Cherlakskiy** Russian Federation
141 K1 **Chermside** *dist* Brisbane, Qnsld Australia
116 H9 **Chernabura I** Alaska U.S.A.
46 G3 **Chernatitsa** *hills* Bulgaria
55 D2 **Chernaya** *R* Russian Federation
52 H5 **Chernaya Kholunitsa** Russian Federation
48 J2 **Chernaya Tisa** *R* Ukraine
Chernenko *see* **Sharypovo**
47 J1 **Chernevo** Bulgaria
54 C5 **Chernigov** Ukraine
59 K3 **Chernigovka** Russian Federation
116 F9 **Cherni I** Alaska U.S.A.
55 C4 **Chernikovsk** Russian Federation
47 H1 **Cherni Lom** *R* Bulgaria
46 F2 **Cherni Vrŭkh** *mt* Bulgaria
53 D8 **Chernobyl'** Ukraine
56 D4 **Chernogorsk** Russian Federation
55 C2 **Chernoistochinsk** Russian Federation
55 G4 **Chernoretskoye** Kazakhstan
55 F4 **Chernousovka** Russian Federation
52 G6 **Chernovskoye** Russian Federation
48 K2 **Chernovtsy** Ukraine
55 E2 **Chernoye** Russian Federation
55 E3 **Chernoye, Oz** *L* Russian Federation
55 C3 **Chernushka** Russian Federation
52 G3 **Chernut'yevo** Russian Federation
31 N1 **Chernyakhovsk** Russian Federation
52 J2 **Chernysheva, Gryada** *ridge* Russian Federation
58 G1 **Chernyshevsk** Russian Federation
31 O1 **Chernyshevskoye** Russian Federation
53 G10 **Chernyye Zemli** Russian Federation
55 C5 **Chernyy Otrog** Russian Federation
53 G9 **Chernyy Yar** Russian Federation
110 J7 **Cherokee** Alabama U.S.A.
99 L7 **Cherokee** Iowa U.S.A.
107 Q4 **Cherokee** Kansas U.S.A.
107 M5 **Cherokee** Oklahoma U.S.A.
109 J5 **Cherokee** Texas U.S.A.
112 D1 **Cherokee Dam** Tennessee U.S.A.
94 D10 **Cherokee L** Tennessee U.S.A.
111 B9 **Cherokee,L** Texas U.S.A.
113 K11 **Cherokee Pt** Bahamas
110 B5 **Cherokees, L O' The** Oklahoma U.S.A.
126 F1 **Cherokee Sound** Great Abaco I Bahamas
55 E2 **Cherpiya** Russian Federation
75 O6 **Cherrapunji** India
20 G4 **Cherrueix** France
137 O4 **Cherry** *isld* Santa Cruz Is
103 K2 **Cherry Cr** Nevada U.S.A.
98 E5 **Cherry Cr** South Dakota U.S.A.
94 H4 **Cherry Creek** New York U.S.A.
103 K1 **Cherry Cr.Mt** Nevada U.S.A.
95 U2 **Cherryfield** Maine U.S.A.
117 O7 **Cherry Point** Alberta Canada
107 P4 **Cherryvale** Kansas U.S.A.
95 N4 **Cherry Valley** New York U.S.A.
112 F2 **Cherryville** North Carolina U.S.A.
56 G3 **Cherskogo,Gora** *mt* Russian Federation
51 O2 **Cherskogo,Khrebet** *mts* Russian Federation
17 H4 **Cherta** Spain
54 M7 **Chertkovo** Russian Federation
54 E1 **Chertolino** Russian Federation
9 F5 **Chertsey** England
144 C5 **Chertsey** New Zealand
52 F6 **Cherusti** Russian Federation
19 O13 **Cheruy,Pt.de** France
52 G4 **Cherva** Russian Federation
48 N3 **Chervonoz-namenka** Ukraine
9 E3 **Cherwell,R** England
94 C3 **Chesaning** Michigan U.S.A.
94 E8 **Chesapeake** Ohio U.S.A.
95 L10 **Chesapeake** Virginia U.S.A.
95 L8 **Chesapeake B** U.S.A.
95 L8 **Chesapeake Beach** Maryland U.S.A.
95 M7 **Chesapeake City** Maryland U.S.A.
94 K9 **Chesdin, L** Virginia U.S.A.
9 F4 **Chesham** England
8 D1 **Cheshire** *co* England
95 O4 **Cheshire** Massachusetts U.S.A.
52 G2 **Chëshskaya Guba** *B* Russian Federation
57 G5 **Cheshtebe** Tajikistan
88 B6 **Chesi,L** Zambia
8 D6 **Chesil Bank** England
120 J8 **Chesley** Ontario Canada
52 F5 **Chesnokovka** Russian Federation
112 F2 **Chesnee** South Carolina U.S.A.
22 H5 **Chesne, le** Ardennes France
21 M4 **Chesne,le** Eure France
122 H9 **Chester** Nova Scotia Canada
8 D1 **Chester** England
110 B6 **Chester** Arkansas U.S.A.
100 D9 **Chester** California U.S.A.
95 P5 **Chester** Connecticut U.S.A.
101 O6 **Chester** Idaho U.S.A.
110 G4 **Chester** Illinois U.S.A.
95 L7 **Chester** *R* Maryland U.S.A.
95 P4 **Chester** Massachusetts U.S.A.
101 P1 **Chester** Montana U.S.A.
98 J9 **Chester** Nebraska U.S.A.
95 M6 **Chester** Pennsylvania U.S.A.
112 F3 **Chester** South Carolina U.S.A.
109 N5 **Chester** Texas U.S.A.
95 P3 **Chester** Vermont U.S.A.
94 K9 **Chester** Virginia U.S.A.
122 H9 **Chester Basin** Nova Scotia Canada
9 E1 **Chesterfield** England
101 O7 **Chesterfield** Idaho U.S.A.
110 F2 **Chesterfield** Illinois U.S.A.
112 G3 **Chesterfield** South Carolina U.S.A.
94 K9 **Chesterfield** Virginia U.S.A.
137 M5 **Chesterfield, Îles** Coral Sea
115 K5 **Chesterfield Inlet** Northwest Territories Canada
94 F7 **Chesterhill** Ohio U.S.A.
9 F2 **Chesterton** England
99 T8 **Chesterton** Indiana U.S.A.
95 L7 **Chestertown** Maryland U.S.A.
95 O3 **Chestertown** New York U.S.A.
121 P7 **Chesterville** Ontario Canada
111 E11 **Chestnut** Louisiana U.S.A.
94 H6 **Chestnut Ridge** Pennsylvania U.S.A.
144 D5 **Chest Pk** New Zealand
95 R7 **Chesuncook L** Maine U.S.A.
95 M7 **Cheswold** Delaware U.S.A.
55 C3 **Chet'** *R* Russian Federation
68 A7 **Chetamale** Andaman Is
99 P4 **Chetek** Wisconsin U.S.A.
123 L7 **Cheticamp** C Breton I, Nova Scotia
73 L6 **Chetlat** *isld* Lakshadweep Indian Oc
107 P4 **Chetopa** Kansas U.S.A.
76 A5 **Chettlatt** *isld* Indian Oc
125 P8 **Chetumal** Mexico
145 E4 **Chetwode Is** New Zealand
117 N8 **Chetwynd** British Columbia Canada
116 E6 **Chevak** Alaska U.S.A.
19 O17 **Cheval-Blanc** France
22 D5 **Chevallerais, La** Loire-Atlantique France
21 O5 **Chevilly** France
118 L6 **Cheviot** Saskatchewan Canada
144 D5 **Cheviot** New Zealand
13 F3 **Cheviot Hills** England/Scotland
141 G7 **Cheviot Ra** Queensland Australia
21 K6 **Chevré-le-Rouge** France
21 N5 **Chèvre, C. de la** France
111 E12 **Chevreuil, Point** Louisiana U.S.A.
42 B5 **Chevreuse** France
40 E7 **Chevril,L** France
20 G7 **Chevrolière, la** France
88 D9 **Chewa** Mozambique
86 G5 **Ch'ew Bahir** *L* Ethiopia
100 H1 **Chewelah** Washington U.S.A.
8 D5 **Chew valley L** England
107 L6 **Cheyenne** Oklahoma U.S.A.
98 D5 **Cheyenne** *R* South Dakota U.S.A.
108 D4 **Cheyenne** Texas U.S.A.
98 B8 **Cheyenne** Wyoming U.S.A.
107 M3 **Cheyenne Bottoms** Kansas U.S.A.
98 A8 **Cheyenne Pass** Wyoming U.S.A.
106 H3 **Cheyenne Wells** Colorado U.S.A.
18 H8 **Cheylard, le** France
143 C10 **Cheyne B** W Australia Australia
117 M9 **Chezacut** British Columbia Canada
21 P8 **Chezal-Benoit** France
20 E5 **Chèze,la** France
75 L6 **Chhapra** India
74 H6 **Chhatarpur** India
75 L9 **Chhatrapur** India
68 G6 **Chhlong** Cambodia
68 H6 **Chhlong** *R* Cambodia
74 F7 **Chhota Udepur** India
68 G7 **Chhuk** Cambodia
116 H9 **Chiachi I** Alaska U.S.A.
67 G5 **Chia-i** Taiwan
66 D5 **Chia-jen Ts'o** *L* China
40 F7 **Chialamberto** Italy
66 D5 **Chia-man-t'e-k'a-mu Hu** *L* China
87 B9 **Chiange** Angola
68 E2 **Chiang Saen** Thailand
42 E6 **Chiani** *R* Italy
125 N9 **Chiapa del Corzo** Mexico
45 O4 **Chiaravalle** Italy
43 G10 **Chiaravalle Centrale** Italy
41 L5 **Chiareggio** Italy
41 J7 **Chiari** Italy
125 K8 **Chiautla** Mexico
44 F3 **Chiavari** Italy
41 K5 **Chiavenna** Italy
61 O10 **Chiba** *prefect* Japan
61 O10 **Chiba** Japan
61 P13 **Chibana** Okinawa
87 B9 **Chibia** Angola
68 E5 **Chi Bon Dam** Thailand
121 P3 **Chibougamau** *R* Quebec Canada
121 Q3 **Chibougamau** Quebec Canada
88 B8 **Chibuluma** Zambia
60 G9 **Chiburi-shima** *isld* Japan
87 F10 **Chibuto** Mozambique
87 E8 **Chibwe** Zambia
99 T8 **Chicago** Illinois U.S.A.
105 **Chicago** *conurbation* Illinois U.S.A.
99 T8 **Chicago Heights** Illinois U.S.A.
122 F5 **Chic-Chocs, Rés. Faun. de** Quebec Canada
117 F7 **Chichagof I** Alaska U.S.A.
85 C2 **Chichaoua** Morocco
21 K8 **Chiché** France
65 C4 **Chicheng** China
125 P7 **Chichén Itza** *ruins* Mexico
9 F6 **Chichester** England
142 C5 **Chichester Ra** W Australia Australia
142 B5 **Chichester Ra Nat Park** W Australia Australia
61 N10 **Chichibu** Japan
61 M9 **Chichibu Tama Nat. Park** Japan
56 C3 **Chichka-Yul** *R* Russian Federation
95 K9 **Chickahominy** *R* Virginia U.S.A.
112 B3 **Chickamauga** Georgia U.S.A.
112 B3 **Chickamauga Dam** Tennessee U.S.A.
111 H10 **Chickasawhay** *R* Mississippi U.S.A.
107 O7 **Chickasaw Nat. Recreation Area** Oklahoma U.S.A.
107 N6 **Chickasha** Oklahoma U.S.A.
116 R4 **Chicken** Alaska U.S.A.
8 D5 **Chicklade** England
16 C8 **Chiclana de la Frontera** Spain
128 C5 **Chiclayo** Peru
133 D6 **Chico** *R* Argentina
71 E2 **Chico** *R* Luzon Philippines
102 C2 **Chico** California U.S.A.
100 H4 **Chico** Oregon U.S.A.
109 K2 **Chico** Texas U.S.A.
133 C7 **Chicoana** Argentina
123 M4 **Chicobi,L** Quebec Canada
87 F10 **Chicomo** Mozambique
125 K7 **Chicontepec** Mexico
95 P4 **Chicopee** Massachusetts U.S.A.
121 T4 **Chicoutimi** Quebec Canada
121 T5 **Chicoutimi** *R* Quebec Canada
89 G4 **Chicualacuala** Mozambique
76 D5 **Chidambaram** India
9 F5 **Chiddingfold** England
105 N5 **Chidester** Arkansas U.S.A.
115 N5 **Chidley,C** Quebec Canada
100 F1 **Chief Joseph Dam** Washington U.S.A.
113 E8 **Chiefland** Florida U.S.A.
120 J8 **Chiefs Pt** Ontario Canada
67 B5 **Chiem Hoa** Vietnam
37 O7 **Chiemsee** *L* Germany
124 E4 **Chiengi** Zambia
68 D3 **Chieng-Mai** Thailand
41 O5 **Chienis** *R* Italy
42 F5 **Chienti** *R* Italy
44 C1 **Chieri** Italy
22 K5 **Chiers** *R* France
44 L7 **Chiese** Italy
41 M5 **Chiese** *R* Italy
42 F5 **Chieti** Italy
22 F2 **Chièvres** Belgium
130 H5 **Chifre,Serra do** *mts* Brazil
57 G2 **Chiganak** Kazakhstan
61 N10 **Chigasaki** Japan
116 J8 **Chiginigak Vol., Mt** Alaska U.S.A.
54 D7 **Chigirin** Ukraine
116 J8 **Chigmit Mts** Alaska U.S.A.
122 H8 **Chignecto B** Nova Scotia/New Bruns Canada
116 H8 **Chignik** Alaska U.S.A.
19 Q13 **Chignin** France
121 R3 **Chigoubiche, L** Quebec Canada
87 F10 **Chigubo** Mozambique
66 E6 **Chigu Co** *L* China
9 G4 **Chigwell** England
Chihli,G. of *see* **Bo Hai**
124 F3 **Chihuahua** Mexico
124 F3 **Chihuido Medio** *pk* Argentina
57 D3 **Chiili** Kazakhstan
67 C6 **Chikan** China
107 N5 **Chikaskia** *R* Okla/Kansas U.S.A.
76 C4 **Chik Ballapur** India
52 C6 **Chikhachevo** Russian Federation
60 O3 **Chikuju-misaki** *C* Japan
76 B4 **Chikmagalur** India
55 F3 **Chikoy** *R* Russian Federation
68 G6 **Chikreng** *R* Cambodia
60 D12 **Chikugo** *R* Japan
60 D12 **Chikugo** Japan
116 H6 **Chikuminuk L** Alaska U.S.A.
61 N9 **Chikuma** *R* Japan
88 E10 **Chikwawa** Malawi
117 L9 **Chilanko Forks** British Columbia Canada
74 F1 **Chilas** Kashmir
83 J10 **Chilaw** Sri Lanka
128 C6 **Chilca, Pta. de** *pt* Peru
102 D2 **Chilcoot** California U.S.A.
117 M10 **Chilcotin** *R* British Columbia Canada
141 K3 **Chilcott I** Gt Barrier Reef Aust
141 K7 **Childers** Queensland Australia
111 K8 **Childersburg** Alabama U.S.A.
108 G1 **Childress** Texas U.S.A.
103 M9 **Childs** Arizona U.S.A.
113 F10 **Childs** Florida U.S.A.
133 C6 **Chile** *rep* S America
128 C5 **Chilete** Peru
76 C3 **Chilgājūr** India
9 G5 **Chilham** England
110 C3 **Chilhowee** Missouri U.S.A.
94 F10 **Chilhowie** Virginia U.S.A.
116 K6 **Chilikadrotna** *R* Alaska U.S.A.
75 L9 **Chilika Lake** India
87 E8 **Chililabombwe** Zambia
89 G2 **Chilimanzi** Zimbabwe
59 H1 **Chi-li-u Ho** *R* China
117 F6 **Chilkat** *R* Alaska U.S.A.
117 M10 **Chilko** *R* British Columbia Canada
141 G3 **Chillagoe** Queensland Australia
131 A6 **Chillán** Chile
140 B5 **Chilla Well** N Terr Australia
21 P5 **Chilleurs-aux-Bois** France
99 R9 **Chillicothe** Illinois U.S.A.
110 C2 **Chillicothe** Missouri U.S.A.
94 D7 **Chillicothe** Ohio U.S.A.
109 H1 **Chillicothe** Texas U.S.A.
139 G6 **Chillingollah** Victoria Australia
100 D1 **Chilliwack** British Columbia Canada
19 P13 **Chilly** France
101 M5 **Chilly** Idaho U.S.A.
116 J6 **Chilnuk Mts** Alaska U.S.A.
133 C6 **Chiloé** *prov* Chile
135 R14 **Chiloe, I. de** Chile
88 C8 **Chilonga** Zambia
87 F8 **Chilongazi** Zambia
100 D7 **Chiloquin** Oregon U.S.A.
125 K9 **Chilpancingo** Mexico
139 H6 **Chiltern** Victoria Australia
9 F4 **Chiltern Hills** England
99 S5 **Chilton** Wisconsin U.S.A.
88 D9 **Chilumba** Malawi
67 G4 **Chi-lung** Taiwan
88 F9 **Chilwa,L** Malawi
9 E6 **Chilworth** England
125 M9 **Chimalapa** Mexico
88 F9 **Chimanimani** Zimbabwe
87 F10 **Chimanimani Nat. Park** Zimbabwe
22 G3 **Chimay** Belgium
106 E6 **Chimayo** New Mexico U.S.A.
57 A4 **Chimbay** Uzbekistan
128 C4 **Chimborazo** *mt* Ecuador
128 C5 **Chimbote** Peru
88 C8 **Chimbwin-gombi** *mt* Zambia
52 G5 **Chimeyevo** Russian Federation
57 F4 **Chimion** Kirghizia
48 M4 **Chimishliya** Moldova
57 E4 **Chimkent** Kazakhstan
123 P4 **Chimney Cove** Newfoundland Canada
108 B3 **Chimney Peak** New Mexico U.S.A.
106 E9 **Chimney Pk** New Mexico U.S.A.
83 J12 **Chimney Rocks** Seychelles
87 F9 **Chimoio** Mozambique
118 E9 **Chin** Alberta Canada
65 F7 **Chin** *isld* S Korea
58 D4 **China** *rep* E Asia
95 S2 **China** Maine U.S.A.
68 C4 **China Bakir** *R* Burma
124 G5 **Chinacates** Mexico
112 G2 **China Grove** North Carolina U.S.A.
125 L3 **Chinandega** Nicaragua
102 F9 **China Pt** California U.S.A.
109 M6 **China Spring** Texas U.S.A.
108 D5 **Chinati Mts** Texas U.S.A.
57 E4 **Chinaz** Uzbekistan
120 J7 **Chin, Cape** Ontario Canada
128 C6 **Chincha Alta** Peru
117 O6 **Chinchaga** *R* Alberta Canada
128 C6 **Chincha, Is** Peru
141 K7 **Chinchilla** Queensland Australia
17 F6 **Chinchilla de Monte Aragón** Spain
128 C4 **Chinchipe** *R* Ecuador/Peru
16 E4 **Chinchón** Spain
95 M9 **Chincoteague** Virginia U.S.A.
95 M8 **Chincoteague B** Maryland U.S.A.
87 G9 **Chinde** Mozambique
73 P4 **Chindwin** *R* Burma
61 P14 **Chinen** Okinawa
88 E8 **Chinengue** Mozambique
66 B4 **Chinese Turkestan** *reg* Xinjiang Uygur Zizhiqu China
67 D1 **Chinghai** *prov* *see* **Qinghai** *prov*
55 B5 **Chingirlau** Kazakhstan
88 A8 **Chingola** Zambia
87 B8 **Chingoroi** Angola
88 C9 **Chinguni** Zambia
73 P4 **Chin Hills** Burma
88 C10 **Chinhoyi** Zimbabwe
116 K8 **Chiniak,C** Alaska U.S.A.
Chining *see* **Jining**
74 E3 **Chiniot** Pakistan
125 M5 **Chinipas** Mexico
116 L7 **Chinitna B** Alaska U.S.A.
65 G7 **Chinju** S Korea
86 D4 **Chinko** *R* Cent Afr Republic
103 P5 **Chinle** Arizona U.S.A.
103 P5 **Chinle Valley** Arizona U.S.A.
103 P5 **Chinle Wash** Arizona U.S.A.
67 G4 **Chin-men** Taiwan
67 F4 **Chin-men** *isld* Taiwan
143 C10 **Chinocup, L** W Australia Australia
21 L7 **Chinon** France
118 G7 **Chinook** Alberta Canada
101 Q1 **Chinook** Montana U.S.A.
100 C3 **Chinook Pass** Washington U.S.A.
103 M7 **Chino Valley** Arizona U.S.A.
87 F8 **Chinsali** Zambia
88 D8 **Chinsali** Zambia
68 A1 **Chin State** Burma
75 P8 **Chin State** *prov* Burma
76 E1 **Chintalnar** India
88 E7 **Chintheche** Malawi
126 G10 **Chinú** Colombia
22 J4 **Chiny** Belgium
55 G3 **Chinyavino** Russian Federation
42 E3 **Chioggia** Italy
Chios *isld* *see* **Khios** *isld*
88 D9 **Chipata** Zambia
87 E9 **Chipepo** Zambia
88 E10 **Chiperone** *mt* Mozambique
119 T1 **Chipewyan,L** Manitoba Canada
117 R7 **Chipewyan Lake** Alberta Canada
87 E8 **Chipili** Zambia
67 B1 **Chiping** China
88 E8 **Chipinge** Zimbabwe
117 Q9 **Chip Lake** Alberta Canada
111 L11 **Chipley** Florida U.S.A.
111 M9 **Chipley** Georgia U.S.A.
74 E10 **Chiplun** India
122 G7 **Chipman** New Brunswick Canada
120 D3 **Chipman L** Ontario Canada
88 E8 **Chipoka** Malawi
111 L11 **Chipola** *R* Florida U.S.A.
88 A9 **Chiposhya, L** Zambia
68 G7 **Chi Pou** Cambodia
121 L9 **Chippawa** Ontario Canada
8 D5 **Chippenham** England
99 L4 **Chippewa** *R* Minnesota U.S.A.
99 P5 **Chippewa Falls** Wisconsin U.S.A.
99 P4 **Chippewa Lake** Wisconsin U.S.A.
13 F6 **Chipping** England
9 E3 **Chipping Campden** England
9 E4 **Chipping Norton** England
8 D4 **Chipping Sodbury** England
46 F1 **Chiprovtsi** Bulgaria
128 C6 **Chiquian** Peru
128 D2 **Chiquinquirá** Colombia
131 F6 **Chiquita, L. Mar** Buenos Aires Argentina
128 F7 **Chiquitos, Llanos de** Bolivia
128 B4 **Chira** *R* Peru
76 E3 **Chirala** India
87 F9 **Chiramba** Mozambique
88 E9 **Chirambirá, Pta** *pt* Colombia
77 J2 **Chiras** Afghanistan
57 E4 **Chirchik** Uzbekistan
87 F10 **Chiredzi** Zimbabwe
89 G3 **Chiredzi** *R* Zimbabwe
109 N4 **Chireno** Texas U.S.A.
111 B10 **Chireno** Texas U.S.A.
84 E5 **Chirfa** Niger
103 P9 **Chiricahua Nat.Mon** Arizona U.S.A.
103 P10 **Chiricahua Pk** Arizona U.S.A.
126 H10 **Chiriguaná** Colombia
116 K9 **Chirikof I** Alaska U.S.A.
75 P8 **Chiringa** Bangladesh
125 N5 **Chiriqui,G.de** Panama
75 K7 **Chirmiri** India
47 J1 **Chirnogeni** Romania
13 F2 **Chirnside** Scotland
15 F5 **Chirnside** Borders Scotland
88 E10 **Chiromo** Malawi
46 G2 **Chirpan** Bulgaria
Chirua, L *see* **Chilwa, L**
87 E9 **Chirundu** Zimbabwe
22 D4 **Chiry-Ourscamps** France
88 B9 **Chisamba** Zambia
116 R5 **Chisana** Alaska U.S.A.
116 Q6 **Chisana Glacier** Alaska U.S.A.
44 B2 **Chisane** *R* Italy
119 R4 **Chisel Lake** Manitoba Canada
88 D6 **Chisenga** Malawi
55 C4 **Chishmy** Russian Federation
118 C4 **Chisholm** Alberta Canada
95 R2 **Chisholm** Maine U.S.A.
99 O2 **Chisholm** Minnesota U.S.A.
74 E4 **Chishtian Mandi** Pakistan
67 B2 **Chishui** China
67 E4 **Chishui** China
67 B3 **Chishui He** *R* China
88 B7 **Chisi** *isld* Zambia
Chisimaio *see* **Kismaayo**
87 F8 **Chisimba Falls** Zambia
57 B4 **Chisimbay** Uzbekistan
Chişinău *see* **Kishinev**
48 G4 **Chişineu-Criş** Romania
108 D6 **Chisos Mts** Texas U.S.A.
108 C5 **Chispa Cr** Texas U.S.A.
116 P5 **Chistochina** Alaska U.S.A.
55 G4 **Chisto-ozernoye** Russian Federation
52 H6 **Chistopol'** Russian Federation
55 E4 **Chistopol'ye** Kazakhstan
55 E4 **Chistovo** Russian Federation
55 F4 **Chistyakovskoye** Kazakhstan
88 E8 **Chiteulu** *isld* Mozambique
58 F1 **Chita** Russian Federation
87 B9 **Chitado** Angola
116 L4 **Chitanana** *R* Alaska U.S.A.
58 C5 **Chi-t'ang** China
61 K11 **Chita wan** *G* Japan
52 G4 **Chitayevo** Russian Federation
118 K5 **Chitek** Saskatchewan Canada
119 S6 **Chitek L** Manitoba Canada
87 C8 **Chitembo** Angola
45 L4 **Chitignano** Italy
116 P6 **Chitina** Alaska U.S.A.
116 Q6 **Chitina** *R* Alaska U.S.A.
56 G5 **Chitinskaya Oblast'** *prov* Russian Federation
60 P3 **Chitose** Japan
76 C3 **Chitradurga** India
74 J6 **Chitrakut** India
74 D1 **Chitral** Pakistan
125 O6 **Chitré** Panama
75 O7 **Chittagong** Bangladesh
75 M7 **Chittaranjan** India
74 F6 **Chittaurgarh** India
143 B9 **Chittering** W Australia Australia
76 D4 **Chittoor** India
76 C5 **Chittur** India
89 G1 **Chitungwiza** Zimbabwe
88 F8 **Chiuledzi** *R* Mozambique
87 D9 **Chiume** Angola
42 D5 **Chiusa** Italy
41 O6 **Chiusi** Italy
45 L4 **Chiusi di Verna** Italy
87 G8 **Chiuta, L** Malawi
88 E9 **Chiuta,L** Mozambique
17 G5 **Chiva** Spain
40 G7 **Chivasso** Italy
124 C4 **Chivato,Pt** *C* Mexico
128 D7 **Chivay** Peru
87 B9 **Chivemba** Angola
89 G2 **Chivhu** Zimbabwe
131 E5 **Chivilcoy** Argentina
22 F4 **Chivy** France
67 D6 **Chixi** China
125 O10 **Chixoy** *R* Guatemala
89 E1 **Chizarira Hills** Zimbabwe
52 F2 **Chizha** Russian Federation
Chizhou *see* **Guichi**
60 H10 **Chizu** Japan
28 C4 **Chkalovo** Kazakhstan
57 H6 **Chkalovsk** Tajikistan
52 D2 **Chkalovskiy** Russian Federation
31 J5 **Chlumec nad Cidlinou** Czech Rep
31 M5 **Chmielnik** Poland
65 F5 **Cho** *isld* N Korea
65 G7 **Ch'o** *isld* S Korea
68 G6 **Choam Ksan** Cambodia
131 B3 **Choapo,R** Chile
87 D9 **Chobe Nat. Park** Botswana
9 F5 **Chobham** England
68 G2 **Cho Bo** Vietnam
31 J5 **Choceň** Czech Rep
122 B2 **Chochocouane** *R* Quebec Canada
67 B6 **Cho Chu** Vietnam
31 J4 **Chocianów** Poland
128 C2 **Chocó** *div* Colombia
103 J8 **Chocolate Mts** Arizona U.S.A.
103 J8 **Chocolate Mts** California U.S.A.
95 Q3 **Chocorua** New Hampshire U.S.A.
112 K2 **Chocowinity** North Carolina U.S.A.
111 L10 **Choctaw** Oklahoma U.S.A.
111 K11 **Choctawhatchee B** Florida U.S.A.
37 O3 **Chodov** Czech Rep
31 K3 **Chodzież** Poland
133 D5 **Choele Choel** Argentina
88 C9 **Chofombo** Mozambique
68 H7 **Cho Giua** Vietnam
119 N5 **Choiceland** Saskatchewan Canada
137 M3 **Choiseul** *isld* Solomon Is
133 F8 **Choiseul Sd** Falkland Is
19 Q12 **Choisy** France
22 D5 **Choisy-au-Bac** France
124 E4 **Choix** Mexico
31 H3 **Chojna** Poland
31 K2 **Chojnice** Poland
31 J4 **Chojnów** Poland
61 O6 **Chōkai-san** *mt* Japan
86 G3 **Ch'ok'ē Mts** Ethiopia
98 K4 **Chokio** Minnesota U.S.A.
55 G5 **Chokpar** Kazakhstan
57 H4 **Choktal** Kirghizia
51 O1 **Chokurdakh** Russian Federation
87 F10 **Chókwé** Mozambique
102 D6 **Cholame** California U.S.A.
102 D6 **Cholame Cr** California U.S.A.
133 C4 **Cholchagua** *prov* Chile
21 J7 **Cholet** France
13 F3 **Chollerford** England
68 H7 **Cho Lon** Vietnam
57 H4 **Cholpon** Kirghizia
57 F4 **Cholpon-Ata** Kirghizia
125 K8 **Cholula** Mexico
125 L3 **Choluleca** Honduras
87 E9 **Choma** Zambia
68 F7 **Chomna** Cambodia
68 G2 **Cho Moi** Vietnam
75 N5 **Chomo Lhari** *mt* Bhutan/China
68 D3 **Chom Thong** Thailand
37 P3 **Chomutov** Czech Rep
56 H1 **Chona** *R* Russian Federation
68 E6 **Chon Buri** Thailand
68 E4 **Chon Daen** Thailand
128 B4 **Chone** Ecuador
67 F3 **Chong'an** China
67 G1 **Chongde** China
65 H4 **Ch'ŏngjin** N Korea
65 F5 **Chŏngju** N Korea
65 G6 **Ch'ŏngju** S Korea
68 F6 **Chong Kal** Cambodia
65 C4 **Chongli** China
67 G1 **Chongming** China
67 G1 **Chongming Dao** *isld* China
67 A1 **Chongqing** China
67 B2 **Chongqing** China
67 E3 **Chongren** China
67 E4 **Chongshi** China
88 E8 **Chongwe** *R* Zambia
67 C2 **Chongyang** China
67 F3 **Chongyang Xi** *R* China
67 E4 **Chongyi** China
56 D5 **Chongyz-Tayga, Gora** *mt* Russian Federation
68 H1 **Chongzuo** China
67 B7 **Chŏnju** S Korea
133 C6 **Chonos,Arch.de los** *islds* Chile
125 N9 **Chontalpa** Mexico
68 H7 **Chon Thanh** Vietnam
75 M4 **Cho Oyu** *pk* China/Nepal
48 G2 **Chop** Ukraine
13 G5 **Chop Gate** England
68 H7 **Cho Phuoc Hai** Vietnam
130 D9 **Chopim** *R* Brazil
130 D9 **Chopinzinho** Brazil
95 M8 **Choptank** *R* Maryland U.S.A.
56 F3 **Chora** *R* Russian Federation
68 G1 **Cho Ra** Vietnam
33 T7 **Chorin** Germany
16 E5 **Chorito, Sa. del** *mts* Spain
57 F5 **Chorku** Kirghizia
13 F6 **Chorley** England
131 B2 **Choros** *R* Chile
131 B2 **Choros,I.de los** Chile
31 O2 **Choroszcz** Poland
141 G6 **Chorregon** Queensland Australia
128 C6 **Chorrillos** Peru
130 G10 **Chorrochó** Brazil
48 K1 **Chortkov** Ukraine
31 M2 **Chorzele** Poland
31 L5 **Chorzów** Poland
Chŏsen-kaikyō *see* **Nishi-suido**
61 O10 **Chōshi** Japan
133 C5 **Chos Malal** Argentina
65 G5 **Chosan-Man** *B* N Korea
31 J2 **Choszczno** Poland
128 C5 **Chota** Peru
74 G8 **Chota Nagpur** *reg* India
101 N2 **Choteau** Montana U.S.A.
107 P5 **Choteau** Oklahoma U.S.A.
31 J6 **Chotěbor** Czech Rep
37 P4 **Chotěšov** Czech Rep
85 E2 **Chott ech Chergui** *salt lake* Algeria
85 E1 **Chott El Hodna** *marsh* Algeria
85 F2 **Chott El Jerid** *salt flats* Tunisia
85 F2 **Chott Melrhir** *salt flats* Algeria
21 L7 **Chouzé-sur-Loire** France
21 N6 **Chouzy-sur-Cisse** France
112 L1 **Chowan** *R* North Carolina U.S.A.
102 D4 **Chowchilla** California U.S.A.
138 F5 **Chowilla Dam** South Australia Australia
117 O9 **Chown,Mt** Alberta Canada
58 F2 **Choybalsan** Mongolia
40 C3 **Choye** France
65 A1 **Choyr** Mongolia
31 K6 **Chřiby** *dist* Czech Rep
109 L5 **Chriesman** Texas U.S.A.
99 T10 **Chrisman** Illinois U.S.A.
89 F6 **Chrissiesmeer** S Africa
144 D5 **Christabel, L** New Zealand
127 P6 **Christchurch** *parish* Barbados
9 E6 **Christchurch** England
144 B4 **Christchurch** New Zealand
116 P3 **Christian** Alaska U.S.A.
89 D6 **Christiana** S Africa
94 J7 **Christiana** Pennsylvania U.S.A.
115 N3 **Christian,C** Northwest Territories Canada
120 K8 **Christian I** Ontario Canada
94 C6 **Christiansburg** Ohio U.S.A.
110 M1 **Christiansburg** Ohio U.S.A.
94 G9 **Christiansburg** Virginia U.S.A.
28 C6 **Christiansfeld** Denmark
115 O4 **Christianshåb** Greenland
28 C4 **Christianshede** Denmark
27 H16 **Christiansø** *isld* Denmark
127 M6 **Christiansted** Virgin Is
69 C8 **Christie I** Burma
119 V2 **Christie L** Manitoba Canada
101 Q2 **Christina** Montana U.S.A.
118 G3 **Christina,L** Alberta Canada
100 G1 **Christina L** British Columbia Canada
144 B6 **Christina, Mt** New Zealand
118 G3 **Christina R** Alberta Canada
108 F5 **Christine** Texas U.S.A.
142 F4 **Christmas Creek** W Australia Australia
Christmas I *see* **Kiritimati**
83 M9 **Christmas I** Indian Oc
120 H2 **Christopher Falls** Ontario Canada
143 G6 **Christopher, L** W Australia Australia
108 G4 **Christoval** Texas U.S.A.
130 G4 **Christóvão Pereira,Pte** Brazil
106 D4 **Chromo** Colorado U.S.A.
31 J6 **Chrudim** Czech Rep
31 L5 **Chrzanow** Poland
57 G3 **Chu** Kazakhstan
57 F3 **Chu** *R* Kazakhstan/Kirghizia
125 O10 **Chuacús,Sa.de** *ra* Guatemala
67 F2 **Chuankeng** China
67 G1 **Chuansha** China
57 J1 **Chubartau** Kazakhstan
103 J7 **Chubbuck** California U.S.A.
61 L9 **Chubu-Sangaku Nat. Park** Japan
133 D6 **Chubut** *R* Argentina
133 C6 **Chubut** *prov* Argentina
Chuchow *see* **Zhuzhou**
103 J8 **Chuckwalla Mts** California U.S.A.
133 E4 **Chucul** Argentina
37 P5 **Chudenice** Czech Rep
55 D4 **Chudinovo** Russian Federation
8 C6 **Chudleigh** England
141 G4 **Chudleigh Park** Queensland Australia
120 K6 **Chudleigh River Valley** Ontario Canada
52 D5 **Chudovo** Russian Federation
Chudskoye, Ozero *see* **Peipus, L**
116 M7 **Chugach Is** Alaska U.S.A.
116 O6 **Chugach Mts** Alaska U.S.A.
60 F11 **Chugoku sanchi** *mts* Japan
Chuguchak *see* **Tacheng**
56 C4 **Chugunash** Russian Federation
55 F3 **Chugunly** Russian Federation
54 H7 **Chuguyev** Ukraine
98 B8 **Chugwater** Wyoming U.S.A.
98 B8 **Chugwater Cr** Wyoming U.S.A.
103 N9 **Chuichu** Arizona U.S.A.
59 L1 **Chukchagirskoye, Oz** *L* Russian Federation
147 O3 **Chukchi Sea** Arctic Oc
52 F5 **Chukhloma** Russian Federation
52 F5 **Chukhlomskoye, Oz** *L* Russian Federation
116 A3 **Chukotskiy Poluostrov** Russian Federation
56 G2 **Chula** *R* Russian Federation
112 D6 **Chula** Georgia U.S.A.
99 N10 **Chula** Missouri U.S.A.
94 K9 **Chula** Virginia U.S.A.
57 E3 **Chulak-Kurgan** Kazakhstan
52 G3 **Chulasa** Russian Federation
102 G9 **Chula Vista** California U.S.A.
116 N5 **Chulitna** *R* Alaska U.S.A.
51 M3 **Chul'man** Russian Federation
8 C6 **Chulmleigh** England
128 B5 **Chulucanas** Peru
58 D2 **Chuluut Gol** *R* Mongolia
56 B3 **Chulym** Russian Federation
56 D3 **Chulym** *R* Russian Federation
56 C5 **Chulyshman** *R* Russian Federation
56 C5 **Chulyshmanskiy Khrebet** *mts* Russian Federation
74 H2 **Chumar** Kashmir
133 D3 **Chumbicha** Argentina
56 C6 **Chumek** Kazakhstan
47 H2 **Chumerna** *mt* Bulgaria
59 L1 **Chumikan** Russian Federation
68 D7 **Chumphon** Thailand
68 E5 **Chum Saeng** Thailand
111 J11 **Chumuckla** Florida U.S.A.
56 B4 **Chumysh** *R* Russian Federation
56 E2 **Chuna** *R* Russian Federation
67 F2 **Chun'an** China
65 G6 **Ch'unch'ŏn** S Korea
111 H11 **Chunchula** Alabama U.S.A.
75 N7 **Chunchura** India
Chungking *see* **Chongqing**
66 C6 **Chung-pa** China
68 K3 **Chung-yüan** China
65 H3 **Chunhua** China
56 E1 **Chunku** *R* Russian Federation
58 D6 **Chün-lien** China
67 C1 **Chunmuying** China
83 K8 **Chunnakam** Sri Lanka
56 E2 **Chunoyar** Russian Federation
56 E1 **Chunya** *R* Russian Federation
88 D6 **Chunya** Tanzania
59 J3 **Chunyang** China
69 G8 **Chuoi,Hon** *isld* Vietnam
52 D2 **Chupa** Russian Federation
127 O1 **Chupara Pt** Trinidad
128 D6 **Chuquibambilla** Peru
133 D2 **Chuquicamata** Chile
128 E7 **Chuquisaca** *dept* Bolivia
52 H6 **Chur** Russian Federation
41 L4 **Chur** Switzerland
52 J5 **Churaki** Russian Federation
51 N2 **Churapcha** Russian Federation
55 C3 **Churayevo** Russian Federation
119 Q8 **Churchbridge** Saskatchewan Canada
95 L8 **Church Creek** Maryland U.S.A.
94 E10 **Church Hill** Tennessee U.S.A.
115 N7 **Churchill** *R* Labrador, Nfld Canada
115 K6 **Churchill** Manitoba Canada
118 L3 **Churchill** *R* Saskatchewan Canada
8 D5 **Churchill** England
101 M7 **Churchill** Idaho U.S.A.
118 J2 **Churchill L** Saskatchewan Canada
95 R7 **Churchill L** Maine U.S.A.
146 D11 **Churchill Mts** Antarctica
117 L6 **Churchill Pk** British Columbia Canada
119 W1 **Churchill R** Manitoba Canada
8 C6 **Churchingford** England
111 D11 **Church Point** Louisiana U.S.A.
122 F9 **Church Pt** Nova Scotia Canada
98 G1 **Churchs Ferry** North Dakota U.S.A.
8 D2 **Church Stretton** England
94 K3 **Churchville** New York U.S.A.
94 H8 **Churchville** Virginia U.S.A.
99 M7 **Churdan** Iowa U.S.A.
56 D5 **Chureg-Tag,Gora** *mt* Russian Federation
41 K3 **Churfirsten** *mt* Switzerland
75 K6 **Churhat** India
52 F3 **Churkino** Russian Federation
74 F4 **Churu** India
94 B5 **Churubusco** Indiana U.S.A.
128 E1 **Churuguara** Venezuela
55 C4 **Chusheviyy** Russian Federation
106 B5 **Chuska Mts** Ariz/New Mex U.S.A.
55 C2 **Chusovaya** *R* Russian Federation
55 C2 **Chusovoy** Russian Federation
52 J4 **Chusovskoy** Russian Federation
57 F4 **Chust** Uzbekistan
122 D4 **Chute-aux-Outardes** Quebec Canada
122 A4 **Chute-des-Passes** Quebec Canada
134 F7 **Chuuk** *islds* Micronesia
52 J4 **Chuval** Russian Federation
52 G6 **Chuvashskaya Respublika** Russian Federation
67 F1 **Chu Xian** China
61 N9 **Chūzenji-ko** *L* Japan
37 P3 **Chyše** Czech Rep
88 F3 **Chyulu Ra** Kenya
70 M9 **Ciamis** Java
45 N6 **Ciampino** Italy
70 L9 **Cianjur** Java
42 C4 **Ciano d'Enza** Italy
130 O7 **Cibecue** Arizona U.S.A.
70 L9 **Cibinong** Java
48 H5 **Cibinului,Munții** *mts* Romania
103 K8 **Cibola** Arizona U.S.A.
70 L9 **Ci Buni** *R* Java
124 D2 **Cibuta** Mexico
42 F3 **Čičarija** *mt* Croatia
45 R8 **Cicciano** Italy
94 A6 **Cicero** Indiana U.S.A.
95 L3 **Cicero** New York U.S.A.
129 L6 **Cícero Dantas** Brazil
46 E1 **Čičevac** Serbia Yugoslavia
67 G1 **Cicheng** China
17 F2 **Cidacos** *R* Spain
70 L9 **Cidaun** Java
78 D1 **Cide** Turkey
31 J5 **Cidlina** *R* Czech Rep
31 M3 **Ciechanów** Poland
31 N3 **Ciechanowiec** Poland
31 L3 **Ciechocinek** Poland

126 E4 **Ciego de Avila** Cuba
70 L9 **Ciemas** Java
128 D1 **Ciénaga** Colombia
126 G10 **Ciénaga de Oro** Colombia
126 G10 **Ciénaga Grande** *marshy lake* Colombia
106 E9 **Cienega** New Mexico U.S.A.
124 H5 **Ciénega del Carmen** Mexico
124 H5 **Cieneguilla** Mexico
124 D3 **Cieneguita** Mexico
126 D3 **Cienfuegos** Cuba
22 J3 **Ciergnon** Belgium
31 O5 **Cieszanow** Poland
31 L6 **Cieszyn** Poland
17 G6 **Cieza** Spain
31 M6 **Ciężkowice** Poland
47 M10 **Çiftalan** Turkey
47 L5 **Çifteler** Turkey
17 F4 **Cifuentes** Spain
70 K9 **Cigeulis** Java
40 H7 **Cigliano** Italy
17 F5 **Cigüela** *R* Spain
78 D2 **Cihanbeyli** Turkey
124 G8 **Cihuatlán** Mexico
16 D5 **Cijara, Embalse de** *res* Spain
70 M9 **Cikalong** Java
46 D4 **Çikës, Mal i** *mt* Albania
70 M9 **Cilacap** Java
70 L9 **Cilangkahan** Java
78 J1 **Cildir G** *L* Turkey
67 D2 **Cili** China
8 C3 **Cilycwm** Wales
103 J6 **Cima** California U.S.A.
70 L9 **Cimahi** Java
70 M9 **Ci Manuk** *R* Java
106 C3 **Cimarron** Colorado U.S.A.
107 K4 **Cimarron** Kansas U.S.A.
106 F5 **Cimarron** New Mexico U.S.A.
107 M5 **Cimarron** *R* Okla/Kansas U.S.A.
31 O2 **Cimochy** Poland
42 D4 **Cimone, M** *mt* Italy
48 H4 **Cîmpeni** Romania
48 H4 **Cîmpia Turzii** Romania
48 K5 **Cîmpina** Romania
48 J5 **Cîmpulung** Romania
48 K3 **Cîmpulung Moldovenesc** Romania
48 K4 **Cîmpuri** Romania
128 E2 **Cinaruco** *R* Venezuela
18 F10 **Cinca** *R* Spain
42 H5 **Cincar** *mt* Bosnia-Herzegovina
99 O9 **Cincinnati** Iowa U.S.A.
94 C7 **Cincinnati** Ohio U.S.A.
95 M4 **Cincinnatus** New York U.S.A.
126 E4 **Cinco-Balas, Cayo** *islds* Cuba
116 H8 **Cinder** *R* Alaska U.S.A.
8 D4 **Cinderford** England
48 K5 **Cîndeşti** Romania
48 H5 **Cîndrelu** *mt* Romania
47 J7 **Çine** *R* Turkey
47 J7 **Çine** Turkey
22 J3 **Ciney** Belgium
16 B3 **Cinfães** Portugal
70 F5 **Cinoko, Tanjong** *C* Sulawesi
21 L7 **Cinq Mars** France
68 A7 **Cinque I** Andaman Is
129 J5 **Cinta,Serra da** *mts* Brazil
85 A4 **Cintra, G.de** Western Sahara
45 O6 **Ciociaria** Italy
48 J6 **Ciolăneşti** Romania
70 M9 **Cipatuja** Java
67 E3 **Ciping** China
21 K5 **Ciral** France
17 G4 **Cirat** Spain
146 E12 **Circe, Dome** *ice dome* Antarctica
43 E7 **Circeo, M** *mt* Italy
43 E7 **Circeo, M** *lighthouse* Italy
116 P4 **Circle** Alaska U.S.A.
98 A2 **Circle** Montana U.S.A.
94 E7 **Circleville** Ohio U.S.A.
103 M3 **Circleville** Utah U.S.A.
70 M9 **Cirebon** Java
9 E4 **Cirencester** England
69 E13 **Cirenti** Sumatra
21 P3 **Cires-les-Mello** France
19 K4 **Cirey** France
36 B6 **Cirey-sur-Vezouse** France
44 C1 **Ciriè** Italy
18 E8 **Ciron** *R* France
21 N8 **Ciron** France
44 G3 **Cisa, Passo di** Italy
99 S9 **Cisco** Illinois U.S.A.
109 J3 **Cisco** Texas U.S.A.
103 P3 **Cisco** Utah U.S.A.
Ciskei *see* **Eastern Cape**
48 K5 **Cislău** Romania
33 N4 **Cismar** Germany
31 N6 **Cisna** Poland
48 J5 **Cisnadie** Romania
110 H3 **Cisne** Illinois U.S.A.
128 C2 **Cisneros** Colombia
133 C6 **Cisnes** *R* Chile
70 L9 **Cisompet** Java
100 D3 **Cispus** *R* Washington U.S.A.
100 D3 **Cispus Pass** Washington U.S.A.
21 N6 **Cisse** *R* France
37 O3 **Čistá** Czech Rep
109 K6 **Cistern** Texas U.S.A.
45 N6 **Cisterna di Latina** Italy
16 D2 **Cistierna** Spain
129 G3 **Citare** *R* Brazil
125 L8 **Citlaltépetl** Mexico
113 E8 **Citra** Florida U.S.A.
111 H10 **Citronelle** Alabama U.S.A.
87 C12 **Citrusdal** S Africa
42 D3 **Cittadella** Italy
42 E6 **Citta della Pieve** Italy
42 E5 **Città di Castello** Italy
43 G10 **Cittanova** Italy
142 A1 **City Beach** *dist* Perth, W Aust Australia
113 G9 **City Point** Florida U.S.A.
48 K5 **Ciucaşu** *mt* Romania
48 H4 **Ciucea** Romania
48 K4 **Ciucului Muntii** *mt* Romania
108 G6 **Ciudad Acuña** Mexico
125 J8 **Ciudad Altamirano** Mexico
128 F2 **Ciudad Bolívar** Venezuela
109 J9 **Ciudad Camargo** Mexico
124 G4 **Ciudad Camargo** Mexico
125 O8 **Ciudad del Carmen** Mexico
130 C9 **Ciudad del Este** Paraguay
124 G3 **Ciudad Delicias** Mexico
17 K4 **Ciudadela** Spain
127 N10 **Ciudad Guayana** Venezuela
124 F3 **Ciudad Guerrero** Mexico
124 H8 **Ciudad Guzmán** Mexico
125 N10 **Ciudad Hidalgo** Mexico
106 D10 **Ciudad Juárez** Mexico
124 H5 **Ciudad Lerdo** Mexico
125 L6 **Ciudad Madero** Mexico
125 K6 **Ciudad Mante** Mexico
124 E4 **Ciudad Obregón** Mexico
128 F2 **Ciudad Piar** Venezuela
16 E6 **Ciudad Real** *prov* Spain
16 E6 **Ciudad Real** Spain
16 C4 **Ciudad Rodrigo** Spain
125 N10 **Ciudad Tecún Umán** Mexico
Ciudad Trujillo *see* **Santo Domingo** Dominican Rep
125 K6 **Ciudad Victoria** Mexico
48 G4 **Ciumeghiu** Romania
48 L5 **Ciuşlea** Romania
47 K5 **Civan Dağı** *mt* Turkey
42 E2 **Cividale del F** Italy
42 E6 **Civita Castellana** Italy
42 F5 **Civitanova Marche** Italy
44 L5 **Civitavecchia** *lighthouse* Italy
45 L3 **Civitelia di Romagna** Italy
45 O6 **Civitella Roveto** Italy
44 B1 **Civrari Monte** Italy
18 F6 **Civray** France
21 P8 **Civray** Cher France
47 K6 **Çivril** Turkey
67 G1 **Cixi** China
65 C6 **Ci Xian** China
78 J3 **Cizre** Turkey
12 C2 **Clachan** Scotland
100 C4 **Clackamas** *R* Oregon U.S.A.
143 B9 **Clackline** W Australia Australia
9 H4 **Clacton-on-Sea** England
12 C1 **Cladich** Scotland
107 M3 **Claflin** Kansas U.S.A.
100 J1 **Clagstone** Idaho U.S.A.
20 E6 **Claie,R** France
21 L8 **Clain** *R* France
119 N6 **Clair** Saskatchewan Canada
6 J2 **Clair** *oil rig* North Sea
68 G1 **Claire** *R* Vietnam
98 J4 **Claire City** South Dakota U.S.A.
117 R6 **Claire, L** Alberta Canada
108 G2 **Clairemont** Texas U.S.A.
94 H6 **Clairton** Pennsylvania U.S.A.
19 J6 **Clairvaux** France
21 N8 **Claise** *R* France
100 A1 **Clallam Bay** Washington U.S.A.
18 H5 **Clamecy** France
102 G2 **Clan Alpine Mts** Nevada U.S.A.
101 N3 **Clancy** Montana U.S.A.
144 C6 **Clandeboye** New Zealand
118 F5 **Clandonald** Alberta Canada
9 E4 **Clanfield** England
111 K9 **Clanton** Alabama U.S.A.
119 S8 **Clanwilliam** Manitoba Canada
87 C12 **Clanwilliam** S Africa
12 C2 **Claonaig** Scotland
9 F5 **Clapham** England
13 F5 **Clapham** N Yorks England
44 B3 **Clapier, Mt** France
141 F4 **Clara** *R* Queensland Australia
14 D3 **Clara** Ireland
113 D8 **Clara** Florida U.S.A.
99 L5 **Clara City** Minnesota U.S.A.
68 C7 **Clara I** Burma
141 F4 **Claraville** Queensland Australia
138 E5 **Clare** South Australia Australia
9 G3 **Clare** England
14 C3 **Clare** *R* Ireland
14 C4 **Clare** *co* Ireland
99 M7 **Clare** Iowa U.S.A.
94 C3 **Clare** Michigan U.S.A.
14 C4 **Clarecastle** Ireland
139 G5 **Clare Corner** New South Wales Australia
14 A3 **Clare I** Ireland
142 A2 **Claremont** *dist* Perth, W Aust Australia
127 K2 **Claremont** Jamaica
95 P3 **Claremont** New Hampshire U.S.A.
98 H4 **Claremont** South Dakota U.S.A.
141 G2 **Claremont Is** Gt Barrier Reef Australia
14 C3 **Claremorris** Ireland
139 L3 **Clarence** *R* New South Wales Australia
144 D5 **Clarence** New Zealand
99 P8 **Clarence** Iowa U.S.A.
99 O10 **Clarence** Missouri U.S.A.
110 D2 **Clarence Cannon Res** Missouri U.S.A.
146 D3 **Clarence I** South Shetland Is Antarctica
133 C8 **Clarence,I** Chile
140 B1 **Clarence Str** N Terr Australia
117 G8 **Clarence Str** Alaska U.S.A.
126 G3 **Clarence Town** Long I Bahamas
121 O8 **Clarendon** Ontario Canada
127 K3 **Clarendon** *parish* Jamaica
110 E7 **Clarendon** Arkansas U.S.A.
94 H5 **Clarendon** Pennsylvania U.S.A.
108 G1 **Clarendon** Texas U.S.A.
123 S5 **Clarenville** Newfoundland Canada
118 D8 **Claresholm** Alberta Canada
19 P16 **Claret** France
98 B6 **Clareton** Wyoming U.S.A.
32 H9 **Clarholz** Germany
141 F4 **Clarina** *R* Queensland Australia
99 L9 **Clarinda** Iowa U.S.A.
127 M10 **Clarines** Venezuela
94 H5 **Clarington** Pennsylvania U.S.A.
99 N7 **Clarion** Iowa U.S.A.
94 H5 **Clarion** *R* Pennsylvania U.S.A.
94 H5 **Clarion** Pennsylvania U.S.A.
126 H4 **Clarion Bank** Bahamas
145 E2 **Claris** New Zealand
107 O7 **Clarita** Oklahoma U.S.A.
102 H8 **Clark** *L* California U.S.A.
101 T9 **Clark** Colorado U.S.A.
110 D2 **Clark** Missouri U.S.A.
98 J5 **Clark** South Dakota U.S.A.
101 N4 **Clark Canyon Res** Montana U.S.A.
103 M7 **Clarkdale** Arizona U.S.A.
141 G4 **Clarke** *R* Queensland Australia
122 F3 **Clarke City** Quebec Canada
139 J8 **Clarke I** Tasmania Australia
118 K4 **Clarke L** Saskatchewan Canada
141 J5 **Clarke Ra** Queensland Australia
141 H4 **Clarke River** Queensland Australia
112 D3 **Clarkesville** Georgia U.S.A.
98 L5 **Clarkfield** Minnesota U.S.A.
100 J1 **Clark Fork** Idaho U.S.A.
117 Q12 **Clark Fork** *R* Idaho U.S.A.
112 E4 **Clark Hill Dam** Georgia U.S.A.
112 E4 **Clark Hill L** *res* Georgia U.S.A.
100 J2 **Clarkia** Idaho U.S.A.
116 K6 **Clark,L** Alaska U.S.A.
117 M3 **Clark,Mt** Northwest Territories Canada
103 J6 **Clark Mt** California U.S.A.
106 E1 **Clark Pk** Colorado U.S.A.
120 J8 **Clark Pt** Ontario Canada
111 D9 **Clarks** Louisiana U.S.A.
98 J8 **Clarks** Nebraska U.S.A.
101 Q5 **Clarks** *R* Wyoming U.S.A.
110 H6 **Clarksburg** Tennessee U.S.A.
94 G7 **Clarksburg** West Virginia U.S.A.
111 F7 **Clarksdale** Mississippi U.S.A.
99 N6 **Clarks Grove** Minnesota U.S.A.
122 G10 **Clark's Harbour** Nova Scotia Canada
110 K1 **Clarks Hill** Indiana U.S.A.
144 C6 **Clarks Junction** New Zealand
121 L9 **Clarkson** Ontario Canada
98 J8 **Clarkson** Nebraska U.S.A.
142 E4 **Clarkson, Mt** W Australia Australia
116 H7 **Clarks Point** Alaska U.S.A.
94 D4 **Clarkston** Michigan U.S.A.
101 O3 **Clarkston** Montana U.S.A.
100 H3 **Clarkston** Washington U.S.A.
127 K2 **Clark's Town** Jamaica
144 B7 **Clarksville** New Zealand
110 C6 **Clarksville** Arkansas U.S.A.
110 F2 **Clarksville** Illinois U.S.A.
99 O7 **Clarksville** Iowa U.S.A.
94 B4 **Clarksville** Michigan U.S.A.
110 J5 **Clarksville** Tennessee U.S.A.
109 M2 **Clarksville** Texas U.S.A.
94 J10 **Clarksville** Virginia U.S.A.
112 J3 **Clarkton** North Carolina U.S.A.
109 K8 **Clarkwood** Texas U.S.A.
100 E5 **Clarno** Oregon U.S.A.
129 H7 **Claro** *R* Brazil
22 E3 **Clary** France
141 H6 **Claude** *R* Queensland Australia
108 C8 **Claude** Texas U.S.A.
130 G7 **Cláudio** Brazil
32 M8 **Clauen** Germany
37 O2 **Claussnitz** Germany
33 M9 **Clausthal-Zellerfeld** Germany
71 E1 **Claveria** Luzon Philippines
118 L8 **Clavet** Saskatchewan Canada
19 N14 **Claveyson** France
112 F5 **Claxton** Georgia U.S.A.
102 C3 **Clay** California U.S.A.
110 J4 **Clay** Kentucky U.S.A.
109 L5 **Clay** Texas U.S.A.
94 F8 **Clay** West Virginia U.S.A.
107 N2 **Clay Center** Kansas U.S.A.
98 H9 **Clay Center** Nebraska U.S.A.
110 H3 **Clay City** Illinois U.S.A.
110 J2 **Clay City** Indiana U.S.A.
110 N4 **Clay City** Kentucky U.S.A.
9 E1 **Clay Cross** England
118 J9 **Claydon** Saskatchewan Canada
9 H3 **Claydon** England
18 H6 **Clayette, la** France
103 L5 **Clayhole Wash** *creek* Arizona U.S.A.
118 J1 **Clay L** Ontario Canada
6 K4 **Claymore** *oil rig* North Sea
107 P5 **Claymore** Oklahoma U.S.A.
117 L11 **Clayoquot** British Columbia Canada
103 O8 **Claypool** Arizona U.S.A.
103 O7 **Clay Springs** Arizona U.S.A.
94 G6 **Claysville** Pennsylvania U.S.A.
138 E3 **Clayton** *R* South Australia Australia
9 F6 **Clayton** England
111 L10 **Clayton** Alabama U.S.A.
112 D3 **Clayton** Georgia U.S.A.
101 L5 **Clayton** Idaho U.S.A.
99 Q9 **Clayton** Illinois U.S.A.
110 K2 **Clayton** Indiana U.S.A.
107 K2 **Clayton** Kansas U.S.A.
106 G5 **Clayton** New Mexico U.S.A.
95 L2 **Clayton** New York U.S.A.
112 J2 **Clayton** North Carolina U.S.A.
107 P7 **Clayton** Oklahoma U.S.A.
95 R7 **Clayton Lake** Maine U.S.A.
13 F6 **Clayton-le-Moors** England
94 G9 **Claytor Lake** Virginia U.S.A.
95 M4 **Clayville** New York U.S.A.
131 F4 **Clé** *R* Argentina
107 O7 **Clear Boggy Cr** Oklahoma U.S.A.
99 L2 **Clearbrook** Minnesota U.S.A.
144 C6 **Clearburn** New Zealand
14 B5 **Clear,C** Ireland
94 G8 **Clearco** West Virginia U.S.A.
103 O7 **Clear Cr** *R* Arizona U.S.A.
101 T5 **Clear Cr** Wyoming U.S.A.
100 B8 **Clear Creek** California U.S.A.
116 O7 **Cleare,C** Alaska U.S.A.
99 M9 **Clearfield** Iowa U.S.A.
94 J5 **Clearfield** Pennsylvania U.S.A.
101 N8 **Clearfield** Utah U.S.A.
108 G3 **Clear Fork** *R* Texas U.S.A.
117 O7 **Clear Hills** Alberta Canada
14 B5 **Clear I** Ireland
119 S8 **Clear L** Manitoba Canada
121 N7 **Clear, L** Ontario Canada
102 B2 **Clear L** California U.S.A.
99 N6 **Clear L** Iowa U.S.A.
109 P4 **Clear L** Louisiana U.S.A.
99 N4 **Clear L** Minnesota U.S.A.
98 K5 **Clear L** South Dakota U.S.A.
103 M2 **Clear L** Utah U.S.A.
99 O4 **Clear L** Wisconsin U.S.A.
100 D8 **Clear L. Res** California U.S.A.
101 T5 **Clearmont** Wyoming U.S.A.
117 O7 **Clear Prairie** Alberta Canada
117 N10 **Clearwater** British Columbia Canada
113 E10 **Clearwater** Florida U.S.A.
100 J3 **Clearwater** *R* Idaho U.S.A.
100 K3 **Clearwater** Idaho U.S.A.
107 N4 **Clearwater** Kansas U.S.A.
98 H7 **Clearwater** Nebraska U.S.A.
119 Q4 **Clearwater L. Prov. Park** Manitoba Canada
100 K3 **Clearwater Mts** Idaho U.S.A.
118 B6 **Clearwater R** Alberta Canada
110 F4 **Clearwater Res** Missouri U.S.A.
99 L2 **Clearwter** *R* Minnesota U.S.A.
143 D7 **Cleaver, Mt** W Australia Australia
107 O2 **Cleburne** Kansas U.S.A.
109 K3 **Cleburne** Texas U.S.A.
21 K4 **Clécy** France
8 B4 **Cleddau, R** Wales
20 B4 **Cléder** France
8 D3 **Clee Hill** England
100 D2 **Cle Elum L** Washington U.S.A.
13 H6 **Cleethorpes** England
7 L8 **Cleeton** *gas field* North Sea
118 H5 **Cleeves** Saskatchewan Canada
40 B1 **Clefmont** France
21 K6 **Clefs** France
109 J7 **Clegg** Texas U.S.A.
20 D5 **Cléguérec** France
140 B6 **Cleland Hills** N Terr Australia
22 K4 **Clemency** Luxembourg
102 C3 **Clements** California U.S.A.
115 N1 **Clements Markham Inlet** Northwest Territories Canada
122 G9 **Clementsport** Nova Scotia Canada
122 G9 **Clementsvale** Nova Scotia Canada
94 F8 **Clendenin** West Virginia U.S.A.
94 F6 **Clendening Res** Ohio U.S.A.
8 D3 **Cleobury Mortimer** England
71 D5 **Cleopatra Needle** *mt* Philippines
107 M5 **Cleo Springs** Oklahoma U.S.A.
21 L7 **Cléré** France
21 N2 **Clères** France
121 M4 **Cléricy** Quebec Canada
40 D2 **Clerjus, Le** France
142 C3 **Clerke Reef** Indian Oc
133 J9 **Clerke Rocks** S Georgia
141 J6 **Clermont** Queensland Australia
122 B6 **Clermont** Quebec Canada
21 P3 **Clermont** Oise France
113 F9 **Clermont** Florida U.S.A.
99 P6 **Clermont** Iowa U.S.A.
94 J5 **Clermont** Pennsylvania U.S.A.
21 K6 **Clermont-Créans** France
19 J3 **Clermont en Argonne** France
18 H7 **Clermont Ferrand** France
18 H9 **Clermont l'Herault** France
121 L4 **Clerval** Quebec Canada
40 D3 **Clerval** France
22 L3 **Clervaux** Luxembourg
21 O3 **Cléry-en-Vexin** France
21 O6 **Cléry-St. André** France
22 D4 **Clery-sur-Somme** France
42 D2 **Cles** Italy
21 K8 **Clessé** France
138 D5 **Cleve** South Australia Australia
8 D5 **Clevedon** England
13 G4 **Cleveland** *co* England
110 D6 **Cleveland** Arkansas U.S.A.
113 F11 **Cleveland** Florida U.S.A.
112 D3 **Cleveland** Georgia U.S.A.
101 O7 **Cleveland** Idaho U.S.A.
99 N5 **Cleveland** Minnesota U.S.A.
111 F8 **Cleveland** Mississippi U.S.A.
101 Q1 **Cleveland** Montana U.S.A.
95 M3 **Cleveland** New York U.S.A.
112 G2 **Cleveland** North Carolina U.S.A.
98 G3 **Cleveland** North Dakota U.S.A.
94 F5 **Cleveland** Ohio U.S.A.
107 O5 **Cleveland** Oklahoma U.S.A.
112 E2 **Cleveland** South Carolina U.S.A.
112 C2 **Cleveland** Tennessee U.S.A.
109 M5 **Cleveland** Texas U.S.A.
103 O2 **Cleveland** Utah U.S.A.
99 T6 **Cleveland** Wisconsin U.S.A.
141 H4 **Cleveland, C** Queensland Australia
13 G4 **Cleveland Hills** England
130 D10 **Clevelândia** Brazil
101 M1 **Cleveland,Mt** Montana U.S.A.
113 G11 **Clewiston** Florida U.S.A.
9 H2 **Cley** England
14 A3 **Clifden** Ireland
144 A7 **Clifden** New Zealand
106 B9 **Cliff** New Mexico U.S.A.
100 D3 **Cliffdell** Washington U.S.A.
71 D5 **Cliff Head** Philippines
101 O5 **Cliff Lake** Montana U.S.A.
94 D3 **Clifford** Michigan U.S.A.
98 J2 **Clifford** North Dakota U.S.A.
94 H9 **Clifford** Virginia U.S.A.
99 Q4 **Clifford** Wisconsin U.S.A.
100 H7 **Cliffs** Idaho U.S.A.
112 F2 **Cliffside** North Carolina U.S.A.
141 K8 **Clifton** Queensland Australia
113 K9 **Clifton** New Providence I Bahamas
8 D5 **Clifton** England
103 P8 **Clifton** Arizona U.S.A.
99 T9 **Clifton** Illinois U.S.A.
107 N2 **Clifton** Kansas U.S.A.
95 N6 **Clifton** New Jersey U.S.A.
98 B6 **Clifton** Wyoming U.S.A.
94 H9 **Clifton Forge** Virginia U.S.A.
138 E2 **Clifton Hills** South Australia Australia
113 K9 **Clifton Pt** New Providence I Bahamas
118 J9 **Climax** Saskatchewan Canada
106 D2 **Climax** Colorado U.S.A.
111 M11 **Climax** Georgia U.S.A.
94 B4 **Climax** Michigan U.S.A.
98 K2 **Climax** Minnesota U.S.A.
112 C2 **Clinch** *R* Tennessee U.S.A.
94 E9 **Clinchco** Virginia U.S.A.
94 E10 **Clinch Mt** Tenn/Virg U.S.A.
94 E10 **Clinchport** Virginia U.S.A.
117 P9 **Cline, Mt** Alberta Canada
37 K1 **Clingen** Germany
112 D2 **Clingmans Dome** Tennessee U.S.A.
108 A4 **Clint** Texas U.S.A.
117 N10 **Clinton** British Columbia Canada
120 J9 **Clinton** Ontario Canada
144 B7 **Clinton** New Zealand
110 D6 **Clinton** Arkansas U.S.A.
95 P5 **Clinton** Connecticut U.S.A.
99 S9 **Clinton** Illinois U.S.A.
99 T10 **Clinton** Indiana U.S.A.
99 Q8 **Clinton** Iowa U.S.A.
110 H5 **Clinton** Kentucky U.S.A.
111 E11 **Clinton** Louisiana U.S.A.
95 S2 **Clinton** Maine U.S.A.
95 Q4 **Clinton** Massachusetts U.S.A.
94 D4 **Clinton** Michigan U.S.A.
98 K4 **Clinton** Minnesota U.S.A.
111 F9 **Clinton** Mississippi U.S.A.
110 C3 **Clinton** Missouri U.S.A.
101 M3 **Clinton** Montana U.S.A.
95 M3 **Clinton** New York U.S.A.
107 M6 **Clinton** Oklahoma U.S.A.
112 F3 **Clinton** South Carolina U.S.A.
112 C1 **Clinton** Tennessee U.S.A.
99 S7 **Clinton** Wisconsin U.S.A.
114 J5 **Clinton-Colden L** Northwest Territories Canada
114 E5 **Clinton Creek** Yukon Territory Canada
99 S5 **Clintonville** Wisconsin U.S.A.
103 N7 **Clints Well** Arizona U.S.A.
110 C1 **Clio** Iowa U.S.A.
94 D3 **Clio** Michigan U.S.A.
112 H3 **Clio** South Carolina U.S.A.
21 N8 **Clion** France
135 Q7 **Clipperton** *atoll* Pacific Oc
15 B3 **Clisham Mt** Lewis Scotland
20 H7 **Clisson** France
13 F6 **Clitheroe** England
118 D6 **Clive** Alberta Canada
145 F3 **Clive** New Zealand
101 M9 **Clive** Utah U.S.A.
117 O4 **Clive L** Northwest Territories Canada
118 J6 **Cloan** Saskatchewan Canada
14 D3 **Cloghan** Ireland
14 D2 **Clogher** N Ireland
14 E3 **Clogher Hd** Ireland
20 C6 **Clohars** France
140 F5 **Clonagh** Queensland Australia
14 C5 **Clonakilty** Ireland
14 C5 **Clonakilty B** Ireland
140 F4 **Cloncurry** *R* Queensland Australia
140 F5 **Cloncurry** Queensland Australia
14 E3 **Clondalkin** Ireland
14 E4 **Clonegal** Ireland
14 D2 **Clones** Ireland
59 J3 **Clŏngjin** N Korea
14 D4 **Clonmel** Ireland
99 L4 **Clontarf** Minnesota U.S.A.
117 L11 **Clo-oose** British Columbia Canada
9 F3 **Clophill** England
32 H7 **Cloppenburg** Germany
99 O3 **Cloquet** Minnesota U.S.A.
130 B9 **Clorinda** Argentina
12 E3 **Closeburn** Scotland
123 L3 **Cloudberry Pt** Quebec Canada
106 E9 **Cloudcroft** New Mexico U.S.A.
101 S5 **Cloud Pk** Wyoming U.S.A.
145 E4 **Cloudy Bay** New Zealand
116 J5 **Cloudy Mt** Alaska U.S.A.
121 L4 **Cloutier** Quebec Canada
20 H8 **Clouzeaux, les** France
121 P4 **Clova** Quebec Canada
15 E4 **Clova** Scotland
8 B5 **Clovelly** England
13 F2 **Clovenfords** Scotland
112 F2 **Clover** South Carolina U.S.A.
94 J10 **Clover** Virginia U.S.A.
102 A3 **Cloverdale** California U.S.A.
110 K2 **Cloverdale** Indiana U.S.A.
106 B10 **Cloverdale** New Mexico U.S.A.
110 K4 **Cloverport** Kentucky U.S.A.
106 G7 **Clovis** New Mexico U.S.A.
8 D3 **Clows Top** England
21 N6 **Cloyes** France
14 C5 **Cloyne** Ireland
21 O8 **Cluis** France
48 H4 **Cluj** *reg* Romania
48 H4 **Cluj-Napoca** Romania
8 C3 **Clun** England
139 G7 **Clunes** Victoria Australia
140 E6 **Cluny** Queensland Australia
118 E8 **Cluny** Alberta Canada
102 H1 **Cluro** Nevada U.S.A.
40 E5 **Cluses** France
41 L6 **Clusone** Italy
120 J3 **Clute** Ontario Canada
144 B6 **Clutha** *R* New Zealand
144 A6 **Clutha/Central Otago** *admin region* New Zealand
144 B7 **Clutha R** New Zealand
99 O7 **Clutier** Iowa U.S.A.
117 P3 **Clut L** Northwest Territories Canada
143 F6 **Clutterbuck Hills** W Australia Australia
8 C1 **Clwyd** *R* Wales
8 C1 **Clwyd** *co* Wales
113 D7 **Clyattville** Georgia U.S.A.
8 C4 **Clydach** Wales
118 D4 **Clyde** Alberta Canada
115 N3 **Clyde** Northwest Territories Canada
144 B6 **Clyde** New Zealand
6 M6 **Clyde** *oil rig* North Sea
107 N2 **Clyde** Kansas U.S.A.
95 L3 **Clyde** New York U.S.A.
98 H1 **Clyde** North Dakota U.S.A.
94 E5 **Clyde** Ohio U.S.A.
109 H3 **Clyde** Texas U.S.A.
12 D2 **Clydebank** Scotland
12 D3 **Clyde,Firth of** Scotland
121 O7 **Clyde Forks** Ontario Canada
101 P4 **Clyde Park** Montana U.S.A.
122 G10 **Clyde R** Nova Scotia Canada
12 D2 **Clyde,R** Scotland
144 B7 **Clydevale** New Zealand
99 S6 **Clyman** Wisconsin U.S.A.
94 H6 **Clymer** Pennsylvania U.S.A.
8 B1 **Clynnog-fawr** Wales
8 C3 **Clyro** Wales
8 C6 **Clyst Honiton** England
16 C4 **Coa** *R* Portugal
103 H8 **Coachella** California U.S.A.
123 M3 **Coacoachou L** Quebec Canada
108 F3 **Coahoma** Texas U.S.A.
124 H4 **Coahuila** *state* Mexico
117 K5 **Coal** *R* Br Col/Yukon Terr Canada
94 F8 **Coal** *R* West Virginia U.S.A.
99 S8 **Coal City** Illinois U.S.A.
124 H8 **Coalcomán de Matamoros** Mexico
116 Q4 **Coal Creek** Alaska U.S.A.
118 E9 **Coaldale** Alberta Canada
102 G3 **Coaldale** Nevada U.S.A.
144 C5 **Coalgate** New Zealand
107 O7 **Coalgate** Oklahoma U.S.A.
94 E8 **Coal Grove** Ohio U.S.A.
110 C6 **Coal Hill** Arkansas U.S.A.
144 A7 **Coal I** New Zealand
102 D5 **Coalinga** California U.S.A.
101 T9 **Coalmont** Colorado U.S.A.
94 J6 **Coalport** Pennsylvania U.S.A.
117 K6 **Coal River** British Columbia Canada
94 E7 **Coalton** Ohio U.S.A.
9 E2 **Coalville** England
101 O9 **Coalville** Utah U.S.A.
98 A4 **Coalwood** Montana U.S.A.
127 L5 **Coamo** Puerto Rico
128 F4 **Coari** Brazil
144 C6 **Coastal North Otago** *admin region* New Zealand
117 G7 **Coast Mts** British Columbia Canada
141 K7 **Coast Ra** Queensland Australia
141 K7 **Coast Ra** *mts* Queensland Australia
100 B9 **Coast Range** *mts* U.S.A.
102 A1 **Coast Rge** California U.S.A.
12 E2 **Coatbridge** Scotland
125 L8 **Coatepec** Mexico
95 M6 **Coatesville** Pennsylvania U.S.A.
121 T7 **Coaticook** Quebec Canada
107 M4 **Coats** Kansas U.S.A.
112 J2 **Coats** North Carolina U.S.A.
115 L5 **Coats I** Northwest Territories Canada
146 E7 **Coats Land** Antarctica
110 D1 **Coatsville** Iowa U.S.A.
125 M8 **Coatzacoalcos** Mexico
121 L5 **Cobalt** Ontario Canada
101 L4 **Cobalt** Idaho U.S.A.
125 O10 **Cobán** Guatemala
139 H4 **Cobar** New South Wales Australia
139 J6 **Cobargo** New South Wales Australia
99 Q7 **Cobb** Wisconsin U.S.A.
139 J6 **Cobberas,Mt** Victoria Australia
143 F6 **Cobb, L** W Australia Australia
9 E6 **Cobblers Corner** England
145 D4 **Cobb Res** New Zealand
139 G7 **Cobden** Victoria Australia
121 O7 **Cobden** Ontario Canada
110 G4 **Cobden** Illinois U.S.A.
122 J8 **Cobequid B** Nova Scotia Canada
122 J8 **Cobequid Mts** Nova Scotia Canada
14 C5 **Cóbh** Ireland
140 B1 **Cobham B** N Terr Australia
128 E6 **Cobija** Bolivia
95 N4 **Cobleskill** New York U.S.A.
121 M8 **Coboconk** Ontario Canada
121 M9 **Cobourg** Ontario Canada
140 B1 **Cobourg Pen** N Terr Australia
143 B6 **Cobra** W Australia Australia
139 H6 **Cobram** New South Wales Australia
101 L8 **Cobre** Nevada U.S.A.
127 L2 **Cobre, R** Jamaica
87 F8 **Cobue** Mozambique
37 K3 **Coburg** Germany
100 B5 **Coburg** Oregon U.S.A.
115 M2 **Coburg I** Northwest Territories Canada
16 D3 **Coca** Spain
128 D7 **Cocachacra** Peru
128 D6 **Cocamá** Peru
42 C2 **Coca, Pzo. di** Italy
45 M3 **Coccolia** Italy
17 G6 **Cocentaina** Spain
128 E7 **Cochabamba** Bolivia
128 C3 **Cocha, L** Colombia
127 N9 **Coche, I** Venezuela
106 D3 **Cochetopa Pass** Colorado U.S.A.
76 C6 **Cochin** India
68 G7 **Cochin** *reg* Vietnam
128 E8 **Cochinoca** Argentina
126 D3 **Cochinos, B. de** Cuba
103 P9 **Cochise** Arizona U.S.A.
103 P9 **Cochise Head** *mt* Arizona U.S.A.
106 D6 **Cochiti L** New Mexico U.S.A.
112 D5 **Cochran** Georgia U.S.A.
118 C7 **Cochrane** Alberta Canada
120 J3 **Cochrane** Ontario Canada
133 C7 **Cochrane, L** Chile/Arg
94 G5 **Cochranton** Pennsylvania U.S.A.
33 O9 **Cochstedt** Germany
142 E3 **Cockatoo I** W Australia Australia
15 E3 **Cock Bridge** Scotland
141 G3 **Cockburn** *R* Queensland Australia
138 F4 **Cockburn** South Australia Australia
133 C8 **Cockburn, Canal** *str* Chile
127 J4 **Cockburn Harbour** Turks & Caicos Is
120 G7 **Cockburn I** Ontario Canada
140 B6 **Cockburn, Mt** N Terr Australia
140 A7 **Cockburn, Mt** N Terr Australia
142 G3 **Cockburn Ra** W Australia Australia
142 A3 **Cockburn Sd** W Australia Australia
13 F2 **Cockburnspath** Scotland
126 G2 **Cockburn Town** San Salvador Bahamas
13 F2 **Cockenzie** Scotland
13 F6 **Cockerham** England
13 E4 **Cockermouth** England
95 L7 **Cockeysville** Maryland U.S.A.
143 F9 **Cocklebiddy** W Australia Australia
127 J2 **Cockpit** *pk* Jamaica
127 J2 **Cockpit Country, The** *reg* Jamaica
109 N9 **Cockrell Hill** Texas U.S.A.
15 F5 **Cocksburnpath** Scotland
89 D9 **Cockscomb** *mt* S Africa
129 J5 **Côco** *R* Brazil
125 M2 **Coco** *R* Honduras/Nicaragua
113 G9 **Cocoa** Florida U.S.A.
113 G9 **Cocoa Beach** Florida U.S.A.
126 E3 **Coco, Cayo** *isld* Cuba
111 F12 **Cocodrie** Louisiana U.S.A.
100 J1 **Cocolalla** Idaho U.S.A.
103 M6 **Coconino Plat** Arizona U.S.A.
139 H5 **Cocoparra Rge** New South Wales Australia
71 E5 **Cocoro** *isld* Philippines
127 P2 **Cocos B** Trinidad
81 G6 **Cocos I** Indian Oc
90 A8 **Cocos I** Pacific Oc
90 A8 **Cocos Ridge** Pacific Oc
83 L13 **Cocotte, Mt** Mauritius
124 H7 **Cocula** Mexico
6 M5 **Cod** *oil rig* North Sea
43 C8 **Coda Cavallo, C** Sardinia
48 L4 **Codăeşti** Romania
128 F4 **Codajas** Brazil
107 L2 **Codell** Kansas U.S.A.
118 L8 **Coderre** Saskatchewan Canada
119 N5 **Codette** Saskatchewan Canada
144 A7 **Codfish I** New Zealand
115 N6 **Cod I** Labrador, Nfld Canada
9 F4 **Codicote** England
42 E4 **Codigoro** Italy
48 J5 **Codlea** Romania
129 K4 **Codó** Brazil
44 G1 **Codogno** Italy
127 N6 **Codrington** Barbuda W Indies
123 N6 **Codroy** Newfoundland Canada
123 O5 **Codroy Pond** Newfoundland Canada
48 G4 **Codrului Muntii** *mts* Romania
122 G8 **Cody** New Brunswick Canada
98 E7 **Cody** Nebraska U.S.A.
101 Q5 **Cody** Wyoming U.S.A.
94 E10 **Coeburn** Virginia U.S.A.
121 N8 **Coe Hill** Ontario Canada
141 F2 **Coen** *R* Queensland Australia
141 G2 **Coen** Queensland Australia
32 F9 **Coesfeld** Germany
83 H5 **Coëtivy Is** Seychelles Indian Oc
100 J2 **Coeur d'Alene** Idaho U.S.A.
22 E5 **Coeuvres et Valsery** France
25 G3 **Coevorden** Netherlands
21 K5 **Coevrons, les** *mts* France
20 G8 **Coëx** France
112 E6 **Coffee** Georgia U.S.A.
117 D4 **Coffee Creek** Yukon Territory Canada
101 P2 **Coffee Creek** Montana U.S.A.
110 G2 **Coffeen** Illinois U.S.A.
111 L10 **Coffee Springs** Alabama U.S.A.
111 G8 **Coffeeville** Mississippi U.S.A.
107 P4 **Coffeyville** Kansas U.S.A.
138 D5 **Coffin B** South Australia Australia
123 L6 **Coffin I** Madeleine Is, Quebec Canada
139 L4 **Coffs Harbour** New South Wales Australia
17 G5 **Cofrentes** Spain
48 M6 **Cogealac** Romania
9 G4 **Coggeshall** England
42 B3 **Coggiola** Italy
99 P7 **Coggon** Iowa U.S.A.
43 B8 **Coghinas** *R* Sardinia
43 C8 **Coghinas, L.d** Sardinia
142 G4 **Coghlan, Mt** W Australia Australia
18 E7 **Cognac** France
40 F6 **Cogne, V.de** Italy
44 E3 **Cogoleto** Italy
16 E4 **Cogolludo** Spain
41 N5 **Cógolo** Italy
98 J3 **Cogswell** North Dakota U.S.A.
101 T2 **Cohagen** Montana U.S.A.
20 E5 **Cohiniac** France
94 K4 **Cohocton** New York U.S.A.
95 K4 **Cohocton** *R* New York U.S.A.
95 O4 **Cohoes** New York U.S.A.
139 G6 **Cohuna** Victoria Australia
112 C3 **Cohutta** Georgia U.S.A.
125 O6 **Coiba, I** Panama
133 C8 **Coig** *R* Argentina
21 O4 **Coignières** France
133 C7 **Coihaique** Chile
76 C5 **Coimbatore** India
129 G7 **Coimbra** Brazil
16 B4 **Coimbra** Portugal
16 D8 **Coin** Spain
110 A1 **Coin** Iowa U.S.A.
128 E7 **Coipasa, L** Bolivia
Coire *see* **Chur** Switzerland
19 N15 **Coiron, Mts du** France
128 E2 **Cojedes** *state* Venezuela
128 B3 **Cojimies** Ecuador
48 H4 **Cojocna** Romania
127 J9 **Cojoro** Venezuela
133 D7 **Cojudo Blanco** *mt* Argentina
47 N10 **Cok** *R* Turkey
99 M4 **Cokato** Minnesota U.S.A.
94 G6 **Cokeburg** Pennsylvania U.S.A.
101 P7 **Cokeville** Wyoming U.S.A.
26 O2 **Cokkarassa** *mt* Norway
139 G7 **Colac** Victoria Australia
144 A7 **Colac** New Zealand
131 B2 **Colanguil, Cerro de** *mt* Argentina
130 H6 **Colatina** Brazil
36 F2 **Cölbe** Germany
146 B10 **Colbeck, C** Antarctica
100 H2 **Colbert** Washington U.S.A.
33 P8 **Colbitz** Germany
33 P8 **Colbitz-Letzlinger Heide** Germany
121 N8 **Colborne** Ontario Canada
107 J2 **Colby** Kansas U.S.A.
99 Q5 **Colby** Wisconsin U.S.A.
128 D7 **Colca** *R* Peru
9 G4 **Colchester** England
95 P5 **Colchester** Connecticut U.S.A.
99 Q9 **Colchester** Illinois U.S.A.
8 D5 **Cold Ashton** England
116 F9 **Cold B** Alaska U.S.A.
44 B2 **Col de Longet** France
94 J4 **Colden** New York U.S.A.
13 F4 **Cold Fell** *mt* England
13 F2 **Coldingham** Scotland
37 O1 **Colditz** Germany
118 G4 **Cold L** Alberta Canada
119 Q3 **Cold L** Manitoba Canada
99 M4 **Cold Spring** Minnesota U.S.A.
109 M5 **Coldspring** Texas U.S.A.
13 F2 **Coldstream** Scotland
121 L8 **Coldwater** Ontario Canada
107 L4 **Coldwater** Kansas U.S.A.
94 C5 **Coldwater** Michigan U.S.A.
111 F7 **Coldwater** *R* Mississippi U.S.A.
110 M1 **Coldwater** Ohio U.S.A.
108 C7 **Coldwater Cr** Texas/Okla U.S.A.
120 D4 **Coldwell** Ontario Canada
139 H8 **Colebrook** Tasmania Australia
121 T8 **Colebrook** New Hampshire U.S.A.
110 C3 **Cole Camp** Missouri U.S.A.
116 Q2 **Coleen** *R* Alaska U.S.A.
8 D4 **Coleford** England
94 J5 **Colegrove** Pennsylvania U.S.A.
141 F2 **Coleman** *R* Queensland Australia
118 C9 **Coleman** Alberta Canada
113 E9 **Coleman** Florida U.S.A.
94 C3 **Coleman** Michigan U.S.A.
109 H4 **Coleman** Texas U.S.A.
22 B2 **Colembert** France
138 F6 **Coleraine** Victoria Australia
121 T7 **Coleraine** Quebec Canada
14 E1 **Coleraine** N Ireland
99 N2 **Coleraine** Minnesota U.S.A.
118 G9 **Coleridge** Alberta Canada
98 J7 **Coleridge** Nebraska U.S.A.
139 J8 **Coles B** Tasmania Australia
89 D8 **Colesberg** S Africa
8 E4 **Colesborne** England
9 E2 **Coleshill** England
128 D7 **Coles, Pta** *C* Peru
118 H7 **Coleville** Saskatchewan Canada
102 E3 **Coleville** California U.S.A.
119 O9 **Colfax** Saskatchewan Canada
102 D2 **Colfax** California U.S.A.
110 H1 **Colfax** Illinois U.S.A.
110 K1 **Colfax** Indiana U.S.A.
99 N8 **Colfax** Iowa U.S.A.
111 D10 **Colfax** Louisiana U.S.A.
106 F5 **Colfax** New Mexico U.S.A.
100 H3 **Colfax** Washington U.S.A.
99 P4 **Colfax** Wisconsin U.S.A.
119 O9 **Colgate** Saskatchewan Canada
133 D7 **Colhué Huapí, L** Argentina
131 B5 **Coliauco** Argentina
131 B7 **Colico, L** Chile
25 A5 **Colijnsplaat** Netherlands
124 H8 **Colima** Mexico
129 K5 **Colinas** Brazil
13 F1 **Colinsburgh** Scotland
118 D4 **Colinton** Alberta Canada
13 E2 **Colinton** Scotland
12 C2 **Colintraive** Scotland
15 B4 **Coll** *isld* Scotland
139 H4 **Collabah** New South Wales Australia
139 J3 **Collarenebri** New South Wales Australia
106 C2 **Collbran** Colorado U.S.A.
42 D5 **Colle di Val d'Elsa** Italy
89 F3 **Colleen Bawn** Zimbabwe
116 O4 **College** Alaska U.S.A.
110 M2 **College Corner** Indiana U.S.A.
110 K6 **College Grove** Tennessee U.S.A.
111 M8 **College Park** Georgia U.S.A.
95 L7 **College Park** Maryland U.S.A.
100 G3 **College Place** Washington U.S.A.
109 L5 **College Station** Texas U.S.A.
45 P6 **Collelongo** Italy
139 H3 **Collerina** New South Wales Australia
42 C5 **Collesalvetti** Italy
45 J4 **Collesalvetti** Italy
45 R7 **Colle Sannita** Italy
109 N9 **Colleyville** Texas U.S.A.
45 N6 **Colli Albani** Italy
139 J4 **Collie** New South Wales Australia
143 B10 **Collie** W Australia Australia
143 B10 **Collie Cardiff** W Australia Australia
142 E3 **Collier B** W Australia Australia
113 F12 **Collier City** Florida U.S.A.
143 C6 **Collier Ra** *mts* W Australia Australia
110 G6 **Collierville** Tennessee U.S.A.
8 B6 **Colliford L** England
12 E3 **Collin** Scotland
45 J3 **Collina, Passo di** Italy
20 E5 **Collinée** France
21 O3 **Collines-du-Vexin, Plaine et** France
9 E5 **Collingbourne Kingston** England
9 F1 **Collingham** England
13 G6 **Collingham** England
95 N7 **Collingswood** New Jersey U.S.A.
141 F5 **Collingwood** Queensland Australia
120 K8 **Collingwood** Ontario Canada
145 D4 **Collingwood** New Zealand
112 E5 **Collins** Georgia U.S.A.
111 G10 **Collins** Mississippi U.S.A.
110 C4 **Collins** Missouri U.S.A.
101 O2 **Collins** Montana U.S.A.
94 J4 **Collins** New York U.S.A.
114 J3 **Collinson Pen** Northwest Territories Canada
111 E9 **Collinston** Louisiana U.S.A.
14 E3 **Collinstown** Ireland
141 J5 **Collinsville** Queensland Australia
111 L7 **Collinsville** Alabama U.S.A.
110 G3 **Collinsville** Illinois U.S.A.
107 P5 **Collinsville** Oklahoma U.S.A.
110 J6 **Collinwood** Tennessee U.S.A.
41 M6 **Collio** Italy
120 J1 **Collis** Ontario Canada
37 Q1 **Cölln** Germany
19 Q18 **Collobrières** France
131 B8 **Collon Cura** *R* Argentina
14 C2 **Collooney** Ireland
107 K2 **Collyer** Kansas U.S.A.
40 F1 **Colmar** France
37 J5 **Colmberg** Germany
133 E3 **Colmena** Argentina
16 E8 **Colmenar** Spain
16 E4 **Colmenar de Oreja** Spain
16 E4 **Colmenar Vieja** Spain
109 N5 **Colmesneil** Texas U.S.A.
12 D3 **Colmonell** Scotland
21 J5 **Colmont** *R* France
106 F5 **Colmor** New Mexico U.S.A.
13 F6 **Colne** England
9 G4 **Colne, R** England
124 A2 **Colnett, C** Mexico
139 K5 **Colo** *R* New South Wales Australia
99 N7 **Colo** Iowa U.S.A.
41 O7 **Cologna** Italy
45 K1 **Cologna Veneta** Italy
Cologne *see* **Köln**
99 N5 **Cologne** Minnesota U.S.A.
94 A4 **Coloma** Michigan U.S.A.
99 R5 **Coloma** Wisconsin U.S.A.
21 K3 **Colombelles** France
40 A1 **Colombey les Deux Églises** France
129 J8 **Colombia** Brazil
108 H8 **Colombia** Mexico
128 C3 **Colombia** *rep* S America
90 B7 **Colombian Basin** Atlantic Oc
121 N4 **Colombiere** Quebec Canada
83 J11 **Colombo** Sri Lanka
20 G3 **Colomby** France
98 G6 **Colome** South Dakota U.S.A.
133 E4 **Colón** Argentina
126 D3 **Colón** Cuba
125 P5 **Colón** Panama
94 B5 **Colon** Michigan U.S.A.
138 B4 **Colona** South Australia Australia
126 G3 **Colonel Hill** Crooked I Bahamas
131 F5 **Colonia** Uruguay
133 D5 **Colonia Catriel** Argentina
131 D7 **Colonia Choele Choel** *isld* Argentina
133 F4 **Colonia del Sac** Uruguay
124 E2 **Colonia Díaz** Mexico
133 D7 **Colonia las Heras** Argentina
95 K8 **Colonial Beach** Virginia U.S.A.
94 K9 **Colonial Heights** Virginia U.S.A.
95 L9 **Colonial Nat. Hist. Park** Virginia U.S.A.
130 H4 **Colônia, R** Brazil
125 M2 **Colón, Montañas de** *ra* Honduras
43 H9 **Colonna, C** Italy
119 M7 **Colonsay** Saskatchewan Canada
15 B4 **Colonsay** *isld* Scotland
107 P3 **Colony** Kansas U.S.A.
131 D7 **Colorada Grande, L** Argentina
127 N10 **Coloradito** Venezuela
131 B5 **Colorado** *R* Chile

106 B2 **Colorado** *state* U.S.A.
103 L5 **Colorado** *R* Arizona U.S.A.
106 B2 **Colorado** *R* Colorado U.S.A.
109 J4 **Colorado** *R* Texas U.S.A.
103 J10 **Colorado, Cerro** *pk* Mexico
108 G3 **Colorado City** Texas U.S.A.
131 E7 **Colorado, Delta del R** Argentina
106 B2 **Colorado Nat.Mon** Colorado U.S.A.
103 N5 **Colorado Plat** Arizona U.S.A.
103 K7 **Colorado R.Aqueduct** California U.S.A.
106 F3 **Colorado Springs** Colorado U.S.A.
16 C4 **Colorico da Beira** Portugal
45 H2 **Colorno** Italy
19 Q17 **Colostre** *R* France
125 L10 **Colotepec** Mexico
124 H6 **Colotlán** Mexico
20 E6 **Colpo** France
120 K8 **Colpoys B** Ontario Canada
133 D1 **Colquechaca** Bolivia
111 M10 **Colquitt** Georgia U.S.A.
9 F2 **Colsterworth** England
101 T4 **Colstrip** Montana U.S.A.
108 D8 **Coltexo** Texas U.S.A.
9 H2 **Coltishall** England
102 G7 **Colton** California U.S.A.
95 L8 **Colton** Maryland U.S.A.
95 N2 **Colton** New York U.S.A.
98 K6 **Colton** South Dakota U.S.A.
103 O2 **Colton** Utah U.S.A.
100 H3 **Colton** Washington U.S.A.
117 O10 **Columbia** *R* British Columbia Canada
111 L10 **Columbia** Alabama U.S.A.
113 E7 **Columbia** Florida U.S.A.
110 F3 **Columbia** Illinois U.S.A.
94 B9 **Columbia** Kentucky U.S.A.
111 D9 **Columbia** Louisiana U.S.A.
95 L7 **Columbia** Maryland U.S.A.
111 G10 **Columbia** Mississippi U.S.A.
110 D3 **Columbia** Missouri U.S.A.
112 L2 **Columbia** North Carolina U.S.A.
95 L6 **Columbia** Pennsylvania U.S.A.
112 F3 **Columbia** South Carolina U.S.A.
98 H4 **Columbia** South Dakota U.S.A.
110 J6 **Columbia** Tennessee U.S.A.
94 J9 **Columbia** Virginia U.S.A.
100 E4 **Columbia** *R* Wash/Oregon U.S.A.
117 O11 **Columbia** *R* Wash/Br Col U.S.A./Canada
100 F2 **Columbia Basin** *reg* Washington U.S.A.
115 N1 **Columbia, C** Northwest Territories Canada
94 B5 **Columbia City** Indiana U.S.A.
95 L8 **Columbia, Dist. of (D.C.)** U.S.A.
101 L1 **Columbia Falls** Montana U.S.A.
116 O6 **Columbia Glacier** Alaska U.S.A.
117 Q10 **Columbia Lake** British Columbia Canada
117 P9 **Columbia, Mt** Br Col/Alberta Canada
114 G7 **Columbia Mts** British Columbia Canada
111 K8 **Columbiana** Alabama U.S.A.
94 G6 **Columbiana** Ohio U.S.A.
100 E2 **Columbia River** Washington U.S.A.
98 H4 **Columbia Road Res** South Dakota U.S.A.
95 O4 **Columbiaville** New York U.S.A.
106 D1 **Columbine** Colorado U.S.A.
101 T6 **Columbine** Wyoming U.S.A.
89 A9 **Columbine, C** S Africa
17 H5 **Columbretes, I** Spain
111 M9 **Columbus** Georgia U.S.A.
110 L2 **Columbus** Indiana U.S.A.
107 Q4 **Columbus** Kansas U.S.A.
111 H8 **Columbus** Mississippi U.S.A.
101 Q4 **Columbus** Montana U.S.A.
98 J8 **Columbus** Nebraska U.S.A.
106 C10 **Columbus** New Mexico U.S.A.
98 D1 **Columbus** North Dakota U.S.A.
94 D7 **Columbus** Ohio U.S.A.
109 L6 **Columbus** Texas U.S.A.
99 R6 **Columbus** Wisconsin U.S.A.
126 G3 **Columbus Bank** Bahamas
99 P8 **Columbus City** Iowa U.S.A.
126 G2 **Columbus Mon** San Salvador Bahamas
126 G2 **Columbus Pt** Cat I Bahamas
127 M2 **Columbus Pt** Tobago
102 B2 **Colusa** California U.S.A.
12 E4 **Colvend** Scotland
94 J6 **Colver** Pennsylvania U.S.A.
145 E2 **Colville** New Zealand
116 L2 **Colville** *R* Alaska U.S.A.
100 H1 **Colville** Washington U.S.A.
114 G4 **Colville L** Northwest Territories Canada
143 F8 **Colville, Lake** W Australia Australia
137 Q8 **Colville Ridge** *sea feature* Pacific Oc
13 F3 **Colwell** England
99 O6 **Colwell** Iowa U.S.A.
8 C1 **Colwyn Bay** Wales
8 C6 **Colyford** England
45 M2 **Comacchio** Italy
125 O10 **Comalapa** Guatemala
125 N8 **Comalcalco** Mexico
131 B8 **Comallo** *R* Argentina
48 K6 **Comana** Romania
107 N7 **Comanche** Oklahoma U.S.A.
109 J4 **Comanche** Texas U.S.A.
146 D3 **Comandante Ferraz** *Brazil Base* Antarctica
133 D7 **Comandante Luis Piedrabuena** Argentina
133 D4 **Comandante Salas** Argentina
48 K4 **Comănești** Romania
48 K5 **Comarnic** Romania
125 L2 **Comayagua** Honduras
16 B4 **Comba Dão** Portugal
112 G5 **Combahee** *R* South Carolina U.S.A.
133 C4 **Combarbala** Chile
40 C2 **Combeaufontaine** France
8 B5 **Combe Martin** England
120 H10 **Comber** Ontario Canada
14 F2 **Comber** N Ireland
121 N7 **Combermere** Ontario Canada
68 A3 **Combermere B** Burma
109 K9 **Combes** Texas U.S.A.
22 D3 **Combles** France
69 F12 **Combol** *isld* Indonesia
20 G5 **Combourg** France
139 L4 **Comboyne** New South Wales Australia
21 N5 **Combres** France
20 B6 **Combrit** France
94 D9 **Combs** Kentucky U.S.A.
131 D4 **Comechingones, Sa. de** *ra* Argentina
38 G8 **Comeglians** Italy
38 G8 **Comelico** Italy
130 E6 **Comendador Gomes** Brazil
111 L9 **Comer** Alabama U.S.A.
112 D3 **Comer** Georgia U.S.A.
14 D4 **Comeragh Mts** Ireland
130 H5 **Comercinho** Brazil
98 B1 **Comertown** Montana U.S.A.
141 J6 **Comet** *R* Queensland Australia
141 J6 **Comet** Queensland Australia
109 J6 **Comfort** Texas U.S.A.
99 M5 **Comfrey** Minnesota U.S.A.
75 O7 **Comilla** Bangladesh
22 E2 **Comines** France
43 F12 **Comino** *isld* Malta
43 C8 **Comino, C** Sardinia
94 C2 **Comins** Michigan U.S.A.
43 F12 **Comiso** Sicily
125 N9 **Comitán de Domínguez** Mexico
20 C5 **Commana** France
121 L7 **Commanda** Ontario Canada
18 G6 **Commentry** France
20 G8 **Commequiers** France
21 J5 **Commer** France
112 D3 **Commerce** Georgia U.S.A.
107 Q5 **Commerce** Oklahoma U.S.A.
109 M2 **Commerce** Texas U.S.A.
106 F2 **Commerce City** Colorado U.S.A.
19 J4 **Commercy** France
45 J1 **Commessaggio** Italy
121 S4 **Commissaires, Lac des** Quebec Canada
115 L4 **Committee B** Northwest Territories Canada
146 D14 **Commonwealth B** Antarctica
138 C3 **Commonwealth Hill** South Australia Australia
139 K6 **Commonwealth Terr** New South Wales Australia
41 K6 **Como** Italy
106 E2 **Como** Colorado U.S.A.
111 G7 **Como** Mississippi U.S.A.
133 D7 **Comodoro Rivadavia** Argentina
41 K5 **Como, Lago di** Italy
124 D4 **Comondú** Mexico
125 J7 **Comonfort** Mexico
76 C6 **Comorin, C** India
81 B7 **Comoro Ridge** Indian Oc
87 G10 **Comoros** *rep* Indian Oc
118 G7 **Compeer** Alberta Canada
22 D5 **Compiègne** France
22 D5 **Compiègne, Forêt de** France
124 G7 **Compostela** Mexico
71 G7 **Compostela** Mindanao Philippines
130 F9 **Comprida, I** São Paulo Brazil
102 A2 **Comptche** California U.S.A.
102 F8 **Compton** California U.S.A.
99 R8 **Compton** Illinois U.S.A.
12 E1 **Comrie** Scotland
95 O3 **Comstock** New York U.S.A.
108 F6 **Comstock** Texas U.S.A.
45 O4 **Cona** Italy
66 E5 **Co Nag** *L* China
85 B7 **Conakry** Guinea
133 D6 **Cona Niyeo** Argentina
112 C3 **Conasauga** *R* Georgia U.S.A.
98 D6 **Conata** South Dakota U.S.A.
45 N4 **Conca** *R* Italy
108 H6 **Concan** Texas U.S.A.
20 C6 **Concarneau** France
130 H9 **Conceição** Paraíba Brazil
130 H6 **Conceição da Barra** Brazil
130 E6 **Conceiçao das Alagoas** Brazil
129 J5 **Conceiçao do Araguaia** Brazil
130 G6 **Conceição do Mato Dentro** Brazil
133 D3 **Concepción** Argentina
128 E6 **Concepcíon** Beni Bolivia
128 F7 **Concepción** Santa Cruz Bolivia
131 A6 **Concepción** Chile
124 C2 **Concepcion** *R* Mexico
130 B8 **Concepción** *dept* Paraguay
130 B8 **Concepción** Paraguay
131 A6 **Concepción, B. del** Chile
133 B8 **Concepción, Can** *str* Chile
130 C10 **Concepción de la Sierra** Argentina
124 J5 **Concepción del Oro** Mexico
131 F4 **Concepción del Uruguay** Argentina
128 F7 **Concepción, L** Bolivia
124 D4 **Concepción, Pta** *C* Mexico
99 M9 **Conception** Missouri U.S.A.
123 U6 **Conception B** Newfoundland Canada
87 B10 **Conception B** Namibia
123 T6 **Conception Harb** Newfoundland Canada
126 G3 **Conception I** Bahamas
83 K12 **Conception I** Mahé I Indian Oc
124 G6 **Concha** Mexico
130 E8 **Conchas** Brazil
106 F6 **Conchas** New Mexico U.S.A.
106 F6 **Conchas Lake** New Mexico U.S.A.
21 M4 **Conches** France
133 D2 **Conchi** Chile
124 G4 **Concho** Mexico
103 P7 **Concho** Arizona U.S.A.
107 N6 **Concho** Oklahoma U.S.A.
108 G4 **Concho** *R* Texas U.S.A.
108 B7 **Conchos, Rio** Mexico
102 B4 **Concord** California U.S.A.
111 M8 **Concord** Georgia U.S.A.
94 C4 **Concord** Michigan U.S.A.
98 K7 **Concord** Nebraska U.S.A.
95 Q3 **Concord** New Hampshire U.S.A.
112 G2 **Concord** North Carolina U.S.A.
95 Q2 **Concord** Vermont U.S.A.
131 F3 **Concordia** Argentina
130 D10 **Concórdia** Brazil
124 F6 **Concordia** Mexico
107 N2 **Concordia** Kansas U.S.A.
110 C3 **Concordia** Missouri U.S.A.
45 J2 **Concórdia sulla Secchia** Italy
100 D1 **Concrete** Washington U.S.A.
68 G3 **Con Cuong** Vietnam
101 O7 **Conda** Idaho U.S.A.
141 K7 **Condamine** *R* Queensland Australia
141 K7 **Condamine** Queensland Australia
18 G7 **Condat** France
129 L6 **Cónde** Brazil
98 H4 **Conde** South Dakota U.S.A.
88 E9 **Condédzi** *R* Mozambique
125 L3 **Condega** Nicaragua
21 M5 **Condé-sur-Huîsne** France
22 F3 **Condé-sur-l'Escaut** France
21 J4 **Condé-sur-Noireau** France
21 O4 **Condé-sur-Vesgres** France
21 H3 **Condé-sur-Vire** France
130 H4 **Condeúba** Brazil
139 H5 **Condobolin** New South Wales Australia
18 F9 **Condom** France
100 E4 **Condon** Oregon U.S.A.
142 C5 **Condon Creek** *B* W Australia Australia
128 C4 **Condor, Cord. del** *mts* Ecuador/Peru
12 D2 **Condorrat** Scotland
19 N14 **Condrieu** France
22 J3 **Condroz** Belgium
142 E3 **Cone B** W Australia Australia
111 K10 **Conecuh** *R* Alabama U.S.A.
42 E3 **Conegliano** Italy
17 J5 **Conejera** *isld* Balearic Is
106 D4 **Conejos** Colorado U.S.A.
94 H6 **Conemaugh** *R* Pennsylvania U.S.A.
45 O4 **Cónero, M** *mt* Italy
133 E6 **Conesa** Argentina
94 K4 **Conesus L** New York U.S.A.
99 P8 **Conesville** Iowa U.S.A.
94 F6 **Conesville** Ohio U.S.A.
123 Q4 **Coney Arm** Newfoundland Canada
90 C1 **Coney I** Bermuda
95 O6 **Coney Island** New York U.S.A.
40 D2 **Conflans** France
19 J3 **Conflans-Jarny** France
21 P4 **Conflans-Ste. Honorine** France
21 P2 **Conflans-Ste. Honorine Villers-Bretonneux** France
94 H7 **Confluence** Pennsylvania U.S.A.
18 F6 **Confolens** France
103 L2 **Confusion Range** Utah U.S.A.
130 B9 **Confuso, R** Paraguay
14 B3 **Cong** Ireland
112 G4 **Congaree** *R* South Carolina U.S.A.
112 G4 **Congaree Swamp Nat. Mon** South Carolina U.S.A.
67 D5 **Conghua** China
67 C4 **Congjiang** China
8 D1 **Congleton** England
86 C6 **Congo** *rep* W Africa
85 C6 **Congo** *R* West Africa
Congo (Brazzaville) *rep see* **Congo** *rep*
Congo (Kinshasa) *rep see* **Zaïre** *rep*
130 G7 **Congonhas** Brazil
8 D5 **Congresbury** England
118 L9 **Congress** Saskatchewan Canada
21 H6 **Congrier** France
68 J5 **Cong Tum** Vietnam
20 D7 **Conguel, Pte. de** France
133 C6 **Cónico** *mt* Chile/Arg
21 N5 **Conie** *R* France
106 E2 **Conifer** Colorado U.S.A.
9 F1 **Coningsby** England
13 G6 **Conisbrough** England
140 B5 **Coniston** N Terr Australia
120 K6 **Coniston** Ontario Canada
13 E5 **Coniston** England
141 G4 **Conjuboy** Queensland Australia
118 F3 **Conklin** Alberta Canada
108 B7 **Conlen** Texas U.S.A.
21 K5 **Conlie** France
40 C4 **Conliège** France
120 K4 **Connaught** Ontario Canada
14 B3 **Connaught** *prov* Ireland
142 E6 **Connaughton, Mt** W Australia Australia
19 N16 **Connaux** France
94 G5 **Conneaut** Ohio U.S.A.
94 G5 **Conneautville** Pennsylvania U.S.A.
95 P3 **Connecticut** *R* U.S.A.
95 O5 **Connecticut** *state* U.S.A.
15 C4 **Connel Ferry** Scotland
100 G3 **Connell** Washington U.S.A.
94 H6 **Connellsville** Pennsylvania U.S.A.
141 F6 **Connemara** Queensland Australia
14 B3 **Connemara** *dist* Ireland
101 L4 **Conner** Montana U.S.A.
138 B2 **Conner, Mt** N Terr Australia
140 B7 **Conner, Mt** N Terr Australia
21 M5 **Connerre** France
94 B7 **Connersville** Indiana U.S.A.
14 B2 **Conn, L** Ireland
142 F2 **Connor, Mt** W Australia Australia
122 D6 **Connors** New Brunswick Canada
141 J5 **Connors Ra** *mts* Queensland Australia
128 C4 **Cononaco** *R* Ecuador
112 F2 **Conover** North Carolina U.S.A.
99 R3 **Conover** Wisconsin U.S.A.
33 S6 **Conow** Germany
20 G6 **Conquereuil** France
118 K7 **Conquest** Saskatchewan Canada
20 A5 **Conquet, le** France
130 F6 **Conquista** Brazil
101 O1 **Conrad** Montana U.S.A.
139 J7 **Conran, C** Victoria Australia
99 Q4 **Conrath** Wisconsin U.S.A.
109 M5 **Conroe** Texas U.S.A.
109 M5 **Conroe, L** Texas U.S.A.
45 L2 **Consandolo** Italy
121 N9 **Consecon** Ontario Canada
130 G7 **Conselheiro Lafaiete** Brazil
45 L3 **Conselice** Italy
45 L1 **Conselve** Italy
22 J5 **Consenvoye** France
13 G4 **Consett** England
95 M6 **Conshohocken** Pennsylvania U.S.A.
22 H4 **Cons-la-Grandville** France
126 C3 **Consolación del Sur** Cuba
69 H8 **Con Son** *isld* Vietnam
69 H8 **Con Son** Vietnam
118 G6 **Consort** Alberta Canada
95 M3 **Constableville** New York U.S.A.
Constance *see* **Konstanz**
143 E6 **Constance Headland** *hill* W Australia Australia
Constance, L *see* **Bodensee**
128 F5 **Constância dos Baetas** Brazil
48 M6 **Constanța** Romania
16 D7 **Constantina** Spain
85 F1 **Constantine** Algeria
94 B5 **Constantine** Michigan U.S.A.
116 H7 **Constantine, C** Alaska U.S.A.
117 C5 **Constantine, Mt** Yukon Territory Canada
Constantinople *see* **İstanbul**
127 N4 **Constant, Morne** *hill* Guadeloupe W Indies
127 L2 **Constant Spring** Jamaica
131 A5 **Constitución** Chile
141 J6 **Consuelo** Queensland Australia
118 H9 **Consul** Saskatchewan Canada
101 L8 **Contact** Nevada U.S.A.
130 G7 **Contagalo** Brazil
128 D5 **Contamana** Peru
128 F3 **Contão** Brazil
131 D4 **Contara** *R* Argentina
45 M1 **Contarina** Italy
129 K6 **Cóntas** *R* Brazil
21 O2 **Conteville** France
40 F5 **Conthey** Switzerland
21 J6 **Contigné** France
103 O10 **Continental** Arizona U.S.A.
94 C5 **Continental** Ohio U.S.A.
106 C4 **Continental Res** Colorado U.S.A.
95 Q3 **Contoocook** New Hampshire U.S.A.
125 Q7 **Contoy, I** Mexico
16 E8 **Contraviesa, Sa** *mts* Spain
121 R7 **Contrecoeur** Quebec Canada
133 C8 **Contreras, I** Chile
21 N7 **Contres** Loir-et-Cher France
22 H5 **Contreuve** France
40 C1 **Contrexéville** France
130 G6 **Contria** Brazil
118 F7 **Control** Alberta Canada
36 C5 **Contwig** Germany
114 J4 **Contwoyto L** Northwest Territories Canada
21 P2 **Conty** France
126 H10 **Convención** Colombia
43 H8 **Conversano** Italy
94 B6 **Converse** Indiana U.S.A.
111 C10 **Converse** Louisiana U.S.A.
94 C6 **Convoy** Ohio U.S.A.
110 D6 **Conway** Arkansas U.S.A.
99 M9 **Conway** Iowa U.S.A.
110 D4 **Conway** Missouri U.S.A.
95 Q3 **Conway** New Hampshire U.S.A.
112 K1 **Conway** North Carolina U.S.A.
98 J1 **Conway** North Dakota U.S.A.
112 H4 **Conway** South Carolina U.S.A.
8 C1 **Conway B** Wales
141 J5 **Conway, C** Queensland Australia
138 D3 **Conway, L** South Australia Australia
110 D6 **Conway, L** Arkansas U.S.A.
140 C6 **Conway, Mt** N Terr Australia
95 Q2 **Conway, N** New Hampshire U.S.A.
144 D5 **Conway R** New Zealand
107 N4 **Conway Springs** Kansas U.S.A.
8 B4 **Conwil Elvet** Wales
8 C1 **Conwy** Wales
8 C1 **Conwy R** Wales
112 C4 **Conyers** Georgia U.S.A.
22 K3 **Coo** Belgium
138 C3 **Coober Pedy** South Australia Australia
9 G6 **Cooden** England
142 A3 **Coogee** *dist* Perth, W Aust Australia
142 A3 **Coogee L** W Australia Australia
142 C5 **Cooglegong** W Australia Australia
141 J7 **Coogoon** *R* Queensland Australia
140 C2 **Cooinda** N Terr Australia
138 B4 **Cook** South Australia Australia
99 O2 **Cook** Minnesota U.S.A.
99 K9 **Cook** Nebraska U.S.A.
133 C9 **Cook, B.de** Chile
117 K10 **Cook, C** British Columbia Canada
101 Q4 **Cooke City** Montana U.S.A.
143 B9 **Cooke, Mt** W Australia Australia
94 B10 **Cookeville** Tennessee U.S.A.
9 F4 **Cookham** England
146 D13 **Cook Ice Shelf** Antarctica
118 D5 **Cooking L** Alberta Canada
116 L7 **Cook Inlet** Alaska U.S.A.
134 L10 **Cook Is** Pacific Oc
144 C5 **Cook, Mt** New Zealand
117 D5 **Cook, Mt** Alaska/Yukon Terr U.S.A./Canada
99 U4 **Cooks** Michigan U.S.A.
123 Q2 **Cook's Hbr** Newfoundland Canada
121 T7 **Cookshire** Quebec Canada
141 H2 **Cook's Passage** Queensland Australia
106 C9 **Cooks Pk** New Mexico U.S.A.
121 L8 **Cookstown** Ontario Canada
14 E2 **Cookstown** N Ireland
145 E4 **Cook Strait** New Zealand
141 H3 **Cooktown** Queensland Australia
141 H7 **Cooladdi** Queensland Australia
139 J4 **Coolah** New South Wales Australia
139 H5 **Coolamon** New South Wales Australia
139 L3 **Coolangatta** New South Wales Australia
141 L8 **Coolangatta** Queensland Australia
143 C8 **Coolarda** *hill* W Australia Australia
142 A2 **Coolbellup, L** W Australia Australia
112 G2 **Cooleemee** North Carolina U.S.A.
143 D9 **Coolgardie** W Australia Australia
140 B3 **Coolibah** N Terr Australia
103 N9 **Coolidge** Arizona U.S.A.
112 D6 **Coolidge** Georgia U.S.A.
109 L4 **Coolidge** Texas U.S.A.
127 P4 **Coolidge** *airport* Antigua W Indies
103 O8 **Coolidge Dam** Arizona U.S.A.
143 B8 **Coolimba** W Australia Australia
100 J1 **Coolin** Idaho U.S.A.
141 K8 **Coolmunda Dam** Queensland Australia
142 A4 **Cooloongup, L** W Australia Australia
94 F7 **Coolville** Ohio U.S.A.
143 B7 **Coolyun Well** W Australia Australia
139 J6 **Cooma** New South Wales Australia
14 A5 **Coomacarrea** *mt* Ireland
9 E5 **Coombe Bissett** England
8 D4 **Coombe Hill** England
143 B9 **Coomberdale** W Australia Australia
139 J4 **Coonabarabran** New South Wales Australia
138 F6 **Coonalpyn** South Australia Australia
139 J4 **Coonamble** New South Wales Australia
143 E9 **Coonana** W Australia Australia
138 F6 **Coonawarra** South Australia Australia
138 F5 **Coonbah Roadhouse** New South Wales Australia
138 D4 **Coondambo** South Australia Australia
Coondapoor *see* **Kundāpura**
142 C5 **Coongan, R** W Australia Australia
141 H8 **Coongoola** Queensland Australia
138 C2 **Coongra** *R* South Australia Australia
138 F2 **Cooninnie, L** South Australia Australia
76 C5 **Coonoor** India
99 M8 **Coon Rapids** Iowa U.S.A.
99 N4 **Coon Rapids** Minnesota U.S.A.
140 C1 **Cooper** *R* N Terr Australia
129 G8 **Cooper** Paraguay
109 M2 **Cooper** Texas U.S.A.
141 F7 **Cooper Cr** Qnsld/S Aust Australia
141 F7 **Cooper Creek** *R* Queensland Australia
144 A6 **Cooper I** New Zealand
143 G7 **Cooper, Mt** W Australia Australia
139 L4 **Coopernook** New South Wales Australia
141 K2 **Coopers Plains** *dist* Brisbane, Qnsld Australia
113 K11 **Cooper's Town** Bahamas
126 F1 **Coopers Town** Great Abaco I Bahamas
95 M4 **Cooperstown** New York U.S.A.
98 H2 **Cooperstown** North Dakota U.S.A.
94 B3 **Coopersville** Michigan U.S.A.
127 O3 **Coora** Trinidad
138 B4 **Coorabie** South Australia Australia
140 F6 **Coorabulka** Queensland Australia
143 B7 **Coor-de-Wandy** *mt* W Australia Australia
138 E6 **Coorong, The** *L* South Australia Australia
143 B8 **Coorow** W Australia Australia
141 L7 **Cooroy** Queensland Australia
111 L7 **Coosa** *R* Alabama U.S.A.
112 C3 **Coosawattee** *R* Georgia U.S.A.
112 F5 **Coosawhatchie** *R* South Carolina U.S.A.
100 A6 **Coos Bay** Oregon U.S.A.
139 J5 **Cootamundra** New South Wales Australia
14 E2 **Cootehill** Ireland
141 K7 **Cooyar** Queensland Australia
131 B6 **Copahué** *pk* Chile
133 C5 **Copahue** *mt* Chile/Arg
100 A2 **Copalis Beach** Washington U.S.A.
109 K7 **Copano B** Texas U.S.A.
100 C8 **Copco** California U.S.A.
106 H2 **Cope** Colorado U.S.A.
128 F4 **Copea, Paraná** *R* Brazil
113 F12 **Copeland** Florida U.S.A.
100 J1 **Copeland** Idaho U.S.A.
107 K4 **Copeland** Kansas U.S.A.
94 B2 **Copemish** Michigan U.S.A.
Copenhagen *see* **København**
95 M3 **Copenhagen** New York U.S.A.
133 E5 **Copetonas** Argentina
139 K3 **Copeton Res.** New South Wales Australia
133 C3 **Copiapó** Chile
133 D3 **Copiapo** *vol* Chile
15 F2 **Copinsay** Scotland
138 E4 **Copley** South Australia Australia
128 D6 **Coporaque** Peru
45 L2 **Copparo** Italy
120 G3 **Coppell** Ontario Canada
109 N8 **Coppell** Texas U.S.A.
129 G2 **Coppename** *R* Suriname
32 L8 **Coppenbrügge** Germany
116 P5 **Copper** *R* Alaska U.S.A.
109 K4 **Copperas Cove** Texas U.S.A.
100 G1 **Copper Butte** *mt* Washington U.S.A.
116 P6 **Copper Center** Alaska U.S.A.
120 J6 **Copper Cliff** Ontario Canada
99 T2 **Copper Hbr** Michigan U.S.A.
138 C3 **Copper Hill** South Australia Australia
114 H4 **Coppermine** Northwest Territories Canada
120 F6 **Coppermine Pt** *C* Ontario Canada
117 N11 **Copper Mt** British Columbia Canada
100 K8 **Copper Mt** Nevada U.S.A.
117 Q5 **Copp L** Northwest Territories Canada
48 J4 **Copșa Mică** Romania
131 B6 **Copulhue, Paso del** Arg/Chile
75 L3 **Coqên** China
22 B2 **Coquelles** France
13 G3 **Coquet I** England
13 G3 **Coquet, R** England
Coquilhatville *see* **Mbandaka**
100 A6 **Coquille** Oregon U.S.A.
131 B2 **Coquimbo** Chile
101 P7 **Cora** Wyoming U.S.A.
46 G1 **Corabia** Romania
130 G5 **Coração de Jesus** Brazil
139 L3 **Coraki** New South Wales Australia
120 J2 **Coral** Ontario Canada
71 C6 **Coral B** Palawan Philippines
113 L9 **Coral Harbour** New Providence I Bahamas
115 L5 **Coral Harbour** Northwest Territories Canada
137 K4 **Coral Sea Islands Terr** Australasia
99 P8 **Coralville Lake** *res* Iowa U.S.A.
101 L1 **Coram** Montana U.S.A.
139 G7 **Corangamite, L** Victoria Australia
129 G3 **Corantijn** *R* Suriname
94 G6 **Coraopolis** Pennsylvania U.S.A.
43 G7 **Corato** Italy
20 C5 **Coray** France
21 P4 **Corbeil-Essonnes** France
19 P13 **Corbelin** France
22 F5 **Corbény** France
120 K8 **Corbetton** Ontario Canada
21 P2 **Corbie** France
20 F3 **Corbiere** Channel Is
18 G10 **Corbières** *reg* France
18 H5 **Corbigny** France
94 C10 **Corbin** Kentucky U.S.A.
123 R7 **Corbin Hd** Newfoundland Canada
45 M1 **Córbola** Italy
16 D7 **Corbones** *R* Spain
13 F4 **Corbridge** England
9 F2 **Corby** Lincs England
9 F2 **Corby** Northants England
36 B7 **Corcieux** France
102 E5 **Corcoran** California U.S.A.
20 G8 **Corcoué-sur-Logne** France
133 C6 **Corcovado** *mt* Chile
133 C6 **Corcovado, Golfo** Chile
16 A2 **Corcubion** Spain
112 D6 **Cordele** Georgia U.S.A.
107 M6 **Cordell** Oklahoma U.S.A.
20 G7 **Cordemais** France
18 G8 **Cordes** France
129 J5 **Cordilheiras, Serra das** *mts* Brazil
16 D1 **Cordillera Cantábrica** *mts* Spain
128 C3 **Cordillera Central** *mts* Colombia
127 J5 **Cordillera Central** *mts* Dominican Rep
125 O5 **Cordillera Central** *mts* Panama
128 C5 **Cordillera Central** *mts* Peru
71 E2 **Cordillera Central** *mts* Luzon Philippines
127 J10 **Cordillera de Mérida** *mts* Venezuela
128 C3 **Cordillera Occidental** *mts* Colombia
128 D2 **Cordillera Oriental** *mts* Colombia
71 F5 **Cordilleras Ra** Panay Philippines
138 F2 **Cordillo Downs** South Australia Australia
130 G6 **Cordisburgo** Brazil
131 D3 **Córdoba** Argentina
131 D4 **Cordoba** *prov* Argentina
128 C2 **Córdoba** *div* Colombia
125 L8 **Cordoba** Mexico
16 D7 **Córdoba** *prov* Spain
16 D7 **Córdoba** Spain
131 D3 **Cordoba, Sierra de** *ra* Argentina
128 C6 **Córdova** Peru
111 J8 **Cordova** Alabama U.S.A.
116 P6 **Cordova** Alaska U.S.A.
99 Q8 **Cordova** Illinois U.S.A.
121 N8 **Cordova Mines** Ontario Canada
116 P6 **Cordova Pk** Alaska U.S.A.
45 J3 **Coreglia Antelminelli** Italy
140 F4 **Corella** *R* Queensland Australia
140 D4 **Corella L** N Terr Australia
141 G5 **Corfield** Queensland Australia
45 P5 **Corfinio** Italy
Corfu *isld* Greece *see* **Kérkira** *isld*
94 J4 **Corfu** New York U.S.A.
100 F3 **Corfu** Washington U.S.A.
16 C2 **Corgo** Spain
130 C6 **Corguinho** Brazil
45 N6 **Cori** Italy
16 C5 **Coria** Spain
16 C7 **Coria del R** Spain
45 N4 **Coriano** Italy
121 O3 **Coribelle** Quebec Canada
139 K5 **Coricudgy** *mt* New South Wales Australia
43 H9 **Corigliano Calabro** Italy
45 O4 **Corinaldo** Italy
141 K2 **Corinda** *dist* Brisbane, Qnsld Australia
140 E4 **Corinda** Queensland Australia
141 K3 **Coringa Is** Gt Barrier Reef Aust
141 K3 **Coringa Is** Coral Sea
139 H8 **Corinna** Tasmania Australia
101 N8 **Corinne** Utah U.S.A.
Corinth *see* **Kórinthos**
101 S4 **Corinth** Montana U.S.A.
95 O3 **Corinth** New York U.S.A.
Corinth, Gulf of *see* **Korinthiakós Kólpos**
143 C9 **Corinthian** W Australia Australia
130 G6 **Corinto** Brazil
130 C6 **Corixinha, R** Brazil
14 C5 **Cork** *co* Ireland
14 C5 **Cork** Ireland
20 D5 **Corlay** France
43 E11 **Corleone** Sicily
47 J3 **Çorlu** Turkey
123 P4 **Cormack** Newfoundland Canada
123 Q5 **Cormack** *mt* Newfoundland Canada
21 O5 **Cormainville** France
21 L3 **Cormeilles** France
21 M7 **Cormery** France
22 F5 **Cormicy** France
123 L2 **Cormier, L** Quebec Canada
21 J3 **Cormolain** France
119 R4 **Cormorant** Manitoba Canada
6 L1 **Cormorant** *oil rig* North Sea
123 L4 **Cormorant Pt** Anticosti I, Quebec
107 M6 **Corn** Oklahoma U.S.A.
41 M6 **Corna** Italy
45 P6 **Còrnacchia, Monte** Italy
32 H7 **Cornau** Germany
21 K7 **Corne** France
112 D3 **Cornelia** Georgia U.S.A.
133 G2 **Cornélio Procópio** Brazil
99 S9 **Cornell** Illinois U.S.A.
99 P4 **Cornell** Wisconsin U.S.A.
123 P5 **Corner Brook** Newfoundland Canada
139 H7 **Corner Inlet** Victoria Australia
110 K6 **Cornersville** Tennessee U.S.A.
111 D9 **Corney L** Louisiana U.S.A.
103 P6 **Cornfields** Arizona U.S.A.
13 F2 **Cornhill-on-Tweed** England
20 H5 **Cornille** France
40 E2 **Cornimont** France
119 P9 **Corning** Saskatchewan Canada
110 F5 **Corning** Arkansas U.S.A.
99 M9 **Corning** Iowa U.S.A.
107 O2 **Corning** Kansas U.S.A.
99 L9 **Corning** Missouri U.S.A.
95 K4 **Corning** New York U.S.A.
94 E7 **Corning** Ohio U.S.A.
Corn Is *see* **Maiz, Is. del**
141 G5 **Cornish** *R* Queensland Australia
95 P3 **Cornish Flat** New Hampshire U.S.A.
142 F5 **Cornish, Mt** W Australia Australia
45 J3 **Corno alle Scale** *mt* Italy
42 F6 **Corno, M** *mt* Italy
20 B5 **Cornouaille** *reg* France
21 J6 **Cornuaille, la** France
100 H4 **Cornucopia** Oregon U.S.A.
99 P3 **Cornucopia** Wisconsin U.S.A.
18 H9 **Cornus** France
121 Q7 **Cornwall** Ontario Canada
8 B7 **Cornwall** *co* England
115 K2 **Cornwallis I** Northwest Territories Canada
138 D5 **Corny Pt** South Australia Australia
127 K9 **Coro** Venezuela
130 G6 **Coroaci** Brazil
129 K4 **Coroatá** Brazil
87 B9 **Coroca** *R* Angola
128 E7 **Corocoro** Bolivia
128 E7 **Coroico** Bolivia
130 F6 **Coromandel** Brazil
145 E2 **Coromandel** New Zealand
76 E5 **Coromandel Coast** India
145 E2 **Coromandel Peninsula** New Zealand
21 J7 **Coron** France
71 E4 **Coron** Philippines
138 F4 **Corona** New South Wales Australia
102 G8 **Corona** California U.S.A.
106 E7 **Corona** New Mexico U.S.A.
119 M9 **Coronach** Saskatchewan Canada
102 G9 **Coronado** California U.S.A.
71 F7 **Coronado B** Mindanao Philippines
125 N5 **Coronado, B.de** Costa Rica
113 G8 **Coronado Beach** Florida U.S.A.
103 O10 **Coronado Nat. Mem** Arizona U.S.A.
118 F6 **Coronation** Alberta Canada
114 H4 **Coronation G** Northwest Territories Canada
146 E3 **Coronation I** S Orkney Is Antarctica
142 E2 **Coronation Is** W Australia Australia
71 E5 **Coron B** Philippines
71 E5 **Coron Delian** *isld* Philippines
131 A6 **Coronel** Chile
133 E5 **Coronel Dorrego** Argentina
130 G6 **Coronel Fabriciano** Brazil
130 C9 **Coronel Oviedo** Paraguay
130 C4 **Coronel Ponce** Brazil
131 E6 **Coronel Pringles** Argentina
131 E6 **Coronel Suárez** Argentina
133 F5 **Coronel Vidal** Argentina
144 B6 **Coronet Pk** New Zealand
128 D7 **Coropuna** *mt* Peru
46 D4 **Çorovodë** Albania
139 H6 **Corowa** New South Wales Australia
126 G10 **Corozal** Colombia
127 O1 **Corozal Pt** Trinidad
20 G6 **Corps-Nuds** France
130 C10 **Corpus** Argentina
109 K8 **Corpus Christi** Texas U.S.A.
133 D1 **Corque** Bolivia
101 L6 **Corral** Idaho U.S.A.
16 E5 **Corralde Almaguer** Spain
124 G5 **Corrales** Mexico
16 D3 **Corrales** Spain
133 F4 **Corrales** Uruguay
126 D3 **Corralillo** Cuba
124 F2 **Corralitos** Mexico
143 B7 **Corrandibby Ra** *mts* W Australia Australia
14 B3 **Corraun** Ireland
14 B3 **Corraun Pen** Ireland
99 L7 **Correctionville** Iowa U.S.A.
71 E3 **Corregidor** Luzon Philippines
130 E5 **Córrego do Ouro** Brazil
129 J6 **Corrente** Brazil
130 D6 **Corrente, R** Goiás Brazil
43 F12 **Correnti, C.I. de** Sicily
129 K6 **Correntina** Brazil
106 C7 **Correo** New Mexico U.S.A.
18 G7 **Corrèze** *dept* France
18 G7 **Corrèze** *R* France
45 K1 **Corezzo** Italy
45 M1 **Corrézzola** Italy
14 B3 **Corrib, L** Ireland
12 C2 **Corrie** Scotland
130 B10 **Corrientes** Argentina
131 F2 **Corrientes** *prov* Argentina
133 F3 **Corrientes** *R* Argentina
128 C4 **Corrientes** *R* Peru
133 F5 **Corrientes, C** Argentina
126 B4 **Corrientes, C** Cuba
124 G7 **Corrientes, C** Mexico
109 N5 **Corrigan** Texas U.S.A.
143 C9 **Corrigin** W Australia Australia
139 K5 **Corrimal** New South Wales Australia
13 H6 **Corringham** England
14 B4 **Corrofin** Ireland
94 H5 **Corry** Pennsylvania U.S.A.
139 J6 **Corryong** Victoria Australia
12 C1 **Corryvreckan, Str.of** Scotland
18 L11 **Corse-du-Sud** *dept* Corsica
20 F5 **Corseul** France
12 C3 **Corsewall Pt** Scotland
8 D5 **Corsham** England
18 L10 **Corsica** *isld* France
98 H6 **Corsica** South Dakota U.S.A.
109 L3 **Corsicana** Texas U.S.A.
12 E3 **Corsock Br** Scotland
8 D5 **Corston** England
13 E2 **Corstorphine** Scotland
115 P5 **Cort Adelaer, Kap** *C* Greenland
103 N9 **Cortaro** Arizona U.S.A.
16 C7 **Cortegana** Spain
130 J10 **Cortès** Brazil
106 B4 **Cortez** Colorado U.S.A.
102 H1 **Cortez** Nevada U.S.A.
38 F8 **Cortina d'Ampezzo** Italy
98 K9 **Cortland** Nebraska U.S.A.
95 L4 **Cortland** New York U.S.A.
94 G5 **Cortland** Ohio U.S.A.
9 H2 **Corton** England
42 D5 **Cortona** Italy
85 B6 **Corubal** *R* Guinea/Guinea-Bissau
16 B6 **Coruche** Portugal
78 H1 **Çoruh** *R* Turkey
15 B3 **Coruisk, L** Scotland
78 E1 **Çorum** Turkey
130 B6 **Corumbá** Brazil
130 E4 **Corumbá de Goiás** Brazil
130 E6 **Corumbaíba** Brazil
130 E5 **Corumbá, R** Brazil
130 H5 **Corumbaú, Pta. do** *C* Brazil
128 F6 **Corumbiara** *R* Brazil
128 F2 **Corumo** *R* Venezuela
16 B1 **Coruña** *prov* Spain
94 C4 **Corunna** Michigan U.S.A.
130 H11 **Coruripe** Brazil
101 L3 **Corvallis** Montana U.S.A.
100 B5 **Corvallis** Oregon U.S.A.
38 E8 **Corvara in Badia** Italy
32 K9 **Corvey** Germany
8 C2 **Corwen** Wales
107 M4 **Corwin** Kansas U.S.A.
116 E7 **Corwin, C** Alaska U.S.A.
101 P4 **Corwin Springs** Montana U.S.A.
94 A8 **Corydon** Indiana U.S.A.
110 K3 **Corydon** Indiana U.S.A.
99 N9 **Corydon** Iowa U.S.A.
110 J4 **Corydon** Kentucky U.S.A.
94 J5 **Corydon** Pennsylvania U.S.A.
9 G5 **Coryton** England
21 K6 **Corzé** France
Cos *isld see* **Kos** *isld*
124 F5 **Cosalá** Mexico
125 M8 **Cosamaloapan** Mexico
43 G9 **Cosenza** Italy
9 E6 **Cosham** England
94 F6 **Coshocton** Ohio U.S.A.
81 B6 **Cosmoledo Is** Indian Oc
143 E8 **Cosmo Newberry** W Australia Australia
99 M5 **Cosmos** Minnesota U.S.A.
18 G5 **Cosne** France
18 G6 **Cosne-d'Allier** France
102 G5 **Coso Junction** California U.S.A.
133 E4 **Cosquin** Argentina
21 J6 **Cossé-le-Vivien** France
21 O6 **Cosson** *R* France
109 K6 **Cost** Texas U.S.A.
17 G7 **Costa Blanca** *reg* Spain
17 K3 **Costa Brava** *reg* Spain
16 C7 **Costa de la Luz** *reg* Spain
17 F8 **Costa del Sol** Spain
45 L1 **Costa di Rovigo** Italy
113 E11 **Costa I, La** Florida U.S.A.
102 G8 **Costa Mesa** California U.S.A.
125 M4 **Costa Rica** *rep* Central America
124 C2 **Costa Rica** Mexico
123 K3 **Costebelle, L** Quebec Canada
94 J5 **Costello** Pennsylvania U.S.A.
Costermansville *see* **Bukavu**
48 J6 **Costeșhi** Romania
95 T1 **Costigan** Maine U.S.A.
106 E5 **Costilla** New Mexico U.S.A.
33 Q9 **Coswig** Germany
71 G7 **Cotabato** Mindanao Philippines
128 E8 **Cotagaita** Bolivia
128 D7 **Cotahuasi** Peru
102 B3 **Cotati** California U.S.A.
130 H6 **Cotaxé, R** Brazil
121 Q7 **Côteau Station** Quebec Canada
118 K7 **Coteau, The** Saskatchewan Canada
126 G5 **Coteaux** Haiti
111 E12 **Cote Blanche B** Louisiana U.S.A.
44 B4 **Côte d'Azur** France
19 J5 **Côte d'Or** *dept* France
19 J5 **Côte d'Or** France
20 G3 **Cotentin** *pen* France
18 C4 **Côtes d'Armor** *dept* France
141 J6 **Cotherstone** Queensland Australia
13 F4 **Cotherstone** England
19 Q18 **Cotignac** France
45 L3 **Cotignola** Italy
128 F3 **Cotinga** *R* Brazil
85 E7 **Cotonou** Benin
128 C4 **Cotopaxi** *vol* Ecuador
106 E3 **Cotopaxi** Colorado U.S.A.
9 E4 **Cotswold Hills** England
100 B6 **Cottage Grove** Oregon U.S.A.
112 G5 **Cottageville** South Carolina U.S.A.
94 F8 **Cottageville** West Virginia U.S.A.
31 H4 **Cottbus** Germany
123 T5 **Cottel I** Newfoundland Canada
9 G3 **Cottenham** England
110 D5 **Cotter** Arkansas U.S.A.
83 M14 **Cotter, C** Mauritius
142 A2 **Cottesloe Beach** *dist* Perth, W Aust Australia
9 F2 **Cottesmore** England
129 H3 **Cottica** Suriname
13 H6 **Cottingham** England
99 O2 **Cotton** Minnesota U.S.A.
140 E6 **Cottonbush Cr** Queensland Australia
111 J8 **Cottondale** Alabama U.S.A.
111 L11 **Cottondale** Florida U.S.A.
140 D1 **Cotton I** N Terr Australia
119 V3 **Cotton L** Manitoba Canada
110 E6 **Cotton Plant** Arkansas U.S.A.
111 D11 **Cottonport** Louisiana U.S.A.
109 O3 **Cotton Valley** Louisiana U.S.A.
111 L10 **Cottonwood** Alabama U.S.A.
103 N7 **Cottonwood** Arizona U.S.A.
100 C9 **Cottonwood** California U.S.A.
100 J3 **Cottonwood** Idaho U.S.A.
99 M5 **Cottonwood** *R* Minnesota U.S.A.
98 E6 **Cottonwood** South Dakota U.S.A.
109 H3 **Cottonwood** Texas U.S.A.
103 L6 **Cottonwood Cliffs** Arizona U.S.A.
107 O3 **Cottonwood Falls** Kansas U.S.A.
103 O6 **Cottonwood Wash** *R* Arizona U.S.A.
127 J5 **Cotuí** Dominican Rep
109 H7 **Cotulla** Texas U.S.A.
18 E7 **Coubre, Pointe de la** *pt* France
142 F3 **Couchman Ra** W Australia Australia
22 E4 **Coucy-le-Château Auffrique** France
21 N7 **Couddes** France
22 C1 **Coudekerque-Branche** France
99 P4 **Couderay** Wisconsin U.S.A.
94 J5 **Coudersport** Pennsylvania U.S.A.
21 O3 **Coudray-St. Germer, le** France
21 M6 **Coudrecieux** France
21 N4 **Coudres** France
122 B6 **Coudres, I.aux** Quebec Canada

138 D6 Coüedic, C.de South Australia Australia
20 G7 Couëron France
21 J5 Couesmes-Vaucé France
20 H5 Couesnon R France
20 H7 Couffé France
100 C3 Cougar Washington U.S.A.
18 F6 Couhé France
14 A5 Coulagh B Ireland
21 L5 Coulans France
15 C2 Coulbeag Mt Scotland
100 F2 Coulee City Washington U.S.A.
100 G1 Coulee Dam Washington U.S.A.
100 G1 Coulee Dam Nat. Recreation Area Washington U.S.A.
21 L5 Coulimer France
146 C12 Coulman I Antarctica
21 O6 Coulmiers France
22 B2 Coulogne France
21 O4 Coulombs Eure France
121 O6 Coulonge R Quebec Canada
18 E6 Coulonges-Sur-l'Autize France
21 K8 Coulonges Thouarsais France
21 H4 Coulouvray-Boisbenâtre France
119 R9 Coulter Manitoba Canada
102 D4 Coulterville California U.S.A.
110 G3 Coulterville Illinois U.S.A.
116 F4 Council Alaska U.S.A.
100 J5 Council Idaho U.S.A.
99 L8 Council Bluffs Iowa U.S.A.
107 O3 Council Grove Kansas U.S.A.
8 D2 Cound England
107 N7 Countyline Oklahoma U.S.A.
15 E4 Coupar Angus Scotland
123 Q7 Coupe, C Langlade I Atlantic Oc
100 C1 Coupeville Washington U.S.A.
109 K5 Coupland Texas U.S.A.
22 B2 Couple, Mt France
21 K5 Couptrain France
117 S3 Courageous L Northwest Territories Canada
21 P5 Courances France
122 B8 Courcelles Quebec Canada
21 L5 Courcemont France
21 N6 Cour Cheverny France
21 K5 Courcité France
21 L5 Courgains France
27 M16 Courland Lagoon Lithuania/Rus Fed
21 J8 Courlay France
18 H7 Courpière France
22 D3 Courrières France
18 H9 Coursan France
21 K3 Courseulles France
18 H5 Courson les Carrières France
21 N5 Courtalain France
40 F3 Courtelary Switzerland
117 L11 Courtenay British Columbia Canada
98 H2 Courtenay North Dakota U.S.A.
18 G7 Courtine, la France
110 J7 Courtland Alabama U.S.A.
107 N2 Courtland Kansas U.S.A.
99 M5 Courtland Minnesota U.S.A.
95 K10 Courtland Virginia U.S.A.
14 C5 Courtmacsherry Ireland
109 L5 Courtney Texas U.S.A.
21 L4 Courtomer France
Courtrai see Kortrijk
22 H2 Court Saint-Etienne Belgium
118 L8 Courval Saskatchewan Canada
21 N5 Courville France
109 O3 Coushatta Louisiana U.S.A.
83 J12 Cousin I Seychelles
22 G3 Cousolre France
21 M8 Coussay-les-Bois France
19 O17 Coustellet France
87 D9 Coutada do Mucusso Angola
20 H3 Coutances France
21 K4 Couterne France
22 J2 Couthuin Belgium
18 E7 Coutras France
101 N1 Coutts Alberta Canada
21 K7 Coutures France
127 O2 Couva Trinidad
20 G2 Couville France
22 H3 Couvin Belgium
22 F4 Couvron-et-Aumencourt France
48 K5 Covasna Romania
48 K5 Covasna reg Romania
109 N1 Cove Arkansas U.S.A.
100 H4 Cove Oregon U.S.A.
112 K2 Cove City North Carolina U.S.A.
103 M3 Cove Fort Utah U.S.A.
100 B10 Covelo California U.S.A.
94 K7 Cove Mt Pennsylvania U.S.A.
126 G10 Coveñas Colombia
9 E3 Coventry England
95 L8 Cove Point Maryland U.S.A.
107 M2 Covert Kansas U.S.A.
94 A4 Covert Michigan U.S.A.
94 J9 Covesville Virginia U.S.A.
16 B4 Covilhã Portugal
116 K7 Coville, L Alaska U.S.A.
112 D4 Covington Georgia U.S.A.
99 T9 Covington Indiana U.S.A.
94 C7 Covington Kentucky U.S.A.
111 F11 Covington Louisiana U.S.A.
99 S3 Covington Michigan U.S.A.
94 C6 Covington Ohio U.S.A.
107 N5 Covington Oklahoma U.S.A.
110 G6 Covington Tennessee U.S.A.
109 K3 Covington Texas U.S.A.
94 G9 Covington Virginia U.S.A.
120 G5 Cow R Ontario Canada
15 C4 Cowal Scotland
139 J5 Cowal, L New South Wales Australia
119 R6 Cowan Manitoba Canada
110 K6 Cowan Tennessee U.S.A.
140 E4 Cowan Downs Queensland Australia
138 F6 Cowangie Victoria Australia
118 K4 Cowan L Saskatchewan Canada
143 D9 Cowan, Lake W Australia Australia
101 P4 Cowan, Mt Montana U.S.A.
121 S7 Cowansville Quebec Canada
138 D3 Coward Springs South Australia Australia
58 C5 Cowargarzê China
138 E2 Cowarie South Australia Australia
9 F2 Cowbit England
103 L2 Cowboy Pass Utah U.S.A.
8 C5 Cowbridge Wales
143 B9 Cowcowing L W Australia Australia
100 G2 Cow Cr Washington U.S.A.
110 H2 Cowden Illinois U.S.A.
13 E1 Cowdenbeath Scotland
101 T9 Cowdrey Colorado U.S.A.
138 D5 Cowell South Australia Australia
94 G8 Cowen West Virginia U.S.A.
139 H7 Cowes Victoria Australia
9 E6 Cowes England
107 P6 Coweta Oklahoma U.S.A.
9 F6 Cowfold England
123 P4 Cow Head Newfoundland Canada
100 E8 Cow Head L California U.S.A.
100 A1 Cowichan, L British Columbia Canada
140 A6 Cowle, Mt N Terr Australia
98 H9 Cowles Nebraska U.S.A.
106 E6 Cowles New Mexico U.S.A.
141 G7 Cowley Queensland Australia
118 D9 Cowley Alberta Canada
101 R5 Cowley Wyoming U.S.A.
100 C3 Cowlitz R Washington U.S.A.
100 D3 Cowlitz Pass Washington U.S.A.
94 H8 Cowpasture R Virginia U.S.A.
112 F2 Cowpens South Carolina U.S.A.
112 F2 Cowpens Nat.Bat.Site South Carolina U.S.A.
139 J5 Cowra New South Wales Australia
130 G4 Coxa, R Brazil
139 H9 Cox Bight Tasmania Australia
13 G4 Coxhoe England
130 C4 Coxibó do Ouro Brazil
130 C6 Coxim Brazil
123 O2 Coxipi L Quebec Canada
130 C4 Coxipó da Ponté Brazil
143 F6 Cox,Mt W Australia Australia
140 D3 Cox R N Terr Australia
95 O4 Coxsackie New York U.S.A.
75 O8 Cox's Bazar Bangladesh
123 P4 Cox's Cove Newfoundland Canada
108 B6 Coyame Mexico
108 D5 Coyanosa Cr Texas U.S.A.
21 P3 Coye-la-Forêt France
107 N6 Coyle Oklahoma U.S.A.
102 C4 Coyote California U.S.A.
102 H6 Coyote L California U.S.A.
102 F5 Coyote Peak California U.S.A.
103 L9 Coyote Pk Arizona U.S.A.
124 D5 Coyote, Pta C Mexico
124 F6 Coyotitán Mexico
98 G9 Cozad Nebraska U.S.A.
44 B2 Cozie Alpi mt Italy
124 C2 Cozón, Cerro mt Mexico
125 Q7 Cozumel, I.de Mexico
100 F3 Crab Cr Washington U.S.A.
141 F1 Crab I Queensland Australia
139 J4 Craboon New South Wales Australia
94 C9 Crab Orchard Kentucky U.S.A.
112 C2 Crab Orchard Tennessee U.S.A.
110 G4 Crab Orchard L Illinois U.S.A.
127 H2 Crab Pond Pt Jamaica
139 H7 Crab Pt Victoria Australia
8 B6 Crackington Haven England
8 D2 Crackleybank England
Cracow see Kraków
141 K7 Cracow Queensland Australia
139 H8 Cradle, Mt Tasmania Australia
138 E4 Cradock South Australia Australia
89 D9 Cradock S Africa
117 G8 Craig Alaska U.S.A.
101 S9 Craig Colorado U.S.A.
113 G13 Craig Florida U.S.A.
99 L9 Craig Missouri U.S.A.
101 O2 Craig Montana U.S.A.
98 K8 Craig Nebraska U.S.A.
15 E3 Craigellachie Scotland
13 E1 Craigend Scotland
15 C5 Craighouse Scotland
12 D2 Craigie Scotland
144 C5 Craigieburn New Zealand
100 J3 Craigmont Idaho U.S.A.
116 R6 Craig, Mt Alaska U.S.A.
118 E7 Craigmyle Alberta Canada
13 E1 Craigrothie Scotland
94 H8 Craigsville Virginia U.S.A.
14 D4 Craiguenamanagh Ireland
119 M7 Craik Saskatchewan Canada
13 F1 Crail Scotland
37 J5 Crailsheim Germany
48 H6 Craiova Romania
13 E2 Cramond Scotland
121 Q8 Cranberry, L New York U.S.A.
119 Q4 Cranberry Portage Manitoba Canada
9 E6 Cranborne England
143 C10 Cranbrook W Australia Australia
117 Q11 Cranbrook British Columbia Canada
9 G5 Cranbrook England
119 R8 Crandall Manitoba Canada
98 J4 Crandall South Dakota U.S.A.
109 L3 Crandall Texas U.S.A.
99 S4 Crandon Wisconsin U.S.A.
127 P6 Crane Barbados
110 C5 Crane Missouri U.S.A.
98 B2 Crane Montana U.S.A.
100 G6 Crane Oregon U.S.A.
108 E4 Crane Texas U.S.A.
100 J5 Crane Cr.Res Idaho U.S.A.
118 H8 Crane L Saskatchewan Canada
119 M9 Crane Valley Saskatchewan Canada
109 K4 Cranfills Gap Texas U.S.A.
9 F5 Cranleigh England
100 A8 Crannell California U.S.A.
13 F2 Cranshaws Scotland
95 Q5 Cranston Rhode I U.S.A.
13 H6 Cranswick England
21 J6 Craon France
22 F5 Craonne France
18 H7 Craponne-sur-Arzon France
98 H1 Crary North Dakota U.S.A.
146 D10 Crary Ice Rise ice rise Antarctica
146 B8 Crary Mts Antarctica
48 H3 Crasna R Romania
48 L4 Crasna Romania
48 H3 Crasnei, Muntii mt Romania
100 C7 Crater L Oregon U.S.A.
100 C7 Crater Lake Nat. Park Oregon U.S.A.
100 D9 Crater Peak mt California U.S.A.
101 M6 Craters of the Moon Nat.Mon Idaho U.S.A.
43 G9 Crati R Italy
130 G9 Crato Brazil
21 L7 Cravant-les Coteaux Indre-et-Loire France
119 N8 Craven Saskatchewan Canada
130 F7 Cravinhos Brazil
128 D2 Cravo Norte R Colombia
6 L3 Crawford oil rig North Sea
12 E3 Crawford Scotland
112 D4 Crawford Georgia U.S.A.
111 H8 Crawford Mississippi U.S.A.
98 C7 Crawford Nebraska U.S.A.
109 K4 Crawford Texas U.S.A.
12 E3 Crawfordjohn Scotland
140 B3 Crawford,Mt N Terr Australia
95 Q2 Crawford Notch New Hampshire U.S.A.
71 D5 Crawford Pt Philippines
110 K1 Crawfordsville Indiana U.S.A.
111 M11 Crawfordville Florida U.S.A.
112 E4 Crawfordville Georgia U.S.A.
9 F5 Crawley England
8 C4 Cray Wales
9 G5 Crayford England
116 P4 Crazy Mts Alaska U.S.A.
101 P3 Crazy Mts Montana U.S.A.
101 P4 Crazy Pk Montana U.S.A.
101 T5 Crazy Woman Cr Wyoming U.S.A.
15 D4 Creag Meagaidh mt Scotland
143 B6 Cream, R W Australia Australia
20 G3 Créances France
118 L4 Crean L Saskatchewan Canada
40 A5 Crêches France
22 B3 Crécy-en-Pontieu France
22 F4 Crécy-sur-Serre France
8 C6 Crediton England
12 D4 Cree Bridge Scotland
106 D4 Creede Colorado U.S.A.
112 J1 Creedmoor North Carolina U.S.A.
101 R9 Creek Colorado U.S.A.
94 H6 Creekside Pennsylvania U.S.A.
113 L9 Creek Village New Providence I Bahamas
114 J6 Cree L Saskatchewan Canada
124 F4 Creel Mexico
119 O9 Creelman Saskatchewan Canada
120 K8 Creemore Ontario Canada
12 D3 Cree, R Scotland
114 J6 Cree River Saskatchewan Canada
12 D4 Creetown Scotland
37 J5 Creglingen Germany
119 P4 Creighton Saskatchewan Canada
98 H7 Creighton Nebraska U.S.A.
120 J6 Creighton Mine Ontario Canada
21 P3 Creil France
44 G1 Crema Italy
47 R14 Cremasti Rhodes Greece
19 O13 Crémieu France
118 C7 Cremona Alberta Canada
44 G1 Crémona Italy
111 F7 Crenshaw Mississippi U.S.A.
18 E8 Créon France
48 F5 Crepaja Serbia Yugoslavia
129 G5 Crepori R Brazil
22 D5 Crépy-en-Valois France
120 K6 Crerar Ontario Canada
42 F4 Cres Croatia
98 G4 Cresbard South Dakota U.S.A.
107 N6 Crescent Oklahoma U.S.A.
113 G10 Crescent Beach Florida U.S.A.
112 J4 Crescent Beach South Carolina U.S.A.
100 A8 Crescent City California U.S.A.
139 K4 Crescent Head New South Wales Australia
113 F8 Crescent L Florida U.S.A.
100 D6 Crescent L Oregon U.S.A.
100 B1 Crescent, L Washington U.S.A.
100 E9 Crescent Mills California U.S.A.
103 J6 Crescent Pk Nevada U.S.A.
99 O6 Cresco Iowa U.S.A.
45 L2 Crespino Italy
8 B4 Cresselly Wales
109 K3 Cresson Texas U.S.A.
139 H8 Cressy Tasmania Australia
139 G7 Cressy Victoria Australia
19 O15 Crest France
94 E6 Crestline Ohio U.S.A.
100 J1 Creston British Columbia Canada
123 R6 Creston Newfoundland Canada
99 M8 Creston Iowa U.S.A.
101 L1 Creston Montana U.S.A.
100 G2 Creston Washington U.S.A.
101 S8 Creston Wyoming U.S.A.
106 E3 Crestone Pk Colorado U.S.A.
111 K11 Crestview Florida U.S.A.
110 J6 Crestview Tennessee U.S.A.
119 M8 Crestwynd Saskatchewan Canada
112 L2 Creswell North Carolina U.S.A.
100 B6 Creswell Oregon U.S.A.
115 K3 Creswell B Northwest Territories Canada
140 D4 Creswell Downs N Terr Australia
139 G7 Creswick Victoria Australia
19 J6 Crêt de la Neige mt France
Crete isld see Kríti isld
99 T8 Crete Illinois U.S.A.
98 K9 Crete Nebraska U.S.A.
98 H3 Crete North Dakota U.S.A.
46 G9 Crete, Sea of Greece
21 J3 Creully France
17 K2 Creus, C Spain
18 G6 Creuse dept France
21 N8 Creuse R France
37 M4 Creussen Germany
37 J1 Creuzburg Germany
45 K2 Crevalcore Italy
21 P2 Crèvecoeur-le-Grand France
21 L3 Crêvecœur France
17 G6 Crevillente Spain
41 H5 Crevola Italy
8 D1 Crewe England
94 J9 Crewe Virginia U.S.A.
8 D6 Crewkerne England
12 D1 Crianlarich Scotland
8 B2 Criccieth Wales
9 E1 Crich England
118 K9 Crichton Saskatchewan Canada
133 H3 Criciuma Brazil
9 E3 Crick England
8 C4 Crickhowell Wales
9 E4 Cricklade England
94 C6 Cridersville Ohio U.S.A.
12 E1 Crieff Scotland
21 N1 Criel-sur-Mer France
15 E6 Criffell mt Scotland
42 F3 Crikvenica Croatia
117 E6 Crillon, Mt Alaska U.S.A.
99 O1 Crilly Ontario Canada
Crimea see Krymskaya Oblast'
37 N2 Crimmitschau Germany
12 C1 Crinan Scotland
15 C4 Crinan Canal Scotland
106 E3 Cripple Creek Colorado U.S.A.
116 J5 Cripple Landing Alaska U.S.A.
9 G6 Cripps's Corner England
21 L2 Criquetot-l'Esneval France
48 G4 Crişana Romania
130 F5 Cristalina Brazil
129 H6 Cristalino R Brazil
38 F8 Cristallo mt Italy
126 H10 Cristóbal Colón, Pico mt Colombia
48 J4 Cristuru Secuiesc Romania
48 G4 Crişul Alb R Romania
48 G4 Crişul Negru R Romania
48 H4 Crişul Repede R Romania
94 C8 Crittenden Kentucky U.S.A.
33 P5 Crivitz Germany
99 S4 Crivitz Wisconsin U.S.A.
46 E3 Crna R Macedonia
38 L9 Črna Slovenia
Crna Gora see Montenegro
46 E2 Crna Gora mt Macedonia/Serbia
46 E2 Crna Trava Serbia Yugoslavia
46 D3 Crni Drim R Macedonia
38 M9 Črni-vrh mt Slovenia
14 B3 Croagh Patrick Mt Ireland
139 J7 Croajingolong Nat. Park Victoria Australia
42 G4 Croatia rep S Europe
41 O5 Croce, C mt Italy
43 G11 Croce, S., C Sicily
110 D4 Crocker Missouri U.S.A.
70 D2 Crocker Ra Borneo
12 E3 Crocketford Scotland
109 M4 Crockett Texas U.S.A.
9 G5 Crockham Hill England
21 K4 Crocy France
38 F8 Croda Rossa mt Italy
110 J4 Crofton Kentucky U.S.A.
98 J7 Crofton Nebraska U.S.A.
142 D5 Crofton,Mt W Australia Australia
95 M3 Croghan New York U.S.A.
19 O18 Croisette, C France
20 E7 Croisic,le France
22 D3 Croisilles France
145 D4 Croisilles Harbour New Zealand
127 H5 Croix des Bouquets Haiti
19 P15 Croix Haute, Col de la pass France
21 H5 Croixille,la France
21 M7 Croix,la France
122 B2 Croix, L.à la Quebec Canada
122 E8 Croix R New Brunswick Canada
22 D5 Croix-St.Ouen, la France
21 N3 Croix-st.Leufroy,la France
120 K8 Croker, Cape Ontario Canada
140 B2 Croker Hill N Terr Australia
140 C1 Croker I N Terr Australia
15 D3 Cromarty Scotland
15 D3 Cromarty Firth Scotland
138 B2 Crombie, Mt South Australia Australia
119 Q9 Cromer Manitoba Canada
9 H2 Cromer England
144 B6 Cromwell New Zealand
99 O3 Cromwell Minnesota U.S.A.
144 C5 Cronadun New Zealand
37 K5 Cronheim Germany
13 F5 Crook Cumbria England
13 G4 Crook Durham England
98 D9 Crook Colorado U.S.A.
107 K4 Crooked Cr Kansas U.S.A.
100 G7 Crooked Cr Oregon U.S.A.
126 G3 Crooked I Bahamas
126 G3 Crooked I.Passage Bahamas
123 Q5 Crooked L Newfoundland Canada
113 F10 Crooked L Florida U.S.A.
117 M8 Crooked R British Columbia Canada
100 E5 Crooked R Oregon U.S.A.
119 O6 Crooked River Saskatchewan Canada
13 F2 Crookham England
14 B5 Crookhaven Ireland
109 M2 Crook, L Texas U.S.A.
13 F5 Crooklands England
12 E1 Crook of Devon Scotland
98 K2 Crookston Minnesota U.S.A.
98 F7 Crookston Nebraska U.S.A.
94 E7 Crooksville Ohio U.S.A.
139 J5 Crookwell New South Wales Australia
14 C4 Croom Ireland
113 E9 Croom Florida U.S.A.
139 K3 Croppa Cr New South Wales Australia
9 E3 Cropredy England
123 R2 Croque Newfoundland Canada
141 G3 Crosbie R Queensland Australia
99 N3 Crosby Minnesota U.S.A.
111 E10 Crosby Mississippi U.S.A.
98 C1 Crosby North Dakota U.S.A.
109 M6 Crosby Texas U.S.A.
108 F2 Crosbyton Texas U.S.A.
8 D5 Cross England
85 F7 Cross R Nigeria
20 F7 Crossac France
12 C2 Crossaig Scotland
87 B10 Cross, C Namibia
113 D8 Cross City Florida U.S.A.
111 E8 Crossett Arkansas U.S.A.
13 F4 Cross Fell England
118 C7 Crossfield Alberta Canada
13 E1 Crossgates Scotland
8 C3 Cross Gates Wales
8 B4 Cross Hands Wales
113 K12 Cross Harbour Bahamas
14 C5 Crosshaven Ireland
12 D3 Crosshill Scotland
112 F3 Cross Hill South Carolina U.S.A.
113 K11 Crossing Rocks Bahamas
121 O8 Cross, L Ontario Canada
111 C9 Cross L Louisiana U.S.A.
119 U4 Cross Lake Manitoba Canada
144 D5 Crossley, Mt New Zealand
118 D4 Cross L. Prov. Park Alberta Canada
12 B5 Crossmaglen N Ireland
103 K7 Crossman Pk Arizona U.S.A.
12 E4 Crossmichael Scotland
14 B2 Crossmolina Ireland
106 B1 Cross Mountain Colorado U.S.A.
109 H3 Cross Plains Texas U.S.A.
94 B1 Cross Village Michigan U.S.A.
110 L6 Crossville Tennessee U.S.A.
116 P5 Crosswind L Alaska U.S.A.
45 J2 Crostolo R Italy
94 E3 Croswell Michigan U.S.A.
110 L3 Crothersville Indiana U.S.A.
43 H9 Crotone Italy
21 O1 Crotoy,le France
37 O3 Crottendorf Germany
100 K5 Crouch Idaho U.S.A.
9 G4 Crouch, R England
22 E5 Crouy France
21 L7 Crouzilles France
101 S4 Crow Agency Montana U.S.A.
139 H4 Crowal R New South Wales Australia
9 G5 Crowborough England
8 C5 Crowcombe England
106 F1 Crow Cr Colorado U.S.A.
111 F7 Crowder Mississippi U.S.A.
107 P6 Crowder Oklahoma U.S.A.
118 F1 Crowduck L. Manitoba Canada
139 L4 Crowdy Hd New South Wales Australia
108 H2 Crowell Texas U.S.A.
139 G7 Crowes Victoria Australia
101 Q6 Crowheart Wyoming U.S.A.
139 H4 Crowl R New South Wales Australia
9 F2 Crowland England
13 H6 Crowle England
106 G3 Crowley Colorado U.S.A.
111 D11 Crowley Louisiana U.S.A.
102 F4 Crowley, L California U.S.A.
94 E8 Crown City Ohio U.S.A.
103 M7 Crown King Arizona U.S.A.
106 B6 Crown Point New Mexico U.S.A.
95 O3 Crown Point New York U.S.A.
115 L4 Crown Prince Frederick I Northwest Territories Canada
127 M2 Crown Pt Tobago
99 T8 Crown Pt Indiana U.S.A.
101 O3 Crow Peak Montana U.S.A.
141 K7 Crow's Nest Queensland Australia
118 C9 Crowsnest Pass Alberta/Br Col Canada
99 M3 Crow Wing R Minnesota U.S.A.
13 G4 Croxdale England
8 B5 Croyde England
141 F4 Croydon Queensland Australia
142 C5 Croydon W Australia Australia
9 F5 Croydon England
144 B7 Croydon New Zealand
83 L13 Croy, Î de Kerguelen Indian Oc
94 J8 Crozet Virginia U.S.A.
81 D9 Crozet Basin Indian Oc
81 C10 Crozet, Îs Indian Oc
81 B10 Crozet Plateau Indian Oc
114 G2 Crozier Chan Northwest Territories Canada
20 B5 Crozon France
19 N15 Cruas France
126 D3 Cruces Cuba
128 C2 Cruces, Pta pt Colombia
22 L4 Cruchten Luxembourg
94 H7 Crucible Pennsylvania U.S.A.
15 G3 Cruden B Scotland
8 D2 Crudgington England
8 D4 Crudwell England
111 F8 Cruger Mississippi U.S.A.
21 M4 Crûlai France
14 E2 Crumlin N Ireland
100 F7 Crump L Oregon U.S.A.
19 Q12 Cruseilles France
22 K5 Crusnes France
133 E4 Cruz Argentina
133 G3 Cruz Alta Brazil
131 D3 Cruz del Eje Argentina
130 G8 Cruzeiro Brazil
133 G2 Cruzeiro do Oeste Brazil
128 D5 Cruzeiro do Sul Brazil
133 C3 Cruz Grande Chile
128 C3 Cruz, La Colombia
18 G9 Cruzy France
117 M8 Crysdale, Mt British Columbia Canada
106 C2 Crystal R Colorado U.S.A.
103 K5 Crystal Nevada U.S.A.
98 J1 Crystal North Dakota U.S.A.
113 E9 Crystal B Florida U.S.A.
138 E5 Crystal Brook South Australia Australia
119 T9 Crystal City Manitoba Canada
108 H7 Crystal City Texas U.S.A.
99 S3 Crystal Falls Michigan U.S.A.
99 S7 Crystal L Illinois U.S.A.
99 U5 Crystal L Michigan U.S.A.
99 N6 Crystal Lake Iowa U.S.A.
113 E9 Crystal River Florida U.S.A.
119 M6 Crystal Springs Saskatchewan Canada
111 F9 Crystal Springs Mississippi U.S.A.
99 U6 Crystal Valley Michigan U.S.A.
48 F4 Csanytelek Hungary
48 E3 Csepel Sziget R Hungary
48 F4 Csongrád co Hungary
48 F4 Csongrád Hungary
48 D3 Csorna Hungary
48 F4 Csorvas Hungary
48 E3 Csóványos mt Hungary
48 D4 Csurgó Hungary
127 L9 Cúa Venezuela
88 F9 Cuambo Mozambique
87 D9 Cuando R Angola
87 C9 Cuangar Angola
87 C7 Cuango Angola
86 C7 Cuango Zaire
87 B7 Cuanza R Angola
67 A7 Cua Rao Vietnam
133 F4 Cuareim Brazil
131 F3 Cuaro R Uruguay
133 E4 Cuarto R Argentina
124 H4 Cuatro Ciénegas de Carranza Mexico
68 H4 Cua Tung Vietnam
124 F3 Cuauhtémoc Mexico
124 G8 Cuautitlán Mexico
125 K8 Cuautla Mexico
16 B6 Cuba Portugal
110 F1 Cuba Illinois U.S.A.
107 N2 Cuba Kansas U.S.A.
110 E3 Cuba Missouri U.S.A.
106 D5 Cuba New Mexico U.S.A.
94 J4 Cuba New York U.S.A.
126 D4 Cuba rep W Indies
103 M10 Cubabi, Cerro pk Mexico
99 Q7 Cuba City Wisconsin U.S.A.
127 M9 Cubagua, I Venezuela
143 B10 Cuballing W Australia Australia
87 C9 Cubango R Angola
130 F8 Cubatão Brazil
119 N4 Cub Hills Saskatchewan Canada
127 K10 Cubiro Venezuela
48 J6 Cuca Romania
133 C6 Cucao, B.de Chile
133 F4 Cuchilla de Haedo hills Uruguay
9 F5 Cuckfield England
9 E1 Cuckney England
94 K9 Cuckoo Virginia U.S.A.
87 C8 Cucumbi Angola
124 D2 Cucurpe Mexico
128 D2 Cúcuta Colombia
99 T7 Cudahy Wisconsin U.S.A.
76 D5 Cuddalore India
76 D3 Cuddapah India
141 F7 Cuddapan,L Queensland Australia
102 G6 Cuddeback L California U.S.A.
113 F13 Cudjoe Key isld Florida U.S.A.
119 M6 Cudworth Saskatchewan Canada
143 C7 Cue W Australia Australia
16 E3 Cuéllar Spain
128 C4 Cuenca Ecuador
71 E4 Cuenca Philippines
17 F4 Cuenca Spain
17 F5 Cuenca prov Spain
124 H5 Cuencamé de Ceniceros Mexico
17 F4 Cuenca, Serrania de mts Spain
125 K8 Cuernavaca Mexico
109 K6 Cuero Texas U.S.A.
19 Q18 Cuers France
106 F6 Cuervo New Mexico U.S.A.
102 D6 Cuesta Pass California U.S.A.
126 G4 Cueto Cuba
17 F7 Cuevas del Almanzora Spain
133 E2 Cuevo Bolivia
22 E5 Cuffies France
123 N2 Cuff L Quebec Canada
19 P18 Cuges-les-Pins France
48 H5 Cugir Romania
43 B8 Cuglieri Sardinia
20 G5 Cuguen France
130 C4 Cuiabá Brazil
14 D2 Cuilcagh mt N Ireland
15 B3 Cuillin Hills Scotland
87 C7 Cuilo R Angola
59 J2 Cuiluan China
87 C8 Cuima Angola
22 D2 Cuinchy France
36 B4 Cuint Germany
22 E5 Cuise-la-Motte France
130 H9 Cuité Brazil
130 H6 Cuité, R Brazil
87 C9 Cuito R Angola
87 C9 Cuito Cuanavale Angola
128 F4 Cuiuni R Brazil
110 E2 Cuivre R Missouri U.S.A.
71 E7 Cujangan isld Philippines
48 H6 Cujmir Romania
69 F10 Cukai Malaysia
78 J3 Çukurca Turkey
68 H4 Cu Lai Vietnam
18 G6 Culan France
68 J5 Cu Lao Bo Bai isld Vietnam
68 J5 Cu Lao Cham isld Vietnam
68 J7 Cu Lao Hon isld Vietnam
68 J5 Cu Lao Re isld Vietnam
71 F5 Culasi Panay Philippines
98 B1 Culbertson Montana U.S.A.
98 F9 Culbertson Nebraska U.S.A.
139 H6 Culcairn New South Wales Australia
22 G4 Cul-des-Sarts Belgium
106 E4 Culebra Pk Colorado U.S.A.
16 C3 Culebra, Sa de la mts Spain
25 D5 Culemborg Netherlands
87 C9 Culevai Angola
141 H8 Culgoa R N S W/Qnsld Australia
139 H3 Culgoa, R New S Wales/Queensland
124 F5 Culiacán Mexico
124 F5 Culiacancito Mexico
71 D5 Culion Philippines
129 H6 Culiseu R Brazil
17 F7 Cúllar de Baza Spain
139 J5 Cullarin Rge New South Wales Australia
15 F3 Cullen Scotland
17 G5 Cullera Spain
107 M4 Cullison Kansas U.S.A.
111 K7 Cullman Alabama U.S.A.
141 G5 Culloden R Queensland Australia
8 C6 Cullompton England
125 M2 Culmi Honduras
8 D3 Culmington England
19 P13 Culoz France
94 J8 Culpeper Virginia U.S.A.
128 A7 Culpepper isld Galapagos Is
15 E5 Culter Fell Scotland
129 H6 Culuene R Brazil
99 U8 Culver Indiana U.S.A.
107 N3 Culver Kansas U.S.A.
100 D5 Culver Oregon U.S.A.
144 D5 Culverden New Zealand
143 E10 Culver,Pt W Australia Australia
129 K4 Cuma, B.de Brazil
47 H4 Cumalı Turkey
128 F1 Cumana Venezuela
127 N9 Cumanacoa Venezuela
47 J6 Cumaovası Turkey
130 E6 Cumari Brazil
117 L11 Cumberland British Columbia Canada
99 M8 Cumberland Iowa U.S.A.
94 D9 Cumberland Kentucky U.S.A.
94 J7 Cumberland Maryland U.S.A.
94 F7 Cumberland Ohio U.S.A.
110 J5 Cumberland R Tennessee U.S.A.
94 J9 Cumberland Virginia U.S.A.
99 O4 Cumberland Wisconsin U.S.A.
Cumberland, C see Nahoï, C
110 J5 Cumberland City Tennessee U.S.A.
94 D10 Cumberland Gap Tenn/Virg U.S.A.
119 P5 Cumberland House Saskatchewan Canada
113 F7 Cumberland I Georgia U.S.A.
141 J5 Cumberland Is Queensland Australia
119 P4 Cumberland L Saskatchewan Canada
94 B10 Cumberland, L Kentucky U.S.A.
110 L5 Cumberland, L Kentucky U.S.A.
94 D10 Cumberland Mt Tennessee U.S.A.
115 N4 Cumberland Pen Northwest Territories Canada
111 K7 Cumberland Plateau Alabama U.S.A.
99 R2 Cumberland Pt Michigan U.S.A.
94 D10 Cumberland R Kentucky U.S.A.
94 J7 Cumberland Res Pennsylvania U.S.A.
115 N4 Cumberland Sound Northwest Territories Canada
140 D1 Cumberland Str N Terr Australia
12 E2 Cumbernauld Scotland
139 J3 Cumborah New South Wales Australia
133 C7 Cumbrera mt Chile
13 E4 Cumbria co England
76 D3 Cumbum India
109 M2 Cumby Texas U.S.A.
44 B2 Cumiana Italy
129 G4 Cumina R Brazil
129 G3 Cuminapanema R Brazil
13 E4 Cummertrees Scotland
112 C3 Cumming Georgia U.S.A.
102 A2 Cummings California U.S.A.
98 J2 Cummings North Dakota U.S.A.
138 D5 Cummins South Australia Australia
142 F4 Cummins Ra W Australia Australia
139 J5 Cumnock New South Wales Australia
12 D3 Cumnock Scotland
124 E2 Cumpas Mexico
78 D3 Çumra Turkey
124 E3 Cumuripa Mexico
130 H5 Cumuruxatiba Brazil
127 O2 Cumuto Trinidad
126 E3 Cunagua Cuba
129 H3 Cunani Brazil
124 D6 Cuñaño Mexico
131 G3 Cuñapiru R Uruguay
133 C5 Cunco Chile
142 D5 Cuncudgerie Hill W Australia Australia
143 B9 Cunderdin W Australia Australia
128 D3 Cundinamarca div Colombia
87 B9 Cunene R Angola
44 C3 Cúneo Italy
138 C4 Cungena South Australia Australia
17 H6 Cunillera isld Balearic Is
18 H7 Cunlhat France
141 H8 Cunnamulla Queensland Australia
107 M4 Cunningham Kansas U.S.A.
100 G3 Cunningham Washington U.S.A.
127 O2 Cunupia Trinidad
21 K7 Cuon France
119 N8 Cupar Saskatchewan Canada
13 E1 Cupar Scotland
128 C2 Cupica, G.de Colombia
46 E1 Čuprija Serbia Yugoslavia
100 J4 Cuprum Idaho U.S.A.
124 D5 Cupula, P Mexico
71 B1 Cur Halmahera Indonesia
129 G7 Curabá R Brazil
129 L5 Curaçá Brazil
126 B1 Curaçao isld Neth Antilles
131 B7 Curacáutin Chile
131 D7 Curaco, R Argentina
131 E6 Cura Malal, Cerro pk Argentina
133 C5 Curanilahue Chile
128 C4 Curaray R Peru/Ecuador
131 B4 Curaumilla, Pta de C Chile
48 K6 Curcani Romania
21 K7 Curçay-sur-Dive France
138 D4 Curdlawidny Lagoon South Australia Australia
9 E2 Curdworth England
18 H5 Cure R France
106 C3 Curecanti Nat. Recreation Area Colorado U.S.A.
83 M13 Curepipe Mauritius
133 C5 Curepto Chile
127 O10 Curiapo Venezuela
131 B5 Curico Chile
131 D8 Curico, L Argentina
128 E4 Curicuriari R Brazil
83 J12 Curieuse I Seychelles
130 J9 Curimataú R Brazil
143 A7 Curious,Mt W Australia Australia
128 D3 Curiplaya Colombia
133 H3 Curitiba Brazil
130 E10 Curitibanos Brazil
100 G1 Curlew Washington U.S.A.
141 J5 Curlew I Queensland Australia
139 K4 Curlewis New South Wales Australia
111 H12 Curlew Is Louisiana U.S.A.
116 F5 Curlew L Alaska U.S.A.
123 L3 Curlew Pt Quebec Canada
123 O5 Curling Newfoundland Canada
138 E4 Curnamona South Australia Australia
44 F2 Curone R Italy
139 K4 Currabubula New South Wales Australia
130 H9 Currais Novas Brazil
138 C2 Curralulla R South Australia Australia
121 Q7 Curran Ontario Canada
94 D2 Curran Michigan U.S.A.
103 J3 Currant Nevada U.S.A.
139 G4 Curranyalpa New South Wales Australia
141 F7 Currawilla Queensland Australia
126 F2 Current Eleuthera Bahamas
110 E4 Current R Missouri U.S.A.
113 L12 Current I Bahamas
139 G7 Currie Tasmania Australia
13 E2 Currie Scotland
99 L5 Currie Minnesota U.S.A.
103 K1 Currie Nevada U.S.A.
112 J3 Currie North Carolina U.S.A.
138 B2 Currie Cr., The South Australia Australia
119 U1 Currie L Manitoba Canada
140 B7 Currie,Mt N Terr Australia
112 L1 Currituck North Carolina U.S.A.
112 M1 Currituck Sound North Carolina U.S.A.
139 K6 Currockbilly, Mt New South Wales Australia
110 E2 Curryville Missouri U.S.A.
37 L2 Cursdorf Germany
45 L1 Curtarolo Italy
48 J5 Curtea de Argeş Romania
48 G4 Curtici Romania
143 D9 Curtin W Australia Australia
100 B6 Curtin Oregon U.S.A.
140 B7 Curtin Springs N Terr Australia
16 B1 Curtis Spain
111 C9 Curtis Louisiana U.S.A.
99 V3 Curtis Michigan U.S.A.
98 F9 Curtis Nebraska U.S.A.
141 L6 Curtis Chan Gt Barrier Reef Australia
139 H7 Curtis Group islds Tasmania Australia
141 K6 Curtis I Queensland Australia
137 R8 Curtis I Kermadec Is Pacific Oc
94 D2 Curtisville Michigan U.S.A.
129 G4 Curuá Brazil
129 H5 Curuaés R Brazil
129 H3 Curuá, I Brazil
129 G3 Curuapanema R Brazil
128 D5 Curuçá R Brazil
129 J4 Curuca Brazil
133 F2 Curuguaty Paraguay
69 F14 Curup Sumatra
129 J4 Cururupu Brazil
131 F2 Curuzú Cuatiá Argentina
129 K7 Curvelo Brazil
94 J6 Curwensville Pennsylvania U.S.A.
14 E1 Cushendall N Ireland
14 E1 Cushendun N Ireland
99 M3 Cushing Minnesota U.S.A.
107 O6 Cushing Oklahoma U.S.A.
111 B10 Cushing Texas U.S.A.
110 E6 Cushman Arkansas U.S.A.
101 Q3 Cushman Montana U.S.A.
100 A6 Cushman Oregon U.S.A.
100 B2 Cushman, L Washington U.S.A.
124 F3 Cusihuiráchic Mexico
45 H3 Cusna, Mt Italy
18 H6 Cusset France
112 C5 Cusseta Georgia U.S.A.
99 O1 Cusson Minnesota U.S.A.
144 D5 Cust New Zealand
101 S3 Custer Montana U.S.A.
98 C6 Custer South Dakota U.S.A.
107 M6 Custer City Oklahoma U.S.A.
45 J1 Custoza Italy
117 O8 Cutbank R Alberta Canada
101 N1 Cut Bank Montana U.S.A.
119 P5 Cut Beaver L Saskatchewan Canada
111 A8 Cuthand Cr Texas U.S.A.
112 C6 Cuthbert Georgia U.S.A.
98 H6 Cuthbert South Dakota U.S.A.
108 F3 Cuthbert Texas U.S.A.
140 E4 Cuthbert, Mt Queensland Australia
45 J3 Cutigliano Italy
118 H6 Cut Knife Saskatchewan Canada
120 H6 Cutler Ontario Canada
116 H3 Cutler R Alaska U.S.A.
102 E5 Cutler California U.S.A.
95 T9 Cutler Maine U.S.A.
14 C3 Cutra, L Ireland
22 E4 Cuts France
139 H3 Cuttaburra R New South Wales Australia
75 L8 Cuttack India
103 O8 Cutter Arizona U.S.A.
81 H7 Cuvier Basin Indian Oc
143 A6 Cuvier,C W Australia Australia
145 E2 Cuvier I New Zealand
87 C8 Cuvo R Angola
32 J5 Cuxhaven Germany
Cu Xu, I see Quan Dao Co To
94 F5 Cuyahoga R Ohio U.S.A.
94 F5 Cuyahoga Falls Ohio U.S.A.
102 E6 Cuyama R California U.S.A.
71 E3 Cuyapo Luzon Philippines
71 E5 Cuyo isld Philippines
71 E5 Cuyo East Passage Philippines
71 E5 Cuyo West Passage Philippines
99 N3 Cuyuna Minnesota U.S.A.
128 G2 Cuyuni R Guyana
125 N2 Cuyu Tigni Nicaragua
128 E8 Cuzco mt Bolivia
128 D6 Cuzco Peru
42 H5 Čvrsnica mt Bosnia-Herzegovina
8 C4 Cwmbran Wales
88 B3 Cyangugu Rwanda
31 H3 Cybinka Poland
Cyclades islds see Kikládhes islds
139 H9 Cygnet Tasmania Australia
119 W2 Cygnet L Manitoba Canada
138 D6 Cygnet River South Australia Australia
118 B5 Cynthia Alberta Canada
110 M3 Cynthiana Kentucky U.S.A.
110 G4 Cypress Illinois U.S.A.
111 C10 Cypress Louisiana U.S.A.
109 M6 Cypress Texas U.S.A.
111 A8 Cypress Cr Texas U.S.A.
109 N3 Cypress Cr., Lit Texas U.S.A.
118 H9 Cypress Hills Saskatchewan Canada
118 G9 Cypress Hills Interprovincial Parks Alberta Canada
113 F9 Cypress L Florida U.S.A.
119 S9 Cypress River Manitoba Canada
79 D4 Cyprus rep Mediterranean Sea
84 G4 Cyrenaica reg Libya
Cyrene see Shaḥḥāt
77 A5 Cyrus oil well Persian Gulf
115 N5 Cyrus Field B Northwest Territories Canada
22 E2 Cysoing France
31 J2 Czaplinek Poland
118 G6 Czar Alberta Canada
31 M4 Czarna R Poland
31 O2 Czarna Blatestocka Poland
31 K2 Czarne Poland
31 K3 Czarnków Poland
31 M6 Czarny Dunajec Poland
31 M6 Czchów Poland
Czechoslovakia see Czech Republic and Slovakia
31 J6 Czech Rep rep Europe
31 K3 Czempin Poland
31 O3 Czeremcha Poland
Czernowitz see Chernovtsy
31 K2 Czersk Poland
31 J3 Czerwiensk Poland
31 L5 Czestochowa Poland
31 J2 Człopa Poland
31 K2 Człuchów Poland
31 N3 Czyżew Poland

D

36 D2 **Daaden** Germany
65 F2 **Da'an** China
71 F5 **Daanbantayan** Cebu Philippines
122 B7 **Daaquam** Quebec Canada
67 B2 **Daba** China
79 F7 **Dabāb, J. Ed** *mt* Jordan
127 J9 **Dabajuro** Venezuela
85 D7 **Dabakala** Ivory Coast
58 D4 **Daban Shan** *mt* China
48 E3 **Dabas** Hungary
67 C1 **Daba Shan** *mts* China
86 G3 **Dabat** Ethiopia
128 C2 **Dabeiba** Colombia
68 C4 **Dabein** Burma
33 P5 **Dabel** Germany
74 E7 **Dabhoi** India
31 H2 **Dąbie** Poland
67 E1 **Dabie Shan** *mts* China
79 G10 **Dabl Mushāsh** *well* Saudi Arabia
36 C6 **Dabo** France
85 B6 **Dabola** Guinea
85 D7 **Dabou** Ivory Coast
85 D7 **Daboya** Ghana
36 C1 **Dabringhausen** Germany
31 O2 **Dąbrowa** Poland
31 L5 **Dąbrowa Górnicza** Poland
31 M2 **Dąbrówno** Poland
65 D7 **Dabu** China
67 E4 **Dabu** China
65 F2 **Dabusu Pao** *L* China
Dacca *see* **Dhaka**
65 C5 **Dachang** China
37 L7 **Dachau** Germany
37 L7 **Dachauer Moos** *marshes* Germany
37 K4 **Dachsbach** Germany
38 J7 **Dachstein** *mt* Austria
38 J7 **Dachstein-Gebirge** *mts* Austria
31 J6 **Dačice** Czech Rep
107 M5 **Dacoma** Oklahoma U.S.A.
128 G3 **Dadanawa** Guyana
79 H2 **Dādāt** Syria
78 D1 **Daday** Turkey
113 E9 **Dade City** Florida U.S.A.
111 L9 **Dadeville** Alabama U.S.A.
74 B4 **Dadhar** Pakistan
65 D7 **Dadian** China
65 G3 **Dadianzi** China
71 C3 **Dadi, Tg** *C* W Irian
68 J1 **Dadong** China
18 G9 **Dadou** *R* France
27 H11 **Dådran** Sweden
74 E8 **Dadra & Nagar Haveli** *Union Terr* India
74 G4 **Dadri** India
74 B5 **Dadu** Pakistan
68 H7 **Da Dung** *R* Vietnam
48 L6 **Dăeni** Romania
65 C4 **Da'erhao** China
140 D7 **Daer,Mt** N Terr Australia
71 F3 **Daet** Philippines
67 B3 **Dafang** China
80 F1 **Dafna** Israel
119 N7 **Dafoe** Saskatchewan Canada
68 B4 **Daga** *R* Burma
27 C11 **Dagali** Norway
85 A5 **Dagana** Senegal
47 K5 **Dağardı** Turkey
71 A1 **Dagasuli** Indonesia
30 D1 **Dagebüll** Germany
9 G4 **Dagenham** England
53 G11 **Dagestanskaya Respublika** Russian Federation
102 H7 **Daggett** California U.S.A.
99 T4 **Daggett** Michigan U.S.A.
78 K5 **Daghgharah, Al** Iraq
27 G12 **Daglösen** Sweden
98 B1 **Dagmar** Montana U.S.A.
65 D5 **Dagu** China
67 A3 **Daguan** China
21 K7 **Daguenière,la** France
71 E2 **Dagupan** Luzon Philippines
94 J5 **Dagus Mines** Pennsylvania U.S.A.
68 C4 **Dagwin** Burma
141 G4 **Dagworth** Queensland Australia
66 E6 **Dagzê** China
79 E10 **Dahab** Egypt
117 L4 **Dahadinni** *R* Northwest Territories Canada
86 H2 **Dahalak' Archipelago** Eritrea
67 D5 **Dahao Dao** *isld* China
65 J1 **Dahezhen** China
59 H2 **Da Hinggan Ling** *mt ra* China
32 G10 **Dahle** Germany
36 B3 **Dahleim** Germany
33 R10 **Dahlen** Germany
33 N6 **Dahlenburg** Germany
33 S8 **Dahlewitz** Germany
95 K8 **Dahlgren** Virginia U.S.A.
112 C3 **Dahlonega** Georgia U.S.A.
33 O4 **Dahme** Germany
33 T8 **Dahme** *R* Germany
33 S9 **Dahme** Germany
33 R5 **Dahmen** Germany
33 O4 **Dahmeshöved** Germany
36 D5 **Dahn** Germany
72 F3 **Dahnā, Ad** *reg* Saudi Arabia
74 F7 **Dāhod** India
78 J3 **Dahok** Iraq
Dahomey *rep see* **Benin, Rep. of**
66 B4 **Dahongliutan** China
65 E4 **Dahongqi** China
67 D1 **Dahong Shan** *mts* China
33 N7 **Dähre** Germany
78 J3 **Dahūk** *prov* Iraq
78 J3 **Dahuk** Iraq
65 E4 **Dahushan** China
139 G5 **Dahwilly** New South Wales Australia
71 O8 **Dai** *isld* Indonesia
48 K7 **Daia** Romania
65 C5 **Daicheng** China
65 B4 **Dai Hai** *L* China
69 G13 **Daik** Indonesia
68 C4 **Daik-U** Burma
75 J4 **Dailekh** Nepal
121 T3 **Dailleboust, L** Quebec Canada
60 G9 **Daimanji-san** *mt* Japan
16 E5 **Daimiel** Spain
109 N2 **Daingerfield** Texas U.S.A.
61 K10 **Dainichiga-take** *pk* Japan
66 F5 **Dainkog** China
141 H3 **Daintree** *R* Queensland Australia
141 H3 **Daintree** Queensland Australia
61 K11 **Daiō** Japan
65 E2 **Daiqin Tal** China
Dairen *see* **Dalian**
84 J4 **Dairût** Egypt
100 D7 **Dairy** Oregon U.S.A.
143 B7 **Dairy Creek** W Australia Australia
60 G10 **Dai-sen** *mt* Japan
60 G10 **Dai sen-Oki Nat. Park** Japan
109 N5 **Daisetta** Texas U.S.A.
67 G1 **Dai Shan** *isld* China
67 G1 **Daishan** China
129 K5 **Dais Irmaos, Serra** *mts* Brazil
100 G1 **Daisy** Washington U.S.A.
58 F4 **Dai Xian** China
Daiyue *see* **Shanyin**
67 F4 **Daiyun Shan** *mts* China
127 J5 **Dajabón** Dominican Rep
140 E5 **Dajarra** Queensland Australia
58 D5 **Dajin Chuan** *R* China
67 G2 **Dajing** China
45 P1 **Dajla** Croatia
70 D5 **Daju** Kalimantan
85 A6 **Dakar** Senegal
67 D4 **Dakengkou** China
67 D5 **Dakengkou** China
68 H5 **Dak Gle** Vietnam
85 A4 **Dakhla, Ad** Western Sahara
84 H4 **Dakhla Oasis** Egypt
68 H5 **Dak Kon** Vietnam
69 A9 **Dakoank** Nicobar Is
85 F6 **Dakoro** Niger
99 R7 **Dakota** Illinois U.S.A.
99 P6 **Dakota** Minnesota U.S.A.
99 M7 **Dakota City** Iowa U.S.A.
98 K7 **Dakota City** Nebraska U.S.A.
46 D2 **Dakovica** Serbia Yugoslavia
48 E5 **Dakovo** Croatia
28 D3 **Dal** Denmark
27 E11 **Dal** Norway
87 D8 **Dala** Angola
27 J11 **Dalä** *L* Sweden
41 L3 **Dalaas Tal** Austria
85 B6 **Dalaba** Guinea
65 A4 **Dalad Qi** China
Dalai *see* **Da'an**
Dalai Nor *L see* **Hulun Nur** *L*
58 G3 **Dalai Nur** *L* China
27 G11 **Dala-Järna** Sweden
78 B3 **Dalaman** *R* Turkey
58 D3 **Dalandzadgad** Mongolia
71 E5 **Dalanganem** *islds* Philippines
27 K12 **Dalarö** Sweden
70 B3 **Dalat** Sarawak
68 J7 **Da Lat** Vietnam
71 C6 **Dalawan B** Philippines
77 J5 **Dalbandin** Pakistan
15 E6 **Dalbeattie** Scotland
141 H5 **Dalbeg** Queensland Australia
27 F13 **Dalbosjön** *L* Sweden
141 K7 **Dalby** Queensland Australia
28 F5 **Dalby** Denmark
27 F11 **Dalby** Sweden
12 D5 **Dalby** I of Man U.K.
28 E3 **Dalbyneder** Denmark
28 E3 **Dalbyover** Denmark
27 A10 **Dale** Norway
27 A11 **Dale** Norway
110 K3 **Dale** Indiana U.S.A.
100 G5 **Dale** Oregon U.S.A.
94 J6 **Dale** Pennsylvania U.S.A.
109 K6 **Dale** Texas U.S.A.
8 A4 **Dale** Wales
110 L5 **Dale Hollow L** Kentucky/Tennessee
118 D8 **Dalemead** Alberta Canada
143 B9 **Dale,Mt** W Australia Australia
25 G3 **Dalen** Netherlands
28 B7 **Daler** Denmark
31 M5 **Daleszyce** Poland
68 A2 **Dalet** *R* Burma
68 A3 **Dalet** Burma
68 A2 **Daletme** Burma
110 L1 **Daleville** Indiana U.S.A.
27 H10 **Dalfors** Sweden
25 F4 **Dalfsen** Netherlands
143 B8 **Dalgaranger Hill** W Australia Australia
139 J6 **Dalgety** New South Wales Australia
12 E1 **Dalginross** Scotland
141 F5 **Dalgonally** Queensland Australia
108 B7 **Dalhart** Texas U.S.A.
114 G3 **Dalhousie, C** Northwest Territories Canada
65 A7 **Dali** China
59 H4 **Dalian** China
58 D6 **Daliang Shan** China
65 E5 **Dalian Wan** *B* China
71 G7 **Daliao** Philippines
106 D7 **Dalies** New Mexico U.S.A.
65 A6 **Dali He** *R* China
Dalinghe *see* **Jin Xian**
80 D3 **Daliyat el Karmil** Israel
65 G4 **Dalizi** China
48 E5 **Dalj** Croatia
15 E5 **Dalkeith** Scotland
14 E3 **Dalkey** Ireland
141 K7 **Dallarnil** Queensland Australia
119 U7 **Dallas** Manitoba Canada
111 M8 **Dallas** Georgia U.S.A.
100 B5 **Dallas** Oregon U.S.A.
109 N10 **Dallas** Texas U.S.A.
99 P4 **Dallas** Wisconsin U.S.A.
99 N8 **Dallas Center** Iowa U.S.A.
99 P9 **Dallas City** Illinois U.S.A.
95 L7 **Dallastown** Pennsylvania U.S.A.
102 D4 **Dallas Warner Res** California U.S.A.
100 D4 **Dalles, The** Oregon U.S.A.
117 G8 **Dall I** Alaska U.S.A.
116 F6 **Dall L** Alaska U.S.A.
116 N3 **Dall Mt** Alaska U.S.A.
85 E6 **Dallol Bosso** *watercourse* Niger
77 C7 **Dalmā** *isld* U.A.E.
133 E4 **Dalmacio Velez Sarsfield** Argentina
12 D1 **Dalmally** Scotland
42 G4 **Dalmatia** *reg* Croatia
55 D3 **Dalmatovo** Russian Federation
12 D3 **Dalmellington** Scotland
118 L6 **Dalmeny** Saskatchewan Canada
28 G6 **Dalmose** Denmark
12 D2 **Dalmuir** Scotland
59 L3 **Dal'negorsk** Russian Federation
59 K2 **Dal'nerechensk** Russian Federation
52 F6 **Dal'neye-Konstantinovo** Russian Federation
52 E1 **Dal'niye Zelentsy** Russian Federation
85 C7 **Daloa** Ivory Coast
67 C5 **Dalongdong Shuiku** *res* China
67 B3 **Dalou Shan** *mt ra* China
121 M4 **Dalquier** Quebec Canada
118 D7 **Dalroy** Alberta Canada
15 D5 **Dalry** Dumfries & Galloway Scotland
15 D5 **Dalry** Strathclyde Scotland
141 H4 **Dalrymple** Queensland Australia
15 D5 **Dalrymple** Scotland
141 J5 **Dalrymple,Mt** Queensland Australia
29 K11 **Dalsbruk** Finland
28 S9 **Dalsmynni** Iceland
13 F4 **Dalston** England
75 L6 **Dāltenganj** India
120 F4 **Dalton** Ontario Canada
13 E3 **Dalton** Scotland
112 C3 **Dalton** Georgia U.S.A.
95 O4 **Dalton** Massachusetts U.S.A.
98 D8 **Dalton** Nebraska U.S.A.
95 M5 **Dalton** Pennsylvania U.S.A.
115 R4 **Dalton, Kap** *C* Greenland
69 E12 **Daludalu** Sumatra
65 F5 **Dalu Dao** *isld* China
28 E6 **Dalum** Denmark
68 E2 **Daluo** China
65 H2 **Daluolemi** China
65 G1 **Daluozhen** China
71 E1 **Dalupiri** *isld* Philippines
71 G4 **Dalupiri** Philippines
12 E3 **Dalveen P** Scotland
28 S9 **Dalvík** Iceland
143 B9 **Dalwallinu** W Australia Australia
15 D4 **Dalwhinnie** Scotland
36 F1 **Dalwigksthal** Germany
109 N9 **Dalworthington Gardens** Texas U.S.A.
140 B2 **Daly** *R* N Terr Australia
102 B4 **Daly City** California U.S.A.
140 B2 **Daly R** N Terr Australia
140 B2 **Daly River** N Terr Australia
140 D1 **Daly River Aboriginal Land** N Terr Australia
140 C3 **Daly Waters** N Terr Australia
98 D5 **Dalzell** South Dakota U.S.A.
79 G10 **'Damaj, Bargā** *hill* Saudi Arabia
74 E8 **Daman** India
79 A7 **Damanhûr** Egypt
65 C4 **Damaqun Shan** *mt ra* China
71 B3 **Damar** *isld* Indonesia
71 O8 **Damar** *isld* Indonesia
107 L2 **Damar** Kansas U.S.A.
86 C5 **Damara** Cent Afr Republic
87 B10 **Damara** *homeland* Namibia
89 A4 **Damaraland** *tribal area* Namibia
95 S2 **Damariscotta L** Maine U.S.A.
Damas *see* **Dimashq**
Damascus *see* **Dimashq**
110 D6 **Damascus** Arkansas U.S.A.
95 K7 **Damascus** Maryland U.S.A.
94 F10 **Damascus** Virginia U.S.A.
131 B5 **Damas, Paso de las** Chile/Arg
86 B3 **Damaturu** Nigeria
77 C2 **Damavand** Iran
87 C7 **Damba** Angola
36 C7 **Dambach** France
83 K10 **Dambulla** Sri Lanka
68 J4 **Dam Cau Hai** Vietnam
126 G5 **Dame Marie** Haiti
20 E6 **Damgan** France
77 D1 **Dāmghān** Iran
28 A4 **Damhus Å** *R* Denmark
65 D3 **Damiao** China
48 L4 **Dămienești** Romania
21 L5 **Damigni** France
65 C6 **Daming** China
67 C5 **Daming Shan** *mts* China
80 F5 **Damiya** Jordan
80 F5 **Damiya Br** Jordan
71 E8 **Dammai** *isld* Philippines
77 B6 **Dammām, Ad** Saudi Arabia
21 O5 **Dammarie** France
18 G3 **Dammartin-en-Goële** France
22 E1 **Damme** Belgium
32 H7 **Damme** Germany
74 H7 **Damoh** India
109 M6 **Damon** Texas U.S.A.
85 D7 **Damongo** Ghana
79 F5 **Damour** Lebanon
70 F4 **Dampelas, Tg** *C* Celebes
22 K4 **Dampicourt** Belgium
142 B5 **Dampier** W Australia Australia
142 B5 **Dampier Arch** W Australia Australia
142 E4 **Dampier Downs** W Australia Australia
40 C2 **Dampierre-sur-Saône** France
71 C3 **Dampir, Selat** *str* W Irian
70 O10 **Dampit** Java
28 J7 **Damsholte** Denmark
19 J3 **Damvillars** France
21 N4 **Damville** France
22 J5 **Dâmvillers** France
80 F1 **Dan** Israel
112 H1 **Dan** *R* North Carolina U.S.A.
94 J10 **Dan** *R* Virginia U.S.A.
119 M6 **Dana** Saskatchewan Canada
71 K10 **Dana** *isld* Indonesia
79 F8 **Danā** Jordan
99 S9 **Dana** Illinois U.S.A.
110 J2 **Dana** Indiana U.S.A.
85 C7 **Danané** Ivory Coast
68 J4 **Da Nang** Vietnam
75 L6 **Danapur** India
116 G9 **Dana Vol** Alaska U.S.A.
58 D5 **Danba** China
85 F6 **Danbatta** Nigeria
95 O5 **Danbury** Connecticut U.S.A.
98 F9 **Danbury** Nebraska U.S.A.
95 Q3 **Danbury** New Hampshire U.S.A.
109 M6 **Danbury** Texas U.S.A.
99 O4 **Danbury** Wisconsin U.S.A.
103 J7 **Danby L** California U.S.A.
119 T6 **Dancing Point** Manitoba Canada
143 B9 **Dandaragan** W Australia Australia
74 J4 **Dandel Dhura** Nepal
76 B3 **Dandeli** India
139 H7 **Dandenong** Victoria Australia
59 H3 **Dandong** China
74 E2 **Dandot** Pakistan
121 Q5 **Dandurand, L** Quebec Canada
99 R6 **Dane** Wisconsin U.S.A.
147 E10 **Daneborg** Greenland
109 L6 **Danevang** Texas U.S.A.
65 A8 **Danfeng** China
67 E6 **Dangan Liedao** *isld* China
57 E5 **Dangara** Tajikistan
65 J2 **Dangbizhen** China
Dangcheng *see* **Xiangshan**
87 B7 **Dange** Angola
21 N5 **Dangeau** France
140 B1 **Danger Pt** *inlet* N Terr Australia
89 A10 **Danger Pt** S Africa
21 M8 **Dangé-St-Romain** France
21 L5 **Dangeul** France
66 F4 **Dang He** *R* China
86 G3 **Dangila** Ethiopia
68 G5 **Dangrek, Chaine des** *mts* Cambodia
125 P9 **Dangriga** Belize
65 C7 **Dangshan** China
67 F1 **Dangtu** China
21 O3 **Dangu** France
67 D1 **Dangyang** China
68 J7 **Da Nhim** *R* Vietnam
113 G11 **Dania** Florida U.S.A.
101 P7 **Daniel** Wyoming U.S.A.
42 E2 **Daniele del Friuli, S** Italy
122 D3 **Daniel-Johnston Dam** Quebec Canada
143 D10 **Daniell** W Australia Australia
144 D5 **Daniells, L** New Zealand
123 P3 **Daniels Harbour** Newfoundland Canada
118 J1 **Daniels L** Ontario Canada
95 Q5 **Danielson** Connecticut U.S.A.
112 D3 **Danielsville** Georgia U.S.A.
52 F5 **Danilov** Russian Federation
42 J6 **Danilovgrad** Montenegro Yugoslavia
55 F4 **Danilovka** Kazakhstan
52 J3 **Danilovka** Russian Federation
52 E3 **Danilovo** Russian Federation
58 F4 **Daning** China
67 C1 **Daningchang** China
Danjiang *see* **Leishan**
68 J6 **Dan Kia** Vietnam
67 A1 **Danleng** China
98 H8 **Dannebrog** Nebraska U.S.A.
115 Q4 **Dannebrog Ø** *isld* Greenland
28 G7 **Dannemare** Denmark
27 J11 **Dannemora** Sweden
95 O2 **Dannemora** New York U.S.A.
33 O6 **Dannenberg** Germany
33 S6 **Dannenwalde** Germany
100 H7 **Danner** Oregon U.S.A.
145 F4 **Dannevirke** New Zealand
68 E4 **Dan Sai** Thailand
144 C6 **Danseys Pass** New Zealand
67 E5 **Danshui** China
68 B4 **Danson B** Burma
94 C4 **Dansville** Michigan U.S.A.
94 K4 **Dansville** New York U.S.A.
94 E10 **Dante** Virginia U.S.A.
76 E1 **Dantewara** India
Dantu *see* **Zhenjiang**
Danube *R* Austria/Germany *see* **Donau** *R*
Danube *R* Bulgaria/Yugoslavia *see* **Dunav** *R*
Danube *R* Hungary *see* **Duna** *R*
Danube *R* Romania *see* **Dunărea** *R*
Danube *R* Slovakia *see* **Dunaj** *R*
68 B4 **Danubyu** Burma
70 D4 **Danumparai** Kalimantan
110 G1 **Danvers** Illinois U.S.A.
99 L4 **Danvers** Minnesota U.S.A.
101 Q2 **Danvers** Montana U.S.A.
121 S7 **Danville** Quebec Canada
110 C6 **Danville** Arkansas U.S.A.
112 D5 **Danville** Georgia U.S.A.
99 T9 **Danville** Illinois U.S.A.
110 K2 **Danville** Indiana U.S.A.
95 R2 **Danville** Maine U.S.A.
94 E6 **Danville** Ohio U.S.A.
95 L6 **Danville** Pennsylvania U.S.A.
95 P2 **Danville** Vermont U.S.A.
94 H10 **Danville** Virginia U.S.A.
94 F8 **Danville** West Virginia U.S.A.
21 J4 **Danvou-la-Ferrière** France
67 C7 **Dan Xian** China
67 F1 **Danyang** China
21 N6 **Danzé** France
67 B3 **Danzhai** China
67 C5 **Danzhu** China
Danzig *see* **Gdańsk**
98 G3 **Danzig** North Dakota U.S.A.
31 L1 **Danzig, G. of** Poland
71 E5 **Dao** Panay Philippines
16 B4 **Dão** *R* Portugal
Daokou *see* **Hua Xian**
21 J6 **Daon** France
20 B5 **Daoulas** France
85 D3 **Daoura** *watercourse* Algeria/Morocco
68 J2 **Dao Vinh Thuc** *isld* Vietnam
67 D4 **Dao Xian** China
67 B2 **Daozhen** China
71 G6 **Dapa** Philippines
85 E6 **Dapaog** Togo
111 J11 **Daphne** Alabama U.S.A.
71 F6 **Dapiak, Mt** Philippines
65 E4 **Dapingfang** China
71 F6 **Dapitan** Philippines
74 E10 **Dapoli** India
118 D4 **Dapp** Alberta Canada
Dapu *see* **Liucheng**
66 F4 **Da Qaidam** China
65 E5 **Daqin Dao** *isld* China
59 J2 **Daqing** China
65 F1 **Daqing** China
65 A4 **Daqing Shan** *mt ra* China
65 B4 **Daqing Shan** *mts* China
Daqin Tal *see* **Naiman Qi**
67 G1 **Daqu Shan** *isld* China
85 A5 **Dara** Senegal
79 G6 **Dar'ā** Syria
77 D5 **Dārāb** Iran
48 K2 **Darabani** Romania
71 F5 **Daraga** Philippines
85 G2 **Daraj** Libya
48 J1 **Darakhov** Ukraine
71 G5 **Daram** *isld* Philippines
77 B3 **Daran** Iran
48 D5 **Darány** Hungary
58 F1 **Darasun** Russian Federation
85 G6 **Darazo** Nigeria
52 B6 **Darbėnai** Lithuania
101 L3 **Darby** Montana U.S.A.
116 F4 **Darby C** Alaska U.S.A.
116 F4 **Darby Mts** Alaska U.S.A.
33 N6 **Darchau** Germany
142 E3 **D'Arcole Is** W Australia Australia
117 M10 **D'Arcy** British Columbia Canada
118 J7 **D'Arcy** Saskatchewan Canada
110 C6 **Dardanelle** Arkansas U.S.A.
102 E3 **Dardanelle** California U.S.A.
Dardanelles *str see* **Çanakkale Boğazi** *str*
33 N9 **Dardesheim** Germany
46 C1 **Đarđevica Tara** Montenegro Yugoslavia
Dar el Beida *see* **Casablanca**
86 D4 **Dar-el-Kouti** *dist* Cent Afr Republic
88 G5 **Dar es Salaam** Tanzania
144 D5 **Darfield** New Zealand
Darfur *prov* Sudan *see* **Northern and Southern Darfur** *provs*
74 D1 **Dargai** Pakistan
57 B4 **Darganata** Turkmenistan
145 D1 **Dargaville** New Zealand
21 O1 **Dargnies** France
139 H6 **Dargo** Victoria Australia
33 R5 **Dargun** Germany
58 E2 **Darhan** Mongolia
59 F3 **Darhan Muminggan Lianheqi** China
47 N11 **Darıca** Turkey
112 F6 **Darien** Georgia U.S.A.
126 F10 **Darién, G.del** Colombia/Panama
125 Q5 **Darién, Serranía del** *ra* Panama
71 E2 **Darigayos Pt** Luzon Philippines
55 B5 **Dar'inskoye** Kazakhstan
125 L3 **Darío** Nicaragua
66 D6 **Dārjiling** India
143 B10 **Darkan** W Australia Australia
138 D5 **Darke Peak** South Australia Australia
77 A4 **Darkhazineh** Iran
58 C5 **Darlag** China
138 F5 **Darling** *R* South Australia Australia
141 J8 **Darling Downs** *reg* Queensland Australia
119 T9 **Darlingford** Manitoba Canada
115 M1 **Darling Pen** Northwest Territories Canada
13 G5 **Darlington** England
101 M6 **Darlington** Idaho U.S.A.
99 M9 **Darlington** Missouri U.S.A.
112 H3 **Darlington** South Carolina U.S.A.
99 Q7 **Darlington** Wisconsin U.S.A.
139 H5 **Darlington Pt** New South Wales Australia
143 D8 **Darlot, L** W Australia Australia
31 J1 **Darłowo** Poland
48 K3 **Dărmănești** Romania
77 F3 **Darmiān** Iran
118 L8 **Darmody** Saskatchewan Canada
36 F4 **Darmstadt** Germany
84 G3 **Darnah** Libya
111 E9 **Darnell** Louisiana U.S.A.
21 N3 **Darnetal** France
139 G5 **Darnick** New South Wales Australia
114 G4 **Darnley B** Northwest Territories Canada
146 J11 **Darnley, C** Antarctica
17 G3 **Daroda** Spain
57 F5 **Daroot-Korgon** Kirghizia
52 G5 **Darovskoy** Russian Federation
141 G6 **Darr** *R* Queensland Australia
141 K2 **Darra** Brisbane, Qnsld Australia
77 F1 **Darreh Gaz** Iran
100 D1 **Darrington** Washington U.S.A.
86 D4 **Dar Rounga** *reg* Cent Afr Republic
108 D7 **Darrouzett** Texas U.S.A.
76 D3 **Darsi** India
30 G1 **Darsser Ort** *C* Germany
9 G5 **Dartford** England
138 F7 **Dartmoor** Victoria Australia
8 C6 **Dartmoor Forest** England
141 H7 **Dartmouth** *L* Queensland Australia
122 J9 **Dartmouth** Nova Scotia Canada
8 C7 **Dartmouth** England
122 H4 **Dartmouth R** Quebec Canada
139 J6 **Dartmouth Res** Victoria Australia
31 J1 **Dartowo** Poland
8 C6 **Dart, R** England
14 C2 **Dartry Mts** Ireland
136 J3 **Daru** Papua New Guinea
71 B1 **Daruba** Halmahera Indonesia
66 E5 **Darum Tso** *L* China
42 H3 **Daruvar** Croatia
15 D5 **Darvel** Scotland
13 F6 **Darwen** England
77 J4 **Darweshan** Afghanistan
140 B1 **Darwin** N Terr Australia
133 F8 **Darwin** Falkland Is
102 G5 **Darwin** California U.S.A.
88 C10 **Darwin** *dist* Zimbabwe
133 C7 **Darwin, Can** *str* Chile
146 D11 **Darwin Glacier** *glacier* Antarctica
78 K3 **Daryācheh-ye Orūmīyeh** *L* Iran
77 C7 **Dās** *isld* U.A.E.
22 L3 **Dasburg** Germany
75 L8 **Dashapalla** India
67 C1 **Dashennongjia** *mt* China
65 A4 **Dashetai** China
Dashiqiao *see* **Yingkou**
65 E1 **Dashizhai** China
77 E1 **Dasht** Iran
77 H7 **Dasht** *R* Pakistan
77 C2 **Dasht-e-Kavir** Iran
77 G7 **Dashtiari** Iran
65 C3 **Dashui Nur** China
120 J9 **Dashwood** Ontario Canada
37 L7 **Dasing** Germany
71 E7 **Dassalan** *isld* Philippines
32 L9 **Dassel** Germany
99 M4 **Dassel** Minnesota U.S.A.
33 N5 **Dassow** Germany
77 E2 **Dastgardān** Iran
70 D4 **Datadian** Kalimantan
70 D4 **Datagenojang** Kalimantan
65 C4 **Datan** China
68 J1 **Datang** China
47 J8 **Datça** Turkey
9 F5 **Datchet** England
60 O3 **Date** Japan
103 L7 **Date Cr** Arizona U.S.A.
103 L9 **Dateland** Arizona U.S.A.
74 H6 **Datia** India
67 F4 **Datian** China
106 C7 **Datil** New Mexico U.S.A.
67 F1 **Datong** China
65 F1 **Datong** Heilongjiang China
65 B4 **Datong** Shanxi China
58 C4 **Datong Shan** *mt ra* China
140 F6 **Datson,Mt** Queensland Australia
59 M2 **Datta** Russian Federation
32 F9 **Datteln** Germany
69 J12 **Datu** *isld* Indonesia
69 J11 **Datuk, Tanjong** *C* Indonesia/Malaysia
65 J2 **Daubikhe** *R* Russian Federation
74 D2 **Daud Khel** India
32 K7 **Dauelsen** Germany
115 N1 **Daugaard Jensen Land** Greenland
28 D5 **Daugård** Denmark
52 C6 **Daugava** *R* Latvia
52 C6 **Daugav'pils** Latvia
77 K1 **Daulatabad** Afghanistan
74 F9 **Daulatabad** India
128 C4 **Daule** Ecuador
41 M3 **Daumen** *mt* Germany
21 K6 **Daumeray** France
36 B3 **Daun** Germany
74 F9 **Daund** India
68 C6 **Daung Kyun** *isld* Burma
119 R7 **Dauphin** Manitoba Canada
95 L6 **Dauphin** Pennsylvania U.S.A.
19 O14 **Dauphiné** *prov* France
111 H11 **Dauphin I** Alabama U.S.A.
119 S7 **Dauphin L** Manitoba Canada
85 F6 **Daura** Nigeria
74 G5 **Dausa** India
15 E3 **Dava** Scotland
76 B3 **Davangere** India
71 G7 **Davao** Mindanao Philippines
71 G7 **Davao Gulf** Mindanao Philippines
12 C3 **Davarr I** Scotland
121 S6 **Daveluyville** Quebec Canada
22 D4 **Davenescourt** France
121 M4 **Davengus** Quebec Canada
116 J5 **Davenport** Alaska U.S.A.
102 B4 **Davenport** California U.S.A.
113 F9 **Davenport** Florida U.S.A.
99 Q8 **Davenport** Iowa U.S.A.
98 J9 **Davenport** Nebraska U.S.A.
95 N4 **Davenport** New York U.S.A.
107 O6 **Davenport** Oklahoma U.S.A.
100 G2 **Davenport** Washington U.S.A.
141 F6 **Davenport Downs** Queensland Australia
140 A6 **Davenport Hills** N Terr Australia
140 B5 **Davenport,Mt** N Terr Australia
140 C5 **Davenport Ra** N Terr Australia
9 E3 **Daventry** England
80 E3 **Daverat** Israel
32 K7 **Daverden** Germany
125 N5 **David** Panama
98 J8 **David City** Nebraska U.S.A.
146 D12 **David Glacier** *glacier* Antarctica
146 H13 **David I** Antarctica
119 M7 **Davidson** Saskatchewan Canada
112 G2 **Davidson** North Carolina U.S.A.
107 L7 **Davidson** Oklahoma U.S.A.
140 B5 **Davidson,Mt** N Terr Australia
116 Q2 **Davidson Mts** Alaska U.S.A.
8 B6 **Davidstow** England
113 G11 **Davie** Florida U.S.A.
138 A2 **Davies, Mt** South Australia Australia
26 A10 **Davik** Norway
109 K5 **Davilla** Texas U.S.A.
119 N8 **Davin** Saskatchewan Canada
146 J11 **Davis** *Australia Base* Antarctica
119 M5 **Davis** Saskatchewan Canada
102 C3 **Davis** California U.S.A.
99 R7 **Davis** Illinois U.S.A.
107 N7 **Davis** Oklahoma U.S.A.
98 K6 **Davis** South Dakota U.S.A.
94 H7 **Davis** West Virginia U.S.A.
112 E5 **Davisboro** Georgia U.S.A.
99 N9 **Davis City** Iowa U.S.A.
100 E8 **Davis Creek** California U.S.A.
103 K6 **Davis Dam** Arizona U.S.A.
115 N6 **Davis Inlet** Labrador, Nfld Canada
94 H7 **Davis, Mt** Pennsylvania U.S.A.
108 C5 **Davis Mts** Texas U.S.A.
94 D3 **Davison** Michigan U.S.A.
146 J13 **Davis Sea** Antarctica
115 O4 **Davis Str** Greenland/Canada
110 E4 **Davisville** Missouri U.S.A.
55 C4 **Davlekanovo** Russian Federation
41 L4 **Davos** Switzerland
79 F2 **Davudi Dağı** *mts* Turkey
94 F9 **Davy** West Virginia U.S.A.
56 G5 **Davydov, Gora** *mt* Russian Federation
143 D9 **Davyhurst** W Australia Australia
65 F3 **Dawa** China
65 E4 **Dawa** China
86 H5 **Dawa** *R* Ethiopia
Dawei *see* **Tavoy**
141 K6 **Dawes Ra** Queensland Australia
77 B7 **Dawḩah, Ad** Qatar
68 D4 **Dawlan** Burma
8 C6 **Dawlish** England
110 C2 **Dawn** Missouri U.S.A.
108 E1 **Dawn** Texas U.S.A.
68 C4 **Dawna Ra** Burma
141 J6 **Dawson** *R* Queensland Australia
117 D3 **Dawson** Yukon Territory Canada
111 M10 **Dawson** Georgia U.S.A.
98 K5 **Dawson** Minnesota U.S.A.
98 G3 **Dawson** North Dakota U.S.A.
107 P5 **Dawson** Oklahoma U.S.A.
109 L4 **Dawson** Texas U.S.A.
119 R6 **Dawson Bay** Manitoba Canada
117 N8 **Dawson Creek** British Columbia Canada
117 Q5 **Dawson Landing** Northwest Territories Canada
117 Q5 **Dawson Lodge** Northwest Territories Canada
117 P10 **Dawson, Mt** British Columbia Canada
117 D4 **Dawson Range** Yukon Territory Canada
110 J4 **Dawson Springs** Kentucky U.S.A.
141 K7 **Dawson Vale** Queensland Australia
111 M7 **Dawsonville** Georgia U.S.A.
67 E1 **Dawu** China
79 H4 **Daww, Ad** *depression* Syria
18 E9 **Dax** France
67 B1 **Da Xian** China
68 H1 **Daxin** China
65 E6 **Daxindian** China
65 C5 **Daxing** China
59 J3 **Daxinggou** China
36 E5 **Daxlanden** Germany
67 C4 **Daxu** China
67 C5 **Daxuan** China
Daxue *see* **Wencheng**
58 D4 **Daxue Shan** *mt ra* China
58 D5 **Daxue Shan** *mt ra* China
67 F3 **Daxu Shan** *pass* China
100 D8 **Day** California U.S.A.
113 D7 **Day** Florida U.S.A.
57 B4 **Dayakhatyn** Turkmenistan
65 F4 **Dayang He** *R* China
67 C5 **Dayao Shan** *mts* China
67 E5 **Daya Wan** *B* China
67 E1 **Daye** China
67 A1 **Dayi** China
67 B4 **Dayi** China
Dayishan *see* **Guanyun**
139 G6 **Daylesford** Victoria Australia
102 G5 **Daylight Pass** California U.S.A.
133 F4 **Dayman** *R* Uruguay
131 F3 **Dayman, Cuchilla del** *mts* Uruguay
143 D9 **Day, Mt** W Australia Australia
67 C2 **Dayong** China
79 G5 **Dayr 'Alī** Syria
79 G4 **Dayr 'Aṭiyah** Syria
78 H4 **Dayr az Zawr** Syria
79 H2 **Dayr Ḩāfir** Syria
79 G3 **Dayr Shumayyil al Taḥtāni** Syria
100 B7 **Days Creek** Oregon U.S.A.
118 E6 **Daysland** Alberta Canada
99 M7 **Dayton** Iowa U.S.A.
94 J4 **Dayton** New York U.S.A.
94 C7 **Dayton** Ohio U.S.A.
94 H6 **Dayton** Pennsylvania U.S.A.
112 B2 **Dayton** Tennessee U.S.A.
109 N5 **Dayton** Texas U.S.A.
100 H3 **Dayton** Washington U.S.A.
101 S5 **Dayton** Wyoming U.S.A.
113 F8 **Daytona Beach** Florida U.S.A.
67 E4 **Dayu** China
67 E4 **Dayu Ling** *mt* China
58 G4 **Da Yunhe** *R* China
100 F5 **Dayville** Oregon U.S.A.
98 H2 **Dazey** North Dakota U.S.A.
67 F4 **Dazhang Xi** *R* China
67 B1 **Dazhu** China
47 K7 **Dazkırı** Turkey
67 B2 **Dazu** China
89 D8 **De Aar** S Africa
99 T3 **Dead** *R* Michigan U.S.A.
116 N1 **Deadhorse** Alaska U.S.A.
101 Q5 **Dead Indian Pk** Wyoming U.S.A.
111 L11 **Dead L** Florida U.S.A.
113 D8 **Deadman B** Florida U.S.A.
103 H7 **Deadman L** California U.S.A.
126 G3 **Deadman's Cay** Long I Bahamas
103 K6 **Dead Mts** Cal/Nev U.S.A.
95 R1 **Dead R** Maine U.S.A.
80 E8 **Dead Sea** Israel/Jordan
95 R8 **Deadwater L** Maine U.S.A.
98 C5 **Deadwood** South Dakota U.S.A.
100 K5 **Deadwood Res** Idaho U.S.A.
140 C2 **Deaf Adder Cr** N Terr Australia
143 G9 **Deakin** W Australia Australia
140 B4 **Deakin,Mt** N Terr Australia
9 H5 **Deal** England
95 L8 **Deale** Maryland U.S.A.
139 H7 **Deal I** Tasmania Australia
95 M8 **Deal Island** Maryland U.S.A.
58 G6 **De'an** China
110 D1 **Dean** Iowa U.S.A.
117 K9 **Dean Ch** British Columbia Canada
141 H5 **Deane,Mt** Queensland Australia
8 D4 **Dean, Forest of** England
131 D3 **Deán Funes** Argentina
146 B9 **Dean I** *isld* Antarctica
143 E10 **Dean,Mt** W Australia Australia
117 L9 **Dean R** British Columbia Canada
95 M4 **Deansboro** New York U.S.A.
94 D4 **Dearborn** Michigan U.S.A.
110 B2 **Dearborn** Missouri U.S.A.
107 P4 **Dearing** Kansas U.S.A.
100 J3 **Deary** Idaho U.S.A.
114 G4 **Dease Arm** *B* Northwest Territories Canada
116 K1 **Dease Inlet** Alaska U.S.A.
117 J6 **Dease Lake** British Columbia Canada
147 G2 **Dease Str** Northwest Territories Canada
102 G5 **Death Valley** California U.S.A.
21 L3 **Deauville** France
101 R5 **Deaver** Wyoming U.S.A.
70 B4 **Debak** Sarawak
54 K8 **Debal'tsevo** Ukraine
67 B5 **Debao** China
46 D3 **Debar** Macedonia
116 H4 **Debauch Mt** Alaska U.S.A.
84 J6 **Debba, Ed** Sudan
80 F1 **Debbe** *R* Israel
118 L5 **Debden** Saskatchewan Canada
127 O3 **Débé** Trinidad
122 E7 **Debec** New Brunswick Canada
80 E1 **Debel et Emmeya** Lebanon
9 H3 **Debenham** England
9 H3 **Deben, R** England
106 B2 **De Beque** Colorado U.S.A.
109 N3 **De Berry** Texas U.S.A.
52 H5 **Debessy** Russian Federation
31 N5 **Dębica** Poland
31 N4 **Dęblin** Poland
31 K1 **Dębnica Kaszubska** Poland
31 H3 **Dębno** Poland
85 D5 **Débó, L** Mali
143 C9 **Deborah,L** W Australia Australia
142 F3 **Deborah,Mt** W Australia Australia
116 O5 **Deborah, Mt** Alaska U.S.A.
100 K2 **De Borgia** Montana U.S.A.
48 F6 **Debrc** Serbia Yugoslavia
86 G4 **Debre Birhan** Ethiopia
48 G3 **Debrecen** Hungary
86 G3 **Debre Mark'os** Ethiopia
86 G3 **Debre Tabor** Ethiopia
71 E2 **Debutunan Pt** Luzon Philippines
46 D2 **Dečani** Serbia Yugoslavia
111 K7 **Decatur** Alabama U.S.A.
110 B5 **Decatur** Arkansas U.S.A.
111 M8 **Decatur** Georgia U.S.A.
99 S10 **Decatur** Illinois U.S.A.
110 H2 **Decatur** Illinois U.S.A.
94 C6 **Decatur** Indiana U.S.A.
99 N9 **Decatur** Iowa U.S.A.
94 B4 **Decatur** Michigan U.S.A.
111 G9 **Decatur** Mississippi U.S.A.
98 K7 **Decatur** Nebraska U.S.A.
109 K2 **Decatur** Texas U.S.A.
110 H6 **Decaturville** Tennessee U.S.A.
18 G8 **Decazeville** France
76 C4 **Deccan** *plateau* India
121 M5 **Decelles, Lac** Quebec Canada
89 C3 **Deception** *watercourse* Botswana
115 M5 **Déception** Quebec Canada
146 C3 **Deception Island** S Shetland Is Antarctica
Dechen Dzong *see* **Dagzê**
122 E2 **Dechêne, L** Quebec Canada
110 K6 **Decherd** Tennessee U.S.A.
22 E3 **Dechy** France
118 F1 **Decimal** Manitoba Canada
43 B9 **Decimomannu** Sardinia
31 H5 **Děčín** Czech Rep
117 F7 **Decision, C** Alaska U.S.A.
18 H6 **Decize** France
119 R8 **Decker** Manitoba Canada
110 J3 **Decker** Indiana U.S.A.
101 T4 **Decker** Montana U.S.A.
106 E2 **Deckers** Colorado U.S.A.
25 C2 **De Cocksdorp** Netherlands
140 C1 **De Courcy Hd** N Terr Australia
48 E4 **Decs** Hungary
48 J4 **Deda** Romania
Dedap *see* **Penasi, Pulau**
9 E4 **Deddington** England
Dedéagach *see* **Alexandroúpolis**
33 N8 **Dedeleben** Germany
33 T6 **Dedelow** Germany
99 M8 **Dedham** Iowa U.S.A.
46 E3 **Dedino** Macedonia
130 F9 **Dedo de Deus** *mt* Brazil
85 D6 **Dedougou** Burkina
52 C6 **Dedovichi** Russian Federation
100 B9 **Dedrick** California U.S.A.
55 B5 **Dedurovka** Kazakhstan
83 J10 **Deduru Oya** *R* Sri Lanka
56 E1 **Dedushka, Porog** *falls* Russian Federation
88 E9 **Dedza** Malawi
15 F3 **Dee** *R* Scotland
14 C4 **Deel** *R* Ireland
112 H2 **Deep** *R* North Carolina U.S.A.
Deep Bay Malawi *see* **Chilumba**
122 G9 **Deep Brook** Nova Scotia Canada
100 J7 **Deep Cr** Idaho U.S.A.
94 H7 **Deep Creek L** Maryland U.S.A.
103 L2 **Deep Creek Ra** Utah U.S.A.
107 O6 **Deep Fork** *R* Oklahoma U.S.A.
112 F1 **Deep Gap** North Carolina U.S.A.
121 N6 **Deep River** Ontario Canada
95 P5 **Deep River** Connecticut U.S.A.
99 O8 **Deep River** Iowa U.S.A.
100 B3 **Deep River** Washington U.S.A.
102 G4 **Deep Sp** California U.S.A.
139 K3 **Deepwater** New South Wales Australia
110 C3 **Deepwater** Missouri U.S.A.
140 C6 **Deep Well** N Terr Australia
8 C1 **Dee, R** England/Wales
12 E4 **Dee, R** Scotland
110 C6 **Deer** Arkansas U.S.A.
100 D9 **Deer Cr** California U.S.A.
99 L3 **Deer Cr** Minnesota U.S.A.
98 F9 **Deer Cr** Nebraska U.S.A.
101 T7 **Deer Cr** Wyoming U.S.A.
107 N5 **Deer Creek** Oklahoma U.S.A.
103 N1 **Deer Cr.Res** Utah U.S.A.
107 J3 **Deerfield** Kansas U.S.A.
113 G11 **Deerfield Beach** Florida U.S.A.
122 F9 **Deer I** New Brunswick Canada
116 F9 **Deer I** Alaska U.S.A.
95 T2 **Deer I** Maine U.S.A.
116 F3 **Deering** Alaska U.S.A.
98 E1 **Deering** North Dakota U.S.A.
138 A2 **Deering Hills** South Australia Australia
143 G7 **Deering,Mt** W Australia Australia
123 P4 **Deer Lake** Newfoundland Canada
22 E2 **Deerlijk** Belgium
101 N3 **Deer Lodge** Montana U.S.A.
111 H10 **Deer Park** Alabama U.S.A.
100 H2 **Deer Park** Washington U.S.A.
117 O11 **Deer Pk** British Columbia Canada
123 S5 **Deer Pond** Newfoundland Canada
99 N2 **Deer River** Minnesota U.S.A.
99 T3 **Deerton** Michigan U.S.A.
106 F2 **Deer Trail** Colorado U.S.A.
99 N3 **Deerwood** Minnesota U.S.A.
111 F7 **Deeson** Mississippi U.S.A.
100 K8 **Deeth** Nevada U.S.A.
Defeng *see* **Liping**
38 F8 **Defereggengeb** *mt* Austria
38 F8 **Defereggental** *V* Austria
95 M2 **Deferiet** New York U.S.A.
133 F5 **Defferrari** Argentina
99 L8 **Defiance** Iowa U.S.A.
94 C5 **Defiance** Ohio U.S.A.
111 K11 **De Funiak Springs** Florida U.S.A.
16 B6 **Degebe** *R* Portugal
27 G16 **Degeberga** Sweden
86 H4 **Degeh Bur** Ethiopia
85 F8 **Degema** Nigeria
27 G12 **Degerfors** Sweden
146 A6 **De Gerlache Seamounts** *seamounts* Antarctica
37 O6 **Deggendorf** Germany
36 H6 **Deggingen** Germany
47 J6 **Degirmendere** Turkey
99 L4 **De Graff** Minnesota U.S.A.
110 N1 **Degraff** Ohio U.S.A.
111 C7 **De Gray Res** Arkansas U.S.A.
142 C5 **De Grey** W Australia Australia
98 G5 **De Grey** South Dakota U.S.A.
142 D5 **De Grey R** W Australia Australia
55 D3 **Degtyarsk** Russian Federation
22 E1 **De Haan** Belgium
86 H2 **Dehalak' Desēt** *isld* Eritrea
77 C4 **Deh Bīd** Iran
77 B4 **Deh-Dasht** Iran
74 E8 **Dehej** India
85 G2 **Dehiba** Tunisia
74 H3 **Dehra Dun** India
75 L6 **Dehri** India
36 E3 **Dehrn** Germany
77 F4 **Deh Salm** Iran
67 F4 **Dehua** China
59 J3 **Dehui** China
36 E5 **Deidesheim** Germany
86 E4 **Deim Zubeir** Sudan
37 M5 **Deining** Germany
25 E2 **Deinum** Netherlands
22 F2 **Deinze** Belgium
80 F4 **Deir Abu Said** Jordan
80 F4 **Deir es Samadiya** Jordan
80 D5 **Deir Istiya** Jordan
80 E6 **Deir Mar Jiryis** Jordan
80 D4 **Deir Sharal** Jordan
32 K8 **Deister** *hills* Germany
48 H3 **Dej** Romania
46 D3 **Dêja** *mt* Albania
71 B2 **Dejailolo, Selat** *str* Indonesia
28 A5 **Dejbjerg** Denmark
27 F12 **Deje** Sweden
86 G3 **Dejen** Ethiopia
67 C2 **Dejiang** China
99 S8 **De Kalb** Illinois U.S.A.
111 H9 **De Kalb** Mississippi U.S.A.
109 N2 **De Kalb** Texas U.S.A.

95 M2 **De Kalb Junc** New York U.S.A.
59 M1 **De Kastri** Russian Federation
86 G2 **Dek'emhāre** Eritrea
86 D6 **Dekese** Zaire
86 C4 **Dékoa** Cent Afr Republic
25 C2 **De Koog** Netherlands
111 G12 **Delacroix** Louisiana U.S.A.
106 F4 **Delagua** Colorado U.S.A.
100 J6 **Delamar** Idaho U.S.A.
103 K4 **Delamar Mts** Nevada U.S.A.
140 B3 **Delamere** N Terr Australia
113 F8 **De Land** Florida U.S.A.
102 E6 **Delano** California U.S.A.
103 M3 **Delano Peak** Utah U.S.A.
77 H3 **Delārām** Afghanistan
118 K4 **Delaronde L** Saskatchewan Canada
110 G1 **Delavan** Illinois U.S.A.
99 S7 **Delavan** Wisconsin U.S.A.
95 N5 **Delaware** *R* U.S.A.
95 M7 **Delaware** *state* U.S.A.
107 P2 **Delaware** *R* Kansas U.S.A.
94 D6 **Delaware** Ohio U.S.A.
107 P5 **Delaware** Oklahoma U.S.A.
145 D4 **Delaware B** New Zealand
95 M7 **Delaware B** U.S.A.
95 M7 **Delaware City** Delaware U.S.A.
108 C4 **Delaware Cr** Texas/New Mex U.S.A.
94 D6 **Delaware Res** Ohio U.S.A.
118 E9 **Del Bonita** Alberta Canada
32 J9 **Delbrück** Germany
118 D6 **Delburne** Alberta Canada
111 E12 **Delcambre** Louisiana U.S.A.
106 F4 **Delcarbon** Colorado U.S.A.
46 F3 **Delčevo** Macedonia
87 E8 **Delcommune, L** Zaire
25 G4 **Delden** Netherlands
119 R9 **Deleau** Manitoba Canada
139 J6 **Delegate** New South Wales Australia
25 F2 **De Leien** Netherlands
40 F3 **Delémont** Switzerland
109 J3 **De Leon** Texas U.S.A.
29 H11 **Delet Teili** *chan* Finland
22 C2 **Delettes** France
102 B2 **Delevan** California U.S.A.
94 J4 **Delevan** New York U.S.A.
130 F7 **Delfinópolis** Brazil
25 B5 **Delfshaven** Netherlands
25 B4 **Delft** Netherlands
83 J8 **Delft** *isld* Sri Lanka
25 G2 **Delfzijl** Netherlands
100 A9 **Delgada, Pt** California U.S.A.
133 E6 **Delgada, Pta** Argentina
88 H7 **Delgado, C** Mozambique
86 F1 **Delgo** Sudan
120 K10 **Delhi** Ontario Canada
74 G4 **Delhi** India
99 P7 **Delhi** Iowa U.S.A.
111 E9 **Delhi** Louisiana U.S.A.
107 L6 **Delhi** Oklahoma U.S.A.
70 K9 **Deli** *isld* Java
118 E7 **Delia** Alberta Canada
107 P2 **Delia** Kansas U.S.A.
129 H3 **Delices** Fr Guiana
109 O1 **Delight** Arkansas U.S.A.
77 B3 **Delijan** Iran
46 E1 **Deli Jovan** *mt* Serbia Yugoslavia
58 C4 **Delingha** China
118 K7 **Delisle** Saskatchewan Canada
140 B2 **Delissaville** N Terr Australia
69 D11 **Delitua** Sumatra
33 Q9 **Delitzsch** Germany
110 F6 **Dell** Arkansas U.S.A.
101 N5 **Dell** Montana U.S.A.
36 C2 **Dellbrück** Germany
40 E2 **Delle** France
101 N9 **Delle** Utah U.S.A.
103 L5 **Dellenbaugh, Mt** Arizona U.S.A.
26 J10 **Dellen, N** *L* Sweden
32 L9 **Delligsen** Germany
100 B9 **Del Loma** California U.S.A.
98 K6 **Dell Rapids** South Dakota U.S.A.
107 L2 **Dellvale** Kansas U.S.A.
85 E1 **Dellys** Algeria
102 G9 **Del Mar** California U.S.A.
99 Q7 **Delmar** Iowa U.S.A.
95 M8 **Delmar** Maryland U.S.A.
118 J6 **Delmas** Saskatchewan Canada
32 J6 **Delmenhorst** Germany
130 H10 **Delmiro Gouveia** Brazil
98 H6 **Delmont** South Dakota U.S.A.
103 K4 **Delmues** Nevada U.S.A.
42 F3 **Delnice** Croatia
106 D4 **Del Norte** Colorado U.S.A.
116 F2 **De Long Mts** Alaska U.S.A.
139 H8 **Deloraine** Tasmania Australia
119 R9 **Deloraine** Manitoba Canada
13 F6 **Delph** England
46 E6 **Delphi** Greece
110 K1 **Delphi** Indiana U.S.A.
107 N2 **Delphos** Kansas U.S.A.
94 C6 **Delphos** Ohio U.S.A.
113 G11 **Delray Beach** Florida U.S.A.
124 D2 **Del Río** Mexico
108 G6 **Del Rio** Texas U.S.A.
26 J10 **Delsbo** Sweden
106 B3 **Delta** Colorado U.S.A.
110 G4 **Delta** Missouri U.S.A.
94 C5 **Delta** Ohio U.S.A.
95 L7 **Delta** Pennsylvania U.S.A.
103 M2 **Delta** Utah U.S.A.
119 T8 **Delta Beach** Manitoba Canada
141 F3 **Delta Downs** Queensland Australia
116 O4 **Delta Junction** Alaska U.S.A.
102 C4 **Delta Mendota Canal** California U.S.A.
95 M3 **Delta Res** New York U.S.A.
95 L9 **Deltaville** Virginia U.S.A.
94 B4 **Delton** Michigan U.S.A.
139 K3 **Delungra** New South Wales Australia
74 D8 **Delvada** India
109 K5 **Del Valle** Texas U.S.A.
32 K4 **Delve** Germany
46 D5 **Delvinákion** Greece
46 D5 **Delvinë** Albania
108 G2 **Delwin** Texas U.S.A.
48 J2 **Delyatin** Ukraine
55 B4 **Dema** *R* Russian Federation
118 K8 **Demaine** Saskatchewan Canada
70 N9 **Demak** Java
16 E2 **Demando, S. de la** *mts* Spain
116 R2 **Demarcation Pt** Alaska U.S.A.
86 D7 **Demba** Zaire
86 D4 **Dembia** Cent Afr Republic
86 F4 **Dembī Dolo** Ethiopia
48 G2 **Demecser** Hungary
22 J2 **Demer** *R* Belgium
Demerara *see* **Georgetown** Guyana
54 C1 **Demidov** Russian Federation
55 D3 **Demina** Russian Federation
106 C9 **Deming** New Mexico U.S.A.
100 C1 **Deming** Washington U.S.A.
128 F3 **Demini** *R* Brazil
79 B2 **Demirçat** Turkey
47 K5 **Demirci** Turkey
47 N11 **Demirciler** Turkey
47 J6 **Demirköprü Baraji** *L* Turkey
47 J3 **Demirköy** Turkey
33 S5 **Demmin** Germany
128 F5 **Democracia** Brazil
111 J9 **Demopolis** Alabama U.S.A.
68 C3 **Demoso** Burma
143 E10 **Dempster, Pt** W Australia Australia
74 H2 **Dêmqog** India
55 F2 **Dem'yanka** *R* Russian Federation
52 D5 **Demyansk** Russian Federation
55 E2 **Dem'yanskoye** Russian Federation
22 E3 **Denain** France
86 H3 **Denakil** *tribal dist* Eritrea/Ethiopia
116 O5 **Denali** Alaska U.S.A.
116 M5 **Denali Nat Park and Preserve** Alaska U.S.A.
86 H4 **Denan** Ethiopia
114 J7 **Denare Beach** Saskatchewan Canada
57 E5 **Denau** Uzbekistan
121 N7 **Denbigh** Ontario Canada
8 C1 **Denbigh** Wales
116 G4 **Denbigh, C** Alaska U.S.A.
25 B5 **Den Bommel** Netherlands
25 C2 **Den Burg** Netherlands
68 E4 **Den Chai** Thailand
69 J14 **Dendang** Indonesia
22 G2 **Dender** *R* Belgium
22 G2 **Denderleeuw** Belgium
22 G1 **Dendermonde** Belgium
25 D3 **Den Dever** Netherlands
86 G4 **Dendi** *mt* Ethiopia
118 K8 **Dendron** Saskatchewan Canada
25 H4 **Denekamp** Netherlands
55 C1 **Denezhkin Kamen', G** *mt* Russian Federation
65 B7 **Dengfeng** China
58 E3 **Dengkou** China
66 F5 **Dêngqên** China
58 F5 **Deng Xian** China
65 C4 **Dengyoufang** China
65 E6 **Dengzhou** China
24 A2 **Den Haag** *conurbation* Netherlands
143 A7 **Denham** W Australia Australia
9 F4 **Denham** England
140 E3 **Denham I** Queensland Australia
141 J5 **Denham Ra** Queensland Australia
143 A7 **Denham Sd** W Australia Australia
111 F11 **Denham Springs** Louisiana U.S.A.
25 C3 **Den Helder** Netherlands
118 K6 **Denholm** Saskatchewan Canada
13 F3 **Denholm** Scotland
17 G7 **Denia** Spain
138 C4 **Denial Bay** South Australia Australia
122 C6 **Deniau** Quebec Canada
139 G6 **Deniliquin** New South Wales Australia
100 G7 **Denio** Oregon U.S.A.
83 J12 **Denis I** Seychelles
99 L7 **Denison** Iowa U.S.A.
109 L2 **Denison** Texas U.S.A.
107 O8 **Denison Dam** Oklahoma U.S.A.
140 B5 **Denison, Mt** N Terr Australia
116 K7 **Denison, Mt** Alaska U.S.A.
142 G4 **Denison Plains** W Australia Australia
141 J4 **Denison Pt** Queensland Australia
52 J2 **Denisovka** Komi Respublika Russian Federation
83 K11 **Deniyaya** Sri Lanka
47 K7 **Denizli** Turkey
37 L6 **Denkendorf** Germany
139 K4 **Denman** New South Wales Australia
146 H13 **Denman Glacier** Antarctica
143 B10 **Denmark** W Australia Australia
122 J8 **Denmark** Nova Scotia Canada
28 **Denmark** *kingdom* N W Europe
100 A7 **Denmark** Oregon U.S.A.
112 F4 **Denmark** South Carolina U.S.A.
99 T5 **Denmark** Wisconsin U.S.A.
115 R4 **Denmark Str** Greenland/Iceland
20 G3 **Denneville** France
33 S9 **Dennewitz** Germany
94 F6 **Dennison** Ohio U.S.A.
95 R5 **Dennis Port** Massachusetts U.S.A.
144 C4 **Denniston** New Zealand
94 H10 **Denniston** Virginia U.S.A.
12 E1 **Denny** Scotland
100 B9 **Denny** California U.S.A.
12 E2 **Dennyloanhead** Scotland
95 U2 **Dennysville** Maine U.S.A.
70 P10 **Denpasar** Bali Indonesia
70 G6 **Densongi** Sulawesi
13 F5 **Dent** England
100 J3 **Dent** Idaho U.S.A.
48 G5 **Denta** Romania
40 G5 **Dent Blanche** *mt* Switzerland
40 E5 **Dent du Midi** *mt* Switzerland
9 H5 **Denton** England
112 E6 **Denton** Georgia U.S.A.
94 E8 **Denton** Kentucky U.S.A.
95 M8 **Denton** Maryland U.S.A.
109 K2 **Denton** Texas U.S.A.
137 L3 **D'Entrecasteaux Is** Papua New Guinea
106 E2 **Denver** Colorado U.S.A.
100 J4 **Denver** Idaho U.S.A.
94 A6 **Denver** Indiana U.S.A.
99 O7 **Denver** Iowa U.S.A.
95 L6 **Denver** Pennsylvania U.S.A.
108 E3 **Denver City** Texas U.S.A.
118 H6 **Denzil** Saskatchewan Canada
86 B4 **Déo** *R* Cameroon
74 G4 **Deoband** India
75 M6 **Deogarh** India
68 J4 **Deo Hai Van** Vietnam
74 E9 **Deolali** India
21 O8 **Déols** France
68 J6 **Deo Ma** Vietnam
22 D1 **De Panne** Belgium
25 E5 **De Peel** Netherlands
99 S5 **De Pere** Wisconsin U.S.A.
94 J4 **Depew** New York U.S.A.
107 O6 **Depew** Oklahoma U.S.A.
65 C6 **Deping** China
22 F2 **De Pinte** Belgium
70 L9 **Depok** Java
109 M2 **Deport** Texas U.S.A.
95 M4 **Deposit** New York U.S.A.
128 F3 **Depósito** Brazil
95 Q4 **Depot** New Hampshire U.S.A.
120 K7 **Depot Harbour** Ontario Canada
86 D2 **Depression du Murdi** Chad
9 E5 **Deptford** England
142 C5 **Depuch I** W Australia Australia
99 R8 **Depue** Illinois U.S.A.
25 G2 **De Punt** Netherlands
51 O2 **Deputatskiy** Russian Federation
58 C6 **Dêqên** China
67 G1 **Deqing** China
67 D5 **Deqing** China
111 B7 **De Queen** Arkansas U.S.A.
111 C11 **De Quincy** Louisiana U.S.A.
77 L5 **Dera Bugti** Pakistan
74 D3 **Dera Ghazi Khan** Pakistan
74 D3 **Dera Ismail Khan** Pakistan
46 D2 **Đeravica** *mt* Serbia Yugoslavia
48 L1 **Derazhnya** Ukraine
33 Q8 **Derben** Germany
78 M1 **Derbent** Russian Federation
86 D4 **Derbisaka** Cent Afr Republic
139 J8 **Derby** Tasmania Australia
142 E3 **Derby** W Australia Australia
9 E2 **Derby** England
95 O5 **Derby** Connecticut U.S.A.
99 N9 **Derby** Iowa U.S.A.
107 N4 **Derby** Kansas U.S.A.
109 H7 **Derby** Texas U.S.A.
95 P2 **Derby Center** Vermont U.S.A.
9 E1 **Derbyshire** *co* England
16 D9 **Derdara** Morocco
48 G3 **Derecske** Hungary
47 K8 **Dereköy** Turkey
47 M10 **Dereköy** *R* Turkey
78 A1 **Derekoy** Turkey
33 N8 **Der Elm** *hills* Germany
33 N9 **Derenburg** Germany
52 D4 **Derevyanka** Russian Federation
14 D2 **Derg** *R* N Ireland
54 H6 **Dergachi** Ukraine
14 D2 **Derg, L** Ireland
32 H5 **Der Hohe Weg** *sandbank* Germany
111 C11 **De Ridder** Louisiana U.S.A.
25 C3 **De Rijp** Netherlands
139 G7 **Derinallum** Victoria Australia
47 N11 **Derince** Turkey
86 H5 **Derkali** Kenya
54 L8 **Derkul** *R* Rus Fed/Ukraine
46 G1 **Dermantsi** Bulgaria
37 J2 **Dermbach** Germany
111 E8 **Dermott** Arkansas U.S.A.
Derna *see* **Darnah**
87 C11 **Dernberg, C** Namibia
32 M8 **Derneburg** Germany
111 F12 **Dernieres, Is** Louisiana U.S.A.
138 C2 **De Rose Hill** South Australia Australia
20 G3 **Déroute,Pass de la** France
14 D3 **Derravaragh, L** Ireland
86 J5 **Derri** Somalia
95 Q4 **Derry** New Hampshire U.S.A.
106 C9 **Derry** New Mexico U.S.A.
94 H6 **Derry** Pennsylvania U.S.A.
140 D5 **Derry Downs** N Terr Australia
14 C2 **Derryveagh Mts** Ireland
36 D1 **Derschlag** Germany
9 G2 **Dersingham** England
86 G2 **Derudeb** Sudan
95 M4 **De Ruyter** New York U.S.A.
20 G6 **Derval** France
46 E6 **Dervéni** Greece
42 H4 **Derventa** Bosnia-Herzegovina
140 B6 **Derwent** N Terr Australia
139 H8 **Derwent** *R* Tasmania Australia
118 F5 **Derwent** Alberta Canada
12 E4 **Derwent, R** England
13 E4 **Derwent Water** *L* England
55 E5 **Derzhavinsk** Kazakhstan
133 D4 **Desaguadero** *R* Argentina
131 B5 **Desague, Cerro** *pk* Argentina
110 E7 **Des Arc** Arkansas U.S.A.
110 F4 **Des Arc** Missouri U.S.A.
102 G2 **Desatoya Mts** Nevada U.S.A.
9 F3 **Desborough** England
130 B5 **Descalvado** Mato Grosso Brazil
130 F7 **Descalvado** São Paulo Brazil
124 A1 **Descanso** Mexico
102 H9 **Descanso** California U.S.A.
21 M8 **Descartes** France
121 S6 **Deschaillons** Quebec Canada
100 E4 **Deschutes** *R* Oregon U.S.A.
109 J3 **Desdemona** Texas U.S.A.
86 G3 **Desē** Ethiopia
45 M1 **Dese** *R* Italy
133 P7 **Deseado** Argentina
41 N7 **Desenzano del Garda** Italy
103 M2 **Deseret** Utah U.S.A.
101 N9 **Deseret Pk** Utah U.S.A.
121 N8 **Deseronto** Ontario Canada
103 J8 **Desert Center** California U.S.A.
102 H8 **Desert Hot Springs** California U.S.A.
121 O6 **Desért, L** Quebec Canada
101 M8 **Desert Pk** Utah U.S.A.
103 J5 **Desert Ra** Nevada U.S.A.
100 G8 **Desert Valley** Nevada U.S.A.
103 N5 **Desert View** Arizona U.S.A.
127 M4 **Deshaies** Guadeloupe W Indies
67 A3 **Deshengpo** China
98 J9 **Deshler** Nebraska U.S.A.
94 D5 **Deshler** Ohio U.S.A.
74 E5 **Deshnok** India
77 H4 **Deshu** Afghanistan
124 B1 **Desierto de Altar** *desert* Mexico
17 H4 **Desierto de las Palmas** Spain
98 E1 **Des Lacs** *R* North Dakota U.S.A.
118 D3 **Desmarais** Alberta Canada
121 O3 **Desmaraisville** Quebec Canada
100 J2 **Desmet** Idaho U.S.A.
101 L3 **De Smet** Montana U.S.A.
98 J5 **De Smet** South Dakota U.S.A.
130 B10 **Desmochados** Paraguay
99 M7 **Des Moines** *R* Iowa U.S.A.
99 N8 **Des Moines** Iowa U.S.A.
99 L6 **Des Moines** *R* Minnesota U.S.A.
106 G5 **Des Moines** New Mexico U.S.A.
54 B6 **Desna** *R* Ukraine
54 E2 **Desnogorsk** Russian Federation
133 C8 **Desolación, I** Chile
71 G5 **Desolation Pt** Philippines
110 G4 **De Soto** Illinois U.S.A.
107 Q3 **De Soto** Kansas U.S.A.
110 F3 **De Soto** Missouri U.S.A.
99 P6 **De Soto** Wisconsin U.S.A.
113 F10 **De Soto City** Florida U.S.A.
16 E6 **Despeñaperros, Pto. de** Spain
99 T7 **Des Plaines** Illinois U.S.A.
48 G6 **Despotovac** Serbia Yugoslavia
83 H5 **Desroches** *isld* Seychelles
33 Q9 **Dessau** Germany
40 E3 **Dessoubre** *R* France
111 K11 **Destin** Florida U.S.A.
31 K5 **Deštná** *mt* Poland
138 E6 **D'Estrees, B** South Australia Australia
117 D5 **Destruction Bay** Yukon Territory Canada
100 A2 **Destruction I** Washington U.S.A.
143 G6 **Destruction,Mt** W Australia Australia
22 B2 **Desvres** France
48 G5 **Deta** Romania
87 E9 **Dete** Zimbabwe
32 G6 **Detern** Germany
121 N7 **Detlor** Ontario Canada
32 J9 **Detmold** Germany
94 D1 **Detour Passage** Michigan U.S.A.
99 U4 **Detour, Pt** Michigan U.S.A.
94 D1 **Detour Village** Michigan U.S.A.
94 D4 **Detroit** Michigan U.S.A.
109 M2 **Detroit** Texas U.S.A.
122 H4 **Détroit d'Honguedo** Quebec Canada
99 L3 **Detroit Lakes** Minnesota U.S.A.
94 D4 **Detroit R** Michigan U.S.A.
100 C5 **Detroit Res** Oregon U.S.A.
37 J4 **Dettelbach** Germany
36 G6 **Dettenhausen** Germany
36 H3 **Detter** Germany
36 F7 **Dettingen** Baden-Württemberg Germany
36 G3 **Dettingen** Bayern Germany
36 C6 **Dettwiller** France
68 G5 **Det Udom** Thailand
48 E2 **Detva** Slovakia
74 G8 **Deūlgaon Rāja** India
25 E6 **Deurne** Netherlands
37 Q2 **Deutsch-Einsiedel** Germany
33 R7 **Deutschhof** Germany
48 D3 **Deutschkreutz** Austria
37 P2 **Deutsch-Neudorf** Germany
122 B2 **Deux Décharges, L** Quebec Canada
121 M6 **Deux Rivieres** Ontario Canada
18 E6 **Deux-Sèvres** *dept* France
48 H5 **Deva** Romania
16 D1 **Deva** *R* Spain
110 E7 **De Valls Bluff** Arkansas U.S.A.
48 F3 **Dévaványa** Hungary
47 L8 **Devecitaşi Adası** *isld* Turkey
48 D3 **Devecser** Hungary
78 E2 **Develi** Turkey
25 F4 **Deventer** Netherlands
112 D4 **Devereux** Georgia U.S.A.
86 H4 **De Verme Falls** Ethiopia
6 L1 **Deveron** *oil rig* North Sea
15 F3 **Deveron** *R* Scotland
46 E1 **Devica** *mt* Serbia Yugoslavia
74 D5 **Devikot** India
21 N3 **Deville** France
116 E3 **Devil Mt** Alaska U.S.A.
145 D4 **Devil River Pk** New Zealand
108 F5 **Devils** *R* Texas U.S.A.
14 D4 **Devilsbit Mt** Ireland
8 C3 **Devils Bridge** Wales
102 E6 **Devils Den** California U.S.A.
15 E4 **Devil's Elbow** Scotland
116 K5 **Devils Elbow** *V* Alaska U.S.A.
102 E3 **Devils Gate** California U.S.A.
89 E1 **Devil's Gorge** Zambia
6 L6 **Devil's Hole** North Sea
99 Q2 **Devils I** Michigan U.S.A.
110 H4 **Devil's Kitchen L** Illinois U.S.A.
98 H1 **Devils Lake** North Dakota U.S.A.
100 K8 **Devils L. Res** Nevada U.S.A.
117 G6 **Devils Paw** *mt* Br Col/Alaska Canada/U.S.A.
102 E4 **Devils Pk** California U.S.A.
103 J7 **Devils Playground** *desert* California U.S.A.
126 G2 **Devil's Point** Cat I Bahamas
102 E4 **Devils Postpile Nat.Mon** California U.S.A.
101 O8 **Devils Slide** Utah U.S.A.
139 H7 **Devils Tower** *isld* Tasmania Australia
98 B5 **Devils Tower** Wyoming U.S.A.
46 G3 **Devin** Bulgaria
109 J6 **Devine** Texas U.S.A.
80 C8 **Devira** Israel
9 E5 **Devizes** England
74 F6 **Devli** India
107 M7 **Devol** Oklahoma U.S.A.
46 D4 **Devoll** *R* Albania
118 D5 **Devon** Alberta Canada
120 G5 **Devon** Ontario Canada
8 C6 **Devon** *co* England
101 O1 **Devon** Montana U.S.A.
115 L2 **Devon I** Northwest Territories Canada
139 H8 **Devonport** Tasmania Australia
8 B7 **Devonport** England
80 E3 **Devora** Israel
78 D1 **Devrek** *R* Turkey
78 D1 **Devrez** *R* Turkey
89 G2 **Devuli** *R* Zimbabwe
52 H6 **Devyaternya** Russian Federation
52 E4 **Devyatiny** Russian Federation
55 E2 **Devyatkova** Russian Federation
70 F7 **Dewakang Besar** *isld* Indonesia
70 F7 **Dewakang Ketjil** *isld* Indonesia
107 P6 **Dewar** Oklahoma U.S.A.
118 H7 **Dewar Lake** Saskatchewan Canada
74 G7 **Dewas** India
69 B11 **Dewa, Tanjong** *C* Indonesia
118 G5 **Dewberry** Alberta Canada
98 H9 **Deweese** Nebraska U.S.A.
103 M7 **Dewey** Arizona U.S.A.
107 P5 **Dewey** Oklahoma U.S.A.
98 C6 **Dewey** South Dakota U.S.A.
94 E9 **Dewey Res** Kentucky U.S.A.
22 E1 **De Wielingen** Belgium/Neths
118 C8 **De Winton** Alberta Canada
111 E7 **De Witt** Arkansas U.S.A.
94 C4 **De Witt** Michigan U.S.A.
110 C2 **De Witt** Missouri U.S.A.
98 K9 **De Witt** Nebraska U.S.A.
95 L3 **De Witt** New York U.S.A.
13 G6 **Dewsbury** England
67 F2 **Dexing** China
111 D7 **Dexter** Arkansas U.S.A.
99 M8 **Dexter** Iowa U.S.A.
107 O4 **Dexter** Kansas U.S.A.
95 S1 **Dexter** Maine U.S.A.
94 D4 **Dexter** Michigan U.S.A.
99 O6 **Dexter** Minnesota U.S.A.
110 G5 **Dexter** Missouri U.S.A.
108 C2 **Dexter** New Mexico U.S.A.
95 L2 **Dexter** New York U.S.A.
109 L2 **Dexter** Texas U.S.A.
113 F8 **Dexter, L** Florida U.S.A.
99 Q5 **Dexterville** Wisconsin U.S.A.
138 B3 **Dey-Dey, L** South Australia Australia
22 L3 **Deyfeldt** Belgium
77 E3 **Deyhuk** Iran
57 C5 **Deynau** Turkmenistan
136 H3 **Deyong, Tanjung** *C* W Irian
77 B6 **Deyyer** Iran
117 E5 **Dezadeash L** Yukon Territory Canada
77 A3 **Dezfūl** Iran
77 B4 **Dez Gerd** Iran
65 C6 **Dezhou** China
41 M6 **Dezzo** Italy
46 E7 **Dháfni** Greece
79 G6 **Dhahab, Wādī adh** *watercourse* Syria
Dhahran *see* **Z̧ahrān, Az**
75 O7 **Dhaka** Bangladesh
79 D3 **Dhali** Cyprus
75 J8 **Dhamtari** India
75 M7 **Dhanbad** India
74 J4 **Dhangarhi** Nepal
109 H6 **D'Hanis** Texas U.S.A.
75 M5 **Dhankuta** Nepal
76 D6 **Dhanushkodi** India
74 F7 **Dhar** India
76 C5 **Dharapuram** India
75 K7 **Dharmajaygarh** India
76 D4 **Dharmapuri** India
76 C3 **Dharmavaram** India
74 G2 **Dharmshāla** India
86 A1 **Dharoor** *R* Somalia
85 C5 **Dhar Oualata** *plateau* Mauritania
76 B3 **Dhārwād** India
66 C6 **Dhaulagiri** *mt* Nepal
74 G5 **Dhaulpur** India
75 L8 **Dhenkanal** India
47 H7 **Dhenoúsa** *isld* Greece
46 D4 **Dhërmi** Albania
46 E5 **Dheskáti** Greece
46 G8 **Dhespotikó** *isld* Greece
40 A4 **Dheune** *R* France
80 G7 **Dhiban** Jordan
46 F7 **Dhídhimoi** Greece
47 H3 **Dhidhimótikhon** Greece
46 G9 **Dhíkti Ori** *mt* Crete Greece
46 G7 **Dhílos** *isld* Greece
46 E7 **Dhimitsána** Greece
78 L6 **Dhī Qar** *prov* Iraq
80 F8 **Dhira** Jordan
46 F6 **Dhírfis** *mt* Greece
47 H7 **Dhodhekánisos** *islds* Greece
74 G5 **Dholpur** India
46 E5 **Dhomokós** Greece
76 C3 **Dhone** India
74 D8 **Dhoraji** India
46 G3 **Dhoxáton** Greece
46 G7 **Dhragonísi** *isld* Greece
47 O12 **Dhráhstis, Akra** *C* Greece
74 D7 **Dhrangadhra** India
46 F5 **Dhrépanon, Ákr** *C* Greece
46 D5 **Dhrin** *R* Albania
75 N5 **Dhuburi** India
Dhufar *see* **Z̧ufār**
21 O6 **Dhuison** France
74 F8 **Dhule** India
74 E2 **Dhulian** Pakistan
86 B2 **Dhuudo** Somalia
46 E6 **Dhytikí Ellas** *admin region* Greece
46 E4 **Dhytikí Makedhonía** *admin region* Greece
46 G9 **Día** *isld* Crete Greece
129 H2 **Diable, I.du** Fr Guiana
40 F5 **Diablerets** *mt* Switzerland
100 D1 **Diablo L** Washington U.S.A.
127 K2 **Diablo, Mt** Jamaica
108 C4 **Diablo, Sa** *mts* Texas U.S.A.
127 O7 **Diablotin, Morne** *hill* Dominica
99 M9 **Diagonal** Iowa U.S.A.
85 B6 **Dialakoto** Senegal
131 E4 **Diamante** Argentina
133 D4 **Diamante** *R* Argentina
141 F6 **Diamantina** *R* Queensland Australia
129 K7 **Diamantina** Brazil
130 G6 **Diamantina** Minas Gerais Brazil
141 F6 **Diamantina Lakes** Queensland Australia
129 G6 **Diamantino** Brazil
130 C4 **Diamantino** Mato Grosso Brazil
130 D5 **Diamantino** Mato Grosso Brazil
110 B5 **Diamond** Missouri U.S.A.
118 E9 **Diamond City** Alberta Canada
75 N7 **Diamond Harb** India
144 D5 **Diamond Harbour** New Zealand
102 S12 **Diamond Hd** Hawaiian Is
141 K3 **Diamond Islets** Gt Barrier Reef Australia
100 C6 **Diamond L** Oregon U.S.A.
103 J2 **Diamond Mts** Nevada U.S.A.
100 C6 **Diamond Peak** *mt* Oregon U.S.A.
103 J2 **Diamond Pk** Nevada U.S.A.
102 D3 **Diamond Springs** California U.S.A.
101 P8 **Diamondville** Wyoming U.S.A.
94 G8 **Diana** West Virginia U.S.A.
141 J3 **Diana Bank** Gt Barrier Reef Aust
28 G5 **Dianaland** Denmark
67 C6 **Dianbai** China
Dianbu *see* **Feidong**
67 A4 **Dian Chi** *L* China
67 B1 **Dianjiang** China
44 D4 **Diano Marina** Italy
129 J6 **Dianópolis** Brazil
65 H2 **Diaoling** China
85 E6 **Diapaga** Burkina
71 F2 **Diapitan B** Luzon Philippines
46 F4 **Diavata** Greece
68 A6 **Diavolo, Mt** Andaman Is
65 A5 **Dibabu** China
87 D7 **Dibaya** Zaire
86 D3 **Dibbis** Sudan
66 F6 **Dibhuk Pass** India/Burma
86 B4 **Dibi** Cameroon
109 N4 **Diboll** Texas U.S.A.
66 E6 **Dibrugarh** India
75 Q5 **Dibrugarh** India
71 E3 **Dicapanisan Pt** Luzon Philippines
Diciosănmârtin *see* **Tîrnăveni**
98 E9 **Dickens** Nebraska U.S.A.
108 G2 **Dickens** Texas U.S.A.
95 R6 **Dickey** Maine U.S.A.
98 H3 **Dickey** North Dakota U.S.A.
98 D3 **Dickinson** North Dakota U.S.A.
109 M6 **Dickinson** Texas U.S.A.
9 H3 **Dickleburgh** England
36 D3 **Dickscheid-Geroldstein** Germany
110 J5 **Dickson** Tennessee U.S.A.
95 M5 **Dickson City** Pennsylvania U.S.A.
78 H3 **Dicle** *R* Turkey
45 L4 **Dicomano** Italy
71 F1 **Didacas** *isld* Luzon Philippines
9 E4 **Didcot** England
85 C6 **Didiéni** Mali
109 L8 **Dido** Texas U.S.A.
118 C7 **Didsbury** Alberta Canada
74 F5 **Didwana** India
121 S4 **Didyme** Quebec Canada
19 O15 **Die** France
89 G5 **Die Berg** *mt* S Africa
36 B5 **Diebling** France
85 D6 **Diébougou** Burkina
36 F4 **Dieburg** Germany
118 K7 **Diefenbaker, L** Saskatchewan Canada
33 N6 **Die Göhrde** *reg* Germany
131 F3 **Diego Lamas** Uruguay
133 D9 **Diego Ramírez, Is** Chile
Diego Suarez *see* **Antsiranana**
30 D1 **Die Halligen** *inlet* Germany
32 L8 **Diekholzen** Germany
22 L4 **Diekirch** Luxembourg
20 G2 **Diélette** France
32 H8 **Dielingen** Germany
85 C6 **Diema** Mali
32 K9 **Diemel** *R* Germany
36 C6 **Diemeringen** France
68 F2 **Dien Bien Phu** Vietnam
68 G3 **Dien Chau** Vietnam
32 J8 **Diepenau** Germany
25 G4 **Diepenheim** Netherlands
32 H7 **Diepholz** Germany
21 N2 **Dieppe** France
127 P4 **Dieppe Bay Town** St Kitts W Indies
36 D2 **Dierdorf** Germany
25 F4 **Dieren** Netherlands
33 Q4 **Dierhagen** Germany
36 D2 **Dieringhausen** Germany
109 N1 **Dierks** Arkansas U.S.A.
65 F2 **Di'er Songhua Jiang** *R* China
33 N7 **Diesdorf** Germany
41 J2 **Diessenhofen** Switzerland
22 J2 **Diest** Belgium
110 H2 **Dieterich** Illinois U.S.A.
37 K3 **Dietersdorf** Germany
37 M5 **Dietfurt** Germany
41 H3 **Dietikon** Switzerland
101 L7 **Dietrich** Idaho U.S.A.
36 F3 **Dietzenbach** Germany
19 O15 **Dieulefit** France
19 K4 **Dieuze** France
25 F3 **Dieverbrug** Netherlands
36 B2 **Die Ville** *reg* Germany
36 E3 **Diez** Germany
65 D7 **Difang** China
22 K4 **Differdange** Luxembourg
67 F1 **Digang** China
75 Q5 **Digboi** India
122 G9 **Digby** Nova Scotia Canada
9 F1 **Digby** England
83 M14 **Digby, C** Kerguelen Indian Oc
122 F9 **Digby Neck** Nova Scotia Canada
107 K3 **Dighton** Kansas U.S.A.
95 Q5 **Dighton** Massachusetts U.S.A.
94 B2 **Dighton** Michigan U.S.A.
74 G9 **Diglur** India
19 Q16 **Digne** France
21 N4 **Digny** France
18 H6 **Digoin** France
71 F2 **Digollorin Pt** Luzon Philippines
71 G7 **Digos** Mindanao Philippines
74 G8 **Digras** India
136 H3 **Digul** *R* W Irian
86 H5 **Diinsoor** Somalia
71 E5 **Diit** *isld* Philippines
22 H2 **Dijle** *R* Belgium
19 J5 **Dijon** France
86 C4 **Dik** Chad
89 E4 **Dikabeye** Botswana
26 H6 **Dikanäs** Sweden
86 H3 **Dikhil** Djibouti
47 H5 **Dikili** Turkey
79 B7 **Dîkirnis** Egypt
22 D2 **Dikkebus** Belgium
67 F3 **Dikou** China
83 K11 **Dikoya** Sri Lanka
55 D2 **Dikoye, Oz** *L* Russian Federation
22 D1 **Diksmuide** Belgium
50 H1 **Dikson** Russian Federation
50 G1 **Dikson, Ostrov** *isld* Russian Federation
86 B3 **Dikwa** Nigeria
47 J7 **Dilek Dağ** *mt* Turkey
71 M9 **Dili** Timor Indonesia
106 E6 **Dilia** New Mexico U.S.A.
68 A6 **Diligent Str** Andaman Is
68 J7 **Di Linh** Vietnam
47 N11 **Diliskelesi Ist** *lighthouse* Turkey
119 M8 **Dilke** Saskatchewan Canada
103 O6 **Dilkon** Arizona U.S.A.
36 E2 **Dill** *R* Germany
118 G6 **Dillberry L. Prov Park** Alberta Canada
107 L6 **Dill City** Oklahoma U.S.A.
36 E2 **Dillenburg** Germany
98 K9 **Diller** Nebraska U.S.A.
109 H7 **Dilley** Texas U.S.A.
86 E3 **Dilling** Sudan
36 B5 **Dillingen** Germany
116 H7 **Dillingham** Alaska U.S.A.
118 H3 **Dillon** Saskatchewan Canada
106 D2 **Dillon** Colorado U.S.A.
101 N4 **Dillon** Montana U.S.A.
112 H3 **Dillon** South Carolina U.S.A.
144 D5 **Dillon Cone** *mt* New Zealand
94 E6 **Dillon Res** Ohio U.S.A.
95 K6 **Dillsburg** Pennsylvania U.S.A.
94 J9 **Dillwyn** Virginia U.S.A.
87 D8 **Dilolo** Zaire
75 P6 **Dimapur** India
124 F6 **Dimas** Mexico
79 G5 **Dimashq** Syria
86 D7 **Dimbelenge** Zaire
85 D7 **Dimbokro** Ivory Coast
138 F6 **Dimboola** Victoria Australia
48 J5 **Dîmbo Viţa** *R* Romania
48 J6 **Dîmboviţa** *reg* Romania
141 H3 **Dimbulah** Queensland Australia
54 J8 **Dimitrov** Ukraine
54 E8 **Dimitrova** Ukraine
47 H2 **Dimitrovgrad** Bulgaria
53 G7 **Dimitrovgrad** Russian Federation
46 F1 **Dimitrovgrad** Serbia Yugoslavia
46 G2 **Dimitrov, Yazovir G.** *res* Bulgaria
108 E1 **Dimmitt** Texas U.S.A.
98 H6 **Dimock** South Dakota U.S.A.
79 F7 **Dīmona** Israel
46 F1 **Dimovo** Bulgaria
71 G5 **Dinagat** *isld* Philippines
71 G5 **Dinagat Sound** Philippines
75 N6 **Dinajpur** Bangladesh
20 F5 **Dinan** France
22 H3 **Dinant** Belgium
47 L6 **Dinar** Turkey
42 G4 **Dinara Planina** *R* Bosnia-Herzegovina/Croatia
20 F4 **Dinard-St.Enogat** France
86 F3 **Dinder** *R* Sudan
76 C5 **Dindigul** India
109 K7 **Dinero** Texas U.S.A.
86 C7 **Dinga** Zaire
71 E3 **Dingalan B** Luzon Philippines
68 K3 **Ding'an** China
58 E4 **Dingbian** China
32 E9 **Dingden** Germany
20 G5 **Dingé** France
33 M10 **Dingelstädt** Germany
33 O9 **Dingelstedt** Germany
48 K3 **Dîngeni** Romania
75 M4 **Dinggyê** China
67 G1 **Dinghai** China
101 O7 **Dingle** Idaho U.S.A.
14 A4 **Dingle B** Ireland
67 E4 **Dingnan** China
141 J6 **Dingo** Queensland Australia
37 O6 **Dingolfing** Germany
71 E1 **Dingras** Luzon Philippines
65 C7 **Dingtao** China
85 B6 **Dinguiraye** Guinea
123 M7 **Dingwall** C Breton I, Nova Scotia
15 D3 **Dingwall** Scotland
58 D4 **Dingxi** China
65 C5 **Ding Xian** China
65 B5 **Dingxiang** China
65 C5 **Dingxing** China
65 E6 **Dingzi Gang** *B* China
69 H8 **Dinh An, Cua** *river mouth* Vietnam
67 B6 **Dinh Lap** Vietnam
25 H4 **Dinkel** *R* Netherlands
37 J5 **Dinkelsbühl** Germany
37 K7 **Dinkelscherben** Germany
32 H7 **Dinklage** Germany
103 O5 **Dinnebito Wash** *creek* Arizona U.S.A.
13 G3 **Dinnington** England
87 E10 **Dinokwe** Botswana
118 K1 **Dinorwic L** Ontario Canada
101 Q9 **Dinosaur Nat.Mon** Utah/Colo U.S.A.
78 J4 **Dīn, Şalāḩ ad** *prov* Iraq
32 E9 **Dinslaken** Germany
118 K7 **Dinsmore** Saskatchewan Canada
113 F7 **Dinsmore** Florida U.S.A.
70 K8 **Dintiteladas** *C* Sumatra
102 E5 **Dinuba** California U.S.A.
94 K9 **Dinwiddie** Virginia U.S.A.
25 F5 **Dinxperlo** Netherlands
27 G15 **Diö** Sweden
85 C6 **Dioila** Mali
116 C4 **Diomede Is** Bering Str
51 S2 **Diomida, Ostrova** *islds* Russian Federation
22 H3 **Dion** Belgium
86 D2 **Diona** Chad
130 D10 **Dionisio Cerqueira** Brazil
130 D5 **Diorama** Brazil
48 F2 **Diósgyör** Hungary
85 A6 **Diouloulou** Senegal
85 C6 **Dioura** Mali
85 A6 **Diourbel** Senegal
74 C6 **Diplo** Pakistan
71 F6 **Dipolog** Mindanao Philippines
22 L4 **Dippach** Luxembourg
12 C2 **Dippen** Scotland
12 C3 **Dippin** Scotland
144 B6 **Dipton** New Zealand
74 D1 **Dir** Pakistan
27 B13 **Dirdal** Norway
141 G2 **Direction,C** Queensland Australia
83 M8 **Direction I** Cocos Is Indian Oc
86 H4 **Dirē Dawa** Ethiopia
125 L4 **Diriamba** Nicaragua
87 D9 **Dirico** Angola
43 F11 **Dirillo** *R* Sicily
143 A7 **Dirk Hartog I** W Australia Australia
84 E6 **Dirkou** Niger
25 B5 **Dirksland** Netherlands
13 F1 **Dirleton** Scotland
36 C5 **Dirmingen** Germany
86 E3 **Dirra** Sudan
141 J8 **Dirranbandi** Queensland Australia
103 O3 **Dirty Devil** *R* Utah U.S.A.
102 T13 **Disappearing I** Hawaiian Is
131 H6 **Disappointment, C** S Georgia
100 A3 **Disappointment, C** Washington U.S.A.
135 N9 **Disappointment Is** Tuamotu Arch Pacific Oc
143 E6 **Disappointment,L** W Australia Australia
139 K6 **Disaster B** New South Wales Australia
100 F1 **Disautel** Washington U.S.A.
37 J6 **Dischingen** Germany
117 Q4 **Discovery** Northwest Territories Canada
138 F7 **Discovery B** S Aust/Vict Australia
127 K1 **Discovery Bay** Jamaica
100 C2 **Discovery Bay** Washington U.S.A.
100 C1 **Discovery I** Washington U.S.A.
90 J13 **Discovery Tablemount** S Atlantic Oc
142 E5 **Discovery Well** W Australia Australia
41 J4 **Disentis** Switzerland
13 G5 **Dishforth** England
116 J5 **Dishkakat** Alaska U.S.A.
116 J5 **Dishna** *R* Alaska U.S.A.
80 F1 **Dishon** *R* Israel
80 F1 **Dishon** Israel
115 O4 **Disko** *isld* Greenland
115 O4 **Diskofjord** Greenland
119 M8 **Disley** Saskatchewan Canada
140 F4 **Dismal** *R* Queensland Australia
98 F8 **Dismal** *R* Nebraska U.S.A.
95 L10 **Dismal Swamp** Virginia U.S.A.
52 C6 **Disna** Belarus
22 K2 **Dison** Belgium
95 K9 **Disputanta** Virginia U.S.A.
121 T7 **Disraëli** Quebec Canada
9 H3 **Diss** England
21 L8 **Dissay** France
21 L6 **Dissay-sous-Courcillon** France
32 H8 **Dissen** Germany
122 C4 **Dissimieux, L** Quebec Canada
100 C6 **Disston** Oregon U.S.A.
79 A7 **Disûq** Egypt
9 F6 **Ditchling** England
33 O9 **Ditfurt** Germany
32 K4 **Dithmarschen** *reg* Germany
43 F11 **Dittaino** *R* Sicily
36 G6 **Ditzingen** Germany
74 D8 **Diu** India
71 G6 **Diuata Mts** Mindanao Philippines
21 K7 **Dive** *R* France
52 D5 **Divenskaya** Russian Federation
121 L6 **Diver** Ontario Canada
110 G2 **Divernon** Illinois U.S.A.
142 G3 **Diversion Dam** W Australia Australia
109 H2 **Diversion L** Texas U.S.A.
21 K3 **Dives** *R* France
21 K3 **Dives sur Mer** France
20 G2 **Divette** *R* France
26 L3 **Dividal** *R* Norway
106 E3 **Divide** Colorado U.S.A.
141 H6 **Dividing Range** Queensland Australia
71 F2 **Divilacan B** Luzon Philippines
87 F10 **Divinhe** Mozambique
130 G7 **Divinopólis** Brazil
22 C3 **Divion** France
100 F8 **Division Peak** *mt* Nevada U.S.A.
53 F10 **Divnoye** Russian Federation
85 C7 **Divo** Ivory Coast
78 G2 **Divriği** Turkey
74 B5 **Diwana** Pakistan
78 K6 **Dīwānīyah, Ad** Iraq
121 O4 **Dix** Quebec Canada
98 C8 **Dix** Nebraska U.S.A.
95 R2 **Dixfield** Maine U.S.A.
111 K8 **Dixiana** Alabama U.S.A.
111 K10 **Dixie** Alabama U.S.A.
113 D7 **Dixie** Georgia U.S.A.
100 K4 **Dixie** Idaho U.S.A.
100 G3 **Dixie** Washington U.S.A.
100 G5 **Dixie Pass** Oregon U.S.A.
102 F2 **Dixie Valley** Nevada U.S.A.
121 Q5 **Dix Milles, L.des** Quebec Canada
95 S2 **Dixmont** Maine U.S.A.
95 O2 **Dix Mt** New York U.S.A.
Dixmude *see* **Diksmuide**
102 C3 **Dixon** California U.S.A.
99 R8 **Dixon** Illinois U.S.A.
110 D4 **Dixon** Missouri U.S.A.
101 L2 **Dixon** Montana U.S.A.
98 K7 **Dixon** Nebraska U.S.A.
106 E5 **Dixon** New Mexico U.S.A.
101 S8 **Dixon** Wyoming U.S.A.
117 G8 **Dixon Entrance** *str* Br Col/Alaska Canada/U.S.A.
111 J9 **Dixons Mills** Alabama U.S.A.
117 P7 **Dixonville** Alberta Canada
94 H6 **Dixonville** Pennsylvania U.S.A.
67 A4 **Dixu** China
121 T7 **Dixville** Quebec Canada
78 K5 **Diyālá** *prov* Iraq
78 H3 **Diyarbakır** Turkey
65 H3 **Diyingou** China
74 B9 **Diz** Pakistan
77 H6 **Diz** Pakistan
67 C2 **Dizhuang** China
8 B6 **Dizzard Pt** England
86 B5 **Dja** *R* Cameroon
84 E5 **Djado** Niger
84 E5 **Djado, Pl.du** Niger
71 A2 **Djailolo** Halmahera Indonesia
Djailolo Gilolo *isld see* **Halmahera** *isld*
Djajapura *see* **Jayapura**
86 B6 **Djambala** Congo
69 F13 **Djambi** *prov* Sumatra
70 L9 **Djampang-Kulon** Java
85 F4 **Djanet** Algeria
70 E6 **Djangeru** Kalimantan
70 E3 **Djanlonong** Kalimantan
85 E3 **Djaret** *watercourse* Algeria
70 L9 **Djatinegara** Java
70 M9 **Djatiwangi** Java
86 B2 **Djbella** Niger
69 G13 **Djebus** Indonesia
86 C3 **Djédaa** Chad
85 E2 **Djedi** *watercourse* Algeria
85 E2 **Djelfa** Algeria
86 E4 **Djéma** Cent Afr Republic
70 F7 **Djeneponto** Sulawesi
Djerba, I de *see* **Jerba, I de**
86 B4 **Djérem** *R* Cameroon
Djezair, El *see* **Alger**
85 D6 **Djibasso** Burkina
85 D6 **Djibo** Burkina
86 H3 **Djibouti** Djibouti
86 H3 **Djibouti** *rep* N E Africa
86 D7 **Djokopunda** Zaire
86 D5 **Djolu** Zaire
70 D7 **Djorong** Kalimantan
86 B6 **Djoué** *R* Congo
85 C5 **Djouf, El** *reg* Mauritania/Mali
85 E7 **Djougou** Benin
86 B5 **Djoum** Cameroon
86 C2 **Djourab** *dist* Chad
86 F5 **Djugu** Zaire
29 T9 **Djupivogur** Iceland
27 H11 **Djura** Sweden
27 K12 **Djursholm** Sweden
28 E4 **Djursland** *reg* Denmark
111 G10 **D'Lo** Mississippi U.S.A.
51 O1 **Dmitriya Lapteva, Proliv** *str* Russian Federation
55 G3 **Dmitriyevka** Russian Federation
54 G4 **Dmitriyev-L'govskiy** Russian Federation
54 J1 **Dmitrov** Russian Federation
54 D6 **Dmitrovka** Ukraine

54 G4 **Dmitrovsk-Orlovskiy** Russian Federation
54 B4 **Dnepr** *R* Belarus/Rus Fed etc
54 F8 **Dneprodzerzhinsk** Ukraine
54 G8 **Dnepropetrovsk** Ukraine
54 F9 **Dneprorudnoye** Ukraine
53 C7 **Dneprovskaya Nizmennost** *lowland* Belarus/Ukraine
54 C10 **Dneprovskiy Liman** *lagoon* Ukraine
53 C9 **Dnestr** *R* Europe
48 M4 **Dnestrovsk** Moldova
48 N4 **Dnestrovskiy Liman** *lagoon* Ukraine
Dnieper *R see* **Dnepr** *R*
Dniester *R see* **Dnestr** *R*
52 C5 **Dno** Russian Federation
77 K2 **Doāb Mekh-i-Zarīn** Afghanistan
122 F7 **Doaktown** New Brunswick Canada
70 E7 **Doangdoangan Besar** *isld* Indonesia
70 E7 **Doangdoangan Ketjil** *isld* Indonesia
67 B6 **Doan Hung** Vietnam
86 C4 **Doba** Chad
33 Q5 **Dobbertin** Germany
138 E2 **Dobbie, L** South Australia Australia
140 E6 **Dobbie,Mt** N Terr Australia
109 M5 **Dobbin** Texas U.S.A.
31 M6 **Dobczyce** Poland
52 B6 **Dobele** Latvia
37 P1 **Döbeln** Germany
33 T9 **Doberlug Kirchhain** Germany
31 J3 **Dobiegniew** Poland
133 E5 **Doblas** Argentina
136 G3 **Dobo** Moluccas Indonesia
48 E6 **Doboj** Bosnia-Herzegovina
112 F6 **Doboy Sd** Georgia U.S.A.
31 J2 **Dobra** Poland
37 M3 **Döbraberg** *mt* Germany
37 P4 **Dobřany** Czech Rep
38 J8 **Dobratsch** *mt* Austria
31 M2 **Dobre Miasto** Poland
48 G4 **Dobresti** Romania
48 H6 **Dobreta-Turnu-Severin** Romania
38 J8 **Döbriach** Austria
47 J1 **Dobrich** Bulgaria
33 S9 **Döbrichau** Germany
46 F3 **Dobrinishte** Bulgaria
31 H6 **Dobříš** Czech Rep
33 Q8 **Dobritz** Germany
31 L5 **Dobrodzień** Poland
31 O6 **Dobromil** Ukraine
54 J8 **Dobropol'ye** Ukraine
48 J6 **Dobroteşti** Romania
54 F2 **Dobroye** Russian Federation
54 C4 **Dobrush** Belarus
54 C4 **Dobryanka** Ukraine
31 L3 **Dobrzyn** Poland
48 F2 **Dobšiná** Slovakia
144 C5 **Dobson** New Zealand
144 B6 **Dobson** *R* New Zealand
112 G1 **Dobson** North Carolina U.S.A.
8 B7 **Dobwalls** England
127 N1 **Docas del Dragón** *chan* Trinidad/Ven
71 D7 **Doc Can** *isld* Sulu Arch Philippines
130 G6 **Doce, R** Brazil
143 G6 **Docker Cr** W Australia Australia
140 A6 **Docker River** N Terr Australia
9 G2 **Docking** England
26 H9 **Dockmyr** Sweden
142 F4 **Dockrell, Mt** W Australia Australia
26 K8 **Docksta** Sweden
36 B3 **Dockweiler** Germany
109 H10 **Doctor Cos** Mexico
143 E8 **Doctor Hicks Ra** W Australia Australia
Doctor Petru Groza *see* **Ştei**
121 P3 **Doda, L** Quebec Canada
76 C4 **Dod Ballapur** India
13 F2 **Doddington** England
109 O2 **Doddridge** Arkansas U.S.A.
118 E5 **Dodds** Alberta Canada
Dodecanese *islds see* **Dhodhekánisos** *islds*
98 K8 **Dodge** Nebraska U.S.A.
98 D2 **Dodge** North Dakota U.S.A.
99 O5 **Dodge Center** Minnesota U.S.A.
107 K4 **Dodge City** Kansas U.S.A.
99 Q7 **Dodgeville** Wisconsin U.S.A.
8 B7 **Dodman Pt** England
88 E5 **Dodoma** Tanzania
33 O6 **Dodow** Germany
118 J7 **Dodsland** Saskatchewan Canada
109 P3 **Dodson** Louisiana U.S.A.
101 R1 **Dodson** Montana U.S.A.
47 K5 **Dodurga** Turkey
22 G1 **Doel** Belgium
112 D6 **Doerun** Georgia U.S.A.
25 F4 **Doesburg** Netherlands
25 F5 **Doetinchem** Netherlands
71 J5 **Dofa** Indonesia
36 F6 **Doffingen** Germany
66 D5 **Dogai Coring** *L* China
47 H6 **Doğanbey Burun** *C* Turkey
78 G1 **Doğankent** Turkey
79 F2 **Doğankent** Turkey
117 M10 **Dog Creek** British Columbia Canada
66 E5 **Dogên Co** *L* China
47 L5 **Döğer** Turkey
7 M8 **Dogger Bank** North Sea
127 N5 **Dog I** Lesser Antilles
144 B7 **Dog I** New Zealand
113 C8 **Dog I** Florida U.S.A.
119 T7 **Dog L** Manitoba Canada
99 R1 **Dog L** Ontario Canada
44 C2 **Dogliani** Italy
38 H9 **Dogna** Italy
60 G9 **Dōgo** *isld* Japan
85 E6 **Dogondoutchi** Niger
60 G10 **Dōgo-yama** *mt* Japan
118 C7 **Dog Pound** Alberta Canada
126 E2 **Dog Rocks** Bahamas
78 K2 **Doğubayazit** Turkey
127 P4 **Dogwood Pt** Nevis W Indies
Doha *see* **Dawḩah, Ad**
Dohad *see* **Dāhod**
75 P7 **Dohazar** Bangladesh
121 S5 **Doheny** Quebec Canada
33 N4 **Döhnsdorf** Germany
71 A1 **Doi** Indonesia
68 D3 **Doi Saket** Thailand
22 H3 **Doische** Belgium
130 E8 **Dois Córregos** Brazil
46 F3 **Dojran** Macedonia
46 F3 **Dojrawsko ezero** *L* Macedonia
27 D11 **Dokka** Norway
26 M4 **Dokkas** Sweden
28 E3 **Dokkedal** Denmark
25 E2 **Dokkum** Netherlands
55 D5 **Dokuchayevka** Kazakhstan
54 J9 **Dokuchayevsk** Ukraine
136 H3 **Dolak** *isld* W Irian
98 H5 **Doland** South Dakota U.S.A.
121 S4 **Dolbeau** Quebec Canada
32 G9 **Dolberg** Germany
20 G4 **Dol-de Bretagne** France
19 J5 **Dôle** France
125 N5 **Dolega** Panama
42 G3 **Dolenjske Toplice** Slovenia
8 C3 **Dolfor** Wales
8 C2 **Dolgellau** Wales
95 N3 **Dolgeville** New York U.S.A.
116 G9 **Dolgoi I** Alaska U.S.A.
55 E3 **Dolgovskoye** Russian Federation
48 H2 **Dolgoye** Ukraine
43 C9 **Dolianova** Sardinia
48 H2 **Dolina** Ukraine
59 M2 **Dolinsk** Russian Federation
54 D8 **Dolinskaya** Ukraine
71 A3 **Dolit** Indonesia
46 F1 **Dolj** Romania
46 E1 **Doljevac** Serbia Yugoslavia
38 G8 **Döllach** Austria
12 E1 **Dollar** Scotland
118 J9 **Dollard** Saskatchewan Canada
122 F3 **Dollard, L** Quebec Canada
15 E5 **Dollar Law** *mt* Scotland
32 F6 **Dollart** *inlet* Germany/Neths
32 M8 **Dollbergen** Germany
33 P8 **Dolle** Germany
146 D5 **Dolleman I** Antarctica
28 C4 **Dollerup** Denmark
37 L6 **Dollnstein** Germany
21 M5 **Dollon** France
37 K1 **Döllstädt** Germany
46 G1 **Dolna Mitropbliya** Bulgaria
46 E3 **Dolneni** Macedonia
46 G1 **Dolni Dŭbnik** Bulgaria
37 Q2 **Dolní Jiřetín** Czech Rep
31 J6 **Dolní Královice** Czech Rep
37 O3 **Dolní Žandov** Czech Rep
45 M1 **Dolo** Italy
70 F5 **Dolo** Sulawesi
19 P13 **Dolomieu** France
42 D2 **Dolomitiche, Alpi** Italy
Dolonnur *see* **Duolun**
86 H5 **Dolo Odo** Ethiopia
131 F6 **Dolores** Argentina
125 P9 **Dolores** Guatemala
17 G6 **Dolores** Spain
131 F4 **Dolores** Uruguay
106 B3 **Dolores** *R* Colorado U.S.A.
106 B4 **Dolores** Colorado U.S.A.
125 J7 **Dolores Hidalgo** Mexico
133 F8 **Dolphin, C** Falkland Is
127 H1 **Dolphin Hd** *hill* Jamaica
87 B11 **Dolphin Hd** Namibia
142 B5 **Dolphin I** W Australia Australia
13 E2 **Dolphinton** Scotland
114 H4 **Dolphin & Union Str** Northwest Territories Canada
38 G8 **Dölsach** Austria
31 K4 **Dolsk** Poland
68 G3 **Do Luong** Vietnam
21 M7 **Dolus-le-Sec** France
8 C1 **Dolwyddelan** Wales
136 H2 **Dom** *mt* W Irian
122 H2 **Domagaya L** Labrador, Nfld Canada
119 U9 **Domain** Manitoba Canada
47 K5 **Domaniç** Turkey
47 K5 **Domaniç Dağı** *mt* Turkey
21 P1 **Domart-en-Ponthieu** France
37 O5 **Domažlice** Czech Rep
55 C5 **Dombarovskiy** Russian Federation
26 D9 **Dombås** Norway
19 K4 **Dombasle** France
87 B8 **Dombe Grande** Angola
140 A2 **Dombey,C** N Terr Australia
48 E4 **Dombóvár** Hungary
48 G2 **Dombrád** Hungary
37 J5 **Dombühl** Germany
25 A5 **Domburg** Netherlands
103 K9 **Dome** Arizona U.S.A.
117 N9 **Dome Creek** British Columbia Canada
40 E7 **Dôme-de-Chasseforêt** France
103 K8 **Dome Rock Mts** Arizona U.S.A.
144 D5 **Domett** New Zealand
145 D4 **Domett, Mt** New Zealand
36 B6 **Domèvre** France
21 J4 **Domfront** France
106 D6 **Domingo** New Mexico U.S.A.
127 O7 **Dominica** *isld* Lesser Antilles
127 J5 **Dominican Rep** W Indies
123 M7 **Dominion** C Breton I, Nova Scotia
115 M4 **Dominion, C** Northwest Territories Canada
119 U9 **Dominion City** Manitoba Canada
123 L1 **Dominion L** Labrador, Nfld Canada
115 O7 **Domino** Labrador, Nfld Canada
33 O6 **Dömitz** Germany
21 H4 **Domjean** France
130 G6 **Dom Joaquim** Brazil
41 K4 **Domleschg** *R* Switzerland
18 F8 **Domme** France
25 D6 **Dommel** *R* Netherlands
33 R9 **Dommitzsch** Germany
86 A2 **Domo** Ethiopia
54 J1 **Domodedovo** Russian Federation
41 H5 **Domodossola** Italy
21 P3 **Domont** France
146 E14 **Domont d'Urville Sea** Antarctica
40 D1 **Dompaire** France
21 H5 **Dompierre-du-Chemin** France
22 B3 **Dompierre-sur-Authie** France
20 H8 **Dompierre-sur-Yon** France
36 B7 **Domptail** France
71 J9 **Dompu** Sumbawa Indonesia
119 M6 **Domremy** Saskatchewan Canada
26 K8 **Domsjö** Sweden
88 E9 **Domue** *pk* Mozambique
131 B6 **Domuyo** *pk* Argentina
141 K8 **Domville** *mt* Queensland Australia
141 K8 **Domville,Mt** Queensland Australia
46 F6 **Domvraína** Greece
42 F2 **Domžale** Slovenia
141 J5 **Don** *R* Queensland Australia
20 G6 **Don** *R* France
22 D2 **Don** France
124 E4 **Don** Mexico
54 L5 **Don** *R* Russian Federation
15 F3 **Don** *R* Scotland
106 D9 **Dona Ana** New Mexico U.S.A.
45 M1 **Donada** Italy
14 F2 **Donaghadee** N Ireland
139 G6 **Donald** Victoria Australia
121 M8 **Donald** Ontario Canada
118 E6 **Donalda** Alberta Canada
144 A6 **Donald, Mt** New Zealand
140 F4 **Donaldson** Queensland Australia
109 P1 **Donaldson** Arkansas U.S.A.
98 K1 **Donaldson** Minnesota U.S.A.
111 E11 **Donaldsonville** Louisiana U.S.A.
112 C6 **Donalsonville** Georgia U.S.A.
14 E3 **Donard** Ireland
124 G5 **Donato Guerra** Mexico
38 L5 **Donau** *R* Austria
37 L6 **Donau** *R* Germany
41 J2 **Donaueschingen** Germany
37 L6 **Donaumoos** *reg* Germany
37 K6 **Donauried** *reg* Germany
37 N5 **Donaustauf** Germany
37 K6 **Donauwörth** Germany
118 K7 **Donavon** Saskatchewan Canada
38 M7 **Donawitz** Austria
54 J8 **Donbass (Donetskiy Ugol'nyy Basseyn)** Ukraine
16 D6 **Don Benito** Spain
140 B1 **Don,C** N Terr Australia
13 G6 **Doncaster** England
95 K8 **Doncaster** Maryland U.S.A.
22 H4 **Donchery** France
22 K4 **Doncols** Luxembourg
87 B7 **Dondo** Angola
87 F9 **Dondo** Mozambique
71 E6 **Dondonay** *isld* Philippines
70 G4 **Dondo, Teluk** *B* Sulawesi
70 G4 **Dondo, Tg** *C* Sulawesi
73 N7 **Dondra Head** *C* Sri Lanka
48 L2 **Dondyushany** Moldova
14 C2 **Donegal** Ireland
14 D2 **Donegal** *co* Ireland
14 C2 **Donegal Bay** *B* Ireland
14 B4 **Donegal Pt** Ireland
110 K5 **Donelson** Tennessee U.S.A.
14 C4 **Doneraile** Ireland
54 J8 **Donetsk** Ukraine
53 E9 **Donetskiy Kryazh** *mts* Rus Fed/Ukraine
127 J2 **Don Figuerero Mts** Jamaica
86 B4 **Donga** *R* Nigeria
59 K2 **Dong'an** China
67 D3 **Dong'an** China
68 J5 **Dong An** Vietnam
143 A8 **Dongara** W Australia
74 J8 **Dongargarh** India
66 D4 **Dongbolhai Shan** *mts* China
Dongchangshou *see* **Xinle**
Dongcun *see* **Haiyang**
68 H2 **Dong Dang** Vietnam
65 C6 **Dong'e** China
25 C5 **Dongen** Netherlands
20 F7 **Donges** France
68 J3 **Dongfang** China
65 J1 **Dongfanghong** China
65 F3 **Dongfeng** China
70 F5 **Donggala** Sulawesi
58 C4 **Donggi Cona** *L* China
67 D1 **Donggong** China
65 F4 **Donggou** China
67 E3 **Donggu** China
67 E5 **Dongguan** China
65 C6 **Dongguang** China
68 H4 **Dong Ha** Vietnam
65 D7 **Donghai** China
67 C6 **Donghai Dao** *isld* China
58 D3 **Dong He** *R* China
58 E4 **Dong He** *R* China
68 H4 **Dong Hoi** Vietnam
Donghuang *see* **Xishui** Guizhou
67 C4 **Dongjiang** China
65 H2 **Dongjingcheng** China
70 F6 **Dongkait, Tanjong** *C* Sulawesi
70 G4 **Dongkalang** Sulawesi
68 H1 **Dong Khe** Vietnam
67 C3 **Dongkou** China
67 B4 **Donglan** China
Dongliao *see* **Liaoyuan**
65 F3 **Dongliao He** *R* China
67 B5 **Dongling** China
67 E1 **Dongliu** China
65 C7 **Dongming** China
68 H7 **Dong Nai** *R* Vietnam
59 K2 **Dongning** China
87 C8 **Dongo** Angola
41 K5 **Dongo** Italy
86 C5 **Dongo** Zaire
84 J6 **Dongola** Sudan
86 C5 **Dongou** Congo
68 E4 **Dong Phraya Fai** *ra* Thailand
68 E5 **Dong Phraya Yen** Thailand
Dongping *see* **Anhua**
65 C7 **Dongping** China
65 C6 **Dongping Hu** *L* China
68 H7 **Dong Sai** Vietnam
67 F5 **Dongshan** China
67 F5 **Dongshan Dao** *isld* China
67 E6 **Dongsha Qundao** *isld* China
65 A5 **Dongsheng** China
67 B2 **Dongsheng** China
67 D2 **Dongting Hu** *L* China
67 G3 **Dongtou** China
67 B6 **Dong Trieu** Vietnam
65 D2 **Dong Ujimqin Qi** China
68 G1 **Dong Van** Vietnam
87 D8 **Dongwe** *R* Zambia
67 B2 **Dongxi** China
67 E2 **Dongxiang** China
65 D7 **Dongxi Lian Dao** *isld* China
65 G1 **Dongxing** China
67 B6 **Dongxing** China
67 G2 **Dongyang** China
65 D6 **Dongying** China
67 F1 **Dongzhi** China
109 L4 **Donie** Texas U.S.A.
9 F2 **Donington** England
110 F5 **Doniphan** Missouri U.S.A.
117 D4 **Donjek** *R* Yukon Territory Canada
48 G6 **Donji Milanovac** Serbia Yugoslavia
42 H4 **Donji Vakuf** Bosnia-Herzegovina
18 H6 **Donjon, le** France
99 S3 **Donken** Michigan U.S.A.
26 F5 **Dönna** *isld* Norway
109 J9 **Donna** Texas U.S.A.
121 T6 **Donnacona** Quebec Canada
42 B3 **Donnas** Italy
36 B6 **Donnelay** France
110 G2 **Donnellson** Illinois U.S.A.
117 P8 **Donnelly** Alberta Canada
100 J5 **Donnelly** Idaho U.S.A.
98 K4 **Donnelly** Minnesota U.S.A.
145 D1 **Donnelly's Crossing** New Zealand
102 D2 **Donner Pass** California U.S.A.
38 K7 **Donnersbach** Austria
38 K7 **Donnersbach Wald** Austria
36 D4 **Donnersberg** *mt* Germany
100 G6 **Donner und Blitzen** *R* Oregon U.S.A.
26 F5 **Dönnes** Norway
143 B10 **Donnybrook** W Australia Australia
98 E1 **Donnybrook** North Dakota U.S.A.
19 K4 **Donon** *mt* France
36 C7 **Donon, Col du** *pass* France
94 H6 **Donora** Pennsylvania U.S.A.
140 F4 **Donor's Hill** Queensland Australia
99 T9 **Donovan** Illinois U.S.A.
102 D4 **Don Pedro Res** California U.S.A.
13 G6 **Don, R** England
54 K3 **Donskoy** Russian Federation
54 L6 **Donskoye Belogorye** Russian Federation
28 B5 **Donslund** Denmark
68 C4 **Donthami** *R* Burma
20 G4 **Donville** France
36 H6 **Donzdorf** Germany
18 G7 **Donzenac** France
19 N16 **Donzère** France
18 H5 **Donzy** France
143 C9 **Doodlakine** W Australia Australia
109 H4 **Doole** Texas U.S.A.
142 C5 **Dooleena** *mt* W Australia Australia
98 B1 **Dooley** Montana U.S.A.
121 O6 **Doolittle, L** Quebec Canada
140 E4 **Doomadgee** Queensland Australia
116 M3 **Doonerak, Mt** Alaska U.S.A.
12 D3 **Doon, L** Scotland
12 D3 **Doon, R** Scotland
25 D4 **Doorn** Netherlands
99 T5 **Door Pen** Wisconsin U.S.A.
86 A2 **Dooxo Nugaaleed** *V* Somalia
44 B1 **Dora** Italy
111 J8 **Dora** Alabama U.S.A.
106 G8 **Dora** New Mexico U.S.A.
42 B3 **Dora Baltea** *R* Italy
124 G4 **Dorado** Mexico
142 E5 **Dora,L** W Australia Australia
66 F5 **Doramarkog** China
113 F9 **Dora, Mt** Florida U.S.A.
98 K3 **Doran** Minnesota U.S.A.
27 G15 **Dörarp** Sweden
18 F6 **Dorat, le** France
Dorbiljin *see* **Emin**
Dorbiljin *see* **Emin**
Dorbod *see* **Siziwang Qi**
65 F1 **Dorbod** China
122 H8 **Dorchester** New Brunswick Canada
8 D6 **Dorchester** England
9 E4 **Dorchester** England
98 J9 **Dorchester** Nebraska U.S.A.
99 Q4 **Dorchester** Wisconsin U.S.A.
115 M4 **Dorchester, C** Northwest Territories Canada
89 A4 **Dordabis** Namibia
18 F7 **Dordogne** *dept* France
18 E8 **Dordogne** *R* France
25 C5 **Dordrecht** Netherlands
18 H7 **Dore** *R* France
140 B5 **Doreen, Mt** N Terr Australia
118 K4 **Doré L** Saskatchewan Canada
18 G7 **Dore, Mont** *mt* France
100 C6 **Dorena** Oregon U.S.A.
32 H8 **Dörenberg** *mt* Germany
32 J9 **Dörenhagen** Germany
118 E6 **Dorenlee** Alberta Canada
32 J8 **Dörentrup** Germany
130 F6 **Dores do Indaiá** Brazil
37 N7 **Dorfen** Germany
32 L7 **Dorfmark** Germany
33 R6 **Dorf Zechlin** Germany
43 C8 **Dorgali** Sardinia
77 J4 **Dori** *R* Afghanistan
85 D6 **Dori** Burkina
75 K5 **Dorīghāt** India
89 A8 **Doring** *R* S Africa
118 J4 **Dorintosh** Saskatchewan Canada
120 B4 **Dorion** Ontario Canada
121 Q7 **Dorion** Quebec Canada
140 B2 **Dorisvale** N Terr Australia
9 F5 **Dorking** England
36 B1 **Dormagen** Germany
18 H3 **Dormans** France
19 N13 **D'Or, Mt** France
41 L3 **Dornbirn** Austria
36 E2 **Dornburg** Germany
37 M1 **Dorndorf** Germany
37 J2 **Dorndorf** Germany
48 K3 **Dorneşti** Romania
36 F7 **Dornhan** Germany
15 C3 **Dornie** Scotland
48 J3 **Dornişoara** Romania
33 Q8 **Dörnitz** Germany
15 D3 **Dornoch** Scotland
15 D3 **Dornoch Firth** Scotland
13 E4 **Dornock** Scotland
65 A2 **Dornogovī** *prov* Mongolia
36 F7 **Dornstetten** Germany
32 F5 **Dornum** Germany
48 E3 **Dorog** Hungary
54 E2 **Dorogobuzh** Russian Federation
52 F2 **Dorogorskoye** Russian Federation
48 K3 **Dorohoi** Romania
54 H1 **Dorokhovo** Russian Federation
26 H7 **Dorotea** Sweden
118 E7 **Dorothy** Alberta Canada
52 G5 **Dorovitsa** Russian Federation
32 F7 **Dörpen** Germany
107 M3 **Dorrance** Kansas U.S.A.
143 A7 **Dorre I** W Australia Australia
139 L4 **Dorrigo** New South Wales Australia
8 D2 **Dorrington** England
100 D8 **Dorris** California U.S.A.
100 E8 **Dorris Res** California U.S.A.
121 M7 **Dorset** Ontario Canada
8 D6 **Dorset** *co* England
94 G5 **Dorset** Ohio U.S.A.
95 O3 **Dorset** Vermont U.S.A.
32 E9 **Dorsten** Germany
32 G9 **Dortmund** Germany
32 J5 **Dorum** Germany
86 E5 **Doruma** Zaire
121 R7 **Dorval** Quebec Canada
36 H5 **Dörzbach** Germany
133 D6 **Dos Bahías, C** Argentina
125 P9 **Dos Bocas** Belize
103 P9 **Dos Cabezas** Arizona U.S.A.
77 G2 **Doshakh, Koh-I** *mt* Afghanistan
71 E4 **Dos Hermanas** *isld* Philippines
16 D7 **Dos Hermanas** Spain
68 H2 **Do Son** Vietnam
102 D5 **Dos Palos** California U.S.A.
46 G3 **Dospat** Bulgaria
121 T6 **Dosquet** Quebec Canada
102 A2 **Dos Rios** California U.S.A.
109 H5 **Doss** Texas U.S.A.
33 R6 **Dosse** *R* Germany
85 E6 **Dosso** Niger
45 J1 **Dossobuono** Italy
50 E4 **Dossor** Kazakhstan
28 D3 **Døstrup** Denmark
94 K9 **Doswell** Virginia U.S.A.
111 L10 **Dothan** Alabama U.S.A.
100 B7 **Dothan** Oregon U.S.A.
123 T4 **Doting Cove** Newfoundland Canada
116 P5 **Dot Lake** Alaska U.S.A.
32 H7 **Dötlingen** Germany
101 S10 **Dotsero** Colorado U.S.A.
36 H5 **Döttingen** Germany
21 N8 **Douadic** France
22 E3 **Douai** France
86 A5 **Douala** Cameroon
20 B5 **Douarnenez** France
20 B5 **Douarnenez, Baie de** France
109 N6 **Double Bayou** Texas U.S.A.
126 D3 **Double Headed Shot Cays** *islds* Bahamas
68 C5 **Double I** Burma
141 L7 **Double Island Pt** Queensland Australia
108 G2 **Double Mountain Fork** *R* Texas U.S.A.
102 F6 **Double Mt** California U.S.A.
116 L6 **Double Peak** Alaska U.S.A.
141 H4 **Double Pt** *C* Queensland Australia
111 J7 **Double Springs** Alabama U.S.A.
31 J6 **Doubrava** *R* Czech Rep
19 J6 **Doubs** *R* France
40 D3 **Doubs** *dept* France
40 F3 **Doubs** *R* Switzerland
142 E3 **Doubtful B** W Australia Australia
143 C10 **Doubtful Island B** W Australia Australia
144 A6 **Doubtful Sd** New Zealand
145 D1 **Doubtless B** New Zealand
40 C4 **Doucier** France
21 M2 **Doudeville** France
99 O9 **Douds** Iowa U.S.A.
21 K7 **Doué-la-Fontaine** Maine-et-Loire France
85 D6 **Douentza** Mali
144 A7 **Doughboy Bay** New Zealand
138 D3 **Douglas** *R* South Australia Australia
119 S9 **Douglas** Manitoba Canada
121 O7 **Douglas** Ontario Canada
89 C7 **Douglas** S Africa
12 E3 **Douglas** Scotland
12 D5 **Douglas** I of Man U.K.
117 F6 **Douglas** Alaska U.S.A.
103 P10 **Douglas** Arizona U.S.A.
112 E6 **Douglas** Georgia U.S.A.
99 U7 **Douglas** Michigan U.S.A.
98 K9 **Douglas** Nebraska U.S.A.
98 E2 **Douglas** North Dakota U.S.A.
100 E2 **Douglas** Washington U.S.A.
98 A7 **Douglas** Wyoming U.S.A.
117 J9 **Douglas Chan** British Columbia Canada
106 B2 **Douglas Cr** Colorado U.S.A.
112 D1 **Douglas Dam** Tennessee U.S.A.
94 C1 **Douglas L** Michigan U.S.A.
112 D2 **Douglas L** Tennessee U.S.A.
12 E2 **Douglas Mill** Scotland
143 E8 **Douglas,Mount** W Australia Australia
116 L7 **Douglas, Mt** Alaska U.S.A.
120 J8 **Douglas Pt** Ontario Canada
107 O4 **Douglass** Kansas U.S.A.
122 G6 **Douglastown** New Brunswick Canada
122 H5 **Douglastown** Quebec Canada
111 M8 **Douglasville** Georgia U.S.A.
22 F3 **Doui** Belgium
46 D6 **Doukáton,Akr** *C* Greece
19 J4 **Doulevant le Château** France
21 P1 **Doullens** France
20 H7 **Doulon** France
14 A5 **Doulus Hd** Ireland
86 B5 **Doumé** Cameroon
67 D5 **Doumen** China
67 A5 **Doumuge** China
12 D1 **Doune** Scotland
15 E2 **Dounreay** Scotland
85 C7 **Douobé** *R* Liberia
37 P3 **Doupov** Czech Rep
22 F3 **Dour** France
130 E6 **Dourada, Cachoeira** *rapids* Brazil
129 J6 **Dourada,Serra** *mts* Brazil
130 E5 **Dourada,Serra** *mts* Brazil
130 B6 **Dourados** Brazil
130 C8 **Dourados** Brazil
133 F2 **Dourados** *R* Brazil
130 D8 **Dourados,Serra dos** *mts* Brazil
21 P4 **Dourdan** France
18 G9 **Dourdou** *R* France
22 B3 **Douriez** France
16 C3 **Douro** *R* Portugal
16 B3 **Douro Litoral** *prov* Portugal
Doushi *see* **Gong'an**
19 Q13 **Doussard** France
20 H3 **Douve** *R* France
21 K3 **Douvres-la-Délivrande** France
19 N14 **Doux** *R* France
18 E9 **Douze** *R* France
22 J4 **Douzy** France
45 L3 **Dovadola** Italy
106 B4 **Dove Creek** Colorado U.S.A.
142 C5 **Dove,Mt** W Australia Australia
139 H9 **Dover** Tasmania Australia
28 D4 **Dover** Denmark
9 E1 **Dove,R** England
9 H5 **Dover** England
110 C6 **Dover** Arkansas U.S.A.
95 M7 **Dover** Delaware U.S.A.
113 E9 **Dover** Florida U.S.A.
112 F5 **Dover** Georgia U.S.A.
110 N3 **Dover** Kentucky U.S.A.
95 Q3 **Dover** New Hampshire U.S.A.
95 N6 **Dover** New Jersey U.S.A.
112 K2 **Dover** North Carolina U.S.A.
94 F6 **Dover** Ohio U.S.A.
107 N6 **Dover** Oklahoma U.S.A.
110 J5 **Dover** Tennessee U.S.A.
95 S1 **Dover Foxcroft** Maine U.S.A.
143 F10 **Dover,Pt** W Australia Australia
22 C1 **Dover,Str.of** France/England
38 J9 **Dovje** Slovenia
28 F7 **Dovnsklint** Denmark
26 D9 **Dovre** Norway
26 D9 **Dovrefjell** Norway
26 D9 **Dovrefjell Nat. Park** Norway
88 D8 **Dowa** Malawi
94 A5 **Dowagiac** Michigan U.S.A.
143 B9 **Dowerin** W Australia Australia
Dow, L. *see* **Xau, L.**
8 C4 **Dowlais** Wales
77 J1 **Dowlatābād** Afghanistan
77 H3 **Dowlatābād** Afghanistan
77 E5 **Dowlatābād** Iran
77 J2 **Dowlat Yār** Afghanistan
118 F7 **Dowling** Alberta Canada
14 F2 **Down** *co* N Ireland
99 T8 **Downers Grove** Illinois U.S.A.
102 F8 **Downey** California U.S.A.
101 N7 **Downey** Idaho U.S.A.
141 K1 **Downfall Cr** Brisbane, Qnsld Australia
9 G2 **Downham Market** England
102 D2 **Downieville** California U.S.A.
99 O9 **Downing** Missouri U.S.A.
95 M6 **Downingtown** Pennsylvania U.S.A.
14 F2 **Downpatrick** N Ireland
14 B2 **Downpatrick Hd** Ireland
107 M2 **Downs** Kansas U.S.A.
101 Q6 **Downs Mt** Wyoming U.S.A.
95 M4 **Downsville** New York U.S.A.
9 E5 **Downton** England
117 L9 **Downton,Mt** British Columbia Canada
8 B6 **Downtown** England
99 N7 **Dows** Iowa U.S.A.
77 L2 **Dowshī** Afghanistan
7 L9 **Dowsing Lightship** North Sea
69 C12 **Dowu, Tanjung** *C* Indonesia
102 D1 **Doyle** California U.S.A.
110 L6 **Doyle** Tennessee U.S.A.
144 D5 **Doyleston** New Zealand
95 M6 **Doylestown** Pennsylvania U.S.A.
106 D3 **Doyleville** Colorado U.S.A.
60 F9 **Dōzen** *islds* Japan
59 K4 **Dōzen Nishi Jima** *isld* Japan
111 K10 **Dozier** Alabama U.S.A.
121 N5 **Dozois, Rés** Quebec Canada
21 K3 **Dozulé** France
45 L3 **Dozza** Italy
85 C2 **Drâa** *R* Morocco/Algeria
36 C2 **Drabenderhöhe** Germany
28 F4 **Dråby** Denmark
19 P15 **Drac** *R* France
130 D7 **Dracena** Brazil
46 E3 **Dračevo** Macedonia
36 E5 **Drachenfels** *mt* Germany
25 F2 **Drachten** Netherlands
95 Q4 **Dracut** Massachusetts U.S.A.
28 F6 **Dræby** Denmark
48 L6 **Dragalina** Romania
26 H7 **Dragan** *L* Sweden
48 J6 **Drăgăneşti-Olt** Romania
48 K6 **Drăgăneşti-Vlaşca** Romania
48 J6 **Drăgăşani** Romania
103 O2 **Dragerton** Utah U.S.A.
46 E3 **Dragoevo** Macedonia
46 F2 **Dragoman** Bulgaria
45 K2 **Dragoncello** Italy
Dragon's Mouths *chan see* **Bocas del Dragon**
103 O9 **Dragoon** Arizona U.S.A.
29 K5 **Dragør** Denmark
46 F2 **Dragovistica** Bulgaria
29 J11 **Dragsfjärd** Finland
28 B3 **Dragstrup** Denmark
19 Q17 **Draguignan** France
33 T9 **Drahnsdorf** Germany
100 B6 **Drain** Oregon U.S.A.
22 G4 **Draize** France
139 K3 **Drake** New South Wales Australia
119 M7 **Drake** Saskatchewan Canada
103 M7 **Drake** Arizona U.S.A.
98 A9 **Drake** Colorado U.S.A.
98 F2 **Drake** North Dakota U.S.A.
32 K7 **Drakenburg** Germany
89 F8 **Drakensberg** *mts* S Africa
89 G5 **Drakensberg Garden** S Africa
146 B3 **Drake Passage** Antarctica
100 E7 **Drake Peak** *mt* Oregon U.S.A.
102 B4 **Drakes Bay** California U.S.A.
110 J4 **Drakesboro** Kentucky U.S.A.
94 J10 **Drakes Branch** Virginia U.S.A.
46 G3 **Dráma** Greece
27 D12 **Drammen** Norway
27 D12 **Dramsfj** *inlet* Norway
40 F5 **Drance** *R* Switzerland
48 L4 **Drânceni** Romania
27 D12 **Drangedal** Norway
40 E5 **Dranse** *R* France
33 R6 **Dranse** Germany
32 L9 **Dransfeld** Germany
28 C5 **Drantum** Denmark
112 H1 **Draper** North Carolina U.S.A.
98 F6 **Draper** South Dakota U.S.A.
101 O9 **Draper** Utah U.S.A.
117 D6 **Draper, Mt** Alaska U.S.A.
74 F1 **Dras** Kashmir
38 G8 **Drau** *R* Austria
38 N9 **Drava** *R* Slovenia
42 G2 **Dravograd** Slovenia
31 J2 **Drawa** *R* Poland
31 J2 **Drawsko** Poland
141 K8 **Drayton** Queensland Australia
98 J1 **Drayton** North Dakota U.S.A.
118 B5 **Drayton Val** Alberta Canada
37 O5 **Draženov** Czech Rep
43 B12 **Dréan** Algeria
37 P2 **Drebach** Germany
32 H7 **Drebber** Germany
48 E2 **Drégelypalánk** Hungary
33 M5 **Dreggers** Germany
36 F3 **Dreieichenhain** Germany
Dreihausen *see* **Ebsdorfergrund**
38 F7 **Dreiherrn-Spitze** *mt* Italy/Austria
36 B3 **Dreis** Germany
40 G1 **Dreisam** *R* Germany
37 P6 **Dreitannenriegel** *mt* Germany
28 E7 **Drejø** Denmark
13 F1 **Drem** Scotland
46 F2 **Dren** Bulgaria
33 T6 **Drense** Germany
32 G9 **Drensteinfurt** Germany
25 G3 **Drenthe** *prov* Netherlands
120 H10 **Dresden** Ontario Canada
37 Q1 **Dresden** Germany
107 K2 **Dresden** Kansas U.S.A.
98 H1 **Dresden** North Dakota U.S.A.
94 E6 **Dresden** Ohio U.S.A.
110 H5 **Dresden** Tennessee U.S.A.
52 C6 **Dretun'** Belarus
21 N4 **Dreux** France
26 F10 **Drevsjö** Norway
111 F8 **Drew** Mississippi U.S.A.
100 C7 **Drew** Oregon U.S.A.
33 Q5 **Drewitzer See** *L* Germany
100 G6 **Drewsey** Oregon U.S.A.
100 E7 **Drews Res** Oregon U.S.A.
110 B3 **Drexel** Missouri U.S.A.
31 J3 **Drezdenko** Poland
52 E6 **Drezna** Russian Federation
54 K1 **Drezna** Russian Federation
36 E2 **Driedorf** Germany
113 D7 **Drifton** Florida U.S.A.
118 B3 **Driftpile** Alberta Canada
120 J3 **Driftwood** Ontario Canada
94 J5 **Driftwood** Pennsylvania U.S.A.
101 O6 **Driggs** Idaho U.S.A.
141 J7 **Drillham** Queensland Australia
46 D2 **Drim** *R* Serbia Yugoslavia
14 B5 **Drimoleague** Ireland
46 D2 **Drin** *R* Albania
48 E7 **Drina** *R* Bosnia-Herzegovina/Yugoslavia
32 K9 **Dringenberg** Germany
46 D3 **Drinit, Pellgu i** *B* Albania
46 D3 **Drin i zi** *R* Albania
119 M8 **Drinkwater** Saskatchewan Canada
109 J5 **Dripping Springs** Texas U.S.A.
109 K8 **Driscoll** Texas U.S.A.
52 C6 **Drissa** *R* Belarus
26 D9 **Driva** *R* Norway
26 D9 **Drivstua** Norway
42 G5 **Drniš** Croatia
41 N6 **Dro** Italy
27 E12 **Dröbak** Norway
31 M3 **Drobin** Poland
55 F4 **Drobyshevo** Russian Federation
48 G4 **Drocea** *mt* Romania
32 K5 **Drochtersen** Germany
22 D3 **Drocourt** France
26 H3 **Drog** Norway
32 M6 **Drögen Nindorf** Germany
14 E3 **Drogheda** Ireland
14 E3 **Drogheda B** Ireland
48 H1 **Drogobych** Ukraine
31 O3 **Drohiczyn** Poland
8 D3 **Droitwich** England
48 L2 **Drokiya** Moldova
36 D1 **Drolshagen** Germany
139 H7 **Dromana** Victoria Australia
14 F2 **Dromara** N Ireland
19 O15 **Drôme** *dept* France
21 J3 **Drome** *R* Calvados France
139 K6 **Dromedary,C** New South Wales Australia
33 O8 **Dromling** Germany
14 D3 **Dromod** Ireland
14 D2 **Dromore** N Ireland
14 C2 **Dromore West** Ireland
44 B3 **Dronero** Italy
9 E1 **Dronfield** England
22 F1 **Drongen** Belgium
18 F7 **Dronne** *R* France
146 J8 **Dronning Fabiolafjella** *ra* Antarctica
28 E2 **Dronninglund** Denmark
146 H4 **Dronning Maud Land** Antarctica
146 H7 **Dronning Maud Land** Antarctica
119 Q7 **Dropmore** Manitoba Canada
18 F8 **Dropt** *R* France
31 J7 **Drosendorf** Austria
74 D1 **Drosh** Pakistan
28 G6 **Drøsselbjerg** Denmark
21 N5 **Droué** France
120 E2 **Drowning** *R* Ontario Canada
37 N1 **Droyssig** Germany
21 L3 **Drucourt** France
118 J7 **Druid** Saskatchewan Canada
8 C2 **Druid** Wales
126 A1 **Druif** Aruba W Indies
36 C6 **Drulingen** France
118 E7 **Drumheller** Alberta Canada
14 D4 **Drum Hills** Ireland
14 D3 **Drumlish** Ireland
144 B7 **Drummond** New Zealand
101 M3 **Drummond** Montana U.S.A.
99 P3 **Drummond** Wisconsin U.S.A.
94 D1 **Drummond I** Michigan U.S.A.
95 L10 **Drummond,L** Virginia U.S.A.
140 D4 **Drummond,Mt** N Terr Australia
141 H6 **Drummond Ra** Queensland Australia
121 S7 **Drummondville** Quebec Canada
12 D4 **Drummore** Scotland
15 D3 **Drumnadrochit** Scotland
15 D4 **Drumochter Pass** Scotland
107 O6 **Drumright** Oklahoma U.S.A.
14 C2 **Drumshanbo** Ireland
12 D1 **Drumvaich** Scotland
25 D5 **Drunen** Netherlands
119 V8 **Drunken Point** *C* Manitoba Canada
13 G3 **Druridge B** England
145 E2 **Drury** New Zealand
117 F4 **Drury L** Yukon Territory Canada
36 D6 **Drusenheim** France
31 O1 **Druskininkai** Lithuania
25 E5 **Druten** Netherlands
52 C6 **Druya** Belarus
54 E4 **Druzhba** Ukraine
51 O2 **Druzhina** Russian Federation
55 C3 **Druzhinino** Russian Federation
54 J8 **Druzhkovka** Ukraine
42 G4 **Drvar** Bosnia-Herzegovina
42 G5 **Drvenik** *isld* Croatia
100 B3 **Dryad** Washington U.S.A.
46 G2 **Dryanovo** Bulgaria
117 D6 **Dry B** Alaska U.S.A.
118 J1 **Dryberry L** Ontario Canada
119 Q2 **Drybrough** Manitoba Canada
101 R5 **Dry Cr** Wyoming U.S.A.
118 K1 **Dryden** Ontario Canada
94 D4 **Dryden** Michigan U.S.A.
95 L4 **Dryden** New York U.S.A.
108 E5 **Dryden** Texas U.S.A.
110 E4 **Dry Fork** *R* Missouri U.S.A.
98 A6 **Dry Fork** *R* Wyoming U.S.A.
146 J13 **Drygalski I.** Antarctica
146 C12 **Drygalski Ice Tongue** *ice tongue* Antarctica
8 C3 **Drygarn Fawr** *mt* Wales
127 K2 **Dry Harbour Mts** Jamaica
102 G2 **Dry L** Nevada U.S.A.
122 F1 **Drylake** Labrador, Nfld Canada
103 K5 **Dry Lake** Nevada U.S.A.
103 K4 **Dry Lake Valley** Nevada U.S.A.
12 D1 **Drymen** Scotland
111 D10 **Dry Prong** Louisiana U.S.A.
141 G4 **Dry R** Queensland Australia
140 D1 **Drysdale I** N Terr Australia
142 F2 **Drysdale River Nat Park** W Australia Australia
113 E13 **Dry Tortugas** *islds* Florida U.S.A.
85 G7 **Dschang** Cameroon
99 V5 **Dtblin** Michigan U.S.A.
86 D5 **Dua** *R* Zaire
127 K9 **Duaca** Venezuela
67 C4 **Du'an** China
Duancun *see* **Wuxiang**
95 N2 **Duane** New York U.S.A.
141 J6 **Duaringa** Queensland Australia
127 J5 **Duarte, Pico** *mt* Dominican Rep
130 E8 **Duartina** Brazil
130 D8 **Duas Onças,Ilha das** Brazil
20 D5 **Duault** France
109 P3 **Dubach** Louisiana U.S.A.
77 D7 **Dubai** U.A.E.
100 B9 **Dubakella Mt** California U.S.A.
114 J5 **Dubawnt** *R* Northwest Territories Canada
Dubayy *see* **Dubai**
139 J4 **Dubbo** New South Wales Australia
56 C1 **Dubches** *R* Russian Federation
37 O4 **Dubec** Czech Rep
33 T9 **Duben** Germany
55 C5 **Dubenskiy** Russian Federation
12 B1 **Dubh Artach** *isld* Scotland
48 G1 **Dubiecko** Poland
57 K3 **Dubin** Kazakhstan
124 F2 **Dublán** Mexico
120 J9 **Dublin** Ontario Canada
14 E3 **Dublin** *co* Ireland
14 E3 **Dublin** Ireland
112 E5 **Dublin** Georgia U.S.A.
94 B7 **Dublin** Indiana U.S.A.
111 F7 **Dublin** Mississippi U.S.A.
94 D6 **Dublin** Ohio U.S.A.
109 J3 **Dublin** Texas U.S.A.
52 E6 **Dubna** *R* Russian Federation
54 H2 **Dubna** Russian Federation
101 N5 **Dubois** Idaho U.S.A.
99 K9 **Du Bois** Nebraska U.S.A.
94 J5 **Du Bois** Pennsylvania U.S.A.
101 Q6 **Dubois** Wyoming U.S.A.
48 M3 **Dubossary** Moldova
54 K3 **Dubovka** Russian Federation
85 B7 **Dubréka** Guinea
54 E3 **Dubrovka** Russian Federation
42 J6 **Dubrovnik** Croatia
54 B2 **Dubrovno** Belarus
55 E2 **Dubrovnoye** Russian Federation
119 P8 **Dubuc** Saskatchewan Canada
99 Q7 **Dubuque** Iowa U.S.A.
52 G6 **Dub'yazy** Russian Federation
20 F6 **Duc,Etang au** *L* France
20 H4 **Ducey** France
67 E2 **Duchang** China
121 Q3 **Ducharme** Quebec Canada
30 H5 **Duchcov** Czech Rep
33 T5 **Ducherow** Germany
101 P9 **Duchesne** Utah U.S.A.
140 E5 **Duchess** Queensland Australia
118 F8 **Duchess** Alberta Canada
141 F1 **Ducie** *R* Queensland Australia
135 O11 **Ducie I** Pacific Oc
110 J6 **Duck** *R* Tennessee U.S.A.
119 R6 **Duck Bay** Manitoba Canada
111 G8 **Duck Hill** Mississippi U.S.A.
118 L6 **Duck Lake** Saskatchewan Canada
119 Q7 **Duck Mt** *ra* Manitoba Canada
119 R7 **Duck Mt. Prov. Park** Manitoba Canada
112 C2 **Ducktown** Tennessee U.S.A.
103 J3 **Duckwater** Nevada U.S.A.
103 J3 **Duckwater Pk** Nevada U.S.A.
21 M3 **Duclair** France
102 E6 **Ducor** California U.S.A.
127 L4 **Ducos** Martinique W Indies
9 F2 **Duddington** England
22 L5 **Dudelange** Luxembourg
36 B4 **Dudeldorf** Germany
32 M9 **Duderstadt** Germany
109 P3 **Dudgemona** *R* Louisiana U.S.A.
7 L9 **Dudgeon Lightship** North Sea
50 H2 **Dudinka** Russian Federation
8 D2 **Dudley** England
112 D5 **Dudley** Georgia U.S.A.
110 F5 **Dudley** Missouri U.S.A.
54 G3 **Dudorovskiy** Russian Federation
47 N10 **Dudullu** Turkey
36 C5 **Dudweiler** Germany
51 J1 **Dudypta** *R* Russian Federation
22 E1 **Dudzele** Belgium
85 C7 **Duékoué** Ivory Coast
16 D3 **Dueñas** Spain
16 C2 **Duerna** *R* Spain
17 F3 **Duero** *R* Spain
112 E3 **Due West** South Carolina U.S.A.
146 D10 **Dufek Coast** Antarctica
119 O8 **Duff** Saskatchewan Canada
22 H1 **Duffel** Belgium
138 C2 **Duffield** *R* N Terr Australia
140 C7 **Duffield** N Terr Australia
118 C5 **Duffield** Alberta Canada
137 O3 **Duff Is** Santa Cruz Is
15 E3 **Dufftown** Scotland
122 F2 **Dufresne,L** Quebec Canada
122 G2 **Dufresne Lake** Quebec Canada
100 D4 **Dufur** Oregon U.S.A.
140 F5 **Dugald** *R* Queensland Australia
103 N7 **Dugas** Arizona U.S.A.
111 D9 **Dugdemona** *R* Louisiana U.S.A.
110 J2 **Dugger** Indiana U.S.A.
42 F4 **Dugi O** Croatia
54 H2 **Dugna** Russian Federation
141 G1 **Dugong I** Gt Barrier Reef Aust
118 E6 **Duhamel** Alberta Canada
131 D2 **Duice, R** Argentina
128 E3 **Duida, Co** *mt* Venezuela
141 F2 **Duifken Pt** Queensland Australia
32 L8 **Duingen** Germany
32 E10 **Duisburg** Germany
25 A5 **Duiveland** Netherlands
67 C4 **Dujiang** China
86 H5 **Dujuuma** Somalia
46 E2 **Dukat** Macedonia/Serbia
107 L7 **Duke** Oklahoma U.S.A.
117 H8 **Duke I** Alaska U.S.A.
141 K5 **Duke Is** Queensland Australia
135 N10 **Duke of Gloucester Is** Pacific Oc
142 F4 **Dukes Dome** *mt* W Australia Australia
86 F4 **Duk Faiwil** Sudan
77 B7 **Dukhān** Qatar
53 G8 **Dukhovnitskoye** Russian Federation
54 D1 **Dukhovshchina** Russian Federation
59 L1 **Duki** Russian Federation

31 N6 Dukla Poland
52 C6 Dukstas Lithuania
111 F12 Dulac Louisiana U.S.A.
58 C4 Dulan China
8 B1 Dulas B Wales
71 G7 Dulawan Mindanao Philippines
116 K4 Dulbi R Alaska U.S.A.
106 D5 Dulce New Mexico U.S.A.
80 G7 Duleilat el Muterat Jordan
51 N2 Dulgalakh R Russian Federation
47 J1 Dŭlgopol Bulgaria
141 F1 Dulhunty R Queensland Australia
70 D3 Dulit Ra Sarawak
67 C4 Duliu Jiang R China
71 G5 Duljugan Pt Leyte Philippines
25 F6 Dülken Germany
75 P6 Dullabchara India
98 B6 Dull Center Wyoming U.S.A.
32 F9 Dülmen Germany
67 A5 Dulong China
47 J1 Dulovo Bulgaria
99 O3 Duluth Minnesota U.S.A.
8 C5 Dulverton England
71 F6 Dumaguete Negros Philippines
69 E12 Dumai Sumatra
47 J6 Dumanlı Dağı mt Turkey
71 F7 Dumanquilas B Mindanao Philippines
71 D5 Dumaran isld Philippines
139 K3 Dumaresq R New S Wales/Queensland
111 E8 Dumas Arkansas U.S.A.
108 C8 Dumas Texas U.S.A.
79 G5 Ḍumayr Syria
79 G5 Ḍumayr,Jebel mts Syria
83 K10 Dumbanagala mt Sri Lanka
12 D2 Dumbarton Scotland
48 F2 Ďumbier mt Slovakia
143 C10 Dumbleyung W Australia Australia
143 C10 Dumbleyung, L W Australia Australia
86 B3 Dumboa Nigeria
48 J4 Dumbrăveni Romania
48 L5 Dumbrăveni Romania
69 H12 Dumdum isld Indonesia
12 E3 Dumfries Scotland
15 D5 Dumfries and Galloway reg Scotland
54 G3 Duminichi Russian Federation
48 K5 Dumitreşti Romania
75 M6 Dumka India
119 N9 Dummer Saskatchewan Canada
32 H7 Dümmersee L Germany
71 J4 Dumoga Sulawesi
71 H4 Dumoga Ketjil Sulawesi
121 N6 Dumoine, L Quebec Canada
98 K4 Dumont Minnesota U.S.A.
146 E14 Dumont d'Urville France Base Antarctica
121 O6 Dumont,L Quebec Canada
36 B3 Dümpelfeld Germany
65 J1 Dumune China
79 B7 Dumyât Egypt
48 E4 Duna R Hungary
48 D3 Dunaj R Slovakia
31 M6 Dunajec R Poland
14 E3 Dunany Pt Ireland
48 E4 Dunapataj Hungary
48 L6 Dunărea R Romania
48 E4 Dunaújváros Hungary
48 F5 Dunav R S Europe
46 F1 Dunavtsi Bulgaria
48 K2 Dunayevtsy Ukraine
144 C6 Dunback New Zealand
141 F3 Dunbar Queensland Australia
13 F1 Dunbar Scotland
107 P7 Dunbar Oklahoma U.S.A.
101 N9 Dunbar Utah U.S.A.
94 F8 Dunbar West Virginia U.S.A.
99 S4 Dunbar Wisconsin U.S.A.
118 L7 Dunblane Saskatchewan Canada
12 E1 Dunblane Scotland
14 E3 Dunboyne Ireland
100 B1 Duncan British Columbia Canada
6 M6 Duncan oil rig North Sea
103 P9 Duncan Arizona U.S.A.
98 J8 Duncan Nebraska U.S.A.
107 N7 Duncan Oklahoma U.S.A.
101 Q6 Duncan Wyoming U.S.A.
141 F1 Duncan Is Queensland Australia
117 R4 Duncan L Northwest Territories Canada
140 A3 Duncan, Mt N Terr Australia
14 E4 Duncannon Ireland
95 K6 Duncannon Pennsylvania U.S.A.
68 A7 Duncan Passage Andaman Is
112 C3 Duncan Ridge Georgia U.S.A.
127 K1 Duncans Jamaica
15 E2 Duncansby Hd Scotland
126 G3 Duncan Town Bahamas
109 N10 Duncanville Texas U.S.A.
9 E3 Dunchurch England
13 F6 Duncombe England
9 F6 Duncton England
52 B6 Dundaga Latvia
120 K8 Dundalk Ontario Canada
14 E2 Dundalk Ireland
14 E3 Dundalk B Ireland
147 F6 Dundas Northwest Territories Canada
115 N2 Dundas Greenland
94 E7 Dundas Ohio U.S.A.
117 H8 Dundas I British Columbia Canada
143 D9 Dundas L W Australia Australia
140 B1 Dundas Str N Terr Australia
89 G7 Dundee S Africa
13 F1 Dundee Scotland
94 D5 Dundee Michigan U.S.A.
95 L4 Dundee New York U.S.A.
109 J2 Dundee Texas U.S.A.
26 G5 Dunderlands-dal V Norway
Dund Hot see Zhenglan Qi
141 G8 Dundoo Queensland Australia
12 E4 Dundrennan Scotland
14 F2 Dundrum N Ireland
14 F2 Dundrum B N Ireland
118 L7 Dundurn Saskatchewan Canada
144 C7 Dunedin New Zealand
113 E9 Dunedin Florida U.S.A.
139 J4 Dunedoo New South Wales Australia
57 J1 Dunenbay Kazakhstan
14 D1 Dunfanaghy Ireland
15 E4 Dunfermline Scotland
120 J9 Dungannon Ontario Canada
14 E2 Dungannon N Ireland
74 E7 Dungarpur India
14 D4 Dungarvan Ireland
14 D4 Dungarvan Harb Ireland
9 G6 Dungeness England
133 D8 Dungeness,Pta Arg/Chile
14 E2 Dungiven N Ireland
14 C2 Dungloe Ireland
139 K4 Dungog New South Wales Australia
86 E5 Dungu Zaire
69 F10 Dungun Malaysia
86 G1 Dungunab Sudan
142 G3 Dunham R W Australia Australia
9 F1 Dunham England
59 J3 Dunhua China
58 B3 Dunhuang China
141 J7 Dunkeld Queensland Australia
138 F6 Dunkeld Victoria Australia
15 E4 Dunkeld Scotland
106 E9 Dunken New Mexico U.S.A.
22 C1 Dunkerque France
Dunkirk see Dunkerque
119 M8 Dunkirk Saskatchewan Canada
110 L1 Dunkirk Indiana U.S.A.
101 O1 Dunkirk Montana U.S.A.
121 L10 Dunkirk New York U.S.A.
86 G3 Dunkur Ethiopia
85 D7 Dunkwa Ghana
14 E3 Dún Laoghaire Ireland
99 L8 Dunlap Iowa U.S.A.
107 O3 Dunlap Kansas U.S.A.
106 F7 Dunlap New Mexico U.S.A.
108 G1 Dunlap Texas U.S.A.
14 E3 Dunlavin Ireland
109 J6 Dunlay Texas U.S.A.
14 E3 Dunleer Ireland
18 G6 Dun-le-Palestel France
6 L1 Dunlin oil rig North Sea
119 T4 Dunlop Manitoba Canada
120 J9 Dunlop Ontario Canada
12 D2 Dunlop Scotland
14 B5 Dunmanus B Ireland
14 B5 Dunmanway Ireland
140 C3 Dunmarra Roadhouse N Terr Australia
14 C3 Dunmore Ireland
95 M5 Dunmore Pennsylvania U.S.A.
113 L12 Dunmore Town Bahamas
126 F2 Dunmore Town Eleuthera Bahamas
9 G4 Dunmow England
112 J2 Dunn North Carolina U.S.A.
98 D2 Dunn Center North Dakota U.S.A.
99 M6 Dunnell Minnesota U.S.A.
113 E8 Dunnellon Florida U.S.A.
15 E2 Dunnet B Scotland
15 E2 Dunnet Hd Scotland
12 E1 Dunning Scotland
98 F8 Dunning Nebraska U.S.A.
36 E7 Dunningen Germany
143 C6 Dunns Ra W Australia Australia
120 G6 Dunn Valley Ontario Canada
121 L10 Dunnville Ontario Canada
139 G6 Dunolly Victoria Australia
12 D2 Dunoon Scotland
100 J9 Dunphy Nevada U.S.A.
14 A4 Dunquin Ireland
84 J5 Dunqul Oasis Egypt
120 G4 Dunrankin Ontario Canada
119 S9 Dunrea Manitoba Canada
13 F2 Duns Scotland
144 D5 Dunsandel New Zealand
143 B10 Dunsborough W Australia Australia
98 G1 Dunseith North Dakota U.S.A.
100 C8 Dunsmuir California U.S.A.
9 F4 Dunstable England
144 B6 Dunstan Mts New Zealand
117 O9 Dunster British Columbia Canada
8 C5 Dunster England
31 K7 Dun Streda Slovakia
18 G6 Dun sur Auron France
22 J5 Dun-sur-Meuse France
120 K8 Duntroon Ontario Canada
144 C6 Duntroon New Zealand
36 D6 Duntzenheim France
15 B3 Dunvegan Scotland
15 B3 Dunvegan,L Scotland
123 T6 Dunville Newfoundland Canada
9 H3 Dunwich England
58 G3 Duolun China
76 D3 Dūpādu India
67 D4 Dupang Ling mts China
121 L4 Duparquet Quebec Canada
69 J11 Duperre I Indonesia
94 B8 Dupont Indiana U.S.A.
95 M5 Dupont Pennsylvania U.S.A.
98 E4 Dupree South Dakota U.S.A.
121 L4 Dupuy Quebec Canada
142 B5 Dupuy,C W Australia Australia
101 N1 Dupuyer Montana U.S.A.
130 G8 Duque de Caxias Brazil
133 B8 Duque de York,I Chile
103 O10 Duquesne Arizona U.S.A.
94 H6 Duquesne Pennsylvania U.S.A.
110 G3 Du Quoin Illinois U.S.A.
80 D7 Dura Jordan
41 M2 Durach Germany
142 F3 Durack,R W Australia Australia
142 F3 Durack Ra W Australia Australia
78 E1 Durağan Turkey
141 K7 Durah Queensland Australia
47 J5 Durak Turkey
106 E7 Duran New Mexico U.S.A.
19 Q16 Durance R France
99 R7 Durand Illinois U.S.A.
94 D4 Durand Michigan U.S.A.
99 P5 Durand Wisconsin U.S.A.
124 G5 Durango Mexico
18 D9 Durango Spain
106 C4 Durango Colorado U.S.A.
47 J1 Durankulak Bulgaria
111 G8 Durant Mississippi U.S.A.
107 O8 Durant Oklahoma U.S.A.
16 E3 Duratón R Spain
131 G4 Durazno dept Uruguay
131 G4 Durazno Uruguay
Durazzo see Durrës
89 G7 Durban S Africa
56 C6 Durbat-Daba, Pereval pass Mongolia/Rus Fed
27 M15 Durbe Latvia
94 H8 Durbin West Virginia U.S.A.
22 J3 Durbuy Belgium
16 E8 Dúrcal Spain
36 B2 Düren Germany
75 J8 Durg India
75 M7 Durgapur India
120 K8 Durham Ontario Canada
121 S7 Durham Quebec Canada
13 G4 Durham co England
13 G4 Durham England
102 C2 Durham California U.S.A.
107 N3 Durham Kansas U.S.A.
95 R3 Durham New Hampshire U.S.A.
112 J2 Durham North Carolina U.S.A.
122 F7 Durham Br New Brunswick Canada
141 F7 Durham Downs Queensland Australia
12 E3 Durisdeer Scotland
100 H5 Durkee Oregon U.S.A.
36 E6 Durlach Germany
9 E6 Durlston Hd England
36 E6 Durmersheim Germany
42 J5 Durmitor mt Montenegro Yugoslavia
15 D2 Durness Scotland
38 N5 Durnstein Austria
123 L3 Durocher,L Quebec Canada
38 M6 Durrenstein mt Austria
46 C3 Durrës Albania
46 C3 Durrësit, Gjiri i B Albania
140 F7 Durrie Queensland Australia
14 D4 Durrow Ireland
37 J5 Dürrwangen Germany
14 A5 Dursey Hd Ireland
14 A5 Dursey I Ireland
8 D4 Dursley England
8 C5 Durston England
47 K5 Dursunbey Turkey
21 K6 Durtal France
Duru see Wuchuan
28 B3 Durup Denmark
47 K3 Durusu Gölü L Turkey
79 G6 Durūz, Jabal ad mts Syria
145 D4 D'Urville I New Zealand
77 J2 Durzab Afghanistan
120 D1 Dusey R Ontario Canada
57 A6 Dushak Turkmenistan
67 B4 Dushan China
57 E5 Dushanbe Tajikistan
65 C4 Dushikou China
95 L5 Dushore Pennsylvania U.S.A.
47 J2 Dŭskotna Bulgaria
144 A6 Dusky Sd New Zealand
32 E10 Düsseldorf Germany
25 C5 Dussen Netherlands
41 J4 Düssist mt Switzerland
33 R9 Düssnitz Germany
107 O6 Dustin Oklahoma U.S.A.
83 J9 Dutch B Sri Lanka
Dutch Guiana see Surīname
116 D10 Dutch Harbor Aleutian Is
101 M9 Dutch Mt Utah U.S.A.
89 C4 Dutlwe Botswana
52 J3 Dutovo Russian Federation
85 F6 Dutsan Wai Nigeria
141 G5 Dutton R Queensland Australia
120 J10 Dutton Ontario Canada
101 O2 Dutton Montana U.S.A.
138 D4 Dutton,L South Australia Australia
103 M3 Dutton,Mt Utah U.S.A.
119 N7 Duval Saskatchewan Canada
127 H5 Duvalierville Haiti
121 N6 Duval,L Quebec Canada
55 C3 Duvan Russian Federation
144 D5 Duvauchelle New Zealand
26 F8 Duved Sweden
127 J5 Duvergé Dominican Rep
52 D3 Duvogero Russian Federation
22 D5 Duvy France
95 R4 Duxbury Massachusetts U.S.A.
9 G3 Duxford England
67 B4 Duyang Shan mts China
68 C4 Duyinzeik Burma
67 B3 Duyun China
78 C1 Düzce Turkey
47 H1 Dve Mogili Bulgaria
26 H2 Dverberg Norway
52 F3 Dvina, Severnaya R Russian Federation
52 E2 Dvinskaya Guba B Russian Federation
54 C1 Dvin'ye,Oz L Russian Federation
31 K6 Dvorce Czech Rep
31 J5 Dvůr Králové Czech Rep
88 D8 Dwangwa R Malawi
143 B10 Dwarda W Australia Australia
74 C7 Dwarka India
89 E5 Dwars Berg mts S Africa
143 B10 Dwellingup W Australia Australia
99 S8 Dwight Illinois U.S.A.
107 O3 Dwight Kansas U.S.A.
98 J8 Dwight Nebraska U.S.A.
94 F9 Dwight Virginia U.S.A.
100 K3 Dworshak Res. Idaho U.S.A.
106 C9 Dwyer New Mexico U.S.A.
98 B7 Dwyer Wyoming U.S.A.
54 F3 Dyat'kovo Russian Federation
28 D7 Dybbøl Denmark
28 A3 Dybe Kirke Denmark
28 H6 Dybsø Fjord inlet Denmark
119 R4 Dyce Manitoba Canada
15 F3 Dyce Scotland
99 T5 Dyckesville Wisconsin U.S.A.
110 H5 Dyer Tennessee U.S.A.
114 G2 Dyer B Northwest Territories Canada
120 J7 Dyer Bay Ontario Canada
110 G5 Dyersburg Tennessee U.S.A.
99 P7 Dyersville Iowa U.S.A.
8 B3 Dyfed co Wales
8 B2 Dyfi R Wales
31 J1 Dygowo Poland
31 J7 Dyje R Czech Rep
53 F11 Dykhtau mt Georgia/Rus Fed
22 H2 Dyle R Belgium
9 G5 Dymchurch England
118 K1 Dyment Ontario Canada
8 D4 Dymock England
141 G8 Dynevor Downs Queensland Australia
31 N6 Dynów Poland
102 F4 Dyor Nevada U.S.A.
28 E6 Dyreborg Denmark
26 C8 Dyrnesvågen Norway
26 J2 Dyröy Norway
119 N8 Dysart Saskatchewan Canada
13 E1 Dysart Scotland
99 O7 Dysart Iowa U.S.A.
47 J2 Dyulevo Bulgaria
47 J2 Dyulino Bulgaria
78 L1 Dyul'tydag mt Russian Federation
57 C2 Dyurmen'tyube Kazakhstan
58 D2 Dzaanhushuu Mongolia
58 C2 Dzag Mongolia
58 F3 Dzamïn Üüde Mongolia
87 H10 Dzaoudzi Mayotte Comoros
56 E6 Dzargal Hid Mongolia
58 C2 Dzavhan Gol R Mongolia
30 H5 Džban mt Czech Rep
54 J8 Dzerzhinsk Ukraine
57 K2 Dzerzhinskoye Kazakhstan
59 K1 Dzhagdy,Khrebet mts Russian Federation
56 D5 Dzhakul', Gora mt Russian Federation
57 G4 Dzhalal-Abad Kirghizia
59 H1 Dzhalinda Russian Federation
55 B5 Dzhambeyty Kazakhstan
57 C4 Dzhankel'dy Uzbekistan
57 J2 Dzhansugurov Kazakhstan
56 D5 Dzhebashskiy Khrebet mts Russian Federation
46 G3 Dzhebel Bulgaria
57 J3 Dzhergalan Kirghizia
55 D5 Dzhetygara Kazakhstan
57 C4 Dzhetymtau, Gory mt Uzbekistan
57 D1 Dzhezdy Kazakhstan
57 E1 Dzhezkazgan Kazakhstan
56 G5 Dzhida R Russian Federation
56 F5 Dzhidinskiy,Khrebet mts Mongolia/Rus Fed
57 B4 Dzhigirbent Turkmenistan
57 E4 Dzhizak Uzbekistan
56 D4 Dzhoyskiy Khrebet mts Russian Federation
57 D5 Dzhuma Uzbekistan
57 K2 Dzhungarskiy Alatau, Khrebet mts Kazakhstan
48 L2 Dzhurin Ukraine
57 C2 Dzhusaly Kazakhstan
31 M2 Działdowo Poland
31 M5 Działoszyce Poland
31 L4 Działoszyn Poland
31 L2 Dzierżgoń Poland
31 K5 Dzierżoniów Poland
125 O7 Dzitbalché Mexico
31 H1 Dziwnów Poland
56 E5 Dzöölon Mongolia
52 B6 Džūkste Latvia
66 C3 Dzungaria reg China
66 C2 Dzungarian Gate pass China/Kazakhstan
58 E3 Dzüünbayan Mongolia
65 C1 Dzüünbulag Mongolia
58 B2 Dzüyl Mongolia

E

106 H3 Eads Colorado U.S.A.
103 P7 Eagar Arizona U.S.A.
101 T10 Eagle Colorado U.S.A.
100 J6 Eagle Idaho U.S.A.
110 M3 Eagle R Kentucky U.S.A.
98 K9 Eagle Nebraska U.S.A.
99 S7 Eagle Wisconsin U.S.A.
101 R5 Eagle Wyoming U.S.A.
98 E4 Eagle Butte South Dakota U.S.A.
107 M6 Eagle City Oklahoma U.S.A.
102 G6 Eagle Crags California U.S.A.
121 O6 Eagle Depot Quebec Canada
141 K1 Eagle Farm dist Brisbane, Qnsld Australia
99 N7 Eagle Grove Iowa U.S.A.
99 S2 Eagle Harbor Michigan U.S.A.
139 J9 Eaglehawk Neck Tasmania Australia
119 O1 Eaglehead L Ontario Canada
119 T5 Eagle I Manitoba Canada
118 J1 Eagle L Ontario Canada
100 E9 Eagle L California U.S.A.
95 S6 Eagle L Maine U.S.A.
95 R7 Eagle L Maine U.S.A.
113 F10 Eagle Lake Florida U.S.A.
109 L6 Eagle Lake Texas U.S.A.
103 J8 Eagle Mts California U.S.A.
106 E5 Eagle Nest New Mexico U.S.A.
108 G7 Eagle Pass Texas U.S.A.
100 E8 Eagle Peak mt California U.S.A.
114 F4 Eagle Plain Yukon Territory Canada
100 C7 Eagle Point Oregon U.S.A.
99 S2 Eagle River Michigan U.S.A.
99 R4 Eagle River Wisconsin U.S.A.
94 H9 Eagle Rock Virginia U.S.A.
12 D2 Eaglesham Scotland
137 Q4 Eaglestone Reef Pacific Oc
116 O4 Eagle Summit Alaska U.S.A.
103 L8 Eagle Tail Mts Arizona U.S.A.
109 N1 Eagleton Arkansas U.S.A.
107 Q7 Eagletown Oklahoma U.S.A.
100 E8 Eagleville California U.S.A.
71 L10 Eahun Roti Indonesia
61 O7 Eai-gawa R Japan
68 H6 Ea Kan R Vietnam
9 F4 Ealing England
144 C6 Ealing New Zealand
143 D7 Earaheedy W Australia Australia
8 D3 Eardisland England
117 L11 Ear Lakes Cove British Columbia Canada
110 F6 Earle Arkansas U.S.A.
99 M8 Earlham Iowa U.S.A.
102 E6 Earlimart California U.S.A.
99 L8 Earling Iowa U.S.A.
110 J4 Earlington Kentucky U.S.A.
100 A8 Earl,L California U.S.A.
144 A6 Earl Mts New Zealand
13 F2 Earlston Scotland
121 L5 Earlton Ontario Canada
99 S8 Earlville Illinois U.S.A.
99 P7 Earlville Iowa U.S.A.
13 E1 Earn,Br.of Scotland
117 F4 Earn L Yukon Territory Canada
12 D1 Earn,L Scotland
12 E1 Earn,R Scotland
144 B6 Earnslaw, Mt New Zealand
103 K7 Earp California U.S.A.
13 G3 Earsdon England
9 F6 Easebourne England
13 G4 Easington Durham England
13 J6 Easington Humberside England
13 G5 Easingwold England
112 E3 Easley South Carolina U.S.A.
110 F3 East Alton Illinois U.S.A.
121 T7 East Angus Quebec Canada
146 E12 East Antarctica Antarctica
123 M7 East B C Breton I, Nova Scotia
113 B7 East B Florida U.S.A.
111 G12 East B Louisiana U.S.A.
111 B12 East B Texas U.S.A.
112 G1 East Bend North Carolina U.S.A.
95 L7 East Berlin Pennsylvania U.S.A.
109 L6 East Bernard Texas U.S.A.
9 G6 Eastbourne England
145 G4 Eastbourne New Zealand
94 H6 East Brady Pennsylvania U.S.A.
8 D5 East Brent England
111 J10 East Brewton Alabama U.S.A.
71 G6 East Bucas Philippines
101 O1 East Butte mt Montana U.S.A.
127 J4 East Caicos isld Turks & Caicos Is
145 G2 East Cape New Zealand
145 F3 East Cape admin region New Zealand
99 T8 East Chicago Indiana U.S.A.
64 G4 East China Sea
145 E2 East Coast Bays New Zealand
118 E7 East Coulee Alberta Canada
9 G6 Eastdean England
9 G2 East Dereham England
99 Q7 East Dubuque Illinois U.S.A.
103 K2 East Ely Nevada U.S.A.
118 J9 Eastend Saskatchewan Canada
143 A8 Easter Grp islds W Australia Australia
135 U16 Easter I Pacific Oc
89 E8 Eastern Cape prov S Africa
141 F5 Eastern Creek Queensland Australia
84 J4 Eastern Desert Egypt
86 F4 Eastern Equatoria prov Sudan
76 C4 Eastern Ghats mts India
123 S5 Eastern Meelpaeg L Newfoundland Canada
89 F5 Eastern Transvaal prov S Africa
119 S5 Easterville Manitoba Canada
122 E7 East Florenceville New Brunswick Canada
120 J3 Eastford Ontario Canada
99 Q9 East Galesburg Illinois U.S.A.
102 G2 Eastgate Nevada U.S.A.
East Germany see Germany
101 M1 East Glacier Park Montana U.S.A.
9 F5 East Grinstead England
8 D1 Eastham England
95 P6 East Hampton Long I, New York U.S.A.
95 P4 Easthampton Massachusetts U.S.A.
101 O3 East Helena Montana U.S.A.
9 G6 East Hoathly England
123 L6 East I Madeleine Is, Quebec Canada
9 E4 East Ilsley England
95 P4 East Jaffrey New Hampshire U.S.A.
147 E12 East Jan Mayen Rdg Norwegian Sea
122 J9 East Jeddore Nova Scotia Canada
122 G10 East Jordan Nova Scotia Canada
94 B1 East Jordan Michigan U.S.A.
9 G1 East Keal England
122 G9 East Kemptville Nova Scotia Canada
12 D2 East Kilbride Scotland
95 R6 East L Maine U.S.A.
99 U5 East Lake Michigan U.S.A.
109 J3 Eastland Texas U.S.A.
94 C4 East Lansing Michigan U.S.A.
9 E6 Eastleigh England
110 N1 East Liberty Ohio U.S.A.
13 F2 East Linton Scotland
94 G6 East Liverpool Ohio U.S.A.
89 E9 East London S Africa
94 E8 East Lynn West Virginia U.S.A.
115 M7 Eastmain Quebec Canada
112 D5 Eastman Georgia U.S.A.
141 H6 Eastmere Queensland Australia
143 E8 East, Mt W Australia Australia
8 D3 Eastnor England
99 R9 Easton Illinois U.S.A.
95 Q4 Easton Massachusetts U.S.A.
99 N6 Easton Minnesota U.S.A.
110 B2 Easton Missouri U.S.A.
95 M6 Easton Pennsylvania U.S.A.
100 D2 Easton Washington U.S.A.
112 G4 Eastover South Carolina U.S.A.
East Pakistan see Bangladesh
113 F8 East Palatka Florida U.S.A.
94 G6 East Palestine Ohio U.S.A.
102 B2 East Park Res California U.S.A.
99 N8 East Peru Iowa U.S.A.
117 N8 East Pine British Columbia Canada
123 L6 East Point Madeleine Is, Quebec Canada
121 L1 East Point Ontario Canada
123 L7 East Point Prince Edward I Canada
123 N10 East Point Sable I, Nova Scotia
111 M8 East Point Georgia U.S.A.
94 E9 East Point Kentucky U.S.A.
119 M9 East Poplar Saskatchewan Canada
106 E2 East Portal Colorado U.S.A.
110 G5 East Prairie Missouri U.S.A.
122 G10 East Pubnico Nova Scotia Canada
94 G9 East Rainelle West Virginia U.S.A.
100 H9 East Range Nevada U.S.A.
9 F1 East Retford England
9 H5 Eastry England
110 F3 East St Louis Illinois U.S.A.
147 P5 East Siberian Sea Arctic Oc
139 J7 East Sister I Tasmania Australia
100 K2 East Sister Peak mt Idaho U.S.A.
9 F1 East Stoke England
8 D5 East Stour England
9 G6 East Sussex co England
94 D2 East Tawas Michigan U.S.A.
139 H4 East Toorale New South Wales Australia
119 N4 East Trout L Saskatchewan Canada
99 S7 East Troy Wisconsin U.S.A.
103 N7 East Verde R Arizona U.S.A.
95 M9 Eastville Virginia U.S.A.
13 E1 East Wemyss Scotland
9 E1 East Wood England
138 C2 Eateringinna Cr South Australia Australia
98 B9 Eaton Colorado U.S.A.
110 L1 Eaton Indiana U.S.A.
110 M2 Eaton Ohio U.S.A.
118 H7 Eatonia Saskatchewan Canada
94 C4 Eaton Rapids Michigan U.S.A.
9 F3 Eaton Socon England
112 D4 Eatonton Georgia U.S.A.
100 C3 Eatonville Washington U.S.A.
17 F9 Eau, C. de l' Morocco
99 U7 Eau Claire Michigan U.S.A.
99 P5 Eau Claire R Wisconsin U.S.A.
99 P5 Eau Claire Wisconsin U.S.A.
122 G1 Eau-Claire, L. à l' Labrador, Nfld Canada
115 M6 Eau Claire, L. à l' Quebec Canada
113 G9 Eau Gallie Florida U.S.A.
121 Q3 Eau-Jaune, L. a l' Quebec Canada
21 N2 Eaulne R France
134 E7 Eauripik - New Guinea Rise Pacific Oc
18 F9 Eauze France
141 G2 Ebagoola Queensland Australia
125 K6 Ebano Mexico
36 D1 Ebbe mts Germany
13 H5 Ebberston England
28 D6 Ebberup Denmark
8 C4 Ebbw Vale Wales
86 B5 Ebebiyin Equat Guinea
33 N10 Ebeleben Germany
28 F4 Ebeltoft Denmark
28 F4 Ebeltoft Vig B Denmark
119 P7 Ebenezer Saskatchewan Canada
99 U3 Eben Junction Michigan U.S.A.
94 J6 Ebensburg Pennsylvania U.S.A.
38 J6 Ebensee Austria
37 K3 Ebensfeld Germany
36 G5 Eberbach Germany
78 C2 Eber Gölü Turkey
32 M9 Ebergötzen Germany
37 L4 Ebermannstadt Germany
37 K3 Ebern Germany
36 D4 Ebernburg Germany
110 M4 E Bernstadt Kentucky U.S.A.
36 H6 Ebersbach Germany
36 H3 Ebersburg Germany
37 L3 Ebersdorf Germany
36 F4 Eberstadt Germany
38 L8 Eberstein Austria
33 T7 Eberswalde Germany
60 P2 Ebetsu Japan
55 F4 Ebeyty, Oz L Russian Federation
67 A2 Ebian China
60 D13 Ebino Japan
66 C3 Ebinur Hu L China
79 G3 Ebla anc site Syria
37 J6 Ebnat Germany
41 K3 Ebnat Switzerland
86 D5 Ebola R Zaire
43 G8 Eboli Italy
86 B5 Ebolowa Cameroon
37 K4 Ebrach Germany
9 F2 E Bridgford England
44 F2 Ebro mt Italy
16 E2 Ebro R Spain
16 E2 Ebro, Embalse del res Spain
36 E2 Ebschloh mt Germany
36 F2 Ebsdorfergrund Germany
33 M6 Ebstorf Germany
22 G2 Ecaussines Belgium
13 E3 Ecclefechan Scotland
13 F2 Eccles Scotland
94 F9 Eccles West Virginia U.S.A.
13 G6 Ecclesfield England
8 D2 Eccleshall England
127 P2 Ecclesville Trinidad
47 H4 Eceabat Turkey
40 E4 Echallens Switzerland
21 L4 Échauffour France
85 E1 Ech Cheliff Algeria
67 E1 Echeng China
101 U5 Echeta Wyoming U.S.A.
19 P14 Échirolles France
61 J10 Echizen-misaki C Japan
99 L5 Echo Minnesota U.S.A.
100 F4 Echo Oregon U.S.A.
101 O9 Echo Utah U.S.A.
103 K5 Echo B Nevada U.S.A.
120 G6 Echo Bay Ontario Canada
103 N5 Echo Cliffs Arizona U.S.A.
139 H8 Echo,L Tasmania Australia
121 P5 Échouani L Quebec Canada
122 H4 Echouerie, L' Quebec Canada
119 O8 Echo Valley Prov. Park Saskatchewan Canada
25 E6 Echt Netherlands
15 F3 Echt Scotland
32 M9 Echte Germany
25 F3 Echten Netherlands
22 L4 Echternach Luxembourg
139 G6 Echuca Victoria Australia
36 F3 Echzell Germany
16 D7 Écija Spain
36 H5 Eckartshausen Germany
98 H3 Eckelson North Dakota U.S.A.
37 L4 Eckental Germany
30 E1 Eckernförde Germany
109 J5 Eckert Texas U.S.A.
13 F3 Eckford Scotland
8 D3 Eckington England
9 E1 Eckington England
12 C1 Eck,L Scotland
98 D9 Eckley Colorado U.S.A.
94 F9 Eckman West Virginia U.S.A.
118 C6 Eckville Alberta Canada
32 H5 Eckwarderhörne Germany
111 K9 Eclectic Alabama U.S.A.
143 C11 Eclipse I W Australia Australia
140 B5 Eclipse, Mt N Terr Australia
115 M3 Eclipse Sound Northwest Territories Canada
21 L6 Écommoy France
110 L2 Economy Indiana U.S.A.
121 O5 Écorces,L.aux Quebec Canada
21 O3 Ecos France
21 K4 Écouché France
21 N3 Ecouis France
21 L4 Écouves, Forêt d' France
22 J4 Ecouviez Belgium
22 C2 Ecques France
20 G3 Ecréhou, les English Chan
111 G7 Ecru Mississippi U.S.A.
128 C4 Ecuador rep S America
21 N7 Écueillé France
123 K9 Ecum Secum Nova Scotia Canada
86 H3 Ēd Eritrea
143 B8 Edah W Australia Australia
118 J5 Edam Saskatchewan Canada
25 D3 Edam Netherlands
15 F1 Eday Scotland
118 E6 Edberg Alberta Canada
109 K9 Edcouch Texas U.S.A.
6 N6 Edda oil rig North Sea
86 E3 Ed Da'ein Sudan
86 F3 Ed Damazin Sudan
86 F2 Ed Damer Sudan
86 F2 Ed Debba Sudan
32 K5 Eddelak Germany
123 Q2 Eddies Cove Newfoundland Canada
13 E2 Eddleston Scotland
15 C2 Eddrachillis B Scotland
86 F3 Ed Dueim Sudan
100 K2 Eddy Montana U.S.A.
109 K4 Eddy Texas U.S.A.
8 B7 Eddystone Lt. Ho English Chan
139 J8 Eddystone Pt Tasmania Australia
99 O8 Eddyville Iowa U.S.A.
110 H4 Eddyville Kentucky U.S.A.
98 G8 Eddyville Nebraska U.S.A.
25 E4 Ede Netherlands
85 E7 Ede Nigeria
86 B5 Edéa Cameroon
27 G11 Edebäck Sweden
27 K11 Edebo Sweden
130 E5 Edéia Brazil
48 F2 Edelény Hungary
143 A7 Edel Land pen W Australia Australia
139 J6 Eden New South Wales Australia
119 S8 Eden Manitoba Canada
101 O2 Eden Montana U.S.A.
94 J4 Eden New York U.S.A.
94 H10 Eden North Carolina U.S.A.
112 H1 Eden North Carolina U.S.A.
98 J4 Eden South Dakota U.S.A.
108 H4 Eden Texas U.S.A.
101 O8 Eden Utah U.S.A.
99 S6 Eden Wisconsin U.S.A.
101 Q7 Eden Wyoming U.S.A.
9 G5 Edenbridge England
89 D7 Edenburg S Africa
144 B7 Edendale New Zealand
14 D3 Edenderry Ireland
13 F6 Edenfield England
138 F6 Edenhope Victoria Australia
120 J8 Edenhurst Ontario Canada
36 E5 Edenkoben Germany
119 R2 Eden L Manitoba Canada
9 G5 Eden,R England
71 N9 Eden,Tg C Indonesia
112 L1 Edenton North Carolina U.S.A.
94 C3 Edenville Michigan U.S.A.
119 N8 Edenwold Saskatchewan Canada
36 E1 Eder R Germany
36 G1 Edermünde Germany
33 O10 Edersleben Germany
36 F1 Ederstausee res Germany
36 G1 Edertal Germany
27 F13 Edet, L Sweden
32 G6 Edewecht Germany
32 G6 Edewechterdamm Germany
101 R4 Edgar Montana U.S.A.
98 J9 Edgar Nebraska U.S.A.
111 F11 Edgard Louisiana U.S.A.
142 D5 Edgar, Mt W Australia Australia
142 E4 Edgar Ra W Australia Australia
110 E4 Edgar Springs Missouri U.S.A.
95 R5 Edgartown Massachusetts U.S.A.
109 M9 Edgecliff Texas U.S.A.
145 F2 Edgecumbe New Zealand
112 F4 Edgefield South Carolina U.S.A.
119 O8 Edgeley Saskatchewan Canada
98 H3 Edgeley North Dakota U.S.A.
115 N5 Edgell I Northwest Territories Canada
110 D6 Edgemont Arkansas U.S.A.
98 C6 Edgemont South Dakota U.S.A.
50 B1 Edgeöya isld Spitzbergen
109 O5 Edgerly Louisiana U.S.A.
118 G6 Edgerton Alberta Canada
94 C5 Edgerton Ohio U.S.A.
99 R7 Edgerton Wisconsin U.S.A.
101 T6 Edgerton Wyoming U.S.A.
113 G9 Edgewater Florida U.S.A.
117 O11 Edgewood British Columbia Canada
110 H3 Edgewood Illinois U.S.A.
95 L7 Edgewood Maryland U.S.A.
106 D6 Edgewood New Mexico U.S.A.
109 M3 Edgewood Texas U.S.A.
9 F4 Edgware England
80 C8 Edh Dhahiriya Jordan
46 E4 Édhessa Greece
144 B6 Edievale New Zealand
36 C3 Ediger-Eller Germany
84 F5 Edimpi Chad
99 N5 Edina Minnesota U.S.A.
94 G5 Edinboro Pennsylvania U.S.A.
99 R10 Edinburg Illinois U.S.A.
111 G9 Edinburg Mississippi U.S.A.
98 J1 Edinburg North Dakota U.S.A.
109 J9 Edinburg Texas U.S.A.
94 J8 Edinburg Virginia U.S.A.
13 E2 Edinburgh Scotland
110 L2 Edinburgh Indiana U.S.A.
141 H7 Edinburgh, Mt Queensland Australia
22 F2 Edingen Belgium
47 H3 Edirne Turkey
102 F6 Edison California U.S.A.
106 F3 Edison Colorado U.S.A.
111 M10 Edison Georgia U.S.A.
112 G4 Edisto R South Carolina U.S.A.
112 G5 Edisto Island South Carolina U.S.A.
138 E6 Edithburgh South Australia Australia
117 P9 Edith Cavell,Mt Alberta Canada
101 O3 Edith, Mt Montana U.S.A.
143 D7 Edith Withnell, L W Australia Australia
85 F3 Edjeleh Algeria
143 D8 Edjudina W Australia Australia
13 G3 Edlingham England
38 O6 Edlitz Austria
95 M4 Edmeston New York U.S.A.
107 L2 Edmond Kansas U.S.A.
107 N6 Edmond Oklahoma U.S.A.
100 C2 Edmonds Washington U.S.A.
141 H3 Edmonton Queensland Australia
118 D5 Edmonton Alberta Canada
9 F4 Edmonton England
94 C3 Edmore Michigan U.S.A.
98 H1 Edmore North Dakota U.S.A.
122 D6 Edmundston New Brunswick Canada
109 L7 Edna Texas U.S.A.
13 F2 Ednam Scotland
27 J13 Ed, O Sweden
61 N10 Edo-gawa R Japan
27 M14 Edole Latvia
42 C2 Edolo Italy
26 C8 Edoy isld Norway
47 J5 Edremit Turkey
47 H5 Edremit Körfezi B Turkey
58 C3 Edrengiyn Nuruu mt Mongolia
109 K8 Edroy Texas U.S.A.
27 K12 Edsbro Sweden
27 H13 Edsbruk Sweden
27 H10 Edsbyn Sweden
26 J8 Edsele Sweden
58 D3 Edsin Gol China
117 P9 Edson Alberta Canada
107 J2 Edson Kansas U.S.A.
27 J14 Ed, V Sweden
118 E4 Edwand Alberta Canada
139 G6 Edward R New South Wales Australia
140 D2 Edward I N Terr Australia
120 B4 Edward I Ontario Canada
88 B2 Edward, L Zaire
140 B6 Edward, Mt N Terr Australia
141 F2 Edward River Queensland Australia
102 G7 Edwards California U.S.A.
99 Q8 Edwards R Illinois U.S.A.
111 F9 Edwards Mississippi U.S.A.
95 M2 Edwards New York U.S.A.
94 A5 Edwardsburg Michigan U.S.A.
138 D3 Edwards Creek South Australia Australia
144 B7 Edwardson, C New Zealand
144 A6 Edwardson Sd New Zealand
108 G5 Edwards Plateau Texas U.S.A.
110 G3 Edwardsville Illinois U.S.A.
146 K10 Edward VIII Ice Shelf Antarctica
146 B10 Edward VII Peninsula Antarctica
15 F4 Edzell Scotland
117 H7 Edziza, Mt British Columbia Canada
22 F1 Eeklo Belgium
100 B9 Eel R California U.S.A.
94 B6 Eel R Indiana U.S.A.
25 G2 Eelde Netherlands
25 D4 Eem R Netherlands
25 D4 Eem Meer Netherlands
25 G2 Eemshaven Netherlands
89 B6 Eenzamheid Pan salt lake S Africa
22 E1 Eernegem Belgium
137 O5 Éfaté isld Vanuatu
38 K5 Eferding Austria
99 N2 Effie Minnesota U.S.A.
99 P6 Effigy Mounds Nat. Mon. Iowa U.S.A.
110 H2 Effingham Illinois U.S.A.
107 P2 Effingham Kansas U.S.A.
48 M6 Eforie Romania
80 D7 Efrata Jordan
71 B3 Ef Torobi isld W Irian
28 B5 Eg Denmark
28 E4 Egå Denmark
18 D10 Ega R Spain
43 E10 Egadi, I Sicily
133 F5 Egaña Argentina
103 K2 Egan Range Nevada U.S.A.
121 N7 Eganville Ontario Canada
85 F7 Egbe Nigeria
98 B8 Egbert Wyoming U.S.A.
28 H5 Egebjerg Denmark
115 O4 Egedesminde Greenland
116 J7 Egegik B Alaska U.S.A.
98 G1 Egeland North Dakota U.S.A.
33 O9 Egeln Germany
28 D7 Egen Denmark
28 F4 Egens Denmark
28 E3 Egense Denmark
37 J6 Eger R Germany
48 F3 Eger Hungary
28 D7 Egernsund Denmark
27 A13 Egersund Norway
143 C6 Egerton, Mt W Australia Australia
32 M6 Egestorf Germany
41 L3 Egg Austria
27 D11 Eggedal Norway
31 J7 Eggenburg Austria
37 O7 Eggenfelden Germany
33 U5 Eggesin Germany
28 G6 Eggeslevmagle Denmark
99 T4 Egg Harbor Wisconsin U.S.A.
95 N7 Egg Harbor City New Jersey U.S.A.
95 N7 Egg Harbor, Gt New Jersey U.S.A.
95 N7 Egg Harbor, Little New Jersey U.S.A.
116 G5 Egg I Alaska U.S.A.
139 G7 Egg Lagoon Tasmania Australia
13 G4 Eggleston England
37 N6 Eggmühl Germany
37 L4 Eggolsheim Germany
9 F5 Egham England
22 H2 Eghezee Belgium
28 G6 Egholm isld Denmark
28 D2 Egholm isld Nordjylland Denmark
15 F1 Egilsay Scotland
142 C5 Eginbah W Australia Australia
85 D3 Eglab,El reg Algeria
18 G7 Egletons France
36 G1 Egling Germany
13 G3 Eglingham England
144 B6 Eglinton R New Zealand
114 H2 Eglinton I Northwest Territories Canada
41 J2 Eglisau Switzerland
37 L4 Egloffstein Germany
25 C3 Egmond aan Zee Netherlands
122 H7 Egmont B Prince Edward I Canada
113 E10 Egmont Key isld Florida U.S.A.
Egmont, Mt see Taranaki, Mt
145 E3 Egmont Village New Zealand
28 J6 Egøje Denmark
118 D4 Egremont Alberta Canada
47 L6 Eğret Turkey
47 L7 Eğridir Turkey
78 C2 Egridir Gölü L Turkey
47 K5 Eğrigöz Dağı mt Turkey
13 H5 Egton England
28 C5 Egtved Denmark
71 E7 Eguet Pt Philippines
19 O17 Eguilles France
18 G6 Éguzon France
28 C6 Egvad Denmark
48 F3 Egyek Hungary
84 H4 Egypt rep Africa
112 F5 Egypt Georgia U.S.A.
111 H8 Egypt Mississippi U.S.A.
109 L6 Egypt Texas U.S.A.
79 F4 Ehden Lebanon

36 H7 **Ehingen** Germany
33 Q8 **Ehle** *R* Germany
32 K10 **Ehlen** Germany
36 F6 **Ehningen** Germany
33 N7 **Ehra-Lessien** Germany
113 E9 **Ehren** Florida U.S.A.
103 K8 **Ehrenberg** Arizona U.S.A.
140 B6 **Ehrenberg Ra** N Terr Australia
36 D3 **Ehrenbreitstein** Germany
32 J7 **Ehrenburg** Germany
37 O2 **Ehrenfriedersdorf** Germany
112 F4 **Ehrhardt** South Carolina U.S.A.
36 E2 **Ehringshausen** Germany
60 D14 **Ei** Japan
36 E2 **Eibach** Germany
36 E2 **Eibelshausen** Germany
37 J4 **Eibelstadt** Germany
37 O3 **Eibenstock** Germany
25 G4 **Eibergen** Netherlands
38 M8 **Eibiswald** Austria
33 O8 **Eichenbarleben** Germany
37 O6 **Eichendorf** Germany
37 M5 **Eichhofen** Germany
32 M10 **Eichsfeld** *mts* Germany
37 L6 **Eichstätt** Germany
40 G1 **Eichstetten** Germany
36 F5 **Eichtersheim** Germany
33 T8 **Eichwalde** Germany
36 H2 **Eichzell** Germany
32 M7 **Eicklingen** Germany
27 D12 **Eidanger** Norway
26 B9 **Eide** Norway
32 J4 **Eider** Germany
32 L4 **Eider** *R* Germany
6 F1 **Eiði** Faeroes
26 G3 **Eidsfjord** Norway
27 D12 **Eidsfoss** Norway
27 F11 **Eidskog** Norway
26 C9 **Eidsvåg** Norway
141 K7 **Eidsvold** Queensland Australia
27 E11 **Eidsvoll** Norway
25 C2 **Eierlandse Gat** Netherlands
36 B3 **Eifel** *mts* Germany
89 F2 **Eiffel Flats** Zimbabwe
37 J1 **Eigenrieden** Germany
40 G4 **Eiger** *mt* Switzerland
15 B4 **Eigg** *isld* Scotland
113 J11 **Eight Mile Rock** Bahamas
146 B7 **Eights Coast** Antarctica
142 D4 **Eighty Mile Beach** W Australia Australia
26 A10 **Eikefjord** Norway
27 D12 **Eikeren** *R* Norway
26 C9 **Eikesdalsvatn** *L* Norway
139 H6 **Eildon** Victoria Australia
33 R10 **Eilenburg** Germany
129 G3 **Eilerts de Haan Geb** *mts* Suriname
33 O8 **Eilsleben** Germany
32 L8 **Eime** Germany
33 M7 **Eimke** Germany
27 E11 **Eina** Norway
141 G4 **Einasleigh** Queensland Australia
32 L9 **Einbeck** Germany
25 D6 **Eindhoven** Netherlands
32 L4 **Einfeld** Germany
68 B4 **Einme** Burma
36 C5 **Einöd** Germany
37 P6 **Einödsriegel** *mt* Germany
Einsiedel *see* **Deutsch-Einsiedel**
79 F8 **Ein Yahav** Israel
120 G4 **Eire River** Ontario Canada
128 E5 **Eirunepe** Brazil
22 L4 **Eisch** *R* Luxembourg
22 K2 **Eisden** Belgium
25 E7 **Eisden** Netherlands
36 C4 **Eisen** Germany
37 J2 **Eisenach** Germany
36 E4 **Eisenberg** Germany
37 M2 **Eisenberg** Germany
38 L6 **Eisenerz** Austria
38 L7 **Eisenerzer-Alpen** *mts* Austria
106 E2 **Eisenhower Tunnel** Colorado U.S.A.
38 J8 **Eisenhut** *mt* Austria
31 H3 **Eisenhüttenstadt** Germany
38 L8 **Eisenkappel** Austria
48 D3 **Eisenstadt** Austria
38 J8 **Eisentratten** Austria
38 L5 **Eisenwurzen** *reg* Austria
36 D2 **Eiserfeld** Germany
37 K3 **Eisfeld** Germany
33 P9 **Eisleben** Germany
36 H6 **Eislingen** Germany
37 L6 **Eitensheim** Germany
36 H2 **Eiterfeld** Germany
36 C2 **Eitorf** Germany
17 G2 **Ejea de los Caballeros** Spain
87 G12 **Ejeda** Madagascar
28 D5 **Ejer Bavnehoj** *hill* Denmark
28 B3 **Ejerslev** Denmark
127 J10 **Ejido** Venezuela
65 A5 **Ejin Horo Qi** China
65 C2 **Ej Nur** China
28 B3 **Ejsing** Denmark
28 C5 **Ejstrup** Denmark
85 D7 **Ejura** Ghana
98 B4 **Ekalaka** Montana U.S.A.
27 J15 **Ekby** Sweden
22 E2 **Eke** Belgium
29 K12 **Ekenäs** Finland
22 G1 **Ekeren** Belgium
145 E4 **Eketahuna** New Zealand
26 N5 **Ekfors** Sweden
46 D6 **Ekhinádhes** *isld* Greece
46 G3 **Ekhínos** Greece
55 G5 **Ekibastuz** Kazakhstan
59 K1 **Ekimchan** Russian Federation
116 N6 **Eklutna** Alaska U.S.A.
6 N6 **Ekofisk** *oil rig* North Sea
27 J12 **Ekoln** *L* Sweden
22 F1 **Eksaarde** Belgium
27 G11 **Ekshärad** Sweden
27 G14 **Eksjö** Sweden
26 L7 **Ekträsk** Sweden
115 L7 **Ekwan** *R* Ontario Canada
116 J7 **Ekwok** Alaska U.S.A.
68 C3 **Ela** Burma
El Aaiún *see* **Laâyoune**
46 F8 **Elafónisos** *isld* Greece
111 F7 **Elaine** Arkansas U.S.A.
80 E5 **El 'Ajâjira** Jordan
103 H10 **El Alamo** Mexico
75 K10 **Elamanchili** India
99 R5 **Eland** Wisconsin U.S.A.
89 E5 **Elands** *R* S Africa
89 C8 **Elands Berg** *mt* S Africa
8 C3 **Elan Valley Reservoirs** Wales
43 B13 **El Aouinet** Algeria
41 L4 **Ela, Piz** *mt* Switzerland
16 D7 **El Arahal** Spain
124 C4 **El Arco** Mexico
80 F5 **El Ardah** Jordan
141 H4 **El Arish** Queensland Australia
46 E5 **Elassón** Greece
79 E9 **Elat** Israel
46 F6 **Elátia** Greece
86 E2 **El Atrun Oasis** Sudan
80 D7 **El 'Azar** Jordan
78 G2 **Elâziğ** Turkey
111 K10 **Elba** Alabama U.S.A.
101 M7 **Elba** Idaho U.S.A.
98 H8 **Elba** Nebraska U.S.A.
94 J3 **Elba** New York U.S.A.
42 C6 **Elba, I.d'** Italy
126 H10 **El Banco** Colombia
16 D4 **El Barco de Avila** Spain
46 D3 **Elbasan** Albania
127 K10 **El Baúl** Venezuela
32 J5 **Elbe** *est* Germany
33 M6 **Elbe** *R* Germany
33 N5 **Elbe-Lübeck Kanal** Germany
79 G4 **El Beqa'a** *R* Lebanon
110 J3 **Elberfield** Indiana U.S.A.
32 F8 **Elbergen** Germany
99 O7 **Elberon** Iowa U.S.A.
109 J2 **Elbert** Texas U.S.A.
99 U5 **Elberta** Michigan U.S.A.
106 D2 **Elbert,Mt** Colorado U.S.A.
112 E3 **Elberton** Georgia U.S.A.
21 N3 **Elbeuf** France
33 N9 **Elbingerode** Germany
78 F2 **Elbistan** Turkey
31 L1 **Elblag** Poland
17 F6 **El Bonillo** Spain
124 H6 **El Bordo** Mexico
16 D9 **El Borj** Morocco
118 L7 **Elbow** Saskatchewan Canada
113 L11 **Elbow Cay** *isld* Bahamas
98 K4 **Elbow L** Minnesota U.S.A.
118 C8 **Elbow R** Alberta Canada
124 J6 **El Bozal** Mexico
53 F11 **El'brus** *mt* Russian Federation
86 E4 **El Buheyrat** *prov* Sudan
25 E4 **Elburg** Netherlands
16 E3 **El Burgo de Osma** Spain
100 K9 **Elburz** Nevada U.S.A.
77 B1 **Elburz Mountains** Iran
102 H9 **El Cajon** California U.S.A.
128 F2 **El Callao** Venezuela
16 D5 **El Campillo de la Jara** Spain
109 L6 **El Campo** Texas U.S.A.
102 H9 **El Capitan Res** California U.S.A.
128 C2 **El Carmen** Colombia
124 G5 **El Casco** Mexico
17 G3 **El Castellar** Spain
103 J9 **El Centro** California U.S.A.
128 F7 **El Cerro** Bolivia
16 C7 **El Cerro de Andévalo** Spain
124 F3 **El Charco** Mexico
17 G6 **Elche** Spain
17 F6 **Elche de la Sierra** Spain
125 N9 **El Chichón** *vol* Mexico
124 G3 **El Chilicote** Mexico
127 K9 **El Chino** Venezuela
99 R4 **Elcho** Wisconsin U.S.A.
140 D1 **Elcho I** N Terr Australia
133 E2 **El Chorro** Argentina
124 H5 **El Cobre** Mexico
128 D2 **El Cocuy** Colombia
126 C3 **El Cotorro** Cuba
126 G4 **El Cristo** Cuba
108 B5 **El Cuervo** Mexico
32 L8 **Eldagsen** Germany
124 C2 **El Dátil** Mexico
33 Q6 **Elde** *R* Germany
33 O6 **Eldena** Germany
138 F4 **Elder,L** South Australia Australia
99 R5 **Elderon** Wisconsin U.S.A.
6 N6 **Eldfisk** *oil rig* North Sea
126 A4 **El Díaz** Mexico
126 G10 **El Difícil** Colombia
33 M7 **Eldingen** Germany
124 G8 **El Divisadero** Mexico
128 C3 **El Diviso** Colombia
124 B2 **El Doctor** Mexico
99 O9 **Eldon** Iowa U.S.A.
110 D3 **Eldon** Missouri U.S.A.
100 B2 **Eldon** Washington U.S.A.
99 N7 **Eldora** Iowa U.S.A.
130 C10 **Eldorado** Argentina
130 E9 **Eldorado** Brazil
114 J6 **Eldorado** Saskatchewan Canada
124 F5 **Eldorado** Mexico
109 P2 **El Dorado** Arkansas U.S.A.
110 H4 **Eldorado** Illinois U.S.A.
107 O4 **El Dorado** Kansas U.S.A.
107 L7 **Eldorado** Oklahoma U.S.A.
108 G5 **Eldorado** Texas U.S.A.
128 F2 **El Dorado** Venezuela
89 G1 **Eldorado** Zimbabwe
100 D1 **Eldorado,Mt** Washington U.S.A.
103 K6 **Eldorado Mts** Nevada U.S.A.
110 B4 **El Dorado Springs** Missouri U.S.A.
88 E1 **Eldoret** Kenya
98 K2 **Eldred** Minnesota U.S.A.
95 N5 **Eldred** New York U.S.A.
94 J5 **Eldred** Pennsylvania U.S.A.
27 F15 **Eldsberga** Sweden
100 H2 **Eleanor** Washington U.S.A.
143 D10 **Eleanora Pk** W Australia Australia
102 E3 **Eleanor, L** California U.S.A.
89 E4 **Elebe** *mt* Botswana
109 J1 **Electra** Texas U.S.A.
101 P5 **Electric Pk** Mont/Wyoming U.S.A.
135 O1 **Eleele** Hawaiian Is
52 B6 **Eleja** Latvia
48 G4 **Elek** Hungary
54 K1 **Elektrogorsk** Russian Federation
54 K1 **Elektrostal'** Russian Federation
22 J2 **Elemalle** Belgium
47 H2 **Elena** Bulgaria
128 D4 **El Encanto** Colombia
33 N9 **Elend** Germany
106 C8 **Elephant Butte** New Mexico U.S.A.
106 C8 **Elephant Butte Res** New Mexico U.S.A.
68 G7 **Elephant, Chaine de l'** *mts* Cambodia
146 D3 **Elephant I** South Shetland Is Antarctica
83 K8 **Elephant Pass** Sri Lanka
116 G3 **Elephant Point** Alaska U.S.A.
46 F3 **Eleshnitsa** Bulgaria
128 E3 **El Esmeralda** Venezuela
128 C3 **El Espinal** Colombia
56 H4 **Elesun** Russian Federation
84 J5 **Elet, Wadi** *watercourse* Sudan
85 F1 **El Eulma** Algeria
113 L12 **Eleuthera I** Bahamas
99 P5 **Eleva** Wisconsin U.S.A.
106 E3 **Eleven Mile Canyon Res** Colorado U.S.A.
110 E5 **Eleven Point** *R* Missouri U.S.A.
46 F6 **Elevsís** Greece
22 H2 **Elewijt** Belgium
20 C5 **Elez** *R* France
80 G2 **El Fahham** Syria
43 C12 **El Fahs** Tunisia
86 E3 **El Fasher** Sudan
16 D9 **El Fendek** Morocco
16 B1 **El Ferrol** Spain
117 E6 **Elfin Cove** Alaska U.S.A.
119 O7 **Elfros** Saskatchewan Canada
86 H4 **El Fud** Ethiopia
124 E4 **El Fuerte** Mexico
86 E3 **El Fula** Sudan
80 D5 **El Fundug** Jordan
26 E9 **Elgå** Norway
26 E9 **Elgepiggen** *mt* Norway
37 K2 **Elgersburg** Germany
86 F3 **El Geteina** Sudan
86 F3 **El Gezira** *prov* Sudan
80 F5 **El Ghor** Jordan
119 R9 **Elgin** Manitoba Canada
122 G8 **Elgin** New Brunswick Canada
15 E3 **Elgin** Scotland
103 O10 **Elgin** Arizona U.S.A.
99 S7 **Elgin** Illinois U.S.A.
99 P7 **Elgin** Iowa U.S.A.
98 H8 **Elgin** Nebraska U.S.A.
103 K4 **Elgin** Nevada U.S.A.
98 E3 **Elgin** North Dakota U.S.A.
107 M7 **Elgin** Oklahoma U.S.A.
100 H4 **Elgin** Oregon U.S.A.
109 K5 **Elgin** Texas U.S.A.
103 O3 **Elgin** Utah U.S.A.
141 H5 **Elgin Downs** Queensland Australia
86 F5 **Elgon, Mt** Uganda
17 H2 **El Grado** Spain
124 G8 **El Grullo** Mexico
128 D3 **El Guamo** Colombia
84 H4 **El Harra** Egypt
86 F3 **El Hawata** Sudan
85 E3 **El Homr** Algeria
87 D7 **Elias Garcia** Angola
127 J5 **Elías Piña** Dominican Rep
109 J3 **Eliasville** Texas U.S.A.
108 D2 **Elida** New Mexico U.S.A.
119 U9 **Elie** Manitoba Canada
13 F1 **Elie** Scotland
46 F6 **Elikón** *mt* Greece
29 M11 **Elimäki** Finland
46 F2 **Elin Pelin** Bulgaria
95 R3 **Eliot** Maine U.S.A.
29 O10 **Elisenvaara** Russian Federation
129 K5 **Eliseu Martins** Brazil
80 E6 **Elisha'** Jordan
53 F10 **Elista** Russian Federation
106 F2 **Elizabeth** Colorado U.S.A.
99 Q7 **Elizabeth** Illinois U.S.A.
109 P5 **Elizabeth** Louisiana U.S.A.
95 N6 **Elizabeth** New Jersey U.S.A.
94 F7 **Elizabeth** West Virginia U.S.A.
112 L1 **Elizabeth City** North Carolina U.S.A.
95 R5 **Elizabeth Is** Massachusetts U.S.A.
142 F3 **Elizabeth, Mt** W Australia Australia
122 F6 **Elizabeth,Mt** New Brunswick Canada
101 P9 **Elizabeth Mt** Utah U.S.A.
137 M7 **Elizabeth Reef** Pacific Oc
143 B7 **Elizabeth Spring** W Australia Australia
94 E10 **Elizabethton** Tennessee U.S.A.
94 B7 **Elizabethtown** Indiana U.S.A.
94 B9 **Elizabethtown** Kentucky U.S.A.
95 O2 **Elizabethtown** New York U.S.A.
112 J3 **Elizabethtown** North Carolina U.S.A.
95 L6 **Elizabethtown** Pennsylvania U.S.A.
Elizabethville *see* **Lubumbashi**
95 L6 **Elizabethville** Pennsylvania U.S.A.
138 E6 **Eliza,L** South Australia Australia
18 D9 **Elizondo** Spain
124 G4 **El Jaralito** Mexico
86 F3 **El Jebelein** Sudan
126 E4 **El Jíbaro** Cuba
31 N2 **Ełk** Poland
102 A2 **Elk** California U.S.A.
110 B5 **Elk** *R* Missouri U.S.A.
108 B3 **Elk** New Mexico U.S.A.
95 M7 **Elk** *R* Penn/Maryland U.S.A.
110 K6 **Elk** *R* Tennessee U.S.A.
94 F8 **Elk** *R* West Virginia U.S.A.
101 P6 **Elk** Wyoming U.S.A.
99 P7 **Elkader** Iowa U.S.A.
86 F2 **El Kamlin** Sudan
101 R5 **Elk Basin** Wyoming U.S.A.
100 K4 **Elk City** Idaho U.S.A.
107 P4 **Elk City** Kansas U.S.A.
107 L6 **Elk City** Oklahoma U.S.A.
102 B2 **Elk Creek** California U.S.A.
140 D5 **Elkedra** N Terr Australia
43 B12 **El Kef** Tunisia
85 C2 **El Kelaâ des Srarhna** Morocco
86 H4 **Ēl Kerē** Ethiopia
102 C3 **Elk Grove** California U.S.A.
86 F2 **El Khandaq** Sudan
79 E7 **El Kharrûba** Egypt
94 B5 **Elkhart** Indiana U.S.A.
107 J4 **Elkhart** Kansas U.S.A.
109 M4 **Elkhart** Texas U.S.A.
99 T6 **Elkhart Lake** Wisconsin U.S.A.
101 S9 **Elkhead Mts** Colorado U.S.A.
119 Q9 **Elkhorn** Manitoba Canada
99 L8 **Elk Horn** Iowa U.S.A.
98 H7 **Elkhorn** *R* Nebraska U.S.A.
99 S7 **Elkhorn** Wisconsin U.S.A.
47 H2 **Elkhovo** Bulgaria
112 G1 **Elkin** North Carolina U.S.A.
118 E5 **Elk I. Nat. Park** Alberta Canada
108 C2 **Elkins** New Mexico U.S.A.
94 H8 **Elkins** West Virginia U.S.A.
94 B2 **Elk L** Michigan U.S.A.
120 K5 **Elk Lake** Ontario Canada
95 K4 **Elkland** Pennsylvania U.S.A.
110 K7 **Elkmont** Alabama U.S.A.
106 D1 **Elk Mt** Colorado U.S.A.
101 T8 **Elk Mt** Wyoming U.S.A.
100 K1 **Elko** British Columbia Canada
100 K9 **Elko** Nevada U.S.A.
101 P8 **Elkol** Wyoming U.S.A.
86 H4 **Ēl K'oran** Ethiopia
101 N3 **Elk Park** Montana U.S.A.
112 F1 **Elk Park** North Carolina U.S.A.
118 G5 **Elk Point** Alberta Canada
98 K7 **Elk Pt** South Dakota U.S.A.
118 C9 **Elk R** British Columbia Canada
99 N4 **Elk R** Minnesota U.S.A.
94 B2 **Elk Rapids** Michigan U.S.A.
43 C12 **El Krib** Tunisia
100 J3 **Elk River** Idaho U.S.A.
43 B13 **El Ksour** Tunisia
106 B1 **Elk Springs** Colorado U.S.A.
113 F8 **Elkton** Florida U.S.A.
110 J5 **Elkton** Kentucky U.S.A.
95 M7 **Elkton** Maryland U.S.A.
99 O6 **Elkton** Minnesota U.S.A.
100 B6 **Elkton** Oregon U.S.A.
98 K5 **Elkton** South Dakota U.S.A.
110 K6 **Elkton** Tennessee U.S.A.
94 J8 **Elkton** Virginia U.S.A.
79 E9 **El Kuntilla** Egypt
94 C10 **Elk Valley** Tennessee U.S.A.
110 G4 **Elkville** Illinois U.S.A.
79 G4 **El Laboue** Lebanon
86 E3 **El Lagowa** Sudan
83 K10 **Ellamulla** Sri Lanka
12 C1 **Ellanbeich** Scotland
13 G6 **Elland** England
143 A7 **Ellavalla** W Australia Australia
113 D7 **Ellaville** Florida U.S.A.
111 M9 **Ellaville** Georgia U.S.A.
20 D5 **Elle** *R* France
37 N3 **Ellefeld** Germany
114 J2 **Ellef Ringnes I** Northwest Territories Canada
143 C10 **Elleker** W Australia Australia
95 O2 **Ellenburg** New York U.S.A.
95 M8 **Ellendale** Delaware U.S.A.
111 F12 **Ellendale** Louisiana U.S.A.
98 H3 **Ellendale** North Dakota U.S.A.
103 O3 **Ellen,Mt** Utah U.S.A.
95 P2 **Ellen,Mt** Vermont U.S.A.
143 C10 **Ellen Pk** W Australia Australia
13 E4 **Ellen,R** England
100 E2 **Ellensburg** Washington U.S.A.
32 H6 **Ellenserdamm** Germany
113 E10 **Ellenton** Florida U.S.A.
95 N5 **Ellenville** New York U.S.A.
36 C3 **Ellenz-Poltersdorf** Germany
112 G2 **Eller** North Carolina U.S.A.
112 H2 **Ellerbe** North Carolina U.S.A.
113 E7 **Ellerbee** Florida U.S.A.
36 D4 **Ellerspring** *mt* Germany
144 B6 **Ellery, L** New Zealand
139 J6 **Ellery,Mt** Victoria Australia
8 D2 **Ellesmere** England
115 L2 **Ellesmere I** Northwest Territories Canada
144 D5 **Ellesmere, L** New Zealand
8 D1 **Ellesmere Port** England
110 K2 **Ellettsville** Indiana U.S.A.
22 F2 **Ellezelles** Belgium
20 C5 **Elliant** France
Ellice Is. *see* **Tuvalu** *islds state*
95 L7 **Ellicott City** Maryland U.S.A.
94 J4 **Ellicottville** New York U.S.A.
28 D3 **Ellidshøj** Denmark
112 C3 **Ellijay** Georgia U.S.A.
28 E2 **Elling** Denmark
28 F6 **Ellinge** Denmark
37 K5 **Ellingen** Germany
13 G3 **Ellington** England
110 F4 **Ellington** Missouri U.S.A.
107 M3 **Ellinwood** Kansas U.S.A.
89 E8 **Elliot** S Africa
95 L8 **Elliot** Maryland U.S.A.
112 G3 **Elliot** South Carolina U.S.A.
142 E4 **Elliot Lake** W Australia Australia
120 H6 **Elliot Lake** Ontario Canada
141 H4 **Elliot, Mt** Queensland Australia
140 C3 **Elliott** N Terr Australia
99 L8 **Elliott** Iowa U.S.A.
98 J3 **Elliott** North Dakota U.S.A.
113 G12 **Elliott Key** *isld* Florida U.S.A.
122 H4 **Ellis B** Quebec Canada
89 E4 **Ellisras** S Africa
138 C5 **Elliston** South Australia Australia
123 T5 **Elliston** Newfoundland Canada
101 N3 **Elliston** Montana U.S.A.
94 G9 **Elliston** Virginia U.S.A.
111 G10 **Ellisville** Mississippi U.S.A.
143 G8 **Ell, L** W Australia Australia
38 F6 **Ellmau** Austria
36 F6 **Ellmendingen** Germany
15 F3 **Ellon** Scotland
74 F8 **Ellora** India
112 G4 **Elloree** South Carolina U.S.A.
33 N9 **Ellrich** Germany
118 E4 **Ellscott** Alberta Canada
110 F5 **Ellsinore** Missouri U.S.A.
107 M3 **Ellsworth** Kansas U.S.A.
95 T2 **Ellsworth** Maine U.S.A.
99 L6 **Ellsworth** Minnesota U.S.A.
98 D7 **Ellsworth** Nebraska U.S.A.
99 O5 **Ellsworth** Wisconsin U.S.A.
109 J1 **Ellsworth,L** Oklahoma U.S.A.
146 B7 **Ellsworth Land** Antarctica
146 C7 **Ellsworth Mts** Antarctica
37 J6 **Ellwangen** Germany
94 G6 **Ellwood City** Pennsylvania U.S.A.
32 H6 **Ellwürden** Germany
32 K5 **Elm** Germany
41 K4 **Elm** Switzerland
99 O6 **Elma** Iowa U.S.A.
100 B2 **Elma** Washington U.S.A.
133 C6 **El Maitén** Argentina
47 K8 **Elmalı** Turkey
86 F3 **El Manaquil** Sudan
124 A2 **El Maneadero** Mexico
124 G5 **El Martínez** Mexico
109 L7 **Elmaton** Texas U.S.A.
103 J9 **El Mayor** Mexico
79 D7 **El Mazâr** Egypt
112 K2 **Elm City** North Carolina U.S.A.
98 G9 **Elm Cr** Nebraska U.S.A.
118 D1 **Elm Creek** Manitoba Canada
107 N6 **Elm Cr.Res.,E** Oklahoma U.S.A.
108 A2 **Elmendorf** New Mexico U.S.A.
127 J9 **El Mene de Mauroa** Venezuela
32 M5 **Elmenhorst** Germany
99 O10 **Elmer** Missouri U.S.A.
95 M7 **Elmer** New Jersey U.S.A.
109 H1 **Elmer** Oklahoma U.S.A.
100 G1 **Elmer City** Washington U.S.A.
43 B13 **El Meskiana** Algeria
99 T8 **Elmhurst** Illinois U.S.A.
79 F4 **El Mīna** Lebanon
123 K7 **Elmira** Prince Edward I Canada
102 C3 **Elmira** California U.S.A.
94 C1 **Elmira** Michigan U.S.A.
95 L4 **Elmira** New York U.S.A.
103 M8 **El Mirage** Arizona U.S.A.
98 H4 **Elm L** South Dakota U.S.A.
109 K4 **Elm Mott** Texas U.S.A.
107 N3 **Elmo** Kansas U.S.A.
99 L9 **Elmo** Missouri U.S.A.
101 T8 **Elmo** Wyoming U.S.A.
16 E4 **El Molar** Spain
108 G7 **El Moral** Mexico
139 G6 **Elmore** Victoria Australia
111 K9 **Elmore** Alabama U.S.A.
99 M6 **Elmore** Minnesota U.S.A.
94 D5 **Elmore** Ohio U.S.A.
109 K1 **Elmore City** Oklahoma U.S.A.
106 B6 **El Morro Nat.Mon** New Mexico U.S.A.
122 J9 **Elmsdale** Nova Scotia Canada
32 L5 **Elmshorn** Germany
98 D5 **Elm Springs** South Dakota U.S.A.
36 D5 **Elmstein** Germany
122 J8 **Elmsvale** Nova Scotia Canada
86 E3 **El Muglad** Sudan
120 J8 **Elmwood** Ontario Canada
110 G1 **Elmwood** Illinois U.S.A.
107 K5 **Elmwood** Oklahoma U.S.A.
99 O5 **Elmwood** Wisconsin U.S.A.
18 G10 **Elne** France
71 D5 **El Nido** Philippines
118 D7 **Elnora** Alberta Canada
110 J3 **Elnora** Indiana U.S.A.
86 F3 **El Obeid** Sudan
111 G12 **Eloi Bay** Louisiana U.S.A.
80 D1 **Elon** Israel
80 E5 **Elon Moré** Jordan
110 K6 **Elora** Tennessee U.S.A.
20 B5 **Elorn** *R* France
128 C4 **El Oro** *prov* Ecuador
125 J8 **El Oro** Mexico
124 F6 **Elota** Mexico
103 N9 **Eloy** Arizona U.S.A.
124 G5 **El Palmito** Mexico
128 F2 **El Pao** Venezuela
16 E4 **El Pardo** Spain
99 R9 **El Paso** Illinois U.S.A.
108 A4 **El Paso** Texas U.S.A.
131 B4 **El Peñón** *pk* Chile
14 C3 **Elphin** Ireland
141 J5 **Elphinstone** Queensland Australia
119 R8 **Elphinstone** Manitoba Canada
127 N9 **El Pilar** Venezuela
133 E2 **El Pintado** Argentina
83 K11 **Elpitiya** Sri Lanka
102 E4 **El Portal** California U.S.A.
128 C5 **El Portugues** Peru
108 B4 **El Porvenir** Mexico
16 D5 **El Puente del Arzobispo** Spain
16 C8 **El Puerto de Sta. Maria** Spain
80 D5 **Elqana** Jordan
80 E1 **El Qouzah** Lebanon
131 B2 **Elqui** *R* Chile
79 E8 **El Quşeima** Egypt
79 F9 **El Quweira** Jordan
124 G6 **El Regocijo** Mexico
108 F7 **El Remolino** Mexico
125 J6 **El Retorno** Mexico
116 N5 **Elridge Glacier** Alaska U.S.A.
106 D5 **El Rito** New Mexico U.S.A.
16 C7 **El Ronquillo** Spain
99 M4 **Elrosa** Minnesota U.S.A.
118 J7 **Elrose** Saskatchewan Canada
99 Q6 **Elroy** Wisconsin U.S.A.
124 H6 **El Rucio** Mexico
117 F4 **Elsa** Yukon Territory Canada
42 D5 **Elsa** *R* Italy
109 K9 **Elsa** Texas U.S.A.
124 G6 **El Salto** Mexico
125 P11 **El Salvador** *rep* Central America
71 G6 **El Salvador** Mindanao Philippines
120 H4 **Elsas** Ontario Canada
108 A6 **El Sauz** Mexico
109 J9 **El Sauz** Texas U.S.A.
25 E4 **Elsberg** *hill* Netherlands
110 F2 **Elsberry** Missouri U.S.A.
32 K6 **Elsdorf** Germany
32 H8 **Else** *R* Germany
22 L3 **Elsenborn** Belgium
36 F5 **Elsenz** *R* Germany
140 C2 **Elsey** N Terr Australia
26 G5 **Elsfjord** Norway
32 H6 **Elsfleth** Germany
98 E9 **Elsie** Nebraska U.S.A.
100 B4 **Elsie** Oregon U.S.A.
103 M3 **Elsinore** Utah U.S.A.
102 G8 **Elsinore L** California U.S.A.
25 E7 **Elsloo** Netherlands
98 F7 **Elsmere** Nebraska U.S.A.
107 P4 **Elsmore** Kansas U.S.A.
33 Q9 **Elsnigk** Germany
130 C10 **El Soberbio** Argentina
127 M10 **El Socorro** Venezuela
127 L10 **El Sombrero** Venezuela
116 K1 **Elson Lagoon** Alaska U.S.A.
25 E4 **Elspeet** Netherlands
25 E5 **Elst** Netherlands
9 F5 **Elstead** England
33 R9 **Elster** Germany
33 Q10 **Elster** *R* Germany
37 N2 **Elsterberg** Germany
33 T10 **Elsterwerda** Germany
145 F3 **Elsthorpe** New Zealand
9 F4 **Elstree** England
108 A6 **El Sueco** Mexico
124 G8 **El Tabaco** Mexico
16 C2 **El Teleno** *mt* Spain
25 F5 **Elten** Germany
37 O2 **Elterlein** Germany
9 G5 **Eltham** England
145 E3 **Eltham** New Zealand
79 E9 **El Thamad** Egypt
128 F2 **El Tigre** Venezuela
9 F3 **Eltisley** England
37 K4 **Eltmann** Germany
128 E2 **El Tocuyo** Venezuela
109 P5 **Elton** Louisiana U.S.A.
100 G3 **Eltopia** Washington U.S.A.
133 C3 **El toro** Chile
102 G8 **El Toro** California U.S.A.
133 C3 **El Tránsito** Chile
124 C2 **El Tren** Mexico
124 D6 **El Triunfo** Mexico
118 K1 **Eltrut L** Ontario Canada
127 O2 **El Tucuche** *mt* Trinidad
133 C8 **El Turbio** Argentina
36 E3 **Eltville** Germany
76 E2 **Eluru** India
119 Q9 **Elva** Manitoba Canada
52 C5 **Elva** Estonia
106 D5 **El Vado** New Mexico U.S.A.
128 C2 **El Valle** Colombia
127 L9 **El Valle** Venezuela
12 E3 **Elvanfoot** Scotland
79 E2 **Elvanlı** Turkey
27 E10 **Elvdal** Norway
26 N2 **Elvebakken** Norway
20 E6 **Elven** France
27 E11 **Elverum** Norway
125 L3 **El Viejo** Nicaragua
128 D2 **El Vigia** Venezuela
128 D5 **Elvira** Brazil
114 J3 **Elvira,C** Northwest Territories Canada
142 B5 **Elvire, Mt** W Australia Australia
143 C8 **Elvire, Mt** W Australia Australia
142 G4 **Elvire, R** W Australia Australia
44 D1 **Elvo** *R* Italy
133 C4 **El Volcán** Chile
86 H5 **El Wak** Kenya
101 O1 **Elwell, L** *res* Montana U.S.A.
99 S8 **Elwood** Illinois U.S.A.
94 B6 **Elwood** Indiana U.S.A.
110 B2 **Elwood** Missouri U.S.A.
98 G9 **Elwood** Nebraska U.S.A.
9 G3 **Ely** England
99 P8 **Ely** Iowa U.S.A.
99 P2 **Ely** Minnesota U.S.A.
103 K2 **Ely** Nevada U.S.A.
80 D3 **Elyaqim** Israel
138 C3 **Ely Hill** South Australia Australia
99 N5 **Elysian** Minnesota U.S.A.
36 E3 **Elz** Germany
40 H1 **Elz** *R* Germany
36 E7 **Elzach** Germany
124 G5 **El Zape** Mexico
32 L7 **Elze** Germany
27 G10 **Emådalen** Sweden
137 O5 **Émaé** *isld* Vanuatu
77 D1 **Emāmrūd** Iran
27 H14 **Emån** *R* Sweden
130 D5 **Emas, Parque Nacional das** Brazil
50 E4 **Emba** *R* Kazakhstan
57 A1 **Emba** Kazakhstan
122 G1 **Embar** Labrador, Nfld Canada
133 E2 **Embarcación** Argentina
110 H2 **Embarras** *R* Illinois U.S.A.
117 R6 **Embarras Portage** Alberta Canada
99 O2 **Embarrass** Minnesota U.S.A.
98 J3 **Embden** North Dakota U.S.A.
60 P1 **Embetsu** Japan
128 D5 **Embira** *R* Brazil
101 R5 **Emblem** Wyoming U.S.A.
13 G3 **Embleton** England
47 U14 **Embóna** Rhodes Greece
130 F6 **Emborcação, Represa** *res* Brazil
121 P7 **Embrun** Ontario Canada
88 F2 **Embu** Kenya
32 F6 **Emden** Germany
99 R9 **Emden** Illinois U.S.A.
67 A2 **Emei** China
67 A2 **Emei Shan** *mt* China
80 F1 **Emeq Ḥula** Israel
80 D2 **'Emeq Zevulun** Israel
98 J2 **Emerado** North Dakota U.S.A.
141 J6 **Emerald** Queensland Australia
114 H2 **Emerald I** Northwest Territories Canada
71 D5 **Emergency Pt** Philippines
142 E3 **Emeriau Pt** W Australia Australia
115 N7 **Emeril** Labrador, Nfld Canada
119 U9 **Emerson** Manitoba Canada
99 L8 **Emerson** Iowa U.S.A.
98 K7 **Emerson** Nebraska U.S.A.
98 J6 **Emery** South Dakota U.S.A.
47 K5 **Emet** Turkey
101 P4 **Emigrant** Montana U.S.A.
102 D2 **Emigrant Gap** California U.S.A.
100 J9 **Emigrant Pass** Nevada U.S.A.
101 P4 **Emigrant Pk** Montana U.S.A.
103 J4 **Emigrant Valley** Nevada U.S.A.
86 C2 **Emi Koussi** *mt* Chad
42 D4 **Emilia-Romagna** *prov* Italy
40 F6 **Emilius, M** Italy
57 L2 **Emin** China
66 C2 **Emin** China
47 J2 **Emine,N** Bulgaria
94 B8 **Eminence** Kentucky U.S.A.
110 E4 **Eminence** Missouri U.S.A.
47 J2 **Eminska Planina** *plateau* Bulgaria
47 K7 **Emir** *R* Turkey
78 C2 **Emirdag** Turkey
139 J7 **Emita** Flinders I, Tasmania Australia
94 H5 **Emlenton** Pennsylvania U.S.A.
32 E7 **Emlichheim** Germany
27 H15 **Emmaboda** Sweden
126 B1 **Emmastad** Curaçao Neth Antilles
27 N13 **Emmaste** Estonia
95 M6 **Emmaus** Pennsylvania U.S.A.
139 K3 **Emmaville** New South Wales Australia
40 G4 **Emme** *R* Switzerland
118 L3 **Emmeline L** Saskatchewan Canada
25 E3 **Emmeloord** Netherlands
25 G3 **Emmen** Netherlands
41 H3 **Emmen** Switzerland
40 G4 **Emmen Tal** Switzerland
25 F5 **Emmerich** Germany
28 B7 **Emmerlev** Denmark
32 K8 **Emmern** Germany
38 M5 **Emmersdorf** Austria
28 B7 **Emmerske** Denmark
32 K8 **Emmerthal** Germany
32 K9 **Emmerthal** Germany
141 G6 **Emmet** Queensland Australia
100 J6 **Emmet** Idaho U.S.A.
98 H7 **Emmet** Nebraska U.S.A.
99 M6 **Emmetsburg** Iowa U.S.A.
107 O2 **Emmett** Kansas U.S.A.
76 C3 **Emmiganuru** India
95 K7 **Emmitsburg** Maryland U.S.A.
103 O1 **Emmons,Mt** Utah U.S.A.
99 N1 **Emo** Ontario Canada
48 F3 **Emöd** Hungary
109 M3 **Emory** Texas U.S.A.
108 D6 **Emory Pk** Texas U.S.A.
124 D4 **Empalme** Mexico
89 G7 **Empangeni** S Africa
32 K7 **Empede** Germany
133 F3 **Empedrado** Argentina
25 F5 **Empel** Germany
112 D5 **Empire** Georgia U.S.A.
99 U5 **Empire** Michigan U.S.A.
100 F9 **Empire** Nevada U.S.A.
100 A6 **Empire** Oregon U.S.A.
106 F1 **Empire Res** Colorado U.S.A.
42 D5 **Empoli** Italy
107 O3 **Emporia** Kansas U.S.A.
94 K10 **Emporia** Virginia U.S.A.
94 J5 **Emporium** Pennsylvania U.S.A.
118 G8 **Empress** Alberta Canada
22 J3 **Emptinne** Belgium
19 N14 **Empurany** France
98 G2 **Emrick** North Dakota U.S.A.
32 F6 **Ems** *R* Germany
32 F8 **Emsbüren** Germany
32 F9 **Emscher** *R* Germany
121 L7 **Emsdale** Ontario Canada
32 G8 **Emsdetten** Germany
32 G6 **Ems-Jade Kanal** Germany
37 K4 **Emskirchen** Germany
32 F7 **Emslage** Germany
36 G1 **Emstal** Germany
32 H7 **Emstek** Germany
9 F6 **Emsworth** England
65 G3 **Emu** China
141 F3 **Emu Ck** Queensland Australia
61 L10 **Ena** Japan
27 J10 **Enånger** Sweden
80 D4 **'Enav** Jordan
80 C3 **'En Ayyala** Israel
101 T8 **Encampment** Wyoming U.S.A.
17 H4 **Encanade** *mt* Spain
108 B6 **Encantada** Mexico
124 B2 **Encantada, Cerro de la** Mexico
131 H3 **Encantadas,Sa** *mts* Brazil
124 C4 **Encantado, Cerro** *mt* Mexico
71 E3 **Encanto,C** Luzon Philippines
124 H7 **Encarnación** Mexico
130 C10 **Encarnación** Paraguay
118 E8 **Enchant** Alberta Canada
85 D7 **Enchi** Ghana
106 C5 **Encinada Mesa** *tableland* New Mexico U.S.A.
109 H7 **Encinal** Texas U.S.A.
108 A6 **Encinillas** Mexico
102 G8 **Encinitas** California U.S.A.
108 B1 **Encino** New Mexico U.S.A.
108 B2 **Encinoso** New Mexico U.S.A.
128 D2 **Encontrados** Venezuela
138 E6 **Encounter B** South Australia Australia
133 G4 **Encruzilhada do Sul** Brazil
48 G2 **Encs** Hungary
117 L8 **Endako** British Columbia Canada
69 F11 **Endau** *R* Malaysia
69 F11 **Endau** Malaysia
71 K9 **Ende** *isld* Flores Indonesia
99 R6 **Endeavor** Wisconsin U.S.A.
141 H3 **Endeavour** Queensland Australia
119 P6 **Endeavour** Saskatchewan Canada
141 F1 **Endeavour Str** Queensland Australia
108 A8 **Endee** New Mexico U.S.A.
71 K9 **Endeh** Indonesia
28 E5 **Endelave** Denmark
134 K8 **Enderbury I** Phoenix Is Pacific Oc
117 O10 **Enderby** British Columbia Canada
142 B5 **Enderby I** W Australia Australia
146 J10 **Enderby Land** Antarctica
98 J3 **Enderlin** North Dakota U.S.A.
98 E9 **Enders Res** Nebraska U.S.A.
118 E7 **Endiang** Alberta Canada
95 L4 **Endicott** New York U.S.A.
100 H3 **Endicott** Washington U.S.A.
117 G7 **Endicott Arm** *pen* Alaska U.S.A.
116 L3 **Endicott Mts** Alaska U.S.A.
117 G4 **End,Mt** Yukon Territory Canada
8 D1 **Endon** England
80 E3 **'En Dor** Israel
140 C1 **Endyalgout I** N Terr Australia
128 D6 **Ene** *R* Peru
143 B8 **Eneabba** W Australia Australia
55 C5 **Energetik** Russian Federation
54 F9 **Energodar** Ukraine
134 G7 **Enewetak** *atoll* Marshall Is
47 H4 **Enez** Turkey
78 A1 **Enez** Turkey
79 F4 **Enfe** Lebanon
43 C12 **Enfida** Tunisia
122 J9 **Enfield** Nova Scotia Canada
9 F4 **Enfield** England
110 H3 **Enfield** Illinois U.S.A.
95 P3 **Enfield** New Hampshire U.S.A.
112 K1 **Enfield** North Carolina U.S.A.
127 K5 **Engaño, C** Dominican Rep
71 E1 **Engaño,C** Luzon Philippines
60 R1 **Engaru** Japan
28 B7 **Enge** Germany
80 E8 **En Gedi** Israel
41 H4 **Engelberg** Switzerland
112 M2 **Engelhard** North Carolina U.S.A.
38 J5 **Engelhartszell** Austria
53 G8 **Engel's** Russian Federation
36 C2 **Engelskirchen** Germany
41 J2 **Engen** Germany
130 C4 **Engenho** Brazil
138 D3 **Engenina** *R* South Australia Australia
32 J8 **Enger** Germany
26 E10 **Engerdal** Norway
27 F10 **Engeren,L** Norway
36 D3 **Engers** Germany
28 C4 **Engesvang** Denmark
80 F2 **'En Gev** Israel
Enghien *see* **Edingen**
21 P4 **Enghien-les-Bains** France
117 F6 **Engineer** British Columbia Canada
22 J2 **Engis** Belgium
70 B4 **Engkilili** Sarawak
8 D3 **England** U.K.
111 E7 **England** Arkansas U.S.A.
106 C8 **Engle** New Mexico U.S.A.
123 Q3 **Englee** Newfoundland Canada
119 N6 **Englefield** Saskatchewan Canada
117 K10 **Englewood** British Columbia Canada
106 F2 **Englewood** Colorado U.S.A.
113 E11 **Englewood** Florida U.S.A.
107 L4 **Englewood** Kansas U.S.A.
112 C2 **Englewood** Tennessee U.S.A.
110 K3 **English** Indiana U.S.A.
122 E4 **English Bay** Quebec Canada
116 L7 **English Bay** Alaska U.S.A.
7 H13 **English Channel** England/France
146 C6 **English Coast** Antarctica
140 D1 **English Company's Is** N Terr Australia
127 P4 **English Harbour Town** Antigua W Indies
123 R6 **English Harbour W** Newfoundland Canada
119 N1 **English River** Ontario Canada
52 D2 **Engozero** Russian Federation
36 G7 **Engstingen** Germany
17 G6 **Énguera** Spain
52 B6 **Engure** Latvia
80 D3 **'En Ha'Emeq** Israel
80 D2 **'En HaMifraz** Israel
80 E3 **'En Ḥarod** Israel
79 F8 **'En Hazeva** Israel
80 C3 **'En Hod** Israel
98 B2 **Enid** Montana U.S.A.
107 N5 **Enid** Oklahoma U.S.A.
111 G7 **Enid L** Mississippi U.S.A.
142 B5 **Enid, Mt** W Australia Australia
118 A3 **Enilda** Alberta Canada
36 G7 **Eningen** Germany
60 P3 **Eniwa** Japan
60 P3 **Eniwa dake** *mt* Japan
85 C5 **Enji** Mauritania
80 C3 **'En Karmel** Israel
36 D5 **Enkenbach-Alsenborn** Germany
25 D3 **Enkhuizen** Netherlands
36 C4 **Enkirch** Germany
27 J12 **Enköping** Sweden
128 G8 **En Madrejón** Paraguay
114 J5 **Ennadai** Northwest Territories Canada
86 E3 **En Nahud** Sudan
86 D2 **Ennedi** *plateau* Chad
14 D3 **Ennell,L** Ireland
32 F10 **Ennepetal** Germany
127 H5 **Ennery** Haiti
139 H3 **Enngonia** New South Wales Australia
32 H9 **Ennigerloh** Germany
98 D5 **Enning** South Dakota U.S.A.
27 E13 **Enningdal** Norway
14 C4 **Ennis** Ireland
101 O4 **Ennis** Montana U.S.A.
109 L3 **Ennis** Texas U.S.A.
14 E4 **Enniscorthy** Ireland
14 D2 **Enniskillen** N Ireland
14 B4 **Ennistimon** Ireland
80 D1 **Enn Nâqoûra** Lebanon
38 K6 **Ennstaler Alpen** *mts* Austria
80 G4 **En Nu'eiyima** Jordan
29 P9 **Eno** Finland
108 E2 **Enochs** Texas U.S.A.
141 K1 **Enoggera** *dist* Brisbane, Qnsld Australia
69 F13 **Enok** Sumatra
98 J8 **Enola** Nebraska U.S.A.
29 O9 **Enonkoski** Finland
29 K3 **Enontekiö** Finland
112 F3 **Enoree** *R* South Carolina U.S.A.
112 F3 **Enoree** South Carolina U.S.A.
95 P2 **Enosburg Falls** Vermont U.S.A.
67 D5 **Enping** China
70 F6 **Enrekang** Sulawesi
71 E2 **Enrile** Luzon Philippines
127 J5 **Enriquillo, Lago de** Dominican Rep
25 E3 **Ens** Netherlands
139 J6 **Ensay** Victoria Australia
25 G4 **Enschede** Netherlands
36 B5 **Ensdorf** Germany
32 H10 **Ense** Germany
133 F4 **Ensenada** Argentina
124 A2 **Ensenada** Mexico
106 D5 **Ensenada** New Mexico U.S.A.
126 B3 **Ensenada de Guadiana** *B* Cuba
36 C5 **Ensheim** Germany
80 D4 **'En Shemer** Israel
67 C1 **Enshi** China
118 D8 **Ensign** Alberta Canada
107 K4 **Ensign** Kansas U.S.A.
99 U4 **Ensign** Michigan U.S.A.
19 K5 **Ensisheim** France
28 F4 **Enslev** Denmark
9 E4 **Enstone** England
86 F5 **Entebbe** Uganda
37 N4 **Entenbühl** *mt* Germany
12 E3 **Enterkinfoot** Scotland
117 P5 **Enterprise** Northwest Territories Canada
121 O8 **Enterprise** Ontario Canada
111 L10 **Enterprise** Alabama U.S.A.
107 N3 **Enterprise** Kansas U.S.A.
111 H9 **Enterprise** Mississippi U.S.A.
100 H4 **Enterprise** Oregon U.S.A.
103 L4 **Enterprise** Utah U.S.A.
71 D5 **Enterprise Pt** Philippines
100 E2 **Entiat Mts** Washington U.S.A.
70 C4 **Entimau, Bt** *mt* Sarawak
17 F8 **Entinas,Pta. De Las** Spain
133 D8 **Entrada,Pta** Argentina
18 H5 **Entrains** France
21 J6 **Entrammes** France
140 A3 **Entrance I** N Terr Australia
18 G8 **Entraygues** France
143 B10 **Entrecasteaux, Pt.d'** W Australia Australia
137 N5 **Entrecasteaux, Récifs D'** *reefs* New Caledonia
83 J14 **Entre-Deux** Réunion Indian Oc
123 L6 **Entré, I. d'** Madeleine Is, Quebec Canada
129 H5 **Entre Rios** Brazil
130 G7 **Entre Rios de Minas** Brazil
36 F6 **Entringen** Germany
103 M7 **Entro** Arizona U.S.A.
89 E2 **Entuba** Zimbabwe
118 C5 **Entwistle** Alberta Canada
85 F7 **Enugu** Nigeria
100 D2 **Enumclaw** Washington U.S.A.
21 N2 **Envermeu** France
27 H11 **Enviken** Sweden
8 D3 **Enville** England
128 D5 **Envira** Brazil
67 B1 **Enyang** China
48 E4 **Enying** Hungary
144 C5 **Enys, Mt** New Zealand
36 F6 **Enz** *R* Germany
45 H2 **Enza** *R* Italy
80 E8 **'En Zafzafa** Israel
61 M10 **Enzan** Japan
37 M6 **Enzelhausen** Germany
36 E6 **Enzklösterle** Germany
80 B7 **En Ẕurim** Israel
36 F6 **Enzweihingen** Germany
111 D11 **Eola** Louisiana U.S.A.
110 E2 **Eolia** Missouri U.S.A.
21 L3 **Epaignes** France
45 P8 **Epameo, M** *mt* Italy
21 K4 **Epaney** France
46 F4 **Epanomí** Greece
32 F8 **Epe** Germany
25 E4 **Epe** Netherlands
133 E5 **Epecuén,L** Argentina
22 E3 **Epéhy** France
140 D5 **Epenarra** N Terr Australia
22 C2 **Éperlecques** France
18 H3 **Épernay** France
87 B9 **Epernbe** Namibia
21 O4 **Épernon** France
111 H9 **Epes** Alabama U.S.A.
21 J8 **Epesses, les** France
36 C7 **Epfig** France
138 E2 **Ephemeral Lakes** South Australia Australia

N2 **Ephraim** Utah U.S.A.
L6 **Ephrata** Pennsylvania U.S.A.
F2 **Ephrata** Washington U.S.A.
O5 **Épi** *isld* Vanuatu
G10 **Epidendron** *isld* Mozambique
F7 **Epídhavros** Greece
O6 **Epieds** France
G3 **Épila** Spain
K4 **Epinal** France
F8 **Epine, l'** Vendée France
G5 **Epiniac** France
J6 **Epiphany** South Dakota U.S.A.
C4 **Episkopi** Cyprus
O4 **Epône** France
B5 **Eppelborn** Germany
P2 **Eppendorf** Germany
F4 **Eppes** France
G3 **Eppe-Sauvage** France
G4 **Epping** England
Q3 **Epping** New Hampshire U.S.A.
C1 **Epping** North Dakota U.S.A.
F5 **Eppingen** Germany
E3 **Eppstein** Germany
A4 **Epsie** Montana U.S.A.
F5 **Epsom** England
M6 **Epuisay** France
C10 **Epukiro** Namibia
H6 **Epworth** England
Q7 **Epworth** Iowa U.S.A.
C4 **Eqlīd** Iran
H4 **Equality** Illinois U.S.A.
D5 **Equateur** *prov* Zaire
E4 **Equatoria** *prov* Sudan
L9 **Equatorial Chan** Maldives
F8 **Equatorial Guinea** *rep* W Africa
G2 **Equeurdreville** France
M5 **Equmunk** Pennsylvania U.S.A.
O4 **Era** Japan
E4 **Era** *watercourse* Sudan
H7 **Erac** *R* Queensland Australia
C6 **Eran** Palawan Philippines
C6 **Eran Bay** Palawan Philippines
D12 **Erath** Louisiana U.S.A.
F1 **Erbaa** Turkey
D5 **Erbach** *R* Germany
H7 **Erbach** Baden-Württemberg Germany
G4 **Erbach** Hessen Germany
G1 **Erba, Jebel** *mt* Sudan
N4 **Erbendorf** Germany
N4 **Erben Tablemount** Pacific Oc
C4 **Erbes Kopf** *mt* Germany
H6 **Erbray** France
D4 **Ercheu** France
J2 **Erciş** Turkey
E2 **Erciyas Dag** Turkey
Q8 **Ercolana** Italy
E3 **Ercsi** Hungary
E3 **Erd** Hungary
H2 **Erdaohezi** China
G3 **Erdao Jiang** *R* China
J4 **Erdek** Turkey
J4 **Erdek Körfezi** *B* Turkey
E2 **Erdemli** Turkey
F6 **Erdenet** Mongolia
D6 **Erdeven** France
D2 **Erdi** *dist* Chad
M7 **Erding** Germany
M7 **Erdinger Moos** *marsh* Germany
E2 **Erdington** England
P2 **Erdmansdorf** Germany
B3 **Erdorf** Germany
H6 **Erdre** *R* France
F5 **Éréac** France
F2 **Erebato** *R* Venezuela
D11 **Erebus, Mt** *vol* Ross I Antarctica
K6 **Erech** Iraq
D10 **Erechim** Brazil
G2 **Ereentsav** Mongolia
Ereğli *see* **Marmaraereğlisi**
C1 **Ereğli** Turkey
H7 **Ereke** Indonesia
L7 **Eren** *R* Turkey
K8 **Eren Dağ** *mt* Turkey
D2 **Eren Gobi** China
B3 **Erenhot** China
Erenköy *see* **İntepe**
N11 **Erenköy** Turkey
G4 **Erepecu, L** Brazil
D3 **Eresma** *R* Spain
H5 **Eressós** Greece
B7 **Erez** Israel
K3 **Erezée** Belgium
K4 **Erfde** Germany
E7 **Erfenis Dam** *res* S Africa
A4 **Erfenzi** China
D2 **Erfoud** Morocco
B2 **Erft** *R* Germany
B2 **Erftstadt** Germany
L2 **Erfurt** Germany
D4 **Ergak-Targak-Tayga, Khrebet** *mts* Russian Federation
G2 **Ergani** Turkey
D4 **Erg Chech** *desert region* Mali/Algeria
C2 **Erg du Djourab** *dist* Chad
A3 **Ergel** Mongolia
H3 **Ergene** *R* Turkey
D3 **Erg er Raoui** *desert region* Algeria
C3 **Erg Iguid** *sand desert* Algeria/Mauritania
E1 **Erginskiy Sor, Oz** *L* Russian Federation
C6 **Ergli** Latvia
N6 **Ergolding** Germany
N6 **Ergoldsbach** Germany
G1 **Ergu** China
B6 **Ergué-Armel** France
C3 **Erguig** *R* Chad
Ergun He *R see* **Argun** *R*
H1 **Ergun Youqi** China
H1 **Ergun Zuoqi** China
O7 **Erharting** Germany
D2 **Eria** *R* Spain
G2 **Eriba** Sudan
A6 **Ericeira** Portugal
K7 **Erichshagen** Germany
L6 **Erick** Oklahoma U.S.A.
S8 **Erickson** Manitoba Canada
G2 **Eric L** Quebec Canada
N1 **Ericsburg** Minnesota U.S.A.
H8 **Ericson** Nebraska U.S.A.
A9 **Erie** Colorado U.S.A.
Q8 **Erie** Illinois U.S.A.
P4 **Erie** Kansas U.S.A.
D5 **Erie** Michigan U.S.A.
J2 **Erie** North Dakota U.S.A.
G4 **Erie** Pennsylvania U.S.A.
J10 **Erieau** Ontario Canada
G4 **Erie,L** U.S.A./Canada
H1 **Erikli** Turkey
O12 **Erikoúsa** *isld* Greece
T8 **Eriksdale** Manitoba Canada
E7 **Erímanthos** *mt* Greece
R4 **Erimo-misaki** *C* Japan
C3 **Erin** France
P7 **Ering** Germany
H15 **Eringsboda** Sweden
N3 **Erin Pt** Trinidad
A3 **Eriskay** *isld* Scotland
G5 **Erith** England
F6 **Erithraí** Greece
G2 **Eritrea** *rep* Africa
F6 **Erkelenz** Germany
K12 **Erken** Sweden
T8 **Erkner** Germany
G2 **Erkowit** Sudan
E10 **Erkrath** Germany
F6 **Erl** Austria
Erlangdiang *see* **Dawu**
L4 **Erlangen** Germany
C7 **Erlanger** Kentucky U.S.A.
M5 **Erlauf** *R* Austria
N3 **Erlbach** Germany
C7 **Erldunda** N Terr Australia
F3 **Erlensee** Germany

111 C8 **Erling,L** Arkansas U.S.A.
65 G3 **Erlong Shan** *mt* China
38 F8 **Erlsbach** Austria
25 E4 **Ermelo** Netherlands
89 F6 **Ermelo** S Africa
78 D3 **Ermenek** Turkey
79 D2 **Ermenek** *R* Turkey
71 M9 **Ermera** Indonesia
Ermoúpolis *see* **Síros**
33 O9 **Ermsleben** Germany
138 B2 **Ernabella** South Australia Australia
138 B2 **Ernabella** *R* South Australia Australia
76 C6 **Ernakulam** India
36 E1 **Erndtebrück** Germany
14 C2 **Erne** *R* Ireland
21 J5 **Ernée** France
21 J5 **Ernée** *R* France
14 D2 **Erne,L.Lower** N Ireland
14 D2 **Erne,L.Upper** N Ireland
143 E7 **Ernest Giles Ra** W Australia Australia
144 A7 **Ernest Is** New Zealand
135 M12 **Ernest Legouve Reef** Pacific Oc
117 G8 **Ernest Sd** Alaska U.S.A.
118 L8 **Ernfold** Saskatchewan Canada
45 O6 **Ernici, Monti** *mt* Italy
36 G4 **Ernstthal** Germany
76 C5 **Erode** India
78 J2 **Erois** Turkey
141 G7 **Eromanga** Queensland Australia
111 D9 **Eros** Louisiana U.S.A.
36 B2 **Erp** Germany
22 G3 **Erquelinnes** Belgium
20 F4 **Erquy** France
20 F4 **Erquy, C.d'** France
143 B7 **Errabiddy Hills** W Australia Australia
85 D2 **Er Rachidia** Morocco
86 F3 **Er Rahad** Sudan
80 G6 **Er Rajib** Jordan
88 F10 **Errego** Mozambique
14 C1 **Errigal** *mt* Ireland
28 G7 **Errindlev** Denmark
14 A2 **Erris Hd** Ireland
28 D5 **Erritsø** Denmark
111 G12 **Errol I** Louisiana U.S.A.
137 O5 **Erromango** *isld* Vanuatu
86 F3 **Er Roseires** Sudan
46 D4 **Ersekë** Albania
118 E6 **Erskine** Alberta Canada
142 F4 **Erskine, Mount** W Australia Australia
26 M6 **Ersnäs** Sweden
36 D7 **Erstein** France
19 L4 **Ersteir** France
36 H3 **Erthal** Germany
54 M5 **Ertil'** Russian Federation
66 D2 **Ertix He** *R* China
47 J5 **Ertugrul** Turkey
22 F1 **Ertvelde** Belgium
145 E3 **Erua** New Zealand
138 E4 **Erudina** South Australia Australia
27 H12 **Ervalla** Sweden
21 K6 **Erve** *R* France
37 Q2 **Ervěnice** Czech Rep
22 D3 **Ervillers** France
112 J2 **Erwin** North Carolina U.S.A.
112 E1 **Erwin** Tennessee U.S.A.
32 H9 **Erwitte** Germany
119 P6 **Erwood** Saskatchewan Canada
8 C3 **Erwood** Wales
33 O8 **Erxleben** Germany
46 D3 **Erzen** *R* Albania
37 N3 **Erzgebirge** Germany
56 E5 **Erzin** Russian Federation
79 G2 **Erzin** Turkey
78 G2 **Erzincan** Turkey
78 H2 **Erzurum** Turkey
52 B6 **Erzvilkas** Lithuania
60 P4 **Esan-misaki** *C* Japan
21 J3 **Esaue** *R* France
28 A6 **Esbjerg** Denmark
107 M2 **Esbon** Kansas U.S.A.
17 G2 **Esca** *R* Spain
18 E10 **Esca** *R* Spain
130 J10 **Escada** Brazil
103 N4 **Escalante** *R* Utah U.S.A.
103 N4 **Escalante** Utah U.S.A.
103 L4 **Escalante Des** Utah U.S.A.
131 A8 **Escalera,Pta** Chile
124 G4 **Escalón** Mexico
16 E4 **Escalona** Spain
111 J11 **Escambia** *R* Florida U.S.A.
99 T3 **Escanaba** *R* Michigan U.S.A.
99 T4 **Escanaba** Michigan U.S.A.
125 O8 **Escárcega** Mexico
21 H7 **Escarpière, l'** France
22 E3 **Escaut** *R* France
36 E3 **Esch** Germany
22 L5 **Esch** Luxembourg
36 G4 **Eschau** Germany
36 F3 **Eschborn** Germany
22 K4 **Eschdorf** Luxembourg
32 E7 **Eschebrügge** Germany
32 M7 **Eschede** Germany
37 L4 **Eschenau** Germany
37 M4 **Eschenbach** Germany
36 E2 **Eschenberg** Germany
32 L9 **Eschershausen** Germany
40 G4 **Escholzmatt** Switzerland
116 G3 **Eschscholtz B** Alaska U.S.A.
22 K4 **Esch-sur-la-Sûre** Luxembourg
37 J1 **Eschwege** Germany
25 F7 **Eschweiler** Germany
127 K5 **Escocesa, B** Dominican Rep
130 H5 **Escondido** Brazil
102 G8 **Escondido** California U.S.A.
20 F7 **Escoublac** France
122 C5 **Escoumins,R** Quebec Canada
21 P5 **Escrennes** France
13 G6 **Escrick** England
124 G6 **Escuinapa de Hidalgo** Mexico
122 F5 **Escuminac** Quebec Canada
122 H6 **Escuminac, Pt** New Brunswick Canada
86 B5 **Eséka** Cameroon
Eşen *see* **Kestep**
47 N10 **Esenceli** Turkey
32 G5 **Esens** Germany
17 H2 **Esera** *R* Spain
77 B3 **Eşfahān** Iran
16 E3 **Esgueva** *R* Spain
80 B8 **Eshbol** Israel
80 B8 **Eshel Ha Nasi** Israel
9 F5 **Esher** England
77 L1 **Eshkamesh** Afghanistan
57 F6 **Eshkāshem** Afghanistan
87 F11 **Eshowe** S Africa
Esh Shem *see* **Dimashq**
77 B2 **Eshtehard** Iran
80 D8 **Eshtemoa** Jordan
87 E10 **Esigodini** Zimbabwe
42 E5 **Esino** *R* Italy
141 K7 **Esk** Queensland Australia
139 H8 **Esk** *R* Tasmania Australia
116 N6 **Eska** Alaska U.S.A.
118 L8 **Eskbank** Saskatchewan Canada
145 F3 **Eskdale** New Zealand
13 E5 **Eskdale Green** England
14 C2 **Eske, L** Ireland
47 K7 **Eskere** Turkey
29 T9 **Eskifjordhur** Iceland
28 H5 **Eskildstrup** Denmark
28 H7 **Eskilstrup** Denmark
27 H12 **Eskilstuna** Sweden
122 J3 **Eskimo I** Quebec Canada
114 F4 **Eskimo Lakes** Northwest Territories Canada
115 K5 **Eskimo Point** Northwest Territories Canada
78 D1 **Eskipazar** Turkey
47 L5 **Eskişehir** Turkey
13 H5 **Esk,R** England
15 E5 **Esk,R** Scotland
107 O3 **Eskridge** Kansas U.S.A.
16 D2 **Esla** *R* Spain

16 D3 **Esla, Embalse del** *res* Spain
78 L4 **Eslamabad-e Gharb** Iran
77 G2 **Eslām Qal'eh** Afghanistan
37 O4 **Eslarn** Germany
32 H10 **Eslohe** Germany
27 F16 **Eslöv** Sweden
47 K6 **Eşme** Turkey
141 G4 **Esmeralda** Queensland Australia
126 E4 **Esmeralda** Cuba
133 B7 **Esmeralda, I** Chile
128 C3 **Esmeraldas** Ecuador
98 G1 **Esmond** North Dakota U.S.A.
98 J5 **Esmond** South Dakota U.S.A.
120 D2 **Esnagami L** Ontario Canada
120 F4 **Esnagi L** Ontario Canada
22 J2 **Esnaux** Belgium
27 E11 **Espa** Norway
127 J8 **Espada,Pta** Colombia
18 G8 **Espalion** France
17 H6 **Espalmador** *isld* Balearic Is
120 J6 **Espanola** Ontario Canada
128 B8 **Española** *isld* Galapagos Is
113 F8 **Espanola** Florida U.S.A.
106 D6 **Espanola** New Mexico U.S.A.
19 P17 **Esparron** France
102 B3 **Esparto** California U.S.A.
125 M5 **Esparza** Costa Rica
28 E6 **Espe** Denmark
27 D10 **Espedals-vatn** *L* Norway
32 J8 **Espelkamp** Germany
116 E3 **Espenberg,C** Alaska U.S.A.
37 N1 **Espenhain** Germany
88 F8 **Esperança** Mozambique
143 D10 **Esperance** W Australia Australia
143 D10 **Esperance B** W Australia Australia
146 D3 **Esperanza** *Argentina Base* Graham Land Antarctica
131 E3 **Esperanza** Argentina
124 E4 **Esperanza** Mexico
113 K7 **Esperanza** Puerto Rico
108 B4 **Esperanza** Texas U.S.A.
125 M2 **Esperanza, Sa. de la** *ra* Honduras
29 K5 **Espergærde** Denmark
45 P7 **Esperia** Italy
16 A6 **Espichel,C** Portugal
16 D6 **Espiel** Spain
130 E10 **Espigão,Serra do** *mts* Brazil
16 D2 **Espigüete** *mt* Spain
128 D6 **Espinar** Peru
19 Q16 **Espinasses** France
124 J4 **Espinazo** Mexico
130 G6 **Espinhaço,Serra,do** *mt* Brazil
16 B4 **Espinho** Portugal
131 G2 **Espinilho, Serra do** *ra* Brazil
130 G4 **Espinosa** Brazil
130 H6 **Espirito Santo** *state* Brazil
124 D5 **Espíritu Santo** *isld* Mexico
137 O5 **Espiritu Santo** *isld* Vanuatu
125 Q8 **Espíritu Santo, B. del** Mexico
133 D8 **Espíritu Santo,C** Chile/Arg
71 G4 **Espiritu Santo,C** Philippines
125 P7 **Espita** Mexico
123 R6 **Espoir, B. d'** Newfoundland Canada
16 B3 **Esposende** Portugal
40 D2 **Esprels** France
87 F10 **Espungabera** Mozambique
100 F3 **Esquatzel Coulee** *R* Washington U.S.A.
124 E2 **Esqueda** Mexico
133 C6 **Esquel** Argentina
22 C2 **Esquelbecq** France
100 B1 **Esquimalt** British Columbia Canada
117 M11 **Esquimalt** British Columbia Canada
133 F3 **Esquina** Argentina
29 K4 **Esrum Sø** *L* Denmark
55 D1 **Ess** *R* Russian Federation
80 F3 **Es Samt** Jordan
80 D8 **Es Samu** Jordan
85 C2 **Essaouira** Morocco
80 G3 **Es Sarih** Jordan
21 O4 **Essarts-le-Roi, les** France
20 H8 **Essarts, les** Vendée France
21 L4 **Essay** France
85 E2 **Es Seggeur** *watercourse* Algeria
32 L7 **Essel** Germany
22 G1 **Essen** Belgium
32 G7 **Essen** Niedersachsen Germany
32 E10 **Essen** Nordrhein-Westfalen Germany
37 N6 **Essenbach** Germany
143 D6 **Essendon, Mt** W Australia Australia
120 H10 **Essex** Ontario Canada
9 G4 **Essex** *co* England
103 J7 **Essex** California U.S.A.
95 P5 **Essex** Connecticut U.S.A.
99 L9 **Essex** Iowa U.S.A.
101 M1 **Essex** Montana U.S.A.
95 O2 **Essex** New York U.S.A.
95 O2 **Essex Junct** Vermont U.S.A.
94 D3 **Essexville** Michigan U.S.A.
37 M6 **Essing** Germany
37 J6 **Essingen** Germany
36 G6 **Esslingen** Germany
21 P4 **Essonne** *dept* France
21 P5 **Essonne** *R* France
52 D4 **Essoyla** Russian Federation
100 C4 **Estacada** Oregon U.S.A.
16 B1 **Estaca de Bares, Pta. de la** Spain
106 G8 **Estacado, Llano** *plain* New Mex/Tex U.S.A.
103 K10 **Estacion Doctor** Mexico
103 K10 **Estacion France** Mexico
103 K9 **Estación Mèdanos** Mexico
133 E8 **Estados, I. de los** Argentina
18 G10 **Estagel** France
71 F2 **Estagno Pt** Luzon Philippines
77 D5 **Eştahbānāt** Iran
120 K6 **Estaire** Ontario Canada
22 D2 **Estaires** France
129 L6 **Estância** Brazil
108 A1 **Estancia** New Mexico U.S.A.
17 F7 **Estancias, Sierra de las** *mts* Spain
77 G4 **Estand, Kūh-e-** *mt* Iran
125 O9 **Estapilla** Mexico
16 B4 **Estarreja** Portugal
18 F10 **Estats, Pic d'** *mt* Spain
40 E4 **Estavayer le Lac** Switzerland
89 F7 **Estcourt** S Africa
32 L6 **Este** *R* Germany
42 D3 **Este** Italy
125 L3 **Estelí** Nicaragua
17 F2 **Estella** Spain
98 K5 **Estelline** South Dakota U.S.A.
16 D5 **Estena** *R* Spain
16 D7 **Estepa** Spain
16 D8 **Estepona** Spain
133 G4 **Este, Pta. del** Uruguay
116 N4 **Ester** Alaska U.S.A.
98 A7 **Esterbrook** Wyoming U.S.A.
119 P8 **Esterhazy** Saskatchewan Canada
18 H4 **Esternay** France
113 F11 **Estero** Florida U.S.A.
102 C6 **Estero B** California U.S.A.
133 C8 **Estero Obstrucción** Chile
125 K6 **Esteros** Mexico
133 E2 **Esteros** Paraguay
133 F3 **Esteros del Iberá** *swamp* Argentina
18 F10 **Esterri de Aneu** Spain
32 G6 **Esterwegen** Germany
98 A9 **Estes Pk** Colorado U.S.A.
119 P9 **Estevan** Saskatchewan Canada
117 J9 **Estevan Group** *islds* British Columbia Canada
117 K11 **Estevan Point** British Columbia Canada
118 G7 **Esther** Alberta Canada
99 M6 **Estherville** Iowa U.S.A.

112 F5 **Estill** South Carolina U.S.A.
18 H4 **Estissac** France
119 N8 **Estlin** Saskatchewan Canada
118 J7 **Eston** Saskatchewan Canada
52 B5 **Estonia** *rep* E Europe
16 A6 **Estoril** Portugal
19 Q17 **Estoublon** France
22 C2 **Estree Blanche** France
22 D5 **Estrées St. Denis** France
133 G4 **Estreíto** Brazil
130 F6 **Estrêla do Indaiá** Brazil
130 F6 **Estrêla do Sul** Brazil
16 B4 **Estrela, Sa. da** *mts* Portugal
103 M9 **Estrella** Arizona U.S.A.
102 D6 **Estrella** *R* California U.S.A.
103 M8 **Estrella,Sierra** *mt* Arizona U.S.A.
129 K6 **Estrelto, Serra do** *mts* Brazil
16 A6 **Estremadura** *prov* Portugal
16 B6 **Estremoz** Portugal
129 J5 **Estrondo, Serra do** *mts* Brazil
28 E3 **Estruplund** Denmark
118 H8 **Estuary** Saskatchewan Canada
28 B3 **Estvad** Denmark
48 E3 **Esztergom** Hungary
20 E4 **Étables** France
138 E3 **Etadunna** South Australia Australia
115 M2 **Etah** Greenland
19 J3 **Etain** France
22 K4 **Étalle** Belgium
123 N3 **Etamamiou,R** Quebec Canada
123 N3 **Etamamu** Quebec Canada
123 N3 **Etamamu R** Quebec Canada
21 P5 **Etampes** France
138 F2 **Etamunbanie,L** South Australia Australia
80 B7 **Etan** Israel
18 H6 **Étang** France
123 L6 **Étang-du-Nord** Madeleine Is, Quebec Canada
22 B2 **Étaples** France
74 H6 **Etawa** India
119 V1 **Etawney L** Manitoba Canada
124 E4 **Etchojoa** Mexico
20 D6 **Etel** France
27 K14 **Etelhem** Gotland Sweden
85 E5 **Etelia** Mali
32 K7 **Etelsen** Germany
122 B5 **Eternité,L** Quebec Canada
146 C5 **Eternity Ra** Antarctica
98 H6 **Ethan** South Dakota U.S.A.
22 K4 **Ethe** Belgium
111 E11 **Ethel** Louisiana U.S.A.
111 G8 **Ethel** Mississippi U.S.A.
110 D2 **Ethel** Missouri U.S.A.
94 F9 **Ethel** West Virginia U.S.A.
119 R7 **Ethelbert** Manitoba Canada
140 A5 **Ethel Cr** N Terr Australia
141 G3 **Ethel Cr** Queensland Australia
142 D6 **Ethel Creek** W Australia Australia
143 C6 **Ethel R** W Australia Australia
111 H8 **Ethelsville** Alabama U.S.A.
119 N6 **Ethelton** Saskatchewan Canada
141 G4 **Etheridge** *R* Queensland Australia
101 R6 **Ethete** Wyoming U.S.A.
86 G4 **Ethiopia** *socialist state* Africa
101 N1 **Ethridge** Montana U.S.A.
47 H5 **Etili** Turkey
40 F5 **Etivaz, l'** *L* Switzerland
116 J2 **Etivluk** *R* Alaska U.S.A.
27 D10 **Etna** *R* Norway
95 S2 **Etna** Maine U.S.A.
101 M8 **Etna** Utah U.S.A.
43 F11 **Etna, Monte** *vol* Sicily
27 A12 **Etne** Norway
27 D11 **Etnedal** Norway
121 L9 **Etobicoke** Ontario Canada
111 B10 **Etoile** Texas U.S.A.
116 D6 **Etolin,C** Alaska U.S.A.
117 G7 **Etolin I** Alaska U.S.A.
116 E6 **Etolin Str** Alaska U.S.A.
119 P6 **Etomami** Saskatchewan Canada
141 J5 **Eton** Queensland Australia
120 F5 **Eton** Ontario Canada
9 F5 **Eton** England
22 K5 **Eton** France
87 C9 **Etosha Nat. Park** Namibia
87 C9 **Etosha Pan** Namibia
112 B3 **Etowah** *R* Georgia U.S.A.
112 C2 **Etowah** Tennessee U.S.A.
22 F4 **Etreaupont** France
21 P5 **Etrechy** France
22 E4 **Etreillers** France
21 O3 **Étrépagny** France
21 L2 **Étretat** France
22 F4 **Etreux** France
22 D3 **Étricourt-Manancourt** France
40 A4 **Etrigny** France
46 F2 **Etropole** Bulgaria
22 F3 **Etrœungt** France
22 L4 **Ettelbrück** Luxembourg
36 D7 **Ettenheim** Germany
25 C5 **Etten-Leur** Netherlands
37 L1 **Ettersburg** Germany
100 A9 **Ettersburg** California U.S.A.
37 J2 **Etterwinden** Germany
9 E3 **Ettington** England
37 O6 **Ettling** Germany
36 E6 **Ettlingen** Germany
142 C5 **Ettrick** W Australia Australia
144 B6 **Ettrick** New Zealand
99 P5 **Ettrick** Wisconsin U.S.A.
15 E5 **Ettrick Pen** *mt* Scotland
13 E3 **Ettrick Water** Scotland
80 G6 **Et Tuneib** Jordan
80 G3 **Et Turra** Jordan
26 N5 **Etu-Aapua** *mt* Sweden
9 E2 **Etwall** England
124 G7 **Etzatlán** Mexico
37 P1 **Etzdorf** Germany
118 F9 **Etzikom** Alberta Canada
118 F9 **Etzikom Coulee** *R* Alberta Canada
21 N1 **Eu** France
137 S6 **'Eua** *isld* Tonga
139 H5 **Euabalong** New South Wales Australia
94 C9 **Eubank** Kentucky U.S.A.
36 H4 **Eubigheim** Germany
Euboea *isld see* **Évvoia** *isld*
143 G9 **Eucla** W Australia Australia
98 K2 **Euclid** Minnesota U.S.A.
94 F5 **Euclid** Ohio U.S.A.
139 J6 **Eucumbene,L** New South Wales Australia
122 G3 **Eudites,L.des** Quebec Canada
111 E8 **Eudora** Arkansas U.S.A.
138 E5 **Eudunda** South Australia Australia
37 J3 **Euerdorf** Germany
111 L10 **Eufala** Alabama U.S.A.
107 P6 **Eufaula** Oklahoma U.S.A.
107 P6 **Eufaula L** Oklahoma U.S.A.
43 G10 **Eufemia,S.,Golfo di** Italy
45 L1 **Euganei, Colli** *hills* Italy
100 B5 **Eugene** Oregon U.S.A.
124 B4 **Eugenia, Pta** *C* Mexico
130 C8 **Eugênio Penzo** Brazil
29 K8 **Eugmo** *isld* Finland
139 J5 **Eugowra** New South Wales Australia
37 O1 **Eula** *R* Germany
109 N9 **Euless** Texas U.S.A.
141 H8 **Eulo** Queensland Australia
112 F6 **Eulonia** Georgia U.S.A.
139 J4 **Eumaungerie** New South Wales Australia
16 B1 **Eume** *R* Spain
141 J5 **Eungella** Queensland Australia
111 D11 **Eunice** Louisiana U.S.A.
108 D3 **Eunice** New Mexico U.S.A.
22 L2 **Eupen** Belgium
78 J5 **Euphrates** *R* S W Asia
111 G8 **Eupora** Mississippi U.S.A.
27 M10 **Eura** Finland

29 J10 **Eurajoki** Finland
18 F3 **Eure** *dept* France
21 N3 **Eure** *R* France
18 F4 **Eure-et-Loir** *dept* France
115 L1 **Eureka** Northwest Territories Canada
100 A9 **Eureka** California U.S.A.
99 R9 **Eureka** Illinois U.S.A.
107 O4 **Eureka** Kansas U.S.A.
101 L1 **Eureka** Montana U.S.A.
103 J2 **Eureka** Nevada U.S.A.
98 G4 **Eureka** South Dakota U.S.A.
101 N10 **Eureka** Utah U.S.A.
100 G3 **Eureka** Washington U.S.A.
116 O6 **Eureka Lodge** Alaska U.S.A.
117 O7 **Eureka River** Alberta Canada
115 L2 **Eureka Snd** Northwest Territories Canada
110 C5 **Eureka Springs** Arkansas U.S.A.
102 G4 **Eureka Valley** California U.S.A.
138 F4 **Eurinilla** *R* South Australia Australia
138 F4 **Euriowie** New South Wales Australia
139 H6 **Euroa** Victoria Australia
23 F2 **Euro Disney** France
141 J7 **Eurombah** *R* Queensland Australia
141 J7 **Eurombah** Queensland Australia
81 B8 **Europa** *isld* Mozambique Chan
16 D8 **Europa Pt** Gibraltar
25 B5 **Europoort** Netherlands
61 J11 **Eushimi** Japan
36 B2 **Euskirchen** Germany
109 L3 **Eustace** Texas U.S.A.
113 F9 **Eustis** Florida U.S.A.
98 F9 **Eustis** Nebraska U.S.A.
139 G5 **Euston** New South Wales Australia
111 J9 **Eutaw** Alabama U.S.A.
112 G4 **Eutawville** South Carolina U.S.A.
33 N4 **Eutin** Germany
36 F7 **Eutingen** Germany
117 K9 **Eutsuk L** British Columbia Canada
33 R9 **Eutzsch** Germany
13 F6 **Euxton** England
111 E10 **Eva** Louisiana U.S.A.
108 C7 **Eva** Oklahoma U.S.A.
140 C4 **Eva Downs** N Terr Australia
87 C9 **Evale** Angola
99 M5 **Evan** Minnesota U.S.A.
139 H8 **Evandale** Tasmania Australia
100 H1 **Evans** Washington U.S.A.
118 B5 **Evansburg** Alberta Canada
115 L1 **Evans,C** Northwest Territories Canada
94 G6 **Evans City** Pennsylvania U.S.A.
139 L3 **Evans Head** New South Wales Australia
146 C7 **Evans Ice Stream** *ice stream* Antarctica
115 M7 **Evans,L** Quebec Canada
117 O9 **Evans,Mt** Alberta Canada
106 E2 **Evans,Mt** Colorado U.S.A.
101 M3 **Evans, Mt** Montana U.S.A.
115 L5 **Evans Str** Northwest Territories Canada
99 T7 **Evanston** Illinois U.S.A.
101 P8 **Evanston** Wyoming U.S.A.
120 H7 **Evansville** Ontario Canada
116 M3 **Evansville** Alaska U.S.A.
110 G3 **Evansville** Illinois U.S.A.
110 J3 **Evansville** Indiana U.S.A.
99 L3 **Evansville** Minnesota U.S.A.
99 R7 **Evansville** Wisconsin U.S.A.
101 T7 **Evansville** Wyoming U.S.A.
109 J4 **Evant** Texas U.S.A.
94 B3 **Evart** Michigan U.S.A.
94 D10 **Evarts** Kentucky U.S.A.
18 G6 **Evaux** France
47 H5 **Evciler** Turkey
99 O2 **Eveleth** Minnesota U.S.A.
138 C3 **Evelyn Ck** South Australia Australia
140 C2 **Evelyn, Mt** N Terr Australia
26 J3 **Evenes** Norway
110 E5 **Evening Shade** Arkansas U.S.A.
56 D1 **Evenkiyskiy Avtonomnyy Okrug** *dist* Russian Federation
80 E1 **Even Menahem** Israel
51 P2 **Evensk** Russian Federation
80 C4 **Even Yehuda** Israel
141 G2 **Eve Pk** Queensland Australia
22 G3 **Evêque** Belgium
120 B4 **Everard** Ontario Canada
138 D4 **Everard,L** South Australia Australia
140 C6 **Everard, Mt** N Terr Australia
138 B2 **Everard,Mt** South Australia Australia
138 C2 **Everard Ra** South Australia Australia
28 H6 **Everdrup** Denmark
22 G2 **Evere** Belgium
107 P2 **Everest** Kansas U.S.A.
75 M5 **Everest, Mt** China/Nepal
94 J6 **Everett** Pennsylvania U.S.A.
100 C2 **Everett** Washington U.S.A.
112 F6 **Everett City** Georgia U.S.A.
95 O4 **Everett, Mt** Massachusetts U.S.A.
22 F1 **Evergem** Belgium
113 F12 **Everglades** Florida U.S.A.
113 G12 **Everglades Nat. Park** Florida U.S.A.
111 K10 **Evergreen** Alabama U.S.A.
106 E2 **Evergreen** Colorado U.S.A.
112 J3 **Evergreen** North Carolina U.S.A.
109 M10 **Everman** Texas U.S.A.
27 G16 **Everöd** Sweden
32 H10 **Eversberg** Germany
32 K6 **Eversen** Germany
141 G6 **Evesham** Queensland Australia
118 H6 **Evesham** Saskatchewan Canada
9 E3 **Evesham** England
40 D5 **Evian-les-Bains** France
29 K8 **Evijärvi** Finland
85 G8 **Evinayong** Mbini Equat Guinea
46 E6 **Évinos** *R* Greece
27 C13 **Evje** Norway
80 D2 **Evlayim** Israel
40 G5 **Evolène** Switzerland
16 B6 **Évora** Portugal
20 G5 **Evran** France
21 K3 **Evrecy** France
47 H4 **Evreşe** Turkey
21 N3 **Évreux** France
21 K5 **Évron** France
80 D2 **Evron** Israel
46 E3 **Évropos** Greece
47 H3 **Évros** *R* Greece
46 E7 **Evrótas** *R* Greece
21 P4 **Evry** France
79 C3 **Evrykhou** Cyprus
46 G6 **Évvoia** *isld* Greece
102 R12 **Ewa** Hawaiian Is
102 R12 **Ewa Bch** Hawaiian Is
100 H2 **Ewan** Washington U.S.A.
116 P5 **Ewan L** Alaska U.S.A.
127 K2 **Ewarton** Jamaica
86 B6 **Ewc** Congo
9 F5 **Ewell** England
36 E2 **Ewersbach** Germany
94 D8 **Ewing** Kentucky U.S.A.
99 P9 **Ewing** Missouri U.S.A.
98 H7 **Ewing** Nebraska U.S.A.
146 D5 **Ewing I** Antarctica
140 D6 **Ewing, Mt** N Terr Australia
66 D3 **Ewirgol** China
128 E6 **Exaltación** Bolivia
118 G7 **Excel** Alberta Canada
110 B2 **Excelsior** Missouri U.S.A.

102 E3 **Excelsior Mt** California U.S.A.
102 F3 **Excelsior Mts** Nevada U.S.A.
117 F6 **Excursion** Alaska U.S.A.
37 K3 **Exdorf** Germany
146 B8 **Executive Committee Ra** Antarctica
99 P4 **Exeland** Wisconsin U.S.A.
8 C5 **Exe,R** England
120 J9 **Exeter** Ontario Canada
8 C6 **Exeter** England
102 E5 **Exeter** California U.S.A.
110 C5 **Exeter** Missouri U.S.A.
98 J9 **Exeter** Nebraska U.S.A.
95 R4 **Exeter** New Hampshire U.S.A.
117 S3 **Exeter L** Northwest Territories Canada
8 C5 **Exford** England
99 M8 **Exira** Iowa U.S.A.
99 O9 **Exline** Iowa U.S.A.
25 G3 **Exloo** Netherlands
21 L4 **Exmes** France
8 C6 **Exminster** England
8 C5 **Exmoor Forest** England
95 M9 **Exmore** Virginia U.S.A.
142 A5 **Exmouth** W Australia Australia
8 C6 **Exmouth** England
142 A5 **Exmouth Gulf** W Australia Australia
117 Q3 **Exmouth L** Northwest Territories Canada
81 H7 **Exmouth Plateau** Indian Oc
46 E8 **Éxo Nímfi** Greece
141 J6 **Expedition Ra** Queensland Australia
123 R5 **Exploits R** Newfoundland Canada
118 B7 **Exshaw** Alberta Canada
32 K8 **Extertal** Germany
8 C5 **Exton** England
16 C5 **Extremadura** *reg* Spain
128 D6 **Extremo** Brazil
126 F2 **Exuma Sd** Bahamas
116 P6 **Eyak** Alaska U.S.A.
80 C5 **Eyal** Israel
88 E3 **Eyasi,L** Tanzania
27 C13 **Eydehamn** Norway
9 F2 **Eye** England
9 H3 **Eye** England
118 L8 **Eyebrow** Saskatchewan Canada
13 F2 **Eyemouth** Scotland
18 G7 **Eygurande** France
28 S10 **Eyjafjalla** *ice cap* Iceland
28 S8 **Eyjafjördhur** *inlet* Iceland
86 A2 **Eyl** Somalia
18 F8 **Eymet** France
18 G7 **Eymoutiers** France
9 E4 **Eynsham** England
99 O6 **Eyota** Minnesota U.S.A.
28 S10 **Eyrarbakki** Iceland
140 E6 **Eyre** *R* Queensland Australia
143 F9 **Eyre** W Australia Australia
118 H7 **Eyre** Saskatchewan Canada
14 C3 **Eyrecourt** Ireland
138 E4 **Eyre,Mt** South Australia Australia
144 B6 **Eyre Mts** New Zealand
138 D3 **Eyre North, L** South Australia Australia
138 D5 **Eyre Pen** South Australia Australia
138 D3 **Eyre South, L** South Australia Australia
119 R1 **Eyrie L** Manitoba Canada
37 L5 **Eysölden** Germany
32 K7 **Eystrup** Germany
6 F1 **Eysturoy** *isld* Faeroes
19 N14 **Eyzin** France
47 H5 **Ezine** Turkey
77 A3 **Ezna** Iran

F

134 C12 **Faaone** Tahiti Pacific Oc
45 J2 **Fabbrico** Italy
108 A4 **Fabens** Texas U.S.A.
27 D10 **Fåberg** Norway
117 P4 **Faber L** Northwest Territories Canada
121 L5 **Fabre** Quebec Canada
42 E5 **Fabriano** Italy
130 E9 **Fábrica de Papel** Brazil
48 L6 **Făcăeni** Romania
128 D3 **Facatativa** Colombia
141 K6 **Facing I** Queensland Australia
18 E8 **Facture** France
133 C7 **Facundo** Argentina
86 D2 **Fada** Chad
85 E6 **Fada N'Gourma** Burkina
51 K1 **Faddeya,Zaliv** *G* Russian Federation
51 O1 **Fadeyevskiy, Ostrov** *isld* Russian Federation
73 L7 **Fadippolu Atoll** Maldives
42 D4 **Faenza** Italy
115 O5 **Færingehavn** Greenland
6 E1 **Faeroe Bank** N Atlantic Oc
6 F1 **Faeroes** *islds* N Atlantic Oc
86 C4 **Fafa** *R* Cent Afr Republic
85 E5 **Fafa** Mali
71 C3 **Fafanlap** W Irian
16 B3 **Fafe** Portugal
86 H4 **Fafen** *watercourse* Ethiopia
48 J5 **Făgăraş** Romania
48 J5 **Făgăraşului, Muntii** *mts* Romania
26 G10 **Fågelsjö** Sweden
27 H14 **Fagerhult** Sweden
27 H12 **Fagersta** Sweden
48 G5 **Făget** Romania
48 H3 **Făgetului, Muntii** *mts* Romania
45 L3 **Faggiola, M** *mt* Italy
85 F6 **Faggo** Nigeria
71 C3 **Fagita** W Irian
45 P5 **Fagnano Alto** Italy
133 D8 **Fagnano, L** Chile/Arg
22 G3 **Fagnes** Belgium
85 D5 **Faguibine,L** Mali
77 F5 **Fahraj** Iran
41 O5 **Fai Della Paganella** Italy
41 J5 **Faido** Switzerland
Faifo *see* **Hoi An**
121 O4 **Faillon,L** Quebec Canada
106 D9 **Fairacres** New Mexico U.S.A.
141 J6 **Fairbairn Res** Queensland Australia
103 O10 **Fairbank** Arizona U.S.A.
99 O7 **Fairbank** Iowa U.S.A.
116 O4 **Fairbanks** Alaska U.S.A.
95 R2 **Fairbanks** Maine U.S.A.
109 M6 **Fairbanks** Texas U.S.A.
112 H3 **Fair Bluff** North Carolina U.S.A.
94 C7 **Fairborn** Ohio U.S.A.
111 M8 **Fairburn** Georgia U.S.A.
98 C6 **Fairburn** South Dakota U.S.A.
99 S9 **Fairbury** Illinois U.S.A.
98 J9 **Fairbury** Nebraska U.S.A.
94 H7 **Fairchance** Pennsylvania U.S.A.
99 Q5 **Fairchild** Wisconsin U.S.A.
98 H1 **Fairdale** North Dakota U.S.A.
144 C4 **Fairdown** New Zealand
144 B7 **Fairfax** New Zealand
111 L9 **Fairfax** Alabama U.S.A.
99 M5 **Fairfax** Minnesota U.S.A.
99 L9 **Fairfax** Missouri U.S.A.
107 O5 **Fairfax** Oklahoma U.S.A.
112 F5 **Fairfax** South Carolina U.S.A.
98 H6 **Fairfax** South Dakota U.S.A.
95 O2 **Fairfax** Vermont U.S.A.
100 C2 **Fairfax** Washington U.S.A.
127 P6 **Fairfield** Barbados
111 K8 **Fairfield** Alabama U.S.A.
102 B3 **Fairfield** California U.S.A.
95 O5 **Fairfield** Connecticut U.S.A.

101 L6 **Fairfield** Idaho U.S.A.
110 H3 **Fairfield** Illinois U.S.A.
99 P8 **Fairfield** Iowa U.S.A.
95 S2 **Fairfield** Maine U.S.A.
101 N2 **Fairfield** Montana U.S.A.
98 H9 **Fairfield** Nebraska U.S.A.
98 C2 **Fairfield** North Dakota U.S.A.
95 K7 **Fairfield** Pennsylvania U.S.A.
109 L4 **Fairfield** Texas U.S.A.
95 P2 **Fairfield** Vermont U.S.A.
100 H2 **Fairfield** Washington U.S.A.
119 T7 **Fairford** Manitoba Canada
9 E4 **Fairford** England
110 C4 **Fair Grove** Missouri U.S.A.
95 R5 **Fairhaven** Massachusetts U.S.A.
95 L3 **Fair Haven** New York U.S.A.
95 O3 **Fair Haven** Vermont U.S.A.
100 B1 **Fairholm** Washington U.S.A.
118 J5 **Fairholme** Saskatchewan Canada
113 B12 **Fairhope** Alabama U.S.A.
15 A2 **Fair I** Scotland
71 C5 **Fairie Queen** Philippines
107 Q5 **Fairland** Oklahoma U.S.A.
144 C6 **Fairlie** New Zealand
12 D2 **Fairlie** Scotland
141 G3 **Fairlight** Queensland Australia
141 G5 **Fairlight** Queensland Australia
119 Q9 **Fairlight** Saskatchewan Canada
144 B6 **Fairlight** New Zealand
99 M6 **Fairmont** Minnesota U.S.A.
98 J9 **Fairmont** Nebraska U.S.A.
112 H3 **Fairmont** North Carolina U.S.A.
107 N5 **Fairmont** Oklahoma U.S.A.
94 G7 **Fairmont** West Virginia U.S.A.
117 Q10 **Fairmont Hot Springs** British Columbia Canada
118 H7 **Fairmount** Saskatchewan Canada
111 M7 **Fair Mount** Georgia U.S.A.
94 B6 **Fairmount** Indiana U.S.A.
95 M8 **Fairmount** Maryland U.S.A.
98 K3 **Fairmount** North Dakota U.S.A.
115 M5 **Fair Ness** *C* Northwest Territories Canada
13 F2 **Fairnilee** Scotland
110 E6 **Fairoaks** Arkansas U.S.A.
102 C3 **Fair Oaks** California U.S.A.
99 T8 **Fair Oaks** Indiana U.S.A.
106 E2 **Fairplay** Colorado U.S.A.
110 C4 **Fair Play** Missouri U.S.A.
107 L2 **Fairport** Kansas U.S.A.
99 U4 **Fairport** Michigan U.S.A.
95 K3 **Fairport** New York U.S.A.
95 L9 **Fair Port** Virginia U.S.A.
94 F5 **Fairport Harbor** Ohio U.S.A.
141 G3 **Fairview** Queensland Australia
117 O7 **Fairview** Alberta Canada
99 Q9 **Fairview** Illinois U.S.A.
107 P2 **Fairview** Kansas U.S.A.
94 C2 **Fairview** Michigan U.S.A.
98 B2 **Fairview** Montana U.S.A.
107 M5 **Fairview** Oklahoma U.S.A.
94 G4 **Fairview** Pennsylvania U.S.A.
98 K6 **Fairview** South Dakota U.S.A.
103 N2 **Fairview** Utah U.S.A.
94 G7 **Fairview** West Virginia U.S.A.
117 D6 **Fairweather,C** Alaska U.S.A.
117 E6 **Fairweather,Mt** Br Col/Alaska Canada/U.S.A.
119 N5 **Fairy Glen** Saskatchewan Canada
74 E3 **Faisalabad** India
112 J2 **Faison** North Carolina U.S.A.
22 H4 **Faissault** France
98 D4 **Faith** South Dakota U.S.A.
79 A9 **Faiyûm,El** Egypt
66 C6 **Faizabad** India
127 M5 **Fajardo** Puerto Rico
135 N10 **Fakarava** *atoll* Tuamotu Arch Pacific Oc
9 G2 **Fakenham** England
136 G2 **Fakfak** W Irian
28 J6 **Fakse** Denmark
28 J6 **Fakse Ladeplads** Denmark
65 F3 **Faku** China
21 K4 **Falaise** France
117 P5 **Falaise L** Northwest Territories Canada
46 F3 **Falakrón** *mt* Greece
68 A1 **Falam** Burma
80 D5 **Falama** Jordan
48 L4 **Fălciu** Romania
106 F3 **Falcon** Colorado U.S.A.
128 D1 **Falcón** *state* Venezuela
45 O4 **Falconara Marittima** Italy
120 K6 **Falconbridge** Ontario Canada
17 G9 **Falcon,C** Algeria
43 B8 **Falcone,C.del** Sardinia
94 H4 **Falconer** New York U.S.A.
109 H9 **Falcon L** Texas/Mexico U.S.A./Mexico
28 E6 **Faldsled** Denmark
85 B6 **Falémé** *R* Senegal/Mali
52 H5 **Falenki** Russian Federation
27 H13 **Falerum** Sweden
48 L3 **Faleshty** Moldova
109 J8 **Falfurrias** Texas U.S.A.
117 P8 **Falher** Alberta Canada
100 A9 **Falk** California U.S.A.
121 L7 **Falkenberg** Ontario Canada
37 N4 **Falkenberg** Germany
33 T7 **Falkenberg** Brandenburg Germany
33 S9 **Falkenberg** Brandenburg Germany
37 O7 **Falkenberg** Niederbayern Germany
27 F15 **Falkenberg** Sweden
33 Q6 **Falkenhagen** Germany
33 S7 **Falkensee** Germany
37 N3 **Falkenstein** Germany
37 O5 **Falkenstein** Germany
12 E2 **Falkirk** Scotland
117 O10 **Falkland** British Columbia Canada
13 E1 **Falkland** Scotland
131 G8 **Falkland Is** Atlantic Oc
133 E8 **Falkland Sd** Falkland Is
110 H7 **Falkner** Mississippi U.S.A.
46 F8 **Falkonéra** *isld* Greece
27 F13 **Falköping** Sweden
111 K7 **Falkville** Alabama U.S.A.
125 P9 **Fallabón** Guatemala
102 G8 **Fallbrook** California U.S.A.
100 D2 **Fall City** Washington U.S.A.
99 P5 **Fall Creek** Wisconsin U.S.A.
33 N8 **Fallersleben** Germany
26 L6 **Fällfors** Sweden
28 E5 **Falling** Denmark
32 L7 **Fallingbostel** Germany
15 C3 **Fall of Glomach** Scotland
98 A3 **Fallon** Montana U.S.A.
102 F2 **Fallon** Nevada U.S.A.
95 Q5 **Fall River** Massachusetts U.S.A.
100 D8 **Fall River Mills** California U.S.A.
107 O4 **Fall R.Res** Kansas U.S.A.
95 N5 **Fallsburg, S** New York U.S.A.
95 K8 **Falls Church** Virginia U.S.A.
99 L9 **Falls City** Nebraska U.S.A.
100 B5 **Falls City** Oregon U.S.A.
109 J7 **Falls City** Texas U.S.A.
94 J5 **Falls Cr** Pennsylvania U.S.A.
15 E5 **Falls of Clyde** Scotland
15 D3 **Falls of Foyers** Scotland
78 J5 **Fallūjah, Al** Iraq
22 H3 **Falmagne** Belgium
9 F6 **Falmer** England
8 A7 **Falmouth** England
127 J1 **Falmouth** Jamaica
94 C8 **Falmouth** Kentucky U.S.A.
95 R5 **Falmouth** Massachusetts U.S.A.
94 B2 **Falmouth** Michigan U.S.A.

94 K8 **Falmouth** Virginia U.S.A.
127 P4 **Falmouth** Antigua W Indies
95 R3 **Falmouth-Foreside** Maine U.S.A.
8 B7 **Fal,R** England
89 A10 **False B** S Africa
116 F9 **False Pass** Aleutian Is
141 F2 **False Pera Hd** Queensland Australia
94 D1 **False Presque I** Michigan U.S.A.
17 H3 **Falset** Spain
127 J5 **Falso, C** Dominican Rep
124 E6 **Falso,C** Mexico
133 D9 **Falso C. de Hornos** Chile
28 H7 **Falster** *isld* Denmark
29 K6 **Falsterbo** Sweden
13 F3 **Falstone** England
42 D5 **Falterona, M** *mt* Italy
48 K3 **Fălticeni** Romania
27 H11 **Falun** Sweden
79 D3 **Famagusta** Cyprus
86 F3 **Famaka** Sudan
133 D3 **Famatina** Argentina
133 D3 **Famatina, Sa. de** *mts* Argentina
22 J3 **Famenne** Belgium
143 E7 **Fame Ra** W Australia Australia
143 F6 **Family Well** W Australia Australia
71 C3 **Fam, Kepulauan** *isld* W Irian
102 E6 **Famoso** California U.S.A.
71 C2 **Fan** *isld* W Irian
14 D1 **Fanad Hd** Ireland
145 E1 **Fanal I** New Zealand
45 J3 **Fanano** Italy
67 F1 **Fanchang** China
110 H5 **Fancy Farm** Kentucky U.S.A.
87 H12 **Fandriana** Madagascar
47 R14 **Fánes** Rhodes Greece
86 F4 **Fangak** Sudan
58 F5 **Fangcheng** China
67 C6 **Fangcheng** China
67 C1 **Fangdou Shan** *mts* China
28 E6 **Fangel** Denmark
65 B5 **Fanglan** China
65 B6 **Fangshan** China
67 C1 **Fang Xian** China
65 G2 **Fangzheng** China
65 D6 **Fangzi** China
65 F3 **Fanjiatun** China
111 B12 **Fannett** Texas U.S.A.
111 G9 **Fannin** Mississippi U.S.A.
109 K7 **Fannin** Texas U.S.A.
Fanning I *see* **Tabuaeran**
77 F6 **Fannuj** Iran
117 L11 **Fanny Bay** British Columbia Canada
119 U9 **Fannystelle** Manitoba Canada
28 A6 **Fanø** *isld* Denmark
42 E5 **Fano** Italy
65 B5 **Fanshi** China
68 F1 **Fan Si Pan** *mt* Vietnam
65 C7 **Fan Xian** China
20 D5 **Faouët,le** France
20 B5 **Faou,le** France
80 F8 **Faqu** Jordan
79 B8 **Fâqûs** Egypt
80 F4 **Fara** Jordan
146 C4 **Faraday** *U.K. Base* Graham Land Antarctica
141 H6 **Faraday, Mt** Queensland Australia
86 E5 **Faradje** Zaire
87 H12 **Farafangana** Madagascar
45 Q8 **Faraglioni** Italy
77 H3 **Farāh** Afghanistan
77 H3 **Farah Rud** *R* Afghanistan
45 N5 **Fara in Sabina** Italy
102 A4 **Farallon Is** California U.S.A.
85 D6 **Faramana** Burkina
85 B6 **Faranah** Guinea
86 H2 **Farasān, Jazā'ir** *isld* Red Sea
77 G3 **Farāt** *prov* Afghanistan
84 J5 **Farâyid,G.El** *mt* Egypt
28 C4 **Fårbæk** Denmark
110 E2 **Farber** Missouri U.S.A.
26 J6 **Fårberg** Sweden
48 J3 **Farcău** *mt* Romania
85 C3 **Farciya, Al** Western Sahara
16 E7 **Fardes** *R* Spain
28 A4 **Fåre** Denmark
36 B5 **Fareberswiller** France
9 E6 **Fareham** England
28 H6 **Farendløse** Denmark
28 G5 **Fårevejle** Denmark
116 L5 **Farewell** Alaska U.S.A.
145 D4 **Farewell, C** New Zealand
98 K3 **Fargo** North Dakota U.S.A.
107 L5 **Fargo** Oklahoma U.S.A.
29 K4 **Farhult** Sweden
28 C7 **Fårhus** Denmark
80 F5 **Fari'a el Jiftlick** Jordan
121 Q3 **Faribault** Quebec Canada
99 N5 **Faribault** Minnesota U.S.A.
75 N7 **Faridpur** Bangladesh
84 G3 **Farigh** *watercourse* Libya
16 A5 **Farilhões** *isld* Portugal
26 H10 **Färilla** Sweden
85 A6 **Farim** Guinea-Bissau
9 E4 **Faringdon** England
27 K12 **Faringe** Sweden
106 E4 **Farista** Colorado U.S.A.
27 H15 **Färjestaden** Sweden
80 D5 **Farkha** Jordan
118 H1 **Farlane** Ontario Canada
141 J5 **Farleigh** Queensland Australia
121 O6 **Farley** Quebec Canada
99 P7 **Farley** Iowa U.S.A.
106 F5 **Farley** New Mexico U.S.A.
98 J6 **Farmer** South Dakota U.S.A.
99 S9 **Farmer City** Illinois U.S.A.
109 O8 **Farmers Branch** Texas U.S.A.
99 T10 **Farmersburg** Indiana U.S.A.
99 P7 **Farmersburg** Iowa U.S.A.
109 L2 **Farmersville** Texas U.S.A.
111 D9 **Farmerville** Louisiana U.S.A.
95 N6 **Farmingdale** New Jersey U.S.A.
98 D6 **Farmingdale** South Dakota U.S.A.
117 N8 **Farmington** British Columbia Canada
102 D4 **Farmington** California U.S.A.
99 Q9 **Farmington** Illinois U.S.A.
99 P9 **Farmington** Iowa U.S.A.
95 R2 **Farmington** Maine U.S.A.
99 N5 **Farmington** Minnesota U.S.A.
110 F4 **Farmington** Missouri U.S.A.
95 Q3 **Farmington** New Hampshire U.S.A.
106 B5 **Farmington** New Mexico U.S.A.
101 O9 **Farmington** Utah U.S.A.
100 H2 **Farmington** Washington U.S.A.
94 G7 **Farmington** West Virginia U.S.A.
94 B6 **Farmland** Indiana U.S.A.
98 C2 **Farm Unit** North Dakota U.S.A.
112 K2 **Farmville** North Carolina U.S.A.
94 J9 **Farmville** Virginia U.S.A.
98 F9 **Farnam** Nebraska U.S.A.
9 F5 **Farnborough** England
8 D1 **Farndon** England
7 K7 **Farne Deep** North Sea
13 G2 **Farne Is** England
112 C2 **Farner** Tennessee U.S.A.
27 C10 **Farnes** Norway
121 S7 **Farnham** Quebec Canada
9 F5 **Farnham** England
94 H4 **Farnham** New York U.S.A.
117 P10 **Farnham,Mt** British Columbia Canada
9 G5 **Farningham** England
13 F6 **Farnworth** England
129 G4 **Faro** Brazil
117 G4 **Faro** Yukon Territory Canada
28 H7 **Farø** *isld* Denmark
16 B7 **Faro** Portugal
27 K14 **Fårö** *isld* Gotland Sweden
71 G6 **Farol Pt** Philippines
43 G10 **Faro,Pta d** Sicily
86 B4 **Faro R** Cameroon
16 B2 **Faro, Sa del** *mts* Spain
27 K14 **Fårösund** Gotland Sweden
87 J10 **Farquhar Is** Br Indian Oc Terr
83 H6 **Farquhar Is** Seychelles Indian Oc
143 E7 **Farquharson Tableland** W Australia Australia
141 F6 **Farrars Cr** Queensland Australia
26 H5 **Farras** *mt* Sweden
77 C5 **Farrāshband** Iran
94 G5 **Farrell** Pennsylvania U.S.A.
121 P7 **Farrellton** Quebec Canada
8 D5 **Farrington Gurney** England
28 C6 **Farris** Denmark
77 C5 **Fārs** Iran
46 E5 **Fársala** Greece
77 H3 **Fārsī** Afghanistan
28 C3 **Farsø** Denmark
99 O8 **Farson** Iowa U.S.A.
101 Q7 **Farson** Wyoming U.S.A.
27 B13 **Farsund** Norway
130 D10 **Fartura,Serra da** *mts* Brazil
28 D4 **Fårvang** Denmark
115 P6 **Farvel,Kap** *C* Greenland
94 C3 **Farwell** Michigan U.S.A.
98 H8 **Farwell** Nebraska U.S.A.
108 D1 **Farwell** Texas U.S.A.
77 J2 **Fāryab** *prov* Afghanistan
77 C5 **Fasā** Iran
43 H8 **Fasano** Italy
109 J7 **Fashing** Texas U.S.A.
79 A10 **Fashn,El** Egypt
28 B5 **Faster** Denmark
28 C4 **Fasterholt** Denmark
14 B5 **Fastnet Rock** Ireland
74 F7 **Fatehabad** India
74 H5 **Fatehgarh** India
45 O7 **Fate, Mt. delle** Italy
54 G4 **Fatezh** Russian Federation
78 J4 **Fathan,Al** Iraq
121 P3 **Father,L** Quebec Canada
120 J7 **Fathom Five National Marine Park** *nat park* Ontario Canada
123 L6 **Fatima** Madeleine Is, Quebec Canada
16 B5 **Fatima** Portugal
78 F1 **Fatsa** Turkey
135 N9 **Fatu Hiva** *isld* Marquesas Is Pacific Oc
86 C6 **Fatunda** Zaire
110 B2 **Faucett** Missouri U.S.A.
40 D6 **Faucigny** *dist* France
19 K4 **Faucilles, Mts** France
45 J4 **Fauglia** Italy
40 G4 **Faulhorn** *mt* Switzerland
98 G4 **Faulkton** South Dakota U.S.A.
111 J9 **Faunsdale** Alabama U.S.A.
22 C2 **Fauquembergues** France
117 O11 **Fauquier** British Columbia Canada
48 L5 **Făurei** Romania
89 D7 **Fauresmith** S Africa
26 H4 **Fauske** Norway
118 B3 **Faust** Alberta Canada
95 N2 **Faust** New York U.S.A.
101 N9 **Faust** Utah U.S.A.
21 M2 **Fauville** France
43 F11 **Favara** Sicily
19 Q13 **Faverges** France
21 O4 **Faverolles** Eure France
9 G5 **Faversham** England
43 E11 **Favignana, I** Sicily
28 C4 **Favrholt** Denmark
77 A5 **Faw, Al** Iraq
118 C4 **Fawcett** Alberta Canada
118 D3 **Fawcett L** Alberta Canada
9 E6 **Fawley** England
115 L7 **Fawn** *R* Ontario Canada
28 R9 **Faxa-flói** *B* Iceland
26 J8 **Faxälven** *R* Sweden
27 F10 **Faxfj** *mt* Norway
107 M6 **Fay** Oklahoma U.S.A.
86 C2 **Faya-Largeau** Chad
54 F2 **Fayansovyy** Russian Federation
85 B4 **Faydat as Sadra** Western Sahara
20 G7 **Fay-de-Bretagne** France
21 J7 **Faye-d'Anjou** France
119 Q3 **Faye Lake** Manitoba Canada
21 L8 **Faye-la-Vineuse** France
111 J8 **Fayette** Alabama U.S.A.
99 P7 **Fayette** Iowa U.S.A.
99 U4 **Fayette** Michigan U.S.A.
111 E10 **Fayette** Mississippi U.S.A.
110 D2 **Fayette** Missouri U.S.A.
94 C5 **Fayette** Ohio U.S.A.
103 N2 **Fayette** Utah U.S.A.
110 B5 **Fayetteville** Arkansas U.S.A.
111 M8 **Fayetteville** Georgia U.S.A.
112 J2 **Fayetteville** North Carolina U.S.A.
110 N2 **Fayetteville** Ohio U.S.A.
110 K6 **Fayetteville** Tennessee U.S.A.
109 L6 **Fayetteville** Texas U.S.A.
94 F8 **Fayetteville** West Virginia U.S.A.
22 F3 **Fay le Franc** Belgium
109 J9 **Faysville** Texas U.S.A.
80 G1 **Fazārah** Syria
74 F3 **Fazilka** India
85 B4 **Fdérik** Mauritania
14 B4 **Feale** *R* Ireland
102 C3 **Feather** *R* California U.S.A.
102 C2 **Feather Falls** California U.S.A.
145 E4 **Featherston** New Zealand
139 H6 **Feathertop,Mt** Victoria Australia
101 K6 **Featherville** Idaho U.S.A.
144 A6 **Febrero Pt** New Zealand
21 L2 **Fécamp** France
40 F1 **Fecht** *R* France
133 F4 **Federación** Argentina
98 A8 **Federal** Wyoming U.S.A.
99 M2 **Federal Dam** Minnesota U.S.A.
95 M8 **Federalsburg** Maryland U.S.A.
27 A11 **Fedje** *isld* Norway
98 J5 **Fedora** South Dakota U.S.A.
14 B3 **Feeagh,L** Ireland
36 D7 **Fegersheim** France
28 B3 **Feggesund** *chan* Denmark
20 F6 **Fégréac** France
48 H2 **Fehérhyarmat** Hungary
30 F1 **Fehmarn** *isld* Germany
33 R7 **Fehrbellin** Germany
38 O8 **Fehring** Austria
130 H8 **Feia, Lagoa** *L* Brazil
65 C6 **Feicheng** China
67 F1 **Feidong** China
65 C7 **Fei Huang** *R* China
128 D5 **Feijó** Brazil
67 D5 **Feilai Xia** *R* China
145 E4 **Feilding** New Zealand
Feira *see* **Luangwa** Zambia
129 L6 **Feira de Santana** Brazil
38 J8 **Feistritz** Austria
38 K8 **Feistritz-im-Ros** Austria
67 F1 **Feixi** China
65 D7 **Fei Xian** China
65 C6 **Feixiang** China
129 K8 **Feja, L** Brazil
48 E3 **Fejér** *co* Hungary
28 G7 **Fejø** *isld* Denmark
28 F4 **Fejrup** Denmark
48 D5 **Fekete Viz** *R* Hungary
17 K5 **Felanitx** Majorca
9 F5 **Felbridge** England
99 T3 **Felch** Michigan U.S.A.
36 G2 **Feldatal** Germany
38 N8 **Feldbach** Austria
28 F4 **Feldballe** Denmark
33 S6 **Feldberg** Germany
40 H2 **Feldberg** *mt* Germany
28 C3 **Feldingbjerg** Denmark
41 L3 **Feldkirch** Austria
131 F3 **Feliciano** *R* Argentina
83 J12 **Felicité I** Seychelles
94 C8 **Felicity** Ohio U.S.A.
73 L8 **Felidu Atoll** Maldives
130 G6 **Felixlândia** Brazil
106 F8 **Felix,R** New Mexico U.S.A.
108 C3 **Felix, Rio** New Mexico U.S.A.
9 H4 **Felixstowe** England
108 B5 **Félix U. Gómez** Mexico
36 B4 **Fell** Germany
36 G6 **Fellbach** Germany
18 G7 **Felletin** France
13 G4 **Felling** England
127 M2 **Fellowship** Jamaica
113 G10 **Fellsmere** Florida U.S.A.
45 K2 **Felonica** Italy
9 F6 **Felpham** England
36 G1 **Felsberg** Germany
28 C7 **Felsted** Denmark
108 B7 **Felt** Oklahoma U.S.A.
13 G3 **Felton** England
102 B4 **Felton** California U.S.A.
111 L8 **Felton** Georgia U.S.A.
98 K2 **Felton** Minnesota U.S.A.
42 D2 **Feltre** Italy
28 G7 **Femer Bælt** *str* Denmark/Germany
28 F4 **Femmøller** Denmark
28 H7 **Femø** *isld* Denmark
28 G7 **Femø Sund** *chan* Denmark
26 E9 **Femund** Norway
26 F9 **Femundsmarka Nat. Park** Norway
87 G13 **Fenambosy, Fenambosy** *pt* Madagascar
106 B7 **Fence Lake** New Mexico U.S.A.
65 B7 **Fencheng** China
121 M8 **Fenelon Falls** Ontario Canada
79 F2 **Fener Burun** *C* Turkey
36 B6 **Fénétrange** France
21 J6 **Feneu** France
59 H3 **Fengcheng** China
67 E2 **Fengcheng** China
67 D5 **Fengchuan** China
67 B2 **Fengdu** China
58 F4 **Fengfeng** China
67 B3 **Fenggang** China
67 G2 **Fenghua** China
67 C3 **Fenghuang** China
67 C1 **Fengjie** *R* China
67 D5 **Fengkai** China
65 F2 **Fengle** China
67 D1 **Fengle** China
67 E5 **Fengliang** China
65 A7 **Fenglingdu** China
65 D5 **Fengnan** China
65 C4 **Fengning** China
67 G2 **Fengqiao** China
65 C7 **Fengqiu** China
65 D5 **Fengrun** China
65 D4 **Fengshan** China
67 B4 **Fengshan** China
58 G4 **Fengtai** China
67 F4 **Fengting** China
67 B5 **Fengwu** China
65 C7 **Feng Xian** China
67 G1 **Fengxian** China
58 E5 **Fengxiang** China
67 E2 **Fengxin** China
Fengyi *see* **Zheng'an**
Fengyizhen *see* **Maowen**
67 G4 **Feng-Yuan** Taiwan
65 B4 **Fengzhen** China
65 B6 **Fen He** *R* China
116 H2 **Feniak L** Alaska U.S.A.
21 K8 **Fenioux** France
14 B4 **Fenit** Ireland
100 J4 **Fenn** Idaho U.S.A.
99 Q7 **Fennimore** Wisconsin U.S.A.
94 A4 **Fennville** Michigan U.S.A.
9 F3 **Fenny Stratford** England
87 H11 **Fenoarivo Atsinanana** Madagascar
28 H6 **Fensmark** Denmark
9 F3 **Fenstanton** England
119 M6 **Fenton** Saskatchewan Canada
109 P5 **Fenton** Louisiana U.S.A.
94 D4 **Fenton** Michigan U.S.A.
95 L10 **Fentress** Virginia U.S.A.
135 L10 **Fenua Ura** *isld* Society Is Pacific Oc
121 L9 **Fenwick** Ontario Canada
13 G2 **Fenwick** England
12 D2 **Fenwick** Strathclyde Scotland
94 G8 **Fenwick** West Virginia U.S.A.
119 O7 **Fenwood** Saskatchewan Canada
99 Q5 **Fenwood** Wisconsin U.S.A.
65 B6 **Fenxi** China
65 B6 **Fenyang** China
67 E3 **Fenyi** China
22 H3 **Fépin** France
26 E9 **Feragen** *L* Norway
100 J3 **Ferdinand** Idaho U.S.A.
110 K3 **Ferdinand** Indiana U.S.A.
33 T5 **Ferdinandshof** Germany
18 H4 **Fère-Champenoise** France
77 A5 **Fereidoon** *oil well* Persian Gulf
20 F7 **Férel** France
22 E4 **Fère,La** France
26 E8 **Feren** *L* Norway
45 O6 **Ferentino** Italy
57 F4 **Fergana** Uzbekistan
57 K6 **Fergana Basin** Tajikistan/Uzbekistan
57 G4 **Ferganskiy Khr** *mts* Kirghizia
101 Q2 **Fergus** Montana U.S.A.
98 K3 **Fergus Falls** Minnesota U.S.A.
140 B2 **Fergusson** *R* N Terr Australia
118 E6 **Ferintosh** Alberta Canada
85 C7 **Ferkessédougou** Ivory Coast
120 B2 **Ferland** Ontario Canada
14 D2 **Fermanagh** *co* N Ireland
20 H2 **Fermanville** France
121 P6 **Ferme Neuve** Quebec Canada
33 S9 **Fermerswalde** Germany
45 N4 **Fermignano** Italy
42 F5 **Fermo** Italy
16 C3 **Fermoselle** Spain
14 C4 **Fermoy** Ireland
128 A8 **Fernandina** *isld* Galapagos Is
113 F7 **Fernandina Beach** Florida U.S.A.
90 G9 **Fernando de Noronha** *isld* Atlantic Oc
130 E7 **Fernandópolis** Brazil
Fernando Póo *isld see* **Bioko**
16 D7 **Fernán Núñez** Spain
130 G5 **Fernão Dias** Brazil
100 C1 **Ferndale** Washington U.S.A.
98 H4 **Ferney** South Dakota U.S.A.
9 F5 **Fernhurst** England
118 B9 **Fernie** British Columbia Canada
141 H8 **Fernlee** Queensland Australia
102 E2 **Fernley** Nevada U.S.A.
41 N3 **Fern Pass** Austria
100 B5 **Fern Ridge Res** Oregon U.S.A.
14 E4 **Ferns** Ireland
144 D5 **Fernside** New Zealand
36 F2 **Fernwald** Germany
100 J2 **Fernwood** Idaho U.S.A.
111 F10 **Fernwood** Mississippi U.S.A.
123 P2 **Ferolle Pt** Newfoundland Canada
47 H4 **Férrai** Greece
42 D4 **Ferrara** Italy
17 G9 **Ferrat,C** Algeria
44 B4 **Ferrat,Cape** France
43 C9 **Ferrato,C** Sardinia
16 B6 **Ferreira do Alentejo** Portugal
129 H3 **Ferreira Gomes** Brazil
130 D7 **Ferreiros** Brazil
20 H5 **Ferré, le** France
128 C5 **Ferreñafe** Peru
18 E8 **Ferret,C** France
40 F6 **Ferret,Col** *pass* Switz/Italy
19 K5 **Ferreue** France
111 E10 **Ferriday** Louisiana U.S.A.
118 C6 **Ferrier** Alberta Canada
21 K4 **Ferrière-aux-Étangs,la** France
21 K8 **Ferriere,la** Deux Sèvres France
20 H8 **Ferrière,la** Vendée France
21 M7 **Ferrière-Larçon** France
18 G4 **Ferrières** France
21 O2 **Ferrières-en-Bray** France
21 M4 **Ferrière-sur-Risle,la** France
28 A3 **Ferring** Denmark
28 A3 **Ferring Sø** Denmark
99 P9 **Ferris** Illinois U.S.A.
95 O2 **Ferrisburg** Vermont U.S.A.
101 S7 **Ferris Mts** Wyoming U.S.A.
28 F6 **Ferritslev** Denmark
43 C7 **Ferro,C** Sardinia
130 G6 **Ferros** Brazil
123 N2 **Ferru,L** Quebec Canada
43 B8 **Ferru, M** *mt* Sardinia
94 G10 **Ferrum** Virginia U.S.A.
116 N5 **Ferry** Alaska U.S.A.
99 U6 **Ferry** Michigan U.S.A.
13 G6 **Ferrybridge** England
123 U6 **Ferryland** Newfoundland Canada
107 P5 **Ferry Res** Oklahoma U.S.A.
99 U6 **Ferrysburg** Michigan U.S.A.
8 B4 **Ferryside** Wales
99 P6 **Ferryville** Wisconsin U.S.A.
55 C4 **Fershampenuaz** Russian Federation
28 H5 **Ferslev** Denmark
21 P5 **Ferté-Alais,la** France
21 M5 **Ferté-Bernard,la** France
21 M4 **Ferté-Fresnel, la** France
18 H4 **Ferté Gaucher,La** France
21 O7 **Ferté-Imbault,la** France
22 F4 **Ferté, la** France
21 K4 **Ferté-Macé,la** France
21 O6 **Ferté-St.Aubin,la** France
21 O6 **Ferté-St. Cyr,la** France
18 H4 **Ferté sur Jouarre, la** France
21 M4 **Ferté-Vidame,la** France
98 K2 **Fertile** Minnesota U.S.A.
48 D3 **Fertöszentmiklos** Hungary
Fertö Tór *see* **Neusiedler See**
21 L3 **Fervaques** France
41 M3 **Ferwall Gruppe** *mt* Austria
25 E2 **Ferwerd** Netherlands
85 C2 **Fès** Morocco
86 C7 **Feshi** Zaire
98 G2 **Fessenden** North Dakota U.S.A.
19 P15 **Festre, Col du** *pass* France
22 D2 **Festubert** France
110 F3 **Festus** Missouri U.S.A.
48 L6 **Fetești** Romania
14 D4 **Fethard** Ireland
47 K8 **Fethiye** Turkey
47 K8 **Fethiye Körfezi** *B* Turkey
43 A12 **Fetzara, L** Algeria
37 L5 **Feucht** Germany
41 N3 **Feuchten** Austria
37 J5 **Feuchtwangen** Germany
118 K7 **Feudal** Saskatchewan Canada
21 O3 **Feuillie, la** France
123 M3 **Feu, L. du** Quebec Canada
21 O2 **Feuquières** France
21 O1 **Feuquières-en-Vimeu** France
18 H7 **Feurs** France
77 L1 **Feyzābād** Afghanistan
77 F2 **Feyzābād** Iran
84 E4 **Fezzan** *reg* Libya
8 C2 **Ffestiniog** Wales
8 C4 **Fforest Fawr** *mts* Wales
133 D3 **Fiambalá** Argentina
45 O5 **Fiamignano** Italy
87 H11 **Fianarantsoa** Madagascar
86 C4 **Fianga** Chad
40 F7 **Fiano** Italy
48 G5 **Fibiș** Romania
45 K2 **Ficarolo** Italy
86 G4 **Fichē** Ethiopia
123 R2 **Fichot I** Newfoundland Canada
37 M3 **Fichtelberg** Germany
37 O3 **Fichtelberg** *mt* Germany
37 M3 **Fichtelfebirge** *mts* Germany
37 J5 **Fichtenau** Germany
89 E7 **Ficksburg** S Africa
44 H2 **Fidenza** Italy
119 V1 **Fidler L** Manitoba Canada
135 O4 **Fieberling Table Mt** Pacific Oc
106 C7 **Field** New Mexico U.S.A.
94 G10 **Fieldale** Virginia U.S.A.
140 B1 **Field I** N Terr Australia
118 K6 **Fielding** Saskatchewan Canada
100 G7 **Fields** Oregon U.S.A.
100 A9 **Fields Landing** California U.S.A.
139 H8 **Field West Mt** Tasmania Australia
48 J5 **Fieni** Romania
22 B2 **Fiennes** France
46 D4 **Fier** Albania
19 P13 **Fier** *R* France
42 D2 **Fiera di Primiero** Italy
106 B9 **Fierro** New Mexico U.S.A.
13 E1 **Fife** *reg* Scotland
109 H4 **Fife** Texas U.S.A.
119 M9 **Fife L** Saskatchewan Canada
13 F1 **Fife Ness** Scotland
139 J5 **Fifield** New South Wales Australia
99 Q4 **Fifield** Wisconsin U.S.A.
101 R5 **Fifteen Mile Cr** Wyoming U.S.A.
17 G9 **Figalo,C** Algeria
43 C8 **Figari,C** Sardinia
18 G8 **Figeac** France
27 J14 **Figeholm** Sweden
45 K4 **Figline Valdarno** Italy
127 P4 **Fig Tree** Nevis W Indies
16 B4 **Figuera da Foz** Portugal
16 B5 **Figuera dos Vinhos** Portugal
17 J2 **Figueras** Spain
Figueres *see* **Figueras**
85 D2 **Figuig** Morocco
137 Q5 **Fiji** *islds* Pacific Oc
17 F7 **Filabres, Sierra de los** *mts* Spain
129 J5 **Filadélfia** Brazil
128 F8 **Filadelfia** Paraguay
48 F2 **Filakovo** Slovakia
146 E7 **Filchner Ice Shelf** Antarctica
36 G6 **Filderstadt** Germany
27 C10 **Filefj** *mt* Norway
119 R4 **File L** Manitoba Canada
101 L7 **Filer** Idaho U.S.A.
45 O6 **Filettino** Italy
13 H5 **Filey** England
46 D5 **Filiátes** Greece
46 E7 **Filiatrá** Greece
43 F10 **Filicudi, I** Italy
85 E6 **Filingué** Niger
31 O1 **Filipów** Poland
27 G12 **Filipstad** Sweden
41 L4 **Filisur** Switzerland
48 H6 **Fillași** Romania
22 C3 **Fillièvres** France
119 O9 **Fillmore** Saskatchewan Canada
102 F7 **Fillmore** California U.S.A.
94 J4 **Fillmore** New York U.S.A.
98 G1 **Fillmore** North Dakota U.S.A.
103 M3 **Fillmore** Utah U.S.A.
36 H6 **Fils** *R* Germany
28 C5 **Filskov** Denmark
28 A5 **Filsø** Denmark
8 D4 **Filton** England
86 H4 **Filtu** Ethiopia
146 H6 **Fimbulheimen** *ra* Antarctica
146 H6 **Fimbulisen** *ice shelf* Antarctica
42 D4 **Finale Emilia** Italy
44 D3 **Finale Ligure** Italy
17 F7 **Fiñana** Spain
94 H9 **Fincastle** Virginia U.S.A.
121 P7 **Finch** Ontario Canada
9 F4 **Finchley** England
28 C4 **Finderup** Denmark
15 E3 **Findhorn** *R* Scotland
15 E3 **Findhorn** Scotland
78 H1 **Fındıklı** Turkey
79 E2 **Fındıkpınarı** Turkey
119 M8 **Findlater** Saskatchewan Canada
99 S10 **Findlay** Illinois U.S.A.
94 D5 **Findlay** Ohio U.S.A.
117 P10 **Findlay,Mt** British Columbia Canada
9 F6 **Findon** England
9 F3 **Finedon** England
139 J8 **Fingal** Tasmania Australia
98 J3 **Fingal** North Dakota U.S.A.
110 H6 **Finger** Tennessee U.S.A.
115 K7 **Finger L** Ontario Canada
95 L4 **Finger Lakes** New York U.S.A.
14 E3 **Finglas** Ireland
88 C9 **Fingoe** *mt* Mozambique
88 C9 **Fingoe** Mozambique
47 L8 **Finike** Turkey
47 P12 **Finiq** Albania
16 A2 **Finisterre,C** Spain
138 D2 **Finke** *R* N Terr Australia
140 C7 **Finke** N Terr Australia
138 D2 **Finke Flood Flats** South Australia Australia
140 C6 **Finke Gorge** N Terr Australia
138 C4 **Finke,Mt** South Australia Australia
140 D7 **Finke, R** N Terr Australia
29 L8 **Finland** *rep* N Europe
99 P2 **Finland** Minnesota U.S.A.
52 C5 **Finland, Gulf of** Estonia/Finland/Rus Fed
114 G6 **Finlay** *R* British Columbia Canada
99 O3 **Finlayson** Minnesota U.S.A.
98 J2 **Finley** North Dakota U.S.A.
109 M1 **Finley** Oklahoma U.S.A.
119 O2 **Finmark** Ontario Canada
14 D2 **Finn** *R* Ireland
12 D1 **Finnart** Scotland
118 E7 **Finnegan** Alberta Canada
26 H4 **Finneid** Norway
36 D1 **Finnentrop** Germany
26 L7 **Finnforsfallet** Sweden
141 H3 **Finnigan, Mt** Queensland Australia
140 B2 **Finniss** *R* N Terr Australia
138 C5 **Finniss,C** South Australia Australia
26 O1 **Finnmark** *county* Norway
26 N2 **Finnmarksvidda** *reg* Norway
116 J6 **Finn Mt** Alaska U.S.A.
27 F11 **Finnskog** Norway
27 F11 **Finnskoga,S** Sweden
26 K2 **Finnsnes** Norway
26 M6 **Finnträsk** Sweden
33 T7 **Finow** Germany
33 T7 **Finowfurt** Germany
33 T7 **Finow Kanal** Germany
27 H13 **Finspång** Sweden
40 H4 **Finsteraarhorn** *mt* Switzerland
33 T9 **Finsterwalde** Germany
15 E1 **Finstown** Scotland
29 H11 **Finström** Finland
36 E4 **Finthen** Germany
14 D2 **Fintona** N Ireland
12 D1 **Fintry** Scotland
142 C5 **Finucane I** W Australia Australia
141 F5 **Finucane Ra** Queensland Australia
40 F5 **Fionnay** Switzerland
15 C3 **Fionn Loch** *L* Scotland
12 B1 **Fionphort** Scotland
45 J2 **Fiorano Modenese** Italy
144 A6 **Fiordland Nat. Park** New Zealand
44 G2 **Fiorenzuola d'Arda** Italy
45 N4 **Fiorenzuola di Focara** Italy
88 C5 **Fip** Tanzania
78 G2 **Firat** *R* Turkey
102 D5 **Firebaugh** California U.S.A.
116 M6 **Fire I** Alaska U.S.A.
42 D5 **Firenze** Italy
42 D4 **Firenzuola** Italy
98 E4 **Firesteel** South Dakota U.S.A.
48 H3 **Firiza** Romania
133 E4 **Firmat** Argentina
18 H7 **Firminy** France
118 L9 **Fir Mt** Saskatchewan Canada
74 H5 **Firozabad** India
77 H2 **Firozkoh** *reg* Afghanistan
74 F3 **Firozpur** India
112 F2 **First R** North Carolina U.S.A.
116 R2 **Firth** *R* Alaska/Yukon Terr U.S.A./Canada
77 C5 **Firūzābād** Iran
37 K7 **Fischach** Germany
36 C4 **Fischbach** Germany
38 M7 **Fischbacher Alpen** *mts* Austria
33 Q7 **Fischbeck** Germany
36 E2 **Fischelbach** Germany
41 M3 **Fischen** Germany
109 J6 **Fischer** Texas U.S.A.
32 K6 **Fischerhude** Germany
33 S6 **Fischerwall** Germany
89 A5 **Fish** *watercourse* Namibia
9 E6 **Fishbourne** England
102 E4 **Fish Camp** California U.S.A.
116 L1 **Fish Cr** Alaska U.S.A.
101 M6 **Fish Cr.Res** Idaho U.S.A.
113 F10 **Fisheating Cr** Florida U.S.A.
121 N4 **Fisher** Quebec Canada
111 C10 **Fisher** Louisiana U.S.A.
98 K2 **Fisher** Minnesota U.S.A.
119 U7 **Fisher Branch** Manitoba Canada
146 H10 **Fisher Glacier** Antarctica
143 A9 **Fisherman I** W Australia Australia
95 M9 **Fishermans I** Virginia U.S.A.
115 L5 **Fisher Str** Northwest Territories Canada
116 E9 **Fisher Vol** Aleutian Is
8 B4 **Fishguard** Wales
8 A3 **Fishguard B** England
95 L8 **Fishing Creek** Maryland U.S.A.
117 M4 **Fish L** Northwest Territories Canada
116 M4 **Fish L** Alaska U.S.A.
103 N3 **Fish L** Utah U.S.A.
94 D3 **Fish Pt** Michigan U.S.A.
102 A3 **Fish Rock** California U.S.A.
101 Q4 **Fishtail** Montana U.S.A.
101 M4 **Fishtrap** Montana U.S.A.
94 E9 **Fishtrap L** Kentucky U.S.A.
46 D6 **Fiskárdho** Greece
28 C3 **Fiskbæk** Denmark
95 P4 **Fiskdale** Massachusetts U.S.A.
118 J7 **Fiske** Saskatchewan Canada
146 D6 **Fiske, C** Antarctica
115 O5 **Fiskenæsset** Greenland
28 S9 **Fiskivötn** *lakes* Iceland
22 F5 **Fismes** France
95 Q4 **Fitchburg** Massachusetts U.S.A.
86 C3 **Fitri, L** Chad
28 C5 **Fitting** Denmark
9 F6 **Fittleworth** England
128 D6 **Fitzcarrald** Peru
143 C10 **Fitzgerald** *R* W Australia Australia
117 R6 **Fitzgerald** Alberta Canada
112 D6 **Fitzgerald** Georgia U.S.A.
143 C10 **Fitzgerald River Nat Park** W Australia Australia
109 L1 **Fitzhugh** Oklahoma U.S.A.
117 K10 **Fitzhugh Sd** British Columbia Canada
22 C5 **Fitz James** France
140 B2 **Fitzmaurice** *R* N Terr Australia
121 S5 **Fitzpatrick** Quebec Canada
133 D7 **Fitz Roy** Argentina
141 K6 **Fitzroy** *R* Queensland Australia
133 C7 **Fitz Roy** *mt* Chile/Arg
142 F4 **Fitzroy Crossing** W Australia Australia
121 O7 **Fitzroy Harbour** Ontario Canada
141 H3 **Fitzroy I** Queensland Australia
142 E4 **Fitzroy R** W Australia Australia
120 J7 **Fitzwilliam I** Ontario Canada
42 E7 **Fiuggi** Italy
45 J3 **Fiumalbo** Italy
Fiume *see* **Rijeka**
42 E7 **Fiumicino** Italy
45 M3 **Fiumi Uniti** *R* Italy
144 A6 **Five Fingers Pen** New Zealand
122 H8 **Five Islands** Nova Scotia Canada
101 R6 **Fivemile Cr** Wyoming U.S.A.
14 D2 **Fivemiletown** N Ireland
144 B6 **Five Rivers** New Zealand
88 B4 **Fizi** Zaire
26 L4 **Fjällåsen** Sweden
26 G6 **Fjällfjällen** *mt* Sweden
26 F9 **Fjällnäs** Sweden
28 H7 **Fjelde** Denmark
28 F3 **Fjellerup** Denmark
28 E6 **Fjelsted** Denmark
28 D6 **Fjelstrup** Denmark
28 C2 **Fjerritslev** Denmark
27 B10 **Fjordane** *reg* Norway
27 B13 **Fjotland** Norway
27 D11 **Flå** Norway
37 K5 **Flachslanden** Germany
28 A3 **Flade Sø** Denmark
28 B6 **Fladså** *R* Denmark
37 J2 **Fladungen** Germany
106 G2 **Flagler** Colorado U.S.A.
113 F8 **Flagler Beach** Florida U.S.A.
103 N6 **Flagstaff** Arizona U.S.A.
95 R1 **Flagstaff L** Maine U.S.A.
100 E7 **Flagstaff L** Oregon U.S.A.
100 K1 **Flagstone** British Columbia Canada
28 G6 **Flakkebjerg** Denmark
26 F3 **Flakstad** Norway
27 B11 **Flåm** Norway
20 G2 **Flamanville** France
99 Q4 **Flambeau** *R* Wisconsin U.S.A.
99 Q3 **Flambeau Res** Wisconsin U.S.A.
13 H5 **Flamborough Hd** England
133 C3 **Flamenco** Chile
131 E8 **Flamenco, I** Argentina
33 R9 **Fläming** *reg* Germany
101 Q8 **Flaming Gorge Res** Utah/Wyoming U.S.A.
113 G12 **Flamingo** Florida U.S.A.
18 F10 **Flamisell** *R* Spain
36 C2 **Flammersfeld** Germany
127 O2 **Flanagin Town** Trinidad
99 O1 **Flanders** Ontario Canada
22 D2 **Flandre** *prov* France
22 E3 **Flandre** France
98 K5 **Flandreau** South Dakota U.S.A.
102 E1 **Flanigan** Nevada U.S.A.
38 H6 **Flankenmarkt** Austria
26 K8 **Flärke** Sweden
98 E3 **Flasher** North Dakota U.S.A.
26 H7 **Flåsjön** *L* Sweden
117 K5 **Flat** *R* Northwest Territories Canada
94 B3 **Flat** *R* Michigan U.S.A.
109 K4 **Flat** Texas U.S.A.
123 O5 **Flat Bay** Newfoundland Canada
118 C4 **Flatbush** Alberta Canada
111 J8 **Flat Creek** Alabama U.S.A.
101 L2 **Flathead L** Montana U.S.A.
101 L1 **Flathead Mts** Montana U.S.A.
117 Q11 **Flathead R** Idaho U.S.A.
5 C5 **Flat Holm** *isld* Bristol Channel England
141 J5 **Flat I** Queensland Australia
118 E4 **Flat L** Alberta Canada
144 A6 **Flat Mt** New Zealand
109 K6 **Flatonia** Texas U.S.A.
110 F4 **Flat River** Missouri U.S.A.
110 J3 **Flat Rock** Illinois U.S.A.
94 B7 **Flat Rock** Indiana U.S.A.
141 H2 **Flattery, C** Queensland Australia
100 A1 **Flattery,C** Washington U.S.A.
38 K8 **Flattnitz** Austria
94 F9 **Flat Top** West Virginia U.S.A.
101 R3 **Flatwillow** Montana U.S.A.
94 G8 **Flatwoods** West Virginia U.S.A.
41 O3 **Flaurling** Austria
27 C12 **Flåv** *L* Norway
28 E2 **Flavenskjold** Denmark
22 F4 **Flavigny le Grd. et Beaurain** France
22 E4 **Flavy le Martel** France
8 D5 **Flax Bourton** England
118 H7 **Flaxcombe** Saskatchewan Canada
116 P1 **Flaxman I** Alaska U.S.A.
98 D1 **Flaxton** North Dakota U.S.A.
98 A1 **Flaxville** Montana U.S.A.
20 B4 **Flèche** *R* France
21 K6 **Flèche, La** France
33 O8 **Flechtingen** Germany
113 K9 **Fleeming Pt** New Providence I Bahamas
118 F6 **Fleet** Alberta Canada
9 G2 **Fleet Hargate** England
141 H5 **Fleetwood** Queensland Australia
13 E6 **Fleetwood** England
95 M6 **Fleetwood** Pennsylvania U.S.A.
36 G5 **Flein** Germany
95 N4 **Fleischmanns** New York U.S.A.
27 B13 **Flekkefjord** Norway
27 C13 **Flekkeröy** *isld* Norway
Flemhude *see* **Quarnbek**
119 Q8 **Fleming** Saskatchewan Canada
98 D9 **Fleming** Colorado U.S.A.
94 D8 **Flemingsburg** Kentucky U.S.A.
95 N6 **Flemington** New Jersey U.S.A.
90 F4 **Flemish Cap** Atlantic Oc
28 E6 **Flemløse** Denmark
27 J12 **Flen** Sweden
29 K4 **Fleninge** Sweden
28 C7 **Flensburg** Germany
28 D7 **Flensburger Förde** *inlet* Denmark/Germany
21 N7 **Fléré-la-Rivière** France
21 J4 **Flers** France
22 D3 **Flers** France
101 N2 **Flesher** Montana U.S.A.
120 K8 **Flesherton** Ontario Canada
112 E2 **Fletcher** North Carolina U.S.A.
107 M7 **Fletcher** Oklahoma U.S.A.
94 D2 **Fletcher Pond** Michigan U.S.A.
146 C7 **Fletcher Promontory** *pen* Antarctica
9 F2 **Fletton** England
18 F9 **Fleurance** France
123 Q3 **Fleur de Lys** Newfoundland Canada
122 H2 **Fleur-de-May,L** Labrador, Nfld Canada
40 E4 **Fleurier** Switzerland
22 H3 **Fleurus** Belgium
21 N3 **Fleury-sur-Andelle** France
68 G1 **Fleuve Rouge** *R* Vietnam
25 D3 **Flevoland** *prov* Netherlands
36 H3 **Flieden** Germany
41 K4 **Flims** Switzerland
9 G5 **Flimwell** England
140 F4 **Flinders** *R* Queensland Australia
143 B10 **Flinders B** W Australia Australia
141 G2 **Flinders Group** *islds* Gt Barrier Reef Aust
139 J7 **Flinders I** Tasmania Australia
141 J4 **Flinder's Passage** Australia
141 J4 **Flinders Reefs** Gt Barrier Reef Aust
138 E4 **Flinders Rge** South Australia Australia
22 E3 **Flines-le-Râches** France
119 Q4 **Flin Flon** Manitoba Canada
110 K7 **Flint** *R* Alabama U.S.A.
111 M10 **Flint** *R* Georgia U.S.A.
94 D3 **Flint** Michigan U.S.A.
8 C1 **Flint** Wales
107 O4 **Flint Hills** Kansas U.S.A.
135 M9 **Flint I** Pacific Oc
120 E3 **Flint L** Ontario Canada
118 L9 **Flintoft** Saskatchewan Canada
141 J8 **Flinton** Queensland Australia
110 D5 **Flippin** Arkansas U.S.A.
112 C4 **Flirt** *R* Georgia U.S.A.
27 F11 **Flisa** Norway
27 H14 **Fliseryd** Sweden
17 H3 **Flix** Spain
13 H6 **Flixborough** England
21 P1 **Flixecourt** France
22 H4 **Flize** France
13 G6 **Flockton Moor** England
111 J11 **Flomaton** Florida U.S.A.
108 G1 **Flomot** Texas U.S.A.
36 E4 **Flonheim** Germany
67 D1 **Flood Basin** *L* Hubei China
146 B9 **Flood Ra** Antarctica
99 O3 **Floodwood** Minnesota U.S.A.
110 H3 **Flora** Illinois U.S.A.
94 A6 **Flora** Indiana U.S.A.
111 F9 **Flora** Mississippi U.S.A.
100 H4 **Flora** Oregon U.S.A.
18 H8 **Florac** France
111 K10 **Florala** Alabama U.S.A.
113 E9 **Floral City** Florida U.S.A.
142 B5 **Flora, Mt** W Australia Australia
141 H3 **Flora Pass** Gt Barrier Reef Aust
140 E4 **Floraville** Queensland Australia
142 A1 **Floreat Park** *dist* Perth, W Aust Australia
22 H3 **Floreffe** Belgium
Florence *see* **Firenze**
110 J7 **Florence** Alabama U.S.A.
103 N8 **Florence** Arizona U.S.A.
106 E3 **Florence** Colorado U.S.A.
100 J4 **Florence** Idaho U.S.A.
107 O3 **Florence** Kansas U.S.A.
94 C8 **Florence** Kentucky U.S.A.
111 F9 **Florence** Mississippi U.S.A.
101 L3 **Florence** Montana U.S.A.
95 N6 **Florence** New Jersey U.S.A.
100 A6 **Florence** Oregon U.S.A.
112 H3 **Florence** South Carolina U.S.A.
98 J4 **Florence** South Dakota U.S.A.
109 K5 **Florence** Texas U.S.A.
99 S4 **Florence** Wisconsin U.S.A.
103 N8 **Florence Junc** Arizona U.S.A.
102 F4 **Florence L** California U.S.A.
128 F8 **Florencia** Argentina
128 C3 **Florencia** Colombia
22 H3 **Florennes** Belgium
22 J4 **Florenville** Belgium
131 F5 **Flores** *R* Argentina
85 A1 **Flores** *isld* Azores Atlantic Oc
130 H9 **Flores** Brazil
125 P9 **Flores** Guatemala
71 K9 **Flores** *isld* Indonesia
131 F4 **Flores** *dept* Uruguay
48 L3 **Floreshty** Moldova
117 K11 **Flores I** British Columbia Canada
71 J8 **Flores Sea** Indonesia
130 H10 **Floresta** Brazil
109 J6 **Floresville** Texas U.S.A.
108 E3 **Florey** Texas U.S.A.
129 K5 **Floriano** Brazil
128 E5 **Floriano Peixoto** Brazil
130 E10 **Florianopólis** Brazil
126 E4 **Florida** Cuba
137 N3 **Florida** *isld* Solomon Is
131 G5 **Florida** Uruguay
113 B12 **Florida** *state* U.S.A.
94 C5 **Florida** Ohio U.S.A.
113 G12 **Florida B** Florida U.S.A.
113 F13 **Florida Keys** *islds* Florida U.S.A.
113 H12 **Florida,Str.of** U.S.A./Bahamas
130 B10 **Florida,V** Paraguay
43 G11 **Floridia** Sicily
109 O4 **Florien** Louisiana U.S.A.
46 E4 **Flórina** Greece
99 O9 **Floris** Iowa U.S.A.
106 E3 **Florissant** Colorado U.S.A.
106 E3 **Florissant Fossilbeds Nat. Mon.** Colorado U.S.A.
26 A10 **Florø** Norway
36 G3 **Flörsbach** Germany
47 M11 **Florya** Turkey
37 N4 **Floss** Germany
37 N4 **Flossenbürg** Germany
15 F2 **Flotta** Scotland
118 J4 **Flotten L** Saskatchewan Canada
103 M3 **Flowell** Utah U.S.A.
120 J7 **Flowerpot I. Nat. Park** Ontario Canada
123 Q2 **Flower's Cove** Newfoundland Canada
98 K7 **Floyd** *R* Iowa U.S.A.
108 D1 **Floyd** New Mexico U.S.A.
108 F2 **Floydada** Texas U.S.A.
103 M6 **Floyd,Mt** Arizona U.S.A.
27 D11 **Fluberg** Norway
41 L4 **Flüela Pass** Switzerland
21 O6 **Fluery les Aubrais** France
25 E3 **Fluessen** *R* Netherlands
71 A3 **Fluk** Indonesia
111 F11 **Fluker** Louisiana U.S.A.
20 G5 **Flume** *R* France
17 G3 **Flumen** *R* Spain
43 B9 **Fluminimaggiore** Sardinia
36 F7 **Fluorn** Germany
Flushing Netherlands *see* **Vlissingen**
94 D3 **Flushing** Michigan U.S.A.
94 F6 **Flushing** Ohio U.S.A.
108 F3 **Fluvanna** Texas U.S.A.
18 G10 **Fluvia** *R* Spain
28 C4 **Fly** Denmark
136 J3 **Fly** *R* Indonesia/Papua New Guinea
83 M9 **Flying Fish Cove** Christmas I Indian Oc
140 C2 **Flying Fox Cr** N Terr Australia
28 A4 **Flynder Kirke** Denmark
28 B3 **Flynder Sø** *L* Denmark
6 M6 **Flyndre** *oil rig* North Sea
109 L4 **Flynn** Texas U.S.A.
140 C4 **Flynn Mem** N Terr Australia
119 O7 **Foam Lake** Saskatchewan Canada
73 L9 **Foa Mulaku I** Maldives
47 H6 **Foça** Turkey
22 J3 **Focant** Belgium
45 H3 **Foce d. Radici** *mt* Italy
15 E3 **Fochabers** Scotland
42 E4 **Foci del Po** Italy
48 L5 **Focșani** Romania
28 H6 **Fodby** Denmark
21 P7 **Foëcy** France
140 D3 **Foelsche** *R* N Terr Australia
67 D5 **Fogang** China
140 B2 **Fog B** N Terr Australia
57 E4 **Fogelevo** Kazakhstan
43 G7 **Foggia** Italy

42 E5 **Foglia** *R* Italy
45 N7 **Fogliano** *L* Italy
29 H11 **Föglö** Finland
123 S4 **Fogo** Newfoundland Canada
88 G10 **Fogo** *isld* Mozambique
123 S4 **Fogo,C** Newfoundland Canada
28 C4 **Fogstrup** Denmark
38 L7 **Fohnsdorf** Austria
28 A7 **Föhr** *isld* Germany
45 R7 **Foiana in Val Fortore** Italy
14 A5 **Foilclogh** *mt* Ireland
15 D2 **Foinaven,Mt** Scotland
18 G10 **Foix** France
52 H6 **Foki** Russian Federation
54 F3 **Fokina, imeni** Russian Federation
54 F3 **Fokino** Russian Federation
26 D9 **Fokstua** Norway
26 G4 **Folda** *inlet* Norway
48 F4 **Földeák** Hungary
26 F7 **Foldereid** Norway
28 B6 **Foldingbro** Denmark
28 C6 **Folding Kirke** Denmark
28 B6 **Fole** Denmark
46 G8 **Folégandros** *isld* Greece
89 E3 **Foley** Botswana
111 J11 **Foley** Alabama U.S.A.
113 D7 **Foley** Florida U.S.A.
99 N4 **Foley** Minnesota U.S.A.
120 H4 **Foleyet** Ontario Canada
115 M4 **Foley I** Northwest Territories Canada
27 B11 **Folgefonna** *gla* Norway
116 J5 **Folger** Alaska U.S.A.
146 G14 **Folger, Cape** *C* Antarctica
20 B4 **Folgoët, le** France
42 E6 **Foligno** Italy
9 H5 **Folkestone** England
9 F2 **Folkingham** England
113 E7 **Folkston** Georgia U.S.A.
112 K3 **Folkstone** North Carolina U.S.A.
26 D9 **Folla** *R* Norway
26 D9 **Folldal** Norway
28 E4 **Følle** Denmark
25 E3 **Follega** Netherlands
28 G5 **Føllenslev** Denmark
20 H4 **Folligny** France
26 G8 **Föllinge** Sweden
27 E12 **Follo** Norway
42 D6 **Follonica** Italy
112 H5 **Folly Beach** South Carolina U.S.A.
100 G6 **Follyfarm** Oregon U.S.A.
102 C3 **Folsom** California U.S.A.
111 F11 **Folsom** Louisiana U.S.A.
106 G5 **Folsom** New Mexico U.S.A.
102 C3 **Folsom L** California U.S.A.
48 L5 **Folteşti** Romania
126 E3 **Fómento** Cuba
52 F6 **Fominki** Russian Federation
52 G2 **Fominskaya** Russian Federation
52 F5 **Fominskoye** Russian Federation
99 M7 **Fonda** Iowa U.S.A.
95 N4 **Fonda** New York U.S.A.
98 F1 **Fonda** North Dakota U.S.A.
114 J6 **Fond-du-Lac** Saskatchewan Canada
99 S6 **Fond du Lac** Wisconsin U.S.A.
94 D10 **Fonde** Kentucky U.S.A.
21 M7 **Fondettes** France
43 E7 **Fondi** Italy
45 O7 **Fondi, L. di** Italy
26 E8 **Fongen** *mt* Norway
43 C8 **Fonni** Sardinia
16 C1 **Fonsagrada** Spain
28 D6 **Fønsskov** Denmark
22 G3 **Fontaine** Belgium
21 N6 **Fontaine** Loir-et-Cher France
18 G4 **Fontainebleau** France
19 O17 **Fontaine-de-Vaucluse** France
40 B2 **Fontaine-Française** France
21 M3 **Fontaine-l'Abbé** France
21 N2 **Fontaine-le-Bourg** France
21 M2 **Fontaine-le-Dun** France
40 B3 **Fontaine-lès-Dijon** France
21 K6 **Fontaine-Milon** France
21 L6 **Fontaine-St. Martin,la** France
133 C6 **Fontana,L** Argentina
112 D2 **Fontana L** North Carolina U.S.A.
45 P6 **Fontana Liri** Italy
45 L3 **Fontanelice** Italy
117 N6 **Fontas** British Columbia Canada
40 D7 **Fontcouvert** France
38 F7 **Fonte** Italy
128 E4 **Fonte Boa** Brazil
128 G6 **Fonte do Pau d'Água** Brazil
18 E6 **Fontenay-le-Comte** France
21 O3 **Fontenay-St.Père** France
123 L2 **Fonteneau,L** Quebec Canada
122 H5 **Fontenelle** Quebec Canada
101 P7 **Fontenelle Fork** *R* Wyoming U.S.A.
101 P7 **Fontenelle Res** Wyoming U.S.A.
22 E2 **Fontenoy** Belgium
21 L7 **Fontevrault l'Abbaye** France
8 D6 **Fontmell Magna** England
22 L5 **Fontoy** France
137 S5 **Fonualei** *isld* Tonga
48 D4 **Fonyód** Hungary
Foochow *see* **Fuzhou** Fujian
103 M2 **Fool Cr.Res** Utah U.S.A.
117 P9 **Foothills** Alberta Canada
99 R7 **Footville** Wisconsin U.S.A.
41 H5 **Foppiano** Italy
27 J14 **Föra** Sweden
107 O5 **Foraker** Oklahoma U.S.A.
116 M5 **Foraker,Mt** Alaska U.S.A.
19 K3 **Forbach** France
36 E6 **Forbach** Germany
139 J5 **Forbes** New South Wales Australia
99 O2 **Forbes** Minnesota U.S.A.
98 H4 **Forbes** North Dakota U.S.A.
117 P10 **Forbes, Mt** Alberta Canada
85 F7 **Forcados** Nigeria
19 Q18 **Forcalqueiret** France
19 P17 **Forcalquier** France
38 E8 **Forchetta** *mt* Italy
37 L4 **Forchheim** Germany
36 H5 **Forchtenberg** Germany
13 F2 **Ford** England
107 L4 **Ford** Kansas U.S.A.
94 C9 **Ford** Kentucky U.S.A.
99 T3 **Ford** *R* Michigan U.S.A.
140 A2 **Ford, C** N Terr Australia
102 E6 **Ford City** California U.S.A.
94 H6 **Ford City** Pennsylvania U.S.A.
26 A10 **Förde** Norway
145 E3 **Fordell** New Zealand
33 P9 **Förderstedt** Germany
9 G3 **Fordham** England
9 E6 **Fordingbridge** England
103 J8 **Ford L** California U.S.A.
110 D4 **Fordland** Missouri U.S.A.
31 L2 **Fordon** Poland
146 B9 **Ford Ranges** Antarctica
139 H3 **Ford's Br** New South Wales Australia
110 K4 **Fordsville** Kentucky U.S.A.
109 K6 **Fordtran** Texas U.S.A.
98 J1 **Fordville** North Dakota U.S.A.
111 D8 **Fordyce** Arkansas U.S.A.
98 J7 **Fordyce** Nebraska U.S.A.
26 G5 **Fore** Norway
85 B7 **Forécariah** Guinea
8 C5 **Foreland,The** England
115 Q4 **Forel, Mont** *mt* Greenland
109 N2 **Foreman** Arkansas U.S.A.
118 F9 **Foremost** Alberta Canada
22 G2 **Forest** Belgium
120 H9 **Forest** Ontario Canada
100 J3 **Forest** Idaho U.S.A.
111 G9 **Forest** Mississippi U.S.A.
94 D6 **Forest** Ohio U.S.A.
118 E6 **Forestburg** Alberta Canada
109 K2 **Forestburg** Texas U.S.A.
110 F6 **Forest City** Arkansas U.S.A.
99 N6 **Forest City** Iowa U.S.A.
112 F2 **Forest City** North Carolina U.S.A.
95 M5 **Forest City** Pennsylvania U.S.A.
142 B3 **Forestdale** *dist* Perth, W Aust Australia
95 O3 **Forest Dale** Vermont U.S.A.
109 O1 **Forester** Arkansas U.S.A.
94 E3 **Forester** Michigan U.S.A.
100 B9 **Forest Glen** California U.S.A.
101 Q3 **Forestgrove** Montana U.S.A.
100 B4 **Forest Grove** Oregon U.S.A.
102 D2 **Foresthill** California U.S.A.
111 D10 **Forest Hill** Louisiana U.S.A.
109 M9 **Forest Hill** Texas U.S.A.
141 G4 **Forest Home** Queensland Australia
139 J8 **Forestier, C** Tasmania Australia
139 J9 **Forestier Pen** Tasmania Australia
99 O4 **Forest Lake** Minnesota U.S.A.
15 D4 **Forest of Atholl** Scotland
99 N4 **Foreston** Minnesota U.S.A.
95 M3 **Forestport** New York U.S.A.
98 J1 **Forest River** North Dakota U.S.A.
9 G5 **Forest Row** England
122 C5 **Forestville** Quebec Canada
102 B3 **Forestville** California U.S.A.
94 E3 **Forestville** Michigan U.S.A.
94 H4 **Forestville** New York U.S.A.
20 C6 **Forêt, B.de la** *B* France
19 J3 **Forêt d'Argonne** France
20 C6 **Forêt, la** France
21 P5 **Forêt-Ste Croix, la** France
18 H7 **Forez, Mts du** France
15 F4 **Forfar** Scotland
118 K7 **Forgan** Saskatchewan Canada
107 K5 **Forgan** Oklahoma U.S.A.
20 E5 **Forges, les** France
21 O2 **Forges-les-Eaux** France
121 O4 **Forget** Quebec Canada
119 P9 **Forget** Saskatchewan Canada
41 N2 **Forggen See** *L* Germany
45 P8 **Forio** Italy
110 G6 **Forked Deer** *R* Tennessee U.S.A.
119 R7 **Fork River** *R* Manitoba Canada
100 A2 **Forks** Washington U.S.A.
144 C5 **Forks, The** New Zealand
94 J9 **Fork Union** Virginia U.S.A.
42 E4 **Forlì** Italy
45 M3 **Forlimpopoli** Italy
14 E4 **Forlorn Pt** Ireland
98 J3 **Forman** North Dakota U.S.A.
13 E6 **Formby** England
138 D6 **Formby B** South Australia Australia
13 E6 **Formby Pt** England
45 M5 **Formello** Italy
17 H6 **Formentera** *isld* Balearic Is
21 O2 **Formerie** France
43 F7 **Formia** Italy
130 F7 **Formiga** Brazil
126 G5 **Formigas Bank** Caribbean
45 J2 **Formigine** Italy
45 L2 **Formignana** Italy
21 J3 **Formigny** France
26 F7 **Formofoss** Norway
Formosa *see* **Taiwan**
133 F3 **Formosa** Argentina
129 J6 **Formosa** *R* Brazil
129 J7 **Formosa** Brazil
129 J6 **Formosa do Rio Prêto** Brazil
129 G6 **Formosa, Serra** *mts* Brazil
Formosa Strait *see* **Taiwan Str**
130 F4 **Formoso** Brazil
107 M2 **Formoso** Kansas U.S.A.
28 F4 **Fornæs** *C* Denmark
17 K4 **Fornells** Menorca
38 G8 **Forni Avoltri** Italy
6 F1 **Føroyar** *islds* N Atlantic Oc
15 E3 **Forres** Scotland
143 G9 **Forrest** W Australia Australia
119 S9 **Forrest** Manitoba Canada
99 S9 **Forrest** Illinois U.S.A.
146 E7 **Forrestal Ra** Antarctica
117 G8 **Forrester I** Alaska U.S.A.
142 C2 **Forrestfield** *dist* Perth, W Aust Australia
143 G8 **Forrest Lakes** W Australia Australia
143 G6 **Forrest, Mt** W Australia Australia
99 R7 **Forreston** Illinois U.S.A.
142 G3 **Forrest River Mission** W Australia Australia
26 J9 **Fors** Sweden
26 J3 **Forsa** Norway
26 J10 **Forsa** Sweden
108 F3 **Forsan** Texas U.S.A.
27 B13 **Forsand** Norway
141 G4 **Forsayth** Queensland Australia
27 J11 **Forsbacka** Sweden
27 F12 **Forshaga** Sweden
27 F13 **Forshem** Sweden
27 F15 **Förslöv** Sweden
27 K11 **Forsmark** Sweden
26 J8 **Forsmo** Sweden
26 K5 **Forsnäs** Sweden
26 C8 **Forsnes** Norway
29 K11 **Forssa** Finland
31 H4 **Forst** Germany
139 L4 **Forster** New South Wales Australia
112 D4 **Forsyth** Georgia U.S.A.
99 S10 **Forsyth** Illinois U.S.A.
101 T3 **Forsyth** Montana U.S.A.
121 O4 **Forsythe** Quebec Canada
145 E4 **Forsyth I** New Zealand
140 E3 **Forsyth Is** Queensland Australia
141 G6 **Forsyth Ra** Queensland Australia
74 E4 **Fort Abbas** Pakistan
111 E10 **Fort Adams** Mississippi U.S.A.
115 L7 **Fort Albany** Ontario Canada
129 L4 **Fortaleza** Brazil
128 E5 **Fortaleza de Ituxi** Brazil
122 G9 **Fort Anne Nat. Hist. Park** Nova Scotia Canada
Fort Archambault *see* **Sarh**
94 J7 **Fort Ashby** West Virginia U.S.A.
118 C4 **Fort Assiniboine** Alberta Canada
99 S7 **Fort Atkinson** Wisconsin U.S.A.
15 D3 **Fort Augustus** Scotland
87 E12 **Fort Beaufort** S Africa
122 H8 **Fort Beau Sejour Nat. Hist. Park** New Brunswick Canada
101 R1 **Fort Belknap Agency** Montana U.S.A.
111 M9 **Fort Benning** Georgia U.S.A.
101 P2 **Fort Benton** Montana U.S.A.
100 E8 **Fort Bidwell** California U.S.A.
118 K3 **Fort Black** Saskatchewan Canada
103 P9 **Fort Bowie Nat. Hist. Site** Arizona U.S.A.
102 A2 **Fort Bragg** California U.S.A.
110 J3 **Fort Branch** Indiana U.S.A.
101 P8 **Fort Bridger** Wyoming U.S.A.
99 K8 **Fort Calhoun** Nebraska U.S.A.
Fort Carnot *see* **Ikongo**
Fort Charlet *see* **Djanet**
Fort Chimo *see* **Kuujjuaq**
117 R6 **Fort Chipewyan** Alberta Canada
98 E2 **Fort Clark** North Dakota U.S.A.
107 M6 **Fort Cobb** Oklahoma U.S.A.
98 A9 **Fort Collins** Colorado U.S.A.
140 F5 **Fort Constantine** Queensland Australia
121 O7 **Fort Coulonge** Quebec Canada
95 N2 **Fort Covington** New York U.S.A.
Fort Dauphin *see* **Tôlañaro**
111 L9 **Fort Davis** Alabama U.S.A.
108 D5 **Fort Davis** Texas U.S.A.
108 D5 **Fort Davis Nat. Hist. Site** Texas U.S.A.
103 P6 **Fort Defiance** Arizona U.S.A.
127 L4 **Fort de France** Martinique W Indies
111 K10 **Fort Deposit** Alabama U.S.A.
100 A8 **Fort Dick** California U.S.A.
99 M7 **Fort Dodge** Iowa U.S.A.
110 J5 **Fort Donelson Nat Mil Park** Tennessee U.S.A.
113 G10 **Fort Drum** Florida U.S.A.
9 E3 **Fort Dunlop** England
123 P2 **Forteau** Labrador, Nfld Canada
130 B6 **Forte Coimbra** Brazil
44 H4 **Forte dei Marmi** Italy
121 L10 **Fort Erie** Ontario Canada
142 B5 **Fortescue R** W Australia Australia
142 C5 **Fortescue, R** W Australia Australia
95 L9 **Fort Eustis** Virginia U.S.A.
95 T7 **Fort Fairfield** Maine U.S.A.
112 K4 **Fort Fisher** North Carolina U.S.A.
Fort Flatters *see* **Bordj Omar Driss**
99 N1 **Fort Frances** Ontario Canada
117 M3 **Fort Franklin** Northwest Territories Canada
117 L8 **Fort Fraser** British Columbia Canada
112 F6 **Fort Frederica Nat. Mon** Georgia U.S.A.
111 L10 **Fort Gaines** Georgia U.S.A.
Fort Garaud *see* **Fdérik**
106 E4 **Fort Garland** Colorado U.S.A.
118 B1 **Fort Garry** Manitoba Canada
94 E8 **Fort Gay** West Virginia U.S.A.
115 M7 **Fort George** Quebec Canada
15 D3 **Fort George** Scotland
107 P6 **Fort Gibson** Oklahoma U.S.A.
107 P5 **Fort Gibson L** Oklahoma U.S.A.
114 G4 **Fort Good Hope** Northwest Territories Canada
113 F10 **Fort Green** Florida U.S.A.
138 F3 **Fort Grey** New South Wales Australia
109 H3 **Fort Griffin** Texas U.S.A.
12 E2 **Forth** Scotland
Fort Hall *see* **Murang'a** Kenya
101 N6 **Fort Hall** Idaho U.S.A.
13 F1 **Forth, Firth of** Scotland
115 L7 **Fort Hope** Ontario Canada
12 D1 **Forth, R** Scotland
103 O10 **Fort Huachuca** Arizona U.S.A.
121 S6 **Fortierville** Quebec Canada
6 L5 **Forties** *oil rig* North Sea
122 H9 **Forties Settlement** Nova Scotia Canada
103 K3 **Fortification Ra** Nevada U.S.A.
128 F8 **Fortin Carlos Antonio López** Paraguay
101 L1 **Fortine** Montana U.S.A.
128 G8 **Fortin Falcón** Paraguay
133 F2 **Fortin Gen. Caballero** Paraguay
128 F8 **Fortin General Eugenio Garay** Paraguay
128 F8 **Fortin Infante Rivarola** Paraguay
122 E3 **Fortin, L** Quebec Canada
133 E3 **Fortin Lavalle** Argentina
128 F8 **Fortin Linares** Paraguay
133 F2 **Fortin Madrejón** Paraguay
128 F7 **Fortin Ravelo** Bolivia
128 G8 **Fortin Rojas Silva** Paraguay
128 F7 **Fortin Suárez Arana** Bolivia
128 G7 **Fortin Teniente Américo Picco** Paraguay
Fort Jameson Zambia *see* **Chipata**
113 E13 **Fort Jefferson Nat.Mon** Florida U.S.A.
Fort Johnston *see* **Mangochi**
100 C8 **Fort Jones** California U.S.A.
118 G4 **Fort Kent** Alberta Canada
95 S6 **Fort Kent** Maine U.S.A.
100 C7 **Fort Klamath** Oregon U.S.A.
94 B9 **Fort Knox** Kentucky U.S.A.
Fort Lallemande *see* **Belhirane**
Fort Lamy *see* **N'djamena**
98 B7 **Fort Laramie** Wyoming U.S.A.
98 B7 **Fort Laramie Nat. Hist. Mon.** Wyoming U.S.A.
107 L3 **Fort Larned Nat. Hist. Site** Kansas U.S.A.
113 G11 **Fort Lauderdale** Florida U.S.A.
112 G3 **Fort Lawn** South Carolina U.S.A.
100 C2 **Fort Lewis** Washington U.S.A.
117 M5 **Fort Liard** Northwest Territories Canada
127 J5 **Fort Liberté** Haiti
98 F3 **Fort Lincoln** North Dakota U.S.A.
112 C2 **Fort Loudon Lake** Tennessee U.S.A.
98 B9 **Fort Lupton** Colorado U.S.A.
106 G3 **Fort Lyon** Colorado U.S.A.
108 G5 **Fort McKavett** Texas U.S.A.
117 S7 **Fort MacKay** Alberta Canada
101 S5 **Fort Mackenzie** Wyoming U.S.A.
118 D9 **Fort Macleod** Alberta Canada
Fort McMahon *see* **El Homr**
118 F2 **Fort McMurray** Alberta Canada
114 F4 **Fort McPherson** Northwest Territories Canada
99 P9 **Fort Madison** Iowa U.S.A.
22 B3 **Fort Mahon Plage** France
Fort Manning *see* **Mchinji**
113 F8 **Fort Matanzas Nat.Mon** Florida U.S.A.
113 F10 **Fort Meade** Florida U.S.A.
112 G2 **Fort Mill** South Carolina U.S.A.
98 C9 **Fort Morgan** Colorado U.S.A.
106 G1 **Fort Morgan** Colorado U.S.A.
113 F11 **Fort Myers** Florida U.S.A.
113 E11 **Fort Myers Beach** Florida U.S.A.
117 M6 **Fort Nelson** British Columbia Canada
117 L3 **Fort Norman** Northwest Territories Canada
113 F10 **Fort Ogden** Florida U.S.A.
43 G7 **Fortore** *R* Italy
111 L7 **Fort Payne** Alabama U.S.A.
101 T2 **Fort Peck L** *res* Montana U.S.A.
113 G10 **Fort Pierce** Florida U.S.A.
98 F5 **Fort Pierre** South Dakota U.S.A.
Fort Pierre Bordes *see* **Tin Zaouaten**
95 N4 **Fort Plain** New York U.S.A.
117 P5 **Fort Providence** Northwest Territories Canada
112 G5 **Fort Pulaski Nat. Mon** Georgia U.S.A.
119 O8 **Fort Qu' Appelle** Saskatchewan Canada
112 M2 **Fort Raleigh Nat.Hist.Site** North Carolina U.S.A.
116 F9 **Fort Randall** Alaska U.S.A.
98 H6 **Fort Randall Dam** South Dakota U.S.A.
94 C6 **Fort Recovery** Ohio U.S.A.
114 J5 **Fort Reliance** Northwest Territories Canada
117 R5 **Fort Resolution** Northwest Territories Canada
101 Q5 **Fortress Mt** Wyoming U.S.A.
123 M8 **Fortress of Louisburg Nat. Hist. Park** C Breton I, Nova Scotia
98 F3 **Fort Rice** North Dakota U.S.A.
107 O2 **Fort Riley** Kansas U.S.A.
99 M3 **Fort Ripley** Minnesota U.S.A.
87 E10 **Fort Rixon** Zimbabwe
98 C7 **Fort Robinson** Nebraska U.S.A.
100 D6 **Fort Rock** Oregon U.S.A.
144 B7 **Fortrose** New Zealand
Fort Rosebery Zambia *see* **Mansa**
102 A3 **Fort Ross** California U.S.A.
Fort Rousset *see* **Owando**
121 M1 **Fort Rupert** Quebec Canada
117 L8 **Fort St. James** British Columbia Canada
117 N7 **Fort St. John** British Columbia Canada
Fort Sandeman *see* **Zhob**
118 D5 **Fort Saskatchewan** Alberta Canada
107 Q4 **Fort Scott** Kansas U.S.A.
115 L6 **Fort Severn** Ontario Canada
100 B9 **Fort Seward** California U.S.A.
107 M7 **Fort Sill** Oklahoma U.S.A.
117 N5 **Fort Simpson** Northwest Territories Canada
114 G5 **Fort Smith** *dist* Northwest Territories Canada
117 R5 **Fort Smith** Northwest Territories Canada
107 Q6 **Fort Smith** Arkansas U.S.A.
101 T8 **Fort Steele** Wyoming U.S.A.
108 E5 **Fort Stockton** Texas U.S.A.
108 C1 **Fort Sumner** New Mexico U.S.A.
112 H5 **Fort Sumter Nat.Mon** South Carolina U.S.A.
107 L5 **Fort Supply** Oklahoma U.S.A.
108 E7 **Fort Supply Res** Oklahoma U.S.A.
103 P8 **Fort Thomas** Arizona U.S.A.
98 G5 **Fort Thompson** South Dakota U.S.A.
107 P7 **Fort Towson** Oklahoma U.S.A.
27 C10 **Fortun** Norway
17 G6 **Fortuna** Spain
100 A9 **Fortuna** California U.S.A.
98 C1 **Fortuna** North Dakota U.S.A.
116 F6 **Fortuna Lodge** Alaska U.S.A.
123 R6 **Fortune** Newfoundland Canada
106 E6 **Fort Union Nat.Mon** New Mexico U.S.A.
112 D5 **Fort Valley** Georgia U.S.A.
117 Q6 **Fort Vermilion** Alberta Canada
Fort Victoria *see* **Masvingo**
94 B7 **Fortville** Indiana U.S.A.
111 K11 **Fort Walton Beach** Florida U.S.A.
101 R6 **Fort Washakie** Wyoming U.S.A.
94 B5 **Fort Wayne** Indiana U.S.A.
113 E8 **Fort White** Florida U.S.A.
118 A2 **Fort Whyte** Manitoba Canada
15 C4 **Fort William** Scotland
109 M10 **Fort Worth** Texas U.S.A.
98 F3 **Fort Yates** North Dakota U.S.A.
116 R5 **Fortymile** *R* Alaska U.S.A.
116 R5 **Fort Yukon** Alaska U.S.A.
77 D6 **Forūr, Jazīreh-ye** *isld* Iran
22 J2 **Forville** Belgium
119 N9 **Forward** Saskatchewan Canada
52 H5 **Fosforitnaya** Russian Federation
67 D5 **Foshan** China
115 L2 **Fosheim Pen** Northwest Territories Canada
26 D8 **Fosna** Norway
26 E7 **Fosnes** Norway
107 L6 **Foss** Oklahoma U.S.A.
44 C2 **Fossano** Italy
22 H3 **Fosse** Belgium
100 E4 **Fossil** Oregon U.S.A.
101 P8 **Fossil** Wyoming U.S.A.
101 P8 **Fossil Butte Nat. Mon.** Wyoming U.S.A.
142 F4 **Fossil Downs** W Australia Australia
121 L6 **Fossmill** Ontario Canada
42 E5 **Fossombrone** Italy
119 O6 **Fosston** Saskatchewan Canada
99 L2 **Fosston** Minnesota U.S.A.
139 H7 **Foster** Victoria Australia
121 S7 **Foster** Quebec Canada
98 J7 **Foster** Nebraska U.S.A.
100 C5 **Foster** Oregon U.S.A.
147 E10 **Foster Bugt** Greenland
99 T4 **Foster City** Michigan U.S.A.
117 D6 **Foster, Mt.** Yukon Territory Canada
118 J8 **Fosterton** Saskatchewan Canada
110 K6 **Fosterville** Tennessee U.S.A.
94 D5 **Fostoria** Ohio U.S.A.
109 M5 **Fostoria** Texas U.S.A.
67 F4 **Fotan** China
142 F5 **Fotheringham, Mt** W Australia Australia
21 O2 **Foucarmont** France
36 C7 **Fouday** France
20 B6 **Fouesnant** France
86 B6 **Fougamou** Gabon
20 H5 **Fougères** France
83 K13 **Fougères,Pl.des** Réunion Indian Oc
40 D2 **Fougerolles** France
21 J5 **Fougerolles-du-Plessis** France
21 P2 **Fouilloy** France
109 O2 **Fouke** Arkansas U.S.A.
68 B3 **Foul** *isld* Burma
84 K5 **Foul Bay** Egypt
9 G4 **Foulness Pt** England
13 E5 **Foulney** *isld* England
144 C4 **Foulwind, C** New Zealand
86 B4 **Foumban** Cameroon
85 D3 **Foum el Hassan** Morocco
85 C2 **Foum Zguid** Morocco
146 D8 **Foundation Ice Stream** *ice stream* Antarctica
106 F3 **Fountain** Colorado U.S.A.
99 U5 **Fountain** Michigan U.S.A.
99 O6 **Fountain** Minnesota U.S.A.
112 K2 **Fountain** North Carolina U.S.A.
103 N2 **Fountain Grn** Utah U.S.A.
111 E8 **Fountain Hill** Arkansas U.S.A.
112 E3 **Fountain Inn** South Carolina U.S.A.
16 B7 **Foupana** *R* Portugal
140 D3 **Four Archers** *mt* N Terr Australia
18 E7 **Fouras** France
101 U1 **Four Buttes** Montana U.S.A.
21 M5 **Fourche, la** France
110 B7 **Fourche la Fave** *R* Arkansas U.S.A.
19 J4 **Fourchies, Mts des** France
123 M8 **Fourchu** C Breton I, Nova Scotia
103 P4 **Four Corners** Utah U.S.A.
98 B5 **Four Corners** Wyoming U.S.A.
140 A1 **Fourcroy, C** N Terr Australia
20 E7 **Four, le** *isld* France
22 G3 **Fourmies** France
83 K14 **Fournaise, Piton de la** *vol* Réunion Indian Oc
46 E5 **Fournás** Greece
83 L13 **Fourneau** *isld* Mauritius
123 P2 **Fournel, L** Quebec Canada
22 D2 **Fournes-en-Weppes** France
122 G2 **Fournier, L** Quebec Canada
47 H7 **Foúrnoi** *isld* Greece
127 K3 **Four Paths** Jamaica
19 N17 **Fourques** France
13 F3 **Fourstones** England
99 R3 **Fourteenmile Pt** Michigan U.S.A.
85 B6 **Fouta Djalon** *mt reg* Guinea
85 B5 **Fouta Ferlo** *reg* Senegal
8 D5 **Fovant** England
144 A7 **Foveaux Strait** New Zealand
28 C3 **Fovlum** Denmark
8 B7 **Fowey** England
113 G12 **Fowey Rocks** Florida U.S.A.
126 F2 **Fowl Cay** *isld* Bahamas
106 F3 **Fowler** Colorado U.S.A.
99 T9 **Fowler** Indiana U.S.A.
107 K4 **Fowler** Kansas U.S.A.
94 C3 **Fowler** Michigan U.S.A.
101 O1 **Fowler** Montana U.S.A.
146 C7 **Fowler Peninsula** *pen* Antarctica
138 B4 **Fowler Pt** South Australia Australia
138 B4 **Fowlers B** South Australia Australia
138 F4 **Fowlers Gap** New South Wales Australia
109 J7 **Fowlerton** Texas U.S.A.
94 C4 **Fowlerville** Michigan U.S.A.
110 G6 **Fowlkes** Tennessee U.S.A.
111 M11 **Fowlstown** Georgia U.S.A.
77 A1 **Fowman** Iran
115 K6 **Fox** *R* Manitoba Canada
99 S8 **Fox** *R* Illinois U.S.A.
99 U3 **Fox** *R* Michigan U.S.A.
99 T4 **Fox** Michigan U.S.A.
99 P9 **Fox** *R* Missouri U.S.A.
100 F5 **Fox** Oregon U.S.A.
99 S5 **Fox** *R* Wisconsin U.S.A.
123 L4 **Fox B** Anticosti I, Quebec
94 H5 **Foxburg** Pennsylvania U.S.A.
117 P8 **Fox Creek** Alberta Canada
115 M4 **Foxe Basin** Northwest Territories Canada
115 L4 **Foxe Chan** Northwest Territories Canada
115 M5 **Foxe Pen** Northwest Territories Canada
119 M5 **Foxford** Saskatchewan Canada
14 B3 **Foxford** Ireland
123 R1 **Fox Harbour** Labrador, Nfld Canada
13 H5 **Foxholes** England
98 K3 **Foxhome** Minnesota U.S.A.
116 P8 **Fox Islands** *isld* Aleutian Is
143 C10 **Fox, L** W Australia Australia
99 S7 **Fox Lake** Illinois U.S.A.
99 S6 **Fox Lake** Wisconsin U.S.A.
101 T8 **Foxpark** Wyoming U.S.A.
144 C5 **Fox Peak** *mt* New Zealand
123 L4 **Fox Pt** Anticosti I, Quebec
117 L7 **Fox R** British Columbia Canada
145 E4 **Foxton** New Zealand
118 H8 **Fox Valley** Saskatchewan Canada
119 Q8 **Foxwarren** Manitoba Canada
111 G10 **Foxworth** Mississippi U.S.A.
15 D3 **Foyers** Scotland
14 D2 **Foyle** *R* N Ireland
14 D1 **Foyle, L** Ireland
14 B4 **Foynes** Ireland
16 C1 **Foz** Spain
130 D9 **Foz de Areia, Représa de** *res* Brazil
87 B9 **Foz do Cunene** Angola
128 D5 **Foz do Gregório** Brazil
130 C9 **Foz do Iguaçú** Brazil
128 F5 **Foz do Jamari** Brazil
128 D5 **Foz do Jordao** Brazil
128 E4 **Foz do Jutaí** Brazil
128 E4 **Foz do Mamoriá** Brazil
128 D5 **Foz do Riozinho** Brazil
67 E1 **Foziling Shuiku** *res* China
128 E5 **Foz Tarauacá** Brazil
95 L6 **Frackville** Pennsylvania U.S.A.
8 B7 **Fraddon** England
17 H3 **Fraga** Spain
36 B7 **Fraize** France
22 F3 **Frameries** Belgium
95 Q4 **Framingham** Massachusetts U.S.A.
9 H3 **Framlingham** England
36 G3 **Frammersbach** Germany
146 J10 **Framnes Mts** Antarctica
31 O5 **Frampol** Poland
130 F7 **Franca** Brazil
83 M14 **Francais, Port-aux-** *France Base* Kerguelen Indian Oc
43 H8 **Francavilla Fontana** Italy
18 **France** *rep* W Europe
147 F10 **France, Ile de** Greenland
138 F6 **Frances** South Australia Australia
117 J5 **Frances** *R* Yukon Territory Canada
100 B3 **Frances** Washington U.S.A.
140 B2 **Frances Creek** N Terr Australia
117 J5 **Frances L** Yukon Territory Canada
101 N1 **Frances, L** Montana U.S.A.
127 K5 **Francés Viejo, C** Dominican Rep
99 U9 **Franceville** Indiana U.S.A.
86 B6 **Franceville** Gabon
19 J6 **Franche Comté** *prov* France
119 O8 **Francis** Saskatchewan Canada
107 O7 **Francis** Oklahoma U.S.A.
98 G6 **Francis Case, L** South Dakota U.S.A.
128 D4 **Francisco de Orellana** Peru
124 H5 **Francisco I. Madero** Coahuila Mexico
124 G5 **Francisco I. Madero** Durango Mexico
130 C9 **Francisco, S** *R* Brazil
130 G5 **Francisco Sá** Brazil
123 R1 **Francis Harbour** Labrador, Nfld Canada
95 Q1 **Francis, L** New Hampshire U.S.A.
89 E3 **Francistown** Botswana
123 Q6 **François** Newfoundland Canada
117 K8 **François L** British Columbia Canada
127 M4 **François, Le** Martinique W Indies
45 L2 **Francolino** Italy
22 K2 **Francorchamps** Belgium
101 Q6 **Francs Pk** Wyoming U.S.A.
21 N7 **Francueil** France
25 E2 **Franeker** Netherlands
118 C9 **Frank** Alberta Canada
36 F1 **Frankenau** Germany
36 F2 **Frankenbach** Germany
37 P2 **Frankenberg** Germany
36 F1 **Frankenberg/Eder** Germany
37 J5 **Frankenhardt** Germany
37 J5 **Frankenhöhe** *mts* Germany
94 D3 **Frankenmuth** Michigan U.S.A.
36 D5 **Frankenstein** Germany
36 E4 **Frankenthal** Germany
37 M3 **Frankenwald** *mts* Germany
127 K2 **Frankfield** Jamaica
121 N8 **Frankford** Ontario Canada
110 E2 **Frankford** Missouri U.S.A.
94 G9 **Frankford** West Virginia U.S.A.
94 A6 **Frankfort** Indiana U.S.A.
107 O2 **Frankfort** Kansas U.S.A.
94 C8 **Frankfort** Kentucky U.S.A.
99 U5 **Frankfort** Michigan U.S.A.
95 M3 **Frankfort** New York U.S.A.
94 D7 **Frankfort** Ohio U.S.A.
98 H5 **Frankfort** South Dakota U.S.A.
36 F3 **Frankfurt am Main** Germany
31 H3 **Frankfurt an der Oder** Germany
37 K6 **Fränkische Alb** *mts* Germany
37 L4 **Fränkische Schweiz** *reg* Germany
139 J7 **Frankland, C** Tasmania Australia
111 L8 **Franklin** Georgia U.S.A.
101 O7 **Franklin** Idaho U.S.A.
94 A7 **Franklin** Indiana U.S.A.
110 K5 **Franklin** Kentucky U.S.A.
111 E12 **Franklin** Louisiana U.S.A.
95 T2 **Franklin** Maine U.S.A.
95 Q4 **Franklin** Massachusetts U.S.A.
101 Q3 **Franklin** Montana U.S.A.
98 H9 **Franklin** Nebraska U.S.A.
95 Q3 **Franklin** New Hampshire U.S.A.
95 N5 **Franklin** New Jersey U.S.A.
95 M4 **Franklin** New York U.S.A.
112 D2 **Franklin** North Carolina U.S.A.
94 C7 **Franklin** Ohio U.S.A.
94 H5 **Franklin** Pennsylvania U.S.A.
110 K6 **Franklin** Tennessee U.S.A.
109 L4 **Franklin** Texas U.S.A.
95 L10 **Franklin** Virginia U.S.A.
94 H8 **Franklin** West Virginia U.S.A.
114 G3 **Franklin B** Northwest Territories Canada
100 G1 **Franklin D. Roosevelt L** Washington U.S.A.
99 R8 **Franklin Grove** Illinois U.S.A.
138 D5 **Franklin Harb** South Australia Australia
146 C11 **Franklin I** Antarctica
120 K7 **Franklin I** Ontario Canada
103 J1 **Franklin L** Nevada U.S.A.
117 L3 **Franklin Mts** Northwest Territories Canada
144 A6 **Franklin Mts** New Zealand
116 P2 **Franklin Mts** Alaska U.S.A.
116 H1 **Franklin, Pt** Alaska U.S.A.
139 J8 **Franklin Snd** Tasmania Australia
115 K3 **Franklin Str** Northwest Territories Canada
111 F11 **Franklinton** Louisiana U.S.A.
112 J1 **Franklinton** North Carolina U.S.A.
94 J4 **Franklinville** New York U.S.A.
112 H2 **Franklinville** North Carolina U.S.A.
100 J6 **Franklin Whitney** *airport* Idaho U.S.A.
144 D5 **Franklyn, Mt** New Zealand
37 J3 **Fränk Saale** *R* Germany
139 H7 **Frankston** Victoria Australia
109 M3 **Frankston** Texas U.S.A.
99 T7 **Franksville** Wisconsin U.S.A.
144 B6 **Frankton** New Zealand
101 R5 **Frannie** Wyoming U.S.A.
87 B10 **Fransfontein** Namibia
26 H9 **Frånsta** Sweden
9 G5 **Frant** England
37 N3 **Františkovy Lázně** Czech Rep
147 L11 **Frantsa-Iosifa, Zemlya** Arctic Oc
120 F4 **Franz** Ontario Canada
33 R4 **Franzburg** Germany
144 C5 **Franz Josef Gla** New Zealand
Franz Josef Land *see* **Frantsa-Iosifa, Zemlya**
38 G7 **Franz-Josefs Höhe** *mt* Austria
43 B9 **Frasca, C. d** Sardinia
42 E7 **Frascati** Italy
100 C1 **Fraser** *R* British Columbia Canada
106 E2 **Fraser** Colorado U.S.A.
87 D12 **Fraserburg** S Africa
15 F3 **Fraserburgh** Scotland
120 J3 **Fraserdale** Ontario Canada
141 L7 **Fraser I** Queensland Australia
143 C7 **Fraser, Mt** W Australia Australia
143 E9 **Fraser Range** W Australia Australia
69 E11 **Fraser's Hill** Malaysia
145 F3 **Frasertown** New Zealand
119 U8 **Fraserwood** Manitoba Canada
46 D4 **Frashër** Albania
48 K6 **Frăsinet** Romania
19 K6 **Frasne** France
22 F2 **Frasnes-les-Buissenal** Belgium
25 F5 **Frasselt** Germany
45 J3 **Frassinoro** Italy
120 F5 **Frater** Ontario Canada
45 L1 **Fratta Polesine** Italy
41 J2 **Frauenfeld** Switzerland
33 S10 **Frauenhain** Germany
37 O5 **Frauenstein** *mt* Germany
37 K2 **Frauenwald** Germany
28 E6 **Fraugde** Denmark
131 F4 **Fray Bentos** Uruguay
21 N5 **Frazé** France
99 L3 **Frazee** Minnesota U.S.A.
101 T1 **Frazer** Montana U.S.A.
142 A6 **Frazer I** W Australia Australia
120 B3 **Frazer L** Ontario Canada
36 B2 **Frechen** Germany
16 D2 **Frechilla** Spain
32 G9 **Freckenhorst** Germany
99 S2 **Freda** Michigan U.S.A.
98 E3 **Freda** North Dakota U.S.A.
36 E1 **Fredeburg** Germany
32 L9 **Freden** Germany
29 K5 **Fredensborg** Denmark
94 C2 **Frederic** Michigan U.S.A.
99 O4 **Frederic** Wisconsin U.S.A.
95 M7 **Frederica** Delaware U.S.A.
28 D5 **Fredericia** Denmark
99 Q9 **Frederick** Illinois U.S.A.
95 K7 **Frederick** Maryland U.S.A.
107 L7 **Frederick** Oklahoma U.S.A.
98 H4 **Frederick** South Dakota U.S.A.
120 J3 **Frederick House** *R* Ontario Canada
137 L6 **Frederick Reef** Coral Sea
99 O7 **Fredericksburg** Iowa U.S.A.
95 L6 **Fredericksburg** Pennsylvania U.S.A.
109 J5 **Fredericksburg** Texas U.S.A.
94 K8 **Fredericksburg** Virginia U.S.A.
117 F7 **Frederick Sd** Alaska U.S.A.
110 F4 **Fredericktown** Missouri U.S.A.
94 E6 **Fredericktown** Ohio U.S.A.
122 F8 **Fredericton** New Brunswick Canada
122 F8 **Fredericton Junct** New Brunswick Canada
28 C4 **Frederiks** Denmark
29 K5 **Frederiksberg** Denmark
28 C5 **Frederikshåb** Denmark
115 P5 **Frederikshåb** Greenland
115 O5 **Frederikshåb Isblink** Greenland
28 F2 **Frederikshavn** Denmark
28 H5 **Frederikssund** Denmark
113 L8 **Frederiksted** Virgin Is
28 J5 **Frederiksværk** Denmark
128 C2 **Fredonia** Colombia
103 M5 **Fredonia** Arizona U.S.A.
107 P4 **Fredonia** Kansas U.S.A.
110 H4 **Fredonia** Kentucky U.S.A.
94 H4 **Fredonia** New York U.S.A.
98 G3 **Fredonia** North Dakota U.S.A.
26 K7 **Fredrika** Sweden
27 E12 **Fredrikstad** Norway
110 E3 **Freeburg** Missouri U.S.A.
95 K6 **Freeburg** Pennsylvania U.S.A.
100 J4 **Freedom** Idaho U.S.A.
110 K2 **Freedom** Indiana U.S.A.
107 L5 **Freedom** Oklahoma U.S.A.
100 E9 **Freedonyer Peak** *mt* California U.S.A.
95 N6 **Freehold** New Jersey U.S.A.
94 C3 **Freeland** Michigan U.S.A.
95 M5 **Freeland** Pennsylvania U.S.A.
138 E4 **Freeling Heights** *mt* South Australia Australia
140 C6 **Freeling Mt** N Terr Australia
102 E3 **Freel Peak** California U.S.A.
123 T4 **Freels, C** Newfoundland Canada
118 B4 **Freeman** *R* Alberta Canada
98 J6 **Freeman** South Dakota U.S.A.
110 K1 **Freeman, L** Indiana U.S.A.
111 G12 **Freemason I** Louisiana U.S.A.
122 F9 **Freeport** Nova Scotia Canada
111 K11 **Freeport** Florida U.S.A.
99 R7 **Freeport** Illinois U.S.A.
95 R3 **Freeport** Maine U.S.A.
94 F6 **Freeport** Ohio U.S.A.
94 H6 **Freeport** Pennsylvania U.S.A.
109 M7 **Freeport** Texas U.S.A.
113 J11 **Freeport City** Grand Bahama I
109 J8 **Freer** Texas U.S.A.
99 U5 **Freesoil** Michigan U.S.A.
126 F2 **Freetown** Eleuthera Bahamas
122 J7 **Freetown** Prince Edward I Canada
85 B7 **Freetown** Sierra Leone
94 A8 **Freetown** Indiana U.S.A.
127 P4 **Freetown** Antigua W Indies
95 L4 **Freeville** New York U.S.A.
16 C6 **Fregenal de la Sierra** Spain
138 B2 **Fregon** South Australia Australia
20 F4 **Fréhel** France
20 F4 **Fréhel, C** France
26 C8 **Frei** Norway
36 G6 **Freiberg** Germany
37 P2 **Freiberg** Germany
37 O1 **Freiberger Mulde** *R* Germany
40 G1 **Freiburg** Germany
32 K10 **Freienhagen** Germany
32 H10 **Freienohl** Germany
36 G3 **Freiensteinau** Germany
37 M4 **Freihung** Germany
36 D2 **Freilingen** Germany
133 C3 **Freirina** Chile
36 C4 **Freisen** Germany
37 M7 **Freising** Germany
38 L4 **Freistadt** Austria
16 C3 **Freixo de Espada à Cinta** Portugal
28 D2 **Frejlev** Denmark
143 B9 **Fremantle** W Australia Australia
94 C5 **Fremont** Indiana U.S.A.
99 V6 **Fremont** Michigan U.S.A.
98 K8 **Fremont** Nebraska U.S.A.
112 K2 **Fremont** North Carolina U.S.A.
94 D5 **Fremont** Ohio U.S.A.
103 O3 **Fremont** *R* Utah U.S.A.
101 N8 **Fremont I** Utah U.S.A.
101 Q7 **Fremont L** Wyoming U.S.A.
106 D2 **Fremont Pass** Colorado U.S.A.
101 Q6 **Fremont Pk** Wyoming U.S.A.
20 F4 **Frênaye, B.de la** France
112 D2 **French Broad** *R* Tennessee U.S.A.
94 D9 **Frenchburg** Kentucky U.S.A.
94 G5 **French Cr** Pennsylvania U.S.A.
100 J4 **French Creek** Idaho U.S.A.
102 T13 **French Frigate Shoals** Hawaiian Is
100 G7 **Frenchglen** Oregon U.S.A.
129 H3 **French Guiana** *French dept* S America
100 C9 **French Gulch** California U.S.A.
139 H7 **French I** Victoria Australia
110 K3 **French Lick** Indiana U.S.A.
102 F2 **Frenchman** Nevada U.S.A.
95 T2 **Frenchman Bay** Maine U.S.A.
118 H5 **Frenchman Butte** Saskatchewan Canada
139 H8 **Frenchman Cap** Tasmania Australia
101 S1 **Frenchman Cr** Mont/Sask U.S.A./Canada
103 J5 **Frenchman Flat** *dry lake* Nevada U.S.A.
98 E9 **Frenchman Fork** *R* Nebraska U.S.A.
118 J9 **Frenchman R** Saskatchewan Canada
123 O4 **Frenchman's Cove** Newfoundland Canada
14 C3 **Frenchpark** Ireland
145 D4 **French Pass** New Zealand
French Terr. of the Afars and the Issas (FTAI) *see* **Djibouti** *rep*
95 M6 **Frenchtown** New Jersey U.S.A.
22 B2 **Frencq** France
19 Q14 **Frêne, Pic du** *mt* France
21 M3 **Freneuse-sur-Risle** France
37 K4 **Frensdorf** Germany
31 L6 **Frenštát** Czech Rep
32 G8 **Freren** Germany
143 D7 **Frere Ra** W Australia Australia
129 H5 **Fresco** *R* Brazil
14 D4 **Freshford** Ireland
144 B6 **Freshford Plain** New Zealand
9 E6 **Freshwater** England
100 A9 **Freshwater** California U.S.A.
21 L5 **Fresnay** France
21 L5 **Fresnaye-sur-Chédouet, la** France
40 C2 **Fresnes** France
22 F3 **Fresnes-sur-L'Escaut** France
124 H6 **Fresnillo de González Echeverría** Mexico
102 E4 **Fresno** *R* California U.S.A.
102 E5 **Fresno** California U.S.A.
101 P1 **Fresno Res** Montana U.S.A.
21 N2 **Fresnoy-Folny** France
22 E4 **Fresnoy-le-Grand** France
40 C4 **Fresse, Mt.de** France
21 O1 **Fressenneville** France
27 B10 **Fresvik** Norway
21 N6 **Fréteval** France
27 B11 **Fretheim** Norway
19 J5 **Fretigney** France
20 A5 **Fret,le** France
13 E1 **Freuchie** Scotland
36 G4 **Freudenberg** Baden-Württemberg Germany
36 D2 **Freudenberg** Nordrhein-Westfalen Germany
36 E7 **Freudenstadt** Germany
22 C3 **Frévent** France
140 D4 **Frewena Roadhouse** N Terr Australia
94 H4 **Frewsburg** New York U.S.A.
37 M1 **Freyburg** Germany
143 A10 **Freycinet, C** W Australia Australia
143 A7 **Freycinet Estuary** *inlet* W Australia Australia
139 J8 **Freycinet Pen** Tasmania Australia
33 Q6 **Freyenstein** Germany

36 B5 Freyming France
37 L5 Freystadt Germany
30 H7 Freyung Germany
85 B6 Fria Guinea
87 B9 Fria, C Namibia
102 E5 Friant California U.S.A.
102 E5 Friant Dam California U.S.A.
102 E6 Friant-Kern Canal California U.S.A.
127 P4 Friar's B., North St Kitts W Indies
83 L10 Friar's Hood mt Sri Lanka
111 F7 Friars Port Mississippi U.S.A.
131 D2 Frias Argentina
40 F4 Fribourg Switzerland
36 E3 Frickhofen Germany
22 D3 Fricourt France
100 B1 Friday Harbour Washington U.S.A.
141 F1 Friday I Queensland Australia
13 H5 Fridaythorpe England
38 O7 Friedberg Austria
37 K7 Friedberg Bayern Germany
36 F3 Friedberg Hessen Germany
33 P9 Friedeburg Germany
38 M4 Friedersbach Austria
33 T8 Friedersdorf Germany
32 L10 Friedland Germany
33 T5 Friedland Germany
37 K2 Friedrichroda Germany
36 F3 Friedrichsdorf Germany
33 T7 Friedrichsfelde Germany
41 K2 Friedrichshafen Germany
33 T8 Friedrichshagen Germany
32 J4 Friedrichskoog Germany
33 P5 Friedrichsruhe Germany
30 E1 Friedrichstadt Germany
33 T6 Friedrichswalde Germany
37 K2 Friedrichswerth Germany
36 G2 Frielendorf Germany
107 K3 Friend Kansas U.S.A.
98 J9 Friend Nebraska U.S.A.
Friendly Is see Tonga
127 K2 Friendship pk Jamaica
95 S3 Friendship Maine U.S.A.
94 J4 Friendship New York U.S.A.
94 D8 Friendship Ohio U.S.A.
99 R6 Friendship Wisconsin U.S.A.
70 C2 Friendship Shoal S China Sea
94 H7 Friendsville Maryland U.S.A.
27 D12 Frierfjord inlet Norway
94 F10 Fries Virginia U.S.A.
38 K8 Friesach Austria
33 R7 Friesack Germany
25 F2 Friesche Gat Netherlands
36 D7 Friesenheim Germany
28 A7 Friesische Inseln islds Germany
25 E2 Friesland Netherlands
32 G6 Friesoythe Germany
83 J12 Frigate isld Seychelles
6 M3 Frigg oil rig North Sea
45 J3 Frignano Italy
9 H4 Frinton-on-Sea England
124 H6 Frío Mexico
109 J7 Frio R Texas U.S.A.
130 H8 Frio, C Brazil
15 F4 Friockheim Scotland
108 E1 Frio Draw R New Mex/Tex U.S.A.
36 F6 Friolzheim Germany
22 L4 Frisange Luxembourg
109 L2 Frisco Texas U.S.A.
111 J10 Frisco City Alabama U.S.A.
103 L3 Frisco Mt Utah U.S.A.
108 C8 Fritch Texas U.S.A.
8 B6 Frithelstock Stone England
36 G1 Fritzlar Germany
42 E2 Friuli-Venezia-Giulia prov Italy
21 O1 Friville-Escarbotin France
12 E5 Frizington England
26 D8 Froan isld Norway
119 P9 Frobisher Saskatchewan Canada
115 N5 Frobisher Bay Northwest Territories Canada
114 J6 Frobisher L Saskatchewan Canada
8 D1 Frodsham England
19 P14 Froges France
118 G5 Frog L L Alberta Canada
26 D8 Frohavet inlet Norway
37 O1 Frohburg Germany
33 S7 Frohnau Germany
33 P8 Frohse Germany
98 B1 Froid Montana U.S.A.
22 G3 Froid-Chapelle Belgium
130 F5 Fróis Brazil
21 P2 Froissy France
36 B2 Froitzheim Germany
52 H4 Frolovskaya Russian Federation
55 E1 Froly Russian Federation
101 R4 Fromberg Montana U.S.A.
31 M1 Frombork Poland
138 E3 Frome R South Australia Australia
8 D5 Frome England
127 H1 Frome Jamaica
138 E4 Frome Downs South Australia Australia
138 E4 Frome, L South Australia Australia
22 D2 Fromelles France
21 K4 Fromentel France
20 F8 Fromentine France
32 G10 Fröndenberg Germany
36 F2 Fronhausen Germany
16 B5 Fronteira Portugal
18 E6 Frontenay Rohan-Rohan France
37 O6 Frontenhausen Germany
125 N8 Frontera Mexico
124 E2 Fronteras Mexico
118 J9 Frontier Saskatchewan Canada
101 P8 Frontier Wyoming U.S.A.
18 H9 Frontignan France
106 E1 Front Range Colorado U.S.A.
94 J8 Front Royal Virginia U.S.A.
28 F6 Frørup Denmark
33 O9 Frose Germany
43 E7 Frosinone Italy
28 B3 Frøslev Denmark
20 G7 Frossay France
109 L3 Frost Texas U.S.A.
26 E8 Frosta Norway
94 J7 Frostburg Maryland U.S.A.
113 F10 Frostproof Florida U.S.A.
28 B2 Frøstrup Denmark
26 G7 Frostviken Sweden
37 K2 Fröttstädt Germany
19 K4 Frouard France
119 O9 Froude Saskatchewan Canada
27 H12 Frövi Sweden
9 E5 Froxfield England
26 C8 Fröya isld Norway
26 B8 Fröyabanken Norway
22 C3 Fruges France
106 B2 Fruita Colorado U.S.A.
111 H10 Fruitdale Alabama U.S.A.
98 C5 Fruitdale South Dakota U.S.A.
100 J5 Fruitland Idaho U.S.A.
106 B5 Fruitland New Mexico U.S.A.
101 P9 Fruitland Utah U.S.A.
144 B6 Fruitlands New Zealand
100 J5 Fruitvale Idaho U.S.A.
48 K3 Frumuşica Romania
Frunze see Bishkek
54 F8 Frunzenskiy Ukraine
48 M3 Frunzovka Ukraine
48 F5 Fruška Gora mt Serbia Yugoslavia
130 E7 Frutal Brazil
40 G4 Frutigen Switzerland
102 B2 Fruto California U.S.A.
54 K1 Fryanovo Russian Federation
98 C3 Fryburg North Dakota U.S.A.
48 E1 Frýdek Mistek Czech Rep
95 R2 Fryeburg Maine U.S.A.
27 F11 Fryksände Sweden
46 E5 Ftéri mt Greece
67 F3 Fu'an China
45 J4 Fucecchio Italy
Fucheng see Qiongshan
65 C6 Fucheng China
65 B7 Fucheng China
36 E2 Fuchskauten mt Germany
60 G11 Fuchū Japan
67 D4 Fuchuan China
59 G6 Fuchun Jiang R China
42 F7 Fucino, Piana del Italy
61 P5 Fudai Japan
67 G3 Fuding China
16 D8 Fuengirola Spain
108 G7 Fuente Mexico
17 G7 Fuente Alamo de Murcia Spain
16 C6 Fuente de Cantos Spain
16 C4 Fuenteguinaldo Spain
16 D6 Fuenteobejuna Spain
16 D3 Fuentesaúco Spain
17 G3 Fuentes de Ebro Spain
16 C4 Fuentes de Oñoro Spain
130 B7 Fuerte Olimpo Paraguay
85 B3 Fuerteventura isld Canary Is
71 E1 Fuga isld Luzon Philippines
38 E7 Fügen Austria
28 H6 Fuglebjerg Denmark
6 F1 Fugloy isld Faeroes
26 L1 Fuglöy isld Norway
28 F7 Fuglsbølle Denmark
65 C7 Fugou China
65 B5 Fugu China
Fuguo see Zhanhua
66 D2 Fuhai China
77 A5 Fuḩayḩīl, Al Kuwait
33 Q9 Fuhne R Germany
32 L7 Fuhrberg Germany
21 H7 Fuilet, le France
77 E7 Fujairah U.A.E.
Fujayrah, Al see Fujairah
67 F3 Fujian prov China
67 B1 Fu Jiang R China
61 M11 Fujieda Japan
61 M10 Fuji Hakone Izu Nat. Park Japan
61 M10 Fuji-kawa R Japan
59 K2 Fujin China
61 M10 Fujinomiya Japan
61 N9 Fujioka Japan
61 O5 Fujisaki Japan
61 M10 Fuji-san vol Japan
61 N10 Fujisawa Japan
61 M10 Fujiyoshida Japan
61 N5 Fukaura Japan
61 N9 Fukaya Japan
Fukien prov see Fujian
60 J10 Fukuchiyama Japan
60 B13 Fukue Japan
60 B13 Fukue-jima isld Japan
61 K9 Fukui Japan
60 D12 Fukuma Japan
61 K9 Fukuno Japan
60 D12 Fukuoka Japan
61 N6 Fukura Japan
61 L11 Fukuroi Japan
61 O8 Fukushima prefect Japan
60 O4 Fukushima Hokkaido Japan
61 O8 Fukushima Honshu Japan
60 G11 Fukuyama Honshu Japan
60 D14 Fukuyama Kyūshū Japan
60 H10 Fukuzaki Japan
85 B6 Fulacunda Guinea-Bissau
77 C1 Fulād Mahalleh Iran
36 H2 Fulda R Germany
36 H2 Fulda Germany
99 L6 Fulda Minnesota U.S.A.
36 G1 Fuldabrück Germany
13 G6 Fulford England
58 D6 Fulin China
67 B2 Fuling China
67 F3 Fuling China
141 F5 Fullarton R Queensland Australia
127 N3 Fullarton Trinidad
102 G8 Fullerton California U.S.A.
94 E8 Fullerton Kentucky U.S.A.
109 P4 Fullerton Louisiana U.S.A.
98 H8 Fullerton Nebraska U.S.A.
6 M6 Fulmar oil rig North Sea
65 F2 Fulongquan China
48 E4 Fülöpszállás Hungary
41 O3 Fulpmes Austria
111 J10 Fulton Alabama U.S.A.
111 C8 Fulton Arkansas U.S.A.
99 Q8 Fulton Illinois U.S.A.
94 A6 Fulton Indiana U.S.A.
107 Q3 Fulton Kansas U.S.A.
110 H5 Fulton Kentucky U.S.A.
111 C11 Fulton Louisiana U.S.A.
111 H7 Fulton Mississippi U.S.A.
110 E3 Fulton Missouri U.S.A.
95 L3 Fulton New York U.S.A.
94 E6 Fulton Ohio U.S.A.
98 J6 Fulton South Dakota U.S.A.
95 N4 Fultonham New York U.S.A.
95 N4 Fultonville New York U.S.A.
27 F10 Fuluälven R Sweden
27 F10 Fulufj mt Sweden
27 F10 Fulunäs Sweden
22 H4 Fumay France
18 F8 Fumel France
41 N5 Fumo, Mt Italy
61 N10 Funabashi Japan
137 Q3 Funafuti atoll Tuvalu
60 E14 Funahiki Japan
Funan see Fusui
65 F4 Funan China
26 F9 Funäsdalen Sweden
85 A2 Funchal Madeira
16 B7 Funcheira Portugal
126 G9 Fundación Colombia
130 H6 Fundão Brazil
124 E4 Fundición Mexico
38 E8 Fundres Italy
48 K6 Fundulea Romania
41 N3 Fundus Feiler mt Austria
122 G8 Fundy, B. of Nova Scotia/New Bruns Canada
122 G8 Fundy Nat. Park New Brunswick Canada
Funen isld see Fyn isld
102 H5 Funeral Peak California U.S.A.
87 F10 Funhalouro Mozambique
65 D5 Funing China
67 B5 Funing China
98 G9 Funk Nebraska U.S.A.
123 T4 Funk I Newfoundland Canada
141 J5 Funnel R Queensland Australia
117 F6 Funter Alaska U.S.A.
85 F6 Funtua Nigeria
65 C5 Fuping China
65 A7 Fuping China
67 F4 Fuqing China
112 J2 Fuquay Springs North Carolina U.S.A.
88 D9 Furancungo Mozambique
60 Q2 Furano Japan
59 J2 Furao China
46 G1 Furculeşti Romania
80 C3 Fureidis Israel
60 Q3 Furenai Japan
60 T2 Füren ko L Japan
29 K5 Furesø L Denmark
36 G5 Fürfeld Baden-Württemberg Germany
36 D4 Fürfeld Rheinland-Pfalz Germany
77 D5 Furg Iran
112 F5 Furman South Carolina U.S.A.
52 F6 Furmanov Russian Federation
57 G3 Furmanovka Kazakhstan
12 C1 Furnace Scotland
130 F7 Furnas, Barragem dam Brazil
139 J8 Furneaux Group islds Tasmania Australia
138 F6 Furner South Australia Australia
Furnes see Veurne
27 E11 Furnes Norway
118 H5 Furness Saskatchewan Canada
67 B2 Furong Jiang R China
67 E3 Furong Shan mt China
32 G7 Fürstenau Germany
33 S6 Fürstenberg Germany
36 F1 Fürstenberg Germany
38 O7 Fürstenfeld Austria
37 L7 Fürstenfeldbrück Germany
30 H3 Fürstenwalde Germany
33 T6 Fürstenwerder Germany
37 P6 Fürstenzell Germany
36 F4 Fürth Germany
37 O5 Furth im Wald Germany
41 H1 Furtwangen Germany
60 O2 Furuhira Japan
61 O7 Furukawa Japan
61 L9 Furukawa Japan
115 L4 Fury & Hecla Str Northwest Territories Canada
27 A11 Fusa Norway
128 D3 Fusagasuga Colombia
45 Q8 Fusaro L Italy
43 G9 Fuscaldo Italy
38 G7 Fusch Austria
32 M8 Fuse R Germany
65 B6 Fushan China
65 E6 Fushan China
68 J3 Fushan China
13 E2 Fushiebridge Scotland
61 K9 Fushiki Japan
59 H3 Fushun China
67 A2 Fushun China
45 L3 Fusignano Italy
118 H7 Fusilier Saskatchewan Canada
Fusin see Fuxin
45 M1 Fusina Italy
41 J5 Fusio Switzerland
59 J3 Fusong China
41 N2 Füssen Germany
28 D4 Fussing Sø L Denmark
67 B5 Fusui China
61 L11 Futagawa Japan
60 E12 Futago-san mt Japan
60 D11 Futaoi-jima isld Japan
45 K3 Futa, Passo di Italy
61 O5 Futatsui Japan
61 N13 Futatsu-ne rocks Japan
61 P13 Futemma Okinawa
61 N10 Futtsu Japan
137 R4 Futuna isld Îles de Horn Pacific Oc
67 F3 Futun Xi R China
79 A7 Fuwa Egypt
65 E5 Fu Xian China
67 A4 Fuxian Hu L China
65 E3 Fuxin China
Fuxing see Wangmo
58 G5 Fuyang China
67 F1 Fuyang China
67 F5 Fuyang China
67 G3 Fuying Dao isld China
59 H2 Fuyu China
59 K2 Fuyuan China
67 A4 Fuyuan China
66 D2 Fuyun China
48 F3 Füzesabony Hungary
48 G3 Füzesgyarmat Hungary
67 F3 Fuzhou Fujian China
67 E2 Fuzhou Jiangxi China
65 E5 Fuzhoucheng China
9 E4 Fyfield England
9 G4 Fyfield Essex England
28 E6 Fyn isld Denmark
28 E6 Fyn co Denmark
12 C1 Fyne, L Scotland
28 D7 Fynshav Denmark
28 F5 Fynshoved C Denmark
27 C12 Fyresv L Norway
127 O3 Fyzabad Trinidad

G

86 A2 Gaalkacyo Somalia
70 C4 Gaat R Sarawak
52 D4 Gabanova Russian Federation
123 M8 Gabarouse C Breton I, Nova Scotia
17 J3 Gabarras, Mts Spain
18 F9 Gabarret France
102 G3 Gabbs Nevada U.S.A.
102 F3 Gabbs Valley Ra Nevada U.S.A.
87 B8 Gabela Angola
Gaberones see Gaborone
85 F2 Gabès Tunisia
85 G2 Gabès, Golfe de Tunisia
84 J5 Gabgaba, Wadi watercourse Sudan
102 C5 Gabilan Ra California U.S.A.
31 M3 Gąbin Poland
145 G3 Gable End Foreland New Zealand
117 K9 Gable Mt British Columbia Canada
139 J7 Gabo isld Victoria Australia
28 C6 Gabol Denmark
86 B6 Gabon rep Equat Africa
89 D5 Gaborone Botswana
95 N2 Gabriels New York U.S.A.
16 C4 Gabriel y Galán, Embalse res Spain
77 F7 Gābrik Iran
46 G2 Gabrovo Bulgaria
85 B6 Gabú Guinea-Bissau
83 L14 Gaby isld Kerguelen Indian Oc
21 L4 Gacé France
77 B4 Gach Sārān Iran
20 F6 Gacilly, la France
98 G3 Gackle North Dakota U.S.A.
48 E7 Gacko Bosnia-Herzegovina
85 B3 Ga'da, Al Western Sahara
76 B3 Gadag India
86 G2 Gadamai Sudan
28 C5 Gadbjerg Denmark
26 G7 Gäddede Sweden
32 J8 Gadderbaum Germany
33 O5 Gadebusch Germany
80 D3 Gadish Israel
17 F8 Gador, Sierra de Spain
80 F1 Gadot Israel
118 E6 Gadsby Alberta Canada
111 L8 Gadsden Alabama U.S.A.
103 K9 Gadsden Arizona U.S.A.
28 J5 Gadstrup Denmark
76 C2 Gadwal India
54 F6 Gadyach Ukraine
89 G2 Gadzema Zimbabwe
86 C5 Gadzi Cent Afr Republic
20 F5 Gaël France
48 J6 Găeşti Romania
43 F7 Gaeta Italy
45 P8 Gaeta, Gulf of Italy
112 F2 Gaffney South Carolina U.S.A.
71 A2 Gafi isld Indonesia
38 L6 Gaflenz Austria
85 F2 Gafsa Tunisia
57 E4 Gafurov Tajikistan
57 H6 Gafurov Tajikistan
71 B3 Gag isld Indonesia
54 F1 Gagarin Russian Federation
106 B9 Gage New Mexico U.S.A.
107 L5 Gage Oklahoma U.S.A.
122 H7 Gage, C Prince Edward I Canada
99 R4 Gagen Wisconsin U.S.A.
19 O15 Gagère, P. de la mt France
122 F8 Gagetown New Brunswick Canada
36 E6 Gaggenau Germany
52 F6 Gagino Russian Federation
27 H11 Gagnef Sweden
85 C7 Gagnoa Ivory Coast
122 D2 Gagnon Quebec Canada
121 P6 Gagnon, L Quebec Canada
52 H4 Gagshor Russian Federation
66 F4 Gahe China
38 N6 Gahns mt Austria
89 A6 Gaiab watercourse Namibia
130 B5 Gaiba L Bolivia/Brazil
75 N6 Gaibanda Bangladesh
48 L4 Găiceana Romania
47 H10 Gaïdhouronísi isld Crete Greece
38 J8 Gail R Austria
36 H6 Gaildorf Germany
18 G9 Gaillac France
122 E1 Gaillarbois, L Quebec Canada
21 O2 Gailléfontaine France
21 N3 Gaillon France
38 G8 Gailtaler Alpen mts Austria
133 D6 Gaiman Argentina
37 L6 Gaimersheim Germany
94 B10 Gainesboro Tennessee U.S.A.
111 H9 Gainesville Alabama U.S.A.
113 E8 Gainesville Florida U.S.A.
109 K2 Gainesville Texas U.S.A.
13 G4 Gainford England
119 Q9 Gainsborough Saskatchewan Canada
13 H6 Gainsborough England
47 P13 Gáïos Greece
138 D4 Gairdner Lake South Australia Australia
15 C3 Gairloch Scotland
15 C4 Gairlochy Scotland
15 E3 Gairn R Scotland
38 L7 Gaishorn Austria
95 K7 Gaithersburg Maryland U.S.A.
65 E4 Gai Xian China
70 P9 Gajam Indonesia
76 B3 Gajendragara India
89 C6 Gakarosa mt S Africa
116 P5 Gakona Alaska U.S.A.
52 E4 Gakugsa Russian Federation
66 D6 Gala China
15 F5 Gala R Scotland
57 C5 Galaasiya Uzbekistan
77 H2 GāLā, Band-i- mts Afghanistan
83 K10 Galagedera Sri Lanka
118 F6 Galahad Alberta Canada
79 B9 Galâla el Baharîya, G. el mts Egypt
79 C10 Galâla el Qiblîya, G. el mts Egypt
17 G4 Galamocha Spain
88 G3 Galana R Kenya
69 G12 Galang Besar isld Indonesia
26 N3 Galanito Norway
48 D2 Galanta Slovakia
128 A7 Galapagos Is Pacific Oc
13 F2 Galashiels Scotland
101 O1 Galata Montana U.S.A.
46 F7 Galatás Greece
145 F3 Galatea New Zealand
106 G3 Galatea Colorado U.S.A.
137 R8 Galathea Depth Pacific Oc
48 L5 Galati Romania
110 H4 Galatia Illinois U.S.A.
107 M3 Galatia Kansas U.S.A.
43 J8 Galatina Italy
Galatz see Galati
19 O14 Galaure R France
94 G10 Galax Virginia U.S.A.
46 E6 Galaxídhion Greece
47 N10 Galaza Burun C Turkey
141 F3 Galbraith Queensland Australia
124 J5 Gal. Cepeda Mexico
26 C10 Galdhöpiggen mt Norway
124 F2 Galeana Mexico
130 G8 Galeào Brazil
45 L4 Galeata Italy
77 C6 Galeh Dār Iran
71 A2 Galela Indonesia
116 J4 Galena Alaska U.S.A.
99 Q7 Galena Illinois U.S.A.
107 Q4 Galena Kansas U.S.A.
95 M7 Galena Maryland U.S.A.
110 C5 Galena Missouri U.S.A.
109 G9 Galena Park Texas U.S.A.
33 T5 Galenbecker See L Germany
127 P3 Galeota Pt Trinidad
17 F7 Galera Spain
128 B3 Galera, Pta pt Ecuador
131 A8 Galera, Pta. de la Chile
99 Q9 Galesburg Illinois U.S.A.
94 B4 Galesburg Michigan U.S.A.
99 P5 Galesville Wisconsin U.S.A.
120 K1 Galeton Ontario Canada
98 B9 Galeton Colorado U.S.A.
94 K5 Galeton Pennsylvania U.S.A.
83 J13 Galets, Pte des Réunion Indian Oc
13 F6 Galgate England
83 K10 Galgiriya mt Sri Lanka
117 M11 Galiano I British Columbia Canada
19 Q14 Galibier, Col du pass France
100 B7 Galice Oregon U.S.A.
48 J1 Galich Ukraine
46 F1 Galiche Bulgaria
52 F5 Galichskoye, Oz L Russian Federation
16 B2 Galicia Spain
99 U8 Galien Michigan U.S.A.
141 H5 Galilee, L Queensland Australia
80 F2 Galilee, Sea of Israel
127 L2 Galina Pt Jamaica
94 E6 Galion Ohio U.S.A.
127 M4 Galion, Baie du Martinique W Indies
123 O2 Galissonnière, L.la Quebec Canada
43 C11 Galite, La Tunisia
103 O9 Galiurov Mts Arizona U.S.A.
140 D1 Galiwinku N Terr Australia
55 D3 Galkino Russian Federation
86 G3 Gallabat Sudan
42 B3 Gallarate Italy
21 O4 Gallardon France
99 N10 Gallatin Missouri U.S.A.
101 O4 Gallatin R Montana U.S.A.
110 K5 Gallatin Tennessee U.S.A.
109 M4 Gallatin Texas U.S.A.
101 O4 Gallatin Gateway Montana U.S.A.
101 O4 Gallatin Pk Montana U.S.A.
101 P4 Gallatin Ra Mont/Wyoming U.S.A.
83 K11 Galle Sri Lanka
17 G3 Gállego R Spain
133 C8 Gallegos R Argentina
106 G6 Gallegos New Mexico U.S.A.
45 J4 Galleno Italy
123 O2 Gallet L Quebec Canada
14 C5 Galley Hd Ireland
45 J3 Gallicano Italy
45 N6 Gallicano nel Lazio Italy
46 F4 Gallikós R Greece
33 Q5 Gallin Germany
106 D5 Gallina Pk New Mexico U.S.A.
44 D3 Gallinara isld Italy
106 E6 Gallinas New Mexico U.S.A.
108 B1 Gallinas Peak New Mexico U.S.A.
128 D1 Gallinas, Pta C Colombia
43 H8 Gallipoli Italy
Gallipoli Turkey see Gelibolu
94 E8 Gallipolis Ohio U.S.A.
94 J6 Gallitzin Pennsylvania U.S.A.
26 L4 Gällivare Sweden
45 Q7 Gallo Italy
17 F4 Gallo R Spain
26 H9 Gällö Sweden
43 E10 Gallo, C Sicily
17 F4 Gallocanta, L.de Spain
41 M5 Gallo, Lago di Italy
106 B8 Gallo Mts New Mexico U.S.A.
95 L3 Galloo I New York U.S.A.
7 M11 Galloper Lightship North Sea
15 D6 Galloway Scotland
27 F14 Gällstad Sweden
106 B6 Gallup New Mexico U.S.A.
17 G3 Gallur Spain
45 K4 Galluzzo Italy
85 F6 Galmi Niger
139 J5 Galong New South Wales Australia
83 K9 Galoya Sri Lanka
83 L10 Gal Oya R Sri Lanka
83 L10 Gal Oya Nat. Park Sri Lanka
124 H5 Gal. Simon Bolívar Mexico
28 C6 Galsted Denmark
12 D2 Galston Scotland
26 J9 Galström Sweden
102 C3 Galt California U.S.A.
99 N9 Galt Missouri U.S.A.
85 B3 Galtat Zemmour Western Sahara
28 D4 Galten Denmark
26 N1 Galten Norway
124 F3 Gal. Trías Mexico
41 M4 Galtür Austria
14 C4 Galtymore mt Ireland
99 R8 Galva Illinois U.S.A.
94 A6 Galveston Indiana U.S.A.
111 B12 Galveston Texas U.S.A.
131 E4 Galvez Argentina
14 B3 Galway co Ireland
14 B3 Galway Ireland
14 B3 Galway Bay Ireland
71 B3 Gam isld Indonesia
71 C3 Gam isld W Irian
21 O2 Gamaches France
61 L11 Gamagōri Japan
131 E8 Gama, I Argentina
94 B10 Gamaliel Kentucky U.S.A.
71 G4 Gamay Bay Philippines
75 N4 Gamba China
85 D6 Gambaga Ghana
21 O4 Gambais France
45 J4 Gambassi Terme Italy
45 R6 Gambatesa Italy
86 F4 Gambēla Ethiopia
116 B5 Gambell St Lawrence I, Alaska U.S.A.
45 M3 Gambettola Italy
85 A6 Gambia R The Gambia/Senegal
85 A6 Gambia, The rep W Africa
94 E6 Gambier Ohio U.S.A.
140 B1 Gambier, C N Terr Australia
138 D6 Gambier Is South Australia Australia
135 R15 Gambier Is Pacific Oc
113 L9 Gambier Village New Providence I Bahamas
124 F9 Gamboa Panama
86 C6 Gamboma Congo
141 G3 Gamboola Queensland Australia
86 C5 Gamboula Cent Afr Republic
71 H4 Gambuta mt Sulawesi
Gamcaka see Lelai
130 J10 Gameleira Brazil
71 A2 Gamkunoro Gunung mt Indonesia
71 A2 Gamlaba Indonesia
27 H14 Gamleby Sweden
26 M6 Gammelstad Sweden
36 G7 Gammertingen Germany
16 D4 Gamo R Spain
83 K10 Gampola Sri Lanka
77 G5 Gamshadzai K mts Iran
66 F5 Gamtog China
26 Q1 Gamvik Norway
18 E9 Gan France
73 L9 Gan Maldives
37 O6 Ganacker Germany
103 P6 Ganado Arizona U.S.A.
109 L6 Ganado Texas U.S.A.
121 O8 Gananoque Ontario Canada
67 C7 Gancheng China
Gand see Gent
87 B8 Ganda Angola
70 F6 Gandadiwata G mt Sulawesi
87 D7 Gandajika Zaire
74 B4 Gandava Pakistan
123 S5 Gander Newfoundland Canada
123 S4 Gander Bay Newfoundland Canada
32 J6 Ganderkesee Germany
123 R5 Gander R Newfoundland Canada
17 H3 Gandesa Spain
74 D7 Gāndhīdhām India
74 E7 Gāndhīnagar India
74 F6 Gāndhi Sāgar L India
17 G6 Gandia Spain
28 E2 Gandrup Denmark
103 L2 Gandy Utah U.S.A.
77 B5 Ganēveh Iran
83 K10 Ganewatta Sri Lanka
74 H5 Gangā R India
74 G9 Gangakher India
Gangā, Mouths of the see Ganges, Mouths of the
133 D6 Gan Gan Argentina
74 E4 Ganganagar India
68 B1 Gangaw Burma
76 C3 Gangawati India
75 R6 Gangaw Range Burma
66 C5 Gangdisê Shan mt ra China
25 F7 Gangelt Germany
Ganges R see Gangā R
18 H9 Ganges France
75 N8 Ganges, Mouths of the Bangladesh/India
27 F14 Gånghester Sweden
37 O7 Gangkofen Germany
65 F4 Gangou China
75 N5 Gangtok India
65 A6 Ganguyi China
67 E3 Gan Jiang R China
Ganjig see Horqin Zuoyi Houqi
139 H5 Ganmam New South Wales Australia
18 H6 Gannat France
6 L5 Gannet oil rig North Sea
145 E2 Gannet I New Zealand
101 L6 Gannett Idaho U.S.A.
101 Q6 Gannett Pk Wyoming U.S.A.
80 C5 Ganne Yehuda Israel
98 G5 Gannvalley South Dakota U.S.A.
80 C6 Gan Shelomo Israel
58 C3 Gansu prov China
85 C7 Ganta Liberia
Gantang see Taiping
143 A8 Gantheaume B W Australia Australia
138 E6 Gantheaume, C South Australia Australia
142 D4 Gantheaume Pt W Australia Australia
69 J14 Gantung Indonesia
67 E4 Gan Xian China
58 E4 Ganyanchi China
80 B6 Gan Yavne Israel
87 D11 Ganyesa S Africa
65 D7 Ganyu China
65 D4 Ganzhao China
Ganzhe see Minhou
67 E4 Ganzhou China
33 Q6 Ganzlin Germany
85 D5 Gao Mali
67 E2 Gao'an China
Gaobeidian see Xincheng
65 C5 Gaocheng China
67 F1 Gaochun China
Gaocun see Mayang
65 B5 Gaocun China
67 D5 Gaohe China
67 E1 Gaohebu China
65 A5 Gaojiabu China
65 A7 Gaoling China
67 B4 Gaolou Ling mt China
65 D6 Gaomi China
67 E4 Gaopi China
65 B7 Gaoping China
65 D6 Gaoqing China
67 C3 Gaosha China
65 B4 Gaoshan China
65 E3 Gaotaishan China
65 C6 Gaotang China
85 D6 Gaoua Burkina
85 B6 Gaoual Guinea
67 A2 Gao Xian China
65 C7 Gaoxianji China
58 G4 Gaoyang China
65 C6 Gaoyi China
59 G5 Gaoyou China
59 G5 Gaoyou Hu L China
67 C6 Gaozhou China
19 Q15 Gap France
71 E3 Gapan Luzon Philippines
19 P18 Gapeau R France
66 C5 Gar China
85 F3 Gara Brune Algeria
86 A2 Garadag Somalia
43 C11 Garaet Ichkeul L Tunisia
139 J3 Garah New South Wales Australia
47 H1 Gara Khitrino Bulgaria
14 C3 Gara, L Ireland
130 H10 Garanhuns Brazil
71 H9 Garantah Indonesia
130 F5 Garapuava Brazil
86 D4 Garba Cent Afr Republic
107 N5 Garber Oklahoma U.S.A.
100 B9 Garberville California U.S.A.
9 G3 Garboldisham England
130 E8 Garça Brazil
130 D4 Garças R Brazil
37 M7 Garching Germany
106 E4 Garcia Colorado U.S.A.
16 D5 García de Sola, Embalse de res Spain
130 D7 Garcias Brazil
18 H8 Gard dept France
18 H9 Gard R France
41 N6 Garda, Lago di Italy
19 O18 Gardanne France
98 J1 Gardar North Dakota U.S.A.
27 J15 Gårdby Sweden
33 O7 Gardelegen Germany
99 U4 Garden Michigan U.S.A.
100 J6 Gardena Idaho U.S.A.
98 F1 Gardena North Dakota U.S.A.
111 K7 Garden City Alabama U.S.A.
107 K4 Garden City Kansas U.S.A.
110 B3 Garden City Missouri U.S.A.
112 F5 Garden City South Carolina U.S.A.
98 J5 Garden City South Dakota U.S.A.
108 F4 Garden City Texas U.S.A.
101 O8 Garden City Utah U.S.A.
109 H7 Gardendale Texas U.S.A.
102 G8 Garden Grove California U.S.A.
99 N9 Garden Grove Iowa U.S.A.
142 A3 Garden I W Australia Australia
143 B9 Garden I W Australia Australia
99 V4 Garden I Michigan U.S.A.
111 G12 Garden I Bay Louisiana U.S.A.
140 B1 Garden Point N Terr Australia
119 V9 Gardenton Manitoba Canada
100 K5 Garden Valley Idaho U.S.A.
77 L3 Gardēz Afghanistan
120 J3 Gardiner Ontario Canada
95 S2 Gardiner Maine U.S.A.
101 P4 Gardiner Montana U.S.A.
106 F5 Gardiner New Mexico U.S.A.
100 A6 Gardiner Oregon U.S.A.
118 L7 Gardiner Dam Saskatchewan Canada
140 C5 Gardiner, Mt N Terr Australia
142 G4 Gardiner Ra Australia
95 P5 Gardiners I New York U.S.A.
140 B6 Gardiner's Range N Terr Australia
32 J4 Garding Germany
106 E4 Gardner Colorado U.S.A.
113 F10 Gardner Florida U.S.A.
99 S8 Gardner Illinois U.S.A.
95 P4 Gardner Massachusetts U.S.A.
95 U2 Gardner L Maine U.S.A.
102 E3 Gardnerville Nevada U.S.A.
31 K1 Gardno, Jezioro L Poland
27 G13 Gårdsjö Sweden
26 H6 Gardsjönas Sweden
27 J15 Gärdslösa Sweden
Gardula see Gīdolē
12 D1 Gare L Scotland
12 D1 Garelochhead Scotland
42 H3 Garešnica Croatia
44 D3 Garessio Italy
85 F3 Garet el Djenoun mt Algeria
45 H3 Garfagnane R Italy
110 C5 Garfield Arkansas U.S.A.
112 E5 Garfield Georgia U.S.A.
107 L3 Garfield Kansas U.S.A.
101 N9 Garfield Utah U.S.A.
100 H2 Garfield Washington U.S.A.
101 N5 Garfield Mt Idaho/Montana U.S.A.
46 E7 Gargaliánoi Greece
16 D5 Gargáligas R Spain
42 G7 Gargano, Promontorio del prom Italy
120 E5 Gargantua, C Ontario Canada
26 N2 Gargia Norway
41 N6 Gargnano Italy
26 J6 Gargnäs Sweden
13 F6 Gargrave England
12 D1 Gargunnock Scotland
52 B6 Gargždai Lithuania
74 H7 Garhakota India
55 D2 Gari Russian Federation
100 B4 Garibaldi Oregon U.S.A.
117 M11 Garibaldi Prov. Park British Columbia Canada
43 F7 Garigliano R Italy
15 F3 Garioch Scotland
88 G2 Garissa Kenya
119 R7 Garland Manitoba Canada
107 Q4 Garland Kansas U.S.A.
98 K9 Garland Nebraska U.S.A.
112 J3 Garland North Carolina U.S.A.
94 H5 Garland Pennsylvania U.S.A.
109 O9 Garland Texas U.S.A.
101 N8 Garland Utah U.S.A.
101 R5 Garland Wyoming U.S.A.
44 E1 Garlasco Italy
12 D4 Garlieston Scotland
18 E9 Garlin France
111 K10 Garlrand Alabama U.S.A.
32 M6 Garlstorf Germany
57 F5 Garm Tajikistan
41 O3 Garmisch-Partenkirchen Germany
77 H4 Garmsel reg Afghanistan
20 G8 Garnache, la France
99 P7 Garnavillo Iowa U.S.A.
122 J2 Garneau, R Quebec Canada
101 Q3 Garneill Montana U.S.A.
99 N6 Garner Iowa U.S.A.
112 J2 Garner North Carolina U.S.A.
118 E4 Garner Lake Prov. Park pk Alberta Canada
101 M3 Garnet Montana U.S.A.
115 M4 Garnet Bay Northwest Territories Canada
107 P3 Garnett Kansas U.S.A.
18 F9 Garonne R France
130 E11 Garopaba Brazil
74 F6 Garoth India
86 B4 Garoua Cameroon
86 B4 Garoua Boulai Cameroon
119 V3 Garraway Manitoba Canada
32 H7 Garrel Germany
98 K6 Garretson South Dakota U.S.A.
94 B5 Garrett Indiana U.S.A.
94 H7 Garrett Pennsylvania U.S.A.
101 U7 Garrett Wyoming U.S.A.
94 F5 Garrettsville Ohio U.S.A.
119 N5 Garrick Saskatchewan Canada
99 O7 Garrison Iowa U.S.A.
94 D8 Garrison Kentucky U.S.A.
99 N3 Garrison Minnesota U.S.A.
101 N3 Garrison Montana U.S.A.
95 O5 Garrison New York U.S.A.
98 E2 Garrison North Dakota U.S.A.
109 N4 Garrison Texas U.S.A.
103 L3 Garrison Utah U.S.A.
98 E2 Garrison Dam North Dakota U.S.A.
16 C5 Garrovillas Spain
15 D4 Garry L Scotland
115 K4 Garry L Northwest Territories Cañada
101 S4 Garryowen Montana U.S.A.
88 H3 Garsen Kenya
28 D5 Gårslev Denmark
27 G16 Gärsnäs Sweden
118 G2 Garson L Alberta Canada
32 M7 Garssen Germany
38 F7 Garsstein mt Austria
13 F6 Garstang England
13 F6 Garston England
144 B6 Garston New Zealand
18 F6 Gartempe R France
8 C3 Garth Wales
8 C2 Garthmyl Wales
Gartok see Garyarsa
33 O6 Gartow Germany
31 H2 Gartz Germany
70 M9 Garut Java
13 F2 Garvald Scotland
15 D3 Garve Scotland
144 B6 Garvie Mts New Zealand
31 N4 Garwolin Poland
100 J2 Garwood Idaho U.S.A.
109 L6 Garwood Texas U.S.A.
98 C9 Gary Colorado U.S.A.
99 T8 Gary Indiana U.S.A.
98 K2 Gary Minnesota U.S.A.
98 K5 Gary South Dakota U.S.A.
109 N3 Gary Texas U.S.A.
94 F9 Gary West Virginia U.S.A.
66 C5 Garyarsa China
60 F11 Garyū zan mt Japan
33 Q6 Garz Germany
58 C5 Garzê China
128 C3 Garzón Colombia
50 E5 Gasan-Kuli Turkmenistan
33 Q10 Gaschwitz Germany
45 J4 Gasciana Terme Italy
94 B6 Gas City Indiana U.S.A.
18 E9 Gascogne prov France
18 D8 Gascogne, G. de France/Spain
110 E3 Gasconade R Missouri U.S.A.
122 H5 Gascons Quebec Canada
98 C3 Gascoyne North Dakota U.S.A.
143 B7 Gascoyne Junction W Australia Australia
143 B6 Gascoyne, Mt W Australia Australia
143 A6 Gascoyne, R W Australia Australia
Gascuña, Golfo de see Gascogne, G.de
86 G2 Gash R Eritrea
85 G7 Gashaka Nigeria
74 G1 Gasherbrum mt Kashmir
85 G6 Gashua Nigeria
Gashuun Nuur L see Gaxun Nur
26 H4 Gaskacok mt Norway
21 O3 Gasny France
126 E4 Gaspar Cuba
127 J5 Gaspar Hernández Dominican Rep
113 E11 Gasparilla isld Florida U.S.A.
69 H14 Gaspar, Selat str Indonesia
122 H5 Gaspé Quebec Canada
122 H5 Gaspé, B. de Quebec Canada
122 H5 Gaspé, C Quebec Canada
122 F5 Gaspé Pen Quebec Canada
122 H9 Gaspereau L Nova Scotia Canada
122 G7 Gaspereau Forks New Brunswick Canada
122 F5 Gaspésie, Parc de la Quebec Canada
100 B8 Gasquet California U.S.A.
61 O7 Gassan mt Japan
94 G8 Gassaway West Virginia U.S.A.
25 G3 Gasselte Netherlands
85 F2 Gassi, El Algeria
40 G7 Gassino Tor Italy
44 C1 Gassino Torinese Italy
85 G7 Gassol Nigeria
103 J5 Gass Pk Nevada U.S.A.
28 E3 Gassum Denmark
38 H7 Gasteiner Tal Austria
100 B4 Gaston Oregon U.S.A.
112 F2 Gastonia North Carolina U.S.A.
94 J10 Gaston, L Virginia U.S.A.
47 O12 Gastoúri Greece
133 D6 Gastre Argentina
17 F8 Gata, C.de Spain
117 K6 Gataga R British Columbia Canada
48 G5 Gătaia Romania
16 C4 Gata, Sa. de mts Spain
52 D5 Gatchina Russian Federation
108 D7 Gate Oklahoma U.S.A.
94 E10 Gate City Virginia U.S.A.
12 D4 Gatehouse of Fleet Scotland
100 C5 Gates Oregon U.S.A.
13 G4 Gateshead England
116 L3 Gates of the Arctic Nat Park and Preserve Alaska U.S.A.
101 O3 Gates of the Mts pass Montana U.S.A.
112 L1 Gatesville North Carolina U.S.A.
109 K4 Gatesville Texas U.S.A.
106 B3 Gateway Colorado U.S.A.
100 K1 Gateway Montana U.S.A.
100 D5 Gateway Oregon U.S.A.
21 L7 Gâtine reg France
121 P5 Gatineau R Quebec Canada
121 P7 Gatineau Quebec Canada
21 J8 Gâtine Hauteurs de hills France
112 D2 Gatlinburg Tennessee U.S.A.
80 D1 Ga'ton Israel
Gatooma see Kadoma
33 S8 Gatow Germany
61 N7 Gatsugi Japan
20 H2 Gatteville France
41 H6 Gattinara Italy
141 K8 Gatton Queensland Australia
124 E9 Gatun Panama
125 O5 Gatún L Panama
9 F5 Gatwick Airport England
36 E4 Gau-Algesheim Germany
21 H8 Gaubretiére, la France
16 D8 Gaucin Spain
16 D6 Gaudalmeliato R Spain
77 H5 Gaud-I-Zirreh salt desert Afghanistan
123 K3 Gaudreault, L Quebec Canada
119 U1 Gauer L Manitoba Canada
Gauhati see Guwahati
26 E9 Gauldalen R Norway
94 F8 Gauley Bridge West Virginia U.S.A.
21 M5 Gault, le France
123 R6 Gaultois Newfoundland Canada
21 N5 Gault-St.Denis, le France
69 F13 Gaung Sumatra
36 E4 Gau-Odernheim Germany
66 D6 Gauri Sankar mt Nepal/China
27 D10 Gausdal, Ö Norway
27 D10 Gausdal, V Norway
27 C12 Gausta mt Norway
77 G7 Gavāter Iran
77 C6 Gāvbandī Iran
77 C6 Gavbus Kūh-e mt Iran
46 F10 Gavdhopoúlu isld Greece
46 G10 Gávdhos isld Crete Greece
18 E9 Gave de Pau R France
130 H4 Gavião, R Brazil
106 C5 Gavilan New Mexico U.S.A.

D7 Gaviota California U.S.A.
E5 Gāv Koshī Iran
J11 Gävle Sweden
J11 Gävlebukten B Sweden
H4 Gavray France
G6 Gavre, le France
E6 Gavrilov Yam Russian Federation
F5 Gavrino Russian Federation
G7 Gávrion Greece
G8 Gawilgarh India
E5 Gawler South Australia Australia
D4 Gawler Ranges South Australia Australia
H8 Gåxsjö Sweden
D3 Gaxun Nur L China
S2 Gay Michigan U.S.A.
L6 Gaya India
E6 Gaya Niger
F6 Gaya Nigeria
H3 Gaya R Spain
H3 Gaya He R China
F2 Gaya, Pulau isld Sabah
E3 Gaydon England
M2 Gaylord Kansas U.S.A.
C1 Gaylord Michigan U.S.A.
M5 Gaylord Minnesota U.S.A.
A7 Gaylord Oregon U.S.A.
K7 Gayndah Queensland Australia
H4 Gayny Russian Federation
M2 Gaysin Ukraine
Q6 Gays Mills Wisconsin U.S.A.
E5 Gayutino Russian Federation
J7 Gayville South Dakota U.S.A.
M2 Gayvoron Ukraine
E7 Gaza Egypt
F6 Gazaoua Niger
A7 Gaza Strip Israel
C8 Gazelle California U.S.A.
O4 Gazeran France
D4 Gazgan Uzbekistan
F3 Gaziantep Turkey
D3 Gazipaşa Turkey
C4 Gazli Uzbekistan
J1 Gazoldo degli Ippoliti Italy
K1 Gazzo Veronese Italy
J1 Gazzuolo Italy
C7 Gbanga Liberia
F7 Gboko Nigeria
L1 Gdańsk Poland
C5 Gdov Russian Federation
L1 Gdynia Poland
B7 Ge'a Israel
B3 Gearhart Oregon U.S.A.
E7 Gearhart Mt Oregon U.S.A.
M6 Geary Oklahoma U.S.A.
B3 Gebe isld Indonesia
K1 Gebesee Germany
N11 Gebze Turkey
G3 Gedaref Sudan
F3 Geddes R Queensland Australia
H6 Geddes South Dakota U.S.A.
F3 Geddington England
G3 Gedern Germany
H7 Gedesby Denmark
L9 Gede, Tg C Java
C4 Gedhus Denmark
H4 Gedinne Belgium
K5 Gediz Turkey
J6 Gediz R Turkey
H4 Gedlegubē Ethiopia
Gedong see Fangshan
B4 Gedong Sarawak
H7 Gedser Denmark
C3 Gedsted Denmark
K8 Gedungpakuan Sumatra
E4 Geegully Ck W Australia Australia
H1 Geel Belgium
G7 Geelong Victoria Australia
A8 Geelvink Chan W Australia Australia
A7 Geel Vloer S Africa
D6 Geers Ferry L Arkansas U.S.A.
C5 Geertruidenberg Netherlands
J5 Geestekanal Germany
J5 Geestenseth Germany
M6 Geesthacht Germany
J2 Geetbets Belgium
H9 Geeveston Tasmania Australia
M3 Gefell Germany
C7 Gefen Israel
M3 Gefrees Germany
E2 Gegenmiao China
D5 Gegu China
G7 Gehaku lighthouse S Korea
G2 Gehau Germany
N7 Gehée France
L8 Gehrden Germany
F1 Ge Hu L China
G6 Geidam Nigeria
P3 Geierspitze mt Austria
B2 Geikie I Ontario Canada
G2 Geikie Ra Queensland Australia
F7 Geilenkirchen Germany
C11 Geilo Norway
R5 Geilow Germany
E5 Geinsheim Germany
B9 Geiranger Norway
N6 Geiselhöring Germany
J4 Geiselwind Germany
M6 Geisenfeld Germany
N7 Geisenhausen Germany
D3 Geisenheim Germany
J2 Geisingen Germany
F7 Geislingen Germany
H6 Geislingen an der Steige Germany
J1 Geismar Germany
D6 Geispolsheim France
D3 Geita Tanzania
O1 Geithain Germany
D12 Geithus Norway
G6 Geittind mt Norway
R5 Gejiu China
F11 Gela R Sicily
F11 Gela Sicily
J4 Geladī Ethiopia
F3 Gelai mt Tanzania
Q4 Gelbensande Germany
J4 Gelchsheim Germany
F3 Gelderingen Netherlands
F4 Gelderland Netherlands
D5 Geldermalsen Netherlands
F5 Geldern Germany
E6 Geldrop Netherlands
J5 Gelembe Turkey
O2 Gelenau Germany
M8 Gelert Ontario Canada
H4 Gelibolu Turkey
D1 Gelicek Turkey
H1 Gelinbuğday Turkey
J2 Gelinden Belgium
F4 Geling China
J4 Gelinsoor Somalia
L9 Gelinting Flores Indonesia
G3 Gelnhausen Germany
C6 Gelså R Denmark
Gelsdorf see Grafschaft
F9 Gelsenkirchen Germany
D6 Gelsted Denmark
D7 Gelting Germany
G14 Gelumbang Sumatra
E8 Gem Alberta Canada
K2 Gem Kansas U.S.A.
F11 Gemas Malaysia
H2 Gembloux Belgium
E9 Gemen Germany
C5 Gemena Zaire
P18 Gémenos France
F2 Gemerek Turkey
H3 Gemerī Häyk' L Ethiopia
E5 Gemert Netherlands
K4 Gemlik Körfezi B Turkey
K2 Gemmenich Belgium
F5 Gemmingen Germany
E2 Gemona del Friuli Italy
E7 Gémozac France
J4 Gemsa Egypt
89 B5 Gemsbok Nat. Park Botswana
36 B2 Gemünd Germany
36 H3 Gemünden Bayern Germany
36 F2 Gemünden Hessen Germany
36 D4 Gemünden Rheinland-Pfalz Germany
70 E7 Gemuru Kalimantan
86 H4 Genalē R Ethiopia
22 G2 Genappe Belgium
27 F16 Genarp Sweden
45 N6 Genazzano Italy
78 H2 Genç Turkey
18 F6 Gençay France
25 F5 Gendringen Netherlands
107 N7 Gene Autry Oklahoma U.S.A.
86 D3 Geneina Sudan
25 F3 Genemuiden Netherlands
133 E5 General Acha Argentina
133 E5 General Alvear Argentina
131 C5 General Alvear Mendoza Argentina
130 C9 General Aquvino Paraguay
133 E4 General Arenales Argentina
130 C10 General Artigas Paraguay
146 E6 General Belgrano II Argentina Base Antarctica
146 D3 General Bernardo O'Higgins Chile Base Graham Land Antarctica
130 D4 General Caneiro Brazil
133 E3 General Capdevila Argentina
102 F5 General Grant Grove Sctn California U.S.A.
133 F5 General Guido Argentina
17 G5 Generalísimo, Emb. de Spain
133 F3 General José de San Martín Argentina
133 E5 General La Madrid Argentina
133 F5 General Lavalle Argentina
71 G6 General Luna Philippines
71 G5 General MacArthur Philippines
133 F5 General Madariaga Argentina
128 E8 General Martin M. de Güemes Argentina
130 B10 General Paz Argentina
133 C6 General Paz, L Argentina
146 C5 General San Martín Argentina Base Antarctica
71 G7 General Santos Philippines
47 J1 General Toshevo Bulgaria
109 H9 General Treviño Mexico
133 E5 General Viamonte Argentina
100 J3 Genesee Idaho U.S.A.
94 D3 Genesee Michigan U.S.A.
94 K4 Genesee R New York U.S.A.
99 Q8 Geneseo Illinois U.S.A.
107 M3 Geneseo Kansas U.S.A.
94 K4 Geneseo New York U.S.A.
20 G7 Geneston France
20 H4 Genêts France
Geneva see Genève
111 L10 Geneva Alabama U.S.A.
111 M9 Geneva Georgia U.S.A.
94 C6 Geneva Indiana U.S.A.
98 J9 Geneva Nebraska U.S.A.
94 G5 Geneva Ohio U.S.A.
109 O4 Geneva Texas U.S.A.
Geneva, L see Léman, Lac
99 S7 Geneva, L Wisconsin U.S.A.
120 J6 Geneva Lake Mine Ontario Canada
40 D5 Genève Switzerland
36 E7 Gengenbach Germany
68 D1 Gengma China
Genhe see Ergun Zuoqi
59 H1 Gen He R China
120 J3 Genier Ontario Canada
16 E7 Genil R Spain
21 N7 Génillé France
58 E4 Genjiawan China
22 K2 Genk Belgium
60 D12 Genkai-nada sea Japan
40 B3 Genlis France
25 E5 Gennep Netherlands
28 C6 Genner Denmark
21 K7 Gennes Maine-et-Loire France
21 J6 Gennes Mayenne France
21 H6 Gennes-sur-Seiche France
21 L6 Genneteil France
21 P4 Gennevilliers France
Genoa see Genova
139 J6 Genoa Victoria Australia
106 G2 Genoa Colorado U.S.A.
113 E7 Genoa Florida U.S.A.
99 S7 Genoa Illinois U.S.A.
98 J8 Genoa Nebraska U.S.A.
102 E2 Genoa Nevada U.S.A.
94 D5 Genoa Ohio U.S.A.
99 P6 Genoa Wisconsin U.S.A.
99 S7 Genoa City Wisconsin U.S.A.
101 O1 Genou Montana U.S.A.
21 O7 Genouilly Cher France
44 E3 Genova Italy
128 B7 Genovesa isld Galapagos Is
51 P1 Genriyetty, Ostrov isld Russian Federation
22 F1 Gent Belgium
70 P9 Genteng Indonesia
70 L9 Genteng Java
33 Q8 Genthin Germany
111 K12 Gentilly New Orleans, Louisiana U.S.A.
69 H11 Genting isld Indonesia
118 B1 Gent Lon Manitoba Canada
29 K5 Gentofte Denmark
110 B5 Gentry Arkansas U.S.A.
99 M9 Gentry Missouri U.S.A.
45 N6 Genzano di Roma Italy
48 H5 Geoagiu Romania
143 B10 Geographe B W Australia Australia
143 A6 Geographe Chan W Australia Australia
107 M2 Geographic Center of US Kansas U.S.A.
22 H3 Geopinnes Belgium
138 D3 George R South Australia Australia
115 N6 George R Quebec Canada
83 M14 George C Kerguelen Indian Oc
89 C9 George S Africa
116 J5 George R Alaska U.S.A.
99 L6 George Iowa U.S.A.
123 L8 George B Nova Scotia Canada
140 B6 George Gills Ra N Terr Australia
139 J6 George, L New South Wales Australia
138 F6 George, L South Australia Australia
142 E5 George, L W Australia Australia
99 W3 George, L Ontario Canada
88 C1 George, L Uganda
116 N6 George, L Alaska U.S.A.
113 F8 George, L Florida U.S.A.
37 L5 Georgensgmünd Germany
37 K2 Georgenthal Germany
90 C4 Georges Bank Atlantic Oc
144 A6 George Sd New Zealand
90 A11 Georgetown Ascension I
141 G4 Georgetown Queensland Australia
138 E5 Georgetown South Australia Australia
139 H8 George Town Tasmania Australia
122 K7 Georgetown Prince Edward I Canada
129 G2 Georgetown Guyana
69 E10 Georgetown Malaysia
144 C6 Georgetown New Zealand
127 O8 Georgetown St Vincent
85 B6 Georgetown The Gambia
110 E6 Georgetown Arkansas U.S.A.
102 D3 Georgetown California U.S.A.
95 M8 Georgetown Delaware U.S.A.
113 F8 Georgetown Florida U.S.A.
111 L10 Georgetown Georgia U.S.A.
101 O7 Georgetown Idaho U.S.A.
99 T10 Georgetown Illinois U.S.A.
94 C8 Georgetown Kentucky U.S.A.
111 F10 Georgetown Mississippi U.S.A.
94 D8 Georgetown Ohio U.S.A.
112 H4 Georgetown South Carolina U.S.A.
109 K5 Georgetown Texas U.S.A.
126 D5 George Town Grand Cayman W Indies
121 S7 Georgeville Quebec Canada
146 C6 George VI Sound Antarctica
146 D13 George V Land Antarctica
109 J7 George West Texas U.S.A.
112 C5 Georgia state U.S.A.
53 F12 Georgia rep W Asia
111 K10 Georgiana Alabama U.S.A.
120 J7 Georgian B Ontario Canada
117 L11 Georgia, St. of British Columbia Canada
140 E5 Georgina R N Terr Australia
140 E5 Georgina R N Terr/Queensland Australia
140 E5 Georgina R Queensland Australia
140 E4 Georgina Cr N Terr Australia
47 J2 Georgi Traykov Bulgaria
Georgiu-Dezh see Liski
53 F11 Georgiyevsk Russian Federation
32 F7 Georgsdorf Germany
32 F6 Georgsheil Germany
32 H8 Georgsmarienhütte Germany
146 G6 Georg von Neumayer Germany Base Antarctica
41 N4 Gepatschhaus Austria
21 J4 Ger France
28 E2 Gerå R Denmark
37 K2 Gera R Germany
37 N2 Gera Germany
22 F2 Geraardsbergen Belgium
36 H5 Gerabronn Germany
119 Q8 Gerald Saskatchewan Canada
110 E3 Gerald Missouri U.S.A.
143 A8 Geraldine W Australia Australia
144 C6 Geraldine New Zealand
101 P2 Geraldine Montana U.S.A.
51 S2 Geral'd, Ostrov islds Russian Federation
143 A8 Geraldton W Australia Australia
120 C3 Geraldton Ontario Canada
120 D3 Geraldton Ontario Canada
130 E10 Geral, Serra mts Brazil
80 B8 Gerar R Israel
19 K4 Gérardmer France
143 E7 Gerard, Mt W Australia Australia
80 G4 Gerasa Jordan
55 F2 Gerasimovka Russian Federation
100 C9 Gerber California U.S.A.
100 D7 Gerber Res Oregon U.S.A.
33 P9 Gerbstedt Germany
36 H4 Gerchsheim Germany
78 H3 Gercuş Turkey
116 L6 Gerdine, Mt Alaska U.S.A.
78 D1 Gerede Turkey
77 J4 Gereshk Afghanistan
17 F7 Gérgal Spain
40 A4 Gergy France
37 K3 Gerhardtsgereuth Germany
69 E10 Gerik Malaysia
98 C8 Gering Nebraska U.S.A.
37 O1 Geringswalde Germany
100 F9 Gerlach Nevada U.S.A.
48 F1 Gerlachovsky mt Slovakia
36 H4 Gerlachsheim Germany
28 H5 Gerlev Denmark
28 G6 Gerlev Denmark
36 G6 Gerlingen Germany
38 E7 Gerlostal R Austria
133 E4 Germania Argentina
117 L8 Germansen Landing British Columbia Canada
110 G3 Germantown Illinois U.S.A.
95 K7 Germantown Maryland U.S.A.
95 O4 Germantown New York U.S.A.
94 C7 Germantown Ohio U.S.A.
110 G6 Germantown Tennessee U.S.A.
30 D5 Germany rep Europe
47 J7 Germencik Turkey
37 L7 Germering Germany
36 E5 Germersheim Germany
89 F6 Germiston S Africa
28 C5 Gerndrup Denmark
36 E6 Gernsbach Germany
36 F4 Gernsheim Germany
61 L10 Gero Japan
70 P10 Gerokgak Bali Indonesia
36 B3 Gerolstein Germany
37 J4 Gerolzhofen Germany
100 G1 Gerome Washington U.S.A.
17 J2 Gerona prov Spain
17 J2 Gerona Spain
17 J3 Gerona Spain
103 O8 Geronimo Arizona U.S.A.
107 M7 Geronimo Oklahoma U.S.A.
139 K5 Gerringong New South Wales Australia
18 F9 Gers dept France
18 F9 Gers R France
36 H3 Gersfeld Germany
36 F4 Gersprenz R Germany
37 J6 Gerstetten Herbrechtingen Germany
37 K7 Gersthofen Germany
37 J2 Gerstingen Germany
116 P5 Gerstle R Alaska U.S.A.
33 T6 Gerswalde Germany
140 B3 Gertrude, Mt N Terr Australia
48 K2 Gertsa Ukraine
80 C4 Gerulim Israel
19 O15 Gervanne R France
66 C5 Gêrzê China
78 E1 Gerze Turkey
37 N7 Gerzen Germany
32 E9 Gescher Germany
32 J9 Geseke Germany
80 D1 Gesher HaZiv Israel
22 H4 Gespunsart France
37 K7 Gessertshausen Germany
44 B3 Gesso R Italy
21 H7 Gesté France
28 C5 Gesten Denmark
86 H4 Gestro, Wabē R Ethiopia
26 H8 Gesunden L Sweden
29 H11 Geta Finland
16 E4 Getafe Spain
100 H8 Getchell Mine Nevada U.S.A.
22 J2 Gete R Belgium
123 M3 Gethsémani Quebec Canada
28 A3 Gettrup Denmark
95 K7 Gettysburg Pennsylvania U.S.A.
98 G5 Gettysburg South Dakota U.S.A.
67 B4 Getu He R China
130 D10 Getúlio Vargas Brazil
146 B8 Getz Ice Shelf Antarctica
107 N4 Geuda Springs Kansas U.S.A.
69 C11 Geumapang R Sumatra
69 C10 Geumpang Sumatra
69 C10 Geureudong, Gunung mt Sumatra
139 J4 Geurie New South Wales Australia
80 C3 Geva' Karmel Israel
32 F10 Gevelsberg Germany
80 B7 Gever'am Israel
20 G5 Geveze France
33 S5 Gevezin Germany
46 E3 Gevgelija Macedonia
19 K6 Gex France
79 C2 Geydik Dağ mt Turkey
37 O2 Geyer Germany
36 G4 Geyersberg mt Germany
47 H5 Geyikli Turkey
101 P2 Geyser Montana U.S.A.
81 B7 Geyser, Banc du Madagascar
28 S9 Geysir Iceland
47 L4 Geyve Turkey
84 D3 Ghadāmis Libya
80 G2 Ghadir al Bustan Syria
73 N3 Ghaghara R India
85 D7 Ghana rep W Africa
84 E5 Ghanīmah, Jabal Bin mts Libya
89 B3 Ghanzi Botswana
89 C4 Ghanzi dist Botswana
80 E7 Ghar R Jordan
78 K6 Gharab Iraq
85 E2 Ghardaia Algeria
43 B12 Ghardimaou Tunisia
43 C11 Ghar El Melh Tunisia
84 J4 Gharib, Gebel Egypt
84 E3 Gharyan Libya
84 E5 Ghāt Libya
75 M7 Ghatsila India
86 E4 Ghazāl, Al prov Sudan
17 F9 Ghazaouet Algeria
74 G4 Ghaziabad India
77 L3 Ghaznī prov Afghanistan
77 K3 Ghaznī prov Afghanistan
77 K3 Ghazoor Afghanistan
99 O2 Gheen Minnesota U.S.A.
Ghent see Gent
94 B8 Ghent Kentucky U.S.A.
99 L5 Ghent Minnesota U.S.A.
Gheorghe Gheorghiu-Dei see Oneşti
48 K4 Gheorgheni Romania
48 H3 Gherla Romania
43 B8 Ghilarza Sardinia
48 K4 Ghimeş Făget Romania
133 C7 Ghio, L Argentina
22 F2 Ghislenghien Belgium
77 J3 Ghizao Afghanistan
118 L1 Ghost R Ontario Canada
117 Q4 Ghost L Northwest Territories Canada
117 P9 Ghost Mt British Columbia Canada
77 J2 Ghowr prov Afghanistan
86 E3 Ghubaysh Sudan
Ghudamis see Ghadāmis
79 H4 Ghunthur Syria
77 G2 Ghūriān Afghanistan
22 D1 Ghyvelde France
68 H7 Gia Dinh Vietnam
68 H6 Gia Nghia Vietnam
42 D6 Giannutri, I.di Italy
89 F7 Giants Castle mt S Africa
14 E1 Giant's Causeway N Ireland
83 K9 Giants Tank L Sri Lanka
70 P10 Gianyar Indonesia
69 G8 Gia Rai Vietnam
43 G11 Giarre Sicily
18 G7 Giat France
44 B1 Giaveno Italy
126 F4 Gibara Cuba
98 H9 Gibbon Nebraska U.S.A.
100 G4 Gibbon Oregon U.S.A.
101 M4 Gibbons Pass Montana U.S.A.
101 M4 Gibbonsville Idaho U.S.A.
142 F3 Gibb River W Australia Australia
99 S3 Gibbs City Michigan U.S.A.
146 D3 Gibbs I S Shetland Is Antarctica
143 C10 Gibbs, Mt W Australia Australia
87 C11 Gibeon Namibia
26 K2 Gibostad Norway
16 C7 Gibraleón Spain
16 D8 Gibraltar colony S W Europe
127 J10 Gibraltar Venezuela
16 D9 Gibraltar, Str of Spain/Africa
111 C9 Gibsland Louisiana U.S.A.
100 C8 Gibson California U.S.A.
112 E4 Gibson Georgia U.S.A.
101 Q3 Gibson Montana U.S.A.
94 D5 Gibsonburg Ohio U.S.A.
99 S9 Gibson City Illinois U.S.A.
143 D6 Gibson Des W Australia Australia
117 M11 Gibsons British Columbia Canada
143 D10 Gibson Soak W Australia Australia
113 E10 Gibsonton Florida U.S.A.
112 H1 Gibsonville North Carolina U.S.A.
58 B2 Gichgeniyn Nuruu mt Mongolia
52 H5 Gidayevo Russian Federation
79 D8 Giddi, G el Egypt
109 L5 Giddings Texas U.S.A.
26 K8 Gideă Sweden
26 K8 Gideå R Sweden
110 G5 Gideon Missouri U.S.A.
141 F6 Gideon, Mt Queensland Australia
138 F3 Gidgealpa Gas Field South Australia Australia
143 F8 Gidgi, L W Australia Australia
31 L5 Gidle Poland
86 G4 Gīdolē Ethiopia
36 H4 Giebelstadt Germany
32 M9 Gieboldehausen Germany
18 G5 Gien France
37 J6 Giengen Germany
19 Q18 Giens France
19 N13 Gier R France
33 P7 Giesenslage Germany
36 F2 Giessen Germany
25 G2 Gieten Netherlands
25 F3 Giethoorn Netherlands
84 J4 Gifatin I Egypt
13 F2 Gifford Scotland
113 G10 Gifford Florida U.S.A.
99 N7 Gifford Iowa U.S.A.
100 G1 Gifford Washington U.S.A.
33 N8 Gifhorn Germany
61 K10 Gifu Japan
124 D5 Giganta, Sa de la Mexico
124 E9 Gigante Panama
124 G3 Gigantes, Llanos de los Mexico
15 C5 Gigha isld Scotland
42 D6 Giglio, I. del Italy
18 H9 Gignac France
19 P17 Gignac France
19 O18 Gignac France
40 F6 Gignod Italy
16 D1 Gijón Spain
103 P9 Gila R Arizona U.S.A.
106 B9 Gila New Mexico U.S.A.
103 M9 Gila Bend Arizona U.S.A.
103 L8 Gila Bend Mts Arizona U.S.A.
106 B8 Gila Cliff Dwellings Nat.Mon New Mexico U.S.A.
103 K9 Gila Mts Arizona U.S.A.
78 K4 Gilān-e Gharb Iran
121 R5 Gilardo Dam Quebec Canada
71 B2 Gila, Tanjong C Indonesia
48 H4 Gilău Romania
141 F3 Gilbert R Queensland Australia
103 N8 Gilbert Arizona U.S.A.
99 O2 Gilbert Minnesota U.S.A.
102 G3 Gilbert Nevada U.S.A.
94 F9 Gilbert West Virginia U.S.A.
137 P2 Gilbert Is Pacific Oc
117 L10 Gilbert, Mt British Columbia Canada
116 O6 Gilbert, Mt Alaska U.S.A.
111 H10 Gilbertown Alabama U.S.A.
101 P9 Gilbert Pk Utah U.S.A.
119 R7 Gilbert Plains Manitoba Canada
141 G4 Gilbert River Queensland Australia
28 J4 Gilbjerghoved C Denmark
129 J5 Gilbués Brazil
98 J1 Gilby North Dakota U.S.A.
98 B9 Gilcrest Colorado U.S.A.
13 G6 Gildersome England
26 G4 Gildeskal Norway
101 P1 Gildford Montana U.S.A.
88 G10 Gilé Mozambique
95 R2 Gilead Maine U.S.A.
98 J9 Gilead Nebraska U.S.A.
143 G6 Giles W Australia Australia
143 G7 Giles W Australia Australia
108 G1 Giles Texas U.S.A.
143 C8 Giles, L W Australia Australia
140 B5 Giles Ra N Terr Australia
84 H5 Gilf Kebir Plateau Egypt
139 K3 Gilgai New South Wales Australia
139 J4 Gilgandra New South Wales Australia
80 E6 Gilgat Jordan
139 J3 Gil Gil R New South Wales Australia
88 F2 Gilgil Kenya
74 F1 Gilgit Kashmir
139 H4 Gilgunnia New South Wales Australia
117 J9 Gil I British Columbia Canada
70 P10 Gilimanuk Bali Indonesia
79 D2 Gilindire Turkey
46 D1 Giljeva Planina mt Serbia Yugoslavia
98 B9 Gill Colorado U.S.A.
115 K6 Gillam Manitoba Canada
28 J4 Gilleleje Denmark
143 E7 Gillen, L W Australia Australia
140 C6 Gillen, Mt N Terr Australia
138 D4 Gilles, L South Australia Australia
103 M8 Gillespie Arizona U.S.A.
110 G2 Gillespie Illinois U.S.A.
144 B5 Gillespies Pt New Zealand
111 E7 Gillett Arkansas U.S.A.
95 L5 Gillett Pennsylvania U.S.A.
109 K6 Gillett Texas U.S.A.
99 S5 Gillett Wisconsin U.S.A.
98 A5 Gillette Wyoming U.S.A.
109 N1 Gillham Arkansas U.S.A.
26 G9 Gillhov Sweden
110 C2 Gilliam Missouri U.S.A.
141 F5 Gilliat R Queensland Australia
141 F5 Gilliat Queensland Australia
13 G5 Gilling England
8 D5 Gillingham England
9 G5 Gillingham England
109 O5 Gillis Louisiana U.S.A.
14 C2 Gill, L Ireland
146 J11 Gillock I isld Antarctica
99 T4 Gills Rock Wisconsin U.S.A.
22 G3 Gilly Belgium
99 S9 Gilman Illinois U.S.A.
99 O8 Gilman Iowa U.S.A.
101 N2 Gilman Montana U.S.A.
99 Q4 Gilman Wisconsin U.S.A.
110 C1 Gilman City Missouri U.S.A.
109 N3 Gilmer Texas U.S.A.
101 M5 Gilmore Idaho U.S.A.
99 M7 Gilmore City Iowa U.S.A.
121 N8 Gilmour Ontario Canada
86 F4 Gilo R Ethiopia
48 H6 Gilort R Romania
117 N9 Gilpin British Columbia Canada
118 L8 Gilroy Saskatchewan Canada
102 C4 Gilroy California U.S.A.
28 R9 Gilsfjördhur inlet Iceland
13 F3 Gilsland England
98 H9 Giltner Nebraska U.S.A.
8 C4 Gilwern Wales
51 M3 Gilyuy R Russian Federation
86 D3 Gimbala mt Sudan
127 O8 Gimie mt St Lucia
101 L6 Gimlet Idaho U.S.A.
119 V8 Gimli Manitoba Canada
27 K11 Gimo Sweden
52 D3 Gimoly Russian Federation
18 F9 Gimone R France
18 F9 Gimont France
26 G3 Gimsöy Norway
80 C6 Gimzo Israel
19 P17 Ginasservis France
141 J6 Gindie Queensland Australia
76 D4 Gingee India
36 H6 Gingen Germany
127 J2 Ginger Hill Jamaica
141 K6 Gin Gin Queensland Australia
143 B9 Gingin W Australia Australia
71 G6 Gingoog B Philippines
86 H4 Ginir Ethiopia
80 E3 Ginnegar Israel
28 F4 Ginnerup Denmark
80 F2 Ginnosar Israel
43 H8 Ginosa Italy
61 P13 Ginowan Okinawa
16 B2 Ginzo de Limia Spain
45 K3 Giogo di Casaglia Italy
45 K3 Giogo di Scarperia Italy
45 P6 Gioia dei Marsi Italy
43 G10 Gioia,G.di Italy
45 Q7 Gioia Sannitica Italy
46 E6 Gióna mt Greece
41 J5 Giornico Switzerland
43 H9 Giovanni in Fiore, S Italy
45 K4 Giovi mt Italy
139 H7 Gippsland Victoria Australia
139 J7 Gippsland Basin Oil & Gas Fields Victoria Australia
142 A6 Giralia W Australia Australia
31 N6 Giraltovce Slovakia
40 D1 Girancourt France
77 F5 Giran Rig mt Iran
99 R10 Girard Illinois U.S.A.
107 Q4 Girard Kansas U.S.A.
94 G5 Girard Ohio U.S.A.
94 G4 Girard Pennsylvania U.S.A.
108 G2 Girard Texas U.S.A.
128 D3 Girardot Colombia
15 F3 Girdle Ness Scotland
78 G1 Giresun Turkey
84 J4 Girga Egypt
74 D8 Gir Hills India
86 C5 Giri R Zaire
75 M6 Giridih India
139 H4 Girilambone New South Wales Australia
83 K10 Giriulla Sri Lanka
19 K5 Giromagny France
Girona see Gerona
18 E7 Gironde R France
18 E8 Gironde dept France
17 J2 Gironella Spain
18 G9 Girou R France
119 V9 Giroux Manitoba Canada
130 C11 Giruá Brazil
15 D5 Girvan R Scotland
15 D5 Girvan Scotland
119 M7 Girvin Saskatchewan Canada
108 E4 Girvin Texas U.S.A.
116 H4 Gisasa R Alaska U.S.A.
145 G3 Gisborne New Zealand
13 F6 Gisburn England
123 S6 Gisburn L Newfoundland Canada
117 M8 Giscome British Columbia Canada
103 N7 Gisela Arizona U.S.A.
88 B2 Gisenye Rwanda
26 A9 Giske isld Norway
28 F6 Gislev Denmark
28 H5 Gislinge Denmark
21 O3 Gisors France
37 K1 Gispersleben Germany
57 E5 Gissar Tajikistan
57 E5 Gissarskiy Khrebet mts Tajikistan/Uzbekistan
22 D1 Gistel Belgium
88 B3 Gitega Burundi
32 M9 Gittelde Germany
Giuba R see Jubba R
41 N6 Giudicarie Val Italy
45 Q8 Giugliano in Campo Italy
45 O6 Giuliano di Roma Italy
42 F6 Giulianova Italy
48 J3 Giumalău mt Romania
48 L6 Giurgeni Romania
48 K4 Giurgeului, Muntii mts Romania
47 H1 Giurgiu Romania
48 K6 Giurgiu reg Romania
80 C3 Giv'at 'Ada Israel
80 C5 Giv'atayim Israel
28 C5 Give Denmark
22 D3 Givenchy-en-Gohelle France
22 H3 Givet Belgium
19 N13 Givors France
22 G3 Givry Belgium
19 J6 Givry France
40 A4 Givry France
28 C5 Givskud Denmark
89 F4 Giyani S Africa
79 B8 Giza, El Egypt
21 L7 Gizeux France
57 C4 Gizhduvan Uzbekistan
51 Q2 Gizhiga Russian Federation
22 F4 Gizy France
31 N1 Gizycko Poland
27 C10 Gjende L Norway
27 C10 Gjendesheim Norway
28 E3 Gjerlev Denmark
28 D4 Gjern Denmark
28 F3 Gjerrild Denmark
27 C13 Gjerstad Norway
26 F7 Gjersvik Norway
26 D9 Gjevil-vatn L Norway
46 D4 Gjirokastër Albania
115 K4 Gjoa Haven Northwest Territories Canada
28 D2 Gjøl Denmark
28 C3 Gjørup Denmark
27 C13 Gjovdal Norway
27 E11 Gjövik Norway
46 C4 Gjuhëzës, Kepi i C Albania
22 H2 Glabbeek Zuurbemde Belgium
123 N7 Glace Bay Nova Scotia Canada
20 G2 Glacerie, la France
117 P10 Glacier British Columbia Canada
117 E6 Glacier B Alaska U.S.A.
117 E6 Glacier Bay Nat. Park Alaska U.S.A.
117 E6 Glacier Bay Nat Park and Preserve Alaska U.S.A.
116 O6 Glacier I Alaska U.S.A.
116 Q4 Glacier Mt Alaska U.S.A.
117 O10 Glacier Nat. Park British Columbia Canada
101 M1 Glacier Nat. Park Montana U.S.A.
100 D1 Glacier Peak Washington U.S.A.
115 M2 Glacier Str Northwest Territories Canada
36 B2 Gladbach Germany
32 E9 Gladbeck Germany
99 O7 Gladbrook Iowa U.S.A.
107 L2 Glade Kansas U.S.A.
36 F2 Gladenbach Germany
106 B3 Glade Park Colorado U.S.A.
94 F10 Glade Spring Virginia U.S.A.
109 N3 Gladewater Texas U.S.A.
119 N9 Gladmar Saskatchewan Canada
26 E6 Gladstad Norway
141 K6 Gladstone Queensland Australia
138 E5 Gladstone South Australia Australia
139 J8 Gladstone Tasmania Australia
119 T8 Gladstone Manitoba Canada
145 E4 Gladstone New Zealand
99 T4 Gladstone Michigan U.S.A.
110 B2 Gladstone Missouri U.S.A.
98 D3 Gladstone North Dakota U.S.A.
94 C3 Gladwin Michigan U.S.A.
94 H8 Glady West Virginia U.S.A.
94 H9 Gladys Virginia U.S.A.
117 G6 Gladys L British Columbia Canada
28 G6 Glænø isld Denmark
27 F12 Glafsfj L Sweden
118 K7 Glamis Saskatchewan Canada
15 F4 Glamis Scotland
103 J8 Glamis California U.S.A.
42 H4 Glamoe Bosnia-Herzegovina
28 E6 Glamsbjerg Denmark
38 K8 Glan R Austria
36 D4 Glan R Germany
71 G8 Glan Mindanao Philippines
27 H13 Glan L Sweden
14 B4 Glanaruddery Mts Ireland
19 P15 Glandage France
19 Q14 Glandon, Col du pass France
32 G8 Glandorf Germany
32 G8 Glane R Germany
38 K8 Glanegg Austria
41 J4 Glärnisch mt Switzerland
41 K3 Glarus Switzerland
107 N2 Glasco Kansas U.S.A.
95 O4 Glasco New York U.S.A.
99 R9 Glasford Illinois U.S.A.
127 H1 Glasgow Jamaica
12 D2 Glasgow Scotland
94 B10 Glasgow Kentucky U.S.A.
110 D2 Glasgow Missouri U.S.A.
101 T1 Glasgow Montana U.S.A.
94 H9 Glasgow Virginia U.S.A.
38 M8 Glashutten Austria
133 D6 Glasier Argentina
118 J5 Glaslyn Saskatchewan Canada
15 E4 Glas Maol mt Scotland
119 M9 Glasnevin Saskatchewan Canada
95 M7 Glassboro New Jersey U.S.A.
108 D5 Glass Mts Texas U.S.A.
8 D5 Glastonbury England
41 J3 Glatt R Switzerland
37 N2 Glauchau Germany
47 H1 Glavinitsa Bulgaria
108 D7 Glazier Texas U.S.A.
52 H5 Glazov Russian Federation
31 K2 Głda R Poland
110 H5 Gleason Tennessee U.S.A.
99 R4 Gleason Wisconsin U.S.A.
94 K5 Gleasonton Pennsylvania U.S.A.
103 P10 Gleeson Arizona U.S.A.
37 K3 Gleichberg mt Germany
118 D8 Gleichen Alberta Canada
33 P10 Gleina Germany
38 L7 Glein Alpe mts Austria
38 N7 Gleisdorf Austria
28 B5 Glejbjerg Denmark
98 C7 Glen Nebraska U.S.A.
95 Q2 Glen New Hampshire U.S.A.
100 A6 Glenada Oregon U.S.A.
15 D3 Glen Affric Scotland
145 E2 Glen Afton New Zealand
121 P7 Glen Almond Quebec Canada
112 F2 Glen Alpine North Carolina U.S.A.
20 C6 Glénans, Iles de France
15 D5 Glen App Scotland
144 B6 Glenaray New Zealand
14 F2 Glenarm N Ireland
12 D1 Glen Artney Scotland
119 O8 Glenavon Saskatchewan Canada
144 C6 Glenavy New Zealand
143 D7 Glenayle W Australia Australia
118 K9 Glenbain Saskatchewan Canada
12 C2 Glenbarr Scotland
139 K4 Glenbawn Reservoir New South Wales Australia
119 S9 Glenboro Manitoba Canada
145 E2 Glenbrook New Zealand
143 B7 Glenburgh W Australia Australia
98 E1 Glenburn North Dakota U.S.A.
138 F6 Glenburnie South Australia Australia
123 P4 Glenburnie Newfoundland Canada
95 L7 Glen Burnie Maryland U.S.A.
118 K5 Glenbush Saskatchewan Canada
15 D3 Glen Cannich Scotland
103 N5 Glen Canyon Arizona U.S.A.
103 N4 Glen Canyon Nat. Recreation Area Utah U.S.A.
15 C3 Glen Carron R Scotland
13 E1 Glencarse Scotland
15 E4 Glen Clova Scotland
138 F6 Glencoe South Australia Australia
120 J10 Glencoe Ontario Canada
89 G7 Glencoe S Africa
111 L8 Glencoe Alabama U.S.A.
99 M5 Glencoe Minnesota U.S.A.
106 E8 Glencoe New Mexico U.S.A.
98 F4 Glencross South Dakota U.S.A.
103 M8 Glendale Arizona U.S.A.
102 F7 Glendale California U.S.A.
111 K11 Glendale Florida U.S.A.
107 N3 Glendale Kansas U.S.A.
103 K5 Glendale Nevada U.S.A.
94 C7 Glendale Ohio U.S.A.
100 B7 Glendale Oregon U.S.A.
94 G7 Glendale West Virginia U.S.A.
117 L10 Glendale Cove British Columbia Canada
12 C1 Glendaruel Scotland
139 K5 Glen Davis New South Wales Australia
106 E1 Glendevey Colorado U.S.A.
12 E1 Glendevon Scotland
98 B2 Glendive Montana U.S.A.
98 A7 Glendo Wyoming U.S.A.
118 F4 Glendon Alberta Canada
111 F8 Glendora Mississippi U.S.A.
14 C2 Glendowan Mts Ireland
141 H4 Gleneagle Queensland Australia
15 E4 Gleneagles Scotland
107 M2 Glen Elder Kansas U.S.A.
138 E5 Glenelg South Australia Australia
138 F6 Glenelg R Victoria Australia
15 C3 Glenelg Scotland
119 S8 Glenella Manitoba Canada
119 P9 Glen Ewen Saskatchewan Canada
12 D1 Glen Falloch Scotland
13 E1 Glenfarg Scotland
95 M3 Glenfield New York U.S.A.
98 H2 Glenfield North Dakota U.S.A.
15 C4 Glenfinnan Scotland
109 L6 Glen Flora Texas U.S.A.
14 D1 Glengad Hd Ireland
14 B5 Glengariff Ireland
15 C3 Glen Garry R Scotland
15 D4 Glen Garry Scotland
143 C7 Glengarry Ra W Australia Australia
127 L2 Glengoffe Jamaica
140 E6 Glengyle Queensland Australia
144 B7 Glenham New Zealand
98 F4 Glenham South Dakota U.S.A.
140 C6 Glen Helen N Terr Australia
140 C6 Glen Helen Gorge N Terr Australia
145 D4 Glenhope New Zealand
139 K3 Glen Innes New South Wales Australia
118 K8 Glen Kerr Saskatchewan Canada
99 V5 Glen L Michigan U.S.A.
12 D4 Glenluce Scotland
139 G4 Glen Lyon New South Wales Australia
15 D4 Glen Lyon Scotland
95 L5 Glen Lyon Pennsylvania U.S.A.
145 E2 Glen Massey New Zealand
109 P5 Glenmora Louisiana U.S.A.
15 D3 Glen More Scotland
141 J7 Glenmorgan Queensland Australia
15 D3 Glen Moriston Scotland
102 B2 Glenn California U.S.A.
116 P5 Glennallen Alaska U.S.A.
14 C3 Glennamaddy Ireland
139 H7 Glennie isld Victoria Australia
94 D2 Glennie Michigan U.S.A.
103 P9 Glenn, Mt Arizona U.S.A.
100 K7 Glenns Ferry Idaho U.S.A.
102 F6 Glennville California U.S.A.
112 F6 Glennville Georgia U.S.A.
12 D1 Glen Ogle Scotland
144 B7 Glenomaru New Zealand
117 H7 Glenora British Columbia Canada
139 H8 Glenorchy Tasmania Australia
144 B6 Glenorchy New Zealand
15 D4 Glen Orchy Scotland
141 F4 Glenore Queensland Australia
144 B7 Glenore New Zealand
140 E6 Glenormiston Queensland Australia
139 L4 Glenreagh New South Wales Australia
108 A8 Glenrio New Mex/Tex U.S.A.
121 Q7 Glen Robertson Ontario Canada
98 A7 Glenrock Wyoming U.S.A.
109 K3 Glen Rose Texas U.S.A.
13 E1 Glenrothes Scotland
142 F3 Glenroy W Australia Australia
95 O3 Glens Falls New York U.S.A.
15 E4 Glen Shee Scotland
118 L7 Glenside Saskatchewan Canada
15 D4 Glen Spean Scotland
28 D3 Glenstrup Sø L Denmark
101 T1 Glentana Montana U.S.A.
14 C2 Glenties Ireland
144 C5 Glentunnel New Zealand
118 L9 Glentworth Saskatchewan Canada
98 E3 Glen Ullin North Dakota U.S.A.
15 D3 Glen Urquhart Scotland
120 K5 Glenvale Ontario Canada
99 T7 Glenview Illinois U.S.A.
99 N6 Glenville Minnesota U.S.A.
98 H9 Glenville Nebraska U.S.A.
94 G8 Glenville West Virginia U.S.A.
112 D2 Glenville L North Carolina U.S.A.
123 S5 Glenwood Newfoundland Canada
111 K10 Glenwood Alabama U.S.A.
111 C7 Glenwood Arkansas U.S.A.
112 E5 Glenwood Georgia U.S.A.
94 B7 Glenwood Indiana U.S.A.
99 L8 Glenwood Iowa U.S.A.
99 L4 Glenwood Minnesota U.S.A.
99 O9 Glenwood Missouri U.S.A.
106 B8 Glenwood New Mexico U.S.A.
112 F2 Glenwood North Carolina U.S.A.
100 B4 Glenwood Oregon U.S.A.
103 N3 Glenwood Utah U.S.A.
100 D3 Glenwood Washington U.S.A.
94 E8 Glenwood West Virginia U.S.A.
99 O4 Glenwood Wisconsin U.S.A.
106 C2 Glenwood Springs Colorado U.S.A.
118 D9 Glenwoodville Alberta Canada
28 F4 Glesborg Denmark
33 N4 Gleschendorf Germany
41 H4 Gletsch Switzerland
118 H7 Glidden Saskatchewan Canada
99 Q3 Glidden Wisconsin U.S.A.
100 B6 Glide Oregon U.S.A.
33 S8 Glienick Germany
33 S7 Glienicke Germany
14 B4 Glin Ireland
32 M5 Glinde Germany

31 M3 **Glinojeck** Poland
48 J1 **Glinyany** Ukraine
26 G9 **Glissjöberg** Sweden
26 C10 **Glittertind** *mt* Norway
31 L5 **Gliwice** Poland
46 D4 **Gllavë** Albania
103 O8 **Globe** Arizona U.S.A.
48 C3 **Gloggnitz** Austria
31 J4 **Głogów** Poland
31 K5 **Głogówek** Poland
31 N5 **Głogów Małopolski** Poland
33 Q8 **Gloine** Germany
20 D5 **Glomel** France
26 G5 **Glomfjord** Norway
26 ·E9 **Glomma** *R* Norway
26 L6 **Glommerstrask** Sweden
27 J15 **Glönminge** Sweden
130 H10 **Glória** Brazil
106 E6 **Glorieta** New Mexico U.S.A.
87 H10 **Glorieuses, Is** Indian Oc
116 C6 **Glory of Russia C** Alaska U.S.A.
21 L3 **Glos** France
21 M4 **Glos-la-Ferrière** France
13 G6 **Glossop** England
21 M3 **Glos-sur-Risle** France
111 E10 **Gloster** Mississippi U.S.A.
29 K5 **Glostrup** Denmark
52 G3 **Glotovo** Russian Federation
139 K4 **Gloucester** New South Wales Australia
8 D4 **Gloucester** England
95 R4 **Gloucester** Massachusetts U.S.A.
95 L9 **Gloucester** Virginia U.S.A.
95 M7 **Gloucester City** New Jersey U.S.A.
141 J4 **Gloucester I** Queensland Australia
94 E7 **Glouster** Ohio U.S.A.
123 P5 **Glover I** Newfoundland Canada
95 N3 **Gloversville** New York U.S.A.
33 Q7 **Glöwen** Germany
31 M4 **Główno** Poland
54 M8 **Glubokiy** Russian Federation
56 B5 **Glubokoye** Kazakhstan
31 K5 **Głuchołazy** Poland
28 D7 **Glucksburg** Germany
32 K5 **Glückstadt** Germany
28 D5 **Glud** Denmark
28 C4 **Gludsted** Denmark
54 E5 **Glukhov** Ukraine
52 F6 **Glukhovo** Russian Federation
69 B10 **Glumpangminyeuk** Sumatra
29 K5 **Glumslöv** Sweden
28 H6 **Glumsø** Denmark
13 F6 **Glusburn** England
55 E4 **Glyadyanskoye** Russian Federation
48 K2 **Glyboka** Ukraine
8 B1 **Glyder Fawr** *mt* Wales
143 E6 **Glynde Hill** W Australia Australia
95 L7 **Glyndon** Maryland U.S.A.
98 K3 **Glyndon** Minnesota U.S.A.
28 B3 **Glyngøre** Denmark
8 C4 **Glynneath** Wales
8 C4 **Glyntawe** Wales
31 J7 **Gmünd** Austria
38 J6 **Gmunden** Austria
33 P9 **Gnadau** Germany
94 F6 **Gnadenhutten** Ohio U.S.A.
26 J9 **Gnarp** Sweden
32 K6 **Gnarrenburg** Germany
38 N8 **Gnas** Austria
27 J12 **Gnesta** Sweden
28 G4 **Gniben** *C* Denmark
31 L2 **Gniew** Poland
31 K3 **Gniezno** Poland
33 M4 **Gnissau** Germany
46 E2 **Gnjilane** Serbia Yugoslavia
33 R5 **Gnoien** Germany
8 D2 **Gnosall** England
37 K5 **Gnotzheim** Germany
143 C10 **Gnowangerup** W Australia
143 B9 **Gnuka** W Australia
32 L4 **Gnutz** Germany
76 A3 **Goa, Daman & Diu** *terr* India
139 K6 **Goalen Head** New South Wales Australia
75 O5 **Goalpara** India
71 H9 **Goang** Indonesia
12 C2 **Goat Fell** *mt* Scotland
13 H5 **Goathland** England
101 M1 **Goat Mt** Montana U.S.A.
87 F11 **Goba** Mozambique
89 A4 **Gobabis** Namibia
58 D3 **Gobi Desert** Mongolia
60 J12 **Gobō** Japan
8 C2 **Gobowen** England
25 F5 **Goch** Germany
87 C10 **Gochas** Namibia
86 G4 **Gocho** Ethiopia
36 F5 **Gochsheim** Germany
79 C2 **Göçuk** Turkey
9 F5 **Godalming** England
74 J9 **Godavari** *R* India
76 F2 **Godavari, Mouths of the** India
122 E4 **Godbout** Quebec Canada
122 E4 **Godbout, R** Quebec Canada
117 E7 **Goddard** Alaska U.S.A.
107 N4 **Goddard** Kansas U.S.A.
36 F4 **Goddelau-Wolfskehlen** Germany
46 F1 **Godech** Bulgaria
27 H13 **Godegård** Sweden
32 K9 **Godelheim** Germany
47 L8 **Gödene** Turkey
120 J9 **Goderich** Ontario Canada
21 L2 **Goderville** France
22 D2 **Godewaersvelde** France
121 O8 **Godfrey** Ontario Canada
110 F3 **Godfrey** Illinois U.S.A.
115 O4 **Godhavn** Greenland
74 E7 **Godhra** India
109 K3 **Godley** Texas U.S.A.
144 C5 **Godley Gl** New Zealand
144 C5 **Godley R** New Zealand
9 F3 **Godmanchester** England
71 J5 **Godo** *mt* Indonesia
48 E3 **Gödöllö** Hungary
9 E6 **Godshill** England
115 K7 **Gods L** Manitoba Canada
9 F5 **Godstone** England
115 O5 **Godthåb** Greenland
112 J2 **Godwin** North Carolina U.S.A.
Godwin Austen *mt see* **K2** *mt*
25 A5 **Goedereede** Netherlands
121 O3 **Goeland** Quebec Canada
25 A5 **Goeree** Netherlands
25 A6 **Goes** Netherlands
107 P2 **Goff** Kansas U.S.A.
95 Q3 **Goffstown** New Hampshire U.S.A.
120 J5 **Gogama** Ontario Canada
60 F10 **Gō-gawa** *R* Japan
99 R3 **Gogebic** Michigan U.S.A.
99 R3 **Gogebic Range** *mts* Michigan U.S.A.
37 K7 **Goggingen** Germany
41 H5 **Goglio** Italy
7 L10 **Gog Magog Hills** England
36 B6 **Gogney** France
22 F3 **Gognies-Chaussée** Belgium
142 F4 **Gogo** W Australia Australia
31 K5 **Gogolin** Poland
86 E4 **Gogrial** Sudan
33 Q9 **Gohrau** Germany
33 N6 **Göhrde** Germany
130 J9 **Goiana** Brazil
130 E6 **Goiandira** Brazil
130 E4 **Goianésia** Brazil
130 E5 **Goiânia** Brazil
130 J9 **Goianinha** *lighthouse* Brazil
130 E4 **Goiás** Brazil
130 D5 **Goiás** *state* Brazil
130 E6 **Goiatuba** Brazil
12 D1 **Goil, L** Scotland
130 D9 **Goio Erê** Brazil
25 D5 **Goirle** Netherlands
45 J1 **Goito** Italy
86 G4 **Gojeb** *R* Ethiopia
61 J11 **Gojō** Japan
61 O6 **Gojōme** Japan
47 K5 **Gök** *R* Turkey
76 B2 **Gokak** India
47 K7 **Gökbel** *mt* Turkey
47 H4 **Gökçeada** *isld* Turkey
47 K5 **Gökçedağ** Turkey
79 C2 **Gökdere** *str* Turkey
32 K4 **Gokels** Germany
78 E1 **Gökirmak** *R* Turkey
78 A3 **Gökova Körfezi** Turkey
77 H7 **Gokprosh Hills** Pakistan
78 D3 **Göksu** *R* Turkey
78 F2 **Göksun** Turkey
68 C1 **Gokteik** Burma
47 K7 **Göktepe** Turkey
47 K8 **Gök Tepe** *mt* Turkey
79 C2 **Göktepe** Turkey
87 E9 **Gokwe** Zimbabwe
27 C11 **Gol** Norway
75 P5 **Golaghat** India
80 G2 **Golan** Syria
31 K3 **Golańcz** Poland
77 E6 **Golāshkerd** Iran
54 D10 **Golaya Pristan'** Ukraine
77 E5 **Golbaf** Iran
77 L2 **Golbahār** Afghanistan
38 G8 **Gölbnerjoch** *mt* Austria
74 H10 **Golconda** India
110 H4 **Golconda** Illinois U.S.A.
100 H9 **Golconda** Nevada U.S.A.
Gölcük *see* **Etili**
47 N11 **Gölcük** Turkey
94 K5 **Gold** Pennsylvania U.S.A.
31 N1 **Gołdap** Poland
100 A7 **Gold Beach** Oregon U.S.A.
33 P7 **Goldbeck** Germany
33 Q5 **Goldberg** Germany
123 L8 **Goldboro** Nova Scotia Canada
101 O1 **Gold Butte** Montana U.S.A.
141 L8 **Gold Coast** Queensland Australia
28 C7 **Goldelund** Germany
117 P10 **Golden** British Columbia Canada
98 A10 **Golden** Colorado U.S.A.
100 K4 **Golden** Idaho U.S.A.
110 E1 **Golden** Illinois U.S.A.
145 D4 **Golden Bay** New Zealand
110 B4 **Golden City** Missouri U.S.A.
100 E4 **Goldendale** Washington U.S.A.
144 D4 **Golden Downs** New Zealand
33 N10 **Goldene Aue** Germany
102 B4 **Golden Gate** California U.S.A.
102 B4 **Golden Gate Nat. Recreation Area** California U.S.A.
103 J4 **Golden Gate Ra** Nevada U.S.A.
127 M3 **Golden Grove** Jamaica
121 N7 **Golden Lake** Ontario Canada
111 F12 **Golden Meadow** Louisiana U.S.A.
110 H5 **Golden Pond** Kentucky U.S.A.
118 H8 **Golden Prairie** Saskatchewan Canada
127 P4 **Golden Rock** *airport* St Kitts W Indies
101 N8 **Golden Spike Nat. Hist. Site** Utah U.S.A.
32 H7 **Goldenstedt** Germany
14 C4 **Golden Vale** Ireland
123 K8 **Goldenville** Nova Scotia Canada
99 N7 **Goldfield** Iowa U.S.A.
102 G4 **Goldfield** Nevada U.S.A.
109 J7 **Goldfinch** Texas U.S.A.
101 M9 **Gold Hill** Utah U.S.A.
102 G4 **Gold Point** Nevada U.S.A.
118 K1 **Gold Rock** Ontario Canada
119 R1 **Goldsand L** Manitoba Canada
95 M7 **Goldsboro** Maryland U.S.A.
112 K2 **Goldsboro** North Carolina U.S.A.
108 E4 **Goldsmith** Texas U.S.A.
102 H6 **Goldstone L** California U.S.A.
142 C5 **Goldsworthy** W Australia Australia
142 C5 **Goldsworthy, Mt** W Australia Australia
109 J4 **Goldthwaite** Texas U.S.A.
112 F3 **Goldville** South Carolina U.S.A.
78 J1 **Göle** Turkey
85 E2 **Golea, El** Algeria
89 G6 **Golela** S Africa
31 H2 **Goleniów** Poland
102 E7 **Goleta** California U.S.A.
16 C7 **Golfo de Cádiz** Spain
43 E10 **Golfo di Castellammare** Sicily
43 E7 **Golfo di Gaeta** Italy
44 E3 **Golfo di Genova** Italy
45 N1 **Golfo di Venezia** Adriatic Sea
47 K7 **Gölgel Dağ** *mts* Turkey
138 F5 **Gol Gol** New South Wales Australia
109 K7 **Goliad** Texas U.S.A.
46 D1 **Golija Planina** *mt* Serbia Yugoslavia
65 E2 **Golin Baixing** China
Gollel *see* **Lavumisa**
33 T6 **Gollin** Germany
38 H6 **Golling** Austria
33 S10 **Gollmberg** *pk* Germany
33 T9 **Gollmitz** Germany
47 J6 **Gölmarmara** Turkey
33 S8 **Golmberg** *pk* Germany
37 M2 **Golmsdorf** Germany
66 E4 **Golmud** China
71 E4 **Golo** *isld* Philippines
52 H1 **Golodnaya Guba, Oz** *L* Russian Federation
57 E4 **Golodnaya Step'** Kazakhstan/Uzbekistan
86 H4 **Gololcha** Ethiopia
88 E9 **Golomoti** Malawi
48 N2 **Golovanevsk** Ukraine
116 F4 **Golovin** Alaska U.S.A.
60 T2 **Golovnino** Kuril Is Russian Federation
77 B3 **Golpāyegān** Iran
47 L4 **Gölpazarı** Turkey
116 G5 **Golsovia** Alaska U.S.A.
15 E3 **Golspie** Scotland
33 T9 **Golssen** Germany
28 D2 **Gølstrup** Denmark
107 M5 **Goltry** Oklahoma U.S.A.
31 L2 **Gołub** Poland
55 F4 **Golubovka** Kazakhstan
89 F3 **Golulu Ruins** Zimbabwe
87 B7 **Golungo Alto** Angola
98 C3 **Golva** North Dakota U.S.A.
46 G3 **Golyam Perelik** *mt* Bulgaria
31 M3 **Gołymin** Poland
54 C2 **Golynki** Russian Federation
55 E3 **Golyshmanovo** Russian Federation
33 R8 **Golzow** Germany
88 B2 **Goma** Zaire
85 G6 **Gombe** Nigeria
44 H4 **Gombo** Italy
70 M9 **Gombong** Java
47 H5 **Gömeç** Turkey
54 B4 **Gomel'** Belarus
85 A3 **Gomera** *isld* Canary Is
124 H5 **Gómez Palacio** Mexico
125 K4 **Gómez, Presa M.R.** *res* Mexico
20 F5 **Gommené** France
33 P8 **Gommern** Germany
66 C5 **Gomo** China
71 A3 **Gomumu** *isld* Indonesia
127 H5 **Gonaïves** Haiti
51 M3 **Gonam** *R* Russian Federation
89 G3 **Gona-re-zhou Game Res.** Zimbabwe
126 H5 **Gonâve, Île de la** Haiti
48 G2 **Gönc** Hungary
19 Q14 **Goncelin** France
74 D8 **Gondal** India
36 F5 **Gondelsheim** Germany
86 G3 **Gonder** Ethiopia
74 J8 **Gondia** India
19 J4 **Gondrecourt** France
80 F1 **Gonen** Israel
47 J4 **Gönen** *R* Turkey
47 J4 **Gönen** Turkey
19 Q18 **Gonfaron** France
21 L2 **Gonfreville l'Orcher** France
83 K11 **Gongala** *mt* Sri Lanka
67 D1 **Gong'an** China
66 E5 **Gongbo'gyamda** China
67 C4 **Gongcheng** China
75 O4 **Gonggar** China
58 D6 **Gongga Shan** *mt* China
57 K3 **Gongliu** China
Gonglüe *see* **Donggu**
85 G6 **Gongola** *R* Nigeria
139 H4 **Gongolgon** New South Wales Australia
67 D3 **Gongpingxu** China
67 D2 **Gongtian** China
65 B7 **Gong Xian** China
65 D4 **Gongyingzi** China
Gongzhuling *see* **Huaide**
31 O2 **Goniądz** Poland
88 G4 **Gonja** Tanzania
36 G7 **Gönningen** Germany
46 E5 **Gónnos** Greece
61 P5 **Gonohe** Japan
60 C12 **Gōnoura** Japan
40 D3 **Gonsans** France
99 L2 **Gonvick** Minnesota U.S.A.
45 J2 **Gonzaga** Italy
102 C5 **Gonzales** California U.S.A.
109 K6 **Gonzales** Texas U.S.A.
36 C4 **Gonzerath** Germany
86 H6 **Goob Weyn** Somalia
94 K9 **Goochland** Virginia U.S.A.
146 F14 **Goodenough, C** Antarctica
121 M8 **Gooderham** Ontario Canada
119 O7 **Goodeve** Saskatchewan Canada
94 B1 **Good Hart** Michigan U.S.A.
99 V4 **Good Hbr. B** Michigan U.S.A.
89 B8 **Goodhope** S Africa
116 E4 **Goodhope** *R* Alaska U.S.A.
116 F3 **Goodhope B** Alaska U.S.A.
87 C12 **Good Hope, C. of** S Africa
117 L10 **Good Hope, Mt** British Columbia Canada
87 C11 **Goodhouse** S Africa
99 O5 **Goodhue** Minnesota U.S.A.
101 L7 **Gooding** Idaho U.S.A.
107 J2 **Goodland** Kansas U.S.A.
119 R9 **Goodlands** Manitoba Canada
83 M12 **Goodlands** Mauritius
110 K5 **Goodlettsville** Tennessee U.S.A.
99 S4 **Goodman** Wisconsin U.S.A.
116 F7 **Goodnews B** Alaska U.S.A.
108 C8 **Goodnight** Texas U.S.A.
139 H3 **Goodooga** New South Wales Australia
140 B2 **Goodparla** N Terr Australia
116 P4 **Goodpaster** *R* Alaska U.S.A.
106 F3 **Good Pasture** Colorado U.S.A.
98 B9 **Goodrich** Colorado U.S.A.
100 J5 **Goodrich** Idaho U.S.A.
98 F2 **Goodrich** North Dakota U.S.A.
111 B11 **Goodrich** Texas U.S.A.
99 Q4 **Goodrich** Wisconsin U.S.A.
140 B1 **Goodrich Bank** N Terr Australia
117 P10 **Goodsir, Mt** British Columbia Canada
118 H4 **Goodsoil** Saskatchewan Canada
119 P7 **Good Spirit L** Saskatchewan Canada
103 J6 **Goodsprings** Nevada U.S.A.
119 O9 **Goodwater** Saskatchewan Canada
111 K8 **Good Water** Alabama U.S.A.
107 J5 **Goodwell** Oklahoma U.S.A.
8 A3 **Goodwick** Wales
121 L4 **Goodwin** Ontario Canada
103 M7 **Goodwin** Arizona U.S.A.
98 K5 **Goodwin** South Dakota U.S.A.
7 M11 **Goodwin Sands** English Chan
144 C6 **Goodwood** New Zealand
9 F6 **Goodwood Park** England
13 H6 **Goole** England
139 H5 **Goolgowi** New South Wales Australia
139 J4 **Goolma** New South Wales Australia
139 J5 **Gooloogong** New South Wales Australia
138 E6 **Goolwa** South Australia Australia
140 C1 **Goomadeer** *R* N Terr Australia
143 B9 **Goomalling** W Australia Australia
139 H3 **Goombalie** New South Wales Australia
141 K7 **Goombungee** Queensland Australia
141 K7 **Goomeri** Queensland Australia
141 K8 **Goondiwindi** Queensland Australia
143 D9 **Goongarrie** W Australia Australia
143 D8 **Goongarrie, L** W Australia Australia
141 J5 **Goonyella** Queensland Australia
25 G4 **Goor** Netherlands
117 P8 **Goose** *R* Alberta Canada
115 N7 **Goose Bay** Labrador, Nfld Canada
144 D5 **Goose Bay** New Zealand
101 R5 **Gooseberry Cr** Wyoming U.S.A.
118 G6 **Gooseberry L. Prov. Park** Alberta Canada
123 R2 **Goose Cove** Newfoundland Canada
101 M7 **Goose Cr** Idaho U.S.A.
112 G4 **Goose Creek** South Carolina U.S.A.
101 M8 **Goose Cr. Mts** Utah U.S.A.
101 T7 **Goose Egg** Wyoming U.S.A.
116 F9 **Goose I** Alaska U.S.A.
119 Q4 **Goose L** Manitoba Canada
100 E8 **Goose L** California U.S.A.
76 C3 **Gooty** India
75 L9 **Gopalpur** India
31 L3 **Gopło, Jezioro** *L* Poland
36 H6 **Göppingen** Germany
103 K10 **Gora** *isld* Mexico
31 K4 **Góra** Poland
31 N4 **Gora Kalwaria** Poland
75 K5 **Gorakhpur** India
42 J5 **Goransko** Montenegro Yugoslavia
48 E7 **Goražde** Bosnia-Herzegovina
113 K11 **Gorda Cay** *isld* Bahamas
128 D7 **Gorda, Pta** *C* Chile
19 O17 **Gordes** France
47 J6 **Gördes** Turkey
86 D4 **Gordil** Cent Afr Republic
28 B6 **Gørding** Denmark
111 J8 **Gordo** Alabama U.S.A.
139 H8 **Gordon** *R* Tasmania Australia
13 F2 **Gordon** Scotland
116 R2 **Gordon** Alaska U.S.A.
106 F4 **Gordon** Colorado U.S.A.
112 D5 **Gordon** Georgia U.S.A.
98 D7 **Gordon** Nebraska U.S.A.
109 J3 **Gordon** Texas U.S.A.
99 P3 **Gordon** Wisconsin U.S.A.
13 E3 **Gordon Arms** Scotland
140 B1 **Gordon B** N Terr Australia
140 B3 **Gordon Cr** N Terr Australia
98 E7 **Gordon Cr** Nebraska U.S.A.
142 G4 **Gordon Downs** W Australia Australia
139 H8 **Gordon L.** Tasmania Australia
118 G2 **Gordon, L** Alberta Canada
117 R4 **Gordon L** Northwest Territories Canada
117 F4 **Gordon Landing** Yukon Territory Canada
94 B10 **Gordonsville** Tennessee U.S.A.
94 J8 **Gordonsville** Virginia U.S.A.
141 H3 **Gordonvale** Queensland Australia
86 C4 **Goré** Chad
86 G4 **Gorē** Ethiopia
144 B7 **Gore** New Zealand
107 P6 **Gore** Oklahoma U.S.A.
120 H7 **Gore Bay** Ontario Canada
144 D5 **Gore Bay** New Zealand
13 E2 **Gorebridge** Scotland
109 H2 **Goree** Texas U.S.A.
54 J2 **Gorelki** Russian Federation
95 Q2 **Gore Mt** Vermont U.S.A.
140 E4 **Gore Pt** Queensland Australia
116 M7 **Gore Pt** Alaska U.S.A.
106 D2 **Gore Ra** Colorado U.S.A.
110 H4 **Goreville** Illinois U.S.A.
20 F3 **Gorey** Channel Is
14 E4 **Gorey** Ireland
77 D1 **Gorgān** Iran
147 K11 **Gorga, Zemlya** *isld* Russian Federation
83 K14 **Gorge** *R* Réunion Indian Oc
142 C5 **Gorge Ra** W Australia Australia
141 H4 **Gorge Ra., The** Queensland Australia
128 C3 **Gorgona** *isld* Colombia
42 C5 **Gorgona, I.di** Italy
41 K6 **Gorgonzola** Italy
86 G3 **Gorgora** Ethiopia
85 G6 **Gorgoram** Nigeria
101 O9 **Gorgorza** Utah U.S.A.
107 L3 **Gorham** Kansas U.S.A.
95 R3 **Gorham** Maine U.S.A.
95 Q2 **Gorham** New Hampshire U.S.A.
95 K4 **Gorham** New York U.S.A.
53 F12 **Gori** Georgia
46 D4 **Goricë** Albania
99 O9 **Gorin** Missouri U.S.A.
25 C5 **Gorinchem** Netherlands
9 E4 **Goring** England
27 H10 **Göringen** Sweden
78 L2 **Goris** Armenia
52 E6 **Goritsy** Russian Federation
42 F3 **Gorizia** Italy
42 G3 **Gorjanci** *mts* Yugoslavia
52 G3 **Gorka** Russian Federation
75 L4 **Gorkhā** Nepal
Gor'kiy *see* **Nizhniy Novgorod**
Gor'kovskaya Oblast' *see* **Nizhegorodskaya Oblast'**
52 F6 **Gor'kovskoye Vodokhranilishche** *res* Russian Federation
33 O6 **Gorleben** Germany
9 H2 **Gorleston** England
28 G5 **Gørlev** Denmark
31 N6 **Gorlice** Poland
52 F3 **Gorlichevskaya** Russian Federation
31 H4 **Görlitz** Germany
28 J5 **Gørløse** Denmark
33 O6 **Gorlosen** Germany
98 F5 **Gorman** South Dakota U.S.A.
109 J3 **Gorman** Texas U.S.A.
94 H7 **Gormania** Maryland U.S.A.
139 H8 **Gormanston** Tasmania Australia
43 F11 **Gornalunga** *R* Sicily
47 H1 **Gorna Oryakhovitsa** Bulgaria
55 E2 **Gornaya Subbota** Russian Federation
65 J2 **Gorniye Klyuchi** Russian Federation
46 D1 **Gornji Milanovac** Serbia Yugoslavia
42 H5 **Gornji Vakuf** Bosnia-Herzegovina
56 C5 **Gorno-Altaysk** Russian Federation
56 C5 **Gorno-Altayskaya Avtonomnyy Oblast'** Russian Federation
57 G5 **Gorno-Badakhshanskaya Avtonomnyy Oblast'** *prov* Tajikistan
56 H2 **Gorno-Chuyskiy** Russian Federation
55 E2 **Gorno Slinkina** Russian Federation
52 G1 **Gornostal'ya Guba** *B* Russian Federation
54 M8 **Gornyatskiy** Russian Federation
29 P2 **Gornyy** Russian Federation
48 N1 **Gornyy Tikich** *R* Ukraine
45 M2 **Goro** Italy
48 J2 **Gorodenka** Ukraine
52 F6 **Gorodets** Russian Federation
52 F1 **Gorodetskiy, Mys Bol'shoy** *C* Russian Federation
54 C7 **Gorodishche** Ukraine
52 D6 **Gorodnya** Russian Federation
54 A1 **Gorodok** Belarus
136 K3 **Goroka** Papua New Guinea
138 F6 **Goroke** Victoria Australia
52 F6 **Gorokhovets** Russian Federation
87 F9 **Gorongosa** Mozambique
71 H4 **Gorontalo** Sulawesi
31 M1 **Górowo Iławeckie** Poland
25 F2 **Gorredijk** Netherlands
120 J9 **Gorrie** Ontario Canada
21 J5 **Gorron** France
33 S9 **Görsdorf** Germany
54 K8 **Gorskoye** Ukraine
25 F4 **Gorssel** Netherlands
14 C3 **Gort** Ireland
14 C1 **Gortahork** Ireland
14 B3 **Gorumna I** Ireland
130 G4 **Gorutuba, R** Brazil
57 A2 **Gory Chushkakul'** *mt* Kazakhstan
53 C8 **Goryn'** *R* Belarus/Ukraine
31 M5 **Góry Świętokrzyskie** *mts* Poland
42 E6 **Gorzano, M** *mt* Italy
33 Q8 **Görzke** Germany
31 L4 **Gorzów** Poland
31 J3 **Gorzów Wielkopolski** Poland
Gosainthan *mt see* **Xixabangma Feng**
9 F2 **Gosberton** England
37 M2 **Göschwitz** Germany
61 N8 **Gosen** Japan
139 K5 **Gosford** New South Wales Australia
102 E5 **Goshen** California U.S.A.
94 B5 **Goshen** Indiana U.S.A.
95 N5 **Goshen** New York U.S.A.
100 B6 **Goshen** Oregon U.S.A.
101 O10 **Goshen** Utah U.S.A.
94 H9 **Goshen** Virginia U.S.A.
61 O5 **Goshogawara** Japan
127 N4 **Gosier** Guadeloupe W Indies
33 M9 **Goslar** Germany
20 H5 **Gosné** France
142 C2 **Gosnells** *dist* Perth, W Aust Australia
42 G4 **Gospić** Croatia
9 E6 **Gosport** England
110 K2 **Gosport** Indiana U.S.A.
111 G10 **Goss** Mississippi U.S.A.
33 Q9 **Gossa** Germany
41 K3 **Gossau** Switzerland
22 G3 **Gosselies** Belgium
26 B9 **Gossen** *isld* Norway
140 C4 **Gosse R** N Terr Australia
86 E4 **Gossinga** Sudan
38 J6 **Gossl** Austria
38 H8 **Gössnitz** Austria
37 N2 **Gössnitz** Germany
46 D3 **Gostivar** Macedonia
38 L6 **Göstling** Austria
38 L6 **Göstlinger Alpen** *mts* Austria
31 K4 **Gostyn** Poland
31 L3 **Gostynin** Poland
27 H13 **Göta Kanal** Sweden
107 M6 **Gotebo** Oklahoma U.S.A.
27 E14 **Göteborg** Sweden
27 E13 **Göteborgs Och Bohus** *county* Sweden
85 G7 **Gotel Mts** Nigeria
61 M10 **Gotemba** Japan
37 K2 **Gotha** Germany
27 K14 **Gothem** Gotland Sweden
98 F9 **Gothenburg** Nebraska U.S.A.
85 E6 **Gothéye** Niger
27 K14 **Gotland** *isld* Sweden
27 K14 **Gotland** *county* Sweden
27 H12 **Götlunda** Sweden
60 B12 **Gotō-rettō** *islds* Japan
71 B2 **Gotowasi** Indonesia
46 F3 **Gotse Delchev** Bulgaria
27 K13 **Gotska Sandön** *isld* Sweden
60 F10 **Gōtsu** Japan
44 G3 **Gottero** *mt* Italy
37 O6 **Gotteszell** Germany
36 F2 **Göttingen** Hessen Germany
32 L9 **Göttingen** Niedersachsen Germany
26 K8 **Gottne** Sweden
117 M10 **Gott Pk** British Columbia Canada
28 C2 **Gøttrup** Denmark
Gottwaldov *see* **Zlín**
Gotval'd *see* **Zmiyev**
41 L3 **Götzis** Austria
20 D5 **Gouarec** France
65 E4 **Goubangzi** China
25 C4 **Gouda** Netherlands
86 C4 **Goudeï** Chad
22 F4 **Goudelancourt** France
9 G5 **Goudhurst** England
85 B6 **Goudiry** Senegal
85 G6 **Goudoumaria** Niger
120 F4 **Goudreau** Ontario Canada
25 B5 **Goudswaard** Netherlands
20 G4 **Gouesnière, la** France
20 B5 **Gouesnou** France
20 E5 **Gouet** *R* France
20 C5 **Gouézec** France
112 E4 **Gough** Georgia U.S.A.
90 J13 **Gough I** S Atlantic Oc
118 E6 **Gough L** Alberta Canada
40 D2 **Gouhenans** France
121 Q4 **Gouin, Rés** Quebec Canada
120 F6 **Goulais River** Ontario Canada
139 K4 **Goulburn** *R* New South Wales Australia
139 J5 **Goulburn** New South Wales Australia
140 C1 **Goulburn Is** N Terr Australia
121 T7 **Gould** Quebec Canada
111 E8 **Gould** Arkansas U.S.A.
106 D1 **Gould** Colorado U.S.A.
107 L7 **Gould** Oklahoma U.S.A.
99 V3 **Gould City** Michigan U.S.A.
146 D9 **Gould Coast** Antarctica
143 B7 **Gould, Mt** W Australia Australia
85 C6 **Goumbou** Mali
46 E4 **Gouménissa** Greece
40 E3 **Goumois** France
85 D5 **Goundam** Mali
86 C4 **Goundi** Chad
46 E7 **Goúra** Greece
86 C2 **Gouradi** Chad
20 F5 **Gouray, le** France
18 F8 **Gourdon** France
85 G6 **Gouré** Niger
21 K8 **Gourgé** France
20 C5 **Gourin** France
120 F4 **Gourlay L** Ontario Canada
85 D5 **Gourma Rharous** Mali
21 O3 **Gournay-en-Bray** France
86 C2 **Gouro** Chad
12 D2 **Gourock** Scotland
139 J6 **Gourock Rge** New South Wales Australia
118 K9 **Gouverneur** Saskatchewan Canada
95 M2 **Gouverneur** New York U.S.A.
47 O12 **Gouviá** Greece
21 P3 **Gouvieux** France
20 G3 **Gouville** France
22 K3 **Gouvy** Belgium
127 P5 **Gouyave** Grenada
22 E3 **Gouzeaucourt** France
18 G6 **Gouzon** France
119 N7 **Govan** Saskatchewan Canada
12 D2 **Govan** Scotland
140 D1 **Gove** N Terr Australia
107 K3 **Gove** Kansas U.S.A.
20 G5 **Goven** France
118 H9 **Govenlock** Saskatchewan Canada
140 D1 **Gove Pen** N Terr Australia
48 J2 **Goverla** *mt* Ukraine
130 H6 **Governador Valadares** Brazil
100 D4 **Government Camp** Oregon U.S.A.
71 G7 **Governor Generoso** Philippines
122 K8 **Governor, L** Nova Scotia Canada
113 L12 **Governor's Harbour** Bahamas
145 D4 **Gowanbridge** New Zealand
94 J4 **Gowanda** New York U.S.A.
141 G6 **Gowan Ra** Queensland Australia
110 B2 **Gower** Missouri U.S.A.
8 B4 **Gower Inn** Wales
120 K5 **Gowganda** Ontario Canada
14 D3 **Gowna, L** Ireland
99 M7 **Gowrie** Iowa U.S.A.
131 F2 **Goya** Argentina
127 N4 **Goyave** Guadeloupe W Indies
138 C2 **Goyder** *R* N Terr Australia
140 D2 **Goyder** *R* N Terr Australia
138 E2 **Goyder Lagoon** South Australia Australia
123 M3 **Goyelle, L** Quebec Canada
128 C6 **Goyllarisquizga** Peru
47 L4 **Göynük** Turkey
61 P6 **Goyō-zan** *mt* Japan
86 D3 **Goz-Beïda** Chad
66 C4 **Gozha Co** *L* China
43 F12 **Gozo** *isld* Malta
86 G2 **Goz Regeb** Sudan
89 D9 **Graaff Reinet** S Africa
36 E5 **Graben-Neudorf** Germany
85 C8 **Grabo** Ivory Coast
46 F9 **Graboúsa** *isld* Crete Greece
55 F4 **Grabovo** Kazakhstan
33 O6 **Grabow** Germany
33 P6 **Grabow** Mecklenburg-Vorpommern Germany
33 P8 **Grabow** Sachsen-Anhalt Germany
31 L4 **Grabów** Poland
42 G4 **Gračac** Croatia
48 E6 **Gračanica** Bosnia-Herzegovina
21 O7 **Graçay** France
101 O7 **Grace** Idaho U.S.A.
98 H2 **Grace City** North Dakota U.S.A.
121 O6 **Gracefield** Quebec Canada
143 C10 **Grace, L** W Australia Australia
122 G1 **Grace L** Labrador, Nfld Canada
107 M6 **Gracemont** Oklahoma U.S.A.
141 K2 **Graceville** *dist* Brisbane, Qnsld Australia
111 L11 **Graceville** Florida U.S.A.
98 K4 **Graceville** Minnesota U.S.A.
110 J5 **Gracey** Kentucky U.S.A.
38 O8 **Grad** Slovenia
48 E6 **Gradačac** Bosnia-Herzegovina
129 H5 **Gradaús, Serra dos** *mts* Brazil
26 H5 **Graddis** Norway
16 D2 **Gradefes** Spain
46 E3 **Gradeska Pl** *mt* Macedonia
48 H5 **Grădistea Muncelului** Romania
33 S9 **Graditz** Germany
70 P10 **Gradjagan** Java
42 E3 **Grado** Italy
16 C1 **Grado** Spain
46 E3 **Gradsko** Macedonia
111 E7 **Grady** Arkansas U.S.A.
108 D1 **Grady** New Mexico U.S.A.
28 A5 **Grådyb** *chan* Denmark
102 D2 **Graeagle** California U.S.A.
28 C5 **Grædstrup** Denmark
28 H7 **Grænge** Denmark
28 J4 **Græsted** Denmark
99 M6 **Graettinger** Iowa U.S.A.
37 P6 **Grafenau** Germany
37 L4 **Gräfenberg** Germany
33 Q9 **Gräfenhainichen** Germany
37 K2 **Gräfenroda** Germany
38 M5 **Grafenschlag** Austria
37 L2 **Gräfenthal** Germany
37 K1 **Gräfentonna** Germany
37 M4 **Grafenwöhr** Germany
38 N5 **Grafenwörth** Austria
36 D6 **Graffenstaden** Germany
Gräfinau *see* **Angstedt-Gräfinau**
37 O6 **Grafling** Germany
109 J3 **Graford** Texas U.S.A.
32 F10 **Grafrath** Germany
36 C2 **Grafschaft** Germany
139 L3 **Grafton** New South Wales Australia
110 F3 **Grafton** Illinois U.S.A.
95 O4 **Grafton** New York U.S.A.
98 J1 **Grafton** North Dakota U.S.A.
94 E5 **Grafton** Ohio U.S.A.
94 G7 **Grafton** West Virginia U.S.A.
99 T6 **Grafton** Wisconsin U.S.A.
141 H3 **Grafton, C** Queensland Australia
133 C8 **Grafton, Is** Chile
103 K3 **Grafton, Mt** Nevada U.S.A.
141 H3 **Grafton Pass** Gt Barrier Reef Australia
45 R8 **Gragnano** Italy
117 M7 **Graham** *R* British Columbia Canada
119 N1 **Graham** Ontario Canada
109 J2 **Graham** Texas U.S.A.
117 G9 **Graham I** British Columbia Canada
115 K2 **Graham I** Northwest Territories Canada
118 C2 **Graham L** Alberta Canada
95 T2 **Graham L** Maine U.S.A.
146 C4 **Graham Land** *pen* Antarctica
103 P9 **Graham, Mt** Arizona U.S.A.
89 E9 **Grahamstown** S Africa
95 N5 **Grahamsville** New York U.S.A.
42 J6 **Grahovo** Montenegro Yugoslavia
42 A3 **Graie, Alpi** Italy
14 E4 **Graigue** Ireland
107 K2 **Grainfield** Kansas U.S.A.
118 D7 **Grainger** Alberta Canada
98 E9 **Grainton** Nebraska U.S.A.
129 J5 **Grajau** Brazil
31 N2 **Grajewo** Poland
52 H6 **Grakhovo** Russian Federation
16 B4 **Gralheira, Sa** *mts* Portugal
28 C6 **Gram** Denmark
46 F1 **Gramada** Bulgaria
18 G8 **Gramat** France
47 J2 **Gramatikovo** Bulgaria
32 H7 **Gramke** Germany
43 F11 **Grammichele** Sicily
Grammont *see* **Geraardsbergen**
33 R4 **Grammow** Germany
15 F3 **Grampian** *reg* Scotland
15 D4 **Grampian Mt** Scotland
138 F6 **Grampians** *mts* Victoria Australia
25 G3 **Gramsbergen** Netherlands
46 D4 **Gramsh** Albania
33 U6 **Gramzow** Germany
44 B3 **Grana** *R* Italy
126 G10 **Granada** Colombia
125 M4 **Granada** Nicaragua
16 E7 **Granada** Spain
16 E7 **Granada** *prov* Spain
106 H3 **Granada** Colorado U.S.A.
16 C4 **Granadilla** Spain
133 D7 **Gran Altiplanicie Central** *plain* Argentina
14 D3 **Granard** Ireland
45 K2 **Granarolo dell'Emilia** Italy
38 G7 **Granat-Spitze** *mt* Austria
133 D7 **Gran Baja** *hills* Argentina
131 C7 **Gran Bajo Salitroso** *salt lake* Argentina
109 K3 **Granbury** Texas U.S.A.
121 S7 **Granby** Quebec Canada
106 E1 **Granby** Colorado U.S.A.
110 B5 **Granby** Missouri U.S.A.
98 A9 **Granby, L** Colorado U.S.A.
85 A3 **Gran Canaria** *isld* Canary Is
40 B2 **Grancey** France
133 E3 **Gran Chaco** *reg* Argentina
127 O2 **Gran Couva** Trinidad
111 E12 **Grand** *R* Louisiana U.S.A.
99 M9 **Grand** *R* Missouri U.S.A.
98 E4 **Grand** *R* South Dakota U.S.A.
20 H6 **Grand-Auverne** France
119 P1 **Grand B** Ontario Canada
113 J11 **Grand Bahama** *isld* Bahamas
123 R6 **Grand Bank** Newfoundland Canada
90 E4 **Grand Banks of Nfld** Atlantic Oc
85 D8 **Grand Bassam** Ivory Coast
122 F8 **Grand Bay** New Brunswick Canada
119 V8 **Grand Beach** Manitoba Canada
119 V8 **Grand Beach Prov. Park** Manitoba Canada
120 J9 **Grand Bend** Ontario Canada
94 D4 **Grand Blanc** Michigan U.S.A.
19 Q13 **Grand Bornand** France
127 N5 **Grand Bourg** Guadeloupe W Indies
123 O6 **Grand Bruit** Newfoundland Canada
127 J4 **Grand Caicos** *isld* Turks & Caicos Is
21 H3 **Grandcamp-Maisy** France
65 D7 **Grand Canal** China
14 D3 **Grand Canal** Ireland
111 C9 **Grand Cane** Louisiana U.S.A.
19 Q17 **Grand Cañon du Verdon** France
103 M5 **Grand Canyon** *gorge* Arizona U.S.A.
103 M5 **Grand Canyon Nat. Park** Arizona U.S.A.
103 M5 **Grand Canyon Village** Arizona U.S.A.
113 J10 **Grand Cays** *islds* Bahamas
118 G4 **Grand Centre** Alberta Canada
85 C8 **Grand Cess** Liberia
20 E6 **Grand Champ** France
20 G7 **Grand-champ** France
111 D12 **Grand Cheniere** Louisiana U.S.A.
19 P13 **Grand Colombier** *mt* France
100 F2 **Grand Coulee** Washington U.S.A.
21 N3 **Grand Couronne** France
21 O2 **Grandcourt** France
127 N4 **Grand Cul de Sac Marin** *B* Guadeloupe W Indies
128 C6 **Grande** *R* Peru
131 G3 **Grande** *R* Uruguay
122 G6 **Grande-Anse** New Brunswick Canada
127 O4 **Grande Anse** Guadeloupe W Indies
133 D8 **Grande, B** Argentina
121 U4 **Grande-Baie** Quebec Canada
45 M2 **Grande Bonificazione Ferrarese** Italy
20 F7 **Grande Brière** *reg* France
83 K14 **Grande Brûlé** Réunion Indian Oc
19 P14 **Grande Chartreuse** *mts* France
133 D5 **Grande Colorado** *R* Argentina
18 H8 **Grande Combe, la** France
131 H2 **Grande, Coxilha** *mt* Brazil
131 G4 **Grande, Cuchilla** *ra* Uruguay
129 G4 **Grande do Curuai, L** Brazil
122 H5 **Grande Grève** Quebec Canada
129 K8 **Grande, I** Brazil
20 C4 **Grande, I** France
45 M3 **Grande, M** *mt* Italy
128 F7 **Grande, Monte** *mts* Bolivia
128 F7 **Grande O'Guapay** *R* Bolivia
117 O8 **Grande Prairie** Alberta Canada
127 M2 **Grande, R** Jamaica
86 B2 **Grand Erg de Bilma** Niger
85 E2 **Grand Erg Occidental** *desert* Algeria
122 H5 **Grande Rivière** Quebec Canada
127 P1 **Grande Rivière** Trinidad
127 L4 **Grande Rivière** Martinique W Indies
127 H5 **Grande Rivière du Nord** Haiti
100 H4 **Grande Ronde** *R* Oregon U.S.A.
122 C5 **Grandes Bergeronnes** Quebec Canada
21 M2 **Grandes Dalles, les** France
129 K5 **Grande, Serra** *mts* Brazil
121 S6 **Grandes Piles** Quebec Canada
21 N2 **Grandes Ventes, les** France
123 L7 **Grand Etang** C Breton I, Nova Scotia
127 P5 **Grand Etang** *L* Grenada
127 N4 **Grande Terre** *isld* Guadeloupe W Indies
122 G4 **Grande Vallée** Quebec Canada
127 N3 **Grande Vigie,Pte.de la** Guadeloupe W Indies
122 E6 **Grand Falls** New Brunswick Canada
123 R5 **Grand Falls** Newfoundland Canada
103 N6 **Grand Falls** Arizona U.S.A.
108 E4 **Grandfalls** Texas U.S.A.
112 F1 **Grandfather Mt** North Carolina U.S.A.
107 M7 **Grandfield** Oklahoma U.S.A.
100 G1 **Grand Forks** British Columbia Canada
98 J2 **Grand Forks** North Dakota U.S.A.
22 C1 **Grand Fort Philippe** France
20 G6 **Grand Fougeray, le** France
95 N4 **Grand Gorge** New York U.S.A.
127 J5 **Grand Gosier** Haiti
22 K3 **Grand-Halleux** Belgium
122 F9 **Grand Harbour** New Brunswick Canada
99 U6 **Grand Haven** Michigan U.S.A.
111 G11 **Grand I** Louisiana U.S.A.
99 U3 **Grand I** Michigan U.S.A.
98 H9 **Grand I** Nebraska U.S.A.
121 M9 **Grand I** New York U.S.A.
113 F8 **Grandin** Florida U.S.A.
110 F5 **Grandin** Missouri U.S.A.
98 J2 **Grandin** North Dakota U.S.A.
117 O3 **Grandin, Lac** Northwest Territories Canada
111 G12 **Grand Isle** Louisiana U.S.A.
95 O2 **Grand Isle** Vermont U.S.A.
131 F7 **Grand Jason** *isld* Falkland Is
99 M7 **Grand Junct** Iowa U.S.A.
106 B2 **Grand Junction** Colorado U.S.A.
94 A4 **Grand Junction** Michigan U.S.A.
110 G6 **Grand Junction** Tennessee U.S.A.
101 N3 **Grand Kohrs Ranch Nat. Hist. Site** Montana U.S.A.
122 E8 **Grand L** New Brunswick Canada
123 P4 **Grand L** Newfoundland Canada
94 D1 **Grand L** Michigan U.S.A.
94 C6 **Grand L** Ohio U.S.A.
122 F2 **Grand Lac Germain** Quebec Canada
106 E1 **Grand Lake** Colorado U.S.A.
111 C11 **Grand Lake** Louisiana U.S.A.
95 S7 **Grand Lakes L** Maine U.S.A.
94 C4 **Grand Ledge** Michigan U.S.A.
20 G7 **Grand Lieu, Lac de** France
28 H5 **Grandløse** Denmark
95 S7 **Grand L Seboeis** Maine U.S.A.
21 L6 **Grand-Lucé, le** France
99 V3 **Grand Marais** Michigan U.S.A.
99 Q2 **Grand Marais** Minnesota U.S.A.
111 M13 **Grand Marais State Park** St Louis
121 S6 **Grand-Mère** Quebec Canada
106 C2 **Grand Mesa** Colorado U.S.A.
122 E2 **Grandmesnil, L** Quebec Canada
117 P10 **Grand Mt** British Columbia Canada
123 R2 **Grandois** Newfoundland Canada
16 B6 **Grândola** Portugal
16 B6 **Grândola, Sa. de** *mt* Portugal
117 E6 **Grand Pacific Glacier** British Colombia Canada
110 C2 **Grand Pass** Missouri U.S.A.
99 R2 **Grand Portage** Minnesota U.S.A.
109 L3 **Grand Prairie** Texas U.S.A.
109 N9 **Grand Prairie** Texas U.S.A.
22 H5 **Grandpré** France
21 M8 **Grand Pressigny, le** France
21 N3 **Grand Quevilly** France
94 F5 **Grand R** Ohio U.S.A.
119 S5 **Grand Rapids** Manitoba Canada
94 B4 **Grand Rapids** Michigan U.S.A.
99 N2 **Grand Rapids** Minnesota U.S.A.
22 G3 **Grandrieu** Belgium
18 H8 **Grandrieu** France
123 M8 **Grand River** C Breton I, Nova Scotia
99 N9 **Grand River** Iowa U.S.A.
100 B4 **Grand Ronde** Oregon U.S.A.
127 P5 **Grand Roy** Grenada
42 A3 **Grand St. Bernard, Col du** *pass* Switz/Italy
109 M3 **Grand Saline** Texas U.S.A.
129 H3 **Grand Santi** Fr Guiana
40 E4 **Grandson** Switzerland
111 G12 **Grand Terre Is** Louisiana U.S.A.
101 P6 **Grand Teton** *mt* Wyoming U.S.A.
101 P6 **Grand Teton Nat. Park** Wyoming U.S.A.

7 J4 **Grand Turk I** Turks & Caicos Is
6 B2 **Grand Valley** Colorado U.S.A.
9 R7 **Grandview** Manitoba Canada
0 J7 **Grand View** Idaho U.S.A.
0 B3 **Grandview** Missouri U.S.A.
9 K3 **Grandview** Texas U.S.A.
0 F3 **Grandview** Washington U.S.A.
4 B4 **Grandville** Michigan U.S.A.
6 B7 **Grandvillers** France
1 O2 **Grandvilliers** France
3 L5 **Grand Wash** *creek* Arizona U.S.A.
3 L6 **Grand Wash Cliffs** Arizona U.S.A.
9 N15 **Grâne** France
6 F6 **Grane** Norway
7 G3 **Grañén** Spain
4 B2 **Granero** *mt* Italy
1 N5 **Granet, L** Quebec Canada
4 C4 **Graney, L** Ireland
7 G11 **Grangarde** Sweden
8 D4 **Grangca** China
7 H11 **Grängeberg** Sweden
7 H1 **Grange Hill** Jamaica
0 E5 **Grange, Mont de** *mt* France
2 E1 **Grangemouth** Scotland
9 P9 **Granger** Missouri U.S.A.
9 K5 **Granger** Texas U.S.A.
0 E3 **Granger** Washington U.S.A.
1 Q8 **Granger** Wyoming U.S.A.
6 B7 **Granges-sur-Vologne** France
0 J4 **Grangeville** Idaho U.S.A.
6 J8 **Graninge** Sweden
7 L7 **Granite** Oklahoma U.S.A.
0 G5 **Granite** Oregon U.S.A.
8 A8 **Granite** Wyoming U.S.A.
7 L10 **Granite Bay** British Columbia Canada
1 M12 **Granite City** St Louis
0 F3 **Granite City** Illinois U.S.A.
9 L5 **Granite Falls** Minnesota U.S.A.
2 F2 **Granite Falls** North Carolina U.S.A.
0 D1 **Granite Falls** Washington U.S.A.
6 N7 **Granite I** Alaska U.S.A.
9 T3 **Granite I** Michigan U.S.A.
0 H9 **Granite Mt** Nevada U.S.A.
3 J7 **Granite Mts** California U.S.A.
3 D7 **Granite Peak** W Australia Australia
2 H6 **Granite Peak** California U.S.A.
0 H8 **Granite Peak** *mt* Nevada U.S.A.
1 Q4 **Granite Pk** Montana U.S.A.
1 M9 **Granite Pk** Utah U.S.A.
1 R7 **Granite Pk** Wyoming U.S.A.
9 T3 **Granite Pt** Michigan U.S.A.
6 Q6 **Granite Range** Alaska U.S.A.
0 F9 **Granite Range** Nevada U.S.A.
3 L8 **Granite Reef Aqueduct** Arizona U.S.A.
0 B5 **Granites, The** *pk* N Terr Australia
2 F4 **Graniteville** South Carolina U.S.A.
0 G9 **Granito** Brazil
4 C4 **Granity** New Zealand
9 K4 **Granja** Brazil
7 J5 **Granja, Pta. de la** Dominican Rep
7 J14 **Grankullavik** Sweden
3 D6 **Gran Laguna Salada** *L* Argentina
8 F9 **Granlea** Alberta Canada
3 E6 **Gran Lorenzo** Argentina
6 G8 **Granlunda** Sweden
4 F3 **Gran Morelos** Mexico
7 G13 **Gränna** Sweden
1 B7 **Grannis** Arkansas U.S.A.
8 E1 **Grano** North Dakota U.S.A.
7 J3 **Granollers** Spain
2 A3 **Gran Paradiso** *mt* Italy
3 E5 **Gran Pico** Argentina
2 D2 **Gran Pilastro** *mt* Italy/Austria
3 E4 **Gran Pinto** Argentina
4 B2 **Gran Queyron** *mt* Italy/France
3 D5 **Gran Roca** Argentina
2 F6 **Gran Sasso d'Italia** Italy
3 S6 **Gransee** Germany
0 D2 **Grant** Ontario Canada
3 G10 **Grant** Florida U.S.A.
9 M8 **Grant** Iowa U.S.A.
4 B3 **Grant** Michigan U.S.A.
1 M4 **Grant** Montana U.S.A.
8 E9 **Grant** Nebraska U.S.A.
7 P8 **Grant** Oklahoma U.S.A.
9 M9 **Grant City** Missouri U.S.A.
3 D7 **Grant Duff Ra** W Australia Australia
9 F2 **Grantham** England
6 B9 **Grant I** *isld* Antarctica
0 C1 **Grant I** N Terr Australia
7 P3 **Grant L** Northwest Territories Canada
6 E4 **Grantley Hbr** Alaska U.S.A.
3 E8 **Grant, Mt** W Australia Australia
0 J9 **Granton** Ontario Canada
3 E2 **Granton** Scotland
9 Q5 **Granton** Wisconsin U.S.A.
5 E3 **Grantown on Spey** Scotland
2 E4 **Grant Ra** W Australia Australia
3 J3 **Grant Ra** Nevada U.S.A.
6 K7 **Granträsk** Sweden
6 M6 **Grants** Alaska U.S.A.
6 C6 **Grants** New Mexico U.S.A.
9 O4 **Grantsburg** Wisconsin U.S.A.
1 L3 **Grantsdale** Montana U.S.A.
3 F2 **Grantshouse** Scotland
0 B7 **Grants Pass** Oregon U.S.A.
1 N9 **Grantsville** Utah U.S.A.
4 F8 **Grantsville** West Virginia U.S.A.
1 M8 **Grantville** Georgia U.S.A.
0 G4 **Granville** France
9 R8 **Granville** Illinois U.S.A.
9 L7 **Granville** Iowa U.S.A.
5 O3 **Granville** New York U.S.A.
8 F1 **Granville** North Dakota U.S.A.
4 E6 **Granville** Ohio U.S.A.
4 K6 **Granville** Pennsylvania U.S.A.
2 G9 **Granville Ferry** Nova Scotia Canada
3 E5 **Gran Villegas** Argentina
9 R2 **Granville L** Manitoba Canada
3 P6 **Granzin** Germany
0 G5 **Grão Mogol** Brazil
9 M4 **Grapeland** Texas U.S.A.
2 F7 **Grapevine** California U.S.A.
9 N8 **Grapevine** Texas U.S.A.
9 K3 **Grapevine Res** Texas U.S.A.
2 D3 **Grappa, Monte** *mt* Italy
6 G5 **Grappler Bk** Caribbean
7 H11 **Gräsberg** Sweden
2 M8 **Grasdorf** Germany
7 F10 **Graskop** S Africa
4 H5 **Gras,L.de** Northwest Territories Canada
3 E5 **Grasmere** England
7 K11 **Gräsö** Sweden
5 M2 **Grass** *R* New York U.S.A.
1 R6 **Grass Creek** Wyoming U.S.A.
4 B4 **Grasse** France
1 M3 **Grasset, L** Quebec Canada
3 G5 **Grassington** England
0 C8 **Grass Lake** California U.S.A.
8 F2 **Grassland** Texas U.S.A.
8 K9 **Grasslands Nat Park** Saskatchewan Canada
5 E4 **Grassmere, L** New Zealand
3 D10 **Grass Patch** W Australia Australia
9 T3 **Grass R** Manitoba Canada
101 R2 **Grassrange** Montana U.S.A.
119 Q4 **Grass River Prov. Park** Manitoba Canada
102 C2 **Grass Valley** California U.S.A.
100 E4 **Grass Valley** Oregon U.S.A.
139 G8 **Grassy** Tasmania Australia
98 C2 **Grassy Butte** North Dakota U.S.A.
126 F3 **Grassy Cr** Andros Bahamas
118 G7 **Grassy Island L** Alberta Canada
94 G8 **Grassy Knob** *mt* West Virginia U.S.A.
118 F9 **Grassy Lake** Alberta Canada
28 D7 **Gråsten** Denmark
27 F13 **Grästorp** Sweden
26 J3 **Gratangen** Norway
123 U5 **Grate's Cove** Newfoundland Canada
99 R7 **Gratiot** Wisconsin U.S.A.
94 C7 **Gratis** Ohio U.S.A.
26 L6 **Gråträsk** Sweden
28 D4 **Grauballe** Denmark
41 K4 **Graubünden** *canton* Switzerland
18 H9 **Grau-du-Roi,le** France
17 H2 **Graus** Spain
131 H2 **Gravata** Brazil
25 E5 **Grave** Netherlands
118 L9 **Gravelbourg** Saskatchewan Canada
22 C2 **Gravelines** France
21 H5 **Gravelle, la** France
87 F10 **Gravelotte** S Africa
121 L8 **Gravenhurst** Ontario Canada
36 F3 **Grävenwiesbach** Germany
101 L3 **Grave Pk** Idaho U.S.A.
18 E7 **Grave, Pte de** *C* France
139 K3 **Gravesend** New South Wales Australia
9 G5 **Gravesend** England
19 N17 **Graveson** France
110 B5 **Gravette** Arkansas U.S.A.
21 N3 **Gravigny** France
21 L2 **Graville** France
43 G8 **Gravina di Puglia** Italy
99 M9 **Gravity** Iowa U.S.A.
28 D3 **Gravlev** Denmark
26 E7 **Gravvik** Norway
99 V5 **Grawn** Michigan U.S.A.
119 N8 **Gray** Saskatchewan Canada
19 J5 **Gray** France
112 D4 **Gray** Georgia U.S.A.
95 R3 **Gray** Maine U.S.A.
108 D7 **Gray** Oklahoma U.S.A.
100 A3 **Grayland** Washington U.S.A.
117 L6 **Grayling** *R* British Columbia Canada
94 C2 **Grayling** Michigan U.S.A.
116 R3 **Grayling Fk.** *R* Alaska U.S.A.
13 F5 **Grayrigg** England
100 A3 **Grays Harbor** Washington U.S.A.
101 O6 **Grays L** Idaho U.S.A.
119 P8 **Grayson** Saskatchewan Canada
94 E8 **Grayson** Kentucky U.S.A.
111 D9 **Grayson** Louisiana U.S.A.
120 A2 **Grayson L** Ontario Canada
106 E2 **Grays Pk** Colorado U.S.A.
94 B1 **Grays Reef** Michigan U.S.A.
100 B3 **Grays River** Washington U.S.A.
9 G5 **Grays Thurrock** England
111 K11 **Grayton Beach** Florida U.S.A.
110 H3 **Grayville** Illinois U.S.A.
54 G6 **Grayvoron** Russian Federation
38 M7 **Graz** Austria
16 D8 **Grazalema** Spain
46 E2 **Grdelica** Serbia Yugoslavia
13 G6 **Greasbrough** England
117 M4 **Greasy L** Northwest Territories Canada
138 B5 **Great Australian Bight** Australia
9 G4 **Great Baddow** England
113 J12 **Great Bahama Bank** Bahamas
145 E2 **Great Barrier I** New Zealand
136 **Great Barrier Reef** Australia
141 H3 **Great Barrier Reef Marine Park** Queensland Australia
95 O4 **Great Barrington** Massachusetts U.S.A.
141 H4 **Great Basalt Wall** Queensland Australia
103 H1 **Great Basin** Nevada U.S.A.
117 L3 **Great Bear** *R* Northwest Territories Canada
114 H4 **Great Bear L** Northwest Territories Canada
107 M3 **Great Bend** Kansas U.S.A.
98 K3 **Great Bend** North Dakota U.S.A.
89 A9 **Great Berg** *R* S Africa
15 B2 **Great Bernera** *isld* Scotland
14 A4 **Great Blasket I.** Ireland
122 F3 **Great Boule I** Quebec Canada
123 R2 **Great Brehat** Newfoundland Canada
8 D1 **Great Budworth** England
123 Q5 **Great Burnt L.** Newfoundland Canada
89 A7 **Great Bushman Land** *reg* S Africa
94 J7 **Great Cacapon** West Virginia U.S.A.
9 F2 **Great Casterton** England
9 G3 **Great Chesterford** England
123 T7 **Great Colinet I.** Newfoundland Canada
12 D2 **Great Cumbrae** *isld* Scotland
9 F2 **Great Dalby** England
118 K6 **Great Deer** Saskatchewan Canada
101 S9 **Great Divide** Colorado U.S.A.
139 **Great Dividing Ra** Australia
13 H5 **Great Driffield** England
120 H7 **Great Duck I.** Ontario Canada
Greater Khingan Range *see* **Da Hinggan Ling**
13 F6 **Greater Manchester** *co* England
145 D1 **Great Exhibition Bay** New Zealand
126 F3 **Great Exuma** *isld* Bahamas
101 O2 **Great Falls** Montana U.S.A.
112 G3 **Great Falls** South Carolina U.S.A.
110 L6 **Great Falls Dam** Tennessee U.S.A.
110 L6 **Great Falls L** Tennessee U.S.A.
89 E9 **Great Fish** *R* S Africa
6 N6 **Great Fisher Bank** North Sea
89 E9 **Great Fish Pt.** *lighthouse* S Africa
145 E4 **Greatford** New Zealand
127 K3 **Great Goat I** Jamaica
9 F2 **Great Gonerby** England
113 K11 **Great Guana Cay** *isld* Bahamas
9 F5 **Greatham** England
126 F2 **Great Harbour Cay** *isld* Bahamas
144 A6 **Great I** New Zealand
145 D1 **Great I** New Zealand
126 H4 **Great Inagua** *isld* Bahamas
Great Indian Desert *see* **Thar**
113 H11 **Great Isaac I** Bahamas
89 A6 **Great Karas Berg** *mts* Namibia
89 C9 **Great Karoo** *reg* S Africa
89 E9 **Great Kei** *R* S Africa
141 K6 **Great Keppel I** Queensland Australia
139 H8 **Great L** Tasmania Australia
112 K3 **Great L** North Carolina U.S.A.
8 D3 **Great Malvern** England
145 E2 **Great Mercury I** New Zealand
9 F4 **Great Missenden** England
136 J3 **Great NE Channel** Australia/Papua New Guinea
69 A9 **Great Nicobar** *isld* Nicobar Is
9 F4 **Great Offley** England
8 C1 **Great Ormes Head** Wales
95 P6 **Great Peconic B** Long I, New York U.S.A.
127 J3 **Great Pedro Bluff** Jamaica
95 T2 **Great Pond** Maine U.S.A.
95 R5 **Great Pt** Massachusetts U.S.A.
122 G10 **Great Pubnico L** Nova Scotia Canada
127 J2 **Great R** Jamaica
88 E5 **Great Ruaha** *R* Tanzania
95 N3 **Great Sacandaga L** New York U.S.A.
113 J11 **Great Sale Cay** Bahamas
101 N8 **Great Salt L** Utah U.S.A.
101 M9 **Great Salt L.Des** Utah U.S.A.
106 E4 **Great Sand Dunes Nat.Mon** Colorado U.S.A.
118 H8 **Great Sand Hills** Saskatchewan Canada
142 D5 **Great Sandy Desert** W Australia Australia
141 L7 **Great Sandy I** Queensland Australia
9 E5 **Great Shefford** England
9 G3 **Great Shelford** England
89 G4 **Great Shingwidzi** *R* S Africa
114 H5 **Great Slave L** Northwest Territories Canada
112 D2 **Great Smoky Mts** Tenn/N Carolina U.S.A.
117 L7 **Great Snow Mt** British Columbia Canada
7 D13 **Great Sole Bank** Atlantic Oc
95 O6 **Great South Bay** Long I, New York U.S.A.
113 K12 **Great Stirrup Cay** *isld* Bahamas
8 B6 **Great Torrington** England
87 C10 **Great Ums** Namibia
138 B3 **Great Victoria Desert** South Australia Australia
122 J8 **Great Village** Nova Scotia Canada
Great Wall *China Base* Antarctica *see* **Chang Cheng**
9 G4 **Great Waltham** England
95 U2 **Great Wass I** Maine U.S.A.
139 H8 **Great Western Tiers** Tasmania Australia
68 C7 **Great West Torres I** Burma
13 G5 **Great Whernside** *mt* England
9 H2 **Great Yarmouth** England
27 E13 **Grebbestad** Sweden
36 G2 **Grebenau** Germany
36 G3 **Grebenhain** Germany
54 D6 **Grebenka** Ukraine
32 K10 **Grebenstein** Germany
38 K7 **Grebenzen** *mt* Austria
85 F4 **Greboun, Mt** Niger
43 F8 **Greco, Torre del** Italy
37 L5 **Greding** Germany
16 D4 **Gredos, Sa. de** *mts* Spain
28 B6 **Gredstedbro** Denmark
46 E6 **Greece** *rep* S Europe
98 B9 **Greeley** Colorado U.S.A.
98 H8 **Greeley** Nebraska U.S.A.
115 L1 **Greely Fiord** Northwest Territories Canada
50 F1 **Greem Bell, Ostrov** *isld* Russian Federation
107 O2 **Green** Kansas U.S.A.
112 E2 **Green** *R* North Carolina U.S.A.
113 G11 **Greenacres City** Florida U.S.A.
95 M8 **Greenbackville** Maryland U.S.A.
99 T5 **Green Bay** Wisconsin U.S.A.
94 G8 **Greenbrier** *R* West Virginia U.S.A.
94 D2 **Greenbush** Michigan U.S.A.
98 K1 **Greenbush** Minnesota U.S.A.
143 B10 **Greenbushes** W Australia Australia
139 K6 **Green Cape** New South Wales Australia
110 K2 **Greencastle** Indiana U.S.A.
94 K7 **Greencastle** Pennsylvania U.S.A.
126 F2 **Green Cay** *isld* Bahamas
99 O9 **Green City** Missouri U.S.A.
118 B4 **Green Court** Alberta Canada
113 F8 **Green Cove Springs** Florida U.S.A.
32 L9 **Greene** Germany
99 O7 **Greene** Iowa U.S.A.
95 M4 **Greene** New York U.S.A.
98 E1 **Greene** North Dakota U.S.A.
143 G6 **Greene, Mt** W Australia Australia
112 E1 **Greeneville** Tennessee U.S.A.
102 C5 **Greenfield** California U.S.A.
110 F2 **Greenfield** Illinois U.S.A.
94 B7 **Greenfield** Indiana U.S.A.
99 M8 **Greenfield** Iowa U.S.A.
95 P4 **Greenfield** Massachusetts U.S.A.
110 C4 **Greenfield** Missouri U.S.A.
94 D7 **Greenfield** Ohio U.S.A.
107 M6 **Greenfield** Oklahoma U.S.A.
110 H5 **Greenfield** Tennessee U.S.A.
110 C5 **Green Forest** Arkansas U.S.A.
143 B9 **Green Head** W Australia Australia
127 O2 **Green Hill** Trinidad
140 B1 **Greenhill I** N Terr Australia
143 B9 **Greenhills** W Australia Australia
144 B7 **Greenhills** New Zealand
102 F6 **Greenhorn Mts** California U.S.A.
141 H3 **Green I** Queensland Australia
143 B9 **Green I** W Australia Australia
123 Q2 **Green I** Newfoundland Canada
144 B7 **Green I** New Zealand
116 O6 **Green I** Alaska U.S.A.
121 Q4 **Greening** Quebec Canada
137 L2 **Green Is** Papua New Guinea
127 H1 **Green Island** Jamaica
144 C7 **Green Island** New Zealand
71 D5 **Green Island B** Philippines
144 A7 **Green Islets** New Zealand
117 N10 **Green L** British Columbia Canada
99 S6 **Green L** Wisconsin U.S.A.
118 K4 **Green Lake** Saskatchewan Canada
109 L7 **Green Lake** Texas U.S.A.
115 P2 **Greenland** *isld terr* Arctic
127 P6 **Greenland** Barbados
90 H1 **Greenland Basin** Arctic Oc
90 G2 **Greenland-Iceland Rise** N Atlantic Oc
144 B6 **Greenland Res** New Zealand
147 G10 **Greenland Sea** Arctic Oc
13 F2 **Greenlaw** Scotland
107 O2 **Greenleaf** Kansas U.S.A.
12 E1 **Greenloaning** Scotland
15 E5 **Green Lowther** *mt* Scotland
138 C5 **Greenly I** South Australia Australia
123 P2 **Greenly I** Quebec Canada
145 F3 **Greenmeadows** New Zealand
106 D2 **Green Mt Res** Colorado U.S.A.
95 O3 **Green Mts** Vermont U.S.A.
101 S7 **Green Mts** Wyoming U.S.A.
12 D2 **Greenock** Scotland
14 E2 **Greenore** Ireland
14 E4 **Greenore Pt** Ireland
143 A8 **Greenough** W Australia Australia
116 R2 **Greenough, Mt** Alaska U.S.A.
112 G5 **Green Pond** South Carolina U.S.A.
95 P5 **Greenport** Long I, New York U.S.A.
122 D6 **Green R** New Brunswick Canada
101 Q8 **Green River** Wyoming U.S.A.
94 B9 **Green R. Res** Kentucky U.S.A.
111 J9 **Greensboro** Alabama U.S.A.
111 M11 **Greensboro** Florida U.S.A.
112 D4 **Greensboro** Georgia U.S.A.
112 H1 **Greensboro** North Carolina U.S.A.
95 P2 **Greensboro** Vermont U.S.A.
94 B7 **Greensburg** Indiana U.S.A.
107 L4 **Greensburg** Kansas U.S.A.
94 B9 **Greensburg** Kentucky U.S.A.
111 F11 **Greensburg** Louisiana U.S.A.
94 H6 **Greensburg** Pennsylvania U.S.A.
141 K2 **Greenslopes** *dist* Brisbane, Qnsld Australia
123 T4 **Greenspond** Newfoundland Canada
94 J7 **Green Spring** West Virginia U.S.A.
94 D5 **Green Springs** Ohio U.S.A.
99 O9 **Greentop** Missouri U.S.A.
94 B6 **Greentown** Indiana U.S.A.
113 K11 **Green Turtle Cay** *isld* Bahamas
110 H2 **Greenup** Illinois U.S.A.
141 H4 **Greenvale** Queensland Australia
85 C8 **Greenville** Liberia
111 K10 **Greenville** Alabama U.S.A.
100 E9 **Greenville** California U.S.A.
113 D7 **Greenville** Florida U.S.A.
110 G3 **Greenville** Illinois U.S.A.
110 J4 **Greenville** Kentucky U.S.A.
95 S1 **Greenville** Maine U.S.A.
94 B3 **Greenville** Michigan U.S.A.
111 E8 **Greenville** Mississippi U.S.A.
110 F4 **Greenville** Missouri U.S.A.
95 Q4 **Greenville** New Hampshire U.S.A.
95 N4 **Greenville** New York U.S.A.
112 K2 **Greenville** North Carolina U.S.A.
94 C6 **Greenville** Ohio U.S.A.
94 G5 **Greenville** Pennsylvania U.S.A.
112 E3 **Greenville** South Carolina U.S.A.
109 L2 **Greenville** Texas U.S.A.
94 H8 **Greenville** Virginia U.S.A.
119 N2 **Greenwater L** Ontario Canada
119 O6 **Greenwater L. Prov. Park** Saskatchewan Canada
119 S9 **Greenway** Manitoba Canada
98 G4 **Greenway** South Dakota U.S.A.
9 G5 **Greenwich** England
107 N4 **Greenwich** Kansas U.S.A.
95 O3 **Greenwich** New York U.S.A.
94 E5 **Greenwich** Ohio U.S.A.
103 N3 **Greenwich** Utah U.S.A.
100 G1 **Greenwood** British Columbia Canada
110 B6 **Greenwood** Arkansas U.S.A.
102 D3 **Greenwood** California U.S.A.
95 M8 **Greenwood** Delaware U.S.A.
94 A7 **Greenwood** Indiana U.S.A.
94 C10 **Greenwood** Kentucky U.S.A.
111 C9 **Greenwood** Louisiana U.S.A.
111 F8 **Greenwood** Mississippi U.S.A.
98 K9 **Greenwood** Nebraska U.S.A.
112 E3 **Greenwood** South Carolina U.S.A.
98 H7 **Greenwood** South Dakota U.S.A.
99 Q5 **Greenwood** Wisconsin U.S.A.
111 H8 **Greenwood Springs** Mississippi U.S.A.
100 J3 **Greer** Idaho U.S.A.
112 E3 **Greer** South Carolina U.S.A.
111 C7 **Greeson, L** Arkansas U.S.A.
32 F5 **Greetsiel** Germany
21 M5 **Greez** France
25 F6 **Grefrath** Germany
119 S9 **Gregg** Manitoba Canada
111 B9 **Greggton** Texas U.S.A.
118 F2 **Gregoire L** Alberta Canada
128 D5 **Gregório** *R* Brazil
98 G6 **Gregory** South Dakota U.S.A.
140 E4 **Gregory Downs** Queensland Australia
142 G5 **Gregory L** W Australia Australia
143 C7 **Gregory, L** W Australia Australia
141 G4 **Gregory Ra** Queensland Australia
142 D5 **Gregory Ra** W Australia Australia
113 L12 **Gregory Town** Bahamas
38 H8 **Greifenburg** Austria
41 J3 **Greifensee** *L* Switzerland
33 T6 **Greiffenberg** Germany
33 S4 **Greifswald** Germany
33 T4 **Greifswalder Bodden** Germany
33 T4 **Greifswalder Oie** *isld* Germany
38 K7 **Greimberg** *mt* Austria
38 L5 **Grein** Austria
41 J4 **Greina Pass** Switzerland
38 M5 **Greinerwald** *woods* Austria
37 L5 **Greisselbach** Germany
37 N2 **Greiz** Germany
52 E1 **Gremikha** Russian Federation
33 N4 **Gremsmühlen** Germany
28 F4 **Grenå** Denmark
127 P5 **Grenada** *isld* Lesser Antilles
100 C8 **Grenada** California U.S.A.
111 G8 **Grenada** Mississippi U.S.A.
18 E9 **Grenade** France
18 F9 **Grenade sur Garonne** France
127 O8 **Grenadines, The** *islds* Lesser Antilles
40 F3 **Grenchen** Switzerland
28 C5 **Grene** Denmark
28 F1 **Grenen** *C* Denmark
139 J5 **Grenfell** New South Wales Australia
119 P8 **Grenfell** Saskatchewan Canada
19 P14 **Grenoble** France
107 O4 **Grenola** Kansas U.S.A.
98 C1 **Grenora** North Dakota U.S.A.
26 S2 **Grense/Jakobselv** Norway
127 P5 **Grenville** Grenada
106 G5 **Grenville** New Mexico U.S.A.
98 J4 **Grenville** South Dakota U.S.A.
141 G1 **Grenville C** Queensland Australia
117 J9 **Grenville Chan** British Columbia Canada
117 L10 **Grenville, Mt** British Columbia Canada
19 P17 **Gréoux-les-Bains** France
33 Q9 **Greppin** Germany
33 Q4 **Gresenhorst** Germany
100 C4 **Gresham** Oregon U.S.A.
70 O9 **Gresik** Java
19 P15 **Gresse** France
19 Q13 **Grésy-sur-Isère** France
139 K5 **Greta** New South Wales Australia
13 G5 **Greta Br** England
119 U9 **Gretna** Manitoba Canada
111 G12 **Gretna** Louisiana U.S.A.
111 J13 **Gretna** New Orleans, Louisiana U.S.A.
94 H10 **Gretna** Virginia U.S.A.
13 E3 **Gretna Green** Scotland
37 K1 **Greussen** Germany
45 K4 **Greve** Italy
25 A5 **Grevelingen** Netherlands
32 G8 **Greven** Germany
46 E4 **Grevená** Greece
36 B1 **Grevenbroich** Germany
32 L5 **Grevenkop** Germany
33 O5 **Grevesmühlen** Germany
27 F16 **Grevie** Sweden
29 K4 **Grevie** Sweden
28 H5 **Grevinge** Denmark
101 R5 **Greybull** Wyoming U.S.A.
140 D2 **Grey, C** N Terr Australia
101 Q4 **Greycliff** Montana U.S.A.
99 M4 **Grey Eagle** Minnesota U.S.A.
117 F4 **Grey Hunter Pk** Yukon Territory Canada
123 R3 **Grey I** Newfoundland Canada
123 R3 **Grey Is** Newfoundland Canada
144 C5 **Greymouth** New Zealand
123 Q5 **Grey R** Newfoundland Canada
141 G8 **Grey Ra** Qnsld/N S W
141 G8 **Grey Range** Queensland Australia
101 P6 **Greys** *R* Wyoming U.S.A.
143 A7 **Grey's Plains** W Australia Australia
13 F4 **Greystoke** England
101 R9 **Greystone** Colorado U.S.A.
14 E3 **Greystones** Ireland
145 E4 **Greytown** New Zealand
89 G7 **Greytown** S Africa
22 H2 **Grez-Doiceau** Belgium
21 J6 **Grez-en-Bouère** France
46 D4 **Griba** *mt* Albania
81 F11 **Gribb Seamount** Southern Oc
86 C4 **Gribingui** *R* Cent Afr Republic
52 D2 **Gridino** Russian Federation
102 C2 **Gridley** California U.S.A.
99 S9 **Gridley** Illinois U.S.A.
107 P3 **Gridley** Kansas U.S.A.
87 D11 **Griekwastad** S Africa
25 D2 **Griend** Netherlands
37 P7 **Griesbach** Germany
36 F4 **Griesheim** Germany
41 O3 **Gries im Sellrain** Austria
Griessen *see* **Klettgau**
25 F5 **Grieth** Germany
38 L8 **Griffen** Austria
111 M8 **Griffin** Georgia U.S.A.
113 F9 **Griffin, L** Florida U.S.A.
116 Q1 **Griffin Pt** Alaska U.S.A.
139 H5 **Griffith** New South Wales Australia
115 K3 **Griffith I** Northwest Territories Canada
110 E6 **Griffithville** Arkansas U.S.A.
112 K2 **Grifton** North Carolina U.S.A.
99 Q10 **Griggsville** Illinois U.S.A.
41 K6 **Grigna** *mt* Italy
19 N16 **Grignan** France
18 E8 **Grignols** France
48 M3 **Grigoriopol'** Moldova
25 F2 **Grijpskerk** Netherlands
86 C4 **Grimari** Cent Afr Republic
19 Q18 **Grimaud** France
21 L8 **Grimaudière, la** France
48 K1 **Grimaylov** Ukraine
139 G8 **Grim, C** Tasmania Australia
102 C2 **Grimes** California U.S.A.
100 K5 **Grimes Pass** Idaho U.S.A.
33 R10 **Grimma** Germany
33 S4 **Grimmen** Germany
Grimmenthal *see* **Obermassfeld-Grimmenthal**
33 T7 **Grimnitzsee** Germany
121 L9 **Grimsby** Ontario Canada
13 H6 **Grimsby** England
41 H4 **Grimsel** *mt* Switzerland
28 S8 **Grimsey** *isld* Iceland
117 P7 **Grimshaw** Alberta Canada
27 C13 **Grimstad** Norway
28 B5 **Grimstrup** Denmark
28 R10 **Grindavik** Iceland
40 H4 **Grindelwald** Switzerland
28 C3 **Grinderslev** Denmark
28 B5 **Grindsted Å** Denmark
95 S8 **Grindstone** Maine U.S.A.
94 E2 **Grind Stone City** Michigan U.S.A.
123 L6 **Grindstone Island** Quebec Canada
119 U7 **Grindstone Prov. Park** Manitoba Canada
119 V7 **Grindstone Pt** Manitoba Canada
99 O8 **Grinnell** Iowa U.S.A.
107 K2 **Grinnell** Kansas U.S.A.
115 K2 **Grinnell Pen** Northwest Territories Canada
42 F2 **Grintavec** *mt* Slovenia
13 G5 **Grinton** England
26 C8 **Grip** *lighthouse* Norway
33 O6 **Grippel** Germany
89 F8 **Griqualand E** *reg* S Africa
89 C7 **Griqualand W** *reg* S Africa
40 F6 **Grisanche, Val** Italy
115 L2 **Grise Fiord** Northwest Territories Canada
45 L1 **Grisignano** Italy
69 F14 **Grisik** Sumatra
22 B2 **Gris Nez, C** France
18 F9 **Grisolles** France
27 K11 **Grisslehamn** Sweden
99 L8 **Griswold** Iowa U.S.A.
52 H4 **Griva** Russian Federation
21 P2 **Grivesnes** France
40 F6 **Grivola** *mt* Italy
33 P9 **Grizeline** Germany
85 D3 **Grizim** Algeria
117 N3 **Grizzly Bear Mt** Northwest Territories Canada
26 C9 **Grjotli** Norway
42 G4 **Grmeč Plan** Bosnia-Herzegovina
123 R3 **Groais I** Newfoundland Canada
33 S10 **Gröba** Germany
33 Q10 **Gröbers** Germany
27 M15 **Grobina** Latvia
9 E2 **Groby** England
33 P9 **Gröbzig** Germany
28 B7 **Gröde-Appelland** *isld* Germany
31 O2 **Gródek** Poland
31 K5 **Grodków** Poland
33 S10 **Grödlitz** Germany
31 O2 **Grodno** Belarus
31 J3 **Grodzisk** Poland
31 M3 **Grodzisk Mazowiecki** Poland
89 C8 **Groen** *watercourse* S Africa
22 G2 **Groenendaal** Belgium
25 G4 **Groenlo** Netherlands
109 L4 **Groesbeck** Texas U.S.A.
25 E5 **Groesbeek** Netherlands
25 C3 **Groet** Netherlands
32 K8 **Grohnde** Germany
22 F3 **Groise, la** France
37 N1 **Groitzsch** Germany
20 D6 **Groix** France
20 D6 **Groix, I de** France
31 M4 **Grójec** Poland
43 C12 **Grombalia** Tunisia
28 C7 **Grønå** *R* Denmark
32 L8 **Gronau** Niedersachsen Germany
32 F8 **Gronau** Nordrhein-Westfalen Germany
28 B4 **Grønbjerg** Denmark
26 F7 **Grong** Norway
28 C4 **Grønhøj** Denmark
33 O9 **Gröningen** Germany
25 G2 **Groningen** Netherlands
25 G2 **Groningen** *prov* Netherlands
25 F2 **Groningerwad** Netherlands
119 N5 **Gronlid** Saskatchewan Canada
115 P5 **Grønnedal** Greenland
26 F5 **Grönöy** Norway
27 K12 **Grönskär** *lighthouse* Sweden
27 H14 **Grönskåra** Sweden
28 J7 **Grønsund** *chan* Denmark
89 D9 **Groot** *R* S Africa
140 D2 **Groote Eylandt** *isld* N Terr Australia
25 F2 **Grootegast** Netherlands
89 B9 **Groot Swartberge** *mts* S Africa
89 C8 **Groot Tafelberg** *mt* S Africa
87 D11 **Grootvloer** *L* S Africa
89 B7 **Groot Vloer** S Africa
89 E9 **Groot Winterberg** *mt* S Africa
22 K4 **Grosbous** Luxembourg
20 G8 **Grosbreuil** France
127 O7 **Gros Islet** St Lucia
27 G14 **Grosjö** Sweden
123 P4 **Gros Morne** *pk* Newfoundland Canada
122 G4 **Gros Morne** Quebec Canada
127 H5 **Gros Morne** Haiti
127 L4 **Gros Morne** Martinique W Indies
123 P4 **Gros Morne Nat. Park** Newfoundland Canada
19 J6 **Grosne** *R* France
20 F3 **Grosnez Pt** Channel Is
41 M5 **Grosotto** Italy
123 P3 **Gros Pate** *pk* Newfoundland Canada
113 F7 **Gross** Florida U.S.A.
37 M4 **Gross Albershof** Germany
40 H4 **Gross Aletsch Gl** Switzerland
32 L10 **Grossalmerode** Germany
33 O9 **Gross Alsleben** Germany
33 P8 **Gross Ammensleben** Germany
37 P5 **Gross Arber** *mt* Germany
33 S8 **Grossbeeren** Germany
33 T8 **Grossbesten** Germany
33 M10 **Grossbodungen** Germany
37 O1 **Gross Bothen** Germany
36 G5 **Grossbottwar** Germany
37 L2 **Gross-Breitenbach** Germany
33 T7 **Gross-Dölln** Germany
37 M2 **Gross Ebersdorf** Germany
123 L6 **Grosse I** Madeleine Is, Quebec Canada
36 F2 **Grossenbuseck** Germany
37 K1 **Grossenehrich** Germany
33 O7 **Gross Engersen** Germany
33 T10 **Grossenhain** Germany
32 H7 **Grossenkneten** Germany
37 N2 **Grossenstein** Germany
127 N4 **Grosse Pointe** Guadeloupe W Indies
33 S10 **Grosse Röder** *R* Germany
42 D6 **Grosseto** Italy
51 N4 **Grossevichi** Russian Federation
36 D5 **Gross Eyberg** *mt* Germany
36 E3 **Gross Feldberg** *mt* Germany
33 T6 **Gross Fredenwalde** Germany
36 E4 **Gross-Gerau** Germany
33 M8 **Gross Gleidingen** Germany
38 G7 **Gross-Glockner** Austria
33 P6 **Gross-Godems** Germany
37 N1 **Gross Görschen** Germany
33 N5 **Gross Gronau** Germany
33 M5 **Gross Hansdorf** Germany
37 P2 **Gross Hartmannsdorf** Germany
32 F5 **Grossheide** Germany
37 M1 **Gross Heringen** Germany
33 M7 **Gross-Kain** Germany
36 E4 **Gross Karlbach** Germany
33 O4 **Gross Klützhöved** Germany
37 L2 **Gross Kochberg** Germany
33 Q10 **Gross Korbetha** Germany
33 T8 **Gross Köris** Germany
33 R8 **Gross Kreutz** Germany
37 N6 **Gross Laaber** *R* Germany
37 J4 **Gross-Langheim** Germany
36 H2 **Grosslüder** Germany
33 S8 **Gross-Machnow** Germany
37 M6 **Grossmehring** Germany
33 M7 **Gross-Oesingen** Germany
36 G4 **Grossostheim** Germany
33 M4 **Gross Plöner See** *L* Germany
37 P6 **Gross Rachel** *mt* Germany
38 L6 **Grossraming** Austria
32 M9 **Gross Rhüden** Germany
36 B5 **Grossrosseln** Germany
37 L1 **Gross Rudestedt** Germany
33 T7 **Gross Schönebeck** Germany
33 P7 **Gross Schwechten** Germany
33 T8 **Gross Selchower See** *L* Germany
33 N8 **Gross-Sisbeck** Germany
33 S6 **Gross Stechlinsee** *L* Germany
36 H6 **Gross Süssen** Germany
36 F4 **Gross-Umstadt** Germany
37 P2 **Gross Waltersdorf** Germany
33 P6 **Gross-Warnow** Germany
33 Q6 **Gross Welle** Germany
33 Q7 **Gross Wudicke** Germany
33 R5 **Gross Wüstenfelde** Germany
33 Q8 **Gross Wusterwitz** Germany
33 T7 **Gross Ziethen** Germany
36 F4 **Gross-Zimmern** Germany
36 B6 **Gros Tenquin** France
21 M3 **Gros Theil, le** France
42 F3 **Grosuplje** Slovenia
141 J5 **Grosvenor Downs** Queensland Australia
116 K7 **Grosvenor, L** Alaska U.S.A.
101 P6 **Gros Ventre Ra** Wyoming U.S.A.
32 J9 **Grotenberg** *mt* Germany
22 F2 **Grotenberge** Belgium
22 H1 **Grote Nete** *R* Belgium
95 Q5 **Groton** Connecticut U.S.A.
95 Q4 **Groton** Massachusetts U.S.A.
95 L4 **Groton** New York U.S.A.
98 H4 **Groton** South Dakota U.S.A.
95 P2 **Groton** Vermont U.S.A.
26 G4 **Grötöy** Norway
45 Q8 **Grotta Azzurra** Italy
45 O7 **Grotta delle Capre** Italy
22 J3 **Grotte-de-Han** Belgium
19 N16 **Grottes de St. Marcel** France
94 J8 **Grottoes** Virginia U.S.A.
36 F5 **Grotzingen** Germany
117 P8 **Grouard** Alberta Canada
20 G4 **Grouin, Pte.du** France
120 H4 **Groundhog** *R* Ontario Canada
101 M6 **Grouse** Idaho U.S.A.
101 M8 **Grouse Creek** Utah U.S.A.
25 E2 **Grouw** Netherlands
27 C13 **Grovane** Norway
107 Q5 **Grove** Oklahoma U.S.A.
94 E7 **Grove City** Ohio U.S.A.
94 G5 **Grove City** Pennsylvania U.S.A.
117 O8 **Grovedale** Alberta Canada
140 B2 **Grove Hill** N Terr Australia
111 J10 **Grove Hill** Alabama U.S.A.
28 C4 **Grove Kirke** Denmark
102 D4 **Groveland** California U.S.A.
26 F9 **Grövelsjön** Sweden
146 H11 **Grove Mts** Antarctica
98 B9 **Grover** Colorado U.S.A.
101 P7 **Grover** Wyoming U.S.A.
111 C12 **Groves** Texas U.S.A.
109 M4 **Groveton** Texas U.S.A.
95 Q2 **Groveton** Vermont U.S.A.
145 D4 **Grovetown** New Zealand
112 E4 **Grovetown** Georgia U.S.A.
101 P6 **Grovont** Wyoming U.S.A.
103 L9 **Growler** Arizona U.S.A.
103 L9 **Growler Mts** Arizona U.S.A.
47 J1 **Grozd'ovo** Bulgaria
45 P1 **Groznjan** Croatia
57 F3 **Groznoye** Kirghizia
53 G11 **Groznyy** Russian Federation
41 J4 **Gr. Scheerh** *mt* Switzerland
33 O4 **Grube** Germany
32 L9 **Grubenhagen** Germany
42 H3 **Grubišno Polje** Croatia
37 P6 **Grubweg** Germany
21 M2 **Gruchet-le-Valasse** France
42 J6 **Gruda** Croatia
47 J2 **Grudovo** Bulgaria
31 M2 **Grudusk** Poland
31 L2 **Grudziadz** Poland
128 D8 **Gruesa, Pta** *C* Chile
122 B6 **Grues, I. aux** Quebec Canada
44 C1 **Grugliasco** Italy
12 B2 **Gruinart** Scotland
109 J9 **Grulla** Texas U.S.A.
36 D4 **Grumbach** Germany
43 H7 **Grumo Appula** Italy
27 F12 **Grums** Sweden
37 O2 **Gruna** Germany
15 C3 **Grunard Bay** Scotland
33 T8 **Grunau** Germany
87 C11 **Grünau** Namibia
36 G6 **Grunbach** Germany
36 F2 **Grünberg** Germany
36 G3 **Gründau** Germany
Gründelhardt *see* **Frankenhardt**
26 K8 **Grundsunda** Sweden
26 J8 **Grundtjärn** Sweden
99 O7 **Grundy Center** Iowa U.S.A.
120 K7 **Grundy Lake Prov. Park** Ontario Canada
28 D7 **Grünholz** Germany
124 J5 **Gruñidora** Mexico
33 Q8 **Grüningen** Germany
36 F2 **Grüningen** Germany
36 H4 **Grünsfeld** Germany
36 E4 **Grünstadt** Germany
38 E8 **Gruppo** *mt* Italy
41 L4 **Grüsch** Switzerland
108 C7 **Gruver** Texas U.S.A.
40 F4 **Gruyère, L. de la** Switzerland
52 B6 **Gruzdžiai** Lithuania
54 L4 **Gryazi** Russian Federation
52 F5 **Gryazovets** Russian Federation
31 M6 **Grybów** Poland
27 H11 **Grycksbo** Sweden
31 J2 **Gryfice** Poland
31 H2 **Gryfino** Poland
99 L1 **Grygla** Minnesota U.S.A.
27 G12 **Grythyttehed** Sweden
26 H3 **Grytöy** *L* Norway
26 C9 **Grytten** Norway
131 H6 **Grytviken** S Georgia
31 J2 **Grzmiąca** Poland
41 O3 **Gschnitz** Austria
36 H6 **Gschwend** Germany
40 F5 **Gstaad** Switzerland
40 F5 **Gsteig** Switzerland
19 P15 **Guâ** France
75 L7 **Gua** India
41 O7 **Gua** *R* Italy
128 D3 **Guacamayas** Colombia
126 F4 **Guacanayabo, G.de** Cuba
127 L9 **Guacara** Venezuela
103 M9 **Gu Achi** Arizona U.S.A.
128 D2 **Guachiria** *R* Colombia
130 C8 **Guaçu** Brazil
124 H7 **Guadalajara** Mexico
16 E4 **Guadalajara** Spain
17 F4 **Guadalajara** *prov* Spain
137 M3 **Guadalcanal** *isld* Solomon Is
16 D6 **Guadalcanal** Spain
16 E6 **Guadalén** *R* Spain
17 F7 **Guadalentin** *R* Spain
16 D8 **Guadalete** *R* Spain
16 E8 **Guadalfeo** *R* Spain
16 E8 **Guadalhorce** *R* Spain
16 E6 **Guadalimar** *R* Spain
17 F6 **Guadalmena** *R* Spain
16 D6 **Guadalmez** *R* Spain
17 G3 **Guadalope** *R* Spain
16 D7 **Guadalquivir** *R* Spain
131 C5 **Guadal, Sa. de** Argentina
108 A4 **Guadalupe** Mexico
124 H6 **Guadalupe** Mexico
71 F5 **Guadalupe** Cebu Philippines
102 D7 **Guadalupe** California U.S.A.
109 J6 **Guadalupe** *R* Texas U.S.A.
108 C4 **Guadalupe Pk** Texas U.S.A.
16 D5 **Guadalupe, Sa de** *mts* Spain
124 G5 **Guadalupe Victoria** Durango Mexico
124 F4 **Guadalupe y Calvo** Mexico
16 E4 **Guadarrama, Sa. de** *mts* Spain
17 F5 **Guadazaón** *R* Spain
127 N4 **Guadeloupe** *islds* Lesser Antilles
16 E6 **Guadiana** *R* Portugal/Spain
16 E7 **Guadiano Menor** *R* Spain
16 D6 **Guadiato** *R* Spain
17 F4 **Guadiela** *R* Spain
16 E7 **Guadix** Spain
133 C6 **Guafo** *isld* Chile
127 P2 **Guaico** Trinidad
130 C7 **Guaicuras** Brazil
128 F2 **Guaina** Venezuela
128 E3 **Guainía** *R* Colombia
128 D3 **Guainía** *div* Colombia
130 C9 **Guaíra** Brazil
130 C9 **Guaira** Paraguay
133 C6 **Guaitecas, Is** Chile
126 F4 **Guajaba, Cayo** *isld* Cuba
128 E6 **Guajará Mirim** Brazil
128 E5 **Guajarraã** Brazil
128 F5 **Guajaturaba** Brazil
124 H4 **Guaje, Llano de** *reg* Mexico
125 L2 **Guajiniquil** Honduras
128 D1 **Guajira** *div* Colombia
128 D1 **Guajira, Pena de** *pen* Colombia
102 A3 **Gualala** California U.S.A.
42 E5 **Gualdo Tadino** Italy
131 F4 **Gualeguay** *R* Argentina
131 F4 **Gualeguay** Argentina
133 F4 **Gualeguaychu** Argentina
131 D8 **Gualicho Salina** *salt pan* Argentina
128 E7 **Guallatiri** *mt* Chile
45 J2 **Gualtieri** Italy
134 E6 **Guam** *isld* Mariana Is Pacific Oc
129 J4 **Guamá** *R* Brazil
129 J4 **Guamá** Brazil
127 K9 **Guama** Venezuela
133 B6 **Guamblin, I** Chile
133 E5 **Guamini** Argentina
124 E5 **Guamúchil** Mexico
69 E10 **Gua Musang** Malaysia
65 C5 **Gu'an** China
126 C3 **Guanabacoa** Cuba
130 G8 **Guanabara** Brazil
125 M4 **Guanacaste, Cord. de** *ra* Costa Rica
124 G5 **Guanacevi** Mexico
126 B3 **Guanahacabibes, Pen. de** Cuba
126 C3 **Guanajay** Cuba
124 J7 **Guanajuato** Mexico
129 K6 **Guanambi** Brazil
128 C5 **Guañape, I** Peru
127 O2 **Guanapo** Trinidad
128 E2 **Guanarito** Venezuela
65 B5 **Guancen Shan** *mt ra* China
67 C6 **Guanchang** China
133 D3 **Guandacol** Argentina
65 G3 **Guandi** China
67 C1 **Guandiankou** China
126 B3 **Guane** Cuba
67 B1 **Guang'an** China
67 E3 **Guangchang** China
67 F1 **Guangde** China
65 D3 **Guangdegong** China
67 D5 **Guangdong** *prov* China
67 F2 **Guangfeng** China
67 A1 **Guangfu** China
67 A1 **Guanghan** China
Guanghua *see* **Laohekou**
65 B6 **Guanghua** China
67 E2 **Guangji** China
58 F4 **Guangling** China
65 E5 **Guanglu Dao** *isld* China
67 F1 **Guangming Ding** *mt* China
67 B4 **Guangnan** China

67 D5 **Guangning** China
65 C6 **Guangping** China
65 D6 **Guangrao** China
67 E1 **Guangshan** China
58 F5 **Guangshui** China
67 B5 **Guangxi** *prov* China
67 F1 **Guangyang** China
58 E5 **Guangyuan** China
67 F3 **Guangze** China
67 D5 **Guangzhou** China
65 C6 **Guangzong** China
130 G6 **Guanhães** Brazil
65 D7 **Guanhu** China
127 L5 **Guánica** Puerto Rico
128 F2 **Guanipa** *R* Venezuela
67 D3 **Guanjiazui** China
67 B4 **Guanling** China
67 C1 **Guanmian Shan** *mts* China
65 D7 **Guannan** China
100 F7 **Guano L** Oregon U.S.A.
65 G1 **Guansongzhen** China
Guansuo *see* **Guanling**
128 F1 **Guanta** Venezuela
126 G4 **Guantánamo** Cuba
126 G5 **Guantánamo, B. de** Cuba
65 C6 **Guantao** China
65 C4 **Guanting Shuiku** *res* China
65 C6 **Guan Xian** China
67 A1 **Guan Xian** China
67 D4 **Guanyang** China
65 D7 **Guanyun** China
130 F7 **Guapé** Brazil
128 C3 **Guapi** Colombia
133 G3 **Guaporé** Brazil
130 J9 **Guarabira** Brazil
130 D10 **Guarama** Brazil
130 F8 **Guarantinguetá** Brazil
130 H7 **Guarapari** Brazil
130 D9 **Guarapuava** Brazil
130 E9 **Guaraqueçaba** Brazil
130 E7 **Guararapes** Brazil
130 J10 **Guararapes** Brazil
17 G2 **Guara, Sa. de** Spain
18 E10 **Guara, Sierra de** *mts* Spain
130 E9 **Guaratuba** Brazil
45 O6 **Guarcino** Italy
16 C4 **Guarda** Portugal
17 F7 **Guardal** *R* Spain
130 F5 **Guarda Mor** Brazil
127 L10 **Guardatinajas** Venezuela
13 F1 **Guardbridge** Scotland
133 E6 **Guardia Mitre** Argentina
133 D7 **Guardián, C** Argentina
45 R7 **Guardia Sanframondi** Italy
16 D2 **Guardo** Spain
16 B4 **Guardunha Sa.da** *mts* Portugal
128 F5 **Guariba** *R* Amazonas Brazil
127 L10 **Guárico** *R* Venezuela
128 E2 **Guárico** *state* Venezuela
130 D10 **Guarita** *R* Brazil
124 E5 **Guasave** Mexico
128 C3 **Guascama, Pta** *pt* Colombia
125 K7 **Guasima** Mexico
130 C9 **Guassú, R** Brazil
42 D4 **Guastalla** Italy
125 O10 **Guatemala** *rep* Central America
126 G4 **Guatemala** Cuba
125 O10 **Guatemala** Guatemala
127 L9 **Guatire** Venezuela
128 D3 **Guaviare** *div* Colombia
128 E3 **Guaviare** *R* Colombia
126 F4 **Guayabal** Cuba
128 E2 **Guayabal** Venezuela
128 D3 **Guayabero** *R* Colombia
131 C3 **Guayaguas, Sa. da** *ra* Argentina
127 P3 **Guayaguayare** Trinidad
127 L5 **Guayama** Puerto Rico
128 C4 **Guayaquil** Ecuador
128 B4 **Guayaquil, Golfo de** Ecuador
128 E6 **Guayaramerin** Bolivia
128 B4 **Guayas** *prov* Ecuador
133 B7 **Guayeco Arch** *islds* Chile
124 D4 **Guaymas** Mexico
131 F3 **Guayquiraró, R** Argentina
130 F7 **Guazupé** Brazil
86 G3 **Guba** Ethiopia
87 E8 **Guba** Zaire
67 A2 **Gubai** China
52 J5 **Gubakha** Russian Federation
71 G4 **Gubat** Philippines
42 E5 **Gubbio** Italy
52 J4 **Gubdor** Russian Federation
65 D4 **Gubeikou** China
31 H4 **Guben** Germany
31 H4 **Gubin** Germany
54 J5 **Gubkin** Russian Federation
47 H2 **Gŭbŭbovo** Bulgaria
65 C6 **Gucheng** China
67 D1 **Gucheng** China
17 G4 **Gudar, Sa. de** *mts* Spain
28 F6 **Gudbjerg** Denmark
26 C9 **Gudbrandsdalen** Norway
28 D5 **Gudenå** *R* Denmark
36 G1 **Gudensberg** Germany
36 F4 **Gudernheim** Germany
28 D6 **Guderup** Denmark
27 G16 **Gudhjem** Denmark
28 F6 **Gudme** Denmark
77 J6 **Gudri** *R* Pakistan
65 B7 **Gudui** China
28 G6 **Gudum** Denmark
28 E3 **Gudumholm** Denmark
28 A3 **Gudum Kirke** Denmark
76 D3 **Gudur** India
27 B11 **Gudvangen** Norway
19 K5 **Guebwiller** France
133 C6 **Guechucuicui, Pta** Chile
85 B7 **Guéckédou** Guinea
21 M5 **Gué-de-la-Chaîne** France
21 O4 **Gue-de-Longroi, le** France
20 E6 **Guegon** France
121 N4 **Guéguen** *L* Quebec Canada
20 E6 **Guéhenno** France
16 E7 **Güéjar Sierra** Spain
86 C3 **Guelengdeng** Chad
85 F1 **Guelma** Algeria
85 B3 **Guelmine** Western Sahara
98 H3 **Guelph** North Dakota U.S.A.
85 D5 **Guem** Mali
36 C7 **Guémar** France
20 G6 **Guémene-Penfao** France
20 D5 **Guéméné-sur-Scorff** France
121 P6 **Guenette** Quebec Canada
133 C7 **Guenguel** *R* Argentina
20 G6 **Guenroue** France
20 F6 **Guer** France
16 C6 **Guereña** Spain
20 F7 **Guérande** France
86 C3 **Guéra, Pic de** *mt* Chad
85 E2 **Guerara** Algeria
20 H6 **Guerche-de-Bretagne, la** France
18 G6 **Guerche-sur-l'Aubois, la** France
86 D3 **Guéréda** Chad
18 G6 **Guéret** France
121 L5 **Guerin** Quebec Canada
20 F8 **Guérinière, la** France
20 D5 **Guerlédan, L.de** France
20 D5 **Guern** France
18 D9 **Guernica** Spain
119 M7 **Guernsey** Saskatchewan Canada
98 B7 **Guernsey** Wyoming U.S.A.
20 E3 **Guernsey I** Channel Is
98 B7 **Guernsey Res** Wyoming U.S.A.
21 M4 **Gueroulde, la** France
109 J9 **Guerra** Texas U.S.A.
21 O2 **Guerville** France
85 D4 **Guettara, El** Mali
18 H6 **Gueugnon** France
111 D12 **Gueydan** Louisiana U.S.A.
41 K4 **Güferhorn** *mt* Switzerland
38 E6 **Güffert-Spitze** *mt* Austria
86 G4 **Gugā** *mt* Ethiopia
86 G4 **Guga** *mt* Ethiopia
42 F7 **Guglionesi** Italy
48 H5 **Gugu** *mt* Romania
70 K9 **Guhakolak, Tanjong** *C* Java
33 R6 **Gühlen-Glienecke** Germany
130 C4 **Guia** Brazil
20 G6 **Guichen** France
67 F1 **Guichi** China
125 M9 **Guichicovi** Mexico
20 C4 **Guiclan** France
20 D6 **Guidel** France
86 B4 **Guider** Cameroon
98 H9 **Guide Rock** Nebraska U.S.A.
67 B3 **Guiding** China
45 J1 **Guidizzolo** Italy
67 D3 **Guidong** China
19 P13 **Guiers** *R* France
85 A5 **Guiers, L. de** Senegal
45 J3 **Guiglia** Italy
85 C7 **Guiglo** Ivory Coast
20 G6 **Guignen** France
22 J2 **Guigoven** Belgium
127 L9 **Güigüi** Venezuela
Guihua *see* **Mingxi**
87 F10 **Guija** Mozambique
67 C4 **Gui Jiang** *R* China
67 G2 **Guiji Shan** *mts* China
143 B9 **Guilderton** W Australia Australia
143 B9 **Guildford** W Australia Australia
9 F5 **Guildford** England
95 Q2 **Guildhall** Vermont U.S.A.
65 E1 **Guiler Gol** *R* China
95 P5 **Guilford** Connecticut U.S.A.
95 S1 **Guilford** Maine U.S.A.
112 H1 **Guilford Ct. Ho. Nat. Mil. Park** North Carolina U.S.A.
67 C4 **Guilin** China
20 F6 **Guillac** France
20 F5 **Guilliers** France
20 B6 **Guilvinec, le** France
16 B3 **Guimaraes** Portugal
71 F5 **Guimaras** *isld* Philippines
71 F5 **Guimaras Str** Philippines
20 B5 **Guimiliau** France
111 J8 **Guin** Alabama U.S.A.
125 M3 **Güina** Nicaragua
71 F5 **Guinauayan** *isld* Philippines
126 E3 **Guinchos Cay** *isld* Cuba
102 B3 **Guinda** California U.S.A.
71 G6 **Guindulman** Philippines
85 B6 **Guinea** *rep* W Africa
90 J8 **Guinea Basin** Atlantic Oc
85 A6 **Guinea-Bissau** *rep* W Africa
85 E8 **Guinea, Gulf of** W Africa
122 C3 **Guinecourt, L** Quebec Canada
126 D3 **Güines** Cuba
22 B2 **Guines** France
20 D4 **Guingamp** France
71 F5 **Guintacan** *isld* Philippines
71 F3 **Guintinua** *isld* Philippines
110 E6 **Guion** Arkansas U.S.A.
20 B5 **Guipavas** France
67 C5 **Guiping** China
17 F1 **Guipúzcoa** *prov* Spain
85 D5 **Guir** Mali
126 C3 **Güira de Melena** Cuba
130 D5 **Guiratinga** Brazil
129 H3 **Guisanbourg** Fr Guiana
13 G5 **Guisborough** England
22 E4 **Guiscard** France
20 C5 **Guiscriff** France
22 F4 **Guise** France
13 G6 **Guiseley** England
20 B4 **Guisseny** France
9 G2 **Guist** England
71 G5 **Guiuan** Philippines
22 E4 **Guivry** France
67 F2 **Guixi** China
67 C5 **Gui Xian** China
67 B3 **Guiyang** Guizhou China
67 B3 **Guizhou** *prov* China
74 D7 **Gujarat** *prov* India
74 F2 **Gujranwala** Pakistan
74 F2 **Gujrat** Pakistan
67 C1 **Gujunba** China
103 N9 **Gu Komelik** Arizona U.S.A.
54 L8 **Gukovo** Russian Federation
58 D4 **Gulang** China
139 J4 **Gulargambone** New South Wales Australia
74 G10 **Gulbarga** India
52 C6 **Gulbene** Latvia
57 G4 **Gul'cha** Kirghizia
28 A5 **Guldager** Denmark
28 E5 **Guldbjerg** Denmark
28 H7 **Guldborg** Denmark
36 D4 **Guldental** Germany
27 H12 **Guldsmedshyttan** Sweden
76 B2 **Guledagudda** India
79 E1 **Gülek** Turkey
27 A10 **Gulen** Norway
112 H2 **Gulf** North Carolina U.S.A.
111 J11 **Gulf Beach** Florida U.S.A.
141 G4 **Gulf Highway** Queensland Australia
111 H11 **Gulf Islands Nat Seashore** Mississippi U.S.A.
113 E10 **Gulfport** Florida U.S.A.
111 G11 **Gulfport** Mississippi U.S.A.
Gulf, The *see* **Persian Gulf**
26 R1 **Gulgofjorden** Norway
139 J4 **Gulgong** New South Wales Australia
67 B2 **Gulin** China
57 E4 **Gulistan** Uzbekistan
33 P6 **Gülitz** Germany
Gulja *see* **Yining**
116 P5 **Gulkana** Alaska U.S.A.
118 D6 **Gull** *L* Alberta Canada
27 H15 **Gullabo** Sweden
13 F1 **Gullane** Scotland
119 O1 **Gull Bay** Ontario Canada
28 D4 **Gullev** Denmark
6 L1 **Gullfaks** *oil rig* North Sea
28 S9 **Gullfoss** *waterfall* Iceland
99 V4 **Gull I** Michigan U.S.A.
99 V3 **Gulliver** Michigan U.S.A.
99 M3 **Gull L** Minnesota U.S.A.
118 J8 **Gull Lake** Saskatchewan Canada
26 K6 **Gullön** Sweden
27 G13 **Gullspång** Sweden
26 M5 **Gullträsk** Sweden
47 J7 **Güllük** Turkey
47 J7 **Güllük Körfezi** *B* Turkey
65 F2 **Gulong** China
25 E7 **Gulpen** Netherlands
33 Q7 **Gülper See** *L* Germany
47 H5 **Gülpınar** Turkey
77 G2 **Gulran** Afghanistan
78 E2 **Gülşehir** Turkey
26 J8 **Gulsele** Sweden
57 G2 **Gul'shad** Kazakhstan
33 S5 **Gültz** Germany
86 F5 **Gulu** Uganda
141 J7 **Guluguba** Queensland Australia
140 D1 **Guluwuru I** N Terr Australia
59 H1 **Gulya** Russian Federation
46 G1 **Gulyantsi** Bulgaria
54 H9 **Gulyaypole** Ukraine
33 S4 **Gülzow** Germany
141 G7 **Gumbardo** Queensland Australia
26 M7 **Gumboda** Sweden
140 B5 **Gum Cr** N Terr Australia
85 F6 **Gumel** Nigeria
125 K6 **Gümez** Mexico
16 E3 **Gumiel de Hizán** Spain
75 L7 **Gumla** India
61 M9 **Gumma** *prefect* Japan
36 D1 **Gummersbach** Germany
85 F6 **Gummi** Nigeria
71 E2 **Gumotgong** Luzon Philippines
69 C10 **Gumpang** *R* Sumatra
94 K9 **Gum Spring** Virginia U.S.A.
33 Q7 **Gumtow** Germany
67 A5 **Gumu** China
47 L7 **Gümüşgün** Turkey
78 G1 **Gümüşhane** Turkey
74 G6 **Guna** India
86 G3 **Guna, Terara** *mt* Ethiopia
139 H5 **Gunbar** New South Wales Australia
113 H12 **Gun Cay** Bahamas
58 F1 **Gunda** Russian Federation
139 J6 **Gundagai** New South Wales Australia
37 J6 **Gundelfingen** Germany
36 G5 **Gundelsheim** Germany
28 C3 **Gundersted** Denmark
36 E4 **Gundheim** Germany
70 N9 **Gundik** Java
86 D5 **Gundji** Zaire
28 H7 **Gundslev** Denmark
71 B3 **Gunedidalem** Indonesia
47 K6 **Güney** Turkey
119 N2 **Gunflint** Ontario Canada
86 C7 **Gungu** Zaire
119 U5 **Gunisao** *R* Manitoba Canada
119 V5 **Gunisao** *L* Manitoba Canada
103 L4 **Gunlock** Utah U.S.A.
114 J6 **Gunnar** Saskatchewan Canada
26 J6 **Gunnarn** Sweden
26 M5 **Gunnarsbyn** Sweden
141 H4 **Gunnawarra** Queensland Australia
115 R4 **Gunnbjørn Fjeld** *mt* Greenland
27 J14 **Gunnebo** Sweden
139 K4 **Gunnedah** New South Wales Australia
146 K8 **Gunnerus Ridge** Antarctica
141 J7 **Gunnewin** Queensland Australia
139 J5 **Gunning** New South Wales Australia
8 B7 **Gunnislake** England
106 B3 **Gunnison** *R* Colorado U.S.A.
106 D3 **Gunnison** Colorado U.S.A.
101 N8 **Gunnison I** Utah U.S.A.
140 B1 **Gunn Pt** N Terr Australia
140 E4 **Gunpowder** *R* Queensland Australia
101 N1 **Gunsight** Montana U.S.A.
76 C3 **Guntakal** India
100 B6 **Gunter** Oregon U.S.A.
109 L2 **Gunter** Texas U.S.A.
33 N9 **Güntersberge** Germany
36 E4 **Guntersblum** Germany
111 K7 **Guntersville** Alabama U.S.A.
119 U8 **Gunton** Manitoba Canada
111 H7 **Guntown** Mississippi U.S.A.
76 E2 **Guntur** India
71 N8 **Gunungapi** *isld* Indonesia
70 B3 **Gunung Ayer** Sarawak
70 E6 **Gunungbatubesar** Kalimantan
69 C12 **Gunungsitoli** Indonesia
70 K8 **Gunungsugih** Sumatra
69 D12 **Gunungtua** Sumatra
75 K9 **Gunupur** India
118 J7 **Gunworth** Saskatchewan Canada
143 B9 **Gunyidi** W Australia Australia
37 J7 **Günz** *R* Germany
37 J7 **Günzburg** Germany
37 K5 **Gunzenhausen** Germany
33 N9 **Günzerode** Germany
67 B5 **Guohua** China
65 C4 **Guojiatun** China
Guoluezhen *see* **Lingbao**
58 G5 **Guoyang** China
65 B5 **Guoyangzhen** China
65 D7 **Gupei** China
48 K3 **Gura Humorului** Romania
66 F4 **Gurban Anggir** China
65 B3 **Gurban Obo** China
66 D2 **Gurbantünggüt Shamo** *desert* China
138 E6 **Gurchen B** South Australia Australia
74 F2 **Gurdaspur** India
111 C8 **Gurdon** Arkansas U.S.A.
47 K6 **Güre** Turkey
74 G4 **Gurgaon** India
86 D3 **Gurgei, Jebel** *mt* Sudan
129 K5 **Gurgueia** *R* Brazil
127 N11 **Guri** Venezuela
128 F2 **Guri, Embalse de** *res* Venezuela
130 E6 **Gurinhatã** Brazil
46 D4 **Gur-i-Topit** *mt* Albania
38 J8 **Gurk** *R* Austria
47 H2 **Gurkovo** Bulgaria
38 K8 **Gurktal** *V* Austria
38 J8 **Gurktaler Alpen** *mts* Austria
66 C5 **Gurla Mandhata** *mt* China
57 B4 **Gurlen** Uzbekistan
110 K7 **Gurley** Alabama U.S.A.
98 D8 **Gurley** Nebraska U.S.A.
88 D10 **Guro** Mozambique
59 L1 **Gurskoye** Russian Federation
88 F9 **Gurué** Mozambique
78 F2 **Gürün** Turkey
129 H4 **Gurupá** Brazil
129 J4 **Gurupi** *R* Brazil
129 J6 **Gurupi** Brazil
129 J4 **Gurupi, C** Brazil
87 F9 **Guruve** Zimbabwe
76 D2 **Guruzala** India
58 D3 **Gurvan Sayhan Uul** *mt* Mongolia
50 E4 **Gur'yev** Kazakhstan
56 C4 **Gur'yevsk** Russian Federation
85 F6 **Gusau** Nigeria
33 P8 **Güsen** Germany
31 N1 **Gusev** Russian Federation
59 H4 **Gushan** China
101 Q9 **Gusher** Utah U.S.A.
67 E1 **Gushi** China
61 P14 **Gushikami** Okinawa
61 P13 **Gushikawa** Okinawa
70 E1 **Gusi** Sabah
52 G7 **Gusikha** Russian Federation
46 D2 **Gusinje** Montenegro Yugoslavia
56 G5 **Gusinoozersk** Russian Federation
56 G5 **Gusinoye, Oz** *L* Russian Federation
52 F6 **Gus'Khrustal'nyy** Russian Federation
46 D4 **Gusmar** Albania
67 B2 **Gusong** China
43 B9 **Guspini** Sardinia
48 C3 **Güssing** Austria
45 J1 **Gussola** Italy
27 G11 **Gustav Adolf** Sweden
115 Q4 **Gustav Holm, Kap** *C* Greenland
127 N6 **Gustavia** Lesser Antilles
124 C2 **Gustavo Sotelo** Mexico
117 F6 **Gustavus** Alaska U.S.A.
33 P9 **Güsten** Germany
36 E2 **Gusternhain** Germany
102 C4 **Gustine** California U.S.A.
109 J4 **Gustine** Texas U.S.A.
33 S4 **Gustow** Germany
33 Q5 **Güstrow** Germany
27 H13 **Gusum** Sweden
48 K1 **Gusyatin** Ukraine
36 E7 **Gutach** Germany
66 E6 **Gutarg** China
56 E4 **Gutarskiy Khrebet** *mts* Russian Federation
38 L5 **Gutau** Austria
37 M3 **Gutenfürst** Germany
38 N6 **Gutenstein** Austria
33 P9 **Gütergltick** Germany
32 H9 **Gütersloh** Germany
143 B8 **Gutha** W Australia Australia
110 J5 **Guthrie** Kentucky U.S.A.
99 M2 **Guthrie** Minnesota U.S.A.
98 F1 **Guthrie** North Dakota U.S.A.
107 N6 **Guthrie** Oklahoma U.S.A.
108 G2 **Guthrie** Texas U.S.A.
99 M8 **Guthrie Center** Iowa U.S.A.
119 R3 **Guthrie L** Manitoba Canada
67 F3 **Gutian** China
125 L7 **Gutiérrez Zamora** Mexico
Guting *see* **Yutai**
33 S8 **Gut-Neuhof** Germany
33 Q5 **Gutow** Germany
38 L8 **Guttaring** Austria
99 P7 **Guttenberg** Iowa U.S.A.
87 F9 **Gutu** Zimbabwe
54 G6 **Guty** Ukraine
33 S5 **Gützkow** Germany
80 C7 **Guvrin** *R* Israel
75 O5 **Guwahati** India
36 G1 **Guxhagen** Germany
65 B6 **Gu Xian** China
65 C4 **Guyan** China
128 G3 **Guyana** *rep* S America
94 E8 **Guyandotte** *R* West Virginia U.S.A.
58 F3 **Guyang** China
65 A4 **Guyang** China
121 M4 **Guyenne** Quebec Canada
18 E8 **Guyenne** *prov* France
9 G2 **Guyhirn** England
Guyi *see* **Sanjiang** Guangxi
107 J5 **Guymon** Oklahoma U.S.A.
116 R6 **Guyot Glacier** Alaska U.S.A.
139 K4 **Guyra** New South Wales Australia
123 L8 **Guysborough** Nova Scotia Canada
112 F5 **Guyton** Georgia U.S.A.
79 B2 **Güzelbağ** Turkey
67 C2 **Guzhang** China
58 G5 **Guzhen** China
Guzhou *see* **Rongjiang**
124 F2 **Guzmán, L. de** Mexico
31 N1 **Gvardeysk** Russian Federation
48 K1 **Gvardeyskoye** Ukraine
53 D10 **Gvardeyskoye** Ukraine
48 J2 **Gvozdets** Ukraine
68 B4 **Gwa** Burma
89 E2 **Gwaai** Zimbabwe
139 J4 **Gwabegar** New South Wales Australia
38 G8 **Gwabl** Austria
74 B10 **Gwadar** Pakistan
89 E2 **Gwai** *R* Zimbabwe
8 B1 **Gwalchmai** Wales
143 D8 **Gwalia** W Australia Australia
74 H5 **Gwalior** India
141 J7 **Gwambegwine** Queensland Australia
89 F3 **Gwanda** Zimbabwe
86 E5 **Gwane** Zaire
8 B3 **Gwbert-on-Sea** Wales
68 B2 **Gwebin** Burma
14 C2 **Gweebarra B** Ireland
Gwelo *see* **Gweru**
100 E4 **Gwendolen** Oregon U.S.A.
8 D4 **Gwent** *co* Wales
89 F2 **Gweru** *R* Zimbabwe
89 F2 **Gweru** Zimbabwe
99 T3 **Gwinn** Michigan U.S.A.
98 J3 **Gwinner** North Dakota U.S.A.
139 J3 **Gwydir** *R* New South Wales Australia
8 B1 **Gwynedd** *co* Wales
118 D6 **Gwynne** Alberta Canada
19 J5 **Gy** France
Gya'gya *see* **Saga**
78 L1 **Gyandzha** Azerbaijan
66 C5 **Gyangrang** China
Gyangtse *see* **Gyangzê**
66 D6 **Gyangzê** China
66 D5 **Gyaring Co** *L* China
58 C5 **Gyaring Hu** *L* China
50 G1 **Gydanskiy Poluostrov** *pen* Russian Federation
75 L4 **Gyirong** China
66 F5 **Gyitang** China
8 C2 **Gylchedd** *mt* Wales
115 P5 **Gyldenløves Fjord** Greenland
28 H5 **Gyldenløves Høj** *hill* Denmark
26 N5 **Gyljen** Sweden
28 E5 **Gylling** Denmark
28 E5 **Gylling Næs** Denmark
141 L7 **Gympie** Queensland Australia
68 B3 **Gyobingauk** Burma
61 N9 **Gyōda** Japan
48 F4 **Gyomaendrőd** Hungary
48 F3 **Gyöngyös** *R* Hungary
48 F3 **Gyöngyös** Hungary
48 E4 **Gyönk** Hungary
48 D3 **Györ** Hungary
48 D3 **Györ-Sopron** Hungary
106 D2 **Gypsum** Colorado U.S.A.
107 N3 **Gypsum** Kansas U.S.A.
117 Q5 **Gypsum Pt** Northwest Territories Canada
119 T7 **Gypsumville** Manitoba Canada
28 H5 **Gyrstinge** Denmark
27 J11 **Gysinge** Sweden
46 F2 **Gyueshevo** Bulgaria
48 G4 **Gyula** Hungary
52 D6 **Gzhat'** *R* Russian Federation
Gzhatsk *see* **Gagarin**

H

22 H2 **Haacht** Belgium
37 M4 **Haag** Germany
25 G4 **Haaksbergen** Netherlands
36 C1 **Haan** Germany
137 S5 **Ha'apai Group** *islds* Tonga
29 L8 **Haapajärvi** Finland
29 L9 **Haapamäki** Finland
29 L7 **Haapavesi** Finland
52 B5 **Haapsalu** Estonia
25 C4 **Haarlem** Netherlands
32 G9 **Haarstrang** Germany
144 B5 **Haast** New Zealand
140 B6 **Haast Bluff** N Terr Australia
25 C5 **Haastrecht** Netherlands
140 A6 **Haasts Bluff Aboriginal Land** N Terr Australia
80 G4 **Habaka** Jordan
126 C3 **Habana** Cuba
83 K9 **Habarane** Sri Lanka
86 G5 **Habaswein** Kenya
117 O6 **Habay** Alberta Canada
22 K4 **Habay-la-Neuve** Belgium
78 J5 **Habbamyah** Iraq
32 K10 **Habichtswald** *wood* Germany
75 O6 **Habiganj** Bangladesh
65 C3 **Habirag** China
80 G7 **Habis** *R* Jordan
80 C5 **Habla** Israel
27 K14 **Hablingo** Sweden
27 G14 **Habo** Sweden
59 N3 **Habomai-Shoto** *islds* Kuril Is Pacific Oc
80 C3 **Ha Bonim** Israel
60 P1 **Haboro** Japan
22 L3 **Habscheid** Germany
61 N11 **Habuminato** Japan
131 B7 **Hachado, Paso de** Arg/Chile
32 G10 **Hachen** Germany
36 D2 **Hachenburg** Germany
59 L5 **Hachijō Jima** *isld* Japan
61 N5 **Hachimori** Japan
60 O2 **Hachinai dake** *mt* Japan
59 M3 **Hachinohe** Japan
59 L4 **Hachiōjio** Japan
106 B10 **Hachita** New Mexico U.S.A.
100 D8 **Hackamore** California U.S.A.
26 G9 **Hackås** Sweden
103 L6 **Hackberry** Arizona U.S.A.
111 C12 **Hackberry** Louisiana U.S.A.
107 K3 **Hackberry Cr** Kansas U.S.A.
118 E6 **Hackett** Alberta Canada
110 B6 **Hackett** Arkansas U.S.A.
95 N6 **Hackettstown** New Jersey U.S.A.
111 J7 **Hackleburg** Alabama U.S.A.
138 E4 **Hack, Mt** South Australia Australia
13 H5 **Hackness** England
87 C8 **Haco** Angola
68 H2 **Ha Coi** Vietnam
36 E3 **Hadamar** Germany
80 C5 **Hadar** Israel
98 J7 **Hadar** Nebraska U.S.A.
72 H4 **Ḩadd, Al** Oman
107 N2 **Haddam** Kansas U.S.A.
9 G3 **Haddenham** England
13 F2 **Haddington** Scotland
9 H2 **Haddiscoe** England
112 D4 **Haddock** Georgia U.S.A.
73 L8 **Haddunmahti Atoll** Maldives
85 F6 **Hadejia** *R* Nigeria
27 D11 **Hadeland** Norway
32 J5 **Hadelner Kanal** Germany
32 K4 **Hademarschen** Germany
80 C4 **Ḩadera** Israel
80 C4 **Hadera** *R* Israel
38 N5 **Hadersdorf** Austria
Haderslev *co see* **Sønderjylland** *co*
28 C6 **Haderslev** Denmark
28 B4 **Haderup** Denmark
72 F5 **Hadhramaut** *reg* Yemen
72 G6 **Ḩadīboh** Socotra
79 G3 **Ḩadīdīyah** Syria
43 A11 **Hadid, Ras El** *C* Algeria
85 F1 **Hadid, Ras El** *C* Algeria
78 D3 **Hadım** Turkey
78 J4 **Hadithah, Al** Iraq
9 G3 **Hadleigh** England
9 G4 **Hadleigh** England
114 J3 **Hadley B** Northwest Territories Canada
144 C6 **Hadlow** New Zealand
33 O9 **Hadmersleben** Germany
80 F2 **Ḩad Nes** Syria
26 G3 **Hadsel** Norway
26 G3 **Hädselöy** *isld* Norway
28 E4 **Hadsten** Denmark
28 E3 **Hadsund** Denmark
116 O3 **Hadweenzic** *R* Alaska U.S.A.
131 G3 **Haedo, Cuchilla de** *ra* Uruguay
65 F5 **Haeju** N Korea
80 C7 **Ha-Ela** Israel
28 E6 **Hæsinge** Denmark
41 O3 **Hafelekar Sp** *mt* Austria
80 C6 **Hafez Ḩayyim** Israel
28 R9 **Haffjördhur** *B* Iceland
33 N4 **Haffkrug-Scharbeutz** Germany
115 N2 **Haffner Bjerg** *mt* Greenland
118 K6 **Hafford** Saskatchewan Canada
43 C13 **Haffouz** Tunisia
78 F2 **Hafik** Turkey
74 E2 **Hafizabad** Pakistan
75 P6 **Haflong** India
28 S9 **Hafnarfjördhur** Iceland
38 H7 **Hafner** *mt* Austria
77 A4 **Haft Gel** Iran
77 H2 **Haftqala** *R* Afghanistan
Hafun *see* **Xaafuun** Somalia
86 F3 **Hag Abdullah** Sudan
112 F5 **Hagan** Georgia U.S.A.
27 J11 **Hagaström** Sweden
32 F5 **Hage** Germany
80 D3 **Ha Gelilit** Israel
33 R8 **Hagelsberg** *mt* Germany
116 G7 **Hagemeister I** Alaska U.S.A.
119 M6 **Hagen** Saskatchewan Canada
32 F10 **Hagen** Germany
32 K8 **Hagenburg** Germany
38 H6 **Hagen-Gebirge** *mts* Austria
33 O6 **Hagenow** Germany
101 L7 **Hagerman** Idaho U.S.A.
106 F8 **Hagerman** New Mexico U.S.A.
27 H13 **Hägerstad** Sweden
94 B7 **Hagerstown** Indiana U.S.A.
94 K7 **Hagerstown** Maryland U.S.A.
120 K10 **Hagersville** Ontario Canada
27 G11 **Hagfors** Sweden
26 G8 **Häggenås** Sweden
13 G2 **Haggerston** England
85 B3 **Haggounia, Al** Western Sahara
26 G8 **Häggsjön** Sweden
68 G1 **Ha Giang** Vietnam
48 K4 **Hăgimaş** *mt* Romania
61 L10 **Hagiwara** Japan
8 D3 **Hagley** England
19 K3 **Hagondage** France
112 G3 **Hagood** South Carolina U.S.A.
80 C5 **Ḩagor** Israel
80 F1 **Ha Gosherim** Israel
14 B4 **Hags Hd** Ireland
118 L6 **Hague** Saskatchewan Canada
95 O3 **Hague** New York U.S.A.
98 F3 **Hague** North Dakota U.S.A.
20 G2 **Hague, C. de la** France
19 L4 **Haguenau** France
98 A9 **Hagues Pk** Colorado U.S.A.
Hague, The *see* **Den Haag**
18 E9 **Haguetmau** France
123 O3 **Haha Bay** Quebec Canada
122 B5 **Ha Ha, L** Quebec Canada
80 D6 **Ha Hamisha** Jordan
113 D7 **Hahira** Georgia U.S.A.
37 M4 **Hahnbach** Germany
36 D2 **Hahnbei** Germany
33 M9 **Hahnenklee-Bockswiese** Germany
80 C3 **Ha Ḩoterim** Israel
67 G1 **Hai'an** China
67 C6 **Hai'an** China
65 E4 **Haicheng** China
67 F4 **Haicheng** China
37 N5 **Haidhof** Germany
43 B13 **Haïdra** Tunisia
37 O5 **Haidstein** *mt* Germany
68 H2 **Hai Duong** Vietnam
22 J2 **Haien** Belgium
80 C2 **Ḩaifa** Israel
80 D2 **Ḩaifa, Bay of** Israel
67 E5 **Haifeng** China
143 F9 **Haig** W Australia Australia
36 E2 **Haiger** Germany
36 F7 **Haigerloch** Germany
117 P7 **Haig Lake** Alberta Canada
98 E10 **Haigler** Nebraska U.S.A.
65 D5 **Hai He** *R* China
67 C6 **Haikang** China
60 C12 **Haiki** Japan
69 D9 **Hai,Ko** *isld* Thailand
68 K2 **Haikou** China
135 T3 **Haiku** Hawaiian Is
75 P6 **Hailakandi** India
59 G2 **Hailar** China
101 L6 **Hailey** Idaho U.S.A.
121 L5 **Haileybury** Ontario Canada
107 P7 **Haileyville** Oklahoma U.S.A.
59 J3 **Hailin** China
67 D6 **Hailing Dao** *isld* China
65 J3 **Hailong** China
68 J7 **Hai Long** Vietnam
9 G6 **Hailsham** England
59 J2 **Hailun** China
29 L6 **Hailuoto** *isld* Finland
29 L6 **Hailuoto** Finland
32 M8 **Haimar** Germany
67 G1 **Haimen** China
67 G2 **Haimen** China
67 C7 **Hainan** *prov* China
68 D2 **Hai-nang** Burma
Hainan Strait *see* **Qiongzhou Haixia**
22 F2 **Hainaut** Belgium
22 F3 **Hainaut** France
31 K7 **Hainburg** Austria
117 F6 **Haines** Alaska U.S.A.
100 H5 **Haines** Oregon U.S.A.
113 F9 **Haines City** Florida U.S.A.
117 E5 **Haines Junction** Yukon Territory Canada
22 G3 **Haine-St-Paul** Belgium
38 N5 **Hainfeld** Austria
68 B4 **Haing** *R* Burma
37 P2 **Hainichen** Germany
67 G1 **Haining** China
33 N10 **Hainleite** Germany
37 Q2 **Hainsberg** Germany
94 D4 **Haintramck** Michigan U.S.A.
68 H2 **Haiphong** Vietnam
118 F5 **Hairy Hill** Alberta Canada
65 E3 **Haisgai** China
127 H5 **Haiti** *rep* W Indies
68 J3 **Haitou** China
65 F2 **Haituo** China
103 N9 **Haivana Nakya** Arizona U.S.A.
102 G5 **Haiwee Res** California U.S.A.
65 D5 **Haixing** China
86 G2 **Haiya Junct** Sudan
67 G1 **Haiyan** China
65 E6 **Haiyang** China
65 F5 **Haiyang Dao** *isld* China
Haiyou *see* **Sanmen**
67 B5 **Haiyuan** China
68 H1 **Haiyuan** China
48 G3 **Hajdú-Bihar** *co* Hungary
48 G3 **Hajdúböszörmény** Hungary
48 G3 **Hajdúdorog** Hungary
48 G3 **Hajdúhadház** Hungary
48 G3 **Hajdúnánás** Hungary
48 G3 **Hajdúszoboszló** Hungary
61 M7 **Hajiki-saki** *C* Japan
79 G9 **Ḩājj** Saudi Arabia
31 O3 **Hajnówka** Poland
65 F7 **Hajo** *isld* S Korea
68 A1 **Haka** Burma
135 V5 **Hakalou** Hawaiian Is
80 G3 **Hakama** Jordan
87 E7 **Hakansson** *mts* Zaire
27 F13 **Håkantorp** Sweden
144 A7 **Hakapoua, L** New Zealand
61 N8 **Hakase-yama** *mt* Japan
144 C6 **Hakataramea** New Zealand
60 G11 **Hakata shima** *isld* Japan
131 B8 **Hakelhuincul, Altiplanicie de** *plateau* Argentina
Hakha *see* **Haka**
78 J3 **Hakkâri** Turkey
26 M5 **Hakkas** Sweden
61 J11 **Hakken-zan** *mt* Japan
61 O5 **Hakkōda san** Japan
60 Q1 **Hako dake** *mt* Japan
59 M3 **Hakodate** Japan
60 O4 **Hakodate wan** *B* Japan
61 K9 **Haku-san** *vol* Japan
61 K9 **Hakusan Nat. Park** Japan
Hal *see* **Halle** Belgium
79 H2 **Ḩalab** Syria
78 G4 **Halabiye** Syria
78 K4 **Halabja** Iraq
65 F2 **Halahai** China
86 G1 **Halaib** Sudan
79 D8 **Halâl, G** *mt* Egypt
72 H5 **Halaniyat, Juzur al** *islds* Arabian Sea
48 G3 **Halasto** *L* Hungary
79 G9 **Ḩālat 'Ammār** Saudi Arabia
48 K3 **Hălăuceşti** Romania
135 S2 **Halawa** Hawaiian Is
80 F4 **Halawa** Jordan
135 S2 **Halawa, C** Hawaiian Is
79 G4 **Halba** Lebanon
86 H3 **Halba Desêt** *isld* Red Sea
56 E6 **Halban** Mongolia
33 T8 **Halbe** Germany
33 O9 **Halberstadt** Germany
8 C6 **Halberton** England
119 O9 **Halbrite** Saskatchewan Canada
145 E4 **Halcombe** New Zealand
71 E4 **Halcon, Mt** Philippines
117 P10 **Halcyon Hot Springs** British Columbia Canada
28 E3 **Hald** Århus Denmark
28 C3 **Hald** Viborg Denmark
28 H6 **Haldagerlille** Denmark
27 E12 **Halden** Norway
33 O8 **Haldensleben** Germany
28 C4 **Hald Sø** *L* Denmark
28 E4 **Haldum** Denmark
74 H4 **Haldwani** India
140 D6 **Hale** *R* N Terr Australia
106 H2 **Hale** Colorado U.S.A.
94 D2 **Hale** Michigan U.S.A.
110 C2 **Hale** Missouri U.S.A.
135 T3 **Haleakala Crater** Hawaiian Is
108 F1 **Hale Center** Texas U.S.A.
135 Q2 **Haleiwa** Hawaiian Is
143 B7 **Hale, Mt** W Australia Australia
135 R2 **Halena** Hawaiian Is
112 B2 **Hales Bar Dam** Tennessee U.S.A.
9 D3 **Halesowen** England
9 G5 **Hale Street** England
9 H3 **Halesworth** England
111 J7 **Haleyville** Alabama U.S.A.
144 B7 **Halfmoon Bay** New Zealand
9 E3 **Halford** England
107 K2 **Halford** Kansas U.S.A.
117 M7 **Halfway** *R* British Columbia Canada
94 K7 **Halfway** Maryland U.S.A.
100 H5 **Halfway** Oregon U.S.A.
108 F1 **Halfway** Texas U.S.A.
116 K6 **Halfway Mt** Alaska U.S.A.
25 C4 **Halfweg** Netherlands
80 B7 **Halib** Israel
121 M7 **Haliburton** Ontario Canada
141 H4 **Halifax** Queensland Australia
123 J9 **Halifax** Nova Scotia Canada
13 G6 **Halifax** England
112 K1 **Halifax** North Carolina U.S.A.
95 L6 **Halifax** Pennsylvania U.S.A.
94 H10 **Halifax** Virginia U.S.A.
141 H4 **Halifax B** Queensland Australia
141 H4 **Halifax, Mt** Queensland Australia
29 K11 **Halikko** Finland
77 E5 **Halil** *R* Iran
79 G4 **Halīmah** *mt* Lebanon
70 L9 **Halimun, G** *mt* Java
Haliut *see* **Urad Zhongqi**
76 B3 **Haliyal** India
26 N4 **Halju** *mt* Sweden
28 D6 **Halk** Denmark
116 L1 **Halkett, C** Alaska U.S.A.
118 E6 **Halkirk** Alberta Canada
15 E2 **Halkirk** Scotland
26 O2 **Halkkavàrre** *mt* Norway
101 M3 **Hall** Montana U.S.A.
26 J8 **Hälla** Sweden
9 G6 **Halland** England
26 F8 **Hålland** Sweden
27 F15 **Halland** *county* Sweden
113 G12 **Hallandale** Florida U.S.A.
27 F15 **Hallandsås** *hills* Sweden
29 K4 **Hallands Väderö** *isld* Sweden
138 D5 **Hall B** South Australia Australia
115 N1 **Hall Basin** Canada/Greenland
119 S8 **Hallboro** Manitoba Canada
22 G2 **Halle** Belgium
32 H8 **Halle** Germany
33 P10 **Halle** Germany
27 H15 **Hälleberga** Sweden
120 G3 **Hallebourg** Ontario Canada
28 G5 **Halleby Å** *R* Denmark
100 K9 **Halleck** Nevada U.S.A.
27 G12 **Hällefors** Sweden
38 H6 **Hallein** Austria
26 G8 **Hallen** Sweden
36 F1 **Hallenberg** Germany
21 O2 **Hallencourt** France
28 F4 **Hallendrup** Denmark
33 P10 **Halle-Neustadt** Germany
26 H9 **Hällesjö** Sweden
146 C12 **Hallett, Cape** *C* Antarctica
109 L6 **Hallettsville** Texas U.S.A.
146 F6 **Halley** *U.K. Base* Antarctica
111 E8 **Halley** Arkansas U.S.A.
116 B6 **Hall I** Bering Sea
98 D2 **Halliday** North Dakota U.S.A.
98 A9 **Halligan Res** Colorado U.S.A.
27 D11 **Hallingdalselv** *R* Norway
27 C11 **Hallingskarvet** *mt* Norway
27 B11 **Hallingskeid** Norway
115 L4 **Hall Lake** *L* Northwest Territories Canada
27 J11 **Hållnäs** Sweden
119 V10 **Hallock** Minnesota U.S.A.
118 K8 **Hallonquist** Saskatchewan Canada
115 N5 **Hall Pen** Northwest Territories Canada
110 G6 **Halls** Tennessee U.S.A.
8 C7 **Hallsands** England
27 H12 **Hallsberg** Sweden
142 G4 **Halls Creek** W Australia Australia
138 F6 **Halls Gap** Victoria Australia
37 K4 **Hallstadt** Germany
27 H12 **Hallstahammar** Sweden
106 G3 **Hall Station** Colorado U.S.A.
38 J6 **Hallstatt** Austria
27 K11 **Hallstavik** Sweden
95 M5 **Hallstead** Pennsylvania U.S.A.
111 C9 **Hall Summit** Louisiana U.S.A.
110 D2 **Hallsville** Missouri U.S.A.
109 N3 **Hallsville** Texas U.S.A.
81 A8 **Hall Table Mt** Indian Oc
41 O3 **Halltal** Austria
94 J5 **Hallton** Pennsylvania U.S.A.
22 E2 **Halluin** France
25 E2 **Hallum** Netherlands
28 E2 **Hallund** Denmark
28 C5 **Hallundbæk** Denmark
26 H8 **Hallviken** Sweden
98 K1 **Halma** Minnesota U.S.A.
71 B2 **Halmahera** *isld* Indonesia
71 B3 **Halmahera** *sea* Indonesia
48 H3 **Halmeu** Romania
27 F15 **Halmstad** Sweden
43 C12 **Halq el Oued** Tunisia
28 E2 **Hals** Denmark
26 C8 **Halsa** Norway
37 P2 **Halsbrucke** Germany
36 F2 **Halsdorf** Germany
98 F8 **Halsey** Nebraska U.S.A.
100 B5 **Halsey** Oregon U.S.A.
71 D5 **Halsey Harbour** Philippines
28 H5 **Halsnæs** *pen* Denmark
28 G6 **Halsskov** Denmark
98 K2 **Halstad** Minnesota U.S.A.
9 G4 **Halstead** England
107 N4 **Halstead** Kansas U.S.A.
36 B5 **Halstroff** France
29 L8 **Halsua** Finland
26 E9 **Haltdalen** Norway
26 D7 **Halten** Norway
32 F9 **Haltern** Germany
29 J2 **Halti** *mt* Finland
109 M9 **Haltom City** Texas U.S.A.
13 F4 **Haltwhistle** England
77 C7 **Ḩālūl** *isld* Qatar
71 K10 **Halura** *isld* Indonesia
36 C1 **Halver** Germany
118 L8 **Halvorgate** Saskatchewan Canada
28 D2 **Halvrimmen** Denmark
141 K7 **Haly, Mt** Queensland Australia
22 E4 **Ham** France
80 G3 **Ham** Jordan
60 F12 **Hama** Japan
60 F11 **Hamada** Japan
85 F3 **Hamada de Tinrhert** *stony desert* Algeria
85 D4 **Hamada El Haricha** *reg* Mali
77 A2 **Hamadān** Iran
85 C3 **Hamada Tounassine** *stony desert* Algeria
80 F3 **Ḩamadya** Israel
79 G3 **Ḩamāh** Syria
61 P13 **Hamahika-jima** *isld* Okinawa
61 L11 **Hamakita** Japan
60 P2 **Hamamasu** Japan
59 L5 **Hamamatsu** Japan
60 T2 **Hamanaka** Japan
61 L11 **Hamana ko** *L* Japan
80 C4 **Ha Ma 'Pil** Israel
27 E11 **Hamar** Norway
98 H2 **Hamar** North Dakota U.S.A.
26 H3 **Hamaröy** Norway
60 H10 **Hamasaka** Japan
84 J5 **Hamâta, Gebel** *mt* Egypt
80 F3 **Hamat Gader** Jordan
60 Q1 **Hama-Tombetsu** Japan
36 C5 **Hambach** France
83 L11 **Hambantota** Sri Lanka
98 G2 **Hamberg** North Dakota U.S.A.
32 J6 **Hambergen** Germany
117 O9 **Hamber Prov. Park** British Columbia Canada
9 F5 **Hambledon** England
13 G6 **Hambleton** England
13 G5 **Hambleton Hills** England
100 D8 **Hambone** California U.S.A.
32 L7 **Hambühren** Germany
34 **Hamburg** *conurbation* Germany
111 E8 **Hamburg** Arkansas U.S.A.
100 B8 **Hamburg** California U.S.A.
99 L9 **Hamburg** Iowa U.S.A.
95 N5 **Hamburg** New Jersey U.S.A.
94 J4 **Hamburg** New York U.S.A.
95 M6 **Hamburg** Pennsylvania U.S.A.
20 H4 **Hambye** France
95 M4 **Hamden** New York U.S.A.
94 E7 **Hamden** Ohio U.S.A.
29 L10 **Hame** *prov* Finland
29 K10 **Hämeenkyrö** Finland
29 L11 **Hämeenlinna** Finland
143 A10 **Hamelin B** W Australia Australia
143 A7 **Hamelin Pool** W Australia Australia
32 K8 **Hameln** Germany
101 N6 **Hamer** Idaho U.S.A.
33 O8 **Hamersleben** Germany
142 C5 **Hamersley** W Australia Australia
142 B5 **Hamersley Ra** W Australia
142 B6 **Hamersley Ra. Nat Park** W Australia Australia
33 P7 **Hamerten** Germany
65 G5 **Hamhŭng** N Korea
66 E3 **Hami** China
140 F6 **Hamilton** *R* Queensland Australia
140 F6 **Hamilton** Queensland Australia
138 C2 **Hamilton** *R* South Australia Australia
139 H8 **Hamilton** Tasmania Australia
138 F6 **Hamilton** Victoria Australia
90 B2 **Hamilton** Bermuda
121 L9 **Hamilton** Ontario Canada
145 E2 **Hamilton** New Zealand
12 D2 **Hamilton** Scotland
111 J7 **Hamilton** Alabama U.S.A.
101 S9 **Hamilton** Colorado U.S.A.
111 M9 **Hamilton** Georgia U.S.A.
99 P9 **Hamilton** Illinois U.S.A.
94 C5 **Hamilton** Indiana U.S.A.
107 O4 **Hamilton** Kansas U.S.A.
94 A4 **Hamilton** Michigan U.S.A.
101 L3 **Hamilton** Montana U.S.A.
95 M4 **Hamilton** New York U.S.A.
119 U10 **Hamilton** North Dakota U.S.A.
94 C7 **Hamilton** Ohio U.S.A.
100 F5 **Hamilton** Oregon U.S.A.
109 J4 **Hamilton** Texas U.S.A.
100 D1 **Hamilton** Washington U.S.A.
102 C2 **Hamilton City** California U.S.A.
101 R6 **Hamilton Dome** Wyoming U.S.A.
140 C6 **Hamilton Downs** N Terr Australia
115 O7 **Hamilton Inlet** Labrador, Nfld Canada
111 C7 **Hamilton,L** Arkansas U.S.A.
103 J2 **Hamilton, Mt** Nevada U.S.A.
29 N11 **Hamina** Finland
74 J6 **Hamirpur** India
Hamitabat *see* **İsparta**
94 C5 **Hamler** Ohio U.S.A.
94 A5 **Hamlet** Indiana U.S.A.
98 E9 **Hamlet** Nebraska U.S.A.
112 H3 **Hamlet** North Carolina U.S.A.
138 E5 **Hamley Bridge** South Australia Australia
94 K3 **Hamlin** New York U.S.A.
108 G3 **Hamlin** Texas U.S.A.
94 E8 **Hamlin** West Virginia U.S.A.
94 A2 **Hamlin L** Michigan U.S.A.
32 G9 **Hamm** Germany
17 G9 **Hammam Bou Hadjar** Algeria
43 D12 **Hammamet** Tunisia
85 G1 **Hammamet, G de** Tunisia
85 G1 **Hammam Lif** Tunisia
29 H11 **Hammarland** Finland
27 F11 **Hammarsbyn** Sweden
29 M3 **Hammastunturi** *mt* Finland
22 G1 **Hamme** Belgium

2 J6 Hamme R Germany
8 D4 Hammel Denmark
6 H3 Hammelburg Germany
8 F4 Hammelev Denmark
8 C6 Hammelev Denmark
3 S6 Hammelspring Germany
2 H2 Hamme-Mille Belgium
6 H8 Hammerdal Sweden
7 H14 Hammerfest Norway
8 D3 Hammershøj Denmark
3 C9 Hammersley L W Australia Australia
6 C3 Hammerstein Germany
3 G6 Hammerton England
8 C4 Hammerum Denmark
0 K7 Hammett Idaho U.S.A.
2 E9 Hamminkeln Germany
7 L6 Hammon Oklahoma U.S.A.
8 E4 Hammond South Australia Australia
9 T8 Hammond Illinois U.S.A.
0 H2 Hammond Illinois U.S.A.
1 F11 Hammond Louisiana U.S.A.
8 B4 Hammond Montana U.S.A.
5 M2 Hammond New York U.S.A.
0 B3 Hammond Oregon U.S.A.
9 O5 Hammond Wisconsin U.S.A.
4 D1 Hammond B Michigan U.S.A.
1 F1 Hammond I Queensland Australia
5 K4 Hammondsport New York U.S.A.
2 G8 Hammond Vale New Brunswick Canada
2 C2 Hammonton California U.S.A.
5 N7 Hammonton New Jersey U.S.A.
6 O1 Hamnbukt Norway
6 L2 Hamneidet Norway
6 S1 Hamningberg Norway
8 G7 Ham Ninh Vietnam
1 T7 Ham Nord Quebec Canada
6 L4 Håmojokk Sweden
2 K1 Hamont Belgium
6 G2 Hamoyet, Jebel mt Sudan
3 Q4 Hampden Newfoundland Canada
4 C6 Hampden New Zealand
8 H1 Hampden North Dakota U.S.A.
5 T2 Hampden Highlands Maine U.S.A.
8 C4 Hampen Denmark
6 B6 Hampont France
9 E5 Hampshire co England
2 F8 Hampstead New Brunswick Canada
5 K7 Hampstead Maryland U.S.A.
2 K3 Hampstead North Carolina U.S.A.
2 G8 Hampton New Brunswick Canada
9 F5 Hampton England
1 D8 Hampton Arkansas U.S.A.
3 E8 Hampton Florida U.S.A.
1 M8 Hampton Georgia U.S.A.
9 N7 Hampton Iowa U.S.A.
8 J9 Hampton Nebraska U.S.A.
5 R4 Hampton New Hampshire U.S.A.
0 E6 Hampton Oregon U.S.A.
2 F5 Hampton South Carolina U.S.A.
5 L9 Hampton Virginia U.S.A.
1 P8 Hampton Wyoming U.S.A.
5 P6 Hampton Bays Long I, New York U.S.A.
3 F9 Hampton Tableland W Australia Australia
7 H10 Hamra Sweden
7 J11 Hamränge Sweden
9 G4 Ḩamrāt, Al Syria
1 P7 Hams Fork R Wyoming U.S.A.
9 G5 Hamstreet England
8 H7 Ham Tan Vietnam
5 T3 Hana Hawaiian Is
6 D3 Hanábana R Cuba
5 O1 Hanalei Hawaiian Is
5 T3 Hanamanioa, C Hawaiian Is
5 O1 Hanamaulu Hawaiian Is
5 O1 Hanapepe Hawaiian Is
1 N13 Hanare-iwa islds Japan
6 F3 Hanau Germany
2 S12 Hanauma B Hawaiian Is
1 L5 Hanbury Ontario Canada
7 M10 Hanceville British Columbia Canada
1 K7 Hanceville Alabama U.S.A.
8 F4 Hancheng China
7 D1 Hanchuan China
5 T2 Hancock Maine U.S.A.
4 J7 Hancock Maryland U.S.A.
9 S2 Hancock Michigan U.S.A.
9 L4 Hancock Minnesota U.S.A.
5 P4 Hancock New Hampshire U.S.A.
5 M5 Hancock New York U.S.A.
9 R5 Hancock Wisconsin U.S.A.
3 F10 Hancock, L Florida U.S.A.
1 K11 Handa Japan
8 F4 Handan China
8 B4 Handbjerg Denmark
9 F5 Handcross England
8 J6 Handel Saskatchewan Canada
7 K12 Handen Sweden
8 G4 Handeni Tanzania
8 D3 Handest Denmark
5 D1 Handgai China
9 K3 Handley Texas U.S.A.
9 P9 Handsworth Saskatchewan Canada
2 K4 Hanerau Germany
2 E5 Hanford California U.S.A.
6 B3 Hangal India
8 C5 Hangan Burma
5 G6 Hangang R S Korea
5 F3 Hangaroa New Zealand
7 C11 Hangastöl Norway
5 E3 Hangatiki New Zealand
8 C2 Hangayn Nuruu mt Mongolia
Hangchow see Hangzhou
3 T8 Hangelsberg Germany
7 G14 Hånger Sweden
8 E3 Hanggin Houqi China
4 E8 Hanging Rock Ohio U.S.A.
9 A10 Hangklip, C S Africa
0 H2 Hangman Cr Washington U.S.A.
9 K12 Hango Finland
5 D5 Hangu China
7 D4 Hanguang China
9 H5 Hangzhou China
9 H5 Hangzhou Wan B China
9 F4 Ḩanidiyah, Al Syria
2 M7 Hänigsen Germany
6 H3 Hanīsh al Kabīr islds Red Sea
0 D1 Ḩanita Israel
Hanjiang see Yangzhou
7 F4 Hanjiang China
9 M9 Hankasalmi Finland
5 C4 Hank, El Mauritania
8 J3 Hankinson North Dakota U.S.A.
8 F5 Hankou China
3 O3 Hanksville Utah U.S.A.
8 L7 Hanley Saskatchewan Canada
8 D1 Hanley England
9 L5 Hanley Falls Minnesota U.S.A.
4 D5 Hanmer Springs New Zealand
8 F7 Hanna Alberta Canada
1 P9 Hanna Utah U.S.A.
1 T8 Hanna Wyoming U.S.A.
8 H2 Hannaford North Dakota U.S.A.
9 T10 Hannah North Dakota U.S.A.
0 K1 Hannah B Ontario Canada
9 P10 Hannibal Missouri U.S.A.
9 Q4 Hannibal Wisconsin U.S.A.
8 A4 Hanning Kirke Denmark

142 F3 Hann, Mt W Australia Australia
32 L8 Hannover Germany
98 E2 Hannover North Dakota U.S.A.
140 C6 Hann Ra N Terr Australia
22 J2 Hannut Belgium
27 H16 Hanöbukten B Sweden
68 G2 Hanoi Vietnam
48 D4 Hanót Hungary
120 J8 Hanover Ontario Canada
127 H1 Hanover parish Jamaica
89 D8 Hanover S Africa
107 O2 Hanover Kansas U.S.A.
99 N4 Hanover Minnesota U.S.A.
101 Q2 Hanover Montana U.S.A.
95 P3 Hanover New Hampshire U.S.A.
133 C8 Hanover, I Chile
48 E6 Han Pijesak Bosnia-Herzegovina
48 D3 Hanság Hungary
117 N8 Hansard British Columbia Canada
98 G1 Hansboro North Dakota U.S.A.
120 F3 Hansen Ontario Canada
146 J10 Hansen mts Antarctica
67 F1 Hanshan China
67 D2 Hanshou China
58 E5 Han Shui R China
67 D1 Han Shui R China
74 F4 Hansi India
27 G10 Hansjö Sweden
140 C5 Hanson R N Terr Australia
138 D4 Hanson, L South Australia Australia
119 P4 Hanson L Saskatchewan Canada
28 D5 Hansted Vejle Denmark
28 B2 Hanstholm Denmark
28 B2 Hanstholm Havn C Denmark
65 D2 Han Sum China
22 J3 Han-sur-Lesse Belgium
25 B6 Hansweert Netherlands
Hantan see Handan
66 C3 Hantengri Feng mt Kazakhstan
Hanting see Wei Xian
122 H8 Hantsport Nova Scotia Canada
36 C7 Hantz, Col du pass France
79 H3 Ḩānūbah, Al Syria
65 D2 Han Ul China
20 B5 Hanvec France
67 A1 Hanwang China
83 K11 Hanwella Sri Lanka
58 F5 Hanyang China
57 K4 Hanyaylak China
61 N9 Hanyū Japan
58 D6 Hanyuan China
58 E5 Hanzhong China
65 D7 Hanzhuang China
135 N10 Hao atoll Tuamotu Arch Pacific Oc
65 H1 Haolianghe China
80 F3 Ha On Israel
75 N7 Hāora India
26 N6 Haparanda Sweden
71 B1 Hapo Halmahera Indonesia
9 H2 Happisburgh England
100 B8 Happy Camp California U.S.A.
140 E5 Happy Cr N Terr Australia
144 D5 Hapuku New Zealand
83 L11 Haputale Sri Lanka
79 E9 Ḩaql Saudi Arabia
26 M5 Harads Sweden
86 H4 Hara Fanna Ethiopia
111 H12 Harahan New Orleans, Louisiana U.S.A.
26 B9 Haram Norway
59 M4 Haramachi Japan
86 H4 Hārar Ethiopia
88 C10 Harare Zimbabwe
58 E2 Har-ayrag Mongolia
86 C3 Haraz Djombo Chad
86 D3 Haraz-Mangueigne Chad
80 E8 Har Ben Yai'r Israel
65 G2 Harbin China
27 J11 Harbo Sweden
77 K5 Harboi Hills Pakistan
28 J7 Hårbølle Denmark
22 D4 Harbonnières France
28 A3 Harboør Denmark
28 A3 Harboør Tange pen Denmark
100 A7 Harbor Oregon U.S.A.
94 E3 Harbor Beach Michigan U.S.A.
117 E6 Harbor Pt Alaska U.S.A.
94 B1 Harbor Springs Michigan U.S.A.
13 F3 Harbottle England
123 R6 Harbour Breton Newfoundland Canada
123 S6 Harbour Buffett Newfoundland Canada
113 K12 Harbour Cay, Little isld Bahamas
123 Q3 Harbour Deep Newfoundland Canada
123 T6 Harbour Grace Newfoundland Canada
113 L12 Harbour I Bahamas
123 S6 Harbour Mille Newfoundland Canada
122 H8 Harbourville Nova Scotia Canada
37 K6 Harburg Bayern Germany
32 L6 Harburg Niedersachsen Germany
28 E6 Hårby Denmark
122 G7 Harcourt New Brunswick Canada
103 L7 Harcuvar Mts Arizona U.S.A.
74 G7 Harda Khās India
27 B11 Hardanger Norway
27 B11 Hardanger-fjorden inlet Norway
27 C11 Hardangervidda plateau Norway
27 B11 Hardangervidda Nat. Park Norway
89 A5 Hardap Dam Namibia
111 F9 Hardee Mississippi U.S.A.
112 F5 Hardeeville South Carolina U.S.A.
25 E2 Hardegarijp Netherlands
32 L9 Hardegsen Germany
22 B2 Hardelot-Plage France
25 G3 Hardenberg Netherlands
70 D2 Harden, Bt mt Kalimantan
25 E4 Harderwijk Netherlands
107 J5 Hardesty Oklahoma U.S.A.
142 B6 Hardey, R W Australia Australia
36 H4 Hardheim Germany
110 F2 Hardin Illinois U.S.A.
110 C2 Hardin Missouri U.S.A.
101 S4 Hardin Montana U.S.A.
87 E12 Harding S Africa
99 M3 Harding Minnesota U.S.A.
116 M6 Harding Icefield Alaska U.S.A.
119 T2 Harding L Manitoba Canada
111 L9 Harding, L Georgia U.S.A.
110 K4 Hardinsburg Kentucky U.S.A.
118 F6 Hardisty Alberta Canada
117 P3 Hardisty L Northwest Territories Canada
21 P2 Hardivillers France
100 F4 Hardman Oregon U.S.A.
142 E4 Hardman, Mt W Australia Australia
80 D8 Hardof R Jordan
98 K6 Hardwick Minnesota U.S.A.
95 P2 Hardwick Vermont U.S.A.
8 D4 Hardwicke England
138 D5 Hardwicke B South Australia Australia
119 N9 Hardy Saskatchewan Canada
110 E5 Hardy Arkansas U.S.A.
101 O2 Hardy Montana U.S.A.
Hardy, Mt see Rangipova
133 D9 Hardy, Pen Chile

94 B3 Hardy Res Michigan U.S.A.
123 S5 Hare B Newfoundland Canada
80 E4 Hare Gilboa Israel
26 B9 Hareid Norway
22 E2 Harelbeke Belgium
32 F7 Haren Germany
115 O3 Hareøen isld Greenland
13 G6 Harewood England
79 F5 Harf el Mreffi mt Lebanon
21 L2 Harfleur France
27 K11 Harg Sweden
36 B5 Hargarten aux Mines France
86 H4 Hargele Ethiopia
86 H4 Hargeysa Somalia
48 K4 Harghita, Muntii mt Romania
22 E4 Hargicourt France
109 J9 Hargill Texas U.S.A.
22 J3 Hargimont Belgium
22 H3 Hargnies France
119 Q9 Hargrave Manitoba Canada
119 S4 Hargrave L Manitoba Canada
79 E8 Har Hakippa mt Israel
79 E8 Har Harif Israel
80 D8 Har Ḩezron Israel
66 F4 Har Hu L China
61 M9 Hari Japan
74 H4 Haridwār India
76 B3 Harihar India
144 C5 Harihari New Zealand
79 G2 Hārim Syria
60 H11 Harima-nada sea Japan
25 B5 Haringvliet Netherlands
74 E1 Haripur Pakistan
77 J2 Hari Rud R Afghanistan/Iran
79 G6 Ḩarīr, Wādī adh watercourse Syria
87 C10 Haris Namibia
26 G10 Härjån R Sweden
29 J10 Harjavalta Finland
26 F10 Härjehågna mt Sweden
80 F2 Har Kena'an pk Israel
112 L3 Harkers I North Carolina U.S.A.
99 L8 Harlan Iowa U.S.A.
107 M2 Harlan Kansas U.S.A.
94 D10 Harlan Kentucky U.S.A.
98 G9 Harlan County Lake res Nebraska U.S.A.
22 K4 Harlange Luxembourg
32 G5 Harle Germany
8 B2 Harlech Wales
112 E4 Harlem Georgia U.S.A.
101 R1 Harlem Montana U.S.A.
32 L5 Harlesiel Germany
9 H3 Harleston England
28 D4 Harlev Denmark
28 J6 Hårlev Denmark
112 G4 Harleyville South Carolina U.S.A.
25 D2 Harlingen Netherlands
109 K9 Harlingen Texas U.S.A.
32 G5 Harlinger Land Germany
33 M9 Harlingerode Germany
9 G4 Harlow England
98 G1 Harlow North Dakota U.S.A.
101 Q3 Harlowton Montana U.S.A.
94 H8 Harman West Virginia U.S.A.
47 K5 Harmancık Turkey
26 J10 Harmånger Sweden
25 C4 Harmelen Netherlands
80 E2 Har Meron pk Israel
107 L5 Harmon Oklahoma U.S.A.
118 A2 Harmon R Alberta Canada
95 S2 Harmony Maine U.S.A.
99 O6 Harmony Minnesota U.S.A.
79 E8 Har Natḩa mt Israel
100 F6 Harney Basin reg Oregon U.S.A.
113 F9 Harney, L Florida U.S.A.
100 F6 Harney L Oregon U.S.A.
98 C6 Harney Pk South Dakota U.S.A.
28 E6 Harnorup Denmark
26 J9 Härnösand Sweden
65 E2 Har Nur China
58 B2 Har Nuur L Mongolia
80 E3 Harod R Israel
26 B9 Haröy isld Norway
9 F4 Harpenden England
85 C8 Harper Liberia
107 M4 Harper Kansas U.S.A.
100 H6 Harper Oregon U.S.A.
109 H5 Harper Texas U.S.A.
116 L4 Harper Bend Alaska U.S.A.
117 Q6 Harper Cr Alberta Canada
102 G6 Harper L California U.S.A.
116 Q4 Harper, Mt Alaska U.S.A.
144 C5 Harper Pass New Zealand
94 K7 Harpers Ferry West Virginia U.S.A.
110 J5 Harpeth R Tennessee U.S.A.
8 C6 Harpford England
9 G2 Harpley England
27 F15 Harplinge Sweden
32 J7 Harpstedt Germany
119 M9 Harptree Saskatchewan Canada
65 D4 Harqin China
65 D4 Harqin Qi China
103 L8 Harquahala Mts Arizona U.S.A.
85 E1 Harrach, El Algeria
107 N6 Harrah Oklahoma U.S.A.
26 F7 Harran Norway
37 K3 Harras Germany
28 B3 Harre Denmark
111 D8 Harrell Arkansas U.S.A.
144 D5 Harrelville New Zealand
121 L2 Harricana R Quebec Canada
28 E3 Harridslev Denmark
94 B2 Harrietta Michigan U.S.A.
112 C2 Harriman Tennessee U.S.A.
95 M8 Harrington Delaware U.S.A.
95 U2 Harrington Maine U.S.A.
100 G2 Harrington Washington U.S.A.
123 N3 Harrington-Harbour Quebec Canada
119 P2 Harriot L Saskatchewan Canada
118 K7 Harris Saskatchewan Canada
15 B3 Harris div Scotland
100 B9 Harris California U.S.A.
99 N9 Harris Missouri U.S.A.
110 F6 Harrisburg Arkansas U.S.A.
110 H4 Harrisburg Illinois U.S.A.
98 C8 Harrisburg Nebraska U.S.A.
94 D7 Harrisburg Ohio U.S.A.
100 B5 Harrisburg Oregon U.S.A.
95 L6 Harrisburg Pennsylvania U.S.A.
98 K6 Harrisburg South Dakota U.S.A.
118 H2 Harris Hill Ontario Canada
138 D4 Harris, L South Australia Australia
113 F9 Harris, L Florida U.S.A.
143 C10 Harrismith W Australia Australia
89 F7 Harrismith S Africa
140 A6 Harris, Mt N Terr Australia
144 B6 Harris Mts New Zealand
110 C5 Harrison Arkansas U.S.A.
112 E5 Harrison Georgia U.S.A.
100 J2 Harrison Idaho U.S.A.
94 C2 Harrison Michigan U.S.A.
101 O4 Harrison Montana U.S.A.
98 C7 Harrison Nebraska U.S.A.
98 H6 Harrison South Dakota U.S.A.
116 L1 Harrison B Alaska U.S.A.
111 E10 Harrisonburg Louisiana U.S.A.
94 J8 Harrisonburg Virginia U.S.A.
115 O7 Harrison, C Labrador, Nfld Canada
117 M11 Harrison L British Columbia Canada
83 K12 Harrison, Mt Mahé I Indian Oc
110 B3 Harrisonville Missouri U.S.A.
94 D2 Harrisville Michigan U.S.A.

95 M2 Harrisville New York U.S.A.
94 F7 Harrisville West Virginia U.S.A.
110 K2 Harrodsburg Indiana U.S.A.
94 C9 Harrodsburg Kentucky U.S.A.
13 G6 Harrogate England
98 G5 Harrold South Dakota U.S.A.
109 H1 Harrold Texas U.S.A.
120 H10 Harrow Ontario Canada
9 F4 Harrow England
119 Q8 Harrowby Manitoba Canada
26 H7 Harrsjön Sweden
27 F14 Härryda Sweden
110 C3 Harry S. Truman Res Missouri U.S.A.
98 F9 Harry Strunk L Nebraska U.S.A.
79 E8 Har Saggi mt Israel
32 K6 Harsefeld Germany
32 H9 Harsewinkel Germany
26 L5 Harsprånget Sweden
26 J3 Harstad Norway
32 L8 Harsum Germany
28 A4 Harsyssel reg Denmark
119 M9 Hart Saskatchewan Canada
13 G4 Hart England
99 U6 Hart Michigan U.S.A.
65 E3 Hartao China
89 B7 Hartbees watercourse S Africa
89 E5 Hartbeespoortdam S Africa
38 N7 Hartberg Austria
27 B11 Hårteigen mt Norway
118 C8 Hartell Alberta Canada
22 E5 Hartennes-et-Taux France
36 E2 Hartenrod Germany
37 O2 Hartenstein Germany
37 J5 Hartershofen Germany
15 E5 Hart Fell Scotland
9 G5 Hartfield England
111 L10 Hartford Alabama U.S.A.
109 N1 Hartford Arkansas U.S.A.
95 P5 Hartford Connecticut U.S.A.
107 P3 Hartford Kansas U.S.A.
110 K4 Hartford Kentucky U.S.A.
94 A4 Hartford Michigan U.S.A.
94 E6 Hartford Ohio U.S.A.
112 D2 Hartford Tennessee U.S.A.
99 S6 Hartford Wisconsin U.S.A.
94 B6 Hartford City Indiana U.S.A.
95 P5 Hartford, E Connecticut U.S.A.
37 O1 Hartha Germany
37 O2 Harthau Germany
12 E2 Harthill Scotland
9 E1 Hartington England
98 J7 Hartington Nebraska U.S.A.
80 E2 Har Tir'an Israel
122 D2 Hart-jaune, R Quebec Canada
138 D4 Hart, L South Australia Australia
122 E7 Hartland New Brunswick Canada
8 B6 Hartland England
95 S2 Hartland Maine U.S.A.
8 B5 Hartland Pt England
8 D3 Hartlebury England
13 G4 Hartlepool England
13 G3 Hartley England
99 L6 Hartley Iowa U.S.A.
108 B8 Hartley Texas U.S.A.
117 J9 Hartley Bay British Columbia Canada
9 F5 Hartley Wintney England
100 F2 Hartline Washington U.S.A.
106 H3 Hartman Colorado U.S.A.
37 P5 Hartmanice Czech Rep
37 O2 Hartmannsdorf Germany
36 G3 Hartmannshain Germany
142 E3 Hart, Mt W Australia Australia
119 Q6 Hart Mt Manitoba Canada
100 F7 Hart Mt Oregon U.S.A.
119 R9 Hartney Manitoba Canada
29 M10 Hartola Finland
13 G4 Harton England
106 E2 Hartsel Colorado U.S.A.
111 K7 Hartselle Alabama U.S.A.
37 J6 Härtsfeld mts Germany
107 P7 Hartshorne Oklahoma U.S.A.
138 C4 Harts I South Australia Australia
140 C6 Harts Range Police Station N Terr Australia
112 G3 Hartsville South Carolina U.S.A.
110 K5 Hartsville Tennessee U.S.A.
89 D6 Hartswater S Africa
80 C6 Hartuv Israel
110 D4 Hartville Missouri U.S.A.
98 B7 Hartville Wyoming U.S.A.
112 E3 Hartwell Georgia U.S.A.
112 E3 Hartwell L res South Carolina U.S.A.
120 H3 Harty Ontario Canada
89 D6 Hartz R S Africa
84 F4 Harūj al Aswad, Al Libya
79 G1 Haruniye Turkey
58 B2 Har Us Nuur L Mongolia
80 C7 Ḩaruvit Israel
100 J3 Harvard Idaho U.S.A.
99 S7 Harvard Illinois U.S.A.
98 H9 Harvard Nebraska U.S.A.
116 O6 Harvard Gl Alaska U.S.A.
106 D3 Harvard, Mt Colorado U.S.A.
143 F7 Harvest, Mt W Australia Australia
143 B10 Harvey W Australia Australia
99 T8 Harvey Illinois U.S.A.
99 O8 Harvey Iowa U.S.A.
111 J13 Harvey New Orleans, Louisiana U.S.A.
98 F2 Harvey North Dakota U.S.A.
102 C1 Harvey Mt California U.S.A.
122 F8 Harvey Stn New Brunswick Canada
107 P3 Harveyville Kansas U.S.A.
110 F5 Harviell Missouri U.S.A.
9 E4 Harwell England
9 H4 Harwich England
109 K6 Harwood Texas U.S.A.
36 E4 Harxheim Germany
74 F4 Haryana prov India
80 E8 Har Yonatan Israel
33 N9 Harz mts Germany
33 O9 Harzegerode Germany
79 F8 Hāsā Jordan
72 F4 Hasā, Al reg Saudi Arabia
78 H3 Hasakah, Al Syria
78 E2 Hasan Daği mt Turkey
74 H9 Hasanparti India
80 E7 Hasasa R Jordan
79 F5 Hâsbaiya Lebanon
32 G8 Hasbergen Germany
36 B5 Hasborn-Dautweiler Germany
32 G7 Hase R Germany
37 K2 Hasel R Germany
32 L5 Haseldorf Germany
32 F7 Haselünne Germany
80 D4 Hashimiye Jordan
61 J11 Hashimoto Japan
26 H8 Håsjö Sweden
111 D7 Haskell Arkansas U.S.A.
107 P6 Haskell Oklahoma U.S.A.
108 H2 Haskell Texas U.S.A.
38 K4 Haslach Austria
36 E7 Haslach Germany
27 G16 Hasle Denmark
109 M8 Haslet Texas U.S.A.
28 H6 Haslev Denmark
13 F6 Haslingden England
41 H4 Hasli Tal Switzerland
28 E4 Haslund Denmark
28 E5 Hasmark Denmark
22 E3 Hasnon France
80 D3 Ha Solelim Israel
18 E9 Hasparren France
32 F10 Haspe Germany
80 G2 Haspin Syria
22 E3 Haspres France
76 C4 Hassan India
103 M8 Hassayampa R Arizona U.S.A.
37 K3 Hassberge mts Germany
36 C5 Hassel Germany

26 J9 Hassela Sweden
33 N9 Hasselfelde Germany
115 K2 Hassel Sd Northwest Territories Canada
22 J2 Hasselt Belgium
25 F3 Hasselt Netherlands
28 F4 Hassensør C Denmark
33 N9 Hasserode Germany
37 K3 Hassfurt Germany
17 F10 Hassi Berkane Morocco
85 E2 Hassi-Bou-Zid Algeria
85 E3 Hassi Chebaba Algeria
28 A3 Hassing Denmark
37 L3 Hasslach Germany
33 T6 Hassleben Germany
37 K1 Hassleben Thüringen Germany
27 G15 Hässleholm Sweden
27 G13 Hasslerör Sweden
36 E5 Hassloch Germany
22 H3 Hastière-Lavaux Belgium
139 L4 Hastings R New South Wales Australia
139 H9 Hastings Tasmania Australia
127 P6 Hastings Barbados
121 N8 Hastings Ontario Canada
9 G6 Hastings England
145 F3 Hastings New Zealand
113 F8 Hastings Florida U.S.A.
99 L9 Hastings Iowa U.S.A.
94 B4 Hastings Michigan U.S.A.
99 O5 Hastings Minnesota U.S.A.
98 H9 Hastings Nebraska U.S.A.
107 M7 Hastings Oklahoma U.S.A.
94 J6 Hastings Pennsylvania U.S.A.
28 E6 Håstrup Denmark
27 G15 Hästveda Sweden
106 H3 Hasty Colorado U.S.A.
26 M1 Hasvik Norway
106 G3 Haswell Colorado U.S.A.
79 G2 Hatay Turkey
95 M6 Hatboro Pennsylvania U.S.A.
106 C9 Hatch New Mexico U.S.A.
103 M4 Hatch Utah U.S.A.
140 D5 Hatches Cr N Terr Australia
126 F2 Hatchet Bay Eleuthera Bahamas
110 G6 Hatchie R Tennessee U.S.A.
98 B7 Hat Cr Wyoming U.S.A.
100 D9 Hat Creek California U.S.A.
48 H5 Haţeg Romania
145 F3 Hatepe New Zealand
67 H4 Haterumashima Japan
139 G5 Hatfield New South Wales Australia
119 M7 Hatfield Saskatchewan Canada
9 F4 Hatfield England
111 B7 Hatfield Arkansas U.S.A.
98 K6 Hatfield Minnesota U.S.A.
9 G4 Hatfield Peverel England
101 T3 Hathaway Montana U.S.A.
138 F6 Hatherleigh South Australia Australia
8 B6 Hatherleigh England
9 E1 Hathersage England
74 H5 Hathras India
68 G7 Ha Tien Vietnam
80 G3 Hatim Jordan
68 G3 Ha Tinh Vietnam
71 M9 Hatohudo Indonesia
127 K5 Hato Mayor Dominican Rep
56 C3 Hatskiy Russian Federation
60 F11 Hatsukaichi Japan
138 F5 Hattah Victoria Australia
70 F2 Hattan, Mt Sabah
25 F4 Hattem Netherlands
36 D6 Hatten France
112 M2 Hatteras North Carolina U.S.A.
112 M2 Hatteras Inlet North Carolina U.S.A.
36 E3 Hattersheim Germany
26 G6 Hattfjelldal Norway
111 G10 Hattiesburg Mississippi U.S.A.
36 B6 Hattigny France
28 D5 Hatting Denmark
32 F10 Hattingen Germany
118 H8 Hatton Saskatchewan Canada
21 P3 Hatton France
98 J2 Hatton North Dakota U.S.A.
100 G3 Hatton Washington U.S.A.
68 C6 Hattras Passage Burma
40 F1 Hattstatt France
29 L10 Hattula Finland
126 F4 Hatuey Cuba
145 F4 Hatuma New Zealand
48 F3 Hatvan Hungary
38 O8 Hatzendorf Austria
36 C3 Hatzenport Germany
36 F2 Hatzfeld Germany
22 D2 Haubourdin France
86 A2 Haud reg Ethiopia
80 G4 Haufa Jordan
28 C4 Hauge Denmark
27 C10 Hauge Norway
99 P4 Haugen Wisconsin U.S.A.
27 A12 Haugesund Norway
111 C9 Haughton Louisiana U.S.A.
31 J7 Haugsdorf Austria
29 L10 Hauho Finland
145 E3 Hauhungaroa Ra New Zealand
27 B12 Haukeliseter Norway
29 L6 Haukipudas Finland
29 N9 Haukivesi L Finland
29 N9 Haukivuori Finland
145 F3 Haumoana New Zealand
36 H2 Haune R Germany
36 H2 Hauneck Germany
36 H2 Haunetal Hessen Germany
37 K7 Haunstetten Germany
144 C5 Haupiri, L New Zealand
37 O5 Hauptenberg mt Germany
145 E2 Hauraki Gulf New Zealand
144 A6 Hauroko, L New Zealand
27 A11 Haus Norway
36 E7 Hausach Germany
32 J8 Hausberge Germany
101 O3 Hauser L. Dam Montana U.S.A.
38 H5 Hausruck mts Austria
Haussez Iles d' see Mercury Is
41 K4 Hausstock mt Switzerland
29 O5 Hautajarvi Finland
22 B3 Haut Banc, Pte du France
40 B2 Haut du Sec mt France
18 L10 Haute-Corse dept Corsica
19 O12 Hautecourt France
18 F7 Hautefort France
18 F9 Haute-Garonne dept France
18 H7 Haute-Loire dept France
40 E6 Hauteluce France
19 J4 Haute-Marne dept France
122 D4 Hauterive Quebec Canada
19 Q15 Hautes Alpes dept France
19 J5 Haute-Saône dept France
40 D6 Haute-Savoie dept France
22 L2 Hautes Fagnes Belgium
18 E9 Hautes-Pyrénées dept France
22 H4 Hautes Rivières France
18 F7 Haute-Vienne dept France
20 G4 Hauteville-sur-Mer France
36 B5 Haut-Hombourg France
95 T2 Haut, I. au Maine U.S.A.
22 F3 Hautmont France
19 K5 Haut-Rhin dept France
85 D2 Hauts Plateaux Morocco/Algeria
86 E5 Haut-Zaire prov Zaire
135 Q2 Hauula Hawaiian Is
145 E4 Hauwai New Zealand
Havana Cuba see Habana
110 C6 Havana Arkansas U.S.A.
111 M11 Havana Florida U.S.A.
99 R9 Havana Illinois U.S.A.
107 P4 Havana Kansas U.S.A.
98 J4 Havana North Dakota U.S.A.
9 F6 Havant England
103 K7 Havasu, L Cal/Ariz U.S.A.
28 C3 Havbro Denmark
28 J5 Havdrup Denmark

33 R6 Havel Germany
22 J3 Havelange Belgium
33 Q7 Havelberg Germany
33 R7 Havelland reg Germany
33 R7 Havelland Grosse Haupt-kanal Germany
122 G8 Havelock New Brunswick Canada
121 N8 Havelock Ontario Canada
145 D4 Havelock New Zealand
112 L3 Havelock North Carolina U.S.A.
98 D3 Havelock North Dakota U.S.A.
140 C2 Havelock Falls N Terr Australia
68 A7 Havelock I Andaman Is
145 F3 Havelock North New Zealand
107 N4 Haven Kansas U.S.A.
107 O2 Havensville Kansas U.S.A.
8 B4 Haverfordwest Wales
9 G3 Haverhill England
95 Q4 Haverhill Massachusetts U.S.A.
95 Q3 Haverhill New Hampshire U.S.A.
76 B3 Haveri India
26 H9 Haverö Sweden
22 J3 Haversin Belgium
28 C2 Haverslev Denmark
28 D3 Haverslev Nordjylland Denmark
95 N5 Haverstraw New York U.S.A.
107 L4 Haviland Kansas U.S.A.
94 C5 Haviland Ohio U.S.A.
120 F6 Haviland Bay Ontario Canada
65 B2 Havirga Mongolia
48 K2 Havirna Romania
31 J6 Havlíčkův Brod Czech Rep
28 D6 Havnbjerg Denmark
28 E3 Havndal Denmark
28 B6 Havneby Denmark
28 G5 Havnebyen Denmark
28 G5 Havnsø Denmark
28 B4 Havnstrup Denmark
26 O1 Havoysund Norway
47 J5 Havran Turkey
22 G3 Havre Belgium
101 Q1 Havre Montana U.S.A.
21 L2 Havre Antifer, Pont du France
123 L6 Havre Aubert Madeleine Is, Quebec Canada
28 G6 Havrebjerg Denmark
123 L8 Havre Boucher Nova Scotia Canada
95 L7 Havre de Grace Maryland U.S.A.
122 J3 Havre-St-Pierre Quebec Canada
137 Q8 Havre Trench sea feature Pacific Oc
28 A5 Havrvig Denmark
26 H7 Havsnäs Sweden
78 E1 Havza Turkey
135 U5 Hawaii isld Hawaiian Is
135 Hawaiian Is Pacific Oc
86 B3 Hawal R Nigeria
118 L7 Hawarden Saskatchewan Canada
144 D5 Hawarden New Zealand
98 K6 Hawarden Iowa U.S.A.
8 C1 Hawarden Wales
138 F6 Hawdon, L South Australia Australia
144 B6 Hawea New Zealand
144 B6 Hawea Flat New Zealand
145 E3 Hawera New Zealand
102 G7 Hawes California U.S.A.
110 K4 Hawesville Kentucky U.S.A.
13 F5 Hawes Water England
135 U4 Hawi Hawaiian Is
13 F3 Hawick Scotland
144 B6 Hawkdun Range New Zealand
145 F3 Hawke Bay New Zealand
139 L4 Hawke, C New South Wales Australia
138 E4 Hawker South Australia Australia
138 F3 Hawker Gate New South Wales Australia
145 F3 Hawke's Bay admin region New Zealand
141 F1 Hawkesbury I Queensland Australia
140 C1 Hawkesbury Pt N Terr Australia
139 K5 Hawkesbury R New South Wales Australia
9 G5 Hawkhurst England
103 L4 Hawkins Pk Utah U.S.A.
112 D5 Hawkinsville Georgia U.S.A.
120 F4 Hawk Junct Ontario Canada
118 J1 Hawk Lake Ontario Canada
110 E3 Hawk Point Missouri U.S.A.
94 D1 Hawks Michigan U.S.A.
126 F2 Hawksbill Cay isld Bahamas
13 E5 Hawkshead England
126 G2 Hawks Nest Pt Cat I Bahamas
98 B8 Hawk Springs Wyoming U.S.A.
141 K7 Hawkwood Queensland Australia
106 G4 Hawley Colorado U.S.A.
98 K3 Hawley Minnesota U.S.A.
95 M5 Hawley Pennsylvania U.S.A.
108 H3 Hawley Texas U.S.A.
68 D2 Hawng Luk Burma
13 G6 Haworth England
107 Q8 Haworth Oklahoma U.S.A.
112 H2 Haw R North Carolina U.S.A.
78 H5 Hawran, Wadi Iraq
78 L5 Hawr as S'adiyah L Iraq
13 H5 Hawsker England
113 E8 Hawthorn Florida U.S.A.
102 F3 Hawthorne Nevada U.S.A.
99 P3 Hawthorne Wisconsin U.S.A.
80 D5 Hawwara Jordan
85 B3 Hawza Western Sahara
65 F2 Haxat China
65 B2 Haxat Hudag China
101 T2 Haxby Montana U.S.A.
98 D9 Haxtun Colorado U.S.A.
139 G5 Hay New South Wales Australia
117 N6 Hay R British Columbia Canada
100 H3 Hay Washington U.S.A.
99 P4 Hay R Wisconsin U.S.A.
61 P6 Hayachine-san mt Japan
60 P3 Hayakita Japan
19 K3 Hayange France
60 E12 Hayasui-seto str Japan
101 T9 Haybro Colorado U.S.A.
47 N10 Haydarpaşa Turkey
103 O8 Hayden Arizona U.S.A.
101 S9 Hayden Colorado U.S.A.
100 J2 Hayden L Idaho U.S.A.
141 F4 Haydon Queensland Australia
13 F4 Haydon Br England
20 G3 Haye-du-Puits, la France
21 N3 Haye, la France
20 H4 Haye-Pesnel, la France
115 K6 Hayes R Manitoba Canada
111 D11 Hayes Louisiana U.S.A.
98 E5 Hayes South Dakota U.S.A.
21 M4 Haye-St.Sylvestre, la France
98 E9 Hayes Center Nebraska U.S.A.
116 L6 Hayes Glaciers Alaska U.S.A.
115 N2 Hayes Halvø pen Greenland
68 C7 Hayes I Burma
116 O5 Hayes, Mt Alaska U.S.A.
112 D2 Hayesville North Carolina U.S.A.
13 G6 Hayfield England
99 O6 Hayfield Minnesota U.S.A.
103 J8 Hayfield Res Carolina U.S.A.
102 A1 Hayfork California U.S.A.
13 F5 Haygarth England
36 G7 Hayingen Germany

117 O6 Hay L Alberta Canada
118 D5 Hay Lakes Alberta Canada
8 A7 Hayle England
9 F6 Hayling England
113 E7 Haylow Georgia U.S.A.
141 J5 Hayman I Queensland Australia
94 K8 Haymarket Virginia U.S.A.
140 C6 Hay, Mt N Terr Australia
109 O3 Haynesville Louisiana U.S.A.
95 T8 Haynesville Maine U.S.A.
111 K9 Hayneville Alabama U.S.A.
21 N2 Hayons, les France
8 C3 Hay-on-Wye England
141 J5 Hay Point Queensland Australia
140 D6 Hay R N Terr Australia
47 J3 Hayrabolu R Turkey
47 J3 Hayrabolu Turkey
117 Q5 Hay River Northwest Territories Canada
118 F8 Hays Alberta Canada
107 L3 Hays Kansas U.S.A.
101 R1 Hays Montana U.S.A.
98 D7 Hay Springs Nebraska U.S.A.
100 K8 Haystack Mt Nevada U.S.A.
103 L2 Haystack Pk Utah U.S.A.
118 G6 Hayter Alberta Canada
110 G5 Hayti Missouri U.S.A.
98 J5 Hayti South Dakota U.S.A.
13 H6 Hayton England
102 B4 Hayward California U.S.A.
99 N6 Hayward Minnesota U.S.A.
107 N5 Hayward Oklahoma U.S.A.
99 P4 Hayward Wisconsin U.S.A.
140 B2 Hayward, Mt N Terr Australia
9 F6 Haywards Heath England
119 T9 Haywood Manitoba Canada
80 E2 Hazan Israel
77 J3 Hazarajat reg Afghanistan
94 D9 Hazard Kentucky U.S.A.
95 P4 Hazardville Connecticut U.S.A.
75 L7 Hazāribag India
77 F1 Hazar Masjed, Kūh-e mts Iran
22 D2 Hazebrouck France
98 K1 Hazel Minnesota U.S.A.
98 J5 Hazel South Dakota U.S.A.
119 V9 Hazelridge Manitoba Canada
117 K8 Hazelton British Columbia Canada
107 M4 Hazelton Kansas U.S.A.
98 F3 Hazelton North Dakota U.S.A.
110 E7 Hazen Arkansas U.S.A.
102 E2 Hazen Nevada U.S.A.
98 E2 Hazen North Dakota U.S.A.
116 E6 Hazen B Alaska U.S.A.
115 N1 Hazen, L Northwest Territories Canada
118 K9 Hazenmore Saskatchewan Canada
114 H2 Hazen Str Northwest Territories Canada
80 B8 Haẕerim Israel
25 C4 Hazerswoude Netherlands
112 E2 Hazewood North Carolina U.S.A.
112 E6 Hazlehurst Georgia U.S.A.
111 F10 Hazlehurst Mississippi U.S.A.
95 M6 Hazleton Pennsylvania U.S.A.
142 G5 Hazlett, L W Australia Australia
37 N3 Hazlov Czech Rep
80 F2 Ḩazor Israel
80 F3 HaZore'im Israel
80 C7 He Israel
9 G2 Heacham England
9 G5 Headcorn England
14 B3 Headford Ireland
122 E9 Head Harbor I Maine U.S.A.
140 E5 Headingly Queensland Australia
111 L10 Headland Alabama U.S.A.
144 B6 Headlong Pk New Zealand
138 B4 Head of Bight B South Australia Australia
100 K3 Headquarters Idaho U.S.A.
83 M9 Headridge Hill Christmas I Indian Oc
100 A7 Heads, The C Oregon U.S.A.
99 R4 Heafford Junct Wisconsin U.S.A.
102 B3 Healdsburg California U.S.A.
109 K1 Healdton Oklahoma U.S.A.
139 H7 Healesville Victoria Australia
116 P4 Healy R Alaska U.S.A.
116 N5 Healy Alaska U.S.A.
107 K3 Healy Kansas U.S.A.
116 P5 Healy L Alaska U.S.A.
119 Q3 Heaman Manitoba Canada
9 E1 Heanor England
81 K16 Heard I Southern Oc
81 L16 Heard I. Base Australia Base Heard I. Southern Oc
119 M8 Hearne Saskatchewan Canada
109 L5 Hearne Texas U.S.A.
117 R4 Hearne L Northwest Territories Canada
120 G3 Hearst Ontario Canada
102 A2 Hearst California U.S.A.
146 D5 Hearst I Antarctica
98 D3 Heart R North Dakota U.S.A.
118 F3 Heart L Alberta Canada
101 P5 Heart L Wyoming U.S.A.
118 A3 Heart R Alberta Canada
123 T6 Heart's Content Newfoundland Canada
123 T6 Heart's Delight Newfoundland Canada
98 H9 Heartwell Nebraska U.S.A.
128 E6 Heath R Bolivia/Peru
139 G6 Heathcote Victoria Australia
6 L2 Heather oil rig North Sea
123 O5 Heatherton Newfoundland Canada
9 G6 Heathfield England
123 L4 Heath Pt Anticosti I, Quebec
9 F5 Heathrow Airport England
112 G3 Heath Springs South Carolina U.S.A.
122 F6 Heath Steel Mines New Brunswick Canada
95 L9 Heathsville Virginia U.S.A.
107 Q7 Heavener Oklahoma U.S.A.
109 J8 Hebbronville Texas U.S.A.
13 F6 Hebden Br England
65 C5 Hebei prov China
141 J8 Hebel Queensland Australia
32 L6 Heber Germany
103 O7 Heber Arizona U.S.A.
101 O9 Heber City Utah U.S.A.
110 D6 Heber Springs Arkansas U.S.A.
121 P3 Hébert, L Quebec Canada
121 T4 Hébertville Station Quebec Canada
101 O5 Hebgen L Montana U.S.A.
65 C7 Hebi China
100 B4 Hebo Oregon U.S.A.
115 N6 Hebron Labrador, Nfld Canada
122 F10 Hebron Nova Scotia Canada
80 D7 Hebron Jordan
101 T9 Hebron Colorado U.S.A.
99 S7 Hebron Illinois U.S.A.
99 T8 Hebron Indiana U.S.A.
98 J9 Hebron Nebraska U.S.A.
98 E3 Hebron North Dakota U.S.A.
94 E7 Hebron Ohio U.S.A.
27 J12 Heby Sweden
117 H9 Hecate Str British Columbia Canada
100 A5 Heceta Head Oregon U.S.A.
117 G8 Heceta I Alaska U.S.A.
67 C4 Hechi China
36 F7 Hechingen Germany
22 J1 Hechtel Belgium
32 K5 Hechthausen Germany
36 E4 Hechtsheim Germany
67 B1 Hechuan China
33 T7 Heckelberg Germany
9 F2 Heckington England

33 P9 **Hecklingen** Germany
98 H4 **Hecla** South Dakota U.S.A.
114 H2 **Hecla & Griper B** Northwest Territories Canada
119 V7 **Hecla I** Manitoba Canada
119 V7 **Hecla Prov. Park** Manitoba Canada
122 F9 **Hectanooga** Nova Scotia Canada
144 C4 **Hector** New Zealand
99 M5 **Hector** Minnesota U.S.A.
117 P10 **Hector, Mt** Alberta Canada
145 E4 **Hector, Mt** New Zealand
144 B6 **Hector Mts** New Zealand
127 M2 **Hector's River** Jamaica
27 H12 **Hed** Sweden
61 M11 **Heda** Japan
27 D11 **Hedal** Norway
21 P1 **Hédauville** France
26 K6 **Hedberg** Sweden
27 D12 **Heddal** Norway
36 F4 **Heddesheim** Germany
13 G3 **Heddon on-the-Wall** England
20 G5 **Hédé** France
26 G9 **Hede** Sweden
25 D5 **Hedel** Netherlands
27 H11 **Hedemora** Sweden
32 L10 **Hedemunden** Germany
28 E6 **Heden** Denmark
26 M6 **Heden** Sweden
26 N5 **Hedenäset** Sweden
28 D5 **Hedensted** Denmark
33 O9 **Hedersleben** Germany
27 J11 **Hedesunda** Sweden
26 G9 **Hedeviken** Sweden
144 B7 **Hedgehope** New Zealand
101 Q3 **Hedgesville** Montana U.S.A.
94 J7 **Hedgesville** West Virginia U.S.A.
67 C6 **Hedi Shuiku** *res* China
117 N11 **Hedley** British Columbia Canada
27 E10 **Hedmark** *county* Norway
27 E11 **Hedmark** Norway
61 Q12 **Hedo** Okinawa
61 Q12 **Hedo-misaki** *C* Okinawa
13 H6 **Hedon** England
83 L11 **Hedo Oya** *R* Sri Lanka
99 O8 **Hedrick** Iowa U.S.A.
28 A4 **Hee** Denmark
32 F7 **Heede** Germany
33 T7 **Heegermühle** Germany
32 F8 **Heek** Germany
25 C4 **Heemstede** Netherlands
32 J8 **Heepen** Germany
22 H3 **Heer** Belgium
25 E7 **Heer** Netherlands
25 F4 **Heerde** Netherlands
25 E3 **Heerenveen** Netherlands
25 C3 **Heerhugo-waard** Netherlands
25 E7 **Heerlen** Netherlands
25 E5 **Heesch** Netherlands
25 E6 **Heeze** Netherlands
67 F1 **Hefei** China
67 C2 **Hefeng** China
117 N10 **Heffley** British Columbia Canada
111 L8 **Heflin** Alabama U.S.A.
65 H1 **Hegang** China
61 K8 **Hegura-jima** *isld* Japan
88 E5 **Hehe** Tanzania
26 D10 **Heidal** Norway
80 F8 **Heidan** *R* Jordan
32 K4 **Heide** Germany
37 L5 **Heideck** Germany
36 F5 **Heidelberg** Germany
111 H10 **Heidelberg** Mississippi U.S.A.
87 E11 **Heidelburg** S Africa
110 N4 **Heidelburg** Kentucky U.S.A.
36 F5 **Heidelsheim** Germany
37 M4 **Heide Naab** *R* Germany
37 J6 **Heidenheim** Germany
36 D3 **Heidenrod** Germany
94 B2 **Heights, The** Michigan U.S.A.
60 F12 **Heigun-tō** *isld* Japan
59 J1 **Heihe** China
59 J1 **Hei-ho** China
25 E6 **Heijthuizsen** Netherlands
87 E11 **Heilbron** S Africa
36 G5 **Heilbronn** Germany
38 G7 **Heiligenblut** Austria
33 P4 **Heiligendamm** Germany
30 F1 **Heiligenhafen** Germany
32 M10 **Heiligenstadt** Germany
37 L4 **Heiligenstadt** Germany
65 D7 **Heilin** China
59 H1 **Heilongjiang** *prov* China
59 J1 **Heilong Jiang** *R* China
37 K5 **Heilsbronn** Germany
Heilungkiang *prov see* **Heilongjiang** *prov*
36 B2 **Heimbach** Germany
36 G4 **Heimbuchenthal** Germany
33 N9 **Heimburg** Germany
6 M3 **Heimdal** *oil rig* North Sea
26 D8 **Heimdal** Norway
98 G2 **Heimdal** North Dakota U.S.A.
36 F6 **Heimsheim** Germany
29 O9 **Heinävesi** Finland
36 H1 **Heinebach** Germany
22 L3 **Heinerscheid** Luxembourg
37 L3 **Heinersdorf** Germany
36 C5 **Heinitz** Germany
25 F4 **Heino** Netherlands
29 M10 **Heinola** Finland
33 P8 **Heinrichsburg** Germany
25 F6 **Heinsberg** Germany
118 G5 **Heinsburg** Alberta Canada
33 S9 **Heinsdorf** Germany
68 C5 **Heinz B** Burma
68 C5 **Heinze I** Burma
65 E4 **Heishan** China
65 C3 **Heishantou** China
67 C2 **Heishui** China
118 E6 **Heisler** Alberta Canada
22 E1 **Heist** Belgium
22 H1 **Heist-op-den-Berg** Belgium
80 G3 **Heit** Syria
80 G2 **Heital** Syria
79 D8 **Heitân, G** *mt* Egypt
40 G2 **Heitersheim** Germany
65 F2 **Heiyupao** China
84 H4 **Heiz, El** Egypt
65 A5 **Hejialiang** China
67 B2 **Hejiang** China
67 D5 **He Jiang** *R* China
67 C6 **Hejiang** China
67 D4 **Hejie** China
65 A7 **Hejin** China
28 D6 **Hejls** Denmark
28 C6 **Hejlsminde** Denmark
28 B5 **Hejnsvig** Denmark
28 D6 **Hejsager** Denmark
28 S10 **Hekla** *mt* Iceland
Hekou *see* **Yanshan**
65 B4 **Hekou** China
67 D5 **Hekou** Guangdong China
67 A5 **Hekou** Yunnan China
31 L1 **Hel** Poland
80 E2 **Ḥela** Israel
26 F9 **Helagsfjället** *mt* Sweden
58 E4 **Helan Shan** *mt ra* China
37 K1 **Helbe** *R* Germany
28 E3 **Helberskov** Denmark
33 O9 **Helbra** Germany
22 J1 **Helchteren** Belgium
37 K3 **Heldburg** Germany
36 F3 **Heldenbergen** Germany
127 P3 **Helden's Pt** St Kitts W Indies
33 O10 **Heldrungen** Germany
112 D3 **Helen** Georgia U.S.A.
111 K8 **Helena** Alabama U.S.A.
111 F7 **Helena** Arkansas U.S.A.
100 B9 **Helena** California U.S.A.
112 E5 **Helena** Georgia U.S.A.
101 N3 **Helena** Montana U.S.A.
107 M5 **Helena** Oklahoma U.S.A.
102 G7 **Helendale** California U.S.A.
118 J5 **Helénè L** Saskatchewan Canada
142 E6 **Helen Hill** W Australia Australia
71 C1 **Helen I** Pacific Oc
119 P1 **Helen L** Ontario Canada
141 F5 **Helen, Mt** Queensland Australia
15 D4 **Helensburgh** Scotland
140 C4 **Helen Springs** N Terr Australia
145 E2 **Helensville** New Zealand
33 P10 **Helfta** Germany
26 F6 **Helgeland** *reg* Norway
27 D12 **Helgen** Norway
32 G4 **Helgoländ** *isld* Germany
32 H4 **Helgoländer Bucht** Germany
26 K1 **Helgöy** Norway
65 H1 **Heli** China
79 B8 **Heliopolis** Egypt
26 E8 **Hell** Norway
28 S10 **Hella** Iceland
33 O7 **Hellberg** *hills* Germany
29 K4 **Hellebæk** Denmark
77 B5 **Helleh** *R* Iran
26 J4 **Hellemobotn** Norway
25 F4 **Hellendoorn** Netherlands
36 B3 **Hellenthal** Germany
29 K5 **Hellerup** Denmark
28 J6 **Hellested** Denmark
26 B9 **Hellesylt** Norway
28 E2 **Hellevad** Nordjylland Denmark
28 C6 **Hellevad** Sønderjylland Denmark
26 L2 **Helligskogen** Norway
26 G4 **Helligvoer** *isld* Norway
17 F6 **Hellin** Spain
Hell's Canyon *see* **Snake River Canyon**
127 L3 **Hellshire Hills** Jamaica
28 E2 **Hellum** Denmark
32 K6 **Hellwege** Germany
102 D5 **Helm** California U.S.A.
77 H4 **Helmand** *R* Afghanistan
77 H4 **Helmand** *prov* Afghanistan
32 K9 **Helmarshausen** Germany
37 M3 **Helmbrechts** Germany
33 N10 **Helme** *R* Germany
87 C11 **Helmeringhausen** Namibia
37 J2 **Helmershausen** Germany
9 H3 **Helmingham** England
25 E6 **Helmond** Netherlands
32 J4 **Helmsand** *sandbank* Germany
15 E2 **Helmsdale** *R* Scotland
15 E2 **Helmsdale** Scotland
13 G5 **Helmsley** England
36 F5 **Helmstadt** Germany
33 O8 **Helmstedt** Germany
101 N3 **Helmville** Montana U.S.A.
28 D6 **Helnæs** Denmark
28 E6 **Helnæs Bugt** *B* Denmark
26 P1 **Helnes** Norway
59 J3 **Helong** China
65 F2 **Helong** China
109 J6 **Helotes** Texas U.S.A.
103 O2 **Helper** Utah U.S.A.
33 T6 **Helpter Berge** *pk* Germany
32 L10 **Helsa-Wickenrode** Germany
29 K4 **Helsingborg** Sweden
28 J4 **Helsinge** Denmark
Helsingfors *see* **Helsinki**
29 K4 **Helsingør** Denmark
29 L11 **Helsinki** Finland
9 G6 **Helston** England
32 L7 **Helstorf** Germany
110 K3 **Heltonville** Indiana U.S.A.
130 H5 **Helvécia** Brazil
14 D4 **Helvick Hd** Ireland
84 J4 **Helwan** Egypt
28 D4 **Hem** Vejle Denmark
28 B3 **Hem** Viborg Denmark
118 F7 **Hemaruka** Alberta Canada
37 M5 **Hemau** Germany
32 E9 **Hemden** Germany
9 F4 **Hemel Hempstead** England
25 D3 **Hemelum** Netherlands
32 G10 **Hemer** Germany
102 H8 **Hemet** California U.S.A.
36 B6 **Héming** France
98 C7 **Hemingford** Nebraska U.S.A.
119 Q4 **Heming Lake** Manitoba Canada
112 H4 **Hemingway** South Carolina U.S.A.
141 L1 **Hemmant** *dist* Brisbane, Qnsld Australia
32 J4 **Hemme** Germany
28 F3 **Hemmed** Denmark
32 L8 **Hemmendorf** Germany
28 A5 **Hemmet** Denmark
32 L8 **Hemmingen** Germany
121 R7 **Hemmingford** Quebec Canada
32 K5 **Hemmoor** Germany
26 G5 **Hemnesberget** Norway
111 C10 **Hemphill** Texas U.S.A.
95 O6 **Hempstead** Long I, New York U.S.A.
109 L5 **Hempstead** Texas U.S.A.
9 H2 **Hemsby** England
27 K14 **Hemse** *isld* Gotland Sweden
27 C11 **Hemsedal** Norway
27 C11 **Hemsil** *R* Norway
27 G15 **Hemsjö** Sweden
32 L6 **Hemslingen** Germany
26 K9 **Hemsö** Sweden
13 G6 **Hemsworth** England
65 B7 **Henan** *prov* China
20 F4 **Hénanbihen** France
145 E1 **Hen and Chicken Is** New Zealand
20 F4 **Hénansal** France
16 E4 **Henares** *R* Spain
61 N5 **Henashi-zaki** *C* Japan
140 C6 **Henbury** N Terr Australia
18 D9 **Hendaye** France
22 D3 **Hendecourt-lès Cagnicourt** France
47 L4 **Hendek** Turkey
103 K5 **Henderson** Nevada U.S.A.
95 L3 **Henderson** New York U.S.A.
112 J1 **Henderson** North Carolina U.S.A.
110 H6 **Henderson** Tennessee U.S.A.
109 N3 **Henderson** Texas U.S.A.
94 E8 **Henderson** West Virginia U.S.A.
146 H13 **Henderson I** *isld* Antarctica
135 O11 **Henderson I** Pacific Oc
112 E2 **Hendersonville** North Carolina U.S.A.
77 A4 **Hendījān** Iran
77 A4 **Hendījān** *oil well* Persian Gulf
119 O6 **Hendon** Saskatchewan Canada
9 F4 **Hendon** England
77 C6 **Hendorābī** *isld* Iran
48 J4 **Hendorf** Romania
141 K1 **Hendra** *dist* Brisbane, Qnsld Australia
98 K5 **Hendricks** Minnesota U.S.A.
94 H7 **Hendricks** West Virginia U.S.A.
129 G3 **Hendrik Top** *mt* Suriname
89 D8 **Hendrik Verwoerd Dam** S Africa
8 B4 **Hendy** Wales
101 O8 **Henefer** Utah U.S.A.
65 H2 **Hengdaohezi** China
65 G3 **Hengdaozi** China
67 D3 **Hengdong** China
58 C6 **Hengduan Shan** *mts* China
25 G4 **Hengelo** Netherlands
37 P6 **Hengersberg** Germany
67 F2 **Hengfeng** China
67 A2 **Heng Jiang** *R* China
67 D2 **Henglongqiao** China
Hengnan *see* **Hengyang**
67 D3 **Heng Shan** *mt* China
67 D3 **Hengshan** China
58 G4 **Hengshui** China
37 J5 **Hengstfeld** Germany
67 C5 **Heng Xian** China
67 D3 **Hengyang** China
69 A9 **Henhoaha** Nicobar Is
22 D3 **Hénin-Beaumont** France
144 C6 **Henley** New Zealand
123 R2 **Henley Hbr** Labrador, Nfld Canada
9 E3 **Henley-in-Arden** England
9 F4 **Henley-on-Thames** England
100 C10 **Henleyville** California U.S.A.
9 F3 **Henlow** England
109 J5 **Henly** Texas U.S.A.
27 E12 **Henmes** Norway
61 P13 **Henna** Okinawa
26 H9 **Hennan** Sweden
28 A5 **Henne** Denmark
37 J3 **Henneberg** Germany
20 D6 **Hennebont** France
36 C2 **Hennef** Germany
37 K5 **Hennenbach** Germany
99 R8 **Hennepin** Illinois U.S.A.
21 L3 **Hennequeville** France
107 N5 **Hennessey** Oklahoma U.S.A.
33 S8 **Hennickendorf** Germany
33 S7 **Hennigsdorf** Germany
95 Q3 **Henniker** New Hampshire U.S.A.
110 J1 **Henning** Illinois U.S.A.
99 L3 **Henning** Minnesota U.S.A.
110 G6 **Henning** Tennessee U.S.A.
26 G3 **Henningsvaer** Norway
32 K4 **Hennstedt** Germany
21 P3 **Hénonville** France
77 D6 **Henqam** *isld* Iran
119 M5 **Henribourg** Saskatchewan Canada
22 K2 **Henri-Chapelle** Belgium
109 J2 **Henrietta** Texas U.S.A.
115 L6 **Henrietta Maria, C** Ontario Canada
103 N4 **Henrieville** Utah U.S.A.
117 L7 **Henri, Mt** British Columbia Canada
Henrique de Carvalho *see* **Saurimo**
101 O7 **Henry** Idaho U.S.A.
99 R8 **Henry** Illinois U.S.A.
95 M10 **Henry, C** Virginia U.S.A.
146 D7 **Henry Ice Rise** *ice rise* Antarctica
115 N4 **Henry Kater Pen** Northwest Territories Canada
111 K8 **Henry L** Alabama U.S.A.
68 A6 **Henry Lawrence I** Andaman Is
100 K1 **Henry, Mt** Montana U.S.A.
103 O4 **Henry Mts** Utah U.S.A.
142 B6 **Henry, R** W Australia Australia
101 O5 **Henrys Fork** *R* Idaho U.S.A.
110 L3 **Henryville** Indiana U.S.A.
120 J9 **Hensall** Ontario Canada
110 H4 **Henshaw** Kentucky U.S.A.
102 H8 **Henshaw, L** California U.S.A.
12 E5 **Hensingham** England
142 G3 **Hensman, Mt** W Australia Australia
32 L5 **Henstedt-Ulzburg** Germany
8 D6 **Henstridge** England
58 E2 **Hentiy** Mongolia
58 E2 **Hentiyn Nuruu** *mt* Mongolia
139 H6 **Henty** New South Wales Australia
68 B4 **Henzada** Burma
61 P13 **Henza-jima** *isld* Okinawa
118 L6 **Hepburn** Saskatchewan Canada
67 E1 **Hepeng** China
112 E4 **Hephzibah** Georgia U.S.A.
Heping *see* **Yanhe**
67 E4 **Heping** China
Hepo *see* **Jiexi**
36 B2 **Heppendorf** Germany
36 F4 **Heppenheim** Germany
100 F4 **Heppner** Oregon U.S.A.
80 F2 **Heptapegon** Israel
68 J2 **Hepu** China
120 J8 **Hepworth** Ontario Canada
65 B5 **Hequ** China
27 E11 **Heradsbygd** Norway
141 J3 **Herald Cays** *islds* Gt Barrier Reef Aust
77 H2 **Herāt** Afghanistan
77 G3 **Herāt** *prov* Afghanistan
18 H9 **Hérault** *R* France
18 H9 **Hérault** *dept* France
19 O14 **Herbasse** *R* France
20 F7 **Herbaudiere, Pte,de l'** France
21 N6 **Herbault** France
32 F10 **Herbede** Germany
36 D3 **Herberge, K** *mt* Germany
32 G9 **Herbern** Germany
141 H4 **Herbert** *R* Queensland Australia
118 K8 **Herbert** Saskatchewan Canada
144 C6 **Herbert** New Zealand
68 A7 **Herbertabad** Andaman Is
140 E6 **Herbert Downs** Queensland Australia
140 B4 **Herbert, Mt** N Terr Australia
142 F3 **Herbert, Mt** W Australia Australia
141 H3 **Herberton** Queensland Australia
145 F4 **Herbertville** New Zealand
22 K2 **Herbesthal** Belgium
22 J4 **Herbeumont** Belgium
21 H8 **Herbiers, les** France
20 F7 **Herbignac** France
36 C5 **Herbitzheim** France
119 S4 **Herb L** Manitoba Canada
36 D7 **Herbolzheim** Germany
36 E2 **Herborn** Germany
36 G2 **Herbstein** Germany
31 L5 **Herby** Poland
42 J6 **Herceg-Novi** Montenegro Yugoslavia
115 K6 **Herchmer** Manitoba Canada
36 H4 **Herchsheim** Germany
146 D9 **Hercules Dome** *ice dome* Antarctica
107 O5 **Herd** Oklahoma U.S.A.
32 F10 **Herdecke** Germany
125 M4 **Heredía** Costa Rica
8 D3 **Hereford** England
98 B9 **Hereford** Colorado U.S.A.
108 E1 **Hereford** Texas U.S.A.
8 D3 **Hereford and Worcester** *co* England
47 N11 **Hereke** Turkey
145 D1 **Herekino** New Zealand
16 E5 **Herencia** Spain
40 F5 **Herens, Val. d'** Switzerland
22 H1 **Herentals** Belgium
87 C10 **Herero** *homeland* Namibia
144 B5 **Heretaniwha Pt** New Zealand
28 J6 **Herfølge** Denmark
32 J8 **Herford** Germany
22 L2 **Hergenrath** Belgium
20 G7 **Heric** France
19 K5 **Hericourt** France
33 N10 **Heringen** Germany
107 O3 **Herington** Kansas U.S.A.
22 G2 **Herinnes** Belgium
144 B6 **Heriot** New Zealand
13 F2 **Heriot** Scotland
117 L10 **Heriot Bay** British Columbia Canada
41 K3 **Herisau** Switzerland
146 C7 **Heritage Ra** Antarctica
22 J2 **Herk-de-Stad** Belgium
95 N3 **Herkimer** New York U.S.A.
121 Q9 **Herkimer** New York U.S.A.
37 N2 **Herlasgrün** Germany
58 F2 **Herlen Gol** *R* Mongolia
58 G2 **Herlen He** *R* China
37 J1 **Herleshausen** Germany
29 K5 **Herlev** Denmark
28 H6 **Herlufmagle** Denmark
20 F3 **Herm** *isld* Channel Is
38 H8 **Hermagor** Austria
99 S3 **Herman** Michigan U.S.A.
98 K4 **Herman** Minnesota U.S.A.
98 K8 **Herman** Nebraska U.S.A.
71 D3 **Hermana Mayor** *isld* Philippines
124 J4 **Hermanas** Mexico
106 C10 **Hermanas** New Mexico U.S.A.
110 E3 **Hermann** Missouri U.S.A.
32 M7 **Hermannsberg** Germany
140 C6 **Hermannsburg** N Terr Australia
37 P4 **Heřmanova Hut'** Czech Rep
99 T4 **Hermansville** Michigan U.S.A.
89 A10 **Hermanus** S Africa
111 F10 **Hermanville** Mississippi U.S.A.
79 G4 **Hermel** Lebanon
21 P3 **Hermes** France
36 B4 **Hermeskeil** Germany
22 H3 **Hermeton-sur-Meuse** Belgium
139 H4 **Hermidale** New South Wales Australia
22 E3 **Hermies** France
100 F4 **Hermiston** Oregon U.S.A.
123 R6 **Hermitage** Newfoundland Canada
111 D8 **Hermitage** Arkansas U.S.A.
123 Q3 **Hermitage B** Newfoundland Canada
20 E5 **Hermitage, l'** France
142 B5 **Hermite I** W Australia Australia
133 D9 **Hermite, Is** Chile
21 M6 **Hermites, les** France
140 B2 **Hermit Hill** N Terr Australia
136 K2 **Hermit Is** Bismarck Arch
103 M5 **Hermits Rest** Arizona U.S.A.
108 G3 **Hermleigh** Texas U.S.A.
Hermōn, Mt *see* **Sheikh, J. esh**
22 F5 **Hermonville** France
98 C6 **Hermosa** South Dakota U.S.A.
124 D3 **Hermosillo** Mexico
Hermsdorf *see* **Ottendorf-Okrilla**
130 C9 **Hernandarias** Paraguay
113 E9 **Hernando** Florida U.S.A.
110 G7 **Hernando** Mississippi U.S.A.
102 E5 **Herndon** California U.S.A.
99 M8 **Herndon** Iowa U.S.A.
107 K2 **Herndon** Kansas U.S.A.
110 J5 **Herndon** Kentucky U.S.A.
95 L6 **Herndon** Pennsylvania U.S.A.
94 F9 **Herndon** West Virginia U.S.A.
32 F9 **Herne** Germany
9 H5 **Herne Bay** England
28 B4 **Herning** Denmark
124 C2 **Heroica Caborca** Mexico
37 L4 **Heroldsberg** Germany
22 J2 **Héron** Belgium
100 K1 **Heron** Montana U.S.A.
120 D4 **Heron Bay** Ontario Canada
25 F6 **Herongen** Germany
141 K6 **Heron I** Gt Barrier Reef Aust
144 C5 **Heron, L** New Zealand
99 L6 **Heron L** Minnesota U.S.A.
Herowābād *see* **Khalkhāl**
26 A9 **Heroy** Norway
130 B10 **Herradura** Argentina
16 D5 **Herrara del Duque** Spain
98 F4 **Herreid** South Dakota U.S.A.
36 F6 **Herrenberg** Germany
38 F6 **Herrenchiemsee** Germany
36 E6 **Herrenwies** Germany
133 E3 **Herrera** Argentina
17 G3 **Herrera** *mt* Spain
16 C5 **Herrera de Alcántara** Spain
17 G3 **Herrera de los Navarros** Spain
124 G5 **Herreras** Mexico
28 F6 **Herrested** Denmark
139 J8 **Herrick** Tasmania Australia
98 G6 **Herrick** South Dakota U.S.A.
110 G4 **Herrin** Illinois U.S.A.
123 S4 **Herring Neck** Newfoundland Canada
94 C9 **Herrington L** Kentucky U.S.A.
119 Q2 **Herriot** Manitoba Canada
28 H7 **Herritslev** Denmark
36 H7 **Herrlingen** Germany
27 F13 **Herrljunga** Sweden
36 E4 **Herrnsheim** Germany
36 C4 **Herrstein** Germany
18 G9 **Hers** *R* France
37 L5 **Hersbruck** Germany
36 D1 **Herscheid** Germany
118 J7 **Herschel** Saskatchewan Canada
116 S2 **Herschel** Yukon Territory Canada
99 S8 **Herscher** Illinois U.S.A.
37 J3 **Herschfeld** Germany
22 H1 **Herselt** Belgium
94 B3 **Hersey** Michigan U.S.A.
95 L6 **Hershey** Pennsylvania U.S.A.
28 D5 **Herslev** Denmark
28 D3 **Hersom** Denmark
22 K2 **Herstal** Belgium
9 G6 **Herstmonceux** England
22 E2 **Hertain** Belgium
32 F9 **Herten** Germany
9 F4 **Hertford** England
112 L1 **Hertford** North Carolina U.S.A.
9 F4 **Hertfordshire** *co* England
80 C5 **Ḥerut** Israel
16 D4 **Hervas** Spain
22 K2 **Herve** Belgium
141 L7 **Hervey B** Queensland Australia
121 S6 **Hervey Junction** Quebec Canada
141 H4 **Hervey Ra** Queensland Australia
36 E5 **Herxheim** Germany
33 M9 **Herzberg** Germany
33 S9 **Herzberg** Germany
33 T8 **Herzfelde** Germany
32 G7 **Herzlake** Germany
80 C5 **Herzliyya** Israel
37 K4 **Herzogenaurach** Germany
38 N5 **Herzogenburg** Austria
25 F7 **Herzogenrath** Germany
33 Q6 **Herzsprung** Germany
22 B2 **Hesdigneul-lès-Boulogne** France
22 C3 **Hesdin** France
32 G6 **Hesel** Germany
67 E3 **He Shui** *R* China
67 D5 **Heshui** China
65 B6 **Heshun** China
27 B13 **Heskestad** Norway
98 G2 **Hesper** North Dakota U.S.A.
22 L4 **Hesperange** Luxembourg
102 G7 **Hesperia** California U.S.A.
94 A3 **Hesperia** Michigan U.S.A.
106 B4 **Hesperus** Colorado U.S.A.
106 B4 **Hesperus Pk** Colorado U.S.A.
117 G4 **Hess** *R* Yukon Territory Canada
116 N4 **Hess Cr** Alaska U.S.A.
28 F6 **Hesselager** Denmark
37 K5 **Hesselberg** *mt* Germany
28 H4 **Hesselø** *isld* Denmark
33 N8 **Hessen** Germany
36 F2 **Hessen** *land* Germany
36 F1 **Hessenstein** Germany
36 H5 **Hessenthal** Germany
36 H1 **Hessisch Lichtenau** Germany
117 H4 **Hess Mts** Yukon Territory Canada
107 N3 **Hesston** Kansas U.S.A.
28 J7 **Hestehoved** *C* Denmark
28 R8 **Hesteyri** Iceland
26 F5 **Hestmannen** *isld* Norway
27 G14 **Hestra, N** Sweden
22 G3 **Hestrud** France
102 C4 **Hetch Hetchy** California U.S.A.
94 C2 **Hetherton** Michigan U.S.A.
25 E4 **Het Loo** Netherlands
68 J2 **Hetou** China
22 L5 **Hettange Gde** France
Hettenhausen *see* **Ebersburg**
36 E4 **Hettenleidelheim** Germany
98 D3 **Hettinger** North Dakota U.S.A.
13 G4 **Hetton-le-Hole** England
33 P9 **Hettstedt** Germany
36 F4 **Hetzbach** Germany
36 B4 **Hetzerath** Germany
22 E1 **Het Zoute** Belgium
36 H6 **Heubach** Germany
41 J1 **Heuberg** *dist* Germany
22 C3 **Heuchin** France
33 N9 **Heudeber** Germany
36 C2 **Heumar** Germany
21 N3 **Heuqueville** France
25 D5 **Heusden** Netherlands
37 J3 **Heustreu** Germany
95 M2 **Heuvelton** New York U.S.A.
21 L2 **Hève, C.de la** France
80 E8 **Hever** *R* Jordan
13 F5 **Heversham** England
48 F3 **Heves** Hungary
28 E3 **Hevring Å** *R* Denmark
80 C8 **Hevron** *R* Israel
119 O9 **Heward** Saskatchewan Canada
7 M9 **Hewett** *oil rig* North Sea
13 F4 **Hexham** England
67 F4 **Hexi** China
67 F1 **He Xian** China
67 D4 **He Xian** China
65 D3 **Hexigten Qi** China
109 H5 **Hext** Texas U.S.A.
65 A7 **Heyang** China
47 N11 **Heybeli** *isld* Turkey
47 N11 **Heybeli** Turkey
101 M7 **Heyburn** Idaho U.S.A.
107 O6 **Heyburn Res** Oklahoma U.S.A.
139 H7 **Heyfield** Victoria Australia
13 F5 **Heysham** England
8 D5 **Heytesbury** England
67 E5 **Heyuan** China
138 F7 **Heywood** Victoria Australia
13 F6 **Heywood** England
65 C7 **Heze** China
113 G12 **Hialeah** Florida U.S.A.
79 G5 **Hīānah, Buhayrat al** *L* Syria
112 D3 **Hiawassee** Georgia U.S.A.
107 P2 **Hiawatha** Kansas U.S.A.
103 O2 **Hiawatha** Utah U.S.A.
121 Q5 **Hibbard** Quebec Canada
99 O2 **Hibbing** Minnesota U.S.A.
142 E1 **Hibernia Reef** Timor Sea
60 D11 **Hibiki-nada** *sea* Japan
71 G5 **Hibuson** *isld* Philippines
103 M9 **Hickiwan** Arizona U.S.A.
13 G6 **Hickleton** England
110 G5 **Hickman** Kentucky U.S.A.
98 K9 **Hickman** Nebraska U.S.A.
106 C7 **Hickman** New Mexico U.S.A.
123 T5 **Hickman's Hbr** Newfoundland Canada
107 J4 **Hickok** Kansas U.S.A.
111 G9 **Hickory** Mississippi U.S.A.
112 F2 **Hickory** North Carolina U.S.A.
112 F2 **Hickory, L** North Carolina U.S.A.
110 G6 **Hickory Valley** Tennessee U.S.A.
109 M8 **Hicks** Texas U.S.A.
145 G2 **Hicks Bay** New Zealand
125 P9 **Hicks Cays** *islds* Belize
139 J7 **Hicks, Pt** Victoria Australia
94 C5 **Hicksville** Ohio U.S.A.
109 J4 **Hico** Texas U.S.A.
48 H3 **Hida** Romania
60 Q3 **Hidaka** Japan
60 J12 **Hidaka** *R* Japan
60 R3 **Hidaka-sammyaku** *mts* Japan
124 G4 **Hidalgo de Parral** Mexico
32 J8 **Hiddenhausen** Germany
30 G1 **Hiddensee** *isld* Germany
141 H4 **Hidden Valley** Queensland Australia
32 J9 **Hiddesen** Germany
130 E5 **Hidrolândia** Brazil
130 E4 **Hidrolina** Brazil
20 C5 **Hière** *R* France
21 P1 **Hiermont** France
28 S9 **Hierodhsvótn** *R* Iceland
85 A3 **Hierro** *isld* Canary Is
127 N9 **Hierro, Pto. de** Venezuela
60 F11 **Higashi-Hiroshima** *isld* Japan
61 O13 **Higashi-iwa** *islds* Japan
61 N9 **Higashi-Matsuyama** Japan
61 O7 **Higashine** Japan
61 P13 **Higashi-Onna** Okinawa
61 J11 **Higashi-Ōsaka** Japan
60 C12 **Higashi-suidō** *str* Japan
110 D2 **Higbee** Missouri U.S.A.
94 C2 **Higgins L** Michigan U.S.A.
143 D9 **Higginsville** W Australia Australia
110 C2 **Higginsville** Missouri U.S.A.
9 E1 **Higham** England
9 F3 **Higham Ferrers** England
8 B6 **Highampton** England
106 G4 **Highbee** Colorado U.S.A.
8 D5 **Highbridge** England
95 N6 **High Bridge** New Jersey U.S.A.
12 D3 **High Br. of Ken** Scotland
9 E5 **Highclere** England
99 S5 **High Cliff** Wisconsin U.S.A.
100 E6 **High Desert** Oregon U.S.A.
99 S4 **High Falls Reservoir** Wisconsin U.S.A.
142 B1 **Highgate** *dist* Perth, W Aust Australia
9 G5 **Highgate** England
127 L2 **Highgate** Jamaica
13 F4 **High Hesket** England
119 W3 **High Hill L** Manitoba Canada
99 V4 **High I** Michigan U.S.A.
109 N6 **High Island** Texas U.S.A.
15 C3 **Highland** *reg* Scotland
102 G7 **Highland** California U.S.A.
110 G3 **Highland** Illinois U.S.A.
107 P2 **Highland** Kansas U.S.A.
99 Q6 **Highland** Wisconsin U.S.A.
99 T7 **Highland Park** Illinois U.S.A.
94 D4 **Highland Park** Michigan U.S.A.
109 O9 **Highland Park** Texas U.S.A.
102 E3 **Highland Peak** California U.S.A.
103 K4 **Highland Pk** Nevada U.S.A.
112 D2 **Highlands** North Carolina U.S.A.
109 M6 **Highlands** Texas U.S.A.
95 K9 **Highland Springs** Virginia U.S.A.
117 P6 **High Level** Alberta Canada
98 G5 **Highmore** South Dakota U.S.A.
141 K5 **High Peak I** Queensland Australia
118 K8 **High Point** Saskatchewan Canada
112 H2 **High Point** North Carolina U.S.A.
117 P8 **High Prairie** Alberta Canada
118 D8 **High River** Alberta Canada
119 R3 **Highrock** Manitoba Canada
113 J11 **High Rock** Grand Bahama I
112 G2 **High Rock L** North Carolina U.S.A.
139 H9 **High Rocky Pt** Tasmania Australia
113 E8 **High Springs** Florida U.S.A.
95 N6 **Hightstown** New Jersey U.S.A.
99 S7 **Highwood** Illinois U.S.A.
101 P2 **Highwood** Montana U.S.A.
9 E4 **Highworth** England
9 F4 **High Wycombe** England
124 E5 **Higuera de Zaragoza** Mexico
17 F1 **Higuer, C** Spain
127 L9 **Higuerote** Venezuela
127 K5 **Higüey** Dominican Rep
145 E3 **Hihitahi** New Zealand
27 N13 **Hiiumaa** *isld* Estonia
79 G5 **Hījānah, Al** Syria
17 G3 **Hijar** Spain
69 F14 **Hijau, Gunung** *mt* Sumatra
60 E12 **Hiji** Japan
71 G7 **Hijo** Philippines
60 E12 **Hikari** Japan
60 H11 **Hiketa** Japan
60 J12 **Hiki** *R* Japan
83 J11 **Hikkaduwa** Sri Lanka
103 J4 **Hiko** Nevada U.S.A.
61 K10 **Hikone** Japan
60 D12 **Hiko-san** *mt* Japan
145 E2 **Hikuai** New Zealand
145 E1 **Hikurangi** New Zealand
145 G2 **Hikurangi** *mt* New Zealand
145 E2 **Hikutaia** New Zealand
71 N8 **Hila** Indonesia
70 G7 **Hilahila** Sulawesi
101 S6 **Hiland** Wyoming U.S.A.
36 E1 **Hilchenbach** Germany
118 G8 **Hilda** Alberta Canada
37 K3 **Hildburghausen** Germany
100 D7 **Hildebrand** Oregon U.S.A.
36 B1 **Hilden** Germany
37 J2 **Hilders** Germany
32 L8 **Hildesheim** Germany
98 G9 **Hildreth** Nebraska U.S.A.
101 Q2 **Hilger** Montana U.S.A.
143 B9 **Hill** *R* W Australia Australia
101 O1 **Hill** Montana U.S.A.
95 Q3 **Hill** New Hampshire U.S.A.
127 P6 **Hillaby, Mt** Barbados
78 K5 **Hillah, Al** Iraq
98 E5 **Hilland** South Dakota U.S.A.
27 F14 **Hillared** Sweden
146 D11 **Hillary Coast** Antarctica
125 P9 **Hill Bank** Belize
101 K6 **Hill City** Idaho U.S.A.
107 L2 **Hill City** Kansas U.S.A.
99 N3 **Hill City** Minnesota U.S.A.
98 C6 **Hill City** South Dakota U.S.A.
103 P2 **Hill Cr** Utah U.S.A.
118 C9 **Hillcrest** Alberta Canada
117 Q11 **Hillcrest Creek** Alberta Canada
25 C4 **Hillegom** Netherlands
32 J8 **Hillegossen** Germany
28 J5 **Hillerød** Denmark
28 B2 **Hillerslev** Denmark
28 E6 **Hillerslev** Denmark
28 C7 **Hillerup** Germany
36 B3 **Hillesheim** Germany
26 K2 **Hillesöy** Norway
139 K4 **Hillgrove** New South Wales Australia
141 H4 **Hill Grove** Queensland Australia
144 C6 **Hillgrove** New Zealand
98 J4 **Hillhead** South Dakota U.S.A.
118 E5 **Hilliard** Alberta Canada
113 F7 **Hilliard** Florida U.S.A.
9 G2 **Hillington** England
20 E4 **Hillion** France
94 D1 **Hillman** Michigan U.S.A.
99 N3 **Hillman** Minnesota U.S.A.
143 B9 **Hillman, L** W Australia Australia
118 H5 **Hillmond** Saskatchewan Canada
15 E3 **Hill of Fearn** Scotland
15 D5 **Hill of Stake** *mt* Scotland
98 C9 **Hillrose** Colorado U.S.A.
99 P8 **Hills** Iowa U.S.A.
98 K6 **Hills** Minnesota U.S.A.
112 D4 **Hillsboro** Georgia U.S.A.
110 G2 **Hillsboro** Illinois U.S.A.
99 P9 **Hillsboro** Iowa U.S.A.
107 N3 **Hillsboro** Kansas U.S.A.
110 F3 **Hillsboro** Missouri U.S.A.
95 Q3 **Hillsboro** New Hampshire U.S.A.
106 C9 **Hillsboro** New Mexico U.S.A.
98 J2 **Hillsboro** North Dakota U.S.A.
110 N2 **Hillsboro** Ohio U.S.A.
100 C4 **Hillsboro** Oregon U.S.A.
109 K3 **Hillsboro** Texas U.S.A.
94 G8 **Hillsboro** West Virginia U.S.A.
113 G11 **Hillsboro Can** Florida U.S.A.
122 H8 **Hillsborough** New Brunswick Canada
112 H1 **Hillsborough** North Carolina U.S.A.
122 J7 **Hillsborough B** Prince Edward I Canada
141 J5 **Hillsborough, C** Queensland Australia
36 D3 **Hillscheid** Germany
121 L8 **Hillsdale** Ontario Canada
94 C5 **Hillsdale** Michigan U.S.A.
98 B8 **Hillsdale** Wyoming U.S.A.
142 C5 **Hillside** W Australia Australia
103 M7 **Hillside** Arizona U.S.A.
106 E3 **Hillside** Colorado U.S.A.
120 E3 **Hillsport** Ontario Canada
139 H5 **Hillston** New South Wales Australia
98 G4 **Hillsview** South Dakota U.S.A.
94 G10 **Hillsville** Virginia U.S.A.
112 F5 **Hilltonia** Georgia U.S.A.
110 F2 **Hillview** Illinois U.S.A.
102 D4 **Hilmar** California U.S.A.
102 V14 **Hilo** Hawaiian Is
113 G10 **Hilolo** Florida U.S.A.
37 L5 **Hilpoltstein** Germany
36 F5 **Hilsbach** Germany
8 B7 **Hilsea Pt** England
36 D7 **Hilsenheim** France
94 K3 **Hilton** New York U.S.A.
112 G5 **Hilton Head I** South Carolina U.S.A.
37 L4 **Hiltpoltstein** Germany
32 G9 **Hiltrup** Germany
100 C8 **Hilts** California U.S.A.
29 N10 **Hiltula** Finland
25 D6 **Hilvarenbeck** Netherlands
25 D4 **Hilversum** Netherlands
74 G2 **Himachal Pradesh** *prov* India
74 F1 **Himalayan Mt.Ra.,Great** Asia
29 K7 **Himanka** Finland
46 D4 **Himarë** Albania
145 E4 **Himatangi** New Zealand
33 N6 **Himbergen** Germany
60 H11 **Himeji** Japan
61 P6 **Himekami dake** *mt* Japan
101 R5 **Himes** Wyoming U.S.A.
60 E12 **Hime-shima** *isld* Japan
61 K9 **Himi** Japan
32 K5 **Himmelpforten** Germany
32 K9 **Himmighausen** Germany
79 G4 **Ḥimş** Syria
79 G4 **Ḥimş, Baḥrat** *L* Syria
71 F5 **Himugaan** Philippines
60 D13 **Hinagu** Japan
69 D11 **Hinaikiri** Sumatra
69 C12 **Hinako** *isld* Indonesia
145 E4 **Hinakura** New Zealand
71 G6 **Hinatuan** Philippines
127 J5 **Hinche** Haiti
116 O6 **Hinchinbrook Entrance** *str* Alaska U.S.A.
141 H4 **Hinchinbrook I** Queensland Australia
116 O6 **Hinchinbrook I** Alaska U.S.A.
119 P6 **Hinchliffe** Saskatchewan Canada
9 E2 **Hinckley** England
99 O3 **Hinckley** Minnesota U.S.A.
103 M2 **Hinckley** Utah U.S.A.
95 N3 **Hinckley Res** New York U.S.A.
74 G5 **Hindaun** India
41 M2 **Hindelang** Germany
25 D3 **Hindeloopen** Netherlands
Hindenburg *see* **Lindenhagen**
28 A7 **Hindenburg-damm** *causeway* Germany
26 N6 **Hindersön** *isld* Sweden
109 J7 **Hindes** Texas U.S.A.
9 F5 **Hindhead** England
13 F6 **Hindley** England
138 F6 **Hindmarsh, L** Victoria Australia
8 D5 **Hindon** England
144 C6 **Hindon** New Zealand
144 C6 **Hinds** New Zealand
123 Q4 **Hinds Hill** *pk* Newfoundland Canada
28 F5 **Hindsholm** Denmark
123 P5 **Hinds L** Newfoundland Canada
74 B3 **Hindubagh** Pakistan
72 K1 **Hindu Kush** *mts* Afghanistan
76 C4 **Hindupur** India
118 G5 **Hindville** Alberta Canada
68 G4 **Hine** Laos
95 O2 **Hinesburg** Vermont U.S.A.
117 O7 **Hines Creek** Alberta Canada
112 F6 **Hinesville** Georgia U.S.A.
74 H8 **Hinganghat** India
28 D4 **Hinge** Denmark
101 P1 **Hingham** Montana U.S.A.
77 J7 **Hinglaj** Pakistan
20 F5 **Hinglé, le** France
77 J7 **Hingol** *R* Pakistan
74 G9 **Hingoli** India
102 G7 **Hinkley** California U.S.A.
143 G7 **Hinkley, Mt** W Australia Australia
80 D4 **Ḥinnanit** Jordan
29 J11 **Hinnerjoki** Finland
28 E4 **Hinnerup** Denmark
26 H3 **Hinnöy** *isld* Norway
61 K9 **Hino** *R* Japan
71 F6 **Hinoba-an** Philippines
16 D6 **Hinojosa del Duque** Spain
60 E13 **Hinokage** Japan
60 F10 **Hinomi saki** *C* Japan
99 S8 **Hinsdale** Illinois U.S.A.
95 O4 **Hinsdale** Massachusetts U.S.A.
101 S1 **Hinsdale** Montana U.S.A.
94 J4 **Hinsdale** New York U.S.A.
8 D2 **Hinstock** England
38 F7 **Hinterbichl** Austria
36 E3 **Hintermeilingen** Germany
41 K4 **Hinterrhein** Switzerland
41 O3 **Hinter Riss** Austria
38 K6 **Hinterstoder** Austria
41 P3 **Hinter Tux** Austria
36 D5 **Hinter Weidenthal** Germany
9 H3 **Hintlesham** England
117 P9 **Hinton** Alberta Canada
107 M6 **Hinton** Oklahoma U.S.A.
61 O9 **Hi-numa** Japan
129 J7 **Hiocolândia** Brazil
135 R2 **Hio Pt** Hawaiian Is
124 J5 **Hipólito** Mexico
25 C3 **Hippolytushoef** Netherlands
80 F2 **Hippos** Syria
60 C12 **Hirado** Japan
60 C12 **Hirado-shima** *isld* Japan
85 F4 **Hirafok** Algeria
145 E2 **Hirakimata** New Zealand
75 K8 **Hirakud Res** India
95 R3 **Hiram** Maine U.S.A.
60 C12 **Hira shima** *isld* Japan
60 F10 **Hirata** Japan
61 N10 **Hiratsuka** Japan
124 D5 **Hiray** Mexico
78 D2 **Hirfanli Barajı** *dam* Turkey
48 K3 **Hîrlău** Romania
61 O8 **Hirono** Japan
60 R3 **Hiroo** Japan
61 O5 **Hirosaki** Japan
60 G10 **Hirose** Japan
60 F11 **Hiroshima** Japan
61 P7 **Hirota-wan** *B* Japan
36 F6 **Hirsau** Germany
37 M4 **Hirschau** Germany
37 M3 **Hirschberg** Germany
38 L7 **Hirschegg** Austria
37 O6 **Hirschenstein** *mt* Germany
36 F5 **Hirschhorn** Germany
48 J6 **Hirşeşti** Romania
28 F2 **Hirsholmene** *isld* Denmark
22 G4 **Hirson** France
48 L6 **Hîrşova** Romania
28 D1 **Hirtshals** Denmark
29 M10 **Hirvensalmi** Finland
29 L7 **Hirvineva** Finland
8 C4 **Hirwaun** Wales
61 K11 **Hisai** Japan
60 B13 **Hisaka-jima** *isld* Japan
74 F4 **Hisar** India
77 J2 **Hisar, Koh-i-** *mts* Afghanistan
80 F6 **Hisban** *R* Jordan
27 F15 **Hishult** Sweden
98 E6 **Hisle** South Dakota U.S.A.
80 E6 **Hisma** Jordan
127 J5 **Hispaniola** *isld* W Indies
80 G1 **Hispin** Syria
79 G4 **Ḥisyah** Syria
78 J5 **Hit** Iraq
60 D12 **Hita** Japan
61 O9 **Hitachi** Japan
61 O9 **Hitachi-Ōta** Japan
60 C11 **Hitakatsu** Japan
9 G3 **Hitcham** England
119 O9 **Hitchcock** Saskatchewan Canada
107 M6 **Hitchcock** Oklahoma U.S.A.
98 H5 **Hitchcock** South Dakota U.S.A.
109 M6 **Hitchcock** Texas U.S.A.
9 F4 **Hitchin** England
107 P6 **Hitchita** Oklahoma U.S.A.
103 O4 **Hite** Utah U.S.A.
60 D13 **Hitoyoshi** Japan
26 C8 **Hitra** Norway
32 L6 **Hittfeld** Germany
33 O6 **Hitzacker** Germany
61 N9 **Hiuchiga-take** *mt* Japan
60 G11 **Hiuchi-nada** *sea* Japan
135 N9 **Hiva Oa** *isld* Pacific Oc
60 H12 **Hiwasa** Japan
112 C2 **Hiwassee** *R* N Carolina/Tenn U.S.A.
112 C2 **Hiwassee Lake** North Carolina U.S.A.
141 L5 **Hixson Cay** *isld* Gt Barrier Reef Aust
60 O3 **Hiyama** *prefect* Japan
78 J2 **Hizan** Turkey
28 E2 **Hjallerup** Denmark
27 H12 **Hjälmaren** *L* Sweden
28 C3 **Hjarbæk** Denmark
28 B2 **Hjardemål** Denmark
26 G6 **Hjarfjell** *mt* Norway
28 E5 **Hjarnø** *isld* Denmark
27 C12 **Hjartdal** Norway
28 C6 **Hjarup** Denmark
26 B10 **Hjelle** Norway
28 F4 **Hjelm** *isld* Denmark
29 K7 **Hjelm Bugt** *B* Denmark
27 B12 **Hjelmeland** Norway
26 O1 **Hjelmsöy** *isld* Norway
28 G5 **Hjembæk** Denmark
26 D9 **Hjerkinn** Norway
28 B4 **Hjerm** Denmark
28 C6 **Hjerndrup** Denmark
28 B6 **Hjerpsted** Denmark
28 A5 **Hjerting** Denmark
27 G13 **Hjo** Sweden
28 C4 **Hjøllund** Denmark
28 C6 **Hjordkær** Denmark
Hjørring *co see* **Nordjylland** *co*
28 D2 **Hjørring** Denmark
28 E7 **Hjortø** Denmark
28 E4 **Hjortshøj** Denmark
28 C5 **Hjortsvang** Denmark
26 B9 **Hjörundfjord** Norway
27 D12 **Hjuksebö** Norway
68 D2 **Hka** *R* Burma
68 D2 **Hkok** *R* Burma
68 C4 **Hlegu** Burma
28 S10 **Hlidharendi** Iceland
37 P3 **Hlinec** *R* Czech Rep
31 K7 **Hlohovec** Slovakia
28 A5 **Ho** Denmark
85 E7 **Ho** Ghana
67 B6 **Hoa Binh** Vietnam
89 A4 **Hoachanas** Namibia
118 C6 **Hoadley** Alberta Canada
98 F8 **Hoagland** Nebraska U.S.A.
68 J5 **Hoai Nhon** Vietnam
68 G1 **Hoang Su Phi** Vietnam
87 B9 **Hoanib** *R* Namibia
60 E12 **Hoashi** Japan

01 P6 Hoback R Wyoming U.S.A.
01 P6 Hoback Pk Wyoming U.S.A.
38 F8 Hobart Tasmania Australia
99 T8 Hobart Indiana U.S.A.
07 L6 Hobart Oklahoma U.S.A.
08 D3 Hobbs New Mexico U.S.A.
46 B9 Hobbs Coast Antarctica
11 K7 Hobbs Island Alabama U.S.A.
13 G10 Hobe Sound Florida U.S.A.
12 K1 Hobgood North Carolina U.S.A.
22 G1 Hoboken Belgium
12 E6 Hoboken Georgia U.S.A.
Hobot Xar see Xianghuang Qi
28 D3 Hobro Denmark
01 Q3 Hobson Montana U.S.A.
12 L2 Hobucken North Carolina U.S.A.
28 A5 Ho Bugt B Denmark
27 K15 Hoburgen lighthouse Sweden
36 A2 Hobyo Somalia
71 D5 Hoc isld Philippines
47 K6 Hocalar Turkey
11 B7 Hochatown Oklahoma U.S.A.
38 N8 Hocheck mt Austria
37 C10 Hochfeld Namibia
36 D6 Hochfelden France
38 G7 Hochfilzen Austria
41 N4 Hochfinstermünz Austria
38 F8 Hochgall mt Italy
36 E3 Hochheim Germany
37 K2 Hochheim Germany
09 K6 Hochheim Texas U.S.A.
68 H7 Ho Chi Minh Vietnam
38 K8 Hochobir mt Austria
41 N2 Hoch Platte mt Germany
38 M6 Hochschwab mt Austria
36 D5 Hochspeyer Germany
37 K4 Höchstadt Germany
37 K6 Höchstädt Germany
36 D2 Höchstenbach Germany
44 C5 Hochstetter, L New Zealand
38 K9 Hochstuhl mt Slovenia
36 F5 Hockenheim Germany
94 E7 Hocking R Ohio U.S.A.
94 F7 Hockingport Ohio U.S.A.
09 M5 Hockley Texas U.S.A.
9 E3 Hockley Heath England
9 F4 Hockliffe England
6 N6 Hod oil rig North Sea
28 B5 Hodde Denmark
13 F6 Hodder, R England
9 F4 Hoddesdon England
Hodeida see Ḩudaydah, Al
11 D9 Hodge Louisiana U.S.A.
10 L4 Hodgenville Kentucky U.S.A.
98 B3 Hodges Montana U.S.A.
12 E3 Hodges South Carolina U.S.A.
23 Q4 Hodges Hill pk Newfoundland Canada
02 G8 Hodges, L California U.S.A.
18 L8 Hodgeville Saskatchewan Canada
19 U7 Hodgson Manitoba Canada
40 C3 Hodgson Downs N Terr Australia
85 C5 Hodh reg Mauritania
80 B7 Hodiyya Israel
48 F4 Hódmezővásárhely Hungary
85 E1 Hodna, Mts. du Algeria
8 D2 Hodnet England
31 K7 Hodonín Czech Rep
48 C4 Hodoš Slovenia
28 B4 Hodsager Denmark
16 N3 Hodzana, R Alaska U.S.A.
28 F4 Hoed Denmark
25 A6 Hoedekenskerke Netherlands
20 E7 Hoëdic isld France
06 F4 Hoehne Colorado U.S.A.
25 B5 Hoeksche Waard Netherlands
25 B5 Hoek van Holland Netherlands
19 M6 Hoey Saskatchewan Canada
37 M3 Hof Germany
36 H2 Hofbieber Germany
Hofei see Hefei
36 F6 Höfen Germany
37 J6 Hofen Germany
98 L4 Hoffman Minnesota U.S.A.
12 H2 Hoffman North Carolina U.S.A.
13 K12 Hoffmans Cay isld Bahamas
32 K10 Hofgeismar Germany
36 E3 Hofheim Germany
37 K3 Hofheim Germany
37 P6 Hofkirchen Germany
29 T9 Hofn Iceland
28 S9 Hofsjökull ice cap Iceland
28 S9 Hofsos Iceland
60 E11 Hōfu Japan
29 K4 Höganäs Sweden
39 H7 Hogan Group islds Tasmania Australia
02 D3 Hogan Res California U.S.A.
11 M8 Hogansville Georgia U.S.A.
41 H7 Hoganthulla R Queensland Australia
19 P1 Hogarth Ontario Canada
40 D5 Hogarth, Mt N Terr Australia
16 K3 Hogatza Alaska U.S.A.
16 K3 Hogatza R R Alaska U.S.A.
01 N5 Hogback Mt Montana U.S.A.
27 F12 Hogboda Sweden
27 J14 Högby Sweden
28 C7 Högel Germany
01 R1 Hogeland Montana U.S.A.
27 H12 Högfors Sweden
85 F4 Hoggar mt reg Algeria
19 V1 Hogg L Manitoba Canada
48 J5 Hoghiz Romania
94 B1 Hog I Michigan U.S.A.
95 M9 Hog I Virginia U.S.A.
28 B4 Høgild Denmark
80 C4 Hogla Israel
27 H14 Högsby Sweden
26 H4 Hogsty Reef Bahamas
26 G5 Högtuvbre mt Norway
00 A2 Hoh R Washington U.S.A.
33 R10 Hohburg Germany
36 C3 Hohe Acht mt Germany
41 N3 Hohe Geige mt Austria
37 K6 Hohen-Altheim Germany
38 N6 Hohenberg Austria
37 M3 Hohenberg Germany
33 S9 Hohenbucke Germany
37 M5 Hohenburg Germany
33 N10 Hohenebra Germany
32 M8 Hoheneggelsen Germany
36 H1 Hoheneiche Germany
41 L3 Hohenems Austria
37 M5 Hohenfels Germany
33 Q7 Hohengöhren Germany
36 G6 Hohenheim Germany
37 M7 Hohenkammer Germany
33 Q10 Hohenleina Germany
37 N2 Hohenleuben Germany
32 G10 Hohenlimburg Germany
32 L5 Hohenlockstedt Germany
33 S5 Hohenmocker Germany
37 N1 Hohenmölsen Germany
33 Q7 Hohennauen Germany
36 H2 Hohenroda Germany
33 Q8 Hohenseeden Germany
33 S9 Hohenseefeld Germany
36 E2 Hohensolms Germany
36 H6 Hohenstaufen Germany
36 G7 Hohenstein Germany
37 O2 Hohenstein-Ernstthal Germany
10 J6 Hohenwald Tennessee U.S.A.
37 L6 Hohenwart Germany
32 K9 Hohenwepel Germany
32 L4 Hohenwestedt Germany
33 N6 Hohenzethen Germany
36 F7 Hohenzollern Germany
41 M3 Hoher Ifen mt Austria
41 M3 Hohes Licht mt Austria
37 J5 Hohe Steig mt Germany
38 F7 Hohe Tauern Austria
58 F3 Hohhot China
36 E6 Hohloh mt Germany
33 M7 Hohne Germany
19 K4 Hohneck mt France
33 N6 Hohnstorf Germany
116 J6 Hoholitna R Alaska U.S.A.
32 K4 Hohrr Germany
66 E4 Hoh Sai Hu L China
33 N4 Hohwacht Germany
36 C7 Hohwald France
66 D4 Hoh Xil Shan ra China
68 J5 Hoi An Vietnam
107 M3 Hoisington Kansas U.S.A.
66 F4 Hoit Taria China
67 B6 Hoi-Xuan Vietnam
75 P6 Hojai India
28 E6 Højby Denmark
28 C5 Højen Denmark
28 B7 Højer Denmark
29 K6 Højerup Denmark
60 F12 Hōjō Japan
28 B6 Højrup Denmark
28 C3 Højslev Denmark
68 D2 Hok R Burma
99 P6 Hokah Minnesota U.S.A.
Hokang see Hegang
27 K11 Hökhuvud Sweden
61 N9 Hōki R Japan
145 D1 Hokianga Harbour New Zealand
144 C5 Hokitika New Zealand
60 Q2 Hokkaidō isld Japan
27 D12 Hokksund Norway
61 O9 Hokota Japan
61 K10 Hokunō Japan
61 K10 Hokuriku Tunnel Japan
27 C11 Hol Norway
27 E12 Höland Norway
Holbæk co see Vestjælland co
28 E3 Holbæk Denmark
28 H5 Holbæk Denmark
9 G2 Holbeach England
117 K10 Holberg British Columbia Canada
28 C7 Holbøl Denmark
141 J4 Holbourne I Queensland Australia
139 H6 Holbrook New South Wales Australia
103 O7 Holbrook Arizona U.S.A.
101 N7 Holbrook Idaho U.S.A.
98 F9 Holbrook Nebraska U.S.A.
13 F6 Holcombe England
99 P4 Holcombe Wisconsin U.S.A.
118 E5 Holden Alberta Canada
95 Q4 Holden Massachusetts U.S.A.
110 C3 Holden Missouri U.S.A.
103 M2 Holden Utah U.S.A.
94 E9 Holden West Virginia U.S.A.
107 O6 Holdenville Oklahoma U.S.A.
13 H6 Holderness pen England
119 M8 Holdfast Saskatchewan Canada
99 M4 Holdingford Minnesota U.S.A.
32 H7 Holdorf Germany
98 G9 Holdrege Nebraska U.S.A.
28 G7 Holeby Denmark
113 K12 Hole in the Wall pt Bahamas
27 E12 Hölen Norway
76 C4 Hole Narsipur India
31 K6 Holešov Czech Rep
127 P6 Holetown Barbados
94 C5 Holgate Ohio U.S.A.
126 F4 Holguín Cuba
48 D2 Holič Slovakia
116 H5 Holikachuk Alaska U.S.A.
116 J6 Holitna R Alaska U.S.A.
27 F11 Höljes Sweden
119 T9 Holland Manitoba Canada
9 F2 Holland div England
99 U7 Holland Michigan U.S.A.
98 K5 Holland Minnesota U.S.A.
94 J4 Holland New York U.S.A.
100 B7 Holland Oregon U.S.A.
109 K5 Holland Texas U.S.A.
111 F8 Hollandale Mississippi U.S.A.
127 M3 Holland B Jamaica
120 K8 Holland Centre Ontario Canada
143 C9 Holland,Mt W Australia Australia
141 K2 Holland Park dist Brisbane, Qnsld Australia
25 C5 Hollandsch Diep Netherlands
22 K4 Hollange Belgium
32 M8 Holle Germany
33 N5 Hollenbek Germany
32 L6 Hollenstedt Germany
38 N6 Hollen-Tal V Austria
38 F7 Hollersbach Austria
9 H3 Hollesley B England
94 J3 Holley New York U.S.A.
37 L4 Hollfeld Germany
109 J2 Holliday Texas U.S.A.
94 J6 Hollidaysburg Pennsylvania U.S.A.
107 L7 Hollis Oklahoma U.S.A.
102 C5 Hollister California U.S.A.
101 L7 Hollister Idaho U.S.A.
110 C5 Hollister Missouri U.S.A.
107 M7 Hollister Oklahoma U.S.A.
22 J2 Hollogne-sur-Geer Belgium
111 D10 Holloway Louisiana U.S.A.
29 K6 Höllviken C Sweden
106 H3 Holly Colorado U.S.A.
94 D4 Holly Michigan U.S.A.
111 F9 Holly Bluff Mississippi U.S.A.
144 B6 Hollyford R New Zealand
111 E7 Holly Grove Arkansas U.S.A.
113 F8 Holly Hill Florida U.S.A.
112 G4 Holly Hill South Carolina U.S.A.
112 K3 Holly Ridge North Carolina U.S.A.
110 G7 Holly Springs Mississippi U.S.A.
113 G11 Hollywood Florida U.S.A.
95 L8 Hollywood Maryland U.S.A.
28 D6 Holm Denmark
26 F6 Holm Norway
26 J9 Holm Sweden
106 E5 Holman New Mexico U.S.A.
114 H3 Holman Island Northwest Territories Canada
28 S9 Holmavik Iceland
28 B5 Holme Å R Denmark
99 P6 Holmen Wisconsin U.S.A.
8 D1 Holmes Chapel England
119 V1 Holmes L Manitoba Canada
101 P5 Holmes, Mt Wyoming U.S.A.
141 J3 Holmes Reef Great Barrier Reef Aust
27 D12 Holmestr Norway
119 S9 Holmfield Manitoba Canada
13 G6 Holmfirth England
26 K6 Holmfors Sweden
115 O3 Holm Ø isld Greenland
26 L8 Holmögadd lighthouse Sweden
26 L8 Holmön Sweden
13 J6 Holmpton England
27 D12 Holmsbu Norway
26 J8 Holmsjö Sweden
26 H9 Holmsjön L Sweden
28 A4 Holmsland Klit sand spit Denmark
28 E6 Holmstrup Fyn Denmark
28 G5 Holmstrup Vestjælland Denmark
26 L8 Holmsund Sweden
27 K14 Holmudden lighthouse Gotland Sweden
111 C11 Holmwood Louisiana U.S.A.
37 M5 Holnstein Germany
27 J12 Hölö Sweden
88 C5 Holoholo Tanzania
80 C5 Ḩolon Israel
87 C11 Holoog Namibia
113 F9 Holopaw Florida U.S.A.
80 B6 Ḩolot Ashdod Israel
142 F2 Holothuria Reefs W Australia Australia
80 B6 Ḩolot Yavne Israel
26 E9 Holöydal Norway
141 F2 Holroyd R Queensland Australia
28 B4 Holstebro Denmark
28 B5 Holsted Denmark
120 K8 Holstein Ontario Canada
99 L7 Holstein Iowa U.S.A.
98 H9 Holstein Nebraska U.S.A.
28 G6 Holsteinborg Denmark
115 O4 Holsteinsborg Greenland
112 E1 Holston R Tennessee U.S.A.
94 F10 Holston R Virginia U.S.A.
33 N4 Holst Schweiz Germany
8 B6 Holsworthy England
9 H2 Holt England
111 J8 Holt Alabama U.S.A.
111 K11 Holt Florida U.S.A.
94 C4 Holt Michigan U.S.A.
98 K1 Holt Minnesota U.S.A.
8 D1 Holt Wales
98 G7 Holt Cr Nebraska U.S.A.
29 K5 Holte Denmark
33 O9 Holtemme R Germany
25 F4 Holten Netherlands
101 O3 Holter L. Dam Montana U.S.A.
33 O5 Holthusen Germany
94 B7 Holton Indiana U.S.A.
107 P2 Holton Kansas U.S.A.
94 B3 Holton Michigan U.S.A.
65 D2 Holt Sum China
28 C4 Holtum Å R Denmark
103 J9 Holtville California U.S.A.
120 K4 Holtyre Ontario Canada
135 U5 Holualoa Hawaiian Is
27 C13 Holum Norway
25 E2 Holwerd Netherlands
116 H5 Holy Cross Alaska U.S.A.
8 B1 Holyhead Wales
8 B1 Holyhead B Wales
12 C3 Holy I Scotland
8 B1 Holy I Wales
118 G4 Holyoke Alberta Canada
106 H1 Holyoke Colorado U.S.A.
95 P4 Holyoke Massachusetts U.S.A.
123 T6 Holyrood Newfoundland Canada
107 M3 Holyrood Kansas U.S.A.
37 P4 Holýšov Czech Rep
8 D6 Holywell England
8 C1 Holywell Wales
14 F2 Holywood N Ireland
36 D3 Holzappel Germany
33 S9 Holzdorf Germany
33 P5 Holzendorf Germany
32 H8 Holzhausen Germany
36 D3 Holzhausen Germany
37 K6 Holzheim Germany
32 K9 Holzminden Germany
32 G10 Holzwickede Germany
28 H6 Høm Denmark
86 G6 Homa Bay Kenya
75 Q6 Homalin Burma
36 G1 Homberg Germany
60 R2 Hombetsu Japan
22 E4 Homblières France
85 D5 Hombori Mali
Homburg see Nümbrecht
36 H4 Homburg Bayern Germany
36 C5 Homburg Rheinland-Pfalz Germany
115 N4 Home B Northwest Territories Canada
100 J6 Homedale Idaho U.S.A.
141 H4 Home Hill Queensland Australia
83 M8 Home I Cocos Is Indian Oc
116 M7 Homer Alaska U.S.A.
99 T9 Homer Illinois U.S.A.
111 C9 Homer Louisiana U.S.A.
94 C4 Homer Michigan U.S.A.
94 H6 Homer City Pennsylvania U.S.A.
9 H3 Homersfield England
144 A6 Homer Tun New Zealand
112 E6 Homerville Georgia U.S.A.
80 D4 Homesh Jordan
141 H5 Homestead Queensland Australia
113 G12 Homestead Florida U.S.A.
99 P8 Homestead Iowa U.S.A.
98 B1 Homestead Montana U.S.A.
107 M5 Homestead Oklahoma U.S.A.
100 J4 Homestead Oregon U.S.A.
98 K9 Homestead Nat Mon Nebraska U.S.A.
145 E4 Homewood New Zealand
111 K8 Homewood Alabama U.S.A.
68 A6 Homfray's Str Andaman Is
107 O5 Hominy Oklahoma U.S.A.
26 E9 Hommelfjell mt Norway
26 E8 Hommelvik Norway
25 E3 Hommerts Netherlands
21 L7 Hommes France
74 G10 Homnabad India
89 H5 Homoine Mozambique
48 G6 Homoljske Planina mt Serbia Yugoslavia
71 G5 Homonhon Philippines
48 J4 Homorod Romania
113 E9 Homosassa Florida U.S.A.
Homs see Hims
Homs Libya see Khums, Al
60 F12 Honai Japan
Honan prov see Henan
76 B3 Honavar India
68 G7 Hon Chong Vietnam
102 C2 Honcut California U.S.A.
128 D2 Honda Colombia
71 D6 Honda B Palawan Philippines
125 P8 Hondo R Belize
118 D3 Hondo Alberta Canada
60 D13 Hondo Japan
106 E8 Hondo New Mexico U.S.A.
109 H6 Hondo Texas U.S.A.
22 D2 Hondschoote France
125 L2 Honduras rep Central America
119 Q2 Hone Manitoba Canada
112 E3 Honea Path South Carolina U.S.A.
36 H2 Hönebach Germany
27 D11 Hönefoss Norway
95 M5 Honesdale Pennsylvania U.S.A.
102 A1 Honeydew California U.S.A.
98 J1 Honeyford North Dakota U.S.A.
109 M2 Honey Grove Texas U.S.A.
109 N5 Honey Island Texas U.S.A.
100 E9 Honey L California U.S.A.
120 K8 Honeywood Ontario Canada
21 L3 Honfleur France
28 G5 Høng Denmark
65 G2 Hongai China
68 H2 Hon Gai Vietnam
67 E1 Hong'an China
67 B6 Hon Gay Vietnam
65 B2 Honggor China
67 E5 Honghai Wan B China
58 F5 Hong He R China
67 D2 Honghu China
67 C3 Hongjiang China
67 G6 Hong Kong colony E Asia
67 F4 Honglai China
68 G7 Hong Ngu Vietnam
Hongning see Wulian
58 F2 Hongor Mongolia
65 B2 Hongor Mongolia
67 D7 Hongqizhen China
68 E3 Hongsa Laos
67 B4 Hongshui He R China
65 B6 Hongtong China
61 J12 Hongū Japan
122 H4 Honguedo Passage Canada
66 E3 Hongxing Sichang China
67 A2 Hongya China
58 G5 Hongze Hu L China
137 N3 Honiara Guadalcanal I Solomon Is
9 H2 Honingham England
8 C6 Honiton England
61 O6 Honjō Japan
29 J10 Honkajoki Finland
68 H3 Hon Matt isld Vietnam
68 G3 Hon Me isld Vietnam
76 B3 Honnali India
26 P1 Honningsvåg Norway
102 V13 Honokaa Hawaiian Is
135 S3 Honokahua Hawaiian Is
145 F2 Honokawa New Zealand
135 S3 Honokohau Hawaiian Is
102 S12 Honolulu Hawaiian Is
135 V5 Honomu Hawaiian Is
102 R12 Honouliuli Hawaiian Is
68 H7 Hon Quan Vietnam
17 F5 Honrubia Spain
59 K4 Honshū isld Japan
28 H5 Hønsinge Denmark
135 U6 Honuapo Hawaiian Is
100 D4 Hood, Mt Oregon U.S.A.
143 C10 Hood Pt W Australia Australia
100 D4 Hood River Oregon U.S.A.
100 B2 Hoodsport Washington U.S.A.
32 K10 Hoof Germany
25 C4 Hoofddorp Netherlands
25 A6 Hoofdplaat Netherlands
25 F3 Hooger Smilde Netherlands
25 G3 Hoogeveen Netherlands
25 G2 Hoogezand Netherlands
25 G3 Hooghalen Netherlands
22 D2 Hoogstade Belgium
22 H1 Hoogstraten Belgium
41 K2 Höohster mt Germany
9 F5 Hook England
144 C6 Hook New Zealand
135 U5 Hookena Hawaiian Is
107 J5 Hooker Oklahoma U.S.A.
140 B4 Hooker Creek N Terr Australia
14 E4 Hook Hd Ireland
141 J5 Hook I Queensland Australia
141 L7 Hook Pt Queensland Australia
141 J4 Hook Reef Gt Barrier Reef Aust
109 N2 Hooks Texas U.S.A.
95 Q3 Hooksett New Hampshire U.S.A.
32 H5 Hooksiel Germany
102 V13 Hoolehua Hawaiian Is
117 F6 Hoonah Alaska U.S.A.
100 B8 Hoopa California U.S.A.
106 E4 Hooper Colorado U.S.A.
98 K8 Hooper Nebraska U.S.A.
101 N8 Hooper Utah U.S.A.
100 G3 Hooper Washington U.S.A.
116 D6 Hooper Bay Alaska U.S.A.
95 L8 Hooper I Maryland U.S.A.
99 T9 Hoopeston Illinois U.S.A.
123 Q3 Hooping Hbr Newfoundland Canada
98 J1 Hoople North Dakota U.S.A.
89 D6 Hoopstad S Africa
27 G16 Höör Sweden
25 D3 Hoorn Noord Netherlands
25 C2 Hoorn Texel Netherlands
95 O4 Hoosick Falls New York U.S.A.
118 H7 Hoosier Saskatchewan Canada
98 C4 Hoover South Dakota U.S.A.
103 K5 Hoover Dam Arizona U.S.A.
94 E6 Hoover Res Ohio U.S.A.
94 J6 Hooversville Pennsylvania U.S.A.
78 H1 Hopa Turkey
95 M5 Hop Bottom Pennsylvania U.S.A.
9 E4 Hopcrofts Holt England
117 N11 Hope British Columbia Canada
103 L8 Hope Arizona U.S.A.
111 C8 Hope Arkansas U.S.A.
94 B7 Hope Indiana U.S.A.
107 N3 Hope Kansas U.S.A.
98 J2 Hope North Dakota U.S.A.
127 M2 Hope Bay Jamaica
115 N6 Hopedale Labrador, Nfld Canada
Hopeh prov see Hebei
138 E3 Hope, L South Australia Australia
143 D9 Hope,L W Australia Australia
138 E3 Hopeless, Mt South Australia Australia
112 J3 Hope Mills North Carolina U.S.A.
147 J12 Hopen isld Arctic Oc
144 D5 Hope Pass New Zealand
116 D2 Hope, Pt Alaska U.S.A.
138 F6 Hopetoun Victoria Australia
143 D10 Hopetoun W Australia Australia
113 L11 Hope Town Bahamas
89 D7 Hopetown S Africa
141 H3 Hopevale Queensland Australia
122 K8 Hopewell Nova Scotia Canada
94 J6 Hopewell Pennsylvania U.S.A.
95 K9 Hopewell Virginia U.S.A.
115 M6 Hopewell Is Northwest Territories Canada
103 O6 Hopi Buttes mt Arizona U.S.A.
67 E4 Ho-p'ing China
139 G7 Hopkins R Victoria Australia
94 B4 Hopkins Michigan U.S.A.
99 M9 Hopkins Missouri U.S.A.
143 G6 Hopkins,L W Australia Australia
144 B5 Hopkins, Mt New Zealand
110 J5 Hopkinsville Kentucky U.S.A.
102 A3 Hopland California U.S.A.
68 C2 Hopong Burma
33 T7 Hoppegarten Germany
26 Q1 Hopseidet Norway
32 G8 Hopsten Germany
9 H2 Hopton England
28 C6 Hoptrup Denmark
94 H7 Hopwood Pennsylvania U.S.A.
141 G5 Hopwood,Mt Queensland Australia
100 B2 Hoquiam Washington U.S.A.
107 J3 Horace Kansas U.S.A.
37 P2 Hora Svatého Šebastiána Czech Rep
37 P2 Hora Svaté Katering Czech Rep
111 B8 Horatio Arkansas U.S.A.
30 H6 Horaždovice Czech Rep
36 F7 Horb Germany
28 J7 Horbelev Denmark
37 O7 Horbering Germany
118 B6 Horburg Alberta Canada
13 G6 Horbury England
28 E2 Hørby Nordjylland Denmark
28 D3 Hørby Nordjylland Denmark
27 G16 Hörby Sweden
16 D5 Horcajo de los Montes Spain
16 E5 Horcajo de Santiago Spain
124 G3 Horcasitas Mexico
36 E4 Horchheim Germany
27 A11 Hordaland reg Norway
109 H4 Hords Cr. Res Texas U.S.A.
28 A3 Hørdum Denmark
8 B3 Horeb Wales
88 C6 Hore B Zambia
48 H5 Horezu Romania
48 F4 Horgoš Serbia Yugoslavia
31 J5 Hořice Czech Rep
99 S6 Horicon Wisconsin U.S.A.
58 F3 Horinger China
22 J2 Horion Hozémont Belgium
119 M9 Horizon Saskatchewan Canada
137 S6 Horizon Depth Pacific Oc
31 H4 Horka Germany
9 F5 Horley England
146 D9 Horlick Mts Antarctica
28 E2 Hørmested Denmark
Hormo see Nyima
77 E6 Hormoz isld Iran
77 D6 Hormozgān prov Iran
77 E6 Hormoz, Strait of Iran
31 J7 Horn Austria
28 R8 Horn C Iceland
25 E6 Horn Netherlands
27 H14 Horn Sweden
48 F2 Hornad R Slovakia
26 J5 Hornavan L Sweden
36 C5 Hornbach Germany
32 J9 Horn-Bad Meinog Germany
29 K4 Hornbæk Denmark
111 C10 Hornbeck Louisiana U.S.A.
36 E7 Hornberg Germany
27 G13 Hornborgasjön L Sweden
100 C8 Hornbrook California U.S.A.
33 N8 Hornburg Germany
9 F1 Horncastle England
27 H11 Horndal Sweden
33 N6 Horndorf Germany
28 E1 Horne Denmark
28 B5 Horne Ribe Denmark
32 L5 Horneburg Germany
26 L8 Hörnefors Sweden
28 E6 Horneland Denmark
94 K4 Hornell New York U.S.A.
120 F3 Hornepayne Ontario Canada
110 F5 Hornersville Missouri U.S.A.
27 C13 Hornesund Norway
28 G2 Hornfiskrøn isld Denmark
14 C1 Horn Hd Ireland
33 O8 Hornhsleben Germany
141 F1 Horn I Queensland Australia
111 H11 Horn I Mississippi U.S.A.
31 K6 Horni Benešov Czech Rep
137 R4 Horn, Îles de Îles Wallis Pacific Oc
124 E4 Hornillos Mexico
26 B10 Hornindal Norway
26 B10 Hornindalsvatn L Norway
36 E6 Hornisgrinde mt Germany
37 O3 Horní Slavkov Czech Rep
41 J3 Hörnli mt Switzerland
117 N4 Horn Mts Northwest Territories Canada
116 H6 Horn Mts Alaska U.S.A.
27 C13 Hornnes Norway
133 C6 Hornopiren mt Chile
124 H5 Hornos Mexico
133 D9 Hornos, C. de Chile
21 O2 Hornoy-le Bourg France
117 O4 Horn R Northwest Territories Canada
139 K5 Hornsby New South Wales Australia
110 H6 Hornsby Tennessee U.S.A.
8 B6 Horns Cross England
13 H6 Hornsea England
26 L8 Hörnsjö Sweden
28 E4 Hornslet Denmark
80 E2 Horns of Hittin Israel
37 K1 Hornsömmern Germany
33 P5 Hornstorf Germany
28 D5 Hornstrup Denmark
28 D5 Hornum Vejle Denmark
28 A7 Hørnum Germany
33 S6 Horn Zieritz Germany
60 T1 Horobetsu Japan
60 R3 Horoizumi Japan
60 Q1 Horonai Japan
145 E3 Horopito New Zealand
144 C5 Hororata New Zealand
60 Q3 Horoshiri-dake mt Japan
65 A5 Horo Sum China
30 H6 Hořovice Czech Rep
145 E4 Horowhenua admin region New Zealand
83 K9 Horowupotana Sri Lanka
21 K5 Horps,le France
59 H2 Horqin Youyi Qianqi China
65 E2 Horqin Youyi Zhongqi China
65 F2 Horqin Zouyi Zhongqi China
65 E3 Horqin Zuoyi Houqi China
129 G8 Horqueta Paraguay
133 F2 Horqueta Paraguay
28 H7 Horreby Denmark
27 F14 Horred Sweden
36 B2 Horrem Germany
143 A8 Horrocks W Australia Australia
83 M8 Horsburgh I Cocos Is Indian Oc
37 J1 Hörschel Germany
110 K4 Horse Branch Kentucky U.S.A.
9 G6 Horsebridge E Sussex England
94 B9 Horse Cave Kentucky U.S.A.
106 G3 Horse Cr Colorado U.S.A.
110 B4 Horse Cr Missouri U.S.A.
98 A8 Horse Cr Wyoming U.S.A.
117 N9 Horsefly British Columbia Canada
98 F2 Horsehead L North Dakota U.S.A.
95 L4 Horseheads New York U.S.A.
123 R3 Horse Is Newfoundland Canada
37 J2 Hörsel R Germany
102 D1 Horse L California U.S.A.
37 J2 Hörsel Berge mt Germany
28 D5 Horsens Vejle Denmark
28 E5 Horsens Fjord inlet Denmark
118 F2 Horse, R Alberta Canada
113 D8 Horseshoe Florida U.S.A.
111 L9 Horseshoe Band Nat. Mil. Park Alabama U.S.A.
138 C2 Horseshoe Bend N Terr Australia
140 C7 Horseshoe Bend N Terr Australia
100 J6 Horse Shoe Bend Idaho U.S.A.
127 P4 Horse Shoe Pt St Kitts W Indies
103 N7 Horseshoe Res Arizona U.S.A.
106 B8 Horse Springs New Mexico U.S.A.
138 F6 Horsham Victoria Australia
118 H8 Horsham Saskatchewan Canada
9 F5 Horsham England
29 K5 Hørsholm Denmark
13 G4 Horsley England
28 G7 Horslunde Denmark
37 O4 Horšovský Týn Czech Rep
32 L5 Horst Germany
33 S4 Horst Germany
25 F6 Horst Netherlands
32 G8 Hörstel Germany
25 F6 Hörstgen Germany
32 F8 Horstmar Germany
48 E2 Hor Stubňa Slovakia
27 D12 Horten Norway
112 F6 Hortense Georgia U.S.A.
26 M6 Hortlax Sweden
114 G4 Horton R Northwest Territories Canada
107 P2 Horton Kansas U.S.A.
27 C10 Horungane Norway
28 C7 Hörup Germany
28 G5 Hørve Denmark
27 G15 Hörvik Sweden
13 F6 Horwich England
120 H5 Horwood L Ontario Canada
37 P5 Hory Matky Boží Czech Rep
31 J5 Hory Orlické mts Czech Rep
47 K7 Horzom R Turkey
86 G4 Hosa'ina Ethiopia
36 G3 Hösbach Germany
76 C4 Hosdurga India
70 C3 Hose Mts Sarawak
84 G5 Hosenofu Libya
77 A3 Hoseynābad Iran
111 M11 Hosford Florida U.S.A.
74 C10 Hoshab Pakistan
77 H6 Hoshāb Pakistan
74 G7 Hoshangabad India
74 F3 Hoshiarpur India
98 J7 Hoskins Nebraska U.S.A.
98 G4 Hosmer South Dakota U.S.A.
60 E13 Hososhima Japan
106 C6 Hospah New Mexico U.S.A.
76 C3 Hospet India
14 C4 Hospital Ireland
131 G3 Hospital, Cuchilla del mt Uruguay
29 O6 Hossa Finland
106 B6 Hosta Butte mt New Mexico U.S.A.
133 D9 Hoste, I Chile
18 E8 Hostens France
27 G13 Höstholmen Sweden
37 O4 Hostouň Czech Rep
28 A5 Hostrup Ribe Denmark
28 B7 Hostrup Sønderjylland Denmark
28 D7 Hostrup Germany
28 C7 Hostrup Sø L Denmark
76 C4 Hosur India
26 G8 Hotagen Sweden
61 L9 Hotaka Japan
66 B4 Hotan China
66 C4 Hotan He R China
87 D11 Hotazel S Africa
117 P7 Hotchkiss Alberta Canada
106 C3 Hotchkiss Colorado U.S.A.
102 H3 Hot Creek Ra Nevada U.S.A.
33 O8 Hötensleben Germany
140 B1 Hotham,C N Terr Australia
116 F3 Hotham Inlet Alaska U.S.A.
139 H6 Hotham, Mt Victoria Australia
26 H7 Hoting Sweden
80 E8 Hot Springs Israel
109 O1 Hot Springs nat park Arkansas U.S.A.
111 C7 Hot Springs Arkansas U.S.A.
101 L2 Hot Springs Montana U.S.A.
112 E2 Hot Springs North Carolina U.S.A.
98 C6 Hot Springs South Dakota U.S.A.
108 D6 Hot Springs Texas U.S.A.
94 H9 Hot Springs Virginia U.S.A.
106 D1 Hot Sulphur Springs Colorado U.S.A.
117 O3 Hottah L Northwest Territories Canada
22 J3 Hotton Belgium
108 B5 Hot Wells Texas U.S.A.
32 L6 Hötzingen Germany
28 E2 Hou Denmark
20 E7 Houat isld France
22 D3 Houdain France
21 O4 Houdan France
22 G3 Houdeng Belgium
18 E8 Houeillès France
22 K3 Houffalize Belgium
107 J5 Hough Oklahoma U.S.A.
141 H4 Houghton R Queensland Australia
99 S2 Houghton Michigan U.S.A.
94 J4 Houghton New York U.S.A.
98 H4 Houghton South Dakota U.S.A.
94 C2 Houghton L Michigan U.S.A.
13 G4 Houghton-le-Spring England
145 D1 Houhora New Zealand
80 F1 Houla Lebanon
21 K3 Houlgate France
111 G7 Houlka Mississippi U.S.A.
21 N2 Houlme,le France
95 T7 Houlton Maine U.S.A.
65 B7 Houma China
111 F12 Houma Louisiana U.S.A.
85 G2 Houmt Souk Tunisia
85 D6 Houndé Burkina
9 F5 Hounslow England
18 E7 Hourtin France
95 O5 Housatonic R Connecticut U.S.A.
108 D1 House New Mexico U.S.A.
123 L6 House Hbr Madeleine Is, Quebec Canada
12 D3 House o'-Hill Scotland
118 E3 House R Alberta Canada
103 L2 House Ra Utah U.S.A.
117 K8 Houston British Columbia Canada
99 P6 Houston Minnesota U.S.A.
111 H8 Houston Mississippi U.S.A.
110 E4 Houston Missouri U.S.A.
109 F9 Houston Texas U.S.A.
110 C3 Houstonia Missouri U.S.A.
109 M5 Houston, L Texas U.S.A.
111 C11 Houston R Louisiana U.S.A.
89 F4 Hout R S Africa
89 A10 Hout B S Africa
25 D4 Houten Netherlands
22 J1 Houthalen Belgium
143 A8 Houtman Abrolhos arch W Australia Australia
94 J6 Houtzdale Pennsylvania U.S.A.
22 J3 Houyet Belgium
28 E5 Hov Denmark
29 K4 Hov Sweden
27 G13 Hova Sweden
28 B5 Hovborg Denmark
58 B2 Hovd Mongolia
27 B12 Hovden Norway
26 H9 Hovdsjö Sweden
28 A3 Hove Denmark
28 G5 Høve Vestjælland Denmark
9 F6 Hove England
28 D5 Hovedgård Denmark
32 J9 Hövelhof Germany
28 B5 Hoven Denmark
98 G4 Hoven South Dakota U.S.A.
103 P4 Hovenweep Nat. Mon Utah U.S.A.
28 A4 Hover Denmark
28 A4 Hover Å R Denmark
77 A4 Hoveyzeh Iran
99 R2 Hovland Minnesota U.S.A.
28 C6 Hovslund Denmark
58 D3 Hövüün Mongolia
141 L7 Howard Queensland Australia
107 O4 Howard Kansas U.S.A.
94 E6 Howard Ohio U.S.A.
94 K5 Howard Pennsylvania U.S.A.
98 J5 Howard South Dakota U.S.A.
99 S5 Howard Wisconsin U.S.A.
94 B3 Howard City Michigan U.S.A.
108 F5 Howard Cr Texas U.S.A.
140 D1 Howard I N Terr Australia
99 M4 Howard L Minnesota U.S.A.
116 J2 Howard Pass Alaska U.S.A.
99 T6 Howards Grove Wisconsin U.S.A.
86 D2 Howar, Wadi watercourse Sudan
13 H6 Howden England
101 M6 Howe Idaho U.S.A.
94 B5 Howe Indiana U.S.A.
109 N1 Howe Oklahoma U.S.A.
109 L2 Howe Texas U.S.A.
139 J6 Howe, C New South Wales Australia
83 L13 Howe, Î Kerguelen Indian Oc
94 D4 Howell Michigan U.S.A.
101 N8 Howell Utah U.S.A.
98 J8 Howells Nebraska U.S.A.
138 C2 Howe, Mt South Australia Australia
15 F4 Howe of Mearns Scotland
98 D5 Howes South Dakota U.S.A.
117 M11 Howe Sound British Columbia Canada
121 R7 Howick Quebec Canada
145 E2 Howick New Zealand
141 H2 Howick Group islds Gt Barrier Reef Aust
138 E2 Howitt, L South Australia Australia
139 H6 Howitt, Mt Victoria Australia
95 T1 Howland Maine U.S.A.
137 R1 Howland I Pacific Oc
123 P4 Howley Newfoundland Canada
117 P10 Howser British Columbia Canada
14 E3 Howth Ireland
68 H4 Ho Xa Vietnam
110 F5 Hoxie Arkansas U.S.A.
107 K2 Hoxie Kansas U.S.A.
32 K9 Höxter Germany
66 D2 Hoxtolgay China
15 E2 Hoy Scotland
32 K7 Hoya Germany
31 H4 Hoyerswerda Germany
8 C1 Hoylake England
26 F7 Höylandet Norway
120 J4 Hoyle Ontario Canada
110 G3 Hoyleton Illinois U.S.A.
33 O9 Hoym Germany
16 C4 Hoyos Spain
15 E2 Hoy Snd Scotland
122 F8 Hoyt New Brunswick Canada
107 P2 Hoyt Kansas U.S.A.
29 O9 Höytiäinen L Finland
101 O9 Hoyt Pk Utah U.S.A.
Hpa-an see Pa-an
68 C2 Hpa Lai Burma
68 C3 Hpasawg Burma
37 P4 Hracholuská Nádrž res Czech Rep
31 J5 Hradec Králové Czech Rep
37 P3 Hradiště mt Czech Rep
31 K6 Hranice Czech Rep
Hranice Czech Rep see Rossbach
48 F2 Hriňová Slovakia
31 L7 Hron R Slovakia
37 O3 Hroznetín Czech Rep
31 O5 Hrubieszów Poland
31 J7 Hrušovany Czech Rep
Hrvatska see Croatia
68 C2 Hsa Mong Hkam Burma
66 D5 Hsia-ju Ts'o L China
67 G6 Hsiao-lan Hsü isld Taiwan
58 G5 Hsieh-chia-chi China
68 C2 Hsi Hkip Burma
68 C2 Hsi-hseng Burma
58 G4 Hsin-chi China
58 F4 Hsin-ch'iang China
67 G4 Hsin-chu Taiwan
68 J3 Hsing-ying China
59 H3 Hsin-min China
68 C1 Hsipaw Burma
66 D5 Hsi-tsang Kao-yüan reg China
68 C1 Hsumhsai Burma
68 K2 Hsü-wen China
67 F4 Hua'an China
128 C6 Huacho Peru
65 H1 Huachuan China
128 C5 Huacrachuco Peru
65 C4 Huade China
59 J3 Huadian China
67 G2 Huading Shan mt China
68 D6 Hua Hin Thailand
68 F5 Huai R Thailand
65 C4 Huai'an China
58 G5 Huaibei China
65 F3 Huaide China
65 F3 Huaidezhen China
58 F5 Huai He R China
67 C3 Huaihua China
67 D5 Huaiji China
65 C4 Huailai China
68 F4 Huai Luang R Thailand
58 G5 Huainan China
67 E1 Huaining China
58 F4 Huairen China
65 C4 Huairou China
68 F4 Huai Yang Res Thailand
59 G5 Huaiyin China
67 C4 Huaiyuan China
125 L9 Huajuápan de León Mexico
71 N8 Huaki Indonesia
103 L6 Hualapai Mts Arizona U.S.A.
67 E2 Hualin China
128 C5 Huallaga R Peru
128 C5 Huallanca Peru
65 H1 Huama China
65 H1 Huanan China
128 E7 Huanay Bolivia
128 C6 Huancabamba Pasco Peru
128 C5 Huancabamba Piura Peru
128 E7 Huancane Peru
128 C6 Huancavelica Peru
128 C6 Huancayo Peru
128 E8 Huanchaca Bolivia
128 F6 Huanchaca, Sa. de mts Bolivia
128 C5 Huanchaco Peru
Huang'an see Hong'an
67 G1 Huangang China
Huangcaoba see Qianxinan
58 G5 Huangchuan China
67 E1 Huanggang China
65 D3 Huangganglliang mt China
67 F3 Huanggang Shan mt China
Huang Hai see Yellow Sea
58 D4 Huang He R China
65 D5 Huanghua China
65 C7 Huangkou China
67 E2 Huanglaomen China
65 A7 Huangling China
68 J3 Huangliu China
65 A7 Huanglong China
65 C7 Huanglongsi China
67 E1 Huangmei China
67 C4 Huangmian China
65 G3 Huangnihe China
67 E1 Huangpi China
67 B3 Huangpin China
67 C6 Huangpo China
67 D5 Huangpu China
67 E2 Huangshagang China
67 F1 Huang Shan mts China
67 F2 Huangshan China
65 E6 Huangshanguan China
58 D4 Huang Shui R China
65 G3 Huangsongdian China
65 D4 Huangtuliangzi China
65 E6 Huang Xian China
67 G2 Huangyan China
67 D3 Huangyangsi China
Huangzhou see Huanggang
67 C7 Huangzhu China
67 G1 Huaniao Shan isld China
67 A4 Huaning China
58 E4 Huan Jiang R China
67 C4 Huanjiang China
65 F4 Huanren China
Huanshan see Yuhuan
58 G5 Huanshi China
128 D6 Huanta Peru
65 D6 Huantai China
128 C5 Huánuco Peru
128 D6 Huanzo, Cord. de mts Peru
125 N3 Huaonta Nicaragua
67 G4 Hua-p'ing Hsü isld Taiwan
128 E7 Huara Chile
128 C5 Huaraz Peru
128 C6 Huariaca Peru
128 C6 Huarmey Peru
67 D2 Huarong China
128 C5 Huascarán mt Peru
133 C3 Huasco Chile
131 B2 Huasco, R Chile
67 D3 Huashi China
125 M2 Huaspuc Honduras
124 E4 Huatabampo Mexico
58 E4 Huating China
65 E3 Hua Tugal China
125 L8 Huatusco Mexico
125 K7 Huauchinango Mexico
65 A7 Hua Xian China
65 C7 Hua Xian China
67 D5 Hua Xian China
65 A7 Huayin China
67 B1 Huaying Shan mts China
67 E1 Huayuan China
67 C2 Huayuan China
67 C6 Huazhou China
65 F4 Huazi China
119 O7 Hubbard Saskatchewan Canada
99 N7 Hubbard Iowa U.S.A.
109 L4 Hubbard Texas U.S.A.
109 H3 Hubbard Cr. Res Texas U.S.A.
117 C5 Hubbard Glacier Alaska U.S.A.
94 D2 Hubbard L Michigan U.S.A.
117 D5 Hubbard, Mt Alaska/Yukon Terr U.S.A./Canada
122 H9 Hubbards Nova Scotia Canada
98 J9 Hubbell Nebraska U.S.A.
103 P6 Hubbell Trading Post Nat. Hist. Site Arizona U.S.A.
58 F5 Hubei prov China

41 N3 **Huben** Austria
121 Q7 **Huberdeau** Quebec Canada
33 T7 **Hubertusstock** Germany
76 B3 **Hubli** India
32 J6 **Huchting** Germany
25 F6 **Hückelhoven-Ratheim** Germany
36 C1 **Hückeswagen** Germany
140 D6 **Huckitta** N Terr Australia
9 E1 **Hucknall** England
22 B2 **Hucqueliers** France
72 E6 **Ḥudaydah, Al** Yemen
86 H3 **Ḥudaydah, Al** Yemen
13 G6 **Huddersfield** England
27 J12 **Huddinge** Sweden
32 H6 **Hude** Germany
32 L7 **Hudemühlen** Germany
26 J10 **Hudiksvall** Sweden
20 H4 **Hudimesnil** France
115 K7 **Hudson** Ontario Canada
133 C7 **Hudson** *mt* Chile
106 F1 **Hudson** Colorado U.S.A.
113 E9 **Hudson** Florida U.S.A.
110 G1 **Hudson** Illinois U.S.A.
94 B5 **Hudson** Indiana U.S.A.
99 O7 **Hudson** Iowa U.S.A.
107 M3 **Hudson** Kansas U.S.A.
94 C5 **Hudson** Michigan U.S.A.
95 O3 **Hudson** *R* New York U.S.A.
95 O4 **Hudson** New York U.S.A.
94 F5 **Hudson** Ohio U.S.A.
101 R7 **Hudson** Wyoming U.S.A.
115 L6 **Hudson Bay** Canada
119 P6 **Hudson Bay** Saskatchewan Canada
146 C13 **Hudson, Cape** *C* Antarctica
95 O3 **Hudson Falls** New York U.S.A.
107 P5 **Hudson, L.** Oklahoma U.S.A.
146 B7 **Hudson Mts** Antarctica
117 N7 **Hudson's Hope** British Columbia Canada
115 M5 **Hudson Str** Canada
94 B4 **Hudsonville** Michigan U.S.A.
119 W5 **Hudwin L** Manitoba Canada
68 H4 **Hue** Vietnam
16 C4 **Huebra** *R* Spain
131 B7 **Huechulafquén, L** Argentina
108 B4 **Hueco Mts** Texas U.S.A.
48 H4 **Huedin** Romania
124 G5 **Huehueto, Cerro** *mt* Mexico
125 K7 **Huejutla** Mexico
20 C5 **Huelgoat** France
16 E7 **Huelma** Spain
16 C7 **Huelva** *R* Spain
16 C7 **Huelva** *prov* Spain
16 C7 **Huelva** Spain
68 G4 **Huen** Laos
131 B3 **Huentelauquén** Chile
124 D3 **Huépac** Mexico
133 C6 **Huequi, Pen** Chile
17 F7 **Huércal Overa** Spain
106 F3 **Huerfano** *R* Colorado U.S.A.
131 C3 **Huerta, Sa. de la** *ra* Argentina
17 G6 **Huertas, C. de las** Spain
124 J5 **Huertecillas** Mexico
17 G3 **Huerva** *R* Spain
17 G2 **Huesca** *prov* Spain
17 G2 **Huesca** Spain
17 F7 **Huéscar** Spain
16 D7 **Huesna** *R* Spain
108 B5 **Hueso, Sierra del** *mts* Mexico
125 J8 **Huétamo** Mexico
17 F4 **Huete** Spain
98 F3 **Huff** North Dakota U.S.A.
36 G5 **Hüffenhardt** Germany
98 H4 **Huffton** South Dakota U.S.A.
77 A7 **Hufuf, Al** Saudi Arabia
116 K4 **Huggins I** Alaska U.S.A.
98 F9 **Hugh Butler L** Nebraska U.S.A.
141 G5 **Hughenden** Queensland Australia
118 F6 **Hughenden** Alberta Canada
121 L4 **Hughes** Ontario Canada
110 F7 **Hughes** Arkansas U.S.A.
119 R2 **Hughes R** Manitoba Canada
109 N3 **Hughes Springs** Texas U.S.A.
110 C3 **Hughesville** Missouri U.S.A.
140 C6 **Hugh R** N Terr Australia
118 K7 **Hughton** Saskatchewan Canada
9 F7 **Hugh Town** Isles of Scilly England
75 M8 **Hugli** *R* India
106 G2 **Hugo** Colorado U.S.A.
99 N4 **Hugo** Minnesota U.S.A.
107 P7 **Hugo** Oklahoma U.S.A.
100 B7 **Hugo** Oregon U.S.A.
107 P7 **Hugo L** Oklahoma U.S.A.
107 J4 **Hugoton** Kansas U.S.A.
36 D7 **Hugsweier** Germany
65 B6 **Huguan** China
Huhehot *see* **Hohhot**
58 F3 **Huhehot** China
67 F4 **Hui'an** China
145 F3 **Huiarau Range** New Zealand
67 E4 **Huichang** China
Huicheng *see* **She Xian**
124 H7 **Huicholes, Sa. de los** *mts* Mexico
59 J3 **Hŭich'ŏn** N Korea
67 E5 **Huidong** China
65 G2 **Huifaheng** China
128 C3 **Huila** *div* Colombia
58 G4 **Huimin** China
65 G3 **Huinan** China
67 B3 **Huishui** China
21 L7 **Huismes** France
21 M5 **Huîsne** *R* France
21 N6 **Huisseau-sur-Cosson** France
65 C7 **Huiting** China
67 C3 **Huitong** China
29 K10 **Huittinen** Finland
125 K8 **Huitzuco** Mexico
65 B7 **Hui Xian** China
125 N10 **Huixtla** Mexico
Huiyang *see* **Huizhou**
25 D4 **Huizen** Netherlands
67 E5 **Huizhou** China
58 D2 **Hujirt** Mongolia
145 F3 **Huka Falls** New Zealand
145 E4 **Hukanui** New Zealand
144 C5 **Hukarere** New Zealand
75 R5 **Hukawng Valley** Burma
145 E1 **Hukerenui** New Zealand
67 E2 **Hukou** China
87 D10 **Hukuntsi** Botswana
107 O5 **Hulah** Oklahoma U.S.A.
107 O5 **Hulah L** Oklahoma U.S.A.
59 J2 **Hulan** China
65 F1 **Hulan Ergi** China
65 G1 **Hulan He** *R* China
80 F1 **Ḥulata** Israel
98 B5 **Hulett** Wyoming U.S.A.
Huliao *see* **Dabu**
65 J2 **Hulin** China
65 E2 **Hulin He** *R* China
121 P7 **Hull** Quebec Canada
99 P10 **Hull** Illinois U.S.A.
98 K6 **Hull** Iowa U.S.A.
98 F3 **Hull** North Dakota U.S.A.
109 N5 **Hull** Texas U.S.A.
140 A6 **Hull Cr** N Terr Australia
22 G2 **Hulpe, la** Belgium
28 E1 **Hulsig** Denmark
25 B6 **Hulst** Netherlands
27 H14 **Hultsfred** Sweden
65 E4 **Huludao** China
69 E11 **HUlu Kali, Gunung** Malaysia
58 G2 **Hulun Nur** *L* China
69 E10 **Hulu Soh, Gunung** *mt* Malaysia
59 J1 **Huma** China
127 M5 **Humacao** Puerto Rico
59 H1 **Huma He** *R* China
128 F5 **Humaitá** Brazil
130 B10 **Humaitá** Paraguay
87 D12 **Humansdorp** S Africa
110 C4 **Humansville** Missouri U.S.A.
128 C6 **Humay** Peru
87 C9 **Humbe** Angola
123 P5 **Humbermouth** Newfoundland Canada
13 H6 **Humber, R** England
13 H6 **Humberside** *co* England
99 Q5 **Humbird** Wisconsin U.S.A.
28 F7 **Humble** Denmark
109 M6 **Humble** Texas U.S.A.
106 G9 **Humble City** New Mexico U.S.A.
119 M6 **Humboldt** Saskatchewan Canada
103 M7 **Humboldt** Arizona U.S.A.
99 S10 **Humboldt** Illinois U.S.A.
99 M7 **Humboldt** Iowa U.S.A.
107 P4 **Humboldt** Kansas U.S.A.
102 F1 **Humboldt** *R* Nevada U.S.A.
102 F1 **Humboldt** Nevada U.S.A.
110 H6 **Humboldt** Tennessee U.S.A.
100 A9 **Humboldt B** California U.S.A.
115 N2 **Humboldt Gletscher** *gla* Greenland
102 F2 **Humboldt L** Nevada U.S.A.
144 B6 **Humboldt Mts** New Zealand
100 G9 **Humboldt Range** Nevada U.S.A.
102 F1 **Humboldt Rge** Nevada U.S.A.
102 G2 **Humboldt Salt Marsh** Nevada U.S.A.
94 J8 **Hume** Virginia U.S.A.
141 H7 **Humeburn** Queensland Australia
77 F7 **Hūmedān** Iran
48 G2 **Humenné** Slovakia
139 H6 **Hume Res** New South Wales Australia
99 N9 **Humeston** Iowa U.S.A.
29 K5 **Humlebæk** Denmark
28 B3 **Humlum** Denmark
32 K9 **Humme** Germany
95 L6 **Hummelstown** Pennsylvania U.S.A.
32 G7 **Hümmling** *hills* Germany
144 C6 **Hummock** *mt* New Zealand
127 K10 **Humocaro Bajo** Venezuela
131 A5 **Humos, C** Chile
87 B9 **Humpata** Angola
111 E7 **Humphrey** Arkansas U.S.A.
101 N5 **Humphrey** Idaho U.S.A.
98 J8 **Humphrey** Nebraska U.S.A.
100 D2 **Humphrey** Washington U.S.A.
102 E5 **Humphreys** California U.S.A.
110 C1 **Humphreys** Missouri U.S.A.
103 N6 **Humphreys Pk** Arizona U.S.A.
140 C7 **Humphries, Mt** N Terr Australia
31 J6 **Humpolec** Czech Rep
29 K11 **Humppila** Finland
100 B2 **Humptulips** Washington U.S.A.
140 B2 **Humpty Doo** N Terr Australia
84 F4 **Hūn** Libya
28 S9 **Húna-flói** *B* Iceland
67 C3 **Hunan** *prov* China
65 H3 **Hunchun** China
144 D5 **Hundalee** New Zealand
28 A3 **Hundborg** Denmark
28 B6 **Hunderup** Denmark
28 H5 **Hundested** Denmark
117 N10 **Hundred Mile House** British Columbia Canada
26 M6 **Hundsjö** Sweden
28 E5 **Hundslund** Denmark
38 G7 **Hundstein** *mt* Austria
28 D2 **Hune** Denmark
48 H5 **Hunedoara** *reg* Romania
48 H5 **Hunedoara** Romania
36 H2 **Hünfeld** Germany
36 E3 **Hünfelden** Germany
48 D3 **Hungary** *rep* Europe
26 H9 **Hunge** Sweden
36 F3 **Hungen** Germany
141 G8 **Hungerford** Queensland Australia
9 E5 **Hungerford** England
58 B2 **Hüngiy** Mongolia
65 G5 **Hŭngnam** N Korea
101 L1 **Hungry Horse Dam** Montana U.S.A.
101 M1 **Hungry Horse Res** Montana U.S.A.
68 H2 **Hung Yen** Vietnam
65 B4 **Hun He** *R* China
65 E4 **Hun He** *R* China
65 F4 **Hun Jiang** *R* China
65 G4 **Hunjiang** China
13 H5 **Hunmanby** England
99 P10 **Hunnewell** Missouri U.S.A.
25 F7 **Hünshoven** Germany
9 G2 **Hunstanton** England
28 B2 **Hunstrup** Denmark
76 C4 **Hunsur** India
65 E2 **Hunt** China
109 H5 **Hunt** Texas U.S.A.
120 J3 **Hunta** Ontario Canada
32 H8 **Hunte** *R* Germany
32 H8 **Hunteburg** Germany
139 K4 **Hunter** *R* New South Wales Australia
144 C6 **Hunter** New Zealand
137 P6 **Hunter** *isld* Pacific Oc
110 E6 **Hunter** Arkansas U.S.A.
107 M2 **Hunter** Kansas U.S.A.
98 J2 **Hunter** North Dakota U.S.A.
107 N5 **Hunter** Oklahoma U.S.A.
109 J6 **Hunter** Texas U.S.A.
139 G8 **Hunter I** Tasmania Australia
117 J10 **Hunter I** British Columbia Canada
99 P1 **Hunter I** Ontario Canada
116 M5 **Hunter, Mt** Alaska U.S.A.
144 A6 **Hunter Mts** New Zealand
144 B6 **Hunter R** New Zealand
122 J7 **Hunter River** Prince Edward I Canada
100 G1 **Hunters** Washington U.S.A.
68 A3 **Hunter's B** Burma
144 C6 **Hunter's Hills, The** New Zealand
12 D2 **Hunterston** Scotland
112 G2 **Huntersville** North Carolina U.S.A.
94 G8 **Huntersville** West Virginia U.S.A.
94 B5 **Huntertown** Indiana U.S.A.
145 E3 **Hunterville** New Zealand
110 K3 **Huntingburg** Indiana U.S.A.
121 Q7 **Huntingdon** Quebec Canada
9 F3 **Huntingdon** England
94 J6 **Huntingdon** Pennsylvania U.S.A.
110 H6 **Huntingdon** Tennessee U.S.A.
122 J3 **Hunting I** Quebec Canada
112 G5 **Hunting I** South Carolina U.S.A.
94 B6 **Huntington** Indiana U.S.A.
95 O6 **Huntington** Long I, New York U.S.A.
100 H5 **Huntington** Oregon U.S.A.
111 B10 **Huntington** Texas U.S.A.
103 O2 **Huntington** Utah U.S.A.
94 E8 **Huntington** West Virginia U.S.A.
102 F8 **Huntington Beach** California U.S.A.
102 E4 **Huntington L** California U.S.A.
8 D4 **Huntley** England
101 R4 **Huntley** Montana U.S.A.
98 G9 **Huntley** Nebraska U.S.A.
98 B8 **Huntley** Wyoming U.S.A.
32 H7 **Huntlosen** Germany
145 E2 **Huntly** New Zealand
15 F3 **Huntly** Scotland
117 J5 **Hunt, Mt** Yukon Territory Canada
138 D3 **Hunt Pen** South Australia Australia
101 S5 **Hunts Mt** Wyoming U.S.A.
122 H10 **Hunts Pt** Nova Scotia Canada
121 L7 **Huntsville** Ontario Canada
110 K7 **Huntsville** Alabama U.S.A.
110 C5 **Huntsville** Arkansas U.S.A.
110 D2 **Huntsville** Missouri U.S.A.
109 M5 **Huntsville** Texas U.S.A.
101 O8 **Huntsville** Utah U.S.A.
32 E9 **Hünxe** Germany
88 C10 **Hunyani Rge** *mts* Zimbabwe
65 B5 **Hunyuan** China
66 A4 **Hunza** Kashmir
25 G2 **Hunze** *R* Netherlands
66 C3 **Huocheng** China
65 F1 **Huodifangzi** China
65 B7 **Huojia** China
139 H9 **Huon** *R* Tasmania Australia
68 H4 **Huong Hoa** Vietnam
68 G3 **Huong Khe** Vietnam
68 H8 **Huong My** Vietnam
68 G3 **Huong Son** Vietnam
68 H4 **Huong Thuy** Vietnam
139 H9 **Huonville** Tasmania Australia
65 B6 **Huo Shan** *mt* China
67 E1 **Huoshan** China
67 G5 **Huo-shao Tao** *isld* Taiwan
65 B6 **Huo Xian** China
Hupeh *prov* *see* **Hubei** *prov*
21 O1 **Huppy** France
33 M10 **Hüpstedt** Germany
48 E3 **Hurbanovo** Slovakia
27 E11 **Hurdals** *L* Norway
120 J7 **Hurd, Cape** Ontario Canada
86 B1 **Hurdiyo** Somalia
110 D1 **Hurdland** Missouri U.S.A.
98 F2 **Hurdsfield** North Dakota U.S.A.
65 E3 **Hure Qi** China
80 E1 **Hurfeish** Israel
84 J4 **Hurghada** Egypt
18 G6 **Huriel** France
119 P2 **Hurkett** Ontario Canada
9 F4 **Hurley** England
111 H11 **Hurley** Mississippi U.S.A.
106 B9 **Hurley** New Mexico U.S.A.
98 J6 **Hurley** South Dakota U.S.A.
99 Q3 **Hurley** Wisconsin U.S.A.
12 D2 **Hurlford** Scotland
15 E2 **Hurliness** Scotland
95 M8 **Hurlock** Maryland U.S.A.
143 C10 **Hurlstone, L** W Australia Australia
102 D5 **Huron** California U.S.A.
94 E5 **Huron** Ohio U.S.A.
98 H5 **Huron** South Dakota U.S.A.
99 S3 **Huron B** Michigan U.S.A.
94 E2 **Huron City** Michigan U.S.A.
94 E2 **Huron, L** U.S.A./Canada
99 T3 **Huron Mts** Michigan U.S.A.
103 L4 **Hurricane** Utah U.S.A.
94 E8 **Hurricane** West Virginia U.S.A.
112 E6 **Hurricane Cr** Georgia U.S.A.
126 E3 **Hurricane Flats** Bahamas
110 J6 **Hurricane Mills** Tennessee U.S.A.
9 E5 **Hursley** England
109 M9 **Hurst** Texas U.S.A.
9 E5 **Hurstbourne Tarrant** England
9 G5 **Hurst Green** England
9 F6 **Hurstpierpoint** England
131 B3 **Hurtado** *R* Chile
36 B2 **Hürtgen** Germany
36 B2 **Hürth** Germany
111 L9 **Hurtsboro** Alabama U.S.A.
70 C4 **Hurung, Gunung** *mt* Kalimantan
88 B10 **Hurungwe** *dist* Zimbabwe
144 D5 **Hurunui R** New Zealand
28 E3 **Hurup** Denmark
28 D7 **Hurup** Germany
28 S9 **Husavik** Iceland
9 E3 **Husbands Bosworth** England
28 A4 **Husby** Denmark
71 L10 **Husdale** Indonesia
Hushan *see* **Cixi**
65 H2 **Hushan** China
48 L4 **Huşi** Romania
80 D3 **Ḥusifa** Israel
139 K6 **Huskisson** New South Wales Australia
27 G14 **Huskvarna** Sweden
116 J4 **Huslia** Alaska U.S.A.
80 G4 **Husn** Jordan
101 L2 **Huson** Montana U.S.A.
27 A10 **Husöy** Norway
118 E7 **Hussar** Alberta Canada
26 B9 **Hustadvika** Norway
28 B6 **Husum** Denmark
30 E1 **Husum** Germany
131 H6 **Husvik** S Georgia
58 D2 **Hutag** Mongolia
69 D12 **Hutanopan** Sumatra
109 O10 **Hutchins** Texas U.S.A.
107 N3 **Hutchinson** Kansas U.S.A.
99 M5 **Hutchinson** Minnesota U.S.A.
113 G10 **Hutchinson I** Florida U.S.A.
103 N7 **Hutch Mt** Arizona U.S.A.
68 D4 **Huthi** Burma
59 K2 **Hutou** China
110 J2 **Hutsonville** Illinois U.S.A.
38 H7 **Hüttau** Austria
21 L5 **Hutte, la** France
37 L4 **Hüttenbach** Germany
38 L8 **Hüttenberg** Austria
36 G3 **Hüttengesäss** Germany
37 P6 **Hutthurm** Germany
111 D8 **Huttig** Arkansas U.S.A.
109 K5 **Hutto** Texas U.S.A.
6 L1 **Hutton** *oil rig* North Sea
141 J7 **Hutton, Mt** Queensland Australia
143 E6 **Hutton Ra** W Australia Australia
94 G8 **Huttonsville** West Virginia U.S.A.
40 G3 **Huttwil** Switzerland
66 D3 **Hutubi** China
58 F4 **Hutuo He** *R* China
73 L8 **Huvadu Atoll** Maldives
79 G3 **Ḥuwayz, Al** Syria
118 D7 **Huxley** Alberta Canada
142 F4 **Huxley, Mt** W Australia Australia
144 B6 **Huxley, Mt** New Zealand
116 R6 **Huxley, Mt** Alaska U.S.A.
22 J3 **Huy** Belgium
67 G1 **Huzhou** China
27 E12 **Hvaler** *isld* Norway
28 C3 **Hvalpsund** Denmark
115 M2 **Hvalsund** *sd* Greenland
28 C3 **Hvam** Denmark
42 G5 **Hvar** Croatia
42 H5 **Hvar** *isld* Croatia
28 S10 **Hveragerdhi** Iceland
28 S9 **Hveravellir** Iceland
28 B3 **Hvidbjerg** Denmark
28 B6 **Hviding** Denmark
28 E4 **Hvilsager** Denmark
28 D3 **Hvilsom** Denmark
28 E4 **Hvilsted** Denmark
28 S9 **Hvita** *R* Iceland
27 E12 **Hvitsten** Norway
27 D12 **Hvittingfoss** Norway
Hwainan *see* **Huainan**
89 E2 **Hwange** Zimbabwe
87 E9 **Hwange Nat. Park** Zimbabwe
Hwang Hai *see* **Yellow Sea**
61 P14 **Hyakuna** Okinawa
101 P4 **Hyalite Pk** Montana U.S.A.
100 B9 **Hyampom** California U.S.A.
95 R5 **Hyannis** Massachusetts U.S.A.
98 E8 **Hyannis** Nebraska U.S.A.
58 B2 **Hyargas Nuur** *L* Mongolia
100 C7 **Hyatt Res** Oregon U.S.A.
95 L8 **Hyattsville** Maryland U.S.A.
101 S5 **Hyattville** Wyoming U.S.A.
111 J10 **Hybart** Alabama U.S.A.
121 N7 **Hybla** Ontario Canada
27 H14 **Hycklinge** Sweden
117 G8 **Hydaburg** Alaska U.S.A.
13 F6 **Hyde** England
144 C6 **Hyde** New Zealand
143 C9 **Hyden** W Australia Australia
94 D9 **Hyden** Kentucky U.S.A.
117 H8 **Hyder** Br Col/Alaska Canada/U.S.A.
74 H10 **Hyderabad** India
77 L7 **Hyderabad** Pakistan
Hydra *isld* *see* **Ídhra** *isld*
109 J5 **Hye** Texas U.S.A.
20 H4 **Hyenville** France
19 Q18 **Hyères** France
59 J3 **Hyesan** N Korea
98 A9 **Hygiene** Colorado U.S.A.
117 J5 **Hyland** *R* Yukon Territory Canada
139 L4 **Hyland, Mt** New South Wales Australia
117 J7 **Hyland Post** British Columbia Canada
28 D5 **Hylke** Denmark
28 G7 **Hyllekrog** *C* Denmark
27 A10 **Hyllestad** Norway
28 F4 **Hyllested** Denmark
28 H5 **Hyllinge** Denmark
118 E4 **Hylo** Alberta Canada
27 B12 **Hylsfjorden** *inlet* Norway
110 J2 **Hymera** Indiana U.S.A.
138 F6 **Hynam** South Australia Australia
12 E2 **Hyndford Br** Scotland
94 J7 **Hyndman** Pennsylvania U.S.A.
101 L6 **Hyndman Peak** Idaho U.S.A.
94 K5 **Hyner** Pennsylvania U.S.A.
60 J10 **Hyōgo** *prefect* Japan
86 D4 **Hyrra Banda** Cent Afr Republic
101 O8 **Hyrum** Utah U.S.A.
29 N7 **Hyrynsalmi** Finland
52 C3 **Hyrynsalmi** Finland
101 S3 **Hysham** Montana U.S.A.
117 O8 **Hythe** Alberta Canada
9 H5 **Hythe** England
9 E6 **Hythe** Hampshire England
60 E13 **Hyūga** Japan
29 L11 **Hyvinkää** Finland

I

68 J6 **Ia Ayun** *R* Vietnam
128 E6 **Iaco** *R* Brazil
48 J3 **Iacobeni** Romania
129 K6 **Iaçu** Brazil
94 F9 **Iaeger** West Virginia U.S.A.
36 B7 **Iaintrux** France
48 K6 **Ialomiţa** *reg* Romania
48 K6 **Ialomiţa** *R* Romania
47 R14 **Ialysus** *hist site* Rhodes Greece
113 C7 **Iamonia, L** Florida U.S.A.
48 L5 **Ianca** Romania
88 C7 **Iangano Nat. Park** Zambia
144 C5 **Ianthe, L** New Zealand
48 H4 **Iara** Romania
14 B3 **Iar Connaught** Ireland
129 H3 **Iaripo** Brazil
53 C10 **Iasi** Romania
46 G3 **Íasmos** Greece
111 D10 **Iatt, L** Louisiana U.S.A.
128 E3 **Iauareté** Brazil
52 H4 **Ib** Russian Federation
71 D3 **Iba** Luzon Philippines
85 E7 **Ibadan** Nigeria
128 C3 **Ibagué** Colombia
130 E8 **Ibaiti** Brazil
101 M9 **Ibapah** Utah U.S.A.
46 D1 **Ibar** *R* Serbia Yugoslavia
60 G11 **Ibara** Japan
61 O9 **Ibaraki** *prefect* Japan
128 C3 **Ibarra** Ecuador
32 G8 **Ibbenbüren** Germany
80 G4 **Ibbin** Jordan
86 C5 **Ibenga** *R* Congo
131 F2 **Iberá, Esteros del** *marshes* Argentina
131 F2 **Iberá, L** Argentina
110 D3 **Iberia** Missouri U.S.A.
121 R7 **Iberville** Quebec Canada
26 J3 **Ibestad** Norway
85 F6 **Ibeto** Nigeria
85 F7 **Ibi** Nigeria
129 J7 **Ibiá** Brazil
130 G5 **Ibiaí** Brazil
129 K4 **Ibiapaba, Serra da** *mts* Brazil
131 G3 **Ibicui da Cruz** *R* Brazil
131 G2 **Ibicuí, R** Brazil
133 F4 **Ibicuy** Argentina
61 K10 **Ibigawa** Japan
80 D2 **I'billin** Israel
130 D8 **Ibiporã** Brazil
130 H6 **Ibiraçu** Brazil
130 E10 **Ibirama** Brazil
130 H5 **Ibiranhém** Brazil
131 G3 **Ibirapuita** *R* Brazil
130 E7 **Ibitinga** Brazil
17 H5 **Ibiza** *isld* Balearic Is
80 F8 **Ibn Hammad** Jordan
88 H8 **Ibo** Mozambique
129 K6 **Ibotirama** Brazil
86 D3 **Ibra., Wadi** *watercourse* Sudan
52 G6 **Ibresi** Russian Federation
47 H3 **İbriktepe** Turkey
79 A9 **Ibshawâi** Egypt
9 E6 **Ibsley** England
61 Q12 **Ibu** Okinawa
60 D14 **Ibusuki** Japan
128 E4 **Içá** *R* Brazil
128 C6 **Ica** Peru
128 F3 **Icabaru** *R* Venezuela
127 N3 **Icacos Pt** Trinidad
71 D5 **Icadambanauan** Philippines
131 G2 **Icamaqua** *R* Brazil
128 E3 **Icana** Brazil
103 K5 **Iceberg Canyon** Nev/Ariz U.S.A.
100 G3 **Ice Harbor Dam** Washington U.S.A.
İçel *see* **Mersin**
28 **Iceland** *rep* N Atlantic Oc
90 H2 **Iceland-Faeroe Rise** Atlantic Oc
56 B3 **Icha** *R* Russian Federation
76 B2 **Ichalkaranji** India
37 J7 **Ichenhausen** Germany
60 G11 **Ichi** Japan
60 E13 **Ichifusa-yama** *mt* Japan
61 O10 **Ichihara** Japan
61 P5 **Ichinohe** Japan
59 L4 **Ichinomiya** Japan
54 D6 **Ichnya** Ukraine
22 E1 **Ichtegem** Belgium
37 K2 **Ichtershausen** Germany
130 H7 **Iconha** Brazil
Iconium *see* **Konya**
116 R6 **Icy B** Alaska U.S.A.
116 F1 **Icy Cape** Alaska U.S.A.
117 E6 **Icy Pt** Alaska U.S.A.
109 O3 **Ida** Louisiana U.S.A.
94 D5 **Ida** Michigan U.S.A.
109 N2 **Idabel** Oklahoma U.S.A.
99 L7 **Ida Grove** Iowa U.S.A.
85 F7 **Idah** Nigeria
101 M6 **Idaho** *state* U.S.A.
100 K6 **Idaho City** Idaho U.S.A.
101 N6 **Idaho Falls** Idaho U.S.A.
106 E2 **Idaho Springs** Colorado U.S.A.
106 H2 **Idalia** Colorado U.S.A.
36 C4 **Idar Oberstein** Germany
56 E4 **Idarskoye Belogor'ye** *mts* Russian Federation
36 C4 **Idarwald** *mts* Germany
144 C6 **Ida Valley** New Zealand
27 E12 **Idd** Norway
77 C7 **Idd al Sharqi** *oil well* Persian Gulf
118 F8 **Iddesleigh** Alberta Canada
111 M9 **Ideal** Georgia U.S.A.
52 D3 **Idel'** Russian Federation
85 F4 **Idelès** Algeria
86 B6 **Idemba** Gabon
28 H7 **Idestrup** Denmark
84 J5 **Idfu** Egypt
84 E4 **Idhān Awbārī** Libya
84 E5 **Idhān Murzuq** Libya
46 G9 **Ídhi Óros** *mt* Crete Greece
46 F7 **Ídhra** *isld* Greece
69 C10 **Idi** Sumatra
Idi Amin Dada, L *see* **Edward, L**
45 K3 **Idice** *R* Italy
116 H5 **Iditarod** Alaska U.S.A.
27 H11 **Idkerberget** Sweden
79 G3 **Idlib** Syria
80 C7 **Idna** Jordan
140 C6 **Idracowra** N Terr Australia
26 F10 **Idre** Sweden
102 D5 **Idria** California U.S.A.
52 C6 **Idritsa** Russian Federation
42 C3 **Idro, L. d'** Italy
21 P8 **Ids St. Roch** France
36 E3 **Idstein** Germany
76 C6 **Idukki** India
28 A4 **Idum** Denmark
87 E12 **Idutywa** S Africa
61 P12 **Ie-jima** *isld* Okinawa
45 R6 **Ielsi** Italy
22 H3 **Iemeppe** Belgium
130 D8 **Iepê** Brazil
22 D2 **Ieper** Belgium
47 H9 **Ierápetra** Crete Greece
46 F8 **Iérax, Akr** *C* Greece
59 G2 **I-erh-hsieh** China
46 F4 **Ierissós** Greece
43 C9 **Ierzu** Sardinia
45 O4 **Iesi** Italy
61 P12 **Ie-suidō** *str* Okinawa
48 J5 **Iezeru** *mt* Romania
17 H6 **Ifach, Pta** Spain
87 H12 **Ifanadiana** Madagascar
85 E7 **Ife** Nigeria
85 F5 **Iférouane** Niger
141 F4 **Iffley** Queensland Australia
138 B4 **Ifould L** South Australia Australia
85 C2 **Ifrane** Morocco
85 E5 **Igadiane** *watercourse* Mali
70 B3 **Igan** Sarawak
88 D1 **Iganga** Uganda
16 E10 **Igá, Oued** *R* Morocco
130 J9 **Igaraçu** Brazil
129 J4 **Igarape-Açu** Brazil
147 P14 **Igarka** Russian Federation
130 C9 **Igatimi** Paraguay
74 E9 **Igatpuri** India
71 F5 **Igbon** *isld* Philippines
78 K2 **Iğdir** Turkey
21 M5 **Igé** France
36 B4 **Igel** Germany
27 J10 **Iggesund** Sweden
133 D4 **Iglesia** Argentina
43 B9 **Iglesias** Sardinia
98 C6 **Igloo** South Dakota U.S.A.
147 E4 **Igloolik** Northwest Territories Canada
41 O3 **Igls** Austria
79 D9 **'Igma, Gebel el** *mts* Egypt
115 K8 **Ignace** Ontario Canada
106 C4 **Ignacio** Colorado U.S.A.
124 H5 **Ignacio Allende** Mexico
52 C6 **Ignalina** Lithuania
47 J3 **İğneada** Turkey
68 A7 **Ignoitijala** Andaman Is
76 G5 **Ignoitijala** Andaman Is
102 B1 **Igo** California U.S.A.
71 C3 **Igom** W Irian
87 F7 **Igoma** Tanzania
70 B3 **Igon** *R* Sarawak
46 D5 **Igoumenitsa** Greece
52 H5 **Igra** Russian Federation
130 E9 **Iguaçu, R** Brazil
130 H4 **Iguaí** Brazil
125 K8 **Iguala** Mexico
17 J3 **Igualda** Spain
129 J8 **Iguapé** Brazil
130 D8 **Iguaraçu** Brazil
130 F7 **Iguatama** Brazil
130 C8 **Iguatemi** Brazil
129 L5 **Iguatu** Brazil
Iguazú Falls *see* **Cataratas del Igauzú** *waterfalls*
86 A6 **Iguéla** Gabon
86 A6 **Iguéla, Lagune** *lagoon* Gabon
116 K8 **Igvak, C** Alaska U.S.A.
87 H10 **Iharaña** Madagascar
87 H12 **Ihosy** Madagascar
68 F6 **Ihr** Cambodia
22 L3 **Ihren** Germany
32 F6 **Ihrhove** Germany
40 G1 **Ihringen** Germany
58 E2 **Ihsuuj** Mongolia
29 L6 **Ii** Finland
61 L10 **Iida** Japan
61 N8 **Iide-san** *mt* Japan
29 N2 **Iijärvi** *L* Finland
29 N6 **Iijoki** *R* Finland
52 C5 **Iisaku** Estonia
29 N9 **Iisvesi** Finland
61 M9 **Iiyama** Japan
61 O8 **Iizaka** Japan
60 D12 **Iizuka** Japan
71 K9 **Ija** *isld* Indonesia
70 P9 **Ijang** *isld* Indonesia
85 E7 **Ijebu Ode** Nigeria
25 E2 **IJlst** Netherlands
25 D4 **IJmeer** Netherlands
25 C4 **IJmuiden** Netherlands
25 F3 **Ijonger** *R* Netherlands
25 C4 **Ijsel** *R* Netherlands
25 F4 **IJssel** *R* Netherlands
25 D3 **IJsselmeer** Netherlands
25 C5 **IJsselmonde** Netherlands
25 E3 **IJsselmuiden** Netherlands
25 D4 **IJsselstein** Netherlands
133 G3 **Ijuí** Brazil
131 G2 **Ijuí, R** Brazil
25 A6 **IJzendijke** Netherlands
22 D2 **Ijzer** *R* Belgium
52 H6 **Ik** *R* Russian Federation
29 K10 **Ikaalinen** Finland
144 C5 **Ikamatua** New Zealand
115 O4 **Ikamiut** Greenland
86 D6 **Ikanda** Zaire
47 H7 **Ikaría** *isld* Greece
28 C4 **Ikast** Denmark
56 H4 **Ikatskiy Khrebet** *mts* Russian Federation
145 F3 **Ikawhenua Range** New Zealand
60 J11 **Ikeda** Japan
60 G12 **Ikegawa** Japan
61 P13 **Ikei-jima** *isld* Okinawa
85 E7 **Ikeja** Nigeria
86 D6 **Ikela** Zaire
115 O3 **Ikerasak** Greenland
46 F2 **Ikhtiman** Bulgaria
60 C12 **Iki** *isld* Japan
88 C2 **Ikimba L** Tanzania
60 C12 **Iki-suidō** *str* Japan
116 K8 **Ikolik, C** Alaska U.S.A.
85 F7 **Ikom** Nigeria
88 D6 **Ikomba** Tanzania
87 H12 **Ikongo** Madagascar
87 H11 **Ikopa** *R* Madagascar
116 K1 **Ikpikpuk** *R* Alaska U.S.A.
56 B3 **Iksa** *R* Russian Federation
54 J1 **Iksha** Russian Federation
88 C1 **Ikulwe** Uganda
60 H10 **Ikuno** Japan
60 R2 **Ikutahara** Japan
71 E2 **Ilagan** Philippines
78 L5 **Īlām** Iran
75 M5 **Ilam** Nepal
56 E3 **Ilanskiy** Russian Federation
41 K4 **Ilanz** Switzerland
85 E7 **Ilaro** Nigeria
31 M2 **Iława** Poland
28 E2 **Ilbro** Denmark
138 D2 **Ilbunga** South Australia Australia
8 D5 **Ilchester** England
120 J9 **Ilderton** Ontario Canada
13 G3 **Ilderton** England
118 J3 **Ile-à-la Crosse** Saskatchewan Canada
118 K3 **Ile-à-la-Crosse L** Saskatchewan Canada
48 H3 **Ileanda** Romania
83 L13 **Ile aux Bénitiers** Mauritius
86 D6 **Ilebo** Zaire
21 P3 **Île de France** *reg* France
20 G8 **Île D'Olonne** France
25 E5 **Ileijen** Netherlands
55 B5 **Ilek** Russian Federation
85 E4 **Ilerh** *watercourse* Algeria
127 N5 **Îles des Saintes** Guadeloupe W Indies
85 F7 **Ilesha** Nigeria
52 G6 **Ilet'** *R* Russian Federation
20 B6 **Ile-Tudy** France
33 N9 **Ilfeld** Germany
119 W2 **Ilford** Manitoba Canada
9 G4 **Ilford** England
141 G6 **Ilfracombe** Queensland Australia
8 B5 **Ilfracombe** England
56 F4 **Ilga** *R* Russian Federation
78 D1 **Ilgaz Dağ** Turkey
130 F8 **Ilhabela** Brazil
128 F4 **Ilha Grande** Brazil
130 G8 **Ilha Grande, B. de** Brazil
130 D7 **Ilha Solteíra, Barragem** *dam* Brazil
16 B4 **Ílhavo** Portugal
130 H4 **Ilhéus** Brazil
48 H5 **Ilia** Romania
116 L6 **Iliamna** Alaska U.S.A.
116 K7 **Iliamna L** Alaska U.S.A.
71 L9 **Ili Boleng** *vol* Indonesia
48 N4 **Il'ichevsk** Ukraine
98 C9 **Iliff** Colorado U.S.A.
71 G6 **Iligan** Philippines
71 G6 **Iligan B** Philippines
71 F1 **Iligan Pt** Philippines
86 A2 **Ilig, Raas** *C* Somalia
46 F6 **Ilikí, L** Greece
56 F3 **Ilim** *R* Russian Federation
56 F1 **Ilimpeya** *R* Russian Federation
56 F3 **Ilimskiy, Khrebet** *mts* Russian Federation
71 E4 **Ilin** *isld* Philippines
55 C6 **Il'inka** Kazakhstan
52 F5 **Il'ino-Zaborskoye** Russian Federation
55 C2 **Il'inskiy** Russian Federation
71 E4 **Ilin Str** Philippines
48 M1 **Il'intsy** Ukraine
46 F5 **Iliodhrómia** *isld* Greece
95 M3 **Ilion** New York U.S.A.
42 F3 **Ilirska Bistrica** Slovenia
76 C3 **Ilkal** India
13 G6 **Ilkley** England
36 D7 **Ill** *R* France
128 E7 **Illampu** *mt* Bolivia
17 F4 **Illana** Spain
71 F7 **Illana B** Philippines
131 B3 **Illapel** Chile
131 B3 **Illapel, R** Chile
54 G8 **Illarionovo** Ukraine
41 O7 **Illasi** Italy
41 O6 **Illasi, Val d'** Italy
138 C2 **Illbillee, Mt** South Australia Australia
18 D4 **Ille-et-Vilaine** *dept* France
37 J7 **Iller** *R* Germany
37 J7 **Illertissen** Germany
16 E4 **Illescas** Spain
21 N5 **Illiers-Combray** France
20 F5 **Illifaut** France
128 E7 **Illimani** *mt* Bolivia
36 F6 **Illingen** Germany
99 R9 **Illinois** *state* U.S.A.
110 G1 **Illinois** *R* Illinois U.S.A.
110 B5 **Illinois** *R* Oklahoma U.S.A.
100 B7 **Illinois** *R* Oregon U.S.A.
99 R8 **Illinois & Mississippi Canal** Illinois U.S.A.
110 G2 **Illiopolis** Illinois U.S.A.
128 G3 **Illiwa** *R* Guyana
85 F3 **Illizit** Algeria
36 D6 **Illkirch** France
110 G4 **Illmo** Missouri U.S.A.
140 D6 **Illogwa** *R* N Terr Australia
21 O2 **Illois** France
16 E7 **Illora** Spain
Illorsuit *see* **Ubekendt Ejland**
37 M5 **Illschwang** Germany
28 E6 **Illumø** *isld* Denmark
37 M6 **Ilm** *R* Germany
29 K9 **Ilmajoki** Finland
33 M6 **Ilmenau** *R* Germany
37 K2 **Ilmenau** Germany
52 D5 **Il'men', Ozero** *L* Russian Federation
8 D6 **Ilminster** England
128 D7 **Ilo** Peru
71 F5 **Iloilo** Philippines
29 P9 **Ilomantsi** Finland
85 E7 **Ilorin** Nigeria
54 K9 **Ilovaysk** Ukraine
53 F9 **Ilovlya** Russian Federation
116 L7 **0il Pt** Alaska U.S.A.
33 N8 **Ilse** *R* Germany
33 N9 **Ilsenburg** Germany
36 G5 **Ilsfeld** Germany
36 H5 **Ilshofen** Germany
28 C4 **Ilskov** Denmark
88 D3 **Ilula** Tanzania
Ilulissat *see* **Jakobshavn**
48 J3 **Ilva Mică** Romania
100 A3 **Ilwaco** Washington U.S.A.
52 J4 **Ilych** *R* Russian Federation
52 D6 **Il'yino** Russian Federation
31 N4 **Iłża** Poland
31 N4 **Iłzanka** *R* Poland
59 K5 **Imabari** Japan
60 O4 **Imabetsu** Japan
61 N9 **Imaichi** Japan
61 K10 **Imajō** Japan
124 F5 **Imala** Mexico
78 K6 **Imām al Ḥamzah** Iraq
57 B6 **Imambaba** Turkmenistan
İmamoğlu *see* **Kırmıt**
Iman *see* **Dal'nerechensk**
52 D1 **Imandra** Russian Federation
130 C10 **Iman, Sa. del** *ra* Argentina
55 E4 **Imantau, Oz** *L* Kazakhstan
60 C12 **Imari** Japan
128 F2 **Imataca, Sa de** *mts* Venezuela
29 O10 **Imatra** Finland
61 J10 **Imazu** Japan
79 B8 **Imbâba** Egypt
128 C3 **Imbabura** *prov* Ecuador
127 J5 **Imbert** Dominican Rep
133 H3 **Imbituba** Brazil
130 E9 **Imbituva** Brazil
100 H4 **Imbler** Oregon U.S.A.
110 E5 **Imboden** Arkansas U.S.A.
52 F5 **Imeni-Babushkina** Russian Federation
52 F5 **Imeni Kalinina** Russian Federation
53 F11 **Imeni Lenina, Kanal** *canal* Russian Federation
53 G7 **Imeni Vl Lenina** Russian Federation
128 E3 **Imeri, Sa** *mts* Venezuela
113 F7 **Imeson** *airport* Florida U.S.A.
55 F2 **Imgyt** *R* Russian Federation
86 H4 **Īmī** Ethiopia
46 F7 **Imittós** *mt* Greece
65 G5 **Imjin** *R* N Korea
102 F1 **Imlay** Nevada U.S.A.
98 D6 **Imlay** South Dakota U.S.A.
94 D3 **Imlay City** Michigan U.S.A.
85 A4 **Imlili** *well* Western Sahara
32 K10 **Immenhausen** Germany
41 M2 **Immenstadt** Germany
113 F11 **Immokalee** Florida U.S.A.
100 J4 **Imnaha** Oregon U.S.A.
99 L9 **Imogene** Iowa U.S.A.
45 L3 **Imola** Italy
42 H5 **Imotski** Croatia
128 E5 **Imperatriz** Brazil
44 D4 **Imperia** Italy
119 M7 **Imperial** Saskatchewan Canada
103 J9 **Imperial** California U.S.A.
98 E9 **Imperial** Nebraska U.S.A.
102 G9 **Imperial Beach** California U.S.A.
103 K9 **Imperial Dam** Cal/Ariz U.S.A.
103 J9 **Imperial Valley** California U.S.A.
142 C4 **Imperieuse Reef** W Australia Australia
122 J9 **Imperoyal** Nova Scotia Canada
36 E5 **Impflingen** Germany
86 C5 **Impfondo** Congo
75 P6 **Imphal** India
18 H6 **Imphy** France
52 D4 **Impilakhti** Russian Federation
45 K4 **Impruneta** Italy
80 F8 **Imra** Jordan
47 K4 **İmralı** *isld* Turkey
İmroz *isld* *see* **Gökçeada** *isld*
47 H4 **Imroz** Turkey
41 N3 **Imst** Austria
124 D2 **Imuris** Mexico
71 D5 **Imuruan B** Philippines
116 D4 **Imuruk Basin** Alaska U.S.A.
116 F4 **Imuruk L** Alaska U.S.A.
16 E9 **Imzouren** Morocco
61 L10 **Ina** Japan
31 J2 **Ina** *R* Poland
90 A16 **Inaccessible I** Atlantic Oc
71 D6 **Inagauan** Philippines
61 N8 **Ina-gawa** *R* Japan
127 H4 **Inagua I., Little** Bahamas
61 N12 **Inamba-jima** *isld* Japan
128 D6 **Inambiri** *R* Peru
85 F3 **In Aménas** Algeria
85 E4 **In Amguel** Algeria
70 E1 **Inanam** Sabah
144 C4 **Inangahua Junction** New Zealand
51 K2 **Inarigda** Russian Federation
29 N3 **Inarijärvi** *L* Finland
61 N11 **Inatori** Japan
61 O8 **Inawashiro** Japan
61 O8 **Inawashiro ko** *L* Japan
85 F4 **In Azaoua** Algeria
85 E3 **In Belbel** Algeria
133 D3 **Incahuasi** *mt* Chile/Arg
78 E2 **İncesu** Turkey
14 E4 **Inch** Ireland
100 G1 **Inchelium** Washington U.S.A.
37 L6 **Inchenhofen** Germany
21 O1 **Incheville** France
13 E1 **Inchkeith** *isld* Scotland
15 D2 **Inchnadamph** Scotland
65 G6 **Inch'ŏn** S Korea
116 B3 **Inchoun** Russian Federation
13 E1 **Inchture** Scotland
22 E3 **Inchy** France
45 K4 **Incisa in Valdarno** Italy
89 H5 **Incomati** *R* Mozambique
22 H2 **Incourt** Belgium
18 M11 **Incudine, L'** *mt* Corsica
12 B2 **Indaal, L** Scotland
85 D4 **In Dagouber** Mali
130 D6 **Indaia Grande, R** Brazil
26 J9 **Indal** Sweden
26 H8 **Indalsälven** *R* Sweden
68 C2 **Indaw** Burma
75 R6 **Indawgyi Lake** Burma
124 G5 **Indé** Mexico
7 M9 **Indefatigable** *oil rig* North Sea
102 F5 **Independence** California U.S.A.
99 P7 **Independence** Iowa U.S.A.
107 P4 **Independence** Kansas U.S.A.
111 F11 **Independence** Louisiana U.S.A.
110 B2 **Independence** Missouri U.S.A.
100 B5 **Independence** Oregon U.S.A.
94 F10 **Independence** Virginia U.S.A.
99 P5 **Independence** Wisconsin U.S.A.
147 H9 **Independence Fj** Greenland
100 J8 **Independence Mts** Nevada U.S.A.
69 E13 **Inderapura** Sumatra
69 E13 **Inderapura, Tg** *C* Sumatra
55 B6 **Inderborskiy** Kazakhstan
26 E8 **Inderöy** Norway
55 B6 **Inder, Oz** *L* Kazakhstan
100 D2 **Index** Washington U.S.A.
74 G10 **Indi** India
74 **India** *rep* S Asia
107 M7 **Indiahoma** Oklahoma U.S.A.
117 D4 **Indian** *R* Yukon Territory Canada
95 M2 **Indian** *R* New York U.S.A.
140 D6 **Indiana** N Terr Australia
94 B6 **Indiana** *state* U.S.A.
94 H6 **Indiana** Pennsylvania U.S.A.
81 G11 **Indian-Antarctic Basin** Southern Oc
81 J11 **Indian-Antarctic Ridge** Southern Oc
94 A7 **Indianapolis** Indiana U.S.A.
123 T4 **Indian B** Newfoundland Canada
123 M7 **Indian Brook** Nova Scotia Canada
117 P6 **Indian Cabins** Alberta Canada
115 O7 **Indian Hbr** Labrador, Nfld Canada
122 J9 **Indian Hbr** Nova Scotia Canada
119 O8 **Indian Head** Saskatchewan Canada
95 K8 **Indian Head** Maryland U.S.A.
95 N3 **Indian L** New York U.S.A.
101 P7 **Indian Mt** Wyoming U.S.A.
81 **Indian Ocean**
83 **Indian Ocean Islands**
99 N8 **Indianola** Iowa U.S.A.
111 F8 **Indianola** Mississippi U.S.A.
98 F9 **Indianola** Nebraska U.S.A.
107 P6 **Indianola** Oklahoma U.S.A.
130 F6 **Indianópolis** Brazil
103 L3 **Indian Peak** Utah U.S.A.
101 Q5 **Indian Pk** Wyoming U.S.A.
113 G10 **Indian R** Florida U.S.A.
94 C1 **Indian River** Michigan U.S.A.
113 G9 **Indian River City** Florida U.S.A.
103 J5 **Indian Sp** Nevada U.S.A.
113 G10 **Indian Town** Florida U.S.A.
100 J5 **Indian Valley** Idaho U.S.A.
98 E2 **Indian Villages Nat. Hist. Site** North Dakota U.S.A.
103 O6 **Indian Wells** Arizona U.S.A.
122 A2 **Indicator L** Quebec Canada
52 G1 **Indiga** Russian Federation
147 L15 **Indiga** Russian Federation
51 O2 **Indigirka** *R* Russian Federation
52 G1 **Indigskaya Guba** *B* Russian Federation
48 F5 **Indija** Serbia Yugoslavia
117 Q3 **Indin L** Northwest Territories Canada
103 H8 **Indio** California U.S.A.
109 K9 **Indios** Mexico
137 N4 **Indispensable Reefs** Pacific Oc
70 D7 **Indonesia** *rep* S E Asia
141 K2 **Indooroopilly** *dist* Brisbane, Qnsld Australia
74 F7 **Indore** India
69 F13 **Indragiri** *R* Sumatra
70 M9 **Indramayu** Java
69 E14 **Indrapura** Sumatra
69 E14 **Indrapura, Tanjong** *C* Sumatra
73 N5 **Indravati** *R* India
18 G6 **Indre** *dept* France
20 G7 **Indre** France
21 N7 **Indre** *R* France
18 F5 **Indre-et-Loire** *dept* France
113 G10 **Indrio** Florida U.S.A.
21 N7 **Indrois** *R* France
31 O2 **Indura** Belarus
118 D8 **Indus** Alberta Canada
73 L2 **Indus** *R* S W Asia
74 B6 **Indus, Mouths of** Pakistan
110 F1 **Industry** Illinois U.S.A.
109 L6 **Industry** Texas U.S.A.
89 E8 **Indwe** S Africa

5 F4 **In Ebeggi** Algeria
8 D1 **İnebolu** Turkey
7 J4 **İnecik** Turkey
5 F4 **In Ecker** Algeria
5 E5 **In Edek** Niger
8 B1 **İnegöl** Turkey
1 K9 **Inerie** *mt* Flores Indonesia
1 P8 **Ineuil** France
9 L7 **Inez** Texas U.S.A.
5 G4 **In Ezzane** Algeria
9 B10 **Infanta, C** S Africa
8 F5 **Infernão, Cach** *rapids* Brazil
4 H8 **Infiernillo, L** Mexico
6 D1 **Infiesto** Spain
0 J9 **Ingá** Brazil
9 L11 **Inga** Finland
8 B4 **Ingabu** Burma
5 F5 **Ingal** Niger
0 C5 **Ingallanna** *R* N Terr Australia
4 B7 **Ingalls** Indiana U.S.A.
7 K4 **Ingalls** Kansas U.S.A.
9 T4 **Ingalls** Michigan U.S.A.
0 E10 **Ingalls, Mt** California U.S.A.
5 F3 **Ingaly** Russian Federation
9 G4 **Ingatestone** England
6 H5 **Ingelfingen** Germany
6 E4 **Ingelheim** Germany
2 E2 **Ingelmunster** Belgium
6 C6 **Ingende** Zaire
3 E5 **Ingeniero Luiggi** Argentina
1 E7 **Ingeniero, Pto** Argentina
7 L7 **Ingenika** *R* British Columbia Canada
6 E7 **Ingeramuit** Alaska U.S.A.
7 M5 **Ingersoll** Oklahoma U.S.A.
1 B2 **Inggelang** *isld* Halmahera Indonesia
1 H4 **Ingham** Queensland Australia
3 K11 **Ingiriya** Sri Lanka
3 F5 **Ingleborough** *mt* England
5 N2 **Inglefield Land** Greenland
9 K8 **Ingleside** Texas U.S.A.
3 F5 **Ingleton** England
1 K8 **Inglewood** Queensland Australia
9 G6 **Inglewood** Victoria Australia
5 E3 **Inglewood** New Zealand
0 D1 **Inglis** *isld* N Terr Australia
9 Q8 **Inglis** Manitoba Canada
6 G4 **Inglutalik** *R* Alaska U.S.A.
8 F1 **Ingoda** *R* Russian Federation
8 F1 **Ingolf** Ontario Canada
9 T10 **Ingolfshöfdhi** *C* Iceland
6 C7 **Ingololo** Zaire
7 L6 **Ingolstadt** Germany
8 C3 **Ingomar** South Australia Australia
1 S3 **Ingomar** Montana U.S.A.
3 M7 **Ingonish** C Breton I, Nova Scotia
2 B1 **Ingot** California U.S.A.
6 N1 **Ingöy** Norway
5 N6 **Ingrāj Bāzār** India
9 H5 **Ingram** Texas U.S.A.
9 Q4 **Ingram** Wisconsin U.S.A.
2 J9 **Ingramport** Nova Scotia Canada
1 M8 **Ingrandes** Indre France
1 J7 **Ingrandes** Maine-et-Loire France
1 M8 **Ingrandes** Vienne France
7 P3 **Ingray L** Northwest Territories Canada
1 O6 **Ingré** France
6 J11 **Ingrid Christensen Coast** Antarctica
8 D2 **Ingstrup** Denmark
5 F5 **In Guezzam** Algeria
0 D6 **Inguiniel** France
4 D9 **Ingul** *R* Ukraine
4 E9 **Ingulets** Ukraine
4 D10 **Ingulets** *R* Ukraine
5 F1 **Inguyagun** *R* Russian Federation
9 G6 **Ingwavuma** S Africa
9 K4 **Ingwiller** France
9 H6 **Inhaca Pen** Mozambique
7 G10 **Inhambane** Mozambique
0 C7 **Inhandui, R** Brazil
0 C7 **Inhanduizinho, R** Brazil
8 E10 **Inhangoma I** Mozambique
0 C10 **Inhanhora** *R* Brazil
0 G6 **Inhapim** Brazil
7 G10 **Inharrime** Mozambique
7 L4 **İnhisar** Turkey
0 H4 **Inhobim** Brazil
9 J7 **Inhumas** Brazil
6 L3 **Iniakuk** *R* Alaska U.S.A.
1 K9 **Inielika** *mt* Flores Indonesia
7 F5 **Iniesta** Spain
5 E3 **Inifel, Hassi** Algeria
7 M11 **Iniö** Finland
8 E3 **Inírida** *R* Colombia
4 A3 **Inishark** *isld* Ireland
4 C1 **Inishbofin** *isld* Ireland
4 A3 **Inishbofin** *isld* Ireland
4 B2 **Inishcrone** Ireland
4 B3 **Inisheer** *isld* Ireland
4 A2 **Inishkea** *isld* Ireland
4 B3 **Inishmaan** *isld* Ireland
4 B3 **Inishmore** *isld* Ireland
4 C2 **Inishmurray** *isld* Ireland
4 D1 **Inishowen** *dist* Ireland
4 E1 **Inishowen Hd** Ireland
4 D1 **Inishtrahull** *isld* Ireland
4 A3 **Inishturk** *isld* Ireland
5 D2 **Injgan Sum** China
1 J7 **Injune** Queensland Australia
1 F3 **Inkerman** Queensland Australia
2 H6 **Inkerman** New Brunswick Canada
6 C7 **Inkis** *R* Zaire
6 C7 **Inkisi-Kisantu** Zaire
7 G6 **Inklin** British Columbia Canada
1 N7 **Inkom** Idaho U.S.A.
2 F5 **Inkovo** Russian Federation
8 J1 **Inkster** North Dakota U.S.A.
8 C2 **Inle, L** Burma
8 H7 **Inman** Nebraska U.S.A.
5 N2 **Inman** New York U.S.A.
2 E2 **Inman** South Carolina U.S.A.
1 O3 **Inn** *R* Austria
8 F6 **Inn** *R* Germany
8 F2 **Innamincka** South Australia Australia
15 E5 **Innerleithen** Scotland
Inner Mongolia *aut reg see* **Nei Mongol Zizhiqu**
41 K3 **Inner-Rhoden** *dist* Switzerland
15 C3 **Inner Sound** Scotland
32 M8 **Innerste** *R* Germany
41 H4 **Innertkirchen** Switzerland
38 F8 **Innervillgraten** Austria
6 M6 **Innes** *oilfield* North Sea
26 E8 **Innherad** *reg* Norway
Innien *see* **Aukrug**
14 C5 **Inniscarra Res** Ireland
41 H3 **Innisfail** Queensland Australia
18 D6 **Innisfail** Alberta Canada
18 F5 **Innisfree** Alberta Canada
16 J5 **Innoko** *R* Alaska U.S.A.
60 G11 **Inno-shima** Japan
41 O3 **Innsbruck** Austria
26 K3 **Innset** Norway
26 B10 **Innvik** Norway
16 A3 **Innymney, Gora** *mt* Russian Federation
30 D6 **Inocência** Brazil
07 P5 **Inola** Oklahoma U.S.A.
47 L5 **İnönü** Turkey
31 L3 **Inowrocław** Poland
28 E7 **Inquisivi** Bolivia
85 E3 **In Rhar** Algeria
40 F3 **Ins** Switzerland
85 E3 **In Salah** Algeria
15 F3 **Insch** Scotland
43 A7 **Inscription,C** W Australia Australia
68 B4 **Insein** Burma
37 J2 **Inselsberg** *mt* Germany
19 O7 **Insinger** Saskatchewan Canada
31 J2 **Insko** Poland
36 B6 **Insming** France
Insterburg *see* **Chernyakhovsk**
146 D7 **Institute Ice Stream** *ice stream* Antarctica
118 J9 **Instow** Saskatchewan Canada
8 B5 **Instow** England
48 L6 **Însurăţei** Romania
52 K2 **Inta** Russian Federation
98 B2 **Intake** Montana U.S.A.
57 F1 **Intaly** Kazakhstan
85 E5 **In Tebezas** Mali
47 H4 **İntepe** Turkey
98 E6 **Interior** South Dakota U.S.A.
113 F8 **Interlachen** Florida U.S.A.
139 H8 **Interlaken** Tasmania Australia
40 G4 **Interlaken** Switzerland
99 N1 **International Falls** Minnesota U.S.A.
119 R10 **International Peace Gdn** Canada/U.S.A.
117 O9 **Intersection Mt** Alberta/Br Col Canada
68 A6 **Interview I** Andaman Is
48 K5 **Intorsura Buzăului** Romania
41 J5 **Intragna** Switzerland
32 G8 **Intrup** Germany
52 F2 **Intsy** Russian Federation
61 O10 **Inubō saki** Japan
115 O3 **Inugsulik Bugt** *B* Greenland
115 M6 **Inukjuak** Quebec Canada
133 C8 **Inútil, B** Chile
114 F4 **Inuvik** Northwest Territories Canada
114 F4 **Inuvik** *dist* Northwest Territories Canada
128 D6 **Inuya** *R* Peru
52 J5 **In'va** *R* Russian Federation
15 C4 **Inveraray** Scotland
15 F4 **Inverbervie** Scotland
144 B7 **Invercargill** New Zealand
12 C2 **Invercloy** Scotland
139 K3 **Inverell** New South Wales Australia
15 D3 **Invergordon** Scotland
15 E4 **Inverkeithing** Scotland
12 D2 **Inverkip** Scotland
140 F4 **Inverleigh** Queensland Australia
12 D1 **Inverlochlarig** Scotland
119 O7 **Invermay** Saskatchewan Canada
117 P10 **Invermere** British Columbia Canada
121 T6 **Inverness** Quebec Canada
123 L7 **Inverness** C Breton I, Nova Scotia
15 D3 **Inverness** Scotland
113 E9 **Inverness** Florida U.S.A.
101 P1 **Inverness** Montana U.S.A.
15 D3 **Invershin** Scotland
15 F3 **Inverurie** Scotland
140 A4 **Inverway** N Terr Australia
68 C6 **Investigator Chan** Burma
138 C5 **Investigator Group** *islds* South Australia Australia
138 D6 **Investigator Str** South Australia Australia
68 A7 **Invisible Bank** Andaman Is
120 J10 **Inwood** Ontario Canada
102 C1 **Inwood** California U.S.A.
56 B3 **Inya** *R* Russian Federation
87 F9 **Inyanga** Zimbabwe
87 F9 **Inyanga Nat. Park** Zimbabwe
98 B5 **Inyan Kara Cr** Wyoming U.S.A.
56 G3 **Inyaptuk, Gora** *mt* Russian Federation
102 G6 **Inyokern** California U.S.A.
55 C4 **Inzer** Russian Federation
86 C7 **Inzia** *R* Zaire
20 D6 **Inzinzac-Lochrist** France
46 D5 **Ioánnina** Greece
38 H9 **Iôf di Montasio** *mt* Italy
47 H9 **Ioinianísia** *isld* Greece
61 N13 **Iō-Jima** *isld* Japan
52 E1 **Iokanga** Russian Federation
106 C3 **Iola** Colorado U.S.A.
107 P4 **Iola** Kansas U.S.A.
109 L5 **Iola** Texas U.S.A.
45 L2 **Iolanda di Savoia** Italy
57 B6 **Iolotan'** Turkmenistan
123 M8 **Iona** C Breton I, Nova Scotia
12 B1 **Iona** *isld* Scotland
101 O6 **Iona** Idaho U.S.A.
99 L6 **Iona** Minnesota U.S.A.
98 G6 **Iona** South Dakota U.S.A.
87 B9 **Iona Nat. Park** Angola
47 J1 **Ion Corvin** Romania
102 G3 **Ione** Nevada U.S.A.
100 F4 **Ione** Oregon U.S.A.
100 H1 **Ione** Washington U.S.A.
48 J6 **Ioneşti** Romania
47 H6 **Ionia** *hist reg* Turkey
99 O6 **Ionia** Iowa U.S.A.
94 B3 **Ionia** Michigan U.S.A.
110 C3 **Ionia** Missouri U.S.A.
Ionian Is *see* **Iónioi Nísoi**
43 H10 **Ionian Sea** S Europe
46 D5 **Iónioi Nísoi** *islds* Greece
116 A4 **Ioniveen** *R* Russian Federation
78 K1 **Iori** *R* Azerbaijan/Georgia
46 G8 **Íos** *isld* Greece
52 H3 **Iosser** Russian Federation
99 N7 **Iowa** *state* U.S.A.
99 N7 **Iowa** *R* Iowa U.S.A.
111 C11 **Iowa** Louisiana U.S.A.
99 P8 **Iowa City** Iowa U.S.A.
99 N7 **Iowa Falls** Iowa U.S.A.
109 J2 **Iowa Park** Texas U.S.A.
124 G7 **Ipala** Mexico
83 K9 **Ipalogama** Sri Lanka
130 E5 **Ipameri** Brazil
130 H6 **Ipanema** Brazil
130 H10 **Ipanema** *R* Brazil
130 H8 **Ipanguacu** Brazil
99 Q9 **Ipava** Illinois U.S.A.
48 E2 **Ipel'** *R* Slovakia
116 E2 **Ipewik** *R* Alaska U.S.A.
37 J4 **Iphofen** Germany
128 C3 **Ipiales** Colombia
129 L6 **Ipiau** Brazil
Ipin *see* **Yibin**
128 E4 **Ipiranga** Amazonas Brazil
130 E9 **Ipiranga** Paraná Brazil
128 D5 **Ipixuna** Amazonas Brazil
128 F5 **Ipixuna** *R* Amazonas Brazil
69 E10 **Ipoh** Malaysia
130 J10 **Ipojuca** *R* Brazil
71 C6 **Ipolote B** Palawan Philippines
129 H7 **Iporá** Brazil
130 E9 **Iporanga** Brazil
120 J9 **Ipperwash Prov. Park** Ontario Canada
37 J4 **Ippesheim** Germany
86 D4 **Ippy** Cent Afr Republic
78 A1 **İpsala** Turkey
141 L8 **Ipswich** Queensland Australia
9 H3 **Ipswich** England
127 J2 **Ipswich** Jamaica
95 R4 **Ipswich** Massachusetts U.S.A.
98 G4 **Ipswich** South Dakota U.S.A.
129 K4 **Ipu** Brazil
54 C4 **Iput'** *R* Belarus/Rus Fed
58 B4 **Iqe** China
66 E4 **Iqe** China
128 D8 **Iquique** Chile
128 D4 **Iquitos** Peru
80 F6 **'Ira** Jordan
108 F5 **Iraan** Texas U.S.A.
61 L11 **Irago-misaki** Japan
130 D10 **Irai** Brazil
46 G8 **Iráklia** *isld* Greece
46 G9 **Iráklion** Crete
130 C9 **Irala** Paraguay
77 C4 **Iran** *rep* S W Asia
130 D10 **Irani** *R* Brazil
77 G6 **Irānshahr** Iran
128 F1 **Irapa** Venezuela
124 J7 **Irapuato** Mexico
78 H5 **Iraq** *rep* S W Asia
95 P2 **Irasburg** Vermont U.S.A.
129 H3 **Iratapuru** *R* Brazil
130 E9 **Iratí** Brazil
133 G3 **Irati** Brazil
17 G2 **Irati** *R* Spain
84 E4 **Irāwan** Libya
52 J3 **Irayel'** Russian Federation
Irbenskiy Proliv *see* **Kura Kurk**
80 G3 **Irbid** Jordan
55 D2 **Irbit** *R* Russian Federation
55 D3 **Irbit** Russian Federation
9 G1 **Irby** England
38 K7 **Irdning** Austria
54 C7 **Irdyn'** Ukraine
109 K4 **Iredell** Texas U.S.A.
109 K4 **Ireland** Texas U.S.A.
90 A2 **Ireland I** Bermuda
14 **Ireland, Rep of**
14 E3 **Ireland's Eye** *isld* Ireland
55 C3 **Iren** *R* Russian Federation
98 J6 **Irene** South Dakota U.S.A.
98 K7 **Ireton** Iowa U.S.A.
57 B1 **Irgiz** *R* Kazakhstan
85 F5 **Irhazer Wan Agadez** *V* Niger
85 C2 **Irhil M'Goun** *mt* Morocco
136 G2 **Irian Jaya** *prov* Indonesia
86 D2 **Iriba** Chad
129 G3 **Iricoumé, Serra** *mts* Brazil
71 F4 **Iriga** Philippines
55 C5 **Iriklinskiy** Russian Federation
87 G7 **Iringa** Tanzania
67 H4 **Iriomote-shima** *isld* Japan
125 M2 **Iriona** Honduras
129 H5 **Iriri** *R* Brazil
139 H8 **Irishtown** Tasmania Australia
56 E2 **Irkineyeva** *R* Russian Federation
56 F5 **Irkutsk** Russian Federation
56 F3 **Irkutskaya Oblast'** Russian Federation
118 F6 **Irma** Alberta Canada
99 R4 **Irma** Wisconsin U.S.A.
36 E2 **Irmgarteichen** Germany
112 F3 **Irmo** South Carolina U.S.A.
20 G5 **Irodouer** France
20 A5 **Iroise** *G* France
86 C3 **Iro, L** Chad
138 D4 **Iron Baron** South Australia Australia
120 G6 **Iron Bridge** Ontario Canada
8 D2 **Ironbridge** England
110 J6 **Iron City** Tennessee U.S.A.
121 M8 **Irondale** Ontario Canada
110 F4 **Irondale** Missouri U.S.A.
94 G6 **Irondale** Ohio U.S.A.
138 D4 **Iron Knob** South Australia Australia
99 S4 **Iron Mountain** Michigan U.S.A.
100 A7 **Iron Mt** Oregon U.S.A.
103 L4 **Iron Mt** Utah U.S.A.
98 G5 **Iron Nation** South Dakota U.S.A.
141 G2 **Iron Range** Queensland Australia
99 S6 **Iron Ridge** Wisconsin U.S.A.
99 S3 **Iron River** Michigan U.S.A.
99 P3 **Iron River** Wisconsin U.S.A.
94 B2 **Irons** Michigan U.S.A.
100 H5 **Ironside** Oregon U.S.A.
103 L4 **Iron Sp** Utah U.S.A.
94 B1 **Ironton** Michigan U.S.A.
110 F4 **Ironton** Missouri U.S.A.
94 E8 **Ironton** Ohio U.S.A.
99 Q3 **Ironwood** Michigan U.S.A.
99 T9 **Iroquois** *R* Illinois U.S.A.
98 J5 **Iroquois** South Dakota U.S.A.
120 K4 **Iroquois Falls** Ontario Canada
71 G4 **Irosin** Philippines
61 M11 **Irō zaki** *C* Japan
45 R8 **Irpinia** Italy
68 B4 **Irrawaddy** *prov* Burma
68 B5 **Irrawaddy** *R* Burma
68 B5 **Irrawaddy, Mouths of** Burma
36 B4 **Irrel** Germany
118 D7 **Irricana** Alberta Canada
85 D5 **Irrigi** *reg* Mali/Mauritania
56 D3 **Irsha** Russian Federation
48 H2 **Irshava** Ukraine
52 G4 **Irta** Russian Federation
13 F3 **Irthing, R** England
55 D3 **Irtyash, Oz** *L* Russian Federation
55 E2 **Irtysh** *R* Russian Federation
55 F4 **Irtysh** Russian Federation
55 G4 **Irtyshsk** Kazakhstan
86 E5 **Irumu** Zaire
17 F1 **Irún** Spain
17 F2 **Irurzun** Spain
18 D10 **Irurzun** Spain
128 E8 **Iruya** Argentina
Irves Šaurums *see* **Kura Kurk**
118 G9 **Irvine** Alberta Canada
15 D5 **Irvine** *R* Scotland
15 D5 **Irvine** Scotland
110 N4 **Irvine** Kentucky U.S.A.
141 H3 **Irvinebank** Queensland Australia
14 D2 **Irvinestown** N Ireland
107 O2 **Irving** Kansas U.S.A.
109 N9 **Irving** Texas U.S.A.
143 F7 **Irving, Mt** W Australia Australia
110 K4 **Irvington** Kentucky U.S.A.
95 L9 **Irvington** Virginia U.S.A.
94 J6 **Irvona** Pennsylvania U.S.A.
13 F6 **Irwell, R** England
143 B8 **Irwin** W Australia Australia
101 O6 **Irwin** Idaho U.S.A.
99 L8 **Irwin** Iowa U.S.A.
98 D7 **Irwin** Nebraska U.S.A.
112 D5 **Irwinton** Georgia U.S.A.
138 F5 **Irymple** Victoria Australia
141 J6 **Isaac** *R* Queensland Australia
117 N9 **Isaac L** British Columbia Canada
123 L8 **Isaacs Hbr** Nova Scotia Canada
17 G2 **Isaba** Spain
107 M4 **Isabel** Kansas U.S.A.
98 E4 **Isabel** South Dakota U.S.A.
71 E7 **Isabela** Philippines
71 F5 **Isabela** Negros Philippines
127 L5 **Isabela** Puerto Rico
126 D3 **Isabela de Sagua** Cuba
128 A8 **Isabela, Isla** Galapagos Is
125 M3 **Isabelia, Cord** *ra* Nicaragua
119 Q8 **Isabella** Manitoba Canada
102 F6 **Isabella** California U.S.A.
99 P2 **Isabella** Minnesota U.S.A.
142 F5 **Isabella, L** W Australia Australia
48 L5 **Isaccea** Romania
147 N11 **Isachenko, Ostrov** *isld* Russian Federation
114 J2 **Isachsen** Northwest Territories Canada
28 R8 **Isafjardhardjup** *inlet* Iceland
28 R8 **Isafjördhur** Iceland
60 D13 **Isahaya** Japan
52 F3 **Isakogorka** Russian Federation
48 H6 **Işalniţat** Romania
87 H12 **Isalo, Parc National de L'** *nat park* Madagascar
86 D5 **Isangi** Zaire
37 N7 **Isar** *R* Germany
42 D2 **Isarco** *R* Italy
46 E7 **Isari** Greece
41 O2 **Isar Tal** Germany
111 J7 **Isbell** Alabama U.S.A.
22 C2 **Isbergues** France
15 G1 **Isbister** Scotland
40 C1 **Isches** France
41 M3 **Ischgl** Austria
45 P8 **Ischia** Italy
142 F3 **Isdell,R** W Australia Australia
21 P6 **Isdes** France
59 L5 **Ise** Japan
28 H5 **Isefjord** *inlet* Denmark
41 O3 **Isel Berg** *mt* Austria
81 H14 **Iselin Seamount** Southern Oc
36 D3 **Isenburg** Germany
33 N8 **Isenbüttel** Germany
33 N7 **Isenhagen** Germany
28 C4 **Isenvad** Denmark
42 C3 **Iseo** Italy
42 C3 **Iseo, L. d'** Italy
19 O14 **Isère** *R* France
19 P14 **Isère** *dept* France
32 G10 **Iserlohn** Germany
32 L8 **Isernhagen** Germany
43 F7 **Isernia** Italy
61 N9 **Isesaki** Japan
61 K11 **Ise shima Nat. Park** Japan
55 E3 **Isetskoye** Russian Federation
61 K11 **Ise-wan** *B* Japan
85 E7 **Iseyin** Nigeria
Isfahan *see* **Eşfahān**
57 E5 **Isfana** Kirghizia
57 F4 **Isfara** Tajikistan
80 D3 **Isfiya** Israel
52 J4 **Isherim, Gora** *mt* Russian Federation
128 G3 **Isherton** Guyana
88 C7 **Ishiba Ngandu** Zambia
67 H4 **Ishigaki** Japan
67 H4 **Ishigaki-shima** *isld* Japan
61 K9 **Ishika** *prefect* Japan
60 P2 **Ishikari** Japan
60 R2 **Ishikari dake** *mt* Japan
59 M3 **Ishikari-wan** *B* Japan
55 E5 **Ishim** *R* Kazakhstan/Rus Fed
55 E3 **Ishim** Russian Federation
55 C4 **Ishimbay** Russian Federation
55 F3 **Ishimskaya Step** *steppe* Russian Federation
55 E5 **Ishimskoye** Kazakhstan
59 M4 **Ishinomaki** Japan
60 G12 **Ishizuchi-san** *mt* Japan
21 H4 **Isigny-le-Buat** France
21 H3 **Isigny sur Mer** Calvados France
47 J4 **Işıklar Dağı** *mts* Turkey
86 G6 **Isiolo** Kenya
87 F11 **Isipingo Bch** S Africa
86 E5 **Isiro** Zaire
141 G6 **Isisford** Queensland Australia
86 G1 **Is, Jebel** *mt* Sudan
55 E3 **Iska** *R* Russian Federation
80 D5 **Iskāka** Jordan
57 E4 **Iskander** Uzbekistan
47 J8 **İskandil Burun** *C* Turkey
78 F3 **İskenderun** Turkey
78 E1 **İskilip** Turkey
57 G4 **Iski-Naukat** Kirghizia
56 B4 **Iskitim** Russian Federation
46 G1 **Iskŭr** *R* Bulgaria
46 F2 **Iskŭr, Yazovir** *res* Bulgaria
117 H7 **Iskut** *R* British Columbia Canada
117 J7 **Iskut** British Columbia Canada
119 O3 **Iskwatam L** Saskatchewan Canada
15 E4 **Isla** *R* Scotland
78 F3 **Islâhiye** Turkey
74 E2 **Islamabad** Pakistan
113 G13 **Islamorada** Florida U.S.A.
117 N5 **Island** *R* Northwest Territories Canada
110 J4 **Island** Kentucky U.S.A.
71 D6 **Island B** Palawan Philippines
100 H4 **Island City** Oregon U.S.A.
120 J3 **Island Falls** Ontario Canada
119 P3 **Island Falls** Saskatchewan Canada
95 S7 **Island Falls** Maine U.S.A.
141 K5 **Island Hd** Queensland Australia
95 N7 **Island Heights** New Jersey U.S.A.
115 K7 **Island L** Manitoba Canada
120 K7 **Island L** Ontario Canada
138 D4 **Island Lagoon** South Australia Australia
99 W3 **Island Lake** Ontario Canada
100 B9 **Island Mountain** California U.S.A.
101 O5 **Island Park** Idaho U.S.A.
123 Q5 **Island Pond** *L* Newfoundland Canada
95 Q2 **Island Pond** Vermont U.S.A.
143 B9 **Island Pt** W Australia Australia
123 O4 **Islands, Bay of** Newfoundland Canada
145 E1 **Islands, Bay of** New Zealand
16 B2 **Islas Cíes** Spain
127 M5 **Isla Verde** *airport* Puerto Rico
118 G5 **Islay** Alberta Canada
15 B5 **Islay** *isld* Scotland
18 F7 **Isle** *R* France
99 N3 **Isle** Minnesota U.S.A.
21 P3 **Isle-Adam,l'** France
123 O6 **Isle aux Morts** Newfoundland Canada
95 T2 **Isleboro** Maine U.S.A.
18 F9 **Isle en Dodon, L'** France
18 F9 **Isle Jourdain, L'** Gers France
18 F6 **Isle Jourdain, L'** Vienne France
118 H4 **Isle, Lac des** Saskatchewan Canada
122 A5 **Isle Maligne** Quebec Canada
112 F6 **Isle of Hope** Georgia U.S.A.
15 G2 **Isle of Noss** Scotland
12 D4 **Isle of Whithorn** Scotland
99 S1 **Isle Royale** Michigan U.S.A.
22 G5 **Isles-sur-Suippes** France
18 H5 **Isle-sur-Serein, L'** France
106 D7 **Isleta** New Mexico U.S.A.
102 C3 **Isleton** California U.S.A.
122 C5 **Isle Verte** Quebec Canada
9 E4 **Islip** England
127 N3 **Islote Pt** Trinidad
128 E7 **Isluga** *vol* Chile
133 D1 **Isluga** *mt* Chile
131 F4 **Ismael Cortinas** Uruguay
84 J3 **Ismâ'ilîya** Egypt
37 M7 **Ismaning** Germany
98 B3 **Ismay** Montana U.S.A.
78 A2 **Ismir Körfezi** Turkey
84 J4 **Isna** Egypt
87 H12 **Isoanala** Madagascar
29 J9 **Isojoki** Finland
87 F8 **Isoka** Zambia
29 J8 **Isokyrö** Finland
41 O7 **Isola** Italy
111 F8 **Isola** Mississippi U.S.A.
45 P6 **Isola d. Liri** Italy
45 M5 **Isola Farnese** Italy
87 H12 **Isola, Massif de L'** *mts* Madagascar
45 K1 **Isola Rizza** Italy
20 C6 **Isole** *R* France
110 L5 **Isoline** Tennessee U.S.A.
45 J1 **Isorella** Italy
29 N6 **Iso-syöte** *mt* Finland
78 C3 **İsparta** Turkey
78 C3 **İsparta** *R* Turkey
47 M10 **Ispartakula** Turkey
47 H1 **Isperikh** Bulgaria
78 H1 **İspir** Turkey
80 **Israel** *state* S W Asia
143 E10 **Israelite B** W Australia Australia
20 H6 **Issé** France
28 F4 **Issehoved** *C* Denmark
143 A8 **Isseka** W Australia Australia
25 F5 **Isselburg** Germany
85 C7 **Issia** Ivory Coast
71 H4 **Issimu** Sulawesi Indonesia
18 H7 **Issoire** France
19 Q18 **Issole** *R* France
21 O8 **Issoudun** France
25 F5 **Issum** Germany
57 H4 **Issyk-Kul'** Kirghizia
57 H4 **Issyk-Kul, Ozero** *L* Kirghizia
57 J4 **Issyk-Kul'skaya Oblast'** Kirghizia
77 L2 **Istalif** Afghanistan
47 M10 **İstanbul** Turkey
120 J7 **Isthmus Bay** Ontario Canada
46 F6 **Istiaía** Greece
128 C2 **Istmina** Colombia
42 F3 **Istra** *pen* Croatia
54 H1 **Istra** Russian Federation
19 N18 **Istres** France
47 Q14 **Ístrios** Rhodes Greece
61 M11 **Isu hantō** *pen* Japan
55 C5 **Isyangulovo** Russian Federation
130 B9 **Itá** Paraguay
129 L6 **Itabaiana** Brazil
130 H7 **Itabapoana** Brazil
130 E8 **Itaberá** Brazil
130 E5 **Itaberaí** Brazil
129 K7 **Itabira** Brazil
130 G7 **Itabirito** Brazil
128 F4 **Itaboca** Brazil
129 L6 **Itabuna** Brazil
129 J5 **Itacajá** Brazil
129 H5 **Itacajuna** *R* Brazil
130 G4 **Itacarambi** Brazil
129 L6 **Itacaré** Brazil
128 G4 **Itacoatiara** Brazil
128 D5 **Itacuai** *R* Brazil
130 C9 **Itacurubí del Rosario** Paraguay
130 H6 **Itaguaçu** Brazil
130 D8 **Itaguaje** Brazil
129 J6 **Itaguari** *R* Brazil
130 E8 **Itaí** Brazil
130 E10 **Itaiópolis** Brazil
129 G4 **Itaituba** Brazil
130 E10 **Itajai Acú, R** Brazil
129 J8 **Itajuba** Brazil
130 H4 **Itajuipe** Brazil
61 O10 **Itako** Japan
Itala *see* **Cadale**
42 **Italy** *rep* S Europe
109 L3 **Italy** Texas U.S.A.
130 G5 **Itamarandiba** Brazil
129 J4 **Itamatare** Brazil
130 H6 **Itambacuri** Brazil
129 K7 **Itambé** Brazil
130 G6 **Itambe, P. de** *mt* Brazil
60 J11 **Itami** Japan
130 F9 **Itanhaém** Brazil
129 K7 **Itanhém** *R* Brazil
129 H3 **Itany** *R* Suriname
130 H5 **Itaobim** Brazil
129 J6 **Itapaci** Brazil
130 E6 **Itapajipe** Brazil
129 L5 **Itaparica, Barragem de** *dam* Brazil
130 H4 **Itapebi** Brazil
130 F7 **Itapecerica** Brazil
129 K4 **Itapecuru Mirim** Brazil
130 H7 **Itapemirim** Brazil
129 K8 **Itaperuna** Brazil
129 K7 **Itapetinga** Brazil
129 J8 **Itapetininga** Brazil
129 J8 **Itapeva** Brazil
129 G3 **Itapi** *R* Brazil
129 K5 **Itapicura** *R* Brazil
129 J5 **Itapicuru, Serra do** *mts* Brazil
128 F5 **Itapinima** Brazil
129 L4 **Itapipoca** Brazil
128 G4 **Itapira** Brazil
130 E10 **Itapocu, R** Brazil
130 E7 **Itápolis** Brazil
130 H9 **Itaporanga** Brazil
130 C10 **Itapuá** *reg* Paraguay
129 H7 **Itapuranga** Brazil
131 G2 **Itaqui** Brazil
133 F2 **Itaquyry** Paraguay
129 J8 **Itararé** Brazil
74 G7 **Itarsi** India
130 D6 **Itarumã** Brazil
109 K3 **Itasca** Texas U.S.A.
99 L2 **Itasca State Park** Minnesota U.S.A.
131 A6 **Itata, R** Chile
130 F8 **Itatiba** Brazil
131 F2 **Itati, L** Argentina
130 E8 **Itatinga** Brazil
128 F5 **Itatuba** Brazil
130 E5 **Itauçu** Brazil
130 G7 **Itaúna** Brazil
129 L7 **Itaúnas** Brazil
130 H6 **Itaúnas** Brazil
9 E5 **Itchin, R** England
55 F4 **Itemgen, Oz** *L* Kazakhstan
Ithaca *isld* Greece *see* **Itháki** *isld*
94 C3 **Ithaca** Michigan U.S.A.
95 L4 **Ithaca** New York U.S.A.
46 D6 **Itháki** *isld* Greece
8 C3 **Ithon, R** Wales
115 O4 **Itilleq** Greenland
86 D5 **Itimbiri** *R* Zaire
130 H5 **Itinga** Brazil
129 H7 **Itiquira** Brazil
129 K6 **Itiúba, Serra de** *mts* Brazil
116 M2 **Itkillik** *R* Alaska U.S.A.
61 N11 **Itō** Japan
61 L8 **Itoigawa** Japan
86 D6 **Itoko** Zaire
61 P14 **Itoman** Okinawa
21 N4 **Iton** *R* France
45 P7 **Itri** Italy
79 A9 **Itsa** Egypt
111 F8 **Itta Bena** Mississippi U.S.A.
25 E6 **Ittervoort** Netherlands
43 B8 **Ittiri** Sardinia
Ittoqqortoormiit *see* **Scoresbysund**
130 F8 **Itu** Brazil
131 G2 **Itú** *R* Brazil
129 J7 **Ituiutaba** Brazil
88 A3 **Itula** Zaire
88 E5 **Itumba** Tanzania
129 J7 **Itumbiara** Brazil
130 E6 **Itumbiara, Barragem** *dam* Brazil
119 O7 **Ituna** Saskatchewan Canada
128 G2 **Ituni** Guyana
130 E10 **Ituporanga** Brazil
128 E8 **Iturbe** Argentina
130 C10 **Iturbe** Paraguay
59 N3 **Iturup, Ostrov** *isld* Russian Federation
130 F7 **Ituverava** Brazil
130 C10 **Ituzalngo** Argentina
37 K3 **Itz** *R* Germany
32 L5 **Itzehoe** Germany
32 K5 **Itzwärden** Germany
88 D6 **Iufira** *R* Malawi
110 H3 **Iuka** Illinois U.S.A.
107 M4 **Iuka** Kansas U.S.A.
110 H7 **Iuka** Mississippi U.S.A.
130 H7 **Iúna** Brazil
112 E3 **Iva** South Carolina U.S.A.
129 H8 **Ivaí** *R* Brazil
29 N3 **Ivalo** Finland
29 N3 **Ivalojoki** *R* Finland
48 E7 **Ivančići** Bosnia-Herzegovina
52 C5 **Ivangorod** Russian Federation
46 D2 **Ivangrad** Montenegro Yugoslavia
139 G5 **Ivanhoe** New South Wales Australia
142 G3 **Ivanhoe** W Australia Australia
120 H4 **Ivanhoe** *R* Ontario Canada
98 K5 **Ivanhoe** Minnesota U.S.A.
94 G10 **Ivanhoe** Virginia U.S.A.
54 M1 **Ivanishchi** Russian Federation
48 F7 **Ivanjica** Serbia Yugoslavia
53 B9 **Ivano-Frankovsk** Ukraine
48 L1 **Ivanopol'** Ukraine
55 B4 **Ivanovka** Russian Federation
55 G3 **Ivanovka** Omskaya obl Russian Federation
52 F6 **Ivanovo** Russian Federation
54 J1 **Ivanteyvka** Russian Federation
53 C7 **Ivatsevichi** Belarus
47 H3 **Ivaylovgrad** Bulgaria
55 D1 **Ivdel'** Russian Federation
33 R5 **Ivenack** Germany
99 S10 **Ivesdale** Illinois U.S.A.
17 H8 **Ivi, C** Algeria
86 B5 **Ivindo** *R* Gabon
9 F4 **Ivinghoe** England
129 H8 **Ivinheima** *R* Brazil
52 E4 **Ivinskiy Razliv, Vodokhranilishche** *res* Russian Federation
116 N2 **Ivishak** *R* Alaska U.S.A.
115 P5 **Ivittuut** Greenland
Iviza *see* **Ibiza**
95 L10 **Ivor** Virginia U.S.A.
85 C7 **Ivory Coast** *rep* W Africa
27 G15 **Ivösjön** Sweden
54 F3 **Ivot** Russian Federation
42 B3 **Ivrea** Italy
47 J5 **İvrindi** Turkey
21 N4 **Ivry-la-Bataille** France
115 M5 **Ivugivik** Quebec Canada
116 S2 **Ivvavik Park** Yukon Canada
8 C7 **Ivybridge** England
94 F8 **Ivydale** West Virginia U.S.A.
61 O7 **Iwadeyama** Japan
61 O7 **Iwai-gawa** *R* Japan
61 P6 **Iwaizumi** Japan
61 O5 **Iwaki** *R* Japan
61 O9 **Iwaki** Japan
61 O5 **Iwaki-san** *mt* Japan
59 K5 **Iwakuni** Japan
60 P2 **Iwamizawa** Japan
70 D3 **Iwan** *R* Kalimantan
60 O3 **Iwanai** Japan
61 O7 **Iwanuma** Japan
61 O9 **Iwase** Japan
61 M9 **Iwasuge-yama** *mt* Japan
61 L11 **Iwata** Japan
61 P6 **Iwate** Japan
60 H11 **Iwaya** Japan
85 E7 **Iwo** Nigeria
Iwo Jima *see* **Iō-Jima**
140 C6 **Iwupataka** N Terr Australia
22 E3 **Iwuy** France
128 E6 **Ixiamas** Bolivia
125 K8 **Ixtaccihuatl** *vol* Mexico
125 M9 **Ixtepec, Ciudad** Mexico
124 H8 **Ixtlahuacán** Mexico
124 G7 **Ixtlán del Río** Mexico
9 G3 **Ixworth** England
56 F4 **Iya** *R* Russian Federation
55 E3 **Iyevlevo** Russian Federation
60 G12 **Iyomishima** Japan
60 F12 **Iyo-nada** *sea* Japan
56 C4 **Iyus** Russian Federation
48 J3 **Iza** *R* Romania
125 P10 **Izabal, L. de** Guatemala
17 G2 **Izalzu** Spain
116 F6 **Izaviknek** *R* Alaska U.S.A.
57 K5 **Izbaskan** Uzbekistan
31 O5 **Izbica** Poland
54 E1 **Izdeshkovo** Russian Federation
22 E2 **Izegem** Belgium
19 O14 **Izeron** France
52 H6 **Izhevsk** Russian Federation
52 H2 **Izhma** Russian Federation
53 C10 **Izmail** Ukraine
78 A2 **Izmir** Turkey
Izmit *see* **Kocaeli**
78 C1 **Izmit** Turkey
47 N11 **İzmit Körfezi** *B* Turkey
16 E7 **Iznajar** Spain
16 E7 **Iznalloz** Spain
78 B1 **Iznik** Turkey
78 B1 **Iznik Gölü** Turkey
53 F10 **Izobil'nyy** Russian Federation
128 F7 **Izozog, Bañados de** Bolivia
79 G6 **Izra'** Syria
48 E4 **Izsák** Hungary
60 C11 **Izuhara** Japan
60 D13 **Izumi** Japan
61 O7 **Izumi** Japan
60 J11 **Izumi-ōtsu** Japan
60 F10 **Izumo** Japan
61 M8 **Izumozaki** Japan
55 D3 **Izumrud** Russian Federation
55 F6 **Izumrudnyy** Kazakhstan
57 F1 **Izumrudnyy** Kazakhstan
61 N11 **Izu-shotō** *islds* Japan
50 H1 **Izvestiy Tsentral'nogo Ispolnitel'nogo Komiteta, Ostrova** *isld* Russian Federation
48 K3 **Izvoru Muntelui, Lacul** *L* Romania
57 A2 **Izyndy** Kazakhstan
54 J7 **Izyum** Ukraine

J

29 M10 **Jaala** Finland
29 L5 **Jaatila** Finland
77 E2 **Jaba** *R* Iran
80 G1 **Jabā** Syria
77 C7 **Jabal az Zannah** U.A.E.
16 E6 **Jabalón** *R* Spain
74 H7 **Jabalpur** India
22 E1 **Jabbeke** Belgium
33 R5 **Jabel** Germany
140 C2 **Jabiru** N Terr Australia
79 F3 **Jablah** Syria
46 D3 **Jablanica** Albania
46 E2 **Jablanica** *R* Serbia Yugoslavia
31 J5 **Jablonec nad Nisou** Czech Rep
31 K7 **Jablonica** Slovakia
31 L2 **Jabłonowo** Poland
31 L6 **Jablunkov** Czech Rep
129 M5 **Jaboatão** Brazil
129 J8 **Jaboticabal** Brazil
69 G13 **Jabung, Tanjung** *C* Sumatra
128 F5 **Jaburu** Brazil
17 G2 **Jaca** Spain
130 B6 **Jacadigo** *L* Brazil
130 G4 **Jacaraci** Brazil
129 K6 **Jacaré** *R* Brazil
129 G5 **Jacareacanga** Brazil
130 F8 **Jacareí** Brazil
128 G5 **Jacaretinga** Brazil
130 E8 **Jacarezinho** Brazil
133 D4 **Jachal** Argentina
37 O3 **Jáchymov** Czech Rep
130 H5 **Jacinto** Brazil
109 M5 **Jacinto, S** *R* Texas U.S.A.
128 F5 **Jaciparaná** Brazil
120 D4 **Jackfish** Ontario Canada
118 J5 **Jackfish L** Saskatchewan Canada
117 R6 **Jackfish River** Alberta Canada
119 U7 **Jackhead Harbour** Manitoba Canada
115 N6 **Jack Lane B** Labrador, Nfld Canada
95 R1 **Jackman** Maine U.S.A.
100 E1 **Jack Mt** Washington U.S.A.
120 C3 **Jackpine** Ontario Canada
141 G3 **Jack R** Queensland Australia
112 C1 **Jacksboro** Tennessee U.S.A.
109 J2 **Jacksboro** Texas U.S.A.
94 K6 **Jacks Mt** Pennsylvania U.S.A.
141 J7 **Jackson** Queensland Australia
111 J10 **Jackson** Alabama U.S.A.
102 D3 **Jackson** California U.S.A.
112 D4 **Jackson** Georgia U.S.A.
94 D9 **Jackson** Kentucky U.S.A.
111 E11 **Jackson** Louisiana U.S.A.
111 F9 **Jackson** Mississippi U.S.A.
110 G4 **Jackson** Missouri U.S.A.
101 M4 **Jackson** Montana U.S.A.
112 K1 **Jackson** North Carolina U.S.A.
94 E7 **Jackson** Ohio U.S.A.
112 F4 **Jackson** South Carolina U.S.A.
110 H6 **Jackson** Tennessee U.S.A.
94 H8 **Jackson** *R* Virginia U.S.A.
101 P6 **Jackson** Wyoming U.S.A.
117 L10 **Jackson Bay** British Columbia Canada
144 B5 **Jackson Bay** New Zealand
145 E4 **Jackson, C** New Zealand
110 M1 **Jackson Cen** Ohio U.S.A.
106 B4 **Jackson Gulch Res** Colorado U.S.A.
113 C7 **Jackson, L** Florida U.S.A.
112 D4 **Jackson L** Georgia U.S.A.
101 P6 **Jackson L** Wyoming U.S.A.
143 C9 **Jackson, Mt** W Australia Australia
100 G8 **Jackson Mts** Nevada U.S.A.
141 F8 **Jackson Oil Field** Queensland Australia
144 A6 **Jackson Peaks** New Zealand
99 T5 **Jacksonport** Wisconsin U.S.A.
111 G9 **Jackson Prairie** Mississippi U.S.A.
106 F1 **Jackson Res** Colorado U.S.A.
144 C5 **Jacksons** New Zealand
123 Q4 **Jackson's Arm** Newfoundland Canada
111 L8 **Jacksonville** Alabama U.S.A.
110 D7 **Jacksonville** Arkansas U.S.A.
113 F7 **Jacksonville** Florida U.S.A.
99 Q10 **Jacksonville** Illinois U.S.A.
110 D2 **Jacksonville** Missouri U.S.A.
112 K3 **Jacksonville** North Carolina U.S.A.
100 C7 **Jacksonville** Oregon U.S.A.
109 M4 **Jacksonville** Texas U.S.A.
113 F7 **Jacksonville Beach** Florida U.S.A.
127 H5 **Jacmel** Haiti
124 G4 **Jaco** Mexico
74 C4 **Jacobabad** Pakistan
129 K6 **Jacobina** Brazil
103 M5 **Jacob L** Arizona U.S.A.
80 E5 **Jacob's Well** Jordan
124 H8 **Jacona** Mexico
121 T5 **Jacques Cartier, L** Quebec Canada
122 G4 **Jacques Cartier, Mt** Quebec Canada
122 F6 **Jacquet R** New Brunswick Canada
130 J9 **Jacú** *R* Brazil
130 F7 **Jacuí** Minas Gerais Brazil
131 H2 **Jacui** *R* Rio Grande do Sul Brazil
131 H2 **Jacui** Rio Grande do Sul Brazil
129 L6 **Jacuípe** *R* Brazil
103 H9 **Jacumba** California U.S.A.
129 H4 **Jacunda** *R* Brazil
129 J4 **Jacundá** Brazil
130 F9 **Jacupiranga** Brazil
129 E4 **Jaçura** Brazil
80 G8 **Jad'a** Jordan
48 E6 **Jadar** *R* Serbia Yugoslavia
32 H6 **Jade** *R* Germany
32 H6 **Jade** Germany
85 C2 **Jadida, El** Morocco
87 E8 **Jadotville** Zaire
31 N3 **Jadów** Poland
17 F4 **Jadraque** Spain
84 E3 **Jādū** Libya
28 H5 **Jægerspris** Denmark
22 F3 **Jaeibise** Belgium
83 J10 **Ja-Ela** Sri Lanka
143 C8 **Jaellan Hill** W Australia Australia
71 E3 **Jaen** Luzon Philippines
16 E7 **Jaén** *prov* Spain
16 E7 **Jaén** Spain
27 A13 **Jaeren** *R* Norway
26 F7 **Jaevsjo** Norway
77 A2 **Ja'farābād** Iran
80 C5 **Jaffa** Israel
138 E6 **Jaffa, C** South Australia Australia
83 K8 **Jaffna** Sri Lanka
75 K9 **Jagdalpur** India
75 J5 **Jagdishpur** India
87 E11 **Jagersfontein** S Africa
84 G4 **Jaghbūb, Al** Libya
116 Q2 **Jago** *R* Alaska U.S.A.
36 H5 **Jagst** *R* Germany
37 J5 **Jagstzell** Germany
74 H9 **Jagtial** India
129 K6 **Jaguaquara** Brazil
131 H4 **Jaguarão** Brazil
131 G2 **Jaguari** *R* Brazil
129 H8 **Jaguariaiva** Brazil
129 L5 **Jaguaribe** *R* Brazil
131 C2 **Jagüe, R** Argentina
126 D3 **Jagüey Grande** Cuba
140 B1 **Jahleel, Pt** N Terr Australia
78 K7 **Jahmah** Iraq
48 E7 **Jahorina** *mt* Bosnia-Herzegovina
77 C5 **Jahrom** Iran
74 G3 **Jaijon** India
75 P6 **Jaintia Hills** India
74 F5 **Jaipur** India
74 D5 **Jaisalmer** India
42 H4 **Jajce** Bosnia-Herzegovina
75 M8 **Jajpur** India
63 **Jakarta** *conurbation* Indonesia
70 L9 **Jakarta** Java
84 G4 **Jakharrah** Libya
26 J5 **Jäkkvik** Sweden
71 N9 **Jako** *isld* Timor
26 S2 **Jakobselv** *R* Norway/Rus Fed
115 O4 **Jakobshavn** Greenland
29 K8 **Jakobstad** Finland
46 E3 **Jakupica** Macedonia
106 G9 **Jal** New Mexico U.S.A.
77 H6 **Jāla** Iran
58 G2 **Jalai Nur** China
77 L2 **Jalalabad** Afghanistan
74 F3 **Jalandhar** India
125 L3 **Jalapa** Nicaragua
125 L8 **Jalapa Enríquez** Mexico
29 K9 **Jalasjärvi** Finland
74 H5 **Jalaun** India
140 C2 **Jalboi** *R* N Terr Australia
130 E7 **Jales** Brazil
75 M8 **Jaleshwar** India
74 F8 **Jalgaon** India
22 K2 **Jalhay** Belgium
78 L6 **Jalibah** Iraq
86 B4 **Jalingo** Nigeria
124 G8 **Jalisco** *state* Mexico
21 J7 **Jallais** France
74 F9 **Jalna** India
17 F3 **Jalón** *R* Spain
Jalo Oasis *see* **Jālu**
74 E6 **Jalor** India
124 H7 **Jalostotitlán** Mexico
124 H7 **Jalpa** Mexico
75 N5 **Jalpaiguri** India
124 K7 **Jalpan** Mexico
77 L2 **Jalrez** Afghanistan
84 G4 **Jālu** Libya
84 G4 **Jālu** *oilfield* Libya
78 K4 **Jalūlā** Iraq
84 G4 **Jālu, Waḩat** *oasis* Libya
77 G2 **Jam** *reg* Iran
128 B4 **Jama** Ecuador
86 H5 **Jamaame** Somalia
126 G4 **Jamaica** Cuba
95 P3 **Jamaica** Vermont U.S.A.
127 K2 **Jamaica** W Indies
126 G5 **Jamaica Chan** Caribbean
27 M13 **Jämaja** Estonia
75 N6 **Jamalpur** Bangladesh
75 M6 **Jamalpur** India
126 A2 **Jamanota** *hill* Aruba W Indies
129 G5 **Jamanxim** *R* Brazil
128 F5 **Jamari** Brazil
66 C2 **Jamati** China
139 K5 **Jamberoo** New South Wales Australia
69 F13 **Jambi** Sumatra
141 K6 **Jambin** Queensland Australia
69 C10 **Jamboaye** *R* Sumatra
70 E1 **Jambongan** *isld* Sabah
122 F4 **Jambon, Pte** Quebec Canada
70 E5 **Jambu** Kalimantan

69 C10 Jambuair, Tanjung C Sumatra
110 C5 James R Missouri U.S.A.
98 H3 James R North Dakota U.S.A.
98 J6 James R South Dakota U.S.A.
115 L7 James B Canada
95 N6 Jamesburg New Jersey U.S.A.
112 K2 James City North Carolina U.S.A.
94 J5 James City Pennsylvania U.S.A.
112 F2 James, L North Carolina U.S.A.
99 N9 Jameson Missouri U.S.A.
115 R3 Jameson Land Greenland
143 G7 Jameson Ra W Australia Australia
99 N10 Jamesport Missouri U.S.A.
113 L12 James Pt Bahamas
140 D5 James R N Terr Australia
95 L9 James R Virginia U.S.A.
140 C6 James Ranges N Terr Australia
146 D4 James Ross I Antarctica
115 K4 James Ross Str Northwest Territories Canada
138 E5 Jamestown South Australia Australia
90 A13 Jamestown St Helena
110 K2 Jamestown Indiana U.S.A.
107 N2 Jamestown Kansas U.S.A.
94 B4 Jamestown Michigan U.S.A.
94 H4 Jamestown New York U.S.A.
98 H3 Jamestown North Dakota U.S.A.
94 D7 Jamestown Ohio U.S.A.
94 G5 Jamestown Pennsylvania U.S.A.
95 Q5 Jamestown Rhode I U.S.A.
112 H4 Jamestown South Carolina U.S.A.
94 C10 Jamestown Tennessee U.S.A.
95 L9 Jamestown Nat. Hist. Site Virginia U.S.A.
95 L4 Jamesville New York U.S.A.
112 L2 Jamesville North Carolina U.S.A.
22 J5 Jametz France
139 H6 Jamieson Victoria Australia
100 H5 Jamieson Oregon U.S.A.
29 K10 Jämijärvi Finland
125 L9 Jamilzepec Mexico
98 G7 Jamison Nebraska U.S.A.
76 B2 Jamkhandi India
74 F9 Jamkhed India
76 D3 Jammalamadugu India
28 C2 Jammerbugt B Denmark
28 F5 Jammerland Bugt B Denmark
74 F2 Jammu Kashmir
Jammu and Kashmir see Kashmir
74 G1 Jammu and Kashmir prov India/Pakistan
74 D7 Jamnagar India
31 J1 Jamno, Jezioro L Poland
22 J4 Jamoigne Belgium
71 K8 Jampea Indonesia
74 D4 Jampur Pakistan
29 L10 Jämsä Finland
29 L10 Jämsänkoski Finland
75 M7 Jamshedpur India
26 F8 Jämtland Sweden
26 H8 Jämtl Sikås Sweden
71 C3 Jamtup, Tg C W Irian
70 E3 Jamuk, G mt Kalimantan
102 H9 Jamul California U.S.A.
75 N6 Jamuna R Bangladesh
128 C3 Jamundí Colombia
75 M5 Janakpur Nepal
129 K7 Janaúba Brazil
129 H3 Janaucu, I Brazil
130 E5 Jandaia Brazil
142 B3 Jandakot dist Perth, W Aust Australia
142 B3 Jandakot, L W Australia Australia
77 D2 Jandaq Iran
28 A5 Janderup Denmark
128 E5 Jandiatuba R Brazil
141 K7 Jandowae Queensland Australia
94 G7 Jane Lew West Virginia U.S.A.
144 B6 Jane Pk New Zealand
100 E9 Janesville California U.S.A.
99 O7 Janesville Iowa U.S.A.
99 N5 Janesville Minnesota U.S.A.
99 R7 Janesville Wisconsin U.S.A.
130 D10 Jangada Brazil
130 C7 Jango Brazil
60 J10 Jango hantō pen Japan
69 G13 Jang, Tanjung C Indonesia
33 S8 Jänickendorf Germany
46 E2 Janjevo Serbia Yugoslavia
89 D6 Jan Kemp S Africa
119 P4 Jan L Saskatchewan Canada
90 H1 Jan Mayen isld Arctic Oc
77 G2 Jannatabad Iran
124 E2 Janos Mexico
48 E4 Jánoshalma Hungary
48 D3 Jánosháza Hungary
37 P5 Janovice nad Uhlavou Czech Rep
33 S5 Janow Germany
31 K3 Janowiec Poland
31 N5 Janów Lubelski Poland
31 O3 Janów Podlaski Poland
119 N7 Jansen Saskatchewan Canada
98 K9 Jansen Nebraska U.S.A.
130 G4 Januária Brazil
21 O5 Janville France
20 H6 Janzé France
130 G5 Jaoquim Felício Brazil
74 F7 Jaora India
61 Japan empire E Asia
59 K3 Japan, Sea of E Asia
29 N9 Jäppilä Finland
128 E4 Japurá Brazil
127 J5 Jarabacoa Dominican Rep
78 F3 Jarābulus Syria
129 J7 Jaraguá Brazil
130 E10 Jaraguá do Sul Brazil
130 C7 Jaraguari Brazil
130 E10 Jaraguá Serra mts Brazil
16 D5 Jaraicejo Spain
16 E4 Jarama R Spain
133 D7 Jaramillo Argentina
16 D4 Jarandilla Spain
129 H4 Jarauçu R Brazil
100 K7 Jarbidge R Idaho U.S.A.
100 K8 Jarbidge Nevada U.S.A.
27 J11 Järbo Sweden
130 G9 Jardim Ceará Brazil
130 C7 Jardim Mato Grosso Brazil
130 H9 Jardim do Seridó Brazil
141 F1 Jardine R Queensland Australia
122 E6 Jardine Brook New Brunswick Canada
141 G1 Jardine River Nat. Park Queensland Australia
126 E4 Jardines de la Reina, Arch. de las islds Cuba
130 E6 Jardinésia Brazil
130 F7 Jardinópolis Brazil
27 H14 Järeda Sweden
27 E11 Jaren Norway
38 N8 Jarenina Slovenia
58 G2 Jargalant Mongolia
21 P6 Jargeau France
129 H3 Jari R Brazil
128 F4 Jari, L Brazil
33 S5 Jarmen Germany
27 J12 Järna Sweden
18 E7 Jarnac France
27 H13 Järnlunden L Sweden
71 F5 Jaro Panay Philippines
31 K4 Jarocin Poland
31 J5 Jaroměř Czech Rep
31 J6 Jaroměřice Czech Rep
126 F4 Jaronu Cuba
31 O5 Jaroslaw Poland
106 E4 Jaroso Colorado U.S.A.
26 F8 Järpen Sweden
80 F8 Jarra R Jordan
94 K10 Jarratt Virginia U.S.A.
26 K5 Jarre mt Sweden
109 K5 Jarrell Texas U.S.A.
68 F3 Jarres, Plaine des Laos
118 F6 Jarrow Alberta Canada
13 G4 Jarrow England
128 F6 Jaru Brazil
65 E2 Jarud Qi China
52 C5 Järva-Jaani Estonia
118 D4 Jarvie Alberta Canada
134 B3 Jarvis I Pacific Oc
26 H10 Järvsö Sweden
21 K6 Jarzé France
48 F5 Jaša Tomic Serbia Yugoslavia
74 D7 Jasdan India
33 T8 Jasdorf Germany
85 E7 Jasikan Ghana
77 E7 Jāsk Iran
31 N6 Jasło Poland
119 O7 Jasmin Saskatchewan Canada
30 H1 Jasmund pen Germany
133 E8 Jason Is Falkland Is
146 D4 Jason Pen Antarctica
110 J2 Jasonville Indiana U.S.A.
117 O9 Jasper Alberta Canada
121 P8 Jasper Ontario Canada
111 J8 Jasper Alabama U.S.A.
110 C5 Jasper Arkansas U.S.A.
106 D4 Jasper Colorado U.S.A.
113 E7 Jasper Florida U.S.A.
111 M7 Jasper Georgia U.S.A.
110 K3 Jasper Indiana U.S.A.
94 C5 Jasper Michigan U.S.A.
98 K6 Jasper Minnesota U.S.A.
110 B4 Jasper Missouri U.S.A.
94 K4 Jasper New York U.S.A.
112 B2 Jasper Tennessee U.S.A.
111 C11 Jasper Texas U.S.A.
117 O9 Jasper Nat. Park Alberta Canada
78 K5 Jassan Iraq
Jassy see Iasi
31 L1 Jastarnia Poland
46 E1 Jastrebac mt Serbia Yugoslavia
31 K2 Jastrowie Poland
48 F3 Jászapáti Hungary
48 F3 Jászarokszállás Hungary
48 F3 Jászberény Hungary
48 F3 Jászfényszaru Hungary
48 F3 Jászladány Hungary
129 H7 Jataí Brazil
128 G4 Jatapu R Brazil
76 B2 Jath India
70 M9 Jatibarang Java
126 E4 Jatibonico Cuba
17 G6 Játiva Spain
129 H4 Jatobá Brazil
80 D4 Jatt Israel
128 F5 Jatuarana Brazil
33 T5 Jatzke Germany
33 T5 Jatznick Germany
128 F4 Jaú R Brazil
129 J8 Jaú Brazil
128 F3 Jauaperi R Brazil
22 H2 Jauche Belgium
126 G4 Jauco Cuba
20 D4 Jaudy R France
128 C6 Jauja Peru
21 L8 Jaulnay France
128 G5 Jauna R Brazil
21 L8 Jaunay Clan France
52 B6 Jaunjelgava Latvia
52 C6 Jaunpiebalga Latvia
75 K6 Jaunpur India
38 L8 Jauntal V Austria
129 G7 Jauru R Brazil
130 D6 Jauru, R Brazil
22 D5 Jaux France
Java isld see Jawa
76 D4 Javadi Hills India
129 J6 Javaés, Serra dos mts Brazil
17 G4 Javalambre, Sierra de mts Spain
128 D4 Javari R Brazil/Peru
70 M8 Java Sea Indonesia
136 D4 Java Trench Indian Oc
17 H6 Jávea Spain
Javhlant see Uliastay
133 C7 Javier B Chile
48 E6 Javor mts Bosnia-Herzegovina
48 E2 Javoria mt Slovakia
38 K9 Javornik Slovenia
48 E1 Javorniky mt Czech Rep/Slovakia
26 M6 Jävre Sweden
21 K5 Javron-les-Chapelles France
70 Jawa isld Indonesia
80 G6 Jawa Jordan
79 H2 Jawbān Bayk Syria
86 J5 Jawhar Somalia
31 J4 Jawor Poland
31 L5 Jaworzno Poland
107 Q5 Jay Oklahoma U.S.A.
75 N5 Jayanti India
136 H2 Jaya Pk mt W Irian
136 J2 Jayapura W Irian
98 B7 Jay Em Wyoming U.S.A.
33 P7 Jayenitz Germany
75 K9 Jaypur India
79 G5 Jayrūd Syria
9 H4 Jaywick Sands England
78 H4 Jazirah, Al Iraq
124 J5 Jazminal Mexico
77 F6 Jaz Murian, Hamun-e L Iran
79 F4 Jbail Lebanon
79 F4 Jdaidet Ghazir Lebanon
85 B3 Jdiriya Western Sahara
103 J6 Jean Nevada U.S.A.
109 J2 Jean Texas U.S.A.
111 E12 Jeanerette Louisiana U.S.A.
122 E1 Jean L Quebec Canada
111 G12 Jean Lafitte Nat. Hist. Park Louisiana U.S.A.
117 N5 Jean Marie River Northwest Territories Canada
6 M6 Jeanne oil rig North Sea
94 H6 Jeannette Pennsylvania U.S.A.
127 H5 Jean Rabel Haiti
13 G5 Jeater Houses England
77 F5 Jebāl Bārez, Kūh-e mts Iran
85 E7 Jebba Nigeria
80 F1 Jebel Lebanon
86 E2 Jebel Abyad Plateau Sudan
16 D9 Jebha Morocco
28 B3 Jebjerg Denmark
88 E8 Jeci mt Mozambique
119 P7 Jedburgh Saskatchewan Canada
13 F2 Jedburgh Scotland
Jedda see Jiddah
94 E3 Jeddo Michigan U.S.A.
43 C12 Jedeida Tunisia
13 F3 Jedfoot Br Scotland
31 M5 Jędrzejów Poland
31 N2 Jedwabne Poland
117 H9 Jedway British Columbia Canada
29 M4 Jeesiö Finland
33 O6 Jeetze R Germany
33 O7 Jeetze Germany
99 L5 Jeffers Minnesota U.S.A.
106 E2 Jefferson Colorado U.S.A.
112 D3 Jefferson Georgia U.S.A.
94 K7 Jefferson Maryland U.S.A.
94 G5 Jefferson Ohio U.S.A.
107 N5 Jefferson Oklahoma U.S.A.
100 C5 Jefferson Oregon U.S.A.
98 K7 Jefferson South Dakota U.S.A.
111 B9 Jefferson Texas U.S.A.
99 S6 Jefferson Wisconsin U.S.A.
110 D3 Jefferson City Missouri U.S.A.
101 N3 Jefferson City Montana U.S.A.
112 D1 Jefferson City Tennessee U.S.A.
101 O4 Jefferson Island Montana U.S.A.
100 D5 Jefferson, Mt Oregon U.S.A.
94 B8 Jeffersontown Kentucky U.S.A.
110 L3 Jeffersontown Kentucky U.S.A.
112 D5 Jeffersonville Georgia U.S.A.
94 B8 Jeffersonville Indiana U.S.A.
95 N5 Jeffersonville New York U.S.A.
94 D7 Jeffersonville Ohio U.S.A.
95 P2 Jeffersonville Vermont U.S.A.
101 S7 Jeffrey City Wyoming U.S.A.
71 C3 Jef Lio W Irian
85 E6 Jega Nigeria
28 B3 Jegindø isld Denmark
18 F9 Jegun France
77 G4 Jehīle Pūzak L Iran
28 B7 Jejsing Denmark
130 C9 Jejui Guazú, R Paraguay
52 C6 Jēkabpils Latvia
112 F6 Jekyll I Georgia U.S.A.
86 H4 Jeldēsa Ethiopia
31 J5 Jelenia Góra Poland
52 B6 Jelgava Latvia
120 C3 Jellicoe Ontario Canada
28 C5 Jelling Denmark
102 B1 Jelly California U.S.A.
31 L5 Jełowa Poland
27 E12 Jelöy isld Norway
28 C6 Jels Denmark
27 B12 Jelsa Norway
48 F2 Jelšava Slovakia
69 G11 Jemaja Indonesia
22 F3 Jemappes Belgium
70 O10 Jember Java
33 N8 Jembke Germany
85 G1 Jem, El Tunisia
22 J3 Jemelle Belgium
106 D6 Jemez R New Mexico U.S.A.
106 D6 Jemez Pueblo New Mexico U.S.A.
106 D6 Jemez Springs New Mexico U.S.A.
32 F6 Jemgum Germany
43 D13 Jemmel Tunisia
31 J6 Jemnice Czech Rep
70 E5 Jempang, Danao L Kalimantan
122 F8 Jemseg New Brunswick Canada
37 M2 Jena Germany
111 D10 Jena Louisiana U.S.A.
38 E7 Jenbach Austria
80 E4 Jenin Jordan
94 F9 Jenkinjones West Virginia U.S.A.
94 E9 Jenkins Kentucky U.S.A.
99 M3 Jenkins Minnesota U.S.A.
140 A7 Jenkins,Mt N Terr Australia
118 F8 Jenner Alberta Canada
102 A3 Jenner California U.S.A.
117 H6 Jennings R British Columbia Canada
113 D7 Jennings Florida U.S.A.
107 K2 Jennings Kansas U.S.A.
111 D11 Jennings Louisiana U.S.A.
107 O5 Jennings Oklahoma U.S.A.
127 O4 Jennings Antigua W Indies
114 J4 Jenny Lind I Northwest Territories Canada
139 K5 Jenolan Caves New South Wales Australia
101 Q9 Jensen Utah U.S.A.
113 G10 Jensen Beach Florida U.S.A.
115 P5 Jensen Nunatakker pk Greenland
115 L4 Jens Munk I Northwest Territories Canada
70 N9 Jepara Java
138 F6 Jeparit Victoria Australia
29 K8 Jeppo Finland
129 K6 Jequie Brazil
130 G5 Jequitai Brazil
129 K7 Jequitinhonha Brazil
85 D2 Jerada Morocco
69 F11 Jerantut Malaysia
85 G2 Jerba, I de Tunisia
126 G5 Jérémie Haiti
129 L6 Jeremoabo Brazil
71 H9 Jerewan Indonesia
124 H6 Jerez de García Salinas Mexico
16 C8 Jerez de la Frontera Spain
16 C6 Jerez de los Caballeros Spain
141 H6 Jericho Queensland Australia
80 E6 Jericho Jordan
33 Q8 Jerichow Germany
129 K4 Jericoaquara, Pta C Brazil
69 G14 Jerigi Sumatra
26 N5 Jerijärvi Sweden
70 B3 Jerijih, Tanjong C Sarawak
139 H6 Jerilderie New South Wales Australia
29 L4 Jerisjärvi L Finland
130 E4 Jeroaquara Brazil
120 H5 Jerome Ontario Canada
103 M7 Jerome Arizona U.S.A.
101 L7 Jerome Idaho U.S.A.
129 H7 Jerônimo, Serra do mts Brazil
143 C10 Jerramungup W Australia Australia
20 F3 Jersey isld Channel Is
95 N6 Jersey City New Jersey U.S.A.
95 K5 Jersey Shore Pennsylvania U.S.A.
110 F2 Jerseyville Illinois U.S.A.
28 E2 Jerslev Denmark
28 C6 Jerstal Denmark
16 D4 Jerte R Spain
70 D2 Jerudong Brunei
129 K5 Jerumenha Brazil
28 E1 Jerup Denmark
80 D6 Jerusalem Israel
145 E3 Jerusalem New Zealand
140 D6 Jervais Ra N Terr Australia
139 K6 Jervis Bay New South Wales Australia
138 E6 Jervis, C South Australia Australia
117 M10 Jervis Inlet British Columbia Canada
140 D6 Jervois Ra N Terr Australia
33 N8 Jerxheim Germany
36 G2 Jesberg Germany
37 P3 Jesenice Czech Rep
42 F2 Jesenice Slovenia
31 K5 Jeseník Czech Rep
48 F2 Jesenské Slovakia
33 Q8 Jeserig Germany
33 R10 Jesewitz Germany
Jesselton see Kota Kinabalu
27 E11 Jessheim Norway
98 H2 Jessie North Dakota U.S.A.
33 Q9 Jessnitz Germany
113 F9 Jessup, L Florida U.S.A.
32 L6 Jesteburg Germany
112 F6 Jesup Georgia U.S.A.
99 O7 Jesup Iowa U.S.A.
133 E4 Jesús María Argentina
124 H7 Jesús María Mexico
126 F4 Jesús Menéndez Cuba
107 M5 Jet Oklahoma U.S.A.
119 Q2 Jetait Manitoba Canada
94 J9 Jetersville Virginia U.S.A.
20 F3 Jethou isld Channel Is
107 L3 Jetmore Kansas U.S.A.
37 J7 Jettingen Germany
37 L7 Jetzendorf Germany
22 G3 Jeumont France
32 L4 Jevenau R Germany
32 L4 Jevenstedt Germany
32 G5 Jever Germany
48 D1 Jevíčko Czech Rep
27 D11 Jevnaker Norway
98 C6 Jewel Cave Nat. Mon South Dakota U.S.A.
99 N7 Jewell Iowa U.S.A.
107 M2 Jewell Kansas U.S.A.
100 B4 Jewell Oregon U.S.A.
110 H2 Jewett Illinois U.S.A.
94 G6 Jewett Ohio U.S.A.
109 L4 Jewett Texas U.S.A.
95 Q5 Jewett City Connecticut U.S.A.
46 D2 Jezerce mt Albania
37 P5 Jezerni mt Czech Rep
42 H4 Jezero Bosnia-Herzegovina
31 M2 Jeziorak, Jezioro L Poland
31 M2 Jeziorany Poland
31 L4 Jeziorsko, Jezioro res Poland
31 P1 Jeznas Lithuania
31 M4 Jeżów Poland
79 F5 Jezzine Lebanon
74 F7 Jhabua India
74 G4 Jhajjar India
74 G6 Jhalawar India
74 E3 Jhang Maghiana Pakistan
74 H6 Jhansi India
75 M5 Jhapa Nepal
74 E2 Jhelum India
74 E2 Jhelum R Pakistan
74 F4 Jhunjhunūn India
65 E3 Jiade He R China
67 G1 Jiading China
67 C4 Jiagui China
67 D4 Jiahe China
Jiaji see Qionghai
67 A2 Jiajiang China
58 E5 Jialing Jiang R China
59 K2 Jiamusi China
65 H1 Jiamusi China
65 G4 Ji'an China
67 E3 Ji'an China
65 D4 Jianchang China
65 F4 Jianchang China
67 F2 Jiande China
67 B2 Jiang'an China
67 B2 Jiangbei China
68 E1 Jiangcheng China
67 C3 Jiangdong China
67 F1 Jiangdu China
67 C6 Jianghong China
67 D4 Jianghua China
67 B2 Jiangjin China
Jiangkou see Fengkai
67 D1 Jiangkou China
67 C3 Jiangkou China
67 F3 Jiangle China
67 D1 Jiangling China
67 D5 Jiangmen China
67 F1 Jiangpu China
67 F2 Jiangshan China
58 G5 Jiangsu prov China
67 E3 Jiangxi prov China
65 B7 Jiang Xian China
67 F1 Jiangxiang China
67 G1 Jiangyin China
67 D4 Jiangyong China
67 A1 Jiangyou China
67 C3 Jianhe China
67 D2 Jianli China
67 E3 Jianning China
67 F3 Jian'ou China
65 D4 Jianping China
65 D5 Jianping China
67 C1 Jianshi China
67 A5 Jianshui China
58 D5 Jianyang China
67 F3 Jianyang China
65 B6 Jiaocheng China
59 J3 Jiaohe China
65 B6 Jiaokou China
67 E4 Jiaoling China
65 E7 Jiaonan China
65 D6 Jiao Xian China
58 F4 Jiaozuo China
65 G3 Jiapigou China
58 G5 Jiashan China
67 G1 Jiashan China
57 H5 Jiashi China
65 D7 Jiawang China
65 A5 Jia Xian China
65 B7 Jia Xian China
59 H5 Jiaxing China
67 C4 Jiaya China
59 K2 Jiayin China
67 D2 Jiayu China
58 C4 Jiayuguan China
65 E7 Jiazohou Wan B China
77 B7 Jiban, Al Saudi Arabia
129 J7 Jibao, Serra do mts Brazil
88 G6 Jibondo isld Tanzania
48 H3 Jibou Romania
67 B3 Jichang China
31 J5 Jičín Czech Rep
86 G1 Jiddah Saudi Arabia
65 H2 Jidong China
Jiehu see Yinan
26 L2 Jiekkevarre mt Norway
67 E5 Jieshi China
67 E5 Jieshi Wan B China
26 O2 Jiesjavrre L Norway
67 E5 Jiexi China
65 B6 Jiexiu China
143 D6 Jiggalong W Australia Australia
100 K9 Jiggs Nevada U.S.A.
67 E1 Jigong Shan mt China
79 H4 Jihar, Wādī el watercourse Syria
31 J6 Jihlava Czech Rep
31 H6 Jihočesky reg Czech Rep
31 J6 Jihomoravský reg Czech Rep
85 F1 Jijel Algeria
48 L3 Jijia R Romania
86 H4 Jijiga Ethiopia
80 G3 Jijjin Jordan
17 G6 Jijona Spain
48 K6 Jilava Romania
86 H5 Jilib Somalia
59 H2 Jilin prov China
65 G3 Jilin China
65 F3 Jilin Hada Ling mt ra China
59 H1 Jiliu He R China
17 G4 Jiloca R Spain
116 M3 Jim R Alaska U.S.A.
86 G4 Jima Ethiopia
69 G14 Jimar Sumatra
142 F5 Jimberingga W Australia Australia
48 F5 Jimbolia Romania
141 L8 Jimboomba Queensland Australia
16 D8 Jimena de la Frontera Spain
124 G4 Jiménez Mexico
140 C2 Jim Jim Cr N Terr Australia
65 E6 Jimo China
65 C6 Jinan China
65 B7 Jincheng China
139 J6 Jindabyne New South Wales Australia
37 O3 Jindřichovice Czech Rep
31 J6 Jindřichův Hradec Czech Rep
67 E2 Jing'an China
67 F1 Jingde China
67 F2 Jingdezhen China
Jingfeng see Hexigten Qi
65 D5 Jinghai China
65 E6 Jinghaiwei China
58 E5 Jing He R China
66 C3 Jinghe China
68 E2 Jinghong China
67 G1 Jingjiang China
65 B5 Jingle China
67 D1 Jingmen China
Jingping see Pinglu
65 G2 Jingpo China
65 G3 Jingpo Hu L China
58 F5 Jing Shan mt ra China
67 D1 Jingshan China
58 D4 Jingtai China
65 C6 Jing Xian China
67 F1 Jing Xian China
59 H2 Jingxing China
67 A2 Jingyan China
65 A7 Jingyang China
65 G3 Jingyu China
58 D4 Jingyuan China
Jingzhou see Jiangling
67 F2 Jinhua China
65 C7 Jining China
65 B4 Jining Nei Monggol Zizhiqu China
88 D1 Jinja-Bugembe Uganda
67 E2 Jin Jiang R China
67 C3 Jin Jiang R China
67 F4 Jinjiang China
67 D2 Jinjing China
65 E6 Jinkou China
67 E1 Jinkou China
67 F4 Jinlong Jiang R China
67 C7 Jinmu Jiao China
68 J3 Jinmu Jiao C China
125 M3 Jinotega Nicaragua
125 L4 Jinotepe Nicaragua
67 C3 Jinping China
68 F1 Jinping China
Jinsha see Nantong
67 B3 Jinsha China
58 C6 Jinsha Jiang R China
Jinshan see Harqin Qi
67 G1 Jinshan China
67 D2 Jinshi China
67 F1 Jintan China
67 A1 Jintang China
67 C5 Jintian Shuiku res China
71 F5 Jintotolo isld Philippines
71 F5 Jintotolo Ch Philippines
59 H3 Jinxi China
67 E3 Jinxi China
67 F3 Jin Xi China
67 B5 Jinxi China
65 E4 Jin Xian China
65 C5 Jin Xian China
65 E5 Jin Xian China
67 E2 Jinxian China
65 C7 Jinxiang China
67 G3 Jinxiang China
67 C4 Jinxiu China
67 G2 Jinyun China
67 E1 Jinzhai China
65 E4 Jinzhou China
65 E5 Jinzhou Wan B China
128 B4 Jipijapa Ecuador
126 F4 Jiquaní Cuba
130 H5 Jiquitaia Brazil
77 C7 Jirāb, Al isld U.A.E.
143 F9 Jirina Rockholes rockhole W Australia Australia
65 D2 Jirin Gol China
37 P3 Jirkov Czech Rep
48 L5 Jirlău Romania
86 A2 Jirriiban Somalia
65 A7 Jishan China
67 C2 Jishou China
67 E3 Jishui China
79 G3 Jisr ash Shughūr Syria
16 C2 Jistredo, Sa. de mts Spain
143 C10 Jitarning W Australia Australia
Jitian see Lianshan
69 E9 Jitra Malaysia
48 H6 Jiu R Romania
Jiucheng see Wucheng
67 A1 Jiuding Shan mt China
58 G6 Jiujiang China
67 E2 Jiujiang China
67 D1 Jiukou China
67 E4 Jiulian Shan mts China
67 E2 Jiuling Shan mt ra China
58 C4 Jiuquan China
65 E6 Jiurongcheng China
59 J3 Jiutai China
67 C4 Jiuwan Dashan mts China
65 C5 Jiuwuqing China
65 C5 Jiuxincheng China
67 B4 Jiuxu China
67 F1 Jiuyuhang China
67 B4 Jiuzhou China
77 G7 Jiwani Iran
74 B10 Jiwani Pakistan
65 H2 Jixi China
67 F1 Jixi China
59 K2 Jixian China
65 D4 Ji Xian China
65 A6 Ji Xian China
65 C6 Ji Xian China
65 C7 Ji Xian China
65 D6 Jiyang China
65 B7 Jiyuan China
79 F7 Jiza Jordan
80 G7 Jiza Jordan
65 C6 Jize China
31 H5 Jizera R Czech Rep
60 G10 Jizō zaki C Japan
86 E1 J. Kissu mt Sudan
120 G1 Joab L Ontario Canada
130 D10 Joaçaba Brazil
33 T7 Joachimsthal Germany
130 H5 Joaíma Brazil
85 A6 Joal-Fadiout Senegal
129 L5 Joao Camara Brazil
129 J4 João Coelho Brazil
131 H4 João Maria, Albardão do Brazil
130 E10 João Paulo R Brazil
130 J9 João Pessoa Brazil
130 F5 João Pinheiro Brazil
111 B10 Joaquin Texas U.S.A.
126 F4 Jobabo Cuba
61 O9 Jōban Japan
71 G6 Jobo Pt Mindanao Philippines
20 G2 Jobourg France
102 F2 Job Pk Nevada U.S.A.
120 D2 Jobrin Ontario Canada
38 F7 Jochberg Austria
16 E7 Jódar Spain
74 E5 Jodhpur India
74 D7 Jodiya Bandar India
22 H2 Jodoigne Belgium
123 S4 Joe Batt's Arm Newfoundland Canada
29 O9 Joensuu Finland
106 H2 Joes Colorado U.S.A.
26 G6 Joeström Sweden
61 M8 Jōetsu Japan
87 F10 Jofane Mozambique
106 E7 Joffre New Mexico U.S.A.
117 Q10 Joffre, Mt British Columbia Canada
61 L9 Joganji R Japan
75 M5 Jogbani India
65 C3 Jogdor China
52 C5 Jõgeva Estonia
122 H8 Joggins Nova Scotia Canada
74 G3 Jogindarnagar India
120 E2 Jog L Ontario Canada
38 N7 Joglland Austria
61 K9 Jōhana Japan
32 J9 Johannaberg Germany
89 A1 Johannesburg S Africa
102 G6 Johannesburg California U.S.A.
37 O3 Johanngeorgenstadt Germany
115 M2 Johan Pen Northwest Territories Canada
60 F13 Jōhen Japan
116 L3 John R Alaska U.S.A.
122 J8 John, C Nova Scotia Canada
127 M2 John Crow Mts Jamaica
100 E4 John Day R Oregon U.S.A.
100 G5 John Day Oregon U.S.A.
100 E5 John Day Fossil Beds Nat. Mon. Oregon U.S.A.
117 Q6 John d'Or Prairie Alberta Canada
113 G9 John F. Kennedy Space Center Florida U.S.A.
94 J10 John H. Kerr Res N Carolina/Virg U.S.A.
106 H3 John Martin Res Colorado U.S.A.
142 G3 John,Mt W Australia Australia
15 E2 John O'Groats Scotland
107 P3 John Redmond Res Kansas U.S.A.
107 J4 Johnson Kansas U.S.A.
99 K9 Johnson Nebraska U.S.A.
94 J5 Johnsonburg Pennsylvania U.S.A.
95 M4 Johnson City New York U.S.A.
94 E10 Johnson City Tennessee U.S.A.
109 J5 Johnson City Texas U.S.A.
99 S6 Johnson Cr Wisconsin U.S.A.
117 G5 Johnsons Crossing Yukon Territory Canada
127 P4 Johnsons Pt Antigua W Indies
112 H4 Johnsonville South Carolina U.S.A.
112 F4 Johnston South Carolina U.S.A.
8 A4 Johnston Wales
110 H4 Johnston City Illinois U.S.A.
15 D5 Johnstone Scotland
117 K10 Johnstone Str British Columbia Canada
88 B7 Johnston Falls Zambia
143 D9 Johnston,L W Australia Australia
143 C8 Johnston Ra W Australia Australia
14 E3 Johnstown Ireland
98 F7 Johnstown Nebraska U.S.A.
95 N4 Johnstown New York U.S.A.
94 E6 Johnstown Ohio U.S.A.
94 J6 Johnstown Pennsylvania U.S.A.
94 E9 John W Flannagan Res Virginia U.S.A.
61 P5 Jōhōji Japan
69 F12 Johor Malaysia
69 F12 Johor Baharo Malaysia
37 P2 Jöhstadt Germany
52 C5 Jõhvi Estonia
18 H5 Joigny France
110 F6 Joiner Arkansas U.S.A.
130 E10 Joinville Brazil
19 J4 Joinville France
146 D3 Joinville I Antarctica
125 K8 Jojutla Mexico
26 N5 Jokk Sweden
26 L5 Jokkmokk Sweden
27 C10 Jokuleggi mt Norway
29 T9 Jökulsá á Fjöllum R Iceland
29 T9 Jökulsa o Bru R Iceland
78 K2 Jolfā Iran
99 S8 Joliet Illinois U.S.A.
101 Q4 Joliet Montana U.S.A.
121 R6 Joliette Quebec Canada
119 U10 Joliette North Dakota U.S.A.
142 A1 Jolimont dist Perth, W Aust Australia
99 M7 Jolley Iowa U.S.A.
117 S3 Jolly L Northwest Territories Canada
71 E7 Jolo Philippines
102 C6 Jolon California U.S.A.
26 B10 Jölstervatn L Norway
26 G7 Joma mt Norway
29 H11 Jomala Finland
71 F3 Jomalig isld Luzon Philippines
70 O9 Jombang Java
66 F5 Jomda China
71 A3 Jome Indonesia
27 D13 Jomfruland isld Norway
52 B6 Jonava Lithuania
22 F5 Jonchery-sur-Vesle France
7 E13 Jones Bank Atlantic Oc
110 F6 Jonesboro Arkansas U.S.A.
111 M8 Jonesboro Georgia U.S.A.
110 G4 Jonesboro Illinois U.S.A.
109 P3 Jonesboro Louisiana U.S.A.
95 U2 Jonesboro Maine U.S.A.
112 H2 Jonesboro North Carolina U.S.A.
100 H6 Jonesboro Oregon U.S.A.
112 E1 Jonesboro Tennessee U.S.A.
109 K4 Jonesboro Texas U.S.A.
116 N1 Jones Is Alaska U.S.A.
146 B7 Jones Mts Antarctica
95 U2 Jonesport Maine U.S.A.
83 M9 Jones Pt Christmas I Indian Oc
115 L2 Jones Sound Northwest Territories Canada
111 F7 Jonestown Mississippi U.S.A.
94 B7 Jonesville Indiana U.S.A.
111 E10 Jonesville Louisiana U.S.A.
94 C5 Jonesville Michigan U.S.A.
112 F3 Jonesville South Carolina U.S.A.
94 D10 Jonesville Virginia U.S.A.
86 F4 Jonglei prov Sudan
52 B6 Joniskis Lithuania
27 G14 Jönköping Sweden
27 G14 Jönköping county Sweden
121 T4 Jonquière Quebec Canada
29 K4 Jönstorp Sweden
18 E7 Jonzac France
110 B4 Joplin Missouri U.S.A.
101 P1 Joplin Montana U.S.A.
80 B5 Joppa Israel
110 H4 Joppa Illinois U.S.A.
141 H6 Jordan R Queensland Australia
80 F1 Jordan R Israel/Jordan
80 Jordan kingdom S W Asia
99 N5 Jordan Minnesota U.S.A.
101 T2 Jordan Montana U.S.A.
95 L3 Jordan New York U.S.A.
100 H7 Jordan R Oregon U.S.A.
129 K7 Jordânia Brazil
122 G9 Jordan L Nova Scotia Canada
111 K9 Jordan L Alabama U.S.A.
48 F1 Jordanow Poland
100 H7 Jordan Valley Oregon U.S.A.
130 D9 Jordão, R Brazil
28 C3 Jordbro Å R Denmark
33 R5 Jördenstorf Germany
27 F10 Jordet Norway
28 E6 Jordløse Denmark
28 C5 Jordrup Denmark
28 B6 Jordsand isld Denmark
26 P2 Jorgastak Norway
133 B8 Jorge Montt, I Chile
75 Q5 Jorhat India
32 L5 Jork Germany
57 F6 Jorm Afghanistan
26 G7 Jormlien Sweden
26 L6 Jörn Sweden
106 C9 Jornada del Muerto reg New Mexico U.S.A.
27 B12 Jörpeland Norway
21 K4 Jort France
85 F7 Jos Nigeria
71 G8 Jose Abad Santos Mindanao Philippines
133 C6 José de San Martín Argentina
129 J8 José dos Campos Brazil
130 C5 Joselândia Brazil
133 E5 José Maria Blanco Argentina
27 B12 Josenfjord inlet Norway
71 F3 Jose Pañganiban Philippines
100 J4 Joseph Idaho U.S.A.
100 H4 Joseph Oregon U.S.A.
142 G2 Joseph Bonaparte G Australia
142 G2 Joseph Bonaparte Gulf Australia
103 O7 Joseph City Arizona U.S.A.
6 M6 Josephine oil rig North Sea
115 N7 Joseph L Labrador, Nfld Canada
123 K4 Joseph Pt Anticosti I, Quebec
144 B6 Josephville New Zealand
61 M9 Jō-Shin-Etsu Nat. Park Japan
109 K3 Joshua Texas U.S.A.
102 H7 Joshua Tree California U.S.A.
21 O6 Josnes France
36 H3 Jossatal Germany
20 E6 Josselin France
26 E7 Jössund Nord-Tröndelag Norway
26 D8 Jössund Sör-Tröndelag Norway
26 B10 Jostedal Norway
26 B10 Jostedalsbreen gla Norway
48 F2 Josvafö Hungary
26 N2 Jotkajavrre Norway
27 C10 Jotunheimen mt Norway
79 F5 Jouaiya Lebanon
21 O4 Jouars France
21 K4 Joué-du-Bois France
21 M7 Joué-lès-Tours France
20 H7 Joué-sur-Erdre France
19 K3 Jœuf France
29 N6 Joukokylä Finland
113 J12 Joulters Cays islds Bahamas
79 F5 Jôunié Lebanon
109 J7 Jourdanton Texas U.S.A.
25 E3 Joure Netherlands
118 B3 Joussard Alberta Canada
121 M3 Joutel Quebec Canada
29 M10 Joutsa Finland
29 N5 Joutsijärvi Finland
40 D4 Joux, L.de Switzerland
21 O4 Jouy France
21 O6 Jouy-le-Potier France
126 D3 Jovellanos Cuba
75 P6 Jowai India
77 J1 Jowzjān prov Afghanistan
14 B3 Joyce's Country Ireland
117 G4 Joy, Mt Yukon Territory Canada
60 O3 Jōzankei Japan
31 N4 Józefów Poland
110 K5 J. Percy Priest L Tennessee U.S.A.
71 B3 Ju isld Indonesia
124 H5 Juan Aldama Mexico
65 C7 Juancheng China
141 J7 Juandah R Queensland Australia
127 K2 Juan de Bolas pk Jamaica
100 A1 Juan de Fuca, Str. of Canada/U.S.A.
87 G11 Juan de Nova isld Madagascar
133 A9 Juan Fernández, Is Pacific Oc
127 N9 Juangriego Venezuela
88 G6 Juani isld Tanzania
128 C5 Juanjui Peru
29 N8 Juankoski Finland
44 B4 Juan les Pins France
124 E2 Juan M. Ortíz Mexico
131 B2 Juan Soldado, C.de Chile
133 B7 Juan Stuven, I Chile
133 F5 Juárez Argentina
103 J9 Juárez, Sa ra Mexico
129 K5 Juazeiro Brazil
130 G9 Juàzeiro do Norte Brazil
86 F5 Juba Sudan
77 A6 Jubayl, Al Saudi Arabia
80 G5 Jubba Jordan
86 H5 Jubba R Somalia
80 G1 Jubbāta el Khashab Syria
123 R5 Jubilee L Newfoundland Canada
143 F8 Jubilee Lake W Australia Australia
102 H6 Jubilee Peak California U.S.A.
21 K5 Jublains France
85 B3 Juby, Cap C Morocco
17 F5 Júcar R Spain
36 B1 Jüchen Germany
124 H7 Juchipila Mexico
125 M9 Juchitán Mexico
124 H7 Juchitlán Mexico
129 K7 Jucurucú R Brazil
98 H3 Jud North Dakota U.S.A.
99 R7 Juda Wisconsin U.S.A.
80 B7 Judaea Israel
79 G5 Judaydat al Wadī Syria
123 S6 Jude I Newfoundland Canada
80 D2 Judeida Israel
37 L3 Judenbach Germany
38 L7 Judenburg Austria
146 B16 Judge and Clerk Is islds S Pacific Oc
123 L8 Judique C Breton I, Nova Scotia
101 Q2 Judith R Montana U.S.A.
101 Q2 Judith Basin reg Montana U.S.A.
101 Q3 Judith Gap Montana U.S.A.
98 E3 Judson North Dakota U.S.A.
Juegang see Rudong
28 E5 Juelsminde Denmark
130 H5 Juerana Brazil
128 F4 Jufari R Brazil
84 F4 Jufrah Oasis, Al Libya
20 F5 Jugon-les-Lacs France
65 E4 Juhua Dao isld China
21 H6 Juigné-des-Moutiers France
18 F7 Juillac France
21 P4 Juine R France
32 E5 Juist isld Germany
32 F5 Juist Germany
129 K8 Juiz de Fora Brazil
65 D3 Jujinchang China
69 E13 Jujuhan R Sumatra
19 O12 Jujurieux France
128 E8 Jujuy prov Argentina
26 L7 Juken Sweden
26 L4 Jukkasjärvi Sweden
67 D3 Jukoupu China
26 H6 Juktån R Sweden
128 E8 Julaca Bolivia
98 D9 Julesburg Colorado U.S.A.
128 E7 Julí Peru
141 F5 Julia R Queensland Australia
128 D7 Juliaca Peru
141 F5 Julia Creek Queensland Australia
100 J3 Juliaetta Idaho U.S.A.
102 H8 Julian California U.S.A.
115 P5 Julianehåb Greenland
14 E3 Julianstown Ireland
36 B2 Jülich Germany
42 E2 Julijske A mts Slovenia
124 G3 Julimes Mexico
80 D2 Jūlis Israel
27 H12 Julita Sweden
140 E5 Julius L. Queensland Australia
20 G4 Jullouville France
Jullundur see Jalandhar
28 D4 Julsø L Denmark
65 C6 Julu China
80 G8 Jumaiyil Jordan
86 H6 Jumba Somalia
117 P10 Jumbo Mt British Columbia Canada
21 K7 Jumelles France
21 J7 Jumellière,la France
22 G3 Jumet Belgium
21 M3 Jumièges France
17 G6 Jumilla Spain
75 K4 Jumla Nepal
74 D8 Junagadh India
65 D7 Junan China
65 D2 Jun Bulen China
124 D5 Juncal Mexico
131 D8 Juncal, L Argentina
108 H5 Junction Texas U.S.A.
103 M3 Junction Utah U.S.A.
140 C1 Junction B N Terr Australia
111 D8 Junction City Arkansas U.S.A.
111 M9 Junction City Georgia U.S.A.
107 O2 Junction City Kansas U.S.A.
94 C9 Junction City Kentucky U.S.A.
110 M4 Junction City Kentucky U.S.A.
100 B5 Junction City Oregon U.S.A.
99 R5 Junction City Wisconsin U.S.A.
141 G6 Jundah Queensland Australia
65 C4 Jundu Shan mt ra China
117 F6 Juneau Alaska U.S.A.
99 S6 Juneau Wisconsin U.S.A.
139 J5 Junee New South Wales Australia
113 F10 June in Winter, L Florida U.S.A.
102 E4 June Lake California U.S.A.
65 A5 Jungar Qi China
40 G4 Jungfrau mt Switzerland
40 G4 Jungfraujoch Switzerland
22 L4 Junglinster Luxembourg
100 G9 Jungo Nevada U.S.A.

98 H9 **Juniata** Nebraska U.S.A.
95 K6 **Juniata** *R* Pennsylvania U.S.A.
131 E5 **Junin** Argentina
128 D7 **Junín** Chile
128 C6 **Junin** Peru
133 C5 **Junín de los Andes** Argentina
94 H8 **Junior** West Virginia U.S.A.
95 T1 **Junior L** Maine U.S.A.
122 E7 **Juniper** New Brunswick Canada
103 L6 **Juniper Mts** Arizona U.S.A.
102 C5 **Junipero Sierra Pk** California U.S.A.
61 O5 **Jūni sho** Japan
22 G5 **Juniville** France
116 O2 **Junjik** *R* Alaska U.S.A.
36 B3 **Jünkerath** Germany
26 H5 **Junkerdal** Norway
67 A2 **Junlian** China
108 F5 **Juno** Texas U.S.A.
118 K5 **Junor** Saskatchewan Canada
26 M4 **Junosuando** Sweden
26 J8 **Junsele** Sweden
67 E2 **Junshan Hu** *L* China
16 A5 **Junto** *mt* Portugal
65 A5 **Juntuliang** China
100 G6 **Juntura** Oregon U.S.A.
29 O6 **Juntusranta** Finland
29 O9 **Juojärvi** *L* Finland
26 N5 **Juoksengi** Sweden
130 H6 **Juparaña, Lagoa** *L* Brazil
130 D7 **Jupia** Brazil
130 D7 **Jupiá, Barragem** *dam* Brazil
22 K2 **Jupille** Belgium
21 L6 **Jupilles** France
113 G11 **Jupiter** Florida U.S.A.
122 J4 **Jupiter R** Quebec Canada
129 J8 **Juquiá** Brazil
86 E4 **Jur** *R* Sudan
40 C4 **Jura** *dept* France
15 C4 **Jura** Scotland
40 F3 **Jura** *canton* Switzerland
128 C2 **Jurado** Colombia
31 L5 **Jura Krakowska** *reg* Poland
130 G5 **Juramento** Brazil
52 B6 **Jurbarkas** Lithuania
12 D5 **Jurby** I of Man U.K.
79 F8 **Jurf ed Darāwīsh** Jordan
65 E2 **Jurh** China
143 B9 **Jurien** W Australia Australia
143 B9 **Jurien B** W Australia Australia
48 M6 **Jurilovca** Romania
52 B6 **Jurmala** Latvia
67 F1 **Jurong** China
38 N9 **Juršinci** Slovenia
128 E4 **Juruá** Brazil
128 D5 **Juruá** *R* Brazil
128 G6 **Juruena** Brazil
129 G4 **Juruti** Brazil
29 J9 **Jurva** Finland
61 O5 **Jūsan-ko** *L* Japan
127 N10 **Jusepín** Venezuela
79 G4 **Jūsīyah** Syria
19 J5 **Jussey** France
119 S8 **Justice** Manitoba Canada
108 F2 **Justiceburg** Texas U.S.A.
109 K2 **Justin** Texas U.S.A.
133 D4 **Justo Daract** Argentina
128 E5 **Jutaí** Brazil
33 S9 **Jüterbog** Germany
130 C8 **Juti** Brazil
125 L2 **Juticalpa** Honduras
26 J5 **Jutis** Sweden
Jutland *see* **Jylland**
26 E10 **Jutulhugget** *pass* Norway
146 H6 **Jutulstraumen** *ice stream* Antarctica
29 O8 **Juuka** Finland
29 N10 **Juva** Finland
126 C4 **Juventud, Isla de la** Cuba
21 H5 **Juvigné** France
21 H4 **Juvigny-le-Tertre** France
21 J4 **Juvigny-sous-Andaine** France
21 P4 **Juvisy** France
28 B6 **Juvre** Denmark
70 N9 **Juwana** Java
79 H5 **Juwayf, Al** Syria
65 D7 **Ju Xian** China
65 C7 **Juye** China
77 F2 **Jūymand** Iran
40 A1 **Juzennecourt** France
Jye Kundo *see* **Yushu**
28 B4 **Jylland** *reg* Denmark
29 M9 **Jyväskylä** Finland

K

66 B4 **K2** *mt* Kashmir/China
85 E6 **Ka** *R* Nigeria
102 S11 **Kaaawa** Hawaiian Is
89 B7 **Kaaing Veld** *plateau* S Africa
57 A5 **Kaakhka** Turkmenistan
102 R11 **Kaala** *pk* Hawaiian Is
26 L4 **Kaalasjarvi** *L* Sweden
135 U6 **Kaalualu** Hawaiian Is
29 N2 **Kaamanen** Finland
86 H6 **Kaambooni** Somalia
89 C7 **Kaap Plato** S Africa
33 O6 **Kaarssen** Germany
29 N9 **Kaavi** Finland
48 G3 **Kaba** Hungary
70 G7 **Kabaena** *isld* Sulawesi
85 B7 **Kabala** Sierra Leone
86 F5 **Kabalega Falls** Uganda
86 E7 **Kabalo** Zaire
88 A4 **Kabambare** Zaire
69 D11 **Kabanjahe** Sumatra
85 D5 **Kabara** Mali
53 F11 **Kabardino Balkarskaya Respublika** Russian Federation
88 B3 **Kabare** Zaire
86 F5 **Kabarole** Uganda
71 F7 **Kabasalang** Philippines
60 C13 **Kaba shima** *isld* Japan
68 C3 **Kabaung** *R* Burma
85 F7 **Kabba** Nigeria
26 G3 **Kabelvåg** *lighthouse* Norway
120 E4 **Kabenung L** Ontario Canada
70 G4 **Kabetan. I** Sulawesi
99 O1 **Kabetogama** Minnesota U.S.A.
99 N1 **Kabetogama L** Minnesota U.S.A.
120 F3 **Kabinakagami** *R* Ontario Canada
86 D7 **Kabinda** Zaire
71 M9 **Kabir** Indonesia
79 F3 **Kabīr** *R* Syria/Lebanon
57 E5 **Kabla** Tajikistan
47 J2 **Kableshkovo** Bulgaria
86 C4 **Kabo** Cent Afr Republic
87 D8 **Kabompo** *R* Zambia
70 B4 **Kabong** Sarawak
87 E7 **Kabongo** Zaire
68 C6 **Kabosa I.** Burma
85 G1 **Kaboudia, Rass** *C* Tunisia
52 E5 **Kabozha** Russian Federation
80 D1 **Kabri** Israel
77 F1 **Kabūd Gonbad** Iran
71 E2 **Kabugao** Philippines
77 L2 **Kābul** Afghanistan
77 L2 **Kābul** *prov* Afghanistan
80 D2 **Kābūl** Israel
88 C2 **Kabula** Uganda
87 E8 **Kabunda** Zaire
88 B7 **Kabunda** Zambia
71 H9 **Kabunduk** Indonesia
86 F2 **Kabushiya** Sudan
88 B9 **Kabwe** Zambia
55 F3 **Kabyrdak** Russian Federation
55 D5 **Kabyrga** *R* Kazakhstan
46 E2 **Kačanik** Serbia Yugoslavia
71 B3 **Kacepi** Indonesia
87 F8 **Kachalola** Zambia
74 C7 **Kachchh, Gulf of** India
74 C6 **Kachchh, Rann of** India
116 M7 **Kachemak B** Alaska U.S.A.
100 D2 **Kachess L** Washington U.S.A.
85 F7 **Kachia** Nigeria
75 R5 **Kachin State** *prov* Burma
55 G4 **Kachiry** Kazakhstan
55 C2 **Kachkanar** Russian Federation
56 G4 **Kachug** Russian Federation
78 H1 **Kaçkar Dağlar** *mt* Turkey
60 J11 **Kada** Japan
68 C4 **Kadaingti** Burma
76 A5 **Kadamatt** *isld* Indian Oc
86 F5 **Kadam Mt** Uganda
37 P3 **Kadaň** Czech Rep
68 D6 **Kadan Kyun** *isld* Burma
70 D7 **Kadapongan** *isld* Indonesia
48 D4 **Kadarkút** Hungary
71 H7 **Kadatung** *isld* Indonesia
137 Q5 **Kadavu** *isld* Fiji
41 H2 **Kadelburg** Germany
61 P13 **Kadena** Okinawa
71 K9 **Kadesa** Indonesia
143 F7 **Kadgo L** W Australia Australia
78 K5 **Kādhimain** Iraq
74 E7 **Kadi** India
85 C6 **Kadiana** Mali
46 F3 **Kadijica** *mt* Macedonia
47 N11 **Kadıköy** Turkey
138 E5 **Kadina** South Australia Australia
78 D2 **Kadınhanı** Turkey
74 F9 **Kadirabad** India
47 J8 **Kadírga Burun** *C* Turkey
76 D3 **Kadiri** India
78 F3 **Kadirli** Turkey
70 G7 **Kadjang** Sulawesi
73 L6 **Kadmat** *isld* Lakshadweep Indian Oc
52 F5 **Kadnikov** Russian Federation
68 C4 **Kado** Burma
60 E13 **Kadogawa** Japan
98 E6 **Kadoka** South Dakota U.S.A.
89 F2 **Kadoma** Zimbabwe
68 B5 **Kadonkani** Burma
46 E3 **Kadrifakovo** Macedonia
86 E3 **Kadugli** Sudan
86 A3 **Kaduna** Nigeria
76 C4 **Kadur** India
52 E5 **Kaduy** Russian Federation
56 E5 **Kadyr-Egi-Tayga, Khrebet** *mts* Russian Federation
52 F5 **Kadyy** Russian Federation
57 H4 **Kadzhi-Say** Kirghizia
85 B5 **Kaedi** Mauritania
123 R5 **Kaegudeck L** Newfoundland Canada
86 B3 **Kaélé** Cameroon
145 D1 **Kaeo** New Zealand
28 D6 **Kærum** Denmark
65 G5 **Kaesŏng** N Korea
87 D7 **Käfakumba** Zaire
85 F7 **Kafanchan** Nigeria
85 A6 **Kaffrine** Senegal
71 C3 **Kafiau** *isld* W Irian
46 G7 **Kafiréos, Porthmós** *str* Greece
46 G6 **Kafirévs, Akr** *C* Greece
26 L2 **Kåfjord** *inlet* Norway
26 N2 **Kåfjord** Norway
80 E1 **Kafra** Lebanon
80 D5 **Kafr 'Abbush** Jordan
80 D5 **Kafr 'Ain** Jordan
79 G3 **Kafr Buhum** Syria
80 F6 **Kafrein** *R* Jordan
79 A7 **Kafr el Dauwâr** Egypt
80 D4 **Kafr-el-Labad** Jordan
79 A7 **Kafr el Sheik** Egypt
79 A8 **Kafr el Zaiyât** Egypt
80 D2 **Kafr Mandā** Israel
80 C5 **Kafr Qāsim** Israel
80 D4 **Kafr Qud** Jordan
80 D4 **Kafr Ra'i** Jordan
80 D4 **Kafr Rumman** Jordan
79 G4 **Kafrūn Bashūr** Syria
80 D5 **Kafr Zibad** Jordan
88 B9 **Kafue** Zambia
87 E8 **Kafue Nat. Park** Zambia
87 E7 **Kafulwe** Zambia
55 C4 **Kaga** Russian Federation
86 C4 **Kaga Bandoro** Cent Afr Republic
60 G10 **Kagami** Japan
57 C5 **Kagan** Uzbekistan
116 G7 **Kagati L** Alaska U.S.A.
60 G11 **Kagawa** *prefect* Japan
120 H7 **Kagawong** Ontario Canada
26 M7 **Kåge** Sweden
88 C2 **Kagera** *reg* Tanzania
88 C2 **Kagera National Park** Rwanda
28 J5 **Kagerup** Denmark
120 C2 **Kagianagami L** Ontario Canada
120 D3 **Kagiano L** Ontario Canada
47 M10 **Kâğithane** Turkey
78 J1 **Kağızman** Turkey
69 D13 **Kagologolo** Indonesia
60 D14 **Kagoshima** Japan
48 L5 **Kagul** Moldova
48 L5 **Kagul, Ozero** *L* Ukraine
116 L8 **Kaguyak** Alaska U.S.A.
70 D6 **Kahajan** *R* Kalimantan
70 E5 **Kahala** Kalimantan
135 O1 **Kahala Pt** Hawaiian Is
102 S12 **Kahaluu** Hawaiian Is
88 D3 **Kahama** Tanzania
74 C4 **Kahan** Pakistan
102 S11 **Kahana** Hawaiian Is
145 F3 **Kaharoa** *mt* New Zealand
71 A2 **Kahatola** *isld* Halmahera Indonesia
87 C7 **Kahemba** Zaire
102 R12 **Kahe Pt** Hawaiian Is
144 A6 **Kaherekoau Mts** New Zealand
116 M5 **Kahiltna Gl** Alaska U.S.A.
36 G3 **Kahl** *R* Germany
37 M2 **Kahla** Germany
36 F1 **Kahler-Asten** *mt* Germany
100 G3 **Kahlotus** Washington U.S.A.
121 R7 **Kahnawake** Quebec Canada
117 N6 **Kahntah** British Columbia Canada
77 E6 **Kahnuj** Iran
110 E1 **Kahoka** Missouri U.S.A.
61 K9 **Kahoku-gata** *L* Japan
102 V13 **Kahoolawe** *isld* Hawaiian Is
29 J2 **Kahperusvaara** *mt* Finland
78 F3 **Kahramanmaraş** Turkey
135 Q1 **Kahuku** Hawaiian Is
102 S11 **Kahuku Pt** Hawaiian Is
135 T3 **Kahului** Hawaiian Is
Kahutara Pt *see* **Table Cape**
88 B3 **Kahuzi-Biega, Parc National** *nat park* Zaire
85 E7 **Kaiama** Nigeria
144 D5 **Kaiapoi** New Zealand
119 O1 **Kaiashk** *R* Ontario Canada
103 M5 **Kaibab Plat** Arizona U.S.A.
60 J10 **Kaibara** Japan
103 N5 **Kaibito Plat** Arizona U.S.A.
66 D3 **Kaidu He** *R* China
128 G2 **Kaieteur Falls** Guyana
65 C7 **Kaifeng** China
145 D1 **Kaihu** New Zealand
67 F2 **Kaihua** China
145 E3 **Kai-Iwi** New Zealand
67 B1 **Kaijiang** China
136 G3 **Kai, Kep** *islds* Moluccas Indonesia
145 D1 **Kaikohe** New Zealand
67 B3 **Kaikou** China
144 D5 **Kaikoura** New Zealand
144 D5 **Kaikoura Range** New Zealand
Kailas Range *see* **Gangdisê Shan**
36 G4 **Kailbach** Germany
67 B3 **Kaili** China
65 E3 **Kailu** China
102 S12 **Kailua** Hawaiian Is
135 T5 **Kailua** Hawaiian Is
145 E2 **Kaimai Ra** New Zealand
46 E4 **Kaïmakchalán** *mt* Greece
136 G2 **Kaimana** W Irian
145 E3 **Kaimanawa Mts** New Zealand
144 C5 **Kaimata** New Zealand
60 D14 **Kaimon-dake** *pk* Japan
135 V5 **Kaimu** Hawaiian Is
27 N13 **Käina** Estonia
38 M7 **Kainach** *R* Austria
135 U5 **Kainaliu** Hawaiian Is
60 J11 **Kainan** Japan
46 G3 **Kainchal** *mt* Greece
57 G3 **Kainda** Kirghizia
68 B2 **Kaing** Burma
145 F3 **Kaingaroa Forest** New Zealand
145 F3 **Kaingaroa Plat.** New Zealand
38 J6 **Kainisch** Austria
85 E6 **Kainji Res** Nigeria
71 H7 **Kaioba** Indonesia
145 E2 **Kaipara Flats** New Zealand
103 N4 **Kaiparowits Plat** Utah U.S.A.
65 D5 **Kaiping** China
67 D5 **Kaiping** China
29 N4 **Kairala** Finland
43 C13 **Kairouan** Tunisia
38 F6 **Kaiser-Gebirge** *mts* Austria
102 E4 **Kaiser Pk** California U.S.A.
36 C3 **Kaisersesch** Germany
36 D5 **Kaiserslautern** Germany
40 G1 **Kaiserstuhl** *mt* Germany
32 E10 **Kaiserswerth** Germany
60 F11 **Kaita** Japan
145 D1 **Kaitaia** New Zealand
144 B7 **Kaitangata** New Zealand
145 F3 **Kaitawa** New Zealand
145 D4 **Kaiteriteri** New Zealand
74 G4 **Kaithal** India
145 E4 **Kaitoki** New Zealand
Kaitong *see* **Tongyu**
26 L4 **Kaitum** Sweden
26 K4 **Kaitumälven** *R* Sweden
26 K4 **Kaitumj** Sweden
26 L3 **Kaivare** *mt* Sweden
145 E2 **Kaiwaka** New Zealand
71 N9 **Kaiwatu** Indonesia
102 V13 **Kaiwi Ch** Hawaiian Is
67 C1 **Kai Xian** China
67 B3 **Kaiyang** China
59 H3 **Kaiyuan** China
67 A5 **Kaiyuan** China
116 H5 **Kaiyuh Mts** Alaska U.S.A.
60 J11 **Kaizuka** Japan
70 E3 **Kaja** Kalimantan
29 N7 **Kajaani** Finland
141 F5 **Kajabbi** Queensland Australia
77 J3 **Kajaki Dam** Afghanistan
71 L9 **Kajan** *isld* Indonesia
69 E11 **Kajang** Malaysia
88 F2 **Kajiado** Kenya
61 M10 **Kajikazawa** Japan
60 D14 **Kajiki** Japan
71 A2 **Kajoa** *isld* Halmahera Indonesia
86 F5 **Kajo Kaji** Sudan
71 K8 **Kajuadi** *isld* Indonesia
85 F6 **Kajuru** Nigeria
86 F3 **Kaka** Sudan
103 M9 **Kaka** Arizona U.S.A.
70 F3 **Kakaban** *isld* Kalimantan
119 O2 **Kakabeka Falls** Ontario Canada
71 L8 **Kakabia** *isld* Indonesia
140 C2 **Kakadu Nat Park** N Terr Australia
118 J1 **Kakagi L** Ontario Canada
145 E3 **Kakahi** New Zealand
71 G7 **Kakal** *R* Mindanao Philippines
70 F5 **Kakali** Sulawesi
87 D11 **Kakamas** S Africa
88 E1 **Kakamega** Kenya
69 A8 **Kakana** Nicobar Is
144 C6 **Kakanui** New Zealand
135 T3 **Kaka Pt** Hawaiian Is
145 E3 **Kakaramea** New Zealand
85 B7 **Kakata** Liberia
145 E3 **Kakatahi** New Zealand
57 D5 **Kakaydy** Uzbekistan
60 F11 **Kake** Japan
117 G7 **Kake** Alaska U.S.A.
61 M11 **Kakegawa** Japan
56 E5 **Ka-Khem** *R* Russian Federation
116 K7 **Kakhonak** Alaska U.S.A.
54 E10 **Kakhovka** Ukraine
54 E10 **Kakhovskoye Vdkhr** *res* Ukraine
77 F2 **Kakht** Iran
77 B5 **Kākī** Iran
76 F2 **Kākināda** India
117 P5 **Kakisa L** Northwest Territories Canada
61 M8 **Kakizaki** Japan
60 H11 **Kakogawa** Japan
55 E4 **Kak, Oz** *L* Kazakhstan
85 D7 **Kakpin** Ivory Coast
66 B3 **Kak Shaal Too, Khrebet** *mts* Kazakhstan
116 Q1 **Kaktovik** Alaska U.S.A.
61 O8 **Kakuda** Japan
61 O6 **Kakumagawa** Japan
61 O6 **Kakunodate** Japan
70 C3 **Kakus** *R* Sarawak
86 E7 **Kakuyu** Zaire
117 O8 **Kakwa** *R* Alberta Canada
48 F3 **Kál** Hungary
43 D13 **Kalaâ Kebira** Tunisia
Kalaallit Nunaat *see* **Greenland**
43 B13 **Kalaat Es Senam** *mt* Tunisia
71 M9 **Kalabahi** Indonesia
46 E5 **Kalabáka** Greece
70 E2 **Kalaban** Sabah
138 F4 **Kalabity** South Australia Australia
87 D8 **Kalabo** Zambia
54 N6 **Kalach** Russian Federation
55 F3 **Kalachinsk** Russian Federation
53 F9 **Kalach-na-donu** Russian Federation
54 M6 **Kalachskaya Vozvyshennost'** *uplands* Russian Federation
68 A2 **Kaladan** Burma
121 N8 **Kaladar** Ontario Canada
102 V14 **Kalae** Hawaiian Is
70 G6 **Kalaena** *R* Sulawesi
47 R14 **Kaláfou** Rhodes Greece
68 C1 **Kalagwe** Burma
89 B4 **Kalahari Desert** Botswana
89 B6 **Kalahari Game Res** S Africa
89 B5 **Kalahari Gemsbok Nat. Park** S Africa
57 F5 **Kalai-Khumb** Tajikistan
57 B6 **Kala-I-Mor** Turkmenistan
29 K7 **Kalajoki** Finland
29 L8 **Kalajoki** *R* Finland
58 G1 **Kalakan** Russian Federation
135 O1 **Kalalau Lookout** Hawaiian Is
70 G5 **Kalaliok** Sulawesi
74 E1 **Kalam** Pakistan
100 C3 **Kalama** Washington U.S.A.
46 E7 **Kalámai** Greece
Kalamata Greece *see* **Kalámai**
94 B4 **Kalamazoo** Michigan U.S.A.
70 D7 **Kalambau** *isld* Indonesia
87 F7 **Kalambo Falls** Tanzania
46 D6 **Kálamos** *isld* Greece
46 F6 **Kálamos** Greece
143 B9 **Kalamunda** W Australia Australia
138 E3 **Kalamurra, L** South Australia Australia
143 B9 **Kalannie** W Australia Australia
29 J11 **Kalanti** Finland
71 K8 **Kalao** *isld* Indonesia
71 G7 **Kalaong** Mindanao Philippines
71 K8 **Kalaotoa** *isld* Indonesia
83 K9 **Kala Oya** *R* Sri Lanka
69 G13 **Kalapa** Indonesia
58 G1 **Kalar** *R* Russian Federation
48 L3 **Kalarash** Moldova
26 H9 **Kälarne** Sweden
83 L9 **Kal Aru** *R* Sri Lanka
74 B4 **Kalat** Pakistan
77 G6 **Kalateh-Masjed** Iran
135 S2 **Kalaupapa** Hawaiian Is
53 F10 **Kalaus** *R* Russian Federation
47 R14 **Kalavardha** Rhodes Greece
46 E6 **Kalávrita** Greece
68 C2 **Kalaw** Burma
83 K9 **Kalawewa** Sri Lanka
36 H3 **Kalbach** Germany
143 A8 **Kalbarri** W Australia Australia
143 A8 **Kalbarri Nat Park** W Australia Australia
33 O7 **Kalbe** Germany
56 B6 **Kalbinskiy Khrebet** *mts* Kazakhstan
77 F2 **Kalbū** Iran
42 F3 **Kalce** Slovenia
55 B5 **Kaldygayty** *R* Kazakhstan
47 K7 **Kale** Turkey
78 D1 **Kalecik** Turkey
71 H7 **Kaledupa** *isld* Indonesia
68 C5 **Kalegauk I** Burma
88 E6 **Kalehe** Zaire
68 B3 **Kaleindaung** *inlet* Burma
86 D6 **Kalema** Zaire
88 B4 **Kalémié** Zaire
32 K7 **Kalenberg** *reg* Germany
31 L5 **Kalety** Poland
94 B2 **Kaleva** Michigan U.S.A.
29 P6 **Kalevala** Russian Federation
28 S10 **Kalfafell** Iceland
52 E3 **Kalgachikha** Russian Federation
Kalgan *see* **Zhangjiakou**
58 G3 **Kalgan** China
143 C10 **Kalgan,R** W Australia Australia
108 F2 **Kalgary** Texas U.S.A.
116 M6 **Kalgin I** Alaska U.S.A.
143 D9 **Kalgoorlie** W Australia Australia
46 E4 **Kalí** Greece
47 L6 **Kalı** *R* Turkey
46 E6 **Kaliakoúdha** *mt* Greece
47 J1 **Kaliakra, N** Bulgaria
70 K8 **Kalianda** Sumatra
70 O9 **Kalianget** Indonesia
55 F4 **Kalibek, Oz** *L* Kazakhstan
71 F5 **Kalibo** Philippines
94 C6 **Kalida** Ohio U.S.A.
69 D14 **Kaliet** Indonesia
86 E6 **Kalima** Zaire
70 **Kalimantan** Borneo
70 B4 **Kalimantan Barat** Borneo
70 D6 **Kalimantan Selatan** Kalimantan
70 C5 **Kalimantan Tengah** Kalimantan
70 E3 **Kalimantan Timur** Kalimantan
47 H8 **Kálimnos** *isld* Greece
75 N5 **Kālīmpang** India
71 H7 **Kalingsusuh Tk** *B* Indonesia
Kalinin *see* **Tver'**
57 E5 **Kalininabad** Tajikistan
27 L17 **Kaliningrad** Russian Federation
55 C3 **Kalinino** Russian Federation
53 F8 **Kalininsk** Russian Federation
Kaliniskaya Oblast' *see* **Tverskaya Oblast'**
48 E7 **Kalinovik** Bosnia-Herzegovina
55 C6 **Kalinovka** Kazakhstan
48 M1 **Kalinovka** Ukraine
55 D3 **Kalinovo** Russian Federation
70 O10 **Kalisat** Java
101 L1 **Kalispell** Montana U.S.A.
31 L4 **Kalisz** Poland
53 F9 **Kalitva** *R* Russian Federation
88 C4 **Kaliua** Tanzania
26 N6 **Kalix** Sweden
26 N5 **Kalix älv** *R* Sweden
26 L4 **Kalixfors** Sweden
74 G3 **Kalka** India
55 G5 **Kalkaman** Kazakhstan
47 K8 **Kalkan** Turkey
25 F5 **Kalkar** Germany
94 B2 **Kalkaska** Michigan U.S.A.
33 T8 **Kalkberge** Germany
87 C10 **Kalkfeld** Namibia
Kalkfontein *see* **Tsootsha**
33 O5 **Kalkhorst** Germany
47 J5 **Kalkım** Turkey
89 A5 **Kalk Plateau** Namibia
87 C10 **Kalkrand** Namibia
83 L10 **Kalkudah** Sri Lanka
138 D2 **Kallakoopah** *R* South Australia Australia
52 C5 **Kallaste** Estonia
29 N9 **Kallavesi** *L* Finland
33 O7 **Kallehne** Germany
32 H10 **Kallenhardt** Germany
32 J8 **Kalletal** Germany
37 P2 **Kallich** Czech Rep
47 V16 **Kallidhiés** Rhodes Greece
80 F7 **Kallirhoe Hot Sp** Jordan
46 D3 **Kallmet** Albania
37 M5 **Kallmünz** Germany
47 H5 **Kalloní** Greece
47 H5 **Kallonís Kólpos** Greece
26 F8 **Kallsjön** Sweden
29 O5 **Kallunki** Finland
57 D2 **Kalmakkyrgan** *R* Kazakhstan
27 H14 **Kalmar** *county* Sweden
27 H15 **Kalmar** Sweden
27 H15 **Kalmarsund** *chan* Sweden
36 E5 **Kalmit** *mt* Germany
53 E10 **Kal'mius** *R* Ukraine
22 H1 **Kalmthout** Belgium
83 L10 **Kalmunai** Sri Lanka
55 B6 **Kalmykovo** Kazakhstan
53 G9 **Kalmytskaya Respublika** Russian Federation
48 E4 **Kalocsa** Hungary
46 G2 **Kalofer** Bulgaria
135 S3 **Kalohi Ch** Hawaiian Is
79 C3 **Kalokhorio** Cyprus
74 E7 **Kalol** India
87 E9 **Kalomo** Zambia
46 F4 **Kalón** Greece
99 P8 **Kalona** Iowa U.S.A.
117 K9 **Kalone Peak** British Columbia Canada
71 F3 **Kalongkooan** *isld* Luzon Philippines
71 F3 **Kalotkot** *isld* Luzon Philippines
28 E4 **Kalø Vig** *B* Denmark
46 G2 **Kaloyanovc** Bulgaria
73 L6 **Kalpeni I** Lakshadweep Indian Oc
74 H5 **Kalpi** India
57 J4 **Kalpin** China
83 J9 **Kalpitiya** Sri Lanka
28 E5 **Kalsenakke** Denmark
77 E1 **Kāl-Shūr, Rūd-e** *R* Iran
6 F1 **Kalsoy** *isld* Faeroes
116 H4 **Kaltag** Alaska U.S.A.
56 C4 **Kaltan** Russian Federation
41 M3 **Kalte Berg** *mt* Austria
37 M4 **Kaltenbrunn** Germany
32 L5 **Kaltenkirchen** Germany
37 J2 **Kaltennordheim** Germany
37 J2 **Kaltensundheim** Germany
54 H2 **Kaluga** Russian Federation
83 K11 **Kalu Ganga** *R* Sri Lanka
70 E7 **Kalukalukuang** *isld* Indonesia
70 F6 **Kaluku** Sulawesi
70 D3 **Kalulong, Bt** *mt* Sarawak
87 E8 **Kalulushi** Zambia
142 F2 **Kalumburu** W Australia Australia
70 F6 **Kalumpang** Sulawesi
28 G5 **Kalundborg** Denmark
28 F5 **Kalundborg Fjord** *inlet* Denmark
88 D6 **Kalungu** *R* Zambia
88 B6 **Kalungwishi** *R* Zambia
70 E1 **Kalupis Falls** Sabah
48 J1 **Kalush** Ukraine
31 N3 **Kałuszyn** Poland
83 J11 **Kalutara** Sri Lanka
53 D7 **Kaluzhskaya Oblast'** *prov* Russian Federation
31 O1 **Kalvarija** Lithuania
28 J6 **Kalvehave** Denmark
29 K8 **Kälviä** Finland
29 N10 **Kalvitsa** Finland
29 L10 **Kalvola** Finland
28 B6 **Kalvslund** Denmark
38 L7 **Kalwang** Austria
55 C1 **Kal'ya** Russian Federation
74 E9 **Kalyan** India
76 C3 **Kalyāndurg** India
74 G10 **Kalyani** India
52 H5 **Kama** *R* Russian Federation
55 G3 **Kama** Novosibirskaya obl Russian Federation
55 D1 **Kama** Sverdlovskaya obl Russian Federation
86 B1 **Kamada** Niger
60 E13 **Kamae** Japan
61 P6 **Kamaishi** Japan
61 N13 **Kama iwa** *islds* Iwo Jima Japan
135 S2 **Kamakou** *pk* Hawaiian Is
61 N10 **Kamakura** Japan
70 O9 **Kamal** Indonesia
74 E3 **Kamalia** Pakistan
135 S3 **Kamalo** Hawaiian Is
85 B7 **Kamalu** Sierra Leone
68 C4 **Kamamaung** Burma
78 D2 **Kaman** Turkey
87 D8 **Kamapanda** Zambia
72 E5 **Kamarān** *isld* Yemen
77 K2 **Kamard** *reg* Afghanistan
74 H9 **Kamareddi** India
75 N7 **Kamarhati** India
74 B9 **Kamarod** Pakistan
101 O9 **Kamas** Utah U.S.A.
87 E9 **Kamativi** Zimbabwe
119 P2 **Kamatsi L** Saskatchewan Canada
60 H11 **Kamatsushima** Japan
143 D9 **Kambalda** W Australia Australia
52 G1 **Kambal'nitskiye Koshki, Ova** *islds* Russian Federation
76 C6 **Kambam** India
69 E13 **Kambang** Sumatra
70 M9 **Kambangan** *isld* Java
71 H7 **Kambara** Indonesia
52 H6 **Kambarka** Russian Federation
85 B7 **Kambia** Sierra Leone
83 M8 **Kambling** *isld* Cocos Is Indian Oc
65 H4 **Kambo Ho** *mt* N Korea
70 F6 **Kambuno** *mt* Sulawesi
51 Q3 **Kamchatka** *pen* Russian Federation
51 Q3 **Kamchatskaya Oblast'** *prov* Russian Federation
47 J1 **Kamchiya** *R* Bulgaria
47 H2 **Kamchiya, Yazovir** *res* Bulgaria
52 F4 **Kamchuga** Russian Federation
61 N8 **Kameda** Japan
100 G4 **Kamela** Oregon U.S.A.
32 G9 **Kamen** Germany
52 D6 **Kamenets** Russian Federation
48 K2 **Kamenets-Podol'skiy** Ukraine
46 D4 **Kamenicë** Albania
42 F4 **Kamenjak. Rt** *C* Croatia
52 H1 **Kamenka** Russian Federation
52 F2 **Kamenka** Russian Federation
56 E2 **Kamenka** *R* Russian Federation
53 B8 **Kamenka-Bugskaya** Ukraine
54 F9 **Kamenka-Dneprovskaya** Ukraine
56 B4 **Kamen'na-Obi** Russian Federation
29 O11 **Kamennogorsk** Russian Federation
52 D3 **Kamennoye, Oz** *L* Russian Federation
47 J2 **Kameno** Bulgaria
54 M9 **Kamenolomni** Russian Federation
59 K3 **Kamen Rybolov** Russian Federation
56 G5 **Kamensk** Russian Federation
55 E3 **Kamenskoye** Russian Federation
53 F9 **Kamensk-Shakhtinskiy** Russian Federation
55 D3 **Kamensk-Ural'skiy** Russian Federation
31 O3 **Kamenyuki** Belarus
30 H4 **Kamenz** Germany
61 J10 **Kameoka** Japan
12 C2 **Kames** Scotland
54 N1 **Kameshkovo** Russian Federation
74 H3 **Kamet** *mt* India/Xizang Zizhiqu
61 K11 **Kameyama** Japan
100 J3 **Kamiah** Idaho U.S.A.
31 K2 **Kamien** Poland
31 J5 **Kamienna Góra** Poland
31 H2 **Kamień Pomorski** Poland
31 L4 **Kamieńsk** Poland
87 C12 **Kamieskroon** S Africa
89 A8 **Kamies Sektor Berg** *mt* S Africa
60 Q2 **Kami-Furano** Japan
60 Q2 **Kamikawa** *prefect* Japan
60 C14 **Kami-Koshiki-jima** *isld* Japan
140 F4 **Kamileroi** Queensland Australia
114 J5 **Kamilukuak L** Northwest Territories Canada
87 D7 **Kamina** Zaire
115 K5 **Kaminak L** Northwest Territories Canada
99 R1 **Kaministikwia** Ontario Canada
60 C11 **Kami no-shima** *isld* Japan
115 K5 **Kaminuriak L** Northwest Territories Canada
61 L9 **Kamioka** Japan
47 Q14 **Kamiros** *hist site* Rhodes Greece
116 L7 **Kamishak B** Alaska U.S.A.
60 R2 **Kami-Shihoro** Japan
Kamishli *see* **Qāmishlī, Al**
88 B3 **Kamituga** Zaire
61 O13 **Kamiyama-jima** *isld* Okinawa
60 R1 **Kami-Yūbetsu** Japan
57 F3 **Kamkaly** Kazakhstan
56 C5 **Kamlak** Russian Federation
117 N10 **Kamloops** British Columbia Canada
68 B3 **Kamma** Burma
29 P7 **Kammenoye, Oz** *L* Russian Federation
60 E12 **Kammon Kaikyō** *str* Japan
60 D12 **Kammon Tunnels** Japan
60 J10 **Kammuri shima** *isld* Japan
60 F11 **Kammuri-yama** *mt* Japan
42 F2 **Kamnik** Slovenia
56 H3 **Kamniokan** Russian Federation
78 K1 **Kamo** Armenia
61 M8 **Kamo** Japan
145 E1 **Kamo** New Zealand
56 E1 **Kamo** *R* Russian Federation
128 G3 **Kamoa Mts** Guyana
60 O2 **Kamoenai** Japan
61 O10 **Kamogawa** Japan
60 H11 **Kamojima** Japan
122 C6 **Kamouraska** Quebec Canada
38 N4 **Kamp** *R* Austria
69 G13 **Kampa** Indonesia
86 F5 **Kampala** Uganda
69 E12 **Kamparkiri** *R* Sumatra
36 D3 **Kamp-Bornhofen** Germany
28 A7 **Kampen** Germany
25 E3 **Kampen** Netherlands
86 E6 **Kampene** Zaire
22 H2 **Kampenhout** Belgium
38 M5 **Kamp, Gr** *R* Austria
68 D4 **Kamphaeng Phet** Thailand
88 B6 **Kampinda** Zambia
88 B7 **Kampolombo, L** Zambia
68 G7 **Kampong Cham** Cambodia
68 G6 **Kampong Chhnang** Cambodia
68 G7 **Kampot** Cambodia
85 D6 **Kampti** Burkina
Kampuchea *rep see* **Cambodia**
99 N7 **Kamrar** Iowa U.S.A.
119 Q7 **Kamsack** Saskatchewan Canada
52 G6 **Kamskoye Ust'ye** Russian Federation
74 H8 **Kāmthi** India
119 P2 **Kamuchawie L** Saskatchewan Canada
60 Q3 **Kamui-dake** *mt* Japan
46 E4 **Kamvoúnia, Óri** *mts* Greece
53 G8 **Kamyshin** Russian Federation
55 D3 **Kamyshlov** Russian Federation
57 B2 **Kamyshlybash** Kazakhstan
55 D5 **Kamyshnoye** Kazakhstan
54 F6 **Kamyshnya** Ukraine
54 H9 **Kamysh-Zarya** Ukraine
68 B1 **Kan** Burma
85 G6 **Kan** Nigeria
56 D3 **Kan** *R* Russian Federation
89 E2 **Kana** *R* Zimbabwe
103 M4 **Kanab** Utah U.S.A.
103 M5 **Kanab Cr** Arizona U.S.A.
70 C3 **Kana, Bt** *mt* Sarawak
61 O5 **Kanagi** Japan
42 F2 **Kanal** Slovenia
46 F5 **Kanália** Greece
69 A9 **Kanalla** Nicobar Is
118 C8 **Kananaskis L** Alberta Canada
86 D7 **Kananga** Zaire
55 C4 **Kananikol'skoye** Russian Federation
103 L4 **Kanarraville** Utah U.S.A.
52 G6 **Kanash** Russian Federation
46 F5 **Kanastraion, Ákr** *C* Greece
116 K8 **Kanatak** Alaska U.S.A.
52 H4 **Kanava** Russian Federation
99 N7 **Kanawha** Iowa U.S.A.
109 M2 **Kanawha** Texas U.S.A.
94 E8 **Kanawha** *R* West Virginia U.S.A.
94 F7 **Kanawha, Little** *R* West Virginia U.S.A.
61 M11 **Kanaya** Japan
61 K9 **Kanazawa** Japan
61 K9 **Kanazu** Japan
75 Q7 **Kanbalu** Burma
68 C5 **Kanbauk** Burma
68 D5 **Kanchanaburi** Thailand
Kanchenjunga *see* **Kanychenjunga**
57 J1 **Kanchingiz, Khrebet** *mt* Kazakhstan
76 D4 **Kanchipuram** India
60 D12 **Kanda** Japan
74 B4 **Kanda** Pakistan
77 J4 **Kandahār** Afghanistan
77 J4 **Kandahār** *prov* Afghanistan
119 N7 **Kandahar** Saskatchewan Canada
52 D2 **Kandalaksha** Russian Federation
52 D2 **Kandalalakshskaya Guba** *B* Russian Federation
69 C11 **Kandang** Sumatra
70 D6 **Kandangan** Kalimantan
46 F9 **Kándanos** Crete Greece
52 B6 **Kandava** Latvia
36 E5 **Kandel** Germany
40 G2 **Kandern** Germany
28 E1 **Kandestederne** Denmark
74 C4 **Kandhkot** Pakistan
85 E6 **Kandi** Benin
76 D2 **Kandi** India
77 K5 **Kandi** Pakistan
116 R4 **Kandik** *R* Alaska U.S.A.
47 L3 **Kandıra** Turkey
70 G4 **Kandi, Tg** *C* Sulawesi
74 D7 **Kandla** India
139 J5 **Kandos** New South Wales Australia
87 H11 **Kandreho** Madagascar
55 B4 **Kandry** Russian Federation
76 D3 **Kandukur** India
83 K10 **Kandy** Sri Lanka
110 F2 **Kane** Illinois U.S.A.
94 J5 **Kane** Pennsylvania U.S.A.
101 R5 **Kane** Wyoming U.S.A.
115 M2 **Kane Basin** Canada/Greenland
116 G7 **Kanektok** *R* Alaska U.S.A.
86 C3 **Kanem** *dist* Chad
102 S12 **Kaneohe** Hawaiian Is
102 S12 **Kaneohe Bay** Hawaiian Is
54 C7 **Kanev** Ukraine
52 E2 **Kanevka** Russian Federation
54 C7 **Kanevskoye Vodokhranilishche** *res* Ukraine
61 O7 **Kaneyama** Japan
42 F3 **Kanfanar** Croatia
87 D10 **Kang** Botswana
115 O4 **Kangaamiut** Greenland
Kangaarsussiaq *see* **Parry, Kap**
115 O4 **Kangaatsiak** Greenland
85 C6 **Kangaba** Mali
78 F2 **Kangal** Turkey
77 C6 **Kangan** Iran
69 E9 **Kangar** Malaysia
138 D6 **Kangaroo I** South Australia Australia
140 E4 **Kangaroo Pt** Queensland Australia
29 L7 **Kangas** Finland
29 N9 **Kangaslampi** Finland
29 M9 **Kangasniemi** Finland
77 A2 **Kangāvar** Iran
48 M4 **Kangaz** Moldova
65 C4 **Kangbao** China
75 N5 **Kangchenjunga** *mt* Nepal/India
58 D5 **Kangding** China
70 P9 **Kangean** *isld* Indonesia
115 N4 **Kangeeak Pt** Northwest Territories Canada
Kangeq *C see* **Cort Adelaer, Kap**
Kanger Iussuaq *see* **Søndre Strømfjord**
Kangerlua *see* **Kobberminebugt**
115 Q4 **Kangerlussuaq** *inlet* Greenland
Kangersuatsiaq *see* **Prøven**
115 Q4 **Kangertittivatsiaq** *inlet* Greenland
86 G5 **Kangetet** Kenya
59 J3 **Kanggye** N Korea
Kangikajik *C see* **Brewster, Kap**
Kangilinnguit *see* **Grønnedal**
115 M5 **Kangiqsujuaq** Quebec Canada
65 B5 **Kangjiahui** China
65 G1 **Kangjinjing** China
59 J4 **Kangnŭng** S Korea
86 B5 **Kango** Gabon
61 N13 **Kangoku-iwa** *islds* Iwo Jima Japan
26 N4 **Kangosfors** Sweden
65 F3 **Kangping** China
75 J3 **Kangrinboqê Feng** *mt* Xizang Zizhiqu
71 E8 **Kang Tipayan Dakula** *isld* Philippines
Kan-hsien *see* **Ganzhou**
68 B1 **Kani** Burma
87 D7 **Kaniama** Zaire
57 F4 **Kanibadam** Tajikistan
144 C5 **Kaniere** New Zealand
144 C5 **Kaniere, L** New Zealand
76 D3 **Kanigiri** India
57 D4 **Kanimekh** Uzbekistan
52 F1 **Kanin Nos, Mys** *C* Russian Federation
52 F1 **Kanin, Poluostrov** *pen* Russian Federation
52 F1 **Kaninskiy Bereg** *coast* Russian Federation
61 O5 **Kanita** Japan
26 N5 **Kaniulasjärvi** Sweden
138 F6 **Kaniva** Victoria Australia
48 F4 **Kanjiža** Serbia Yugoslavia
29 J10 **Kankaanpää** Finland
99 S8 **Kankakee** *R* Illinois U.S.A.
85 C6 **Kankan** Guinea
75 J8 **Kanker** India
83 J8 **Kankesanturai** Sri Lanka
29 L4 **Kankonen** Finland
74 E6 **Kankroli** India
68 D7 **Kanmaw Kyun** *isld* Burma
56 D5 **Kanmegirskiy Khrebet** *mts* Russian Federation
27 G15 **Kånna** Sweden
112 G2 **Kannapolis** North Carolina U.S.A.
22 K2 **Kanne** Belgium
74 G7 **Kannod** India
29 L9 **Kannonkoski** Finland
Kannur *see* **Cannanore**
29 K8 **Kannus** Finland
71 J6 **Kano** *isld* Indonesia
60 E11 **Kano** Japan
85 F6 **Kano** Nigeria
107 K2 **Kanona** Kansas U.S.A.
55 G5 **Kanonerka** Kazakhstan
60 G11 **Kanonji** Japan
126 B2 **Kanon, Pt** Curaçao Neth Antilles
107 M3 **Kanopolis** Kansas U.S.A.
103 M3 **Kanosh** Utah U.S.A.
70 C3 **Kanowit** Sarawak
60 D14 **Kanoya** Japan
74 J5 **Kanpur** India
107 K3 **Kansas** *state* U.S.A.
99 T10 **Kansas** Illinois U.S.A.
107 P2 **Kansas** *R* Kansas U.S.A.
107 Q5 **Kansas** Oklahoma U.S.A.
107 Q2 **Kansas City** Kansas U.S.A.
110 B2 **Kansas City** Missouri U.S.A.
67 E4 **Kanshi** China
56 E3 **Kansk** Russian Federation
56 E4 **Kanskoye Belogor'ye** *mts* Russian Federation
88 A5 **Kansonge** Zaire
Kansu *prov see* **Gansu**
57 G3 **Kant** Kirghizia
29 N9 **Kantala** Finland
85 E6 **Kantchari** Burkina
85 E6 **Kanté** Togo
68 G5 **Kantharalak** Thailand
75 M8 **Kānthi** India
116 M4 **Kantishna** *R* Alaska U.S.A.
134 A6 **Kanton I** *isld* Phoenix Is Pacific Oc
61 M10 **Kanto sanchi** *mts* Japan
68 C2 **Kantulong** Burma
14 C4 **Kanturk** Ireland
77 J5 **Kanuk** Afghanistan
102 S11 **Kanuku** Hawaiian Is
128 G3 **Kanuku Mts** Guyana
61 N9 **Kanuma** Japan
87 C11 **Kanus** Namibia
116 M3 **Kanuti** *R* Alaska U.S.A.
89 D5 **Kanye** Botswana
68 B3 **Kanyinngu** Burma
68 C3 **Kanyutkwin** Burma
38 J8 **Kanzel** *mt* Austria
87 E8 **Kanzenze** Zaire
137 R5 **Kao** *isld* Tonga
87 B9 **Kaoko Veld** *reg* Namibia
85 A6 **Kaolack** Senegal
47 J1 **Kaolinovo** Bulgaria
87 D8 **Kaoma** Zambia
65 F2 **Kaoshan** China
102 V13 **Kapaa** Hawaiian Is
102 V13 **Kapaau** Hawaiian Is
74 E7 **Kapadvanj** India
57 J2 **Kapal** Kazakhstan
71 O9 **Kapala** *isld* Indonesia
71 A3 **Kapalabuaya** Indonesia
71 M9 **Kapan** Timor Indonesia
87 D7 **Kapanga** Zaire
87 F7 **Kapatu** Zambia
66 B3 **Kapchagay** Kazakhstan
57 H3 **Kapchagayskoye Vdkhr.** *res* Kazakhstan
22 G1 **Kapellen** Belgium
25 F5 **Kapellen** Germany
86 G5 **Kapenguria** Kenya
38 M7 **Kapfenberg** Austria
88 E9 **Kapichira Falls** *waterfall* Malawi
47 J4 **Kapıdağı Yar** *pen* Turkey
70 G5 **Kapinyu, Tanjong** *C* Sulawesi
87 E8 **Kapiri Mposhi** Zambia
77 L2 **Kāpīsā** *prov* Afghanistan
115 L7 **Kapiskau** Ontario Canada
70 C4 **Kapit** Sarawak
54 C8 **Kapitanovka** Ukraine
145 E4 **Kapiti I** New Zealand
111 D11 **Kaplan** Louisiana U.S.A.
31 H7 **Kaplice** Czech Rep
69 D8 **Kapoe** Thailand
86 F5 **Kapoeta** Sudan
135 V5 **Kapoho** Hawaiian Is
71 L9 **Kapondai, Tanjong** Indonesia
145 E3 **Kaponga** New Zealand
70 F7 **Kapoposang** *isld* Indonesia
48 E4 **Kapos** *R* Hungary
48 D4 **Kaposvár** Hungary
71 C3 **Kapotjol** W Irian
74 B10 **Kappar** Pakistan
28 G7 **Kappel** Denmark
36 C3 **Kappel** Germany
28 D7 **Kappeln** Germany
36 E6 **Kappelrodeck** Germany
27 K14 **Kappelshamn** *isld* Gotland Sweden
41 M3 **Kappl** Austria
38 G7 **Kaprun** Austria
Kapsukas *see* **Marijampolė**
88 C9 **Kapsuku** *mt* Zimbabwe
70 B4 **Kapuas** *R* Kalimantan
70 D5 **Kapuas** *R* Kalimantan
70 C4 **Kapuas Hulu, Peg** Kalimantan
138 E5 **Kapunda** South Australia Australia
145 E3 **Kapuni** New Zealand
74 F3 **Kapurthala** India
120 H3 **Kapuskasing** Ontario Canada
120 H4 **Kapuskasing** *R* Ontario Canada
139 K4 **Kaputar** *mt* New South Wales Australia
48 D3 **Kapuvár** Hungary
56 H4 **Kapylyushi, Oz** *L* Russian Federation
66 B4 **Kaqung** China
85 E7 **Kara** Togo
78 G2 **Kara** *R* Turkey
79 G6 **Karā', Arḑ al** Syria
57 G5 **Karaart** Tajikistan
57 G3 **Kara Balta** Kirghizia
54 K1 **Karabanovo** Russian Federation
57 H2 **Karabas** Kazakhstan
57 C5 **Karabekaul** Turkmenistan
47 J4 **Karabiğa** Turkey
57 C6 **Karabil', Vozvyshennost'** *uplands* Turkmenistan
78 D1 **Karabük** Turkey
57 J4 **Karabulak** China
46 C4 **Karaburun** Albania
47 H6 **Kara Burun** *C* Turkey
47 H6 **Karaburun** Turkey
47 J8 **Kara Burun** *C* Turkey
55 D6 **Karabutak** Kazakhstan
47 J4 **Karacabey** Turkey
47 J3 **Karacaköy** Turkey
79 C2 **Karaçal Tepe** *mt* Turkey
47 J3 **Karacaoğlan** Turkey
47 K7 **Karacasu** Turkey

53 F11 Karachayevo-Cherkesskaya Avtonomnyy Oblast' Russian Federation
54 F3 Karachev Russian Federation
74 B6 Karachi Pakistan
76 B2 Karad India
78 D3 Kara Dağ mt Turkey
57 G4 Karadar'ya R Kirghizia
47 M11 Karadeniz Boğazı str Turkey
55 F2 Karagach Russian Federation
55 F6 Karaganda Kazakhstan
57 H1 Karagayly Kazakhstan
51 Q4 Karaginskiy, Ostrova islds Russian Federation
47 K8 Kara Göl L Turkey
56 B5 Karaguzhikha Kazakhstan
47 K6 Karahalh Turkey
47 J7 Karahayıt Turkey
55 C3 Karaidel' Russian Federation
76 D5 Kāraikāl India
Kara Irtysh R see Ertix He
79 F1 Karaisalı Turkey
70 E4 Karaitan Kalimantan
83 J9 Karaitivu Sri Lanka
77 B2 Karaj Iran
79 F7 Karak Jordan
47 H6 Karaka Burun C Turkey
57 A3 Karakalpakskaya Respublika Uzbekistan
57 C2 Karaketken Kazakhstan
143 B9 Karakin Ls W Australia Australia
57 E2 Karakoin, Ozero L Kazakhstan
57 H4 Karakolka Kirghizia
74 F1 Karakoram ra Kashmir
74 G1 Karakoram Pass Kashmir
85 B5 Karakoro R Mauritania/Mali
58 D2 Karakorum Mongolia
55 G5 Karakul Kazakhstan
55 F4 Kara-Kuga Kazakhstan
57 G4 Kara Kul' Kirghizia
57 C5 Karakul' Uzbekistan
52 H6 Karakulino Russian Federation
57 G5 Kara-Kul', Ozero L Tajikistan
55 D4 Karakul'skoye Russian Federation
57 C5 Karakumskiy Kanal Turkmenistan
50 E5 Karakumy Turkmenistan
57 A5 Karakumy, Peski desert Turkmenistan
60 D14 Karakuni-dake mt Japan
38 M8 Karalpe mts Austria
143 C7 Karalundi W Australia Australia
70 F6 Karam R Sulawesi
80 F6 Karama Jordan
47 K7 Karaman Turkey
47 K7 Karamanlı Turkey
66 C2 Karamay China
145 D4 Karamea New Zealand
70 D7 Karamian isld Indonesia
47 L6 Karamık Gölü L Turkey
66 C4 Karamiran He R China
66 D4 Karamiran Shankou pass China
86 F5 Karamoja dist Uganda
47 K4 Karamürsel Turkey
78 L4 Karand Iran
69 G14 Karangagung Sumatra
70 K8 Karangan Sumatra
144 B5 Karangarua R New Zealand
70 P10 Karangasem Indonesia
70 M9 Karangbolong Tanjong C Java
70 F7 Karang Bril Indonesia
70 F5 Karang, Tg C Sulawesi
74 G8 Karanja India
47 J7 Karaova Turkey
57 G2 Karaoy Kazakhstan
57 D3 Karaozek Kazakhstan
47 J1 Karapelit Bulgaria
78 D3 Karapınar Turkey
145 E2 Karapiro New Zealand
66 C4 Karasay China
47 K5 Karasay Kirghizia
89 A7 Karasburg Namibia
147 M12 Kara Sea Arctic Oc
55 G5 Karashoky Kazakhstan
26 O2 Karasjok Norway
26 O2 Karasjokka R Norway
55 G5 Karasor Kazakhstan
55 F4 Karasu Kokchetavskaya obl Kazakhstan
55 D5 Karasu Kustanayskaya Kazakhstan
47 L3 Karasu Turkey
78 H1 Karasu R Turkey
57 F4 Karasuk Russian Federation
56 B4 Karasuk R Russian Federation
61 O9 Karasuyama Japan
55 E2 Karas'ye, Oz L Russian Federation
57 L1 Karatal Kazakhstan
57 H2 Karatal R Kazakhstan
78 E3 Karataş Turkey
57 F3 Kara Tau Kazakhstan
68 D7 Karathuri Burma
83 J9 Karativu isld Sri Lanka
27 K5 Karatjaur L Sweden
55 B6 Karatobe Kazakhstan
57 B2 Karatobe, Mys C Kazakhstan
55 D5 Karatomarskoye Vodokhranilishche res Kazakhstan
60 C12 Karatsu Japan
57 A2 Karatup, Poluostrov pen Kazakhstan
55 E6 Karaturgay R Kazakhstan
Karaul see Qongkol
57 J1 Karaul Kazakhstan
50 H1 Karaul Russian Federation
57 A3 Kara-uzyak Uzbekistan
46 E5 Karáva mt Greece
57 F4 Karavan Kirghizia
46 C4 Karavastasë, Këneta e Albania
79 C4 Karavostasi Cyprus
70 L9 Karawang Java
70 L8 Karawang Tg. C Java
38 K8 Karawanken mt Austria
57 F2 Karazhal Kazakhstan
57 G2 Karazhingil Kazakhstan
78 J5 Karbalā' prov Iraq
78 J5 Karbala Iraq
36 F3 Karben Germany
26 H10 Kårböle Sweden
33 Q6 Karbow-Vietlübbe Germany
55 G6 Karbushevka Kazakhstan
28 B3 Karby Denmark
48 F3 Karcag Hungary
46 E8 Kardhamíla Greece
46 F6 Kardhamíla Greece
46 E5 Kardhítsa Greece
26 N5 Kardis Sweden
52 B5 Kärdla Estonia
138 B2 Karee N Terr Australia
52 D3 Karel'skaya Masel'ga Russian Federation
52 D3 Karel'skaya Respublika Russian Federation
87 F7 Karema Tanzania
Karen State see Kayin State
85 C4 Karet Mauritania
145 F2 Karewa I New Zealand
55 C5 Kargala Russian Federation
57 G1 Kargaly Kazakhstan
55 D3 Kargapolye Russian Federation
56 B3 Kargat R Russian Federation
Karghalik see Yecheng
78 E1 Kargı Turkey
52 E4 Kargopol' Russian Federation
33 R6 Kargow Germany
31 J3 Kargowa Poland
85 G6 Kargueri Niger
117 G8 Karheen Alaska U.S.A.
29 M11 Karhula Finland
88 B10 Kariba Zimbabwe
88 B10 Kariba Dam Zimbabwe/Zambia
88 B10 Kariba,L Zimbabwe/Zambia
60 N3 Kariba yama mt Japan
87 C10 Karibib Namibia
89 C9 Kariega watercourse S Africa
29 M2 Karigasniemi Finland
29 J9 Karijoki Finland
145 D1 Karikari, C New Zealand
86 F2 Karima Sudan
75 P6 Karimganj India
74 H9 Karimnagar India
69 F12 Karimun Besar isld Indonesia
70 N8 Karimundjawa isld Indonesia
70 N8 Karimundjawa, Pulau Pulau islds Indonesia
86 A1 Karin Somalia
145 E2 Karioi mt New Zealand
145 E3 Karioi New Zealand
29 K11 Karis Finland
28 J6 Karise Denmark
88 E6 Karisimbi. Mt Zaire
46 G6 Káristos Greece
144 C6 Karitane New Zealand
76 B4 Karkal India
Karkamiş see Barak
136 K2 Karkar isld Papua New Guinea
57 H1 Karkaralinsk Kazakhstan
77 F7 Kārkīn Dar Iran
29 L11 Karkkila Finland
29 L11 Kärkölä Finland
138 D5 Karkoo South Australia Australia
Karlá L see Voïvis L
54 G5 Karla Libknekhta Russian Federation
57 G6 Karla Marksa, Pik mt Tajikistan
28 F4 Karlby Denmark
26 R1 Karlebotn Norway
27 H2 Karleby Denmark
31 J1 Karlino Poland
Karl-Marx-Stadt see Chemnitz
42 G4 Karlobag Croatia
54 G7 Karlovka Ukraine
46 G2 Karlovo Bulgaria
37 O3 Karlovy Vary Czech Rep
26 K8 Karlsbäck Sweden
36 E6 Karlsbad Germany
36 E6 Karlsberg Sweden
27 G13 Karlsborg Sweden
37 L7 Karlsfeld Germany
32 K9 Karlshafen Germany
26 N5 Karlshamn Sweden
27 G12 Karlskoga Sweden
27 H15 Karlskrona Sweden
26 L1 Karlsöy Norway
36 E5 Karlsruhe Germany
98 F1 Karlsruhe North Dakota U.S.A.
27 F12 Karlstad Sweden
98 K1 Karlstad Minnesota U.S.A.
36 H4 Karlstadt Germany
116 K8 Karluk L Alaska U.S.A.
57 D5 Karlyuk Turkmenistan
76 B1 Karmala India
52 E6 Karmanovo Russian Federation
80 D8 Karmel Jordan
80 C2 Karmel, Cape Israel
80 C6 Karmé Yosēf Israel
80 E2 Karmi'el Israel
80 B7 Karmiyya Israel
27 A12 Karmöy isld Norway
109 N3 Karnack Texas U.S.A.
110 H4 Karnak Illinois U.S.A.
74 G4 Karnal India
74 G4 Karnataka prov India
109 K7 Karnes City Texas U.S.A.
38 G8 Karnische Alpen mts Austria
47 H2 Karnobat Bulgaria
27 E13 Kärnsj L Sweden
38 H8 Kärnten Austria
87 E9 Karoi Zimbabwe
77 L2 Karokh Afghanistan
31 M2 Karokpi Burma
68 C5 Karompalompo isld Indonesia
71 K8 Karona Fall Guyana
128 G3 Karonga Malawi
88 D6 Karonie W Australia Australia
143 D9 Karool-Döbö Kirghizia
57 H4 Karoo National Park S Africa
89 C9 Karoonda South Australia Australia
138 E6 Káros isld Greece
47 H8 Karossa Sulawesi Indonesia
70 F5 Karossa, Tg C Indonesia
71 J9 Karousádhes Greece
47 O12 Karow Germany
33 Q5 Kárpathos isld Greece
47 J9 Kárpathos Kárpathos I Greece
47 J9 Karpathos Str Greece
46 D6 Karpenision Greece
41 K4 Kärpf mt Switzerland
37 P7 Karpfham Germany
55 C2 Karpinsk Russian Federation
52 F3 Karpogory Russian Federation
55 D2 Karpunino Russian Federation
55 C3 Karpushikha Russian Federation
79 C2 Karpuz R Turkey
47 J7 Karpuzlu Turkey
142 A1 Karrakatta dist Perth, W Aust Australia
142 B5 Karratha W Australia Australia
115 O3 Karrats Fjord Greenland
28 H6 Karrebæk Denmark
28 H6 Karrebæksminde Denmark
28 G6 Karrebæksminde Bugt B Denmark
89 B8 Karreeberge mts S Africa
143 B10 Karridale W Australia Australia
78 J1 Kars Turkey
57 D1 Karsakpay Kazakhstan
119 S2 Karsakuwigamak L Manitoba Canada
29 M8 Kärsämäki Finland
52 C6 Kārsava Latvia
57 D5 Karshi Uzbekistan
57 D5 Karshinskaya Step' Uzbekistan
75 N5 Kārsiyāng India
53 E1 Karskiye Vorota, Proliv str Russian Federation
33 P6 Karstädt Germany
28 B5 Karstoft Denmark
28 L9 Karstula Finland
26 H10 Karsvall Sweden
47 J7 Kartal mt Greece
47 N11 Kartal Turkey
55 D4 Kartaly Russian Federation
55 D4 Kartayêl Russian Federation
94 J5 Karthaus Germany
94 J5 Karthaus Pennsylvania U.S.A.
29 N9 Karttula Finland
31 L1 Kartuzy Poland
88 C8 Karubwe Zambia
61 M9 Karuizawa Japan
75 Q9 Karulbie Rockhole rockhole W Australia Australia
140 F3 Karumba Queensland Australia
77 A4 Karun R Iran
27 H11 Karungi Sweden
71 J9 Karuni Indonesia
142 G3 Karunjie W Australia Australia
106 G3 Karval Colorado U.S.A.
74 K9 Karvia Finland
26 K2 Kårvik Norway
31 L6 Karviná Czech Rep
76 B3 Karwar India
76 B3 Karwendel Geb mts Austria
41 O3 Karym Russian Federation
55 E1 Kås Denmark
28 D2 Kas R Russian Federation
56 C2 Kaş Turkey
47 K8 Kaş Turkey
88 C6 Kasaba B Zambia
86 D6 Kasai prov Zaire
87 D7 Kasai R Zaire
87 D8 Kasaji Zaire
61 O9 Kasama Japan
88 C7 Kasama Zambia
57 D5 Kasan Uzbekistan
88 C6 Kasanga Tanzania
57 F4 Kasansay Uzbekistan
76 B4 Kasaragod India
75 O7 Kasba Bangladesh
114 J5 Kasba L Northwest Territories Canada
27 G16 Kåseberga Sweden
60 D14 Kaseda Japan
116 F1 Kasegaluk Lag Alaska U.S.A.
87 E8 Kasempa Zambia
37 L3 Kasendorf Germany
88 B7 Kasenga Zaire
86 F5 Kasenyi Zaire
86 F5 Kasese Uganda
77 B5 Kāserūn Iran
86 C1 Kasese Uganda
86 B5 Kasese Zaire
83 E3 Kaset Wisai Thailand
119 N2 Kashabowie Ontario Canada
77 B2 Kāshān Iran
Kashgar see Kashi
66 B4 Kashi China
61 J11 Kashihara Japan
60 D12 Kashima Japan
52 E6 Kashin Russian Federation
74 H4 Kashipur India
54 K2 Kashira Russian Federation
119 O1 Kashishibog L Ontario Canada
61 M8 Kashiwazaki Japan
58 D4 Kashkadar'in-skaya Oblast Uzbekistan
57 G2 Kashkanteniz Kazakhstan
52 D4 Kashkany Russian Federation
52 E2 Kashkarantsy Russian Federation
57 H4 Kashkasu Kirghizia
77 F2 Kāshmar Iran
66 B5 Kashmir prov India/Pakistan
74 C4 Kashmor Pakistan
88 G3 Kasigao mt Kenya
70 G5 Kasimbar Sulawesi
71 A3 Kasiruta isld Indonesia
110 G2 Kaskaskia R Illinois U.S.A.
26 K6 Kasker Sweden
29 J9 Kaskinen Finland
Kaskö see Kaskinen
68 F7 Kas Kong Cambodia
55 D3 Kasli Russian Federation
117 P11 Kaslo British Columbia Canada
69 F14 Kasmaran Sumatra
70 C5 Kasongan Kalimantan
86 E6 Kasongo Zaire
87 C7 Kasongo-Lunda Zaire
47 H9 Kásos isld Greece
47 H9 Kásos Str Greece
47 J1 Kaspichan Bulgaria
54 C1 Kaspiya R Belarus/Rus Fed
68 H6 Kas Preas Cambodia
68 F7 Kas Prins isld Cambodia
68 F6 Kas Rong isld Cambodia
68 F7 Kas Rong Sam Lem isld Cambodia
86 G2 Kassala Sudan
46 F4 Kassándra Greece
32 L10 Kassel Germany
85 F1 Kasserine Tunisia
47 O12 Kassiópi Greece
68 F7 Kas Smach isld Cambodia
99 O5 Kasson Minnesota U.S.A.
78 D1 Kastamonu Turkey
47 H6 Kastaneai Greece
28 E3 Kastbjerg Denmark
36 E3 Kastel Germany
46 C3 Kastellaun Germany
46 F9 Kastélli Crete Greece
46 G9 Kastéllion Crete Greece
47 J8 Kastellórizon isld Greece
36 B1 Kaster Germany
22 H1 Kasterlee Belgium
37 M5 Kastl Germany
27 H15 Kastlösa Sweden
33 N5 Kastorf Germany
46 D4 Kastoria Greece
46 E5 Kastoría, L Greece
46 G5 Kástron Límnos I Greece
46 F4 Kástron Nigrita Greece
46 D5 Kastrosikiá Greece
29 K5 Kastrup Denmark
80 D2 Kasubuchi Japan
60 D12 Kasuga Japan
61 K10 Kasugai Japan
61 O9 Kasumiga-ura L Japan
70 E5 Kasungan Kalimantan
87 F8 Kasungu Malawi
88 F8 Kasupe Malawi
74 F3 Kasur Pakistan
87 G6 Katagum Nigeria
95 S8 Katahdin, Mt Maine U.S.A.
86 D6 Katako-Kombe Zaire
46 E7 Katákolon Greece
116 P2 Katakturuk R Alaska U.S.A.
116 P2 Katalla Alaska U.S.A.
86 D7 Katanda Zaire
56 F2 Katanga R Russian Federation
74 H8 Katangi India
53 G1 Katangli Russian Federation
143 C10 Katanning W Australia Australia
75 J4 Katarnian Ghat India
77 L5 Katastāri Greece
61 J10 Katata Japan
88 C6 Katavi Nat. Park Tanzania
77 L3 Katāwāz-Urgan Afghanistan
57 B5 Kataysk Russian Federation
69 A9 Katchall isld Nicobar Is
38 J7 Katchberg Austria
88 C6 Katchiungo Angola
116 F8 Kateel R Alaska U.S.A.
119 O8 Katepwa Saskatchewan Canada
46 F4 Kateríni Greece
25 E6 Katerveer Netherlands
117 G7 Kates Needle mt British Columbia Canada
75 K7 Katghora India
75 K5 Katha Burma
84 J4 Katherina, Gebel hill Egypt
140 B2 Katherine N Terr Australia
140 C2 Katherine R N Terr Australia
71 H8 Kathgodam India
74 D7 Kathiawar reg India
83 L9 Kathiraveli Sri Lanka
113 E9 Kathleen Florida U.S.A.
140 B3 Kathleen Falls N Terr Australia
143 D7 Kathleen Valley W Australia Australia
75 L5 Kathmandu Nepal
118 D7 Kathryn Alberta Canada
98 H3 Kathryn North Dakota U.S.A.
74 F2 Kathua Kashmir
85 D6 Kati Mali
75 L5 Katibas R Sarawak
75 M6 Katihar India
145 E2 Katikati New Zealand
87 D9 Katima Mulilo Namibia
119 S5 Katimik L Manitoba Canada
85 D7 Katiola Ivory Coast
29 L7 Kätkätunturi mt Finland
89 A8 Katkop Hills S Africa
48 M5 Katlabuk, Oz L Ukraine
32 M9 Katlenburg Germany
116 K7 Katmai Nat Park and Preserve Alaska U.S.A.
116 K7 Katmai Vol., Mt Alaska U.S.A.
74 J7 Katni India
46 E7 Káto Akhaia Greece
46 F5 Katokhi Greece
88 C9 Katondwe Zambia
47 H5 Káto Nevrokópion Greece
139 K5 Katoomba New South Wales Australia
70 G5 Katoposa, Gunung mt Sulawesi
46 F4 Káto Stavrós Greece
55 C4 Katov-Ivanovsk Russian Federation
31 L5 Katowice Poland
75 N7 Kātoya India
47 L7 Katranc Dağ mt Turkey
27 H10 Katrineberg Sweden
27 H13 Katrineholm Sweden
12 D1 Katrine, L Scotland
85 F6 Katsina Nigeria
61 P13 Katsuren-zaki C Okinawa
61 O9 Katsuta Japan
61 O10 Katsuura Japan
61 N10 Katsuyama Japan
61 K9 Katsuyama Fukui Japan
60 G10 Katsuyama Okayama Japan
57 D5 Kattakurgan Uzbekistan
142 F5 Kattamudda Well W Australia Australia
29 K4 Kattarp Sweden
47 J9 Kattavia Rhodes Greece
47 Q15 Kattavia Rhodes Greece
120 K3 Kattawagami L Ontario Canada
28 E3 Kattegat str Denmark
32 G8 Kattenvenne Germany
27 K14 Katthammarsvik isld Gotland Sweden
28 D5 Kattrup Denmark
88 A8 Katue R Zambia
87 E7 Katumba Zaire
88 D7 Katumbi Malawi
56 C5 Katun' R Russian Federation
83 J10 Katunayaka Sri Lanka
56 C6 Katunskiy Khr mts Russian Federation
88 B2 Katwe Uganda
25 B4 Katwijk aan Zee Netherlands
31 K4 Katy Wrocł Poland
36 G5 Katzenbuckel mt Germany
36 D3 Katzenelnbogen Germany
37 L2 Katzhütte Germany
71 A2 Kau Halmahera Indonesia
135 V5 Kauai Channel Hawaiian Is
102 V13 Kauai isld Hawaiian Is
102 V13 Kauai Ch Hawaiian Is
144 B7 Kauana New Zealand
36 D3 Kaub Germany
89 D2 Kaucaca Pans Botswana
135 U6 Kau Desert Hawaiian Is
41 N2 Kaufbeuren Germany
41 N1 Kaufering Germany
109 L3 Kaufman Texas U.S.A.
32 L10 Kaufungen Germany
29 K8 Kauhava Finland
135 T6 Kauiki Hd Hawaiian Is
145 E2 Kaukapakapa New Zealand
99 S5 Kaukauna Wisconsin U.S.A.
135 U6 Kaula isld Hawaiian Is
102 U13 Kaulakahi Ch Hawaiian Is
135 U5 Kauluoa Pt Hawaiian Is
135 O1 Kaumakani Hawaiian Is
38 N5 Kaumberg Austria
135 R2 Kaunakakai Hawaiian Is
135 U6 Kauna Pt Hawaiian Is
53 B7 Kaunas Lithuania
29 L11 Kauniainen Finland
145 E3 Kaupokonui Stream New Zealand
85 F6 Kaura Namoda Nigeria
48 M4 Kaushany Moldova
29 K8 Kaustinen Finland
22 L4 Kautenbach Luxembourg
71 A2 Kau, Tk B Halmahera Indonesia
26 N3 Kautokeino Norway
68 D7 Kau-ye Kyun isld Burma
47 K5 Kavacık Turkey
46 E3 Kavadarci Macedonia
46 C4 Kavajë Albania
47 J7 Kavaklıdere Turkey
59 K3 Kavalerovo Russian Federation
76 E3 Kavali India
46 G4 Kavála Greece
87 C9 Kavango R Namibia
87 C9 Kavango homeland Namibia
73 L6 Kavaratti isld Lakshadweep Indian Oc
47 J1 Kavarna Bulgaria
33 Q4 Kavelstorf Germany
136 L2 Kavieng New Ireland
116 O2 Kavik R Alaska U.S.A.
27 F16 Kävlinge Sweden
47 P13 Kavos Greece
47 H9 Kavoúsi Crete Greece
88 C5 Kavu R Tanzania
80 D2 Kavul Israel
87 B8 Kavungo Angola
129 H3 Kaw Fr Guiana
121 M7 Kawagama L Ontario Canada
61 N10 Kawagoe Japan
61 N10 Kawaguchi Japan
60 N10 Kawahara Japan
61 M7 Kawaharada Japan
135 U4 Kawaihae Hawaiian Is
135 U4 Kawaihoa Pt Hawaiian Is
135 O1 Kawaikini pk Hawaiian Is
102 R11 Kawailoa Bch Hawaiian Is
145 E1 Kawakawa New Zealand
145 E4 Kawakawa B New Zealand
60 E13 Kawakita Japan
61 O8 Kawamata Japan
88 B6 Kawambwa Zambia
61 K9 Kawana Japan
71 J4 Kawangkoan Sulawesi
60 G11 Kawanoe Japan
144 B6 Kawarau R New Zealand
75 J7 Kawardha India
121 M8 Kawartha Lakes Ontario Canada
61 N10 Kawasaki Japan
60 D11 Kawashiri-misaki C Japan
71 H5 Kawatop Sulawesi Indonesia
60 O4 Kawauchi Japan
145 E2 Kawau I New Zealand
107 O5 Kaw City Oklahoma U.S.A.
71 J4 Kawe isld Indonesia
102 E5 Kaweah R California U.S.A.
145 E3 Kaweka mt New Zealand
135 O1 Kawela B Hawaiian Is
145 E3 Kawerau New Zealand
145 E3 Kawhia New Zealand
145 E4 Kawhia Harbour New Zealand
102 H4 Kawich Ra Nevada U.S.A.
88 C6 Kawimbe Zambia
119 S4 Kawinaw L Manitoba Canada
71 J9 Kawindua Sumbawa Indonesia
68 D4 Kawkareik Burma
107 N5 Kaw L Oklahoma U.S.A.
68 C5 Kawludo Burma
68 D6 Kawmapyin Burma
68 D7 Kawthaung Burma
66 B4 Kaxgar He R China
52 J3 Kay Russian Federation
86 F2 Kaya Burkina
68 C3 Kayah State Burma
116 P7 Kayak I Alaska U.S.A.
78 D1 Kayalar Turkey
47 N11 Kayali Dag mt Turkey
77 F7 Kayan Burma
70 E3 Kayan R Kalimantan
70 E3 Kayankulam India
71 J5 Kayasa Indonesia
57 E3 Kaybagar, Oz L Kazakhstan
101 T6 Kaycee Wyoming U.S.A.
68 D6 Kaydan Kyun isld Burma
103 O5 Kayenta Arizona U.S.A.
120 D2 Kayedon L Ontario Canada
85 B5 Kayes Mali
94 F8 Kayford West Virginia U.S.A.
57 F5 Kaygy Kazakhstan
68 D4 Kayin State Burma
47 J6 Kayışlar Turkey
57 J4 Kaymanachikha Kazakhstan
55 G2 Kaymysovy Russian Federation
37 N2 Kayna Germany
48 M4 Kaynary Moldova
116 S2 Kay Pt Yukon Territory Canada
129 G3 Kayser Geb mts Suriname
78 E2 Kayseri Turkey
101 O8 Kaysville Utah U.S.A.
69 G14 Kayuagung Sumatra
119 M9 Kayville Saskatchewan Canada
121 P7 Kazabazua Quebec Canada
56 G3 Kazachinskoye Russian Federation
78 K1 Kazakh Azerbaijan
57 A3 Kazakhdar'ya Uzbekistan
57 D1 Kazakhskiy Melkosopochnik reg Kazakhstan
57 B2 Kazakhstan rep C Asia
57 B2 Kazalinsk Kazakhstan
115 K5 Kazan R Northwest Territories Canada
52 G6 Kazan' Russian Federation
52 G6 Kazanka R Russian Federation
46 G2 Kazanlŭk Bulgaria
54 K3 Kazanovka Russian Federation
55 E3 Kazanskoye Russian Federation
57 G4 Kazarman Kirghizia
48 M1 Kazatin Ukraine
47 H5 Kaz Dağı mt Turkey
55 E5 Kazgorodok Kazakhstan
55 F4 Kazgorodok Kokchetavskaya obl Kazakhstan
52 H4 Kazhym Russian Federation
31 N4 Kazimierz Poland
48 F2 Kazincbarcika Hungary
54 L3 Kazinka Russian Federation
37 P4 Kaznějov Czech Rep
61 N9 Kazo Japan
86 D7 Kazumba Zaire
61 O5 Kazuno Japan
50 F2 Kazym R Russian Federation
56 D4 Kazyr R Russian Federation
77 G4 Kbash Afghanistan
31 K3 Kcynia Poland
37 P5 Kdyně Czech Rep
46 G7 Kéa isld Greece
135 V5 Keaau Hawaiian Is
14 E2 Keady N Ireland
135 T5 Keahole Pt Hawaiian Is
135 S3 Kealaikahiki Pt Hawaiian Is
102 V14 Kealakekue B Hawaiian Is
135 U5 Kealia Hawaiian Is
102 R11 Keamapapa Pt Hawaiian Is
103 O6 Keams Canyon Arizona U.S.A.
Kéamu isld see Anatom isld
121 L7 Kearney Ontario Canada
98 G9 Kearney Nebraska U.S.A.
102 F5 Kearsarge Pass California U.S.A.
109 O3 Keatchie Louisiana U.S.A.
100 H5 Keating Oregon U.S.A.
94 K5 Keating Pennsylvania U.S.A.
118 K6 Keatley Saskatchewan Canada
113 D8 Keatons Beach Florida U.S.A.
135 V5 Keaukaha Hawaiian Is
78 G2 Keban Baraji res Turkey
68 H2 Ke Bao, I de Vietnam
17 F10 Kebdana, Jbel mts Morocco
85 A5 Kébemer Senegal
85 F2 Kebili Tunisia
86 D3 Kebkabiya Sudan
26 K4 Kebnekaise Sweden
70 M9 Kebonen Java
69 F14 Kebur Sumatra
48 E4 Kecel Hungary
60 C11 Kechi Japan
117 K6 Kechika R British Columbia Canada
47 L7 Keçiborlu Turkey
48 F4 Kecskemet Hungary
69 E9 Kedah prov Malaysia
52 B6 Kédainiai Lithuania
100 E9 Keddie California U.S.A.
80 F1 Kedesh Naphtali Israel
122 F7 Kedgewick New Brunswick Canada
70 O9 Kediri Java
85 B6 Kédougou Senegal
46 E4 Kedriki Makedhonia admin region Greece
141 K1 Kedron dist Brisbane, Qnsld Australia
111 D7 Kedron Arkansas U.S.A.
141 K1 Kedron Brook Brisbane, Qnsld Australia
55 D3 Kedrovoye Russian Federation
55 E1 Kedrovyy Russian Federation
70 B4 Kedukul Kalimantan
70 M9 Kedungwuni Java
52 J4 Kedvavom Russian Federation
117 N10 Keefers British Columbia Canada
117 J4 Keele Pk Yukon Territory Canada
119 M8 Keeler Saskatchewan Canada
118 J4 Keeley L Saskatchewan Canada
Keeling Is see Cocos Is
123 T5 Keels Newfoundland Canada
71 D7 Keenapusan Philippines
102 F6 Keene California U.S.A.
95 P4 Keene New Hampshire U.S.A.
95 O2 Keene New York U.S.A.
111 L7 Keener Alabama U.S.A.
98 B9 Keenesburg Colorado U.S.A.
14 C4 Keeper Hill Ireland
141 F2 Keer-weer,C Queensland Australia
95 O2 Keeseville New York U.S.A.
89 A6 Keetmanshoop Namibia
115 K5 Keewatin dist Northwest Territories Canada
118 H1 Keewatin Ontario Canada
99 N2 Keewatin Minnesota U.S.A.
46 D5 Kefalí, Kep C Albania
46 D6 Kefallinía isld Greece
71 M9 Kefamenanu Timor Indonesia
80 C6 Kefar Bilu Israel
80 F1 Kefar Blum Israel
80 C7 Kefar Daniyyel Israel
80 D6 Kefar 'Ezyon Jordan
80 F2 Kefar Gallim Israel
80 C6 Kefar Gil'adi Israel
80 C6 Kefar Habad Israel
80 C6 Kefar Ha Maccabi Israel
80 B6 Kefar Ha Nagid Israel
80 F2 Kefar HaNasi Israel
80 B7 Kefar Ha No'ar Nizzanim Israel
80 C5 Kefar Hess Israel
80 C5 Kefar Mallal Israel
80 C7 Kefar Menahem Israel
Kefar Qēsem see Kafr Qāsim
80 D1 Kefar Rosh HaNiqra Israel
80 D5 Kefar Ruppin Israel
80 C7 Kefar Rut Jordan
80 E1 Kefar Sava Israel
80 C8 Kefar Szold Israel
80 C5 Kefar Tappuah Jordan
80 E4 Kefar Tavor Israel
80 C4 Kefar Uriyya Israel
80 C4 Kefar Vitkin Israel
80 C4 Kefar Ya'vetz Israel
80 C4 Kefar Yona Israel
80 E6 Kefar Zekharya Israel
80 C7 Kefer Monash Israel
85 F7 Keffi Nigeria
47 H7 Kefken Adasi isld Turkey
28 R9 Keflavik Iceland
83 K10 Kegalla Sri Lanka
123 L3 Kégashka, L Quebec Canada
123 L3 Kegaska Quebec Canada
28 D7 Kegnæs Denmark
117 O8 Keg River Alberta Canada
84 F5 Keguer Terbi mt Chad
52 B6 Kegums Latvia
9 E2 Kegworth England
32 K5 Kehdingen Das Alte Ld reg Germany
84 J6 Keheili Sudan
77 C3 Kehl Iran
36 D6 Kehl Germany
52 C5 Kehra Estonia
36 C3 Kehrig Germany
13 G6 Keighley England
52 B5 Keila Estonia
86 E3 Keilak, L Sudan
86 C4 Keita R Chad
85 F6 Keïta Niger
29 M8 Keitele Finland
138 F6 Keith South Australia Australia
117 M3 Keith Arm B Northwest Territories Canada
117 N9 Keithley Creek British Columbia Canada
110 G3 Keithsburg Illinois U.S.A.
109 O3 Keithville Louisiana U.S.A.
135 N1 Kekaha Hawaiian Is
57 H4 Kékaygyr Kirghizia
145 E5 Kekerengu New Zealand
115 N4 Kekertuk Northwest Territories Canada
48 F3 Kékes mt Hungary
71 B3 Kekik isld Indonesia
83 K9 Kekirawa Sri Lanka
47 K8 Kekova Adası isld Turkey
74 F6 Kekri India
86 H4 K'elafo Ethiopia
73 L7 Kelai isld Maldives
65 B5 Kelan China
69 E11 Kelang Malaysia
69 F9 Kelantan R Malaysia
69 E10 Kelantan prov Malaysia
70 F7 Kelara R Sulawesi
69 J13 Kelawar isld Indonesia
36 B3 Kelberg Germany
33 O10 Kelbra Germany
38 F7 Kelchsau Austria
14 E3 Keld England
52 F3 Kel'da R Russian Federation
29 K6 Keldby Denmark
80 C8 Kelekh R Israel
57 E4 Keles Kazakhstan
47 K5 Keles Turkey
118 J7 Kelfield Saskatchewan Canada
112 K1 Kelford North Carolina U.S.A.
37 M6 Kelheim Germany
43 D12 Kelibia Tunisia
77 K1 Kelif Turkmenistan
57 C6 Kelifskiy Uzboy Turkmenistan
98 B9 Kelim Colorado U.S.A.
71 K9 Keli Mutu mt Flores Indonesia
36 E3 Kelkheim Germany
78 G1 Kelkit Turkey
86 B6 Kellé Congo
95 M9 Keller Virginia U.S.A.
100 G1 Keller Washington U.S.A.
143 C9 Kellerberrin W Australia Australia
117 N4 Keller L Northwest Territories Canada
118 K2 Keller L Saskatchewan Canada
33 N4 Kellersee Germany
99 M9 Kellerton Iowa U.S.A.
114 G3 Kellet, C Northwest Territories Canada
94 H5 Kellettville Pennsylvania U.S.A.
94 E5 Kelleys I Ohio U.S.A.
119 O7 Kelliher Saskatchewan Canada
99 M2 Kelliher Minnesota U.S.A.
32 L5 Kellinghusen Germany
41 M1 Kellmünz Germany
100 J2 Kellogg Idaho U.S.A.
99 O8 Kellogg Iowa U.S.A.
29 O5 Kelloselkä Finland
14 E3 Kells Ireland
15 D5 Kells Range Scotland
140 E6 Kelly R Queensland Australia
116 F2 Kelly R Alaska U.S.A.
110 J5 Kelly Kentucky U.S.A.
111 D10 Kelly Louisiana U.S.A.
101 P6 Kelly Wyoming U.S.A.
140 B4 Kelly Hills N Terr Australia
117 K3 Kelly L Northwest Territories Canada
9 F3 Kelmarsh England
52 B6 Kelme Lithuania
48 K2 Kel'mentsy Ukraine
142 C3 Kelmscott dist Perth, W Aust Australia
86 C4 Kélo Chad
26 M3 Kelottijarvi L Sweden
117 O11 Kelowna British Columbia Canada
8 D1 Kelsall England
36 F3 Kelsbach Germany
119 V2 Kelsey Manitoba Canada
117 L10 Kelsey Bay British Columbia Canada
119 Q5 Kelsey L Manitoba Canada
102 B3 Kelseyville California U.S.A.
119 Q9 Kelso Saskatchewan Canada
144 B6 Kelso New Zealand
13 F2 Kelso Scotland
103 J6 Kelso California U.S.A.
98 J2 Kelso North Dakota U.S.A.
100 C3 Kelso Washington U.S.A.
9 E1 Kelstedge England
28 H5 Kelstrup Denmark
28 D6 Kelstrupstrand Denmark
101 M8 Kelton Utah U.S.A.
109 N4 Keltys Texas U.S.A.
69 F11 Keluang Malaysia
70 O9 Kelud G mt Java
9 G4 Kelvedon England
103 O8 Kelvin Arizona U.S.A.
119 O6 Kelvington Saskatchewan Canada
119 P1 Kelvin I Ontario Canada
119 S8 Kelwood Manitoba Canada
52 D3 Kem' Russian Federation
52 E4 Kema R Russian Federation
71 J4 Kema Sulawesi
70 D3 Kemabung Sabah
78 G2 Kemah Turkey
78 G2 Kemaliye Turkey
47 J6 Kemalpasa Turkey
117 K9 Kemano British Columbia Canada
69 F10 Kemaman Malaysia
70 B4 Kembayan Kalimantan
86 C5 Kembe Cent Afr Republic
33 R9 Kemberg Germany
53 D3 Kemchug R Russian Federation
47 K8 Kemer Turkey
47 L8 Kemer Lycia Turkey
47 K7 Kemer Baraji L Turkey
47 M10 Kemerburgaz Turkey
56 C3 Kemerovo Russian Federation
56 C4 Kemerovskaya Oblast' prov Russian Federation
29 L6 Kemi Finland
29 N5 Kemijärvi Finland
29 M5 Kemijoki R Finland
101 P8 Kemmerer Wyoming U.S.A.
37 M4 Kemnath Germany
119 R9 Kemnay Manitoba Canada
33 T4 Kemnitz Germany
109 L3 Kemp Texas U.S.A.
29 L7 Kempele Finland
25 F6 Kempen Germany
22 H1 Kempenich Germany
22 H1 Kempenland reg Belgium
36 C4 Kempfeld Germany
22 J1 Kempisch Kan Belgium
109 H2 Kemp, L Texas U.S.A.
146 J10 Kemp Land Antarctica
146 E15 Kemp Pen Antarctica
126 F2 Kemp's Bay Andros Bahamas
139 L4 Kempsey New South Wales Australia
36 D4 Kempten Germany
41 M2 Kempten Germany
121 Q5 Kempt, L Quebec Canada
139 H8 Kempton Tasmania Australia
99 S9 Kempton Illinois U.S.A.
98 J2 Kempton North Dakota U.S.A.
121 P7 Kemptville Ontario Canada
70 N8 Kemudjan isld Indonesia
85 D2 Kenadsa Algeria
116 M6 Kenai Alaska U.S.A.
116 N6 Kenai Fjords Nat Park Alaska U.S.A.
116 N6 Kenai L Alaska U.S.A.
116 N6 Kenai Pen Alaska U.S.A.
70 K8 Kenam, Tg C Sumatra
86 F4 Kenamuke Swamp Sudan
118 L7 Kenaston Saskatchewan Canada
70 D3 Kenawang, Bt mt Sarawak
94 J10 Kenbridge Virginia U.S.A.
70 O10 Kencong Java
139 L4 Kendal New South Wales Australia
119 O8 Kendal Saskatchewan Canada
13 F5 Kendal England
127 K2 Kendal Jamaica
70 N9 Kendal Java
141 F2 Kendall R Queensland Australia
113 G12 Kendall Florida U.S.A.
107 J4 Kendall Kansas U.S.A.
94 J3 Kendall New York U.S.A.
115 L5 Kendall, C Northwest Territories Canada
145 D4 Kendall, Mt New Zealand
94 B5 Kendallville Indiana U.S.A.
71 H6 Kendari Sulawesi
143 C10 Kendenup W Australia Australia
86 C3 Kendigué Chad
75 M8 Kendrāpārha India
100 J3 Kendrick Idaho U.S.A.
103 N6 Kendrick Pk Arizona U.S.A.
75 L8 Kendujhargarh India
57 L1 Kendyrlik Kazakhstan
139 J4 Kenebri New South Wales Australia
109 K7 Kenedy Texas U.S.A.
107 O7 Kenefick Oklahoma U.S.A.
98 F4 Kenel South Dakota U.S.A.
85 B7 Kenema Sierra Leone
70 B4 Kenepai mt Kalimantan
145 D4 Kenepuru Sound New Zealand
98 H9 Kenesaw Nebraska U.S.A.
53 B6 Kenga R Russian Federation
86 C6 Kenge Zaire
57 A3 Kenges Uzbekistan
26 N4 Kengis Sweden
68 G4 Keng Kaboa Laos
68 G4 Keng Kok Laos
68 E2 Keng Lap Burma
68 D1 Keng Lon Burma
68 E3 Keng Tawng Burma
68 D2 Kengtung Burma
87 D11 Kenhardt S Africa
116 L6 Kenibuna L Alaska U.S.A.
85 B6 Keniéba Mali
9 E3 Kenilworth England
70 E2 Keningau Sabah
85 C2 Kénitra Morocco
12 D3 Ken, L Scotland
67 E1 Kenli China
112 J2 Kenly North Carolina U.S.A.
14 B5 Kenmare Ireland
98 E1 Kenmare North Dakota U.S.A.
14 A5 Kenmare, R Ireland
141 K2 Kenmore dist Brisbane, Qnsld Australia
15 E4 Kenmore Scotland
108 D2 Kenna New Mexico U.S.A.
94 F8 Kenna West Virginia U.S.A.
95 R1 Kennebago Lake Maine U.S.A.
95 S2 Kennebec R Maine U.S.A.
98 G6 Kennebec South Dakota U.S.A.
95 R3 Kennebunk Maine U.S.A.
109 M10 Kennedale Texas U.S.A.
141 H4 Kennedy Queensland Australia
119 P8 Kennedy Saskatchewan Canada
98 J1 Kennedy Minnesota U.S.A.
98 F7 Kennedy Nebraska U.S.A.
94 J4 Kennedy New York U.S.A.
115 N1 Kennedy Channel Canada/Greenland
141 G4 Kennedy Highway Queensland Australia
119 P5 Kennedy L Saskatchewan Canada
117 D5 Kennedy, Mt Yukon Territory Canada
141 G3 Kennedy R Queensland Australia
143 B6 Kennedy Ra W Australia Australia
145 E2 Kennedy's B New Zealand
95 M7 Kennedyville Maryland U.S.A.
111 F11 Kenner Louisiana U.S.A.
111 H12 Kenner New Orleans, Louisiana U.S.A.
122 J8 Kennetcook Nova Scotia Canada
143 B6 Kenneth Ra W Australia Australia
9 E5 Kennet, R England
110 F5 Kennett Missouri U.S.A.
100 F3 Kennewick Washington U.S.A.
110 G1 Kenney Illinois U.S.A.
117 L9 Kenney Dam British Columbia Canada
116 Q6 Kennicott Alaska U.S.A.
9 H3 Kenninghall England
137 M6 Kenn Reef Coral Sea
100 D7 Keno Oregon U.S.A.
120 E2 Kenogami R Ontario Canada
121 T4 Kénogami L res Quebec Canada
120 J4 Kenogamissi L Ontario Canada
117 F4 Keno Hill Yukon Territory Canada
118 H1 Kenora Ontario Canada
99 T7 Kenosha Wisconsin U.S.A.
94 E8 Kenova West Virginia U.S.A.
52 E4 Kenozero, Oz L Russian Federation
12 D3 Ken, R Scotland
98 H2 Kensal North Dakota U.S.A.
127 H5 Kenscoff Haiti
111 E7 Kensett Arkansas U.S.A.
99 N6 Kensett Iowa U.S.A.
122 J7 Kensington Prince Edward I Canada
107 M2 Kensington Kansas U.S.A.
9 G5 Kent co England
95 O5 Kent Connecticut U.S.A.
99 K1 Kent Iowa U.S.A.
98 K3 Kent Minnesota U.S.A.
94 F5 Kent Ohio U.S.A.
100 E4 Kent Oregon U.S.A.
100 C2 Kent Washington U.S.A.
57 G1 Kentau Kazakhstan
120 H10 Kent Bridge Ontario Canada
94 B3 Kent City Michigan U.S.A.
9 G3 Kentford England
139 H7 Kent Gr islds Tasmania Australia
68 E4 Ken Thao Thailand
71 J7 Kentiolo isld Indonesia
122 G7 Kent Junction New Brunswick Canada
99 T9 Kentland Indiana U.S.A.
13 F5 Kentmere England
99 S3 Kenton Manitoba Canada
99 S3 Kenton Michigan U.S.A.
94 D6 Kenton Ohio U.S.A.
106 H5 Kenton Oklahoma U.S.A.
110 H6 Kenton Tennessee U.S.A.
29 P7 Kentozero Russian Federation

4 J4 Kent Pen Northwest Territories Canada
J4 Kentucky state U.S.A.
H5 Kentucky L Kentucky/Tenn U.S.A.
M3 Kentucky R Kentucky U.S.A.
2 H8 Kentville Nova Scotia Canada
F11 Kentwood Louisiana U.S.A.
7 J2 Kentyubek, Poluostrov pen Kazakhstan
9 Q7 Kenville Manitoba Canada
2 C2 Kenwick dist Perth, W Aust Australia
6 G5 Kenya rep Africa
Kenya, Mt see Kirinyaga
3 F2 Kenya National Park Kenya
9 F10 Kenyir, Tasek res Malaysia
3 E9 Kenyon Alberta Canada
6 D5 Kenyon Pen Antarctica
N10 Ken-zaki C Japan
5 F6 Kenzharyk' Kazakhstan
6 D7 Kenzingen Germany
5 T3 Keokea Hawaiian Is
E1 Keokuk Iowa U.S.A.
2 S12 Keolu Hills Hawaiian Is
3 G3 Keo Neua, Col de mt Laos
Keos isld Greece see Kéa isld
D1 Keosauqua Iowa U.S.A.
3 B9 Keota Colorado U.S.A.
9 P8 Keota Iowa U.S.A.
7 Q6 Keota Oklahoma U.S.A.
3 G7 Kep Cambodia
2 D2 Kepa Russian Federation
7 A4 Këpekli Turkmenistan
7 J5 Kepez Dağı mt Turkey
2 F2 Kepina Russian Federation
4 A6 Kepler Mts New Zealand
K4 Kępno Poland
3 E8 Keppel isld Falkland Is
K6 Keppel B Queensland Australia
7 J5 Kepsut Turkey
6 B5 Kerala prov India
9 G6 Kerang Victoria Australia
6 F7 Keratéa Greece
2 C5 Keraudren,C W Australia Australia
9 L11 Kerava Finland
B7 Kerby Oregon U.S.A.
3 E10 Kerch' Ukraine
5 D2 Kerchel' Russian Federation
2 H4 Kerchem'ya Russian Federation
2 J5 Kerchevskiy Russian Federation
6 F4 Kerdhíllion mt Greece
6 K3 Kerema Papua New Guinea
F1 Keremeos British Columbia Canada
C3 Kerem Maharal Israel
6 G2 Keren Eritrea
9 L3 Kerens Texas U.S.A.
5 E2 Kerepehi New Zealand
2 E2 Kerets, Mys C Russian Federation
2 G3 Kerga Russian Federation
D5 Kergrist-Moëlou France
3 M14 Kerguelen Is Indian Oc
M16 Kerguelen Plateau Southern Oc
D10 Kerguelen Ridge Indian Oc
5 N5 Kerhonkson New York U.S.A.
6 D7 Kerí Greece
3 E2 Kerichot Kenya
D5 Kerien France
5 D1 Kerikeri New Zealand
9 O10 Kerimäki Finland
9 E13 Kerinci, Danau L Sumatra
9 E13 Kerinci, Gunung mt Sumatra
3 D4 Kerka R Hungary
5 F6 Kerken Germany
5 G2 Kerkenah, Iles Tunisia
9 L4 Kerkhoven Minnesota U.S.A.
2 H3 Kerki Russian Federation
7 D5 Kerkichi Turkmenistan
6 F3 Kerkinítis, L Greece
7 O12 Kérkira Greece
7 O13 Kérkira isld Greece
5 F7 Kerkrade Netherlands
B4 Kerlouan France
7 R8 Kermadec Is Pacific Oc
7 E4 Kerman Iran
2 D5 Kerman California U.S.A.
7 F5 Kerman Desert Iran
7 H2 Kermen Bulgaria
3 D4 Kermit Texas U.S.A.
4 E9 Kermit West Virginia U.S.A.
2 F6 Kern R California U.S.A.
D5 Kernascléden France
6 B2 Kernen Germany
2 G1 Kernersville North Carolina U.S.A.
B7 Kernot Ra N Terr Australia
2 F6 Kernville California U.S.A.
2 H4 Kercs Russian Federation
5 C7 Kérouané Guinea
6 B2 Kerpen Germany
3 M4 Kerpineny Moldova
6 D11 Kerr, C Antarctica
2 C1 Kerrera isld Scotland
3 B7 Kerrick Texas U.S.A.
3 F8 Kerr, L Florida U.S.A.
3 H7 Kerrobert Saskatchewan Canada
5 D1 Kerr Pt New Zealand
4 H9 Kerrs Creek Virginia U.S.A.
G6 Kerrville Tennessee U.S.A.
9 H5 Kerrville Texas U.S.A.
4 A4 Kerry co Ireland
8 C3 Kerry Wales
4 B4 Kerry Hd Ireland
Kersaint, I.du see Dao Vinh Thuc
6 F1 Kersey Colorado U.S.A.
2 G3 Kershaw South Carolina U.S.A.
8 F6 Kerteminde Denmark
9 F10 Kertih Malaysia
0 O9 Kertosono Java
6 E9 Kert, Oued R Morocco
0 Q10 Keruak Indonesia
8 F2 Keruguya Kenya
9 E10 Keruh Malaysia
Kerulen R see Herlen He R
5 F5 Kervenheim Germany
0 D6 Kervignac France
5 D3 Kerzaz Australia
6 H2 Kerzell Germany
F4 Kerzers Switzerland
2 F6 Kerzhenets R Russian Federation
0 K2 Kesagami L Ontario Canada
9 O10 Kesälahti Finland
8 A1 Kesan Turkey
1 L4 Kesch, Piz mt Switzerland
1 P7 Kesennuma Japan
9 J2 Keshan China
9 S5 Keshena Wisconsin U.S.A.
2 D4 Keskozero Russian Federation
2 E5 Kesova Gora Russian Federation
7 K4 Kestel Turkey
7 L7 Kestelovasi Gölü L Turkey
2 D2 Kesten'ga Russian Federation
7 K8 Kestep Turkey
5 E5 Kesteren Netherlands
6 D3 Kestert Germany
9 M7 Kestilä Finland
3 E4 Keswick England
2 F8 Keswick Rdg New Brunswick Canada
8 D4 Keszthely Hungary
6 C2 Ket' R Russian Federation
5 E7 Kéta Ghana
9 E14 Ketahun Sumatra
0 O9 Ketapang Java
9 E13 Ketaun Sumatra
7 H8 Ketchikan Alaska U.S.A.
1 L6 Ketchum Idaho U.S.A.
7 P5 Ketchum Oklahoma U.S.A.
8 F4 Ketchum Mt Texas U.S.A.
5 D7 Kété Ghana
25 E3 Ketelmeer Netherlands
74 B6 Keti Bandar Pakistan
116 H2 Ketik R Alaska U.S.A.
66 C3 Ketmen', Khr mts China/Kazakhstan
85 E7 Kétou Benin
31 N1 Kętrzyn Poland
36 E3 Kettenbach Germany
9 F3 Kettering England
28 D7 Ketting Denmark
28 H7 Kettinge Denmark
13 E1 Kettle Scotland
99 O3 Kettle R Minnesota U.S.A.
100 G1 Kettle R Washington U.S.A.
94 K5 Kettle Cr Pennsylvania U.S.A.
100 G1 Kettle Falls Washington U.S.A.
102 E5 Kettleman City California U.S.A.
100 G1 Kettle R. Range mts Washington U.S.A.
13 F5 Kettlewell England
9 F2 Ketton England
32 E10 Kettwig Germany
70 B4 Ketungau R Kalimantan
33 R8 Ketzin Germany
95 K4 Keuka L New York U.S.A.
33 N10 Keula Germany
55 F2 Keum R Russian Federation
29 L9 Keuruuselkä L Finland
55 E1 Keushki Russian Federation
25 F5 Kevelaer Germany
110 H4 Kevil Kentucky U.S.A.
101 O1 Kevin Montana U.S.A.
121 M4 Kewagama Quebec Canada
99 R8 Kewanee Illinois U.S.A.
111 H9 Kewanee Mississippi U.S.A.
94 A5 Kewanna Indiana U.S.A.
71 L9 Kewapante Indonesia
99 T5 Kewaunee Wisconsin U.S.A.
99 S3 Keweenaw B Michigan U.S.A.
99 S2 Keweenaw Pen Michigan U.S.A.
98 F6 Keya Paha R South Dakota U.S.A.
98 F6 Keyapaha South Dakota U.S.A.
119 S8 Keyes Manitoba Canada
106 H5 Keyes Oklahoma U.S.A.
110 G3 Keyesport Illinois U.S.A.
98 B5 Keyhole Res Wyoming U.S.A.
120 K7 Key Junction Ontario Canada
14 C2 Key, L Ireland
113 G12 Key Largo Florida U.S.A.
140 A2 Keyling Inlet N Terr Australia
95 K7 Keymar Maryland U.S.A.
8 D5 Keynsham England
100 C2 Keyport Washington U.S.A.
94 J7 Keyser West Virginia U.S.A.
99 O8 Keystone Iowa U.S.A.
98 E8 Keystone Nebraska U.S.A.
107 O5 Keystone Oklahoma U.S.A.
98 C6 Keystone South Dakota U.S.A.
94 F9 Keystone West Virginia U.S.A.
113 F8 Keystone Heights Florida U.S.A.
107 O5 Keystone L Oklahoma U.S.A.
103 N10 Keystone Pk Arizona U.S.A.
119 M8 Keystown Saskatchewan Canada
112 E4 Keysville Georgia U.S.A.
94 J9 Keysville Virginia U.S.A.
113 F13 Key West Florida U.S.A.
9 E2 Keyworth England
52 H5 Kez Russian Federation
95 R3 Kezar Falls Maine U.S.A.
95 R2 Kezar L Maine U.S.A.
31 M6 Kežmarok Slovakia
89 B5 Kgalagadi dist Botswana
89 E5 Kgatleng reg Botswana
89 C5 Kgokong Botswana
89 B5 Kgothi Botswana
52 H2 Khabarikha Russian Federation
59 L2 Khabarovsk Russian Federation
55 E5 Khabay R Kazakhstan
78 H4 Khabur R Syria
77 E7 Khābūrah, Al Oman
52 E3 Khachela Russian Federation
74 E9 Khadki India
53 E11 Khadyzhensk Russian Federation
77 C5 Khafr Iran
77 H4 Khairabad Afghanistan
74 C5 Khairpur Pakistan
74 H6 Khajurāho anc site India
56 C4 Khakasskaya Avtonomnyy Oblast' Russian Federation
87 D10 Khakhea Botswana
57 C5 Khalach Turkmenistan
77 A4 Khalafābād Iran
74 G1 Khalatse Kashmir
55 C5 Khalilovo Russian Federation
78 K5 Khālis, Al Iraq
78 M3 Khalkhāl Iran
46 F5 Khálki Greece
47 J8 Khálki isld Greece
46 F6 Khalkís Greece
80 E5 Khallat El Fūla Jordan
75 L9 Khallikot India
50 F2 Khal'mer-Yu Russian Federation
52 G5 Khalturin Russian Federation
75 J7 Khamaria India
74 E8 Khambhat, Gulf of India
89 F2 Khami R Zimbabwe
47 H9 Khamili isld Greece
68 G3 Kham Keut Laos
76 E2 Khammam India
68 H5 Khampho R Laos
56 E4 Khamsara R Russian Federation
77 A1 Khamseh Iran
57 F4 Khamza Uzbekistan
77 L2 Khānābād Afghanistan
76 B3 Khanapur India
78 K4 Khānaqin Iraq
139 J6 Khancoban New South Wales Australia
84 J6 Khandaq, El Sudan
47 H9 Khandrá Crete Greece
74 G8 Khandwa India
74 B3 Khanewal Pakistan
55 D1 Khangokurt Russian Federation
68 J6 Khanh Hoa Vietnam
69 G8 Khanh Hung Vietnam
47 G9 Khaniá Crete Greece
74 H2 Khaniadhana India
54 H2 Khanino Russian Federation
46 F4 Khanion, Kólpos B Crete Greece
57 B4 Khanka Uzbekistan
Khankendy see Stepanakert
74 D4 Khanpur Pakistan
79 G3 Khān Shaykhūn Syria
86 A1 Khansir, Ras C Somalia
57 G3 Khantau Kazakhstan
51 J2 Khantayskoye, Ozero L Russian Federation
55 E1 Khanty-Mansiysk Russian Federation
55 E1 Khanty-Mansiyskiy Avtonomnyy Okrug dist Russian Federation
68 D4 Khanu Thailand
80 G1 Khān 'Urayníbah Syria
79 E7 Khān Yūnis Egypt
80 F4 Khanzira Jordan
69 D8 Khao Chum Thong Thailand
74 G1 Khapalu Kashmir
58 F2 Khapcheranga Russian Federation
75 M6 Kharagpur India
77 J5 Kharan Pakistan
74 A4 Kharan Kalat Pakistan
84 J4 Khârga, El Egypt
84 J5 Khârga Oasis Egypt
56 H4 Kharga, Oz L Russian Federation
79 D8 Kharîm, G mt Egypt
72 F4 Kharj, Al reg Saudi Arabia
77 B5 Khārk isld Iran
54 H6 Khar'kov Ukraine
52 E1 Kharlovka Russian Federation
52 D4 Kharlu Russian Federation
47 H3 Kharmanli Bulgaria
77 L3 Kharoti reg Afghanistan
52 F5 Kharovsk Russian Federation
147 Q7 Kharstan Russian Federation
86 F2 Khartoum Sudan
54 K8 Khartsyzsk Ukraine
52 J2 Kharuta Russian Federation
65 H3 Khasan Russian Federation
77 H4 Khash Afghanistan
77 G5 Khāsh Iran
86 G2 Khashem el Girba Sudan
77 H4 Khash Rud R Afghanistan
78 J1 Khashuri Georgia
46 E5 Khasiá Óri Greece
75 O6 Khāsi Hills India
47 H3 Khaskovo Bulgaria
51 K1 Khatanga Russian Federation
51 L1 Khatangskiy Zaliv G Russian Federation
52 J2 Khatayakha Russian Federation
57 D5 Khatyrchi Uzbekistan
57 D5 Khaudag Uzbekistan
57 E4 Khavast Uzbekistan
68 C5 Khawsa Burma
57 F5 Khaydarken Kirghizia
57 B4 Khazar-Asp Uzbekistan
57 E5 Khazora Tajikistan
68 G3 Khe Bo Vietnam
74 E10 Khed India
68 G2 Khe Long Vietnam
52 D4 Khelyulya Russian Federation
56 D5 Khemchik R Russian Federation
56 D5 Khemchikskiy, Khr mts Russian Federation
85 C2 Khemisset Morocco
68 G4 Khemmarat Thailand
85 D4 Khenachich, El reg Mali
85 F1 Khenchela Algeria
68 A2 Khenkhar Burma
53 D10 Kherson Ukraine
51 J1 Kheta R Russian Federation
52 D2 Khetolambina Russian Federation
74 F5 Khetri India
68 E5 Khiaw, Khao mt Thailand
29 O10 Khiitola Russian Federation
46 F7 Khiliomódhion Greece
56 G5 Khilok R Russian Federation
56 H5 Khilok Russian Federation
52 E6 Khimki Russian Federation
56 C5 Khindiktig Khol', Oz L Russian Federation
46 D6 Khionáta Greece
47 H6 Khíos isld Greece
79 H3 Khirbat Isrīyah Syria
80 D8 Khirbet Deir Razih Jordan
80 G4 Khirbet el Kufeirat Jordan
80 F4 Khirbet el Wahadina Jordan
80 G4 Khirbet Harqala Jordan
80 D5 Khirbet Isla Jordan
80 D5 Khirbet Listib Jordan
80 F4 Khirbet Mar Ilyas Jordan
46 G2 Khisarya Bulgaria
57 B4 Khiva Uzbekistan
47 H1 Khlebarovo Bulgaria
46 F6 Khlomón mt Greece
48 L1 Khmel'nik Ukraine
48 K1 Khmel'nitskiy Ukraine
Khmer Rep see Cambodia
69 G8 Khoai, Hon isld Vietnam
48 J1 Khodorov Ukraine
57 D5 Khodzhambas Turkmenistan
57 E4 Khodzhent Tajikistan
57 A4 Khodzheyli Uzbekistan
54 K5 Khokhol'skiy Russian Federation
77 K1 Kholm Afghanistan
52 D6 Kholm Russian Federation
52 F3 Kholmogorskaya Russian Federation
59 M2 Kholmsk Russian Federation
56 D5 Khol'-Oozhu Russian Federation
56 F5 Kholtoson Russian Federation
56 B5 Kholzun, Khr mts Kazakhstan/Rus Fed
77 A1 Khoman Iran
87 C10 Khomas Hochland dist Namibia
77 B3 Khomeyn Iran
77 B3 Khomeyni Shahr Iran
87 F8 Khondowe Malawi
88 E10 Khonjeni Malawi
77 C6 Khonj, Kūhe-e mt Iran
68 F4 Khon Kaen Thailand
53 F8 Khoper R Russian Federation
59 L2 Khor R Russian Federation
59 L2 Khor Russian Federation
46 E7 Khóra Greece
77 E2 Khorāsan prov Iran
46 G9 Khóra Sfakíon Crete Greece
75 L8 Khordha India
52 J2 Khoreyver Russian Federation
57 B4 Khorezmskaya Oblast' prov Uzbekistan
57 C2 Khorkhut Kazakhstan
54 K1 Khorlovo Russian Federation
57 F6 Khorog Tajikistan
54 E7 Khorol R Ukraine
54 E7 Khorol Ukraine
55 G4 Khorosheye Russian Federation
77 A3 Khorramābād Iran
77 A4 Khorramshahr Iran
52 J2 Khoseda Khard Russian Federation
77 F3 Khosf Iran
74 B3 Khost Pakistan
Khotan see Hotan
54 D3 Khotimsk Belarus
48 K2 Khotin Ukraine
54 K1 Khot'kovo Russian Federation
116 H4 Khotol mt Alaska U.S.A.
85 C2 Khouribga Morocco
77 L3 Khowst Afghanistan
77 L3 Khowst reg Afghanistan
53 F12 Khrami R Georgia
52 F6 Khrapovitskaya Russian Federation
54 M5 Khrenovoye Russian Federation
68 A2 Khreum Burma
46 G4 Khrisoúpolis Greece
46 G8 Khristianá isld Greece
48 M2 Khristinovka Ukraine
52 G4 Khristoforovo Russian Federation
55 C5 Khrom-Tau Kazakhstan
79 C3 Khrysokhou B Cyprus
47 H7 Khtapodhiá isld Greece
77 B6 Khubar, Al Saudi Arabia
56 G5 Khudanskiy Khrebet mts Russian Federation
77 K6 Khude Hills Pakistan
56 D4 Khudoyelanskoye Russian Federation
84 G5 Khufrah Oasis,Al Libya
68 G5 Khu Khan Thailand
75 N7 Khulna Bangladesh
84 E3 Khums, Al Libya
79 H4 Khunayzir, Jebel al mts Syria
Khungari see Gurskoye
74 F1 Khunjerab Pass China/India
77 B3 Khunsar Iran
75 L7 Khunti India
77 J3 Khurd, Koh-i- mt Afghanistan
74 G4 Khurja India
74 E2 Khushab Pakistan
79 F6 Khushnīyah, Al Syria
48 H2 Khust Ukraine
86 E3 Khuwei Sudan
57 E5 Khuybyshevsk Tajikistan
77 A4 Khuzestan Iran
56 G4 Khuzhir Russian Federation
77 G2 Khvāf Iran
77 D3 Khvor Iran
78 K2 Khvoy Iran
46 G3 Khvoyna Bulgaria
52 D5 Khvoynaya Russian Federation
77 L1 Khwāja-i-Ghar Afghanistan
77 L1 Khwaja Muhammad Range Afghanistan
74 D1 Khyber Pass Afghanistan/Pakistan
48 H1 Khyrov Ukraine
139 K5 Kiama New South Wales Australia
71 G7 Kiamba Mindanao Philippines
88 F2 Kiambu Kenya
107 P7 Kiamichi Mts Oklahoma U.S.A.
121 P6 Kiamika Quebec Canada
Kiangsi prov see Jiangxi prov
Kiangsu prov see Jiangsu prov
29 O6 Kiantajärvi L Finland
119 U2 Kiask L Manitoba Canada
28 B4 Kibæk Denmark
86 F5 Kibanga Uganda
86 B6 Kibangou Congo
71 G7 Kibawe Mindanao Philippines
88 F4 Kibaya Tanzania
26 S1 Kiberg Norway
85 D7 Kibi Ghana
87 G7 Kibiti Tanzania
86 E6 Kibombo Zaire
88 C3 Kibondo Tanzania
57 E4 Kibray Uzbekistan
86 G4 Kibre Mengist Ethiopia
79 E10 Kibrīt, J. al Saudi Arabia
88 C3 Kibungu Rwanda
46 D3 Kičevo Macedonia
86 C2 Kichi Kichi Chad
52 G4 Kichmenga R Russian Federation
52 G5 Kichmengskiy Gorodok Russian Federation
52 H7 Kichuy Russian Federation
52 H7 Kichuy R Russian Federation
99 Q6 Kickapoo R Wisconsin U.S.A.
117 P10 Kicking Horse Pass British Columbia Canada
85 E5 Kidal Mali
98 J4 Kidder South Dakota U.S.A.
8 D3 Kidderminster England
86 F5 Kidepo Nat. Park Kenya
85 B6 Kidira Senegal
9 E4 Kidlington England
145 F3 Kidnappers, C New Zealand
70 C3 Kidurong, Tg C Sarawak
8 B4 Kidwelly Wales
98 F2 Kief North Dakota U.S.A.
32 M4 Kiel Germany
99 S6 Kiel Wisconsin U.S.A.
31 M5 Kielce Poland
13 F3 Kielder England
13 F3 Kielder Res England
22 G1 Kieldrecht Belgium
30 E1 Kieler Bucht B Germany
138 D5 Kielpa South Australia Australia
67 B6 Kien An Vietnam
69 G8 Kien Hung Vietnam
37 N1 Kieritzsch Germany
36 D1 Kierspe Germany
109 O9 Kiest Park Texas U.S.A.
Kiev see Kiyev
139 H6 Kiewa R Victoria Australia
85 B5 Kiffa Mauritania
46 F6 Kifissós R Greece
78 K5 Kifl, Al Iraq
88 C2 Kigali Rwanda
116 K2 Kigalik R Alaska U.S.A.
116 E4 Kigluaik Mts Alaska U.S.A.
88 B4 Kigoma Tanzania
88 C4 Kigoma dist Tanzania
70 C5 Kihambatang Kalimantan
141 F7 Kihee Queensland Australia
27 M13 Kihelkonna Estonia
145 E3 Kihikihi New Zealand
29 K4 Kihlanki Finland
29 K9 Kihniö Finland
102 V14 Kiholo Hawaiian Is
29 K11 Kiikala Finland
29 K10 Kiikoinen Finland
135 N1 Kii Landing Hawaiian Is
29 N3 Kiilopää mt Finland
29 M6 Kiiminki Finland
61 K11 Kii-Nagashima Japan
61 J12 Kii Sanchi mts Japan
60 H12 Kii suidō str Japan
116 K6 Kijik Alaska U.S.A.
61 Q12 Kijoka Okinawa
59 J6 Kikai-shima isld Japan
116 L2 Kikiakrorak R Alaska U.S.A.
48 F5 Kikinda Serbia Yugoslavia
46 G7 Kikládhes islds Greece
52 G6 Kiknur Russian Federation
60 O4 Kikonai Japan
136 J3 Kikori Papua New Guinea
60 D13 Kikuchi Japan
89 D8 Kikvors Berg S Africa
121 M6 Kikwissi, L Quebec Canada
86 C7 Kikwit Zaire
27 F12 Kil Sweden
27 J13 Kila Sweden
101 L1 Kila Montana U.S.A.
27 J10 Kilafors Sweden
113 L9 Kilarney, L New Providence I Bahamas
135 O1 Kilauea Hawaiian Is
102 V14 Kilauea Crater Hawaiian Is
14 D3 Kilbeggan Ireland
12 C2 Kilberry Scotland
15 C5 Kilbrennan Snd Scotland
116 G6 Kilbuck Mts Alaska U.S.A.
122 E7 Kilburn New Brunswick Canada
12 C2 Kilchattan Scotland
12 B2 Kilchoman Scotland
12 C1 Kilchrenan Scotland
65 H4 Kilchu N Korea
52 H7 Kilchuy Russian Federation
13 F1 Kilconquhar Scotland
14 D3 Kilcormac Ireland
141 K7 Kilcoy Queensland Australia
14 E3 Kilcullen Ireland
117 K9 Kildala Arm R British Columbia Canada
13 G5 Kildale England
14 E3 Kildare co Ireland
14 E3 Kildare Ireland
109 N3 Kildare Texas U.S.A.
122 J7 Kildare, C Prince Edward I Canada
28 J5 Kildebrønde Denmark
52 D1 Kil'din, Ostrov isld Russian Federation
117 L11 Kildonan British Columbia Canada
118 B1 Kildonan Manitoba Canada
87 F9 Kildonan Zimbabwe
86 C7 Kilembe Zaire
28 A3 Kilen L Denmark
14 B4 Kilfenora Ireland
12 C2 Kilfinan Scotland
14 C4 Kilfinnane Ireland
14 B5 Kilgarvan Ireland
101 O5 Kilgore Idaho U.S.A.
98 F7 Kilgore Nebraska U.S.A.
111 B9 Kilgore Texas U.S.A.
13 H5 Kilham England
85 E7 Kilibo Benin
47 K4 Kılıç Turkey
47 H2 Kilifarevo Bulgaria
88 G3 Kilifi Kenya
88 F3 Kilimanjaro mt Tanzania
137 M2 Kilinailau Is Papua New Guinea
15 C4 Kilinelfort Scotland
52 B5 Kilingi-Nõmme Estonia
83 K8 Kilinochchi Sri Lanka
78 F3 Kilis Turkey
116 L8 Kiliuda B Alaska U.S.A.
48 M5 Kiliya Ukraine
14 B4 Kilkee Ireland
14 F2 Kilkeel N Ireland
14 D4 Kilkenny co Ireland
14 D4 Kilkenny Ireland
12 C3 Kilkenzie Scotland
8 B6 Kilkhampton England
14 B3 Kilkieran B Ireland
46 F4 Kilkís Greece
141 K7 Kilkivan Queensland Australia
14 E3 Kill Ireland
14 B2 Killala Ireland
14 B2 Killala B Ireland
120 D3 Killala L Ontario Canada
121 N7 Killaloe Ontario Canada
14 C4 Killaloe Ireland
119 P8 Killaly Saskatchewan Canada
118 F6 Killam Alberta Canada
140 B3 Killarney N Terr Australia
141 K8 Killarney Queensland Australia
119 S9 Killarney Manitoba Canada
120 J7 Killarney Ontario Canada
14 B4 Killarney Ireland
120 J6 Killarney Prov. Park Ontario Canada
14 A3 Killary Hbr Ireland
14 D2 Killashandra Ireland
118 L9 Killdeer Saskatchewan Canada
98 D2 Killdeer North Dakota U.S.A.
99 O8 Killduff Iowa U.S.A.
12 D1 Killearn Scotland
109 K4 Killeen Texas U.S.A.
47 J5 Killer R Turkey
15 E4 Killiecrankie, Pass of Scotland
116 K2 Killik Bend Alaska U.S.A.
14 C3 Killimor Ireland
15 D4 Killin Scotland
26 E9 Killingdal Norway
46 E7 Killíni Greece
46 E7 Killini mt Greece
14 B4 Killorglin Ireland
14 C2 Killybegs Ireland
14 F2 Killyleagh N Ireland
14 C4 Kilmallock Ireland
15 B3 Kilmaluag Scotland
13 F1 Kilmany Scotland
12 D2 Kilmarnock Scotland
95 L9 Kilmarnock Virginia U.S.A.
12 C1 Kilmartin Scotland
52 H6 Kil'mez Russian Federation
111 G8 Kilmichael Mississippi U.S.A.
12 C1 Kilmichael Glassary Scotland
139 G6 Kilmore Victoria Australia
12 C2 Kilmory Scotland
12 D1 Kilmun Scotland
13 E4 Kilnhill England
12 C1 Kilninver Scotland
13 J6 Kilnsea England
88 F6 Kilombero R Tanzania
88 F5 Kilosa Tanzania
29 H2 Kilpisjärvi Finland
29 L7 Kilpua Finland
29 Q2 Kilp'yavr Russian Federation
14 E2 Kilrea N Ireland
14 B4 Kilrush Ireland
9 E3 Kilsby England
12 D2 Kilsyth Scotland
76 A5 Kiltān isld Indian Oc
73 L6 Kiltan isld Lakshadweep Indian Oc
14 C3 Kiltimagh Ireland
26 M5 Kilvo Sweden
87 E7 Kilwa Zaire
88 B6 Kilwa isld Zambia
88 G6 Kilwa Kisiwani Tanzania
88 G6 Kilwa Kivinje Tanzania
88 G6 Kilwa Masoko Tanzania
12 D2 Kilwinning Scotland
106 G4 Kim Colorado U.S.A.
101 M7 Kimama Idaho U.S.A.
70 D2 Kimanis B Sabah
138 D5 Kimba South Australia Australia
98 C8 Kimball Nebraska U.S.A.
98 H6 Kimball South Dakota U.S.A.
94 F9 Kimball West Virginia U.S.A.
116 P5 Kimball, Mt Alaska U.S.A.
99 L8 Kimballton Iowa U.S.A.
86 C7 Kimbao Zaire
117 Q11 Kimberley British Columbia Canada
120 K8 Kimberley Ontario Canada
89 D7 Kimberley S Africa
141 H3 Kimberley,C Queensland Australia
142 E3 Kimberley Downs W Australia Australia
142 F3 Kimberley Plateau W Australia Australia
143 C7 Kimberley Ra W Australia Australia
101 L7 Kimberly Idaho U.S.A.
103 J2 Kimberly Nevada U.S.A.
99 S5 Kimberly Wisconsin U.S.A.
9 F3 Kimbolton England
145 E4 Kimbolton New Zealand
88 D5 Kimbu Tanzania
46 G6 Kími Greece
29 K11 Kimito Finland
118 A3 Kimiwan Lake Alberta Canada
110 F3 Kimmswick Missouri U.S.A.
46 G8 Kímolos isld Greece
61 M7 Kimpoku-san mt Japan
52 E6 Kimry Russian Federation
27 H13 Kimstad Sweden
71 H5 Kimtom Sulawesi
52 F2 Kimzha Russian Federation
68 B1 Kin Burma
61 P13 Kin Okinawa
61 P13 Kina Okinawa
70 E1 Kinabalu mt Sabah
70 E2 Kinabatangan R Sabah
70 F2 Kinabatangan, Kualu est Sabah
47 N11 Kinali isld Turkey
88 F2 Kinangop, Mt Kenya
47 H8 Kínaros isld Greece
70 D2 Kinarut Sabah
117 O10 Kinbasket British Columbia Canada
117 O9 Kinbasket L Canada
118 F8 Kinbrook I. Prov. Pk Alberta Canada
118 K9 Kincaid Saskatchewan Canada
107 P3 Kincaid Kansas U.S.A.
120 J8 Kincardine Ontario Canada
12 E1 Kincardine Scotland
117 J8 Kincolith British Columbia Canada
141 J7 Kincora Gas Field Queensland Australia
15 E3 Kincraig Scotland
87 E7 Kinda Zaire
94 E3 Kinde Michigan U.S.A.
33 O10 Kindelbrück Germany
109 P5 Kinder Louisiana U.S.A.
36 C3 Kinderbeuern Germany
118 J7 Kindersley Saskatchewan Canada
85 B6 Kindia Guinea
57 G3 Kindiktas, Gory mts Kazakhstan
98 J3 Kindred North Dakota U.S.A.
86 E6 Kindu Zaire
116 G7 Kinegnak Alaska U.S.A.
53 H7 Kinel' R Russian Federation
53 H7 Kinel'-Cherkasy Russian Federation
52 F6 Kineshma Russian Federation
140 C1 King R N Terr Australia
140 E6 King R Queensland Australia
141 G2 King R Queensland Australia
141 K7 Kingaroy Queensland Australia
133 C6 King, Canal str Chile
114 J2 King Christian I Northwest Territories Canada
102 C5 King City California U.S.A.
99 M9 King City Missouri U.S.A.
117 K10 Kingcome Inlet British Columbia Canada
116 F9 King Cove Alaska U.S.A.
146 F1 King Edward Point U.K. Base S Georgia S Atlantic Oc
142 F3 King Edward R W Australia Australia
95 R2 Kingfield Maine U.S.A.
107 N6 Kingfisher Oklahoma U.S.A.
146 D3 King George I South Shetland Is Antarctica
115 M6 King George Is Northwest Territories Canada
135 N10 King George Is Tuamotu Arch Pacific Oc
118 B8 King George, Mt British Columbia Canada
117 D5 King George, Mt Yukon Territory Canada
142 F2 King George R W Australia Australia
143 C11 King George Sd W Australia Australia
131 H6 King Haakon B S Georgia
142 E5 King Hill W Australia Australia
120 C3 Kinghorn Ontario Canada
13 E1 Kinghorn Scotland
King I see Kaydan Kyun
139 G7 King I Tasmania Australia
117 K9 King I British Columbia Canada
52 C5 Kingisepp Russian Federation
Kingisseppa see Kuressaare
100 G8 King Lear mt Nevada U.S.A.
146 J12 King Leopold & Queen Astrid Coast Antarctica
142 E3 King Leopold Ra W Australia Australia
118 E5 Kingman Alberta Canada
103 K6 Kingman Arizona U.S.A.
107 M4 Kingman Kansas U.S.A.
95 T1 Kingman Maine U.S.A.
141 H7 King, Mt Queensland Australia
142 C5 King, Mt W Australia Australia
108 E4 King Mt Texas U.S.A.
86 E6 Kingombe Zaire
138 D4 Kingoonya South Australia Australia
146 B7 King Pen Antarctica
139 H8 King, R Tasmania Australia
142 G3 King, R W Australia Australia
102 D5 Kings R California U.S.A.
100 G8 Kings R Nevada U.S.A.
116 J7 King Salmon Alaska U.S.A.
13 F1 Kingsbarns Scotland
8 C7 Kingsbridge England
102 E5 Kingsburg California U.S.A.
109 K6 Kingsbury Texas U.S.A.
106 D1 Kings Canyon Colorado U.S.A.
102 F4 Kings Canyon Nat Park California U.S.A.
9 E5 Kingsclere England
139 L3 Kingscliff-Fingal New South Wales Australia
138 D6 Kingscote South Australia Australia
14 E3 Kingscourt Ireland
145 E2 Kingseat New Zealand
146 D3 King Sejong Korea Base Antarctica
9 G5 Kingsferry Bridge England
9 F5 Kingsfold England
109 P2 Kingsland Arkansas U.S.A.
113 F7 Kingsland Georgia U.S.A.
9 F4 Kings Langley England
99 L7 Kingsley Iowa U.S.A.
94 B2 Kingsley Michigan U.S.A.
98 E8 Kingsley Dam Nebraska U.S.A.
9 G2 King's Lynn England
137 P2 Kingsmill Group islds Kiribati
112 F2 Kings Mt North Carolina U.S.A.
95 O6 Kings Park Long I, New York U.S.A.
101 P9 Kings Pks Utah U.S.A.
122 H8 Kingsport Nova Scotia Canada
94 E10 Kingsport Tennessee U.S.A.
142 E3 Kings Sd W Australia Australia
8 C6 Kingsteignton England
138 E6 Kingston South Australia Australia
139 H9 Kingston Tasmania Australia
121 O8 Kingston Ontario Canada
9 F5 Kingston England
127 L3 Kingston Jamaica
144 B6 Kingston New Zealand
137 O7 Kingston Norfolk I Pacific Oc
110 C5 Kingston Arkansas U.S.A.
110 B2 Kingston Missouri U.S.A.
95 R4 Kingston New Hampshire U.S.A.
95 N5 Kingston New York U.S.A.
94 E7 Kingston Ohio U.S.A.
107 O7 Kingston Oklahoma U.S.A.
95 M5 Kingston Pennsylvania U.S.A.
100 C2 Kingston Washington U.S.A.
94 F9 Kingston West Virginia U.S.A.
9 E4 Kingston Lisle England
103 J6 Kingston Pk California U.S.A.
13 H6 Kingston upon Hull England
13 F4 Kingstown England
127 O8 Kingstown St Vincent
112 H4 Kingstree South Carolina U.S.A.
120 H10 Kingsville Ontario Canada
94 G5 Kingsville Ohio U.S.A.
109 K8 Kingsville Texas U.S.A.
8 C7 Kingswear England
8 C3 Kington England
86 C7 Kinguji Zaire
15 D3 Kingussie Scotland
115 K4 King William I Northwest Territories Canada
89 E9 King William's Town S Africa
94 H7 Kingwood West Virginia U.S.A.
87 E8 Kiniama Zaire
47 J5 Kınık Turkey
119 M6 Kinistino Saskatchewan Canada
61 P7 Kinka-san C Japan
87 H11 Kinkony, Farihy L Madagascar
122 J7 Kinkora Prince Edward I Canada
145 E3 Kinleith New Zealand
118 K6 Kinley Saskatchewan Canada
144 B6 Kinloch New Zealand
15 C3 Kinlochewe Scotland
15 D4 Kinlochleven Scotland
15 D4 Kinloch Rannoch Scotland
68 B3 Kinmaw Burma
61 P13 Kin-misaki C Okinawa
121 M8 Kinmount Ontario Canada
110 H3 Kinmundy Illinois U.S.A.
27 F14 Kinna Sweden
117 P11 Kinnaird British Columbia Canada
15 F3 Kinnairds Hd Scotland
101 R6 Kinnear Wyoming U.S.A.
80 F3 Kinneret Israel
80 B8 Kinneret-Negev-Conduit Israel
83 L9 Kinniyai Sri Lanka
29 L8 Kinnula Finland
60 J11 Kino R Japan
61 K10 Kinomoto Japan
119 Q1 Kinoosa Manitoba Canada
60 H10 Kinosaki Japan
13 E1 Kinglassie Scotland
13 E1 Kinross Scotland
7 E11 Kinsale oil rig Celtic Sea
14 C5 Kinsale Ireland
95 L8 Kinsale Virginia U.S.A.
14 C5 Kinsale, Old Hd of C Ireland
118 F5 Kinsella Alberta Canada
101 U3 Kinsey Montana U.S.A.
86 C6 Kinshasa Zaire
60 C11 Kin Shimo no-shima Japan
107 L4 Kinsley Kansas U.S.A.
94 G5 Kinsman Ohio U.S.A.
112 K2 Kinston North Carolina U.S.A.
107 P6 Kinta Oklahoma U.S.A.
70 P10 Kintamani, G mt Indonesia
85 C6 Kintinnian Guinea
101 L1 Kintla Pk Montana U.S.A.
70 D6 Kintop Kalimantan
15 F3 Kintore Scotland
138 B2 Kintore, Mt South Australia Australia
140 A6 Kintore Ra N Terr Australia
12 C2 Kintyre pen Scotland
68 B1 Kinu Burma
61 N9 Kinu R Japan
118 B3 Kinuso Alberta Canada
14 C3 Kinvarra Ireland
61 P13 Kin wan B Okinawa
86 F5 Kinyeti mt Sudan
55 C6 Kinzhaly Kazakhstan
36 D7 Kinzig R Baden-Württemberg Germany
36 G3 Kinzig R Hessen Germany
100 E5 Kinzua Oregon U.S.A.
71 N9 Kio Indonesia
100 F3 Kiona Washington U.S.A.
121 M6 Kiosk Ontario Canada
106 F2 Kiowa Colorado U.S.A.
107 M4 Kiowa Kansas U.S.A.
107 P7 Kiowa Oklahoma U.S.A.
119 Q3 Kipahigan L Manitoba Canada
135 T3 Kipahulu Hawaiian Is
46 E7 Kiparissia Greece
46 E7 Kiparissiakós Kolpos B Greece
121 M6 Kipawa Quebec Canada
88 C5 Kipili Tanzania
86 H6 Kipini Kenya
119 P8 Kipling Saskatchewan Canada
116 E7 Kipnuk Alaska U.S.A.
118 E9 Kipp Alberta Canada
12 D1 Kippen Scotland
36 D7 Kippenheim Germany
123 O5 Kippens Newfoundland Canada
95 M9 Kiptopeke Virginia U.S.A.
87 E8 Kipushi Zaire
47 M10 Kıraçköy Turkey
60 H12 Kiragawa Japan
79 D1 Kıraman Turkey
75 J8 Kirandul India
76 E1 Kirandul India
47 H4 Kirazh Turkey
Kirberg see Hünfelden
120 F6 Kirby Ontario Canada
9 H4 Kirby England
111 C7 Kirby Arkansas U.S.A.
101 R6 Kirby Wyoming U.S.A.
111 C11 Kirbyville Texas U.S.A.
38 N8 Kirchbach Austria
38 M5 Kirchberg Austria
37 O2 Kirchberg Germany
36 H5 Kirchberg Baden-Württemberg Germany
36 C4 Kirchberg Rheinland-Pfalz Germany
33 O5 Kirchdorf Germany
37 P6 Kirchdorf Germany
37 M4 Kirchenlaibach Germany
37 M3 Kirchenlamitz Germany
36 D2 Kirchen-Sieg Germany
36 G6 Kirchentellinsfurt Germany
37 M4 Kirchenthumbach Germany
33 T9 Kirchhain Germany
36 F2 Kirchhain Germany
37 K1 Kirchheilingen Germany
36 G5 Kirchheim Germany
36 D4 Kirchheim Bolanden Germany
32 E9 Kirchhellen Germany
36 E1 Kirchhundem Germany
33 O6 Kirch Jesar Germany
32 H6 Kirchkimmen Germany
37 K3 Kirchlauter Germany
32 J8 Kirchlengern Germany
32 K7 Kirchlinteln Germany
38 K5 Kirchschlag Austria
32 J7 Kirchweyhe Germany
32 J6 Kirchwistedt Germany
47 J5 Kireç Turkey
33 Q5 Kireh Grubenhagen Germany
56 G3 Kirenga R Russian Federation
47 K7 Kirenis R Turkey
56 G2 Kirensk Russian Federation
55 E6 Kirey R Kazakhstan
54 J3 Kireyevsk Russian Federation
83 K11 Kirgalpotta mt Sri Lanka
57 F4 Kirghizia rep C Asia
55 G6 Kirgiziya Kazakhstan
55 B4 Kirgiz-Miyaki Russian Federation
86 C6 Kiri Zaire
137 Q2 Kiribati rep Pacific Oc
86 A2 Kiridh Somalia
89 A6 Kiriis Ost Namibia
78 F3 Kırıkhan Turkey
78 D2 Kırıkkale Turkey
145 E1 Kirikopuni New Zealand
29 O11 Kirillovskoye Russian Federation
Kirin see Jilin
83 L11 Kirindi Oya R Sri Lanka
88 F2 Kirinyaga Kenya
145 E1 Kiripa New Zealand
52 D5 Kirishi Russian Federation
60 D14 Kirishima-Ōmuta Nat. Park Japan
135 U10 Kiritimati isld Pacific Oc
136 L3 Kiriwina Is Papua New Guinea
106 H2 Kirk Colorado U.S.A.
98 C8 Kirk Nebraska U.S.A.
100 D7 Kirk Oregon U.S.A.
47 L5 Kırka Turkey
47 J5 Kırkağaç Turkey
12 E4 Kirkbean Scotland
13 E4 Kirkbride England
13 F5 Kirkby Lonsdale England
13 H5 Kirkbymoorside England
13 F5 Kirkby Stephen England
118 D8 Kirkcaldy Alberta Canada
13 E1 Kirkcaldy Scotland
12 C4 Kirkcolm Scotland
12 D4 Kirkcowan Scotland
12 D4 Kirkcudbright Scotland
12 D4 Kirkcudbright B Scotland
13 G6 Kirk Deighton England
28 F6 Kirkeby Fyn Denmark
28 B6 Kirkeby Sønderjylland Denmark
28 G5 Kirke Helsinge Denmark
28 H5 Kirke Hvalsø Denmark
28 H5 Kirke Hyllinge Denmark
119 Q8 Kirkella Manitoba Canada
36 C5 Kirkel-Neuhausel Germany
26 R2 Kirkenes Norway
28 H5 Kirke Såby Denmark
28 G6 Kirke Stillinge Denmark
26 K3 Kirkestind mt Norway
12 E2 Kirkfieldbank Scotland
13 F6 Kirkham England
12 D4 Kirkinner Scotland
12 D2 Kirkintilloch Scotland
29 L11 Kirkkonummi Finland
12 E3 Kirkland Scotland

103 M7 **Kirkland** Arizona U.S.A.
99 S7 **Kirkland** Illinois U.S.A.
120 K4 **Kirkland Lake** Ontario Canada
47 J3 **Kirklarelı** Turkey
94 A6 **Kirklin** Indiana U.S.A.
9 F1 **Kirklington** England
13 G5 **Kirklington** N Yorks England
12 E2 **Kirkliston** Scotland
144 C6 **Kirkliston Range** New Zealand
99 L8 **Kirkman** Iowa U.S.A.
12 D3 **Kirkmichael** Scotland
13 F4 **Kirkoswald** England
12 D3 **Kirkoswald** Scotland
13 E3 **Kirkpatrick-Fleming** Scotland
146 D10 **Kirkpatrick, Mt** Antarctica
13 F5 **Kirkstone Pass** England
110 D1 **Kirksville** Missouri U.S.A.
78 K4 **Kirkūk** Iraq
15 F2 **Kirkwall** Scotland
89 D9 **Kirkwood** S Africa
102 B2 **Kirkwood** California U.S.A.
95 M4 **Kirkwood** New York U.S.A.
98 E5 **Kirley** South Dakota U.S.A.
79 F1 **Kırmıt** Turkey
36 C4 **Kirn** Germany
12 D2 **Kirn** Scotland
54 F2 **Kirov** Kaluga Russian Federation
52 G5 **Kirov** Kirovskaya obl Russian Federation
Kirovabad *see* **Gyandzha**
78 K1 **Kirovakan** Armenia
55 D3 **Kirovo** Russian Federation
54 D8 **Kirovograd** Ukraine
52 D1 **Kirovsk** Russian Federation
52 G5 **Kirovskaya Oblast'** *prov* Russian Federation
57 E5 **Kirovskiy** Tajikistan
118 G7 **Kirriemuir** Alberta Canada
15 E4 **Kirriemuir** Scotland
52 H5 **Kirs** Russian Federation
78 E2 **Kırşehir** Turkey
87 D11 **Kirstonia** S Africa
98 B7 **Kirtley** Wyoming U.S.A.
13 H6 **Kirton** England
9 F2 **Kirton Holme** England
36 G2 **Kirtorf** Germany
26 L4 **Kiruna** Sweden
86 E6 **Kirundu** Zaire
144 D5 **Kirwee** New Zealand
107 M2 **Kirwin** Kansas U.S.A.
61 N9 **Kiryū** Japan
54 K1 **Kirzhach** Russian Federation
27 H14 **Kisa** Sweden
61 N6 **Kisakata** Japan
87 G7 **Kisaki** Tanzania
46 F9 **Kisámou, K** *B* Crete Greece
86 E5 **Kisangani** Zaire
71 N9 **Kisar** *isld* Indonesia
116 G6 **Kisaralik** *R* Alaska U.S.A.
69 D11 **Kisaran** Sumatra
61 N10 **Kisarazu** Japan
48 D3 **Kisbér** Hungary
119 P9 **Kisbey** Saskatchewan Canada
56 C4 **Kiselevsk** Russian Federation
74 F5 **Kishangarh** India
85 E7 **Kishi** Nigeria
55 F4 **Kishikaroy, Oz** *L* Kazakhstan
48 M3 **Kishinev** Moldova
60 J11 **Kishiwada** Japan
74 F2 **Kishtwar** Kashmir
Kisi *see* **Jixi**
88 G3 **Kisigau Mt** Kenya
88 E5 **Kisigo** *R* Tanzania
88 E2 **Kisii** Kenya
119 T4 **Kiskittogisu L** Manitoba Canada
119 T4 **Kiskitto L** Manitoba Canada
48 D4 **Kiskomárom** Hungary
48 E4 **Kiskörei-viztárole** *L* Hungary
48 F3 **Kisköreiviztároló** *L* Hungary
48 F4 **Kiskundorozsma** Hungary
48 F4 **Kiskunfélegyháza** Hungary
48 E4 **Kiskunhalas** Hungary
48 F4 **Kiskunmajsa** Hungary
53 F11 **Kislovodsk** Russian Federation
86 H6 **Kismaayo** Somalia
61 L10 **Kiso** Japan
61 L10 **Kiso-Fukushima** Nagano Japan
61 L10 **Kiso-sammyaku** *mts* Japan
48 E3 **Kispest** Hungary
117 J8 **Kispiox** *R* British Columbia Canada
28 H5 **Kisserup** Denmark
85 B7 **Kissidougou** Guinea
113 F9 **Kissimmee** Florida U.S.A.
113 F10 **Kissimmee** *R* Florida U.S.A.
119 Q3 **Kississing L** Manitoba Canada
41 L2 **Kisslegg** Germany
84 H5 **Kissu, Jebel** *mt* Sudan
26 L3 **Kistefjell** *mt* Norway
48 F4 **Kistelek** Hungary
48 F2 **Kisterenye** Hungary
26 O1 **Kistrand** Norway
48 F3 **Kisújszállás** Hungary
88 E2 **Kisumu** Kenya
48 G2 **Kisvárda** Hungary
79 G5 **Kiswah, Al** Syria
85 C6 **Kita** Mali
57 D5 **Kitab** Uzbekistan
60 H12 **Kitagawa** Japan
61 O9 **Kita-Ibaraki** Japan
26 L5 **Kitajaur** Sweden
61 P6 **Kitakami** Japan
61 N8 **Kitakata** Japan
60 D12 **Kita-Kyūshū** Japan
86 G5 **Kitale** Kenya
60 R2 **Kitami** Japan
60 Q1 **Kitami-sanchi** *mts* Japan
61 N9 **Kitamoto** Japan
88 G7 **Kitangari** Tanzania
61 N13 **Kitano-hana** *C* Japan
61 O9 **Kita-ura** *L* Japan
61 J12 **Kitayama** *R* Japan
48 M5 **Kitay, Ozero** *L* Ukraine
106 H3 **Kit Carson** Colorado U.S.A.
120 K9 **Kitchener** Ontario Canada
112 E5 **Kite** Georgia U.S.A.
29 P9 **Kitee** Finland
86 F5 **Kitgum** Uganda
46 F6 **Kithairón** *mt* Greece
46 F8 **Kíthira** *isld* Greece
46 G7 **Kíthnos** *isld* Greece
120 H3 **Kitigan** Ontario Canada
114 H3 **Kitikmeot** *dist* Northwest Territories Canada
80 G4 **Kitim** Jordan
117 J8 **Kitimat** British Columbia Canada
117 J9 **Kitimat Mill** Alberta Canada
29 M3 **Kitinen** *R* Finland
29 M4 **Kitinen** *R* Finland
52 C1 **Kitinen** *R* Finland
46 E2 **Kitka** *mt* Serbia Yugoslavia
46 F4 **Kítros** Greece
118 G5 **Kitscoty** Alberta Canada
48 K2 **Kitsman'** Ukraine
60 E12 **Kitsuki** Japan
61 O9 **Kitsuregawa** Japan
138 E3 **Kittakittaooloo, L** South Australia Australia
94 H6 **Kittanning** Pennsylvania U.S.A.
95 N5 **Kittatinny Mts** New Jersey U.S.A.
33 R5 **Kittendorf** Germany
95 R3 **Kittery** Maine U.S.A.
29 L4 **Kittilä** Finland
112 M1 **Kitty Hawk** North Carolina U.S.A.
88 G2 **Kitui** Kenya
88 D5 **Kitunda** Tanzania
117 J8 **Kitwanga** British Columbia Canada
88 B8 **Kitwe-Nkana** Zambia
38 F7 **Kitzbüheler Alpen** *mts* Austria
37 J4 **Kitzingen** Germany
27 M10 **Kiukainen** Finland
116 L7 **Kiukpalik I** Alaska U.S.A.
68 D3 **Kiu Lom Dam** Thailand
86 E7 **Kiumbi** Zaire
29 M8 **Kiuruvesi** Finland
116 A4 **Kivak** Russian Federation
116 E3 **Kivalina** Alaska U.S.A.
53 C8 **Kivertsy** Ukraine
116 E3 **Kividlo** Alaska U.S.A.
29 L8 **Kivijärvi** Finland
27 G17 **Kivik** Sweden
52 C5 **Kiviõli** Estonia
46 E4 **Kivotós** Greece
88 B2 **Kivu, Lac** Zaire/Rwanda
145 D4 **Kiwi** New Zealand
56 C3 **Kiya** *R* Russian Federation
55 E6 **Kiyakty, Oz** *L* Kazakhstan
61 O14 **Kiyan** Okinawa
61 O14 **Kiyan-zaki** *C* Okinawa
54 B6 **Kiyev** Ukraine
55 F5 **Kiyevka** Kazakhstan
54 B5 **Kiyevskoy Vdkr** *res* Ukraine
47 J3 **Kiyiköy** Turkey
47 L5 **Kıyır** *R* Turkey
118 H7 **Kiyiu L** Saskatchewan Canada
55 E5 **Kiyma** Kazakhstan
52 J5 **Kizel** Russian Federation
52 F4 **Kizema** Russian Federation
47 M11 **Kızıl Adalar** *islds* Turkey
79 D2 **Kızıl Burun** *C* Turkey
79 D2 **Kızılca** Turkey
47 K7 **Kızılcabölük** Turkey
47 K7 **Kızılcadağ** Turkey
47 K8 **Kızılca Dağ** *mt* Turkey
78 D1 **Kızılcahamam** Turkey
47 K7 **Kızılhişar** Turkey
78 E1 **Kızılırmak** *R* Turkey
47 L7 **Kızılkaya** Turkey
55 C5 **Kizil'skoye** Russian Federation
47 N11 **Kiziltoprak** Turkey
79 C1 **Kızılyaka** Turkey
56 D4 **Kizir** *R* Russian Federation
53 G11 **Kizlyar** Russian Federation
50 E5 **Kizyl-Arvat** Turkmenistan
26 M2 **Kjaekan** Norway
28 C4 **Kjellerup** Denmark
26 P1 **Kjelvik** Norway
26 G4 **Kjerringöy** Norway
26 Q1 **Kjöllefjord** Norway
71 J4 **Klabat** *mt* Sulawesi
48 E6 **Kladanj** Bosnia-Herzegovina
30 H5 **Kladno** Czech Rep
48 H6 **Kladovo** Serbia Yugoslavia
37 O4 **Kladruby** Czech Rep
70 E2 **Klagan** Sabah
38 K8 **Klagenfurt** Austria
103 P6 **Klagetoh** Arizona U.S.A.
52 B6 **Klaipėda** Lithuania
28 D5 **Klakring** Denmark
6 F1 **Klaksvik** Faeroes
100 A8 **Klamath** California U.S.A.
100 B8 **Klamath** *R* California U.S.A.
100 D7 **Klamath Falls** Oregon U.S.A.
100 B8 **Klamath Mts** California U.S.A.
100 C8 **Klamath River** California U.S.A.
71 C3 **Klamono** W Irian
70 D4 **Klampo** Kalimantan
117 J7 **Klappan** *R* British Columbia Canada
27 F12 **Klarä** *R* Sweden
27 F11 **Klarabro** Sweden
27 F11 **Klarälven** *R* Sweden
37 P3 **Klášterec** Czech Rep
70 N9 **Klaten** Java
37 P5 **Klatovy** Czech Rep
38 O5 **Klausen-Leopoldsdorf** Austria
41 J4 **Klausen P** *mt* Switzerland
117 G8 **Klawock** Alaska U.S.A.
31 K3 **Kłecko** Poland
31 L3 **Kleczew** Poland
122 J3 **Kleczkowski L** Quebec Canada
117 L10 **Kleena Kleene** British Columbia Canada
101 S5 **Kleenburn** Wyoming U.S.A.
33 S5 **Kleeth** Germany
25 F5 **Klefe** Germany
28 S9 **Kleifar** Iceland
101 R3 **Klein** Montana U.S.A.
33 P6 **Kleinberge** Germany
22 J1 **Kleine-Brogel** Belgium
33 S9 **Kleine Elster** *R* Germany
32 J9 **Kleinenberg** Germany
22 H1 **Kleine Nete** *R* Belgium
33 R8 **Klein Kreutz** Germany
37 N6 **Klein Laaber** *R* Germany
36 F2 **Klein Linden** Germany
89 B9 **Klein Roggeveld Berge** *mts* S Africa
89 B9 **Klein Swartberge** *mts* S Africa
33 N5 **Klein Thurow** Germany
33 Q8 **Klein Wusterwitz** Germany
38 N6 **Klein Zell** Austria
28 D3 **Klejtrup** Denmark
42 H4 **Klekovača** *mt* Bosnia-Herzegovina
99 N6 **Klemme** Iowa U.S.A.
22 E1 **Klemskerke** Belgium
117 J9 **Klemtu** British Columbia Canada
48 F6 **Klenak** Serbia Yugoslavia
33 N7 **Klenze** Germany
89 E6 **Klerksdorp** S Africa
116 G3 **Klery Creek** Alaska U.S.A.
54 E3 **Kletnya** Russian Federation
53 F9 **Kletskiy** Russian Federation
41 H2 **Klettgau** *R* Germany
33 T9 **Klettwitz** Germany
100 D3 **Klickitat** *R* Washington U.S.A.
79 E3 **Klidhes Is** Cyprus
33 Q7 **Klietz** Germany
28 C2 **Klim** Denmark
31 N5 **Klimontów** Poland
54 C3 **Klimovichi** Belarus
52 H5 **Klimovka** Russian Federation
54 D4 **Klimovo** Russian Federation
54 J1 **Klimovsk** Russian Federation
26 G6 **Klimpfjäll** Sweden
54 H1 **Klin** Russian Federation
117 L10 **Klinaklini** *R* British Columbia Canada
112 F4 **Kline** South Carolina U.S.A.
71 G8 **Kling** Mindanao Philippines
36 G4 **Klingenberg** Germany
37 Q2 **Klingenberg** Germany
36 D5 **Klingenmünster** Germany
37 N3 **Klingenthal** Germany
70 B4 **Klingkang Ra** Sarawak
41 H2 **Klingnau** Germany
33 R6 **Klink** Germany
37 O3 **Klínovec** *mt* Czech Rep
28 E5 **Klinte** Denmark
27 K14 **Klintehamn** Sweden
54 D4 **Klintsy** Russian Federation
47 H5 **Klió** Greece
27 F15 **Klippan** Sweden
89 A8 **Kliprug Berg** *mt* S Africa
46 G2 **Klisura** Bulgaria
28 B2 **Klitmøller** Denmark
28 B7 **Klixbüll** Germany
42 H4 **Ključ** Bosnia-Herzegovina
31 L5 **Kłobuck** Poland
121 M6 **Klock** Ontario Canada
33 U6 **Klockow** Germany
31 L3 **Kłodawa** Poland
31 K5 **Kłodzko** Poland
27 E11 **Klöfta** Norway
117 F6 **Klondike Gold rush National Historic Park** Alaska U.S.A.
25 B6 **Kloosterzande** Netherlands
46 D3 **Klos** Albania
41 L3 **Kloster** *R* Austria
33 S7 **Klosterfelde** Germany
28 A4 **Klosterhede Plantage** Denmark
41 M3 **Klösterle** Austria
33 Q6 **Kloster Malchow** Germany
33 O9 **Kloster Mansfeld** Germany
31 J7 **Klosterneuburg** Austria
36 E6 **Klosterreichenbach** Germany
41 L4 **Klosters** Switzerland
33 S8 **Kloster Zinna** Germany
27 H12 **Kloten** Sweden
36 C3 **Klotten** Germany
33 O7 **Klötze** Germany
28 C5 **Klovborg** Denmark
26 G9 **Klövsjö** Sweden
117 D5 **Kluane** Yukon Territory Canada
117 D5 **Kluane Nat. Park** Yukon Territory Canada
31 L5 **Kluczbork** Poland
117 F6 **Klukwan** Alaska U.S.A.
70 E6 **Klumpang, Teluk** *B* Kalimantan
25 C5 **Klundert** Netherlands
70 P10 **Klungkung** Indonesia
36 C1 **Kluppelberg** Germany
116 P6 **Klutina L** Alaska U.S.A.
26 L7 **Klutmark** Sweden
33 O5 **Klütz** Germany
52 H7 **Klyavlino** Russian Federation
52 F6 **Klyazma** *R* Russian Federation
52 F2 **Klyuchevaya** Russian Federation
51 Q3 **Klyuchevskaya Sopka** *mt* Russian Federation
55 D2 **Klyuchi** Russian Federation
55 G4 **Klyuchi** Russian Federation
56 C2 **Klyuvinka** Russian Federation
27 B13 **Knabengruber** Norway
38 J7 **Knallstein, Gross** *mt* Austria
99 O5 **Knapp** Wisconsin U.S.A.
13 G5 **Knaresborough** England
13 F4 **Knarsdale** England
37 M2 **Knau** Germany
9 F4 **Knebworth** England
32 H5 **Knechtsand** *sandbank* Germany
118 K3 **Knee L** Saskatchewan Canada
33 N7 **Knesebeck** Germany
22 E1 **Knesselare** Belgium
37 K4 **Knetsgau** Germany
117 L9 **Knewstubb L** British Columbia Canada
46 G1 **Knezha** Bulgaria
98 D2 **Knife** *R* North Dakota U.S.A.
116 K7 **Knife Pk** Alaska U.S.A.
99 P3 **Knife River** Minnesota U.S.A.
101 P8 **Knight** Wyoming U.S.A.
116 O6 **Knight I** Alaska U.S.A.
117 K10 **Knight Inlet** British Columbia Canada
8 C3 **Knighton** Wales
94 B7 **Knightstown** Indiana U.S.A.
110 J2 **Knightsville** Indiana U.S.A.
42 G4 **Knin** Croatia
32 H5 **Kniphausen** Germany
109 H6 **Knippa** Texas U.S.A.
38 L7 **Knittelfeld** Austria
27 J12 **Knivsta** Sweden
46 E1 **Knjaževac** Serbia Yugoslavia
110 F5 **Knobel** Arkansas U.S.A.
142 G2 **Knob Pk** W Australia Australia
14 C3 **Knock** Ireland
14 B5 **Knockboy** *mt* Ireland
14 B5 **Knockbrack** *mt* Ireland
14 E1 **Knocklayd** *mt* N Ireland
14 D4 **Knockmealdown Mts** Ireland
14 B5 **Knockowen** *mt* Ireland
22 E1 **Knokke** Belgium
29 O5 **Knolayarvi** Russian Federation
101 M9 **Knolls** Utah U.S.A.
29 L10 **Knorevesi** Finland
28 E2 **Knøsen** *hill* Denmark
46 G9 **Knossos** Crete Greece
108 F3 **Knott** Texas U.S.A.
9 E3 **Knowle** England
107 K5 **Knowles** Oklahoma U.S.A.
146 D5 **Knowles, Cape** *C* Antarctica
121 S7 **Knowlton** Quebec Canada
99 R5 **Knowlton** Wisconsin U.S.A.
99 U8 **Knox** Indiana U.S.A.
98 G1 **Knox** North Dakota U.S.A.
94 H5 **Knox** Pennsylvania U.S.A.
117 G8 **Knox, C** Graham I, Br Col Canada
110 E1 **Knox City** Missouri U.S.A.
108 H2 **Knox City** Texas U.S.A.
146 G13 **Knox Coast** Antarctica
102 B3 **Knoxville** California U.S.A.
99 Q9 **Knoxville** Illinois U.S.A.
99 N8 **Knoxville** Iowa U.S.A.
111 E10 **Knoxville** Mississippi U.S.A.
94 K5 **Knoxville** Pennsylvania U.S.A.
112 C1 **Knoxville** Tennessee U.S.A.
83 K10 **Knuckles** *mt* Sri Lanka
115 N2 **Knud Rasmussen Land** Greenland
28 H6 **Knudshoved** *C* Denmark
36 G2 **Knüllwald** Germany
8 D1 **Knutsford** England
52 D2 **Knyazhaya Guba** Russian Federation
52 F5 **Knyazhevo** Russian Federation
87 D12 **Knysna** S Africa
31 O2 **Knyszyn** Poland
29 M2 **Koarvikods** *mt* Finland
69 H14 **Koba** Indonesia
60 D14 **Koba** Japan
28 H6 **Kobanke** *hill* Denmark
69 D8 **Ko Ban Sa Ket** Thailand
42 F2 **Kobarid** Slovenia
60 D13 **Kobayashi** Japan
115 P5 **Kobberminebugt** *B* Greenland
28 C3 **Kobberup** Denmark
Kobdo Jargalant *see* **Hovd**
71 A2 **Kobe** Halmahera Indonesia
60 J11 **Kōbe** Japan
28 G7 **Købelev** Denmark
54 F7 **Kobelyaki** Ukraine
89 A8 **Kobe Mts** S Africa
29 K5 **København** Denmark
38 H5 **Kobernausser Wald** *reg* Austria
36 C3 **Kobern-Gondorf** Germany
67 H4 **Kōbi-sho** *isld* Japan
36 D3 **Koblenz** Germany
86 F4 **Kobowem Swamp** Sudan
52 E5 **Kobozha** *R* Russian Federation
52 H4 **Kobra** Russian Federation
52 H5 **Kobra** *R* Russian Federation
61 M10 **Kobuchizawa** Japan
116 H3 **Kobuk** *R* Alaska U.S.A.
116 J3 **Kobuk** Alaska U.S.A.
116 H3 **Kobuk Valley Nat Park** Alaska U.S.A.
31 K4 **Kobylin** Poland
47 K8 **Koca** *R* Turkey
Kocaeli *see* **Izmit**
46 E3 **Kočani** Macedonia
47 J7 **Koçarlı** Turkey
47 L6 **Koca Tepe** *mt* Turkey
48 F6 **Koceljevo** Serbia Yugoslavia
42 F3 **Kočevje** Slovenia
75 N5 **Koch Bihār** India
52 F4 **Kochen'ga** Russian Federation
36 H5 **Kocher** *R* Germany
46 F2 **Kocherinovo** Bulgaria
54 M4 **Kochetovka** Russian Federation
52 H5 **Kochevo** Russian Federation
115 M4 **Koch I** Northwest Territories Canada
60 F11 **Kōchi** Japan
60 G12 **Kōchi** *prefect* Japan
60 G12 **Kōchi** Japan
61 P14 **Kochinada** Okinawa
52 D3 **Kochkoma** Russian Federation
57 H4 **Kochkorka** Kirghizia
52 K2 **Kochmes** Russian Federation
101 O4 **Koch Mt** Montana U.S.A.
53 G11 **Kochubey** Russian Federation
31 K4 **Kocie Góry** *mts* Poland
31 N4 **Kock** Poland
33 O7 **Köckte** Germany
48 E4 **Kocsola** Hungary
52 J3 **Kodachdikost** Russian Federation
76 C5 **Kodaikanal** India
60 O4 **Kodamari misaki** *C* Japan
75 L6 **Kodarma** India
83 L9 **Koddiyar B** Sri Lanka
31 O4 **Kodeń** Poland
116 L8 **Kodiak** Alaska U.S.A.
116 L8 **Kodiak I** Alaska U.S.A.
83 K8 **Kodikamam** Sri Lanka
52 F4 **Kodima** Russian Federation
74 D8 **Kodinar** India
52 E3 **Kodino** Russian Federation
76 D5 **Kodiyakkari** India
86 F4 **Kodok** Sudan
60 O4 **Kodomari** Japan
48 M2 **Kodyma** Ukraine
102 G6 **Koehn L** California U.S.A.
22 D1 **Koekelare** Belgium
22 J1 **Koersel** Belgium
87 C11 **Koës** Namibia
60 P1 **Koetoi** Japan
103 L8 **Kofa Mts** Arizona U.S.A.
37 N6 **Köfering** Germany
87 E11 **Koffiefontein** S Africa
85 D7 **Koforidua** Ghana
61 M10 **Kōfu** Japan
47 K8 **Kofu Tepe** *mt* Turkey
61 N9 **Koga** Japan
141 K7 **Kogan** Queensland Australia
28 J6 **Køge** Denmark
29 K6 **Køge Bugt** *B* Denmark
52 J3 **Kogel'** *R* Russian Federation
48 M4 **Kogil'nik** *R* Moldova/Ukraine
116 H6 **Kogrukluk** *R* Alaska U.S.A.
60 D11 **Kogushi** Japan
74 D2 **Kohat** Pakistan
52 B5 **Kohila** Estonia
75 Q6 **Kohima** India
68 G6 **Koh Ker** Cambodia
146 B8 **Kohler Ra** Antarctica
74 C4 **Kohlu** Pakistan
37 O1 **Kohren Sahlis** Germany
77 G2 **Kohsun** Afghanistan
68 F7 **Koh Tang** *isld* Cambodia
52 C5 **Kohtla-Järve** Estonia
145 E3 **Kohuratahi** New Zealand
61 M8 **Koide** Japan
116 R6 **Koidern** Yukon Territory Canada
69 A8 **Koihoa** Nicobar Is
52 H3 **Koin** *R* Russian Federation
78 K3 **Koi Sanjaq** Iraq
29 P8 **Koitere** *L* Finland
29 L5 **Koivu** Finland
65 G7 **Kŏje** *isld* S Korea
31 K6 **Kojetín** Czech Rep
60 N4 **Ko jima** *isld* Japan
143 B10 **Kojonup** W Australia Australia
95 S1 **Kokadjo** Maine U.S.A.
83 L10 **Kokagala** *mt* Sri Lanka
86 G4 **K'ok'a Häyk'** *L* Ethiopia
55 D6 **Kokalaat** Kazakhstan
57 F4 **Kokand** Uzbekistan
117 P11 **Kokanee Glacier Nat. Park** British Columbia Canada
57 B2 **Kokaral** Kazakhstan
48 F2 **Kokava** Slovakia
60 J11 **Kokawa** Japan
56 C5 **Kokbesh** Russian Federation
57 F6 **Kokcha** *R* Afghanistan
55 E4 **Kokchetav** Kazakhstan
29 K10 **Kokemäenjoki** *R* Finland
29 J10 **Kokemäki** Finland
136 H2 **Kokenau** W Irian
54 A2 **Kokhanovo** Belarus
80 B7 **Kokhav** Israel
80 E6 **Kokhav HaShaḥar** Jordan
80 C5 **Kokhav Ya'ir** Jordan
29 K8 **Kokkola** Finland
85 E6 **Koko** Nigeria
136 K3 **Kokoda** Papua New Guinea
102 S12 **Koko Head** Hawaiian Is
116 F2 **Kokolik** *R* Alaska U.S.A.
94 A6 **Kokomo** Indiana U.S.A.
144 C6 **Kokonga** New Zealand
Koko Nor *L* *see* **Qinghai Hu** *L*
52 C4 **Kokonselka** *L* Finland
54 F4 **Kokorevka** Russian Federation
69 B11 **Kokos** *isld* Indonesia
116 K4 **Kokrines Hills** Alaska U.S.A.
57 E4 **Koksaray** Kazakhstan
52 G6 **Kokshaga** *R* Russian Federation
52 F4 **Kokshen'ga** *R* Russian Federation
22 D1 **Koksijde** Belgium
115 N6 **Koksoak** *R* Quebec Canada
54 M8 **Koksovyy** Russian Federation
89 F8 **Kokstad** S Africa
60 D14 **Kokubu** Japan
60 D12 **Kokura** Japan
70 G7 **Koku, Tg** *C* Sulawesi
116 H7 **Kokwok** *R* Alaska U.S.A.
57 G4 **Kok-Yangak** Kirghizia
52 D1 **Kola** Russian Federation
70 G7 **Kolaka** Sulawesi
71 F6 **Kolambugan** Mindanao Philippines
76 D4 **Kolar** India
76 D4 **Kolar Gold Fields** India
29 K4 **Kolari** Finland
Kolarovgrad *see* **Shumen**
48 D3 **Kolárovo** Slovakia
26 F8 **Kolåsen** Sweden
46 D2 **Kolašin** Montenegro Yugoslavia
27 H12 **Kolbäck** Sweden
71 M10 **Kolbano** Timor
38 H8 **Kölbnitz** Austria
26 D9 **Kolbotn** Norway
31 N5 **Kolbuszowa** Poland
28 F5 **Kolby** Denmark
52 E6 **Kol'chugino** Russian Federation
85 A6 **Kolda** Senegal
28 B3 **Koldby** Denmark
28 C6 **Kolding** Denmark
86 E5 **Kole** Zaire
135 T3 **Kolekole** *pk* Hawaiian Is
48 M4 **Kolesnoye** Ukraine
37 P5 **Koleveč** Czech Rep
52 C5 **Kolga laht** *G* Estonia
50 D2 **Kolguyev Ostrov** *isld* Russian Federation
76 B2 **Kolhapur** India
29 O8 **Koli** Finland
48 L5 **Kolibash** Moldova
116 J7 **Koliganek** Alaska U.S.A.
47 R14 **Kolímbia** Rhodes Greece
31 J5 **Kolín** Czech Rep
101 Q2 **Kolin** Montana U.S.A.
28 F4 **Kolind** Denmark
37 P5 **Kolinec** Czech Rep
28 C4 **Kølkær** Denmark
121 N7 **Kol. Kienitz** Ontario Canada
33 T7 **Kol Kienitz** Germany
Kollam *see* **Quilon**
37 L1 **Kölleda** Germany
76 C4 **Kollegal** India
76 D5 **Kollidam** *R* India
46 E7 **Kollínai** Greece
25 F2 **Kollum** Netherlands
28 C4 **Kollund** Ringkøbing Denmark
28 C7 **Kollund** Sønderjylland Denmark
36 B2 **Köln** Germany
31 N2 **Kolno** Poland
31 L3 **Koło** Poland
135 O1 **Koloa** Hawaiian Is
31 J1 **Kołobrzeg** Poland
33 S9 **Kolochau** Germany
54 D2 **Kolodnya** Russian Federation
52 F5 **Kologriv** Russian Federation
71 B3 **Kolok** Indonesia
85 C6 **Kolokani** Mali
137 M3 **Kolombangara** *isld* Solomon Is
56 B2 **Kolominskiye Grivy** Russian Federation
54 K1 **Kolomna** Russian Federation
48 J2 **Kolomyya** Ukraine
70 G6 **Kolonedale** Sulawesi
134 F7 **Kolonia** Micronesia
71 B2 **Kolorai** *isld* Halmahera Indonesia
55 F3 **Kolosovka** Russian Federation
Kolozsvar *see* **Cluj-Napoca**
52 E5 **Kolp'** *R* Russian Federation
56 B2 **Kolpashevo** Russian Federation
33 R6 **Kölpin-See** *L* Germany
33 Q10 **Kölsa** Germany
26 G9 **Kolsätt** Sweden
52 D1 **Kol'skiy Poluostrov** *pen* Russian Federation
52 D1 **Kol'skiy Zaliv** *G* Russian Federation
28 F6 **Kølstrup** Denmark
27 H12 **Kolsva** Sweden
52 A3 **Kol'tsovo** Russian Federation
48 F6 **Kolubara** *R* Serbia Yugoslavia
145 D1 **Koluikohu** New Zealand
73 L8 **Kolumadulu Atoll** Maldives
31 M4 **Koluszki** Poland
55 E5 **Koluton** Kazakhstan
52 J1 **Kolva** *R* Komi Respublika Russian Federation
52 J4 **Kolva** *R* Permskaya obl Russian Federation
26 E7 **Kolvereid** Norway
26 O1 **Kolvik** Norway
52 D2 **Kolvitsa** Russian Federation
87 E8 **Kolwezi** Zaire
54 K1 **Kolyberovo** Russian Federation
51 P2 **Kolyma** *R* Russian Federation
54 H1 **Kolyubakino** Russian Federation
147 P2 **Kolyuchinskaya** Russian Federation
116 A3 **Kolyuchinskaya Guba** *G* Russian Federation
56 B5 **Kolyvan'** Russian Federation
27 G14 **Kölzby** Sweden
46 F1 **Kom** *mt* Bulgaria
68 D5 **Koma** Burma
86 G4 **Koma** Ethiopia
61 P6 **Kōma** Japan
85 G6 **Komadugu Gana** *R* Nigeria
61 L10 **Komagane** Japan
60 O3 **Komaga-take** *mt* Hokkaido Japan
61 N8 **Komaga-take** *mt* Honshu Japan
26 N1 **Komagfjord** Norway
26 S1 **Komagvaer** Norway
55 C2 **Komarikhinskiy** Russian Federation
119 U8 **Komarno** Manitoba Canada
48 E3 **Komárno** Slovakia
48 E3 **Komárom** *co* Hungary
48 E3 **Komárom** Hungary
89 G6 **Komati** *R* Swaziland
89 G5 **Komatipoort** S Africa
103 M8 **Komatke** Arizona U.S.A.
61 K9 **Komatsu** Ishikawa Japan
61 O7 **Komatsu** Yamagata Japan
71 L8 **Komba** *isld* Indonesia
71 J4 **Kombot** Sulawesi
46 E5 **Kombóti** Greece
28 E3 **Komdrup** Denmark
88 D2 **Kome I** Uganda
89 E9 **Komga** S Africa
61 O5 **Kominato** Japan
52 H5 **Komi-Permyatskiy Avtonomnyy Okrug** *dist* Russian Federation
52 H3 **Komi Respublika** Russian Federation
48 E2 **Komjatice** Slovakia
48 E4 **Komló** Hungary
53 E9 **Kommunarsk** Ukraine
57 F5 **Kommunizma, Pik** *mt* Tajikistan
71 J9 **Komodo** *isld* Indonesia
85 D7 **Komoé** *R* Ivory Coast
85 D7 **Komoé Nat. Park** Ivory Coast
84 J5 **Kôm Ombo** Egypt
61 M9 **Komoro** Japan
46 G3 **Komotiní** Greece
46 D2 **Komovi** *mt* Montenegro Yugoslavia
89 D8 **Kompas Berg** *mt* S Africa
68 G6 **Kompong Kleang** Cambodia
68 F7 **Kompong Som** Cambodia
68 G7 **Kompong Speu** Cambodia
68 G6 **Kompong Sralao** Cambodia
68 G6 **Kompong Thom** Cambodia
68 G6 **Kompong Trabek** Cambodia
68 G7 **Kompong Trach** Cambodia
68 G7 **Kompong Tralach** Cambodia
48 M4 **Komrat** Moldova
89 B9 **Komsbergeskarp** *mts* S Africa
55 D4 **Komsomolets** Kazakhstan
51 J1 **Komsomolets, Ostrov** *isld* Russian Federation
52 F6 **Komsomol'sk** Russian Federation
54 E8 **Komsomol'sk** Ukraine
55 D1 **Komsomol'skiy** Russian Federation
54 K9 **Komsomol'skoye** Ukraine
59 L1 **Komsomol'skoye-na-Amure** Russian Federation
103 M10 **Kom Vo** Arizona U.S.A.
53 G12 **Konagkend** Azerbaijan
52 E6 **Konakovo** Russian Federation
75 M9 **Konārka** India
77 B5 **Konār Takhteh** Iran
109 L1 **Konawa** Oklahoma U.S.A.
42 H3 **Končanica** Croatia
55 E2 **Konda** *R* Russian Federation
71 C3 **Konda** W Irian
76 E1 **Kondagaon** India
121 O6 **Kondiaronk, L** Quebec Canada
143 C10 **Kondinin** W Australia Australia
88 E4 **Kondoa** Tanzania
52 D4 **Kondopoga** Russian Federation
48 F4 **Kondoros** Hungary
54 G2 **Kondrovo** Russian Federation
86 B3 **Konduga** Nigeria
143 B9 **Kondut** W Australia Australia
56 D2 **Konduyak** Russian Federation
77 L1 **Kondūz** Afghanistan
77 L1 **Kondūz** *prov* Afghanistan
52 J3 **Konetsbor** Russian Federation
52 E4 **Konevo** Russian Federation
28 H6 **Køng** Denmark
85 D7 **Kong** Ivory Coast
116 R2 **Kongakut** *R* Alaska U.S.A.
115 Q4 **Kong Christian IX Land** Greenland
115 R3 **Kong Christian X Land** Greenland
28 B6 **Kongeå** *R* Denmark
29 K5 **Kongens Lyngby** Denmark
115 P5 **Kong Frederik VI Kyst** *coast* Greenland
29 M9 **Konginkangas** Finland
68 F7 **Kong Kaôh Kong** Cambodia
50 B1 **Kong Karls Land** *isld* Spitzbergen
70 E4 **Kong Kat** *mt* Kalimantan
70 E4 **Kongkemul** *mt* Kalimantan
87 D9 **Kongola** Namibia
86 E7 **Kongolo** Zaire
86 F4 **Kongor** Sudan
147 E10 **Kong Oscars Fj** Greenland
26 J3 **Kongsbakktind** *mt* Norway
27 D12 **Kongsberg** Norway
26 R1 **Kongsfjord** *inlet* Norway
26 R1 **Kongsfjord** Norway
28 B6 **Kongsmark** Denmark
26 F7 **Kongsmoen** Norway
28 J6 **Kongsted** Denmark
27 E11 **Kongsvinger** Norway
66 B4 **Kongur Shan** *mt* China
88 F5 **Kongwa** Tanzania
31 M5 **Koniecpol** Poland
36 H4 **Königheim** Germany
36 F6 **Königsbach** Germany
Königsberg *see* **Kaliningrad**
36 D4 **Königsberg** *mt* Germany
37 J6 **Königsbronn** Germany
33 T10 **Königsbrück** Germany
37 K7 **Königsbrunn** Germany
41 O2 **Königsdorf** Germany
37 L2 **Königsee** Germany
37 L4 **Königsfeld** Germany
Königshofen *see* **Lauda-Königshofen**
36 H4 **Königshofen** Germany
33 N8 **Königslutter** Germany
36 F5 **Königsstuhl** *mt* Germany
36 E3 **Königstein** Germany
38 L5 **Königswiesen** Austria
36 C2 **Königswinter** Germany
33 T8 **Königs Wusterhausen** Germany
31 L3 **Konin** Poland
145 E4 **Konini** New Zealand
46 D5 **Konispol** Albania
42 H5 **Konjic** Bosnia-Herzegovina
88 B1 **Konjo** *tribal dist* Zaire
48 E6 **Konjuh** *mt* Bosnia-Herzegovina
26 M3 **Konkämä Älv** *R* Sweden/Finland
88 A8 **Konkola** Zambia
85 B6 **Konkouré** *R* Guinea
33 P9 **Könnern** Germany
37 N3 **Konnersreuth** Germany
29 M9 **Konnevesi** Finland
85 D7 **Konongo** Ghana
88 C5 **Konongo** Tanzania
61 N9 **Kōnosu** Japan
54 E5 **Konotop** Ukraine
66 D3 **Konqi He** *R* China
85 C7 **Konsankoro** Guinea
31 M4 **Końskie** Poland
53 F10 **Konstantinovsk** Russian Federation
41 K2 **Konstanz** Germany
85 F6 **Kontagora** Nigeria
86 B4 **Kontcha** Cameroon
22 G1 **Kontich** Belgium
29 N7 **Kontiomäki** Finland
47 O12 **Kontókali** Greece
116 L6 **Kontrashibuna L** Alaska U.S.A.
68 J6 **Kontum, Plat. du** Vietnam
52 F2 **Konushin, Mys** *C* Russian Federation
78 D3 **Konya** Turkey
36 B4 **Konz** Germany
88 F2 **Konza** Kenya
37 O5 **Konzell** Germany
55 C2 **Konzhakovskiy Kamen', G** *mt* Russian Federation
25 C4 **Koog** Netherlands
116 C5 **Kookooligit Mts** St Lawrence I, Alaska U.S.A.
143 D8 **Kookynie** W Australia Australia
140 D2 **Koolatong** *R* N Terr Australia
102 S11 **Koolauloa** Hawaiian Is
102 S12 **Koolaupoko** Hawaiian Is
142 B6 **Kooline** W Australia
140 E6 **Koolivoo,L** Queensland Australia
143 C9 **Koolyanobbing** W Australia Australia
143 G9 **Koonalda** South Australia Australia
142 B6 **Koorabooka** *R* W Australia Australia
143 B6 **Koorabooka** W Australia Australia
143 B9 **Koorda** W Australia Australia
142 B5 **Koordarrie** W Australia Australia
29 T8 **Kópasker** Iceland
48 L2 **Kopaygorod** Ukraine
144 A7 **Kopeka B** New Zealand
33 T8 **Kopenick** Germany
26 K8 **Köpmanholmen** Sweden
27 F10 **Kopparberg** *county* Sweden
79 C2 **Köprülü** Turkey
145 E2 **Kopu** New Zealand
145 E4 **Kopuaranga** New Zealand
77 C4 **Kor** *R* Iran
86 H4 **K'orahē** Ethiopia
47 O12 **Korakiána** Greece
75 K7 **Korba** India
32 J10 **Korbach** Germany
100 B9 **Korbel** California U.S.A.
69 E10 **Korbu, G.** *mt* Malaysia
46 D4 **Korcë** Albania
42 H6 **Korčula** Croatia
36 B4 **Kordel** Germany
77 A2 **Kordestān** Iran
77 D1 **Kord Kūy** Iran
Kordofan *prov* Sudan *see* **Northern and Southern Kordofan** *provs*
77 G6 **Kords** *reg* Iran
59 H4 **Korea Bay** China/Korea
65 G4 **Korea, North** *rep* E Asia
65 H6 **Korea, South** *rep* E Asia
52 D2 **Korelaksha** Russian Federation
52 J4 **Korelino** Russian Federation
54 F5 **Korenevo** Russian Federation
146 D7 **Korff Ice Rise** *ice rise* Antarctica
26 G5 **Korgen** Norway
85 C7 **Korhogo** Ivory Coast
60 D14 **Kori** Japan
46 F4 **Korinós** Greece
28 E6 **Korinth** Denmark
46 E6 **Korinthiakós Kólpos** *G* Greece
46 F7 **Kórinthos** Greece
46 D2 **Koritnik** *mt* Serbia Yugoslavia
Koritsa *see* **Korcë**
61 O8 **Kōriyama** Japan
55 D4 **Korkino** Russian Federation
47 L7 **Korkuteli** Turkey
66 D3 **Korla** China
54 B3 **Korma** Belarus
120 G5 **Kormak** Ontario Canada
48 D3 **Körmend** Hungary
55 F3 **Kormilovka** Russian Federation
42 G5 **Kornat** *isld* Croatia
37 L5 **Kornburg** Germany
25 F7 **Kornelimünster** Germany
37 K1 **Körner** Germany
48 L3 **Korneshty** Moldova
55 E4 **Korneyevka** Kazakhstan
55 F5 **Korneyevka** Kazakhstan
27 E13 **Kornsjö** Norway
28 C3 **Kornum** Denmark
36 G6 **Kornwestheim** Germany
70 G5 **Koro** *R* Sulawesi
54 J6 **Korocha** Russian Federation
78 C1 **Köröglu D** Turkey
88 G4 **Korogwe** Tanzania
138 F7 **Koroit** Victoria Australia
144 D4 **Koromiko** New Zealand
113 F8 **Korona** Florida U.S.A.
85 E7 **Koronga** *mt* Togo
139 G6 **Korong Vale** Victoria Australia
46 E8 **Koróni** Greece
46 F4 **Korónia, L** Greece
31 K2 **Koronowo** Poland
54 D5 **Korop** Ukraine
48 J2 **Koropets** Ukraine
46 F7 **Koropí** Greece
134 D7 **Koror** Palau Pacific Oc
48 F4 **Körös** *R* Hungary
53 C8 **Korosten** Ukraine
53 C8 **Korostyshev** Ukraine
86 C2 **Koro Toro** Chad
54 L6 **Korotoyak** Russian Federation
116 G9 **Korovin I** Alaska U.S.A.
29 M9 **Korpilahti** Finland
26 N5 **Korpilombolo** Sweden
29 J11 **Korpo** Finland
59 M2 **Korsakov** Russian Federation
27 H14 **Korsberga** Sweden
36 B1 **Korschenbroich** Germany
28 H5 **Korshage** *C* Denmark
48 J2 **Korshev** Ukraine
28 E3 **Korsholm** *isld* Denmark
27 H11 **Korsnäs** Sweden
26 H3 **Korsnes** Norway
28 G6 **Korsør** Denmark
54 C7 **Korsun' Shevchenkovskiy** Ukraine
22 E1 **Kortemark** Belgium
29 K8 **Kortesjärvi** Finland
22 J2 **Kortessem** Belgium
27 G12 **Kortfors** Sweden
25 A5 **Kortgene** Netherlands
52 H4 **Kortkeros** Russian Federation
22 E2 **Kortrijk** Belgium
52 F5 **Kortsovo** Russian Federation
47 J5 **Korucu** Turkey
139 H7 **Korumburra** Victoria Australia
29 O3 **Korvatunturi** *mt* Finland
29 O4 **Korya** Russian Federation
52 G4 **Koryazhma** Russian Federation
54 D5 **Koryukovka** Ukraine
47 J8 **Kos** *isld* Greece
52 H5 **Kosa** Russian Federation
53 E10 **Kosa Arabatskaya Strelka** *spit* Ukraine
55 D5 **Kosagal** Kazakhstan
61 L11 **Kosai** Japan
61 O5 **Kosaka** Japan
69 E8 **Ko Samui** *isld* Thailand
57 D1 **Kosay** Kazakhstan
54 J2 **Kosaya Gora** Russian Federation
56 E2 **Kosaya, Shiv** Russian Federation
57 C4 **Kosboget** Uzbekistan
37 M6 **Kösching** Germany
31 K3 **Kościan** Poland
31 K1 **Kościerzyna** Poland
111 G8 **Kosciusko** Mississippi U.S.A.
117 G7 **Kosciusko I** Alaska U.S.A.
139 J6 **Kosciusko, Mt** New South Wales Australia
139 J6 **Kosciusko Nat Park** New South Wales Australia
33 S10 **Koselitz** Germany
33 U4 **Koserow** Germany
56 B1 **Koses** *R* Russian Federation
76 C2 **Kosgi** India
56 C6 **Kosh Agach** Russian Federation
55 D2 **Koshay** Russian Federation
57 G4 **Kosh-Dëbë** Kirghizia
60 S2 **Koshikawa** Japan
60 C14 **Koshiki-kaikyō** *str* Japan
60 C14 **Koshiki-rettō** *islds* Japan
110 E5 **Koshkonong** Missouri U.S.A.
57 K2 **Koshkorkol', Ozero** *L* Kazakhstan
57 B4 **Kosh-Kupyr** Uzbekistan
61 M9 **Kōshoku** Japan
57 D4 **Koshrabad** Uzbekistan
48 G2 **Košice** Slovakia
68 E6 **Ko Si Chang** *isld* Thailand
76 C3 **Kosigi** India
89 H6 **Kosi L** S Africa
55 C5 **Kos-Istek** Kazakhstan
48 E5 **Koška** Croatia
123 R6 **Koskaecodde L** Newfoundland Canada
29 K11 **Koski** Finland
26 M5 **Koskivaara** Sweden
57 D1 **Koskol'** Kazakhstan
57 H3 **Koskuduk** Kazakhstan
26 L4 **Koskullskulle** Sweden
52 G3 **Koslan** Russian Federation
52 G2 **Kosma** *R* Russian Federation
48 J2 **Kosmach** Ukraine
100 C3 **Kosmos** Washington U.S.A.
59 J4 **Kosŏng** N Korea
48 J2 **Kosov** Ukraine
46 D2 **Kosovo** *aut rep* Serbia Yugoslavia
46 E2 **Kosovo Polje** Serbia Yugoslavia
33 S10 **Kossdorf** Germany
109 L4 **Kosse** Texas U.S.A.
33 P9 **Kösseln** Germany
37 O1 **Kössern** Germany
37 P7 **Kösslarn** Germany
31 N3 **Kossów** Poland
27 H15 **Kosta** Sweden
33 T9 **Kostebrau** Germany
46 F2 **Kostenets** Bulgaria
28 J7 **Koster** Denmark
54 L1 **Kosterevo** Russian Federation
48 L2 **Kosteshty-Synka, Vodokhranilishche** *res* Moldova
48 L3 **Kostesty** Moldova
86 F3 **Kosti** Sudan
46 F2 **Kostinbrod** Bulgaria
50 H2 **Kostino** Russian Federation
52 D3 **Kostomuksha** Russian Federation
52 F5 **Kostroma** Russian Federation
52 F5 **Kostromskaya Oblast'** *prov* Russian Federation
31 H3 **Kostrzyn** Poland
54 D3 **Kostyukovichi** Belarus
54 B4 **Kostyukovka** Belarus
61 L9 **Kosugi** Japan
52 J2 **Kos'yu** Russian Federation
52 J2 **Kos'yuvom** Russian Federation
31 J1 **Koszalin** Poland
48 D3 **Kőszeg** Hungary
75 K7 **Kota** India
70 K8 **Kotaagung** Sumatra
69 F9 **Kota Baharu** Malaysia
70 B5 **Kotabaru** Kalimantan
70 E6 **Kotabaru** Kalimantan
69 C11 **Kotabaru** Sumatra
69 E13 **Kotabaru** Sumatra
70 E1 **Kota Belud** Sabah
70 C6 **Kotabesi** Kalimantan
70 K8 **Kotabumi** Sumatra
70 E2 **Kota Kinabalu** Sabah
29 O4 **Kotala** Finland
71 J4 **Kotamubagu** Sulawesi
76 F1 **Kotapārh** India
69 E12 **Kotapinang** Sumatra
69 E12 **Kotatengah** Sumatra
69 F12 **Kota Tinggi** Malaysia
70 B6 **Kotawaringin** Kalimantan
117 N6 **Kotcho** *R* British Columbia Canada
47 H2 **Kotel** Bulgaria
53 F9 **Kotel'nikovo** Russian Federation
51 N1 **Kotel'nyy, Ostrov** *isld* Russian Federation
145 F3 **Kotemaori** New Zealand
33 P9 **Köthen** Germany
74 F3 **Kot Kapura** India
52 H2 **Kotkino** Russian Federation
55 G2 **Kotkino** Russian Federation
52 G4 **Kotlas** Russian Federation
29 O11 **Kotlin, O** *isld* Russian Federation
28 S10 **Kötlutangi** *C* Iceland
52 C5 **Kotly** Russian Federation
60 G11 **Kotohira** Japan
60 P2 **Kotoni** Japan
42 J6 **Kotor** Montenegro Yugoslavia

42 H4 **Kotor Varoš** Bosnia-Herzegovina
53 C10 **Kotovsk** Ukraine
74 C6 **Kotri** Pakistan
57 A1 **Kotr-Tas** Kazakhstan
38 H8 **Kötschach** Austria
74 J10 **Kottagudem** India
75 K10 **Kottakota** India
76 C6 **Kottayam** India
83 J11 **Kotte** Sri Lanka
86 D4 **Kotto** *R* Cent Afr Republic
26 H8 **Köttsjön** Sweden
76 C3 **Kotturu** India
51 K1 **Kotuy** *R* Russian Federation
48 M3 **Kotyuzhany** Moldova
116 F3 **Kotzebue** Alaska U.S.A.
116 E3 **Kotzebue Sd** Alaska U.S.A.
37 Q1 **Kötzschenbroda** Germany
37 O5 **Kötzting** Germany
85 E6 **Kouandé** Benin
86 D4 **Kouango** Cent Afr Republic
86 C2 **Kouba Modounga** Chad
85 D6 **Koudougou** Burkina
89 A9 **Koue Bokkeveld** *reg* S Africa
89 D8 **Koueveld Berge** *mts* S Africa
47 H10 **Koufonísi** *isld* Crete Greece
47 H8 **Koufonísia** *isld* Greece
89 C9 **Kougaberge** *mts* S Africa
86 B6 **Koulamoutou** Gabon
85 C6 **Koulikoro** Mali
141 J5 **Koumala** Queensland Australia
66 E3 **Koumenzi** China
86 C4 **Koumra** Chad
86 C3 **Koungouri** Chad
48 C1 **Kounice** Czech Rep
47 H8 **Kounoupói** *isld* Greece
57 G2 **Kounradskiy** Kazakhstan
111 B11 **Kountze** Texas U.S.A.
85 D6 **Koupela** Burkina
Kouqian *see* **Yongji**
61 Q12 **Kouri-jima** *isld* Okinawa
84 F5 **Kourizo, Passe de** Chad
29 H2 **Kourou** Fr Guiana
85 C6 **Kouroussa** Guinea
89 B9 **Kousberg** *mt* S Africa
85 C5 **Koussa** Mauritania
86 B3 **Kousséri** Cameroon
85 C6 **Koutiala** Mali
85 C7 **Kouto** Ivory Coast
46 F7 **Koutsopódhi** Greece
29 M11 **Kouvola** Finland
86 C6 **Kouyou** *R* Congo
56 F2 **Kova** *R* Russian Federation
47 H2 **Kovachevo** Bulgaria
48 F5 **Kovačica** Serbia Yugoslavia
46 C1 **Kovač Planina** *mt* Montenegro Yugoslavia
52 D2 **Kovda** Russian Federation
52 D2 **Kovdozero, Oz** *L* Russian Federation
55 E1 **Kovenskaya** *R* Russian Federation
52 F6 **Kovernino** Russian Federation
29 P9 **Kovero** Finland
48 F6 **Kovin** Serbia Yugoslavia
46 D1 **Kovren** Montenegro Yugoslavia
52 G1 **Kovriga, Gora** *mt* Russian Federation
54 N1 **Kovrov** Russian Federation
52 E5 **Kovzha** *R* Russian Federation
52 E4 **Kovzhskoye, Oz** *L* Russian Federation
44 C5 **Kowai Bush** New Zealand
31 L3 **Kowal** Poland
31 L2 **Kowalewo** Poland
71 J9 **Kowangge** Sumbawa Indonesia
44 C5 **Kowhitirangi** New Zealand
20 C2 **Kowkash** Ontario Canada
57 G6 **Kowloon** Hong Kong
55 G6 **Koyandy** Kazakhstan
61 J11 **Kōyasan** Japan
47 K8 **Koyceğiz** Turkey
47 J8 **Köyceğiz Gölü** *L* Turkey
52 F2 **Koyda** Russian Federation
52 H4 **Koygorodok** Russian Federation
46 G1 **Koynare** Bulgaria
52 G3 **Koynas** Russian Federation
61 O6 **Koyoshi-gawa** *R* Japan
52 J4 **Koyp, Gora** *mt* Russian Federation
54 L9 **Koysug** Russian Federation
57 D4 **Koytash** Uzbekistan
6 G4 **Koyuk** Alaska U.S.A.
6 L3 **Koyukuk** *R* Alaska U.S.A.
6 J4 **Koyukuk I** Alaska U.S.A.
78 F1 **Koyulhisar** Turkey
5 C2 **Koyva** *R* Russian Federation
9 P7 **Koyvayarvi** Russian Federation
1 J12 **Koza** *R* Japan
0 C11 **Kō-zaki** *C* Japan
0 G11 **Kōzan** Japan
8 E3 **Kozan** Turkey
6 E4 **Kozáni** Greece
2 H3 **Kozara** Bosnia-Herzegovina
8 E2 **Kozárovce** Slovakia
4 C6 **Kozelets** Ukraine
4 E7 **Kozel'shchina** Ukraine
4 G2 **Kozel'sk** Russian Federation
5 E5 **Kozhakol', Oz** *L* Kazakhstan
5 G3 **Kozhevnikovo** Russian Federation
Kozhikode *see* **Calicut**
2 J2 **Kozhim** Russian Federation
2 J2 **Kozhimvom** Russian Federation
2 E3 **Kozhozero, Oz** *L* Russian Federation
2 E3 **Kozhposelok** Russian Federation
5 G3 **Kozhurla** Russian Federation
2 J2 **Kozhva** Russian Federation
2 J3 **Kozhymiz, Gora** *mt* Russian Federation
1 N4 **Kozienice** Poland
2 F3 **Kozina** Slovenia
6 E3 **Kozjak** *mt* Macedonia
L5 **Koźle** Poland
6 F1 **Kozloduy** Bulgaria
6 G1 **Kozlovets** Bulgaria
4 M6 **Kozlovka** Russian Federation
8 C1 **Kozlu** Turkey
K4 **Koźmin** Poland
7 E3 **Kozmoldak** Kazakhstan
8 J1 **Kozova** Ukraine
J4 **Kozuchów** Poland
N11 **Kōzu-shima** *isld* Japan
5 E7 **Kpalime** Togo
5 D7 **Kpandu** Ghana
9 E8 **Kraai** *R* S Africa
8 O6 **Kraak** Germany
5 B6 **Krabbendijke** Netherlands
8 D7 **Kra Buri** Thailand
7 M2 **Kraftsdorf** Germany
0 N9 **Kragan** Java
8 C4 **Kragelund** Denmark
8 G7 **Kragenæs** Denmark
7 D13 **Kragerö** Norway
8 F6 **Kragujevac** Serbia Yugoslavia
6 G4 **Krahenberg** Germany
7 K2 **Krahnberg** *mt* Germany
6 F5 **Kraich** *R* Germany
6 F5 **Kraichtal** Germany
8 Q7 **Kra, Isthmus of** Thailand
2 G3 **Krajina** *reg* Croatia/Yugoslavia
K9 **Krakatau** *isld* Sumatra
A9 **Kråkenes** Norway
F6 **Krakor** Cambodia
H1 **Krakovets** Ukraine
Q5 **Krakow** Germany
M5 **Kraków** Poland
F6 **Kralanh** Cambodia
G2 **Král Chlmec** Slovakia
K8 **Kralendijk** Bonaire Neth Antilles
K5 **Králiky** Czech Rep
46 D1 **Kraljevo Vrnjacka** Serbia Yugoslavia
48 E1 **Kralovany** Slovakia
37 Q4 **Kralovice** Czech Rep
37 P3 **Kralupy** Severočesky Czech Rep
69 G11 **Kramat** Indonesia
98 F1 **Kramer** North Dakota U.S.A.
26 J9 **Kramfors** Sweden
68 E6 **Kram, Ko** *isld* Thailand
26 S1 **Krampenes** Norway
25 F5 **Kranenburg** Germany
26 H8 **Krångede** Sweden
46 E5 **Kraniá** Greece
37 L2 **Kranichfeld** Germany
46 F7 **Kranídhion** Greece
42 F2 **Kranj** Slovenia
38 J9 **Kranjska-Gord** Slovenia
31 K5 **Krapkowice** Poland
29 K4 **Krapperup** Sweden
52 G4 **Krasavino** Russian Federation
54 K1 **Krashy Oktyabr'** Russian Federation
48 K1 **Krasilov** Ukraine
50 E1 **Krasino** Russian Federation
59 K3 **Kraskino** Russian Federation
52 C6 **Krāslava** Latvia
37 O3 **Kraslice** Czech Rep
31 N5 **Krasnik** Poland
31 N4 **Kraśnik Fabryczny** Poland
37 O3 **Krásno** Czech Rep
55 E4 **Krasnoarmeyesk** Kazakhstan
54 K1 **Krasnoarmeysk** Russian Federation
58 G1 **Krasnoarmeysk** Russian Federation
54 J8 **Krasnoarmeysk** Ukraine
55 D4 **Krasnoarmeyskiy** Kustanayskaya Kazakhstan
52 G4 **Krasnoborsk** Russian Federation
31 O5 **Krasnobród** Poland
53 E11 **Krasnodar** Russian Federation
53 E10 **Krasnodarskiy Kray** *reg* Russian Federation
54 L8 **Krasnodon** Ukraine
52 D5 **Krasnofarfornyy** Russian Federation
52 C6 **Krasnogorodskoye** Russian Federation
59 M2 **Krasnogorsk** Russian Federation
55 D4 **Krasnogorskiy** Chelyabinskaya obl Russian Federation
52 H5 **Krasnogorskoye** Russian Federation
54 G7 **Krasnograd** Ukraine
55 D3 **Krasnogvardeyskiy** Russian Federation
55 B5 **Krasnokholm** Orenburgskaya obl Russian Federation
55 G4 **Krasnokutsk** Pavlodarskaya obl Kazakhstan
54 G6 **Krasnokutsk** Ukraine
55 E1 **Krasnoleninskiy** Russian Federation
54 L5 **Krasnolesniyy** Russian Federation
31 N1 **Krasnoles'ye** Russian Federation
54 J7 **Krasnooskol'skoye Vodokhranilishche** *res* Ukraine
52 C4 **Krasnoostrovskiy** Russian Federation
54 H7 **Krasnopavlovka** Ukraine
54 C3 **Krasnopol'ye** Belarus
54 K7 **Krasnorechenskoye** Ukraine
53 F9 **Krasnoslobodsk** Russian Federation
55 D2 **Krasnotur'insk** Russian Federation
55 C3 **Krasnoufimsk** Russian Federation
55 D2 **Krasnoural'sk** Russian Federation
55 C4 **Krasnousol'skiy** Russian Federation
52 J4 **Krasnovishersk** Russian Federation
50 E4 **Krasnovodsk** Turkmenistan
55 F3 **Krasnoyarka** Omskaya obl Russian Federation
55 D2 **Krasnoyarka** Sverdlovskaya obl Russian Federation
56 D3 **Krasnoyarsk** Russian Federation
54 K4 **Krasnoye** Russian Federation
48 J1 **Krasnoye** Ukraine
54 M1 **Krasnoye Ekho** Russian Federation
57 B6 **Krasnoye Znamya** Turkmenistan
52 H4 **Krasnozatonskiy** Russian Federation
55 G4 **Krasnozerskoye** Russian Federation
55 C4 **Krasnoznamenskiy** Bashkirskaya Respublika Russian Federation
55 E5 **Krasnoznamenskoye** Tselinogradskaya obl Kazakhstan
52 H6 **Krasny Bor** Russian Federation
54 J8 **Krasny Liman** Ukraine
54 K8 **Krasny Luch** Ukraine
54 N1 **Krasny Mayak** Russian Federation
31 O5 **Krasnystaw** Poland
54 L1 **Krasny Tkach** Russian Federation
54 C2 **Krasnyy** Russian Federation
52 G6 **Krasnyye-Baki** Russian Federation
48 M3 **Krasnyye Okna** Ukraine
52 E5 **Krasnyye Tkachi** Russian Federation
52 E5 **Krasnyy Kholm** Tverskaya obl Russian Federation
55 C3 **Krasnyy-Klyuch** Russian Federation
55 D3 **Krasnyy Oktyabr** Russian Federation
52 E5 **Krasnyy Pereval** Russian Federation
55 F3 **Krasnyy Yar** Omskaya obl Russian Federation
55 D2 **Krasnyy Yar** Sverdlovskaya obl Russian Federation
68 H6 **Kratie** Cambodia
46 E2 **Kratovo** Macedonia
38 L7 **Kraubath** Austria
41 K1 **Krauchenwies** Germany
115 O3 **Kraulshavn** Greenland
36 H5 **Krautheim** Germany
32 K5 **Krautsand** Germany
107 P7 **Krebs** Oklahoma U.S.A.
25 G6 **Krefeld** Germany
28 J5 **Kregme** Denmark
36 F4 **Krehberg** *mt* Germany
32 L9 **Kreiensen** Germany
116 D5 **Krekatok I** Alaska U.S.A.
46 F1 **Kremena** Bulgaria
54 E7 **Kremenchug** Ukraine
54 D7 **Kremenchugskoye Vdkhr** *res* Ukraine
54 K7 **Kremennaya** Ukraine
46 F2 **Kremikovtsi** Bulgaria
101 P1 **Kremlin** Montana U.S.A.
33 N8 **Kremlingen** Germany
33 S7 **Kremmen** Germany
106 D1 **Kremmling** Colorado U.S.A.
32 K5 **Krempe** Germany
38 M5 **Krems** *R* Austria
38 N5 **Krems** Austria
116 D9 **Krenitzin Is** Aleutian Is
33 Q10 **Krensitz** Germany
48 E7 **Kreševo** Bosnia-Herzegovina
56 B3 **Kreshchenskoye** Russian Federation
46 F3 **Kresna** Bulgaria
108 F1 **Kress** Texas U.S.A.
52 D6 **Kresti** Russian Federation
54 G7 **Krestische** Ukraine
52 H2 **Krestovka** Russian Federation
51 H1 **Kresty** Russian Federation
27 M16 **Kretinga** Lithuania
41 P2 **Kreuth** Germany
36 B2 **Kreuzau** Germany
41 O3 **Kreuzeck** *mt* Germany
38 H8 **Kreuzeck-Gruppe** *mts* Austria
38 L5 **Kreuzen** Austria
38 E7 **Kreuzjoch** *mt* Austria
41 K2 **Kreuzlingen** Switzerland
36 E2 **Kreuztal** Germany
86 A5 **Kribi** Cameroon
54 C3 **Krichev** Belarus
46 G2 **Krichim** Bulgaria
28 A3 **Krik** Denmark
28 A3 **Krik Vig** *B* Denmark
38 F7 **Krimml** Austria
38 F7 **Krimmler Fälle** Austria
38 F7 **Krimmler Tal** *R* Austria
26 D10 **Kringen** Norway
46 E6 **Krionéri** Greece
46 F9 **Kriós, Akr** *C* Crete Greece
76 C2 **Krishna** *R* India
76 D4 **Krishnagiri** India
75 N7 **Krishnanagar** India
27 H14 **Kristdala** Sweden
17 G9 **Kristel** Algeria
27 H15 **Kristianopel** Sweden
27 C13 **Kristiansand** Norway
27 F15 **Kristianstad** *county* Sweden
27 G15 **Kristianstad** Sweden
26 C8 **Kristiansund** Norway
29 J9 **Kristiinankaupunki** Finland
27 G12 **Kristinehamn** Sweden
28 E4 **Kristrup** Denmark
46 G9 **Kríti** *isld* Greece
48 M3 **Kriulyany** Moldova
46 E2 **Kriva** *R* Macedonia
48 E6 **Krivaja** *R* Bosnia-Herzegovina
46 E2 **Kriva Palanka** Macedonia
46 F1 **Krivodol** Bulgaria
48 N3 **Krivoye Ozero** Ukraine
54 E9 **Krivoy Rog** Ukraine
52 G5 **Krivyachka** Russian Federation
42 F3 **Krk** Croatia
42 G5 **Krka** *R* Croatia
31 J5 **Krkonoše** *mts* Czech Rep
31 K5 **Krnov** Czech Rep
31 K4 **Krobia** Poland
27 D11 **Kröderen** Norway
28 B5 **Krogager** Denmark
37 P1 **Krögis** Germany
28 E5 **Krogsbølle** Denmark
37 O6 **Kröhstorf** Germany
70 M9 **Kroja** Java
27 H13 **Krokek** Sweden
26 G6 **Kroken** Norway
89 E5 **Krokodil** *R* S Africa
26 G8 **Krokom** Sweden
31 L1 **Krokowa** Poland
26 J7 **Kroksjö** Sweden
54 E5 **Krolevets** Ukraine
36 D2 **Krombach** Germany
48 D1 **Kroměříž** Czech Rep
25 D5 **Kromme Rijn** *R* Netherlands
37 L3 **Kronach** Germany
119 N8 **Kronau** Saskatchewan Canada
36 E3 **Kronberg** Germany
37 P3 **Krondorf** Czech Rep
36 B3 **Kronenberg** Germany
68 H5 **Krong Poko** *R* Vietnam
27 G15 **Kronoberg** *county* Sweden
29 K8 **Kronoby** Finland
146 F6 **Kronprinsess Märtha Kyst** *coast* Antarctica
115 Q4 **Kronprins Frederiks Bjerge** *mts* Greenland
29 O12 **Kronshtadt** Russian Federation
68 D5 **Kronwa** Burma
37 N7 **Kronwinkl** Germany
89 E6 **Kroonstad** S Africa
55 C3 **Kropachevo** Russian Federation
33 P4 **Kröpelin** Germany
53 F10 **Kropotkin** Russian Federation
29 K4 **Kropp** Sweden
33 O9 **Kroppenstedt** Germany
33 R9 **Kropstädt** Germany
33 T4 **Kröslin** Germany
31 L3 **Krośniewice** Poland
37 M2 **Krossen** Germany
31 K4 **Krotoszyn** Poland
41 O2 **Krotten Kopf** *mt* Germany
111 E11 **Krotz Springs** Louisiana U.S.A.
46 F3 **Kroúsia** *mt* Greece
46 D2 **Krrab** *mt* Albania
36 C3 **Kruft-Mendig** Germany
89 G4 **Kruger Nat. Park** S Africa
89 E6 **Krugersdorp** S Africa
70 K8 **Krui** Sumatra
22 F2 **Kruishoutem** Belgium
46 D3 **Krujë** Albania
109 K2 **Krum** Texas U.S.A.
38 O6 **Krumbach** Austria
37 J7 **Krumbach** Germany
46 D2 **Krume** Albania
36 D1 **Krummenerl** Germany
32 F6 **Krummhörn** Germany
33 T4 **Krummin** Germany
47 H3 **Krumovgrad** Bulgaria
41 O2 **Krün** Germany
Krungkao *see* **Ayutthaya**
Krung Thep *see* **Bangkok**
68 E6 **Krung Thep** Thailand
48 E6 **Krupanj** Serbia Yugoslavia
48 E2 **Krupina** Slovakia
116 F3 **Krusenstern, C** Alaska U.S.A.
46 E1 **Kruševac** Serbia Yugoslavia
46 E3 **Kruševo** Macedonia
Krušné Hory *mts see* **Erzgebirge**
52 C6 **Krustpils** Latvia
52 H3 **Krutaya** Russian Federation
19 K5 **Kruth** France
55 D4 **Krutoyarskiy** Russian Federation
117 F7 **Kruzof I** Alaska U.S.A.
118 K6 **Krydor** Saskatchewan Canada
27 H11 **Krylbo** Sweden
31 P5 **Krylów** Poland
53 D10 **Krymskaya Oblast'** *prov* Ukraine
48 F1 **Krynica** Poland
31 O2 **Krynki** Poland
37 P3 **Kryry** Czech Rep
54 J1 **Kryukovo** Russian Federation
56 E4 **Kryzhina, Khr** *mts* Russian Federation
48 M2 **Kryzhopol'** Ukraine
31 L5 **Krzepice** Poland
31 N5 **Krzeszów** Poland
31 M5 **Krzeszowice** Poland
31 K4 **Krzywin** Poland
31 J3 **Krzyż** Poland
85 D3 **Ksabi** Algeria
85 C4 **Ksalb Ounane, El** Mali
85 E1 **Ksar el Boukhari** Algeria
16 D9 **Ksar el Kebir** Morocco
16 D9 **Ksar Sghir** Morocco
16 D9 **Ksar Sghir Oued Laou** Morocco
52 J4 **Ksenofontova** Russian Federation
85 E2 **Ksour, Mts. des** Algeria
52 F6 **Kstovo** Russian Federation
79 C4 **Ktima** Cyprus
69 D9 **Kuah** Malaysia
67 A4 **Kuaize He** *R* China
70 B6 **Kualajelai** Kalimantan
69 E10 **Kuala Kangsar** Malaysia
70 D6 **Kualakapuas** Kalimantan
69 F10 **Kuala Kerai** Malaysia
70 C6 **Kualakuagan** Kalimantan
70 C5 **Kualakurun** Kalimantan
69 C10 **Kualalangsa** Sumatra
69 F10 **Kuala Lipis** Malaysia
69 E11 **Kuala Lumpur** Malaysia
69 E9 **Kuala Nerang** Malaysia
70 C6 **Kualapembuang** Kalimantan
70 D2 **Kuala Penyu** Sabah
69 F11 **Kuala Pilah** Malaysia
135 S2 **Kualapuu** Hawaiian Is
70 C6 **Kualasampit** Kalimantan
69 E11 **Kuala Selangor** Malaysia
69 F10 **Kuala Terengganu** Malaysia
69 F13 **Kualatungkal** Sumatra
70 E2 **Kuamut** *R* Sabah
70 E2 **Kuamut** Sabah
65 D4 **Kuancheng** China
71 H4 **Kuandang, Tk** *B* Sulawesi Indonesia
59 H3 **Kuandian** China
Kuang-chou *see* **Guangzhou**
69 F11 **Kuantan** Malaysia
145 E2 **Kuaotunu** New Zealand
53 G12 **Kuba** Azerbaijan
53 F11 **Kuban'** *R* Russian Federation
78 G4 **Kubar, el** Syria
79 H3 **Kubaybāt** Syria
26 K8 **Kubbe** Sweden
86 D3 **Kubbum** Sudan
52 F4 **Kubena** *R* Russian Federation
52 E5 **Kubenskoye, Oz** *L* Russian Federation
52 G6 **Kubnya** *R* Russian Federation
60 G12 **Kubokawa** Japan
79 A8 **Kubra, El** Egypt
47 H1 **Kubrat** Bulgaria
69 J13 **Kubu** Indonesia
70 P10 **Kubu** Indonesia
70 D3 **Kubuang** Kalimantan
58 F1 **Kubukhay** Russian Federation
70 D4 **Kubumesaäi** Kalimantan
48 G6 **Kučevo** Serbia Yugoslavia
52 F2 **Kuchema** Russian Federation
36 H6 **Kuchen** Germany
41 M3 **Kuchen Spitze** *mt* Austria
70 B4 **Kuching** Sarawak
60 D13 **Kuchinotsu** Japan
60 F10 **Kuchitagi** Japan
55 G4 **Kuchukskoye, Oz** *L* Russian Federation
48 M3 **Kuchurgan** *R* Ukraine
Kucing *see* **Kuching**
33 N5 **Kücknitz** Germany
47 M10 **Küçükçekmece** Turkey
47 M10 **Küçükçekmece Gölu** Turkey
47 M11 **Küçükçekmece Koya** *crater* Turkey
47 J6 **Küçük Menderes** *R* Turkey
83 K11 **Kuda** *R* Sri Lanka
61 P14 **Kudaka-jima** *isld* Okinawa
60 E11 **Kudamatsu** Japan
70 B5 **Kudangan** Kalimantan
69 F12 **Kudap** Sumatra
70 E1 **Kudat** Sabah
68 B1 **Kudaw** Burma
55 C4 **Kudeyevskiy** Russian Federation
116 F9 **Kudiakof Is** Alaska U.S.A.
31 O1 **Kudirkos Naumiestis** Lithuania
80 G1 **Kudnah** Syria
116 G8 **Kudobin Is** Alaska U.S.A.
57 E5 **Kuduk** Afghanistan
70 N9 **Kudus** Java
52 H5 **Kudymkar** Russian Federation
80 D4 **Kufairāt** Jordan
47 K6 **Kûfi** *R* Turkey
80 F4 **Kufr Alma** Jordan
80 F4 **Kufrinja** *R* Jordan
80 F4 **Kufrinja** Jordan
80 G3 **Kufr Jayiz** Jordan
80 G4 **Kufr Khal** Jordan
80 G3 **Kufr Kifiya** Jordan
80 F4 **Kufr Rakib** Jordan
80 G3 **Kufr Saum** Jordan
38 F6 **Kufstein** Austria
60 F11 **Kuga** Japan
57 D5 **Kugitangtau, Khr** *mts* Turkmenistan
116 F4 **Kugruk** *R* Alaska U.S.A.
37 L7 **Kühbach** Germany
33 Q6 **Kuhbier** Germany
77 A2 **Kūh-e Alvand** Iran
77 K2 **Kūh-e-Bābā** *mts* Afghanistan
77 C4 **Kūh-e Būl** *mt* Iran
77 B3 **Kūh-e Karkas** Iran
78 L2 **Kuhha-ye Sabalan** *mt* Iran
33 T4 **Kühlenhagen** Germany
29 L10 **Kuhmalahti** Finland
29 O7 **Kuhmo** Finland
77 F6 **Kūhrān, Kūh-e** *mt* Iran
33 Q5 **Kuhs** Germany
32 J6 **Kuhstedt** Germany
87 C11 **Kuibis** Namibia
87 C10 **Kuiseb** *R* Namibia
87 C8 **Kuito** Angola
117 F7 **Kuiu I** Alaska U.S.A.
29 L6 **Kuivajoki** *R* Finland
29 L6 **Kuivaniemi** Finland
59 J4 **Kujang-dong** N Korea
61 O9 **Kuji-gawa** Japan
60 E12 **Kujū-san** *mt* Japan
116 G1 **Kuk** *R* Alaska U.S.A.
116 M7 **Kukak** Alaska U.S.A.
116 K7 **Kukaklek L** Alaska U.S.A.
116 G6 **Kukaklik L** Alaska U.S.A.
120 H4 **Kukatush** Ontario Canada
143 C10 **Kukerin** W Australia Australia
46 D2 **Kukës** Albania
29 L5 **Kukkola** Finland
52 H6 **Kukmor** Russian Federation
52 E5 **Kukoboy** Russian Federation
116 F2 **Kukpowruk** *R* Alaska U.S.A.
116 E2 **Kukpuk** *R* Alaska U.S.A.
135 U4 **Kukuihaele** Hawaiian Is
135 O1 **Kukuiula** Hawaiian Is
118 K1 **Kukukus L** Ontario Canada
83 K11 **Kukulugala** *mt* Sri Lanka
69 F12 **Kukup** Malaysia
70 D6 **Kukusan, G** *mt* Kalimantan
55 C2 **Kukushtan** Russian Federation
89 B4 **Kul** Botswana
46 F1 **Kula** Bulgaria
47 K6 **Kula** Turkey
48 F5 **Kula** Serbia Yugoslavia
69 D12 **Kulabu, Gunung** *mt* Sumatra
74 D3 **Kulachi** Pakistan
57 A2 **Kulandy** Kazakhstan
57 A2 **Kulandy, Poluostrov** *pen* Kazakhstan
55 F6 **Kulanutpes** *R* Kazakhstan
71 E7 **Kulassein** *isld* Philippines
46 F3 **Kulata** Bulgaria
70 F5 **Kulawi** Sulawesi Indonesia
27 M15 **Kuldiga** Latvia
117 K8 **Kuldo** British Columbia Canada
57 C4 **Kul'dzhuktau, Gory** *mt* Uzbekistan
52 F6 **Kulebaki** Russian Federation
54 G8 **Kulebovka** Ukraine
42 G4 **Kulen Vakuf** Bosnia-Herzegovina
55 D4 **Kulevchi** Russian Federation
140 C7 **Kulgera** N Terr Australia
52 H5 **Kuligi** Russian Federation
48 J1 **Kulikov** Ukraine
69 E10 **Kulim** Malaysia
143 C10 **Kulin** W Australia Australia
56 G1 **Kulingda** Russian Federation
143 B9 **Kulja** W Australia Australia
139 G4 **Kulkyne** *R* New South Wales Australia
29 K4 **Kulla Gunnarstorp** Sweden
29 K4 **Kullen** *mt* Sweden
32 M10 **Küllstedt** Germany
74 G3 **Kullu** India
98 H3 **Kulm** North Dakota U.S.A.
37 M4 **Kulmain** Germany
37 L3 **Kulmbach** Germany
52 F3 **Kuloy** Russian Federation
52 F4 **Kuloy** *R* Russian Federation
138 E5 **Kulpara** South Australia Australia
95 L6 **Kulpmont** Pennsylvania U.S.A.
38 G7 **Kuls** Austria
50 E4 **Kul'sary** Kazakhstan
36 H4 **Külsheim** Germany
56 G5 **Kul'skiy Stanok** Russian Federation
29 M3 **Kultala** Finland
75 M7 **Kulti** India
26 H7 **Kultsjöluspen** Sweden
26 G6 **Kultsjön** *L* Sweden
33 R10 **Kültzschau** Germany
78 D2 **Kulu** Turkey
55 G4 **Kulunda** Russian Federation
56 B4 **Kulunda** *R* Russian Federation
57 E5 **Kulyab** Tajikistan
47 J6 **Kum** *R* Turkey
60 F12 **Kuma** Japan
53 G11 **Kuma** *R* Russian Federation
60 D13 **Kuma-gawa** *R* Japan
61 N9 **Kumagaya** Japan
70 B6 **Kumai** Kalimantan
70 B6 **Kumai, Teluk** *B* Kalimantan
55 C5 **Kumak** *R* Russian Federation
55 D5 **Kumak** Russian Federation
60 D13 **Kumamoto** Japan
83 L11 **Kumana** Sri Lanka
48 F7 **Kumanica** Serbia Yugoslavia
61 K12 **Kumano** Japan
46 E2 **Kumanovo** Macedonia
70 D6 **Kumap** *R* Kalimantan
144 C5 **Kumara** New Zealand
51 M3 **Kumara** Russian Federation
144 C5 **Kumara Junction** New Zealand
85 D7 **Kumasi** Ghana
74 H3 **Kumaun** *reg* India
86 A5 **Kumba** Cameroon
76 D5 **Kumbakonam** India
47 L5 **Kümbet** Turkey
83 L11 **Kumbukkan Oya** *R* Sri Lanka
59 J4 **Kŭmch'ŏn** S Korea
47 L6 **Kumdanlı** Turkey
47 N10 **Kumdere** Turkey
55 C4 **Kumertau** Russian Federation
86 F5 **Kumi** Uganda
60 H10 **Kumihama** Japan
55 E2 **Kuminskiy** Russian Federation
47 H5 **Kumkale** Turkey
27 H12 **Kumla** Sweden
29 H11 **Kumlinge** Finland
116 J8 **Kumliun, C** Alaska U.S.A.
79 G2 **Kumlu** Turkey
47 L8 **Kumluca** Turkey
33 R5 **Kummerow** Germany
33 R4 **Kummerow** Mecklenburg-Vorpommern Germany
33 R5 **Kummerower See** *L* Germany
37 M5 **Kümmersbruck** Germany
33 S8 **Kummersdorf** Germany
65 G7 **Kūmo** *isld* S Korea
57 D2 **Kumola** *R* Kazakhstan
75 R5 **Kumon Range** Burma
68 F4 **Kumphawapi** Thailand
76 B3 **Kumta** India
135 V5 **Kumukahi, C** Hawaiian Is
Kumush *see* **Kümüx**
66 D3 **Kümüx** China
68 C3 **Kun** *R* Burma
116 J2 **Kuna** *R* Alaska U.S.A.
143 E6 **Kunanaggi Well** W Australia Australia
74 D1 **Kunar** Afghanistan
55 D3 **Kunashak** Russian Federation
60 T1 **Kunashir Ostrov** *isld* Russian Federation
52 C5 **Kunda** Estonia
76 B4 **Kundāpura** India
88 A6 **Kundelungu** *mt* Zaire
86 E3 **Kundi, L** Sudan
143 D10 **Kundip** W Australia Australia
55 D4 **Kundravy** Russian Federation
Kunduk *see* **Kogil'nik**
69 F12 **Kundur** *isld* Indonesia
66 C3 **Künes He** *R* China
27 E14 **Kungälv** Sweden
Kunges *R see* **Künes He**
117 H9 **Kunghit I** British Columbia Canada
57 K3 **Kung-liu** China
57 A3 **Kungrad** Uzbekistan
27 F14 **Kungsbacka** Sweden
27 J11 **Kungsgården** Sweden
27 H12 **Kungsör** Sweden
86 C5 **Kungu** Zaire
Kungur *mt see* **Kongur Shan** *mt*
55 C2 **Kungur** Russian Federation
68 C4 **Kungyangon** Burma
48 F3 **Kunhegyes** Hungary
68 D2 **Kunhing** Burma
61 Q12 **Kunigami** Okinawa
60 E13 **Kunimi-dake** *mt* Japan
70 M9 **Kuningan** Java
67 C5 **Kunlun Guan** *pass* China
48 F3 **Kunmadaras** Hungary
67 A4 **Kunming** China
60 R2 **Kunneppu** Japan
25 E3 **Kunnre** Netherlands
60 O3 **Kunnui** *R* Japan
6 F1 **Kunoy** *isld* Faeroes
65 G7 **Kunsan** S Korea
67 G1 **Kunshan** China
48 F4 **Kunszentmárton** Hungary
48 E3 **Kunszentmiklós** Hungary
52 E6 **Kuntsevo** Russian Federation
143 C9 **Kununoppin** W Australia Australia
142 G3 **Kununurra** W Australia Australia
52 D6 **Kunya** Russian Federation
57 A4 **Kunya Urgench** Turkmenistan
65 E6 **Kunyu Shan** *mts* China
36 H5 **Künzelsau** Germany
67 G2 **Kuocang Shan** *mts* China
52 C2 **Kuolayarvi** Russian Federation
29 N9 **Kuopio** Finland
29 N2 **Kuorboaivi** *mt* Finland
29 K9 **Kuortane** Finland
29 M10 **Kuortti** Finland
26 L5 **Kuouka** Sweden
26 L3 **Kuoutatjärro** *mt* Sweden
42 G3 **Kupa** *R* Croatia/Slovenia
71 L10 **Kupang** Timor Indonesia
71 L10 **Kupang, Tk** *B* Timor Indonesia
116 N1 **Kuparuk** *R* Alaska U.S.A.
37 M3 **Kupferberg** Germany
36 H5 **Kupferzell** Germany
55 G4 **Kupino** Russian Federation
52 B6 **Kupiškis** Lithuania
36 E6 **Kuppenheim** Germany
117 G7 **Kupreanof I** Alaska U.S.A.
116 H9 **Kupreanof Pt** Alaska U.S.A.
116 L7 **Kupreanof St** Alaska U.S.A.
37 L3 **Küps** Germany
54 J7 **Kupyansk** Ukraine
54 J7 **Kupyansk-Uzlovoy** Ukraine
66 C3 **Kuqa** China
59 L1 **Kur** *R* Russian Federation
78 J1 **Kura** *R* Turkey
57 G3 **Kuragaty** Kazakhstan
60 F11 **Kurahashi-jima** *isld* Japan
27 M14 **Kura Kurk** *str* Latvia
70 E6 **Kurambu** Kalimantan
57 E4 **Kuramins'kiy Khr** *mts* Tajikistan etc
60 C12 **Kuramoto** Japan
55 C5 **Kurashasay** Kazakhstan
60 G11 **Kurashiki** Japan
142 G4 **Kura Soak** W Australia Australia
60 G10 **Kurayoshi** Japan
56 C5 **Kurayskiy Khr** *mts* Russian Federation
56 G5 **Kurba** *R* Russian Federation
54 G5 **Kurchatov** Russian Federation
56 B6 **Kurchum** *R* Kazakhstan
57 H3 **Kurday** Kazakhstan
78 G2 **Kurdistan** *reg* Turkey/Iraq/Iran
74 F9 **Kurduvadi** India
46 G3 **Kŭrdzhali** Bulgaria
46 G3 **Kŭrdzhali, Yazovir** *res* Bulgaria
60 F11 **Kure** Japan
134 J5 **Kure Atoll** Hawaiian Is U.S.A.
80 F4 **Kureiyima** Jordan
52 B5 **Kuressaare** Estonia
51 J2 **Kureyka** *R* Russian Federation
55 F5 **Kurgal'dzhinskiy** Kazakhstan
55 E3 **Kurgan** Russian Federation
55 D3 **Kurganskaya Oblast'** *prov* Russian Federation
57 K6 **Kurgantepa** Uzbekistan
57 E5 **Kurgan-Tyube** Tajikistan
57 D1 **Kurgasyn** Kazakhstan
137 P1 **Kuria** *isld* Kiribati
Kuria Muria Islands *see* **Khurīyā Murīyā, Jazā'ir** *islds*
43 D13 **Kuriat, Is.** Tunisia
29 J9 **Kurikka** Finland
61 O7 **Kurikoma-yama** *mt* Japan
Kuril Is *see* **Kuril'skiye Ostrova**
52 F5 **Kurilovo** Russian Federation
59 N2 **Kuril'sk** Russian Federation
51 O4 **Kuril'skiye Ostrova** Russian Federation
145 F3 **Kuripapango** New Zealand
Kurisches Haff *see* **Courland lagoon**
60 P2 **Kuriyama** Japan
29 O10 **Kurkiyoki** Russian Federation
56 C5 **Kurkurabazhi, Gora** *mt* Russian Federation
84 J5 **Kurkur Oasis** Egypt
52 F6 **Kurlovskiy** Russian Federation
86 F3 **Kurmuk** Sudan
36 F5 **Kürnbach** Germany
76 D3 **Kurnool** India
61 O9 **Kurobane** Japan
61 L9 **Kurobe** Japan
61 L9 **Kurobe No. 4 Dam** Japan
60 D12 **Kurogi** Japan
61 O5 **Kuroishi** Japan
61 O9 **Kuroiso** Japan
119 O7 **Kuroki** Saskatchewan Canada
60 O3 **Kuromatsunai** Japan
60 G10 **Kurosaka** Japan
Kurósių Marios *see* **Courland lagoon**
54 K1 **Kurovskoye** Russian Federation
144 C6 **Kurow** New Zealand
31 N4 **Kurów** Poland
139 K5 **Kurri Kurri** New South Wales Australia
54 H5 **Kursk** Russian Federation
53 F11 **Kurskaya** Russian Federation
53 E8 **Kurskaya Oblast'** *prov* Russian Federation
Kurškiy Zaliv *see* **Courland lagoon**
46 E1 **Kuršumlija** Serbia Yugoslavia
57 A4 **Kurt** Turkmenistan
55 D4 **Kurtamysh** Russian Federation
36 C1 **Kürten** Germany
47 K8 **Kurtoğlu Burun** *C* Turkey
56 D5 **Kurtushibinskiy, Khr** *mts* Russian Federation
29 K10 **Kuru** Finland
78 G2 **Kuruçay** Turkey
47 H4 **Kuru Dağı** *mt* Turkey
57 E6 **Kuruk** Afghanistan
47 N10 **Kuruköy** Turkey
66 D3 **Kuruktag** *mts* China
89 C6 **Kuruman** S Africa
60 D12 **Kurume** Japan
58 F1 **Kurumkan** Russian Federation
83 K10 **Kurunegala** Sri Lanka
116 K2 **Kurupa Lakes** Alaska U.S.A.
61 O10 **Kururi** Japan
52 J4 **Kur'ya** Russian Federation
68 G7 **Kus** Cambodia
86 G5 **Kusa** Ethiopia
47 J7 **Kuşadasi** Turkey
70 D6 **Kusan, Peg** *mt* Kalimantan
117 E5 **Kusawa L** Yukon Territory Canada
60 G10 **Kuse** Japan
36 C4 **Kusel** Germany
33 O7 **Kusey** Germany
26 L7 **Kusfors** Sweden
47 J4 **Kuş Gölü** *L* Turkey
52 E6 **Kushalino** Russian Federation
52 E3 **Kushereka** Russian Federation
61 P12 **Kushi** Okinawa
61 K11 **Kushida-gawa** *R* Japan
60 D14 **Kushikino** Japan
60 E14 **Kushima** Japan
61 J12 **Kushimoto** Japan
60 R2 **Kushiro** *prefect* Japan
60 S3 **Kushiro** Japan
57 C6 **Kushka** Turkmenistan
52 F3 **Kushkushara** Russian Federation
48 H2 **Kushnitsa** Ukraine
116 P6 **Kushtaka L** Alaska U.S.A.
75 N7 **Kushtia** Bangladesh
53 H9 **Kushum** *R* Kazakhstan
55 C2 **Kushva** Russian Federation
116 G6 **Kuskokwim** *R* Alaska U.S.A.
116 F7 **Kuskokwim B** Alaska U.S.A.
116 H6 **Kuskokwim Mts** Alaska U.S.A.
116 F6 **Kuskovak** Alaska U.S.A.
75 K4 **Kusma** Nepal
60 S2 **Kussharo ko** *L* Japan
29 L4 **Küstala** Finland
55 D4 **Kustanay** Kazakhstan
26 J5 **Kustarakaise** *mt* Sweden
29 J11 **Kustavi** Finland
70 Q10 **Kuta** Indonesia
85 F7 **Kuta** Nigeria
56 G3 **Kuta** *R* Russian Federation
69 C10 **Kutabagok** Sumatra
71 J4 **Kutabunan** Sulawesi
47 K5 **Kütahya** Turkey
53 F12 **Kutaisi** Georgia
78 K5 **Kūt, Al** Iraq
57 E2 **Kutansor, Ozero** *L* Kazakhstan
145 F3 **Kutarere** New Zealand
56 E5 **Ku Tayga, Khrebet** *mts* Russian Federation
106 G3 **Kutch** Colorado U.S.A.
60 O3 **Kutchan** Japan
54 K9 **Kuteynikovo** Ukraine
42 H3 **Kutina** Croatia
68 F4 **Kut Khao** Thailand
68 F7 **Kut, Ko** *isld* Thailand
31 J6 **Kutná Hóra** Czech Rep
31 L3 **Kutno** Poland
70 M9 **Kutoadjo** Java
69 C11 **Kutobangun** Sumatra
69 C11 **Kutocane** Sumatra
76 E1 **Kutru** India
89 D4 **Kutse** Botswana
89 D4 **Kutse Game Res** Botswana
26 N3 **Kuttainen** Sweden
110 H4 **Kuttawa** Kentucky U.S.A.
88 F5 **Kutu** Tanzania
86 C6 **Kutu** Zaire
56 F4 **Kutulik** Russian Federation
86 D3 **Kutum** Sudan
56 D4 **Kuturchinskoye Belog** *mt* Russian Federation
31 O1 **Kutuzovo** Russian Federation
48 J2 **Kuty** Ukraine
37 J3 **Kützberg** Germany
95 M6 **Kutztown** Pennsylvania U.S.A.
115 N6 **Kuujjuaq** Quebec Canada
29 L4 **Kuusajoki** Finland
29 O6 **Kuusamo** Finland
29 M11 **Kuusankoski** Finland
52 H5 **Kuva** Russian Federation
55 C5 **Kuvandyk** Russian Federation
87 C8 **Kuvango** Angola
29 P2 **Kuvets'yarvi, Ozero** *L.* Russian Federation
28 S9 **Kuvikur** Iceland
52 D6 **Kuvshinovo** Russian Federation
Kuwait *see* **Kuwayt, Al**
77 A5 **Kuwait** *state* Persian Gulf
61 K10 **Kuwana** Japan
78 L5 **Kuwayt, Al** Iraq
77 A5 **Kuwayt, Al** Kuwait
52 F2 **Kuya** Russian Federation
Kuybyshev *see* **Samara**
55 G3 **Kuybyshev** Russian Federation
Kuybyshevskaya Oblast' *see* **Samarskaya Oblast'**
55 E4 **Kuybyshevskiy** Kazakhstan
55 C3 **Kuyeda** Russian Federation
65 A5 **Kuye He** *R* China
26 S2 **Kuyets'yarvi, Oz** *L* Russian Federation
66 D3 **Kuytun** China
55 D5 **Kuyukkol', Oz** *L* Kazakhstan
128 G3 **Kuyuwini** *R* Guyana
56 C3 **Kuzbass** *basin* Russian Federation
116 E4 **Kuzitrin** *R* Alaska U.S.A.
53 G7 **Kuznetsk** Russian Federation
56 C3 **Kuznetskiy Alatau** *mt* Russian Federation
55 D2 **Kuznetsovo** Russian Federation
52 E2 **Kuzomen** Russian Federation
26 H3 **Kvaefjord** Norway
26 M1 **Kvaenangen** *inlet* Norway
26 M2 **Kvaenangen** Norway
26 M2 **Kvaenangsbotn** Norway
28 H6 **Kværkeby** Denmark
28 F6 **Kværndrup** Denmark
28 C7 **Kværs** Denmark
26 N1 **Kvalöya** *isld* Norway
26 K1 **Kvalöy, N** *isld* Norway
26 K2 **Kvalöy, S** *isld* Norway
26 N1 **Kvalsund** Norway
26 D10 **Kvam** Norway
55 C5 **Kvarkeno** Russian Federation
27 G15 **Kvarnamåla** Sweden
26 G7 **Kvarnbergsvattnet** *L* Sweden
42 F4 **Kvarner** *chan* Croatia
42 F4 **Kvarnerić** *chan* Croatia
27 J13 **Kvarsebo** Sweden
27 C11 **Kvenna** *R* Norway
26 C8 **Kvernes** Norway
26 L2 **Kvesmenas** Norway
29 J8 **Kvevlax** Finland
116 J7 **Kvichak** Alaska U.S.A.
26 G6 **Kvigtind** *mt* Norway
26 J5 **Kvikkjock** Sweden
26 D9 **Kvikne** Norway
27 B13 **Kvina** *R* Norway
27 B13 **Kvinesdal** Norway
27 B12 **Kvinnherad** Norway
27 G12 **Kvistbro** Sweden
29 K5 **Kvistofta** Sweden
26 C8 **Kvisvik** Norway
27 C12 **Kviteseid** Norway
26 R1 **Kvitnes** Norway
147 K11 **Kvitøya** *isld* Spitzbergen
27 A12 **Kvitsöy** *isld* Norway
28 A5 **Kvong** Denmark
28 D4 **Kvorning** Denmark
117 L7 **Kwadacha Wilderness Prov. Park** British Columbia Canada
134 G7 **Kwajalein** *atoll* Marshall Is
129 G2 **Kwakoegron** Suriname
69 D11 **Kwala** Sumatra
88 G4 **Kwale** Kenya
85 F7 **Kwale** Nigeria
86 C6 **Kwamouth** Zaire
71 H4 **Kwandang** Sulawesi
Kwangchow *see* **Guangzhou**
65 G7 **Kwangju** S Korea
86 C6 **Kwango** *R* Zaire
Kwangsi *aut reg see* **Guangxi**
Kwangtung *prov see* **Guangdong** *prov*
86 F5 **Kwania, L** Uganda
120 H1 **Kwataboahegan** *R* Ontario Canada
89 C2 **Kwa Thema** S Africa
89 G7 **KwaZulu-Natal** *prov* S Africa
Kweichow *prov see* **Guizhou**
Kweilin *see* **Guilin**
Kweiyang *see* **Guiyang**
89 F2 **Kwekwe** Zimbabwe
89 D5 **Kweneng** *dist* Botswana
87 C7 **Kwenge** *R* Zaire
116 G6 **Kwethluk** Alaska U.S.A.
31 L2 **Kwidzyn** Poland
116 D7 **Kwigamiuk** Alaska U.S.A.
116 F7 **Kwigillingok** Alaska U.S.A.
116 E5 **Kwiguk** Alaska U.S.A.
116 E5 **Kwikpak** Alaska U.S.A.
87 C7 **Kwilu** *R* Zaire
142 A4 **Kwinana** W Australia Australia
31 J4 **Kwisa** *R* Poland
128 G3 **Kwitaro** *R* Guyana
143 C10 **Kwobrup** W Australia Australia
136 G2 **Kwoka** *mt* W Irian
26 D7 **Kya** *isld* Norway
86 C4 **Kyabé** Chad
141 G7 **Kyabra** Queensland Australia
139 H6 **Kyabram** Victoria Australia
68 B2 **Kyadet** Burma
68 B3 **Kyagu** Burma
68 C4 **Kyaikkami** Burma
68 B4 **Kyaiklat** Burma
68 C4 **Kyaikto** Burma
68 D5 **Kya-in Seikkyi** Burma
88 C2 **Kyaka** Tanzania
56 G5 **Kyakhta** Russian Federation
139 G5 **Kyalite** New South Wales Australia
138 D5 **Kyancutta** South Australia Australia
52 E3 **Kyanda** Russian Federation
52 D3 **Kyargozero** Russian Federation
68 C3 **Kyaukhnyat** Burma
68 B3 **Kyaukkyi** Burma
68 C1 **Kyaukme** Burma
68 B1 **Kyaukmyaung** Burma
68 A3 **Kyaukpyu** Burma
68 C2 **Kyaukse** Burma
68 A2 **Kyauktaw** Burma
68 B2 **Kyaukyit** Burma
68 B4 **Kyaunggon** Burma
138 F6 **Kybybolite** South Australia Australia
26 G7 **Kycklingvattnet** Sweden
68 C3 **Kyebogyi** Burma
144 C6 **Kyeburn** New Zealand
68 D5 **Kyeikdon** Burma
68 D4 **Kyeikywa** Burma
68 B3 **Kyeintali** Burma
33 O10 **Kyffhäuser** *mt* Germany
143 E7 **Kyffin-Thomas Hill** W Australia Australia
28 F5 **Kyholm** *isld* Denmark
68 C3 **Kyidaunggan** Burma
58 D4 **Kyikug** China
68 A2 **Kyindwe** Burma
31 K6 **Kyjov** Czech Rep
118 J8 **Kyle** Saskatchewan Canada

98 D6 Kyle South Dakota U.S.A.
109 K6 Kyle Texas U.S.A.
101 T8 Kyle Wyoming U.S.A.
15 C3 Kyleakin Scotland
87 F10 Kyle Dam Zimbabwe
15 D2 Kyle of Durness Scotland
15 C3 Kyle of Lochalsh Scotland
15 D2 Kyle of Tongue Scotland
12 C2 Kyles of Bute chan Scotland
36 B3 Kyll R Germany
36 B3 Kyllburg Germany
29 N10 Kymi prov Finland
29 M11 Kymijoki R Finland
55 C2 Kyn Russian Federation
139 G6 Kyneton Victoria Australia
37 O3 Kynšperk nad Ohři Czech Rep
141 F5 Kynuna Queensland Australia
61 P12 Kyoda Okinawa
86 F5 Kyoga, L Uganda
60 J10 Kyōga-misaki C Japan
139 L3 Kyogle New South Wales Australia
65 F5 Kyŏmip'o N Korea
68 D4 Kyondo Burma
141 H5 Kyong Queensland Australia
68 C2 Kyong Burma
60 J10 Kyōto prefect Japan
62 Kyōto conurbation Japan
55 E6 Kypshak, Oz L Kazakhstan
79 D3 Kyrenia Cyprus
Kyrgyzstan see Kirghizia
33 Q7 Kyritz Germany
Kyrkslätt see Kirkkonummi
29 J8 Kyröjoki R Finland
29 K10 Kyrösjärvi L Finland
52 J3 Kyrta Russian Federation
55 D2 Kyrtym'ya Russian Federation
55 C2 Kyr'ya Russian Federation
55 G3 Kyshtovka Russian Federation
55 D3 Kyshtym Russian Federation
68 G3 Ky Son Vietnam
52 G3 Kyssa Russian Federation
79 D3 Kythrea Cyprus
55 C2 Kytlym Russian Federation
57 H3 Kyungëy-Ala-Too, Khrebet mts Kazakhstan/Kirghizia
68 D5 Kyungyaung Burma
68 C7 Kyun Pila islds Burma
117 K10 Kyuquot British Columbia Canada
60 D13 Kyūshū isld Japan
60 E13 Kyūshū-sanchi mts Japan
46 F2 Kyustendil Bulgaria
51 M1 Kyusyur Russian Federation
139 H6 Kywong New South Wales Australia
29 L8 Kyyjärvi Finland
56 D5 Kyzyl Russian Federation
57 E1 Kyzyldyykan Kazakhstan
56 E5 Kyzyl-Khem R Russian Federation
57 J2 Kyzylkiya Kazakhstan
57 F4 Kyzyl-Kiya Kirghizia
57 E1 Kyzyl-Kommuna Kazakhstan
57 C4 Kyzylkum, Peski desert Kazakhstan/Uzbekistan
57 G5 Kyzylrabot Tajikistan
55 F5 Kyzyltas Kazakhstan
57 H1 Kyzyltu Kazakhstan
57 D1 Kyzyluy Kazakhstan
57 C1 Kyzylzhar Kazakhstan
57 E1 Kyzylzhar Kazakhstan
57 J3 Kyzylzhide Kazakhstan
57 D3 Kzyl-Orda Kazakhstan
55 F4 Kzyltu Kazakhstan

L

31 J7 Laa Austria
37 M5 Laaber Germany
36 C3 Laacher See L Germany
33 Q5 Laage Germany
25 F4 Laag Keppel Netherlands
124 C4 La Angostura Mexico
29 N3 Laanila Finland
131 A7 La Araucanía prov Chile
86 A2 Laascaanood Somalia
86 A1 Laas Dhuura Somalia
86 A1 Laasgoray Somalia
86 A1 Laaso Dawaco Somalia
36 E2 Laasphe Germany
127 N9 La Asunción Venezuela
135 R2 Laau Pt Hawaiian Is
85 B3 Laâyoune W Sahara
108 E7 La Babia Mexico
110 F3 Labadie Missouri U.S.A.
7 E12 Labadie Bank Atlantic Oc
111 F12 Labadieville Louisiana U.S.A.
121 U4 La Baie Quebec Canada
71 L9 Labala Indonesia
19 P12 Labalme France
79 F8 Labān Jordan
16 D2 La Baneza Spain
124 H7 La Barca Mexico
101 P7 La Barge Wyoming U.S.A.
137 Q5 Labasa Vanua Levu Fiji
19 P17 La Bastide-des-Jourdans France
18 G8 Labastide Murat France
19 Q13 La Bathie France
19 Q15 La Bâtie-Neuve France
68 A2 Labawa Burma
52 H2 Labazhskoye Russian Federation
26 J5 Labbas Sweden
80 D1 Labbouna Lebanon
26 R3 Labdshy'aur, Oz L Russian Federation
31 J5 Labe R Czech Rep
85 B6 Labé Guinea
19 Q17 La Bégude Blanche France
121 Q6 Labelle Quebec Canada
99 P9 La Belle Missouri U.S.A.
71 H6 Labengke isld Sulawesi
19 Q15 La Bérarde France
117 F5 Laberge, L Yukon Territory Canada
131 E7 Laberinto, Pta Argentina
37 N6 Laberweinting Germany
70 D2 Labi Brunei
117 L5 La Biche R Yukon Terr/Br Col Canada
71 B2 Labilabi Halmahera Indonesia
42 F3 Labin Croatia
69 F11 Labis Malaysia
127 M9 La Blanquilla, I Venezuela
71 F3 Labo Philippines
71 H5 Labobo isld Indonesia
103 J10 La Bomba Mexico
101 U7 Labonte Cr Wyoming U.S.A.
124 G4 La Boquilla Mexico
48 G1 Laborec R Slovakia
143 C7 Labouchere, Mt W Australia Australia
79 G4 Laboué Lebanon
18 E8 Labouheyre France
133 E4 Laboulaye Argentina
115 N7 Labrador dist Newfoundland Canada
115 N7 Labrador City Labrador, Nfld Canada
115 O6 Labrador Sea Nfld/Greenland
128 F5 Labrea Brazil
128 B4 La Brea, Cer. de hill Peru
124 E5 La Brecha Mexico
18 E8 Labrède France
122 C4 Labrieville Quebec Canada
18 E8 Labrit France
118 E1 La Broquerie Manitoba Canada
22 B3 Labroye France
18 G9 Labruguière France
70 G5 Labuanbajo Sulawesi
136 F2 Labuha Moluccas Indonesia
70 K9 Labuhan Java
71 J9 Labuhanbadjo Sumba Indonesia
69 E11 Labuhanbilik Sumatra
69 C11 Labuhanhaji Sumatra
70 K8 Labuhanmeringgai Sumatra
69 D11 Labuhanruku Sumatra
71 H9 Labuhansepakah Indonesia
19 P14 La Buisse France
70 E2 Labuk R Sabah
70 E1 Labuk, Telukan B Sabah
68 B4 Labutta Burma
138 D4 Labyrinth, L South Australia Australia
50 F2 Labytnangi Russian Federation
46 D3 Laç Albania
118 J8 Lacadena Saskatchewan Canada
124 G5 La Cadena Mexico
22 L2 La Calamine Belgium
122 J3 Lac Allard Quebec Canada
111 D10 Lacamp Louisiana U.S.A.
18 E8 Lacanau France
128 F2 La Canoa Venezuela
125 O9 Lacantum R Mexico
18 G8 Lacapelle-Marival France
131 B8 Lacar, L Argentina
133 E4 La Carlota Argentina
71 F5 La Carlota Negros Philippines
16 E6 La Carolina Spain
18 G9 Lacaune France
Laccadive Is see Lakshadweep
122 B8 Lac-Droiet Quebec Canada
99 R4 Lac du Flambeau Wisconsin U.S.A.
13 H6 Laceby England
125 L2 La Ceiba Honduras
128 D2 La Ceiba Venezuela
138 E6 Lacepede B South Australia Australia
142 D3 Lacepede Is W Australia Australia
100 C2 Lacey Washington U.S.A.
19 Q14 La Chambre France
52 E4 Lacha, Oz L Russian Federation
21 O3 Lachapelle-aux-Pots France
19 O15 La Chapelle-en-Vercors France
128 C6 Lachay, Pta pt Peru
36 E5 Lachen Germany
41 J3 Lachen Switzerland
94 D1 Lachine Michigan U.S.A.
139 H5 Lachlan R New South Wales Australia
125 P5 La Chorrera Panama
33 M7 Lachte R Germany
121 Q7 Lachute Quebec Canada
19 P18 La Ciotat France
94 J4 Lackawanna New York U.S.A.
118 E4 Lac la Biche Alberta Canada
117 N10 Lac La Hache British Columbia Canada
119 M3 Lac la Ronge Saskatchewan Canada
100 J1 Laclede Idaho U.S.A.
99 N10 Laclede Missouri U.S.A.
19 Q13 La Clusaz France
133 D3 La Cocha Argentina
8 D5 Lacock England
121 R7 Lacolle Quebec Canada
124 D3 La Colorada Mexico
118 D6 Lacombe Alberta Canada
111 G11 Lacombe Louisiana U.S.A.
99 R8 Lacon Illinois U.S.A.
99 N8 Lacona Iowa U.S.A.
95 L3 Lacona New York U.S.A.
43 C9 Laconi Sardinia
95 Q3 Laconia New Hampshire U.S.A.
113 E9 Lacoochee Florida U.S.A.
130 B9 La Cordillera dept Paraguay
121 N4 Lacorne Quebec Canada
16 B1 Lá Coruña Spain
109 J6 Lacoste Texas U.S.A.
19 O14 La Côte St. André France
127 J2 Lacovia Jamaica
98 K4 Lac Qui Parle Minnesota U.S.A.
98 E6 Lacreek L South Dakota U.S.A.
126 A3 Lacre Pt Bonaire W Indies
99 P6 La Crescent Minnesota U.S.A.
99 O1 La Croix,L Ontario Canada
99 U8 La Crosse Indiana U.S.A.
107 L3 La Crosse Kansas U.S.A.
94 J10 La Crosse Virginia U.S.A.
99 P6 La Crosse Wisconsin U.S.A.
133 F3 La Cruz Argentina
125 M4 La Cruz Costa Rica
124 G4 La Cruz Mexico
124 F6 La Cruz Mexico
120 G3 Lac Ste. Thérèse Ontario Canada
108 E7 La Cuesta Mexico
133 C5 La Cueva Chile
106 E6 La Cueva New Mexico U.S.A.
119 N6 Lac Vert Saskatchewan Canada
107 Q3 La Cygne Kansas U.S.A.
130 H5 Ladainha Brazil
74 G1 Ladakh Range Kashmir
54 D6 Ladan' Ukraine
69 D9 Ladang, Ko isld Thailand
129 G7 Ladário Brazil
70 K9 Lada, Teluk B Java
9 E3 Ladbroke England
99 R8 Ladd Illinois U.S.A.
107 J3 Ladder Cr Kansas U.S.A.
110 E2 Laddonia Missouri U.S.A.
111 E8 Ladelle Arkansas U.S.A.
28 C7 Ladelund Germany
126 C4 La Demajagua Cuba
36 F5 Ladenburg Germany
127 O4 La Désirade isld Guadeloupe W Indies
79 F3 Ladhiqīyah, Al Syria
46 E7 Ládhon R Greece
83 J12 La Digue isld Seychelles
28 D4 Lading Denmark
89 B9 Ladismith S Africa
77 G5 Ladīz Iran
98 C4 Ladner South Dakota U.S.A.
48 G6 Ladne Vode Serbia Yugoslavia
74 F5 Ladnun India
8 B7 Ladock England
Ladoga L see Ladozhskoye Oz
110 K2 Ladoga Indiana U.S.A.
109 M2 Ladonia Texas U.S.A.
128 D2 La Dorada Colombia
52 D4 Ladozhskoye Oz L Russian Federation
106 C7 Ladrones Pk New Mexico U.S.A.
116 R5 Ladue R Alaska/Yukon Terr U.S.A./Canada
124 E3 La Dura Mexico
52 D4 Ladva Vetka Russian Federation
115 L2 Lady Ann Str Northwest Territories Canada
15 E4 Ladybank Scotland
139 J8 Lady Barron Tasmania Australia
89 E7 Ladybrand S Africa
142 F5 Lady Edith L W Australia Australia
141 L6 Lady Elliot I Gt Barrier Reef Aust
120 K5 Lady Evelyn L Ontario Canada
100 B1 Ladysmith British Columbia Canada
89 F7 Ladysmith S Africa
99 P4 Ladysmith Wisconsin U.S.A.
55 E5 Ladyzhenka Kazakhstan
48 M2 Ladyzhin Ukraine
136 K3 Lae Papua New Guinea
68 E3 Lae Thailand
28 C5 Læborg Denmark
22 G2 Laeken Belgium
69 D8 Laem Ao Kham C Thailand
68 F6 Laem Ngop Thailand
69 D8 Laem Sui C Thailand
17 G6 La Encina Spain
127 L10 La Encrucijada Venezuela
27 B10 Laerdalsöyri Norway
128 F8 La Esmeralda Paraguay
28 G2 Læsø isld Denmark
28 F2 Læsø Rende str Denmark
133 D5 La Esperanza Argentina
126 F4 La Esperanza Cuba
16 B2 La Estrada Spain
26 P2 Laevajoki Norway
131 D3 La Falda Argentina
95 M2 La Fargeville New York U.S.A.
19 Q18 La Farlède France
111 L9 Lafayette Alabama U.S.A.
106 E2 Lafayette Colorado U.S.A.
112 B3 Lafayette Georgia U.S.A.
110 K1 Lafayette Indiana U.S.A.
111 E11 Lafayette Louisiana U.S.A.
99 M5 Lafayette Minnesota U.S.A.
94 B10 Lafayette Tennessee U.S.A.
95 Q2 Lafayette, Mt New Hampshire U.S.A.
126 B3 La Fé Cuba
126 C4 La Fé Cuba
109 K9 La Feria Texas U.S.A.
121 M4 Laferte Quebec Canada
85 F7 Lafia Nigeria
85 F7 Lafiagi Nigeria
121 N3 Laflamme R Quebec Canada
118 L9 Lafleche Saskatchewan Canada
38 O7 Lafnitz R Austria
94 C10 La Follette Tennessee U.S.A.
121 M5 Laforce Quebec Canada
120 J5 Laforest Ontario Canada
18 F8 Lafrançaise France
112 E3 La France South Carolina U.S.A.
36 C6 Lafrimbole France
16 C4 La Fuente de San Esteban Spain
69 A9 Laful Nicobar Is
124 G5 La Gallega Mexico
14 E2 Lagan R N Ireland
27 G15 Lagan R Sweden
16 B2 La Gañiza Spain
36 B6 Lagarde France
41 N6 Lagarina, Val Italy
106 D4 La Garita Mts Colorado U.S.A.
129 H8 Lagarto, Serra do mts Brazil
85 B3 Lag'Ayda Western Sahara
32 J8 Lage Germany
la Geltrú see Geltrú
26 D10 Lågen R Norway
32 L5 Lägerdorf Germany
54 H7 Lagery Ukraine
12 C2 Lagg Scotland
15 D3 Laggan Scotland
12 B2 Laggan B Scotland
77 L2 Laghmān prov Afghanistan
85 E2 Laghouat Algeria
46 C3 Lagjit, kepi i C Albania
40 B6 Lagnieu France
16 B7 Lagôa Portugal
130 G6 Lagoa Santa Brazil
130 E4 Lagolândia Brazil
43 G8 Lagonegro Italy
71 F4 Lagonoy Gulf Philippines
133 C7 Lago Posadas Argentina
85 E7 Lagos Nigeria
16 B7 Lagos Portugal
45 M2 Lagosanto Italy
100 G4 La Grande Oregon U.S.A.
115 M7 La Grande 2, Réservoir res Quebec Canada
115 M7 La Grande 3, Réservoir res Quebec Canada
115 M7 La Grande-Riviére R Quebec Canada
142 D4 Lagrange W Australia Australia
111 L8 La Grange Georgia U.S.A.
94 B5 Lagrange Indiana U.S.A.
94 B8 La Grange Kentucky U.S.A.
99 P9 La Grange Missouri U.S.A.
112 K2 La Grange North Carolina U.S.A.
94 E5 Lagrange Ohio U.S.A.
109 L6 La Grange Texas U.S.A.
98 B8 La Grange Wyoming U.S.A.
128 F2 La Gran Sabana reg Venezuela
19 Q14 La Grave France
83 M13 Lagrave mt Mauritius
20 G6 La Grigonnais France
127 J10 La Grita Venezuela
27 L12 Lågskär Finland
29 H11 Lågskär lighthouse Finland
127 L9 La Guaira Venezuela
133 D3 La Guardia Argentina
16 B3 La Guardia Portugal
17 F2 Laguardia Spain
16 C2 La Gudiña Spain
18 G8 Laguiole France
133 H3 Laguna Brazil
42 E3 Laguna Italy
106 C6 Laguna New Mexico U.S.A.
141 L7 Laguna B Queensland Australia
102 G8 Laguna Beach California U.S.A.
103 O5 Laguna Cr Arizona U.S.A.
103 K9 Laguna Dam Cal/Ariz U.S.A.
102 H9 Laguna Mts California U.S.A.
128 C5 Lagunas Peru
71 J9 Lagunda, Tanjong C Sumbawa Indonesia
133 E1 Lagunillas Bolivia
127 J9 Lagunillas Venezuela
65 F4 Lagushao China
70 F2 Lahad Datu Sabah
70 F2 Lahad Datu, Telukan B Sabah
68 F1 Lahadi China
135 S3 Lahaina Hawaiian Is
99 Q9 La Harpe Illinois U.S.A.
69 F14 Lahat Sumatra
70 K7 Lahat Sumatra
80 C8 Lahav Israel
122 H9 La Have Nova Scotia Canada
80 F1 Lahavot HaBashan Israel
32 J8 Lahde Germany
124 D4 La Higuera Mexico
77 B1 Lāhījān Iran
102 R12 Lahilahi Pt Hawaiian Is
37 K3 Lahm Germany
30 D5 Lahn Germany
36 E2 Lahn R Germany
36 F2 Lahntal Germany
27 F15 Laholm Sweden
27 F15 Laholmsbukten Sweden
71 F4 Lahong Philippines
102 E2 Lahontan Res Nevada U.S.A.
74 F3 Lahore Pakistan
36 D7 Lahr Germany
32 M8 Lahstedt Germany
29 M11 Lahti Finland
124 G8 La Huerta Mexico
80 G8 Lahun Jordan
71 F4 Lahuy isld Philippines
86 C4 Lai Chad
67 F1 Lai'an China
133 F3 La Iberá L Argentina
67 C5 Laibin China
68 F2 Lai Chau Vietnam
36 H7 Laichingen Germany
141 K8 Laidley Queensland Australia
102 S11 Laie Hawaiian Is
67 C2 Laifeng China
22 H4 Laifour France
21 H5 Laignelet France
18 H5 Laignes France
44 D4 Laigueglia Italy
29 J9 Laihia Finland
68 C2 Lai-Hka Burma
68 C2 Lai-Hsak Burma
21 O6 Lailly-en-Val France
71 E1 Lai-Lo Luzon Philippines
71 H7 Laimea Sulawesi
47 H3 Lainá Greece
38 L6 Lainbach Austria
89 B9 Laingsburg S Africa
94 C4 Laingsburg Michigan U.S.A.
26 K6 Lainijaur Sweden
26 M4 Lainio Sweden
26 M3 Lainio älv R Sweden
118 L6 Laird Saskatchewan Canada
98 D9 Laird Colorado U.S.A.
15 D2 Lairg Scotland
71 G7 Lais Mindanao Philippines
70 G4 Lais Sulawesi
86 G5 Laisamis Kenya
52 G6 Laishevo Russian Federation
65 C5 Laishui China
21 K4 Laison R France
18 G8 Laissac France
26 J5 Laisvall Sweden
20 C6 Laïta R France
26 K4 Laitaure L Sweden
29 J11 Laitila Finland
65 D6 Laiwu China
65 E6 Laixi China
71 E4 Laiya Philippines
59 H4 Laiyang China
65 C5 Laiyuan China
21 K3 Laize R France
65 D6 Laizhou Wan B China
79 G6 Lajā, Al mts Syria
131 B6 Laja, L. de Chile
133 D5 La Japonesa Argentina
131 A6 Laja, R Chile
106 E4 La Jara Colorado U.S.A.
70 E7 Lajar, Tg C Kalimantan
19 Q16 La Javie France
130 F9 Laje dos Santos isld Brazil
71 O8 Lajeni Indonesia
130 E10 Lajes Brazil
108 D6 Lajitas Texas U.S.A.
133 E2 Lajitas, Las Argentina
48 F6 Lajkovac Serbia Yugoslavia
102 G9 La Jolla California U.S.A.
119 N8 Lajord Saskatchewan Canada
48 F3 Lajosmizse Hungary
124 F4 La Joya Mexico
106 D7 La Joya New Mexico U.S.A.
128 F7 La Junta Bolivia
124 F3 La Junta Mexico
106 G4 La Junta Colorado U.S.A.
26 J8 Lakasjö Sweden
26 M5 Lakaträsk Sweden
101 O5 Lake Idaho U.S.A.
94 B3 Lake Michigan U.S.A.
100 E6 Lake Oregon U.S.A.
113 F9 Lake Alfred Florida U.S.A.
119 N9 Lake Alma Saskatchewan Canada
109 P5 Lake Arthur Louisiana U.S.A.
106 F8 Lake Arthur New Mexico U.S.A.
98 K5 Lake Benton Minnesota U.S.A.
143 C10 Lake Biddy W Australia Australia
139 G6 Lake Boga Victoria Australia
98 K1 Lake Bronson Minnesota U.S.A.
143 C9 Lake Brown W Australia Australia
137 R5 Lakebu isld Fiji
113 E7 Lake Butler Florida U.S.A.
143 C10 Lake Camm W Australia Australia
109 O5 Lake Charles Louisiana U.S.A.
100 E1 Lake Chelan Nat. Recreation Area Washington U.S.A.
110 F6 Lake City Arkansas U.S.A.
100 E8 Lake City California U.S.A.
106 C3 Lake City Colorado U.S.A.
113 E7 Lake City Florida U.S.A.
99 M7 Lake City Iowa U.S.A.
94 B2 Lake City Michigan U.S.A.
99 O5 Lake City Minnesota U.S.A.
94 G4 Lake City Pennsylvania U.S.A.
112 H4 Lake City South Carolina U.S.A.
98 J4 Lake City South Dakota U.S.A.
94 C10 Lake City Tennessee U.S.A.
116 L6 Lake Clark Nat Park and Preserve Alaska U.S.A.
144 C5 Lake Coleridge New Zealand
110 F7 Lake Cormorant Mississippi U.S.A.
100 J8 Lake Cr Nevada U.S.A.
99 M5 Lake Crystal Minnesota U.S.A.
99 R6 Lake Delton Wisconsin U.S.A.
118 F5 Lake Eliza Alberta Canada
102 G8 Lake Elsinore California U.S.A.
145 E4 Lake Ferry New Zealand
141 G2 Lakefield Queensland Australia
121 M8 Lakefield Ontario Canada
99 L6 Lakefield Minnesota U.S.A.
141 G2 Lakefield Nat. Park Queensland Australia
99 T7 Lake Forest Illinois U.S.A.
99 S7 Lake Geneva Wisconsin U.S.A.
106 E3 Lake George Colorado U.S.A.
95 O3 Lake George New York U.S.A.
115 N5 Lake Harbour Northwest Territories Canada
101 U8 Lake Hattie Res Wyoming U.S.A.
103 K7 Lake Havasu City Arizona U.S.A.
102 F7 Lake Hughes California U.S.A.
95 N6 Lakehurst New Jersey U.S.A.
109 M6 Lake Jackson Texas U.S.A.
143 C10 Lake King W Australia Australia
112 D6 Lakeland Georgia U.S.A.
119 N6 Lake Lenore Saskatchewan Canada
99 S2 Lake Linden Michigan U.S.A.
117 P10 Lake Louise Alberta Canada
140 B5 Lake Mackay Aboriginal Land N Terr Australia
108 C8 Lake Meredith Recreation Area Texas U.S.A.
99 N6 Lake Mills Iowa U.S.A.
94 G5 Lake Milton Ohio U.S.A.
116 L5 Lake Minchumina Alaska U.S.A.
95 S1 Lake Moxie Maine U.S.A.
140 E5 Lake Nash N Terr Australia
37 P5 Laken Berg mt Czech Rep/Germany
9 G3 Lakenheath England
94 B4 Lake Odessa Michigan U.S.A.
99 M1 Lake of the Woods L Ontario Canada
94 D4 Lake Orion Michigan U.S.A.
100 C4 Lake Oswego Oregon U.S.A.
107 Q5 Lake O' The Cherokees L Oklahoma U.S.A.
109 N3 Lake O'The Pines L Texas U.S.A.
101 P5 Lake Outlet Wyoming U.S.A.
144 B5 Lake Paringa New Zealand
113 G11 Lake Park Florida U.S.A.
113 D7 Lake Park Georgia U.S.A.
99 L6 Lake Park Iowa U.S.A.
113 F10 Lake Placid Florida U.S.A.
95 O2 Lake Placid New York U.S.A.
102 B2 Lakeport California U.S.A.
113 F11 Lakeport Florida U.S.A.
94 E3 Lakeport Michigan U.S.A.
98 J5 Lake Preston South Dakota U.S.A.
111 E9 Lake Providence Louisiana U.S.A.
144 C6 Lake Pukaki New Zealand
100 F9 Lake Range mts Nevada U.S.A.
115 L7 Lake River Ontario Canada
139 J7 Lakes Entrance Victoria Australia
102 E4 Lakeshore California U.S.A.
103 P7 Lakeside Arizona U.S.A.
102 H9 Lakeside California U.S.A.
98 D7 Lakeside Nebraska U.S.A.
101 N8 Lakeside Utah U.S.A.
120 F5 Lake Superior Prov. Park Ontario Canada
144 C5 Lake Tekapo New Zealand
101 O8 Laketown Utah U.S.A.
121 M7 Lake Traverse Ontario Canada
118 L8 Lake Valley Saskatchewan Canada
106 C9 Lake Valley New Mexico U.S.A.
109 J5 Lake Victor Texas U.S.A.
99 L7 Lake View Iowa U.S.A.
94 B3 Lakeview Michigan U.S.A.
101 O5 Lakeview Montana U.S.A.
100 E7 Lakeview Oregon U.S.A.
112 H3 Lake View South Carolina U.S.A.
109 N9 Lakeview Texas U.S.A.
111 E8 Lake Village Arkansas U.S.A.
95 O5 Lakeville Connecticut U.S.A.
94 A5 Lakeville Indiana U.S.A.
99 N5 Lakeville Minnesota U.S.A.
94 K4 Lakeville New York U.S.A.
113 F10 Lake Wales Florida U.S.A.
98 G2 Lake Williams North Dakota U.S.A.
102 F8 Lakewood California U.S.A.
106 E2 Lakewood Colorado U.S.A.
95 N6 Lakewood New Jersey U.S.A.
106 F9 Lakewood New Mexico U.S.A.
94 H4 Lakewood New York U.S.A.
94 F5 Lakewood Ohio U.S.A.
113 G11 Lake Worth Florida U.S.A.
47 Q15 Lakhaniá Rhodes Greece
52 D4 Lakhdenpokh'ya Russian Federation
74 J5 Lakhimpur India
80 B6 Lakhish Israel
80 C7 Lakhish R Israel
80 C7 Lakhish Israel
74 C7 Lakhpat India
107 J4 Lakin Kansas U.S.A.
54 L1 Lakinsk Russian Federation
47 P13 Lákka Greece
74 D2 Lakki Pakistan
71 M9 Laklo R Timor
71 K9 Lakohembi Sumba Indonesia
28 A6 Lakoik Denmark
47 O12 Lákones Greece
46 F8 Lakonikós Kólpos B Greece
71 O9 Lakor isld Indonesia
85 C7 Lakota Ivory Coast
99 M6 Lakota Iowa U.S.A.
98 H1 Lakota North Dakota U.S.A.
68 G3 Lak Sao Laos
26 P1 Lakse Fjord inlet Norway
26 O1 Lakselv Norway
26 F6 Laksfors Norway
76 A5 Lakshadweep islds Indian Oc
71 F7 Lala Mindanao Philippines
88 C8 Lala Zambia
87 B7 Lalama Angola
47 H3 Lâlapaşa Turkey
86 B5 Lalare Gabon
87 G8 Lalaúa Mozambique
18 G8 Lalbenque France
77 E5 Lāleh Zar, Kūh-e mt Iran
33 Q5 Lalendorf Germany
46 C3 Lalëzit, Gjiri i B Albania
77 A3 Lāli Iran
128 B4 La Libertad Ecuador
125 O9 La Libertad Guatemala
133 C4 La Ligua Chile
71 N8 Laliki Indonesia
71 H6 Lalimboee Sulawesi
65 G2 Lalin China
16 B2 Lalin Spain
18 F8 Lalinde France
65 G2 Lalin He R China
74 H6 Lalitpur India
19 P15 Lalley France
70 G7 Laloa Sulawesi
118 H2 La Loche West Saskatchewan Canada
52 G4 Lal'sk Russian Federation
124 H6 La Luz Mexico
37 P5 Lam Germany
52 E6 Lama R Russian Federation
128 D3 La Macarena Colombia
106 D5 La Madera New Mexico U.S.A.
65 D4 Lamadong China
124 J4 Lamadrid Mexico
70 E2 Lamag Sabah
68 C5 Lamaing Burma
68 D6 Lamaingkaw Burma
71 L9 Lamakera Indonesia
122 B6 La Malbaie Quebec Canada
123 R7 Lamaline Newfoundland Canada
45 J3 Lama Mocogno Italy
124 H5 La Mancha Mexico
17 F5 La Mancha reg Spain
125 M4 La Mansión Costa Rica
110 C6 Lamar Arkansas U.S.A.
106 H3 Lamar Colorado U.S.A.
110 G7 Lamar Mississippi U.S.A.
110 B4 Lamar Missouri U.S.A.
98 E9 Lamar Nebraska U.S.A.
107 O6 Lamar Oklahoma U.S.A.
112 G3 Lamar South Carolina U.S.A.
101 P5 Lamar R Wyoming U.S.A.
40 C1 Lamarche France
40 A2 Lamargelle France
133 D5 Lamarque Argentina
109 N6 La Marque Texas U.S.A.
122 B6 Lamartine Quebec Canada
125 L2 La Masica Honduras
19 N15 Lamastre France
126 G4 La Maya Cuba
69 B11 Lamayang Indonesia
20 E5 Lamballe France
86 B6 Lambaréné Gabon
130 F7 Lambari Brazil
70 G7 Lambasina isld Sulawesi
128 B5 Lambayeque dept Peru
14 E3 Lambay I Ireland
70 D5 Lambeng Kalimantan
9 G5 Lamberhurst England
112 F6 Lambert Georgia U.S.A.
111 F7 Lambert Mississippi U.S.A.
98 B2 Lambert Montana U.S.A.
142 B5 Lambert, C W Australia Australia
146 H10 Lambert Glacier Antarctica
99 L5 Lamberton Minnesota U.S.A.
87 C12 Lamberts B S Africa
95 N6 Lambertville New Jersey U.S.A.
19 O17 Lambesc France
120 J10 Lambeth Ontario Canada
46 E7 Lámbia Greece
9 E5 Lambourn England
36 E5 Lambrecht Germany
41 K7 Lambro R Italy
94 G10 Lambsburg Virginia U.S.A.
14 A5 Lambs Hd Ireland
36 E4 Lambsheim Germany
121 T7 Lambton Quebec Canada
114 G3 Lambton, C Northwest Territories Canada
70 G7 Lambuya Sulawesi
68 F5 Lam Chi R Thailand
68 G5 Lam Dom Noi R Thailand
69 C11 Lame Sumatra
101 T4 Lame Deer Montana U.S.A.
16 B3 Lamego Portugal
127 N4 Lamentin Guadeloupe W Indies
122 H6 Lameque New Brunswick Canada
122 H6 Lamèque, Ile New Brunswick Canada
133 D3 La Merced Argentina
138 F6 Lameroo South Australia Australia
102 G9 La Mesa California U.S.A.
106 D9 La Mesa New Mexico U.S.A.
108 F3 Lamesa Texas U.S.A.
43 F7 La Meta mt Italy
20 G5 La Meziére France
46 E6 Lamia Greece
127 K10 La Miel Venezuela
71 G7 Lamigan Pt Mindanao Philippines
15 E5 Lamington Scotland
124 D3 La Misa Mexico
71 F7 Lamitan Philippines
85 B3 Lamjaybir Western Sahara
109 J4 Lamkin Texas U.S.A.
71 C3 Lamlam Indonesia
15 C5 Lamlash Scotland
144 B6 Lammerlaw Range New Zealand
141 G5 Lammermoor Queensland Australia
15 F5 Lammermuir Hills Scotland
25 F7 Lammersdorf Germany
27 G14 Lammhult Sweden
29 L10 Lammi Finland
68 G5 Lam Nam Mun R Thailand
21 M5 Lamnay France
99 R8 La Moille Illinois U.S.A.
103 J1 Lamoille Nevada U.S.A.
95 P2 Lamoille R Vermont U.S.A.
110 F1 La Moine R Illinois U.S.A.
100 G2 Lamona Washington U.S.A.
71 E3 Lamon B Luzon Philippines
42 D4 Lamone R Italy
70 O9 Lamongan Java
110 C1 Lamoni Iowa U.S.A.
118 E5 Lamont Alberta Canada
102 F6 Lamont California U.S.A.
113 D7 Lamont Florida U.S.A.
101 O6 Lamont Idaho U.S.A.
99 P7 Lamont Iowa U.S.A.
107 N5 Lamont Oklahoma U.S.A.
101 S7 Lamont Wyoming U.S.A.
124 G3 La Morita Mexico
19 P14 La Morte France
22 J4 Lamorteau Belgium
121 M4 La Motte Quebec Canada
21 P6 Lamotte-Beuvron France
19 P15 La Motte d'Aveillans France
19 P13 La Motte-Servolex France
98 H3 La Moure North Dakota U.S.A.
68 F4 Lam Pao Res Thailand
109 J4 Lampasas Texas U.S.A.
109 K5 Lampasas R Texas U.S.A.
20 A5 Lampaul-Plouarzel France
125 K4 Lampazos Mexico
43 E13 Lampedusa, I. di Italy
36 E4 Lampertheim Germany
33 T10 Lampërtswalde Germany
8 B3 Lampeter Wales
8 B4 Lamphey Wales
46 F5 Lampinoú Greece
43 E13 Lampione, I. di Italy
68 F5 Lam Plai R Thailand
119 P9 Lampman Saskatchewan Canada
45 J4 Lamporecchio Italy
9 F3 Lamport England
52 F2 Lampozhnya Russian Federation
29 O6 Lämpsä Finland
70 K8 Lampung prov Sumatra
70 K8 Lampung Teluk B Sumatra
68 G5 Lam Si Bai R Thailand
32 M9 Lamspringe Germany
32 K5 Lamstedt Germany
68 B3 Lamu Burma
86 H6 Lamu Kenya
19 P15 La Mure France
19 N12 Lamure-sur-Azergues France
106 E6 Lamy New Mexico U.S.A.
141 G5 Lana Queensland Australia
42 D2 Lana Italy
135 S3 Lanai isld Hawaiian Is
135 S3 Lanai City Hawaiian Is
135 S3 Lanaihale pk Hawaiian Is
22 K2 Lanaken Belgium
74 H1 Lanak Pass Kashmir/Xizang Zizhiqu
71 G7 Lanao L Mindanao Philippines
121 O7 Lanark Ontario Canada
12 E2 Lanark Scotland
113 C8 Lanark Florida U.S.A.
99 R7 Lanark Illinois U.S.A.
70 E2 Lanas Sabah
68 C7 Lanbi Kyun isld Burma
71 F6 Lanboyan Pt Mindanao Philippines
68 D1 Lancang China
Lancang Jiang R see Mekong
13 F6 Lancashire co England
121 Q7 Lancaster Ontario Canada
13 F5 Lancaster England
102 F7 Lancaster California U.S.A.
110 M4 Lancaster Kentucky U.S.A.
98 K1 Lancaster Minnesota U.S.A.
110 D1 Lancaster Missouri U.S.A.
95 Q2 Lancaster New Hampshire U.S.A.
94 J4 Lancaster New York U.S.A.
94 E7 Lancaster Ohio U.S.A.
95 L6 Lancaster Pennsylvania U.S.A.
112 G3 Lancaster South Carolina U.S.A.
109 L3 Lancaster Texas U.S.A.
95 L9 Lancaster Virginia U.S.A.
99 Q7 Lancaster Wisconsin U.S.A.
115 L3 Lancaster Sd Northwest Territories Canada
98 B6 Lance Cr Wyoming U.S.A.
143 B9 Lancelin W Australia Australia
143 B9 Lancelin I W Australia Australia
143 E7 Lancelot, Mt W Australia Australia
19 O16 Lance, Mt. de la France
118 J8 Lancer Saskatchewan Canada
21 O1 Lanchères France
13 G4 Lanchester England
66 C5 Lan-chia Ts'o L China
48 J2 Lanchin Ukraine
Lanchow see Lanzhou
42 F6 Lanciano Italy
20 F4 Lancieux France
94 C10 Lancing Tennessee U.S.A.
19 O17 Lançon France
31 N5 Łańcut Poland
27 D11 Land reg Norway
98 F1 Landa North Dakota U.S.A.
32 K10 Landau Hessen Germany
36 E5 Landau Rheinland-Pfalz Germany
21 H5 Landéan France
41 N3 Landeck Austria
26 G4 Landegode isld Norway
20 C5 Landeleau France
21 H4 Landelles-et-Coupigny France
22 J2 Landen Belgium
140 C5 Lander R N Terr Australia
101 R7 Lander Wyoming U.S.A.
20 B5 Landerneau France
140 B5 Lander R N Terr Australia
27 F14 Landeryd Sweden
18 E8 Landes reg France
18 E8 Landes dept France
21 N6 Landes Loir-et-Cher France
94 H8 Landes West Virginia U.S.A.
28 G7 Landet Denmark
17 G5 Landete Spain
20 D6 Landévant France
20 B5 Landevennec France
20 G8 Landevieille France
68 A6 Landfall I Andaman Is
133 C8 Landfall, I Chile
9 E6 Landford England
33 S5 Landgraben R Germany
32 J5 Land Hadeln Germany
69 E13 Landik, Gunung mt Sumatra
74 D1 Landi Khana Pakistan
77 H4 Landi Md. Amin Khan Afghanistan
119 U3 Landing L Manitoba Canada
118 J6 Landis Saskatchewan Canada
112 G2 Landis North Carolina U.S.A.
20 B5 Landivisiau France
21 H5 Landivy France
112 F3 Lando South Carolina U.S.A.
99 R3 Land O Lakes Wisconsin U.S.A.
143 B7 Landor W Australia Australia
26 G8 Landösjön L Sweden
22 F3 Landrecies France
22 J5 Landres Ardennes France
22 K5 Landres Meurthe-et-Moselle France
121 N4 Landrienne Quebec Canada
142 F4 Landrigan Cliffs W Australia Australia
38 F8 Landro Italy
112 E2 Landrum South Carolina U.S.A.
40 E6 Landry France
26 M5 Landså Sweden
33 Q9 Landsberg Germany
41 N1 Landsberg Germany
141 G5 Landsborough R Queensland Australia
144 B5 Landsborough R New Zealand
114 G2 Lands End C Northwest Territories Canada
9 F7 Land's End England
37 N6 Landshut Germany
29 K5 Landskrona Sweden
36 D5 Landstuhl Germany
20 C5 Landudal France
20 B6 Landudec France
101 R2 Landusky Montana U.S.A.
32 L10 Landwehrhagen Germany
37 N3 Landwüst Germany
112 H4 Lane South Carolina U.S.A.
98 H5 Lane South Dakota U.S.A.
109 L6 Lane City Texas U.S.A.
22 G3 Laneffe Belgium
99 P6 Lanesboro Minnesota U.S.A.
111 L9 Lanett Alabama U.S.A.
22 D5 Laneuvilleroy France
22 J5 Laneuville-sur-Meuse France
20 E5 Lanfains France
Lanfeng see Lankao
118 G7 Lanfine Alberta Canada
119 N9 Lang Saskatchewan Canada
28 F6 Langå Denmark
66 C5 La'nga Co L China
16 E3 Langa de Duero Spain
46 F4 Langadhás Greece
46 E7 Langádhia Greece
29 T8 Langanes pen Iceland
86 G4 Langano Hāyk' L Ethiopia
71 H7 Langara Sulawesi
117 G8 Langara I British Columbia Canada
77 A1 Langarūd Iran
119 P8 Langbank Saskatchewan Canada
67 B6 Lang Chanh Vietnam
Lang-ch'u Ho see Sutlej
111 L9 Langdale Alabama U.S.A.
118 D8 Langdon Alberta Canada
107 M4 Langdon Kansas U.S.A.
98 H1 Langdon North Dakota U.S.A.
13 F4 Langdon Beck England
18 H7 Langeac France
21 L7 Langeais France
89 A9 Langeberg mts S Africa
89 C7 Langebergen mts S Africa
19 P18 L'Ange, Col de France
28 F7 Langeland isld Denmark
29 L10 Längelmäki Finland
29 L10 Längelmävesi L Finland
33 M9 Langelsheim Germany
22 D2 Langemark Belgium
32 J5 Langen Germany
36 F4 Langen Hessen Germany
37 P2 Langenau Germany
37 J7 Langenau Germany
32 F10 Langenberg Germany
37 N2 Langenberg Thüringen Germany
37 M4 Langenbruck Germany
119 Q8 Langenburg Saskatchewan Canada
36 H5 Langenburg Germany
26 H2 Langenes lighthouse Norway
28 B7 Langeness isld Germany
32 L8 Langenhagen Germany
28 B7 Langenhorn Germany
37 O6 Langenisarhofen Germany
38 N5 Langenlois Austria
36 D4 Langenlonsheim Germany
33 S9 Langennaundorf Germany
36 G3 Langenselbold Germany
37 J5 Langensteinach Germany
36 F6 Langensteinbach Germany
40 G3 Langenthal Switzerland
38 N6 Langenwang Austria
37 K5 Langenzenn Germany
32 F5 Langeoog Germany
28 E2 Lange-Rak inlet Denmark
28 F6 Langeskov Denmark
28 H5 Langesø L Denmark
27 D12 Langesund Norway
27 D13 Langesundsfjord inlet Norway
26 B9 Langevag Norway
37 K2 Langewiesen Germany
21 N5 Langey France
Langfang see Anci
26 M1 Langfjord Norway
26 Q1 Langfjord inlet Finnmark Norway
26 C9 Langfjord inlet Möre og Romsdal Norway
98 J4 Langford South Dakota U.S.A.
32 H7 Langförden Germany
69 E12 Langgam Sumatra
69 D12 Langgapayung Sumatra
118 L6 Langham Saskatchewan Canada
44 D2 Langhe Italy
44 H2 Langhirano Italy
68 C2 Langhko Burma
15 F5 Langholm Scotland
28 S9 Langjokull ice cap Iceland
69 C10 Langka Sumatra
69 D9 Langkawi isld Malaysia
69 D8 Lang Kha Toek, Khao mt Thailand
70 E1 Langkon Sabah
123 Q7 Langlade isld Atlantic Oc
121 P4 Langlade Quebec Canada
100 C1 Langley Washington U.S.A.
28 A5 Langli isld Denmark
141 H7 Langlo R Queensland Australia
141 H7 Langlo Crossing Queensland Australia
141 H7 Langlo Downs Queensland Australia
100 A7 Langlois Oregon U.S.A.
121 N4 Langlois Village Quebec Canada
32 H5 Langlütjensand sandbank Germany
36 D4 Langmeil Germany
40 G4 Langnau Switzerland
28 J7 Langø isld Denmark
18 H8 Langogne France
18 E8 Langon France
20 G6 Langon Ille-et-Vilaine France
28 F5 Langør Denmark
26 G3 Langöy isld Norway
8 D5 Langport England
37 N6 Langquaid Germany
40 B2 Langres France
40 B2 Langres, Plat. de France
21 K3 Langrune France
119 T8 Langruth Manitoba Canada
69 C10 Langsa Sumatra
69 C10 Langsa, Teluk B Sumatra
26 J8 Långsele Sweden

26 H7 **Långseleån** *R* Sweden
58 E3 **Lang Shan** *mt ra* China
27 H11 **Långshyttan** Sweden
28 D5 **Langskov** Denmark
67 B6 **Lang Son** Vietnam
13 H5 **Langtoft** England
26 L6 **Långträsk** Sweden
108 F6 **Langtry** Texas U.S.A.
18 H8 **Languedoc** *prov* France
20 E4 **Langueux** France
20 D6 **Languidic** France
110 F6 **L'Anguille** *R* Arkansas U.S.A.
37 J1 **Langula** Germany
32 H5 **Langwarden** Germany
13 F4 **Langwathby** England
32 K7 **Langwedel** Germany
9 F1 **Langworth** England
67 F1 **Langxi** China
67 F2 **Langxi** China
58 E5 **Langzhong** China
20 B5 **Lanhouarneau** France
67 G5 **Lan Hsü** *isld* Taiwan
121 L5 **Laniel** Quebec Canada
119 N7 **Lanigan** Saskatchewan Canada
102 S12 **Lanikai** Hawaiian Is
20 A5 **Lanildut** France
133 C5 **Lanín** *mt* Argentina
131 B7 **Lanín, Vol** Arg/Chile
8 B7 **Lanivet** England
70 C4 **Lanjak** Kalimantan
70 B4 **Lanjak, Bt** *mt* Sarawak
32 E10 **Lank** Germany
65 C7 **Lankao** China
33 T7 **Lanke** Germany
98 J1 **Lankin** North Dakota U.S.A.
22 K1 **Lanklaar** Belgium
20 E4 **Lanloup** France
20 C4 **Lanmeur** France
26 M3 **Lannavaara** Sweden
18 F9 **Lannemezan** France
20 A4 **Lannilis** France
20 D4 **Lannion** France
22 E2 **Lannoy** France
17 H3 **La Noguera** *dist* Spain
121 R7 **Lanoraie** Quebec Canada
124 F6 **La Noria** Mexico
48 K1 **Lanovtsy** Ukraine
95 M6 **Lansdale** Pennsylvania U.S.A.
121 P8 **Lansdowne** Ontario Canada
115 L7 **Lansdowne House** Ontario Canada
99 S3 **L'Anse** Michigan U.S.A.
123 Q2 **L'Anse-Amour** Labrador, Nfld Canada
123 P2 **L'Anse au Loup** Quebec Canada
123 R2 **L'anse-Au-Meadow** Newfoundland Canada
33 R5 **Lansen** Germany
19 P14 **Lans en Vercors** France
98 E1 **Lansford** North Dakota U.S.A.
95 M6 **Lansford** Pennsylvania U.S.A.
67 D4 **Lanshan** China
99 P6 **Lansing** Iowa U.S.A.
07 Q2 **Lansing** Kansas U.S.A.
94 C4 **Lansing** Michigan U.S.A.
12 F1 **Lansing** North Carolina U.S.A.
31 K6 **Lanškroun** Czech Rep
40 E7 **Lanslebourg** France
19 P14 **Lans, Mts de** France
69 D9 **Lanta Ko** Thailand
69 D9 **Lanta, Ko** *isld* Thailand
21 O7 **Lanthenay** France
Lantian *see* **Lianyuan**
65 A7 **Lantian** China
98 E4 **Lantry** South Dakota U.S.A.
43 C9 **Lanusei** Sardinia
71 G6 **Lanuza** Mindanao Philippines
20 E6 **Lanvaux, Landes de** *reg* France
20 B5 **Lanvéoc** France
20 E4 **Lanvollon** France
65 G1 **Lanxi** China
67 E1 **Lanxi** China
65 B5 **Lan Xian** China
33 P6 **Lanz** Germany
85 B3 **Lanzarote** *isld* Canary Is
58 D4 **Lanzhou** China
65 F2 **Lanzijing** China
71 E1 **Laoag** Luzon Philippines
71 G4 **Laoang** Philippines
67 A5 **Lao Cai** Vietnam
67 A4 **Laochang** China
66 C2 **Laofengkou** China
65 D4 **Laoguo** China
59 G3 **Laoha He** *R* China
58 F5 **Laohekou** China
58 F5 **Lao-ho-k'ou** China
14 D4 **Laois** *co* Ireland
65 G4 **Laoling** China
Laolong *see* **Longchuan**
22 F4 **Laon** France
99 S4 **Laona** Wisconsin U.S.A.
21 N4 **Laons** France
27 L9 **La Orchila, I** Venezuela
28 C6 **La Oroya** Peru
68 F3 **Laos** *rep* S E Asia
65 E6 **Laoshan** China
65 E5 **Laotie Shan** *C* China
65 E5 **Laotieshan Shuidao** *str* China
16 D9 **Laou, Oued** *R* Morocco
65 G2 **Laoye Ling** *mts* China
65 H3 **Laoye Ling** *mts* China
71 E8 **Lapac** *isld* Philippines
37 G8 **Lapala** Mozambique
18 H6 **Lapalisse** France
35 A3 **La Palma** *isld* Canary Is
25 P9 **La Palma** Guatemala
16 C7 **La Palma del Concado** Spain
31 C6 **La Pampa** *prov* Argentina
02 D6 **La Panza** California U.S.A.
02 D6 **La Panza Ra** California U.S.A.
28 F2 **La Paragua** Venezuela
17 F4 **La Paraleja** *L* Spain
16 D4 **La Paramera de Avila** Spain
71 D7 **Laparan** *isld* Sulu Arch
24 G6 **La Parilla** Mexico
33 D4 **La Paz** Argentina
31 F3 **La Paz** Entre Rios Argentina
28 E7 **La Paz** *R* Bolivia
28 E7 **La Paz** Bolivia
24 D5 **La Paz** Mexico
94 A5 **Lapaz** Indiana U.S.A.
27 H9 **La Paz** Venezuela
28 E4 **La Pedrera** Colombia
94 D3 **Lapeer** Michigan U.S.A.
94 B6 **Lapel** Indiana U.S.A.
33 E4 **La Pelada** Argentina
24 G3 **La Perla** Mexico
9 U3 **La Perouse** Manitoba Canada
2 T13 **La Pérouse Pinnacle** Hawaiian Is
9 M2 **La Pérouse Strait** Japan/Rus Fed
71 A2 **Lapi** Halmahera Indonesia
24 H7 **La Piedad** Mexico
0 D6 **Lapine** Oregon U.S.A.
1 G5 **Lapinin** Bohol Philippines
9 N8 **Lapinlahti** Finland
9 D3 **Lapithos** Cyprus
1 F11 **Laplace** Louisiana U.S.A.
8 D4 **Lap Lae** Thailand
2 D1 **Laplandiya** Russian Federation
1 F5 **La Plata** Argentina
5 L8 **La Plata** Maryland U.S.A.
9 O9 **La Plata** Missouri U.S.A.
3 O6 **La Poile B** Newfoundland Canada
9 Q3 **La Pointe** Wisconsin U.S.A.
6 D2 **La Pola de Gordón** Spain
2 F3 **Lapominka** Russian Federation
8 H7 **Laporte** Saskatchewan Canada
2 D2 **La Porte** California U.S.A.
9 U8 **La Porte** Indiana U.S.A.
9 M2 **Laporte** Minnesota U.S.A.
95 L5 **Laporte** Pennsylvania U.S.A.
109 N6 **La Porte** Texas U.S.A.
99 O7 **La Porte City** Iowa U.S.A.
70 F7 **Laposa, Bk** *mt* Sulawesi
36 C7 **Lapoutroie** France
48 G6 **Lapovo** Serbia Yugoslavia
29 K8 **Lappajärvi** Finland
29 N10 **Lappeenranta** Finland
29 J9 **Lappfjärd** Finland
27 M10 **Lappi** Finland
29 J10 **Lappi Kauttua** Finland
26 L3 **Lappland** Sweden/Finland
26 N2 **Lappojavrre** *L* Norway
26 N5 **Lappträsk** Sweden
121 R7 **Laprairie** Quebec Canada
101 U7 **La Prele Cr** Wyoming U.S.A.
133 E5 **Laprida** Argentina
108 H7 **La Pryor** Texas U.S.A.
47 H4 **Lâpseki** Turkey
54 J2 **Laptevo** Russian Federation
51 M1 **Laptev Sea** Russian Federation
29 K9 **Lapua** Finland
29 K8 **Lapuanjoki** *R* Finland
16 E5 **La Puebla de Montalbán** Spain
127 J10 **La Puerta** Venezuela
128 B4 **La Puntilla** *pt* Ecuador
124 C4 **La Purisima** Mexico
100 A2 **La Push** Washington U.S.A.
48 H3 **Lăpusului, Muntii** *mts* Romania
31 O3 **Łapy** Poland
84 H5 **Laqiya Arba'in** Sudan
128 E8 **La Quiaca** Argentina
42 E6 **L'Aquila** Italy
77 D6 **Lār** Iran
16 C9 **Larache** Morocco
19 P16 **Laragne** France
77 E6 **Larak** *isld* Iran
128 D6 **Laramate** Peru
16 D7 **La Rambla** Spain
98 A7 **Laramie** *R* Wyoming U.S.A.
98 A8 **Laramie** Wyoming U.S.A.
98 A7 **Laramie Pk** *mt* Wyoming U.S.A.
130 F8 **Laranjal Paulista** Brazil
130 D9 **Laranjeiras do Sul** Brazil
130 E8 **Laranjinha, R** Brazil
71 L9 **Larantuka** Flores Indonesia
19 O15 **La Raye** *mt* France
15 E4 **Larbert** Scotland
19 N13 **L'Arbresle** France
127 H5 **L'Arcahaie** Haiti
21 J5 **Larchamp** France
121 L4 **Larder Lake** Ontario Canada
47 R14 **Lárdhos** Rhodes Greece
47 V17 **Lárdhos, Akr** Rhodes Greece
123 M8 **L'Ardoise** C Breton I, Nova Scotia
21 P4 **Lardy** France
16 E1 **Laredo** Spain
99 N9 **Laredo** Missouri U.S.A.
109 H8 **Laredo** Texas U.S.A.
121 L4 **La Reine** Quebec Canada
48 K2 **Larga** Moldova
Largeau *see* **Faya-Largeau**
122 J3 **Large I** Quebec Canada
18 H8 **Largentière** France
15 F4 **Largo** Scotland
113 E10 **Largo** Florida U.S.A.
126 D4 **Largo, Cayo** *isld* Cuba
13 F1 **Largo Ward** Scotland
15 D5 **Largs** Scotland
45 J4 **Lari** Italy
70 F5 **Lariang** *R* Sulawesi
70 F5 **Lariang** Sulawesi
46 F6 **Lárimna** Greece
98 J2 **Larimore** North Dakota U.S.A.
42 F7 **Larino** Italy
131 C2 **La Rioja** Argentina
17 F2 **La Rioja** *prov* Spain
46 E5 **Lárisa** Greece
77 D6 **Laristan** Iran
119 T9 **La Rivière** Manitoba Canada
98 E3 **Lark** North Dakota U.S.A.
74 C5 **Larkana** Pakistan
12 E2 **Larkhall** Scotland
123 O4 **Lark Harb** Newfoundland Canada
110 K7 **Larkinsville** Alabama U.S.A.
141 H3 **Lark Pass** Gt Barrier Reef Aust
9 G3 **Lark, R** England
106 F2 **Larkspur** Colorado U.S.A.
9 G3 **Larling** England
55 F2 **Larlomkiny** Russian Federation
20 D6 **Larmar-Plage** France
79 D4 **Larnaca** Cyprus
14 F2 **Larne** N Ireland
107 L3 **Larned** Kansas U.S.A.
14 F2 **Larne L** N Ireland
16 D2 **La Robla** Spain
19 P15 **La Roche-des-Arnauds** France
18 H5 **Laroche-Migennes** France
19 Q14 **La Rochette** France
22 L4 **Larochette** Luxembourg
17 F5 **La Roda** Spain
16 D7 **La Roda de A** Spain
127 K5 **La Romana** Dominican Rep
70 G6 **Larompong** Sulawesi
119 M3 **La Ronge** Saskatchewan Canada
124 J5 **La Rosa** Mexico
111 F12 **La Rose** Louisiana U.S.A.
124 J3 **La Rosita** Mexico
142 C5 **Larrey Pt** W Australia Australia
140 C3 **Larrimah** N Terr Australia
123 L8 **Larry's R** Nova Scotia Canada
146 D4 **Larsen Ice Shelf** Antarctica
101 T1 **Larslan** Montana U.S.A.
29 K8 **Larsmo** Finland
119 N1 **Larson** Ontario Canada
109 M3 **La Rue** Texas U.S.A.
18 E10 **Laruns** France
27 D12 **Larvik** Norway
56 B1 **Lar'yak** Russian Federation
55 G1 **Lar'yegan** *R* Russian Federation
124 G6 **Las Adjuntas** Mexico
103 P3 **La Sal** Utah U.S.A.
119 U9 **La Salle** Manitoba Canada
120 G10 **La Salle** Ontario Canada
98 B9 **La Salle** Colorado U.S.A.
99 R8 **La Salle** Illinois U.S.A.
16 E8 **Las Alpujarras** *dist* Spain
70 D4 **Lasan** Kalimantan
124 D2 **La Sangre** Mexico
106 G3 **Las Animas** Colorado U.S.A.
121 L4 **La Sarre** Quebec Canada
19 Q16 **La Saulce** France
128 E1 **Las Aves, Is** Venezuela
17 G2 **Las Bardenas** *reg* Spain
38 L5 **Lasberg** Austria
28 D4 **Låsby** Denmark
127 J5 **Lascahobas** Haiti
133 E3 **Las Cejas** Argentina
139 G6 **Lascelles** Victoria Australia
123 R4 **La Scie** Newfoundland Canada
133 C5 **Las Coloradas** Neuquén Argentina
124 F3 **Las Cruces** Mexico
106 D9 **Las Cruces** New Mexico U.S.A.
127 J5 **La Selle** *mt* Haiti
131 B2 **La Serena** Chile
16 D6 **La Serena** *reg* Spain
108 F8 **Las Esperanzas** Mexico
124 J4 **Las Esperanzas** Mexico
19 P18 **La Seyne** France
131 F6 **Las Flores** Argentina
16 E5 **Las Guadalerzas** *reg* Spain
118 H5 **Lashburn** Saskatchewan Canada
77 G4 **Lāsh-ē Joveyn** Afghanistan
68 C1 **Lashio** Burma
77 J4 **Lashkar Gāh** Afghanistan
54 N2 **Lashma** Russian Federation
16 C4 **Las Hurdes** Spain
43 G9 **La Sila** *dist* Italy
31 L2 **Łasin** Poland
31 L4 **Łask** Poland
31 L2 **Laskowice** Poland
133 C5 **Las Lajas** Argentina
128 F8 **Las Lajitas** Argentina
128 F8 **Las Lomitas** Argentina
16 C7 **Las Marismas** *dist* Spain
133 D7 **Las Martinetas** Argentina
127 L10 **Las Mercedes** Venezuela
124 G3 **Las Mesteñas** Mexico
124 G4 **Las Nieves** Mexico
16 E6 **La Solana** Spain
71 H6 **Lasolo, Tk** *B* Sulawesi
19 O14 **La Sône** France
38 F8 **Lasorling** *mt* Austria
85 A3 **Las Palmas de Gran Canaria** Canary Is
106 C8 **Las Palomas** New Mexico U.S.A.
44 G3 **La Spezia** Italy
117 L11 **Lasqueti I** British Columbia Canada
16 E4 **Las Rozas** Spain
33 N5 **Lassahn** Germany
33 T5 **Lassan** Germany
130 G5 **Lassance** Brazil
21 K5 **Lassay-les-Châteaux** France
26 M5 **Lassbyn** Sweden
100 D9 **Lassen Peak** *mt* California U.S.A.
100 D9 **Lassen Vol. Nat. Park** California U.S.A.
22 D4 **Lassigny** France
38 L6 **Lassing** Austria
146 D6 **Lassiter Coast** Antarctica
38 K7 **Lassnitz-Dorf** Austria
38 N7 **Lassnitzhöhe** Austria
121 R7 **L'Assomption** Quebec Canada
13 E2 **Lasswade** Scotland
21 J4 **Lassy** France
133 D3 **Lastarria** *mt* Chile/Arg
106 G2 **Last Chance** Colorado U.S.A.
13 H5 **Lastingham** England
119 N7 **Last Mountain** Saskatchewan Canada
119 M7 **Last Mountain L** Saskatchewan Canada
Lastoursville *see* **Bonda**
42 H6 **Lastovo** *isld* Croatia
32 G7 **Lastrup** Germany
126 F4 **Las Tunas** Cuba
124 E3 **Las Varas** Mexico
124 G3 **Las Varas** Mexico
124 G7 **Las Varas** Mexico
103 J5 **Las Vegas** Nevada U.S.A.
106 E6 **Las Vegas** New Mexico U.S.A.
128 C4 **Latacunga** Ecuador
146 C5 **Latady I** Antarctica
Latakia *see* **Ladhiqīyah, Al**
29 J3 **Latäseno** *R* Finland
121 L5 **Latchford** Ontario Canada
137 S5 **Late** *isld* Tonga
109 M4 **Latexo** Texas U.S.A.
143 B8 **Latham** W Australia Australia
99 R10 **Latham** Illinois U.S.A.
21 L7 **Lathan** *R* France
32 F7 **Lathen** Germany
15 E2 **Latheron** Scotland
110 B2 **Lathrop** Missouri U.S.A.
102 H5 **Lathrop Wells** Nevada U.S.A.
26 J7 **Latikberg** Sweden
21 L8 **Latillé** France
43 E7 **Latina** Italy
45 N6 **Latina Scalo** Italy
106 E5 **Latir Pk** New Mexico U.S.A.
54 K5 **Latnaya** Russian Federation
133 D4 **La Toma** Argentina
48 H2 **Latoritsa** *R* Ukraine
128 E1 **La Tortuga** *isld* Venezuela
142 D4 **Latouche Treville, C** W Australia
19 O13 **La Tour du Pin** France
121 P3 **La Trève, L** Quebec Canada
127 L4 **La Trinité** Martinique W Indies
139 H8 **Latrobe** Tasmania Australia
94 H6 **Latrobe** Pennsylvania U.S.A.
131 C2 **La Troya, R** Argentina
112 H3 **Latta** South Carolina U.S.A.
94 C5 **Latty** Ohio U.S.A.
71 M9 **Latuna** Indonesia
121 S5 **La Tuque** Quebec Canada
74 G9 **Latur** India
27 M15 **Latvia** *rep* E Europe
85 G7 **Lau** Nigeria
36 G2 **Laubach** Hessen Germany
36 D3 **Laubach** Rheinland-Pfalz Germany
137 R6 **Lau Basin** Pacific Oc
21 H6 **Laubrières** France
36 E3 **Laubuseschbach** Germany
128 E7 **Lauca** *R* Bolivia
37 M1 **Laucha** Germany
33 T9 **Lauchhammer** Germany
37 J6 **Lauchheim** Germany
36 H4 **Lauda-Königshofen** Germany
27 C13 **Laudal** Norway
36 H5 **Laudenbach** Germany
119 R9 **Lauder** Manitoba Canada
13 F2 **Lauder** Scotland
139 J9 **Lauderdale** Tasmania Australia
111 H9 **Lauderdale** Mississippi U.S.A.
19 N16 **Laudun** France
32 K8 **Lauenau** Germany
32 L6 **Lauenbruck** Germany
33 N6 **Lauenburg** Germany
32 K9 **Lauenförde** Germany
32 L8 **Lauenstein** Germany
37 J3 **Lauer** *R* Germany
37 L5 **Lauf** Germany
36 G3 **Laufach** Germany
38 G6 **Laufen** Germany
40 F3 **Laufen** Switzerland
36 G5 **Lauffen** Germany
8 B4 **Laugharne** Wales
99 U3 **Laughing Fish Pt** Michigan U.S.A.
140 C6 **Laughlen Mt** N Terr Australia
106 F5 **Laughlin Pk** New Mexico U.S.A.
9 G6 **Laughton** England
37 J6 **Lauingen** Germany
29 M9 **Laukaa** Finland
70 G4 **Laulalang** Sulawesi
18 H5 **Laumes, les** France
68 D7 **Laun** Thailand
20 B5 **Launay, P** France
121 M4 **Launay Sta** Quebec Canada
139 H8 **Launceston** Tasmania Australia
8 B6 **Launceston** England
14 B4 **Laune** *R* Ireland
68 C6 **Launglon Bok** *islds* Burma
131 A8 **La Unión** Chile
106 D10 **La Union** New Mexico U.S.A.
127 L10 **La Unión** Venezuela
22 H4 **Launois-sur-Vence** France
38 K8 **Launsdorf** Austria
135 V4 **Laupahoehoe** Hawaiian Is
36 H7 **Laupheim** Germany
71 E3 **Laur** Luzon Philippines
141 G3 **Laura** Queensland Australia
138 E5 **Laura** South Australia Australia
118 K7 **Laura** Saskatchewan Canada
140 A4 **Laura Cr** N Terr Australia
128 E2 **La Urbana** Venezuela
28 D4 **Laurbjerg** Denmark
95 M8 **Laurel** Delaware U.S.A.
94 B7 **Laurel** Indiana U.S.A.
95 L7 **Laurel** Maryland U.S.A.
111 G10 **Laurel** Mississippi U.S.A.
101 R4 **Laurel** Montana U.S.A.
130 B10 **Laureles** Paraguay
111 K11 **Laurel Hill** Florida U.S.A.
94 H6 **Laurel Hill** Pennsylvania U.S.A.
94 E7 **Laurelville** Ohio U.S.A.
15 F4 **Laurencekirk** Scotland
99 M7 **Laurens** Iowa U.S.A.
95 M4 **Laurens** New York U.S.A.
112 E3 **Laurens** South Carolina U.S.A.
121 R7 **Laurentides** Quebec Canada
121 T5 **Laurentides, Réserve Faunique des** Quebec Canada
43 G8 **Laurenzana** Italy
43 G8 **Lauria** Italy
146 E3 **Laurie I** *isld* S Orkney Is Antarctica
119 P2 **Laurie L** Saskatchewan Canada
143 E7 **Laurie, Mt** W Australia Australia
119 Q2 **Laurie R** Manitoba Canada
119 S8 **Laurier** Manitoba Canada
121 T6 **Laurierville** Quebec Canada
12 D4 **Laurieston** Scotland
139 L4 **Laurieton** New South Wales Australia
29 L6 **Laurila** Finland
101 N4 **Laurin** Montana U.S.A.
112 H3 **Laurinburg** North Carolina U.S.A.
19 O17 **Lauris** France
144 C5 **Lauriston** New Zealand
29 N10 **Lauritsala** Finland
99 S2 **Laurium** Michigan U.S.A.
45 R8 **Lauro** Italy
43 F11 **Lauro, M** *mt* Sicily
133 H3 **Lauro Muller** Brazil
40 E4 **Lausanne** Switzerland
37 L3 **Lauscha** Germany
70 E6 **Laut** *isld* Kalimantan
19 Q14 **Lautaret, Col du** *pass* France
131 A7 **Lautaro** Chile
33 M9 **Lautenthal** Germany
36 D5 **Lauter** *R* Germany
37 O2 **Lauter** Germany
37 M5 **Lauterach** *R* Germany
36 E7 **Lauterbach** Baden-Württemberg Germany
36 G2 **Lauterbach** Hessen Germany
37 O1 **Lauterbach** Sachsen Germany
36 E6 **Lauterbourg** France
36 D4 **Lauterecken** Germany
37 M5 **Lauterhofen** Germany
36 G2 **Lautertal** Germany
37 K3 **Lautertal** Germany
29 L6 **Lautiosaari** Finland
70 D7 **Laut Kecil, Kepulauan** *islds* Indonesia
41 J1 **Lautlingen** Germany
18 G9 **Lautrec** France
70 D6 **Laut, Selat** *str* Kalimantan
69 C10 **Lauttawar,Danau** *L* Sumatra
26 E7 **Lauvsnes** Norway
25 F2 **Lauwers** Netherlands
25 F2 **Lauwers Zee** Netherlands
18 F8 **Lauzerte** France
121 T6 **Lauzon** Quebec Canada
100 D8 **Lava Beds Nat. Mon** California U.S.A.
109 L6 **Lavaca** *R* Texas U.S.A.
109 **Lavaca B** Texas U.S.A.
22 J3 **Lavacherie** Belgium
44 F3 **Lavagna** *R* Italy
44 F3 **Lavagna** Italy
101 O7 **Lava Hot Springs** Idaho U.S.A.
21 J5 **Laval** France
19 P18 **La Valette** France
99 Q6 **La Valle** Wisconsin U.S.A.
131 G5 **Lavalleja** *dept* Uruguay
122 C5 **Laval, R** Quebec Canada
38 L8 **Lavamünd** Austria
77 C6 **Lavan** Iran
45 L3 **Lavane, M** *mt* Italy
26 J3 **Lavangen** Norway
38 L8 **Lavant** *R* Austria
121 O7 **Lavant** Ontario Canada
9 F6 **Lavant** England
38 L8 **Lavanttal** *V* Austria
131 A6 **Lavaplé, Pta** *C* Chile
18 F8 **Lavardac** France
21 M6 **Lavardin** France
21 M5 **Lavaré** France
77 D4 **Lavar Meydan** *salt lake* Iran
18 G9 **Lavaur** France
21 L8 **Lavausseau** France
102 C5 **Laveaga Pk** California U.S.A.
16 D2 **La Vecilla** Spain
127 J5 **La Vega** Dominican Rep
124 H7 **La Vega** Mexico
128 E1 **La Vela** Venezuela
18 G10 **Lavelanet** France
16 D3 **La Vellés** Spain
28 D4 **Laven** Denmark
9 G3 **Lavenham** England
41 J6 **Laveno** Italy
22 D2 **Laventie** France
130 B10 **La Verá** *L* Paraguay
103 L4 **La Verkin** Utah U.S.A.
107 L5 **Laverne** Oklahoma U.S.A.
109 J6 **La Vernia** Texas U.S.A.
143 D8 **Laverton** W Australia Australia
106 E4 **La Veta** Colorado U.S.A.
71 G4 **Lavezares** Philippines
45 L2 **Lavezzola** Italy
29 K10 **Lavia** Finland
124 H4 **La Víbora** Mexico
121 M7 **Lavieille, L** Ontario Canada
27 A10 **Lavik** Norway
128 C5 **La Viña** Peru
101 R3 **Lavina** Montana U.S.A.
8 D5 **Lavington** England
112 D3 **Lavonia** Georgia U.S.A.
109 L2 **Lavon Res** Texas U.S.A.
118 F5 **Lavoy** Alberta Canada
130 G7 **Lavras** Brazil
130 H9 **Lavras da Mangabeira** Brazil
55 D4 **Lavrent'yevka** Kazakhstan
26 J7 **Lavsjö** Sweden
87 F11 **Lavumisa** Swaziland
88 C8 **Lavusi** *mt* Zambia
109 L7 **La Ward** Texas U.S.A.
70 D2 **Lawas** Sarawak
70 G6 **Lawata** Sulawesi
71 H7 **Lawele** Indonesia
100 G6 **Lawen** Oregon U.S.A.
119 V4 **Lawford L** Manitoba Canada
141 K6 **Lawgi** Queensland Australia
71 B3 **Lawin** *isld* Indonesia
70 C4 **Lawit, G** *mt* Sarawak
69 F10 **Lawit, Gunung** *mt* Malaysia
68 C2 **Lawksawk** Burma
99 N3 **Lawler** Minnesota U.S.A.
123 R7 **Lawn** Newfoundland Canada
108 H3 **Lawn** Texas U.S.A.
112 F2 **Lawndale** North Carolina U.S.A.
140 E4 **Lawn Hill** Queensland Australia
85 D6 **Lawra** Ghana
144 B6 **Lawrence** New Zealand
94 A7 **Lawrence** Indiana U.S.A.
107 P3 **Lawrence** Kansas U.S.A.
95 Q4 **Lawrence** Massachusetts U.S.A.
98 H9 **Lawrence** Nebraska U.S.A.
94 B7 **Lawrenceburg** Indiana U.S.A.
94 C8 **Lawrenceburg** Kentucky U.S.A.
110 J6 **Lawrenceburg** Tennessee U.S.A.
122 E8 **Lawrence Stn** New Brunswick Canada
122 G9 **Lawrencetown** Nova Scotia Canada
122 J9 **Lawrencetown** Nova Scotia Canada
112 D4 **Lawrenceville** Georgia U.S.A.
110 J3 **Lawrenceville** Illinois U.S.A.
95 L5 **Lawrenceville** Pennsylvania U.S.A.
94 K10 **Lawrenceville** Virginia U.S.A.
143 D7 **Lawrence Wells, Mt** W Australia Australia
102 F4 **Laws** California U.S.A.
118 L8 **Lawson** Saskatchewan Canada
110 B2 **Lawson** Missouri U.S.A.
113 E7 **Lawtey** Florida U.S.A.
94 B4 **Lawton** Michigan U.S.A.
98 H1 **Lawton** North Dakota U.S.A.
107 M7 **Lawton** Oklahoma U.S.A.
27 G12 **Laxå** Sweden
12 D5 **Laxey** I of Man U.K.
9 H3 **Laxfield** England
15 G2 **Laxo** Scotland
26 G8 **Laxsjö** Sweden
21 H8 **Lay** *R* France
101 S9 **Lay** Colorado U.S.A.
52 J2 **Laya** *R* Russian Federation
52 G1 **Laydennyy, Mys** *C* Russian Federation
21 P5 **Laye** *R* France
139 G7 **Layers Hill** Victoria Australia
111 K9 **Lay L** Alabama U.S.A.
21 J7 **Layon** *R* France
78 M2 **Laysār** Iran
55 E2 **Laytamak** Russian Federation
101 N8 **Layton** Utah U.S.A.
83 K12 **Lazare, Pt** Mahé I Indian Oc
48 F6 **Lazarevac** Serbia Yugoslavia
57 A3 **Lazareva, Oz** *isld* Uzbekistan
146 J7 **Lazarevisen** *ice shelf* Antarctica
146 J6 **Lazarev Sea** Antarctica
124 B2 **Lázaro Cárdenas** Mexico
124 H8 **Lázaro Cárdenas** Mexico
31 O1 **Lazdijai** Lithuania
21 P7 **Lazenay** France
42 E6 **Lazio** *prov* Italy
37 O3 **Lázně Kynžvart** Czech Rep
59 K3 **Lazo** Russian Federation
13 F4 **Lazonby** England
48 L3 **Lazovsk** Moldova
9 F1 **Lea** England
100 C5 **Leaburg** Oregon U.S.A.
68 F6 **Leach** Cambodia
110 F6 **Leachville** Arkansas U.S.A.
98 C5 **Lead** South Dakota U.S.A.
13 E2 **Leadburn** Scotland
9 F1 **Leadenham** England
9 G4 **Leaden Roding** England
118 H8 **Leader** Saskatchewan Canada
15 E5 **Leadhills** Scotland
101 M5 **Leadore** Idaho U.S.A.
139 J4 **Leadville** New South Wales Australia
106 D2 **Leadville** Colorado U.S.A.
115 M6 **Leaf** *R* Quebec Canada
99 R7 **Leaf River** Illinois U.S.A.
9 G1 **Leake** England
142 F4 **Leake, Mt** W Australia Australia
143 C7 **Leake, Mt** W Australia Australia
111 H10 **Leakesville** Mississippi U.S.A.
108 H6 **Leakey** Texas U.S.A.
111 G10 **Leal** *R* Mississippi U.S.A.
98 H2 **Leal** North Dakota U.S.A.
133 D3 **Leales** Argentina
142 B5 **Leal, Mt** W Australia Australia
120 H10 **Leamington** Ontario Canada
145 E2 **Leamington** New Zealand
103 M2 **Leamington** Utah U.S.A.
9 E3 **Leamington Spa, Royal** England
9 E3 **Leam,R** England
67 E3 **Le'an** China
12 C1 **Leanach** Scotland
109 K5 **Leander** Texas U.S.A.
130 C10 **Leandro N.Alem** Argentina
14 B4 **Leane,L** Ireland
67 F2 **Le'an Jiang** *R* China
9 F4 **Lea, R** England
142 A5 **Learmonth** W Australia Australia
111 M10 **Leary** Georgia U.S.A.
9 F1 **Leasingham** England
118 L5 **Leask** Saskatchewan Canada
9 F5 **Leatherhead** England
101 M5 **Leatherman Pk** Idaho U.S.A.
110 K3 **Leavenworth** Indiana U.S.A.
107 P2 **Leavenworth** Kansas U.S.A.
100 E2 **Leavenworth** Washington U.S.A.
102 E3 **Leavitt Pk** California U.S.A.
31 K1 **Łeba** Poland
36 B5 **Lebach** Germany
70 L9 **Lebak** Java
71 G7 **Lebak** Mindanao Philippines
100 B3 **Lebam** Washington U.S.A.
46 E2 **Lebane** Serbia Yugoslavia
86 B5 **Lebango** Congo
79 F4 **Lebanon** *rep* S W Asia
110 G3 **Lebanon** Illinois U.S.A.
110 K1 **Lebanon** Indiana U.S.A.
107 M2 **Lebanon** Kansas U.S.A.
110 L4 **Lebanon** Kentucky U.S.A.
110 D4 **Lebanon** Missouri U.S.A.
98 F9 **Lebanon** Nebraska U.S.A.
95 Q3 **Lebanon** New Hampshire U.S.A.
94 C7 **Lebanon** Ohio U.S.A.
100 C5 **Lebanon** Oregon U.S.A.
95 L6 **Lebanon** Pennsylvania U.S.A.
98 G4 **Lebanon** South Dakota U.S.A.
110 K5 **Lebanon** Tennessee U.S.A.
94 E10 **Lebanon** Virginia U.S.A.
94 B9 **Lebanon Junc** Kentucky U.S.A.
113 E8 **Lebanon Stn** Florida U.S.A.
55 F3 **Lebazh'ye** Russian Federation
19 P18 **Le Beausset** France
102 F7 **Lebec** California U.S.A.
55 E3 **Lebedevka** Russian Federation
54 F6 **Lebedin** Ukraine
54 L3 **Lebedyan'** Russian Federation
48 D3 **Lébénymiklós** Hungary
26 Q1 **Lebesby** Norway
71 H7 **Lebo** Indonesia
107 P3 **Lebo** Kansas U.S.A.
89 G4 **Lebombo Mts** Mozambique
68 A2 **Lebon** Burma
31 K1 **Lębork** Poland
71 M9 **Lebos** Timor
19 Q14 **Le Bourg d'Oisans** France
19 P13 **Le Bourget** France
122 H6 **Le Bouthillier** New Brunswick Canada
89 F5 **Lebowakgomo** S Africa
119 O8 **Lebret** Saskatchewan Canada
16 C8 **Lebrija** Spain
31 K1 **Łebsko, Jezioro** *L* Poland
133 C5 **Lebu** Chile
33 S9 **Lebusa** Germany
28 E7 **Leby** Denmark
55 G5 **Lebyazh'ye** Kazakhstan
52 G6 **Lebyazh'ye** Kirovskaya obl Russian Federation
55 E3 **Lebyazh'ye** Kurganskaya obl Russian Federation
71 N9 **Leça** Timor
19 Q18 **Le Canadel** France
43 J8 **Lecce** Italy
41 K6 **Lecco** Italy
41 K6 **Lecco, Lago di** Italy
99 N5 **Le Center** Minnesota U.S.A.
37 K7 **Lech** *R* Germany
67 D4 **Lechang** China
41 N2 **Lechbruck** Germany
19 J3 **Le Chesne** France
41 N1 **Lechfeld** *plain* Germany
48 J3 **Lechința** Romania
9 E4 **Lechlade** England
41 M3 **Lech Tal** *V* Austria
41 M3 **Lechtaler Alpen** *mt* Austria
17 G3 **Leciñena** Spain
28 B7 **Leck** Germany
22 E3 **Lecluse** France
111 D10 **Lecompte** Louisiana U.S.A.
13 H6 **Leconfield** England
18 H6 **Le Creusot** France
18 F9 **Lectoure** France
18 D9 **Lecumberri** Spain
31 O4 **Łęczna** Poland
31 L3 **Łęczyca** Poland
52 F4 **Led** *R* Russian Federation
32 G6 **Leda** *R* Germany
69 F11 **Ledang, Gunung** Malaysia
8 D3 **Ledbury** England
16 C3 **Ledesma** Spain
143 C10 **Ledge Pt** W Australia Australia
101 O1 **Ledger** Montana U.S.A.
87 B7 **Ledo, C** Angola
68 J3 **Ledong** China
41 N6 **Ledro,L.di** Italy
118 D5 **Leduc** Alberta Canada
31 K2 **Lędyczek** Poland
28 D4 **Lee** Denmark
103 P10 **Lee** Arizona U.S.A.
113 D7 **Lee** Florida U.S.A.
99 S8 **Lee** Illinois U.S.A.
95 O4 **Lee** Massachusetts U.S.A.
94 H6 **Leechburg** Pennsylvania U.S.A.
119 P7 **Leech L** Saskatchewan Canada
99 M2 **Leech L** Minnesota U.S.A.
41 N2 **Leeder** Germany
142 B1 **Leederville** *dist* Perth, W Aust Australia
108 E8 **Leedey** Oklahoma U.S.A.
13 G6 **Leeds** England
111 K8 **Leeds** Alabama U.S.A.
98 G1 **Leeds** North Dakota U.S.A.
103 L4 **Leeds** Utah U.S.A.
95 R2 **Leeds Junct** Maine U.S.A.
8 D1 **Leek** England
25 F2 **Leek** Netherlands
94 B2 **Leelanau L** Michigan U.S.A.
143 A8 **Leeman** W Australia Australia
13 G5 **Leeming** England
142 F2 **Leeming,Mt** W Australia Australia
25 E6 **Leende** Netherlands
9 E6 **Lee-on-the-Solent** England
110 F4 **Leeper** Missouri U.S.A.
94 H5 **Leeper** Pennsylvania U.S.A.
32 F6 **Leer** Germany
22 G2 **Leerbeek** Belgium
25 D5 **Leerdam** Netherlands
113 F9 **Leesburg** Florida U.S.A.
112 C6 **Leesburg** Georgia U.S.A.
101 L4 **Leesburg** Idaho U.S.A.
94 D7 **Leesburg** Ohio U.S.A.
109 M3 **Leesburg** Texas U.S.A.
94 K7 **Leesburg** Virginia U.S.A.
32 K7 **Leese** Germany
110 B3 **Lees Summit** Missouri U.S.A.
143 D7 **Lee Steere Ra** W Australia Australia
144 D5 **Leeston** New Zealand
109 O4 **Leesville** Louisiana U.S.A.
112 F4 **Leesville** South Carolina U.S.A.
109 K6 **Leesville** Texas U.S.A.
94 H9 **Leesville L.** Virginia U.S.A.
94 F6 **Leesville Res** Ohio U.S.A.
139 H5 **Leeton** New South Wales Australia
94 G6 **Leetonia** Ohio U.S.A.
94 B2 **Leetsville** Michigan U.S.A.
25 E2 **Leeuwarden** Netherlands
143 B10 **Leeuwin,C** W Australia Australia
102 E4 **Lee Vining** California U.S.A.
127 N5 **Leeward Is** W Indies
32 M5 **Leezen** Germany
20 E4 **Leff** *R* France
22 D1 **Leffinge** Belgium
86 C6 **Lefini** *R* Congo
79 C3 **Lefka** Cyprus
79 D4 **Lefkara** Cyprus
79 D3 **Lefkoniko** Cyprus
22 E3 **Leforest** France
71 C3 **Lef Pale** *isld* W Irian
121 L8 **Lefroy** Ontario Canada
143 D9 **Lefroy,L** W Australia Australia
119 T2 **Leftrook L** Manitoba Canada
118 D5 **Legal** Alberta Canada
120 E2 **Legarde** *R* Ontario Canada
121 R6 **Legaré,L** Quebec Canada
71 F4 **Legaspi** Philippines
9 G1 **Legbourne** England
32 F8 **Legden** Germany
20 G8 **Légé** Loire-Atlantique France
142 B5 **Legendre I** W Australia Australia
19 P14 **Le Genevrey** France
Leghorn *see* **Livorno**
31 M3 **Legionowo** Poland
121 T4 **Le Gîte** Quebec Canada
22 K4 **Léglise** Belgium
45 K1 **Legnago** Italy
41 J6 **Legnano** Italy
45 L1 **Legnaro** Italy
31 J4 **Legnica** Poland
41 K5 **Legnone** *mt* Italy
56 B4 **Legostayevo** Russian Federation
48 D4 **Legrad** Croatia
102 D4 **Le Grand** California U.S.A.
143 E10 **Le Grand,C** W Australia Australia
19 O14 **Le Grand Serre** France
20 D4 **Léguer** *R* France
140 A3 **Legune** N Terr Australia
74 G1 **Leh** Kashmir
21 L3 **Le Havre** France
37 L3 **Lehesten** Germany
101 O9 **Lehi** Utah U.S.A.
107 O7 **Lehigh** Oklahoma U.S.A.
109 L1 **Lehigh** Oklahoma U.S.A.
95 M6 **Lehighton** Pennsylvania U.S.A.
48 K6 **Lehliu** Romania
100 G4 **Lehman** Oregon U.S.A.
103 K3 **Lehman Caves Nat. Mon.** Nevada U.S.A.
33 R8 **Lehnin** Germany
20 F5 **Lehon** France
98 G3 **Lehr** North Dakota U.S.A.
37 K5 **Lehrberg** Germany
33 N8 **Lehre** Germany
32 L8 **Lehrte** Germany
33 O6 **Lehsen** Germany
29 K9 **Lehtimäki** Finland
67 E2 **Lehua** China
102 U13 **Lehua I** Hawaiian Is
74 D3 **Leiah** Pakistan
37 O6 **Leiblfing** Germany
38 N8 **Leibnitzer** Austria
67 A2 **Leibo** China
33 T8 **Leibsch** Germany
9 E2 **Leicester** England
9 E2 **Leicestershire** *co* England
140 C5 **Leichardt, Mt** N Terr Australia
140 E4 **Leichhardt** *R* Queensland Australia
140 E4 **Leichhardt Falls** Queensland Australia
141 H5 **Leichhardt Ra** Queensland Australia
36 C1 **Leichlingen** Germany
68 K2 **Lei-chou** China
25 C4 **Leiden** Netherlands
22 E2 **Leie** *R* Belgium
33 M8 **Leiferde** Germany
138 E4 **Leigh** *R* South Australia Australia
9 G5 **Leigh** England
145 E2 **Leigh** New Zealand
138 E4 **Leigh Creek** South Australia Australia
14 E4 **Leighlinbridge** Ireland
110 J7 **Leighton** Alabama U.S.A.
142 A2 **Leighton Beach** *dist* Perth, W Aust Australia
9 F4 **Leighton Buzzard** England
21 L8 **Leigne-sur-Usseau** France
22 J3 **Leignon** Belgium
27 B10 **Leikanger** Norway
68 C3 **Leiktho** Burma
33 O9 **Leimbach** Germany
36 D5 **Leimen** Germany
25 C4 **Leimuiden** Netherlands
37 K2 **Leina** *R* Germany
118 K8 **Leinan** Saskatchewan Canada
32 L8 **Leine** *R* Germany
33 M10 **Leinefelde** Germany
36 G6 **Leinfelden-Echterdingen** Germany
14 D3 **Leinster** *prov* Ireland
14 E4 **Leinster** *mt* Ireland
37 J7 **Leipheim** Germany
26 M4 **Leipojärvi** Sweden
94 D5 **Leipsic** Ohio U.S.A.
118 J6 **Leipzig** Saskatchewan Canada
33 Q10 **Leipzig** Germany
26 G4 **Leiranger** Norway
26 N1 **Leirbotn** Norway
16 B5 **Leiria** Portugal
26 R1 **Leirpollen** Norway
27 A12 **Leirvik** Norway
22 D2 **Leisele** Belgium
67 C3 **Leishan** China
67 D3 **Lei Shui** *R* China
138 B3 **Leisler Hills** South Australia Australia
140 A6 **Leisler,Mt** N Terr Australia
37 O1 **Leisnig** Germany
9 H3 **Leiston** England
110 K4 **Leitchfield** Kentucky U.S.A.
101 T5 **Leiter** Wyoming U.S.A.
13 E2 **Leith** Scotland
98 E3 **Leith** North Dakota U.S.A.
48 C3 **Leitha** *R* Austria
144 D5 **Leithfield** New Zealand
9 F5 **Leith Hill** England
14 C2 **Leitrim** *co* Ireland
33 P8 **Leitzkau** Germany
29 M10 **Leivonmäki** Finland
14 E3 **Leixlip** Ireland
67 D3 **Leiyang** China
Leizhou *see* **Haikang**
67 C6 **Leizhou Bandao** *pen* China
67 C6 **Leizhou Wan** *inlet* China
25 C5 **Lek** *R* Netherlands
26 E6 **Leka** *isld* Norway
46 G3 **Lekáni** Greece
Lekemti *see* **Nek'emtē** Ethiopia
46 E7 **Lekhainá** Greece
46 E4 **Lékhovon** Greece
16 C9 **Lekkous, Oued** *R* Morocco
27 G11 **Leksand** Sweden
29 P8 **Leksozero, Ozero** *L* Russian Federation
26 E8 **Leksvik** Norway
71 B2 **Lelai, Tanjong** *C* Indonesia
127 L4 **Le Lamentin** Martinique W Indies
99 N6 **Leland** Iowa U.S.A.
99 V4 **Leland** Michigan U.S.A.
111 F8 **Leland** Mississippi U.S.A.
27 E12 **Lelången** *L* Sweden
19 Q18 **Le Lavandou** France
133 C6 **Leleque** Argentina
Leli *see* **Tianlin**
108 G1 **Lelia Lake** Texas U.S.A.
48 E7 **Lelija** *mt* Bosnia-Herzegovina
65 D6 **Leling** China
71 C3 **Lelintah** W Irian
28 J6 **Lellinge** Denmark
71 L9 **Lelogama** Timor Indonesia
127 L4 **Le Lorrain** Martinique W Indies
19 Q18 **Le Luc** France
25 D3 **Lelystad** Netherlands
28 A4 **Lem** Denmark
43 F11 **Le Madonie** *mts* Sicily
133 E8 **Le Maire, Estrecho de** *str* Argentina
7 M9 **Leman Bank** *oil rig* North Sea
40 D5 **Léman,Lac** Switz/France
21 L5 **Le Mans** France
94 K7 **Lemasters** Pennsylvania U.S.A.
38 J5 **Lembach** Austria
36 D5 **Lembach** France
70 Q10 **Lembar** Indonesia
71 J4 **Lembeh** *isld* Sulawesi
Lemberg *see* **L'vov**
119 O8 **Lemberg** Saskatchewan Canada
36 C5 **Lemberg** France
36 D5 **Lemberg** Germany
32 H7 **Lembruch** Germany
70 E3 **Lembu** Kalimantan
70 E2 **Lembubut** Kalimantan
69 C10 **Lembu,Gunung** *mt* Sumatra
130 F8 **Leme** São Paulo Brazil
19 N17 **Le Merle** France
71 E4 **Lemery** Philippines
32 H8 **Lemforde** Germany
32 J8 **Lemgo** Germany
101 M5 **Lemhi** Idaho U.S.A.
101 M5 **Lemhi Ra** Idaho U.S.A.
121 S6 **Lemieux** Quebec Canada
115 N5 **Lemieux Is** Northwest Territories Canada
106 D7 **Lemitar** New Mexico U.S.A.
32 K7 **Lemke** Germany
29 M3 **Lemmenjoki** *R* Finland
29 L3 **Lemmenjoki Nat. Park** Finland
25 E3 **Lemmer** Netherlands
28 D4 **Lemming** Denmark
98 D4 **Lemmon** South Dakota U.S.A.
103 O9 **Lemmon, Mt** Arizona U.S.A.
Lemnos *isld* Greece *see* **Límnos** *isld*
126 H5 **Le Môle St. Nicolas** Haiti
111 G9 **Lemon** Mississippi U.S.A.
102 E5 **Lemoore** California U.S.A.
127 L4 **Le Morne Rouge** Martinique W Indies
98 E8 **Lemoyne** Nebraska U.S.A.
125 P11 **Lempa** *R* El Salvador
29 K10 **Lempäälä** Finland
18 H7 **Lempdes** France
117 O9 **Lempriere** British Columbia Canada
118 H8 **Lemsford** Saskatchewan Canada
85 B3 **Lemsid** Western Sahara
43 G7 **Le Murge** *dist* Italy
19 Q18 **Le Muy** France
28 A3 **Lemvig** Denmark
32 J6 **Lemwerder** Germany
68 B4 **Lemyethna** Burma
56 G3 **Lena** *R* Russian Federation
99 R7 **Lena** Illinois U.S.A.
109 P4 **Lena** Louisiana U.S.A.
111 G9 **Lena** Mississippi U.S.A.
100 F4 **Lena** Oregon U.S.A.
99 S5 **Lena** Wisconsin U.S.A.
101 Q9 **Lena, Mt** Utah U.S.A.
71 H9 **Lenangguar** Indonesia
107 P5 **Lenapah** Oklahoma U.S.A.
129 K4 **Lençíos Marahenses, Parque Nacional dos** Brazil
21 L8 **Lencloître** France
38 H7 **Lend** Austria
12 D3 **Lendalfoot** Scotland
29 P8 **Lendery** Russian Federation
45 L1 **Lendinara** Italy
118 K6 **Leney** Saskatchewan Canada
33 M8 **Lengede** Germany
37 P2 **Lengefeld** Germany
32 G8 **Lengerich** Germany
66 E4 **Lenghu** China
58 D4 **Lenglong Ling** *mt ra* China
67 D3 **Lengshuijiang** China
131 B3 **Lengua de Vaca,Pta** Chile
65 E4 **Lengzipu** China
9 G5 **Lenham** England
27 H15 **Lenhovda** Sweden
70 D5 **Lenili** Kalimantan
Leninabad Tajikistan *see* **Khodzhent**
57 A3 **Leninabad** Uzbekistan
78 J1 **Leninakan** Armenia
57 G5 **Lenina, Pik** *mt* Tajikistan
36 B6 **Léning** France
Leningrad *see* **Sankt-Peterburg**
52 D5 **Leningradskaya Oblast'** *prov* Russian Federation
Lenin I.V. Kanal *see* **Volgo-Balt**
56 B5 **Leninogorsk** Kazakhstan

55 C4 **Leninsk** Chelyabinskaya obl Russian Federation
57 A4 **Leninsk** Turkmenistan
55 G5 **Leninskiy** Kazakhstan
52 G6 **Leninskiy** Mariyskaya Respublika Russian Federation
54 J2 **Leninskiy** Tul'skaya obl Russian Federation
56 B4 **Leninsk-Kuznetskiy** Russian Federation
55 E4 **Leninskoye** Kazakhstan
57 G4 **Leninskoye** Kirghizia
52 G5 **Leninskoye** Kirovskaya obl Russian Federation
48 G3 **Leninváros** Hungary
88 B9 **Lenje** Zambia
55 H4 **Len'ki** Russian Federation
142 E3 **Lennard,R** W Australia Australia
27 E12 **Lennartsfors** Sweden
36 E1 **Lenne** *R* Germany
101 P3 **Lennep** Montana U.S.A.
36 E1 **Lennestadt** Germany
143 F7 **Lennis Hills** W Australia Australia
98 K6 **Lennox** South Dakota U.S.A.
133 D9 **Lennox, I** Chile/Arg
12 D2 **Lennoxtown** Scotland
121 T7 **Lennoxville** Quebec Canada
56 F4 **Leno-Angarskoye Plato** *plateau* Russian Federation
112 F2 **Lenoir** North Carolina U.S.A.
112 C2 **Lenoir City** Tennessee U.S.A.
107 K2 **Lenora** Kansas U.S.A.
119 R9 **Lenore** Manitoba Canada
119 M6 **Lenore L** Saskatchewan Canada
100 F2 **Lenore, L** Washington U.S.A.
112 D6 **Lenox** Georgia U.S.A.
99 M9 **Lenox** Iowa U.S.A.
95 O4 **Lenox** Massachusetts U.S.A.
22 F2 **Lens** Belgium
22 D3 **Lens** France
33 N4 **Lensahn** Germany
26 D8 **Lensvik** Norway
25 E5 **Lent** Netherlands
37 L6 **Lenting** Germany
43 F11 **Lentini** Sicily
29 O7 **Lentüra** Finland
26 K2 **Lenvik** Norway
68 D7 **Lenya** Burma
33 O6 **Lenzen** Germany
12 D2 **Lenzie** Scotland
85 D6 **Léo** Burkina
38 M7 **Leoben** Austria
127 H5 **Léogane** Haiti
38 G7 **Leogang** Austria
38 G7 **Leoganger** Austria
70 G4 **Leok** Sulawesi Indonesia
8 D3 **Leominster** England
95 Q4 **Leominster** Massachusetts U.S.A.
18 E9 **Léon** France
20 A5 **Léon** *reg* France
124 J7 **Leon** Mexico
125 L3 **León** Nicaragua
16 D2 **León** *prov* Spain
16 D2 **León** Spain
99 N9 **Leon** Iowa U.S.A.
107 O4 **Leon** Kansas U.S.A.
94 F8 **Leon** West Virginia U.S.A.
109 M4 **Leona** Texas U.S.A.
109 H7 **Leona** *R* Texas U.S.A.
94 D4 **Leonard** Michigan U.S.A.
99 O10 **Leonard** Missouri U.S.A.
98 J3 **Leonard** North Dakota U.S.A.
109 L2 **Leonard** Texas U.S.A.
89 A4 **Leonardville** Namibia
107 O2 **Leonardville** Kansas U.S.A.
79 E3 **Leonarisso** Cyprus
36 G6 **Leonberg** Germany
36 F5 **Leonbronn** Germany
19 O15 **Léoncel** France
131 B2 **Leoncito,L** Argentina
128 F8 **Leon,Co** *mt* Paraguay
108 E4 **Leon Cr** Texas U.S.A.
46 E5 **Leondári** Greece
139 H7 **Leongatha** Victoria Australia
46 F7 **Leonídhion** Greece
16 C2 **León, Montañas de** *mts* Spain
143 D8 **Leonora** W Australia Australia
109 J6 **Leon Springs** Texas U.S.A.
116 F9 **Leontovitch,C** Alaska U.S.A.
142 F4 **Leopold Downs** W Australia Australia
130 G7 **Leopoldina** Brazil
129 J7 **Leopoldo de Bulhões** Brazil
22 J1 **Leopoldsburg** Belgium
33 T5 **Leopoldshagen** Germany
40 G1 **Leopoldskan** *canal* Germany
Leopoldville *see* **Kinshasa**
107 J3 **Leoti** Kansas U.S.A.
118 K5 **Leoville** Saskatchewan Canada
48 L4 **Leovo** Moldova
125 M5 **Lepanto** Costa Rica
110 F6 **Lepanto** Arkansas U.S.A.
69 H14 **Lepar** *isld* Indonesia
125 L2 **Lepaterique** Honduras
87 E10 **Lephepe** Botswana
67 F2 **Leping** China
45 O6 **Lepini, Mti** *mts* Italy
121 R7 **L'Epiphanie** Quebec Canada
55 D1 **Leplya** *R* Russian Federation
71 H7 **Lepolepo** Sulawesi
42 B2 **Lepontine,Alpi** *mts* Italy
70 G7 **Leppangeng** Sulawesi
29 N9 **Leppävirta** Finland
145 E3 **Lepperton** New Zealand
122 F8 **Lepreau** New Brunswick Canada
122 F8 **Lepreau, Pt** New Brunswick Canada
57 J2 **Lepsa** *R* Kazakhstan
48 E4 **Lepsény** Hungary
57 K2 **Lepsinsk** Kazakhstan
57 J2 **Lepsy** Kazakhstan
19 O17 **Le Puy Ste Réparade** France
95 L5 **Le Raysville** Pennsylvania U.S.A.
33 M9 **Lerbach** Germany
29 K4 **Lerberget** Sweden
28 D4 **Lerbjerg** Denmark
43 F11 **Lercara Friddi** Sicily
86 B4 **Léré** Chad
70 F5 **Lereh, Tanjong** *C* Sulawesi
121 T5 **Le Relais** Quebec Canada
29 K4 **Lerhamn** Sweden
141 G5 **Lerida** Queensland Australia
128 D3 **Lérida** Colombia
17 H3 **Lérida** *prov* Spain
17 H3 **Lérida** Spain
28 C3 **Lerkenfeld Å** *R* Denmark
16 E2 **Lerma** Spain
53 F11 **Lermontov** Russian Federation
41 N3 **Lermoos** Austria
99 S10 **Lerna** Illinois U.S.A.
21 L7 **Lerné** France
127 L4 **Le Robert** Martinique W Indies
47 H7 **Léros** *isld* Greece
119 O7 **Leross** Saskatchewan , Canada
19 J4 **Lérouville** France
119 N7 **Leroy** Saskatchewan Canada
99 S9 **Le Roy** Illinois U.S.A.
99 N9 **Le Roy** Iowa U.S.A.
107 P3 **Le Roy** Kansas U.S.A.
94 B2 **Le Roy** Michigan U.S.A.
99 O6 **Le Roy** Minnesota U.S.A.
94 J4 **Leroy** New York U.S.A.
101 P8 **Le Roy** Wyoming U.S.A.
40 D1 **Lerrain** France
27 F14 **Lerum** Sweden
15 G2 **Lerwick** Scotland
21 N3 **Léry** France
111 G12 **Lery,L** Louisiana U.S.A.
48 G4 **Leş** Romania
41 J6 **Lesa** Italy
19 P13 **Les Abrets** France
38 G8 **Lesach Tal** *V* Austria
38 G8 **Lesachtal** Austria
19 N18 **Le Salin de Giraud** France
19 P13 **Les Avenières** France
19 N17 **Les Baux** France
Lesbos *isld see* **Lésvos** *isld*
13 G3 **Lesbury** England
83 M13 **L'Escalier** Mauritius
18 E9 **Lescar** France
126 H5 **Les Cayes** Haiti
143 B9 **Leschenault, C** W Australia Australia
122 B6 **Les Éboulements** Quebec Canada
19 P14 **Les Echelles** France
122 C5 **Les Escoumins** Quebec Canada
122 D6 **Les Étroits** Quebec Canada
67 A2 **Leshan** China
20 E3 **Les Hanois Lt.Ho** English Chan
40 G5 **Les Haudères** Switzerland
52 G3 **Leshukonskoye** Russian Federation
69 C11 **Lesikin** Indonesia
44 F2 **Lésima** *mt* Italy
42 G7 **Lesina,L.di** Italy
26 C9 **Lesja** Norway
26 C9 **Lesjaskog** Norway
26 C9 **Lesjaskogsvatn** *L* Norway
27 G12 **Lesjöfors** Sweden
31 N6 **Lesko** Poland
46 E1 **Leskovac** Serbia Yugoslavia
146 G2 **Leskov I** S Sandwich Is S Atlantic Oc
46 D4 **Leskovik** Albania
13 E1 **Leslie** Scotland
110 D6 **Leslie** Arkansas U.S.A.
112 C6 **Leslie** Georgia U.S.A.
101 M6 **Leslie** Idaho U.S.A.
94 C4 **Leslie** Michigan U.S.A.
119 O7 **Leslie Stn** Saskatchewan Canada
118 C6 **Leslieville** Alberta Canada
12 E2 **Lesmahagow** Scotland
127 N4 **Les Mangles** Guadeloupe
19 P16 **Les Mées** France
19 Q16 **Les Monges** *mt* France
31 O3 **Lesnaya** *R* Belarus
20 B4 **Lesneven** France
48 E6 **Lešnica** Serbia Yugoslavia
55 E3 **Lesnoy** Russian Federation
52 D2 **Lesnoy** Murmanskaya obl Russian Federation
52 E5 **Lesnoye** Russian Federation
59 M2 **Lesogorsk** Russian Federation
52 C4 **Lesogorskiy** Russian Federation
56 D2 **Lesosibirsk** Russian Federation
89 E7 **Lesotho** *kingdom* Africa
65 J2 **Lesozavodsk** Russian Federation
18 E7 **Lesparre-Medoc** France
19 O18 **Les-Pennes-Mirabeau** France
83 K12 **L'Espérance** Mahé I Indian Oc
22 F4 **Lesquielles-St Germain** France
38 J7 **Lessach** Austria
127 N5 **Les Saintes** *islds* Guadeloupe W Indies
20 G3 **Lessay** France
22 J3 **Lesse** *R* Belgium
32 M8 **Lesse** Germany
27 H15 **Lessebo** Sweden
127 N6 **Lesser Antilles** *islds* W Indies
Lesser Khingan Range *see* **Xiao Hinggan Ling**
117 Q8 **Lesser Slave L** Alberta Canada
118 C3 **Lesser Slave R** Alberta Canada
22 F2 **Lessines** Belgium
41 O6 **Lessini** *mt* Italy
40 G7 **Lessolo** Italy
98 K6 **Lester** Iowa U.S.A.
98 H9 **Lester** Nebraska U.S.A.
94 F9 **Lester** West Virginia U.S.A.
99 M5 **Lester Prairie** Minnesota U.S.A.
98 J6 **Lesterville** South Dakota U.S.A.
29 L8 **Lestijärvi** Finland
119 N7 **Lestock** Saskatchewan Canada
127 L4 **Les Trois Îlets** Martinique W Indies
99 N5 **Le Sueur** Minnesota U.S.A.
142 F2 **Lesueur I** W Australia Australia
143 B9 **Lesueur, Mt** W Australia Australia
70 D4 **Lesung, Bt** *mt* Kalimantan
47 H5 **Lésvos** *isld* Greece
12 C4 **Leswalt** Scotland
31 K4 **Leszno** Poland
89 G4 **Letaba** *R* S Africa
111 K9 **Letchatchee** Alabama U.S.A.
98 H6 **Letcher** South Dakota U.S.A.
9 F4 **Letchworth** England
119 U9 **Letellier** Manitoba Canada
100 J6 **Letha** Idaho U.S.A.
118 E9 **Lethbridge** Alberta Canada
123 T5 **Lethbridge** Newfoundland Canada
71 N9 **Leti** *isld* Indonesia
48 L1 **Letichev** Ukraine
128 E4 **Leticia** Colombia
71 N9 **Leti, Kepulauan** *islds* Indonesia
65 D5 **Leting** China
37 P4 **Letiny** Czech Rep
52 G5 **Letka** *R* Russian Federation
32 G10 **Letmathe** Germany
52 D3 **Letnerechenskiy** Russian Federation
46 G1 **Letnitsa** Bulgaria
52 D2 **Letnyaya-Reka** Russian Federation
52 E3 **Letnyaya Zolotitsa** Russian Federation
38 F8 **Le Tofane** *mt* Italy
19 P14 **Le Touvet** France
68 B4 **Letpadan** Burma
139 G5 **Lette** New South Wales Australia
14 D2 **Letterkenny** Ireland
8 B4 **Letterston** Wales
94 B7 **Letts** Indiana U.S.A.
69 G11 **Letung** Indonesia
17 F6 **Letur** Spain
33 O8 **Letzlingen** Germany
48 J6 **Leu** Romania
87 D8 **Leua** Angola
37 N2 **Leubnitz** Germany
18 H10 **Leucate** France
15 F4 **Leuchars** Scotland
37 N4 **Leuchtenberg** Germany
37 M2 **Leuchtenburg** Germany
102 G8 **Leucidia** California U.S.A.
22 G3 **Leugnies** France
20 C5 **Leuhan** France
40 G5 **Leuk** Switzerland
40 G5 **Leukerbad** Switzerland
36 E2 **Leun** Germany
33 Q10 **Leuna** Germany
37 M3 **Leupoldsdorf** Germany
69 B10 **Leupung** Sumatra
141 J6 **Leura** Queensland Australia
69 C11 **Leuser,Gunung** *mt* Sumatra
48 L4 **Leusheny** Moldova
55 E2 **Leushi** Russian Federation
55 E2 **Leushinskiy Tuman, Oz** *L* Russian Federation
33 O6 **Leussow** Germany
41 O3 **Leutasch** Austria
37 L2 **Leutenberg** Germany
37 J5 **Leutershausen** Germany
41 M2 **Leutkirch** Germany
38 M8 **Leutschach** Austria
22 H2 **Leuven** Belgium
22 F2 **Leuze** Belgium
120 J6 **Levack** Ontario Canada
46 F6 **Levádhia** Greece
19 Q18 **Le Val** France
46 C4 **Levan** Albania
103 N2 **Levan** Utah U.S.A.
26 E8 **Levanger** Norway
44 B1 **Levanna** *mt* Italy
40 F7 **Levanna, M** Italy
107 J2 **Levant** Kansas U.S.A.
19 Q18 **Levant,I.du** France
44 F3 **Levanto** Italy
43 E10 **Levanzo, I. di** Sicily
21 J5 **Levare** France
127 M4 **Le Vauclin** Martinique W Indies
55 E1 **Levdym** Russian Federation
108 E2 **Levelland** Texas U.S.A.
144 C6 **Levels** New Zealand
13 H6 **Leven** England
13 E1 **Leven** Scotland
41 J5 **Leventina, Valle** Switzerland
142 E3 **Lévêque,C** W Australia Australia
98 B6 **Leverett** Wyoming U.S.A.
36 B1 **Leverkusen** Germany
117 P3 **Lever L** Northwest Territories Canada
32 H8 **Levern** Germany
9 F4 **Leverstock Green** England
21 N5 **Lèves** France
48 E2 **Levice** Slovakia
41 O5 **Levico** Italy
55 C2 **Levikha** Russian Federation
145 E4 **Levin** New Zealand
52 F5 **Levinskoye** Russian Federation
140 B6 **Levi Ra** N Terr Australia
121 T6 **Lévis** Quebec Canada
94 E9 **Levisa Fork** *R* Kentucky U.S.A.
47 H7 **Levítha** *isld* Greece
95 N6 **Levittown** Pennsylvania U.S.A.
46 G9 **Lévka Óri** *mt* Crete Greece
46 F9 **Lévka Óri National Park** Crete Greece
46 D6 **Levkás** *isld* Greece
47 P13 **Levkimmi** Greece
31 M6 **Levoča** Slovakia
85 A4 **Lévrier,B.du** Mauritania
28 C4 **Levring** Denmark
21 O8 **Levroux** France
46 G1 **Levski** Bulgaria
106 F5 **Levy** New Mexico U.S.A.
20 H2 **Levy,C** France
113 E8 **Levy,L** Florida U.S.A.
71 J9 **Lewa** Indonesia
98 F7 **Lewanna** Nebraska U.S.A.
68 C3 **Lewe** Burma
98 D8 **Lewellen** Nebraska U.S.A.
9 F6 **Lewes** England
142 D5 **Lewin,Mt** W Australia Australia
15 B2 **Lewis** *dist* Scotland
99 L8 **Lewis** Iowa U.S.A.
94 K6 **Lewis** Pennsylvania U.S.A.
100 D3 **Lewis** *R* Washington U.S.A.
98 J7 **Lewis and Clark L** South Dakota U.S.A.
138 D3 **Lewis B** South Australia Australia
110 K5 **Lewisburg** Kentucky U.S.A.
94 C7 **Lewisburg** Ohio U.S.A.
95 K6 **Lewisburg** Pennsylvania U.S.A.
110 K6 **Lewisburg** Tennessee U.S.A.
94 G9 **Lewisburg** West Virginia U.S.A.
123 O5 **Lewis Hills** Newfoundland Canada
68 A6 **Lewis Inlet** Andaman Is
101 P5 **Lewis L** Wyoming U.S.A.
144 D5 **Lewis Pass** New Zealand
123 R4 **Lewisporte** Newfoundland Canada
142 G5 **Lewis Ra** W Australia Australia
101 M1 **Lewis Ra** Montana U.S.A.
94 J5 **Lewis Run** Pennsylvania U.S.A.
103 O10 **Lewis Sps** Arizona U.S.A.
100 J3 **Lewiston** Idaho U.S.A.
95 R2 **Lewiston** Maine U.S.A.
94 C2 **Lewiston** Michigan U.S.A.
110 E1 **Lewiston** Missouri U.S.A.
94 J3 **Lewiston** New York U.S.A.
112 K1 **Lewiston** North Carolina U.S.A.
101 O8 **Lewiston** Utah U.S.A.
99 Q9 **Lewistown** Illinois U.S.A.
101 Q2 **Lewistown** Montana U.S.A.
111 C8 **Lewisville** Arkansas U.S.A.
101 N6 **Lewisville** Idaho U.S.A.
99 M6 **Lewisville** Minnesota U.S.A.
94 K5 **Lewisville** Pennsylvania U.S.A.
109 L2 **Lewisville** Texas U.S.A.
109 L2 **Lewisville, L** Texas U.S.A.
33 P6 **Lewitz** Germany
71 L9 **Lewoleba** Indonesia
71 L9 **Lewotobi** *mt* Flores Indonesia
119 N8 **Lewvan** Saskatchewan Canada
111 F7 **Lexa** Arkansas U.S.A.
99 S9 **Lexington** Illinois U.S.A.
94 B8 **Lexington** Indiana U.S.A.
94 C8 **Lexington** Kentucky U.S.A.
94 E3 **Lexington** Michigan U.S.A.
111 F8 **Lexington** Mississippi U.S.A.
110 C2 **Lexington** Missouri U.S.A.
98 G9 **Lexington** Nebraska U.S.A.
112 G2 **Lexington** North Carolina U.S.A.
109 K1 **Lexington** Oklahoma U.S.A.
100 F4 **Lexington** Oregon U.S.A.
112 F4 **Lexington** South Carolina U.S.A.
110 H6 **Lexington** Tennessee U.S.A.
109 K5 **Lexington** Texas U.S.A.
94 H9 **Lexington** Virginia U.S.A.
95 L8 **Lexington Park** Maryland U.S.A.
98 J1 **Leyden** North Dakota U.S.A.
95 M3 **Leyden,W** New York U.S.A.
67 B4 **Leye** China
83 L13 **Leygues** Kerguelen Indian Oc
13 F6 **Leyland** England
18 E8 **Leyre** *R* France
9 G5 **Leysdown** England
71 G5 **Leyte** *isld* Philippines
71 G5 **Leyte Gulf** Philippines
19 N16 **Lez** *R* France
31 N5 **Leżajsk** Poland
20 D4 **Lèzardrieux** France
18 E6 **Lezay** France
52 F5 **Lezha** Russian Federation
46 D3 **Lezhë** Albania
67 B1 **Lezhi** China
52 F6 **Lezhnevo** Russian Federation
18 G9 **Lézignan** France
18 H7 **Lezoux** France
17 F6 **Lezuza** Spain
99 R3 **L. Gogebic** Michigan U.S.A.
54 G5 **L'gov** Russian Federation
54 G5 **L'govskiy** Russian Federation
66 E5 **Lhari** China
143 A7 **Lharidon Bight** W Australia Australia
Lhariguo *see* **Lhari**
66 E6 **Lhasa** China
Lhatse Dzong *see* **Lhazê**
66 D6 **Lhazê** China
Lho Dzong *see* **Lhorong**
69 B10 **Lhokkreut** Sumatra
69 C10 **Lhokseumawe** Sumatra
69 C10 **Lhoksukon** Sumatra
66 F5 **Lhorong** China
Liancheng *see* **Qinglong**
67 E4 **Liancheng** China
21 P3 **Liancourt** France
Liancourt Rocks *see* **Tok-to**
22 B2 **Liane** *R* France
71 H5 **Liang** Indonesia
71 G6 **Lianga** Mindanao Philippines
65 B4 **Liangcheng** China
65 D7 **Liangcheng** China
58 E5 **Liangdang** China
67 C2 **Lianghekou** China
Liangjiayoufang *see* **Youyu**
71 E8 **Liang Liang** Philippines
67 B1 **Liangping** China
70 D4 **Liangpran, Bukit** *mt* Kalimantan
Liangshizhen *see* **Shaodong**
67 D4 **Liangtan** China
69 E11 **Liang Timur, Gunung** *mt* Malaysia
67 A4 **Liangwang Shan** *mts* China
67 E1 **Liangzi Hu** *L* China
67 D3 **Lianhua** China
67 E5 **Lianhua Shan** *mts* China
67 F3 **Lianjiang** China
67 B4 **Lian Jiang** *R* China
68 K2 **Lianjiang** China
65 H1 **Lianjiangkou** China
67 D4 **Liannan** China
67 E4 **Lianping** China
67 D4 **Lianshan** China
65 F4 **Lianshanguan** China
67 D3 **Lian Shui** *R* Hunan China
68 E6 **Liant** *C* Thailand
67 D5 **Liantan** China
Liantang *see* **Nanchang**
67 D1 **Liantuo** China
67 D4 **Lian Xian** China
67 D3 **Lianyuan** China
65 D7 **Lianyungang** China
Lianzhou *see* **Lian Xian**
Lianzhou *see* **Hepu**
65 H2 **Lianzhushan** China
58 G4 **Liaocheng** China
59 H4 **Liaodong** *pen* China
59 H3 **Liaodong Wan** *B* China
59 H3 **Liao He** *R* China
65 E4 **Liaoning** *prov* China
Liaotung *pen see* **Liaodong** *pen*
Liaotung, Gulf of *see* **Liaodong Wan**
59 H3 **Liaoyang** China
65 F3 **Liaoyangwopu** China
59 J3 **Liaoyuan** China
65 E4 **Liaozhong** China
47 O12 **Liapádhes** Greece
117 M5 **Liard** *R* Br Col/N W Terr Canada
117 J5 **Liard** *R* Yukon Territory Canada
117 M5 **Liard Ra** Northwest Territories Canada
117 K6 **Liard River** British Columbia Canada
77 K7 **Liari** Pakistan
22 G4 **Liart** France
69 H14 **Liat** *isld* Indonesia
79 F5 **Liban, Jebel** *mts* Lebanon
117 Q11 **Libby** Idaho U.S.A.
100 K1 **Libby** Montana U.S.A.
86 C5 **Libenge** Zaire
107 K4 **Liberal** Kansas U.S.A.
110 B4 **Liberal** Missouri U.S.A.
116 H2 **Liberator L** Alaska U.S.A.
129 H6 **Liberdade** *R* Brazil
130 G8 **Liberdade** Brazil
31 J5 **Liberec** Czech Rep
85 C7 **Liberia** *rep* W Africa
127 P4 **Liberta** Antigua W Indies
128 C5 **Libertad** *dept* Peru
127 K10 **Libertad** Venezuela
133 E2 **Libertador Gen. San Martín** Argentina
124 C3 **Libertad,Pto** Mexico
13 E2 **Liberton** Scotland
116 R4 **Liberty** Alaska U.S.A.
110 E2 **Liberty** Illinois U.S.A.
94 B7 **Liberty** Indiana U.S.A.
110 M4 **Liberty** Kentucky U.S.A.
111 F10 **Liberty** Mississippi U.S.A.
110 B2 **Liberty** Missouri U.S.A.
98 K9 **Liberty** Nebraska U.S.A.
95 N5 **Liberty** New York U.S.A.
112 H2 **Liberty** North Carolina U.S.A.
95 K5 **Liberty** Pennsylvania U.S.A.
109 N5 **Liberty** Texas U.S.A.
100 E2 **Liberty** Washington U.S.A.
94 C5 **Liberty Center** Ohio U.S.A.
112 G3 **Liberty Hill** South Carolina U.S.A.
109 K5 **Liberty Hill** Texas U.S.A.
95 K7 **Libertytown** Maryland U.S.A.
99 T7 **Libertyville** Illinois U.S.A.
99 O9 **Libertyville** Iowa U.S.A.
22 J4 **Libin** Belgium
37 Q4 **Liblín** Czech Rep
71 F4 **Libmanan** Philippines
67 B4 **Libo** China
71 B3 **Libobo, Tg** *C* Indonesia
46 D4 **Libohovë** Albania
69 D9 **Libong,Ko** *isld* Thailand
86 B5 **Liboumba** *R* Gabon
18 E8 **Libourne** France
22 J4 **Libramont** Belgium
46 D3 **Librazhd** Albania
131 F2 **Libres,P.de los** Argentina
86 A5 **Libreville** Gabon
71 G7 **Libuganon** *R* Mindanao Philippines
84 F4 **Libya** *rep* Africa
84 G4 **Libyan Desert** Libya
84 H3 **Libyan Plateau** Egypt
47 N11 **Libyssa** *hist site* Turkey
43 F11 **Licata** Sicily
36 F2 **Lich** Germany
65 B6 **Licheng** China
65 C6 **Licheng** China
9 E2 **Lichfield** England
145 E3 **Lichfield** New Zealand
88 E8 **Lichinga** Mozambique
36 E6 **Lichtenau** Baden-Württemberg Germany
32 J9 **Lichtenau** Nordrhein-Westfalen Germany
37 P2 **Lichtenberg** Germany
37 M3 **Lichtenberg** Germany
89 E6 **Lichtenburg** S Africa
36 G7 **Lichtenstein** Germany
37 O2 **Lichtenstein** Germany
37 N2 **Lichtentanne** Germany
36 E6 **Lichtenthal** Germany
25 G5 **Lichtenvoorde** Netherlands
33 S8 **Lichterfelde** Germany
22 E1 **Lichtervelde** Belgium
67 C1 **Lichuan** China
67 E3 **Lichuan** China
110 E4 **Licking** Missouri U.S.A.
94 D8 **Licking R** Kentucky U.S.A.
42 G4 **Ličko Petrovo Selo** Bosnia-Herzegovina
43 F8 **Licosa,P** Italy
22 B2 **Licques** France
53 C7 **Lida** Belarus
102 G4 **Lida** Nevada U.S.A.
65 E6 **Lidao** China
99 M7 **Lidderdale** Iowa U.S.A.
15 F5 **Liddesdale Valley** Scotland
26 L7 **Liden** Sweden
26 J9 **Liden** Sweden
98 J3 **Lidgerwood** North Dakota U.S.A.
27 F15 **Lidhult** Sweden
27 K12 **Lidingo** Sweden
27 F13 **Lidköping** Sweden
26 M3 **Lidnatjärro** *mt* Sweden
45 M1 **Lido** Italy
42 E7 **Lido di Ostia** Italy
31 M2 **Lidzbark** Poland
31 M1 **Lidzbark Warmiński** Poland
20 E5 **Lié** *R* France
32 K9 **Liebenau** Hessen Germany
32 K7 **Liebenau** Niedersachsen Germany
37 M2 **Liebengrün** Germany
118 H8 **Liebenthal** Saskatchewan Canada
33 S7 **Liebenwalde** Germany
33 S9 **Liebenwerda** Germany
140 B6 **Liebig, Mt** N Terr Australia
144 C5 **Liebig Range** New Zealand
48 G5 **Liebling** Romania
41 L3 **Liechtenstein** *princ* Europe
26 M3 **Liedakka** Sweden
22 K2 **Liège** Belgium
21 N7 **Liège, le** France
29 P8 **Lieksa** Finland
32 G8 **Lienen** Germany
Lienyünkang *see* **Lianyungang**
27 M15 **Liepāja** Latvia
33 S5 **Liepen** Germany
36 C7 **Liepvre** France
22 H1 **Lier** Belgium
27 E11 **Lier** Norway
22 K3 **Lierneux** Belgium
22 K2 **Liers** Belgium
21 O3 **Lierville** France
36 D3 **Liesenfeld** Germany
38 J8 **Lieser** *R* Austria
36 B3 **Lieser** *R* Germany
29 K11 **Liesjärvi Nat. Park** Finland
22 F4 **Liesse** France
25 E6 **Liessel** Netherlands
40 G3 **Liestal** Switzerland
48 L5 **Lieşti** Romania
21 M3 **Lieurey** France
21 L3 **Lieuvin** France
22 D3 **Liévin** France
121 P7 **Lièvre** *R* Quebec Canada
122 B6 **Lievres, I. aux** Quebec Canada
38 K6 **Liezen** Austria
71 M9 **Lifan** Indonesia
14 E3 **Liffey** *R* Ireland
19 J4 **Liffol le Grand** France
14 D2 **Lifford** Ireland
20 H5 **Liffre** France
78 J6 **Lifiyah, Al** Saudi Arabia
137 O6 **Lifu** Îles Loyauté Pacific Oc
133 D6 **Lifue Mahuida** *mt* Argentina
45 Q8 **Li Galli** Italy
71 F4 **Ligao** Philippines
Ligen-i Shkodrës *see* **Skadarsko Jez**
65 B7 **Ligeta** China
65 E6 **Ligezhuang** China
26 L5 **Ligga** Sweden
8 A7 **Ligger Bay** England
109 H7 **Light** Texas U.S.A.
143 E8 **Lightfoot L** W Australia Australia
113 C8 **Lighthouse Pt** Florida U.S.A.
142 F4 **Lightjack Hill** W Australia Australia
119 N2 **Light L** Ontario Canada
139 J3 **Lightning Rdg** New South Wales Australia
20 H7 **Ligne** France
21 K4 **Lignieres** France
21 P8 **Lignières** France
21 K4 **Lignières-Orgères** France
98 D1 **Lignite** North Dakota U.S.A.
20 D5 **Lignol** France
94 K8 **Lignum** Virginia U.S.A.
22 H3 **Ligny** Belgium
19 J4 **Ligny en Barrois** France
21 O6 **Ligny-le-Ribault** France
45 H3 **Ligonchio** Italy
88 G9 **Ligonha** *R* Mozambique
94 B5 **Ligonier** Indiana U.S.A.
94 H6 **Ligonier** Pennsylvania U.S.A.
46 F7 **Ligoúrion** Greece
65 D7 **Ligouyi** China
131 B4 **Ligua,B de la** Chile
21 M7 **Ligueil** France
124 D5 **Ligui** Mexico
44 F2 **Ligure** *reg* Italy
44 D3 **Ligure** Italy
44 E4 **Ligurian Sea** Italy
103 K9 **Ligurta** Arizona U.S.A.
137 L2 **Lihir Group** Bismarck Arch
28 B3 **Lihme** Denmark
22 D4 **Lihons** France
141 K3 **Lihou Reef** Coral Sea
141 K3 **Lihou Reef & Cays** Gt Barrier Reef Aust
102 V13 **Lihue** Hawaiian Is
52 B5 **Lihula** Estonia
52 D1 **Liinakhamari** Russian Federation
65 D6 **Lijin** China
68 F3 **Lik** *R* Laos
86 D5 **Likati** Zaire
117 N9 **Likely** British Columbia Canada
100 E8 **Likely** California U.S.A.
52 E6 **Likhoslavl'** Russian Federation
54 M8 **Likhovskoy** Russian Federation
54 K1 **Likino-Dulevo** Russian Federation
71 M9 **Likisia** Timor
46 D3 **Likmetaj** Albania
86 C6 **Likouala** *R* Congo
69 J12 **Liku** Indonesia
70 D2 **Liku** Sarawak
71 J4 **Likupang** Sulawesi
110 G5 **Lilbourn** Missouri U.S.A.
28 B2 **Lildstrand** Denmark
143 F8 **Lilian, Pt** W Australia Australia
38 N5 **Lilienfeld** Austria
32 J6 **Lilienthal** Germany
67 D3 **Liling** China
22 H1 **Lille** Belgium
22 E2 **Lille** France
28 B4 **Lilleå** *R* Denmark
28 D6 **Lille Bælt** *chan* Denmark
21 M2 **Lillebonne** France
27 D10 **Lillehammer** Norway
22 C2 **Lillers** France
27 C13 **Lillesand** Norway
27 E12 **Lilleström** Norway
28 E3 **Lille Vildmose** Denmark
26 G10 **Lillhärdal** Sweden
26 G8 **Lillholmsjön** Sweden
26 K6 **Lillholmträsk** Sweden
123 L2 **Lillian L** Quebec Canada
109 P3 **Lillie** Louisiana U.S.A.
13 F3 **Lilliesleaf** Scotland
112 J2 **Lillington** North Carolina U.S.A.
107 O2 **Lillis** Kansas U.S.A.
22 G1 **Lillo** Belgium
16 E5 **Lillo** Spain
117 M10 **Lillooet** *R* British Columbia Canada
117 N10 **Lillooet** British Columbia Canada
94 J6 **Lilly** Pennsylvania U.S.A.
88 D8 **Lilongwe** Malawi
88 E8 **Lilongwe** *R* Malawi
71 F6 **Liloy** Mindanao Philippines
98 J4 **Lily** South Dakota U.S.A.
138 F5 **Lilydale** South Australia Australia
139 H8 **Lilydale** Tasmania Australia
48 F7 **Lim** *R* Serbia Yugoslavia
130 C8 **Lima** Paraguay
128 C6 **Lima** Peru
16 B3 **Lima** *R* Portugal
27 F11 **Lima** Sweden
99 P9 **Lima** Illinois U.S.A.
101 N5 **Lima** Montana U.S.A.
94 K4 **Lima** New York U.S.A.
94 C6 **Lima** Ohio U.S.A.
133 C4 **Limache** Chile
130 G7 **Lima Duarte** Brazil
80 D1 **Liman** Israel
70 N9 **Liman, G** *mt* Java
48 F1 **Limanowa** Poland
71 N8 **Limar** Indonesia
133 C4 **Limari** *R* Chile
131 B3 **Limari,R** Chile
69 G12 **Limas** Indonesia
79 E2 **Limas** *R* Turkey
71 G6 **Limasawa** *isld* Philippines
79 D4 **Limassol** Cyprus
14 E1 **Limavady** N Ireland
21 O4 **Limay** France
133 D5 **Limay Mahuida** Argentina
131 C7 **Limay,R** Argentina
36 C5 **Limbach** Germany
37 O2 **Limbach** Germany
37 O2 **Limbach-Oberfrohna** Germany
70 D2 **Limbang** *R* Sarawak
43 C8 **Limbara, Monte** *mt* Sardinia
52 B6 **Limbaži** Latvia
85 F8 **Limbe** Cameroon
127 H5 **Limbé** Haiti
88 E9 **Limbe** Malawi
71 H4 **Limboto** Sulawesi
71 H4 **Limboto, Danau** *L* Sulawesi
22 K2 **Limbourg** Belgium
70 F7 **Limbung** Sulawesi
70 D6 **Limbungan** Kalimantan
140 A3 **Limbunya** N Terr Australia
57 J6 **Limbur** Uzbekistan
22 J2 **Limburg** *prov* Belgium
36 E3 **Limburg** Germany
25 E6 **Limburg** *prov* Netherlands
144 B7 **Limchills** New Zealand
100 H5 **Lime** Oregon U.S.A.
27 F11 **Limedsforsen** Sweden
116 K6 **Lime Hills** Alaska U.S.A.
130 F8 **Limeira** Brazil
45 L1 **Limena** Italy
46 G4 **Limenária** Greece
47 H7 **Limén Vathéos** Greece
118 L9 **Limerick** Saskatchewan Canada
14 C4 **Limerick** *co* Ireland
14 C4 **Limerick** Ireland
95 R3 **Limerick** Maine U.S.A.
20 F6 **Limerzel** France
22 J4 **Limes** Belgium
99 O6 **Lime Springs** Iowa U.S.A.
113 F10 **Limestone** Florida U.S.A.
95 T7 **Limestone** Maine U.S.A.
94 J4 **Limestone** New York U.S.A.
119 W2 **Limestone L** Manitoba Canada
119 T5 **Limestone Pt** Manitoba Canada
21 M2 **Limésy** France
28 B3 **Limfjorden** *inlet* Denmark
29 K5 **Limhamn** Sweden
16 B2 **Limia** *R* Spain
Limín *isld see* **Thásos** *isld*
26 G7 **Limingen** *L* Norway
29 L7 **Liminka** Finland
41 H3 **Limmat** *R* Switzerland
25 C3 **Limmen** Netherlands
140 D2 **Limmen Bight** N Terr Australia
140 D3 **Limmen Bight R** N Terr Australia
46 F6 **Límni** Greece
46 G5 **Límnos** *isld* Greece
129 L5 **Limoeiro** Brazil
129 L5 **Limoeiro do Norte** Brazil
121 P7 **Limoges** Ontario Canada
18 F7 **Limoges** France
125 N5 **Limón** Costa Rica
125 M2 **Limón** Honduras
106 G2 **Limon** Colorado U.S.A.
128 F7 **Limoquije** Bolivia
18 F7 **Limousin** *reg* France
18 G9 **Limoux** France
108 D5 **Limpia Cr** Texas U.S.A.
8 D5 **Limpley Stoke** England
89 E4 **Limpopo** *R* Botswana
9 G5 **Limpsfield** England
45 P1 **Limski Zaljev** Croatia
67 C4 **Limu** China
28 D4 **Lina** Denmark
26 L4 **Linaälv** Sweden
26 M5 **Lina älv** *R* Sweden
67 F1 **Lin'an** China
71 F7 **Linao B** Mindanao Philippines
71 D5 **Linapacan** *isld* Philippines
71 D5 **Linapacan Str** Philippines
131 B5 **Linares** Chile
131 B6 **Linares** *prov* Chile
125 K5 **Linares** Mexico
16 E6 **Linares** Spain
21 P4 **Linas** France
43 B9 **Linas, M** *mt* Sardinia
70 D3 **Linau Balui Plateau** Sarawak
67 E3 **Linchuan** China
133 E4 **Lincoln** Argentina
9 F1 **Lincoln** England
144 A4 **Lincoln** New Zealand
111 K8 **Lincoln** Alabama U.S.A.
102 C3 **Lincoln** California U.S.A.
95 M8 **Lincoln** Delaware U.S.A.
99 R9 **Lincoln** Illinois U.S.A.
107 M2 **Lincoln** Kansas U.S.A.
95 T1 **Lincoln** Maine U.S.A.
94 D2 **Lincoln** Michigan U.S.A.
99 M3 **Lincoln** Minnesota U.S.A.
101 N3 **Lincoln** Montana U.S.A.
98 K9 **Lincoln** Nebraska U.S.A.
95 Q2 **Lincoln** New Hampshire U.S.A.
106 E8 **Lincoln** New Mexico U.S.A.
110 K3 **Lincoln City** Indiana U.S.A.
100 A5 **Lincoln City** Oregon U.S.A.
98 J9 **Lincoln Cr** Nebraska U.S.A.
138 E4 **Lincoln Gap** South Australia Australia
9 F1 **Lincolnshire** *co* England
112 E4 **Lincolnton** Georgia U.S.A.
112 F2 **Lincolnton** North Carolina U.S.A.
123 L8 **Lincolnville** Nova Scotia Canada
95 S2 **Lincolnville** Maine U.S.A.
100 G3 **Lind** Washington U.S.A.
140 E6 **Linda** *R* Queensland Australia
52 F6 **Linda** Nizhegorodskaya obl Russian Federation
13 F5 **Lindale** England
111 L7 **Lindale** Georgia U.S.A.
109 M3 **Lindale** Texas U.S.A.
27 A11 **Lindas** Norway
33 Q8 **Lindau** Germany
41 L2 **Lindau** Germany
118 G5 **Lindbergh** Alberta Canada
98 B8 **Lindbergh** Wyoming U.S.A.
101 M2 **Lindbergh L** Montana U.S.A.
28 A4 **Linde** Denmark
28 F7 **Lindelse** Denmark
141 J5 **Lindeman I** Queensland Australia
32 L8 **Linden** Germany
128 G2 **Linden** Guyana
111 J9 **Linden** Alabama U.S.A.
94 J4 **Linden** New York U.S.A.
112 J2 **Linden** North Carolina U.S.A.
110 J6 **Linden** Tennessee U.S.A.
111 B8 **Linden** Texas U.S.A.
37 K3 **Lindenau Friedrichshall** Germany
33 Q6 **Lindenberg** Germany
28 D3 **Lindenborg Å** *R* Denmark
36 F4 **Lindenfels** Germany
33 T6 **Lindenhagen** Germany
33 Q9 **Lindenhayn** Germany
115 P5 **Lindenow Fjord** Greenland
25 F6 **Lindern** Germany
32 G7 **Lindern** Germany
143 B10 **Lindesay, Mt** W Australia Australia
27 H12 **Lindesberg** Sweden
27 B14 **Lindesnes** *lighthouse* Norway
9 F5 **Lindfield** England
27 G12 **Lindfors** Sweden
28 F5 **Lindholm** *isld* Denmark
88 F6 **Lindi** *reg* Tanzania
88 G6 **Lindi** Tanzania
86 E5 **Lindi** *R* Zaire
65 F1 **Lindian** China
13 G2 **Lindisfarne** England
144 B6 **Lindis Valley** New Zealand
28 C5 **Lindknud** Denmark
106 D1 **Lindland** Colorado U.S.A.
36 C1 **Lindlar** Germany
32 K8 **Lindnorst** Germany
106 G2 **Lindon** Colorado U.S.A.
13 E1 **Lindores** Scotland
47 V17 **Líndos** Rhodes Greece
33 R7 **Lindow** Germany
36 B6 **Lindre,Etg de** *L* France
121 M8 **Lindsay** Ontario Canada
102 E5 **Lindsay** California U.S.A.
101 U2 **Lindsay** Montana U.S.A.
98 J8 **Lindsay** Nebraska U.S.A.
107 N7 **Lindsay** Oklahoma U.S.A.
143 D7 **Lindsay Gordon, L** W Australia Australia
140 A6 **Lindsay, Mt** N Terr Australia
107 N3 **Lindsborg** Kansas U.S.A.
94 D5 **Lindsey** Ohio U.S.A.
33 P7 **Lindstedt** Germany
83 K11 **Lindula** Sri Lanka
28 D3 **Lindum** Denmark
37 P4 **Líně** Czech Rep
94 G5 **Linesville** Pennsylvania U.S.A.
111 L8 **Lineville** Alabama U.S.A.
99 N9 **Lineville** Iowa U.S.A.
56 B4 **Linevo** Russian Federation
58 F4 **Linfen** China
68 J3 **Lingao** China
71 E2 **Lingayen** Luzon Philippines
71 E2 **Lingayen Gulf** Luzon Philippines
65 B7 **Lingbao** China
27 J10 **Lingbo** Sweden
65 B7 **Lingchuan** China
67 C4 **Lingchuan** China
21 N8 **Lingé** France
25 D5 **Linge** *R* Netherlands
32 F7 **Lingen** Germany
69 G13 **Lingga** Indonesia
70 B4 **Lingga** Sarawak
69 G13 **Lingga,Kep** *islds* Indonesia
27 H11 **Linghed** Sweden
70 E3 **Lingkas** Kalimantan
98 B7 **Lingle** Wyoming U.S.A.
86 D5 **Lingomo** Zaire
58 F4 **Lingqiu** China
68 J1 **Lingshan** China
65 E7 **Lingshan Dao** *isld* China
65 B6 **Lingshi** China
101 O3 **Lingshire** Montana U.S.A.
65 C5 **Lingshou** China
68 K3 **Lingshui** China
76 C2 **Lingsugur** India
67 D7 **Lingtou** China
43 G11 **Linguaglossa** Sicily
85 B5 **Linguère** Senegal
67 C4 **Lingui** China
Lingxi *see* **Yongshun**
65 C6 **Ling Xian** China
67 D3 **Ling Xian** China
67 B4 **Lingyang** China
65 D4 **Lingyuan** China
67 B4 **Lingyun** China
67 G2 **Linhai** China
130 H6 **Linhares** Brazil
68 G3 **Linh Cam** Vietnam
65 D7 **Linhong Kou** *B* China
122 B7 **Liniere** Quebec Canada
21 O7 **Liniez** France
65 G4 **Linjiang** China
67 G2 **Lin Jiang** *R* China
65 F4 **Linjiatai** China
65 A7 **Linjin** China
36 E5 **Linkenheim** Germany
27 H13 **Linköping** Sweden
59 K2 **Linkou** China
67 A3 **Linkou** China
52 B6 **Linkuva** Lithuania
67 D2 **Linli** China
15 E5 **Linlithgow** Scotland
32 E10 **Linn** Germany
107 N2 **Linn** Kansas U.S.A.
110 E3 **Linn** Missouri U.S.A.
109 J9 **Linn** Texas U.S.A.
29 N9 **Linnansaari Nat. Park** Finland
95 S7 **Linneus** Maine U.S.A.
99 N10 **Linneus** Missouri U.S.A.
8 A4 **Linney Hd** Wales
25 F7 **Linnich** Germany
100 C9 **Linn,Mt** California U.S.A.
15 E4 **Linn of Dee** Scotland
43 E13 **Linosa, I. di** Italy
33 R6 **Linow** Germany
Linping *see* **Yuhang**
65 B7 **Linqi** China
65 C6 **Linqing** China
65 D6 **Linqu** China
65 B7 **Linru** China
130 E7 **Lins** Brazil
32 K7 **Linsburg** Germany
26 G9 **Linsell** Sweden
65 A7 **Lin Shan** *hist site* China
67 B2 **Linshizhen** China
65 D7 **Linshu** China
67 B1 **Linshui** China
127 L2 **Linstead** Jamaica
71 J9 **Lintah,Selat** *str* Indonesia
58 D5 **Lintan** China
58 D4 **Lintao** China
41 K3 **Linth** *R* Switzerland
41 J4 **Linthal** Switzerland
119 O6 **Lintlaw** Saskatchewan Canada
121 S5 **Linton** Quebec Canada
145 E4 **Linton** New Zealand
110 J2 **Linton** Indiana U.S.A.
98 F3 **Linton** North Dakota U.S.A.
65 A7 **Lintong** China
32 E10 **Lintorf** Germany
33 R7 **Linum** Germany
112 F1 **Linville** North Carolina U.S.A.
94 J8 **Linville** Virginia U.S.A.
107 P2 **Linwood** Kansas U.S.A.
94 D3 **Linwood** Michigan U.S.A.
98 K8 **Linwood** Nebraska U.S.A.
67 D4 **Linwu** China
58 G3 **Linxi** China
58 D4 **Linxia** China
65 A6 **Lin Xian** China
67 D2 **Linxiang** China
65 C6 **Linyi** China
65 A7 **Linyi** China
65 D7 **Linyi** China
38 K5 **Linz** Austria
36 C2 **Linz** Germany
65 C6 **Linzhang** China
65 D6 **Linzi** China
70 D3 **Lio Matoh** Sarawak
21 J6 **Lion-d' Angers, le** France
89 G1 **Lion's Den** Zimbabwe
120 J8 **Lions Head** Ontario Canada
21 K3 **Lion-sur-Mer** France
71 N8 **Lioppa** Indonesia
86 C5 **Liouesso** Congo
54 B1 **Liozno** Belarus
42 G4 **Lipa** Bosnia-Herzegovina
71 E4 **Lipa** Philippines
65 J3 **Lipadiya** Russian Federation
109 J3 **Lipan** Texas U.S.A.
43 F10 **Lipari, I** *islds* Italy
43 F10 **Lipari, I** Italy
69 E12 **Lipatkain** Sumatra
29 O9 **Liperi** Finland
54 L4 **Lipetsk** Russian Federation
9 F5 **Liphook** England
31 H2 **Lipiany** Poland
52 E4 **Lipin Bor** Russian Federation
67 C3 **Liping** China
48 K2 **Lipkany** Moldova
46 E2 **Lipljan** Serbia Yugoslavia
48 D1 **Lipnik** Czech Rep
48 L6 **Lipniţa** Romania
31 L3 **Lipno** Poland
89 F3 **Lipokolo Hills** Botswana
48 G4 **Lipova** Romania
48 M1 **Lipovets** Ukraine
32 H9 **Lippe** *R* Germany
32 H9 **Lipperode** Germany
32 H9 **Lippetal** Germany
32 H9 **Lippstadt** Germany
108 D7 **Lipscomb** Texas U.S.A.
31 O2 **Lipsk** Poland
47 H7 **Lipsói** *isld* Greece
119 O8 **Lipton** Saskatchewan Canada
48 F1 **Liptovský Mikuláš** Slovakia
139 H7 **Liptrap,C** Victoria Australia
67 C4 **Lipu** China
86 F5 **Lira** Uganda
71 M8 **Liran** *isld* Indonesia
86 C6 **Liranga** Congo
128 D6 **Lircay** Peru
21 H7 **Liré** France
45 O6 **Liri** *R* Italy
45 P7 **Liri** Italy
69 F13 **Lirik** Sumatra
55 D4 **Lisakovsk** Kazakhstan
86 D5 **Lisala** Zaire
127 O2 **Lisas B** Trinidad
16 A6 **Lisboa** Portugal

99 S8 Lisbon Illinois U.S.A.
95 Q2 Lisbon New Hampshire U.S.A.
95 M2 Lisbon New York U.S.A.
98 J3 Lisbon North Dakota U.S.A.
94 G6 Lisbon Ohio U.S.A.
95 R2 Lisbon Falls Maine U.S.A.
14 E2 Lisburn N Ireland
16 D2 Lisburne,C Alaska U.S.A.
14 B4 Liscannor B Ireland
98 D8 Lisco Nebraska U.S.A.
23 K8 Liscomb Nova Scotia Canada
14 B3 Lisdoonvarna Ireland
28 H4 Liseleje Denmark
67 D1 Lishan China
65 B6 Lishi China
65 F3 Lishu China
67 C2 Li Shui R China
67 F1 Lishui Jiangsu China
67 G2 Lishui Zhejiang China
54 K8 Lisichansk Ukraine
18 L9 Lisieux Saskatchewan Canada
21 L3 Lisieux France
56 C2 Lisitsa R Russian Federation
8 B7 Liskeard England
54 L6 Liski Russian Federation
95 L4 Lisle New York U.S.A.
18 G9 Lisle sur Tarn France
11 H9 Lisman Alabama U.S.A.
23 K8 Lismore Nova Scotia Canada
14 D4 Lismore Ireland
15 C4 Lismore isld Scotland
14 D2 Lisnaskea N Ireland
21 H3 Lison France
21 N3 Lisors France
42 G3 Lissadell W Australia Australia
25 C4 Lisse Netherlands
28 A6 List Germany
27 B13 Lista isld Norway
27 B13 Listerfj inlet Norway
40 E7 Listore R Queensland Australia
14 B4 Listowel Ireland
41 H7 Listowel Downs Queensland Australia
56 C6 Listvyaga,Khr mts Kazakhstan/Rus Fed
56 G5 Listvyanka Russian Federation
26 G8 Lit Sweden
58 D5 Litang China
67 C5 Litang China
58 D6 Litang Qu R China
79 F5 Lītāni R Lebanon
9 G2 Litcham England
00 E9 Litchfield California U.S.A.
95 O5 Litchfield Connecticut U.S.A.
10 G2 Litchfield Illinois U.S.A.
94 C4 Litchfield Michigan U.S.A.
99 M4 Litchfield Minnesota U.S.A.
98 G8 Litchfield Nebraska U.S.A.
03 M8 Litchfield Pk Arizona U.S.A.
98 H3 Litchville North Dakota U.S.A.
48 K3 Liteni Romania
18 E8 Lit et Mixe France
46 D7 Lithakiá Greece
46 G6 Lithári,Akr C Greece
39 K5 Lithgow New South Wales Australia
46 G10 Líthinon, Akr C Crete Greece
27 M16 Lithuania rep E Europe
37 P4 Litice Czech Rep
42 F2 Litija Slovenia
48 L1 Litin Ukraine
95 L6 Lititz Pennsylvania U.S.A.
6 F1 Litla Dimun isld Faeroes
86 A6 Lit. Loango Nat. Park Gabon
46 F4 Litókhoron Greece
31 H5 Litoměřice Czech Rep
31 J6 Litomyšl Czech Rep
59 K2 Litovko Russian Federation
27 J12 Litslena Sweden
10 D6 Little R Arkansas U.S.A.
12 E4 Little R Georgia U.S.A.
10 J5 Little R Kentucky U.S.A.
11 D10 Little R Louisiana U.S.A.
12 J2 Little R North Carolina U.S.A.
07 O6 Little R Oklahoma U.S.A.
09 M1 Little R Oklahoma U.S.A.
09 L5 Little R Texas U.S.A.
68 A7 Little Andaman isld Andaman Is
99 T4 Little Bay de Noc Michigan U.S.A.
23 R4 Little Bay Is Newfoundland Canada
19 N4 Little Bear L Saskatchewan Canada
01 P3 Little Belt Mts Montana U.S.A.
01 S4 Little Bighorn Battlefield Nat. Mon Montana U.S.A.
01 S4 Little Bighorn River Montana U.S.A.
16 Q3 Little Black R Alaska U.S.A.
13 F6 Littleborough England
18 E8 Little Bow Prov. Park Alberta Canada
18 D8 Little Bow R Alberta Canada
23 R2 Little Brehat Newfoundland Canada
17 R5 Little Buffalo R Northwest Territories Canada
19 V7 Little Bullhead Manitoba Canada
23 R4 Little Burnt Bay Newfoundland Canada
9 G3 Littlebury England
89 A7 Little Bushman Land reg S Africa
99 S5 Little Chute Wisconsin U.S.A.
03 N6 Little Colorado R Arizona U.S.A.
03 M4 Little Creek Pk Utah U.S.A.
20 J7 Little Current Ontario Canada
11 B9 Little Cypress Cr Texas U.S.A.
38 F6 Little Desert Victoria Australia
16 C3 Little Diomede isld Alaska U.S.A.
01 T2 Little Dry Cr Montana U.S.A.
99 M4 Little Falls Minnesota U.S.A.
95 N4 Little Falls New York U.S.A.
03 L5 Littlefield Arizona U.S.A.
08 E2 Littlefield Texas U.S.A.
99 N1 Little Fork R Minnesota U.S.A.
99 N1 Little Fork Minnesota U.S.A.
17 N10 Little Fort British Columbia Canada
10 G4 Little Grassy L Illinois U.S.A.
6 K4 Little Halibut Bank North Sea
9 F6 Littlehampton England
13 L11 Little Harbour Bahamas
89 A6 Little Karas Berg mts Namibia
89 B9 Little Karoo reg S Africa
16 H9 Little Koniuji I Alaska U.S.A.
02 G6 Little L California U.S.A.
11 F12 Little L Louisiana U.S.A.
27 H2 Little London Jamaica
01 M5 Little Lost R Idaho U.S.A.
01 N7 Little Malad R Idaho U.S.A.
22 E2 Little Manicouagan,L Quebec Canada
95 L5 Little Meadows Pennsylvania U.S.A.
15 N7 Little Mecatina R Quebec/Labrador Canada
98 A7 Little Medicine Wyoming U.S.A.
10 M2 Little Miami R Ohio U.S.A.
15 B3 Little Minch chan Hebrides Scotland
98 B5 Little Missouri R Wyoming U.S.A.
69 A9 Little Nicobar isld Nicobar Is
107 Q3 Little Osage R Kansas/Missouri U.S.A.
112 H3 Little Pee Dee R South Carolina U.S.A.
9 G3 Littleport England
98 A5 Little Powder R Wyoming U.S.A.
123 Q5 Little R Newfoundland Canada
144 D5 Little River New Zealand
111 J10 Little River Alabama U.S.A.
107 N3 Little River Kansas U.S.A.
112 J4 Little River Inlet North Carolina U.S.A.
110 D7 Little Rock Arkansas U.S.A.
102 G7 Littlerock California U.S.A.
88 E6 Little Ruaha R Tanzania
99 U6 Little Sable Pt Michigan U.S.A.
110 C4 Little Sac R Missouri U.S.A.
117 F4 Little Salmon L Yukon Territory Canada
103 M4 Little Salt L Utah U.S.A.
119 T1 Little Sand L Manitoba Canada
101 Q7 Little Sandy Cr Wyoming U.S.A.
112 E6 Little Satilla R Georgia U.S.A.
99 L7 Little Sioux R Iowa U.S.A.
117 P8 Little Smoky River Alberta Canada
101 R9 Little Snake R Colorado U.S.A.
9 G6 Littlestone-on-Sea England
95 K7 Littlestown Pennsylvania U.S.A.
99 T5 Little Suamico Wisconsin U.S.A.
122 F7 Little S.W. Miramichi R New Brunswick Canada
112 C2 Little Tennessee R Tennessee U.S.A.
127 N1 Little Tobago isld Tobago
106 E2 Littleton Colorado U.S.A.
99 Q9 Littleton Illinois U.S.A.
95 Q2 Littleton New Hampshire U.S.A.
112 K1 Littleton North Carolina U.S.A.
94 G7 Littleton West Virginia U.S.A.
95 N2 Little Tupper L New York U.S.A.
94 J4 Little Valley New York U.S.A.
100 K7 Little Valley Cr Idaho U.S.A.
111 J7 Littleville Alabama U.S.A.
110 H3 Little Wabash R Illinois U.S.A.
9 G4 Little Waltham England
98 E6 Little White R South Dakota U.S.A.
101 L6 Little Wood R Idaho U.S.A.
8 D2 Littleworth England
78 J4 Little Zab R Iraq
67 C4 Liucheng China
67 B3 Liuchong He R China
Liuchuan see Jianhe
67 B2 Liudu China
67 B3 Liuguang China
65 E3 Liu He R China
65 F3 Liu He R China
65 F3 Liuhe China
67 B1 Liuhechang China
67 G2 Liuheng Dao isld China
65 E2 Liuhu China
67 D1 Liujiachang China
67 C4 Liu Jiang R China
88 E7 Liuli Tanzania
65 C5 Liulihezhen China
67 B4 Liuma China
Liupai see Tian'e
67 D1 Liushuigou China
67 C4 Liutang China
67 D2 Liuyang China
67 D2 Liuyang He R China
67 B4 Liuzhai China
Liuzhangzhen see Qinghe
Liuzhangzhen see Yuanqu
67 C4 Liuzhou China
65 C7 Liuzhuang China
48 H3 Livade Romania
52 C6 Līvāni Latvia
21 L3 Livarot France
118 J5 Livelong Saskatchewan Canada
116 N4 Livengood Alaska U.S.A.
42 E3 Livenza R Italy
102 C2 Live Oak California U.S.A.
113 E7 Live Oak Florida U.S.A.
142 E4 Liveringa W Australia Australia
102 C4 Livermore California U.S.A.
99 M7 Livermore Iowa U.S.A.
110 J4 Livermore Kentucky U.S.A.
95 R2 Livermore Falls Maine U.S.A.
108 C5 Livermore, Mt Texas U.S.A.
139 K5 Liverpool New South Wales Australia
140 C1 Liverpool R N Terr Australia
122 H9 Liverpool Nova Scotia Canada
11 B2 Liverpool conurbation England
95 L3 Liverpool New York U.S.A.
114 G3 Liverpool B Northwest Territories Canada
115 M3 Liverpool,C Northwest Territories Canada
139 K4 Liverpool Plains New South Wales Australia
139 K4 Liverpool Ra mts New South Wales Australia
143 F7 Livesey Ra W Australia Australia
19 P14 Livet France
41 M4 Livigno Italy
125 P10 Livingston Guatemala
15 E5 Livingston Scotland
111 H9 Livingston Alabama U.S.A.
110 M4 Livingston Kentucky U.S.A.
111 F11 Livingston Louisiana U.S.A.
101 P4 Livingston Montana U.S.A.
109 N5 Livingston Texas U.S.A.
99 Q7 Livingston Wisconsin U.S.A.
144 C6 Livingstone New Zealand
89 D1 Livingstone Zambia
117 F5 Livingstone Creek Yukon Territory Canada
88 C8 Livingstone Memorial Zambia
144 B6 Livingstone Mts New Zealand
88 E6 Livingstone Mts Tanzania
118 C8 Livingstone Ra Alberta Canada
146 C3 Livingston I S Shetland Is Antarctica
87 F8 Livingstonia Malawi
95 N5 Livingston Manor New York U.S.A.
42 H5 Livno Bosnia-Herzegovina
54 J4 Livny Russian Federation
28 B3 Livø isld Denmark
29 M6 Livojoki R Finland
111 E11 Livonia Louisiana U.S.A.
94 D4 Livonia Michigan U.S.A.
99 O9 Livonia Missouri U.S.A.
44 H4 Livorno Italy
18 H7 Livradois,Mts.du France
133 F4 Livramento Brazil
20 H5 Livré France
19 N15 Livron France
87 G7 Liwale Tanzania
88 G6 Liwale Tanzania
31 N3 Liwiec R Poland
67 E2 Lixi China
65 C5 Li Xian China
67 D2 Li Xian Hunan China
67 A1 Li Xian Sichuan China
36 B5 Lixing les St.Avold France
46 D6 Lixoúrion Greece
67 F1 Liyang China
67 C4 Liyong China
9 G7 Lizard pen England
129 J5 Lizarda Brazil
101 Q7 Lizard Head Pk Wyoming U.S.A.
141 H2 Lizard I Gt Barrier Reef Aust
112 D5 Lizella Georgia U.S.A.
94 F8 Lizemores West Virginia U.S.A.
52 D4 Lizhma Russian Federation
18 F7 Lizonne R France
121 S4 Lizotte Quebec Canada
110 K2 Lizton Indiana U.S.A.
45 J3 Lizzano in Belvedere Italy
27 F10 Ljöra R Norway
28 S9 Ljosafoss Iceland
42 H4 Ljubija Bosnia-Herzegovina
42 J6 Ljubinje Bosnia-Herzegovina
46 C1 Ljubišnja mt Bosnia-Herzegovina/Yugoslavia
42 F2 Ljubljana Slovenia
46 E2 Ljuboten mt Serbia Yugoslavia
48 E6 Ljubovija Serbia Yugoslavia
42 H5 Ljubuški Bosnia-Herzegovina
27 K14 Ljugarn Gotland Sweden
26 H9 Ljunga Sweden
26 H9 Ljungan R Sweden
26 H9 Ljungaverk Sweden
27 G15 Ljungby Sweden
27 G15 Ljungby, Ö Sweden
26 F9 Ljungdalen Sweden
26 H10 Ljusdal Sweden
26 H9 Ljusnan R Sweden
27 J10 Ljusne Sweden
27 K12 Ljusterö Sweden
133 C5 Llaima mt Chile
131 B7 Llaima,Vol Chile
8 B2 Llanaelhaearn Wales
8 B3 Llanarth Wales
8 B2 Llanbedr Wales
8 B2 Llanbedrog Wales
8 B1 Llanberis Wales
8 C3 Llanbister Wales
131 B5 Llancanelo, L Argentina
131 C5 Llancanelo,Salina Argentina
8 C5 Llandaf Wales
8 C4 Llandarcy Wales
8 B4 Llanddarog Wales
8 B4 Llandefeilog Wales
8 B1 Llandegai Wales
8 D4 Llandegfedd Resr. res Wales
8 B4 Llandeilo Wales
8 B4 Llandissilio Wales
8 C4 Llandovery Wales
8 B4 Llandowror Wales
8 C2 Llandrillo Wales
8 C3 Llandrindod Wells Wales
8 C1 Llandudno Wales
8 B3 Llandyssul Wales
8 B4 Llanelli Wales
8 C2 Llanelltyd Wales
8 B1 Llanerchymedd Wales
16 D1 Llanes Spain
8 B1 Llanfaethlu Wales
8 C1 Llanfairfechan Wales
8 C1 Llanfair Talhaiarn Wales
8 B3 Llanfarian Wales
8 C1 Llanferres Wales
8 C2 Llanfyllin Wales
8 C2 Llangadfan Wales
8 C4 Llangadog Wales
8 C3 Llangammarch Wells Wales
8 B1 Llangefni Wales
8 B3 Llangeler Wales
8 B2 Llangelynin Wales
8 C1 Llangernyw Wales
8 C2 Llangollen Wales
8 C3 Llangurig Wales
8 C2 Llangynog Wales
8 C3 Llanidloes Wales
8 B3 Llanilar Wales
8 B1 Llanllyfni Wales
8 B4 Llanmadog Wales
124 D2 Llano Mexico
109 H5 Llano R Texas U.S.A.
109 J5 Llano Texas U.S.A.
124 G6 Llano Grande Mexico
128 D2 Llanos prairies Colombia/Venezuela
17 H3 Llanos de Urgel reg Spain
131 C3 Llanos,Sa.de los mts Argentina
133 C6 Llanquihue prov Chile
131 A8 Llanquihue,L Chile
141 F5 Llanrheidol Queensland Australia
8 B4 Llanrhidian Wales
8 B3 Llanrhystyd Wales
8 C1 Llanrwst Wales
18 H10 Llansa Spain
8 C1 Llansannan Wales
8 B3 Llansantffraid Wales
8 B4 Llanstephan Wales
8 C4 Llanthony Wales
8 C4 Llantrisant Wales
8 C4 Llanwrda Wales
8 C3 Llanwrtyd Wells Wales
8 B3 Llanybydder Wales
8 C2 Llanymynech England
77 E5 Llazārān, Kūh-e mt Iran
8 B3 Llechryd Wales
Lleida see Lérida
17 H3 Llena,Sierra de la mts Spain
16 C6 Llerena Spain
133 C4 Llico Chile
17 G5 Lliria Spain
17 J3 Llobregat R Spain
17 J3 Lloret de Mar Spain
101 Q1 Lloyd Montana U.S.A.
141 G2 Lloyd B Queensland Australia
117 L7 Lloyd George, Mt British Columbia Canada
118 H5 Lloydminster Alberta/Sask Canada
127 K2 Lluidas Vale Jamaica
133 D2 Llullaillaco mt Arg/Chile
128 E7 Lluta R Chile
8 B2 Llwyngwril Wales
8 C3 Llyswen Wales
128 E8 Loa R Chile
103 N3 Loa Utah U.S.A.
70 E5 Loakulu Kalimantan
99 R10 Loami Illinois U.S.A.
130 D8 Loanda Brazil
86 D6 Loanga R Zaire
86 B6 Loango Congo
13 E2 Loanhead Scotland
110 G2 Loann Illinois U.S.A.
44 D3 Loano Italy
71 G6 Loay Philippines
52 H5 Loban' R Russian Federation
54 K3 Lobanovo Russian Federation
70 G6 Lobata Sulawesi
89 D5 Lobatse Botswana
31 H4 Löbau Germany
86 C5 Lobaye R Cent Afr Republic
22 G3 Lobbes Belgium
37 M2 Lobeda Germany
33 P9 Löbejün Germany
37 M3 Lobenstein Germany
133 F5 Lobería Argentina
31 J2 Łobez Poland
87 B8 Lobito Angola
33 R4 Löbnitz Germany
54 J1 Lobnya Russian Federation
85 C7 Lobo R Ivory Coast
16 C6 Lobón Spain
27 H10 Lobonäs Sweden
131 F5 Lobos Argentina
124 D4 Lobos isld Mexico
128 D7 Lobos,C Chile
124 C3 Lobos,C Mexico
126 F3 Lobos Cay isld Cuba
128 B5 Lobos de Tierra isld Peru
133 D6 Lobos,Pta Argentina
131 A5 Lobos,Pta Colchagua Chile
37 N1 Lobstädt Germany
115 N7 Lobstick L Labrador, Nfld Canada
33 Q8 Loburg Germany
55 D2 Lobva Russian Federation
31 K2 Łobżenica Poland
40 G7 Locana Italy
41 J5 Locarno Switzerland
67 B6 Loc Binh Vietnam
32 K8 Loccum Germany
15 D4 Lochaber Scotland
122 K8 Lochaber Mines Nova Scotia Canada
15 C4 Lochaline Scotland
120 F4 Lochalsh Ontario Canada
15 C2 Loch Assynt Scotland
15 C4 Loch Awe Scotland
15 A3 Loch Boisdale Outer Hebrides Scotland
15 C3 Loch Broom Scotland
15 C4 Lochbuie Scotland
15 C3 Loch Clunie Scotland
15 D4 Lochearnhead Scotland
15 C4 Loch Eil Scotland
25 F4 Lochem Netherlands
15 D2 Loch Eriboll Scotland
15 D4 Loch Ericht Scotland
15 B2 Loch Erisort Scotland
21 M7 Loches France
21 N7 Loché-sur-Indrois France
15 C4 Loch Etive Scotland
15 C3 Loch Ewe Scotland
15 E4 Loch Faskally Scotland
15 C4 Loch Fyne Scotland
12 C1 Lochgilphead Scotland
15 C4 Lochgilphead Scotland
15 D3 Loch Glass Scotland
12 D1 Lochgoilhead Scotland
15 C3 Loch Hourn Scotland
144 B7 Lochie New Zealand
15 C2 Loch Inchard Scotland
15 C2 Lochinver Scotland
15 D4 Loch Laggan Scotland
15 B2 Loch Langavat Scotland
15 C2 Loch Laxford Scotland
15 E4 Loch Leven Scotland
15 D4 Loch Lochy Scotland
15 D4 Loch Long Scotland
15 C3 Loch Loyne Scotland
12 E3 Lochmaben Scotland
15 E5 Lochmaben Scotland
15 A3 Lochmaddy Outer Hebrides Scotland
15 C3 Loch Maree Scotland
15 C3 Loch Monar Scotland
15 C4 Loch Morar Scotland
15 D2 Loch More Scotland
144 B6 Lochnagar L New Zealand
15 E4 Lochnagar mt Scotland
15 D2 Loch Naver Scotland
15 D3 Loch Ness Scotland
15 D3 Loch Oich Scotland
15 C3 Loch Quoich Scotland
15 D4 Loch Rannoch Scotland
12 C2 Lochranza Scotland
22 F1 Lochristi Belgium
15 C4 Loch Sheil Scotland
15 D2 Loch Shin Scotland
15 C4 Loch Sunart Scotland
15 D4 Loch Tay Scotland
15 C3 Loch Torridon Scotland
68 J2 Lo Chuc San isld Vietnam
15 D4 Loch Vennacher Scotland
12 D2 Lochwinnoch Scotland
138 D5 Lock South Australia Australia
95 L4 Locke New York U.S.A.
100 H1 Locke Washington U.S.A.
122 G10 Lockeport Nova Scotia Canada
109 J4 Locker Texas U.S.A.
15 E5 Lockerbie Scotland
142 A5 Locker Pt W Australia Australia
103 J3 Lockes Nevada U.S.A.
111 B8 Lockesburg Arkansas U.S.A.
109 H1 Lockett Texas U.S.A.
139 H6 Lockhart New South Wales Australia
111 K10 Lockhart Alabama U.S.A.
98 K2 Lockhart Minnesota U.S.A.
112 F3 Lockhart South Carolina U.S.A.
109 K6 Lockhart Texas U.S.A.
141 G2 Lockhart River Queensland Australia
94 K5 Lock Haven Pennsylvania U.S.A.
143 B6 Lockier Ra W Australia Australia
108 F1 Lockney Texas U.S.A.
33 P6 Löcknitz R Germany
99 S8 Lockport Illinois U.S.A.
111 F12 Lockport Louisiana U.S.A.
94 J3 Lockport New York U.S.A.
99 P9 Lockridge Iowa U.S.A.
119 N7 Lockwood Saskatchewan Canada
110 C4 Lockwood Missouri U.S.A.
116 J3 Lockwood Hills Alaska U.S.A.
19 K5 Locle, Le France
20 D7 Locmaria Belle Isle, Nfld France
20 E6 Locmaria Morbihan France
20 E6 Locmariaquer France
20 E6 Locminé France
68 H7 Loc Ninh Vietnam
107 N7 Loco Oklahoma U.S.A.
101 P3 Loco Mt Montana U.S.A.
20 C4 Locquirec France
43 G10 Locri Italy
20 B5 Locronan France
20 B6 Loctudy France
99 N9 Locust Cr R Missouri U.S.A.
111 K7 Locust Fork R Alabama U.S.A.
94 D8 Locust Grove Ohio U.S.A.
107 P5 Locust Grove Oklahoma U.S.A.
80 C6 Lod Israel
99 S9 Loda Illinois U.S.A.
26 B10 Lodalskåpa mt Norway
139 G6 Loddon R Victoria Australia
9 H2 Loddon England
33 P10 Lodersleben Germany
18 H9 Lodève France
52 D4 Lodeynoye-Pole Russian Federation
101 Q1 Lodge Cr Mont/Sask U.S.A./Canada
101 S4 Lodge Grass Montana U.S.A.
117 E6 Lodge, Mt Br Col/Alaska Canada/U.S.A.
98 D8 Lodgepole Nebraska U.S.A.
98 C8 Lodgepole Cr Nebraska U.S.A.
98 B8 Lodgepole Cr Wyoming U.S.A.
74 D4 Lodhran Pakistan
41 L7 Lodi Italy
102 C3 Lodi California U.S.A.
94 E5 Lodi Ohio U.S.A.
99 R6 Lodi Wisconsin U.S.A.
26 G4 Løding Norway
26 H3 Lödingen Norway
86 D6 Lodja Zaire
71 A3 Lodji Indonesia
88 E3 Lodmalasin mt Tanzania
18 D10 Lodosa Spain
40 D3 Lods France
86 G5 Lodwar Kenya
31 L4 Łódź Poland
16 E4 Loeches Spain
86 F4 Loelli Sudan
25 F4 Loenen Netherlands
26 B10 Loenvatn L Norway
21 P2 Loeuilly France
38 G6 Lofer Austria
38 G6 Loferer St Ulrich Austria
36 E6 Loffenau Germany
15 E1 L. of Harray Scotland
26 F3 Lofoten islds Norway
26 F9 Lofsdalen Sweden
28 B5 Loft Denmark
27 J14 Loftahammar Sweden
13 G5 Lofthouse England
13 H4 Loftus England
143 C6 Lofty Ra W Australia Australia
141 H5 Logan R Queensland Australia
141 L8 Logan R Queensland Australia
99 L8 Logan Iowa U.S.A.
107 L2 Logan Kansas U.S.A.
101 O4 Logan Montana U.S.A.
98 F8 Logan Nebraska U.S.A.
106 G6 Logan New Mexico U.S.A.
101 O8 Logan Utah U.S.A.
94 F9 Logan West Virginia U.S.A.
98 K8 Logan Cr Nebraska U.S.A.
103 K5 Logandale Nevada U.S.A.
116 R6 Logan Glacier Alaska/Yukon Terr U.S.A./Canada
118 F3 Logan L Alberta Canada
122 E5 Logan,Mt Quebec Canada
117 C5 Logan,Mt Yukon Territory Canada
100 E1 Logan, Mt Washington U.S.A.
117 K5 Logan Mts Yukon Terr/N W Terr Canada
101 M1 Logan Pass Montana U.S.A.
94 A6 Logansport Indiana U.S.A.
111 B10 Logansport Louisiana U.S.A.
95 K5 Loganton Pennsylvania U.S.A.
99 Q6 Loganville Wisconsin U.S.A.
98 A9 Logcabin Colorado U.S.A.
26 K8 Logde älv R Sweden
100 F5 Logdell Oregon U.S.A.
87 B7 Loge R Angola
21 L2 Loges, les France
8 D2 Loggerheads England
55 D3 Loginovo Russian Federation
86 B3 Logone R Cameroon
21 N5 Logron France
17 F2 Logroño Spain
16 D5 Logrosan Spain
28 C3 Løgstør Denmark
28 C3 Løgstrup Denmark
28 E4 Løgten Denmark
20 D4 Loguivy-Plougras France
28 B6 Løgumkloster Denmark
28 F6 Lohals Denmark
80 D2 Loḥame HaGeta'ot Israel
75 L7 Lohardaga India
20 G6 Lohéac France
32 L10 Lohfelden Germany
37 M7 Lohhof Germany
29 L5 Lohijärvi Finland
29 L11 Lohja Finland
101 Q1 Lohman Montana U.S.A.
33 Q5 Lohmen Germany
109 H4 Lohn Texas U.S.A.
36 E3 Löhnberg Germany
32 J8 Löhne Germany
36 D4 Lohnsfeld Germany
70 G6 Loholoho Sulawesi
36 H4 Lohr Germany
36 F2 Lohra Germany
99 M7 Lohrville Iowa U.S.A.
29 K7 Lohtaja Finland
68 C2 Loi-ai Burma
45 K3 Loiano Italy
38 K8 Loibl Pass Austria/Italy
21 J6 Loigne France
68 C3 Loikaw Burma
68 C3 Loi Lan mt Burma
68 C2 Loi-Lem Burma
68 D1 Loi Lun Burma
29 K11 Loimaa Finland
18 G4 Loing R France
21 L6 Loir R France
18 H7 Loire R France
21 K7 Loire R France
21 J6 Loiré Maine-et-Loire France
18 D5 Loire-Atlantique dept France
18 G5 Loiret dept France
18 F5 Loir-et-Cher dept France
21 J5 Loiron France
41 O2 Loisach R Germany
68 C2 Loi Sang mt Burma
22 J5 Loison R France
40 B4 Loisy France
33 S5 Loitz Germany
128 C4 Loja prov Ecuador
16 E7 Loja Spain
28 C6 Løjt Denmark
86 F5 Loka Sudan
29 J11 Lokalahti Finland
70 E2 Lokan R Sabah
86 E6 Lokandu Zaire
29 N4 Lokantekojärvi L Finland
70 D6 Lokbatu Kalimantan
52 H4 Lokchim R Russian Federation
22 D2 Loker Belgium
22 F1 Lokeren Belgium
37 O3 Loket Czech Rep
54 E6 Lokhvitsa Ukraine
86 G5 Lokichar Kenya
70 G5 Lokilalaki, G mt Sulawesi
86 G5 Lokitaung Kenya
29 N4 Lokka Finland
28 D2 Løkken Denmark
26 D8 Lökken Norway
52 D6 Loknya Russian Federation
86 A4 Loko Nigeria
86 D6 Lokolo R Zaire
53 C7 Lokoml'skoye, Ozero L Belarus
86 C6 Lokoro R Zaire
55 F1 Lokosovo Russian Federation
54 F4 Lokot' Russian Federation
52 C5 Loksa Estonia
59 K1 Lokshak Russian Federation
115 N5 Loks Land Northwest Territories Canada
86 E4 Lol R Sudan
71 J4 Lolak Sulawesi
121 P4 Lola, L Quebec Canada
100 A9 Loleta California U.S.A.
20 H4 Lolif France
88 E3 Loliondo Tanzania
28 G7 Lolland isld Denmark
36 F2 Lollar Germany
101 L3 Lolo Montana U.S.A.
71 B2 Lolobata Halmahera Indonesia
71 A2 Loloda Halmahera Indonesia
71 A2 Loloda,Tk B Halmahera Indonesia
71 A1 Loloda Utara, Pulau Pulau islds Halmahera Indonesia
86 B5 Lolodorf Cameroon
52 H4 Lolog R Russian Federation
101 L3 Lolo Hot Springs Montana U.S.A.
69 C12 Lolomoyo Indonesia
101 L3 Lolo Pass Idaho/Montana U.S.A.
71 M9 Lolotoi Indonesia
69 C12 Lolowau Indonesia
46 F1 Lom Bulgaria
37 O4 Lom Czech Rep
37 P4 Lom mt Czech Rep
26 C10 Lom Norway
106 B2 Loma Colorado U.S.A.
101 P2 Loma Montana U.S.A.
98 H1 Loma North Dakota U.S.A.
16 E6 Loma de Chiclana Spain
16 E6 Loma de Úbeda Spain
88 B10 Lomagundi dist Zimbabwe
86 E6 Lomami R Zaire
85 B7 Loma Mts Sierra Leone/Guinea
99 N1 Loman Minnesota U.S.A.
131 D6 Loma Negra,Planicie de la plain Argentina
133 D6 Lomas Coloradas hills Argentina
130 B10 Lomas de Vallejos Argentina
133 F4 Lomas de Zamora Argentina
142 E3 Lombadina W Australia Australia
101 O3 Lombard Montana U.S.A.
129 H3 Lombarda, Serra mts Brazil
42 C3 Lombardia prov Italy
22 D1 Lombardsijde Belgium
18 F9 Lombez France
71 L9 Lomblen isld Indonesia
70 Q10 Lombok Indonesia
70 P10 Lombok,Selat str Indonesia
21 L5 Lombron France
85 E7 Lomé Togo
86 D6 Lomela Zaire
109 J4 Lometa Texas U.S.A.
86 B5 Lomié Cameroon
99 S6 Lomira Wisconsin U.S.A.
37 P1 Lommatzsch Germany
22 D2 Lomme France
22 J1 Lommel Belgium
118 E8 Lomond Alberta Canada
123 P4 Lomond Newfoundland Canada
6 M5 Lomond oil rig North Sea
15 E4 Lomond Hills Scotland
12 D1 Lomond, Loch L Scotland
52 D6 Lomonosovo Russian Federation
55 E4 Lomonosovskaya Kazakhstan
52 F3 Lomovoye Russian Federation
68 H6 Lomphat Cambodia
70 G7 Lompobattang, G mt Sulawesi
102 D7 Lompoc California U.S.A.
68 E4 Lom Sak Thailand
26 C10 Lomseggja mt Norway
26 J7 Lomsjö Sweden
31 N2 Łomza Poland
106 E7 Lon New Mexico U.S.A.
94 J7 Lonaconing Maryland U.S.A.
74 E9 Lonāvale India
28 A5 Lønborg Denmark
133 C5 Loncoche Chile
133 C5 Loncopue Argentina
22 F2 Londerzeel Belgium
120 J9 Londesborough Ontario Canada
21 N2 Londinières France
120 J10 London Ontario Canada
10 London conurbation England
110 C6 London Arkansas U.S.A.
94 C9 London Kentucky U.S.A.
94 D7 London Ohio U.S.A.
109 H5 London Texas U.S.A.
122 J8 Londonderry Nova Scotia Canada
14 D1 Londonderry N Ireland
14 D2 Londonderry co N Ireland
95 Q4 Londonderry New Hampshire U.S.A.
95 P3 Londonderry Vermont U.S.A.
142 F2 Londonderry, C W Australia Australia
133 C9 Londonderry, I Chile
Londorf see Rabenau
130 D8 Londrina Brazil
107 N7 Lone Grove Oklahoma U.S.A.
120 J7 Lonely I Ontario Canada
102 G4 Lone Mt Nevada U.S.A.
109 M3 Lone Oak Texas U.S.A.
102 F5 Lone Pine California U.S.A.
101 L2 Lonepine Montana U.S.A.
118 H5 Lone Rock Saskatchewan Canada
100 F4 Lonerock Oregon U.S.A.
99 Q6 Lone Rock Wisconsin U.S.A.
101 P8 Lonetree Wyoming U.S.A.
98 F2 Lonetree Res North Dakota U.S.A.
107 L7 Lone Wolf Oklahoma U.S.A.
87 C8 Longa Angola
129 K4 Longa R Brazil
46 E8 Longá Greece
70 D3 Longagung Kalimantan
70 D3 Long Akah Sarawak
67 B5 Long'an China
141 F5 Longara Queensland Australia
45 L1 Longara Italy
45 L1 Longare Italy
42 E2 Longarone Italy
133 C5 Longavi mt Chile
127 K3 Long B Jamaica
70 D3 Longbawan Kalimantan
127 M2 Long Bay Jamaica
112 J4 Long Bay South Carolina U.S.A.
144 C6 Longbeach New Zealand
102 F8 Long Beach California U.S.A.
95 O6 Long Beach Long I, New York U.S.A.
111 G11 Long Beach Mississippi U.S.A.
100 A3 Long Beach Washington U.S.A.
9 F2 Long Bennington England
70 D3 Longberini Kalimantan
70 E3 Longbia Kalimantan
113 E10 Longboat Key isld Florida U.S.A.
70 D4 Longboh Kalimantan
95 N6 Long Branch New Jersey U.S.A.
8 D5 Longbridge Deverill England
145 E4 Longburn New Zealand
8 D6 Long Burton England
22 K3 Longchamps Belgium
67 B2 Longchang China
67 E4 Longchuan China
9 E3 Long Compton England
138 C3 Long Cr South Australia Australia
119 O9 Long Cr Saskatchewan Canada
98 C1 Long Cr North Dakota U.S.A.
100 F5 Long Creek Oregon U.S.A.
68 H4 Long Dai Vietnam
107 M5 Longdale Oklahoma U.S.A.
58 E4 Longde China
9 E2 Longdon England
9 E2 Long Eaton England
40 B3 Longecourt France
95 M5 Long Eddy New York U.S.A.
36 B1 Longerich Germany
95 R1 Long Falls Dam Maine U.S.A.
108 E5 Longfellow Texas U.S.A.
144 D5 Longfellow, Mt New Zealand
65 G2 Longfengshan Shuiku res China
139 H8 Longford Tasmania Australia
14 D3 Longford co Ireland
14 D3 Longford Ireland
145 D4 Longford New Zealand
107 N2 Longford Kansas U.S.A.
13 F2 Longformacus Scotland
6 K5 Long Forties bank North Sea
13 G3 Longframlington England
65 G3 Longgang Shan mt ra China
70 E4 Longgi R Kalimantan
65 C4 Longguan China
65 C7 Longguji China
67 C7 Longgun China
67 F4 Longhai China
9 E6 Longham England
123 T6 Long Harbour Newfoundland Canada
13 G3 Longhorsley England
13 G3 Longhoughton England
65 D4 Longhua China
67 D3 Longhui China
112 J1 Longhurst North Carolina U.S.A.
68 A6 Long I Andaman Is
141 J5 Long I Queensland Australia
126 G3 Long I Bahamas
115 M7 Long I Northwest Territories Canada
122 F9 Long I Nova Scotia Canada
83 K12 Long I Mahé I Indian Oc
144 A6 Long I New Zealand
136 K3 Long I Papua New Guinea
95 P6 Long I New York U.S.A.
100 A3 Long I Washington U.S.A.
127 M4 Long, I Martinique W Indies
70 E5 Longikis Kalimantan
70 D5 Longiram Kalimantan
95 P5 Long I Sd Conn/New York U.S.A.
107 L2 Long Island Kansas U.S.A.
59 H2 Longjiang China
67 B4 Long Jiang R China
65 H3 Longjing China
21 P4 Longjumeau France
Longjuzhai see Danfeng
36 C4 Longkamp Germany
70 D4 Longkay Kalimantan
65 E6 Longkou China
122 F6 Long L New Brunswick Canada
120 D3 Long L Ontario Canada
116 K6 Long L Alaska U.S.A.
95 S6 Long L Maine U.S.A.
94 B2 Long L Michigan U.S.A.
99 M3 Long L Minnesota U.S.A.
95 N2 Long L New York U.S.A.
98 G3 Long L North Dakota U.S.A.
122 J1 Long, Lac Labrador, Nfld Canada
120 D3 Longlac Ontario Canada
95 N3 Long Lake New York U.S.A.
99 S4 Long Lake Wisconsin U.S.A.
70 D3 Long Lama Sarawak
8 D5 Longleat House England
67 B3 Longli China
22 J4 Longlier Belgium
67 B4 Longlin China
12 D1 Long, Loch L Scotland
118 E4 Long L. Prov. Park Alberta Canada
100 F2 Long L.Res Washington U.S.A.
70 E3 Longmalinau Kalimantan
9 G3 Long Melford England
67 C6 Longmen China
65 A7 Longmen Shan mts China
98 A9 Longmont Colorado U.S.A.
70 D3 Long Murum Sarawak
67 E4 Longnan China
70 D4 Longnawan Kalimantan
21 O4 Longnes France
9 E1 Longnor England
21 M4 Longny France
43 H9 Longobucco Italy
88 F2 Longonot,Mt Kenya
70 D4 Longpahangai Kalimantan
69 H8 Long Phu Vietnam
98 G7 Long Pine Nebraska U.S.A.
Longping see Luodian
99 S8 Long Point Illinois U.S.A.
120 K10 Long Point B Ontario Canada
123 U6 Long Pond Newfoundland Canada
22 E5 Longpont France
123 Q5 Long Pound res Newfoundland Canada
99 M4 Long Prairie Minnesota U.S.A.
21 O1 Longpré-les-Corps-Saints France
119 T5 Long Pt Manitoba Canada
123 O5 Long Pt Newfoundland Canada
144 A7 Long Pt New Zealand
71 D6 Long Pt Philippines
70 D3 Longpujungan Kalimantan
67 F2 Longquan China
67 F3 Longquan Xi R China
123 P4 Long Range Mts Newfoundland Canada
141 G6 Longreach Queensland Australia
142 F2 Long Reef W Australia Australia
13 F6 Longridge England
112 J4 Longs South Carolina U.S.A.
144 A7 Long Sd New Zealand
70 E3 Longsegah Kalimantan
67 D2 Longshan China
67 C4 Longsheng China
67 D5 Longsheng China
Longshi see Ninggang
98 A9 Longs Peak mt Colorado U.S.A.
140 B6 Longs Ra N Terr Australia
9 H3 Long Stratton England
9 G2 Long Sutton England
67 B2 Longtan China
70 D3 Long Teru Sarawak
67 C3 Longtian China
117 P3 Longtom L Northwest Territories Canada
100 K6 Long Tom Res Idaho U.S.A.
141 H5 Longton Queensland Australia
8 D2 Longton England
13 F6 Longton Lancs England
107 O4 Longton Kansas U.S.A.
13 F2 Longtown England
110 G4 Longtown Missouri U.S.A.
83 M14 Longue isld Kerguelen Indian Oc
21 P2 Longueau France
22 D5 Longueil-St.Marie France
21 K7 Longué-Jumelles France
22 D3 Longueval France
18 H4 Longueville Seine-et-Marne France
21 N2 Longueville Seine-Inférieure France
19 J3 Longuyon France
98 E6 Longvalley South Dakota U.S.A.
102 F4 Long Valley Res California U.S.A.
40 B3 Longvic France
118 C8 Longview Alberta Canada
109 N3 Longview Texas U.S.A.
100 C3 Longview Washington U.S.A.
109 O5 Longville Louisiana U.S.A.
22 K3 Longvilly Belgium
70 E4 Longwai Kalimantan
65 J2 Longwangmiao China
65 F5 Longwangmiao China
113 F9 Longwood Florida U.S.A.
111 E8 Longwood Mississippi U.S.A.
108 G3 Longworth Texas U.S.A.
22 K4 Longwy France
58 D5 Longxi China
Longxian see Wengyuan
58 E5 Long Xian China
67 B2 Longxing China
Longxu see Cangwu
68 G7 Long Xuyen Vietnam
67 F4 Longyan China
65 C6 Longyao China
147 H11 Longyearbyen Spitzbergen
67 F2 Longyou China
67 B5 Longzhou China
45 K1 Lonigo Italy
32 G7 Löningen Germany
21 J4 Lonlay-L'Abbaye France
25 G4 Lonneker Netherlands
33 S10 Lonnewitz Germany
22 H4 Lonny France
110 E7 Lonoke Arkansas U.S.A.
26 H5 Lönsdal Norway
99 N5 Lonsdale Minnesota U.S.A.
139 G6 Lonsdale L Victoria Australia
36 H6 Lonsee Germany
26 D9 Lönset Norway
28 D2 Lønstrup Denmark
129 H4 Lontra Brazil
130 D7 Lontra, R Brazil
22 C2 Looberghe France
71 F4 Looc Philippines
8 B7 Looe, E England
110 K3 Loogootee Indiana U.S.A.
107 M6 Lookeba Oklahoma U.S.A.
94 C4 Lookingglass R Michigan U.S.A.
100 D8 Lookout California U.S.A.
116 H5 Lookout Mt Alaska U.S.A.
102 F5 Lookout Mt California U.S.A.
112 B3 Lookout Mt Georgia U.S.A.
106 B6 Lookout Mt New Mexico U.S.A.
100 K2 Lookout Pass Mont/Idaho U.S.A.
141 H2 Lookout Pt Queensland Australia
141 L7 Lookout, Pt Queensland Australia
94 D2 Lookout, Pt Michigan U.S.A.
100 C6 Lookout Pt.Res Oregon U.S.A.
116 H2 Lookout Ridge Alaska U.S.A.
112 F2 Lookout Shoal North Carolina U.S.A.
118 D5 Looma Alberta Canada
118 J9 Loomis Saskatchewan Canada

98 G9 Loomis Nebraska U.S.A.
100 F1 Loomis Washington U.S.A.
117 Q7 Loon R Alberta Canada
120 B4 Loon Ontario Canada
123 S4 Loon Bay Newfoundland Canada
143 F9 Loongana W Australia Australia
95 R7 Loon L Maine U.S.A.
118 H4 Loon Lake Saskatchewan Canada
22 C2 Loon Plage France
119 Q2 Loon R Manitoba Canada
117 N9 Loos British Columbia Canada
110 G6 Loosahatchie R Tennessee U.S.A.
22 D3 Loos-en-Gohelle France
54 F4 Lopandino Russian Federation
55 E4 Lopatki Russian Federation
68 E5 Lop Buri Thailand
59 H1 Lopcha Russian Federation
71 F4 Lopez Philippines
86 A6 Lopez, C Gabon
25 C5 Lopik Netherlands
Lop Nor L see Lop Nur L
66 E3 Lop Nur L China
71 H9 Lopok Indonesia
86 D5 Lopori R Zaire
26 M1 Loppa Norway
26 M1 Lopphavet chan Norway
52 G3 Loptyuga Russian Federation
31 M5 Łopuszno Poland
52 H4 Lopydino Russian Federation
20 C5 Loqueffret France
138 C3 Lora R South Australia Australia
16 D7 Lora del Rio Spain
77 J5 Lora, Hamun-i- Pakistan
94 E5 Lorain Ohio U.S.A.
99 P9 Loraine Illinois U.S.A.
98 E1 Loraine North Dakota U.S.A.
77 L4 Loralai Pakistan
70 G6 Lorana Sulawesi
131 A5 Lora, Pta Chile
77 K4 Lorba R Afghanistan
17 F7 Lorca Spain
36 H6 Lorch Baden-Württemberg Germany
36 D3 Lorch Hessen Germany
26 C9 Lord R Norway
137 M8 Lord Howe I Pacific Oc
137 M7 Lord Howe Seamounts Pacific Oc
68 C7 Lord Loughborough I Burma
115 K4 Lord Mayor B Northwest Territories Canada
106 B9 Lordsburg New Mexico U.S.A.
118 L7 Loreburn Saskatchewan Canada
36 D3 Loreley cliffs Germany
130 F8 Lorena Brazil
109 K4 Lorena Texas U.S.A.
41 H3 Lorenzago di Cadore Italy
33 S10 Lorenzkirch Germany
101 O6 Lorenzo Idaho U.S.A.
98 C8 Lorenzo Nebraska U.S.A.
131 F4 Lorenzo Geyres Uruguay
45 M1 Loreo Italy
77 A3 Lorestan Iran
130 B10 Loreto Argentina
124 D4 Loreto Mexico
130 B8 Loreto Paraguay
128 C5 Loreto dept Peru
71 G5 Loreto Philippines
99 Q4 Loretta Wisconsin U.S.A.
119 V9 Lorette Manitoba Canada
121 T6 Loretteville Quebec Canada
94 B9 Loretto Kentucky U.S.A.
110 J6 Loretto Tennessee U.S.A.
19 Q18 Lorgues France
126 G10 Lorica Colombia
20 D6 Lorient France
121 Q7 L'Orignal Ontario Canada
99 M8 Lorimor Iowa U.S.A.
141 F2 Lorim Point Queensland Australia
48 F3 Lőrinci Hungary
101 S1 Loring Montana U.S.A.
112 J3 Loris South Carolina U.S.A.
119 O8 Lorlie Saskatchewan Canada
111 E10 Lorman Mississippi U.S.A.
22 B2 Lormel, Pte de France
18 H5 Lormes France
15 C4 Lorn Scotland
143 D7 Lorna Glen W Australia Australia
140 D4 Lorne R N Terr Australia
141 H6 Lorne Queensland Australia
122 F6 Lorne New Brunswick Canada
135 L11 L'Orne Bank Pacific Oc
15 C1 Lorn, Firth of Scotland
45 L4 Loro Ciuffenna Italy
20 H7 Loroux-Bottereau, le France
36 G6 Lorquin France
40 G2 Lörrach Germany
140 E4 Lorraine Queensland Australia
36 B5 Lorraine hist reg France
107 M3 Lorraine Kansas U.S.A.
121 L5 Lorrainville Quebec Canada
36 F4 Lorsch Germany
28 B3 Lørslev Denmark
13 E4 Lorton England
32 G7 Lorup Germany
26 H10 Los Sweden
128 C5 Los Alamos Mexico
102 D7 Los Alamos California U.S.A.
106 D6 Los Alamos New Mexico U.S.A.
131 B5 Los Angeles Chile
124 H3 Los Angeles Mexico
104 Los Angeles conurbation California U.S.A.
109 H7 Los Angeles Texas U.S.A.
102 F6 Los Angeles Aqueduct California U.S.A.
126 D3 Los Arabos Cuba
17 F4 Losares mt Spain
70 M9 Losari Java
17 F4 Los Baños Mexico
102 D4 Los Banos California U.S.A.
128 F8 Los Blancos Argentina
124 D2 Los Chirriones Mexico
131 C3 Los Colorados Argentina
109 J9 Los Comales Mexico
124 D5 Los Dolores Mexico
109 J9 Los Ebanos Texas U.S.A.
38 K6 Losenstein Austria
17 F7 Los Filabres mts Spain
109 K9 Los Fresnos Texas U.S.A.
102 C4 Los Gatos California U.S.A.
22 L3 Losheim Belgium
36 B5 Losheim Germany
128 F1 Los Hermanos islds Venezuela
109 H10 Los Herreras Mexico
124 F3 Los Hoyos Mexico
27 G15 Loshult Sweden
31 O3 Łosice Poland
85 B7 Los, Iles de Guinea
42 F4 Lošinj isld Croatia
56 C2 Losinoborskoye Russian Federation
55 D3 Losinyy Russian Federation
89 F5 Loskop Dam S Africa
131 A8 Los Lagos prov Chile
108 A4 Los Médanos Mexico
124 E5 Los Mochis Mexico
100 C9 Los Molinos California U.S.A.
131 B3 Los Molles, R Chile
27 D10 Losna Norway
16 D5 Los Navalmorales Spain
28 D5 Løsning Denmark
102 D7 Los Olivos California U.S.A.
126 C3 Los Palacios Cuba
16 D6 Los Pedroches reg Spain
124 D3 Los Pocitos Mexico
133 C3 Los Pozos Chile
124 H8 Los Reyes Mexico
128 C4 Los Rios R Ecuador
128 C4 Los Rios prov Ecuador
127 L9 Los Roques, Is Venezuela
127 L8 Los Roques Trench Caribbean
37 L1 Lossa Germany
16 C6 Los Santos de Maimona Spain
36 E7 Lossburg Germany
15 E3 Lossie R Scotland
15 E3 Lossiemouth Scotland
37 O2 Lössnitz Germany
101 S6 Lost Cabin Wyoming U.S.A.
94 J8 Lost City West Virginia U.S.A.
101 R7 Lost Cr Wyoming U.S.A.
127 L9 Los Teques Venezuela
127 N9 Los Testigos islds Venezuela
102 E6 Lost Hills California U.S.A.
133 E3 Los Tigres Argentina
100 H4 Lostine Oregon U.S.A.
111 E12 Lost L Louisiana U.S.A.
94 J8 Lost River West Virginia U.S.A.
101 M5 Lost River Ra Idaho U.S.A.
107 O3 Lost Springs Kansas U.S.A.
98 B7 Lost Springs Wyoming U.S.A.
101 M4 Lost Trail Pass Idaho/Montana U.S.A.
8 B7 Lostwithiel England
98 D1 Lostwood North Dakota U.S.A.
71 B1 Losuwo Halmahera Indonesia
133 C4 Los Vilos Chile
16 E5 Los Yebenes Spain
18 G8 Lot dept France
18 G8 Lot R France
131 A6 Lota Chile
86 F5 Lotagipi Swamp Sudan
68 A1 Lotaw Burma
18 F8 Lot et Garonne dept France
77 F1 Lotfābād Iran
101 O1 Lothair Montana U.S.A.
15 E5 Lothian reg Scotland
21 O8 Lothiers France
86 D6 Loto Zaire
54 G1 Lotoshino Russian Federation
89 E4 Lotsane R Botswana
40 G5 Lötschberg Tunnel Switzerland
40 G5 Lötschen R Switzerland
54 G8 Lotsmano-Kamenka Ukraine
109 K4 Lott Texas U.S.A.
52 C1 Lotta R Russian Federation
37 N3 Lottengrün Germany
41 J5 Lottigna Switzerland
112 F5 Lotts Cr Georgia U.S.A.
88 D2 Lotui isld Uganda
101 M6 Lotus Idaho U.S.A.
99 S9 Lotus Illinois U.S.A.
21 K6 Louailles France
68 F3 Louang-Phrabang Laos
20 D4 Louannec France
21 M7 Louans France
20 D4 Louargat France
86 B6 Loubomo Congo
20 E5 Loudéac France
46 E4 Loudhias R Greece
86 B6 Loudima Zaire
95 Q3 Loudon New Hampshire U.S.A.
112 C2 Loudon Tennessee U.S.A.
94 E6 Loudonville Ohio U.S.A.
21 L7 Loudun France
21 K6 Loué France
40 C3 Loue R France
85 B5 Louga Senegal
9 E2 Loughborough England
118 F6 Lougheed Alberta Canada
114 F2 Lougheed I Northwest Territories Canada
8 B4 Loughor Wales
14 C3 Loughrea Ireland
19 J6 Louhans France
111 G9 Louin Mississippi U.S.A.
94 E8 Louisa Kentucky U.S.A.
94 J8 Louisa Virginia U.S.A.
142 E3 Louisa Downs W Australia Australia
70 C1 Louisa Reef S China Sea
123 N8 Louisbourg C Breton I, Nova Scotia
107 Q3 Louisburg Kansas U.S.A.
112 J1 Louisburg North Carolina U.S.A.
123 L8 Louisdale C Breton I, Nova Scotia
109 L6 Louise Texas U.S.A.
117 P5 Louise Falls Northwest Territories Canada
117 H9 Louise I British Columbia Canada
117 P10 Louise, L Alberta Canada
116 O5 Louise, L Alaska U.S.A.
121 S6 Louiseville Quebec Canada
137 L4 Louisiade Arch islds Papua New Guinea
111 E11 Louisiana state U.S.A.
110 E2 Louisiana Missouri U.S.A.
109 O6 Louisiana Pt Louisiana U.S.A.
89 F4 Louis Trichardt S Africa
111 L10 Louisville Alabama U.S.A.
98 A10 Louisville Colorado U.S.A.
112 E4 Louisville Georgia U.S.A.
94 B8 Louisville Kentucky U.S.A.
111 G8 Louisville Mississippi U.S.A.
99 L9 Louisville Nebraska U.S.A.
94 F6 Louisville Ohio U.S.A.
115 M7 Louis XIV, Pte Quebec Canada
52 D2 Loukhi Russian Federation
16 B7 Loule Portugal
30 H5 Louny Czech Rep
98 H8 Loup City Nebraska U.S.A.
21 N5 Loupe, la France
22 J5 Louppy-sur-Loison France
22 E3 Lourches France
123 N5 Lourdes Newfoundland Canada
18 F9 Lourdes France
130 B5 Lourenço R Brazil
Lourenço Marques see Maputo
16 A6 Loures Portugal
16 A5 Lourinhã Portugal
46 D5 Loúros Greece
21 J6 Louroux-Beconnais, le France
21 P5 Loury France
16 B4 Lousã Portugal
118 D6 Lousana Alberta Canada
16 B4 Lousa, Serra Da mts Portugal
6 B2 Lousy Bank N Atlantic Oc
139 H4 Louth New South Wales Australia
13 H6 Louth England
14 E3 Louth co Ireland
14 E3 Louth Ireland
46 E7 Loutrá Dhytikí Ellás Greece
46 F6 Loutrá Evvoia Greece
47 O12 Loútsai Greece
Louvain see Leuven
22 K4 Louveigne Belgium
21 P1 Louvencourt France
21 N3 Louverne France
22 G3 Louvière, La Belgium
21 N3 Louviers France
106 E2 Louviers Colorado U.S.A.
20 H5 Louvigné-de-Bais France
20 H4 Louvigné-du-Désert France
21 P3 Louvres France
28 H6 Lov Denmark
26 M7 Lövånger Sweden
48 E3 Lovasberény Hungary
48 D3 Lovászpatona Hungary
54 B1 Lovat' R Russian Federation
26 K6 Lövberg Sweden
26 H8 Lövberga Sweden
42 J6 Lovćen mt Montenegro Yugoslavia
119 N5 Love Saskatchewan Canada
28 G5 Løve Denmark
68 F6 Lovea Cambodia
46 G1 Lovech Bulgaria
109 O9 Love Field Airport Texas U.S.A.
28 C3 Løvel Denmark
109 M4 Lovelady Texas U.S.A.
98 A9 Loveland Colorado U.S.A.
94 C7 Loveland Ohio U.S.A.
106 E2 Loveland Pass Colorado U.S.A.
101 R5 Lovell Wyoming U.S.A.
94 C2 Lovells Michigan U.S.A.
100 G9 Lovelock Nevada U.S.A.
103 O1 Lovenia, Mt Utah U.S.A.
95 L7 Love Point Maryland U.S.A.
42 C3 Lovere Italy
118 H7 Loverna Saskatchewan Canada
113 D7 Lovett Florida U.S.A.
26 F10 Lövhögen Sweden
26 N4 Lovikka Sweden
106 F9 Loving New Mexico U.S.A.
109 J2 Loving Texas U.S.A.
94 J9 Lovingston Virginia U.S.A.
99 S10 Lovington Illinois U.S.A.
106 G9 Lovington New Mexico U.S.A.
16 B3 Lovios Spain
29 M11 Lovisa Finland
26 J5 Lövnäs Sweden
28 C4 Lovns Bredning B Denmark
30 H5 Lovosice Czech Rep
52 E1 Lovozero Russian Federation
52 E1 Lovozero, Ozero L Russian Federation
45 P1 Lovre ćica Croatia
48 F5 Lovrin Romania
26 H7 Lövsjön Sweden
26 F5 Lovunden isld Norway
103 L1 Low Utah U.S.A.
86 E6 Lowa Zaire
144 B6 Lowburn New Zealand
120 K4 Low Bush River Ontario Canada
115 L5 Low, C Northwest Territories Canada
99 P8 Lowden Iowa U.S.A.
100 E6 Low Desert Oregon U.S.A.
9 F1 Lowdham England
103 P10 Lowell Arizona U.S.A.
110 B5 Lowell Arkansas U.S.A.
100 K3 Lowell Idaho U.S.A.
99 T8 Lowell Indiana U.S.A.
95 Q4 Lowell Massachusetts U.S.A.
94 B4 Lowell Michigan U.S.A.
94 F7 Lowell Ohio U.S.A.
100 C6 Lowell Oregon U.S.A.
100 J6 Lowell, L Idaho U.S.A.
33 S7 Löwenberg Germany
28 C7 Löwenstedt Germany
36 G5 Löwenstein Germany
117 P11 Lower Arrow L British Columbia Canada
98 G5 Lower Brule South Dakota U.S.A.
101 P5 Lower Falls Wyoming U.S.A.
119 V8 Lower Ft.Garry Manitoba Canada
103 L6 Lower Granite Gorge Arizona U.S.A.
145 G4 Lower Hutt New Zealand
123 U6 Lower Island Cove Newfoundland Canada
100 D8 Lower Klamath L California U.S.A.
102 B3 Lower L California U.S.A.
117 F5 Lower Laberge Yukon Territory Canada
115 K4 Lower Macdougall L Northwest Territories Canada
122 G6 Lower Neguac New Brunswick Canada
122 G10 Lower Ohio Nova Scotia Canada
135 T3 Lower Paia Hawaiian Is
117 J6 Lower Post British Columbia Canada
99 L2 Lower Red L Minnesota U.S.A.
101 O5 Lower Red Rock L Montana U.S.A.
115 N5 Lower Savage Is Northwest Territories Canada
122 G10 Lower West Pubnico Nova Scotia Canada
15 F1 Lower Whitehall Scotland
110 H5 Lowes Kentucky U.S.A.
9 H3 Lowestoft England
77 L2 Lowgar R Afghanistan
77 L3 Lowgar prov Afghanistan
139 H8 Low Head Tasmania Australia
146 C3 Low I isld Antarctica
13 G2 Lowick England
13 E5 Lowick Br England
31 M3 Łowicz Poland
141 H3 Low Is Queensland Australia
100 K5 Lowman Idaho U.S.A.
111 K9 Lowndesboro Alabama U.S.A.
83 M9 Low Pt Christmas I Indian Oc
139 H9 Low Rocky Pt Tasmania Australia
110 C3 Lowry City Missouri U.S.A.
87 H10 Lowry, Iles Madagascar
112 F3 Lowrys South Carolina U.S.A.
13 F4 Lowther England
115 K3 Lowther I Northwest Territories Canada
121 P9 Lowville New York U.S.A.
125 L9 Loxicha Mexico
111 J11 Loxley Alabama U.S.A.
138 F5 Loxton South Australia Australia
99 Q5 Loyal Wisconsin U.S.A.
118 F7 Loyalist Alberta Canada
94 D10 Loyall Kentucky U.S.A.
95 K5 Loyalsock Cr Pennsylvania U.S.A.
102 D2 Loyalton California U.S.A.
98 G4 Loyalton South Dakota U.S.A.
Loyang see Luoyang
137 O6 Loyauté, Is Pacific Oc
54 B5 Loyev Belarus
52 G4 Loyma Russian Federation
52 H5 Loyno Russian Federation
51 H2 Lozarevo Bulgaria
18 H8 Lozère dept France
18 H8 Lozère, Mt France
48 E6 Loznica Serbia Yugoslavia
47 H1 Loznitsa Bulgaria
54 H8 Lozovaya Ukraine
55 G4 Lozovoye Kazakhstan
55 D1 Loz'va R Russian Federation
86 C5 Lua R Zaire
87 C8 Luacano Angola
87 D7 Luachimo Angola
69 D13 Luahasibuka Indonesia
88 F10 Lualaba R Zaire
86 E6 Luala R Mozambique
86 E6 Lualaba R Zaire
87 F8 Luambe Zambia
87 D9 Luampa Zambia
58 G5 Lu'an China
127 J2 Luana Pt Jamaica
68 F2 Luan Chau Vietnam
67 C5 Luancheng Guangxi China
65 B8 Luancheng China
87 B7 Luanda Angola
87 C8 Luando R Angola
71 O9 Luang isld Indonesia
68 D7 Luang, Khao mt Thailand
69 E9 Luang, Thale L Thailand
87 C7 Luangue R Angola
88 D7 Luangwa R Zambia
88 C8 Luangwa Zambia
67 F1 Luan He R China
65 F3 Luannan China
88 B9 Luano Zambia
88 D4 Luanping China
88 B8 Luanshya Zambia
65 D5 Luan Xian China
88 B8 Luapula R Zaire
88 B7 Luapula Zambia
16 C1 Luarca Spain
70 C4 Luar, D L Kalimantan
87 D8 Luashi Zaire
87 F8 Luatize R Mozambique
87 D8 Luau Angola
85 F8 Luba Bioko Equat Guinea
125 P9 Lubaantum Belize
31 O5 Lubaczów Poland
87 C7 Lubalo Angola
31 J4 Lubań Poland
31 J4 Lubāna Latvia
52 C6 Lubānasezers L Latvia
71 E4 Lubang Philippines
87 B8 Lubango Angola
87 C7 Lubansenshi R Zambia
87 E7 Lubao Zaire
33 Q8 Lübars Germany
31 O4 Lubartów Poland
31 M2 Lubawa Poland
32 J8 Lübbecke Germany
33 T9 Lübben Germany
33 T9 Lübbenau Germany
108 F2 Lubbock Texas U.S.A.
139 G6 Lubeck Victoria Australia
33 N5 Lübeck Germany
33 O4 Lübecker Bucht Germany
86 D6 Lubefu Zaire
37 P3 Lubenec Czech Rep
55 B5 Lubenka Kazakhstan
88 B2 Lubero Zaire
19 O17 Lubéron, Montagne du mts France
88 C8 Lubi R Zambia
71 E5 Lubic isld Philippines
118 B2 Lubicon L Alberta Canada
31 J2 Lubie, Jezioro L Poland
31 L3 Lubień Poland
87 D7 Lubilash R Zaire
31 J4 Lubiń Poland
31 O4 Lublin Poland
99 Q4 Lublin Wisconsin U.S.A.
31 L5 Lubliniec Poland
33 T4 Lubmin Germany
31 J3 Lubnaig, L Scotland
54 D6 Lubny Ukraine
70 B4 Lubok Anto Sarawak
29 P8 Lubosalma Russian Federation
17 F7 Lubrín Spain
31 H4 Lubsko Poland
33 O7 Lübtheen Germany
71 E2 Lubuagan Luzon Philippines
71 E2 Lubudi R Zaire
87 E7 Lubudi Zaire
70 K8 Lubukbatang Sumatra
69 F14 Lubuklinggau Sumatra
69 D11 Lubukpakam Sumatra
69 E12 Lubuksikaping Sumatra
87 E8 Lubumbashi Zaire
86 E6 Lubutu Zaire
37 N3 Luby Czech Rep
33 Q6 Lübz Germany
21 K3 Luc Calvados France
87 C7 Lucala Angola
120 J9 Lucan Ontario Canada
14 E3 Lucan Ireland
116 R6 Lucania, Mt Yukon Territory Canada
43 G8 Lucano, Appennino mts Italy
129 G6 Lucas Brazil
99 N8 Lucas Iowa U.S.A.
107 M2 Lucas Kansas U.S.A.
94 E6 Lucas Ohio U.S.A.
142 G5 Lucas, L W Australia Australia
126 E1 Lucaya Grand Bahama I
21 N7 Luçay-le-Mâle France
71 E3 Lucban Luzon Philippines
45 J4 Lucca Italy
98 J1 Lucca North Dakota U.S.A.
13 J3 Luce Bay Scotland
129 G3 Luce R Suriname
127 H1 Lucea Jamaica
15 D6 Luce B Scotland
111 H11 Lucedale Mississippi U.S.A.
130 E7 Lucélia Brazil
71 E4 Lucena Philippines
17 G4 Lucena del Cid Spain
16 D6 Lucena, Sa. de mts Spain
48 F2 Lučenec Slovakia
43 G7 Lucera Italy
Lucerne see Luzern
102 B2 Lucerne California U.S.A.
99 N9 Lucerne Missouri U.S.A.
100 E1 Lucerne Washington U.S.A.
101 R6 Lucerne Wyoming U.S.A.
102 H6 Lucerne L California U.S.A.
102 H7 Lucerne Valley California U.S.A.
108 A5 Lucero Mexico
106 C8 Lucero New Mexico U.S.A.
122 A5 Luceville Quebec Canada
65 B6 Lucheng China
67 B4 Lucheng China
88 E9 Luchenza Malawi
21 L6 Luché-Pringé France
111 F11 Lucher Louisiana U.S.A.
54 B2 Luchesa R Belarus
21 P1 Lucheux France
33 O7 Lüchow Germany
68 K1 Luchuan China
21 P1 Luchy France
102 C5 Lucia California U.S.A.
121 M2 Lucie, L Quebec Canada
100 J4 Lucile Idaho U.S.A.
16 C2 Lucillo Spain
103 M1 Lucin Utah U.S.A.
141 H4 Lucinda Queensland Australia
94 H5 Lucinda Pennsylvania U.S.A.
138 F6 Lucindale South Australia Australia
87 B8 Lucira Angola
99 O4 Luck Wisconsin U.S.A.
37 N1 Lucka Germany
33 T9 Luckau Germany
33 S8 Luckenwalde Germany
143 E8 Lucky, Mt W Australia Australia
141 K6 Lucknow Queensland Australia
120 J9 Lucknow Ontario Canada
74 J5 Lucknow India
118 K8 Lucky Lake Saskatchewan Canada
100 K6 Lucky Peak Res Idaho U.S.A.
118 F9 Lucky Strike Alberta Canada
20 H5 Luçon France
94 H9 Lucone ne Marsi Italy
18 E5 Lucquy France
22 G4 Lucrecia, C Cuba
126 G4 Lucs-sur-Boulogne, les France
20 H8 Lucusse Angola
87 D8 Lucy New Mexico U.S.A.
106 E7 Lucy Creek N Terr Australia
140 B6 Lucy Yen Vietnam
68 G1 Lucy, Mt N Terr Australia
140 C6 Lüda see Dalian
13 H6 Ludborough England
98 H3 Ludden North Dakota U.S.A.
21 L6 Lude, le France
107 K2 Ludell Kansas U.S.A.
32 G10 Lüdenscheid Germany
33 P7 Lüderitz Germany
89 A5 Lüderitz Namibia
120 K7 Ludgate Ontario Canada
9 E5 Ludgershall England
74 F3 Ludhiana India
32 F9 Lüdinghausen Germany
99 U6 Ludington Michigan U.S.A.
122 F7 Ludlow New Brunswick Canada
8 D3 Ludlow England
103 H7 Ludlow California U.S.A.
106 F4 Ludlow Colorado U.S.A.
99 S9 Ludlow Illinois U.S.A.
94 J5 Ludlow Pennsylvania U.S.A.
98 C4 Ludlow South Dakota U.S.A.
95 P3 Ludlow Vermont U.S.A.
47 H1 Ludogorie Bulgaria
52 C5 Ludoni Russian Federation
112 F6 Ludowici Georgia U.S.A.
36 E5 Ludswigshöhe Germany
48 J4 Luduș Romania
27 H11 Ludvika Sweden
36 H2 Ludwigsau Germany
36 G6 Ludwigsburg Germany
37 M3 Ludwigschorgast Germany
36 E5 Ludwigshafen Germany
37 L5 Ludwigs Kanal canal Germany
33 O6 Ludwigslust Germany
37 L3 Ludwigstadt Germany
52 C6 Ludza Latvia
86 D7 Luebo Zaire
109 H3 Lueders Texas U.S.A.
86 E6 Lueki Zaire
87 C8 Luena Angola
87 D8 Luena R Angola
87 D8 Luena R Zambia
88 D10 Luenha R Mozambique
128 F2 Luepa Venezuela
87 D7 Lueta Zaire
87 D9 Lueti R Zambia
58 E5 Lüeyang China
67 E5 Lufeng China
88 D6 Lufira R Malawi
111 B10 Lufkin Texas U.S.A.
88 C6 Lufubu R Zambia
88 B10 Lufya R Zambia
48 F6 Lug R Serbia Yugoslavia
52 C5 Luga R Russian Federation
52 D5 Luga Russian Federation
88 B4 Lugamba Zaire
41 J5 Lugano Switzerland
42 B3 Lugano, L. di Italy
54 L8 Lugansk Ukraine
126 F4 Lugareño Cuba
32 K9 Lügde Germany
88 F10 Lugela R Mozambique
88 F10 Lugela Mozambique
88 F9 Lugenda R Mozambique
144 B6 Luggate New Zealand
8 D3 Lugg, R England
Lugh Ferrandi see Luuq
14 E4 Lugnaquilla mt Ireland
41 K4 Lugnezer Tal Switzerland
45 L3 Lugo Italy
16 B1 Lugo prov Spain
16 B1 Lugo Spain
48 G6 Lugoj Romania
55 E1 Lugovskoy Russian Federation
12 D2 Lugton Scotland
86 E6 Lugulu R Zaire
71 E8 Lugus isld Philippines
70 G6 Luha isld Celebes
29 M10 Luhanka Finland
72 E5 Luḥayyah, Al Yemen
67 F1 Luhe China
32 M6 Luhe R Germany
37 N4 Luhe Germany
65 D1 Luhin Sum China
33 M4 Lühmannsdorf Germany
87 C7 Lui R Angola
88 D10 Luia R Mozambique
87 D9 Luiana Angola
Luichow Pen see Leizhou Bandao
Luik see Liège
86 D6 Luilaka R Zaire
15 C4 Luing isld Scotland
42 B2 Luino Italy
29 N4 Luira R Finland
124 E4 Luis Mexico
130 E10 Luis Alves Brazil
130 H9 Luis Gomes Brazil
87 E8 Luishia Zaire
124 H5 Luis Moya Mexico
146 F7 Luitpold Coast Antarctica
87 D7 Luiza Zaire
131 F5 Luján R Argentina
133 D4 Luján Argentina
67 F1 Lujiang China
67 C5 Lujing China
70 Q10 Luk Indonesia
37 P3 Luka Czech Rep
87 E8 Lukafu Zaire
88 A8 Lukanga R Zambia
88 A8 Lukanga Sw Zambia
143 B7 Luke, Mt W Australia Australia
86 C6 Lukenie R Zaire
52 F6 Lukh Russian Federation
55 E4 Lukhovitsy Russian Federation
46 G3 Lūki Bulgaria
41 J4 Lukmanier Pass Switzerland
86 C6 Lukolela Zaire
67 D3 Lukou China
46 G1 Lukovit Bulgaria
46 D3 Lukovo Macedonia
31 N4 Łuków Poland
52 F6 Lukoyanov Russian Federation
86 B7 Lukula Zaire
88 B8 Lukulu Zambia
87 G7 Lukuledi R Tanzania
88 A8 Lukulu Zambia
88 B8 Lukulu R Zambia
87 G7 Lukumburu Tanzania
88 D8 Lukuzye R Zambia
112 D3 Lula Georgia U.S.A.
111 F7 Lula Mississippi U.S.A.
26 M6 Luleå Sweden
26 M6 Lule älv R Sweden
47 J3 Lüleburgaz Turkey
87 D7 Lulenge R Angola
67 A4 Luliang China
65 B6 Lüliang Shan ra China
111 F12 Luling Louisiana U.S.A.
109 K6 Luling Texas U.S.A.
65 D5 Lulong China
86 C5 Lulonga R Zaire
113 E7 Lulu Florida U.S.A.
86 D7 Lulua R Zaire
Luluabourg see Kananga
8 D6 Lulworth Cove England
143 C7 Lulworth, Mt W Australia Australia
70 O10 Lumajang Java
70 E2 Lumaku mt Sabah
70 D2 Lumaku mt Sabah
70 O10 Lumajang Java
87 D8 Lumbala Kaquengue Angola
87 D8 Lumbala N'guimbo Angola
112 H3 Lumber R North Carolina U.S.A.
112 E6 Lumber City Georgia U.S.A.
94 J6 Lumber City Pennsylvania U.S.A.
94 G7 Lumberport West Virginia U.S.A.
111 G10 Lumberton Mississippi U.S.A.
106 D5 Lumberton New Mexico U.S.A.
112 H3 Lumberton North Carolina U.S.A.
18 E10 Lumbier Spain
70 E2 Lumbis Kalimantan
88 H9 Lumbo Mozambique
52 F1 Lumbovka Russian Federation
16 C4 Lumbrales Spain
22 C2 Lumbres France
28 E6 Lumby Denmark
75 P6 Lumding India
14 D2 Lumijoki Finland
88 E8 Lumimba R Zambia
22 J2 Lummen Belgium
29 H11 Lumparland Finland
111 M9 Lumpkin Georgia U.S.A.
28 H5 Lumsås Denmark
123 T4 Lumsden Newfoundland Canada
119 N8 Lumsden Saskatchewan Canada
144 B6 Lumsden New Zealand
15 F3 Lumsden Scotland
69 F10 Lumut Malaysia
70 D5 Lumut, Bt mt Kalimantan
71 E2 Luna Luzon Philippines
106 B8 Luna New Mexico U.S.A.
131 G2 Luna, L Argentina
67 A4 Lunan China
15 F4 Lunan B Scotland
71 F7 Lunan Philippines
117 L10 Lund British Columbia Canada
28 D5 Lund Denmark
27 F16 Lund Sweden
103 J3 Lund Nevada U.S.A.
103 L3 Lund Utah U.S.A.
27 J13 Lunda Sweden
88 B7 Lunda Chishinga Zambia
29 K5 Lundåkrabukten B Sweden
119 T8 Lundar Manitoba Canada
87 F8 Lundazi Zambia
88 D8 Lundazi R Zambia
118 C9 Lundbreck Alberta Canada
28 H6 Lundby Denmark
28 A5 Lunde Denmark
28 F6 Lundeborg Denmark
28 C6 Lunderskov Denmark
27 B13 Lunde-Vatn L Norway
28 C3 Lunde Denmark
28 D5 Lundum Denmark
8 B5 Lundy isld England
32 J6 Lüne R Germany
33 M6 Lüne Germany
36 B3 Lünebach Germany
33 M6 Lüneburg Germany
32 J8 Lüneburger Heide reg Germany
18 H9 Lunel France
32 G9 Lünen Germany
122 H9 Lunenburg Nova Scotia Canada
95 Q2 Lunenburg Vermont U.S.A.
21 M2 Luneray France
41 L3 Lüner See L Austria
21 P8 Lunery France
19 K4 Lunéville France
87 D8 Lunga R Zambia
68 H1 Lung-chou China
66 C5 Lungdo China
66 C5 Lunggar China
44 G3 Lungiana Italy
26 H8 Lungsjön Sweden
27 G12 Lungsund Sweden
88 C8 Lungu Zambia
87 C8 Lungue Bungo R Angola
102 F3 Luning Nevada U.S.A.
71 H9 Lunjuk Sumbawa Indonesia
15 G2 Lunna Scotland
32 F8 Lünne Germany
85 B7 Lunsar Sierra Leone
88 B8 Lunsemfwa R Zambia
66 C3 Luntai China
38 M6 Lunz am See Austria
37 O2 Lunzenau Germany
48 D3 Lunzi R China
67 C4 Luocheng China
58 E4 Luochuan China
67 B4 Luodian China
67 D5 Luoding China
65 A7 Luo He R China
65 B7 Luo He R China
67 A1 Luojiang China
67 D5 Luojing China
67 B2 Luolong China
65 A7 Luonan China
26 M4 Luongasunturi mt Sweden
88 B7 Luongo R Zambia
65 B7 Luoning China
67 A4 Luoping China
67 C4 Luoqing Jiang R China
67 C4 Luorong China
67 E1 Luoshan China
67 D2 Luoshan China
67 E1 Luotian China
65 E1 Luotuobozi China
67 B1 Luowenba China
65 B7 Luoyang China
67 F3 Luoyuan China
86 B6 Luozi Zaire
88 D6 Lupa R Tanzania
88 D8 Lupachi R Malawi
89 E2 Lupane Zimbabwe
89 F2 Lupani R Zimbabwe
71 D7 Lupa pula Philippines
70 B4 Lupar R Sarawak
31 K1 Łupawa R Poland
37 M5 Lupburg Germany
48 H5 Lupeni Romania
127 J5 Luperon Dominican Rep
41 J1 Lupfen mt Germany
87 G8 Lupilichi Mozambique
67 B3 Luping China
87 C8 Lupire Angola
42 F3 Lupoglav Croatia
54 B3 Lupolovo Belarus
71 G7 Lupon Mindanao Philippines
33 R10 Luppa Germany
110 D3 Lupus Missouri U.S.A.
87 D7 Luputa Zaire
52 H4 Lup'ya R Russian Federation
130 B9 Luque Paraguay
107 M2 Luray Kansas U.S.A.
94 J8 Luray Virginia U.S.A.
112 E2 Lure, L North Carolina U.S.A.
19 P16 Lure, Mt de France
14 E2 Lurgan N Ireland
128 E7 Luribay Bolivia
128 C6 Luricacha Peru
87 H8 Lurio Mozambique
26 F5 Lurøy Norway
19 P17 Lurs France
110 C6 Lurton Arkansas U.S.A.
21 P7 Lury sur-Arnon France
88 B9 Lusaka Zambia
86 D6 Lusambo Zaire
88 C3 Lusanga Zaire
86 B6 Lusangazi Zambia
20 G8 Lusanger France
117 P9 Luscar Alberta Canada
118 H6 Luseland Saskatchewan Canada
88 C6 Lusenga Plain Nat. Park Zambia
75 P7 Lushai Hills India
65 D6 Lu Shan mt China
58 F5 Lushi China
143 B8 Lush, Mt W Australia Australia
88 G4 Lushoto Tanzania
65 E5 Lüshun China
67 G1 Lusi R Java
70 N9 Lusi R Java
21 O6 Lusignan France
94 K9 Lusk Wyoming U.S.A.
98 B7 Lus-la-Croix Haute France
19 P15 Luson Italy
38 E8 Lusong Zhou
26 L4 Luspebryggan Sweden
15 D4 Luss Scotland
18 F6 Lussac les Châteaux France
12 C3 Lussa, L Scotland
129 H8 Lussanvira Brazil
78 J6 Lussuf, Al Iraq
141 J7 Lussvale Queensland Australia
36 E5 Lustadt Germany
41 L3 Lustenau Austria
37 J5 Lustenau Germany
27 B10 Luster Norway
22 H3 Lustin Belgium
101 U1 Lustre Montana U.S.A.
Lu-tao see Nunghe
77 E3 Lut, Dasht-e desert Iran
87 D8 Lutembo Angola
110 G4 Lutesville Missouri U.S.A.
99 N8 Luther Iowa U.S.A.
107 N6 Luther Oklahoma U.S.A.
109 J3 Lutie Texas U.S.A.
33 N4 Lütjenburg Germany
9 F4 Luton England
40 E4 Lutry Switzerland
87 C7 Lutshima R Zaire
32 M9 Lutter am Barenberge Germany
32 M7 Lutterloh Germany
9 E3 Lutterworth England
22 G3 Luttre Belgium
112 D1 Luttrell Tennessee U.S.A.
36 C1 Lütringhausen Germany
54 L8 Lutugino Ukraine
113 E9 Lutz Florida U.S.A.
32 L6 Lutzelbourg France
36 C6 Lutzelhouse France
33 Q10 Lützen Germany
36 B3 Lutzerath Germany
33 O5 Lützow Germany
146 J8 Lützow-Holmbukta B Antarctica
29 N11 Luumäki Finland
86 H5 Luuq Somalia
29 N5 Luusua Finland
111 K10 Luverne Alabama U.S.A.
99 M7 Luverne Iowa U.S.A.
98 K6 Luverne Minnesota U.S.A.
98 J2 Luverne North Dakota U.S.A.
29 J10 Luvia Finland
26 K5 Luvos Sweden
29 P7 Luvozero Russian Federation
87 E7 Luvua R Zaire
87 D8 Luvuei Angola
88 F6 Luwegu R Tanzania
88 C8 Luwingu Zambia
71 B2 Luwo isld Halmahera Indonesia
68 J1 Luwu China
70 B5 Luwuhuyu Kalimantan
71 H5 Luwuk Sulawesi
88 D7 Luwumbu R Zambia
111 J8 Luxapallila R Alabama U.S.A.
22 L4 Luxembourg Grand Duchy Europe
22 L4 Luxembourg Luxembourg
99 P7 Luxemburg Iowa U.S.A.
40 D2 Luxeuil-les-Bains France
67 C2 Luxi China
67 A4 Luxi China
67 B2 Lu Xian China
84 J4 Luxor Egypt
18 E9 Luy R France
21 M7 Luynes France
18 E10 Luz France
52 G4 Luza Russian Federation
52 J2 Luza R Komi Respublika Russian Federation
21 P3 Luzarches France
18 F8 Luzech France
21 N8 Luzeret France
41 H3 Luzern Switzerland
94 C2 Luzerne Michigan U.S.A.
95 O3 Luzerne New York U.S.A.
67 C4 Luzhai China
67 B3 Luzhi China
67 B2 Luzhou China
130 F5 Luziânia Brazil
21 N7 Luzillé France
31 H6 Lužnice R Czech Rep
71 E2 Luzon Philippines
18 H6 Luzy France
45 J2 Luzzara Italy
48 J1 L'vov Ukraine
88 B7 Lwela R Zambia
88 C7 Lwitikila R Zambia
31 J3 Lwówek Poland
31 J4 Lwówek Śląski Poland
51 L4 Lyadiny Russian Federation
48 L2 Lyadova R Ukraine
147 Q7 Lyakhovskiye Os isld Russian Federation
144 A6 Lyall, Mt New Zealand
Lyallpur see Faisalabad
57 E5 Lyal'-Mikar Uzbekistan
55 D2 Lyalya R Russian Federation
55 F1 Lyamin R Russian Federation
57 D4 Lyangar Uzbekistan
52 D4 Lyaskelya Russian Federation
47 H1 Lyaskovets Bulgaria
106 C5 Lybrook New Mexico U.S.A.
15 E2 Lybster Scotland
28 C3 Lyby Denmark
106 H4 Lycan Colorado U.S.A.
33 S6 Lychen Germany
52 D5 Lychkovo Russian Federation
47 K8 Lycia Turkey
Lyck see Ełk
26 K7 Lycksele Sweden
9 G6 Lydd England
Lydda see Lod
119 T3 Lyddal Manitoba Canada
146 F6 Lyddan Ice Rise ice rise Antarctica
89 G5 Lydenburg S Africa
8 B6 Lydford England
8 D2 Lydham England
47 J6 Lydia hist reg Turkey
112 G3 Lydia South Carolina U.S.A.
119 V8 Lydiatt Manitoba Canada
8 D4 Lydney England
8 B6 Lyd, R England
28 A5 Lydum Denmark
21 N7 Lye France
145 D4 Lyell New Zealand
140 B6 Lyell Brown, Mt N Terr Australia
117 H9 Lyell I British Columbia Canada
139 H8 Lyell, Mt Tasmania Australia
111 L7 Lyerly Georgia U.S.A.
26 K2 Lyfjord Norway
109 K9 Lyford Texas U.S.A.
113 K9 Lyford Cay isld New Providence I Bahamas
27 B13 Lygna R Norway
95 L6 Lykens Pennsylvania U.S.A.
52 D5 Lykoshino Russian Federation
99 O6 Lyle Minnesota U.S.A.
100 D4 Lyle Washington U.S.A.
112 D5 Lyles Tennessee U.S.A.
119 Q9 Lyleton Manitoba Canada
111 G11 Lyman Mississippi U.S.A.
107 O5 Lyman Oklahoma U.S.A.
112 E3 Lyman South Carolina U.S.A.
101 P8 Lyman Wyoming U.S.A.
117 O8 Lymburn Alberta Canada
95 P3 Lyme New Hampshire U.S.A.
8 D6 Lyme B England
8 D6 Lyme Regis England
9 H5 Lyminge England
9 E6 Lymington England
31 M1 Łyna R Poland
28 H5 Lynæs Denmark
98 H7 Lynch Nebraska U.S.A.
94 D7 Lynchburg Ohio U.S.A.
110 K6 Lynchburg Tennessee U.S.A.
94 H9 Lynchburg Virginia U.S.A.
112 G3 Lynches R South Carolina U.S.A.
95 R2 Lynchville Maine U.S.A.
141 G3 Lynd R Queensland Australia
141 G4 Lynd Queensland Australia
100 C1 Lynden Washington U.S.A.
141 G4 Lyndhurst Queensland Australia
138 E4 Lyndhurst South Australia Australia
9 E6 Lyndhurst England
144 C5 Lyndhurst New Zealand
143 B6 Lyndon W Australia Australia
107 P3 Lyndon Kansas U.S.A.
95 P2 Lyndon Vermont U.S.A.
109 J5 Lyndon B. Johnson, L Texas U.S.A.
143 A6 Lyndon, R W Australia Australia
94 J3 Lyndonville New York U.S.A.
95 P2 Lyndonville Vermont U.S.A.
28 A5 Lyne Denmark
13 E2 Lyne Scotland
28 F4 Lyngby Denmark
29 J14 Lyngdal Norway
28 D4 Lyngbygd Å R Denmark
27 B13 Lyngdal Norway
28 H6 Lynge Denmark
26 L2 Lyngen Norway
27 D13 Lyngør Norway
28 A3 Lyngs Denmark
28 G6 Lyngs Denmark
26 L2 Lyngseidet Norway
26 L2 Lyngsfjord inlet Norway
142 D3 Lynher Reef W Australia Australia
8 C5 Lynmouth England
111 J7 Lynn Alabama U.S.A.
94 C6 Lynn Indiana U.S.A.
95 R4 Lynn Massachusetts U.S.A.
101 M8 Lynn Utah U.S.A.
117 F6 Lynn Canal Alaska U.S.A.
103 M2 Lynndyl Utah U.S.A.
111 L11 Lynn Haven Florida U.S.A.
119 Q2 Lynn Lake Manitoba Canada
99 O8 Lynnville Iowa U.S.A.
110 J6 Lynnville Tennessee U.S.A.

143 A8 Lynton W Australia Australia
8 C5 Lynton England
28 E6 Lyø Denmark
18 N13 Lyon France
94 C2 Lyon Manor Michigan U.S.A.
95 O2 Lyon Mountain New York U.S.A.
18 H7 Lyonnais, Mts.du France
Lyons see Lyon
138 C4 Lyons South Australia Australia
98 A9 Lyons Colorado U.S.A.
112 E5 Lyons Georgia U.S.A.
110 J3 Lyons Indiana U.S.A.
107 M3 Lyons Kansas U.S.A.
94 C4 Lyons Michigan U.S.A.
98 K8 Lyons Nebraska U.S.A.
95 L3 Lyons New York U.S.A.
94 C5 Lyons Ohio U.S.A.
100 C5 Lyons Oregon U.S.A.
98 K6 Lyons South Dakota U.S.A.
109 L5 Lyons Texas U.S.A.
99 S7 Lyons Wisconsin U.S.A.
95 M3 Lyons Falls New York U.S.A.
21 N3 Lyons-la-Forêt France
143 B6 Lyons, R W Australia Australia
137 L2 Lyra Reef Bismarck Arch
22 D2 Lys R France
42 B3 Lys R Italy
31 H5 Lysá Czech Rep
27 B12 Lyse Norway
27 B13 Lysefjorden inlet Norway
27 E13 Lysekil Sweden
79 D3 Lysi Cyprus
101 S6 Lysite Wyoming U.S.A.
40 F3 Lyss Switzerland
121 T6 Lyster Quebec Canada
55 C2 Lys'va Russian Federation
27 F11 Lysvik Sweden
53 F8 Lysyye Gory Russian Federation
8 D6 Lytchett England
13 E6 Lytham St.Anne's England
68 J5 Ly Tin Vietnam
109 J6 Lytle Texas U.S.A.
144 B4 Lyttleton New Zealand
117 N10 Lytton British Columbia Canada
121 O6 Lytton Quebec Canada
102 B3 Lytton California U.S.A.
52 D5 Lyuban' Russian Federation
48 N3 Lyubashevka Ukraine
52 E6 Lyubertsu Russian Federation
54 J1 Lyubertsy Russian Federation
52 F5 Lyubim Russian Federation
47 H3 Lyubimets Bulgaria
55 C2 Lyubimova Russian Federation
55 F3 Lyubinskiy Russian Federation
52 D5 Lyublino Russian Federation
54 F3 Lyubokhna Russian Federation
54 G7 Lyubotin Ukraine
54 F3 Lyudinovo Russian Federation
52 H6 Lyuk Russian Federation
52 G6 Lyunda R Russian Federation
52 J2 Lyzha R Russian Federation

M

68 D1 Ma R Burma
80 F3 Ma'ad Jordan
79 B9 Ma'âdi Egypt
80 F3 Ma'agan Israel
80 C3 Ma'agan Mikha'el Israel
87 H8 Maaia Mozambique
135 T3 Maalaea Hawaiian Is
80 E6 Ma'alé Adummim Jordan
80 D7 Ma'alé 'Amos Jordan
73 L7 Maalosmadulu Atoll Maldives
79 F8 Ma'ān Jordan
29 N8 Maaninka Finland
58 E2 Maanït Mongolia
29 O8 Maanselkä Finland
58 G5 Ma'anshan China
71 F5 Ma-ao Negros Philippines
25 E6 Maarheeze Netherlands
79 G2 Ma'arrat al Ikhwān Syria
79 G3 Ma'arrat an Nu'mān Syria
25 D4 Maarsbergen Netherlands
25 D5 Maarsser Netherlands
25 D4 Maartensdijk Netherlands
25 D5 Maas R Netherlands
25 E6 Maasbracht Netherlands
22 K1 Maaseik Belgium
22 K2 Maasmechelen Belgium
25 B5 Maassluis Netherlands
25 E7 Maastricht Netherlands
139 H9 Maatsuyker Is Tasmania Australia
Maba see Qujiang
71 B2 Maba Halmahera Indonesia
87 F10 Mabalane Mozambique
109 L3 Mabank Texas U.S.A.
80 C4 Ma'barot Israel
71 F4 Mabatobato Philippines
6 M4 Mabel oil rig North Sea
99 P6 Mabel Minnesota U.S.A.
138 C3 Mabel Creek South Australia Australia
142 G3 Mabel Downs W Australia Australia
119 O2 Mabella Ontario Canada
94 F9 Maben West Virginia U.S.A.
121 O8 Maberly Ontario Canada
122 K2 Mabille, L Quebec Canada
28 B4 Måbjerg Denmark
9 G1 Mablethorpe England
123 L7 Mabou C Breton I, Nova Scotia
85 D5 Mabrouk Mali
84 E5 Mabrous Niger
84 F4 Mabruk Libya
100 E3 Mabton Washington U.S.A.
89 D5 Mabule Botswana
61 P14 Mabuni Okinawa
84 G4 Ma'būs Yūsuf well Libya
89 C5 Mabutsane Botswana
133 C7 Maca mt Chile
122 E8 McAdam New Brunswick Canada
143 B7 Macadam Plains W Australia Australia
140 A2 Macadam Ra N Terr Australia
130 H8 Macaé Brazil
130 J8 Macaiba Brazil
71 G6 Macajalar B Philippines
109 M1 McAlester Oklahoma U.S.A.
139 J5 Macalister, Mt New South Wales Australia
109 J9 McAllen Texas U.S.A.
101 O4 McAllister Montana U.S.A.
113 E7 McAlpin Florida U.S.A.
114 J4 MacAlpine L Northwest Territories Canada
121 L4 Macamic Quebec Canada
Macan, Kepulauan isld see Taka' Bonerate, Kepulauan
67 D5 Macao terr E Asia
16 B5 Macão Portugal
128 E5 Macapá Amazonas Brazil
130 H4 Macarani Brazil
127 O10 Macareo R Venezuela
141 F3 Macaroni Queensland Australia
138 F7 Macarthur Victoria Australia
100 D8 McArthur California U.S.A.
94 E7 McArthur Ohio U.S.A.
140 D3 McArthur R N Terr Australia
140 D3 McArthur River N Terr Australia
94 A4 Macatawa Michigan U.S.A.
Macau see Macao
129 L5 Macau Brazil
119 Q8 McAuley Manitoba Canada
137 R8 Macauley I Kermadec Is Pacific Oc
94 B2 McBain Michigan U.S.A.
110 D3 McBaine Missouri U.S.A.
112 F4 McBean Georgia U.S.A.
112 G3 McBee South Carolina U.S.A.
119 U6 McBeth Pt Manitoba Canada
117 N9 McBride British Columbia Canada
133 F8 Macbride Hd Falkland Is
100 J5 McCall Idaho U.S.A.
108 E4 McCamey Texas U.S.A.
101 N7 McCammon Idaho U.S.A.
122 H8 Maccan Nova Scotia Canada
98 J1 McCanna North Dakota U.S.A.
44 M6 Maccarese Italy
117 H9 McCauley I British Columbia Canada
100 B2 McCleary Washington U.S.A.
112 H4 McClellanville South Carolina U.S.A.
113 E7 MacClenny Florida U.S.A.
8 D1 Macclesfield England
123 S5 Maccles L Newfoundland Canada
114 J3 McClintock Ch Northwest Territories Canada
142 F4 McClintock Ra W Australia Australia
100 C8 McCloud California U.S.A.
140 C1 McCluer I N Terr Australia
94 D5 McClure Ohio U.S.A.
95 K6 McClure Pennsylvania U.S.A.
102 D4 McClure, L California U.S.A.
114 H3 McClure Str Northwest Territories Canada
118 H3 McClusker R Saskatchewan Canada
98 F2 McClusky North Dakota U.S.A.
111 F10 McComb Mississippi U.S.A.
94 D5 McComb Ohio U.S.A.
98 D8 McConaughy, L Nebraska U.S.A.
117 M3 McConnell Range Northwest Territories Canada
94 J7 McConnellsburg Pennsylvania U.S.A.
98 F9 McCook Nebraska U.S.A.
111 G8 McCool Mississippi U.S.A.
98 J9 McCool Junct Nebraska U.S.A.
118 L9 McCord Saskatchewan Canada
112 E4 McCormick South Carolina U.S.A.
106 D2 McCoy Colorado U.S.A.
107 L3 McCracken Kansas U.S.A.
119 S8 McCreary Manitoba Canada
110 E3 McCredie Missouri U.S.A.
110 E6 McCrory Arkansas U.S.A.
115 M3 Macculloch, C Northwest Territories Canada
103 J6 McCullough Ridge Nevada U.S.A.
110 B6 McCurtain Oklahoma U.S.A.
109 K5 McDade Texas U.S.A.
117 J6 McDame British Columbia Canada
100 H8 McDermitt Nevada U.S.A.
94 D8 McDermott Ohio U.S.A.
120 B3 Macdiarmid Ontario Canada
100 C8 Macdoel California U.S.A.
107 J2 McDonald Kansas U.S.A.
81 E11 Macdonald Is Indian Oc
143 G6 Macdonald, L W Australia Australia
101 M1 McDonald, L Montana U.S.A.
100 E9 McDonald Peak mt California U.S.A.
101 M2 McDonald Pk Montana U.S.A.
142 E3 Macdonald Ra W Australia Australia
101 L1 Macdonald Range British Columbia Canada
138 E3 McDonnell R South Australia Australia
140 B6 MacDonnell Ranges N Terr Australia
112 C4 McDonough Georgia U.S.A.
138 D3 McDouall Peak South Australia Australia
115 K7 MacDowell L Ontario Canada
103 N8 McDowell Pk Arizona U.S.A.
15 F3 MacDuff Scotland
16 C3 Macedo de Chavaleiros Portugal
95 K3 Macedon New York U.S.A.
46 E3 Macedonia rep S Europe
99 L8 Macedonia Iowa U.S.A.
139 G7 Macedon, Mt Victoria Australia
130 J10 Maceió Alagoas Brazil
87 G8 Maceloge Mozambique
85 C7 Macenta Guinea
42 E5 Macerata Italy
100 G5 McEwen Oregon U.S.A.
110 J5 McEwen Tennessee U.S.A.
101 T8 McFadden Wyoming U.S.A.
99 M9 McFall Missouri U.S.A.
107 O2 McFarland Kansas U.S.A.
138 D4 Macfarlane, L South Australia Australia
144 B5 Macfarlane, Mt New Zealand
106 B6 McGaffey New Mexico U.S.A.
118 J7 McGee Saskatchewan Canada
107 P7 McGee Creek Res Oklahoma U.S.A.
111 E8 McGehee Arkansas U.S.A.
103 K2 McGill Nevada U.S.A.
100 K1 McGillvray Range mts British Columbia Canada
14 B5 Macgillycuddy's Reeks mts Ireland
116 K5 McGrath Alaska U.S.A.
95 L4 McGraw New York U.S.A.
119 T9 MacGregor Manitoba Canada
94 E3 McGregor Michigan U.S.A.
99 N3 McGregor Minnesota U.S.A.
109 K4 McGregor Texas U.S.A.
118 E8 McGregor L Alberta Canada
117 N8 McGregor R British Columbia Canada
141 F7 McGregor Ra Queensland Australia
98 C8 McGrew Nebraska U.S.A.
101 L4 McGuire, Mt Idaho U.S.A.
77 K5 Mach Pakistan
89 F7 Machache Mt Lesotho
128 C4 Machachi Ecuador
130 F7 Maçhado Brazil
80 F7 Machaerus Jordan
87 F10 Machaila Mozambique
88 F2 Machakos Kenya
128 C4 Machala Ecuador
70 C4 Machan Sarawak
67 B3 Machangping China
133 E2 Macharetí Bolivia
140 E6 Machattie L Queensland Australia
22 G5 Machault France
87 F10 Machaze Mozambique
20 G8 Machecoul France
112 D4 Machen Georgia U.S.A.
67 E1 Macheng China
99 S7 McHenry Illinois U.S.A.
111 G11 McHenry Mississippi U.S.A.
76 D2 Macherla India
33 R10 Machern Germany
95 U2 Machias Maine U.S.A.
95 S7 Machias R Maine U.S.A.
17 F1 Machichaco, C Spain
76 E2 Machilipatnam India
88 G6 Mchinja Tanzania
88 D8 Mchinji Malawi
127 H9 Machiques Venezuela
12 C2 Machrie Scotland
12 C3 Machrihanish Scotland
8 C2 Machynlleth Wales
87 F10 Macia Mozambique
Macias Nguema Biyogo see Bioko
141 G2 McIlwraith Ra Queensland Australia
48 L5 Măcin Romania
85 C6 Macina reg Mali
120 J3 Mc. Innes Ontario Canada
99 O6 McIntire Iowa U.S.A.
118 J1 McIntosh Ontario Canada
98 E4 McIntosh South Dakota U.S.A.
143 F7 Macintosh Ra W Australia Australia
120 B3 McIntyre B Ontario Canada
141 K8 Macintyre Brook Queensland Australia
106 B2 Mack Colorado U.S.A.
119 O6 McKague Saskatchewan Canada
141 J5 Mackay Queensland Australia
101 M6 Mackay Idaho U.S.A.
114 H5 MacKay L Northwest Territories Canada
120 D3 McKay L Ontario Canada
142 G5 Mackay, L N Terr/W Aust
142 D5 Mackay, Mt W Australia Australia
117 R7 McKay R Alberta Canada
143 D6 McKay Ra W Australia Australia
137 S2 McKean I Phoenix Is Pacific Oc
94 H6 McKeesport Pennsylvania U.S.A.
94 G6 McKees Rocks Pennsylvania U.S.A.
33 T10 Mäckenberg Germany
133 E4 Mackenna Argentina
33 N9 Mackenrode Germany
141 J6 Mackenzie R Queensland Australia
114 G5 Mackenzie R Northwest Territories Canada
111 K10 McKenzie Alabama U.S.A.
98 F3 McKenzie North Dakota U.S.A.
110 H5 McKenzie Tennessee U.S.A.
146 J11 Mackenzie B Antarctica
114 F4 Mackenzie B Yukon Territory Canada
100 C5 McKenzie Bridge Oregon U.S.A.
114 H2 Mackenzie King I Northwest Territories Canada
119 N2 McKenzie L Ontario Canada
119 P4 McKenzie L Saskatchewan Canada
117 H3 Mackenzie Mts Yukon Terr/N W Terr Canada
100 D5 McKenzie Pass Oregon U.S.A.
119 S1 MacKerracher L Manitoba Canada
144 B6 McKerrow, L New Zealand
94 C1 Mackinac Michigan U.S.A.
94 C1 Mackinac, Str. of Michigan U.S.A.
99 R9 Mackinaw R Illinois U.S.A.
99 R9 Mackinaw Illinois U.S.A.
94 C1 Mackinaw City Michigan U.S.A.
141 F5 McKinlay R Queensland Australia
141 F5 McKinlay Queensland Australia
116 M5 McKinley, Mt Alaska U.S.A.
110 M4 McKinney Kentucky U.S.A.
109 L2 McKinney Texas U.S.A.
107 J3 McKinney, L Kansas U.S.A.
144 A6 McKinnon Pass New Zealand
146 D5 Mackintosh, Cape C Antarctica
139 H8 Mackintosh L. Tasmania Australia
120 B3 McKirdy Ontario Canada
102 E6 McKittrick California U.S.A.
118 H6 Macklin Saskatchewan Canada
119 Q2 McKnight L Manitoba Canada
38 O8 Mačkovci Slovenia
94 F7 Macksburg Ohio U.S.A.
101 O5 Macks Inn Idaho U.S.A.
139 L4 Macksville New South Wales Australia
107 M4 Macksville Kansas U.S.A.
141 F6 Mackunda R Queensland Australia
111 H10 McLain Mississippi U.S.A.
116 O5 Maclaren R Alaska U.S.A.
138 E6 McLaren Vale South Australia Australia
142 E4 McLarty Hills W Australia Australia
142 D5 McLarty, Mt W Australia Australia
118 G6 McLaughlin Alberta Canada
98 F4 McLaughlin South Dakota U.S.A.
119 U5 McLaughlin R Manitoba Canada
139 L3 Maclean New South Wales Australia
119 N8 McLean Saskatchewan Canada
99 R9 McLean Illinois U.S.A.
118 H2 McLean L Saskatchewan Canada
110 H3 McLeansboro Illinois U.S.A.
87 E12 Maclear S Africa
88 E8 Maclear, C Malawi
139 L4 Macleay R New South Wales Australia
118 A3 McLennan Alberta Canada
119 N3 McLennan Lake Saskatchewan Canada
98 J3 McLeod North Dakota U.S.A.
114 J5 McLeod B Northwest Territories Canada
143 A6 Macleod, L W Australia Australia
117 M8 McLeod Lake British Columbia Canada
118 B5 McLeod R Alberta Canada
68 C7 McLeods I Burma
110 A2 McLouth Kansas U.S.A.
118 K8 McMahon Saskatchewan Canada
94 G7 McMechen West Virginia U.S.A.
83 M9 McMicken Pt Christmas I Indian Oc
141 G1 Macmillan R Queensland Australia
117 F4 Macmillan R Yukon Territory Canada
99 V3 McMillan Michigan U.S.A.
106 F9 McMillan, L New Mexico U.S.A.
140 C6 McMinns Cr N Terr Australia
100 B4 McMinnville Oregon U.S.A.
110 L6 McMinnville Tennessee U.S.A.
118 J7 McMorran Saskatchewan Canada
118 F1 McMunn Manitoba Canada
146 D11 McMurdo U.S.A. Base Antarctica
117 O10 McMurphy British Columbia Canada
100 C1 McMurray Washington U.S.A.
111 E10 McNair Mississippi U.S.A.
103 P7 McNary Arizona U.S.A.
108 B4 McNary Texas U.S.A.
100 F4 McNary Dam Oregon U.S.A.
103 P10 McNeal Arizona U.S.A.
111 C8 McNeil Arkansas U.S.A.
109 K5 McNeil Texas U.S.A.
111 G11 McNeill Mississippi U.S.A.
119 Q7 MacNutt Saskatchewan Canada
122 G10 McNutt I Nova Scotia Canada
128 D1 Macollo, Pta C Venezuela
110 F1 Macomb Illinois U.S.A.
107 O6 Macomb Oklahoma U.S.A.
43 B8 Macomer Sardinia
88 H8 Macomia Mozambique
22 G3 Maçon Belgium
19 J6 Mâcon France
112 D5 Macon Georgia U.S.A.
99 S10 Macon Illinois U.S.A.
111 H8 Macon Mississippi U.S.A.
99 O10 Macon Missouri U.S.A.
98 G9 Macon Nebraska U.S.A.
87 D8 Macondo Angola
119 O9 Macoun Saskatchewan Canada
107 N3 McPherson Kansas U.S.A.
142 D5 Macpherson, Mt W Australia Australia
141 L8 Macpherson Ra N S W/Qnsld Australia
68 A7 Macpherson's Str Andaman Is
139 J4 MacQuarie R New South Wales Australia
139 H8 Macquarie R Tasmania Australia
139 H8 Macquarie Harbour Tasmania Australia
81 J12 Macquarie I S Pacific Oc
146 B16 Macquarie Island Australia Base Antarctica
139 K5 Macquarie, L New South Wales Australia
139 J4 Macquarie Marshes New South Wales Australia
139 J5 Macquarie, Mt New South Wales Australia
134 H14 Macquarie Ridge S Pacific Oc
22 G4 Macquenoise Belgium
117 E4 McQuesten R Yukon Territory Canada
117 E4 McQuesten Yukon Territory Canada
112 E5 McRae Georgia U.S.A.
144 D5 McRae, L New Zealand
142 C5 McRae, Mt W Australia Australia
144 C6 Macraes Flat New Zealand
94 E9 McRoberts Kentucky U.S.A.
146 J11 MacRobertson Land Antarctica
14 C5 Macroom Ireland
118 K7 Macrorie Saskatchewan Canada
119 N9 McTaggart Saskatchewan Canada
71 G5 Mactan isld Philippines
118 D1 McTavish Manitoba Canada
128 D3 Macujer Colombia
71 G4 Maculiv Philippines
138 D2 Macumba R South Australia Australia
95 M6 Macungie Pennsylvania U.S.A.
128 D6 Macusani Peru
87 G9 Macuse Mozambique
125 N9 Macuspana Mexico
124 E4 Macuzari, Presa res Mexico
119 Q2 McVeigh Manitoba Canada
94 E9 McVeigh Kentucky U.S.A.
117 N3 McVicar Arm inlet Northwest Territories Canada
98 H2 McVille North Dakota U.S.A.
121 M4 McWatters Quebec Canada
111 J10 McWilliams Alabama U.S.A.
86 A4 Mada R Nigeria
80 G7 Madaba Jordan
86 D2 Madadi Chad
87 H11 Madagascar rep Indian Oc
81 C8 Madagascar Basin Indian Oc
76 C4 Madakasira India
70 E1 Madalon mt Sabah
84 E5 Madama Niger
46 G3 Madan Bulgaria
76 D4 Madanapalle India
136 K3 Madang Papua New Guinea
85 F6 Madaoua Niger
75 O7 Madaripur Bangladesh
85 F6 Madarounfa Niger
121 M7 Madawaska Ontario Canada
121 N7 Madawaska R Ontario Canada
95 S6 Madawaska Maine U.S.A.
122 D6 Madawaska R Quebec Canada
68 C1 Madaya Burma
43 C7 Maddalena, la Sardinia
45 Q7 Maddaloni Italy
143 C10 Madden, Mt W Australia Australia
142 C2 Maddington dist Perth, W Aust Australia
98 G2 Maddock North Dakota U.S.A.
85 A2 Madeira isld Atlantic Oc
128 F5 Madeira R Brazil
128 F5 Madeirinho R Brazil
41 M3 Madelegabel mt Austria
21 M5 Madeleine-Bouvet, la France
123 L6 Madeleine, Iles de la Quebec Canada
18 H6 Madeleine, Mts.de la France
99 M5 Madelia Minnesota U.S.A.
100 E8 Madeline California U.S.A.
99 Q3 Madeline I Wisconsin U.S.A.
78 G2 Maden Turkey
57 J1 Madeniyet Kazakhstan
124 E3 Madera Mexico
102 D5 Madera California U.S.A.
94 J6 Madera Pennsylvania U.S.A.
102 E5 Madera Canal California U.S.A.
108 E5 Madera Mt Texas U.S.A.
29 M4 Madetkoski Finland
32 J10 Madfeld Germany
76 A3 Madgaon India
119 Q7 Madge L Saskatchewan Canada
83 J12 Madge Rocks Seychelles
75 M5 Madhubani India
74 G7 Madhya Pradesh prov India
65 H3 Madida China
128 E6 Madidi R Bolivia
70 C4 Madi, Dtt Kalimantan
138 E3 Madigan Gulf South Australia Australia
76 B4 Madikeri India
109 L1 Madill Oklahoma U.S.A.
86 C6 Madimba Zaire
72 D4 Madīnah, Al Saudi Arabia
86 H3 Madinat ash Sha'ab Yemen
81 C5 Madingley Rise Indian Oc
86 B6 Madingo-Kayes Congo
86 B6 Madingou Congo
78 G4 Ma'din Jadīd Syria
118 J7 Madison Saskatchewan Canada
111 M12 Madison St Louis
110 K7 Madison Alabama U.S.A.
110 F6 Madison Arkansas U.S.A.
113 D7 Madison Florida U.S.A.
112 D4 Madison Georgia U.S.A.
107 O3 Madison Kansas U.S.A.
98 K4 Madison Minnesota U.S.A.
110 D2 Madison Missouri U.S.A.
101 O4 Madison R Montana U.S.A.
98 J8 Madison Nebraska U.S.A.
112 H1 Madison North Carolina U.S.A.
94 F5 Madison Ohio U.S.A.
98 J5 Madison South Dakota U.S.A.
110 K5 Madison Tennessee U.S.A.
94 J8 Madison Virginia U.S.A.
94 F8 Madison West Virginia U.S.A.
99 R6 Madison Wisconsin U.S.A.
94 H9 Madison Heights Virginia U.S.A.
101 P5 Madison Junct Wyoming U.S.A.
101 O4 Madison Ra Montana U.S.A.
110 J4 Madisonville Kentucky U.S.A.
111 F11 Madisonville Louisiana U.S.A.
112 C2 Madisonville Tennessee U.S.A.
109 M5 Madisonville Texas U.S.A.
71 K10 Madita Sumba Indonesia
70 N9 Madiun Java
8 D3 Madley England
143 E6 Madley, Mt W Australia Australia
121 N8 Madoc Ontario Canada
98 A1 Madoc Montana U.S.A.
86 G5 Mado Gashi Kenya
52 C6 Madona Latvia
100 B9 Mad R California U.S.A.
47 J5 Madra Dağı mt Turkey
76 E4 Madras India
100 D5 Madras Oregon U.S.A.
128 E6 Madre de Dios R Bolivia/Peru
128 D6 Madre de Dios dept Peru
133 B8 Madre de Dios, I Chile
125 L5 Madre. Laguna Mexico
109 K9 Madre, Laguna Texas U.S.A.
124 F4 Madre Occidental, Sierra mts Mexico
18 G10 Madrès mt France
71 F2 Madre, Sierra mts Luzon Philippines
71 G6 Madrid Mindanao Philippines
16 E4 Madrid prov Spain
16 E4 Madrid Spain
99 N8 Madrid Iowa U.S.A.
98 E9 Madrid Nebraska U.S.A.
106 D6 Madrid New Mexico U.S.A.
95 M2 Madrid New York U.S.A.
71 F5 Madridejos Philippines
16 E5 Madridejos Spain
16 D3 Madrigal de las Atlas Torres Spain
16 E6 Madrona, Sa mts Spain
128 G4 Madruba, L Brazil
126 D3 Madruga Cuba
79 E11 Madsûs, G mt Egypt
71 K8 Madu isld Indonesia
71 E5 Maducang isld Philippines
28 A4 Madum Denmark
28 D3 Madum Sø Denmark
143 F9 Madura W Australia Australia
70 O9 Madura isld Indonesia
76 D6 Madurai India
70 O9 Madura, Selat str Java
83 L10 Maduru Oya R Sri Lanka
52 H4 Madzha Russian Federation
47 H3 Madzharovo Bulgaria
60 D12 Maebaru Japan
61 N9 Maebashi Japan
68 C3 Mae Hong Son Thailand
61 O13 Mae-jima isld Okinawa
68 D5 Mae Khlong R Thailand
69 D8 Mae Kirirath R Thailand
27 C12 Mael Norway
68 D3 Mae Lao R Thailand
20 D5 Maël-Carhaix France
68 D3 Mae Li R Thailand
17 H3 Maella Spain
20 D5 Maël-Pestivien France
69 D8 Mae Luang R Thailand
68 F4 Mae Nam R Thailand
68 E3 Mae Nam Ing R Thailand
68 F5 Mae Nam Mun R Thailand
68 E3 Mae Nam Nan R Thailand
68 D3 Mae Nam Ping R Thailand
68 E3 Mae Nam Yom R Thailand
68 D3 Mae Rim Thailand
48 K5 Măeruş Romania
103 P1 Maeser Utah U.S.A.
8 C4 Maesteg Wales
45 M2 Maestra, Pta Italy
126 F4 Maestra, Sierra mts Cuba
71 E4 Maestre de Campo isld Philippines
137 O5 Maéwo isld Vanuatu
71 A2 Mafa Halmahera Indonesia
88 H10 Mafameda isld Mozambique
119 Q6 Mafeking Manitoba Canada
89 E7 Mafeteng Lesotho
139 H7 Maffra Victoria Australia
88 G5 Mafia Channel Tanzania
88 G5 Mafia,I Tanzania
89 D5 Mafikeng S Africa
88 E8 Mafinto Mozambique
67 E1 Ma-fou China
130 E10 Mafra Brazil
16 A6 Mafra Portugal
89 F2 Mafungabusi Plateau Zimbabwe
51 P3 Magadan Russian Federation
51 P2 Magadanskaya Oblast' Russian Federation
88 F2 Magadi L Kenya
88 F2 Magadi Kenya
122 E8 Magaguadavic L New Brunswick Canada
133 C8 Magallanes prov Chile
71 F4 Magallanes Philippines
133 C8 Magallanes, Estrecho de chan Chile
71 F5 Magallon Negros Philippines
71 C3 Magamo W Irian
126 G10 Magangué Colombia
128 C2 Magangue Colombia
85 F6 Magaria Niger
61 Q12 Magari-zaki C Okinawa
71 E2 Magat R Luzon Philippines
89 G4 Magato Mts S Africa
110 C6 Magazine Mt Arkansas U.S.A.
85 B7 Magburaka Sierra Leone
59 J1 Magdagachi Russian Federation
37 L2 Magdala Germany
128 F6 Magdalena Bolivia
126 D2 Magdalena div Colombia
128 C3 Magdalena R Colombia
124 D2 Magdalena Sonora Mexico
106 C7 Magdalena New Mexico U.S.A.
133 C6 Magdalena, I Chile
124 C5 Magdalena, I Mexico
70 E2 Magdalena, Mt Sabah
Magdalen Is see Madeleine, Iles de la
33 P8 Magdeburg Germany
33 Q8 Magdeburgerforth Germany
141 K3 Magdelaine Cays islds Gt Barrier Reef Aust
33 O9 Mägdesprung Germany
80 C5 Magdi'el Israel
111 G10 Magee Mississippi U.S.A.
14 F2 Magee, I N Ireland
116 K7 Mageik Vol Alaska U.S.A.
70 N9 Magelang Java
133 D8 Magellan, Str. of Chile
80 A8 Magen Israel
80 E3 Magen Shaul Israel
41 J7 Magenta Italy
143 C10 Magenta, L W Australia Australia
41 K3 Magereu mt Switzerland
26 P1 Mageröya isld Norway
80 D4 Maggal Israel
41 J5 Maggia, Val Switzerland
44 F2 Maggiorasca mt Italy
41 J6 Maggiore, Lago Italy
43 F7 Maggiore, M mt Italy
127 J2 Maggotty Jamaica
79 A10 Maghâgha Egypt
79 D8 Maghâra, G mt Egypt
14 A4 Magharee Is Ireland
14 E2 Maghera N Ireland
14 E2 Magherafelt N Ireland
17 F10 Maghnia Algeria
84 H3 Maghra, El Egypt
13 F6 Maghull England
101 L6 Magic Res Idaho U.S.A.
14 E1 Magilligan Pt N Ireland
16 E7 Mágina mt Spain
56 G3 Magistral'nyy Russian Federation
48 E6 Maglaj Bosnia-Herzegovina
40 E5 Magland France
29 K6 Magleby Denmark
29 K7 Magleby isld Denmark
28 G7 Maglehöjstrand Denmark
45 M6 Magliana Italy
45 O5 Magliano de Marsi Italy
48 E7 Maglić mt Bosnia-Herzegovina
43 J8 Maglie Italy
103 N8 Magma Arizona U.S.A.
18 F6 Magnac-Laval France
98 J7 Magnet Nebraska U.S.A.
121 L7 Magnetawan Ontario Canada
146 K10 Magnet B Antarctica
141 H4 Magnetic I Queensland Australia
55 C3 Magnitka Russian Federation
55 C4 Magnitogorsk Russian Federation
109 O2 Magnolia Arkansas U.S.A.
111 F10 Magnolia Mississippi U.S.A.
112 J3 Magnolia North Carolina U.S.A.
109 M5 Magnolia Texas U.S.A.
27 F12 Magnor Norway
6 L1 Magnus oil rig North Sea
21 O3 Magny-en-Vexin France
21 K3 Magny-la-Campagne France
88 C9 Magoe Mozambique
121 S7 Magog Quebec Canada
8 D4 Magor Wales
47 O12 Magouládhes Greece
120 F4 Magpie Ontario Canada
122 H3 Magpie Quebec Canada
122 H2 Magpie L Quebec Canada
120 F4 Magpie Mine Ontario Canada
122 H2 Magpie R Quebec Canada
44 G3 Magra, R Italy
118 E9 Magrath Alberta Canada
41 O5 Magrè sulla Strada del Vino Italy
17 G5 Magro R Spain
102 G4 Magruder Mt Nevada U.S.A.
71 E2 Magsingal Luzon Philippines
28 C6 Magstrup Denmark
67 A5 Maguan China
129 J4 Maguari, C Brazil
89 H5 Magude Mozambique
67 D5 Magui China
86 B3 Magumeri Nigeria
Magway see Magwe
68 B2 Magwe Burma
68 A2 Magyichaung Burma
78 K3 Mahābād Iran
74 E10 Mahabaleshwar India
Mahabalipuram see Māmallapuram
87 G12 Mahabo Madagascar
74 E9 Mahad India
86 A3 Mahaddayweyne Somalia
74 H7 Mahadeo Hills India
94 J6 Mahaffey Pennsylvania U.S.A.
86 F5 Mahagl Zaire
87 H11 Mahajamba, Helodrano B Madagascar
87 H11 Mahajanga Madagascar
70 D4 Mahakam R Kalimantan
89 E4 Mahalapye Botswana
46 E6 Mahalás Greece
88 C5 Mahale Mountains National Park Tanzania
79 B8 Mahalla, El Egypt
77 B3 Mahallāt Iran
70 O10 Mahameru, G mt Java
77 E4 Mahān Iran
75 K8 Mahanadi R India
71 G5 Mahanay isld Philippines
95 L6 Mahanoy City Pennsylvania U.S.A.
65 G3 Mahao China
83 J10 Maha Oya R Sri Lanka
74 E9 Maharashtra prov India
75 K8 Mahasamund India
68 F4 Maha Sarakham Thailand
98 J10 Mahaska Kansas U.S.A.
87 H11 Mahavavy R Madagascar
87 H11 Mahavelona Madagascar
83 K10 Mahaweli Ganga R Sri Lanka
68 G4 Mahaxay Laos
74 H10 Mahbubabad India
76 C2 Mahbubnagar India
77 D7 Mahḑah Oman
85 G1 Mahdia Tunisia
76 B5 Mahe India
83 J12 Mahé isld Seychelles
83 M13 Mahebourg Mauritius
88 F6 Mahenge Tanzania
144 C6 Maheno New Zealand
120 J3 Maher Ontario Canada
74 E7 Mahesāna India
74 F7 Maheshwar India
145 F3 Mahia New Zealand
74 E9 Mahim India
144 C5 Mahinapua, L New Zealand
144 B6 Mahinerangi, L New Zealand
80 G6 Mahis Jordan
87 F11 Mahlabatini S Africa
68 B2 Mahlaing Burma
33 S8 Mahlow Germany
33 P8 Mahlwinkel Germany
75 J5 Mahmudabad India
77 L2 Mahmūde 'Erāqī Afghanistan
48 M5 Mahmudia Romania
47 M10 Mahmutbe Turkey
79 C2 Mahmutlar Turkey
47 N10 Mahmutşevketpaşa Turkey
83 K10 Maho Sri Lanka
74 H6 Mahoba India
145 E3 Mahoenui New Zealand
100 F8 Mahogany Peak mt Nevada U.S.A.
99 S9 Mahomet Illinois U.S.A.
17 K5 Mahón Menorca
122 H9 Mahone Bay Nova Scotia Canada
117 L3 Mahony L Northwest Territories Canada
17 F5 Mahora Spain
85 G2 Mahrès Tunisia
98 F4 Mahto South Dakota U.S.A.
145 E4 Mahuri New Zealand
74 D8 Mahuva India
137 P1 Maiana atoll Kiribati
71 M9 Maibang Indonesia
61 K10 Maibara Japan
48 L5 Măicăneşti Romania
19 K5 Maich France
40 E3 Maiche France
68 J2 Maichen China
68 J2 Mai-ch'u China
129 H3 Maicuru R Brazil
142 C1 Maida Vale W Australia Australia
112 F2 Maiden North Carolina U.S.A.
8 D5 Maiden Bradley England
9 F4 Maidenhead England
8 D6 Maiden Newton England
99 O5 Maiden Rock Wisconsin U.S.A.
12 D3 Maidens Scotland
71 A2 Maidi Halmahera Indonesia
118 H5 Maidstone Saskatchewan Canada
9 G5 Maidstone England
86 B3 Maidugun Nigeria
42 F6 Maiella, M.della Italy
41 L3 Maienfeld Switzerland
21 P2 Maignelay France
128 E2 Maigualida, Sierra mts Venezuela
14 C4 Maigue R Ireland
74 J8 Maikala Range India
36 E5 Maikammer Germany
86 E6 Maiko, Parc Nacional de nat park Zaire
69 D14 Maileppe Indonesia
102 R12 Maili Hawaiian Is
21 N4 Maillebois France
21 M3 Mailleraye-sur-Seine, la France
22 D3 Mailly Maillet France
74 E4 Mailsi Pakistan
144 C5 Maimai New Zealand
127 J5 Maimon, B.de Dominican Rep
37 K3 Main R Germany
80 F7 Ma'in Jordan
14 E2 Main R N Ireland
123 N8 Main-à-Dieu C Breton I, Nova Scotia
37 J4 Mainbernheim Germany
123 Q2 Main Brook Newfoundland Canada
37 M6 Mainburg Germany
118 K8 Main Centre Saskatchewan Canada
120 J7 Main Channel Cave I Ontario Canada
86 C6 Mai Ndombe, L Zaire
37 L5 Main-Donau-Kanal Germany
Maindong see Coqên
121 O9 Main Duck I Ontario Canada
20 H4 Maine R France
20 H8 Maine R France
21 J5 Maine reg France
21 J7 Maine R France
95 R1 Maine state U.S.A.
103 N6 Maine Arizona U.S.A.
95 L4 Maine New York U.S.A.
18 E5 Maine-et-Loire dept France
85 G6 Mainé-Soroa Niger
110 M2 Maineville Ohio U.S.A.
68 D6 Maingy isld Burma
36 H5 Mainhardt Germany
71 G6 Mainit, L Mindanao Philippines
15 G2 Mainland Shetland Scotland
140 C2 Mainoru N Terr Australia
74 H5 Mainpuri India
138 F4 Main Range Barrier New South Wales Australia
122 F7 Main S.W. Miramichi R New Brunswick Canada
36 F3 Maintal Germany
21 O4 Maintenon France
87 G11 Maintirano Madagascar
123 Q4 Main Topsail pk Newfoundland Canada
29 N7 Mainua Finland
74 D2 Mainwali Pakistan
36 E3 Mainz Germany
45 R8 Maiori Italy
133 C4 Maipo R Chile
133 D4 Maipo mt Chile/Arg
131 B5 Maipo, Vol pk Arg/Chile
133 F5 Maipu Argentina
127 L9 Maiquetia Venezuela
44 B3 Maira R Italy
75 P5 Mairabari India
37 L7 Maisach Germany
20 H7 Maisdon-sur-Sèvre France
126 G4 Maisí Cuba
126 G4 Maisí, Pta. de Cuba
122 G6 Maisonnette New Brunswick Canada
21 P4 Maisons-Laffitte France
38 N4 Maissau Austria
21 P5 Maisse France
22 J4 Maissin Belgium
139 K5 Maitland New South Wales Australia
138 D5 Maitland South Australia Australia
122 J8 Maitland Nova Scotia Canada
99 L9 Maitland Missouri U.S.A.
122 G9 Maitland Br Nova Scotia Canada
143 D7 Maitland, L W Australia Australia
143 C7 Maitland, Mt W Australia Australia
142 B5 Maitland, R W Australia Australia
70 E2 Maitland Ra Sabah
146 H7 Maitri India Base Antarctica
140 C2 Maiwok R N Terr Australia
61 P7 Maiya Japan
140 A4 Maiyu, Mt N Terr Australia
75 O4 Maizhokunggar China
36 B6 Maizières-les-Vic France
125 N3 Maiz, Is. del Nicaragua
60 J10 Maizuru Japan
128 D2 Majagual Colombia
70 M9 Majalengka Java
74 G9 Mājalgaon India
128 F3 Majari R Brazil
26 F6 Majavatn L Norway
28 H7 Majbølle Denmark
80 E5 Majdal Bani Fadil Jordan
80 F8 Majdalein Jordan
31 N5 Majdan Poland
48 G6 Majdanpek Serbia Yugoslavia
80 D2 Majd el Kurum Israel
80 G1 Majdūliyah Syria
130 G8 Majé Brazil
70 F6 Majene Sulawesi
48 E6 Majevica mts Bosnia-Herzegovina
86 G4 Maji Ethiopia
67 B3 Majiang China
67 D5 Majiang China
67 A4 Majie China
67 F2 Majin China
67 D2 Majitang China
118 H7 Major Saskatchewan Canada
Majorca isld see Mallorca
89 F6 Majuba Hill S Africa
Majunga see Mahajanga
134 H7 Majuro atoll Marshall Is
89 B5 Majwane Pan Botswana
85 B6 Maka Senegal
61 P14 Makabe Okinawa
102 R12 Makaha Hawaiian Is
70 F6 Makale Sulawesi
69 E14 Makalo Indonesia
75 M5 Makalu mt China/Nepal
87 F7 Makambako Tanzania
86 C5 Makanza Zaire
135 U4 Makapala Hawaiian Is
102 S12 Makapuu Hd Hawaiian Is
145 E2 Makarau New Zealand
144 B7 Makarewa New Zealand
52 J2 Makarikha Russian Federation
144 B6 Makarora R New Zealand
59 M2 Makarov Russian Federation
42 H5 Makarska Croatia
52 G3 Makar-Yb Russian Federation
52 G5 Makar'ye Russian Federation
Makassar see Ujung Pandang
70 F5 Makassar Str Indonesia
89 H6 Makatini Flats reg S Africa
135 T3 Makawao Hawaiian Is
71 C3 Makbon W Irian
Makedonija see Macedonia
135 N10 Makemo atoll Pacific Oc
85 B7 Makeni Sierra Leone
145 F2 Maketu New Zealand
54 K8 Makeyevka Ukraine
89 D3 Makgadikgadi salt pans Botswana
Makharadze see Ozurgety
16 D9 Makhazen, Oued R Morocco
55 D2 Makhnevo Russian Federation
55 E4 Makhorovka Kazakhstan
80 F3 Makhraba Jordan
61 M8 Maki Japan
71 A2 Makian Halmahera Indonesia
144 C6 Makikihi New Zealand
119 S8 Makinak Manitoba Canada
55 F4 Makinsk Kazakhstan
115 M2 Makinson Inlet Northwest Territories Canada
26 S1 Makkaur Norway
25 F3 Makkinga Netherlands
115 O6 Makkovik Labrador, Nfld Canada
25 D2 Makkum Netherlands
48 F4 Makó Hungary
120 C1 Makokibatan L Ontario Canada
87 F7 Makongolosi Tanzania
145 F3 Makorako mt New Zealand
98 E2 Makoti North Dakota U.S.A.
145 F4 Makotuku New Zealand
86 C5 Makoua Congo
31 L6 Makov Slovakia

31 M6 **Maków** Poland
31 N3 **Maków Mazowiecki** Poland
80 D2 **Makr** Israel
47 H8 **Makrá** *isld* Greece
74 F5 **Makrana** India
77 J7 **Makran Coast Range** Pakistan
47 H4 **Mákri** Greece
76 E1 **Makri** India
46 G7 **Makronísi** *isld* Greece
52 J3 **Maksim** Russian Federation
56 C2 **Maksimkin Yar** Russian Federation
85 F1 **Makthar** Tunisia
78 K2 **Maku** Iran
70 C4 **Makup, Bt** *mt* Kalimantan
60 D14 **Makurazaki** Japan
86 A4 **Makurdi** Nigeria
55 E3 **Makushino** Russian Federation
116 D10 **Makushin Vol** Aleutian Is
88 D7 **Makutu Mts** Zambia
118 H4 **Makwa L** Saskatchewan Canada
89 G1 **Makwiro** Zimbabwe
128 C6 **Mala** Peru
71 G7 **Malabang** Mindanao Philippines
113 G9 **Malabar** Florida U.S.A.
76 B5 **Malabar Coast** India
70 L9 **Malabar, G** *mt* Java
85 F8 **Malabo** Fernando Póo Equat Guinea
71 C6 **Malabuñgan** Palawan Philippines
69 E11 **Malacca, Str. of** Malaysia
118 H1 **Malachi** Ontario Canada
31 K7 **Malacky** Slovakia
101 N7 **Malad City** Idaho U.S.A.
17 H2 **Maladeta** Spain
31 L6 **Malá Fatra** *mts* Slovakia
16 D8 **Málaga** *prov* Spain
16 E8 **Málaga** Spain
100 E2 **Malaga** Washington U.S.A.
88 C4 **Malagarasi** Tanzania
Malagasy Rep *see* **Madagascar**
16 E5 **Malagón** Spain
71 K9 **Malahar** Indonesia
14 E3 **Malahide** Ireland
87 G12 **Malaimbandy** Madagascar
137 N3 **Malaita** *isld* Solomon Is
71 J9 **Malaka** *mt* Sumbawa Indonesia
86 F4 **Malakal** Sudan
42 G4 **Mala Kapela** *mts* Croatia
109 L3 **Malakoff** Texas U.S.A.
71 B2 **Malaku** *islds* Indonesia
137 O5 **Malakula** *isld* Vanuatu
45 L2 **Malalbergo** Italy
71 A3 **Malamala** *isld* Indonesia
70 G6 **Malamala** Sulawesi
71 E7 **Malamaui** *isld* Philippines
45 M1 **Malamocco** Italy
71 D5 **Malampaya Snd** Philippines
141 H3 **Malanda** Queensland Australia
70 O10 **Malang** Java
88 E6 **Malangali** Tanzania
70 M9 **Malangbong** Java
26 K2 **Malangen** *inlet* Norway
26 K2 **Malangen** Norway
26 J2 **Malangsgrunnen** *shoal* Norway
75 L5 **Malangwa** Nepal
71 F7 **Malanipa** *isld* Philippines
87 C7 **Malanje** Angola
20 F6 **Malansac** France
71 D6 **Malanut B** Philippines
85 E6 **Malanville** Benin
65 D4 **Malanyu** China
131 C3 **Malanzaán, Sa. de** *mts* Argentina
76 C5 **Malappuram** India
27 J12 **Mälaren** *L* Sweden
131 B5 **Malargue** *R* Argentina
133 D5 **Malargue** Argentina
129 H3 **Malaripo** Brazil
121 M4 **Malartic** Quebec Canada
70 F7 **Malasoro, Tk** *B* Sulawesi
117 C6 **Malaspina Gl** Alaska U.S.A.
144 A6 **Malaspina Reach** New Zealand
117 L11 **Malaspina Str** British Columbia Canada
26 K6 **Malåtrask** Sweden
78 G2 **Malatya** Turkey
19 O16 **Malaucène** France
21 N2 **Malaunay** France
70 E1 **Malawali** *isld* Sabah
88 D8 **Malawi** *rep* Africa
Malawi, L *see* **Nyasa, L**
29 J9 **Malax** Finland
55 D1 **Malaya Sos'va** *R* Russian Federation
52 D5 **Malaya Vishera** Russian Federation
77 A2 **Malāyer** Iran
141 J4 **Malay Reef** Gt Barrier Reef Aust
69 **Malaysia** S E Asia
69 E10 **Malaysia, Peninsular** S E Asia
14 B4 **Mal B** Ireland
122 H5 **Mal Baie** Quebec Canada
122 B6 **Malbaie** *R* Quebec Canada
131 B6 **Malbarco, L** Argentina
140 F5 **Malbon** Queensland Australia
38 J9 **Malborghetto** Italy
31 L1 **Malbork** Poland
41 N6 **Malcesine** Italy
33 R5 **Malchin** Germany
33 Q6 **Malchow** Germany
143 D8 **Malcolm** W Australia Australia
116 R2 **Malcolm** *R* Yukon Territory Canada
68 D7 **Malcolm I** Burma
143 E10 **Malcolm,Pt** W Australia Australia
99 O8 **Malcom** Iowa U.S.A.
22 E1 **Maldegem** Belgium
95 Q4 **Malden** Massachusetts U.S.A.
110 G5 **Malden** Missouri U.S.A.
100 H2 **Malden** Washington U.S.A.
94 F8 **Malden** West Virginia U.S.A.
135 M8 **Malden I** Pacific Oc
73 L8 **Maldive Is** *rep* Indian Oc
43 B9 **Mal di Ventre, I. di** Sardinia
73 L9 **Maldive Ridge** Indian Oc
9 G4 **Maldon** England
131 G5 **Maldonado** *dept* Uruguay
131 G5 **Maldonado** Uruguay
41 N5 **Male** Italy
73 L8 **Male** Maldives
46 F8 **Maléa, Akr** *C* Greece
47 H5 **Maléa, Akr** Turkey
74 F8 **Malegaon** India
70 G6 **Malehu** Sulawesi
48 D2 **Malé Karpaty** Slovakia
121 P4 **Mâle, L.du** Quebec Canada
88 F9 **Malema** Mozambique
87 E7 **Malemba Nkulu** Zaire
46 F9 **Máleme** Crete
52 E3 **Malen'ga** Russian Federation
33 N4 **Malente** Germany
74 F3 **Maler Kotla** India
47 H9 **Máles** Crete Greece
21 P5 **Malesherbes** France
20 F6 **Malestroit** France
54 K3 **Malevka** Russian Federation
89 B10 **Malgas** S Africa
37 O6 **Malgersdorf** Germany
86 E2 **Malha** Sudan
13 F5 **Malham** England
100 H5 **Malheur** Oregon U.S.A.
100 H6 **Malheur** *R* Oregon U.S.A.
83 K12 **Malheureu, Cap** Mahé I Indian Oc
100 G6 **Malheur L** Oregon U.S.A.
66 F6 **Mali** *R* Burma
85 D5 **Mali** *rep* W Africa
71 M9 **Maliana** Indonesia
21 K6 **Malicorne-sur-Sarthe** France
71 F7 **Maligoy B** Mindanao Philippines
80 F4 **Malih** *R* Jordan
19 Q16 **Malijai** France
70 D6 **Maliku** Kalimantan
71 H5 **Maliku** Sulawesi
68 D6 **Mali Kyun** *isld* Burma
70 G6 **Malili** Sulawesi
27 H14 **Målilla** Sweden
88 B5 **Malimba** *mts* Zaire
70 K9 **Malimping** Java
100 D7 **Malin** Oregon U.S.A.
71 G5 **Malinao Inlet** Philippines
71 F6 **Malindang, Mt** Mindanao Philippines
88 H3 **Malindi** Kenya
48 F2 **Malinec** Slovakia
Malines *see* **Mechelen**
70 G4 **Maling, G** *mt* Sulawesi
27 H12 **Malingsbo** Sweden
14 D1 **Malin Hd** Ireland
48 K3 **Mălini** Romania
14 C2 **Malin More** Ireland
70 F7 **Malino** Sulawesi
54 H7 **Malinovka** Ukraine
55 G5 **Malinovoye Ozero** *L* Russian Federation
68 G1 **Malipo** China
42 F4 **Mali Rajinac** *mt* Croatia
71 G7 **Malita** Mindanao Philippines
71 G5 **Malitbog** Leyte Philippines
68 D7 **Maliwun** Burma
106 G9 **Maljamar** New Mexico U.S.A.
48 F6 **Maljen** *mt* Serbia Yugoslavia
80 F3 **Malka** Jordan
53 F11 **Malka** *R* Russian Federation
47 J2 **Malkapapiye** Bulgaria
74 G8 **Malkapur** India
47 H4 **Malkara** Turkey
56 G5 **Malkhanskiy Khr** *mts* Russian Federation
31 N3 **Małkinia** Poland
80 F1 **Malkiyya** Israel
139 J7 **Mallacoota** Victoria Australia
118 F4 **Mallaig** Alberta Canada
15 C3 **Mallaig** Scotland
99 M7 **Mallard** Iowa U.S.A.
84 J4 **Mallawi** Egypt
131 A7 **Malleco** *prov* Chile
19 O17 **Mallemort** France
37 N6 **Mallersdorf** Germany
41 N4 **Malles Venosta** Italy
130 E9 **Mallét** Brazil
142 C5 **Mallina** W Australia Australia
28 E4 **Malling** Denmark
38 H8 **Mallnitz** Austria
17 J5 **Mallorca** *isld* Balearic Is
94 F9 **Mallory** West Virginia U.S.A.
121 P8 **Mallorytown** Ontario Canada
14 C4 **Mallow** Ireland
142 E5 **Mallowa Well** W Australia Australia
8 B1 **Malltraeth B** Wales
8 C2 **Mallwyd** Wales
22 F5 **Malmaison, la** France
27 G14 **Malmbäck** Sweden
26 L4 **Malmberget** Sweden
22 L3 **Malmédy** Belgium
8 D4 **Malmesbury** England
89 A9 **Malmesbury** S Africa
26 K6 **Malmesjaure** *L* Sweden
27 J12 **Malmköping** Sweden
29 K5 **Malmö** Sweden
27 F16 **Malmöhus** *county* Sweden
126 A2 **Malmok** *pt* Bonaire Neth Antilles
52 H6 **Malmyzh** Russian Federation
26 G3 **Malnes** Norway
137 O5 **Malo** *isld* Vanuatu
54 H4 **Maloarkhangel'sk** Russian Federation
129 G3 **Maloca** Amapá Brazil
129 H5 **Maloca** Pará Brazil
41 L5 **Maloggia** Switzerland
71 E3 **Malolos** Luzon Philippines
55 C2 **Malomal'sk** Russian Federation
88 E9 **Malombe,L** Malawi
47 H2 **Malomir** Bulgaria
47 R14 **Malóna** Rhodes Greece
121 N8 **Malone** Ontario Canada
113 B7 **Malone** Florida U.S.A.
95 N2 **Malone** New York U.S.A.
109 L4 **Malone** Texas U.S.A.
98 F8 **Maloney Res** Nebraska U.S.A.
67 A4 **Malong** China
87 D8 **Malonga** Zaire
26 N6 **Malören** Sweden
31 P4 **Malorita** Belarus
52 E3 **Maloshuyka** Russian Federation
89 F7 **Maloti Mts** Lesotho
100 F1 **Malott** Washington U.S.A.
26 A10 **Målöy** Norway
54 H1 **Maloyaroslavets** Russian Federation
55 E2 **Maloye Gorodishche** Russian Federation
52 H1 **Malozemel'skaya Tundra** *plain* Russian Federation
106 C10 **Malpais** New Mexico U.S.A.
138 F5 **Malpas** South Australia Australia
8 D1 **Malpas** England
124 H6 **Malpaso** Mexico
90 A8 **Malpelo I** Pacific Oc
122 J7 **Malpeque B** Prince Edward I Canada
16 D5 **Malpica** Spain
16 B1 **Malpica de Bergantiños** Spain
131 B4 **Malpo** *R* Chile
73 L5 **Malprabha** *R* India
74 F5 **Malpura** India
36 E6 **Malsch** Germany
31 H7 **Malše** *R* Czech Rep
26 K2 **Målselv** *R* Norway
26 K2 **Målselv** Norway
36 H1 **Malsfeld** Germany
77 A7 **Malsūnīyah, Al** Saudi Arabia
38 J8 **Malta** Austria
43 F13 **Malta** *rep* Mediterranean Sea
106 D2 **Malta** Colorado U.S.A.
101 M7 **Malta** Idaho U.S.A.
101 S1 **Malta** Montana U.S.A.
94 F7 **Malta** Ohio U.S.A.
43 F12 **Malta Ch** Mediterranean Sea
87 C10 **Maltahöhe** Namibia
38 H7 **Maltatel** *V* Austria
9 G1 **Maltby** England
13 G6 **Maltby** S Yorks England
144 C5 **Malte Brun** *mt* New Zealand
47 N11 **Maltepe** Turkey
121 L9 **Malton** *airport* Ontario Canada
13 H5 **Malton** England
48 K6 **Malu** Romania
71 D5 **Malubutglubut** *isld* Philippines
85 F6 **Malumfashi** Nigeria
70 F6 **Malunda** Sulawesi
27 G11 **Malung** Sweden
41 K5 **Malvaglia** Switzerland
76 A2 **Malvan** India
127 J2 **Malvern** Jamaica
127 J3 **Malvern** *pk* Jamaica
109 P1 **Malvern** Arkansas U.S.A.
99 L9 **Malvern** Iowa U.S.A.
94 F6 **Malvern** Ohio U.S.A.
8 D3 **Malvern Wells** England
20 G7 **Malville** France
Malvinas, Is *see* **Falkland Is.**
74 F7 **Malwa Plateau** India
83 K9 **Malwatu Oya** *R* Sri Lanka
78 K1 **Maly Kavkaz** *mts* Armenia/Azerbaijan
55 E1 **Malyy Atlym** Russian Federation
55 F1 **Malyy Balyk** *R* Russian Federation
55 G4 **Malyye Chany, Oz** *L* Russian Federation
52 G6 **Malyy Kundysh** *R* Russian Federation
51 O1 **Malyy Lyakhovski,Ostrov** *isld* Russian Federation
51 K1 **Malyy Taymyr, Ostrov** *isld* Russian Federation
55 G2 **Malyy Yugan** *R* Russian Federation
56 H2 **Mama** *R* Russian Federation
56 H2 **Mama** Russian Federation
52 H6 **Mamadysh** Russian Federation
48 M6 **Mamaia** Romania
120 F5 **Mamainse Point** Ontario Canada
145 F3 **Mamaku** New Zealand
76 E4 **Māmallapuram** India
145 D1 **Mamaranui** New Zealand
70 F6 **Mamasa** Sulawesi
71 D7 **Mambahenauhan** *isld* Philippines
71 G6 **Mambajao** Philippines
89 F3 **Mambala Cave** Zimbabwe
86 E5 **Mambasa** Zaire
136 H2 **Mamberamo** *R* W Irian
86 C4 **Mambéré** *R* Cent Afr Republic
70 F6 **Mambi** Sulawesi
79 H2 **Mambij** Syria
71 E4 **Mamburao** Philippines
118 K1 **Mameigwess L** Ontario Canada
83 J12 **Mamelle** *isld* Seychelles
118 D6 **Ma-Me-O Beach** Alberta Canada
118 D5 **Ma-Me-O Beach Prov. Park** Alberta Canada
22 K4 **Mamer** Luxembourg
21 L5 **Mamers** France
86 A4 **Mamfé** Cameroon
128 F4 **Mamia, L** Brazil
40 D3 **Mamirolle** France
55 E4 **Mamlyutka** Kazakhstan
120 F2 **Mammamattawa** Ontario Canada
28 D4 **Mammen** Denmark
37 L7 **Mammendorf** Germany
37 O6 **Mamming** Germany
43 G10 **Mammola** Italy
94 F8 **Mammoth** West Virginia U.S.A.
110 K4 **Mammoth Cave** Kentucky U.S.A.
101 P5 **Mammoth Hot Springs** Wyoming U.S.A.
102 F4 **Mammoth lakes** California U.S.A.
110 E5 **Mammoth Spring** Arkansas U.S.A.
126 G9 **Mamonal** Colombia
130 G4 **Mamonas** Brazil
31 M1 **Mamo-novo** Russian Federation
128 E6 **Mamore** *R* Bolivia/Brazil
128 F4 **Mamoré, L** Brazil
85 B6 **Mamou** Guinea
111 D11 **Mamou** Louisiana U.S.A.
87 H11 **Mampikohy** Madagascar
16 D1 **Mampodre** *mt* Spain
85 D7 **Mampong** Ghana
83 J9 **Mampuri** Sri Lanka
31 N1 **Mamry,Jezioro** *L* Poland
15 C3 **Mam Soul** *mt* Scotland
Mamuji *see* **Yucheng**
70 F6 **Mamuji** Sulawesi
87 D10 **Mamuno** Botswana
55 C5 **Mamyt** Kazakhstan
85 C7 **Man** Ivory Coast
94 F9 **Man** West Virginia U.S.A.
129 H3 **Mana** *R* Fr Guiana
135 N1 **Mana** Hawaiian Is
56 D3 **Mana** *R* Russian Federation
128 B4 **Manabi** Ecuador
128 F4 **Manacapuru** Brazil
128 F4 **Manacapuru,L.Grande de** Brazil
17 K5 **Manacor** Majorca
71 J4 **Manado** Sulawesi
71 J4 **Manadotua** *isld* Sulawesi
22 G3 **Manage** Belgium
140 D3 **Managoora** N Terr Australia
125 L3 **Managua** Nicaragua
145 E4 **Mana I** New Zealand
145 E3 **Manaia** New Zealand
87 H12 **Manakara** Madagascar
144 D5 **Manakau** *mt* New Zealand
145 E4 **Manakau** New Zealand
136 K2 **Manam** *isld* Papua New Guinea
76 D6 **Manamadurai** India
77 B6 **Manāmah,Al** Bahrain
87 G11 **Manambaho** *R* Madagascar
127 N10 **Mánamo** *R* Venezuela
71 E5 **Manamoc** *isld* Philippines
102 S12 **Manana** Hawaiian Is
87 H11 **Mananara** Madagascar
139 G6 **Manangatang** Victoria Australia
87 H12 **Mananjary** Madagascar
128 F2 **Manano,Caño** *creek* Venezuela
85 B6 **Manantali, Lac de** *res* Mali
76 C5 **Mānantavādi** India
87 H12 **Manantenina** Madagascar
144 A6 **Manapouri** New Zealand
66 D3 **Manas** China
Manasarowar Lake *see* **Mapam Yumco**
74 H3 **Mana Shankou** *pass* India/China
66 D3 **Manas He** *R* China
66 D2 **Manas Hu** *L* China
75 L4 **Manaslu** *mt* Nepal
95 N6 **Manasquan** New Jersey U.S.A.
106 E4 **Manassa** Colorado U.S.A.
94 K8 **Manassas** Virginia U.S.A.
71 M9 **Manatang** Indonesia
127 L5 **Manatí** Puerto Rico
128 G4 **Manaus** Brazil
78 C3 **Manavgat** Turkey
99 S5 **Manawa** Wisconsin U.S.A.
119 P3 **Manawan L** Saskatchewan Canada
145 E2 **Manawaru** New Zealand
145 F4 **Manawatu** *admin region* New Zealand
145 E4 **Manawatu R** New Zealand
71 G7 **Manay** Mindanao Philippines
140 B2 **Manbulloo** N Terr Australia
94 C2 **Mancelona** Michigan U.S.A.
16 E7 **Mancha Real** Spain
18 E3 **Manche** *dept* France
21 P5 **Manchecourt** France
74 H9 **Mancheral** India
11 E2 **Manchester** *conurbation* England
127 K3 **Manchester** *parish* Jamaica
102 A3 **Manchester** California U.S.A.
95 P5 **Manchester** Connecticut U.S.A.
112 C5 **Manchester** Georgia U.S.A.
110 F2 **Manchester** Illinois U.S.A.
99 P7 **Manchester** Iowa U.S.A.
107 N2 **Manchester** Kansas U.S.A.
110 N4 **Manchester** Kentucky U.S.A.
94 C4 **Manchester** Michigan U.S.A.
95 Q4 **Manchester** New Hampshire U.S.A.
95 K4 **Manchester** New York U.S.A.
94 D8 **Manchester** Ohio U.S.A.
107 M5 **Manchester** Oklahoma U.S.A.
95 L6 **Manchester** Pennsylvania U.S.A.
110 K6 **Manchester** Tennessee U.S.A.
95 O3 **Manchester** Vermont U.S.A.
37 M6 **Manching** Germany
127 M2 **Manchioneal** Jamaica
65 E1 **Manchuria** *reg* China
42 D6 **Manciano** Italy
128 B4 **Máncora** Peru
106 B4 **Mancos** Colorado U.S.A.
77 B5 **Mand** *R* Iran
87 F8 **Manda** Tanzania
130 D8 **Mandaguari** Brazil
80 F3 **Mandah** Jordan
69 F13 **Mandah** Sumatra
88 D7 **Manda Hd** Zambia
77 G3 **Mandal** Afghanistan
58 D2 **Mandal** Mongolia
27 B13 **Mandal** Norway
68 C2 **Mandalay** Burma
78 A3 **Mandalaya** *isld* Turkey
58 E2 **Mandalgovī** Mongolia
78 K5 **Mandalī** Iraq
27 B13 **Mandalsåni** *R* Norway
Mandalt *see* **Sonid Zuoqi**
98 F3 **Mandan** North Dakota U.S.A.
69 E12 **Mandau** Sumatra
36 C5 **Mandelbachtal** Germany
127 K2 **Mandeville** Jamaica
144 B7 **Mandeville** New Zealand
111 F11 **Mandeville** Louisiana U.S.A.
69 F10 **Mandi Angin, Gunung** *mt* Malaysia
130 B6 **Mandioré, Lagoa** *L* Bolivia/Brazil
74 J7 **Mandla** India
69 J12 **Mandor** Indonesia
46 F6 **Mandoúdhion** Greece
74 F6 **Mandsaur** India
143 B10 **Mandurah** W Australia Australia
48 K5 **Maneciu** Romania
41 N6 **Manerba del Garda** Italy
17 G7 **Manga del Mar Menor** Spain
145 E3 **Mangakino** New Zealand
76 E2 **Mangalagiri** India
76 B4 **Mangalore** India
145 E4 **Mangamahoe** New Zealand
145 E3 **Mangamahu** New Zealand
144 D5 **Mangamaunu** New Zealand
145 D1 **Mangamuka** New Zealand
145 E3 **Mangapehi** New Zealand
145 E4 **Mangatainoka** New Zealand
145 E3 **Mangaweka** New Zealand
145 E2 **Mangawhai** New Zealand
142 A4 **Mangles B** W Australia Australia
66 E4 **Mangnai** China
85 E6 **Mango** Togo
88 E9 **Mangochi** Malawi
87 G12 **Mangoky** *R* Madagascar
145 D1 **Mangonui** New Zealand
87 H12 **Mangoro** Madagascar
74 D8 **Māngral** India
113 J11 **Mangrove Cay** *isld* Bahamas
126 F2 **Mangrove Cay** Andros Bahamas
71 E4 **Mangsoagui Pt** Philippines
130 H10 **Manguaba,L** Brazil
16 B4 **Mangualde** Portugal
86 D3 **Mangueigne** Chad
131 H4 **Mangueira, L** Brazil
130 D9 **Mangueirinha** Brazil
84 E5 **Mangueni,Pl.du** Niger
59 H1 **Mangui** China
87 G7 **Mangula** Tanzania
108 E9 **Mangum** Oklahoma U.S.A.
67 A5 **Manhao** China
99 T8 **Manhattan** Illinois U.S.A.
107 O2 **Manhattan** Kansas U.S.A.
101 O4 **Manhattan** Montana U.S.A.
102 G3 **Manhattan** Nevada U.S.A.
22 K3 **Manhay** Belgium
130 H7 **Manhuaçu** Brazil
130 H6 **Manhuaçu,R** Brazil
113 L12 **Man I** Bahamas
87 E7 **Mani** Zaire
87 H11 **Mania** *R* Madagascar
42 E2 **Maniago** Italy
88 E8 **Maniamba** Mozambique
87 F9 **Manica** Mozambique
71 G5 **Manicani** *isld* Philippines
122 D4 **Manic Deux Dam** Quebec Canada
128 F5 **Manicoré** *R* Brazil
122 D3 **Manicouagan** Quebec Canada
122 D4 **Manicouagan Pen** Quebec Canada
122 D4 **Manicouagan R** Quebec Canada
122 D2 **Manicouagan, Res** Quebec Canada
141 K6 **Manifold, C** Queensland Australia
119 V7 **Manigotagan** Manitoba Canada
Maniitsoq *see* **Sukkertoppen Iskappe**
71 E3 **Manila** Luzon Philippines
110 F6 **Manila** Arkansas U.S.A.
101 Q9 **Manila** Utah U.S.A.
71 E3 **Manila B** Luzon Philippines
139 J5 **Manildra** New South Wales Australia
139 K4 **Manilla** New South Wales Australia
99 L8 **Manilla** Iowa U.S.A.
70 F5 **Manimbaja,Tg** *C* Sulawesi
69 E13 **Manindjan,Danau** *L* Sumatra
87 H11 **Maningory** Madagascar
140 C1 **Maningrida** N Terr Australia
85 C6 **Maninian** Ivory Coast
69 E13 **Maninjau Danau** *L* Sumatra
73 P4 **Manipur** *R* Burma
75 P6 **Manipur** *prov* India
47 J6 **Manisa** Turkey
17 G5 **Manises** Spain
12 D5 **Man,Isle of** U.K.
70 B6 **Manismata** Kalimantan
94 B2 **Manistee** *R* Michigan U.S.A.
99 U5 **Manistee** Michigan U.S.A.
99 U3 **Manistique** *R* Michigan U.S.A.
99 U4 **Manistique** Michigan U.S.A.
99 V3 **Manistique L** Michigan U.S.A.
99 R9 **Manito** Illinois U.S.A.
114 J6 **Manitoba** Canada
119 S7 **Manitoba, L** Manitoba Canada
118 H6 **Manito L** Saskatchewan Canada
119 T9 **Manitou** Manitoba Canada
109 J1 **Manitou** Oklahoma U.S.A.
119 M7 **Manitou Bch** Saskatchewan Canada
99 T2 **Manitou I** Michigan U.S.A.
99 W4 **Manitou Island, North** Michigan U.S.A.
99 W4 **Manitou Island, South** Michigan U.S.A.
120 J7 **Manitou L** Ontario Canada
122 G3 **Manitou,L** Quebec Canada
120 H7 **Manitoulin I** Ontario Canada
122 G2 **Manitou R** Quebec Canada
106 F3 **Manitou Springs** Colorado U.S.A.
120 E3 **Manitouwadge** Ontario Canada
120 J7 **Manitowaning** Ontario Canada
120 F4 **Manitowik L** Ontario Canada
99 T5 **Manitowoc** Wisconsin U.S.A.
121 P6 **Maniwaki** Quebec Canada
128 C2 **Manizales** Colombia
80 G6 **Manja** Jordan
87 G12 **Manja** Madagascar
143 B10 **Manjimup** W Australia Australia
38 M5 **Mank** Austria
107 M2 **Mankato** Kansas U.S.A.
99 N5 **Mankato** Minnesota U.S.A.
89 G6 **Mankayane** Swaziland
86 B5 **Mankim** Cameroon
109 J2 **Mankins** Texas U.S.A.
85 C7 **Mankono** Ivory Coast
118 K9 **Mankota** Saskatchewan Canada
48 N2 **Man'kovka** Ukraine
83 K8 **Mankulam** Sri Lanka
95 M3 **Manlius** New York U.S.A.
17 J2 **Manlleu** Spain
139 K5 **Manly** New South Wales Australia
145 E2 **Manly** New Zealand
99 N6 **Manly** Iowa U.S.A.
74 F8 **Manmad** India
139 K3 **Mann** *R* New South Wales Australia
140 C2 **Mann** *R* N Terr Australia
138 F4 **Mannahill** South Australia Australia
83 J9 **Mannar** Sri Lanka
73 M7 **Mannar,G.of** India/Sri Lanka
76 D5 **Mannargudi** India
83 J8 **Mannar I** Sri Lanka
36 F5 **Mannheim** Germany
14 A3 **Mannin B** Ireland
139 K4 **Manning** *R* New South Wales Australia
117 P7 **Manning** Alberta Canada
109 P1 **Manning** Arkansas U.S.A.
99 L8 **Manning** Iowa U.S.A.
98 D2 **Manning** North Dakota U.S.A.
112 G4 **Manning** South Carolina U.S.A.
109 N4 **Manning** Texas U.S.A.
117 N11 **Manning Prov. Park** British Columbia Canada
94 G7 **Mannington** West Virginia U.S.A.
9 H4 **Manningtree** England
140 A7 **Mann, Mt** N Terr Australia
140 A7 **Mann Ranges** N Terr/S Aust Australia
112 M2 **Manns Harbor** North Carolina U.S.A.
95 L3 **Mannsville** New York U.S.A.
43 C9 **Mannu** *R* Sardinia
43 B8 **Mannu,C** Sardinia
138 E5 **Mannum** South Australia Australia
118 F5 **Mannville** Alberta Canada
85 B7 **Mano** Sierra Leone
128 E5 **Manoa** Bolivia
80 B8 **Manoah** *R* Israel
127 N1 **Man of War B** Tobago
116 H7 **Manokotak** Alaska U.S.A.
136 G2 **Manokwari** W Irian
46 E6 **Manolás** Greece
87 G12 **Manombo** Madagascar
88 A5 **Manono** Zaire
119 Q9 **Manor** Saskatchewan Canada
112 E6 **Manor** Georgia U.S.A.
109 K5 **Manor** Texas U.S.A.
8 B4 **Manorbier** Wales
144 B6 **Manorburn Res** New Zealand
14 C2 **Manorhamilton** Ireland
85 B7 **Mano River** Liberia
68 D7 **Manoron** Burma
19 P17 **Manosque** France
21 M4 **Manou** France
121 Q5 **Manouane** Quebec Canada
122 B3 **Manouane L** Quebec Canada
61 M8 **Mano-wan** *B* Japan
68 C1 **Man Pan** Burma
134 K9 **Manra** *isld* Phoenix Is Pacific Oc
17 J3 **Manresa** Spain
88 B7 **Mansa** Zambia
85 A6 **Mansaba** Guinea-Bissau
85 A6 **Mansa Konko** The Gambia
71 E4 **Mansalay B** Philippines
71 H5 **Mansalean** Indonesia
68 C1 **Man Sam** Burma
142 G4 **Mansbridge, Mt** W Australia Australia
115 L5 **Mansel I** Northwest Territories Canada
33 O9 **Mansfeld** Germany
139 H6 **Mansfield** Victoria Australia
9 E1 **Mansfield** England
110 B6 **Mansfield** Arkansas U.S.A.
112 D4 **Mansfield** Georgia U.S.A.
99 S9 **Mansfield** Illinois U.S.A.
109 O3 **Mansfield** Louisiana U.S.A.
95 Q4 **Mansfield** Massachusetts U.S.A.
110 D4 **Mansfield** Missouri U.S.A.
94 E6 **Mansfield** Ohio U.S.A.
98 H4 **Mansfield** South Dakota U.S.A.
109 K3 **Mansfield** Texas U.S.A.
100 F2 **Mansfield** Washington U.S.A.
95 P2 **Mansfield,Mt** Vermont U.S.A.
21 L6 **Mansigne** France
56 D4 **Manskoye Belogor'ye** *mts* Russian Federation
18 F7 **Mansle** France
99 M7 **Manson** Iowa U.S.A.
100 E2 **Manson** Washington U.S.A.
117 L8 **Manson Creek** British Columbia Canada
130 C4 **Manso,R** Brazil
80 D1 **Mansoyra** Israel
8 D6 **Manston** England
111 D10 **Mansura** Louisiana U.S.A.
79 B7 **Mansûra,El** Egypt
128 B4 **Manta** Ecuador
71 C6 **Mantalingajan, Mt** Palawan Philippines
70 E1 **Mantanani Besar** *isld* Sabah
86 D6 **Mantantale** Zaire
65 H4 **Mantap-san** *mt* N Korea
71 J5 **Mantarara** Indonesia
118 H7 **Mantario** Saskatchewan Canada
128 C6 **Mantaro** *R* Peru
102 C4 **Manteca** California U.S.A.
111 G8 **Mantee** Mississippi U.S.A.
71 J4 **Mantehase** *isld* Sulawesi
37 N4 **Mantel** Germany
130 H6 **Mantena** Brazil
99 T8 **Manteno** Illinois U.S.A.
112 M2 **Manteo** North Carolina U.S.A.
107 J4 **Manter** Kansas U.S.A.
21 O4 **Mantes-la-Jolie** France
25 E2 **Mantgum** Netherlands
74 H9 **Manthani** India
21 M7 **Manthelan** France
103 N2 **Manti** Utah U.S.A.
130 F8 **Mantiqueira,Serra da** *mts* Brazil
100 D9 **Manton** California U.S.A.
94 B2 **Manton** Michigan U.S.A.
65 B5 **Mantou Shan** *mt ra* China
45 J1 **Mantova** Italy
29 L11 **Mäntsälä** Finland
29 L10 **Mänttä** Finland
126 B3 **Mantua** Cuba
Mantua Italy *see* **Mantova**
94 F5 **Mantua** Ohio U.S.A.
141 H6 **Mantuan Downs** Queensland Australia
52 F5 **Manturovo** Russian Federation
29 J10 **Mäntyluoto** Finland
128 D6 **Manú** Peru
Manuan *see* **Manouane**
122 B3 **Manuanis,L** Quebec Canada
71 F6 **Manucan** Mindanao Philippines
129 J5 **Manuel Alves** *R* Brazil
106 B6 **Manuelito** New Mexico U.S.A.
130 D9 **Manuel Ribas** Brazil
133 C8 **Manuel Rodríguez, I** Chile
128 E5 **Manuel Urbano** Brazil
129 H5 **Manuelzinho** Brazil
71 H6 **Manui** *isld* Indonesia
77 E6 **Manūjān** Iran
145 G2 **Manukau** New Zealand
145 E2 **Manukau Hbr** New Zealand
70 F2 **Manuk Manka** Philippines
138 E4 **Manunda** *R* South Australia Australia
145 E3 **Manunui** New Zealand
71 C3 **Manuran** *isld* W Irian
128 E6 **Manuripe** *R* Bolivia/Peru
136 K2 **Manus** *isld* Bismarck Arch
145 E3 **Manutahi** New Zealand
138 E3 **Manuwalkaninna** South Australia Australia
98 J1 **Manvel** North Dakota U.S.A.
76 C3 **Manvi** India
98 B7 **Manville** Wyoming U.S.A.
109 O4 **Many** Louisiana U.S.A.
52 K4 **Man'ya** Russian Federation
88 B10 **Manyangau** *mt* Zimbabwe
88 G3 **Manyara,L** Tanzania
47 J4 **Manyas** Turkey
118 G9 **Manyberries** Alberta Canada
54 M9 **Manych** *R* Russian Federation
118 G8 **Many Island I** Alberta Canada
88 E4 **Manyoni** Tanzania
141 K6 **Many Peaks** Queensland Australia
143 C10 **Many Peaks, Mt** W Australia Australia
79 B7 **Manzala,El** Egypt
84 J3 **Manzala, L** Egypt
89 E2 **Manzamnyama** *R* Zimbabwe
16 E5 **Manzanares** Spain
127 P2 **Manzanilla B** Trinidad
126 F4 **Manzanillo** Cuba
124 G8 **Manzanillo** Mexico
106 D7 **Manzano** New Mexico U.S.A.
131 A8 **Manzano,B del** Chile
106 G3 **Manzanola** Colorado U.S.A.
106 D7 **Manzano Mts** New Mexico U.S.A.
58 G2 **Manzhouli** China
79 G7 **Manzil** Jordan
89 G6 **Manzini** Swaziland
Manzovka *see* **Sibirtsevo**
86 C3 **Mao** Chad
65 G2 **Mao'ershan** China
136 H2 **Maoke, Pegunungan** *ra* W Irian
65 F4 **Maokui Shan** *mt* China
65 G3 **Maolin** China
67 C6 **Maoming** China
80 D8 **Ma'on** Jordan
67 C1 **Maoping** China
67 G6 **Mao-pi T'ou** *C* Taiwan
67 B3 **Maotai** China
67 A1 **Maowen** China
65 F2 **Maoxing** China
80 F4 **Ma'oz** Israel
87 F10 **Mapai** Mozambique
66 C5 **Mapam Yumco** *L* China
70 G5 **Mapane** Sulawesi
71 D7 **Mapin** Philippines
67 D1 **Maping** China
128 F2 **Mapire** Venezuela
129 H3 **Mapireme** Brazil
128 E7 **Mapiri** *R* La Paz Bolivia
128 F4 **Mapixari, L** Brazil
99 L7 **Maple** *R* Iowa U.S.A.
94 C3 **Maple** *R* Michigan U.S.A.
118 H9 **Maple Creek** Saskatchewan Canada
99 N6 **Maple Island** Minnesota U.S.A.
111 K9 **Maplesville** Alabama U.S.A.
122 H8 **Mapleton** Nova Scotia Canada
99 L7 **Mapleton** Iowa U.S.A.
95 S7 **Mapleton** Maine U.S.A.
99 N6 **Mapleton** Minnesota U.S.A.
100 B5 **Mapleton** Oregon U.S.A.
100 C2 **Maple Valley** Washington U.S.A.
95 L3 **Maple View** New York U.S.A.
141 F1 **Mapoon** Queensland Australia
69 G12 **Mapor** *isld* Indonesia
144 C5 **Mapourika, L** New Zealand
13 H6 **Mappleton** England
129 G4 **Mapuera** *R* Brazil
87 F11 **Maputo** Mozambique
89 H6 **Maputo** *R* Mozambique
80 F8 **Maqam en Nabi Yusha** Jordan
78 H6 **Maqar an Naam** Iraq
46 D3 **Maqellarë** Albania
58 C5 **Maqên Gangri** *mt* China
65 H2 **Maqiaohe** China
79 E10 **Maqnā** Saudi Arabia
66 C6 **Maquan He** *R* China
71 G4 **Maqueda Chan** Philippines
122 H5 **Maquereau Pte.au** Quebec Canada
133 D6 **Maquinchao** Argentina
131 B8 **Maquinchao, R** Argentina
99 Q7 **Maquoketa** Iowa U.S.A.
99 Q9 **Maquon** Illinois U.S.A.
70 G7 **Mara** Sulawesi
127 J9 **Mara** Venezuela
128 E4 **Maraa** Brazil
129 J5 **Marabá** Brazil
70 D6 **Marabahan** Kalimantan
40 B2 **Marac** France
127 J9 **Maracaibo** Venezuela
127 J9 **Maracaibo, L. de** Venezuela
129 H3 **Maracá, Ilha de** Amapá Brazil
128 F3 **Maracá, Ilha de** Roraima Brazil
133 F2 **Maracaju** Brazil
130 C7 **Maracaju,Serra de** *mts* Brazil
129 J4 **Maracana** Brazil
127 O2 **Maracas B** Trinidad
127 L9 **Maracay** Venezuela
84 F4 **Marādah** Libya
85 F6 **Maradi** Niger
145 E3 **Maraetai** New Zealand
78 L3 **Marāgheh** Iran
130 J10 **Maragogi** Brazil
144 D4 **Marahau** New Zealand
128 E3 **Marahuaca,Co** *mt* Venezuela
65 E2 **Marain Sum** China
110 A3 **Marais des Cygnes** *R* Kansas/Missouri U.S.A.
21 L3 **Marais-Vernier** France
129 J4 **Marajó,I.de** Brazil
86 G5 **Maralal** Kenya
55 G4 **Maraldy** Kazakhstan
86 C4 **Marali** Cent Afr Republic
137 N3 **Maramasike** *isld* Solomon Is
Maramba *see* **Livingstone** Zambia
48 H3 **Maramures** *old prov* Romania
69 F11 **Maran** Malaysia
103 N9 **Marana** Arizona U.S.A.
140 C2 **Maranboy** N Terr Australia
17 F3 **Maranchón** Spain
78 K2 **Marand** Iran
45 J2 **Maranello** Italy
68 D7 **Marang** Burma
69 F10 **Marang** Malaysia
129 L4 **Maranguape** Brazil
129 J4 **Maranhão** *state* Brazil
130 E4 **Maranhão** *R* Brazil
141 J7 **Maranoa** *R* Queensland Australia
45 Q8 **Marano di Napoli** Italy
128 D4 **Marañón** *R* Peru
18 E6 **Marans** France
40 A1 **Maranville** France
16 B3 **Marão, Sa do** *mts* Portugal
129 G3 **Marapi** *R* Brazil
43 B8 **Marargiu, C** Sardinia
128 E5 **Marari** Brazil
144 B6 **Mararoa** *R* New Zealand
70 F7 **Marasende** *isld* Indonesia
48 L5 **Mărăşeşti** Romania
71 C6 **Marasi B** Palawan Philippines
16 B6 **Marateca** Portugal
46 D7 **Marathiás,Akr** *C* Greece
120 D4 **Marathon** Ontario Canada
46 F6 **Marathón** Greece
113 F13 **Marathon** Florida U.S.A.
95 L4 **Marathon** New York U.S.A.
108 D5 **Marathon** Texas U.S.A.
99 R5 **Marathon** Wisconsin U.S.A.
70 F3 **Maratua** *isld* Indonesia
129 L6 **Maraú** Brazil
128 E3 **Marauaí** *R* Brazil
127 O2 **Maraval** Trinidad
108 E6 **Maravillas Cr** Texas U.S.A.
71 G7 **Marawi** Mindanao Philippines
38 M5 **Marbach** Austria
36 F2 **Marbach** Germany
22 K4 **Marbehan** Belgium
106 C2 **Marble** Colorado U.S.A.
100 H1 **Marble** Washington U.S.A.
142 C5 **Marble Bar** W Australia Australia
103 N5 **Marble Canyon** Arizona U.S.A.
110 B6 **Marble City** Oklahoma U.S.A.
109 J5 **Marble Falls** Texas U.S.A.
87 E10 **Marble Hall** S Africa
99 P10 **Marblehead** Illinois U.S.A.
95 R4 **Marblehead** Massachusetts U.S.A.
94 E5 **Marblehead** Ohio U.S.A.
99 O7 **Marble Rock** Iowa U.S.A.
121 T7 **Marbleton** Quebec Canada
101 P7 **Marbleton** Wyoming U.S.A.
36 F2 **Marburg** Germany
95 K8 **Marbury** Maryland U.S.A.
26 G8 **Marby** Sweden
48 D3 **Marcal** *R* Hungary
47 J7 **Marçal Dağ** *mt* Turkey
48 D4 **Marcali** Hungary
45 J1 **Marcaria** Italy
122 F2 **Marceau,L** Quebec Canada
118 L6 **Marcelin** Saskatchewan Canada
110 D2 **Marceline** Missouri U.S.A.
133 G3 **Marcelino Ramos** Brazil
110 E6 **Marcella** Arkansas U.S.A.
94 B4 **Marcellus** Michigan U.S.A.
100 G2 **Marcellus** Washington U.S.A.
45 O5 **Marcetelli** Italy
9 G2 **March** England
21 M4 **Marchainville** France
118 E2 **Marchand** Manitoba Canada
138 E4 **Marchant Hill** South Australia Australia
40 D3 **Marchaux** France
18 F6 **Marche** *reg* France
45 N4 **Marche** *reg* Italy
22 J3 **Marche-en-Famenne** Belgium
128 A7 **Marchena** *isld* Galapagos Is
16 D7 **Marchena** Spain
21 N6 **Marchenoir** France
20 H3 **Marchésieux** France
127 P6 **Marchfield** Barbados
22 E3 **Marchiennes-Ville** France
22 J3 **Marchin** Belgium
140 D1 **Marchinbar I** N Terr Australia
131 E3 **Mar Chiquita, L** Córdoba Argentina
45 Q7 **Marcianise** Italy
18 H6 **Marcigny** France
18 G8 **Marcillac** France
21 J5 **Marcille-la-Ville** France
20 H4 **Marcilly** Manche France
21 O7 **Marcilly-en-Gault** France
21 P6 **Marcilly-en-Villette** France
21 N4 **Marcilly-sur-Eure** France
40 G1 **Marckolsheim** France
122 J1 **Marc,L** Labrador, Nfld Canada
113 F12 **Marco** Florida U.S.A.
110 J3 **Marco** Indiana U.S.A.
43 G9 **Marco Argentano, S** Italy
22 E3 **Marcoing** France
100 C5 **Marcola** Oregon U.S.A.
21 M6 **Marçon** France
118 C1 **Marconi** Manitoba Canada
22 K3 **Marcourt** Belgium
19 Q16 **Marcoux** France
99 L7 **Marcus** Iowa U.S.A.
100 G1 **Marcus** Washington U.S.A.
116 O6 **Marcus Baker,Mt** Alaska U.S.A.
134 G5 **Marcus I** Pacific Oc
95 M3 **Marcy** New York U.S.A.
95 O2 **Marcy, Mt** New York U.S.A.
80 D5 **Marda** Jordan
74 E1 **Mardan** Pakistan
131 F6 **Mar del Plata** Argentina
9 G5 **Marden** England
142 B5 **Mardie** W Australia Australia
78 H3 **Mardin** Turkey
26 M5 **Mårdsel** Sweden
26 K7 **Mårdsele** Sweden
26 J7 **Mardsjö** Sweden
26 H8 **Mårdsjön** Sweden
71 A2 **Mare** *isld* Halmahera Indonesia
137 O6 **Maré** *isld* Îles Loyauté Pacific Oc
126 F5 **Marea de Portillo** Cuba
45 M3 **Marecchia** *R* Italy
130 J10 **Marechal Deodoro** Brazil
141 H3 **Mareeba** Queensland Australia
86 A3 **Mareeq** Somalia
86 A2 **Mareer-Gur** Somalia
118 H7 **Marengo** Saskatchewan Canada
41 N7 **Marengo** Italy
110 K3 **Marengo** Indiana U.S.A.
99 P8 **Marengo** Iowa U.S.A.
94 E6 **Marengo** Ohio U.S.A.
100 G2 **Marengo** Washington U.S.A.
99 Q3 **Marengo** Wisconsin U.S.A.
99 R3 **Marenisco** Michigan U.S.A.
18 E7 **Marennes** France
145 E2 **Mareretu** New Zealand
9 G6 **Maresfield** England
43 E11 **Marettimo, I** Sicily
22 E3 **Maretz** France
18 F7 **Mareuil** France
21 P8 **Mareuil-sur-Arnon** France
20 H8 **Mareuil-sur-Lay** France
108 C5 **Marfa** Texas U.S.A.
66 D4 **Margai Caka** *L* China
75 M1 **Margai Caka** *L* China
8 C4 **Margam** Wales
123 L7 **Margaree Harbour** C Breton I, Nova Scotia
123 L7 **Margaree I** Nova Scotia Canada
123 M7 **Margaree Valley** C Breton I, Nova Scotia
138 D3 **Margaret** *R* South Australia Australia
108 H1 **Margaret** Texas U.S.A.
141 G1 **Margaret Bay** Queensland Australia
117 K10 **Margaret Bay** British Columbia Canada
117 Q6 **Margaret L** Alberta Canada
117 P3 **Margaret L** Northwest Territories Canada
142 C5 **Margaret, Mt** W Australia Australia
143 B10 **Margaret R** W Australia Australia
95 N4 **Margaretville** New York U.S.A.
130 C7 **Margarida** Brazil
127 N9 **Margarita I. de** Venezuela
46 D5 **Margarítion** Greece
139 H9 **Margate** Tasmania Australia
9 H5 **Margate** England
89 G8 **Margate** S Africa
95 N7 **Margate City** New Jersey U.S.A.
18 H8 **Margeride, Mts de la** France
Margherita *see* **Jamaame** Somalia
48 G3 **Marghita** Romania
118 F3 **Margie** Alberta Canada
99 N1 **Margie** Minnesota U.S.A.
57 F4 **Margilan** Uzbekistan
48 G5 **Margina** Romania
48 G5 **Margita** Serbia Yugoslavia
119 O7 **Margo** Saskatchewan Canada
77 H4 **Margo, Dasht-i-** *desert* Afghanistan
71 F7 **Margosatubig** Mindanao Philippines
94 C2 **Margrethe, L** Michigan U.S.A.
117 M9 **Marguerite** British Columbia Canada
146 C5 **Marguerite B** Antarctica
22 J4 **Margut** France
80 F3 **Marhaba** Jordan
122 F5 **Maria** Quebec Canada
124 F7 **María Cleofas, I** Mexico
28 D3 **Mariager** Denmark
32 M7 **Mariaglück** Germany
140 D2 **Maria I** N Terr Australia
139 J8 **Maria I** Tasmania Australia
68 C7 **Maria I** Burma
36 C3 **Maria Laach** Germany
38 G8 **Maria Luggau** Austria
124 F7 **María Madre, I** Mexico
124 F7 **María Magdalena, I** Mexico

3 K8 Maria Mts California U.S.A.
1 J5 Marian Queensland Australia
0 G7 Mariana Brazil
8 E3 Mariana Lake Alberta Canada
6 C3 Marianao Cuba
5 Q5 Mariani India
7 P4 Marian L Northwest Territories Canada
0 F7 Marianna Arkansas U.S.A.
3 B7 Marianna Florida U.S.A.
7 H14 Mariannelund Sweden
7 O4 Marianské Lázně Czech Rep
9 T9 Mariapolis Manitoba Canada
1 N1 Marias R Montana U.S.A.
7 F7 Maria,Sierra de mts Spain
4 F7 Marias, Islas islds Mexico
1 M1 Marias Pass Montana U.S.A.
8 F6 Mariastein Austria
5 M12 Maria Theresa Reef Pacific Oc
5 D1 Maria van Diemen, C New Zealand
8 M6 Mariazell Austria
9 T5 Maribel Wisconsin U.S.A.
Maribo co see Storstrøm co
8 G7 Maribo Denmark
8 N8 Maribor Slovenia
1 E4 Maricaban isld Philippines
9 E5 Marico R Botswana
3 M8 Maricopa Arizona U.S.A.
3 E6 Maricopa California U.S.A.
3 M8 Maricopa Mts Arizona U.S.A.
Maricourt see Kangiqsujuaq
6 E5 Maridi Sudan
8 E4 Marié R Brazil
3 K12 Marie Anne I Seychelles
6 C8 Marie Byrd Land Antarctica
6 A8 Marie Byrd Seamount seamount Antarctica
7 H13 Mariedam Sweden
7 J12 Mariefred Sweden
7 N5 Marie Galante isld Guadeloupe W Indies
7 L11 Mariehamn Finland
8 G4 Marie L Alberta Canada
6 C3 Mariel Cuba
Marienbad see Mariánské Lázně
2 L8 Marienberg Germany
7 P2 Marienberg Germany
5 G3 Marienberg Netherlands
2 H3 Marienbourg Belgium
Marienburg see Malbork
6 C2 Marienburg Nordrhein-Westfalen Germany
7 N3 Marieney Germany
2 F5 Marienhafe Germany
6 C1 Marienheide Germany
8 G7 Marienleuchte C Germany
9 A5 Mariental Namibia
7 J3 Marienthal Kansas U.S.A.
4 H5 Marienville Pennsylvania U.S.A.
0 B1 Marie Shoal N Terr Australia
7 G13 Mariestad Sweden
2 C4 Marietta Georgia U.S.A.
4 F7 Marietta Ohio U.S.A.
9 K2 Marietta Oklahoma U.S.A.
2 E2 Marietta South Carolina U.S.A.
R7 Marieville Quebec Canada
9 O18 Marignane France
J6 Marigné Maine-et-Loire France
L6 Marigné Sarthe France
0 H3 Marigny France
7 N5 Marigot Saint Martin W Indies
5 A3 Mariinsk Russian Federation
5 C3 Mariinsk Russian Federation
5 D4 Mariinskoye Russian Federation
2 G6 Mariinsky Posad Russian Federation
O1 Marijampolė Lithuania
J5 Marikasu,Tg C Indonesia
0 D8 Marila Brazil
3 H2 Marília Brazil
2 C5 Marillana W Australia Australia
0 E7 Marimbondo Cachoeira rapids Brazil
0 D5 Marimun Kalimantan
6 B2 Marín Spain
7 M4 Marin Martinique W Indies
2 C5 Marina California U.S.A.
4 H3 Marina di Carrara Italy
4 H3 Marina di Massa Italy
4 H4 Marina di Pisa Italy
5 M3 Marina di Ravenna Italy
3 G2 Marina Fall Guyana
3 C7 Mar'ina Gorka Belarus
E4 Marinduque isld Philippines
0 G3 Marine Illinois U.S.A.
3 F8 Marineland Florida U.S.A.
P3 Marines France
9 T4 Marinette Wisconsin U.S.A.
9 H8 Maringá Brazil
6 D5 Maringa R Zaire
E11 Maringouin Louisiana U.S.A.
7 F9 Maringue Mozambique
6 B5 Marinha Grande Portugal
4 J9 Mar'inka Ukraine
2 E7 Marino Italy
3 E3 Marinuma Colombia
J9 Marion Alabama U.S.A.
0 F6 Marion Arkansas U.S.A.
7 Q11 Marion Idaho U.S.A.
0 H4 Marion Illinois U.S.A.
4 B6 Marion Indiana U.S.A.
9 P7 Marion Iowa U.S.A.
7 O3 Marion Kansas U.S.A.
0 H4 Marion Kentucky U.S.A.
D9 Marion Louisiana U.S.A.
5 U2 Marion Maine U.S.A.
4 B2 Marion Michigan U.S.A.
H9 Marion Mississippi U.S.A.
L1 Marion Montana U.S.A.
3 F9 Marion Nebraska U.S.A.
2 E2 Marion North Carolina U.S.A.
3 H3 Marion North Dakota U.S.A.
4 D6 Marion Ohio U.S.A.
2 H3 Marion South Carolina U.S.A.
3 J6 Marion South Dakota U.S.A.
9 J6 Marion Texas U.S.A.
4 F10 Marion Virginia U.S.A.
9 S5 Marion Wisconsin U.S.A.
9 J8 Marion B Tasmania Australia
0 E6 Marion Downs Queensland Australia
J9 Marion Junction Alabama U.S.A.
K4 Marion Reef Gt Barrier Reef Aust
L4 Marion Reef Coral Sea
0 C4 Marionville Missouri U.S.A.
3 E2 Maripa Venezuela
G5 Maripipi isld Philippines
2 D4 Mariposa R California U.S.A.
2 E4 Mariposa California U.S.A.
0 G4 Marisa Sulawesi
3 E2 Mariscal Estigarribia Paraguay
0 G3 Marissa Illinois U.S.A.
6 G2 Maritsa R Bulgaria
7 R14 Marítsa Rhodes Greece
4 B3 Marittime, Alpi mts Italy/France
2 G6 Mari Turek Russian Federation
4 J9 Mariupol' Ukraine
7 O10 Mariusa R Venezuela
3 L4 Marīvān Iran
2 G6 Mariyskaya Respublika Russian Federation
7 J4 Marja Afghanistan
4 G3 Marj, Al Libya
7 A5 Marjan, Al oil well Persian Gulf
6 N5 Marjärv Sweden
9 F5 Marjayoûn Lebanon
5 C5 Mark R Netherlands
0 G6 Marka Jordan
6 H5 Marka Somalia
26 E8 Markabygd Norway
56 C6 Markakal', Oz L Kazakhstan
52 J4 Markalasta Russian Federation
58 C6 Markam China
76 D3 Markapur India
77 A2 Markazī prov Iran
120 K8 Markdale Ontario Canada
41 K2 Markdorf Germany
110 F6 Marked Tree Arkansas U.S.A.
25 G4 Markelo Netherlands
28 G7 Markelsdorfe Huk C Germany
25 D4 Marken Netherlands
25 D3 Markermeer Netherlands
99 S6 Markesan Wisconsin U.S.A.
9 F2 Market Deeping England
8 D2 Market Drayton England
9 F3 Market Harborough England
14 E2 Markethill N Ireland
13 H6 Market Rasen England
9 E1 Market Warsop England
13 H6 Market Weighton England
36 G6 Markgröningen Germany
121 L9 Markham Ontario Canada
109 L7 Markham Texas U.S.A.
100 B3 Markham Washington U.S.A.
9 F1 Markham Moor England
146 D10 Markham, Mt Antarctica
31 N3 Marki Poland
119 N8 Markinch Saskatchewan Canada
15 E4 Markinch Scotland
33 T8 Märkisch Buchholz Germany
66 B4 Markit China
26 M4 Markitta Sweden
102 E3 Markleeville California U.S.A.
37 O6 Marklkofen Germany
37 N3 Markneukirchen Germany
26 J4 Markotjåkko mt Sweden
33 Q10 Markrapstädt Germany
111 F7 Marks Mississippi U.S.A.
8 D5 Marksbury England
120 K6 Markstay Ontario Canada
9 G4 Marks Tey England
37 J2 Marksuhl Germany
111 D10 Marksville Louisiana U.S.A.
37 J5 Marktbergel Germany
37 J4 Markt Bibart Germany
37 J4 Marktbreit Germany
37 L3 Marktgraitz Germany
36 H4 Marktheidenfeld Germany
37 L7 Markt Indersdorf Germany
37 O7 Marktl Germany
37 M3 Marktleugast Germany
37 J6 Marktoffingen Germany
37 N3 Marktredwitz Germany
37 M3 Marktschorgast Germany
37 J4 Marktsteft Germany
38 M7 Markt-Übelbach Austria
110 E2 Mark Twain L Missouri U.S.A.
41 N1 Markt Wald Germany
37 L3 Marktzeuln Germany
99 O3 Markville Minnesota U.S.A.
32 F9 Marl Germany
107 N5 Marland Oklahoma U.S.A.
143 B8 Marlandy Hill W Australia Australia
121 N8 Marlbank Ontario Canada
95 P4 Marlboro New Hampshire U.S.A.
141 J6 Marlborough Queensland Australia
9 E5 Marlborough England
128 G2 Marlborough Guyana
145 D4 Marlborough admin region New Zealand
95 Q4 Marlborough Massachusetts U.S.A.
22 F4 Marle France
33 S8 Marlendorf Germany
33 S8 Marlenfelde Germany
94 D3 Marlette Michigan U.S.A.
19 O12 Marlieux France
109 L4 Marlin Texas U.S.A.
94 G8 Marlinton West Virginia U.S.A.
139 J7 Marlo Victoria Australia
22 J3 Marloie Belgium
9 F4 Marlow England
33 R4 Marlow Germany
95 P3 Marlow New Hampshire U.S.A.
109 K1 Marlow Oklahoma U.S.A.
22 F4 Marly France
27 J10 Marma Sweden
110 F5 Marmaduke Arkansas U.S.A.
21 P7 Marmagne Cher France
18 F8 Marmande France
47 J4 Marmara Adası isld Turkey
47 J4 Marmara Denizi Turkey
47 J4 Marmaraereğlisi Turkey
47 J6 Marmara Gölü L Turkey
Marmara, Sea of see Marmara Denizi
47 J8 Marmaris Turkey
98 C3 Marmarth North Dakota U.S.A.
26 K3 Mårmatj mt Sweden
94 E4 Marme City Michigan U.S.A.
16 B2 Marmed,Sa des S mts Spain
128 F5 Marmelos R Brazil
94 F8 Marmet West Virginia U.S.A.
121 P4 Marmette,L Quebec Canada
118 L1 Marmion L res Ontario Canada
143 C8 Marmion, Mt W Australia Australia
45 J1 Marmirolo Italy
42 D2 Marmolada mt Italy
16 E6 Marmolejo Spain
116 L7 Marmot B Alaska U.S.A.
125 M9 Mar Muerto B Mexico
19 J5 Marnay France
18 H4 Marne dept France
40 B1 Marne R France
32 K5 Marne Germany
36 B6 Marne, Canal de la France
36 D4 Marnheim Germany
33 P6 Marnitz Germany
139 G6 Marnoo Victoria Australia
145 F3 Maroa New Zealand
99 S9 Maroa Illinois U.S.A.
87 H11 Maroantsetra Madagascar
74 C2 Marobi Pakistan
22 F3 Maroilles France
37 K3 Maroldsweisach Germany
21 L5 Marolles-les-Braults France
87 H10 Maromandia Madagascar
21 N3 Maromme France
21 O8 Mâron Indre France
89 G2 Marondera Zimbabwe
47 H4 Marónia Greece
18 G7 Maronne R France
141 L7 Maroochydore Queensland Australia
143 B6 Maroonah W Australia Australia
127 J2 Maroon Town Jamaica
70 F7 Maros R Sulawesi
70 F7 Maros Sulawesi
145 E1 Marotiri Is New Zealand
86 B3 Maroua Cameroon
20 E5 Maroué France
121 L4 Marouf Jct Quebec Canada
22 D3 Marœuil France
129 H3 Marouini R Fr Guiana
87 H11 Marovoay Madagascar
78 H4 Marqādah Syria
110 F4 Marquano Missouri U.S.A.
135 U13 Marquesas Is Pacific Oc
113 E13 Marquesas Keys islds Florida U.S.A.
130 G8 Marquês de Valençá Brazil
118 D1 Marquette Manitoba Canada
99 P6 Marquette Iowa U.S.A.
107 N3 Marquette Kansas U.S.A.
99 T3 Marquette Michigan U.S.A.
99 U6 Marquette R Michigan U.S.A.
98 H8 Marquette Nebraska U.S.A.
106 C6 Marquez New Mexico U.S.A.
109 L4 Marquez Texas U.S.A.
17 F1 Marquina Spain
22 E3 Marquion France
119 M8 Marquis Saskatchewan Canada
22 B2 Marquise France
139 G4 Marra New South Wales Australia
139 H4 Marra R New South Wales Australia
89 H5 Marracuene Mozambique
45 L3 Marradi Italy
143 B10 Marradong W Australia Australia
86 D3 Marra, Jebel mts Sudan
140 B2 Marrakai N Terr Australia
85 C2 Marrakech Morocco
85 E2 Marraket, Hassi Algeria
139 H5 Marrar New South Wales Australia
139 G8 Marrawah Tasmania Australia
28 H7 Marrebæk Denmark
138 E3 Marree South Australia Australia
111 J13 Marrero New Orleans, Louisiana U.S.A.
87 G9 Marromeu Mozambique
16 D8 Marroqui,Pta Spain
88 F8 Marrupa Mozambique
94 G6 Mars Pennsylvania U.S.A.
84 K4 Marsá Alam Egypt
17 F9 Marsa Ben Mehidi Algeria
86 G5 Marsabit Kenya
Marsa Brega see Al Burayqah
20 G6 Marsac-sur-Don France
130 F8 Mar,Sa.do mts Brazil
36 B6 Marsal France
43 E11 Marsala Sicily
19 N15 Marsanne France
139 J5 Marsden New South Wales Australia
118 H6 Marsden Saskatchewan Canada
13 G4 Marsden England
25 C3 Marsdiep chan Netherlands
19 O18 Marseille France
21 O2 Marseille-en-Beauvaisis France
19 N18 Marseille-Rhône, Canal France
Marseilles France see Marseille
99 S8 Marseilles Illinois U.S.A.
94 D6 Marseilles Ohio U.S.A.
98 B3 Marsh Montana U.S.A.
79 E10 Marshah, J mt Saudi Arabia
118 H5 Marshall Saskatchewan Canada
110 D6 Marshall Arkansas U.S.A.
99 T10 Marshall Illinois U.S.A.
94 C4 Marshall Michigan U.S.A.
99 L5 Marshall Minnesota U.S.A.
110 C2 Marshall Missouri U.S.A.
112 E2 Marshall North Carolina U.S.A.
98 D2 Marshall North Dakota U.S.A.
107 N5 Marshall Oklahoma U.S.A.
109 N3 Marshall Texas U.S.A.
94 K8 Marshall Virginia U.S.A.
101 U7 Marshall Wyoming U.S.A.
139 J7 Marshall B Tasmania Australia
134 G7 Marshall Is rep Pacific Oc
120 C2 Marshall L Ontario Canada
99 O7 Marshalltown Iowa U.S.A.
8 D3 Marshbrook England
8 D5 Marshfield England
110 D4 Marshfield Missouri U.S.A.
99 Q5 Marshfield Wisconsin U.S.A.
113 K11 Marsh Harbour Great Abaco I Bahamas
95 L5 Marsh Hill Pennsylvania U.S.A.
95 T7 Mars Hill Maine U.S.A.
111 D12 Marsh Island Louisiana U.S.A.
117 F5 Marsh L Yukon Territory Canada
98 K4 Marsh Lake Minnesota U.S.A.
101 Q9 Marsh Pk Utah U.S.A.
112 G3 Marshville North Carolina U.S.A.
100 J6 Marsing Idaho U.S.A.
13 G4 Marske-by-the-Sea England
98 C7 Marsland Nebraska U.S.A.
19 J3 Mars la Tour France
28 E4 Mårslet Denmark
28 F6 Marslev Denmark
25 E2 Marssum Netherlands
27 J12 Märsta Sweden
28 F7 Marstal Denmark
28 E7 Marstal Bugt B Denmark
101 Q8 Marston Wyoming U.S.A.
27 E14 Marstrand Sweden
28 C6 Marstrup Denmark
55 D1 Marsyaty Russian Federation
109 L4 Mart Texas U.S.A.
42 D6 Marta R Italy
68 C4 Martaban Burma
73 Q5 Martaban,G.of Burma
21 L8 Martaizé France
70 D6 Martapura Kalimantan
70 K8 Martapura Sumatra
18 G8 Martel France
22 K4 Martelange Belgium
45 M1 Martellago Italy
41 N4 Martello, Val Italy
47 H1 Marten Bulgaria
99 N8 Martensdale Iowa U.S.A.
17 G5 Martés,Sierra mts Spain
139 J4 Marthaguy R New South Wales Australia
110 E3 Marthasville Missouri U.S.A.
95 R5 Marthas Vineyard Massachusetts U.S.A.
36 B6 Marthille France
126 F4 Martí Cuba
45 M5 Martignano,L.di Italy
21 J5 Martigné France
21 K7 Martigné Briand France
20 H6 Martigné-Ferchaud France
40 F5 Martigny Switzerland
40 C1 Martigny-les-Bains France
19 O18 Martigues France
16 D9 Martil Morocco
31 L6 Martin Slovakia
17 G4 Martin R Spain
116 N4 Martin Alaska U.S.A.
94 E9 Martin Kentucky U.S.A.
94 B4 Martin Michigan U.S.A.
98 E6 Martin South Dakota U.S.A.
110 H5 Martin Tennessee U.S.A.
41 M4 Martina Switzerland
43 H8 Martina Franca Italy
145 E4 Martinborough New Zealand
109 K6 Martindale Texas U.S.A.
125 L7 Martínez Mexico
102 B3 Martinez California U.S.A.
32 M10 Martinfeld Germany
130 F6 Martinho Campos Brazil
127 L4 Martinique isld Lesser Antilles
111 L9 Martin L Alabama U.S.A.
130 D8 Martinópolis Brazil
146 B8 Martin Pen Antarctica
116 Q1 Martin Pt Alaska U.S.A.
144 A6 Martins B New Zealand
38 M5 Martinsberg Austria
Martinsbrück see Martina
110 E2 Martinsburg Missouri U.S.A.
95 M3 Martinsburg New York U.S.A.
94 E6 Martinsburg Ohio U.S.A.
94 J6 Martinsburg Pennsylvania U.S.A.
94 K7 Martinsburg West Virginia U.S.A.
101 P3 Martinsdale Montana U.S.A.
94 G6 Martins Ferry Ohio U.S.A.
99 T10 Martinsville Illinois U.S.A.
94 A7 Martinsville Indiana U.S.A.
94 H10 Martinsville Virginia U.S.A.
20 G2 Martinvast France
21 N8 Martizay France
9 H3 Martlesham England
8 D6 Martock England
28 F5 Martofte Denmark
9 F1 Marton England
145 E4 Marton New Zealand
17 J3 Martorell Spain
16 E7 Martos Spain
117 O4 Martre, Lac La Northwest Territories Canada
117 P4 Martre, Lac la Northwest Territories Canada
29 N4 Martti Finland
29 K11 Marttila Finland
55 C5 Martuk Kazakhstan
52 J2 Martyn Russian Federation
80 G3 Maru Jordan
70 B6 Marua Kalimantan
77 H2 Maruchak Afghanistan
70 D2 Marudi Sarawak
70 E1 Marudu Bay Sabah
77 K4 Maruf Afghanistan
60 G11 Marugame Japan
144 D5 Maruia New Zealand
144 D5 Maruia Springs New Zealand
129 L6 Maruim Brazil
139 J5 Marulan New South Wales Australia
28 J4 Mårum Denmark
25 F2 Marum Netherlands
145 F3 Marumaru New Zealand
140 C2 Marumba Mt N Terr Australia
88 B5 Marungu mts Zaire
61 K9 Maruoka Japan
77 D4 Marvast Iran
27 C11 Mår-vatn L Norway
18 H8 Marvejols France
111 F7 Marvell Arkansas U.S.A.
143 C9 Marvel Loch W Australia Australia
22 J5 Marville France
98 K4 Marvin South Dakota U.S.A.
106 C1 Marvine Colorado U.S.A.
103 N3 Marvine,Mt Utah U.S.A.
77 H2 Marwa Afghanistan
74 E6 Marwar India
118 G5 Marwayne Alberta Canada
15 E1 Marwick Hd Orkney Scotland
32 G6 Marx Germany
33 S9 Marxdorf Germany
37 M3 Marxgrün Germany
77 G1 Mary Turkmenistan
55 F3 Mar'yanovka Russian Federation
139 G6 Maryborough New South Wales Australia
141 L7 Maryborough Queensland Australia
87 D11 Marydale S Africa
55 E4 Mar'yevka Kazakhstan
119 Q9 Maryfield Saskatchewan Canada
117 L6 Mary Henry,Mt British Columbia Canada
12 D2 Maryhill Scotland
111 E10 Mary,L Mississippi U.S.A.
95 K7 Maryland state U.S.A.
89 G1 Maryland Zimbabwe
108 G3 Maryneal Texas U.S.A.
12 E4 Maryport England
141 K7 Mary R Queensland Australia
123 R1 Mary's Hbr Labrador, Nfld Canada
100 K8 Marys R Nevada U.S.A.
123 R6 Marystown Newfoundland Canada
103 M3 Marysvale Utah U.S.A.
122 F8 Marysville New Brunswick Canada
101 O5 Marysville Idaho U.S.A.
107 O2 Marysville Kansas U.S.A.
94 E4 Marysville Michigan U.S.A.
94 D6 Marysville Ohio U.S.A.
100 C1 Marysville Washington U.S.A.
141 H4 Maryvale Queensland Australia
141 K8 Maryvale Queensland Australia
99 M9 Maryville Missouri U.S.A.
112 D2 Maryville Tennessee U.S.A.
45 K3 Marzabotto Italy
85 D5 Marzafal Mali
130 E5 Marzagão Brazil
33 R8 Marzahna Germany
33 R7 Marzahne Germany
20 F6 Marzan France
128 C2 Marzo,C Colombia
70 O9 Mas R Java
69 D13 Masa isld Indonesia
Masada see Meẓada
80 F1 Mas'ada Syria
88 E2 Masai Mara Game Reserve Kenya
88 E2 Masai Mara National Reserve nat park Kenya
88 F4 Masai Steppe Tanzania
88 C2 Masaka Uganda
86 C3 Masalasef Chad
70 D7 Masalembu Besar isld Indonesia
70 D7 Masalembu Kecil isld Indonesia
70 G6 Masamba Sulawesi
65 G7 Masan S Korea
71 N8 Masapun Indonesia
95 S7 Masardis Maine U.S.A.
113 E9 Masaryktown Florida U.S.A.
88 G7 Masasi Tanzania
Mas Atierra isld see Robinson Crusoe isld
71 F4 Masbate isld Philippines
32 F9 Masbeck Germany
17 H9 Mascara Algeria
81 C7 Mascarene Basin Indian Oc
81 C7 Mascarene Is Indian Oc
81 C7 Mascarene Rge Indian Oc
98 G9 Mascot Nebraska U.S.A.
112 D1 Mascot Tennessee U.S.A.
130 H4 Mascote Brazil
110 G3 Mascoutah Illinois U.S.A.
18 F9 Mas d'Azil, le France
118 K9 Masefield Saskatchewan Canada
70 E3 Ma Sekatok Kalimantan
71 O9 Masela isld Indonesia
38 N7 Masenberg mt Austria
45 L1 Masera di P Italy
121 P4 Masères,L Quebec Canada
89 E7 Maseru Lesotho
40 E2 Masevaux France
13 G5 Masham England
65 H2 Mashan China
67 C5 Mashan China
80 G1 Mashāraḩ Syria
80 E7 Mashash R Jordan
87 F9 Mashava Zimbabwe
80 F2 Mashfa Syria
77 F1 Mashhad Iran
85 E7 Mashi R Nigeria
60 P2 Mashike Japan
77 E5 Mashīz Iran
77 H5 Māshkei, Hāmūn-i- marsh Pakistan
77 H6 Mashkel R Pakistan
120 F5 Mashkode Ontario Canada
88 C10 Mashonaland Central prov Zimbabwe
88 D10 Mashonaland East prov Zimbabwe
88 B10 Mashonaland West prov Zimbabwe
89 C6 Mashowing watercourse S Africa
95 R5 Mashpee Massachusetts U.S.A.
60 S2 Mashū-ko L Japan
26 N2 Masi Norway
124 E4 Masiáca Mexico
86 C6 Masi-Manimba Zaire
70 F5 Masimbu Sulawesi
86 F5 Masindi Uganda
71 D3 Masinloc Luzon Philippines
72 H4 Maşīrah isld Oman
77 B4 Masiri Iran
89 G5 Masitonto R S Africa
77 A4 Masjed Soleymān Iran
125 P9 Maskall Belize
78 G3 Maskanah Syria
121 R6 Maskinongé Quebec Canada
14 B3 Mask,L Ireland
29 J11 Masku Finland
47 J2 Maslen Nos, N. Bulgaria
55 D1 Maslovo Russian Federation
56 B4 Maslyanino Russian Federation
55 F3 Maslyanskiy Russian Federation
28 H7 Masnedssund Denmark
22 E3 Masnieres France
87 I11 Masoala, Tanjona C Madagascar
110 H3 Mason Illinois U.S.A.
94 C4 Mason Michigan U.S.A.
102 E3 Mason Nevada U.S.A.
110 M2 Mason Ohio U.S.A.
110 G6 Mason Tennessee U.S.A.
109 H5 Mason Texas U.S.A.
99 P3 Mason Wisconsin U.S.A.
101 P7 Mason Wyoming U.S.A.
144 A7 Mason Bay New Zealand
99 R9 Mason City Illinois U.S.A.
99 N6 Mason City Iowa U.S.A.
98 G8 Mason City Nebraska U.S.A.
117 M7 Mason Creek British Columbia Canada
88 F3 Masongaleni Kenya
71 J5 Masoni isld Indonesia
143 C8 Mason, L W Australia Australia
94 H7 Masontown Pennsylvania U.S.A.
94 H7 Masontown West Virginia U.S.A.
26 O1 Måsöy isld Norway
77 F7 Masqat Oman
99 R3 Mass Michigan U.S.A.
44 H3 Massa Italy
95 P4 Massachusetts state U.S.A.
95 R4 Massachusetts B U.S.A.
45 H4 Massaciuccoli,L.di Italy
100 F8 Massacre L Nevada U.S.A.
80 F3 Massada Israel
106 B1 Massadona Colorado U.S.A.
45 M2 Massa Fiscáglia Italy
86 C3 Massaguet Chad
86 C3 Massakoti Chad
45 L3 Massa Lombarda Italy
45 Q8 Massa Lubrense Italy
42 D5 Massa Marittima Italy
87 F10 Massanga Mozambique
87 F10 Massangena Mozambique
94 J8 Massanutten Mt Virginia U.S.A.
129 K4 Massape Brazil
94 K8 Massaponax Virginia U.S.A.
45 H4 Massarosa Italy
18 F10 Massat France
55 D1 Massava Russian Federation
Massawa see Mits'iwa
21 O7 Massay France
37 J3 Massbach Germany
99 M8 Massena Iowa U.S.A.
95 N2 Massena New York U.S.A.
86 C3 Massénya Chad
20 G6 Masserac France
117 G9 Masset British Columbia Canada
18 F9 Masseube France
120 H6 Massey Ontario Canada
18 H7 Massiac France
45 P7 Massico, M mt Italy
94 H9 Massies Mill Virginia U.S.A.
18 H7 Massif Central plateau France
18 F10 Massif de Néouvieille mt France
86 D4 Massif des Bongos mts Cent Afr Republic
19 Q18 Massif des Maures mts France
85 F4 Massif de Tarazit mts Niger
85 G5 Massif de Termit mts Niger
19 O15 Massif du Diois mts France
19 Q15 Massif du Pelvoux mts France
86 D4 Massif du Tondou mts Cent Afr Republic
94 F6 Massillon Ohio U.S.A.
87 G10 Massinga Mozambique
89 G4 Massingir Mozambique
121 P7 Masson Quebec Canada
146 H13 Masson I Antarctica
80 C7 Massu'a Israel
74 B4 Mastang Pakistan
27 K14 Mästerby Sweden
145 E4 Masterton New Zealand
95 P6 Mastic Beach Long I, New York U.S.A.
126 E2 Mastic Point Andros Bahamas
47 H6 Mástikho,Akr C Greece
37 P3 Maštov Czech Rep
74 E1 Mastuj Pakistan
60 E11 Masuda Japan
Masulipatnam see Machilipatnam
89 G3 Masvingo Zimbabwe
89 G3 Masvingo prov Zimbabwe
79 G3 Maşyāf Syria
46 D3 Mat R Albania
68 F5 Mat R Thailand
133 C7 Mata Amarilla Argentina
89 E2 Matabeleland North prov Zimbabwe
89 F3 Matabeleland South prov Zimbabwe
71 H4 Matabulawa mt Sulawesi
88 F8 Mataca Mozambique
120 K5 Matachewan Ontario Canada
86 B7 Matadi Zaire
118 K8 Matador Saskatchewan Canada
108 G1 Matador Texas U.S.A.
125 M3 Matagalpa Nicaragua
121 N3 Matagami Quebec Canada
109 M7 Matagorda Texas U.S.A.
109 L7 Matagorda I Texas U.S.A.
130 H10 Mata Grande Brazil
145 F3 Matahina New Zealand
145 E3 Matahiwi New Zealand
134 C12 Mataiea Tahiti Pacific Oc
145 F4 Mataikona New Zealand
69 H11 Matak isld Indonesia
139 H5 Matakana New South Wales Australia
145 E2 Matakana New Zealand
145 F2 Matakana I New Zealand
145 G2 Matakaoa Pt New Zealand
144 D5 Matakitaki R New Zealand
145 D4 Matakitaki New Zealand
145 E2 Matakohe New Zealand
87 C8 Matala Angola
85 B5 Matam Senegal
145 E2 Matamata New Zealand
145 F4 Matamau New Zealand
85 F6 Matameye Niger
95 N5 Matamoras Pennsylvania U.S.A.
124 H5 Matamoros Coahuila Mexico
125 L5 Matamoros Tamaulipas Mexico
70 G6 Matana, Danao L Sulawesi
71 F7 Matanal Pt Philippines
84 G5 Ma'ṭan as Sārah Libya
84 G5 Ma'ṭan Bishrah well Libya
88 G6 Matandu R Tanzania
122 E5 Matane Quebec Canada
122 E5 Matane R Quebec Canada
122 F5 Matane, Rés. Faun. de Quebec Canada
145 E2 Matangi New Zealand
145 E2 Matangi I New Zealand
113 J10 Matanilla Reef Bahamas
116 O6 Matanuska mt Alaska U.S.A.
126 D3 Matanzas Cuba
113 F8 Matanzas Inlet Florida U.S.A.
131 C6 Matanzilla, Pampa de la plain Argentina
129 H5 Matão, Serra do mts Brazil
Matapán, C Greece see Taínaron, Akr
122 F6 Matapedia Quebec Canada
122 E5 Matapedia L Quebec Canada
122 E5 Matapedia R Quebec Canada
16 D3 Matapozuelos Spain
131 B5 Mataquito R Chile
83 K12 Matara Sri Lanka
70 Q10 Mataram Indonesia
128 D7 Matarani Peru
140 C2 Mataranka N Terr Australia
71 H6 Matarape,Tk B Sulawesi
17 J3 Mataró Spain
145 E3 Mataroa New Zealand
70 G6 Matarombeo R Sulawesi
17 F3 Mata,Sierra de la mts Spain
70 D7 Matasiri isld Indonesia
145 F2 Matata New Zealand
87 E12 Matatiele S Africa
144 B7 Mataura New Zealand
137 R4 Mata-Utu Îles Wallis Pacific Oc
145 F3 Matawai New Zealand
121 R6 Matawin R Quebec Canada
57 J2 Matay Kazakhstan
57 E5 Matcha Tajikistan
121 N5 Matchi-Manitou, L Quebec Canada
128 F6 Mategua Bolivia
125 J6 Matehuala Mexico
89 G3 Mateke Hills Zimbabwe
127 P1 Matelot Trinidad
145 E3 Matemateaonga Ra New Zealand
88 H8 Matemo isld Mozambique
43 H8 Matera Italy
45 Q7 Matese L Italy
45 Q7 Matese, Monti del mts Italy
48 G3 Mátészalka Hungary
43 C11 Mateur Tunisia
129 K7 Mateus R Brazil
129 L7 Mateus Brazil
94 E9 Matewan West Virginia U.S.A.
107 O3 Matfield Green Kansas U.S.A.
26 J9 Matfors Sweden
18 E7 Matha France
102 E4 Mather California U.S.A.
94 G7 Mather Pennsylvania U.S.A.
74 E9 Matheran India
99 Q8 Matherville Illinois U.S.A.
120 K4 Matheson Ontario Canada
106 G2 Matheson Colorado U.S.A.
119 V7 Matheson Island Manitoba Canada
111 K9 Mathews Alabama U.S.A.
95 L9 Mathews Virginia U.S.A.
109 K7 Mathis Texas U.S.A.
111 G8 Mathiston Mississippi U.S.A.
80 F8 Mathlutha Jordan
21 N2 Mathonville France
139 G6 Mathoura New South Wales Australia
8 A4 Mathry Wales
74 G5 Mathura India
71 G7 Mati Mindanao Philippines
125 M9 Matías Romero Mexico
145 E3 Matiere New Zealand
20 F4 Matignon France
22 E4 Matigny France
16 D4 Matilla de los Caños del Rio Spain
120 H6 Matinenda L Ontario Canada
134 C13 Matiti Tahiti Pacific Oc
89 E5 Matlabas R S Africa
119 V8 Matlock Manitoba Canada
100 B2 Matlock Washington U.S.A.
9 E1 Matlock Bath England
94 F9 Matoaka West Virginia U.S.A.
129 G6 Mato Grosso reg Brazil
130 D4 Mato Grosso,Chapada de hills Brazil
130 C7 Mato Grosso do Sul state Brazil
130 C4 Mato Grosso,Planalto de plateau Brazil
122 C2 Matonipi L Quebec Canada
122 C2 Matonipis L Quebec Canada
89 F3 Matopo Hills Nat. Park Zimbabwe
87 E10 Matopos Nat. Park Zimbabwe
130 D10 Matos Costa Brazil
16 B3 Matosinhos Portugal
Matou see Qiu Xian
86 B6 Matouti, Pto Gabon
130 G4 Mato Verde Minas Gerais Brazil
48 F3 Mátra mts Hungary
72 H4 Maṭraḥ Oman
27 F11 Matrand Norway
83 K13 Mât, R. du Réunion Indian Oc
27 A11 Matre Norway
41 O3 Matrei am Brenner Austria
89 A9 Matroos Berg mt S Africa
59 M2 Matrosov Russian Federation
84 H3 Matrûh Egypt
61 N10 Matsudo Japan
59 K4 Matsue Japan
60 O4 Matsumae Japan
61 L9 Matsumoto Japan
60 G11 Matsunaga Japan
61 K11 Matsusaka Japan
61 M9 Matsushiro Japan
67 G3 Ma-tsu Tao isld Taiwan
61 K9 Matsutō Japan
60 C12 Matsuura Japan
61 P7 Matsuyama Honshu Japan
60 F12 Matsuyama Shikoku Japan
61 M11 Matsuzaki Japan
120 J4 Mattagami Heights Ontario Canada
120 J5 Mattagami L Ontario Canada
120 H2 Mattagami R Ontario Canada
112 L2 Mattamuskeet L North Carolina U.S.A.
76 C6 Mattancheri India
95 K9 Mattaponi R Virginia U.S.A.
121 M6 Mattawa Ontario Canada
95 T1 Mattawamkeag Maine U.S.A.
89 E3 Mattengwe R Botswana
40 G6 Matterhorn mt Switzerland
100 H4 Matterhorn mt Oregon U.S.A.
48 C3 Mattersburg Austria
137 P6 Matthew isld Pacific Oc
126 H4 Matthew Town Great Inagua I Bahamas
103 M7 Matthie Arizona U.S.A.
120 G3 Mattice Ontario Canada
38 H5 Mattig R Austria
95 P6 Mattituck Long I, New York U.S.A.
26 G8 Mattmar Sweden
102 A1 Mattole R California U.S.A.
99 S10 Mattoon Illinois U.S.A.
110 H4 Mattoon Kentucky U.S.A.
99 R4 Mattoon Wisconsin U.S.A.
113 E7 Mattox Georgia U.S.A.
115 K4 Matty I Northwest Territories Canada
70 B3 Matu Sarawak
128 C6 Matucana Peru
144 B6 Matukituki R New Zealand
Matūn see Khowst reg
145 D1 Matupia I New Zealand
56 C4 Matur Russian Federation
127 P2 Matura Trinidad
127 N10 Maturín Venezuela
55 B4 Matveyevka Russian Federation
54 K9 Matveyev Kurgan Russian Federation
75 K6 Mau India
87 G8 Maua Mozambique
71 M9 Maubara Timor
18 F10 Mauberme, Pic de mt France/Spain
22 G4 Maubert-Fontaine France
22 F3 Maubeuge France
68 B4 Maubin Burma
18 E9 Maubourguet France
12 D3 Mauchline Scotland
94 A8 Mauckport Indiana U.S.A.
107 O6 Maud Oklahoma U.S.A.
109 N2 Maud Texas U.S.A.
146 G6 Maudheimvidda ra Antarctica
101 O3 Maudlow Montana U.S.A.
90 J15 Maud Rise S Atlantic Oc
146 J5 Maud Rise seamount S Atlantic Oc
87 F10 Mau-é-ele Mozambique
129 G4 Maués Brazil
134 A1 Maugaafi pk Western Samoa
94 K7 Maugansville Maryland U.S.A.
20 H7 Mauges, Les reg France
12 D5 Maughold Hd I of Man U.K.
135 T3 Maui isld Hawaiian Is
70 L9 Mauk Java
36 F6 Maulbronn Germany
22 E3 Maulde France
131 A5 Maule prov Chile
131 B5 Maule R Chile
21 O4 Maule France
21 J8 Mauléon France
18 E9 Mauléon Licharre France
21 J7 Maulévrier France
14 B2 Maumakeogh mt Ireland
94 D5 Maumee Ohio U.S.A.
94 D5 Maumee Bay Michigan/Ohio U.S.A.
110 D7 Maumelle, L Arkansas U.S.A.
71 L9 Maumere Flores Indonesia
14 B3 Maumturk Mts Ireland
21 H7 Maumusson France
87 D9 Maun Botswana
135 U5 Mauna Kea pk Hawaiian Is
135 R2 Mauna Loa Hawaiian Is
135 U5 Mauna Loa vol Hawaiian Is
102 S12 Maunalua Bay Hawaiian Is
116 K3 Mauneluk R Alaska U.S.A.
145 F3 Maungaharuru Ra New Zealand
145 F3 Maungahaumi mt New Zealand
145 F3 Maungapohatu New Zealand
145 F3 Maungataniwha mt New Zealand
145 E1 Maungatapere New Zealand
145 E2 Maungaturoto New Zealand
68 A2 Maungdaw Burma
68 C5 Maungmagan islds Burma
68 D6 Maungthama Burma
114 G4 Maunoir,L Northwest Territories Canada
138 D6 Maupertuis B South Australia Australia
100 D4 Maupin Oregon U.S.A.
38 E7 Maurach Austria
19 Q16 Maure,Col de pass France
20 G6 Maure-de-Bretagne France
6 M4 Maureen oil rig North Sea
111 F11 Maurepas,L Louisiana U.S.A.
18 G7 Mauriac France
145 E4 Mauriceville New Zealand
111 C11 Mauriceville Texas U.S.A.
121 R6 Mauricie, Parc Nat. de la Québec Canada
19 Q14 Maurienne dist France
40 D7 Maurienne V France
98 D4 Maurine South Dakota U.S.A.
85 B4 Mauritania rep W Africa
83 L12 Mauritius isld Indian Oc
20 F5 Mauron France
18 G8 Maurs France
19 N17 Maussane France
99 Q6 Mauston Wisconsin U.S.A.
38 N5 Mautern Austria
38 J7 Mauterndorf Austria
38 L5 Mauthausen Austria
40 B2 Maûtz France
19 N14 Mauves France
18 F9 Mauvezin France
18 E6 Mauzé France
21 K8 Mauzé Thouarsais France
128 E3 Mavaca R Venezuela
21 N6 Maves-Pontijou France
87 D9 Mavinga Angola
127 L2 Mavis Bank Jamaica
144 B6 Mavora L, N New Zealand
46 F5 Mavrovqúni mt Greece
46 D3 Mavrovsko ezero L Macedonia
88 D9 Mavudzi R Mozambique
88 C10 Mavuradonha Mts Zimbabwe
70 C4 Mawa, Bt mt Kalimantan
71 H7 Mawasangka Indonesia
68 C3 Mawchi Burma
68 D7 Mawdaung pass Burma/Thailand
119 R4 Mawdesley L Manitoba Canada
118 L8 Mawer Saskatchewan Canada
144 C5 Mawheraiti New Zealand
68 D4 Mawkhi Burma
68 C2 Mawkmai Burma
75 Q7 Mawlaik Burma
Mawlamyine see Mawkhi
78 J3 Mawşil, Al Iraq
146 K10 Mawson Australia Base Antarctica
146 J11 Mawson Coast Antarctica
146 H10 Mawson Escarpt Antarctica
146 C13 Mawson Pen Antarctica
98 E9 Max Nebraska U.S.A.
98 E2 Max North Dakota U.S.A.
86 A3 Maxaas Somalia
98 E1 Maxbass North Dakota U.S.A.
20 F6 Maxent France
112 D4 Maxeys Georgia U.S.A.
117 M6 Maxhamish L British Columbia Canada
37 N5 Maxhütte-Haidof Germany
36 E5 Maximiliansau Germany
94 G10 Max Meadows Virginia U.S.A.
29 J8 Maxmo Finland
118 L9 Maxstone Saskatchewan Canada
112 H3 Maxton North Carolina U.S.A.
121 Q7 Maxville Ontario Canada
113 E7 Maxville Florida U.S.A.
101 M3 Maxville Montana U.S.A.
102 B2 Maxwell California U.S.A.
99 N8 Maxwell Iowa U.S.A.
98 F8 Maxwell Nebraska U.S.A.
106 F5 Maxwell New Mexico U.S.A.
12 E3 Maxwelltown Scotland
141 G5 Maxwelton Queensland Australia
101 M5 May Idaho U.S.A.
108 E7 May Oklahoma U.S.A.
109 J4 May Texas U.S.A.
59 K1 Maya R Russian Federation
55 C4 Mayachnyy Russian Federation
78 H4 Mayādīn, Al Syria
126 H3 Mayaguana Passage Bahamas
127 L5 Mayagüez Puerto Rico
85 F6 Mayahi Niger
55 C5 Mayakskiy Russian Federation
17 H3 Mayals Spain
77 D1 Mayamey Iran
80 D3 May 'Ami Israel
125 P9 Maya Mts Belize
80 F1 Ma'yan Barukh Israel
67 C3 Mayang China
126 G4 Mayari Cuba
127 P3 Mayaro co Trinidad
94 D4 Maybee Michigan U.S.A.
106 B1 Maybell Colorado U.S.A.
12 D3 Maybole Scotland
86 G3 Maych'ew Ethiopia
86 A1 Mayd Somalia
52 F2 Mayda Russian Federation
79 G2 Maydān Ikbis Syria
77 L2 Maydān Shahr Afghanistan
127 K3 May Day Mts Jamaica
109 M4 Maydelle Texas U.S.A.
139 H9 Maydena Tasmania Australia
86 A1 Mayd, Jasiired isld Somalia
36 C3 Mayen Germany

18 E4 **Mayenne** *dept* France
21 J5 **Mayenne** France
21 J5 **Mayenne** *R* France
90 H1 **Mayen Ridge** Arctic Oc
103 M7 **Mayer** Arizona U.S.A.
118 B5 **Mayerthorpe** Alberta Canada
112 G4 **Mayesville** South Carolina U.S.A.
21 L6 **Mayet** France
107 P2 **Mayetta** Kansas U.S.A.
118 K5 **Mayfair** Saskatchewan Canada
9 E1 **Mayfield** England
9 G5 **Mayfield** England
144 C5 **Mayfield** New Zealand
100 K6 **Mayfield** Idaho U.S.A.
110 H5 **Mayfield** Kentucky U.S.A.
107 L6 **Mayfield** Oklahoma U.S.A.
95 M5 **Mayfield** Pennsylvania U.S.A.
103 N2 **Mayfield** Utah U.S.A.
110 D7 **Mayflower** Arkansas U.S.A.
111 H8 **Mayhew** Mississippi U.S.A.
106 E9 **Mayhill** New Mexico U.S.A.
65 G2 **Mayi He** *R* China
13 F1 **May, I. of** Scotland
55 G5 **Maykain** Kazakhstan
57 H2 **Maykamys** Kazakhstan
53 F11 **Maykop** Russian Federation
52 J5 **Maykor** Russian Federation
110 L5 **Mayland** Tennessee U.S.A.
142 B1 **Maylands** *dist* Perth, W Aust Australia
57 C2 **Maylibash** Kazakhstan
57 D2 **Maylykum** Kazakhstan
56 C5 **Mayma** Russian Federation
57 F3 **Maymak** Kazakhstan
118 K6 **Maymont** Saskatchewan Canada
68 C1 **Maymyo** Burma
99 P7 **Maynard** Iowa U.S.A.
143 C8 **Maynard Hills** W Australia Australia
141 F6 **Mayne** *R* Queensland Australia
121 N7 **Maynooth** Ontario Canada
14 E3 **Maynooth** Ireland
51 R2 **Maynopil'gyn** Russian Federation
117 F4 **Mayo** Yukon Territory Canada
14 B3 **Mayo** *co* Ireland
128 C5 **Mayo** *R* Peru
113 D7 **Mayo** Florida U.S.A.
95 L8 **Mayo** Maryland U.S.A.
71 G7 **Mayo B** Mindanao Philippines
86 B4 **Mayo Daga** Nigeria
94 G10 **Mayodan** North Carolina U.S.A.
71 F4 **Mayon** *mt* Philippines
17 F4 **Mayor** *R* Spain
16 D2 **Mayorga** Spain
145 F2 **Mayor I** New Zealand
133 E2 **Mayor Pablo Lagerenza** Paraguay
87 H10 **Mayotte** *isld* Comoros
127 K3 **May Pen** Jamaica
113 F7 **Mayport** Florida U.S.A.
142 E3 **May R** W Australia
71 E1 **Mayraira Pt** Luzon Philippines
38 E7 **Mayrhofen** Austria
78 L5 **Maysān** *prov* Iraq
55 G2 **Maysk** Russian Federation
54 M9 **Mayskiy** Russian Federation
59 J1 **Mayskiy** Amurskaya obl Russian Federation
55 G5 **Mayskoye** Kazakhstan
95 N7 **Mays Landing** New Jersey U.S.A.
21 J7 **May-sur-Evre, le** France
112 D3 **Maysville** Georgia U.S.A.
94 D8 **Maysville** Kentucky U.S.A.
99 M10 **Maysville** Missouri U.S.A.
112 K3 **Maysville** North Carolina U.S.A.
107 N7 **Maysville** Oklahoma U.S.A.
71 D5 **Maytiguid** Philippines
68 A2 **Mayu** *R* Burma
86 B6 **Mayumba** Gabon
94 D3 **Mayville** Michigan U.S.A.
94 H4 **Mayville** New York U.S.A.
98 J2 **Mayville** North Dakota U.S.A.
100 E4 **Mayville** Oregon U.S.A.
99 S6 **Mayville** Wisconsin U.S.A.
98 F9 **Maywood** Nebraska U.S.A.
133 E5 **Maza** Argentina
98 G1 **Maza** North Dakota U.S.A.
88 A9 **Mazabuka** Zambia
129 H4 **Mazagão** Brazil
22 H5 **Mazagran** France
46 G2 **Mazalat** *mt* Bulgaria
100 E1 **Mazama** Washington U.S.A.
18 G9 **Mazamet** France
78 B1 **Māzandarān** *prov* Iran
21 M6 **Mazange** France
124 J5 **Mazapil** Mexico
79 F7 **Mazār** Jordan
43 E11 **Mazara del Vallo** Sicily
77 K1 **Mazār-e-Sharif** Afghanistan
16 D9 **Mazari,C** Morocco
130 D7 **Mazarredo** Argentina
17 G7 **Mazarrón** Spain
80 F8 **Mazar Saiyidna Suleiman** Jordan
128 F2 **Mazaruni** *R* Guyana
124 D3 **Mazatán** Mexico
125 O10 **Mazatenango** Guatemala
124 F6 **Mazatlán** Mexico
103 N7 **Mazatzal Pk** Arizona U.S.A.
77 B3 **Mazdaj** Iran
52 B6 **Mazeikiai** Lithuania
118 D8 **Mazeppa** Alberta Canada
21 L7 **Mazières** Touraine France
52 B5 **Mazirbe** Latvia
80 C6 **Mazliah** Israel
99 R6 **Mazomanie** Wisconsin U.S.A.
99 S8 **Mazon** Illinois U.S.A.
88 C10 **Mazowe** *R* Zimbabwe
88 E2 **Mazowe** Zimbabwe
80 F8 **Mazra'** Jordan
86 E3 **Mazrub** Sudan
87 E10 **Mazunga** Zimbabwe
22 H4 **Mazures, les** France
31 M2 **Mazury** *reg* Poland
89 G6 **Mbabane** Swaziland
86 C5 **Mbaéré** *R* Cent Afr Republic
85 D7 **Mbahiakro** Ivory Coast
86 C5 **Mbaiki** Cent Afr Republic
88 C8 **Mbala** Zambia
87 E10 **Mbalabala** Zimbabwe
88 E2 **Mbale** Uganda
86 B5 **Mbalmayo** Cameroon
86 B4 **Mbam** *R* Cameroon
87 F8 **Mbamba B** Tanzania
86 C5 **Mbandaka** Zaire
86 B5 **Mbanga** Cameroon
86 B7 **M'banza Congo** Angola
86 B7 **Mbanza-Ngungu** Zaire
88 C2 **Mbarara** Uganda
88 F6 **Mbarika** *mt* Tanzania
89 F9 **Mbashe** S Africa
88 G6 **Mbemkuru** *R* Tanzania
86 D6 **Mbeya** *mt* Tanzania
88 D6 **Mbeya** Tanzania
Mbini *see* **Río Muni**
87 F10 **Mbizi** Zimbabwe
86 C4 **Mbo** Cent Afr Republic
85 A6 **Mbour** Senegal
85 B5 **Mbout** Mauritania
86 C4 **Mbrés** Cent Afr Republic
87 B7 **M'Bridge** *R* Angola
86 D7 **Mbuji-Mayi** Zaire
86 F5 **Mbulamuti** Uganda
88 E3 **Mbulu** Tanzania
88 F6 **Mbungu** Tanzania
133 F3 **Mburucuyá** Argentina
117 F5 **M'Clintock** Yukon Territory Canada
115 M1 **M'Clintock, C** Northwest Territories Canada
115 L1 **M'Clintock Inlet** Northwest Territories Canada
85 C3 **Mdakane, Hassi** Algeria
43 B12 **M'Daourouch** Algeria
85 C4 **Mdennah** Mali/Mauritania
68 J6 **Mdrak** Vietnam
119 M6 **Meacham** Saskatchewan Canada
100 G4 **Meacham** Oregon U.S.A.
120 G3 **Mead** Ontario Canada
100 H2 **Mead** Washington U.S.A.
116 K1 **Meade** *R* Alaska U.S.A.
107 K4 **Meade** Kansas U.S.A.
101 O7 **Meade Pk** Idaho U.S.A.
103 K5 **Mead,L** Nev/Ariz U.S.A.
103 K6 **Mead, L. National Recreational Area** Arizona U.S.A.
143 A7 **Meadow** W Australia Australia
98 D4 **Meadow** South Dakota U.S.A.
108 E2 **Meadow** Texas U.S.A.
94 G9 **Meadow Bridge** West Virginia U.S.A.
109 M9 **Meadowbrook** Texas U.S.A.
94 G9 **Meadow Creek** West Virginia U.S.A.
98 B7 **Meadowdale** Wyoming U.S.A.
118 J4 **Meadow Lake** Saskatchewan Canada
99 O2 **Meadowlands** Minnesota U.S.A.
118 H4 **Meadow L. Prov. Park** Saskatchewan Canada
119 S7 **Meadow Portage** Manitoba Canada
100 J5 **Meadows** Idaho U.S.A.
103 K4 **Meadow Val.Mts** Nevada U.S.A.
103 K5 **Meadow Val.Wash** *R* Nevada U.S.A.
110 C2 **Meadville** Missouri U.S.A.
98 G7 **Meadville** Nebraska U.S.A.
94 G5 **Meadville** Pennsylvania U.S.A.
120 K8 **Meaford** Ontario Canada
122 J9 **Meaghers Grant** Nova Scotia Canada
60 R2 **Me-akan dake** *mt* Japan
16 B4 **Mealhada** Portugal
13 E4 **Mealsgate** England
115 N7 **Mealy Mts** Labrador, Nfld Canada
141 J7 **Meandarra** Queensland Australia
117 P6 **Meander River** Alberta Canada
100 B4 **Meares,Cape** Oregon U.S.A.
80 C3 **Me 'Arot Karmel** Israel
99 U6 **Mears** Michigan U.S.A.
15 C3 **Measach Falls** Scotland
9 E2 **Measham** England
14 E3 **Meath** *co* Ireland
119 M5 **Meath Park** Saskatchewan Canada
18 G4 **Meaux** France
112 H1 **Mebane** North Carolina U.S.A.
17 G9 **Mebtoub** *R* Algeria
71 H7 **Mebula** Indonesia
70 P10 **Mebulu,Tg** *C* Bali Indonesia
101 S2 **Mecaha** Montana U.S.A.
123 O3 **Mecatina I.,Gt** Quebec Canada
123 N3 **Mecatina I.,Little** Quebec Canada
123 M1 **Mecatina,Riv.du Petite** Quebec Canada
86 G1 **Mecca** Saudi Arabia
103 H8 **Mecca** California U.S.A.
95 R2 **Mechanic Falls** Maine U.S.A.
94 D6 **Mechanicsburg** Ohio U.S.A.
95 K6 **Mechanicsburg** Pennsylvania U.S.A.
95 L8 **Mechanicsville** Maryland U.S.A.
95 O4 **Mechanicville** New York U.S.A.
111 F12 **Mechant,L** Louisiana U.S.A.
22 G1 **Mechelen** Belgium
85 D2 **Mecheria** Algeria
36 B2 **Mechernich** Germany
122 F5 **Méchins,Les** Quebec Canada
37 Q3 **Mecholupy** Czech Rep
17 F10 **Mechra Saf Saf** Morocco
33 M6 **Mechtersen** Germany
47 H4 **Mecidiye** Turkey
37 P5 **Měčin** Czech Rep
41 L2 **Meckenbeuren** Germany
36 C2 **Meckenheim** Germany
36 E5 **Meckenheim** Germany
36 F5 **Meckesheim** Germany
33 O5 **Mecklenburg** Germany
30 F1 **Mecklenburger Bucht** *B* Germany
33 P5 **Mecklenburg-Vorpommern** *land* Germany
88 G9 **Meconta** Mozambique
94 B3 **Mecosta** Michigan U.S.A.
48 E4 **Mecsek** *mts* Hungary
88 G9 **Mecuburi** *R* Mozambique
88 H8 **Mecufi** Mozambique
87 G8 **Mecula** Mozambique
16 C4 **Meda** Portugal
42 G4 **Medak** Croatia
74 H9 **Medak** India
69 D11 **Medan** Sumatra
71 H9 **Medang** *isld* Indonesia
124 D4 **Médano** Mexico
133 E5 **Médanos** Argentina
133 D7 **Medanosa,Pta** Argentina
99 U8 **Medaryville** Indiana U.S.A.
17 K2 **Medas** *isld* Spain
83 K9 **Medawachchiya** Sri Lanka
144 D5 **Medbury** New Zealand
95 U1 **Meddybemps L** Maine U.S.A.
85 E1 **Médéa** Algeria
36 F1 **Medebach** Germany
41 J4 **Medel** *mt* Switzerland
28 C7 **Medelby** Germany
128 C2 **Medellín** Colombia
32 J5 **Medem** *R* Germany
25 D3 **Medemblik** Netherlands
85 G2 **Medenine** Tunisia
85 A5 **Mederdra** Mauritania
22 L4 **Medernach** Luxembourg
79 E1 **Medetsiz Tepe** *mt* Turkey
95 Q4 **Medford** Massachusetts U.S.A.
107 N5 **Medford** Oklahoma U.S.A.
100 C7 **Medford** Oregon U.S.A.
99 Q4 **Medford** Wisconsin U.S.A.
116 K5 **Medfra** Alaska U.S.A.
48 L6 **Medgidia** Romania
99 P8 **Mediapolis** Iowa U.S.A.
48 J4 **Mediaş** Romania
100 H2 **Medical Lake** Washington U.S.A.
45 L3 **Medicina** Italy
101 T8 **Medicine Bow** *R* Wyoming U.S.A.
101 T8 **Medicine Bow** Wyoming U.S.A.
106 D1 **Medicine Bow Mts** Wyo/Colo U.S.A.
101 T8 **Medicine Bow Pk** Wyoming U.S.A.
118 G8 **Medicine Hat** Alberta Canada
100 D8 **Medicine L** California U.S.A.
98 B1 **Medicine L** Montana U.S.A.
107 M4 **Medicine Lodge** Kansas U.S.A.
109 H1 **Medicine Mound** Texas U.S.A.
118 C6 **Medicine R** Alberta Canada
98 B3 **Medicine Rocks** Montana U.S.A.
Medina *see* **Madīnah, Al**
143 B9 **Medina** W Australia Australia
130 H5 **Medina** Brazil
94 J3 **Medina** New York U.S.A.
98 G3 **Medina** North Dakota U.S.A.
94 F5 **Medina** Ohio U.S.A.
110 H6 **Medina** Tennessee U.S.A.
109 H6 **Medina** Texas U.S.A.
17 F3 **Medinaceli** Spain
16 D3 **Medina del Campo** Spain
16 D3 **Medina de Rioseco** Spain
131 F2 **Medina,L** Argentina
16 D8 **Medina Sidonia** Spain
33 N6 **Medingen** Germany
75 M7 **Medinīpur** India
84 F2 **Mediterranean Sea** Europe/Africa
85 F1 **Medjerda** *R* Tunisia
43 B12 **Medjerda, Monts de la** Algeria/Tunisia
118 G4 **Medley** Alberta Canada
55 C5 **Mednogorsk** Russian Federation
18 E7 **Medoc** *reg* France
45 J1 **Médole** Italy
110 H6 **Medon** Tennessee U.S.A.
119 R9 **Medora** Manitoba Canada
110 F2 **Medora** Illinois U.S.A.
107 N3 **Medora** Kansas U.S.A.
98 C3 **Medora** North Dakota U.S.A.
86 B5 **Médouneu** Gabon
20 F5 **Médréac** France
118 J5 **Medstead** Saskatchewan Canada
122 E8 **Meductic** New Brunswick Canada
Medu Kongkar *see* **Maizhokunggar**
46 E2 **Medveda** Serbia Yugoslavia
55 E2 **Medvedchikovo** Russian Federation
52 E6 **Medveditsa** *R* Russian Federation
52 H6 **Medvedok** Russian Federation
51 J1 **Medvezhiy Yar** Russian Federation
59 L2 **Medvezh'ya, Gora** *mt* Russian Federation
55 F3 **Medvezh'ye** Russian Federation
52 D3 **Medvezh'yegorsk** Russian Federation
95 T1 **Medway** Maine U.S.A.
9 G5 **Medway,R** England
83 M9 **Medwin Pt** Christmas I Indian Oc
54 G2 **Medyn** Russian Federation
48 L1 **Medzhibozh** Ukraine
31 N6 **Medzilaborce** Slovakia
141 L1 **Meeandah** *dist* Brisbane, Qnsld Australia
143 B7 **Meeberrie** W Australia Australia
37 K3 **Meeder** Germany
143 C7 **Meekatharra** W Australia Australia
106 C1 **Meeker** Colorado U.S.A.
107 O6 **Meeker** Oklahoma U.S.A.
123 Q5 **Meelpaeg L** *res* Newfoundland Canada
37 N2 **Meerane** Germany
36 B3 **Meerfeld** Germany
25 F5 **Meerlo** Netherlands
25 E7 **Meerssen** Netherlands
74 G4 **Meerut** India
101 R5 **Meeteetse** Wyoming U.S.A.
118 E6 **Meeting Cr** Alberta Canada
14 E4 **Meeting of the Waters** Ireland
118 K5 **Meetoos** Saskatchewan Canada
33 R5 **Meetschow** Germany
22 K1 **Meeuwen** Belgium
80 B7 **Mefallesim** Israel
86 G5 **Mēga** Ethiopia
69 E14 **Mega** *isld* Indonesia
71 C3 **Mega** W Irian
80 C3 **Megadim** Israel
18 H7 **Megal** *mt* France
86 H4 **Megalo** Ethiopia
47 J8 **Megálo Khorió** Tílos I Greece
46 E7 **Megalópolis** Greece
46 D6 **Meganisi** *mt* Greece
122 B8 **Mégantic** Quebec Canada
122 B8 **Megantic,L** Quebec Canada
46 F6 **Mégara** Greece
109 J2 **Megargel** Texas U.S.A.
46 E5 **Mégdhova** *R* Greece
25 E5 **Megen** Netherlands
40 E6 **Megève** France
36 E1 **Meggen** Germany
13 E3 **Megget Res** Scotland
112 G5 **Meggett** South Carolina U.S.A.
85 F2 **Meghaiēr, El** Algeria
75 O6 **Meghalaya** *prov* India
75 O6 **Meghna** *R* Bangladesh
121 P4 **Mégiscane, L** Quebec Canada
100 B3 **Megler** Washington U.S.A.
52 F2 **Megra** Arkhangel'skaya obl Russian Federation
52 E4 **Megra** Vologodskaya obl Russian Federation
48 G6 **Mehadia** Romania
26 Q1 **Mehamn** Norway
77 C2 **Mehdi Shahr** Iran
48 H6 **Mehedinti** *reg* Romania
74 G8 **Mehekar** India
94 J9 **Meherrin** Virginia U.S.A.
94 J10 **Meherrin** *R* Virginia U.S.A.
37 N2 **Mehitheuer** Germany
75 K5 **Mehndawal** India
78 L5 **Mehran** Iran
36 B3 **Mehren** Germany
36 B4 **Mehring** Germany
77 D4 **Mehriz** Iran
77 L2 **Mehtar Lām** Afghanistan
21 P7 **Mehun-sur-Yèvre** France
130 E5 **Meia Ponte,R** Brazil
67 D2 **Meichengzhen** China
67 E1 **Meichuan** China
8 C2 **Meifod** Wales
86 B4 **Meiganga** Cameroon
114 J1 **Meighen I** Northwest Territories Canada
112 C6 **Meigs** Georgia U.S.A.
25 E6 **Meijel** Netherlands
67 E5 **Mei Jiang** *R* China
117 O7 **Meikle** *R* Alberta Canada
68 B2 **Meiktila** Burma
Meilin *see* **Gan Xian**
20 G5 **Meillac** France
20 H6 **Meilleraye-de-Bretagne,la** France
117 L5 **Meilleur Cr** Northwest Territories Canada
33 N8 **Meine** Germany
33 M8 **Meinersen** Germany
36 D1 **Meinerzhagen** Germany
37 J2 **Meiningen** Germany
16 C1 **Meira, Sa. de** *mts* Spain
41 H4 **Meiringen** Switzerland
80 C3 **Me'ir Shefeya** Israel
36 D4 **Meisenheim** Germany
67 A1 **Meisham** China
Meishan *see* **Jinzhai**
67 E1 **Meishan Shuiku** *res* China
80 E1 **Meiss ej Jabal** Lebanon
37 P1 **Meissen** Germany
32 L7 **Meissendorf** Germany
36 H1 **Meissner** *mt* Germany
67 B3 **Meitan** China
37 K6 **Meitingen** Germany
Meixian *see* **Meizhou**
65 E2 **Meiyao** China
67 E4 **Meizhou** China
43 C12 **Mejerda** *R* Tunisia
43 C12 **Mejez El Bab** Tunisia
133 C2 **Mejillones** Chile
28 B4 **Mejrup** Denmark
86 B5 **Mékambo** Gabon
120 F5 **Mekatina** Ontario Canada
86 G3 **Mek'elē** Ethiopia
55 D3 **Mekhonskoye** Russian Federation
74 C3 **Mekhtar** Pakistan
98 J1 **Mekinock** North Dakota U.S.A.
85 C2 **Meknès** Morocco
68 G6 **Mekong** *R* S E Asia
70 G7 **Mekongga, Tk** *B* Sulawesi
69 H8 **Mekong, Mouths of the** Vietnam
116 D6 **Mekoryuk** Alaska U.S.A.
85 E6 **Mekrou** *R* Benin/Niger
69 F11 **Melaka** Malaysia
69 G13 **Melalo, Tanjong** *C* Indonesia
46 G9 **Mélambes** Crete Greece
134 E8 **Melanesia** Pacific Oc
137 P4 **Melanesian Border Plat** Pacific Oc
70 D2 **Melapap** Sabah
70 E2 **Melaut** *mt* Sabah
118 L9 **Melaval** Saskatchewan Canada
70 C5 **Melawi** *R* Kalimantan
21 J7 **Melay** Maine-et-Loire France
100 J6 **Melba** Idaho U.S.A.
33 M6 **Melbeck** Germany
9 G3 **Melbourn** England
138 C7 **Melbourne** Victoria Australia
9 E2 **Melbourne** England
113 G9 **Melbourne** Florida U.S.A.
99 N8 **Melbourne** Iowa U.S.A.
113 G9 **Melbourne Beach** Florida U.S.A.
26 G3 **Melbu** Norway
28 H5 **Melby** Denmark
99 N8 **Melcher** Iowa U.S.A.
120 D2 **Melchett L** Ontario Canada
124 J5 **Melchor Ocampo** Coahuila Mexico
124 H8 **Melchor Ocampo** Michigan U.S.A.
26 D8 **Meldal** Norway
26 M6 **Melderstein** Sweden
45 M3 **Meldola** Italy
32 K4 **Meldorf** Germany
112 F5 **Meldrim** Georgia U.S.A.
120 G7 **Meldrum Bay** Ontario Canada
80 D3 **Melea** Israel
119 U8 **Meleb** Manitoba Canada
44 F1 **Melegnano** Italy
46 G9 **Melékhas, Akr** *C* Crete Greece
52 J5 **Melekhina** Russian Federation
87 G9 **Melela** *R* Mozambique
52 F6 **Melenki** Russian Federation
55 D3 **Melent'yevskoye** Russian Federation
20 G5 **Melesse** France
21 L4 **Mêle-sur-Sarthe,le** France
55 C4 **Meleuz** Russian Federation
45 P6 **Melfa** *R* Italy
95 M9 **Melfa** Virginia U.S.A.
86 C3 **Melfi** Chad
43 G8 **Melfi** Italy
119 N6 **Melfort** Saskatchewan Canada
20 C6 **Melgven** France
28 E2 **Melholt** Denmark
26 D8 **Melhus** Norway
36 F4 **Melibocus** *mt* Germany
21 M4 **Melicourt** France
130 E9 **Mel, I. do** Brazil
46 E7 **Meligalá** Greece
71 H5 **Melilis** *isld* Indonesia
85 D1 **Melilla** *Spanish exclave* Morocco
133 C6 **Melimoyu** *mt* Chile
144 B6 **Melina, Mt** New Zealand
48 H6 **Melineşti** Romania
70 E5 **Melintang, D** *L* Kalimantan
133 C4 **Melipilla** Chile
119 R9 **Melita** Manitoba Canada
43 G11 **Melito di Porto Salvo** Italy
54 G10 **Melitopol'** Ukraine
38 M5 **Melk** Austria
86 G5 **Melka Guba** Ethiopia
8 D5 **Melksham** England
44 H1 **Mella** *R* Italy
26 K8 **Mellansel** Sweden
26 H9 **Mellansjö** Sweden
22 F2 **Melle** Belgium
32 H8 **Melle** Germany
43 B12 **Mellégue** *R* Tunisia
99 Q3 **Mellen** Wisconsin U.S.A.
32 L7 **Mellendorf** Germany
27 F13 **Mellerud** Sweden
18 E6 **Melle S. Bretonne** France
98 H4 **Mellette** South Dakota U.S.A.
16 B2 **Mellid** Spain
22 K4 **Mellier** Belgium
37 L2 **Mellingen** Germany
137 M5 **Mellish Rise** Coral Sea
86 E3 **Mellit** Sudan
13 F6 **Mellor Brook** England
32 H5 **Mellun** *isld* Germany
111 E7 **Mellwood** Arkansas U.S.A.
13 F4 **Melmerby** England
46 F3 **Melnik** Bulgaria
31 H5 **Mělník** Czech Rep
48 K2 **Mel'nitsa-Podol'skaya** Ukraine
131 G4 **Melo** Uruguay
52 G2 **Melogorskoye** Russian Federation
71 A3 **Meloku** Indonesia
71 K9 **Melolo** Sumba Indonesia
54 M7 **Melovoye** Ukraine
26 F5 **Melöy** Norway
116 K4 **Melozitna** *R* Alaska U.S.A.
20 D6 **Melrand** France
22 J3 **Melreux** Belgium
17 G9 **Melrir** *R* Algeria
143 D8 **Melrose** W Australia Australia
123 K8 **Melrose** Nova Scotia Canada
13 F2 **Melrose** Scotland
100 J3 **Melrose** Idaho U.S.A.
99 M4 **Melrose** Minnesota U.S.A.
101 N4 **Melrose** Montana U.S.A.
106 G7 **Melrose** New Mexico U.S.A.
100 B6 **Melrose** Oregon U.S.A.
99 P5 **Melrose** Wisconsin U.S.A.
101 S3 **Melstone** Montana U.S.A.
99 U3 **Melstrand** Michigan U.S.A.
36 H1 **Melsungen** Germany
70 E2 **Melta, Mt** Sabah
29 L5 **Meltaus** Finland
13 G6 **Meltham** England
9 F2 **Melton Mowbray** England
88 G10 **Meluli** *R* Mozambique
68 A2 **Melun** Burma
18 G4 **Melun** France
86 F3 **Melut** Sudan
107 P3 **Melvern** Kansas U.S.A.
15 E2 **Melvich** Scotland
119 P8 **Melville** Saskatchewan Canada
111 E11 **Melville** Louisiana U.S.A.
101 Q3 **Melville** Montana U.S.A.
98 G2 **Melville** North Dakota U.S.A.
140 D1 **Melville B** N Terr Australia
115 N2 **Melville Bugt** *B* Greenland
141 G2 **Melville, C** Queensland Australia
71 C6 **Melville, Cape** Philippines
114 G4 **Melville Hills** Northwest Territories Canada
140 B1 **Melville I** N Terr Australia
114 H2 **Melville I** Northwest Territories Canada
115 O7 **Melville, L** Labrador, Nfld Canada
115 L4 **Melville Pen** Northwest Territories Canada
142 A1 **Melville Water** *B* Perth, W Aust Australia
109 H4 **Melvin** Texas U.S.A.
119 R1 **Melvin L** Manitoba Canada
14 C2 **Melvin, L** Ireland
48 E4 **Mélykút** Hungary
68 H6 **Meman** Cambodia
88 H9 **Memba** Mozambique
71 J9 **Memboro** Sumba Indonesia
22 H4 **Membre** France
21 M7 **Membrolle,la** France
Memel *see* **Klaipėda**
32 E5 **Memmert** *isld* Germany
41 M2 **Memmingen** Germany
70 D2 **Mempakul** Sabah
69 J12 **Mempawah** Indonesia
84 J4 **Memphis** *ruins* Egypt
99 O9 **Memphis** Missouri U.S.A.
110 G6 **Memphis** Tennessee U.S.A.
108 G1 **Memphis** Texas U.S.A.
121 S8 **Memphremagog, L** Vermont U.S.A.
122 H7 **Memramcook** New Brunswick Canada
60 R3 **Memuro** Japan
71 M9 **Ména** Timor Indonesia
54 D5 **Mena** Ukraine
110 B7 **Mena** Arkansas U.S.A.
80 F3 **Menaḥemya** Israel
99 L3 **Menahga** Minnesota U.S.A.
8 B1 **Menai Brigde** Wales
8 B1 **Menai Str** Wales
85 E5 **Menaka** Mali
101 O4 **Menard** Montana U.S.A.
108 H5 **Menard** Texas U.S.A.
99 S5 **Menasha** Wisconsin U.S.A.
123 L2 **Menaskwagama, L** Quebec Canada
45 M2 **Menate** Italy
69 H14 **Mendanau** *isld* Indonesia
130 G6 **Mendanha** Brazil
69 H12 **Mendarik** Indonesia
70 C6 **Mendawai** Kalimantan
18 H8 **Mende** France
86 G4 **Mendebo Mts** Ethiopia
56 D3 **Mendel'** *R* Russian Federation
32 G10 **Menden** Germany
111 G10 **Mendenhall** Mississippi U.S.A.
116 D7 **Mendenhall, C** Alaska U.S.A.
47 K6 **Menderes** *R* Turkey
55 E5 **Mendesh** Kazakhstan
71 E3 **Mendez-Nuñez** Luzon Philippines
118 H8 **Mendham** Saskatchewan Canada
136 J3 **Mendi** Papua New Guinea
8 D5 **Mendip Hills** England
100 A9 **Mendocino, C** California U.S.A.
135 N4 **Mendocino Seascarp** Pacific Oc
94 B4 **Mendon** Michigan U.S.A.
110 M1 **Mendon** Ohio U.S.A.
139 J4 **Mendooran** New South Wales Australia
102 D5 **Mendota** California U.S.A.
99 R8 **Mendota** Illinois U.S.A.
108 D8 **Mendota** Texas U.S.A.
99 R6 **Mendota, L** Wisconsin U.S.A.
131 C4 **Mendoza** Argentina
131 C5 **Mendoza** *prov* Argentina
128 C5 **Mendoza** Peru
16 B6 **Mendro** *mt* Portugal
20 F5 **Ménéac** France
44 G2 **Menegosa** *mt* Italy
127 J10 **Mene Grande** Venezuela
47 J6 **Menemen** Turkey
22 E2 **Menen** Belgium
21 P6 **Ménestreau** France
21 P7 **Ménétréol-sous-Sancerre** France
20 B5 **Ménez Hom** *mt* France
20 F5 **Menez, Landes du** *reg* France
43 E11 **Menfi** Sicily
70 D1 **Mengalum** *isld* S China Sea
58 G5 **Mengcheng** China
65 D5 **Mengcun** China
41 K1 **Mengen** Germany
32 J10 **Mengeringhausen** Germany
36 E2 **Mengerskirchen** Germany
70 K8 **Menggala** Sumatra
68 E2 **Menghai** China
65 H1 **Mengjiagang** China
67 C5 **Mengjiang** China
65 A5 **Mengjiawan** China
65 B7 **Mengjin** China
70 D6 **Mengkatip** Kalimantan
70 B4 **Mengkiang** *R* Kalimantan
37 N6 **Mengkofen** Germany
70 G6 **Mengkoka, Gunung** *mt* Sulawesi
68 E2 **Mengla** China
68 D1 **Menglian** China
68 E1 **Mengman** China
67 C4 **Mengshan** China
68 E1 **Mengwang** China
65 B7 **Meng Xian** China
65 D7 **Mengyin** China
68 E2 **Mengyuan** China
67 A5 **Mengzi** China
115 N7 **Menihek, Lac** Labrador, Nfld Canada
83 L11 **Menik Ganga** *R* Sri Lanka
21 N3 **Menilles** France
36 B7 **Ménil-sur-Bélvitte** France
Menin *see* **Menen**
139 G4 **Menindee** New South Wales Australia
138 E6 **Meningie** South Australia Australia
21 K7 **Ménitre,la** France
70 E4 **Menjapa, Gt** *mt* Kalimantan
51 M2 **Menkere** Russian Federation
112 B3 **Menlo** Georgia U.S.A.
99 M8 **Menlo** Iowa U.S.A.
107 K2 **Menlo** Kansas U.S.A.
102 B4 **Menlo Pk** California U.S.A.
21 P4 **Mennecy** France
21 O7 **Mennetou-sur-Cher** France
98 J6 **Menno** South Dakota U.S.A.
12 E3 **Mennock P** Scotland
99 T4 **Menominee** *R* Michigan U.S.A.
99 S6 **Menomonee Falls** Wisconsin U.S.A.
99 P5 **Menomonie** Wisconsin U.S.A.
17 K4 **Menorca** *isld* Balearic Is
19 P15 **Mens** France
70 E3 **Mensalong** Kalimantan
47 N10 **Menşari** Turkey
55 G3 **Men'shchikovo** Russian Federation
66 C5 **Men-shih** China
32 G7 **Menslage** Germany
12 E1 **Menstrie** Scotland
28 H6 **Menstrup** Denmark
70 C5 **Mentaja** *R* Kalimantan
45 N5 **Mentana** Italy
70 E2 **Mentapok** Sabah
70 E3 **Mentarang** *R* Kalimantan
116 Q5 **Mentasta Mts** Alaska U.S.A.
69 D13 **Mentawai, Kepulauan** *island group* Indonesia
69 F11 **Mentekab** Malaysia
19 Q13 **Menthon** France
69 G14 **Mentok** Sumatra
44 B4 **Menton** France
94 A5 **Mentone** Indiana U.S.A.
108 D4 **Mentone** Texas U.S.A.
98 K2 **Mentor** Minnesota U.S.A.
94 F5 **Mentor** Ohio U.S.A.
65 C5 **Mentougou** China
70 C5 **Mentubar** *R* Kalimantan
89 D9 **Mentz, L** S Africa
70 C5 **Menukung** Kalimantan
58 E2 **Menza** *R* Mongolia
56 G5 **Menza** *R* Russian Federation
56 G6 **Menza** Russian Federation
43 C11 **Menzel Bourguiba** Tunisia
52 H6 **Menzelinsk** Russian Federation
43 D12 **Menzel Temime** Tunisia
143 D8 **Menzies** W Australia Australia
146 H10 **Menzies,Mt** Antarctica
Menzingen *see* **Kraichtal**
21 N8 **Méobecq** France
9 G5 **Meopham** England
124 G3 **Meoqui** Mexico
118 J5 **Meota** Saskatchewan Canada
25 F3 **Meppel** Netherlands
32 F7 **Meppen** Germany
17 H3 **Mequinenza** Spain
99 T6 **Mequon** Wisconsin U.S.A.
21 O6 **Mer** France
52 F5 **Mera** *R* Russian Federation
47 H9 **Merabéllou, Kólpos** *B* Crete Greece
70 E4 **Merah** Kalimantan
70 K8 **Merak** Java
26 E8 **Meråker** Norway
138 B3 **Meramangye, L** South Australia Australia
110 F3 **Meramec Park** Missouri U.S.A.
Meran *see* **Merano**
41 O4 **Merano** Italy
70 P9 **Merapi, G** *mt* Java
69 E13 **Merapi, Gunung** *mt* Sumatra
123 S6 **Merasheen** Newfoundland Canada
70 D6 **Meratus, Peg** *mts* Kalimantan
136 J3 **Merauke** W Irian
69 F12 **Merbau** Sumatra
138 F5 **Merbein** Victoria Australia
22 G3 **Merbes-le-Château** Belgium
70 P10 **Merbuk** *mt* Indonesia
45 M4 **Mercato Saraceno** Italy
102 D4 **Merced** *R* California U.S.A.
102 D4 **Merced** California U.S.A.
131 B3 **Mercedario, Cerro** *mt* Chile/Arg
131 D4 **Mercedes** Argentina
131 F5 **Mercedes** Buenos Aires Argentina
131 F2 **Mercedes** Corrientes Argentina
131 F4 **Mercedes** Uruguay
109 K9 **Mercedes** Texas U.S.A.
133 C3 **Merceditas** Chile
145 E2 **Mercer** New Zealand
99 N9 **Mercer** Missouri U.S.A.
98 F2 **Mercer** North Dakota U.S.A.
94 G5 **Mercer** Pennsylvania U.S.A.
110 H6 **Mercer** Tennessee U.S.A.
99 Q3 **Mercer** Wisconsin U.S.A.
94 J7 **Mercersburg** Pennsylvania U.S.A.
22 G2 **Merchtem** Belgium
121 O6 **Mercier Dam** Quebec Canada
117 P9 **Mercoal** Alberta Canada
45 R8 **Mercogliano** Italy
103 M1 **Mercur** Utah U.S.A.
48 H5 **Mercurea** Romania
19 Q13 **Mercury** France
109 H4 **Mercury** Texas U.S.A.
145 E2 **Mercury Is** New Zealand
114 H3 **Mercy B** Northwest Territories Canada
115 N5 **Mercy, C** Northwest Territories Canada
20 H3 **Merderet** *R* France
20 F5 **Merdrignac** France
8 D5 **Mere** England
21 P7 **Méreau** France
86 G3 **Mereb** *R* Eritrea/Ethiopia
95 Q3 **Meredith** New Hampshire U.S.A.
133 E8 **Meredith, C** Falkland Is
108 C8 **Meredith, L** Texas U.S.A.
99 Q10 **Meredosia** Illinois U.S.A.
85 E3 **Meredoua** Algeria
54 H7 **Merefa** Ukraine
85 C5 **Mereié, El** *reg* Mauritania/Mali
137 O4 **Méré Lava** *isld* Vanuatu
36 E3 **Merenberg** Germany
56 B4 **Meret'** Russian Federation
21 P5 **Méréville** France
9 G5 **Mereworth** England
Merga *see* **Nukheila**
68 D6 **Mergui** Burma
68 C7 **Mergui Arch** Burma
138 F5 **Meribah** South Australia Australia
47 H3 **Meriç** *R* Greece
47 H3 **Meriç** Turkey
118 H7 **Merid** Saskatchewan Canada
125 P7 **Mérida** Mexico
16 C6 **Mérida** Spain
128 D2 **Mérida** Venezuela
95 O5 **Meriden** Connecticut U.S.A.
107 P2 **Meriden** Kansas U.S.A.
95 P3 **Meriden** New Hampshire U.S.A.
98 B8 **Meriden** Wyoming U.S.A.
102 C2 **Meridian** California U.S.A.
100 J6 **Meridian** Idaho U.S.A.
111 H9 **Meridian** Mississippi U.S.A.
95 L3 **Meridian** New York U.S.A.
109 K4 **Meridian** Texas U.S.A.
137 O4 **Mérig** *isld* Vanuatu
21 M8 **Merigny** France
29 J10 **Merikarvia** Finland
139 J6 **Merimbula** New South Wales Australia
141 J4 **Merinda** Queensland Australia
19 O17 **Mérindol** France
37 L7 **Mering** Germany
138 F5 **Meringur** Victoria Australia
138 F6 **Merino** Victoria Australia
106 G1 **Merino** Colorado U.S.A.
70 C3 **Merit** Sarawak
141 J7 **Merivale** *R* Queensland Australia
57 G3 **Merke** Kazakhstan
22 D2 **Merkem** Belgium
37 K5 **Merkendorf** Germany
26 H5 **Merkenes** Sweden
31 P1 **Merkine** Lithuania
37 O3 **Merklín** Czech Rep
37 P4 **Merklín** Czech Rep
22 G1 **Merksem** Belgium
22 H1 **Merksplas** Belgium
55 E2 **Merkushino** Tyumenskaya obl Russian Federation
36 C3 **Merl** Germany
45 K1 **Merlara** Italy
21 L4 **Merlerault,le** France
22 B3 **Merlimont** France
120 H10 **Merlin** Ontario Canada
100 B7 **Merlin** Oregon U.S.A.
141 F2 **Merluna** Queensland Australia
69 F13 **Merlung** Sumatra
142 C3 **Mermaid Reef** Indian Oc
111 C12 **Mermentau** *R* Louisiana U.S.A.
28 J6 **Mern** Denmark
98 G8 **Merna** Nebraska U.S.A.
101 P7 **Merna** Wyoming U.S.A.
69 A9 **Meroe** *isld* Nicobar Is
143 D8 **Merolia** W Australia Australia
80 E2 **Meron** Israel
86 F2 **Merowe** Sudan
143 C9 **Merredin** W Australia Australia
110 B2 **Merriam** Kansas U.S.A.
15 D5 **Merrick Mt** Scotland
121 P8 **Merrickville** Ontario Canada
98 H3 **Merricourt** North Dakota U.S.A.
98 K7 **Merrill** Iowa U.S.A.
94 C3 **Merrill** Michigan U.S.A.
111 H11 **Merrill** Mississippi U.S.A.
100 D7 **Merrill** Oregon U.S.A.
99 R4 **Merrill** Wisconsin U.S.A.
99 Q5 **Merrillan** Wisconsin U.S.A.
99 R6 **Merrimac** Wisconsin U.S.A.
95 Q3 **Merrimack** *R* New Hamps/Mass U.S.A.
98 E7 **Merriman** Nebraska U.S.A.
117 N10 **Merritt** British Columbia Canada
98 F7 **Merritt Res** Nebraska U.S.A.
139 K4 **Merriwa** New South Wales Australia
111 E9 **Mer Rouge** Louisiana U.S.A.
9 F5 **Merrow** England
139 J4 **Merrygoen** New South Wales Australia
109 O5 **Merryville** Louisiana U.S.A.
86 H3 **Mersa Fatma** Eritrea
22 L4 **Mersch** Luxembourg
9 G4 **Mersea I** England
33 P10 **Merseburg** Germany
17 G9 **Mers el Kébir** Algeria
8 D1 **Mersey, R** England
13 F6 **Merseyside** *co* England
Mersin *see* **İçel**
79 E2 **Mersin** Turkey
69 F11 **Mersing** Malaysia
21 N1 **Mers-les-Bains** France
52 B6 **Mērsrags** Latvia
21 O8 **Mers-sur-Indre** France
74 F5 **Merta** India
8 C4 **Merthyr Tydfil** Wales
37 K6 **Mertingen** Germany
16 B7 **Mértola** Portugal
8 B6 **Merton** England
143 D8 **Mertondale** W Australia Australia
146 D14 **Mertz Glacier** Antarctica
108 G4 **Mertzon** Texas U.S.A.
21 P3 **Méru** France
88 F1 **Meru** Kenya
88 F3 **Meru** *mt* Tanzania
74 C8 **Merui** Pakistan
70 G4 **Merunu** Sulawesi
70 E2 **Merutai** Sabah
22 D2 **Merville** France
118 J5 **Mervin** Saskatchewan Canada
100 C4 **Merwin, L** Washington U.S.A.
18 H4 **Méry-sur-Seine** France
78 E1 **Merzifon** Turkey
36 B5 **Merzig** Germany
146 D5 **Merz Peninsula** *pen* Antarctica
71 B2 **Mesa** Halmahera Indonesia
17 F3 **Mesa** *R* Spain
103 N8 **Mesa** Arizona U.S.A.
100 J5 **Mesa** Idaho U.S.A.
106 F8 **Mesa** New Mexico U.S.A.
99 N2 **Mesabi Ra** *mts* Minnesota U.S.A.
43 H8 **Mesagne** Italy
117 Q3 **Mesa L** Northwest Territories Canada
116 K6 **Mesa Mt** Alaska U.S.A.
47 Q14 **Mesanagrós** Rhodes Greece
69 G12 **Mesanak** *isld* Indonesia
20 H7 **Mésanger** France
70 D2 **Mesapo** Sabah
46 G10 **Mesarás, Kólpos** *B* Crete Greece
106 B4 **Mesa Verde Nat. Park** Colorado U.S.A.
103 O10 **Mescal** Arizona U.S.A.
106 E8 **Mescalero** New Mexico U.S.A.
32 H10 **Meschede** Germany
26 J7 **Meselefors** Sweden
68 C3 **Mesenan** Burma
48 H3 **Meseşului, Muntii** *mts* Romania
128 F2 **Meseta del Cerro Jaua** *mts* Venezuela
52 G6 **Mesha** *R* Russian Federation
54 L1 **Meshcherskaya Nizina** *lowland* Russian Federation
54 G2 **Meshchovsk** Russian Federation
52 H3 **Meshchura** Russian Federation
Meshed *see* **Mashhad**
57 B4 **Meshekli** Uzbekistan
116 H8 **Meshik** Alaska U.S.A.
86 E4 **Meshra er Req** Sudan
94 B2 **Mesick** Michigan U.S.A.
117 L7 **Mesilinka** *R* British Columbia Canada
106 D9 **Mesilla** New Mexico U.S.A.
80 C6 **Mesillat Ẓiyyon** Israel
28 F5 **Mesinge** Denmark
21 J6 **Meslay-du-Maine** France
27 E10 **Mesna** *L* Norway
21 N2 **Mesnières-en-Béthune** France
21 J4 **Mesnil-Auzouf,le** France
21 P2 **Mesnil-St.Firmin,le** France
20 H3 **Mesnil-Vigot,le** France
21 K4 **Mesnil-Villement,le** France
41 K5 **Mesocco** Switzerland
45 M2 **Mésola** Italy
41 K5 **Mesolcina, Valle** Switzerland
46 E6 **Mesolóngion** Greece
78 J4 **Mesopotamia** Iraq
20 F7 **Mesquer** France
130 G6 **Mesquita** Brazil
103 K5 **Mesquite** Nevada U.S.A.
106 D9 **Mesquite** New Mexico U.S.A.
109 O9 **Mesquite** Texas U.S.A.
103 J6 **Mesquite L** California U.S.A.
20 G6 **Messac** France
Messalo *R see* **Mualo** *R*
87 G8 **Messalo** *R* Mozambique
22 K4 **Messancy** Belgium
85 F2 **Messaoud, Hassi** Algeria
33 P7 **Messdorf** Germany
21 J4 **Messei** France
Messick *see* **Poquoson**
133 C7 **Messie, Can** *str* Chile
89 F4 **Messina** S Africa
43 G10 **Messina** Sicily
22 J4 **Messincourt** France
121 O6 **Messines** Quebec Canada
13 H6 **Messingham** England
46 E7 **Messíni** Greece
46 E8 **Messiniakós Kólpos** *B* Greece
41 K2 **Messkirch** Germany
47 O12 **Messongí** Greece
Mesta *R see* **Néstos** *R*
46 F3 **Mesta** *R* Bulgaria
16 E6 **Mestanza** Spain
33 P5 **Mestlin** Germany
42 G3 **Mesto, N** Slovenia
37 P4 **Město-Touškov** Czech Rep
42 E3 **Mestre** Italy
45 L1 **Mestrino** Italy
128 D3 **Meta** *div* Colombia
45 Q8 **Meta** Italy
110 D3 **Meta** Missouri U.S.A.
128 E2 **Meta** *R* Venezuela/Colombia
115 N5 **Meta Incognita Pen** Northwest Territories Canada
111 F11 **Metairie** Louisiana U.S.A.
111 H12 **Metairie** New Orleans, Louisiana U.S.A.
120 C2 **Meta L** Ontario Canada
48 H4 **Metalici, Muntii** *mts* Romania
117 P11 **Metaline Falls** Washington U.S.A.
42 D5 **Metallifere, Colline** *hills* Italy
99 R9 **Metamora** Illinois U.S.A.
133 E3 **Metán** Argentina
70 D6 **Metangai** Kalimantan
87 F8 **Metangula** Mozambique
43 H8 **Metaponto** Italy
80 C8 **Metar** Israel
42 E5 **Metauro** *R* Italy
80 E3 **Metav** Israel
122 F9 **Meteghan** Nova Scotia Canada
32 F8 **Metelen** Germany
86 G3 **Metema** Ethiopia
141 J6 **Meteor** *R* Queensland Australia
90 G14 **Meteor Depth** S Atlantic Oc
90 K14 **Meteor Seamount** S Atlantic Oc
22 D2 **Méteren** France
46 F7 **Méthana** Greece
119 S7 **Methley** Manitoba Canada
46 E8 **Methóni** Greece
100 E1 **Methow** *R* Washington U.S.A.
95 Q4 **Methuen** Massachusetts U.S.A.
142 E3 **Methuen,Mt** W Australia Australia
144 C5 **Methven** New Zealand
12 E1 **Methven** Scotland
143 D7 **Methwin,Mt** W Australia Australia
9 G2 **Methwold** England
119 N1 **Metionga L** Ontario Canada
118 G6 **Metiskow** Alberta Canada
122 E5 **Metis L** Quebec Canada
42 H5 **Metković** Croatia
117 H8 **Metlakatla** Alaska U.S.A.
85 F2 **Metlaoui** Tunisia
38 K8 **Metnitz** Austria
46 D2 **Metohija** *mts* Serbia Yugoslavia
46 D2 **Metohija** Serbia Yugoslavia
100 D5 **Metolius** Oregon U.S.A.
46 E1 **Metovnica** Serbia Yugoslavia
70 K8 **Metro** Sumatra
110 H4 **Metropolis** Illinois U.S.A.
29 N6 **Metsäkylä** Finland
25 F2 **Metslawier** Netherlands
46 E5 **Métsovon** Greece

37 O6 Metten Germany
36 B4 Mettendorf Germany
112 E5 Metter Georgia U.S.A.
22 H3 Mettet Belgium
32 G8 Mettingen Germany
36 B4 Mettlach Germany
32 E10 Mettmann Germany
36 B4 Mettnich Germany
21 M7 Mettray France
76 C5 Mettuppalaiyam India
76 C5 Mettur India
88 H7 Metudo isld Mozambique
79 F5 Metulla Israel
19 K3 Metz France
40 F1 Metzeral France
22 L5 Metzervisse France
36 G6 Metzingen Germany
20 F5 Meu R France
88 G9 Meucate Mozambique
36 D3 Meudt Germany
69 C10 Meulaboh Sumatra
21 O3 Meulan France
22 E2 Meulebeke Belgium
21 L4 Meulles France
21 O6 Meung-sur-Loire France
69 C10 Meureudu Sumatra
40 A4 Meursault France
19 K4 Meurthe R France
36 B6 Meurthe et Moselle dept France
22 H3 Meuse R Belgium
19 J3 Meuse R France
19 J4 Meuse dept France
37 N1 Meuselwitz Germany
21 O7 Meusnes France
8 B7 Mevagissey England
80 D6 Meva Horon Jordan
80 C6 Meva Modiin Jordan
13 G6 Mexborough England
109 L4 Mexia Texas U.S.A.
129 J3 Mexiana isld Brazil
103 J9 Mexicali Mexico
103 P4 Mexican Hat Utah U.S.A.
124 F3 Mexicanos, Lago de los Mexico
103 P5 Mexican Water Arizona U.S.A.
125 K8 México Mexico
124 G6 Mexico rep N America
94 A6 Mexico Indiana U.S.A.
95 R2 Mexico Maine U.S.A.
110 E2 Mexico Missouri U.S.A.
95 L3 Mexico New York U.S.A.
125 M6 Mexico, G. of Mexico
40 B6 Meximieux France
71 E3 Meycawayan Luzon Philippines
77 D5 Meydān-e-Gel salt lake Iran
33 Q6 Meyenburg Germany
94 H7 Meyersdale Pennsylvania U.S.A.
18 G7 Meymac France
77 J2 Meymaneh Afghanistan
77 B3 Meymeh Iran
118 L8 Meyronne Saskatchewan Canada
18 H8 Meyrueis France
18 G7 Meyssac France
80 E8 Mezada Israel
80 F2 Mezar Syria
125 N9 Mezcalapa R Mexico
46 F1 Mezdra Bulgaria
18 H9 Mèze France
19 Q17 Mézel France
52 G3 Mezen' R Russian Federation
52 F2 Mezen' Arkhangel'skaya obl Russian Federation
52 F2 Mezenskaya Guba B Russian Federation
80 D4 Mezer Israel
54 C1 Mezha R Russian Federation
52 G3 Mezhdurechensk Russian Federation
56 C4 Mezhdurechensk Russian Federation
55 E2 Mezhdurechenskiy Russian Federation
31 N1 Mezhdurech'ye Russian Federation
50 D1 Mezhdusharskiy Ostrov isld Russian Federation
48 H2 Mezhgor'ye Ukraine
42 F2 Mežica Slovenia
21 K3 Mézidon-Canon France
21 N8 Mézières-en-Brenne France
21 O4 Mézières-sur-Seine France
31 H6 Mezimostí Czech Rep
18 F8 Mézin France
54 M1 Mezinovskiy Russian Federation
48 G4 Mezőberény Hungary
48 F3 Mezőcsát Hungary
48 F4 Mezőhegyes Hungary
48 F4 Mezőkovacsháza Hungary
48 F3 Mezőkövesd Hungary
18 E8 Mézos France
48 F3 Mezőtúr Hungary
124 G6 Mezquital R Mexico
124 G6 Mezquital Mexico
124 H6 Mezquitic Mexico
41 N5 Mezzana Italy
45 M3 Mezzano Italy
41 O4 Mezzaselva Italy
45 M2 Mezzogoro Italy
41 K5 Mezzola, Lago di Italy
41 L5 Mezzoldo Italy
42 D2 Mezzolombardo Italy
89 G7 Mfolozi R S Africa
52 D5 Mga Russian Federation
74 F10 Mhasvad India
89 G6 Mhlume Swaziland
125 L9 Miahuatlán de Porfirio Diaz Mexico
16 D5 Miajadas Spain
119 T9 Miami Manitoba Canada
103 O8 Miami Arizona U.S.A.
113 G12 Miami Florida U.S.A.
94 C7 Miami R Ohio U.S.A.
107 Q5 Miami Oklahoma U.S.A.
108 D8 Miami Texas U.S.A.
113 G12 Miami Beach Florida U.S.A.
113 G11 Miami Canal Florida U.S.A.
94 C6 Miami, Great R Ohio U.S.A.
94 C7 Miami, Little R Ohio U.S.A.
94 C7 Miamisburg Ohio U.S.A.
113 G12 Miami Shores Florida U.S.A.
113 G12 Miami Springs Florida U.S.A.
65 B7 Mianchi China
78 L3 Miandowab Iran
87 H11 Miandrivazo Madagascar
77 A1 Mïāneh Iran
67 E4 Mian Shui R China
58 E5 Mian Xian China
67 D1 Mianyang China
67 A1 Mianzhu China
65 E6 Miao Dao isld China
65 E5 Miaodao Qundao islds China
65 H3 Miaoling China
67 B3 Miao Ling mt ra China
67 C4 Miaoping China
87 H11 Miarinarivo Madagascar
55 D3 Miass R Russian Federation
31 K1 Miastko Poland
117 O9 Mica Dam British Colombia Canada
103 O9 Mica Mt Arizona U.S.A.
58 E5 Micang Shan mt ra China
113 E8 Micanopy Florida U.S.A.
128 C3 Micay Colombia
113 C7 Miccosukee Florida U.S.A.
52 H3 Michaichmon' Russian Federation
48 G2 Michal'any Slovakia
48 G2 Michalovce Slovakia
118 C9 Michel British Columbia Canada
118 H3 Michel Saskatchewan Canada
38 N5 Michelbach Austria
36 E3 Michelbach Germany
116 Q2 Michelson, Mt Alaska U.S.A.
36 G4 Michelstadt Germany
33 S8 Michendorf Germany
127 K5 Miches Dominican Rep
118 E7 Michichi Alberta Canada
112 J1 Michie, L North Carolina U.S.A.
99 S3 Michigamme Michigan U.S.A.
99 S3 Michigamme L Michigan U.S.A.
99 S3 Michigamme Res Michigan U.S.A.
94 A1 Michigan state U.S.A.
98 H1 Michigan North Dakota U.S.A.
94 C4 Michigan Center Michigan U.S.A.
99 U8 Michigan City Indiana U.S.A.
94 A4 Michigan, L U.S.A.
110 K1 Michigantown Indiana U.S.A.
120 F5 Michipicoten Ontario Canada
31 N4 Michów Poland
47 J2 Michurin Bulgaria
54 M4 Michurinsk Russian Federation
13 F4 Mickle Fell mt England
9 E3 Mickleton England
127 O8 Micoud St Lucia
134 F7 Micronesia Pacific Oc
69 H11 Midai isld Indonesia
119 O9 Midale Saskatchewan Canada
100 J8 Midas Nevada U.S.A.
90 E6 Mid-Atlantic Ridge Atlantic Oc
12 E2 Mid Calder Scotland
25 A6 Middelburg Netherlands
87 D12 Middelburg S Africa
89 D8 Middelburg Eastern Cape S Africa
89 F5 Middelburg N Transvaal S Africa
25 B5 Middelharnis Netherlands
22 D1 Middelkerke Belgium
89 B9 Middel Roggeveld reg S Africa
87 E10 Middelwit S Africa
25 C3 Middenbeemster Netherlands
90 A7 Middle America Trench Pacific Oc
68 A6 Middle Andaman isld Andaman Is
138 D5 Middleback, Mt South Australia Australia
95 R5 Middleboro Massachusetts U.S.A.
94 G7 Middlebourne West Virginia U.S.A.
118 F1 Middlebro Manitoba Canada
95 K6 Middleburg Pennsylvania U.S.A.
94 K8 Middleburg Virginia U.S.A.
95 N4 Middleburgh New York U.S.A.
94 B5 Middlebury Indiana U.S.A.
95 O2 Middlebury Vermont U.S.A.
108 G4 Middle Concho R Texas U.S.A.
28 D5 Middlefart Denmark
144 A6 Middle Fiord New Zealand
13 G5 Middleham England
143 E10 Middle I W Australia Australia
69 C8 Middle I Thailand
90 B16 Middle I Tristan da Cunha
94 D1 Middle I Michigan U.S.A.
100 F8 Middle L Nevada U.S.A.
119 M6 Middle Lake Saskatchewan Canada
98 G8 Middle Loup R Nebraska U.S.A.
144 C6 Middlemarch New Zealand
8 D6 Middlemarsh England
94 J3 Middleport New York U.S.A.
94 E8 Middleport Ohio U.S.A.
83 M9 Middle Pt Christmas I Indian Oc
94 C6 Middle Pt Ohio U.S.A.
98 K1 Middle R Minnesota U.S.A.
123 R5 Middle Rge Newfoundland Canada
95 L7 Middle River Maryland U.S.A.
118 G8 Middle Sand Hills, The Alberta Canada
94 D10 Middlesboro Kentucky U.S.A.
13 G4 Middlesbrough England
125 P9 Middlesex Belize
95 K4 Middlesex New York U.S.A.
141 F5 Middleton Queensland Australia
122 G9 Middleton Nova Scotia Canada
13 F5 Middleton Cumbria England
13 F6 Middleton Greater Manchester England
13 H6 Middleton Humberside England
100 J6 Middleton Idaho U.S.A.
94 C3 Middleton Michigan U.S.A.
110 H6 Middleton Tennessee U.S.A.
99 R6 Middleton Wisconsin U.S.A.
116 P7 Middleton I Alaska U.S.A.
13 F4 Middleton in Teesdale England
8 C2 Middletown England
95 P5 Middletown Connecticut U.S.A.
95 M7 Middletown Delaware U.S.A.
94 B6 Middletown Indiana U.S.A.
94 K7 Middletown Maryland U.S.A.
95 N5 Middletown New York U.S.A.
110 M2 Middletown Ohio U.S.A.
95 L6 Middletown Pennsylvania U.S.A.
8 D2 Middletown Wales
94 B4 Middleville Michigan U.S.A.
95 N3 Middleville New York U.S.A.
108 B8 Middle Water Texas U.S.A.
8 D1 Middlewich England
122 H9 Middlewood Nova Scotia Canada
85 D2 Midelt Morocco
109 L7 Midfield Texas U.S.A.
8 C4 Mid Glamorgan co Wales
145 E3 Midhirst New Zealand
121 L8 Midhurst Ontario Canada
9 F6 Midhurst England
18 G9 Midi, Canal du France
18 E10 Midi d'Ossau, Pic du mt France
18 F10 Midi du Bigorre, Pic du mt France
143 B9 Midland W Australia Australia
110 B6 Midland Arkansas U.S.A.
103 K8 Midland California U.S.A.
94 J7 Midland Maryland U.S.A.
94 C3 Midland Michigan U.S.A.
98 E5 Midland South Dakota U.S.A.
108 E4 Midland Texas U.S.A.
111 L10 Midland City Alabama U.S.A.
89 F2 Midlands prov Zimbabwe
14 C5 Midleton Ireland
109 K3 Midlothian Texas U.S.A.
94 K9 Midlothian Virginia U.S.A.
32 J5 Midlum Germany
111 F8 Midnight Mississippi U.S.A.
87 H12 Midongy Atsimo Madagascar
60 D13 Midori-kawa R Japan
18 E9 Midouze R France
134 G5 Mid-Pacific Mountains Pacific Oc
71 G7 Midsayap Philippines
100 J5 Midvale Idaho U.S.A.
101 O9 Midvale Utah U.S.A.
112 E5 Midville Georgia U.S.A.
117 O11 Midway British Columbia Canada
111 L9 Midway Alabama U.S.A.
112 F6 Midway Georgia U.S.A.
94 C8 Midway Kentucky U.S.A.
109 M4 Midway Texas U.S.A.
135 U2 Midway Is atoll Hawaiian Is
116 O1 Midway Is Alaska U.S.A.
122 E1 Midway L Quebec Canada
143 E6 Midway Well W Australia Australia
101 T6 Midwest Wyoming U.S.A.
107 N6 Midwest City Oklahoma U.S.A.
25 F2 Midwolde Netherlands
78 H3 Midyat Turkey
15 G1 Mid Yell Scotland
46 F1 Midžor mt Serbia Yugoslavia
61 K11 Mie prefect Japan
31 M5 Miechów Poland
40 F3 Miécourt Switzerland
31 J3 Międzychód Poland
31 K5 Międzylesie Poland
31 O4 Międzyrzec Poland
31 J3 Międzyrzecz Poland
31 K4 Miejska Gorka Poland
29 L5 Miekojärvi L Finland
18 F9 Miélan France
31 N5 Mielec Poland
41 N3 Mieminger Kette mt Austria
27 G15 Mien L Sweden
139 H8 Miena Tasmania Australia
67 G4 Mien-hua Hsü isld Taiwan
109 H9 Mier Mexico
106 D7 Miera New Mexico U.S.A.
48 K4 Miercurea-Ciuc Romania
16 D1 Mieres Spain
26 N2 Mieron Norway
38 E6 Miesbach Germany
86 H4 Mī 'ēso Ethiopia
33 O8 Mieste Germany
31 H3 Mieszkowice Poland
94 K6 Mifflin Pennsylvania U.S.A.
95 K6 Mifflinburg Pennsylvania U.S.A.
95 K6 Mifflintown Pennsylvania U.S.A.
83 L9 Migaswewa Sri Lanka
80 F2 Migdal Israel
80 D3 Migdal Ha'Émeq Israel
80 D7 Migdal Oz Jordan
80 D7 Migdal'Oz Jordan
77 F4 Mighān Iran
45 L2 Migliarino Italy
21 L8 Mignaloux Beauvoir France
45 P7 Mignano Italy
44 G2 Mignano, L. di Italy
21 N8 Migné Indre France
21 L8 Migné-Auxances Vienne France
44 L5 Mignone R Italy
122 F5 Miguasha-Ouest Quebec Canada
124 H5 Miguel Auza Mexico
88 H2 Migwani Kenya
68 B3 Migyaunye Burma
48 K3 Mihăileni Romania
60 G11 Mihara Japan
61 N11 Mihara-yama vol Japan
61 O8 Miharu Japan
37 J1 Mihla Germany
60 G10 Miho wan B Japan
40 D5 Mijoux France
119 P7 Mikado Saskatchewan Canada
94 D2 Mikado Michigan U.S.A.
60 P2 Mikasa Japan
61 K9 Mikawa Japan
61 L11 Mikawa-wan B Japan
Mikha Tskhakaya see Senaki
54 L2 Mikhaylov Russian Federation
46 F1 Mikhaylovgrad Bulgaria
146 J12 Mikhaylov I Antarctica
48 L1 Mikhaylovka Ukraine
47 H2 Mikhaylovo Bulgaria
55 C3 Mikhaylovsk Russian Federation
55 G4 Mikhaylovskiy Altayskiy Kray Russian Federation
80 C4 Mikhmoret Israel
79 E9 Mikhrot Timna Israel
88 H7 Mikindani Tanzania
100 E4 Mikkalo Oregon U.S.A.
29 N10 Mikkeli Finland
117 Q7 Mikkwa R Alberta Canada
31 N2 Mikołajki Poland
31 L5 Mikołow Poland
46 G1 Mikre Bulgaria
46 E4 Mikrï Préspa L Greece
47 H3 Mikrón Dhérion Greece
52 G1 Mikulkin, Mys C Russian Federation
48 D2 Mikulov Czech Rep
87 G7 Mikumi Tanzania
88 F5 Mikumi Nat. Park Tanzania
61 N8 Mikuni sammyaku mts Japan
61 N12 Mikura-jima isld Japan
99 N4 Milaca Minnesota U.S.A.
73 L7 Miladunmadulu Atoll Maldives
130 H9 Milagres Brazil
Milan see Milano
122 A8 Milan Quebec Canada
94 B7 Milan Indiana U.S.A.
107 N4 Milan Kansas U.S.A.
94 D4 Milan Michigan U.S.A.
99 L4 Milan Minnesota U.S.A.
99 N9 Milan Missouri U.S.A.
94 E5 Milan Ohio U.S.A.
110 H6 Milan Tennessee U.S.A.
100 H2 Milan Washington U.S.A.
138 E6 Milang South Australia Australia
88 E10 Milange Mozambique
39 Milano conurbation Italy
109 L5 Milano Texas U.S.A.
17 G4 Milares R Spain
47 J7 Milâs Turkey
43 G10 Milazzo Sicily
98 K4 Milbank South Dakota U.S.A.
95 U2 Milbridge Maine U.S.A.
94 A4 Milburg Michigan U.S.A.
144 B7 Milburn New Zealand
9 G3 Mildenhall England
120 J8 Mildmay Ontario Canada
118 K5 Mildred Saskatchewan Canada
98 A3 Mildred Montana U.S.A.
95 L5 Mildred Pennsylvania U.S.A.
117 R7 Mildred Lake Alberta Canada
138 F5 Mildura Victoria Australia
67 A4 Mile China
46 F5 Miléai Greece
127 J2 Mile Gully Jamaica
141 K7 Miles Queensland Australia
100 G2 Miles Washington U.S.A.
101 U3 Miles City Montana U.S.A.
21 L5 Milesse,la France
119 N9 Milestone Saskatchewan Canada
43 G10 Mileto Italy
45 Q7 Miletto, M mt Italy
143 B7 Mileura W Australia Australia
31 H6 Milevsko Czech Rep
9 F5 Milford Surrey England
102 D1 Milford California U.S.A.
95 O5 Milford Connecticut U.S.A.
95 M8 Milford Delaware U.S.A.
99 T9 Milford Illinois U.S.A.
94 B5 Milford Indiana U.S.A.
99 L6 Milford Iowa U.S.A.
107 O2 Milford Kansas U.S.A.
95 T2 Milford Maine U.S.A.
95 Q4 Milford Massachusetts U.S.A.
94 D4 Milford Michigan U.S.A.
98 J9 Milford Nebraska U.S.A.
95 Q4 Milford New Hampshire U.S.A.
95 N4 Milford New York U.S.A.
109 L3 Milford Texas U.S.A.
103 L3 Milford Utah U.S.A.
94 K8 Milford Virginia U.S.A.
94 D6 Milford Center Ohio U.S.A.
8 A4 Milford Haven Wales
9 E6 Milford on Sea England
144 A6 Milford Sound New Zealand
140 F4 Milgarra Queensland Australia
143 C8 Milgoo, Mt W Australia Australia
143 C7 Milgun W Australia Australia
85 E1 Miliana Algeria
43 C12 Miliane R Tunisia
31 K4 Milicz Poland
140 B1 Milikapiti N Terr Australia
143 B9 Miling W Australia Australia
140 C1 Milingimbi N Terr Australia
20 A5 Milizac France
51 P3 Milkovo Russian Federation
118 F9 Milk R Alberta/Montana Canada/U.S.A.
127 K3 Milk River Bath Jamaica
86 E2 Milk, Wadi el watercourse Sudan
25 E5 Mill Netherlands
141 H4 Millaa Millaa Queensland Australia
21 O7 Millançay France
99 O9 Millard Missouri U.S.A.
141 H5 Millaroo Queensland Australia
98 H3 Millarton North Dakota U.S.A.
94 H9 Millboro Virginia U.S.A.
121 M8 Millbrook Ontario Canada
95 O5 Millbrook New York U.S.A.
102 F1 Mill City Nevada U.S.A.
100 C5 Mill City Oregon U.S.A.
102 C1 Mill Creek California U.S.A.
109 L1 Mill Creek Oklahoma U.S.A.
94 H8 Mill Creek West Virginia U.S.A.
112 D4 Milledgeville Georgia U.S.A.
99 R8 Milledgeville Illinois U.S.A.
101 O2 Millegan Montana U.S.A.
99 N3 Mille Lacs L Minnesota U.S.A.
119 N2 Mille Lacs, Lac des Ontario Canada
112 F5 Millen Georgia U.S.A.
138 D3 Miller R South Australia Australia
110 C4 Miller Missouri U.S.A.
98 G9 Miller Nebraska U.S.A.
98 H5 Miller South Dakota U.S.A.
124 B3 Miller, Desembarcadero de Mexico
116 Q6 Miller, Mt Alaska U.S.A.
54 M8 Millerovo Russian Federation
103 O10 Miller Pk Arizona U.S.A.
102 G3 Millers Nevada U.S.A.
94 B5 Millersburg Indiana U.S.A.
110 M3 Millersburg Kentucky U.S.A.
94 D1 Millersburg Michigan U.S.A.
94 F6 Millersburg Ohio U.S.A.
95 L6 Millersburg Pennsylvania U.S.A.
138 D4 Millers Creek South Australia Australia
95 P4 Millers Falls Massachusetts U.S.A.
111 J9 Millers Ferry Alabama U.S.A.
144 B6 Miller's Flat New Zealand
12 D2 Millerston Scotland
94 H6 Millerstown Pennsylvania U.S.A.
108 H4 Millersview Texas U.S.A.
122 G7 Millerton New Brunswick Canada
144 C4 Millerton New Zealand
95 O5 Millerton New York U.S.A.
102 E4 Millerton L California U.S.A.
123 Q5 Millertown Newfoundland Canada
123 Q4 Millertown Junct Newfoundland Canada
118 D5 Millet Alberta Canada
94 E9 Millet West Virginia U.S.A.
102 G2 Millett Nevada U.S.A.
109 H7 Millett Texas U.S.A.
18 G7 Millevaches, Plateau de France
14 D1 Millford Ireland
94 K5 Mill Hall Pennsylvania U.S.A.
146 H13 Mill I Antarctica
115 M5 Mill I Northwest Territories Canada
100 E6 Millican Oregon U.S.A.
109 L5 Millican Texas U.S.A.
138 F6 Millicent South Australia Australia
118 F8 Millicent Alberta Canada
143 D8 Millicent,Mt W Australia Australia
111 K11 Milligan Florida U.S.A.
98 J9 Milligan Nebraska U.S.A.
106 F1 Milliken Colorado U.S.A.
95 M7 Millington Maryland U.S.A.
94 D3 Millington Michigan U.S.A.
110 G6 Millington Tennessee U.S.A.
95 S8 Millinocket Maine U.S.A.
141 K8 Millmerran Queensland Australia
13 E5 Millom England
12 D2 Millport Scotland
111 H8 Millport Alabama U.S.A.
95 L4 Millport New York U.S.A.
111 H10 Millry Alabama U.S.A.
141 G5 Mills R Queensland Australia
106 F5 Mills New Mexico U.S.A.
101 T7 Mills Wyoming U.S.A.
109 J3 Millsap Texas U.S.A.
102 B2 Millsaps California U.S.A.
95 M8 Millsboro Delaware U.S.A.
94 G7 Millsboro Pennsylvania U.S.A.
117 O5 Mills L Northwest Territories Canada
99 Q5 Millston Wisconsin U.S.A.
142 B5 Millstream W Australia Australia
14 B4 Millstreet Ireland
8 C2 Milltir Cerig mt Wales
122 E8 Milltown New Brunswick Canada
123 R6 Milltown Newfoundland Canada
14 B4 Milltown Malbay Ireland
141 F4 Millungera Queensland Australia
102 B4 Mill Valley California U.S.A.
122 H9 Mill Village Nova Scotia Canada
122 E7 Millville New Brunswick Canada
94 C7 Millville Ohio U.S.A.
95 L5 Millville Pennsylvania U.S.A.
109 N2 Millwood Res Arkansas U.S.A.
21 P5 Milly-la-Forêt France
143 B7 Milly Milly W Australia Australia
21 P3 Milly-sur Thérain France
33 T6 Milmersdorf Germany
13 E1 Milnathort Scotland
115 R3 Milne Land Greenland
112 C4 Milner Georgia U.S.A.
101 L7 Milner Idaho U.S.A.
118 E1 Milner Ridge Manitoba Canada
120 K6 Milnet Ontario Canada
12 D2 Milngavie Scotland
98 J3 Milnor North Dakota U.S.A.
13 F5 Milnthorpe England
118 E8 Milo Alberta Canada
88 E6 Milo Tanzania
99 N8 Milo Iowa U.S.A.
95 S1 Milo Maine U.S.A.
100 B7 Milo Oregon U.S.A.
135 U6 Milolii Hawaiian Is
31 M2 Miłomłyn Poland
46 G8 Mílos isld Greece
31 K3 Miłosław Poland
33 Q7 Milow Germany
31 L6 Milówka Poland
138 F3 Milparinka New South Wales Australia
102 C4 Milpitas California U.S.A.
110 L2 Milroy Indiana U.S.A.
94 K6 Milroy Pennsylvania U.S.A.
37 O5 Miltach Germany
36 G4 Miltenberg Germany
139 K6 Milton New South Wales Australia
122 H9 Milton Nova Scotia Canada
144 B7 Milton New Zealand
12 D2 Milton Scotland
95 M8 Milton Delaware U.S.A.
111 J11 Milton Florida U.S.A.
99 Q10 Milton Illinois U.S.A.
110 D1 Milton Iowa U.S.A.
107 N4 Milton Kansas U.S.A.
95 R3 Milton Maine U.S.A.
94 H10 Milton North Carolina U.S.A.
98 J1 Milton North Dakota U.S.A.
95 L5 Milton Pennsylvania U.S.A.
95 O2 Milton Vermont U.S.A.
94 E8 Milton West Virginia U.S.A.
99 S7 Milton Wisconsin U.S.A.
8 B6 Milton Abbot England
139 J3 Milton Downs New South Wales Australia
100 G4 Milton Freewater Oregon U.S.A.
12 D3 Miltonish Scotland
9 F3 Milton Keynes England
107 N2 Miltonvale Kansas U.S.A.
86 C3 Miltou Chad
33 S4 Miltzow Germany
67 D2 Miluo China
8 C5 Milverton England
99 T6 Milwaukee Wisconsin U.S.A.
127 K5 Milwaukee Depth Caribbean
60 E13 Mimitsu Japan
18 E8 Mimizan France
60 O4 Mimmaya Japan
31 H5 Mimoň Czech Rep
86 B6 Mimongo Gabon
60 H10 Mimuro yama mt Japan
102 A2 Mina California U.S.A.
102 F3 Mina Nevada U.S.A.
77 A5 Mina' al Ahmadi Iran
77 E6 Mīnāb Iran
60 J12 Minabe Japan
124 F3 Miñaca Mexico
119 T4 Minago R Manitoba Canada
71 H4 Minahassa Peninsula Sulawesi Indonesia
77 D7 Mina Jebel Ali U.A.E.
79 H2 Mīnakh Syria
118 H1 Minaki Ontario Canada
100 H4 Minam Oregon U.S.A.
60 D13 Minamata Japan
61 L10 Minami Alps Nat. Park Japan
85 C6 Mina, Mt Mali
126 F4 Minas Cuba
69 E12 Minas Sumatra
131 G5 Minas Uruguay
77 A5 Mina' Sa'ud Kuwait
122 H8 Minas Basin Nova Scotia Canada
126 C3 Minas de Matahambre Cuba
16 C7 Minas de Riotinto Spain
16 C7 Minas de Tharsis Spain
130 F5 Minas Gerais state Brazil
129 K7 Minas Novas Brazil
130 G5 Minas Novas Brazil
125 P10 Minas, Sa. de las mts Guatemala
98 C8 Minatare Nebraska U.S.A.
120 B2 Minataree Ontario Canada
125 M9 Minatitlán Mexico
68 B2 Minbu Burma
118 F5 Minburn Alberta Canada
99 M8 Minburn Iowa U.S.A.
68 A2 Minbya Burma
116 M5 Minchumina, L Alaska U.S.A.
45 J1 Mincio R Italy
107 N6 Minco Oklahoma U.S.A.
31 M6 Minčol mt Slovakia
71 G7 Mindanao Philippines
71 G6 Mindanao Sea Philippines
138 F5 Mindarie South Australia Australia
68 A2 Mindat Sakan Burma
37 J7 Mindel R Germany
41 M1 Mindelheim Germany
121 M8 Minden Ontario Canada
32 J8 Minden Germany
111 C9 Minden Louisiana U.S.A.
98 G9 Minden Nebraska U.S.A.
102 E3 Minden Nevada U.S.A.
94 F9 Minden West Virginia U.S.A.
94 E3 Minden City Michigan U.S.A.
142 B5 Minderoo W Australia Australia
68 B3 Mindon Burma
138 F5 Mindona L New South Wales Australia
71 E4 Mindoro isld Philippines
71 E4 Mindoro Str Philippines
48 H5 Mîndra Romania
48 F4 Mindszent Hungary
55 C4 Mindyak Russian Federation
60 E11 Mine Japan
99 O1 Mine Centre Ontario Canada
14 D5 Mine Hd Ireland
8 C5 Minehead England
130 D5 Mineiros Brazil
21 J3 Mine,la France
99 L8 Mineola Iowa U.S.A.
109 M3 Mineola Texas U.S.A.
101 P4 Miner Montana U.S.A.
102 C1 Mineral California U.S.A.
109 K7 Mineral Texas U.S.A.
94 K8 Mineral Virginia U.S.A.
100 C3 Mineral Washington U.S.A.
125 K7 Mineral del Monte Mexico
103 M3 Mineral Mts Utah U.S.A.
99 Q7 Mineral Pt Wisconsin U.S.A.
109 O2 Mineral Springs Arkansas U.S.A.
109 J3 Mineral Wells Texas U.S.A.
45 K2 Minerbio Italy
103 M3 Minersville Utah U.S.A.
94 F6 Minerva Ohio U.S.A.
137 R6 Minerva Rfs Pacific Oc
43 G7 Minervino Murge Italy
95 L3 Minetto New York U.S.A.
94 E8 Minford Ohio U.S.A.
68 C4 Mingaladon Burma
122 H3 Mingan Quebec Canada
122 J3 Mingan Chan Quebec Canada
122 J3 Mingan Is Quebec Canada
138 F4 Mingary South Australia Australia
67 D5 Mingcheng China
78 L1 Mingechaur Azerbaijan
78 L1 Mingechaurskoye Vdkhr res Azerbaijan
141 H4 Mingela Queensland Australia
143 B8 Mingenew W Australia Australia
140 E5 Mingera R Queensland Australia
68 B1 Mingin Burma
75 Q6 Mingin Range Burma
67 B5 Mingjiang China
58 G5 Ming-kuang China
17 G5 Minglanilla Spain
67 C4 Minglun China
99 N8 Mingo Iowa U.S.A.
107 K2 Mingo Kansas U.S.A.
94 G6 Mingo Junct Ohio U.S.A.
87 G8 Mingoyo Tanzania
67 A1 Mingshan China
Mingshui see Zhangqiu
65 F1 Mingshui China
109 J3 Mingus Texas U.S.A.
67 F3 Mingxi China
68 G8 Minh Hoa, Hon isld Vietnam
68 B4 Minhla Burma
16 B3 Minho prov Portugal
16 B2 Minho R Spain/Portugal
127 K2 Minho, R Jamaica
67 F3 Minhou China
20 G4 Miniac Morvan France
46 E1 Minićevo Serbia Yugoslavia
73 L7 Minicoy I Lakshadweep Indian Oc
101 M7 Minidoka Idaho U.S.A.
99 R9 Minier Illinois U.S.A.
143 E8 Minigwal,L W Australia Australia
143 A6 Minilya W Australia Australia
143 A6 Minilya R W Australia Australia
110 K4 Mining City Res Kentucky U.S.A.
119 Q8 Miniota Manitoba Canada
83 K10 Minipe Sri Lanka
123 L1 Minipi L Labrador, Nfld Canada
118 H4 Ministikwan L Saskatchewan Canada
17 F3 Ministra, Sierra Spain
119 Q6 Minitonas Manitoba Canada
58 D5 Min Jiang R China
67 F3 Min Jiang R China
140 C1 Minjilang N Terr Australia
102 E5 Minkler California U.S.A.
48 L2 Min'kovtsy Ukraine
57 G4 Min-Kush Kirghizia
138 D5 Minlaton South Australia Australia
85 F7 Minna Nigeria
146 D11 Minna Bluff pt Antarctica
61 P12 Minna-jima isld Okinawa
107 N2 Minneapolis Kansas U.S.A.
99 N4 Minneapolis Minnesota U.S.A.
119 S8 Minnedosa Manitoba Canada
107 L4 Minneola Kansas U.S.A.
99 N3 Minnesota state U.S.A.
99 M5 Minnesota R Minnesota U.S.A.
99 P5 Minnesota City Minnesota U.S.A.
99 N6 Minnesota Lake Minnesota U.S.A.
27 E11 Minnesund Norway
99 N5 Minnetonka Minnesota U.S.A.
118 B7 Minnewanka, L Alberta Canada
99 L4 Minnewaska L Minnesota U.S.A.
98 G1 Minnewaukan North Dakota U.S.A.
143 B6 Minnie Creek W Australia Australia
141 H7 Minnie Downs Queensland Australia
142 B5 Minnie,Mt W Australia Australia
138 D5 Minnipa South Australia Australia
120 G4 Minnipuka Ontario Canada
118 K1 Minnitaki L Ontario Canada
61 K10 Mino Japan
16 B2 Miño R Spain
61 M10 Minobu Japan
99 R4 Minocqua Wisconsin U.S.A.
61 K10 Minokamo Japan
61 K11 Minokuchi Japan
99 P3 Minong Wisconsin U.S.A.
99 R9 Minonk Illinois U.S.A.
99 S8 Minooka Illinois U.S.A.
40 A2 Minot France
98 E1 Minot North Dakota U.S.A.
67 F3 Minqing China
65 C7 Minquan China
20 F4 Minquiers,les English Chan
32 G5 Minsen Germany
65 A4 Minsheng Canal China
53 C7 Minsk Belarus
31 N3 Mińsk Mazowieckie Poland
9 H5 Minster England
94 C6 Minster Ohio U.S.A.
74 F1 Mintaka Pass China/Kashmir
111 J9 Minter Alabama U.S.A.
111 F8 Minter City Mississippi U.S.A.
119 S9 Minto Manitoba Canada
122 F7 Minto New Brunswick Canada
117 E4 Minto Yukon Territory Canada
114 J3 Minto Hd Northwest Territories Canada
114 H3 Minto Inlet Northwest Territories Canada
115 M6 Minto, L Quebec Canada
98 B1 Minton Saskatchewan Canada
106 D2 Minturn Colorado U.S.A.
45 P7 Minturno Italy
79 A8 Minûf Egypt
56 D4 Minusinsk Russian Federation
58 D5 Min Xian China
79 A10 Minya, El Egypt
79 B8 Minya el Qamn Egypt
Minya Konka mt see Gongga Shan mt
55 C3 Min'yar Russian Federation
138 F6 Minyip Victoria Australia
68 B1 Minywa Burma
94 C2 Mio Michigan U.S.A.
83 J10 Mi Oya R Sri Lanka
78 K5 Miqdādiyah Iraq
123 Q6 Miquelon isld Atlantic Oc
123 Q6 Miquelon Miquelon I Atlantic Oc
121 O3 Miquelon Quebec Canada
123 Q6 Miquelon, C Miquelon I Atlantic Oc
118 E5 Miquelon Prov. Park Alberta Canada
123 N7 Mira C Breton I, Nova Scotia
45 M1 Mira Italy
16 B7 Mira R Portugal
17 G5 Mira Spain
19 P17 Mirabeau France
130 G5 Mirabela Brazil
45 R7 Mirabella Eclano Italy
130 G7 Miracema Brazil
129 J5 Mirador, Parque Nacional de Brazil
128 D2 Miraflores Boyaca Colombia
124 E6 Miraflores Mexico
102 G7 Mirage L California U.S.A.
130 G7 Miraí Brazil
76 B2 Miraj India
130 G5 Miralta Brazil
19 O17 Miràmas France
18 E7 Mirambeau France
122 G6 Miramichi B New Brunswick Canada
18 F8 Miramont de Guyenne France
133 F5 Miranda Argentina
145 E2 Miranda New Zealand
128 E1 Miranda state Venezuela
17 F2 Miranda de E.Haro Spain
16 C3 Miranda do D Portugal
141 F3 Miranda Downs Queensland Australia
130 C6 Miranda, R Brazil
18 F9 Mirande France
16 C3 Mirandela Portugal
109 J8 Mirando City Texas U.S.A.
45 K2 Mirandola Italy
130 D7 Mirandópolis Brazil
45 M1 Mirano Italy
130 E8 Mirante Serra do mts Brazil
60 F11 Mirasaka Japan
17 G5 Mira, Sierra de mts Spain
130 E7 Mirassol Brazil
16 C2 Miravalles mt Spain
46 E3 Miravci Macedonia
77 L2 Mīr Bacheh Kowt Afghanistan
25 E3 Mirdum Netherlands
21 K6 Miré France
86 G1 Mirear I Egypt
127 H5 Mirebalais Haiti
19 J5 Mirebeau Côte-d'Or France
21 L8 Mirebeau Vienne France
18 G9 Mirepoix France
54 E7 Mirgorod Ukraine
70 D2 Miri Sarawak
141 K6 Miriam Vale Queensland Australia
85 A5 Mirik, C Mauritania
127 K9 Mirimire Venezuela
131 H4 Mirim, L Brazil/Uruguay
131 F2 Miriñay, R Argentina
141 G8 Mirintu R Queensland Australia
128 D4 Miriti-Paraná R Colombia
77 G5 Mīrjāveh Iran
80 D4 Mirka Jordan
45 P1 Mirna R Croatia
146 H13 Mirnyy Rus Fed Base Antarctica
56 H1 Mirnyy Russian Federation
40 E3 Miroir, Mt France
144 D5 Miromiro mt New Zealand
119 P3 Mirond L Saskatchewan Canada
54 B7 Mironovka Ukraine
31 J2 Mirosławiec Poland
33 R6 Mirow Germany
77 L7 Mirpur Khas Pakistan
140 D7 Mirranponga Pongunna L N Terr Australia
85 F6 Mirria Niger
118 D6 Mirror Alberta Canada
48 J6 Mîrşani Romania
56 D5 Mirskoy Khrebet mts Russian Federation
141 H5 Mirtna Queensland Australia
46 F7 Mirtoan Sea Greece
59 J4 Miryang S Korea
56 E1 Miryuginskiy Porog falls Russian Federation
57 B5 Mirzachiria Turkmenistan
75 K6 Mirzapur India
45 O4 Misa R Italy
60 G11 Mi-saki C Japan
60 F12 Misaki Japan
61 L10 Misakubo Japan
45 N4 Misano Monte Italy
61 P13 Misato Okinawa
61 P5 Misawa Japan
32 L8 Misburg Germany
40 G5 Mischabel mt Switzerland
122 J7 Miscouche Prince Edward I Canada
122 H6 Miscou I New Brunswick Canada
122 H5 Miscou, Pt New Brunswick Canada
127 P4 Misery, Mt St Kitts W Indies
80 F1 Misgav 'Am Israel
69 A9 Misha Nicobar Is
77 A5 Mish'ab, Al U.A.E.
128 D6 Mishahua R Peru
65 H2 Mishan China
94 A5 Mishawaka Indiana U.S.A.
116 G2 Misheguk Mt Alaska U.S.A.
56 F4 Mishelevka Russian Federation
120 E4 Mishibishu L Ontario Canada
99 T5 Mishicot Wisconsin U.S.A.
60 E11 Mi shima isld Japan
61 M10 Mishima Japan
55 C3 Mishkino Bashkirskaya Respublika Russian Federation
55 D3 Mishkino Sverdlovskaya obl Russian Federation
80 F7 Mishmaqa Jordan
80 C6 Mishmar 'Ayyalon Israel
80 B8 Mishmar Ha Negev Israel
80 F1 Mishmar Ha Yarden Israel
121 P5 Mishomis Quebec Canada
52 J2 Mishvan' Russian Federation
80 E4 Misilya Jordan
137 L4 Misima isld Louisiade Arch
128 E6 Misión Cavinas Bolivia
130 C10 Misiones prov Argentina
130 B10 Misiones dept Paraguay
130 C10 Misiones, Sa.de ra Argentina
88 B4 Misisi Zaire
125 N2 Miskito, Cayos islds Nicaragua
48 F2 Miskolc Hungary
38 M9 Mislinja Slovenia
79 G5 Mismīyah, Al Syria
60 G10 Misogu chi Japan
71 C3 Misoöl isld W Irian
99 Q2 Misquah Hills Minnesota U.S.A.
84 F3 Mişrātah Libya
84 F3 Mişrātah, Ra's C Libya
120 F4 Missanabie Ontario Canada
130 G9 Missão Velhá Brazil
20 F7 Missillac France
120 G4 Missinaibi L Ontario Canada
120 H2 Missinaibi R Ontario Canada
100 C1 Mission British Columbia Canada
98 F6 Mission South Dakota U.S.A.
109 J9 Mission Texas U.S.A.
117 M11 Mission City British Columbia Canada
98 J7 Mission Hill South Dakota U.S.A.
101 M2 Mission Range Montana U.S.A.
121 L1 Missisicabi R Quebec Canada
120 G6 Mississagi R Ontario Canada
121 L9 Mississauga Ontario Canada
94 B6 Mississinewa L Indiana U.S.A.
110 L1 Mississinewa L Indiana U.S.A.
111 F9 Mississippi state U.S.A.
111 E10 Mississippi R U.S.A.
111 G12 Mississippi Delta Louisiana U.S.A.
121 O7 Mississippi, L Ontario Canada
111 H11 Mississippi Sound Mississippi U.S.A.
Missolonghi Greece see Mesolóngion
120 H4 Missonga Ontario Canada
101 L3 Missoula Montana U.S.A.
110 C3 Missouri state U.S.A.
110 C2 Missouri R Missouri U.S.A.
109 O2 Missouri, Lit R Arkansas U.S.A.
98 F3 Missouri Res North Dakota U.S.A.
99 L8 Missouri Valley Iowa U.S.A.
141 H5 Mistake Cr Queensland Australia
140 A3 Mistake Creek N Terr Australia
123 K2 Mistanipisipou R Quebec Canada
121 S4 Mistassini Quebec Canada
115 M7 Mistassini, Lac Quebec Canada
119 O6 Mistatim Saskatchewan Canada
121 M3 Mistawak L Quebec Canada
31 K7 Mistelbach Austria
27 J14 Misterhult Sweden
126 C5 Misteriosa Bank Caribbean
8 D6 Misterton England
128 D7 Misti mt Peru
122 E5 Mistigougèche L Quebec Canada
37 P3 Misto Czech Rep
131 D3 Mistolar, L Argentina
26 E10 Mistra R Norway
43 F11 Mistretta Sicily
117 H8 Misty Fjords Nat Mon Alaska U.S.A.
60 E11 Misumi Japan
60 D13 Misumi Japan
60 E13 Mitai Japan
127 P2 Mitan Trinidad
124 G7 Mita, Pta.de C Mexico
8 D4 Mitcheldean England
141 J7 Mitchell Queensland Australia
120 J9 Mitchell Ontario Canada
8 A7 Mitchell England
110 K3 Mitchell Indiana U.S.A.
98 C8 Mitchell Nebraska U.S.A.
100 E5 Mitchell Oregon U.S.A.
98 H6 Mitchell South Dakota U.S.A.
111 K9 Mitchell L Alabama U.S.A.
94 B2 Mitchell, L Michigan U.S.A.
112 E2 Mitchell, Mt North Carolina U.S.A.
140 A1 Mitchell Pt N Terr Australia
141 F3 Mitchell River Queensland Australia
14 C4 Mitchelstown Ireland

121 Q5 **Mitchinamecus, L** Quebec Canada
74 C6 **Mithi** Pakistan
47 H5 **Míthimna** Greece
71 B2 **Miti** isld Halmahera Indonesia
47 H5 **Mitilíni** Greece
52 G2 **Mitina** Russian Federation
119 S4 **Mitishto R** Manitoba Canada
117 G7 **Mitkof I** Alaska U.S.A.
79 C8 **Mitla Pass** Egypt
61 O9 **Mito** Japan
86 A5 **Mitra** mt Equat Guinea
137 P4 **Mitre** isld Santa Cruz Is
145 E4 **Mitre, Mt** New Zealand
144 A6 **Mitre Pk** New Zealand
52 J3 **Mitrofan-Dikost** Russian Federation
116 H9 **Mitrofania I** Alaska U.S.A.
46 D2 **Mitrovica** Serbia Yugoslavia
46 D5 **Mitsikéli** R Greece
86 G2 **Mits'iwa** Eritrea
86 H2 **Mits'iwa Channel** Eritrea
60 F11 **Mitsu** Japan
60 F12 **Mitsuhama** Japan
60 Q3 **Mitsuishi** Japan
60 H11 **Mitsuishi** Japan
61 N9 **Mitsukaidō** Japan
61 M8 **Mitsuke** Japan
60 R2 **Mitsumata** Japan
139 K5 **Mittagong** New South Wales Australia
141 F4 **Mittagong** Queensland Australia
41 L3 **Mittagspitze** mt Austria
139 J6 **Mitta Mitta** Victoria Australia
41 N4 **Mittelberg** Austria
37 J5 **Mittelfranken** dist Bayern Germany
40 F4 **Mittelland** dist Switzerland
32 H8 **Mittellandkanal** Germany
33 R8 **Mittelmark** reg Germany
36 H3 **Mittelsinn** Germany
41 O3 **Mittenwald** Germany
33 T8 **Mittenwalde** Germany
38 M6 **Mitterbach** Austria
37 O6 **Mitterfels** Germany
38 G7 **Mitter Pinzgau** V Austria
36 B6 **Mittersheim** France
37 N4 **Mitterteich** Germany
140 D4 **Mittiebah** R N Terr Australia
37 O2 **Mittweida** Germany
128 D3 **Mitú** Colombia
88 B3 **Mitumba** mts Zaire
87 E7 **Mitwaba** Zaire
55 D1 **Mityayevo** Russian Federation
86 B5 **Mitzic** Gabon
61 N10 **Miura** Japan
54 K9 **Mius** R Rus Fed/Ukraine
54 K9 **Miusskiy Liman** lagoon Russian Federation
65 B7 **Mi Xian** China
38 M7 **Mixnitz** Austria
61 K11 **Miya-gawa** R Japan
61 O7 **Miyagi** prefect Japan
61 Q12 **Miyagi** Okinawa
61 P13 **Miyagusuku-jima** isld Okinawa
78 G4 **Miyāh, Wadi Al** Syria
61 N11 **Miyake-jima** isld Japan
61 P6 **Miyako** Japan
60 E14 **Miyakonojō** Japan
55 B6 **Miyaly** Kazakhstan
60 E13 **Miyazaki** prefect Japan
60 E14 **Miyazaki** Japan
60 J10 **Miyazu** Japan
60 F11 **Miyoshi** Japan
65 C4 **Miyun** China
65 D4 **Miyun Shuiku** res China
86 G4 **Mīzan Teferī** Ethiopia
84 E3 **Mizdah** Libya
111 G10 **Mize** Mississippi U.S.A.
14 B5 **Mizen Hd** Cork Ireland
14 E4 **Mizen Hd** Wicklow Ireland
65 A6 **Mizhi** China
48 K6 **Mizil** Romania
46 F1 **Miziya** Bulgaria
75 P7 **Mizoram** prov India
99 M2 **Mizpah** Minnesota U.S.A.
79 E7 **Mizpe Ramon** Israel
61 P6 **Mizusawa** Japan
26 K9 **Mjällom** Sweden
88 C1 **Mjanji** Uganda
27 F14 **Mjöbäck** Sweden
27 H13 **Mjölby** Sweden
28 B6 **Mjolden** Denmark
27 D12 **Mjöndalen** Norway
27 F14 **Mjörn** L Sweden
27 E11 **Mjösa** L Norway
88 C9 **Mkokomo** mt Zambia
88 G4 **Mkokotoni** Tanzania
88 B8 **Mkuku** Zambia
87 E8 **Mkushi** Zambia
88 B8 **Mkushi** R Zambia
89 H6 **Mkuze** S Africa
31 H5 **Mladá Boleslav** Czech Rep
48 F6 **Mladenovac** Serbia Yugoslavia
37 P4 **Mladotice** Czech Rep
88 C5 **Mlala Hills** Tanzania
48 G6 **Mlava** R Serbia Yugoslavia
31 M2 **Mława** Poland
88 G10 **M'lela** R Mozambique
87 G7 **Mlimba** Tanzania
42 H6 **Mljet** isld Croatia
88 E7 **Mlowe** Malawi
89 D5 **Mmabatho** S Africa
89 E3 **Mmashoro** Botswana
37 O3 **Mnichov** Czech Rep
31 H5 **Mnichovo Hradiště** Czech Rep
48 F2 **Mnišek** Slovakia
26 K8 **Mo** Sweden
128 D5 **Moa** R Brazil
71 N9 **Moa** isld Indonesia
85 B7 **Moa** R Sierra Leone/Guinea
103 P3 **Moab** Utah U.S.A.
126 G4 **Moa Grande, Cayo** isld Cuba
141 F1 **Moa I** Queensland Australia
119 U3 **Moak L** Manitoba Canada
139 G6 **Moama** New South Wales Australia
89 H5 **Moamba** Mozambique
144 C5 **Moana** New Zealand
138 F3 **Moanba, L** South Australia Australia
86 B6 **Moanda** Gabon
86 B7 **Moanda** Zaire
103 K5 **Moapa** Nevada U.S.A.
71 N8 **Moapora** isld Indonesia
14 D3 **Moate** Ireland
88 D10 **Moatize** Mozambique
145 E3 **Moawhango** New Zealand
87 E7 **Moba** Zaire
61 O10 **Mobara** Japan
77 B3 **Mobārakeh** Iran
86 D5 **Mobaye** Cent Afr Republic
86 D5 **Mobayi-Mbongo** Zaire
110 D2 **Moberly** Missouri U.S.A.
117 N8 **Moberly Lake** British Columbia Canada
120 E4 **Mobert** Ontario Canada
111 H11 **Mobile** Alabama U.S.A.
103 M8 **Mobile** Arizona U.S.A.
111 J11 **Mobile Pt** Alabama U.S.A.
141 G7 **Moble** R Queensland Australia
71 F4 **Mobo** Philippines
28 A4 **Møborg** Denmark
98 F4 **Mobridge** South Dakota U.S.A.
Mobutu, L see **Albert, L**
127 J5 **Moca** Dominican Rep
129 J4 **Mocajuba** Brazil
Moçambique see **Mozambique**
88 H9 **Moçambique** dist Mozambique
Moçâmedes see **Namibe**
95 L5 **Mocanaqua** Pennsylvania U.S.A.
103 M5 **Moccasin** Arizona U.S.A.
101 Q2 **Moccasin** Montana U.S.A.
68 G2 **Moc Chau** Vietnam
125 Q7 **Mocche** Mexico
Mocha see **Mukha, Al**
131 A7 **Mocha** isld Chile
124 E5 **Mochicahui** Mexico
127 K2 **Mocho Mts** Jamaica
89 E5 **Mochudi** Botswana
88 H7 **Mocímboa da Praia** Mozambique
48 H4 **Mociu** Romania
27 G15 **Möckeln** L Sweden
33 P8 **Möckern** Germany
95 M9 **Mockhorn** isld Virginia U.S.A.
106 D8 **Mockingbird Gap** gap New Mexico U.S.A.
27 J15 **Möckleby, N** Sweden
27 H15 **Möckleby, S** Sweden
36 G5 **Mockmühl** Germany
33 R9 **Mockrehna** Germany
112 G2 **Mocksville** North Carolina U.S.A.
100 A2 **Moclips** Washington U.S.A.
128 C3 **Mocoa** Colombia
130 F7 **Mococa** Brazil
131 F3 **Mocoretá** R Argentina
124 F5 **Mocorito** Mexico
124 F2 **Moctezuma** Chihuahua Mexico
124 E3 **Moctezuma** Sonora Mexico
88 F10 **Mocuba** Mozambique
40 E7 **Modane** France
83 K9 **Modaragam Aru** R Sri Lanka
74 E7 **Modasa** India
22 J3 **Modave** Belgium
8 C7 **Modbury** England
89 D7 **Modder** R S Africa
106 F4 **Model** Colorado U.S.A.
45 J2 **Modena** Italy
45 J3 **Modena** prov Italy
103 L4 **Modena** Utah U.S.A.
19 L4 **Moder** R France
38 K7 **Moderbrugg** Austria
102 C4 **Modesto** California U.S.A.
43 F12 **Modica** Sicily
45 L3 **Modigliana** Italy
80 C6 **Modi'im** Israel
86 D5 **Modjamboli** Zaire
94 B6 **Modoc** Indiana U.S.A.
107 J3 **Modoc** Kansas U.S.A.
112 E4 **Modoc** South Carolina U.S.A.
100 D7 **Modoc Point** Oregon U.S.A.
58 E2 **Modot** Mongolia
36 B2 **Mödrath** Germany
48 E6 **Modriča** Bosnia-Herzegovina
48 E2 **Modrý Kameň** Slovakia
68 J5 **Mo Đuc** Vietnam
139 H7 **Moe** Victoria Australia
145 E2 **Moehau** mt New Zealand
20 C6 **Moelan** France
8 B1 **Moelfre** Wales
8 C2 **Moel Sych** mt Wales
27 E11 **Moelv** Norway
129 H2 **Moengo** Suriname
103 N5 **Moenkopi** Arizona U.S.A.
144 B5 **Moeraki, L** New Zealand
22 F1 **Moerbeke** Belgium
25 C5 **Moerdijk** Netherlands
22 D1 **Moere** Belgium
20 G7 **Moëre,la** France
145 E1 **Moerewa** New Zealand
145 E3 **Moeroa** New Zealand
Moero, Lac see **Mweru, L**
13 E3 **Moffat** Scotland
106 E3 **Moffat** Colorado U.S.A.
144 B6 **Moffat Pk** New Zealand
98 F3 **Moffit** North Dakota U.S.A.
48 H3 **Moftin** Romania
74 F3 **Moga** India
Mogadiscio see **Muqdisho**
Mogadishu see **Muqdisho**
94 F5 **Mogadore** Ohio U.S.A.
16 C3 **Mogadouro** Portugal
89 F4 **Mogalakwena** R S Africa
61 N7 **Mogami-gawa** R Japan
67 F1 **Mogan Shan** mt China
75 R6 **Mogaung** Burma
28 B7 **Møgeltønder** Denmark
17 G6 **Mogente** Spain
36 H6 **Mögglingen** Germany
60 C13 **Mogi** Japan
129 J8 **Mogi das Cruzes** Brazil
31 M4 **Mogielnica** Poland
130 F7 **Mogi Guaçu** R Brazil
54 H9 **Mogila-Bel'mak Gora** mt Ukraine
54 B3 **Mogilëv** Belarus
48 L2 **Mogilev-Podol'skiy** Ukraine
139 J3 **Mogil-Mogil** New South Wales Australia
31 K3 **Mogilno** Poland
130 F8 **Mogi Mirim** Brazil
88 H9 **Mogincual** Mozambique
45 J2 **Móglia** Italy
42 E3 **Mogliano Veneto** Italy
45 M1 **Mogliano Veneto** Italy
46 D4 **Moglicë** Albania
19 N12 **Mogneneins** France
59 G1 **Mogocha** Russian Federation
68 C1 **Mogok** Burma
89 E4 **Mogol** R S Africa
106 B8 **Mogollon** New Mexico U.S.A.
106 B8 **Mogollon Mts** New Mexico U.S.A.
103 O7 **Mogollon Rim** tableland Arizona U.S.A.
106 D4 **Mogote** Colorado U.S.A.
56 F5 **Mogoyty** Russian Federation
16 C7 **Moguer** Spain
143 B9 **Mogumber** W Australia Australia
48 E5 **Mohács** Hungary
145 F3 **Mohaka** New Zealand
98 E1 **Mohall** North Dakota U.S.A.
17 H9 **Mohammadia** Algeria
85 C2 **Mohammedia** Morocco
103 K6 **Mohave, L** Nev/Ariz U.S.A.
103 K7 **Mohave Mts** Cal/Ariz U.S.A.
103 L9 **Mohawk** Arizona U.S.A.
99 S2 **Mohawk** Michigan U.S.A.
95 N4 **Mohawk** R New York U.S.A.
103 L9 **Mohawk Mts** Arizona U.S.A.
59 H1 **Mohe** China
27 G14 **Moheda** Sweden
87 D9 **Mohembo** Botswana
74 C5 **Mohenjo Daro** anc site Pakistan
14 B4 **Moher, Cliffs of** Ireland
116 D6 **Mohican, C** Alaska U.S.A.
14 D3 **Mohill** Ireland
100 J3 **Mohler** Idaho U.S.A.
32 H10 **Möhne** R Germany
32 H10 **Möhnesee** Germany
32 H10 **Möhnestausee** L Germany
27 G13 **Moholm** Sweden
20 E5 **Mohon** France
103 L7 **Mohon Pk** Arizona U.S.A.
88 G6 **Mohoro** Tanzania
124 H4 **Mohovano Ranch** Mexico
37 J2 **Möhra** Germany
36 G6 **Möhringen** Germany
28 D7 **Mohrkirch** Germany
27 B13 **Moi** Norway
16 B4 **Moimenta da Beira** Portugal
66 C5 **Moincêr** China
21 H7 **Moine** R France
95 N2 **Moira** New York U.S.A.
26 G5 **Mo i Rana** Norway
19 P14 **Moirans** France
46 G9 **Moíres** Crete Greece
52 C5 **Mõisaküla** Estonia
20 H6 **Moisdon** France
55 G2 **Moiseyevka** Russian Federation
122 F3 **Moisie** Quebec Canada
19 Q17 **Moissac** France
86 C4 **Moissala** Chad
21 O3 **Moisson** France
21 N6 **Moisy** France
27 K12 **Möja** Sweden
17 F7 **Mojácar** Spain
102 F6 **Mojave** California U.S.A.
102 G7 **Mojave** R California U.S.A.
102 G6 **Mojave Desert** California U.S.A.
60 E12 **Moji** Japan
130 F8 **Moji das Cruzes** Brazil
120 B2 **Mojikit L** Ontario Canada
86 G4 **Mojo** Ethiopia
71 H9 **Mojo** isld Indonesia
86 F5 **Mojo** Uganda
70 O9 **Mojokerto** Java
128 E7 **Mojos, Llanos de** plain Bolivia
129 J4 **Moju** R Brazil
61 O9 **Mōka** Japan
145 E3 **Mokai** New Zealand
75 L6 **Mokāma** India
110 E3 **Mokane** Missouri U.S.A.
102 S12 **Mokapu Pen** Hawaiian Is
145 E3 **Mokau** New Zealand
102 D3 **Mokelumne** R California U.S.A.
89 F7 **Mokhotlong** mt Lesotho
55 F3 **Mokhovoy Prival** Russian Federation
27 J11 **Möklinta** Sweden
85 G1 **Moknine** Tunisia
145 E1 **Mokohinau Is** New Zealand
145 E3 **Mokoia** New Zealand
75 Q5 **Mokokchung** India
86 B3 **Mokolo** Cameroon
144 B7 **Mokoreta** New Zealand
144 B7 **Mokotua** New Zealand
65 G7 **Mokp'o** S Korea
46 D2 **Mokra Gora** mt Montenegro/Serbia Yugoslavia
48 F5 **Mokrin** Serbia Yugoslavia
55 E3 **Mokrousovo** Russian Federation
29 L8 **Möksy** Finland
102 S11 **Mokuauia I** Hawaiian Is
135 U5 **Mokuaweoweo Crater** Hawaiian Is
102 R11 **Mokuleia** Hawaiian Is
102 S12 **Mokulua Is** Hawaiian Is
22 J1 **Mol** Belgium
20 F6 **Molac** France
100 C4 **Molalla** Oregon U.S.A.
125 K7 **Molango** Mexico
46 F8 **Moláoi** Greece
42 F4 **Molat** isld Croatia
70 G6 **Molawe** Sulawesi
21 J3 **Molay-Littry, le** France
32 G7 **Molbergen** Germany
28 B5 **Mølby** Denmark
8 C1 **Mold** Wales
48 G2 **Moldava nad Bodvon** Slovakia
Moldavia rep E Europe see **Moldova**
48 K4 **Moldavia** reg Romania
26 B9 **Molde** Norway
53 C10 **Moldova** rep E Europe
48 K3 **Moldova** R Romania
48 J5 **Moldoveanu** mt Romania
48 K3 **Moldoviţa** Romania
28 D3 **Møldrup** Denmark
40 D5 **Môle** mt France
20 A5 **Molène** isld France
89 D5 **Molepolole** Botswana
8 C6 **Mole, R** England
9 F5 **Mole, R** England
144 D5 **Molesworth** New Zealand
43 H7 **Molfetta** Italy
133 C5 **Molina** Chile
17 F4 **Molina de Aragón** Spain
17 G6 **Molina de Segura** Spain
99 Q8 **Moline** Illinois U.S.A.
107 O4 **Moline** Kansas U.S.A.
94 B4 **Moline** Michigan U.S.A.
45 L2 **Molinella** Italy
38 E8 **Molini** Italy
124 D3 **Molino** Mexico
111 J11 **Molino** Florida U.S.A.
42 F7 **Molise** prov Italy
40 D2 **Mollans** France
29 K4 **Mölle** Sweden
28 C5 **Møllebjerg** hill Denmark
33 S6 **Möllenbeck** Germany
128 D7 **Mollendo** Peru
33 R5 **Möllenhagen** Germany
143 C9 **Mollerin L** W Australia Australia
28 D4 **Mollerup** Denmark
17 H3 **Mollerusa** Spain
26 O2 **Mollesjok** Norway
21 P2 **Molliens-Dreuil** France
12 D2 **Mollinsburn** Scotland
26 M2 **Mollius** mt Norway
33 N5 **Mölln** Germany
33 S5 **Mölln** Germany
38 G8 **Molltal** V Austria
27 F14 **Mölndal** Sweden
54 G9 **Molochansk** Ukraine
53 E10 **Molochnyy, Liman** Ukraine
88 G10 **Molocue** R Mozambique
146 K9 **Molodezhnaya** Rus Fed Base Antarctica
54 D8 **Molodezhnoye** Ukraine
55 F5 **Molodezhnyy** Kazakhstan
56 B2 **Molodezhnyy** Russian Federation
55 F4 **Molodogvardeyskoye** Kazakhstan
52 D6 **Molodoy-Tud** Russian Federation
52 E5 **Mologa** R Russian Federation
102 V13 **Molokai** isld Hawaiian Is
135 S3 **Molokini** isld Hawaiian Is
52 E5 **Molokovo** Russian Federation
52 G5 **Moloma** R Russian Federation
139 J5 **Molong** New South Wales Australia
89 B6 **Molopo** R S Africa
46 F6 **Mólos** Greece
86 C5 **Moloundou** Cameroon
28 F4 **Mols B** hill Denmark
89 F5 **Molsgat** S Africa
36 D6 **Molsheim** France
118 E1 **Molson** Manitoba Canada
119 V4 **Molson L** Manitoba Canada
101 R4 **Molt** Montana U.S.A.
87 E12 **Molteno** S Africa
Moluccas see **Malaku** islds
88 G10 **Moma** Mozambique
51 O2 **Moma** R Russian Federation
86 D6 **Moma** Zaire
139 G4 **Momba** New South Wales Australia
88 D6 **Momba** R Tanzania
45 N4 **Mombaroccio** Italy
88 G4 **Mombasa** Kenya
60 R1 **Mombetsu** Japan
60 Q3 **Mombetsu** Japan
130 D6 **Mombuca, Serra da** mts Brazil
46 G3 **Momchilgrad** Bulgaria
99 T8 **Momence** Illinois U.S.A.
22 G3 **Momignies** Belgium
36 D6 **Mommenheim** France
70 G5 **Momo** Sulawesi
71 F4 **Mompog Passage** Philippines
86 D5 **Mompono** Zaire
126 G10 **Mompós** Colombia
68 B2 **Mon** R Burma
68 C3 **Mon** Burma
29 K7 **Møn** isld Denmark
127 L2 **Mona** Jamaica
103 N2 **Mona** Utah U.S.A.
94 G6 **Monaca** Pennsylvania U.S.A.
15 A3 **Monach I** Outer Hebrides Scotland
44 B4 **Monaco** princ W Europe
15 D3 **Monadhliath Mts** Scotland
29 J8 **Monå Fjärd** inlet Finland
128 F2 **Monagas** state Venezuela
14 E2 **Monaghan** co Ireland
14 E2 **Monaghan** Ireland
108 E4 **Monahans** Texas U.S.A.
127 L5 **Mona, I** Puerto Rico
98 H3 **Monango** North Dakota U.S.A.
87 C7 **Mona Quimbundo** Angola
118 D9 **Monarch** Alberta Canada
106 D3 **Monarch** Colorado U.S.A.
101 P2 **Monarch** Montana U.S.A.
117 L10 **Monarch Mt** British Columbia Canada
103 N2 **Mona Res** Utah U.S.A.
117 O10 **Monashee Mts** British Columbia Canada
14 D3 **Monasterevin** Ireland
18 H8 **Monastier, le** France
43 D13 **Monastir** Tunisia
48 J1 **Monastyriska** Ukraine
55 D2 **Monastyrskoye** Russian Federation
44 C2 **Moncalieri** Italy
16 B2 **Monção** Portugal
17 F3 **Moncayo, Sierra del** Spain
22 F4 **Monceau-le-Neuf** France
38 L5 **Mönchdorf** Austria
52 D1 **Monchegorsk** Russian Federation
36 B1 **Mönchengladbach** Germany
30 H1 **Mönchgut** pen Germany
16 B7 **Monchique** Portugal
101 R1 **Monchy** Saskatchewan Canada
112 G4 **Moncks Corner** South Carolina U.S.A.
124 J4 **Monclova** Mexico
20 E5 **Moncontour** Côtes d'Armor France
21 K8 **Moncontour** Vienne France
122 A5 **Moncouche, L** Quebec Canada
21 J8 **Moncoutant** France
122 H7 **Moncton** New Brunswick Canada
130 D10 **Mondai** Brazil
99 L8 **Mondamin** Iowa U.S.A.
45 N4 **Mondavio** Italy
130 C9 **Monday, R** Paraguay
16 B4 **Mondego** R Portugal
16 B4 **Mondego, C** Portugal
16 E4 **Mondéjar** Spain
21 K3 **Mondeville** France
89 G3 **Mondi** R Zimbabwe
89 G6 **Mondlo** S Africa
86 C3 **Mondo** Chad
45 O4 **Mondolfo** Italy
16 C1 **Mondoñedo** Spain
22 L4 **Mondorf-les-Bains** Luxembourg
21 M6 **Mondoubleau** France
44 C3 **Mondovi** Italy
99 P5 **Mondovi** Wisconsin U.S.A.
19 N16 **Mondragon** France
45 P7 **Mondragone** Italy
143 E10 **Mondrain I** W Australia Australia
41 P3 **Mondschein Spitze** mt Austria
38 H6 **Mondsee** Austria
127 K2 **Moneague** Jamaica
44 F3 **Moneglia** Italy
18 E9 **Monein** France
46 F8 **Monemvasía** Greece
94 H9 **Moneta** Virginia U.S.A.
101 S6 **Moneta** Wyoming U.S.A.
110 C5 **Monett** Missouri U.S.A.
110 F6 **Monette** Arkansas U.S.A.
42 F3 **Monfalcone** Italy
68 D3 **Mon Fang** Thailand
44 C2 **Monferrato** dist Italy
86 D5 **Monga** Zaire
95 N5 **Mongaup Vall** New York U.S.A.
68 H2 **Mong Cai** Vietnam
142 A1 **Monger L** Perth, W Aust Australia
143 B8 **Monger, L** W Australia Australia
68 D2 **Mong Hai** Burma
68 D2 **Mong Hang** Burma
45 K3 **Monghidoro** Italy
68 E2 **Mong Hkan** Burma
68 D2 **Mong Hkok** Burma
68 D2 **Mong Hpayak** Burma
68 D2 **Mong Hsat** Burma
68 C2 **Mong Hsawk** Burma
68 D2 **Mong Hsu** Burma
44 C3 **Mongioie** mt Italy
68 F6 **Mongkol Borey** Cambodia
68 D3 **Mong Kyawt** Burma
68 D2 **Mong La** Burma
68 E2 **Mong Lin** Burma
68 E2 **Mong Loi** Burma
68 C1 **Mong Long** Burma
68 C2 **Mong Long** Burma
68 C3 **Mong Mau** Burma
68 C2 **Mong Nai** Burma
68 D2 **Mong Nawng** Burma
17 H6 **Mongo** mt Spain
94 B5 **Mongo** Indiana U.S.A.
58 C2 **Mongolia** rep Asia
Mongolküre see **Zhaosu**
85 G8 **Mongomo** Mbini Equat Guinea
142 F3 **Mongona,Mt** W Australia Australia
86 B3 **Mongonu** Nigeria
68 C3 **Mong Pai** Burma
68 D2 **Mong Pan** Burma
68 D1 **Mong Pat** Burma
68 D1 **Mong Pawk** Burma
68 C2 **Mong Pawn** Burma
68 D2 **Mong Ping** Burma
68 D2 **Mong Pu** Burma
68 D2 **Mong Pu-awn** Burma
124 H9 **Mongrove, Pta** C Mexico
68 D2 **Mong Ton** Burma
68 D2 **Mong Tum** Burma
68 C1 **Mong Tung** Burma
87 D9 **Mongu** Zambia
38 F8 **Monguelfo** Italy
68 E2 **Mong Un** Burma
68 D1 **Mong Yai** Burma
68 D2 **Mong Yang** Burma
68 D2 **Mong Yawn** Burma
68 E2 **Mong Yawng** Burma
95 S3 **Monhegan I** Maine U.S.A.
37 K6 **Monheim** Bayern Germany
36 B1 **Monheim** Nordrhein-Westfalen Germany
113 E7 **Moniac** Georgia U.S.A.
12 E3 **Moniaive** Scotland
19 O16 **Monieux** France
13 F1 **Monifieth** Scotland
18 H7 **Monistrol-sur-Loire** France
118 G7 **Monitor** Alberta Canada
102 H3 **Monitor** pk Nevada U.S.A.
14 C3 **Monivea** Ireland
28 B7 **Mönkebüll** Germany
140 F6 **Monkira** Queensland Australia
86 D6 **Monkoto** Zaire
120 J9 **Monkton** Ontario Canada
12 D3 **Monkton** Scotland
99 Q9 **Monmouth** Illinois U.S.A.
95 R2 **Monmouth** Maine U.S.A.
8 D4 **Monmouth** Wales
117 M10 **Monmouth, Mt** British Columbia Canada
21 L4 **Monnai** France
21 M7 **Monnaie** France
25 D3 **Monnickendam** Netherlands
85 E7 **Mono** R Togo
102 F3 **Mono L** California U.S.A.
47 U17 **Monólithos** Rhodes Greece
95 S5 **Monomoy Pt** Massachusetts U.S.A.
99 U9 **Monon** Indiana U.S.A.
99 P6 **Monona** Iowa U.S.A.
94 G7 **Monongah** West Virginia U.S.A.
94 H6 **Monongahela** Pennsylvania U.S.A.
43 H8 **Monopoli** Italy
48 E3 **Monor** Hungary
127 N1 **Monos I** Trinidad
86 D2 **Monou** Chad
17 G6 **Monóvar** Spain
144 A6 **Monowai** New Zealand
98 H7 **Monowi** Nebraska U.S.A.
18 F8 **Monpont** France
36 C3 **Monreal** Germany
17 G4 **Monreal del Campo** Spain
43 E10 **Monreale** Sicily
102 A2 **Monroe** California U.S.A.
112 D4 **Monroe** Georgia U.S.A.
94 C6 **Monroe** Indiana U.S.A.
99 N8 **Monroe** Iowa U.S.A.
111 D9 **Monroe** Louisiana U.S.A.
94 D5 **Monroe** Michigan U.S.A.
95 N5 **Monroe** New York U.S.A.
112 G3 **Monroe** North Carolina U.S.A.
100 B5 **Monroe** Oregon U.S.A.
95 L5 **Monroe** Pennsylvania U.S.A.
98 J6 **Monroe** South Dakota U.S.A.
103 M3 **Monroe** Utah U.S.A.
94 H9 **Monroe** Virginia U.S.A.
100 D2 **Monroe** Washington U.S.A.
99 R7 **Monroe** Wisconsin U.S.A.
99 P10 **Monroe City** Missouri U.S.A.
113 F9 **Monroe, L** Florida U.S.A.
110 K2 **Monroe L** Indiana U.S.A.
111 J10 **Monroeville** Alabama U.S.A.
94 C6 **Monroeville** Indiana U.S.A.
94 E5 **Monroeville** Ohio U.S.A.
85 B7 **Monrovia** Liberia
102 G7 **Monrovia** California U.S.A.
17 G4 **Monroyo** Spain
22 F3 **Mons** Belgium
16 C4 **Monsanto** Portugal
130 H6 **Monsarás, Pta. de** Brazil
22 L2 **Monschau** Germany
71 H7 **Monse** Indonesia
42 D3 **Monselice** Italy
36 E4 **Monsheim** Germany
29 K7 **Møns Klint** cliffs Denmark
95 P4 **Monson** Massachusetts U.S.A.
68 C3 **Mon State** Burma
28 C4 **Mønsted** Denmark
25 B4 **Monster** Netherlands
27 H14 **Mönsterås** Sweden
45 J4 **Monsummano Terme** Italy
22 K3 **Mont** Belgium
36 D3 **Montabaur** Germany
41 L3 **Montafon** V Austria
45 K1 **Montagnana** Italy
89 B9 **Montagu** S Africa
122 K7 **Montague** Prince Edward I Canada
100 C8 **Montague** California U.S.A.
94 A3 **Montague** Michigan U.S.A.
109 K2 **Montague** Texas U.S.A.
139 K6 **Montague I** New South Wales Australia
103 K10 **Montague, I** Mexico
116 O6 **Montague I** Alaska U.S.A.
143 C7 **Montague Ra** W Australia Australia
142 F2 **Montague Sd** W Australia Australia
116 N7 **Montague Str** Alaska U.S.A.
146 G3 **Montagu I** S Sandwich Is S Atlantic Oc
20 H8 **Montaigu** France
18 F8 **Montaigu-de-Quercy** France
40 D7 **Montaimont** France
45 J4 **Montaione** Italy
70 D5 **Montalat** R Kalimantan
17 G4 **Montalbán** Spain
127 K9 **Montalbán** Venezuela
45 K4 **Montale** Italy
16 B3 **Montalegre** Portugal
40 B6 **Montalieu** France
19 O13 **Montalieu Vercieu** France
43 G10 **Montalto** mt Italy
21 L8 **Montamise** France
101 P3 **Montana** state U.S.A.
116 N5 **Montana** Alaska U.S.A.
40 G7 **Montanaro** Italy
16 C5 **Montánchez** Spain
121 T5 **Mont-Apica** Quebec Canada
18 G5 **Montargis** France
21 P3 **Montataire** France
18 F9 **Montauban** France
20 F5 **Montauban-de-Bretagne** France
21 J5 **Montaudin** France
18 H5 **Montbard** France
40 C3 **Montbarrey** France
21 M7 **Montbazon** France
40 E2 **Montbéliard** France
109 N6 **Mont Belvieu** Texas U.S.A.
40 D4 **Montbenoit** France
20 H7 **Montbert** France
40 E6 **Mont Blanc** mt France
17 H3 **Montblanch** Spain
Montblanc Vilanovai see **Montblanch Vilanuevay**
40 D3 **Montbozon** France
21 H4 **Montbray** France
18 H7 **Montbrison** France
Montcalm, L see **Dogai Coring**
18 F10 **Montcalm, Pic** mt France
21 J4 **Montchamp** France
22 G4 **Montcornet** France
18 E9 **Mont de Marsan** France
22 D4 **Montdidier** France
43 G9 **Montea** mt Italy
110 L6 **Monteagle** Tennessee U.S.A.
129 H4 **Monte Alegre** Brazil
17 G6 **Montealegre del Castillo** Spain
130 E6 **Monte Alegre de Minas** Brazil
130 G4 **Monte Azul** Brazil
121 Q7 **Montebello** Quebec Canada
142 B5 **Monte Bello Is** W Australia Australia
45 K1 **Montebello Vic** Italy
42 E3 **Montebelluna** Italy
20 H3 **Montebourg** France
45 N4 **Montecalvo in Foglia** Italy
45 S7 **Montecalvo Irpino** Italy
133 G3 **Montecarlo** Argentina
44 B4 **Monte-Carlo** Monaco
129 J7 **Monte Carmelo** Brazil
45 O4 **Montecarotto** Italy
131 F3 **Monte Caseros** Argentina
45 J4 **Montecatini Terme** Italy
45 J2 **Montécchio Emilia** Italy
45 K1 **Montecchio Maggiore** Italy
45 H2 **Montecchio nell'Emilia** Italy
45 N5 **Montecélio** Italy
18 F9 **Montech** France
112 H3 **Monte Clare** South Carolina U.S.A.
45 R8 **Montecorvino Rovella** Italy
45 J3 **Montecreto** Italy
127 J5 **Montecristi** Dominican Rep
128 F6 **Monte Cristo** Bolivia
42 C6 **Montecristo, I.di** Italy
41 O4 **Montecroce, Pta di** mt Italy
124 H6 **Monte Escobedo** Mexico
45 M4 **Montefeltro** Italy
45 J3 **Montefiorino** Italy
45 R8 **Monteforte Irpina** Italy
16 E7 **Montefrio** Spain
127 J1 **Montego Bay** Jamaica
45 M4 **Monte Grimano** Italy
130 H9 **Monteiro** Brazil
140 B3 **Montejinnie** N Terr Australia
45 O6 **Montelanico** Italy
131 E6 **Monte, L.del** Argentina
19 N15 **Montélimar** France
129 G8 **Monte Lindo** Paraguay
108 G6 **Montell** Texas U.S.A.
45 S8 **Montella** Italy
16 D8 **Montellanto** Spain
101 L8 **Montello** Nevada U.S.A.
99 R6 **Montello** Wisconsin U.S.A.
45 K4 **Montelupo Fiorentino** Italy
45 R8 **Montemárano** Italy
45 O4 **Montemarciano** Italy
133 D6 **Montemayor, Meseta de** hills Argentina
45 L4 **Montemignaio** Italy
45 R7 **Montemiletto** Italy
125 K5 **Montemorelos** Mexico
45 K4 **Montemurio** Italy
21 J5 **Montenay** France
18 E7 **Montendre** France
46 C2 **Montenegro** reg Yugoslavia
46 C2 **Montenegro** rep Yugoslavia
20 F6 **Monteneuf** France
42 D6 **Montepescali** Italy
127 K5 **Monte Plata** Dominican Rep
45 O4 **Monteporzio** Italy
88 G8 **Montepuez** Mozambique
42 D5 **Montepulciano** Italy
18 G4 **Montereau** France
45 K3 **Monterenzio** Italy
102 C5 **Monterey** California U.S.A.
99 U8 **Monterey** Indiana U.S.A.
110 L5 **Monterey** Tennessee U.S.A.
94 H8 **Monterey** Virginia U.S.A.
102 B5 **Monterey B** California U.S.A.
126 G10 **Montería** Colombia
128 F7 **Montero** Bolivia
21 N2 **Montérolier** France
45 M5 **Monterosi** Italy
44 M5 **Monterosi, L** Italy
45 N5 **Monterotondo** Italy
125 J5 **Monterrey** Mexico
42 G7 **Monte S. Angelo** Italy
100 B3 **Montesano** Washington U.S.A.
130 G11 **Monte Santo** Brazil
130 F7 **Monte Santo de Minas** Brazil
45 R7 **Montesarchio** Italy
45 O7 **Monte S. Biágio** Italy
129 K7 **Montes Claros** Brazil
45 J3 **Montese** Italy
45 O4 **Montesicuro** Italy
45 K4 **Montespértoli** Italy
18 F9 **Montesquieu-Volvestre** France
18 H6 **Montet, le** France
19 N16 **Monteux** France
111 K8 **Montevallo** Alabama U.S.A.
42 D5 **Montevarchi** Italy
45 K3 **Monteveglio** Italy
45 O5 **Monte Velino** Italy
131 G5 **Montevideo** Uruguay
99 L5 **Montevideo** Minnesota U.S.A.
101 N6 **Monteview** Idaho U.S.A.
106 D4 **Monte Vista** Colorado U.S.A.
103 L8 **Montezuma** Arizona U.S.A.
112 C5 **Montezuma** Georgia U.S.A.
99 T10 **Montezuma** Indiana U.S.A.
99 O8 **Montezuma** Iowa U.S.A.
107 K4 **Montezuma** Kansas U.S.A.
106 E6 **Montezuma** New Mexico U.S.A.
103 N7 **Montezuma Castle Nat.Mon** Arizona U.S.A.
102 G4 **Montezuma Pk** Nevada U.S.A.
20 H2 **Montfarville** France
21 H7 **Montfaucon** Maine-et-Loire France
22 J5 **Montfaucon** Meuse France
19 P14 **Montferrat** France
21 O4 **Montfort-l'Amaury** France
21 L5 **Montfort-le-Rotrou** France
20 G5 **Montfort-sur-Meu** France
21 M3 **Montfort-sur-Risle** France
19 N17 **Montfrin** France
111 K9 **Montgomery** Alabama U.S.A.
111 D10 **Montgomery** Louisiana U.S.A.
94 C5 **Montgomery** Michigan U.S.A.
99 N5 **Montgomery** Minnesota U.S.A.
109 M5 **Montgomery** Texas U.S.A.
94 F8 **Montgomery** West Virginia U.S.A.
8 C2 **Montgomery** Wales
110 E3 **Montgomery City** Missouri U.S.A.
100 D9 **Montgomery Creek** California U.S.A.
142 E3 **Montgomery I** W Australia Australia
18 E7 **Montguyon** France
22 H4 **Monthermé** France
40 E5 **Monthey** Switzerland
22 H5 **Monthois** France
40 C1 **Monthureux-sur-Saône** France
43 C8 **Monti** Sardinia
111 E8 **Monticello** Arkansas U.S.A.
113 D7 **Monticello** Florida U.S.A.
112 D4 **Monticello** Georgia U.S.A.
110 H1 **Monticello** Illinois U.S.A.
110 K1 **Monticello** Indiana U.S.A.
99 P7 **Monticello** Iowa U.S.A.
110 M5 **Monticello** Kentucky U.S.A.
95 T7 **Monticello** Maine U.S.A.
99 N4 **Monticello** Minnesota U.S.A.
111 F10 **Monticello** Mississippi U.S.A.
110 E1 **Monticello** Missouri U.S.A.
106 C8 **Monticello** New Mexico U.S.A.
95 N5 **Monticello** New York U.S.A.
103 P4 **Monticello** Utah U.S.A.
99 R7 **Monticello** Wisconsin U.S.A.
45 J1 **Montichiari** Italy
43 C8 **Monti del Gennargentu** Sardinia
131 F3 **Montiel, Cuchilla de** mts Argentina
21 O8 **Montierchaume** France
19 J4 **Montier en Der** France
22 D5 **Montiers** France
18 F7 **Montignac** France
18 F7 **Montignac-Charente** France
21 H4 **Montigny** Manche France
36 B6 **Montigny** Meurthe-et-Moselle France
40 B2 **Montigny-le-Roi** France
16 B6 **Montijo** Portugal
16 C6 **Montijo** Spain
125 O6 **Montijo, G.de** Panama
16 D7 **Montilla** Spain
21 O8 **Montipouret** France
45 N5 **Monti Sabini** Italy
130 D5 **Montividiu** Brazil
21 L2 **Montivilliers** France
21 J7 **Montjean** Maine-et-Loire France
21 J5 **Montjean** Mayenne France
21 H4 **Montjoie** France
122 D5 **Mont-Joli** Quebec Canada
138 F2 **Montkeleary** R South Australia Australia
21 N5 **Montlandon** France
121 P6 **Mont-Laurier** Quebec Canada
40 E3 **Montlebon** France
21 P4 **Montlhéry** France
18 E7 **Montlieu** France
122 G4 **Mont Louis** Quebec Canada
18 G10 **Mont Louis** France
18 G6 **Montluçon** France
19 O13 **Montluel** France
122 B7 **Montmagny** Quebec Canada
20 G4 **Montmartin-sur-Mer** France
119 O8 **Montmartre** Saskatchewan Canada
22 J4 **Montmédy** France
19 Q14 **Montmélian** France
40 A5 **Montmerle** France
19 Q17 **Montmeyan** France
19 N15 **Montmeyran** France
18 H4 **Montmirail** Marne France
21 M5 **Montmirail** Sarthe France
18 F7 **Montmoreau St Cybard** France
21 P4 **Montmorency** France
122 A6 **Montmorency, R** Quebec Canada
18 F6 **Montmorillon** France
19 P16 **Montmorin** France
141 K6 **Monto** Queensland Australia
20 F7 **Montoir-de-Bretagne** France
21 M6 **Montoire-sur-le-Loir** France
45 M3 **Montone** R Italy
16 E6 **Montoro** Spain
99 O8 **Montour** Iowa U.S.A.
95 L4 **Montour Falls** New York U.S.A.
21 J8 **Montournais** France
95 L5 **Montoursville** Pennsylvania U.S.A.
106 F6 **Montoya** New Mexico U.S.A.
127 J2 **Montpelier** Jamaica
101 O7 **Montpelier** Idaho U.S.A.
110 L1 **Montpelier** Indiana U.S.A.
98 H3 **Montpelier** North Dakota U.S.A.
94 C5 **Montpelier** Ohio U.S.A.
95 P2 **Montpelier** Vermont U.S.A.
121 P7 **Montpellier** Quebec Canada
18 H9 **Montpellier** France
40 B4 **Montpont** France
120 K5 **Montreal** R Ontario Canada
121 R7 **Montréal** Quebec Canada
18 G9 **Montréal** France
99 Q3 **Montreal** Wisconsin U.S.A.
120 F5 **Montreal I** Ontario Canada
119 M4 **Montreal Lake** Saskatchewan Canada
119 M4 **Montreal R** Saskatchewan Canada
120 F5 **Montreal River** Ontario Canada
18 G9 **Montredon Labessonié** France
18 F9 **Montrejeau** France
21 N7 **Montrésor** France
22 B3 **Montreuil** France
21 K7 **Montreuil Bellay** France
21 K5 **Montreuil-le-Chetif** France
20 G5 **Montreuil-sur-Ille** France
40 E5 **Montreux** Switzerland
21 H7 **Montrevault** France
21 N7 **Montrichard** France
19 P18 **Montrieux le Vieux** France
6 L5 **Montrose** oil rig North Sea
15 F4 **Montrose** Scotland
111 E8 **Montrose** Arkansas U.S.A.
106 C3 **Montrose** Colorado U.S.A.
110 H2 **Montrose** Illinois U.S.A.
99 P9 **Montrose** Iowa U.S.A.
98 C7 **Montrose** Nebraska U.S.A.
95 L5 **Montrose** Pennsylvania U.S.A.
98 J6 **Montrose** South Dakota U.S.A.
95 L8 **Montross** Virginia U.S.A.
22 G3 **Mont. St.Christophe** Belgium
22 H2 **Mont.St.Guibert** Belgium
22 G2 **Mont-St.Jean** Belgium
22 K4 **Mont St.Martin** France
20 G4 **Mont-St. Michel, B. du** France
20 G4 **Mont-St.Michel, le** France
21 J4 **Montsecret** France
17 H2 **Montseny** mt Spain
17 J3 **Montseny, Sierra de** mts Spain
127 N6 **Montserrat** isld Lesser Antilles
17 J3 **Montserrat** dist Spain
129 H3 **Montsinery** Fr Guiana
21 L7 **Montsoreau** France
21 P3 **Montsoult** France
115 N8 **Monts, Pointe des** Quebec Canada
21 L8 **Mont-sur-Guesnes** France
21 J5 **Montsûrs** France
121 Q6 **Mont Tremblant** Quebec Canada
21 L4 **Montviette** France
95 P5 **Montville** Connecticut U.S.A.
106 F2 **Monument** Colorado U.S.A.
107 J2 **Monument** Kansas U.S.A.
108 D3 **Monument** New Mexico U.S.A.
100 F5 **Monument** Oregon U.S.A.
116 F4 **Monument Mt** Alaska U.S.A.
103 O4 **Monument V** Utah/Ariz U.S.A.
86 D5 **Monveda** Zaire
21 N2 **Monville** France
68 B1 **Monywa** Burma
41 K6 **Monza** Italy
87 E9 **Monze** Zambia
17 H3 **Monzón** Spain
45 K3 **Monzuno** Italy
109 K4 **Moody** Texas U.S.A.
95 O2 **Mooers** New York U.S.A.
138 E3 **Moolawatana** South Australia Australia
138 E2 **Moolionburrinna, L** South Australia Australia
138 F3 **Moomba Oil & Gas Field** South Australia Australia
139 J3 **Moomin** R New South Wales Australia
138 D4 **Moonaree** South Australia Australia
120 H3 **Moonbeam** Ontario Canada
140 F7 **Moonda L** Queensland Australia
141 J8 **Moonie** R Queensland Australia
141 K8 **Moonie** Queensland Australia
103 O1 **Moon L.Res** Utah U.S.A.
139 K4 **Moonoi Ra** mts New South Wales Australia
138 D5 **Moonta** South Australia Australia
143 B9 **Moora** W Australia Australia
140 F7 **Mooraberree** Queensland Australia
98 B5 **Moorcroft** Wyoming U.S.A.
101 M6 **Moore** Idaho U.S.A.
101 Q3 **Moore** Montana U.S.A.
107 N6 **Moore** Oklahoma U.S.A.
109 H6 **Moore** Texas U.S.A.
134 A11 **Moorea** isld Society Is Pacific Oc
116 J5 **Moore Creek** Alaska U.S.A.
98 F9 **Moorefield** Nebraska U.S.A.
94 J7 **Moorefield** West Virginia U.S.A.
113 F11 **Moore Haven** Florida U.S.A.
143 C8 **Moore, L** W Australia Australia
108 E7 **Mooreland** Oklahoma U.S.A.
140 D2 **Moore, Mt** N Terr Australia
143 E7 **Moore, Mt** W Australia Australia
143 C9 **Moore, Mt** W Australia Australia
143 A8 **Moore, Pt** W Australia Australia
95 Q2 **Moore Res** Vermont U.S.A.
112 J3 **Moores Cr. Nat. Mil. Park** North Carolina U.S.A.
113 K11 **Moore's I** Bahamas
122 E8 **Moore's Mills** New Brunswick Canada
110 K2 **Mooresville** Indiana U.S.A.
112 G2 **Mooresville** North Carolina U.S.A.
98 J3 **Mooreton** North Dakota U.S.A.
127 M2 **Moore Town** Jamaica
13 E2 **Moorfoot Hills** Scotland
98 K3 **Moorhead** Minnesota U.S.A.
111 F8 **Moorhead** Mississippi U.S.A.
101 U4 **Moorhead** Montana U.S.A.
109 O3 **Mooringsport** Louisiana U.S.A.
121 N6 **Moor Lake** Ontario Canada
99 M7 **Moorland** Iowa U.S.A.
110 J4 **Moorman** Kentucky U.S.A.
139 G5 **Moornanyah L** New South Wales Australia
87 F7 **Moorokosa** Zambia
141 K2 **Moorooka** dist Brisbane, Qnsld Australia
140 D1 **Mooroongga I** N Terr Australia
139 H6 **Mooroopna** Victoria Australia
102 F7 **Moorpark** California U.S.A.
22 G2 **Moorsel** Belgium
22 E2 **Moorslede** Belgium
89 F5 **Moos** R S Africa
37 N4 **Moosbach** Germany
32 L9 **Moosberg** mt Germany
37 M7 **Moosburg** Germany
120 J2 **Moose** R Ontario Canada
101 P6 **Moose** Wyoming U.S.A.
120 K1 **Moose Factory** Ontario Canada
95 S1 **Moosehead L** Maine U.S.A.
119 O2 **Moose Hill** Ontario Canada
119 T7 **Moosehorn** Manitoba Canada
119 U7 **Moose I** Manitoba Canada
119 M8 **Moose Jaw** Saskatchewan Canada
119 N8 **Moosejaw Cr** Saskatchewan Canada
99 O3 **Moose L** Minnesota U.S.A.
119 R5 **Moose Lake** Manitoba Canada
95 R2 **Mooselookmeguntic L** Maine U.S.A.
119 P9 **Moose Mt. Prov. Park** Saskatchewan Canada

119 W2 Moose Nose L Manitoba Canada
116 N6 Moose Pass Alaska U.S.A.
120 J2 Moose River Ontario Canada
37 N6 Moosham Germany
38 M8 Mooskirchen Austria
119 Q8 Moosomin Saskatchewan Canada
120 K1 Moosonee Ontario Canada
95 Q5 Moosup Connecticut U.S.A.
89 G7 Moot R S Africa
138 F4 Mootwingee New South Wales Australia
87 G9 Mopeia Mozambique
85 D6 Mopti Mali
77 K3 Moqor Afghanistan
99 P3 Moquah Wisconsin U.S.A.
128 D7 Moquegua dept Peru
128 D7 Moquegua Peru
48 E3 Mór Hungary
86 B3 Mora Cameroon
16 B6 Mora Portugal
16 E5 Mora Spain
27 G10 Mora Sweden
100 J6 Mora Idaho U.S.A.
99 N4 Mora Minnesota U.S.A.
106 E6 Mora New Mexico U.S.A.
46 C2 Morača R Montenegro Yugoslavia
131 B5 Mora, Cerro pk Arg/Chile
74 H4 Moradabad India
16 B5 Moradal, Sa. do mts Portugal
130 F6 Morada Nova de Minas Brazil
17 H3 Mora de Ebro Spain
17 G4 Mora de Rubielos Spain
87 G11 Morafenobe Madagascar
31 M2 Morąg Poland
83 K11 Moragala Sri Lanka
133 C6 Moraleda, Canal str Chile
109 L6 Morales Texas U.S.A.
87 H11 Moramanga Madagascar
110 A4 Moran Kansas U.S.A.
109 H3 Moran Texas U.S.A.
101 P6 Moran Wyoming U.S.A.
141 J5 Moranbah Queensland Australia
21 K6 Morannes France
43 G9 Morano Cal Italy
126 G6 Morant Cays reefs W Indies
16 C1 Morás C Spain
15 E4 Moras R Spain
16 E4 Morata de T Spain
17 F6 Moratalla Spain
83 J11 Moratuwa Sri Lanka
31 K7 Morava R Czech Rep/ Slovakia
48 G6 Morava R Serbia Yugoslavia
48 D1 Moravia old reg Czech Rep
99 O9 Moravia Iowa U.S.A.
95 L4 Moravia New York U.S.A.
46 D1 Moravica R Serbia Yugoslavia
31 K6 Moravice R Czech Rep
31 K6 Moravská Třebová Czech Rep
31 J6 Moravské Budějovice Czech Rep
143 B8 Morawa W Australia Australia
128 G2 Morawhanna Guyana
141 H5 Moray Downs Queensland Australia
15 E3 Moray Firth Scotland
140 B3 Moray Ra N Terr Australia
36 C4 Morbach Germany
22 C2 Morbecque France
41 L5 Morbegno Italy
74 D7 Morbi India
20 E6 Morbihan, le B France
27 H15 Mörbylånga Sweden
18 E8 Morcenx France
45 N4 Morciano di Romagna Italy
124 G5 Morcillo Mexico
45 R7 Morcone Italy
9 F2 Morcott England
59 H1 Mordaga China
20 G5 Mordelles France
98 H1 Morden Manitoba Canada
122 H8 Morden Nova Scotia Canada
139 H7 Mordialloc Victoria Australia
52 H4 Mordino Russian Federation
53 F7 Mordovskaya Respublika Russian Federation
116 E9 Mordvinof, C Aleutian Is
31 N3 Mordy Poland
20 A6 Moréac France
98 E4 Moreau R South Dakota U.S.A.
111 E10 Moreauville Louisiana U.S.A.
13 F3 Morebattle Scotland
13 F5 Morecambe England
7 H9 Morecambe oil rig Irish Sea
16 E7 Moreda Spain
139 J3 Moree New South Wales Australia
21 N6 Morée France
141 G2 Morehead R Queensland Australia
94 D8 Morehead Kentucky U.S.A.
112 L3 Morehead City North Carolina U.S.A.
110 G5 Morehouse Missouri U.S.A.
128 F4 Moreira Brazil
101 N6 Moreland Idaho U.S.A.
124 J8 Morelia Mexico
141 G6 Morella Queensland Australia
124 H6 Morelos Mexico
74 H5 Morena India
102 H9 Morena Res California U.S.A.
16 C7 Morena, Sa mts Spain
103 P8 Morenci Arizona U.S.A.
94 C5 Morenci Michigan U.S.A.
48 K6 Moreni Romania
124 D3 Moreno Mexico
26 C9 More og Romsdal reg Norway
145 F3 Morere New Zealand
12 E4 Moresby England
22 K2 Moresnet Belgium
40 B6 Morestel France
18 G4 Moret France
141 L7 Moreton B Queensland Australia
8 C6 Moretonhampstead England
141 L7 Moreton I Queensland Australia
9 E4 Moreton in Marsh England
95 P2 Moretown Vermont U.S.A.
21 P2 Moreuil France
40 D4 Morez France
36 F4 Mörfelden Germany
29 M3 Morgam Viibus mt Finland
138 E5 Morgan South Australia Australia
112 C6 Morgan Georgia U.S.A.
109 K3 Morgan Texas U.S.A.
101 O8 Morgan Utah U.S.A.
110 J4 Morganfield Kentucky U.S.A.
102 C4 Morgan Hill California U.S.A.
109 J3 Morgan Mill Texas U.S.A.
140 D4 Morgan, Mt N Terr Australia
102 F4 Morgan, Mt California U.S.A.
113 K12 Morgan's Bluff Bahamas
112 F2 Morganton North Carolina U.S.A.
110 K2 Morgantown Indiana U.S.A.
110 K4 Morgantown Kentucky U.S.A.
111 F10 Morgantown Mississippi U.S.A.
94 H7 Morgantown West Virginia U.S.A.
111 E11 Morganza Louisiana U.S.A.
20 A5 Morgat France
40 E4 Morges Switzerland
40 F6 Morgex Italy
21 O3 Morgny France
36 B6 Morhange France
22 K4 Morhet Belgium
122 K2 Morhiban, L.de Quebec Canada
66 E3 Mori China
41 N6 Mori Italy
60 O3 Mori Japan
127 M2 Moriah Tobago
95 O2 Moriah New York U.S.A.
103 K2 Moriah, Mt Nevada U.S.A.
22 H3 Morialme Belgium
108 A1 Moriarty New Mexico U.S.A.
141 H8 Moriarty's Ra Queensland Australia
117 K8 Morice L British Columbia Canada
128 D3 Morichal Colombia
45 N5 Moricone Italy
118 J4 Morin Creek Saskatchewan Canada
59 H2 Morin Dawa China
32 L9 Moringen Germany
52 D5 Morino Russian Federation
118 D5 Morinville Alberta Canada
61 P6 Morioka Japan
124 E3 Moris Mexico
139 K5 Morisset New South Wales Australia
122 B7 Morisset Sta Quebec Canada
32 L8 Moritzberg Germany
37 L5 Moritzberg mt Germany
61 O6 Moriyashi-zan mt Japan
138 F5 Morkalla Victoria Australia
28 E4 Mørke Denmark
52 G6 Morki Russian Federation
28 G5 Mørkøv Denmark
21 M5 Morlaix France
107 K2 Morland Kansas U.S.A.
36 F4 Mörlenbach Germany
118 C7 Morley Alberta Canada
13 G6 Morley England
106 F4 Morley Colorado U.S.A.
110 G4 Morley Missouri U.S.A.
117 G5 Morley River Yukon Territory Canada
45 N5 Morlupe Italy
43 G9 Mormanno Italy
19 O16 Mormoiron France
103 N7 Mormon L Arizona U.S.A.
101 L4 Mormon Mt Idaho U.S.A.
103 K5 Mormon Mts Nevada U.S.A.
19 N13 Mornant France
19 N16 Mornas France
83 M14 Morne, Pte Kerguelen Indian Oc
141 F7 Morney R Queensland Australia
141 F7 Morney Queensland Australia
140 F4 Morning Inlet R Queensland Australia
141 K1 Morningside dist Brisbane, Qnsld Australia
99 P8 Morning Sun Iowa U.S.A.
140 E3 Mornington Queensland Australia
140 E3 Mornington I Queensland Australia
133 B7 Mornington, I Chile
46 E6 Mórnos R Greece
28 F2 Mornshausen Germany
37 L6 Mörnsheim Germany
110 F7 Moro Arkansas U.S.A.
100 E4 Moro Oregon U.S.A.
136 K3 Morobe Papua New Guinea
85 C3 Morocco kingdom N Africa
99 T9 Morocco Indiana U.S.A.
88 F5 Morogoro Tanzania
71 F7 Moro Gulf Philippines
89 C6 Morokweng S Africa
124 J7 Moroleón Mexico
71 J7 Moromaho isld Indonesia
87 G12 Morombe Madagascar
126 E3 Morón Cuba
58 D2 Mörön Mongolia
40 F3 Moron mt Switzerland
127 K9 Morón Venezuela
128 C4 Morona Ecuador
128 C4 Morona-Santiago prov Ecuador
87 G12 Morondava Madagascar
17 F3 Morón de Almazán Spain
16 D7 Morón de la Frontera Spain
87 G10 Moroni Comoros
103 N2 Moroni Utah U.S.A.
66 E5 Moron Us He R China
61 K11 Morosaki Japan
71 B1 Morotai isld Halmahera Indonesia
48 E5 Morović Serbia Yugoslavia
70 G5 Morowali Sulawesi
55 D2 Morozkovo Russian Federation
120 J10 Morpeth Ontario Canada
13 G3 Morpeth England
79 C3 Morphou B Cyprus
94 D6 Morral Ohio U.S.A.
130 E9 Morretes Brazil
99 L10 Morrill Kansas U.S.A.
98 C8 Morrill Nebraska U.S.A.
110 D6 Morrilton Arkansas U.S.A.
118 E7 Morrin Alberta Canada
130 E5 Morrinhos Brazil
145 E2 Morrinsville New Zealand
119 U9 Morris Manitoba Canada
99 S8 Morris Illinois U.S.A.
99 L4 Morris Minnesota U.S.A.
95 M4 Morris New York U.S.A.
107 P6 Morris Oklahoma U.S.A.
95 K5 Morris Pennsylvania U.S.A.
121 P8 Morrisburg Ontario Canada
112 H5 Morris I South Carolina U.S.A.
138 B2 Morris, Mt South Australia Australia
142 D4 Morris, Mt W Australia Australia
99 R8 Morrison Illinois U.S.A.
107 O5 Morrison Oklahoma U.S.A.
110 L6 Morrison Tennessee U.S.A.
144 C6 Morrisons New Zealand
94 C6 Morrisonville Illinois U.S.A.
113 E8 Morriston Florida U.S.A.
8 C4 Morriston Wales
103 M8 Morristown Arizona U.S.A.
99 N5 Morristown Minnesota U.S.A.
95 N6 Morristown New Jersey U.S.A.
95 M2 Morristown New York U.S.A.
98 E4 Morristown South Dakota U.S.A.
112 D1 Morristown Tennessee U.S.A.
95 M4 Morrisville New York U.S.A.
95 N6 Morrisville Pennsylvania U.S.A.
95 P2 Morrisville Vermont U.S.A.
94 K8 Morrisville Virginia U.S.A.
130 E7 Morro Brazil
130 F6 Morro Agudo Brazil
102 D6 Morro B California U.S.A.
131 H7 Morro d'Anta Brazil
131 A8 Morro del Compas C Chile
129 G6 Morro Do Sinal Brazil
133 C3 Morro, Pta Chile
131 D4 Morro, Sa. del pk Argentina
126 G10 Morrosquillo, G. de Colombia
111 D11 Morrow Louisiana U.S.A.
94 D7 Morrow Ohio U.S.A.
88 E10 Morrumbala Mozambique
87 G10 Morrumbene Mozambique
28 B3 Mors isld Denmark
20 H2 Morsalines France
36 D2 Morsbach Germany
36 E3 Mörsch Germany
37 M2 Mörsdorf Germany
118 K8 Morse Saskatchewan Canada
111 D11 Morse Louisiana U.S.A.
108 C7 Morse Texas U.S.A.
53 F7 Morshansk Russian Federation
52 D3 Morskaya Maselga Russian Federation
27 E11 Morskogen Norway
33 O8 Morsleben Germany
120 J8 Morson Ontario Canada
43 B13 Morsott Algeria
140 E4 Morstone Queensland Australia
28 A7 Morsum Germany
26 H4 Morsvik Norway
140 F5 Mort R Queensland Australia
36 B7 Mortagne R France
21 M4 Mortagne-au-Perche France
127 J10 Mortagne-sur-Sèvre France
16 B4 Mortágua Portugal
21 J4 Mortain France
138 C5 Mortana South Australia Australia
41 J7 Mortara Italy
40 E3 Morteau France
21 K4 Morteaux-Coulibœuf France
16 E4 Mortehoe England
130 G7 Mortes R Brazil
129 H6 Mortes, Rio das R Brazil
22 F4 Mortiers France
8 D3 Mortimers Cross England
118 L8 Mortlach Saskatchewan Canada
139 G7 Mortlake Victoria Australia
99 R9 Morton Illinois U.S.A.
99 M5 Morton Minnesota U.S.A.
111 G9 Morton Mississippi U.S.A.
108 E2 Morton Texas U.S.A.
100 C3 Morton Washington U.S.A.
139 J5 Morton Nat Park New South Wales Australia
110 J4 Mortons Gap Kentucky U.S.A.
21 L4 Mortrée France
22 G1 Mortsel Belgium
28 E6 Morud Denmark
127 O3 Moruga Trinidad
139 H5 Morundah New South Wales Australia
139 K6 Moruya New South Wales Australia
18 H5 Morvan mts France
141 H7 Morven Queensland Australia
144 C6 Morven New Zealand
15 E2 Morven mt Scotland
113 D7 Morven Georgia U.S.A.
112 G3 Morven North Carolina U.S.A.
15 C4 Morvern Scotland
8 D2 Morville England
56 B3 Moryakovskiy Zaton Russian Federation
52 F2 Morzhovets, Os isld Russian Federation
116 F9 Morzhovoi B Alaska U.S.A.
54 F2 Mosal'sk Russian Federation
28 E1 Mosbjerg Denmark
101 S2 Mosby Montana U.S.A.
Moscow see Moskva
100 J3 Moscow Idaho U.S.A.
107 J4 Moscow Kansas U.S.A.
110 F3 Moscow Missouri U.S.A.
110 M3 Moscow Ohio U.S.A.
95 M5 Moscow Pennsylvania U.S.A.
110 G6 Moscow Tennessee U.S.A.
146 F14 Moscow University Ice Shelf ice shelf Antarctica
146 E14 Mose, C Antarctica
36 C3 Mosel R Germany
37 N2 Mosel Germany
94 K9 Moseley Virginia U.S.A.
36 C3 Mosel Kern Germany
36 B5 Moselle dept France
40 E1 Moselle R France
111 G10 Moselle Mississippi U.S.A.
40 E2 Moselotte R France
123 K9 Moser River Nova Scotia Canada
106 G5 Moses New Mexico U.S.A.
100 F2 Moses Coulee R Washington U.S.A.
100 H9 Moses, Mt Nevada U.S.A.
116 F4 Moses Point Alaska U.S.A.
60 P2 Moseushi Japan
52 G2 Moseyevo Russian Federation
144 C6 Mosgiel New Zealand
52 F4 Mosha R Russian Federation
52 C5 Moshchnyy, Ostrov isld Russian Federation
112 E1 Mosheim Tennessee U.S.A.
120 F4 Mosher Ontario Canada
88 F3 Moshi Tanzania
52 F6 Moshok Russian Federation
52 H3 Mosh'yuga Russian Federation
33 Q9 Mosigkau Germany
31 K3 Mosina Poland
99 R5 Mosinee Wisconsin U.S.A.
26 F6 Mosjøen Norway
55 F3 Moskalenki Russian Federation
59 M1 Moskal'vo Russian Federation
98 B5 Moskee Wyoming U.S.A.
26 F4 Moskenes Norway
26 F4 Moskenesöy isld Norway
26 F4 Moskenstraumen isld Norway
26 M4 Moskijärvi Sweden
26 L6 Moskosel Sweden
29 M4 Moskuvaara Finland
49 Moskva conurbation Russian Federation
54 G1 Moskva R Russian Federation
56 D4 Moskva, Gora mt Russian Federation
54 J1 Moskvy, Kanal Imeni Russian Federation
42 H3 Moslavačka Gora mt Croatia
21 N7 Mosnes France
41 O4 Moso Italy
87 E10 Mosomane Botswana
48 D3 Mosonmagyaróvar Hungary
89 D5 Mosopa Botswana
54 C6 Mospino Ukraine
128 C3 Mosquera Colombia
125 M2 Mosquitia reg Honduras
130 C9 Mosquito R Brazil
94 F5 Mosquito Cr.Res Ohio U.S.A.
113 G9 Mosquito Lagoon Florida U.S.A.
125 N3 Mosquitos, Costa de Nicaragua
27 E12 Moss Norway
130 E5 Mossâmedes Brazil
118 L9 Mossbank Saskatchewan Canada
15 G2 Mossbank Scotland
144 B6 Mossburn New Zealand
89 C10 Mosselbaai S Africa
86 B6 Mossendjo Congo
139 G5 Mossgiel New South Wales Australia
36 G7 Mössingen Germany
119 T1 Moss L Manitoba Canada
13 F6 Mossley England
141 H3 Mossman Queensland Australia
28 D4 Mossø L Denmark
129 L5 Mossoró Brazil
13 F3 Mosspaul Scotland
111 H11 Moss Point Mississippi U.S.A.
88 H9 Mossuril Mozambique
139 K5 Moss Vale New South Wales Australia
113 A7 Mossy Head Florida U.S.A.
119 Q6 Mossy Pt Manitoba Canada
119 O4 Mossy R Saskatchewan Canada
100 C3 Mossyrock Washington U.S.A.
47 H3 Most Bulgaria
30 H5 Most Czech Rep
17 H9 Mostaganem Algeria
42 H5 Mostar Bosnia-Herzegovina
31 O6 Mostiska Ukraine
55 C3 Mostovaya Russian Federation
55 E3 Mostovskoye Russian Federation
31 P2 Mosty Belarus
70 F2 Mostyn Sabah
8 C1 Mostyn Wales
27 C12 Mös-vatn L Norway
26 E8 Mosvik Norway
86 G3 Mot'a Ethiopia
86 C5 Motaba R Congo
17 F5 Mota del Cuervo Spain
16 D3 Mota del Marqués Spain
125 O10 Motagua R Guatemala
27 H13 Motala Sweden
127 J10 Motatán Venezuela
61 O9 Motegi Japan
20 G8 Mothe-Achard, la France
116 J8 Mother Goose L Alaska U.S.A.
12 E2 Motherwell Scotland
58 D5 Motian Ling mt ra China
40 F4 Môtier Switzerland
75 L5 Motihari India
71 A2 Moti, I California U.S.A.
17 F5 Motilla del Palancar Spain
145 F2 Motiti I New Zealand
27 G12 Motjärnshyttan Sweden
99 M3 Motley Minnesota U.S.A.
89 F3 Motloutse R Botswana
89 E5 Motokwe Botswana
60 O4 Motomachi Japan
71 J4 Motongkat Sulawesi
52 D1 Motovskiy Zaliv G Russian Federation
42 F3 Motovun Croatia
60 G12 Motoyama Japan
61 N13 Moto-yama pk Iwo Jima Japan
61 P7 Motoyoshi Japan
16 E8 Motril Spain
48 H6 Motru Romania
61 N3 Motsuta misaki C Japan
98 D3 Mott North Dakota U.S.A.
45 J1 Motteggiana Italy
20 E5 Motte, la France
36 H3 Motten Germany
41 M2 Motteville France
145 F3 Motu New Zealand
145 G3 Motu Ahiauru New Zealand
145 D4 Motueka New Zealand
145 F2 Motuhora I New Zealand
144 D5 Motukarara New Zealand
145 D1 Motukawanui I New Zealand
Motukorea I see Browns I
144 D5 Motunau Beach New Zealand
144 D5 Motunau I New Zealand
135 L10 Motu One isld Society Is Pacific Oc
145 G3 Motuoroi I New Zealand
145 D4 Motupiko New Zealand
145 F2 Motu R New Zealand
145 D1 Moturoa Is New Zealand
145 E3 Motutaiko I New Zealand
145 D1 Motutangi New Zealand
145 E2 Motutapu I New Zealand
28 E3 Mou Denmark
122 C2 Mouchalagane R. Quebec Canada
21 H8 Mouchamps France
127 J4 Mouchoir Passage Caribbean
46 G6 Moúdhros Greece
85 B5 Moudjéria Mauritania
40 E4 Moudon Switzerland
86 B6 Mouila Gabon
21 J8 Mouilleron-en-Pareds France
86 D4 Mouka Cent Afr Republic
139 G6 Moulamein New South Wales Australia
16 C10 Moulay-Bouselham Morocco
114 H2 Mould Bay Northwest Territories Canada
127 N4 Moule Guadeloupe W Indies
86 H3 Moulhoule Djibouti
21 M4 Moulicent France
21 L7 Moulihierne France
18 H6 Moulins Allier France
21 K5 Moulins Sarthe France
18 H6 Moulins-Engilbert France
21 L4 Moulins-la-Marche France
21 O7 Moulins-sur-Cephons France
68 C4 Moulmein Burma
85 D2 Moulouya, Oued R Morocco
111 J7 Moulton Alabama U.S.A.
101 M7 Moulton Idaho U.S.A.
110 D1 Moulton Iowa U.S.A.
109 K6 Moulton Texas U.S.A.
112 D6 Moultrie Georgia U.S.A.
112 G4 Moultrie, L South Carolina U.S.A.
86 B6 Mounana Gabon
46 D6 Moúnda, Akr C Greece
111 F8 Mound Bayou Mississippi U.S.A.
110 G4 Mound City Illinois U.S.A.
110 B3 Mound City Kansas U.S.A.
99 L9 Mound City Missouri U.S.A.
98 F4 Mound City South Dakota U.S.A.
94 D7 Mound City Nat.Mon Ohio U.S.A.
86 C4 Moundou Chad
107 N3 Mound Ridge Kansas U.S.A.
110 G4 Mounds Illinois U.S.A.
107 O6 Mounds Oklahoma U.S.A.
94 G7 Moundsville West Virginia U.S.A.
110 A4 Mound Valley Kansas U.S.A.
111 J9 Moundville Alabama U.S.A.
68 F6 Moung Cambodia
68 B5 Moung Hat Hin Laos
98 J1 Mountain North Dakota U.S.A.
94 G7 Mountain West Virginia U.S.A.
108 A1 Mountainair New Mexico U.S.A.
8 C4 Mountain Ash Wales
100 K8 Mountain City Nevada U.S.A.
109 N10 Mountain Creek L Texas U.S.A.
109 N1 Mountain Fork R Oklahoma U.S.A.
110 D4 Mountain Grove Missouri U.S.A.
110 D5 Mountain Home Arkansas U.S.A.
100 K6 Mountain Home Idaho U.S.A.
109 H5 Mountain Home Texas U.S.A.
103 O1 Mountain Home Utah U.S.A.
112 G2 Mountain Island L North Carolina U.S.A.
117 P9 Mountain Park Alberta Canada
109 J1 Mountain Park Oklahoma U.S.A.
109 O1 Mountain Pine Arkansas U.S.A.
118 D9 Mountain View Alberta Canada
135 V5 Mountain View Hawaiian Is
110 E6 Mountain View Arkansas U.S.A.
110 E5 Mountain View Missouri U.S.A.
107 M6 Mountain View Oklahoma U.S.A.
101 P8 Mountainview Wyoming U.S.A.
116 F5 Mountain Village Alaska U.S.A.
95 K7 Mount Airy Maryland U.S.A.
112 G1 Mount Airy North Carolina U.S.A.
99 S4 Mountan Wisconsin U.S.A.
100 C4 Mount Angel Oregon U.S.A.
144 B6 Mount Aspiring Nat. Park New Zealand
118 B8 Mount Assiniboine Prov Park Br Col/Alberta Canada
99 R10 Mount Auburn Illinois U.S.A.
143 B6 Mount Augustus W Australia Australia
89 F8 Mount Ayliff S Africa
99 M9 Mount Ayr Iowa U.S.A.
138 E6 Mount Barker South Australia Australia
143 C10 Mount Barker W Australia Australia
142 F3 Mount Barnett W Australia Australia
14 C3 Mount Bellew Br Ireland
138 F3 Mount Browne New South Wales Australia
145 E4 Mount Bruce New Zealand
139 H6 Mount Buller Victoria Australia
120 J4 Mount Byers Ontario Canada
109 L4 Mount Calm Texas U.S.A.
141 H3 Mount Carbine Queensland Australia
123 T6 Mount Carmel Newfoundland Canada
110 J3 Mount Carmel Illinois U.S.A.
95 L6 Mount Carmel Pennsylvania U.S.A.
99 R7 Mount Carroll Illinois U.S.A.
140 C7 Mount Cavenagh N Terr Australia
98 H9 Mount Clare Nebraska U.S.A.
94 G7 Mount Clare West Virginia U.S.A.
143 C7 Mount Clere W Australia Australia
144 C5 Mount Cook New Zealand
141 H5 Mount Coolon Queensland Australia
88 C10 Mount Darwin Zimbabwe
140 B5 Mount Denison N Terr Australia
95 T2 Mount Desert I Maine U.S.A.
95 T3 Mount Desert Rock Maine U.S.A.
108 A7 Mount Dora New Mexico U.S.A.
140 B5 Mount Doreen N Terr Australia
141 H5 Mount Douglas Queensland Australia
138 D2 Mount Dutton South Australia Australia
138 D4 Mount Eba South Australia Australia
140 C7 Mount Ebenezer N Terr Australia
117 F7 Mount Edgecumbe Alaska U.S.A.
117 H7 Mount Edziza Prov. Park British Columbia Canada
101 P9 Mount Emmons Utah U.S.A.
141 G5 Mount Emu Plains Queensland Australia
109 N4 Mount Enterprise Texas U.S.A.
140 C6 Mount Ertwa N Terr Australia
89 F8 Mount Fletcher S Africa
89 F8 Mount Frere S Africa
138 F6 Mount Gambier South Australia Australia
141 H4 Mount Garnet Queensland Australia
112 H2 Mount Gilead North Carolina U.S.A.
94 E6 Mount Gilead Ohio U.S.A.
141 L2 Mount Gravatt dist Brisbane, Qnsld Australia
136 J3 Mount Hagen Papua New Guinea
106 C1 Mount Harris Colorado U.S.A.
100 C8 Mount Hebron California U.S.A.
95 N6 Mount Holly New Jersey U.S.A.
94 K6 Mount Holly Pennsylvania U.S.A.
138 D5 Mount Hope South Australia Australia
107 N4 Mount Hope Kansas U.S.A.
99 R6 Mount Horeb Wisconsin U.S.A.
142 F3 Mount House W Australia Australia
141 F7 Mount Howitt Queensland Australia
144 C5 Mount Hutt New Zealand
109 O1 Mount Ida Arkansas U.S.A.
100 J4 Mount Idaho Idaho U.S.A.
140 E5 Mount Isa Queensland Australia
94 J8 Mount Jackson Virginia U.S.A.
94 J5 Mount Jewett Pennsylvania U.S.A.
120 H6 Mount L Ontario Canada
141 K6 Mount Larcom Queensland Australia
83 J11 Mount Lavinia Sri Lanka
142 B1 Mount Lawley dist Perth, W Aust Australia
138 E6 Mount Lofty Ra S Australia Australia
141 H5 Mount McConnell Queensland Australia
143 C8 Mount Magnet W Australia Australia
139 G4 Mount Manara New South Wales Australia
141 G6 Mount Marlow Queensland Australia
145 F2 Mount Maunganui New Zealand
100 E9 Mount Meadows Res California U.S.A.
14 D3 Mountmellick Ireland
141 H3 Mount Molloy Queensland Australia
102 F4 Mount Montgomery Nevada U.S.A.
141 K6 Mount Morgan Queensland Australia
110 C1 Mount Moriah Missouri U.S.A.
99 R7 Mount Morris Illinois U.S.A.
94 K4 Mount Morris New York U.S.A.
139 G4 Mount Murchison New South Wales Australia
106 D2 Mount of the Holy Cross Colorado U.S.A.
110 G2 Mount Olive Illinois U.S.A.
111 G10 Mount Olive Mississippi U.S.A.
110 M3 Mount Olivet Kentucky U.S.A.
110 N2 Mount Orab Ohio U.S.A.
121 S7 Mount Orford, Parc de Quebec Canada
141 K7 Mount Perry Queensland Australia
99 P9 Mount Pleasant Iowa U.S.A.
94 C3 Mount Pleasant Michigan U.S.A.
94 H6 Mount Pleasant Pennsylvania U.S.A.
110 J6 Mount Pleasant Tennessee U.S.A.
109 N2 Mount Pleasant Texas U.S.A.
103 N2 Mount Pleasant Utah U.S.A.
95 M5 Mount Pocono Pennsylvania U.S.A.
99 R9 Mount Pulaski Illinois U.S.A.
100 D3 Mount Rainier Nat.Pk Washington U.S.A.
14 D3 Mountrath Ireland
117 O10 Mount Revelstoke Nat. Park British Columbia Canada
106 C10 Mount Riley New Mexico U.S.A.
98 C6 Mount Rushmore Nat.Mem South Dakota U.S.A.
100 C3 Mount St. Helens Nat. Vol Mon Washington U.S.A.
140 B3 Mount Sanford N Terr Australia
94 J7 Mount Savage Maryland U.S.A.
9 F7 Mount's B England
109 M3 Mount Selman Texas U.S.A.
140 C7 Mount Squires N Terr Australia
99 Q10 Mount Sterling Illinois U.S.A.
110 M3 Mount Sterling Kentucky U.S.A.
94 D7 Mount Sterling Ohio U.S.A.
122 K7 Mount Stewart Prince Edward I Canada
94 H7 Mount Storm West Virginia U.S.A.
142 B5 Mount Stuart W Australia Australia
141 G5 Mount Sturgeon Queensland Australia
141 G4 Mount Surprise Queensland Australia
140 D6 Mount Swan N Terr Australia
103 L5 Mount Trumbull Arizona U.S.A.
122 J9 Mount Uniacke Nova Scotia Canada
94 K6 Mount Union Pennsylvania U.S.A.
143 C6 Mount Vernon W Australia Australia
111 J10 Mount Vernon Alabama U.S.A.
110 D6 Mount Vernon Arkansas U.S.A.
112 E5 Mount Vernon Georgia U.S.A.
110 H3 Mount Vernon Illinois U.S.A.
110 J4 Mount Vernon Indiana U.S.A.
99 P8 Mount Vernon Iowa U.S.A.
110 M4 Mount Vernon Kentucky U.S.A.
110 C4 Mount Vernon Missouri U.S.A.
95 O6 Mount Vernon New York U.S.A.
94 E6 Mount Vernon Ohio U.S.A.
100 F5 Mount Vernon Oregon U.S.A.
98 H6 Mount Vernon South Dakota U.S.A.
109 M2 Mount Vernon Texas U.S.A.
95 K8 Mount Vernon Virginia U.S.A.
100 C1 Mount Vernon Washington U.S.A.
94 D6 Mount Victory Ohio U.S.A.
140 B6 Mount Wedge N Terr Australia
138 D5 Mount Wedge South Australia Australia
111 K9 Mount Willing Alabama U.S.A.
138 C3 Mount Willoughby South Australia Australia
142 B1 Mount Yokine dist Perth, W Aust Australia
110 H2 Mount Zion Illinois U.S.A.
99 P9 Mount Zion Iowa U.S.A.
141 J6 Moura Queensland Australia
128 D5 Moura R Brazil
16 C6 Moura Portugal
85 C6 Mourdiah Mali
19 N17 Mouriès France
141 H4 Mourilyan Harbour Queensland Australia
14 D2 Mourne R N Ireland
14 E2 Mourne Mts N Ireland
15 G2 Mousa isld Shetland Scotland
22 E2 Mouscron Belgium
98 E1 Mouse R North Dakota U.S.A.
18 F7 Mousin reg France
36 B6 Moussey Moselle France
36 C7 Moussey Vosges France
86 C3 Moussoro Chad
20 D4 Mousterus France
19 Q17 Moustiers France
12 E3 Mouswald Scotland
36 C6 Mouterhouse France
40 D4 Mouthe France
40 D3 Mouthier France
40 F3 Moutier Switzerland
40 E7 Moutiers France
21 M5 Moutiers-au-Perche France
70 G4 Moutong Sulawesi
21 P3 Mouy France
22 J5 Mouzay France
22 H4 Mouzon France
124 E3 Movas Mexico
14 D1 Moville Ireland
99 L7 Moville Iowa U.S.A.
142 E3 Mowanjum W Australia Australia
141 K7 Mowbullan, Mt Queensland Australia
99 S10 Moweaqua Illinois U.S.A.
145 E3 Mowhanau New Zealand
100 D6 Mowich Oregon U.S.A.
100 D3 Moxee City Washington U.S.A.
130 H10 Moxotó,R Brazil
14 B3 Moy R Ireland
17 J3 Moyá Spain
106 F6 Moya R New Mexico U.S.A.
124 H7 Moyahua Mexico
86 G5 Moyale Kenya
85 B7 Moyamba Sierra Leone
21 L3 Moyaux France
22 E4 Moy-de-l'Aisne France
65 E6 Moye Dao isld China
36 B7 Moyenmoutier France
83 K12 Moyenne isld Mahé I Indian Oc
21 O1 Moyenneville France
36 B6 Moyenvic France
117 O9 Moyie British Columbia Canada
100 J1 Moyie Springs Idaho U.S.A.
86 C4 Moyo Chad
128 C5 Moyobamba Peru
86 C3 Moyto Chad
57 E2 Moyynkum desert Kazakhstan
57 G3 Moyynkum Kazakhstan
57 E3 Moyynkum, Peski desert Kazakhstan
57 G2 Moyynty Kazakhstan
87 G9 Mozambique rep Africa
81 B9 Mozambique Ridge Indian Oc
120 H6 Mozhabong L Ontario Canada
52 E6 Mozhaysk Russian Federation
52 H6 Mozhga Russian Federation
77 G2 Mozhnābād Iran
68 B1 Mozo Burma
45 J1 Mozzecane Italy
87 E7 Mpala Zaire
88 D7 Mpandamatenga Botswana
88 E9 Mpika Zambia
88 C6 Mporokoso Zambia
86 C6 M'Pouya Congo
85 D7 Mpraeso Ghana
87 F7 Mpulungu Zambia
87 G7 Mpwapwa Tanzania
31 N2 Mrągowo Poland
55 C4 Mrakovo Russian Federation
123 Mras-Su R Russian Federation
85 C4 Mreiti,El Mauritania
88 C10 Mrewa Zimbabwe
42 H4 Mrkonjić Grad Bosnia-Herzegovina
31 J5 Mrlina R Czech Rep
31 J1 Mrzeżyno Poland
43 D13 M'saken Tunisia
31 H5 Mšeno Czech Rep
52 D5 Msta R Russian Federation
52 C2 Mstislavl' Belarus
31 M4 Mszczonów Poland
88 C5 Mtakuja Tanzania
89 G6 Mtambama Mt Swaziland
88 H5 Mtambo R Tanzania
89 F8 Mtata S Africa
120 J10 Mt. Brydges Ontario Canada
103 M4 Mt Carmel Utah U.S.A.
89 G8 Mtentu S Africa
144 C5 Mt Hutt New Zealand
89 G3 Mtilikwe R Zimbabwe
141 G6 Mt Marlow Queensland Australia
144 C5 Mt Somers New Zealand
87 F11 Mtubatuba S Africa
89 F8 Mtwara reg Tanzania
88 H7 Mtwara Tanzania
16 B7 Mu mt Portugal
88 G7 Mualo R Mozambique
88 C8 Muamadzi R Zambia
21 K3 Muance R France
68 F6 Muang Cambodia
68 E4 Muang Botene Thailand
68 G5 Muang Bua Thailand
68 E5 Muang Chainat Thailand
68 E3 Muang Chaiyaphum Thailand
68 E4 Muang Chiang Khan Thailand
68 D3 Muang Chiang Rai Thailand
68 G4 Muang Hinboun Laos
68 F4 Muang Kalasin Thailand
68 G5 Muang Khong Laos
68 G5 Muang Khong-Xedon Laos
68 D4 Muang Kosamphi Thailand
69 D8 Muang Krabi Thailand
68 D3 Muang Lampang Thailand
68 D3 Muang Lamphun Thailand
68 E4 Muang Loei Thailand
68 D3 Muang Long Thailand
68 G4 Muang Nakhon Phanom Thailand
68 D5 Muang Nakhon Sawan Thailand
68 D3 Muang Ngao Thailand
68 E3 Muang Oi Thailand
68 G4 Muang Phaluka Thailand
68 D3 Muang Phan Thailand
68 F4 Muang Phannanikhom Thailand
68 D3 Muang Phayao Thailand
68 E4 Muang Phetchabun Thailand
68 E4 Muang Phichai Thailand
68 E4 Muang Phichit Thailand
68 E3 Muang Phrae Thailand
68 G4 Muang Renu Nakhon Thailand
68 F5 Muang Roi Et Thailand
68 F4 Muang Sakon Nakhon Thailand
68 G5 Muang Sam Sip Thailand
68 G5 Muang Si Chalalai Thailand
68 F4 Muang Song Thailand
68 D4 Muang Thoen Thailand
69 F11 Muar R Malaysia
69 F11 Muar Malaysia
70 D2 Muara Brunei
70 E3 Muara Kalimantan
70 E4 Muaraancalong Kalimantan
70 E4 Muaraatap Kalimantan
70 K9 Muarabinuangeun Java
69 F13 Muarabulian Sumatra
69 E13 Muarabungo Sumatra
70 K8 Muaradua Sumatra
69 F14 Muaraenim Sumatra
70 D5 Muarainu Kalimantan
70 E5 Muarajawa Kalimantan
70 E5 Muarakaman Kalimantan
70 C5 Muarakayang Kalimantan
69 E13 Muaralabuh Sumatra
69 F14 Muaralakitan Sumatra
70 D5 Muaralaung Kalimantan
70 E4 Muaraleesan Kalimantan
70 E4 Muaramayang Kalimantan
70 E4 Muaranawai Kalimantan
69 F14 Muararupit Sumatra
70 F3 Muarasabak Sumatra
69 D13 Muarasiberut Indonesia
69 D13 Muarasigep Indonesia
69 D12 Muarasipongi Sumatra
69 D12 Muarasoma Sumatra
70 F4 Muaras Rf Indonesia
69 F13 Muaratebo Sumatra
69 F13 Muaratembesi Sumatra
70 D5 Muaratewe Kalimantan
70 E4 Muarawahau Kalimantan
71 A3 Muari Halmahera Indonesia
57 D5 Mubarek Uzbekistan
77 A7 Mubarraz,Al Saudi Arabia
88 C1 Mubende Uganda
80 G5 Mubis Jordan
79 F8 Mubrak, J mt Jordan
69 H11 Mubur isld Indonesia
142 C5 Muccan W Australia Australia
36 C2 Much Germany
117 K11 Muchalat British Columbia Canada
15 F3 Muchalls Scotland
143 B9 Muchea W Australia Australia
33 P10 Mücheln Germany
88 C8 Muchinga Escarpment Zambia
52 G3 Muchkas Russian Federation
67 A2 Muchuan China
8 D2 Much Wenlock England
15 B4 Muck isld Inner Hebrides Scotland
141 J7 Muckadilla Queensland Australia
14 D1 Muckish Mt Ireland
15 G1 Muckle Flugga isld Shetland Scotland
15 G2 Muckle Roe isld Shetland Scotland
9 E2 Muckley Corner England
14 C2 Muckros Hd Ireland
88 H8 Mucojo Mozambique
87 D8 Muconda Angola
130 H6 Mucuri Brazil
130 H5 Mucuri,R Brazil
87 D9 Mucusso Angola
69 E10 Muda R Malaysia
80 G7 Mudaiyina Jordan
65 H2 Mudan Jiang R China
65 H2 Mudanjiang China
47 K4 Mudanya Turkey
47 N10 Mudarri Turkey
36 G4 Mudau Germany
79 F9 Mudawwara, Al Jordan
98 D4 Mud Butte South Dakota U.S.A.
98 G8 Mud Cr Nebraska U.S.A.
76 C2 Muddebihal India
26 L5 Muddus Nat. Park Sweden
107 O7 Muddy Boggy Cr Oklahoma U.S.A.
103 N3 Muddy Cr Utah U.S.A.
101 T7 Muddy Cr Wyoming U.S.A.
101 P8 Muddy Cr Wyoming U.S.A.
101 S8 Muddy Cr Wyoming U.S.A.
101 S7 Muddy Gap pass Wyoming U.S.A.
118 H6 Muddy L Saskatchewan Canada
103 K5 Muddy Pk Nevada U.S.A.
33 M7 Müden Germany
139 J4 Mudgee New South Wales Australia
141 H6 Mudge, Mt Queensland Australia
76 B2 Mudhol India
74 G9 Mudhol Andhra Pradesh India
101 N6 Mud L Idaho U.S.A.
101 Q1 Mud L Montana U.S.A.
102 G4 Mud L Nevada U.S.A.
98 H4 Mud L.Res South Dakota U.S.A.
68 C4 Mudon Burma
47 L4 Mudurnu R Turkey
52 E3 Mud'yuga Russian Federation
88 D10 Mudzi R Zimbabwe
21 K3 Mue R France
88 G7 Mueda Mozambique
20 F5 Muel France
17 G4 Muela de Ares mt Spain
17 G3 Muela,Sierra de la Spain
142 G4 Mueller, Mt W Australia Australia
142 F4 Mueller Ra W Australia Australia
141 F6 Muellers Ra Queensland Australia
119 N6 Muenster Saskatchewan Canada
109 K2 Muenster Texas U.S.A.
125 N2 Muerto,Cayo isld Nicaragua
126 D2 Muertos Cays reefs Bahamas
52 G3 Muftyuga Russian Federation
88 B8 Mufulira Zambia

67 E2 **Mufu Shan** mts Jiangxi/Hubei China
67 B5 **Mugang** China
16 B5 **Muge** Portugal
87 G9 **Mugeba** Mozambique
45 K4 **Mugello** Italy
33 S10 **Mügeln** Germany
37 L4 **Muggendorf** Germany
79 H9 **Mughayrā', Al** Saudi Arabia
59 K5 **Mugi** Japan
16 A1 **Mugía** Spain
88 B5 **Mugila** mts Zaire
47 J7 **Muğla** Turkey
47 H2 **Mŭglizh** Bulgaria
57 A1 **Mugodzhary** mts Kazakhstan
18 E9 **Mugron** France
75 K4 **Mugu** Nepal
86 G1 **Muhammad Qol** Sudan
77 B6 **Muharraq,Al** Bahrain
36 F6 **Mühlacker** Germany
36 H2 **Mühlbach** Germany
33 S10 **Mühlberg** Brandenburg Germany
37 K2 **Mühlberg** Thüringen Germany
38 G5 **Mühldorf** Germany
41 K3 **Mühlehorn** Switzerland
33 S7 **Mühlenbeck** Germany
33 O5 **Mühlen Eichsen** Germany
37 J1 **Mühlhausen** Germany
37 K4 **Mühlhausen** Germany
36 C4 **Mühlheim** Germany
146 H6 **Mühlig-Hofmannfjella** mts Antarctica
37 M2 **Mühltroff** Germany
29 M7 **Muhos** Finland
38 H7 **Muhr** Austria
80 D3 **Muhraqa** Israel
36 F7 **Mühringen** Germany
52 B5 **Muhu** Estonia
88 C2 **Muhutwe** Tanzania
88 F7 **Muhuwesi** R Tanzania
69 G8 **Mui Bai Bung** Vietnam
68 J4 **Mui Chon May Dong** C Vietnam
68 J7 **Mui da Vaich** C Vietnam
25 D4 **Muiden** Netherlands
21 O6 **Muides-sur-Loire** France
68 J7 **Mui Dinh** C Vietnam
21 N3 **Muids** France
61 M8 **Muikamachi** Japan
71 B3 **Muilijk** isld Indonesia
14 E4 **Muine Bheag** Ireland
94 C3 **Muir** Michigan U.S.A.
88 D10 **Muira** R Mozambique
13 F1 **Muirdrum** Scotland
117 E6 **Muir Gl** Alaska U.S.A.
13 E1 **Muirhead** Scotland
12 D3 **Muirkirk** Scotland
143 B10 **Muir, L** W Australia Australia
143 G7 **Muir, Mt** W Australia Australia
142 A5 **Muiron I., N** W Australia Australia
102 B4 **Muir Woods Nat.Mon** California U.S.A.
87 G8 **Muite** Mozambique
68 J6 **Mui Yen** C Vietnam
125 Q7 **Mujeres, I** Mexico
80 F8 **Mujib** R Jordan
87 D8 **Mujimbeji** Zambia
70 C3 **Mujong** R Sarawak
48 H2 **Mukachevo** Ukraine
70 C3 **Mukah** Sarawak
72 F6 **Mukallā, Al** Yemen
80 E6 **Mukallik** R Jordan
60 P3 **Mukawa** Japan
60 Q3 **Mu-kawa** R Japan
80 F7 **Mukawir** Jordan
86 G1 **Mukawwar I** Sudan
68 G4 **Mukdahan** Thailand
Mukden see **Shenyang**
13 F5 **Muker** England
72 E6 **Mukha, Al** Yemen
86 H3 **Mukhā, Al** Yemen
84 G3 **Mukhaylī, Al** Libya
74 G9 **Mukher** India
80 E6 **Mukhmas** Jordan
58 F1 **Mukhor-Konduy** Russian Federation
143 C9 **Mukinbudin** W Australia Australia
69 D9 **Muk,Ko** isld Thailand
69 E14 **Mukomuko** Sumatra
33 P9 **Mukrena** Germany
57 D5 **Mukry** Turkmenistan
75 K4 **Muktinath** Nepal
86 D7 **Mukumbi** Zaire
86 G5 **Mukutan** Kenya
119 U5 **Mukutawa R** Manitoba Canada
87 D9 **Mukwe** Namibia
99 S7 **Mukwonago** Wisconsin U.S.A.
17 G6 **Mula** Spain
73 L8 **Mulaku Atoll** Maldives
57 J2 **Mulaly** Kazakhstan
65 G2 **Mulan** China
71 F4 **Mulanay** Philippines
88 E9 **Mulanje** mt Malawi
88 E10 **Mulanje** Malawi
129 H4 **Mulata** Brazil
124 E3 **Mulatos** Mexico
125 Q5 **Mulatupo Sasardi** Panama
110 B6 **Mulberry** Arkansas U.S.A.
110 C6 **Mulberry** R Arkansas U.S.A.
113 F10 **Mulberry** Florida U.S.A.
110 K1 **Mulberry** Indiana U.S.A.
107 Q4 **Mulberry** Kansas U.S.A.
110 B4 **Mulberry** Missouri U.S.A.
111 K8 **Mulberry Fork** R Alabama U.S.A.
110 G3 **Mulberry Grove** Illinois U.S.A.
116 K6 **Mulchatna** R Alaska U.S.A.
133 C5 **Mulchen** Chile
37 P2 **Mulda** Germany
28 E3 **Muldbjerge** hill Denmark
33 Q9 **Mulde** R Germany
101 M6 **Muldoon** Idaho U.S.A.
108 E5 **Mule Cr** Texas U.S.A.
98 B6 **Mule Cr** Wyoming U.S.A.
106 B8 **Mule Creek** New Mexico U.S.A.
124 C4 **Mulegé** Mexico
80 G7 **Muleih** Jordan
88 C8 **Mulembo** R Zambia
86 D6 **Mulenda** Zaire
71 K9 **Mules** isld Flores Indonesia
108 E1 **Muleshoe** Texas U.S.A.
87 G9 **Mulevala** Mozambique
36 H5 **Mulfingen** Germany
142 C5 **Mulga Downs** W Australia Australia
140 B7 **Mulga Park** N Terr Australia
138 C4 **Mulgathing** South Australia Australia
138 C4 **Mulgathing Rocks** mt South Australia Australia
123 L8 **Mulgrave** Nova Scotia Canada
116 F3 **Mulgrave Hills** Alaska U.S.A.
143 C6 **Mulgul** W Australia Australia
16 E7 **Mulhacén** mt Spain
107 N5 **Mulhall** Oklahoma U.S.A.
32 E10 **Mülheim** Germany
40 F2 **Mulhouse** France
65 H2 **Muling** China
65 D6 **Muling Guan** pass China
65 J2 **Muling He** R China
138 E3 **Mulka** South Australia Australia
76 B4 **Mulki** India
15 C4 **Mull** isld Scotland
14 B4 **Mullaghareirk Mts** Ireland
83 K8 **Mullaittivu** Sri Lanka
139 J4 **Mullaley** New South Wales Australia
100 K2 **Mullan** Idaho U.S.A.
98 E7 **Mullen** Nebraska U.S.A.
109 J4 **Mullen** Texas U.S.A.
139 H4 **Mullengudgery** New South Wales Australia
94 F9 **Mullens** West Virginia U.S.A.
140 C6 **Muller** R N Terr Australia
70 C4 **Muller,Peg** mts Kalimantan
113 E10 **Mullet Key** isld Florida U.S.A.
94 C1 **Mullett L** Michigan U.S.A.
143 B8 **Mullewa** W Australia Australia
15 F1 **Mull Head** Orkney Scotland
40 G2 **Müllheim** Germany
95 N7 **Mullica** R New Jersey U.S.A.
140 E6 **Mulligan** R Queensland Australia
14 D3 **Mullingar** Ireland
112 H3 **Mullins** South Carolina U.S.A.
107 L4 **Mullinville** Kansas U.S.A.
139 J5 **Mullion Creek** New South Wales Australia
83 K8 **Mulliyavalai** Sri Lanka
15 D6 **Mull of Galloway** Scotland
15 C5 **Mull of Kintyre** Scotland
12 B2 **Mull of Oa** Scotland
27 G14 **Mullsjö** Sweden
15 C4 **Mull, Sound of** Scotland
139 L3 **Mullumbimby** New South Wales Australia
80 F6 **Mul Nevo** Jordan
87 E9 **Mulobezi** Zambia
87 C9 **Mulondo** Angola
87 E7 **Mulongo** Zaire
138 E3 **Muloorina** South Australia Australia
14 D1 **Mulroy B** Ireland
21 L6 **Mulsanne** France
33 P5 **Mulsow** Germany
74 D3 **Multan** Pakistan
55 F1 **Multanovy** Russian Federation
29 L9 **Multia** Finland
26 J8 **Multrå** Sweden
70 D2 **Mulu, G** mt Sarawak
130 J9 **Mulungu** Brazil
107 N4 **Mulvane** Kansas U.S.A.
119 T8 **Mulvihill** Manitoba Canada
139 G4 **Mulyah,Mt** New South Wales Australia
55 E1 **Mulym'ya** R Russian Federation
138 F4 **Mulyungarie** South Australia Australia
8 C4 **Mumbles** Wales
87 B8 **Mumbondo** Angola
87 C8 **Mumbué** Angola
87 E8 **Mumbwa** Zambia
87 E8 **Mumena** Zaire
109 L5 **Mumford** Texas U.S.A.
69 D9 **Mum Nauk,Laem** C Thailand
71 H7 **Muna** isld Indonesia
125 P7 **Muna** Mexico
67 B5 **Munankwan Lin** pass Vietnam/China
141 G2 **Munburra** Queensland Australia
37 M3 **Münchberg** Germany
30 H3 **Müncheberg** Germany
39 **München** conurbation Germany
37 M2 **Münchenbernsdorf** Germany
36 F2 **Münchhausen** Germany
117 L6 **Muncho Lake** British Columbia Canada
37 N5 **Münchshofen** Germany
37 O6 **Münchshofen** Germany
37 M6 **Münchsmünster** Germany
110 L1 **Muncie** Indiana U.S.A.
140 E7 **Muncoonie, L** Queensland Australia
95 L5 **Muncy** Pennsylvania U.S.A.
118 E5 **Mundare** Alberta Canada
109 H2 **Munday** Texas U.S.A.
99 S7 **Mundelein** Illinois U.S.A.
83 J10 **Mundel L** Sri Lanka
32 L10 **Münden** Germany
98 J10 **Munden** Kansas U.S.A.
36 H7 **Munderkingen** Germany
9 H2 **Mundesley** England
9 G2 **Mundford** England
143 D6 **Mundiwindi** W Australia Australia
141 F4 **Mundjuro** R Queensland Australia
17 F6 **Mundo** R Spain
129 K6 **Mundo Nôvo** Brazil
143 G9 **Mundrabilla** W Australia Australia
141 K7 **Mundubbera** Queensland Australia
56 C4 **Mundybash** Russian Federation
46 D3 **Munella** mt Albania
17 F5 **Munera** Spain
110 L4 **Munfordville** Kentucky U.S.A.
141 J7 **Mungallala** Queensland Australia
141 H8 **Mungallala** R Queensland Australia
141 G3 **Mungana** Queensland Australia
87 F9 **Mungari** Mozambique
142 C5 **Mungaroona Ra** W Australia Australia
56 D5 **Mungash-Kul', Gora** mt Russian Federation
86 E5 **Mungbere** Zaire
75 J7 **Mungeli** India
75 M6 **Munger** India
94 D3 **Munger** Michigan U.S.A.
138 E3 **Mungerannie** South Australia Australia
69 J12 **Mungguresak, Tanjong** C Indonesia
141 J8 **Mungindi** Queensland Australia
87 C8 **Munhango** Angola
Munich Germany see **München**
98 H1 **Munich** North Dakota U.S.A.
88 B8 **Muniengashi** R Zaire
17 G3 **Muniesa** Spain
130 H7 **Muniz Freire** Brazil
28 H5 **Munke Bjergby** Denmark
28 F6 **Munkebo** Denmark
27 E13 **Munkedal** Sweden
26 G8 **Munkflohögen** Sweden
27 G12 **Munkfors** Sweden
28 A7 **Munkmarsch** Germany
26 M6 **Munksund** Sweden
56 F5 **Munku-Sardyk,Gora** mt Mongolia/Rus Fed
37 J3 **Münnerstadt** Germany
22 J4 **Muno** Belgium
71 E3 **Muñoz** Luzon Philippines
133 C8 **Muñoz Gamero, Pen** Chile
139 J8 **Munro,Mt** Tasmania Australia
36 H7 **Münsingen** Germany
118 E7 **Munson** Alberta Canada
111 K11 **Munson** Florida U.S.A.
40 F1 **Munster** France
32 M7 **Münster** Niedersachsen Germany
32 G9 **Münster** Nordrhein-Westfalen Germany
14 B4 **Munster** prov Ireland
41 H5 **Münster** Switzerland
36 C3 **Münstermaifeld** Germany
143 C9 **Muntadgin** W Australia Australia
70 F4 **Munte** Sulawesi
48 H4 **Muntelui Mare** mt Romania
70 P10 **Muntjar** Java
87 E9 **Munyati** R Zimbabwe
36 F3 **Münzenberg** Germany
26 N4 **Muodoslompolo** Sweden
29 O6 **Muojärvi** L Finland
68 F1 **Muong Boum** Vietnam
68 F2 **Muong Hiem** Laos
68 F2 **Muong Hun Xieng Hung** Laos
68 F3 **Muong Khao** Laos
68 F2 **Muong Khoua** Laos
68 G1 **Muong Khuong** Vietnam
68 E3 **Muong Ki** Laos
68 G3 **Muong Lam** Vietnam
68 E3 **Muong Liep** Laos
68 E2 **Muong Louang Namtha** Laos
68 H7 **Muong Man** Vietnam
68 F3 **Muong May** Laos
68 F3 **Muong Moc** Laos
68 F2 **Muong Ngoi** Laos
68 F1 **Muong Nhie** Vietnam
68 H4 **Muong Nong** Laos
68 E3 **Muong Oua** Laos
68 E1 **Muong ou Neua** Laos
68 E1 **Muong ou Tay** Laos
68 E3 **Muong Pa** Laos
68 G4 **Muong Phalane** Laos
68 E3 **Muong Phiang** Laos
68 E2 **Muong Sai** Laos
68 E3 **Muong Saiapoun** Laos
68 E2 **Muong Sing** Laos
68 F2 **Muong Son** Laos
68 G4 **Muong Song Khone** Laos
68 F3 **Muong Soui** Laos
68 F3 **Muong Soum** Laos
68 F1 **Muong Te** Vietnam
68 E3 **Muong Tha Deua** Laos
68 E3 **Muong Thong** Laos
68 F2 **Muong Va** Laos
Muong Xen see **Ky Son**
29 K4 **Muonio** Finland
26 N3 **Muonio älv** R Sweden/Finland
29 K4 **Muoniojoki** R Finland
26 N4 **Muonionalusta** Sweden
71 B2 **Muor** isld Halmahera Indonesia
41 J4 **Muotathal** Switzerland
88 B9 **Mupata Gorge** Zambia
65 E6 **Muping** China
80 G4 **Muqbilla** Jordan
86 J5 **Muqdisho** Somalia
130 H7 **Muqui** Brazil
38 J7 **Mur** R Austria
56 E2 **Mura** R Russian Federation
48 C4 **Mura** R Slovenia
80 G1 **Murāba 'āt** Syria
47 J6 **Muradiye** Turkey
45 L4 **Muraglione,Pso.di** pass Italy
61 N7 **Murakami** Japan
48 D4 **Murakeresztúr** Hungary
133 C7 **Murallón** mt Chile/Arg
61 N8 **Muramatsu** Japan
88 F2 **Murang'a** Kenya
45 M1 **Murano** Italy
52 G5 **Murashi** Russian Federation
18 G7 **Murat** France
78 H2 **Murat** R Turkey
78 J2 **Murat** R Turkey
47 K6 **Murat Dağı** Turkey
47 J3 **Muratlı** Turkey
38 K7 **Murau** Austria
77 C7 **Murban** U.A.E.
16 C3 **Murça** Portugal
77 B3 **Murcheh Khvort** Iran
33 T5 **Murchin** Germany
139 H6 **Murchison** Victoria Australia
145 D4 **Murchison** New Zealand
6 M1 **Murchison** oil rig North Sea
Murchison Falls Uganda see **Kabalega Falls**
143 B7 **Murchison, Mt** W Australia Australia
144 C5 **Murchison, Mt** New Zealand
145 D4 **Murchison, Mt** New Zealand
144 A6 **Murchison Mts** New Zealand
143 A8 **Murchison, R** W Australia Australia
140 C5 **Murchison Ra** N Terr Australia
89 G4 **Murchison Ra** S Africa
88 E9 **Murchison Rapids** Malawi
17 F6 **Murcia** reg Spain
17 F7 **Murcia** prov Spain
17 G7 **Murcia** Spain
71 F6 **Murcielagos B** Mindanao Philippines
18 G8 **Mur-de-Barrez** France
20 E5 **Mur-de-Bretagne** France
21 O7 **Mur-de-Sologne** France
98 F6 **Murdo** South Dakota U.S.A.
141 G2 **Murdoch Pt** Queensland Australia
122 G5 **Murdochville** Quebec Canada
113 E10 **Murdock** Florida U.S.A.
61 M9 **Mure** Japan
21 O4 **Mureaux, Les** France
38 N8 **Mureck** Austria
47 J4 **Mürefte** Turkey
86 G4 **Murel** Ethiopia
48 J4 **Mureş** R Romania
48 J4 **Mureş** reg Romania
18 F9 **Muret** France
111 C7 **Murfreesboro** Arkansas U.S.A.
95 K10 **Murfreesboro** North Carolina U.S.A.
110 K6 **Murfreesboro** Tennessee U.S.A.
36 E6 **Murg** R Germany
57 G5 **Murgab** R Tajikistan
57 G5 **Murgab** Tajikistan
46 D5 **Murgána** mt Greece
46 F2 **Murgash** mt Bulgaria
140 C1 **Murgenella Cr** N Terr Australia
48 L4 **Murgeni** Romania
77 H2 **Murghab** R Afghanistan
74 C3 **Murgha Kibzai** Pakistan
48 K4 **Murgoci** mt Romania
141 K7 **Murgon** Queensland Australia
143 B7 **Murgoo** W Australia Australia
58 D4 **Muri** China
75 L7 **Muri** India
130 G7 **Muriaé** Brazil
70 N9 **Muria, Gunung** mt Java
16 C2 **Murias de Paredes** Spain
87 D7 **Muriege** Angola
118 G4 **Muriel L** Alberta Canada
60 R2 **Murii-dake** mt Japan
119 O2 **Murill** Ontario Canada
17 G2 **Murillo de Gállego** Spain
20 G6 **Murin, L. de** France
33 R6 **Müritz** L Germany
145 F3 **Muriwai** New Zealand
26 L5 **Murjek** Sweden
36 B3 **Mürlenbach** Germany
52 D1 **Murmansk** Russian Federation
52 D1 **Murmanskaya Oblast'** prov Russian Federation
52 D1 **Murmashi** Russian Federation
54 M2 **Murmino** Russian Federation
41 O2 **Murnau** Germany
18 L11 **Muro, Cap di** C Corsica
102 G7 **Muroc L** California U.S.A.
52 F6 **Murom** Russian Federation
55 G3 **Muromtsevo** Russian Federation
60 O3 **Muroran** Japan
16 A2 **Muros** Spain
60 H12 **Muroto** Japan
60 H12 **Muroto-zaki** Japan
60 N3 **Murotsu-shima** isld Japan
48 L2 **Murovanyye Kurilovtsy** Ukraine
31 K3 **Murowana Goslina** Poland
60 E12 **Murozumi** Japan
100 J6 **Murphy** Idaho U.S.A.
112 C2 **Murphy** North Carolina U.S.A.
100 B7 **Murphy** Oregon U.S.A.
102 D3 **Murphys** California U.S.A.
110 G4 **Murphysboro** Illinois U.S.A.
141 H8 **Murra Murra** Queensland Australia
139 G6 **Murray** R New South Wales Australia
99 N8 **Murray** Iowa U.S.A.
110 H5 **Murray** Kentucky U.S.A.
99 K9 **Murray** Nebraska U.S.A.
103 N1 **Murray** Utah U.S.A.
138 E6 **Murray Bridge** South Australia Australia
94 E7 **Murray City** Ohio U.S.A.
135 L5 **Murray Deep** Pacific Oc
140 C5 **Murray Downs** N Terr Australia
122 K7 **Murray Hbr** Prince Edward I Canada
123 K8 **Murray Hd** Prince Edward I Canada
83 M9 **Murray Hill** pk Christmas I Indian Oc
107 N7 **Murray,L** Oklahoma U.S.A.
112 F3 **Murray, L** South Carolina U.S.A.
143 B10 **Murray, R** W Australia Australia
117 N8 **Murray R** British Columbia Canada
143 G7 **Murray Ra** W Australia Australia
122 K7 **Murray River** Prince Edward I Canada
89 C8 **Murraysburg** S Africa
135 M5 **Murray Seascarp** Pacific Oc
138 E5 **Murray Town** South Australia Australia
138 F6 **Murrayville** Victoria Australia
99 Q10 **Murrayville** Illinois U.S.A.
112 H4 **Murrells Inlet** South Carolina U.S.A.
40 G4 **Mürren** Switzerland
36 H6 **Murrhardt** Germany
139 J5 **Murringo** New South Wales Australia
143 D8 **Murrin Murrin** W Australia Australia
14 B3 **Murrisk** mts Ireland
139 G5 **Murrumbidgee** R New South Wales Australia
139 J5 **Murrumburrah & Harden** New South Wales Australia
139 K4 **Murrurundi** New South Wales Australia
19 O17 **Murs** France
38 O8 **Murska Sobota** Slovenia
74 G8 **Murtajāpur** India
38 K7 **Mur Tal** V Austria
41 M4 **Murtarol,Piz** mt Italy
101 L7 **Murtaugh** Idaho U.S.A.
139 G4 **Murtee** New South Wales Australia
40 F4 **Murten See** L Switzerland
42 G5 **Murter** isld Croatia
138 F3 **Murteree,L** South Australia Australia
117 O9 **Murtle L** British Columbia Canada
138 F6 **Murtoa** Victoria Australia
29 O6 **Murtovaara** Finland
74 E9 **Murud** India
70 D3 **Murud** mt Kalimantan
65 E3 **Muruin Sum Shuiku** res China
70 D5 **Murui, R** Kalimantan
70 D4 **Murung,R** Kalimantan
145 F3 **Murupara** New Zealand
128 F3 **Murupu** Brazil
109 N3 **Murvaul Res** Texas U.S.A.
22 K5 **Murville** France
74 J7 **Murwara** India
139 L3 **Murwillumbah** New South Wales Australia
52 G5 **Murygino** Russian Federation
38 M6 **Mürzsteg** Austria
38 M7 **Murz Tal** V Austria
84 E4 **Murzuq** Libya
38 N6 **Mürzzuchlag** Austria
78 H2 **Muş** Turkey
86 D6 **Musadi** Zaire
79 D10 **Mûsa, G** mt Egypt
74 C3 **Musa Khel Bazar** Pakistan
47 N10 **Musaköyalçaği Burun** C Turkey
46 F2 **Musala** mt Bulgaria
69 D12 **Musala** isld Sumatra
59 J3 **Musan** N Korea
77 E6 **Musandam** pen Oman
77 J3 **Musa Qala** Afghanistan
77 B7 **Musay'īd** Qatar
Muscat see **Masqat**
99 P8 **Muscatine** Iowa U.S.A.
Muscat & Oman sultanate see **Oman**
110 J7 **Muscle Shoals** Alabama U.S.A.
99 Q6 **Muscoda** Wisconsin U.S.A.
95 S3 **Muscongus B** Maine U.S.A.
88 C9 **Muse** R Mozambique
80 G8 **Museitiba** Jordan
141 G2 **Musgrave** Queensland Australia
138 B2 **Musgrave Ranges** South Australia Australia
123 S5 **Musgravetown** Newfoundland Canada
89 G3 **Mushandike Dam** Zimbabwe
80 G8 **Musheirifa** Jordan
14 C5 **Musheramore** mt Ireland
86 C6 **Mushie** Zaire
28 G6 **Musholm** isld Denmark
103 L6 **Music Mt** Arizona U.S.A.
103 N2 **Musinia Pk** Utah U.S.A.
117 M5 **Muskeg** R Northwest Territories Canada
99 L1 **Muskeg B** Minnesota U.S.A.
95 R5 **Muskeget Chan** Massachusetts U.S.A.
119 O1 **Muskeg L** Ontario Canada
94 A3 **Muskegon** R Michigan U.S.A.
94 A3 **Muskegon** Michigan U.S.A.
94 A3 **Muskegon Heights** Michigan U.S.A.
26 H4 **Musken** Norway
94 F7 **Muskingum** R Ohio U.S.A.
27 K13 **Muskö** Sweden
110 A6 **Muskogee** Oklahoma U.S.A.
121 L7 **Muskoka,L** Ontario Canada
101 S6 **Muskrat Cr** Wyoming U.S.A.
77 F6 **Mūskutān** Iran
118 C2 **Muskwa R** Alberta Canada
79 H2 **Muslimīyah** Syria
52 H6 **Muslyumovo** Russian Federation
86 G2 **Musmar** Sudan
80 D3 **Musmus** Israel
88 D2 **Musoma** Tanzania
45 M1 **Musone** R Italy
45 O4 **Musone** Italy
123 L3 **Musquanus L** Quebec Canada
123 L3 **Musquaro** Quebec Canada
122 F8 **Musquash** New Brunswick Canada
122 J8 **Musquodoboit** Nova Scotia Canada
122 J9 **Musquodoboit Hbr** Nova Scotia Canada
28 H7 **Musse** Denmark
25 H3 **Mussel Aa** R Netherlands
13 E2 **Musselburgh** Scotland
101 R3 **Musselshell** Montana U.S.A.
101 S3 **Musselshell** R Montana U.S.A.
87 C8 **Mussende** Angola
18 F7 **Mussidan** France
43 F11 **Mussomeli** Sicily
47 K4 **Mustafakemalpaşa** Turkey
47 K5 **Mustafakemalpaşa** R Turkey
86 H4 **Mustahīl** Ethiopia
75 K4 **Mustang** Nepal
107 N6 **Mustang** Oklahoma U.S.A.
108 E3 **Mustang Cr** Texas U.S.A.
109 K8 **Mustang I** Texas U.S.A.
55 B5 **Mustayevo** Russian Federation
133 D7 **Muster,L** Argentina
98 K4 **Mustinka** R Minnesota U.S.A.
127 O8 **Mustique** isld Lesser Antilles
27 M13 **Mustjala** Estonia
52 C5 **Mustla** Estonia
29 N3 **Mustola** Finland
13 H5 **Muston** England
52 C5 **Mustvee** Estonia
65 H4 **Musu-dan** C N Korea
139 K4 **Muswellbrook** New South Wales Australia
48 F1 **Muszyna** Poland
84 H4 **Mut** Egypt
78 D3 **Mut** Turkey
38 M8 **Muta** Slovenia
88 C1 **Mutai** Uganda
89 G4 **Mutale** R S Africa
87 E8 **Mutanda** Zambia
Mutankiang see **Mudanjiang**
88 E10 **Mutarara** Mozambique
87 F9 **Mutare** Zimbabwe
37 O4 **Mutěnín** Czech Rep
88 C10 **Mutepatepa** Zimbabwe
78 K6 **Muthanna, Al** prov Iraq
12 E1 **Muthill** Scotland
71 M9 **Mutis** mt Timor Indonesia
52 J2 **Mutnyy-Materik** Russian Federation
88 D10 **Mutoko** Zimbabwe
87 D7 **Mutombo Mukulu** Zaire
138 F4 **Mutooroo** South Australia Australia
88 C10 **Mutorashanga** Zimbabwe
65 D4 **Mutoudeng** China
65 D3 **Mutougou** China
45 R7 **Mutria, M** mt Italy
87 G10 **Mutsamudu** Comoros
87 D8 **Mutshatsha** Zaire
60 P4 **Mutsu** Japan
61 O5 **Mutsu-wan** B Japan
141 G6 **Muttaburra** Queensland Australia
40 G1 **Muttersholtz** France
36 E5 **Mutterstadt** Germany
41 M4 **Muttler** mt Switzerland
123 O3 **Mutton Bay** Quebec Canada
144 B7 **Muttonbird Is.** New Zealand
14 B4 **Mutton I** Ireland
107 L5 **Mutual** Oklahoma U.S.A.
87 G8 **Mutuala** Mozambique
129 H7 **Mutum** Mato Grosso Brazil
130 H6 **Mutum** Minas Gerais Brazil
128 F5 **Mutumparaná** Brazil
83 L9 **Mutur** Sri Lanka
36 C6 **Mutzig** France
33 R10 **Mutzschen** Germany
29 M9 **Muurame** Finland
29 L5 **Muurola** Finland
65 A5 **Mu Us Shamo** desert China
58 F1 **Muya** R Russian Federation
88 C3 **Muyinga** Burundi
125 M3 **Muy Muy** Nicaragua
57 A3 **Muynak** Uzbekistan
87 E7 **Muyumba** Zaire
67 C1 **Muyuping** China
74 E1 **Muzaffarabad** Kashmir
74 D3 **Muzaffargarh** Pakistan
74 G4 **Muzaffarnagar** India
75 L5 **Muzaffarpur** India
130 F7 **Muzambinho** Brazil
57 K4 **Muzat He** R China
50 F2 **Muzhi** Russian Federation
20 F6 **Muzillac** France
40 A3 **Muzin** R France
117 G8 **Muzon, C** Alaska U.S.A.
108 F8 **Múzquiz** Mexico
66 C4 **Muztag** mt China
66 D4 **Muztag** mt China
66 B4 **Muztagata** mt China
88 E8 **Mvera** Malawi
86 E4 **Mvolo** Sudan
87 G7 **Mvomero** Tanzania
86 B6 **M'Vouti** Congo
89 G2 **Mvuma** Zimbabwe
88 C10 **Mvurwi Ra** mts Zimbabwe
87 G10 **Mwali** isld Comoros
88 D7 **Mwambwa** R Zambia
88 D3 **Mwanza** Tanzania
88 D6 **Mwaya** Tanzania
14 B3 **Mweelrea** mts Ireland
86 D6 **Mweka** Zaire
87 D7 **Mwene Ditu** Zaire
87 F10 **Mwenezi** Zimbabwe
89 G3 **Mwenezi** R Zimbabwe
89 G3 **Mwenezi** Zimbabwe
88 B3 **Mwenga** Zaire
88 G6 **Mwera** Tanzania
89 G2 **Mwerihari** R Zimbabwe
88 B6 **Mweru, L** Zaire/Zambia
88 B6 **Mweru Wantipa** Zambia
89 F3 **Mwewe** R Zimbabwe
87 D7 **Mwimba** Zaire
87 D8 **Mwinilunga** Zambia
68 B2 **Myaing** Burma
113 E10 **Myakka** Florida U.S.A.
113 E10 **Myakka City** Florida U.S.A.
52 E5 **Myaksa** Russian Federation
31 H3 **Myálibórz** Poland
139 K4 **Myall L** New South Wales Australia
68 B3 **Myanaung** Burma
52 D3 **Myanduselga** Russian Federation
Myanmar see **Burma**
54 G2 **Myatlevo** Russian Federation
68 A2 **Myaungbwe** Burma
68 B4 **Myaungmya** Burma
68 D4 **Myawadi** Burma
46 F7 **Mycenae** Greece
68 A2 **Myebon** Burma
117 G8 **Myers Chuck** Alaska U.S.A.
95 L6 **Myerstown** Pennsylvania U.S.A.
68 B2 **Myingyan** Burma
68 C2 **Myinkyado** Burma
68 D6 **Myinmoletkat** mt Burma
68 B2 **Myinmu** Burma
68 B2 **Myitche** Burma
68 D5 **Myitta** Burma
68 C2 **Myittha** Burma
48 D2 **Myjava** Slovakia
26 F5 **Myken** lighthouse Norway
6 E1 **Mykines** isld Faeroes
52 H2 **Myla** Russian Federation
37 N2 **Mylau** Germany
29 M11 **Myllykoski** Finland
98 G1 **Mylo** North Dakota U.S.A.
75 O6 **Mymensingh** Bangladesh
29 J11 **Mynämäki** Finland
57 G2 **Mynaral** Kazakhstan
57 C4 **Mynbulak** Uzbekistan
8 B3 **Mynydd Bach** mts Wales
8 C3 **Mynydd Eppynt** mts Wales
68 A2 **Myohaung** Burma
68 B2 **Myohla** Burma
68 B2 **Myotha** Burma
68 B2 **Myothit** Burma
47 K8 **Myra** Turkey
109 K2 **Myra** Texas U.S.A.
141 F3 **Myra Vale** Queensland Australia
27 B11 **Myrdal** Norway
28 S10 **Myrdalsjökull** ice cap Iceland
26 H3 **Myre** Norway
27 G14 **Myresjö** Sweden
26 L6 **Myrheden** Sweden
118 F5 **Myrnam** Alberta Canada
119 U9 **Myrtle** Manitoba Canada
121 M8 **Myrtle** Ontario Canada
100 J3 **Myrtle** Idaho U.S.A.
111 G7 **Myrtle** Mississippi U.S.A.
112 J4 **Myrtle Beach** South Carolina U.S.A.
100 B6 **Myrtle Cr** Oregon U.S.A.
139 H6 **Myrtleford** Victoria Australia
100 A6 **Myrtle Point** Oregon U.S.A.
138 E4 **Myrtle Springs** South Australia Australia
141 L1 **Myrtletown** Queensland Australia
65 H3 **Mys Gamova** lighthouse Russian Federation
52 E5 **Myshkino** Russian Federation
47 J5 **Mysia** hist reg Turkey
56 C4 **Myski** Russian Federation
31 M6 **Myślenice** Poland
76 C4 **Mysore** India
147 P3 **Mys Shmidta** Russian Federation
26 G9 **Myssjo** Sweden
119 U3 **Mystery L** Manitoba Canada
112 D6 **Mystic** Georgia U.S.A.
99 O9 **Mystic** Iowa U.S.A.
52 H4 **Mysy** Permskaya obl Russian Federation
31 L5 **Myszków** Poland
31 N2 **Myszyniec** Poland
52 F6 **Myt** Russian Federation
68 H7 **My Tho** Vietnam
54 J1 **Mytishchi** Russian Federation
101 P9 **Myton** Utah U.S.A.
68 J6 **My Trach** Vietnam
29 T9 **Myvatn** L Iceland
57 H1 **Myylybulak** Kazakhstan
37 O4 **Mže** R Czech Rep
85 C4 **Mzereb,El** Mali
88 D7 **Mzimba** Malawi
89 F8 **Mzimvubu** R S Africa
88 E7 **Mzuzu** Malawi

N

37 M5 **Naab** R Germany
25 B5 **Naaldwijk** Netherlands
135 U6 **Naalehu** Hawaiian Is
80 C6 **Na'an** Israel
86 E4 **Naandi** Sudan
29 J11 **Naantali** Finland
25 D4 **Naarden** Netherlands
14 E3 **Naas** Ireland
29 N2 **Näätämönjoki** R Finland
89 A7 **Nababeep** S Africa
16 B5 **Nabaõ** R Portugal
75 K9 **Nabarangapur** India
61 K11 **Nabari** Japan
140 C1 **Nabarlek** N Terr Australia
71 F5 **Nabas** Panay Philippines
80 G1 **Nab'as Şakhr** Syria
79 F5 **Nabatīyet Ett Tahta** Lebanon
143 D7 **Nabberu, L** W Australia Australia
71 E2 **Nabbuan** Luzon Philippines
37 N5 **Nabburg** Germany
52 H6 **Naberezhnyye Chelny** Russian Federation
116 Q5 **Nabesna Gl** Alaska U.S.A.
43 D12 **Nabeul** Tunisia
139 K4 **Nabiac** New South Wales Australia
130 B7 **Nabileque,R** Brazil
136 H2 **Nabire** W Irian
123 K3 **Nabisipi R** Quebec Canada
79 F5 **Nabi Younés, Ras en** C Lebanon
80 E5 **Nablus** Jordan
79 E10 **Nabq** Egypt
71 F6 **Nabulao B** Negros Philippines
68 D5 **Nabule** Burma
88 H9 **Nacala** Mozambique
88 H9 **Nacala-a-Velha** Mozambique
125 L3 **Nacaome** Honduras
67 B5 **Nacham** Vietnam
100 E3 **Naches** Washington U.S.A.
100 D2 **Naches Pass** Washington U.S.A.
87 G8 **Nachingwea** Tanzania
74 D5 **Nāchna** India
66 E5 **Na Ch'u** R China
68 A7 **Nachuge** Andaman Is
102 C6 **Nacimiento** R California U.S.A.
102 C6 **Nacimiento Res** California U.S.A.
33 R7 **Nackel** Germany
103 P10 **Naco** Mexico
111 B10 **Nacogdoches** Texas U.S.A.
68 B6 **Nacondam I** Andaman Is
124 E2 **Nacozari de García** Mexico
Nada see **Dan Xian**
103 L3 **Nada** Utah U.S.A.
61 M8 **Nadachi** Japan
124 J4 **Nadadores** Mexico
67 B6 **Nadang** China
99 T4 **Nadeau** Michigan U.S.A.
Nådendal see **Naantali**
55 D4 **Nadezhdinka** Kazakhstan
137 Q5 **Nadi** Viti Levu Fiji
74 E7 **Nadiad** India
48 F4 **Nădlac** Romania
85 D1 **Nador** Morocco
48 G3 **Nádudvar** Hungary
77 C3 **Nadūshan** Iran
52 D3 **Nadvoitsy** Russian Federation
48 J2 **Nadvornaya** Ukraine
50 G2 **Nadym** Russian Federation
27 A13 **Naerbö** Norway
26 E7 **Naeröy** Norway
29 K5 **Nærum** Denmark
28 B5 **Næsbjerg** Denmark
28 C3 **Næsborg** Denmark
28 H6 **Næsby** Denmark
28 E6 **Næsbyhoved** Denmark
28 A3 **Næs Sund** inlet Denmark
28 H6 **Næstelsø** Denmark
28 H6 **Næstved** Denmark
68 A2 **Naf** R Burma
101 M7 **Naf** Idaho U.S.A.
85 G6 **Nafada** Nigeria
77 A4 **Naft-e Safīd** Iran
78 K4 **Naft Shahr** Iran
77 J6 **Nāg** Pakistan
71 F4 **Naga** Philippines
120 F3 **Nagagami** Ontario Canada
120 F3 **Nagagamisis L** Ontario Canada
60 F12 **Nagahama** Japan
75 Q5 **Nagaland** prov India
139 H6 **Nagambie** Victoria Australia
61 O13 **Nagannu-jima** isld Okinawa
61 L9 **Nagano** prefect Japan
61 M9 **Nagano** Japan
61 M9 **Naganohara** Japan
61 M8 **Nagaoka** Japan
75 P5 **Nagaon** India
76 D5 **Nagappattinam** India
76 E1 **Nāgāram** India
76 D2 **Nāgārjuna Sāgar** res India
76 D2 **Nagar Karnul** India
74 D6 **Nagar Parkar** Pakistan
60 C12 **Nagasaki** prefect Japan
60 C13 **Nagasaki** Japan
60 D14 **Nagasaki-bana** Japan
60 F12 **Naga-shima** isld Japan
60 D13 **Naga shima** isld Japan
60 E12 **Nagasu** Japan
60 E11 **Nagato** Japan
74 E5 **Nagaur** India
Nagchu Dzong see **Nagqu**
76 C6 **Nagercoil** India
26 H9 **Naggen** Sweden
74 H4 **Nagina** India
75 Q5 **Nāginimāra** India
61 P12 **Nago** Okinawa
74 J6 **Nagod** India
36 F6 **Nagold** R Germany
36 F6 **Nagold** Germany
78 L2 **Nagornyy Karabakh** aut reg Azerbaijan
52 H5 **Nagorsk** Russian Federation
61 P13 **Nago-wan** B Okinawa
61 K10 **Nagoya** Japan
74 H8 **Nagpur** India
66 E5 **Nagqu** China
29 J11 **Nagu** Finland
127 K5 **Nagua** Dominican Rep
71 E2 **Naguilian** Luzon Philippines
71 G4 **Nagumbuaya Pt** Philippines
48 D4 **Nagyatád** Hungary
48 D4 **Nagybajom** Hungary
48 G3 **Nagyecsed** Hungary
48 G3 **Nagykálló** Hungary
48 D4 **Nagykanizsa** Hungary
48 F3 **Nagykáta** Hungary
48 F3 **Nagykörös** Hungary
48 G3 **Nagyléta** Hungary
48 E3 **Nagymaros** Hungary
Nagyvárad see **Oradea**
66 F4 **Nagza** China
61 P13 **Naha** Okinawa
70 D4 **Nahabuan** Kalimantan
80 D3 **Nahalal** Israel
80 C7 **Naḥalat** Israel
80 C8 **Naḥal Eshkolot** Jordan
80 E4 **Naḥal Ginnat** Jordan
80 E4 **Naḥal 'Irit** Jordan
80 C8 **Naḥal Negohot** Jordan
80 C8 **Naḥal Zohar** Jordan
74 G3 **Nahan** India
117 M5 **Nahanni Butte** Northwest Territories Canada
117 L5 **Nahanni Nat. Park** Northwest Territories Canada
80 D1 **Nahariyya** Israel
77 A2 **Nahāvand** Iran
36 C4 **Nahbollenbach** Germany
36 C4 **Nahe** R Germany
80 G4 **Nahla** Jordan
137 O4 **Nahoï, C** Vanuatu
21 O7 **Nahon** R France
79 H2 **Nahr Sājūr** R Syria
80 C3 **Naḥsholim** Israel
131 B8 **Nahuel Huapi, L** Argentina
133 D6 **Nahuel Niyeu** Argentina
112 E6 **Nahunta** Georgia U.S.A.
71 E3 **Naic** Luzon Philippines
124 G4 **Naica** Mexico
119 N6 **Naicam** Saskatchewan Canada
66 E4 **Naij Tal** China
71 L9 **Naikliu** Timor Indonesia
37 M3 **Naila** Germany
65 D4 **Nailin** China
8 D5 **Nailsea** England
8 D4 **Nailsworth** England
65 E3 **Naiman Qi** China
66 E3 **Naimin Bulak** spring China
115 N6 **Nain** Labrador, Nfld Canada
77 C3 **Nā'īn** Iran
74 J7 **Nainpur** India
21 L8 **Naintré** France
120 J6 **Nairn** Ontario Canada
15 E3 **Nairn** Scotland
143 B7 **Nairn, Mt** W Australia Australia
15 D3 **Nairn,R** Scotland
88 F2 **Nairobi** Kenya
52 B5 **Naissaar** isld Estonia
88 F2 **Naivasha** Kenya
20 E6 **Naizin** France
77 B3 **Najafābād** Iran
78 J6 **Najaf, An** prov Iraq
78 K6 **Najaf, An** Iraq
126 F4 **Najasa** R Cuba
17 F2 **Nájera** Spain
17 F2 **Najerilla** R Spain
65 H3 **Najin** N Korea
77 B2 **Najmabad** Iran
60 H12 **Naka** R Japan
60 C13 **Nakadōri shima** isld Japan
60 C12 **Nakagumi** Japan
61 P13 **Nakagusuku-wan** B Okinawa
61 N7 **Nakajō** Japan
60 C14 **Naka koshiki jima** isld Japan
60 D12 **Nakama** Japan
61 O9 **Nakaminato** Japan
60 F13 **Nakamura** Japan
60 E14 **Nakamura** Japan
61 M9 **Nakano** Japan
61 M9 **Nakanojō** Japan
60 G9 **Nakano-shima** isld Japan
67 H4 **Nakanougan-jima** isld Japan
61 Q12 **Nakaoshi** Okinawa
77 L3 **Naka Pass** Afghanistan
61 O5 **Nakasato** Japan
60 R3 **Nakasatsunai** Japan
60 T2 **Naka-shibetsu** Japan
55 D2 **Nakatay** Russian Federation
60 Q1 **Naka-Tombetsu** Japan
60 E12 **Nakatsu** Japan
61 L10 **Nakatsugawa** Japan
60 G10 **Naka-umi** Japan
116 J8 **Nakchamik I** Alaska U.S.A.
116 O6 **Naked I** Alaska U.S.A.
86 G2 **Nak'fa** Eritrea
78 K2 **Nakhichevan** Azerbaijan
78 K2 **Nakhichevanskaya Respublika** Azerbaijan
84 J4 **Nakhl** Egypt
65 J3 **Nakhodka** Russian Federation
68 E5 **Nakhon Nayok** Thailand
68 D6 **Nakhon Pathom** Thailand
68 F5 **Nakhon Ratchasima** Thailand
69 E8 **Nakhon Si Thammarat** Thailand
68 E4 **Nakhon Thai** Thailand
59 L2 **Nakhtakhe** Russian Federation
61 P12 **Nakijin** Okinawa
117 G6 **Nakina** British Columbia Canada
120 D2 **Nakina** Ontario Canada
29 K3 **Näkkälä** Finland
29 J10 **Nakkila** Finland
31 K2 **Nakło** Poland
116 J7 **Naknek** Alaska U.S.A.
61 O9 **Nakoso** Japan
67 F3 **Nakou** China
Naksho Biru see **Biru**
28 G7 **Nakskov** Denmark
26 G9 **Näkten** L Sweden
65 G7 **Naktong** R S Korea
88 F2 **Nakuru** Kenya
88 E2 **Nakuru, L** Kenya
117 P10 **Nakusp** British Columbia Canada
68 C1 **Na-lang** Burma
58 E2 **Nalayh** Mongolia
53 F11 **Nal'chik** Russian Federation
74 G10 **Naldurg** India
76 D2 **Nalgonda** India
22 G3 **Nalinnes** Belgium
76 D3 **Nallamala Hills** India
94 G8 **Nallen** West Virginia U.S.A.
21 M8 **Nalliers** Vienne France
78 C1 **Nallıhan** Turkey
87 D9 **Nalolo** Zambia
6 M2 **N Alwyn** oil rig North Sea
68 C1 **Nam** R Burma
68 F3 **Nam** R Laos
65 G5 **Nam** R N Korea
60 C12 **Nama** Japan
87 C9 **Namacunde** Angola
88 F10 **Namacurra** Mozambique
118 D8 **Namaka** Alberta Canada
118 K2 **Namakan L** Minnesota/Ontario U.S.A./Canada
77 F4 **Namakiār-e Shadād** salt lake Iran
77 E2 **Namak, Kavīr-e** salt waste Iran
69 H14 **Namang** Indonesia
57 F4 **Namangan** Uzbekistan
88 G8 **Namapa** Mozambique
88 G9 **Namaponda** Mozambique
87 C11 **Namaqualand** tribal area Namibia
87 C12 **Namaqualand** dist S Africa
88 F9 **Namarroi** Mozambique
86 F5 **Namasagali** Uganda
87 E9 **Nambala** Zambia
68 E2 **Nam Beng** R Laos
141 L7 **Nambour** Queensland Australia
139 L4 **Nambucca Heads** New South Wales Australia
68 G3 **Nam Ca Dinh** R Laos
69 G8 **Nam Can** Vietnam
66 E5 **Nam Co** L China
26 F7 **Namdalen** V Norway
26 E7 **Namdalseid** Norway
68 G2 **Nam Ðing** Vietnam
88 G8 **Namecala** Mozambique
99 P3 **Namekagon** R Wisconsin U.S.A.
61 L9 **Namerikawa** Japan
48 E1 **Námestovo** Slovakia
88 G9 **Nametil** Mozambique
119 P4 **Namew L** Saskatchewan Canada
68 F2 **Nam Het** R Laos
68 D2 **Nam Hsin** R Burma
87 B10 **Namib Des** Namibia
87 B9 **Namibe** Angola
87 B10 **Namib Game Res.** Namibia
87 C10 **Namibia** rep Africa
88 F9 **Namicunde** Mozambique
61 O8 **Namie** Japan
61 O5 **Namioka** Japan
56 D6 **Namir** Mongolia
87 C11 **Namisis** mt Namibia
66 F6 **Namjagbarwa Feng** mt China

68 F3 Nam Khan R Laos
68 D2 Nam Kok R Thailand
68 C1 Namlan Burma
68 C2 Namlang R Burma
68 E2 Nam Loi R Burma
68 E2 Nam Ma R Laos
68 C3 Nammekon Burma
68 G3 Nam Muone R Laos
68 F1 Nam Na R Vietnam
68 E2 Nam Ngaou R Laos
68 F2 Nam Noud R Vietnam
139 J4 Namoi R New South Wales Australia
68 G4 Nam One R Laos
68 E1 Nam Ou R Laos
85 D2 Namous watercourse Algeria
118 A2 Nampa Alberta Canada
29 M5 Nampa Finland
100 J6 Nampa Idaho U.S.A.
85 C5 Nampala Mali
68 E4 Nam Pa Sak R Thailand
68 E4 Nam Pat Thailand
68 F4 Nam Phong Thailand
65 F5 Namp'o N Korea
22 B3 Nampont France
88 G9 Nampula Mozambique
68 G4 Nam Pung Res Thailand
26 F7 Namsen R Norway
68 F2 Nam Seng R Laos
26 E7 Namsos Norway
68 F2 Nam Suong R Laos
26 G7 Namsvatn L Norway
68 C2 Nam Teng Burma
68 E2 Nam Tha Laos
68 G4 Nam Theun R Laos
68 C2 Namtok Burma
68 D5 Nam Tok Thailand
68 D1 Namton Burma
51 M2 Namtsy Russian Federation
88 F9 Namuli mt Mozambique
87 G8 Namuno Mozambique
83 L11 Namunukula mt Sri Lanka
22 H3 Namur Belgium
121 Q7 Namur Quebec Canada
117 R7 Namur L Alberta Canada
87 C9 Namutoni Namibia
87 E9 Namwala Zambia
68 D4 Nam Wang R Thailand
88 E9 Namwera Malawi
31 L4 Namysłaki Poland
31 K4 Namysłów Poland
68 E3 Nan Thailand
100 B1 Nanaimo British Columbia Canada
102 R12 Nanakuli Hawaiian Is
65 H4 Nanam N Korea
67 F4 Nan'an China
67 B6 Nanan China
141 K7 Nanango Queensland Australia
67 F5 Nan'ao China
61 K8 Nanao Japan
67 F5 Nan'ao Dao isld China
61 L8 Nanao wan B Japan
61 K8 Nanatsu-jima isld Japan
67 B3 Nanbai China
67 B1 Nanbazhen China
67 B1 Nanbu China
21 P7 Nançay France
59 J2 Nancha China
67 E2 Nanchang China
65 E6 Nanchangshan Dao isld China
67 E3 Nancheng China
67 B1 Nanchong China
69 A9 Nancowry isld Nicobar Is
19 K4 Nancy France
144 A6 Nancy Sd New Zealand
74 H3 Nanda Devi mt India
67 B4 Nandan China
74 G9 Nānded India
139 K4 Nandewar Ra mts New South Wales Australia
37 M6 Nandlstadt Germany
22 J3 Nandrin Belgium
67 C7 Nandu Jiang R China
74 F8 Nandurbar India
76 D3 Nandyal India
36 D4 Nane R Germany
65 F4 Nanfen China
67 E3 Nanfeng China
67 D5 Nanfeng China
75 P4 Nang China
70 C4 Nangabadau Kalimantan
70 B6 Nangabulik Kalimantan
86 B5 Nanga Eboko Cameroon
70 C4 Nangahbunut Kalimantan
70 C4 Nangahdangkan Kalimantan
70 B5 Nangah Dedai Kalimantan
70 C4 Nangahembaloh Kalimantan
70 B4 Nangahkantuk Kalimantan
70 B4 Nangahketungau Kalimantan
70 B5 Nangahmau Kalimantan
70 B4 Nangah Merakai Kalimantan
70 B5 Nangahpinoh Kalimantan
70 C5 Nangahserawai Kalimantan
70 C4 Nangahsuruk Kalimantan
70 C4 Nangahtempuai Kalimantan
74 G3 Nangal India
71 E5 Nangalao isld Philippines
74 F1 Nanga Parbat mt Kashmir
71 K9 Nangarendi Indonesia
77 L2 Nangarhār prov Afghanistan
70 B5 Nangataman Kalimantan
69 K13 Nangatayap Indonesia
68 D7 Nangin Burma
18 G4 Nangis France
65 G5 Nangnim Sanmaek mts N Korea
65 C6 Nangong China
76 C6 Nanguneri India
87 D9 Nangweshi Zambia
Nanhaoqian see Shangyi
65 C6 Nanhe China
67 D1 Nan He R China
67 G1 Nanhui China
66 F4 Nan Hulsan Hu L China
76 C4 Nanjangud India
58 E5 Nanjiang China
67 D2 Nanjiangqiao China
Nanjie see Guangning
67 F1 Nanjing China
67 F4 Nanjing China
67 E4 Nankang China
67 C6 Nankang China
Nanking see Nanjing
65 C4 Nankouzhen China
65 C6 Nanle China
67 F1 Nanling China
67 D4 Nan Ling mts China
Nanma see Yiyuan
67 G2 Nanma China
67 E3 Nanmiao Jiangxi China
37 L7 Nannhofen Germany
143 C7 Nannine W Australia Australia
67 C5 Nanning China
143 B10 Nannup W Australia Australia
127 M2 Nanny Town hist site Jamaica
115 P5 Nanortalik Greenland
67 A4 Nanpan Jiang R China
75 J5 Nanpara India
67 F5 Nanpeng Liedao islds China
65 C5 Nanpi China
65 H3 Nanping China
68 E3 Nan Poui R Laos
65 D5 Nanpu China
67 F3 Nanpu Xi R China
Nanqiao see Fengxian
67 F4 Nanri Dao isld China
68 C2 Nansang Burma
134 D4 Nansei Shoto Ridge Pacific Oc
134 D5 Nansei Shoto Tr Pacific Oc
51 J5 Nan Shan mt ra China
66 E3 Nanshankou China
88 D3 Nansio Tanzania
143 A8 Nanson W Australia Australia
18 H8 Nant France
112 D2 Nantahala L North Carolina U.S.A.
115 M5 Nantais,L Quebec Canada
21 P4 Nanterre France
122 A8 Nantes Quebec Canada
20 G7 Nantes France
8 C4 Nant-garw Wales
70 K8 Nanti mt Sumatra
67 G2 Nantian China
18 F6 Nantiat France
120 K10 Nanticoke Ontario Canada
95 M8 Nanticoke R Delaware/Maryland U.S.A.
95 L5 Nanticoke Pennsylvania U.S.A.
8 C4 Nant Moel Wales
118 D8 Nanton Alberta Canada
67 G1 Nantong China
40 C5 Nantua France
95 R5 Nantucket I Massachusetts U.S.A.
88 G8 Nantulo Mozambique
8 D1 Nantwich England
94 J6 Nanty Glo Pennsylvania U.S.A.
137 Q3 Nanumanga isld Tuvalu
137 Q3 Nanumea isld Tuvalu
130 H5 Nanuque Brazil
116 M2 Nanushuk R Alaska U.S.A.
142 B5 Nanutarra W Australia Australia
65 B6 Nanweiquan China
67 A2 Nanxi China
67 D2 Nan Xian China
67 C5 Nanxiang China
67 E4 Nanxiong China
58 F5 Nanyang China
67 C2 Nanyaojie China
65 C7 Nanyi China
67 F1 Nanyi Hu China
61 O7 Nan'yō Japan
65 C5 Nanyuan China
88 F1 Nanyuki Kenya
65 F4 Nanzamu China
67 D1 Nanzhang China
67 G3 Nanzhen China
17 H6 Nao,C.de la Spain
115 M7 Naococane,L Quebec Canada
61 M8 Naoetsu Japan
75 N6 Naogaon Bangladesh
74 C6 Naokot Pakistan
59 K2 Naoli He R China
77 G3 Naomid, Dasht-e desert Iran
101 O8 Naomi Pk Utah U.S.A.
46 E4 Náousa Greece
67 C6 Naozhou Dao isld China
102 B3 Napa California U.S.A.
71 H7 Napabalana Indonesia
122 F7 Napadogan New Brunswick Canada
121 O8 Napanee Ontario Canada
116 G6 Napaskiak Alaska U.S.A.
115 O4 Napasoq Greenland
100 C3 Napavine Washington U.S.A.
71 F4 Napayauan Philippines
68 G3 Nape Laos
99 S8 Naperville Illinois U.S.A.
123 O2 Napetipi R Quebec Canada
40 G4 Napf mt Switzerland
145 F3 Napier New Zealand
99 L9 Napier Missouri U.S.A.
142 F2 Napier Broome B W Australia Australia
140 A4 Napier, Mt N Terr Australia
146 K10 Napier Mts Antarctica
140 D1 Napier Pen N Terr Australia
142 E3 Napier Ra W Australia Australia
121 R7 Napierville Quebec Canada
119 R9 Napinka Manitoba Canada
Naples see Napoli Italy
113 F11 Naples Florida U.S.A.
95 K4 Naples New York U.S.A.
109 N2 Naples Texas U.S.A.
67 B5 Napo China
68 G1 Napo China
128 C4 Napo prov Ecuador
128 C4 Napo R Peru/Ecuador
94 B7 Napoleon Indiana U.S.A.
98 G3 Napoleon North Dakota U.S.A.
94 C5 Napoleon Ohio U.S.A.
111 E12 Napoleonville Louisiana U.S.A.
43 G7 Napoletano, Appennino mts Italy
45 Q8 Napoli Italy
98 G9 Naponee Nebraska U.S.A.
135 U5 Napoopoo Hawaiian Is
131 E7 Naposta R Argentina
141 F8 Nappamerry Queensland Australia
94 A5 Nappanee Indiana U.S.A.
140 C6 Napperby N Terr Australia
110 C2 Napton Missouri U.S.A.
78 K3 Naqadeh Iran
79 F8 Naqb Ishtar Jordan
79 C9 Naqb Malba mt Egypt
61 J11 Nara Japan
85 C5 Nara Mali
139 G7 Naracoopa Tasmania Australia
138 F6 Naracoorte South Australia Australia
139 H5 Naradhan New South Wales Australia
117 O11 Naramata British Columbia Canada
83 K10 Narammala Sri Lanka
65 C2 Naran Bulag China
113 G12 Naranja Florida U.S.A.
124 E5 Naranjo Mexico
76 E2 Naraspur India
69 E9 Narathiwat Thailand
106 G6 Nara Visa New Mexico U.S.A.
75 O7 Narayanganj Bangladesh
76 C2 Narayanpet India
Narbada R see Narmada R
18 H9 Narbonne France
9 G2 Narborough England
16 C1 Narcea R Spain
43 J8 Nardò Italy
8 B7 Nare Head England
143 C9 Narembeen W Australia Australia
74 H3 Narendranagar India
90 D6 Nares Deep Atlantic Oc
115 M2 Nares Str Canada/Greenland
143 E9 Naretha W Australia Australia
31 O3 Narew Poland
65 G3 Narhong China
65 A5 Narin China
66 E4 Narin Gol R China
128 C3 Nariño div Colombia
61 O10 Narita Japan
127 P2 Nariva co Trinidad
127 P2 Nariva Swamp Trinidad
60 G11 Nariwa Japan
124 D4 Narizon pt Mexico
107 N2 Narka Kansas U.S.A.
29 M5 Narkaus Finland
26 N5 Narken Sweden
74 F7 Narmada R India
42 E6 Narni Italy
71 F5 Naro isld Philippines
52 K2 Narodnaya, Gora mt Russian Federation
89 A7 Naroegas S Africa
54 H1 Naro-Fominsk Russian Federation
88 E2 Narok Kenya
16 B1 Naron Spain
139 K6 Narooma New South Wales Australia
74 F2 Narowal Pakistan
29 J9 Närpes Finland
139 K4 Narrabri New South Wales Australia
139 J4 Narrabri West New South Wales Australia
95 Q5 Narragansett Rhode I U.S.A.
139 J3 Narran R New South Wales Australia
139 H5 Narrandera New South Wales Australia
139 H3 Narran,L New South Wales Australia
117 N8 Narraway R British Columbia Canada
141 H6 Narrien Ra Queensland Australia
143 B10 Narrogin W Australia Australia
139 J4 Narromine New South Wales Australia
100 G6 Narrows Oregon U.S.A.
94 G9 Narrows Virginia U.S.A.
95 M5 Narrowsburg New York U.S.A.
142 B1 Narrows, The str Perth, W Aust Australia
127 P4 Narrows,The chan St Kitts W Indies
143 B7 Narryer, Mt W Australia Australia
115 P5 Narsalik Greenland
115 P5 Narsaq Greenland
115 P5 Narsarsuaq Greenland
37 O1 Narsdorf Germany
74 G7 Narsinghgarh India
75 K10 Narsipatnam India
65 C3 Nart China
46 C4 Nartës, Gjoli i isld Albania
61 O7 Naruko Japan
131 F2 Narunjito, L Argentina
60 B13 Naru-shima isld Japan
61 O10 Narutō Japan
60 H11 Naruto-kaikyō str Japan
52 C5 Narva Estonia
52 C5 Narva Bay Estonia/Rus Fed
71 E2 Narvacan Luzon Philippines
26 J3 Narvik Norway
Narvskiy Zaliv see Narva Bay
74 G4 Narwana India
74 G6 Narwar India
140 C6 Narwietooma N Terr Australia
52 H1 Nar'yan-Mar Russian Federation
141 F8 Naryilco Queensland Australia
56 B6 Narymskiy Khrebet mts Kazakhstan
57 H4 Naryn Kirghizia
57 G4 Naryn Ugyut R Kirghizia
54 G4 Naryshkino Russian Federation
27 G11 Nås Sweden
85 F7 Nasarawa Nigeria
48 J3 Năsăud Romania
26 M5 Näsberg Sweden
18 H8 Nasbinals France
144 C6 Naseby New Zealand
107 M5 Nash Oklahoma U.S.A.
8 C5 Nash Wales
122 F6 Nash Cr New Brunswick Canada
116 D6 Nash Harbor Alaska U.S.A.
140 E5 Nash, L Queensland Australia
8 C5 Nash Pt Wales
99 O7 Nashua Iowa U.S.A.
101 T1 Nashua Montana U.S.A.
95 Q4 Nashua New Hampshire U.S.A.
111 C8 Nashville Arkansas U.S.A.
112 D6 Nashville Georgia U.S.A.
110 G3 Nashville Illinois U.S.A.
94 A7 Nashville Indiana U.S.A.
107 M4 Nashville Kansas U.S.A.
94 B4 Nashville Michigan U.S.A.
112 J2 Nashville North Carolina U.S.A.
94 E6 Nashville Ohio U.S.A.
110 K5 Nashville Tennessee U.S.A.
99 N2 Nashwauk Minnesota U.S.A.
48 E5 Našice Croatia
29 K10 Näsijärvi L Finland
74 E8 Nasik India
70 B4 Nasilat Kalimantan
86 F4 Nasir Sudan
79 A8 Nasr Egypt
79 H4 Naşrānī, Jebel an mts Syria
117 J8 Nass R British Columbia Canada
141 F3 Nassau R Queensland Australia
113 L9 Nassau New Providence I Bahamas
36 D3 Nassau Germany
98 K4 Nassau Minnesota U.S.A.
95 O4 Nassau New York U.S.A.
133 D9 Nassau,B.de Chile
113 F7 Nassau Sd Florida U.S.A.
95 M9 Nassawadox Virginia U.S.A.
33 T10 Nasseböhla Germany
37 L6 Nassenfels Germany
33 S7 Nassenheide Germany
84 J5 Nasser, L Egypt
27 G14 Nässjö Sweden
22 J3 Nassogne Belgium
38 N6 Nasswald Austria
115 M6 Nastapoka Is Northwest Territories Canada
36 D3 Nastätten Germany
71 E3 Nasugbu Luzon Philippines
61 N8 Nasu-Yumoto Japan
52 D6 Nasva Russian Federation
26 J10 Näsviken Sweden
87 E10 Nata Botswana
89 E3 Nata R Botswana
Natal see KwaZulu-Natal
141 H5 Natal R Queensland Australia
128 F5 Natal Brazil
69 D12 Natal Sumatra
90 M13 Natal Basin Indian Oc
141 H5 Natal Downs Queensland Australia
109 J6 Natalia Texas U.S.A.
55 C3 Natalinsk Russian Federation
77 B3 Naţanz Iran
123 L3 Natashquan Quebec Canada
123 L3 Natashquan R Quebec/Labrador Canada
116 K3 Natavukti L Alaska U.S.A.
116 R6 Natazhat Mt Alaska U.S.A.
111 E10 Natchez Mississippi U.S.A.
111 C10 Natchitoches Louisiana U.S.A.
139 H6 Nathalia Victoria Australia
115 R3 Nathorsts Land Greenland
106 D3 Nathrop Colorado U.S.A.
124 J5 Natillas Mexico
138 F6 Natimuk Victoria Australia
116 R4 Nation Alaska U.S.A.
101 L2 National Bison Ra Montana U.S.A.
102 G9 National City California U.S.A.
86 C3 National Park Chad
117 L8 Nation R British Columbia Canada
123 K4 Natiskotek B Anticosti I, Quebec
141 H6 Native Companion Cr Queensland Australia
124 B4 Natividad isld Mexico
129 J6 Natividade Brazil
68 C5 Natkyizin Burma
107 M2 Natoma Kansas U.S.A.
124 E3 Nátora Mexico
61 O7 Natori Japan
22 J3 Natoye Belgium
101 T6 Natrona Wyoming U.S.A.
88 F3 Natron L Tanzania
61 O8 Natsui-gawa R Japan
68 B3 Nattalin Burma
83 J10 Nattandiya Sri Lanka
29 N3 Nattaset mt Finland
68 C3 Nattaung mt Burma
26 L5 Nattavaara Sweden
37 O6 Natternberg Germany
37 J6 Nattheim Germany
27 H15 Nättraby Sweden
69 H10 Natuna Besar isld Indonesia
69 H11 Natuna, Kepulauan islds Indonesia
69 H10 Natuna Utara isld Indonesia
95 M2 Natural Bridge New York U.S.A.
94 H9 Natural Bridge Virginia U.S.A.
103 O4 Natural Br.Nat.Mon Utah U.S.A.
108 F3 Natural Dam L Texas U.S.A.
143 B10 Naturaliste, C W Australia Australia
143 A7 Naturaliste Chan W Australia Australia
81 H9 Naturaliste Plateau Indian Oc
106 B3 Naturita Colorado U.S.A.
99 V3 Naubinway Michigan U.S.A.
87 C10 Nauchas Namibia
121 T4 Naudville Quebec Canada
33 R7 Nauen Germany
130 E10 Naufragados, Pta Dos C Brazil
95 O5 Naugatuck Connecticut U.S.A.
71 E4 Naujan Philippines
29 N8 Naulavaara mt Finland
87 B9 Naulila Angola
36 G1 Naumburg Germany
37 M1 Naumburg Germany
68 C4 Naunglon Burma
68 C3 Naungpale Burma
33 R10 Naunhof Germany
80 G6 Na'ur Jordan
36 D2 Nauroth Germany
137 O2 Nauru rep Pacific Oc
55 D5 Naurzum Kazakhstan
26 A10 Naustdal Norway
26 C9 Nauste Norway
128 D4 Nauta Peru
75 K5 Nautanwa India
89 A6 Naute Dam Namibia
111 J8 Nauvoo Alabama U.S.A.
99 P9 Nauvoo Illinois U.S.A.
108 G7 Nava Mexico
57 F5 Navabad Tajikistan
57 E5 Navabadskiy Tajikistan
16 D3 Nava de Rey Spain
16 E5 Navahermosa Spain
103 P6 Navajo Arizona U.S.A.
103 M4 Navajo L Utah U.S.A.
103 O4 Navajo Mt Utah U.S.A.
103 O5 Navajo Nat.Mon Arizona U.S.A.
103 N5 Navajo Pt Arizona U.S.A.
106 C5 Navajo Res Colo/New Mex U.S.A.
16 E4 Navalcarnero Spain
16 D5 Navalmoral de la Mata Spain
86 E5 Nava R Zaire
133 D9 Navarino, I Chile
17 F2 Navarra prov Spain
139 G6 Navarre Victoria Australia
94 F6 Navarre Ohio U.S.A.
102 A2 Navarro R California U.S.A.
102 A2 Navarro California U.S.A.
109 L4 Navarro Mills Res Texas U.S.A.
109 L5 Navasota Texas U.S.A.
126 G5 Navassa I Caribbean
45 P5 Navelli Italy
9 F1 Navenby England
16 C1 Navia R Spain
16 C1 Navia Spain
109 L6 Navidad R Texas U.S.A.
127 K4 Navidad Bank Caribbean
130 H10 Navio R Brazil
54 F4 Navlya R Russian Federation
54 F4 Navlya Russian Federation
48 M6 Năvodari Romania
57 D4 Navoi Uzbekistan
124 E4 Navojoa Mexico
124 F5 Navolato Mexico
52 F5 Navoloki Russian Federation
46 E6 Návpaktos Greece
46 F7 Návplion Greece
28 B4 Navr Denmark
85 D6 Navrongo Ghana
74 E8 Navsari India
75 N6 Nawabganj Bangladesh
75 J5 Nawabganj India
74 C5 Nawabshah Pakistan
75 L6 Nawada India
77 K3 Nāwah Afghanistan
83 K10 Nawalapitiya Sri Lanka
84 F3 Nawfalīyah,an Libya
68 D1 Nawng-Hpa Burma
68 C1 Nawngkio Burma
68 D1 Nawngleng Burma
67 B2 Naxi China
46 G7 Náxos Greece
47 H7 Náxos isld Greece
18 E9 Nay France
16 E4 Nayacerrada, Pto. de pk Spain
75 L8 Nayagarh India
124 G6 Nayar Mexico
124 G7 Nayarit state Mexico
77 E3 Nay Band Iran
9 G4 Nayland England
113 D7 Naylor Georgia U.S.A.
110 F5 Naylor Missouri U.S.A.
67 B3 Nayong China
59 M3 Nayoro Japan
76 D4 Nāyudupeta India
129 L6 Nazaré Brazil
16 A5 Nazaré Portugal
130 J9 Nazaré da Mata Brazil
22 F2 Nazareth Belgium
76 C6 Nazareth India
80 E3 Nazareth Israel
95 M6 Nazareth Pennsylvania U.S.A.
130 E5 Nazário Brazil
54 N2 Nazarovka Russian Federation
56 D3 Nazarovo Krasnoyarskiy Kray Russian Federation
55 F3 Nazarovo Tyumenskaya obl Russian Federation
124 G5 Nazas Mexico
128 D6 Nazca Peru
59 J6 Naze Japan
9 H4 Naze,The C England
47 J7 Nazilli Turkey
56 A1 Nazinskaya R Russian Federation
75 Q5 Nazira India
75 O7 Nazir Hat Bangladesh
117 M9 Nazko British Columbia Canada
80 A7 Nazla Israel
80 D4 Nazlat Jordan
86 G4 Nazrēt Ethiopia
67 B4 Nazuo China
72 H4 Nazwá Oman
55 E1 Nazym R Russian Federation
55 F3 Nazyvayevsk Russian Federation
37 J1 Nazza Germany
6 L4 N Brae oil rig North Sea
89 F3 Ncema Dam Zimbabwe
88 A8 Nchanga Zambia
89 B4 Ncojane Botswana
87 B7 N'dalatando Angola
85 E6 Ndali Benin
71 L10 Ndao isld Indonesia
86 D4 Ndéle Cent Afr Republic
86 B6 Ndendé Gabon
137 O4 Ndeni isld Santa Cruz Is
86 B5 Ndikiniméki Cameroon
86 B6 Ndindi Gabon
86 C3 Ndjamena Chad
86 B6 Ndjolé Gabon
86 B6 Ndogo, Lagune lagoon Gabon
88 B8 Ndola Zambia
71 K9 Ndona Flores Indonesia
86 B6 N'Dongo Congo
26 E8 Nea Norway
141 J7 Neabul R Queensland Australia
46 D5 Néa Filippías Greece
14 E2 Neagh,L N Ireland
107 O4 Neal Kansas U.S.A.
140 B6 Neale,L N Terr Australia
138 D3 Neales R South Australia Australia
46 F4 Neá Moudhaniá Greece
48 K4 Neamţ reg Romania
20 F5 Néant France
21 O6 Néant R France
15 G2 Neap Shetland Scotland
47 H9 Neápolis Crete Greece
46 E4 Neápolis Dhytikí Makedhonía Greece
46 F8 Neápolis Pelopónnisos Greece
46 F6 Néa Psará Greece
116 J9 Near Is Aleutian Is
8 C4 Neath Wales
21 O4 Neauphle-le-Château France
47 H3 Néa Víssi Greece
85 D6 Nebbou Burkina
52 G3 Nebdino Russian Federation
28 A7 Nebel Germany
33 Q5 Nebel R Germany
41 M3 Nebelhorn mt Germany
43 B12 Nebeur Tunisia
43 C12 Nebhana R Tunisia
141 H8 Nebine R Queensland Australia
50 E5 Nebit-Dag Turkmenistan
141 J5 Nebo Queensland Australia
52 D5 Nebolchi Russian Federation
80 F6 Nebo, Mt Jordan
103 N2 Nebo,Mt Utah U.S.A.
33 P10 Nebra Germany
98 G8 Nebraska state U.S.A.
99 L9 Nebraska City Nebraska U.S.A.
43 F11 Nebrodi,Monti Sicily
99 Q5 Necedah Wisconsin U.S.A.
117 L9 Nechako R British Columbia Canada
98 J1 Neche North Dakota U.S.A.
109 M4 Neches R Texas U.S.A.
128 D2 Nechi R Colombia
33 T6 Nechlin Germany
36 F7 Neckar R Germany
36 F5 Neckarbischofsheim Germany
36 G5 Neckarelz Germany
36 F5 Neckargemünd Germany
36 F5 Neckarsteinach Germany
36 G5 Neckarsulm Germany
102 U13 Necker I Hawaiian Is
144 B7 Neck, The New Zealand
131 F7 Necochea Argentina
37 P4 Nečtiny Czech Rep
86 B6 Necuto Angola
21 K4 Nécy France
16 B1 Neda Spain
33 S5 Neddemin Germany
121 L5 Nedelec Quebec Canada
46 G3 Nedelino Bulgaria
106 E2 Nederland Colorado U.S.A.
109 N6 Nederland Texas U.S.A.
25 E5 Neder Rijn R Netherlands
25 E6 Nederweert Netherlands
142 A2 Nedlands dist Perth, W Aust Australia
33 Q8 Nedlitz Germany
66 E6 Nêdong China
17 F9 Nedroma Algeria
31 L5 Nedza Poland
25 G4 Neede Netherlands
9 H3 Needham Market England
101 Q5 Needle Mt Wyoming U.S.A.
103 K7 Needles California U.S.A.
145 E2 Needles Pt New Zealand
9 E6 Needles, The rocks England
109 M6 Needville Texas U.S.A.
119 S9 Neelin Manitoba Canada
101 N7 Neely Idaho U.S.A.
110 F5 Neelyville Missouri U.S.A.
130 B10 Neembucú dept Paraguay
99 S5 Neenah Wisconsin U.S.A.
119 S8 Neepawa Manitoba Canada
25 E6 Neer Netherlands
106 H3 Nee Res Colorado U.S.A.
115 M3 Neergaard L Northwest Territories Canada
22 J1 Neerpelt Belgium
22 J2 Neerwinden Belgium
28 A4 Nees Denmark
112 F4 Neeses South Carolina U.S.A.
55 F2 Nefedovo Russian Federation
85 F2 Nefta Tunisia
57 F4 Nefteabad Tajikistan
52 H6 Neftekamsk Russian Federation
8 B2 Nefyn Wales
43 C12 Nefza Tunisia
87 C7 Negage Angola
85 C6 Negala Mali
83 K10 Negama Sri Lanka
70 P10 Negara Bali Indonesia
70 D6 Negara R Kalimantan
70 D6 Negara Kalimantan
99 T3 Negaunee Michigan U.S.A.
80 B7 Negba Israel
86 G4 Negelē Ethiopia
69 F11 Negeri Sembilan Malaysia
79 E8 Negev mt reg Israel
130 C8 Negla R Paraguay
48 J5 Negoiu mt Romania
87 G8 Negomano Mozambique
83 J10 Negombo Sri Lanka
48 H6 Negotin Serbia Yugoslavia
46 E3 Negotino Macedonia
73 P5 Negrais,C Burma
131 H5 Negra o de los Difuntos, L Uruguay
143 D7 Negrara,R W Australia Australia
130 G6 Negra,Serra mts Brazil
16 B2 Negreira Spain
48 J6 Negreni Romania
18 G8 Nègrepelisse France
48 L4 Negreşti Romania
48 H3 Negreşti-Oaş Romania
127 H1 Negril Pt.N Jamaica
128 F4 Negro R Brazil
16 D9 Negro,C Morocco
94 H7 Negro Mt Penn/Maryland U.S.A.
131 C7 Negro,R Argentina
130 B9 Negro,R Paraguay
131 F4 Negro,R Uruguay
71 F5 Negros isld Philippines
47 J1 Negru Vodă Romania
100 B4 Nehalem Oregon U.S.A.
80 C5 Nehalim Israel
77 G4 Nehbandān Iran
59 H2 Nehe China
32 G10 Neheim-Hüsten Germany
48 K5 Nehoiaşu Romania
20 G3 Néhou France
33 R4 Nehringen Germany
80 C7 Neḥusha Israel
137 S5 Neiafu Tonga
127 J5 Neiba Dominican Rep
33 R10 Neichen Germany
52 C1 Neiden Norway
118 K8 Neidpath Saskatchewan Canada
101 P3 Neihart Montana U.S.A.
58 F4 Neihuang China
65 C7 Neihuang China
67 B2 Neijiang China
Neikiang see Neijiang
16 E2 Neila,Sa.de mts Spain
118 H6 Neilburg Saskatchewan Canada
68 A7 Neill I Andaman Is
99 Q5 Neillsville Wisconsin U.S.A.
123 M7 Neil's Harbour C Breton I, Nova Scotia
100 B2 Neilton Washington U.S.A.
58 E3 Nei Mongol Zizhiqu aut reg China
33 N8 Neindorf Germany
36 G5 Neipperg Germany
65 C6 Neiqiu China
31 H4 Neisse R Germany/Poland
128 C3 Neiva Colombia
37 O3 Nejdek Czech Rep
86 G4 Nejo Ethiopia
86 G4 Nek'emtē Ethiopia
53 F8 Nekhayevskiy Russian Federation
98 H1 Nekoma North Dakota U.S.A.
99 R5 Nekoosa Wisconsin U.S.A.
28 G5 Nekselø isld Denmark
27 H16 Neksø Denmark
27 C13 Nelaug Norway
141 F5 Nelia Queensland Australia
52 D6 Nelidovo Russian Federation
54 D1 Nelidovo Russian Federation
98 J7 Neligh Nebraska U.S.A.
142 E3 Nellie,Mt W Australia Australia
139 K6 Nelligen New South Wales Australia
76 D3 Nellore India
59 L2 Nel'ma Russian Federation
52 F5 Nel'sha Russian Federation
138 F7 Nelson Victoria Australia
117 P11 Nelson British Columbia Canada
13 F6 Nelson England
145 D4 Nelson New Zealand
103 L6 Nelson Arizona U.S.A.
102 C2 Nelson California U.S.A.
98 H9 Nelson Nebraska U.S.A.
103 K6 Nelson Nevada U.S.A.
112 J2 Nelson North Carolina U.S.A.
95 K5 Nelson Pennsylvania U.S.A.
99 P5 Nelson Wisconsin U.S.A.
8 C4 Nelson Wales
144 D4 Nelson Bays admin region New Zealand
138 F7 Nelson,C Victoria Australia
144 C5 Nelson Creek New Zealand
133 C8 Nelson,Estrecho chan Chile
117 M6 Nelson Forks British Columbia Canada
119 T3 Nelson House Manitoba Canada
116 E6 Nelson I Alaska U.S.A.
145 D4 Nelson Lakes Nat. Park New Zealand
119 V3 Nelson R Manitoba Canada
101 S1 Nelson Res Montana U.S.A.
94 E7 Nelsonville Ohio U.S.A.
89 G5 Nelspruit S Africa
52 J4 Nem R Russian Federation
85 C5 Néma Mauritania
52 H5 Nema Russian Federation
99 O3 Nemadji R Minnesota U.S.A.
99 L9 Nemaha Nebraska U.S.A.
76 C6 Nemam India
31 O2 Neman R Belarus
52 B6 Neman Russian Federation
52 F5 Nemda R Russian Federation
52 H3 Nemed Russian Federation
120 G5 Nemegos Ontario Canada
120 G4 Nemegosenda L Ontario Canada
119 M3 Nemeiban Saskatchewan Canada
46 D4 Nëmerçkë Albania
52 D1 Nemetskiy, Mys C Russian Federation
45 N6 Nemi L Italy
48 K4 Nemira mt Romania
48 M2 Nemirov Ukraine
115 M7 Nemiscau Quebec Canada
18 G4 Nemours France
71 L10 Nemperola Indonesia
52 B6 Nemunas R Lithuania
60 S2 Nemuro prefect Japan
60 T2 Nemuro Japan
60 T1 Nemuro-kaikyō str Japan/Rus Fed
14 C4 Nenagh Ireland
116 N4 Nenana Alaska U.S.A.
41 L3 Nendeln Liechtenstein
9 F2 Nene, R England
59 H2 Nen Jiang R China
59 J2 Nenjiang China
36 B4 Nennig Germany
36 H1 Nentershausen Germany
13 F4 Nenthead England
98 E7 Nenzel Nebraska U.S.A.
41 L3 Nenzing Austria
107 P4 Neodesha Kansas U.S.A.
99 S10 Neoga Illinois U.S.A.
99 L8 Neola Iowa U.S.A.
103 O1 Neola Utah U.S.A.
47 H7 Néon Karlóvasi Greece
99 S5 Neopit Wisconsin U.S.A.
130 H11 Neópolis Brazil
107 P4 Neosho R Kansas/Okla U.S.A.
99 S6 Neosho Wisconsin U.S.A.
80 E7 Ne'ot Adummim Jordan
80 F2 Ne'ot Golan Israel
80 F1 Ne'ot Mordekhay Israel
56 G2 Nepa R Russian Federation
75 K4 Nepal kingdom S Asia
75 J5 Nepalganj India
103 N2 Nephi Utah U.S.A.
14 B2 Nephin mt Ireland
14 B2 Nephin Beg mt Ireland
121 N8 Nephton Ontario Canada
45 M5 Nepi Italy
37 P3 Nepomyšl Czech Rep
119 N9 Neptune Saskatchewan Canada
113 F7 Neptune Beach Florida U.S.A.
138 D6 Neptune Is South Australia Australia
146 E8 Neptune Ra Antarctica
31 L4 Ner R Poland
42 E6 Nera R Italy
48 G6 Nera R Romania
18 F8 Nérac France
116 D6 Neragon I Alaska U.S.A.
58 G1 Nercha R Russian Federation
33 R10 Nerchau Germany
58 G1 Nerchinsk Russian Federation
59 G1 Nerchinsky Zavod Russian Federation
68 C7 Nerchus Passage Burma
52 J5 Nerdva Russian Federation
52 F5 Nerekhta Russian Federation
37 J6 Neresheim Germany
42 H5 Neretva R Bosnia-Herzegovina/Croatia
87 D9 Neriquinha Angola
52 B6 Neris R Lithuania
116 H7 Nerka,L Alaska U.S.A.
52 E6 Nerl' Russian Federation
52 F6 Nerl' Russian Federation
45 N5 Nerola Italy
18 G5 Nerondes France
45 N4 Nerone, M mt Italy
130 E5 Nerópolis Brazil
52 J3 Neroyka, Gora mt Russian Federation
17 F6 Nerpio Spain
142 E4 Nerrima W Australia Australia
54 E4 Nerussa R Russian Federation
16 C7 Nerva Spain
44 F3 Nervi Italy
52 K2 Ner'yuvom Russian Federation
25 E2 Nes Netherlands
27 D11 Nesbyen Norway
95 L5 Nescopeck Pennsylvania U.S.A.
47 J2 Nesebŭr Bulgaria
52 C6 Neshcherdo Oz L Belarus
80 D2 Nesher Israel
116 A3 Neshkan Alaska U.S.A.
99 R6 Neshkoro Wisconsin U.S.A.
111 G9 Neshoba Mississippi U.S.A.
29 T9 Neskaupsstadhur Iceland
27 D13 Neslandsvatn Norway
22 D4 Nesle France
123 N3 Nesle,L Quebec Canada
26 F5 Nesna Norway
26 F5 Nesöy isld Norway
100 G1 Nespelem Washington U.S.A.
45 O5 Nespolo Italy
19 O16 Nesque R France
107 L3 Ness City Kansas U.S.A.
37 K1 Nesse R Germany
26 R1 Nesseby Norway
117 F6 Nesselrode,Mt Br Col/Alaska Canada/U.S.A.
18 F10 Neste R France
31 O1 Nesterov Russian Federation
120 G6 Nesterville Ontario Canada
52 G6 Nestiary Russian Federation
127 P2 Nestor Trinidad
118 J1 Nestor Falls Ontario Canada
99 S3 Nestoria Michigan U.S.A.
46 E4 Nestórion Greece
46 G3 Néstos R Greece
27 A11 Nesttun Norway
80 C6 Nes Ẓiyyona Israel
80 C4 Netanya Israel
107 P2 Netawaka Kansas U.S.A.
95 N6 Netcong New Jersey U.S.A.
32 K9 Nethe R Germany
118 H7 Netherhill Saskatchewan Canada
25 Netherlands kingdom Europe
127 K8 Netherlands Antilles W Indies
8 C5 Nether Stowey England
145 E2 Netherton New Zealand
15 E3 Nethy Bridge Scotland
80 C6 Netiva Israel
80 C7 Netiv HaLamed Israel
80 B8 Netivot Israel
43 H9 Neto R Italy
36 E2 Netphen Germany
37 J1 Netra Germany
75 O6 Netrakona Bangladesh
36 C3 Nette R Germany
36 B3 Nettersheim Germany
25 F6 Nettetal Germany
115 M4 Nettilling L Northwest Territories Canada
99 N1 Nett L Minnesota U.S.A.
9 F4 Nettlebed England
120 K4 Nettle Lakes Prov. Park Ontario Canada
110 F6 Nettleton Arkansas U.S.A.
111 H7 Nettleton Mississippi U.S.A.
45 N7 Nettuno Italy
125 N9 Netzahualcoyotl, Presa res Mexico
37 N2 Netzschkau Germany
36 H1 Neu Germany
32 G7 Neu Arenberg Germany
37 N5 Neubäu Germany
32 H9 Neubeckum Germany
21 M3 Neuborg,le France
33 S5 Neubrandenburg Germany
32 J7 Neubruchhausen Germany
36 H4 Neubrunn Germany
33 P4 Neubukow Germany
33 P5 Neuburg Germany
37 L6 Neuburg Germany
40 E3 Neuchâtel canton Switzerland
40 E3 Neuchâtel Switzerland
40 E4 Neuchâtel, Lac de Switzerland
32 M9 Neuckrug Germany
119 P8 Neudorf Saskatchewan Canada
37 M3 Neudrossenfeld Germany
32 L10 Neu-Eichenberg Germany
36 F6 Neuenburg Baden-Württemberg Germany
32 G6 Neuenburg Niedersachsen Germany
32 E7 Neuenhaus Germany
32 J6 Neuenkirchen Niedersachsen Germany
32 F8 Neuenkirchen Nordrhein-Westfalen Germany
32 G10 Neuenrade Germany
36 G5 Neuenstadt Germany
36 H5 Neuenstein Germany
36 G2 Neuental Germany
32 J5 Neuenwalde Germany
37 M7 Neufahrn Germany
40 G1 Neuf Brisach France
22 J4 Neufchateau Belgium
19 J4 Neufchâteau France
21 L5 Neufchâtel Sarthe France
21 N2 Neufchâtel-en-Bray France
22 B2 Neufchâtel-Hardelot France
22 F5 Neufchâtel-sur-Aisne France
38 K5 Neufelden Austria
36 G6 Neuffen Germany
21 O3 Neuf-Marché France
36 G7 Neufra Germany
41 N2 Neugablonz Germany
33 S6 Neuglobsow Germany
32 G5 Neuharlingersiel Germany
33 N6 Neuhaus Germany
37 M4 Neuhaus Bayern Germany
32 K5 Neuhaus Niedersachsen Germany
36 G6 Neuhausen Germany
37 P2 Neuhausen Germany
33 S8 Neuhof Germany
38 K5 Neuhofen Austria
36 G5 Neuhütten Germany
21 N8 Neuillay-les-Bois France
21 M4 Neuilly Orne France
21 P3 Neuilly-en-Thelle France
21 H3 Neuilly-la-Forêt France
36 F3 Neu-Isenburg Germany
33 R5 Neukalen Germany
33 O6 Neu Kaliss Germany
38 F7 Neukirchen Austria
37 O2 Neukirchen Germany
33 O4 Neukirchen Schleswig-Holstein Germany
37 N5 Neukirchen Balbini Germany
32 L6 Neukloster Germany
33 P5 Neukloster Germany
21 M6 Neullé-Pont-Pierre France
20 E5 Neulliac France
37 N2 Neumark Germany
38 H6 Neumarkt Salzburg Austria
38 K7 Neumarkt Steiermark Austria
37 L5 Neumarkt Germany
37 O7 Neumarkt-St Veit Germany
32 L4 Neumünster Germany
37 N5 Neunburg Germany
21 O6 Neung-sur-Beuvron France
38 O6 Neunkirchen Austria
36 C2 Neunkirchen Germany
36 D2 Neunkirchen Nordrhein-Westfalen Germany
36 E2 Neunkirchen Rheinland-Pfalz Germany
36 C5 Neunkirchen Saarland Germany
37 O7 Neuötting Germany
131 B7 Neuquén terr Argentina
131 C7 Neuquén Argentina
131 B7 Neuquén, R Argentina
33 R7 Neuruppin Germany
37 K7 Neusäss Germany
112 L3 Neuse R North Carolina U.S.A.
48 D3 Neusiedla Austria
48 D3 Neusiedler See Austria
36 B1 Neuss Germany
18 H7 Neussargues France
48 C3 Neustadt Austria
33 Q7 Neustadt Brandenburg Germany
36 G2 Neustadt Hessen Germany
36 H3 Neustadt Hessen Germany
36 G4 Neustadt Hessen Germany
36 E5 Neustadt Rheinland-Pfalz Germany
37 K2 Neustadt Thüringen Germany
37 M2 Neustadt Thüringen Germany
37 K4 Neustadt an der Aisch Germany
37 N4 Neustadt an der Waldnaab Germany
37 L3 Neustadt bei Coburg Germany
33 P6 Neustadt-Glewe Germany
32 G6 Neustadt-gödens Germany
37 M7 Neustift Germany
33 S6 Neustrelitz Germany
37 J7 Neu Ulm Germany
22 D2 Neuve Chapelle France
21 M4 Neuve-Lyre,la France
40 F3 Neuveville Switzerland
18 G7 Neuvic France
109 N4 Neuville Texas U.S.A.
21 P5 Neuville-aux-Bois France
21 L8 Neuville-de-Poitou Vienne France
22 G5 Neuville-en-Tourne-à-Fuy France
19 O12 Neuville-les-Dames France

21 N2 **Neuville-les-Dieppe** France
21 K8 **Neuvy Bouin** France
21 M6 **Neuvy-le-Roi** France
21 O8 **Neuvy Pailloux** France
21 O8 **Neuvy St. Sépulchre** France
21 P7 **Neuvy-sur-Barangeon** France
33 O8 **Neuwegersleben** Germany
36 E6 **Neuweier** Germany
32 H5 **Neuwerk** *isld* Germany
36 C3 **Neuwied** Germany
36 C6 **Neuwiller** France
32 L6 **Neu-Wulmstorf** Germany
52 D5 **Neva** *R* Russian Federation
27 G11 **Neva** Sweden
99 R4 **Neva** Wisconsin U.S.A.
102 F2 **Nevada** *state* U.S.A.
99 N7 **Nevada** Iowa U.S.A.
110 B4 **Nevada** Missouri U.S.A.
109 L2 **Nevada** Texas U.S.A.
102 C2 **Nevada City** California U.S.A.
128 D2 **Nevada de Cocuy,Sa** *mts* Colombia
124 H8 **Nevada de Colima** Mexico
16 E7 **Nevada, Sierra** *mts* Spain
131 C5 **Nevado, Cerro** *pk* Argentina
131 B6 **Nevados Chillán** *mt* Chile
131 C5 **Nevado, Sierra del** *ra* Argentina
54 A1 **Nevel'** Russian Federation
59 M2 **Nevel'sk** Russian Federation
59 H1 **Never** Russian Federation
8 B3 **Nevern** Wales
26 F6 **Nevernes** Norway
18 H5 **Nevers** France
139 J4 **Nevertire** New South Wales Australia
48 E7 **Nevesinje** Bosnia-Herzegovina
20 C6 **Névez** France
45 H2 **Neviano d'Arduini** Italy
32 F10 **Neviges** Germany
118 K9 **Neville** Saskatchewan Canada
21 M2 **Neville** France
112 F5 **Nevils** Georgia U.S.A.
53 F11 **Nevinnomyssk** Russian Federation
79 E9 **Neviot** Egypt
118 D6 **Nevis** Alberta Canada
127 P4 **Nevis** *isld* Lesser Antilles
99 M3 **Nevis** Minnesota U.S.A.
127 P4 **Nevis Pk** Nevis W Indies
80 E6 **Nevit HaGedud** Jordan
78 E2 **Nevşehir** Turkey
65 J2 **Nevskoye** Russian Federation
55 D2 **Nev'yansk** Russian Federation
103 J9 **New** *R* California U.S.A.
112 F1 **New** *R* North Carolina U.S.A.
94 F9 **New** *R* Virginia/W Virginia U.S.A.
12 E4 **New Abbey** Scotland
95 S3 **Newagen** Maine U.S.A.
87 G8 **Newala** Tanzania
94 B8 **New Albany** Indiana U.S.A.
111 G7 **New Albany** Mississippi U.S.A.
95 L5 **New Albany** Pennsylvania U.S.A.
99 P6 **New Albin** Iowa U.S.A.
99 S4 **Newald** Wisconsin U.S.A.
9 E5 **New Alresford** England
141 J8 **New Angledool** New South Wales Australia
9 F1 **Newark** England
110 E6 **Newark** Arkansas U.S.A.
102 B4 **Newark** California U.S.A.
95 M7 **Newark** Delaware U.S.A.
99 S8 **Newark** Illinois U.S.A.
98 G9 **Newark** Nebraska U.S.A.
95 N6 **Newark** New Jersey U.S.A.
95 K3 **Newark** New York U.S.A.
94 E6 **Newark** Ohio U.S.A.
95 L4 **Newark Valley** New York U.S.A.
110 G3 **New Athens** Illinois U.S.A.
99 P4 **New Auburn** Wisconsin U.S.A.
111 G10 **New Augusta** Mississippi U.S.A.
94 E4 **New Baltimore** Michigan U.S.A.
94 J7 **New Baltimore** Pennsylvania U.S.A.
95 R5 **New Bedford** Massachusetts U.S.A.
100 C4 **Newberg** Oregon U.S.A.
99 Q10 **New Berlin** Illinois U.S.A.
95 M4 **New Berlin** New York U.S.A.
111 J9 **Newbern** Alabama U.S.A.
112 K2 **New Bern** North Carolina U.S.A.
110 G5 **Newbern** Tennessee U.S.A.
102 H7 **Newberry** California U.S.A.
113 E8 **Newberry** Florida U.S.A.
110 J3 **Newberry** Indiana U.S.A.
99 V3 **Newberry** Michigan U.S.A.
112 F3 **Newberry** South Carolina U.S.A.
94 H5 **New Bethlehem** Pennsylvania U.S.A.
13 G3 **Newbiggin by-the-Sea** England
13 E3 **Newbigging** Scotland
110 D3 **New Bloomfield** Missouri U.S.A.
99 R4 **Newbold** Wisconsin U.S.A.
121 O8 **Newboro** Ontario Canada
8 B1 **Newborough** Wales
99 Q8 **New Boston** Illinois U.S.A.
109 N2 **New Boston** Texas U.S.A.
109 J6 **New Braunfels** Texas U.S.A.
94 C6 **New Bremen** Ohio U.S.A.
12 E3 **New Bridge** Scotland
8 C3 **Newbridge** Wales
118 G7 **New Brigden** Alberta Canada
136 K3 **New Britain** *isld* Papua New Guinea
95 P5 **New Britain** Connecticut U.S.A.
111 L10 **New Brockton** Alabama U.S.A.
122 F7 **New Brunswick** *prov* Canada
95 N6 **New Brunswick** New Jersey U.S.A.
9 H3 **New Buckenham** England
99 U8 **New Buffalo** Michigan U.S.A.
99 O8 **Newburg** Iowa U.S.A.
110 E4 **Newburg** Missouri U.S.A.
94 K6 **Newburg** Pennsylvania U.S.A.
94 H7 **Newburg** West Virginia U.S.A.
121 O8 **Newburgh** Ontario Canada
15 F3 **Newburgh** Scotland
15 E4 **Newburgh** Fife Scotland
110 J4 **Newburgh** Indiana U.S.A.
95 N5 **Newburgh** New York U.S.A.
123 T5 **New Burnt Cove** Newfoundland Canada
9 E5 **Newbury** England
95 R4 **Newburyport** Massachusetts U.S.A.
85 E6 **New Bussa** Nigeria
137 N6 **New Caledonia** *isld* Pacific Oc
95 O5 **New Canaan** Connecticut U.S.A.
99 P10 **New Canton** Illinois U.S.A.
122 G5 **New Carlisle** Quebec Canada
94 C7 **New Carlisle** Ohio U.S.A.
139 K5 **Newcastle** New South Wales Australia
122 G6 **Newcastle** New Brunswick Canada
121 M9 **Newcastle** Ontario Canada
14 E3 **Newcastle** Ireland
127 L2 **Newcastle** Jamaica
14 F2 **Newcastle** N Ireland
89 F6 **Newcastle** S Africa
102 C3 **Newcastle** California U.S.A.
106 C2 **New Castle** Colorado U.S.A.
94 B7 **New Castle** Indiana U.S.A.
110 L3 **New Castle** Kentucky U.S.A.
98 K7 **Newcastle** Nebraska U.S.A.
95 M7 **New Castle** New Jersey U.S.A.
107 N6 **Newcastle** Oklahoma U.S.A.
94 G6 **New Castle** Pennsylvania U.S.A.
109 J2 **Newcastle** Texas U.S.A.
103 L4 **Newcastle** Utah U.S.A.
94 G9 **New Castle** Virginia U.S.A.
98 B6 **Newcastle** Wyoming U.S.A.
127 P4 **Newcastle** Nevis W Indies
141 G1 **Newcastle B** Queensland Australia
122 F7 **Newcastle Br** New Brunswick Canada
8 B3 **Newcastle Emlyn** Wales
118 E7 **Newcastle Mine** Alberta Canada
141 G4 **Newcastle Ra** Queensland Australia
15 F5 **Newcastleton** Scotland
8 D1 **Newcastle Under Lyme** England
13 G4 **Newcastle-upon-Tyne** England
140 C3 **Newcastle Waters** N Terr Australia
14 B4 **Newcastle West** Ireland
9 F5 **New Chapel** England
106 B5 **Newcomb** New Mexico U.S.A.
94 F6 **Newcomerstown** Ohio U.S.A.
94 F7 **New Concord** Ohio U.S.A.
12 D3 **New Cumnock** Scotland
12 D3 **New Dailly** Scotland
119 R8 **Newdale** Manitoba Canada
101 O6 **Newdale** Idaho U.S.A.
118 E9 **New Dayton** Alberta Canada
15 F3 **New Deer** Scotland
143 C10 **Newdegate** W Australia Australia
76 **New Delhi** India
117 P11 **New Denver** British Columbia Canada
111 M7 **New Echota Nat.Mon** Georgia U.S.A.
111 D8 **New Edinburg** Arkansas U.S.A.
113 E7 **Newell** Georgia U.S.A.
99 L7 **Newell** Iowa U.S.A.
112 G2 **Newell** North Carolina U.S.A.
98 C5 **Newell** South Dakota U.S.A.
112 F4 **New Ellenton** South Carolina U.S.A.
143 F6 **Newell,L** W Australia Australia
118 E8 **Newell L** Alberta Canada
111 E9 **Newellton** Louisiana U.S.A.
98 D3 **New England** North Dakota U.S.A.
139 K4 **New England Ra** *mts* New South Wales Australia
90 D4 **New England Seamount Chain** Atlantic Oc
116 F7 **Newenham,C** Alaska U.S.A.
8 D4 **Newent** England
94 A3 **New Era** Michigan U.S.A.
80 F3 **Newe Ur** Israel
80 C3 **Newe Yam** Israel
94 J3 **Newfane** New York U.S.A.
95 P3 **Newfane** Vermont U.S.A.
141 K1 **New Farm** *dist* Brisbane, Qnsld Australia
95 R3 **Newfield** Maine U.S.A.
95 M7 **Newfield** New Jersey U.S.A.
117 P8 **New Fish Creek** Alberta Canada
110 E3 **New Florence** Missouri U.S.A.
98 K1 **Newfolden** Minnesota U.S.A.
9 E6 **New Forest** England
95 Q3 **Newfound L** New Hampshire U.S.A.
115 N6 **Newfoundland** *prov* Canada
123 P5 **Newfoundland** *isld* Newfoundland Canada
95 M5 **Newfoundland** Pennsylvania U.S.A.
90 F4 **Newfoundland Basin** Atlantic Oc
90 E4 **Newfoundland Rise** Atlantic Oc
110 D2 **New Franklin** Missouri U.S.A.
95 L7 **New Freedom** Pennsylvania U.S.A.
8 A4 **Newgale** Wales
12 D3 **New Galloway** Scotland
118 B9 **Newgate** British Columbia Canada
137 M3 **New Georgia** *isld* Solomon Is
122 H9 **New Germany** Nova Scotia Canada
99 R7 **New Glarus** Wisconsin U.S.A.
122 K8 **New Glasgow** Nova Scotia Canada
95 R3 **New Gloucester** Maine U.S.A.
127 O3 **New Grant** Trinidad
136 J3 **New Guinea** *isld* S E Asia
109 M6 **Newgulf** Texas U.S.A.
100 D1 **Newhalem** Washington U.S.A.
116 K7 **Newhalen** Alaska U.S.A.
102 F7 **Newhall** California U.S.A.
116 F5 **New Hamilton** Alaska U.S.A.
95 Q4 **New Hampshire** *state* U.S.A.
99 O6 **New Hampton** Iowa U.S.A.
99 M9 **New Hampton** Missouri U.S.A.
95 S3 **New Harbor** Maine U.S.A.
110 J3 **New Harmony** Indiana U.S.A.
95 O5 **New Hartford** Connecticut U.S.A.
9 G6 **Newhaven** England
95 P5 **New Haven** Connecticut U.S.A.
94 B5 **New Haven** Indiana U.S.A.
110 E3 **New Haven** Missouri U.S.A.
94 F8 **New Haven** West Virginia U.S.A.
98 B5 **New Haven** Wyoming U.S.A.
117 K8 **New Hazelton** British Columbia Canada
New Hebrides *see* **Vanuatu**
13 F6 **New Hey** England
13 H6 **New Holland** England
99 R9 **New Holland** Illinois U.S.A.
99 S6 **New Holstein** Wisconsin U.S.A.
109 O1 **Newhope** Arkansas U.S.A.
12 E2 **Newhouse** Scotland
111 E12 **New Iberia** Louisiana U.S.A.
9 H5 **Newington** England
112 F5 **Newington** Georgia U.S.A.
137 L2 **New Ireland** *isld* Bismarck Arch
95 N7 **New Jersey** *state* U.S.A.
94 H6 **New Kensington** Pennsylvania U.S.A.
95 L9 **New Kent** Virginia U.S.A.
106 F6 **Newkirk** New Mexico U.S.A.
107 N5 **Newkirk** Oklahoma U.S.A.
143 E8 **Newland Ra** W Australia Australia
98 E3 **New Leipzig** North Dakota U.S.A.
94 E7 **New Lexington** Ohio U.S.A.
99 Q6 **New Lisbon** Wisconsin U.S.A.
121 L5 **New Liskeard** Ontario Canada
99 P9 **New London** Iowa U.S.A.
99 M4 **New London** Minnesota U.S.A.
99 P10 **New London** Missouri U.S.A.
95 P3 **New London** New Hampshire U.S.A.
94 E5 **New London** Ohio U.S.A.
99 S5 **New London** Wisconsin U.S.A.
12 D4 **New Luce** Scotland
110 G5 **New Madrid** Missouri U.S.A.
12 E2 **Newmains** Scotland
143 C6 **Newman** W Australia Australia
145 E4 **Newman** New Zealand
102 C4 **Newman** California U.S.A.
99 T10 **Newman** Illinois U.S.A.
106 D9 **Newman** New Mexico U.S.A.
98 J8 **Newman Gr** Nebraska U.S.A.
142 C6 **Newman,Mt** W Australia Australia
123 T5 **Newman's Cove** Newfoundland Canada
141 K1 **Newmarket** *dist* Brisbane, Qnsld Australia
121 L8 **Newmarket** Ontario Canada
9 G3 **Newmarket** England
14 B4 **Newmarket** Ireland
127 J2 **Newmarket** Jamaica
110 K7 **New Market** Alabama U.S.A.
99 M9 **New Market** Iowa U.S.A.
95 Q3 **Newmarket** New Hampshire U.S.A.
94 J8 **New Market** Virginia U.S.A.
94 E7 **New Marshfield** Ohio U.S.A.
94 G7 **New Martinsville** West Virginia U.S.A.
94 F7 **New Matamoras** Ohio U.S.A.
100 J5 **New Meadows** Idaho U.S.A.
102 D4 **New Melones Res** California U.S.A.
106 D6 **New Mexico** *state* U.S.A.
94 C7 **New Miami** Ohio U.S.A.
95 O5 **New Milford** Connecticut U.S.A.
95 M5 **New Milford** Pennsylvania U.S.A.
12 D2 **Newmilns** Scotland
108 E2 **New Moore** Texas U.S.A.
111 M8 **Newnan** Georgia U.S.A.
113 E8 **Newnan L** Florida U.S.A.
139 K5 **Newnes** New South Wales Australia
8 D4 **Newnham** England
143 B9 **New Norcia** W Australia Australia
139 H8 **New Norfolk** Tasmania Australia
118 E6 **New Norway** Alberta Canada
111 F11 **New Orleans** Louisiana U.S.A.
119 O6 **New Osgoode** Saskatchewan Canada
95 K7 **New Oxford** Pennsylvania U.S.A.
95 N5 **New Paltz** New York U.S.A.
94 C7 **New Paris** Ohio U.S.A.
94 A8 **New Pekin** Indiana U.S.A.
94 F6 **New Philadelphia** Ohio U.S.A.
100 E7 **New Pine Creek** Oregon U.S.A.
15 F3 **New Pitsligo** Scotland
145 E3 **New Plymouth** New Zealand
100 J6 **New Plymouth** Idaho U.S.A.
122 H5 **Newport** Quebec Canada
8 D2 **Newport** England
9 G4 **Newport** England
9 E6 **Newport** England
14 B3 **Newport** Ireland
127 K3 **Newport** Jamaica
126 B2 **New Port** Curaçao Neth Antilles
110 E6 **Newport** Arkansas U.S.A.
99 T10 **Newport** Indiana U.S.A.
110 M2 **Newport** Kentucky U.S.A.
94 D5 **Newport** Michigan U.S.A.
99 O5 **Newport** Minnesota U.S.A.
98 G7 **Newport** Nebraska U.S.A.
95 P3 **Newport** New Hampshire U.S.A.
95 M7 **Newport** New Jersey U.S.A.
112 L3 **Newport** North Carolina U.S.A.
100 A5 **Newport** Oregon U.S.A.
95 K6 **Newport** Pennsylvania U.S.A.
95 Q5 **Newport** Rhode I U.S.A.
112 D2 **Newport** Tennessee U.S.A.
109 J2 **Newport** Texas U.S.A.
95 P2 **Newport** Vermont U.S.A.
100 H1 **Newport** Washington U.S.A.
8 B3 **Newport** Wales
8 D4 **Newport** Wales
8 B3 **Newport B** Wales
102 G8 **Newport Beach** California U.S.A.
95 L10 **Newport News** Virginia U.S.A.
13 F1 **Newport-on-Tay** Scotland
9 F3 **Newport Pagnell** England
113 E9 **New Port Richey** Florida U.S.A.
112 D1 **New Powell** Tennessee U.S.A.
99 N5 **New Prague** Minnesota U.S.A.
113 L9 **New Providence** *isld* Bahamas
8 A7 **Newquay** England
8 B3 **New Quay** Wales
113 E8 **New R** Florida U.S.A.
8 C3 **New Radnor** Wales
106 G1 **New Raymer** Colorado U.S.A.
99 N6 **New Richland** Minnesota U.S.A.
122 G5 **New Richmond** Quebec Canada
94 C8 **New Richmond** Ohio U.S.A.
99 O4 **New Richmond** Wisconsin U.S.A.
110 M5 **New River** Tennessee U.S.A.
112 K3 **New River Inlet** North Carolina U.S.A.
111 E11 **New Roads** Louisiana U.S.A.
98 G2 **New Rockford** North Dakota U.S.A.
9 G6 **New Romney** England
14 E4 **New Ross** Ireland
110 K2 **New Ross** Indiana U.S.A.
140 A3 **Newry** N Terr Australia
14 E2 **Newry** N Ireland
95 R2 **Newry** Maine U.S.A.
94 J6 **Newry** Pennsylvania U.S.A.
14 E2 **Newry Canal** N Ireland
98 E3 **New Salem** North Dakota U.S.A.
94 H7 **New Salem** Pennsylvania U.S.A.
13 E1 **New Scone** Scotland
99 O8 **New Sharon** Iowa U.S.A.
New Siberian Is *see* **Novosibirskiye Ostrova**
113 G8 **New Smyrna Beach** Florida U.S.A.
139 G5 **New South Wales** *state* Australia
94 E7 **New Straitsville** Ohio U.S.A.
85 D7 **New Tamale** Ghana
94 D10 **New Tazewell** Tennessee U.S.A.
116 E6 **Newtok** Alaska U.S.A.
9 G2 **Newton** England
13 E3 **Newton** Scotland
111 L10 **Newton** Alabama U.S.A.
110 H3 **Newton** Illinois U.S.A.
99 N8 **Newton** Iowa U.S.A.
107 N3 **Newton** Kansas U.S.A.
95 Q4 **Newton** Massachusetts U.S.A.
111 G9 **Newton** Mississippi U.S.A.
112 F2 **Newton** North Carolina U.S.A.
109 O5 **Newton** Texas U.S.A.
8 C6 **Newton Abbot** England
13 E4 **Newton Arlosh** England
95 M2 **Newton Falls** New York U.S.A.
94 G5 **Newton Falls** Ohio U.S.A.
8 B7 **Newton Ferrers** England
112 J2 **Newton Grove** North Carolina U.S.A.
94 K6 **Newton Hamilton** Pennsylvania U.S.A.
13 F6 **Newton-le-Willows** England
12 D2 **Newton Mearns** Scotland
15 D3 **Newtonmore** Scotland
101 O8 **Newton Res** Utah U.S.A.
12 D4 **Newton Stewart** Scotland
123 T4 **Newtown** Newfoundland Canada
110 C1 **Newtown** Missouri U.S.A.
95 K9 **Newtown** Virginia U.S.A.
8 C3 **Newtown** Wales
14 E2 **Newtownabbey** N Ireland
14 F2 **Newtownards** N Ireland
14 D2 **Newtownbutler** N Ireland
14 E2 **Newtownhamilton** N Ireland
14 E3 **Newtown Mt.Kennedy** Ireland
98 D2 **New Town Sanish** North Dakota U.S.A.
14 D2 **Newtown Stewart** N Ireland
99 M5 **New Ulm** Minnesota U.S.A.
109 L6 **New Ulm** Texas U.S.A.
98 D5 **New Underwood** South Dakota U.S.A.
111 L10 **Newville** Alabama U.S.A.
102 B2 **Newville** California U.S.A.
94 K6 **Newville** Pennsylvania U.S.A.
99 N8 **New Virginia** Iowa U.S.A.
94 E6 **New Washington** Ohio U.S.A.
123 M7 **New Waterford** C Breton I, Nova Scotia
109 M5 **New Waverly** Texas U.S.A.
117 J11 **New Westminster** British Columbia Canada
95 K7 **New Windsor** Maryland U.S.A.
123 S4 **New World I** Newfoundland Canada
100 F8 **New Year L** Nevada U.S.A.
96 **New York** *conurbation*
95 K4 **New York** *state* U.S.A.
103 J6 **New York Mts** California U.S.A.
144 **New Zealand** *dominion* S W Pacific
94 C5 **Ney** Ohio U.S.A.
52 F5 **Neya** Russian Federation
8 B4 **Neyland** Wales
77 D5 **Neyrīz** Iran
77 F1 **Neyshābūr** Iran
76 D5 **Neyveli** India
55 D2 **Neyvo Shaytanskiy** Russian Federation
31 H6 **Nežárka** *R* Czech Rep
54 C5 **Nezhin** Ukraine
100 J3 **Nezperce** Idaho U.S.A.
61 N7 **Nezugaseki** Japan
86 C6 **N'Gabé** Congo
88 E10 **N'gabu** Malawi
68 D5 **Nga Chong,Khao** *mt* Burma/Thailand
68 H5 **Ngac Linh** *mt* Vietnam
71 J9 **Ngadubolu** Sumba Indonesia
68 A2 **Ngahan** Burma
144 C5 **Ngahere** New Zealand
71 K10 **Ngalu** Indonesia
145 E3 **Ngamatapouri** New Zealand
145 F3 **Ngamatea Swamp** New Zealand
66 F5 **Ngamda** China
87 D10 **Ngami, L** Botswana
66 C5 **Ngangla Ringco** *L* China
74 J2 **Nganglong Kangri** *mt ra* China
75 M3 **Ngangzê Co** *L* China
70 N9 **Nganjuk** Java
68 G3 **Ngan Pha** *R* Vietnam
68 G3 **Ngan Sau** *R* Vietnam
68 G1 **Ngan Son** Vietnam
86 C6 **N'Gao** Congo
86 B4 **Ngaoundéré** Cameroon
144 C6 **Ngapara** New Zealand
68 B2 **Ngape** Burma
144 C6 **Ngapuna** New Zealand
70 K8 **Ngaras** Sumatra
145 E3 **Ngaroma** New Zealand
145 E2 **Ngaruawahia** New Zealand
145 F3 **Ngaruroro R** New Zealand
145 D1 **Ngataki** New Zealand
145 F3 **Ngatapo** New Zealand
145 E2 **Ngatea** New Zealand
68 B4 **Ngathainggyaung** Burma
145 E3 **Ngatira** New Zealand
145 E3 **Ngauruhoe** *vol* New Zealand
68 D7 **Ngawan Chaung** *R* Burma
145 F2 **Ngawaro** New Zealand
70 N9 **Ngawi** Java
68 B4 **Ngayok B** Burma
Ngemda *see* **Ngamda**
89 G2 **Ngezi** *R* Zimbabwe
89 G3 **Ngezi** *R* Zimbabwe
89 G3 **Ngezi** Zimbabwe
89 G2 **Ngezi Dam** Zimbabwe
Nghia Hung *see* **Thai Hoa**
68 G2 **Nghia Lô** Vietnam
71 M9 **Ngilmina** Indonesia
70 O9 **Ngimbang** Java
88 F6 **Ngindo** Tanzania
86 C5 **Ngoko** *R* Congo
87 E9 **Ngoma** Zambia
88 F2 **Ngong** Kenya
145 F3 **Ngongotaha** New Zealand
88 D7 **Ngoni** Malawi
66 F5 **Ngoring Hu** *L* China
88 E3 **Ngorongoro Crater** Tanzania
71 A2 **Ngotakiaha** Halmahera Indonesia
86 B6 **Ngounié** *R* Gabon
86 B2 **N'Gourti** Niger
88 B3 **Ngozi** Burundi
86 B3 **N'Guigmi** Niger
140 B1 **Nguiu** N Terr Australia
140 C2 **Ngukurr** N Terr Australia
68 F3 **Ngum** *R* Laos
71 K10 **Ngundju,Tg** *C* Sumba Indonesia
145 E1 **Ngunguru** New Zealand
88 E7 **Nguni** Tanzania
70 O10 **Ngunut** Java
85 G6 **Nguru** Nigeria
67 B5 **Nguyen Binh** Vietnam
89 B4 **Ngwatlhe Pan** Botswana
87 G10 **Nhachengue** Mozambique
128 G6 **Nhambiquara** Brazil
129 G4 **Nhamunda** Brazil
67 A6 **Nhan Nghia** Vietnam
68 J6 **Nha Trang** Vietnam
74 E9 **Nhava-Sheva** India
130 C6 **Nhecolândia** Brazil
68 F3 **Nhiep** *R* Laos
138 F6 **Nhill** Victoria Australia
68 G4 **Nhommarath** Laos
140 D1 **Nhulunbuy** N Terr Australia
68 G3 **Nhu Xuan** Vietnam
144 B7 **Niagara** New Zealand
98 H1 **Niagara** North Dakota U.S.A.
99 S4 **Niagara** Wisconsin U.S.A.
121 L9 **Niagara Falls** Ontario Canada
94 J3 **Niagara Falls** New York U.S.A.
121 L9 **Niagara-on-the-Lake** Ontario Canada
70 C3 **Niah** Sarawak
85 C7 **Niakaramandougou** Ivory Coast
85 E6 **Niamey** Niger
86 E5 **Niangara** Zaire
85 D5 **Niangaye,L** Mali
85 C7 **Niangbo,Pic de** *mt* Ivory Coast
85 D6 **Niangoloko** Burkina
110 D4 **Niangua** *R* Missouri U.S.A.
Niangxi *see* **Xinshao**
86 E5 **Nia Nia** Zaire
95 P5 **Niantic** Connecticut U.S.A.
65 E1 **Nianzishan** China
101 L2 **Niarada** Montana U.S.A.
86 B6 **Niari** *R* Congo
69 C12 **Nias** *isld* Indonesia
88 F8 **Niassa** Mozambique
46 F8 **Niata** Greece
101 R4 **Nibbe** Montana U.S.A.
28 D3 **Nibe** Denmark
28 D2 **Nibe Bredning** *B* Denmark
121 R3 **Nicabau** Quebec Canada
125 L3 **Nicaragua** *rep* Central America
125 M4 **Nicaragua, Lac de** Nicaragua
95 T1 **Nicatous L**
44 B4 **Nice** France
102 B2 **Nice** California U.S.A.
111 K11 **Niceville** Florida U.S.A.
115 M7 **Nichicun, L** Quebec Canada
60 E11 **Nichihara** Japan
112 E6 **Nicholls** Georgia U.S.A.
99 P8 **Nichols** Iowa U.S.A.
95 L4 **Nichols** New York U.S.A.
140 E4 **Nicholson** *R* Queensland Australia
142 G4 **Nicholson** W Australia Australia
143 B7 **Nicholson Ra** W Australia Australia
95 N2 **Nicholville** New York U.S.A.
99 O1 **Nickel L** Ontario Canada
129 G2 **Nickerie** *R* Suriname
107 M3 **Nickerson** Kansas U.S.A.
142 B5 **Nickol B** W Australia Australia
122 F3 **Nicman** Quebec Canada
69 A8 **Nicobar Is** Bay of Bengal
117 N10 **Nicola** British Columbia Canada
121 S6 **Nicolet** Quebec Canada
99 M5 **Nicollet** Minnesota U.S.A.
Nicomedia *see* **Kocaeli**
78 D4 **Nicosia** Cyprus
43 F11 **Nicosia** Sicily
43 G10 **Nicotera** Italy
125 M4 **Nicoya** Costa Rica
125 M5 **Nicoya,Pen.de** Costa Rica
122 E6 **Nictau** New Brunswick Canada
31 M5 **Nida** *R* Poland
76 E2 **Nidadavole** India
40 F3 **Nidau** Switzerland
36 F3 **Nidda** *R* Germany
36 G3 **Nidda** Germany
36 F3 **Niddatal** Germany
36 B2 **Nideggen** Germany
27 C13 **Nidelv** *R* Norway
41 H4 **Nidwalden** *canton* Switzerland
31 M2 **Nidzica** Poland
30 D1 **Niebüll** Germany
36 G1 **Niedenstein** Germany
37 N6 **Niederaichbach** Germany
37 L6 **Niederarnbach** Germany
36 H2 **Nieder Aula** Germany
37 N6 **Niederbayern** *dist* Germany
36 C3 **Niederbieber** Germany
19 L4 **Niederbronn** France
33 O6 **Nieder Elde** *R* Germany
36 G2 **Nieder Gemünden** Germany
33 R9 **Niedergörsdorf** Germany
36 C2 **Niederkassel** Germany
25 F6 **Niederkrüchten** Germany
36 D3 **Nieder Lahnstein** Germany
32 J10 **Nieder Marsberg** Germany
33 M6 **Nieder Marschacht** Germany
36 H5 **Niedernhall** Germany
36 E3 **Niedernhausen** Germany
36 E4 **Nieder Olm** Germany
36 E3 **Nieder Ouembach** Germany
32 J7 **Niedersachsen** *land* Germany
36 D2 **Nieder Schelden** Germany
36 E3 **Niederselters** Germany
32 J10 **Niedersfeld** Germany
36 H5 **Niederstetten** Germany
37 J6 **Niederstotzingen** Germany
36 D4 **Niederwald** Germany
36 E2 **Nieder Weidbach** Germany
36 F2 **Nieder Weimar** Germany
37 P2 **Niederwiesa** Germany
36 F3 **Nieder Wöllstadt** Germany
36 C3 **Nieder Zissen** Germany
33 T8 **Nieder Zittau** Germany
32 K9 **Nieheim** Germany
98 K2 **Nielsville** Minnesota U.S.A.
88 B4 **Niemba** Zaire
88 B5 **Niemba** *R* Zaire
33 Q9 **Niemberg** Germany
31 K5 **Niemcza** Poland
33 R8 **Niemegk** Germany
26 N5 **Niemis** Sweden
26 M5 **Niemisel** Sweden
31 K5 **Niemodlin** Poland
33 N7 **Nienbergen** Germany
32 F8 **Nienborg** Germany
32 K7 **Nienburg** Germany
33 P9 **Nienburg** Germany
33 N5 **Niendorf** Germany
31 M5 **Niepołomice** Poland
22 D2 **Nieppe** France
25 F5 **Niers** *R* Germany
36 E4 **Nierstein** Germany
31 H4 **Niesky** Germany
31 L3 **Nieszawa** Poland
85 C7 **Niete, Mt** Liberia
33 P10 **Nietleben** Germany
20 H8 **Nieul le Dolent** France
129 G2 **Nieuw Amsterdam** Suriname
25 D4 **Nieuwegein** Netherlands
25 B5 **Nieuwe Maas** Netherlands
25 C5 **Nieuwendijk** Netherlands
25 D4 **Nieuwersluis** Netherlands
32 F6 **Nieuweschans** Germany
25 H2 **Nieuweschans** Netherlands
22 D2 **Nieuwkerke** Belgium
25 C4 **Nieuwkoop** Netherlands
129 G2 **Nieuw Nickerie** Suriname
25 G2 **Nieuwolda** Netherlands
22 D1 **Nieuwpoort** Belgium
25 C5 **Nieuwpoort** Netherlands
25 E6 **Nieuwstadt** Netherlands
25 C4 **Nieuw-Vennep** Netherlands
18 H5 **Nièvre** *dept* France
122 G6 **Nigadoo** New Brunswick Canada
78 E3 **Niğde** Turkey
85 F5 **Niger** *rep* W Africa
85 B6 **Niger** *R* W Africa
85 F7 **Nigeria** *rep* W Africa
85 F8 **Niger,Mouths of the** Nigeria
144 B6 **Nightcaps** New Zealand
100 F1 **Nighthawk** Washington U.S.A.
141 G2 **Night I** Great Barrier Reef Aust
Nightingale I *see* **Bach Long Vi,I.**
90 B16 **Nightingale I** Tristan da Cunha
116 K2 **Nigu** *R* Alaska U.S.A.
21 O8 **Niherne** France
102 U13 **Nihoa** Hawaiian Is
131 C5 **Nihuili, Embalse del** *res* Argentina
61 N8 **Niigata** Japan
60 G12 **Niihama** Japan
135 N1 **Niihau** *isld* Hawaiian Is
61 N11 **Nii-jima** *isld* Japan
60 Q3 **Niikappu** *R* Japan
60 G10 **Niimi** Japan
60 D4 **Niitomi** Japan
61 N8 **Niitsu** Japan
17 F8 **Níjar** Spain
25 F2 **Nijega** Netherlands
60 S2 **Nijibetsu** Japan
79 F8 **Nijil** Jordan
25 D4 **Nijkerk** Netherlands
25 E5 **Nijmegen** Netherlands
25 F4 **Nijverdal** Netherlands
116 K6 **Nikabuna Lakes** Alaska U.S.A.
Nikaria *isld see* **Ikaría** *isld*
26 S2 **Nikel'** Russian Federation
55 C5 **Nikel'tau** Kazakhstan
71 M9 **Nikiniki** Timor Indonesia
46 F4 **Nikitas** Greece
52 D6 **Nikitinka** Russian Federation
54 K8 **Nikitovka** Ukraine
85 E7 **Nikki** Benin
61 N9 **Nikkō** Japan
61 N9 **Nikkō Nat. Park** Japan
40 G5 **Niklaus** Switzerland
116 K5 **Nikolai** Alaska U.S.A.
48 H1 **Nikolayev** Ukraine
54 D10 **Nikolayev** Ukraine
55 E4 **Nikolayevka** Kazakhstan
53 G8 **Nikolayevsk** Russian Federation
55 D4 **Nikolayevskiy** Russian Federation
59 M1 **Nikolayevsk-na-Amure** Russian Federation
52 G5 **Nikol'sk** Russian Federation
52 F5 **Nikolskoye** Russian Federation
55 C5 **Nikol'skoye** Russian Federation
88 C3 **Nikonga** *R* Tanzania
46 G1 **Nikopol** Bulgaria
54 F9 **Nikopol'** Ukraine
78 F1 **Niksar** Turkey
77 G6 **Nīkshahr** Iran
42 J6 **Nikšić** Montenegro Yugoslavia
137 S2 **Nikumaroro** *isld* Phoenix Is Pacific Oc
71 O8 **Nila** *isld* Indonesia
103 J8 **Niland** California U.S.A.
73 L8 **Nilande Atoll** Maldives
83 L9 **Nilaveli** Sri Lanka
84 J4 **Nile** *R* N E Africa
86 F2 **Nile** *prov* Sudan
102 B4 **Niles** California U.S.A.
107 N3 **Niles** Kansas U.S.A.
94 A5 **Niles** Michigan U.S.A.
94 G5 **Niles** Ohio U.S.A.
121 N6 **Nilgaut, L** Quebec Canada
76 C5 **Nilgiri Hills** India
116 E6 **Nilikluguk** Alaska U.S.A.
57 K3 **Nilka** China
29 N8 **Nilsiä** Finland
47 K4 **Nilüfer** *R* Turkey
57 F5 **Nil'van** Tajikistan
83 K11 **Nilwala** *R* Sri Lanka
28 D5 **Nim** Denmark
74 F6 **Nimach** India
85 C7 **Nimba, Mts** Guinea/Liberia/Ivory Co
142 E6 **Nimberra Well** W Australia Australia
139 L3 **Nimbin** New South Wales Australia
18 H9 **Nîmes** France
47 O12 **Nímfai** Greece
74 F5 **Nimka Thana** India
139 J6 **Nimmitabel** New South Wales Australia
101 M3 **Nimrod** Montana U.S.A.
Nimrod Bay *see* **Xiangshan Gang**
110 C7 **Nimrod L** Arkansas U.S.A.
144 C6 **Nimrod, Mt** New Zealand
109 O1 **Nimrod Res** Arkansas U.S.A.
77 H4 **Nīmrūz** *prov* Afghanistan
28 F4 **Nimtofte** Denmark
42 G4 **Nin** Croatia
78 H4 **Nīnawá** *prov* Iraq
71 F4 **Nin Bay** Philippines
87 D8 **Ninda** Angola
141 J8 **Nindigully** Queensland Australia
73 L7 **Nine Degree Chan** Lakshadweep Indian Oc
13 E2 **Nine Mile Burn** Scotland
139 G4 **Nine Mile L** New South Wales Australia
103 H2 **Ninemile Pk** Nevada U.S.A.
108 D6 **Nine Point Mesa** *mt* Texas U.S.A.
119 S9 **Ninette** Manitoba Canada
139 J7 **Ninety Mile Beach** Victoria Australia
145 D1 **Ninety Mile Beach** New Zealand
112 E3 **Ninety Six** South Carolina U.S.A.
94 G7 **Ninevah** Pennsylvania U.S.A.
133 E6 **Ninfas,Pta** Argentina
9 G6 **Ninfield** England
143 A6 **Ningaloo** W Australia Australia
59 J3 **Ning'an** China
67 G2 **Ningbo** China
65 D4 **Ningcheng** China
67 F3 **Ningde** China
67 E3 **Ningdu** China
67 D3 **Ninggang** China
67 F1 **Ningguo** China
67 G2 **Ninghai** China
65 D5 **Ninghe** China
Ning-hsia *see* **Yinchuan**
67 E3 **Ninghua** China
58 F4 **Ningjin** China
65 C6 **Ningjin** China
66 F5 **Ningjing Shan** *ra* China
65 C7 **Ningling** China
67 B5 **Ningming** China
Ningpo *see* **Ningbo**
Ningsia *aut reg see* **Ningxia**
65 B5 **Ningwu** China
58 E4 **Ningxia** *aut reg* China
67 D2 **Ningxiang** China
65 C7 **Ningyang** China
67 D4 **Ningyuan** China
67 B6 **Ninh Binh** Vietnam
68 J6 **Ninh Hoa** Vietnam
6 L2 **Ninian** *oil rig* North Sea
116 M6 **Ninilchik** Alaska U.S.A.
142 C5 **Niningarra** W Australia Australia
107 N7 **Ninnekah** Oklahoma U.S.A.
107 N4 **Ninnescah** *R* Kansas U.S.A.
146 D14 **Ninnis Glacier** Antarctica
111 C9 **Ninock** Louisiana U.S.A.
61 P5 **Ninohe** Japan
60 E14 **Ninokata** Japan
22 G2 **Ninove** Belgium
130 C7 **Nioaque** Brazil
94 H4 **Niobe** New York U.S.A.
98 E7 **Niobrara** *R* Nebraska U.S.A.
98 J7 **Niobrara** Nebraska U.S.A.
86 C6 **Nioki** Zaire
85 B6 **Niokolo-koba,Parc Nat.du** Senegal
85 A6 **Nioro du Rip** Senegal
85 C5 **Nioro du Sahel** Mali
18 E6 **Niort** France
Nios *isld see* **Íos** *isld*
99 P9 **Niota** Illinois U.S.A.
112 C2 **Niota** Tennessee U.S.A.
85 C5 **Niout** Mauritania
76 B2 **Nipani** India
71 H6 **Nipanipa,Tg** *C* Sulawesi
119 N5 **Nipawin** Saskatchewan Canada
119 N4 **Nipawin Prov.Park** Saskatchewan Canada
120 B3 **Nipigon** Ontario Canada
120 C4 **Nipigon B** Ontario Canada
120 B3 **Nipigon, Lake** Ontario Canada
118 H3 **Nipin R** Saskatchewan Canada
118 C3 **Nipisi R** Alberta Canada
122 G6 **Nipisquit,B** New Brunswick Canada
121 L6 **Nipissing Junc** Ontario Canada
120 K6 **Nipissing,L** Ontario Canada
122 F3 **Nipissis L** Quebec Canada
122 F3 **Nipissis R** Quebec Canada
122 G3 **Nipisso L** Quebec Canada
102 D6 **Nipomo** California U.S.A.
103 J6 **Nipton** California U.S.A.
84 J5 **Niqrûb el Fuqâni, Gebel** *mt* Egypt
126 F4 **Niquero** Cuba
80 E6 **Niran** Jordan
61 M10 **Nirasaki** Japan
80 C3 **Nir 'Ezyon** Israel
80 B6 **Nir Gallim** Israel
80 B7 **Nir Hen** Israel
74 H9 **Nirmal** India
75 M5 **Nirmali** India
80 B8 **Nir Moshe** Israel
94 B3 **Nirvana** Michigan U.S.A.
80 C6 **Nir Zevi** Israel
46 E1 **Niš** Serbia Yugoslavia
16 B5 **Nisa** Portugal
72 F6 **Nişāb** Yemen
46 F1 **Nisava** *R* Serbia Yugoslavia
95 K5 **Nisbet** Pennsylvania U.S.A.
60 O3 **Niseko** Japan
67 C2 **Nishi** China
61 P5 **Nishi-Hōji** Japan
60 J11 **Nishinomiya** Japan
60 F9 **Nishino-shima** *isld* Japan
61 L11 **Nishio** Japan
60 C13 **Nishi-Sonogi-hantō** *pen* Japan
60 C11 **Nishi-suidō** *str* Japan
60 H10 **Nishiwaki** Japan
116 H6 **Nishlik L** Alaska U.S.A.
99 L8 **Nishnabotna, E** *R* Iowa U.S.A.
99 L8 **Nishnabotna, W** *R* Iowa U.S.A.
130 J9 **Nísia Floresta** Brazil
48 J3 **Nisipitul** Romania
47 J8 **Nísiros** *isld* Greece
31 N5 **Nisko** Poland
98 C5 **Nisland** South Dakota U.S.A.
117 D4 **Nisling** *R* Yukon Territory Canada
48 L3 **Nisporeny** Moldova
100 C3 **Nisqually** *R* Washington U.S.A.
27 F15 **Nissan** *R* Sweden
27 C12 **Nissedal** Norway
27 C12 **Nisserv** *L* Norway
28 A3 **Nissum Bredning** *B* Denmark
28 A4 **Nissum Fjord** *inlet* Denmark
117 G5 **Nisutlin** *R* Yukon Territory Canada
115 M7 **Nitchequon** Quebec Canada
130 G8 **Niterói** Brazil
15 E5 **Nith,R** Scotland
15 E5 **Nithsdale** Scotland
71 M9 **Nitibe** Timor
80 G7 **Nitil** Jordan
100 A1 **Nitinat L** British Columbia Canada
9 E6 **Niton** England
31 L7 **Nitra** *R* Slovakia
48 E2 **Nitra** Slovakia
94 F8 **Nitro** West Virginia U.S.A.
55 D2 **Nitsa** *R* Russian Federation
29 N2 **Nitsjärvi** *L* Finland
37 N5 **Nittenau** Germany
37 M5 **Nittendorf** Germany
137 R5 **Niuafo'ou** *isld* Pacific Oc
137 S5 **Niuatoputapu** *isld* Pacific Oc
137 T5 **Niue** *isld* Pacific Oc
137 Q4 **Niulakita** *isld* Tuvalu
65 F4 **Niumaowu** China
69 F13 **Niur, Pulau** *isld* Sumatra
Niushan *see* **Donghai**
137 Q3 **Niutao** *isld* Tuvalu
65 E4 **Niuzhuang** China
29 K5 **Nivå** Denmark
29 L8 **Nivala** Finland
141 H7 **Nive** *R* Queensland Australia
18 E9 **Nive** *R* France
141 H7 **Nive Downs** Queensland Australia
22 G2 **Nivelles** Belgium
18 H5 **Nivernais** *prov* France
118 D1 **Niverville** Manitoba Canada
21 P3 **Nivillers** France
102 G4 **Nivloc** Nevada U.S.A.
40 B6 **Nivolas-Vermelle** France
52 D2 **Nivskiy** Russian Federation
74 J7 **Niwas** India
102 E2 **Nixon** Nevada U.S.A.
109 K6 **Nixon** Texas U.S.A.
47 N11 **Niyandros** *isld* Turkey
70 B4 **Niyat, Gunung** *mt* Kalimantan
74 H9 **Nizamabad** India
52 F6 **Nizhegorodskaya Oblast'** *prov* Russian Federation
52 E3 **Nizhmozero** Russian Federation
56 G3 **Nizhneangarsk** Russian Federation
52 H2 **Nizhne Bugayevo** Russian Federation
54 L9 **Nizhne Gnilovskoy** Russian Federation
52 H6 **Nizhnekamsk** Russian Federation
52 H6 **Nizhnekamskoye Vodokhranilishche** *res* Russian Federation
55 B4 **Nizhne-troitskiy** Russian Federation
56 E4 **Nizhneudinsk** Russian Federation
55 G1 **Nizhnevartovsk** Russian Federation
55 B4 **Nizhneye Il'yasovo** Russian Federation
52 D2 **Nizhneye Kuyto, Oz** *L* Russian Federation
52 F6 **Nizhniy Novgorod** Russian Federation
55 C2 **Nizhniy Tagil** Russian Federation
52 H6 **Nizhniy Takanysh** Russian Federation
56 F5 **Nizhniy Torey** Russian Federation
52 E2 **Nizhniy Vyalozerskiy** Russian Federation
52 G4 **Nizhniy Yenangsk** Russian Federation
55 E2 **Nizhnyaya Aremzyan** Russian Federation
55 C3 **Nizhnyaya Irga** Russian Federation
55 F3 **Nizhnyaya Omka** Russian Federation
52 J3 **Nizhnyaya-Omra** Russian Federation
52 G2 **Nizhnyaya Pesha** Russian Federation
56 E3 **Nizhnyaya Pomya** Russian Federation
55 D2 **Nizhnyaya Salda** Russian Federation
55 G4 **Nizhnyaya Suyetka** Russian Federation
55 E2 **Nizhnyaya Tavda** Russian Federation
52 F3 **Nizhnyaya Toyma** *R* Russian Federation
56 G1 **Nizhnyaya Tunguska** *R* Russian Federation
55 C2 **Nizhnyaya Tura** Russian Federation
52 H4 **Nizhnyaya Voch'** Russian Federation
52 F2 **Nizhnyaya Zolotitsa** Russian Federation
29 Q4 **Nizh Pirengskoye Ozero** *L* Russian Federation
56 G2 **Nizh Tunguska** *R* Russian Federation
116 Q6 **Nizina** Alaska U.S.A.
78 F3 **Nizip** Turkey
31 L7 **Nízké Tatry** *mts* Slovakia
48 F2 **Nižm Medzev** Slovakia
22 G4 **Nizy-le-Comte** France
44 D2 **Nizza** Italy
79 E8 **Nizzana** *hist site* Israel
80 C4 **Nizzane 'Oz** Israel
80 B7 **Nizzanim** Israel
70 D4 **Njaän** *mt* Kalimantan
87 G10 **Njazidja** *isld* Comoros
42 J6 **Njegoš** *mt* Montenegro Yugoslavia
87 G7 **Njinjo** Tanzania
87 D9 **Njoko** *R* Zambia
88 E5 **Njombe** *R* Tanzania
88 E6 **Njombe** Tanzania
88 G10 **Njoro** *isld* Mozambique
26 J9 **Njurundabommen** Sweden
27 J10 **Njutånger** Sweden
89 G7 **Nkandla** S Africa
88 D7 **Nkanka** *R* Zambia
88 E7 **Nkhata B** Malawi
88 E8 **Nkhotakota** Malawi
86 A6 **Nkomi, Lagune** *lagoon* Gabon
86 A5 **Nkongsamba** Cameroon
88 D5 **Nkululu** *R* Tanzania
28 A4 **No** Denmark

21 P3 **Noailles** France
75 O7 **Noakhali** Bangladesh
45 M1 **Noale** Italy
128 C3 **Noanama** Colombia
95 Q5 **Noank** Connecticut U.S.A.
26 O3 **Noarvas** *mt* Norway
40 F7 **Noasca** Italy
116 F3 **Noatak** Alaska U.S.A.
116 G3 **Noatak Nat Preserve** Alaska U.S.A.
14 E3 **Nobber** Ireland
120 K7 **Nobel** Ontario Canada
60 E13 **Nobeoka** Japan
110 H3 **Noble** Illinois U.S.A.
107 N6 **Noble** Oklahoma U.S.A.
118 D9 **Nobleford** Alberta Canada
111 E7 **Noble Lake** Arkansas U.S.A.
94 A6 **Noblesville** Indiana U.S.A.
60 P3 **Noboribetsu** Japan
130 C4 **Nobres** Brazil
141 G8 **Noccundra** Queensland Australia
21 M5 **Noce** France
41 O5 **Noce** *R* Italy
45 R8 **Nocera Inferiore** Italy
44 H2 **Noceto** Italy
124 H7 **Nochistlán** Mexico
141 G8 **Nockatunga** Queensland Australia
109 K2 **Nocona** Texas U.S.A.
48 J5 **Nocrich** Romania
61 P5 **Noda** Japan
133 D7 **Nodales,B.de los** Argentina
99 M8 **Nodaway** *R* Iowa U.S.A.
99 M9 **Nodaway** Iowa U.S.A.
98 B7 **Node** Wyoming U.S.A.
20 G6 **Noé-Blanche** France
130 D4 **Noedori** *R* Brazil
110 B5 **Noel** Missouri U.S.A.
123 Q5 **Noel Paul's Brook** Newfoundland Canada
120 K6 **Noelville** Ontario Canada
22 D3 **Noeux les Mines** France
124 D2 **Nogales** Sonora Mexico
125 L8 **Nogales** Vera Cruz Mexico
103 O10 **Nogales** Arizona U.S.A.
116 J6 **Nogamut** Alaska U.S.A.
45 K1 **Nogara** Italy
18 E9 **Nogaro** France
31 L1 **Nogat** *R* Poland
60 D12 **Nōgata** Japan
40 B1 **Nogent en Bassigny** France
21 L5 **Nogent-le-Bernard** France
21 O4 **Nogent-le-Roi** France
21 M5 **Nogent-le-Rotrou** France
21 P3 **Nogent-sur-Oise** France
18 H4 **Nogent-sur-Seine** France
54 K1 **Noginsk** Russian Federation
59 M1 **Nogliki** Russian Federation
40 C4 **Nogno** France
141 K7 **Nogo** *R* Queensland Australia
141 J6 **Nogoa** *R* Queensland Australia
61 K10 **Nōgohaku-san** *mt* Japan
131 F4 **Nogoya** *R* Argentina
48 E3 **Nógrád** *co* Hungary
16 C3 **Nogueira** *mt* Portugal
17 H2 **Noguera Pallarésa** *R* Spain
17 H2 **Noguera Ribagorzana** *R* Spain
21 O8 **Nohant Vicq** France
74 F4 **Nohar** India
61 P5 **Noheji** Japan
36 C4 **Nohfelden** Germany
36 B3 **Nohn** Germany
121 N6 **Noire** *R* Quebec Canada
67 A6 **Noire** *R* Vietnam
16 E9 **Noire, Pt** Morocco
20 C5 **Noires,Mtgnes** France
20 F7 **Noirmoutier** France
20 F8 **Noirmoutier,Ile de** France
20 C5 **Noir,Mt** France
21 K8 **Noirterre** France
17 H9 **Noisy les Bains** Algeria
61 N11 **Nojima-zaki** *C* Japan
61 M9 **Nojiri-ko** *L* Japan
87 D9 **Nokaneng** Botswana
29 K10 **Nokia** Finland
74 B8 **Nok Kundi** Pakistan
77 H5 **Nok Kundi** Pakistan
144 B6 **Nokomai** New Zealand
119 N7 **Nokomis** Saskatchewan Canada
110 G2 **Nokomis** Illinois U.S.A.
86 C5 **Nola** Cent Afr Republic
45 R8 **Nola** Italy
119 O2 **Nolalu** Ontario Canada
98 J2 **Nolan** North Dakota U.S.A.
108 G3 **Nolan** Texas U.S.A.
28 E5 **Nølev** Denmark
44 D3 **Noli** Italy
112 E1 **Nolichucky** *R* Tennessee U.S.A.
112 E1 **Nolichucky Dam** Tennessee U.S.A.
52 G5 **Nolinsk** Russian Federation
21 N3 **Nolléval** France
6 F1 **Nólsoy** *isld* Faeroes
69 E9 **Nol,Thale** *L* Thailand
66 E3 **Nom** China
111 L11 **Noma** Florida U.S.A.
60 D14 **Noma-misaki** *C* Japan
95 R5 **No Mans Land** *isld* Massachusetts U.S.A.
116 E4 **Nome** Alaska U.S.A.
98 J3 **Nome** North Dakota U.S.A.
116 E4 **Nome C** Alaska U.S.A.
19 K4 **Nomeny** France
121 P6 **Nominingue** Quebec Canada
60 C13 **Nomo-zaki** *C* Japan
87 C10 **Nomtsas** Namibia
137 S6 **Nomuka** *isld* Tonga
114 J5 **Nonacho L** Northwest Territories Canada
21 N4 **Nonancourt** France
21 J3 **Nonant** France
21 L4 **Nonant-le-Pin** France
45 K2 **Nonantola** Italy
52 H2 **Nonburg** Russian Federation
65 F2 **Nong'an** China
68 F3 **Nong Het** Laos
68 F5 **Nong Hong** Thailand
68 F4 **Nong Khai** Thailand
87 F11 **Nongoma** S Africa
19 N15 **Nonières** France
Nonni *R see* **Nen Jiang** *R*
138 D4 **Nonning** South Australia Australia
138 D4 **Nonning,Mt** South Australia Australia
36 B4 **Nonnweiler** Germany
130 D10 **Nonoaí** Brazil
124 F4 **Nonoava** Mexico
71 G6 **Nonoc** *isld* Philippines
137 P2 **Nonouti** *atoll* Kiribati
119 W2 **Nonsuch** Manitoba Canada
68 E6 **Nonthaburi** Thailand
18 F7 **Nontron** France
116 K7 **Nonvianuk L** Alaska U.S.A.
143 B7 **Nookawarra** W Australia Australia
138 D2 **Noolyeanna,L** South Australia Australia
140 B2 **Noonamah** N Terr Australia
98 C1 **Noonan** North Dakota U.S.A.
143 C9 **Noongaar** W Australia Australia
142 E4 **Noonkanbah** W Australia Australia
141 H8 **Noorama** *R* Queensland Australia
25 A5 **Noord-Beveland** Netherlands
25 D5 **Noord-Brabant** Netherlands
25 C5 **Noordeloos** Netherlands
25 C3 **Noord-Holland** Netherlands
25 E3 **Noordoost Polder** Netherlands
126 A1 **Noord Pt** Curaçao Neth Antilles
25 B4 **Noordwijk aan zee** Netherlands
7 N9 **Noordwinning** *oil rig* North Sea
25 F3 **Noordwolde** Netherlands
25 C4 **Noordzee-Kanaal** Netherlands
29 J10 **Noormarkku** Finland
116 G3 **Noorvik** Alaska U.S.A.
141 L7 **Noosa Heads** Queensland Australia
117 K11 **Nootka** British Columbia Canada
117 K11 **Nootka I** British Columbia Canada
103 H5 **Nopah Ra** California U.S.A.
99 T4 **Noquebay,L** Wisconsin U.S.A.
119 O6 **Nora** Saskatchewan Canada
59 J1 **Nora** *R* Russian Federation
27 H12 **Nora** Sweden
98 J9 **Nora** Nebraska U.S.A.
28 D3 **Nørager** Denmark
86 G2 **Nora I** Eritrea
71 G7 **Norala** Mindanao Philippines
121 L4 **Noranda** Quebec Canada
99 O6 **Nora Springs** Iowa U.S.A.
98 G4 **Norbeck** South Dakota U.S.A.
27 H11 **Norberg** Sweden
110 C2 **Norborne** Missouri U.S.A.
107 K2 **Norcatur** Kansas U.S.A.
42 E6 **Norcia** Italy
143 D9 **Norcott,Mt** W Australia Australia
111 M8 **Norcross** Georgia U.S.A.
18 H2 **Nord** *dept* France
27 D12 **Nordaguta** Norway
26 K7 **Nordanås** Sweden
27 D11 **Nord-Aurdal** Norway
50 B1 **Nordaustlandet** *isld* Spitzbergen
28 D6 **Nordborg** Denmark
28 F5 **Nordby** Denmark
28 A6 **Nordby** Denmark
Nord Cap *see* **Horn**
26 B9 **Norddal** Norway
32 F5 **Norddeich** Germany
28 A7 **Norddorf** Germany
32 L7 **Norddrebber** Germany
118 B6 **Nordegg R** Alberta Canada
9 G2 **Nordelph** England
32 F5 **Norden** Germany
37 K6 **Nordendorf** Germany
32 H5 **Nordenham** Germany
51 J1 **Nordenshel'da Arkhipelag** Russian Federation
117 E5 **Nordenskiold** *R* Yukon Territory Canada
28 A7 **Norder Aue** *chan* Germany
32 J5 **Nordergründe** *sandbank* Germany
32 F5 **Norderney** *isld* Germany
32 F5 **Norderney** Germany
26 A10 **Nordfjord** *reg* Norway
26 A10 **Nordfjord** *inlet* Norway
26 B10 **Nordfjordeid** Norway
26 H4 **Nordfold** Norway
30 D1 **Nord-friesische Inseln** *islds* Germany
28 B7 **Nordfriesland** *reg* Germany
37 M3 **Nordhalben** Germany
33 N10 **Nordhausen** Germany
109 K7 **Nordheim** Texas U.S.A.
32 J5 **Nordholz** Germany
27 A11 **Nordhordland** *reg* Norway
32 F8 **Nordhorn** Germany
26 K9 **Nordingrå** Sweden
80 C4 **Nordiyya** Israel
28 C3 **Nordjylland** *co* Denmark
26 P1 **Nordkapp** *C* Norway
26 Q1 **Nordkinn** Norway
26 L2 **Nordkjosbotn** Norway
26 F6 **Nordland Fylker** Norway
26 G7 **Nordli** Norway
37 K6 **Nördlingen** Germany
26 K8 **Nordmaling** Sweden
100 J1 **Nordman** Idaho U.S.A.
27 G12 **Nordmark** Sweden
27 D11 **Nordmarka** *reg* Norway
26 B9 **Nordmöre** *reg* Norway
98 F7 **Nordon** Nebraska U.S.A.
32 K4 **Nord-Ostsee Kanal** Germany
28 F2 **Nordre Rønner** *isld* Denmark
115 O4 **Nordre Strømfjord** *inlet* Greenland
32 E9 **Nordrhein Westfalen** *land* Germany
28 C7 **Nord Schleswig** Germany
28 B6 **Nord Slesvig** *reg* Denmark
32 L8 **Nord-Stemmen** Germany
30 D1 **Nordstrand** *isld* Germany
26 E7 **Nord-Tröndelag Fylker** Norway
51 L1 **Nordvik** Russian Federation
32 F8 **Nordwalde** Germany
14 D4 **Nore** *R* Ireland
27 C11 **Nore** Norway
27 D11 **Norefjell** *mt* Norway
122 E1 **Nore,L** Quebec Canada
120 K4 **Norembego** Ontario Canada
17 K2 **Norfeo,C** Spain
9 H2 **Norfolk** *co* England
110 D5 **Norfolk** Arkansas U.S.A.
95 O5 **Norfolk** Connecticut U.S.A.
98 J7 **Norfolk** Nebraska U.S.A.
95 L10 **Norfolk** Virginia U.S.A.
137 O7 **Norfolk I** Pacific Oc
110 D5 **Norfolk L** Arkansas U.S.A.
25 F2 **Norg** Netherlands
13 F2 **Norham** England
109 K9 **Norias** Texas U.S.A.
61 L9 **Norikura-dake** *mt* Japan
51 H2 **Noril'sk** Russian Federation
141 G8 **Norley** Queensland Australia
112 J1 **Norlina** North Carolina U.S.A.
45 N6 **Norma** Italy
110 K7 **Normal** Alabama U.S.A.
99 S9 **Normal** Illinois U.S.A.
141 F4 **Norman** *R* Queensland Australia
111 C7 **Norman** Arkansas U.S.A.
98 H9 **Norman** Nebraska U.S.A.
107 N6 **Norman** Oklahoma U.S.A.
141 G2 **Normanby** *R* Queensland Australia
13 H5 **Normanby** England
145 E3 **Normanby** New Zealand
141 K5 **Normanby Ra** Queensland Australia
21 H4 **Normandie** *reg* France
20 H4 **Normandie, Collines de** *hills* France
121 S4 **Normandin** Quebec Canada
110 K6 **Normandy** Tennessee U.S.A.
109 L4 **Normangee** Texas U.S.A.
143 E7 **Norman Hurst,Mt** W Australia Australia
112 F2 **Norman, L** North Carolina U.S.A.
109 K7 **Normanna** Texas U.S.A.
141 K2 **Norman Park** *dist* Brisbane, Qnsld Australia
141 F4 **Normanton** Queensland Australia
117 K3 **Norman Wells** Northwest Territories Canada
121 L4 **Normetal** Quebec Canada
143 B10 **Nornalup** W Australia Australia
124 F4 **Norogachic** Mexico
111 D8 **Norphlet** Arkansas U.S.A.
119 Q7 **Norquay** Saskatchewan Canada
133 C5 **Norquin** Argentina
133 C6 **Norquinco** Argentina
29 J8 **Norra Kvarken** *chan* Finland/Sweden
27 J10 **Norrala** Sweden
27 G15 **Norraryd** Sweden
26 J4 **Norrbotten** *reg* Sweden
28 D4 **Nørreå** *R* Denmark
28 C5 **Nørre Bramdrup** Denmark
28 A5 **Nørre Nebel** Denmark
22 C2 **Norrent-Fontès** France
28 D2 **Nørre Saltum** Denmark
28 D2 **Nørresundby** Denmark
26 M6 **Norrfjärden** Sweden
26 K8 **Norrfors** Sweden
26 J9 **Norrhassel** Sweden
95 S2 **Norridgewock** Maine U.S.A.
99 Q9 **Norris** Illinois U.S.A.
101 O4 **Norris** Montana U.S.A.
98 E6 **Norris** South Dakota U.S.A.
112 C1 **Norris** Tennessee U.S.A.
101 P5 **Norris** Wyoming U.S.A.
123 R4 **Norris Arm** Newfoundland Canada
110 H4 **Norris City** Illinois U.S.A.
112 C1 **Norris Dam** Tennessee U.S.A.
112 D1 **Norris Lake** Tennessee U.S.A.
123 P4 **Norris Point** Newfoundland Canada
95 M6 **Norristown** Pennsylvania U.S.A.
27 H13 **Norrköping** Sweden
29 H8 **Norrskär** *lighthouse* Finland
27 J11 **Norrsundet** Sweden
27 K12 **Norrtälje** Sweden
26 H6 **Norrvik** Sweden
27 F12 **Norsä** *R* Sweden
143 D9 **Norseman** W Australia Australia
145 F4 **Norsewood** New Zealand
27 H13 **Norsholm** Sweden
27 D12 **Norsjö** *L* Norway
26 K7 **Norsjö** Sweden
26 Q1 **Norskholmen** Norway
28 B2 **Nors Sø** *L* Denmark
129 H3 **Norte,C** Brazil
128 D2 **Norte de Santander** *div* Colombia
32 L9 **Nörten Hardenburg** Germany
133 E6 **Norte,Pta** Argentina
131 D3 **Norte,Sa de** *ra* Argentina
128 G6 **Norte,Serra do** *mts* Brazil
111 J8 **North** *R* Alabama U.S.A.
112 F4 **North** South Carolina U.S.A.
94 C5 **North Adams** Michigan U.S.A.
13 G5 **Northallerton** England
143 B9 **Northam** W Australia Australia
98 F1 **North America, Center of** North Dakota U.S.A.
90 C6 **North American Basin** Atlantic Oc
143 A8 **Northampton** W Australia Australia
9 F3 **Northampton** England
95 P4 **Northampton** Massachusetts U.S.A.
141 H6 **Northampton Downs** Queensland Australia
9 F3 **Northamptonshire** *co* England
68 A6 **North Andaman** *isld* Andaman Is
94 K8 **North Anna** *R* Virginia U.S.A.
95 S2 **North Anson** Maine U.S.A.
117 Q4 **North Arm** *inlet* Northwest Territories Canada
112 E4 **North Augusta** Georgia U.S.A.
115 N6 **North Aulatsivik I** Labrador, Nfld Canada
94 D5 **North Baltimore** Ohio U.S.A.
118 J6 **North Battleford** Saskatchewan Canada
123 O6 **North Bay** Newfoundland Canada
121 L6 **North Bay** Ontario Canada
98 K8 **North Bend** Nebraska U.S.A.
100 A6 **North Bend** Oregon U.S.A.
13 F1 **North Berwick** Scotland
99 L9 **Northboro** Iowa U.S.A.
139 H4 **North Bourke** New South Wales Australia
118 H2 **North Branch** Ontario Canada
94 D3 **North Branch** Michigan U.S.A.
99 O4 **North Branch** Minnesota U.S.A.
121 N8 **North Brook** Ontario Canada
13 H5 **North Burton** England
123 M6 **North,C** C Breton I, Nova Scotia
127 J4 **North Caicos** *isld* Turks & Caicos Is
108 B7 **North Canadian** *R* Oklahoma U.S.A.
145 D1 **North Cape** New Zealand
137 P8 **North Cape Rise** *sea feature* Pacific Oc
115 L7 **North Caribou L** Ontario Canada
112 E2 **North Carolina** *state* U.S.A.
100 D1 **North Cascades Nat. Park** Washington U.S.A.
113 H12 **North Cat Cay** *isld* Bahamas
113 L9 **North Cay** *isld* New Providence I Bahamas
14 F1 **North Chan** N Ireland/ Scotland
120 G6 **North Channel** Ontario Canada
112 H5 **North Charleston** South Carolina U.S.A.
13 G2 **North Charlton** England
99 T7 **North Chicago** Illinois U.S.A.
143 B10 **Northcliffe** W Australia Australia
108 F4 **North Concho** *R* Texas U.S.A.
100 A3 **North Cove** Washington U.S.A.
95 N3 **North Creek** New York U.S.A.
98 F2 **North Dakota** *state* U.S.A.
122 F8 **North Devon** New Brunswick Canada
9 F5 **North Downs** England
94 H4 **North East** Pennsylvania U.S.A.
95 R8 **North East Carry** Maine U.S.A.
141 L5 **North-East Cay** *isld* Gt Barrier Reef Aust
90 G3 **North Eastern Atlantic Basin** Atlantic Oc
122 A3 **Northeast Mistassibi R** Quebec Canada
126 F2 **Northeast Providence Chan** Bahamas
123 R1 **Northeast Pt** Belle Isle, Nfld
83 M9 **North East Pt** *C* Christmas I Indian Oc
32 L9 **Northeim** Germany
99 O8 **North English** Iowa U.S.A.
86 E2 **Northern** *prov* Sudan
123 T5 **Northern Bight** Newfoundland Canada
89 A7 **Northern Cape** *prov* S Africa
86 E2 **Northern Darfur** *prov* Sudan
113 L12 **Northern Eleuthera** *dist* Bahamas
122 F9 **Northern Hd** New Brunswick Canada
119 U1 **Northern Indian L** Manitoba Canada
12 A4 **Northern Ireland** U.K.
86 E2 **Northern Kordofan** *prov* Sudan
99 Q1 **Northern Light L** Ontario Canada
134 E6 **Northern Mariana Is** Pacific Oc
83 M9 **Northern Plateau** Christmas I Indian Oc
127 O2 **Northern Range** Trinidad
Northern Sporades *islds see* **Voríai Sporádhes** *islds*
138 B1 **Northern Territory** Australia
89 F4 **Northern Transvaal** *prov* S Africa
139 H8 **North Esk** *R* Tasmania Australia
9 E3 **Northfield** England
95 P4 **Northfield** Massachusetts U.S.A.
99 N5 **Northfield** Minnesota U.S.A.
95 P2 **Northfield** Vermont U.S.A.
144 A6 **North Fiord** New Zealand
99 S6 **North Fond du Lac** Wisconsin U.S.A.
9 H5 **North Foreland** *hd* England
102 E4 **North Fork** California U.S.A.
101 M4 **North Fork** Idaho U.S.A.
100 K8 **North Fork** Nevada U.S.A.
94 B1 **North Fox I** Michigan U.S.A.
99 R6 **North Freedom** Wisconsin U.S.A.
120 J2 **North French** *R* Ontario Canada
13 H6 **North Frodingham** England
141 K1 **Northgate** *dist* Brisbane, Qnsld Australia
119 P9 **Northgate** Saskatchewan Canada
13 G3 **Northgate** England
95 P5 **North Haven** Connecticut U.S.A.
144 D5 **North Hd.** New Zealand
122 F9 **North Head** New Brunswick Canada
123 O4 **North Head** Newfoundland Canada
141 H2 **North Horn** *C* Gt Barrier Reef Aust
86 G5 **North Horr** Kenya
83 J12 **North I** Seychelles
112 H4 **North I** South Carolina U.S.A.
9 G6 **Northiam** England
145 E3 **North Island** New Zealand
71 E6 **North Islet** Philippines
103 O6 **North Jadito Canyon** *R* Arizona U.S.A.
83 M8 **North Keeling I** Cocos Is Indian Oc
115 L2 **North Kent I** Northwest Territories Canada
94 G5 **North Kingsville** Ohio U.S.A.
119 V1 **North Knife L** Manitoba Canada
59 J3 **North Korea** *rep* E Asia
North Land *see* **Severnaya Zemlya**
145 D1 **Northland** *admin region* New Zealand
99 T3 **Northland** Michigan U.S.A.
103 J5 **North Las Vegas** Nevada U.S.A.
9 E4 **Northleach** England
99 U8 **North Liberty** Indiana U.S.A.
110 D7 **North Little Rock** Arkansas U.S.A.
98 H8 **North Loup** *R* Nebraska U.S.A.
98 H8 **North Loup** Nebraska U.S.A.
88 D7 **North Luangwa Nat. Park** Zambia
70 C2 **North Luconia Shoals** S China Sea
106 C2 **North Mam Pk** Colorado U.S.A.
94 B5 **North Manchester** Indiana U.S.A.
99 U4 **North Manitou I** Michigan U.S.A.
113 G12 **North Miami** Florida U.S.A.
15 B2 **North Minch** Scotland
142 E4 **North, Mt** W Australia Australia
94 A3 **North Muskegon** Michigan U.S.A.
112 J4 **North Myrtle Beach** South Carolina U.S.A.
117 L4 **North Nahanni** *R* Northwest Territories Canada
113 G11 **North New River Can** Florida U.S.A.
94 E5 **North Olmsled** Ohio U.S.A.
99 M2 **Northome** Minnesota U.S.A.
8 C1 **Northop** Wales
North Ossetia *see* **Severo-Osetinskaya Respublika**
102 F4 **North Palisade** *pk* California U.S.A.
98 D8 **North Platte** *R* Nebraska U.S.A.
98 F8 **North Platte** Nebraska U.S.A.
101 T8 **North Platte** *R* Wyoming U.S.A.
116 O4 **North Pole** Alaska U.S.A.
122 J8 **Northport** Nova Scotia Canada
111 J8 **Northport** Alabama U.S.A.
99 V4 **Northport** Michigan U.S.A.
98 C8 **Northport** Nebraska U.S.A.
100 H1 **Northport** Washington U.S.A.
100 H4 **North Powder** Oregon U.S.A.
99 S7 **North Prairie** Wisconsin U.S.A.
139 J7 **North Pt** Flinders I, Tasmania Australia
122 H6 **North Pt** Prince Edward I Canada
83 J12 **North Pt** Mahé I Indian Oc
94 D1 **North Pt** Michigan U.S.A.
100 B3 **North R** Washington U.S.A.
142 A4 **North Rankin Gas Field** W Australia Australia
68 A6 **North Reef I** Andaman Is
109 M9 **North Richland Hills** Texas U.S.A.
123 M7 **North River Bridge** C Breton I, Nova Scotia
15 C1 **North Rona** Scotland
15 F1 **North Ronaldsay** Orkney Scotland
15 F1 **North Ronaldsay Firth** Orkney Scotland
122 J7 **North Rustico** Prince Edward I Canada
102 C2 **North San Juan** California U.S.A.
100 C5 **North Santiam** *R* Oregon U.S.A.
118 B6 **North Sask R** Alberta Canada
90 J3 **North Sea** W Europe
68 A7 **North Sentinel I** Andaman Is
13 G3 **North Shields** England
102 G2 **North Shoshone Pk** Nevada U.S.A.
99 O8 **North Skunk** *R* Iowa U.S.A.
116 M1 **North Slope** Alaska U.S.A.
117 P7 **North Star** Alberta Canada
110 M1 **North Star** Ohio U.S.A.
141 L8 **North Stradbroke I** Queensland Australia
109 M2 **North Sulphur** *R* Texas U.S.A.
123 M7 **North Sydney** C Breton I, Nova Scotia
8 C6 **North Tawton** England
144 A7 **North Trap** *islds* New Zealand
71 E7 **North Ubian** *isld* Philippines
15 A3 **North Uist** *isld* Scotland
141 J5 **Northumberland** *islds* Queensland Australia
13 F3 **Northumberland** *co* England
138 F7 **Northumberland,C** South Australia Australia
122 H7 **Northumberland Str** Nova Scotia Canada
117 G10 **North Vancouver** British Columbia Canada
71 D5 **North Verde** Philippines
117 P6 **North Vermilion** Alberta Canada
94 B7 **North Vernon** Indiana U.S.A.
95 N3 **Northville** New York U.S.A.
98 H4 **Northville** South Dakota U.S.A.
9 H2 **North Walsham** England
116 R5 **Northway Junc** Alaska U.S.A.
89 C6 **North West** *prov* S Africa
116 B5 **Northwest C.** St Lawrence I, Alaska U.S.A.
113 K11 **Northwest Cay** *isld* Bahamas
74 D2 **North West Frontier Prov** Pakistan
142 B5 **North West I** W Australia Australia
126 E1 **Northwest Providence Chan** Bahamas
83 M9 **North-West Pt** *C* Christmas I Indian Oc
115 N7 **North West River** Labrador, Nfld Canada
123 N2 **Northwest St.Augustin R** Quebec Canada
114 H4 **Northwest Territories** *prov* Canada
8 D1 **Northwich** England
112 F1 **North Wilkesboro** North Carolina U.S.A.
99 N6 **Northwood** Iowa U.S.A.
98 J2 **Northwood** North Dakota U.S.A.
120 C9 **North York** Ontario Canada
13 G5 **North Yorkshire** *co* England
109 L5 **North Zulch** Texas U.S.A.
32 G6 **Nortmoor** Germany
122 G8 **Norton** New Brunswick Canada
94 E10 **Norton** Virginia U.S.A.
89 G1 **Norton** Zimbabwe
116 G4 **Norton B** Alaska U.S.A.
116 E5 **Norton Sound** Alaska U.S.A.
107 P2 **Nortonville** Kansas U.S.A.
98 H3 **Nortonville** North Dakota U.S.A.
32 L4 **Nortorf** Germany
32 G7 **Nortrup** Germany
20 H7 **Nort-sur-Erdre** France
28 E5 **Norup** Denmark
116 K3 **Norutak L** Alaska U.S.A.
146 G6 **Norvegia Kapp** *C* Antarctica
36 B2 **Nörvenich** Germany
102 F8 **Norwalk** California U.S.A.
95 O5 **Norwalk** Connecticut U.S.A.
99 N8 **Norwalk** Iowa U.S.A.
99 U5 **Norwalk** Michigan U.S.A.
94 E5 **Norwalk** Ohio U.S.A.
99 Q6 **Norwalk** Wisconsin U.S.A.
99 P8 **Norway** Iowa U.S.A.
95 R2 **Norway** Maine U.S.A.
99 T4 **Norway** Michigan U.S.A.
112 F4 **Norway** South Carolina U.S.A.
68 H2 **Norway** *isld* Vietnam
26 **Norway** *kingdom* W Europe
119 U5 **Norway House** Manitoba Canada
115 K2 **Norwegian B** Northwest Territories Canada
147 E13 **Norwegian Basin** Arctic Oc
147 E12 **Norwegian Sea** Arctic Oc
120 K10 **Norwich** Ontario Canada
9 H2 **Norwich** England
95 P5 **Norwich** Connecticut U.S.A.
107 N4 **Norwich** Kansas U.S.A.
95 M4 **Norwich** New York U.S.A.
141 J6 **Norwich Park** Queensland Australia
15 G1 **Norwick** Scotland
121 N8 **Norwood** Ontario Canada
95 Q4 **Norwood** Massachusetts U.S.A.
95 N2 **Norwood** New York U.S.A.
112 G2 **Norwood** North Carolina U.S.A.
71 E3 **Norzagaray** Luzon Philippines
60 T2 **Nosappu-misaki** *C* Japan
36 G2 **Nösberts** Germany
61 N5 **Noshiro** Japan
52 G4 **Noshul'** Russian Federation
55 E2 **Noska** *R* Russian Federation
89 B5 **Nosop** *R* Botswana
52 E3 **Nosovshchina** Russian Federation
77 F5 **Nosratābād** Iran
130 H11 **Nossa Senhora das Dores** Brazil
130 C4 **Nossa Senhora do Livramento** Brazil
27 F13 **Nossebro** Sweden
22 H2 **Nossegem** Belgium
37 P1 **Nossen** Germany
33 Q5 **Nossentin** Germany
89 A4 **Nossob** Namibia
87 G11 **Nosy Barren** Madagascar
87 H10 **Nosy Be** *isld* Madagascar
87 H10 **Nosy Lava** Madagascar
87 H10 **Nosy Mitsio** *isld* Madagascar
87 H10 **Nosy Radamà** Madagascar
87 H12 **Nosy Varika** Madagascar
111 L9 **Notasulga** Alabama U.S.A.
103 L2 **Notch Pk** Utah U.S.A.
31 K2 **Noteć** *R* Poland
80 F1 **Notera** Israel
100 B5 **Noti** Oregon U.S.A.
46 E3 **Notia** Greece
114 H6 **Notikewin** Alberta Canada
117 O7 **Notikewin** *R* Alberta Canada
46 G8 **Nótion Aiyaíon** *admin region* Greece
43 G12 **Noto** Sicily
27 D12 **Notodden** Norway
43 G12 **Noto, Golfo di** Sicily
61 K8 **Noto-hantō** *pen* Japan
61 L8 **Noto-jima** *isld* Japan
60 S1 **Notoro-ko** *L* Japan
60 S1 **Notoro-misaki** *C* Japan
Notozero, Oz. *see* **Verkhnetulomskoye, Vodokhranilishche**
122 H7 **Notre Dame** New Brunswick Canada
122 A8 **Notre Dame** Quebec Canada
123 R4 **Notre Dame B** Newfoundland Canada
21 L4 **Notre Dame-de-Courson** France
21 M3 **Notre Dame de Gravenchon** France
115 M5 **Notre Dame de Koartáo** Quebec Canada
121 S4 **Notre-Dame-de-la-Doré** Quebec Canada
119 T9 **Notre Dame de Lourdes** Manitoba Canada
20 F8 **Notre Dame-de-Monts** France
121 P6 **Notre Dame du Laus** Quebec Canada
121 L5 **Notre Dame du-Nord** Quebec Canada
122 A5 **Notre Dame du Rosaire** Quebec Canada
85 E7 **Notsé** Togo
60 T2 **Notsuke-saki** *C* Japan
60 T2 **Notsuke-suidō** *str* Japan/ Rus Fed
120 K8 **Nottawasaga Bay** Ontario Canada
121 M2 **Nottaway R** Quebec Canada
27 H14 **Nottebäck** Sweden
112 C3 **Nottely L** Georgia U.S.A.
27 E12 **Nötteröy** *isld* Norway
9 E1 **Nottingham** *co* England
9 E2 **Nottingham** England
115 M5 **Nottingham Island** Northwest Territories Canada
27 G15 **Nöttja** Sweden
37 K2 **Nottleben** Germany
94 K10 **Nottoway** *R* Virginia U.S.A.
100 J6 **Notus** Idaho U.S.A.
85 A4 **Nouadhibou** Mauritania
85 A5 **Nouakchott** Mauritania
21 P6 **Nouan-le-Fuzelier** France
21 N7 **Nouans-les-Fontaines** France
21 O6 **Nouan-sur-Loire** France
22 J5 **Nouart** France
137 O6 **Nouméa** New Caledonia
85 D6 **Nouna** Burkina
89 D8 **Noupoort** S Africa
115 M7 **Nouveau-Comptoir** Quebec Canada
115 M5 **Nouveau Québec, Cratèr du** Quebec Canada
115 M5 **Nouveau Québec, Cratére du** Canada
122 D4 **Nouvel,L** Quebec Canada
Nouvelle Calédonie *isld see* **New Caledonia**
115 M5 **Nouvelle-France,Cap de** Quebec Canada
18 H9 **Nouvelle, la** France
122 F5 **Nouvelle,R** Quebec Canada
21 O1 **Nouvion-en-Pontheiu** France
22 F3 **Nouvion-en-Thiérache,Le** France
21 M6 **Nouzilly** France
22 H4 **Nouzonville** France
71 M9 **Nova Anadia** Timor
48 E2 **Nová Baňa** Slovakia
87 B7 **Nova Caipemba** Angola
48 H5 **Novaci** Romania
45 M4 **Novafeltria** Italy
130 G8 **Nova Friburgo** Brazil
Nova Gaia *see* **Cambundi-Catembo**
42 H3 **Nova Gradiška** Croatia
130 G8 **Nova Iguaçu** Brazil
129 K5 **Nova Iorque** Brazil
130 G6 **Nova Lima** Brazil
87 C8 **Nova Lisboa** Angola
87 F10 **Nova Mambone** Mozambique
128 G4 **Nova Olinda do Norte** Brazil
129 K5 **Nova Pilão Arcado** Brazil
41 J7 **Novara** Italy
129 K5 **Nova Remanso** Brazil
129 K4 **Nova Russas** Brazil
122 G9 **Nova Scotia** *prov* Canada
129 K5 **Nova Sento Sé** Brazil
41 K5 **Novate** Italy
102 B3 **Novato** California U.S.A.
130 E10 **Nova Trento** Brazil
48 F7 **Nova Varš** Serbia Yugoslavia
128 F6 **Nova Vida** Brazil
55 C5 **Novaya Akkermanovka** Russian Federation
55 E3 **Novaya Aptula** Russian Federation
56 F3 **Novaya Igirma** Russian Federation
54 E10 **Novaya Kakhovka** Ukraine
53 F8 **Novaya Kriusha** Russian Federation
55 D2 **Novaya Lyala** Russian Federation
51 O1 **Novaya Sibir', Ostrov** *isld* Russian Federation
56 E3 **Novaya Solyanka** Russian Federation
48 J1 **Novaya Strelishcha** Ukraine
48 L2 **Novaya Ushitsa** Ukraine
55 E3 **Novaya Zaimka** Russian Federation
50 E1 **Novaya Zemlya** *isld* Russian Federation
47 H2 **Nova Zagora** Bulgaria
45 J2 **Novellara** Italy
110 D1 **Novelty** Missouri U.S.A.
45 L1 **Noventa V** Italy
33 N7 **Növenthien** Germany
48 E3 **Nové Zámky** Slovakia
52 D5 **Novgorod** Russian Federation
54 E5 **Novgorod Severskiy** Ukraine
52 D5 **Novgorodskaya Oblast'** *prov* Russian Federation
47 J1 **Novgradets** Bulgaria
44 E2 **Novi** Italy
109 H4 **Novice** Texas U.S.A.
45 J2 **Novi di Modena** Italy
42 F3 **Novigrad** Croatia
42 G4 **Novigrad** Croatia
46 F2 **Novi Iskŭr** Bulgaria
48 F4 **Novi Kneževac** Serbia Yugoslavia
59 M2 **Novikovo** Russian Federation
45 N4 **Novilara** Italy
124 G6 **Novillero** Mexico
99 O9 **Novinger** Missouri U.S.A.
22 G4 **Novion-Porcien** France
47 J1 **Novi Pazar** Bulgaria
46 D1 **Novi Pazar** Serbia Yugoslavia
48 F5 **Novi Sad** Serbia Yugoslavia
42 F3 **Novi Vinodolski** Croatia
54 N1 **Novki** Russian Federation
28 B4 **Nøvling** Denmark
129 H4 **Nôvo Acôrdo** Brazil
53 F10 **Novoaleksandrovsk** Russian Federation
55 C5 **Novoalekseyevka** Kazakhstan
56 B4 **Novoaltaysk** Russian Federation
52 B4 **Novoandreyevka** Russian Federation
128 F5 **Novo Aripuana** Brazil
53 D9 **Novo Arkhangelsk** Ukraine
55 D2 **Novoasbest** Russian Federation
54 K9 **Novoazovsk** Ukraine
54 C4 **Novobelitsa** Belarus
55 C3 **Novobelokatay** Russian Federation
55 E3 **Novoberezovka** Russian Federation
55 D3 **Novoburino** Russian Federation
54 M9 **Novocherkassk** Russian Federation
55 F5 **Novodolinka** Kazakhstan
52 D6 **Novo Dugino** Russian Federation
52 F3 **Novodvinsk** Arkhangel'skaya obl Russian Federation
53 C8 **Novograd-Volynskiy** Ukraine
53 C7 **Novogrudok** Belarus
54 J2 **Novogurovskiy** Russian Federation
131 H2 **Novo Hamburgo** Brazil
59 L1 **Novoilinovka** Russian Federation
55 F5 **Novoishimka** Kazakhstan
56 F4 **Novokadinskiy** Russian Federation
53 G7 **Novokashpirskiy** Russian Federation
57 B2 **Novokazalinsk** Kazakhstan
53 F8 **Novokhopersk** Russian Federation
59 J1 **Novokiyevskiy Uval** Russian Federation
56 C4 **Novokuznetsk** Russian Federation
129 H3 **Novo, L** Brazil
146 H7 **Novolazarevskaya** *Rus Fed Base* Antarctica
43 J8 **Novoli** Italy
71 M9 **Novo Luso** Timor
54 L2 **Novomichurinsk** Russian Federation
53 E11 **Novomikhaylovskiy** Russian Federation
48 F5 **Novo Miloševo** Serbia Yugoslavia
54 C8 **Novomirgorod** Ukraine
54 K2 **Novomoskovsk** Russian Federation
54 G8 **Novomoskovsk** Ukraine
55 E3 **Novonikolskoye** Russian Federation
55 C5 **Novoorsk** Russian Federation
52 C6 **Novopolotsk** Belarus
Novo Redondo *see* **Sumbe**
56 B4 **Novoromanovka** Russian Federation
53 E11 **Novorossiysk** Russian Federation
55 C5 **Novorossiyskoye** Kazakhstan
54 M3 **Novoryazhsk** Russian Federation
55 F5 **Novorybinka** Kazakhstan
51 K1 **Novorybnoye** Russian Federation
52 C6 **Novorzhev** Russian Federation
52 H7 **Novo Sakhcha** Russian Federation
48 K2 **Novoselitsa** Ukraine
55 B5 **Novosergiyevka** Russian Federation
54 L9 **Novoshakhtinsk** Russian Federation
52 H6 **Novo Sheshminsk** Russian Federation
56 B4 **Novosibirsk** Russian Federation
55 G3 **Novosibirskaya Oblast'** *prov* Russian Federation
51 O1 **Novosibirskiye Ostrova** *islds* Russian Federation
54 J4 **Novosil'** Russian Federation
55 D3 **Novosineglazovskiy** Russian Federation
52 D6 **Novosokol'niki** Russian Federation
55 C5 **Novotroitsk** Russian Federation
55 G3 **Novotroitsk** Novosibirskaya obl Russian Federation
57 G3 **Novotroitskoye** Kazakhstan
54 K2 **Novougol'nyy** Russian Federation
54 C8 **Novoukrainka** Ukraine
55 C5 **Novouralets** Russian Federation
53 G8 **Novo Uzensk** Russian Federation
55 F4 **Novovarshavka** Russian Federation
55 G2 **Novovaya Vasyugan** Russian Federation
54 L5 **Novovoronezhskiy** Russian Federation
52 G5 **Novo-Vyatsk** Russian Federation
56 D2 **Novoyeniseysk** Russian Federation
56 F3 **Novoye Prirech'ye** Russian Federation
52 E6 **Novozavidovskiy** Russian Federation
52 H3 **Novozhilovskaya** Russian Federation
42 H3 **Novska** Croatia
31 L6 **Novy Bohumin** Czech Rep
31 J5 **Nový Bydžov** Czech Rep
22 G4 **Novy-Chevrières** France
54 K8 **Novy Donbass** Ukraine
54 F7 **Novye Sanzhary** Ukraine
48 D1 **Nový Jičin** Czech Rep
54 J6 **Novy Oskol** Russian Federation
52 D1 **Novyy** Russian Federation
52 H2 **Novyy Bor** Russian Federation
54 D9 **Novyy Bug** Ukraine
54 B3 **Novyy Bykhov** Belarus
54 D6 **Novyy Bykov** Ukraine
48 M4 **Novyye Aneny** Moldova
55 E1 **Novyy Karymkary** Russian Federation
55 E2 **Novyy Katysh** Russian Federation
50 G2 **Novyy Port** Russian Federation
52 G6 **Novyy Tor'yal** Russian Federation
56 H3 **Novyy Uoyan** Russian Federation
50 G2 **Novyy Urengoy** Russian Federation
31 J5 **Nowa Ruda** Poland
31 J4 **Nowa Sól** Poland
107 P5 **Nowata** Oklahoma U.S.A.
77 A2 **Nowbarān** Iran
31 L2 **Nowe** Poland
142 E5 **No.34 Well** W Australia Australia
142 F5 **No.37 Well** W Australia Australia
142 F5 **No.41 Well** W Australia Australia
142 F5 **No.45 Well** W Australia Australia
31 M2 **Nowe Miasto** Poland
Nowgong *see* **Nagaon**
116 K4 **Nowitna** *R* Alaska U.S.A.
31 J2 **Nowógard** Poland
31 N2 **Nowogród** Poland
31 J4 **Nowogrodziec** Poland
101 S5 **Nowood Cr** Wyoming U.S.A.
139 K5 **Nowra** New South Wales Australia
77 A5 **Nowruz** *oil well* Persian Gulf
77 B1 **Now Shahr** Iran
74 E1 **Nowshera** Pakistan
31 O2 **Nowy Dwór** Poland
31 M3 **Nowy Dwor** Poland
31 L1 **Nowy Dwór Gdański** Poland
31 M5 **Nowy Korczyn** Poland
48 F1 **Nowy Sącz** Poland
48 F1 **Nowy Targ** Poland
31 J3 **Nowy Tomysl** Poland
111 G9 **Noxapater** Mississippi U.S.A.
95 L5 **Noxen** Pennsylvania U.S.A.
100 K2 **Noxon** Montana U.S.A.
111 H8 **Noxubee** *R* Mississippi U.S.A.
16 B2 **Noya** Spain
17 J3 **Noya** *R* Spain
20 F6 **Noyal Muzillac** France
20 E6 **Noyalo** France
20 E5 **Noyal-Pontivy** France
20 G5 **Noyal-sur-Vilaine** France
21 J6 **Noyant-la-Gravoyère** France
21 K7 **Noyant-la-Plaine** France
21 L6 **Noyant-sous-le-Lude** France
21 P2 **Noye** *R* France
21 O1 **Noyelles-sur-Mer** France
21 K6 **Noyen** France
21 N7 **Noyers-sur-Cher** Loir-et-Cher France
117 G8 **Noyes I** Alaska U.S.A.
102 A2 **Noyo** California U.S.A.
22 E4 **Noyon** France
123 O2 **Noyrot,L** Quebec Canada
20 G6 **Nozay** France
86 C6 **N'Sah** Congo
88 E10 **Nsanje** Malawi
85 D7 **Nsawam** Ghana
88 C9 **Nsenga** Zambia
87 E9 **Nsiza** Zimbabwe
89 F2 **Nsiza** *R* Zimbabwe
88 E9 **Ntcheu** Malawi
86 B5 **Ntem** *R* Cameroon
83 L13 **Nuageuses** *isld* Kerguelen Indian Oc
21 J7 **Nuaillé** Maine-et-Loire France
52 C3 **Nuasjärvi** *L* Finland
84 J5 **Nuba, L** Sudan
86 F3 **Nuba Mts** Sudan
84 J5 **Nubian Des** Sudan
100 D8 **Nubieber** California U.S.A.
131 B6 **Nuble** *R* Chile
131 B6 **Nuble** *prov* Chile
48 H4 **Nucet** Romania
65 D2 **Nudam** China
65 A3 **Nüden** Mongolia
141 K1 **Nudgee** *dist* Brisbane, Qnsld Australia
109 J7 **Nueces** *R* Texas U.S.A.
21 J8 **Nueil-sur-Argent** France
21 K7 **Nueil-sur-Layon** France
115 K5 **Nueltin L** Northwest Territories Canada
65 E4 **Nü'erhe** China
128 F8 **Nueva Asunción** *dept* Paraguay
124 F2 **Nueva Casas Grandes** Mexico
109 H9 **Nueva Ciudad** Mexico
125 K4 **Nueva Ciudad Guerrero** Mexico
128 F1 **Nueva Esparta** *state* Venezuela
128 F7 **Nueva Esperanza** Bolivia
130 C8 **Nueva Germania** Paraguay
126 C4 **Nueva Gerona** Cuba
133 D9 **Nueva, I** Chile/Arg
133 C5 **Nueva Imperial** Chile
133 C6 **Nueva Lubecka** Argentina
124 J4 **Nueva Rosita** Mexico
133 E5 **Nueve de Julio** Argentina
126 F4 **Nuevitas** Cuba

71 F5 **Nuevo** Cebu Philippines
133 E6 **Nuevo,G** Argentina
124 G5 **Nuevo Ideal** Mexico
125 K4 **Nuevo Laredo** Mexico
109 H8 **Nuevo Laredo** Texas U.S.A.
125 J5 **Nuevo Leon** *state* Mexico
128 C4 **Nuevo Rocafuerte** Ecuador
141 J6 **Nuga Nuga, L** Queensland Australia
84 J5 **Nugrus,Gebel** *mt* Egypt
137 L2 **Nuguria Is** Bismarck Arch
145 F3 **Nuhaka** New Zealand
137 Q3 **Nui** *atoll* Tuvalu
68 H5 **Nui Ti On** *mt* Vietnam
18 H5 **Nuits** France
19 J5 **Nuits St.Georges** France
66 E5 **Nu Jiang** *R* China
116 M7 **Nuka I** Alaska U.S.A.
138 D4 **Nukey Bluff** South Australia Australia
80 G8 **Nukheila** *R* Jordan
86 E2 **Nukheila** Sudan
137 R6 **Nuku'alofa** *isld* Tonga
137 Q3 **Nukufetau** *atoll* Tuvalu
135 N9 **Nuku Hiva** *isld* Marquesas Is Pacific Oc
137 Q3 **Nukulaelae** *atoll* Tuvalu
137 M2 **Nukumanu Is** Solomon Is
137 Q2 **Nukunau** *isld* Kiribati
57 A4 **Nukus** Uzbekistan
17 G5 **Nules** Spain
142 D5 **Nullagine** W Australia Australia
142 D5 **Nullagine R** W Australia Australia
138 B4 **Nullarbor** South Australia Australia
138 B4 **Nullarbor Nat Park** South Australia Australia
143 F9 **Nullarbor Plain** S/W Australia Australia
65 D4 **Nulu'erhu Shan** *mt ra* China
43 B8 **Nulvi** Sardinia
61 L8 **Numaho** Japan
61 P6 **Numakunai** Japan
141 G8 **Numalla, L** Queensland Australia
86 B4 **Numan** Nigeria
45 O4 **Numana** Italy
17 F3 **Numancia** Spain
25 B5 **Numansdorp** Netherlands
60 P2 **Numata** Japan
86 E4 **Numatinna** *R* Sudan
61 M10 **Numazu** Japan
36 D2 **Nümbrecht** Nordrhein-Westfalen Germany
140 D2 **Numbulwar** N Terr Australia
27 D11 **Numedal** *V* Norway
27 D12 **Numedalsågen** *R* Norway
136 G2 **Numfor** *isld* W Irian
29 K11 **Nummi** Finland
139 H6 **Numurkah** Victoria Australia
116 J7 **Nunachuak** Alaska U.S.A.
116 F6 **Nunapitchuk** Alaska U.S.A.
116 E6 **Nunavakanuk L** Alaska U.S.A.
114 J4 **Nunavut** *reg* Northwest Territories Canada
94 K4 **Nunda** New York U.S.A.
141 K1 **Nundah** *dist* Brisbane, Qnsld Australia
139 K4 **Nundle** New South Wales Australia
138 B4 **Nundroo** South Australia Australia
9 E2 **Nuneaton** England
143 C9 **Nungarin** W Australia Australia
65 D2 **Nungnain Sum** China
87 G8 **Nungo** Mozambique
116 E7 **Nunivak I** Alaska U.S.A.
106 F1 **Nunn** Colorado U.S.A.
110 J6 **Nunnelly** Tennessee U.S.A.
8 D5 **Nunney** England
25 E4 **Nunspeet** Netherlands
138 F4 **Nuntherungie** New South Wales Australia
70 E3 **Nunukan** *isld* Kalimantan
59 H2 **Nuomin He** *R* China
43 C8 **Nuoro** Sardinia
26 L5 **Nuortikon** Sweden
137 O4 **Nupani** Santa Cruz Is
128 C2 **Nuquí** Colombia
57 G1 **Nura** *R* Kazakhstan
57 G1 **Nura** Kazakhstan
Nurakita *see* **Niulakita**
57 D4 **Nuratau, Khr** *mts* Uzbekistan
57 D4 **Nuratau, Khrebet** *mts* Uzbekistan
36 B3 **Nürburg** Germany
78 F3 **Nur Daları** *mts* Turkey
44 G2 **Nure** *R* Italy
57 E5 **Nurek** Tajikistan
57 E5 **Nurek Vodokhranilishche** *res* Tajikistan
Nuremberg *see* **Nürnberg**
95 L6 **Nuremburg** Pennsylvania U.S.A.
21 N8 **Nuret-le-Ferron** France
124 E3 **Nuri** Mexico
138 E5 **Nuriootpa** South Australia Australia
74 D1 **Nuristan** *reg* Afghanistan
52 H7 **Nurlat** Russian Federation
52 G6 **Nurlaty** Russian Federation
29 O8 **Nurmes** Finland
29 K9 **Nurmo** Finland
37 L5 **Nürnberg** Germany
71 G7 **Nuro** Mindanao Philippines
138 A3 **Nurrari Lakes** South Australia Australia
43 C9 **Nurri** Sardinia
36 G6 **Nürtingen** Germany
66 E4 **Nur Turu** China
31 O3 **Nurzec** *R* Poland
71 H9 **Nusa Tenggara Barat** Indonesia
71 K9 **Nusa Tenggara Timur** Indonesia
78 H3 **Nusaybin** Turkey
79 G3 **Nusayrīyah, Jebel al** *mts* Syria
116 J6 **Nushagak** *R* Alaska U.S.A.
116 H7 **Nushagak B** Alaska U.S.A.
116 H7 **Nushagak Pen** Alaska U.S.A.
66 F6 **Nu Shan** *mt ra* China
74 B4 **Nushki** Pakistan
33 N5 **Nusse** Germany
115 N6 **Nutak** Labrador, Nfld Canada
33 S8 **Nuthe** *R* Germany
119 O6 **Nut L** Saskatchewan Canada
9 G5 **Nutley** England
128 E2 **Nutrias** Venezuela
14 E2 **Nutts Corner** N Ireland
140 C3 **Nutwood Downs** N Terr Australia
116 Q5 **Nutzotin Mts** Alaska U.S.A.
115 O3 **Nuugaabsiaq** Greenland
Nuuk *see* **Godthåb**
29 M5 **Nuupas** Finland
Nuussuaq *see* **Kraulshavn**
115 O3 **Nuussuaq** *area* Greenland
115 O3 **Nuussuaq** *pen* Greenland
75 K4 **Nuwakot** Nepal
83 K11 **Nuwara Eliya** Sri Lanka
79 E10 **Nuweiba el Muzeina** Egypt
89 B9 **Nuweveldreeks** *mts* S Africa
116 J7 **Nuyakuk** *R* Alaska U.S.A.
116 H7 **Nuyakuk,L** Alaska U.S.A.
138 C4 **Nuyts Arch** South Australia Australia
138 B4 **Nuyts,C** South Australia Australia
143 B11 **Nuyts, Pt** W Australia Australia
122 F6 **N.W. Miramichi R** New Brunswick Canada
87 E9 **Nxai Pan National Park** Botswana
143 C10 **Nyabing** W Australia Australia
88 B3 **Nyabisindu** Rwanda
101 M1 **Nyack** Montana U.S.A.
88 D10 **Nyaderi** *R* Zimbabwe
139 G6 **Nyah** Victoria Australia
88 F1 **Nyahururu** Kenya
66 D6 **Nyainqêntanglha Shan** *ra* China
88 D3 **Nyakabindi** Tanzania
26 K8 **Nyåker** Sweden
55 D1 **Nyaksimvol'** Russian Federation
86 D3 **Nyala** Sudan
66 D6 **Nyalam** China
88 D3 **Nyalikungu** Tanzania
55 E1 **Nyalinskoye** Russian Federation
87 E9 **Nyamandhlovu** Zimbabwe
88 C10 **Nyamanji** *mt* Zimbabwe
88 D10 **Nyamapanda** Zimbabwe
87 D8 **Nyamboma Falls** Zambia
86 E4 **Nyamlell** Sudan
87 G8 **Nyamtumba** Tanzania
Nyanda *see* **Masvingo**
52 F4 **Nyandoma** Russian Federation
88 C10 **Nyangadzi** *R* Zimbabwe
88 D10 **Nyangadzi** *R* Zimbabwe
143 F8 **Nyanga, L** W Australia Australia
88 E10 **Nyanja** Malawi
87 F8 **Nyanji** Zambia
52 H4 **Nyanyayel'** Russian Federation
70 E4 **Nyapa, Gunung** *mt* Kalimantan
117 R5 **Nyarling** *R* Northwest Territories Canada
88 E7 **Nyasa** *tribe* Tanzania
88 E7 **Nyasa,L** Malawi/Moz
Nyasaland *see* **Malawi**
52 H2 **Nyashabozh** Russian Federation
68 B3 **Nyaungbinzeik** Burma
68 C4 **Nyaunglebin** Burma
68 B2 **Nyaungu** Burma
55 C3 **Nyazepetrovsk** Russian Federation
87 F9 **Nyazura** Zimbabwe
89 G2 **Nyazvidzi** *R* Zimbabwe
28 F6 **Nyborg** Denmark
26 R1 **Nyborg** Norway
27 H15 **Nybro** Sweden
50 G2 **Nyda** Russian Federation
27 G14 **Nydala** Sweden
115 O1 **Nyeboe Land** Greenland
Nyenchen Tanglha Range *see* **Nyainqêntanglha Shan**
86 F4 **Nyerol** Sudan
27 G11 **Nyhammar** Sweden
29 K4 **Nyhamn** Sweden
26 H9 **Nyhem** Sweden
88 D6 **Nyiha** Tanzania
66 D5 **Nyima** China
87 F8 **Nyimba** Zambia
66 E6 **Nyingchi** China
48 G3 **Nyíradony** Hungary
48 G3 **Nyírbátor** Hungary
48 G3 **Nyíregyháza** Hungary
88 F3 **Nyiri Desert** Kenya
86 G5 **Nyiru** *mt* Kenya
29 K8 **Nykarleby** Finland
27 H13 **Nykil** Sweden
28 J5 **Nykøbing** Denmark
28 H7 **Nykøbing** Falster Denmark
28 B3 **Nykøbing** Mors Denmark
27 J13 **Nyköping** Sweden
27 G12 **Nykroppa** Sweden
89 F5 **Nyl** *R* S Africa
26 J8 **Nyland** Sweden
89 F5 **Nylstroom** S Africa
26 K6 **Nylund** Sweden
139 H4 **Nymagee** New South Wales Australia
139 L3 **Nymboida** New South Wales Australia
139 L3 **Nymborda** *R* New South Wales Australia
31 J5 **Nymburk** Czech Rep
7 F11 **Nymphe Bank** Atlantic Oc
27 J13 **Nynäshamn** Sweden
139 H4 **Nyngan** New South Wales Australia
21 J6 **Nyoiseau** France
86 B5 **Nyong** *R* Cameroon
19 O16 **Nyons** France
37 P4 **Nýřany** Czech Rep
52 J4 **Nyrob** Russian Federation
37 P5 **Nýrsko** Czech Rep
26 R2 **Nyrud** Norway
31 K5 **Nysa** Poland
27 F11 **Nyskoga** Sweden
100 H6 **Nyssa** Oregon U.S.A.
Nystad *see* **Uusikaupunki**
55 C2 **Nyta** Russian Federation
52 H5 **Nytva** Russian Federation
61 N5 **Nyūdō zaki** *C* Japan
52 G3 **Nyukhcha** Arkhangel'skaya obl Russian Federation
52 E3 **Nyukhcha** Karel'skaya Respublika Russian Federation
52 D3 **Nyuk, Oz** *L* Russian Federation
52 F4 **Nyuksenitsa** Russian Federation
59 H1 **Nyukzha** *R* Russian Federation
51 L2 **Nyurba** Russian Federation
55 E1 **Nyurkoy** Russian Federation
69 H14 **Nyurun** Indonesia
52 H4 **Nyuvchim** Russian Federation
56 H1 **Nyuya** *R* Russian Federation
88 D4 **Nzega** Tanzania
85 C7 **Nzérékoré** Guinea
87 B7 **N'Zeto** Angola
87 G10 **Nzwane** *isld* Comoros

O

98 G6 **Oacoma** South Dakota U.S.A.
98 F5 **Oahe Dam** South Dakota U.S.A.
98 F5 **Oahe, L** South Dakota U.S.A.
102 S11 **Oahu** *isld* Hawaiian Is
103 N7 **Oak** *R* Arizona U.S.A.
60 S2 **O-akan-dake** *mt* Japan
122 E8 **Oak B** New Brunswick Canada
138 F5 **Oakbank** South Australia Australia
95 R5 **Oak Bluffs** Massachusetts U.S.A.
112 G2 **Oakboro** North Carolina U.S.A.
119 R8 **Oakburn** Manitoba Canada
112 K2 **Oak City** North Carolina U.S.A.
103 M2 **Oak City** Utah U.S.A.
109 N9 **Oak Cliff** Texas U.S.A.
101 T9 **Oak Creek** Colorado U.S.A.
102 D4 **Oakdale** California U.S.A.
111 D11 **Oakdale** Louisiana U.S.A.
98 J7 **Oakdale** Nebraska U.S.A.
98 H3 **Oakes** North Dakota U.S.A.
100 H2 **Oakesdale** Washington U.S.A.
140 F7 **Oakes, Mt** Queensland Australia
141 K7 **Oakey** Queensland Australia
99 S6 **Oakfield** Wisconsin U.S.A.
99 R9 **Oakford** Illinois U.S.A.
111 E9 **Oak Grove** Louisiana U.S.A.
9 F2 **Oakham** England
94 D5 **Oak Harbor** Ohio U.S.A.
113 G9 **Oak Hill** Florida U.S.A.
107 N2 **Oak Hill** Kansas U.S.A.
94 E8 **Oak Hill** Ohio U.S.A.
94 F9 **Oak Hill** West Virginia U.S.A.
119 R9 **Oak Lake** Manitoba Canada
102 B4 **Oakland** California U.S.A.
99 S10 **Oakland** Illinois U.S.A.
99 L8 **Oakland** Iowa U.S.A.
95 S2 **Oakland** Maine U.S.A.
94 H7 **Oakland** Maryland U.S.A.
111 G7 **Oakland** Mississippi U.S.A.
98 K8 **Oakland** Nebraska U.S.A.
100 B6 **Oakland** Oregon U.S.A.
95 M5 **Oakland** Pennsylvania U.S.A.
110 G6 **Oakland** Tennessee U.S.A.
109 L6 **Oakland** Texas U.S.A.
110 J3 **Oakland City** Indiana U.S.A.
113 G11 **Oakland Park** Florida U.S.A.
139 H6 **Oaklands** New South Wales Australia
99 T8 **Oak Lawn** Illinois U.S.A.
145 E1 **Oakleigh** New Zealand
102 C4 **Oakley** California U.S.A.
101 M7 **Oakley** Idaho U.S.A.
107 K2 **Oakley** Kansas U.S.A.
94 C3 **Oakley** Michigan U.S.A.
112 C3 **Oakman** Georgia U.S.A.
94 H6 **Oakmont** Pennsylvania U.S.A.
119 R8 **Oakner** Manitoba Canada
142 D5 **Oakover, R** W Australia Australia
141 G4 **Oak Park** Queensland Australia
112 E5 **Oakpark** Georgia U.S.A.
119 T8 **Oak Pt** Manitoba Canada
111 E9 **Oak Ridge** Louisiana U.S.A.
110 G4 **Oak Ridge** Missouri U.S.A.
100 C6 **Oakridge** Oregon U.S.A.
112 C1 **Oak Ridge** Tennessee U.S.A.
119 R8 **Oak River** Manitoba Canada
145 D3 **Oakura** New Zealand
138 F5 **Oakvale** South Australia Australia
119 T9 **Oakville** Manitoba Canada
121 L9 **Oakville** Ontario Canada
109 J7 **Oakville** Texas U.S.A.
141 H7 **Oakwood** Queensland Australia
110 J1 **Oakwood** Illinois U.S.A.
110 E2 **Oakwood** Missouri U.S.A.
94 C5 **Oakwood** Ohio U.S.A.
107 M6 **Oakwood** Oklahoma U.S.A.
144 C6 **Oamaru** New Zealand
61 O10 **Ōami** Japan
144 D5 **Oaro** New Zealand
71 F4 **Oas** Philippines
60 F11 **Ōasa** Japan
102 G4 **Oasis** California U.S.A.
101 L8 **Oasis** Nevada U.S.A.
146 C13 **Oates Land** Antarctica
139 H8 **Oatlands** Tasmania Australia
103 K6 **Oatman** Arizona U.S.A.
125 L9 **Oaxaca de Juárez** Mexico
56 B4 **Ob'** *R* Russian Federation
120 F3 **Oba** Ontario Canada
120 E3 **Obakamiga L** Ontario Canada
120 F4 **Oba L** Ontario Canada
86 B5 **Obala** Cameroon
121 Q3 **Obalski** Quebec Canada
61 J10 **Obama** Japan
118 J6 **Oban** Saskatchewan Canada
15 C4 **Oban** Scotland
61 O7 **Obanazawa** Japan
106 G6 **Obar** New Mexico U.S.A.
120 E4 **Obatanga Prov. Park** Ontario Canada
121 Q3 **Obatogamau L** Quebec Canada
26 L8 **Obbola** Sweden
38 L7 **Obdach** Austria
117 P9 **Obed** Alberta Canada
38 J5 **Ober** *dist* Austria
40 G3 **Ober Aargau** *dist* Switzerland
30 F8 **Oberammergau** Germany
37 Q1 **Oberau** Germany
41 O2 **Oberau** Germany
36 H2 **Oberaula** Germany
36 H3 **Oberbach** Germany
38 E5 **Oberbayern** *dist* Germany
25 F6 **Oberbruch-Dremmen** Germany
39 C2 **Oberbrunn** Germany
36 H7 **Oberdischingen** Germany
38 H8 **Ober-Drau-Tal** *V* Austria
37 J4 **Obereisenheim** Germany
37 J2 **Oberellen** Germany
41 L4 **Oberengadin** *dist* Switzerland
38 K7 **Oberenns Tal** Austria
37 K3 **Oberessfeld** Germany
37 P1 **Ober Eula** Germany
37 L4 **Oberfranken** *dist* Germany
Oberfrohna *see* **Limbach-Oberfrohna**
38 H8 **Obergailtal** *V* Austria
41 O4 **Obergurgl** Austria
41 L4 **Oberhalbstein** *R* Switzerland
36 E7 **Oberharmersbach** Germany
36 C6 **Oberhaslach** France
32 E10 **Oberhausen** Germany
36 F3 **Oberhausen** Hessen Germany
36 E4 **Ober Hilbersheim** Germany
37 K2 **Oberhof** Germany
36 E6 **Oberkirch** Germany
36 F3 **Oberkleen** Germany
37 J6 **Ober-Kochen** Germany
37 M3 **Ober Kotzau** Germany
37 J3 **Ober Lauringen** Germany
36 H6 **Oberlenningen** Germany
107 K2 **Oberlin** Kansas U.S.A.
111 D11 **Oberlin** Louisiana U.S.A.
94 E5 **Oberlin** Ohio U.S.A.
36 H7 **Ober Marchthal** Germany
32 J10 **Ober Marsberg** Germany
37 J2 **Obermassfeld-Grimmenthal** Germany
36 D4 **Ober Moschel** Germany
36 C7 **Obernai** France
36 G4 **Obernburg** Germany
32 K8 **Obernkirchen** Germany
139 J5 **Oberon** New South Wales Australia
98 G2 **Oberon** North Dakota U.S.A.
39 C2 **Oberpfaffenhofen** Germany
37 M5 **Oberpfalz** *dist* Germany
37 N4 **Oberpfalzer Wald** *mts* Germany
36 C2 **Oberpleis** Germany
36 F4 **Ober Ramstadt** Germany
41 K3 **Oberri** Switzerland
37 O3 **Ober Rittersgrün** Germany
33 P10 **Ober Röblingen** Germany
36 F3 **Ober Rosbach** Germany
36 G5 **Ober Schefflenz** Germany
40 F4 **Ober Simmen Tal** Switzerland
36 H5 **Obersontheim** Germany
33 N10 **Oberspier** Germany
41 M3 **Oberstdorf** Germany
36 D5 **Obersteinbach** France
37 J3 **Obertheres** Germany
37 N6 **Obertraubling** Germany
37 O7 **Ober Trennbach** Germany
33 T6 **Oberueckersee** *L* Germany
36 F3 **Oberursel** Germany
37 N5 **Oberviechtach** Germany
41 H4 **Oberwald** Switzerland
38 O7 **Oberwart** Austria
36 D3 **Oberwesel** Germany
37 O3 **Oberwiesenthal** Germany
36 C2 **Oberwinter** Germany
38 K7 **Oberwölz** Austria
71 A3 **Obi** *isld* Indonesia
60 E14 **Obi** Japan
129 G4 **Obidos** Brazil
16 A5 **Obidos** Portugal
60 R3 **Obihiro** Japan
71 A3 **Obi,Kep** *isld* Indonesia
71 A3 **Obilatu** *isld* Indonesia
38 F5 **Obing** Germany
110 G5 **Obion** Tennessee U.S.A.
19 P15 **Obiou, l'** *mt* France
110 J3 **Oblong** Illinois U.S.A.
59 K2 **Obluch'ye** Russian Federation
54 H1 **Obninsk** Russian Federation
86 H3 **Obock** Djibouti
54 A1 **Obol'** *R* Belarus
120 A3 **Obonga L** Ontario Canada
70 D2 **Obong, G** *mt* Sarawak
31 K3 **Oborniki** Poland
52 F1 **Obornyy, Mys** *C* Russian Federation
86 C6 **Obouya Mossaka** Congo
54 H5 **Oboyan'** Russian Federation
52 F3 **Obozerskiy** Russian Federation
124 E4 **Obregón, Presa** *res* Mexico
120 K5 **O'Brien** Ontario Canada
42 G4 **Obrovac** Croatia
137 M6 **Observatoire, Caye de l'** *islds* Coral Sea
117 H8 **Observatory Inlet** British Columbia Canada
54 D1 **Obsha** *R* Russian Federation
55 B5 **Obshchiy Syrt** *reg* Russian Federation
101 L5 **Obsidian** Idaho U.S.A.
50 G2 **Obskaya Guba** *G* Russian Federation
85 D7 **Obuasi** Ghana
52 J5 **Obva** *R* Russian Federation
41 H4 **Obwalden** *canton* Switzerland
52 G4 **Ob'yachevo** Russian Federation
16 E2 **Oca** *R* Spain
113 E8 **Ocala** Florida U.S.A.
124 E3 **Ocampo** Chihuahua Mexico
124 H4 **Ocampo** Coahuila Mexico
16 E2 **Oca,Mt.de** Spain
126 H10 **Ocaña** Colombia
16 E5 **Ocaña** Spain
106 E5 **Ocate** New Mexico U.S.A.
45 L2 **Occhiobello** Italy
95 M8 **Ocean City** Maryland U.S.A.
95 N7 **Ocean City** New Jersey U.S.A.
100 A2 **Ocean City** Washington U.S.A.
117 K9 **Ocean Falls** British Columbia Canada
95 N7 **Ocean Gate** New Jersey U.S.A.
Ocean I *see* **Banaba**
101 R6 **Ocean L** Wyoming U.S.A.
102 D6 **Oceano** California U.S.A.
90 F5 **Oceanographer Fracture** Atlantic Oc
100 A3 **Ocean Park** Washington U.S.A.
102 G8 **Oceanside** California U.S.A.
100 B4 **Oceanside** Oregon U.S.A.
111 H11 **Ocean Springs** Mississippi U.S.A.
95 M8 **Ocean View** Delaware U.S.A.
16 E3 **Ocejón,Pic** *mt* Spain
108 G4 **O. C. Fisher L** Texas U.S.A.
54 C10 **Ochakov** Ukraine
53 F11 **Ochamchira** Georgia
56 H1 **Ochchuguy Botuobuya** *R* Russian Federation
52 H5 **Ocher** Russian Federation
60 C12 **Ōchi** Japan
60 G10 **Ochiai** Japan
60 T2 **Ochiishi-misaki** *C* Japan
15 E4 **Ochil Hills** Scotland
15 D5 **Ochiltree** Scotland
113 C7 **Ochlocknee** Georgia U.S.A.
111 M11 **Ochlockonee** *R* Florida U.S.A.
100 E5 **Ochoco Res** Oregon U.S.A.
32 G6 **Ocholt** Germany
113 F12 **Ochopee** Florida U.S.A.
127 K2 **Ocho Rios** Jamaica
119 S7 **Ochre River** Manitoba Canada
40 F4 **Ochsen** *mt* Switzerland
37 J4 **Ochsenfurt** Germany
41 L1 **Ochsenhausen** Germany
37 M3 **Ochsenkopf** *mt* Germany
32 L5 **Ochsenzoll** Germany
36 C3 **Ochtendung** Germany
33 O8 **Ochtmersleben** Germany
32 F8 **Ochtrup** Germany
112 D6 **Ocilla** Georgia U.S.A.
27 J11 **Ockelbo** Sweden
28 B7 **Ockholm** Germany
9 F5 **Ockley** England
48 J4 **Ocland** Romania
112 D4 **Ocmulgee** *R* Georgia U.S.A.
112 D5 **Ocmulgee Nat Mon** Georgia U.S.A.
48 H4 **Ocna Mureș** Romania
48 J5 **Ocna Sibiului** Romania
48 H3 **Ocna Sugătag** Romania
48 J5 **Ocnele Mari** Romania
113 F9 **Ocoee** Florida U.S.A.
112 C2 **Ocoee** Tennessee U.S.A.
128 D7 **Ocoña** Peru
112 E5 **Oconee** *R* Georgia U.S.A.
110 G2 **Oconee** Illinois U.S.A.
98 J8 **Oconee** Nebraska U.S.A.
141 G5 **O'Connell** *R* Queensland Australia
98 G8 **Oconto** Nebraska U.S.A.
99 T5 **Oconto** Wisconsin U.S.A.
99 S5 **Oconto Falls** Wisconsin U.S.A.
124 E5 **Ocoroni** Mexico
125 M3 **Ocotal** Nicaragua
124 H7 **Ocotlán** Mexico
125 N9 **Ocozocoautla** Mexico
22 J3 **Ocquier** Belgium
112 M2 **Ocracoke** North Carolina U.S.A.
48 E3 **Ocsa** Hungary
48 F4 **Öcsöd** Hungary
20 G2 **Octeville** Manche France
21 L2 **Octeville** Seine-Inférieure France
120 D3 **Octopus** Ontario Canada
127 L9 **Ocumare del Tuy** Venezuela
71 M9 **Ocussi Ambeno** Timor
27 F14 **Od** Sweden
85 D7 **Oda** Ghana
60 F10 **Ōda** Japan
28 S9 **Odádhahraun** *lava field* Iceland
61 K11 **Ōdaigahara-zan** *mt* Japan
61 O8 **Odaka** Japan
27 E11 **Odal,N** Norway
27 E11 **Odal,S** Norway
99 Q3 **Odanah** Wisconsin U.S.A.
61 O5 **Ōdate** Japan
61 N10 **Odawara** Japan
27 B11 **Odda** Norway
86 G1 **Odda,Jebel** *mt* Sudan
28 E3 **Odde** Denmark
28 E5 **Odder** Denmark
27 C13 **Oddernes** Norway
99 L7 **Odebolt** Iowa U.S.A.
16 B7 **Odeleite** Portugal
99 S8 **Odell** Illinois U.S.A.
98 K9 **Odell** Nebraska U.S.A.
109 H1 **Odell** Texas U.S.A.
37 L7 **Odelzhausen** Germany
109 K8 **Odem** Texas U.S.A.
16 B7 **Odemira** Portugal
47 J6 **Ödemş** Turkey
110 C7 **Oden** Arkansas U.S.A.
36 D4 **Odenbach** Germany
89 E6 **Odendaalsrus** S Africa
36 F5 **Odenheim** Germany
36 B1 **Odenkirchen** Germany
Odense *co see* **Fyn** *co*
28 E6 **Odense** Denmark
28 F5 **Odense Fjord** *inlet* Denmark
36 G4 **Odenwald** *mts* Germany
Oder *R see* **Odra** *R*
33 U7 **Oderberg** Germany
33 T8 **Oderin** Germany
36 E4 **Odernheim** Germany
33 T8 **Oder-Spree-Kanal** Germany
42 E3 **Oderzo** Italy
27 G13 **Ödeshög** Sweden
121 O8 **Odessa** Ontario Canada
119 O8 **Odessa** Saskatchewan Canada
48 N4 **Odessa** Ukraine
110 C3 **Odessa** Missouri U.S.A.
95 L4 **Odessa** New York U.S.A.
108 E4 **Odessa** Texas U.S.A.
100 G2 **Odessa** Washington U.S.A.
55 F4 **Odesskoye** Russian Federation
20 C5 **Odet** *R* France
119 T3 **Odhill** Manitoba Canada
87 E10 **Odiakwe** Botswana
85 C7 **Odienné** Ivory Coast
9 F5 **Odiham** England
6 M2 **Odin** *oil rig* North Sea
110 G3 **Odin** Illinois U.S.A.
54 J1 **Odintsovo** Russian Federation
48 L5 **Odobești** Romania
31 K4 **Odolanów** Poland
21 J3 **Odon** *R* France
110 K3 **Odon** Indiana U.S.A.
108 F3 **O'Donnell** Texas U.S.A.
25 G3 **Odoorn** Netherlands
48 J4 **Odorheiu Secuiesc** Romania
31 J4 **Odra** *R* Poland
16 E2 **Odra** *R* Spain
25 F6 **Odt** Germany
112 E6 **Odum** Georgia U.S.A.
48 E5 **Odžaci** Serbia Yugoslavia
33 O8 **Oebisfelde** Germany
37 J2 **Oechsen** Germany
22 E1 **Oedelem** Belgium
37 P2 **Oederan** Germany
32 E9 **Oeding** Germany
36 E1 **Oedingen** Germany
129 K5 **Oeiras** Brazil
16 A6 **Oeiras** Portugal
16 B7 **Oeiras** *R* Portugal
32 H9 **Oelde** Germany
98 C6 **Oelrichs** South Dakota U.S.A.
37 N3 **Oelsnitz** Germany
99 P7 **Oelwein** Iowa U.S.A.
37 L2 **Oelze** Germany
135 O11 **Oeno** *atoll* Pacific Oc
140 C1 **Oenpelli** N Terr Australia
32 F9 **Oer-Erkenschwick** Germany
32 J9 **Oerlinghausen** Germany
37 L3 **Oeslau** Germany
71 M9 **Oessilo** Timor
36 E3 **Oestrich-Winkel** Germany
133 E3 **Oetling** Argentina
37 K6 **Oettingen** Germany
32 H10 **Oeventrop** Germany
111 G9 **Ofahoma** Mississippi U.S.A.
43 G7 **Ofanto** *R* Italy
80 B8 **Ofaqim** Israel
41 M5 **Ofenpass** Italy
80 C3 **Ofer** Israel
14 D3 **Offaly** *co* Ireland
36 F3 **Offenbach am Main** Germany
36 D7 **Offenburg** Germany
26 G8 **Offerdal** Sweden
112 E6 **Offerman** Georgia U.S.A.
138 B2 **Officer Cr.,The** South Australia Australia
37 J7 **Offingen** Germany
21 N2 **Offranville** France
36 E4 **Offstein** Germany
47 H8 **Ofidhoúsa** *isld* Greece
79 E11 **Ofira** Egypt
26 J3 **Ofotfjord** *inlet* Norway
80 D6 **Ofra** Jordan
61 N6 **Oga** Japan
70 D4 **Oga** *R* Kalimantan
86 J4 **Ogadēn** *reg* Ethiopia
120 E2 **Ogahalla** Ontario Canada
61 N6 **Oga-hantō** *pen* Japan
61 K10 **Ōgaki** Japan
107 L3 **Ogallah** Kansas U.S.A.
98 E8 **Ogallala** Nebraska U.S.A.
54 J3 **Ogarevka** Russian Federation
59 M6 **Ogasawara-shoto** Japan
121 M5 **Ogascanan, L** Quebec Canada
61 O7 **Ogawara** Japan
61 P5 **Ogawara ko** *L* Japan
85 E7 **Ogbomosho** Nigeria
9 E5 **Ogbourne St.George** England
123 L8 **Ogden** Nova Scotia Canada
110 J1 **Ogden** Illinois U.S.A.
99 M7 **Ogden** Iowa U.S.A.
107 O2 **Ogden** Kansas U.S.A.
101 O8 **Ogden** Utah U.S.A.
117 G6 **Ogden,Mt** Br Col/Alaska Canada/U.S.A.
95 M2 **Ogdensburg** New York U.S.A.
112 F5 **Ogeechee** *R* Georgia U.S.A.
119 N9 **Ogema** Saskatchewan Canada
98 K2 **Ogema** Minnesota U.S.A.
32 G5 **Ogenbargen** Germany
36 B6 **Ogéviller** France
41 K6 **Oggiono** Italy
61 M8 **Ogi** Japan
120 F6 **Ogidaki** Ontario Canada
103 K9 **Ogilby** California U.S.A.
143 A8 **Ogilvie** W Australia Australia
99 N4 **Ogilvie** Minnesota U.S.A.
114 F5 **Ogilvie Mts** Yukon Territory Canada
61 Q12 **Ōgimi** Japan
98 D6 **Oglala** South Dakota U.S.A.
99 R8 **Oglesby** Illinois U.S.A.
109 K4 **Oglesby** Texas U.S.A.
112 C5 **Oglethorpe** Georgia U.S.A.
55 F3 **Oglukhino** Russian Federation
141 J6 **Ogmore** Queensland Australia
55 G2 **Ognev Yar** Russian Federation
19 J5 **Ognon** *R* France
70 G4 **Ogoamas, G** *mt* Celebes
59 K1 **Ogodzha** Russian Federation
85 F7 **Ogoja** Nigeria
120 C2 **Ogoki L** Ontario Canada
120 D2 **Ogoki R** Ontario Canada
120 B2 **Ogoki Res** Ontario Canada
86 A6 **Ogooué** *R* Gabon
46 F1 **Ogosta** *R* Bulgaria
70 G4 **Ogotomubu** Sulawesi
61 K9 **Ogoya** Japan
143 B9 **O'Grady, L** W Australia Australia
47 H3 **Ogražden** *hills* Greece
46 F3 **Ogražden Planina** *mt* Macedonia
52 B6 **Ogre** Latvia
61 N10 **Oguchi Dam** Japan
85 D4 **Oguilet Khenachich** Mali
124 F4 **Oguivo** Mexico
85 E7 **Ogun** *R* Nigeria
60 E12 **Oguni** Japan
95 R3 **Ogunquit** Maine U.S.A.
85 F7 **Ogwashi-Uku** Nigeria
145 D1 **Ohaeawai** New Zealand
144 A6 **Ohai** New Zealand
145 E3 **Ohakune** New Zealand
86 D2 **O Haouach** *dist* Chad
61 O10 **Ōhara** Japan
61 P6 **Ōhasama** Japan
60 P4 **Ōhata** Japan
118 E6 **Ohaton** Alberta Canada
145 E4 **Ohau** New Zealand
144 B6 **Ohau, L** New Zealand
145 E2 **Ohaupo** New Zealand
32 G7 **Ohe** *R* Germany
22 J3 **Ohey** Belgium
131 B5 **O'Higgins** *prov* Chile
133 C7 **O'Higgins, L** Chile/Arg
133 C7 **O'Higgins Pirámide** *mt* Chile
145 E2 **Ohinewai** New Zealand
145 E3 **Ohingaiti** New Zealand
94 C6 **Ohio** *state* U.S.A.
110 H4 **Ohio** *R* U.S.A.
99 R8 **Ohio** Illinois U.S.A.
94 C8 **Ohio** *R* Indiana U.S.A.
94 C6 **Ohio City** Ohio U.S.A.
32 G10 **Ohle** Germany
36 F2 **Ohm** *R* Germany
33 M8 **Ohof** Germany
116 G6 **Ohogamiut** Alaska U.S.A.
112 E5 **Ohoopee** *R* Georgia U.S.A.
145 F2 **Ohope** New Zealand
33 N7 **Ohrdorf** Germany
37 K2 **Ohrdruf** Germany
37 O3 **Ohře** *R* Czech Rep
33 O8 **Ohre** *R* Germany
46 D3 **Ohrid** Macedonia
46 D3 **Ohridsko ezero** *L* Albania/Macedonia
36 H5 **Öhringen** Germany
36 G5 **Ohrnberg** Germany
26 N5 **Ohtanajärvi** Sweden
145 E3 **Ohura** New Zealand
129 H3 **Oiapoque** Fr Guiana
66 E6 **Oiga** China
22 H3 **Oignies** Belgium
29 M6 **Oijärvi** Finland
106 G9 **Oil Center** New Mexico U.S.A.
102 F6 **Oil City** California U.S.A.
111 C9 **Oil City** Louisiana U.S.A.
94 H5 **Oil City** Pennsylvania U.S.A.
120 H10 **Oil Springs** Ontario Canada
107 O5 **Oilton** Oklahoma U.S.A.
109 J8 **Oilton** Texas U.S.A.
94 K9 **Oilville** Virginia U.S.A.
47 H6 **Oinoúsa** *isld* Greece
58 C6 **Oi Qu** *R* China
61 P5 **Oirase-gawa** *R* Japan
21 K8 **Oiron** France
25 D5 **Oirschot** Netherlands
19 Q14 **Oisans** *dist* France
18 G3 **Oise** *dept* France
21 P3 **Oise** *R* France
21 O2 **Oisemont** France
21 J5 **Oisseau** France
21 N3 **Oissel** France
25 D5 **Oisterwijk** Netherlands
127 P6 **Oistins** Barbados
22 E3 **Oisy-le-Verger** France
60 E12 **Ōita** Japan
46 E6 **Oíti** *mt* Greece
48 K4 **Oituz** *pass* Romania
60 P3 **Oiwake** Japan
102 E7 **Ojai** California U.S.A.
27 G11 **Öje** Sweden
61 J11 **Ōji** Japan
60 B12 **Ojika-jima** *isld* Japan
124 G3 **Ojinaga** Mexico
61 M8 **Ojiya** Japan
124 H6 **Ojocaliente** Mexico
106 B7 **Ojo Caliente** New Mexico U.S.A.
133 E3 **Ojo de Agua** Argentina
124 F3 **Ojo de Laguna** Mexico
124 C4 **Ojo de Liebre** Mexico
16 E5 **Ojos del Guadiana** *mt* Spain
133 D3 **Ojos del Salado, Nev** *mt* Chile/Arg
17 F4 **Ojos Negros** Spain
113 G12 **Ojus** Florida U.S.A.
27 F10 **Öjvallberget** Sweden
121 Q7 **Oka** Quebec Canada
54 G4 **Oka** *R* Russian Federation
56 F4 **Oka** *R* Russian Federation
87 C10 **Okahandja** Namibia
145 E1 **Okahu** New Zealand
145 E3 **Okahukura** New Zealand
145 E3 **Okaiawa** *R* New Zealand
145 D1 **Okaihau** New Zealand
115 N6 **Okak Is** Labrador, Nfld Canada
113 F11 **Okaloacoochee Slough** *swamp* Florida U.S.A.
117 O10 **Okanagan Centre** British Columbia Canada
117 O11 **Okanagan Falls** British Columbia Canada
86 B6 **Okanda Nat. Park** Gabon
100 F1 **Okanogan** Washington U.S.A.
100 F1 **Okanogan Range** Wash/Br Col U.S.A./Canada
74 E3 **Okara** Pakistan
107 N6 **Okarche** Oklahoma U.S.A.
144 C5 **Okarito** New Zealand
60 D14 **Okasaki** Japan
145 F3 **Okataina L** New Zealand
145 D3 **Okato** New Zealand
111 G10 **Okatoma** *R* Mississippi U.S.A.
87 C9 **Okaukuejo** Namibia
87 D9 **Okavango Basin** Botswana
60 D12 **Ōkawa** Japan
61 N8 **Ō-kawa** *R* Japan
110 G3 **Okawville** Illinois U.S.A.
107 P6 **Okay** Oklahoma U.S.A.
61 L9 **Okaya** Japan
60 G11 **Okayama** *prefect* Japan
60 G11 **Okayama** Japan
61 L11 **Okazaki** Japan
113 G10 **Okeechobee** Florida U.S.A.
113 G11 **Okeechobee,L** Florida U.S.A.
107 M5 **Okeene** Oklahoma U.S.A.
113 E7 **Okefenokee Swamp** Georgia U.S.A.
8 B6 **Okehampton** England
107 O6 **Okemah** Oklahoma U.S.A.
85 F7 **Okene** Nigeria
33 N8 **Oker** *R* Germany
33 M9 **Oker** Germany
60 R2 **Oketo** Japan
98 K10 **Oketo** Kansas U.S.A.
74 C7 **Okha** India
59 M1 **Okha** Russian Federation
75 M5 **Okhaldhunga** Nepal
46 G6 **Ókhi** *mt* Greece
51 O3 **Okhotsk** Russian Federation
59 N1 **Okhotskoye More** *sea* E Asia
Okhotsk,Sea of *see* **Okhotskoye More**
60 G9 **Oki** *islds* Japan
89 A7 **Okiep** S Africa
85 F7 **Okigwi** Nigeria
61 P13 **Okinawa** *isld* Japan
61 P13 **Okinawa** Okinawa
60 D11 **Okino-shima** *isld* Japan
60 F13 **Okino-shima** Japan
56 E4 **Okinskiy Khrebet** *mts* Russian Federation
85 E7 **Okitipupa** Nigeria
68 B4 **Okkan** Burma
107 N6 **Oklahoma** *state* U.S.A.
107 N6 **Oklahoma City** Oklahoma U.S.A.
109 H1 **Oklaunion** Texas U.S.A.
113 F8 **Oklawaha** *R* Florida U.S.A.
107 P6 **Okmulgee** Oklahoma U.S.A.
48 L2 **Oknitsa** Moldova
48 K2 **Okno** Ukraine
99 L6 **Okoboji L** Iowa U.S.A.
98 F5 **Okobojo** South Dakota U.S.A.
145 E3 **Okoia** New Zealand
111 H7 **Okolona** Mississippi U.S.A.
86 B6 **Okondja** Gabon
112 D4 **Okonee, L** Georgia U.S.A.
31 K2 **Okonek** Poland
60 R1 **Okoppe** Japan
145 E2 **Okoroire** New Zealand
118 D8 **Okotoks** Alberta Canada
86 B6 **Okoyo** Congo
85 E7 **Okpara** *R* Benin/Nigeria
98 F6 **Okreek** South Dakota U.S.A.
28 A5 **Oksby** Denmark
26 C9 **Oksendal** Norway
26 M1 **Öksfjord** Norway
26 M1 **Öksfjord-jökel** *mt* Norway
52 H1 **Oksino** Russian Federation
54 M3 **Oksko-Donskaya Ravnina** *plain* Russian Federation
26 G3 **Öksnes** Norway
52 E3 **Oksovskiy** Russian Federation
26 G5 **Okstinderne** *mt* Norway
107 P6 **Oktaha** Oklahoma U.S.A.
68 C3 **Oktwin** Burma
55 C6 **Oktyabr'sk** Kazakhstan
56 B6 **Oktyabr'skiy** Kazakhstan
55 D4 **Oktyabr'skiy** Kustanayskaya Kazakhstan
56 E2 **Oktyabr'skiy** Russian Federation
55 C3 **Oktyabr'skiy** Bashkirskaya Respublika Russian Federation
55 D3 **Oktyabr'skiy** Chelyabinskaya obl Russian Federation
52 F5 **Oktyabr'skiy** Kostromskaya obl Russian Federation
55 E2 **Oktyabr'skiy** Tyumenskaya obl Russian Federation
57 E5 **Oktyabr'skiy** Tajikistan
55 E5 **Oktyabr'skoye** Turgayskaya obl Kazakhstan
55 D4 **Oktyabr'skoye** Chelyabinskaya obl Russian Federation
55 E1 **Oktyabr'skoye** Khanty-Mansiyskiy aut ok Russian Federation
55 C4 **Oktyabr'skoye** Orenburgskaya obl Russian Federation
54 D10 **Oktyabr'skoye** Ukraine
51 J1 **Oktyabr'skoy Revolyutsii, Os** *isld* Russian Federation
61 Q12 **Oku** Okinawa
60 D13 **Ōkuchi** Japan
144 D5 **Okuku** *R* New Zealand
52 D5 **Okulovka** Russian Federation
144 B5 **Okuru** New Zealand
60 N3 **Okushiri-kaikyō** *str* Japan
60 N3 **Okushiri-tō** *isld* Japan
89 B4 **Okwa** *watercourse* Botswana
110 C6 **Ola** Arkansas U.S.A.
100 J5 **Ola** Idaho U.S.A.
28 S8 **Olafsfjordhur** Iceland
28 R9 **Olafsvik** Iceland
80 D1 **Olailé** Israel
16 C7 **Olalla de Cala, Sta** Spain
95 T1 **Olamon** Maine U.S.A.
28 D2 **Øland** *reg* Denmark
27 J15 **Oland** *isld* Sweden
29 P5 **Olanga** *R* Finland/Rus Fed
52 D2 **Olanga** Russian Federation
112 H4 **Olanta** South Carolina U.S.A.
18 G9 **Olargues** France
138 C2 **Olarinna** *R* South Australia Australia
138 F4 **Olary** South Australia Australia
107 Q3 **Olathe** Kansas U.S.A.
131 E6 **Olavarria** Argentina
31 K5 **Oława** Poland
103 N8 **Olberg** Arizona U.S.A.
37 P2 **Olbernhau** Germany
37 L1 **Olbersleben** Germany
43 C8 **Olbia** Sardinia
37 L7 **Olching** Germany
94 J3 **Olcott** New York U.S.A.
126 E3 **Old Bahama Chan** Caribbean
14 D3 **Oldcastle** Ireland
142 F4 **Old Cherrabun** W Australia Australia
141 F6 **Old Cork** Queensland Australia
116 R3 **Old Crow** Yukon Territory Canada
116 R2 **Old Crow** *R* Alaska/Yukon Terr U.S.A./Canada
88 E3 **Oldeani** Tanzania
109 J3 **Olden** Texas U.S.A.
32 H6 **Oldenbrok** Germany
33 N4 **Oldenburg** Germany
33 N6 **Oldendorf** Germany
33 N7 **Oldenstadt** Germany
25 G4 **Oldenzaal** Netherlands
32 F6 **Oldersum** Germany
26 B10 **Oldevatn** *L* Norway
101 P5 **Old Faithful** Wyoming U.S.A.
95 M3 **Old Forge** New York U.S.A.
95 M5 **Old Forge** Pennsylvania U.S.A.
112 E2 **Old Fort** North Carolina U.S.A.
123 O2 **Old Fort Bay** Quebec Canada
143 C8 **Old Gidgee** W Australia Australia
108 G2 **Old Glory** Texas U.S.A.
13 F6 **Oldham** England
98 J5 **Oldham** South Dakota U.S.A.
116 L8 **Old Harbor** Alaska U.S.A.
127 K3 **Old Harbour** Jamaica
110 K5 **Old Hickory L** Tennessee U.S.A.
117 L8 **Old Hogem** British Columbia Canada
9 F3 **Old Hurst** England
33 O10 **Oldisleben** Germany
116 P2 **Old John L** Alaska U.S.A.
95 P5 **Old Lyme** Connecticut U.S.A.
15 F3 **Oldmeldrum** Scotland
110 F3 **Old Monroe** Missouri U.S.A.
95 R3 **Old Orchard Beach** Maine U.S.A.
123 T5 **Old Perlican** Newfoundland Canada
123 L3 **Old Post Pt** Quebec Canada
116 R3 **Old Rampart** Alaska U.S.A.
113 G12 **Old Rhodes Key** *isld* Florida U.S.A.
127 O5 **Old Road** Antigua W Indies
127 P4 **Old Road Town** St Kitts W Indies
118 C7 **Olds** Alberta Canada
95 R2 **Old Speck Mt** Maine U.S.A.
9 F3 **Old Stratford** England
28 A7 **Oldsum** Germany
113 E10 **Old Tampa B** Florida U.S.A.
138 E4 **Old Telichie** South Australia Australia
113 D8 **Old Town** Florida U.S.A.
95 T2 **Old Town** Maine U.S.A.
88 E3 **Olduvai Gorge** Tanzania
118 L8 **Old Wives L** Saskatchewan Canada
116 H5 **Old Woman** *R* Alaska U.S.A.
103 J7 **Old Woman Mts** California U.S.A.
65 A2 **Öldziyt** Mongolia
94 J4 **Olean** New York U.S.A.
122 H7 **O'Leary** Prince Edward I Canada
31 N1 **Olecko** Poland
16 B5 **Oleiros** Portugal
59 G1 **Olekminski Stanovik** *mt ra* Russian Federation
52 G3 **Olema** Russian Federation
27 A12 **Ölen** Norway
100 D7 **Olene** Oregon U.S.A.
52 D1 **Olenegorsk** Russian Federation
51 L2 **Olenek** *R* Russian Federation
52 D6 **Olenino** Russian Federation
52 E2 **Olenitsa** Russian Federation
55 B5 **Olenty** *R* Kazakhstan
18 E7 **Oléron,Ile d'** France
48 J1 **Olesko** Ukraine
31 K4 **Oleśnica** Poland
31 L5 **Oleśno** Poland
45 O6 **Olevano Romano** Italy
100 E4 **Olex** Oregon U.S.A.
32 F9 **Olfen** Germany
59 L3 **Ol'ga** Russian Federation
113 F11 **Olga** Florida U.S.A.
98 H1 **Olga** North Dakota U.S.A.
116 K8 **Olga B** Alaska U.S.A.
121 N3 **Olga,L** Quebec Canada
140 B7 **Olga, Mt** N Terr Australia
54 J9 **Ol'ginka** Ukraine
66 D2 **Ölgiy** Mongolia
28 B5 **Ølgod** Denmark
48 M2 **Ol'gopol'** Ukraine
16 B7 **Olhão** Portugal
29 L6 **Olhava** Finland
85 E7 **Oli** *R* Benin/Nigeria
138 A2 **Olia Chain** *mts* N Terr Australia
140 A7 **Olia Chain** *mts* N Terr Australia
17 H2 **Oliana** Spain
42 F4 **Olib** *isld* Croatia
17 G4 **Oliete** Spain
87 C10 **Olifants** *R* Namibia
89 A5 **Olifants** *watercourse* Namibia
89 G5 **Olifants** *R* S Africa
89 A8 **Olifants** S Africa
87 D11 **Olifantshoek** S Africa
89 A9 **Olifants R. Berge** *mts* S Africa
131 G4 **Olimar** *R* Uruguay
46 E7 **Olimbía** Greece
46 E4 **Ólimbos** *mt* Greece
133 F2 **Olimpo** Paraguay
99 P7 **Olin** Iowa U.S.A.
100 C9 **Olinda** California U.S.A.
141 G1 **Olinda Ent** Gt Barrier Reef Aust
129 L6 **Olindina** Brazil

141 G5 **Olio** Queensland Australia
17 F2 **Olite** Spain
17 G6 **Oliva** Spain
131 B2 **Oliva, Cord. de** *mt ra* Arg/Chile
16 C6 **Oliva de Mérida** Spain
131 B3 **Olivares,Cerro del** *pk* Arg/Chile
17 F5 **Olivares de Júcar** Spain
98 A4 **Olive** Montana U.S.A.
110 G7 **Olive Branch** Mississippi U.S.A.
94 D8 **Olive Hill** Kentucky U.S.A.
130 G7 **Oliveira** Brazil
16 B4 **Oliveira de Azemeis** Portugal
16 B4 **Oliveira do Hospital** Portugal
112 J2 **Olive, Mt** North Carolina U.S.A.
Olivenca *see* **Lupilichi**
16 C6 **Olivenza** Spain
117 O11 **Oliver** British Columbia Canada
112 F5 **Oliver** Georgia U.S.A.
21 O6 **Olivet** France
94 C4 **Olivet** Michigan U.S.A.
98 J6 **Olivet** South Dakota U.S.A.
99 M5 **Olivia** Minnesota U.S.A.
109 L7 **Olivia** Texas U.S.A.
144 B6 **Olivine Range** New Zealand
41 J5 **Olivone** Switzerland
31 L1 **Oliwa** Poland
65 D3 **Olji Moron He** *R* China
54 L6 **Ol'khovatka** Russian Federation
55 D3 **Ol'khovka** Russian Federation
31 M5 **Olkusz** Poland
111 D10 **Olla** Louisiana U.S.A.
133 D2 **Ollague** *vol* Bolivia/Chile
9 E1 **Ollerton** England
98 B3 **Ollie** Montana U.S.A.
29 N2 **Ollila** Finland
131 B3 **Ollita, Cord. de** *ra* Arg/Chile
131 B3 **Ollitas** *pk* Argentina
27 G12 **Ölme** Sweden
16 D3 **Olmeda** Spain
131 D4 **Olmos,L** Argentina
9 F3 **Olney** England
110 H3 **Olney** Illinois U.S.A.
101 L1 **Olney** Montana U.S.A.
109 J2 **Olney** Texas U.S.A.
106 G3 **Olney Springs** Colorado U.S.A.
26 K8 **Olofsfors** Sweden
27 G15 **Olofström** Sweden
123 M3 **Olomane R** Quebec Canada
86 C6 **Olombo** Congo
48 D1 **Olomouc** Czech Rep
41 K7 **Olona** *R* Italy
48 M4 **Oloneshty** Moldova
52 D4 **Olonets** Russian Federation
71 E3 **Olongapo** Luzon Philippines
70 D5 **Olongliko** Kalimantan
20 G8 **Olonne-sur-Mer** France
18 G9 **Olonzac** France
18 E9 **Oloron-St.Marie** France
17 J2 **Olot** Spain
37 O3 **Olovi** Czech Rep
48 E6 **Olovo** Bosnia-Herzegovina
58 G1 **Olovyannaya** Russian Federation
36 D1 **Olpe** Germany
107 O3 **Olpe** Kansas U.S.A.
41 P3 **Olperer** *mt* Austria
107 O2 **Olsburg** Kansas U.S.A.
31 L6 **Olše** *R* Czech Rep
54 G6 **Ol'shany** Ukraine
25 F4 **Olst** Netherlands
31 M2 **Olsztyn** Poland
31 M2 **Olsztynek** Poland
48 K4 **Olt** *R* Romania
40 G3 **Olten** Switzerland
48 K6 **Oltenița** Romania
133 D6 **Olte,Sa.de** *mts* Argentina
48 H6 **Olteț** *R* Romania
108 E1 **Olton** Texas U.S.A.
78 H1 **Oltu** Turkey
67 G6 **O-luan-pi** *C* Taiwan
113 E7 **Olustee** Florida U.S.A.
107 L7 **Olustee** Oklahoma U.S.A.
71 F7 **Olutanga** *isld* Philippines
33 P8 **Olvenstedt** Germany
16 D8 **Olvera** Spain
46 E7 **Olympia** Greece
100 C2 **Olympia** Washington U.S.A.
100 B2 **Olympic Mts** Washington U.S.A.
100 A2 **Olympic Nat. Park** Washington U.S.A.
100 B2 **Olympic Nat. Park** Washington U.S.A.
Olympus *mt* Cyprus *see* **Troödos** *mt*
Olympus *mt* Greece *see* **Ólimbos** *mt*
100 B2 **Olympus,Mt** Washington U.S.A.
95 M5 **Olyphant** Pennsylvania U.S.A.
51 Q2 **Olyutorskiy** Russian Federation
36 B3 **Olzheim** Germany
56 B3 **Om'** *R* Russian Federation
60 O4 **Ōma** Japan
52 G2 **Oma** Russian Federation
111 F10 **Oma** Mississippi U.S.A.
61 L9 **Ōmachi** Japan
61 M11 **Omae zaki** *C* Japan
14 D2 **Omagh** N Ireland
128 D4 **Omaguas** Peru
110 C5 **Omaha** Arkansas U.S.A.
99 L8 **Omaha** Nebraska U.S.A.
109 N2 **Omaha** Texas U.S.A.
126 F4 **Omaja** Cuba
100 F1 **Omak** Washington U.S.A.
144 B6 **Omakau** New Zealand
145 F4 **Omakere** New Zealand
72 H5 **Oman** *sultanate* Arabian Pen
77 F7 **Oman, Gulf of** Iran/Oman
145 D1 **Omapere, L** New Zealand
94 E9 **Omar** West Virginia U.S.A.
144 B6 **Omarama** New Zealand
87 C10 **Omaruru** Namibia
128 D7 **Omate** Peru
71 J9 **Omatema** Indonesia
60 O4 **Ōma-zaki** *C* Japan
120 C2 **Ombabika** Ontario Canada
120 B2 **Ombabika B** Ontario Canada
71 M9 **Ombai,Selat** *str* Indonesia
61 N11 **Ombase-jima** *isld* Japan
8 D3 **Ombersley** England
69 C12 **Ombolata** Indonesia
86 A6 **Omboue** Gabon
45 J4 **Ombrone** *R* Italy
66 D5 **Ombu** China
86 F2 **Omdurman** Sudan
61 N10 **Ōme** Japan
111 L10 **Omega** Alabama U.S.A.
112 D6 **Omega** Georgia U.S.A.
107 M6 **Omega** Oklahoma U.S.A.
121 M8 **Omemee** Ontario Canada
98 F1 **Omemee** North Dakota U.S.A.
94 B1 **Omena** Michigan U.S.A.
80 C8 **'Omer** Israel
94 D2 **Omer** Michigan U.S.A.
47 J5 **Ömerköy** Turkey
47 N10 **Ömerli Baraji** *dam* Turkey
14 A3 **Omey I** Ireland
86 G3 **Om Häjer** Eritrea
61 L8 **Ōmi** Japan
22 D4 **Omiecourt** France
144 D5 **Omihi** New Zealand
60 P4 **Ōminato** Japan
117 L8 **Omineca** *R* British Columbia Canada
117 K7 **Omineca Mts** British Columbia Canada
42 H5 **Omis** Croatia
60 E11 **Ōmi-shima** *isld* Japan
60 F11 **Ōmi-shima** *isld* Japan
61 N10 **Ōmiya** Japan
117 F7 **Ommaney,C** Alaska U.S.A.
114 J3 **Ommanney B** Northwest Territories Canada
28 B5 **Omme Å** *R* Denmark
25 F3 **Ommen** Netherlands
28 G6 **Omø** Denmark
86 G4 **Omo** *R* Ethiopia
43 B8 **Omodeo, L** Sardinia
51 P2 **Omolon** *R* Russian Federation
51 N2 **Omoloy** *R* Russian Federation
61 O6 **Omono-gawa** *R* Japan
22 H4 **Omont** France
20 G2 **Omonville-la Rogue** France
61 O6 **Ōmori** Japan
61 P6 **Omoto** Japan
61 P6 **Omoto-gawa** *R* Japan
99 S5 **Omro** Wisconsin U.S.A.
55 F3 **Omsk** Russian Federation
55 G3 **Omskaya Oblast'** *prov* Russian Federation
68 D1 **O-mu** Burma
60 Q1 **Ōmu** Japan
31 N2 **Omulew** *R* Poland
83 L10 **Omuna** Sri Lanka
60 C13 **Ōmura** Japan
60 C13 **Ōmura wan** *B* Japan
47 H1 **Omurtag** Bulgaria
60 D12 **Ōmuta** Japan
55 E3 **Omutinskiy** Russian Federation
52 H5 **Omutninsk** Russian Federation
26 B9 **Ona** Norway
56 C5 **Ona** *R* Russian Federation
16 E2 **Oña** Spain
113 F10 **Ona** Florida U.S.A.
107 O2 **Onaga** Kansas U.S.A.
61 P7 **Onagawahama** Japan
61 P7 **Onagawa-wan** *B* Japan
61 O9 **Onahama** Japan
98 G4 **Onaka** South Dakota U.S.A.
120 J2 **Onakawana** Ontario Canada
120 J1 **Onakwehegan** *R* Ontario Canada
100 C3 **Onalaska** Washington U.S.A.
99 P6 **Onalaska** Wisconsin U.S.A.
120 C2 **Onaman L** Ontario Canada
99 N3 **Onamia** Minnesota U.S.A.
95 M9 **Onancock** Virginia U.S.A.
70 F6 **Onang** Sulawesi
86 B6 **Onangue, L** Gabon
120 J5 **Onaping L** Ontario Canada
110 H1 **Onarga** Illinois U.S.A.
121 U3 **Onatchiway,L** Quebec Canada
124 F2 **Oñate** Mexico
124 E3 **Onavas** Mexico
98 K7 **Onawa** Iowa U.S.A.
94 C1 **Onaway** Michigan U.S.A.
87 B9 **Oncocua** Angola
17 G5 **Onda** Spain
87 C9 **Ondangwa** Namibia
31 N6 **Ondava** *R* Slovakia
25 G2 **Onderdendam** Netherlands
87 C9 **Ondjiva** Angola
85 E7 **Ondo** Nigeria
58 F2 **Öndörhaan** Mongolia
65 E2 **Ondor Had** China
73 L8 **One and Half Degree Chan** Indian Oc
113 E10 **Oneco** Florida U.S.A.
Onega *L* *see* **Onezhskoye, Oz**
52 E3 **Onega** Russian Federation
52 E4 **Onega** *R* Russian Federation
44 D4 **Oneglia** Italy
141 H2 **One & Half Mile Opening** *str* Gt Barrier Reef Aust
99 Q8 **Oneida** Illinois U.S.A.
99 P7 **Oneida** Iowa U.S.A.
94 D9 **Oneida** Kentucky U.S.A.
95 M3 **Oneida** New York U.S.A.
110 M5 **Oneida** Tennessee U.S.A.
95 L3 **Oneida L** New York U.S.A.
98 H7 **O'Neill** Nebraska U.S.A.
145 D4 **Onekaka** New Zealand
94 A2 **Onekama** Michigan U.S.A.
86 D6 **Onema** Zaire
111 K8 **Oneonta** Alabama U.S.A.
95 M4 **Oneonta** New York U.S.A.
145 E1 **Onerahi** New Zealand
145 E2 **Oneroa I** New Zealand
118 J1 **One Sided Lake** Ontario Canada
48 K4 **Onești** Romania
52 E4 **Onezhskoye,Oz** *L* Russian Federation
145 F3 **Ongaonga** New Zealand
9 G4 **Ongar** England
145 E3 **Ongarue** New Zealand
89 C8 **Ongers** *watercourse* S Africa
143 C10 **Ongerup** W Australia Australia
65 B3 **Onggon Ul** China
19 P16 **Ongles** France
65 D3 **Ongniud Qi** China
76 E3 **Ongole** India
56 G4 **Onguren** Russian Federation
15 C4 **Onich** Scotland
98 G5 **Onida** South Dakota U.S.A.
87 G12 **Onilahy** *R* Madagascar
118 H5 **Onion Lake** Saskatchewan Canada
60 P1 **Onishika** Japan
122 A3 **Onistagan L** Quebec Canada
85 F7 **Onitsha** Nigeria
21 N1 **Onival** France
29 N8 **Onkivesi** *L* Finland
95 M9 **Onley** Virginia U.S.A.
61 P13 **Onna** Okinawa
61 P13 **Onna-dake** *mt* Okinawa
22 F3 **Onnaing** France
60 O4 **Ōno** Japan
60 E11 **Onoda** Japan
61 N11 **Ōnohara-jima** *isld* Japan
137 R6 **Ono-i-lau** *isld* Pacific Oc
145 E4 **Onoke, L** New Zealand
60 G11 **Onomichi** Japan
58 G1 **Onon** *R* Russian Federation
69 C12 **Ononamolo** Indonesia
94 C4 **Onondaga** Michigan U.S.A.
58 F2 **Onon Gol** *R* Mongolia
61 O8 **Ono-Niimachi** Japan
59 M1 **Onor** Russian Federation
128 E2 **Onoto** Venezuela
137 Q2 **Onotoa** *atoll* Kiribati
118 C5 **Onoway** Alberta Canada
28 F5 **Onsbjerg** Denmark
16 B2 **Ons., I.de** Spain
28 H7 **Ønslev** Denmark
142 B5 **Onslow** W Australia Australia
112 K3 **Onslow B** North Carolina U.S.A.
144 B6 **Onslow, L** New Zealand
94 C4 **Onsted** Michigan U.S.A.
36 G7 **Onstmettingen** Germany
25 H2 **Onstwedde** Netherlands
61 L10 **Ontake-san** *mt* Japan
115 K7 **Ontario** *prov* Canada
102 G7 **Ontario** California U.S.A.
100 J5 **Ontario** Oregon U.S.A.
99 Q6 **Ontario** Wisconsin U.S.A.
94 J3 **Ontario,L** U.S.A./Canada
17 G6 **Onteniente** Spain
99 R3 **Ontonagon** Michigan U.S.A.
137 M3 **Ontong Java Is** Solomon Is
17 G6 **Ontur** Spain
60 O4 **Onuma** Japan
111 F9 **Onward** Mississippi U.S.A.
102 F6 **Onyx** California U.S.A.
21 N6 **Onzain** France
138 E5 **Oodla Wirra** South Australia Australia
138 D2 **Oodnadatta** South Australia Australia
135 V4 **Ookala** Hawaiian Is
138 B4 **Ooldea** South Australia Australia
138 B4 **Ooldea Ra** South Australia Australia
110 K3 **Oolitic** Indiana U.S.A.
107 P5 **Oologah** Oklahoma U.S.A.
107 P5 **Oologah L** Oklahoma U.S.A.
25 B5 **Ooltgensplaat** Netherlands
140 C6 **Ooraminna Ra** N Terr Australia
140 D5 **Ooratippra** *R* N Terr Australia
140 D5 **Ooratippra** N Terr Australia
141 F5 **Oorindi** Queensland Australia
111 L7 **Oostanaula** *R* Georgia U.S.A.
25 A6 **Oostburg** Netherlands
22 D2 **Oost Cappel** France
22 D1 **Oostduinkerke** Belgium
25 E4 **Oostelijk-Flevoland** Netherlands
22 D1 **Oostende** Belgium
25 E5 **Oosterbeër** Netherlands
25 D2 **Oosterend** Netherlands
25 C5 **Oosterhout** Netherlands
25 A5 **Oosterschelde** Netherlands
25 F3 **Oosterwolde** Netherlands
22 F2 **Oosterzele** Belgium
25 D3 **Oosthuizen** Netherlands
25 F2 **Oostmahoorn** Netherlands
22 H1 **Oostmalle** Belgium
22 F1 **Oost Vlaanderen** Belgium
25 D2 **Oost Vlieland** Netherlands
25 B5 **Oostvoorne** Netherlands
25 G4 **Ootmarsum** Netherlands
117 L9 **Ootsa Lake** British Columbia Canada
119 S2 **Opachuanau L** Manitoba Canada
102 R11 **Opaeula** *R* Hawaiian Is
47 H1 **Opaka** Bulgaria
145 E4 **Opaki** New Zealand
118 D5 **Opal** Alberta Canada
124 H5 **Opal** Mexico
101 P8 **Opal** Wyoming U.S.A.
51 P3 **Opala** Russian Federation
86 D6 **Opala** Zaire
31 J3 **Opalenica** Poland
113 G12 **Opa-Locka** Florida U.S.A.
83 K11 **Opanake** Sri Lanka
86 F5 **Opari** Sudan
52 G5 **Oparino** Russian Federation
120 H3 **Opasatika** Ontario Canada
120 G3 **Opasatika L** Ontario Canada
42 F3 **Opatija** Croatia
31 N5 **Opatów** Poland
31 L4 **Opatówek** Poland
31 K5 **Opava** *R* Czech Rep
31 K6 **Opava** Czech Rep
121 P3 **Opawica, L** Quebec Canada
111 L9 **Opelika** Alabama U.S.A.
111 D11 **Opelousas** Louisiana U.S.A.
120 D2 **Opemisha** Ontario Canada
144 B5 **Open Bay Is** New Zealand
121 M7 **Opeongo L** Ontario Canada
22 F2 **Ophasselt** Belgium
101 T1 **Opheim** Montana U.S.A.
100 A7 **Ophir** Oregon U.S.A.
101 N9 **Ophir** Utah U.S.A.
69 E12 **Ophir, Gunung** *mt* Sumatra
22 K1 **Ophoven** Belgium
142 C6 **Ophthalmia Ra** W Australia Australia
45 P6 **Opi** Italy
86 E5 **Opienge** Zaire
144 C6 **Opihi R** New Zealand
36 B1 **Opladen** Germany
85 F8 **Opobo** Nigeria
52 C6 **Opochka** Russian Federation
122 F1 **Opocopa L** Quebec Canada
31 M4 **Opoczno** Poland
124 D3 **Opodepe** Mexico
31 K5 **Opole** Poland
145 F3 **Oponae** New Zealand
145 D1 **Opononi** New Zealand
54 F7 **Oposhnya** Ukraine
145 F3 **Opotiki** New Zealand
145 E2 **Opoutere** New Zealand
111 K10 **Opp** Alabama U.S.A.
61 P7 **Oppa-gawa** *R* Japan
61 P7 **Oppa-wan** *B* Japan
26 D9 **Oppdal** Norway
45 K1 **Oppeano** Italy
33 T9 **Oppelhaun** Germany
36 E7 **Oppenau** Germany
36 E4 **Oppenheim** Germany
36 G6 **Oppenweiler** Germany
28 J5 **Oppe Sundby** Denmark
27 D10 **Oppland** *county* Norway
119 Q4 **Optic Lake** Manitoba Canada
107 J5 **Optima** Oklahoma U.S.A.
145 E1 **Opua** New Zealand
145 E1 **Opuawhanga** New Zealand
145 D3 **Opunake** New Zealand
124 E2 **Oputo** Mexico
87 B9 **Opuwo** Namibia
22 G2 **Opwijk** Belgium
99 Q9 **Oquawka** Illinois U.S.A.
124 D2 **Oquitoa** Mexico
95 R2 **Oquossoc** Maine U.S.A.
55 C5 **Or'** *R* Kazakhstan/Rus Fed
27 G15 **Ör** Sweden
41 O5 **Ora** Italy
84 F4 **Ora** Libya
143 D9 **Ora Banda** W Australia Australia
127 L2 **Oracabessa** Jamaica
103 O9 **Oracle** Arizona U.S.A.
48 G3 **Oradea** Romania
18 F7 **Oradour-sur-Vayres** France
29 T9 **Oræfajökull** *ice cap* Iceland
74 H6 **Orai** India
103 O6 **Oraibi** Arizona U.S.A.
103 O5 **Oraibi Wash** *creek* Arizona U.S.A.
29 M4 **Orajärvi** *L* Finland
29 L5 **Orajärvi** Finland
98 C6 **Oral** South Dakota U.S.A.
85 D1 **Oran** Algeria
110 G4 **Oran** Missouri U.S.A.
139 J5 **Orange** New South Wales Australia
19 N16 **Orange** France
87 C11 **Orange** *R* S Africa/Namibia
102 G8 **Orange** California U.S.A.
95 P4 **Orange** Massachusetts U.S.A.
109 O5 **Orange** Texas U.S.A.
94 J8 **Orange** Virginia U.S.A.
111 J11 **Orange Beach** Alabama U.S.A.
112 G4 **Orangeburg** South Carolina U.S.A.
129 H3 **Orange,C** Brazil
126 E2 **Orange Cay** *isld* Bahamas
113 F9 **Orange City** Florida U.S.A.
116 Q3 **Orange Cr** Alaska U.S.A.
123 L8 **Orangedale** C Breton I, Nova Scotia
113 F7 **Orangedale** Florida U.S.A.
95 N6 **Orange, E** New Jersey U.S.A.
89 D7 **Orange Free State** *prov* S Africa
129 G3 **Orange Gebergte** *mts* Suriname
109 K8 **Orange Grove** Texas U.S.A.
113 E8 **Orange L** Florida U.S.A.
113 F7 **Orange Park** Florida U.S.A.
99 R7 **Orangeville** Illinois U.S.A.
103 N2 **Orangeville** Utah U.S.A.
145 E3 **Orangimea** New Zealand
71 E3 **Orani** Luzon Philippines
43 C8 **Orani** Sardinia
33 Q9 **Oranienbaum** Germany
33 S7 **Oranienburg** Germany
80 D3 **Oranim** Israel
87 C11 **Oranjemund** Namibia
126 A1 **Oranjestad** Aruba W Indies
127 N6 **Oranjestad** St Eustatius W Indies
14 C3 **Oranmore** Ireland
133 E2 **Orán, N** Argentina
Orantes *R* *see* **'Āsi** *R*
143 G6 **Orantjugurr,L** W Australia Australia
80 C3 **Or'Aqiva** Israel
144 C6 **Orari** New Zealand
71 G4 **Oras** Philippines
71 G4 **Oras B** Philippines
48 E5 **Orašje** Bosnia-Herzegovina
48 H5 **Orăștie** Romania
48 H3 **Orașu Nou** Romania
124 H5 **Oratario** Mexico
48 M1 **Oratov** Ukraine
31 L6 **Orava** *R* Slovakia
29 J8 **Oravais** Finland
48 G5 **Oravița** Romania
31 L6 **Oravská Magura** *mts* Slovakia
144 A7 **Orawia** New Zealand
18 H9 **Orb** *R* France
44 E2 **Orba** *R* Italy
66 C5 **Orba Co** *L* China
21 L3 **Orbec** France
42 D6 **Orbetello** Italy
21 N7 **Orbigny** France
16 D2 **Orbigo** *R* Spain
94 K6 **Orbisonia** Pennsylvania U.S.A.
139 J7 **Orbost** Victoria Australia
28 F5 **Ørby** Denmark
27 F14 **Örby** Sweden
27 J11 **Örbyhus** Sweden
116 O6 **Orca B** Alaska U.S.A.
146 E3 **Orcadas** *Argentina Base* S Orkney Is S Atlantic Oc
146 G4 **Orcadas Seamounts, Islas** *seamounts* Antarctica
21 L8 **Orches** France
113 G10 **Orchid Island** Florida U.S.A.
128 E1 **Orchila, La** *isld* Venezuela
16 B1 **Órdenes** Spain
103 M4 **Orderville** Utah U.S.A.
28 B3 **Ørding** Denmark
142 F3 **Ord,Mt** W Australia Australia
102 H7 **Ord Mt** California U.S.A.
52 D3 **Ordozero** Russian Federation
142 G3 **Ord River** W Australia Australia
78 F1 **Ordu** Turkey
78 K2 **Ordubail** Azerbaijan
16 E2 **Orduña** Spain
106 G3 **Ordway** Colorado U.S.A.
98 H4 **Ordway** South Dakota U.S.A.
Ordzhonikidze *see* **Vladikavkaz**
55 D4 **Ordzhonikidze** Kazakhstan
56 C4 **Ordzhonikidzevskiy** Russian Federation
28 E5 **Ore** Denmark
26 C9 **Öre** Norway
26 K7 **Oreälv** *R* Sweden
100 J6 **Oreana** Idaho U.S.A.
102 F1 **Oreana** Nevada U.S.A.
27 G12 **Örebro** *county* Sweden
27 H12 **Örebro** Sweden
109 N3 **Ore City** Texas U.S.A.
100 E6 **Oregon** *state* U.S.A.
99 R7 **Oregon** Illinois U.S.A.
110 A2 **Oregon** Missouri U.S.A.
99 R7 **Oregon** Wisconsin U.S.A.
100 B7 **Oregon Caves Nat. Mon** Oregon U.S.A.
100 C4 **Oregon City** Oregon U.S.A.
112 M2 **Oregon Inlet** North Carolina U.S.A.
27 K11 **Öregrund** Sweden
54 G9 **Orekhov** Ukraine
46 G1 **Orekhovitsa** Bulgaria
55 F3 **Orekhovo** Russian Federation
52 E6 **Orekhovo Zuyevo** Russian Federation
54 B2 **Orekhovsk** Belarus
54 H4 **Orël** Orlovskaya obl Russian Federation
52 J5 **Orël** Permskaya obl Russian Federation
54 F8 **Orel'** *R* Ukraine
98 C7 **Orella** Nebraska U.S.A.
128 C5 **Orellana** Peru
16 D5 **Orellana, Embalse de** *res* Spain
53 E7 **Orel Oblast'** *prov* Russian Federation
59 L1 **Orel', Oz** *L* Russian Federation
103 N1 **Orem** Utah U.S.A.
47 J7 **Ören** Turkey
55 C5 **Orenburg** Russian Federation
50 E3 **Orenburgskaya Oblast'** *prov* Russian Federation
16 B2 **Orense** *prov* Spain
16 B2 **Orense** Spain
46 F6 **Oreoí** Greece
144 A7 **Orepuki** New Zealand
47 H3 **Orestiás** Greece
29 K5 **Öresund** *str* Sweden/Denmark
80 G1 **Oretal** Syria
144 B7 **Oreti R** New Zealand
145 E2 **Orewa** New Zealand
22 J2 **Oreye** Belgium
139 J8 **Orford** Tasmania Australia
9 H3 **Orford** England
95 P3 **Orford** New Hampshire U.S.A.
141 G1 **Orford Ness** Queensland Australia
9 H3 **Orford Ness** England
106 D9 **Organ** New Mexico U.S.A.
106 D9 **Organ** *mt* New Mexico U.S.A.
126 C3 **Organos, Sa. de los** *hills* Cuba
103 M9 **Organ Pipe Cactus Nat. Mon** Arizona U.S.A.
16 E5 **Orgaz** Spain
21 P4 **Orge** *R* France
40 C4 **Orgelet** France
21 O5 **Orgères-en-Beauce** France
21 O4 **Orgeval** France
48 M3 **Orgeyev** Moldova
45 K1 **Orgiano** Italy
16 E8 **Órgiva** Spain
47 N10 **Örgök Burun** *C* Turkey
65 B3 **Orgon Tal** China
52 F6 **Orgtrud** Russian Federation
77 L3 **Orgūn** Afghanistan
47 K5 **Orhaneli** *R* Turkey
47 K5 **Orhaneli** Turkey
47 K4 **Orhangazi** Turkey
Orhanie *see* **Botevgrad**
47 J5 **Orhanlar** Turkey
58 D2 **Orhon Gol** *R* Mongolia
17 F1 **Oria** *R* Spain
17 F7 **Oria** Spain
52 G5 **Orichi** Russian Federation
100 A8 **Orick** California U.S.A.
141 G8 **Orient** Queensland Australia
106 E3 **Orient** Colorado U.S.A.
99 M8 **Orient** Iowa U.S.A.
98 G5 **Orient** South Dakota U.S.A.
108 G4 **Orient** Texas U.S.A.
100 G1 **Orient** Washington U.S.A.
112 L2 **Oriental** North Carolina U.S.A.
120 B3 **Orient Bay** Ontario Canada
95 P5 **Orient I** New York U.S.A.
138 F3 **Orientos** New South Wales Australia
141 F8 **Orientos** Queensland Australia
22 G4 **Origny-en-Thiérache** France
22 E4 **Origny-St.-Benoîte** France
17 G6 **Orihuela** Spain
121 L8 **Orillia** Ontario Canada
29 M11 **Orimattila** Finland
98 A7 **Orin** Wyoming U.S.A.
48 K2 **Orinin** Ukraine
128 F2 **Orinoco** *R* Venezuela
128 F2 **Orinoco, Mouths of the** Venezuela
43 G8 **Oriolo** Italy
118 G9 **Orion** Alberta Canada
99 Q8 **Orion** Illinois U.S.A.
98 J3 **Oriska** North Dakota U.S.A.
95 M4 **Oriskany Falls** New York U.S.A.
75 K8 **Orissa** *prov* India
43 B9 **Oristano** Sardinia
43 B9 **Oristano, G. di** Sardinia
128 E2 **Orituco** *R* Venezuela
29 O9 **Orivesi** *L* Finland
129 G4 **Oriximiná** Brazil
125 L8 **Orizaba** Mexico
47 J2 **Orizare** Bulgaria
42 J6 **Orjen** *mt* Bosnia-Herzegovina
26 D8 **Orkdalen** *V* Norway
27 F15 **Örkelljunga** Sweden
27 G15 **Örkened** Sweden
26 D9 **Orkla** *R* Norway
118 K9 **Orkney** Saskatchewan Canada
87 E11 **Orkney** S Africa
15 F1 **Orkney** *isld* Scotland
37 M2 **Orla** *R* Germany
31 K4 **Orla** *R* Poland
108 D4 **Orla** Texas U.S.A.
37 M2 **Orlamünde** Germany
102 B2 **Orland** California U.S.A.
94 B5 **Orland** Indiana U.S.A.
95 T2 **Orland** Maine U.S.A.
113 F9 **Orlando** Florida U.S.A.
107 N5 **Orlando** Oklahoma U.S.A.
43 F10 **Orlando, C.d'** Sicily
21 N5 **Orléanais** *reg* France
21 O6 **Orléans** France
100 B8 **Orleans** California U.S.A.
110 K3 **Orleans** Indiana U.S.A.
95 S5 **Orleans** Massachusetts U.S.A.
98 K1 **Orleans** Minnesota U.S.A.
98 G9 **Orleans** Nebraska U.S.A.
95 P2 **Orleans** Vermont U.S.A.
121 U6 **Orleans, Île d'** Quebec Canada
Orléansville *see* **Ech Cheliff**
31 J5 **Orlice** *R* Czech Rep
56 E5 **Orlik** Russian Federation
31 L6 **Orlová** Czech Rep
56 C2 **Orlovka** Russian Federation
55 F3 **Orlovo** Russian Federation
53 E7 **Orlovskaya Oblast'** *prov* Russian Federation
52 F2 **Orlovskiy, Mys** *C* Russian Federation
21 P4 **Orly** *airport* France
74 C10 **Ormara** Pakistan
13 G4 **Ormesby** England
36 C5 **Ormesheim** Germany
21 M8 **Ormes,les** France
119 M9 **Ormiston** Saskatchewan Canada
71 G5 **Ormoc** Philippines
145 F3 **Ormond** New Zealand
113 F8 **Ormond** Florida U.S.A.
113 F8 **Ormond Beach** Florida U.S.A.
145 F4 **Ormondville** New Zealand
38 O9 **Ormož** Slovenia
99 M6 **Ormsby** Minnesota U.S.A.
99 R4 **Ormsby** Wisconsin U.S.A.
26 H7 **Ormsjö** Sweden
13 F6 **Ormskirk** England
121 R7 **Ormstown** Quebec Canada
19 J4 **Ornain** *R* France
19 K5 **Ornans** France
41 H6 **Ornavasso** Italy
37 K5 **Ornbau** Germany
18 E4 **Orne** *dept* France
21 L5 **Orne** *R* France
31 M1 **Orneta** Poland
27 K12 **Orno** Sweden
26 K8 **Örnsköldsvik** Sweden
28 H5 **Orø** Denmark
41 L5 **Orobie, Alpi** *mt* Italy
42 C2 **Orobie, Alpi** *mts* Italy
51 M3 **Orochen** Russian Federation
128 D3 **Orocué** Colombia
85 D6 **Orodara** Burkina
100 J3 **Orofino** Idaho U.S.A.
102 G7 **Oro Grande** California U.S.A.
100 K4 **Orogrande** Idaho U.S.A.
106 D9 **Orogrande** New Mexico U.S.A.
61 P13 **Oroku** Okinawa
122 F8 **Oromocto** New Brunswick Canada
122 F8 **Oromocto L** New Brunswick Canada
79 F8 **Oron** Israel
134 K9 **Orona** *isld* Phoenix Is Pacific Oc
121 M9 **Orono** Ontario Canada
95 T2 **Orono** Maine U.S.A.
110 B4 **Oronogo** Missouri U.S.A.
12 B1 **Oronsay** *isld* Scotland
16 D5 **Oropesa** Spain
127 P2 **Oropuche** *R* Trinidad
59 H1 **Oroqen Zizhiqi** China
71 F6 **Oroquieta** Mindanao
129 L5 **Orós, Açude** *res* Brazil
43 C8 **Orosei** Sardinia
43 C8 **Orosei, G.di** Sardinia
48 F4 **Orosháza** Hungary
48 E3 **Oroszlany** Hungary
51 P2 **Orotukan** Russian Federation
145 E4 **Oroua R** New Zealand
100 H8 **Orovada** Nevada U.S.A.
102 C2 **Oroville** California U.S.A.
100 F1 **Oroville** Washington U.S.A.
101 U7 **Orpha** Wyoming U.S.A.
141 H4 **Orpheus I** Queensland Australia
21 O4 **Orphin** France
19 P16 **Orpierre** France
98 J1 **Orr** North Dakota U.S.A.
107 N7 **Orr** Oklahoma U.S.A.
28 B4 **Ørre** Denmark
27 H15 **Orrefors** Sweden
15 D3 **Orrin** *R* Scotland
98 F1 **Orrin** North Dakota U.S.A.
119 U2 **Orr L** Manitoba Canada
26 G10 **Orrmosjön** *L* Sweden
138 E4 **Orroroo** South Australia Australia
27 J11 **Orrskog** Sweden
94 K6 **Orrstown** Pennsylvania U.S.A.
94 F6 **Orrville** Ohio U.S.A.
27 G10 **Orsa** Sweden
44 H3 **Orsaro** *mt* Italy
21 P4 **Orsay** France
9 G5 **Orsett** England
54 B2 **Orsha** Belarus
52 G6 **Orshanka** Russian Federation
27 H15 **Örsjö** Sweden
55 C5 **Orsk** Russian Federation
27 F13 **Örslösa** Sweden
28 E2 **Ørsø** Denmark
48 G6 **Orșova** Romania
32 E9 **Orsoy** Germany
26 B9 **Örsta** Norway
27 J12 **Örsundsbro** Sweden
47 K8 **Ortaca** Turkey
47 J7 **Ortaklar** Turkey
80 G1 **Or Tal** Syria
41 H6 **Orta, L. d'** Italy
26 K7 **Ortäsk** Sweden
42 E6 **Orte** Italy
16 B1 **Ortegal, C** Spain
36 G3 **Ortenberg** Germany
37 P6 **Ortenburg** Germany
30 F1 **Orth** Germany
18 E9 **Orthez** France
45 L4 **Ortignano Raggiolo** Italy
16 B1 **Ortigueira** Spain
28 E5 **Ørting** Denmark
100 C2 **Orting** Washington U.S.A.
124 D3 **Ortiz** Mexico
106 D4 **Ortiz** Colorado U.S.A.
128 E2 **Ortiz** Venezuela
41 N4 **Ortles** *mt* Italy
37 O2 **Ortmannsdorf** Germany
127 P3 **Ortoire R** Trinidad
128 E6 **Orton** *R* Bolivia
13 F5 **Orton** England
42 F6 **Ortona** Italy
98 K4 **Ortonville** Minnesota U.S.A.
57 H4 **Orto-Tokoy** Kirghizia
33 T10 **Ortrand** Germany
32 M7 **Ortze** *R* Germany
51 M2 **Orulgan, Khrebet** *mt* Russian Federation
28 E2 **Ørum** Denmark
28 D4 **Ørum** Denmark
78 K3 **Orūmīyeh** Iran
78 K3 **Orūmīyeh, Daryācheh-ye** *L* Iran
133 D1 **Oruro** Bolivia
145 D1 **Oruru** New Zealand
27 E13 **Orust** *isld* Sweden
77 J3 **Orūzgān** Afghanistan
77 J3 **Orūzgān** *prov* Afghanistan
20 G7 **Orvault** France
42 E6 **Orvieto** Italy
146 D6 **Orville Coast** Antarctica
21 O4 **Orvilliers** France
45 N5 **Orvinio** Italy
94 K5 **Orviston** Pennsylvania U.S.A.
95 L3 **Orwell** New York U.S.A.
94 G5 **Orwell** Ohio U.S.A.
95 O3 **Orwell** Vermont U.S.A.
58 G2 **Orxon Gol** *R* China
46 F1 **Oryakhovo** Bulgaria
41 L7 **Orzinuovi** Italy
31 M2 **Orzyc** *R* Poland
31 N2 **Orzysz** Poland
26 E9 **Os** Norway
27 G14 **Os** Sweden
27 E10 **Osa** *R* Norway
119 O9 **Osage** Saskatchewan Canada
99 O6 **Osage** Iowa U.S.A.
107 O5 **Osage** Oklahoma U.S.A.
98 B6 **Osage** Wyoming U.S.A.
107 P3 **Osage City** Kansas U.S.A.
110 D4 **Osage Fork** *R* Missouri U.S.A.
62 **Ōsaka** *conurbation* Japan
55 F5 **Osakarovka** Kazakhstan
99 L4 **Osakis** Minnesota U.S.A.
99 L4 **Osakis L** Minnesota U.S.A.
107 Q3 **Osawatomie** Kansas U.S.A.
120 E3 **Osawin** *R* Ontario Canada
142 F2 **Osborne Is** W Australia Australia
27 G15 **Osby** Sweden
142 F4 **Oscar Ra** W Australia Australia
110 G6 **Osceola** Arkansas U.S.A.
99 N8 **Osceola** Iowa U.S.A.
110 C3 **Osceola** Missouri U.S.A.
98 J8 **Osceola** Nebraska U.S.A.
94 J6 **Osceola** Pennsylvania U.S.A.
99 O4 **Osceola** Wisconsin U.S.A.
33 S10 **Oschatz** Germany
33 O8 **Oschersleben** Germany
94 D2 **Oscoda** Michigan U.S.A.
106 D8 **Oscura** New Mexico U.S.A.
26 E7 **Osen** Norway
54 K2 **Osetr** *R* Russian Federation
60 B13 **Ōse-zaki** *C* Japan
94 B7 **Osgood** Indiana U.S.A.
110 C1 **Osgood** Missouri U.S.A.
121 P7 **Osgoode Station** Ontario Canada
100 H8 **Osgood Mts** Nevada U.S.A.
57 G4 **Osh** Kirghizia
55 F3 **Osha** *R* Russian Federation
87 C9 **Oshakati** Namibia
60 O3 **Oshamambe** Japan
121 M9 **Oshawa** Ontario Canada
60 P1 **Oshidomari** Japan
61 P7 **Oshika-Hantō** *pen* Japan
59 J6 **O-shima** *isld* Japan
61 N11 **Ō-shima** *isld* Japan
98 D8 **Oshkosh** Nebraska U.S.A.
99 S6 **Oshkosh** Wisconsin U.S.A.
52 J2 **Oshkur'ya** Russian Federation
55 D1 **Oshmar'ye** Russian Federation
78 K3 **Oshnoviyeh** Iran
85 E7 **Oshogbo** Nigeria
98 B5 **Oshoto** Wyoming U.S.A.
77 A3 **Oshtorān Kūh** *mt* Iran
52 K2 **Oshvor** Russian Federation
86 C6 **Oshwe** Zaire
46 G1 **Osica** Romania
48 J6 **Osica de Jos** Romania
48 E5 **Osijek** Croatia
45 O4 **Osimo** Italy
56 C4 **Osinniki** Russian Federation
54 B2 **Osintorf** Belarus
74 E5 **Osiyān** India
26 N3 **Oskal** Norway
99 O8 **Oskaloosa** Iowa U.S.A.
107 P2 **Oskaloosa** Kansas U.S.A.
27 H14 **Oskarshamn** Sweden
27 F15 **Oskarström** Sweden
121 P4 **Oskelaneo** Quebec Canada
54 J7 **Oskol** *R* Rus Fed/Ukraine
31 J6 **Oslava** *R* Czech Rep
118 L6 **Osler** Saskatchewan Canada
27 E12 **Oslo** Norway
98 J1 **Oslo** Minnesota U.S.A.
71 F6 **Oslob** Cebu Philippines
27 E13 **Oslofjord** *inlet* Norway
28 C2 **Øsløs** Denmark
54 E2 **Os'ma** *R* Russian Federation
74 G9 **Osmanabad** India
78 E1 **Osmancık** Turkey
47 K4 **Osmaneli** Turkey
52 C5 **Osmino** Russian Federation
27 J13 **Ösmo** Sweden
98 J7 **Osmond** Nebraska U.S.A.
98 H1 **Osnabrock** North Dakota U.S.A.
32 H8 **Osnabrück** Germany
31 H3 **Ośno** Poland
46 E2 **Osogovske Planina** *mt* Macedonia
41 N7 **Osone** *R* Italy
60 O4 **Osore yama** *mt* Japan
131 A8 **Osorno** *prov* Chile
131 A8 **Osorno** Chile
16 E2 **Osorno** Spain
131 A8 **Osorno, Vol** *pk* Chile
133 C6 **Osorro** *mt* Chile
100 F1 **Osoyoos** British Columbia Canada
44 C4 **Ospedaletti** Italy
117 M7 **Ospika** *R* British Columbia Canada
113 E10 **Osprey** Florida U.S.A.
141 H2 **Osprey Reef** Gt Barrier Reef Aust
9 G5 **Ospringe** England
25 E5 **Oss** Netherlands
46 F5 **Óssa** *mt* Greece
112 F6 **Ossabaw I** Georgia U.S.A.
139 H8 **Ossa, Mt** Tasmania Australia
16 B6 **Ossa, Sa. d'** *mts* Portugal
85 F7 **Osse** *R* Nigeria
99 P5 **Osseo** Wisconsin U.S.A.
38 J8 **Ossiach** Austria
99 P6 **Ossian** Iowa U.S.A.
94 D2 **Ossineke** Michigan U.S.A.
95 O5 **Ossining** New York U.S.A.
95 Q3 **Ossipee L** New Hampshire U.S.A.
27 E10 **Os-sjöen** *L* Norway
32 J8 **Ossning** *hills* Germany
41 H5 **Ossola, Val d'** Italy
51 Q3 **Ossora** Russian Federation
71 N9 **Ossu** Timor
121 M5 **Ostaboningue, L** Quebec Canada
77 A2 **Ostan-e Markazi** Iran
52 E6 **Ostashevo** Russian Federation
52 D6 **Ostashkov** Russian Federation
26 H9 **Östavall** Sweden
32 G8 **Ostbevern** Germany
32 K5 **Oste** *R* Germany
113 F9 **Osteen** Florida U.S.A.
45 L2 **Ostellato** Italy
32 K5 **Osten** Germany
Ostend *see* **Oostende**
32 L7 **Ostenholz** Germany
41 K6 **Osteno** Italy
54 D3 **Oster** *R* Belarus/Rus Fed
33 P7 **Osterburg** Germany
94 J6 **Osterburg** Pennsylvania U.S.A.
36 G5 **Osterburken** Germany
27 J11 **Österby** Sweden
27 H14 **Österbymo** Sweden
32 H8 **Ostercappeln** Germany
27 G10 **Österdalälven** *R* Sweden
32 E5 **Osterems** *est* Germany
27 H13 **Östergotland** *county* Sweden
37 P6 **Osterhofen** Germany
32 J6 **Osterholz-Scharmbeck** Germany
38 H6 **Osterhorn Gruppe** *mts* Austria
28 D3 **Øster Hornum** Nordjylland Denmark
27 J11 **Österlövsta** Sweden
26 J7 **Österoret** Sweden
32 M9 **Osterode** Germany
27 A11 **Osteröy** *isld* Norway
38 H5 **Osterreich** *dist* Austria
26 G8 **Östersund** Sweden
28 H7 **Øster Ulslev** Denmark
27 J11 **Östervåla** Sweden
33 N9 **Osterwieck** Germany
36 G6 **Ostfildern** Germany
27 E12 **Östfold** *reg* Norway
32 F5 **Ostfriesische Inseln** *islds* Germany
32 F6 **Ostfriesland** *reg* Germany
32 G6 **Ostgrossefehn** Germany
27 K11 **Östhammar** Sweden
36 C7 **Ostheim** France
37 J3 **Ostheim** Germany
45 M6 **Ostia** Italy
45 K1 **Ostiglia** Italy
27 F11 **Östmark** Sweden
33 R5 **Ost Peene** *R* Germany
45 O4 **Ostra** Italy
94 D6 **Ostrander** Ohio U.S.A.
37 P1 **Ostrau** Germany
31 L6 **Ostrava** Czech Rep
45 O4 **Ostra Vetere** Italy
31 M2 **Ostróda** Poland
31 N2 **Ostrołęka** Poland
120 J5 **Ostrom** Ontario Canada
37 O3 **Ostrov** Czech Rep
48 L6 **Ostrov** Romania
52 C6 **Ostrov** Russian Federation
55 F3 **Ostrovnaya** Russian Federation
51 Q2 **Ostrovnoye** Russian Federation
65 J3 **Ostrov Russkiy** *isld* Russian Federation
31 K4 **Ostrów** Poland
31 N5 **Ostrowiec** Poland
31 O4 **Ostrów Lubelski** Poland
31 N3 **Ostrów Mazowiecka** Poland
28 C3 **Østrup** Denmark
37 P5 **Ostrý** *mt* Czech Rep
31 K4 **Ostrzeszów** Poland
33 O5 **Ostseebad Boltenhagen** Germany
33 Q4 **Ostseebad Graal-Müritz** Germany
33 P4 **Ostseebad Kühlungsborn** Germany
33 P4 **Ostseebad Nienhagen** Germany
33 P4 **Ostseebad Rerik** Germany
43 H8 **Ostuni** Italy
52 D6 **Osuga** *R* Russian Federation
100 F3 **O'Sullivan Dam** Washington U.S.A.
120 D2 **O'Sullivan, L** Ontario Canada
121 P5 **O'Sullivan, L** Quebec Canada
46 D4 **Osum** *R* Albania
46 G1 **Osŭm** *R* Bulgaria
60 D14 **Ōsumi-hantō** *pen* Japan
16 D7 **Osuna** Spain
52 C6 **Osveya** Belarus
13 G5 **Oswaldkirk** England
94 J5 **Oswayo** Pennsylvania U.S.A.
95 M2 **Oswegalchie** *R* New York U.S.A.
99 S8 **Oswego** Illinois U.S.A.
107 P4 **Oswego** Kansas U.S.A.
101 U1 **Oswego** Montana U.S.A.
95 L3 **Oswego** New York U.S.A.
8 C2 **Oswestry** England
31 L5 **Oświęcim** Poland
111 F10 **Osyka** Mississippi U.S.A.
60 F11 **Ōta** *R* Japan
61 N9 **Ōta** Japan
144 D7 **Otago Peninsula** New Zealand
144 C6 **Otaio** New Zealand
60 F11 **Ōtake** Japan
145 E3 **Otakeho** New Zealand
61 M10 **Ōtaki** Japan
145 E4 **Otaki** New Zealand
61 O8 **Ōtakine-yama** *mt* Japan
145 F3 **Otane** New Zealand
145 F2 **Otanewainuku** New Zealand
29 N7 **Otanmäki** Finland
83 K9 **Otappuwa** Sri Lanka
57 H3 **Otar** Kazakhstan
60 O2 **Otaru** Japan
144 B7 **Otatara** New Zealand
144 B7 **Otautau** New Zealand
30 H6 **Otava** *R* Czech Rep
128 C3 **Otavalo** Ecuador
87 C9 **Otavi** Namibia
87 B9 **Otchinjau** Angola
95 M4 **Otego** New York U.S.A.
144 C6 **Otekaieke** New Zealand
48 F5 **Otelec** Romania
48 G5 **Oțelu Roșu** Romania
144 C6 **Otematata** New Zealand
52 C5 **Otepää** Estonia
22 K5 **Othain** *R* France
22 J2 **Othée** Belgium
18 H4 **Othe, Forêt d'** France
100 F3 **Othello** Washington U.S.A.
27 K14 **Othem** Sweden
8 D5 **Othery** England
46 C5 **Othonoí** *isld* Greece
46 F5 **Óthris** *mt* Greece
70 F5 **Oti** Sulawesi
85 E7 **Oti** *R* W Africa
124 G5 **Otinapa** Mexico
144 C5 **Otira** New Zealand
106 H1 **Otis** Colorado U.S.A.
107 L3 **Otis** Kansas U.S.A.
95 O4 **Otis** Massachusetts U.S.A.
95 L4 **Otisco L** New York U.S.A.
122 B1 **Otish Mts** Quebec Canada
95 N5 **Otisville** New York U.S.A.
87 C10 **Otjiwarongo** Namibia
31 K5 **Otmuchów** Poland
60 O3 **Otobe-dake** *mt* Japan
42 G4 **Otočac** Croatia
99 K9 **Otoe** Nebraska U.S.A.
60 R2 **Otofuke** Japan
60 Q1 **Otoineppu** Japan
145 F3 **Otoko** New Zealand
145 E3 **Otorohanga** New Zealand
119 P5 **Otosquen** Saskatchewan Canada
27 C13 **Otra** *R* Norway
126 B1 **Otrabanda** Curaçao Neth Antilles
54 H3 **Otradinskiy** Russian Federation
43 J8 **Otranto** Italy
43 J8 **Otranto, C.d'** Italy
46 C4 **Otranto, Str of** Adriatic Sea
94 C2 **Otsego** Michigan U.S.A.
95 N4 **Otsego I** New York U.S.A.
94 C2 **Otsego Lake** Michigan U.S.A.
95 M4 **Otselic, South** New York U.S.A.
60 R3 **Ōtsu** Hokkaido Japan
61 J10 **Ōtsu** Honshu Japan
61 P6 **Ōtsuchi-wan** *B* Japan
61 M10 **Ōtsuki** Japan
26 C10 **Otta** *R* Norway
26 D10 **Otta** Norway
22 L5 **Ottange** France
27 F16 **Ottarp** Sweden
45 Q8 **Ottaviano** Italy
120 D9 **Ottawa** Ontario Canada
99 S8 **Ottawa** Illinois U.S.A.
107 P3 **Ottawa** Kansas U.S.A.
94 C5 **Ottawa** Ohio U.S.A.
115 L6 **Ottawa Is** Northwest Territories Canada
121 L6 **Ottawa R** Ontario/Quebec
32 K9 **Ottbergen** Germany
27 H15 **Ottenby** Sweden
36 H5 **Ottendorf** Germany
37 M2 **Ottendorf-Okrilla** Germany
36 E6 **Ottenhöfen** Germany
38 M5 **Ottenshlag** Austria
32 K9 **Ottenstein** Niedersachsen Germany

32 E8 **Ottenstein** Nordrhein-Westfalen Germany
101 T4 **Otter** Montana U.S.A.
110 J1 **Otterbein** Indiana U.S.A.
36 D4 **Otterberg** Germany
13 F3 **Otterburn** England
118 D1 **Otterburne** Manitoba Canada
113 E8 **Otter Creek** Florida U.S.A.
103 N3 **Otter Cr Res** Utah U.S.A.
38 E6 **Otterfing** Germany
116 D8 **Otter I** Pribilof Is Bering Sea
120 D4 **Otter I** Ontario Canada
119 N3 **Otter L** Saskatchewan Canada
94 D3 **Otter Lake** Michigan U.S.A.
25 E4 **Otterlo** Netherlands
32 J5 **Otterndorf** Germany
26 E7 **Otteröy** Norway
26 B9 **Otteröy** *isld* Norway
32 K6 **Ottersberg** Germany
9 F5 **Ottershaw** England
33 P8 **Ottersleben** Germany
15 G1 **Otterswick** Scotland
98 K3 **Otter Tail** *R* Minnesota U.S.A.
99 L3 **Otter Tail L** Minnesota U.S.A.
28 E5 **Otterup** Denmark
8 B6 **Ottery, R** England
8 C6 **Ottery St. Mary** England
119 P7 **Otthon** Saskatchewan Canada
22 H2 **Ottignies** Belgium
57 H4 **Ottik** Kirghizia
109 L4 **Otto** Texas U.S.A.
101 R5 **Otto** Wyoming U.S.A.
37 M7 **Ottobrunn** Germany
115 L1 **Otto Fiord** Northwest Territories Canada
94 C6 **Ottoville** Ohio U.S.A.
36 C7 **Ottrott** France
99 O8 **Ottumwa** Iowa U.S.A.
98 E5 **Ottumwa** South Dakota U.S.A.
36 C5 **Ottweiler** Germany
118 K2 **Otukamanoan L** Ontario Canada
144 B6 **Oturehua** New Zealand
85 F7 **Oturkpo** Nigeria
94 D8 **Otway** Ohio U.S.A.
133 C8 **Otway, B** Chile
139 G7 **Otway, C** Victoria Australia
31 N3 **Otwock** Poland
48 J2 **Otynya** Ukraine
41 N3 **Ötz** Austria
36 B1 **Otzenrath** Germany
41 N3 **Ötztal** Austria
41 N4 **Ötztaler Alpen** *mt* Austria
111 D8 **Ouachita** *R* Arkansas U.S.A.
110 C7 **Ouachita, L** Arkansas U.S.A.
109 N1 **Ouachita Mts** Ark/Okla U.S.A.
86 D3 **Ouadai** *dist* Chad
85 B4 **Ouadane** Mauritania
86 D4 **Ouadda** Cent Afr Republic
85 D6 **Ouagadougou** Burkina
85 D6 **Ouahigouya** Burkina
86 D4 **Ouaka** *R* Cent Afr Republic
85 C5 **Oualata** Mauritania
85 E4 **Ouallene** Algeria
86 D4 **Ouanda Djallé** Cent Afr Republic
86 D5 **Ouango** Cent Afr Republic
85 C7 **Ouangolodougou** Ivory Coast
18 H5 **Ouanne** *R* France
85 F3 **Ouan Taredert** Algeria
129 H3 **Ouaqui** Fr Guiana
85 C4 **Ouarane** *reg* Mauritania
121 Q6 **Ouareau, L** Quebec Canada
85 F2 **Ouargla** Algeria
85 C3 **Ouarkziz, Jbel** *mt reg* Morocco/Algeria
21 O5 **Ouarville** France
85 C2 **Ouarzazate** Morocco
86 D5 **Oubangui** *R* Cent Afr Republic/Zaire
40 B3 **Ouche** *R* France
21 N6 **Oucques** France
25 A5 **Ouddorp** Netherlands
25 B5 **Oude** *R* Netherlands
25 F5 **Oude Ijssel** *R* Netherlands
22 D1 **Oudekapelle** Belgium
22 F2 **Oudenaarde** Belgium
25 C5 **Oudenbosch** Netherlands
25 H2 **Oude Pekela** Netherlands
25 C4 **Oude Rijn** Netherlands
25 C2 **Oudeschild** Netherlands
25 F3 **Oude Smildervaart** *R* Netherlands
25 C4 **Oudewater** Netherlands
22 L3 **Oudler** Belgium
20 H7 **Oudon** France
21 J6 **Oudon** *R* France
68 G7 **Oudong** Cambodia
89 C9 **Oudtshoorn** S Africa
85 F2 **Oued, El** Algeria
17 H9 **Oued Taria** Algeria
85 C2 **Oued Zem** Morocco
85 E7 **Ouémé** *R* Benin
20 A5 **Ouessant, I.d'** France
86 C5 **Ouesso** Congo
83 L14 **Ouest, î de l'** Kerguelen Indian Oc
71 F5 **Ouezon** Negros Philippines
85 C2 **Ouezzane** Morocco
22 J3 **Ouffet** Belgium
14 B3 **Oughterard** Ireland
40 C3 **Ougney** France
86 C4 **Ouham** *R* Cent Afr Republic
85 E7 **Ouidah** Benin
119 P2 **Ouimet** Ontario Canada
124 E4 **Ouiriego** Mexico
18 H9 **Ouissac** France
21 K3 **Ouistreham** France
85 C5 **Oujaf** Mauritania
85 D2 **Oujda** Morocco
29 L7 **Oulainen** Finland
29 O5 **Oulanka Nat. Park** Finland
21 N8 **Oulches** France
85 E2 **Ouled-Nail, Mts. des** Algeria
19 N13 **Oullins** France
85 C2 **Oulmès** Morocco
13 G6 **Oulton** England
29 L6 **Oulu** Finland
29 M7 **Oulujoki** *R* Finland
86 D2 **Oum Chalouba** Chad
85 C3 **Oum el Guebor** Algeria
85 C2 **Oum er Rbia** *R* Morocco
86 C3 **Oum Hadjer** Chad
29 K3 **Ounasjärvi** *L* Finland
29 L4 **Ounasjoki** *R* Finland
29 K3 **Ounastunturi** *mt* Finland
9 F3 **Oundle** England
98 C1 **Oungre** Saskatchewan Canada
86 D2 **Ounianga Kébir** Chad
86 D2 **Ounianga Sérir** Chad
85 C6 **Ouolodo** Mali
61 Q12 **Ōura-wan** *B* Okinawa
106 C3 **Ouray** Colorado U.S.A.
103 P1 **Ouray** Utah U.S.A.
28 F6 **Oure** Denmark
84 F5 **Ouri** Chad
129 K5 **Ouricuri** Brazil
130 H9 **Ouricuri, R** Brazil
130 E8 **Ourinhos** Brazil
16 B7 **Ourique** Portugal
130 F8 **Ouro Fino** Brazil
130 G7 **Ouro Prêto** Brazil
22 K3 **Ourthe** *R* Belgium
21 M2 **Ourville** France
139 H8 **Ouse** Tasmania Australia
9 G2 **Ouse, R** England
13 G6 **Ouse, R** N Yorks England
20 E5 **Oust** *R* France
121 M6 **Outaouais, R des** Quebec Canada
122 C3 **Outardes Quatre, Res** Quebec Canada
122 D4 **Outardes, R. aux** Quebec Canada
122 D4 **Outardes Trois Dam** Quebec Canada
21 P5 **Outarville** France
85 D2 **Outat-Oulad-el-Haj** Morocco
6 B2 **Outer Bailey** N Atlantic Oc
15 A3 **Outer Hebrides** Scotland
102 F8 **Outer Santa Barbara Chan** California U.S.A.
7 M8 **Outer Silver Pit** North Sea
13 F5 **Outhgill** England
87 C10 **Outjo** Namibia
118 K7 **Outlook** Saskatchewan Canada
101 V1 **Outlook** Montana U.S.A.
29 O9 **Outokumpu** Finland
144 C6 **Outram** New Zealand
22 B2 **Outreau** France
15 G2 **Out Skerries** *isld* Scotland
19 O16 **Ouveze** *R* France
138 F6 **Ouyen** New South Wales Australia
21 O6 **Ouzouer-le-Marché** France
79 D2 **Ovacık** Turkey
44 E2 **Ovada** Italy
131 B3 **Ovalle** Chile
108 H3 **Ovalo** Texas U.S.A.
87 B9 **Ovamboland** *tribal area* Namibia
101 M2 **Ovando** Montana U.S.A.
16 B4 **Ovar** Portugal
38 G9 **Ovaro** Italy
47 H2 **Ovcharitsa, Yazovir** *res* Bulgaria
28 D3 **Ove** Denmark
32 H6 **Ovelgönne** Germany
139 H6 **Ovens** *R* Victoria Australia
36 C2 **Overath** Germany
107 P3 **Overbrook** Kansas U.S.A.
25 B5 **Overflakkee** Netherlands
119 Q5 **Overflowing R** Manitoba Canada
26 G9 **Överhogdal** Sweden
22 H2 **Overijse** Belgium
25 F4 **Overijssel** *prov* Netherlands
26 N5 **Överkalix** Sweden
28 C3 **Overlade** Denmark
107 Q3 **Overland Park** Kansas U.S.A.
98 F1 **Overly** North Dakota U.S.A.
29 J9 **Övermark** Finland
131 B5 **Overo, Vol** Argentina
22 J1 **Overpelt** Belgium
9 E5 **Overton** England
98 G9 **Overton** Nebraska U.S.A.
103 K5 **Overton** Nevada U.S.A.
109 N3 **Overton** Texas U.S.A.
8 D2 **Overton** Wales
26 N5 **Övertorneå** Sweden
27 H14 **Överum** Sweden
26 G5 **Över-uman** *L* Sweden
111 G10 **Ovett** Mississippi U.S.A.
106 H1 **Ovid** Colorado U.S.A.
101 O7 **Ovid** Idaho U.S.A.
94 C3 **Ovid** Michigan U.S.A.
95 L4 **Ovid** New York U.S.A.
16 C1 **Oviedo** *prov* Spain
16 D1 **Oviedo** Spain
113 F9 **Oviedo** Florida U.S.A.
26 G9 **Oviken** Sweden
45 P5 **Ovindoli** Italy
52 E5 **Ovinishche** Russian Federation
26 K8 **Öv Nyland** Sweden
26 O3 **Øvre Anarjokka Nat. Park** Norway
27 B13 **Övrebygd** Norway
26 L3 **Øvre Dividal Nat. Park** Norway
26 L6 **Övre Grundsel** Sweden
26 R2 **Øvre Pasvik Nat. Park** Norway
27 B13 **Öv-Sirdal** Norway
26 H8 **Övsjö** Sweden
28 A5 **Ovtrup** Denmark
145 F4 **Owahanga** New Zealand
144 B7 **Owaka** New Zealand
87 C9 **Owambo** *homeland* Namibia
86 C6 **Owando** Congo
61 O5 **Ōwani** Japan
95 L4 **Owasco L** New York U.S.A.
61 K11 **Owase** Japan
107 P5 **Owasso** Oklahoma U.S.A.
99 N5 **Owatonna** Minnesota U.S.A.
77 H2 **Owbeh** Afghanistan
95 L4 **Owego** New York U.S.A.
36 G6 **Owen** Germany
99 Q5 **Owen** Wisconsin U.S.A.
142 A3 **Owen Anchorage** W Australia Australia
86 F5 **Owen Falls D** Uganda
68 C7 **Owen I** Burma
14 B2 **Owenmore** *R* Ireland
145 D4 **Owen, Mt** New Zealand
145 D4 **Owen River** New Zealand
102 F4 **Owens** *R* California U.S.A.
94 F8 **Owens** West Virginia U.S.A.
110 J4 **Owensboro** Kentucky U.S.A.
102 G5 **Owens L** California U.S.A.
120 K8 **Owen Sound** Ontario Canada
140 C6 **Owen Springs** N Terr Australia
136 K3 **Owen Stanley Ra** Papua New Guinea
110 J3 **Owensville** Indiana U.S.A.
110 E3 **Owensville** Missouri U.S.A.
110 M3 **Owenton** Kentucky U.S.A.
102 F5 **Owenyo** California U.S.A.
9 E6 **Ower** England
85 F7 **Owerri** Nigeria
145 E3 **Owhango** New Zealand
117 K10 **Owikeno L** British Columbia Canada
94 D8 **Owingsville** Kentucky U.S.A.
36 F5 **Öwisheim** Germany
106 E1 **Owl Canyon** Colorado U.S.A.
101 R6 **Owl Cr** Wyoming U.S.A.
101 R6 **Owl-Creek Mts** Wyoming U.S.A.
118 F4 **Owl R** Alberta Canada
85 F7 **Owo** Nigeria
94 C3 **Owosso** Michigan U.S.A.
100 J8 **Owyhee** Nevada U.S.A.
100 H6 **Owyhee** Oregon U.S.A.
29 T8 **Øxarfjørdhur** *B* Iceland
27 G10 **Oxberg** Sweden
119 P9 **Oxbow** Saskatchewan Canada
100 J5 **Oxbow Dam** Oregon U.S.A.
111 F7 **Oxbow L** Mississippi U.S.A.
118 K1 **Oxdrift** Ontario Canada
27 J13 **Oxelösund** Sweden
122 J8 **Oxford** Nova Scotia Canada
9 E4 **Oxford** England
144 D5 **Oxford** New Zealand
111 L8 **Oxford** Alabama U.S.A.
101 N7 **Oxford** Idaho U.S.A.
110 J1 **Oxford** Indiana U.S.A.
99 P8 **Oxford** Iowa U.S.A.
107 N4 **Oxford** Kansas U.S.A.
95 R2 **Oxford** Maine U.S.A.
95 L8 **Oxford** Maryland U.S.A.
95 Q4 **Oxford** Massachusetts U.S.A.
94 D4 **Oxford** Michigan U.S.A.
111 G7 **Oxford** Mississippi U.S.A.
98 G9 **Oxford** Nebraska U.S.A.
95 M4 **Oxford** New York U.S.A.
112 J1 **Oxford** North Carolina U.S.A.
94 C7 **Oxford** Ohio U.S.A.
99 R6 **Oxford** Wisconsin U.S.A.
141 J5 **Oxford Downs** Queensland Australia
119 W4 **Oxford House** Manitoba Canada
101 N7 **Oxford Pk** Idaho U.S.A.
9 E4 **Oxfordshire** *co* England
46 E5 **Oxiá** *mt* Greece
140 E4 **Oxide, Mt** Queensland Australia
46 G6 **Oxílithos** Greece
125 P7 **Oxkutzcab** Mexico
141 K2 **Oxley** Brisbane, Qnsld Australia
139 G5 **Oxley** New South Wales Australia
139 K4 **Oxleys Pk** New South Wales Australia
14 C2 **Ox Mts** Ireland
102 E7 **Oxnard** California U.S.A.
9 E1 **Oxton** England
8 B4 **Oxwich** Wales
56 D4 **Oya** *R* Russian Federation
70 B3 **Oya** Sarawak
70 C3 **Oya** *R* Sarawak
61 K9 **Oyabe** Japan
61 M10 **Oyama** Shizuoka Japan
61 N9 **Oyama** Tochigi Japan
61 N7 **Ōyama** Yamagata Japan
60 D13 **Ōyano shima** *isld* Japan
129 H3 **Oyapock, B. d'** Fr Guiana
57 L1 **Oychilik** Kazakhstan
86 B5 **Oyem** Gabon
118 G7 **Oyen** Alberta Canada
22 C2 **Oye Plage** France
27 E12 **Oyeren** *L* Norway
56 B3 **Oyesh** *R* Russian Federation
26 J3 **Öyjord** Norway
15 D3 **Oykel** *R* Scotland
51 O2 **Oymyakon** Russian Federation
85 E7 **Oyo** Nigeria
128 C6 **Oyón** Peru
40 C5 **Oyonnax** France
21 M8 **Oyré** France
109 M6 **Oyster Cr** Texas U.S.A.
68 A2 **Oyster I** Burma
100 A3 **Oysterville** Washington U.S.A.
57 G3 **Oytal** Kazakhstan
32 K6 **Oyten** Germany
79 C2 **Oyuklu Dağ Tepe** *mt* Turkey
51 N2 **Oyun Khomoto** Russian Federation
78 J2 **Özalp** Turkey
71 F6 **Ozamiz** Mindanao Philippines
111 L10 **Ozark** Alabama U.S.A.
110 C6 **Ozark** Arkansas U.S.A.
110 C4 **Ozark** Missouri U.S.A.
110 C6 **Ozark lake** Arkansas U.S.A.
110 C5 **Ozark Plateau** Missouri U.S.A.
110 C3 **Ozarks, L. of the** Missouri U.S.A.
48 F2 **Ózd** Hungary
80 B7 **Ozem** Israel
55 F3 **Ozernoye** Russian Federation
55 D4 **Ozernyy** Kustanayskaya Kazakhstan
54 D1 **Ozernyy** Smolenskaya obl Russian Federation
55 D3 **Ozernyy** Sverdlovskaya obl Russian Federation
55 G3 **Ozero Karachi** Russian Federation
65 J2 **Ozero Khanka** *L* China/Rus Fed
46 E6 **Ozerós, L** Greece
31 N1 **Ozersk** Russian Federation
54 K2 **Ozery** Russian Federation
100 A1 **Ozette, L** Washington U.S.A.
54 K2 **Ozherel'ye** Russian Federation
51 O2 **Ozhogino** Russian Federation
43 C8 **Ozieri** Sardinia
31 L5 **Ozimek** Poland
108 F5 **Ozona** Texas U.S.A.
48 E4 **Ozora** Hungary
31 L4 **Ozorków** Poland
55 C5 **Ozorodnyy** Kazakhstan
86 A6 **Ozouri** Gabon
60 F12 **Ōzu** Japan
60 D13 **Ōzu** *R* Japan
60 E11 **Ozuki** Japan
48 K5 **Ozun** Romania
78 J1 **Ozurgety** Georgia
45 K3 **Ozzano dell'Emilia** Italy

P

80 B8 **Pa'ame Tashaz** Israel
Paamiut *see* **Frederikshåb**
68 C4 **Pa-an** Burma
37 L6 **Paar** *R* Germany
33 R7 **Paaren** Germany
89 A9 **Paarl** S Africa
29 O3 **Paatsjoki** *R* Finland
135 U4 **Paauilo** Hawaiian Is
29 L7 **Paavola** Finland
15 A3 **Pabbay** *isld* Outer Hebrides Scotland
70 P9 **Pabean** Indonesia
31 L4 **Pabjanice** Poland
77 K6 **Pab Range** Pakistan
128 F6 **Pacaás Novos, Sa. dos** *mts* Brazil
129 H4 **Pacajá** *R* Brazil
128 F3 **Pacaraima, Sa** *mts* Brazil/Venezuela
128 C5 **Pacasmayo** Peru
20 G5 **Pace** France
111 F8 **Pace** Mississippi U.S.A.
67 F5 **Pa'-chao Hsü** *isld* Taiwan
124 E2 **Pacheco** Chihuahua Mexico
124 H5 **Pacheco** Zacatecas Mexico
100 A1 **Pachena Pt** British Columbia Canada
124 F3 **Pachera** Mexico
43 G12 **Pachino** Sicily
128 D5 **Pachitea** *R* Peru
125 K7 **Pachuca** Mexico
111 H9 **Pachuta** Mississippi U.S.A.
102 D3 **Pacific** California U.S.A.
110 F3 **Pacific** Missouri U.S.A.
135 L14 **Pacific Antarctic Ridge** Pacific Oc
100 A2 **Pacific Beach** Washington U.S.A.
100 B4 **Pacific City** Oregon U.S.A.
101 Q7 **Pacific Cr** Wyoming U.S.A.
102 C5 **Pacific Grove** California U.S.A.
135 **Pacific Ocean**
117 L11 **Pacific Rim Nat Park** British Columbia Canada
71 G5 **Pacijan** *isld* Philippines
70 P9 **Pacinan, Tanjong** *C* Java
70 D4 **Pacingapan, Bukit** *mt* Kalimantan
145 E4 **Packakariki** New Zealand
38 L7 **Pack Alpe** *mts* Austria
138 F4 **Packsaddle** New South Wales Australia
111 D10 **Packton** Louisiana U.S.A.
99 O8 **Packwood** Iowa U.S.A.
100 D3 **Packwood** Washington U.S.A.
112 E2 **Pacolet** *R* South Carolina U.S.A.
112 F3 **Pacolet Mills** South Carolina U.S.A.
31 J6 **Pacov** Czech Rep
123 R4 **Pacquet** Newfoundland Canada
98 C5 **Pactola** South Dakota U.S.A.
135 Q15 **Pactolus Bank** Pacific Oc
130 G5 **Pacui** *R* Brazil
21 N3 **Pacy-sur-Eure** France
31 K5 **Paczków** Poland
71 H6 **Padabale** *isld* Sulawesi
71 G7 **Padada** Mindanao Philippines
70 G7 **Padamarang** *isld* Sulawesi
71 K8 **Padang** Indonesia
69 F12 **Padang** Riau Arch Indonesia
69 E13 **Padang** Sumatra
69 E13 **Padangpanjang** Sumatra
69 D12 **Padangsidimpuan** Sumatra
69 B10 **Padangtiji** Sumatra
69 J13 **Padangtikar** Indonesia
52 D3 **Padany** Russian Federation
70 D2 **Padas** *R* Sabah
29 L10 **Padasjoki** Finland
128 F3 **Padauiri** *R* Brazil
68 B3 **Padaung** Burma
83 K9 **Padawiya Tank** Sri Lanka
141 K1 **Paddington** *dist* Brisbane, Qnsld Australia
117 P7 **Paddle Prairie** Alberta Canada
119 M5 **Paddockwood** Saskatchewan Canada
71 H6 **Padea Besar** *isld* Indonesia
94 G7 **Paden City** West Virginia U.S.A.
32 J9 **Paderborn** Germany
48 G5 **Padeş** *mt* Romania
13 F6 **Padiham** England
128 F7 **Padilla** Bolivia
48 L6 **Padina** Romania
26 J4 **Padjelanta Nat. Park** Sweden
115 K5 **Padlei** Northwest Territories Canada
115 N4 **Padloping Island** Northwest Territories Canada
122 E5 **Padoue** Quebec Canada
36 B7 **Padoux** France
45 L1 **Padova** Italy
109 K9 **Padre I** Texas U.S.A.
16 B2 **Padrón** Spain
8 B6 **Padstow** England
138 F6 **Padthaway** South Australia Australia
Padua *see* **Padova**
75 K9 **Pādua** India
110 H4 **Paducah** Kentucky U.S.A.
108 G1 **Paducah** Texas U.S.A.
45 R7 **Paduli** Italy
56 C3 **Padunskaya** Russian Federation
145 F2 **Paengaroa** New Zealand
65 F6 **Paengnyŏng-do** *isld* S Korea
145 E2 **Paeroa** New Zealand
44 B2 **Paesana** Italy
45 R8 **Paestum** Italy
71 E3 **Paete** Luzon Philippines
87 F10 **Pafuri** Mozambique
42 F4 **Pag** *isld* Croatia
42 G4 **Pag** Croatia
71 L9 **Paga** Flores Indonesia
129 H4 **Paga Centa** Brazil
70 L9 **Pagadenbaru** Java
71 F7 **Pagadian** Mindanao Philippines
69 E14 **Pagai Selatan** *isld* Indonesia
69 E14 **Pagai Utara** *isld* Indonesia
68 B2 **Pagan** Burma
45 R8 **Pagani** Italy
70 K7 **Pagaralam** Sumatra
46 F5 **Pagasitikós, Kólpos** *B* Greece
70 C6 **Pagatan** Kalimantan
70 D6 **Pagatan** Kalimantan
119 P2 **Pagato R** Saskatchewan Canada
71 F4 **Pagbulungan Pt** Philippines
103 N5 **Page** Arizona U.S.A.
98 H7 **Page** Nebraska U.S.A.
98 J2 **Page** North Dakota U.S.A.
107 Q7 **Page** Oklahoma U.S.A.
52 B6 **Pagėgiai** Lithuania
112 G3 **Pageland** South Carolina U.S.A.
142 E3 **Page, Mt** W Australia Australia
69 G14 **Pagerdewa** Sumatra
141 K4 **Paget Cay** *isld* Gt Barrier Reef Australia
68 A6 **Paget I** Andaman Is
131 H6 **Paget, Mt** S Georgia
77 L2 **Paghman** Afghanistan
42 D6 **Paglia** *R* Italy
101 S9 **Pagoda Pk** Colorado U.S.A.
47 H7 **Pagóndhas** Greece
70 D2 **Pagonprick, G** *mt* Sarawak
134 D1 **Pago Pago** Amer Samoa
106 C4 **Pagosa Springs** Colorado U.S.A.
106 C6 **Paguate** New Mexico U.S.A.
71 H4 **Pagujaman** *R* Sulawesi
120 D3 **Pagwachuan** Ontario Canada
120 E3 **Pagwachuan** *R* Ontario Canada
120 E2 **Pagwa River** Ontario Canada
116 K3 **Pah** *R* Alaska U.S.A.
102 V14 **Pahala** Hawaiian Is
73 R8 **Pahang** *R* Malaysia
69 F11 **Pahang, S** *R* Malaysia
145 E4 **Pahaoa R** New Zealand
69 J12 **Pahauman** Indonesia
144 A7 **Pahia** New Zealand
144 A7 **Pahia Pt** New Zealand
145 E4 **Pahiatua** New Zealand
76 G4 **Pahlāgaon** Andaman Is
135 V5 **Pahoa** Hawaiian Is
77 G2 **Pahra** Afghanistan
103 J4 **Pahranagat L** Nevada U.S.A.
103 J4 **Pahranagat Ra** Nevada U.S.A.
103 K4 **Pahrock Ra** Nevada U.S.A.
103 J5 **Pahrump** Nevada U.S.A.
101 M5 **Pahsimeroi** *R* Idaho U.S.A.
102 H4 **Pahute Mesa** Nevada U.S.A.
100 F8 **Pahute Peak** *mt* Nevada U.S.A.
135 T3 **Paia** Hawaiian Is
130 B6 **Paiaguás** Brazil
67 G4 **Pai-ch'üan Lieh-tao** *islds* Taiwan
52 C5 **Paide** Estonia
109 K5 **Paige** Texas U.S.A.
8 C7 **Paignton** England
145 E1 **Paihia** New Zealand
29 M10 **Päijänne** *reg* Finland
68 F6 **Pailin** Cambodia
Pailing *see* **Chun'an**
135 S3 **Pailolo Ch** Hawaiian Is
9 E3 **Pailton** England
20 F7 **Paimbœuf** France
116 G5 **Paimiut** Alaska U.S.A.
20 D4 **Paimpol** France
20 F5 **Paimpont** France
69 E13 **Painan** Sumatra
120 H10 **Paincourt** Ontario Canada
133 C8 **Paine** *mt* Chile
99 S2 **Painesdale** Michigan U.S.A.
94 F5 **Painesville** Ohio U.S.A.
103 N5 **Painted Des** Arizona U.S.A.
103 L8 **Painted Rock Res** Arizona U.S.A.
37 M6 **Painten** Germany
138 E4 **Painter, Mt** South Australia Australia
119 T3 **Paint L** Manitoba Canada
120 J8 **Paisley** Ontario Canada
12 D2 **Paisley** Scotland
100 E7 **Paisley** Oregon U.S.A.
29 M2 **Paistunturit** *mt* Finland
17 F2 **País Vasco** *reg* Spain
128 B5 **Paita** Peru
70 E1 **Paitan, Telukan** *B* Sabah
26 K4 **Paittasjärbi** *L* Sweden
16 B4 **Paiva** *R* Portugal
21 M8 **Paizey-le-Sec** France
69 E11 **Pajakbaru** Sumatra
69 E13 **Pajakumbuh** Sumatra
26 N4 **Pajala** Sweden
16 D1 **Pajares, Pto. de** Spain
106 D7 **Pajarito** New Mexico U.S.A.
131 B2 **Pajaros** *isld* Chile
129 L5 **Pajeu** Brazil
130 H10 **Pajeú, R** Brazil
48 D4 **Páka** Hungary
69 F10 **Paka** Malaysia
68 B2 **Pakangyi** Burma
128 F2 **Pakaraima Mts** Guyana
119 N1 **Pakashkhan L** *isld* Ontario Canada
56 E3 **Pakateyevo** Russian Federation
68 E3 **Pak Beng** Laos
121 O7 **Pakenham** Ontario Canada
145 D1 **Pakenui** New Zealand
57 G4 **Pakhtaabad** Uzbekistan
74 A4 **Pakistan** *rep* Asia
69 D11 **Pakkat** Sumatra
68 E3 **Pak Khop** Laos
68 E3 **Pak Lay** Laos
Paknampho *see* **Muang Nakhon Sawan**
68 E3 **Pak Niam** Laos
68 B2 **Pakokku** Burma
145 D1 **Pakotai** New Zealand
69 E8 **Pak Phanang** Thailand
69 E9 **Pak Phayun** Thailand
42 H3 **Pakrac** Croatia
48 E4 **Paks** Hungary
68 F3 **Pak Sane** Laos
68 G5 **Pakse** Laos
68 E2 **Pak Tha** Laos
77 L3 **Paktīā** Afghanistan
77 L3 **Paktīkā** *prov* Afghanistan
70 C3 **Paku** *R* Sarawak
70 G6 **Pakue** Sulawesi
119 T4 **Pakwa L** Manitoba Canada
89 F4 **Pakwe** *R* Botswana
86 F5 **Pakwich** Uganda
68 D6 **Pala** Burma
86 C4 **Pala** Chad
102 G8 **Pala** California U.S.A.
70 L9 **Palabuhanratu** Java
70 L9 **Palabuhanratu, Teluk** *B* Java
109 L7 **Palacios** Texas U.S.A.
127 L10 **Palacios** Venezuela
133 D6 **Palacios, L** Argentina
17 K3 **Palafrugell** Spain
42 G6 **Palagruža** *isld* Croatia
46 F7 **Palaiá** Greece
45 J4 **Paláia** Italy
47 H9 **Palaiókastron** Crete Greece
46 F9 **Palaiokhóra** Crete Greece
46 D6 **Pálairos** Greece
21 P4 **Palaiseau** France
20 D7 **Palais, le** Belle Isle, Nfld France
Palakkad *see* **Palghat**
89 F4 **Palala** *R* S Africa
68 A7 **Palalankwe** Andaman Is
46 E5 **Palamás** Greece
71 A3 **Palamea** Indonesia
17 K3 **Palamós** Spain
47 J6 **Palamut** Turkey
139 J7 **Palana** Tasmania Australia
71 F2 **Palanan** Luzon Philippines
17 G5 **Palancia** *R* Spain
52 B6 **Palanga** Lithuania
77 G4 **Palangān, Kūh-e-** *mts* Iran
70 C6 **Palangka Raya** Kalimantan
76 C5 **Palani** India
76 G5 **Palankwe** Andaman Is India
16 D2 **Palanquinos** Spain
70 F7 **Palanro** Sulawesi
135 S3 **Palaoa Pt** Hawaiian Is
71 G4 **Palapag** Philippines
89 E4 **Palapye** Botswana
70 G4 **Palasa** Sulawesi
16 B2 **Palas de Rey** Spain
113 F8 **Palatka** Florida U.S.A.
56 B6 **Palattsy** Kazakhstan
108 F8 **Palau** Mexico
134 D7 **Palau** *islds* Caroline Is Pacific Oc
43 C7 **Palau** Sardinia
71 F1 **Palaui** *isld* Luzon Philippines
71 D3 **Palauig** Luzon Philippines
68 D6 **Palauk** Burma
70 K8 **Palausekopong, Tanjong** *C* Sumatra
83 J10 **Palavi** Sri Lanka
68 D6 **Palaw** Burma
71 D6 **Palawan** *isld* Philippines
71 C6 **Palawan Passage** Philippines
76 C6 **Pālayankottai** India
43 F11 **Palazzolo Acreide** Sicily
41 L6 **Palazzolo sull Oglio** Italy
45 L3 **Palazzuolo sul Sénio** Italy
133 D1 **Palca** Chile
52 B5 **Paldiski** Estonia
68 B2 **Pale** Burma
70 G4 **Paleleh** Sulawesi
69 G14 **Palembang** Sumatra
38 K6 **Palen** *R* Austria
16 D2 **Palencia** *prov* Spain
103 J8 **Palen L** California U.S.A.
47 O12 **Paleokastritsa** Greece
79 D4 **Paleokhorio** Cyprus
43 E10 **Palermo** Sicily
102 C2 **Palermo** California U.S.A.
98 D1 **Palermo** North Dakota U.S.A.
128 E8 **Palestina** Chile
110 J3 **Palestine** Illinois U.S.A.
109 M4 **Palestine** Texas U.S.A.
110 M1 **Palestine Hill** Ohio U.S.A.
109 M3 **Palestine, L** Texas U.S.A.
45 N6 **Palestrina** Italy
68 A2 **Paletwa** Burma
76 C5 **Palghat** India
143 B6 **Palgrave, Mt** W Australia
45 O6 **Paliano** Italy
83 K8 **Pali Aru** *R* Sri Lanka
70 P9 **Paliat** *isld* Indonesia
71 G7 **Palimbang** Mindanao Philippines
70 E1 **Palin, Mt** Sabah
43 G8 **Palinuro, C** Italy
106 B2 **Palisade** Colorado U.S.A.
98 E9 **Palisade** Nebraska U.S.A.
103 H1 **Palisade** Nevada U.S.A.
101 O6 **Palisades Res** Idaho U.S.A.
127 L3 **Palisadoes** *airport* Jamaica
22 J4 **Paliseul** Belgium
109 J8 **Palito Blanco** Texas U.S.A.
26 K5 **Paljaape** *mt* Sweden
29 L10 **Pälkäne** Finland
83 J8 **Palk Bay** Sri Lanka
52 F5 **Palkino** Russian Federation
75 K9 **Pālkohda** India
83 J8 **Palk Str** India/Sri Lanka
83 K8 **Pallai** Sri Lanka
Pallanza *see* **Verbania**
Palla Rd *see* **Dinokwe** Botswana
18 F10 **Pallaresa** *R* Spain
29 L3 **Pallas-Ounastunturi Nat. Park.** Finland
29 L3 **Pallastunturi** *mt* Finland
83 K10 **Pallegama** Sri Lanka
26 K3 **Pallemtjåkko** *mt* Sweden
46 C3 **Pallës, Bishti i** *C* Albania
21 H7 **Pallet, le** France
18 E6 **Pallice, la** France
36 B4 **Pallien** Germany
70 G7 **Pallima** Sulawesi
Pallíni Greece *see* **Kassándra**
143 C10 **Pallinup, R** W Australia Australia
145 E4 **Palliser Bay** New Zealand
20 G8 **Palluau** France
21 N8 **Palluau-sur-Indre** France
88 H7 **Palma** Mozambique
106 E6 **Palma** New Mexico U.S.A.
17 J5 **Palma, B. de** Majorca
45 R8 **Palma Camp** Italy
17 J5 **Palma de Mallorca** Majorca
43 F11 **Palma di Montechiaro** Sicily
80 B6 **Palmaḥim** Israel
127 H9 **Palmar** *R* Venezuela
133 G4 **Palmares do Sul** Brazil
126 G4 **Palmarito del Cauto** Cuba
43 E8 **Palmarola, I** Italy
129 J6 **Palmas** Brazil
85 C8 **Palmas, C** Liberia
43 B10 **Palmas, G. di** Sardinia
128 E1 **Palma Sola** Venezuela
126 G4 **Palma Soriano** Cuba
87 B7 **Palmas, Pta. das** Angola
142 A4 **Palm Beach** W Australia Australia
113 G11 **Palm Beach** Florida U.S.A.
102 F7 **Palmdale** California U.S.A.
113 F11 **Palmdale** Florida U.S.A.
102 H8 **Palm Desert** California U.S.A.
133 G3 **Palmeira** Brazil
146 C4 **Palmer** *U.S.A. Base* Antarctica
141 G3 **Palmer** *R* Queensland Australia
118 L9 **Palmer** Saskatchewan Canada
116 N6 **Palmer** Alaska U.S.A.
99 R10 **Palmer** Illinois U.S.A.
99 M7 **Palmer** Iowa U.S.A.
99 T3 **Palmer** Michigan U.S.A.
98 H8 **Palmer** Nebraska U.S.A.
110 L6 **Palmer** Tennessee U.S.A.
109 L3 **Palmer** Texas U.S.A.
146 C6 **Palmer Land** Antarctica
140 C6 **Palmer R** N Terr Australia
144 C6 **Palmerston** New Zealand
141 J5 **Palmerston, C** Queensland Australia
145 E4 **Palmerston North** New Zealand
95 M6 **Palmerton** Pennsylvania U.S.A.
140 C6 **Palmer Valley** N Terr Australia
141 G3 **Palmerville** Queensland Australia
113 E10 **Palmetto** Florida U.S.A.
112 C4 **Palmetto** Georgia U.S.A.
126 F2 **Palmetto Pt** Eleuthera Bahamas
127 N6 **Palmetto Pt** Barbuda W Indies
113 E9 **Palm Harbor** Florida U.S.A.
43 G10 **Palmi** Italy
128 C3 **Palmira** Colombia
126 D3 **Palmira** Cuba
141 H4 **Palm Is** Queensland Australia
124 G6 **Palmito del Verde, I** Mexico
94 E3 **Palms** Michigan U.S.A.
112 H5 **Palms, I of** South Carolina U.S.A.
102 H8 **Palm Springs** California U.S.A.
141 J7 **Palm Tree Cr** Queensland Australia
140 C6 **Palm Valley** N Terr Australia
Palmyra *see* **Tadmur**
110 G2 **Palmyra** Illinois U.S.A.
99 P10 **Palmyra** Missouri U.S.A.
98 K9 **Palmyra** Nebraska U.S.A.
95 N7 **Palmyra** New Jersey U.S.A.
95 K3 **Palmyra** New York U.S.A.
95 L6 **Palmyra** Pennsylvania U.S.A.
110 J5 **Palmyra** Tennessee U.S.A.
94 J9 **Palmyra** Virginia U.S.A.
99 S7 **Palmyra** Wisconsin U.S.A.
135 U7 **Palmyra I** *atoll* Pacific Oc
12 E4 **Palnackie** Scotland
52 J4 **Pal'niki** Russian Federation
42 E7 **Palo** Italy
71 G5 **Palo** Leyte Philippines
70 F5 **Palo** Sulawesi
99 P7 **Palo** Iowa U.S.A.
102 B4 **Palo Alto** California U.S.A.
125 Q6 **Palo de las Letras** Panama
108 B8 **Palo Duro Cr** Texas U.S.A.
108 C7 **Paloduro Cr** Texas/Okla U.S.A.
70 B3 **Paloh** Sarawak
86 F3 **Paloich** Sudan
29 K3 **Palojärvi** Finland
29 K3 **Palojoensuu** Finland
29 K3 **Palojoki** *R* Finland
102 H8 **Palomar Mt** California U.S.A.
103 L9 **Palomas** Arizona U.S.A.
45 N5 **Palombara Sabina** Italy
17 G4 **Palomera, Sa** *mts* Spain
109 J3 **Palo Pinto** Texas U.S.A.
70 G6 **Palopo** Sulawesi
133 F3 **Palo Santo** Argentina
17 G7 **Palos, C. de** Spain
127 O3 **Palo Seco** Trinidad
100 H3 **Palouse** Washington U.S.A.
103 M8 **Palo Verde** Arizona U.S.A.
103 K8 **Palo Verde** California U.S.A.
141 F6 **Palparara** Queensland Australia
27 H12 **Pålsboda** Sweden
29 N7 **Paltamo** Finland
38 H5 **Palting** Austria
71 K9 **Palu** *isld* Flores Indonesia
70 F5 **Palu** *R* Sulawesi
127 N10 **Palúa** Venezuela
71 E4 **Paluan** Philippines
83 K9 **Palugassegama** Sri Lanka
57 C5 **Pal'vart** Turkmenistan
85 E6 **Pama** Burkina
71 L10 **Pamana** Indonesia
71 L9 **Pamana Besar** *isld* Flores Indonesia
70 L9 **Pamanukan** Java
83 J8 **Pamban** *isld* India
70 F4 **Pambero** Sulawesi
118 K9 **Pambrun** Saskatchewan Canada
139 J6 **Pambula** New South Wales Australia
38 M8 **Pameče** Slovenia
70 O9 **Pamekasan** Java
70 L9 **Pameungpeuk** Java
18 G9 **Pamiers** France
46 E7 **Pámisos** *R* Greece
112 L2 **Pamlico R** North Carolina U.S.A.
68 E4 **Pamong D.Site** Thailand
133 D4 **Pampa de las Salinas** Argentina
70 G7 **Pampanua** Sulawesi
128 D6 **Pampas** Peru
133 E5 **Pampas, Plains** Argentina
16 B4 **Pampilhosa da Serra** Portugal
16 B4 **Pampilhosa do Botão** Portugal
94 J9 **Pamplin City** Virginia U.S.A.
128 D2 **Pamplona** Colombia
71 F6 **Pamplona** Negros Philippines
17 F2 **Pamplona** Spain
33 O5 **Pampow** Germany
70 E6 **Pamukan, Teluk** *B* Kalimantan
47 K7 **Pamukkale** Turkey
47 L4 **Pamukova** Turkey
95 K9 **Pamunkey** *R* Virginia U.S.A.
99 R10 **Pana** Illinois U.S.A.
71 F7 **Panabutan B** Mindanao Philippines
103 K4 **Panaca** Nevada U.S.A.
120 J6 **Panache, L** Ontario Canada
83 J11 **Panadura** Sri Lanka
71 D6 **Panagtaran** *pt* Palawan Philippines
46 G2 **Panagyurishte** Bulgaria
70 K9 **Panaitan** *isld* Java
76 A3 **Panaji** India
46 E6 **Panakhaikón** *mt* Greece
125 O5 **Panama** *rep* Central America
125 P5 **Panamá** Panama
94 H4 **Panama** New York U.S.A.
107 Q6 **Panama** Oklahoma U.S.A.
124 E10 **Panama Canal** Central America
113 B7 **Panama City** Florida U.S.A.
125 P5 **Panamá, Golfo de** Panama
102 G5 **Panamint V** California U.S.A.
71 G6 **Panaon** *isld* Philippines
43 G10 **Panarea, I** Italy
45 K2 **Panaro** *R* Italy
70 O9 **Panarukan** Java
71 G4 **Panay** Philippines
71 F5 **Panay** *isld* Philippines
71 F5 **Panay Gulf** Philippines
46 G4 **Panayía** Greece
103 J3 **Pancake Ra** Nevada U.S.A.
20 G6 **Pancé** France
48 F6 **Pančevo** Serbia Yugoslavia
46 D1 **Pančiće** *mt* Serbia Yugoslavia
48 L5 **Panciu** Romania
69 D11 **Pancurbatu** Sumatra
87 F10 **Panda** Mozambique
108 F5 **Pandale** Texas U.S.A.
71 G3 **Pandan** Catanduanes Philippines
71 F5 **Pandan** Panay Philippines
70 C3 **Pandan** Sarawak
71 C6 **Pandanan** *isld* Palawan Philippines
71 F5 **Pandan Bay** Panay Philippines
70 K8 **Pandan, Bt** *mt* Sumatra
70 D5 **Pandang** Kalimantan
141 F3 **Pandanus** *R* Queensland Australia
87 F10 **Pande** Mozambique
133 C3 **Pan de Azúcar** Chile
71 F5 **Pan de Azucar** Philippines
70 L9 **Pandeglang** Java
130 G4 **Pandeiros** *R* Brazil
138 E2 **Pandie Pandie** South Australia Australia
70 F3 **Pandjang** *isld* Kalimantan
70 G4 **Pandjang, Tg** *C* Sulawesi
128 E6 **Pando** *dept* Bolivia
133 F4 **Pando** Uruguay
47 O12 **Pandokrátor** *mt* Greece
125 N5 **Pandora** Costa Rica
141 G1 **Pandora Ent** Gt Barrier Reef Aust
71 E7 **Panducan** *isld* Philippines
8 D4 **Pandy** Wales
52 B6 **Panevėžys** Lithuania
138 D4 **Paney** South Australia Australia
66 C3 **Panfilov** Kazakhstan
57 H3 **Panfilova, Imeni** Kazakhstan
86 E5 **Panga** Zaire
46 F4 **Pangaion** *mt* Greece
70 M9 **Pangandaran** Java
88 F4 **Pangani** *R* Tanzania
88 G4 **Pangani** Tanzania
71 F4 **Panganiran** Philippines
9 E5 **Pangbourne** England
110 E6 **Pangburn** Arkansas U.S.A.
70 F5 **Pangean** Sulawesi
68 D1 **Panghsang** Burma
86 E6 **Pangi** Zaire
70 O9 **Pangkah, Tg** *C* Java
70 F7 **Pangkajene** Sulawesi
70 B6 **Pangkalanbuun** Kalimantan
69 E11 **Pangkalanlunang** Sumatra
69 D10 **Pangkalansusu** Sumatra
69 H14 **Pangkalpinang** Sumatra
71 H5 **Pangkalsiang, Tg** *C* Sulawesi
71 F6 **Panglao** *isld* Philippines
68 C2 **Panglong** Burma
119 N9 **Pangman** Saskatchewan Canada
115 N4 **Pangnirtung** Northwest Territories Canada
70 L9 **Pangrongo, G** *mt* Java
68 C2 **Pangtara** Burma
133 C5 **Panguipulli** *mt* Chile
131 A7 **Panguipulli, L** Chile
103 M4 **Panguitch** Utah U.S.A.
70 B6 **Pangujon, Tanjong** *C* Kalimantan
71 E7 **Pangutaran** *isld* Philippines
71 E7 **Pangutaran Group** *islds* Philippines
88 E7 **Pangwa** Tanzania
68 D1 **Pang Yang** Burma
87 F9 **Panhalonga** Zimbabwe
108 C8 **Panhandle** Texas U.S.A.
65 A7 **Panhe** China
136 H2 **Paniai, Danau** *L* W Irian
86 D7 **Pania Mutembo** Zaire
137 N6 **Panié, Mt** New Caledonia
71 G5 **Paninihian Pt** Samar Philippines
71 D6 **Panitan** Palawan Philippines
77 K2 **Panjāb** Afghanistan
Panjang *isld* Cocos Is *see* **West I**
69 J11 **Panjang** *isld* Indonesia
69 F8 **Panjang, Hon** *isld* G of Thailand
77 J6 **Panjgur** Pakistan
77 L2 **Panjshir** *reg* Afghanistan
60 Q1 **Panke-zan** *mt* Japan
116 F9 **Pankof, C** Aleutian Is
33 S7 **Pankow** Germany
85 F7 **Pankshin** Nigeria
65 H3 **Pan Ling** *mts* China
142 B5 **Pannawonica** W Australia Australia
20 H7 **Pannecé** France
25 F5 **Pannerden** Netherlands
102 D5 **Panoche** California U.S.A.
70 B5 **Panopah** Kalimantan
99 M8 **Panora** Iowa U.S.A.
133 G2 **Panorama** Brazil
141 J6 **Panorama, Mt** Queensland Australia
55 F3 **Panovo** Russian Federation
52 D2 **Panozero** Russian Federation
65 E4 **Panshan** China
65 G3 **Panshi** China
70 E6 **Pantai** Kalimantan
69 E13 **Pantaicermin, Gunung** *mt* Sumatra
129 G7 **Pantanal de São Lourénço** *swamp* Brazil
130 B5 **Pantanal Matogrossense, Parque Nacional do** Brazil
68 B4 **Pantanaw** Burma
103 O9 **Pantano** Arizona U.S.A.
18 F10 **Pantano de Tremp** *L* Spain
71 M9 **Pantar** *isld* Indonesia
112 L2 **Pantego** North Carolina U.S.A.
109 M9 **Pantego** Texas U.S.A.
43 E12 **Pantelleria, I. di** Italy
41 N6 **Pantena, Val** Italy
110 J4 **Panther** *R* Kentucky U.S.A.
74 H4 **Pantnagar** India
128 C4 **Pantoja** Peru
69 C10 **Pantonlabu** Sumatra
125 K6 **Pánuco** Mexico
67 A4 **Pan Xian** China
67 D5 **Panyu** China
54 H8 **Panyutino** Ukraine
87 C7 **Panzi** Zaire
Paoki *see* **Baoji**
43 G9 **Paola** Italy
107 Q3 **Paola** Kansas U.S.A.
98 D9 **Paoli** Colorado U.S.A.
110 K3 **Paoli** Indiana U.S.A.
107 N7 **Paoli** Oklahoma U.S.A.
106 C3 **Paonia** Colorado U.S.A.
134 A11 **Paopao** Moorea Pacific Oc
Paotow *see* **Baotou**
135 U6 **Papa** Hawaiian Is
48 D3 **Pápa** Hungary
135 V4 **Papaaloa** Hawaiian Is
46 F8 **Papadhiánika** Greece
125 M4 **Papagayo, Golfo de** Costa Rica
135 V5 **Papaikou** Hawaiian Is
144 C6 **Papakaio** New Zealand
145 E2 **Papakura** New Zealand
43 G8 **Papa, Monte del** Italy
125 L7 **Papantla** Mexico
70 D2 **Papar** Sabah
145 F3 **Paparatu** New Zealand
75 K9 **Pāparhāhāndi** India
145 E2 **Paparoa** New Zealand
144 C5 **Paparoa National Park** New Zealand
144 C5 **Paparoa Range** New Zealand
46 E6 **Pápas, Akr** Greece
15 G2 **Papa Stour** *isld* Scotland
145 G2 **Papatoetoe** New Zealand
144 B7 **Papatowai** New Zealand
15 F1 **Papa Westray** Orkney Scotland
135 M10 **Papeete** Tahiti Pacific Oc
32 F6 **Papenburg** Germany
25 C5 **Papendrecht** Netherlands
79 C4 **Paphos** Cyprus
124 E3 **Papigochic** *R* Mexico
121 P7 **Papineauville** Quebec Canada
133 C3 **Paposo** Chile
45 M2 **Papozze** Italy
37 J2 **Pappenheim** Germany
37 K6 **Pappenheim** Germany
15 C5 **Paps of Jura** *mt* Scotland
136 J3 **Papua, G. of** Papua New Guinea
136 K3 **Papua New Guinea** *state* S W Pacific
141 H3 **Papuan Passage** Gt Barrier Reef Aust
42 H3 **Papuk** *mt* Croatia
68 C3 **Papun** Burma
140 B6 **Papunya** N Terr Australia
128 E3 **Papuri** *R* Brazil/Colombia
48 J5 **Păpuşa** *mt* Romania
8 B7 **Par** England
129 H4 **Para** *state* Brazil
129 J4 **Pará** *R* Brazil

56 B2 **Parabel'** *R* Russian Federation
143 B6 **Paraburdoo** W Australia Australia
71 F3 **Paracale** Philippines
128 C6 **Paracas, Pena de** *pen* Peru
130 F5 **Paracatu** Brazil
138 E4 **Parachilna** South Australia Australia
46 E1 **Paraćin** Serbia Yugoslavia
98 E4 **Parade** South Dakota U.S.A.
130 G6 **Pará de Minas** Brazil
126 A1 **Paradera** Aruba W Indies
121 O4 **Paradis** Quebec Canada
144 B6 **Paradise** New Zealand
102 C2 **Paradise** California U.S.A.
107 M2 **Paradise** Kansas U.S.A.
101 L2 **Paradise** Montana U.S.A.
109 K2 **Paradise** Texas U.S.A.
101 O8 **Paradise** Utah U.S.A.
118 H5 **Paradise Hill** Saskatchewan Canada
116 H5 **Paradise Hill** Alaska U.S.A.
113 L9 **Paradise I.** New Providence I Bahamas
102 G3 **Paradise Pk** Nevada U.S.A.
118 G5 **Paradise Valley** Alberta Canada
100 H8 **Paradise Valley** Nevada U.S.A.
71 J9 **Parado** Sumbawa Indonesia
75 M8 **Pārādwīp** India
110 K2 **Paragon** Indiana U.S.A.
103 M4 **Paragonah** Utah U.S.A.
110 F5 **Paragould** Arkansas U.S.A.
128 F6 **Paraguá** *R* Bolivia
128 F2 **Paragua** *R* Venezuela
130 E8 **Paraguaca Paulista** Brazil
129 L6 **Paraguaçu** *R* Brazil
133 F2 **Paraguai** *R* Paraguay
127 J9 **Paraguaipoa** Venezuela
127 J9 **Paraguaná, Pen. de** Venezuela
130 B10 **Paraguari** *dept* Paraguay
133 F3 **Paraguay** *R* Paraguay
133 F2 **Paraguay** *rep* S America
130 H9 **Paraíba** *state* Brazil
130 G8 **Paraiba do Sul** Brazil
130 H7 **Paraíba, R** Brazil
Parainen *see* **Pargas**
133 G1 **Paraísa** Brazil
85 E7 **Parakou** Benin
138 D4 **Parakylia** South Australia Australia
75 L9 **Paralākhemundi** India
76 D6 **Paramakkudi** India
129 G2 **Paramaribo** Suriname
20 G4 **Paramé** France
131 B4 **Paramillos, Sa. de los** *mts* Argentina
129 K6 **Paramirim** Brazil
46 D5 **Paramithiá** Greece
128 C6 **Paramonga** Peru
133 E4 **Paraná** Argentina
130 D9 **Paraná** *state* Brazil
130 B10 **Paraná** *R* Brazil
130 E9 **Paranaguá** Brazil
133 G1 **Paranaíba** Brazil
130 E6 **Paranaiba, R** Brazil
131 F4 **Paraná Ibicuy** *R* Argentina
131 F2 **Paraná, L** Argentina
129 G2 **Paranam** Suriname
129 H8 **Paranapanema** *R* Brazil
131 F3 **Paraná, R** Argentina
133 G2 **Paranaval** Brazil
46 G3 **Paranéstion** Greece
70 N8 **Parang** *isld* Indonesia
71 E8 **Parang** Philippines
86 F5 **Paranga** Uganda
83 K8 **Parangi Aru** *R* Sri Lanka
76 D5 **Parangipettai** India
83 K8 **Paranthan** Sri Lanka
130 G6 **Paraopeba** Brazil
145 E4 **Paraparaumu** New Zealand
128 F8 **Parapeti** *R* Bolivia
46 F8 **Parapóla** *isld* Greece
128 E2 **Paraque, Cerro** *mt* Venezuela
71 G5 **Parasan** *isld* Philippines
138 E4 **Paratoo** South Australia Australia
129 H5 **Parauapebas** *R* Brazil
18 H6 **Paray-le-Monial** France
56 B3 **Parbig** *R* Russian Federation
122 J3 **Parc Archipelago Mingan** *nat park* Quebec Canada
21 L7 **Parçay-les-Pins** France
20 H5 **Parcé** Ille-et-Vilaine France
21 K6 **Parcé** Sarthe France
55 E5 **Parchevka** Kazakhstan
33 P6 **Parchim** Germany
45 O7 **Parco Naz. del Circeo** Italy
22 C3 **Parcq, le** France
31 O4 **Parczew** Poland
102 D3 **Pardee Res** California U.S.A.
99 R6 **Pardeeville** Wisconsin U.S.A.
80 C4 **Pardes Hanna-Karkur** Israel
129 H8 **Pardo** *R* Brazil
130 F4 **Pardo** *R* Minas Gerais Brazil
131 H2 **Pardo** *R* Rio Grande do Sul Brazil
142 C5 **Pardoo** W Australia Australia
130 D7 **Pardo, R** Mato Grosso Brazil
31 J5 **Pardubice** Czech Rep
70 O9 **Pare** Java
129 G6 **Parecis** Brazil
128 F6 **Parecis, Sa. dos** *mts* Brazil
133 D3 **Pareditas** Argentina
145 D1 **Parengarenga Harbour** New Zealand
70 C6 **Parenggean** Kalimantan
21 K5 **Parennes** France
121 Q5 **Parent** Quebec Canada
18 E8 **Parentis en Born** France
121 O4 **Parent L** Quebec Canada
144 C6 **Pareora** New Zealand
70 F7 **Parepare** Sulawesi
33 P8 **Parey** Germany
52 F5 **Parfen'yevo** Russian Federation
46 D5 **Párga** Greece
29 J11 **Pargas** Finland
52 D4 **Pargolovo** Russian Federation
127 P4 **Parham** Antigua W Indies
103 N4 **Paria** *R* Utah U.S.A.
128 F1 **Paria, G. of** Venezuela/Trinidad
128 F2 **Pariaguán** Venezuela
69 E13 **Pariaman** Sumatra
128 F1 **Paria, Pen. de** Venezuela
103 M5 **Paria Plat** Arizona U.S.A.
128 E4 **Paricá, L** Brazil
70 G5 **Parigi** Sulawesi
21 L6 **Parigné-l'Eveque** France
128 G2 **Parika** Guyana
144 D5 **Parikawa** New Zealand
145 E3 **Parikino** New Zealand
29 O10 **Parikkala** Finland
128 F3 **Parima, Sa** *mts* Brazil/Venezuela
128 D7 **Parinacocha, L** Peru
128 D4 **Parinari** Peru
128 B4 **Pariñas, Pta** Peru
48 L4 **Parincea** Romania
138 F5 **Paringa** South Australia Australia
129 G4 **Parintins** Brazil
23 **Paris** *conurbation* France
110 C6 **Paris** Arkansas U.S.A.
101 O7 **Paris** Idaho U.S.A.
99 T10 **Paris** Illinois U.S.A.
110 M3 **Paris** Kentucky U.S.A.
110 E2 **Paris** Missouri U.S.A.
110 H5 **Paris** Tennessee U.S.A.
109 M2 **Paris** Texas U.S.A.
95 L3 **Parish** New York U.S.A.
99 W3 **Parisienne, Ile** Ontario Canada
69 E10 **Parit Buntar** Malaysia
71 L10 **Pariti** Timor Indonesia
55 D4 **Parizh** Russian Federation
26 N4 **Parkajoki** Sweden
29 K9 **Parkano** Finland
118 L8 **Parkbeg** Saskatchewan Canada
110 K4 **Park City** Kentucky U.S.A.
101 R4 **Park City** Montana U.S.A.
103 N1 **Park City** Utah U.S.A.
106 E3 **Parkdale** Colorado U.S.A.
100 D4 **Parkdale** Oregon U.S.A.
103 K7 **Parker** Arizona U.S.A.
106 F2 **Parker** Colorado U.S.A.
101 O6 **Parker** Idaho U.S.A.
107 Q3 **Parker** Kansas U.S.A.
98 J6 **Parker** South Dakota U.S.A.
110 L1 **Parker City** Indiana U.S.A.
94 H5 **Parker City** Pennsylvania U.S.A.
103 K7 **Parker Dam** California U.S.A.
143 D9 **Parker Hill** W Australia Australia
140 E3 **Parker Pt** Queensland Australia
143 C9 **Parker Range** W Australia Australia
99 O7 **Parkersburg** Iowa U.S.A.
94 F7 **Parkersburg** West Virginia U.S.A.
99 L3 **Parkers Prairie** Minnesota U.S.A.
119 O7 **Parkerview** Saskatchewan Canada
139 J5 **Parkes** New South Wales Australia
95 M6 **Parkesburg** Pennsylvania U.S.A.
99 Q4 **Park Falls** Wisconsin U.S.A.
102 D6 **Parkfield** California U.S.A.
12 E3 **Parkgate** Scotland
95 L8 **Park Hall** Maryland U.S.A.
57 E5 **Parkhar** Tajikistan
120 J9 **Parkhill** Ontario Canada
26 K5 **Parkijaur** *L* Sweden
110 F6 **Parkin** Arkansas U.S.A.
118 E9 **Park Lake Prov. Park** Alberta Canada
118 D8 **Parkland** Alberta Canada
119 Q9 **Parkman** Saskatchewan Canada
101 S5 **Parkman** Wyoming U.S.A.
99 L3 **Park Rapids** Minnesota U.S.A.
99 T8 **Park Ridge** Illinois U.S.A.
98 J1 **Park River** North Dakota U.S.A.
103 N6 **Parks** Arizona U.S.A.
98 E9 **Parks** Nebraska U.S.A.
111 L13 **Parks Airport** St Louis
118 L5 **Parkside** Saskatchewan Canada
95 M9 **Parksley** Virginia U.S.A.
140 C6 **Parks, Mt** N Terr Australia
109 K2 **Park Springs** Texas U.S.A.
37 N4 **Parkstein** Germany
98 J6 **Parkston** South Dakota U.S.A.
95 L7 **Parkton** Maryland U.S.A.
112 H3 **Parkton** North Carolina U.S.A.
101 M8 **Park Valley** Utah U.S.A.
106 D1 **Park View Mt** Colorado U.S.A.
100 D3 **Parkway** Washington U.S.A.
26 K5 **Pärlälven** *R* Sweden
127 M1 **Parlatuvier** Tobago
74 G9 **Parli Vaijnāth** India
45 H2 **Parma** *R* Italy
45 H2 **Parma** Italy
100 J6 **Parma** Idaho U.S.A.
94 C4 **Parma** Michigan U.S.A.
110 G5 **Parma** Missouri U.S.A.
94 F5 **Parma** Ohio U.S.A.
129 K6 **Parnaguá** Brazil
129 K4 **Parnaiba** Brazil
129 J5 **Parnaíba** *R* Brazil
46 F6 **Parnassós** *mt* Greece
144 D5 **Parnassus** New Zealand
99 O8 **Parnell** Iowa U.S.A.
99 M9 **Parnell** Missouri U.S.A.
108 G1 **Parnell** Texas U.S.A.
46 F6 **Párnis** *mt* Greece
46 F7 **Párnon Óros** *mts* Greece
52 B5 **Pärnu** Estonia
52 B5 **Pärnu laht** *G* Estonia
144 C5 **Paroa** New Zealand
59 M1 **Paromay** Russian Federation
110 D7 **Paron** Arkansas U.S.A.
141 G8 **Paroo** *R* Queensland Australia
139 G4 **Paroo Chan** New South Wales Australia
77 G2 **Paropamisus** *mts* Afghanistan
70 F6 **Paroreang, Bk** *mt* Sulawesi
46 G7 **Páros** *isld* Greece
127 J3 **Parottee Pt** Jamaica
103 M4 **Parowan** Utah U.S.A.
129 H6 **Parque Indigena do Xingu** *nat park* Brazil
99 T8 **Parr** Indiana U.S.A.
112 F3 **Parr** South Carolina U.S.A.
8 C5 **Parracombe** England
133 C5 **Parral** Chile
139 K5 **Parramatta** New South Wales Australia
95 M9 **Parramore I** Virginia U.S.A.
124 H5 **Parras de la Fuente** Mexico
8 D5 **Parrett, R** England
111 J8 **Parrish** Alabama U.S.A.
113 E10 **Parrish** Florida U.S.A.
112 G5 **Parris I** South Carolina U.S.A.
112 C6 **Parrott** Georgia U.S.A.
94 G9 **Parrott** Virginia U.S.A.
122 H8 **Parrsboro** Nova Scotia Canada
119 N9 **Parry** Saskatchewan Canada
115 L4 **Parry B** Northwest Territories Canada
120 K7 **Parry I** Ontario Canada
114 H2 **Parry Is** Northwest Territories Canada
115 M2 **Parry, Kap** Greenland
127 N3 **Parrylands** Trinidad
142 B5 **Parry Ra** W Australia Australia
77 B6 **Pars** *oil well* Persian Gulf
33 N7 **Parsau** Germany
37 M5 **Parsberg** Germany
41 M3 **Parseier Spitze** *mt* Austria
98 D2 **Parshall** North Dakota U.S.A.
103 K3 **Parsnip Pk** Nevada U.S.A.
107 P4 **Parsons** Kansas U.S.A.
110 H6 **Parsons** Tennessee U.S.A.
94 H7 **Parsons** West Virginia U.S.A.
123 P3 **Parson's Pond** Newfoundland Canada
43 E11 **Partanna** Sicily
26 J4 **Pårtefjället** *mt* Sweden
36 E4 **Partenheim** Germany
21 K8 **Parthenay** France
46 F7 **Parthénion** Greece
124 D5 **Partida** *isld* Mexico
43 E10 **Partinico** Sicily
56 D2 **Partizansk** Russian Federation
59 K3 **Partizansk** Russian Federation
120 K2 **Partridge** *R* Ontario Canada
107 M4 **Partridge** Kansas U.S.A.
123 R5 **Partridgeberry Hills** Newfoundland Canada
119 U1 **Partridge Breast L** Manitoba Canada
123 Q3 **Partridge Pt** Newfoundland Canada
129 H4 **Paru** *R* Brazil
145 E1 **Parua Bay** New Zealand
77 L2 **Parvan** *prov* Afghanistan
66 C6 **Paryang** China
27 H15 **Påryd** Sweden
89 E6 **Parys** S Africa
102 G7 **Pasadena** California U.S.A.
109 G9 **Pasadena** Texas U.S.A.
128 B4 **Pasado, C** Ecuador
133 E3 **Pasaje** *R* Argentina
124 H5 **Pasaje** Mexico
106 G5 **Pasamonte** New Mexico U.S.A.
70 F5 **Pasangkaiu** Sulawesi
69 E14 **Pasarbantal** Sumatra
77 C4 **Pasargadae** Iran
69 E14 **Pasarseblat** Sumatra
71 H7 **Pasarwadjo** Indonesia
111 H11 **Pascagoula** *R* Mississippi U.S.A.
121 N4 **Pascalis** Quebec Canada
48 K3 **Paşcani** Romania
128 C6 **Pasco** *dept* Peru
100 F3 **Pasco** Washington U.S.A.
95 Q5 **Pascoag** Rhode I U.S.A.
130 H5 **Pascoal, Mte** Brazil
142 B5 **Pascoe I** W Australia Australia
140 E3 **Pascoe Inlet** Queensland Australia
141 G2 **Pascoe, R** Queensland Australia
120 A2 **Pascopee** Ontario Canada
133 C7 **Pascua** *R* Chile
18 G2 **Pas-de-Calais** *dept* France
22 C3 **Pas en Artois** France
33 T5 **Pasewalk** Germany
52 D4 **Pasha** Russian Federation
52 J3 **Pashnya** Russian Federation
71 E3 **Pasig** Luzon Philippines
71 J4 **Pasige** *isld* Indonesia
78 H1 **Pasinler** Turkey
70 O10 **Pasirian** Java
69 E12 **Pasirpangarayan** Sumatra
69 F10 **Pasir Putih** Malaysia
71 K8 **Pasitelu, Pulau Pulau** *islds* Indonesia
27 H14 **Påskallavik** Sweden
102 B2 **Paskenta** California U.S.A.
31 M1 **Pasłęk** Poland
143 E10 **Pasley, C** W Australia Australia
29 L4 **Pasmajärvi** Finland
42 G5 **Pašman** *isld* Croatia
138 E4 **Pasmore** *R* South Australia Australia
77 H7 **Pasni** Pakistan
133 D6 **Paso de Indios** Argentina
125 M4 **Paso del Cascal** *mt* Nicaragua
133 F3 **Paso de los Libres** Argentina
133 F4 **Paso de los Toros** Uruguay
130 B10 **Paso de Patria** Paraguay
68 B2 **Pasok** Burma
133 C6 **Paso Limay** Argentina
125 M2 **Paso Reál** Honduras
133 C7 **Paso Rio Mayo** Argentina
102 D6 **Paso Robles** California U.S.A.
122 G5 **Paspébiac** Quebec Canada
119 M8 **Pasqua** Saskatchewan Canada
119 O5 **Pasquia Hills** Saskatchewan Canada
119 Q5 **Pasquia R** Manitoba Canada
112 L1 **Pasquotank R** North Carolina U.S.A.
77 C5 **Pas Rūdak** Iran
95 T1 **Passadumkeag** Maine U.S.A.
20 F8 **Passage du Gois** France
120 B4 **Passage I** Ontario Canada
99 S1 **Passage I** Michigan U.S.A.
113 E10 **Pass-a-Grille Beach** Florida U.S.A.
95 N6 **Passaic** New Jersey U.S.A.
21 J4 **Passais** France
38 H4 **Passau** Germany
40 D2 **Passavant** France
111 G11 **Pass Christian** Mississippi U.S.A.
101 T8 **Pass Cr** Wyoming U.S.A.
22 E2 **Passendale** Belgium
43 G12 **Passero, C** Sicily
123 Q6 **Pass I** Newfoundland Canada
71 F5 **Passi** Philippines
41 O4 **Passiria, Val** Italy
99 S1 **Pass L** Ontario Canada
120 B4 **Pass Lake** Ontario Canada
15 C4 **Pass of Brander** Scotland
133 H2 **Passos** Brazil
128 C4 **Pastaza** *prov* Ecuador
122 F3 **Pasteur, L** Quebec Canada
128 C3 **Pasto** Colombia
116 F5 **Pastol B** Alaska U.S.A.
9 H2 **Paston** England
103 P5 **Pastora Pk** Arizona U.S.A.
129 K5 **Pastos Bons** Brazil
71 E1 **Pasuquin** Luzon Philippines
70 O9 **Pasuruan** Java
52 B6 **Pasvalys** Lithuania
52 C1 **Pasvikelv** *R* Norway
119 O6 **Paswegin** Saskatchewan Canada
31 M2 **Pasym** Poland
48 F3 **Pásztó** Hungary
86 D4 **Pata** Cent Afr Republic
71 E8 **Pata** *isld* Philippines
133 C7 **Patagonia** *terr* Chile/Arg
103 O10 **Patagonia** Arizona U.S.A.
100 H3 **Pataha** *R* Washington U.S.A.
77 K1 **Pata Kesar** Afghanistan
130 G10 **Patamuté** Brazil
75 L5 **Patan** Nepal
71 B2 **Patani** Indonesia
95 L7 **Patapsco** *R* Maryland U.S.A.
21 O5 **Patay** France
138 F6 **Patchewollock** Victoria Australia
95 P6 **Patchogue** Long I, New York U.S.A.
88 H3 **Pate** *isld* Kenya
145 E3 **Patea** New Zealand
144 C6 **Patearoa** New Zealand
85 F7 **Pategi** Nigeria
43 F11 **Paternò** Sicily
45 R8 **Paternopoli** Italy
100 F1 **Pateros** Washington U.S.A.
141 H8 **Paterson** *R* Queensland Australia
95 N6 **Paterson** New Jersey U.S.A.
100 F4 **Paterson** Washington U.S.A.
144 B7 **Paterson Inlet** New Zealand
142 D5 **Paterson Ra** W Australia Australia
25 G2 **Paterswolde** Netherlands
74 F2 **Pathankot** India
74 F9 **Pathardi** India
Pathein *see* **Bassein**
101 T7 **Pathfinder Res** Wyoming U.S.A.
13 F2 **Pathhead** Lothian Scotland
12 D3 **Pathhead** Strathclyde Scotland
68 D7 **Pathiu** Thailand
119 N6 **Pathlow** Saskatchewan Canada
74 G9 **Pathri** India
68 E5 **Pathum Thani** Thailand
70 N9 **Pati** Java
128 C3 **Patia** *R* Colombia
74 G3 **Patiala** India
143 F6 **Patience Well** W Australia Australia
70 G7 **Patiro Tg** *C* Sulawesi
128 C6 **Pativilca** Peru
70 N10 **Patjitan** Java
75 Q5 **Pātkai Bum** *reg* India
109 M2 **Pat Mayse Res** Texas U.S.A.
47 H7 **Pátmos** *isld* Greece
111 C8 **Patmos** Arkansas U.S.A.
75 L6 **Patna** India
12 D3 **Patna** Scotland
75 K8 **Patnagarh** India
71 F3 **Patnanongan** *isld* Luzon Philippines
78 J2 **Patnos** Turkey
145 F3 **Patoka** New Zealand
110 G3 **Patoka** Illinois U.S.A.
110 K3 **Patoka** *R* Indiana U.S.A.
99 M7 **Paton** Iowa U.S.A.
130 H9 **Patos** Brazil
129 J7 **Patos de Minas** Brazil
127 N1 **Patos, I** Trinidad
100 C1 **Patos I** Washington U.S.A.
131 H3 **Patos, Lagoa dos** Brazil
108 A5 **Patos, Laguna de** Mexico
131 E3 **Patos, L. de los** Santa Fé Argentina
131 B3 **Patos, R. de los** Argentina
133 D4 **Patquía** Argentina
46 E6 **Pátrai** Greece
Patras Greece *see* **Pátrai**
28 R9 **Patreksfjördhur** *inlet* Iceland
118 F8 **Patricia** Alberta Canada
98 E6 **Patricia** South Dakota U.S.A.
140 B5 **Patricia, Mt** N Terr Australia
133 B7 **Patricio Lynch, I** Chile
13 G5 **Patrick Brompton** England
121 T7 **Patrie, La** Quebec Canada
110 M3 **Patriot** Indiana U.S.A.
133 H1 **Patrocinio** Brazil
111 K10 **Patsaliga** *R* Alabama U.S.A.
41 O3 **Patscherkofel** *mt* Austria
52 C1 **Patsoyoki** *R* Russian Federation
43 C8 **Pattada** Sardinia
57 D6 **Pattakesar** Uzbekistan
70 F7 **Pattalasa** Sulawesi Indonesia
76 C6 **Pattanapuram** India
69 E9 **Pattani** *R* Thailand
69 E9 **Pattani** Thailand
95 S7 **Patten** Maine U.S.A.
32 L8 **Pattensen** Germany
13 F5 **Patterdale** England
102 C4 **Patterson** California U.S.A.
112 E6 **Patterson** Georgia U.S.A.
101 M5 **Patterson** Idaho U.S.A.
111 E12 **Patterson** Louisiana U.S.A.
94 H7 **Patterson Cr** West Virginia U.S.A.
117 F3 **Patterson, Mt** Yukon Territory Canada
102 E5 **Patterson Mt** California U.S.A.
99 V4 **Patterson, Pt** Michigan U.S.A.
71 N9 **Patti** Indonesia
43 F10 **Patti** Sicily
140 B4 **Pattie Cr** N Terr Australia
43 G10 **Patti, G. di** Sicily
80 B8 **Pattish** *R* Israel
111 F10 **Pattison** Mississippi U.S.A.
94 J6 **Patton** Pennsylvania U.S.A.
99 M9 **Pattonsburg** Missouri U.S.A.
130 H9 **Patu** Brazil
78 H2 **Patu** Turkey
75 O7 **Patuakhali** Bangladesh
118 K3 **Patuanak** Saskatchewan Canada
48 H6 **Pătuele** Romania
70 L9 **Patuha, G** *mt* Java
117 J7 **Patullo, Mt** British Columbia Canada
144 D4 **Paturau River** New Zealand
145 F3 **Patutahi** New Zealand
145 E3 **Patutu** *mt* New Zealand
95 L8 **Patuxent** *R* Maryland U.S.A.
146 E8 **Patuxent Ra** Antarctica
18 E9 **Pau** France
145 D1 **Paua** New Zealand
129 J5 **Pau D'Arco** Brazil
21 O7 **Paudy** France
121 O7 **Paugan Falls** Quebec Canada
18 E7 **Pauillac** France
128 E5 **Pauini** Brazil
68 B2 **Pauk** Burma
68 A2 **Pauktaw** Burma
101 M7 **Paul** Idaho U.S.A.
38 H8 **Paularo** Italy
114 G4 **Paulatuk** Northwest Territories Canada
103 M7 **Paulden** Arizona U.S.A.
94 C5 **Paulding** Ohio U.S.A.
18 H9 **Paulhan** France
115 N6 **Paul I** Labrador, Nfld Canada
116 H9 **Paul I** Alaska U.S.A.
100 F5 **Paulina** Oregon U.S.A.
33 R7 **Paulinenaue** Germany
Paulis *see* **Isiro**
130 J9 **Paulista** Brazil
129 K5 **Paulistana** Brazil
99 L7 **Paullina** Iowa U.S.A.
41 K7 **Paullo** Italy
21 N8 **Paulnay** France
130 H10 **Paulo Alfonso, Cachoeira de** *falls* Brazil
25 C3 **Paulowna** Netherlands
107 N7 **Pauls Valley** Oklahoma U.S.A.
37 M5 **Paulushofen** Germany
20 G8 **Paulx** France
68 C4 **Paung** Burma
68 B3 **Paungde** Burma
74 H8 **Pauni** India
74 H3 **Pauri** India
37 M2 **Pausa** Germany
128 D7 **Pausa** Peru
33 S7 **Pausin** Germany
128 D2 **Pauto** *R* Colombia
26 J7 **Pauträsk** Sweden
22 G5 **Pauvres** France
135 T3 **Pauwela** Hawaiian Is
103 M3 **Pavant Ra** Utah U.S.A.
55 C2 **Pavda** Russian Federation
46 G2 **Pavel Banya** Bulgaria
54 L3 **Pavelets** Russian Federation
44 F1 **Pavia** Italy
117 N10 **Pavilion** British Columbia Canada
94 K4 **Pavilion** New York U.S.A.
101 R6 **Pavillion** Wyoming U.S.A.
21 M2 **Pavilly** France
27 M15 **Pāvilosta** Latvia
52 G5 **Pavino** Russian Federation
46 G1 **Pavlikeni** Bulgaria
55 G4 **Pavlodar** Kazakhstan
116 G9 **Pavlof** Alaska U.S.A.
116 F9 **Pavlof Harbour** Aleutian Is
116 G9 **Pavlof Vol** Alaska U.S.A.
54 G8 **Pavlograd** Ukraine
55 F4 **Pavlogradka** Russian Federation
55 F5 **Pavlovka** Kazakhstan
55 C3 **Pavlovka** Bashkirskaya Respublika Russian Federation
52 F6 **Pavlovo** Russian Federation
56 B4 **Pavlovsk** Altayskiy Kray Russian Federation
52 D5 **Pavlovsk** Leningradskaya obl Russian Federation
55 D4 **Pavlovskiy** Kazakhstan
52 H5 **Pavlovskiy** Permskaya obl Russian Federation
113 D7 **Pavo** Georgia U.S.A.
45 J3 **Pavullo nel Frignano** Italy
107 O5 **Pawhuska** Oklahoma U.S.A.
119 Q3 **Pawistik** Manitoba Canada
95 O3 **Pawlet** Vermont U.S.A.
8 D5 **Pawlett** England
112 H4 **Pawleys Island** South Carolina U.S.A.
68 C3 **Pawn** *R* Burma
99 R10 **Pawnee** Illinois U.S.A.
107 O5 **Pawnee** Oklahoma U.S.A.
109 K7 **Pawnee** Texas U.S.A.
99 L9 **Pawnee City** Nebraska U.S.A.
98 C9 **Pawnee Cr** Colorado U.S.A.
107 L3 **Pawnee Rock** Kansas U.S.A.
94 B4 **Paw Paw** Michigan U.S.A.
94 J7 **Paw Paw** West Virginia U.S.A.
95 Q5 **Pawtucket** Rhode I U.S.A.
46 G9 **Paximádhia** *isld* Crete Greece
Paxoi *see* **Paxos**
47 P13 **Paxos** *isld* Greece
116 P5 **Paxson** Alaska U.S.A.
116 P5 **Paxson L** Alaska U.S.A.
99 S9 **Paxton** Illinois U.S.A.
98 E8 **Paxton** Nebraska U.S.A.
68 C4 **Payagyi** Burma
71 A2 **Payahe** Halmahera Indonesia
79 G2 **Payas** Turkey
58 E3 **Pa-yen-kao-le** China
40 E4 **Payerne** Switzerland
100 J5 **Payette** *R* Idaho U.S.A.
100 J5 **Payette** Idaho U.S.A.
109 L3 **Pay Hubbard, L** Texas U.S.A.
50 F2 **Pay-Khoy, Khrebet** *mt* Russian Federation
112 D5 **Payne** Georgia U.S.A.
94 C5 **Payne** Ohio U.S.A.
115 M6 **Payne, L** Quebec Canada
102 C1 **Paynes Cr** California U.S.A.
143 C8 **Payne's Find** W Australia Australia
99 M4 **Paynesville** Minnesota U.S.A.
118 J5 **Paynton** Saskatchewan Canada
131 F4 **Paysandu** Uruguay
21 K3 **Pays-d'Auge** *reg* France
21 O2 **Pays-de-Bray** *reg* France
19 N13 **Pays de Dombes** *reg* France
40 F5 **Pays d'Enhaut** Switzerland
103 N7 **Payson** Arizona U.S.A.
103 N1 **Payson** Utah U.S.A.
57 K6 **Paytug** Uzbekistan
131 B6 **Payún** *vol* Argentina
70 C3 **Payung Tanjong** *C* Sarawak
131 B6 **Payún Matru, Cerros** *hills* Argentina
77 A4 **Pāzanūn** Iran
46 G2 **Pazardzhik** Bulgaria
47 J5 **Pazarköy** Turkey
47 J6 **Pazaryeri** Turkey
124 D5 **Paz, B. de la** Mexico
128 D2 **Paz de Rio** Colombia
42 F3 **Pazin** Croatia
41 M3 **Paznauntal** Austria
52 D5 **Pchevzha** Russian Federation
31 M6 **Pcim** Poland
46 E2 **Pčinja** *R* Macedonia/Serbia
68 D6 **Pe** Burma
111 L10 **Pea** *R* Alabama U.S.A.
117 R6 **Peace Point** Alberta Canada
118 A2 **Peace R** Alberta Canada
117 M7 **Peace R** Br Col/Alberta Canada
113 F10 **Peace R** Florida U.S.A.
117 P7 **Peace River** Alberta Canada
117 O11 **Peachland** British Columbia Canada
103 L6 **Peach Sp** Arizona U.S.A.
94 B2 **Peacock** Michigan U.S.A.
141 J5 **Peak Downs** Queensland Australia
138 D3 **Peake** *R* South Australia Australia
71 D5 **Peaked Pt** Philippines
140 B3 **Peake, Mt** N Terr Australia
143 C7 **Peak Hill** W Australia Australia
102 E7 **Peak Mt** California U.S.A.
141 J6 **Peak Ra** Queensland Australia
103 P3 **Peale, Mt** Utah U.S.A.
100 B9 **Peanut** California U.S.A.
118 D9 **Pearce** Alberta Canada
103 P10 **Pearce** Arizona U.S.A.
140 A2 **Pearce Pt** N Terr Australia
111 C7 **Pearcy** Arkansas U.S.A.
116 H1 **Peard B** Alaska U.S.A.
110 C5 **Pea Ridge Nat. Mil. Park** Arkansas U.S.A.
119 P2 **Pearl** Ontario Canada
110 F2 **Pearl** Illinois U.S.A.
111 F9 **Pearl** Mississippi U.S.A.
111 G11 **Pearl** *R* Miss/Louisiana U.S.A.
109 G10 **Pearland** Texas U.S.A.
134 K5 **Pearl and Hermes Atoll** Hawaiian Is U.S.A.
102 S12 **Pearl City** Hawaiian Is
99 R7 **Pearl City** Illinois U.S.A.
102 S12 **Pearl Hbr** Hawaiian Is
144 A7 **Pearl I** New Zealand
109 H7 **Pearsall** Texas U.S.A.
112 E6 **Pearson** Georgia U.S.A.
138 C5 **Pearson Is** South Australia Australia
119 V2 **Pearson L** Manitoba Canada
114 J2 **Peary Ch** Northwest Territories Canada
109 H1 **Pease** *R* Texas U.S.A.
20 F6 **Péaule** France
99 S3 **Peavy Falls Res** Michigan U.S.A.
142 C5 **Peawah, R** W Australia Australia
88 G10 **Pebane** Mozambique
128 D4 **Pebas** Peru
133 F8 **Pebble I** Falkland Is
70 G5 **Pebengko** Sulawesi
46 D2 **Peć** Serbia Yugoslavia
111 D12 **Pecan Island** Louisiana U.S.A.
130 E9 **Peças, I. das** Brazil
99 R7 **Pecatonica** *R* Illinois U.S.A.
99 R7 **Pecatonica** Illinois U.S.A.
45 J4 **Péccioli** Italy
48 L5 **Pechea** Romania
48 J2 **Pechenezhin** Ukraine
54 H6 **Pechenezhskoye Vodokhranilishche** *res* Ukraine
29 P2 **Pechenga** Russian Federation
55 D1 **Pecherakh** Russian Federation
52 J2 **Pechora** Russian Federation
52 J3 **Pechora** *R* Russian Federation
50 E2 **Pechorskaya Guba** *sea* Russian Federation
52 C5 **Pechory** Russian Federation
48 G4 **Pecica** Romania
100 B7 **Peck** Oregon U.S.A.
33 S5 **Peckatel** Germany
32 K9 **Peckelsheim** Germany
43 B9 **Pecora, C** Sardinia
43 G10 **Pecoraro, M** *mt* Italy
106 E6 **Pecos** New Mexico U.S.A.
106 F6 **Pecos** *R* New Mexico U.S.A.
108 D4 **Pecos** Texas U.S.A.
108 F5 **Pecos** *R* Texas/Mexico U.S.A./Mexico
106 E6 **Pecos Nat. Mon** New Mexico U.S.A.
48 E4 **Pécs** Hungary
48 E4 **Pécsvárad** Hungary
110 B3 **Peculiar** Missouri U.S.A.
125 O6 **Pedasí** Panama
139 H9 **Pedder, L** Tasmania Australia
100 B5 **Pedee** Oregon U.S.A.
127 J5 **Pedernales** Dominican Rep
124 F3 **Pedernales** Mexico
127 N10 **Pedernales** Venezuela
28 H6 **Pedersborg** Denmark
70 L9 **Pedes** Java
79 C4 **Pedhoulas** Cyprus
138 D2 **Pedirka** South Australia Australia
71 A2 **Pediwang** Indonesia
129 K7 **Pedra Azul** Brazil
130 J9 **Pedra, Pta. de** *C* Brazil
128 F6 **Pedras Negras** Brazil
124 H5 **Pedriceña** Mexico
129 J5 **Pedro Afonso** Brazil
126 E6 **Pedro Bank** Caribbean
116 K7 **Pedro Bay** Alaska U.S.A.
126 D3 **Pedro Betancourt** Cuba
126 F6 **Pedro Cays** *reefs* Caribbean
140 D7 **Peebles, Mt** N Terr Australia
142 B5 **Peedamulla** W Australia Australia
12 D5 **Peel** I of Man U.K.
144 C5 **Peel, Mt** New Zealand
103 M7 **Peeples Valley** Arizona U.S.A.
117 Q7 **Peerless L** Alberta Canada
118 A5 **Peers** Alberta Canada
139 G4 **Peery, L** New South Wales Australia
106 G1 **Peetz** Colorado U.S.A.
98 K4 **Peever** South Dakota U.S.A.
144 D5 **Pegasus Bay** New Zealand
37 N1 **Pegau** Germany
38 M7 **Peggau** Austria
44 E3 **Pegli** Italy
37 M4 **Pegnitz** Germany
17 G6 **Pego** Spain
45 J2 **Pegognaga** Italy
101 O7 **Pegram** Idaho U.S.A.
13 G3 **Pegswood** England
69 F13 **Peg Tigabuluh** *mt* Sumatra
68 C4 **Pegu** Burma
69 E13 **Pegunungan Barisan** *mt* Sumatra
69 K12 **Pegunungan Bayang** *mt* Indonesia
68 B3 **Pegu Yoma** *ra* Burma
9 H5 **Pegwell B** England
52 H3 **Pegysh** Russian Federation
46 F3 **Pehčevo** Macedonia
67 B1 **Peijiangchang** China
67 G3 **Pei-Kan-t'ang Tao** *isld* Taiwan
20 F6 **Peillac** France
38 M5 **Peilstein** *mt* Austria
32 M8 **Peine** Germany
133 C8 **Peineta** *mt* Chile
68 B2 **Peinwa** Burma
19 P16 **Peipin** France
Peipsi Järv *see* **Peipus, L**
52 C5 **Peipus, L** Estonia/Rus Fed
41 N2 **Peiting** Germany
133 G2 **Peixe** *R* Brazil
130 C5 **Peixe de Couro, R** Brazil
65 C7 **Pei Xian** China
65 D7 **Pei Xian** China
69 H12 **Pejantan** *isld* Indonesia
48 G6 **Pek** *R* Serbia Yugoslavia
70 F6 **Pekabata** Sulawesi
70 M9 **Pekalongan** Java
69 F11 **Pekan** Malaysia
69 E12 **Pekanbaru** Sumatra
99 R9 **Pekin** Illinois U.S.A.
110 G1 **Pekin** Illinois U.S.A.
98 H2 **Pekin** North Dakota U.S.A.
Peking *see* **Beijing**
117 Q10 **Pekisko** Alberta Canada
29 M5 **Pekkala** Finland
68 C3 **Pekon** Burma
69 E11 **Pelabuhan Kelang** Malaysia
43 E13 **Pelagie, Isole** Italy
45 L4 **Pelago** Italy
46 G5 **Pélagos** *isld* Greece
111 G9 **Pelahatchee** Mississippi U.S.A.
69 F12 **Pelalawan** Sumatra
17 G4 **Pelarda, Sa** *mts* Spain
46 F6 **Pelasyía** Greece
89 F7 **Pelatsoeu** *mt* Lesotho
70 F4 **Pelawanbesar** Kalimantan
31 J2 **Pełczyce** Poland
48 H5 **Peleaga** *mt* Romania
56 H2 **Peleduy** *R* Russian Federation
120 H10 **Pelee Island** Ontario Canada
127 L4 **Pelée, Mt** Martinique W Indies
47 O12 **Pélekas** Greece
71 H5 **Peleng** *isld* Indonesia
71 H5 **Peleng, Selat** *str* Sulawesi
71 H5 **Peleng, Tk** *B* Indonesia
112 C6 **Pelham** Georgia U.S.A.
31 J6 **Pelhřimov** Czech Rep
119 R6 **Pelican B** Manitoba Canada
113 L11 **Pelican Harbour** Bahamas
118 D3 **Pelican L** Alberta Canada
119 S9 **Pelican L** Manitoba Canada
119 O3 **Pelican L** Saskatchewan Canada
99 O1 **Pelican L** Minnesota U.S.A.
99 R4 **Pelican L** Wisconsin U.S.A.
118 E3 **Pelican Portage** Alberta Canada
141 G3 **Pelican R** Queensland Australia
119 R6 **Pelican Rapids** Manitoba Canada
98 K3 **Pelican Rapids** Minnesota U.S.A.
48 L3 **Peliniya** Moldova
59 L1 **Peliny Osipenko, imeni** Russian Federation
112 F4 **Pelion** South Carolina U.S.A.
26 J5 **Peljekaise Nat. Park** Sweden
42 H6 **Pelješac** *pen* Croatia
29 N4 **Pelkosenniemi** Finland
52 D3 **Pelkula** Russian Federation
32 G9 **Pelkum** Germany
43 G8 **Pella** Italy
80 F4 **Pella** Jordan
99 O8 **Pella** Iowa U.S.A.
111 K8 **Pell City** Alabama U.S.A.
133 E5 **Pellegrini** Argentina
133 D5 **Pellegrini, L** Argentina
21 H5 **Pellerine, la** France
20 G7 **Pellerin, le** France
45 M1 **Pellestrina** Italy
119 U2 **Pelletier L** Manitoba Canada
21 N8 **Pellevoisin** France
140 D3 **Pellew C** N Terr Australia
36 B4 **Pellingen** Germany
29 L5 **Pello** Finland
21 K6 **Pellouailles** France
94 C1 **Pellston** Michigan U.S.A.
30 D1 **Pellworm** *isld* Germany
119 Q7 **Pelly** Saskatchewan Canada
117 E4 **Pelly** *R* Yukon Territory Canada
115 L4 **Pelly Bay** Northwest Territories Canada
117 E4 **Pelly Crossing** Yukon Territory Canada
114 J4 **Pelly L** Northwest Territories Canada
117 G5 **Pelly Mts** Yukon Territory Canada
71 J8 **Pelokang** *isld* Indonesia
46 E7 **Pelopónnisos** *admin region* Greece
43 G11 **Peloritani, Mi** *mts* Sicily
145 D4 **Pelorus Sound** New Zealand
131 H3 **Pelotas** Brazil
130 D10 **Pelotas, R.das** Brazil
46 G1 **Pelovo** Bulgaria
31 L2 **Pelplin** Poland
143 A8 **Pelsart Group** *islds* W Australia Australia
33 T5 **Pelsin** Germany
110 C6 **Pelsor** Arkansas U.S.A.
29 L3 **Peltovuoma** Finland
44 B2 **Pelvo d'Elva** *mt* Italy
19 Q15 **Pelvoux, Mt** France
55 D1 **Pelym** *R* Russian Federation
55 D2 **Pelym** Russian Federation
55 D1 **Pelymskiy Tuman, Oz** *L* Russian Federation
8 B7 **Pelynt** England
112 E3 **Pelzer** South Carolina U.S.A.
33 N4 **Pelzerhaken** Germany
120 G5 **Pemache, R** Ontario Canada
95 S1 **Pemadumcook L** Maine U.S.A.
70 M9 **Pemalang** Java
70 M9 **Pemalang, Ujung** *C* Java
71 H5 **Pemali, Tg** *C* Sulawesi
69 J12 **Pemangkat** Indonesia
70 E5 **Pemarung, P** Kalimantan
69 D11 **Pematangsiantar** Sumatra
88 H8 **Pemba** Mozambique
87 E9 **Pemba** Zambia
87 H8 **Pemba, B.de** Mozambique
88 G4 **Pemba I** Tanzania
143 B10 **Pemberton** W Australia Australia
117 M10 **Pemberton** British Columbia Canada
98 H1 **Pembina** *R* Manitoba Canada
119 U10 **Pembina** North Dakota U.S.A.
119 T9 **Pembina Mt** Manitoba Canada
118 B5 **Pembina Oil Fields** Alberta Canada
118 C5 **Pembina Prov. Park** Alberta Canada
118 C4 **Pembina R** Alberta Canada
99 T4 **Pembine** Wisconsin U.S.A.
121 N7 **Pembroke** Ontario Canada
112 F5 **Pembroke** Georgia U.S.A.
110 J5 **Pembroke** Kentucky U.S.A.
112 H3 **Pembroke** North Carolina U.S.A.
94 G9 **Pembroke** Virginia U.S.A.
8 B4 **Pembroke** Wales
133 F8 **Pembroke, C** Falkland Is
144 A6 **Pembroke, Mt** New Zealand
9 G5 **Pembury** England
70 B5 **Pemuar** Kalimantan
127 J5 **Peña** Dominican Rep
106 D6 **Penablanca** New Mexico U.S.A.
95 Q3 **Penacook** New Hampshire U.S.A.
17 G2 **Peña de Oroel** *mt ra* Spain
16 B3 **Penafiel** Portugal
16 E3 **Peñafiel** Spain
17 G4 **Peñagolosa** *mt* Spain
127 O3 **Penal** Trinidad
8 B4 **Penally** Wales
70 D3 **Penambo Ra** Kalimantan
16 C3 **Peña Mira** *mt* Spain
70 E2 **Penampang** Sabah
131 B2 **Peña Negra, Pasco de** Arg/Chile
125 K6 **Peña Nevada, Cerro** *mt* Mexico
Penang *see* **Pinang** *isld*
130 E7 **Penápolis** Brazil
16 D1 **Peña Prieta** *mt* Spain
16 D4 **Peñaranda de Bracamonte** Spain
95 M6 **Pen Argyl** Pennsylvania U.S.A.
139 G5 **Penarie** New South Wales Australia
17 G4 **Peñarroya** *mt* Spain
16 D6 **Peñarroya-Pueblonuevo** Spain
8 C5 **Penarth** Wales
16 C1 **Peña Rubia** *mt* Spain
17 G2 **Peña, Sa. de la** *mts* Spain
124 M4 **Peñas Blancas** Nicaragua
16 D1 **Peñas, C. de** Spain
106 E5 **Penasco** New Mexico U.S.A.
108 C3 **Penasco, Rio** *R* New Mexico U.S.A.
16 E3 **Peñas de Cervera** Spain
17 F6 **Peñas de San Pedro** Spain
133 C7 **Penas, G.de** Chile
69 B10 **Penasi, Pulau** *isld* Sumatra
127 N9 **Peñas, Pta** Venezuela
16 C2 **Peña Trevinca** *mt* Spain
16 D1 **Peña Vieja** *mt* Spain
100 H3 **Penawawa** Washington U.S.A.
65 F4 **Pen-ch'i** China
146 J12 **Penck, C** Antarctica
131 C4 **Pencoso, Alto de** *mt* Argentina
70 C5 **Pendadahian** Kalimantan
46 E4 **Pendálofon** Greece
118 F9 **Pendant d'Oreille** Alberta Canada
86 C4 **Pende** *R* Cent Afr Republic
46 F6 **Pendelikón** *mt* Greece
85 B7 **Pendembu** Sierra Leone
130 H8 **Pendencia** Brazil
142 E3 **Pender** W Australia Australia
98 K7 **Pender** Nebraska U.S.A.
142 E3 **Pender Bay** W Australia Australia
144 A6 **Pender, Mt** New Zealand
47 N11 **Pendik** Turkey
8 B4 **Pendine** Wales
13 F6 **Pendlebury** England
13 F6 **Pendle Hill** England
94 B7 **Pendleton** Indiana U.S.A.
100 G4 **Pendleton** Oregon U.S.A.
112 E3 **Pendleton** South Carolina U.S.A.
117 J6 **Pendleton, Mt** British Columbia Canada
69 F14 **Pendopo** Sumatra
100 H1 **Pend Oreille** *R* Washington U.S.A.
117 P11 **Pend Oreille, L** Idaho U.S.A.
101 N1 **Pendroy** Montana U.S.A.
69 J13 **Penebangan** *isld* Indonesia
16 B3 **Peneda** *mt* Portugal
129 L6 **Penedo** Brazil
20 F7 **Penestin** France
94 J5 **Penfield** Pennsylvania U.S.A.
70 L9 **Pengalengan** Java
67 B1 **Peng'an** China
67 G4 **P'eng-chia Hsü** *isld* Taiwan
86 D7 **Penge** Zaire
67 F5 **P'eng-hu Lieh-tao** *isld* Taiwan
67 F5 **P'eng-hu Tao** *isld* Taiwan
69 J12 **Pengiki** *isld* Indonesia
67 E4 **Pengkou** China
65 E6 **Penglai** China
58 G5 **Peng-pu** China
67 A1 **Pengshan** China
67 C2 **Pengshui** China
139 H8 **Penguin** Tasmania Australia
142 F2 **Penguin Deeps** Timor Sea
67 B1 **Pengxi** China
67 A1 **Peng Xian** China
67 E2 **Pengze** China
130 E10 **Penha** Brazil
20 A5 **Penhir, Pte de** France
118 D6 **Penhold** Alberta Canada
8 D4 **Penhow** Wales
120 F3 **Penhurst** Ontario Canada
44 F2 **Penice** *mt* Italy
16 A5 **Peniche** Portugal
13 E2 **Penicuik** Scotland
70 P10 **Penida** *isld* Indonesia
37 O2 **Penig** Germany
71 G5 **Peninsula Pt** Philippines
69 E10 **Peninsular Malaysia** S E Asia
17 H4 **Peñíscola** Spain
13 G6 **Penistone** England
70 M9 **Penju, Teluk** *B* Java
78 K4 **Penjwin** Iran
38 H8 **Penk** Austria
56 B3 **Pen'ki** Russian Federation
8 D2 **Penkridge** England
8 C1 **Penmaenmawr** Wales
20 B6 **Penmarc'h** France
20 B6 **Penmarc'h, Pte de** France
118 K5 **Penn** Saskatchewan Canada
45 M4 **Pennabilli** Italy
45 L4 **Penna, M** *mt* Italy
118 J8 **Pennant** Saskatchewan Canada
122 J9 **Pennant Pt** Nova Scotia Canada
42 F6 **Penna, Pta. della** Italy
42 F6 **Penne** Italy
18 F8 **Penne d'Agenais** France
146 C11 **Pennell Bank** *sea feature* Antarctica
146 C12 **Pennell Coast** *coast* Antarctica
138 E6 **Penneshaw** South Australia Australia
122 F8 **Pennfield** New Brunswick Canada
40 G5 **Pennine, Alpi** *mts* Switzerland
7 J8 **Pennine Chain** *mts* England
26 G7 **Penningkejsen** *mt* Norway/Sweden
95 N6 **Pennington** New Jersey U.S.A.
109 M4 **Pennington** Texas U.S.A.
94 D10 **Pennington Gap** Virginia U.S.A.
42 E5 **Pennino, M** *mt* Italy
95 M6 **Pennsburg** Pennsylvania U.S.A.
95 M7 **Penns Grove** New Jersey U.S.A.
94 H6 **Pennsylvania** *state* U.S.A.
95 K4 **Penn Yan** New York U.S.A.
12 B1 **Pennyghael** Scotland
115 N4 **Penny Ice Cap** Northwest Territories Canada
146 D11 **Penny Point** *pt* Antarctica
115 K2 **Penny Str** Northwest Territories Canada
52 D6 **Peno** Russian Federation
95 T1 **Penobscot** *R* Maine U.S.A.
95 T2 **Penobscot B** Maine U.S.A.
122 G8 **Penobsquis** New Brunswick Canada
138 F6 **Penola** South Australia Australia
124 G5 **Peñón Blanco** Mexico
138 C4 **Penong** South Australia Australia
125 O5 **Penonomé** Panama

100 C8 **Penoyar** California U.S.A.
8 B2 **Penrhyndeudraeth** Wales
139 K5 **Penrith** New South Wales Australia
13 F4 **Penrith** England
8 A7 **Penryn** England
111 J11 **Pensacola** Florida U.S.A.
113 K10 **Pensacola Cay** Bahamas
146 E8 **Pensacola Mts** Antarctica
119 N8 **Pense** Saskatchewan Canada
8 D5 **Pensford** England
138 F7 **Penshurst** Victoria Australia
9 G5 **Penshurst** England
70 E2 **Pensiangan** Sabah
137 O5 **Pentecost I** Vanuatu
142 G3 **Pentecost, R** W Australia Australia
Pentecôte, Î *see* **Pentecost I**
122 E4 **Pentecôte, L** Quebec Canada
48 K5 **Penteleu** *mt* Romania
117 O11 **Penticton** British Columbia Canada
141 H5 **Pentland** Queensland Australia
15 E2 **Pentland Firth** Scotland
13 E2 **Pentland Hills** Scotland
15 F2 **Pentland Skerries** Orkney Scotland
8 B1 **Pentraeth** Wales
8 C1 **Pentre-Foelas** Wales
94 A3 **Pentwater** Michigan U.S.A.
131 E5 **Penuajo** Argentina
69 G13 **Penuba** Indonesia
69 G14 **Penuguan** Sumatra
69 F10 **Penunjuk, Tanjong** *C* Malaysia
20 D4 **Penvénan** France
68 C3 **Penwegon** Burma
8 C1 **Pen-y-benclog** Wales
8 C3 **Penybont** Wales
8 B1 **Pen-y-groes** Wales
53 F7 **Penza** Russian Federation
119 M7 **Penzance** Saskatchewan Canada
9 F6 **Penzance** England
41 O2 **Penzberg** Germany
51 Q2 **Penzhinskaya Guba** *G* Russian Federation
33 S6 **Penzlin** Germany
100 H3 **Peola** Washington U.S.A.
101 R1 **Peoples Cr** Montana U.S.A.
103 M8 **Peoria** Arizona U.S.A.
99 R9 **Peoria** Illinois U.S.A.
99 T8 **Peotone** Illinois U.S.A.
89 C6 **Pepani** *watercourse* S Africa
85 B7 **Pepel** Sierra Leone
25 F3 **Peperga** Netherlands
145 D4 **Pepin I** New Zealand
99 O5 **Pepin, L** Wisconsin U.S.A.
22 K2 **Pepinster** Belgium
130 D10 **Pepiri Guaçu. R** Brazil
44 B3 **Pépoiri, Mt** France
46 D3 **Peqin** Albania
131 H3 **Pequena, L** Brazil
124 C4 **Pequeña, Pta** *C* Mexico
103 K1 **Pequop Mts** Nevada U.S.A.
99 M3 **Pequot Lakes** Minnesota U.S.A.
37 O7 **Perach** Germany
141 F2 **Pera Hd** Queensland Australia
70 M9 **Perahu, Gunung** *mt* Java
69 E10 **Perai** Malaysia
69 D10 **Perak** *isld* Malaysia
69 E10 **Perak** *prov* Malaysia
46 F6 **Perakhóra** Greece
38 G8 **Peralba** *mt* Italy
106 D7 **Peralta** New Mexico U.S.A.
46 G9 **Pérama** Crete Greece
69 F13 **Peranap** Sumatra
29 M5 **Perä-Posio** Finland
29 K9 **Peräseinäjoki** Finland
80 E3 **Perazon** Israel
122 H5 **Percé** Quebec Canada
21 J3 **Percée, Pte. de la** France
18 G10 **Perche, Col de la** *pass* France
21 M4 **Perche, Coteaux du** *hills* France
8 B2 **Percilan Hd** Wales
45 N5 **Percile** Italy
99 L9 **Percival** Iowa U.S.A.
142 E5 **Percival Ls** W Australia Australia
21 H4 **Percy** France
110 G3 **Percy** Illinois U.S.A.
99 N8 **Percy** Iowa U.S.A.
141 K5 **Percy Is** Queensland Australia
143 D9 **Percy, L** W Australia Australia
133 D6 **Perdido** *R* Argentina
17 H2 **Perdido** *mt* Spain
111 J11 **Perdido** *R* Alabama/Florida U.S.A.
18 F10 **Perdido, M** *mt* Spain
130 B7 **Perdido, R** Brazil
118 K6 **Perdue** Saskatchewan Canada
122 B3 **Perdu, L** Quebec Canada
99 U6 **Pere** *R* Michigan U.S.A.
48 G2 **Perechin** Ukraine
48 J2 **Pereginskoye** Ukraine
50 F2 **Peregrebnoye** Russian Federation
128 C3 **Pereira** Colombia
130 D7 **Pereira Barreto** Brazil
Pereira de Eça *see* **Ondjiva**
129 G5 **Pereirinha** Brazil
17 H4 **Perello** Spain
94 A3 **Pere Marquette** *R* Michigan U.S.A.
146 G13 **Peremennyy, C** Antarctica
48 J1 **Peremyshlyany** Ukraine
143 B8 **Perenjori** W Australia Australia
116 L7 **Perenosa B** Alaska U.S.A.
52 E6 **Pereslavl' Zalesskiy** Russian Federation
45 O5 **Pereto** Italy
48 H2 **Pereval Veretski** *mt* Ukraine
55 B5 **Perevolotskiy** Russian Federation
54 C6 **Pereyaslav Khmel'nitskiy** Ukraine
133 D3 **Pérez** Chile
100 D8 **Perez** California U.S.A.
69 C8 **Perforated I** Thailand
131 E4 **Pergamino** Argentina
Pergamum *see* **Bergama**
45 N4 **Pergola** Italy
52 E4 **Perguba** Russian Federation
99 L3 **Perham** Minnesota U.S.A.
69 F10 **Perhentian Besar** *isld* Malaysia
29 L8 **Perho** Finland
29 L8 **Perhojoki** *R* Finland
48 F4 **Periam** Romania
121 T3 **Péribonca** *R* Quebec Canada
121 S4 **Péribonca** Quebec Canada
122 A3 **Peribonca L** Quebec Canada
133 D2 **Perico** Argentina
124 F5 **Pericos** Mexico
20 H3 **Périers** France
129 J3 **Perigoso, Can** Brazil
18 F7 **Périgueux** France
127 H9 **Perijá, Sa. de** *mts* Colombia/Venezuela
123 P2 **Peril Rock** Quebec Canada
117 F7 **Peril Str** Alaska U.S.A.
72 E6 **Perim** *isld* Yemen
118 C2 **Perimeter Highway** Manitoba Canada
130 H10 **Periquito, Sa do** *mts* Brazil
48 K6 **Periş** Romania
46 E5 **Peristéri** *mt* Greece
133 C7 **Perito Moreno** Argentina
47 P13 **Perivóli** Greece
76 C5 **Periyakulam** India
95 M6 **Perkasie** Pennsylvania U.S.A.
69 G13 **Perkat, Tanjong** *C* Indonesia
112 F5 **Perkins** Georgia U.S.A.
111 C11 **Perkins** Louisiana U.S.A.
99 T4 **Perkins** Michigan U.S.A.
111 G11 **Perkinston** Mississippi U.S.A.
103 M7 **Perkinsville** Arizona U.S.A.
53 F11 **Per Klukhorskiy** *pass* Georgia
42 G5 **Perković** Croatia
22 L5 **Perl** Germany
41 P1 **Perlach** Germany
125 P5 **Perlas, Arch. de las** *islds* Panama
33 P6 **Perleberg** Germany
37 P6 **Perlesreut** Germany
54 K5 **Perlevka** Russian Federation
98 K2 **Perley** Minnesota U.S.A.
48 F5 **Perlez** Serbia Yugoslavia
69 E9 **Perlis** *prov* Malaysia
52 J5 **Perm'** Russian Federation
101 L2 **Perma** Montana U.S.A.
53 F11 **Per Mamisonskiy** *pass* Georgia/Rus Fed
53 F11 **Per Marukhskiy** *pass* Georgia/Rus Fed
52 G5 **Permas** Russian Federation
46 D4 **Përmet** Albania
55 C2 **Permskaya Oblast'** *prov* Russian Federation
Pernambuco *see* **Recife**
130 H9 **Pernambuco** *state* Brazil
138 D4 **Pernatty Lagoon** South Australia Australia
107 N7 **Pernell** Oklahoma U.S.A.
22 C3 **Pernes** France
46 F2 **Pernik** Bulgaria
29 K11 **Perniö** Finland
25 B5 **Pernis** Netherlands
40 C5 **Peron** France
143 A7 **Peron, C** W Australia Australia
140 B2 **Peron Is** N Terr Australia
22 D4 **Péronne** France
22 G3 **Peronnes** Belgium
143 A7 **Peron Pen** W Australia Australia
21 O5 **Péronville** France
18 G10 **Perpignan** France
112 L1 **Perquimans R** North Carolina U.S.A.
8 A7 **Perranporth** England
21 O4 **Perray-en-Yvelines, le** France
20 D5 **Perret** France
21 N3 **Perriers-sur-Andelle** France
109 J2 **Perrin** Texas U.S.A.
113 G12 **Perrine** Florida U.S.A.
102 G8 **Perris** California U.S.A.
40 B2 **Perrogney** France
108 B1 **Perro, Laguna del** New Mexico U.S.A.
121 N4 **Perron** Quebec Canada
20 D4 **Perros-Guirec** France
120 F5 **Perry** Ontario Canada
110 D6 **Perry** Arkansas U.S.A.
113 D7 **Perry** Florida U.S.A.
112 D5 **Perry** Georgia U.S.A.
110 F2 **Perry** Illinois U.S.A.
99 M8 **Perry** Iowa U.S.A.
94 C4 **Perry** Michigan U.S.A.
110 E2 **Perry** Missouri U.S.A.
94 K4 **Perry** New York U.S.A.
107 N5 **Perry** Oklahoma U.S.A.
116 O6 **Perry I** Alaska U.S.A.
120 D2 **Perry L** Ontario Canada
110 A2 **Perry L** Kansas U.S.A.
95 L7 **Perryman** Maryland U.S.A.
94 D5 **Perrysburg** Ohio U.S.A.
108 D7 **Perryton** Texas U.S.A.
118 D4 **Perryvale** Alberta Canada
110 D6 **Perryville** Arkansas U.S.A.
110 G4 **Perryville** Missouri U.S.A.
21 P3 **Persan** France
Persepolis *see* **Takht-e Jamshīd**
128 F6 **Perseverancia** Bolivia
121 O4 **Pershing** Quebec Canada
8 D3 **Pershore** England
54 H8 **Pershotravensk** Ukraine
Persia *see* **Iran**
99 L8 **Persia** Iowa U.S.A.
77 A5 **Persian Gulf** S W Asia
27 J14 **Persnäs** Sweden
139 H8 **Perth** Tasmania Australia
143 B9 **Perth** W Australia Australia
121 O8 **Perth** Ontario Canada
12 E1 **Perth** Scotland
107 N4 **Perth** Kansas U.S.A.
98 G1 **Perth** North Dakota U.S.A.
95 N6 **Perth Amboy** New Jersey U.S.A.
122 E7 **Perth-Andover** New Brunswick Canada
38 L4 **Pertholz** Austria
41 P3 **Pertisau** Austria
52 E3 **Pertominsk** Russian Federation
42 J6 **Pertovac** Montenegro Yugoslavia
21 H5 **Pertre, le** France
29 M10 **Pertunmaa** Finland
52 G5 **Pertyugskiy** Russian Federation
128 D6 **Peru** *rep* S America
99 R8 **Peru** Illinois U.S.A.
94 A6 **Peru** Indiana U.S.A.
99 L9 **Peru** Nebraska U.S.A.
95 O2 **Peru** New York U.S.A.
135 S12 **Peru-Chile Trench** Pacific Oc
42 E5 **Perugia** Italy
129 J8 **Peruibe** Brazil
46 G2 **Perushtitsa** Bulgaria
42 G4 **Perušić** Croatia
22 F3 **Peruwelz** Belgium
78 J3 **Pervari** Turkey
21 L5 **Pervenchères** France
54 G4 **Pervoavgustovskiy** Russian Federation
55 F5 **Pervomayka** Kazakhstan
54 K8 **Pervomaysk** Ukraine
52 H4 **Pervomayskaya** Russian Federation
56 B5 **Pervomayskiy** Kazakhstan
58 G1 **Pervomayskiy** Russian Federation
55 C4 **Pervomayskiy** Bashkirskaya Respublika Russian Federation
55 B5 **Pervomayskiy** Orenburgskaya obl Russian Federation
55 D2 **Pervomayskiy** Sverdlovskaya obl Russian Federation
56 C3 **Pervomayskoye** Russian Federation
51 Q2 **Pervorechenskiy** Russian Federation
55 C3 **Pervoural'sk** Russian Federation
22 H2 **Perwez** Belgium
52 D5 **Pes'** *R* Russian Federation
45 K4 **Pesa** *R* Italy
80 D6 **Pesagot** Jordan
70 B6 **Pesaguan** Kalimantan
45 N4 **Pesaro** Italy
102 B4 **Pescadero** California U.S.A.
Pescadores *islds see* **P'eng-hu Lieh-tao**
128 D7 **Pescadores, Pta** *C* Peru
45 H4 **Pescaglia** Italy
42 F6 **Pescara** *R* Italy
42 F6 **Pescara** Italy
45 P6 **Pescasseroli** Italy
42 G7 **Peschici** Italy
45 J1 **Peschiera del Garda** Italy
45 J4 **Pescia** Italy
45 P5 **Pescina** Italy
45 R7 **Pesco Sannita** Italy
45 P6 **Pescosolido** Italy
52 G2 **Pesha** *R* Russian Federation
74 D1 **Peshawar** Pakistan
46 D3 **Peshkopi** Albania
46 G2 **Peshtera** Bulgaria
99 S4 **Peshtigo** *R* Wisconsin U.S.A.
99 T4 **Peshtigo** Wisconsin U.S.A.
26 J5 **Peskehaure** Sweden
55 E4 **Peski** Kazakhstan
57 B2 **Peski Priaral'skiye Karkumy** Kazakhstan
57 C5 **Peski Sundukli** Turkmenistan
52 H5 **Peskovka** Russian Federation
38 N8 **Pesnica** *R* Slovenia
16 B3 **Péso de Regua** Portugal
110 H2 **Pesotum** Illinois U.S.A.
129 L5 **Pesqueira** Brazil
18 E8 **Pessac** France
33 R7 **Pessin** Germany
48 E3 **Pest** *co* Hungary
48 H6 **Peşteana Jiu** Romania
52 E5 **Pestovo** Russian Federation
52 F6 **Pestyaki** Russian Federation
46 E5 **Péta** Greece
80 C5 **Petah Tiqwa** Israel
29 L9 **Petäjävesi** Finland
71 B2 **Petak, Tg** *C* Halmahera Indonesia
111 G10 **Petal** Mississippi U.S.A.
29 J9 **Petalax** Finland
69 G14 **Petaling** Sumatra
46 G7 **Petalioí** *isld* Greece
46 G7 **Petalión Kólpos** *G* Greece
102 B3 **Petaluma** California U.S.A.
22 K4 **Petange** Luxembourg
70 E6 **Petangis** Kalimantan
127 L9 **Petare** Venezuela
88 C9 **Petauke** Zambia
121 P6 **Petawaga, L** Quebec Canada
121 N7 **Petawawa** Ontario Canada
125 P9 **Petén Itzá, L** Guatemala
99 R5 **Petenwell Lake** *res* Wisconsin U.S.A.
120 G4 **Peterbell** Ontario Canada
138 E5 **Peterborough** South Australia Australia
121 M8 **Peterborough** Ontario Canada
9 F2 **Peterborough** England
95 Q4 **Peterborough** New Hampshire U.S.A.
15 F3 **Peterculter** Scotland
15 G3 **Peterhead** Scotland
146 B6 **Peter I Øy** *isld* Antarctica
13 G4 **Peterlee** England
140 B6 **Petermann Aboriginal Land** N Terr Australia
115 O1 **Petermann Gletscher** *gla* Greenland
143 G6 **Petermann Ra** N Terr/W Aust Australia
131 B5 **Peteroa, Vol** *pk* Arg/Chile
118 H2 **Peter Pond L** Saskatchewan Canada
36 H2 **Petersberg** Germany
117 G7 **Petersburg** Alaska U.S.A.
110 G1 **Petersburg** Illinois U.S.A.
110 J3 **Petersburg** Indiana U.S.A.
94 D5 **Petersburg** Michigan U.S.A.
98 H8 **Petersburg** Nebraska U.S.A.
98 H1 **Petersburg** North Dakota U.S.A.
94 J6 **Petersburg** Pennsylvania U.S.A.
110 K6 **Petersburg** Tennessee U.S.A.
108 F2 **Petersburg** Texas U.S.A.
94 K9 **Petersburg** Virginia U.S.A.
94 H7 **Petersburg** West Virginia U.S.A.
116 M5 **Peters Creek** Alaska U.S.A.
119 V8 **Petersfield** Manitoba Canada
9 F5 **Petersfield** England
32 J8 **Petershagen** Germany
33 T7 **Petershagen** Germany
37 L7 **Petershausen** Germany
99 L7 **Peterson** Iowa U.S.A.
90 D16 **Peter 1st I** Antarctica
116 M5 **Petersville** Alaska U.S.A.
143 E7 **Peterswald Hill** W Australia Australia
123 R4 **Peterview** Newfoundland Canada
43 H9 **Petilia Policastro** Italy
17 G2 **Petilla de Aragón** Spain
111 H11 **Petit Bois I** Mississippi U.S.A.
127 N4 **Petit Bourg** Guadeloupe W Indies
127 N4 **Petit Canal** Guadeloupe W Indies
122 G8 **Petitcodiac** New Brunswick Canada
127 N4 **Petit Cul de Sac Marin** *B* Guadeloupe W Indies
122 G5 **Petite-Cascapédia, Rés. Faun. de la** Quebec Canada
122 E5 **Petite Matane** Quebec Canada
121 Q7 **Petite-Nation, Réserve de la** Quebec Canada
122 B6 **Petite Rivière** Quebec Canada
122 H9 **Petite Rivière Bridge** Nova Scotia Canada
127 H5 **Petite Rivière de l'Artibonite** Haiti
21 M2 **Petites Dalles, les** France
123 M7 **Petit Etang** C Breton I, Nova Scotia
127 O4 **Petite Terre, Îles de la** Guadeloupe W Indies
122 G4 **Petite Vallèe** Quebec Canada
127 H5 **Petit Goâve** Haiti
123 N5 **Petit Jardin** Newfoundland Canada
110 C6 **Petit Jean** *R* Arkansas U.S.A.
95 U2 **Petit Manan Pt** Maine U.S.A.
20 H7 **Petit Mars** France
36 B6 **Petitmont** France
117 N6 **Petitot** *R* British Columbia Canada
122 G6 **Petit Rocher** New Brunswick Canada
29 P9 **Petkeljärvi Nat. Park** Finland
29 M4 **Petkula** Finland
74 E7 **Petlad** India
125 P7 **Peto** Mexico
145 G4 **Petone** New Zealand
133 C4 **Petorca** Chile
94 C1 **Petoskey** Michigan U.S.A.
52 G4 **Petrakovo** Russian Federation
43 F11 **Petralia** Sicily
51 L1 **Petra, Ostrov** *isld* Russian Federation
65 H3 **Petra Velikogo, Zaliv** *B* Russian Federation
45 P7 **Petrella, M** *mt* Italy
121 N9 **Petre, Pt** Ontario Canada
52 J4 **Petretsovo** Russian Federation
45 N4 **Petriano** Italy
46 F3 **Petricn** Bulgaria
141 L2 **Petrie, Mt** Brisbane, Qnsld Australia
103 P6 **Petrified Forest Nat. Park** Arizona U.S.A.
54 F8 **Petrikovka** Ukraine
48 H5 **Petrila** Romania
8 B6 **Petrockstow** England
52 C5 **Petrodvorets** Russian Federation
46 F1 **Petrokhanski P** Bulgaria
52 D5 **Petrokrepost'** Russian Federation
129 L5 **Petrolândia** Brazil
109 J8 **Petroleum** Texas U.S.A.
120 H10 **Petrolia** Ontario Canada
100 A9 **Petrolia** California U.S.A.
109 J2 **Petrolia** Texas U.S.A.
129 K5 **Petrolina** Brazil
46 F6 **Petromagoúla** Greece
52 A4 **Petropavlovka** Russian Federation
56 G5 **Petropavlovka** Russian Federation
55 E4 **Petropavlovsk** Kazakhstan
56 G2 **Petropavlovsk** Russian Federation
51 P3 **Petropavlovsk-Kamchatskiy** Russian Federation
129 K8 **Petrópolis** Brazil
112 C1 **Petros** Tennessee U.S.A.
48 H5 **Petroşani** Romania
48 G6 **Petrovac** Serbia Yugoslavia
48 F5 **Petrovaradin** Serbia Yugoslavia
55 E4 **Petrovka** Kazakhstan
52 E3 **Petrovskiy Yam** Russian Federation
55 C4 **Petrovskoye** Bashkirskaya Respublika Russian Federation
52 E6 **Petrovskoye** Yaroslavskaya obl Russian Federation
56 G5 **Petrovsk-Zabaykal'skiy** Russian Federation
52 D4 **Petrozavodsk** Russian Federation
52 K2 **Petrun'** Russian Federation
48 J3 **Petru Rareş** Romania
Petsamo *see* **Pechenga**
29 N2 **Petsikko** *mt* Finland
25 C3 **Petten** Netherlands
38 K6 **Pettenbach** Austria
14 D2 **Pettigoe** Ireland
110 C6 **Pettigrew** Arkansas U.S.A.
109 K7 **Pettus** Texas U.S.A.
123 U6 **Petty Hbr** Newfoundland Canada
55 E3 **Petukhovo** Russian Federation
9 F6 **Petworth** England
38 L8 **Petzen** *mt* Austria
38 J5 **Peuerbach** Austria
69 C10 **Peuetsagu, Gunung** *mt* Sumatra
116 J8 **Peulik, Mt** Alaska U.S.A.
29 M4 **Peurasuvanto** Finland
26 J5 **Peuraure** Sweden
69 C10 **Peureula** Sumatra
9 G6 **Pevensey** England
94 C3 **Pewamo** Michigan U.S.A.
99 S6 **Pewaukee** Wisconsin U.S.A.
9 E5 **Pewsey** England
32 F6 **Pewsum** Germany
36 B7 **Pexonne** France
19 P18 **Peynier** France
19 P18 **Peypin** France
18 E9 **Peyrehorade** France
18 H8 **Peyreleau** France
19 P13 **Peyrieu** France
19 P17 **Peyrolles-en-Provence** France
19 P16 **Peyruis** France
106 F2 **Peyton** Colorado U.S.A.
52 G2 **Peza** *R* Russian Federation
18 H9 **Pézenas** France
31 K7 **Pezinok** Slovakia
52 H4 **Pezmog** Russian Federation
37 N6 **Pfaffenberg** Germany
37 L6 **Pfaffenhofen an der Ilm** Germany
36 D6 **Pfaffenhoffen** France
41 J3 **Pfäffikon** Switzerland
37 P2 **Pfaffroda** Germany
36 C4 **Pfälzer Bergland** *reg* Germany
36 D5 **Pfalzer Wald** *mts* Germany
36 D3 **Pfalzfeld** Germany
36 F6 **Pfalzgrafenweiler** Germany
37 L6 **Pfalzpaint** Germany
37 O7 **Pfarrkirchen** Germany
37 K3 **Pfarrweisach** Germany
37 N6 **Pfatter** Germany
36 E4 **Pfeddersheim** Germany
37 M6 **Pfeffenhausen** Germany
36 F6 **Pfinztal** Germany
140 C6 **Pfitzner, Mt** N Terr Australia
41 N2 **Pflach** Austria
37 M6 **Pförring** Germany
36 F6 **Pforzheim** Germany
37 N5 **Pfreimd** Germany
36 D4 **Pfrimm** *R* Germany
41 K2 **Pfullendorf** Germany
36 G7 **Pfullingen** Germany
41 N4 **Pfunds** Austria
36 F4 **Pfungstadt** Germany
37 L6 **Pfünz** Germany
74 F3 **Phagwara** India
68 E6 **Phai, Ko** *isld* Thailand
95 T7 **Phair** Maine U.S.A.
74 E5 **Phalodi** India
88 E9 **Phalombe** Malawi
36 C6 **Phalsbourg** France
76 B2 **Phaltan** India
69 D8 **Pha Luai, Ko** *isld* Thailand
69 E8 **Pha Ngan, Ko** *isld* Thailand
69 D8 **Phangnga** Thailand
68 J7 **Phan Ly** Vietnam
68 G5 **Phanom Dang Raek** *mt* Thailand
68 D5 **Phanom Thuan** Thailand
68 J7 **Phan Rang** Vietnam
68 J7 **Phan Ri** Vietnam
68 J7 **Phan Thiet** Vietnam
103 M5 **Phantom Ranch** Arizona U.S.A.
109 J9 **Pharr** Texas U.S.A.
68 H2 **Phat Diem** Vietnam
69 D9 **Phatthalung** Thailand
69 D8 **Phayam, Ko** *isld* Thailand
68 E5 **Phayuhakhiri** Thailand
140 D2 **Phelp** *R* N Terr Australia
94 E9 **Phelps** Kentucky U.S.A.
95 K4 **Phelps** New York U.S.A.
109 M5 **Phelps** Texas U.S.A.
99 R3 **Phelps** Wisconsin U.S.A.
112 L2 **Phelps L** North Carolina U.S.A.
68 F4 **Phen** Thailand
94 J9 **Phenix** Virginia U.S.A.
111 L9 **Phenix City** Alabama U.S.A.
68 D6 **Phet Buri** Thailand
68 H5 **Phia Phay** Laos
111 G9 **Philadelphia** Mississippi U.S.A.
99 P10 **Philadelphia** Missouri U.S.A.
95 M2 **Philadelphia** New York U.S.A.
97 **Philadelphia** *conurbation* Pennsylvania U.S.A.
84 J5 **Philae** *ruins* Egypt
111 J7 **Phil Campbell** Alabama U.S.A.
98 E5 **Philip** South Dakota U.S.A.
137 O7 **Philip I** Pacific Oc
111 F8 **Philipp** Mississippi U.S.A.
Philippeville *see* **Skikda**
22 G3 **Philippeville** Belgium
94 G7 **Philippi** West Virginia U.S.A.
140 E6 **Philippi, L** Queensland Australia
25 A6 **Philippine** Netherlands
71 **Philippines** *rep* E Indies
89 D8 **Philippolis** S Africa
Philippopolis Bulgaria *see* **Plovdiv**
36 E5 **Philippsburg** Germany
121 R7 **Philipsburg** Quebec Canada
101 M3 **Philipsburg** Montana U.S.A.
94 J6 **Philipsburg** Pennsylvania U.S.A.
116 O2 **Philip Smith Mts** Alaska U.S.A.
139 H7 **Phillip I** Victoria Australia
95 R2 **Phillips** Maine U.S.A.
101 R1 **Phillips** Montana U.S.A.
98 H9 **Phillips** Nebraska U.S.A.
108 C8 **Phillips** Texas U.S.A.
99 Q4 **Phillips** Wisconsin U.S.A.
107 L2 **Phillipsburg** Kansas U.S.A.
115 L1 **Phillips Inlet** Northwest Territories Canada
138 C3 **Phillipson, L** South Australia Australia
142 G5 **Phillipson Ra** W Australia Australia
142 F3 **Phillips Ra** W Australia Australia
95 O4 **Philmont** New York U.S.A.
102 A2 **Philo** California U.S.A.
100 B5 **Philomath** Oregon U.S.A.
118 F3 **Philomena** Alberta Canada
115 M3 **Philpots Island** Northwest Territories Canada
94 G10 **Philpott Dam** Virginia U.S.A.
68 G5 **Phimun Mangsahan** Thailand
118 J6 **Phippen** Saskatchewan Canada
106 D1 **Phippsburg** Colorado U.S.A.
68 E4 **Phitsanulok** Thailand
68 G7 **Phnom Penh** Cambodia
67 B6 **Pho Binh Gia** Vietnam
144 D5 **Phoebe** New Zealand
95 N4 **Phoenicia** New York U.S.A.
103 M8 **Phoenix** Arizona U.S.A.
111 G12 **Phoenix** Louisiana U.S.A.
95 L3 **Phoenix** New York U.S.A.
134 K8 **Phoenix Is** Pacific Oc
95 M6 **Phoenixville** Pennsylvania U.S.A.
68 G1 **Pho Lu** Vietnam
68 H4 **Phong Nha** Vietnam
68 F2 **Phongsali** Laos
68 F1 **Phong Tho** Vietnam
68 F3 **Phon Phisai** Thailand
139 G7 **Phoques B** Tasmania Australia
140 E5 **Phosphate Hill** Queensland Australia
68 H7 **Phouc Le** Vietnam
68 D3 **Phrao** Thailand
68 E5 **Phra Phutthabat** Thailand
69 D8 **Phra Saeng** Thailand
69 C8 **Phra Thong, Ko** *isld* Thailand
68 E5 **Phrom Buri** Thailand
47 L6 **Phrygia** Turkey
68 G2 **Phuc Yen** Vietnam
67 B7 **Phu Dien** Vietnam
69 D9 **Phuket, Ko** *isld* Thailand
68 F4 **Phu Khieo** Thailand
75 L8 **Phulabāni** India
67 B6 **Phulang Thuong** Vietnam
68 H4 **Phu Loc** Vietnam
68 G2 **Phu Ly** Vietnam
68 F6 **Phum Bavel** Cambodia
68 G7 **Phum Hay** Cambodia
68 G6 **Phum Khvao** Cambodia
68 G6 **Phum Koulen** Cambodia
68 F6 **Phum Siem** Cambodia
68 F6 **Phum Svai** Cambodia
68 F6 **Phum Treng** Cambodia
68 F6 **Phum Troy Toch** Cambodia
68 J5 **Phu My** Vietnam
68 G2 **Phu Nho Quan** Vietnam
69 D8 **Phun Phin** Thailand
75 N5 **Phuntsholing** Bhutan
69 G8 **Phuoc Long** Vietnam
Phu Qui *see* **Thai Hoa**
68 F7 **Phu Quoc** Vietnam
68 G2 **Phu Tho** Vietnam
129 J5 **Piaca** Brazil
44 G1 **Piacenza** Italy
44 F2 **Piacenza** *prov* Italy
45 L1 **Piacenza d'Adige** Italy
45 J1 **Piadena** Italy
122 B2 **Piakoudie L** Quebec Canada
141 L7 **Pialba** Queensland Australia
139 J4 **Pian** *R* New South Wales Australia
45 P5 **Piana del Fucino** Italy
41 K5 **Pianazzo** Italy
130 H9 **Piancó** *R* Brazil
45 K3 **Pian del Vóglio** Italy
45 L4 **Pian de Sco** Italy
45 M4 **Pian di Meleto** Italy
45 N4 **Pianello** Italy
139 G6 **Piangil** Victoria Australia
45 M1 **Pianiga** Italy
42 G6 **Pianosa** *isld* Adriatic Sea
42 C6 **Pianosa, I** Italy
65 B5 **Pianquan** China
118 H9 **Piapot** Saskatchewan Canada
127 O2 **Piarco** *airport* Trinidad
31 M3 **Piaseczno** Poland
122 K3 **Piashti, L** Quebec Canada
31 O4 **Piaski** Poland
31 L3 **Piątek** Poland
48 K4 **Piatra Neamt** Romania
129 K5 **Piauí** *state* Brazil
129 K5 **Piaui, Sa. do** *mts* Brazil
42 E2 **Piave** *R* Italy
143 B9 **Piawaning** W Australia Australia
45 H3 **Piazza al Serchio** Italy
43 F11 **Piazza Armerina** Sicily
133 C8 **Piazzi** *isld* Chile
45 L1 **Piazzolas B** Italy
86 F4 **Pibor Post** Sudan
118 D4 **Pibroch** Alberta Canada
103 L6 **Pica** Arizona U.S.A.
101 L6 **Picabo** Idaho U.S.A.
103 N9 **Picacho** Arizona U.S.A.
103 K8 **Picacho** California U.S.A.
106 E8 **Picacho** New Mexico U.S.A.
103 N9 **Picacho Res** Arizona U.S.A.
124 B3 **Picachos, Cerro dos** *mt* Mexico
22 D4 **Picardie** France
20 H3 **Picauville** France
111 G11 **Picayune** Mississippi U.S.A.
123 O5 **Piccadilly** Newfoundland Canada
106 B2 **Piceance Cr** Colorado U.S.A.
45 R8 **Picentini, Mti** *mt* Italy
124 F3 **Picháchic** Mexico
133 E2 **Pichanal** Argentina
131 B4 **Pichidangui, B** Chile
133 C4 **Pichilemu** Chile
128 C4 **Pichincha** *prov* Ecuador
52 G6 **Pichkasy** Russian Federation
118 D4 **Pickardville** Alberta Canada
111 F9 **Pickens** Mississippi U.S.A.
112 E3 **Pickens** South Carolina U.S.A.
94 G8 **Pickens** West Virginia U.S.A.
120 K7 **Pickerel** Ontario Canada
99 P1 **Pickerel L** Ontario Canada
13 H5 **Pickering** England
110 B1 **Pickering** Missouri U.S.A.
143 D8 **Pickering, Mt** W Australia Australia
126 D4 **Pickle Bank** Caribbean
115 K7 **Pickle Lake** Ontario Canada
98 H6 **Pickstown** South Dakota U.S.A.
109 M2 **Pickton** Texas U.S.A.
110 H6 **Pickwick L** Tennessee U.S.A.
45 P7 **Pico** Italy
16 D4 **Pico de Almanzor** *mt* Spain
16 E4 **Pico Penalara** *mt* Spain
129 K5 **Picos** Brazil
16 C2 **Picos de Ancares, Sa. de** *mts* Spain
16 C6 **Picos de Aroche** *mt* Spain
21 P2 **Picquigny** France
120 D4 **Pic R** Ontario Canada
139 K5 **Picton** New South Wales Australia
121 N8 **Picton** Ontario Canada
145 E4 **Picton** New Zealand
139 H9 **Picton, Mt** Tasmania Australia
122 K8 **Pictou** Nova Scotia Canada
122 K8 **Pictou I** Nova Scotia Canada
118 E9 **Picture Butte** Alberta Canada
99 U3 **Pictured Rocks Nat. Lakeshore** Michigan U.S.A.
95 L5 **Picture Rocks** Pennsylvania U.S.A.
130 H9 **Picuí** Brazil
131 B7 **Picún Leufú** Argentina
138 B4 **Pidinga** South Australia Australia
45 Q7 **Piedimonte d'Alife** Italy
111 L8 **Piedmont** Alabama U.S.A.
110 F4 **Piedmont** Missouri U.S.A.
112 E3 **Piedmont** South Carolina U.S.A.
98 C5 **Piedmont** South Dakota U.S.A.
94 F6 **Piedmont Res** Ohio U.S.A.
17 F3 **Piedra** *R* Spain
102 E5 **Piedra** California U.S.A.
106 C4 **Piedra** *R* Colorado U.S.A.
16 E5 **Piedrabuena** Spain
16 C2 **Piedrafita, Pto. de** *pass* Spain
16 D4 **Piedrahita** Spain
131 B3 **Piedra Lobos, Pta** Chile
102 C6 **Piedras Blancas Pt** California U.S.A.
125 J3 **Piedras Negras** Mexico
71 D5 **Piedras Point** Philippines
133 F5 **Piedras, Pta** Argentina
128 D6 **Piedras, R.de las** *R* Peru
99 R1 **Pie I** Ontario Canada
31 L5 **Piekary Śląskié** Poland
29 N9 **Pieksämäki** Finland
38 M5 **Pielach** *R* Austria
29 M8 **Pielavesi** *L* Finland
29 O8 **Pielinen** *L* Finland
29 O9 **Pielisjoki** *R* Finland
139 H8 **Pieman R** Tasmania Australia
44 C3 **Piemonte** *reg* Italy
31 M1 **Pieniężno** Poland
22 K5 **Piennes** France
31 J4 **Pieńsk** Poland
36 B2 **Pier** Germany
106 F1 **Pierce** Colorado U.S.A.
113 F10 **Pierce** Florida U.S.A.
100 K3 **Pierce** Idaho U.S.A.
98 J7 **Pierce** Nebraska U.S.A.
13 G4 **Piercebridge** England
110 B5 **Pierce City** Missouri U.S.A.
94 B5 **Pierceton** Indiana U.S.A.
107 K4 **Pierceville** Kansas U.S.A.
102 A2 **Piercy** California U.S.A.
46 E4 **Piéria Óri** Greece
15 F1 **Pierowall** Orkney Scotland
98 J4 **Pierpont** South Dakota U.S.A.
19 J6 **Pierre** France
98 F5 **Pierre** South Dakota U.S.A.
18 F7 **Pierre-Buffière** France
19 P15 **Pierre-Châtel** France
21 P6 **Pierrefitte-sur-Sauldre** France
22 D5 **Pierrefonds** France
120 K3 **Pierre L** Ontario Canada
19 N16 **Pierrelatte** France
22 K5 **Pierrepont** France
121 S6 **Pierreville** Quebec Canada
127 P3 **Pierreville** Trinidad
119 Q9 **Pierson** Manitoba Canada
113 F8 **Pierson** Florida U.S.A.
36 B4 **Piesport** Germany
143 B10 **Piesseville** W Australia Australia
31 K7 **Piešt'any** Slovakia
Pietarsaari *see* **Jakobstad**
89 G7 **Pietermaritzburg** S Africa
89 F4 **Pietersburg** S Africa
22 G3 **Piéton** Belgium
106 B7 **Pie Town** New Mexico U.S.A.
44 D3 **Pietra Ligure** Italy
45 Q7 **Pietramelara** Italy
44 B3 **Pietraporzio** Italy
44 H4 **Pietrasanta** Italy
45 Q7 **Pietravairano** Italy
87 F11 **Piet Retief** S Africa
48 J3 **Pietroşu** *mt* Romania
29 P2 **Piets'yarvi, Oz** *L* Russian Federation
20 G2 **Pieux, les** France
38 F9 **Pieve** Italy
42 E2 **Pieve di Cadore** Italy
45 K2 **Pieve di Cento** Italy
45 J3 **Pievepelago** Italy
45 M4 **Pieve S. Stefano** Italy
Pigádhia *see* **Kárpathos**
94 C1 **Pigeon** *R* Michigan U.S.A.
94 D3 **Pigeon** Michigan U.S.A.
120 H10 **Pigeon B** Ontario Canada
111 K10 **Pigeon Cr** Alabama U.S.A.
140 B3 **Pigeon Hole** N Terr Australia
127 K3 **Pigeon I** Jamaica
118 C5 **Pigeon L** Alberta Canada
121 M8 **Pigeon L** Ontario Canada
127 M2 **Pigeon Pt** Tobago
102 B4 **Pigeon Pt** California U.S.A.
119 V6 **Pigeon R** Manitoba Canada
119 O2 **Pigeon River** Ontario Canada
143 C8 **Pigeon Rocks** W Australia Australia
94 H10 **Pigg** *R* Virginia U.S.A.
110 F5 **Piggott** Arkansas U.S.A.
89 G8 **Pigg's Peak** Swaziland
19 Q18 **Pignans** France
45 P7 **Pignataro Interamna** Italy
45 Q7 **Pignatoro Maggiore** Italy
133 E5 **Pigüe** Argentina
145 D3 **Pihaina** New Zealand
67 E1 **Pi He** *R* China
29 L9 **Pihlajavesi** Finland
29 M8 **Pihtipudas** Finland
56 E4 **Pik Grandioznyy** *mt* Russian Federation
115 P5 **Pikiulleq** *isld* Greenland
31 K2 **Piła** Poland
19 N14 **Pilat, Mt** France
48 F3 **Pilis** Hungary
48 E3 **Pilisvörösvár** Hungary
98 J2 **Pillsbury** North Dakota U.S.A.
102 B2 **Pillsbury, L** California U.S.A.
52 G6 **Pil'na** Russian Federation
8 D4 **Pilning** England
130 F5 **Pilões, Sa. dos** *mts* Brazil
126 F5 **Pilón** Cuba
46 E8 **Pílos** Greece
119 N8 **Pilot Butte** Saskatchewan Canada
110 D3 **Pilot Grove** Missouri U.S.A.
119 T9 **Pilot Mound** Manitoba Canada
112 G1 **Pilot Mountain** North Carolina U.S.A.
102 G3 **Pilot Pk** Nevada U.S.A.
101 Q5 **Pilot Pk** Wyoming U.S.A.
116 J8 **Pilot Point** Alaska U.S.A.
109 L2 **Pilot Point** Texas U.S.A.
100 G4 **Pilot Rock** Oregon U.S.A.
116 F5 **Pilot Station** Alaska U.S.A.
139 J6 **Pilot, The** *mt* New South Wales Australia
133 E2 **Piloya** *R* Bolivia
37 M5 **Pilsach** Germany
Pilsen *see* **Plzeň**
99 T5 **Pilsen** Wisconsin U.S.A.
41 O1 **Pilsen See** *L* Germany
37 O6 **Pilsting** Germany
55 F1 **Pil'tan-Lor, Oz** *L* Russian Federation
27 M14 **Piltene** Latvia
8 D5 **Pilton** England
52 J4 **Pil'va** *R* Russian Federation
31 N6 **Pilzno** Poland
55 F1 **Pim** Russian Federation
103 P9 **Pima** Arizona U.S.A.
138 D4 **Pimba** South Australia Australia
129 G4 **Pimenta** Brazil
128 F6 **Pimenta Bueno** Brazil
127 J5 **Pimental** Dominican Rep
128 C5 **Pimentel** Peru
113 L12 **Pimlico I** Bahamas
71 H4 **Pimpi** Sulawesi
86 D5 **Pimu** Zaire
17 G3 **Pina** Spain
103 L10 **Pinacate, Cerro** *pk* Mexico
124 C2 **Pinacate, Sa. del** *mt* Mexico
103 O9 **Pinaleno Mts** Arizona U.S.A.
71 E4 **Pinamalayan** Philippines
131 G6 **Pinamar** Argentina
69 E10 **Pinang** *isld* Malaysia
70 E2 **Pinangah** Sabah
78 F2 **Pınarbaşı** Turkey
126 C3 **Pinar del Río** Cuba
47 J3 **Pinarhisar** Turkey
138 F3 **Pinaroo, L** New South Wales Australia
133 D4 **Piñas** Argentina
21 L4 **Pin-au-Haras, le** France
45 L2 **Pincara** Italy
9 F2 **Pinchbeck** England
118 D9 **Pincher Creek** Alberta Canada
117 L8 **Pinchi** British Columbia Canada
128 C4 **Pinchincha** *mt* Ecuador
94 D4 **Pinckney** Michigan U.S.A.
110 G3 **Pinckneyville** Illinois U.S.A.
21 J4 **Pinçon, Mt** France
94 C3 **Pinconning** Michigan U.S.A.
48 G4 **Pîncota** Romania
31 M5 **Pińczów** Poland
129 H6 **Pindaiba** Brazil
110 D5 **Pindall** Arkansas U.S.A.
143 B8 **Pindar** W Australia Australia
129 J4 **Pindaré** *R* Brazil
70 G6 **Pindolo** Sulawesi
28 E4 **Pindstrup** Denmark
138 F4 **Pine** *R* New South Wales Australia
103 N7 **Pine** Arizona U.S.A.
100 K6 **Pine** Idaho U.S.A.
94 B2 **Pine** *R* Michigan U.S.A.
99 Q6 **Pine** *R* Wisconsin U.S.A.
111 K10 **Pine Apple** Alabama U.S.A.
111 D7 **Pine Bluff** Arkansas U.S.A.
119 P4 **Pinebluff L** Saskatchewan Canada
98 B8 **Pine Bluffs** Wyoming U.S.A.
123 T7 **Pine, C** Newfoundland Canada
113 F9 **Pinecastle** Florida U.S.A.
111 E7 **Pine City** Arkansas U.S.A.
99 O4 **Pine City** Minnesota U.S.A.
103 H1 **Pine Cr** Nevada U.S.A.
94 K5 **Pine Cr** Pennsylvania U.S.A.
140 B2 **Pine Creek** N Terr Australia
102 E3 **Pinecrest** California U.S.A.
107 P7 **Pine Cr. Res** Oklahoma U.S.A.
16 E2 **Pineda de la S** Spain
117 P9 **Pinedale** Alberta Canada
102 E5 **Pinedale** California U.S.A.
101 Q7 **Pinedale** Wyoming U.S.A.
102 E5 **Pine Flat Res** California U.S.A.
100 G8 **Pine Forest Range** Nevada U.S.A.
52 F3 **Pinega** Russian Federation
52 G3 **Pinega** *R* Russian Federation
140 C6 **Pine Gap** N Terr Australia
143 B8 **Pinegrove** W Australia Australia
95 L6 **Pine Grove** Pennsylvania U.S.A.
140 C5 **Pine Hill** N Terr Australia
118 K3 **Pine House** Saskatchewan Canada
118 L3 **Pine House L** Saskatchewan Canada
112 H2 **Pinehurst** North Carolina U.S.A.
100 C2 **Pinehurst** Washington U.S.A.
118 F4 **Pinehurst L** Alberta Canada
113 E11 **Pine I** Florida U.S.A.
99 O5 **Pine Island** Minnesota U.S.A.
146 B7 **Pine Island B** Antarctica
146 B7 **Pine Island Glacier** *glacier* Antarctica
99 S4 **Pine L** Wisconsin U.S.A.
109 O4 **Pineland** Texas U.S.A.
71 J4 **Pineleng** Sulawesi
144 B6 **Pinelheugh** *mt* New Zealand
113 E10 **Pinellas** *airport* Florida U.S.A.
102 C6 **Pine Mt** California U.S.A.
107 P7 **Pine Mt** Oklahoma U.S.A.
103 L7 **Pine Pk** Arizona U.S.A.
117 Q5 **Pine Point** Northwest Territories Canada
119 P1 **Pine Portage** Ontario Canada
117 Q5 **Pine Pt** Northwest Territories Canada
113 D8 **Pine Pt** Florida U.S.A.
118 D4 **Pine R** Alberta Canada
117 M8 **Pine R** British Columbia Canada
98 D6 **Pine Ridge** South Dakota U.S.A.
119 R7 **Pine River** Manitoba Canada
118 K3 **Pine River** Saskatchewan Canada
99 M3 **Pine River** Minnesota U.S.A.
44 B2 **Pinerolo** Italy
120 J9 **Pinery Prov. Park** Ontario Canada
111 B9 **Pines, L. O'The** Texas U.S.A.
108 C4 **Pine Springs** Texas U.S.A.
89 G7 **Pinetown** S Africa
110 B7 **Pine Valley** Oklahoma U.S.A.
103 L4 **Pine Valley** Utah U.S.A.
103 L4 **Pine Valley Mts** Utah U.S.A.
94 D10 **Pineville** Kentucky U.S.A.
111 D10 **Pineville** Louisiana U.S.A.
110 B5 **Pineville** Missouri U.S.A.
112 G2 **Pineville** North Carolina U.S.A.
94 F9 **Pineville** West Virginia U.S.A.
99 M1 **Pinewood** Ontario Canada
99 L2 **Pinewood** Minnesota U.S.A.
112 G4 **Pinewood** South Carolina U.S.A.
98 K1 **Piney** Manitoba Canada
101 T2 **Piney Buttes** *hills* Montana U.S.A.
110 C6 **Piney Cr** Arkansas U.S.A.
113 D8 **Piney Pt** Florida U.S.A.
58 D4 **Ping'an** China
65 F2 **Ping'an** China
143 C10 **Pingaring** W Australia Australia
67 A5 **Pingbian** China
67 B1 **Pingchang** China
65 D7 **Ping Dao** *isld* China
67 C3 **Pingdeng** China
65 B6 **Pingding** China
Pingdingbu *see* **Guyan**
58 F5 **Pingdingshan** China
65 G1 **Pingding Shan** *mt* China
65 F4 **Pingdingshan** China
65 D6 **Pingdu** China
143 B10 **Pingelly** W Australia Australia
65 F3 **Pinggang** China
65 C7 **Pinggang** China
65 D4 **Pinggu** China
67 B5 **Pingguo** China
67 F4 **Pinghai** China
67 F4 **Pinghe** China
Pinghu *see* **Pingtang**
67 G1 **Pinghu** China
67 D2 **Pingjiang** China
67 C4 **Pingle** China
58 E4 **Pingliang** China
67 D1 **Pinglin** China
65 B5 **Pinglu** China
65 B7 **Pinglu** China
58 E4 **Pingluo** China
Pingma *see* **Tiandong**
75 N6 **Pingna** Bangladesh
67 F3 **Pingnan** China
67 C5 **Pingnan** China
Pingqiao *see* **Xinyang**
65 D4 **Pingquan** China
101 N6 **Pingree** Idaho U.S.A.
98 G2 **Pingree** North Dakota U.S.A.
143 C10 **Pingrup** W Australia Australia
65 C5 **Pingshan** China
67 A2 **Pingshan** China
65 D7 **Pingshang** China
67 D4 **Pingshi** China
67 E4 **Pingshi** China
65 B6 **Pingshun** China
67 F4 **Pingtan** China
67 F4 **Pingtan Dao** *isld* China
67 B4 **Pingtang** China
67 G5 **P'ing-tung** Taiwan
67 D3 **Pingxiang** China
67 B5 **Pingxiang** China
65 F1 **Pingyang** China
67 G3 **Pingyang** China
65 B6 **Pingyao** China
65 D7 **Pingyi** China
65 C6 **Pingyin** China
67 C3 **Pingyong** China
65 C6 **Pingyuan** China
67 E4 **Pingyuan** China
67 A5 **Pingyuanjie** China
130 F8 **Pinhal** Brazil
16 B3 **Pinhão** Portugal
129 J4 **Pinheiro** Brazil
16 C4 **Pinhel** Portugal
69 D12 **Pini** *isld* Indonesia
46 E5 **Piniós** *R* Greece
46 E7 **Piniós** *R* Greece

143 B10 **Pinjarra** W Australia Australia
143 E9 **Pinjin** W Australia Australia
38 O7 **Pinka** *R* Austria
38 O7 **Pinkafeld** Austria
141 K1 **Pinkenba** *dist* Brisbane, Qnsld Australia
140 A3 **Pinkerton Ra** N Terr Australia
118 H7 **Pinkham** Saskatchewan Canada
112 K2 **Pink Hill** North Carolina U.S.A.
117 M7 **Pink Mountain** British Columbia Canada
21 M5 **Pin-la-Garenne, le** France
68 C2 **Pinlaung** Burma
145 D4 **Pinnacle** *mt* New Zealand
116 C6 **Pinnacle I** Bering Sea
102 C5 **Pinnacles Nat. Mon** California U.S.A.
138 F6 **Pinnaroo** South Australia Australia
32 L5 **Pinn Au** *R* Germany
32 L5 **Pinneberg** Germany
106 G1 **Pinneo** Colorado U.S.A.
9 F4 **Pinner** England
33 T5 **Pinnow** Germany
70 B5 **Pinoh** *R* Kalimantan
111 F10 **Pinola** Mississippi U.S.A.
106 F3 **Pinon** Colorado U.S.A.
106 E9 **Pinon** New Mexico U.S.A.
112 H4 **Pinopolis Dam** South Carolina U.S.A.
Pinos, Isla de *see* **Juventud, Isla de la**
102 E7 **Pinos, Mt** California U.S.A.
17 G6 **Pinoso** Spain
125 K9 **Pinotepa Nacional** Mexico
70 G6 **Pinrang** Sulawesi Indonesia
70 F6 **Pinrang** Sulawesi
137 O6 **Pins, Île Des** New Caledonia
53 C8 **Pinsk** Belarus
111 K8 **Pinson** Alabama U.S.A.
110 H6 **Pinson** Tennessee U.S.A.
120 J10 **Pins, Pte. aux** Ontario Canada
128 A7 **Pinta** *isld* Galapagos Is
103 P6 **Pinta** Arizona U.S.A.
133 D2 **Pintados** Chile
103 L9 **Pinta, Sa** Arizona U.S.A.
70 E2 **Pintasan** Sabah
133 E3 **Pinto** Argentina
118 K9 **Pinto Butte** *pk* Saskatchewan Canada
103 J8 **Pinto Mts** California U.S.A.
103 L4 **Pintura** Utah U.S.A.
103 J5 **Pintwater Ra** Nevada U.S.A.
123 Q2 **Pinware R** Labrador, Nfld Canada
12 D3 **Pinwherry** Scotland
143 B8 **Pinyalling** *mt* W Australia Australia
52 G4 **Pinyug** Russian Federation
41 N5 **Pinzolo** Italy
45 M4 **Pióbbico** Italy
103 K4 **Pioche** Nevada U.S.A.
19 N16 **Piolenc** France
42 D6 **Piombino** Italy
94 C5 **Pioneer** Ohio U.S.A.
109 H3 **Pioneer** Texas U.S.A.
101 M4 **Pioneer Mts** Montana U.S.A.
56 C3 **Pioner** Russian Federation
51 J1 **Pioner, Ostrova** *islds* Russian Federation
31 M1 **Pionerskiy** Russian Federation
55 D1 **Pionerskiy** Russian Federation
31 N4 **Pionki** Poland
145 E3 **Piopio** New Zealand
128 F4 **Piorini** *L* Brazil
44 B2 **Piossasco** Italy
31 L3 **Piotrków** Bydgoszcz Poland
31 M4 **Piotrków Trybunalski** Łódź Poland
45 M1 **Piove di Sacco** Italy
65 G3 **Pipa Dingzi** *mt* China
74 E5 **Pipar** India
6 L4 **Piper** *oil rig* North Sea
102 G4 **Piper Pk** Nevada U.S.A.
103 M5 **Pipe Spring Nat. Mon** Arizona U.S.A.
119 R9 **Pipestone** Manitoba Canada
98 K6 **Pipestone** Minnesota U.S.A.
119 Q9 **Pipestone Cr** Manitoba Canada
98 K5 **Pipestone Nat. Mon** Minnesota U.S.A.
145 E3 **Pipipi** *mt* New Zealand
145 E3 **Pipiriki** New Zealand
121 U3 **Pipmuacan, Rés** Quebec Canada
122 B4 **Pipmuacan, Res** Quebec Canada
60 Q2 **Pippu** Japan
20 G6 **Pipriac** France
107 P4 **Piqua** Kansas U.S.A.
110 M1 **Piqua** Ohio U.S.A.
17 F2 **Piqueras, Pto. de** Spain
130 C5 **Piquiri, R** Mato Grosso Brazil
130 D9 **Piquiri, R** Paraná Brazil
85 E7 **Pira** Benin
129 J7 **Piracanjuba** *R* Brazil
130 E5 **Piracanjuba** Brazil
129 J8 **Piracicaba** Brazil
130 G6 **Piracicaba** *R* Brazil
133 F3 **Piracuacito** Argentina
130 F7 **Piraçunungа** Brazil
129 K4 **Piraeuruca** Brazil
46 F7 **Piraiévs** Greece
56 E4 **Piramida, G** *mt* Russian Federation
42 F3 **Piran** Slovenia
129 L5 **Piranhas** Alagoas Brazil
130 D5 **Piranhas** Goiás Brazil
130 D8 **Pirapó, R** Brazil
129 K7 **Pirapora** Brazil
122 A3 **Piraube, L** Quebec Canada
130 C10 **Piray** *R* Argentina
128 F7 **Piray** *R* Bolivia
9 F5 **Pirbright** England
20 H5 **Piré** France
129 J7 **Pires do Rio** Brazil
46 E7 **Pírgos** Greece
46 G9 **Pírgos** Crete Greece
20 E7 **Piriac** France
130 B9 **Piribebuy** Paraguay
46 F3 **Pirin** *plateau* Bulgaria
17 G2 **Pirineos** *mt* Spain
145 E4 **Pirinoa** New Zealand
145 F3 **Piripaua** New Zealand
129 K4 **Piripiri** Brazil
127 M9 **Píritu** Anzoátegui Venezuela
127 K10 **Piritu** Miranda Venezuela
37 N3 **Pirk** Germany
29 K10 **Pirkkala** Finland
36 D5 **Pirmasens** Germany
30 H5 **Pirna** Germany
12 C2 **Pirnmill** Scotland
145 E2 **Pirongia** New Zealand
46 F1 **Pirot** Serbia Yugoslavia
20 G3 **Pirou** France
74 F2 **Pir Panjal Rge** Kashmir
29 M5 **Pirttikoski** Finland
36 F2 **Piru** Moluccas Indonesia
102 F7 **Piru** California U.S.A.
54 D6 **Piryatin** Ukraine
47 H6 **Piryí** Greece
77 J4 **Pirzada** Afghanistan
45 H4 **Pisa** Italy
33 C1 **Pisagua** Chile
71 B3 **Pisang** *isld* Indonesia
44 H3 **Pisanino** *mt* Italy
44 B6 **Pisa Range** New Zealand
70 F1 **Pisau, Tg** *C* Sabah
43 G8 **Pisciotta** Italy
28 C6 **Pisco** Peru
Piscopi *isld see* **Tílos** *isld*
95 N3 **Piseco** New York U.S.A.
30 H6 **Písek** Czech Rep
98 J1 **Pisek** North Dakota U.S.A.
80 F6 **Pisga** Jordan
99 L8 **Pisgah** Iowa U.S.A.
44 C6 **Pisgah, Mt** New Zealand
12 E2 **Pisgah, Mt** North Carolina U.S.A.
77 G6 **Pīshīn** Iran
74 B3 **Pishin** Pakistan
70 G7 **Pising** Sulawesi
103 M9 **Pisinimo** Arizona U.S.A.
102 D6 **Pismo Bch** California U.S.A.
128 F6 **Piso Firme** Bolivia
41 M6 **Pisogne** Italy
85 D6 **Pissila** Burkina
133 D3 **Pissis** *vol* Argentina
29 P6 **Pista** *R* Russian Federation
29 P6 **Pistayarvi** *L* Russian Federation
43 H8 **Pisticci** Italy
45 J4 **Pistoia** Italy
123 R2 **Pistolet B** Newfoundland Canada
100 A7 **Pistol River** Oregon U.S.A.
52 F6 **Pistsovo** Russian Federation
8 C2 **Pistyll Rhaeadr** *mt* Wales
16 E3 **Pisuerga** *R* Spain
31 N2 **Pisz** Poland
100 D8 **Pit** *R* California U.S.A.
85 B6 **Pita** Guinea
122 G1 **Pitaga** Labrador, Nfld Canada
139 G5 **Pitarpunga L** New South Wales Australia
71 G7 **Pitas Pt** Mindanao Philippines
135 U11 **Pitcairn I** Pacific Oc
101 Q5 **Pitchfork** Wyoming U.S.A.
127 O3 **Pitch L** Trinidad
26 M6 **Piteå** Sweden
26 L6 **Piteälv** *R* Sweden
45 J3 **Piteglio** Italy
48 J6 **Pitești** Romania
143 B9 **Pithara** W Australia Australia
21 P5 **Pithiviers** France
42 D6 **Pitigliano** Italy
124 C2 **Pitiquito** Mexico
138 B2 **Pitjantjatjara Lands** South Australia Australia
106 D3 **Pitkin** Colorado U.S.A.
111 D11 **Pitkin** Louisiana U.S.A.
52 D1 **Pitkul'** Russian Federation
52 D4 **Pitkyaranta** Russian Federation
15 E4 **Pitlochry** Scotland
95 M7 **Pitman** New Jersey U.S.A.
87 G12 **Piton des Neiges** *mt* Réunion
111 G11 **Pitre, I. au** Louisiana U.S.A.
13 F1 **Pitscottie** Scotland
9 G4 **Pitsea** England
13 F1 **Pittenweem** Scotland
117 J9 **Pitt I** British Columbia Canada
137 R10 **Pitt I** Chatham Is Pacific Oc
112 H2 **Pittsboro** North Carolina U.S.A.
102 C3 **Pittsburg** California U.S.A.
110 B4 **Pittsburg** Kansas U.S.A.
110 M4 **Pittsburg** Kentucky U.S.A.
121 T7 **Pittsburg** New Hampshire U.S.A.
107 P7 **Pittsburg** Oklahoma U.S.A.
109 N3 **Pittsburg** Texas U.S.A.
94 H6 **Pittsburgh** Pennsylvania U.S.A.
110 E2 **Pittsfield** Illinois U.S.A.
95 S2 **Pittsfield** Maine U.S.A.
95 O4 **Pittsfield** Massachusetts U.S.A.
95 Q3 **Pittsfield** New Hampshire U.S.A.
94 C5 **Pittsford** Michigan U.S.A.
94 K3 **Pittsford** New York U.S.A.
95 O3 **Pittsford** Vermont U.S.A.
95 M5 **Pittston** Pennsylvania U.S.A.
111 L9 **Pittsview** Alabama U.S.A.
95 M8 **Pittsville** Maryland U.S.A.
110 C3 **Pittsville** Missouri U.S.A.
99 Q5 **Pittsville** Wisconsin U.S.A.
141 K8 **Pittsworth** Queensland Australia
100 D8 **Pittville** California U.S.A.
88 E6 **Pitu** *R* Tanzania
Pituffik *see* **Dundas**
140 E6 **Pituri** *R* Queensland Australia
41 N3 **Pitz Tal** Austria
45 J1 **Piú bega** Italy
19 Q17 **Piumoisson** France
128 B4 **Piura** *dept* Peru
128 B5 **Piura** Peru
103 J7 **Piute Mts** California U.S.A.
102 F6 **Piute Pk** California U.S.A.
103 M3 **Piute Res** Utah U.S.A.
75 K4 **Piuthan** Nepal
42 J5 **Piva** *R* Montenegro Yugoslavia
120 G2 **Pivabiska** *R* Ontario Canada
126 G9 **Pivijay** Colombia
31 M6 **Piwniczna** Poland
102 E6 **Pixley** California U.S.A.
46 E5 **Piyaí** Greece
60 Q1 **Piyashiri yama** *mt* Japan
128 E7 **Pizacoma** Peru
52 G5 **Pizhanka** Russian Federation
52 G5 **Pizhma** Russian Federation
41 K4 **Pizol** *mt* Switzerland
43 G10 **Pizzo** Italy
45 O6 **Pizzodeta, M** *mt* Italy
33 Q5 **Plaaz** Germany
20 B4 **Plabennec** France
109 L7 **Placedo** Texas U.S.A.
123 T6 **Placentia** Newfoundland Canada
71 G6 **Placer** Mindanao Philippines
102 F1 **Placeritos** Nevada U.S.A.
102 D3 **Placerville** California U.S.A.
106 B3 **Placerville** Colorado U.S.A.
126 E3 **Placetas** Cuba
46 G2 **Plachkovtsi** Bulgaria
113 E11 **Placida** Florida U.S.A.
113 F10 **Placid, L** Florida U.S.A.
106 D6 **Placitas** New Mexico U.S.A.
46 E3 **Plačkovica** *mt* Macedonia
12 C3 **Pladda I** Scotland
15 C5 **Pladda Lt. Ho** Scotland
40 F4 **Plaffeien** Switzerland
99 Q6 **Plain** Wisconsin U.S.A.
94 D6 **Plain City** Ohio U.S.A.
101 N8 **Plain City** Utah U.S.A.
111 C9 **Plain Dealing** Louisiana U.S.A.
40 E2 **Plain de Corravillers, Le** France
21 J7 **Plaine, la** France
20 F7 **Plaine-sur-Mer, la** France
94 A7 **Plainfield** Indiana U.S.A.
99 O7 **Plainfield** Iowa U.S.A.
95 N6 **Plainfield** New Jersey U.S.A.
99 R5 **Plainfield** Wisconsin U.S.A.
112 C5 **Plains** Georgia U.S.A.
101 L2 **Plains** Montana U.S.A.
108 E2 **Plains** Texas U.S.A.
94 K8 **Plains, The** Virginia U.S.A.
20 E5 **Plaintel** France
110 C6 **Plainview** Arkansas U.S.A.
99 O5 **Plainview** Minnesota U.S.A.
98 J7 **Plainview** Nebraska U.S.A.
108 F1 **Plainview** Texas U.S.A.
95 P5 **Plainville** Connecticut U.S.A.
110 E2 **Plainville** Illinois U.S.A.
107 L2 **Plainville** Kansas U.S.A.
94 B4 **Plainwell** Michigan U.S.A.
18 F9 **Plaisance** France
127 H5 **Plaisance** Haiti
69 G14 **Plaju** Sumatra
46 G4 **Pláka, Akr** *C* Greece
47 H9 **Pláka, Akra** *C* Crete Greece
46 D3 **Plakenska Pl** *mt* Macedonia
118 E4 **Plamondon** Alberta Canada
71 H9 **Plampang** Indonesia
37 O4 **Planá** Czech Rep
102 D4 **Planada** California U.S.A.
129 L5 **Planalto da Borborema** *plateau* Brazil
129 H7 **Planalto de Mato Grosso** *plateau* Brazil
17 G6 **Plana Ó Nueva Tabarca** *isld* Spain
40 E2 **Plancher les Mines** France
40 D4 **Planches-en-Montagne, Les** France
131 B5 **Planchon, Paso de** Chile/Arg
20 F4 **Plancoët** France
19 O15 **Plan-de-Baix** France
19 N17 **Plan d'Orgon** France
17 G9 **Plane** *isld* Algeria
33 R8 **Plane, R** Germany
126 G10 **Planeta Rica** Colombia
137 L3 **Planet Deep** Solomon Sea
37 P5 **Plánice** Czech Rep
37 L4 **Plankenfels** Germany
98 H6 **Plankinton** South Dakota U.S.A.
109 L2 **Plano** Texas U.S.A.
127 M3 **Plantain Garden R** Jamaica
113 E9 **Plant City** Florida U.S.A.
111 K9 **Plantersville** Alabama U.S.A.
111 E11 **Plaquemine** Louisiana U.S.A.
16 C4 **Plasencia** Spain
27 F10 **Plassen** Norway
55 D4 **Plast** Russian Federation
33 R5 **Plasten** Germany
103 J9 **Plaster City** California U.S.A.
37 P4 **Plasy** Czech Rep
43 E11 **Platani** *R* Sicily
133 C2 **Plata, Puerta** Chile
131 G5 **Plata, Rio de la** Arg/Uruguay
19 O14 **Plateau de Chambarand** France
19 J15 **Plateau de Langres** France
19 P16 **Plateau de St. Etienne** France
86 B1 **Plateau du Tchigaï** Niger
85 C3 **Plateau du Tinrhert** *stony desert* Algeria
Plateau of Tibet *see* **Xizang Gaoyuan**
123 T5 **Plate Cove** Newfoundland Canada
124 H6 **Plateros** Mexico
46 F4 **Platí** Greece
46 G4 **Platí Ákra** *C* Greece
46 F5 **Platíkambos** Greece
102 B1 **Platina** California U.S.A.
116 G7 **Platinum** Alaska U.S.A.
118 J7 **Plato** Saskatchewan Canada
126 G10 **Plato** Colombia
110 D4 **Plato** Missouri U.S.A.
56 D5 **Plato Alash** Russian Federation
79 C4 **Platres** Cyprus
37 N4 **Platte** *mt* Germany
99 M9 **Platte** *R* Missouri U.S.A.
98 G9 **Platte** *R* Nebraska U.S.A.
98 H6 **Platte** South Dakota U.S.A.
98 J8 **Platte Center** Nebraska U.S.A.
110 B2 **Platte City** Missouri U.S.A.
106 E2 **Platte Mt** Colorado U.S.A.
98 B9 **Platteville** Colorado U.S.A.
99 Q7 **Platteville** Wisconsin U.S.A.
36 E6 **Plättig** Germany
37 O6 **Plattling** Germany
110 B2 **Plattsburg** Missouri U.S.A.
95 O2 **Plattsburgh** New York U.S.A.
99 K8 **Plattsmouth** Nebraska U.S.A.
33 Q6 **Plau** Germany
33 Q8 **Plaue** Germany
37 K2 **Plaue** Thüringen Germany
37 N3 **Plauen** Germany
46 D2 **Plav** Montenegro Yugoslavia
52 C6 **Pļaviņas** Latvia
42 J6 **Plavnica** Montenegro Yugoslavia
54 J3 **Plavsk** Russian Federation
124 H8 **Playa Azul** Mexico
126 G5 **Playa Daiquirī** Cuba
128 B4 **Playas** Ecuador
106 B10 **Playas L** New Mexico U.S.A.
68 H6 **Play Cu** Vietnam
140 D4 **Playford** *R* N Terr Australia
140 D6 **Playford Mt** N Terr Australia
119 U4 **Playgreen L** Manitoba Canada
124 E5 **Playón** Mexico
98 E1 **Plaza** North Dakota U.S.A.
133 D5 **Plaza Huincul** Argentina
12 E1 **Plean** Scotland
110 M1 **Pleasant** Ohio U.S.A.
95 S5 **Pleasant B** Massachusetts U.S.A.
123 M7 **Pleasant Bay** C Breton I, Nova Scotia
94 F7 **Pleasant City** Ohio U.S.A.
119 N6 **Pleasantdale** Saskatchewan Canada
94 K6 **Pleasant Gap** Pennsylvania U.S.A.
101 O9 **Pleasant Grove** Utah U.S.A.
110 F2 **Pleasant Hill** Illinois U.S.A.
111 C10 **Pleasant Hill** Louisiana U.S.A.
110 B3 **Pleasant Hill** Missouri U.S.A.
94 E6 **Pleasant Hill Res** Ohio U.S.A.
103 M8 **Pleasant, L** Arizona U.S.A.
122 F8 **Pleasant, Mt** New Brunswick Canada
112 H5 **Pleasant, Mt** South Carolina U.S.A.
102 C4 **Pleasanton** California U.S.A.
110 B3 **Pleasanton** Kansas U.S.A.
98 G9 **Pleasanton** Nebraska U.S.A.
109 J7 **Pleasanton** Texas U.S.A.
110 E6 **Pleasant Plains** Arkansas U.S.A.
119 S9 **Pleasant Pt** Manitoba Canada
144 C6 **Pleasant Pt** New Zealand
100 H5 **Pleasant Valley** Oregon U.S.A.
100 G3 **Pleasant View** Washington U.S.A.
99 N8 **Pleasantville** Iowa U.S.A.
95 N7 **Pleasantville** New Jersey U.S.A.
94 H5 **Pleasantville** Pennsylvania U.S.A.
9 E1 **Pleasley** England
110 L3 **Pleasureville** Kentucky U.S.A.
18 G7 **Pleaux** France
37 L4 **Plech** Germany
20 F5 **Plédéliac** France
120 G2 **Pledger L** Ontario Canada
20 E5 **Plédran** France
133 F4 **Pledra Sola** Uruguay
20 D4 **Pléhedel** France
70 D3 **Pleieran** *R* Sarawak
70 D6 **Pleihari** Kalimantan
68 J5 **Plei Herel** Vietnam
68 J6 **Plei Kly** Vietnam
20 G4 **Pleine Fougères** France
37 L5 **Pleinfeld** Germany
20 E3 **Pleinmont Pt** Channel Is
37 P6 **Pleinting** Germany
37 N1 **Pleisse** *R* Germany
68 H5 **Plei Ta Uan** Vietnam
20 F5 **Plélan-le-Grand** France
20 F5 **Plélan-le-Petit** France
20 E5 **Plemet** France
17 F1 **Plencia** Spain
20 F5 **Plenée-Jugon** France
20 E4 **Pléneuf** France
48 H6 **Plentița** Romania
118 J7 **Plenty** Saskatchewan Canada
145 F2 **Plenty, Bay of** New Zealand
140 D6 **Plenty R** N Terr Australia
98 B1 **Plentywood** Montana U.S.A.
20 G4 **Plerguer** France
20 E4 **Plérin** France
20 E6 **Plescop** France
52 F3 **Plesetsk** Russian Federation
55 E3 **Pleshkova** Russian Federation
20 D5 **Plésidy** France
48 F2 **Plešivec** Slovakia
71 J4 **Plesko, Tanjong** *C* Sulawesi
20 F4 **Pleslin-Trivagou** France
20 G6 **Plessé** France
121 T6 **Plessisville** Quebec Canada
20 F5 **Plestan** France
20 C4 **Plestin-les-Greves** France
122 B2 **Pletipi L** Quebec Canada
36 D1 **Plettenberg** Germany
89 C10 **Plettenberg B** S Africa
20 D4 **Pleubian** France
20 G4 **Pleudihen-sur-Rance** France
20 G5 **Pleugueneuc** France
21 M8 **Pleumartin** France
20 C4 **Pleumeur** France
20 F4 **Pleurtuit** France
46 G1 **Pleven** Bulgaria
98 B3 **Plevna** Montana U.S.A.
20 C5 **Pleyben** France
20 C4 **Pleyber-Christ** France
37 N4 **Pleystein** Germany
145 E4 **Plimmerton** New Zealand
48 M1 **Pliskov** Ukraine
42 G4 **Plitvice** Croatia
42 G4 **Pljesivica** *dist* Croatia
48 E7 **Pljevlja** Montenegro Yugoslavia
43 B8 **Ploaghe** Sardinia
36 D7 **Plobsheim** France
42 H5 **Ploča** *lighthouse* Croatia
36 G6 **Plochingen** Germany
31 M3 **Płock** Poland
30 H7 **Plöckenstein** *mt* Czech Rep
22 D2 **Ploegsteert** Belgium
20 D6 **Ploemel** France
20 D6 **Ploemeur** France
20 D5 **Ploërdut** France
20 F6 **Ploërmel** France
20 B6 **Plogastel-St. Germain** France
20 A5 **Plogoff** France
20 B5 **Plogonnec** France
48 K6 **Ploiești** Romania
47 H6 **Plomárion** Greece
18 G7 **Plomb du Cantal** *mt* France
19 K5 **Plombières-les-Bains** France
40 A3 **Plombières-les-Dijon** France
20 B6 **Plomelin** France
139 L4 **Plomer, Pt** New South Wales Australia
20 B6 **Plomeur** France
22 G4 **Plomion** France
33 M4 **Plön** Germany
31 J2 **Płona** *R* Poland
20 B5 **Plonéis** France
20 B6 **Plonéour-Lanvern** France
20 C5 **Plonévez-du-Faou** France
20 B5 **Plonévez-Porzay** France
31 M3 **Płońsk** Poland
48 K5 **Plopeni** Romania
48 H6 **Plopi** Romania
52 D6 **Ploskosh'** Russian Federation
37 N4 **Plössberg** Germany
31 J2 **Płoty** Poland
20 D4 **Plouagat** France
20 D4 **Plouaret** France
20 A5 **Plouarzel** France
20 D6 **Plouay** France
20 F4 **Ploubalay** France
20 E5 **Plœuc** France
31 H5 **Ploučnice** *R* Czech Rep
20 A4 **Ploudalmézeau** France
20 B4 **Ploudaniel** France
20 B5 **Ploudiry** France
20 B4 **Plouénan** France
20 G4 **Plouër-Langrolay-sur-Rance** France
20 B4 **Plouescat** France
20 E4 **Plouézec** France
20 E4 **Plouézec, Pte.de** France
20 B5 **Plougastel-Daoulas** France
20 E5 **Plougenast** France
20 A5 **Plougonvelin** France
20 C4 **Plougonven** France
20 D5 **Plougonver** France
20 E6 **Plougoumelen** France
20 D4 **Plougrescant** France
20 A4 **Plouguerneau** France
20 D5 **Plouguernevel** France
20 E4 **Plouha** France
20 D6 **Plouharnel** France
20 A5 **Plouhinec** Finistère France
20 D6 **Plouhinec** Morbihan France
20 C4 **Plouigneau** France
20 C4 **Ploujean** France
20 D4 **Ploumanac'h** France
20 C4 **Ploumilliau** France
20 A5 **Ploumoguer** France
20 C5 **Plounëour-Ménez** France
20 B4 **Plouneour-Tréz** France
20 C4 **Plounérin** France
20 B4 **Plounévez-Lochrist** France
20 D5 **Plounevez-Quintin** France
20 C5 **Plourach** France
20 D5 **Plouray** France
20 A4 **Plourin** France
20 B4 **Plouvien** France
20 B4 **Plouvorn** France
20 C5 **Plouyé** France
20 B4 **Plouzévéde** France
46 G2 **Plovdiv** Bulgaria
99 M7 **Plover** Iowa U.S.A.
99 R5 **Plover** *R* Wisconsin U.S.A.
99 R5 **Plover** Wisconsin U.S.A.
116 K1 **Plover Is** Alaska U.S.A.
20 B6 **Plozévet** France
36 H6 **Plüderhausen** Germany
119 S8 **Plumas** Manitoba Canada
20 F5 **Plumaugat** France
99 O5 **Plum City** Wisconsin U.S.A.
118 D1 **Plum Coulee** Manitoba Canada
20 E6 **Plumelec** France
20 E6 **Pluméliau** France
20 E6 **Plumelin** France
20 E6 **Plumergat** France
95 P5 **Plum I** New York U.S.A.
20 E5 **Plumieux** France
100 J2 **Plummer** Idaho U.S.A.
116 H6 **Plummer, Mt** Alaska U.S.A.
110 D6 **Plummerville** Arkansas U.S.A.
13 F4 **Plumpton Hd** England
143 F8 **Plumridge Lakes** W Australia Australia
87 E10 **Plumtree** Zimbabwe
20 E6 **Pluneret** France
52 B6 **Plunge** Lithuania
119 M7 **Plunkett** Saskatchewan Canada
100 F7 **Plush** Oregon U.S.A.
20 D6 **Pluvigner** France
36 B4 **Pluwig** Germany
20 D4 **Pluzunet** France
8 B7 **Plymouth** England
127 M2 **Plymouth** Tobago
102 D3 **Plymouth** California U.S.A.
94 A5 **Plymouth** Indiana U.S.A.
99 N6 **Plymouth** Iowa U.S.A.
95 R5 **Plymouth** Massachusetts U.S.A.
98 K9 **Plymouth** Nebraska U.S.A.
95 Q3 **Plymouth** New Hampshire U.S.A.
94 E6 **Plymouth** Ohio U.S.A.
95 M5 **Plymouth** Pennsylvania U.S.A.
101 N8 **Plymouth** Utah U.S.A.
95 P3 **Plymouth** Vermont U.S.A.
99 T6 **Plymouth** Wisconsin U.S.A.
127 O6 **Plymouth** Montserrat W Indies
122 G9 **Plympton** Nova Scotia Canada
8 B7 **Plympton** England
8 C3 **Plynlimon Fawr** *mt* Wales
52 C5 **Plyussa** *R* Russian Federation
52 C5 **Plyussa** Russian Federation
37 P4 **Plzeň** Czech Rep
31 J3 **Pniewy** Poland
85 D6 **Po** Burkina
45 J2 **Po** *R* Italy
71 H5 **Poat** *isld* Sulawesi
139 H8 **Poatina** Tasmania Australia
85 E7 **Pobé** Benin
66 C3 **Pobedy, Pik** *mt* China/Kazakhstan
37 O5 **Poběžovice** Czech Rep
31 K3 **Pobiedziska** Poland
17 J2 **Pobla de Lilleta, L** Spain
17 H2 **Pobla de Segur** Spain
110 F5 **Pocahontas** Arkansas U.S.A.
99 M7 **Pocahontas** Iowa U.S.A.
94 F9 **Pocahontas** Virginia U.S.A.
107 N6 **Pocasse** Oklahoma U.S.A.
94 F8 **Pocatalico** *R* West Virginia U.S.A.
101 N7 **Pocatello** Idaho U.S.A.
31 J6 **Počátky** Czech Rep
131 D3 **Pocha, Sa. de** *mts* Argentina
54 E4 **Pochep** Russian Federation
54 D2 **Pochinok** Russian Federation
38 M5 **Pochlarn** Austria
125 L10 **Pochutla** Mexico
37 P5 **Pocinovice** Czech Rep
37 P2 **Pockau** Germany
37 P7 **Pocking** Germany
13 H6 **Pocklington** England
70 F2 **Pock, Mt** Sabah
128 D7 **Pocoma** Peru
95 M8 **Pocomoke City** Maryland U.S.A.
95 M9 **Pocomoke Sd** Virginia U.S.A.
129 G7 **Poconé** Brazil
95 M6 **Pocono Mts** Pennsylvania U.S.A.
95 M5 **Pocono Pines** Pennsylvania U.S.A.
129 J8 **Pocos de Caldas** Brazil
125 O6 **Pocrí** Panama
125 P9 **Poctún** Guatemala
103 L5 **Pocum Wash** *creek* Arizona U.S.A.
37 P3 **Podbořany** Czech Rep
52 J3 **Podcher'ye** Russian Federation
31 L4 **Poddębice** Poland
118 C4 **Poddle R** Alberta Canada
52 D5 **Poddor'ye** Russian Federation
31 J5 **Poděbrady** Czech Rep
45 M2 **Po delle Tolle** *R* Italy
18 E8 **Podensac** France
48 J1 **Podgaytsy** Ukraine
42 J6 **Podgorica** Montenegro Yugoslavia
54 G8 **Podgornoye** Ukraine
45 M2 **Po di Goro** *R* Italy
76 D3 **Podile** India
45 L2 **Po di Volano** *R* Italy
51 Q2 **Podkagernoye** Russian Federation
56 D1 **Podkamennay** *R* Russian Federation
38 J9 **Podkoren** Slovenia
46 G3 **Podkova** Bulgaria
48 F1 **Podolinec** Slovakia
54 J1 **Podol'sk** Russian Federation
85 B5 **Podor** Senegal
52 G4 **Podosinovets** Russian Federation
42 H4 **Podovi** Bosnia-Herzegovina
52 D4 **Podporozh'ye** Russian Federation
55 E2 **Podrezovo** Russian Federation
56 D2 **Podtesovo** Russian Federation
48 L3 **Podu Iloaiei** Romania
46 E2 **Podujevo** Serbia Yugoslavia
48 L4 **Podu Turcului** Romania
52 F4 **Podyuga** Russian Federation
33 O4 **Poel** *isld* Germany
22 D2 **Poelkapelle** Belgium
140 E7 **Poeppel Corner** N Terr Australia
94 C1 **Poe Reef Lt. Ho** Michigan U.S.A.
144 C5 **Poerua** New Zealand
87 C11 **Pofadder** S Africa
45 O6 **Pofi** Italy
120 J6 **Pogamasing** Ontario Canada
54 E4 **Pogar** Russian Federation
33 S4 **Poggendorf** Germany
42 D5 **Poggibonsi** Italy
45 K4 **Poggio a Caiano** Italy
45 N5 **Poggio Moiano** Italy
45 K2 **Póggio Renatico** Italy
45 K2 **Póggio Rusco** Italy
59 M1 **Pogibi** Russian Federation
48 L6 **Pogoanele** Romania
46 D4 **Pogradec** Albania
45 M2 **Po Grande** *R* Italy
65 H2 **Pogranichnyy** Russian Federation
48 M1 **Pogrebishche** Ukraine
116 E9 **Pogromni Vol** Aleutian Is
32 F6 **Pogum** Germany
71 H5 **Poh** Sulawesi
135 U5 **Pohakuloa** Hawaiian Is
59 J4 **Pohang** S Korea
145 E4 **Pohangina** New Zealand
145 D4 **Pohara** New Zealand
29 K11 **Pohja** Finland
29 O8 **Pohjois-Karjala** *prov* Finland
36 F3 **Pohl-Göns** Germany
36 F2 **Pohlheim** Germany
145 E3 **Pohokura** New Zealand
145 F3 **Pohokura** *mt* New Zealand
48 F2 **Pohorelá** Slovakia
31 K7 **Pohořelice** Czech Rep
38 M9 **Pohorje** *mt* Slovenia
102 V14 **Pohue B** Hawaiian Is
45 K1 **Poiana Magg** Italy
46 F1 **Poiana Mare** Romania
48 K3 **Poiana Teiului** Romania
71 J4 **Poigar** Sulawesi Indonesia
123 O2 **Poincaré, L** Quebec Canada
146 G14 **Poinsett, C** Antarctica
113 G9 **Poinsett, L** Florida U.S.A.
102 D7 **Point Arguello** California U.S.A.
109 M5 **Pointblank** Texas U.S.A.
138 E5 **Point Broughton** South Australia Australia
102 D6 **Point Buchon** California U.S.A.
109 L7 **Point Comfort** Texas U.S.A.
102 D7 **Point Conception** California U.S.A.
123 N3 **Pointe-à Maurier** Quebec Canada
127 O3 **Pointe-á-Pierre** Trinidad
127 N4 **Pointe-á-Pitre** Guadeloupe W Indies
120 K7 **Pointe au Baril Station** Ontario Canada
122 E4 **Pointe aux Anglais** Quebec Canada
121 R7 **Pointe aux Trembles** Quebec Canada
121 S4 **Pointe Bleue** Quebec Canada
122 H7 **Pointe du Chêne** New Brunswick Canada
120 H9 **Point Edward** Ontario Canada
122 D4 **Pointe le Bel** Quebec Canada
86 B6 **Pointe-Noire** Congo
127 M4 **Pointe Noire** Guadeloupe W Indies
22 C1 **Pointe Synthe** France
122 G6 **Pointe Verte** New Brunswick Canada
127 N3 **Point Fortin** Trinidad
123 K8 **Point George, C** Nova Scotia Canada
112 M1 **Point Harbor** North Carolina U.S.A.
139 H8 **Point Hills** Tasmania Australia
116 D2 **Point Hope** Alaska U.S.A.
117 R3 **Point L** Northwest Territories Canada
116 F2 **Point Lay** Alaska U.S.A.
139 L4 **Point Lookout** *mt* New South Wales Australia
95 L8 **Point Lookout** Maryland U.S.A.
94 H7 **Point Marion** Pennsylvania U.S.A.
94 K7 **Point of Rocks** Maryland U.S.A.
101 R8 **Point of Rocks** Wyoming U.S.A.
120 H10 **Point Pelee Nat Park** Ontario Canada
95 N6 **Point Pleasant** New Jersey U.S.A.
94 E8 **Point Pleasant** West Virginia U.S.A.
142 B5 **Point Samson** W Australia Australia
140 B1 **Point Stuart** N Terr Australia
102 C5 **Point Sur** California U.S.A.
138 D5 **Point Turton** South Australia Australia
145 E2 **Point Waikato** New Zealand
68 F6 **Poipet** Cambodia
20 G8 **Poiré-sur-Vie, le** France
52 H6 **Poisevo** Russian Federation
101 S6 **Poison Cr** Wyoming U.S.A.
142 B1 **Poison Gully** *R* Perth, W Aust Australia
121 P6 **Poisson Blanc, L** Quebec Canada
142 C5 **Poissonnier Pt** W Australia Australia
21 P4 **Poissy** France
21 L8 **Poitiers** France
21 J8 **Poitou** *reg* France
142 B5 **Poivre, C** W Australia Australia
21 O2 **Poix-de-Picardie** France
22 J3 **Poix St. Hubert** Belgium
22 H4 **Poix-Terron** France
46 D4 **Pojan** Albania
106 D6 **Pojoaque** New Mexico U.S.A.
102 R12 **Pokai Bay** Hawaiian Is
145 E3 **Pokaka** New Zealand
74 D5 **Pokaran** India
139 J3 **Pokataroo** New South Wales Australia
52 J3 **Pokcha** Russian Federation
145 E2 **Pokeno** New Zealand
75 L4 **Pokhara** Nepal
29 M3 **Pokka** Finland
86 E5 **Poko** Zaire
31 K5 **Pokój** Poland
116 F2 **Poko Mt** Alaska U.S.A.
52 E6 **Pokrov** Russian Federation
55 E5 **Pokrovka** Tselinogradskaya obl Kazakhstan
55 G3 **Pokrovka** Novosibirskaya obl Russian Federation
55 B5 **Pokrovka** Orenburgskaya obl Russian Federation
55 E3 **Pokrovskoye** Russian Federation
52 F3 **Pokshen'ga** *R* Russian Federation
71 E4 **Pola** Philippines
71 E4 **Pola B** Philippines
103 O6 **Polacca** Arizona U.S.A.
103 O6 **Polacca Wasa** *R* Arizona U.S.A.
16 D1 **Pola de Laviana** Spain
16 D1 **Pola de Lena** Spain
16 D1 **Pola de Siero** Spain
31 K4 **Poland** *rep* Europe
95 M3 **Poland** New York U.S.A.
31 K1 **Polanow** Poland
99 S4 **Polar** Wisconsin U.S.A.
101 M4 **Polaris** Montana U.S.A.
78 D2 **Polatlı** Turkey
8 B7 **Polbathick** England
36 C3 **Polch** Germany
133 C5 **Polcura** Chile
31 J2 **Połczyn Zdrój** Poland
52 E3 **Pole** Russian Federation
37 P5 **Poledník** *mt* Czech Rep
80 C5 **Poleg** *R* Israel
9 G6 **Polegate** England
68 H5 **Polei Monu** Vietnam
57 B6 **Polekhatum** Turkmenistan
77 L2 **Pol-e-Khomrī** Afghanistan
37 P5 **Poleň** Czech Rep
45 L2 **Polesella** Italy
31 N1 **Polessk** Russian Federation
53 C8 **Polesye** *marsh* Belarus/Ukraine
55 D3 **Polevskoy** Russian Federation
70 F6 **Polewali** Sulawesi
48 G3 **Polgár** Hungary
48 E3 **Polgárdi** Hungary
86 B4 **Poli** Cameroon
46 G8 **Políaigos** *isld* Greece
43 G8 **Policastro, G. di** Italy
31 H2 **Police** Poland
138 E6 **Policemans Point** South Australia Australia
31 J6 **Polička** Czech Rep
19 J6 **Poligny** France
46 F3 **Políkastron** Greece
47 H5 **Políkhnitos** Greece
71 E3 **Polillo** *isld* Luzon Philippines
45 J3 **Polinago** Italy
38 H8 **Polinik** *mt* Austria
127 L3 **Polink Pt** Jamaica
79 C3 **Polis** Cyprus
71 J4 **Polisan, Tanjong** *C* Sulawesi
52 D5 **Polist'** *R* Russian Federation
52 G3 **Politovo** Russian Federation
98 J8 **Polk** Nebraska U.S.A.
94 H5 **Polk** Pennsylvania U.S.A.
56 D1 **Polkan, Gora** *mt* Russian Federation
113 F9 **Polk City** Florida U.S.A.
33 P7 **Polkritz** Germany
76 C5 **Pollachi** India
37 L5 **Pollanten** Germany
14 E3 **Pollaphuca Res** Ireland
110 F5 **Pollard** Arkansas U.S.A.
38 N7 **Pöllau** Austria
32 K9 **Polle** Germany
122 A1 **Pollet, L** Quebec Canada
43 G9 **Pollino, M** *mt* Italy
33 P7 **Pollitz** Germany
100 J4 **Pollock** Idaho U.S.A.
111 D10 **Pollock** Louisiana U.S.A.
98 F4 **Pollock** South Dakota U.S.A.
142 G6 **Pollock Hills** W Australia Australia
143 E10 **Pollock Reef** W Australia Australia
112 K3 **Pollocksville** North Carolina U.S.A.
118 F7 **Pollockville** Alberta Canada
144 B6 **Pollux** *mt* New Zealand
29 N2 **Polmak** Finland
26 Q1 **Polmak** Norway
12 E2 **Polmont** Scotland
31 J6 **Polná** Czech Rep
52 C5 **Polna** Russian Federation
99 R8 **Polo** Illinois U.S.A.
110 B2 **Polo** Missouri U.S.A.
54 H9 **Pologi** Ukraine
71 G7 **Polomoloc** Mindanao Philippines
54 G2 **Polotnanyy Zavod** Russian Federation
52 C6 **Polotsk** Belarus
55 E4 **Polovinnoye** Russian Federation
52 H3 **Polovniki** Russian Federation
8 B7 **Polperro** England
83 K10 **Polpitigama** Sri Lanka
38 L7 **Pöls** *R* Austria
47 H2 **Polski Gradets** Bulgaria
47 H1 **Polski Trŭmbesh** Bulgaria
101 L2 **Polson** Montana U.S.A.
38 K7 **Pöls-Tal** *V* Austria
52 F2 **Polta** *R* Russian Federation
48 F2 **Poltár** Slovakia
54 F7 **Poltava** Ukraine
55 F4 **Poltavka** Russian Federation
121 P7 **Poltimore** Quebec Canada
52 C5 **Põltsamaa** Estonia
55 E4 **Poludino** Kazakhstan
55 D1 **Polunochnoye** Russian Federation
50 E4 **Poluostrov Buzachi** *pen* Kazakhstan
106 D7 **Polvadera** New Mexico U.S.A.
29 O9 **Polvijärvi** Finland
118 L5 **Polwarth** Saskatchewan Canada
31 L1 **Półwysep Helski** *pen* Poland
55 E1 **Pol'yanovo** Russian Federation
52 D1 **Polyarnyy** Russian Federation
116 N5 **Polychrome Pass** Alaska U.S.A.
46 F4 **Polýiros** Greece
134 K12 **Polynesia** *ethnic reg* Pacific Oc
56 C4 **Polysayevo** Russian Federation
37 N2 **Pölzig** Germany
133 D2 **Poma** Argentina
144 B6 **Pomahaka** *R* New Zealand
133 D3 **Poman** Argentina
16 B7 **Pomarão** Portugal
112 F3 **Pomaria** South Carolina U.S.A.
29 J10 **Pomarkku** Finland
130 G7 **Pomba** *R* Brazil
129 L5 **Pombal** Brazil
16 B5 **Pombal** Portugal
130 D7 **Pombo, R** Brazil
19 O18 **Pomègues, Île** France
31 G2 **Pomerania** *reg* Germany/Poland
99 M7 **Pomercy** Iowa U.S.A.
103 O9 **Pomerene** Arizona U.S.A.
14 E2 **Pomeroy** N Ireland
94 E7 **Pomeroy** Ohio U.S.A.
100 H3 **Pomeroy** Washington U.S.A.
45 M6 **Pomezia** Italy
95 P5 **Pomfret** Connecticut U.S.A.
45 Q8 **Pomigliano d'Arco** Italy
110 C4 **Pomme de Terre** *R* Missouri U.S.A.
37 M5 **Pommelsbrunn** Germany
20 D4 **Pommerit-Jaudy** France
20 D4 **Pommerit-le-Vicomte** France
21 O8 **Pommiers** France
107 P3 **Pomoma** Kansas U.S.A.
141 L7 **Pomona** Queensland Australia
125 P9 **Pomona** Belize
87 C11 **Pomona** Namibia
110 E5 **Pomona** Missouri U.S.A.
47 J2 **Pomorie** Bulgaria
52 E3 **Pomorskiy Bereg** *coast* Russian Federation
48 J1 **Pomoryany** Ukraine
54 C8 **Pomoshnaya** Ukraine
21 K8 **Pompaire** France
113 G11 **Pompano Beach** Florida U.S.A.
45 Q8 **Pompei** Italy
95 L4 **Pompey** New York U.S.A.
142 G3 **Pompeys Pillar** *mt* W Australia Australia
101 S4 **Pompeys Pillar** Montana U.S.A.
95 N5 **Pompton Lakes** New Jersey U.S.A.
88 D10 **Pompué** *R* Mozambique
123 L8 **Pomquet** Nova Scotia Canada
33 R10 **Pomssen** Germany
119 N6 **Ponass L** Saskatchewan Canada
98 K7 **Ponca** Nebraska U.S.A.
107 N5 **Ponca City** Oklahoma U.S.A.
127 L5 **Ponce** Puerto Rico
111 L11 **Ponce de Leon** Florida U.S.A.
113 F12 **Ponce de Leon B** Florida U.S.A.
113 F8 **Ponce de Leon Inlet** Florida U.S.A.
111 F11 **Ponchatoula** Louisiana U.S.A.
124 H7 **Poncitlán** Mexico
107 N5 **Pond Creek** Oklahoma U.S.A.
109 K2 **Ponder** Texas U.S.A.
76 D5 **Pondicherry** India
115 M3 **Pond Inlet** Northwest Territories Canada
89 F8 **Pondoland** *reg* S Africa
100 D8 **Pondosa** California U.S.A.
100 H4 **Pondosa** Oregon U.S.A.
99 M1 **Ponemah** Minnesota U.S.A.
44 E3 **Ponente** Italy
94 B6 **Poneto** Indiana U.S.A.
16 C2 **Ponferrada** Spain
86 A5 **Pongara, Pte** Gabon
145 F4 **Pongaroa** New Zealand
38 H7 **Pongau** *reg* Austria
70 G7 **Pongkolaero** Sulawesi
52 D2 **Pon'goma** Russian Federation
122 H9 **Ponhook L** Nova Scotia Canada
31 N4 **Poniatowa** Poland
33 T10 **Ponickau** Germany
31 K4 **Poniec** Poland
71 H4 **Poniki, Mt** Sulawesi
70 G5 **Ponindilisa, Tg** *C* Sulawesi
68 A2 **Ponnagyun** Burma
68 B1 **Ponnyadaung** *ra* Burma
118 D6 **Ponoka** Alberta Canada
55 B4 **Ponomarevka** Russian Federation
70 N9 **Ponorogo** Java
52 E2 **Ponoy** *R* Russian Federation
52 F2 **Ponoy** Russian Federation
18 E7 **Pons** France
17 H3 **Pons** Spain
45 J4 **Ponsacco** Italy
71 G5 **Ponson** *isld* Philippines
18 E9 **Pontacq** France
130 E9 **Ponta Grossa** Brazil
40 B3 **Pontailler** France
19 J5 **Pontailler-sur-Saône** France
19 O15 **Pontaix** France
22 E3 **Pont-à-Marcq** France
19 J4 **Pont à Mousson** France
129 G8 **Ponta Porá** Brazil
8 C4 **Pontardawe** Wales
8 B4 **Pontarddulais** Wales
19 K6 **Pontarlier** France
45 K4 **Pontassieve** Italy
20 H4 **Pontaubault** France
21 M3 **Pont Audemer** France
18 G7 **Pontaumur** France
20 C6 **Pont-Aven** France
22 F5 **Pontavert** France
121 M1 **Pontax** *R* Quebec Canada
122 K3 **Pontbriand B** Quebec Canada
40 G7 **Pont-Canav** Italy
19 Q14 **Pontcharra** France
111 F11 **Pontchartrain, L** Louisiana U.S.A.
20 F7 **Pont-Château** France
20 B5 **Pont-Croix** France
19 Q17 **Pont-d'Aiguines** France
19 O12 **Pont d'Ain** France
19 O15 **Pont-de-Barret** France
21 M6 **Pont-de-Braye** France
20 B5 **Pont-de-Buis** France
21 N3 **Pont-de-l'Arche** France
40 C4 **Pont-de-Poitte** France
19 J6 **Pont de Vaux** France
19 J6 **Pont de Veyle** France
21 K4 **Pont-d'Ouilly** France
129 J6 **Ponte Alta do Norte** Brazil
42 E2 **Pontebba** Italy
45 R8 **Pontecagnano** Italy
45 P7 **Pontecorvo** Italy
16 B3 **Ponte da Barca** Portugal
129 G6 **Ponte de Pedra** Brazil
45 J4 **Pontedera** Italy
16 B5 **Ponte de Sor** Portugal
16 B3 **Ponte do Lima** Portugal
13 G6 **Pontefract** England
118 K9 **Ponteix** Saskatchewan Canada
45 L2 **Pontelagoscuro** Italy
13 G3 **Ponteland** England
45 R7 **Pontelandolfo** Italy
45 M1 **Pontelongo** Italy
130 G7 **Ponte Nova** Brazil
18 E8 **Pontenx les Forges** France
8 C3 **Ponterwyd** Wales
45 L1 **Ponte San Nicolò** Italy
16 B2 **Pontevedra** *prov* Spain
16 B2 **Pontevedra** Spain
113 F7 **Ponte Vedra Beach** Florida U.S.A.
19 N13 **Pont-Evêque** France

41 M7 **Pontevico** Italy
21 H4 **Pontfarcy** France
22 G5 **Pont Faverger** France
21 N5 **Pontgouin** France
20 E5 **Pont-Hamon** France
21 H3 **Pont-Hébert** France
99 S9 **Pontiac** Illinois U.S.A.
94 D4 **Pontiac** Michigan U.S.A.
70 A5 **Pontianak** Kalimantan
43 E7 **Pontinia** Italy
20 E5 **Pontivy** France
20 B6 **Pont-l'Abbé** France
122 H6 **Pont Lafrance** New Brunswick Canada
40 A1 **Pont la Ville** France
21 L3 **Pont-l'Evêque** France
21 N7 **Pontlevoy** France
20 D5 **Pont-Melvez** France
119 S4 **Ponton** Manitoba Canada
143 E9 **Ponton Ck** W Australia Australia
20 H4 **Pontorson** France
111 G7 **Pontotoc** Mississippi U.S.A.
109 J5 **Pontotoc** Texas U.S.A.
44 G3 **Pontremoli** Italy
41 L4 **Pontresina** Switzerland
8 C3 **Pontrhydfendigaid** Wales
8 B1 **Pont Rhythallt** Wales
20 D4 **Pontrieux** France
119 N5 **Pontrilas** Saskatchewan Canada
8 D4 **Pontrilas** England
121 T6 **Pont Rouge** Quebec Canada
19 N16 **Pont-St. Esprit** France
22 D5 **Pont-Ste. Maxence** France
20 D6 **Pont-Scorff** France
21 J7 **Ponts-de-Cé, les** France
22 F3 **Pont-sur-Sambre** France
18 H4 **Pont-sur-Yonne** France
20 B4 **Pontusval, Pte.de** France
21 L6 **Pontvallain** France
121 M8 **Pontypool** Ontario Canada
8 C4 **Pontypool** Wales
8 C4 **Pontypridd** Wales
145 E2 **Ponui I** New Zealand
101 O4 **Pony** Montana U.S.A.
43 E8 **Ponza, I di** Italy
43 E8 **Ponziane, Isole** *islds* Italy
138 C4 **Poochera** South Australia Australia
13 G6 **Pool** England
138 D2 **Poolawanna L** South Australia Australia
144 B6 **Poolburn Dam** New Zealand
9 E6 **Poole** England
138 F3 **Poole, Mt** New South Wales Australia
112 F5 **Pooler** Georgia U.S.A.
95 K7 **Poolesville** Maryland U.S.A.
15 C3 **Poolewe** Scotland
12 E1 **Pool of Muckart** Scotland
109 K3 **Poolville** Texas U.S.A.
Poona *see* **Pune**
139 G5 **Pooncarie** New South Wales Australia
143 B8 **Poondarrie,Mt** W Australia Australia
139 G4 **Poopelloe, L** New South Wales Australia
128 E7 **Poopó** Bolivia
145 E1 **Poor Knights Is** New Zealand
116 K4 **Poorman** Alaska U.S.A.
86 C7 **Popakabaka** Zaire
129 G3 **Popakai** Suriname
54 K8 **Popasnaya** Ukraine
128 C3 **Popayan** Colombia
27 M14 **Pope** Latvia
103 J8 **Pope** California U.S.A.
111 G7 **Pope** Mississippi U.S.A.
99 N7 **Popejoy** Iowa U.S.A.
58 F1 **Poperechnoye** Russian Federation
22 D2 **Poperinge** Belgium
95 L8 **Popes Creek** Maryland U.S.A.
95 S3 **Popham Beach** Maine U.S.A.
51 K1 **Popigay** *R* Russian Federation
138 F5 **Popiltah** New South Wales Australia
98 A1 **Poplar** Montana U.S.A.
99 P3 **Poplar** Wisconsin U.S.A.
110 F5 **Poplar Bluff** Missouri U.S.A.
101 U1 **Poplar Cr** Montana U.S.A.
119 U6 **Poplar Pt** Manitoba Canada
111 G11 **Poplarville** Mississippi U.S.A.
125 K8 **Popocatepetl** *vol* Mexico
116 G9 **Popof I** Alaska U.S.A.
70 N10 **Popoh** Java
45 P5 **Popoli** Italy
136 K3 **Popondetta** Papua New Guinea
47 H1 **Popovo** Bulgaria
37 M5 **Poppberg** *mt* Germany
25 H4 **Poppe** Netherlands
22 J1 **Poppel** Belgium
37 J3 **Poppenhausen** Germany
45 L4 **Poppi** Italy
31 M6 **Poprad** Slovakia
48 F1 **Poprad** *R* Slovakia
128 E8 **Poquis** *mt* Chile/Arg
95 L9 **Poquoson** Virginia U.S.A.
145 F4 **Porangahau** New Zealand
74 C8 **Porbander** India
117 H9 **Porcher I** British Columbia Canada
54 B1 **Porch'ye** Pskovskaya obl Russian Federation
133 D1 **Porco** Bolivia
16 E7 **Porcuna** Spain
141 G5 **Porcupine** *R* Queensland Australia
116 R3 **Porcupine** *R* Alaska/Yukon Terr U.S.A./Canada
90 H3 **Porcupine Bank** Atlantic Oc
101 T1 **Porcupine Cr** Montana U.S.A.
118 C8 **Porcupine Hills** Alberta Canada
119 Q6 **Porcupine Hills** Manitoba/Sask Canada
99 R3 **Porcupine Mts** Michigan U.S.A.
119 O6 **Porcupine Plain** Saskatchewan Canada
42 E3 **Pordenoné** Italy
46 G1 **Pordim** Bulgaria
42 F3 **Poreč** Croatia
130 D8 **Porecatu** Brazil
55 D2 **Porech'ye** Russian Federation
52 G6 **Poretskoye** Russian Federation
145 E4 **Porewa** New Zealand
85 E6 **Porga** Benin
29 J10 **Pori** Finland
145 F4 **Porirua** New Zealand
80 F3 **Poriyya** Israel
26 L5 **Porjus** Sweden
29 L12 **Porkala** Finland
52 C5 **Porkhov** Russian Federation
128 F1 **Porlamar** Venezuela
41 K5 **Porlezza** Italy
8 C5 **Porlock** England
37 L6 **Pörnbach** Germany
20 F7 **Pornic** France
20 F7 **Pornichet** France
71 G5 **Poro** *isld* Philippines
52 E3 **Porog** Arkhangel'skaya obl Russian Federation
52 J4 **Porog** Komi Respublika Russian Federation
59 M2 **Poronaysk** Russian Federation
68 G6 **Porong** *R* Cambodia
143 C10 **Porongorup** W Australia Australia
60 Q1 **Poronupuri yama** *mt* Japan
145 E3 **Porootarao** New Zealand
46 F7 **Póros** *isld* Greece
60 Q1 **Poroshiri yama** *mt* Japan
52 D3 **Porosozero** Russian Federation
52 H3 **Porozhsk** Russian Federation
56 F3 **Porozhskiy** Russian Federation
146 E14 **Porpoise B** Antarctica
19 Q18 **Porquerolles, I. de** France
120 K4 **Porquis Junct** Ontario Canada
40 F3 **Pörrentruy** Switzerland
45 J3 **Porretta Terme** Italy
16 B2 **Porriño** Spain
26 N1 **Porsa** Norway
26 O1 **Porsangen** *inlet* Norway
27 D12 **Porsgrunn** Norway
20 A4 **Porspoder** France
33 Q9 **Porst** Germany
47 L5 **Porsük** *R* Turkey
128 F7 **Portachuelo** Bolivia
138 E5 **Port Adelaide** South Australia Australia
14 E2 **Portadown** N Ireland
144 B7 **Port Adventure** New Zealand
14 F2 **Portaferry** N Ireland
122 H7 **Portage** Prince Edward I Canada
116 N6 **Portage** Alaska U.S.A.
95 S7 **Portage** Maine U.S.A.
101 O2 **Portage** Montana U.S.A.
94 D5 **Portage** *R* Ohio U.S.A.
94 J6 **Portage** Pennsylvania U.S.A.
101 N8 **Portage** Utah U.S.A.
110 F3 **Portage des Sioux** Missouri U.S.A.
122 G6 **Portage I** New Brunswick Canada
119 T9 **Portage la Prairie** Manitoba Canada
110 G5 **Portageville** Missouri U.S.A.
94 J4 **Portageville** New York U.S.A.
103 P10 **Portal** Arizona U.S.A.
112 F5 **Portal** Georgia U.S.A.
98 D1 **Portal** North Dakota U.S.A.
14 D3 **Portalaoise** Ireland
117 L11 **Port Alberni** British Columbia Canada
139 H7 **Port Albert** Victoria Australia
120 J9 **Port Albert** Ontario Canada
145 E2 **Port Albert** New Zealand
16 C5 **Portalegre** Portugal
106 G7 **Portales** New Mexico U.S.A.
117 F7 **Port Alexander** Alaska U.S.A.
89 E9 **Port Alfred** S Africa
117 K10 **Port Alice** British Columbia Canada
94 J5 **Port Allegany** Pennsylvania U.S.A.
111 E11 **Port Allen** Louisiana U.S.A.
141 K6 **Port Alma** Queensland Australia
117 M11 **Port Angeles** Washington U.S.A.
109 K8 **Port Aransas** Texas U.S.A.
102 A3 **Port Arena** California U.S.A.
14 D3 **Portarlington** Ireland
Port Arthur *see* **Lüshun**
139 J9 **Port Arthur** Tasmania Australia
109 N6 **Port Arthur** Texas U.S.A.
12 B2 **Port Askaig** Scotland
138 D4 **Port Augusta** South Australia Australia
123 N5 **Port-au-Port** *pen* Newfoundland Canada
123 O5 **Port-au-Port** Newfoundland Canada
127 H5 **Port-au-Prince** Haiti
94 D2 **Port Austin** Michigan U.S.A.
32 J8 **Porta Westfalica** Germany
20 G3 **Portbail** France
12 C2 **Port Bannatyne** Scotland
111 E11 **Port Barre** Louisiana U.S.A.
71 D5 **Port Barton** Palawan Philippines
123 L8 **Port Bickerton** Nova Scotia Canada
68 A7 **Port Blair** Andaman Is
109 N6 **Port Bolivar** Texas U.S.A.
17 K2 **Port Bou** Spain/France
85 D8 **Port Bouet** Ivory Coast
140 D2 **Port Bradshaw** *inlet* N Terr Australia
21 J5 **Port Brillet** France
120 J10 **Port Bruce** Ontario Canada
120 K10 **Port Burwell** Ontario Canada
99 Q8 **Port Byron** Illinois U.S.A.
95 L3 **Port Byron** New York U.S.A.
139 G7 **Port Campbell** Victoria Australia
75 N7 **Port Canning** India
121 L7 **Port Carling** Ontario Canada
13 E4 **Port Carlisle** England
122 F3 **Port Cartier** Quebec Canada
144 D7 **Port Chalmers** New Zealand
145 E2 **Port Charles** New Zealand
15 B5 **Port Charlotte** Scotland
95 O6 **Port Chester** New York U.S.A.
111 G12 **Port Chicot I** Louisiana U.S.A.
117 F6 **Port Chilkoot** Alaska U.S.A.
116 D4 **Port Clarence** *hbr* Alaska U.S.A.
117 G9 **Port Clements** British Columbia Canada
141 K5 **Port Clinton** *inlet* Queensland Australia
94 E5 **Port Clinton** Ohio U.S.A.
95 S3 **Port Clyde** Maine U.S.A.
121 L10 **Port Colborne** Ontario Canada
117 M11 **Port Coquitlam** British Columbia Canada
68 A6 **Port Cornwallis** Andaman Is
121 L9 **Port Credit** Ontario Canada
19 Q18 **Port Cros, I. de** France
141 K6 **Port Curtis** *inlet* Queensland Australia
121 L9 **Port Dalhousie** Ontario Canada
122 H5 **Port Daniel** Quebec Canada
139 H9 **Port Davey** Tasmania Australia
19 N18 **Port de Bouc** France
19 N18 **Port de Fos** *hbr* France
102 A1 **Port Delgada** California U.S.A.
127 H5 **Port-de-Paix** Haiti
21 M7 **Port-de-Piles** France
69 E11 **Port Dickson** Malaysia
8 B1 **Port Dinorwic** Wales
141 H3 **Port Douglas** Queensland Australia
120 K10 **Port Dover** Ontario Canada
123 K9 **Port Dufferin** Nova Scotia Canada
111 G12 **Porte a la Hache** Louisiana U.S.A.
Porte d'Annam *see* **Vinh Son**
99 U4 **Porte des Morts** Wisconsin U.S.A.
117 H8 **Port Edward** British Columbia Canada
89 G8 **Port Edward** S Africa
130 G4 **Porteirinha** Brazil
129 H4 **Portel** Brazil
16 B6 **Portel** Portugal
130 H7 **Portela** Brazil
122 H7 **Port Elgin** New Brunswick Canada
120 J8 **Port Elgin** Ontario Canada
127 O8 **Port Elizabeth** Lesser Antilles
89 D9 **Port Elizabeth** S Africa
22 B2 **Portel, le** France
12 B2 **Port Ellen** Scotland
130 B9 **Porteña** *R* Argentina
21 J3 **Port-en-Bessin-Huppain** France
98 K5 **Porter** Minnesota U.S.A.
98 C7 **Porter** Nebraska U.S.A.
106 D6 **Porter** New Mexico U.S.A.
107 P6 **Porter** Oklahoma U.S.A.
112 D4 **Porterdale** Georgia U.S.A.
99 T4 **Porterfield** Wisconsin U.S.A.
12 D5 **Port Erin** I of Man U.K.
117 H6 **Porter Landing** British Columbia Canada
15 G3 **Port Errol** Scotland
87 C12 **Porterville** S Africa
102 E5 **Porterville** California U.S.A.
127 K3 **Port Esquivel** Jamaica
Port Etienne *see* **Nouadhibou**
8 B4 **Port Eynon** Wales
138 F7 **Port Fairy** Victoria Australia
123 L8 **Port Felix** Nova Scotia Canada
145 E2 **Port Fitzroy** New Zealand
Port Francqui *see* **Ilebo**
86 A6 **Port Gentil** Gabon
122 G9 **Port George** Nova Scotia Canada
111 E10 **Port Gibson** Mississippi U.S.A.
12 D2 **Port Glasgow** Scotland
14 E2 **Portglenone** N Ireland
15 E3 **Portgordon** Scotland
145 E4 **Port Gore** New Zealand
116 M7 **Port Graham** Alaska U.S.A.
143 A8 **Port Gregory** *B* W Australia Australia
122 H8 **Port Greville** Nova Scotia Canada
8 C4 **Porth** Wales
85 F8 **Port Harcourt** Nigeria
117 K10 **Port Hardy** British Columbia Canada
145 D4 **Port Hardy** New Zealand
Port Harrison *see* **Inukjuak**
123 L8 **Port Hastings** C Breton I, Nova Scotia
123 L8 **Port Hawkesbury** C Breton I, Nova Scotia
8 C5 **Porthcawl** Wales
8 B2 **Porth Dinlleyn** *B* Wales
142 C5 **Port Hedland** W Australia Australia
127 L3 **Port Henderson** Jamaica
95 O3 **Port Henry** New York U.S.A.
Port Herald *see* **Nsanje**
100 J1 **Porthill** Idaho U.S.A.
8 B2 **Porthmadog** Wales
8 B2 **Porth Neigwl** *B* Wales
123 L8 **Port Hood** C Breton I, Nova Scotia
121 M9 **Port Hope** Ontario Canada
94 E3 **Port Hope** Michigan U.S.A.
123 Q1 **Port Hope Simpson** Labrador, Nfld Canada
102 E7 **Port Hueneme** California U.S.A.
120 H10 **Port Huron** Ontario Canada
94 E4 **Port Huron** Michigan U.S.A.
45 Q8 **Portici** Italy
16 B7 **Portimão** Portugal
29 M5 **Portimo** Finland
12 C1 **Portinnisherrich** Scotland
107 M2 **Portis** Kansas U.S.A.
8 B6 **Port Isaac** England
109 K9 **Port Isabel** Texas U.S.A.
99 T2 **Port Isabelle** Michigan U.S.A.
8 D5 **Portishead** England
139 K5 **Port Jackson** New South Wales Australia
95 O6 **Port Jefferson** Long I, New York U.S.A.
95 N5 **Port Jervis** New York U.S.A.
20 F8 **Port Joinville** France
127 J3 **Port Kaiser** Jamaica
140 A2 **Port Keats** N Terr Australia
139 K5 **Port Kembla** New South Wales Australia
138 C5 **Port Kenney** South Australia Australia
139 J5 **Portland** New South Wales Australia
138 F7 **Portland** Victoria Australia
127 P6 **Portland** Barbados
121 O8 **Portland** Ontario Canada
127 M2 **Portland** *parish* Jamaica
145 E1 **Portland** New Zealand
106 E3 **Portland** Colorado U.S.A.
94 C6 **Portland** Indiana U.S.A.
95 R3 **Portland** Maine U.S.A.
94 C4 **Portland** Michigan U.S.A.
98 J2 **Portland** North Dakota U.S.A.
100 C4 **Portland** Oregon U.S.A.
110 K5 **Portland** Tennessee U.S.A.
109 K8 **Portland** Texas U.S.A.
127 K3 **Portland Bight** Jamaica
8 D7 **Portland, Bill of** *head* England
139 J8 **Portland, C** Tasmania Australia
117 H8 **Portland Canal** Br Col/Alaska Canada/U.S.A.
123 P3 **Portland Cr. Pond** Newfoundland Canada
8 D6 **Portland Hbr** England
145 F3 **Portland I** New Zealand
117 H8 **Portland Inlet** British Columbia Canada
127 K3 **Portland Ridge** Jamaica
141 G2 **Portland Roads** Queensland Australia
126 F6 **Portland Rock** Caribbean
71 E8 **Port Languyan** Philippines
139 H8 **Port Latta** Tasmania Australia
109 L7 **Port Lavaca** Texas U.S.A.
14 D4 **Portlaw** Ireland
144 B4 **Port Levy** New Zealand
95 M3 **Port Leyden** New York U.S.A.
138 D5 **Port Lincoln** South Australia Australia
12 D4 **Port Logan** Scotland
120 K7 **Port Loring** Ontario Canada
20 D6 **Port-Louis** France
83 L12 **Port Louis** Mauritius
127 N4 **Port Louis** Guadeloupe W Indies
140 D3 **Port McArthur** *B* N Terr Australia
138 F7 **Port MacDonnell** South Australia Australia
121 L8 **Port McNicoll** Ontario Canada
139 L4 **Port Macquarie** New South Wales Australia
122 F10 **Port Maitland** Nova Scotia Canada
121 L10 **Port Maitland** Ontario Canada
109 K9 **Port Mansfield** Texas U.S.A.
115 N6 **Port Manvers** Labrador, Nfld Canada
127 L2 **Port Maria** Jamaica
94 J6 **Port Matilda** Pennsylvania U.S.A.
113 G11 **Port Mayaca** Florida U.S.A.
122 H9 **Port Medway** Nova Scotia Canada
117 M11 **Port Mellon** British Columbia Canada
122 H4 **Port Menier** Quebec Canada
116 G8 **Port Moller** Alaska U.S.A.
117 M11 **Port Moody** British Columbia Canada
127 M3 **Port Morant** Jamaica
136 K3 **Port Moresby** Papua New Guinea
123 N7 **Port Morien** C Breton I, Nova Scotia
21 N3 **Port-Mort** France
122 H10 **Port Mouton** Nova Scotia Canada
122 H10 **Port Mouton I** Nova Scotia Canada
141 F1 **Port Musgrave** *inlet* Queensland Australia
15 C4 **Portnacroish** Scotland
12 B2 **Portnahaven** Scotland
20 E6 **Port Navalo** France
109 O6 **Port Neches** Texas U.S.A.
138 D5 **Port Neill** South Australia Australia
126 G3 **Port Nelson** Bahamas
101 N7 **Portneuf** Idaho U.S.A.
122 C5 **Portneuf, R** Quebec Canada
122 C5 **Portneuf-sur-Mer** Quebec Canada
145 G4 **Port Nicholson** New Zealand
138 E6 **Port Noarlunga** South Australia Australia
87 C11 **Port Nolloth** S Africa
95 M7 **Port Norris** New Jersey U.S.A.
115 N6 **Port-Nouveau Québec** Quebec Canada
129 K4 **Pôrto** Brazil
16 B3 **Porto** Portugal
128 E5 **Pôrto Acre** Brazil
130 D7 **Pôrto Alegre** Mato Grosso Brazil
131 H3 **Pôrto Alegre** Rio Grande do Sul Brazil
Porto Alexandre *see* **Tombua**
87 B8 **Porto Amboim** Angola
Porto Amelia *see* **Pemba** Mozambique
129 G6 **Porto Artur** Brazil
144 D7 **Portobello** New Zealand
13 E2 **Portobello** Scotland
130 E10 **Pôrto Belo** Brazil
116 L8 **Port O'Brian** Alaska U.S.A.
43 C7 **Porto Cervo** Sardinia
109 L7 **Port O'Connor** Texas U.S.A.
16 B3 **Porto de Leixões** Portugal
129 H4 **Pôrto de Mos** Brazil
129 H6 **Pôrto dos Meinacos** Brazil
43 F11 **Porto Empedocle** Sicily
128 G7 **Pôrto Espiridião** Brazil
42 C6 **Portoferraio** Elba Italy
44 F3 **Portofino** Italy
12 D1 **Port of Menteith** Scotland
15 B2 **Port of Ness** Scotland
127 O2 **Port of Spain** Trinidad
45 M2 **Porto Garibaldi** Italy
129 H3 **Pôrto Grande** Brazil
42 E3 **Portogruaro** Italy
129 G7 **Pôrto Jofre** Brazil
102 D2 **Portola** California U.S.A.
130 C10 **Porto Luceno** Brazil
29 J9 **Pörtom** Finland
45 L2 **Portomaggiore** Italy
45 J1 **Porto Mantovano** Italy
44 D4 **Porto Maurizio** Italy
88 H9 **Porto Mocambo** Mozambique
129 G8 **Pôrto Murtinho** Brazil
129 J6 **Pôrto Nacional** Brazil
85 E7 **Porto Novo** Benin
113 G8 **Port Orange** Florida U.S.A.
117 M12 **Port Orchard** Washington U.S.A.
42 F5 **Porto Recanati** Italy
100 A7 **Port Orford** Oregon U.S.A.
133 G2 **Pôrto San José** Brazil
42 D6 **Porto San Stefano** Italy
85 A2 **Pôrto Santo** *isld* Madeira
129 H8 **Pôrto São José** Brazil
130 H5 **Pôrto Seguro** Brazil
45 M2 **Porto Tolle** Italy
43 B8 **Porto Torres** Sardinia
133 G3 **Pôrto União** Brazil
128 F5 **Pôrto Velho** Brazil
44 G3 **Portovenere** Italy
128 B4 **Portoviejo** Ecuador
12 C4 **Portpatrick** Scotland
140 B2 **Port Patterson** *inlet* N Terr Australia
144 A7 **Port Pegasus** New Zealand
121 M8 **Port Perry** Ontario Canada
139 G7 **Port Phillip B** Victoria Australia
138 E5 **Port Pirie** South Australia Australia
114 H4 **Port Radium** Northwest Territories Canada
8 A7 **Portreath** England
15 B3 **Portree** Scotland
118 J8 **Portreeve** Saskatchewan Canada
83 M8 **Port Refuge** Cocos Is Indian Oc
100 A1 **Port Renfrew** British Columbia Canada
123 T5 **Port Rexton** Newfoundland Canada
102 A4 **Port Reyes** California U.S.A.
100 B1 **Port Roberts** Washington U.S.A.
144 D5 **Port Robinson** New Zealand
140 D2 **Port Roper** *inlet* N Terr Australia
120 K10 **Port Rowan** Ontario Canada
127 L3 **Port Royal** Jamaica
112 G5 **Port Royal** South Carolina U.S.A.
95 K8 **Port Royal** Virginia U.S.A.
122 G9 **Port Royal Nat. Hist. Park** Ontario Canada
14 E1 **Portrush** N Ireland
79 C7 **Port Said** Egypt
113 B8 **Port St. Joe** Florida U.S.A.
89 F8 **Port St Johns** S Africa
19 N18 **Port St. Louis** France
18 F8 **Port St. Marie** France
20 G7 **Port St.Père** France
20 A4 **Portsall** France
14 D1 **Portsalon** Ireland
94 E3 **Port Sanilac** Michigan U.S.A.
123 P3 **Port Saunders** Newfoundland Canada
Port Say *see* **Marsa Ben Mehdi**
38 K8 **Pörtschach** Austria
89 G8 **Port Shepstone** S Africa
117 H8 **Port Simpson** British Columbia Canada
142 D4 **Port Smith** *B* W Australia Australia
121 O8 **Portsmouth** Ontario Canada
127 O7 **Portsmouth** Dominica
9 E6 **Portsmouth** England
99 L8 **Portsmouth** Iowa U.S.A.
95 R3 **Portsmouth** New Hampshire U.S.A.
112 L2 **Portsmouth** North Carolina U.S.A.
94 E8 **Portsmouth** Ohio U.S.A.
95 Q5 **Portsmouth** Rhode I U.S.A.
95 L10 **Portsmouth** Virginia U.S.A.
12 C1 **Portsonachan** Scotland
15 F3 **Portsoy** Scotland
120 J10 **Port Stanley** Ontario Canada
139 K5 **Port Stephens** New South Wales Australia
141 G2 **Port Stewart** *inlet* Queensland Australia
14 E1 **Port Stewart** N Ireland
86 G2 **Port Sudan** Sudan
8 C4 **Port Talbot** Wales
71 F4 **Port Tambang** Philippines
79 C9 **Port Taufiq** Egypt
127 O2 **Port Tembladora** Trinidad
29 M3 **Porttipahdan tekojärvi** *L* Finland
117 M11 **Port Townsend** Washington U.S.A.
16 B7 **Portugal** *rep* W Europe
83 J9 **Portugal B** Sri Lanka
123 U6 **Portugal Cove** Newfoundland Canada
17 F1 **Portugalete** Spain
128 E2 **Portuguesa** *state* Venezuela
Portuguese Guinea *see* **Guinea-Bissau** *rep*
14 C3 **Portumna** Ireland
123 T5 **Port Union** Newfoundland Canada
18 H10 **Port Vendres** France
102 F8 **Port Vicente** California U.S.A.
88 D1 **Port Victoria** Kenya
137 O5 **Port-Vila** Vanuatu
94 J4 **Portville** New York U.S.A.
138 E5 **Port Vincent** South Australia Australia
52 D1 **Port Vladimir** Russian Federation
138 E5 **Port Wakefield** South Australia Australia
142 F2 **Port Warrender** *inlet* W Australia Australia
99 T6 **Port Washington** Wisconsin U.S.A.
142 B5 **Port Weld** *B* W Australia Australia
116 N6 **Port Wells** *inlet* Alaska U.S.A.
112 F5 **Port Wentworth** Georgia U.S.A.
12 D4 **Port William** Scotland
122 H8 **Port Williams** Nova Scotia Canada
99 P3 **Port Wing** Wisconsin U.S.A.
107 P6 **Porum** Oklahoma U.S.A.
127 K2 **Porus** Jamaica
133 C8 **Porvenir** Chile
108 C5 **Porvenir** Texas U.S.A.
29 M11 **Porvoo** Finland
36 C2 **Porz** Germany
16 E5 **Porzuna** Spain
16 E5 **Porzuna, Sa. de** *mts* Spain
43 C8 **Posada** *R* Sardinia
133 F3 **Posadas** Argentina
16 D7 **Posadas** Spain
41 M5 **Poschiavo** Switzerland
94 D1 **Posen** Michigan U.S.A.
110 J3 **Poseyville** Indiana U.S.A.
52 E5 **Poshekhonye** Russian Federation
119 O1 **Poshkokagan L** Ontario Canada
46 F5 **Posídhion, Ákr** *C* Greece
41 O6 **Posina** *R* Italy
37 O5 **Pösing** Germany
29 N5 **Posio** Finland
45 Q8 **Positano** Italy
70 G5 **Poso** Sulawesi
78 J1 **Posof** Turkey
129 J6 **Posse** Brazil
37 N3 **Posseck** Germany
146 C12 **Possession Is** Antarctica
37 M2 **Pössneck** Germany
21 J7 **Possonnière, la** France
38 M8 **Possruck** Slovenia
109 J3 **Possum Kingdom L** Texas U.S.A.
100 E5 **Post** Oregon U.S.A.
37 N6 **Postau** Germany
37 L5 **Postbauer-Heng** Germany
8 C6 **Postbridge** England
115 M6 **Poste-de-la-Baleine** Quebec Canada
68 H6 **Poste Deshayes** Cambodia
Poste Maurice Cortier *see* **Bidon 5**
83 M12 **Poste, R du** Mauritius
85 E4 **Poste Weygand** Algeria
100 J2 **Post Falls** Idaho U.S.A.
71 J8 **Postiljon Pulau** *isld* Indonesia
89 C7 **Postmasburg** S Africa
129 H6 **Pôsto Alto Manissaua** Brazil
128 C4 **Posto Bobonazo** Peru
42 F3 **Postojna** Slovenia
99 P6 **Postville** Iowa U.S.A.
42 H5 **Posušje** Bosnia-Herzegovina
71 K9 **Pota** Indonesia
124 D4 **Pótam** Mexico
46 G3 **Potamoí** Greece
46 F8 **Potamós** Greece
47 O12 **Potamós** Greece
50 H2 **Potapovo** Russian Federation
128 G2 **Potaro** *R* Guyana
89 E6 **Potchefstroom** S Africa
48 J6 **Potcoava** Romania
130 H5 **Poté** Brazil
107 Q7 **Poteau** *R* Okla/Ark U.S.A.
107 Q6 **Poteau** Oklahoma U.S.A.
109 J6 **Poteet** Texas U.S.A.
130 J8 **Potengi** *R* Brazil
43 G8 **Potenza** Italy
144 A7 **Poteriteri, L** New Zealand
16 D1 **Potes** Spain
89 F5 **Potgietersrus** S Africa
109 J6 **Poth** Texas U.S.A.
100 F2 **Potholes Res** Washington U.S.A.
129 K5 **Poti** *R* Brazil
21 K4 **Potigny** France
85 G6 **Potiskum** Nigeria
71 K9 **Potjo Mandasawu** *mt* Indonesia
100 J3 **Potlatch** Idaho U.S.A.
89 B8 **Potloer** *mt* S Africa
48 K6 **Potlogi** Romania
101 M3 **Potomac** Montana U.S.A.
94 J7 **Potomac S. Branch** *R* West Virginia U.S.A.
133 D1 **Potosí** Bolivia
133 D2 **Potosí** *dept* Bolivia
110 F4 **Potosi** Missouri U.S.A.
103 J6 **Potosi Mt** Nevada U.S.A.
71 F5 **Pototan** Panay Philippines
133 D3 **Potrerillos** Chile
131 B2 **Potro, Cerro de** *pk* Chile
33 S8 **Potsdam** Germany
95 N2 **Potsdam** New York U.S.A.
37 L4 **Pottenstein** Germany
120 K4 **Potter** Ontario Canada
98 C8 **Potter** Nebraska U.S.A.
9 E5 **Potterne** England
9 F4 **Potter's Bar** England
102 A2 **Potter Valley** California U.S.A.
94 C4 **Potterville** Michigan U.S.A.
37 L6 **Pottmes** Germany
9 F3 **Potton** England
109 L2 **Pottsboro** Texas U.S.A.
111 G7 **Potts Camp** Mississippi U.S.A.
95 M6 **Pottstown** Pennsylvania U.S.A.
95 L6 **Pottsville** Pennsylvania U.S.A.
109 J4 **Pottsville** Texas U.S.A.
83 L11 **Pottuvil** Sri Lanka
107 N4 **Potwin** Kansas U.S.A.
21 H6 **Pouancé** France
68 F3 **Pou Bia** *mt* Laos
117 N8 **Pouce Coupé** British Columbia Canada
123 U6 **Pouch Cove** Newfoundland Canada
21 J6 **Poueze la** France
95 O5 **Poughkeepsie** New York U.S.A.
18 H5 **Pougues les Eaux** France
21 N7 **Pouillé** France
18 E9 **Pouillon** France
18 J5 **Pouilly en Auxois** France
21 O7 **Poulaines** France
20 B5 **Pouldergat** France
20 B6 **Pouldreuzic** France
20 C6 **Pouldu,le** France
21 N8 **Pouligny St. Pierre** France
20 F7 **Pouliguen,le** France
122 B5 **Poulin de Courval, L** Quebec Canada
20 C5 **Poullaouen** France
68 J5 **Poulo Canton, Is de** Vietnam
69 G8 **Poulo Dama, Iles** Vietnam
68 J6 **Poulo Gambir, Cu Lao** *isld* Vietnam
95 O3 **Poultney** Vermont U.S.A.
13 E6 **Poulton-le-Fylde** England
68 E4 **Pou Miang** *mt* Thailand
99 S4 **Pound** Wisconsin U.S.A.
9 F5 **Pound Hill** England
19 P18 **Pourcieux** France
145 F4 **Pourerere** New Zealand
145 G3 **Pourewa I** New Zealand
40 E6 **Pourri, Mont** France
21 N2 **Pourville** France
68 F3 **Pou San** *mt* Laos
68 F3 **Pou Sao** *mt* Laos
68 H5 **Pou Set** *mt* Laos
129 G6 **Pouso Alegre** Mato Grosso Brazil
130 F8 **Pouso Alegre** Minas Gerais Brazil
29 O6 **Poussu** Finland
144 A7 **Poutama I** New Zealand
68 F6 **Pouthisat** Cambodia
145 E2 **Pouto** New Zealand
121 Q3 **Poutrincourt, L** Quebec Canada
40 D1 **Pouxeux** France
21 J8 **Pouzauges** France
21 M7 **Pouzay** France
48 E1 **Pov Bystrica** Slovakia
52 D3 **Povenets** Russian Federation
145 F3 **Poverty Bay** New Zealand
9 F5 **Povey Cross** England
45 J2 **Poviglio** Italy
48 F6 **Povlen** *mt* Serbia Yugoslavia
16 B3 **Póvoa de Varzim** Portugal
65 J3 **Povorotnyy, Mys** *C* Russian Federation
115 M5 **Povungnituk** Quebec Canada
121 L6 **Powassan** Ontario Canada
101 T5 **Powder** *R* Wyo/Mont U.S.A.
106 C3 **Powderhorn** Colorado U.S.A.
100 H5 **Powder R** Oregon U.S.A.
98 A4 **Powderville** Montana U.S.A.
141 G7 **Powell** *R* Queensland Australia
98 E5 **Powell** South Dakota U.S.A.
94 D10 **Powell** *R* Tenn/Virg U.S.A.
99 R3 **Powell** Wisconsin U.S.A.
101 R5 **Powell** Wyoming U.S.A.
100 D5 **Powell Butte** Oregon U.S.A.
113 K11 **Powell Cay** *isld* Bahamas
103 O4 **Powell, L** Ariz/Utah U.S.A.
106 D2 **Powell, Mt** Colorado U.S.A.
102 F3 **Powell Mt** Nevada U.S.A.
126 F2 **Powell Pt** Eleuthera Bahamas
117 L10 **Powell River** British Columbia Canada
94 F8 **Powellton** West Virginia U.S.A.
101 O2 **Power** Montana U.S.A.
99 T4 **Powers** Michigan U.S.A.
100 A7 **Powers** Oregon U.S.A.
98 D1 **Powers L** North Dakota U.S.A.
111 C10 **Powhatan** Louisiana U.S.A.
94 K9 **Powhatan** Virginia U.S.A.
107 P2 **Powhattan** Kansas U.S.A.
8 D3 **Powick** England
141 H5 **Powlathanga** Queensland Australia
95 O4 **Pownal** Vermont U.S.A.
8 C3 **Powys** *co* Wales
130 C5 **Poxoreu** *R* Brazil
67 E2 **Poyang Hu** *L* China
111 D7 **Poyen** Arkansas U.S.A.
99 S5 **Poygan, L** Wisconsin U.S.A.
31 K7 **Poysdorf** Austria
124 C5 **Poza Grande** Mexico
78 E3 **Pozantı** Turkey
48 G6 **Požarevac** Serbia Yugoslavia
125 L7 **Poza Rica** Mexico
48 F7 **Požega** Serbia Yugoslavia
Pozen *see* **Poznań**
59 K2 **Pozharskoye** Russian Federation
52 J5 **Pozhva** Russian Federation
22 D3 **Pozières** France
140 D5 **Pozieres,Mt** N Terr Australia
31 K3 **Poznań** Poland
102 D6 **Pozo** California U.S.A.
17 F7 **Pozo Alcón** Spain
133 D2 **Pozo Almonte** Chile
16 D6 **Pozoblanco** Spain
103 J9 **Pozo Cenizo** Mexico
17 F6 **Pozohondo** Spain
103 J9 **Pozo Salado** Mexico
103 N10 **Pozo Verde** Mexico
52 H4 **Poztykeros** Russian Federation
133 D2 **Pozuelos, L. de** Argentina
45 J1 **Pozzolengo** Italy
45 L1 **Pozzonova** Italy
45 Q8 **Pozzuoli** Italy
68 F2 **P. Phac Mo** *mt* Vietnam
85 D7 **Pra** *R* Ghana
69 G14 **Prabumulih** Sumatra
31 L2 **Prabuty** Poland
45 J3 **Pracchia** Italy
68 D7 **Pracham Hiang, Laem** Thailand
30 H7 **Prachatice** Czech Rep
68 E5 **Prachin Buri** Thailand
68 D7 **Prachuap Khiri Khan** Thailand
16 C1 **Pradairo** Spain
31 K5 **Praděd** *mt* Czech Rep
18 G10 **Prades** France
70 P9 **Pradjekan** Java
28 E2 **Præstbro** Denmark
Præstø *co see* **Storstrøm and Roskilde** *counties*
28 J6 **Præsto** Denmark
38 N9 **Pragersk** Slovenia
38 F7 **Prägraten** Austria
Prague *see* **Praha**
107 O6 **Prague** Oklahoma U.S.A.
31 H5 **Praha** Czech Rep
48 K5 **Prahova** Romania
48 K6 **Prahova** *R* Romania
48 H6 **Prahova** Serbia Yugoslavia
85 B8 **Praia** Cape Verde
133 G4 **Praia Albardão** *beach* Brazil
48 J4 **Praid** Romania
129 H4 **Prainha** Brazil
122 B3 **Praires, L. des** Quebec Canada
109 K6 **Prairia Lea** Texas U.S.A.
141 G5 **Prairie** Queensland Australia
100 K6 **Prairie** Idaho U.S.A.
110 F1 **Prairie City** Illinois U.S.A.
100 G5 **Prairie City** Oregon U.S.A.
107 K2 **Prairie Dog Cr** Kansas U.S.A.
108 F1 **Prairie Dog Town Fork** *R* Texas U.S.A.
99 P6 **Prairie du Chien** Wisconsin U.S.A.
99 R6 **Prairie du Sac** Wisconsin U.S.A.
110 B6 **Prairie Grove** Arkansas U.S.A.
109 L4 **Prairie Hill** Texas U.S.A.
119 P6 **Prairie River** Saskatchewan Canada
119 Q7 **Prairies, L of the** Manitoba/Sask Canada
110 J2 **Prairieton** Indiana U.S.A.
107 L2 **Prairie View** Kansas U.S.A.
111 F11 **Prairieville** Louisiana U.S.A.
94 E9 **Praise** Kentucky U.S.A.
68 F5 **Prakhon Chai** Thailand
40 E7 **Pralognan** France
42 E2 **Pramaggiore, Mont** *mt* Italy
70 N9 **Prambanan** Java
37 O3 **Prameny** Czech Rep
69 D8 **Pram, Khao** *mt* Thailand
68 D6 **Pran** *R* Thailand
68 D6 **Pran Buri** Thailand
38 K7 **Prankerhöhe** *mt* Austria
69 D11 **Prapat** Sumatra
40 B2 **Praslay** France
83 J12 **Praslin** *isld* Seychelles
47 Q15 **Prasonísi** *isld* Greece
47 J9 **Prasonísí, Akr** *C* Rhodes Greece
31 L4 **Praszka** Poland
129 J7 **Prata** *R* Brazil
Pratas *isld see* **Dongsha Qundao**
33 R9 **Pratau** Germany
17 J3 **Prat de Llobregat** Spain
41 L4 **Prätigau** *V* Switzerland
45 K4 **Prato** Italy
45 R8 **Prátola Serra** Italy
42 D5 **Pratomagno** *mt* Italy
45 L4 **Pratomagno** Italy
45 H3 **Prato, Mt** Italy
45 L4 **Pratovecchio** Italy
18 G10 **Prats-de-Mollo** France
119 T9 **Pratt** Manitoba Canada
107 M4 **Pratt** Kansas U.S.A.
95 N4 **Prattsville** New York U.S.A.
111 K9 **Prattville** Alabama U.S.A.
40 B2 **Prauthoy** France
31 N1 **Pravdinsk** Russian Federation
54 J1 **Pravdinskiy** Russian Federation
46 F2 **Pravets** Bulgaria
16 C1 **Pravia** Spain
8 C7 **Prawle Pt** England
70 Q10 **Praya** Indonesia
21 N7 **Préaux** France
37 O3 **Přebuz** Czech Rep
20 H4 **Precey** France
52 D6 **Prechistoye** Russian Federation
21 K6 **Précigné** France
21 P3 **Précy-sur-Oise** France
45 L3 **Predappio** Italy
42 D2 **Predazzo** Italy
37 O5 **Predigtstuhl** *mt* Germany
38 M8 **Preding** Austria
38 J7 **Predlitz** Austria
38 F7 **Predoi** Italy
44 E2 **Predosa** Italy
51 O2 **Predporozhnyy** Russian Federation
119 P7 **Preeceville** Saskatchewan Canada
21 K5 **Pré-en-Pail** France
33 M4 **Preetz** Germany
20 F7 **Préfailles** France
31 M1 **Pregolya** *R* Russian Federation
127 J10 **Pregonero** Venezuela
18 E8 **Preignac** France
52 C6 **Preiļi** Latvia
121 M4 **Preissac** Quebec Canada
68 G6 **Prek Kak** Cambodia
68 H6 **Prek Preas** *R* Cambodia
68 G7 **Prek Sandek** Cambodia
68 F7 **Prek Taley** *R* Cambodia
8 B3 **Pren-gwyn** Wales
46 D4 **Prenjas** Albania
33 T6 **Prenzlau** Germany
59 K3 **Preobrazheniye** Russian Federation
42 A3 **Pré-St.-Didier** Italy
144 A7 **Preservation Inlet** New Zealand
130 D8 **Presidente Prudente** Brazil
108 C6 **Presidio** Texas U.S.A.
95 T7 **Presque Isle** Maine U.S.A.
18 F6 **Pressac** France
8 C1 **Prestatyn** Wales
8 C3 **Presteigne** Wales
13 F6 **Preston** England
101 O7 **Preston** Idaho U.S.A.
95 M8 **Preston** Maryland U.S.A.
99 O6 **Preston** Minnesota U.S.A.
110 C4 **Preston** Missouri U.S.A.
103 J3 **Preston** Nevada U.S.A.
107 P6 **Preston** Oklahoma U.S.A.
9 E5 **Preston Candover** England
109 O9 **Preston Hollow** Texas U.S.A.
13 F2 **Prestonpans** Scotland
94 E9 **Prestonsburg** Kentucky U.S.A.
13 F6 **Prestwich** England
12 D3 **Prestwick** Scotland
129 K6 **Preto** *R* Bahia Brazil
129 J7 **Prêto** *R* Minas Gerais Brazil
128 F4 **Prêto do Igapó Açu** *R* Brazil
89 F5 **Pretoria** S Africa
89 E5 **Pretoria-Witwatersrand-Vereeniging** *prov* S Africa
20 H3 **Prétot** France
33 R9 **Prettin** Germany
95 L7 **Prettyboy Res** Maryland U.S.A.
107 M4 **Pretty Prairie** Kansas U.S.A.
33 O7 **Pretzier** Germany
33 R9 **Pretzsch** Germany
21 M8 **Preuilly-sur-Claise** France
38 L8 **Prevalje** Slovenia
46 D6 **Préveza** Greece
106 B6 **Prewitt** New Mexico U.S.A.
106 G1 **Prewitt Res** Colorado U.S.A.
21 N4 **Prey** France
68 G7 **Prey Lovea** Cambodia
68 G7 **Prey Veng** Cambodia
45 P5 **Prezza** Italy
69 B10 **Priala** Sumatra
54 H9 **Priazovskaya Vozvyshenost'** *uplands* Ukraine
116 D8 **Pribilof Is** Bering Sea
30 H6 **Příbram** Czech Rep
122 D5 **Price** Quebec Canada
95 M7 **Price** Maryland U.S.A.
98 F2 **Price** North Dakota U.S.A.
103 O2 **Price** *R* Utah U.S.A.
103 O2 **Price** Utah U.S.A.
68 A6 **Price, C** Andaman Is
106 B1 **Price Creek** Colorado U.S.A.
117 J9 **Price I** British Columbia Canada
111 H11 **Prichard** Alabama U.S.A.
100 K2 **Prichard** Idaho U.S.A.
54 E9 **Prichernomorskaya Nizmennost'** *lowland* Ukraine
37 J4 **Prichsenstadt** Germany
127 P5 **Prickly Pt** Grenada
109 J4 **Priddy** Texas U.S.A.
54 D7 **Pridneprovskaya Nizmennost'** *lowland* Ukraine
54 C8 **Pridneprovskaya Vozvyshennost'** *uplands* Ukraine
17 F4 **Priego** Spain
16 E7 **Priego de C** Spain
27 M15 **Priekule** Latvia
27 M16 **Priekulė** Lithuania
33 Q5 **Priemerburg** Germany
89 C7 **Prieska** S Africa
37 M1 **Priessnitz** Germany
33 T10 **Priestewitz** Germany
100 J1 **Priest L** Idaho U.S.A.
127 M2 **Priestman's River** Jamaica
100 F3 **Priest Rapids** Washington U.S.A.
100 E3 **Priest Rapids Lake** *res* Washington U.S.A.
100 J1 **Priest River** Idaho U.S.A.
117 P11 **Priest River** Idaho U.S.A.
31 L7 **Prievidza** Slovakia
33 Q6 **Prignitz** *reg* Germany
56 C4 **Priiskovyy** Russian Federation
42 H4 **Prijedor** Bosnia-Herzegovina
53 G9 **Prikaspiyskaya Nizmennost** *lowlands* Kazakhstan/Rus Fed
46 E3 **Prilep** Macedonia
54 D6 **Priluki** Ukraine
40 B7 **Primarette** France
118 H6 **Primate** Saskatchewan Canada
37 O4 **Přimda** Czech Rep
20 C4 **Primel,Pte.de** France
20 C4 **Primel-Trégastel** France
126 E4 **Primero de Enero** Cuba
131 D3 **Primero, R** Argentina
139 J8 **Prime Seal I** Tasmania Australia
99 L6 **Primghar** Iowa U.S.A.
52 C4 **Primorsk** Russian Federation
53 E10 **Primorsk** Ukraine
59 K3 **Primorskiy** Russian Federation
56 F5 **Primorskiy Khrebet** *mts* Russian Federation
59 K2 **Primorskiy Kray** *reg* Russian Federation
47 J2 **Primorsko** Bulgaria
48 M5 **Primorskoye** Ukraine
48 N5 **Primorskoye** Ukraine
54 J9 **Primorskoye** Ukraine
122 J7 **Prim, Pt** Prince Edward I Canada
117 F5 **Primrose** *R* Br Col/Yukon Terr Canada
118 H4 **Primrose L** Saskatchewan Canada
36 B5 **Prims** *R* Germany
36 C4 **Primstal** Germany
118 J6 **Prince** Saskatchewan Canada
119 M5 **Prince Albert** Saskatchewan Canada
89 C9 **Prince Albert** S Africa
146 D11 **Prince Albert Mts** Antarctica

118 L5 **Prince Albert Nat. Park** Saskatchewan Canada
114 H3 **Prince Albert Pen** Northwest Territories Canada
114 G3 **Prince Alfred, C** Northwest Territories Canada
115 M4 **Prince Charles I** Northwest Territories Canada
146 H10 **Prince Charles Mts** Antarctica
121 O9 **Prince Edward B** Ontario Canada
122 J7 **Prince Edward I** *prov* Canada
90 M14 **Prince Edward I** Indian Oc
122 J7 **Prince Edward I. Nat. Park** Canada
95 L8 **Prince Frederick** Maryland U.S.A.
142 F3 **Prince Frederick Harb** W Australia Australia
117 M9 **Prince George** British Columbia Canada
114 J2 **Prince Gustaf Adolf Sea** Northwest Territories Canada
116 C4 **Prince of Wales, C** Alaska U.S.A.
141 F1 **Prince of Wales I** Queensland Australia
114 J3 **Prince of Wales I** Northwest Territories Canada
117 G8 **Prince of Wales I** Alaska U.S.A.
114 H3 **Prince of Wales Str** Northwest Territories Canada
114 H2 **Prince Patrick I** Northwest Territories Canada
115 K3 **Prince Regent Inlet** Northwest Territories Canada
142 F3 **Prince Regent R** W Australia Australia
117 H8 **Prince Rupert** British Columbia Canada
130 H9 **Princesa Isabel** Brazil
Princes Is *see* **Kızıl Adalar**
Princes Lake Ontario *see* **Wallace**
9 F4 **Princes Risborough** England
95 M8 **Princess Anne** Maryland U.S.A.
141 G2 **Princess Charlotte B** Queensland Australia
146 H12 **Princess Elizabeth Land** Antarctica
142 F3 **Princess May Ra** W Australia Australia
144 A6 **Princess Mts** New Zealand
143 D7 **Princess Ra** W Australia Australia
117 J9 **Princess Royal I** British Columbia Canada
127 O3 **Prince's Town** Trinidad
9 E3 **Princethorpe** England
117 N11 **Princeton** British Columbia Canada
102 B2 **Princeton** California U.S.A.
99 R8 **Princeton** Illinois U.S.A.
110 J3 **Princeton** Indiana U.S.A.
110 J4 **Princeton** Kentucky U.S.A.
95 U1 **Princeton** Maine U.S.A.
99 T3 **Princeton** Michigan U.S.A.
99 N4 **Princeton** Minnesota U.S.A.
99 N9 **Princeton** Missouri U.S.A.
95 N6 **Princeton** New Jersey U.S.A.
112 J2 **Princeton** North Carolina U.S.A.
94 F9 **Princeton** West Virginia U.S.A.
99 R6 **Princeton** Wisconsin U.S.A.
8 C6 **Princetown** England
121 T6 **Princeville** Quebec Canada
99 R9 **Princeville** Illinois U.S.A.
116 O6 **Prince William Sound** Alaska U.S.A.
86 A5 **Príncipe** *isld* G of Guinea
128 F6 **Principe da Beira** Brazil
100 E5 **Prineville** Oregon U.S.A.
98 C6 **Pringle** South Dakota U.S.A.
108 C8 **Pringle** Texas U.S.A.
19 Q13 **Pringy** France
115 P5 **Prins Christian Sund** Greenland
25 C5 **Prinsenhage** Netherlands
68 C6 **Prinsep I** Burma
146 H7 **Prinsesse Astrid Kyst** *coast* Antarctica
146 J7 **Prinsesse Ragnhild Kyst** *coast* Antarctica
146 J8 **Prins Harald Kyst** *coast* Antarctica
50 A1 **Prins Karls Forland** Spitzbergen
123 L4 **Prinsta B** Anticosti I, Quebec
125 N3 **Prinzapolca** Nicaragua
54 L2 **Priokskiy** Russian Federation
16 B1 **Prior, C** Spain
52 D4 **Priozersk** Russian Federation
52 K3 **Pripolyarnyy Ural** *mts* Russian Federation
53 C8 **Pripyat** *R* Belarus/Ukraine
29 P3 **Prirechnyy** Russian Federation
37 P3 **Přísečnice** Czech Rep
48 J3 **Prislop Pass** Romania
46 E4 **Prispansko ezero** *L* Albania/Greece/Macedonia
46 E2 **Priština** Serbia Yugoslavia
106 H4 **Pritchett** Colorado U.S.A.
33 Q8 **Pritzerbe** Germany
33 O6 **Pritzier** Germany
33 Q6 **Pritzwalk** Germany
19 N15 **Privas** France
45 O7 **Priverno** Italy
45 O6 **Privernum** Italy
42 F3 **Privka** Slovenia
52 F6 **Privolzhsk** Russian Federation
53 G7 **Privolzhskaya Vozvyshennost** *uplands* Russian Federation
53 G7 **Privolzh'ye** Russian Federation
20 D5 **Priziac** France
46 D2 **Prizren** Serbia Yugoslavia
43 E11 **Prizzi** Sicily
48 K1 **Probezhnaya** Ukraine
70 O9 **Probolinggo** Java
37 L2 **Probstzella** Germany
8 B7 **Probus** England
31 J4 **Prochowice** Poland
43 F8 **Procida** *isld* Italy
45 Q8 **Procida** Italy
106 H1 **Proctor** Colorado U.S.A.
109 J4 **Proctor** Texas U.S.A.
95 O3 **Proctor** Vermont U.S.A.
109 J3 **Proctor Res** Texas U.S.A.
95 P3 **Proctorsville** Vermont U.S.A.
16 B5 **Proènca a Nova** Portugal
37 N1 **Profen** Germany
22 H3 **Profondeville** Belgium
125 L2 **Progreso** Honduras
125 P7 **Progreso** Mexico
59 J2 **Progress** Russian Federation
106 E7 **Progresso** New Mexico U.S.A.
56 B6 **Prokhladnoye** Kazakhstan
55 G2 **Prokhorkino Proryto** Russian Federation
54 H5 **Prokhorovka** Russian Federation
46 D2 **Prokletije** Montenegro Yugoslavia
56 C4 **Prokop'yevsk** Russian Federation
46 E1 **Prokuplje** Serbia Yugoslavia
52 D5 **Proletariy** Russian Federation
53 F10 **Proletarsk** Russian Federation
54 K8 **Proletarsk** Ukraine
54 J1 **Proletarskiy** Russian Federation
54 G6 **Proletarskiy** Russian Federation
59 N2 **Proliv Frizi** *str* Russian Federation
50 E1 **Proliv Matochkin Shar** Russian Federation
37 K4 **Prolsdorf** Germany
Prome *see* **Pyè**
99 N9 **Promise City** Iowa U.S.A.
101 N8 **Promontory** Utah U.S.A.
56 C3 **Promyshlennaya** Russian Federation
53 G10 **Promyslovka** Russian Federation
52 F5 **Pronino** Russian Federation
100 G9 **Pronto** Nevada U.S.A.
54 M2 **Pronya** *R* Russian Federation
117 M6 **Prophet River** British Columbia Canada
99 R8 **Prophetstown** Illinois U.S.A.
130 H11 **Propriá** Brazil
33 S10 **Prösen** Germany
141 J5 **Proserpine** Queensland Australia
33 Q9 **Prosigk** Germany
31 K3 **Prosna** *R* Poland
52 H5 **Prosnitsa** Russian Federation
46 F3 **Prosotsáni** Greece
95 M3 **Prospect** New York U.S.A.
94 D6 **Prospect** Ohio U.S.A.
100 C7 **Prospect** Oregon U.S.A.
94 G6 **Prospect** Pennsylvania U.S.A.
127 M3 **Prospect Pt** Jamaica
100 A6 **Prosper** Oregon U.S.A.
112 F3 **Prosperity** South Carolina U.S.A.
98 H9 **Prosser** Nebraska U.S.A.
100 F3 **Prosser** Washington U.S.A.
48 D1 **Prostějov** Czech Rep
141 K7 **Proston** Queensland Australia
52 H2 **Prosunduy** Russian Federation
54 H8 **Prosyanaya** Ukraine
31 M5 **Proszowice** Poland
107 L4 **Protection** Kansas U.S.A.
99 O6 **Protivin** Iowa U.S.A.
54 J2 **Protva** *R* Russian Federation
33 T7 **Prötzel** Germany
47 J1 **Provadiya** Bulgaria
115 O3 **Prøven** Greenland
111 C10 **Provencal** Louisiana U.S.A.
19 O17 **Provence** *prov* France
36 C7 **Provenchères-sur-Fave** France
127 P5 **Providence** Grenada
110 J4 **Providence** Kentucky U.S.A.
112 J1 **Providence** North Carolina U.S.A.
95 Q5 **Providence** Rhode I U.S.A.
101 O8 **Providence** Utah U.S.A.
120 H7 **Providence Bay** Ontario Canada
144 A7 **Providence, C** New Zealand
116 J8 **Providence, C** Alaska U.S.A.
87 J9 **Providence I** Br Indian Oc Terr
103 J7 **Providence Mts** California U.S.A.
127 H4 **Providenciales** *isld* Turks & Caicos Is
128 F6 **Providencia, Sa. da** *mts* Brazil
116 A4 **Provideniya** Russian Federation
141 G2 **Providential Chan** Gt Barrier Reef Aust
95 R4 **Provincetown** Massachusetts U.S.A.
18 H4 **Provins** France
98 C6 **Provo** South Dakota U.S.A.
103 N1 **Provo** Utah U.S.A.
118 G6 **Provost** Alberta Canada
22 D4 **Proyart** France
42 H5 **Prozor** Bosnia-Herzegovina
130 E9 **Prudentópolis** Brazil
94 C2 **Prudenville** Michigan U.S.A.
13 G4 **Prudhoe** England
116 N1 **Prudhoe Bay** Alaska U.S.A.
141 J5 **Prudhoe I** Queensland Australia
115 N2 **Prudhoe Land** Greenland
119 M6 **Prud'homme** Saskatchewan Canada
31 K5 **Prudnik** Poland
54 H6 **Prudyanka** Ukraine
36 B3 **Prüm** Germany
21 M6 **Prunay** France
21 O5 **Prunay-le-Gillon** France
45 J3 **Prunetta** Italy
19 Q15 **Prunières** France
21 P8 **Pruniers** Indre France
21 O7 **Pruniers** Loir-et-Cher France
52 H4 **Prupt** *R* Russian Federation
31 K2 **Pruszcz** Poland
31 M3 **Pruszków** Poland
48 L4 **Prut** *R* Moldova/Romania
48 L3 **Prutul** *R* Romania
41 N3 **Prutz** Austria
52 D4 **Pryazha** Russian Federation
146 J11 **Prydz B** Antarctica
101 R4 **Pryor** Montana U.S.A.
107 P5 **Pryor** Oklahoma U.S.A.
31 M2 **Przasnysz** Poland
31 K2 **Przechlewo** Poland
31 M4 **Przedbórz** Poland
31 O6 **Przemyśl** Poland
31 N5 **Przeworsk** Poland
31 H4 **Przewóz** Poland
57 J4 **Przheval'sk** Kirghizia
31 M4 **Przysucha** Poland
46 F6 **Psakhná** Greece
47 H6 **Psará** *isld* Greece
46 G5 **Psathoúra** *isld* Greece
31 K4 **Psie Pole** Poland
47 R14 **Psíndhos** Rhodes Greece
47 H9 **Psíra** *isld* Greece
52 C5 **Pskov** Russian Federation
52 C5 **Pskovskaya Oblast'** *prov* Russian Federation
52 C5 **Pskovskoye, Ozero** *L* Russian Federation
31 L1 **Pszczółki** Poland
31 L6 **Pszczyna** Poland
53 C7 **Ptich'** *R* Belarus
46 E4 **Ptolemaís** Greece
38 N9 **Ptuj** Slovenia
135 U4 **Puako** Hawaiian Is
116 K8 **Puale B** Alaska U.S.A.
133 E5 **Puán** Argentina
67 C5 **Pubei** China
122 G10 **Pubnico** Nova Scotia Canada
128 C5 **Pucacaca** Peru
128 D5 **Pucallpa** Peru
21 O3 **Puchay** France
38 N6 **Puchberg** Austria
65 A7 **Pucheng** China
65 C7 **Pucheng** China
67 F3 **Pucheng** China
52 F6 **Puchezh** Russian Federation
31 L6 **Puchov** Slovakia
71 E5 **Pucio Pt** Panay Philippines
31 L1 **Puck** Poland
99 R6 **Puckaway L** Wisconsin U.S.A.
9 G4 **Puckeridge** England
111 G9 **Puckett** Mississippi U.S.A.
143 B7 **Puckford,Mt** W Australia Australia
29 M6 **Pudasjärvi** Finland
8 D6 **Puddletown** England
52 H5 **Pudem** Russian Federation
70 E6 **Pudi** Kalimantan
67 B3 **Puding** China
123 Q5 **Pudops L** Newfoundland Canada
52 E4 **Pudozh** Russian Federation
52 E4 **Pudozhgora** Russian Federation
13 G6 **Pudsey** England
125 K8 **Puebla** Mexico
16 D5 **Puebla de Alcocer** Spain
17 F7 **Puebla de Don Fadrique** Spain
16 D5 **Puebla de Don Rodrigo** Spain
16 C2 **Puebla de Sanabria** Spain
16 C2 **Puebla de Trives** Spain
106 F3 **Pueblo** Colorado U.S.A.
106 C5 **Pueblo Bonito** New Mexico U.S.A.
133 C3 **Pueblo Hundido** Chile
100 G7 **Pueblo Mts** Oregon U.S.A.
124 G6 **Pueblo Nuevo** Mexico
125 N9 **Pueblo Viejo** Mexico
125 L6 **Pueblo Viejo, L. de** Mexico
133 D5 **Puelches** Argentina
133 D5 **Puelén** Argentina
16 B2 **Puenteareas** Spain
16 B2 **Puente-Caldelas** Spain
16 D7 **Puente Genil** Spain
103 P7 **Puerco** *R* Arizona U.S.A.
106 C6 **Puerco, R** New Mexico U.S.A.
128 C2 **Puerta Mutis** Colombia
133 C7 **Puerto Aisén** Chile
125 N5 **Puerto Armuelles** Panama
128 C3 **Puerto Asis** Colombia
128 E2 **Puerto Ayacucho** Venezuela
125 P10 **Puerto Barrios** Guatemala
128 D6 **Puerto Bermúdez** Peru
128 D2 **Puerto Berrio** Colombia
133 C7 **Puerto Bertrand** Chile
128 C6 **Puerto Caballas** Peru
128 E1 **Puerto Cabello** Venezuela
125 N2 **Puerto Cabezas** Nicaragua
128 E2 **Puerto Carreño** Colombia
130 B8 **Puerto Casado** Paraguay
128 C5 **Puerto Chicama** Peru
133 C6 **Puerto Cisnes** Chile
133 D8 **Puerto Coig** Argentina
128 D1 **Puerto Colombia** Colombia
125 Q10 **Puerto Cortés** Honduras
128 E1 **Puerto Cumarebo** Venezuela
125 L10 **Puerto Escondido** Mexico
127 J8 **Puerto Estrella** Colombia
128 C5 **Puerto Eten** Peru
133 C5 **Puerto Fuy** Chile
128 F7 **Puerto Grether** Bolivia
133 D8 **Puerto Harberton** Argentina
128 E6 **Puerto Heath** Bolivia
128 D3 **Puerto Huitoto** Colombia
133 E5 **Puerto Ingeniero White** Argentina
128 E3 **Puerto Inírido** Colombia
125 Q7 **Puerto Juárez** Mexico
127 M9 **Puerto La Cruz** Venezuela
128 D4 **Puerto Leguizamo** Colombia
125 N2 **Puerto Lempira** Honduras
16 E6 **Puertollano** Spain
128 D7 **Puerto Lomas** Peru
127 J9 **Puerto López** Colombia
17 F7 **Puerto Lumbreras** Spain
133 D6 **Puerto Madryn** Argentina
128 E6 **Puerto Maldonado** Peru
126 F4 **Puerto Manatí** Cuba
128 D4 **Puerto Miraña** Colombia
133 C6 **Puerto Montt** Chile
133 C8 **Puerto Natales** Chile
128 E2 **Puerto Nuevo** Colombia
133 F3 **Puerto Ocampo** Argentina
128 F2 **Puerto Ordaz** Venezuela
126 F4 **Puerto Padre** Cuba
133 C2 **Puerto Patillos** Chile
124 C2 **Puerto Penasco** Mexico
133 F2 **Puerto Pinasco** Paraguay
133 E6 **Puerto Pirámides** Argentina
128 F1 **Puerto Piritu** Venezuela
127 J5 **Puerto Plata** Dominican Rep
128 D5 **Puerto Portillo** Peru
71 D6 **Puerto Princesa** Palawan Philippines
125 M5 **Puerto Quepos** Costa Rica
128 E6 **Puerto Rico** Bolivia
113 J7 **Puerto Rico** *terr* Caribbean
127 L5 **Puerto Rico Trench** Caribbean
126 G4 **Puerto Samá** Cuba
125 L3 **Puerto Sandino** Nicaragua
130 B8 **Puerto Sastre** Paraguay
128 E6 **Puerto Siles** Bolivia
130 B6 **Puerto Suárez** Bolivia
124 G7 **Puerto Vallarta** Mexico
133 C6 **Puerto Varas** Chile
128 F7 **Puerto Velarde** Bolivia
128 D5 **Puerto Victoria** Peru
128 D2 **Puerto Villamizar** Colombia
133 D7 **Puerto Visser** Argentina
128 D2 **Puerto Wilches** Colombia
133 C7 **Pueyrredón, L** Chile/Arg
25 F7 **Puffendorf** Germany
124 G7 **Puga** Mexico
52 H6 **Pugachevo** Russian Federation
74 E4 **Pugal** India
88 G10 **Puga Puga** *isld* Mozambique
100 C2 **Puget Sound** Washington U.S.A.
19 P13 **Pugieu** France
43 G8 **Puglia** *prov* Italy
71 K9 **Pugubengo** Flores Indonesia
70 K8 **Pugung, G** *mt* Sumatra
122 J8 **Pugwash** Nova Scotia Canada
145 F3 **Puha** New Zealand
135 O1 **Puhi** Hawaiian Is
145 E2 **Puhoi** New Zealand
48 H5 **Pui** Romania
48 L4 **Puiești** Romania
17 J2 **Puigcerda** Spain
71 G7 **Pujada B** Mindanao Philippines
65 G4 **Pujan Res** N Korea
19 N16 **Pujaut** France
67 A1 **Pujiang** China
67 F2 **Pujiang** China
119 Q3 **Pukatawagan** Manitoba Canada
46 D2 **Pukë** Albania
145 G2 **Pukeamaru** *mt* New Zealand
145 E3 **Pukearuhe** New Zealand
145 F3 **Pukehou** New Zealand
145 E2 **Pukekawa** New Zealand
145 E2 **Pukekohe** New Zealand
144 C5 **Pukekura** New Zealand
145 E2 **Pukemiro** New Zealand
145 D1 **Pukenui** New Zealand
145 F3 **Pukeokahu** New Zealand
144 C6 **Pukerangi** New Zealand
144 B7 **Pukerau** New Zealand
145 E3 **Pukeroa** New Zealand
145 G3 **Puketawai** New Zealand
144 D5 **Puketeraki Range** New Zealand
145 F3 **Puketitiri** New Zealand
145 F2 **Puketoetoe** *mt* New Zealand
145 F4 **Puketoi Range** New Zealand
145 E3 **Puketutu** New Zealand
145 F2 **Puketutu I** New Zealand
144 C6 **Pukeuri Junction** New Zealand
29 M11 **Pukkila** Finland
67 F1 **Pukou** China
52 F3 **Puksa** Russian Federation
52 H5 **Puksib** Russian Federation
52 F3 **Puksoozero** Russian Federation
98 G6 **Pukwana** South Dakota U.S.A.
42 F4 **Pula** Croatia
128 E8 **Pulacayo** Bolivia
43 C9 **Pula, C. di** Sardinia
69 C11 **Pulaksama** Sumatra
Pulandian *see* **Xinjin**
71 G6 **Pulangi** *R* Mindanao Philippines
70 D6 **Pulangpisau** Kalimantan
70 K8 **Pulao Seribu** *isld* Sumatra
70 K9 **Pulasari** *mt* Java
71 K8 **Pulasi** *isld* Indonesia
99 O9 **Pulaski** Iowa U.S.A.
95 L3 **Pulaski** New York U.S.A.
110 J6 **Pulaski** Tennessee U.S.A.
94 G9 **Pulaski** Virginia U.S.A.
99 S5 **Pulaski** Wisconsin U.S.A.
69 F13 **Pulaukidjang** Sumatra
70 B4 **Pulaumadjang** Kalimantan
69 E13 **Pulaupunjung** Sumatra
31 N4 **Puławy** Poland
9 F6 **Pulborough** England
76 D3 **Pulivendla** India
76 C6 **Puliyangudi** India
83 K9 **Puliyankulam** Sri Lanka
29 M7 **Pulkkila** Finland
100 H3 **Pullman** Washington U.S.A.
71 E2 **Pulog, Mt** Luzon Philippines
83 K8 **Puloli** Sri Lanka
52 F2 **Pulonga** Russian Federation
52 D1 **Pulozero** Russian Federation
124 D4 **Púlpito, Pta** *C* Mexico
33 T10 **Pulsnitz** *R* Germany
31 M3 **Pułtusk** Poland
66 C4 **Pulu** China
70 P10 **Pulukan** Bali Indonesia
66 E6 **Puma Yumco** *L* China
Pumiao *see* **Yongning**
98 A4 **Pumpkin Cr** Montana U.S.A.
98 C8 **Pumpkin Cr** Nebraska U.S.A.
108 F6 **Pumpville** Texas U.S.A.
8 C3 **Pumsaint** Wales
128 B4 **Puná** *isld* Ecuador
70 G5 **Puna** *R* Sulawesi
144 C5 **Punakaiki** New Zealand
83 L10 **Punani** Sri Lanka
74 F2 **Punch** Kashmir
117 M9 **Punchaw** British Columbia Canada
52 F4 **Punduga** Russian Federation
76 A1 **Pune** India
55 D1 **Punga** *R* Russian Federation
112 L2 **Pungo** North Carolina U.S.A.
59 J3 **Pungsan** N Korea
86 E6 **Punia** Zaire
70 Q10 **Punikan, G** *mt* Indonesia
131 B2 **Punilla, Sa. de la** *mts* Chile
74 F3 **Punjab** *prov* India
74 D3 **Punjab, The** *prov* Pakistan
140 E4 **Punjaub** Queensland Australia
29 O10 **Punkaharju** Finland
29 K10 **Punkalaidun** Finland
119 N7 **Punnichy** Saskatchewan Canada
128 D6 **Puno** *dept* Peru
128 D7 **Puno** Peru
106 D7 **Punta** New Mexico U.S.A.
131 E7 **Punta Alta** Argentina
133 C8 **Punta Arenas** Chile
43 C7 **Puntaccia, Monte** *mt* Sardinia
133 C3 **Punta Colorada** Chile
108 B8 **Punta de Agua Cr.** *R* Texas/New Mex U.S.A.
17 H4 **Punta de la Baña** Spain
125 P9 **Punta Gorda** Belize
125 N4 **Punta Gorda** Nicaragua
100 A9 **Punta Gorda** California U.S.A.
113 E11 **Punta Gorda** Florida U.S.A.
131 G6 **Punta Norte** Argentina
127 J5 **Punta Palenque** Dominican Rep
124 B3 **Punta Prieta** Mexico
125 M5 **Puntarenas** Costa Rica
128 G8 **Punta Rieles** Paraguay
125 N5 **Punta San Pedrillo** Costa Rica
127 M5 **Punta Tuna** Puerto Rico
128 D1 **Punto Fijo** Venezuela
46 G4 **Punto Lágo** Greece
133 D7 **Puntudo, Cerro** *mt* Argentina
116 C5 **Punuk Is** Bering Sea
94 J6 **Punxsutawney** Pennsylvania U.S.A.
68 F6 **Puok** Cambodia
29 N7 **Puolanka** Finland
26 L5 **Puottaure** Sweden
128 E6 **Puoya** *mt* Bolivia
145 D4 **Puponga** New Zealand
58 F6 **Puqi** China
128 D6 **Puquio** Peru
133 D3 **Puquios** Chile
50 G2 **Pur** *R* Russian Federation
128 C3 **Puracé** *vol* Colombia
70 M9 **Purbalingga** Java
107 N7 **Purcell** Oklahoma U.S.A.
116 J3 **Purcell Mt** Alaska U.S.A.
117 P10 **Purcell Mts** British Columbia Canada
100 K1 **Purcell Range** Montana U.S.A.
94 K7 **Purcellville** Virginia U.S.A.
17 F7 **Purchena** Spain
99 N10 **Purdin** Missouri U.S.A.
98 F7 **Purdum** Nebraska U.S.A.
110 C5 **Purdy** Missouri U.S.A.
145 E3 **Pureora** *mt* New Zealand
124 H8 **Purépero** Mexico
145 E1 **Purerua** New Zealand
9 E6 **Purewell** England
106 G4 **Purgatoire** *R* Colorado U.S.A.
116 N3 **Purgatory** Alaska U.S.A.
38 M5 **Purgstall** Austria
75 L9 **Puri** India
128 D3 **Purificación** Colombia
145 E2 **Puriri** New Zealand
9 F5 **Purley** England
25 C3 **Purmerend** Netherlands
74 G9 **Purna** India
138 B2 **Purndu Saltpan** South Australia Australia
52 E3 **Purnema** Russian Federation
75 M6 **Pūrnia** India
118 F9 **Purple Springs** Alberta Canada
128 E4 **Purué** *R* Brazil
70 D5 **Purukcahu** Kalimantan
128 F4 **Purus** *R* Brazil
29 O10 **Puruvesi** *L* Finland
111 G10 **Purvis** Mississippi U.S.A.
46 G2 **Pŭrvomay** Bulgaria
70 L9 **Purwakarta** Java
70 M9 **Purwarejo** Java
70 N9 **Purwodadi** Java
70 M9 **Purwokerto** Java
110 H5 **Puryear** Tennessee U.S.A.
66 B4 **Pusa** China
52 C6 **Puša** Latvia
70 B4 **Pusa** Sarawak
74 G9 **Pusad** India
52 B6 **Pušalotas** Lithuania
65 H7 **Pusan** S Korea
71 G7 **Pusan Pt** Mindanao Philippines
70 B4 **Pusatdamai** Kalimantan
79 D2 **Pusatlı Dağı** *mt* Turkey
65 D6 **Pushang** China
95 T2 **Pushaw L** Maine U.S.A.
52 D5 **Pushkin** Russian Federation
54 J1 **Pushkino** Russian Federation
52 E3 **Pushlakhta** Russian Federation
123 Q6 **Pushthrough** Newfoundland Canada
77 H4 **Pusht-i-Rud** *reg* Afghanistan
120 E4 **Puskaskwa Nat. Park** Ontario Canada
121 O3 **Puskitamika L** Quebec Canada
48 G3 **Püspökladány** Hungary
21 O5 **Pussay** France
22 H4 **Pussemange** Belgium
38 K7 **Pusterwald** Austria
52 C6 **Pustoshka** Russian Federation
102 B3 **Putah Cr** California U.S.A.
67 G5 **Pu-tai** Taiwan
71 M9 **Putain** Timor Indonesia
21 K4 **Putanges-Pont-Ecrepin** France
75 R5 **Putao** Burma
145 E3 **Putaruru** New Zealand
30 G1 **Putbus** Germany
70 P9 **Puteran** *isld* Indonesia
83 K8 **Puthukkudiyiruppu** Sri Lanka
67 F4 **Putian** China
43 H8 **Putignano** Italy
48 J3 **Putila** Ukraine
52 F5 **Putilovo** Russian Federation
70 B6 **Puting Tg** *C* Kalimantan
54 E5 **Putivl'** Ukraine
33 Q6 **Putlitz** Germany
48 K3 **Putna** Romania
95 Q5 **Putnam** Connecticut U.S.A.
108 E8 **Putnam** Oklahoma U.S.A.
109 H3 **Putnam** Texas U.S.A.
112 C6 **Putney** Georgia U.S.A.
98 H4 **Putney** South Dakota U.S.A.
95 P4 **Putney** Vermont U.S.A.
51 J2 **Putorana, Plato** *mt* Russian Federation
145 F3 **Putorino** New Zealand
83 J9 **Puttalam** Sri Lanka
83 J9 **Puttalam Lag** Sri Lanka
22 G1 **Putte** Belgium
36 B5 **Puttelange** France
33 O5 **Püttelkow** Germany
25 E4 **Putten** Netherlands
28 G7 **Puttgarden** Germany
36 B5 **Püttlingen** Germany
128 C3 **Putumayo** *div* Colombia
128 D4 **Putumayo** *R* Peru/Colombia
67 G2 **Putuo** China
67 G1 **Putuo Shan** *isld* China
70 C4 **Putusibau** Kalimantan
33 T5 **Putzar** Germany
135 U5 **Puuanahulu** Hawaiian Is
135 U5 **Puu Hualalei** *crater* Hawaiian Is
135 S3 **Puukoli** Hawaiian Is
29 M10 **Puulavesi** *L* Finland
29 N10 **Puumala** Finland
22 G1 **Puurs** Belgium
135 N1 **Puuwai** Hawaiian Is
Puxian *see* **Pucheng**
65 A6 **Pu Xian** China
117 M12 **Puyallup** Washington U.S.A.
65 C7 **Puyang** China
18 G7 **Puy de Dôme** *dept* France
18 G7 **Puy-de-Sancy** *mt* France
131 A8 **Puyehue, L de** Chile
131 B8 **Puyehue, P. de** Argentina
131 A8 **Puyehue, V** Chile
21 M8 **Puye, La** France
19 Q14 **Puy Gris** *mt* France
18 G9 **Puylaurens** France
18 H7 **Puy, le** France
18 F8 **Puy l'Evêque** France
18 G7 **Puy Mary** *mt* France
21 K7 **Puy Notre Dame, le** France
21 N2 **Puys** France
52 H4 **Puzla** Russian Federation
88 G5 **Pwani** *prov* Tanzania
88 B6 **Pweto** Zaire
68 B2 **Pwinbyu** Burma
8 B2 **Pwllheli** Wales
52 E2 **Pyalitsa** Russian Federation
52 E4 **Pyal'ma** Russian Federation
68 B3 **Pyalo** Burma
68 B5 **Pyamalaw** *R* Burma
52 F6 **Pyana** *R* Russian Federation
57 E6 **Pyandzh** Tajikistan
57 E6 **Pyandzh** *R* Tajikistan/Afghanistan
52 J4 **Pyanteg** Russian Federation
52 D2 **Pyaozero, Oz** *L* Russian Federation
76 C3 **Pyapalli** India
68 B4 **Pyapon** Burma
51 H1 **Pyasina** *R* Russian Federation
53 F11 **Pyatigorsk** Russian Federation
54 E8 **Pyatikhatki** Ukraine
52 H4 **Pyatiqory** Russian Federation
110 D5 **Pyatt** Arkansas U.S.A.
52 H6 **Pychas** Russian Federation
68 B3 **Pyè** Burma
116 M7 **Pye Is** Alaska U.S.A.
29 M9 **Pyhä-Häki Nat. Park** Finland
27 M11 **Pyhajärvi** *L* Finland
29 M8 **Pyhäjärvi** Finland
29 L7 **Pyhäjoki** Finland
29 M7 **Pyhäntä** Finland
29 J11 **Pyhäranta** Finland
29 O9 **Pyhäselkä** Finland
29 M4 **Pyhätunturi Nat. Park** Finland
38 N5 **Pyhra** Austria
68 C3 **Pyinmana** Burma
8 C4 **Pyle** Wales
29 L9 **Pylkönmäki** Finland
94 G5 **Pymatuning Res** Ohio/Penn U.S.A.
69 A9 **Pymgalion Pt** Nicobar Is
59 J3 **Pyŏktong** N Korea
65 F5 **P'yŏngyang** N Korea
100 F9 **Pyramid** Nevada U.S.A.
103 K6 **Pyramid Canyon** Ariz/Nev U.S.A.
139 G6 **Pyramid Hill** Victoria Australia
106 C1 **Pyramid Pk** Colorado U.S.A.
94 A2 **Pyramid Pt** Michigan U.S.A.
102 E2 **Pyramid Rge** Nevada U.S.A.
18 F9 **Pyrénées** *mts* France/Spain
18 E9 **Pyrénées Atlantiques** *dept* France
18 G10 **Pyrénées-Orientales** *dept* France
142 B5 **Pyrton,Mt** W Australia Australia
31 H2 **Pyrzyce** Poland
52 G5 **Pyshchug** Russian Federation
55 D3 **Pyshma** Russian Federation
31 L5 **Pyskowice** Poland
52 C6 **Pytalovo** Russian Federation
121 O6 **Pythonga, L** Quebec Canada
68 C3 **Pyu** *R* Burma
68 C3 **Pyu** Burma
68 C4 **Pyuntaza** Burma
31 K3 **Pyzdry** Poland

Q

Qaanaaq *see* **Thule**
84 E3 **Qaddāhīyah, Al** Libya
74 F3 **Qadian** India
78 K6 **Qādisīyah, Al** *prov* Iraq
77 C1 **Qāem Shahr** Iran
80 G4 **Qafqafa** Jordan
58 G2 **Qagan** China
Qagan Nur *see* **Zhengxiangbai Qi**
65 F2 **Qagan Nur** *L* China
65 B3 **Qagan Nur** China
65 C3 **Qagan Nur** *L* China
65 B4 **Qagan Nur** *L* China
65 D1 **Qagan Qulut** China
65 D3 **Qagan Us** China
65 B4 **Qahar Youyi Houqi** China
65 B4 **Qahar Youyi Qianqi** China
65 B4 **Qahar Youyi Zhongqi** China
Qâhira, El *see* **Cairo**
66 E4 **Qaidam Pendi** *reg* China
66 F4 **Qaidam Shan** *mts* China
77 J4 **Qala Bist** Afghanistan
86 G3 **Qala'en Nahl** Sudan
77 J3 **Qala-i-Ghor** Afghanistan
77 H3 **Qala-i-Kāl** Afghanistan
77 K3 **Qalāt** Afghanistan
79 G4 **Qal 'at al Hisn** Syria
79 F3 **Qal'at al Marqab** Syria
78 H4 **Qal'at as Salihīyah** Syria
80 F4 **Qal'at er Rabad** Jordan
78 L6 **Qal'at Sālih** Iraq
77 J4 **Qal'eh-ye Bost** Afghanistan
77 H2 **Qal'eh-ye Now** Afghanistan
80 C5 **Qalqīlya** Israel
80 E6 **Qalya** Jordan
79 B8 **Qalyûb** Egypt
80 G3 **Qam** Jordan
74 C5 **Qambar** Pakistan
66 F5 **Qamdo** *reg* China
84 F3 **Qaminis** Libya
78 H3 **Qāmishlī, Al** Syria
74 C3 **Qamruddin Karez** Pakistan
80 D5 **Qana** Jordan
86 A1 **Qandala** Somalia
65 C3 **Qangdin Gol** China
65 C3 **Qangdin Sum** China
79 C8 **Qanṭara, El** Egypt
79 G6 **Qanwāt, Al** Syria
Qaqortoq *see* **Julianehåb**
84 H4 **Qara** Egypt
79 F5 **Qaraaoun** Lebanon
77 L2 **Qarah Bāgh** Afghanistan
80 D5 **Qarawat Bani Ḥassan** Jordan
79 G3 **Qardāhah, Al** Syria
86 A2 **Qardho** Somalia
78 L2 **Qareh Su** *R* Iran
79 C10 **Qarn el Kabsh, G** *mt* Egypt
66 D4 **Qarqan He** *R* China
79 F4 **Qartaba** Lebanon
84 E3 **Qaryāt, Al** Libya
79 H4 **Qaryatayn, Al** Syria
80 G7 **Qaryat Falha** Jordan
77 H2 **Qasa Murg** Afghanistan
Qasigiangguit *see* **Christianshåb**
80 F8 **Qasr** Jordan
79 H4 **Qasr al Ḥayr** Syria
79 F8 **Qasr ed Deir, J** *mt* Jordan
84 H4 **Qasr, El** Egypt
78 K4 **Qasr-e-Shirin** Iran
80 G8 **Qasr eth Thuraiya** Jordan
84 H4 **Qasr Farâfra** Egypt
115 P5 **Qassimiut** Greenland
79 G5 **Qatana** Syria
77 B7 **Qatar** *state* Persian Gulf
77 B6 **Qatīf, Al** Saudi Arabia
79 G7 **Qatrāna** Jordan
84 E5 **Qaṭrūn, Al** Libya
84 H4 **Qattara Depression** Egypt
77 F3 **Qāyen** Iran
78 J4 **Qayyarah** Iraq
80 F2 **Qazrin** Syria
77 A1 **Qazvīn** Iran
80 F1 **Qela'** Syria
84 J4 **Qena** Egypt
Qeqertarsuaq *see* **Godhavn**
Qeqertarsuaq *isld* *see* **Disko** *isld*
Qeqertarsuatsiaat *see* **Fiskenæsset**
Qeqertarsuatsiaq *see* **Hareøen**
77 E6 **Qeshm** Iran
77 A1 **Qeydār** Iran
77 C6 **Qeys** *isld* Iran
77 A1 **Qezel Owzan** *R* Iran
79 E8 **Qeẕi'ot** Israel
65 F2 **Qian'an** China
65 D4 **Qian'an** China
67 C3 **Qiancheng** China
65 F2 **Qian Gorlos** China
67 C3 **Qiangu'ao** China
Qianguozhen *see* **Qian Gorlos**
65 D7 **Qiangwei He** *R* China
67 D1 **Qianjiang** China
67 C2 **Qianjiang** *R* China
67 C5 **Qianjiang** China
59 K2 **Qianjin** China
65 F4 **Qian Shan** *mt ra* China
66 E3 **Qianshan** China
67 E1 **Qianshan** China
65 E4 **Qianwei** China
67 A2 **Qianwei** China
65 D4 **Qianxi** China
67 B3 **Qianxi** China
67 A4 **Qianxinan** China
67 C3 **Qianyang** China
65 D3 **Qiaotou** China
67 E3 **Qiaotou** China
67 E1 **Qichun** China
80 F1 **Qidmat Ẕevi** Syria
67 G1 **Qidong** China
67 D3 **Qidong** China
66 D4 **Qiemo** China
67 C2 **Qifeng Guan** *pass* China
65 C6 **Qihe** China
65 B3 **Qihreg** China
58 E6 **Qijiang** China
66 E3 **Qijiaojing** China
Qike *see* **Xunke**
65 D5 **Qikou** China
77 H6 **Qila Lādgasht** Pakistan
65 D4 **Qilaotu Shan** *mt ra* China
74 A8 **Qila Safed** Pakistan
74 C3 **Qila Saifullah** Pakistan
Qili *see* **Shitai**
66 F4 **Qilian Shan** *mt ra* China
65 E4 **Qilihe** China
67 F2 **Qimen** China
65 G1 **Qing'an** China
65 D6 **Qingcheng** China
65 E6 **Qingdao** China
65 E5 **Qingduizi** China
65 C7 **Qingfeng** China
67 A2 **Qingfu** China
65 G1 **Qinggang** China
Qinggil *see* **Qinghe**
65 C7 **Qingguji** China
66 E4 **Qinghai** *prov* China
58 D4 **Qinghai Hu** *L* China
65 H1 **Qinghe** China
65 C6 **Qinghe** China
66 E2 **Qinghe** China
65 F4 **Qinghecheng** China
65 E4 **Qinghemen** China
65 F3 **Qinghe Shuiku** *res* China
67 F2 **Qinghu** China
65 A6 **Qingjian** China
67 C1 **Qing Jiang** *R* China
67 E2 **Qingjiang** China
65 A6 **Qingjian He** *R* China
Qingkou *see* **Ganyu**
67 C7 **Qinglan** China
67 D7 **Qinglan Gang** *inlet* China
67 D4 **Qinglian** China
67 E3 **Qingliu** China
65 D4 **Qinglong** China
67 B4 **Qinglong** China
65 D4 **Qinglong He** *R* China
65 C6 **Qingping** China
68 J2 **Qingping** China
67 G1 **Qingpu** China
67 A2 **Qingshen** China
58 E4 **Qingshui He** *R* China
65 B5 **Qingshuihe** China
67 C3 **Qingshui Jiang** *R* China
67 G2 **Qingtian** China
65 C5 **Qing Xian** China
65 B6 **Qingxu** China
Qingyang *see* **Jinjiang**
58 E4 **Qingyang** China
67 F1 **Qingyang** China
Qingyuan *see* **Yishan**
59 J3 **Qingyuan** China
67 F3 **Qingyuan** China
67 D5 **Qingyuan** China
65 D6 **Qingyun** China
65 B7 **Qin He** *R* China
65 D5 **Qinhuangdao** China
67 C6 **Qin Jiang** *R* China
58 E5 **Qin Ling** *mt ra* China
65 B7 **Qinshui** China
67 C5 **Qintang** China
58 F4 **Qin Xian** China
58 F4 **Qinyang** China
67 G3 **Qinyu** China
65 B6 **Qinyuan** China
67 C6 **Qinzhou** China
68 J2 **Qinzhou Wan** *B* China
68 K3 **Qionghai** China
58 D5 **Qionglai** China
58 D5 **Qionglai Shan** *mt ra* China
67 C7 **Qiongshan** China
67 C7 **Qiongzhong** China
68 J2 **Qiongzhou Haixia** China
67 B1 **Qiping** China
59 H2 **Qiqihar** China
77 C5 **Qīr** Iran
80 D7 **Qiryat Arba'** Jordan
80 D2 **Qiryat Ata** Israel
80 D8 **Qiryatayim** Jordan
80 D2 **Qiryat Bialik** Israel
80 C7 **Qiryat Gat** Israel
80 D2 **Qiryat Motmkin** Israel
80 D5 **Qiryat Netafim** Jordan
80 F1 **Qiryat Shemona** Israel
80 D3 **Qiryat Tiv'on** Israel
80 D2 **Qiryat Yam** Israel
80 D6 **Qiryat Yearim** Israel
67 C6 **Qisha** China
80 D3 **Qishon 'Eneq Yizre'el** Israel
68 J2 **Qishui** China
66 D3 **Qitai** China
65 H2 **Qitaihe** China
67 A4 **Qiubei** China
65 C6 **Qiu Xian** China
65 E6 **Qixia** China
65 B6 **Qi Xian** China
65 C7 **Qi Xian** China
65 B4 **Qixiaying** China
65 J1 **Qixing He** *R* China
65 H1 **Qixingpao** China
67 D3 **Qiyang** China
67 E1 **Qizhou** China
Qogir Feng *mt pk* *see* **K2** *mt*
65 C2 **Qog Ul** China
77 B2 **Qom** Iran
77 B3 **Qomishēh** Iran
Qomolangma Feng *mt* *see* **Everest, Mt**
66 D3 **Qongkol** China
115 O5 **Qoornoq** Greenland
77 A2 **Qorveh** Iran
79 G4 **Qoubaiyat** Lebanon
95 P4 **Quabbin Res** Massachusetts U.S.A.
122 G8 **Quaco Hd** New Brunswick Canada
74 D2 **Quaidabad** Pakistan
102 H6 **Quail Mts** California U.S.A.
143 B9 **Quairading** W Australia Australia
32 G7 **Quakenbrück** Germany
95 M6 **Quakertown** Pennsylvania U.S.A.
45 Q8 **Qualiano** Italy
85 E6 **Quallam** Niger
139 G6 **Quambatook** Victoria Australia
139 J4 **Quambone** New South Wales Australia
140 F5 **Quamby** Queensland Australia
108 H1 **Quanah** Texas U.S.A.
128 F4 **Quanaru, Ilha** Brazil
68 H2 **Quan Dao Co To** *isld* Vietnam
68 J5 **Quang Nam** Vietnam
68 J5 **Quang Ngai** Vietnam
68 H4 **Quang Tri** Vietnam
67 B6 **Quang Yen** Vietnam
67 F1 **Quanjiao** China
69 G8 **Quan Long** Vietnam
67 E4 **Quannan** China
68 F7 **Quan Phu Quoc** *isld* Vietnam
94 K8 **Quantico** Virginia U.S.A.
120 E1 **Quantz L** Ontario Canada
67 C4 **Quanzhou** China
119 O8 **Qu'Appelle** Saskatchewan Canada
119 P8 **Qu'Appelle R** Saskatchewan Canada
118 L7 **Qu'Appelle R. Dam** Saskatchewan Canada
133 F4 **Quaraí** Brazil
131 G3 **Quarai, R** Brazil
32 L4 **Quarnbek** Germany
122 G7 **Quarryville** New Brunswick Canada
95 L7 **Quarryville** Pennsylvania U.S.A.
40 F6 **Quart** Italy
45 L2 **Quartesana** Italy
45 N6 **Quartière Mt. Sacro** Italy
83 M12 **Quartier Militaire** Mauritius
43 C9 **Quartu Sant'Elena** Sardinia
102 H4 **Quartzite Mt** Nevada U.S.A.
102 G2 **Quartz Mt** Nevada U.S.A.
100 G1 **Quartz Mt** Washington U.S.A.
103 K8 **Quartzsite** Arizona U.S.A.
99 P7 **Quasqueton** Iowa U.S.A.
22 G2 **Quatre Bras** Belgium
22 H5 **Quatre-Champs** France
117 K10 **Quatsino** British Columbia Canada
45 H2 **Quattro Castella** Italy
106 G7 **Quay** New Mexico U.S.A.
77 F1 **Qūchān** Iran
101 P8 **Quealy** Wyoming U.S.A.
139 J6 **Queanbeyan** New South Wales Australia
115 M7 **Quebec** *prov* Canada
121 T6 **Québec** Quebec Canada
130 F6 **Quebra Anzol** *R* Brazil
88 D9 **Quebrabasa Rapids** Mozambique
133 E3 **Quebracho Coto** Argentina
131 A8 **Quedal, C. de** Chile
33 O9 **Quedlinburg** Germany
17 G9 **Qued Tlélat** Algeria
95 L8 **Queen Anne** Maryland U.S.A.
117 L10 **Queen Bess, Mt** British Columbia Canada
9 G5 **Queenborough** England
115 M5 **Queen, C** Northwest Territories Canada
133 E8 **Queen Charlotte B** Falkland Is
117 G9 **Queen Charlotte Is** British Columbia Canada
117 J10 **Queen Charlotte Sd** British Columbia Canada
145 E4 **Queen Charlotte Sound** New Zealand
117 K10 **Queen Charlotte Str** British Columbia Canada
99 O9 **Queen City** Missouri U.S.A.
109 N2 **Queen City** Texas U.S.A.
115 K2 **Queen Elizabeth Is** Northwest Territories Canada
146 H12 **Queen Mary Land** Antarctica
117 D5 **Queen Mary, Mt** Yukon Territory Canada
114 J4 **Queen Maud Gulf** Northwest Territories Canada
146 D9 **Queen Maud Mts** Antarctica
13 G6 **Queensbury** England
140 A2 **Queens Chan** N Terr Australia
115 K2 **Queens Chan** Northwest Territories Canada
139 G7 **Queenscliff** Victoria Australia
13 E2 **Queensferry** Scotland
140 F6 **Queensland** *state* Australia
142 B2 **Queens Park** *dist* Perth, W Aust Australia
123 L8 **Queensport** Nova Scotia Canada
139 H8 **Queenstown** Tasmania Australia
118 E8 **Queenstown** Alberta Canada
144 B6 **Queenstown** New Zealand
89 E8 **Queenstown** S Africa
95 L8 **Queenstown** Maryland U.S.A.
100 A2 **Queets** Washington U.S.A.
131 F4 **Queguay Grande** *R* Uruguay
36 E5 **Queich** *R* Germany
16 C2 **Queija, S. de** *mts* Spain
129 L6 **Queimadas** Brazil
87 C7 **Quela** Angola
21 J6 **Quelaines** France
87 B7 **Quele** Angola
88 F10 **Quelimane** Mozambique
124 F6 **Quelite** Mexico
133 C6 **Quellen** Chile
106 B7 **Quemado** New Mexico U.S.A.
108 G7 **Quemado** Texas U.S.A.
20 B5 **Quéménéven** France
Quemoy *see* **Chin-men**
133 E5 **Quemu Quemu** Argentina
22 B3 **Quend** France
9 G4 **Quendon** England
22 B3 **Quend Plage** France
107 P3 **Quenemo** Kansas U.S.A.
111 F10 **Quentin** Mississippi U.S.A.
Que Que *see* **Kwekwe**
133 F5 **Quequén** Argentina
22 C2 **Quercamps** France
130 D8 **Querência do Norte** Brazil
125 J7 **Querétaro** Mexico
33 P10 **Querfurt** Germany
124 D2 **Querobabi** Mexico
20 G2 **Querqueville** France
20 C6 **Querrien** France

21 P2 **Querrieu** France
117 M9 **Quesnel** British Columbia Canada
117 N9 **Quesnel L** British Columbia Canada
22 D4 **Quesnoy** France
22 F3 **Quesnoy, le** France
22 E2 **Quesnoy-sur-Deule, le** France
20 E5 **Quessoy** France
106 E5 **Questa** New Mexico U.S.A.
20 F6 **Questembert** France
133 D2 **Quetena** Bolivia
99 Q1 **Quetico** Ontario Canada
118 L2 **Quetico L** Ontario Canada
99 P1 **Quetico Provincial Park** Ontario Canada
74 B3 **Quetta** Pakistan
20 H2 **Quettehou** France
21 L3 **Quetteville** France
20 H4 **Quettreville** France
111 D11 **Queue de Tortue** *R* Louisiana U.S.A.
21 O4 **Queue-lèz-Yvelines,la** France
21 P2 **Quevauvillers** France
121 O3 **Quévillon** Quebec Canada
125 O10 **Quezaltenango** Guatemala
71 C6 **Quezon** Palawan Philippines
71 E3 **Quezon City** Luzon Philippines
65 D7 **Qufu** China
87 B8 **Quibala** Angola
87 B7 **Quibate** Angola
128 C2 **Quibdó** Colombia
118 J1 **Quibell** Ontario Canada
20 D7 **Quiberon** France
20 D6 **Quiberon,B.de** France
21 M2 **Quiberville** France
127 K10 **Quíbor** Venezuela
87 B7 **Quicama Nat. Park** Angola
68 G3 **Qui Chau** Vietnam
32 L5 **Quickborn** Germany
36 C5 **Quierschied** Germany
117 G5 **Quiet L** Yukon Territory Canada
22 F3 **Quievrain** Belgium
22 E3 **Quiévy** France
118 G2 **Quigley** Alberta Canada
133 F3 **Quiindy** Paraguay
103 M9 **Quijotoa** Arizona U.S.A.
124 F5 **Quilá** Mexico
133 C6 **Quilán, C** Chile
16 E9 **Quilates, C** Morocco
128 D7 **Quilca** Peru
100 C2 **Quilcene** Washington U.S.A.
87 B8 **Quilengues** Angola
133 E4 **Quilino** Argentina
128 D6 **Quillabamba** Peru
128 E7 **Quillacollo** Bolivia
Quillak *see* **Dannebrog Ø**
18 G10 **Quillan** France
21 M3 **Quillebeuf** France
131 B7 **Quillén, L** Argentina
119 N6 **Quill Lake** Saskatchewan Canada
131 B4 **Quillota** Chile
119 N7 **Quillsks L** Saskatchewan Canada
20 G7 **Quilly** France
76 C6 **Quilon** India
141 G7 **Quilpie** Queensland Australia
87 C8 **Quimbango** Angola
20 B5 **Quimerch** France
20 B6 **Quimper** France
20 C6 **Quimperlé** France
71 F3 **Quinabucasan Pt** Philippines
71 F4 **Quinalasag** *isld* Philippines
100 A2 **Quinault** *R* Washington U.S.A.
100 B2 **Quinault** Washington U.S.A.
21 N2 **Quincampoix** France
21 L8 **Quinçay** France
128 D6 **Quince Mil** Peru
102 D2 **Quincy** California U.S.A.
111 M11 **Quincy** Florida U.S.A.
99 P10 **Quincy** Illinois U.S.A.
95 R4 **Quincy** Massachusetts U.S.A.
110 N1 **Quincy** Ohio U.S.A.
100 B3 **Quincy** Oregon U.S.A.
100 F2 **Quincy** Washington U.S.A.
20 H2 **Quineville** France
68 F2 **Quinh Nhai** Vietnam
128 E3 **Quinigua, Cerro** *mts* Venezuela
71 E5 **Quiniluban** *isld* Philippines
109 L3 **Quinlan** Texas U.S.A.
98 D6 **Quinn** South Dakota U.S.A.
103 J4 **Quinn Canyon Ra** Nevada U.S.A.
100 G8 **Quinn River Crossing** Nevada U.S.A.
19 Q17 **Quinson** France
16 E5 **Quintanar de la Orden** Spain
125 P8 **Quintana Roo** *terr* Mexico
107 K2 **Quinter** Kansas U.S.A.
20 E5 **Quintin** France
131 D5 **Quinto** *R* Argentina
17 G3 **Quinto** Spain
119 N7 **Quinton** Saskatchewan Canada
107 P6 **Quinton** Oklahoma U.S.A.
45 L1 **Quinto Vicentino** Italy
8 A7 **Quintrel Downs** England
94 G8 **Quinwood** West Virginia U.S.A.
88 H7 **Quionga** Mozambique
130 J10 **Quipapá** Brazil
87 B8 **Quipungo** Angola
15 B3 **Quirang** Scotland
87 C8 **Quirima** Angola
139 K4 **Quirindi** New South Wales Australia
131 A6 **Quiriquina** *isld* Chile
127 N10 **Quiriquire** Venezuela
120 H6 **Quirke L** Ontario Canada
36 C5 **Quirnbach** Germany
16 C2 **Quiroga** Spain
123 R2 **Quirpon** Newfoundland Canada
123 R2 **Quirpon I** Newfoundland Canada
88 H8 **Quissanga** Mozambique
87 F10 **Quissico** Mozambique
45 J1 **Quistello** Italy
20 D6 **Quistinic** France
87 C8 **Quitapa** Angola
126 D7 **Quita Sueño Bank** Caribbean
130 D6 **Quitéria** *R* Brazil
110 D6 **Quitman** Arkansas U.S.A.
113 D7 **Quitman** Georgia U.S.A.
109 P3 **Quitman** Louisiana U.S.A.
111 H9 **Quitman** Mississippi U.S.A.
109 M3 **Quitman** Texas U.S.A.
128 C4 **Quito** Ecuador
103 M10 **Quitovac** Mexico
21 N3 **Quittebeuf** France
103 M6 **Quivero** Arizona U.S.A.
128 C5 **Quivilla** Peru
129 L4 **Quixadá** Brazil
67 B1 **Qu Jiang** *R* China
67 D4 **Qujiang** China
67 C6 **Qujie** China
67 A4 **Qujing** China
46 D3 **Qukës-Shkumbin** Albania
80 G6 **Quleib** *R* Jordan
66 E4 **Qumar He** *R* China
58 C5 **Qumarlêb** China
89 F8 **Qumbu** S Africa
80 G1 **Qunayţirah, El** Syria
84 G4 **Qunayyin, S. al** Libya
72 E5 **Qunfudhah, Al** Saudi Arabia
66 D5 **Qungtag** China
143 A6 **Quobba,Pt** W Australia Australia
83 M12 **Quoin Channel** Mauritius
140 A2 **Quoin I** N Terr Australia
141 K6 **Quoin I** Queensland Australia
89 A10 **Quoin Pt** S Africa
138 E4 **Quorn** South Australia Australia
119 N1 **Quorn** Ontario Canada
80 G6 **Qureiyat Nafi** Jordan
80 G6 **Qureiyat Salim** Jordan
129 J4 **Qurem** Brazil
84 J4 **Qus** Egypt
80 G1 **Quşaybah** Syria
84 J4 **Quseir** Egypt
77 G6 **Quşr-e-Qand** Iran
67 C1 **Qutang Xia Wu Xia** China
87 E12 **Quthing** Lesotho
79 H2 **Quwayq** *R* Syria
79 B8 **Quweisna** Egypt
65 B7 **Quwo** China
58 E4 **Quwu Shan** *mt ra* China
67 A5 **Quxi** China
Qu Xian *see* **Quzhou**
67 B1 **Qu Xian** China
75 O4 **Qüxü** China
65 C5 **Quyang** China
67 E3 **Quyang** China
67 B7 **Quynh Luu** Vietnam
68 J6 **Quy Nhon** Vietnam
121 O7 **Quyon** Quebec Canada
65 C6 **Quzhou** China
67 F2 **Quzhou** China

R

29 K5 **Rå** Sweden
27 F16 **Råå** Sweden
Raab *see* **Györ**
31 J7 **Raabs** Austria
38 N7 **Raab Tal** *V* Austria
29 L7 **Raahe** Finland
138 F5 **Raak Plain** Victoria Australia
29 O9 **Rääl-kylä** Finland
25 F4 **Raalte** Netherlands
115 L2 **Raanes Pen** Northwest Territories Canada
29 L5 **Raanujärvi** Finland
70 P9 **Raas** *isld* Indonesia
77 A5 **Ra'as Al Khafji** Saudi Arabia
15 B3 **Raasay, Sd of** Scotland
42 F4 **Rab** *isld* Croatia
48 D3 **Rába** *R* Hungary
71 J9 **Raba** Sumbawa Indonesia
80 E4 **Raba** Jordan
48 F1 **Raba** *R* Poland
16 C3 **Rabaçal** *R* Portugal
18 F9 **Rabastens de Bigorre** Hautes-Pyrénées France
85 C2 **Rabat** Morocco
137 L2 **Rabaul** New Britain
Rabbah *see* **'Ammān**
117 K6 **Rabbit** *R* British Columbia Canada
98 D4 **Rabbit Cr** South Dakota U.S.A.
106 D1 **Rabbit Ears Pass** Colorado U.S.A.
145 D4 **Rabbit I** New Zealand
118 K5 **Rabbit Lake** Saskatchewan Canada
117 N5 **Rabbitskin** *R* Northwest Territories Canada
28 D7 **Rabel** Germany
36 F2 **Rabenau** Germany
77 E5 **Rābor** Iran
52 F6 **Rabotki** Russian Federation
37 P3 **Rabštejn** Czech Rep
112 D3 **Rabun, L** Georgia U.S.A.
84 G5 **Rabyānah** *well* Libya
84 G5 **Rabyānah, Ramlat** *sands* Libya
46 D1 **Rača** Serbia Yugoslavia
44 C2 **Racconigi** Italy
99 M8 **Raccoon** *R* Iowa U.S.A.
126 G3 **Raccoon Cay** Bahamas
94 E8 **Raccoon Cr** Ohio U.S.A.
38 N9 **Rače** Slovenia
123 T7 **Race, C** Newfoundland Canada
94 E8 **Raceland** Kentucky U.S.A.
111 F12 **Raceland** Louisiana U.S.A.
113 E7 **Race Pond** Florida U.S.A.
95 R4 **Race Pt** Massachusetts U.S.A.
100 B1 **Race Rocks** British Columbia Canada
101 N3 **Race Track** Montana U.S.A.
80 E1 **Rachaf** Lebanon
79 F5 **Rachaiya** Lebanon
109 J9 **Rachal** Texas U.S.A.
69 D9 **Racha Noi, Ko** *isld* Thailand
69 D9 **Racha Yai, Ko** *isld* Thailand
68 G8 **Rach Gia** Vietnam
31 L5 **Racibórz** Poland
37 P3 **Račic** Czech Rep
94 F8 **Racine** Ohio U.S.A.
99 T7 **Racine** Wisconsin U.S.A.
122 D1 **Racine-de-Bouleau, R** Quebec Canada
120 G4 **Racine L** Ontario Canada
33 Q10 **Rackwitz** Germany
37 O4 **Racovský** *mt* Czech Rep
46 E1 **Radan** *mt* Serbia Yugoslavia
48 K3 **Rădăuţi** Romania
37 P4 **Radbuza** *R* Czech Rep
110 L4 **Radcliff** Kentucky U.S.A.
13 F6 **Radcliffe** England
99 N7 **Radcliffe** Iowa U.S.A.
27 E12 **Råde** Norway
30 H4 **Radeberg** Germany
37 Q1 **Radebeul** Germany
33 T10 **Radeburg** Germany
19 Q18 **Rade d'Hyères** *B* France
33 Q9 **Radegast** Germany
38 M8 **Radel Pass** Austria
36 C1 **Radevormwald** Germany
94 G9 **Radford** Virginia U.S.A.
140 B1 **Radford Pt** N Terr Australia
74 D7 **Radhanpur** India
118 K6 **Radisson** Saskatchewan Canada
99 P4 **Radisson** Wisconsin U.S.A.
101 T10 **Radium** Colorado U.S.A.
98 K1 **Radium** Minnesota U.S.A.
37 N3 **Radiumbad-Brambach** Germany
138 F4 **Radium Hill** *pk* South Australia Australia
117 P10 **Radium Hot Springs** British Columbia Canada
106 D9 **Radium Springs** New Mexico U.S.A.
70 O9 **Radja, I** Indonesia
77 F1 **Rādkān** Iran
Radldorf *see* **Bergstorf**
38 L6 **Radmer-an-dem-Hasel** Austria
47 H2 **Radnevo** Bulgaria
30 H6 **Radnice** Czech Rep
41 J2 **Radolfzell** Germany
31 N4 **Radom** Poland
86 D4 **Radom** Sudan
46 F2 **Radomir** Bulgaria
31 L4 **Radomsko** Poland
37 P3 **Radonice** Czech Rep
31 K7 **Radošina** Slovakia
31 M4 **Radoszyce** Poland
46 E3 **Radoviš** Macedonia
54 L1 **Radovitskiy** Russian Federation
42 F2 **Radovljica** Slovenia
38 H7 **Radstadt** Austria
8 D5 **Radstock** England
38 L9 **Raduha** *mt* Slovenia
42 H5 **Raduša** *mt* Bosnia-Herzegovina
52 B6 **Radviliškis** Lithuania
119 N9 **Radville** Saskatchewan Canada
118 E4 **Radway** Alberta Canada
31 O6 **Radymno** Poland
31 M3 **Radzanów** Poland
31 L3 **Radziejów** Poland
31 N3 **Radzymin** Poland
31 O4 **Radzyń Podlaski** Poland
117 P4 **Rae** Northwest Territories Canada
75 J5 **Rae Bareli** India
112 H3 **Raeford** North Carolina U.S.A.
115 L4 **Rae Isthmus** Northwest Territories Canada
114 H5 **Rae L** Northwest Territories Canada
118 B8 **Rae, Mt** British Columbia Canada
28 B2 **Rær** Denmark
22 L2 **Raeren** Belgium
32 E9 **Raesfeld** Germany
143 D8 **Raeside, L** W Australia Australia
115 K4 **Rae Str** Northwest Territories Canada
145 D1 **Raetea** *mt* New Zealand
145 E3 **Raetihi** New Zealand
131 E3 **Rafaela** Argentina
79 E7 **Rafaḩ** Egypt
86 D5 **Rafaï** Cent Afr Republic
53 C8 **Rafalovka** Ukraine
80 D5 **Rafat** Jordan
17 G5 **Rafelbuñol** Spain
78 J7 **Rafḩā'** Saudi Arabia
77 E4 **Rafsanjān** Iran
101 M7 **Raft** *R* Idaho U.S.A.
119 Q3 **Rafter** Manitoba Canada
101 M8 **Raft R. Mts** Utah U.S.A.
26 H3 **Raftsund** Norway
86 E4 **Raga** Sudan
71 G7 **Ragang, Mt** Philippines
71 F4 **Ragay G** Philippines
28 J4 **Rågeleje** Denmark
33 R6 **Rägelin** Germany
126 G3 **Ragged I** Bahamas
143 E10 **Ragged,Mt** W Australia Australia
127 P6 **Ragged Pt** Barbados
145 E2 **Raglan** New Zealand
8 D4 **Raglan** Wales
111 K8 **Ragland** Alabama U.S.A.
108 D1 **Ragland** New Mexico U.S.A.
145 D4 **Raglan Range** New Zealand
107 M4 **Rago** Kansas U.S.A.
44 G2 **Ragola Monte** Italy
33 R8 **Ragösen** Germany
28 G7 **Rågø Sund** *chan* Denmark
33 Q9 **Raguhn** Germany
26 H8 **Ragunda** Sweden
Ragusa *see* **Dubrovnik**
43 F12 **Ragusa** Sicily
71 H7 **Raha** Indonesia
86 G3 **Rahad** *R* Sudan
86 D3 **Rahad el Berdi** Sudan
Rahaeng *see* **Tak**
80 E8 **Raḩaf** Israel
27 J11 **Råhällan** Sweden
32 J8 **Rahden** Germany
86 E2 **Rahib** Sudan
80 D8 **Rahiya** Jordan
145 D3 **Raholu** New Zealand
74 F9 **Rahuri** India
16 B6 **Raia** *R* Portugal
45 P5 **Raiano** Italy
Raibu *see* **Air**
76 C2 **Raichur** India
71 K10 **Raidjua** *isld* Indonesia
75 K8 **Raigarh** India
102 G2 **Railroad Pass** Nevada U.S.A.
103 J3 **Railroad Valley** Nevada U.S.A.
37 K6 **Rain** Germany
37 N6 **Rain** Germany
37 J6 **Rainau** Germany
138 F6 **Rainbow** Victoria Australia
103 O4 **Rainbow Br. Nat. Mon** Utah U.S.A.
124 E9 **Rainbow City** Panama
111 K8 **Rainbow City** Alabama U.S.A.
141 G1 **Raine I** Gt Barrier Reef Aust
9 G4 **Rainham** England
100 C3 **Rainier** Oregon U.S.A.
100 C3 **Rainier** Washington U.S.A.
100 D3 **Rainier, Mt** Washington U.S.A.
100 B5 **Rainrock** Oregon U.S.A.
94 J7 **Rainsburg** Pennsylvania U.S.A.
94 C1 **Rainy** *R* Michigan U.S.A.
99 M1 **Rainy** *R* Minnesota U.S.A.
118 J2 **Rainy L** Minnesota/Ontario U.S.A./Canada
99 N1 **Rainy Lake** Ontario Canada
100 E1 **Rainy Pass** Washington U.S.A.
116 L5 **Rainy Pass Lodge** Alaska U.S.A.
118 H2 **Rainy R** Ontario Canada
99 M1 **Rainy River** Ontario Canada
29 J8 **Raippaluoto** *isld* Finland
75 J8 **Raipur** India
74 G7 **Raisen** India
27 M11 **Raisio** Finland
22 E3 **Raismes** France
29 N5 **Raistakka** Finland
119 O2 **Raith** Ontario Canada
68 A1 **Raithaw** Burma
145 D4 **Rai Valley** New Zealand
70 F4 **Raja** Kalimantan
70 B5 **Raja, Bt** *mt* Kalimantan
70 C5 **Raja, Bt** *mt* Kalimantan
76 E2 **Rajahmundry** India
76 D3 **Rajampet** India
70 B3 **Rajang** Sarawak
74 D4 **Rajanpur** Pakistan
76 C6 **Rajapalaiyam** India
74 D5 **Rajasthan** *prov* India
69 C11 **Raja, Ujung** *C* Sumatra
46 D2 **Rajë** Albania
75 L6 **Rajgir** India
31 O2 **Rajgród** Poland
80 F5 **Rajib** *R* Jordan
80 F5 **Rajib** Jordan
69 G14 **Rajik** Bangka Indonesia
75 J8 **Rajim** India
74 D7 **Rajkot** India
75 J8 **Raj Nandgaon** India
74 E8 **Rajpipla** India
75 N6 **Rajshahi** Bangladesh
76 D1 **Rajura** India
88 C2 **Rakai** Uganda
144 D5 **Rakaia** New Zealand
Rakata *isld see* **Krakatau** *isld*
145 F3 **Rakauroa** New Zealand
99 N6 **Rake** Iowa U.S.A.
144 A7 **Rakeahua** *mt* New Zealand
56 C6 **Rakhmanoviskoye** Kazakhstan
56 C6 **Rakhmanovskiye Klyuchi** Kazakhstan
48 J2 **Rakhov** Ukraine
77 J6 **Rakhshan** *R* Pakistan
145 E2 **Rakino I** New Zealand
26 L3 **Rakisvaara** *mt* Sweden
70 M8 **Rakit** *isld* Indonesia
71 C7 **Rakit** Sabah
46 G3 **Rakitovo** Bulgaria
145 E2 **Rakitu I** New Zealand
55 C5 **Rakityanka** Russian Federation
Raki-ura *isld see* **Stewart I**
27 E12 **Rakkestad** Norway
69 D8 **Ra, Ko** *isld* Thailand
31 J3 **Rakoniewice** Poland
87 D10 **Rakops** Botswana
30 H5 **Rakovník** Czech Rep
46 G2 **Rakovski** Bulgaria
33 S4 **Rakow** Germany
52 F3 **Rakula** Russian Federation
52 G4 **Rakulka** Russian Federation
52 C5 **Rakvere** Estonia
111 G9 **Raleigh** Mississippi U.S.A.
112 J2 **Raleigh** North Carolina U.S.A.
98 E3 **Raleigh** North Dakota U.S.A.
112 L3 **Raleigh B** North Carolina U.S.A.
101 M1 **Raley** Alberta Canada
70 F7 **Ralla** Sulawesi
108 F2 **Ralls** Texas U.S.A.
99 T3 **Ralph** Michigan U.S.A.
98 C4 **Ralph** South Dakota U.S.A.
107 O5 **Ralston** Oklahoma U.S.A.
95 L5 **Ralston** Pennsylvania U.S.A.
100 G3 **Ralston** Washington U.S.A.
101 R5 **Ralston** Wyoming U.S.A.
117 M5 **Ram** *R* Northwest Territories Canada
79 F9 **Ram** Jordan
119 P7 **Rama** Saskatchewan Canada
80 D4 **Rāma** Jordan
125 M3 **Rama** Nicaragua
78 J5 **Ramādi, Ar** Iraq
106 F2 **Ramah** Colorado U.S.A.
106 B6 **Ramah** New Mexico U.S.A.
16 E1 **Ramales de la Victoria** Spain
129 K6 **Ramalho, Sa. do** *mts* Brazil
133 E4 **Ramalio** Argentina
80 D6 **Ramallah** Jordan
76 D6 **Ramanathapuram** India
75 K8 **Rāmapur** India
89 E3 **Ramaquabane** *R* Zimbabwe
54 E4 **Ramasukha** Russian Federation
80 C5 **Ramatayim** Israel
80 C5 **Ramat Gan** Israel
80 C5 **Ramat Ha Kovesh** Israel
80 C5 **Ramat Ha Sharon** Israel
80 D3 **Ramat HaShofet** Israel
80 E7 **Ramat Qidron** Jordan
80 D2 **Ramat Yoḩanan** Israel
83 K10 **Rambe** Sri Lanka
36 E5 **Ramberg** Germany
36 B7 **Rambervillers** France
83 K9 **Rambewa** Sri Lanka
127 J2 **Ramble** Jamaica
133 D4 **Ramblon** Argentina
21 O4 **Rambouillet** France
33 P6 **Rambow** Germany
76 B3 **Ramdurg** India
123 P6 **Ramea** Newfoundland Canada
139 J7 **Rame Hd** Victoria Australia
52 E6 **Ramenskoye** Russian Federation
111 K9 **Ramer** Alabama U.S.A.
52 E6 **Rameshki** Russian Federation
83 J8 **Rameswaram** India
75 L7 **Ramgarh** India
77 A4 **Rāmhormoz** Iran
44 B2 **Ramière, Punta** *mt* Italy/France
22 H2 **Ramillies-Offus** Belgium
140 D1 **Ramingining** N Terr Australia
109 K10 **Ramírez** Mexico
109 J8 **Ramirez** Texas U.S.A.
109 J9 **Ramirito** Texas U.S.A.
86 H4 **Ramis** *R* Ethiopia
80 E1 **Râmîye** Lebanon
27 G14 **Ramkvilla** Sweden
80 C6 **Ramla** Israel
80 C6 **Ramle** Israel
28 J4 **Ramløse** Denmark
27 G11 **Rämmen** Sweden
75 K6 **Ramnagar** India
27 H12 **Ramnäs** Sweden
89 E3 **Ramokgwebana** Botswana
80 E3 **Ram On** Israel
54 L5 **Ramon'** Russian Federation
102 H8 **Ramona** California U.S.A.
94 B3 **Ramona** Michigan U.S.A.
107 P5 **Ramona** Oklahoma U.S.A.
98 J5 **Ramona** South Dakota U.S.A.
120 K4 **Ramore** Ontario Canada
124 G5 **Ramos** Mexico
71 C6 **Ramos** *isld* Philippines
80 F1 **Ramot Naftali** Israel
87 E10 **Ramotsua** Botswana
116 M4 **Rampart** Alaska U.S.A.
116 R3 **Rampart House** Yukon Territory Canada
13 E5 **Rampside** England
74 H4 **Rampur** India
74 F6 **Rampura** India
68 A3 **Ramree** Burma
142 F4 **Ramsay Ra** W Australia Australia
32 H10 **Ramsbeck** Germany
27 H12 **Ramsberg** Sweden
13 F6 **Ramsbottom** England
32 E9 **Ramsdorf** Germany
32 F7 **Ramsel** Germany
26 H8 **Ramsele** Sweden
112 H2 **Ramseur** North Carolina U.S.A.
120 H5 **Ramsey** Ontario Canada
9 F3 **Ramsey** England
12 D5 **Ramsey** I of Man U.K.
110 G2 **Ramsey** Illinois U.S.A.
95 N5 **Ramsey** New Jersey U.S.A.
8 A4 **Ramsey I** Wales
9 H5 **Ramsgate** England
13 G5 **Ramsgill** England
28 B3 **Ramsing** Denmark
26 H9 **Ramsjö** Sweden
22 D1 **Ramskapelle** Belgium
74 H8 **Ramtek** India
79 G6 **Ramtha** Jordan
71 J9 **Ramu** *mt* Sumbawa Indonesia
136 K3 **Ramu** *R* Papua New Guinea
26 J9 **Ramvik** Sweden
127 M4 **Ramville, I** Martinique
52 B6 **Ramygala** Lithuania
26 G5 **Rana** *inlet* Norway
16 C1 **Rañadoiro, Sa. de** *mts* Spain
26 F5 **Ranafjord** *inlet* Norway
75 N7 **Ranaghat** India
69 J10 **Ranai** Indonesia
145 E3 **Ranana** New Zealand
27 K12 **Rånäs** Sweden
27 E11 **Rånåsfoss** Norway
70 K8 **Ranau, D** *L* Sumatra
131 B5 **Rancagua** Chile
22 G3 **Rance** Belgium
20 G4 **Rance** *R* Côtes d'Armor France
133 G2 **Rancharia** Brazil
117 F5 **Rancheria** Yukon Territory Canada
101 S5 **Ranchester** Wyoming U.S.A.
75 L7 **Ranchi** India
129 G6 **Rancho de Caça dos Tapiúnas** Brazil
124 H6 **Rancho Grande** Mexico
106 E5 **Ranchos de Taos** New Mexico U.S.A.
126 D3 **Rancho Veloz** Cuba
131 A8 **Ranco, L. de** Chile
106 D1 **Rand** Colorado U.S.A.
109 J8 **Randado** Texas U.S.A.
99 N7 **Randall** Iowa U.S.A.
107 M2 **Randall** Kansas U.S.A.
99 M3 **Randall** Minnesota U.S.A.
14 E2 **Randalstown** N Ireland
43 F11 **Randazzo** Sicily
89 A1 **Randburg** S Africa
Randers *co see* **Århus** *co*
28 E4 **Randers** Denmark
37 J4 **Randersacker** Germany
26 L5 **Randijaur** *L* Sweden
100 D3 **Randle** Washington U.S.A.
112 H2 **Randleman** North Carolina U.S.A.
109 J1 **Randlett** Oklahoma U.S.A.
103 P1 **Randlett** Utah U.S.A.
28 E5 **Randlev** Denmark
99 L9 **Randolph** Iowa U.S.A.
107 O2 **Randolph** Kansas U.S.A.
95 S2 **Randolph** Maine U.S.A.
111 G7 **Randolph** Mississippi U.S.A.
98 J7 **Randolph** Nebraska U.S.A.
94 J4 **Randolph** New York U.S.A.
101 O8 **Randolph** Utah U.S.A.
95 P3 **Randolph** Vermont U.S.A.
99 S6 **Randolph** Wisconsin U.S.A.
123 T5 **Random I** Newfoundland Canada
99 T6 **Random Lake** Wisconsin U.S.A.
21 M4 **Randonnai** France
102 G6 **Randsburg** California U.S.A.
27 D11 **Randsfjord** Norway
32 E5 **Randzel** *sandbank* Germany
26 N6 **Råneå** Norway
21 K4 **Rânes** France
118 F5 **Ranfurly** Alberta Canada
144 C6 **Ranfurly** New Zealand
69 E9 **Rangae** Thailand
70 F6 **Rangasa, Tanjong** *C* Sulawesi
70 F6 **Rangas, Tanjong** *C* Sulawesi
145 E3 **Rangataua** New Zealand
145 D1 **Rangaunu Harbour** New Zealand
111 J10 **Range** Alabama U.S.A.
95 R2 **Rangeley** Maine U.S.A.
101 R9 **Rangely** Colorado U.S.A.
109 J3 **Ranger** Texas U.S.A.
94 E8 **Ranger** West Virginia U.S.A.
120 G6 **Ranger L** Ontario Canada
75 O5 **Rangia** India
144 D5 **Rangiora** New Zealand
145 F2 **Rangipoua** New Zealand
145 F3 **Rangitaiki** New Zealand
145 F3 **Rangitaiki R** New Zealand
144 C6 **Rangitata** New Zealand
145 E4 **Rangitikei R** New Zealand
145 E2 **Rangitoto I** New Zealand
145 E3 **Rangitoto Ra** New Zealand
145 G2 **Rangitukia** New Zealand
69 D10 **Rangkalanberandan** Sumatra
70 L9 **Rangkasbitung** Java
Rangoon *see* **Yangon**
68 C4 **Rangoon** *R* Burma
75 N6 **Rangpur** Bangladesh
69 F12 **Rangsang** *isld* Sumatra
33 S8 **Rangsdorf** Germany
28 C6 **Rangstrup** Denmark
76 B3 **Ranibennur** India
99 N1 **Ranier** Minnesota U.S.A.
75 M7 **Raniganj** India
37 M2 **Ranis** Germany
74 E6 **Raniwara** India
140 D5 **Ranken** *R* N Terr Australia
140 D4 **Ranken Store** N Terr Australia
110 J1 **Rankin** Illinois U.S.A.
108 F4 **Rankin** Texas U.S.A.
115 K5 **Rankin Inlet** Northwest Territories Canada
139 H5 **Rankin's Springs** New South Wales Australia
80 B8 **Rannen** Israel
141 K6 **Rannes** Queensland Australia
55 B5 **Ranneye** Russian Federation
15 D4 **Rannoch Moor** Scotland
87 H12 **Ranohira** Madagascar
120 J2 **Ranoke** Ontario Canada
68 D7 **Ranong** Thailand
69 E9 **Ranot** Thailand
26 G6 **Ransarn** *L* Sweden
36 D3 **Ransel** Germany
99 S8 **Ransom** Illinois U.S.A.
107 L3 **Ransom** Kansas U.S.A.
94 K7 **Ranson** West Virginia U.S.A.
36 G3 **Ranstadt** Germany
29 N9 **Rantasalmi** Finland
70 D6 **Rantau** Kalimantan
69 F12 **Rantau** *isld* Sumatra
69 E12 **Rantaukampar** Sumatra
70 E3 **Rantaupandjang** Kalimantan
70 C5 **Rantaupanjang** Kalimantan
69 D11 **Rantauprapat** Sumatra
70 C6 **Rantaupulut** Kalimantan
70 F6 **Rantemario, Gunung** *mt* Sulawesi
70 F6 **Rantepao** Sulawesi
21 P3 **Rantigny** France
110 H1 **Rantoul** Illinois U.S.A.
102 H1 **Rant Pass** Nevada U.S.A.
29 M7 **Rantsila** Finland
29 M6 **Ranua** Finland
131 A8 **Ranue, R** Chile
28 C3 **Ranum** Denmark
78 K3 **Ranya** Iraq
68 G3 **Rao Go** *mt* Laos
65 J1 **Raohe** China
36 B7 **Raon-l'Etape** France
36 C6 **Raon-sur-Plaine** France
67 E5 **Raoping** China
41 O6 **Raossi** Italy
137 R7 **Raoul** *isld* Kermadec Is Pacific Oc
65 C5 **Raoyang** China
144 C5 **Rapahoe** New Zealand
44 F3 **Rapallo** Italy
131 B4 **Rapel** *R* Chile
101 Q4 **Rapelje** Montana U.S.A.
115 N4 **Raper, C** Northwest Territories Canada
94 H9 **Raphine** Virginia U.S.A.
14 D2 **Raphoe** Ireland
116 R3 **Rapid** *R* Alaska U.S.A.
99 M1 **Rapid** *R* Minnesota U.S.A.
94 J8 **Rapidan** Virginia U.S.A.
94 K8 **Rapidan** *R* Virginia U.S.A.
138 E6 **Rapid B** South Australia Australia
119 R8 **Rapid City** Manitoba Canada
98 C5 **Rapid City** South Dakota U.S.A.
121 R5 **Rapide Blanc** Quebec Canada
121 N6 **Rapides des Joachims** Quebec Canada
141 H2 **Rapid Horn** *C* Gt Barrier Reef Aust
99 U4 **Rapid River** Michigan U.S.A.
118 H4 **Rapid View** Saskatchewan Canada
52 C5 **Räpina** Estonia
52 B5 **Rapla** Estonia
95 K8 **Rappahannock** *R* Virginia U.S.A.
70 F6 **Rappang** Sulawesi
41 J3 **Rapperswil** Switzerland
46 F5 **Rapsáni** Greece
128 E6 **Rapulo** *R* Bolivia
71 G4 **Rapu Rapu** Philippines
80 G1 **Raqqādīyah** Syria
95 N2 **Raquette** *R* New York U.S.A.
95 N3 **Raquette Lake** New York U.S.A.
140 D1 **Raragala I** N Terr Australia
71 K9 **Rarakah** *mt* Flores Indonesia
95 N6 **Raritan B** New Jersey U.S.A.
40 G5 **Raron** Switzerland
134 A10 **Rarotonga** *isld* Pacific Oc
42 F3 **Raša** Croatia
71 D6 **Rasa** *isld* Palawan Philippines
79 F3 **Ra's al Basiţ** *C* Syria
77 D7 **Ras al Khaimah** U.A.E.
Ra's al Khaymah *see* **Ras al Khaimah**
131 E8 **Rasa, Pta** *C* Argentina
133 E6 **Rasa, Pta** Argentina
79 G4 **Ras Baalbek** Lebanon
86 G3 **Ras Dashen** *mt* Ethiopia
52 B6 **Raseiniai** Lithuania
80 G4 **Ras el Aqra** Jordan
80 F8 **Ras el Ghor** Jordan
84 H3 **Râs el Kenâyis** *C* Egypt
85 D5 **Ras el Ma** Mali
72 G5 **Ra's Fartak** *C* Yemen
79 D10 **Râs Ghârib** Egypt
86 F3 **Rashad** Sudan
86 G1 **Râs Hadarba** *C* Egypt
79 F8 **Rashādīya** Jordan
79 A7 **Rashîd** Egypt
77 A1 **Rasht** Iran
76 D5 **Rasipuram** India
77 G6 **Rāsk** Iran
46 D1 **Raška** Serbia Yugoslavia
86 G2 **Râs Kasar** *C* Sudan
28 D5 **Raskmølle** Denmark
77 J5 **Raskoh** *reg* Pakistan
84 F3 **Ra's Lānūf** Libya
31 N6 **Raslavice** Slovakia
72 H5 **Ra's Madrakah** *C* Oman
72 G6 **Ra's Māmī** *C* Socotra
79 C9 **Râs Matarma** Egypt
84 J4 **Ras Muhammad** *C* Egypt
85 A4 **Ras Nouadhibou** Mauritania
133 D6 **Raso, C** Argentina
130 H10 **Raso da Catarina** Brazil
143 E8 **Rason L** W Australia Australia
46 F1 **Rasovo** Bulgaria
116 L7 **Raspberry I** Alaska U.S.A.
79 D10 **Râs Shukheir** Egypt
53 F7 **Rasskazov** Russian Federation
26 P1 **Rásstigáisa** *mt* Norway
77 B6 **Ras Tannurah** Saudi Arabia
16 D9 **Ras Targa** Morocco
36 E6 **Rastatt** Germany
28 A4 **Råsted** Denmark
32 H6 **Rastede** Germany
38 M4 **Rastenfeld** Austria
38 E7 **Rastkogel** *mt* Austria
26 M3 **Råstoätno** *R* Sweden
43 B8 **Rasu, M** *mt* Sardinia
80 G4 **Rasun** Jordan
145 E3 **Rata** New Zealand
71 J4 **Ratahan** Sulawesi
70 K8 **Ratai, Gunung** *mt* Sumatra Indonesia
31 H6 **Rataje** Czech Rep
26 L8 **Ratan** Sweden
26 G9 **Rätan** Sweden
74 F4 **Ratangarh** India
68 D6 **Rat Buri** Thailand
55 B4 **Ratchino** Russian Federation
110 C6 **Ratcliff** Arkansas U.S.A.
109 M4 **Ratcliff** Texas U.S.A.
33 N5 **Ratekau** Germany
74 H6 **Rath** India
99 N9 **Rathburn Lake** *res* Iowa U.S.A.
14 E4 **Rathdrum** Ireland
100 J2 **Rathdrum** Idaho U.S.A.
68 A2 **Rathedaung** Burma
33 Q7 **Rathenow** Germany
14 E2 **Rathfriland** N Ireland
14 C4 **Ráth Luirc** Ireland
14 D1 **Rathmelton** Ireland
14 E4 **Rathnew** Ireland
119 T9 **Rathwell** Manitoba Canada
32 E10 **Ratingen** Germany
116 L10 **Rat Is** Aleutian Is
Ratisbon *see* **Regensburg**
119 S2 **Rat L** Manitoba Canada
74 F7 **Ratlam** India
116 C4 **Ratmanova, Ostrov** *isld* Russian Federation
76 A2 **Ratnagiri** India
83 K11 **Ratnapura** Sri Lanka
119 N5 **Ratner** Saskatchewan Canada
106 F5 **Raton** New Mexico U.S.A.
19 O18 **Ratonneau, I** France
106 F4 **Raton Pass** Colorado U.S.A.
115 K7 **Rat Rapids** Ontario Canada
117 R5 **Rat River** Northwest Territories Canada
109 M1 **Rattan** Oklahoma U.S.A.
37 K3 **Rattelsdorf** Germany
38 N7 **Ratten** Austria
38 E7 **Rattenberg** Austria
106 F4 **Rattlesnake Buttes** *mts* Colorado U.S.A.
107 L4 **Rattlesnake Cr** Kansas U.S.A.
100 H7 **Rattlesnake Cr** Oregon U.S.A.
101 S7 **Rattlesnake Ra** Wyoming U.S.A.
123 Q4 **Rattling Brook** Newfoundland Canada
15 G3 **Rattray Head** Scotland
27 H11 **Rättvik** Sweden
33 N5 **Ratzeburg** Germany
33 N5 **Ratzeburger See** *L* Germany
71 B1 **Rau** Halmahera Indonesia
69 E11 **Raub** Malaysia
133 F5 **Rauch** Argentina
22 H4 **Raucourt** France
29 M5 **Raudanjoki** *R* Finland
29 T8 **Raufarhöfn** Iceland
27 E11 **Raufoss** Norway
36 G7 **Rauhe Alb** *mts* Germany
37 K4 **Rauhe Ebrach** *R* Germany
37 K4 **Rauhenebrach** Germany
145 F2 **Raukokore** New Zealand
145 G2 **Raukumara** New Zealand
145 F3 **Raukumara Range** New Zealand
27 C12 **Rauland** Norway
27 M10 **Rauma** Finland
26 C9 **Rauma** *R* Norway
145 E4 **Raumati** New Zealand
36 E6 **Raumünzach** Germany
52 C6 **Rauna** Latvia
27 B11 **Raundal** *R* Norway
70 P10 **Raung, G** *mt* Java
145 E3 **Raurimu** New Zealand
29 K4 **Raus** Sweden
36 F2 **Rauschenberg** Germany
60 T1 **Rausu** Japan
29 M9 **Rautalampi** Finland
26 K3 **Rautasjaure** *L* Sweden
29 N8 **Rautavaara** Finland
29 O10 **Rautjärvi** Finland
101 L2 **Ravalli** Montana U.S.A.
48 E6 **Ravan** *mt* Bosnia-Herzegovina
31 O5 **Rava Russkaya** Ukraine
45 R8 **Ravello** Italy
94 F9 **Raven** Virginia U.S.A.
95 O4 **Ravena** New York U.S.A.
119 O5 **Ravendal** Saskatchewan Canada
102 D1 **Ravendale** California U.S.A.
22 C4 **Ravenel** France
13 E5 **Ravenglass** England
45 L3 **Ravenna** *reg* Italy
45 M3 **Ravenna** Italy
102 F7 **Ravenna** California U.S.A.
110 N4 **Ravenna** Kentucky U.S.A.
98 H8 **Ravenna** Nebraska U.S.A.
94 F5 **Ravenna** Ohio U.S.A.
20 H3 **Ravenoville** France
141 H6 **Ravensbourne** *R* Queensland Australia
33 S6 **Ravensbrück** Germany
41 L2 **Ravensburg** Germany
13 H5 **Ravenscar** England
118 H9 **Ravenscrag** Saskatchewan Canada
141 H4 **Ravenshoe** Queensland Australia
7 L8 **Ravenspurn** *gas field* North Sea
25 E5 **Ravenstein** Netherlands
143 D10 **Ravensthorpe** W Australia Australia
141 H5 **Ravenswood** Queensland Australia
94 F8 **Ravenswood** West Virginia U.S.A.
121 L7 **Ravensworth** Ontario Canada
74 E3 **Ravi** *R* Pakistan
109 L1 **Ravia** Oklahoma U.S.A.
18 H5 **Ravières** France
46 E1 **Ravna Reka** Serbia Yugoslavia
38 L8 **Ravne Na Koroškem** Slovenia
57 C2 **Ravnina Dar'yalytakyr** Kazakhstan
115 K4 **Ravn, Kap** Greenland
28 D3 **Ravnkilde** Denmark
42 H6 **Ravno** Bosnia-Herzegovina
74 E2 **Rawalpindi** Pakistan
117 Q3 **Rawalpindi L** Northwest Territories Canada
31 M4 **Rawa Mazowiecka** Poland
78 K3 **Rawandiz** Iraq
121 R6 **Rawdon** Quebec Canada
119 R4 **Rawebb** Manitoba Canada
145 D1 **Rawene** New Zealand
98 B7 **Rawhide Cr** Wyoming U.S.A.
31 K4 **Rawicz** Poland
69 D9 **Rawi, Ko** *isld* Thailand
143 F9 **Rawlinna** W Australia Australia
101 S8 **Rawlins** Wyoming U.S.A.
143 F7 **Rawlinson, Mt** W Australia Australia
143 G7 **Rawlinson Mt** W Australia Australia
133 D6 **Rawson** Argentina
94 D6 **Rawson** Ohio U.S.A.
38 N6 **Raxalpe** *mts* Austria
116 M4 **Ray** *R* Alaska U.S.A.
99 N1 **Ray** Minnesota U.S.A.
98 C1 **Ray** North Dakota U.S.A.
76 D3 **Rayachoti** India
76 C3 **Rāyadurg** India
75 K9 **Rāyagarha** India
79 G5 **Rayak** Lebanon
26 R3 **Rayakoski** Russian Federation
86 B4 **Ray-Bouba** Cameroon
123 N6 **Ray, C** Newfoundland Canada
59 J2 **Raychikhinsk** Russian Federation
112 D6 **Ray City** Georgia U.S.A.
77 E5 **Rāyen** Iran
55 B4 **Rayevskiy** Russian Federation
54 J8 **Raygorodok** Ukraine
80 G1 **Rayhānīyah** Syria
9 G4 **Rayleigh** England
118 E9 **Raymond** Alberta Canada
102 E4 **Raymond** California U.S.A.
110 G2 **Raymond** Illinois U.S.A.
111 F9 **Raymond** Mississippi U.S.A.
98 B1 **Raymond** Montana U.S.A.
98 J5 **Raymond** South Dakota U.S.A.
109 N3 **Raymond** Texas U.S.A.
100 B3 **Raymond** Washington U.S.A.
139 K5 **Raymond Terrace** New South Wales Australia
109 K9 **Raymondville** Texas U.S.A.
119 N7 **Raymore** Saskatchewan Canada
116 L4 **Ray Mts** Alaska U.S.A.
111 D11 **Rayne** Louisiana U.S.A.
101 P2 **Raynesford** Montana U.S.A.
108 A1 **Rayo** New Mexico U.S.A.
68 E6 **Rayong** Thailand
110 B3 **Raytown** Missouri U.S.A.
66 E5 **Rayü** China
111 E9 **Rayville** Louisiana U.S.A.
77 A2 **Razan** Iran
48 N4 **Razdel'naya** Ukraine
56 D2 **Razdolinsk** Russian Federation
47 H1 **Razgrad** Bulgaria
48 M6 **Razim, Lacul** *L* Romania
46 F3 **Razlog** Bulgaria
20 A5 **Raz, Pte.du** France
110 B1 **Rea** Missouri U.S.A.
142 A1 **Reabold Hill** W Australia Australia
117 D6 **Reaburn, Mt** Alaska U.S.A.
109 O2 **Reader** Arkansas U.S.A.
119 Q5 **Reader L** Manitoba Canada
9 F5 **Reading** England
127 J2 **Reading** Jamaica
94 C5 **Reading** Michigan U.S.A.
99 L6 **Reading** Minnesota U.S.A.
95 M6 **Reading** Pennsylvania U.S.A.
119 M9 **Readlyn** Saskatchewan Canada
95 P4 **Readsboro** Vermont U.S.A.
99 Q6 **Readstown** Wisconsin U.S.A.
109 L4 **Reagan** Texas U.S.A.
128 E7 **Real, Cord** *mts* Bolivia
128 C4 **Real, Cord** *mts* Ecuador
44 C1 **Reale** Italy
133 E5 **Realico** Argentina
109 J8 **Realitos** Texas U.S.A.
68 F7 **Ream** Cambodia
100 H2 **Reardan** Washington U.S.A.
15 G2 **Reawick** Scotland
112 D6 **Rebecca** Georgia U.S.A.
143 D9 **Rebecca, L** W Australia Australia
100 H8 **Rebel Creek** Nevada U.S.A.
33 T5 **Rebelow** Germany
117 P3 **Rebesca L** Northwest Territories Canada
28 D3 **Rebild** Denmark
128 G5 **Reboja, Cachoeira de** Brazil
29 P8 **Reboly** Russian Federation
46 F2 **Rebrovo** Bulgaria
60 P1 **Rebun-suidō** *str* Japan
60 P1 **Rebun-tō** *isld* Japan
133 E5 **Recalde** Argentina
48 G5 **Recaş** Romania
44 F3 **Recco** Italy
40 A2 **Recey** France
19 J5 **Recey-sur-Ource** France
143 D10 **Recherche, Arch.of the** W Australia Australia
36 B6 **Réchicourt le Château** France
54 B4 **Rechitsa** Belarus
33 R6 **Rechlin** Germany
22 L3 **Recht** Belgium
130 J10 **Recife** Brazil
89 D10 **Recife, C** S Africa
83 J12 **Recif I** Seychelles
32 G8 **Recke** Germany
32 F9 **Recklinghausen** Germany
101 U5 **Recluse** Wyoming U.S.A.
22 J4 **Recogne** Belgium
131 F2 **Reconquista** Argentina
19 O15 **Recoubeau** France
146 E7 **Recovery Glacier** Antarctica
133 D3 **Recreo** Argentina
31 J2 **Recz** Poland
110 E6 **Red** *R* Arkansas U.S.A.
98 K2 **Red** *R* Minnesota U.S.A.
69 F10 **Redang** *isld* Malaysia
22 K4 **Redange** Luxembourg
122 G7 **Red Bank** New Brunswick Canada
95 N6 **Red Bank** New Jersey U.S.A.
Red Basin *see* **Sichuan Pendi**
123 Q2 **Red Bay** Labrador, Nfld Canada
120 J8 **Red Bay** Ontario Canada
111 H7 **Red Bay** Alabama U.S.A.
113 B7 **Redbay** Florida U.S.A.
118 K6 **Redberry L** Saskatchewan Canada
109 N10 **Redbird Airport** Texas U.S.A.
143 C6 **Red Bluff** *mt* W Australia Australia
102 B1 **Red Bluff** California U.S.A.
108 D4 **Red Bluff L** Texas/New Mex U.S.A.
9 F4 **Redbourn** England
110 G3 **Red Bud** Illinois U.S.A.
103 M6 **Red Butte** *mt* Arizona U.S.A.
98 A8 **Red Buttes** Wyoming U.S.A.
99 M2 **Redby** Minnesota U.S.A.
13 G4 **Redcar** England
106 D2 **Red Cliff** Colorado U.S.A.
141 L7 **Redcliffe** Queensland Australia
89 F2 **Redcliffe** Zimbabwe
143 D8 **Redcliffe, Mt** W Australia Australia
138 F5 **Red Cliffs** Victoria Australia
111 H11 **Red Cr** Mississippi U.S.A.
101 R8 **Red Cr** Wyoming U.S.A.
95 L3 **Red Creek** New York U.S.A.
118 D6 **Red Deer** Alberta Canada
119 Q6 **Red Deer L** Manitoba Canada
119 P6 **Red Deer R** Saskatchewan Canada
111 D11 **Reddell** Louisiana U.S.A.
13 E4 **Red Dial** England
113 E8 **Reddick** Florida U.S.A.
102 B1 **Redding** California U.S.A.
118 H1 **Reddit** Ontario Canada
9 E3 **Redditch** England
33 O6 **Redefin** Germany
98 E4 **Red Elm** South Dakota U.S.A.
129 K5 **Redenção** Brazil
20 D6 **Redené** France
85 F2 **Redeyef** Tunisia
111 D7 **Redfield** Arkansas U.S.A.
99 M8 **Redfield** Iowa U.S.A.
98 H5 **Redfield** South Dakota U.S.A.
101 L5 **Redfish L** Idaho U.S.A.
108 C6 **Redford** Texas U.S.A.
99 R5 **Redgranite** Wisconsin U.S.A.
75 L8 **Redhākhol** India
9 F5 **Redhill** England
145 D4 **Red Hill** *mt* New Zealand
111 K10 **Red Hills** Alabama U.S.A.
95 O5 **Red Hook** New York U.S.A.
100 H8 **Red House** Nevada U.S.A.

123 S6 **Red I** Newfoundland Canada
98 C4 **Redig** South Dakota U.S.A.
123 Q5 **Red Indian L** Newfoundland Canada
103 O9 **Redington** Arizona U.S.A.
98 C8 **Redington** Nebraska U.S.A.
85 D2 **Redjem Demouch** Algeria
110 L1 **Red Key** Indiana U.S.A.
52 E6 **Redkino** Russian Federation
117 O5 **Redknife** *R* Northwest Territories Canada
103 K6 **Red L** Arizona U.S.A.
115 K7 **Red Lake** Ontario Canada
103 M6 **Red Lake** Arizona U.S.A.
102 G7 **Redlands** California U.S.A.
98 K2 **Red L. Falls** Minnesota U.S.A.
95 L7 **Red Lion** Pennsylvania U.S.A.
101 Q4 **Red Lodge** Montana U.S.A.
118 C7 **Red Lodge Prov. Park** Alberta Canada
145 E2 **Red Mercury I** New Zealand
13 G5 **Redmire** England
110 J2 **Redmon** Illinois U.S.A.
100 D5 **Redmond** Oregon U.S.A.
103 N2 **Redmond** Utah U.S.A.
102 G6 **Red Mt** California U.S.A.
112 C1 **Red Mt** Tennessee U.S.A.
37 L5 **Rednitz** *R* Germany
99 L8 **Red Oak** Iowa U.S.A.
110 A7 **Red Oak** Oklahoma U.S.A.
109 L3 **Red Oak** Texas U.S.A.
20 F6 **Redon** France
127 N6 **Redonda** *isld* Antigua & Barbuda W Indies
16 B2 **Redondela** Spain
16 B6 **Redondo** Portugal
102 F8 **Redondo Beach** California U.S.A.
128 F3 **Redondo, Pico** *mt* Brazil
116 L6 **Redoubt Vol** Alaska U.S.A.
117 O9 **Red Pass** British Columbia Canada
118 J6 **Red Pheasant** Saskatchewan Canada
141 G2 **Red Pt** Queensland Australia
117 J6 **Red R** British Columbia Canada
119 U9 **Red R** Manitoba Canada
111 D10 **Red R** Louisiana U.S.A.
109 J1 **Red R** Texas U.S.A.
Red R Vietnam *see* **Song-koi** *R*
122 E7 **Red Rapids** New Brunswick Canada
101 K4 **Red R. Hot Springs** Idaho U.S.A.
119 P2 **Red Rock** Ontario Canada
103 N9 **Redrock** Arizona U.S.A.
106 B9 **Red Rock** New Mexico U.S.A.
107 N5 **Red Rock** Oklahoma U.S.A.
109 K6 **Red Rock** Texas U.S.A.
117 Q3 **Redrock L** Northwest Territories Canada
99 N8 **Red Rock Res** Iowa U.S.A.
143 G9 **Red Rocks Pt** W Australia Australia
8 A7 **Redruth** England
86 G1 **Red Sea** Africa/Arabian Pen
112 H3 **Red Springs** North Carolina U.S.A.
117 M9 **Redstone** British Columbia Canada
117 K4 **Redstone** *R* Northwest Territories Canada
120 J4 **Redstone** *R* Ontario Canada
101 V1 **Redstone** Montana U.S.A.
124 E9 **Red Tank** Panama
22 J4 **Redu** Belgium
119 Q9 **Redvers** Saskatchewan Canada
118 D5 **Redwater** Alberta Canada
121 L6 **Redwater** Ontario Canada
98 A2 **Redwater** *R* Montana U.S.A.
109 N2 **Redwater** Texas U.S.A.
8 B1 **Red Wharf B** Wales
118 E6 **Red Willow** Alberta Canada
98 E9 **Red Willow Cr** Nebraska U.S.A.
99 O5 **Red Wing** Minnesota U.S.A.
102 B4 **Redwood City** California U.S.A.
99 L5 **Redwood Falls** Minnesota U.S.A.
100 A8 **Redwood Nat. Park** California U.S.A.
102 A2 **Redwood Valley** California U.S.A.
71 C5 **Reed Bank** S China Sea
94 B3 **Reed City** Michigan U.S.A.
98 D3 **Reeder** North Dakota U.S.A.
102 E5 **Reedley** California U.S.A.
101 Q4 **Reedpoint** Montana U.S.A.
106 C8 **Reeds Pk** New Mexico U.S.A.
100 A6 **Reedsport** Oregon U.S.A.
112 E3 **Reedy** *R* South Carolina U.S.A.
94 F8 **Reedy** West Virginia U.S.A.
138 D4 **Reedy Lagoon** South Australia Australia
141 G4 **Reedy Springs** Queensland Australia
144 C5 **Reefton** New Zealand
98 G5 **Ree Heights** South Dakota U.S.A.
14 C3 **Ree, L** Ireland
110 G5 **Reelfoot L** Tennessee U.S.A.
32 G6 **Reepsholt** Germany
28 G5 **Reersø** Denmark
25 F5 **Rees** Germany
94 D3 **Reese** Michigan U.S.A.
100 H9 **Reese** *R* Nevada U.S.A.
103 N8 **Reesor** Ontario Canada
33 P6 **Reetz** Germany
78 G2 **Refahiye** Turkey
111 J8 **Reform** Alabama U.S.A.
133 D3 **Refresco** Chile
27 F6 **Refs** Denmark
27 G14 **Reftele** Sweden
109 K7 **Refugio** Texas U.S.A.
31 J2 **Rega** *R* Poland
120 E4 **Regan** Ontario Canada
80 D3 **Regavim** Israel
37 N5 **Regen** *R* Germany
37 N5 **Regensburg** Germany
37 N5 **Regenstauf** Germany
119 R9 **Regent** Manitoba Canada
120 F5 **Regent** Ontario Canada
85 E3 **Reggane** Algeria
45 L4 **Reggello** Italy
43 G10 **Reggio di Calabria** Italy
45 J2 **Reggiolo** Italy
45 J2 **Reggio nell Emilia** Italy
129 H3 **Regina** Brazil
119 N8 **Regina** Saskatchewan Canada
37 N1 **Regis** Germany
77 J4 **Registan** Afghanistan
20 G3 **Regnéville** France
21 G4 **Régniowez** France
37 K4 **Regnitz** *R* Germany
16 B6 **Reguengos de Monsaraz** Portugal
20 E6 **Reguiny** France
80 D4 **Rehan** Jordan
37 K2 **Rehau** Germany
36 D5 **Rehberg** *mt* Germany
32 H7 **Rehden** Germany
33 Q7 **Rehfeld** Germany
74 H7 **Rehli** India
32 J8 **Rehme** Germany
33 N7 **Rehna** Germany
87 C10 **Rehoboth** Namibia
95 M8 **Rehoboth Beach** Delaware U.S.A.
80 C6 **Rehovot** Israel
36 F3 **Reichelshausen** Germany
37 N2 **Reichenbach** Germany
38 L7 **Reichenfels** Austria
37 J1 **Reichensachsen** Germany
38 F5 **Reichertsheim** Germany
37 L6 **Reichertshofen** Germany
101 N4 **Reichle** Montana U.S.A.
36 D2 **Reichshof** Germany
36 D6 **Reichshoffen** France
143 G9 **Reid** W Australia Australia
118 J8 **Reid L** Saskatchewan Canada
140 B4 **Reid, Mt** N Terr Australia
141 H4 **Reid R** Queensland Australia
112 E5 **Reidsville** Georgia U.S.A.
112 H1 **Reidsville** North Carolina U.S.A.
9 F5 **Reigate** England
21 M7 **Reignac-sur-Indre** Indre-et-Loire France
25 C5 **Reijen** Netherlands
103 O9 **Reiley Pk** Arizona U.S.A.
36 F5 **Reilingen** Germany
19 P17 **Reillanne** France
22 G5 **Reims** France
18 H3 **Reims, Mt de** France
133 C8 **Reina Adelaida, Arch. de la** *islds* Chile
99 O7 **Reinbeck** Iowa U.S.A.
32 M5 **Reinbek** Germany
33 S4 **Reinberg** Germany
119 U6 **Reindeer I** Manitoba Canada
119 Q1 **Reindeer L** Manitoba/Sask Canada
26 F4 **Reine** Norway
140 D6 **Reinecke, Mt** N Terr Australia
27 C11 **Reineskarvet** *mt* Norway
33 M5 **Reinfeld** Germany
145 D1 **Reinga, C** New Zealand
32 L10 **Reinhausen** Germany
36 C5 **Reinheim** Germany
33 S7 **Reinickendorf** Germany
16 E1 **Reinosa** Spain
26 L2 **Reinöy** *isld* Norway
37 P1 **Reinsberg** Germany
36 B4 **Reinsfeld** Germany
33 P5 **Reinstorf** Germany
27 M2 **Reisa** *R* Norway
33 O6 **Reisbach** Germany
29 L8 **Reisjärvi** Finland
38 H8 **Reisseck** *mt* Austria
25 F2 **Reitdiep** *R* Netherlands
38 G6 **Reiter Alpen** *mt* Austria
38 J7 **Reitereck** *mt* Austria
87 E11 **Reitz** S Africa
37 P2 **Reitzenhain** Germany
27 H13 **Rejmyre** Sweden
31 O4 **Rejowiec** Poland
28 B6 **Rejsby** Denmark
27 H12 **Rekarne** Sweden
32 F9 **Reken** Germany
60 R3 **Rekifune-gawa** *R* Japan
109 N4 **Reklaw** Texas U.S.A.
46 E1 **Rekovac** Serbia Yugoslavia
20 B5 **Relecq-Kerhoun,le** France
112 E6 **Relee** Georgia U.S.A.
98 G6 **Reliance** South Dakota U.S.A.
101 Q8 **Reliance** Wyoming U.S.A.
85 E1 **Relizane** Algeria
124 D4 **Rellano** Mexico
36 C2 **Remagen** Germany
21 M5 **Rémalard** France
138 E4 **Remarkable, Mt** South Australia Australia
70 N9 **Rembang** Java
72 F6 **Remchingen** Germany
37 K2 **Remda** Germany
126 E3 **Remedios** Cuba
124 F5 **Remedios** Mexico
32 G6 **Remels** Germany
77 F6 **Remeshk** Iran
22 L4 **Remich** Luxembourg
121 L5 **Rémigny** Quebec Canada
120 H3 **Remi L** Ontario Canada
22 J4 **Remilly-Allicourt** France
99 T9 **Remington** Indiana U.S.A.
94 K8 **Remington** Virginia U.S.A.
40 E1 **Remiremont** France
33 N8 **Remlingen** Germany
100 B6 **Remote** Oregon U.S.A.
22 K3 **Remouchamps** Belgium
19 N17 **Remoulins** France
83 K14 **Remparts, R. des** Réunion Indian Oc
36 H6 **Rems** *R* Germany
36 C1 **Remscheid** Germany
99 L7 **Remsen** Iowa U.S.A.
121 F9 **Remsen** New York U.S.A.
20 E6 **Remungol** France
94 B3 **Remus** Michigan U.S.A.
19 O16 **Rémuzat** France
27 E10 **Rena** Norway
120 G4 **Renabie** Ontario Canada
20 G6 **Renac** France
Renaix *see* **Ronse**
71 D2 **Rena Pt** Luzon Philippines
128 E4 **Renascenca** Brazil
146 C4 **Renaud I** *isld* Antarctica
21 H6 **Renazé** France
36 E6 **Renchen** Germany
26 E10 **Rendal** Norway
32 L4 **Rendsburg** Germany
121 L4 **Renault** Quebec Canada
123 U7 **Renews** Newfoundland Canada
121 O7 **Renfrew** Ontario Canada
12 D2 **Renfrew** Scotland
70 N9 **Rengasdengklok** Java
69 F13 **Rengat** Sumatra
67 C1 **Ren He** *R* China
67 D4 **Renhua** China
67 B3 **Renhuai** China
74 J8 **Renhuai** China
94 G9 **Renick** West Virginia U.S.A.
120 J2 **Renison** Ontario Canada
139 H8 **Renison Bell** Tasmania Australia
86 F3 **Renk** Sudan
29 L11 **Renko** Finland
25 E5 **Renkum** Netherlands
115 R3 **Renland** *reg* Greenland
138 F5 **Renmark** South Australia Australia
65 F1 **Renmin** China
26 D9 **Rennebu** Norway
137 N4 **Rennell** *isld* Solomon Is
22 E1 **Rennerod** Germany
140 C4 **Renner Springs** N Terr Australia
37 L6 **Rennertshofen** Germany
20 G5 **Rennes** France
27 A12 **Rennesöy** *isld* Norway
146 C13 **Rennick Glacier** *glacier* Antarctica
118 F1 **Rennie** Manitoba Canada
38 J7 **Rennweg** Austria
45 L1 **Reno** *R* Italy
102 E2 **Reno** Nevada U.S.A.
99 L4 **Reno, L** Minnesota U.S.A.
122 G7 **Renous** New Brunswick Canada
94 K5 **Renovo** Pennsylvania U.S.A.
119 M7 **Renown** Saskatchewan Canada
65 C5 **Renqiu** China
28 C7 **Rens** Denmark
67 E5 **Renshan** China
67 A2 **Renshou** China
95 O4 **Rensselaer** New York U.S.A.
99 T9 **Rensselaer** Indiana U.S.A.
95 N4 **Rensselaerville** New York U.S.A.
25 E4 **Renswoude** Netherlands
100 C2 **Renton** Washington U.S.A.
37 K3 **Rentweinsdorf** Germany
37 J3 **Rentwertshausen** Germany
99 L5 **Renville** Minnesota U.S.A.
119 R6 **Renwer** Manitoba Canada
22 H4 **Renwez** France
145 D4 **Renwick** New Zealand
99 N7 **Renwick** Iowa U.S.A.
65 C6 **Ren Xian** China
67 D7 **Renxing** China
18 E8 **Réole, la** France
76 E2 **Repalle** India
129 G4 **Repartição** Brazil
37 G4 **Repartimento** Brazil
40 E3 **Repentis, Mt** France
29 J8 **Replot** Finland
55 E1 **Repolovo** Russian Federation
145 F3 **Reporoa** New Zealand
40 E6 **Reposoir, Chaîne de** *mt* France
26 J5 **Reppentjåkko** *mt* Sweden
130 D8 **Reprêsa Ilha Grande** *res* Brazil
130 C9 **Reprêsa Itaipu** *res* Brazil/Paraguay
130 D7 **Reprêsa Pôrto Primavera** *res* Brazil
129 J4 **Represa Tucuruí** *res* Brazil
111 J10 **Repton** Alabama U.S.A.
107 N2 **Republic** Kansas U.S.A.
94 D5 **Republic** Ohio U.S.A.
100 G1 **Republic** Washington U.S.A.
98 H9 **Republican** *R* Nebraska/Kansas U.S.A.
141 J5 **Repulse Bay** Queensland Australia
115 L4 **Repulse Bay** Northwest Territories Canada
26 P1 **Repvåg** Norway
54 K5 **Rep'yevka** Russian Federation
98 F2 **Regan** North Dakota U.S.A.
130 H6 **Reqência** Brazil
98 D3 **Regent** North Dakota U.S.A.
25 G4 **Reqqe** *R* Netherlands
100 A8 **Requa** California U.S.A.
128 D5 **Requena** Peru
17 G5 **Requena** Spain
18 G8 **Réquista** France
21 P7 **Rère** *R* France
145 F3 **Rerewhakaaitu L** New Zealand
15 G2 **Rerwick** Scotland
78 F1 **Reşadiye** Turkey
70 K8 **Resag, G** *mt* Sumatra
102 F7 **Reseda** California U.S.A.
26 J8 **Resele** Sweden
28 C3 **Resen** Denmark
28 C4 **Resen** Denmark
46 E3 **Resen** Macedonia
119 P6 **Reserve** Saskatchewan Canada
111 F11 **Reserve** Louisiana U.S.A.
98 B1 **Reserve** Montana U.S.A.
106 B8 **Reserve** New Mexico U.S.A.
52 F6 **Reshetilovka** Ukraine
54 F7 **Reshetilovka** Ukraine
74 N4 **Resia** Italy
133 F3 **Resistencia** Argentina
48 G5 **Reşiţa** Romania
122 E6 **Resitgouche R** New Brunswick Canada
115 K3 **Resolute** Northwest Territories Canada
144 A6 **Resolution I** New Zealand
115 N5 **Resolution Island** Northwest Territories Canada
115 N6 **Resolution L** Quebec Canada
32 L7 **Resse** Germany
21 P3 **Ressons** France
22 D4 **Ressons-sur-Matz** France
127 K3 **Rest** Jamaica
12 D1 **Rest and be Thankful** *hill* Scotland
122 F5 **Restigouche** Quebec Canada
119 Q9 **Reston** Manitoba Canada
13 F2 **Reston** Scotland
94 K7 **Reston** Virginia U.S.A.
121 L6 **Restoule** Ontario Canada
31 N1 **Reszel** Poland
48 H5 **Retezatului, Munti** *mts* Romania
85 G5 **Rethel** France
32 K7 **Rethem** Germany
18 G7 **Rethem** Germany
46 G9 **Réthimnon** Crete Greece
42 C2 **Retiche, Alpi** *mts* Italy
22 J1 **Retie** Belgium
20 H6 **Retiers** France
118 E8 **Retlaw** Alberta Canada
141 G7 **Retreat** Queensland Australia
108 E8 **Retrop** Oklahoma U.S.A.
48 E3 **Rétság** Hungary
9 G4 **Rettendon** England
36 D3 **Rettert** Germany
38 G6 **Retz** Austria
20 F7 **Retz** *reg* France
36 H4 **Retzbach** Germany
21 M7 **Reugny** Indre-et-Loire France
21 P7 **Reuilly** Indre France
22 L3 **Reuland** Belgium
83 K13 **Réunion** *isld* Indian Oc
17 H3 **Reus** Spain
69 C11 **Reusam, Pulau** *isld* Indonesia
25 D6 **Reusel** Netherlands
41 J4 **Reuss** *R* Switzerland
33 O10 **Reussen** Germany
48 L3 **Reut** *R* Moldova
33 R5 **Reuterstadt Stavenhagen** Germany
37 M3 **Reuth** Germany
37 N4 **Reuth** Germany
36 G7 **Reutlingen** Germany
38 C7 **Reutte** Austria
98 C4 **Reva** South Dakota U.S.A.
80 C6 **Revadim** Israel
40 C6 **Revard** *mt* France
40 C4 **Revel** France
103 H4 **Reveille Pk** Nevada U.S.A.
22 D4 **Revel** France
142 G2 **Reveley I** W Australia Australia
117 O10 **Revelstoke** British Columbia Canada
117 O10 **Revelstoke Dam** British Columbia Canada
118 J6 **Revenue** Saskatchewan Canada
45 K1 **Revere** Italy
9 F1 **Revesby** England
19 J4 **Revigny** France
117 H8 **Revillagigedo I** Alaska U.S.A.
20 H2 **Réville** France
98 K5 **Revillo** South Dakota U.S.A.
24 H4 **Revin** France
79 E7 **Revivim** Israel
28 F5 **Revninge** Denmark
26 O1 **Revsbotn** Norway
26 H9 **Revsund** Sweden
88 D9 **Revubué** *R* Mozambique
94 J5 **Rew** Pennsylvania U.S.A.
74 H7 **Rewa** India
145 E4 **Rewa** *mt* New Zealand
80 B7 **Rewaha** Israel
118 H6 **Reward** Saskatchewan Canada
74 G4 **Rewari** India
99 O1 **Rewey** Wisconsin U.S.A.
101 O6 **Rexburg** Idaho U.S.A.
107 K1 **Rexford** Kansas U.S.A.
101 K1 **Rexford** Montana U.S.A.
22 D2 **Rexpoede** France
122 F7 **Rexton** New Brunswick Canada
80 D2 **Reyba** Israel
29 T9 **Reydharfjördhur** *inlet* Iceland
107 L6 **Reydon** Oklahoma U.S.A.
102 F7 **Reyes Pk** California U.S.A.
29 S7 **Reykir** Iceland
28 R10 **Reykjanesta** *C* Iceland
119 T7 **Reykjavik** Manitoba Canada
28 R9 **Reykjavik** Iceland
128 B1 **Reynaud** Saskatchewan Canada
140 B2 **Reynolds** *R* N Terr Australia
111 M9 **Reynolds** Georgia U.S.A.
101 J6 **Reynolds** Idaho U.S.A.
110 K1 **Reynolds** Indiana U.S.A.
98 J9 **Reynolds** Nebraska U.S.A.
138 D4 **Reynolds, L** South Australia Australia
140 C5 **Reynolds Ra** N Terr Australia
94 J5 **Reynoldsville** Pennsylvania U.S.A.
109 J9 **Reynosa** Mexico
40 B5 **Reyssouze** *R* France
78 K3 **Rezaiyeh** Iran
37 K5 **Rezat** *R* Germany
52 F7 **Reze** France
52 C6 **Rēzekne** Latvia
55 D3 **Rezh** Russian Federation
48 M3 **Rezina** Moldova
47 J3 **Rezvaya** *R* Turkey
41 K5 **Rezzonico** Italy
32 K6 **Rhade** Germany
98 C3 **Rhame** North Dakota U.S.A.
41 L3 **Rhätikon** *mt* Switzerland
36 C4 **Rhaunen** Germany
8 C3 **Rhayader** Wales
32 H9 **Rheda-Wiedenbrück** Germany
32 F6 **Rhede** Niedersachsen Germany
32 E9 **Rhede** Nordrhein-Westfalen Germany
25 F4 **Rheden** Netherlands
9 F3 **Rhee, R** England
119 P7 **Rhein** Saskatchewan Canada
36 E6 **Rhein** *R* W Europe
36 D6 **Rheinau** Germany
36 B2 **Rheinbach** Germany
36 D3 **Rheinböllen** Germany
36 C3 **Rheinbrohl** Germany
25 F6 **Rheindahlen** Germany
32 F8 **Rheine** Germany
41 J2 **Rheinfall** Switzerland
40 G2 **Rheinfelden** Switzerland
32 E10 **Rheinhausen** Germany
36 B3 **Rheinland-Pfalz** *land* Germany
36 E6 **Rheinmünster** Germany
33 R6 **Rheinsberg** Germany
36 E6 **Rheinstetten** Germany
41 L3 **Rhein Tal** *V* Switzerland
36 E5 **Rheinzabern** Germany
42 F6 **Rhêmes, Val de** Italy
85 D3 **Rhemilès** Algeria
32 J10 **Rhena** Germany
25 E5 **Rhenen** Netherlands
36 D3 **Rhens** Germany
36 B1 **Rheydt** Germany
40 G2 **Rhin** *R* France
36 E6 **Rhin** *R* Germany
36 D7 **Rhinau** France
Rhine *R* France *see* **Rhin** *R*
Rhine *R* Germany/Switzerland *see* **Rhein** *R*
112 D6 **Rhine** Georgia U.S.A.
95 O5 **Rhinebeck** New York U.S.A.
99 R4 **Rhinelander** Wisconsin U.S.A.
33 R7 **Rhinkanal** Germany
33 Q7 **Rhinow** Germany
16 E9 **Rhis, Oued** *R* Morocco
41 K6 **Rho** Italy
127 K1 **Rhoades, Pt** Jamaica
95 Q5 **Rhode I** *state* U.S.A.
94 F9 **Rhodell** West Virginia U.S.A.
32 K10 **Rhoden** Germany
Rhodes *isld see* **Ródhos** *isld*
83 L13 **Rhodes** *B* Kerguelen Indian Oc
94 C3 **Rhodes** Michigan U.S.A.
Rhodesia *see* **Zimbabwe**
112 F2 **Rhodhiss L** North Carolina U.S.A.
109 K2 **Rhome** Texas U.S.A.
8 C4 **Rhondda** Wales
19 J7 **Rhône** *dept* France
8 C1 **Rhône** *R* France
19 O13 **Rhône** *R* Switzerland
41 H5 **Rhône, Grand** *R* France
19 N18 **Rhône Valley** France
8 B4 **Rhosili** Wales
8 B1 **Rhosneigr** Wales
8 C1 **Rhos-on-Sea** Wales
85 F2 **Rhourd El Baguel** Algeria
8 C1 **Rhuddlan** Wales
18 G7 **Rhue** *R* France
20 E6 **Rhuis, Presqu'île de** *pen* France
32 M9 **Rhume** *R* Germany
18 D9 **Rhune, la** *mt* France/Spain
8 C3 **Rhydd Hywel** *mt* Wales
8 C3 **Rhyl** Wales
32 G9 **Rhynern** Germany
15 F3 **Rhynie** Scotland
131 E8 **Riachos, I de los** Argentina
16 B2 **Ría de Arosa** *est* Spain
16 A2 **Ría de Corcubión** *est* Spain
16 A1 **Ría de Muros** Spain
16 A2 **Ría de Murosa y Noya** *est* Spain
16 B2 **Ría de Pontevedra** *est* Spain
16 B1 **Ría de Sta. Marta** *est* Spain
16 B2 **Ría de Vigo** *est* Spain
20 H6 **Riallé** France
70 B5 **Riam** Kalimantan
45 N5 **Riano** Italy
16 D2 **Riaño** Spain
19 P17 **Rians** France
8 E3 **Riansares** *R* Spain
20 D6 **Riantec** France
74 F2 **Riasi** Kashmir
69 F12 **Riau, Kep** *islds* Indonesia
16 E3 **Riaza** *R* Spain
16 B2 **Ribadavia** Spain
16 C2 **Ribadeo** Spain
16 D1 **Ribadesella** Spain
17 F2 **Ribagorza** *dist* Spain
128 F4 **Ribamar** Brazil
17 H3 **Ribarroja, Emb. de** *res* Spain
17 J2 **Ribas de Fresser** Spain
130 D7 **Ribas do Rio Pardo** Brazil
16 B4 **Ribatejo** *prov* Portugal
88 G9 **Ribaué** Mozambique
26 K1 **Ribbenesöy** *isld* Norway
13 F6 **Ribble, R** England
28 B6 **Ribe** Denmark
28 B6 **Ribe Å** *R* Denmark
40 F1 **Ribeauville** France
22 D4 **Ribécourt** France
22 D4 **Ribécourt** France
133 H2 **Ribeira** *R* Brazil
133 H2 **Ribeirão Prêto** Brazil
129 J5 **Ribeiro Gonçalves** Brazil
22 E4 **Ribemont** France
43 E11 **Ribera** Sicily
18 F7 **Ribérac** France
128 E6 **Riberalta** Bolivia
19 P16 **Ribiers** France
121 L5 **Rib Lake** Ontario Canada
99 Q4 **Rib Lake** Wisconsin U.S.A.
99 R5 **Rib Mt** Wisconsin U.S.A.
42 F3 **Ribnica** Slovenia
33 Q4 **Ribnitz-Damgarten** Germany
118 F6 **Ribstone Cr** Alberta Canada
118 F6 **Ribstone Cr** Alberta Canada
142 B5 **Rica,Mt** W Australia Australia
109 K8 **Ricardo** Texas U.S.A.
45 M3 **Riccione** Italy
103 K7 **Rice** California U.S.A.
109 L3 **Rice** Texas U.S.A.
112 F6 **Riceboro** Georgia U.S.A.
121 M8 **Rice L** Ontario Canada
99 N1 **Rice L** Minnesota U.S.A.
120 H5 **Rice Lake** Ontario Canada
99 P4 **Rice Lake** Wisconsin U.S.A.
119 N8 **Riceton** Saskatchewan Canada
99 O6 **Riceville** Iowa U.S.A.
18 H5 **Riceys, les** France
118 K6 **Richard** Saskatchewan Canada
110 K6 **Richard City** Tennessee U.S.A.
114 H3 **Richard Collinson Inlet** Northwest Territories Canada
89 H7 **Richards Bay** S Africa
114 F4 **Richards I** Northwest Territories Canada
116 N6 **Richardson** Alaska U.S.A.
109 L3 **Richardson** Texas U.S.A.
109 O8 **Richardson** Texas U.S.A.
114 H3 **Richardson I** Northwest Territories Canada
95 R2 **Richardson Lakes** Maine U.S.A.
143 C8 **Richardson, Mt** W Australia Australia
114 F4 **Richardson Mts** Yukon Terr/N W Terr Canada
144 B6 **Richardson Mts** New Zealand
119 N8 **Richardson Sta** Saskatchewan Canada
85 A5 **Richard Toll** Senegal
98 D3 **Richardton** North Dakota U.S.A.
94 J4 **Richburg** New York U.S.A.
118 F7 **Richdale** Alberta Canada
143 C10 **Riche, C** W Australia Australia
121 R7 **Richelieu** *R* Quebec Canada
21 L7 **Richelieu** France
21 O2 **Richemont** France
123 P3 **Riche Pt** Newfoundland Canada
101 U2 **Richey** Montana U.S.A.
101 L6 **Richfield** Idaho U.S.A.
107 J4 **Richfield** Kansas U.S.A.
103 M3 **Richfield** Utah U.S.A.
95 L4 **Richford** New York U.S.A.
121 S8 **Richford** Vermont U.S.A.
102 E6 **Richgrove** California U.S.A.
110 B3 **Rich Hill** Missouri U.S.A.
122 H7 **Richibucto** New Brunswick Canada
118 F4 **Rich Lake** Alberta Canada
112 C5 **Richland** Georgia U.S.A.
94 B4 **Richland** Michigan U.S.A.
110 D4 **Richland** Missouri U.S.A.
101 T1 **Richland** Montana U.S.A.
95 N7 **Richland** New Jersey U.S.A.
100 H5 **Richland** Oregon U.S.A.
100 F3 **Richland** Washington U.S.A.
99 Q6 **Richland Center** Wisconsin U.S.A.
109 L4 **Richland Cr** Texas U.S.A.
112 K3 **Richlands** North Carolina U.S.A.
94 F9 **Richlands** Virginia U.S.A.
109 J4 **Richland Springs** Texas U.S.A.
118 J7 **Richlea** Saskatchewan Canada
139 K5 **Richmond** New South Wales Australia
141 G5 **Richmond** Queensland Australia
139 H8 **Richmond** Tasmania Australia
121 P7 **Richmond** Ontario Canada
122 H7 **Richmond** Prince Edward I Canada
121 S7 **Richmond** Quebec Canada
9 F5 **Richmond** England
13 G5 **Richmond** North Yorkshire England
127 L2 **Richmond** Jamaica
145 D4 **Richmond** New Zealand
89 C8 **Richmond** S Africa
102 B4 **Richmond** California U.S.A.
110 M2 **Richmond** Indiana U.S.A.
110 M4 **Richmond** Kentucky U.S.A.
95 S2 **Richmond** Maine U.S.A.
99 M4 **Richmond** Minnesota U.S.A.
100 F5 **Richmond** Oregon U.S.A.
109 M6 **Richmond** Texas U.S.A.
103 N1 **Richmond** Utah U.S.A.
94 K9 **Richmond** Virginia U.S.A.
121 L9 **Richmond Hill** Ontario Canada
112 F6 **Richmond Hill** Georgia U.S.A.
142 A4 **Richmond, L** W Australia Australia
139 L3 **Richmond R** New South Wales Australia
139 L3 **Richmond Ra** *mts* New South Wales Australia
95 N4 **Richmondville** New York U.S.A.
118 H8 **Richmound** Saskatchewan Canada
110 B7 **Rich Mt** Arkansas U.S.A.
33 R4 **Richtenberg** Germany
111 H10 **Richton** Mississippi U.S.A.
99 L3 **Richville** Minnesota U.S.A.
110 J5 **Richwood** Ohio U.S.A.
94 G8 **Richwood** West Virginia U.S.A.
99 S6 **Richwood** Wisconsin U.S.A.
110 F3 **Richwoods** Missouri U.S.A.
32 M4 **Rickling** Germany
9 F4 **Rickmansworth** England
17 G3 **Ricla** Spain
106 B4 **Rico** Colorado U.S.A.
40 F5 **Riddes** Switzerland
100 J7 **Riddle** Idaho U.S.A.
100 B7 **Riddle** Oregon U.S.A.
140 C6 **Riddock, Mt** N Terr Australia
121 P7 **Rideau** *R* Ontario Canada
121 O8 **Rideau Canal** Ontario Canada
121 O8 **Rideau, L** Ontario Canada
120 F2 **Ridge** *R* Ontario Canada
98 B4 **Ridge** Montana U.S.A.
102 G6 **Ridgecrest** California U.S.A.
119 N5 **Ridgedale** Saskatchewan Canada
101 N7 **Ridgedale** Idaho U.S.A.
99 T10 **Ridge Farm** Illinois U.S.A.
95 O5 **Ridgefield** Connecticut U.S.A.
111 F9 **Ridgeland** Mississippi U.S.A.
112 F5 **Ridgeland** South Carolina U.S.A.
99 P4 **Ridgeland** Wisconsin U.S.A.
141 K6 **Ridgelands** Queensland Australia
94 J7 **Ridgeley** West Virginia U.S.A.
95 M8 **Ridgely** Maryland U.S.A.
112 F4 **Ridge Spring** South Carolina U.S.A.
120 J10 **Ridgetown** Ontario Canada
98 F4 **Ridgeview** South Dakota U.S.A.
118 E1 **Ridgeville** Manitoba Canada
110 L1 **Ridgeville** Indiana U.S.A.
112 G4 **Ridgeville** South Carolina U.S.A.
110 C1 **Ridgeway** Missouri U.S.A.
112 G3 **Ridgeway** South Carolina U.S.A.
99 Q6 **Ridgeway** Wisconsin U.S.A.
110 G5 **Ridgely** Tennessee U.S.A.
106 C3 **Ridgway** Colorado U.S.A.
110 H4 **Ridgway** Illinois U.S.A.
94 B4 **Ridgway** Montana U.S.A.
119 R8 **Riding Mt** Manitoba Canada
143 D10 **Ridley,Mt** W Australia Australia
142 C5 **Ridley, R** W Australia Australia
118 J7 **Ridpath** Saskatchewan Canada
13 F3 **Ridsdale** England
26 J5 **Riebnes** *L* Sweden
20 F6 **Riec** France
38 H5 **Ried** Austria
37 M5 **Rieden** Germany
37 M6 **Riedenburg** Germany
36 D5 **Riedseltz** France
33 T6 **Riegenwalde** Germany
41 J2 **Riehen** Switzerland
18 B2 **Riel** Manitoba Canada
32 H8 **Riemsloh** Germany
36 H3 **Rieneck** Germany
38 H7 **Rienzi** Mississippi U.S.A.
33 S10 **Riesa** Germany
133 C8 **Riesco, I** Chile
43 F11 **Riesi** Sicily
33 O10 **Riestedt** Germany
52 B7 **Riet** *R* S Africa
52 C6 **Rietavas** Lithuania
32 H9 **Rietberg** Germany
89 B3 **Rietfontein** Namibia
42 E6 **Rieti** Italy
41 O3 **Rietzer Grieskogel** *mt* Austria
18 G8 **Rieupeyroux** France
20 F6 **Rieux** Morbihan France
19 Q17 **Riez** France
22 G4 **Riezes** Belgium
16 D10 **Rif** *dist* Morocco
100 C3 **Riffe Lake** Washington U.S.A.
106 C2 **Rifle** Colorado U.S.A.
94 C2 **Rifle** *R* Michigan U.S.A.
29 T8 **Rifstangi** *C* Iceland
52 B5 **Rīga** Latvia
52 B5 **Riga, Gulf of** Estonia/Latvia
142 B5 **Riga,Mt** W Australia Australia
77 F5 **Rīgān** Iran
Rīgas Jūras Līcis *see* **Rīga, Gulf of**
121 Q7 **Rigaud** Quebec Canada
101 O6 **Rigby** Idaho U.S.A.
110 F2 **Riggston** Illinois U.S.A.
37 M4 **Riglasreuth** Germany
45 K4 **Rignano sull'Arno** Italy
21 L7 **Rigny-Ussé** France
115 O7 **Rigolet** Labrador, Nfld Canada
80 G4 **Rihaba** Jordan
Riia Laht *see* **Rīga, Gulf of**
29 M4 **Riipi** Finland
146 K8 **Riiser-Larsenhalvøya** *pen* Antarctica
146 J7 **Riiser-Larsen Sea** Antarctica
42 F3 **Rijeka** Croatia
25 C5 **Rijsbergen** Netherlands
25 G4 **Rijssen** Netherlands
25 B4 **Rijswijk** Netherlands
48 H2 **Rika** *R* Ukraine
69 C10 **Rikitgaib** Sumatra
60 R2 **Rikubetsu** Japan
61 Q6 **Rikuchū Kaigan Nat. park** Japan
61 P6 **Rikuzen Takata** Japan
46 F2 **Rila** *plateau* Bulgaria
46 F2 **Rila** Bulgaria
110 J2 **Riley** Indiana U.S.A.
107 O2 **Riley** Kansas U.S.A.
106 C7 **Riley** New Mexico U.S.A.
100 F6 **Riley** Oregon U.S.A.
21 L7 **Rillé** France
46 F2 **Rilski Manastir** Bulgaria
128 C4 **Rimachi, L** Peru
145 E1 **Rimariki I** New Zealand
40 B1 **Rimaucourt** France
69 G14 **Rimau, Pulau** *isld* Sumatra
48 F2 **Rimava** *R* Slovakia
118 C6 **Rimbey** Alberta Canada
27 K12 **Rimbo** Sweden
94 H5 **Rimersburg** Pennsylvania U.S.A.
27 H13 **Rimforsa** Sweden
45 N3 **Rimini** Italy
48 L5 **Rimmicu Sărat** Romania
80 E2 **Rimmon** Israel
80 E6 **Rimmonim** Jordan
48 K5 **Rimna** *R* Romania
48 J5 **Rimnicu Vîlcea** Romania
22 H4 **Rimogne** France
122 D5 **Rimouski R** Quebec Canada
36 H4 **Rimpar** Germany
40 G5 **Rimpfischhorn** *mt* Switzerland
75 N4 **Rinbung** China
71 J9 **Rinca** *isld* Indonesia
37 P6 **Rinchnach** Germany
126 A2 **Rincon** Bonaire Neth Antilles
106 C9 **Rincon** New Mexico U.S.A.
133 D2 **Rinconada** Argentina
124 H6 **Rincón de Romos** Mexico
28 A6 **Rindby** Denmark
70 K8 **Rindingan, Bukit** *hill* Sumatra
70 Q10 **Rindjani, Gunung** *mt* Indonesia
28 B4 **Rind Kirke** Denmark
139 J8 **Ringarooma** Tasmania Australia
74 F5 **Ringas** India
28 E6 **Ringe** Denmark
27 D10 **Ringebu** Norway
41 K4 **Ringelspitz** *mt* Switzerland
27 D11 **Ringerike** *L* Norway
12 D4 **Ringford** Scotland
37 J1 **Ringgau** Germany
109 O3 **Ringgold** Louisiana U.S.A.
109 K2 **Ringgold** Texas U.S.A.
28 C5 **Ringive** Denmark
28 A4 **Ringkøbing** Denmark
47 P13 **Ringládhes** Greece
101 P3 **Ringling** Montana U.S.A.
109 K1 **Ringling** Oklahoma U.S.A.
9 G6 **Ringmer** England
109 M1 **Ringold** Oklahoma U.S.A.
27 E11 **Ringsaker** Norway
28 H6 **Ringsted** Denmark
99 M6 **Ringsted** Iowa U.S.A.
27 H13 **Ringstorp** Sweden
26 K2 **Ringvassöy** *isld* Norway
140 C6 **Ringwood** N Terr Australia
9 E6 **Ringwood** England
107 M5 **Ringwood** Oklahoma U.S.A.
46 G7 **Rinia** *isld* Greece
133 C5 **Rinihue** Chile
131 A7 **Riñihue, L** Chile
27 H15 **Rinkabyholm** Sweden
28 D7 **Rinkenæs** Denmark
41 O3 **Rinn** Austria
15 C5 **Rinns Pt** Scotland
27 G16 **Rinsjön** *L* Sweden
32 K8 **Rinteln** Germany
21 M3 **Rinxent** France
99 Q8 **Rio** Illinois U.S.A.
111 G11 **Rio** Louisiana U.S.A.
99 R6 **Rio** Wisconsin U.S.A.
125 P5 **Río Abajo** Panama
130 C5 **Rio Alegre** Brazil
124 G4 **Río Arreola** Mexico
128 C4 **Riobamba** Ecuador
85 F8 **Río Benito** Mbini Equat Guinea
128 E5 **Rio Branco** Brazil
133 G4 **Río Branco** Uruguay
130 E9 **Rio Branco do Sul** Brazil
109 J10 **Río Bravo** Mexico
108 B5 **Río Bravo del Norte** *R* Mexico
133 C6 **Río Bueno** Chile
127 K1 **Rio Bueno** Jamaica
127 N9 **Río Caribe** Venezuela
133 D7 **Río Chico** Argentina
127 M9 **Río Chico** Venezuela
130 F8 **Rio Claro** Brazil
127 P3 **Rio Claro** Trinidad
127 K10 **Rio Claro** Venezuela
131 C5 **Rio Cuarto** Argentina
132 **Rio de Janeiro** *conurbation* Brazil
100 A9 **Rio Dell Scotia** California U.S.A.
128 D2 **Río de Oro** Colombia
85 A4 **Río de Oro, B. de** Western Sahara
131 E2 **Río Dulce** Argentina
125 L4 **Río Frío** Costa Rica
133 C8 **Río Gallegos** Argentina
131 B6 **Río Grande** *R* Argentina
133 F4 **Rio Grande** Brazil
124 H6 **Río Grande** Mexico
125 M3 **Río Grande** *R* Nicaragua
103 O5 **Rio Grande** *R* U.S.A./Mexico
109 J9 **Rio Grande City** Texas U.S.A.
130 H8 **Rio Grande do Norte** Brazil
131 G2 **Rio Grande do Sul** *state* Brazil
106 C4 **Rio Grande Res** Colorado U.S.A.
90 F12 **Rio Grande Rise** Atlantic Oc
109 K10 **Rio Grande Valley** *airport* Texas U.S.A.
127 H9 **Ríohacha** Colombia
108 B2 **Río Hondo** *R* New Mexico U.S.A.
109 K9 **Rio Hondo** Texas U.S.A.
128 C5 **Rioja** Peru
20 D3 **Riom** France
133 C3 **Río Mayo** Argentina
102 C3 **Rio Linda** California U.S.A.
130 B5 **Río Largo** Brazil
133 E3 **Rio Lindo** California U.S.A.
45 L3 **Riolo Terme** Italy
16 B5 **Rio Maior** Portugal
109 J6 **Riomedina** Texas U.S.A.
18 G7 **Riom ès Montagne** France
133 E3 **Rio Muerto** Argentina
133 D1 **Río Mulatos** Bolivia
85 G8 **Río Muni** *prov* Equat Guinea
131 C8 **Río Negro** *prov* Argentina
130 E10 **Rio Negro** Brazil
131 F4 **Río Negro** *dept* Uruguay
131 G4 **Río Negro, Embalse del** *res* Uruguay
130 C6 **Rio Negro, Pantanal do** *swamp* Brazil
43 G8 **Rionero in Vulture** Italy
124 F3 **Río Palacio** Mexico
17 F6 **Riópar** Spain
133 G4 **Río Pardo** Brazil
127 M5 **Río Piedras** Puerto Rico
130 F5 **Rio Prêto, Sa. do** *mts* Brazil
128 E6 **Río Quetena** *R* Bolivia
129 L6 **Rio Real** Brazil
45 J2 **Rio Saliceto** Italy
130 J9 **Rio Tinto** Brazil
100 K8 **Rio Tinto** Nevada U.S.A.
71 C6 **Rio Tuba** Philippines
133 C8 **Río Turbio Mines** Argentina
19 O18 **Riou, I. de** France
128 C3 **Rioverde** Ecuador
125 J7 **Río Verde** Mexico
130 C6 **Rio Verdi de Mato Grosso** Brazil
109 K3 **Rio Vista** Texas U.S.A.
130 C6 **Riozinho, R** Brazil
48 F6 **Ripanj** Serbia Yugoslavia
44 B1 **Riparia** Italy
100 G3 **Riparia** Washington U.S.A.
26 L5 **Ripats** Sweden
122 K2 **Ripault, L** Quebec Canada
45 O4 **Ripe** Italy
45 O6 **Ripi** Italy
71 G6 **Ripley** Ontario Canada
9 E1 **Ripley** England
9 F5 **Ripley** England
13 G5 **Ripley** N Yorks England
103 K8 **Ripley** California U.S.A.
110 H7 **Ripley** Mississippi U.S.A.
94 H4 **Ripley** New York U.S.A.
110 N3 **Ripley** Ohio U.S.A.
107 O5 **Ripley** Oklahoma U.S.A.
110 G6 **Ripley** Tennessee U.S.A.
94 F8 **Ripley** West Virginia U.S.A.
17 J2 **Ripoll** Spain
121 P7 **Ripon** Quebec Canada
13 G5 **Ripon** England
102 C4 **Ripon** California U.S.A.
99 S6 **Ripon** Wisconsin U.S.A.
142 D5 **Ripon Hills** W Australia Australia
99 M8 **Rippey** Iowa U.S.A.
13 G6 **Ripponden** England
100 J4 **Riggins** Idaho U.S.A.
45 N5 **Rignano Flaminio** Italy
28 C5 **Ris** Denmark
42 J6 **Risan** Montenegro Yugoslavia
79 D8 **Risān 'Aneiza** *mt* Egypt
26 H7 **Risbäck** Sweden
18 E9 **Riscle** France
131 B5 **Risco Plateado** *pk* Argentina
28 C6 **Rise** Denmark
26 H7 **Risede** Sweden
28 C3 **Risgårde Bredning** *B* Denmark
47 H2 **Rish** Bulgaria
60 P1 **Rishiri-suidō** *str* Japan
60 P1 **Rishiri-tō** *isld* Japan
80 C5 **Rishon LeZiyyon** Israel
57 J6 **Rishtan** Uzbekistan
112 B3 **Rising Fawn** Georgia U.S.A.
109 J3 **Rising Star** Texas U.S.A.
95 L7 **Rising Sun** Maryland U.S.A.
94 D5 **Rising Sun** Ohio U.S.A.
110 M3 **Rising Sun** Indiana U.S.A.
117 M10 **Riske Creek** British Columbia Canada
21 L3 **Risle** *R* France
42 F3 **Risnjak** *mt* Croatia
48 J5 **Rîşnov** Romania
111 D8 **Rison** Arkansas U.S.A.
27 D13 **Risör** Norway
21 P4 **Ris-Orangis** France
40 D4 **Risoux, Mont** France
26 D8 **Rissa** Norway
145 F3 **Rissington** New Zealand
52 B5 **Rist** Estonia
29 N10 **Ristiina** Finland
29 N7 **Ristijärvi** Finland
28 F7 **Ristinge** Denmark
26 M5 **Risträsk** Sweden
28 E7 **Risum-Lindholm** Germany
108 B8 **Rita Blanca Cr** *R* Texas U.S.A.
70 D4 **Ritan** *R* Kalimantan
142 B5 **Ritchie Reef** W Australia Australia
68 A6 **Ritchie's Arch** Andaman Is
83 K9 **Ritigala** *mt* Sri Lanka
37 J3 **Ritschenhausen** Germany
100 F5 **Ritter** Oregon U.S.A.
32 J6 **Ritterhude** Germany
102 E4 **Ritter, Mt** California U.S.A.
94 F6 **Rittman** Ohio U.S.A.
32 M10 **Rittmarshausen** Germany
100 G2 **Ritzville** Washington U.S.A.
68 D7 **Riu, Laem** Thailand
71 K9 **Riung** Flores Indonesia
41 N6 **Riva** Italy
47 N10 **Riva** Turkey
47 N11 **Riva** *R* Turkey
21 K3 **Riva Bella** France
133 E2 **Rivadavia** Argentina
133 C2 **Rivadavia** Chile
38 F8 **Riva di Tures** Italy
22 K3 **Rivage** Belgium
19 N14 **Rival** *R* France
44 B1 **Rivalta di Torinese** Italy
125 M4 **Rivas** Nicaragua
133 E5 **Rivera** Argentina
131 G3 **Rivera** Uruguay
102 D4 **Riverbank** California U.S.A.
85 C7 **River Cess** Liberia
102 E5 **Riverdale** California U.S.A.
107 N4 **Riverdale** Kansas U.S.A.
101 O2 **Riverdale** Montana U.S.A.
98 G9 **Riverdale** Nebraska U.S.A.
98 E2 **Riverdale** North Dakota U.S.A.
123 L8 **River Denys** C Breton I, Nova Scotia
111 K10 **River Falls** Alabama U.S.A.
99 O5 **River Falls** Wisconsin U.S.A.
123 T7 **Riverhead** Newfoundland Canada
95 P6 **Riverhead** Long I, New York U.S.A.
122 H8 **River Hébert** Nova Scotia Canada
118 L8 **Riverhurst** Saskatchewan Canada
139 H5 **Riverina** *reg* New South Wales Australia
143 D8 **Riverina** W Australia Australia
122 J8 **River John** Nova Scotia Canada
109 L9 **River Oaks** Texas U.S.A.
123 P3 **River of Ponds** Newfoundland Canada
133 C7 **Rivero, I** Chile
122 H9 **Riverport** Nova Scotia Canada
119 R8 **Rivers** Manitoba Canada
144 B6 **Riversdale** New Zealand
145 F4 **Riversdale** New Zealand
89 B10 **Riversdale** S Africa
120 H10 **Riverside** Ontario Canada
102 G8 **Riverside** California U.S.A.
95 L8 **Riverside** Maryland U.S.A.
100 G6 **Riverside** Oregon U.S.A.
109 M5 **Riverside** Texas U.S.A.
101 N8 **Riverside** Utah U.S.A.
101 T8 **Riverside** Wyoming U.S.A.
98 B9 **Riverside Res** Colorado U.S.A.
117 K10 **Rivers Inlet** British Columbia Canada
140 E4 **Riversleigh** Queensland Australia
119 M9 **Rivers, L. of the** Saskatchewan Canada
138 E5 **Riverton** South Australia Australia
119 U8 **Riverton** Manitoba Canada
144 B7 **Riverton** New Zealand
110 G2 **Riverton** Illinois U.S.A.
99 L9 **Riverton** Iowa U.S.A.
98 H9 **Riverton** Nebraska U.S.A.
94 J8 **Riverton** Virginia U.S.A.
101 R6 **Riverton** Wyoming U.S.A.

100 C2 **Riverton Heights** Washington U.S.A.
110 F6 **Rivervale** Arkansas U.S.A.
122 H7 **Riverview** New Brunswick Canada
98 G7 **Riverview** Nebraska U.S.A.
19 P14 **Rives** France
110 G5 **Rives** Tennessee U.S.A.
94 C4 **Rives Junc** Michigan U.S.A.
94 G7 **Rivesville** West Virginia U.S.A.
103 K6 **Riviera** Nevada U.S.A.
109 K8 **Riviera** Texas U.S.A.
113 G11 **Riviera Beach** Florida U.S.A.
44 F3 **Riviera di Levante** Italy
44 D4 **Riviera di Ponente** Italy
21 J4 **Rivière** Orne France
22 D3 **Rivière** Pas-de-Calais France
122 G4 **Rivière à Claude** Quebec Canada
122 J4 **Rivière-à-la-Loutre** Quebec Canada
121 S6 **Rivière à Pierre** Quebec Canada
122 H5 **Rivière-au-Renard** Quebec Canada
122 G3 **Rivière aux Graines** Quebec Canada
121 S5 **Rivière-aux-Rats** Quebec Canada
122 D6 **Rivière Bleue** Quebec Canada
122 K4 **Rivière-de-la-Chaloupe** Quebec Canada
83 M13 **Rivière des Anguilles** Mauritius
122 C6 **Rivière du Loup** Quebec Canada
121 S5 **Rivière du Milieu** Quebec Canada
122 B5 **Rivière du Moulin** Quebec Canada
121 M4 **Rivière Héva** Quebec Canada
122 G4 **Rivière La Madeleine** Quebec Canada
122 B6 **Rivière Ouelle** Quebec Canada
122 E4 **Rivière Pentecôte** Quebec Canada
122 G3 **Rivière Pigou** Quebec Canada
127 M4 **Rivière Pilote** Martinique W Indies
122 H3 **Rivière St. Jean** Quebec Canada
21 L3 **Rivière-St. Sauveur, la** France
127 L4 **Rivière Salée** Martinique W Indies
122 D6 **Rivière-Verte** New Brunswick Canada
122 C6 **Rivière Verte** Quebec Canada
44 C1 **Rivoli** Italy
138 E6 **Rivoli B** South Australia Australia
145 D4 **Riwaka** New Zealand
72 F4 **Riyāḍ, Ar** Saudi Arabia
Riyadh *see* **Riyāḍ, Ar**
71 E3 **Rizal** Luzon Philippines
78 H1 **Rize** Turkey
65 D7 **Rizhao** China
Rizhskiy Zaliv *see* **Riga, Gulf of**
79 E3 **Rizokarpaso** Cyprus
46 E5 **Rízoma** Greece
43 H10 **Rizzuto, C** Italy
27 C12 **Rjukan** Norway
27 B12 **Rjuven** Norway
85 A5 **Rkiz, L** Mauritania
80 E1 **Rmaich** Lebanon
68 H5 **Ro** Vietnam
27 E11 **Roa** Norway
16 E3 **Roa** Spain
110 K2 **Roachdale** Indiana U.S.A.
9 F3 **Roade** England
106 B9 **Road Forks** New Mexico U.S.A.
127 M5 **Road Town** Virgin Is
28 B6 **Roager** Denmark
103 P2 **Roan Cliffs** Utah U.S.A.
106 B2 **Roan Cr** Colorado U.S.A.
112 E1 **Roan Mt** North Carolina U.S.A.
18 H6 **Roanne** France
111 L8 **Roanoke** Alabama U.S.A.
99 R9 **Roanoke** Illinois U.S.A.
94 B6 **Roanoke** Indiana U.S.A.
109 K3 **Roanoke** Texas U.S.A.
94 H9 **Roanoke** Virginia U.S.A.
112 M2 **Roanoke I** North Carolina U.S.A.
112 K1 **Roanoke Rapids** North Carolina U.S.A.
106 B2 **Roan Plateau** Colorado U.S.A.
103 P2 **Roan Plateau** Utah U.S.A.
109 M5 **Roans Prairie** Texas U.S.A.
95 L5 **Roaring Branch** Pennsylvania U.S.A.
112 F1 **Roaring Gap** North Carolina U.S.A.
108 G2 **Roaring Springs** Texas U.S.A.
14 B5 **Roaringwater B** Ireland
77 D4 **Robāt** Iran
77 B2 **Robāt Karīm** Iran
109 J9 **Robberson** Texas U.S.A.
112 H2 **Robbins** North Carolina U.S.A.
139 G8 **Robbins I** Tasmania Australia
112 D2 **Robbinsville** North Carolina U.S.A.
44 E1 **Robbio** Italy
138 E6 **Robe** South Australia Australia
14 B3 **Robe** *R* Ireland
33 R6 **Röbel** Germany
109 O4 **Robeline** Louisiana U.S.A.
138 F4 **Robe, Mt** New South Wales Australia
122 K3 **Robe Noir, L. de la** Quebec Canada
142 B5 **Robe R** W Australia Australia
112 K2 **Robersonville** North Carolina U.S.A.
108 G4 **Robert Lee** Texas U.S.A.
140 B7 **Robert, Mt** N Terr Australia
13 F3 **Roberton** Scotland
101 N6 **Roberts** Idaho U.S.A.
101 Q4 **Roberts** Montana U.S.A.
100 E5 **Roberts** Oregon U.S.A.
123 R4 **Robert's Arm** Newfoundland Canada
9 G6 **Robertsbridge** England
102 H2 **Roberts Cr. Mt** Nevada U.S.A.
111 J11 **Robertsdale** Alabama U.S.A.
26 L7 **Robertsfors** Sweden
110 A6 **Robert S. Kerr Res** Oklahoma U.S.A.
141 K8 **Roberts, Mt** Queensland Australia
101 Q7 **Roberts Mt** Wyoming U.S.A.
141 G4 **Robertson** *R* Queensland Australia
89 A9 **Robertson** S Africa
101 P8 **Robertson** Wyoming U.S.A.
146 C12 **Robertson Bay** Antarctica
146 D4 **Robertson I** Antarctica
142 D6 **Robertson Ra** W Australia Australia
121 T6 **Robertsonville** Quebec Canada
85 B7 **Robertsport** Liberia
138 E5 **Robertstown** South Australia Australia
14 E3 **Robertstown** Ireland
122 G6 **Robertville** New Brunswick Canada
121 S4 **Roberval** Quebec Canada
115 N1 **Robeson Chan** Canada/Greenland
8 B4 **Robeston Wathen** Wales
101 N7 **Robin** Idaho U.S.A.
100 J5 **Robinette** Oregon U.S.A.
13 H5 **Robin Hoods Bay** England
141 J7 **Robinson** *R* Queensland Australia
110 J2 **Robinson** Illinois U.S.A.
98 G2 **Robinson** North Dakota U.S.A.
133 B9 **Robinson Crusoe** *isld* Juan Fernández Is Pacific Oc
138 D2 **Robinson, Mt** South Australia Australia
142 C6 **Robinson, Mt** W Australia Australia
116 Q6 **Robinson Mts** Alaska U.S.A.
143 C7 **Robinson Ras** W Australia Australia
140 D3 **Robinson River** N Terr Australia
122 F6 **Robinsonville** New Brunswick Canada
139 G5 **Robinvale** New South Wales Australia
17 F6 **Robledo** Spain
103 N9 **Robles Pass** Arizona U.S.A.
103 N9 **Robles Ranch** Arizona U.S.A.
118 A1 **Roblin Park** Manitoba Canada
128 G7 **Robore** Bolivia
118 H9 **Robsart** Saskatchewan Canada
117 O9 **Robson, Mt** Alberta/Br Col Canada
117 O9 **Robson, Mt** British Columbia Canada
109 K8 **Robstown** Texas U.S.A.
16 A6 **Roca, C. da** Portugal
119 Q8 **Rocanville** Saskatchewan Canada
129 M4 **Rocas** *isld* Brazil
124 B5 **Rocas Alijos** *isld* Mexico
43 G8 **Roccadaspide** Italy
45 P5 **Rocca di Mezzo** Italy
45 N6 **Rocca di Papa** Italy
45 O6 **Roccagorga** Italy
43 H8 **Rocca Imperiale** Italy
Rocca Littorio *see* **Gaalkacyo**
45 P7 **Roccamonfina** Italy
38 E9 **Rocca Pietore** Italy
45 L3 **Rocca San Casciano** Italy
45 P6 **Roccasecca** Italy
45 N5 **Rocca Sinibalda** Italy
42 D5 **Roccastrada** Italy
44 B1 **Rocciamelone** *mt* Italy
40 E5 **Roc d'Enfer** *mt* France
131 G4 **Rocha** *dept* Uruguay
131 G5 **Rocha** Uruguay
21 K5 **Rochard, Mt** France
13 F6 **Rochdale** England
121 N4 **Rochebaucourt** Quebec Canada
20 F6 **Roche-Bernard, la** France
21 H7 **Roche Blanche, la** France
18 F7 **Rochechouart** France
20 D4 **Roche-Derrien, la** France
22 K3 **Roche-en-Ardenne, La** Belgium
22 J3 **Rochefort** Belgium
18 E7 **Rochefort** France
19 N17 **Rochefort-du-Gard** France
20 F6 **Rochefort-en-Terre** France
18 G7 **Rochefort-Montagne** France
18 F7 **Rochefoucauld, la** France
21 O3 **Roche-Guyon, la** France
22 J4 **Rochehaut** Belgium
113 E8 **Rochelle** Florida U.S.A.
112 D6 **Rochelle** Georgia U.S.A.
99 R8 **Rochelle** Illinois U.S.A.
111 D10 **Rochelle** Louisiana U.S.A.
109 H4 **Rochelle** Texas U.S.A.
18 E6 **Rochelle, la** France
119 P9 **Roche Percee** Saskatchewan Canada
110 D3 **Rocheport** Missouri U.S.A.
21 M8 **Roche-Posay, la** France
127 L4 **Rocher du Diamant** Martinique W Indies
123 O2 **Rocher, L. du** Quebec Canada
117 R5 **Rocher River** Northwest Territories Canada
122 E3 **Rochers, R. aux** Quebec Canada
20 E3 **Roches Douvres** *islds* English Chan
20 H8 **Rocheservière** France
83 M12 **Roches, Plaine des** Mauritius
40 E1 **Rochesson** France
139 G6 **Rochester** Victoria Australia
118 D4 **Rochester** Alberta Canada
9 G5 **Rochester** England
13 F3 **Rochester** Northumberland England
110 G2 **Rochester** Illinois U.S.A.
94 A5 **Rochester** Indiana U.S.A.
94 D4 **Rochester** Michigan U.S.A.
99 O5 **Rochester** Minnesota U.S.A.
95 Q3 **Rochester** New Hampshire U.S.A.
95 K3 **Rochester** New York U.S.A.
121 N9 **Rochester** New York U.S.A.
94 E5 **Rochester** Ohio U.S.A.
94 G6 **Rochester** Pennsylvania U.S.A.
108 H2 **Rochester** Texas U.S.A.
100 B3 **Rochester** Washington U.S.A.
20 H8 **Roche-sur-Yon, La** France
9 G4 **Rochford** England
98 C5 **Rochford** South Dakota U.S.A.
118 B5 **Rochfort Br** Alberta Canada
37 O1 **Rochlitz** Germany
118 E6 **Rochon Sands Prov. Park** Alberta Canada
21 P3 **Rochy-Condé** France
117 K5 **Rock** *R* Yukon Territory Canada
98 K6 **Rock** *R* Iowa/Minnesota U.S.A.
107 O4 **Rock** Kansas U.S.A.
99 T3 **Rock** Michigan U.S.A.
99 S6 **Rock** *R* Wisconsin U.S.A.
6 B5 **Rockall** N Atlantic Oc
90 H3 **Rockall Bank** Atlantic Oc
144 C6 **Rock and Pillar Range** New Zealand
117 L10 **Rock Bay** British Columbia Canada
12 E4 **Rockcliffe** Scotland
101 S1 **Rock Cr** Montana U.S.A.
101 M3 **Rock Cr** Montana U.S.A.
94 G5 **Rock Cr** Ohio U.S.A.
100 E4 **Rock Cr** Oregon U.S.A.
101 T8 **Rock Cr** Wyoming U.S.A.
117 D3 **Rock Creek** Yukon Territory Canada
101 L7 **Rockcreek** Idaho U.S.A.
109 K5 **Rockdale** Texas U.S.A.
146 B10 **Rockefeller Mts** Antarctica
146 C9 **Rockefeller Plat** Antarctica
36 D4 **Rockenhausen** Germany
99 R8 **Rock Falls** Illinois U.S.A.
94 J9 **Rockfish** Virginia U.S.A.
111 K9 **Rockford** Alabama U.S.A.
101 N6 **Rockford** Idaho U.S.A.
99 R7 **Rockford** Illinois U.S.A.
94 B3 **Rockford** Michigan U.S.A.
99 N4 **Rockford** Minnesota U.S.A.
94 C6 **Rockford** Ohio U.S.A.
100 H2 **Rockford** Washington U.S.A.
119 M9 **Rockglen** Saskatchewan Canada
98 H5 **Rockham** South Dakota U.S.A.
141 K6 **Rockhampton** Queensland Australia
140 D4 **Rockhampton Downs** N Terr Australia
99 S1 **Rock Harbor** Michigan U.S.A.
118 J6 **Rockhaven** Saskatchewan Canada
112 F3 **Rock Hill** South Carolina U.S.A.
99 Q8 **Rock I** Illinois U.S.A.
143 B9 **Rockingham** W Australia Australia
112 H3 **Rockingham** North Carolina U.S.A.
141 H4 **Rockingham B** Queensland Australia
121 S7 **Rock Island** Quebec Canada
109 L6 **Rock Island** Texas U.S.A.
98 G1 **Rock L** North Dakota U.S.A.
100 H2 **Rock L** Washington U.S.A.
121 P7 **Rockland** Ontario Canada
101 N7 **Rockland** Idaho U.S.A.
95 S2 **Rockland** Maine U.S.A.
99 R3 **Rockland** Michigan U.S.A.
109 N4 **Rockland** Texas U.S.A.
140 E4 **Rocklands** Queensland Australia
138 F6 **Rocklands Res** Victoria Australia
141 K2 **Rocklea** *dist* Brisbane, Qnsld Australia
142 B6 **Rocklea** W Australia Australia
100 G2 **Rocklyn** Washington U.S.A.
112 B3 **Rockmart** Georgia U.S.A.
117 Q3 **Rocknest L** Northwest Territories Canada
33 R10 **Röcknitz** Germany
95 L8 **Rock Point** Maryland U.S.A.
102 A2 **Rockport** California U.S.A.
110 E2 **Rockport** Illinois U.S.A.
110 J4 **Rockport** Indiana U.S.A.
95 S2 **Rockport** Maine U.S.A.
95 R4 **Rockport** Massachusetts U.S.A.
110 A1 **Rock Port** Missouri U.S.A.
109 K7 **Rockport** Texas U.S.A.
100 D1 **Rockport** Washington U.S.A.
101 U8 **Rock River** Wyoming U.S.A.
113 L13 **Rock Sound** Bahamas
126 F2 **Rock Sound** Eleuthera Bahamas
103 M7 **Rock Springs** Arizona U.S.A.
101 T3 **Rock Springs** Montana U.S.A.
108 G5 **Rocksprings** Texas U.S.A.
101 Q8 **Rock Springs** Wyoming U.S.A.
144 D4 **Rocks Pt.** New Zealand
128 G2 **Rockstone** Guyana
99 R7 **Rockton** Illinois U.S.A.
98 K6 **Rock Valley** Iowa U.S.A.
145 D4 **Rockville** New Zealand
95 P5 **Rockville** Connecticut U.S.A.
110 J2 **Rockville** Indiana U.S.A.
95 K7 **Rockville** Maryland U.S.A.
100 H6 **Rockville** Oregon U.S.A.
112 G5 **Rockville** South Carolina U.S.A.
103 L4 **Rockville** Utah U.S.A.
109 L3 **Rockwall** Texas U.S.A.
99 N7 **Rockwell** Iowa U.S.A.
112 G2 **Rockwell** North Carolina U.S.A.
99 M7 **Rockwell City** Iowa U.S.A.
106 C4 **Rockwood** Colorado U.S.A.
95 S1 **Rockwood** Maine U.S.A.
94 H7 **Rockwood** Pennsylvania U.S.A.
112 C2 **Rockwood** Tennessee U.S.A.
109 H4 **Rockwood** Texas U.S.A.
112 G2 **Rocky** *R* North Carolina U.S.A.
107 L6 **Rocky** Oklahoma U.S.A.
112 E3 **Rocky** *R* South Carolina U.S.A.
100 K6 **Rocky Bar** Idaho U.S.A.
139 H8 **Rocky C** Tasmania Australia
118 D7 **Rockyford** Alberta Canada
106 G3 **Rocky Ford** Colorado U.S.A.
112 F5 **Rocky Ford** Georgia U.S.A.
98 D6 **Rockyford** South Dakota U.S.A.
94 D7 **Rocky Fork Res** Ohio U.S.A.
94 H5 **Rocky Grove** Pennsylvania U.S.A.
143 B10 **Rocky Gully** W Australia Australia
120 H5 **Rocky Island L** Ontario Canada
119 Q4 **Rocky L** Manitoba Canada
112 K2 **Rocky Mount** North Carolina U.S.A.
94 H10 **Rocky Mount** Virginia U.S.A.
118 C6 **Rocky Mountain House** Alberta Canada
101 N2 **Rocky Mt** Montana U.S.A.
98 A9 **Rocky Mt Nat. Park** Colorado U.S.A.
118 B8 **Rocky Mts** British Columbia Canada
106 C1 **Rocky Mts** N America
127 K3 **Rocky Point** Jamaica
95 P6 **Rocky Point** Long I, New York U.S.A.
98 A5 **Rockypoint** Wyoming U.S.A.
113 K11 **Rocky Pt** Bahamas
116 F4 **Rocky Pt** Alaska U.S.A.
94 F5 **Rocky River** Ohio U.S.A.
131 D7 **Ró Colorado** Argentina
20 F3 **Rocque Pt. La** Channel Is
22 H4 **Rocroi** France
37 M2 **Roda** *R* Germany
36 D5 **Rodalben** Germany
27 C11 **Rödberg** Norway
28 G7 **Rødby** Denmark
28 G7 **Rødbyhavn** Denmark
123 Q3 **Roddickton** Newfoundland Canada
28 B3 **Rødding** Denmark
28 C6 **Rødding** Sønderjylland Denmark
27 H15 **Rödeby** Sweden
36 F4 **Rödemark** Germany
25 F2 **Roden** Netherlands
32 K8 **Rodenberg** Germany
27 E12 **Rödenes** Norway
32 H6 **Rodenkirchen** Germany
37 L3 **Rödental** Germany
124 G5 **Rodeo** Mexico
106 B10 **Rodeo** New Mexico U.S.A.
33 S10 **Röderau** Germany
109 O3 **Rodessa** Louisiana U.S.A.
32 K7 **Rodewald** Germany
37 N2 **Rodewisch** Germany
18 G8 **Rodez** France
36 F3 **Rodgau** Germany
36 F2 **Rodheim-Bieber** Germany
46 F4 **Rodholívos** Greece
47 V14 **Ródhos** *isld* Greece
47 V14 **Ródhos** Greece
45 J1 **Rodigo** Italy
37 O5 **Roding** Germany
140 C6 **Rodinga** N Terr Australia
52 J2 **Rodionovo** Russian Federation
28 C4 **Rødkærsbro** Denmark
77 J6 **Rodkhan** Pakistan
48 J3 **Rodnei, Muntii** Romania
120 J10 **Rodney** Ontario Canada
94 B3 **Rodney** Michigan U.S.A.
116 D4 **Rodney, C** Alaska U.S.A.
52 F6 **Rodniki** Russian Federation
55 C5 **Rodnikovka** Kazakhstan
54 D3 **Rodnya** Belarus
139 H7 **Rodondo** *isld* Victoria Australia
46 C3 **Rodonit, kepi i** *C* Albania
13 E3 **Rodono** Scotland
46 G3 **Rodopi Planina** Bulgaria
Rodosto *see* **Tekirdağ**
26 F5 **Rödöy** Norway
128 D5 **Rodrigues** Brazil
81 D7 **Rodrigues I** Indian Oc
28 H7 **Rødsand** *sandbank* Denmark
28 D3 **Rød Sø** Denmark
29 K6 **Rødvig** Denmark
14 E2 **Roe** *R* N Ireland
111 E7 **Roe** Arkansas U.S.A.
142 B5 **Roebourne** W Australia Australia
142 D4 **Roebuck B** W Australia Australia
142 D4 **Roebuck Plains** W Australia Australia
143 E9 **Roe, L** W Australia Australia
21 H6 **Roë, la** France
143 G9 **Roe Plains** W Australia Australia
25 E6 **Roermond** Netherlands
22 D2 **Roesbrugge-Haringe** Belgium
22 E2 **Roeselare** Belgium
115 L5 **Roes Welcome Sound** Northwest Territories Canada
45 L2 **Ro Ferrarese** Italy
109 L1 **Roff** Oklahoma U.S.A.
54 B3 **Rogachev** Belarus
128 E7 **Rogaguado, L** Bolivia
128 E6 **Rogagua, L** Bolivia
27 A12 **Rogaland** *county* Norway
54 H7 **Rogan'** Ukraine
109 O5 **Roganville** Texas U.S.A.
48 J1 **Rogatin** Ukraine
33 P8 **Rogatz** Germany
26 F9 **Rogen** *L* Sweden
121 M5 **Roger, Lac** Quebec Canada
110 B5 **Rogers** Arkansas U.S.A.
98 H2 **Rogers** North Dakota U.S.A.
109 K5 **Rogers** Texas U.S.A.
94 D1 **Rogers City** Michigan U.S.A.
102 G7 **Rogers L.** California U.S.A.
117 P10 **Rogers, Mt** British Columbia Canada
101 L7 **Rogerson** Idaho U.S.A.
122 G7 **Rogersville** New Brunswick Canada
110 J7 **Rogersville** Alabama U.S.A.
110 C4 **Rogersville** Missouri U.S.A.
112 D1 **Rogersville** Tennessee U.S.A.
98 B9 **Roggen** Colorado U.S.A.
33 O5 **Roggendorf** Germany
89 A8 **Roggeveld Berge** *mts* S Africa
8 D4 **Rogiet** Wales
43 G9 **Rogliano** Italy
19 O18 **Rognac** France
26 H4 **Rognan** Norway
19 O17 **Rognes** France
33 O6 **Rögnitz** *R* Germany
44 B2 **Rognosa, Punta** *mt* Italy
46 D1 **Rogozna** *mt* Serbia Yugoslavia
31 K3 **Rogoźno** Poland
100 A7 **Rogue** *R* Oregon U.S.A.
20 E5 **Rohan** France
121 Q3 **Rohault, L** Quebec Canada
33 P6 **Rohlsdorf** Germany
28 J6 **Roholte** Denmark
37 M6 **Rohr** Germany
38 J4 **Rohrbach** Austria
36 C5 **Rohrbach** France
37 O7 **Rohrbach** Germany
33 O7 **Rohrberg** Germany
36 G4 **Rohrbrunn** Germany
74 C5 **Rohri** Pakistan
37 L7 **Röhrmoos** Germany
74 G4 **Rohtak** India
111 E8 **Rohwer** Arkansas U.S.A.
21 L7 **Roiffe** France
22 E4 **Roisel** France
22 F3 **Roisin** Belgium
33 R9 **Roitzsch** Sachsen Germany
33 Q9 **Roitzsch** Sachsen-Anhalt Germany
52 B6 **Roja** Latvia
26 G9 **Röjan** Sweden
133 E4 **Rojas** Argentina
127 L5 **Rojo, C** Puerto Rico
141 G2 **Rokeby** Queensland Australia
119 P7 **Rokeby** Saskatchewan Canada
29 O5 **Rokhmoyva, G** *mt* Russian Federation
52 C6 **Rokiškis** Lithuania
53 C8 **Rokitnoye** Ukraine
77 L2 **Rokkah** Afghanistan
61 P5 **Rokkasho** Japan
26 M6 **Roknäs** Sweden
29 M7 **Rokua Nat. Park** Finland
61 O6 **Rokugō** Japan
61 L8 **Rokugō-saki** *C* Japan
30 H6 **Rokycany** Czech Rep
44 C4 **Rola** *R* Italy
40 B2 **Rolampont** France
118 D1 **Roland** Manitoba Canada
83 L13 **Roland** *isld* Kerguelen Indian Oc
110 D7 **Roland** Arkansas U.S.A.
99 N7 **Roland** Iowa U.S.A.
130 D8 **Rolândia** Brazil
28 D3 **Rold** Denmark
27 B12 **Röldal** Norway
25 G3 **Rolde** Netherlands
98 G1 **Rolette** North Dakota U.S.A.
99 M7 **Rolfe** Iowa U.S.A.
94 J5 **Rolfe** Pennsylvania U.S.A.
141 H6 **Rolfes** Queensland Australia
103 L9 **Roll** Arizona U.S.A.
117 N8 **Rolla** British Columbia Canada
107 J4 **Rolla** Kansas U.S.A.
110 E4 **Rolla** Missouri U.S.A.
98 G1 **Rolla** North Dakota U.S.A.
27 D11 **Rollag** Norway
141 J6 **Rolleston** Queensland Australia
144 D5 **Rolleston** New Zealand
144 C5 **Rolleston, Mt** New Zealand
144 C5 **Rolleston Range** New Zealand
121 L5 **Rollet** Quebec Canada
21 L2 **Rolleville** France
110 L4 **Rolling Fork** *R* Kentucky U.S.A.
111 F9 **Rolling Fork** Mississippi U.S.A.
101 L2 **Rollins** Montana U.S.A.
45 J2 **Rolo** Italy
33 R4 **Rolofshagen** Germany
68 G6 **Rolous** Cambodia
121 N6 **Rolphton** Ontario Canada
28 F6 **Rolsted** Denmark
26 N1 **Rolvsöy** *isld* Norway
28 A3 **Rom** Denmark
141 J7 **Roma** Queensland Australia
71 N8 **Roma** *isld* Indonesia
44 M6 **Roma** Italy
27 K14 **Roma** Sweden
45 H3 **Romagna** *reg* Italy
42 B3 **Romagnano Sesia** Italy
20 H5 **Romagné** France
22 J5 **Romagne-sous-Montfaucon** France
144 B7 **Romahapa** New Zealand
122 J3 **Romaine, R** Quebec Canada
109 H9 **Roma Los Saenz** Texas U.S.A.
46 F1 **Roman** Bulgaria
48 K4 **Roman** Romania
126 F3 **Romana, Cayo** *isld* Cuba
19 P14 **Romanche** *R* France
90 H8 **Romanche Gap** Atlantic Oc
19 N12 **Romanèche-Thorins** France
48 G5 **Romania** *rep* E Europe
113 F12 **Romano, C** Florida U.S.A.
58 F1 **Romanovka** Russian Federation
55 D2 **Romanovo** Russian Federation
36 C6 **Romanswiller** France
116 D6 **Romanzof, C** Alaska U.S.A.
116 Q2 **Romanzof Mts** Alaska U.S.A.
128 F4 **Romão** Brazil
20 H5 **Romazy** France
71 F4 **Romblon** Philippines
Rome *see* **Roma**
111 L7 **Rome** Georgia U.S.A.
95 M3 **Rome** New York U.S.A.
95 L5 **Rome** Pennsylvania U.S.A.
110 K5 **Rome** Tennessee U.S.A.
106 E4 **Romeo** Colorado U.S.A.
94 D4 **Romeo** Michigan U.S.A.
36 E5 **Römerberg** Germany
22 H3 **Romerée** Belgium
27 E11 **Romerike** *reg* Norway
125 K8 **Romero** Mexico
106 E6 **Romeroville** New Mexico U.S.A.
36 H7 **Römerstein** Germany
40 C6 **Romey, Val** France
9 G4 **Romford** England
37 K3 **Römhild** Germany
20 G5 **Romille** France
18 H4 **Romilly** France
21 M3 **Romilly** Eure France
21 N3 **Romilly-sur-Andelle** France
142 F5 **Romily, Mt** W Australia Australia
57 E5 **Romit** Tajikistan
57 C5 **Romitan** Uzbekistan
36 B1 **Rommerskirchen** Germany
94 J7 **Romney** West Virginia U.S.A.
54 E6 **Romny** Ukraine
28 A6 **Rømø** *isld* Denmark
54 E6 **Romodan** Ukraine
21 O7 **Romorantin** France
69 F11 **Rompin** Malaysia
36 G2 **Romrod** Germany
26 C9 **Romsdal** *V* Norway
26 B9 **Romsdalsfjord** *inlet* Norway
9 E6 **Romsey** England
28 F5 **Romsø** *isld* Denmark
94 D4 **Romulus** Michigan U.S.A.
68 H4 **Ron** Vietnam
15 C3 **Rona** *isld* Scotland
101 L2 **Ronan** Montana U.S.A.
28 B3 **Rønbjerg** Denmark
126 D8 **Roncador Bank** Caribbean
129 H6 **Roncador, Sa. do** *mts* Brazil
94 G9 **Ronceverte** West Virginia U.S.A.
20 H4 **Roncey** France
40 E2 **Ronchamp** France
44 M5 **Ronciglione** Italy
45 M3 **Ronco** *R* Italy
45 J1 **Roncoferraro** Italy
45 M3 **Roncofreddo** Italy
22 E2 **Roncq** France
16 D8 **Ronda** Spain
26 D10 **Rondane** Norway
16 D8 **Ronda, Sa. de** *mts* Spain
128 F7 **Rondas-das-Salinas** Brazil
28 E4 **Rønde** Denmark
120 J10 **Rondeau Prov. Park** Ontario Canada
83 L14 **Ronde I** Kerguelen Indian Oc
26 D10 **Rondeslottet** *mt* Norway
128 D2 **Rondón** Colombia
128 F6 **Rondônia** Brazil
130 C5 **Rondonópolis** Brazil
128 F3 **Rondon, Pico** *mt* Brazil
88 G7 **Rondo Plat** Tanzania
36 B2 **Rondorf** Germany
95 N5 **Rondout Res** New York U.S.A.
27 K14 **Ronehamn** Sweden
67 C4 **Rong'an** China
67 B2 **Rongchang** China
65 C5 **Rongcheng** China
65 E6 **Rongcheng** China
67 C4 **Rong Jiang** *R* China
67 C4 **Rongjiang** China
68 A1 **Rongklang Ra** Burma
70 G6 **Rongko** *R* Sulawesi
145 E4 **Rongotea** New Zealand
67 C4 **Rongshui** China
88 H7 **Rongüi** *isld* Mozambique
67 A2 **Rong Xian** China
67 C5 **Rong Xian** China
28 A3 **Rønland** *C* Denmark
27 G16 **Rønne** Denmark
27 F15 **Rönnea** *R* Sweden
37 N2 **Ronneburg** Germany
27 H15 **Ronneby** Sweden
146 C6 **Ronne Entrance** Antarctica
146 D6 **Ronne Ice Shelf** Antarctica
32 L8 **Ronnenberg** Germany
26 G8 **Rönnöfors** Sweden
142 C5 **Ronsard I** W Australia Australia
22 F2 **Ronse** Belgium
129 H6 **Ronuro** *R* Brazil
25 G2 **Roodeschool** Netherlands
110 F2 **Roodhouse** Illinois U.S.A.
22 L4 **Roodt** Luxembourg
89 F4 **Rooiberg** *mt* S Africa
25 B5 **Roosendaal** Netherlands
103 N8 **Roosevelt** Arizona U.S.A.
99 L1 **Roosevelt** Minnesota U.S.A.
109 H1 **Roosevelt** Oklahoma U.S.A.
108 G5 **Roosevelt** Texas U.S.A.
101 P9 **Roosevelt** Utah U.S.A.
100 E4 **Roosevelt** Washington U.S.A.
103 N8 **Roosevelt Dam** Arizona U.S.A.
117 O12 **Roosevelt, F.D., L** Washington U.S.A.
135 L16 **Roosevelt I** Antarctica
146 C10 **Roosevelt I** Antarctica
117 L6 **Roosevelt, Mt** British Columbia Canada
14 D3 **Roosky** Ireland
89 F5 **Roossenekal** *mt* S Africa
117 L4 **Root** *R* Northwest Territories Canada
99 P6 **Root** *R* Minnesota U.S.A.
116 E9 **Rootok I** Aleutian Is
52 B6 **Ropaži** Latvia
52 H3 **Ropcha** Russian Federation
31 N5 **Ropczyce** Poland
140 D2 **Roper** *R* N Terr Australia
112 L2 **Roper** North Carolina U.S.A.
140 C2 **Roper Bar Police Station** N Terr Australia
29 J3 **Ropi** *mt* Finland
36 D6 **Roppenheim** France
18 E8 **Roquefort** France
121 L4 **Roquemaure** Quebec Canada
19 N16 **Roquemaure** France
19 P18 **Roquevaire** France
15 E2 **Rora Head** Scotland
128 F3 **Roraima** *state* Brazil
128 F2 **Roraima** *mt* Guyana
27 F10 **Rörbäcksnäs** Sweden
28 D3 **Rørbæk** Denmark
28 G5 **Rørby** Denmark
89 G7 **Rorke's Drift** S Africa
119 S7 **Rorketon** Manitoba Canada
26 E9 **Röros** Norway
41 L3 **Rorschach** Switzerland
26 H4 **Rörstad** Norway
28 H5 **Rørvig** Denmark
26 E7 **Rörvik** Norway
48 N1 **Ros'** *R* Ukraine
26 G6 **Röså** *R* Norway
43 B12 **Rosa, C** Algeria
122 B7 **Rosaire** Quebec Canada
107 O4 **Rosalia** Kansas U.S.A.
100 H2 **Rosalia** Washington U.S.A.
118 E6 **Rosalind** Alberta Canada
126 D6 **Rosalind Bank** Caribbean
102 F7 **Rosamond** California U.S.A.
102 F7 **Rosamond L** California U.S.A.
40 G6 **Rosa, Monte** *mt* Italy
124 G6 **Rosamorada** Mexico
109 K6 **Rosanky** Texas U.S.A.
41 M3 **Rosanna** *R* Austria
19 P16 **Rosans** France
124 E4 **Rosa, Pta** *C* Mexico
131 E4 **Rosario** Argentina
129 K4 **Rosário** Brazil
128 E8 **Rosario** Chile
124 E4 **Rosario** Mexico
124 B2 **Rosario** Baja California Mexico
124 H4 **Rosario** Coahuila Mexico
130 B9 **Rosario** Paraguay
71 E4 **Rosario** Philippines
127 H9 **Rosario** Venezuela
126 B5 **Rosario Bank** Caribbean
126 D4 **Rosario, Cayo del** Cuba
133 E3 **Rosario de la Frontera** Argentina
133 D2 **Rosario de Lerma** Argentina
133 F4 **Rosario del Tala** Argentina
126 C3 **Rosario, Sa. del** *hills* Cuba
124 B3 **Rosarito** Mexico
124 D4 **Rosarito** Mexico
16 D4 **Rosarito Embalse de** *res* Spain
17 K2 **Rosas** Spain
20 A5 **Roscanvel** France
33 N7 **Rosche** Germany
99 S7 **Roscoe** Illinois U.S.A.
101 Q4 **Roscoe** Montana U.S.A.
95 N5 **Roscoe** New York U.S.A.
98 G4 **Roscoe** South Dakota U.S.A.
108 G3 **Roscoe** Texas U.S.A.
20 C4 **Roscoff** France
14 C3 **Roscommon** *co* Ireland
14 C3 **Roscommon** Ireland
94 C2 **Roscommon** Michigan U.S.A.
14 D4 **Roscrea** Ireland
98 G7 **Rose** Nebraska U.S.A.
127 O7 **Roseau** Dominica
98 K1 **Roseau** *R* Minnesota U.S.A.
139 H8 **Roseberry** Tasmania Australia
100 J5 **Roseberry** Idaho U.S.A.
140 E7 **Roseberth** Queensland Australia
123 O6 **Rose Blanche** Newfoundland Canada
112 J3 **Roseboro** North Carolina U.S.A.
118 D7 **Rosebud** Alberta Canada
110 E3 **Rosebud** Missouri U.S.A.
101 T3 **Rosebud** Montana U.S.A.
108 A8 **Rosebud** New Mexico U.S.A.
98 F6 **Rosebud** South Dakota U.S.A.
109 L4 **Rosebud** Texas U.S.A.
101 T4 **Rosebud Cr** Montana U.S.A.
101 S4 **Rosebud Mts** Montana U.S.A.
100 B6 **Roseburg** Oregon U.S.A.
94 C3 **Rosebush** Michigan U.S.A.
94 C2 **Rose City** Michigan U.S.A.
102 G1 **Rose Creek** Nevada U.S.A.
141 K6 **Rosedale** Queensland Australia
118 E7 **Rosedale** Alberta Canada
110 J2 **Rosedale** Indiana U.S.A.
111 F8 **Rosedale** Mississippi U.S.A.
13 H5 **Rosedale Abbey** England
22 H3 **Rosée** Belgium
38 K8 **Rosegg** Austria
127 J1 **Rose Hall** Jamaica
83 L12 **Rose Hill** Mauritius
99 O8 **Rose Hill** Iowa U.S.A.
112 J3 **Rose Hill** North Carolina U.S.A.
113 K12 **Rose I** Bahamas
111 F11 **Roseland** Louisiana U.S.A.
118 F7 **Rose Lynn** Alberta Canada
118 E8 **Rosemary** Alberta Canada
6 D3 **Rosemary Bank** N Atlantic Oc
142 B5 **Rosemary I** W Australia Australia
99 N5 **Rosemount** Minnesota U.S.A.
102 E2 **Rose, Mt** Nevada U.S.A.
38 J8 **Rosenbach** *mt* Austria
33 O5 **Rosenberg** Germany
36 G5 **Rosenberg** Germany
109 M6 **Rosenberg** Texas U.S.A.
22 C1 **Rosendaël** France
32 F8 **Rosendahl** Germany
110 B1 **Rosendale** Missouri U.S.A.
121 M8 **Roseneath** Ontario Canada
12 D1 **Roseneath** Scotland
36 F7 **Rosenfeld** Germany
32 L6 **Rosengarten** Germany
38 F6 **Rosenheim** Germany
38 M8 **Rosenkopf** *mt* Austria
38 J8 **Rosennock** *mt* Austria
38 K8 **Rosental** *V* Austria
36 F2 **Rosenthal** Germany
109 O5 **Rosepine** Louisiana U.S.A.
117 H8 **Rose Pt** British Columbia Canada
140 D2 **Rose R** N Terr Australia
118 J8 **Roseray** Saskatchewan Canada
126 G3 **Roses** Long I Bahamas
118 K7 **Rosetown** Saskatchewan Canada
141 H5 **Rosetta** *R* Queensland Australia
Rosetta Egypt *see* **Rashîd**
101 M8 **Rosette** Utah U.S.A.
119 O6 **Rose Valley** Saskatchewan Canada
110 F1 **Roseville** Illinois U.S.A.
94 E7 **Roseville** Ohio U.S.A.
118 A5 **Rosewear** Alberta Canada
140 B3 **Rosewood** N Terr Australia
141 K8 **Rosewood** Queensland Australia
101 L7 **Roseworth** Idaho U.S.A.
52 E6 **Roshal'** Russian Federation
109 M6 **Rosharon** Texas U.S.A.
52 C4 **Roshchino** Russian Federation
55 E4 **Roshchinskoye** Kazakhstan
36 C6 **Rosheim** France
80 C5 **Rosh Ha 'Ayin** Israel
77 F2 **Roshkhvär** Iran
98 K4 **Rosholt** South Dakota U.S.A.
99 R5 **Rosholt** Wisconsin U.S.A.
80 F2 **Rosh Pinna** Israel
57 F6 **Roshtkala** Tajikistan
80 D7 **Rosh Ẕurim** Jordan
31 J6 **Rosice** Czech Rep
110 H4 **Rosiclare** Illinois U.S.A.
22 D4 **Rosières-en-Santerre** France
122 H5 **Rosiers, C.des** Quebec Canada
21 K7 **Rosiers, les** France
142 A5 **Rosily I** W Australia Australia
48 J6 **Roșiori de Vede** Romania
46 G1 **Rositsa** *R* Bulgaria
47 J1 **Rositsa** Bulgaria
37 N1 **Rositz** Germany
28 J5 **Roskilde** *co* Denmark
28 J5 **Roskilde** Denmark
33 R8 **Roskow** Germany
103 N9 **Roskruge Mts** Arizona U.S.A.
54 D3 **Roslavl'** Russian Federation
14 D2 **Roslea** N Ireland
28 B3 **Roslev** Denmark
52 F5 **Roslyatino** Russian Federation
98 J4 **Roslyn** South Dakota U.S.A.
100 D2 **Roslyn** Washington U.S.A.
120 C3 **Roslyn L** Ontario Canada
28 F4 **Rosmus** Denmark
28 F5 **Røsnæs** *C* Denmark
21 N8 **Rosnay** France
20 B5 **Rosnoen** France
45 M1 **Rosolina** Italy
20 C6 **Rosporden** France
22 L4 **Rosport** Luxembourg
36 C2 **Rosrath** Germany
139 J8 **Ross** Tasmania Australia
83 L14 **Ross** *mt* Kerguelen Indian Oc
144 C5 **Ross** New Zealand
98 D1 **Ross** North Dakota U.S.A.
101 U6 **Ross** Wyoming U.S.A.
41 K5 **Rossa** Switzerland
37 K3 **Rossach** Germany
43 H9 **Rossano** Italy
14 C2 **Rossan Pt** Ireland
37 N3 **Rossbach** Czech Rep
33 P10 **Rossbach** Germany
111 G9 **Ross Barnett Res** Mississippi U.S.A.
119 R8 **Rossburn** Manitoba Canada
14 B5 **Ross Carbery** Ireland
108 F3 **Ross City** Texas U.S.A.
146 A10 **Ross Dependency** Antarctica
37 J2 **Rossdorf** Germany
121 L7 **Rosseau** Ontario Canada
137 L4 **Rossel** *isld* Louisiade Arch
119 T9 **Rossendale** Manitoba Canada
109 L3 **Rosser** Texas U.S.A.
8 D1 **Rossett** Wales
26 K2 **Rossfjord** Norway
83 M9 **Ross Hill** *mt* Christmas I Indian Oc
146 C11 **Ross I** Antarctica
119 U4 **Ross I** Manitoba Canada
146 C10 **Ross Ice Shelf** Antarctica
22 J4 **Rossignal** Belgium
122 G9 **Rossignol Res** Nova Scotia Canada
94 J6 **Rossiter** Pennsylvania U.S.A.
143 E10 **Rossiter B** W Australia Australia
100 D1 **Ross L** Washington U.S.A.
33 O10 **Rossla** Germany
100 E1 **Ross Lake Nat. Recreation Area** Washington U.S.A.
100 H1 **Rossland** British Columbia Canada
14 E4 **Rosslare** Ireland
33 Q9 **Rosslau** Germany
33 O10 **Rossleben** Germany
145 E4 **Ross, Mt** New Zealand
85 A5 **Rosso** Mauritania
26 H8 **Rossön** Sweden
8 D4 **Ross-on-Wye** England
54 L6 **Rossosh'** Russian Federation
33 R6 **Rossow** Germany
120 C4 **Rossport** Ontario Canada
140 C6 **Ross River** N Terr Australia
117 G4 **Ross River** Yukon Territory Canada
146 B11 **Ross Sea** Antarctica
37 K5 **Rosstal** Germany
108 E7 **Rosston** Oklahoma U.S.A.
33 O9 **Rosstrappe** Germany
26 G6 **Rössvassbukt** Norway
26 G6 **Røssvatnet** *L* Norway
110 J5 **Rossview Res** Tennessee U.S.A.
112 B3 **Rossville** Georgia U.S.A.
110 J1 **Rossville** Illinois U.S.A.
107 P2 **Rossville** Kansas U.S.A.
37 P1 **Rosswein** Germany
117 J8 **Rosswood** British Columbia Canada
26 F4 **Röst** *isld* Norway
26 L3 **Rosta** Norway
26 L3 **Rostaelv** *R* Norway
26 L2 **Rostafjord** *mt* Norway
77 C7 **Rostam** *oil well* Persian Gulf
27 F16 **Röstånga** Sweden
77 L1 **Rostāq** Afghanistan
118 L6 **Rosthern** Saskatchewan Canada
36 C2 **Rostingen** Germany
33 Q4 **Rostock** Germany
26 M3 **Rostonsölkä** *reg* Sweden
52 E6 **Rostov** Russian Federation
53 E10 **Rostov-na-Donu** Russian Federation
53 F10 **Rostovskaya Oblast'** *prov* Russian Federation
20 D5 **Rostrenen** France
28 D3 **Rostrup** Denmark
46 D3 **Rostuša** Macedonia
26 D9 **Röstvangen** Norway
52 H2 **Rosvinskoye** Russian Federation
112 C3 **Roswell** Georgia U.S.A.
108 C2 **Roswell** New Mexico U.S.A.
41 M1 **Rot** *R* Germany
27 G10 **Rot** Sweden
26 F5 **Rota** *C* Norway
16 C8 **Rota** Spain
37 J5 **Rot am See** Germany
108 G3 **Rotan** Texas U.S.A.
37 N5 **Rot Buhl** *mt* Germany
71 L10 **Rote** *isld* Timor Indonesia
80 F4 **Rotem** Jordan
36 H2 **Rotenburg** Hessen Germany
32 K6 **Rotenburg/Wümme** Niedersachsen Germany
38 G8 **Roter Kopf** *mt* Austria
37 L3 **Roter Main** *R* Germany
32 H5 **Roter Sand** Germany
41 L3 **Rote Wand** *mt* Austria
25 F7 **Rotgen** Germany
36 D2 **Roth** Germany
37 N1 **Rötha** Germany
36 E1 **Rothaargebirge** *mts* Germany
36 C7 **Rothau** France
13 G3 **Rothbury** England
99 U6 **Rothbury** Michigan U.S.A.
36 D2 **Rothe Mühle** Germany
37 L5 **Röthenbach** Germany
41 L2 **Röthenbach** Germany
33 P9 **Rothenburg** Germany
37 J5 **Rothenburg ober der Tauber** Germany
20 G4 **Rothéneuf** France
36 H4 **Rothenfels** Germany
36 E6 **Rothenfels** Baden-Württemberg Germany
37 L3 **Rothenkirchen** Germany
33 O10 **Rothenschirmbach** Germany
146 C5 **Rothera** *U.K. Base* Antarctica
13 G6 **Rotherham** England
144 D5 **Rotherham** New Zealand
9 G5 **Rother, R** England
15 E3 **Rothes** Scotland
122 G8 **Rothesay** New Brunswick Canada
12 C2 **Rothesay** Scotland
40 H4 **Rothorn** *mt* Switzerland
98 K3 **Rothsay** Minnesota U.S.A.
146 C5 **Rothschild I** Antarctica
Roti *see* **Rote**
71 L10 **Roti** Indonesia
71 L10 **Roti, Selat** Indonesia
139 H5 **Roto** New South Wales Australia
145 E3 **Rotoaira, L** New Zealand
145 F2 **Rotoehu, L** New Zealand
145 F3 **Rotoiti, L** New Zealand
145 D4 **Rotoiti, L** New Zealand
145 F3 **Rotomahana** New Zealand
145 F3 **Rotoma, L** New Zealand
144 C5 **Rotomanu** New Zealand
43 H8 **Rotondella** Italy
45 O5 **Rotondo, M** *mt* Italy
144 D4 **Rotoroa** New Zealand
145 D4 **Rotoroa, L** New Zealand
145 F3 **Rotorua** New Zealand
145 E2 **Rotowaro** New Zealand
21 K3 **Rots** France
37 O7 **Rott** *R* Germany
41 N2 **Rott** Germany
33 R9 **Rotta** Germany
36 F7 **Rottenburg** Germany
37 J4 **Rottendorf** Germany
38 K6 **Rottenmann** Austria
38 K7 **Rottenmanner Tauern** *mts* Austria
25 C5 **Rotterdam** Netherlands
37 P7 **Rotthalmünster** Germany
9 F6 **Rottingdean** England
36 H4 **Rottingen** Germany
33 N9 **Rottleberode** Germany
143 B9 **Rottnest I** W Australia Australia
33 R8 **Rottstock** Germany
25 G1 **Rottumeroog** *isld* Netherlands
25 F2 **Rottumerplaat** Netherlands
41 J1 **Rottweil** Germany
137 Q4 **Rotuma** *isld* Pacific Oc
37 O5 **Rötz** Germany
20 G7 **Rouans** France
22 E2 **Roubaix** France
19 N15 **Roubion** *R* France
31 H5 **Roudnice** Czech Rep
20 C5 **Roudouallec** France
21 N3 **Rouen** France
40 F2 **Rouffach** France
20 H6 **Rougé** France
40 D3 **Rougemont** France
7 L9 **Rough** *oil rig* North Sea
8 D2 **Roughclose** England
144 B6 **Rough Ridge** New Zealand
110 K4 **Rough River L** Kentucky U.S.A.
19 P18 **Rougiers** France
18 E7 **Rouillac** France
119 N8 **Rouleau** Saskatchewan Canada
Roulers *see* **Roeselare**
94 J5 **Roulette** Pennsylvania U.S.A.
121 L5 **Roulier** Quebec Canada
22 G3 **Rœulx** Belgium
18 F7 **Roumazières** France
116 J4 **Roundabout Mt** Alaska U.S.A.
101 L2 **Round Butte** Montana U.S.A.

123 R4 Round Harbour Newfoundland Canada
118 E5 Round Hill Alberta Canada
141 K6 Round Hill Hd Queensland Australia
87 G12 Round I Mauritius
116 H7 Round I Alaska U.S.A.
109 J5 Round Mountain Texas U.S.A.
139 K4 Round Mt New South Wales Australia
102 G3 Round Mt Nevada U.S.A.
123 R5 Round Pond Newfoundland Canada
95 S3 Round Pond Maine U.S.A.
109 K5 Round Rock Texas U.S.A.
117 R3 Roundrock L Northwest Territories Canada
110 E4 Round Spring Missouri U.S.A.
101 R3 Roundup Montana U.S.A.
119 S9 Rounthwaite Manitoba Canada
129 H3 Roura Fr Guiana
44 B2 Roure Italy
75 L7 Rourkela India
15 F1 Rousay Orkney Scotland
106 F4 Rouse Colorado U.S.A.
94 H5 Rouseville Pennsylvania U.S.A.
142 A2 Rous Hd Perth, W Aust Australia
133 D9 Rous, Pen Chile
19 O17 Roussillon France
22 L5 Roussy-le-Village France
19 P15 Route Napoléon France
21 M3 Routot France
25 F3 Rouveen Netherlands
121 U3 Rouvray, L Quebec Canada
40 A2 Rouvres France
22 H4 Rouvroy-sur-Audry France
22 G3 Roux Belgium
89 E8 Rouxville S Africa
121 M4 Rouyn Quebec Canada
48 L1 Rov R Ukraine
41 M6 Rovato Italy
26 A9 Rovde Norway
52 F4 Rovdino Russian Federation
54 L8 Roven'ki Ukraine
45 J1 Roverbella Italy
41 O6 Rovereto Italy
68 F6 Rovieng Cambodia
45 L1 Rovigo Italy
45 P1 Rovinj Croatia
45 P1 Rovinjsko Selo Croatia
53 C8 Rovno Ukraine
87 G8 Rovuma R Mozambique
99 N7 Rowan Iowa U.S.A.
118 J1 Rowan L Ontario Canada
106 E6 Rowe New Mexico U.S.A.
139 J3 Rowena New South Wales Australia
108 G4 Rowena Texas U.S.A.
112 G4 Rowesville South Carolina U.S.A.
100 K8 Rowland Nevada U.S.A.
94 H7 Rowlesburg West Virginia U.S.A.
118 E7 Rowley Alberta Canada
115 M4 Rowley I Northwest Territories Canada
142 C3 Rowley Shoals W Australia Australia
103 M9 Rowood Arizona U.S.A.
9 E1 Rowsley England
103 K5 Rox Nevada U.S.A.
71 E2 Roxas Luzon Philippines
71 E4 Roxas Mindoro Philippines
71 D5 Roxas Palawan Philippines
71 F5 Roxas Panay Philippines
112 H1 Roxboro North Carolina U.S.A.
127 N2 Roxborough Tobago
140 E6 Roxborough Downs Queensland Australia
144 B6 Roxburgh New Zealand
144 B6 Roxburgh,L New Zealand
95 N4 Roxbury New York U.S.A.
95 P2 Roxbury Vermont U.S.A.
138 D4 Roxby Downs South Australia Australia
27 H13 Roxen L Sweden
111 E10 Roxie Mississippi U.S.A.
109 M2 Roxton Texas U.S.A.
121 S7 Roxton-Sud Quebec Canada
101 N7 Roy Idaho U.S.A.
101 R2 Roy Montana U.S.A.
106 F6 Roy New Mexico U.S.A.
101 N8 Roy Utah U.S.A.
100 C2 Roy Washington U.S.A.
98 H7 Royal Nebraska U.S.A.
14 E3 Royal Canal Ireland
99 U9 Royal Center Indiana U.S.A.
70 C1 Royal Charlotte Reef S China Sea
113 L12 Royal I Bahamas
120 B3 Royal, Mount Ontario Canada
119 P1 Royal, Mt Ontario Canada
89 F7 Royal Natal Nat. Park S Africa
94 D4 Royal Oak Michigan U.S.A.
113 F12 Royal Palm Hammock Florida U.S.A.
113 G12 Royal Palm Ranger Sta Florida U.S.A.
118 C8 Royalties Alberta Canada
9 G5 Royal Tunbridge Wells England
18 E7 Royan France
19 O14 Roybon France
22 D4 Roye France
95 M6 Royersford Pennsylvania U.S.A.
142 C5 Roy Hill W Australia Australia
27 D11 Röykenvik Norway
122 C4 Roy, L Quebec Canada
26 G7 Röyrvik Norway
109 L3 Royse City Texas U.S.A.
26 C10 Röysheim Norway
9 F3 Royston England
112 D3 Royston Georgia U.S.A.
29 L6 Röytta Finland
31 N3 Różan Poland
46 E3 Rožden Macedonia
20 F3 Rozel Channel Is
107 L3 Rozel Kansas U.S.A.
20 G3 Rozel, Pte du France
98 A5 Rozet Wyoming U.S.A.
31 L1 Rozewie C Poland
55 F5 Rozhdestvenka Kazakhstan
52 G5 Rozhdestvenskoye Russian Federation
22 G4 Rozoy France
31 M4 Rozprza Poland
Rozwadów see Stalowa Wola
46 D3 Rrësen Albania
46 E1 Rtanj mt Serbia Yugoslavia
87 B9 Ruacana Namibia
87 G7 Ruaha, Gt R Tanzania
88 E5 Ruaha Nat. Park Tanzania
145 F4 Ruahine Range New Zealand
145 E1 Ruakaka New Zealand
71 J4 Ruang isld Indonesia
145 E3 Ruapehu vol New Zealand
144 B7 Ruapuke I New Zealand
145 F3 Ruatahuna New Zealand
144 C5 Ruatapu New Zealand
71 J9 Rua, Tg C Sumba Indonesia
145 F3 Ruatoki New Zealand
145 G2 Ruatoria New Zealand
145 E2 Ruawai New Zealand
77 C7 Ru'ays, Ar U.A.E.
54 B1 Ruba Belarus
72 F5 Rub al Khālī desert Saudi Arabia
53 G12 Rubas R Russian Federation
33 N9 Rübeland Germany
60 R2 Rubeshibe Japan
54 K7 Rubezhnoye Ukraine
15 C2 Rubha Coigeach Scotland
15 B3 Rubha Hunish Scotland
15 C3 Rubha Reidh Scotland
86 E5 Rubi R Zaire
102 D3 Rubicon R California U.S.A.
45 J2 Rubiera Italy
133 G2 Rubinéia Brazil
124 F3 Rubio Mexico
16 E3 Rubio mt Spain
28 D2 Rubjerg Knude hill Denmark
56 B5 Rubtsovsk Russian Federation
116 K4 Ruby Alaska U.S.A.
103 N10 Ruby Arizona U.S.A.
101 N4 Ruby R Montana U.S.A.
100 H1 Ruby Washington U.S.A.
103 J1 Ruby Dome pk Nevada U.S.A.
103 J1 Ruby L Nevada U.S.A.
103 J1 Ruby Mts Nevada U.S.A.
141 J6 Rubyvale Queensland Australia
103 J1 Ruby Valley Nevada U.S.A.
52 H4 Ruch' Russian Federation
100 B7 Ruch Oregon U.S.A.
67 D4 Rucheng China
52 F2 Ruch'i Russian Federation
Ruchugi see Uvinza
27 H14 Ruda Sweden
138 D5 Rudall South Australia Australia
143 E6 Rudall, R W Australia Australia
142 D5 Rudall River Nat Park W Australia Australia
140 B6 Rudalls R N Terr Australia
77 E6 Rudan Iran
75 J5 Rudauli India
77 H4 Rudbar Afghanistan
77 A1 Rudbār Iran
28 B7 Rudbøl Denmark
118 K6 Ruddell Saskatchewan Canada
22 E1 Ruddervoorde Belgium
119 R3 Ruddock Manitoba Canada
116 P6 Rude R Alaska U.S.A.
38 L8 Ruden Austria
33 T4 Ruden isld Germany
36 H6 Rudersberg Germany
33 T8 Rudersdorf Germany
36 D4 Rüdesheim Germany
31 O6 Rudki Ukraine
28 F7 Rudkøbing Denmark
31 J4 Rudna Poland
59 L3 Rudnaya Pristan' Russian Federation
52 H5 Rudnichnyy Russian Federation
55 D2 Rudnichnyy Sverdlovskaya obl Russian Federation
31 N5 Rudnik Poland
54 C2 Rudnya Russian Federation
55 D4 Rudnyy Kazakhstan
Rudok see Rutog
46 D3 Rudoka Planina mt Macedonia/Serbia
50 E1 Rudol'fa, O isld Russian Federation
Rudolf, L see Turkana, L
37 L2 Rudolstadt Germany
67 G1 Rudong China
46 G3 Rudozem Bulgaria
77 B1 Rūdsar Iran
28 G5 Ruds Vedby Denmark
101 P1 Rudyard Montana U.S.A.
22 B3 Rue France
120 J5 Ruel Ontario Canada
21 P3 Rue St. Pierre, la France
86 F3 Rufa'a Sudan
18 F6 Ruffec France
21 N8 Ruffec Indre France
20 F6 Ruffiac France
20 H6 Ruffigne France
112 G4 Ruffin South Carolina U.S.A.
88 F6 Rufiji R Tanzania
45 K4 Rufina Italy
131 E5 Rufino Argentina
85 A6 Rufisque Senegal
88 C9 Rufunsa R Zambia
100 F1 Rufus Woods L Washington U.S.A.
67 G1 Rugao China
9 E3 Rugby England
98 G1 Rugby North Dakota U.S.A.
9 E2 Rugeley England
30 H1 Rügen isld Germany
144 A7 Rugged Is New Zealand
37 K5 Rügland Germany
21 M4 Rugles France
52 D3 Rug Oz L Russian Federation
52 D3 Rugozero Russian Federation
80 B7 Ruḥama Israel
75 N5 Ruhea Bangladesh
33 N7 Rühen Germany
29 L11 Rühimäki Finland
37 J2 Ruhla Germany
33 T10 Ruhland Germany
33 S7 Ruhleben Germany
37 O6 Ruhmannsfelden Germany
33 P5 Rühn Germany
33 P6 Ruhner Bge mt Germany
32 F10 Ruhr R Germany
35 Ruhr, The reg Germany
88 E6 Ruhudji R Tanzania
88 E7 Ruhuhu R Tanzania
67 G3 Rui'an China
67 E2 Ruichang China
65 A7 Ruicheng China
108 C6 Ruidosa Texas U.S.A.
106 E8 Ruidoso New Mexico U.S.A.
108 B2 Ruidoso New Mexico U.S.A.
67 E4 Ruijin China
80 G7 Ruim el Hiri Jordan
22 E1 Ruiselede Belgium
9 F4 Ruislip England
25 H3 Ruiten Aa R Netherlands
124 G7 Ruiz Mexico
128 C3 Ruiz, Nevada del vol Colombia
80 G7 Rujeim Salim Jordan
46 E2 Rujen mt Macedonia
52 C5 Rūjiena Latvia
70 D5 Rujon Kalimantan
29 O5 Rukatunturi mt Finland
88 C10 Rukovakuona Mts Zimbabwe
88 D7 Rukuru R Malawi
71 H7 Rukuwa Indonesia
88 C5 Rukwa reg Tanzania
88 D5 Rukwa, L Tanzania
107 J2 Ruleton Kansas U.S.A.
111 F8 Ruleville Mississippi U.S.A.
26 G10 Rullbo Sweden
99 L9 Rulo Nebraska U.S.A.
36 E5 Rülzheim Germany
15 B3 Rum isld Scotland
48 F5 Ruma Serbia Yugoslavia
Rumania see Romania
71 J4 Rumbai Sulawesi
140 C7 Rumbalara N Terr Australia
86 E4 Rumbek Sudan
31 H5 Rumburk Czech Rep
126 G3 Rum Cay isld Bahamas
22 E3 Rumegies France
22 L5 Rumelange Luxembourg
47 N10 Rumelifeneri Turkey
95 R2 Rumford Maine U.S.A.
22 G4 Rumigny France
22 E2 Rumillies Belgium
140 B2 Rum Jungle N Terr Australia
80 E2 Rummāna Israel
Rummelsburg see Miastko
60 P2 Rumoi Japan
88 D7 Rumphi Malawi
118 E7 Rumsey Alberta Canada
95 N6 Rumson New Jersey U.S.A.
144 C5 Rumu New Zealand
144 C5 Runanga New Zealand
127 K1 Runaway Bay Jamaica
8 D1 Runcorn England
89 G3 Runde R Zimbabwe
36 C1 Ründeroth Germany
28 D7 Rundhof Germany
26 A9 Rundöy Norway
87 C9 Rundu Namibia
71 J7 Runduma isld Indonesia
29 G8 Rundvik Sweden
71 M8 Rung isld Indonesia
70 C6 Rungan R Kalimantan
109 K7 Runge Texas U.S.A.
29 K5 Rungsted Denmark
88 D5 Rungwa R Tanzania
88 D6 Rungwe pk Tanzania
27 J11 Runhällen Sweden
36 E3 Runkel Germany
27 H11 Runn L Sweden
99 N8 Runnells Iowa U.S.A.
108 E1 Running Water Cr Texas/Okla U.S.A.
119 Q7 Runnymede Saskatchewan Canada
143 E6 Runton Ra W Australia Australia
29 O10 Ruokolahti Finland
66 D4 Ruoqiang China
58 D3 Ruo Shui R China
29 L10 Ruovesi Finland
131 A8 Rupanco, L Chile
139 G6 Rupanyup Victoria Australia
88 D8 Rupashe R Malawi
69 E12 Rupat isld Sumatra
48 J4 Rupea Romania
141 F5 Rupert R Queensland Australia
101 M7 Rupert Idaho U.S.A.
95 O3 Rupert Vermont U.S.A.
94 G9 Rupert West Virginia U.S.A.
121 L1 Rupert B Quebec Canada
121 N1 Rupert, R Quebec Canada
37 L6 Rupertsbuch Germany
146 B9 Ruppert Coast Antarctica
36 G2 Ruppertenrod Germany
36 F2 Ruppertsberg Germany
36 C2 Ruppichteroth Germany
33 S7 Ruppiner Kanal Germany
128 G3 Rupununi R Guyana
80 G2 Ruqqād R Syria
80 G1 Ruqqād Sakhr Syria
25 F6 Rur R Germany
112 G1 Rural Hall North Carolina U.S.A.
94 F10 Rural Retreat Virginia U.S.A.
128 E6 Rurrenabaque Bolivia
28 C6 Rurup Denmark
17 F5 Rus R Spain
71 L9 Rusah isld Indonesia
87 F9 Rusape Zimbabwe
Ruschuk see Ruse
47 H1 Ruse Bulgaria
38 M8 Ruše Slovenia
37 P6 Rusel Germany
146 F6 Rüser-Larsenisen ice shelf Antarctica
14 E3 Rush Ireland
106 F3 Rush Colorado U.S.A.
9 E5 Rushall England
65 E6 Rushan China
57 F5 Rushanskiy Khrebet mts Tajikistan
107 L3 Rush Center Kansas U.S.A.
99 O4 Rush City Minnesota U.S.A.
106 G3 Rush Cr Colorado U.S.A.
9 F3 Rushden England
99 P6 Rushford Minnesota U.S.A.
94 J4 Rushford New York U.S.A.
118 K8 Rush Lake Saskatchewan Canada
107 N7 Rush Springs Oklahoma U.S.A.
110 F1 Rushville Illinois U.S.A.
110 L2 Rushville Indiana U.S.A.
98 D7 Rushville Nebraska U.S.A.
139 H6 Rushworth Victoria Australia
109 M4 Rusk Texas U.S.A.
113 E10 Ruskin Florida U.S.A.
26 K7 Rusksele Sweden
26 K7 Rusksträsk Sweden
98 F2 Ruso North Dakota U.S.A.
129 L4 Russas Brazil
38 H6 Russbachsaag Austria
113 L12 Russel I Bahamas
119 Q8 Russell Manitoba Canada
121 P7 Russell Ontario Canada
145 E1 Russell New Zealand
99 N9 Russell Iowa U.S.A.
107 M3 Russell Kansas U.S.A.
94 E8 Russell Kentucky U.S.A.
99 L5 Russell Minnesota U.S.A.
95 M2 Russell New York U.S.A.
94 H5 Russell Pennsylvania U.S.A.
112 B3 Russell Cave National Monument Alabama U.S.A.
143 E6 Russell Headland mt W Australia Australia
115 K3 Russell I Northwest Territories Canada
137 M3 Russell Is Solomon Is
119 Q2 Russell L Manitoba Canada
117 Q4 Russell L Northwest Territories Canada
143 C7 Russell,Mt W Australia Australia
116 M5 Russell, Mt Alaska U.S.A.
143 E10 Russell Ra W Australia Australia
110 L4 Russell Springs Kentucky U.S.A.
110 N1 Russells Pt Ohio U.S.A.
111 J7 Russellville Alabama U.S.A.
110 D6 Russellville Arkansas U.S.A.
110 K5 Russellville Kentucky U.S.A.
110 D3 Russellville Missouri U.S.A.
94 D8 Russellville Ohio U.S.A.
45 M3 Russi Italy
50 Russian Federation Asia/Europe
116 G6 Russian Mission Alaska U.S.A.
116 H6 Russian Mts Alaska U.S.A.
50 F1 Russkaya Gavan' Russian Federation
55 F4 Russkaya-Polyana Russian Federation
55 D3 Russkaya-Techa Russian Federation
54 M6 Russkaya-Zhuravka Russian Federation
52 H6 Russkiy Aktash Russian Federation
51 J1 Russkiy, Ostrova islds Russian Federation
78 K1 Rustavi Georgia
94 H9 Rustburg Virginia U.S.A.
26 Q1 Rustefjelbma Norway
89 E5 Rustenburg S Africa
32 H5 Rustersiel Germany
100 C7 Rustler Peak mt Oregon U.S.A.
109 P3 Ruston Louisiana U.S.A.
71 A3 Ruta Indonesia
88 C3 Rutana Burundi
16 E7 Rute Spain
27 K14 Rute Sweden
33 S6 Rutenberg Germany
32 F7 Rütenbrock Germany
71 K9 Ruteng Flores Indonesia
146 D7 Rutford Ice Stream ice stream Antarctica
102 A1 Ruth California U.S.A.
103 K2 Ruth Nevada U.S.A.
32 H10 Rüthen Germany
112 F2 Rutherfordton North Carolina U.S.A.
121 L6 Rutherglen Ontario Canada
12 D2 Rutherglen Scotland
94 K9 Ruther Glen Virginia U.S.A.
116 M5 Ruth Glacier Alaska U.S.A.
118 J7 Ruthilda Saskatchewan Canada
8 C1 Ruthin Wales
98 K5 Ruthton Minnesota U.S.A.
141 G6 Ruthven Queensland Australia
99 M6 Ruthven Iowa U.S.A.
88 E7 Rutikira R Tanzania
52 G6 Rutka R Russian Federation
99 R9 Rutland Illinois U.S.A.
98 J3 Rutland North Dakota U.S.A.
94 E7 Rutland Ohio U.S.A.
95 P3 Rutland Vermont U.S.A.
68 A7 Rutland I Andaman Is
141 F3 Rutland Plains Queensland Australia
118 H6 Rutland Station Saskatchewan Canada
9 F2 Rutland Water L England
99 O3 Rutledge Minnesota U.S.A.
110 D1 Rutledge Missouri U.S.A.
66 B5 Rutog China
25 E3 Rutten Netherlands
120 K6 Rutter Ontario Canada
25 F4 Ruurlo Netherlands
87 G7 Ruvu Tanzania
88 G5 Ruvu R Tanzania
88 E7 Ruvuma Tanzania
88 G7 Ruvuma R Tanzania
89 G1 Ruwa Zimbabwe
86 E2 Ruweiba Sudan
88 C1 Ruwenzori Rge mts Uganda
36 B4 Ruwer Germany
87 F9 Ruya R Zimbabwe
65 B7 Ruyang China
67 D4 Ruyuan China
55 E4 Ruzayevka Kazakhstan
48 M1 Ruzhin Ukraine
48 E1 Ružomberok Slovakia
88 B2 Rwanda rep Cent Africa
28 D4 Ry Denmark
28 D2 Ryå Denmark
47 H1 Ryakhovo Bulgaria
144 C5 Ryall,Mt New Zealand
99 P7 Ryan Iowa U.S.A.
109 K1 Ryan Oklahoma U.S.A.
12 C4 Ryan, Loch Scotland
101 T8 Ryan Park Wyoming U.S.A.
101 L6 Ryan Pk Idaho U.S.A.
53 E7 Ryazan' Russian Federation
54 M3 Ryazhsk Russian Federation
Rybach'ye see Issyk-Kul'
37 O3 Rybáře Czech Rep
52 E5 Rybinsk Russian Federation
52 E5 Rybinskoye Vdkhr res Russian Federation
31 L5 Rybnik Poland
48 M3 Rybnitsa Moldova
54 L2 Rybnoye Russian Federation
55 D2 Rychkovo Russian Federation
31 J5 Rychnov Czech Rep
31 L3 Rychwał Poland
33 S4 Ryckgraben R Germany
117 O8 Rycroft Alberta Canada
120 G6 Rydal Bank Ontario Canada
146 C6 Rydberg Peninsula pen Antarctica
28 B4 Ryde Denmark
28 G7 Ryde Denmark
9 E6 Ryde England
98 E2 Ryder North Dakota U.S.A.
100 B3 Ryderwood Washington U.S.A.
27 H14 Ryd, V Sweden
28 D4 Rye Denmark
28 H5 Rye Denmark
9 G6 Rye England
106 F4 Rye Colorado U.S.A.
95 R3 Rye New Hampshire U.S.A.
109 N5 Rye Texas U.S.A.
77 B5 R-ye Dalaki R Iran
101 Q3 Ryegate Montana U.S.A.
100 G9 Rye Patch Nevada U.S.A.
102 F1 Rye Patch Res Nevada U.S.A.
119 Q9 Ryerson Saskatchewan Canada
21 J3 Ryes France
27 A12 Ryfylke Norway
13 G4 Ryhope England
31 N4 Ryki Poland
120 G3 Ryland Ontario Canada
118 E5 Ryley Alberta Canada
54 F5 Ryl'sk Russian Federation
139 J5 Rylstone New South Wales Australia
31 N6 Rymanow Poland
31 K6 Rýmařov Czech Rep
55 F1 Rymovy Russian Federation
31 N2 Ryn Poland
52 E1 Rynda Russian Federation
53 G9 Ryn Peski desert Kazakhstan
28 F4 Ryomgard Denmark
61 P7 Ryōri-zaki C Japan
61 M7 Ryōtsu Japan
31 L2 Rypin Poland
48 L3 Ryshkany Moldova
28 F6 Ryslinge Denmark
32 F6 Rysum Germany
31 M6 Rysy mt Poland/Slovakia
61 O10 Ryūgasaki Japan
31 H3 Rzepin Poland
31 N5 Rzeszów Poland
54 E3 Rzhanitsa Russian Federation
52 D6 Rzhev Russian Federation

S

77 C4 Sa'ādatābād Iran
33 R4 Saal Germany
36 F5 Saal R Germany
37 J3 Saal Germany
38 G7 Saalach R Austria
36 F3 Saalburg Germany
37 M3 Saalburg Germany
33 P9 Saale R Germany
37 M3 Saale R Germany
36 C7 Saales France
37 L2 Saalfeld Germany
40 F5 Saanen Switzerland
117 M11 Saanich British Columbia Canada
36 B5 Saar R Germany
19 K3 Saarbrücken France
36 B5 Saarbrücken Germany
36 B4 Saarburg Germany
27 M14 Sääre Estonia
27 M13 Saaremaa Estonia
29 M5 Saarenkylä Finland
29 O10 Saari Finland
29 L9 Saarijärvi Finland
29 N3 Saariselkä mts Finland
36 B5 Saarland land Germany
115 P5 Saarloq Greenland
36 B5 Saarlouis Germany
33 S8 Saarmund Germany
36 B5 Saar-Wellingen Germany
36 D7 Saasenheim France
40 G5 Saas Tal Switzerland
133 E5 Saavedra Argentina
131 A7 Saavedra, Pto Chile
125 L2 Sabá Honduras
127 N6 Saba isld Lesser Antilles
32 L9 Sababurg Germany
48 F6 Sabac Serbia Yugoslavia
17 J3 Sabadell Spain
70 E2 Sabah state Borneo
69 E11 Sabak Malaysia
71 J8 Sabalana, Kepulauan islds Indonesia
44 M5 Saba, Mt Italy
126 D3 Sabana, Arch. de islds Cuba
127 K5 Sabana de la Mar Dominican Rep
127 J10 Sabana de Mendoza Venezuela
128 D1 Sabanalarga Colombia
127 K9 Sabaneta Venezuela
70 F4 Sabang Sulawesi
70 G6 Sabang Sulawesi
69 B10 Sabang Sumatra
83 K11 Sabaragamuwa reg Sri Lanka
71 J8 Sabaru isld Indonesia
80 D4 Sabastiya Jordan
45 O7 Sabaudia Italy
128 E7 Sabaya Bolivia
41 M6 Sabbia, V Italy
45 H2 Sabbioneta Italy
77 G4 Şāberi, Hāmūn-e L Iran
107 P2 Sabetha Kansas U.S.A.
84 E4 Sabhā Libya
87 F10 Sabi R Zimbabwe
89 G5 Sabie R S Africa
52 B6 Sabile Latvia
45 N5 Sabina Italy
94 D7 Sabina Ohio U.S.A.
124 F2 Sabinal Mexico
109 H6 Sabinal Texas U.S.A.
126 F4 Sabinal, Pen. de Cuba
17 G2 Sabiñánigo Spain
108 F8 Sabinas Mexico
125 J4 Sabinas Hidalgo Mexico
111 C11 Sabine R Louisiana/Texas U.S.A.
111 C12 Sabine L Louisiana U.S.A.
111 C12 Sabine Pass Louisiana U.S.A.
42 E6 Sabini, Monti Italy
79 H2 Sabkhat al Jabbūl Syria
79 H3 Sabkhat al Marāghah salt lake Syria
79 D7 Sabkhet el Bardawîl Egypt
71 E4 Sablayan Philippines
137 M5 Sable isld Coral Sea
123 N10 Sable I Nova Scotia Canada
122 G10 Sable River Nova Scotia Canada
18 D6 Sables-d'Olonne, les France
20 F4 Sables d'Or France
120 H6 Sables, L. aux Ontario Canada
120 H6 Sables, River Aux Ontario Canada
21 K6 Sable-sur-Sarthe France
19 O16 Sablet France
19 N18 Sablon, Pte. du France
19 N14 Sablons France
16 C3 Sabor R Portugal
131 G2 Sá Borja Brazil
94 H7 Sabraton West Virginia U.S.A.
18 E8 Sabres France
146 F14 Sabrina Coast Antarctica
28 E4 Sabro Denmark
16 C4 Sabugal Portugal
99 Q7 Sabula Iowa U.S.A.
70 G5 Sabulu Sulawesi
47 L5 Sabuncu Turkey
70 P9 Sabunten isld Indonesia
Sabzawar see Shīndand
77 E1 Sabzevār Iran
110 C4 Sac R Missouri U.S.A.
128 E7 Sacaca Bolivia
103 N8 Sacaton Arizona U.S.A.
99 L7 Sac City Iowa U.S.A.
43 E7 Sacco R Italy
45 L1 Saccolongo Italy
17 F4 Sacedón Spain
115 K7 Sachigo R Ontario Canada
109 O8 Sachse Texas U.S.A.
37 O2 Sachsen land Germany
33 O8 Sachsen-Anhalt land Germany
36 F1 Sachsenberg Germany
38 H8 Sachsenburg Austria
33 O10 Sachsenburg Germany
32 K8 Sachsenhagen Germany
32 K10 Sachsenhausen Germany
114 G3 Sachs Harbour Northwest Territories Canada
42 E3 Sacile Italy
95 L3 Sackets Harbor New York U.S.A.
122 H8 Sackville New Brunswick Canada
110 B3 Sac, L Missouri U.S.A.
21 P5 Saclas France
95 R3 Saco Maine U.S.A.
101 S1 Saco Montana U.S.A.
71 F7 Sacol isld Philippines
40 B2 Sacquenay France
102 B2 Sacramento R California U.S.A.
102 C3 Sacramento California U.S.A.
108 B3 Sacramento Mts New Mexico U.S.A.
102 B1 Sacramento V California U.S.A.
103 K6 Sacramento Wash R Arizona U.S.A.
16 E8 Sacratif, C Spain
122 D5 Sacré Coeur Quebec Canada
122 C5 Sacré-Coeur Saguenay Quebec Canada
130 F6 Sacremento Brazil
48 G3 Săcueni Romania
18 E10 Sadaba Spain
77 B5 Sa'dabad Iran
72 E5 Şa'dah Yemen
60 F12 Sada-misaki Japan
69 E9 Sadao Thailand
13 G4 Sadberge England
74 D2 Sadda Pakistan
141 G2 Saddle Hill Queensland Australia
142 D4 Saddle Hill W Australia Australia
100 A7 Saddle Mt Oregon U.S.A.
101 Q5 Saddle Mt Wyoming U.S.A.
68 A6 Saddle Pk Andaman Is
68 G7 Sa Dec Vietnam
48 K2 Sadgora Ukraine
127 O3 Sadhoowa Trinidad
94 C8 Sadieville Kentucky U.S.A.
85 B6 Sadiola Mali
74 D4 Sadiqabad Pakistan
16 B6 Sado R Portugal
61 M7 Sado-shima isld Japan
46 G2 Sadovo Bulgaria
74 E6 Sadri India
26 H5 Sadvajaur L Sweden
28 F2 Sæby Nordjylland Denmark
28 G5 Sæby Vestjælland Denmark
28 J6 Sædder Denmark
28 B4 Sædding Denmark
60 E13 Saeki Japan
60 E13 Saeki-wan B Japan
17 F5 Saelices Spain
32 G8 Saerbeck Germany
28 E5 Særslev Denmark
28 E2 Saesing Denmark
22 K4 Saeul Luxembourg
Safad see Zefat
55 D4 Safakulevo Russian Federation
48 F2 Sáfárikovo Slovakia
57 F5 Safed Khirs reg Afghanistan
77 L2 Safed Koh mt Afghanistan
38 O7 Safen R Austria
77 J4 Safer Afghanistan
142 A4 Safety Bay dist W Australia Australia
80 D5 Saffārin Jordan
79 B9 Şaff, El Egypt
27 F12 Säffle Sweden
111 J9 Safford Alabama U.S.A.
103 P9 Safford Arizona U.S.A.
20 G7 Saffré France
9 G3 Saffron Walden England
85 C2 Safi Morocco
77 G4 Safidabeh Iran
77 A1 Safid Rud R Iran
41 K4 Safier Tal Switzerland
130 H6 Safiras, Sa. das mts Brazil
54 K3 Safonovka Russian Federation
52 G2 Safonovo Russian Federation
78 D1 Safranbolu Turkey
27 G11 Säfsnäs Sweden
80 G5 Safut Jordan
66 D6 Saga China
60 D12 Saga prefect Japan
60 D12 Saga Kyūshū Japan
60 G12 Saga Shikoku Japan
60 C11 Saga Tsushima Japan
57 C1 Saga Kazakhstan
61 O7 Sagae Japan
68 B2 Sagaing Burma
59 L5 Sagami-nada B Japan
61 N10 Sagami-wan B Japan
94 H6 Sagamore Pennsylvania U.S.A.
119 N2 Saganaga L Ontario Canada
120 H3 Saganash L Ontario Canada
60 E12 Saganoseki Japan
68 D6 Saganthit Kyun isld Burma
56 E5 Sagan-Tologoy Russian Federation
76 C2 Sagar India
61 M11 Sagara Japan
88 F5 Sagara Tanzania
116 N2 Sagavanirktok R Alaska U.S.A.
32 H7 Sage Germany
101 P8 Sage Wyoming U.S.A.
101 P1 Sage Cr Montana U.S.A.
101 S8 Sage Cr Wyoming U.S.A.
27 G11 Sågen Sweden
71 C3 Sageurin W Irian
26 H4 Sagfjord Norway
26 J5 Saggat L Sweden
95 P6 Sag Harbor Long I, New York U.S.A.
94 D3 Saginaw Michigan U.S.A.
109 L9 Saginaw Texas U.S.A.
94 D3 Saginaw Bay Michigan U.S.A.
88 D2 Sagitu isld Uganda
115 N6 Saglek B Labrador, Nfld Canada
71 H6 Sago isld Indonesia
99 S3 Sagola Michigan U.S.A.
17 F7 Sagra, La mt Spain
130 D7 Sagredo, Reprêsa res Brazil
85 F8 Sagre, Pto.de Bioko Equat Guinea
16 B8 Sagres Portugal
71 L9 Sagu Indonesia
106 D3 Saguache Colorado U.S.A.
126 G4 Sagua de Tánamo Cuba
126 D3 Sagua la Grande Cuba
103 N8 Saguaro L Arizona U.S.A.
103 O9 Saguaro Nat.Mon Arizona U.S.A.
115 M8 Saguenay R Quebec Canada
85 B3 Saguia al Hamra, As R Western Sahara
17 G5 Sagunto Spain
116 N2 Sagwan Alaska U.S.A.
80 G3 Saham Jordan
85 C4 Sahara desert N Africa
79 E10 Sahara, G mt Egypt
74 G4 Saharanpur India
142 E5 Sahara Well W Australia Australia
75 L5 Sahibganj India
28 D4 Sahl Denmark
124 E3 Sahuaripa Mexico
103 O10 Sahuarita Arizona U.S.A.
124 H7 Sahuayo Mexico
136 F4 Sahul Shelf Timor Sea
19 O16 Sahune France
68 J5 Sa Huynh Vietnam
61 L9 Sai R Japan
136 J3 Saibai I Papua New Guinea
69 E9 Sai Buri R Thailand
69 E9 Sai Buri Thailand
85 E2 Saïda Algeria
79 F5 Saïda Lebanon
77 D5 Sa'īdābād Iran
68 F6 Sai Dao Tai, Khao mt Thailand
86 D4 Said Bundas Sudan
75 N6 Saidpur Bangladesh
74 E1 Saidu Pakistan
40 E3 Saignelégier Switzerland
60 G9 Saigō Japan
Saigon see Ho Chi Minh
68 H7 Saigon R Vietnam
29 O4 Saija Finland
60 G12 Saijō Japan
60 C13 Saikai Nat. Park Japan
71 C3 Saileen W Irian
19 O15 Saillans France
71 C3 Sailolo W Irian
100 K7 Sailor Cr Idaho U.S.A.
76 C1 Sailu India
65 F4 Saima China
29 N10 Saimaa L Finland
29 N11 Saimaa Canal Finland/Rus Fed
124 H6 Sain Alto Mexico
77 G5 Saindak Pakistan
78 L3 Sa'īndezh Iran
22 D2 Sainghin-en-Weppes France
22 G3 Sains-du-Nord France
22 F4 Sains-Richaumont France
15 F5 St. Abb's Head Scotland
122 H5 Ste. Adelaide Quebec Canada
121 Q7 Ste.Adèle Quebec Canada
21 L2 Ste.Adresse France
38 N6 St.Aegyd Austria
18 G9 St.Affrique France
121 T6 St.Agapit Quebec Canada
119 U9 Ste.Agathe Manitoba Canada
121 Q6 Ste.Agathe des Monts Quebec Canada
21 M5 St.Agil France
121 L4 Ste.Agnes Quebec Canada
8 A7 St.Agnes England
9 F7 St.Agnes isld Isles of Scilly England
21 N7 St.Aignan France
21 H6 St.Aignan-sur-Roë France
28 D3 Ste. Ajstrup Denmark
20 E4 St.Alban France
19 P13 St.-Alban-Leysee France
40 C6 St.-Alban-Leysse France
123 R6 St.Alban's Newfoundland Canada
9 F4 St.Albans England
95 P2 St.Albans Vermont U.S.A.
94 F8 St.Albans West Virginia U.S.A.
118 D5 St.Albert Alberta Canada
122 C6 St.Alexandre Quebec Canada
121 R6 St.Alexis des Monts Quebec Canada
22 E3 St.Amand-les-Eaux France
21 N6 St. Amand-Longpré France
18 G6 St. Amand Mont Rond France
21 J8 St.Amand-sur-Sèvre France
40 F2 St.Amarin France
121 T4 St.-Ambroise Quebec Canada
21 P8 St.Ambroix Cher France
122 D5 St.Anaclet Quebec Canada
19 N17 St.-Andiol France
38 L8 St. Andra-im-Lavanttal Austria
83 K13 St.André Réunion Indian Oc
83 M12 Saint-André Mauritius
33 M9 St. Andreasberg Germany
19 N13 St.Andre-de-Corcy France
18 E8 St.André-de-Cubzac France
21 N4 St.André-de-l'Eure France
20 F7 St.-André-des-Eaux France
21 N4 St.André,Plaine de France
127 L2 St.Andrew parish Jamaica
127 P2 St.Andrew co Trinidad
111 L11 St.Andrew Florida U.S.A.
123 N6 St.Andrew's Newfoundland Canada
144 C6 St. Andrews New Zealand
13 F1 St.Andrews Scotland
123 M7 St.Andrew's Chan Nova Scotia Canada
113 F7 St.Andrew Sd Georgia U.S.A.
127 K2 St.Ann parish Jamaica
98 F9 St.Ann Nebraska U.S.A.
126 B2 St. Anna-Baai B Curaçao Neth Antilles
119 V9 Ste.Anne Manitoba Canada
21 M4 Ste.Anne France
99 T8 St.Anne Illinois U.S.A.
127 N4 Ste.Anne Guadeloupe W Indies
127 L4 Ste.Anne Martinique W Indies
20 E6 Ste.Anne-d'Auray France
121 U5 Ste.-Anne-de-Beaupré Quebec Canada
121 S6 Ste. Anne de la Pérade Quebec Canada
122 B6 Ste.Anne de la Pocatière Quebec Canada
122 F4 Ste.Anne des Monts Quebec Canada
121 P6 Ste.Anne du Lac Quebec Canada
122 E3 Ste.Anne, L Quebec Canada
118 C5 Ste. Anne, Lac Alberta Canada
122 B6 Ste.Anne, R Quebec Canada
20 F2 St.Annes Channel Is
117 Q9 St.Ann, L Alberta Canada
123 M7 St. Anns Nova Scotia Canada
127 K2 St. Ann's Bay Jamaica
12 E3 St Ann's Bridge Scotland
99 O6 St.Ansgar Iowa U.S.A.
25 E5 St.Anthonis Netherlands
123 R2 St.Anthony Newfoundland Canada
101 O6 St.Anthony Idaho U.S.A.
19 O18 St.Antoine France
41 M3 St.Anton Austria
122 C6 St.Antonin Quebec Canada
18 G8 St.Antonin France
21 O8 St.Août France
21 N3 St.Aquilin-de-Pacy France
139 G6 St.Arnaud Victoria Australia
145 D4 St. Arnaud New Zealand
21 O4 St. Arnoult-en-Yvelines France
122 C6 St.Arsène Quebec Canada
8 C1 St. Asaph Wales
140 B1 St.Asaph B N Terr Australia
18 F7 St.Astier France
122 C6 St.Athanase Quebec Canada
122 B6 St.Aubert Quebec Canada
20 F3 St.Aubin Channel Is
21 K3 St.Aubin Calvados France
20 G5 St.Aubin-d'Aubigné France
21 L3 St.Aubin-de-Scellon France
20 H4 St.Aubin-de-Terregatte France
20 H5 St.Aubin-du-Cormier France
21 N2 St.Aubin-le-Cauf France
123 O2 St.Augustin Quebec Canada
36 C2 St. Augustin Germany
123 O2 St.Augustin B Quebec Canada
87 G12 St.Augustin, B.de Madagascar
21 J7 St.Augustin-des-Bois France
127 O2 St.Augustine Trinidad
113 F8 St.Augustine Florida U.S.A.
123 N2 St.Augustin R Quebec Canada
18 F7 St.Aulaye France
8 B7 St. Austell England
21 M7 St.Avertin France
19 K3 St.Avold France
123 Q2 St. Barbe Newfoundland Canada
121 S6 St.Barnabé Nord Quebec Canada
121 R6 St.Barthélémi Quebec Canada
18 G10 St.Barthélemy France
127 N5 St. Barthélemy isld Lesser Antilles
144 B6 St. Bathans New Zealand
21 P8 St.Baudel France
19 P18 Ste.Baume France
18 F10 St. Béat France
12 E5 St.Bees England
119 M6 St.Benedict Saskatchewan Canada
99 M6 St.Benedict Iowa U.S.A.
21 L8 St.Benoit Vienne France
18 F6 St.-Benoît-du-Sault France
122 B7 St.Benoit Labre Quebec Canada
21 P6 St.Benoît-sur-Loire France
122 H5 Ste.Bernadette Quebec Canada
121 T6 St.Bernard Quebec Canada
144 D5 St. Bernard mt New Zealand
40 F6 St. Bernard, Col du Gd. Switz/Italy
42 A3 St. Bernard, Petit pass Italy/France
110 J2 St.Bernice Indiana U.S.A.
19 P13 St.Beron France
21 J5 St.Berthevin France
36 C7 St.Blaise France
122 D5 Ste.Blandine Quebec Canada
8 B7 St.Blazey England
118 D1 St.Boniface Manitoba Canada
118 L8 St.Boswells Saskatchewan Canada
13 F2 St. Boswells Scotland
21 M7 St. Branchs France
123 T5 St.Brendan's Newfoundland Canada
20 F7 St.Brévin-les-Pins France
20 F4 St.Briac France
20 H5 St.Brice-en-Cogles France
118 B7 St.Bride, Mt Alberta Canada
123 S7 St.Bride's Newfoundland Canada
8 A4 St. Bride's Wales
20 E4 St.Brieuc France
20 E4 St.Brieuc,B.de France
119 N6 St.Brieux Saskatchewan Canada
20 G4 St.Broladre France
121 L5 St. Bruno de Guiques Quebec Canada
21 M6 St.Calais France
119 T9 St.Calude Manitoba Canada
122 B7 St.Camille Quebec Canada
20 E5 St.Caradec France
20 E5 St. Carreuc France
121 S6 St.Casimir Quebec Canada
20 F4 St.Cast France
121 L9 St. Catharines Ontario Canada
127 K2 St. Catherine parish Jamaica
127 P5 St.Catherine, Mt Grenada
112 F6 St.Catherines I Georgia U.S.A.
9 E6 St.Catherines Pt England
122 B8 Ste.Cécile Quebec Canada
18 G8 St. Céré France
18 G7 St.Cernin France
121 R7 St.Césaire Quebec Canada
18 H7 St.Chamond France
118 A1 St.Charles Manitoba Canada
101 O7 St.Charles Idaho U.S.A.
99 S8 St.Charles Illinois U.S.A.
94 C3 St.Charles Michigan U.S.A.
99 O6 St.Charles Minnesota U.S.A.
110 F3 St.Charles Missouri U.S.A.
21 O8 St.Chartier France
19 O13 St. Chef France
18 H8 St. Chély l'Apcher France
21 P4 St.Chéron France
18 G9 St.Chinian France
126 A1 St.Christoffel Berg mt Curaçao Neth Antilles
19 Q15 St.Christophe d'Oisans France
20 G8 St.Christophe-du-Ligneron France
21 O7 St. Christophe-en-Bazelle France
St. Christopher isld see St Kitts
121 T4 St.-Cîour-de-Marie Quebec Canada
21 H3 St.Clair France
94 E4 St.Clair Michigan U.S.A.
99 N5 St.Clair Minnesota U.S.A.
110 F3 St.Clair Missouri U.S.A.
94 E4 St. Clair, L U.S.A./Canada
120 H9 St.Clair R Ontario/Michigan Canada/U.S.A.
21 O3 St.Clair-sur-Epte France
19 J6 St.Claude France
127 N4 St.Claude Guadeloupe W Indies
8 B4 St.Clears Wales
122 C6 St.Clement Quebec Canada
21 J6 St. Clement-de-la-Place France
121 S7 Ste.Clothilde Quebec Canada
113 F9 St.Cloud Florida U.S.A.
99 M4 St.Cloud Minnesota U.S.A.
8 B7 St.Columb England
20 G7 St. Columban France
121 R6 St.Côme Quebec Canada
20 H3 St.Côme-du-Mont France
21 L5 St.Cosme-de-Vair France
122 E8 Ste. Croix New Brunswick Canada

40 D4 **Ste. Croix** Switzerland
99 O4 **St. Croix** *R* Wisconsin U.S.A.
95 T8 **St. Croix** *R* Maine/New Brunswick U.S.A./Canada
36 C7 **Ste.Croix aux Mines** France
113 L8 **St.Croix I** Virgin Is
122 C6 **St.Cyprien** Quebec Canada
18 F8 **St.Cyprien** France
19 P18 **St.Cyr** France
21 K5 **St.Cyr** Mayenne France
21 J4 **St.Cyr-du-Bailleul** France
21 K7 **St.Cyr-en-Bourg** France
21 O6 **St.Cyr-en-Val** France
121 S7 **St.Cyrille** Quebec Canada
121 P4 **St.Cyr, L** Quebec Canada
118 J4 **St. Cyr Lake** Saskatchewan Canada
21 M7 **St.-Cyr-sur-Loire** France
122 B7 **St.Damien** Quebec Canada
127 P1 **St.David** *co* Trinidad
110 F1 **St.David** Illinois U.S.A.
122 A5 **St.David-de-Falardeau** Quebec Canada
123 O5 **St. David's** Newfoundland Canada
8 A4 **St. David's** Wales
90 D1 **St.Davids I** Bermuda
22 G3 **St.Denis** Belgium
121 R7 **St.Denis** Quebec Canada
21 P4 **St. Denis** France
83 J13 **St.-Denis** Réunion Indian Oc
21 K6 **St.Denis-d'Anjou** France
21 J5 **St. Denis-de-Gastines** France
21 O8 **St.Denis-de-Jouhet** France
21 K5 **St.Denis-d'Orques** France
20 H8 **St. Denis la Chevasse** France
21 K5 **St.Denis-sur-Sarthon** France
20 F4 **St.Denoual** France
19 O16 **St.Didier** France
36 B7 **St. Dié** France
19 J4 **St.Dizier** France
20 F6 **St.Dolay** France
20 G5 **St Domineuc** France
19 N14 **St.Donat sur l'Herbasse** France
98 J8 **St.Edward** Nebraska U.S.A.
116 P7 **St.Elias, C** Alaska U.S.A.
117 D5 **St. Elias Mts** Alaska/Yukon Terr U.S.A./Canada
121 S4 **Ste.Elisabeth** Quebec Canada
127 J2 **St.Elizabeth** *parish* Jamaica
110 H2 **St.Elmo** Illinois U.S.A.
122 C5 **St.Eloi** Quebec Canada
18 G6 **St Éloy-les-Mines** France
121 R6 **Ste.Emélie** Quebec Canada
18 H8 **Ste.Enimie** France
20 H3 **Sainteny** France
21 M7 **St.Epain** France
122 B7 **St.Ephrem** Quebec Canada
121 L3 **St.Ephrem de Paradis** Quebec Canada
122 C6 **St.-Epiphane** Quebec Canada
20 G5 **St.Erblon** France
22 F5 **St.Erme-Outre-et-Ramecourt** France
18 E7 **Saintes** France
127 L4 **St. Ésprit, Le** Martinique W Indies
22 B2 **St.Étienne-au-Mont** France
18 E9 **St. Étienne de Baïgorry** France
20 G7 **St.Étienne-de-Montluc** France
19 O14 **St.Étienne de St.Geoirs** France
21 N3 **St.Étienne-du-Rouvray** France
121 M4 **St. Eugène** Quebec Canada
121 S4 **St.-Eugène** Quebec Canada
122 D6 **St.Eusèbe** Quebec Canada
121 R7 **St.Eustache** Quebec Canada
127 N6 **Sint Eustatius** *isld* Lesser Antilles
21 L4 **St.Evroult Notre Dame-du-Bois** France
122 D5 **St.Fabien** Quebec Canada
122 B7 **Ste.Familie** Quebec Canada
121 P6 **Ste.Famille d'Aumond** Quebec Canada
18 H5 **St.Fargeau** France
121 S4 **St.Félicien** Quebec Canada
122 E5 **Ste.Félicité** Quebec Canada
121 R6 **St. Félix de Valois** Quebec Canada
12 D1 **St.Fillans** Scotland
14 A5 **St. Finan's B** Ireland
123 O5 **St.Fintan's** Newfoundland Canada
19 Q15 **St. Firmin** France
20 G8 **Ste. Flaive-des-Loups** France
121 T6 **St.Flavien** Quebec Canada
122 E5 **Ste.Florence** Quebec Canada
20 H8 **St.Florent-des-Bois** France
18 H4 **St.Florentin** France
21 H7 **St.Florent-le-Vieil** France
21 P8 **St.Florent-sur-Cher** France
18 H7 **St.Flour** France
21 N8 **St.Flovier** France
121 T7 **St.Fortunat** Quebec Canada
19 N15 **St.Fortunat** France
121 T6 **Ste. Foy** Quebec Canada
18 F8 **Ste.Foy-la-Grande** France
107 J2 **St.Francis** Kansas U.S.A.
110 F5 **St. Francis** *R* Missouri/Ark U.S.A.
95 R6 **St. Francis** *R* Maine/New Brunswick U.S.A./Canada
89 D10 **St. Francis B** S Africa
123 U6 **St.Francis, C** Newfoundland Canada
89 D10 **St. Francis C** S Africa
138 C4 **St.Francis, I.of** South Australia Australia
110 J3 **St. Francisville** Illinois U.S.A.
111 E11 **St.Francisville** Louisiana U.S.A.
121 S7 **St. François** *R* Quebec Canada
127 N4 **St.François** Guadeloupe W Indies
121 T7 **St. François, L** Quebec Canada
110 F4 **St. Francois Mts** Missouri U.S.A.
121 S7 **St.François Xavier** Quebec Canada
95 S7 **St.Froid L** Maine U.S.A.
21 H8 **St.Fulgent** France
111 E11 **St.Gabriel** Louisiana U.S.A.
121 R6 **St.Gabriel de Brandon** Quebec Canada
122 H5 **St.Gabriel de Gaspé** Quebec Canada
41 K3 **St. Gallen** Switzerland
21 L4 **Ste.Gauburge-Ste.Colombe** France
18 F9 **St.Gaudens** France
21 N8 **St.Gaultier** France
122 B8 **St.Gédéon** Quebec Canada
21 N8 **Ste.Gemme** France
21 P3 **Ste. Geneviève** Oise France
110 F4 **Ste.Genevieve** Missouri U.S.A.
123 P2 **St.Genevieve B** Quebec Canada
18 G8 **St.Geniez** France
21 N8 **St.Genou** France
19 P14 **St Geoire-en-Valdaine** France
141 G3 **St. George** *R* Queensland Australia
141 J8 **St.George** Queensland Australia
127 P6 **St.George** *parish* Barbados
90 C1 **St.George** Bermuda
122 F8 **St.George** New Brunswick Canada
127 O2 **St.George** *co* Trinidad
113 E7 **St.George** Georgia U.S.A.
112 G4 **St.George** South Carolina U.S.A.
103 L4 **St.George** Utah U.S.A.
123 N5 **St.George, C** Newfoundland Canada
139 K6 **St.George Hd** New South Wales Australia
116 D8 **St. George I** Pribilof Is Bering Sea
113 C8 **St.George I** Florida U.S.A.
41 H1 **St.Georgen** Germany
100 A8 **St.George, Pt** California U.S.A.
142 E4 **St.George Ra** W Australia Australia
123 O5 **St.George's** Newfoundland Canada
122 B7 **St.Georges** Quebec Canada
36 B6 **St.Georges** France
129 H3 **St.Georges** Fr Guiana
127 P5 **St.George's** Grenada
123 N5 **St.George's B** Newfoundland Canada
125 P9 **St. Georges Cay** *isld* Belize
7 F11 **St Georges Chan** U.K.
137 L2 **St.George's Channel** Bismarck Arch
14 E5 **St. Georges Channel** Ireland/U.K.
69 A9 **St.George's Channel** Nicobar Is
20 H8 **St.Georges-de-Montaigu** France
20 H4 **St.Georges-de-Reintembault** France
21 M3 **St.Georges-du-Mesnil** France
21 M3 **St. Georges du-Vièvre** France
90 C1 **St.George's I** Bermuda
21 L8 **St.Georges-les-Baillargeaux** France
21 N4 **St.Georges-Motel** Eure France
21 N5 **St.Georges-sur-Eure** France
21 O7 **St.Georges-sur-la Prée** France
21 J7 **St.Georges-sur-Loire** France
22 H3 **St.Gérard** Belgium
121 M4 **St. Gerard-Centre** Quebec Canada
19 N13 **St. Germain au Mt D'Or** France
21 J5 **St.Germain-d'Anxure** France
19 P12 **St. Germain-de-Joux** France
21 M5 **St.Germain-de-la-Coudre** France
18 H6 **St.Germain-des-Fosses** France
19 J6 **St.Germain du Bois** France
122 B7 **Ste.Germaine** Quebec Canada
21 P4 **St. Germain-en-Laye** France
20 G3 **St. Germain, Hâvre de** France
21 L3 **St.Germain-la-Campagne** France
18 G7 **St.Germain-les-Belles** France
20 G3 **St.Germain-sur-Ay** France
8 B7 **St.Germans** England
21 O3 **St. Germer-de-Fly** France
41 N5 **St. Gertrude** Italy
20 G8 **St.Gervais** Vendée France
40 E6 **St. Gervais-les-Bains** France
21 L8 **St. Gervais-les-Trois-Clochers** France
22 F3 **St.Ghislain** Belgium
20 E6 **St.Gildas-de-Rhuis** France
20 F6 **St.Gildas-des-Bois** France
20 F7 **St.Gildas,Pte.de** France
121 T6 **St.-Giles** Quebec Canada
127 N1 **St. Giles Is** Tobago
20 G8 **St. Gilles-Croix-de-Vie** France
20 D5 **St.Gilles-Pligeaux** France
22 G1 **St. Gillis-bij-Dendermonde** Belgium
22 G1 **St.Gillis-Waas** Belgium
18 F10 **St.Girons** France
27 F12 **St.Gla** *L* Sweden
36 D3 **St.Goar** Germany
20 C5 **St.Goazec** France
22 E4 **St.Gobain** France
122 G5 **St.Godefroi** Quebec Canada
41 J4 **St.Gotthard** *pass* Switzerland
8 B4 **St.Govan's Hd** Wales
119 N6 **St.Gregor** Saskatchewan Canada
123 O4 **St.Gregory, Mt** Newfoundland Canada
20 B6 **St.Guénolé** France
121 S7 **St. Guillaume** Quebec Canada
19 Q15 **St. Guillaume, Mt** France
94 C2 **St.Helen** Michigan U.S.A.
90 B14 **St. Helena** *isld* Atlantic Oc
102 B3 **St.Helena** California U.S.A.
89 A9 **St.Helena B** S Africa
90 H10 **St Helena Fracture** Atlantic Oc
94 B1 **St.Helena I** Michigan U.S.A.
112 G5 **St.Helena Sd** South Carolina U.S.A.
122 B6 **Ste.Hélène** Quebec Canada
18 E8 **Ste.Hélène** France
139 J8 **St.Helens** Tasmania Australia
13 F6 **St.Helens** England
100 C4 **St.Helens** Oregon U.S.A.
100 C3 **St.Helens, Mt** Washington U.S.A.
139 J8 **St.Helens Pt** Tasmania Australia
122 H4 **St.Helier** Quebec Canada
20 F3 **St Hélier** Channel Is
121 U6 **Ste.Hénédine** Quebec Canada
121 T6 **St.Henri** Quebec Canada
20 G7 **St.-Herblain** France
121 T7 **St.Herménégilde** Quebec Canada
21 H8 **Ste.Hermine** France
18 G9 **St.Hilaire** France
98 K1 **St.Hilaire** Minnesota U.S.A.
20 G7 **St. Hilaire-de-Chaléons** France
20 H7 **St. Hilaire-de-Loulay** France
20 G8 **St. Hilaire-de-Riez** France
21 H4 **St. Hilaire-du-Harcouet** France
21 K7 **St. Hilaire St. Florent** France
21 O6 **St.Hilaire-St.Mesmin** France
140 D6 **Sainthill,Mt** N Terr Australia
19 K5 **St.Hippolyte** Doubs France
21 N7 **St.Hippolyte** Indre-et-Loire France
18 H9 **St.Hippolyte du Fort** France
122 A5 **St.Honoré** Quebec Canada
122 C6 **St.Honoré** Quebec Canada
21 J3 **Ste.Honorine** France
21 K3 **Ste.Honorine-du-Fay** France
22 J3 **St.Hubert** Belgium
25 F6 **St.Hubert** Germany
29 K5 **St Ibb** Sweden
94 C1 **St.Ignace** Michigan U.S.A.
121 R6 **St.Ignace du Lac** Quebec Canada
120 C4 **St. Ignace, Isle** Ontario Canada
101 L2 **St.Ignatius** Montana U.S.A.
40 E3 **St.Imier** Switzerland
36 C5 **St.Ingbert** Germany
122 B6 **St.Irénée** Quebec Canada
121 L5 **St.Isidore** Quebec Canada
121 T7 **St.Isidore** Quebec Canada
26 K3 **St.Istind** *mt* Norway
8 A7 **St.Ives** England
9 F3 **St.Ives** England
20 C6 **St.Ivy** France
25 E2 **St. Jacobiparochie** Netherlands
122 D6 **St.Jacques** New Brunswick Canada
20 G5 **St.Jacques-de-la-Lande** France
38 F8 **St.Jakob** Austria
118 A1 **St.James** Manitoba Canada
20 H4 **St.James** France
127 J2 **St.James** *parish* Jamaica
99 V4 **St.James** Michigan U.S.A.
99 M5 **St.James** Minnesota U.S.A.
110 E3 **St.James** Missouri U.S.A.
117 H10 **St.James, C** British Columbia Canada
113 E11 **St.James City** Florida U.S.A.
22 D2 **Sint Jan** Belgium
121 L4 **St.Janvier** Quebec Canada
121 R7 **St.Jean** Quebec Canada
21 K5 **St.Jean** France
119 U9 **St.Jean Baptiste** Manitoba Canada
121 S5 **St.Jean Bosco** Quebec Canada
20 E6 **St.Jean-Brévelay** France
18 E7 **St.-Jean-d'Angély** France
21 L5 **St.Jean-d'Asse** France
19 O13 **St.Jean-de-Bournay** France
21 O6 **St.-Jean-de-Braye** France
21 H3 **St.Jean-de-Daye** France
122 C5 **St.Jean de Dieu** Quebec Canada
21 O6 **St.-Jean-de-la-Ruelle** France
19 J5 **St.Jean de Losne** France
18 D9 **St.Jean-de-Luz** France
121 R6 **St. Jean-de-Matha** Quebec Canada
19 Q14 **St.Jean-de-Maurienne** France
20 F8 **St.Jean-de-Monts** France
21 L8 **St.Jean-de-Sauves** France
18 H8 **St.Jean du Gard** France
19 O14 **St.Jean-en-Royans** France
121 S4 **Saint-Jean, Lac** Quebec Canada
20 G4 **St.Jean-le-Thomas** France
18 E9 **St.Jean Pied de Port** France
122 B6 **St.Jean Port Joli** Quebec Canada
122 H3 **St.Jean, R** Quebec Canada
36 B5 **St.Jean Rohrbach** France
20 H5 **St.Jean-sur-Couesnon** France
121 Q7 **St.Jérôme** Quebec Canada
19 N14 **St. Jeure D'Ay** France
109 K2 **St.Jo** Texas U.S.A.
122 B6 **St.Joachim** Quebec Canada
20 F7 **St.Joachim** France
41 O3 **St.Jodok** Austria
110 D5 **St.Joe** Arkansas U.S.A.
100 J2 **St.Joe** Idaho U.S.A.
94 C5 **St.Joe** Indiana U.S.A.
36 E4 **St.Johann** Germany
38 G8 **St. Johann-im-Walde** Austria
127 P6 **St.John** *parish* Barbados
122 F8 **St.John** New Brunswick Canada
107 M3 **St.John** Kansas U.S.A.
95 R7 **St. John** *R* Maine U.S.A.
119 S10 **St.John** North Dakota U.S.A.
103 M1 **St.John** Utah U.S.A.
100 H2 **St.John** Washington U.S.A.
123 P3 **St John B** Newfoundland Canada
123 R3 **St.John, C** Newfoundland Canada
113 L7 **St.John I** Virgin Is
123 S5 **St.John, L** Newfoundland Canada
122 E7 **St. John R** New Brunswick Canada
122 G5 **St. John R** Quebec Canada
123 T6 **St. John's** Newfoundland Canada
103 P7 **St.Johns** Arizona U.S.A.
94 C3 **St.Johns** Michigan U.S.A.
127 P4 **St.John's** Antigua W Indies
95 P2 **St.Johnsbury** Vermont U.S.A.
13 F4 **St.John's Chapel** England
14 C2 **St.John's Pt** Ireland
113 F7 **St.Johns R** Florida U.S.A.
95 N3 **St.Johnsville** New York U.S.A.
20 H3 **St.Jores** France
22 H2 **St.Joris-Winge** Belgium
127 P6 **St.Joseph** *parish* Barbados
121 U6 **St.Joseph** Quebec Canada
83 K14 **St.Joseph** Réunion Indian Oc
127 P2 **St.Joseph** Mayoro Trinidad
127 O2 **St.Joseph** St George Trinidad
111 E10 **St.Joseph** Louisiana U.S.A.
94 A5 **St. Joseph** *R* Michigan U.S.A.
99 U7 **St.Joseph** Michigan U.S.A.
99 M10 **St.Joseph** Missouri U.S.A.
127 L4 **St.Joseph** Martinique W Indies
113 B8 **St. Joseph Bay** Florida U.S.A.
120 G6 **St. Joseph I** Ontario Canada
109 L8 **St. Joseph I** Texas U.S.A.
115 K7 **St. Joseph, L** Ontario Canada
123 T6 **St.Joseph's** Newfoundland Canada
22 B3 **St.Josse** France
20 F5 **St. Jouan-de-l'Isle** France
20 G4 **St Jouan-des-Guerets** France
21 L2 **St.Jouin** France
21 K8 **St.Jouin-de-Marnes** France
121 Q6 **St. Jovite** Quebec Canada
126 A1 **St. Jozefsdal** Curaçao Neth Antilles
19 N14 **St.Julian Molin-Molette** France
40 D5 **St.Julien** France
20 E5 **St.Julien** Côtes d'Armor France
20 H7 **St.Julien-de-Concelles** France
20 G8 **St. Julien-des-Landes** France
20 H6 **St.Julien-de-Vouvantes** France
19 O15 **St.Julien en Quint** France
21 L8 **St.Julien-l'Ars** France
21 L3 **St.Julien-le-Faucon** France
18 F7 **St.Junien** France
9 F7 **St.Just** England
21 P2 **St.Just-en-Chaussée** France
18 H7 **St.Just-en-Chevalet** France
38 M7 **St.Katherein** Austria
15 A1 **St. Kilda** *isld* Scotland
127 P4 **St.Kitts** *isld* Lesser Antilles
127 P4 **St. Kitts-Nevis** *islds* West Indies
126 A1 **St.Kruis** Curaçao Neth Antilles
121 T6 **St.Lambert** Quebec Canada
121 R7 **St.Lambert** Quebec Canada
142 G2 **St.Lambert,C** W Australia Australia
21 K7 **St. Lambert des Levées** France
21 J7 **St.Lambert-du-Lattay** France
111 D11 **St.Landry** Louisiana U.S.A.
119 U8 **St.Laurent** Manitoba Canada
121 L4 **Saint-Laurent** Quebec Canada
19 J6 **St. Laurent** France
129 H2 **St.Laurent** Fr Guiana
18 G10 **St.Laurent de la Salanque** France
19 O13 **St.Laurent-de-Mûre** France
21 H7 **St. Laurent-des-Autels** France
21 O6 **St.Laurent-des-Eaux** France
19 P14 **St.Laurent-du-Pont** France
21 M2 **St.Laurent-en-Caux** France
21 M6 **St.Laurent-en-Gâtines** France
18 E7 **St.Laurent-et-Benon** France
121 U5 **St.Laurent, R** Quebec Canada
21 J3 **St.Laurent-sur-Mer** France
22 K5 **St.Laurent-sur-Othain** France
21 J8 **St. Laurent-sur-Sèvre** France
141 J5 **St.Lawrence** Queensland Australia
123 R7 **St.Lawrence** Newfoundland Canada
95 M2 **St. Lawrence** *R* Canada/U.S.A.
122 K5 **St.Lawrence, G.of** Canada
116 B5 **St.Lawrence I** Bering Sea
121 O8 **St. Lawrence I Nat. Park** Ontario Canada
121 P8 **St.Lawrence Seaway** Canada/U.S.A.
119 Q8 **St.Lazare** Manitoba Canada
22 K4 **St.Léger** Belgium
21 O4 **St.Léger-en-Yvelines** France
22 H1 **St.Lenaarts** Belgium
122 E5 **St.Léon** Quebec Canada
122 E6 **St.-Léonard** New Brunswick Canada
121 S6 **St.Léonard** Quebec Canada
36 B7 **St. Léonard** France
18 G7 **St.-Léonard-de-Noblat** France
9 G6 **St.Leonards** England
121 T4 **St.-Léon-de-Chicoutimi** Quebec Canada
122 B7 **St.Léon de Standon** Quebec Canada
38 L8 **St.Leonhard** Kärnten Austria
38 N4 **St.Leonhard** Nieder Österreich Austria
123 Q1 **St.Lewis R** Labrador, Nfld Canada
121 S7 **St.Liboire** Quebec Canada
18 F8 **Ste. Livrade** France
21 P7 **Ste.Lizaigne** France
18 F9 **St.Lizier** France
21 H3 **St.Lô** France
122 H7 **St.Louis** Prince Edward I Canada
119 M6 **St.Louis** Saskatchewan Canada
83 J14 **St.Louis** Réunion Indian Oc
85 A5 **St.Louis** Mauritania
94 C3 **St.Louis** Michigan U.S.A.
99 O2 **St. Louis** *R* Minnesota U.S.A.
105 **St.Louis** *conurbation* Missouri U.S.A.
127 N4 **St.Louis** Marie Galante W Indies
122 H7 **St.Louis de Kent** New Brunswick Canada
122 D6 **St.Louis du Ha Ha** Quebec Canada
126 H5 **St.Louis du Sud** Haiti
122 B6 **Ste.Louise** Quebec Canada
121 R7 **St.Louis, L** Quebec Canada
36 C5 **St. Louis-lès-Bitche** France
94 E6 **St.Louisville** Ohio U.S.A.
21 K8 **St. Loup-Lamaire** France
40 D2 **St. Loup-sur-Semoise** France
21 N4 **St.Lubin-des-Joncherets** France
127 L4 **Ste.Luce** Martinique W Indies
141 K2 **St.Lucia** *dist* Brisbane, Qnsld Australia
127 O8 **St. Lucia** *isld* Lesser Antilles
87 F11 **St. Lucia, C** S Africa
121 Q6 **Ste.Lucie** Quebec Canada
113 G10 **St. Lucie Canal** Florida U.S.A.
127 P6 **St.Lucy** *parish* Barbados
122 B8 **St.Ludger** Quebec Canada
127 H5 **St.Luis du Nord** Haiti
123 R2 **St Lunaire** Newfoundland Canada
20 F4 **St.Lunaire** France
20 F7 **St.Lyphard** France
127 N5 **Sint Maarten** *isld* Lesser Antilles
25 B5 **St.Maartens-dijk** Netherlands
18 E8 **St. Macaire** Gironde France
21 J7 **St. Macaire-en-Mauges** France
15 G2 **St.Magnus B** Scotland
122 B7 **St.Malachie** Quebec Canada
20 F4 **St.Malo** France
20 G3 **St.Malo-de-la-Lande** France
20 F4 **St.Malo,G.de** France
20 F5 **St.Malon-sur-Mel** France
19 P18 **St.Mandrier** France
20 B5 **St.Marc** Finistère France
20 F7 **St.Marc** Loire-Inférieure France
127 H5 **St.Marc** Haiti
121 S6 **St.Marc des Carrières** Quebec Canada
122 B7 **St.Marcel** Quebec Canada
21 O8 **St.Marcel** Indre France
19 O14 **St.Marcellin** France
21 H3 **St.Marcouf,Is** France
20 H5 **St.Marc-sur-Couesnon** France
22 K4 **St.Mard** Belgium
123 P2 **St.Margaret B** Newfoundland Canada
122 J9 **St.Margaret B** Nova Scotia Canada
38 K8 **St.Margarethen** Austria
32 K5 **St.Margarethen** Germany
9 H5 **St. Margaret's at Cliffe** England
15 F2 **St.Margarets Hope** Scotland
20 F7 **Ste.Marguerite** France
122 F3 **Ste.Marguerite, R** Quebec Canada
122 B5 **Ste.Marguerite, R** Quebec Canada
121 T6 **Ste.Marie** Quebec Canada
83 K13 **Ste.Marie** Réunion Indian Oc
110 H3 **Ste.Marie** Illinois U.S.A.
127 L4 **Ste.Marie** Martinique W Indies
19 K4 **Ste.Marie aux Mines** France
36 C7 **Ste. Marie, Col de** *pass* France
20 H3 **Ste.Marie-du-Mont** France
19 Q17 **St Marie Mourre de Chanier** *mt* France
100 J2 **St.Maries** Idaho U.S.A.
113 C7 **St.Marks** Florida U.S.A.
21 L6 **St. Mars-d'Outille** France
20 H7 **St.Mars-du-Désert** France
21 L5 **St.Mars-la-Brière** France
21 H6 **St.Mars-la-Jaille** France
21 H5 **St.Mars-sur-la-Futaie** France
122 F4 **Ste.Marthe de Gaspé** Quebec Canada
18 E6 **St.Martin** France
19 P17 **St.-Martin** France
20 F6 **St.Martin** Morbihan France
127 N5 **St.Martin** *isld* Lesser Antilles
22 B2 **St.Martin-Boulogne** France
89 A9 **St.Martin, C** S Africa
127 L4 **St. Martin, C** Martinique W Indies
21 O4 **St.Martin-de-Bretencourt** France
19 N17 **St.Martin-de-Crau** France
21 H4 **St.Martin-de-Landelle** France
21 J3 **St.Martin-des-Besaces** France
21 H8 **St.Martin-des-Noyers** France
16 E4 **St.Martín de Valdeiglesias** Spain
19 P14 **St.-Martin-d'Heres** France
19 P12 **St.Martin-du-Fresne** France
19 O12 **St.Martin-du-Mont** France
40 B4 **St.Martin en Bresse** France
21 N2 **St.Martin-en-Campagne** France
99 U4 **St.Martin I** Michigan U.S.A.
119 T7 **St. Martin, L** Manitoba Canada
21 M7 **St. Martin-le-Beau** France
122 G8 **St. Martin's** New Brunswick Canada
9 F7 **St. Martin's** *isld* Isles of Scilly England
68 A2 **St.Martin's I** Burma
20 E3 **St.Martin's Pt** Channel Is
119 T7 **St. Martin Station** Manitoba Canada
111 E11 **St.Martinville** Louisiana U.S.A.
20 F3 **St.Mary** Channel Is
127 L2 **St.Mary** *parish* Jamaica
101 M1 **St. Mary** *R* Montana/Alberta U.S.A./Canada
123 N3 **St. Mary Is** Quebec Canada
101 M1 **St.Mary L** Montana U.S.A.
117 P11 **St. Mary, Mt** British Columbia Canada
144 B6 **St. Mary, Mt** New Zealand
123 N3 **St.Mary Reefs** Quebec Canada
118 D9 **St.Mary Res** Alberta Canada
139 J8 **St.Marys** Tasmania Australia
123 T7 **St.Marys** Newfoundland Canada
9 F7 **St.Mary's** *isld* Isles of Scilly England
15 F2 **St. Marys** Scotland
127 O3 **St. Mary's** Trinidad
116 F5 **St. Marys** Alaska U.S.A.
113 F7 **St. Marys** Georgia U.S.A.
94 B6 **St. Marys** *R* Indiana U.S.A.
107 O2 **St Marys** Kansas U.S.A.
110 G4 **St.Marys** Missouri U.S.A.
94 C6 **St.Marys** Ohio U.S.A.
94 J5 **St.Marys** Pennsylvania U.S.A.
94 F7 **St.Marys** West Virginia U.S.A.
123 T7 **St.Mary's B** Newfoundland Canada
122 F9 **St.Mary's B** Nova Scotia Canada
95 L8 **St. Marys City** Maryland U.S.A.
89 H6 **St.Mary's Hill** S Africa
15 E5 **St. Marys Loch** Scotland
123 K8 **St.Mary's, R** Nova Scotia Canada
113 F7 **St.Marys R** Florida/Georgia U.S.A.
112 G4 **St. Mathews** South Carolina U.S.A.
121 M4 **St.Mathieu** Quebec Canada
20 A5 **St.Mathieu,Pte de** France
20 G8 **St.Mathurin** France
116 C6 **St.Matthew I** Bering Sea
136 K2 **St. Matthias Group** *islds* Bismarck Arch
21 M7 **Ste.Maure-de-Touraine** France
40 E2 **St.Maurice** France
21 K7 **St. Maurice la Fougereuse** Deux Sèvres France
21 M4 **St. Maurice-les-Charencey** France
8 A7 **St. Mawes** England
122 B7 **St. Maxime** Quebec Canada
19 P18 **St.Maximin** France
20 D5 **St.Mayeux** France
22 J4 **St. Médard** Belgium
18 E8 **St Medard en Jalles** France
20 F5 **St.Meen** France
110 K3 **St.Meinrad** Indiana U.S.A.
8 C4 **St.Mellons** Wales
20 G4 **St.Méloir-des-Ondes** France
19 J3 **St. Menehould** France
22 H4 **St.Menges** France
20 H3 **Ste.Mère-Église** France
21 J8 **St.Mesmin** Vendée France
127 P6 **St.Michael** *parish* Barbados
98 H8 **St.Michael** Nebraska U.S.A.
32 K5 **St.Michaelisdonn** Germany
103 P6 **St.Michaels** Arizona U.S.A.
95 L8 **St.Michaels** Maryland U.S.A.
22 G4 **St.Michel** Aisne France
21 H6 **St.Michel** Maine-et-Loire France
20 F7 **St.Michel-Chef-Chef** France
127 H5 **St.Michel de L'Atalaye** Haiti
121 R6 **St.Michel des Saints** Quebec Canada
21 J8 **St.Michel-Mont Mercure** France
20 C5 **St.Michel,Mt** Finistère France
20 C5 **St.Michel,Res.de** France
36 B7 **St.Michel-sur-Meurthe** France
126 B1 **St.Michiel** Curaçao Neth Antilles
19 J4 **St Mihiel** France
22 C2 **St.Momelin** France
13 F1 **St.Monance** Scotland
41 L5 **St.Moritz** Switzerland
20 F7 **St.Nazaire** Loire-Atlantique France
19 O14 **St.Nazaire-en-Royans** France
9 F3 **St.Neots** England
20 B5 **St.Nic** France
126 A2 **Sint Nicolaas** Aruba W Indies
St.Nicolas *see* **St.Niklaas**
21 N2 **St.Nicolas-d'Aliermont** France
20 F6 **St.Nicolas-de-Redon** France
20 D5 **St.Nicolas-du-Pélem** France
22 G1 **St.Niklaas** Belgium
21 P4 **St.-Nom-la-Bretêche** France
119 U9 **St.Norbert** Manitoba Canada
25 F6 **St. Odiliënberg** Netherlands
25 D5 **St.Oedenrode** Netherlands
122 F5 **St.Omer** Quebec Canada
22 C2 **St.Omer** France
145 D4 **St. Omer** New Zealand
21 P2 **St.-Omer-en-Chaussée** France
18 E7 **Saintonge** *prov* France
98 C5 **St.Onge** South Dakota U.S.A.
20 H4 **St.Osvin** France
21 P4 **St.-Ouen** France
21 J5 **St.Ouen-des-Toits** France
21 P3 **St.Ouen-l'Aumône** France
121 R7 **St.Ours** Quebec Canada
122 C6 **St.Pacôme** Quebec Canada
20 G4 **St.Pair** France
18 E9 **St.Palais** France
122 C7 **St.Pamphile** Quebec Canada
18 F7 **St.Pardoux la Rivière** France
94 D6 **St.Paris** Ohio U.S.A.
122 C6 **St.Pascal** Quebec Canada
21 L6 **St. Paterne** Indre-et-Loire France
21 L5 **St. Paterne** Sarthe France
121 N6 **St.Patrice, L-** Quebec Canada
127 O3 **St.Patrick** *co* Trinidad
38 L8 **St.Paul** Austria
118 F4 **St.Paul** Alberta Canada
18 E9 **St.Paul** France
85 C7 **St. Paul** *R* Guinea/Liberia
83 J13 **St.Paul** Réunion Indian Oc
110 C6 **St.Paul** Arkansas U.S.A.
94 B7 **St.Paul** Indiana U.S.A.
107 P4 **St.Paul** Kansas U.S.A.
99 N4 **St.Paul** Minnesota U.S.A.
98 H8 **St.Paul** Nebraska U.S.A.
112 G4 **St.Paul** South Carolina U.S.A.
94 E10 **St.Paul** Virginia U.S.A.
18 G10 **St. Paul de Fenouillet** France
122 C6 **St.-Paul-de-la-Croix** Quebec Canada
122 B7 **St.Paul de Montriny** Quebec Canada
122 C5 **St.Paul du Nord** Quebec Canada
116 D8 **St. Paul I** Pribilof Is Bering Sea
123 M6 **St.Paul I** C Breton I, Nova Scotia
81 E9 **St. Paul, Î** Indian Oc
18 H7 **St.Paulien** France
121 R6 **St.Paulin** Quebec Canada
19 P17 **St.Paul-les-Durance** France
123 P2 **St.Paul R** Quebec Canada
90 G8 **St.Paul Rocks** Atlantic Oc
112 H3 **St.Pauls** North Carolina U.S.A.
127 P4 **St.Pauls** St Kitts W Indies
123 P4 **St.Paul's Inlet** Newfoundland Canada
19 N16 **St Paul-Trois-Châteaux** France
20 G7 **St. Pazanne** France
18 E9 **St.Pé de B** France
21 O5 **St. Peravy-la-Colombe** France
20 F7 **St. Père-en-Retz** France
122 C6 **Ste.Perpétue** Quebec Canada
32 J4 **Sankt Peter** Germany
110 H3 **St.Peter** Illinois U.S.A.
38 K7 **St.Peter-am-Kammersberg** Austria
123 R1 **St.Peter B** Labrador, Nfld Canada
32 J4 **St Peter-Ording** Germany
20 E3 **St. Peter Port** Channel Is
122 H5 **St.Peter, Pt** Quebec Canada
122 K7 **St.Peters** Prince Edward I Canada
123 M8 **St.Peters** C Breton I, Nova Scotia
St.Petersburg *see* **Sankt-Peterburg**
113 E10 **St.Petersburg** Florida U.S.A.
69 J12 **St.Petrus** *isld* Indonesia
20 G8 **St. Philbert-de-Bouaine** France
20 G7 **St. Philbert-de-Grandlieu** France
122 B7 **St.Philémon** Quebec Canada
127 P6 **St. Philip** *parish* Barbados
25 B5 **St.Philipsland** Netherlands
121 S7 **St.Pie** Quebec Canada
123 Q7 **St. Pierre** St. Pierre I Atlantic Oc
119 V9 **St.Pierre** Manitoba Canada
20 D6 **St. Pierre** Morbihan France
83 J14 **St.Pierre** Réunion Indian Oc
127 L4 **St.Pierre** Martinique W Indies
123 Q7 **St. Pierre and Miquelon** *islds* Atlantic Oc
19 Q13 **St Pierre d'Albigny** France
21 N3 **St. Pierre-d'Autils** France
21 M8 **St. Pierre-de-Maillé** France
20 G5 **St. Pierre-de-Plesguen** France
21 M7 **St.-Pierre-des-Corps** France
21 J8 **St. Pierre-des-Echaubrognes** France
21 K5 **St. Pierre-des-Nids** France
21 J8 **St. Pierre-du-Chemin** France
21 N3 **St. Pierre-du-Vauvray** France
20 H2 **St. Pierre-Église** France
21 L2 **St. Pierre-en-Port** France
123 Q7 **St. Pierre, I** Atlantic Oc
81 C6 **St. Pierre I** Indian Oc
121 S6 **St.Pierre, L** Quebec Canada
21 H5 **St. Pierre-la-Cour** France
20 H4 **St. Pierre-Langers** France
18 H6 **St. Pierre le Môutier** France
21 N3 **St. Pierre-lès-Elbeuf** France
20 A5 **St. Pierre-Quilbignon** France
21 K3 **St. Pierre-sur-Dives** France
21 K5 **St. Pierre-sur-Orthe** France
21 H4 **St. Pois** France
21 H6 **St. Poix** France
22 C1 **St.Pol** France
22 C3 **St.Pol** France
20 C4 **St. Pol-de-Leon** France
38 N5 **St.Pölten** Austria
19 K6 **St.Pon, L.de** France
18 G9 **St Pons** France
18 H6 **St.Pourcain-sur-Sioule** France
121 S4 **St.-Prime** Quebec Canada
21 J8 **St. Prouant** France
20 E4 **St. Quay-Portrieux** France
122 E6 **St.Quentin** New Brunswick Canada
22 E4 **St.Quentin** Aisne France
21 J6 **St.-Quentin** Maine-et-Loire France
21 P4 **St. Quentin-en-Yvelines** France
22 B3 **St.Quentin, Pte.de** France
36 C6 **St.Quirin** France
18 H7 **St.Rambert** France
122 B7 **St.Raphaël** Quebec Canada
121 T6 **St.Raymond** Quebec Canada
101 L2 **St.Regis** Montana U.S.A.
95 N2 **St. Regis Falls** New York U.S.A.
121 R7 **St.Rémi** Quebec Canada
19 N17 **St. Rémy** Bouches du Rhône France
21 K4 **St. Rémy** Calvados France
21 L5 **St. Rémy-des-Monts** France
20 G5 **St Remy du Plain** France
21 L5 **St. Rémy-du-Plain** France
21 N4 **St. Rémy-sur-Avre** France
18 H7 **St. Rémy-sur-Durolle** France
20 A5 **St. Renan** France
40 F6 **St.Rhémy** Italy
19 J6 **St. Rigaud, Mt** France
21 O1 **St. Riquier** France
121 R7 **St.Robert** Quebec Canada
122 A8 **St.Romain** Quebec Canada
21 L2 **St. Romain-de-Colbosc** France
21 N7 **St. Romain-sur-Cher** France
121 T6 **St.Romuald** Quebec Canada
141 G4 **St. Ronans** Queensland Australia
121 R7 **Ste.Rose** Quebec Canada
127 N4 **Ste.Rose** Guadeloupe W Indies
119 S7 **Ste.Rose de Lac** Manitoba Canada
122 D6 **Ste.Rose du Dégelé** Quebec Canada
38 N7 **St.Ruprecht-an-der-Raab** Austria
21 N2 **St. Saëns** France
20 E3 **St. Sampson** Channel Is
20 E5 **St. Samson** France
21 P8 **St. Saturnin** France
19 O17 **St.Saturnin d'Apt** France
19 N17 **St Saturnin-lès-Avig-non** France
21 P2 **St. Sauflieu** France
121 Q7 **St.Sauveur** Quebec Canada
19 O16 **St. Sauveur** France
20 B5 **St. Sauveur** Finistère France
21 K4 **St. Sauveur** Orne France
20 H3 **St. Sauveur-Lendelin** France
20 G3 **St. Sauveur-le-Vicomte** France
21 N4 **St. Sauveur-Marville** Eure France
18 E7 **St.Savin** France
21 M8 **St. Savin** Vienne France
21 L4 **Ste. Scolasse** France
20 B5 **St. Segal** France
18 G9 **St.Sernin-sur-Rance** France
20 F4 **St. Servan** France
18 E9 **St.Sever** France
21 H4 **St. Sever-Calvados** France
21 P8 **Ste. Sévère-sur-Indre** Indre France
123 T7 **St.Shott's** Newfoundland Canada
122 C5 **St.Simon** Quebec Canada
22 E4 **St.Simon** France
112 F6 **St. Simons** Georgia U.S.A.
26 J4 **St. Sjöfallets Nat. Park** Sweden
122 E8 **St.Stephen** New Brunswick Canada
112 H4 **St.Stephen** South Carolina U.S.A.
101 R7 **St.Stephens** Wyoming U.S.A.
18 G9 **St.Sulpice** France
21 M4 **St. Sulpice** Orne France
20 G6 **St. Sulpice-des-Landes** France
18 F6 **St. Sulpice Laurière** France
21 K5 **Ste. Suzanne** France
83 K13 **Ste.Suzanne** Réunion Indian Oc
21 K3 **St. Sylvain** France
121 T6 **St.-Sylvestre** Quebec Canada
18 E8 **St.Symphorien** France
117 F6 **St. Terese** Alaska U.S.A.
122 E5 **St.Tharsicius** Quebec Canada
121 S6 **Ste.Thècle** Quebec Canada
20 C4 **St. Thégonnec** France
122 B8 **St. Théophile** Quebec Canada
121 R7 **Ste.Thérèse** Quebec Canada
117 N3 **Ste. Thérèse, Lac** Northwest Territories Canada
40 C1 **St.Thiébault** France
127 P6 **St.Thomas** *parish* Barbados
120 J10 **St.Thomas** Ontario Canada
127 M3 **St.Thomas** *parish* Jamaica
98 J1 **St.Thomas** North Dakota U.S.A.
113 K7 **St.Thomas I** Virgin Is
20 C6 **St Thurien** France
121 S6 **St.Tite** Quebec Canada
122 B6 **St.Tite des Caps** Quebec Canada
40 B5 **St.Trivier de Courtes** France
19 N12 **St. Trivier-Moignans** France
St.Trond *see* **St.Truiden**
22 J2 **St.Truiden** Belgium
8 B2 **St. Tudwal's Is** Wales
27 H11 **St.Tuna** Sweden
122 E5 **St.Ulric** Quebec Canada
122 B6 **St.Urbain** Quebec Canada
21 M2 **St. Vaast** France
20 H2 **St. Vaast-la-Hougue** France
21 M2 **St. Valéry-en-Caux** France
21 O1 **St. Valery-sur-Somme** France
122 B7 **St.Vallier** Quebec Canada
21 K8 **St. Varent** France
38 H7 **St.Veit** Austria
38 K8 **St.Veit-an-der-Glan** Austria
22 D2 **St.Venant** France
20 F5 **St. Véran** Côtes d'Armor France
121 Q6 **Ste.Véronique** Quebec Canada
21 O6 **St. Viâtre** France
20 F7 **St Viaud** France
20 G7 **St. Viaud** France
19 P17 **Ste Victoire, Mt** France
20 F6 **St. Vincent** France
127 O8 **St. Vincent** *isld* Lesser Antilles
21 L6 **St Vincent-de-Larouer** France
18 E9 **St.Vincent-de-Tyrosse** France
138 E5 **St.Vincent, G** South Australia Australia
113 B8 **St. Vincent I** Florida U.S.A.
139 H9 **St.Vincent, Pt** Tasmania Australia
123 T7 **St.Vincent's** Newfoundland Canada
118 A2 **St.Vital** Manitoba Canada
94 C1 **St. Vital Pt** Michigan U.S.A.
22 L3 **St.Vith** Belgium
18 E7 **St.Vivien-de-Médoc** France
106 G7 **St.Vrain** New Mexico U.S.A.
118 H5 **St.Walburg** Saskatchewan Canada
21 M2 **St. Wandrille** France
36 C5 **St.Wendel** Germany
126 A1 **St. Willebrordus** Curaçao Neth Antilles
120 K10 **St.Williams** Ontario Canada
101 S4 **St.Xavier** Montana U.S.A.
18 F7 **St. Yrieix** France
122 H4 **St.Yvon** Quebec Canada
19 P18 **St.Zacharie** France
21 O5 **Sainville** France
134 E6 **Saipan** *isld* Mariana Is Pacific Oc
20 H2 **Saire** *R* France
20 H2 **Saire, Pte. de** France
18 E9 **Saison** *R* France
61 M10 **Saitama** *prefect* Japan
68 A1 **Saitlai** Burma
60 E13 **Saito** Japan
26 N3 **Saivomuotka** Sweden
77 L2 **Saiydabad** Afghanistan
77 L1 **Saiyid** Afghanistan
74 E3 **Saiyidwala** Pakistan
71 B2 **Sajafi** *isld* Indonesia
128 E7 **Sajama** *mt* Bolivia
128 E7 **Sajama** Bolivia
71 B2 **Sajang** *isld* Indonesia
48 F2 **Sajó** *R* Hungary
89 B7 **Sak** *watercourse* S Africa
88 G2 **Saka** Kenya
Saka Dzong *see* **Saga** China
59 L5 **Sakai** Japan
60 G11 **Sakaide** Japan
60 G10 **Sakai Minato** Japan
78 H7 **Sākākah** Saudi Arabia
98 E2 **Sakakawea, L** North Dakota U.S.A.
70 Q9 **Sakala** *isld* Indonesia
61 N7 **Sakamachi** Japan
115 M7 **Sakami, L** Quebec Canada
88 B8 **Sakania** Zaire
47 H3 **Sakar** *hills* Bulgaria
57 C5 **Sakar** Turkmenistan
87 G12 **Sakaraha** Madagascar
57 B5 **Sakar-chaga** Turkmenistan
47 J5 **Sakar Daği** *mt* Turkey
78 C1 **Sakarya** *R* Turkey
78 C2 **Sakarya** *R* Turkey
59 L4 **Sakata** Japan
111 H8 **Sakatonchee** *R* Mississippi U.S.A.
85 E7 **Sakete** Benin
59 M1 **Sakhalin** *isld* Russian Federation
51 O4 **Sakhalinskaya Oblast'** Russian Federation
51 O3 **Sakhalinskiy Zaliv** *B* Russian Federation
85 F2 **Sakhira** Tunisia
54 G7 **Sakhnovshchina** Ukraine
77 B1 **Sakht-Sar** Iran
52 B7 **Šakiai** Lithuania
80 G4 **Sakib** Jordan
60 H12 **Sakihama** Japan
67 H4 **Sakishima-guntō** *islds* Japan
55 C5 **Sakmara** Russian Federation
85 B3 **Sakn, As** Western Sahara
68 C3 **Sa-koi** Burma
95 Q5 **Sakonnet R** Rhode I U.S.A.
87 D12 **Sakrivier** S Africa
28 E5 **Saksild** Denmark
28 H7 **Sakskøbing** Denmark
75 K7 **Sakti** India
51 M1 **Saktyakh** Russian Federation
61 M9 **Saku** Japan
61 L10 **Sakuma** Japan
61 J11 **Sakurai** Japan
60 D14 **Sakura jima** *isld* Japan
27 M10 **Säkylä** Finland
80 G3 **Sal** Jordan
53 F9 **Sal** *R* Russian Federation
48 D2 **Šala** Slovakia
27 J12 **Sala** Sweden
68 F7 **Sala Andong Tuk** Cambodia
71 H6 **Salabangka** *isld* Sulawesi
52 B5 **Salacgriva** Latvia
43 G8 **Sala Consilina** Italy
109 K5 **Salad** Texas U.S.A.
133 C3 **Salada, B** Chile
131 G6 **Salada, L** Buenos Aires Argentina
131 F2 **Salada, L** Corrientes Argentina
124 B1 **Salada, L** Mexico
103 J9 **Salada, Laguna** *L* Mexico
131 E4 **Saladillo** *R* Argentina
131 B2 **Salado** *R* La Rioja Argentina
131 E2 **Salado, R** Santa Fé Argentina

106 C7 **Salado, R** New Mexico U.S.A.
85 D7 **Salaga** Ghana
68 F7 **Sala Hintoun** Cambodia
56 C4 **Salair** Russian Federation
56 C4 **Salairskiy Kryazh** *ridge* Russian Federation
48 H3 **Sălaj** *prov* Romania
70 G7 **Salajar, Selat** *str* Sulawesi
70 L9 **Salak, G** *mt* Java
86 C3 **Salal** Chad
72 G5 **Şalālah** Oman
125 O10 **Salamá** Guatemala
16 C4 **Salamanca** *prov* Spain
16 D4 **Salamanca** Spain
94 J4 **Salamanca** New York U.S.A.
86 C4 **Salamat** *R* Chad
70 D6 **Salamban** Kalimantan
128 C2 **Salamina** Colombia
79 D3 **Salamis** Cyprus
46 F7 **Salamís** Greece
79 H3 **Salamīyah** Syria
94 B6 **Salamonie** *R* Indiana U.S.A.
26 J3 **Salangen** Norway
52 B6 **Salantai** Lithuania
45 K2 **Salara** Italy
48 G3 **Sălard** Romania
133 D2 **Salar de Arizaro** *salt pan* Argentina
133 D2 **Salar de Atacama** *salt pan* Chile
133 D2 **Salar de Cauchari** *salt pan* Argentina
133 D1 **Salar de Coipasa** *salt pan* Bolivia
133 D3 **Salar del Hombre Muerto** *salt pan* Argentina
133 D2 **Salar de Uyuni** *salt pan* Bolivia
16 C1 **Salas** Spain
46 E1 **Salaš** Serbia Yugoslavia
16 E2 **Salas de los Infantes** Spain
18 F9 **Salat** *R* France
70 N9 **Salatiga** Java
18 F10 **Salau, Pont de** *pass* France/Spain
52 H6 **Salaushi** Russian Federation
55 C4 **Salavat** Russian Federation
128 C5 **Salaverry** Peru
133 E3 **Salavina** Argentina
71 C3 **Salawati** *isld* W Irian
71 G6 **Salay** Mindanao Philippines
135 Q11 **Sala y Gómez** *isld* Pacific Oc
Salazar *see* **N'dalatando**
21 P7 **Salbris** France
126 D3 **Sal, Cay** *isld* Bahamas
127 J5 **Salcedo** Dominican Rep
116 P4 **Salcha** *R* Alaska U.S.A.
116 O4 **Salchaket** Alaska U.S.A.
33 P8 **Salchau** Germany
37 O6 **Salching** Germany
46 G1 **Salcia** Romania
8 C7 **Salcombe** England
47 K7 **Salda Gölü** *L* Turkey
16 D2 **Saldaña** Spain
87 C12 **Saldanha** S Africa
41 N4 **Saldura, Pta** *mt* Italy
52 B6 **Saldus** Latvia
139 H7 **Sale** Victoria Australia
68 B2 **Sale** Burma
8 D1 **Sale** England
85 C2 **Salé** Morocco
70 G5 **Salea** Sulawesi
112 C6 **Sale City** Georgia U.S.A.
112 B2 **Sale Creek** Tennessee U.S.A.
77 A2 **Sālehābad** Iran
71 H9 **Saleh, Teluk** *B* Indonesia
147 N15 **Salekhard** Russian Federation
76 D5 **Salem** India
111 L9 **Salem** Alabama U.S.A.
110 E5 **Salem** Arkansas U.S.A.
113 D8 **Salem** Florida U.S.A.
110 H3 **Salem** Illinois U.S.A.
110 K3 **Salem** Indiana U.S.A.
95 R4 **Salem** Massachusetts U.S.A.
110 E4 **Salem** Missouri U.S.A.
95 Q4 **Salem** New Hampshire U.S.A.
95 M7 **Salem** New Jersey U.S.A.
106 C9 **Salem** New Mexico U.S.A.
95 O3 **Salem** New York U.S.A.
94 G6 **Salem** Ohio U.S.A.
100 B5 **Salem** Oregon U.S.A.
112 E3 **Salem** South Carolina U.S.A.
98 J6 **Salem** South Dakota U.S.A.
94 G9 **Salem** Virginia U.S.A.
99 S7 **Salem** Wisconsin U.S.A.
43 E11 **Salemi** Sicily
15 C4 **Salen** Scotland
27 F10 **Sälen** Sweden
142 E3 **Sale, R** W Australia Australia
19 Q17 **Salernes** France
43 F8 **Salerno** Italy
113 G10 **Salerno** Florida U.S.A.
43 F8 **Salerno, Golfo di** Italy
45 L1 **Saletto** Italy
21 P2 **Saleux** France
19 Q12 **Salève, Mt** France
13 F6 **Salford** England
130 H9 **Salgado** *R* Brazil
131 H2 **Salgado Filho** *airport* Brazil
48 F2 **Salgótarján** Hungary
130 G10 **Salgueiro** Brazil
80 E1 **Sâlhâni** Lebanon
79 C8 **Sâlhîya, El** Egypt
127 P2 **Salibea** Trinidad
106 D3 **Salida** Colorado U.S.A.
18 E9 **Salies de Béarn** France
18 F9 **Salies du Salat** France
47 J6 **Salihli** Turkey
87 F8 **Salima** Malawi
70 E3 **Salimbatu** Kalimantan
68 B2 **Salin** *R* Burma
68 B2 **Salin** Burma
107 N3 **Salina** Kansas U.S.A.
110 A5 **Salina** Oklahoma U.S.A.
103 N3 **Salina** Utah U.S.A.
125 M9 **Salina Cruz** Mexico
43 F10 **Salina, I** Italy
133 D4 **Salina La Antigua** *salt pan* Argentina
126 G3 **Salina Pt** Acklins I Bahamas
129 K7 **Salinas** Brazil
128 B4 **Salinas** Ecuador
128 C6 **Salinas** Peru
102 C5 **Salinas** *R* California U.S.A.
102 C5 **Salinas** California U.S.A.
133 D4 **Salinas Grandes** Argentina
106 D7 **Salinas Nat. Mon** New Mexico U.S.A.
108 A1 **Salinas Nat.Mon** New Mexico U.S.A.
131 C3 **Salinas, Pampa de la** Argentina
106 D8 **Salinas Pk** New Mexico U.S.A.
87 B8 **Salinas, Pte. das** Angola
12 E1 **Saline** Scotland
111 D8 **Saline** *R* Arkansas U.S.A.
110 H4 **Saline** *R* Illinois U.S.A.
107 L2 **Saline** *R* Kansas U.S.A.
94 D4 **Saline** Michigan U.S.A.
127 P2 **Saline B** Trinidad
109 P3 **Saline Bayou** *R* Louisiana U.S.A.
109 P4 **Saline L** Louisiana U.S.A.
127 P5 **Salines, Pt** Grenada
102 G5 **Saline V** California U.S.A.
94 G6 **Salineville** Ohio U.S.A.
68 B1 **Salingyi** Burma
133 C3 **Salinitas** Chile
129 J4 **Salinópolis** Brazil
Salisbury *see* **Harare** Zimbabwe
141 K2 **Salisbury** *dist* Brisbane, Qnsld Australia
138 E5 **Salisbury** South Australia Australia
122 G7 **Salisbury** New Brunswick Canada
9 E5 **Salisbury** England
95 O4 **Salisbury** Connecticut U.S.A.
95 M8 **Salisbury** Maryland U.S.A.
110 D2 **Salisbury** Missouri U.S.A.
112 G2 **Salisbury** North Carolina U.S.A.
94 H7 **Salisbury** Pennsylvania U.S.A.
95 O3 **Salisbury** Vermont U.S.A.
115 M5 **Salisbury I** Northwest Territories Canada
86 F5 **Salisbury, L** Uganda
116 O2 **Salisbury, Mt** Alaska U.S.A.
9 E5 **Salisbury Plain** England
48 H5 **Săliste** Romania
129 K6 **Salitre** *R* Brazil
80 G8 **Saliya** Jordan
45 K1 **Salizzole** Italy
112 F4 **Salkehatchie** *R* South Carolina U.S.A.
79 G6 **Şalkhad** Syria
28 D4 **Sall** Denmark
38 L7 **Salla** Austria
29 O5 **Salla** Finland
21 J7 **Salle-de-Vihiers, la** France
17 G2 **Sallent de G** Spain
19 N16 **Salles** France
18 G8 **Salles-Curan** France
112 F4 **Salley** South Carolina U.S.A.
33 T9 **Sallgast** Germany
28 B3 **Salling** *reg* Denmark
107 Q6 **Sallisaw** Oklahoma U.S.A.
86 G2 **Sallom** Sudan
78 K6 **Salman, As** Iraq
78 K2 **Salmās** Iran
17 F4 **Salmerón** Spain
29 N5 **Salmivaara** Finland
100 H1 **Salmo** British Columbia Canada
117 M8 **Salmon** *R* British Columbia Canada
116 Q3 **Salmon** Alaska U.S.A.
101 M4 **Salmon** Idaho U.S.A.
117 O10 **Salmon Arm** British Columbia Canada
123 P2 **Salmon Bay** Quebec Canada
101 L7 **Salmon Cr.Res** Idaho U.S.A.
142 F3 **Salmond R** W Australia Australia
101 L7 **Salmon Falls** Idaho U.S.A.
116 R4 **Salmon Fork** *R* Alaska U.S.A.
143 D10 **Salmon Gums** W Australia Australia
123 T6 **Salmonier** Newfoundland Canada
100 B8 **Salmon Mt** California U.S.A.
122 G7 **Salmon R** New Brunswick Canada
122 K4 **Salmon, R** Quebec Canada
95 M3 **Salmon Res** New York U.S.A.
100 K5 **Salmon River Mts** Idaho U.S.A.
36 G3 **Salmünster** Germany
52 E2 **Sal'nitsa** Russian Federation
42 D3 **Salò** Italy
52 G6 **Salobelyak** Russian Federation
130 C7 **Salobra, R** Brazil
29 L7 **Saloinen** Finland
99 L1 **Salol** Minnesota U.S.A.
103 L8 **Salome** Arizona U.S.A.
127 L4 **Salomon, C** Martinique W Indies
40 C2 **Salon** *R* France
19 O17 **Salon-de-Provence** France
86 D6 **Salonga, Parc Nacional de la** *nat park* Zaire
Salonica *see* **Thessaloníki**
48 G4 **Salonta** Romania
17 H3 **Salou, C** Spain
29 M11 **Salpausselkä** *reg* Finland
53 F10 **Sal'sk** Russian Federation
43 F11 **Salso** *R* Sicily
44 G2 **Salsomaggiore Terme** Italy
80 F5 **Salt** Jordan
103 N8 **Salt** *R* Arizona U.S.A.
110 L3 **Salt** *R* Kentucky U.S.A.
110 E2 **Salt** *R* Missouri U.S.A.
133 D2 **Salta** Argentina
55 F3 **Saltaim, Oz** *L* Russian Federation
8 B7 **Saltash** England
28 G5 **Saltbæk Vig** *lagoon* Denmark
108 B4 **Salt Basin** Texas U.S.A.
13 H4 **Saltburn-by-the-Sea** England
119 P7 **Saltcoats** Saskatchewan Canada
12 D2 **Saltcoats** Scotland
99 R9 **Salt Cr** *R* Illinois U.S.A.
110 G1 **Salt Cr** Illinois U.S.A.
94 E7 **Salt Cr** Ohio U.S.A.
101 T6 **Salt Cr** Wyoming U.S.A.
138 E6 **Salt Creek** South Australia Australia
26 H4 **Saltdal** Norway
108 C4 **Salt Draw** *R* Texas U.S.A.
14 E4 **Saltee Is** Ireland
26 H5 **Saltelv** *R* Norway
26 G4 **Salten** *reg* Norway
28 D4 **Salten Langsø** *L* Denmark
26 G4 **Saltfjord** *inlet* Norway
108 B4 **Salt Flat** Texas U.S.A.
13 J6 **Saltfleet** England
107 M5 **Salt Fork** *R* Oklahoma U.S.A.
108 F2 **Salt Fork** *R* Texas U.S.A.
109 H4 **Salt Gap** Texas U.S.A.
103 N8 **Salt-Gila Aqueduct** Arizona U.S.A.
29 K5 **Saltholm** *isld* Denmark
125 J5 **Saltillo** Mexico
94 J6 **Saltillo** Pennsylvania U.S.A.
110 H6 **Saltillo** Tennessee U.S.A.
106 G9 **Salt L** New Mexico U.S.A.
108 C4 **Salt L** Texas U.S.A.
101 O9 **Salt Lake City** Utah U.S.A.
94 D8 **Salt Lick** Kentucky U.S.A.
133 E4 **Salto** Argentina
130 F8 **Salto** Brazil
42 E6 **Salto** *R* Italy
131 F3 **Salto** *dept* Uruguay
131 F3 **Salto** Uruguay
130 D7 **Salto do Urubupungá** *falls* Brazil
131 F3 **Salto Grande, Embalse de** *res* Arg/Uruguay
45 O5 **Salto, L. del** Italy
26 K4 **Saltoluokta** Sweden
103 J8 **Salton Sea** California U.S.A.
130 D9 **Salto Santiago, Reprêsa de** *res* Brazil
Saltos do Iguaçu *see* **Cataratas del Iguazú** *waterfalls*
107 M5 **Salt Plains L** Oklahoma U.S.A.
127 L3 **Salt Ponds, The** Jamaica
74 E2 **Salt Range** Pakistan
127 K3 **Salt River** Jamaica
127 H5 **Saltrou** Haiti
101 P7 **Salt R. Ra** Wyoming U.S.A.
27 K12 **Saltsjöbaden** Sweden
27 L11 **Saltvik** Finland
94 F10 **Saltville** Virginia U.S.A.
102 F2 **Salt Wells** Nevada U.S.A.
112 E3 **Saluda** *R* South Carolina U.S.A.
112 F3 **Saluda** South Carolina U.S.A.
71 H5 **Salue** *isld* Indonesia
71 H5 **Salue Timpaus, Selat** *str* Indonesia
84 H3 **Salûm** Egypt
45 N4 **Saluoecio** Italy
71 F7 **Saluping** *isld* Philippines
76 F1 **Salur** India
110 C6 **Salus** Arkansas U.S.A.
129 H2 **Salut, I.du** Fr Guiana
44 B2 **Saluzzo** Italy
129 L6 **Salvador** Brazil
118 H6 **Salvador** Saskatchewan Canada
84 E5 **Salvador** Niger
111 F12 **Salvador, L** Louisiana U.S.A.
123 T5 **Salvage** Newfoundland Canada
16 B5 **Salvaterra de Magos** Portugal
125 J7 **Salvatierra** Mexico
103 N3 **Salvation Cr** Utah U.S.A.
141 H6 **Salvator, L** Queensland Australia
18 G8 **Salvetat, la** Aveyron France
18 G9 **Salvetat, la** Hérault France
117 J8 **Salvus** British Columbia Canada
68 C4 **Salween** *R* Burma/Thailand
75 K4 **Salyan** Nepal
94 D9 **Salyersville** Kentucky U.S.A.
55 F1 **Salym** Russian Federation
38 L6 **Salza** *R* Austria
32 F8 **Salzbergen** Germany
38 H6 **Salzburg** Austria
38 H7 **Salzburg** *prov* Austria
32 L9 **Salzderhelden** Germany
33 M8 **Salzgitter** Germany
33 M8 **Salzgitter-Bad** Germany
38 J6 **Salzkammer-gut** *res* Austria
32 J9 **Salzkotten** Germany
33 P9 **Salzmünde** Germany
33 O7 **Salzwedel** Germany
101 O6 **Sam** Idaho U.S.A.
80 G3 **Sama** Jordan
80 G4 **Samad** Jordan
71 J5 **Samada** *isld* Indonesia
16 D1 **Sama de Langreo** Spain
56 E5 **Samagaltay** Russian Federation
84 F4 **Samāh** Libya
80 F2 **Samak** Syria
71 G7 **Samal** *isld* Mindanao Philippines
69 C10 **Samalanga** Sumatra
69 J12 **Samalantan** Indonesia
108 A4 **Samalayuca** Mexico
71 E7 **Samales Group** *islds* Philippines
76 F2 **Samalkot** India
84 J4 **Samâlût** Egypt
127 K5 **Samaná** Dominican Rep
126 H3 **Samana Cay** *isld* Bahamas
78 E3 **Samandağı** Turkey
47 N11 **Samandira** Turkey
77 K1 **Samangān** *prov* Afghanistan
60 Q3 **Samani** Japan
70 N10 **Samanu** Java
121 S3 **Samaqua** *R* Quebec Canada
80 G3 **Samar** Jordan
71 G5 **Samar** *isld* Philippines
53 H7 **Samara** Russian Federation
53 H7 **Samara** *R* Russian Federation
136 L4 **Samarai** Papua New Guinea
80 D4 **Samaria** Jordan
101 N7 **Samaria** Idaho U.S.A.
46 E4 **Samarína** Greece
70 E5 **Samarinda** Kalimantan
57 D5 **Samarkand** Uzbekistan
78 J4 **Sāmarrā'** Iraq
71 G5 **Samar Sea** Philippines
53 G7 **Samarskaya Oblast'** Russian Federation
71 C3 **Samate** W Irian
78 K6 **Samāwah, Aq** Iraq
70 C5 **Samba** *R* Kalimantan
86 D5 **Samba** Equateur Zaire
86 E6 **Samba** Kasai Oriental Zaire
87 C7 **Samba Caju** Angola
71 A3 **Sambaki, Selat** Indonesia
70 F4 **Sambaliung** *mts* Kalimantan
75 L8 **Sambalpur** India
70 G7 **Sambapolulu, G** *mt* Sulawesi
87 J10 **Sambava** Madagascar
25 E5 **Sambeek** Netherlands
74 H4 **Sambhal** India
71 H5 **Sambiat** Sulawesi
21 N7 **Sambin** France
70 F4 **Sambit** *isld* Kalimantan
129 K5 **Sambito** *R* Brazil
70 F6 **Sambo** Sulawesi
70 E5 **Sambodja** Kalimantan
68 H6 **Sambor** Cambodia
48 H1 **Sambor** Ukraine
131 G6 **Samborombón, B** Argentina
22 H3 **Sambre** *R* Belgium
69 F12 **Sambu** Indonesia
70 D5 **Sambuah** Kalimantan
45 J3 **Sambuca Pistojese** Italy
59 J4 **Samchŏk** S Korea
68 D6 **Same** Burma
88 F4 **Same** Tanzania
22 B2 **Samer** France
68 E6 **Samet, Ko** *isld* Thailand
87 E8 **Samfya** Zambia
68 A2 **Sami** Burma
46 D6 **Sámi** Greece
71 H4 **Samia, Tg** *C* Sulawesi Indonesia
128 D5 **Samiria** *R* Peru
85 E5 **Samit** Mali
68 C2 **Samka** Burma
29 K11 **Sammatti** Finland
80 F3 **Sammu'** Jordan
68 F5 **Samnak Kado** Thailand
41 M3 **Samnaun Gruppe** *mt* Austria
80 E6 **Samniya Auja** *R* Jordan
84 F4 **Şamnū** Libya
100 A9 **Samoa** California U.S.A.
Samoa i Sisifo *islds see* **Western Samoa**
42 G3 **Samobor** Croatia
52 F3 **Samoded** Russian Federation
40 E5 **Samoëns** France
46 F2 **Samokov** Bulgaria
68 C2 **Samon** *R* Burma
47 H7 **Sámos** *isld* Greece
Samothrace *see* **Samothráki**
47 H4 **Samothráki** *isld* Anatolikí Makedhonía Kaí Thráki Greece
46 D5 **Samothráki** *isld* Ionian Is Greece
133 E4 **Sampacho** Argentina
70 F6 **Sampaga** Sulawesi
71 E3 **Sampaloc Pt** Luzon Philippines
70 O9 **Sampang** Indonesia
17 G3 **Samper de Calanda** Spain
113 L12 **Samphire Cay** *isld* Bahamas
70 C6 **Sampit** Kalimantan
70 C6 **Sampit, Teluk** *B* Kalimantan
87 E7 **Sampwe** Zaire
80 F8 **Samra** Jordan
109 N4 **Sam Rayburn L** Texas U.S.A.
111 B10 **Sam Rayburn Res** Texas U.S.A.
22 K3 **Samrée** Belgium
68 F6 **Samrong** *R* Cambodia
28 F5 **Samsø** *isld* Denmark
111 K10 **Samson** Alabama U.S.A.
68 G3 **Sam Son** Vietnam
78 F1 **Samsun** Turkey
67 A6 **Sam Teu** Laos
140 C4 **Samuel, Mt** N Terr Australia
47 H1 **Samuil** Bulgaria
56 B3 **Samus'** Russian Federation
68 E6 **Samut Prakan** Thailand
68 E6 **Samut Sakhon** Thailand
68 E6 **Samut Songkhram** Thailand
71 J5 **Samuya** Indonesia
85 D6 **San** Mali
31 N6 **San** *R* Poland
42 H4 **Sana** *R* Bosnia-Herzegovina
72 E5 **Şan'ā'** Yemen
106 D7 **San Acacia** New Mexico U.S.A.
146 H6 **Sanae** *S Africa Base* Antarctica
86 B5 **Sanaga** *R* Cameroon
106 D10 **San Agustin** Mexico
71 G7 **San Agustin, C** Mindanao Philippines
133 D4 **San Agustín de Valle Fértil** Argentina
106 B8 **San Agustin, Plains of** *high plain* New Mexico U.S.A.
116 F9 **Sanak I** Aleutian Is
45 M2 **San Alberto** Italy
79 G5 **Şanamayn, Aş** Syria
135 S12 **San Ambrosio** *isld* Pacific Oc
102 D3 **San Andreas** California U.S.A.
128 D2 **San Andrés** Colombia
125 P9 **San Andrés** Guatemala
106 D9 **San Andres Mts** New Mexico U.S.A.
125 M8 **San Andrés Tuxtla** Mexico
41 K7 **San Angelo** Italy
108 G4 **San Angelo** Texas U.S.A.
126 C3 **San Anton de los Baños** Cuba
125 P9 **San Antonio** Belize
131 B4 **San Antonio** Chile
125 L2 **San Antonio** Honduras
124 E6 **San Antonio** Mexico
71 E2 **San Antonio** Luzon Philippines
113 E9 **San Antonio** Florida U.S.A.
106 D8 **San Antonio** New Mexico U.S.A.
109 J6 **San Antonio** Texas U.S.A.
109 K7 **San Antonio** *R* Texas U.S.A.
128 E3 **San Antonio** Venezuela
17 H6 **San Antonio Abad** Ibiza
71 C6 **San Antonio B** Palawan Philippines
109 L7 **San Antonio B** Texas U.S.A.
133 F5 **San Antonio, C** Argentina
126 B4 **San Antonio, C** Cuba
17 H6 **San Antonio, C** Spain
133 D2 **San Antonio de los Cobres** Argentina
124 E3 **San Antonio del Rio** Mexico
127 N9 **San Antonio de Maturín** Venezuela
127 L10 **San Antonio de Tamanaco** Venezuela
102 G7 **San Antonio, Mt** California U.S.A.
108 B4 **San Antonio Mt** Texas U.S.A.
133 E6 **San Antonio Oeste** Argentina
130 J9 **San Antonio, Pta. de** *C* Brazil
128 E2 **Sanariapo** Venezuela
19 P18 **Sanary** France
111 B10 **San Augustine** Texas U.S.A.
74 G7 **Sanawad** India
16 B7 **San Bartolómeu de Messines** Portugal
45 R7 **San Bartolomew in Galdo** Italy
42 F6 **San Benedetto del Tronto** Italy
45 J1 **San Benedetto Po** Italy
125 P9 **San Benito** Guatemala
102 C5 **San Benito** *R* California U.S.A.
109 K9 **San Benito** Texas U.S.A.
102 D5 **San Benito Mt** California U.S.A.
71 G4 **San Bernadino Str** Philippines
109 M6 **San Bernard** *R* Texas U.S.A.
130 B9 **San Bernardino** Paraguay
102 G7 **San Bernardino** California U.S.A.
103 J8 **San Bernardino Mts** California U.S.A.
41 K5 **San Bernardino P** Switzerland
131 B4 **San Bernardo** Chile
124 G4 **San Bernardo** Mexico
128 C2 **San Bernardo, I.de** Colombia
60 F10 **Sanbe-san** *mt* Japan
45 L2 **San Biagio** Italy
124 G7 **San Blas** Nayarit Mexico
124 E4 **San Blas** Sonora Mexico
113 B7 **San Blas** Florida U.S.A.
125 P5 **San Blas, Archipélago de** *islds* Panama
113 B8 **San Blas, C** Florida U.S.A.
125 P5 **San Blas, Serrania de** *mts* Panama
41 O7 **San Bonifacio** Italy
128 E6 **San Borja** Bolivia
124 C3 **San Borja** Mexico
99 L6 **Sanborn** Iowa U.S.A.
99 L5 **Sanborn** Minnesota U.S.A.
98 H3 **Sanborn** North Dakota U.S.A.
95 Q3 **Sanbornville** New Hampshire U.S.A.
124 J4 **San Buenaventura** Mexico
68 E5 **San Buri** Thailand
128 F8 **San Camilo** Argentina
133 D4 **San Carlos** Argentina
131 B6 **San Carlos** Chile
124 C4 **San Carlos** Baja Cal Sur Mexico
124 H5 **San Carlos** Coahuila Mexico
71 E3 **San Carlos** Luzon Philippines
71 F5 **San Carlos** Negros Philippines
133 G4 **San Carlos** Uruguay
103 O8 **San Carlos** Arizona U.S.A.
127 K10 **San Carlos** Venezuela
131 B8 **San Carlos de Bariloche** Argentina
17 H4 **San Carlos de la Rápita** Spain
128 D2 **San Carlos del Zulia** Venezuela
128 E3 **San Carlos de Rio Negro** Venezuela
124 B3 **San Carlos, Mesa de** *mt* Mexico
103 O8 **San Carlos Res** Arizona U.S.A.
45 K4 **San Casciano in Valdi Pesa** Italy
17 J3 **San Celoní** Spain
18 G5 **Sancergues** France
18 G5 **Sancerre** France
45 K2 **San Cesario sul Panaro** Italy
21 O5 **Sancheville** France
127 K5 **Sánchez** Dominican Rep
106 E4 **Sanchez Res** Colorado U.S.A.
52 G6 **Sanchursk** Russian Federation
125 K7 **San Ciro de Acosta** Mexico
17 F5 **San Clemente** Spain
102 G8 **San Clemente** California U.S.A.
102 F9 **San Clemente** *isld* California U.S.A.
18 G6 **Sancoins** France
71 G6 **Sanco Pt** Mindanao Philippines
130 B10 **San Cosme** Argentina
133 F3 **San Cosme** Paraguay
45 O4 **San Costanzo** Italy
131 E3 **San Cristóbal** Argentina
127 J5 **San Cristóbal** Dominican Rep
128 B8 **San Cristóbal** *isld* Galapagos Is
137 N4 **San Cristobal** Solomon Is
128 D2 **San Cristóbal** Venezuela
125 N9 **San Cristóbal de las Casas** Mexico
103 L9 **San Cristobal Wash** *R* Arizona U.S.A.
45 J4 **San Croce sulee Arno** Italy
133 C4 **San Cruz** Chile
126 E4 **Sancti Spíritus** Cuba
118 J7 **Sanctuary** Saskatchewan Canada
22 K5 **Sancy** France
27 B12 **Sand** Norway
89 F4 **Sand** *R* N Transvaal S Africa
89 E7 **Sand** *R* Orange Free State S Africa
60 J11 **Sanda** Japan
15 C5 **Sanda** *isld* Scotland
28 D6 **Sandager** Denmark
70 F2 **Sandakan** Sabah
70 F2 **Sandakan, Pelabuhan** *hbr* Sabah
68 H6 **Sandan** Cambodia
26 B10 **Sandane** Norway
46 F3 **Sandanski** Bulgaria
65 H2 **Sandaotong** China
65 G1 **Sandaozhen** China
85 B6 **Sandare** Mali
27 J10 **Sandarne** Sweden
106 H4 **Sand Arroyo** *R* Colo/Kansas U.S.A.
33 Q7 **Sandau** Germany
15 F1 **Sanday** Scotland
8 D5 **Sand B** England
8 D1 **Sandbach** England
37 P6 **Sandbach** Germany
27 G15 **Sandbäck** Sweden
12 D2 **Sandbank** Scotland
120 H1 **Sandbank L** Ontario Canada
89 E4 **Sandbult** S Africa
28 G7 **Sandby** Denmark
26 F7 **Sanddöla** *R* Norway
32 H5 **Sande** Germany
26 A9 **Sande** Norway
27 A10 **Sande** Norway
27 D12 **Sandefj** Norway
146 J10 **Sandercock Nunataks** *mt peaks* Antarctica
103 P6 **Sanders** Arizona U.S.A.
100 J2 **Sanders** Idaho U.S.A.
37 M6 **Sandersdorf** Germany
33 P9 **Sandersleben** Germany
113 E7 **Sanderson** Florida U.S.A.
108 E5 **Sanderson** Texas U.S.A.
112 E5 **Sandersville** Georgia U.S.A.
111 H10 **Sandersville** Mississippi U.S.A.
33 M5 **Sandesneben** Germany
28 B5 **Sandet** Denmark
142 D4 **Sandfire Flat Roadhouse** W Australia Australia
118 L3 **Sandfly L** Saskatchewan Canada
94 G8 **Sand Fork** West Virginia U.S.A.
141 L7 **Sandgate** Queensland Australia
9 H5 **Sandgate** England
36 F5 **Sandhausen** Germany
12 D4 **Sandhead** Scotland
26 G4 **Sandhornöy** *isld* Norway
9 F5 **Sandhurst** England
99 Q3 **Sand I** Wisconsin U.S.A.
109 K7 **Sandia** Texas U.S.A.
106 D6 **Sandia Pk** New Mexico U.S.A.
124 G3 **San Diego** Mexico
102 G9 **San Diego** California U.S.A.
109 J8 **San Diego** Texas U.S.A.
102 G8 **San Diego Aqueduct** California U.S.A.
133 D8 **San Diego, C** Argentina
128 F2 **San Diego de Cabrutica** Venezuela
47 L6 **Sandıklı** Turkey
74 J5 **Sandila** India
118 E1 **Sandilands** Manitoba Canada
113 M9 **Sandilands Village** New Providence I Bahamas
21 P6 **Sandillon** France
143 B6 **Sandiman, Mt** W Australia Australia
124 G5 **San Dimas** Mexico
69 E14 **Sanding** *isld* Indonesia
116 D5 **Sand Is** Alaska U.S.A.
52 J2 **Sandivey** *R* Russian Federation
32 H6 **Sandkrug** Germany
38 L4 **Sandl** Austria
120 F5 **Sand Lake** Ontario Canada
110 K7 **Sand Mountain** Alabama U.S.A.
27 C13 **Sandnes** Aust Agder Norway
27 A13 **Sandnes** Rogaland Norway
15 G2 **Sandness** Scotland
26 F5 **Sandnessjöen** Norway
87 D7 **Sandoa** Zaire
31 N5 **Sandomierz** Poland
45 P6 **San Donato Val di Comino** Italy
110 G3 **Sandoval** Illinois U.S.A.
106 D6 **Sandoval** New Mexico U.S.A.
140 D5 **Sandover** *R* N Terr Australia
52 E5 **Sandovo** Russian Federation
68 B3 **Sandoway** Burma
9 E6 **Sandown** England
89 A10 **Sandown B** S Africa
6 F1 **Sandoy** *isld* Faeroes
116 G9 **Sand Point** Alaska U.S.A.
117 P11 **Sandpoint** Idaho U.S.A.
118 F4 **Sand R** Alberta Canada
47 K7 **Sandras Daği** *mt* Turkey
140 E6 **Sandringham** Queensland Australia
9 G2 **Sandringham** England
99 T3 **Sands** Michigan U.S.A.
27 G14 **Sandsjö, N** Sweden
113 G12 **Sands Key** *isld* Florida U.S.A.
117 H9 **Sandspit** British Columbia Canada
38 G8 **Sandspitze** *mt* Austria
101 S2 **Sand Springs** Montana U.S.A.
107 O5 **Sand Springs** Oklahoma U.S.A.
102 F2 **Sand Springs Salt Flat** Nevada U.S.A.
26 D8 **Sandstad** Norway
32 J6 **Sandstedt** Germany
95 K9 **Sandston** Virginia U.S.A.
143 C8 **Sandstone** W Australia Australia
99 O3 **Sandstone** Minnesota U.S.A.
103 M9 **Sand Tanks Mts** Arizona U.S.A.
123 L4 **Sandtop, C** Anticosti I, Quebec
67 B3 **Sandu** China
67 B4 **Sandu** Guizhou China
67 E2 **Sandu** Jiangxi China
94 E3 **Sandusky** Michigan U.S.A.
94 D5 **Sandusky** *R* Ohio U.S.A.
94 E5 **Sandusky** Ohio U.S.A.
28 H6 **Sandved** Denmark
87 C11 **Sandverhaar** Namibia
27 G16 **Sandvig** Denmark
27 D12 **Sandvika** Norway
27 J11 **Sandviken** Sweden
9 H5 **Sandwich** England
99 S8 **Sandwich** Illinois U.S.A.
95 R5 **Sandwich** Massachusetts U.S.A.
115 O7 **Sandwich B** Labrador, Nfld Canada
141 H4 **Sandwich, C** Queensland Australia
15 G2 **Sandwick** Scotland
118 J5 **Sandwith** Saskatchewan Canada
95 R2 **Sandy** *R* Maine U.S.A.
103 J6 **Sandy** Nevada U.S.A.
100 C4 **Sandy** Oregon U.S.A.
103 N1 **Sandy** Utah U.S.A.
119 P3 **Sandy Bay** Saskatchewan Canada
127 H1 **Sandy Bay** Jamaica
118 K1 **Sandybeach L** Ontario Canada
141 L6 **Sandy C** Queensland Australia
139 G8 **Sandy C** Tasmania Australia
101 O9 **Sandy City** Utah U.S.A.
109 L6 **Sandy Cr** Texas U.S.A.
101 Q7 **Sandy Cr** Wyoming U.S.A.
121 O7 **Sandy Creek** Quebec Canada
95 L3 **Sandy Creek** New York U.S.A.
95 O5 **Sandy Hook** Connecticut U.S.A.
94 D8 **Sandy Hook** Kentucky U.S.A.
111 G10 **Sandy Hook** Mississippi U.S.A.
95 N6 **Sandy Hook** *pt* New Jersey U.S.A.
57 C6 **Sandykachi** Turkmenistan
123 Q4 **Sandy L** Newfoundland Canada
115 K7 **Sandy L** Ontario Canada
119 R8 **Sandy Lake** Manitoba Canada
119 O3 **Sandy Narrows** Saskatchewan Canada
112 L2 **Sandy Pt** North Carolina U.S.A.
127 P4 **Sandy Pt** St Kitts W Indies
126 G9 **San Estanislao** Colombia
129 G8 **San Estanislao** Paraguay
71 E2 **San Fabian** Luzon Philippines
45 O7 **San Felice Circeo** Italy
45 K2 **San Felice sul Panaro** Italy
131 B4 **San Felipe** Chile
128 E3 **San Felipe** Colombia
124 B2 **San Felipe** Baja California Mexico
124 F4 **San Felipe** Chihuahua Mexico
127 K9 **San Felipe** Venezuela
126 C4 **San Felipe, Cayos de** *islds* Cuba
17 F4 **San Felipe, Cerro de** *pk* Spain
103 H8 **San Felipe Cr** California U.S.A.
106 D6 **San Felipe Pueblo** New Mexico U.S.A.
17 K3 **San Feliú de Guixols** Spain
17 J3 **San Felíu de Llobregat** Spain
135 S12 **San Félix** *isld* Pacific Oc
131 B5 **San Fernando** Chile
124 B3 **San Fernando** Mexico
71 E2 **San Fernando** Luzon Philippines
16 C8 **San Fernando** Spain
127 O3 **San Fernando** Trinidad
102 F7 **San Fernando** California U.S.A.
128 E2 **San Fernando de Apure** Venezuela
128 E3 **San Fernando de Atabape** Venezuela
26 G9 **Sånfjället** *mt* Sweden
118 D1 **Sanford** Manitoba Canada
106 E4 **Sanford** Colorado U.S.A.
113 F9 **Sanford** Florida U.S.A.
95 R3 **Sanford** Maine U.S.A.
112 H2 **Sanford** North Carolina U.S.A.
108 C8 **Sanford** Texas U.S.A.
94 C3 **Sanford L** Michigan U.S.A.
116 Q5 **Sanford, Mt** Alaska U.S.A.
143 B7 **Sanford, R** W Australia Australia
127 N3 **San Francique** Trinidad
131 E3 **San Francisco** Argentina
106 B8 **San Francisco** *R* Ariz/New Mex U.S.A.
104 **San Francisco** *conurbation* California U.S.A.
127 J9 **San Francisco** Venezuela
102 B4 **San Francisco Bay** California U.S.A.
108 E6 **San Francisco Cr** Texas U.S.A.
124 G4 **San Francisco de Conchos** Mexico
133 E3 **San Francisco del Chanar** Argentina
133 D4 **San Francisco del Monte de Oro** Argentina
124 G4 **San Francisco del Oro** Mexico
124 H7 **San Francisco del Rincón** Mexico
127 J5 **San Francisco de Macoris** Dominican Rep
133 D7 **San Francisco de Paula, C** Argentina
133 G4 **San Gabriel** Brazil
102 G7 **San Gabriel Mts** California U.S.A.
124 C3 **San Gabriel, Pta** *C* Mexico
69 G14 **Sangaigerong** Sumatra
76 B1 **Sangammer** India
74 F9 **Sangamner** India
99 R10 **Sangamon** *R* Illinois U.S.A.
77 J3 **Sangan, Koh-i** *mt* Afghanistan
51 M2 **Sangar** Russian Federation
76 D2 **Sangāreddi** India
70 E5 **Sangasanga** Kalimantan
70 F2 **Sanga Sanga** *isld* Philippines
85 C6 **Sangasso** Mali
22 B2 **Sangatte** France
43 B9 **San Gavino Monreale** Sardinia
128 C4 **Sangay** *vol* Ecuador
71 E7 **Sangboy Island** Philippines
71 J9 **Sangeang** *isld* Indonesia
102 E5 **Sanger** California U.S.A.
98 E2 **Sanger** North Dakota U.S.A.
109 K2 **Sanger** Texas U.S.A.
33 O10 **Sangerhausen** Germany
127 L5 **San Germán** Puerto Rico
65 C4 **Sanggan He** *R* China
71 J9 **Sanggar** Sumbawa Indonesia
71 J9 **Sanggar, Teluk** *B* Indonesia
70 B4 **Sanggau** Kalimantan
69 J12 **Sanggauledo** Indonesia
65 E6 **Sanggou Wan** *B* China
86 C5 **Sangha** *R* Congo
74 C5 **Sānghār** Pakistan
56 B1 **Sangil'ka** *R* Russian Federation
45 R7 **San Giorgio del Sannio** Italy
45 J1 **San Giórgio di Mántova** Italy
42 E3 **San Giorgio di N** Italy
45 K2 **San Giorgio di Piano** Italy
45 R7 **San Giorgio la Molara** Italy
38 E8 **San Giovanni** Italy
45 Q8 **San Giovanni a Teducio** Italy
45 J1 **San Giovanni in Croce** Italy
45 K2 **San Giovanni in Persiceto** Italy
45 K1 **San Giovanni Lupatoto** Italy
43 G10 **San Giovanni, V** Italy
45 L4 **San Giovanni Valdarno** Italy
71 E3 **Sangitan** Luzon Philippines
45 M1 **San Giuliano** Italy
45 H4 **San Giuliano Terme** Italy
45 R8 **San Giuseppe Vesuviano** Italy
45 M4 **San Giustino** Italy
65 G6 **Sangju** S Korea
70 F7 **Sangkarang, Kep** *isld* Sulawesi
68 D5 **Sangkhla Buri** Thailand
70 E4 **Sangkulirang** Kalimantan
70 F4 **Sangkulirang, Teluk** *B* Kalimantan
74 E3 **Sangla** Pakistan
76 B2 **Sangli** India
86 B5 **Sangmélima** Cameroon
89 G4 **Sango** Zimbabwe
45 L4 **San Godenzo** Italy
17 G7 **Sangonera** *R* Spain
102 H7 **San Gorgonio Mt** California U.S.A.
71 B1 **Sangowo** Halmahera Indonesia
106 E5 **Sangre de Cristo Mts** New Mex/Colo U.S.A.
102 B4 **San Gregorio** California U.S.A.
127 P2 **Sangre Grande** Trinidad
42 F6 **Sangro** *R* Italy
74 F3 **Sangrur** India
88 E5 **Sangu** Tanzania
118 C5 **Sangudo** Alberta Canada
129 G6 **Sangue** *R* Brazil
18 E10 **Sangüesa** Spain
41 O7 **Sanguinetto** Italy
Sangyuan *see* **Wuqiao**
67 C2 **Sangzhi** China
Sanhe *see* **Sandu** Guizhou
59 H1 **Sanhe** China
65 D4 **Sanhe** China
67 D1 **Sanhedian** China
59 J1 **Sanhezhan** China
124 D5 **San Hilario** Mexico
59 H1 **San-ho** China
67 D1 **San Hu** *L* China
67 B1 **Sanhuizhen** China
113 E11 **Sanibel I** Florida U.S.A.
130 C10 **San Ignacio** Argentina
128 E6 **San Ignacio** Beni Bolivia
128 F7 **San Ignacio** Santa Cruz Bolivia
124 D2 **San Ignacio** Mexico
124 C4 **San Ignacio, Laguna** Mexico
16 E4 **San Ildefonso** Spain
106 D6 **San Ildefonso** New Mexico U.S.A.
71 F2 **San Ildefonso, C** Luzon Philippines
79 H3 **Saniman, Wādī** *watercourse* Syria
60 H10 **San'in** Japan
106 E4 **San Isabel** Colorado U.S.A.
133 F4 **San Isidro** Argentina
124 H5 **San Isidro** Mexico
71 G5 **San Isidro** Leyte Philippines
33 Q4 **Sanitz** Germany
126 G10 **San Jacinto** Colombia
71 F4 **San Jacinto** Philippines
101 L8 **San Jacinto** Nevada U.S.A.
102 H8 **San Jacinto Mts** California U.S.A.
133 F4 **San Javier** Argentina
124 F4 **San Javier** Mexico
131 F2 **San Javier, R** Argentina
125 J9 **San Jerónimo** Mexico
Sanjiang *see* **Liannan** Guangdong
67 C4 **Sanjiang** China
65 F3 **Sanjiangkou** China
65 F3 **Sanjiazi** China
61 M8 **Sanjō** Japan
128 F6 **San Joaquin** Bolivia
130 C9 **San Joaquin** Paraguay
102 D4 **San Joaquin** *R* California U.S.A.
102 D5 **San Joaquin** California U.S.A.
102 D5 **San Joaquin Valley** California U.S.A.
108 A8 **San Jon** New Mexico U.S.A.
128 C2 **San Jorge** *R* Colombia
133 D7 **San Jorge, G** Argentina
17 H4 **San Jorge, G.de** Spain
131 B4 **San Jose** *vol* Chile
125 M5 **San José** Costa Rica
124 D5 **San José** *isld* Mexico
71 E4 **San Jose** Philippines
131 G5 **San José** *dept* Uruguay
131 G5 **San José** Uruguay
102 C4 **San Jose** California U.S.A.
99 R9 **San Jose** Illinois U.S.A.
106 E6 **San Jose** New Mexico U.S.A.
131 F3 **San José, Cuchilla de** *mts* Uruguay
128 F2 **San José de Amacuro** Venezuela
128 F7 **San José de Chiquitos** Bolivia
124 D3 **San José de Dimas** Mexico
133 F4 **San José de Feliciano** Argentina
124 F4 **San José de Gracia** Sinaloa Mexico
127 M10 **San José de Guaribe** Venezuela
127 J5 **San José de las Matas** Dominican Rep
124 E6 **San José del Cabo** Mexico
128 D3 **San José del Gauviare** Colombia
127 J5 **San José de Ocoa** Dominican Rep
128 D3 **San José de Ocuné** Colombia
106 C6 **San Jose, R** New Mexico U.S.A.
131 B3 **San Juan** *prov* Argentina
131 C3 **San Juan** Argentina
128 F7 **San Juan** Bolivia
128 C3 **San Juan** *R* Colombia
125 M4 **San Juan** *R* Costa Rica
126 D4 **San Juan** *mt* Cuba
127 J5 **San Juan** Dominican Rep
124 F4 **San Juan** Chihuahua Mexico
124 J4 **San Juan** Coahuila Mexico
128 D7 **San Juan** Peru
71 G6 **San Juan** Mindanao Philippines
127 L5 **San Juan** Puerto Rico
102 D6 **San Juan** *R* California U.S.A.
109 J9 **San Juan** Texas U.S.A.
103 P4 **San Juan** *R* Utah U.S.A.
128 E2 **San Juan** Venezuela
102 C5 **San Juan Bautista** California U.S.A.
128 C7 **San Juan, B. de** *B* Peru
133 E8 **San Juan, C** Argentina
102 G8 **San Juan Capistrano** California U.S.A.
124 H5 **San Juan de Guadalupe** Mexico
18 G10 **San Juan de las Abadesas** Spain
124 H8 **San Juan de Lima, Pta** *C* Mexico
125 N4 **San Juan del Norte** Nicaragua
127 K9 **San Juan de los Cayos** Venezuela
124 H7 **San Juan de los Lagos** Mexico
127 L10 **San Juan de los Morros** Venezuela
125 J7 **San Juan del Río** Mexico
100 C1 **San Juan Is** Washington U.S.A.
124 F7 **San Juanito, I** Mexico
106 C4 **San Juan Mts** Colo/New Mex U.S.A.
125 L9 **San Juan Quiotepec** Mexico
131 C3 **San Juan, R** Argentina
126 C3 **San Juan y Martínez** Cuba
133 D7 **San Julián** Argentina
133 E4 **San Justo** Argentina
17 G4 **San Just, Sa. de** *mts* Spain
85 C6 **Sankarani** *R* Guinea/Mali
76 C6 **Sankarankovil** India
76 B2 **Sankeshwar** India
88 E10 **Sankhulani** Malawi
49 **Sankt-Peterburg** *conurbation* Russian Federation
86 D6 **Sankuru** *R* Zaire
45 H2 **San Lazzaro** Italy
102 B4 **San Leandro** California U.S.A.
45 M4 **San Leo** Italy
124 C3 **San Lino, Sa** *mt* Mexico
78 G3 **Şanlıurfa** Turkey
133 E4 **San Lorenzo** Argentina
128 E6 **San Lorenzo** Bolivia
133 C7 **San Lorenzo** *mt* Chile/Arg
128 C3 **San Lorenzo** Ecuador
125 P9 **San Lorenzo** Guatemala
124 C3 **San Lorenzo** *isld* Mexico
124 F3 **San Lorenzo** Mexico
128 E6 **San Lorenzo** Peru
106 C9 **San Lorenzo** New Mexico U.S.A.
127 J10 **San Lorenzo** Venezuela
44 C4 **San Lorenzo al Mare** Italy
128 B4 **San Lorenzo, C** Ecuador
16 E4 **San Lorenzo de El Escorial** Spain
17 F5 **San Lorenzo de la Parrilla** Spain
17 J2 **San Lorenzo de Morunys** Spain
128 C6 **San Lorenzo, I** Peru
45 N4 **San Lorenzo in Campo** Italy
16 C8 **Sanlúcar de Barrameda** Spain
16 C7 **Sanlúcar la Mayor** Spain
128 E8 **San Lucas** Bolivia
124 E6 **San Lucas** Mexico
102 C5 **San Lucas** California U.S.A.
131 C4 **San Luis** *prov* Argentina
131 C4 **San Luis** Argentina
126 G4 **San Luis** Cuba
125 P9 **San Luís** Guatemala
125 J9 **San Luis** Mexico
124 F4 **San Luis** Chihuahua Mexico
124 D3 **San Luís** Sonora Mexico

71 E2 **San Luis** Luzon Philippines
103 K9 **San Luis** Arizona U.S.A.
106 E4 **San Luis** Colorado U.S.A.
127 K9 **San Luis** Venezuela
124 E4 **San Luis Babarocos** Mexico
125 J7 **San Luis de la Paz** Mexico
128 F6 **San Luis, L** Bolivia
103 K9 **San Luis, Mesa de** Mexico
102 D6 **San Luis Obispo** California U.S.A.
109 M6 **San Luis Pass** Texas U.S.A.
106 D3 **San Luis Pk** Colorado U.S.A.
125 J6 **San Luis Potosí** Mexico
102 G8 **San Luis Rey** *R* California U.S.A.
124 B1 **San Luis Rio Colorado** Mexico
131 C4 **San Luis, Sa. de** *mts* Argentina
102 D5 **San Luiz Canal** California U.S.A.
71 E3 **San Marcelino** Luzon Philippines
124 D3 **San Marcial** Mexico
106 C8 **San Marcial** New Mexico U.S.A.
124 D5 **San Marcial, Pta** *C* Mexico
43 B9 **San Marco, C** Sardinia
126 G10 **San Marcos** Colombia
124 C4 **San Marcos** *isld* Mexico
124 G7 **San Marcos** Mexico
109 K6 **San Marcos** Texas U.S.A.
42 E5 **San Marino** *rep* S Europe
128 F6 **San Martin** *R* Bolivia
128 D3 **San Martín** Colombia
128 C5 **San Martin** *dept* Peru
133 C6 **San Martín de los Andes** Argentina
133 C7 **San Martin, L** Chile/Arg
45 L2 **San Martino in Argine** Italy
38 E8 **San Martino in Badia** Italy
45 J2 **San Martino in Rio** Italy
45 K2 **San Martino in Spino** Italy
125 M5 **San Mateo** Costa Rica
17 H4 **San Mateo** Spain
102 B4 **San Mateo** California U.S.A.
106 C6 **San Mateo** New Mexico U.S.A.
127 M10 **San Mateo** Venezuela
106 C8 **San Mateo Pk** New Mexico U.S.A.
128 G7 **San Matías** Bolivia
131 D8 **San Matias, G** Argentina
121 R5 **Sanmaur** Quebec Canada
127 L10 **San Mauricio** Venezuela
44 C1 **San Mauro Torinese** Italy
67 G2 **Sanmen** China
67 G2 **Sanmen Wan** *B* China
65 B7 **Sanmenxia** China
45 K1 **San Michele Extra** Italy
128 F7 **San Miguel** Bolivia
128 C3 **San Miguel** *R* Ecuador
125 Q11 **San Miguel** Honduras
124 D3 **San Miguel** *R* Mexico
124 J5 **San Miguel** Mexico
128 D6 **San Miguel** Peru
71 D6 **San Miguel** *islds* Philippines
103 N10 **San Miguel** Arizona U.S.A.
102 D6 **San Miguel** California U.S.A.
106 B3 **San Miguel** *R* Colorado U.S.A.
71 F4 **San Miguel B** Philippines
109 J9 **San Miguel Camargo** Mexico
109 J7 **San Miguel Cr** Texas U.S.A.
125 J7 **San Miguel de Allende** Mexico
128 E7 **San Miguel de Huachi** Bolivia
133 D3 **San Miguel de Tucumán** Argentina
102 D7 **San Miguel I** California U.S.A.
67 F3 **Sanming** China
45 J4 **San Miniato** Italy
71 E3 **San Narciso** Luzon Philippines
44 E1 **Sannazzaro de 'Burgondi** Italy
42 G7 **Sannicandro Garganico** Italy
131 E4 **San Nicolas** Argentina
124 G5 **San Nicolás** Mexico
71 E1 **San Nicolas** Luzon Philippines
71 E2 **San Nicolas** Luzon Philippines
102 E8 **San Nicolas I** California U.S.A.
45 L2 **San Nicolo Ferrarese** Italy
27 D13 **Sannidal** Norway
51 O1 **Sannikoya, Proliv** *str* Russian Federation
45 R7 **Sannio** *mts* Italy
61 N9 **Sano** Japan
31 N6 **Sanok** Poland
133 D8 **San Pablo** Argentina
128 F7 **San Pablo** *R* Bolivia
133 D2 **San Pablo** Bolivia
71 E3 **San Pablo** Luzon Philippines
124 F4 **San Pablo Balleza** Mexico
124 B4 **San Pablo, Pta** *C* Mexico
124 H6 **San Pascual** Mexico
131 F4 **San Pedro** Buenos Aires Argentina
128 F8 **San Pedro** Jujuy Argentina
130 C10 **San Pedro** Misiones Argentina
124 E4 **San Pedro** Mexico
130 B9 **San Pedro** Paraguay
103 O9 **San Pedro** *R* Arizona U.S.A.
102 F8 **San Pedro** California U.S.A.
128 F2 **San Pedro** Venezuela
71 G5 **San Pedro B** Philippines
131 A8 **San Pedro, B.de** Chile
102 F8 **San Pedro Chan** California U.S.A.
128 D3 **San Pedro de Arimena** Colombia
124 E3 **San Pedro de la Cueva** Mexico
124 H5 **San Pedro de las Colonias** Mexico
128 C5 **San Pedro de Lloc** Peru
17 G7 **San Pedro del Pinatar** Spain
127 K5 **San Pedro de Macoris** Dominican Rep
133 C3 **San Pedro, Pta** *C* Chile
16 C5 **San Pedro, Sa. de** *mts* Spain
125 P10 **San Pedro Sula** Honduras
41 L6 **San Pellegrino Terme** Italy
44 E3 **San Pier d'Arena** Italy
45 K4 **San Piero a Sieve** Italy
99 U8 **San Pierre** Indiana U.S.A.
45 K1 **San Pietro di Morubio** Italy
45 K2 **San Pietro di Piano** Italy
43 H8 **San Pietro, I** Italy
43 B9 **San Pietro, I. di** Sardinia
42 C3 **San Pietro, Pte** Italy
100 G1 **Sanpoil** *R* Washington U.S.A.
45 J2 **San Polo d'Enza** Italy
45 H2 **San Polo d'Enza in Caviano** Italy
45 J2 **San Possidónio** Italy
45 K2 **San Prospero** Italy
15 E5 **Sanquhar** Scotland
124 A2 **San Quintín** Mexico
131 C5 **San Rafael** Argentina
128 F7 **San Rafael** Bolivia
102 B4 **San Rafael** California U.S.A.
106 C6 **San Rafael** New Mexico U.S.A.
103 O2 **San Rafael** *R* Utah U.S.A.
127 K10 **San Rafael** Venezuela
127 K5 **San Rafael, C** Dominican Rep
127 K5 **San Rafael del Yuma** Dominican Rep
103 O3 **San Rafael Knob** *mt* Utah U.S.A.
102 E7 **San Rafael Mts** California U.S.A.
125 M3 **San Ramón** Nicaragua
128 C6 **San Ramón** Peru
67 E5 **Sanrao** China
44 C4 **San Remo** Italy
108 F7 **San Rodrigo** *R* Mexico
127 J8 **San Román, C** Venezuela
16 D8 **San Roque** Spain
108 G5 **San Saba** *R* Texas U.S.A.
109 J4 **San Saba** Texas U.S.A.
126 A3 **San Salvador** *isld* Bahamas
125 P11 **San Salvador** El Salvador
128 A8 **San Salvador** *isld* Galapagos Is
131 F4 **San Salvador** *R* Uruguay
133 D2 **San Salvador de Jujuy** Argentina
133 D8 **San Sebastián** Argentina
85 A3 **San Sebastian** Canary Is
124 C3 **San Sebastián** *isld* Mexico
17 F1 **San Sebastian** Spain
127 L10 **San Sebastián** Venezuela
129 J8 **San Sebastião** Brazil
42 E5 **Sansepolcro** Italy
42 G7 **San Severo** Italy
67 G3 **Sansha** China
66 D3 **Sanshichang** China
67 D5 **Sanshui** China
128 E6 **San Silvestre** Bolivia
127 J10 **San Silvestre** Venezuela
102 C6 **San Simeon** California U.S.A.
103 P9 **San Simon** Arizona U.S.A.
103 P9 **San Simon Cr** Arizona U.S.A.
42 H4 **Sanski Most** Bosnia-Herzegovina
145 E4 **Sanson** New Zealand
108 B6 **San Sostenes** Mexico
44 C4 **San Stefano al Mare** Italy
127 N4 **Sans Toucher** *mt* Guadeloupe W Indies
67 C3 **Sansui** China
128 C5 **Santa** Peru
125 O9 **Santa Amelia** Guatemala
128 E6 **Santa Ana** Bolivia
128 B4 **Santa Ana** Ecuador
125 P11 **Santa Ana** El Salvador
124 D2 **Santa Ana** Mexico
102 G8 **Santa Ana** *R* California U.S.A.
102 G8 **Santa Ana** California U.S.A.
127 M10 **Santa Ana** Venezuela
124 F3 **Santa Ana Babicora** Mexico
102 G8 **Santa Ana Mts** California U.S.A.
44 F1 **Santa Angelo** Italy
109 H4 **Santa Anna** Texas U.S.A.
130 G6 **Santa Bárbara** Brazil
124 G4 **Santa Bárbara** Mexico
102 E7 **Santa Barbara** California U.S.A.
127 N10 **Santa Bárbara** Venezuela
102 D7 **Santa Barbara Ch** California U.S.A.
102 E8 **Santa Barbara I** California U.S.A.
102 E7 **Santa Barbara Res** California U.S.A.
130 D7 **Santa Barbara, Sa de** *mts* Brazil
128 E8 **Santa Catalina** Argentina
133 D3 **Santa Catalina** Chile
124 D5 **Santa Catalina** *isld* Mexico
102 G8 **Santa Catalina, G.of** California U.S.A.
102 F8 **Santa Catalina, I** California U.S.A.
133 G3 **Santa Catarina** *state* Brazil
124 B3 **Santa Catarina** Mexico
124 G5 **Santa Catarina de Tepehuanes** Mexico
126 B1 **Santa Catharina** Curaçao Neth Antilles
128 E4 **Santa Clara** Colombia
126 E3 **Santa Clara** Cuba
103 K10 **Santa Clara** Mexico
133 B9 **Santa Clara** *isld* Juan Fernández Is Pacific Oc
102 B4 **Santa Clara** California U.S.A.
102 E7 **Santa Clara** *R* California U.S.A.
95 N2 **Santa Clara** New York U.S.A.
103 L4 **Santa Clara** Utah U.S.A.
110 K3 **Santa Claus** Indiana U.S.A.
17 J3 **Santa Coloma de Farnés** Spain
16 B1 **Santa Comba** Spain
133 C7 **Santa Cruz** *prov* Argentina
128 F7 **Santa Cruz** Bolivia
128 D5 **Santa Cruz** Amazonas Brazil
130 J9 **Santa Cruz** Rio Grande do Norte Brazil
128 A8 **Santa Cruz** *isld* Galapagos Is
124 D5 **Santa Cruz** *isld* Mexico
128 C5 **Santa Cruz** Peru
71 E2 **Santa Cruz** Luzon Philippines
71 D3 **Santa Cruz** Luzon Philippines
71 E3 **Santa Cruz** Luzon Philippines
71 F6 **Santa Cruz** Negros Philippines
102 B5 **Santa Cruz** California U.S.A.
106 D6 **Santa Cruz** New Mexico U.S.A.
126 A1 **Santa Cruz** Aruba W Indies
130 H5 **Santa Cruz Cabralia** Brazil
85 A3 **Santa Cruz de la Palma** Canary Is
16 E5 **Santa Cruz de la Zarza** Spain
126 F4 **Santa Cruz del Sur** Cuba
16 E6 **Santa Cruz de Mudela** Spain
85 A3 **Santa Cruz de Tenerife** Canary Is
133 G3 **Santa Cruz do Sul** Brazil
137 O4 **Santa Cruz Is** Solomon Is
127 J2 **Santa Cruz Mts** Jamaica
102 B4 **Santa Cruz Mts** California U.S.A.
17 F3 **Santa Cruz, Sa. de** *mts* Spain
79 B8 **Santa, El** Egypt
128 B4 **Santa Elena** Ecuador
109 J9 **Santa Elena** Texas U.S.A.
128 F3 **Santa Elena** Venezuela
128 B4 **Santa Elena, B. de** Ecuador
125 M4 **Santa Elena, C** Costa Rica
100 J2 **Santa Emida** Idaho U.S.A.
16 A2 **Santa Eugenia de Ribeira** Spain
17 G4 **Santa Eulalia** Spain
17 J6 **Santa Eulalia del Rio** Ibiza
131 E3 **Santa Fe** Argentina
133 E4 **Santa Fe** *prov* Argentina
128 A8 **Santa Fe** *isld* Galapagos Is
71 F4 **Santa Fe** Philippines
16 E7 **Santafé** Spain
113 E8 **Santa Fe** *R* Florida U.S.A.
106 E6 **Santa Fe** New Mexico U.S.A.
129 J5 **Santa Filomena** Brazil
124 E6 **Santa Genovéva** *mt* Mexico
124 G4 **Santa Gertrudis** Mexico
129 J4 **Santa Helena** Brazil
58 E5 **Santai** China
133 C8 **Santa Ines, I** Chile
133 D5 **Santa Isabel** Argentina
128 G5 **Santa Isabel** Brazil
Santa Isabel Fernando Póo *see* **Malabo** Bioko
137 M3 **Santa Isabel** *isld* Solomon Is
124 B2 **Santa Isabel, Sa** *mts* Mexico
129 J5 **Santa Isobel do Araguaia** Brazil
129 G5 **Santa Julía** Brazil
130 F6 **Santa Juliana** Brazil
58 D4 **Santala** China
126 B3 **Santa Lucía** Cuba
124 G5 **Santa Lucía** Mexico
131 F2 **Santa Lucia, R** Argentina
131 G5 **Santa Lucia, R** Uruguay
102 C5 **Santa Lucia Rge** California U.S.A.
130 C6 **Santa Luisa, Sa. de** *mts* Brazil
130 H9 **Santa Luzia** Brazil
124 D5 **Santa Margarita** *isld* Mexico
102 D6 **Santa Margarita** California U.S.A.
102 G8 **Santa Margarita** *R* California U.S.A.
44 F3 **Santa Margherita** Italy
133 D3 **Santa María** Argentina
133 D5 **Santa María** *mt* Argentina
131 G3 **Santa Maria** *R* Brazil
128 G4 **Santa Maria** Amazonas Brazil
131 H2 **Santa Maria** Rio Grande do Sul Brazil
128 A8 **Santa María** *isld* Galapagos Is
124 F2 **Santa María** *R* Mexico
103 L7 **Santa Maria** *R* Arizona U.S.A.
102 D7 **Santa Maria** California U.S.A.
137 O4 **Santa Maria** *isld* Vanuatu
87 E8 **Santa Maria** Zambia
131 G5 **Santa Maria, C** Uruguay
43 F7 **Santa Maria Capua Vetere** Italy
126 E3 **Santa Maria, Cayo** *isld* Cuba
16 B7 **Santa Maria, C. de** Portugal
16 B8 **Santa María, C. de** Portugal
130 F4 **Santa Maria, Chapadão de** *hills* Brazil
124 F4 **Santa María de Cuevas** Mexico
127 M10 **Santa Maria de Ipire** Venezuela
124 G5 **Santa María del Oro** Mexico
43 J9 **Santa Maria di Leuca, C** Italy
45 M1 **Santa Maria di Sala** Italy
131 A6 **Santa Maria, I** Chile
103 M7 **Santa Maria Mts** Arizona U.S.A.
128 C6 **Santa Maria, Pta** *C* Peru
130 C7 **Santa Maria, R** Brazil
130 F4 **Santa Maria, Sa. de** *mts* Brazil
131 B6 **Santa Mariá, Vol** Argentina
126 G3 **Santa Marie, C** Long I Bahamas
126 G9 **Santa Marta** Colombia
87 B8 **Santa Marta, C** Angola
126 H9 **Santa Marta, Sa. Nevada de** *mts* Colombia
130 D6 **Santa Martha, Sa. de** *mts* Brazil
Santa Maura *isld* *see* **Levkás**
41 N6 **Sant Ambrogio di Valpolicella** Italy
108 G7 **Santa Mónica** Mexico
102 F7 **Santa Monica** California U.S.A.
109 K9 **Santa Monica** Texas U.S.A.
102 F8 **Santa Monica B** California U.S.A.
102 H8 **Santa Mts** California U.S.A.
70 E5 **Santan** Kalimantan
129 K6 **Santana** Brazil
131 G3 **Santana, Coxilha de** *mt* Brazil/Uruguay
131 G3 **Santana do Livramento** Brazil
128 C3 **Santander** Colombia
128 D2 **Santander** *div* Colombia
16 E1 **Santander** Spain
67 D3 **Santang** China
66 E3 **Santanghu** China
71 G5 **Santa Niño** Samar Philippines
103 N8 **Santan Mt** Arizona U.S.A.
43 B9 **Sant'Antioco** Sardinia
43 B9 **Sant'Antioco, I. di** Sardinia
102 E7 **Santa Paula** California U.S.A.
109 K9 **Santa Perlita** Texas U.S.A.
17 G6 **Santa Pola, C. de** Spain
101 O10 **Santaquin** Utah U.S.A.
16 B5 **Santarem** Portugal
130 J9 **Santa Rita** Brazil
101 N1 **Santa Rita** Montana U.S.A.
127 J9 **Santa Rita** Venezuela
131 D6 **Santa Rosa** Argentina
128 E3 **Santa Rosa** Colombia
130 C10 **Santa Rosa** Paraguay
102 B3 **Santa Rosa** California U.S.A.
108 C1 **Santa Rosa** New Mexico U.S.A.
125 M2 **Santa Rosa de Aguán** Honduras
128 F7 **Santa Rosa de la Roca** Bolivia
125 L3 **Santa Rosa de Lima** El Salvador
111 J11 **Santa Rosa I** Florida U.S.A.
109 H2 **Santa Rosa L** Texas U.S.A.
124 C4 **Santa Rosalía** Mexico
130 C10 **Santa Rosa, R** Brazil
100 H8 **Santa Rosa Range** Nevada U.S.A.
103 N9 **Santa Rosa Wash** *R* Arizona U.S.A.
133 E3 **Santa Sylvina** Argentina
129 J6 **Santa Teresa** *R* Brazil
124 G6 **Santa Teresa** Mexico
43 C7 **Santa Teresa Gallura** Sardinia
129 H6 **Santa Teresinha** Brazil
140 C6 **Santa Theresa** N Terr Australia
133 G4 **Santa Vitória do Palmar** Brazil
43 C9 **Santa Vittoria, Monte** *mt* Sardinia
102 D7 **Santa Ynez** California U.S.A.
102 D7 **Santa Ynez Mts** California U.S.A.
102 H8 **Santa Ysabel** California U.S.A.
112 H4 **Santee** *R* South Carolina U.S.A.
112 H4 **Santee Pt** South Carolina U.S.A.
112 D2 **Santeetlah, L** North Carolina U.S.A.
125 O5 **Sante Fé** Panama
124 A2 **San Telmo** Mexico
124 H8 **San Telmo, Pta** *C* Mexico
45 O5 **Sante Marie** Italy
21 N6 **Santenay** France
42 D4 **Santerno** *R* Italy
21 O5 **Santeuil** France
44 D1 **Santhià** Italy
131 B4 **Santiago** *prov* Chile
131 B4 **Santiago** Chile
127 J5 **Santiago** Dominican Rep
124 D6 **Santiago** Baja California Mexico
124 G8 **Santiago** Colima Mexico
125 O5 **Santiago** Panama
130 C10 **Santiago** Paraguay
128 C4 **Santiago** *R* Peru
16 B2 **Santiago de Compastela** Spain
126 G4 **Santiago de Cuba** Cuba
17 F6 **Santiago de la Espana** Spain
133 E3 **Santiago del Estero** *prov* Argentina
16 B6 **Santiago do Cacem** Portugal
124 G7 **Santiago Ixcuintla** Mexico
108 D6 **Santiago Mts** Texas U.S.A.
124 G5 **Santiago Papasquiaro** Mexico
102 G8 **Santiago Pk** California U.S.A.
124 H7 **Santiago, Rio Grande de** Mexico
128 G7 **Santiago, Serranía de** *mts* Bolivia
124 G5 **Santiaguillo, L. de** Mexico
70 G4 **Santigi** Sulawesi Indonesia
70 G4 **Santiki, Tanjong** *C* Sulawesi
16 E1 **Santillana** Spain
16 E6 **Santisteban del Puerto** Spain
109 J3 **Santo** Texas U.S.A.
130 F8 **Santo Amaro, I. de** Brazil
130 G6 **Santo Antônia** *R* Brazil
128 F5 **Santo Antonio** Brazil
129 K6 **Santo Antônio de Jesus** Brazil
128 E4 **Santo Antônio do Iça** Brazil
86 B7 **Santo Antonio do Zaire** Angola
130 C10 **Santo Cristo** *R* Brazil
87 D9 **Santo Cruz do Cuando** Angola
126 D3 **Santo Domingo** Cuba
127 K5 **Santo Domingo** Dominican Rep
124 B3 **Santo Domingo** Baja California Mexico
124 H3 **Santo Domingo** Coahuila Mexico
126 G4 **Santo Domingo, Cay** *isld* Bahamas
17 F2 **Santo Domingo de la Calza** Spain
124 C5 **Santo Domingo del Pacifico** Mexico
130 G6 **Santo Maria do Suaçuí** Brazil
127 M10 **San Tomé** Venezuela
128 F2 **San Tome de Guayana** Venezuela
16 E1 **Santoña** Spain
65 G3 **Santong He** *R* China
Santorini *isld* *see* **Thíra** *isld*
130 F8 **Santos** Brazil
128 E5 **Santos Dumont** Amazonas Brazil
130 G7 **Santos Dumont** Minas Gerais Brazil
16 D6 **Santos, Sa. de los** *mts* Spain
44 G1 **Santo Stéfano Lodigiano** Italy
16 B3 **Santo Tirso** Portugal
124 F3 **Santo Tomás** Mexico
128 D6 **Santo Tomás** Peru
125 P10 **Santo Tomás de Castilla** Guatemala
133 F3 **Santo Tomé** Argentina
43 C8 **Santu, C. di M** *mt* Sardinia
65 D4 **Santunying** China
103 L6 **Sanup Plat** Arizona U.S.A.
80 D4 **Sa Nur** Jordan
133 C7 **San Valentin** *mt* Chile
21 L2 **Sanvic** France
124 A2 **San Vicente** Mexico
71 F1 **San Vicente** Luzon Philippines
16 A7 **San Vicente, C. de** Portugal
128 C6 **San Vicente de Cañete** Peru
16 E1 **San Vicente de la Barquera** Spain
45 P6 **San Vicenze Falle Roveto** Italy
42 E3 **San Vito al Tag** Italy
43 E10 **San Vito, C** Sicily
38 F9 **San Vito di Cadore-Antelao** Italy
45 N6 **San Vito Romano** Italy
67 C7 **Sanya** China
88 B10 **Sanyati** *R* Zimbabwe
109 H8 **San Ygnacio** Texas U.S.A.
102 G9 **San Ysidro** California U.S.A.
106 D6 **San Ysidro** New Mexico U.S.A.
58 E5 **Sanyuan** China
65 F3 **Sanyuanpu** China
87 C7 **Sanza Pomba** Angola
65 F2 **Sanzhan** China
130 F8 **São Bernardo do Campo** Brazil
87 B7 **São Brás, Cabo de** *C* Angola
130 F8 **São Carlos** Brazil
129 L6 **São Cristóvão** Brazil
129 J6 **São Domingos** Brazil
130 D6 **São Domingos, R** Brazil
129 K7 **São Felippe, Serra de** *mts* Brazil
129 H5 **São Felix do Xingu** Brazil
129 K7 **São Francisco** Brazil
130 F6 **São Francisco** *R* Brazil
130 E10 **São Francisco do Sul** Brazil
130 E10 **Sao Francisco, I.de** Brazil
129 J7 **São Gabriel de Goias** Brazil
87 G7 **Sao Hill** Tanzania
130 D8 **São João** *R* Brazil
129 J6 **São João da Alianca** Brazil
130 F7 **São João da Boa Vista** Brazil
130 G7 **São João del Rei** Brazil
129 K5 **São João do Piauí** Brazil
129 J5 **São João du Araguaia** Brazil
129 K4 **São João, I. de** Brazil
128 F5 **São João, Sa. de** *mts* Brazil
128 E4 **São Joaquim** Brazil
128 E4 **São José** Brazil
128 F3 **São José do Anauá** Brazil
133 G4 **São José do Norte** Brazil
130 E7 **São José do Rio Prêto** Brazil
130 F8 **São José dos Campos** Brazil
130 E9 **São José dos Pinhais** Brazil
133 G3 **São Leopoldo** Brazil
130 C5 **São Lourenço** Brazil
133 G4 **São Lourenço do Sul** Brazil
130 C5 **São Lourenço, Pantanal de** *swamp* Brazil
129 J4 **São Luís** Brazil
128 F5 **São Luis de Cassianá** Brazil
133 G3 **São Luis Gonzaga** Brazil
128 E3 **São Marcelino** Brazil
129 K4 **São Marco, B. de** Brazil
130 F5 **São Marcos, R** Brazil
130 H6 **São Mateus** Brazil
130 F4 **São Miguel** *R* Brazil
127 K5 **Saona, I** Dominican Rep
19 N12 **Saône** *R* France
18 H6 **Saône-et-Loire** *dept* France
71 C3 **Saonek** W Irian
130 F8 **São Paulo** Brazil
128 E4 **São Paulo de Olivença** Brazil
128 F5 **São Pedro** Brazil
129 L5 **São Rafael** Brazil
129 J5 **São Raimundo das Mangabeiras** Brazil
129 K5 **São Raimundo Nonato** Brazil
128 E5 **São Romão** Brazil
129 H5 **São Sebastião** Brazil
130 F7 **São Sebastião do Paraíso** Brazil
130 F8 **São Sebastião, I. de** Brazil
128 F6 **São Simão** *R* Brazil
130 E6 **São Simão, Barragem de** *dam* Brazil
86 A5 **Sao Tome and Principe** *rep* West Africa
130 H7 **São Tomé, C. de** Brazil
19 O15 **Saou** France
68 F7 **Sa Oui** Cambodia
85 D3 **Saoura** *watercourse* Algeria
129 J8 **Sao Vicente** Brazil
68 F1 **Sa Pa** Vietnam
47 H3 **Sápai** Greece
69 D13 **Sapako** Indonesia
47 L4 **Sapanca** Turkey
71 E3 **Sapangbato** Luzon Philippines
46 F2 **Sapareva Banya** Bulgaria
71 J9 **Sape** Sumbawa Indonesia
85 F7 **Sapele** Nigeria
106 E6 **Sapello** New Mexico U.S.A.
112 F6 **Sapelo I** Georgia U.S.A.
16 C4 **Sa. Peña de Francia** *mt* Spain
71 J9 **Sape Selat** Indonesia
71 J9 **Sape Teluk** *B* Indonesia
47 K5 **Şaphane** Turkey
68 G2 **Sa Phin, Pou** *mt* Vietnam
46 E8 **Sapiéntza** *isld* Greece
106 C3 **Sapinero** Colorado U.S.A.
21 L4 **Sap, le** France
71 E2 **Sapocoy, Mt** Luzon Philippines
125 P6 **Sapo, Serranía del** *ra* Panama
128 C5 **Saposoa** Peru
54 M3 **Sapozhok** Russian Federation
98 F10 **Sappa Cr** Kansas U.S.A.
38 G8 **Sappada** Italy
141 J6 **Sapphire** Queensland Australia
101 M3 **Sapphire Mts** Montana U.S.A.
26 M4 **Sappisaasi** Sweden
59 M3 **Sapporo** Japan
43 G8 **Sapri** Italy
129 G4 **Sapucua, L. de** Brazil
70 P9 **Sapudi** *isld* Indonesia
70 E2 **Sapulot** Sabah
107 O5 **Sapulpa** Oklahoma U.S.A.
70 O9 **Sapulu** Java
115 O3 **Saqqaq** Greenland
78 L3 **Saqqez** Iran
78 L3 **Sarab** Iran
68 E5 **Sara Buri** Thailand
106 E6 **Sarafina** New Mexico U.S.A.
108 D4 **Saragosa** Texas U.S.A.
Saragossa *see* **Zaragoza** Spain
128 C4 **Saraguro** Ecuador
29 M7 **Säräisniemi** Finland
48 E7 **Sarajevo** Bosnia-Herzegovina
140 J5 **Saraji** Queensland Australia
77 G1 **Sarakhs** Iran
46 F4 **Saraklí** Greece
55 C5 **Saraktash** Russian Federation
129 G2 **Saramacca R** Suriname
18 F9 **Saramon** France
138 D2 **Sara, Mt** South Australia Australia
57 G1 **Saran'** Kazakhstan
94 B4 **Saranac** Michigan U.S.A.
95 N2 **Saranac Lake** New York U.S.A.
46 D5 **Sarandë** Albania
130 D10 **Sarandi** Brazil
133 F4 **Sarandi del Yi** Uruguay
70 B5 **Saran, G** *mt* Kalimantan
71 G8 **Sarangani** *isld* Mindanao Philippines
75 K8 **Sarangarh** India
53 G7 **Saransk** Russian Federation
59 L2 **Sarapul'skoye** Russian Federation
79 F3 **Sarārā** Syria
113 E10 **Sarasota** Florida U.S.A.
111 B11 **Saratoga** Texas U.S.A.
101 T8 **Saratoga** Wyoming U.S.A.
95 O3 **Saratoga Springs** New York U.S.A.
70 B4 **Saratok** Sarawak
53 G8 **Saratov** Russian Federation
77 H6 **Saravan** Iran
68 H5 **Saravan** Laos
68 D6 **Sarawa** *R* Burma
70 **Sarawak** *state* Malaysia
47 J3 **Saray** Turkey
47 K7 **Sarayköy** Turkey
77 G6 **Sarbāz** Iran
42 D3 **Sarca** *R* Italy
21 P4 **Sarcelles** France
33 T9 **Särchen** Germany
133 C3 **Sarco** Chile
110 B4 **Sarcoxie** Missouri U.S.A.
74 F4 **Sardarshahr** India
43 C8 **Sardegna** *isld* Italy
86 G5 **Sardindida Plain** Kenya
Sardinia *see* **Sardegna**
94 D7 **Sardinia** Ohio U.S.A.
47 J6 **Sardis** Turkey
112 F5 **Sardis** Georgia U.S.A.
111 G7 **Sardis** Mississippi U.S.A.
110 H6 **Sardis** Tennessee U.S.A.
107 P7 **Sardis Lake** Oklahoma U.S.A.
71 J8 **Sarege** *isld* Indonesia
45 K1 **Sarego** Italy
26 J4 **Sarektjåkko** *mt* Sweden
70 D5 **Sarempaka** *mt* Kalimantan
86 G3 **Sarenga** *mt* Ethiopia
41 O4 **Sarentina, V** Italy
42 D2 **Sarentine, Alpi** *mts* Italy
41 O4 **Sarentino** Italy
77 J1 **Sar-e-Pol** Afghanistan
77 K2 **Sar-e Pol** *prov* Afghanistan
111 C9 **Sarepta** Louisiana U.S.A.
77 D4 **Sar e Yazd** Iran
41 K3 **Sargans** Switzerland
90 C6 **Sargasso Sea** Atlantic Oc
55 F3 **Sargatskoye** Russian Federation
21 L5 **Sarge** France
102 C5 **Sargent** California U.S.A.
98 G8 **Sargent** Nebraska U.S.A.
116 N6 **Sargent Icefield** Alaska U.S.A.
106 D3 **Sargents** Colorado U.S.A.
21 M6 **Sargé-sur-Braye** France
74 E2 **Sargodha** Pakistan
86 C4 **Sarh** Chad
85 C2 **Sarhro, Jbel** *mts* Morocco
77 C1 **Sārī** Iran
47 J9 **Sária** *isld* Greece
57 E5 **Sariasiya** Uzbekistan
124 D2 **Sáric** Mexico
116 E9 **Sarichef, C** Aleutian Is
80 D3 **Sarid** Israel
47 K6 **Sarigöl** Turkey
78 J1 **Sarıkamıs** Turkey
78 C2 **Şarikaraağaç** Turkey
79 D2 **Sarıkavac** Turkey
70 B3 **Sarikei** Sarawak
141 J5 **Sarina** Queensland Australia
17 G3 **Sariñena** Spain
77 K2 **Sar-i-Pul** Afghanistan
84 G4 **Sarīr** Libya
109 K8 **Sarita** Texas U.S.A.
59 J4 **Sariwŏn** N Korea
78 C1 **Sarıyar Barajı** *dam* Turkey
29 L7 **Sarjakylä** Finland
20 F3 **Sark** *isld* Channel Is
57 J2 **Sarkand** Kazakhstan
78 F2 **Sarkisla** Turkey
47 J4 **Şarköy** Turkey
18 F8 **Sarlat** France
77 K4 **Sarlath Range** Afghanistan/Pakistan
98 H1 **Sarles** North Dakota U.S.A.
119 T10 **Sarles** North Dakota U.S.A.
52 H6 **Sarmanovo** Russian Federation
48 J4 **Sărmaşu** Romania
136 H2 **Sarmi** W Irian
133 D7 **Sarmiento** Argentina
133 C8 **Sarmiento** *mt* Chile
27 F10 **Särna** Sweden
27 M14 **Sārnate** Latvia
8 B3 **Sarnau** Wales
41 H4 **Sarnen** Switzerland
120 H10 **Sarnia** Ontario Canada
41 L6 **Sarnico** Italy
43 F8 **Sarno** Italy
53 C8 **Sarny** Ukraine
27 E14 **Särö** Sweden
70 G6 **Saroako** Sulawesi
69 F14 **Sarolangun** Sumatra
60 R1 **Saroma-ko** *L* Japan
46 F7 **Saronikós Kólpos** *B* Greece
42 C3 **Saronno** Italy
47 H4 **Saros Körfezi** *B* Turkey
77 L2 **Şarowbī** Afghanistan
46 D2 **Šar Planina** *mt* Macedonia/Serbia
27 E12 **Sarpsborg** Norway
101 T4 **Sarpy** Montana U.S.A.
36 C6 **Sarralbe** France
36 C6 **Sarraltroff** France
19 N14 **Sarras** France
36 C6 **Sarrebourg** France
19 K3 **Sarreguemines** France
16 C2 **Sarria** Spain
19 N16 **Sarrians** France
17 G4 **Sarrión** Spain
80 G5 **Sarrut** Jordan
55 C3 **Sars** Russian Federation
52 H6 **Sarsak Omga** Russian Federation
45 M4 **Sarsina** Italy
22 D3 **Sars, le** France
22 G3 **Sars-Poteries** France
32 L8 **Sarstedt** Germany
22 K2 **Sart** Belgium
74 D5 **Sartanahu** Pakistan
51 N2 **Sartang** *R* Russian Federation
18 F5 **Sarthe** *dept* France
21 K5 **Sarthe** *R* France
20 H4 **Sartilly** France
Sartu *see* **Daqing**
60 R3 **Sarubetsu** *R* Japan
60 F10 **Sarumasay** Japan
75 O5 **Sarupeta** India
79 G3 **Sarūt** *R* Syria
78 L4 **Sarvabad** Iran
48 E4 **Sarviz** *R* Hungary
26 F9 **Särvsjö** Sweden
57 G2 **Sarykomey** Kazakhstan
55 D5 **Sarykopa, Oz** *L* Kazakhstan
55 D5 **Sarymoin, Oz** *L* Kazakhstan
57 J3 **Sary-Ozek** Kazakhstan
57 G2 **Sary-Shagan** Kazakhstan
57 E2 **Sarysu** *R* Kazakhstan
57 G5 **Sary-Tash** Kirghizia
52 J3 **Sar'yudin** Russian Federation
57 B6 **Saryyazinskoye Vodokhranilishche** *res* Turkmenistan
57 H2 **Saryyesik-Atyray** *desert* Kazakhstan
57 J3 **Saryzhaz** Kazakhstan
44 G3 **Sarzana** Italy
20 E6 **Sarzeau** France
124 D2 **Sásabe** Mexico
103 N10 **Sasabe** Arizona U.S.A.
86 H4 **Sasabeneh** Ethiopia
69 D12 **Sasak** Sumatra
75 L6 **Sasaram** India
71 J9 **Sasar Tg** *C* Sumba Indonesia
60 J10 **Sasayama** Japan
40 G1 **Sasbach** Germany
60 C12 **Sasebo** Japan
114 J7 **Saskatchewan** *prov* Canada
119 O5 **Saskatchewan** *R* Canada
118 L6 **Saskatoon** Saskatchewan Canada
119 Q5 **Saskeram L** Manitoba Canada
51 L1 **Saskylakh** Russian Federation
125 M3 **Saslaya** *mt* Nicaragua
89 E6 **Sasolburg** S Africa
109 J6 **Saspamco** Texas U.S.A.
112 E2 **Sassafras Mt** South Carolina U.S.A.
77 C7 **Sassan** *oil well* Persian Gulf
85 C7 **Sassandra** *R* Ivory Coast
85 C8 **Sassandra** Ivory Coast
37 K4 **Sassanfahr** Germany
43 B8 **Sassari** Sardinia
33 S4 **Sassen** Germany
19 P14 **Sassenage** France
32 H9 **Sassenberg** Germany
33 N7 **Sassenburg** Germany
25 C4 **Sassenheim** Netherlands
21 M2 **Sassetot** France
30 H1 **Sassnitz** Germany
45 N4 **Sassocorvaro** Italy
45 K3 **Sasso Marconi** Italy
38 E8 **Sass Rigais** *mt* Italy
45 J2 **Sassuolo** Italy
17 G3 **Sástago** Spain
133 E4 **Sastre** Argentina
60 C11 **Sasuna** Japan
25 A6 **Sas-van Gent** Netherlands
57 K2 **Sasykkol', Ozero** *L* Kazakhstan
48 M5 **Sasyk, Oz** *L* Ukraine
53 D10 **Sasyk, Ozero** *L* Ukraine
85 B6 **Satadougou** Mali
60 D14 **Sata-misaki** *C* Japan
106 B6 **Satan Pass** New Mexico U.S.A.
107 K4 **Satanta** Kansas U.S.A.
76 A2 **Satara** India
114 H2 **Satellite B** Northwest Territories Canada
113 G9 **Satellite Beach** Florida U.S.A.
71 H8 **Satengar** *isld* Indonesia
27 H11 **Säter** Sweden
32 G6 **Saterland** *reg* Germany
112 E6 **Satilla** *R* Georgia U.S.A.
19 N14 **Satillieu** France
128 D6 **Satipo** Peru
26 K4 **Satisjaure** *L* Sweden
55 C4 **Satka** Russian Federation
13 G4 **Satley** England
Satluj *R* *see* **Sutlej** *R*
74 F8 **Satmala Hills** India
71 H9 **Satonda** *isld* Indonesia
86 D6 **Satonga** *R* Zaire
42 H4 **Šator** *mt* Bosnia-Herzegovina
48 G2 **Sátoraljaújhely** Hungary
33 P5 **Satow** Germany
74 F8 **Satpura Range** India
28 D7 **Satrup** Germany
60 D14 **Satsuma-hantō** *pen* Japan
26 N4 **Sattajärvi** Sweden
29 M4 **Sattanen** Finland
41 J3 **Sattel** Switzerland
76 E2 **Sattenapalle** India
68 B3 **Satthwa** Burma
26 J9 **Sättna** Sweden
38 K8 **Sattnitz** *reg* Austria
70 D6 **Satui** Kalimantan
48 H3 **Satu Mare** Romania
69 D9 **Satun** Thailand
100 B1 **Saturna I** British Columbia Canada
100 E3 **Satus** Washington U.S.A.
76 C5 **Satyamangalam** India
55 D2 **Satyga** Russian Federation
38 L8 **Saualpe** *mts* Austria
70 P9 **Saubi** *isld* Indonesia
122 H2 **Saubosq, L** Quebec Canada
124 J5 **Sauceda** Mexico
103 M9 **Sauceda Mts** Arizona U.S.A.
131 E7 **Sauce, R** Argentina
124 G4 **Sauces** Mexico
111 G11 **Saucier** Mississippi U.S.A.
124 G3 **Saucillo** Mexico
27 B12 **Sauda** Norway
128 F5 **Saudade** Brazil
28 S9 **Saudhárkrókur** Iceland
72 E4 **Saudi Arabia** *kingdom*
36 D1 **Sauerland** *reg* Germany
129 G6 **Saueruina** *R* Brazil
71 G7 **Saug** *R* Mindanao Philippines
99 U7 **Saugatuck** Michigan U.S.A.
120 J8 **Saugeen** *R* Ontario Canada
117 K9 **Saugstad, Mt** British Columbia Canada
18 H8 **Saugues** France
129 G4 **Sauiá** Brazil
18 E7 **Saujon** France
99 M4 **Sauk** *R* Minnesota U.S.A.
100 D1 **Sauk** *R* Washington U.S.A.
99 M4 **Sauk Center** Minnesota U.S.A.
99 R6 **Sauk City** Wisconsin U.S.A.
52 B6 **Šaukenai** Lithuania
19 N15 **Saulce** France
22 G4 **Saulces-Monclin** France
21 K5 **Saule, Mt.du** France
41 L1 **Saulgau** Germany
41 O2 **Saulgrub** Germany
18 H5 **Saulieu** France
52 B6 **Saulkrasti** Latvia
122 F9 **Saulnierville** Nova Scotia Canada
19 O16 **Sault** France
122 C5 **Sault au Mouton** Quebec Canada
122 C5 **Sault-aux-Cochons, R** Quebec Canada
120 F6 **Sault Ste. Marie** Ontario Canada
120 F6 **Sault Ste. Marie** Michigan U.S.A.
36 C7 **Saulxures** France
80 G3 **Saum** Jordan
141 L5 **Saumarez Reef** Gt Barrier Reef Aust
127 J5 **Saumâtre, Etang** *L* Haiti
21 N5 **Saumeray** France
136 G3 **Saumlakki** Moluccas Indonesia
21 K7 **Saumur** France
122 K2 **Saumur, L** Quebec Canada
29 N4 **Saunavaara** Finland
118 B6 **Saunders** Alberta Canada
146 C10 **Saunders Coast** *coast* Antarctica
8 B4 **Saundersfoot** Wales
146 G2 **Saunders I** S Sandwich Is S Atlantic Oc
140 B2 **Saunders, Mt** N Terr Australia
8 B5 **Saunton** England
87 D7 **Saurimo** Angola
57 L2 **Saur, Khrebet** *mts* Kazakhstan
41 K4 **Sauronstock** *mt* Switzerland
38 M8 **Sausal** *reg* Austria
102 B4 **Sausalito** California U.S.A.
71 C3 **Sausapor** W Irian
20 H2 **Saussemesnil** France
19 O18 **Sausset-les-Pins** France
40 A3 **Saussy** France
70 G5 **Sausu** Sulawesi
87 C8 **Sautar** Angola
122 H2 **Sauterelles, Lac aux** Quebec Canada
127 P5 **Sauteurs** Grenada
20 G7 **Sautron** France
18 E9 **Sauveterre** France
18 F8 **Sauveterre-de-Guyenne** France
29 K11 **Sauvo** Finland
25 G2 **Sauwerd** Netherlands
20 D7 **Sauzon** France
42 H3 **Sava** *R* Croatia/Slovenia/Yugoslavia
95 L7 **Savage** Maryland U.S.A.
111 F7 **Savage** Mississippi U.S.A.
98 B2 **Savage** Montana U.S.A.
139 H8 **Savage River** Tasmania Australia
101 U6 **Savageton** Wyoming U.S.A.
134 A1 **Savaii** *isld* Western Samoa
85 E7 **Savalou** Benin
122 A2 **Savan'e, R** Quebec Canada
126 A2 **Savaneta** Aruba W Indies
99 Q7 **Savanna** Illinois U.S.A.
107 P7 **Savanna** Oklahoma U.S.A.
112 F5 **Savannah** Georgia U.S.A.
110 B2 **Savannah** Missouri U.S.A.
94 E6 **Savannah** Ohio U.S.A.
112 E3 **Savannah** *R* South Carolina U.S.A.
110 H6 **Savannah** Tennessee U.S.A.
112 F6 **Savannah Beach** Georgia U.S.A.
113 L12 **Savannah Sound** Bahamas
126 F2 **Savannah Sound** Eleuthera Bahamas
68 G4 **Savannakhet** Laos
127 H2 **Savanna la Mar** Jamaica
Sāvantvadi *see* **Vādi**
76 B3 **Savanur** India
26 L8 **Sävar** Sweden
26 L7 **Sävarån** *R* Sweden
40 F6 **Savaranche, V** Italy
26 M6 **Sävast** Sweden
47 J5 **Savaştepe** Turkey
85 E7 **Savé** Benin
18 F9 **Save** *R* France
87 F10 **Save** *R* Mozambique
77 B2 **Sāveh** Iran
85 D7 **Savelugu** Ghana
56 F3 **Savel'yevka** Russian Federation
45 K3 **Savena** *R* Italy
20 G7 **Savenay** France
18 G9 **Saverdun** France
36 C6 **Saverne** France
101 S8 **Savery** Wyoming U.S.A.
44 C2 **Savigliano** Italy
45 M3 **Savignano** Italy
21 L6 **Savigne** France
21 L5 **Savigné-l'Evêque** France
21 L7 **Savigné-sur-Lathan** France
45 K3 **Savigno** Italy
21 L7 **Savigny-en-Véron** Indre-et-Loire France
21 M6 **Savigny-sur-Braye** France
19 Q15 **Savines** France
42 F2 **Savinja** *R* Slovenia
52 H2 **Savino** Russian Federation
52 J3 **Savinobor** Russian Federation
45 M3 **Savio** Italy
45 M4 **Såvio** *R* Italy
29 N10 **Savitaipale** Finland
42 J6 **Šavnik** Montenegro Yugoslavia
120 F3 **Savoff** Ontario Canada
19 K7 **Savoie** *dept* France
117 N10 **Savona** British Columbia Canada
44 D3 **Savona** Italy
95 K4 **Savona** New York U.S.A.
29 O10 **Savonlinna** Finland
29 O9 **Savonranta** Finland
116 B5 **Savoonga** St Lawrence I, Alaska U.S.A.
111 H9 **Savoy** Mississippi U.S.A.
101 R1 **Savoy** Montana U.S.A.
48 N2 **Savran'** Ukraine
27 G14 **Sävsjö** Sweden
27 H15 **Sävsjöström** Sweden
71 K10 **Savu** *isld* Indonesia
42 E3 **Savudrija Rtič** *pt* Croatia
29 N4 **Savukoski** Finland
78 H3 **Savur** Turkey
71 K9 **Savu Sea** Indonesia
80 C5 **Savyon** Israel
68 B2 **Saw** Burma
69 E13 **Sawahlunto** Sumatra
74 G6 **Sawai Madhopur** India
70 M9 **Sawall, G** *mt* Java
70 D5 **Sawan** Kalimantan
68 F4 **Sawang Daen Din** Thailand
68 D4 **Sawankhalok** Thailand
60 O3 **Sawara** Hokkaido Japan
61 O10 **Sawara** Honshu Japan
61 M8 **Sawasaki-bana** *C* Japan
106 D2 **Sawatch Ra** Colorado U.S.A.
121 L1 **Sawayan Pt** Quebec Canada
119 Q1 **Sawbill** Manitoba Canada
84 E4 **Sawdā', Jabal as** *mts* Libya
118 D4 **Sawdy** Alberta Canada
14 D2 **Sawel** *mt* N Ireland
69 A8 **Sawi B** Nicobar Is
80 E5 **Sāwīya** Jordan
107 L4 **Sawlog Cr** Kansas U.S.A.
117 O3 **Sawmill Bay** Northwest Territories Canada
9 G3 **Sawston** England
116 N4 **Sawtooth Mt** Alaska U.S.A.
99 P2 **Sawtooth Mts** Minnesota U.S.A.
101 L6 **Sawtooth Range** Idaho U.S.A.
100 E1 **Sawtooth Range** Washington U.S.A.
Sawu *see* **Savu**
71 L10 **Sawu** Indonesia
107 M4 **Sawyer** Kansas U.S.A.
98 E1 **Sawyer** North Dakota U.S.A.
99 T5 **Sawyer** Wisconsin U.S.A.
100 B8 **Sawyers Bar** California U.S.A.
121 T7 **Sawyerville** Quebec Canada
141 F4 **Saxby** *R* Queensland Australia
141 G5 **Saxby Downs** Queensland Australia
9 F1 **Saxilby** England
9 H3 **Saxmundham** England
26 H7 **Saxnäs** Sweden
99 Q3 **Saxon** Wisconsin U.S.A.
94 J6 **Saxton** Pennsylvania U.S.A.
144 D5 **Saxton Pass** New Zealand
85 E6 **Say** Niger
79 F3 **Şāyā** Syria
81 C6 **Saya de Malha Bank** Indian Oc
57 H2 **Sayak Pervyy** Kazakhstan
128 C6 **Sayán** Peru
56 D4 **Sayano-Shushenskoye Vodokhranilishche** *res* Russian Federation
56 D3 **Sayanskiy** Russian Federation

56 D5 **Sayanskiy Khrebet** *mt* Russian Federation
57 C5 **Sayat** Turkmenistan
125 O9 **Sayaxché** Guatemala
37 P2 **Sayda** Germany
69 C8 **Sayer I** Thailand
72 G5 **Sayḩūt** Yemen
86 H3 **Saylac** Somalia
56 C6 **Saylyugem, Khrebet** *mts* Russian Federation
29 M9 **Säynätsalo** Finland
58 F3 **Saynshand** Mongolia
108 E8 **Sayre** Oklahoma U.S.A.
95 L5 **Sayre** Pennsylvania U.S.A.
124 H8 **Sayula** Mexico
72 F5 **Say'ūn** Yemen
117 L10 **Sayward** British Columbia Canada
46 C4 **Sazan** *isld* Albania
31 J6 **Sázava** *R* Czech Rep
55 C3 **Sazhino** Russian Federation
47 M10 **Sazli** *R* Turkey
47 M10 **Sazlibosna Çitlihan** Turkey
52 E5 **Sazonovo** Russian Federation
85 D3 **Sbaa** Algeria
85 F1 **Sbeitla** Tunisia
6 L4 **S Brae** *oil rig* North Sea
143 D10 **Scaddan** W Australia Australia
20 C5 **Scaër** France
45 R8 **Scafati** Italy
13 E5 **Scafell Pikes** *mt* England
13 H5 **Scalby** England
43 G9 **Scalea** Italy
99 Q7 **Scales Mound** Illinois U.S.A.
15 G2 **Scalloway** Shetland Scotland
15 C3 **Scalpay** *isld* Scotland
116 E6 **Scammon Bay** Alaska U.S.A.
9 F1 **Scampton** England
118 F8 **Scandia** Alberta Canada
107 N2 **Scandia** Kansas U.S.A.
45 J2 **Scandiano** Italy
45 N5 **Scandriglia** Italy
119 V8 **Scanterbury** Manitoba Canada
43 H8 **Scanzano Ionico** Italy
118 F7 **Scapa** Alberta Canada
6 K4 **Scapa** *oil rig* North Sea
15 E2 **Scapa Flow** Orkney Scotland
100 C4 **Scappoose** Oregon U.S.A.
43 F12 **Scaramia, C** Sicily
15 C4 **Scarba** *isld* Scotland
142 A1 **Scarborough** *dist* Perth, W Aust Australia
120 E9 **Scarborough** Ontario Canada
13 H5 **Scarborough** England
127 M2 **Scarborough** Tobago
144 D5 **Scargill** New Zealand
14 A5 **Scariff** *isld* Ireland
15 A2 **Scarp** *isld* Lewis Scotland
Scarpanto *isld see* **Kárpathos** *isld*
22 D3 **Scarpe** *R* France
45 K4 **Scarperia** Italy
119 R9 **Scarth** Manitoba Canada
123 N7 **Scaterie I** C Breton I, Nova Scotia
15 B3 **Scavaig, L** Scotland
138 C5 **Sceale B** South Australia Australia
21 M5 **Sceaux** Sarthe France
42 G5 **Šćedro** *isld* Croatia
98 D6 **Scenic** South Dakota U.S.A.
118 H8 **Sceptre** Saskatchewan Canada
33 N6 **Schaale** *R* Germany
33 N5 **Schaalsee** *L* Germany
38 H6 **Schafberg** *mt* Austria
99 T4 **Schaffer** Michigan U.S.A.
41 J2 **Schaffhausen** Switzerland
28 C7 **Schaffland** Germany
33 P10 **Schafstädt** Germany
25 C3 **Schagen** Netherlands
36 C6 **Schalbach** France
37 P6 **Schalding** Germany
32 G8 **Schale** Germany
37 L3 **Schalkau** Germany
32 G10 **Schalksmühle** Germany
99 L7 **Schaller** Iowa U.S.A.
41 K4 **Schams** *R* Switzerland
32 G8 **Schapen** Germany
38 H5 **Schärding** Austria
32 H5 **Scharhörn** *isld* Germany
33 M6 **Scharnebeck** Germany
41 O3 **Scharnitz** Austria
32 G6 **Scharrel** Germany
36 G1 **Schauenburg** Germany
37 M3 **Schauenstein** Germany
32 K8 **Schaumburg** Germany
36 H6 **Schechingen** Germany
25 G2 **Scheemda** Netherlands
41 K1 **Scheer** Germany
32 K6 **Scheessel** Germany
115 N7 **Schefferville** Quebec Canada
38 M6 **Scheibbs** Austria
37 K4 **Scheinfeld** Germany
22 G1 **Schelde** *R* Belgium
36 H7 **Schelklingen** Germany
103 K2 **Schell Creek Ra** Nevada U.S.A.
95 O4 **Schenectady** New York U.S.A.
32 K4 **Schenefeld** Germany
32 L5 **Schenefeld** Germany
36 H2 **Schenklengsfeld** Germany
32 K9 **Scherfede** Germany
32 E9 **Schermbeck** Germany
25 C3 **Schermerhorn** Netherlands
33 N10 **Schernberg** Germany
22 H2 **Scherpen Heuvel** Belgium
28 D7 **Schersberg** *hill* Germany
109 J6 **Schertz** Texas U.S.A.
41 L3 **Schesaplana** *mt* Austria
37 L4 **Schesslitz** Germany
25 B4 **Scheveningen** Netherlands
38 J7 **Schiadming** Austria
25 B5 **Schiedam** Netherlands
32 K9 **Schieder** Germany
15 D4 **Schiehallion** *mt* Scotland
33 N6 **Schierling** Germany
25 F2 **Schiermonnikoog** Netherlands
25 F2 **Schiermonnokoog** *isld* Netherlands
33 S8 **Schiessplatz** Germany
36 F2 **Schiffenberg** Germany
36 E5 **Schifferstadt** Germany
36 C5 **Schiffweiler** Germany
25 D5 **Schijndel** Netherlands
33 R10 **Schildau** Germany
33 N6 **Schilde** *R* Germany
33 R6 **Schillersdorf** Germany
32 L8 **Schillerslage** Germany
32 H5 **Schillighörn** *pt* Germany
37 J5 **Schillingsfürst** Germany
41 M5 **Schilpario** Italy
36 E7 **Schiltach** Germany
38 N4 **Schiltern** Austria
41 O6 **Schio** Italy
25 F4 **Schipbeek** *R* Netherlands
25 C4 **Schiphol** Netherlands
19 K4 **Schirmeck** France
33 Q10 **Schkeuditz** Germany
37 M1 **Schkölen** Germany
33 T9 **Schlabendorf** Germany
38 J7 **Schladminger Tauern** *mts* Austria
36 E3 **Schlangenbad** Germany
36 C1 **Schlebusch** Germany
30 E1 **Schlei** *R* Germany
36 B2 **Schleiden** Germany
36 E6 **Schleithal** France
37 M2 **Schleiz** Germany
33 P5 **Schlemmin** Germany
30 E1 **Schleswig** Germany
99 L7 **Schleswig** Iowa U.S.A.
32 K4 **Schleswig Holstein** *land* Germany
37 O2 **Schlettau** Germany
37 K2 **Schleusinger-Neundorf** Germany
37 M4 **Schlicht** Germany
33 S9 **Schlieben** Germany
40 G2 **Schliengen** Germany
36 H3 **Schlüchtern** Germany
36 H2 **Schlitz** Germany
32 J9 **Schloss-Holte** Germany
37 L1 **Schlossvippach** Germany
37 K1 **Schlotheim** Germany
40 H2 **Schluchsee** Germany
40 F1 **Schlucht, Col de la** *pass* France
32 K8 **Schlüsselburg** Germany
33 N5 **Schlutup** Germany
36 E1 **Schmallenberg** Germany
33 O7 **Schmarsau** Germany
36 B5 **Schmelz** Germany
37 M5 **Schmidmühlen** Germany
36 B3 **Schmidthein** Germany
37 K2 **Schmiedefeld** Germany
36 F1 **Schmittlotheim** Germany
81 A10 **Schmitt-Ott Seamount** Atlantic Oc
37 N2 **Schmölln** Germany
37 K7 **Schmutter** *R* Germany
37 M4 **Schnabelwaid** Germany
33 P6 **Schnackenburg** Germany
37 N4 **Schnaittenbach** Germany
36 C6 **Schnee Berg** *mt* France
37 O2 **Schneeberg** Germany
37 M3 **Schneeburg** *mt* Germany
32 K7 **Schneeren** Germany
33 O9 **Schneidlingen** Germany
37 J5 **Schnelldorf** Germany
32 L6 **Schneverdingen** Germany
38 K7 **Schöder** Austria
40 G1 **Schöenau** France
99 R5 **Schofield** Wisconsin U.S.A.
135 Q2 **Schofield Barracks** Hawaiian Is
95 N4 **Schoharie** New York U.S.A.
41 P3 **Scholastika** Austria
127 L4 **Schœlcher** Martinique W Indies
33 Q7 **Schollene** Germany
36 G3 **Schöllkrippen** Germany
89 D7 **Scholtzkop** *mt* S Africa
36 F7 **Schömberg** Germany
38 J6 **Schön** *mt* Austria
36 G6 **Schönaich** Germany
36 F5 **Schönau** Germany
37 J2 **Schönau** Germany
36 B3 **Schönau** Nordrhein-Westfalen Germany
22 L3 **Schonberg** Belgium
30 E1 **Schönberg** Germany
33 R7 **Schönberg** Germany
36 H3 **Schondra** Germany
33 P8 **Schönebeck** Germany
33 S8 **Schöneberg** Germany
37 N3 **Schöneck** Germany
36 B3 **Schönecken-Wetteldorf** Germany
33 S8 **Schönefeld** *airport* Germany
36 C5 **Schönenberg-Kubelberg** Germany
33 S9 **Schönewalde** Germany
36 B3 **Schönfeld** Germany
41 N2 **Schongau** Germany
32 L9 **Schönhagen** Germany
33 Q7 **Schönhausen** Germany
37 O3 **Schönheide** Germany
33 N8 **Schöningen** Germany
37 O4 **Schönsee** Germany
36 H5 **Schöntal** Germany
37 O5 **Schönthal** Germany
37 J3 **Schonungen** Germany
33 S7 **Schönwalde** Germany
33 N4 **Schönwalde am Bungsberg** Germany
95 S1 **Schoodic L** Maine U.S.A.
94 B4 **Schoolcraft** Michigan U.S.A.
25 C5 **Schoonhoven** Netherlands
25 C3 **Schoorl** Netherlands
40 G2 **Schopfheim** Germany
33 T7 **Schopfurch** Germany
33 N8 **Schöppenstedt** Germany
32 F8 **Schöppingen** Germany
36 C5 **Schorbach** France
36 H6 **Schorndorf** Germany
32 G5 **Schortens** Germany
36 G3 **Schotten** Germany
139 J8 **Schouten I** Tasmania Australia
25 A5 **Schouwen** Netherlands
100 G2 **Schrag** Washington U.S.A.
36 E7 **Schramberg** Germany
33 P10 **Schraplau** Germany
40 H4 **Schreckhorn** *mt* Switzerland
36 G2 **Schrecksbach** Germany
120 C4 **Schreiber** Ontario Canada
33 Q6 **Schrepkow** Germany
33 N5 **Schretstaken** Germany
36 F5 **Schriesheim** Germany
37 L6 **Schrobenhausen** Germany
95 O3 **Schroon Lake** New York U.S.A.
36 H5 **Schrozberg** Germany
41 L3 **Schruns** Austria
53 B7 **Schuchin** Belarus
103 M9 **Schuchuli** Arizona U.S.A.
32 L8 **Schulenburg** Germany
109 L6 **Schulenburg** Texas U.S.A.
118 G8 **Schuler** Alberta Canada
14 B5 **Schull** Ireland
37 M1 **Schulpforta** Germany
107 P6 **Schulter** Oklahoma U.S.A.
141 K1 **Schultz Can** Brisbane, Qnsld Australia
115 K5 **Schultz L** Northwest Territories Canada
33 T8 **Schulzendorf** Germany
120 J4 **Schumacher** Ontario Canada
33 N8 **Schunter** *R* Germany
40 H4 **Schüpfheim** Switzerland
102 F3 **Schurz** Nevada U.S.A.
41 L2 **Schussen** *R* Germany
36 D7 **Schutterwald** Germany
32 F8 **Schüttorf** Germany
98 J8 **Schuyler** Nebraska U.S.A.
94 J9 **Schuyler** Virginia U.S.A.
95 L6 **Schuylkill Haven** Pennsylvania U.S.A.
33 Q5 **Schwaan** Germany
37 L5 **Schwabach** Germany
37 J7 **Schwaben** *reg* Germany
37 L7 **Schwabhausen** Germany
36 G7 **Schwäbische Alb** *mts* Germany
36 H6 **Schwäbisch Gmünd** Germany
36 H5 **Schwäbisch Hall** Germany
41 K3 **Schwägalp** Switzerland
37 M7 **Schwaig** Germany
36 G5 **Schwaigern** Germany
32 K9 **Schwalenberg** Germany
36 G2 **Schwalm** *R* Germany
38 M8 **Schwanberg** Austria
37 L5 **Schwand** Germany
41 K3 **Schwanden** Switzerland
37 N5 **Schwandorf** Germany
33 O9 **Schwanebeck** Germany
70 C5 **Schwaner Peg** *mts* Kalimantan
32 J6 **Schwanewede** Germany
32 L7 **Schwarmstedt** Germany
33 R6 **Schwarz** Germany
37 L2 **Schwarza** Germany
38 H7 **Schwarzach** Austria
37 N5 **Schwarzach** *R* Germany
37 L2 **Schwarzburg** Germany
33 S9 **Schwarze Elster** *R* Germany
37 M3 **Schwarzenbach** Germany
33 M6 **Schwarzenbek** Germany
37 K4 **Schwarzenberg** Germany
36 G2 **Schwarzenborn** Hessen Germany
36 B3 **Schwarzenborn** Rheinland-Pfalz Germany
40 F4 **Schwarzenburg** Switzerland
37 N5 **Schwarzenfeld** Germany
36 H3 **Schwarzenfels** Germany
36 B3 **Schwarzer Mann** *mt* Germany
37 O5 **Schwarzer Regen** *R* Germany
37 N5 **Schwarzhofen** Germany
40 G5 **Schwarzhorn** *mt* Switzerland
36 E7 **Schwarzwald** *mts* Germany
36 B4 **Schwarzwälder Hochwald** *mts* Germany
116 J3 **Schwatka Mts** Alaska U.S.A.
41 P3 **Schwaz** Austria
31 H2 **Schwedt** Germany
40 F4 **Schwefelberg** Switzerland
36 B4 **Schweich** Germany
36 D7 **Schweighausen** Germany
37 J2 **Schweina** Germany
33 M7 **Schweinau** Germany
37 J3 **Schweinfurt** Germany
33 S9 **Schweinitz** Germany
32 F10 **Schwelm** Germany
Schwenningen *see* **Villingen-Schwenningen**
33 O5 **Schwerin** Germany
33 O5 **Schweriner See** *L* Germany
32 G10 **Schwerte** Germany
36 F5 **Schwetzingen** Germany
33 T5 **Schwichtenberg** Germany
31 H3 **Schwielochsee** *L* Germany
33 R8 **Schwielowsee** *L* Germany
32 K5 **Schwinge** *R* Germany
33 R5 **Schwinkendorf** Germany
33 P9 **Schwittersaf** Germany
41 J3 **Schwyz** Switzerland
43 E11 **Sciacca** Sicily
43 F12 **Scicli** Sicily
21 N2 **Scie** *R* France
9 F7 **Scilly, Isles of** England
31 J4 **Ścinawa** Poland
94 K4 **Scio** New York U.S.A.
94 F6 **Scio** Ohio U.S.A.
94 D8 **Scioto** *R* Ohio U.S.A.
94 E8 **Sciotoville** Ohio U.S.A.
103 M2 **Scipio** Utah U.S.A.
119 R7 **Sclater** Manitoba Canada
8 B4 **Scleddau** Wales
48 H5 **Scoarța** Romania
98 A1 **Scobey** Montana U.S.A.
103 N2 **Scofield Res** Utah U.S.A.
118 E7 **Scollard** Alberta Canada
139 K4 **Scone** New South Wales Australia
15 E4 **Scone** Scotland
111 H9 **Scooba** Mississippi U.S.A.
21 L8 **Scorbé-Clairvaux** France
115 R3 **Scoresby Land** Greenland
115 R3 **Scoresby Sund** *sd* Greenland
115 R3 **Scoresbysund** Greenland
20 D6 **Scorff, R** France
100 G9 **Scossa** Nevada U.S.A.
121 L7 **Scotia** Ontario Canada
102 A1 **Scotia** California U.S.A.
98 H8 **Scotia** Nebraska U.S.A.
100 H1 **Scotia** Washington U.S.A.
117 G6 **Scotia Bay** British Columbia Canada
81 A14 **Scotia Ridge** Antarctica
146 F3 **Scotia Ridge** Antarctica
81 A15 **Scotia Sea** Antarctica
146 E2 **Scotia Sea** Antarctica
15 **Scotland** U.K.
98 J6 **Scotland** South Dakota U.S.A.
109 J2 **Scotland** Texas U.S.A.
112 K1 **Scotland Neck** North Carolina U.S.A.
111 E11 **Scotlandville** Louisiana U.S.A.
122 H8 **Scots B** Nova Scotia Canada
122 K8 **Scotsburn** Nova Scotia Canada
118 J9 **Scotsguard** Saskatchewan Canada
121 T7 **Scotstown** Quebec Canada
138 E4 **Scott** *R* South Australia Australia
143 B10 **Scott** *R* W Australia Australia
118 J6 **Scott** Saskatchewan Canada
100 C8 **Scott** *R* California U.S.A.
112 E5 **Scott** Georgia U.S.A.
111 E8 **Scott** Mississippi U.S.A.
94 C6 **Scott** Ohio U.S.A.
100 C8 **Scott Bar** California U.S.A.
146 D11 **Scott Base** *N Z Base* Antarctica
89 G8 **Scottburgh** S Africa
117 J10 **Scott, C** Vancouver I, Br Col Canada
140 A2 **Scott, Cape** N Terr Australia
107 K3 **Scott City** Kansas U.S.A.
146 D12 **Scott Coast** Antarctica
94 H6 **Scottdale** Pennsylvania U.S.A.
146 D9 **Scott Glacier** Antarctica
146 H13 **Scott Glacier** Antarctica
142 E4 **Scott Headland** *mt* W Australia Australia
115 M3 **Scott Inlet** Northwest Territories Canada
117 J10 **Scott, Is** British Columbia Canada
100 C7 **Scott, Mt** Oregon U.S.A.
146 K9 **Scott Mts** Antarctica
142 D2 **Scott Reef** Indian Oc
94 B4 **Scotts** Michigan U.S.A.
98 C8 **Scottsbluff** Nebraska U.S.A.
98 C8 **Scotts Bluff Nat. Mon** Nebraska U.S.A.
110 K7 **Scottsboro** Alabama U.S.A.
94 B8 **Scottsburg** Indiana U.S.A.
100 B6 **Scottsburg** Oregon U.S.A.
94 J10 **Scottsburg** Virginia U.S.A.
139 J8 **Scottsdale** Tasmania Australia
103 N8 **Scottsdale** Arizona U.S.A.
111 L11 **Scotts Ferry** Florida U.S.A.
127 O7 **Scotts Head** Dominica
123 L7 **Scottsville** C Breton I, Nova Scotia
107 N2 **Scottsville** Kansas U.S.A.
110 K5 **Scottsville** Kentucky U.S.A.
94 J9 **Scottsville** Virginia U.S.A.
94 A3 **Scottville** Michigan U.S.A.
102 G4 **Scottys Castle** California U.S.A.
102 G4 **Scottys Junct** Nevada U.S.A.
15 C2 **Scourie** Scotland
118 L9 **Scout Lake** Saskatchewan Canada
15 E2 **Scrabster** Scotland
7 M10 **Scram** *oil rig* North Sea
110 C6 **Scranton** Arkansas U.S.A.
107 P3 **Scranton** Kansas U.S.A.
98 C3 **Scranton** North Dakota U.S.A.
95 M5 **Scranton** Pennsylvania U.S.A.
95 L3 **Scriba** New York U.S.A.
98 K8 **Scribner** Nebraska U.S.A.
15 B4 **Scridain, Loch** Scotland
44 E2 **Scrivia R** Italy
120 H10 **Scudder** Ontario Canada
121 M8 **Scugog, L** Ontario Canada
13 H6 **Scunthorpe** England
45 O5 **Scurcola Marsicana** Italy
Scutari *see* **Üsküdar**
Scutari Albania *see* **Shkodër**
112 K1 **Seaboard** North Carolina U.S.A.
109 M6 **Seabrook** Texas U.S.A.
143 C9 **Seabrook, L** W Australia Australia
143 C7 **Seabrook, Mt** W Australia Australia
144 C6 **Seacliff** New Zealand
89 D8 **Seacow** *R* S Africa
109 L7 **Seadrift** Texas U.S.A.
139 G7 **Sea Elephant B** Tasmania Australia
9 G6 **Seaford** England
95 M8 **Seaford** Delaware U.S.A.
142 C3 **Seaforth** W Australia Australia
120 J9 **Seaforth** Ontario Canada
127 M3 **Seaforth** Jamaica
119 O4 **Seager Wheeler L** Saskatchewan Canada
108 E3 **Seagraves** Texas U.S.A.
112 H2 **Seagrove** North Carolina U.S.A.
13 G4 **Seaham** England
122 G1 **Seahorse** Labrador, Nfld Canada
115 L5 **Seahorse Pt** Northwest Territories Canada
70 C2 **Seahorse Shoal** S China Sea
13 G2 **Seahouses** England
112 F6 **Sea Island** Georgia U.S.A.
95 N7 **Sea Isle City** New Jersey U.S.A.
115 K6 **Seal** *R* Manitoba Canada
139 G6 **Sea Lake** Victoria Australia
123 R1 **Seal Bight** Labrador, Nfld Canada
89 C10 **Seal C** S Africa
116 H9 **Seal C** Alaska U.S.A.
127 J4 **Seal Cays** *islds* Turks & Caicos Is
122 F9 **Seal Cove** New Brunswick Canada
123 Q4 **Seal Cove** Newfoundland Canada
111 L9 **Seale** Alabama U.S.A.
144 C5 **Seal I** New Zealand
133 F8 **Sea Lion Is** Falkland Is
139 H7 **Seal Is** Victoria Australia
115 M6 **Seal Lakes** Quebec Canada
144 A7 **Seal Pt** New Zealand
100 A5 **Seal Rock** Oregon U.S.A.
109 L6 **Sealy** Texas U.S.A.
144 C5 **Sealy, Mt** New Zealand
144 C5 **Sealy Pass** New Zealand
103 J4 **Seaman Ra** Nevada U.S.A.
13 H5 **Seamer** England
7 M9 **Sean** *oil rig* North Sea
9 H2 **Sea Palling** England
103 K6 **Searchlight** Nevada U.S.A.
120 F6 **Searchmont** Ontario Canada
110 E6 **Searcy** Arkansas U.S.A.
102 G6 **Searles** California U.S.A.
102 G6 **Searles Lake** California U.S.A.
95 T2 **Searsport** Maine U.S.A.
123 N6 **Searston** Newfoundland Canada
12 E5 **Seascale** England
102 C5 **Seaside** California U.S.A.
100 B4 **Seaside** Oregon U.S.A.
95 N7 **Seaside Heights** New Jersey U.S.A.
8 C6 **Seaton** England
100 C2 **Seattle** Washington U.S.A.
117 D5 **Seattle, Mt** Alaska/Yukon Terr U.S.A./Canada
141 H4 **Seaview Ra** Queensland Australia
95 N7 **Seaville, S** New Jersey U.S.A.
144 D5 **Seaward Kaikoura Range** New Zealand
127 P6 **Seawell** *airport* Barbados
71 K10 **Seba** Indonesia
118 C5 **Seba Beach** Alberta Canada
95 R3 **Sebago L** Maine U.S.A.
70 E5 **Sebakung** Kalimantan
89 G2 **Sebakwe** *R* Zimbabwe
70 C6 **Sebangan, Teluk** *B* Kalimantan
68 G4 **Se Bang Fai** *R* Laos
69 G12 **Sebangka** *isld* Indonesia
113 G10 **Sebastian** Florida U.S.A.
109 K9 **Sebastian** Texas U.S.A.
124 B3 **Sebastián Vizcaíno, B** Mexico
95 S2 **Sebasticook L** Maine U.S.A.
102 B3 **Sebastopol** California U.S.A.
111 G9 **Sebastopol** Mississippi U.S.A.
70 E2 **Sebatik** *isld* Borneo
70 C3 **Sebauh** Sarawak
70 B5 **Sebayan, Bukit** *mt* Kalimantan
28 D3 **Sebbersund** Denmark
99 L3 **Sebeka** Minnesota U.S.A.
78 C1 **Seben** Turkey
Sebenico *see* **Sibenik**
124 D4 **Seberi, Cerro** *mt* Mexico
48 H5 **Sebeș** *R* Romania
70 K8 **Sebesi** *isld* Sumatra
48 H5 **Sebeșului, Muntii** *mts* Romania
94 D3 **Sebewaing** Michigan U.S.A.
52 C6 **Sebezh** Russian Federation
78 G1 **Şebinkarahisar** Turkey
48 G4 **Sebis** Romania
85 B4 **Sebkha de Chinchane** Mauritania
85 B4 **Sebkha Oum el Drouss Guebli** Mauritania
85 B4 **Sebkha Oum el Drouss Telli** Mauritania
43 C13 **Sebkhat Kelbia** *L* Tunisia
85 B4 **Sebkhet Idjil** Mauritania
85 E3 **Sebkra Azzel Matti** *salt flats* Algeria
85 C3 **Sebkra de Tindouf** *salt flats* Algeria
17 G9 **Sebkra d'Oran** Algeria
85 E3 **Sebkra Mekerrhane** *salt flats* Algeria
31 H5 **Sebnitz** Germany
95 T1 **Seboeis L** Maine U.S.A.
95 R8 **Seboomook L** Maine U.S.A.
85 C2 **Sebou** *R* Morocco
110 J4 **Sebree** Kentucky U.S.A.
95 K10 **Sebrell** Virginia U.S.A.
113 F10 **Sebring** Florida U.S.A.
94 F6 **Sebring** Ohio U.S.A.
16 D9 **Sebt Beni Zarfet** Morocco
70 K8 **Sebuku** *isld* Indonesia
70 E6 **Sebuku** *isld* Kalimantan
70 B4 **Sebuyau** Sarawak
37 Q4 **Seč** Czech Rep
42 C4 **Secchia** *R* Italy
112 E3 **Secession L** South Carolina U.S.A.
68 G4 **Se Cham** *R* Laos
122 C1 **Séchelles, L** Quebec Canada
128 B5 **Sechura, B. de** Peru
128 B5 **Sechura, Des. de** *desert* Peru
38 L7 **Seckau** Austria
38 L7 **Seckauer Alpen** *mts* Austria
22 E2 **Seclin** France
133 D7 **Seco** *R* Argentina
17 H4 **Seco** *R* Spain
21 K8 **Secondigny** France
118 L8 **Secretan** Saskatchewan Canada
144 A6 **Secretary I** New Zealand
76 D2 **Secunderabad** India
128 E7 **Sécure** *R* Bolivia
48 E3 **Séd** *R* Hungary
52 B6 **Seda** Lithuania
16 B5 **Seda** *R* Portugal
71 L10 **Sedah** Indonesia
118 G7 **Sedalia** Alberta Canada
106 F2 **Sedalia** Colorado U.S.A.
94 D7 **Sedalia** Ohio U.S.A.
76 C2 **Sedam** India
138 E5 **Sedan** South Australia Australia
19 J3 **Sedan** France
107 O4 **Sedan** Kansas U.S.A.
106 G5 **Sedan** New Mexico U.S.A.
56 F3 **Sedannavskaya, Shiver** *falls* Russian Federation
16 E2 **Sedano** Spain
13 F5 **Sedbergh** England
145 E4 **Seddon** New Zealand
115 O2 **Seddon, Kap** *C* Greenland
144 C4 **Seddonville** New Zealand
47 H4 **Seddülbahir** Turkey
79 E8 **Sede Boqer** Israel
80 B7 **Sede Dawid** Israel
80 F1 **Sede Eli'ezer** Israel
80 F4 **Sede Eliyyahu** Israel
47 N11 **Sedef** *isld* Turkey
55 G3 **Sedel'nikovo** Russian Federation
80 C7 **Sede Moshe** Israel
80 F1 **Sede Neḥemya** Israel
19 P16 **Séderon** France
80 B7 **Sederot** Israel
80 D3 **Sede Ya'aqov** Israel
80 G2 **Sede Yaaqov** Syria
80 B8 **Sede Zevi** Israel
9 E3 **Sedgeberrow** England
13 G4 **Sedgefield** England
8 D2 **Sedgley** England
106 H1 **Sedgwick** Colorado U.S.A.
107 N4 **Sedgwick** Kansas U.S.A.
95 T2 **Sedgwick** Maine U.S.A.
69 E12 **Sedinginan** Sumatra
70 E6 **Sedjaka** Kalimantan
31 H6 **Sedlčany** Czech Rep
9 G6 **Sedlescombe** England
119 O8 **Sedley** Saskatchewan Canada
79 F7 **Sedom** Israel
103 N7 **Sedona** Arizona U.S.A.
68 G5 **Se Done** *R* Laos
80 C7 **Sedot Mikha** Israel
80 C4 **Sedot Yam** Israel
100 C1 **Sedro Woolley** Washington U.S.A.
70 E4 **Sedulang** Kalimantan
52 B6 **Šeduva** Lithuania
20 H4 **See** *R* France
33 O4 **Seebad Heringsdorf** Germany
118 C7 **Seebe** Alberta Canada
37 K2 **Seebergen** Germany
33 P10 **Seeburg** Germany
41 O3 **Seefeld** Austria
33 T7 **Seefeld** Germany
40 G2 **Seefelden** Germany
33 O8 **Seehausen** Germany
36 F4 **Seeheim** Germany
87 C11 **Seeheim** Namibia
36 D7 **Seelbach** Germany
101 M2 **Seeley Lake** Montana U.S.A.
121 O8 **Seeleys Bay** Ontario Canada
146 D8 **Seelig, Mt** Antarctica
33 R10 **Seelingstädt** Germany
36 C2 **Seelscheid** Germany
32 L8 **Seelze** Germany
28 B6 **Seem** Denmark
70 P10 **Seemanandjung** Java
33 S10 **Seerhausen** Germany
41 J2 **Seerücken** *mt* Switzerland
21 L4 **Sées** France
32 M9 **Seesen** Germany
41 O2 **Seeshaupt** Germany
38 L7 **Seetaler Alpen** *mts* Austria
32 M6 **Seevetal** Germany
41 K3 **Seez** *R* Switzerland
47 H6 **Seferihisar** Turkey
17 G9 **Sefioun** *R* Algeria
85 D2 **Sefrou** Morocco
144 D5 **Sefton** New Zealand
144 C5 **Sefton, Mt** New Zealand
70 F2 **Segama** *R* Sabah
69 F11 **Segamat** Malaysia
70 M9 **Segara Anakan** Java
48 H6 **Şegarcea** Romania
71 B2 **Segea** Halmahera Indonesia
86 G4 **Segen** *watercourse* Ethiopia
56 F4 **Segentuy** Russian Federation
70 F7 **Segeri** Sulawesi
43 E11 **Segesta** Sicily
71 C3 **Seget** W Irian
52 D3 **Segezha** Russian Federation
57 D3 **Segiz, Ozero** *L* Kazakhstan
20 D5 **Seglien** France
41 K4 **Segnes Pass** Switzerland
45 O6 **Segni** Italy
103 P2 **Sego** Utah U.S.A.
17 G5 **Segorbe** Spain
85 C6 **Segou** Mali
16 E3 **Segovia** *prov* Spain
16 E4 **Segovia** Spain
108 H5 **Segovia** Texas U.S.A.
52 D3 **Segozero, Oz** *L* Russian Federation
21 J6 **Segré** France
17 H2 **Segre** *R* Spain
21 L5 **Segrie** France
84 E5 **Séguedine** Niger
85 C7 **Séguéla** Ivory Coast
124 J5 **Seguín** Mexico
107 K2 **Seguin** Kansas U.S.A.
109 K6 **Seguin** Texas U.S.A.
133 E4 **Segundo** *R* Argentina
106 F4 **Segundo** Colorado U.S.A.
17 F6 **Segura** *R* Spain
17 F6 **Segura, Sa de** *mts* Spain
32 L8 **Sehnde** Germany
71 J5 **Seho** *isld* Indonesia
71 A2 **Sehu** Halmahera Indonesia
74 B5 **Sehwan** Pakistan
100 B8 **Seiad Valley** California U.S.A.
37 L3 **Seibelsdorf** Germany
106 H2 **Seibert** Colorado U.S.A.
127 K5 **Seibo** Dominican Rep
20 H6 **Seiche** *R* France
21 K6 **Seiches** France
80 D4 **Seidā** Jordan
80 F3 **Seidur** Jordan
140 E4 **Seigals Creek** N Terr Australia
122 C1 **Seignelay, R** Quebec Canada
68 B2 **Seikpyu** Burma
68 B2 **Seiktein** Burma
12 C1 **Seil** *isld* Scotland
26 N1 **Seiland** *isld* Norway
18 G7 **Seilhac** France
107 M5 **Seiling** Oklahoma U.S.A.
19 K4 **Seille** *R* France
29 K9 **Seinäjoki** Finland
21 N3 **Seine** *R* France
21 K2 **Seine, B. de la** France
18 H4 **Seine-et-Marne** *dept* France
18 F3 **Seine-Maritime** *dept* France
21 P4 **Seine-St. Denis** *dept* France
20 A5 **Sein, I. de** France
113 E10 **Seista Key** *isld* Florida U.S.A.
38 L5 **Seitenstetten** Austria
18 F10 **Seix** France
69 J12 **Sejangkung** Indonesia
28 G5 **Sejerø** Denmark
28 G5 **Sejerø** *isld* Denmark
28 B3 **Sejerslev** Denmark
28 E3 **Sejflod** Denmark
31 O1 **Sejny** Poland
28 D4 **Sejs** Denmark
28 B6 **Sejstrup** Denmark
70 B5 **Sekadau** Kalimantan
70 D6 **Sekakajang** Kalimantan
69 G13 **Sekanak, Teluk** *B* Sumatra
69 F12 **Sekapil** Sumatra
70 E3 **Sekatak Bengarao** Kalimantan
69 F14 **Sekayu** Sumatra
88 E4 **Sekenke** Tanzania
61 K10 **Seki** Japan
70 K8 **Sekicau** *mt* Sumatra
89 C5 **Sekoma** Botswana
85 D7 **Sekondi** Ghana
86 G3 **Sek'ota** Ethiopia
77 G4 **Sekuheh** Iran
69 J12 **Sekura** Indonesia
69 E14 **Selagan** *R* Sumatra
100 E3 **Selah** Washington U.S.A.
69 J12 **Selakau** Indonesia
70 B4 **Selalang** Sarawak
69 E10 **Selama** Malaysia
69 E11 **Selangor** Malaysia
68 H4 **Se La Nong** *R* Laos
29 M10 **Selänpää** Finland
68 F4 **Selaphum** Thailand
70 D7 **Selatan, Tg** *C* Kalimantan
69 D13 **Selat Bungalaut** *str* Indonesia
69 D13 **Selat Mentawai** *str* Indonesia
69 F12 **Selat Panjang** *R* Sumatra
69 F12 **Selatpanjang** Sumatra
69 D13 **Selat Siberut** *str* Sumatra
69 D14 **Selat Sipura** *str* Indonesia
116 H3 **Selawik** Alaska U.S.A.
116 G3 **Selawik L** Alaska U.S.A.
37 N3 **Selb** Germany
37 M3 **Selbitz** Germany
27 A12 **Selbjörnfj** *inlet* Norway
26 E8 **Selbusjö** *L* Norway
13 G6 **Selby** England
98 F4 **Selby** South Dakota U.S.A.
116 K3 **Selby, L** Alaska U.S.A.
95 M8 **Selbyville** Delaware U.S.A.
28 C3 **Selde** Denmark
107 K2 **Selden** Kansas U.S.A.
123 S4 **Seldom** Newfoundland Canada
116 M7 **Seldovia** Alaska U.S.A.
43 G8 **Sele** *R* Italy
71 C3 **Sele** W Irian
87 E10 **Selebi Phikwe** Botswana
59 K1 **Selemdzha** *R* Russian Federation
47 K6 **Selendi** Turkey
56 G5 **Selenga** *R* Russian Federation
86 C6 **Selenge** Zaire
58 E2 **Selenge Mörön** *R* Mongolia
56 G5 **Selenginsk** Russian Federation
46 D4 **Selenicë** Albania
51 O2 **Selennyakh** *R* Russian Federation
33 M4 **Selent** Germany
33 M4 **Selenter See** *L* Germany
71 C3 **Sele, Selat** *str* W Irian
40 F1 **Sélestat** France
55 F4 **Seleti** *R* Kazakhstan
28 S10 **Selfoss** Iceland
98 F3 **Selfridge** North Dakota U.S.A.
85 B5 **Selibaby** Mauritania
54 F4 **Selichnya** Russian Federation
36 F3 **Seligenstadt** Germany
52 D6 **Seliger, Oz** *L* Russian Federation
103 M6 **Seligman** Arizona U.S.A.
110 C5 **Seligman** Missouri U.S.A.
84 H5 **Selima Oasis** Sudan
70 C4 **Selimbau** Kalimantan
47 J7 **Selimiye** Turkey
85 C6 **Selingue, Lac de** *res* Mali
46 E7 **Selinoús** Greece
95 L6 **Selinsgrove** Pennsylvania U.S.A.
55 F1 **Seliyarovo** Russian Federation
52 D6 **Selizharovo** Russian Federation
33 O9 **Selke** *R* Germany
119 V8 **Selkirk** Manitoba Canada
13 F2 **Selkirk** Scotland
107 J3 **Selkirk** Kansas U.S.A.
94 C2 **Selkirk** Michigan U.S.A.
117 O10 **Selkirk Mts** Br Col/Idaho Canada/U.S.A.
119 S5 **Selkirk T** Manitoba Canada
12 E5 **Sellafield** England
20 G6 **Sel, le** France
21 P2 **Selle** *R* France
100 D2 **Selleck** Washington U.S.A.
94 B8 **Sellersburg** Indiana U.S.A.
21 O7 **Selles-St. Denis** France
21 O7 **Selles-sur-Cher** France
141 H5 **Sellheim** *R* Queensland Australia
40 C4 **Sellières** France
9 G5 **Sellindge** England
41 O3 **Sellrain** Austria
103 N10 **Sells** Arizona U.S.A.
32 F9 **Selm** Germany
111 J9 **Selma** Alabama U.S.A.
111 D10 **Selma** Louisiana U.S.A.
112 J2 **Selma** North Carolina U.S.A.
100 B7 **Selma** Oregon U.S.A.
110 H6 **Selmer** Tennessee U.S.A.
33 N5 **Selmsdorf** Germany
21 N6 **Selommes** France
70 Q10 **Selong** Indonesia
40 B2 **Selongey** France
19 Q16 **Sélonnet** France
88 F6 **Selous Game Res** Tanzania
117 G4 **Selous, Mt** Yukon Territory Canada
71 C3 **Selpele** Indonesia
83 K12 **Sel Pt** Mahé I Indian Oc
9 F6 **Selsey** England
32 K6 **Selsingen** Germany
36 D2 **Selters** Germany
54 F3 **Sel'tso** Russian Federation
52 H6 **Selty** Russian Federation
36 E6 **Seltz** France
33 S5 **Seltz** Germany
69 H10 **Seluan** *isld* Indonesia
69 H14 **Selui** *isld* Indonesia
20 H4 **Selune** *R* France
133 E3 **Selva** Argentina
38 E8 **Selva di V. Gardena** Italy
128 D5 **Selvas** *forests* Brazil
45 L1 **Selvazzano Dentro** Italy
117 H4 **Selwyn Mts** Yukon Territory Canada
140 F5 **Selwyn Ra** Queensland Australia
48 J3 **Selyatin** Ukraine
52 G3 **Sel'yb** Russian Federation
36 E4 **Selz** *R* Germany
98 G2 **Selz** North Dakota U.S.A.
40 F3 **Selzach** Switzerland
38 K6 **Selzthal** Austria
70 E5 **Semajang, D** *L* Kalimantan
21 L5 **Semallé** France
46 D4 **Seman** *R* Albania
70 K8 **Semang Ka, Teluk** *B* Sumatra
79 G2 **Sem'ān, Jebel** *mts* Syria
119 N7 **Semans** Saskatchewan Canada
85 B3 **Semara, Es** Western Sahara
70 N9 **Semarang** Java
71 L10 **Semau** *isld* Timor Indonesia
88 C2 **Sembabule** Uganda
70 E3 **Sembakung** *R* Kalimantan
86 B5 **Sembé** Congo
21 M6 **Semblançay** France
52 F6 **Semenov** Russian Federation
54 D4 **Semenovka** Chernigovskaya obl Ukraine
54 E7 **Semenovka** Poltavskaya obl Ukraine
52 G6 **Semenovo** Russian Federation
52 F5 **Semenovskoye** Kostromskaya obl Russian Federation
52 F5 **Sementsovo** Russian Federation
70 O10 **Semeru** Java
116 J8 **Semidi Is** Alaska U.S.A.
52 F5 **Semigorodnyaya** Russian Federation
54 M9 **Semikarakorsk** Russian Federation
31 J5 **Semily** Czech Rep
111 G10 **Seminary** Mississippi U.S.A.
101 T7 **Seminoe Dam** Wyoming U.S.A.
101 T7 **Seminoe Res** Wyoming U.S.A.
107 O6 **Seminole** Oklahoma U.S.A.
108 E3 **Seminole** Texas U.S.A.
111 M11 **Seminole, L** Georgia U.S.A.
56 C5 **Seminsky Khrebet** *mts* Russian Federation
55 D4 **Semiozernoye** Kazakhstan
56 B5 **Semipalatinsk** Kazakhstan
55 E4 **Semipolka** Kazakhstan
71 E5 **Semirara** *isld* Philippines
77 B4 **Semīrom** Iran
70 C4 **Semitau** Kalimantan
69 H10 **Semium** *isld* Indonesia
55 G5 **Semiyarka** Kazakhstan
55 F5 **Semiz-Bugu** Kazakhstan
33 R4 **Semlow** Germany
33 T7 **Semmelberg** *mt* Germany
38 N6 **Semmering** Austria
86 F1 **Semna** Sudan
77 C2 **Semnān** Iran
20 G6 **Semnon** *R* France
22 J4 **Semois** *R* Belgium
89 F3 **Semokwe** *R* Zimbabwe
70 E1 **Sempang Mangayau, Tg** *C* Sabah
70 F2 **Semporna** Sabah
45 O6 **Semprevisa** *mt* Italy
70 O10 **Sempu** *isld* Java
26 H5 **Semskefjell** *mt* Norway
129 H4 **Sem Tripa** Brazil
88 E3 **Semu** *R* Tanzania
18 H5 **Semur-en-Auxois** France
89 F2 **Semwe** *R* Zimbabwe
52 F2 **Semzha** Russian Federation
128 E6 **Sena** Bolivia
88 E10 **Sena** Mozambique
129 L5 **Senador Pompeu** Brazil
70 E1 **Senaja** Sabah
53 F12 **Senaki** Georgia
128 E5 **Sena Madureira** Brazil
87 D9 **Senango** Zambia
70 B4 **Senaning** Kalimantan
21 O2 **Sénarpont** France
19 O17 **Sénas** France
118 H9 **Senate** Saskatchewan Canada
110 F5 **Senath** Missouri U.S.A.
111 G7 **Senatobia** Mississippi U.S.A.
69 G13 **Senayang** Indonesia
61 O7 **Sendai** Honshu Japan
60 D14 **Sendai** Kyūshū Japan
60 D14 **Sendai-gawa** *R* Japan
87 C11 **Sendelingsdrif** Namibia
37 J7 **Senden** Germany
32 G9 **Sendenhorst** Germany
16 C3 **Sendim** Portugal
70 B5 **Senduruhan** Kalimantan
74 F8 **Sendwha** India
69 E11 **Senebui, Tg** *C* Sumatra
99 S8 **Seneca** Illinois U.S.A.
107 O2 **Seneca** Kansas U.S.A.
110 B5 **Seneca** Missouri U.S.A.
98 F7 **Seneca** Nebraska U.S.A.
100 G5 **Seneca** Oregon U.S.A.
112 E3 **Seneca** South Carolina U.S.A.
98 G4 **Seneca** South Dakota U.S.A.
95 L4 **Seneca L** New York U.S.A.
94 F7 **Seneca Lake** Ohio U.S.A.
94 F7 **Senecaville** Ohio U.S.A.
22 G2 **Seneffe** Belgium
85 B5 **Sénégal** *R* W Africa
85 B6 **Senegal** *rep* W Africa
87 E11 **Senekal** S Africa
99 V3 **Seney** Michigan U.S.A.
30 H4 **Senftenberg** Germany
87 F7 **Senga Hill** Zambia
70 E4 **Sengata** Kalimantan
52 H1 **Sengeyskiy, Ostrov** *isld* Russian Federation
56 E5 **Sengilen, Khrebet** *mts* Russian Federation
38 K6 **Sengsengebirge** *mts* Austria
133 C7 **Senguerr** *R* Argentina
88 B10 **Sengwa** *R* Zimbabwe
32 H5 **Sengwärden** Germany
87 E9 **Sengwe** *R* Zimbabwe
129 K6 **Senhor do Bonfim** Brazil
45 O4 **Senigallia** Italy
45 L3 **Senio** *R* Italy
80 F1 **Senir** Israel
43 G8 **Senise** Italy
42 F4 **Senj** Croatia
26 J2 **Senja** *isld* Norway
67 H4 **Senkaku-shotō** *isld* Japan
52 H2 **Sen'kina** Russian Federation
79 G2 **Senköy** Turkey
118 H6 **Senlac** Saskatchewan Canada
65 H3 **Senlin Shan** *mt* China
68 H6 **Senmonorom** Cambodia
86 F3 **Sennar** Sudan
32 J9 **Senne** *reg* Germany
40 A4 **Sennecey le Grand** France
32 J9 **Sennelager** Germany
28 B3 **Sennels** Denmark
121 N4 **Senneterre** Quebec Canada
21 L2 **Senneville** France
54 A2 **Senno** Belarus
8 C4 **Sennybridge** Wales
133 C8 **Seno Almirantazgo** *G* Chile
68 G4 **Se Noi** *R* Laos
111 M8 **Senoia** Georgia U.S.A.
21 N4 **Senonches** France
19 K4 **Senones** France
133 C8 **Seno Otway** *G* Chile
133 C8 **Seno Skyring** *G* Chile
18 H4 **Sens** France
20 G5 **Sens-de-Bretagne** France
40 F4 **Sense R** Switzerland
48 F5 **Senta** Serbia Yugoslavia
70 B4 **Sentarum** *L* Kalimantan
18 F10 **Sentem** France
103 L9 **Sentinel** Arizona U.S.A.
109 H1 **Sentinel** Oklahoma U.S.A.
98 C3 **Sentinel Butte** North Dakota U.S.A.
117 N8 **Sentinel Pk** British Columbia Canada
146 C7 **Sentinel Ra** Antarctica
124 G7 **Sentispac** Mexico
22 H5 **Senuc** France
70 E4 **Senyiur** Kalimantan
78 H3 **Şenyurt** Turkey
56 C4 **Senzas** Russian Federation
33 R7 **Senzke** Germany
74 H7 **Seoni** India
Seoul *see* **Sŏul**
63 **Seoul** *conurbation* China
70 E5 **Sepan** Kalimantan
70 P9 **Sepandjang** Indonesia
70 C5 **Sepangsimin** Kalimantan
106 B9 **Separ** New Mexico U.S.A.
142 E6 **Separation Well** W Australia Australia
70 E4 **Sepasu** Kalimantan
70 B4 **Sepauk** Kalimantan
130 G8 **Sepetiba, B. de** Brazil
77 C4 **Sepidān** Fārs Iran
136 J2 **Sepik** *R* Papua New Guinea
70 F4 **Sepinang** Kalimantan
70 D3 **Seping** *R* Sarawak
45 R7 **Sepino** Italy
21 M7 **Sepmes** France
31 K2 **Sępolno** Poland
68 H4 **Sepone** Laos
31 N1 **Sępopol** Poland
130 B4 **Sepotuba** *R* Brazil
32 F9 **Seppenrade** Germany
19 N13 **Septême** France
19 O18 **Septêmes les Valdonne** France
46 G2 **Septemvri** Bulgaria
21 O4 **Septeuil** France
21 J5 **Sept-Forges** France
122 F3 **Sept Îles** Quebec Canada
20 D4 **Sept Isles, les** France
122 B2 **Sept-Milles, L** Quebec Canada
16 E3 **Sepúlveda** Spain
70 K8 **Seputih** *R* Sumatra
112 B2 **Sequatchie** *R* Tennessee U.S.A.
16 D3 **Sequillo** *R* Spain
100 B1 **Sequim** Washington U.S.A.
102 F5 **Sequoia Nat. Park** California U.S.A.
71 O9 **Sera** Indonesia
22 G4 **Seraincourt** France
22 K2 **Seraing** Belgium
71 J9 **Seraja** *isld* Indonesia
70 P10 **Seraja, G** *mt* Indonesia
70 M9 **Seraju** *R* Java
57 B6 **Serakhs** Turkmenistan
136 F2 **Seram** *isld* Moluccas Indonesia
136 F2 **Seram Sea** Indonesia
70 L9 **Serang** Java
69 J11 **Serasan** *isld* Indonesia
69 J11 **Seraya** Indonesia
46 D1 **Serbia** *rep* Yugoslavia
45 H4 **Serchio** *R* Italy
86 H3 **Serdo** Ethiopia
53 F7 **Serdobsk** Russian Federation
55 F3 **Serebryanoye** Russian Federation
56 B6 **Serebryansk** Kazakhstan
54 K2 **Serebryanyye Prudy** Russian Federation
88 F5 **Serebu** *mt* Tanzania
52 F5 **Sereda** Russian Federation
54 G2 **Seredeyskiy** Russian Federation
52 C5 **Seredka** Russian Federation
78 D2 **Şereflikoçhisar** Turkey
18 H5 **Serein** *R* France
69 E11 **Seremban** Malaysia
71 C3 **Seremuk** *R* W Irian

88 E3 **Serengeti Nat. Park** Tanzania
88 C8 **Serenje** Zambia
20 F6 **Serent** France
48 K1 **Seret** R Ukraine
56 D3 **Serezh** R Russian Federation
52 F6 **Serezha** R Russian Federation
46 G7 **Serfopoúla** isld Greece
52 G6 **Sergach** Russian Federation
98 K7 **Sergeant Bluff** Iowa U.S.A.
58 E2 **Sergelen** Mongolia
87 E7 **Serge Tshimbo** Zaire
55 E4 **Sergeyevka** Kokchetavskaya obl Kazakhstan
55 G3 **Sergeyevka** Novosibirskaya obl Russian Federation
55 E1 **Serginskiy** Russian Federation
129 L6 **Sergipe** state Brazil
54 K1 **Sergiyev Posad** Russian Federation
52 E2 **Sergozero, Oz** L Russian Federation
70 D2 **Seria** Brunei
41 L6 **Seriana, Val** Italy
69 D11 **Seribudolok** Sumatra
130 H9 **Seridó** R Brazil
21 O3 **Sérifontaine** France
46 G7 **Sérifos** isld Greece
20 C5 **Serignac** France
19 N16 **Sérignan** France
68 D5 **Serim** Burma
142 D2 **Seringapatam Reef** Indian Oc
129 H5 **Seringa, Serra da** mts Brazil
45 R8 **Serino** Italy
41 L7 **Serio** R Italy
85 F4 **Serkout, Dj** mt Algeria
138 E4 **Serle, Mt** South Australia Australia
21 P5 **Sermaises** France
71 O9 **Sermata** isld Indonesia
45 K1 **Sermide** Italy
45 N6 **Sermoneta** Italy
38 H9 **Sernio** mt Italy
33 U6 **Sernitz** R Germany
33 Q8 **Serno** Germany
60 T2 **Sernovodsk** Russian Federation
57 A5 **Sernyy-Zavod** Turkmenistan
31 N3 **Serock** Poland
126 A2 **Seroe Colorado** Aruba W Indies
17 F7 **Serón** Spain
85 F4 **Serouenout** Algeria
55 D2 **Serov** Russian Federation
89 E4 **Serowe** Botswana
16 B7 **Serpa** Portugal
87 C8 **Serpa Pinto** Angola
43 C9 **Serpeddi, Pta** mt Sardinia
116 E4 **Serpentine Hot Springs** Alaska U.S.A.
138 A3 **Serpentine Lakes** South Australia Australia
143 B9 **Serpentine, R** W Australia Australia
122 A3 **Serpent, R. au** Quebec Canada
128 F1 **Serpents Mouth** str Venezuela
17 G6 **Serpis** R Spain
54 J2 **Serpukhov** Russian Federation
21 O2 **Serqueux** Seine-Inférieure France
21 M3 **Serquigny** France
130 H7 **Serra** Brazil
45 L4 **Serra, Alpe di** mts Italy
130 E10 **Serra Alta** Brazil
130 F4 **Serra Bonita** Brazil
130 F4 **Serra das Araras** Brazil
129 H3 **Serra do Navio** Brazil
33 Q5 **Serrahn** Germany
46 F3 **Sérrai** Greece
45 J3 **Serramazzoni** Italy
125 O2 **Serrana Bank** Caribbean
125 P2 **Serranilla Bank** Caribbean
43 G10 **Serra San Bruno** Italy
43 C11 **Serrat, Cape** C Tunisia
45 J4 **Serravalle Pistojese** Italy
22 F4 **Serre** R France
18 G10 **Serrére, Pic de** mt France
19 P16 **Serres** France
133 D4 **Serrezuela** Argentina
19 N14 **Serrières** France
129 L6 **Serrinha** Brazil
45 M4 **Serriola, Bocca** pass Italy
43 B12 **Sers** Tunisia
16 B5 **Sertã** Portugal
130 F7 **Sertãozinho** Brazil
70 K9 **Sertung** isld Sumatra
69 D10 **Seruai** Sumatra
70 C6 **Serujan** R Kalimantan
89 E3 **Serule** Botswana
40 E2 **Servance** France
46 E4 **Sérvia** Greece
100 E5 **Service Creek** Oregon U.S.A.
138 F6 **Serviceton** Victoria Australia
106 E5 **Servilleta** New Mexico U.S.A.
71 N9 **Serwaro** Indonesia
66 F5 **Sêrxü** China
22 G4 **Séry** France
22 E4 **Séry-les-Mezières** France
68 G4 **Se Sang Soi** R Laos
70 E3 **Sesatap** Kalimantan
88 D2 **Sese Is** Uganda
120 K4 **Sesekinika** Ontario Canada
71 A3 **Sesepe** Indonesia
87 B9 **Sesfontein** Namibia
87 D9 **Sesheka** Zambia
41 H7 **Sesia R** Italy
16 A6 **Sesimbra** Portugal
26 N6 **Seskarön** isld Sweden
47 Q14 **Seskli** isld Greece
61 P12 **Sesoko-jima** isld Okinawa
43 F7 **Sessa Aurunca** Italy
36 D6 **Sessenheim** France
110 G3 **Sesser** Illinois U.S.A.
37 K3 **Sesslach** Germany
71 K9 **Sessok** Flores Indonesia
45 M4 **Sestino** Italy
45 K4 **Sesto Fiorentino** Italy
31 O1 **Seštokai** Lithuania
45 J3 **Sestola** Italy
52 E6 **Sestra** R Russian Federation
44 E3 **Sestri** Italy
44 F3 **Sestri Levante** Italy
29 O11 **Sestroretsk** Russian Federation
60 D12 **Setaka** Japan
60 N3 **Setana** Japan
9 G2 **Setchey** England
18 H9 **Sète** France
130 G6 **Sete Lagoas** Brazil
130 D8 **Sete Quedas, Ilha Grande ou** isld Brazil
27 B12 **Setesdal** Norway
94 F8 **Seth** West Virginia U.S.A.
85 F1 **Sétif** Algeria
60 C13 **Seto** Japan
60 F12 **Seto Naikai** sea Japan
60 G11 **Seto Naikai Nat. Park** Japan
68 B4 **Setsan** Burma
85 C2 **Settat** Morocco
86 A6 **Sette Cama** Gabon
119 U1 **Settee L** Manitoba Canada
119 T3 **Setting L** Manitoba Canada
13 F5 **Settle** England
140 E3 **Settlement Cr** Queensland Australia
90 C15 **Settlement of Edinburgh** Tristan da Cunha
16 B6 **Setúbal** Portugal
37 M5 **Seubersdorf** Germany
Seu d'Urgell, la see **Seo de Urgel**
37 K5 **Seukendorf** Germany
55 E1 **Seul'** R Russian Federation
99 V4 **Seul Choix Pt** Michigan U.S.A.
69 B10 **Seulimeum** Sumatra
115 K7 **Seul, Lac** Ontario Canada
21 J3 **Seulles** R France
69 C11 **Seumayan** Sumatra
40 B3 **Seurre** France
78 K1 **Sevan, Ozero** Armenia
53 D11 **Sevastopol'** Ukraine
54 H6 **Sev Donets** R Rus Fed/Ukraine
28 B4 **Sevel** Denmark
100 J4 **Seven Devils Mts** Idaho U.S.A.
140 D3 **Seven Emu** N Terr Australia
14 C5 **Seven Hd** Ireland
122 F3 **Seven Is. Bay** Quebec Canada
106 C6 **Seven Lakes** New Mexico U.S.A.
9 G5 **Sevenoaks** England
118 G9 **Seven Persons** Alberta Canada
109 J7 **Seven Sisters** Texas U.S.A.
112 K2 **Seven Springs** North Carolina U.S.A.
141 K6 **Seventeen Seventy** Queensland Australia
102 F1 **Seven Troughs** Nevada U.S.A.
117 N10 **Seventy Mile House** British Columbia Canada
25 F6 **Sevenum** Netherlands
20 F6 **Sévérac** France
18 H8 **Séverac-le-Château** France
107 P2 **Severance** Kansas U.S.A.
139 K3 **Severn** R New South Wales Australia
121 L8 **Severn** R Ontario Canada
52 J4 **Severnaya Mylva** R Russian Federation
51 K1 **Severnaya Zemlya** arch Arctic Oc
55 G3 **Severnoye** Russian Federation
8 D4 **Severn, R** England
55 D3 **Severnyy** Russian Federation
52 J3 **Severnyy Ural** mts Russian Federation
56 G3 **Severobaykal'sk** Russian Federation
51 L3 **Severo-Baykal'skoye Nagor'ye** uplands Russian Federation
37 P3 **Severocesky Kraj** reg Czech Rep
52 E3 **Severodvinsk** Russian Federation
55 E4 **Severo-Kazakhstanskaya Oblast'** prov Kazakhstan
31 K6 **Severomoravský** reg Czech Rep
52 D1 **Severomorsk** Russian Federation
53 F11 **Severo-Osetinskaya Respublika** Russian Federation
55 C1 **Severouralsk** Russian Federation
54 K2 **Severo Zadonsk** Russian Federation
107 O4 **Severy** Kansas U.S.A.
20 H3 **Séves** R France
29 O2 **Sevettijarvi** Finland
56 D5 **Sevi** Russian Federation
103 M2 **Sevier** R Utah U.S.A.
103 M3 **Sevier** Utah U.S.A.
103 M2 **Sevier Bridge Res** Utah U.S.A.
103 M2 **Sevier Des** Utah U.S.A.
112 D2 **Sevierville** Tennessee U.S.A.
20 F5 **Sévignac** France
22 G4 **Sevigny** France
126 F4 **Sevilla** R Cuba
16 D7 **Sevilla** prov Spain
16 D7 **Sevilla** Spain
46 G2 **Sevlievo** Bulgaria
48 J2 **Sevola** mt Ukraine
21 J8 **Sèvre** R France
18 E6 **Sèvre-Niortaise** R France
40 B5 **Sevron** R France
54 F4 **Sevsk** Russian Federation
85 B7 **Sewa** R Sierra Leone
110 L6 **Sewanee** Tennessee U.S.A.
116 N6 **Seward** Alaska U.S.A.
107 M3 **Seward** Kansas U.S.A.
98 J9 **Seward** Nebraska U.S.A.
107 N6 **Seward** Oklahoma U.S.A.
94 H6 **Seward** Pennsylvania U.S.A.
116 R6 **Seward Glacier** Yukon Terr/Alaska Canada/U.S.A.
146 D6 **Seward Mts** Antarctica
116 E4 **Seward Pen** Alaska U.S.A.
133 C4 **Sewell** Chile
40 E2 **Sewen** France
94 G6 **Sewickley** Pennsylvania U.S.A.
117 O8 **Sexsmith** Alberta Canada
124 G4 **Sextín** Mexico
77 H3 **Seyah Band Koh** mts Afghanistan
43 B12 **Seybouse** R Algeria
83 J12 **Seychelles** rep Indian Oc
33 R9 **Seyda** Germany
52 K2 **Seyda** Russian Federation
29 T9 **Seydhisfjördhur** Iceland
78 C3 **Seydişehir** Turkey
20 G3 **Seye** R France
78 E3 **Seyhan** R Turkey
79 F1 **Seyhan Barajı** res Turkey
47 L5 **Seyit** R Turkey
47 L5 **Seyitgazi** Turkey
54 D5 **Seym** R Ukraine
139 H6 **Seymour** Victoria Australia
95 O5 **Seymour** Connecticut U.S.A.
94 B8 **Seymour** Indiana U.S.A.
110 C1 **Seymour** Iowa U.S.A.
110 D4 **Seymour** Missouri U.S.A.
109 H2 **Seymour** Texas U.S.A.
99 S5 **Seymour** Wisconsin U.S.A.
140 C6 **Seymour Ra** N Terr Australia
19 Q16 **Seyne-les-Alpes** France
42 F3 **Sežana** Slovenia
18 H4 **Sezanne** France
52 D6 **Sezha** R Russian Federation
45 O6 **Sezze** Italy
85 G2 **Sfax** Tunisia
46 F9 **Sfinári** Crete Greece
48 K5 **Sfîntu Gheorghe** Romania
48 M6 **Sfîntu Gheorghe** R Romania
's-Gravenhage see **Den Haag**
25 B5 **'s-Gravenzande** Netherlands
15 D3 **Sgurr Mor** mt Scotland
80 D2 **Sha'ab** Israel
80 F1 **Sha'al** Syria
58 E4 **Shaanxi** prov China
80 F3 **Sha'ar** Israel
87 E7 **Shaba** reg Zaire
Shabani see **Zvishavane**
119 O2 **Shabaqua** Ontario Canada
99 S8 **Shabbona** Illinois U.S.A.
84 H5 **Shab, El** Egypt
53 E10 **Shabel'skoye** Russian Federation
78 K2 **Shabestar** Iran
79 F9 **Shabībī, J. esh** mt Jordan
47 J1 **Shabla** Bulgaria
86 E6 **Shabunda** Zaire
55 D2 **Shaburovo** Russian Federation
67 B3 **Shachang** China
66 B4 **Shache** China
118 J8 **Shackleton** Saskatchewan Canada
146 D11 **Shackleton Coast** Antarctica
146 D10 **Shackleton Glacier** Antarctica
146 H13 **Shackleton Ice Shelf** Antarctica
146 D10 **Shackleton Inlet** Antarctica
146 F7 **Shackleton Ra** Antarctica
78 H3 **Shadādah, Ash** Syria
74 B5 **Shadadkot** Pakistan
68 C3 **Shadaw** Burma
98 D4 **Shadehill Res** South Dakota U.S.A.
67 E3 **Shadi** China
55 D3 **Shadrinsk** Russian Federation
84 J4 **Shadwân** Egypt
111 K10 **Shady Grove** Alabama U.S.A.
113 D7 **Shady Grove** Florida U.S.A.
146 C12 **Shafer Peak** mt Antarctica
57 C4 **Shafirkan** Uzbekistan
55 C4 **Shafranovo** Russian Federation
102 E6 **Shafter** California U.S.A.
101 L9 **Shafter** Nevada U.S.A.
108 C6 **Shafter** Texas U.S.A.
8 D5 **Shaftesbury** England
55 G5 **Shagan** R Kazakhstan
65 E4 **Shagang** China
48 M5 **Shagany, Oz** L Ukraine
Shagedu see **Jungar Qi**
55 F4 **Shaglyteniz, Oz** L Kazakhstan
56 D5 **Shagonar** Russian Federation
144 C6 **Shag R** New Zealand
57 A2 **Shagray, Plato** plateau Kazakhstan
146 E1 **Shag Rocks** S Georgia S Atlantic Oc
76 C2 **Shahabad** India
76 B3 **Shahapur** India
80 B7 **Shaḥar** Israel
74 C6 **Shahbadpur** Pakistan
74 B6 **Shahbandar** Pakistan
75 J7 **Shahdol** India
65 C6 **Shahe** China
65 D6 **Shahe** China
67 E2 **Shahezhen** China
Shahezi see **Wan Xian**
77 K2 **Shah Fuladi** mt Afghanistan
84 G3 **Shaḥḥāt** Libya
Shāhī see **Qāem Shahr**
74 H5 **Shahjahanpur** India
77 E1 **Shāh Jehān, Kuh-e** mts Iran
77 K3 **Shāh Jūy** Afghanistan
65 E4 **Shahousuo** China
74 G7 **Shahpur** India
74 F6 **Shahpura** India
77 J2 **Shahrak** Afghanistan
77 G3 **Shāhrakht** Iran
77 D4 **Shahr-e Bābak** Iran
77 B3 **Shahr-e Kord** Iran
77 B2 **Shahr Rey** Iran
77 D2 **Shahrud Bustam** Iran
77 F5 **Shāh Savāran, Kūh-e** mts Iran
55 D1 **Shaim** Russian Federation
79 H4 **Shā'īr, Jabal** mt Syria
80 G3 **Shajara** Jordan
65 F4 **Shajianzi** China
52 E6 **Shakhovskaya** Russian Federation
57 D5 **Shakhrisabz** Uzbekistan
59 M2 **Shakhtersk** Sakhalin Russian Federation
54 K8 **Shakhtersk** Ukraine
55 F6 **Shakhtinsk** Kazakhstan
54 M9 **Shakhty** Russian Federation
52 G5 **Shakhun'ya** Russian Federation
85 E7 **Shaki** Nigeria
99 N5 **Shakopee** Minnesota U.S.A.
59 L3 **Shakotan misaki** C Japan
55 C4 **Shaksha** Russian Federation
116 G4 **Shaktolik** Alaska U.S.A.
86 G4 **Shala Hāyk'** L Ethiopia
52 F4 **Shalakusha** Russian Federation
117 M10 **Shalalth** British Columbia Canada
65 G2 **Shalan** China
67 D6 **Shalang** China
55 G4 **Shalday** Kazakhstan
52 F6 **Shaldezh** Russian Federation
9 F5 **Shalford** England
52 E4 **Shalgachëva** Russian Federation
57 F2 **Shalgiya** Kazakhstan
80 C8 **Shalhavi** Israel
66 E4 **Shaliangzi** China
77 E4 **Shalidab** Iran
55 D5 **Shalkar Karashatau** L Kazakhstan
55 D5 **Shalkar-Yega-Kara** L Russian Federation
57 J3 **Shalkudysu** Kazakhstan
80 G3 **Shallala** Jordan
112 J4 **Shallotte** North Carolina U.S.A.
108 E2 **Shallowater** Texas U.S.A.
120 J8 **Shallow Lake** Ontario Canada
80 C7 **Shalwa** Israel
55 C3 **Shalya** Russian Federation
56 C4 **Shalym** Russian Federation
88 D5 **Shama** R Tanzania
56 C5 **Shaman, Khrebet** mts Russian Federation
55 C3 **Shamary** Russian Federation
86 F4 **Shambe** Sudan
80 D2 **Shamerat** Israel
75 O5 **Shamgong** Bhutan
77 E6 **Shamīl** Iran
80 F1 **Shamir** Israel
78 K6 **Shamiya Des** Iraq
95 L6 **Shamokin** Pennsylvania U.S.A.
118 L8 **Shamrock** Saskatchewan Canada
113 D8 **Shamrock** Florida U.S.A.
107 O6 **Shamrock** Oklahoma U.S.A.
108 D8 **Shamrock** Texas U.S.A.
88 C10 **Shamva** Zimbabwe
68 C2 **Shan** prov Burma
80 G6 **Sha'nab** Jordan
Shanchengzhen see **Nanjing**
77 G5 **Shāndak** Iran
58 D4 **Shandan** China
65 C3 **Shandian He** R China
12 D1 **Shandon** Scotland
102 D6 **Shandon** California U.S.A.
65 C6 **Shandong** prov China
65 E6 **Shandong Bandao** pen China
87 E9 **Shangani** R Zimbabwe
65 D4 **Shangbancheng** China
67 E1 **Shangcheng** China
65 F3 **Shangchengzhen** China
67 D6 **Shangchuan Dao** isld China
65 B4 **Shangdu** China
Shangdundu see **Linchuan**
67 E2 **Shangfu** China
67 E2 **Shanggao** China
63 **Shanghai** conurbation China
67 G1 **Shanghai** China
67 E4 **Shanghang** China
65 D6 **Shanghe**
65 C4 **Shanghuangqi** China
67 C1 **Shangkan** China
67 C5 **Shanglin** China
87 D9 **Shangombo** Zambia
Shangpaihe see **Feixi**
58 G5 **Shangqiu** China
67 F2 **Shangrao** China
67 B5 **Shangsi** China
Shangxian see **Shangzhou**
65 B5 **Shangyangwu** China
65 C4 **Shangyi** China
67 E4 **Shangyou** China
66 C3 **Shangyou Shuiku** res China
67 G1 **Shangyu** China
59 J2 **Shangzhi** China
58 E5 **Shangzhou** China
65 D5 **Shanhaiguan** China
65 G2 **Shanhetun** China
100 E4 **Shaniko** Oregon U.S.A.
9 E6 **Shanklin** England
67 E2 **Shankou** China
94 J6 **Shanksville** Pennsylvania U.S.A.
145 E4 **Shannon** New Zealand
112 B3 **Shannon** Georgia U.S.A.
99 R7 **Shannon** Illinois U.S.A.
111 H7 **Shannon** Mississippi U.S.A.
14 C4 **Shannon Airport** Ireland
99 M9 **Shannon City** Iowa U.S.A.
14 D2 **Shannon Pot** Ireland
14 C2 **Shannon R** Ireland
Shansi prov see **Shanxi** prov
65 G3 **Shansonggang** China
80 G4 **Shantana** Jordan
51 N3 **Shantarskiye, Ostrova** islds Russian Federation
67 E5 **Shantou** China
Shantung prov see **Shandong** prov
Shantung Peninsula see **Shandong Bandao**
67 E5 **Shanwei** China
58 F4 **Shanxi** prov China
65 C7 **Shan Xian** China
67 F4 **Shanyao** China
58 F4 **Shanyin** China
67 F1 **Shaobo** China
67 D3 **Shaodong** China
67 D3 **Shaoshan** China
67 F3 **Shaowu** China
59 H5 **Shaoxing** China
67 D3 **Shaoyang** China
15 F1 **Shapinsay** Scotland
52 H2 **Shapkina** R Russian Federation
56 C5 **Shapshal'skiy Khrebet** mts Russian Federation
80 D4 **Shaqéd** Jordan
Shara Gol R see **Dang He** R
52 H7 **Sharan** Russian Federation
52 G6 **Sharanga** Russian Federation
121 O8 **Sharbot Lake** Ontario Canada
56 E6 **Sharga** Mongolia
48 L2 **Shargorod** Ukraine
58 D3 **Sharhulsan** Mongolia
60 S2 **Shari** Japan
79 H4 **Sharīfah** Syria
56 G6 **Sharïngol** Mongolia
Shāriqah, Ash see **Sharjah**
77 D7 **Sharjah** U.A.E.
52 H6 **Sharkan** Russian Federation
71 D5 **Shark Fin B** Philippines
52 C6 **Sharkovshchina** Belarus
141 H2 **Shark Reef** Gt Barrier Reef Aust
55 B4 **Sharlyk** Russian Federation
79 F10 **Sharmah** Saudi Arabia
95 O5 **Sharon** Connecticut U.S.A.
112 E4 **Sharon** Georgia U.S.A.
107 M4 **Sharon** Kansas U.S.A.
94 B2 **Sharon** Michigan U.S.A.
98 J2 **Sharon** North Dakota U.S.A.
108 E7 **Sharon** Oklahoma U.S.A.
110 H5 **Sharon** Tennessee U.S.A.
95 P3 **Sharon** Vermont U.S.A.
99 S7 **Sharon** Wisconsin U.S.A.
80 C5 **Sharon, Plain of** Israel
107 J3 **Sharon Springs** Kansas U.S.A.
54 G6 **Sharovka** Ukraine
98 F5 **Sharpe, L** South Dakota U.S.A.
95 L9 **Sharps** Virginia U.S.A.
99 M9 **Sharpsburg** Iowa U.S.A.
94 K7 **Sharpsburg** Maryland U.S.A.
94 A6 **Sharpsville** Indiana U.S.A.
79 F5 **Sharqi, Jebel esh** mts Lebanon
52 G5 **Shar'ya** Russian Federation
56 C3 **Sharypovo** Russian Federation
89 F3 **Shashani** R Zimbabwe
89 E3 **Shashe** Botswana
89 G2 **Shashe** R Zimbabwe
87 E10 **Shashe** R Zimbabwe/Botswana
86 G4 **Shashemenē** Ethiopia
67 D1 **Shashi** China
100 C9 **Shasta L** California U.S.A.
100 C8 **Shasta, Mt** California U.S.A.
67 D4 **Shatian** China
52 F6 **Shatki** Russian Federation
55 D3 **Shatrovo** Russian Federation
108 E7 **Shattuck** Oklahoma U.S.A.
54 L1 **Shatura** Russian Federation
79 F8 **Shaubak** Jordan
57 J2 **Shaukar, Poluostrov** pen Kazakhstan
80 G3 **Shaumar** Jordan
118 J9 **Shaunavon** Saskatchewan Canada
52 D3 **Shaverki** Russian Federation
102 E4 **Shaver L** California U.S.A.
94 H8 **Shavers Fork** R West Virginia U.S.A.
80 D4 **Shavé Shomeron** Jordan
80 D2 **Shave Ẕiyyon** Israel
111 F8 **Shaw** Mississippi U.S.A.
120 K7 **Shawanaga** Ontario Canada
95 N5 **Shawangunk Mts** New York U.S.A.
99 S5 **Shawano** Wisconsin U.S.A.
99 S5 **Shawano L** Wisconsin U.S.A.
121 R7 **Shawbridge** Quebec Canada
8 D2 **Shawbury** England
141 J5 **Shaw I** Queensland Australia
121 S6 **Shawinigan** Quebec Canada
79 H4 **Shawmarīyah, Jabal ash** mt Syria
101 Q3 **Shawmut** Montana U.S.A.
94 E7 **Shawnee** Ohio U.S.A.
107 O6 **Shawnee** Oklahoma U.S.A.
98 A7 **Shawnee** Wyoming U.S.A.
110 H4 **Shawneetown** Illinois U.S.A.
121 O7 **Shawville** Quebec Canada
67 F3 **Sha Xi** R China
67 F3 **Sha Xian** China
67 D1 **Shayang** China
142 D5 **Shay Gap** W Australia Australia
84 J4 **Shayib el Banât, Gebel** mt Egypt
79 G6 **Shaykh Miskīn** Syria
52 J4 **Shaytanovka** Russian Federation
67 G1 **Shazhou** China
57 F5 **Shazud** Tajikistan
54 J3 **Shchekino** Russian Federation
54 K1 **Shchelkovo** Russian Federation
52 H2 **Shchel'yayur** Russian Federation
55 G4 **Shcherbakty** Kazakhstan
54 J1 **Shcherbinka** Russian Federation
54 H5 **Shchigry** Russian Federation
54 C5 **Shchors** Ukraine
54 F8 **Shchorsk** Ukraine
55 F4 **Shchuchinsk** Kazakhstan
55 D3 **Shchuch'ye** Russian Federation
54 M5 **Shchuch'ye** Voronezhskaya obl Russian Federation
55 C3 **Shchuch'ye Ozero** Russian Federation
54 K1 **Shchurovo** Russian Federation
128 G3 **Shea** Guyana
100 H6 **Sheaville** Oregon U.S.A.
119 O2 **Shebandowan L** Ontario Canada
54 H6 **Shebekino** Russian Federation
86 H4 **Shebelē, Wabē** R Ethiopia
77 J1 **Sheberghān** Afghanistan
99 T6 **Sheboygan** Wisconsin U.S.A.
86 B4 **Shebshi Mts** Nigeria
100 B5 **Shedd** Oregon U.S.A.
120 J10 **Shedden** Ontario Canada
122 H7 **Shediac** New Brunswick Canada
14 D3 **Sheelin, L** Ireland
121 N7 **Sheenboro** Quebec Canada
116 Q2 **Sheenjek** R Alaska U.S.A.
117 O9 **Sheep Cr** Alberta Canada
101 U7 **Sheep Cr** Wyoming U.S.A.
14 D1 **Sheep Haven** Ireland
101 T10 **Sheephorn** Colorado U.S.A.
106 C2 **Sheep Mt** Colorado U.S.A.
103 J5 **Sheep Pk** Nevada U.S.A.
103 J5 **Sheep Ra** Nevada U.S.A.
14 B5 **Sheep's Hd** Ireland
118 F7 **Sheerness** Alberta Canada
9 G5 **Sheerness** England
122 K9 **Sheet Harbour** Nova Scotia Canada
80 D2 **Shefar'am** Israel
80 C7 **Shefela** Israel
139 H8 **Sheffield** Tasmania Australia
13 G6 **Sheffield** England
144 D5 **Sheffield** New Zealand
110 J7 **Sheffield** Alabama U.S.A.
99 R8 **Sheffield** Illinois U.S.A.
99 N7 **Sheffield** Iowa U.S.A.
95 O4 **Sheffield** Massachusetts U.S.A.
94 H5 **Sheffield** Pennsylvania U.S.A.
108 F5 **Sheffield** Texas U.S.A.
94 E5 **Sheffield Lake** Ohio U.S.A.
56 B3 **Shegarka** R Russian Federation
52 G3 **Shegmas** Russian Federation
120 J7 **Sheguiandah** Ontario Canada
119 O7 **Sheho** Saskatchewan Canada
67 B1 **Shehong** China
133 C7 **Shehuén** R Argentina
79 F5 **Sheikh, J. esh** mt Lebanon/Syria
120 F3 **Shekak** R Ontario Canada
Shekar Dzong see **Tingri**
Shekhem see **Nablus**
54 M4 **Shekhman'** Russian Federation
74 F3 **Shekhupura** Pakistan
53 G12 **Sheki** Azerbaijan
52 E5 **Sheksna** R Russian Federation
52 E5 **Sheksna** Russian Federation
94 E9 **Shelbiana** Kentucky U.S.A.
110 D2 **Shelbina** Missouri U.S.A.
110 J2 **Shelburn** Indiana U.S.A.
122 G10 **Shelburne** Nova Scotia Canada
120 K8 **Shelburne** Ontario Canada
95 O2 **Shelburne** Vermont U.S.A.
141 G1 **Shelburne B** Queensland Australia
95 P4 **Shelburne Falls** Massachusetts U.S.A.
99 T8 **Shelby** Indiana U.S.A.
99 L8 **Shelby** Iowa U.S.A.
99 U6 **Shelby** Michigan U.S.A.
111 F8 **Shelby** Mississippi U.S.A.
101 O1 **Shelby** Montana U.S.A.
98 J8 **Shelby** Nebraska U.S.A.
112 F2 **Shelby** North Carolina U.S.A.
94 E6 **Shelby** Ohio U.S.A.
110 H2 **Shelbyville** Illinois U.S.A.
110 L2 **Shelbyville** Indiana U.S.A.
110 L3 **Shelbyville** Kentucky U.S.A.
110 E2 **Shelbyville** Missouri U.S.A.
110 K6 **Shelbyville** Tennessee U.S.A.
109 N4 **Shelbyville** Texas U.S.A.
99 T9 **Sheldon** Illinois U.S.A.
99 L6 **Sheldon** Iowa U.S.A.
110 B4 **Sheldon** Missouri U.S.A.
98 J3 **Sheldon** North Dakota U.S.A.
117 H4 **Sheldon, Mt** Yukon Territory Canada
95 P2 **Sheldon Springs** Vermont U.S.A.
122 H3 **Sheldrake** Quebec Canada
56 F5 **Shelekhov** Russian Federation
51 P3 **Shelikhova, Zaliv** B Russian Federation
116 K8 **Shelikof Str** Alaska U.S.A.
99 L3 **Shell** R Minnesota U.S.A.
101 S5 **Shell** Wyoming U.S.A.
111 G12 **Shell Beach** Louisiana U.S.A.
118 L5 **Shellbrook** Saskatchewan Canada
101 R8 **Shell Cr** Wyoming U.S.A.
101 N6 **Shelley** Idaho U.S.A.
139 K5 **Shellharbour** New South Wales Australia
99 P4 **Shell L** Wisconsin U.S.A.
118 K5 **Shell Lake** Saskatchewan Canada
143 F8 **Shell Lakes** W Australia Australia
111 M10 **Shellman** Georgia U.S.A.
119 Q8 **Shellmouth** Manitoba Canada
102 A1 **Shell Mt** California U.S.A.
99 O7 **Shell Rock** Iowa U.S.A.
99 O7 **Shellrock** R Iowa U.S.A.
99 P7 **Shellsburg** Iowa U.S.A.
80 D1 **Shelomi** Israel
58 G1 **Shelopugino** Russian Federation
102 A1 **Shelter Cove** California U.S.A.
95 P5 **Shelter I** Long I, New York U.S.A.
144 B7 **Shelter Pt** New Zealand
95 O5 **Shelton** Connecticut U.S.A.
98 H9 **Shelton** Nebraska U.S.A.
117 M12 **Shelton** Washington U.S.A.
52 E4 **Sheltozero** Russian Federation
78 M1 **Shemakha** Azerbaijan
56 B5 **Shemonaikha** Kazakhstan
52 H6 **Shemordan** Russian Federation
52 G6 **Shemursha** Russian Federation
99 L9 **Shenandoah** Iowa U.S.A.
95 L6 **Shenandoah** Pennsylvania U.S.A.
94 J8 **Shenandoah** Virginia U.S.A.
94 H8 **Shenandoah Mts** W Virginia/Virginia U.S.A.
94 J8 **Shenandoah Nat. Park** Virginia U.S.A.
94 G5 **Shenango Res** Ohio/Penn U.S.A.
57 D1 **Shenber** Kazakhstan
65 B5 **Shenchi** China
86 A4 **Shendam** Nigeria
86 F2 **Shendi** Sudan
65 J1 **Shending Shan** mt China
57 J3 **Shengel'dy** Kazakhstan
46 D3 **Shëngjin** Albania
65 F1 **Shengping** China
67 G1 **Shengsi** China
67 G1 **Shengsi Liedao** islds China
67 G2 **Sheng Xian** China
52 F4 **Shenkursk** Russian Federation
65 A5 **Shenmu** China
67 C1 **Shennongjia** China
Shensi prov see **Shaanxi**
52 H7 **Shentala** Russian Federation
143 E8 **Shenton, Mt** W Australia Australia
Shentza Dzong see **Xainza**
65 C5 **Shen Xian** China
65 C6 **Shen Xian** China
59 H3 **Shenyang** China
65 C5 **Shenze** China
Shenzhen see **Bao'an**
74 G6 **Sheopur** India
118 D7 **Shepard** Alberta Canada
94 C3 **Shepherd** Michigan U.S.A.
101 R4 **Shepherd** Montana U.S.A.
109 M5 **Shepherd** Texas U.S.A.
137 O5 **Shepherd Is** Vanuatu
94 K7 **Shepherdstown** West Virginia U.S.A.
94 B9 **Shepherdsville** Kentucky U.S.A.
117 G7 **Sheppard, Mt** British Columbia Canada
139 H6 **Shepparton** Victoria Australia
9 G5 **Sheppey** isld England
8 D5 **Shepton Mallet** England
80 C7 **Sheqef** Israel
77 K1 **Sherabad** Uzbekistan
115 M3 **Sherard, C** Northwest Territories Canada
55 F4 **Sherbakul'** Russian Federation
8 D6 **Sherborne** England
85 B7 **Sherbro I** Sierra Leone
121 T7 **Sherbrooke** Quebec Canada
122 H9 **Sherbrooke L** Nova Scotia Canada
13 H5 **Sherburn** England
13 G6 **Sherburn** England
99 M6 **Sherburn** Minnesota U.S.A.
95 M4 **Sherburne** New York U.S.A.
86 C1 **Sherda** Chad
9 F5 **Shere** England
84 J6 **Shereik** Sudan
54 J1 **Sheremet'yevo** airport Russian Federation
74 E5 **Shergarh** India
111 D7 **Sheridan** Arkansas U.S.A.
94 A6 **Sheridan** Indiana U.S.A.
94 B3 **Sheridan** Michigan U.S.A.
101 N4 **Sheridan** Montana U.S.A.
100 B4 **Sheridan** Oregon U.S.A.
101 T5 **Sheridan** Wyoming U.S.A.
115 N1 **Sheridan, C** Northwest Territories Canada
106 H3 **Sheridan L** Colorado U.S.A.
101 P5 **Sheridan, Mt** Wyoming U.S.A.
138 D5 **Sheringa** South Australia Australia
9 H2 **Sheringham** England
111 H7 **Sherman** Mississippi U.S.A.
94 H4 **Sherman** New York U.S.A.
109 L2 **Sherman** Texas U.S.A.
95 S8 **Sherman Mills** Maine U.S.A.
103 J1 **Sherman Mt** Nevada U.S.A.
101 O7 **Sherman Pk** Idaho U.S.A.
98 H8 **Sherman Res** Nebraska U.S.A.
77 L2 **Sherpur** Afghanistan
119 Q3 **Sherridon** Manitoba Canada
95 M3 **Sherrill** New York U.S.A.
25 D5 **'s-Hertogenbosch** Netherlands
141 K2 **Sherwood** dist Brisbane, Qnsld Australia
122 J7 **Sherwood** Prince Edward I Canada
98 E1 **Sherwood** North Dakota U.S.A.
108 G4 **Sherwood** Texas U.S.A.
144 C5 **Sherwood Downs** New Zealand
9 E1 **Sherwood Forest** England
52 H6 **Sheshma** R Russian Federation
77 E1 **Sheshtamad** Iran
67 E1 **She Shui** R China
117 H6 **Sheslay** British Columbia Canada
52 H5 **Shestakovo** Russian Federation
99 L5 **Shetek, L** Minnesota U.S.A.
15 G2 **Shetland** reg Scotland
50 E4 **Shevchenko** Kazakhstan
48 M5 **Shevchenko, Liman** B Ukraine
57 B2 **Shevchenko, Zaliv** G Kazakhstan
99 L2 **Shevlin** Minnesota U.S.A.
86 G4 **Shewa Gīmīra** Ethiopia
65 B6 **She Xian** China
67 F2 **She Xian** China
98 G2 **Sheyenne** North Dakota U.S.A.
98 J3 **Sheyenne** R North Dakota U.S.A.
77 C6 **Sheykh Sho'eyb** isld Iran
80 E2 **Shezor** Israel
15 B3 **Shiant** isld Scotland
94 C3 **Shiawassee** R Michigan U.S.A.
61 N8 **Shibata** Japan
65 B4 **Shibatai** China
60 S2 **Shibecha** Japan
60 T2 **Shibetsu** Japan
84 J3 **Shibîn el Kom** Egypt
79 B8 **Shibîn el Qanâtir** Egypt
67 C3 **Shibing** China
61 M9 **Shibukawa** Japan
60 E14 **Shibushi-wan** Japan
65 D6 **Shibuzi** China
67 B3 **Shichang** China
67 E3 **Shicheng** China
61 P5 **Shichinohe** Japan
98 J9 **Shickley** Nebraska U.S.A.
95 L5 **Shickshinny** Pennsylvania U.S.A.
122 F5 **Shickshock Mts** Quebec Canada
Shicun see **Xiangfen**
65 E6 **Shidao** China
65 E6 **Shidao Wan** B China
55 F5 **Shiderty** Kazakhstan
55 F5 **Shiderty** R Kazakhstan
107 O5 **Shidler** Oklahoma U.S.A.
60 H11 **Shido** Japan
15 C3 **Shieldaig** Scotland
140 D2 **Shield, C** N Terr Australia
107 K3 **Shields** Kansas U.S.A.
98 E3 **Shields** North Dakota U.S.A.
67 A1 **Shifang** China
8 D2 **Shifnal** England
61 K10 **Shiga** prefect Japan
Shigatse see **Xigazê**
122 G5 **Shigawake** Quebec Canada
65 A4 **Shiguaigou** China
67 F1 **Shih-chiu Hu** L China
58 G5 **Shi He** R China
66 D3 **Shihezi** China
Shihkiachwang see **Shijiazhuang**
86 J4 **Shiikh** Somalia
61 M8 **Shiiya** Japan
46 D3 **Shijak** Albania
67 A1 **Shijiaba** China
Shijiao see **Fogang**
65 B5 **Shijiazhuang** China
65 C5 **Shijiazhuang** China
67 F1 **Shijiu Hu** China
65 D7 **Shijiusuo** China
60 O3 **Shikabe** Japan
119 N1 **Shikag L** Ontario Canada
60 H11 **Shikama** Japan
68 J2 **Shikang** China
77 L2 **Shikar, Darya-i-** R Afghanistan
76 B3 **Shikarpur** India
74 C5 **Shikarpur** Pakistan
61 N11 **Shikine-jima** isld Japan
60 G12 **Shikoku** isld Japan
60 F12 **Shikoku-sanchi** mts Japan
59 N3 **Shikotan** isld Japan
60 O3 **Shikotsu Toya Nat. Park** Japan
86 H4 **Shilabo** Ethiopia
52 G4 **Shilador** Russian Federation
80 D6 **Shilat** Jordan
55 D5 **Shil'da** Russian Federation
75 N5 **Shiliguri** India
Shiliu see **Changjiang**
59 G1 **Shilka** R Russian Federation
14 E4 **Shillelagh** Ireland
9 E4 **Shillingford** England
120 K4 **Shillington** Ontario Canada
95 M6 **Shillington** Pennsylvania U.S.A.
80 E5 **Shillo** Jordan
75 O6 **Shillong** India
110 H6 **Shiloh Nat. Mil. Park** Tennessee U.S.A.
67 C5 **Shilong** China
67 D5 **Shilong** China
65 A6 **Shilou** China
54 M2 **Shilovo** Russian Federation
Shima see **Longhai**
67 E3 **Shima** China
60 D13 **Shimabara** Japan
61 M11 **Shimada** Japan
60 F10 **Shimane** prefect Japan
59 J1 **Shimanovsk** Russian Federation
60 F13 **Shimanto** Japan
67 D2 **Shimen** China
65 D4 **Shimenzhai** China
61 M11 **Shimizu** Japan
74 G3 **Shimla** India
61 L9 **Shimminato** Japan
61 M11 **Shimoda** Japan
61 O9 **Shimodate** Japan
60 P4 **Shimofuro** Japan
76 B4 **Shimoga** India
60 E11 **Shimogo** Japan
60 Q1 **Shimokawa** Japan
61 O8 **Shimo-kitaba** Japan
60 O4 **Shimokita-hantō** pen Japan
60 C14 **Shimo koshiki jima** isld Japan
61 M9 **Shimonita** Japan
59 K5 **Shimonoseki** Japan
60 D14 **Shimo-Taniguchi** Japan
60 E13 **Shimo-Tashima** Japan
61 N9 **Shimotsuma** Japan
80 D3 **Shimron** Israel
52 D5 **Shimsk** Russian Federation
67 C5 **Shinan** China
59 L4 **Shinano** R Japan
77 H3 **Shīndand** Afghanistan
61 K11 **Shindō** Japan
109 K6 **Shiner** Texas U.S.A.
94 J5 **Shinglehouse** Pennsylvania U.S.A.
145 D4 **Shingle Pk** New Zealand
99 U3 **Shingleton** Michigan U.S.A.
100 D9 **Shingletown** California U.S.A.
61 J12 **Shingū** Japan
120 J5 **Shining Tree** Ontario Canada
61 O7 **Shinjō** Japan
60 E11 **Shin-Nan'yō** Japan
94 G7 **Shinnston** West Virginia U.S.A.
61 M9 **Shinonoi** Japan
79 G4 **Shinshār** Syria
61 L11 **Shinshiro** Japan
60 Q2 **Shintoku** Japan
88 D3 **Shinyanga** Tanzania
61 P7 **Shiogama** Japan
61 L9 **Shiojiri** Japan
61 J12 **Shiono-misaki** C Japan
Shipai see **Huaining**
126 F2 **Ship Chan. Cay** isld Bahamas
123 S6 **Ship Cove** Newfoundland Canada
9 G2 **Shipdham** England
111 H11 **Ship I** Mississippi U.S.A.
52 G4 **Shipitsino** Russian Federation
46 G2 **Shipka P** Bulgaria
74 H3 **Shipki Pass** India/Xizang Zizhiqu
13 G6 **Shipley** England
119 N5 **Shipman** Saskatchewan Canada
94 K6 **Shippensburg** Pennsylvania U.S.A.
106 B5 **Shiprock** New Mexico U.S.A.
121 T4 **Shipshaw Dam** Quebec Canada
111 E13 **Ship Shoal Lt. Hse** Louisiana U.S.A.
13 G5 **Shipton** N Yorks England
9 E4 **Shipton under Wychwood** England
Shipu see **Huanglong**
67 G2 **Shipu** China
67 C3 **Shiqian** China
Shiqiao see **Panyu**
67 D5 **Shiqiao** China
80 A7 **Shiqma** Israel
80 C8 **Shiqma** R Israel
58 E5 **Shiquan** China
66 C5 **Shiquan He** R China
74 H2 **Shiquanhe** China
60 J12 **Shirahama** Japan
60 O4 **Shirakami-misaki** C Japan
61 O8 **Shirakawa** Fukushima, Honshu Japan
61 K9 **Shirakawa** Toyama, Honshu Japan
78 L1 **Shirakskaya Step'** Azerbaijan/Georgia
61 N9 **Shirane-san** mt Tochigi Japan
61 M10 **Shirane san** mt Yamanashi Japan
60 S3 **Shiranuka** Japan
60 P3 **Shiraoi** Japan
146 C10 **Shirase Coast** Antarctica
77 C5 **Shīrāz** Iran
79 B7 **Shirbîn** Egypt
88 E9 **Shire** R Malawi
65 B2 **Shireet** Mongolia
88 E9 **Shire Highlands** Malawi
65 G4 **Shiren** China
60 T1 **Shiretoko misaki** C Japan
60 O3 **Shiribeshi** prefect Japan
57 C3 **Shirikrabat** Kazakhstan
60 O4 **Shiriuchi** Japan
60 P4 **Shiriya-zaki** C Japan
9 E3 **Shirley** England
9 E6 **Shirley** England
110 D6 **Shirley** Arkansas U.S.A.
101 T7 **Shirley Mts** Wyoming U.S.A.
61 O8 **Shiroishi** Japan
54 E9 **Shirokoye** Ukraine
61 K10 **Shirotori** Japan
61 L9 **Shirouma-dake** mt Japan
77 E1 **Shīrvān** Iran
116 E9 **Shishaldin Vol** Aleutian Is
60 H12 **Shishikui** Japan
60 C11 **Shishimi** Japan
116 D3 **Shishmaref** Alaska U.S.A.
116 E3 **Shishmaref Inlet** Alaska U.S.A.
67 D2 **Shishou** China
67 F1 **Shitai** China
61 L10 **Shitara** Japan
74 D5 **Shiv** India
74 G6 **Shivpuri** India
103 L5 **Shivwits Plat** Arizona U.S.A.
67 B6 **Shiwan Dashan** mts China
87 F8 **Shiwa Ngandu** Zambia
67 E4 **Shixing** China
67 B2 **Shiyangchang** China
67 C2 **Shiye** China
Shizhaihe see **Zhenping**
67 C2 **Shizhu** China
Shizilu see **Junan**
67 A4 **Shizong** China
61 P7 **Shizugawa** Japan
58 E4 **Shizuishan** China
65 A6 **Shizuiyi** China
61 O6 **Shizukuishi** Japan
60 Q3 **Shizunai** Japan
59 L5 **Shizuoka** Japan
61 M10 **Shizuoka** prefect Japan
54 B2 **Shklov** Belarus
46 D2 **Shkodër** Albania
46 D3 **Shkumbin** R Albania
52 D5 **Shlino** R Russian Federation
51 J1 **Shmidta, Ostrova** islds Russian Federation
61 L9 **Shō** R Japan
113 A7 **Shoal** R Florida U.S.A.
140 B1 **Shoal B** N Terr Australia
123 T5 **Shoal Harb** Newfoundland Canada
139 K5 **Shoalhaven R** New South Wales Australia
119 U8 **Shoal L** Manitoba Canada
118 F1 **Shoal L** Ontario Canada
110 K3 **Shoals** Indiana U.S.A.
141 K5 **Shoalwater B** Queensland Australia
60 F11 **Shōbara** Japan
60 H11 **Shōdo-shima** isld Japan
9 G4 **Shoeburyness** England
123 R4 **Shoe Cove** Newfoundland Canada
145 E2 **Shoe I** New Zealand
77 F1 **Shoghlābād** Iran
51 K1 **Shokal'skogo, Proliv** str Russian Federation
60 P2 **Shokambetsu dake** mt Japan
57 E6 **Shokh** Tajikistan
60 R1 **Shokotsu** Japan
52 E4 **Shola** R Russian Federation
55 D5 **Sholaksay** Kazakhstan
55 F5 **Sholakshalkar, Oz** L Kazakhstan
142 B5 **Sholl I** W Australia Australia
52 D2 **Shomba** Russian Federation
80 E1 **Shomera** Israel
52 H3 **Shomvukva** Russian Federation
57 A2 **Shomyshkol'** Kazakhstan
88 B9 **Shona** Zambia
55 G5 **Shoptykul'** Kazakhstan

52 G6 **Shora** *R* Russian Federation
76 C5 **Shoranur** India
76 C2 **Shorapur** India
77 J5 **Shorawak** *reg* Afghanistan
9 F6 **Shoreham-by-Sea** England
99 T6 **Shorewood** Wisconsin U.S.A.
55 F5 **Shortandy** Kazakhstan
03 M5 **Short Cr** Arizona U.S.A.
19 Q7 **Shortdale** Manitoba Canada
11 L9 **Shorter** Alabama U.S.A.
38 E2 **Short, L** South Australia Australia
43 C10 **Short, Mt** W Australia Australia
95 K4 **Shortsville** New York U.S.A.
57 A2 **Shoshkakol'** Kazakhstan
02 H6 **Shoshone** California U.S.A.
01 L7 **Shoshone** Idaho U.S.A.
01 R5 **Shoshone** *R* Wyoming U.S.A.
01 Q5 **Shoshone Cavern Nat. Mon** Wyoming U.S.A.
01 P5 **Shoshone L** Wyoming U.S.A.
02 G2 **Shoshone Mts** Nevada U.S.A.
02 H5 **Shoshone Pk** Nevada U.S.A.
01 R6 **Shoshoni** Wyoming U.S.A.
54 E5 **Shostka** Ukraine
9 H4 **Shotley** England
44 B6 **Shotover R** New Zealand
67 F2 **Shouchang** China
67 C4 **Shoucheng** China
65 D6 **Shouguang** China
16 Q3 **Shoulder Mt** Alaska U.S.A.
18 E8 **Shouldice** Alberta Canada
67 F3 **Shouning** China
01 L4 **Shoup** Idaho U.S.A.
65 B6 **Shouyang** China
80 B8 **Shoval** Israel
99 N3 **Shovel L** Minnesota U.S.A.
46 J9 **Showa** *Japan Base* Antarctica
86 G3 **Showak** Sudan
60 O3 **Shōwa-Shinzan** *mt* Japan
03 O7 **Show Low** Arizona U.S.A.
52 F1 **Shoyna** Russian Federation
52 F4 **Shozhma** Russian Federation
54 C7 **Shpola** Ukraine
94 F6 **Shreve** Ohio U.S.A.
11 C9 **Shreveport** Louisiana U.S.A.
8 D2 **Shrewsbury** England
11 H12 **Shrewsbury** New Orleans, Louisiana U.S.A.
9 E5 **Shrewton** England
76 B1 **Shrigonda** India
76 B1 **Shrirampur** India
9 E4 **Shrivenham** England
8 D2 **Shropshire** *co* England
54 K8 **Shterovka** Ukraine
65 G2 **Shuang-ch'eng** China
65 F2 **Shuangchengpu** China
67 D3 **Shuangfeng** China
65 E2 **Shuanggang** China
67 D1 **Shuanggou** China
65 G3 **Shuanghezhen** China
Shuanghuyu *see* **Zizhou**
Shuangjiang *see* **Tongdao**
59 H3 **Shuangliao** China
67 A1 **Shuangliu** China
65 F3 **Shuangshan** China
65 F3 **Shuangyang** China
59 K2 **Shuangyashan** China
55 C6 **Shubar-Kuduk** Kazakhstan
79 H3 **Shubayṯ, Jebel ash** *mts* Syria
22 J8 **Shubenacadie** Nova Scotia Canada
22 J9 **Shubenacadie L** Nova Scotia Canada
99 L9 **Shubert** Nebraska U.S.A.
16 P2 **Shublik Mts** Alaska U.S.A.
79 A7 **Shubra Khît** Egypt
11 H10 **Shubuta** Mississippi U.S.A.
67 E1 **Shucheng** China
80 F6 **Shu'eib** *R* Jordan
80 F6 **Shu'eib Br** Jordan
80 D4 **Shufa** Jordan
57 H5 **Shufu** China
55 G4 **Shuga** Kazakhstan
57 F5 **Shugnan** Tajikistan
57 F5 **Shugnanskiy Khrebet** *mts* Tajikistan
52 D5 **Shugozero** Russian Federation
55 E1 **Shugur** Russian Federation
52 H6 **Shugurovo** Russian Federation
65 D7 **Shu He** *R* China
67 B2 **Shuibatang** China
67 A3 **Shuicheng** China
Shuiji *see* **Laixi**
67 F3 **Shuiji** China
67 F3 **Shuikou** China
67 C4 **Shuikou** China
67 D5 **Shuikou** China
65 G2 **Shuiquliu** China
65 E5 **Shuishiying** China
74 D4 **Shujaabad** Pakistan
74 G7 **Shujalpur** India
55 D1 **Shukhtungort** Russian Federation
00 D1 **Shuksan, Mt** Washington U.S.A.
59 J3 **Shulan** China
57 H5 **Shule** China
58 C3 **Shule He** *R* China
Shulinzhao *see* **Dalad Qi**
99 Q7 **Shullsburg** Wisconsin U.S.A.
65 C6 **Shulu** China
16 G9 **Shumagin Is** Alaska U.S.A.
16 Q3 **Shuman House** Alaska U.S.A.
60 Q1 **Shumarinai** Japan
55 D5 **Shumekty** Kazakhstan
47 H1 **Shumen** Bulgaria
52 G6 **Shumerlya** Russian Federation
55 D3 **Shumikha** Russian Federation
54 A1 **Shumilino** Belarus
52 H4 **Shumino** Russian Federation
56 E4 **Shumskiy** Russian Federation
65 E1 **Shumugou** China
103 O7 **Shumway** Arizona U.S.A.
80 F6 **Shunat Nimrin** Jordan
67 F3 **Shunchang** China
67 D5 **Shunde** China
52 D3 **Shunga** Russian Federation
65 C4 **Shunyi** China
67 B5 **Shuolong** China
58 F4 **Shuo Xian** China
80 F8 **Shuqeiq** *R* Jordan
111 H9 **Shuqualak** Mississippi U.S.A.
77 G4 **Shur** *R* Iran
57 F4 **Shurab** Tajikistan
52 G6 **Shuran** Russian Federation
61 P13 **Shuri** Okinawa
58 F1 **Shurinda** Russian Federation
52 H6 **Shurma** Russian Federation
87 E9 **Shurugwi** Zimbabwe
77 A3 **Shūsh** Iran
78 L2 **Shusha** Azerbaijan
46 D4 **Shushicë** *R* Albania
77 A3 **Shūshtar** Iran
117 O10 **Shuswap L** British Columbia Canada
139 H4 **Shuttleton** New South Wales Australia
80 B8 **Shuva** Israel
52 F6 **Shuya** Ivanovskaya obl Russian Federation
52 D4 **Shuya** Karel'skaya Respublika Russian Federation
116 L7 **Shuyak I** Alaska U.S.A.
65 D8 **Shuyang** China
52 D3 **Shuyeretskoye** Russian Federation
55 G4 **Shuyreksor, Oz** *L* Kazakhstan
52 F5 **Shuyskoye** Russian Federation
61 M11 **Shuzenji** Japan
68 B3 **Shwebandaw** Burma
68 B1 **Shwebo** Burma
68 B3 **Shwedaung** Burma
68 C4 **Shwegun** Burma
68 C4 **Shwegyin** Burma
68 C2 **Shwenyaung** Burma
74 H1 **Shyok** Kashmir
69 D12 **Siabu** Sumatra
77 H6 **Siahan Range** Pakistan
69 E12 **Siak Sri Inderapura** Sumatra
74 F2 **Sialkot** Pakistan
Siam *see* **Thailand**
Sian *see* **Xi'an**
Siangtan *see* **Xiangtan**
47 Q14 **Siánna** Rhodes Greece
31 J1 **Sianów** Poland
69 H11 **Siantan** *isld* Indonesia
69 D8 **Si Ao Ban Don, Laem** Thailand
128 E3 **Siapa** *R* Venezuela
71 G6 **Siargao** *isld* Philippines
95 S5 **Siasconset** Massachusetts U.S.A.
71 E8 **Siasi** Philippines
71 F6 **Siaton** Negros Philippines
52 B6 **Siauliai** Lithuania
84 J4 **Sibâi, Gebel** *mt* Egypt
126 F4 **Sibanicú** Cuba
71 E5 **Sibay** *isld* Philippines
55 C4 **Sibay** Russian Federation
89 H6 **Sibayi** S Africa
118 G7 **Sibbald** Alberta Canada
146 C12 **Sibbald, Cape** *C* Antarctica
29 L11 **Sibbo** Finland
42 G5 **Sibenik** Croatia
69 D13 **Siberut** *isld* Indonesia
74 B4 **Sibi** Pakistan
69 B11 **Sibigo** Indonesia
42 E6 **Sibillini, Monti** Italy
59 K3 **Sibirtsevo** Russian Federation
86 B6 **Sibiti** Congo
48 J5 **Sibiu** Romania
9 G4 **Sible Hedingham** England
99 S9 **Sibley** Illinois U.S.A.
99 L6 **Sibley** Iowa U.S.A.
109 O3 **Sibley** Louisiana U.S.A.
70 G4 **Siboa** Sulawesi
69 D12 **Sibolga, Tel** *B* Sumatra
71 E4 **Sibolon** *isld* Philippines
126 G5 **Siboney** Cuba
69 D11 **Siborongborong** Sumatra
41 M3 **Sibratsgfäll** Austria
75 Q5 **Sibsagar** India
9 G1 **Sibsey** England
70 B3 **Sibu** Sarawak
71 F7 **Sibuco** Mindanao Philippines
71 F7 **Sibuguey Bay** Mindanao Philippines
86 C4 **Sibut** Cent Afr Republic
70 C2 **Sibuti** Sarawak
71 F4 **Sibuyan** *isld* Philippines
48 H4 **Sic** Romania
71 E1 **Sicapoo** *mt* Luzon Philippines
128 E7 **Sicasica** Bolivia
71 F6 **Sicayac** Mindanao Philippines
138 E4 **Siccus** *R* South Australia Australia
68 E6 **Si Chang, Ko** *isld* Thailand
67 A1 **Sichuan** *prov* China
67 B1 **Sichuan Pendi** *basin* China
43 E11 **Sicilia** *isld* Italy
43 D11 **Sicilian Chan** S Europe
Sicily *see* **Sicilia**
111 E10 **Sicily Island** Louisiana U.S.A.
119 R2 **Sickle L** Manitoba Canada
71 F5 **Sicogon** *isld* Philippines
128 D6 **Sicuani** Peru
48 E5 **Šid** Serbia Yugoslavia
71 A2 **Sidangoli** Halmahera Indonesia
47 O12 **Sidari** Greece
85 F5 **Sidawet** Niger
8 D5 **Sidcot** England
9 G5 **Sidcup** England
140 B6 **Siddeley Ra** N Terr Australia
74 E7 **Siddhapur** India
76 D3 **Siddhavattam** India
8 D1 **Siddington** England
76 D1 **Siddipet** India
29 J9 **Sideby** Finland
99 T10 **Sidell** Illinois U.S.A.
70 F6 **Sidenreng, D** *L* Sulawesi
26 K8 **Sidensjö** Sweden
85 D6 **Sidéradougou** Burkina
43 H10 **Siderno Marina** Italy
118 H8 **Sidewood** Saskatchewan Canada
46 G4 **Sidherítis** *isld* Greece
47 H9 **Sídheros, Akra** *C* Crete Greece
75 J6 **Sidhi** India
46 F3 **Sidhirókastron** Greece
17 H8 **Sidi Ali** Algeria
84 H3 **Sidi Barrani** Egypt
85 D1 **Sidi Bel Abbès** Algeria
43 C13 **Sidi Bou Ali** Tunisia
85 B3 **Sidi Ifni** Morocco
85 C2 **Sidi Kacem** Morocco
69 D11 **Sidikalang** Sumatra
85 B4 **Sidi Mhamed** Western Sahara
13 E1 **Sidlaw Hills** Scotland
146 B9 **Sidley, Mt** Antarctica
8 C6 **Sidmouth** England
141 G2 **Sidmouth, C** Queensland Australia
99 S3 **Sidnaw** Michigan U.S.A.
100 B1 **Sidney** British Columbia Canada
117 M11 **Sidney** British Columbia Canada
119 S9 **Sidney** Manitoba Canada
99 S9 **Sidney** Illinois U.S.A.
99 L9 **Sidney** Iowa U.S.A.
98 B2 **Sidney** Montana U.S.A.
98 D8 **Sidney** Nebraska U.S.A.
95 M4 **Sidney** New York U.S.A.
110 M1 **Sidney** Ohio U.S.A.
85 C6 **Sido** Mali
70 G4 **Sidoan** Sulawesi
70 O9 **Sidoardjo** Java
68 B2 **Sidoktaya** Burma
Sidon *see* **Saïda**
84 F3 **Sidrah, As** Libya
130 C7 **Sidrolândia** Brazil
36 C2 **Siebengebirge** *mt* Germany
37 P1 **Siebeniehn** Germany
32 J7 **Siedenburg** Germany
31 N3 **Siedlce** Poland
36 D2 **Sieg** *R* Germany
36 E2 **Siegbach** Germany
36 C2 **Siegburg** Germany
Siegelsdorf *see* **Seukendorf**
37 M6 **Siegenburg** Germany
31 O3 **Siemiatycze** Poland
68 H5 **Siem Pang** Cambodia
68 F6 **Siem Reap** Cambodia
42 D5 **Siena** Italy
31 O5 **Sieniawa** Poland
20 H4 **Sienne** *R* France
29 K4 **Sieppijärvi** Finland
31 L4 **Sieradz** Poland
31 J3 **Sieraków** Poland
22 L5 **Sierck** France
40 F2 **Sierentz** France
31 M3 **Sierpc** Poland
108 B4 **Sierra Blanca** Texas U.S.A.
102 D2 **Sierra Buttes** *pk* California U.S.A.
133 D6 **Sierra Colorada** Argentina
133 D6 **Sierra Grande** Argentina
124 J6 **Sierra Hermosa** Mexico
85 B7 **Sierra Leone** *rep* W Africa
90 H8 **Sierra Leone Basin** Atlantic Oc
90 H8 **Sierra Leone Rise** Atlantic Oc
125 J9 **Sierra Madre del Sur** *mts* Mexico
102 D7 **Sierra Madre Mts** California U.S.A.
125 J5 **Sierra Madre Oriental** *mts* Mexico
124 H4 **Sierra Mojada** Mexico
102 D2 **Sierraville** California U.S.A.
36 D3 **Siershahn** Germany
130 B8 **Siete Puntas, R** Paraguay
33 R6 **Sietow** Germany
48 J4 **Şieu** Romania
45 K4 **Sieve** *R* Italy
33 Q7 **Sieversdorf** Germany
32 M8 **Sievershausen** Germany
29 L8 **Sievi** Finland
67 C5 **Sifang Ling** *mts* China
65 G1 **Sifangtai** China
80 E1 **Sifsufa** Israel
119 R7 **Sifton** Manitoba Canada
117 K7 **Sifton Pass** British Columbia Canada
17 G9 **Sig** Algeria
28 B5 **Sig** Denmark
52 D2 **Sig** Russian Federation
27 D11 **Sigdal** Norway
18 G9 **Sigean** France
110 H2 **Sigel** Illinois U.S.A.
94 H5 **Sigel** Pennsylvania U.S.A.
26 H3 **Sigerfjord** Norway
48 H3 **Sighetu Marmaţiei** Romania
48 J4 **Sighişoara** Romania
47 J4 **Sığırcı** Turkey
69 B10 **Sigli** Sumatra
28 S8 **Siglufjördhur** Iceland
71 F5 **Sigma** Panay Philippines
41 K1 **Sigmaringen** Germany
45 K4 **Signa** Italy
103 L7 **Signal** Arizona U.S.A.
18 G7 **Signal du Luguet** *mt* France
112 B2 **Signal Mt** Tennessee U.S.A.
103 K8 **Signal Pk** Arizona U.S.A.
19 P18 **Signes** France
146 E3 **Signy** *U.K. Base* S Orkney Is S Atlantic Oc
22 G4 **Signy-l'Abbaye** France
22 G4 **Signy-le-petit** France
69 D14 **Sigoisooinan** Indonesia
99 O8 **Sigourney** Iowa U.S.A.
128 C4 **Sigsig** Ecuador
27 J12 **Sigtuna** Sweden
125 L2 **Siguatepeque** Honduras
17 F3 **Sigüenza** Spain
85 C6 **Siguiri** Guinea
103 N3 **Sigurd** Utah U.S.A.
21 N2 **Sigy-en-Bray** France
68 B1 **Sihaung Myauk** Burma
65 D4 **Siheyong** China
41 J3 **Sihl** *R* Switzerland
41 J3 **Sihl See** *L* Switzerland
74 J7 **Sihora** India
67 D5 **Sihui** China
29 J10 **Siikainen** Finland
52 C3 **Siikajoki** *R* Finland
29 N8 **Siilinjärvi** Finland
78 H3 **Siirt** Turkey
69 E13 **Sijunjung** Sumatra
69 E14 **Sikakap** Indonesia
117 M7 **Sikanni Chief** British Columbia Canada
74 F5 **Sikar** India
77 L2 **Sikaram** *mt* Afghanistan
85 C6 **Sikasso** Mali
70 G7 **Sikeli** Sulawesi
110 G5 **Sikeston** Missouri U.S.A.
59 K3 **Sikhote Alin'** *mts* Russian Federation
46 G8 **Síkinos** *isld* Greece
46 F6 **Sikionía** Greece
75 N5 **Sikkim** *prot* India
48 E5 **Siklós** Hungary
116 B5 **Siknik C** Alaska U.S.A.
71 A2 **Siko** *isld* Halmahera Indonesia
70 E1 **Sikuati** Sabah
16 C2 **Sil** *R* Spain
52 B6 **Šilale** Lithuania
41 N4 **Silandro** Italy
70 B4 **Silantek, G** *mt* Sarawak/ Kalimantan
71 G4 **Sila Pt** Philippines
111 H10 **Silas** Alabama U.S.A.
69 B10 **Silawaih Agam** *vol* Sumatra
71 F5 **Silay** Negros Philippines
75 P6 **Silchar** India
26 M1 **Silda** *isld* Norway
47 N10 **Şile** Turkey
22 G3 **Silenrieux** Belgium
27 F12 **Silen, V** *L* Sweden
112 H2 **Siler City** North Carolina U.S.A.
31 K4 **Silesia** *reg* Czech Rep/ Poland
101 R4 **Silesia** Montana U.S.A.
85 E4 **Silet** Algeria
55 F4 **Siletiteniz, Ozero** *L* Kazakhstan
20 D5 **Silfiac** France
74 J4 **Silgarhi** Nepal
83 J12 **Silhouette I** Seychelles
67 C4 **Silian** China
43 C12 **Siliana** Tunisia
99 N2 **Silica** Minnesota U.S.A.
66 D5 **Siling Co** *L* China
43 B9 **Siliqua** Sardinia
47 J1 **Silistra** Bulgaria
47 J3 **Silivri** Turkey
27 G11 **Siljan** *L* Sweden
28 C4 **Silkeborg** Denmark
13 G6 **Silkstone** England
128 E7 **Sillajhuay** *mt* Chile/Bolivia
52 C5 **Sillamäe** Estonia
45 H3 **Sillano** Italy
45 L3 **Sillaro** *R* Italy
21 K5 **Sillé-le-Guillaume** France
38 F8 **Sillian** Austria
21 L4 **Silli-en-Gouffern** France
20 D4 **Sillon-de-Talbert** France
47 H3 **Sílo** *mt* Greece
110 B5 **Siloam Springs** Arkansas U.S.A.
109 N5 **Silsbee** Texas U.S.A.
119 W3 **Silsby L** Manitoba Canada
106 C2 **Silt** Colorado U.S.A.
119 N8 **Silton** Saskatchewan Canada
86 C2 **Siltou** Chad
70 Q10 **Silungblanak** Indonesia
52 B6 **Šilutė** Lithuania
78 H2 **Silvan** Turkey
130 E5 **Silvânia** Brazil
Silva Porto *see* **Kuito**
74 E8 **Silvassa** India
127 K4 **Silver Bank** Caribbean
99 P2 **Silver Bay** Minnesota U.S.A.
103 N9 **Silver Bell** Arizona U.S.A.
101 N3 **Silver Bow** Montana U.S.A.
121 L5 **Silver Centre** Ontario Canada
100 J6 **Silver City** Idaho U.S.A.
111 F8 **Silver City** Mississippi U.S.A.
106 B9 **Silver City** New Mexico U.S.A.
103 M2 **Silver City** Utah U.S.A.
98 J8 **Silver Cr** Nebraska U.S.A.
100 F6 **Silver Cr** Oregon U.S.A.
111 F10 **Silver Creek** Mississippi U.S.A.
94 H4 **Silver Creek** New York U.S.A.
98 A8 **Silver Crown** Wyoming U.S.A.
145 E2 **Silverdale** New Zealand
107 O4 **Silverdale** Kansas U.S.A.
118 F6 **Silver Heights** Alberta Canada
120 B4 **Silver Islet** Ontario Canada
99 T3 **Silver L** Michigan U.S.A.
100 E6 **Silver L** Oregon U.S.A.
100 D6 **Silver Lake** Oregon U.S.A.
123 P4 **Silver Mt** Newfoundland Canada
102 G4 **Silverpeak** Nevada U.S.A.
7 L9 **Silver Pit** North Sea
141 G2 **Silver Plains** Queensland Australia
94 J4 **Silver Springs** New York U.S.A.
141 J8 **Silver Springs Gas Field** Queensland Australia
101 N4 **Silver Star** Montana U.S.A.
117 O10 **Silver Star Prov. Park** British Columbia Canada
117 K10 **Silverthrone Mt** British Columbia Canada
106 C4 **Silverton** Colorado U.S.A.
100 C5 **Silverton** Oregon U.S.A.
108 F1 **Silverton** Texas U.S.A.
100 D1 **Silverton** Washington U.S.A.
128 G4 **Silves** Brazil
16 B7 **Silves** Portugal
131 C4 **Silveyra, L** Argentina
100 F6 **Silvies** *R* Oregon U.S.A.
41 M4 **Silvretta Gruppe** *mt* Switzerland
41 M4 **Silvrettahorn** *mt* Switz/ Austria
80 D6 **Silwād** Jordan
36 B5 **Silwingen** Germany
55 C3 **Sim** Russian Federation
70 B4 **Simanggang** Sarawak
68 E1 **Simao** China
71 F4 **Simara** *isld* Philippines
121 M5 **Simàrd, Lac** Quebec Canada
70 G4 **Simatang** *isld* Sulawesi
47 J4 **Simav** *R* Turkey
47 K5 **Simav** Turkey
47 J5 **Simav Dağlari** *mts* Turkey
47 K5 **Simav Gölü** *L* Turkey
37 O6 **Simbach** Germany
71 E7 **Simbahan** Philippines
79 B8 **Simbillâwein, El** Egypt
45 O6 **Simbruini, Monti** *mt* Italy
120 K10 **Simcoe** Ontario Canada
98 F7 **Simeon** Nebraska U.S.A.
116 H9 **Simeonof I** Alaska U.S.A.
47 H2 **Simeonovgrad** Bulgaria
48 H5 **Simeria** Romania
28 D3 **Simested** Denmark
43 F11 **Simeto** *R* Sicily
69 C11 **Simeuluë** *isld* Indonesia
53 D11 **Simferopol'** Ukraine
47 Q14 **Sími** Greece
47 U14 **Sími** *isld* Greece
46 F3 **Simitli** Bulgaria
102 F7 **Simi Valley** California U.S.A.
Simla *see* **Shimla**
106 F2 **Simla** Colorado U.S.A.
48 H3 **Şimleu Silvaniei** Romania
37 L4 **Simmelsdorf** Germany
40 G4 **Simmental** *R* Switzerland
36 C4 **Simmer** *R* Germany
22 L2 **Simmerath** Germany
36 D4 **Simmern** Germany
111 E11 **Simmesport** Louisiana U.S.A.
118 J9 **Simmie** Saskatchewan Canada
102 E6 **Simmler** California U.S.A.
109 J7 **Simmons** Texas U.S.A.
126 G3 **Simms** Long I Bahamas
101 O2 **Simms** Montana U.S.A.
111 B8 **Simms** Texas U.S.A.
113 K9 **Simms Pt** New Providence I Bahamas
31 O1 **Simnas** Lithuania
29 L6 **Simo** Finland
27 D12 **Simoa** *R* Norway
29 M6 **Simojoki** *R* Finland
29 N11 **Simola** Finland
143 E9 **Simon** W Australia Australia
102 G3 **Simon** Nevada U.S.A.
117 O8 **Simonette** *R* Alberta Canada
119 Q4 **Simonhouse** Manitoba Canada
121 P7 **Simon, L** Quebec Canada
13 G5 **Simon Seat** *mt* England
27 H13 **Simonstorp** Sweden
89 A10 **Simon's Town** S Africa
117 K10 **Simoom Sd** British Columbia Canada
69 G13 **Simpang** Sumatra
69 C11 **Simpangkiri** Sumatra
29 O10 **Simpele** Finland
25 E7 **Simpelveld** Netherlands
129 K5 **Simplício Mendes** Brazil
40 H5 **Simplon Tunnel** Italy/Switz
119 M7 **Simpson** Saskatchewan Canada
107 N2 **Simpson** Kansas U.S.A.
99 O6 **Simpson** Minnesota U.S.A.
101 P1 **Simpson** Montana U.S.A.
140 D6 **Simpson Des** N Terr Australia
138 E2 **Simpson Desert Conservation Park** South Australia Australia
140 E7 **Simpson Desert Nat Park** Queensland Australia
143 F7 **Simpson Hill** W Australia Australia
120 C4 **Simpson I** Ontario Canada
133 C7 **Simpson, I** Chile
117 R5 **Simpson Is** Northwest Territories Canada
115 L4 **Simpson Pen** Northwest Territories Canada
102 H2 **Simpson Pk Mts** Nevada U.S.A.
112 E3 **Simpsonville** South Carolina U.S.A.
27 G16 **Simrishamn** Sweden
100 C8 **Sims** California U.S.A.
100 D5 **Simtustus, L** Oregon U.S.A.
69 C13 **Simuk** *isld* Indonesia
69 D13 **Simulubek** Indonesia
70 B4 **Simunjan** Sarawak
70 F2 **Simunul** *isld* Philippines
69 C11 **Sinabang** Indonesia
69 D11 **Sinabung** *mt* Sumatra
42 G4 **Sinac** Croatia
86 J4 **Sina Dhaqa** Somalia
84 J4 **Sinai** *pen* Egypt
98 J5 **Sinai** South Dakota U.S.A.
48 K5 **Sinaia** Romania
124 F5 **Sinaloa** *state* Mexico
42 D5 **Sinalunga** Italy
127 J9 **Sinamaica** Venezuela
67 C3 **Sinan** China
46 D4 **Sinanaj** Albania
55 D3 **Sinara** *R* Russian Federation
47 O12 **Sinarádhes** Greece
68 B3 **Sinbaungwe** Burma
75 R6 **Sinbo** Burma
68 D6 **Sinbyubyin** Burma
68 D6 **Sinbyudaing** Burma
68 B2 **Sinbyugyun** Burma
126 G10 **Sincé** Colombia
126 G10 **Sincelejo** Colombia
22 E4 **Sinceny** France
101 S8 **Sinclair** Wyoming U.S.A.
112 D4 **Sinclair L** Georgia U.S.A.
117 N9 **Sinclair Mills** British Columbia Canada
138 C4 **Sinclair, Pt** South Australia Australia
15 E2 **Sinclairs B** Scotland
94 H4 **Sinclairville** New York U.S.A.
28 E2 **Sindal** Denmark
71 F6 **Sindañgan** Mindanao Philippines
70 L9 **Sindangbarang** Java
71 K9 **Sindeh, Tk** *B* Flores Indonesia
47 J1 **Sindel** Bulgaria
36 G6 **Sindelfingen** Germany
55 D1 **Sindeya** Russian Federation
76 C2 **Sindgi** India
74 B6 **Sindh** *prov* Pakistan
76 C3 **Sindhnur** India
52 B5 **Sindi** Estonia
47 J5 **Sındırği** Turkey
48 K4 **Sîndominic** Romania
52 H3 **Sindor** Russian Federation
75 M7 **Sindri** India
36 G5 **Sindringen** Germany
54 M9 **Sinegorskiy** Russian Federation
52 H5 **Sinegor'ye** Russian Federation
47 J4 **Sinekçi** Turkey
47 J3 **Sinekli** Turkey
54 G8 **Sinel'nikoyo** Ukraine
16 B7 **Sines** Portugal
29 L5 **Sinettä** Finland
Sinfu *see* **Jianping**
68 D2 **Sing** Burma
86 F3 **Singa** Sudan
68 C2 **Singaingmyo** Burma
69 G12 **Singapore** *rep* S E Asia
69 B14 **Singapore** *city* Singapore
69 F12 **Singapore, Str. of** S E Asia
70 P10 **Singaraja** Indonesia
68 E5 **Sing Buri** Thailand
41 J2 **Singen** Germany
48 J4 **Sîngeorgiu de Pădure** Romania
48 J3 **Sîngeorz-Băi** Romania
111 C11 **Singer** Louisiana U.S.A.
88 E4 **Singida** Tanzania
46 F4 **Singitikós, Kólpos** *G* Greece
75 Q5 **Singkaling Hkamti** Burma
70 G7 **Singkang** Sulawesi
69 E13 **Singkarak** Sumatra
69 G13 **Singkep** Indonesia
69 C11 **Singkil** Sumatra
69 D12 **Singkuang** Sumatra
139 K4 **Singleton** New South Wales Australia
140 C5 **Singleton** N Terr Australia
9 F6 **Singleton** England
109 M5 **Singleton** Texas U.S.A.
140 B5 **Singleton, Mt** N Terr Australia
143 B8 **Singleton, Mt** W Australia Australia
Singora *see* **Songkhla**
68 B1 **Singu** Burma
47 O12 **Siniais** Greece
46 E4 **Siniátsikon** *mt* Greece
71 E3 **Siniloan** Luzon Philippines
Sining *see* **Xining**
Sining Ho *R* *see* **Huang Shui** *R*
70 F5 **Sinio, Gunung** *mt* Sulawesi
43 C8 **Siniscola** Sardinia
55 D5 **Siniy-Shikhan** Russian Federation
70 G7 **Sinjai** Sulawesi
46 C2 **Sinjavina** *mt* Montenegro Yugoslavia
86 G2 **Sinkat** Sudan
Sinkiang *see* **Xinjiang Uygur Zizhiqu**
Sinkiang *aut reg see* **Xinjiang Uygur Zizhiqu**
94 D7 **Sinking Spring** Ohio U.S.A.
65 F5 **Sinmi** *isld* N Korea
36 E2 **Sinn** Germany
36 H3 **Sinn** *R* Germany
129 H2 **Sinnamary** Fr Guiana
76 B1 **Sinnar** India
94 J5 **Sinnemahoning** Pennsylvania U.S.A.
43 H8 **Sinni** *R* Italy
13 H5 **Sinnington** England
36 H3 **Sinntal** Germany
79 A9 **Sinnûris** Egypt
48 M6 **Sinoe, L** Romania
78 E1 **Sinop** Turkey
124 D2 **Sinoquipe** Mexico
131 H2 **Sinos** *R* Brazil
59 J3 **Sinp'o** N Korea
36 F5 **Sinsheim** Germany
36 B4 **Sinspelt** Germany
119 O8 **Sintaluta** Saskatchewan Canada
70 B4 **Sintang** Kalimantan
109 K7 **Sinton** Texas U.S.A.
16 A6 **Sintra** Portugal
59 H3 **Sinŭiju** N Korea
86 A2 **Sinujiif** Somalia
126 G10 **Sinú, R** Colombia
52 C6 **Sinyaya** *R* Russian Federation
36 E6 **Sinzheim** Germany
36 C2 **Sinzig** Germany
28 F7 **Siø** *isld* Denmark
48 E4 **Sió** *R* Hungary
71 F7 **Siocon** Mindanao Philippines
20 G6 **Sion** France
40 F5 **Sion** Switzerland
18 G6 **Sioule** *R* France
98 K6 **Sioux Center** Iowa U.S.A.
98 K7 **Sioux City** Iowa U.S.A.
98 K6 **Sioux Falls** South Dakota U.S.A.
118 L1 **Sioux Lookout** Ontario Canada
99 L7 **Sioux Rapids** Iowa U.S.A.
71 F6 **Sipalay** Negros Philippines
127 O3 **Siparia** Trinidad
Siping *see* **Huangpin**
59 H3 **Siping** China
70 D2 **Sipitang** Sabah
119 U3 **Sipiwesk** Manitoba Canada
146 C10 **Siple Coast** Antarctica
146 A8 **Siple I** *isld* Antarctica
146 A8 **Siple, Mt** Antarctica
29 N11 **Sippola** Finland
111 J7 **Sipsey** Alabama U.S.A.
111 J8 **Sipsey** *R* Alabama U.S.A.
111 J8 **Sipsey Fork** *R* Alabama U.S.A.
69 D14 **Sipura** *isld* Indonesia
71 F6 **Siquijor** Philippines
128 E1 **Siquisique** Venezuela
80 G6 **Sir** *R* Jordan
76 C4 **Sira** India
27 B13 **Sira** *R* Norway
128 D5 **Sira** *mt* Peru
77 D7 **Şir Abū Nu'āyr** *isld* U.A.E.
19 Q15 **Sirac** *mt* France
68 E6 **Si Racha** Thailand
43 G11 **Siracusa** Sicily
117 N9 **Sir Alexander, Mt** British Columbia Canada
85 E6 **Sirba** *watercourse* Niger/ Burkina
123 S4 **Sir Charles Hamilton Sd** Newfoundland Canada
141 G1 **Sir Charles Hardy Is** Gt Barrier Reef Aust
27 B13 **Sirdalsvatn** *L* Norway
118 B8 **Sir Douglas, Mt** Alberta Canada
140 D3 **Sir Edward Pellew Group** *islds* N Terr Australia
99 O4 **Siren** Wisconsin U.S.A.
45 P5 **Sirente, M** *mt* Italy
48 K3 **Siret** *R* Romania
80 F8 **Sirfa** Jordan
140 B1 **Sir George Hope Is** N Terr Australia
142 F2 **Sir Graham Moore Is** W Australia Australia
79 H7 **Sirhān, Wādī** *watercourse* Saudi Arabia
68 E4 **Siri Kit Dam** Thailand
70 B3 **Sirik, Tg** *C* Sarawak
138 D5 **Sir Isaac Pt** South Australia Australia
117 J4 **Sir James McBrien, Mt** Northwest Territories Canada
143 D7 **Sir James, Mt** W Australia Australia
138 D5 **Sir Joseph Banks Group** *islds* South Australia Australia
29 L4 **Sirkka** Finland
29 L5 **Sirkkakoski** Finland
74 G5 **Sir Muttra** India
47 H8 **Sírna** *isld* Greece
78 J3 **Sirnak** Turkey
74 E6 **Sirohi** India
42 H5 **Široki Brijeg** Bosnia-Herzegovina
45 O4 **Sirolo** Italy
69 C12 **Sirombu** Indonesia
76 E1 **Sironcha** India
74 G6 **Sironj** India
46 G7 **Síros** Greece
76 D1 **Sirpur** India
102 F6 **Sirretta Pk** California U.S.A.
77 D7 **Sīrrī, Jazīreh-ye** *isld* Iran
74 F4 **Sirsa** India
117 P10 **Sir Sandford** *mt* British Columbia Canada
117 P10 **Sir Sanford, Mt** British Columbia Canada
76 B3 **Sirsi** India
Sirte *see* **Surt**
84 F3 **Sirte Desert** Libya
84 F3 **Sirte, G. of** Libya
138 A2 **Sir Thomas, Mt** South Australia Australia
71 M9 **Sirung** *isld* Indonesia
117 O9 **Sir Wilfrid Laurier, Mt** British Columbia Canada
141 G2 **Sir William Thompson Ra** Queensland Australia
68 G5 **Sisaket** Thailand
16 B1 **Sisargas** *isld* Spain
87 D11 **Sishen** S Africa
65 D7 **Sishui** China
119 S6 **Sisib L** Manitoba Canada
56 D4 **Sisim** *R* Russian Federation
Sisimiut *see* **Holsteinsborg**
119 Q3 **Sisipuk L** Manitoba Canada
99 S2 **Siskiwit B** Michigan U.S.A.
100 B8 **Siskiyou Mts** Cal/Oregon U.S.A.
124 F4 **Sisogúichic** Mexico
68 F4 **Si Song Khram** Thailand
68 F6 **Sisophon** Cambodia
102 D7 **Sisquoc** California U.S.A.
40 G3 **Sissach** Switzerland
98 J4 **Sisseton** South Dakota U.S.A.
122 E6 **Sisson Branch Res** New Brunswick Canada
22 F4 **Sissonne** France
77 G4 **Sistan, Daryacheh ye** *L* Afghanistan
109 J6 **Sisterdale** Texas U.S.A.
19 P16 **Sisteron** France
68 A7 **Sisters** *islds* Andaman Is
100 D5 **Sisters** Oregon U.S.A.
143 F7 **Sisters, The** *mt* W Australia Australia
83 J12 **Sisters, The** *isld* Seychelles
116 G5 **Sisters, The** *mt* Alaska U.S.A.
94 G7 **Sistersville** West Virginia U.S.A.
36 B3 **Sistig** Germany
45 O7 **Sisto** *R* Italy
52 E5 **Sit** *R* Russian Federation
75 L5 **Sitamarhi** India
70 F2 **Sitangkai** Philippines
74 J5 **Sitapur** India
26 J3 **Sitasjaure** *L* Sweden
89 G6 **Siteki** Swaziland
17 J3 **Sitges** Spain
46 F4 **Sithoniá** Greece
47 H9 **Sitía** Crete Greece
66 E3 **Sitian** China
130 F4 **Sítio da Abadia** Brazil
129 K6 **Sítio de Mato** Brazil
117 F7 **Sitka** Alaska U.S.A.
107 L4 **Sitka** Kansas U.S.A.
116 L8 **Sitkalidak I** Alaska U.S.A.
117 F7 **Sitka Nat Historical Park** Alaska U.S.A.
116 L8 **Sitkinak I** Alaska U.S.A.
100 B6 **Sitkum** Oregon U.S.A.
46 D2 **Sitnica** *R* Serbia Yugoslavia
55 E3 **Sitnikovo** Russian Federation
26 K4 **Sitojaure** *L* Sweden
84 H4 **Sitra** *oasis* Egypt
77 B6 **Sitrah** Bahrain
68 C4 **Sittang** *R* Burma
25 E7 **Sittard** Netherlands
Sitten *see* **Sion**
32 K6 **Sittensen** Germany
9 G5 **Sittingbourne** England
68 A2 **Sittwe** Burma
70 P9 **Situbondo** Java
33 R10 **Sitzenroda** Germany
71 H7 **Siumpu** *isld* Indonesia
125 M3 **Siuna** Nicaragua
29 M6 **Siuruanjoki** *R* Finland
59 J1 **Sivaki** Russian Federation
78 F2 **Sivas** Turkey
53 E10 **Sivash, Zaliv** *B* Ukraine
47 K6 **Sivaslı** Turkey
78 G3 **Siverek** Turkey
52 D5 **Siverskiy** Russian Federation
52 K2 **Sivomaskinskiy** Russian Federation
47 M11 **Sivri** *isld* Turkey
78 C2 **Sivrihisar** Turkey
22 G3 **Sivry** Belgium
22 J5 **Sivry-sur-Meuse** France
84 H4 **Siwa** Egypt
70 G6 **Siwa** Sulawesi
100 A7 **Sixes** Oregon U.S.A.
19 P18 **Six Fours-la-Plage** France
14 C4 **Sixmilebridge** Ireland
111 E12 **Six Mile L** Louisiana U.S.A.
20 F6 **Sixt** Ille-et-Vilaine France
40 E5 **Sixt Vallorcine** France
52 F3 **Siya** Russian Federation
86 G1 **Siyâl I** Egypt
52 G6 **Siyava** Russian Federation
101 M1 **Siyeh, Mt** Montana U.S.A.
56 E5 **Sizim** Russian Federation
59 M1 **Siziman** Russian Federation
65 B4 **Siziwang Qi** China
20 B5 **Sizun** France
52 H2 **Sizyabsk** Russian Federation
28 G5 **Sjælland** *isld* Denmark
28 G5 **Sjællands Odde** *C* Denmark
26 K8 **Själevad** Sweden
46 D1 **Sjenica** Serbia Yugoslavia
26 D10 **Sjoa** *R* Norway
27 G16 **Sjöbo** Sweden
127 M10 **S. José de Guanipa** Venezuela
26 G7 **Sjoutnäs** Sweden
27 F14 **Sjövik** Sweden
26 G7 **Sjulsåsen** Sweden
26 M6 **Sjulsmark** Sweden
26 O2 **Sjusjavrre** Norway
26 F8 **Skäckerfjällen** *mt* Sweden
42 J6 **Skadarsko Jez** *L* Albania/ Yugoslavia
28 G6 **Skælskør** Denmark
28 S10 **Skaftárós** *est* Iceland
27 J14 **Skaftet** Sweden
27 K11 **Skäfthammar** Sweden
28 S9 **Skagafjördhur** *inlet* Iceland
27 C10 **Skagastölstindane** *mt* Norway
28 S9 **Skagastrand** Iceland
28 F1 **Skagen** Denmark
27 G13 **Skagern** *L* Sweden
27 C14 **Skagerrak** *chan* Denmark/ Norway
27 D10 **Skaget** *mt* Norway
100 D1 **Skagit** *R* Washington U.S.A.
117 F6 **Skagway** Alaska U.S.A.
79 D4 **Skala** Cyprus
46 F8 **Skála** Greece
48 K2 **Skala-Podol'skaya** Ukraine
27 F15 **Skälderviken** *B* Sweden
26 K5 **Skalka** *L* Sweden
26 S1 **Skallelv** Norway
28 A5 **Skallingen** *pen* Denmark
27 F14 **Skallsjö** Sweden
27 J13 **Skällvik** Sweden
31 K4 **Skalmierzyce** Poland
37 N3 **Skalná** Czech Rep
28 G7 **Skalø** *isld* Denmark
28 C3 **Skals Å** *R* Denmark
100 C4 **Skamania** Washington U.S.A.
28 E5 **Skamby** Denmark
28 D6 **Skamlingsbanken** *hill* Denmark
Skanderborg *co see* **Vejle** *co*
99 T3 **Skandia** Michigan U.S.A.
27 F16 **Skåne** *physical reg* Sweden
95 L4 **Skaneateles** New York U.S.A.
99 S3 **Skanee** Michigan U.S.A.
26 J3 **Skånland** Norway
28 D4 **Skannerup** Denmark
27 F16 **Skanör** Sweden
26 H7 **Skansholm** Sweden
26 J6 **Skansnäs** Sweden
46 G5 **Skantzoúra** *isld* Greece
27 F13 **Skara** Sweden
27 F13 **Skaraborg** *reg* Sweden
26 F9 **Skardörfjell** *mt* Norway
74 F1 **Skardu** Kashmir
27 M12 **Skärgårdshavets Nat. Park** Finland
27 E11 **Skarnes** Norway
28 E6 **Skarø** *isld* Denmark
28 F6 **Skårop** Denmark
28 B5 **Skarrild** Denmark
26 F9 **Skarsfjället** *mt* Sweden
31 L1 **Skarszewy** Poland
26 J7 **Skarvsjö** Sweden
31 N4 **Skaryszew** Poland
31 M4 **Skarżysko-Kamienna** Poland
28 B5 **Skast** Denmark
26 H10 **Skästra** Sweden
27 G15 **Skatelöv** Sweden
13 F2 **Skateraw** Scotland
27 G12 **Skattkärr** Sweden
27 G10 **Skattungen** *L* Sweden
52 B6 **Skaudvilė** Lithuania
28 B4 **Skave** Denmark
31 M6 **Skawina** Poland
120 K6 **Skead** Ontario Canada
117 J8 **Skeena** *R* British Columbia Canada
117 K8 **Skeena Crossing** British Columbia Canada
117 J7 **Skeena Mts** British Columbia Canada
9 G1 **Skegness** England
28 H6 **Skelby** Denmark
28 H7 **Skelby** Storstrøm Denmark
28 D7 **Skelde** Denmark
140 D3 **Skeleton** *R* N Terr Australia
87 B9 **Skeleton Coast Nat. Park** Namibia
28 C4 **Skelhøje** Denmark
26 L7 **Skellefteå** Sweden
26 L6 **Skellefte älv** *R* Sweden
26 M7 **Skelleftehamm** Sweden
13 F6 **Skelmersdale** England
146 D11 **Skelton Glacier** *glacier* Antarctica
28 E3 **Skelund** Denmark
27 F14 **Skene** Sweden
28 J5 **Skensved** Denmark
46 F6 **Skhimatárion** Greece
46 E8 **Skhíza** *isld* Greece
46 G8 **Skhoinoúsa** *isld* Greece
27 E12 **Ski** Norway
46 F5 **Skíathos** *isld* Greece
107 O5 **Skiatook** Oklahoma U.S.A.
14 B5 **Skibbereen** Ireland
28 B4 **Skibbild** Denmark
28 H5 **Skibby** Denmark
28 C5 **Skibet** Denmark
28 J6 **Skibinge** Denmark
26 L2 **Skibotn** Norway
28 A3 **Skibsted Fjord** Denmark
112 F6 **Skidaway I** Georgia U.S.A.
117 H9 **Skidegate** British Columbia Canada
31 P2 **Skidel'** Belarus
95 L8 **Skidmore** Maryland U.S.A.
109 K7 **Skidmore** Texas U.S.A.
27 D12 **Skien** Norway
31 M4 **Skierniewice** Poland
118 F9 **Skiff** Alberta Canada
29 J11 **Skiftet Kihti** Finland
85 F1 **Skikda** Algeria
116 M6 **Skilak L** Alaska U.S.A.
46 F7 **Skíllaion, Akra** *C* Greece
27 G14 **Skillengaryd** Sweden
110 H3 **Skillet** *R* Illinois U.S.A.
46 D7 **Skinári, Akra** *C* Greece
28 B3 **Skinnerup** Denmark
27 H12 **Skinnskatteberg** Sweden
26 Q1 **Skipagurra** Norway
12 C2 **Skipness** Scotland
144 B6 **Skippers** New Zealand
144 B6 **Skippers Range** New Zealand
13 H6 **Skipsea** England
139 G6 **Skipton** Victoria Australia
13 F6 **Skipton** England
46 G6 **Skíros** *isld* Greece
28 C3 **Skive** Denmark
28 C3 **Skive Fj** *inlet* Denmark
26 C10 **Skjåk** Norway
28 S9 **Skjalfandafljot** *R* Iceland
28 S8 **Skjálfandi** *B* Iceland
26 G5 **Skjelåtind** *mt* Norway
28 D3 **Skjellerup** Denmark
28 A5 **Skjern** Ringkøbing Denmark
28 D4 **Skjern** Viborg Denmark
28 C5 **Skjern Å** *R* Denmark
26 H4 **Skjerstad** Norway
26 L1 **Skjervöy** Norway
28 D4 **Skjød** Denmark
27 A12 **Skjold** Norway
28 B3 **Skjoldborg** Denmark
27 C10 **Skjolden** Norway
28 E7 **Skjoldnæs** *C* Denmark
115 P5 **Skjoldungen** Greenland
26 J3 **Skjomen** Norway
26 H4 **Skjönstå** Norway
26 E6 **Sklinna** *lighthouse* Norway
26 D6 **Sklinnabanken** Norway
48 E1 **Skoczow** Poland
28 C6 **Skodborg** Denmark
28 A5 **Skodsbøl** Denmark
29 K5 **Skodsborg** Denmark
28 E4 **Skødstrup** Denmark
42 F2 **Skofja Loka** Slovenia
26 K9 **Skog** Sweden
26 O2 **Skoganvarre** Norway
26 R2 **Skogerøy** Norway
27 F12 **Skoghall** Sweden
8 A4 **Skokholm I** Wales
99 T8 **Skokie** Illinois U.S.A.
55 D6 **Skol'** Kazakhstan
31 O6 **Skole** Ukraine
48 H1 **Skole** Ukraine
27 H12 **Sköllersta** Sweden
8 A4 **Skomer I** Wales
26 F4 **Skomvoer** Norway
117 Q11 **Skookumchuk** British Columbia Canada
46 F5 **Skópelos** *isld* Greece
46 G6 **Skópelos Kaloyeroi** *isld* Greece
54 L3 **Skopin** Russian Federation
46 E2 **Skopje** Macedonia
31 L2 **Skórcz** Poland
55 F2 **Skorodum** Russian Federation
26 F7 **Skorovatn** Norway
26 J8 **Skorped** Sweden
28 D3 **Skørping** Denmark
28 G7 **Skørringe** Denmark
27 D12 **Skotselv** Norway
28 F7 **Skovballe** Denmark
28 D4 **Skovby** Århus Denmark
28 E5 **Skovby** Fyn Denmark
28 D7 **Skovby** Sønderjylland Denmark
27 G13 **Skövde** Sweden
28 B5 **Skovlund** Denmark
59 H1 **Skovorodino** Russian Federation
95 S2 **Skowhegan** Maine U.S.A.
119 S7 **Skownan** Manitoba Canada
28 C2 **Skræm** Denmark
27 E11 **Skreia** Norway
28 F7 **Skrøbelev** Denmark
26 M5 **Skröven** Sweden
28 C6 **Skrydstrup** Denmark
27 A12 **Skudeneshavn** Norway
27 E12 **Skulerud** Norway
103 H5 **Skull Pk** Nevada U.S.A.
103 M7 **Skull V** Arizona U.S.A.
48 L3 **Skulyany** Moldova
111 G8 **Skuna** *R* Mississippi U.S.A.
110 E1 **Skunk** *R* Iowa U.S.A.
27 M15 **Skuodas** Lithuania
27 F16 **Skurup** Sweden
31 J6 **Skuteč** Czech Rep
27 J11 **Skutskär** Sweden
26 H3 **Skutvik** Norway
6 F1 **Skúvoy** *isld* Faeroes
48 M1 **Skvira** Ukraine
116 M6 **Skwentna** Alaska U.S.A.
31 J3 **Skwierzyna** Poland
15 B3 **Skye, I. of** Scotland
100 D2 **Skykomish** Washington U.S.A.
146 D7 **Skytrain Ice Rise** *ice rise* Antarctica
55 D2 **Sladkovskoye** Russian Federation
28 G6 **Slagelse** Denmark
13 F4 **Slaggyford** England
111 C10 **Slagle** Louisiana U.S.A.
28 H5 **Slaglille** Denmark
26 K6 **Slagnäs** Sweden
70 N9 **Slahung** Java
13 F6 **Slaidburn** England
12 E2 **Slamannan** Scotland

70 M9 **Slamet, G** *mt* Java
48 F2 **Slana** *R* Slovakia
116 P5 **Slana** Alaska U.S.A.
14 E3 **Slane** Ireland
14 E4 **Slaney** *R* Ireland
89 B8 **Slang Berg** *mt* S Africa
28 J5 **Slangerup** Denmark
89 A10 **Slang Kop Pt** S Africa
48 K5 **Slănic** Romania
48 K4 **Slănic-Moldova** Romania
42 H6 **Slano** Croatia
52 C5 **Slantsy** Russian Federation
30 H5 **Slaný** Czech Rep
37 N3 **Slapany** Czech Rep
15 B3 **Slapin, L** Scotland
141 H4 **Slashers Reefs** Gt Barrier Reef Aust
120 D4 **Slate I** Ontario Canada
101 S9 **Slater** Colorado U.S.A.
110 C2 **Slater** Missouri U.S.A.
98 B8 **Slater** Wyoming U.S.A.
102 G6 **Slate Ra** California U.S.A.
111 G8 **Slate Springs** Mississippi U.S.A.
48 J6 **Slatina** Romania
42 H3 **Slatina, P** Croatia
108 F2 **Slaton** Texas U.S.A.
27 H11 **Slättberg** Sweden
26 O1 **Slåtten** Norway
94 G8 **Slatyfork** West Virginia U.S.A.
111 E11 **Slaughter** Louisiana U.S.A.
51 Q2 **Slautnoye** Russian Federation
118 C3 **Slave Lake** Alberta Canada
117 Q5 **Slave Pt** Northwest Territories Canada
117 R5 **Slave R** Northwest Territories Canada
54 C3 **Slavgorod** Belarus
54 G8 **Slavgorod** Dnepropetrovskaya obl Ukraine
31 N1 **Slavinek** Russian Federation
48 D1 **Slavkov** Czech Rep
52 C5 **Slavkovichi** Russian Federation
42 H3 **Slavonia** *reg* Croatia
46 F2 **Slavovvrŭkh** *mt* Bulgaria
42 H3 **Slav Požega** Croatia
48 H2 **Slavskoye** Ukraine
46 G1 **Slavyanovo** Bulgaria
54 J8 **Slavyansk** Ukraine
31 J4 **Sława** Poland
31 O4 **Sławatycze** Poland
31 K1 **Sławno** Poland
31 J2 **Sławoborze** Poland
99 L6 **Slayton** Minnesota U.S.A.
9 F1 **Sleaford** England
138 D6 **Sleaford B** South Australia Australia
116 D4 **Sledge I** Alaska U.S.A.
118 K4 **Sled L** Saskatchewan Canada
13 H5 **Sledmere** England
115 M6 **Sleeper Is** Northwest Territories Canada
99 W5 **Sleeping Bear Dunes Nat. Lakeshore** *nat park* Michigan U.S.A.
94 A2 **Sleeping Bear Pt** Michigan U.S.A.
120 B4 **Sleeping Giant Prov. Park** Ontario Canada
99 M5 **Sleepy Eye** Minnesota U.S.A.
116 J6 **Sleetmute** Alaska U.S.A.
22 F1 **Sleidinge** Belgium
6 M4 **Sleipner** *oil rig* North Sea
70 N9 **Sleman** Java
52 C5 **Slepino** Russian Federation
31 L3 **Ślesin** Poland
146 F7 **Slessor Glacier** Antarctica
28 F4 **Sletterhage** *C* Denmark
28 C2 **Slettestrand** Denmark
26 Q1 **Slettnes** Norway
111 G11 **Slidell** Louisiana U.S.A.
109 K2 **Slidell** Texas U.S.A.
27 D10 **Slidre** Norway
25 C5 **Sliedrecht** Netherlands
14 D2 **Slieve Anierin** *mt* Ireland
14 C3 **Slieve Aughty** *mts* Ireland
14 D2 **Slieve Beagh** *mt* Ireland
14 C4 **Slieve Bernagh** Ireland
14 D3 **Slieve Bloom Mts** Ireland
14 B2 **Slieve Car** *mt* Ireland
14 F2 **Slieve Donard** *mt* N Ireland
14 B3 **Slieve Elva** *mt* Ireland
14 C4 **Slievefelim Cullaun Mts** Ireland
14 B2 **Slieve Gamph** *mt* Ireland
14 E2 **Slieve Gullion** *mt* N Ireland
14 C2 **Slieve League** *mt* Ireland
14 B4 **Slieve Mish** *mts* Ireland
14 B5 **Slieve Miskish** *mt* Ireland
14 A3 **Slievemore** *mt* Ireland
14 D2 **Slievenakilla** *hill* Ireland
14 D4 **Slievenamon** *mt* Ireland
14 D1 **Slieve Snaght** *mt* Ireland
14 C2 **Slieve Tooey** *mt* Ireland
15 B3 **Sligachan** Scotland
14 C2 **Sligo** *co* Ireland
14 C2 **Sligo** Ireland
94 H5 **Sligo** Pennsylvania U.S.A.
28 H6 **Slimminge** Denmark
99 S6 **Slinger** Wisconsin U.S.A.
15 C3 **Slioch Mt** Scotland
145 E2 **Slipper I** New Zealand
94 G5 **Slippery Rock** Pennsylvania U.S.A.
27 K14 **Slite** Sweden
47 H2 **Sliven** Bulgaria
46 F2 **Slivnitsa** Bulgaria
98 K7 **Sloan** Iowa U.S.A.
101 L2 **Sloan** Montana U.S.A.
103 J6 **Sloan** Nevada U.S.A.
102 D2 **Sloat** California U.S.A.
52 H5 **Slobedskoy** Russian Federation
54 M5 **Sloboda** Russian Federation
52 G4 **Slobodchikovo** Russian Federation
48 M3 **Slobodka** Ukraine
48 M4 **Slobodzeya** Moldova
48 L6 **Slobozia** Ialomita Romania
48 J6 **Slobozia** Teleorman Romania
117 P11 **Slocan** British Columbia Canada
25 G2 **Slochteren** Netherlands
111 L10 **Slocomb** Alabama U.S.A.
117 G6 **Sloko** *R* British Columbia Canada
27 F15 **Slömge** Sweden
31 H3 **Słońsk** Poland
25 E3 **Sloten** Netherlands
25 E3 **Sloter Meer** Netherlands
28 G6 **Slots** Denmark
81 B9 **Slot van Capelle** Indian Oc
9 F4 **Slough** England
31 L7 **Slovakia** *rep* Europe
48 F2 **Slovakia** *old reg* Slovakia
42 F3 **Slovenia** *rep* S Europe
Slovenija *see* **Slovenia**
38 N8 **Slovenske Gorice** *mts* Slovenia
48 E2 **Slovenské Pravno** Slovakia
31 L7 **Slovenské Rudohorie** *mts* Slovakia
116 L5 **Slow Fork** *R* Alaska U.S.A.
12 D1 **Sloy, L** Scotland
31 H3 **Słubice** Poland
53 C8 **Sluch'** *R* Ukraine
52 H4 **Sludka** Komi Respublika Russian Federation
25 A6 **Sluis** Netherlands
25 A6 **Sluiskil** Netherlands
31 H4 **Sluknov** Czech Rep
31 K3 **Słupca** Poland
31 K1 **Słupsk** Poland
14 A3 **Slyne Hd** Ireland
111 D8 **Smackover** Arkansas U.S.A.
15 E4 **Sma Glen** Scotland
13 F2 **Smailholm** Scotland
27 G15 **Småland** *physical reg* Sweden
28 G6 **Smålandsfarvandet** Denmark
27 F14 **Smål Burseryd** Sweden
101 N5 **Small** Idaho U.S.A.
119 U1 **Small L** Manitoba Canada
95 S3 **Small Pt** Maine U.S.A.
115 N7 **Smallwood Res** Labrador, Nfld Canada
9 G5 **Smarden** England
119 N5 **Smeaton** Saskatchewan Canada
48 F6 **Smederevo** Serbia Yugoslavia
48 F6 **Smederevska Palanka** Serbia Yugoslavia
27 H11 **Smedjebacken** Sweden
54 C7 **Smela** Ukraine
26 S1 **Smelror** Norway
94 J5 **Smethport** Pennsylvania U.S.A.
59 K2 **Smidovich** Russian Federation
28 J4 **Smidstrup** Denmark
31 K3 **Śmigiel** Poland
118 H7 **Smiley** Saskatchewan Canada
109 K6 **Smiley** Texas U.S.A.
52 C6 **Smiltene** Latvia
46 G3 **Smilyan** Bulgaria
46 G1 **Smirdiasa** Romania
31 J5 **Smiřice** Czech Rep
55 E4 **Smirnovo** Kazakhstan
59 M2 **Smirnykh** Russian Federation
117 Q8 **Smith** Alberta Canada
102 E3 **Smith** Nevada U.S.A.
94 H10 **Smith** *R* Virginia/N Carolina U.S.A.
114 G4 **Smith Arm** *B* Northwest Territories Canada
115 M2 **Smith B** Northwest Territories Canada
116 K1 **Smith B** Alaska U.S.A.
110 G3 **Smithboro** Illinois U.S.A.
140 F3 **Smithburne R** Queensland Australia
107 M2 **Smith Center** Kansas U.S.A.
117 K8 **Smithers** British Columbia Canada
89 E8 **Smithfield** S Africa
98 G9 **Smithfield** Nebraska U.S.A.
112 J2 **Smithfield** North Carolina U.S.A.
94 H7 **Smithfield** Pennsylvania U.S.A.
109 M9 **Smithfield** Texas U.S.A.
101 O8 **Smithfield** Utah U.S.A.
95 L9 **Smithfield** Virginia U.S.A.
94 G7 **Smithfield** West Virginia U.S.A.
68 A6 **Smith I** Andaman Is
146 C3 **Smith I** S Shetland Is Antarctica
115 M5 **Smith I** Northwest Territories Canada
95 M8 **Smith I** Maryland U.S.A.
112 K4 **Smith I** North Carolina U.S.A.
95 M9 **Smith I** Virginia U.S.A.
100 C1 **Smith I** Washington U.S.A.
94 H9 **Smith Mountain Lake** Virginia U.S.A.
146 D6 **Smith Peninsula** *pen* Antarctica
100 J1 **Smith Pk** *mt* Idaho U.S.A.
140 B1 **Smith Pt** *inlet* N Terr Australia
122 J8 **Smith Pt** Nova Scotia Canada
101 O2 **Smith R** Montana U.S.A.
117 K6 **Smith River** British Columbia Canada
100 A8 **Smith River** California U.S.A.
121 O8 **Smiths Falls** Ontario Canada
100 J5 **Smiths Ferry** Idaho U.S.A.
110 K4 **Smiths Grove** Kentucky U.S.A.
7 M10 **Smiths Knoll** *oil rig* North Sea
115 M2 **Smith Sound** Northwest Territories Canada
139 H8 **Smithton** Australia
110 C3 **Smithton** Missouri U.S.A.
139 L4 **Smithtown-Gladstone** New South Wales Australia
111 M10 **Smithville** Georgia U.S.A.
110 B2 **Smithville** Missouri U.S.A.
107 Q7 **Smithville** Oklahoma U.S.A.
110 L6 **Smithville** Tennessee U.S.A.
109 K6 **Smithville** Texas U.S.A.
94 F7 **Smithville** West Virginia U.S.A.
98 C6 **Smithwick** South Dakota U.S.A.
46 D4 **Smlikas** *mt* Greece
102 E1 **Smoke Creek Desert** Nevada U.S.A.
94 H8 **Smoke Hole** West Virginia U.S.A.
117 O8 **Smoky** *R* Alberta Canada
138 C4 **Smoky B** South Australia Australia
139 L4 **Smoky C** New South Wales Australia
123 M7 **Smoky C** Nova Scotia Canada
120 H2 **Smoky Falls** Ontario Canada
106 H2 **Smoky Hill** *R* Colo/Kansas U.S.A.
107 L2 **Smoky Hills** Kansas U.S.A.
118 E4 **Smoky Lake** Alberta Canada
26 C8 **Smöla** *isld* Norway
54 D2 **Smolensk** Russian Federation
53 D7 **Smolenskaya Oblast'** *prov* Russian Federation
54 E2 **Smolensko-Moskovskaya Vozvyshennost'** *upland* Russian Federation
46 G3 **Smolyan** Bulgaria
101 P7 **Smoot** Wyoming U.S.A.
120 J3 **Smooth Rock Falls** Ontario Canada
120 A2 **Smooth Rock L** Ontario Canada
118 L3 **Smoothstone R** Saskatchewan Canada
48 K2 **Smotrich** Ukraine
47 J1 **Smyadovo** Bulgaria
54 G1 **Smychka** Russian Federation
27 F16 **Smygehamn** Sweden
146 C6 **Smyley** *isld* Antarctica
Smyrna *see* **Izmir**
95 M7 **Smyrna** Delaware U.S.A.
112 C4 **Smyrna** Georgia U.S.A.
95 M4 **Smyrna** New York U.S.A.
110 K6 **Smyrna** Tennessee U.S.A.
95 S7 **Smyrna Mills** Maine U.S.A.
29 T9 **Snæfell** *mt* Iceland
12 D5 **Snaefell** *mt* I of Man U.K.
139 H9 **Snag** Tasmania Australia
68 G7 **Snaipol** Cambodia
13 G6 **Snaith** England
101 O6 **Snake** *R* Idaho/Wyoming U.S.A.
98 E7 **Snake** *R* Nebraska U.S.A.
100 G3 **Snake** *R* Washington U.S.A.
103 K2 **Snake Ra** Nevada U.S.A.
100 J4 **Snake R. Canyon** Idaho/ Oregon U.S.A.
101 N6 **Snake R. Plain** Idaho U.S.A.
126 F3 **Snap Pt** Andros Bahamas
28 E5 **Snaptun** Denmark
117 Q3 **Snare L** Northwest Territories Canada
117 P4 **Snare River** Northwest Territories Canada
26 F7 **Snåsa** Norway
26 F8 **Snasahögarna** *mt* Sweden
26 E7 **Snåsavatn** *L* Norway
111 M11 **Sneads** Florida U.S.A.
25 E2 **Sneek** Netherlands
25 E2 **Sneeker Meer** Netherlands
14 B5 **Sneem** Ireland
89 D8 **Sneeuberg** *mts* S Africa
89 A9 **Sneeukop** *mt* S Africa
29 K4 **Snekkersten** Denmark
102 D4 **Snelling** California U.S.A.
28 B5 **Sneum Å** *R* Denmark
54 L8 **Snezhnoye** Ukraine
31 J5 **Sněžka** *mt* Czech Rep
42 F3 **Snežnik** *mt* Slovenia
31 N2 **Śniadowo** Poland
31 N2 **Sniardwy, Jezioro** *L* Poland
31 N7 **Snina** Slovakia
118 A3 **Snipe L** Alberta Canada
15 B3 **Snizort, Loch** Scotland
28 F6 **Snøde** Denmark
28 D5 **Snoghøj** Denmark
26 D9 **Snöhetta** *mt* Norway
100 C2 **Snohomish** Washington U.S.A.
28 J5 **Snoldelev** Denmark
127 M3 **Snook Pt** Jamaica
100 D2 **Snoqualmie Pass** Washington U.S.A.
26 G10 **Snössvallen** Sweden
68 H6 **Snoul** Cambodia
54 D4 **Snov** *R* Rus Fed/Ukraine
94 D3 **Snover** Michigan U.S.A.
116 L6 **Snowcap Mt** Alaska U.S.A.
119 N5 **Snowden** Saskatchewan Canada
100 B8 **Snowden** California U.S.A.
8 B1 **Snowdon** *mt* Wales
114 H5 **Snowdrift** Northwest Territories Canada
119 T9 **Snowflake** Manitoba Canada
103 O7 **Snowflake** Arizona U.S.A.
95 M8 **Snow Hill** Maryland U.S.A.
112 K2 **Snow Hill** North Carolina U.S.A.
146 D4 **Snow Hill I** Antarctica
146 C3 **Snow I** S Shetland Is Antarctica
119 R4 **Snow Lake** Manitoba Canada
111 E7 **Snow Lake** Arkansas U.S.A.
106 C2 **Snowmass Mt** Colorado U.S.A.
121 O8 **Snow Road** Ontario Canada
94 K5 **Snow Shoe** Pennsylvania U.S.A.
100 K1 **Snowshoe Pk** *mt* Montana U.S.A.
138 E5 **Snowtown** South Australia Australia
101 N8 **Snowville** Utah U.S.A.
103 K1 **Snow Water L** Nevada U.S.A.
139 J6 **Snowy Mts** Vict/N S W Australia
48 K2 **Snyatyn** Ukraine
98 K8 **Snyder** Nebraska U.S.A.
107 M7 **Snyder** Oklahoma U.S.A.
108 G3 **Snyder** Texas U.S.A.
27 H12 **Snyten** Sweden
143 E6 **Soakage Well** W Australia Australia
144 A6 **Soaker, Mt** New Zealand
87 H11 **Soalala** Madagascar
40 G7 **Soana, Val di** Italy
87 H11 **Soanierana Ivongo** Madagascar
65 G7 **Soan kundo** *isld* S Korea
100 F2 **Soap Lake** Washington U.S.A.
48 J5 **Soarş** Romania
71 A2 **Soa-Šiu** Halmahera Indonesia
45 K1 **Soave** Italy
15 B3 **Soay** Scotland
41 K5 **Soazza** Switzerland
85 F6 **Soba** Nigeria
86 F4 **Sobat** *prov* Sudan
86 F4 **Sobat** *R* Sudan
36 D4 **Sobernheim** Germany
31 H6 **Soběslav** Czech Rep
54 M1 **Sobinka** Russian Federation
53 H8 **Sobolevo** Russian Federation
60 E13 **Sobo-san** *mt* Japan
38 M8 **Soboth** Austria
31 K5 **Sobótka** Poland
129 K6 **Sobradinho, Barragem de** *res* Brazil
129 K4 **Sobral** Brazil
48 G2 **Sobrance** Slovakia
18 F10 **Sobrarbe** *dist* Spain
68 H1 **Soc Bang Giang** *R* Vietnam
68 H1 **Soc Giang** Vietnam
31 M3 **Sochaczew** Poland
40 E2 **Sochaux** France
53 E11 **Sochi** Russian Federation
112 D4 **Social Circle** Georgia U.S.A.
112 H3 **Society Hill** South Carolina U.S.A.
135 M10 **Society Is** Pacific Oc
Socna *see* **Sūknah**
128 E8 **Socompa** *vol* Chile/Arg
130 F8 **Socorro** Brazil
108 A1 **Socorro** New Mexico U.S.A.
133 B6 **Socorro, I** Chile
Socotra *see* **Suqutrá**
17 F5 **Socuéllamos** Spain
117 M9 **Soda Creek** British Columbia Canada
103 H6 **Soda L** California U.S.A.
29 M4 **Sodankylä** Finland
101 O7 **Soda Springs** Idaho U.S.A.
102 F3 **Sodaville** Nevada U.S.A.
112 B2 **Soddy-Daisy** Tennessee U.S.A.
36 F3 **Södel** Germany
27 K12 **Söderby-Karl** Sweden
26 J9 **Söderfjärden** Sweden
27 J11 **Söderfors** Sweden
27 J10 **Söderhamn** Sweden
27 H13 **Söderköping** Sweden
27 H12 **Södermanland** *reg* Sweden
27 J12 **Södertälje** Sweden
86 E3 **Sodiri** Sudan
86 G4 **Sodo** Ethiopia
95 K3 **Sodus** New York U.S.A.
89 H6 **Sodwana B** S Africa
71 M9 **Soë** Timor Indonesia
60 D12 **Soeda** Japan
87 E10 **Soekmekaar** S Africa
52 B5 **Soela Väin** *chan* Estonia
32 H9 **Soest** Germany
25 D4 **Soest** Netherlands
32 G7 **Soeste** *R* Germany
46 E5 **Sofádhes** Greece
Sofala *see* **Beira** Mozambique
139 J5 **Sofala** New South Wales Australia
79 F5 **Sofar** Lebanon
Sofia *see* **Sofiya**
87 H11 **Sofia** *R* Madagascar
106 G5 **Sofia** New Mexico U.S.A.
46 F7 **Sofikón** Greece
46 F2 **Sofiya** Bulgaria
36 H7 **Söflingen** Germany
52 D2 **Sofporog** Russian Federation
75 P3 **Sog** China
128 D2 **Sogamoso** Colombia
32 G7 **Sögel** Germany
45 M3 **Sogliano al Rubicone** Italy
27 B10 **Sogn** *reg* Norway
27 C13 **Sögne** Norway
27 B10 **Sognefjorden** *inlet* Norway
26 B10 **Sogn og Fjordane** Norway
71 G5 **Sogod** Philippines
55 E1 **Sogom** Russian Federation
47 K7 **Söğüt** Turkey
78 C1 **Söğüt** Turkey
47 K7 **Söğüt Gölü** *L* Turkey
84 J4 **Sohâg** Egypt
75 J7 **Sohagpur** India
9 G3 **Soham** England
137 L3 **Sohano** Bougainville I Papua New Guinea
68 D5 **Sohng Gwe, Khao** *mt* Burma/Thailand
36 H1 **Söhrewald** Germany
65 F7 **Sohŭksan** *isld* S Korea
22 G2 **Soignies** Belgium
21 O7 **Soings-en-Sologne** France
29 L9 **Soini** Finland
22 E5 **Soissons** France
60 G11 **Sōja** Japan
74 E6 **Sojat** India
71 F6 **Sojoton Pt** Philippines
53 H7 **Sok** *R* Russian Federation
78 A3 **Soke** Turkey
46 F4 **Sokhós** Greece
48 L2 **Sokiryany** Ukraine
46 E1 **Soko Banja** Serbia Yugoslavia
85 E7 **Sokodé** Togo
52 F5 **Sokol** Russian Federation
31 O2 **Sokółka** Poland
31 L4 **Sokolniki** Poland
85 C6 **Sokolo** Mali
37 O3 **Sokolov** Czech Rep
55 E3 **Sokolovka** Kazakhstan
52 J2 **Sokolovo** Russian Federation
31 N5 **Sokołów Małopolski** Poland
31 N3 **Sokołów Podlaski** Poland
52 D2 **Sokolozero** Russian Federation
52 F6 **Sokol'skoye** Russian Federation
31 O3 **Sokoły** Poland
115 R4 **Søkongen Ø** *isld* Greenland
61 Q12 **Sokoniya** Okinawa
85 F6 **Sokoto** *R* Nigeria
85 F6 **Sokoto** Nigeria
56 B3 **Sokur** Russian Federation
56 C3 **Sokur** Russian Federation
126 F4 **Sola** Cuba
27 A13 **Sola** Norway
88 F1 **Soiai** Kenya
74 G3 **Solan** India
144 A7 **Solander I** New Zealand
71 E2 **Solano** Luzon Philippines
106 F6 **Solano** New Mexico U.S.A.
76 B2 **Solāpur** India
45 Q8 **Solaro, M** *mt* Italy
41 O3 **Solbad Hall** Austria
26 J8 **Solberg** Sweden
26 J2 **Solbergfjord** *inlet* Norway
27 E12 **Solbergfoss** Norway
28 E3 **Solbjerg** Denmark
28 D4 **Solbjerg Sø** *L* Denmark
48 K3 **Solca** Romania
41 O4 **Sölden** Austria
99 L8 **Soldier** Iowa U.S.A.
107 P2 **Soldier** Kansas U.S.A.
94 D8 **Soldier** Kentucky U.S.A.
31 L2 **Solec Kujawski** Poland
126 G9 **Soledad** Colombia
124 C5 **Soledad** Mexico
102 C5 **Soledad** California U.S.A.
127 N10 **Soledad** Venezuela
128 E5 **Soledade** Brazil
100 A1 **Soleduck** *R* Washington U.S.A.
55 F3 **Solenoye, Ozero** *L* Russian Federation
125 M4 **Solentiname, Is. de** Nicaragua
9 E6 **Solent, The** *chan* England
7 L9 **Sole Pit** North Sea
45 L1 **Solesino** Italy
22 F3 **Solesmes** Nord France
21 K6 **Solesmes** Sarthe France
41 N5 **Sole, Val. di** Italy
29 J8 **Solf** Finland
45 J1 **Solferino** Italy
52 F4 **Solginskiy** Russian Federation
56 D3 **Solgonskiy Kryzah** *ra* Russian Federation
27 A11 **Solheim** Norway
52 F5 **Soligalich** Russian Federation
21 M4 **Soligny-la-Trappe** France
9 E3 **Solihull** England
52 J5 **Solikamsk** Russian Federation
55 B5 **Sol'Iletsk** Russian Federation
43 C12 **Soliman** Tunisia
128 E4 **Solimões** *R* Brazil
36 C1 **Solingen** Germany
127 J10 **Solita** Venezuela
139 L3 **Solitary I, North** New South Wales Australia
139 L4 **Solitary I, South** New South Wales Australia
17 H3 **Solivella** Spain
38 F7 **Söll** Austria
26 J8 **Sollefteå** Sweden
27 J12 **Sollentuna** Sweden
26 D10 **Sollia** Norway
33 R9 **Söllichau** Germany
32 K9 **Solling** *hills* Germany
33 N8 **Söllingen** Germany
36 E3 **Solms** Germany
26 E10 **Söln** *mt* Norway
27 J12 **Solna** Sweden
54 H1 **Solnechnogorsk** Russian Federation
37 K6 **Solnhofen** Germany
26 D10 **Sölnkletten** *mt* Norway
54 H5 **Solntsevo** Russian Federation
70 N9 **Solo** *R* Java
70 G6 **Solo** *R* Sulawesi
45 R8 **Solofra** Italy
21 N7 **Sologne** *reg* France
71 J4 **Solok** Sulawesi
69 E13 **Solok** Sumatra
52 D4 **Solomennoye** Russian Federation
103 P9 **Solomon** Arizona U.S.A.
107 M2 **Solomon** *R* Kansas U.S.A.
107 N3 **Solomon** Kansas U.S.A.
137 M3 **Solomon Is** Pacific Oc
137 L3 **Solomon Sea** Pacific Oc
80 D7 **Solomon's Pools** Jordan
59 H2 **Solon** China
99 P8 **Solon** Iowa U.S.A.
94 F5 **Solon** Ohio U.S.A.
55 F5 **Solonichki** Kazakhstan
54 H6 **Solonitsevka** Ukraine
99 P3 **Solon Springs** Wisconsin U.S.A.
58 G1 **Solontsovo** Russian Federation
45 R7 **Solopaca** Italy
71 L9 **Solor** *isld* Indonesia
17 F3 **Solorio, Sa. del** *mts* Spain
71 L9 **Solor, Kepulauan** *isld* Indonesia
40 F3 **Solothurn** Switzerland
48 J2 **Solotvin** Ukraine
52 E2 **Solovetskiye Ostrova** *islds* Russian Federation
59 H1 **Solov'yevsk** Russian Federation
22 G3 **Solre-le-Château** France
28 J5 **Solrød Strand** Denmark
41 O3 **Solstein** *mt* Austria
42 G5 **Šolta** *isld* Croatia
32 L7 **Soltau** Germany
52 D5 **Soltsy** Russian Federation
27 A10 **Solund** Norway
46 E3 **Solunska** *mt* Macedonia
102 D7 **Solvang** California U.S.A.
95 L3 **Solvay** New York U.S.A.
27 G15 **Sölvesborg** Sweden
52 G4 **Sol'vychegodsk** Russian Federation
15 E6 **Solway Firth** Scotland
87 E8 **Solwezi** Zambia
61 O8 **Sōma** Japan
47 J5 **Soma** Turkey
22 E3 **Somain** France
86 H5 **Somalia** *rep* E Africa
72 G7 **Somali Basin** Indian Oc
70 E3 **Sombang, Gunung** *mt* Kalimantan
87 D7 **Sombo** Angola
48 E5 **Sombor** Serbia Yugoslavia
120 H10 **Sombra** Ontario Canada
22 H2 **Sombreffe** Belgium
124 H6 **Sombrerete** Mexico
127 N5 **Sombrero** *isld* Lesser Antilles
69 A9 **Sombrero Chan** Nicobar Is
113 F13 **Sombrero Key** *isld* Florida U.S.A.
48 H3 **Şomcuţa Mare** Romania
48 H3 **Şomcuta Mare** Romania
25 E6 **Someren** Netherlands
29 K11 **Somero** Finland
99 M7 **Somers** Iowa U.S.A.
101 L1 **Somers** Montana U.S.A.
99 T7 **Somers** Wisconsin U.S.A.
139 H8 **Somerset** Tasmania Australia
119 T9 **Somerset** Manitoba Canada
8 C5 **Somerset** *co* England
106 C3 **Somerset** Colorado U.S.A.
94 C9 **Somerset** Kentucky U.S.A.
95 Q5 **Somerset** Massachusetts U.S.A.
94 E7 **Somerset** Ohio U.S.A.
94 H6 **Somerset** Pennsylvania U.S.A.
109 J6 **Somerset** Texas U.S.A.
87 E12 **Somerset East** S Africa
90 A2 **Somerset I** Bermuda
147 F4 **Somerset I** Northwest Territories Canada
141 L7 **Somerset Res** Queensland Australia
95 P4 **Somerset Res** Vermont U.S.A.
89 A10 **Somerset West** S Africa
95 N7 **Somers Point** New Jersey U.S.A.
95 Q3 **Somersworth** New Hampshire U.S.A.
8 D5 **Somerton** England
103 K9 **Somerton** Arizona U.S.A.
95 Q4 **Somerville** Massachusetts U.S.A.
95 N6 **Somerville** New Jersey U.S.A.
110 G6 **Somerville** Tennessee U.S.A.
109 L5 **Somerville Res** Texas U.S.A.
48 H3 **Someş** *R* Romania
100 B8 **Somesbar** California U.S.A.
48 H4 **Somesul Cald** *R* Romania
48 J3 **Someşul Mare** *R* Romania
77 K7 **Somiani Bay** *B* Pakistan
45 J1 **Sommacompagna** Italy
22 H5 **Sommauthe** France
45 Q8 **Somma Vesuvio** Italy
18 G3 **Somme** *dept* France
21 O1 **Somme** *R* France
22 D4 **Somme** *R* France
22 J3 **Somme-Leuze** Belgium
27 G13 **Sommen** Sweden
27 H13 **Sommen** *L* Sweden
37 L1 **Sömmerda** Germany
18 H4 **Sommesous** France
18 H9 **Sommières** France
68 G2 **Som Mong** Vietnam
48 D4 **Somogy** *co* Hungary
48 D4 **Somogyszob** Hungary
48 D4 **Somogyvár** Hungary
99 S8 **Somonauk** Illinois U.S.A.
16 E3 **Somosierra, Pto. de** Spain
54 L5 **Somovo** Russian Federation
31 L3 **Sompolno** Poland
131 C8 **Somuncurá, Mesa Vol. de** *mt* Argentina
22 G3 **Somzée** Belgium
73 N4 **Son** *R* India
27 E12 **Son** Norway
21 O4 **Sonchamp** France
44 G1 **Soncino** Italy
41 M5 **Sondalo** Italy
52 D3 **Sondaly** Russian Federation
28 C7 **Sønderå** *R* Denmark
28 D7 **Sønderborg** Denmark
28 A6 **Sønderjylland** *co* Denmark
28 D3 **Sønder Onsild** Denmark
33 N10 **Sondershausen** Germany
28 E6 **Søndersø** Denmark
111 E9 **Sondheimer** Louisiana U.S.A.
115 O4 **Søndre Strømfjord** *inlet* Greenland
115 O3 **Søndre Upernavik** Greenland
42 C2 **Sondrio** Italy
25 E5 **Son en Breugel** Netherlands
76 C1 **Sonepet** India
128 E8 **Sonequera** *mt* Bolivia
95 L5 **Sonestown** Pennsylvania U.S.A.
70 C4 **Song** Sarawak
71 A3 **Songa** Indonesia
65 J2 **Song'acha He** *R* China/Rus Fed
88 G6 **Songa Manara** *isld* Tanzania
27 B12 **Songa Totak** *R* Norway
68 J6 **Song Ba** *R* Vietnam
68 H2 **Song Ba Che** *R* Vietnam
67 D3 **Songbai** China
Song Bo *R* *see* **Noire** *R*
68 G2 **Song Boi** *R* Vietnam
67 E1 **Songbu** China
67 A7 **Song Ca** *R* Vietnam
68 J6 **Song Cai** *R* Vietnam
67 B5 **Song Cau** *R* Vietnam
68 J6 **Song Cau** Vietnam
68 G2 **Song Chay** *R* Vietnam
67 A7 **Song Chu** *R* Vietnam
69 H8 **Song Co Chien** *R* Vietnam
69 G8 **Song Cua Lon** *R* Vietnam
88 E7 **Songea** Tanzania
21 O2 **Songeons** France
68 J5 **Song Ha Giao** *R* Vietnam
65 G3 **Songhua Hu** *res* China
65 F2 **Songhua Jiang** *R* China
Songjiachuan *see* **Wubu**
Songjiang *see* **Antu**
67 G1 **Songjiang** China
59 J3 **Sŏngjin** N Korea
67 B2 **Songkan** China
57 G4 **Song-Kël'-Too, Ozero** *L* Kirghizia
69 E9 **Songkhla** Thailand
68 F4 **Song Khram** *R* Thailand
67 A5 **Song-koi** *R* Vietnam
67 E4 **Songkou** China
68 H2 **Song Ky Cung** *R* Vietnam
65 E4 **Song Ling** *mts* China
68 D1 **Songlong** Burma
68 J7 **Song Luy** *R* Vietnam
68 G2 **Song Ma** *R* Vietnam
67 A4 **Songming** China
68 H7 **Song Nha Be** *R* Vietnam
87 B7 **Songo** Angola
86 B7 **Songololo** Zaire
69 G8 **Song Ong Doc** *R* Vietnam
58 D5 **Songpan** China
88 G6 **Song Songo** *isld* Tanzania
67 C2 **Songtao** China
68 J5 **Song Tra Khuc** *R* Vietnam
68 H7 **Song Vam Co Dong** *R* Vietnam
68 H7 **Song Vam Co Tay** *R* Vietnam
88 D6 **Songwe** *R* Tanzania
67 F3 **Song Xi** *R* China
67 F3 **Songxi** China
65 B7 **Song Xian** China
65 F1 **Song Zhan** China
67 D1 **Songzi** China
68 J5 **Son Ha** Vietnam
68 J7 **Son Hai** Vietnam
68 J6 **Son Hoa** Vietnam
65 B3 **Sonid Youqi** China
65 B3 **Sonid Zuoqi** China
74 G4 **Sonīpat** India
29 N8 **Sonkajärvi** Finland
68 F2 **Son La** Vietnam
74 B6 **Sonmiani** Pakistan
38 H7 **Sonnblick, Gross** *mt* Austria
37 L3 **Sonneberg** Germany
37 L3 **Sonnefeld** Germany
37 P6 **Sonnen Wald** *mts* Germany
33 T9 **Sonnewalde** Germany
118 K6 **Sonningdale** Saskatchewan Canada
45 O7 **Sonnino** Italy
129 J5 **Sono** *R* Brazil
60 J10 **Sonobe** Japan
41 J5 **Sonogno** Switzerland
103 M10 **Sonoita** Mexico
103 O10 **Sonoita** Arizona U.S.A.
103 M1 **Sonoita** *R* Utah U.S.A.
103 L10 **Sonoita R** Mexico
102 B3 **Sonoma** California U.S.A.
100 H9 **Sonoma Range** Nevada U.S.A.
123 L8 **Sonora** Nova Scotia Canada
124 D3 **Sonora** *state* Mexico
124 D3 **Sonora** *R* Mexico
103 O8 **Sonora** Arizona U.S.A.
102 D4 **Sonora** California U.S.A.
108 G5 **Sonora** Texas U.S.A.
92 C4 **Sonoran Desert** Cal/Ariz U.S.A.
102 E3 **Sonora Pk** California U.S.A.
25 F5 **Sonsbeck** Germany
56 D4 **Sonskiy** Russian Federation
128 C2 **Sonsón** Colombia
125 P11 **Sonsonate** El Salvador
67 B6 **Son Tay** Vietnam
37 J6 **Sontheim** Germany
41 M2 **Sonthofen** Germany
36 H1 **Sontra** Germany
94 K4 **Sonyea** New York U.S.A.
21 L6 **Sonzay** France
Soochow *see* **Suzhou**
116 C5 **Sooghmeghat** Alaska U.S.A.
117 M11 **Sooke** British Columbia Canada
36 D4 **Soonwald** *mts* Germany
131 G3 **Sopas** *R* Uruguay
113 C7 **Sopchoppy** Florida U.S.A.
107 P7 **Soper** Oklahoma U.S.A.
112 E5 **Soperton** Georgia U.S.A.
68 F3 **Sop Khao** Laos
9 E6 **Sopley** England
86 E4 **Sopo** *R* Sudan
46 G2 **Sopot** Bulgaria
31 L1 **Sopot** Poland
26 M3 **Soppero** Sweden
48 D3 **Sopron** Hungary
123 Q4 **Sop's Arm** Newfoundland Canada
71 J4 **Soputan, G** Sulawesi
102 C5 **Soquel** California U.S.A.
16 B5 **Sor** *R* Portugal
42 F7 **Sora** Italy
27 G14 **Söraby** Sweden
60 Q2 **Sorachi** *R* Japan
75 L9 **Sorada** India
26 J9 **Söråker** Sweden
45 N5 **Soratte, M** *mt* Italy
17 F7 **Sorbas** Spain
16 E3 **Sorbe** *R* Spain
27 F10 **Sörberget** Sweden
12 D4 **Sorbie** Scotland
45 H2 **Sorbolo** Italy
26 H9 **Sörbygden** Sweden
28 G6 **Sørbymagle** Denmark
28 B3 **Sørdbjerg** Denmark
70 L9 **Soreang** Java
121 R6 **Sorel** Quebec Canada
139 J8 **Sorell** Tasmania Australia
139 H8 **Sorell, C** Tasmania Australia
80 B6 **Soreq** *R* Israel
44 G1 **Soresina** Italy
27 B11 **Sörfjorden** Norway
26 E7 **Sör Flatanger** Norway
26 H4 **Sörfold** Norway
26 H7 **Sörfors** Sweden
45 J1 **Sorgà** Italy
43 C8 **Sorgono** Sardinia
18 G9 **Sorgues** *R* France
19 N17 **Sorgues** France
79 E2 **Sorgun** *R* Turkey
44 F3 **Sori** Italy
17 F3 **Soria** *prov* Spain
17 F3 **Soria** Spain
133 F4 **Soriano** *dept* Uruguay
21 M7 **Sorigny** France
69 D12 **Sorikmarapi** *mt* Sumatra
52 E5 **Sorka** Russian Federation
50 A1 **Sörkapp** *isld* Svalbard
26 G7 **Sörli** Norway
26 L8 **Sörmjöle** Sweden
12 D3 **Sorn** Scotland
41 J5 **Sornico** Switzerland
Sorø *co* *see* **Vestjælland** *co*
28 H6 **Sorø** Denmark
130 F8 **Sorocaba** Brazil
52 H6 **Soroch'i Gory** Russian Federation
55 B5 **Sorochinsk** Russian Federation
48 L2 **Soroki** Moldova
48 E3 **Soroksár** Hungary
57 H2 **Sorolen** Kazakhstan
43 F11 **Soro, M** *mt* Sicily
71 C3 **Sorong** W Irian
86 F5 **Soroti** Uganda
26 N1 **Söröya** *isld* Norway
26 N1 **Söröysund** *chan* Norway
32 G10 **Sorpetalsperre** *L* Germany
16 B6 **Sorraia** *R* Portugal
26 K2 **Sörreisa** Norway
139 G7 **Sorrento** Victoria Australia
117 O10 **Sorrento** British Columbia Canada
45 Q8 **Sorrento** Italy
111 F11 **Sorrento** Louisiana U.S.A.
95 T2 **Sorrento** Maine U.S.A.
87 B10 **Sorris-Sorris** Namibia
146 J8 **Sør Rondane** *mts* Antarctica
29 O4 **Sorsatunturi** *mt* Finland
26 J6 **Sorsele** Sweden
56 C4 **Sorsk** Russian Federation
43 B8 **Sorso** Sardinia
71 G4 **Sorsogon** Philippines
18 F10 **Sort** Spain
29 P10 **Sortavala** Russian Federation
26 H3 **Sortland** Norway
52 H4 **Sortopolovskaya** Russian Federation
26 E9 **Sör-Tröndelag** *reg* Norway
28 H7 **Sortsø** Denmark
47 N10 **Sortullu** Turkey
98 D4 **Sorum** South Dakota U.S.A.
28 G7 **Sørup** Denmark
28 D7 **Sörup** Germany
28 B4 **Sørvad** Denmark
26 M1 **Sörvaer** Norway
26 F9 **Sörvattnan** Sweden
Sõrve Väin *see* **Kura Kurk** *str*
52 G5 **Sorvizhi** Russian Federation
17 G2 **Sos del Rey Catolico** Spain
32 M9 **Sose** *R* Germany
131 B5 **Sosneado** *pk* Argentina
54 D5 **Sosnitsa** Ukraine
52 H3 **Sosnogorsk** Russian Federation
52 D3 **Sosnovets** Russian Federation
52 F2 **Sosnovka** Russian Federation
52 G6 **Sosnovka** Chuvashskaya Respublika Russian Federation
29 P11 **Sosnovo** Russian Federation
58 F1 **Sosnovo-Ozerskoye** Russian Federation
52 C5 **Sosnovyy Bor** Russian Federation
55 E1 **Sosnovyy Mys** Russian Federation
31 L5 **Sosnowiec** Poland
29 M7 **Soso** Finland
111 G10 **Soso** Mississippi U.S.A.
42 G2 **Šoštanj** Slovenia
61 Q12 **Sosu** Okinawa
55 D2 **Sos'va** Russian Federation
53 E10 **Sosyka** *R* Russian Federation
78 H2 **Sothan** Turkey
29 N7 **Sotkamo** Finland
125 K6 **Soto la Marina** Mexico
27 A11 **Sotra** *isld* Norway
54 K6 **Sotsgorodok** Russian Federation
20 G2 **Sottevast** France
21 N3 **Sotteville** France
27 L11 **Sottunga** Finland
21 M5 **Souance** France
86 B5 **Souanké** Congo
85 C7 **Soubré** Ivory Coast
22 D3 **Souchez** France
140 D5 **Soudan** N Terr Australia
20 H6 **Soudan** Loire-Inférieure France
95 M6 **Souderton** Pennsylvania U.S.A.
21 P7 **Souesmes** France
86 B5 **Soufflay** Congo
36 D6 **Soufflenheim** France
47 H3 **Souflíon** Greece
127 O8 **Soufrière** St Lucia
127 O8 **Soufrière** *mt* St Vincent
127 N4 **Soufrière** *pk* Guadeloupe W Indies
21 K5 **Sougé-le Ganelon** France
21 O5 **Sougy** France
18 G8 **Souillac** France
83 L13 **Souillac** Mauritius
85 F1 **Souk Ahras** Algeria
16 D10 **Souk-el-Arba-du-Rharb** Morocco
16 D9 **Souk-Sebt-des-Beni-Zarfeto** Morocco
16 D9 **Souk Tolba** Morocco
65 G6 **Sŏul** S Korea
121 Q7 **Soulanges Canal** Quebec Canada
21 J5 **Soulgé-sur-Quette** France
21 L5 **Souligné** France
21 L6 **Souligné** France
20 G8 **Soullans** France
36 D6 **Soultz** France
68 A6 **Sound I** Andaman Is
118 G6 **Sounding L** Alberta Canada
15 A3 **Sound of Barra** Scotland
15 A3 **Sound of Harris** Outer Hebrides Scotland
15 C3 **Sound of Sleat** Scotland
46 F7 **Soúnion, Akra** Greece
79 F5 **Soûr** Lebanon
89 F7 **Sources, Mt. aux** Lesotho
21 J4 **Sourdeval** France
129 J4 **Soure** Brazil
16 B4 **Souré** Portugal
85 E1 **Sour El Ghozlane** Algeria
119 R9 **Souris** Manitoba Canada
123 K7 **Souris** Prince Edward I Canada
119 R10 **Souris** North Dakota U.S.A.
119 O9 **Souris R** Saskatchewan Canada
46 F5 **Soúrpi** Greece
21 O5 **Sours** France
85 C2 **Sous** *R* Morocco
130 H9 **Sousa** Brazil
129 H4 **Sousel** Brazil
43 D13 **Sousse** Tunisia
18 E9 **Soustons** France
18 G6 **Souterraine, la** France
89 **South Africa** *rep*
South African National Antarctic Expedition *see* **Sanae**
9 F5 **Southall** England
9 E3 **Southam** England
98 H1 **Southam** North Dakota U.S.A.
122 H8 **Southampton** Nova Scotia Canada
120 J8 **Southampton** Ontario Canada
9 E6 **Southampton** England
95 P6 **Southampton** Long I, New York U.S.A.
115 L5 **Southampton I** Northwest Territories Canada
68 A6 **South Andaman** *isld* Andaman Is
94 K9 **South Anna** *R* Virginia U.S.A.
102 C6 **South Antonio** *R* California U.S.A.
146 F14 **Southard, C** Antarctica
138 **South Australia** *state* Australia
120 J7 **South B** Ontario Canada
106 C8 **South Baldy** *mt* New Mexico U.S.A.
94 E5 **South Bass I** Ohio U.S.A.
113 G11 **South Bay** Florida U.S.A.
120 H7 **South Baymouth** Ontario Canada
142 A2 **South Beach** *dist* Perth, W Aust Australia
142 B2 **South Belmont** *dist* Perth, W Aust Australia
99 S7 **South Beloit** Illinois U.S.A.
99 U8 **South Bend** Indiana U.S.A.
109 J3 **South Bend** Texas U.S.A.
100 B3 **South Bend** Washington U.S.A.
126 F2 **South Bight** Andros Bahamas
141 J6 **South Blackwater** Queensland Australia
126 G3 **South Bluff** Acklins I Bahamas
94 B2 **South Boardman** Michigan U.S.A.
9 G5 **Southborough** England
94 H10 **South Boston** Virginia U.S.A.
123 N6 **South Branch** Newfoundland Canada
94 D2 **South Branch** Michigan U.S.A.
8 C7 **South Brent** England
144 D5 **Southbridge** New Zealand
95 P4 **Southbridge** Massachusetts U.S.A.
141 K1 **South Brisbane** *dist* Brisbane, Qnsld Australia
123 Q4 **South Brook** Newfoundland Canada
144 D5 **Southbrook** New Zealand
122 H9 **South Brookfield** Nova Scotia Canada
144 C6 **Southburn** New Zealand
127 J4 **South Caicos** *isld* Turks & Caicos Is
112 F3 **South Carolina** *state* U.S.A.
13 H6 **South Cave** England
94 C1 **South Chan** Michigan U.S.A.
94 D7 **South Charleston** Ohio U.S.A.
94 F8 **South Charleston** West Virginia U.S.A.
67 E6 **South China Sea**
95 N2 **South Colton** New York U.S.A.
98 F5 **South Dakota** *state* U.S.A.
94 H4 **South Dayton** New York U.S.A.
13 F3 **Southdean** Scotland
95 P4 **South Deerfield** Massachusetts U.S.A.
9 F6 **South Downs** England
139 H9 **South East C** Tasmania Australia
139 H7 **South East C** Victoria Australia
83 K12 **South East I** Mahé I Indian Oc
135 N15 **South East Pacific Basin** Pacific Oc
114 J6 **Southend** Saskatchewan Canada
9 G4 **Southend** England
12 C3 **Southend** Scotland
99 O8 **South English** Iowa U.S.A.
89 D5 **Southern** *dist* Botswana
144 C5 **Southern Alps** *mts* New Zealand
143 C9 **Southern Cross** W Australia Australia
101 M3 **Southern Cross** Montana U.S.A.
86 D3 **Southern Darfur** *prov* Sudan
8 C5 **Southerndown** Wales
123 T6 **Southern Harbour** Newfoundland Canada
119 S2 **Southern Indian L** Manitoba Canada
86 E3 **Southern Kordofan** *prov* Sudan
81 B11 **Southern Ocean**
111 G10 **Southern Pine Hills** Miss/Ala U.S.A.
112 H2 **Southern Pines** North Carolina U.S.A.
142 B2 **Southern R** Perth, W Aust Australia
142 F5 **South Esk Tablelands** W Australia Australia
119 N8 **Southey** Saskatchewan Canada
110 E2 **South Fabius** *R* Missouri U.S.A.
13 H6 **South Ferriby** England
144 A6 **South Fiord** New Zealand
9 H5 **South Foreland** England

118 J9 South Fork Saskatchewan Canada
100 B9 South Fork California U.S.A.
106 D4 South Fork Colorado U.S.A.
112 F1 South Fork R North Carolina U.S.A.
94 J6 South Fork Pennsylvania U.S.A.
110 G6 South Fork R Tennessee U.S.A.
98 D4 South Fork R South Dakota U.S.A.
99 V4 South Fox I Michigan U.S.A.
110 H5 South Fulton Tennessee U.S.A.
146 F11 South Geomagnetic Pole Antarctica
131 H5 South Georgia S Atlantic Oc
99 O9 South Gifford Missouri U.S.A.
8 C4 South Glamorgan co Wales
110 B3 South Grand R Missouri U.S.A.
123 M7 South Harbour Nova Scotia Canada
107 N4 South Haven Kansas U.S.A.
99 U7 South Haven Michigan U.S.A.
115 K5 South Henik L Northwest Territories Canada
94 J10 South Hill Virginia U.S.A.
94 F10 South Holston L Tenn/Virg U.S.A.
140 C1 South I N Terr Australia
83 M8 South I Cocos Is Indian Oc
119 T2 South Indian L Manitoba Canada
95 P5 Southington Connecticut U.S.A.
144 B5 South Island New Zealand
71 D6 South Islet Sulu Sea
118 F1 South Junc Manitoba Canada
99 T7 South Kenosha Wisconsin U.S.A.
59 J4 South Korea rep Asia
109 M8 Southlake Texas U.S.A.
102 E3 South Lake Tahoe California U.S.A.
144 A6 Southland admin region New Zealand
123 K9 South Lochaber Nova Scotia Canada
98 G8 South Loup R Nebraska U.S.A.
88 C8 South Luangwa Nat. Park Zambia
70 C2 South Luconia Shoals S China Sea
94 D4 South Lyon Michigan U.S.A.
120 K7 Southmag Ontario Canada
146 E14 South Magnetic Pole Antarctica
99 U4 South Manitou I Michigan U.S.A.
95 L10 South Mills North Carolina U.S.A.
99 T7 South Milwaukee Wisconsin U.S.A.
9 G4 Southminster England
141 H4 South Mission Beach Queensland Australia
8 C5 South Molton England
117 H9 South Moresby Nat. Park British Columbia Canada
109 K10 Southmost Texas U.S.A.
95 K6 South Mt Pennsylvania U.S.A.
116 J7 South Naknek Alaska U.S.A.
122 G7 South Nelson New Brunswick Canada
112 F6 South Newport Georgia U.S.A.
95 P5 Southold Long I, New York U.S.A.
90 F15 South Orkney Is S Atlantic Oc
146 E3 South Orkney Is S Atlantic Oc
53 F12 South Ossetia aut reg Georgia
102 B3 South Pablo B California U.S.A.
95 R2 South Paris Maine U.S.A.
94 F7 South Parkersburg West Virginia U.S.A.
101 R7 South Pass Wyoming U.S.A.
101 R7 South Pass City Wyoming U.S.A.
99 R9 South Pekin Illinois U.S.A.
110 L6 South Pittsburg Tennessee U.S.A.
106 E2 South Platte Colorado U.S.A.
146 E9 South Pole Antarctica
120 J4 South Porcupine Ontario Canada
141 L8 Southport Queensland Australia
139 H9 Southport Tasmania Australia
123 T5 Southport Newfoundland Canada
13 E6 Southport England
94 A7 Southport Indiana U.S.A.
112 J4 Southport North Carolina U.S.A.
123 K4 South Pt Anticosti I, Quebec
83 M9 South Pt Christmas I Indian Oc
13 J3 South R North Carolina U.S.A.
99 S2 South Range Michigan U.S.A.
144 A7 South Red Head Pt. New Zealand
113 H12 South Riding Rock Bahamas
121 L7 South River Ontario Canada
95 N6 South River New Jersey U.S.A.
15 F2 South Ronaldsay Scotland
131 J7 South Sandwich Is S Atlantic Oc
102 B4 South San Francisco California U.S.A.
118 J8 South Sask R Saskatchewan Canada
9 E6 Southsea England
119 S1 South Seal R Manitoba Canada
146 C3 South Shetland Is S Atlantic Oc
13 G3 South Shields England
98 K7 South Sioux City Nebraska U.S.A.
98 K6 South Sioux Falls South Dakota U.S.A.
117 P11 South Slocan British Columbia Canada
103 N2 South Tent pk Utah U.S.A.
15 A3 South Uist Scotland
9 F1 Southwell England
South West Africa see Namibia rep
113 K9 South West B New Providence I Bahamas
139 H9 South West C Tasmania Australia
123 K6 Southwest C Madeleine Is, Quebec Canada
144 A7 Southwest Cape New Zealand
113 L8 South West Cape Virgin Is
139 H7 South West I Tasmania Australia
81 C9 South-West Indian Ridge Indian Oc
139 H8 Southwest Nat. Park Tasmania Australia
135 M12 South-West Pacific Basin Pacific Oc
122 J4 Southwest Pt Quebec Canada
126 E6 Southwest Rock Caribbean
139 L4 South West Rocks New South Wales Australia
99 S8 South Wilmington Illinois U.S.A.
9 H3 Southwold England
9 G4 South Woodham Ferrers England
9 G2 South Wootton England
South Yemen see Yemen
13 G6 South Yorkshire co England
89 F4 Soutpansberg mts S Africa
144 B6 Soutra Hill New Zealand
18 H6 Souvigny France
16 B6 Souzel Portugal
48 J4 Sovata Romania
118 K7 Sovereign Saskatchewan Canada
57 G4 Sovetabad Uzbekistan
52 G5 Sovetsk Russian Federation
52 B6 Sovetsk Russian Federation
53 F9 Sovetskaya Russian Federation
59 M2 Sovetskaya Gavan Russian Federation
52 C4 Sovetskiy Leningradskaya obl Russian Federation
55 D1 Sovetskiy Tyumenskaya obl Russian Federation
Soviet Union see Union of Soviet Socialist Republics
28 E5 Søvind Denmark
52 F2 Sovpol'ye Russian Federation
89 D3 Sowa Pan Botswana
119 N1 Sowden L Ontario Canada
13 G6 Sowerby Br England
60 P1 Sōya Japan
60 P1 Sōya-misaki C Japan
52 F2 Soyana R Russian Federation
18 F7 Soyaux France
60 P1 Soya wan B Japan
38 F5 Soyen Germany
19 N15 Soyons France
124 E3 Soyopa Mexico
54 B4 Sozh R Belarus/Rus Fed
52 H5 Sozimskiy Russian Federation
47 J2 Sozopol Bulgaria
22 K3 Spa Belgium
126 B2 Spaanse Baai B Curaçao Neth Antilles
146 C6 Spaatz I isld Antarctica
16 Spain kingdom W Europe
31 M4 Spała Poland
Spalato see Split Croatia
138 E5 Spalding South Australia Australia
119 N6 Spalding Saskatchewan Canada
9 F2 Spalding England
100 J3 Spalding Idaho U.S.A.
98 H8 Spalding Nebraska U.S.A.
37 K5 Spalt Germany
25 C3 Spanbroek Netherlands
33 S7 Spandau Berlin
28 B6 Spandet Denmark
27 H14 Spångenäs Sweden
36 H1 Spangenberg Germany
100 H2 Spangle Washington U.S.A.
94 J6 Spangler Pennsylvania U.S.A.
123 T6 Spaniard's B Newfoundland Canada
120 H6 Spanish Ontario Canada
101 O9 Spanish Fork Utah U.S.A.
106 F4 Spanish Pks Colorado U.S.A.
127 L3 Spanish Town Jamaica
113 L7 Spanish Town Virgin Is
113 L12 Spanish Wells Eleuthera Bahamas
45 Q7 Sparanise Italy
26 E8 Sparbu Norway
28 C4 Sparkær Denmark
111 D8 Sparkman Arkansas U.S.A.
112 D6 Sparks Georgia U.S.A.
98 F7 Sparks Nebraska U.S.A.
102 E2 Sparks Nevada U.S.A.
107 O6 Sparks Oklahoma U.S.A.
99 R8 Sparland Illinois U.S.A.
37 M3 Sparnberg Germany
94 C1 Sparr Michigan U.S.A.
112 E4 Sparta Georgia U.S.A.
110 G3 Sparta Illinois U.S.A.
94 B3 Sparta Michigan U.S.A.
110 C4 Sparta Missouri U.S.A.
94 F10 Sparta North Carolina U.S.A.
100 H5 Sparta Oregon U.S.A.
110 L6 Sparta Tennessee U.S.A.
99 Q6 Sparta Wisconsin U.S.A.
112 F3 Spartanburg South Carolina U.S.A.
94 H5 Spartansburg Pennsylvania U.S.A.
16 D9 Spartel, C Morocco
47 O12 Spartilla Greece
43 G11 Spartivento, C Italy
43 B10 Spartivento, C Sardinia
118 C9 Sparwood British Columbia Canada
54 M1 Spas-Klepiki Russian Federation
56 C4 Spassk Russian Federation
52 D4 Spasskaya Guba Russian Federation
59 K3 Spassk Dal'niy Russian Federation
55 E5 Spasskoye Kazakhstan
54 M2 Spassk-Ryazanskiy Russian Federation
46 F9 Spátha, Akr C Crete Greece
117 J7 Spatsizi Plat. Wilderness Prov. Pk British Columbia Canada
110 A5 Spavinaw, L Oklahoma U.S.A.
36 D3 Spay Germany
109 L6 Speaks Texas U.S.A.
15 D4 Spean Bridge Scotland
98 C5 Spearfish South Dakota U.S.A.
119 T7 Spearhill Manitoba Canada
108 C7 Spearman Texas U.S.A.
107 L4 Spearville Kansas U.S.A.
142 A3 Spearwood dist Perth, W Aust Australia
33 R6 Specker-See L Germany
95 N3 Speculator New York U.S.A.
118 F4 Spedden Alberta Canada
109 M1 Speer Oklahoma U.S.A.
98 B8 Speer Wyoming U.S.A.
118 K6 Speers Saskatchewan Canada
36 B4 Speicher Germany
37 M4 Speichersdorf Germany
37 M7 Speichersee L Germany
127 P6 Speightstown Barbados
116 M6 Spenard Alaska U.S.A.
115 K4 Spence Bay Northwest Territories Canada
101 N5 Spencer Idaho U.S.A.
110 K2 Spencer Indiana U.S.A.
99 L6 Spencer Iowa U.S.A.
95 P4 Spencer Massachusetts U.S.A.
98 H7 Spencer Nebraska U.S.A.
95 L4 Spencer New York U.S.A.
98 J6 Spencer South Dakota U.S.A.
94 F8 Spencer West Virginia U.S.A.
99 Q5 Spencer Wisconsin U.S.A.
138 D6 Spencer, C South Australia Australia
117 E6 Spencer, C Alaska U.S.A.
138 D5 Spencer Gulf South Australia Australia
95 R1 Spencer L Maine U.S.A.
94 K3 Spencerport New York U.S.A.
116 D4 Spencer, Pt Alaska U.S.A.
140 C1 Spencer Ra N Terr Australia
94 C6 Spencerville Ohio U.S.A.
117 N10 Spences Bridge British Columbia Canada
32 H8 Spenge Germany
13 G4 Spennymoor England
144 D5 Spenser Mts New Zealand
33 S8 Sperenberg Germany
27 D11 Sperillen Norway
46 E6 Sperkhiós R Greece
118 D1 Sperling Manitoba Canada
45 O7 Sperlonga Italy
43 B10 Sperone, C Sardinia
14 D2 Sperrin Mts N Ireland
94 J8 Sperryville Virginia U.S.A.
36 G3 Spessart mts Germany
46 F7 Spétsai isld Greece
15 E3 Spey R Scotland
36 E5 Speyer Germany
36 E5 Speyerbach R Germany
127 N1 Speyside Tobago
20 C5 Spézet France
44 G3 Spezia, La Italy
115 M4 Spicer Is Northwest Territories Canada
99 N9 Spickardsville Missouri U.S.A.
32 G5 Spiekeroog Germany
38 N8 Spielfeld Austria
36 C5 Spiesen-Elversberg Germany
44 D2 Spigno R Italy
25 G2 Spijk Netherlands
110 C1 Spikard Missouri U.S.A.
116 R3 Spike Mt Alaska U.S.A.
45 K2 Spilamberto Italy
46 G9 Spíli Crete Greece
42 E2 Spilimbergo Italy
9 G1 Spilsby England
43 G8 Spinazzola Italy
77 K4 Spīn Būldak Afghanistan
22 K5 Spincourt France
112 F2 Spindale North Carolina U.S.A.
45 M1 Spinea Italy
44 F1 Spino d'Adda Italy
89 B8 Spioenberg I mt S Africa
89 A8 Spioenberg II mt S Africa
89 F7 Spioen Kop mt S Africa
99 L6 Spirit L Iowa U.S.A.
100 J2 Spirit Lake Idaho U.S.A.
100 C3 Spirit Lake Washington U.S.A.
117 O8 Spirit River Alberta Canada
145 D1 Spirits B New Zealand
118 K5 Spiritwood Saskatchewan Canada
98 H3 Spiritwood North Dakota U.S.A.
107 Q6 Spiro Oklahoma U.S.A.
52 D6 Spirovo Russian Federation
48 F1 Spišská Belá Slovakia
48 F2 Spišská Nová Ves Slovakia
31 M6 Spišské Podhradie Slovakia
50 A1 Spitsbergen arch Arctic Oc
38 H8 Spittal-an-der-Drau Austria
38 N5 Spitz Austria
28 A4 Spjald Denmark
109 N5 Splendora Texas U.S.A.
42 H5 Split Croatia
122 H8 Split, C Nova Scotia Canada
119 V2 Split L Manitoba Canada
100 G8 Split Pk mt Nevada U.S.A.
38 N9 Spodnje Hoče Slovenia
28 F7 Spodsbjerg Denmark
109 M3 Spofford Texas U.S.A.
13 G6 Spofforth England
100 H2 Spokane Washington U.S.A.
42 E6 Spoleto Italy
118 F7 Spondin Alberta Canada
68 G6 Spong Cambodia
33 S6 Sponholz Germany
22 J3 Spontin Belgium
99 Q9 Spoon R Illinois U.S.A.
99 P4 Spooner Wisconsin U.S.A.
100 E8 Spooner Res California U.S.A.
Sporádes islds see Dhodhekánisos islds
33 P6 Spornitz Germany
28 E4 Sporring Denmark
44 D3 Spotorno Italy
101 U5 Spotted Horse Wyoming U.S.A.
103 J5 Spotted Ra Nevada U.S.A.
118 F1 Sprague Manitoba Canada
111 K9 Sprague Alabama U.S.A.
100 H2 Sprague Washington U.S.A.
99 Q5 Sprague Wisconsin U.S.A.
100 D7 Sprague River Oregon U.S.A.
36 H6 Spraitbach Germany
33 M7 Sprakensehl Germany
100 F5 Spray Oregon U.S.A.
48 E6 Spreča R Bosnia-Herzegovina
54 J4 Spredne Russkaya Vozvyshennost' uplands Russian Federation
31 H4 Spree R Germany
33 T9 Spreewald Germany
36 F1 Spremberg Germany
36 F3 Sprendlingen Hessen Germany
36 E4 Sprendlingen Rheinland-Pfalz Germany
22 K3 Sprimont Belgium
110 E5 Spring R Arkansas U.S.A.
110 B5 Spring R Oklahoma U.S.A.
109 M5 Spring Texas U.S.A.
103 N2 Spring B Utah U.S.A.
89 A7 Springbok S Africa
94 G5 Springboro Pennsylvania U.S.A.
109 L6 Spring Branch Texas U.S.A.
98 C1 Spring Brook North Dakota U.S.A.
118 A3 Springburn Alberta Canada
144 C5 Springburn New Zealand
95 M6 Spring City Pennsylvania U.S.A.
112 C2 Spring City Tennessee U.S.A.
103 N2 Spring City Utah U.S.A.
118 D9 Spring Coulee Alberta Canada
140 E4 Spring Cr N Terr Australia
141 F6 Spring Cr Queensland Australia
98 E9 Spring Cr Nebraska U.S.A.
101 L8 Spring Cr Nevada U.S.A.
145 D4 Spring Creek New Zealand
123 Q4 Springdale Newfoundland Canada
110 B5 Springdale Arkansas U.S.A.
101 P4 Springdale Montana U.S.A.
102 H4 Springdale Nevada U.S.A.
103 M4 Springdale Utah U.S.A.
100 H1 Springdale Washington U.S.A.
32 L8 Springe Germany
106 F5 Springer New Mexico U.S.A.
109 K1 Springer Oklahoma U.S.A.
121 Q3 Springer, Mt Quebec Canada
103 P7 Springerville Arizona U.S.A.
122 G8 Springfield New Brunswick Canada
122 H9 Springfield Nova Scotia Canada
144 C5 Springfield New Zealand
106 H4 Springfield Colorado U.S.A.
113 B7 Springfield Florida U.S.A.
112 F5 Springfield Georgia U.S.A.
101 N6 Springfield Idaho U.S.A.
110 G2 Springfield Illinois U.S.A.
94 B9 Springfield Kentucky U.S.A.
95 P4 Springfield Massachusetts U.S.A.
110 C4 Springfield Missouri U.S.A.
94 D7 Springfield Ohio U.S.A.
100 C5 Springfield Oregon U.S.A.
112 F4 Springfield South Carolina U.S.A.
98 J7 Springfield South Dakota U.S.A.
110 K5 Springfield Tennessee U.S.A.
95 P3 Springfield Vermont U.S.A.
89 D8 Springfontein S Africa
99 Q6 Spring Green Wisconsin U.S.A.
99 P6 Spring Grove Minnesota U.S.A.
95 L7 Spring Grove Pennsylvania U.S.A.
122 H8 Springhill Nova Scotia Canada
111 C9 Springhill Louisiana U.S.A.
110 K6 Spring Hill Tennessee U.S.A.
112 J2 Spring Hope North Carolina U.S.A.
99 U6 Spring Lake Michigan U.S.A.
95 N6 Spring Lake New Jersey U.S.A.
112 H2 Spring Lake North Carolina U.S.A.
108 E1 Springlake Texas U.S.A.
103 J5 Spring Mts Nevada U.S.A.
126 H3 Spring Point Acklins I Bahamas
89 F6 Springs S Africa
95 K6 Springs Pennsylvania U.S.A.
119 P7 Springside Saskatchewan Canada
144 D5 Springs Junction New Zealand
144 D5 Springston New Zealand
141 J6 Springsure Queensland Australia
109 K3 Springtown Texas U.S.A.
140 F6 Springvale Queensland Australia
141 G3 Springvale Queensland Australia
142 G4 Springvale W Australia Australia
95 R3 Springvale Maine U.S.A.
119 M9 Spring Valley Saskatchewan Canada
99 O6 Spring Valley Minnesota U.S.A.
98 G7 Springview Nebraska U.S.A.
111 K8 Springville Alabama U.S.A.
94 J4 Springville New York U.S.A.
101 O9 Springville Utah U.S.A.
118 J7 Springwater Saskatchewan Canada
13 H6 Sproatley England
28 F6 Sprogø isld Denmark
32 L6 Sprötze Germany
94 D2 Spruce Michigan U.S.A.
123 O5 Spruce Brook Newfoundland Canada
121 L7 Sprucedale Ontario Canada
118 D5 Spruce Grove Alberta Canada
94 H8 Spruce Knob mt West Virginia U.S.A.
118 H5 Spruce Lake Saskatchewan Canada
101 L9 Spruce Mt Nevada U.S.A.
112 E2 Spruce Pine North Carolina U.S.A.
103 M4 Spry Utah U.S.A.
25 B5 Spui R Netherlands
43 H9 Spulico, C Italy
109 O3 Spur Texas U.S.A.
118 C3 Spurfield Alberta Canada
111 B11 Spurger Texas U.S.A.
106 B8 Spur Lake New Mexico U.S.A.
116 L6 Spurr, Mt Alaska U.S.A.
46 C2 Spuž Montenegro Yugoslavia
22 H3 Spy Belgium
119 Q8 Spy Hill Saskatchewan Canada
117 M11 Squamish British Columbia Canada
95 Q3 Squam L New Hampshire U.S.A.
95 S7 Squapan L Maine U.S.A.
101 P2 Square Butte Montana U.S.A.
95 S6 Square L Maine U.S.A.
122 D6 Squatteck Quebec Canada
123 L3 Squaw L Quebec Canada
99 M2 Squaw L Minnesota U.S.A.
119 O5 Squaw Rapids Saskatchewan Canada
43 H10 Squillace, Golfo di Italy
43 J8 Squinzano Italy
138 C2 Squires, Mt N Terr Australia
143 G7 Squires,Mt W Australia Australia
120 F2 Squirrel R Ontario Canada
116 G3 Squirrel R Alaska U.S.A.
70 N9 Sragen Java
48 G3 Srbica Macedonia
46 E3 Srbica Serbia Yugoslavia
46 D2 Srbica see Serbia
48 F5 Srbobran Serbia Yugoslavia
68 F7 Srê Âmběl Cambodia
46 C1 Srebrenica Bosnia-Herzegovina
47 J2 Sredetska R Bulgaria
46 G2 Sredna Gora Bulgaria
51 K2 Sredne-Sibirskoye Ploskogor'ye tableland Russian Federation
52 D2 Sredneye Kuyto, Oz L Russian Federation
58 G1 Sredniy Kalar Russian Federation
55 C3 Sredniy Ural ra Russian Federation
53 F10 Sredniy Yegorlyk Russian Federation
46 G2 Srednogorie Bulgaria
53 F9 Srednyaya Akhtuba Russian Federation
55 G2 Sred Vasyugan Russian Federation
68 H6 Sre Khtum Cambodia
31 K3 Śrem Poland
48 F6 Srem Mitrovica Serbia Yugoslavia
48 E6 Srem Raca Serbia Yugoslavia
48 F5 Sremski Karlovci Serbia Yugoslavia
58 G1 Sretensk Russian Federation
74 F4 Sri Düngargarh India
76 F1 Srikakulam India
76 D4 Sri Kālahasti India
83 Sri Lanka rep S Asia
74 E1 Srinagar Kashmir
68 E5 Srinagarind Dam Thailand
76 B4 Sringeri India
76 C6 Srivilliputtur India
42 H4 Srnetica Bosnia-Herzegovina
31 K3 Środa Poland
31 K4 Środa Śląska Poland
75 L7 Srungavarapukota India
141 F3 Staaten R Queensland Australia
141 F3 Staaten River Nat. Park Queensland Australia
26 O1 Stabbursdalen Nat. Park Norway
26 O1 Stabburselv R Norway
33 Q4 Stäbelow Germany
100 D4 Stabler Washington U.S.A.
28 A4 Staby Denmark
120 J5 Stackpool Ontario Canada
15 D1 Stack Skerry isld Scotland
14 B4 Stack's Mts Ireland
16 E4 Sta. Cruz del Retamar Spain
100 E9 Stacy California U.S.A.
112 L3 Stacy North Carolina U.S.A.
32 K5 Stade Germany
22 E2 Staden Belgium
36 F3 Staden Germany
9 E4 Stadhampton England
28 A4 Stadil Denmark
28 A4 Stadil Fjord inlet Denmark
26 A9 Stadlandet Norway
25 G2 Stadskanaal Netherlands
36 F2 Stadt Allendorf Germany
37 N5 Stadtamhof Germany
37 K7 Stadtbergen Germany
32 K8 Stadthagen Germany
37 L2 Stadtilm Germany
36 B3 Stadtkyll Germany
32 H6 Stadtland Germany
37 J3 Stadtlauringen Germany
37 J2 Stadtlengsfeld Germany
32 E8 Stadtlohn Germany
32 L9 Stadtoldendorf Germany
36 G4 Stadtprozelten Germany
37 M2 Stadtroda Germany
37 J4 Stadt Schwarzach Germany
37 M3 Stadtsteinach Germany
15 B4 Staffa isld Scotland
33 R7 Staffelde Germany
37 L3 Staffelstein Germany
44 F2 Staffora R Italy
141 K1 Stafford dist Brisbane, Qnsld Australia
8 D2 Stafford England
107 M4 Stafford Kansas U.S.A.
98 H7 Stafford Nebraska U.S.A.
94 K8 Stafford Virginia U.S.A.
8 D2 Staffordshire co England
95 P5 Stafford Springs Connecticut U.S.A.
70 E6 Stagen Kalimantan
117 Q4 Stagg L Northwest Territories Canada
45 H4 Stagno Italy
9 F3 Stagsden England
33 S4 Stahlbrode Germany
33 S8 Stahnsdorf Germany
52 B5 Staicele Latvia
38 K6 Stainach Austria
9 F5 Staines England
12 D3 Stair Scotland
13 H4 Staithes England
48 G2 Stakčín Slovakia
53 E9 Stakhanov Ukraine
28 B5 Stakroge Denmark
46 E1 Stalać Serbia Yugoslavia
27 J12 Stålboga Sweden
8 D6 Stalbridge England
9 H2 Stalham England
27 B11 Stalheim Norway
Stalingrad see Volgograd
117 L6 Stalin, Mt British Columbia Canada
Stalino see Donetsk
38 H8 Stall Austria
37 O5 Stallwang Germany
31 N5 Stalowa Wola Poland
119 M7 Stalwart Saskatchewan Canada
13 F6 Stalybridge England
46 G2 Stamboliyski Bulgaria
46 G1 Stamboliyski, Yazovir A. res Bulgaria
141 G5 Stamford Queensland Australia
9 F2 Stamford England
95 O5 Stamford Connecticut U.S.A.
95 N4 Stamford New York U.S.A.
98 E6 Stamford South Dakota U.S.A.
108 H3 Stamford Texas U.S.A.
37 L6 Stammham Germany
27 A11 Stamnes Norway
Stampalia isld see Astipálaia isld
100 D2 Stampede Washington U.S.A.
94 C8 Stamping Ground Kentucky U.S.A.
87 C10 Stampriet Namibia
25 E6 Stamproij Netherlands
109 O2 Stamps Arkansas U.S.A.
37 O5 Stamsried Germany
26 G3 Stamsund Norway
94 J8 Stanadsville Virginia U.S.A.
99 M9 Stanberry Missouri U.S.A.
147 Q6 Stanchik Russian Federation
118 E7 Standard Alberta Canada
103 O7 Standard Arizona U.S.A.
87 E11 Standerton S Africa
94 D3 Standish Michigan U.S.A.
101 M8 Standrod Utah U.S.A.
100 F4 Stanfield Oregon U.S.A.
110 K2 Stanford Indiana U.S.A.
110 M4 Stanford Kentucky U.S.A.
101 P2 Stanford Montana U.S.A.
9 G4 Stanford-le-Hope England
8 D3 Stanford on Teme England
27 K14 Stånga Sweden
27 E11 Stange Norway
87 F11 Stanger S Africa
45 L1 Stanghella Italy
26 C9 Stangvik Norway
126 F2 Staniard Cr Andros Bahamas
102 D3 Stanislaus R California U.S.A.
Stanislav see Ivano-Frankovsk
46 F2 Stanke Dimitrov Bulgaria
37 P4 Staňkov Czech Rep
139 H8 Stanley Tasmania Australia
122 F7 Stanley New Brunswick Canada
131 G8 Stanley Falkland Is
15 E4 Stanley Scotland
101 L5 Stanley Idaho U.S.A.
106 E6 Stanley New Mexico U.S.A.
112 F2 Stanley North Carolina U.S.A.
98 D1 Stanley North Dakota U.S.A.
109 M1 Stanley Oklahoma U.S.A.
94 J8 Stanley Virginia U.S.A.
99 Q5 Stanley Wisconsin U.S.A.
119 M3 Stanley Mission Saskatchewan Canada
139 G8 Stanley, Mt Tasmania Australia
88 B1 Stanley, Mt Uganda/Zaire
86 C6 Stanley Pool Zaire
Stanleyville see Kisangani
118 F7 Stanmore Alberta Canada
145 E2 Stanmore Bay New Zealand
99 T2 Stannard Rock Michigan U.S.A.
13 G3 Stannington England
55 F3 Stanovka Russian Federation
55 D2 Stanovoy Russian Federation
51 M3 Stanovoy Khrebet mts Russian Federation
41 P3 Stans Austria
138 E5 Stansbury South Australia Australia
142 G5 Stansmore Ra W Australia Australia
9 G4 Stansted England
141 K8 Stanthorpe Queensland Australia
147 J1 Stanton Northwest Territories Canada
99 L9 Stanton Iowa U.S.A.
94 D9 Stanton Kentucky U.S.A.
99 U5 Stanton Michigan U.S.A.
98 J8 Stanton Nebraska U.S.A.
98 E2 Stanton North Dakota U.S.A.
110 G6 Stanton Tennessee U.S.A.
108 D3 Stanton Texas U.S.A.
6 E6 Stanton Banks Atlantic Oc
56 B3 Stantsionno-Oyashinskiy Russian Federation
94 B3 Stanwood Michigan U.S.A.
117 M11 Stanwood Washington U.S.A.
41 N3 Stanzach Austria
33 N9 Stapelburg Germany
25 F3 Staphorst Netherlands
9 E5 Stapleford England
111 J11 Stapleton Alabama U.S.A.
112 E4 Stapleton Georgia U.S.A.
54 F3 Star' Russian Federation
111 F9 Star Mississippi U.S.A.
112 H2 Star North Carolina U.S.A.
109 J4 Star Texas U.S.A.
31 N4 Starachowice Poland
48 F1 Stara L'ubovňa Slovakia
37 O3 Stará-Role Czech Rep
53 G7 Staraya Drozhzhanoye Russian Federation
53 G8 Staraya Kulatka Russian Federation
52 D5 Staraya Russa Russian Federation
48 L1 Staraya Sinyava Ukraine
48 L2 Staraya Ushitsa Ukraine
55 E1 Staraya Vorpavla Russian Federation
47 H2 Stara Zagora Bulgaria
119 U9 Starbuck Manitoba Canada
99 L4 Starbuck Minnesota U.S.A.
100 G3 Starbuck Washington U.S.A.
135 L9 Starbuck I Pacific Oc
119 N6 Star City Saskatchewan Canada
111 E8 Star City Arkansas U.S.A.
94 A6 Star City Indiana U.S.A.
94 H7 Star City West Virginia U.S.A.
141 G2 Starcke Queensland Australia
8 C6 Starcross England
37 O4 Staré Sedliště Czech Rep
31 J2 Stargard Poland
42 H4 Stari Majdan Bosnia-Herzegovina
31 N6 Starina Slovakia
52 D6 Staritsa Russian Federation
103 O10 Stark Arizona U.S.A.
101 L2 Stark Montana U.S.A.
95 Q2 Stark New Hampshire U.S.A.
55 C6 Star Karabutak Kazakhstan
113 E8 Starke Florida U.S.A.
100 J5 Starkey Idaho U.S.A.
100 G4 Starkey Oregon U.S.A.
109 O5 Starks Louisiana U.S.A.
106 F4 Starkville Colorado U.S.A.
111 H8 Starkville Mississippi U.S.A.
98 H1 Starkweather North Dakota U.S.A.
99 R3 Starlake Wisconsin U.S.A.
41 O1 Starnberg Germany
56 C4 Starobachati Russian Federation
54 K7 Star'obel'sk Ukraine
54 D4 Starodub Russian Federation
31 L2 Starogard Poland
48 M4 Starokazach'ye Ukraine
48 L1 Starokonstantinov Ukraine
53 C9 Starokonstantinov Ukraine
55 F3 Staromalinovka Russian Federation
31 O2 Starosielce Poland
55 F3 Starosoldatskoye Russian Federation
55 C4 Starosubkhangulovo Russian Federation
55 C3 Staroutkinsk Russian Federation
52 G5 Starovercheskaya Russian Federation
52 H6 Staroye Baysarovo Russian Federation
102 F1 Star Pk Nevada U.S.A.
8 C7 Start Pt England
15 F1 Start Pt Scotland
48 F1 Stary Sącz Poland
52 H6 Staryye Zyattsy Russian Federation
52 H6 Staryy Menzelyabash Russian Federation
50 G2 Staryy Nadym Russian Federation
54 J5 Staryy Oskol Russian Federation
52 D5 Staryy Ryad Russian Federation
31 O6 Staryy Sambor Ukraine
48 H1 Staryy Sambor Ukraine
33 P9 Stassfurt Germany
31 N5 Staszów Poland
99 N7 State Center Iowa U.S.A.
94 K6 State College Pennsylvania U.S.A.
111 H10 State Line Mississippi U.S.A.
Staten I Argentina see Estados, I de los
95 N6 Staten I New York U.S.A.
112 F5 Statesboro Georgia U.S.A.
112 G2 Statesville North Carolina U.S.A.
6 M1 Statfjord oil rig North Sea
27 D12 Stathelle Norway
33 S10 Stauchitz Germany
36 F2 Staufenberg Germany
100 E6 Stauffer Oregon U.S.A.
8 D4 Staunton England
110 G2 Staunton Illinois U.S.A.
94 H8 Staunton Virginia U.S.A.
27 A13 Stavanger Norway
22 H3 Stave Belgium
117 M11 Stave L British Columbia Canada
9 E1 Staveley England
13 F5 Staveley Cumbria England
22 K3 Stavelot Belgium
118 D8 Stavely Alberta Canada
33 S5 Staven Germany
25 B5 Stavenisse Netherlands
28 A5 Stavning Denmark
28 F3 Stavnshoved C Denmark
25 D3 Stavoren Netherlands
28 J6 Stavreby Denmark
28 F6 Stavreshoved C Denmark
53 F10 Stavropol' Russian Federation
55 E4 Stavropolka Kazakhstan
53 F10 Stavropol'skaya Vozvyshennost' uplands Russian Federation
53 F11 Stavropol'skiy Kray reg Russian Federation
46 G5 Stavrós Greece
46 G9 Stavrós, Akra C Crete Greece
46 G3 Stavroúpolis Greece
139 G6 Stawell Victoria Australia
31 N2 Stawiski Poland
31 L4 Stawiszyn Poland
120 K8 Stayner Ontario Canada
100 C5 Stayton Oregon U.S.A.
45 H4 Stazzema Italy
101 R2 Steamboat Nevada U.S.A.
106 D1 Steamboat Springs Colorado U.S.A.
94 C10 Stearns Kentucky U.S.A.
31 M2 Stębark Poland
116 F5 Stebbins Alaska U.S.A.
33 Q7 Stechow Germany
41 J2 Steckborn Switzerland
28 B7 Stedesand Germany
116 R4 Steel Creek Alaska U.S.A.
111 K8 Steele Alabama U.S.A.
110 G5 Steele Missouri U.S.A.
98 G3 Steele North Dakota U.S.A.
98 K9 Steele City Nebraska U.S.A.
146 D5 Steele I Antarctica
117 C5 Steele,Mt Yukon Territory Canada
110 G3 Steeleville Illinois U.S.A.
120 D4 Steel R Ontario Canada
95 L6 Steelton Pennsylvania U.S.A.
110 E4 Steelville Missouri U.S.A.
25 E3 Steenbergen Netherlands
89 G5 Steenkamps Berg mts S Africa
22 G2 Steenkerque Belgium
117 P6 Steen River Alberta Canada
25 D6 Steensel Netherlands
100 G7 Steens Mt Oregon U.S.A.
115 O2 Steenstrup Gletscher gla Greenland
22 D2 Steenvoorde France
22 D2 Steenwerck France
25 F3 Steenwijk Netherlands
119 M5 Steep Cr Saskatchewan Canada
119 O3 Steephill L Saskatchewan Canada
131 F7 Steeple Jason isld Falkland Is
71 D6 Steep Pt Philippines
119 T7 Steep Rock Manitoba Canada
118 K2 Steep Rock Ontario Canada
143 B6 Steere, Mt W Australia Australia
13 G6 Steeton England
48 L3 Stefăneşti Romania
43 F10 Stefano di Cam., S Sicily
146 K10 Stefansson B Antarctica
147 H3 Stefansson I Northwest Territories Canada
133 C6 Steffen mt Chile/Arg
36 F2 Steffenberg Germany
98 C8 Stegall Nebraska U.S.A.
28 J7 Stege Denmark
28 J6 Stege Bugt B Denmark
33 P8 Stegelitz Germany
29 K7 Stege Nor L Denmark
99 T8 Steger Illinois U.S.A.
87 F11 Stegi Swaziland
33 S8 Steglitz Berlin
100 E1 Stehekin Washington U.S.A.
48 G4 Ştei Romania
38 L7 Steiermark prov Austria
37 J4 Steigerwald hills Germany
37 L5 Stein Germany
37 L3 Steinach Germany
37 J5 Steinach Germany
36 H3 Steinau Germany
99 K9 Steinauer Nebraska U.S.A.
118 E1 Steinbach Manitoba Canada
36 E6 Steinbach Germany
37 J2 Steinbach Germany
37 K2 Steinbach Hallenberg Germany
28 D7 Steinberg Germany
38 G6 Steinberge Austria
36 C6 Steinbourg France
129 H6 Steinen R Brazil
38 G7 Steinernes Meer mts Austria
32 H7 Steinfeld Germany
22 K4 Steinfort Luxembourg
32 H8 Steinhagen Germany
113 D8 Steinhatchee Florida U.S.A.
87 C10 Steinhausen Namibia
37 L3 Steinheid Germany
36 F3 Steinheim Germany
33 M5 Steinhorst Germany
32 K8 Steinhuder Meer L Germany
32 L5 Steinkirchen Germany
26 E8 Steinkjer Norway
87 C11 Steinkopf S Africa
38 L7 Steinplan mt Austria
106 B9 Steins New Mexico U.S.A.
36 F5 Steinsfurt Germany
37 L3 Steinwiesen Germany
22 G1 Stekene Belgium
99 L9 Stella Nebraska U.S.A.
112 K3 Stella North Carolina U.S.A.
122 K8 Stellarton Nova Scotia Canada
45 K2 Stellata Italy
32 M6 Stelle Germany
87 C12 Stellenbosch S Africa
116 Q6 Steller, Mt Alaska U.S.A.
42 D2 Stelvio, Passo di Italy
112 J1 Stem North Carolina U.S.A.
32 K7 Stemmen Germany
26 C8 Stemshaug Norway
32 H8 Stemwede Germany
22 J5 Stenay France
28 A3 Stenbjerg Denmark
33 P7 Stendal Germany
52 B6 Stende Latvia
28 D5 Stenderup Denmark
28 D7 Stenderup Germany
119 P7 Stenen Saskatchewan Canada
28 E2 Stenhøj Denmark
138 D6 Stenhouse B South Australia Australia
28 D3 Stenild Denmark
28 H5 Stenlille Denmark
28 J5 Stenløse Denmark
15 G2 Stenness Shetland Scotland
15 E1 Stenness,L.of Orkney Scotland
47 P13 Stenón Kerkiras, Vório chan Greece/Albania
26 J6 Stensele Sweden
27 G14 Stensjön Sweden
27 G13 Stenstorp Sweden
28 E6 Stenstrup Denmark
26 L5 Stenträsk Sweden
27 E13 Stenungsund Sweden
28 F4 Stenvad Denmark
78 L2 Stepanakert Azerbaijan
78 K1 Stepanavan Armenia
55 C5 Stepanovka Kazakhstan
33 O5 Stepenitz R Germany
33 P6 Stepenitz R Germany
37 O6 Stephansposching Germany
98 K1 Stephen Minnesota U.S.A.
109 O2 Stephens Arkansas U.S.A.
94 J7 Stephens City Virginia U.S.A.
138 F4 Stephens Creek New South Wales Australia
117 H8 Stephens I British Columbia Canada
115 K6 Stephens L Manitoba Canada
119 W2 Stephens L Manitoba Canada
99 T4 Stephenson Michigan U.S.A.
145 D1 Stephenson I New Zealand
117 G7 Stephens Pass Alaska U.S.A.
123 O5 Stephenville Newfoundland Canada
109 J3 Stephenville Texas U.S.A.
123 O5 Stephenville Crossing Newfoundland Canada
57 D5 Step' Karnabchul' Uzbekistan
55 F5 Stepnogorsk Kazakhstan
57 G3 Stepnoye Kirghizia
55 F4 Stepnyak Kazakhstan
116 G9 Stepovak B Alaska U.S.A.
28 C6 Stepping Denmark
103 K2 Steptoe Nevada U.S.A.
36 H3 Sterbfritz Germany
46 E6 Stereá Elláš admin region Greece
87 E12 Sterkstroom S Africa
108 F1 Sterley Texas U.S.A.
55 C4 Sterlibashevo Russian Federation
106 G1 Sterling Colorado U.S.A.
99 R8 Sterling Illinois U.S.A.
107 M3 Sterling Kansas U.S.A.
94 C2 Sterling Michigan U.S.A.
98 K9 Sterling Nebraska U.S.A.
98 F3 Sterling North Dakota U.S.A.
109 J1 Sterling Oklahoma U.S.A.
103 N2 Sterling Utah U.S.A.
108 G4 Sterling City Texas U.S.A.
94 D4 Sterling Heights Michigan U.S.A.
55 C4 Sterlitamak Russian Federation
33 P5 Sternberg Germany
31 K6 Šternberk Czech Rep
22 H2 Sterrebeek Belgium
52 E4 Steshevskaya Russian Federation
31 K3 Stęszew Poland
41 K1 Stetten Germany
Stettin see Szczecin
33 U5 Stettiner Haff Germany
118 E6 Stettler Alberta Canada
99 U3 Steuben Michigan U.S.A.
99 Q6 Steuben Wisconsin U.S.A.
94 G6 Steubenville Ohio U.S.A.
33 Q9 Steutz Germany
9 F4 Stevenage England
120 E3 Stevens Ontario Canada
145 D4 Stevens, Mt New Zealand
138 C2 Stevenson R South Australia Australia
119 U9 Stevenson Manitoba Canada
110 L7 Stevenson Alabama U.S.A.
100 D4 Stevenson Washington U.S.A.
119 W5 Stevenson L Manitoba Canada
99 R5 Stevens Pt Wisconsin U.S.A.
12 D2 Stevenston Scotland
116 N4 Stevens Village Alaska U.S.A.
94 A4 Stevensville Michigan U.S.A.
32 F9 Stever R Germany
118 F8 Steveville Prov.Pk Alberta Canada
29 K6 Stevns pen Denmark
22 J2 Stevoort Belgium
99 S8 Steward Illinois U.S.A.
110 H2 Stewardson Illinois U.S.A.
141 G2 Stewart R Queensland Australia
117 H8 Stewart British Columbia Canada

117 D4 Stewart Yukon Territory Canada
99 M5 Stewart Minnesota U.S.A.
102 E2 Stewart Nevada U.S.A.
140 C1 Stewart, C N Terr Australia
144 A7 Stewart I New Zealand
137 N3 Stewart Is Pacific Oc
143 C10 Stewart, Mt W Australia Australia
15 D5 Stewarton Scotland
95 L7 Stewartstown Pennsylvania U.S.A.
110 B2 Stewartsville Missouri U.S.A.
127 K2 Stewart Town Jamaica
118 K8 Stewart Valley Saskatchewan Canada
99 O6 Stewartville Minnesota U.S.A.
122 J8 Stewiacke Nova Scotia Canada
32 K7 Steyerberg Germany
9 F6 Steyning England
8 A4 Steynton Wales
38 K5 Steyr Austria
121 S7 St-Hyacinthe Quebec Canada
45 L4 Stia Italy
8 B6 Stibb Cross England
100 K5 Stibnite Idaho U.S.A.
9 G1 Stickford England
32 G6 Stickhausen Germany
9 G1 Stickney England
98 H6 Stickney South Dakota U.S.A.
33 N9 Stiege Germany
25 E2 Stiens Netherlands
45 L2 Stienta Italy
107 P6 Stigler Oklahoma U.S.A.
43 G8 Stigliano Italy
26 J9 Stigsjö Sweden
117 H7 Stikine R Alaska/Br Col U.S.A./Canada
117 H6 Stikine Ranges British Columbia Canada
117 G7 Stikine Str Alaska U.S.A.
108 F4 Stiles Texas U.S.A.
110 K2 Stilesville Indiana U.S.A.
46 F6 Stilis Greece
28 D4 Stilling Denmark
13 G5 Stillington England
99 R7 Stillman Valley Illinois U.S.A.
99 O4 Stillwater Minnesota U.S.A.
101 L1 Stillwater R Montana U.S.A.
102 F2 Stillwater Nevada U.S.A.
107 N5 Stillwater Oklahoma U.S.A.
102 F2 Stillwater Ra Nevada U.S.A.
43 H10 Stilo, Pta Italy
48 J5 Stilpeni Romania
110 B6 Stilwell Oklahoma U.S.A.
46 E7 Stimfalías, L Greece
101 M1 Stimson,Mt Montana U.S.A.
12 D3 Stinchar,R Scotland
98 E9 Stinking Water Cr Nebraska U.S.A.
46 E3 Štip Macedonia
46 G6 Stira Greece
140 C5 Stirling N Terr Australia
138 E5 Stirling South Australia Australia
118 E9 Stirling Alberta Canada
121 N8 Stirling Ontario Canada
144 B7 Stirling New Zealand
12 E1 Stirling Scotland
100 D10 Stirling City California U.S.A.
143 C9 Stirling, Mt W Australia Australia
143 C10 Stirling Ra W Australia Australia
44 H2 Stirone R Italy
98 J3 Stirum North Dakota U.S.A.
100 K3 Stites Idaho U.S.A.
119 V3 Stitt Manitoba Canada
99 Q7 Stitzer Wisconsin U.S.A.
27 K14 Stjärnarve Sweden
26 N1 Stjernöya isld Norway
26 E8 Stjördalselv R Norway
26 E8 Stjördalshalsen Norway
18 E6 St-Maixent-l'École France
121 R5 St-Maurice, Parc du Quebec Canada
121 R5 St-Maurice, Parc du Québec Canada
13 E2 Stobo Scotland
41 K2 Stockach Germany
27 G14 Stockaryd Sweden
9 E5 Stockbridge England
95 O4 Stockbridge Massachusetts U.S.A.
94 C4 Stockbridge Michigan U.S.A.
94 E8 Stockdale Ohio U.S.A.
109 K6 Stockdale Texas U.S.A.
33 N5 Stockelsdorf Germany
48 C2 Stockerau Austria
36 B6 Stock,Etang du L France
101 O2 Stockett Montana U.S.A.
98 J9 Stockham Nebraska U.S.A.
37 L3 Stockheim Germany
119 P8 Stockholm Saskatchewan Canada
27 J12 Stockholm county Sweden
27 K12 Stockholm Sweden
95 S6 Stockholm Maine U.S.A.
40 G4 Stockhorn mt Switzerland
139 J5 Stockinbingal New South Wales Australia
13 F6 Stockport England
94 F7 Stockport Ohio U.S.A.
139 K5 Stockton New South Wales Australia
119 S9 Stockton Manitoba Canada
144 C4 Stockton New Zealand
111 J10 Stockton Alabama U.S.A.
102 C4 Stockton California U.S.A.
99 Q7 Stockton Illinois U.S.A.
107 L2 Stockton Kansas U.S.A.
95 M8 Stockton Maryland U.S.A.
110 C4 Stockton Missouri U.S.A.
101 N9 Stockton Utah U.S.A.
99 Q3 Stockton I Wisconsin U.S.A.
116 O1 Stockton Is Alaska U.S.A.
110 C4 Stockton L Missouri U.S.A.
13 G4 Stockton-on-Tees England
95 T2 Stockton Springs Maine U.S.A.
98 F9 Stockville Nebraska U.S.A.
31 N4 Stoczek Łukowski Poland
37 P4 Stod Czech Rep
26 F7 Stod Norway
99 P6 Stoddard Wisconsin U.S.A.
26 J9 Stöde Sweden
68 H6 Stoeng Treng Cambodia
15 C2 Stoer,Pt of Scotland
28 C4 Stoholm Denmark
145 D4 Stoke New Zealand
9 G2 Stoke Ferry England
8 C7 Stoke Fleming England
9 F4 Stokenchurch England
8 D1 Stoke-on-Trent England
120 J7 Stokes Bay Ontario Canada
112 H1 Stokesdale North Carolina U.S.A.
143 D10 Stokes Inlet W Australia Australia
145 E4 Stokes, Mt New Zealand
139 G8 Stokes Pt Tasmania Australia
140 B3 Stokes Ra N Terr Australia
53 C8 Stokhod R Ukraine
28 G7 Stokkemarke Denmark
28 S10 Stokkseyri Iceland
26 D7 Stokksund Norway
26 G3 Stokmarknes Norway
42 H5 Stolac Bosnia-Herzegovina
25 F7 Stolberg Germany
33 P9 Stolberg Germany
147 Q8 Stolbovoy,Ostrov Russian Federation
48 F2 Stolica mt Slovakia
37 O2 Stollberg Germany
32 H5 Stollhamm Germany
Stolp see Słupsk
90 A16 Stoltenhoff I Tristan da Cunha
32 K7 Stolzenau Germany
36 D3 Stolzenfels Germany
46 F5 Stómion Greece
36 B1 Stommeln Germany
8 D2 Stone England
94 G5 Stoneboro Pennsylvania U.S.A.
9 E3 Stonebridge England
106 F3 Stone City Colorado U.S.A.
121 N6 Stonecliffe Ontario Canada
100 F7 Stone Corral L Oregon U.S.A.
122 A7 Stoneham Quebec Canada
98 C9 Stoneham Colorado U.S.A.
95 N7 Stone Harbor New Jersey U.S.A.
15 F4 Stonehaven Scotland
141 G6 Stonehenge Queensland Australia
9 E5 Stonehenge anc mon England
8 D4 Stonehouse England
99 P4 Stone L Wisconsin U.S.A.
112 C4 Stone Mt Georgia U.S.A.
117 L6 Stone Mt. Prov. Park British Columbia Canada
110 K6 Stones River Nat. Battlefield Tennessee U.S.A.
118 D1 Stonewall Manitoba Canada
111 H9 Stonewall Mississippi U.S.A.
109 L1 Stonewall Oklahoma U.S.A.
109 J5 Stonewall Texas U.S.A.
121 L9 Stoney Creek Ontario Canada
12 D4 Stoneykirk Scotland
26 J2 Stonglandet Norway
106 H4 Stonington Colorado U.S.A.
95 Q5 Stonington Connecticut U.S.A.
99 R10 Stonington Illinois U.S.A.
95 T2 Stonington Maine U.S.A.
119 M8 Stony Beach Saskatchewan Canada
94 K10 Stony Creek Virginia U.S.A.
8 D3 Stony Cross England
102 B2 Stonyford California U.S.A.
127 L2 Stony Hill Jamaica
118 D1 Stony Mountain Manitoba Canada
118 D5 Stony Plain Alberta Canada
95 N5 Stony Point New York U.S.A.
112 F2 Stony Point North Carolina U.S.A.
144 C6 Stony R New Zealand
114 J6 Stony Rapids Saskatchewan Canada
116 J6 Stony River Alaska U.S.A.
9 F3 Stony Stratford England
120 H1 Stooping R Ontario Canada
32 L4 Stör R Germany
28 C4 Storå R Denmark
27 H12 Storå Sweden
26 G8 Storåbränna Sweden
6 F1 Stora Dimun isld Faeroes
27 E12 Stora Le L Sweden
26 L5 Stora Lule älv R Sweden
26 K4 Stora Lulevatten L Sweden
26 F9 Storån R Sweden
26 J4 Stora Sjöfallet L Sweden
26 K6 Storavan L Sweden
26 K6 Storberg Sweden
27 L11 Storby Finland
27 A12 Stord Norway
26 B9 Stordal Möre og Romsdal Norway
26 E8 Stordal Sör-Tröndelag Norway
28 D3 Store Arden Denmark
28 F5 Store Bælt chan Denmark
26 G6 Store Börgefjell mt Norway
27 H14 Storebro Sweden
28 B6 Store Darum Denmark
28 G5 Store Fuglede Denmark
28 K6 Store Heddinge Denmark
26 C7 Store Jyndevad Denmark
29 K7 Storeklint cliffs Denmark
147 F10 Store Koldewey isld Greenland
26 P1 Storelv R Norway
27 E10 Stor-Elvdal Norway
29 K5 Store Magleby Denmark
28 H5 Store Merløse Denmark
26 R1 Store Molvik Norway
26 D8 Stören Norway
28 E7 Store Rise Denmark
28 J6 Store Spjellerup Denmark
28 J6 Store Tårnby Denmark
28 D2 Store Vildmose Denmark
26 H6 Storfjellet,N mt Sweden
26 G6 Storfjellet,S mt Sweden
26 B9 Storfjord inlet Norway
26 G5 Storfosshei Norway
26 H8 Storhögen Sweden
26 A9 Storholmen Norway
26 G7 Storjorm L Sweden
33 P5 Storkanal Germany
114 G3 Storkerson B Northwest Territories Canada
26 F8 Storlien Sweden
26 K7 Storlögda Sweden
32 L5 Stormarn reg Germany
139 J9 Storm B Tasmania Australia
89 E8 Stormberge mts S Africa
99 M7 Storm L Iowa U.S.A.
118 K1 Stormy L Ontario Canada
119 P7 Stornoway Saskatchewan Canada
15 B2 Stornoway Scotland
52 H4 Storozhevsk Russian Federation
48 K2 Storozhinets Ukraine
26 F8 Storrensjön L Sweden
9 F6 Storrington England
15 B3 Storr,The mt Scotland
27 E11 Stor-s L Norway
26 L7 Storsävarträsk Sweden
26 F9 Storsjö Sweden
27 E10 Stor-sjöen L Norway
27 F10 Storsjøen Sweden
27 J11 Storsjön L Gävleborg Sweden
26 F9 Storsjön L Jämtland Sweden
26 H6 Storstrøm co Denmark
28 H7 Storstrømmen chan Denmark
119 Q9 Storthoaks Saskatchewan Canada
26 J6 Storuman Sweden
27 G10 Storvarden mt Sweden
26 F9 Storvigelen mt Norway
27 J11 Storvik Sweden
26 J6 Stor-vindein L Sweden
28 E2 Storvorde Denmark
101 T5 Story Wyoming U.S.A.
99 N8 Story City Iowa U.S.A.
133 B7 Stosch, I Chile
37 M1 Stössen Germany
26 F5 Stött Norway
41 N2 Stotten Germany
37 L1 Stotternheim Germany
28 D5 Stouby Denmark
121 L9 Stouffville Ontario Canada
119 O9 Stoughton Saskatchewan Canada
95 Q4 Stoughton Massachusetts U.S.A.
99 R7 Stoughton Wisconsin U.S.A.
22 K3 Stoumont Belgium
47 G3 Stoupi Greece
8 D3 Stourbridge England
8 D3 Stourport England
9 H5 Stour,R England
8 D3 Stourton England
94 E7 Stoutsville Ohio U.S.A.
26 D9 Støvring Denmark
28 E3 Støvring Denmark
12 F4 Stow Scotland
95 P2 Stowe Vermont U.S.A.
109 N6 Stowell Texas U.S.A.
9 G3 Stowmarket England
9 E4 Stow on the Wold England
26 E6 Stoy Denmark
59 K1 Stoyba Russian Federation
46 C2 Stožac mt Montenegro Yugoslavia
45 M1 Stra Italy
33 R9 Straach Germany
14 D2 Strabane N Ireland
12 C1 Strachur Scotland
14 D3 Stradbally Ireland
45 H3 Stradella Italy
38 N8 Straden Austria
9 G2 Stradsett England
25 F6 Straelen Germany
110 C4 Strafford Missouri U.S.A.
139 H8 Strahan Tasmania Australia
103 N4 Straight Cliffs Utah U.S.A.
22 J4 Straimont Belgium
12 D3 Straiton Scotland
30 H6 Strakonice Czech Rep
47 H2 Straldzha Bulgaria
33 S4 Stralsund Germany
27 E10 Strand Hedmark Norway
27 A12 Strand Rogaland Norway
89 A10 Strand S Africa
26 B9 Stranda Norway
28 C3 Strandby Nordjylland Denmark
28 F2 Strandby Vendsyssel Denmark
98 J9 Strang Nebraska U.S.A.
113 J10 Strangers Cay isld Bahamas
14 F2 Strangford N Ireland
14 F2 Strangford L N Ireland
27 J12 Strängnäs Sweden
27 H13 Strångsjö Sweden
140 C3 Strangways R N Terr Australia
140 C6 Strangways Ra N Terr Australia
14 D2 Stranorlar Ireland
118 J7 Stranraer Saskatchewan Canada
12 C4 Stranraer Scotland
119 N7 Strasbourg Saskatchewan Canada
36 D6 Strasbourg France
33 T5 Strasburg Germany
106 F2 Strasburg Colorado U.S.A.
110 H2 Strasburg Illinois U.S.A.
98 F3 Strasburg North Dakota U.S.A.
94 F6 Strasburg Ohio U.S.A.
94 J8 Strasburg Virginia U.S.A.
48 M3 Strasheny Moldova
38 N8 Strass Steiermark Austria
38 E7 Strass Tirol Austria
27 H12 Stråssa Sweden
38 K8 Strassburg Austria
36 C2 Strassenhaus Germany
38 M7 Strassgang Austria
37 O6 Strasskirchen Germany
38 H6 Strasswalchen Austria
139 H7 Stratford Victoria Australia
122 A8 Stratford Quebec Canada
145 E3 Stratford New Zealand
95 O5 Stratford Connecticut U.S.A.
99 N7 Stratford Iowa U.S.A.
95 Q2 Stratford New Hampshire U.S.A.
109 L1 Stratford Oklahoma U.S.A.
98 H4 Stratford South Dakota U.S.A.
108 B7 Stratford Texas U.S.A.
99 Q5 Stratford Wisconsin U.S.A.
9 E3 Stratford-on-Avon England
9 H4 Stratford St. Mary England
138 E6 Strathalbyn South Australia Australia
15 D5 Strathaven Scotland
12 D2 Strathblane Scotland
15 D2 Strath Brora Scotland
15 C3 Strath Carron Scotland
119 R8 Strathclair Manitoba Canada
15 D5 Strathclyde reg Scotland
117 L11 Strathcona Prov. Park British Columbia Canada
15 E3 Strath Dearn Scotland
15 D3 Strath Farrar Scotland
15 E2 Strath Halladale Scotland
141 G3 Strathleven Queensland Australia
123 L7 Strathlorne Nova Scotia Canada
13 E1 Strathmiglo Scotland
141 G4 Strathmore Queensland Australia
118 D7 Strathmore Alberta Canada
15 E4 Strathmore dist Scotland
117 M9 Strathnaver British Columbia Canada
15 D3 Strathpeffer Scotland
120 J10 Strathroy Ontario Canada
15 D2 Strathy Pt Scotland
12 D1 Strathyre Scotland
8 B6 Stratton England
106 H2 Stratton Colorado U.S.A.
95 R1 Stratton Maine U.S.A.
98 E9 Stratton Nebraska U.S.A.
37 O6 Straubing Germany
26 G4 Straumen Norway
30 H3 Strausberg Germany
108 A3 Strauss New Mexico U.S.A.
37 K1 Straussfurt Germany
101 Q3 Straw Montana U.S.A.
110 E5 Strawberry R Arkansas U.S.A.
103 J2 Strawberry Nevada U.S.A.
100 G5 Strawberry Mt Oregon U.S.A.
99 P7 Strawberry Pt Iowa U.S.A.
101 P9 Strawberry Res Utah U.S.A.
121 R5 Strawhat Depot Quebec Canada
99 S9 Strawn Illinois U.S.A.
109 J3 Strawn Texas U.S.A.
37 O4 Stráž Czech Rep
47 H1 Strazhitsa Bulgaria
31 K7 Strážnice Czech Rep
31 M6 Štrba Slovakia
138 C5 Streaky B South Australia Australia
118 G5 Streamstown Alberta Canada
9 F5 Streatham England
8 E4 Streatley England
99 S8 Streator Illinois U.S.A.
31 H6 Středočeský reg Czech Rep
31 K7 Středoslovenský reg Slovakia
8 D5 Street England
98 G3 Streeter North Dakota U.S.A.
109 H5 Streeter Texas U.S.A.
109 L4 Streetman Texas U.S.A.
13 G5 Strensall England
33 S10 Strehla Germany
48 H5 Strei R Romania
143 E9 Streich Mound W Australia Australia
37 L4 Streitberg Germany
48 G5 Strejeşti Romania
37 P4 Střela R Czech Rep
46 G2 Strelcha Bulgaria
54 K5 Streletskaya Russian Federation
33 S6 Strelitz-Alt Germany
56 D2 Strelka Russian Federation
28 B5 Strellev Kirke Denmark
142 C5 Strelley W Australia Australia
142 C5 Strelley R W Australia Australia
52 E2 Strel'na R Russian Federation
52 E2 Strel'na Russian Federation
52 C5 Strenči Latvia
41 M3 Strengen Austria
27 C12 Strengen Norway
13 G5 Strensall England
46 E2 Strešer mt Serbia Yugoslavia
54 B4 Streshin Belarus
9 G3 Stretham England
43 G10 Stretto di Messina Sicily
8 D1 Stretton England
9 E2 Stretton England
9 F2 Stretton England
37 J3 Streu R Germany
37 K3 Streufdorf Germany
6 F1 Streymoy isld Faeroes
55 G1 Strezhevoy Russian Federation
28 D5 Strib Denmark
37 P4 Stříbro Czech Rep
15 F3 Strichen Scotland
120 J3 Strickland Ontario Canada
25 C5 Strijen Netherlands
109 N4 Striker Cr.Res Texas U.S.A.
26 G5 Strimasund Sweden
46 F3 Strimón R Greece
46 F4 Strimonikós,Kólpos G Greece
12 C2 Striven,L Scotland
48 E5 Strizivojna Croatia
46 D7 Strofádhes isld Greece
32 J7 Ströhen Germany
54 H6 Stroitel' Russian Federation
14 C3 Strokestown Ireland
33 T6 Strom R Germany
15 E2 Stroma isld Orkney Scotland
32 H9 Stromberg Nordrhein-Westfalen Germany
36 D4 Stromberg Rheinland-Pfalz Germany
43 G10 Stromboli, I Italy
118 E6 Strome Alberta Canada
15 C3 Stromeferry Scotland
26 L7 Strömfors Sweden
15 E2 Stromness Orkney Scotland
131 H6 Stromness S Georgia
131 H6 Stromness B S Georgia
26 J10 Strömsbruck Sweden
98 J8 Stromsburg Nebraska U.S.A.
27 E13 Strömstad Sweden
26 H8 Strömsund Sweden
26 H8 Strömsvattudal L Sweden
12 D1 Stronachlachar Scotland
98 A5 Stroner Wyoming U.S.A.
111 D8 Strong Arkansas U.S.A.
95 R1 Strong Maine U.S.A.
111 H8 Strong Mississippi U.S.A.
107 O3 Strong City Kansas U.S.A.
107 L6 Strong City Oklahoma U.S.A.
118 L7 Strongfield Saskatchewan Canada
99 Q9 Stronghurst Illinois U.S.A.
47 O12 Strongili Greece
43 H9 Strongoli Italy
94 F5 Strongsville Ohio U.S.A.
15 F1 Stronsay Scotland
15 F1 Stronsay Firth Scotland
9 G5 Strood England
31 K6 Stropkov Slovakia
112 F3 Strother South Carolina U.S.A.
139 K4 Stroud New South Wales Australia
8 D4 Stroud England
107 O6 Stroud Oklahoma U.S.A.
139 K4 Stroud Road New South Wales Australia
95 M6 Stroudsburg Pennsylvania U.S.A.
138 F6 Struan South Australia Australia
15 E4 Struan Scotland
32 G6 Strücklingen Germany
38 L5 Strudengau V Austria
28 B3 Struer Denmark
46 D3 Struga Macedonia
52 C5 Strugi-Krasnyye Russian Federation
89 B10 Struisbaai S Africa
14 D2 Strule R N Ireland
99 P5 Strum Wisconsin U.S.A.
47 F3 Struma R Bulgaria
8 A3 Strumble Head Wales
46 F3 Strumica Macedonia
46 F3 Strumitsa R Macedonia
54 K1 Strunino Russian Federation
120 E4 Struthers Ontario Canada
94 G5 Struthers Ohio U.S.A.
37 P3 Stružná Czech Rep
47 G2 Stryama R Bulgaria
46 G2 Stryama Bulgaria
101 L1 Stryker Montana U.S.A.
94 C5 Stryker Ohio U.S.A.
31 M4 Strykow Poland
28 F7 Stryno Denmark
26 B10 Strynvatn L Norway
31 O6 Stryy R Ukraine
48 H1 Stryy Ukraine
31 J5 Strzegom Poland
31 J3 Strzelce Poland
31 L5 Strzelce Poland
138 F3 Strzelecki Cr South Australia Australia
140 C5 Strzelecki, Mt N Terr Australia
139 J8 Strzelecki Pk Tasmania Australia
31 K5 Strzelin Poland
31 L3 Strzelno Poland
31 N6 Strzyżów Poland
141 K7 Stuart R Queensland Australia
113 G10 Stuart Florida U.S.A.
99 M8 Stuart Iowa U.S.A.
98 G7 Stuart Nebraska U.S.A.
109 L1 Stuart Oklahoma U.S.A.
94 G10 Stuart Virginia U.S.A.
140 B6 Stuart Bluff Ra N Terr Australia
138 D3 Stuart Creek South Australia Australia
116 F5 Stuart I Alaska U.S.A.
117 L8 Stuart L British Columbia Canada
100 E2 Stuart, Mt Washington U.S.A.
144 A6 Stuart Mts New Zealand
140 B1 Stuart Pt N Terr Australia
138 C3 Stuart Rge South Australia Australia
139 J5 Stuart Town New South Wales Australia
38 K8 Stubalper Alpen mt Austria
41 O3 Stubai Tal Austria
41 O3 Stubaier Alpen mts Austria
38 L7 Stub Alpe mts Austria
28 J7 Stubbekøbing Denmark
32 H6 Stubben Germany
28 H5 Stubberød Sø L Denmark
28 F4 Stubbe Sø L Denmark
83 M9 Stubbings Pt Christmas I Indian Oc
41 M3 Stuben Austria
38 N7 Stubenberg Austria
38 M6 Stübming R Austria
47 H3 Studen Kladenets, Yazovir res Bulgaria
38 N7 Studenzen Austria
140 B5 Studholme Hills N Terr Australia
144 C6 Studholme Junction New Zealand
144 C6 Studholme, Mt New Zealand
46 G1 Studina Romania
9 E6 Studland England
28 B4 Studsgård Denmark
32 L8 Stugun Sweden
32 J6 Stuhr Germany
28 G6 Stukenbrock Germany
9 G3 Stump Cross England
112 M2 Stumpy Point North Carolina U.S.A.
33 Q9 Stumsdorf Germany
68 G6 Stung Chinle R Cambodia
68 G6 Stung Sen R Cambodia
26 G6 Stuorajavrre L Norway
26 N2 Stupendous Mt British Columbia Canada
117 L9 Stupendous Mt British Columbia Canada
54 K2 Stupino Russian Federation
37 P3 Stura R Italy
40 G7 Stura di Ala R Italy
44 B1 Stura di Demonte R Italy
44 B3 Stura di V,Grande R Italy
40 G7 Stura di Viu R Italy
146 C13 Sturge I Antarctica
120 K6 Sturgeon R Ontario Canada
94 C2 Sturgeon R Michigan U.S.A.
110 D2 Sturgeon Missouri U.S.A.
119 U6 Sturgeon B Manitoba Canada
94 B1 Sturgeon B Michigan U.S.A.
99 T5 Sturgeon Bay Wisconsin U.S.A.
99 T5 Sturgeon Bay Canal Wisconsin U.S.A.
120 D6 Sturgeon Falls Ontario Canada
117 P8 Sturgeon L Alberta Canada
121 M8 Sturgeon L Ontario Canada
119 U3 Sturgeon Landing Manitoba Canada
118 C5 Sturgeon R Alberta Canada
118 L5 Sturgeon R Saskatchewan Canada
119 P7 Sturgis Saskatchewan Canada
110 J4 Sturgis Kentucky U.S.A.
94 B5 Sturgis Michigan U.S.A.
111 G8 Sturgis Mississippi U.S.A.
107 N6 Sturgis Oklahoma U.S.A.
98 C5 Sturgis South Dakota U.S.A.
44 E3 Sturla Italy
8 D6 Sturminster Newton England
48 E3 Štúrovo Slovakia
9 H5 Sturry England
138 D6 Sturt B South Australia Australia
142 G4 Sturt Cr R W Australia Australia
142 G4 Sturt Creek W Australia Australia
141 F8 Sturt Des Qnsld/S Aust Australia
99 T7 Sturtevant Wisconsin U.S.A.
138 F3 Sturt, Mt New South Wales Australia
138 F3 Sturt Nat Park New South Wales Australia
140 C3 Sturt Plain N Terr Australia
36 D5 Stürzelbronn France
36 E5 Stutensee Germany
89 E9 Stutterheim S Africa
36 G6 Stuttgart Germany
111 E7 Stuttgart Arkansas U.S.A.
107 L2 Stuttgart Kansas U.S.A.
37 K2 Stützerbach Germany
26 H9 Styggberg Sweden
28 R8 Stykkishólmur Iceland
130 G6 Suaçui Grande, R Brazil
71 M9 Suai Indonesia
70 C3 Suai Sarawak
86 G2 Suakin Sudan
99 T5 Suamico Wisconsin U.S.A.
124 E3 Suaqui Mexico
128 D2 Suárez R Colombia
70 L9 Subang Java
71 F4 Suban Pt Philippines
52 C6 Subate Latvia
77 A5 Şubayhiyah, Aş Kuwait
45 L4 Subbiano Italy
80 F5 Subeihi Jordan
57 J4 Subexi China
69 J11 Subi isld Indonesia
142 A1 Subiaco dist Perth, W Aust Australia
42 E7 Subiaco Italy
69 J1 Subi Kecil isld Indonesia
101 M7 Sublett Idaho U.S.A.
99 R8 Sublette Illinois U.S.A.
107 K4 Sublette Kansas U.S.A.
109 L6 Sublime Texas U.S.A.
48 F4 Subotica Serbia Yugoslavia
65 D2 Subrag China
118 J8 Success Saskatchewan Canada
110 D4 Success Missouri U.S.A.
44 H3 Succiso,Alpe di mt Italy
20 G7 Sucé France
48 F1 Sucha Poland
Suchan see Partizansk
31 J2 Suchan Poland
31 H7 Suchdol Czech Rep
31 M4 Suchedniów Poland
Suchow see Xuzhou
31 O2 Suchowola Poland
25 F6 Süchteln Germany
100 C1 Sucia I Washington U.S.A.
14 C3 Suck R Ireland
100 H6 Sucker Cr Oregon U.S.A.
116 Q7 Suckling,C Alaska U.S.A.
33 P6 Suckow Germany
128 F7 Sucre Bolivia
126 G10 Sucre Colombia
128 D2 Sucre div Colombia
128 C4 Sucumbíos prov Ecuador
128 G5 Sucunduri R Brazil
130 D7 Sucuriu R Brazil
52 G5 Suda Russian Federation
86 E3 Sudan rep Africa
108 E1 Sudan Texas U.S.A.
52 F5 Suday Russian Federation
55 B5 Sud'bodarovka Russian Federation
120 J6 Sudbury Ontario Canada
9 G3 Sudbury England
86 E4 Sudd dist Sudan
128 G2 Suddie Guyana
33 O6 Sude R Germany
28 D7 Süderbrarup Germany
28 B7 Süderburg Germany
33 M7 Süderhastedt Germany
32 K4 Süderhöft Germany
32 J4 Süder Lügum Germany
28 B7 Sudilova Russian Federation
52 E6 Sudislavl' Russian Federation
52 F5 Südlohn Germany
32 E9 Sudogda Russian Federation
52 F6 Sudost' R Russian Federation
54 E4 Sud Ouest, Pte Mauritius
83 L13 Sudr Egypt
79 C9 Suðureyri Iceland
6 F1 Suðuroy Faeroes
6 F1 Suðuroyarfjørður fj Faeroes
54 G5 Sudzha Russian Federation
59 K3 Sudzukhe Russian Federation
17 G5 Sueca Spain
46 G2 Suedinenie Bulgaria
80 G8 Su'eida R Jordan
80 F8 Su'eidat Jordan
117 G8 Suemez I Alaska U.S.A.
108 D6 Sue Pk Texas U.S.A.
55 E3 Suer' R Russian Federation
21 N6 Suèvres France
79 C5 Suez Egypt
79 C8 Suez Canal Egypt
79 C8 Suez,G.of Egypt
84 J4 Suf Jordan
80 G4 Suffield Alberta Canada
118 F8 Suffolk co England
9 H3 Suffolk Montana U.S.A.
101 Q2 Suffolk Virginia U.S.A.
95 L10 Suga-jima isld Japan
61 K11 Sugar Idaho U.S.A.
101 O6 Sugar R Wisconsin U.S.A.
99 R7 Sugar City Colorado U.S.A.
106 G3 Sugar Grove Pennsylvania U.S.A.
94 H5 Sugar Grove Virginia U.S.A.
94 F10 Sugar Land Texas U.S.A.
109 M6 Sugarloaf mt Brazil
132 C2 Sugarloaf Hill W Australia Australia
143 C6 Sugarloaf Key isld Florida U.S.A.
113 F13 Sugarloaf Pt New South Wales Australia
139 L4 Sugar Loaf Pt St Helena
90 A13 Sugbuhan Pt Philippines
71 G5 Sugenheim Germany
37 J4 Suggi L Saskatchewan Canada
119 P4 Sugi Indonesia
69 F12 Sugi Japan
60 J10 Suğla Gölü L Turkey
78 D3 Sugoy R Russian Federation
51 P2 Sugut R Sabah
70 E1 Sugut, Tanjung C Sabah
70 E1 Suhait China
46 G1 Şuhār Oman
77 E7 Suhl Germany
37 J2 Suhopolje Croatia
42 H3 Suhr R Switzerland
40 H3 Suhut Turkey
74 C4 Sui Pakistan
129 H6 Suiá-Missu R Brazil
100 E1 Suiattle Pass Washington U.S.A.
67 F2 Suichang China
67 E3 Suichuan China
58 F4 Suide China
65 H2 Suifenhe China
65 H3 Suifen He China
74 D6 Suigam India
65 G1 Suihua China
67 A2 Sui Jiang R China
59 J2 Suileng China
58 E5 Suining China
58 G5 Suining China
128 E8 Suipacha Bolivia
22 G5 Suippe R France
14 D4 Suir R Ireland
60 T2 Suishō tō isld Russian Federation
95 L8 Suitland Maryland U.S.A.
68 K2 Suixi China
65 C7 Sui Xian China
67 D1 Sui Xian China
67 B2 Suiyanchang China
67 B3 Suiyang China
40 B2 Suize R France
59 H3 Suizhong China
74 F5 Sujangarh India
Suji see Haixing
70 L9 Sukabumi Java
70 K8 Sukadana Sumatra
61 O8 Sukagawa Japan
70 L9 Sukanegara Java
69 K14 Sukaraja Indonesia
70 B6 Sukaramai Kalimantan
70 F2 Sukau Sabah
29 N8 Sukeva Finland
51 L2 Sukhana Russian Federation
65 J1 Sukhanovka Russian Federation
46 G1 Sukhindol Bulgaria
54 G2 Sukhinichi Russian Federation
54 K3 Sukhodol'skiy Russian Federation
52 F5 Sukhona R Russian Federation
68 D4 Sukhothai Thailand
55 D3 Sukhoy Log Russian Federation
53 F11 Sukhumi Georgia
115 O4 Sukkertoppen Iskappe ice field Greenland
74 C5 Sukkur Pakistan
76 E1 Sukma India
84 E4 Süknah Libya
70 O9 Sukodadi Java
70 N9 Sukohardjo Java
70 N9 Sukolilo Java
71 H5 Sukon Sulawesi
69 D9 Sukon,Ko isld Thailand
33 P5 Sukow Germany
52 F6 Sukpay Datani Russian Federation
87 C10 Sukses Namibia
55 C3 Suksun Russian Federation
60 F13 Sukumo Japan
60 F13 Sukumo-wan B Japan
117 N8 Sukunka R British Columbia Canada
26 F8 Sul Norway
27 A10 Sula isld Norway
54 D7 Sula R Ukraine
101 M4 Sula Montana U.S.A.
125 L2 Sulaco Honduras
74 C4 Sulaiman Range Pakistan
53 G11 Sulak Russian Federation
71 K9 Sula,Kep isld Indonesia
52 F4 Sulanda R Russian Federation
15 B1 Sular Sgeir isld Scotland
70 Q10 Sulat isld Indonesia
71 G5 Sulat Samar Philippines
71 A2 Sulat, Bukit mt Halmahera Indonesia
116 K4 Sulatna R Alaska U.S.A.
116 K4 Sulatna Alaska U.S.A.
70 Sulawesi isld Indonesia
71 G7 Sulawesi Selatan Sulawesi
71 H4 Sulawesi Utara Sulawesi
78 K4 Sulaymānīyah, As Iraq
77 A7 Şulb, Aş plain Saudi Arabia
27 B12 Suldal Norway
27 B12 Suldalsvatn Norway
28 D3 Suldrup Denmark
31 J3 Sulechów Poland
31 J3 Sulecin Poland
77 C1 Suledeh Iran
31 M4 Sulejów Poland
31 N3 Sulejówek Poland
31 M4 Sulejowskie, Jezioro res Poland
70 F4 Suleman Teluk B Kalimantan
27 B12 Suleskar Norway
15 D1 Sule Skerry isld Scotland
32 M5 Sülfeld Germany
66 E4 Suli Hu L China
69 E13 Sulik Sumatra
85 B7 Sulima Sierra Leone
48 M5 Sulina R Romania
48 M5 Sulina Romania
32 J7 Sulingen Germany
48 K3 Sulita Romania
26 H4 Sulitjelma Norway
29 N10 Sulkava Finland
128 B4 Sullana Peru
111 H8 Sulligent Alabama U.S.A.
99 S10 Sullivan Illinois U.S.A.
110 E3 Sullivan Missouri U.S.A.
117 K10 Sullivan Bay British Columbia Canada
Sullivan I see Lanbi Kyun
118 F6 Sullivan L Alberta Canada
15 G12 Sullom Voe B Shetland Scotland
99 O8 Sully Iowa U.S.A.
21 P6 Sully-la Chapelle France
21 P6 Sully-sur-Loire France
28 N8 Sulm R Austria
42 F6 Sulmona Italy
109 O5 Sulphur Louisiana U.S.A.
100 G9 Sulphur Nevada U.S.A.
109 L1 Sulphur Oklahoma U.S.A.
109 N2 Sulphur R Texas/Louisiana U.S.A.
103 M3 Sulphurdale Utah U.S.A.
109 N3 Sulphur Springs Texas U.S.A.
108 E3 Sulphur Springs Cr Texas U.S.A.
28 D2 Sulsted Denmark
120 H5 Sultan Ontario Canada
78 C2 Sultan Dağları mts Turkey
47 J7 Sultanhisar Turkey
75 K5 Sultanpur India
36 B1 Sultan Germany
71 F7 Sulu Arch isld Philippines
70 G1 Sulu Arch isids Philippines
116 K5 Sulukna R Alaska U.S.A.
84 G3 Suluq Libya
57 D3 Sulutobe Kazakhstan
57 E5 Sulyukta Kirghizia
36 F7 Sulz Germany
41 O3 Sulzau Austria
36 H5 Sulzbach Baden-Württemberg Germany
36 C5 Sulzbach Saarland Germany
37 M5 Sulzbach-Rosenberg Germany
41 L2 Sulzberg Austria
41 M2 Sulzberg Germany
146 B10 Sulzberger B Antarctica
37 L5 Sulzbürg Germany
37 K3 Sülzdorf Germany
37 J5 Sulzer Germany
117 C5 Sulzer, Mt Alaska U.S.A.
36 F5 Sulzfeld Germany
37 J4 Sulzheim Germany
37 J3 Sulzthal Germany
71 H4 Sumalata Sulawesi Indonesia
70 E1 Sumangat, Tanjung C Sabah
70 E1 Sumangat, Tanjung Sabah
100 C1 Sumas Washington U.S.A.
69 D11 Sumatera isld Indonesia
69 E13 Sumatera Barat prov Sumatra
69 F14 Sumatera Selatan prov Sumatra
69 D11 Sumatera Utara prov Sumatra
Sumatra see Sumatera
113 C7 Sumatra Florida U.S.A.
101 S3 Sumatra Montana U.S.A.
128 G5 Sumaúma Brazil
71 J9 Sumba isld Indonesia
71 J9 Sumba,Selat str Indonesia
71 H9 Sumbawa isld Indonesia
71 H9 Sumbawabesar Indonesia
88 C5 Sumbawanga Tanzania
87 B8 Sumbe Angola
70 N9 Sumbing, G mt Java
69 E13 Sumbing Gunung mt Sumatra
15 G2 Sumburgh Hd Scotland
117 G7 Sumdum Alaska U.S.A.
130 H9 Sumé Brazil
70 L9 Sumedang Java
48 D4 Sümeg Hungary
70 O9 Sumenep Indonesia
78 M1 Sumgait Azerbaijan
29 M9 Sumiainen Finland
40 G3 Sumiswald Switzerland
111 J8 Sumiton Alabama U.S.A.
55 E3 Sumki Russian Federation
55 E2 Sumkino Russian Federation
98 K10 Summerfield Kansas U.S.A.
94 F7 Summerfield Ohio U.S.A.
108 F1 Summerfield Texas U.S.A.
123 S4 Summerford Newfoundland Canada
15 C2 Summer I Scotland
99 U4 Summer I Michigan U.S.A.
100 E7 Summer L Oregon U.S.A.
117 O11 Summerland British Columbia Canada
94 B10 Summer Shade Kentucky U.S.A.
123 P4 Summerside Newfoundland Canada
122 J7 Summerside Prince Edward I Canada
110 E4 Summersville Missouri U.S.A.
94 G8 Summersville West Virginia U.S.A.
112 G4 Summerton South Carolina U.S.A.
112 E5 Summertown Georgia U.S.A.
123 T5 Summerville Newfoundland Canada
112 B3 Summerville Georgia U.S.A.
94 H5 Summerville Pennsylvania U.S.A.
112 G4 Summerville South Carolina U.S.A.
120 F5 Summit Ontario Canada
145 F4 Summit mt New Zealand
116 N5 Summit Alaska U.S.A.
101 M1 Summit Montana U.S.A.
106 B9 Summit New Mexico U.S.A.
100 B5 Summit Oregon U.S.A.
98 J4 Summit South Dakota U.S.A.
103 M4 Summit Utah U.S.A.
94 B2 Summit City Michigan U.S.A.
116 P5 Summit L Alaska U.S.A.
100 F8 Summit L Nevada U.S.A.
117 L6 Summit Lake British Columbia Canada
102 H2 Summit Mt Nevada U.S.A.
106 D4 Summit Pk Colorado U.S.A.
106 D4 Summitville Colorado U.S.A.
94 B6 Summitville Indiana U.S.A.
110 L6 Summitville Tennessee U.S.A.
144 B4 Sumner New Zealand
110 J3 Sumner Illinois U.S.A.
99 O7 Sumner Iowa U.S.A.
110 C2 Sumner Missouri U.S.A.
144 D5 Sumner, L New Zealand
117 G7 Sumner Str Alaska U.S.A.
61 N8 Sumon-dake mt Japan
48 D5 Sumony Hungary
60 H11 Sumoto Japan
70 F7 Sumpangbinangae Sulawesi
31 K6 Šumperk Czech Rep
100 G5 Sumpter Oregon U.S.A.
111 G10 Sumrall Mississippi U.S.A.
52 E3 Sumskiy Posad Russian Federation
112 G4 Sumter South Carolina U.S.A.
54 F6 Sumy Ukraine
52 H5 Suna Russian Federation
88 C4 Suna Tanzania
60 P2 Sunagawa Japan
101 R9 Sunbeam Colorado U.S.A.
101 L5 Sunbeam Idaho U.S.A.
94 C10 Sunbright Tennessee U.S.A.
101 O1 Sunburst Montana U.S.A.
139 G7 Sunbury Victoria Australia
95 L10 Sunbury North Carolina U.S.A.
94 E6 Sunbury Ohio U.S.A.
95 L6 Sunbury Pennsylvania U.S.A.
37 N6 Sünching Germany
133 E3 Suncho Corral Argentina
89 E5 Sun City S Africa
107 M4 Sun City Kansas U.S.A.
95 Q3 Suncook New Hampshire U.S.A.
98 B5 Sundance Wyoming U.S.A.
70 D2 Sundar Sarawak
75 N8 Sundarbans tidal forest India/Bangladesh
70 K9 Sunda,Selat str Sumatra
140 C3 Sunday Cr N Terr Australia
89 D9 Sunday R S Africa
142 E3 Sunday Str W Australia Australia
28 B3 Sundby Denmark
27 J12 Sundbyberg Sweden
121 L8 Sunderland Ontario Canada
13 G4 Sunderland England
32 H10 Sundern Germany
28 D7 Sundeved reg Denmark
40 F2 Sundgau reg France
70 N9 Sundoro, G mt Java
138 C2 Sundown South Australia Australia
118 E1 Sundown Manitoba Canada
108 E2 Sundown Texas U.S.A.
118 C7 Sundre Alberta Canada
27 K15 Sundre Sweden
121 L7 Sundridge Ontario Canada
28 C4 Sunds Denmark
26 J9 Sundsbruk Sweden
26 H8 Sundsjö Sweden
27 C12 Sundsli Norway
28 C3 Sundstrup Denmark
26 J9 Sundsvall Sweden
32 G10 Sundwig Germany
94 B4 Sunfield Michigan U.S.A.
111 F8 Sunflower Mississippi U.S.A.
69 E12 Sungaiapit Sumatra
70 B4 Sungai Ayak Kalimantan
69 E13 Sungaidareh Sumatra
69 F12 Sungaiguntung Sumatra
69 E13 Sungaikabung Sumatra
69 H13 Sungailiat Indonesia
69 E13 Sungailimau Sumatra
70 D5 Sungaipinang Kalimantan
69 J12 Sungaipinyuh Indonesia
69 B10 Sungairaya Sumatra
69 F13 Sungaisalak Sumatra
69 G14 Sungaiselan Indonesia
Sungari R see Songhua Jiang
69 E10 Sungei Patani Malaysia
70 F7 Sungguminasa Sulawesi
86 E3 Sungikai Sudan
67 D3 Sung-pai China
69 G14 Sungsang Sumatra
47 H2 Sungurlare Bulgaria
78 E1 Sungurlu Turkey
120 C2 Suni Ontario Canada
70 E2 Suniatan Besar, G mt Sabah
65 C5 Suning China
37 P3 Suniperk Czech Rep
42 H3 Sunja Croatia
94 B7 Sunman Indiana U.S.A.
26 C9 Sunndal R Norway
26 C9 Sunndalsöra Norway
27 F12 Sunne Sweden
27 H10 Sunnersta Sweden
27 J12 Sunnersta Sweden
27 A10 Sunnfjord Norway
27 A12 Sunnhordland reg Norway
113 F11 Sunniland Florida U.S.A.
26 B9 Sunnmöre Norway
141 K2 Sunnybank dist Brisbane, Qnsld Australia
122 K8 Sunnybrae Nova Scotia Canada
118 C5 Sunnybrook Alberta Canada
26 B9 Sunnyliven Norway
118 F7 Sunnynook Alberta Canada
123 T6 Sunnyside Newfoundland Canada
103 J3 Sunnyside Nevada U.S.A.

103 O2 **Sunnyside** Utah U.S.A.
100 E3 **Sunnyside** Washington U.S.A.
102 B4 **Sunnyvale** California U.S.A.
99 R6 **Sun Prairie** Wisconsin U.S.A.
108 C7 **Sunray** Texas U.S.A.
116 N6 **Sunrise** Alaska U.S.A.
103 O6 **Sunrise** Arizona U.S.A.
98 B7 **Sunrise** Wyoming U.S.A.
101 O2 **Sun River** Montana U.S.A.
111 D11 **Sunset** Louisiana U.S.A.
109 K2 **Sunset** Texas U.S.A.
102 R11 **Sunset Beach** Hawaiian Is
103 N6 **Sunset Crater Nat.Mon** Arizona U.S.A.
117 P8 **Sunset House** Alberta Canada
103 N6 **Sunshine** Arizona U.S.A.
101 Q5 **Sunshine** Wyoming U.S.A.
118 K1 **Sunstrum** Ontario Canada
51 L2 **Suntar** Russian Federation
32 K8 **Süntel** *hills* Germany
85 D7 **Sunyani** Ghana
37 M7 **Sünzhausen** Germany
67 B6 **Suoi Rut** Vietnam
29 M9 **Suolahti** Finland
26 N2 **Suolovuobme** Norway
29 N10 **Suomenniemi** Finland
119 O2 **Suomi** Ontario Canada
29 O7 **Suomussalmi** Finland
60 E12 **Suō-nada** *sea* Japan
29 N9 **Suonenjoki** Finland
29 M10 **Suonne** *L* Finland
29 N3 **Suorsapää** *mt* Finland
26 K4 **Suorva** Sweden
52 D4 **Suoyarvi** Russian Federation
Suozhen *see* **Huantai**
103 M5 **Supai** Arizona U.S.A.
75 M5 **Supaul** India
128 C6 **Supe** Peru
118 H7 **Superb** Saskatchewan Canada
57 D5 **Superfosfatnyy** Uzbekistan
103 N8 **Superior** Arizona U.S.A.
106 E2 **Superior** Colorado U.S.A.
101 L2 **Superior** Montana U.S.A.
98 J9 **Superior** Nebraska U.S.A.
99 O3 **Superior** Wisconsin U.S.A.
101 R8 **Superior** Wyoming U.S.A.
45 J1 **Superiore,L** Italy
99 R2 **Superior,L** U.S.A./Canada
68 E5 **Suphan Buri** Thailand
78 J2 **Süphan D** *mt* Turkey
45 O6 **Supino** Italy
100 F5 **Suplee** Oregon U.S.A.
54 C7 **Supoy** *R* Ukraine
33 N8 **Süpplingen** Germany
31 O2 **Supraśl** Poland
48 H3 **Supuru** Romania
72 G6 **Suqutrá** *isld* Indian Oc
52 G3 **Sura** Russian Federation
52 G6 **Sura** *R* Russian Federation
27 H12 **Sura** Sweden
74 B4 **Surab** Pakistan
70 O9 **Surabaja** Java
77 F7 **Sūrak** Iran
70 N9 **Surakarta** Java
84 E3 **Sūr al Jīn** *watercourse* Libya
70 F5 **Suramana** Sulawesi
40 B5 **Suran** *R* France
79 G3 **Şūrān** Syria
48 E2 **Šurany** Slovakia
141 J7 **Surat** Queensland Australia
74 E8 **Surat** India
74 E4 **Suratgarhi** India
69 D8 **Surat Thani** Thailand
31 O3 **Suraż** Poland
54 D4 **Surazh** Russian Federation
141 H6 **Surbiton** Queensland Australia
9 F5 **Surbiton** England
48 F6 **Surčin** Serbia Yugoslavia
78 K4 **Sūrdāsh** Iraq
21 L4 **Surdon** France
48 H3 **Surduc** Romania
46 E2 **Surdulica** Serbia Yugoslavia
22 L4 **Sure** *R* Luxembourg
48 H5 **Şureanu** Romania
74 D7 **Surendranagar** India
41 K4 **Surettahorn** *mt* Switzerland
102 D7 **Surf** California U.S.A.
95 N7 **Surf City** New Jersey U.S.A.
117 J9 **Surf Inlet** British Columbia Canada
112 J4 **Surfside Beach** South Carolina U.S.A.
18 E6 **Surgères** France
126 C3 **Surgidero de Batabanó** Cuba
55 F1 **Surgut** Russian Federation
50 H2 **Surgutikha** Russian Federation
76 D2 **Suriapet** India
61 N13 **Suribachi-yama** *mt* Japan
71 G6 **Surigao** Mindanao Philippines
71 G5 **Surigao Str** Philippines
68 F5 **Surin** Thailand
83 L13 **Surinam** Mauritius
129 G3 **Suriname** *rep* S America
129 G2 **Suriname** Suriname
99 S4 **Suring** Wisconsin U.S.A.
128 D2 **Suripá** *R* Venezuela
57 D5 **Surkhandar'inskaya Oblast** *prov* Uzbekistan
77 C4 **Surmāq** Iran
26 C9 **Surnadalsöra** Norway
117 G6 **Surprise** British Columbia Canada
98 J8 **Surprise** Nebraska U.S.A.
121 Q3 **Surprise,L.de la** Quebec Canada
133 F5 **Sur,Pta** Argentina
112 E6 **Surrency** Georgia U.S.A.
9 F5 **Surrey** *co* England
98 E1 **Surrey** North Dakota U.S.A.
95 L9 **Surry** Virginia U.S.A.
40 H3 **Sursee** Switzerland
84 F3 **Surt** Libya
20 G3 **Surtainville** France
28 S10 **Surtsey** *isld* Iceland
71 N9 **Surubec,Danau** *L* Timor
78 G3 **Sürüç** Turkey
61 M11 **Suruga-wan** *B* Japan
69 F14 **Surulangun** Sumatra
71 G7 **Surup** Mindanao Philippines
20 E6 **Surzur** France
28 H6 **Suså** *R* Denmark
44 B1 **Susa** Italy
60 E11 **Susa** Japan
42 G6 **Sušac** *isld* Croatia
84 G3 **Sūsah** Libya
60 G12 **Susaki** Japan
60 J12 **Susami** Japan
57 G4 **Susamyr** Kirghizia
102 D1 **Susan** *R* California U.S.A.
77 A4 **Sūsangerd** Iran
52 F5 **Susanino** Russian Federation
102 D1 **Susanville** California U.S.A.
100 G5 **Susanville** Oregon U.S.A.
78 F1 **Suşehri** Turkey
33 N4 **Süsel** Germany
37 Q5 **Sušice** Czech Rep
80 F2 **Susitha** Syria
116 M6 **Susitna** Alaska U.S.A.
116 O5 **Susitna L** Alaska U.S.A.
69 D9 **Suso** Thailand
58 G5 **Susong** China
67 E1 **Susong** China
61 M10 **Susono** Japan
95 L5 **Susquehanna** *R* Pennsylvania U.S.A.
95 M5 **Susquehanna** Pennsylvania U.S.A.
33 P10 **Süsser See** *L* Germany
122 G8 **Sussex** New Brunswick Canada
95 N5 **Sussex** New Jersey U.S.A.
101 T6 **Sussex** Wyoming U.S.A.
25 E6 **Susteren** Netherlands
45 K1 **Sustinente** Italy
117 K7 **Sustut Pk** British Columbia Canada
70 E2 **Susul** Sabah
116 K5 **Susulatna** *R* Alaska U.S.A.
51 O2 **Susuman** Russian Federation
71 A1 **Susupu** Halmahera Indonesia
47 J5 **Susurluk** Turkey
100 F10 **Sutcliffe** Nevada U.S.A.
48 L5 **Şuteşti** Romania
87 D12 **Sutherland** S Africa
99 L7 **Sutherland** Iowa U.S.A.
98 E8 **Sutherland** Nebraska U.S.A.
143 F7 **Sutherland Ra** W Australia Australia
98 E8 **Sutherland Res** Nebraska U.S.A.
144 A6 **Sutherland Sd** New Zealand
100 B6 **Sutherlin** Oregon U.S.A.
56 D5 **Sut-Khol'** Russian Federation
74 F3 **Sutlej** *R* India
74 E3 **Sutlej** *R* Pakistan
79 D2 **Sütluce** Turkey
102 D3 **Sutter Cr** California U.S.A.
9 F2 **Sutterton** England
121 L8 **Sutton** Ontario Canada
121 S7 **Sutton** Quebec Canada
9 G3 **Sutton** England
9 F5 **Sutton** England
144 C6 **Sutton** New Zealand
98 J9 **Sutton** Nebraska U.S.A.
98 H2 **Sutton** North Dakota U.S.A.
94 G8 **Sutton** West Virginia U.S.A.
121 L5 **Sutton Bay** Ontario Canada
9 E2 **Sutton Coldfield** England
9 E1 **Sutton-in-Ashfield** England
94 G8 **Sutton Res** West Virginia U.S.A.
9 E5 **Sutton Scotney** England
141 H5 **Suttor** *R* Queensland Australia
116 J8 **Sutwik I** Alaska U.S.A.
89 D9 **Suurberge** *mts* S Africa
52 C5 **Suure-Jaani** Estonia
137 Q5 **Suva** Viti Levu Fiji
46 E1 **Suva Pl** *mt* Serbia Yugoslavia
46 D2 **Suva Reka** Serbia Yugoslavia
29 N9 **Suvasvesi** *L* Finland
Suvla, C *see* **Büyük Kemikli Br.**
54 H2 **Suvorov** Russian Federation
47 J1 **Suvorovo** Bulgaria
48 M5 **Suvorovo** Ukraine
61 M9 **Suwa** Japan
61 M9 **Suwa ko** *L* Japan
70 D5 **Suwakong** Kalimantan
31 O1 **Suwałki** Poland
68 F5 **Suwannaphum** Thailand
113 D8 **Suwannee** Florida U.S.A.
119 R2 **Suwannee L** Manitoba Canada
113 E7 **Suwanoochee Cr** Georgia U.S.A.
78 H4 **Suwar** Syria
70 E4 **Suwaran, G** *mt* Kalimantan
79 G6 **Suwaydā', As** Syria
80 G2 **Suwaysah** Syria
80 F6 **Suweima** Jordan
Suweis,El *see* **Suez**
Su Xian *see* **Suzhou**
88 A9 **Suye,L** Zambia
55 D1 **Suyevatpaul** Russian Federation
57 E3 **Suzak** Kazakhstan
83 M14 **Suzanne,Pte** Kerguelen Indian Oc
52 F6 **Suzdal'** Russian Federation
19 N16 **Suze la Rousse** France
21 L6 **Suze-sur-Sarthe, la** France
58 G5 **Suzhou** China
59 H5 **Suzhou** China
40 B3 **Suzon** *R* France
121 T4 **Suzor Côté** Quebec Canada
61 L8 **Suzu** Japan
61 K11 **Suzuka** Japan
61 L8 **Suzu-misaki** *C* Japan
56 B4 **Suzun** Russian Federation
45 J2 **Suzzara** Italy
27 H10 **Svabensverk** Sweden
28 H6 **Sværdborg** Denmark
26 P1 **Svaerholtklubben** *C* Norway
26 H9 **Svågan** *R* Sweden
26 H5 **Svaipa** *mt* Sweden
147 H12 **Svalbard** *arch* Arctic Oc
28 G5 **Svallerup** Denmark
48 H2 **Svalyava** Ukraine
27 H16 **Svaneke** Denmark
28 E6 **Svanninge** Denmark
27 F12 **Svanskog** Sweden
26 N5 **Svanstein** Sweden
26 R2 **Svanvik** Norway
54 F5 **Svapa** *R* Russian Federation
26 M4 **Svappavaara** Sweden
29 K11 **Svartå** Finland
27 G12 **Svartå** Sweden
26 N5 **Svartbyn** Sweden
115 O3 **Svartenhuk Halvö** *pen* Greenland
26 G5 **Svartisen** *mt* Norway
26 M6 **Svartlå** Sweden
27 H11 **Svartnäs** Sweden
26 M6 **Svartöstaden** Sweden
54 K7 **Svatovo** Ukraine
27 D10 **Svatsum** Norway
68 G7 **Svay Rieng** Cambodia
52 G5 **Svecha** Russian Federation
27 F16 **Svedala** Sweden
26 L7 **Svedun** Sweden
26 G9 **Sveg** Sweden
26 A10 **Svelgen** Norway
27 D12 **Svelvik** Norway
52 C6 **Švenčionėliai** Lithuania
Svendborg *co see* **Fyn** *co*
28 F6 **Svendborg** Denmark
27 F14 **Svenljunga** Sweden
27 H12 **Svennevad** Sweden
26 F6 **Svenningdal** Norway
100 B3 **Svensen** Oregon U.S.A.
26 J2 **Svensgrunnen** *shoal* Norway
28 D6 **Svenstrup** Sønderjylland Denmark
Sverdlovsk *see* **Yekaterinburg**
55 D2 **Sverdlovskaya Oblast'** *prov* Russian Federation
115 K1 **Sverdrup Chan** Northwest Territories Canada
50 G1 **Sverdrup, Ostrov** *isld* Russian Federation
42 G5 **Svetac** *isld* Croatia
46 E3 **Sveti Nikola** Macedonia
59 L2 **Svetlaya** Russian Federation
53 C8 **Svetlogorsk** Belarus
31 M1 **Svetlogorsk** Russian Federation
51 J2 **Svetlogorsk** Russian Federation
31 M1 **Svetloye** Russian Federation
31 M1 **Svetlyy** Russian Federation
51 L3 **Svetlyy** Russian Federation
52 C4 **Svetogorsk** Russian Federation
46 E1 **Svetozarevo** Serbia Yugoslavia
37 P5 **Švihov** Czech Rep
48 G6 **Svilajnac** Serbia Yugoslavia
47 H3 **Svilengrad** Bulgaria
28 F6 **Svindinge** Denmark
28 G5 **Svinninge** Denmark
6 F1 **Svínoy** *isld* Faeroes
52 D4 **Svir'** *R* Russian Federation
52 D4 **Sviritsa** Russian Federation
56 F4 **Svirsk** Russian Federation
52 D4 **Svir'stroy** Russian Federation
46 G1 **Svishtov** Bulgaria
53 C7 **Svisloch'** *R* Belarus
31 J6 **Svitavy** Czech Rep
52 G6 **Sviyaga** *R* Russian Federation
59 J1 **Svobodnyy** Russian Federation
46 F2 **Svoge** Bulgaria
28 J5 **Svogerslev** Denmark
37 O4 **Svojšin** Czech Rep
26 G3 **Svolvaer** Norway
31 J6 **Svratka** *R* Czech Rep
46 E1 **Svrljig** Serbia Yugoslavia
46 E1 **Svrljiške Pl** *mt* Serbia Yugoslavia
52 F5 **Svyatogor'ye** Russian Federation
52 E1 **Svyatoy Nos, Mys** *C* Russian Federation
52 D4 **Svyatozero** Russian Federation
68 C3 **Swa** *R* Burma
9 G2 **Swaffham** England
141 K5 **Swain Reefs** Gt Barrier Reef Aust
112 E5 **Swainsboro** Georgia U.S.A.
134 B4 **Swains I** Pacific Oc
87 B10 **Swakopmund** Namibia
9 G5 **Swale,R** England
137 O4 **Swallow Is** Santa Cruz Is
70 C1 **Swallow Reef** S China Sea
106 F3 **Swallows** Colorado U.S.A.
118 D7 **Swalwell** Alberta Canada
9 E6 **Swanage** England
142 A2 **Swanbourne Beach** *dist* Perth, W Aust Australia
139 G6 **Swan Hill** Victoria Australia
118 B4 **Swan Hills** Alberta Canada
139 J8 **Swan Is** Tasmania Australia
126 C6 **Swan Is** W Indies
117 J8 **Swan, L** British Columbia Canada
98 G4 **Swan L** South Dakota U.S.A.
119 T9 **Swan Lake** Manitoba Canada
101 M2 **Swan Lake** Montana U.S.A.
112 E2 **Swannanoa** North Carolina U.S.A.
119 Q6 **Swan Plain** Saskatchewan Canada
142 E3 **Swan Pt** W Australia Australia
112 L2 **Swanquarter** North Carolina U.S.A.
143 B9 **Swan R** W Australia Australia
118 B3 **Swan R** Alberta Canada
138 E5 **Swan Reach** South Australia Australia
119 Q6 **Swan River** Manitoba Canada
99 N2 **Swan River** Minnesota U.S.A.
112 K3 **Swansboro** North Carolina U.S.A.
139 K5 **Swansea** New South Wales Australia
139 J8 **Swansea** Tasmania Australia
103 L7 **Swansea** Arizona U.S.A.
112 F4 **Swansea** South Carolina U.S.A.
8 C4 **Swansea** Wales
95 T2 **Swans I** Maine U.S.A.
118 K7 **Swanson** Saskatchewan Canada
117 J9 **Swanson Bay** British Columbia Canada
98 E9 **Swanson Res** Nebraska U.S.A.
98 J9 **Swanton** Nebraska U.S.A.
94 D5 **Swanton** Ohio U.S.A.
121 R8 **Swanton** Vermont U.S.A.
33 S4 **Swantow** Germany
139 K3 **Swan Vale** New South Wales Australia
101 O6 **Swan Valley** Idaho U.S.A.
99 M4 **Swanville** Minnesota U.S.A.
89 A10 **Swartberg** *mt* S Africa
103 L2 **Swasey Pk** Utah U.S.A.
120 K4 **Swastika** Ontario Canada
89 G6 **Swaziland** *kingdom* Africa
99 M6 **Swea City** Iowa U.S.A.
26 **Sweden** *kingdom* W Europe
95 M7 **Swedesboro** New Jersey U.S.A.
85 D7 **Swedru** Ghana
12 C2 **Sween, L** Scotland
109 M6 **Sweeny** Texas U.S.A.
140 E3 **Sweers I** Queensland Australia
100 J6 **Sweet** Idaho U.S.A.
101 O1 **Sweetgrass** Montana U.S.A.
111 D7 **Sweet Home** Arkansas U.S.A.
100 C5 **Sweet Home** Oregon U.S.A.
109 L6 **Sweet Home** Texas U.S.A.
110 C3 **Sweet Springs** Missouri U.S.A.
107 L6 **Sweetwater** Oklahoma U.S.A.
112 C2 **Sweet Water** Tennessee U.S.A.
108 G3 **Sweetwater** Texas U.S.A.
101 R7 **Sweetwater** *R* Wyoming U.S.A.
87 D12 **Swellendam** S Africa
108 G2 **Swenson** Texas U.S.A.
31 J5 **Świdnica** Poland
31 O4 **Świdnik** Poland
31 J2 **Świdwin** Poland
31 J3 **Świebodzin** Poland
31 L2 **Świecie** Poland
116 K6 **Swift** *R* Alaska U.S.A.
95 R2 **Swift** *R* Maine U.S.A.
123 S6 **Swift Current** Newfoundland Canada
118 K8 **Swiftcurrent** Saskatchewan Canada
116 L5 **Swift Fork** *R* Alaska U.S.A.
110 E6 **Swifton** Arkansas U.S.A.
100 C3 **Swift Res** Washington U.S.A.
117 H5 **Swift River** Yukon Territory Canada
100 A1 **Swiftsure Bank Lightship** British Columbia Canada
14 D1 **Swilly,L** Ireland
8 C5 **Swimbridge** England
9 E4 **Swindon** England
9 F2 **Swineshead** England
14 C3 **Swinford** Ireland
106 G3 **Swink** Colorado U.S.A.
31 H2 **Swinoujście** Poland
13 F2 **Swinton** Scotland
40 F4 **Switzerland** *rep* Europe
15 E2 **Swona** *isld* Orkney Scotland
14 E3 **Swords** Ireland
141 F5 **Swords Ra** Queensland Australia
52 D4 **Syamozero, Oz** *L* Russian Federation
52 F4 **Syamzha** Russian Federation
52 D5 **Syas'** *R* Russian Federation
52 D4 **Syas'stroy** Russian Federation
52 G5 **Syava** Russian Federation
98 A8 **Sybille Cr** Wyoming U.S.A.
14 A4 **Sybil Pt** Ireland
111 K8 **Sycamore** Alabama U.S.A.
99 S8 **Sycamore** Illinois U.S.A.
94 D6 **Sycamore** Ohio U.S.A.
112 F4 **Sycamore** South Carolina U.S.A.
52 D6 **Sychevka** Russian Federation
31 K4 **Sycow** Poland
56 D4 **Syda** *R* Russian Federation
121 O8 **Sydenham** Ontario Canada
9 G2 **Syderstone** England
139 K5 **Sydney** New South Wales Australia
123 M7 **Sydney** Nova Scotia Canada
98 B2 **Sydney** Montana U.S.A.
140 E3 **Sydney I** Queensland Australia
123 M7 **Sydney Mines** Nova Scotia Canada
115 P5 **Sydproven** Greenland
32 J7 **Syke** Germany
98 G2 **Sykeston** North Dakota U.S.A.
94 J5 **Sykesville** Pennsylvania U.S.A.
52 H4 **Syktyvkar** Russian Federation
111 K8 **Sylacauga** Alabama U.S.A.
110 D6 **Sylamore** Arkansas U.S.A.
26 F8 **Sylene** *mt* Norway
75 O6 **Sylhet** Bangladesh
28 A7 **Sylt** *isld* Germany
26 B9 **Sylte** Norway
26 S1 **Sylterfjord** *inlet* Norway
55 C3 **Sylva** Russian Federation
112 D2 **Sylva** North Carolina U.S.A.
94 J7 **Sylvan** Pennsylvania U.S.A.
107 M2 **Sylvan Grove** Kansas U.S.A.
143 D6 **Sylvania** W Australia Australia
119 N6 **Sylvania** Saskatchewan Canada
112 F5 **Sylvania** Georgia U.S.A.
94 D5 **Sylvania** Ohio U.S.A.
118 C6 **Sylvan Lake** Alberta Canada
101 P5 **Sylvan Pass** Wyoming U.S.A.
112 D6 **Sylvester** Georgia U.S.A.
140 D4 **Sylvester, L** N Terr Australia
123 R5 **Sylvester,Mt** Newfoundland Canada
107 M4 **Sylvia** Kansas U.S.A.
117 L6 **Sylvia,Mt** British Columbia Canada
56 C1 **Sym** *R* Russian Federation
15 E5 **Symington** Scotland
124 H5 **Symon** Mexico
8 D4 **Symonds Yat** England
71 F4 **Syndicate** Philippines
142 F3 **Synnot,Mt** W Australia Australia
142 F3 **Synnot Ra** W Australia Australia
56 H3 **Synnyr, Khrebet** *mts* Russian Federation
54 N2 **Syntul** Russian Federation
52 J2 **Synya** Russian Federation
55 E1 **Syn'yakha** *R* Russian Federation
Syowa *see* **Showa**
Syracuse Italy *see* **Siracusa**
94 B5 **Syracuse** Indiana U.S.A.
107 J3 **Syracuse** Kansas U.S.A.
98 K9 **Syracuse** Nebraska U.S.A.
121 O9 **Syracuse** New York U.S.A.
101 N8 **Syracuse** Utah U.S.A.
57 E4 **Syrdarinsk. Obl** Uzbekistan
57 D3 **Syrdar'ya** *R* Kazakhstan etc
57 E4 **Syrdar'ya** Uzbekistan
57 D4 **Syr Dar'ya Oblast'** *prov* Uzbekistan
79 G4 **Syria** *rep* S W Asia
68 C4 **Syriam** Burma
Syrian Desert *see* **Badiet esh Sham**
55 E1 **Syrkovoye, Oz** *L* Russian Federation
28 G2 **Syr Odde** *C* Denmark
54 L4 **Syrskiy** Russian Federation
55 D3 **Sysert'** Russian Federation
95 T1 **Sysladobsis L** Maine U.S.A.
52 H4 **Sysola** *R* Russian Federation
9 E2 **Syston** England
56 D4 **Systyg-Khem** Russian Federation
52 D6 **Syt'kovo** Russian Federation
55 F1 **Sytomino** Russian Federation
52 F4 **Syuma** *R* Russian Federation
52 H6 **Syumsi** Russian Federation
52 H6 **Syun'** *R* Russian Federation
46 F3 **Syutkya** *mt* Bulgaria
53 G7 **Syzran'** Russian Federation
48 E4 **Szabadszállás** Hungary
48 G2 **Szabolcsszatmár** *co* Hungary
31 L4 **Szadek** Poland
31 K2 **Szamocin** Poland
48 G2 **Szamosszeg** Hungary
31 K3 **Szamotuły** Poland
48 D3 **Szany** Hungary
48 F4 **Szarvas** Hungary
31 O5 **Szczebrzeszyn** Poland
31 H2 **Szczecin** Poland
31 K2 **Szczecinek** Poland
31 M5 **Szczekociny** Poland
31 L4 **Szczerców** Poland
31 N5 **Szczucin** Poland
31 N2 **Szczuczyn** Poland
31 M2 **Szczytno** Poland
Szechwan *prov see* **Sichuan** *prov*
48 F2 **Szécsény** Hungary
48 F4 **Szeged** Hungary
48 G3 **Szeghalom** Hungary
48 E3 **Székesfehérvár** Hungary
48 F2 **Szendrö** Hungary
48 E3 **Szentendre** Hungary
48 F4 **Szentes** Hungary
48 C4 **Szentgotthárd** Hungary
48 D4 **Szentlörinc** Hungary
48 G2 **Szerencs** Hungary
48 D3 **Szigetköz** *dist* Hungary
48 D4 **Szigetvár** Hungary
48 F2 **Szikszó** Hungary
31 J5 **Szklarska Poreba** Poland
31 N2 **Szkwa** *R* Poland
31 J4 **Szlichtyngowa** Poland
48 E3 **Szob** Hungary
48 F3 **Szolnok** Hungary
48 D3 **Szombathely** Hungary
31 J4 **Szprotawa** Poland
31 M2 **Szreńsk** Poland
31 L2 **Sztum** Poland
31 K2 **Szubin** Poland
31 M4 **Szydłowiec** Poland

T

79 F5 **Taalabaya** Lebanon
71 E3 **Taal,L** Luzon Philippines
48 E4 **Tab** Hungary
71 F4 **Tabaco** Philippines
128 F5 **Tabajara** Brazil
70 P10 **Tabanan** Indonesia
70 P16 **Tabanan** Bali Indonesia
70 D4 **Tabang** *R* Kalimantan
70 E4 **Tabang** Kalimantan
85 E5 **Tabankort** Mali
89 F8 **Tabankulu** S Africa
127 O2 **Tabaquite** Trinidad
137 L2 **Tabar Is** Bismarck Arch
43 B12 **Tabarka** Tunisia
77 E3 **Ţabas** Iran
77 G3 **Ţabas** Iran
124 H7 **Tabasco** Mexico
125 N8 **Tabasco** *state* Mexico
52 G6 **Tabashino** Russian Federation
123 N3 **Tabatière,La** Quebec Canada
128 E4 **Tabatinga** Brazil
68 B1 **Tabayin** Burma
71 E2 **Tabayoa, Mt** Philippines
68 G6 **Tabeng** Cambodia
118 E9 **Taber** Alberta Canada
27 G14 **Taberg** Sweden
17 F7 **Tabernas** Spain
17 G5 **Tabernes de Valldigna** Spain
16 D10 **Taberrant** Morocco
17 G9 **Tabia** Algeria
101 P9 **Tabiona** Utah U.S.A.
69 F13 **Tabir** *R* Sumatra
71 F4 **Tablas** *isld* Philippines
131 B3 **Tablas,C** Chile
71 E4 **Tablas Strait** Philippines
89 A9 **Table B** S Africa
139 H8 **Table C** Tasmania Australia
145 G3 **Table Cape** New Zealand
71 D6 **Table Hd** Philippines
144 A7 **Table Hill** New Zealand
68 A6 **Table I** Andaman Is
68 H2 **Table,I.de la** Vietnam
142 F3 **Tableland** W Australia Australia
87 C12 **Table Mt** S Africa
116 Q2 **Table Mt** Alaska U.S.A.
71 D5 **Table Pt** Philippines
83 K14 **Table Pt.de la** Réunion Indian Oc
101 R8 **Table Rock** Wyoming U.S.A.
110 C5 **Table Rock Res** Missouri U.S.A.
141 G4 **Tabletop, Mt** Queensland Australia
130 C6 **Taboco,R** Brazil
31 H6 **Tábor** Czech Rep
51 P1 **Tabor** Russian Federation
99 L9 **Tabor** Iowa U.S.A.
98 J7 **Tabor** South Dakota U.S.A.
88 D4 **Tabora** Tanzania
88 D4 **Tabora** *reg* Tanzania
112 J3 **Tabor City** North Carolina U.S.A.
80 E3 **Tabor, Mt** Israel
118 E9 **Tabor Prov. Park** Alberta Canada
55 D2 **Tabory** Russian Federation
85 C8 **Tabou** Ivory Coast
78 L2 **Tabrīz** Iran
68 G2 **Ta Bu** Vietnam
135 U9 **Tabuaeran** *atoll* Pacific Oc
79 G10 **Tabūk** Saudi Arabia
60 E12 **Tabuka** Japan
139 L3 **Tabulam** New South Wales Australia
71 H5 **Tabulan** Sulawesi
129 G5 **Tabuleiro** Brazil
55 G4 **Tabuny** Russian Federation
45 R7 **Taburno, M** *mt* Italy
122 G6 **Tabusintac R** New Brunswick Canada
69 D12 **Tabuyung** Sumatra
88 B6 **Tabwe** Zambia
27 K12 **Täby** Sweden
130 H10 **Tacaratú** Brazil
66 C2 **Tacheng** China
67 G4 **Ta-chia** Taiwan
60 C13 **Tachibana-wan** *B* Japan
61 N10 **Tachikawa** Japan
128 D2 **Táchira** *state* Venezuela
37 O4 **Tachov** Czech Rep
70 G7 **Tacipi** Sulawesi
139 L4 **Tacking Pt** New South Wales Australia
71 G5 **Tacloban** Philippines
133 C1 **Tacna** Peru
103 K9 **Tacna** Arizona U.S.A.
21 O4 **Tacoignières** France
117 M12 **Tacoma** Washington U.S.A.
133 E3 **Tacŏ Pozo** Argentina
128 E7 **Tacora** *mt* Chile
130 E7 **Tacquaritinga** Brazil
130 B10 **Tacuaras** Paraguay
131 G3 **Tacuarembó** Uruguay
131 H4 **Tacuari,R** Uruguay
130 C8 **Tacuatí** Paraguay
124 E3 **Tacupeto** Mexico
61 N8 **Tadami** *R* Japan
13 G6 **Tadcaster** England
85 F4 **Tadeinte** *watercourse* Algeria
85 E3 **Tadémaït,Pl.du** Algeria
85 B5 **Tadjakant** Mauritania
85 E3 **Tadjmout** Algeria
86 H3 **Tadjoura** Djibouti
9 E3 **Tadmarton** England
145 D4 **Tadmor** New Zealand
78 G4 **Tadmur** Syria
60 Q2 **Tadoshi** Japan
60 G11 **Tadotsu** Japan
122 C5 **Tadoussec** Quebec Canada
76 D3 **Tadpatri** India
65 F6 **Taech'ŏngdo** *isld* S Korea
65 G5 **Taedong** *R* N Korea
65 G7 **Taegu** S Korea
65 F7 **Taehŭksan** *isld* S Korea
65 G6 **Taejon** S Korea
28 J7 **Tæro** *isld* Denmark
137 S5 **Tafahi** *isld* Pacific Oc
17 F2 **Tafalla** Spain
85 F4 **Tafasaset** *watercourse* Algeria
126 A1 **Tafelberg** *mt* Curaçao Neth Antilles
16 E9 **Tafersite** Morocco
8 C4 **Taff,R** Wales
79 F8 **Tafila** Jordan
85 C7 **Tafiré** Ivory Coast
26 B9 **Tafjord** Norway
17 F9 **Tafna** *R* Algeria
106 F5 **Tafoya** New Mexico U.S.A.
85 C3 **Tafraoute** Morocco
102 E6 **Taft** California U.S.A.
107 P6 **Taft** Oklahoma U.S.A.
109 K8 **Taft** Texas U.S.A.
77 G5 **Taftan, Kūh-e-** *mt* Iran
95 P5 **Taftville** Connecticut U.S.A.
69 A9 **Tafwap** Nicobar Is
75 N5 **Taga** Bhutan
48 J4 **Ţaga** Romania
116 H4 **Tagagawik** *R* Alaska U.S.A.
61 P7 **Tagajō** Japan
53 E10 **Taganrog** Russian Federation
54 K9 **Taganrogskiy Zaliv** *G* Rus Fed/Ukraine
85 A4 **Tagarzimat** Western Sahara
71 E3 **Tagaytay City** Philippines
71 F6 **Tagbilaran** Philippines
85 D2 **Taghit** Algeria
117 F6 **Tagish L** British Columbia Canada
45 O5 **Tagliacozzo** Italy
42 E2 **Tagliamento** *R* Italy
45 M1 **Táglio di Po** Italy
22 G5 **Tagnon** France
71 F6 **Tagolo Pt** Philippines
85 C3 **Tagounite** Morocco
26 J8 **Tågsjöberg** Sweden
129 J6 **Taguatinga** Brazil
71 F5 **Tagubanhan** *isld* Philippines
61 L11 **Taguchi** Japan
71 E2 **Tagudin** Philippines
137 L4 **Tagula** *isld* Louisiade Arch
98 E1 **Tagus** North Dakota U.S.A.
144 B7 **Tahakopa** New Zealand
69 G10 **Tahan, Gunung** Malaysia
61 L11 **Tahara** Japan
85 F4 **Tahat** *mt* Algeria
145 D1 **Taheke** New Zealand
77 C6 **Tāheri** Iran
117 G6 **Tahi** *R* British Columbia Canada
135 M10 **Tahiti** *isld* Pacific Oc
110 B6 **Tahlequah** Oklahoma U.S.A.
117 H6 **Tahltan** British Columbia Canada
102 D2 **Tahoe City** California U.S.A.
114 J4 **Tahoe L** Northwest Territories Canada
102 D2 **Tahoe L** California U.S.A.
102 D3 **Tahoe Valley** California U.S.A.
108 F2 **Tahoka** Texas U.S.A.
100 A2 **Taholah** Washington U.S.A.
145 E3 **Tahora** New Zealand
145 F4 **Tahoraiti** New Zealand
85 F6 **Tahoua** Niger
99 V3 **Tahquamenon Falls** Michigan U.S.A.
59 H2 **Ta-hsing-an Ling** China
59 H2 **Ta Hsing-an-Ling Shan-mo** *ra* China
117 K11 **Tahsis** British Columbia Canada
67 F5 **Ta Hsü** *isld* Taiwan
84 J4 **Tahta** Egypt
47 L8 **Tahtali Dağ** *mt* Turkey
78 E2 **Tahtali Dağları** *mts* Turkey
117 K9 **Tahtsa** *R* British Columbia Canada
128 D6 **Tahuamanu** *R* Peru
145 E2 **Tahuna** New Zealand
85 C7 **Tai** Ivory Coast
65 E4 **Tai'an** China
65 C6 **Tai'an** China
134 D12 **Taiarapu, Presqu'ile de** *pen* Tahiti Pacific Oc
67 F2 **Taibai** China
106 F7 **Taiban** New Mexico U.S.A.
17 F6 **Taibilla,Sa de** *mts* Spain
58 G3 **Taibus Qi** China
65 C4 **Taibus Qi** China
67 G1 **Taicang** China
67 G4 **T'ai-chung** Taiwan
144 C6 **Taieri** *airport* New Zealand
Taigong *see* **Taijiang**
65 B6 **Taigu** China
65 B5 **Taihang Shan** *mt ra* China
65 B7 **Taihang Shan** *ra* China
145 E3 **Taihape** New Zealand
67 E3 **Taihe** China
61 Q12 **Taiho** Okinawa
67 E1 **Taihu** China
67 G1 **Tai Hu** *L* China
67 C3 **Taijiang** China
Taikang *see* **Dorbod**
65 C7 **Taikang** China
60 R3 **Taiki** Japan
68 B4 **Taikkyi** Burma
59 H2 **Tailai** China
69 D13 **Taileleo** Indonesia
138 E6 **Tailem Bend** South Australia Australia
36 G7 **Tailfingen** Germany
21 K4 **Taillebois** France
19 P14 **Taillefer** *mt* France
20 H5 **Taillis** France
15 D3 **Tain** Scotland
46 E8 **Taínaron, Akr** *C* Greece
67 F3 **Taining** China
19 N14 **Tain l'Hermitage** France
67 G5 **T'ain-nan** Taiwan
130 G4 **Taiobeiras** Brazil
70 G5 **Taipa** Sulawesi
29 O9 **Taipale** Finland
29 N10 **Taipalsaari** Finland
67 G4 **T'ai-pei** Taiwan
67 F1 **Taiping** China
67 B5 **Taiping** China
67 C5 **Taiping** China
69 E10 **Taiping** Malaysia
59 H3 **Taipingchuan** China
65 G3 **Taipingchuan** China
65 F4 **Taipingshao** China
130 J8 **Taipu** Brazil
61 O8 **Taira** Japan
61 Q12 **Taira** Okinawa
60 O4 **Tairadate kaikyō** Japan
145 E2 **Tairua** New Zealand
60 N3 **Taisei** Japan
60 Q2 **Taisetsuzan Nat.Park** Japan
60 F10 **Taisha** Japan
67 D5 **Taishan** China
67 F3 **Taishun** China
69 E14 **Taitaitanopo** *isld* Indonesia
133 C7 **Taitao, Pen. de** Chile
65 D4 **Taitouying** China
52 C2 **Taivalkoski** Finland
27 M11 **Taivassalo** Finland
67 G5 **Taiwan** *rep* E Asia
Taiwan Haixia *see* **Taiwan Str**
67 F4 **Taiwan Strait** China/Taiwan
67 G1 **Tai Xian** China
67 G1 **Taixing** China
46 E7 **Taïyetos** *mt* Greece
80 E3 **Taiyiba** Israel
80 D4 **Taiyiba** Israel
80 F3 **Taiyiba** *R* Jordan
65 B6 **Taiyuan** China
65 B6 **Taiyue Shan** *mt* China
Taizhou *see* **Linhai**
67 G1 **Taizhou** China
67 G2 **Taizhou Wan** *B* China
65 F4 **Taizi He** *R* China
72 E6 **Ta'izz** Yemen
86 H3 **Ta'izz** Yemen
84 E5 **Tajarhī** Libya
84 G5 **Tāj, At** Libya
69 H14 **Tajem, Gunung** *mt* Indonesia
43 B13 **Tajerouine** Tunisia
57 E5 **Tajikistan** *rep* C Asia
61 N8 **Tajima** Japan
61 L10 **Tajimi** Japan
106 D7 **Tajique** New Mexico U.S.A.
124 C2 **Tajito** Mexico
16 E4 **Tajo** *R* Spain
70 N9 **Taju** Java
17 F4 **Tajuna** *R* Spain
68 D4 **Tak** Thailand
71 K8 **Taka' Bonerate, Kepulauan** *islds* Indonesia
61 M8 **Takada** Japan
61 P7 **Takagi** Japan
61 O9 **Takahagi** Japan
61 J10 **Takahama** Japan
60 G11 **Takahashi** Japan
61 O8 **Takahata** Japan
60 E13 **Takajō** Japan
145 D4 **Takaka** New Zealand
46 E7 **Táka, L** Greece
83 K12 **Takamaka** Mahé I Indian Oc
60 H11 **Takamatsu** Japan
60 E13 **Takamori** Japan
61 O5 **Takanosu** Japan
61 K9 **Takaoka** Japan
145 F4 **Takapau** New Zealand
145 F1 **Takapuna** New Zealand
70 F7 **Taka Rewataya** *reef* Indonesia
60 H11 **Takasago** Japan
59 L4 **Takasaki** Japan
60 C12 **Taka shima** *isld* Saga Japan
60 E11 **Taka shima** *isld* Shimane Japan
89 B4 **Takatshwaane** Botswana
61 J11 **Takatsuki** Japan
145 E2 **Takatu Pt.** New Zealand
88 G3 **Takaungu** Kenya
68 D2 **Ta-Kaw** Burma
60 D12 **Takawa** Japan
61 L9 **Takayama** Japan
60 D14 **Takazaki** Japan
60 E14 **Takazaki** Japan
69 F9 **Tak Bai** Thailand
60 E13 **Takeda** Japan
61 K10 **Takefu** Japan
60 F11 **Takehara** Japan
9 G4 **Takeley** England
69 C10 **Takengon** Sumatra
68 G7 **Takeo** Cambodia
60 D12 **Takeo** Japan
60 C11 **Takeshiki** Japan
Take-shima *see* **Tok-to**
77 A1 **Takestān** Iran
60 E12 **Taketazu** Japan
71 C3 **Takeum** W Irian
78 K7 **Takhadid** Iraq
77 L1 **Takhār** *prov* Afghanistan
57 A4 **Takhiatash** Uzbekistan
117 F5 **Takhini** *R* Yukon Territory Canada
57 A4 **Takhta** Turkmenistan
57 C6 **Takhta-Bazar** Turkmenistan
55 E4 **Takhtabrod** Kazakhstan
57 B3 **Takhtakupyr** Uzbekistan
77 C5 **Takht-e Jamshīd** Iran
114 H4 **Takijug L** Northwest Territories Canada
60 Q2 **Takikawa** Japan
100 B7 **Takilma** Oregon U.S.A.
60 R1 **Takinoue** Japan
119 R3 **Takipy** Manitoba Canada
70 D6 **Takisung** Kalimantan
144 A6 **Takitimu Mts** New Zealand
117 L8 **Takla Landing** British Columbia Canada
66 B4 **Taklimakan Shamo** *reg* China
57 E5 **Takob** Tajikistan
85 D8 **Takoradi** Ghana
116 J5 **Takotna** Alaska U.S.A.
145 D1 **Takou B** New Zealand
116 F6 **Takslesluk L** Alaska U.S.A.
117 G6 **Taku** British Columbia Canada
60 D12 **Taku** Japan
69 D8 **Takua Pa** Thailand
117 F5 **Taku Arm** *L* Br Col/Yukon Terr Canada
69 D8 **Takua Thung** Thailand
117 F6 **Taku Glacier** Br Col/Alaska Canada/U.S.A.
85 F7 **Takum** Nigeria
74 E2 **Talagang** Pakistan
133 D6 **Talagapa** Argentina
68 H7 **Ta Lai** Vietnam
83 J8 **Talaimannar** Sri Lanka
85 F5 **Talak** *reg* Niger
107 P5 **Talala** Oklahoma U.S.A.
16 E10 **Talamagait** Morocco
69 F14 **Talang** Sumatra
70 K8 **Talangbatu** Sumatra
69 G14 **Talangbetutu** Sumatra
69 F14 **Talanglambangantir** Sumatra
69 G14 **Talangpulaukabung** Sumatra
128 B4 **Talara** Peru
77 H7 **Talar-i-Band** *mts* Pakistan
57 F3 **Talas** Kirghizia
136 L3 **Talasea** New Britain
57 F4 **Talasskiy Alatau, Khr** *mts* Kazakhstan/Uzbekistan etc
70 G5 **Talatakoh** *isld* Sulawesi
79 G4 **Ţal at Mūsá** *mt* Lebanon
16 D5 **Talavera de la Reina** Spain
130 C10 **Talavera,I** Paraguay
140 F4 **Talawanta** Queensland Australia
71 G7 **Talayan** Philippines
65 G3 **Talazhan** China
79 G4 **Talbīsah** Syria
142 F2 **Talbot, C** W Australia Australia
113 F7 **Talbot I** Florida U.S.A.
115 M2 **Talbot Inlet** Northwest Territories Canada
119 S4 **Talbot L** Manitoba Canada
143 F7 **Talbot, Mt** W Australia Australia
139 J4 **Talbragar** New South Wales Australia
131 B5 **Talca** *prov* Chile
131 B5 **Talca** Chile
131 A6 **Talcahuano** Chile
131 B4 **Talca,Pta** Chile
109 M2 **Talco** Texas U.S.A.
94 G9 **Talcott** West Virginia U.S.A.
52 E6 **Taldom** Russian Federation
141 F4 **Taldora** Queensland Australia
57 A3 **Taldyk** Uzbekistan
57 J3 **Taldy-Kurgan** Kazakhstan
77 B4 **Tal-e Khosravī** Iran
100 C7 **Talent** Oregon U.S.A.
8 C2 **Talerddig** Wales
8 C4 **Talgarth** Wales
76 B3 **Talguppa** India
138 C5 **Talia** South Australia Australia
71 G5 **Talibon** Bohol Philippines
110 A7 **Talihina** Oklahoma U.S.A.
76 C2 **Talikota** India
71 G7 **Talikua** *isld* Mindanao Philippines
86 F4 **Tali Post** Sudan
71 F5 **Talisay** Cebu Philippines
70 F4 **Talisayan** Kalimantan
71 G6 **Talisayan** Philippines
71 J4 **Talisei** *isld* Indonesia
55 D1 **Talitsa** Sverdlovskaya obl Russian Federation
55 D3 **Talitsa** Sverdlovskaya obl Russian Federation
54 M4 **Talitskiy Chamlyk** Russian Federation
33 N5 **Talkau** Germany
116 N5 **Talkeetna Mts** Alaska U.S.A.
79 B7 **Talkha** Egypt
29 N3 **Talkkunapää** *mt* Finland
77 B3 **Talkuncheh** Iran
45 L4 **Talla** Italy
84 G5 **Ţallāb, Aţ** Libya
111 K8 **Talladega** Alabama U.S.A.
111 G10 **Tallahala** *R* Mississippi U.S.A.
111 M11 **Tallahassee** Florida U.S.A.
111 F7 **Tallahatchie** *R* Mississippi U.S.A.
139 H6 **Tallangatta** Victoria Australia
111 K9 **Tallapoosa** *R* Alabama U.S.A.
111 L8 **Tallapoosa** Georgia U.S.A.
19 Q16 **Tallard** France
26 H10 **Tallåsen** Sweden
80 G1 **Tall ash Sha'ar** *mt* Syria
111 L9 **Tallassee** Alabama U.S.A.
143 B8 **Tallering Pk** W Australia Australia
8 C4 **Talley** Wales
78 H4 **Tall Fadghāmī** Syria
52 B5 **Tallinn** Estonia
26 M5 **Talljäry** Sweden
79 G4 **Tall Kalakh** Syria
40 D6 **Talloires** France
14 C4 **Tallow** Ireland
119 P6 **Tall Pines** Saskatchewan Canada
80 G3 **Tall Shihāb** Syria
110 G2 **Tallula** Illinois U.S.A.
111 E9 **Tallulah** Louisiana U.S.A.
119 O9 **Talmage** Saskatchewan Canada
102 A2 **Talmage** California U.S.A.
107 N2 **Talmage** Kansas U.S.A.
99 L9 **Talmage** Nebraska U.S.A.
40 B3 **Talmay** France
56 B4 **Tal'menka** Russian Federation
80 B7 **Talmey Yafe** Israel
18 D6 **Talmont** France
48 N2 **Tal'noye** Ukraine
74 F8 **Taloda** India
86 F3 **Talodi** Sudan
107 M5 **Taloga** Oklahoma U.S.A.
70 F4 **Talok** Kalimantan
68 D2 **Ta-Long** Burma
77 L1 **Tāloqān** Afghanistan
106 E5 **Talpa** New Mexico U.S.A.
108 H4 **Talpa** Texas U.S.A.
124 G7 **Talpa de Allende** Mexico
127 O2 **Talparo R** Trinidad
111 M11 **Talquin,L** Florida U.S.A.
80 C6 **Tal Shahar** Israel
52 B6 **Talsi** Latvia
26 L7 **Tålsmark** Sweden
133 C3 **Taltal** Chile
69 D12 **Talu** Sumatra
71 H4 **Taludaä** Sulawesi
70 G4 **Taluditi** Sulawesi
71 E8 **Talue** *isld* Philippines
68 G3 **Ta Lus,C** Vietnam
41 O4 **Talvera** *R* Italy
26 N1 **Talvik** Norway
141 J8 **Talwood** Queensland Australia
56 F5 **Tal'yany** Russian Federation
139 G4 **Talyawalka** *R* New South Wales Australia
8 C3 **Talybont** Wales
8 C1 **Tal-y-cafn** Wales
52 J3 **Talyy** Russian Federation
61 M9 **Tama** Japan
61 N10 **Tama** *R* Japan
99 O8 **Tama** Iowa U.S.A.
70 D3 **Tamabo Ra** Sarawak
68 B1 **Tamadaw** Burma
143 A7 **Tamala** W Australia Australia
85 D7 **Tamale** Ghana
16 C4 **Tamames** Spain
60 D13 **Tamana** Japan
130 J10 **Tamandare** Brazil
140 B4 **Tamani Desert** N Terr Australia
60 G11 **Tamano** Japan
85 F4 **Tamanrasset** Algeria
70 G5 **Tamanusi** Sulawesi
95 M6 **Tamaqua** Pennsylvania U.S.A.
45 L2 **Tamara** Italy
100 J5 **Tamarack** Idaho U.S.A.
99 N3 **Tamarack** Minnesota U.S.A.
60 E13 **Tamarai** Japan
17 H3 **Tamarite de Litera** Spain
110 G3 **Tamaroa** Illinois U.S.A.
41 J5 **Tamaro,Mt** Switzerland
139 H8 **Tamar R** Tasmania Australia
8 B6 **Tamar,R** England
60 G11 **Tamashima** Japan
48 E4 **Tamási** Hungary
Tamatave *see* **Toamasina**
61 O9 **Tamatsukuri** Japan
128 D5 **Tamaya** *R* Peru
85 A4 **Tamayya** Western Sahara
124 F5 **Tamazula** Mexico
124 H8 **Tamazula de Gordiano** Mexico
125 K7 **Tamazunchale** Mexico
37 K2 **Tambach Dietharz** Germany
85 B6 **Tambacounda** Senegal

71 K8 **Tambalongang** *isld* Indonesia
70 B5 **Tambangmunjul** Kalimantan
69 F14 **Tambangsawah** Sumatra
88 E10 **Tambara** Mozambique
130 J9 **També** Brazil
70 G7 **Tambea** Sulawesi
69 H12 **Tambelan Besar** *isld* Indonesia
69 H12 **Tambelan, Kepulauan** *islds* Indonesia
143 C10 **Tambellup** W Australia Australia
87 E9 **Tambero** Zambia
70 O9 **Tamberu** Java
131 B2 **Tambillos,Nevado de los** *pk* Chile
141 H6 **Tambo** Queensland Australia
128 D7 **Tambo** *R* Peru
128 C6 **Tambo de Mora** Peru
71 G6 **Tambog Pt** Mindanao Philippines
70 G6 **Tamboli** Sulawesi
124 G5 **Tambor** Mexico
139 H6 **Tamboritha,Mt** Victoria Australia
53 F7 **Tambov** Russian Federation
16 B2 **Tambre,R** Spain
142 C5 **Tambrey** W Australia Australia
70 F5 **Tambulan** Sulawesi
70 E2 **Tambunan** Sabah
86 E4 **Tambura** Sudan
70 F4 **Tambu, Tk** *B* Sulawesi
83 K9 **Tambutta** Sri Lanka
70 E1 **Tambuyukon, G** *mt* Sabah
85 B5 **Tamchakett** Mauritania
55 C6 **Tamdy** Kazakhstan
57 C4 **Tamdybulak** Uzbekistan
57 C4 **Tamdytau, Gory** *mt* Uzbekistan
128 D2 **Tame** Colombia
16 B3 **Tâmega** *R* Portugal
133 C7 **Tamel Aike** Argentina
Tamenghest *see* **Tamanrasset**
85 F5 **Tamgak, Mts** Niger
57 E2 **Tamgaly, Ozero** *L* Kazakhstan
125 L7 **Tamiahua,L.de** Mexico
113 F12 **Tamiami Canal** Florida U.S.A.
69 C10 **Tamiang** *R* Sumatra
76 C5 **Tamil Nadu** *prov* India
78 J4 **Ta'mīm, At** *prov* Iraq
41 K4 **Tamina** *R* Switzerland
70 D6 **Taminglayang** Kalimantan
84 G3 **Tamīnī,At** Libya
41 K4 **Tamins** Switzerland
58 D2 **Tamirin Gol** *R* Mongolia
48 F5 **Tamis** *R* Serbia Yugoslavia
52 E3 **Tamitsa** Russian Federation
57 C1 **Tamkamys** Kazakhstan
68 J5 **Tam Ky** Vietnam
71 F5 **Tamlang** Negros Philippines
45 R7 **Tammaro** *R* Italy
Tammerfors *see* **Tampere**
110 G4 **Tamms** Illinois U.S.A.
113 E10 **Tampa** Florida U.S.A.
107 N3 **Tampa** Kansas U.S.A.
70 K8 **Tampang** Sumatra
29 K10 **Tampere** Finland
125 L6 **Tampico** Mexico
99 R8 **Tampico** Illinois U.S.A.
101 T1 **Tampico** Montana U.S.A.
69 F11 **Tampin** Malaysia
69 C13 **Tampines** *dist* Singapore
69 C10 **Tamporbur** Sumatra
68 J5 **Tam Quan** Vietnam
80 D2 **Tamra** Israel
58 G2 **Tamsagbulag** Mongolia
75 Q6 **Tamu** Burma
71 E7 **Tamuk** *isld* Philippines
139 K4 **Tamworth** New South Wales Australia
121 O8 **Tamworth** Ontario Canada
9 E2 **Tamworth** England
95 Q3 **Tamworth** New Hampshire U.S.A.
68 F6 **Tamyong** *R* Cambodia
57 H1 **Tan** Kazakhstan
116 Q6 **Tana** *R* Alaska U.S.A.
60 J12 **Tanabe** Japan
130 E7 **Tanabi** Brazil
26 Q1 **Tana-Bru** Norway
116 Q5 **Tanacross** Alaska U.S.A.
116 Q5 **Tanada L** Alaska U.S.A.
26 Q1 **Tanafjord** *inlet* Norway
43 G8 **Tanagro** *R* Italy
61 O8 **Tanagura** Japan
86 G3 **Tana Hāyk'** *L* Ethiopia
69 D13 **Tanahbala** *isld* Indonesia
71 K8 **Tanahdjampea** *isld* Indonesia
70 E5 **Tanahgrogot** Kalimantan
71 K10 **Tanahkadukung** Indonesia
68 D13 **Tanahmasa** *isld* Indonesia
70 E3 **Tanahmerah** Kalimantan
69 F9 **Tanah Merah** Malaysia
26 R1 **Tanahorn** *mt* Norway
69 E12 **Tanahputih** Sumatra
70 M9 **Tanah,Tg** *C* Java
70 F7 **Tanakeke** *isld* Sulawesi
70 F6 **Tanambung** Sulawesi
136 J3 **Tanamerah** W Irian
140 A4 **Tanami** N Terr Australia
71 J4 **Tanamon** Sulawesi
68 H7 **Tan An** Vietnam
116 L4 **Tanana** Alaska U.S.A.
116 N4 **Tanana** *R* Alaska U.S.A.
Tananarive *see* **Antananarivo**
18 H8 **Tanargue, Mt** France
44 E2 **Tanaro** *R* Italy
84 E4 **Tanārūt** Libya
71 G5 **Tanauan** Leyte Philippines
141 F7 **Tanbar** Queensland Australia
21 L3 **Tancarville** France
61 P13 **Tancha** Okinawa
65 D7 **Tancheng** China
59 J3 **Tanch'ŏn** N Korea
124 H8 **Tancitario,Cerro de** *mt* Mexico
125 K7 **Tancuayalab** Mexico
75 K5 **Tanda** India
71 G6 **Tandag** Mindanao Philippines
48 L6 **Ţăndărei** Romania
70 E1 **Tandek** Sabah
28 D6 **Tanderup** Denmark
131 F6 **Tandil** Argentina
131 F6 **Tandil, Sa del** *ra* Argentina
70 F3 **Tandjungbatu** Kalimantan
69 J11 **Tandjung Blitung** Indonesia
70 L9 **Tandjungpriok** Java
70 C5 **Tandjungpusu** Kalimantan
74 C6 **Tando Adam** Pakistan
74 C6 **Tando Muhammad Khan** Pakistan
138 F4 **Tandou L** New South Wales Australia
55 G3 **Tandovo, Oz** *L* Russian Federation
14 E2 **Tandragee** N Ireland
27 G10 **Tandsjöborg** Sweden
28 D7 **Tandslet** Denmark
71 E8 **Tandubatu** *isld* Philippines
76 C2 **Tandur** India
145 F3 **Taneatua** New Zealand
59 K5 **Tanega-shima** *isld* Japan
61 P5 **Taneichi** Japan
Tanen *mt see* **Taunggyi** *mt*
71 A3 **Taneti** Halmahera Indonesia
31 O5 **Tanew** *R* Poland
95 K7 **Taneytown** Maryland U.S.A.
85 E4 **Tanezrouft** *reg* Algeria
84 E4 **Tanezzuft** *watercourse* Libya/Algeria
88 G4 **Tanga** Tanzania
75 N6 **Tangail** Bangladesh
137 L2 **Tanga Is** Bismarck Arch
83 K11 **Tangalla** Sri Lanka
Tanganyika *see* **Tanzania**
88 B5 **Tanganyika,L** E Africa
130 D10 **Tangará** Brazil
67 D3 **Tangdukou** China
28 D4 **Tange Å** *R* Denmark
146 K9 **Tange Promontory** *pen* Antarctica
16 D9 **Tanger** Morocco
70 L9 **Tangerang** Java
33 P8 **Tangerhütte** Germany
33 P7 **Tangermünde** Germany
28 D4 **Tange Sø** *L* Denmark
58 G4 **Tanggu** China
66 D5 **Tanggula Shan** *ra* China
66 E5 **Tanggula Shankou** *pass* China
58 F5 **Tang He** China
65 C5 **Tang He** *R* China
122 K9 **Tangier** Nova Scotia Canada
122 K9 **Tangier Grand L** Nova Scotia Canada
95 M9 **Tangier I** Virginia U.S.A.
145 E4 **Tangimoana** New Zealand
111 F11 **Tangipahoa** *R* Louisiana U.S.A.
70 G6 **Tangkeleboke, G** *mt* Sulawesi
70 K8 **Tangkittebak, Gunung** *mt* Sumatra
70 L9 **Tangkuban Perahu** *mt* Java
66 D5 **Tang-ku-la-yu-mu Ts'o** *L* China
109 L5 **Tanglewood** Texas U.S.A.
Tanglha Range *see* **Tanggula Shan**
66 F5 **Tangmai** China
141 G5 **Tangorin** Queensland Australia
145 D1 **Tangowahine** New Zealand
67 C6 **Tangpeng** China
66 D5 **Tangra Yumco** *L* China
69 B10 **Tangse** Sumatra
65 D5 **Tangshan** China
67 A3 **Tangtang** China
67 C3 **Tangtou** China
67 E5 **Tangtouxia** China
71 F5 **Tangub** Negros Philippines
85 E6 **Tanguiéta** Benin
56 F3 **Tanguy** Russian Federation
59 J2 **Tangwanghe** China
67 F2 **Tangxi** China
65 C5 **Tang Xian** China
67 D1 **Tangxianzhen** China
68 D1 **Tang-Yan** Burma
67 C2 **Tangyan He** *R* China
58 F4 **Tangyin** China
65 C7 **Tangyin** China
65 H1 **Tangyuan** China
29 N4 **Tanhua** Finland
68 G7 **Tani** Cambodia
61 K10 **Tanigumi** Japan
136 G3 **Tanimbar, Kep** *islds* Moluccas Indonesia
40 E5 **Taninges** France
Tanintharyi *see* **Tenasserim**
60 D14 **Taniyama** Japan
71 F6 **Tanjay** Philippines
70 D6 **Tanjung** Kalimantan
69 G13 **Tanjung** Sumatra
69 F12 **Tanjungbalai** Kepulauan Riau Indonesia
69 D11 **Tanjungbalai** Sumatra
69 F12 **Tanjungbatu** Indonesia
69 F13 **Tanjungbojo** Sumatra
70 F4 **Tanjungbuaya** *isld* Kalimantan
70 K7 **Tanjungenim** Sumatra
70 E6 **Tanjunggaru** Kalimantan
70 K8 **Tanjungkarang Telukbetung** Sumatra
69 H14 **Tanjung-pandan** Indonesia
69 G12 **Tanjungpinang** Indonesia
69 D11 **Tanjungpura** Sumatra
69 G14 **Tanjungraja** Sumatra
70 E3 **Tanjungredeb** Kalimantan
69 J13 **Tanjungsaleh** *isld* Indonesia
69 J13 **Tanjungsatai** Indonesia
70 E3 **Tanjungselor** Kalimantan
74 D2 **Tank** Pakistan
138 E3 **Tankamarinna,L** South Australia Australia
29 N3 **Tankapirtti** Finland
108 G4 **Tankersly** Texas U.S.A.
56 G5 **Tankhoy** Russian Federation
68 B3 **Tanlwe** *R* Burma
68 J7 **Tan My** Vietnam
37 O7 **Tann** Bayern Germany
37 J2 **Tann** Hessen Germany
37 M3 **Tanna** Germany
137 O5 **Tanna** *isld* Vanuatu
15 F4 **Tannadice** Scotland
22 H4 **Tannay** France
33 N9 **Tanne** Germany
95 N4 **Tannersville** New York U.S.A.
95 M5 **Tannersville** Pennsylvania U.S.A.
37 N4 **Tännesberg** Germany
37 J6 **Tannhausen** Germany
41 M1 **Tannheim** Germany
29 M6 **Tannila** Finland
119 N1 **Tannin** Ontario Canada
80 C3 **Tanninim** Israel
28 E1 **Tannis Bugt** *B* Denmark
28 E1 **Tannisby** Denmark
37 L2 **Tannroda** Germany
85 D7 **Tano** *R* Ghana
71 F5 **Tañon Str** Philippines
85 F6 **Tanout** Niger
68 G1 **Tan Quang** Vietnam
124 H4 **Tanque Alvarez** Mexico
125 K7 **Tanquian** Mexico
79 F2 **Tanrıverdı** Turkey
75 K5 **Tansing** Nepal
79 A8 **Tanta** Egypt
68 B1 **Tantabin** Sagaing Burma
68 C3 **Tantabin** Tenasserim Burma
119 Q8 **Tantallon** Saskatchewan Canada
85 B3 **Tan-Tan** Morocco
138 F6 **Tantanoola** South Australia Australia
Tantung *see* **Dandong**
140 C3 **Tanumbirini** N Terr Australia
116 E6 **Tanunak** Alaska U.S.A.
138 E5 **Tanunda** South Australia Australia
55 C3 **Tanyp** *R* Russian Federation
88 C4 **Tanzania** *rep* Africa
117 H6 **Tanzilla** *R* British Columbia Canada
65 E2 **Tao'an** China
67 G2 **Taohua Dao** *isld* China
Taohuaping *see* **Longhui**
67 D2 **Taojiang** China
68 D7 **Tao,Ko** *isld* Thailand
65 D7 **Taoluo** China
Taonan *see* **Tao'an**
99 O6 **Taopi** Minnesota U.S.A.
43 G11 **Taormina** Sicily
106 E5 **Taos** New Mexico U.S.A.
85 D4 **Taoudenni** Mali
85 D2 **Taounate** Morocco
85 D2 **Taourirt** Morocco
85 D2 **Taouz** Morocco
67 D2 **Taoyuan** China
55 E3 **Tap** *R* Russian Federation
52 C5 **Tapa** Estonia
71 E8 **Tapaan Passage** Philippines
125 N10 **Tapachula** Mexico
69 E10 **Tapah** Malaysia
129 G5 **Tapajós** *R* Brazil
69 C11 **Tapaktuan** Sumatra
133 E5 **Tapalquén** Argentina
69 E14 **Tapan** Sumatra
129 G3 **Tapanahoni** *R* Suriname
125 M9 **Tapanatapec** Mexico
144 B6 **Tapanui** New Zealand
69 D12 **Tapanuli, Teluk** *B* Sumatra
128 F5 **Tapauá** Brazil
145 D4 **Tapawera** New Zealand
130 H9 **Taperoá** Brazil
131 H3 **Tapes, Pta. de** *C* Brazil
37 K6 **Tapfheim** Germany
74 F8 **Tāpi** *R* India
71 F7 **Tapiantana** *isld* Philippines
128 D5 **Tapiche** *R* Peru
70 B5 **Tapinbini** Kalimantan
29 L11 **Tapiola** Finland
128 E3 **Tapirapeó, Sa** *mts* Venezuela/Brazil
130 B4 **Tapirapuã** Brazil
69 F10 **Tapis** *mt* Malaysia
124 E4 **Tapizuelas** Mexico
75 M5 **Taplejung** Nepal
48 D4 **Tapolca** Hungary
68 D2 **Ta-Pom** Burma
95 L9 **Tappahannock** Virginia U.S.A.
70 F6 **Tappalang** Sulawesi
94 F6 **Tappan Res** Ohio U.S.A.
98 G3 **Tappen** North Dakota U.S.A.
28 J6 **Tappernøje** Denmark
60 O4 **Tappi zaki** *C* Japan
60 P1 **Tappu** Japan
28 C6 **Taps** Denmark
55 D1 **Tapsuy** *R* Russian Federation
145 E2 **Tapu** New Zealand
145 D4 **Tapuaenuku** *mt* New Zealand
71 E8 **Tapul** Philippines
69 D12 **Tapulonanjing** *mt* Sumatra
68 B3 **Tapun** Burma
128 F4 **Tapurucuara** Brazil
133 G3 **Taquara** Brazil
130 D7 **Taquaraçu** *R* Brazil
130 D4 **Taquara,Sa.da** *mts* Brazil
131 H2 **Taquari** *R* Brazil
130 C6 **Taquari,Pantanal do** *swamp* Brazil
112 K2 **Tar** *R* North Carolina U.S.A.
141 K7 **Tara** Queensland Australia
120 J8 **Tara** Ontario Canada
71 E4 **Tara** *isld* Philippines
55 F3 **Tara** Russian Federation
55 G3 **Tara** *R* Russian Federation
48 E7 **Tara** *mt* Serbia Yugoslavia
85 G7 **Taraba** *R* Nigeria
84 E3 **Tarābulus** Libya
128 E3 **Taracua** Brazil
145 F3 **Taradale** New Zealand
84 E4 **Tarāghin** Libya
60 D13 **Taragi** Japan
139 J6 **Tarago** New South Wales Australia
14 E3 **Tara Hill** Ireland
26 L5 **Tårajaure** Sweden
70 E3 **Tarakan** Kalimantan
77 K3 **Tarakki** *reg* Afghanistan
47 L4 **Taraklı** Turkey
48 M4 **Tarakliya** Moldova
145 D4 **Tarakohe** New Zealand
139 J5 **Taralga** New South Wales Australia
144 C5 **Taramakau R** New Zealand
71 M9 **Taramana** Indonesia
139 J5 **Tarana** New South Wales Australia
145 E3 **Taranaki** *admin region* New Zealand
145 E3 **Taranaki, Mt** New Zealand
16 E4 **Tarancón** Spain
145 E1 **Taranga I** New Zealand
76 D5 **Tarangambadi** India
55 D4 **Taranovskoye** Kazakhstan
15 A3 **Taransay** *isld* Scotland
43 H8 **Taranto** Italy
43 H8 **Taranto,G.di** Italy
128 E7 **Tarapacá** *prov* Chile
145 F3 **Taraponui** *mt* New Zealand
128 C5 **Tarapoto** Peru
18 H7 **Tarare** France
145 E4 **Tararua Range** New Zealand
69 A8 **Tarāsa Dwīp** Nicobar Is
19 N17 **Tarascon** France
48 N1 **Tarashcha** Ukraine
41 M4 **Tarasp** Switzerland
85 F3 **Tarat** Algeria
128 D5 **Tarauacá** Brazil
17 F4 **Taravilla** Spain
134 J8 **Tarawa** *atoll* Kiribati
145 F3 **Tarawera L** New Zealand
145 F3 **Tarawera, Mt** New Zealand
17 F3 **Tarazona** Spain
17 F5 **Tarazona de la Mancha** Spain
29 K5 **Tårbæk** Denmark
57 K2 **Tarbagatay, Khrebet** *mts* Kazakhstan
14 B4 **Tarbert** Ireland
15 B3 **Tarbert** Harris Scotland
12 C2 **Tarbert** Strathclyde Scotland
12 B2 **Tarbert,L** Scotland
18 F9 **Tarbes** France
12 D3 **Tarbolton** Scotland
112 K2 **Tarboro** North Carolina U.S.A.
141 F5 **Tarbrax** Queensland Australia
48 K4 **Tarcăului,Munţii** *mts* Romania
138 C4 **Tarcoola** South Australia Australia
139 H4 **Tarcoon** New South Wales Australia
138 C2 **Tarcoonyinna** *R* South Australia Australia
139 J6 **Tarcutta** New South Wales Australia
18 E9 **Tardets-Sorholus** France
17 G3 **Tardienta** Spain
21 J8 **Tardière,la** France
18 F7 **Tardoire** *R* France
59 L2 **Tardoki-Yami, Gora** *mt* Russian Federation
143 B8 **Tardun** W Australia Australia
139 L4 **Taree** New South Wales Australia
139 G4 **Tarella** New South Wales Australia
26 N4 **Tärendö** Sweden
40 E7 **Tarentaise** *dist* France
94 H6 **Tarentum** Pennsylvania U.S.A.
85 B3 **Tarfaya** Morocco
65 F1 **Targan** China
16 E10 **Targuist** Morocco
112 J3 **Tarheel** North Carolina U.S.A.
84 E3 **Tarhūnah** Libya
65 A4 **Tarian Gol** China
16 D8 **Tarifa** Spain
71 F2 **Tarigtig Pt** Philippines
133 E2 **Tarija** *prov* Bolivia
133 E2 **Tarija** Bolivia
76 B4 **Tarikere** India
145 E3 **Tariki** New Zealand
72 F5 **Tarīm** Yemen
Tarim Basin *see* **Tarim Pendi**
88 F6 **Tarime** Tanzania
66 D3 **Tarim He** *R* China
66 C3 **Tarim Pendi** *basin* China
77 J3 **Tarīn Kowt** Afghanistan
Tari Nor *see* **Dalai Nur** *L*
89 D9 **Tarka** *R* S Africa
87 E12 **Tarkastad** S Africa
110 A1 **Tarkio** Missouri U.S.A.
101 L2 **Tarkio** Montana U.S.A.
50 G2 **Tarko-Sale** Russian Federation
85 D7 **Tarkwa** Ghana
133 C7 **Tar,L** Argentina
71 E3 **Tarlac** Philippines
15 F3 **Tarland** Scotland
13 F6 **Tarleton** England
140 D5 **Tarlton Downs** N Terr Australia
28 B5 **Tarm** Denmark
128 C6 **Tarma** Peru
32 K6 **Tarmstedt** Germany
18 F9 **Tarn** *R* France
18 G9 **Tarn** *dept* France
48 F3 **Tarna** *R* Hungary
26 H6 **Tärnaby** Sweden
77 K3 **Tarnak** *R* Afghanistan
18 F8 **Tarn-et-Garonne** *dept* France
18 H8 **Tarn,Gorges du** France
31 N5 **Tarnobrzeg** Poland
52 F4 **Tarnogskiy Gorodok** Russian Federation
119 M6 **Tarnopo** Saskatchewan Canada
33 Q5 **Tarnow** Germany
31 M5 **Tarnow** Poland
31 L5 **Tarnowskie Gory** Poland
27 J11 **Tärnsjö** Sweden
44 H2 **Taro** *R* Italy
54 F8 **Taromskoye** Ukraine
141 J7 **Taroom** Queensland Australia
85 C2 **Taroudannt** Morocco
28 C7 **Tarp** Germany
140 D4 **Tarpaulin Swamp** N Terr Australia
109 H6 **Tarpley** Texas U.S.A.
113 E9 **Tarpon Springs** Florida U.S.A.
8 D1 **Tarporley** England
113 L12 **Tarpum Bay** Eleuthera Bahamas
44 L5 **Tarquinia** Italy
80 D7 **Tarqumiya** Jordan
17 H3 **Tarragona** *prov* Spain
17 H3 **Tarragona** Spain
139 H8 **Tarraleah** Tasmania Australia
139 H4 **Tarran Hills** New South Wales Australia
111 K8 **Tarrant City** Alabama U.S.A.
8 D6 **Tarrant Hinton** England
140 E3 **Tarrant,Pt** Queensland Australia
144 B6 **Tarras** New Zealand
17 J3 **Tarrasa** Spain
26 J4 **Tarrekaise** *mt* Sweden
41 N3 **Tarrenz** Austria
106 E2 **Tarryall** Colorado U.S.A.
112 E5 **Tarrytown** Georgia U.S.A.
95 O5 **Tarrytown** New York U.S.A.
17 F9 **Tarsa,C** Algeria
45 P1 **Tarski Zaljev** *B* Croatia
84 F5 **Tarso Taro** *mt* Chad
86 C1 **Tarso Tieroko** *mt* Chad
78 E3 **Tarsus** Turkey
79 E1 **Tarsus** *R* Turkey
133 E2 **Tartagal** Argentina
6 L4 **Tartan** *oil rig* North Sea
45 J1 **Tártaro** *R* Italy
18 E9 **Tartas** France
56 A3 **Tartas** *R* Russian Federation
52 C5 **Tartu** Estonia
79 F4 **Tarţūs** Syria
80 C6 **Tarum** Israel
60 P3 **Tarumae-san** *mt* Japan
130 H6 **Tarumirim** Brazil
60 D14 **Tarumizu** Japan
54 J2 **Tarusa** Russian Federation
69 D9 **Tarutao,Ko** *isld* Thailand
48 M4 **Tarutino** Ukraine
69 D11 **Tarutung** Sumatra
26 D8 **Tarva** *isld* Norway
38 J9 **Tarvisio** Italy
56 E5 **Tarys-Arzhan** Russian Federation
120 K5 **Tarzwell** Ontario Canada
108 B6 **Tasajera, Sa** *mts* Mexico
57 G2 **Tasaral** Kazakhstan
84 E4 **Tasāwah** Libya
57 D3 **Tas Buget** Kazakhstan
121 M4 **Taschereau** Quebec Canada
107 K2 **Tasco** Kansas U.S.A.
69 F11 **Tasek Dampar** Malaysia
117 M10 **Taseko, Mt** British Columbia Canada
56 D2 **Taseyeva** *R* Russian Federation
76 B2 **Tasgaon** India
58 A2 **Tashanta** Russian Federation
57 A4 **Tashauz** Turkmenistan
75 O5 **Tashigang** Bhutan
57 E4 **Tashkent** Uzbekistan
57 C6 **Tashkepri** Turkmenistan
57 F4 **Tash-Kumyr** Kirghizia
55 B5 **Tashla** Russian Federation
120 C2 **Tashota** Ontario Canada
56 C4 **Tashtagol** Russian Federation
56 C4 **Tashtyp** Russian Federation
70 M9 **Tasikmalaja** Java
70 L9 **Tasikmalaya** Java
80 G2 **Tasil** Syria
28 F7 **Tåsinge** *isld* Denmark
115 O3 **Tasiusaq** Greenland
26 H7 **Tåsjö** Sweden
26 H7 **Tåsjön** *L* Sweden
85 G5 **Tasker** Niger
47 N11 **Taşkopru** Turkey
56 E5 **Taskyl,Khrebet** *mts* Russian Federation
78 J2 **Taşlıçay** Turkey
144 D4 **Tasman** New Zealand
145 D4 **Tasman Bay** New Zealand
139 H9 **Tasman Hd** Tasmania Australia
139 H8 **Tasmania** *state* Australia
145 D4 **Tasman Mountains** New Zealand
144 C5 **Tasman, Mt** New Zealand
139 J9 **Tasman Pen** Tasmania Australia
134 G13 **Tasman Plateau** Pacific Oc
137 M9 **Tasman Sea** Pacific Oc
48 H3 **Tăşnad** Romania
85 F5 **Tassara** Niger
19 J5 **Tasselot, Mt** France
115 M6 **Tassialouc,L** Quebec Canada
85 E5 **Tassili du Hoggar** *plateau* Algeria
85 F3 **Tassili-n'-Ajjer** *plateau* Algeria
28 J5 **Tåstrup** Denmark
51 M2 **Tas Tumus** Russian Federation
57 E3 **Tasty** Kazakhstan
79 D2 **Taşucu** Turkey
85 C3 **Tata** Morocco
71 H5 **Tataba** Sulawesi Indonesia
48 E3 **Tatabánya** Hungary
71 E7 **Tatalan** *isld* Philippines
122 J8 **Tatamagouche** Nova Scotia Canada
85 G2 **Tataouine** Tunisia
48 M5 **Tatarbunary** Ukraine
47 H3 **Tatarlar** Turkey
55 G3 **Tatarsk** Russian Federation
52 H6 **Tatarskaya Respublika** Russian Federation
59 M1 **Tatarskiy Proliv** *str* Russian Federation
Tatarstan *see* **Tatarskaya Respublika**
70 C3 **Tatau** Sarawak
141 G3 **Tate** *R* Queensland Australia
89 E3 **Tate** *R* Botswana
119 N7 **Tate** Saskatchewan Canada
112 C3 **Tate** Georgia U.S.A.
61 O6 **Tateai** Japan
140 C2 **Tate Bluff** *hill* N Terr Australia
60 O4 **Tateura** Japan
61 L9 **Tate yama** *mt* Japan
61 N11 **Tateyama** Japan
117 P5 **Tathlina L** Northwest Territories Canada
139 K6 **Tathra** New South Wales Australia
116 O6 **Tatitlek** Alaska U.S.A.
117 L10 **Tatla Lake** British Columbia Canada
117 K7 **Tatlatui Prov. Park** British Columbia Canada
116 K5 **Tatlawiksuk** *R* Alaska U.S.A.
117 L10 **Tatlayoko Lake** British Columbia Canada
117 M10 **Tatlow, Mt** British Columbia Canada
101 R5 **Tatman Mt** Wyoming U.S.A.
116 K6 **Tatna L** Alaska U.S.A.
115 K6 **Tatnam,C** Manitoba Canada
139 H6 **Tatong** Victoria Australia
Tatra *mts see* **Tatry**
66 D4 **Tatrang** China
31 M6 **Tatry** *mts* Poland/Slovakia
117 E6 **Tatshenshini** *R* British Columbia Canada
77 K7 **Tatta** Pakistan
9 F1 **Tattershall** England
57 G3 **Tatty** Kazakhstan
130 F8 **Tatuí** Brazil
131 B2 **Tatul,Sa de** *mts* Chile
108 D2 **Tatum** New Mexico U.S.A.
109 N3 **Tatum** Texas U.S.A.
107 N7 **Tatums** Oklahoma U.S.A.
Tatung *see* **Datong**
139 H6 **Tatura** Victoria Australia
129 K5 **Tauá** Brazil
128 F4 **Tauapeçaçu** Brazil
37 L2 **Taubach** Germany
130 F8 **Taubaté** Brazil
36 H5 **Tauber** *R* Germany
33 R10 **Taucha** Germany
38 H7 **Tauerin Tunnel** Austria
37 N7 **Taufkirchen** Germany
36 G2 **Taufstein** *mt* Germany
128 G3 **Tauini** *R* Brazil
145 E2 **Taukoa** New Zealand
20 C4 **Taulé** France
19 N16 **Taulignan** France
28 D5 **Taulov** Denmark
145 E3 **Taumarunui** New Zealand
128 D5 **Taumaturgo** Brazil
110 F4 **Taum Sauk Mt** Missouri U.S.A.
130 C7 **Taunay** Brazil
89 D6 **Taung** S Africa
68 C5 **Taungbon** Burma
68 B2 **Taungdwingyi** Burma
68 C2 **Taung-Gyi** Burma
68 D3 **Taunggyi** *mt* Burma/Thailand
68 C2 **Taunglau** Burma
68 C4 **Taungnyo A** *ra* Burma
68 B2 **Taungtha** Burma
68 B3 **Taungup** Burma
74 D3 **Taunsa** Pakistan
8 C5 **Taunton** England
95 Q5 **Taunton** Massachusetts U.S.A.
95 R5 **Taunton,E** Massachusetts U.S.A.
36 E3 **Taunus** *mts* Germany
145 E2 **Taupiri** New Zealand
145 F3 **Taupo** New Zealand
52 B6 **Tauragė** Lithuania
145 E3 **Taurakawa** *mt* New Zealand
145 F2 **Tauranga** New Zealand
121 R6 **Taureau, L** Quebec Canada
145 D1 **Tauroa Pt** New Zealand
55 F2 **Taurovy** Russian Federation
Taurus Mts *see* **Toroslar Dağlari**
17 G3 **Tauste** Spain
144 B7 **Tautuku Peninsula** New Zealand
137 M2 **Tauu Is** Papua New Guinea
115 K5 **Tavani** Northwest Territories Canada
40 F3 **Tavannes** Switzerland
113 F9 **Tavares** Florida U.S.A.
45 K4 **Tavarnelles Val di Pesa** Italy
47 K7 **Tavas** Turkey
22 F4 **Tavaux** France
55 D2 **Tavda** *R* Russian Federation
55 E2 **Tavda** Russian Federation
26 L7 **Tavelsjö** Sweden
41 J5 **Taverne** Switzerland
45 K1 **Tavernelle** Italy
115 M4 **Taverner B** Northwest Territories Canada
19 Q17 **Tavernes** France
113 G12 **Tavernier** Florida U.S.A.
21 P3 **Taverny** Val d'Oise France
88 F3 **Taveta** Kenya
137 R5 **Taveuni** *isld* Fiji
56 G6 **Tavin** Mongolia
16 B7 **Tavira** Portugal
8 B6 **Tavistock** England
43 C8 **Tavolara, I** Sardinia
55 G4 **Tavolzhan** Kazakhstan
16 B4 **Távora** *R* Portugal
68 D5 **Tavoy** Burma
Tavoy I *see* **Mali Kyun**
68 D6 **Tavoy Pt** Burma
65 H3 **Tavrichanka** Russian Federation
55 F4 **Tavricheskoye** Russian Federation
47 N11 **Tavşancıl** Turkey
47 K5 **Tavşanlı** Turkey
47 N11 **Tavşanlı** Turkey
26 L3 **Tavvaätno** *R* Sweden
145 G4 **Tawa** New Zealand
109 M3 **Tawakoni, L** Texas U.S.A.
94 D2 **Tawas City** Michigan U.S.A.
118 D4 **Tawatinaw** Alberta Canada
70 E2 **Tawau** Sabah
70 E2 **Tawau, Telukan** *B* Kalimantan
86 E3 **Taweisha** Sudan
8 C4 **Tawe,R** Wales
145 E1 **Tawhiti Rahi I** New Zealand
70 F2 **Tawitawi** Philippines
8 B5 **Taw,R** England
67 G5 **Ta-wu** Taiwan
84 F3 **Tāwurghā, Sabkhat** *salt flat* Libya
38 G7 **Taxenbach** Austria
27 J12 **Taxinge** Sweden
66 B4 **Taxkorgan** China
128 C5 **Tayabamba** Peru
71 E4 **Tayabas B** Philippines
69 K13 **Tayan** Indonesia
52 D1 **Taybola** Russian Federation
86 H5 **Tayeeglow** Somalia
13 E1 **Tay,Firth of** Scotland
56 C3 **Tayga** Russian Federation
12 C2 **Tayinloan** Scotland
143 D10 **Tay,L** W Australia Australia
140 C5 **Taylor** *R* N Terr Australia
117 N7 **Taylor** British Columbia Canada
103 O7 **Taylor** Arizona U.S.A.
109 O2 **Taylor** Arkansas U.S.A.
111 G7 **Taylor** Mississippi U.S.A.
110 E2 **Taylor** Missouri U.S.A.
98 G8 **Taylor** Nebraska U.S.A.
109 K5 **Taylor** Texas U.S.A.
100 D2 **Taylor** Washington U.S.A.
99 P5 **Taylor** Wisconsin U.S.A.
144 C5 **Taylor, Mt** New Zealand
106 C6 **Taylor, Mt** New Mexico U.S.A.
116 J6 **Taylor Mts** Alaska U.S.A.
106 D3 **Taylor Park Res** Colorado U.S.A.
112 B3 **Taylor Ridge** Georgia U.S.A.
112 E3 **Taylors** South Carolina U.S.A.
142 B3 **Taylors Crossing** W Australia Australia
106 F5 **Taylor Springs** New Mexico U.S.A.
94 B8 **Taylorsville** Kentucky U.S.A.
111 G10 **Taylorsville** Mississippi U.S.A.
112 F2 **Taylorsville** North Carolina U.S.A.
94 F7 **Taylorsville** Ohio U.S.A.
110 G2 **Taylorville** Illinois U.S.A.
122 F7 **Taymouth** New Brunswick Canada
51 K2 **Taymura** *R* Russian Federation
51 K1 **Taymyr,Ozero** *L* Russian Federation
51 J1 **Taymyr,Poluostrov** *pen* Russian Federation
55 E4 **Tayncha** Kazakhstan
68 H7 **Tay Ninh** Vietnam
12 C1 **Taynuilt** Scotland
71 G6 **Tayoloan** *R* Mindanao Philippines
13 F1 **Tayport** Scotland
15 E4 **Tay,R** Scotland
56 E3 **Tayshet** Russian Federation
58 C2 **Tayshir** Mongolia
15 E4 **Tayside** *reg* Scotland
71 E3 **Taytay** Luzon Philippines
71 D5 **Taytay** Palawan Philippines
71 G5 **Taytay Pt** Philippines
77 G2 **Tayyebād** Iran
79 E10 **Ţayyib al Ism** Saudi Arabia
50 H2 **Taz** *R* Russian Federation
85 D2 **Taza** Morocco
85 F5 **Tazalc** Niger
61 O6 **Tazawa ko** *L* Japan
112 D1 **Tazewell** Tennessee U.S.A.
94 F9 **Tazewell** Virginia U.S.A.
65 F1 **Tazicheng** China
116 K7 **Tazimina Lakes** Alaska U.S.A.
84 G4 **Tāzirbū** Libya
48 K4 **Tazlău** *R* Romania
116 O6 **Tazlina L** Alaska U.S.A.
50 G2 **Tazovskaya Guba** *G* Russian Federation
50 G2 **Tazovskiy** Russian Federation
66 F6 **Tazungdam** Burma
61 K8 **Tazuruhama** Japan
78 K1 **Tbilisi** Georgia
85 E7 **Tchaourou** Benin
86 B6 **Tchibanga** Gabon
84 E5 **Tchigaï, Plat. du** Chad/Niger
68 J2 **Tching Lan Xan** *isld* Vietnam
85 F5 **Tchin-Tabaradene** Niger
86 B4 **Tcholliré** Cameroon
111 F8 **Tchula** Mississippi U.S.A.
31 L1 **Tczew** Poland
128 E4 **Tea** *R* Brazil
98 K6 **Tea** South Dakota U.S.A.
48 J4 **Teaca** Romania
124 G6 **Teacapán** Mexico
108 D3 **Teague** New Mexico U.S.A.
109 L4 **Teague** Texas U.S.A.
143 D7 **Teague,L** W Australia Australia
13 G4 **Team Valley** England
144 A6 **Te Anau** New Zealand
145 E3 **Te Anga** New Zealand
45 Q7 **Teano** Italy
101 T6 **Teapot Dome** *hill* Wyoming U.S.A.
145 G2 **Te Araroa** New Zealand
145 E2 **Te Aroha** New Zealand
140 C5 **Tea Tree** N Terr Australia
145 E3 **Te Awamutu** New Zealand
16 D8 **Teba** Spain
69 J12 **Tebas** Indonesia
85 F1 **Tebessa** Algeria
130 B10 **Tebicuary** Paraguay
69 D11 **Tebingtinggi** Sumatra
69 E13 **Tebo** *R* Sumatra
43 C12 **Tébourba** Tunisia
43 C12 **Téboursouk** Tunisia
69 F12 **Tebrau** Malaysia
53 G11 **Tebulosmta** *mt* Georgia/Rus Fed
18 G10 **Tech** *R* France
55 D3 **Techa** *R* Russian Federation
85 D7 **Techiman** Ghana
47 J1 **Techirghiol** Romania
144 D5 **Technical, Mt** New Zealand
33 Q6 **Techow** Germany
79 G1 **Tecirli** Turkey
36 G6 **Teck** Germany
133 C6 **Tecka** Argentina
32 G8 **Tecklenburg** Germany
27 F16 **Teckomatorp** Sweden
124 G7 **Tecolotlán** Mexico
124 H8 **Tecomán** Mexico
103 H6 **Tecopa** California U.S.A.
124 F4 **Tecorichic** Mexico
124 E3 **Tecoripa** Mexico
125 J9 **Tecpan** Mexico
124 G6 **Tecuala** Mexico
48 L5 **Tecuci** Romania
120 H10 **Tecumseh** Ontario Canada
94 D4 **Tecumseh** Michigan U.S.A.
110 D5 **Tecumseh** Missouri U.S.A.
98 K9 **Tecumseh** Nebraska U.S.A.
107 O6 **Tecumseh** Oklahoma U.S.A.
8 C6 **Tedburn St Mary** England
70 P16 **Tedjakula** Indonesia
57 B5 **Tedzhen** Turkmenistan
77 G1 **Tedzhen** Turkmenistan
56 D5 **Teeli** Russian Federation
118 D6 **Tees** Alberta Canada
13 G5 **Tees,R** England
120 J9 **Teeswater** Ontario Canada
71 D6 **Teeth,The** *mt* Palawan Philippines
128 F4 **Tefe** Brazil
47 K7 **Tefenni** Turkey
26 L8 **Teg** Sweden
70 M9 **Tegal** Java
33 S7 **Tegel** Germany
25 F6 **Tegelen** Netherlands
41 P2 **Tegernsee** *L* Germany
85 F6 **Tegina** Nigeria
70 K8 **Tegineneng** Sumatra
141 H8 **Tego** Queensland Australia
125 L2 **Tegucigalpa** Honduras
85 F5 **Teguiddan Tessoum** Niger
89 E3 **Tegwani** *R* Zimbabwe
102 F6 **Tehachapi** California U.S.A.
102 F7 **Tehachapi Mts** California U.S.A.
102 B1 **Tehama** California U.S.A.
102 B2 **Tehama-Colusa Canal** California U.S.A.
145 E2 **Te Hana** New Zealand
145 D1 **Te Hapua** New Zealand
145 F3 **Te Haroto** New Zealand
145 F3 **Te Hauke** New Zealand
115 K4 **Tehek L** Northwest Territories Canada
77 B2 **Tehrān** Iran
77 B2 **Tehrān** *prov* Iran
125 L8 **Tehuacán** Mexico
125 M9 **Tehuantepec** Mexico
37 L2 **Teichel** Germany
8 C3 **Teifi** *R* Wales
8 C6 **Teignmouth** England
8 C6 **Teign,R** England
20 G6 **Teillay** France
20 H7 **Teille** France
21 J4 **Teilleul,le** France
61 Q12 **Teima** Okinawa
Teinach *see* **Bad Teinach-Zavelstein**
36 F6 **Teinach** Germany
37 N6 **Teisbach** Germany
29 K10 **Teisko** Finland
88 G3 **Teita Hills** Kenya
12 D1 **Teith,R** Scotland
48 H4 **Teius** Romania
130 H9 **Teixeira** Brazil
Teixeira de Sousa *see* **Luau**
130 G7 **Teixeiras** Brazil
130 E9 **Teixeira Soares** Brazil
16 E8 **Tejeda,Sa** *mts* Spain
16 B5 **Tejo** *R* Portugal
124 F3 **Tejolocachic** Mexico
102 F7 **Tejon Pk** California U.S.A.
130 E6 **Tejuco,R** Brazil
125 J8 **Tejupilco** Mexico
145 F2 **Te Kaha** New Zealand
98 K8 **Tekamah** Nebraska U.S.A.
145 D1 **Te Kao** New Zealand
145 F3 **Te Karaka** New Zealand
145 E2 **Te Kauwhata** New Zealand
145 E3 **Te Kawa** New Zealand
47 N10 **Teke** Turkey
57 J3 **Tekeli** Kazakhstan
55 F4 **Teke, Oz** *L* Kazakhstan
57 K3 **Tekes** China
66 C3 **Tekes** *R* Kazakhstan
57 K3 **Tekes He** *R* China
86 G3 **Tekezē** *R* Ethiopia
144 C5 **Te Kinga** New Zealand
47 J4 **Tekirdağ** Turkey
145 D3 **Te Kiri** New Zealand
68 A2 **Teknaf** Burma
100 H2 **Tekoa** Washington U.S.A.
144 D5 **Tekoa, Mt** New Zealand
94 C4 **Tekonsha** Michigan U.S.A.
145 D2 **Te Kopuru** New Zealand
86 D2 **Tekro** Chad
71 H5 **Teku** Sulawesi
145 E3 **Te Kuiti** New Zealand
125 Q10 **Tela** Honduras
80 E3 **Tel 'Adashim** Israel
69 C10 **Telagatujuh** Sumatra
17 G10 **Télagh** Algeria
80 B7 **Telamim** Israel
69 G12 **Telan** *isld* Indonesia
116 L6 **Telaquana,L** Alaska U.S.A.
80 B6 **Tel Ashdod** Israel
80 B7 **Tel Ashqelon** Israel
53 G12 **Telavi** Georgia
80 C5 **Tel Aviv** Israel
80 C7 **Tel Azeqa** Israel
56 C4 **Tel'bes** Russian Federation
80 F3 **Tel Bet She'an** Israel
80 C7 **Tel Bet Shemesh** Israel
80 F3 **Tel Bet Yerah** Israel
31 J6 **Telč** Czech Rep
48 J3 **Telciu** Romania
80 C8 **Tel Devir** Israel
70 C6 **Telegapulang** Kalimantan
117 H7 **Telegraph Creek** British Columbia Canada
80 F6 **Teleilet el Ghassul** Jordan
27 C12 **Telemark** *prov* Norway
70 E4 **Telen** *R* Kalimantan
48 L3 **Teleneshty** Moldova
48 J6 **Teleorman** *R* Romania
109 L2 **Telephone** Texas U.S.A.
102 G5 **Telescope Pk** California U.S.A.
127 P5 **Telescope Pt** Grenada
129 G5 **Teles Pires** *R* Brazil
56 C5 **Teletskoye, Oz** *L* Russian Federation
80 C8 **Tel Eyton** Israel
142 D5 **Telfer Mining Centre** W Australia Australia
8 D2 **Telford** England
80 D4 **Tel Gat** Israel
20 B5 **Telgruc** France
32 G9 **Telgte** Germany
80 F1 **Tel Ḥazor** Israel
85 B6 **Télimélé** Guinea
80 F2 **Tel Kinnerot** Israel
78 J3 **Tel Kotchek** Syria
117 K8 **Telkwa** British Columbia Canada
108 G1 **Tell** Texas U.S.A.
80 C7 **Tel Lakhish** Israel
22 K5 **Tellancourt Villers** France
110 K4 **Tell City** Indiana U.S.A.
80 F5 **Tell Deir'Alla** Jordan
26 L5 **Tellejåkk** Sweden
116 D4 **Teller** Alaska U.S.A.
76 B5 **Tellicherry** India
112 C2 **Tellico L** Tennessee U.S.A.
112 C2 **Tellico Plains** Tennessee U.S.A.
122 F3 **Tellier** Quebec Canada
22 J3 **Tellin** Belgium
32 K4 **Tellingstedt** Germany
80 C5 **Tel Litwinsky** Israel
80 F6 **Tell Nimrin** Jordan
106 C4 **Telluride** Colorado U.S.A.
57 B4 **Tel'mansk** Turkmenistan
80 C7 **Tel Maresha** Israel
58 C2 **Telmen Nuur** *L* Mongolia
80 B8 **Tel Mifsah** Israel
80 C4 **Tel Mond** Israel
69 D13 **Telo** Indonesia
100 H4 **Telocaset** Oregon U.S.A.
69 B14 **Telok Blangah** *dist* Singapore
125 K8 **Teloloapán** Mexico
52 J3 **Tel'poziz, Gora** *mt* Russian Federation
80 F1 **Tel Qedesh** Israel
80 A8 **Tel Re'im** Israel
133 D6 **Telsen** Argentina
80 C2 **Tel Shiqmona** Israel
80 C8 **Tel Shoqet** Israel
52 B6 **Telšiai** Lithuania
120 E3 **Teltaka** Ontario Canada
33 S8 **Teltow** Germany
70 E3 **Telukbajur** Kalimantan
69 E13 **Telukbayur** Sumatra
70 K8 **Telukbetung** Sumatra
69 J10 **Telukbutun** Indonesia
69 C12 **Telukdalam** Indonesia
69 E10 **Teluk Intan** Malaysia
69 E13 **Telukkuantan** Sumatra
70 B5 **Telukmelan** Kalimantan
70 L9 **Teluknaga** Java
69 J13 **Telukpakedai** Indonesia
69 F12 **Teluksabah** Sumatra
85 F5 **Telwes** Niger
80 C8 **Tel Ziqlag** Israel
85 E7 **Tema** Ghana
69 J12 **Temaju** *isld* Indonesia
94 K9 **Teman** Virginia U.S.A.
70 N9 **Temanggung** Java
85 F4 **Temasint** Algeria
69 E14 **Tembesi** *R* Sumatra
69 F13 **Tembilahan** Sumatra
102 D6 **Temblor Rge** California U.S.A.
87 C7 **Tembo Aluma** Angola
89 E8 **Tembuland** *dist* S Africa
102 G8 **Temecula** California U.S.A.
56 E5 **Temenchulu,Gora** *mt* Russian Federation
69 E10 **Temengor, Tasek** *res* Malaysia
8 D3 **Teme,R** England
48 F5 **Temerin** Serbia Yugoslavia
69 F11 **Temerluh** Malaysia
69 F10 **Temiang, Bukit** *hill* Malaysia
71 C3 **Teminabuan** W Irian
57 A1 **Temir** Kazakhstan
56 C4 **Temirtau** Russian Federation
122 A2 **Temiscamie L** Quebec Canada
122 A2 **Temiscamie R** Quebec Canada
121 L6 **Témiscaming** Quebec Canada
121 L5 **Témiscamingue, L** Quebec Canada
122 D6 **Temiscouata L** Quebec Canada
121 L6 **Témiskaming** Quebec Canada
69 G12 **Temiyang** *isld* Indonesia
139 G8 **Temma** Tasmania Australia
56 F5 **Temnik** *R* Russian Federation
139 J5 **Temora** New South Wales Australia
124 F3 **Temósachic** Mexico
103 N8 **Tempe** Arizona U.S.A.
70 F7 **Tempe, L** *isld* Sulawesi
33 S8 **Tempelhof** Germany
94 D5 **Temperance** Michigan U.S.A.
69 F13 **Tempino** Sumatra
43 C8 **Tempio Paus** Sardinia
95 R2 **Temple** Maine U.S.A.
94 C2 **Temple** Michigan U.S.A.
109 J1 **Temple** Oklahoma U.S.A.
95 M6 **Temple** Pennsylvania U.S.A.
109 K4 **Temple** Texas U.S.A.
141 G1 **Temple B** Queensland Australia
8 B3 **Temple Bar** Wales
20 G7 **Temple-de-Bretagne, le** France
140 B6 **Temple Downs** N Terr Australia
9 H5 **Temple Ewell** England
14 D4 **Templemore** Ireland
13 F4 **Temple Sowerby** England
140 E5 **Templeton** *R* Queensland Australia
102 D6 **Templeton** California U.S.A.
94 H6 **Templeton** Pennsylvania U.S.A.
8 B4 **Templeton** Wales
22 E2 **Templeuve** Belgium
33 T6 **Templin** Germany
87 C8 **Tempué** Angola
33 P5 **Tempzin** Germany
55 E2 **Temryak, Oz** *L* Russian Federation
22 G1 **Temse** Belgium
131 A7 **Temuco** Chile
144 C6 **Temuka** New Zealand
98 F3 **Temvik** North Dakota U.S.A.
55 C4 **Temyasovo** Russian Federation
128 C4 **Tena** Ecuador
102 H1 **Tenabo** Nevada U.S.A.
124 G8 **Tenacatita** Mexico
109 N4 **Tenaha** Texas U.S.A.
117 F7 **Tenakee Springs** Alaska U.S.A.
29 K11 **Tenala** Finland
76 E2 **Tenali** India
124 G7 **Tenamaxtlán** Mexico
145 D4 **Te Namu** New Zealand
68 D6 **Tenasserim** Burma
73 Q6 **Tenasserim** *R* Burma
68 C6 **Tenasserim I** Burma
68 E5 **Tenasserim State** Burma

19 P13 Tenay France
8 D3 Tenbury Wells England
8 B4 Tenby Wales
120 G6 Tenby Bay Ontario Canada
18 H7 Tence France
86 H3 Tendaho Ethiopia
73 P7 Ten Degree Ch Andaman/Nicobar Is
86 F3 Tendelti Sudan
61 O7 Tendō Japan
101 M5 Tendoy Idaho U.S.A.
85 D2 Tendrara Morocco
40 D4 Tendre, Mt Switzerland
9 H4 Tendring England
21 O8 Tendu France
Tenedos see Bozcaada
85 G4 Ténéré du Tafassasset reg Niger
85 A3 Tenerife isld Canary Is
85 E1 Ténès Algeria
47 H2 Tenevo Bulgaria
71 J4 Tenga Sulawesi
71 L9 Tengahdai Flores Indonesia
70 N9 Tengah, Jawa prov Java
Tengchow see Penglai
70 E5 Tenggarong Kalimantan
70 O9 Tengger Java
69 F10 Tenggul isld Malaysia
70 E1 Tenghilan Sabah
55 E5 Tengiz, Oz L Kazakhstan
71 E7 Tengolan isld Philippines
67 C7 Tengqiao China
65 D7 Teng Xian China
67 C5 Teng Xian China
27 G14 Tenhult Sweden
44 B3 Tenibres mt Italy/France
146 D3 Teniente Jubany Argentina Base Antarctica
146 D3 Teniente Rodolfo Marsh Chile Base Antarctica
100 C3 Tenino Washington U.S.A.
55 F3 Tenis, Oz L Russian Federation
55 D4 Teniz, Oz L Kazakhstan
76 C6 Tenkasi India
52 G6 Ten'ki Russian Federation
107 Q6 Tenkiller Ferry L Oklahoma U.S.A.
85 D6 Tenkodogo Burkina
69 A9 Tenlaa Nicobar Is
123 Q2 Ten Mile L Newfoundland Canada
42 F5 Tenna R Italy
100 D8 Tennant California U.S.A.
140 C4 Tennant Creek N Terr Australia
38 H6 Tennen-Geb mts Austria
110 H6 Tennessee state U.S.A.
106 D2 Tennessee Pass Colorado U.S.A.
110 J6 Tennessee R Tennessee U.S.A.
26 F4 Tennholmen Norway
112 E5 Tennille Georgia U.S.A.
29 O4 Tenniöjoki R Finland
144 D5 Tennyson, L New Zealand
131 B5 Teno R Chile
29 M2 Tenojoki R Finland
70 D2 Tenom Sabah
125 O9 Tenosique Mexico
61 J11 Tenri Japan
61 L11 Tenryū Japan
111 E9 Tensas R Louisiana U.S.A.
111 J11 Tensaw R Alabama U.S.A.
100 J2 Tensed Idaho U.S.A.
85 C2 Tensift R Morocco
99 M2 Tenstrike Minnesota U.S.A.
70 G5 Tenteno Sulawesi
143 B10 Tenterden W Australia Australia
9 G5 Tenterden England
139 K3 Tenterfield New South Wales Australia
113 F12 Ten Thousand Is Florida U.S.A.
70 G4 Tentolomatinan mt Sulawesi
124 H7 Teocaltiche Mexico
45 M3 Teodorano Italy
130 H5 Teófilo Otôni Brazil
48 K1 Teofipol' Ukraine
71 E7 Teomabal isld Philippines
125 L8 Teotitlan Mexico
71 O8 Tepa Indonesia
124 E3 Tepache Mexico
29 L3 Tepasto Finland
124 H7 Tepatitlán de Morelos Mexico
46 E2 Tepe mt Serbia Yugoslavia
125 K8 Tepeji Mexico
57 B3 Tepekul' Uzbekistan
46 D4 Tepelenë Albania
37 O4 Tepelská Plošina mts Czech Rep
47 N11 Tepeoren Turkey
70 E4 Tepianlangsat Kalimantan
124 G7 Tepic Mexico
37 O4 Teplá Czech Rep
30 H5 Teplice Czech Rep
37 O3 Teplička Czech Rep
48 M2 Teplik Ukraine
52 H4 Teplogorka Russian Federation
54 K8 Teplogorsk Ukraine
124 C2 Tepoca, C Mexico
145 F3 Te Pohue New Zealand
145 G3 Te Puia Springs New Zealand
145 F2 Te Puke New Zealand
80 D7 Teqoa Jordan
124 H7 Tequila Mexico
17 J3 Ter R Spain
85 E6 Téra Niger
16 B6 Tera R Portugal
16 C3 Tera R Spain
25 C4 Ter Aar Netherlands
61 M8 Teradomari Japan
61 P7 Teraike Japan
42 F6 Teramo Italy
139 G7 Terang Victoria Australia
25 H3 Ter Apel Netherlands
77 L5 Teratani R Pakistan
71 O8 Terbang Selatan Indonesia
71 O8 Terbang Utara isld Indonesia
25 F5 Terborg Netherlands
78 H2 Tercan Turkey
78 H2 Tercan Barajı dam Turkey
21 M8 Tercé France
133 E4 Tercero R Argentina
106 E4 Tercio Colorado U.S.A.
48 H2 Tereblya R Ukraine
48 K1 Terebovlya Ukraine
48 G5 Teregova Romania
53 G11 Terek R Russian Federation
56 E5 Tere-Khol',Oz L Russian Federation
54 C4 Terekhovka Belarus
56 C5 Terektinskiy Khrebet mts Russian Federation
122 J9 Terence B Nova Scotia Canada
69 F10 Terengganu state Malaysia
130 C7 Terenos Brazil
57 C2 Terenozek Kazakhstan
55 C5 Terensay Russian Federation
69 J13 Terentang Indonesia
70 E5 Terentang,P Kalimantan
130 D9 Teresa Cristina Brazil
53 G8 Tereshka R Penzenskaya obl Russian Federation
129 K5 Teresina Brazil
129 H3 Teresinha Brazil
128 E3 Teresita Colombia
130 G8 Teresópolis Brazil
31 O3 Terespol Poland
139 J3 Terewah I New South Wales Australia
16 B7 Terge R Portugal
22 E4 Tergnier France
85 C4 Terhazza Mali
52 E1 Teriberka Russian Federation
108 D6 Terlingua Texas U.S.A.
78 F1 Terme Turkey
41 O5 Termeno sulla Strada del Vino Italy
77 K1 Termez Uzbekistan
40 E7 Termignon France
143 D10 Termination I W Australia Australia
21 O5 Terminiers France
43 F11 Termini Imerese Sicily
42 E6 Terminillo mt Italy
45 R8 Terminio, M mt Italy
125 O8 Términos,L.de Mexico
100 E9 Termo California U.S.A.
42 F7 Termoli Italy
Termonde see Dendermonde
6 L1 Tern oil rig North Sea
71 A2 Ternate Halmahera Indonesia
83 J12 Ternay,C Mahé I Indian Oc
83 K12 Ternay Pass Mahé I Indian Oc
38 K6 Ternberg Austria
28 E3 Terndrup Denmark
25 A6 Terneuzen Netherlands
59 L2 Terney Russian Federation
8 D2 Ternhill England
102 T13 Tern I Hawaiian Is
42 E6 Terni Italy
48 K1 Ternopol' Ukraine
54 G8 Ternovka Ukraine
54 D9 Ternovka Ukraine
145 E3 Te Roti New Zealand
16 D10 Teroual Morocco
138 E5 Terowie South Australia Australia
59 M2 Terpeniya,Mys C Russian Federation
55 E3 Terpugovo Russian Federation
94 H7 Terra Alta West Virginia U.S.A.
102 E6 Terra Bella California U.S.A.
117 J8 Terrace British Columbia Canada
120 C4 Terrace Bay Ontario Canada
143 D8 Terraces, The hills W Australia Australia
45 O7 Terracina Italy
89 C5 Terra Firma S Africa
109 K2 Terral Oklahoma U.S.A.
43 B9 Terralba Sardinia
123 S5 Terra Nova Newfoundland Canada
45 L4 Terranuova Bracc Italy
18 F7 Terrasson France
124 F3 Terrazas Mexico
146 D15 Terre Adélie Antarctica
146 E13 Terre Adélie Antarctica
100 D5 Terrebonne Oregon U.S.A.
111 F12 Terrebonne B Louisiana U.S.A.
127 N5 Terre de Bas isld Guadeloupe W Indies
127 N5 Terre de Haut isld Guadeloupe W Indies
110 J2 Terre Haute Indiana U.S.A.
109 L3 Terrell Texas U.S.A.
123 S6 Terrenceville Newfoundland Canada
101 N6 Terreton Idaho U.S.A.
20 H3 Terrette R France
139 K5 Terrigal New South Wales Australia
40 F3 Terri, Mt Switzerland
111 F9 Terry Mississippi U.S.A.
101 U3 Terry Montana U.S.A.
55 E6 Tersakkan R Kazakhstan
25 D2 Terschelling isld Netherlands
25 D2 Terschellinger Wad Netherlands
86 C3 Tersef Chad
57 H4 Terskey Ala-Too Khrebet mts Kirghizia
52 E2 Terskiy Bereg coast Russian Federation
43 C9 Tertenia Sardinia
57 H3 Teru-Aygyr Kirghizia
17 G4 Teruel prov Spain
47 J1 Tervel Bulgaria
29 M9 Tervo Finland
29 L5 Tervola Finland
22 H2 Tervuren Belgium
42 H4 Tešanj Bosnia-Herzegovina
107 N2 Tescott Kansas U.S.A.
86 G2 Teseney Eritrea
52 F6 Tesha R Russian Federation
116 L1 Teshekpuk L Alaska U.S.A.
60 S2 Teshikaga Japan
60 H11 Te-shima isld Japan
60 Q1 Teshio R Japan
60 Q2 Teshio dake mt Japan
60 P1 Teshio-sanchi mts Japan
46 E1 Tešica Serbia Yugoslavia
117 F5 Teslin R Yukon Territory Canada
117 G5 Teslin L Br Col/Yukon Terr Canada
130 E4 Tesouras, R Brazil
130 D5 Tesouro Brazil
52 D5 Tesovo Netyl'skiy Russian Federation
17 G9 Tessala, Mt.du Algeria
85 E4 Tessalit Mali
85 F6 Tessaoua Niger
118 K7 Tessier Saskatchewan Canada
33 Q4 Tessin Germany
21 H4 Tessy France
43 C7 Testa, C Sardinia
42 G7 Testa del Gargano Italy
18 E8 Teste-de-Buch, la France
32 L6 Testedt Germany
43 C12 Testour Tunisia
9 E5 Test, R England
106 E6 Tesuque New Mexico U.S.A.
18 G10 Tet R France
48 D3 Tét Hungary
117 L9 Tetachuck L British Columbia Canada
122 F6 Tetagouche R New Brunswick Canada
125 J9 Tetala Mexico
17 F4 Tetas de Viana mt Spain
133 C2 Tetas, Pta Chile
8 D4 Tetbury England
88 D10 Tete Mozambique
123 N3 Tete à la Baleine Quebec Canada
69 C12 Tetehosi Indonesia
117 O9 Tete Jaune Cache British Columbia Canada
145 F3 Te Teko New Zealand
36 B5 Téterchen France
56 F1 Tetere R Russian Federation
33 R5 Teterow Germany
46 G2 Teteven Bulgaria
48 M1 Tetiyev Ukraine
116 Q5 Tetlin Alaska U.S.A.
101 O2 Teton R Montana U.S.A.
101 O6 Tetonia Idaho U.S.A.
101 P6 Teton Ra Wyoming U.S.A.
16 D9 Tétouan Morocco
46 D2 Tetovo Macedonia
46 E7 Tetráyi mt Greece
37 L3 Tettau Germany
32 G5 Tettens Germany
52 G7 Tetyushi Russian Federation
37 N1 Teuchern Germany
133 E3 Teuco R Argentina
38 N7 Teufelstein mt Austria
128 E5 Teuini Brazil
43 B10 Teulada Sardinia
124 H7 Teul de G. Ortega Mexico
119 U8 Teulon Manitoba Canada
71 O8 Teun isld Indonesia
69 B10 Teunom R Sumatra
69 B10 Teunom Sumatra
33 T8 Teupitz Germany
60 P1 Teuri-tō isld Japan
37 L3 Teuschnitz Germany
32 H8 Teutoburger Wald Germany
29 J9 Teuva Finland
26 H9 Tevansjö Sweden
20 B4 Téven-Kerbrat France
45 M6 Tevere R Italy
144 B6 Teviot New Zealand
15 F5 Teviotdale V Scotland
13 F3 Teviot, R Scotland
55 F2 Tevriz Russian Federation
144 A7 Te Waewae Bay New Zealand
70 C5 Tewah Kalimantan
141 L7 Tewantin Queensland Australia
70 D5 Teweh R Kalimantan
145 E3 Te Wera New Zealand
145 F3 Te Whaiti New Zealand
145 E4 Te Wharau New Zealand
8 D4 Tewkesbury England
117 L11 Texada I British Columbia Canada
12 B2 Texa I Scotland
109 O2 Texarkana Texas/Ark U.S.A.
141 K8 Texas Queensland Australia
109 Texas state U.S.A.
109 N6 Texas City Texas U.S.A.
25 C2 Texel isld Netherlands
25 C2 Texelstroom Netherlands
108 C7 Texhoma Texas/Okla U.S.A.
108 D1 Texico New Mexico U.S.A.
108 B7 Texline Texas U.S.A.
125 K8 Texmelucan Mexico
109 L2 Texoma, L Oklahoma U.S.A.
108 F4 Texon Texas U.S.A.
56 D1 Teya Russian Federation
67 A1 Te-yang China
52 F6 Teykovo Russian Federation
77 J3 Teyvareh Afghanistan
52 F6 Teza R Russian Federation
125 L8 Teziutlán Mexico
75 P5 Tezpur India
87 E11 Thabana Ntlenyana mt Lesotho
89 E7 Thaba Putsoa mt Lesotho
68 B4 Thabaung Burma
87 E10 Thabazimbi S Africa
68 C1 Thabeikkyin Burma
79 E10 Thabt, G. el mt Egypt
68 C2 Thabyedaung Burma
109 K2 Thackerville Oklahoma U.S.A.
Tha Han see Lop Buri
67 B6 Thai Binh Vietnam
68 H4 Thai Duong Thung Vietnam
68 G3 Thai Hoa Vietnam
68 E5 Thailand kingdom S E Asia
73 R6 Thailand, G. of Thailand
69 D8 Thai Muang Thailand
67 B6 Thai Nguyen Vietnam
69 D8 Tha Khanon Thailand
68 G4 Thakhek Laos
38 G8 Thal Austria
37 J2 Thal Germany
74 D2 Thal Pakistan
85 F1 Thala Tunisia
69 D8 Thalang Thailand
66 F6 Thala Pass China/Burma
Thalassery see Telicherry
33 O9 Thale Germany
69 E9 Thale Luang Thailand
36 B4 Thalfang Germany
38 H6 Thalgau Austria
37 O2 Thalheim Germany
41 K4 Thalkirch Switzerland
141 J8 Thallon Queensland Australia
112 F6 Thalmann Georgia U.S.A.
37 L5 Thalmässing Germany
84 F4 Thamad Bu, Hashīshah Libya
89 D5 Thamaga Botswana
9 F4 Thame England
120 H10 Thames R Ontario Canada
145 E2 Thames New Zealand
120 J9 Thamesford Ontario Canada
9 G4 Thames, R England
145 F2 Thames Valley admin region New Zealand
120 J10 Thamesville Ontario Canada
68 D6 Thamihla Kyun isld Burma
84 F3 Thāmit, Wadi Libya
37 K1 Thamsbrück Germany
26 D8 Thamshamn Norway
68 C4 Thanatpin Burma
68 C5 Thanbyuzayat Burma
76 A1 Thāne India
68 J5 Thang Binh Vietnam
142 D4 Thangoo W Australia Australia
141 K6 Thangool Queensland Australia
68 G3 Thanh Hoa Vietnam
68 H2 Thanh Moi Vietnam
68 G1 Thanh Thuy Vietnam
76 D5 Thanjavur India
Thanlwin R see Salween R
40 F2 Thann France
38 F5 Thann Germany
37 J7 Thannhausen Germany
77 K7 Thano Bula Khan Pakistan
36 C7 Thanville France
40 D1 Thaon France
19 K4 Thaon les Vosages France
68 E4 Tha Pla Thailand
69 D8 Thap Put Thailand
68 D7 Thap Sakae Thailand
73 L3 Thar desert India
37 Q2 Tharandt Germany
74 D5 Thar Desert India
141 G8 Thargomindah Queensland Australia
68 B4 Tharrawaddy Burma
68 B4 Tharrawaw Burma
78 J5 Tharthar Basin Iraq
46 G4 Thásos isld Greece
9 E5 Thatcham England
103 P9 Thatcher Arizona U.S.A.
106 F4 Thatcher Colorado U.S.A.
101 O7 Thatcher Idaho U.S.A.
67 B5 That Khe Vietnam
68 C4 Thaton Burma
68 F5 Tha Tum Thailand
18 H9 Thau, Étang de L France
68 D4 Thaungyin R Thailand
68 C6 Thayawthadang-yi Kyun isld Burma
110 E5 Thayer Missouri U.S.A.
68 D6 Thayetchaung Burma
68 B3 Thayetmyo Burma
101 P7 Thayne Wyoming U.S.A.
68 A3 Thazi Arakan Burma
68 B2 Thazi Magwe Burma
68 C2 Thazi Mandalay Burma
9 E5 Theale England
103 M9 Theba Arizona U.S.A.
Thebes see Thívai
84 J4 Thebes ruins Egypt
110 G4 Thebes Illinois U.S.A.
120 J9 Thedford Ontario Canada
98 F7 Thedford Nebraska U.S.A.
32 K7 Thedinghausen Germany
139 K5 The Entrance New South Wales Australia
68 B3 Thegon Burma
98 K1 Theif River Falls Minnesota U.S.A.
21 P7 Theillay France
20 H6 Theil, le Ille-et-Vilaine France
21 M5 Theil, le Orne France
68 D7 Theinkun Burma
68 C4 Theinzeik Burma
37 N1 Theissen Germany
20 E6 Theix France
114 J5 Thekulthili L Northwest Territories Canada
8 C6 Thelbridge England
6 L4 Thelma oil rig North Sea
113 E7 Thelma Georgia U.S.A.
114 J5 Thelon R Northwest Territories Canada
28 D4 Them Denmark
37 K3 Themar Germany
21 N8 Thenay Indre France
21 N7 Thenay Loir-et-Cher France
21 K8 Thénezay France
18 F7 Thenon France
141 K7 Theodore Queensland Australia
119 P7 Theodore Saskatchewan Canada
111 H11 Theodore Alabama U.S.A.
128 F6 Theodore Roosevelt R Brazil
103 N8 Theodore Roosevelt L Arizona U.S.A.
98 C2 Theodore Roosevelt Nat. Mem. Park North Dakota U.S.A.
140 B5 Theo, Mt N Terr Australia
21 P3 Therain R France
141 J6 Theresa R Queensland Australia
95 M2 Theresa New York U.S.A.
99 S6 Theresa Wisconsin U.S.A.
83 K12 Thérèse isld Mahé I Indian Oc
118 F4 Therien Alberta Canada
111 F12 Theriot Louisiana U.S.A.
46 F4 Thermaïkós, Kólpos B Greece
103 L3 Thermo Utah U.S.A.
46 E6 Thérmon Greece
46 F6 Thermopílai Greece
101 R6 Thermopolis Wyoming U.S.A.
139 H6 The Rock New South Wales Australia
146 F7 Theron Mts Antarctica
22 C2 Thérouanne France
21 N7 Thésée France
114 G3 Thesiger B Northwest Territories Canada
46 E5 Thessalía admin region Greece
120 G6 Thessalon Ontario Canada
46 F4 Thessaloníki Greece
9 G3 Thetford England
121 T6 Thetford Mines Quebec Canada
68 B5 Thetkethaung R Burma
119 P3 The Two Rivers Saskatchewan Canada
21 O5 Theuville France
22 K2 Theux Belgium
127 N5 The Valley Anguilla Lesser Antilles
138 C4 Thevenard South Australia Australia
142 A5 Thevenard I W Australia Australia
21 P8 Thevet St. Julien France
109 M5 The Woodlands Texas U.S.A.
19 P16 Thèze France
46 D5 Thiamis R Greece
21 L3 Thiberville France
111 F12 Thibodaux Louisiana U.S.A.
21 M3 Thibouville France
119 T3 Thicket Portage Manitoba Canada
8 D6 Thickthorn England
118 E2 Thickwood Hills Alberta Canada
100 H4 Thief V.Res Oregon U.S.A.
146 D8 Thiel Mts Antarctica
100 C6 Thielsen, Mt Oregon U.S.A.
Thielt see Tielt
99 T6 Thiensville Wisconsin U.S.A.
22 F4 Thiérache France
18 H7 Thiers France
37 N3 Thiersheim Germany
85 A6 Thies Senegal
43 B8 Thiesi Sardinia
33 T4 Thiessow Germany
88 F2 Thika Kenya
73 L7 Thiladunmathi Atoll Maldives
21 O3 Thilliers-en-Vexin, les France
40 E2 Thillot, le France
21 N4 Thimert-Gâtelles France
75 N5 Thimphu Bhutan
28 R9 Thingeyri Iceland
28 S9 Thingvellir Iceland
22 H4 Thin le-Moutier France
137 O6 Thio New Caledonia
19 K3 Thionville France
85 D6 Thiou Burkina
46 G8 Thíra isld Greece
46 G8 Thirasía isld Greece
21 J8 Thiré France
21 N5 Thiron-Gardais France
13 G5 Thirsk England
13 G3 Thirston England
143 D9 Thirsty, Mt W Australia Australia
120 K7 Thirty Thousand Is Ontario Canada
Thiruvananthapuram see Trivandrum
Thisted co see Viborg co
28 B3 Thisted Denmark
29 T8 Thistilfjördhur B Iceland
6 L1 Thistle oil rig North Sea
101 O10 Thistle Utah U.S.A.
117 D4 Thistle Creek Yukon Territory Canada
138 D5 Thistle I South Australia Australia
68 B1 Thitseingyi Burma
46 F6 Thívai Greece
21 N5 Thivars France
18 F7 Thiviers France
18 H6 Thizy France
28 S9 Thjórsá R Iceland
19 Q16 Thoard France
68 E3 Thoeng Thailand
89 F4 Thohoyandou S Africa
21 O4 Thoiry France
19 N12 Thoissey France
25 B5 Tholen Netherlands
36 C5 Tholey Germany
19 P18 Tholonet France
107 M6 Thomas Oklahoma U.S.A.
94 H7 Thomas West Virginia U.S.A.
102 E4 Thomas A Edison, L California U.S.A.
113 K11 Thomas B Bahamas
115 K1 Thomas Hubbard, C Northwest Territories Canada
108 F3 Thomas, J.B., L Texas U.S.A.
138 E2 Thomas, L South Australia Australia
144 D5 Thomas, Mt New Zealand
102 H8 Thomas Mt California U.S.A.
111 J9 Thomaston Alabama U.S.A.
112 C5 Thomaston Georgia U.S.A.
95 S2 Thomaston Maine U.S.A.
109 K7 Thomaston Texas U.S.A.
14 D4 Thomastown Ireland
111 G9 Thomastown Mississippi U.S.A.
111 J10 Thomasville Alabama U.S.A.
113 D7 Thomasville Georgia U.S.A.
110 E5 Thomasville Missouri U.S.A.
112 G2 Thomasville North Carolina U.S.A.
21 N4 Thomer-la-Sogne France
127 J5 Thomonde Haiti
117 N10 Thompson R British Columbia Canada
119 U3 Thompson Manitoba Canada
95 Q5 Thompson Connecticut U.S.A.
99 N6 Thompson Iowa U.S.A.
99 U4 Thompson Michigan U.S.A.
110 C1 Thompson R Missouri U.S.A.
98 J2 Thompson North Dakota U.S.A.
95 M5 Thompson Pennsylvania U.S.A.
103 P3 Thompson Utah U.S.A.
100 K2 Thompson Falls Montana U.S.A.
142 B3 Thompson L W Australia Australia
117 R4 Thompson Lake Northwest Territories Canada
114 H5 Thompson Landing Northwest Territories Canada
138 B1 Thompson, Mt N Terr Australia
140 B6 Thompson, Mt N Terr Australia
116 P6 Thompson Pass Alaska U.S.A.
109 M6 Thompsons Texas U.S.A.
144 A6 Thompson Sd New Zealand
Thompson's Falls see Nyahururu
95 P4 Thompsonville Connecticut U.S.A.
99 V5 Thompsonville Michigan U.S.A.
141 G6 Thomson R Queensland Australia
99 Q8 Thomson Illinois U.S.A.
144 B6 Thomson Mts New Zealand
139 H7 Thomson Res Victoria Australia
68 E6 Thon Buri Thailand
40 D6 Thônes France
68 C4 Thongwa Burma
40 D5 Thonon-les-Bains France
18 G9 Thoré R France
21 M6 Thore France
106 B6 Thoreau New Mexico U.S.A.
21 L6 Thorée France
40 D5 Thorens les Glières France
Thorez see Torez
118 D4 Thorhild Alberta Canada
20 H8 Thorigny Vendée France
28 S9 Thórisvatn L Iceland
141 G8 Thorlindah, L Queensland Australia
13 G4 Thornaby England
9 H2 Thornage England
94 B4 Thornapple R Michigan U.S.A.
94 K8 Thornburg Virginia U.S.A.
120 K8 Thornbury Ontario Canada
8 D4 Thornbury England
144 B7 Thornbury New Zealand
109 K5 Thorndale Texas U.S.A.
13 H6 Thorne England
102 F3 Thorne Nevada U.S.A.
9 F2 Thorney England
12 D1 Thornhill Central Scotland
12 E3 Thornhill Dumfries & Galloway Scotland
13 E6 Thornton England
13 E1 Thornton Scotland
109 P2 Thornton Arkansas U.S.A.
106 F2 Thornton Colorado U.S.A.
99 N7 Thornton Iowa U.S.A.
109 L4 Thornton Texas U.S.A.
100 H2 Thornton Washington U.S.A.
141 F4 Thorntonia Queensland Australia
110 K1 Thorntown Indiana U.S.A.
138 D6 Thorny Passage South Australia Australia
121 L9 Thorold Ontario Canada
Thorout see Torhout
100 E2 Thorp Washington U.S.A.
99 Q5 Thorp Wisconsin U.S.A.
145 D4 Thorpe New Zealand
9 H3 Thorpeness England
28 E4 Thorsager Denmark
118 C5 Thorsby Alberta Canada
146 J8 Thorshavnheiane mts Antarctica
29 T8 Thórshöfn Iceland
28 D4 Thorsø Denmark
119 U1 Thorsteinson L Manitoba Canada
8 C6 Thorverton England
68 G7 Thot Not Vietnam
21 K7 Thouarcé France
21 K8 Thouaret R France
21 K8 Thouars France
21 J8 Thouarsais-Bouildroux France
21 K8 Thouet R France
142 C5 Thouin,C W Australia Australia
46 E7 Thouría Greece
20 H6 Thourie France
22 D5 Thourotte France
95 L2 Thousand Is Ontario/New York Canada/U.S.A.
103 N3 Thousand Lake Mt Utah U.S.A.
102 F7 Thousand Oaks California U.S.A.
101 L8 Thousand Spring Cr Nevada U.S.A.
101 L7 Thousand Springs Idaho U.S.A.
47 H3 Thrace Turkey
109 K5 Thrall Texas U.S.A.
100 E3 Thrall Washington U.S.A.
9 F3 Thrapston England
139 J6 Thredbo New South Wales Australia
8 C3 Three Cocks Wales
101 K7 Three Creek Idaho U.S.A.
101 O4 Three Forks Montana U.S.A.
118 D7 Three Hills Alberta Canada
139 G8 Three Hummock I Tasmania Australia
110 J5 Three I.Res Tennessee U.S.A.
9 F2 Threekingham England
137 O8 Three Kings Basin Pacific Oc
145 D1 Three Kings Is New Zealand
140 D3 Three Knobs mt N Terr Australia
99 R4 Three Lakes Wisconsin U.S.A.
141 G2 Three Mile 0pening, First & Second straits Gt Barrier Reef Aust
99 U8 Three Oaks Michigan U.S.A.
68 D5 Three Pagodas Pass Burma/Thailand
119 T3 Threepoint L Manitoba Canada
85 D8 Three Points, C Ghana
102 F5 Three Rivers California U.S.A.
94 B5 Three Rivers Michigan U.S.A.
106 D8 Three Rivers New Mexico U.S.A.
109 J7 Three Rivers Texas U.S.A.
123 N5 Three Rock Cove Newfoundland Canada
141 G1 Three Sisters islds Queensland Australia
100 D5 Three Sisters mts Oregon U.S.A.
143 B8 Three Springs W Australia Australia
140 C4 Three Ways Roadhouse N Terr Australia
13 E4 Threlkeld England
Thrissur see Trichur
109 H2 Throckmorton Texas U.S.A.
68 F5 Throm Cambodia
143 E8 Throssell, L W Australia Australia
143 E7 Throssell, Mt W Australia Australia
142 D5 Throssel Ra W Australia Australia
68 J5 Thu Bon R Vietnam
68 H7 Thu Dao Mot Vietnam
139 J5 Thuddungra New South Wales Australia
18 H8 Thueyte France
40 E6 Thuile, la Italy
22 G3 Thuin Belgium
115 N2 Thule Greenland
115 N2 Thule Air Base Greenland
146 G3 Thule, Southern isld S Sandwich Is Atlantic Oc
37 O2 Thum Germany
101 P5 Thumb Wyoming U.S.A.
144 C5 Thumbs, The mt New Zealand
40 G4 Thun Switzerland
141 G7 Thunda Queensland Australia
119 O2 Thunder Ontario Canada
94 D2 Thunder B Michigan U.S.A.
99 R1 Thunder Bay Ontario Canada
98 D4 Thunder Butte Cr South Dakota U.S.A.
120 G2 Thunderhouse Falls Ontario Canada
126 D6 Thunder Knoll Caribbean
118 C4 Thunder L. Prov. Park Alberta Canada
116 G2 Thunder Mt Alaska U.S.A.
36 H4 Thüngen Germany
69 D8 Thung Maphrao Thailand
69 D8 Thung Song Thailand
69 D9 Thung Wa Thailand
75 O5 Thunkar Bhutan
40 B4 Thurey France
33 R5 Thürikow Germany
41 L3 Thüringen Austria
37 K2 Thüringen land Germany
37 J2 Thüringer Wald mts Germany
19 N13 Thurins France
14 D4 Thurles Ireland
8 C7 Thurlestone England
139 G3 Thurloo Downs New South Wales Australia
101 T3 Thurlow Montana U.S.A.
37 L3 Thurnau Germany
28 F6 Thurø Denmark
13 E4 Thursby England
141 F1 Thursday I Queensland Australia
121 P7 Thurso Quebec Canada
15 E2 Thurso R Scotland
15 E2 Thurso Scotland
146 B7 Thurston I Antarctica
21 K4 Thury-Harcourt France
117 K7 Thutade L British Columbia Canada
146 B8 Thwaites Glacier glacier Antarctica
28 A3 Thy reg Denmark
141 G7 Thylungra Queensland Australia
87 G9 Thyolo Malawi
139 K4 Tia New South Wales Australia
127 J9 Tía Juana Venezuela
65 G3 Tianboashan China
67 B5 Tiandeng China
67 B5 Tiandong China
67 B4 Tian'e China
53 F12 Tianeti Georgia
67 C4 Tianhe China
65 D5 Tianjin China
58 C4 Tianjun China
67 B4 Tianlin China
67 D1 Tianmen China
65 H3 Tianqiaoling China
Tianshan see Ar Horquin Qi
66 C3 Tian Shan ra China/Kazakhstan
58 E5 Tianshui China
67 G2 Tiantai China
67 B5 Tianyang China
Tianyi see Ningcheng
Tianzhen see Gaoqing
65 C4 Tianzhen China
67 C3 Tianzhu China
134 C11 Tiarel Tahiti Pacific Oc
85 E1 Tiaret Algeria
141 L7 Tiaro Queensland Australia
85 D7 Tiassalé Ivory Coast
130 E9 Tibagi Brazil
86 B4 Tibati Cameroon
13 E3 Tibbie Shiels Inn Scotland
Tiber R see Tevere R
80 F2 Tiberias Israel
80 F2 Tiberias, L Israel
86 C1 Tibesti reg Chad
84 F5 Tibesti, Sarīr Libya
Tibet aut reg see Xizang Zizhiqu
121 N4 Tiblemont Quebec Canada
48 J3 Ţibleşului, Muntii mts Romania
138 F3 Tibooburra New South Wales Australia
75 K4 Tibrikot Nepal
124 C3 Tiburón isld Mexico
71 F4 Ticao isld Philippines
9 G5 Ticehurst England
47 H1 Ticha, Yazovir res Bulgaria
121 O8 Tichborne Ontario Canada
85 C5 Tichitt Mauritania
85 B4 Tichla Western Sahara
44 E1 Ticino R Italy
41 J5 Ticino canton Switzerland
13 G6 Tickhill England
9 E2 Ticknall England
48 H6 Ticleni Romania
95 O3 Ticonderoga New York U.S.A.
27 G13 Tidaholm Sweden
122 F6 Tide Hd New Brunswick Canada
118 F8 Tide L Alberta Canada
69 A9 Tiden Nicobar Is
100 B5 Tidewater Oregon U.S.A.
85 E3 Tidikelt reg Algeria
94 H5 Tidioute Pennsylvania U.S.A.
85 B5 Tidjikja Mauritania
122 H8 Tidnish Nova Scotia Canada
44 F2 Tidone R Italy
71 A2 Tidore Halmahera Indonesia
85 A5 Tidra, I Mauritania
9 E5 Tidworth England
85 D6 Tiébélé Burkina
85 C7 Tiébissou Ivory Coast
33 T7 Tiefensee Germany
36 C6 Tieffenbach France
116 P6 Tiekel Alaska U.S.A.
25 D5 Tiel Netherlands
65 G1 Tieli China
65 F3 Tieling China
22 E1 Tielt Belgium
85 C7 Tiéme Ivory Coast
22 H2 Tienen Belgium
Tientsin see Tianjin
67 B6 Tien Yen Vietnam
89 D9 Tier Berg mt S Africa
21 K6 Tiercé France
27 J11 Tierp Sweden
106 D5 Tierra New Mexico U.S.A.
125 L8 Tierra Blanca Mexico
133 D8 Tierra del Fuego, I.Grande de Arg/Chile
101 U8 Tie Siding Wyoming U.S.A.
16 D4 Tiétar R Spain
130 E7 Tietê R Brazil
130 F8 Tietê Brazil
138 B2 Tietkens, Mt South Australia Australia
100 E3 Tieton Washington U.S.A.
100 D3 Tieton Res Washington U.S.A.
138 C2 Tieyon South Australia Australia
45 Q7 Tifata, M mt Italy
6 L4 Tiffany oil rig North Sea
100 F1 Tiffany Mt Washington U.S.A.
99 P8 Tiffin Iowa U.S.A.
94 D5 Tiffin Ohio U.S.A.
17 H10 Tiffrit Algeria
112 D6 Tifton Georgia U.S.A.
70 D2 Tiga isld Sabah
116 E9 Tigalda I Aleutian Is
100 C4 Tigard Oregon U.S.A.
112 F3 Tiger R South Carolina U.S.A.
100 H1 Tiger Washington U.S.A.
99 R5 Tigerton Wisconsin U.S.A.
15 C5 Tighnabruaich Scotland
51 P3 Tigil Russian Federation
56 B5 Tigiretskiy Khrebet mts Kazakhstan/Rus Fed
112 E4 Tignall Georgia U.S.A.
86 B4 Tignère Cameroon
42 A3 Tignes, Bge. de France
122 H7 Tignish Prince Edward I Canada
128 C4 Tigre R Peru
127 N10 Tigre R Venezuela
125 K6 Tigre, Cerro del mt Mexico
131 B3 Tigre, Sa ra Argentina
78 J4 Tigris R Iraq
85 F3 Tiguentourine Algeria
86 C2 Tigui Chad
21 P6 Tigy France
79 D9 Tih, Gebel el plateau Egypt
145 E3 Tihoi New Zealand
28 B4 Tihøje hill Denmark
106 D6 Tijeras New Mexico U.S.A.
124 A1 Tijuana Mexico
130 E10 Tijucas Brazil
122 G3 Tika Quebec Canada
125 P9 Tikal anc site Guatemala
74 H6 Tikamgarh India
116 H6 Tikchik L Alaska U.S.A.
53 F10 Tikhoretsk Russian Federation
52 D5 Tikhvin Russian Federation
145 G2 Tikitiki New Zealand
145 F3 Tikokino New Zealand
137 O4 Tikopia isld Santa Cruz Is
78 J4 Tikrit Iraq
52 D3 Tiksha Russian Federation
52 D2 Tikshozero, Oz L Russian Federation
51 M1 Tiksi Russian Federation
71 H4 Tilamuta Sulawesi
141 H8 Tilbooroo Queensland Australia
25 D5 Tilburg Netherlands
120 H10 Tilbury Ontario Canada
9 G5 Tilbury England
133 D2 Tilcara Argentina
138 F3 Tilcha South Australia Australia
110 G3 Tilden Illinois U.S.A.
98 J7 Tilden Nebraska U.S.A.
109 J7 Tilden Texas U.S.A.
48 G3 Tileagd Romania
85 D3 Tilemsī el Fasi Algeria
85 E5 Tilemsi, Vallée du Mali
98 C5 Tilford South Dakota U.S.A.
74 H5 Tilhar India
51 Q2 Tilichiki Russian Federation
68 B2 Tilin Burma
85 E6 Tillabéri Niger
100 B4 Tillamook Oregon U.S.A.
100 A4 Tillamook Rock Oregon U.S.A.
69 A8 Tillanchāng Dwīp Nicobar Is
21 O5 Tillay le Peneux France
27 J12 Tillberge Sweden
40 B3 Tille R France
112 G2 Tillery, L North Carolina U.S.A.
118 F8 Tilley Alberta Canada
85 E5 Tillia Niger
12 E1 Tillicoultry Scotland
21 H7 Tillières France
21 N4 Tillières-sur-Avre France
28 G7 Tillitse Denmark
112 F5 Tillman South Carolina U.S.A.
113 L11 Tilloo Cay isld Bahamas
13 G2 Till, R England
120 K10 Tillsonburg Ontario Canada
21 J3 Tilly-sur-Seulles France
71 M9 Tilomar Timor
47 J8 Tílos isld Greece
139 G4 Tilpa New South Wales Australia
85 E2 Tilrhemt Algeria
9 E5 Tilshead England
119 Q9 Tilston Manitoba Canada
123 S4 Tilting Newfoundland Canada
110 J1 Tilton Illinois U.S.A.
95 Q3 Tilton New Hampshire U.S.A.
70 G5 Tily mt Sulawesi
28 A4 Tim Denmark
54 J5 Tim Russian Federation
121 L5 Timagami Ontario Canada
52 G2 Timanskiy Kryazh ra Russian Federation
144 C6 Timaru New Zealand
53 E10 Timashevsk Russian Federation
46 G9 Timbákion Crete Greece
111 F12 Timbalier I Louisiana U.S.A.
70 F2 Timbang isld Sabah
130 J9 Timbaúba Brazil
85 C5 Timbédra Mauritania
100 B4 Timber Oregon U.S.A.
140 B3 Timber Creek Police Station N Terr Australia
98 E4 Timber L South Dakota U.S.A.
112 J1 Timberlake North Carolina U.S.A.
102 H4 Timber Mt Nevada U.S.A.
139 G7 Timboon Victoria Australia
130 E10 Timbo, R Brazil
Timbuktu see Tombouctou
70 F2 Timbun Mata Sabah
85 F3 Timellouline Algeria
85 D5 Timetrine Mts Mali
46 D5 Tímfi, Óros mt Greece
46 E6 Timfristós mt Greece
85 F5 Timia Niger
85 E3 Timimoun Algeria
Timiris, C see Mirik, C
57 E3 Timirlanovka Kazakhstan
55 E4 Timiryazevo Kazakhstan
56 B3 Timiryazevskiy Russian Federation
48 G5 Timiş R Romania
48 G5 Timişoara Romania
55 D1 Timkapaul' Russian Federation
33 N5 Timmendorfer Strand Germany
27 G13 Timmersdala Sweden
85 F5 Timmersoi watercourse Niger
115 P5 Timmiarmiut Greenland
120 J4 Timmins Ontario Canada
112 H3 Timmonsville South Carolina U.S.A.
46 E1 Timok R Serbia Yugoslavia
129 K5 Timon Brazil
71 M9 Timor isld E Indies
136 E4 Timor Trough Timor Sea
52 E4 Timoshino Russian Federation
133 E5 Timote Argentina
127 J10 Timotes Venezuela
103 J4 Timpahute Ra Nevada U.S.A.
101 O9 Timpanogos Cave Nat. Mon Utah U.S.A.
143 E7 Timperley Ra W Australia Australia
101 N9 Timpie Utah U.S.A.
109 N4 Timpson Texas U.S.A.
26 J9 Timrå Sweden
80 D3 Timrat Israel
28 B4 Timring Denmark
110 K6 Tim's Ford L Tennessee U.S.A.
112 A2 Tims Ford L Tennessee U.S.A.
52 H4 Timsher Russian Federation
57 E3 Timur Kazakhstan
70 O9 Timur, Jawa prov Java
144 D5 Timutimu Headland New Zealand
89 F8 Tina R S Africa
71 G8 Tinaca Pt Mindanao Philippines
127 K10 Tinaco Venezuela
71 F3 Tinaga isld Philippines
71 G5 Tinago Leyte Philippines
14 E4 Tinahely Ireland
124 J5 Tinaja Mexico
137 O4 Tinakula isld Santa Cruz Is
85 G4 Tin Alkoum Algeria
127 K10 Tinaquillo Venezuela
48 G4 Tinca Romania
141 L7 Tin Can Bay Queensland Australia
21 J4 Tinchebray France
22 C3 Tincques France
100 K7 Tindall Idaho U.S.A.
76 D4 Tindivanam India
70 K9 Tindjil isld Java
85 C3 Tindouf Algeria
86 D2 Tine Sudan
85 E4 Tinef Algeria
102 F4 Tinemaha Res California U.S.A.
16 C1 Tineo Spain
85 C3 Tinfouchy Algeria
85 F3 Tin Fouye Algeria
141 L1 Tingalpa dist Brisbane, Qnsld Australia
69 G11 Tinggi isld Malaysia
139 K3 Tingha New South Wales Australia
75 K4 Tingjegaon Nepal

28 C7 **Tinglev** Denmark
99 M9 **Tingley** Iowa U.S.A.
128 C5 **Tingo María** Peru
67 C3 **Tingping** China
85 C6 **Tingrela** Ivory Coast
66 D6 **Tingri** China
67 E2 **Tingsiqiao** China
27 G15 **Tingsryd** Sweden
133 D4 **Tinguiririca** *mt* Chile/Arg
26 C9 **Tingvoll** Norway
121 T7 **Tingwick** Quebec Canada
Tingzhou *see* **Changting**
129 L6 **Tinharé, I.de** Brazil
67 B7 **Tinh Gia** Vietnam
145 F3 **Tiniroto** New Zealand
70 D3 **Tinjar** *R* Sarawak
144 D5 **Tinline, Mt** New Zealand
27 C11 **Tinn** Norway
141 H8 **Tinnenburra** Queensland Australia
27 D12 **Tinnoset** Norway
27 D12 **Tinnsjö** *L* Norway
44 G3 **Tino, I.di** Italy
70 G4 **Tinompo** Sulawesi
46 G7 **Tínos** *isld* Greece
85 E4 **Ti-n Rerhoh** Algeria
111 D8 **Tinsman** Arkansas U.S.A.
142 C5 **Tinstane, Mt** W Australia Australia
75 Q5 **Tinsukia** India
8 B6 **Tintagel** England
98 K3 **Tintah** Minnesota U.S.A.
85 F4 **Tin Tarabine** *watercourse* Algeria
20 G5 **Tinténiac** France
8 D4 **Tintern** England
22 K4 **Tintigny** Belgium
133 E3 **Tintina** Argentina
138 F6 **Tintinara** South Australia Australia
16 C7 **Tinto** *R* Spain
15 E5 **Tinto, Mt** Scotland
145 F4 **Tinui** New Zealand
144 C5 **Tinwald** New Zealand
85 E4 **Tin Zaouaten** Algeria/Mali
86 H3 **T'ī'o** Eritrea
111 D10 **Tioga** Louisiana U.S.A.
98 D1 **Tioga** North Dakota U.S.A.
95 K5 **Tioga** Pennsylvania U.S.A.
109 L2 **Tioga** Texas U.S.A.
94 G8 **Tioga** West Virginia U.S.A.
69 G11 **Tioman** *isld* Malaysia
120 H4 **Tionaga** Ontario Canada
41 N5 **Tione** Italy
42 D2 **Tione di Trento** Italy
100 D8 **Tionesta** California U.S.A.
94 H5 **Tionesta** Pennsylvania U.S.A.
94 A5 **Tippecanoe** Indiana U.S.A.
99 U9 **Tippecanoe** *R* Indiana U.S.A.
14 C4 **Tipperary** Ireland
14 D4 **Tipperary** *co* Ireland
111 F8 **Tippo** Mississippi U.S.A.
102 E5 **Tipton** California U.S.A.
110 K1 **Tipton** Indiana U.S.A.
107 M2 **Tipton** Kansas U.S.A.
110 D3 **Tipton** Missouri U.S.A.
109 H1 **Tipton** Oklahoma U.S.A.
103 K6 **Tipton, Mt** Arizona U.S.A.
110 G5 **Tiptonville** Tennessee U.S.A.
120 D4 **Tip Top Hill** Ontario Canada
9 G4 **Tiptree** England
76 C4 **Tiptur** India
128 E3 **Tiquié** *R* Brazil
80 C5 **Tira** Israel
129 J4 **Tiracambu, Sa.do** *mts* Brazil
79 E11 **Tirān** *isld* Saudi Arabia
46 D3 **Tiranë** Albania
41 M5 **Tirano** Italy
83 K9 **Tirappane** Sri Lanka
53 C10 **Tiraspol'** Moldova
80 C2 **Tirat Karmel** Israel
80 F4 **Tirat Zevi** Israel
145 E2 **Tirau** New Zealand
145 F4 **Tiraumea** New Zealand
47 J6 **Tire** Turkey
78 G1 **Tirebolu** Turkey
15 B4 **Tiree** *isld* Scotland
85 B4 **Tires** *reg* Western Sahara
48 J6 **Tîrgovişte** Romania
48 L5 **Tîrgu Bujor** Romania
48 H6 **Tîrgu Cărbuneşti** Romania
48 L3 **Tîrgu Frumos** Romania
48 H5 **Tîrgu Jiu** Romania
48 H3 **Tîrgu Lăpuş** Romania
48 J4 **Tîrgu Mureş** Romania
48 K3 **Tîrgu Neamt** Romania
48 K4 **Tîrgu Ocna** Romania
48 K4 **Tîrgu Secuiesc** Romania
47 K4 **Tirilye** Turkey
145 E2 **Tiritiri** New Zealand
Tirlemont *see* **Tienen**
55 C4 **Tirlyanskiy** Russian Federation
48 J4 **Tîrnava Mare** *R* Romania
48 J4 **Tîrnava Mică** *R* Romania
48 J4 **Tîrnăveni** Romania
46 E5 **Tírnavos** Greece
94 E6 **Tiro** Ohio U.S.A.
38 F8 **Tirol** *prov* Austria
41 O4 **Tirolo** Italy
80 C6 **Tirosh** Israel
86 D4 **Tiroungoulou** Cent Afr Republic
45 H4 **Tirrenia** Italy
37 N4 **Tirschenreuth** Germany
43 B8 **Tirso** *R* Sardinia
43 B8 **Tirso, L. del** Sardinia
28 G7 **Tirsted** Denmark
131 A7 **Tirua, Pta** Chile
76 D6 **Tiruchchendur** India
76 D5 **Tiruchchirāppalli** India
83 L10 **Tirukkovil** Sri Lanka
76 C6 **Tirunelveli** India
128 D5 **Tiruntán** Peru
76 D4 **Tirupati** India
76 D4 **Tiruppattur** India
76 C5 **Tiruppur** India
76 D4 **Tiruvannamalai** India
48 H2 **Tisa** *R* Ukraine
119 N6 **Tisdale** Saskatchewan Canada
111 H7 **Tishomingo** Mississippi U.S.A.
109 L1 **Tishomingo** Oklahoma U.S.A.
79 G6 **Ţisīyah** Syria
99 R8 **Tiskilwa** Illinois U.S.A.
28 C6 **Tislund** Denmark
27 H13 **Tisnaren** *L* Sweden
31 J6 **Tišnov** Czech Rep
48 F2 **Tisovec** Slovakia
83 L11 **Tissamaharama** Sri Lanka
9 E1 **Tissington** England
27 E12 **Tistedal** Norway
48 F3 **Tisza** *R* Hungary
48 F4 **Tiszaföldvár** Hungary
31 N8 **Tiszavasvari** Hungary
85 E3 **Tit** Algeria
116 K2 **Titaluk** *R* Alaska U.S.A.
146 E9 **Titan Dome** *ice dome* Antarctica
9 E6 **Titchfield** England
128 E7 **Titicaca, L** Peru/Bolivia
116 L4 **Titna** *R* Alaska U.S.A.
Titograd *see* **Podgorica**
99 M6 **Titonka** Iowa U.S.A.
52 D1 **Titovka** *R* Russian Federation
26 C8 **Titran** Norway
94 C3 **Tittabawassee** *R* Michigan U.S.A.
37 L6 **Titting** Germany
38 G5 **Tittmoning** Germany
48 K6 **Titu** Romania
86 E5 **Titule** Zaire
113 G9 **Titusville** Florida U.S.A.
94 H5 **Titusville** Pennsylvania U.S.A.
85 A6 **Tivaouane** Senegal
27 G13 **Tived** Sweden
122 F9 **Tiverton** Nova Scotia Canada
120 J8 **Tiverton** Ontario Canada
8 C6 **Tiverton** England
95 Q5 **Tiverton** Rhode I U.S.A.
45 N6 **Tivoli** Italy
95 O4 **Tivoli** New York U.S.A.
109 L7 **Tivoli** Texas U.S.A.
70 G5 **Tiwad** Sulawesi
71 H7 **Tiworo, Selat** *str* Indonesia
68 D6 **Ti-ywa** Burma
124 H7 **Tizapán el Alto** Mexico
17 H9 **Tizi** Algeria
16 E10 **Tizi-Ifri** Morocco
125 P7 **Tizimín** Mexico
85 C3 **Tiznit** Morocco
124 J5 **Tizoc** Mexico
16 E10 **Tiztoutine** Morocco
28 B6 **Tjæreborg** Denmark
28 G6 **Tjæreby** Denmark
27 H13 **Tjällmo** Sweden
70 L9 **Tjamara** Java
26 K5 **Tjåmotis** Sweden
71 L10 **Tjamplong** Timor Indonesia
70 K9 **Tjankuang Tg** *C* Java
26 L4 **Tjårro Keble** *mt* Sweden
26 J5 **Tjeggelvas** *L* Sweden
26 H3 **Tjeldöy** *isld* Norway
28 D3 **Tjele** Denmark
70 D4 **Tjemaru, G** *mt* Kalimantan
71 J9 **Tjempi, Teluk** *B* Sumbawa Indonesia
70 F6 **Tjenrana** Sulawesi
70 N9 **Tjepu** Java
70 M9 **Tjereme** *mt* Java
25 E3 **Tjeuke Meer** Netherlands
70 L9 **Tjiandjur** Java
70 L9 **Tjibadak** Java
70 L9 **Tjibatu** Java
70 L9 **Tjibuni** *R* Java
70 M9 **Tjidjulang** Java
70 L9 **Tjidua** Java
70 L9 **Tjihara** Java
70 L9 **Tjikadjang** Java
70 L9 **Tjikampek** Java
70 M9 **Tjilatjap** Java
70 M9 **Tjiledug** Java
70 L9 **Tjimahi** Java
70 G6 **Tjimpu** Sulawesi
70 K8 **Tjina, Tg** *C* Sumatra
70 M9 **Tjipatudjah** Java
70 M9 **Tjirebon** Java
70 L9 **Tjitarum** *R* Java
27 E12 **Tjöme** *isld* Norway
27 E13 **Tjörn** *isld* Sweden
28 B4 **Tjørring** Denmark
26 F6 **Tjötta** Norway
53 F11 **Tkvarcheli** Georgia
125 L9 **Tlacolula de Matamoros** Mexico
125 M8 **Tlacotalpan** Mexico
125 K8 **Tlalnepantla** Mexico
125 K8 **Tlálpam** Mexico
68 A1 **Tlangtlang** Burma
125 L8 **Tlapacoyán** Mexico
124 H7 **Tlaquepaque** Mexico
125 K8 **Tlaxcala** Mexico
85 D2 **Tlemcen** Algeria
85 E5 **Tlemcès** Niger
48 J2 **Tlumach** Ukraine
31 N3 **Tłuszcz** Poland
52 E6 **T'ma** *R* Russian Federation
84 F4 **Tmassah** Libya
85 D4 **Tni Haïa** Algeria
68 C4 **To** *R* Burma
126 G4 **Toa** *R* Cuba
117 L6 **Toad River** British Columbia Canada
87 H11 **Toamasina** Madagascar
101 L9 **Toana** *mt ra* Nevada U.S.A.
45 J3 **Toano** Italy
95 L9 **Toano** Virginia U.S.A.
145 F3 **Toatoa** New Zealand
133 E5 **Toay** Argentina
70 F5 **Toaya** Sulawesi
61 K11 **Toba** Japan
69 D11 **Toba, Danau** *L* Sumatra
127 M1 **Tobago** *isld* W Indies
117 L10 **Toba Inlet** British Columbia Canada
77 K4 **Toba & Kakar Ranges** Pakistan
78 G4 **Tobaqah** Syria
101 L9 **Tobar** Nevada U.S.A.
17 F6 **Tobarra** Spain
60 D12 **Tobata** Japan
14 C2 **Tobbercurry** Ireland
71 H7 **Tobea** *isld* Indonesia
140 E5 **Tobermorey** N Terr Australia
141 G7 **Tobermory** Queensland Australia
120 J7 **Tobermory** Ontario Canada
15 B4 **Tobermory** Scotland
60 P2 **Tōbetsu** Japan
98 J9 **Tobias** Nebraska U.S.A.
61 N14 **Tobiishi-hana** *C* Iwo Jima Japan
115 R3 **Tobin, Kap** *C* Greenland
142 F5 **Tobin,L** W Australia Australia
119 O5 **Tobin L** Saskatchewan Canada
102 G1 **Tobin, Mt** Nevada U.S.A.
122 E6 **Tobique R** New Brunswick Canada
61 N6 **Tobi-shima** *isld* Japan
69 H14 **Toboali** Indonesia
55 D4 **Tobol** Kazakhstan
55 E2 **Tobol'sk** Russian Federation
68 J6 **To Bong** Vietnam
71 F5 **Toboso** Negros Philippines
Tobruk *see* **Tubruq**
95 M5 **Tobyhanna** Pennsylvania U.S.A.
52 H2 **Tobysh** *R* Russian Federation
52 H3 **Tobysh** Russian Federation
129 J5 **Tocantínia** Brazil
129 J5 **Tocantinópolis** Brazil
129 J4 **Tocantins** *R* Brazil
129 J6 **Tocantins** *state* Brazil
112 D3 **Toccoa** Georgia U.S.A.
41 H5 **Toce** *R* Italy
61 N9 **Tochigi** Japan
61 M8 **Tochio** Japan
133 D2 **Toco** Chile
133 C2 **Tocopilla** Chile
133 D2 **Tocorpuri** *mt* Chile/Bolivia
139 H6 **Tocumwal** New South Wales Australia
127 K9 **Tocuyo** *R* Venezuela
127 K9 **Tocuyo de la Costa** Venezuela
74 F5 **Toda** India
26 C9 **Todal** Norway
116 L3 **Todatonten** Alaska U.S.A.
140 B2 **Todd,Mt** N Terr Australia
122 F7 **Todd Mt** New Brunswick Canada
140 C6 **Todd R** N Terr Australia
143 F7 **Todd Ra** W Australia Australia
32 M5 **Todesfelde** Germany
13 F1 **Todhills** Scotland
42 E6 **Todi** Italy
41 J4 **Tödi** *mt* Switzerland
138 C2 **Todmorden** South Australia Australia
13 F6 **Todmorden** England
61 Q6 **Todoga-saki** *C* Japan
60 P4 **Todohokke** Japan
131 A8 **Todos los Santos, L** Chile
129 L6 **Todos os Santos, B. de** Brazil
124 D6 **Todos Santos** Mexico
56 E5 **Todzha, Oz** *L* Russian Federation
14 B5 **Toe Hd** Ireland
68 D5 **Toe Jaga, Khao** *mt* Burma/Thailand
144 B7 **Toetoes B** New Zealand
118 E5 **Tofield** Alberta Canada
117 L11 **Tofino** British Columbia Canada
26 F9 **Töfsingdalens Nat. Park** Sweden
27 F14 **Tofta** Sweden
27 E12 **Tofte** Norway
28 C6 **Toftlund** Denmark
116 M4 **Tofty** Alaska U.S.A.
137 R5 **Tofua** *isld* Tonga
Tōfutsu *see* **Sernovodsk**
61 O10 **Tōgane** Japan
41 H5 **Togano, Monte** Italy
41 K3 **Toggenburg** *mt* Switzerland
61 K8 **Togi** Japan
116 G7 **Togiak** Alaska U.S.A.
70 G5 **Togian Kep** *isld* Sulawesi
37 O7 **Töging** Germany
60 C13 **Togitsu** Japan
86 G2 **Togni** Sudan
119 Q7 **Togo** Saskatchewan Canada
85 E7 **Togo** *rep* W Africa
Togrog Ul *see* **Qahar Youyi Qianqi**
65 B4 **Togtoh** China
61 P12 **Toguchi** Okinawa
56 B3 **Toguchin** Russian Federation
56 E4 **Togul'skiy Khrebet** *mts* Russian Federation
57 B2 **Togyz** Kazakhstan
102 E1 **Tohakum Pk** Nevada U.S.A.
74 F4 **Tohana** India
106 B6 **Tohatchi** New Mexico U.S.A.
70 C4 **Tohenbatu** *mt* Sarawak
134 A11 **Tohiea** *pk* Moorea Pacific Oc
29 P9 **Tohmajärvi** Finland
29 L8 **Toholampi** Finland
113 F9 **Tohopekaliga, L** Florida U.S.A.
61 M11 **Toi** Japan
68 A7 **Toibalewe** Andaman Is
29 K10 **Toijala** Finland
71 H5 **Toili** Sulawesi
99 P2 **Toimi** Minnesota U.S.A.
60 E14 **Toi-misaki** Japan
71 L10 **Toineke** Indonesia
29 K9 **Toisvesi** *L* Finland
29 M9 **Toivakka** Finland
99 S3 **Toivola** Michigan U.S.A.
102 G2 **Toiyabe Ra** Nevada U.S.A.
70 G5 **Toja** Sulawesi
60 G11 **Tōjō** Japan
30 H6 **Tok** *mt* Czech Rep
145 E3 **Tokaanu** New Zealand
60 R2 **Tokachi** *prefect* Japan
60 Q2 **Tokachi dake** *mt* Japan
48 G2 **Tokajo** Hungary
70 G5 **Tokala, G** *mt* Sulawesi
61 M8 **Tōkamachi** Japan
144 B7 **Tokanui** New Zealand
86 G2 **Tokar** Sudan
59 J5 **Tokara-retto** *islds* Japan
55 F5 **Tokarevka** Kazakhstan
52 D4 **Tokari** Russian Federation
52 G5 **Tokarikha** Russian Federation
78 F1 **Tokat** Turkey
145 D2 **Tokatoka** New Zealand
65 F6 **Tŏkchŏk-kundo** *B* S Korea
70 G6 **Toke** Sulawesi
134 K9 **Tokelau** *islds* Pacific Oc
101 P9 **Tokewanna Pk** Utah U.S.A.
56 E1 **Tokhoma** *R* Russian Federation
61 L10 **Toki** Japan
98 H2 **Tokio** North Dakota U.S.A.
116 Q5 **Tok Junc** Alaska U.S.A.
27 D12 **Tokke-Vatn** *L* Norway
116 M4 **Toklat** Alaska U.S.A.
Tokmak *see* **Eşme**
57 H3 **Tokmak** Kirghizia
54 G9 **Tokmak** Ukraine
145 E3 **Toko** New Zealand
145 E4 **Tokomaru** New Zealand
145 G3 **Tokomaru Bay** New Zealand
60 S1 **Tokoro** Japan
145 E3 **Tokoroa** New Zealand
84 G3 **Tokrah** Libya
57 H1 **Tokrau** *R* Kazakhstan
52 E3 **Toksha-Kuznetsova** Russian Federation
66 D3 **Toksun** China
59 K4 **Tok-to** *isld* Japan/Korea
57 G4 **Toktogul Vdkhr** Kirghizia
57 G5 **Toktomush** Tajikistan
57 K2 **Tokty** Kazakhstan
59 K1 **Tokur** Russian Federation
60 H11 **Tokushima** Japan
60 E11 **Tokuyama** Japan
89 G3 **Tokwe** *R* Zimbabwe
62 **Tōkyō** *conurbation* Japan
61 N10 **Tōkyō-wan** *B* Japan
77 K2 **Tokzār** Afghanistan
145 G3 **Tolaga Bay** New Zealand
87 H13 **Tôlañaro** Madagascar
106 G7 **Tolar** New Mexico U.S.A.
109 K3 **Tolar** Texas U.S.A.
78 K1 **Tolavi** Georgia
55 C4 **Tolbazy** Russian Federation
Tolbukhin *see* **Dobrich**
130 D9 **Toledo** Brazil
133 C3 **Toledo** Chile
16 E5 **Toledo** *prov* Spain
16 E5 **Toledo** Spain
110 H2 **Toledo** Illinois U.S.A.
99 O7 **Toledo** Iowa U.S.A.
94 D5 **Toledo** Ohio U.S.A.
100 B5 **Toledo** Oregon U.S.A.
100 C3 **Toledo** Washington U.S.A.
109 O4 **Toledo Bend Res** Louisiana U.S.A.
16 D5 **Toledo, Montes de** *mts* Spain
42 E5 **Tolentino** Italy
44 L5 **Tolfa, Mt.della** Italy
27 G14 **Tolg** Sweden
26 E9 **Tolga** Norway
87 G12 **Toliara** Madagascar
128 C3 **Tolima** *vol* Colombia
128 C3 **Tolima** *div* Colombia
70 G4 **Tolitoli** Sulawesi
27 G16 **Tollarp** Sweden
33 S5 **Tollense** *R* Germany
33 S5 **Tollensesee** *L* Germany
103 M8 **Tolleson** Arizona U.S.A.
98 E1 **Tolley** North Dakota U.S.A.
102 E4 **Tollhouse** California U.S.A.
28 H5 **Tølløse** Denmark
52 C5 **Tolmachevo** Russian Federation
42 E2 **Tolmezzo** Italy
42 F2 **Tolmin** Slovenia
48 E4 **Tolna** *co* Hungary
48 E4 **Tolna** Hungary
28 E2 **Tolne** Denmark
86 C6 **Tolo** Zaire
54 A2 **Tolochin** Belarus
110 H2 **Tolono** Illinois U.S.A.
17 F1 **Tolosa** Spain
116 N4 **Tolovana** *R* Alaska U.S.A.
65 G7 **Tolsan** *isld* S Korea
15 B2 **Tolsta Head** Scotland
48 K2 **Tolstoye** Ukraine
103 N9 **Toltec** Arizona U.S.A.
133 C5 **Toltén** Chile
131 A7 **Toltén, R** Chile
126 G10 **Tolú** Colombia
125 K8 **Toluca** Mexico
99 R8 **Toluca** Illinois U.S.A.
29 P5 **Tolvand, Ozero** *L* Russian Federation
52 D4 **Tolvayarvi** Russian Federation
52 E4 **Tolvuya** Russian Federation
55 A4 **Tol'yatti** Russian Federation
55 D5 **Tolybay** Kazakhstan
56 B3 **Tom'** *R* Russian Federation
99 Q6 **Tomah** Wisconsin U.S.A.
99 R4 **Tomahawk** Wisconsin U.S.A.
60 P3 **Tomakomai** Japan
70 G5 **Tomali** Sulawesi
60 P1 **Tomamae** Japan
128 F4 **Tomar** Brazil
57 H2 **Tomar** Kazakhstan
16 B5 **Tomar** Portugal
Tomari *see* **Golovnino**
60 N3 **Tomari** Japan
59 M2 **Tomari** Russian Federation
46 D1 **Tomaševo** Montenegro Yugoslavia
31 O4 **Tomashevka** Ukraine
48 M2 **Tomashpol'** Ukraine
130 E8 **Tomasina** Brazil
31 O5 **Tomaszów Lubelski** Poland
31 M4 **Tomaszów Mazowiecka** Poland
15 D3 **Tomatin** Scotland
124 G8 **Tomatlán** Mexico
38 O9 **Tomaz** Slovenia
31 O4 **Tomazy** Poland
109 M5 **Tomball** Texas U.S.A.
60 F10 **Tombara** Japan
86 F4 **Tombe** Sudan
111 H8 **Tombigbee** *R* Mississippi U.S.A.
71 H5 **Tombila** *mt* Sulawesi
87 B7 **Tomboco** Angola
130 G7 **Tombos** Brazil
85 D5 **Tombouctou** Mali
103 O10 **Tombstone** Arizona U.S.A.
87 B9 **Tombua** Angola
131 A6 **Tome** Chile
71 J7 **Tomea** *isld* Indonesia
27 G16 **Tomelilla** Sweden
57 D3 **Tomenaryk** Kazakhstan
80 E5 **Tomer** Jordan
121 L6 **Tomiko** Ontario Canada
139 J4 **Tomingley** New South Wales Australia
70 G4 **Tomini** Sulawesi
70 G5 **Tomini, Teluk** *B* Sulawesi
15 E3 **Tomintoul** Scotland
61 O8 **Tomioka** Japan
42 H5 **Tomislavgrad** Yugoslavia
143 G7 **Tomkinson Ras** S/W Australia Australia
26 F5 **Tomma** *isld* Norway
28 C2 **Tømmerby** Denmark
28 E6 **Tommerup** Denmark
51 M3 **Tommot** Russian Federation
128 E2 **Tomo** *R* Colombia
60 G11 **Tomo** Japan
124 F3 **Tomóchic** Mexico
60 H11 **Tomogashima-suidō** *str* Japan
70 G6 **Tompira** Sulawesi
118 J8 **Tompkins** Saskatchewan Canada
94 C4 **Tompkins Center** Michigan U.S.A.
110 L5 **Tompkinsville** Kentucky U.S.A.
70 F5 **Tompo** Sulawesi
143 C6 **Tom Price** W Australia Australia
142 C6 **Tom Price,Mt** W Australia Australia
66 D5 **Tomra** China
86 H4 **Tomsa** Ethiopia
56 C3 **Tomsk** Russian Federation
56 B2 **Tomskaya Oblast** *prov* Russian Federation
83 M9 **Tom's Ridge** Christmas I Indian Oc
95 N6 **Toms River** New Jersey U.S.A.
Tömük *see* **Elvanlı**
60 Q2 **Tomuraushi yama** *mt* Japan
Tomur Feng *see* **Pobedy, Pik**
116 Q6 **Tom White, Mt** Alaska U.S.A.
124 F4 **Tónachic** Mexico
125 N9 **Tonalá** Mexico
103 O5 **Tonalea** Arizona U.S.A.
42 D2 **Tonale, Pso. di** Italy
61 K9 **Tonami** Japan
128 E4 **Tonantins** Brazil
100 F1 **Tonasket** Washington U.S.A.
121 M9 **Tonawanda** New York U.S.A.
9 G5 **Tonbridge** England
60 J12 **Tonda** Japan
71 J4 **Tondano** Sulawesi
16 B4 **Tondela** Portugal
Tønder *co see* **Sønderjylland** *co*
28 B7 **Tønder** Denmark
120 E3 **Tondern** Ontario Canada
85 E4 **Tondjara** *watercourse* Algeria
88 C10 **Tondongwe** *mt* Zimbabwe
36 B3 **Tondorf** Germany
61 N9 **Tone** *R* Japan
61 O10 **Tone-gawa** *R* Japan
8 C5 **Tone, R** England
139 G4 **Tonga** New South Wales Australia
137 S6 **Tonga** *kingdom* Pacific Oc
86 F4 **Tonga** Sudan
88 B10 **Tonga** Zambia
89 G7 **Tongaat** S Africa
145 D4 **Tonga I** New Zealand
139 G4 **Tonga L** New South Wales Australia
139 G6 **Tongala** Victoria Australia
67 F4 **Tong'an** China
110 A2 **Tonganoxie** Kansas U.S.A.
145 E3 **Tongaporutu** New Zealand
145 E3 **Tongariro** *mt* New Zealand
145 E3 **Tongariro** *admin region* New Zealand
137 R6 **Tongatapu Group** Tonga
58 F5 **Tongbai Shan** *mt ra* China
Tongcheng *see* **Dong'e**
67 E1 **Tongcheng** China
67 D2 **Tongcheng** China
58 E4 **Tongchuan** China
67 C3 **Tongdao** China
22 J2 **Tongeren** Belgium
67 E2 **Tonggu** China
65 A7 **Tongguan** China
67 A4 **Tonghai** China
59 J2 **Tonghe** China
59 J3 **Tonghua** China
59 K2 **Tongjiang** China
67 B1 **Tongjiang** China
59 J2 **Tongken He** *R* China
67 B6 **Tong King, G. of** Vietnam
70 G5 **Tongko** Sulawesi
12 D4 **Tongland** Scotland
67 B2 **Tongliang** China
59 H3 **Tongliao** China
67 F1 **Tongling** China
67 F2 **Tonglu** China
67 B1 **Tongnan** China
68 H6 **Tong Noy** Cambodia
87 G12 **Tongobory** Madagascar
131 B3 **Tongoi, Bahia** Chile
133 C4 **Tongoy** Chile
Tongquan *see* **Malong**
71 E7 **Tongquil** *isld* Philippines
67 C3 **Tongren** China
Tongres *see* **Tongeren**
Tongshan *see* **Xuzhou**
67 E2 **Tongshan** China
68 J3 **Tongshi** China
68 D2 **Tongta** Burma
58 C5 **Tongtian He** *R* China
15 D2 **Tongue** Scotland
101 U3 **Tongue** *R* Montana U.S.A.
126 F2 **Tongue of the Ocean** *chan* Bahamas
101 T4 **Tongue R.Res** Montana U.S.A.
65 C5 **Tong Xian** China
67 G1 **Tongxiang** China
65 D3 **Tongxing** China
65 C7 **Tongxu** China
65 F2 **Tongyu** China
65 F4 **Tongyuanpu** China
67 B4 **Tongzhou** China
67 B2 **Tongzi** China
6 L4 **Toni** *oil rig* North Sea
99 R8 **Tonica** Illinois U.S.A.
124 E3 **Tónichi** Mexico
124 H8 **Tonila** Mexico
86 E4 **Tonj** Sudan
74 F5 **Tonk** India
77 B1 **Tonkābon** Iran
107 N5 **Tonkawa** Oklahoma U.S.A.
52 G6 **Tonkino** Russian Federation
68 H6 **Tonle Kong** *R* Laos/Cambodia
68 G7 **Tonle Sap** *R* Cambodia
18 E7 **Tonnay-Charente** France
18 F8 **Tonneins** France
28 D5 **Tønning** Denmark
32 J4 **Tönning** Germany
102 G3 **Tonopah** Nevada U.S.A.
60 H11 **Tonoshō** Japan
20 D4 **Tonquédec** France
27 D12 **Tönsberg** Norway
27 B13 **Tonstad** Norway
131 B3 **Tontal, Sa** *ra* Argentina
103 N8 **Tonto Basin** Arizona U.S.A.
103 O8 **Tonto Nat.Mon** Arizona U.S.A.
116 L5 **Tonzona** *R* Alaska U.S.A.
141 J8 **Toobeah** Queensland Australia
143 B9 **Toodyay** W Australia Australia
101 N9 **Tooele** Utah U.S.A.
141 K7 **Toogoolawah** Queensland Australia
139 G6 **Tooleyone** New South Wales Australia
143 G9 **Toolgana Rockhole** *rockhole* W Australia Australia
138 D5 **Tooligie** South Australia Australia
116 N2 **Toolik** *R* Alaska U.S.A.
138 F6 **Toolondo** Victoria Australia
139 J6 **Tooma** *R* New South Wales Australia
141 G7 **Toompine** Queensland Australia
139 H7 **Toora** Victoria Australia
141 F5 **Toorak** Queensland Australia
56 E5 **Toora-Khem** Russian Federation
141 K2 **Toowong** *dist* Brisbane, Qnsld Australia
141 K8 **Toowoomba** Queensland Australia
116 J1 **Topagoruk** *R* Alaska U.S.A.
48 L6 **Topalu** Romania
17 F7 **Topares, Sa.de** *mts* Spain
103 N10 **Topawa** Arizona U.S.A.
102 E3 **Topaz L** California U.S.A.
33 T8 **Töpchin** Germany
13 G5 **Topcliffe** England
94 B5 **Topeka** Indiana U.S.A.
107 P2 **Topeka** Kansas U.S.A.
124 F5 **Topia** Mexico
56 C3 **Topki** Russian Federation
48 G1 **Topl'a** *R* Slovakia
118 C4 **Topland** Alberta Canada
117 K8 **Topley Lodge** British Columbia Canada
46 E1 **Toplica** *R* Serbia Yugoslavia
48 J4 **Topliţa** Romania
131 A5 **Topocalma, Pta** Chile
103 K7 **Topock** Arizona U.S.A.
48 F6 **Topola** Serbia Yugoslavia
46 E3 **Topolčane** Macedonia
48 E2 **Topol'čany** Slovakia
29 O10 **Topol'ki** Russian Federation
46 G2 **Topolnitsa** *R* Bulgaria
124 E5 **Topolobampo** Mexico
48 J6 **Topoloveni** Romania
47 H2 **Topolovgrad** Bulgaria
38 L9 **Topolšica** Slovenia
106 D1 **Toponas** Colorado U.S.A.
52 E5 **Topornya** Russian Federation
52 D2 **Topozero, Ozero** *L* Russian Federation
100 E3 **Toppenish** Washington U.S.A.
47 J1 **Topraisar** Romania
57 B4 **Toprak-kala** Uzbekistan
52 F3 **Topsa** Russian Federation
95 U1 **Topsfield** Maine U.S.A.
8 C6 **Topsham** England
95 R3 **Topsham** Maine U.S.A.
140 B3 **Top Springs** N Terr Australia
95 M6 **Topton** Pennsylvania U.S.A.
103 L4 **Toquerville** Utah U.S.A.
102 G3 **Toquima Ra** Nevada U.S.A.
86 F4 **Tor** Ethiopia
6 N6 **Tor** *oil rig* North Sea
17 H3 **Torá** Spain
71 J4 **Torawitan, Tg** *B* Sulawesi
123 L8 **Tor B** Nova Scotia Canada
47 J6 **Torbalı** Turkey
77 F2 **Torbat-e-Ḩeydarīyeh** Iran
77 G2 **Torbat-e Jām** Iran
123 U6 **Torbay** Newfoundland Canada
123 L8 **Tor Bay** Nova Scotia Canada
143 C11 **Torbay B** W Australia Australia
27 F10 **Torberget** Norway
116 L6 **Torbert, Mt** Alaska U.S.A.
52 D5 **Torbino** Russian Federation
94 B1 **Torch L** Michigan U.S.A.
8 C7 **Torcross** England
21 N2 **Torcy-le-Grand** France
16 D3 **Tordesillas** Spain
26 N6 **Töre** Sweden
27 G13 **Töreboda** Sweden
28 H7 **Toreby** Denmark
27 F15 **Torekov** Sweden
29 K4 **Torekov** Sweden
145 F2 **Torere** New Zealand
27 J12 **Toresund** Sweden
17 F3 **Torete** *R* Spain
54 K8 **Torez** Ukraine
21 H7 **Torfou** France
33 S9 **Torgau** Germany
33 U5 **Torgelow** Germany
26 F6 **Torghatten** *isld* Norway
53 G8 **Torgun** *R* Russian Federation
27 H15 **Torhamn** Sweden
22 E1 **Torhout** Belgium
61 O10 **Toride** Japan
21 J3 **Torigny-sur-Vire** France
44 C1 **Torino** Italy
86 F5 **Torit** Sudan
130 D5 **Torixoreu** Brazil
52 D5 **Torkovichi** Russian Federation
29 N3 **Törmänen** Finland
8 D5 **Tormarton** England
55 G1 **Tormemtor, Ozero** *L* Russian Federation
142 E3 **Torment, Pt** W Australia Australia
16 D4 **Tormes** *R* Spain
117 Q11 **Tornado Mt** Alberta/Br Col Canada
28 D1 **Tornby** Denmark
Torneå *see* **Tornio**
26 M4 **Torne älv** *R* Sweden
32 L5 **Tornesch** Germany
26 K3 **Torneträsk** *L* Sweden
26 L3 **Torneträsk** Sweden
115 N6 **Torngat Mts** Quebec/ Labrador Canada
48 F7 **Tornik** *mt* Serbia Yugoslavia
108 A4 **Tornillo** Texas U.S.A.
28 C4 **Torning** Denmark
29 L6 **Tornio** Finland
29 L6 **Tornionjoki** *R* Finland
33 S6 **Tornow** Germany
133 E5 **Tornquist** Argentina
28 D6 **Torø** *isld* Denmark
60 S2 **Tōro** Japan
16 D3 **Toro** Spain
131 B2 **Toro, Cerro de** *pk* Arg/Chile
48 J3 **Toroiaga** *mt* Romania
48 F3 **Törökszentmiklós** Hungary
46 F4 **Toronaíos Kólpos** *G* Greece
139 K5 **Toronto** New South Wales Australia
121 D9 **Toronto** Ontario Canada
107 P4 **Toronto** Kansas U.S.A.
94 G6 **Toronto** Ohio U.S.A.
52 D6 **Toropets** Russian Federation
124 H5 **Toro, Pico del** *mt* Mexico
102 H8 **Toro Pk** California U.S.A.
131 B4 **Toro, Pta** Chile
88 E1 **Tororo** Uganda
78 D3 **Toros Dağlari** *mts* Turkey
15 F3 **Torphins** Scotland
52 F6 **Torpino** Russian Federation
8 B7 **Torpoint** England
26 H9 **Torpshammar** Sweden
133 G4 **Torquato Severo** Brazil
139 G7 **Torquay** Victoria Australia
98 C1 **Torquay** Saskatchewan Canada
8 C7 **Torquay** England
12 B3 **Torr** N Ireland
121 L8 **Torrance** Ontario Canada
102 F8 **Torrance** California U.S.A.
16 B6 **Torrão** Portugal
45 Q8 **Torre Annunziata** Italy
41 O6 **Torrebelvicino** Italy
17 H4 **Torreblanca** Spain
17 F2 **Torrecilla en Cameros** Spain
45 Q8 **Torre del Greco** Italy
44 F1 **Torre del Mangano** Italy
16 C3 **Torre de Moncorvo** Portugal
44 H4 **Torre di Lago Puccini** Italy
16 E7 **Torredonjimeno** Spain
45 L1 **Torréglia** Italy
16 C5 **Torrejoncillo** Spain
16 E1 **Torrelavega** Spain
42 G7 **Torremaggiore** Italy
16 E8 **Torremolinos** Spain
141 H5 **Torrens** *R* Queensland Australia
141 H5 **Torrens Cr** Queensland Australia
138 E4 **Torrens, L** South Australia Australia
17 G5 **Torrente** Spain
124 H5 **Torreón** Mexico
17 G7 **Torre Pacheco** Spain
133 H3 **Tôrres** Brazil
124 D3 **Torres** Mexico
16 E9 **Torres de Aleală** Morocco
137 O4 **Torres Is** Vanuatu
16 B5 **Torres Novas** Portugal
141 F1 **Torres Strait** Queensland Australia
16 A5 **Torres Vedras** Portugal
17 G7 **Torrevieja** Spain
103 N3 **Torrey** Utah U.S.A.
45 N5 **Torricella in Sabina** Italy
8 B6 **Torridge, R** England
45 L1 **Torri di Quartesolo** Italy
28 E5 **Torrild** Denmark
28 C5 **Tørring** Denmark
139 K3 **Torrington** New South Wales Australia
118 D7 **Torrington** Alberta Canada
95 O5 **Torrington** Connecticut U.S.A.
98 B7 **Torrington** Wyoming U.S.A.
98 B7 **Torrington, S** Wyoming U.S.A.
140 C1 **Tor Rock** *mt* N Terr Australia
26 F8 **Torröjen** *L* Sweden
16 E8 **Torrox** Spain
27 H11 **Torsåker** Sweden
27 H15 **Torsås** Sweden
27 G15 **Torsås, V** Sweden
26 F9 **Torsborg** Sweden
27 F11 **Torsby** Sweden
27 H12 **Torshälla** Sweden
6 F1 **Tórshavn** Faeroes
26 J2 **Torsken** Norway
26 L1 **Torsvåg** Norway
57 E3 **Tortkol'** Kazakhstan
55 F5 **Tortkuduk** Kazakhstan
43 F11 **Torto** *R* Sicily
113 L7 **Tortola** *isld* Virgin Is
131 B2 **Tortolas, Cerro las** *pk* Arg/Chile
44 E2 **Tortona** Italy
17 H4 **Tortosa** Spain
127 H4 **Tortue, Île de la** Haiti
77 D2 **Ţorūd** Iran
70 G5 **Torue** Sulawesi
31 L2 **Toruń** Poland
27 F15 **Torup** Sweden
52 C5 **Tõrva** Estonia
27 G13 **Torved** Sweden
13 E5 **Torver** England
26 J7 **Torvsjö** Sweden
121 M8 **Tory Hill** Ontario Canada
14 C1 **Tory I** Ireland
48 G2 **Torysa** *R* Slovakia
31 J3 **Torzym** Poland
60 G12 **Tosa** Japan
60 F13 **Tosa-Shimizu** Japan
60 G12 **Tosa-wan** *B* Japan
60 G12 **Tosa-Yamada** Japan
87 D11 **Tosca** S Africa
45 K4 **Toscana** *reg* Italy
42 C5 **Toscano, Arch** *islds* Italy
124 D5 **Tosca, Pta** *C* Mexico
41 N6 **Toscolano-Moderno** Italy
26 F6 **Tosen** Norway
26 F6 **Tosenfjord** *inlet* Norway
41 N3 **Tösens** Austria
61 K11 **Tōshi-jima** *isld* Japan
61 N11 **To-shima** *isld* Japan
61 P5 **Tōshima-yama** *mt* Japan
52 D5 **Tosno** Russian Federation
58 C4 **Toson Hu** *L* China
58 C2 **Tosontsengel** Mongolia
26 F9 **Tossåsen** Sweden
45 L3 **Tossignano** Italy
133 E3 **Tostado** Argentina
101 O3 **Toston** Montana U.S.A.
60 D12 **Tosu** Japan
78 D1 **Tosya** Turkey
31 L5 **Toszek** Poland
17 F7 **Totana** Spain
83 K11 **Totapola** *mt* Sri Lanka
144 C5 **Totara Flat** New Zealand
145 D1 **Totara North** New Zealand
145 D4 **Totaranui** New Zealand
27 E11 **Toten** *reg* Norway
32 L6 **Tötensen** Germany
21 N2 **Tôtes** France
38 J6 **Totes Gebirge** *mts* Austria
48 F4 **Tótkomlós** Hungary
9 E1 **Totley** England
8 C7 **Totnes** England
129 G2 **Totness** Suriname
89 C6 **Toto** *mt* S Africa
144 B6 **Totoko Pk** New Zealand
125 L9 **Totolápam** Mexico
131 B2 **Totoralillo** Chile
85 C7 **Totota** Liberia
146 G14 **Totten Glacier** Antarctica
139 H4 **Tottenham** New South Wales Australia
121 L8 **Tottenham** Ontario Canada
9 E6 **Totton** England
59 K4 **Tottori** Japan
60 G10 **Tottori** *prefect* Japan
119 M6 **Totzke** Saskatchewan Canada
85 C7 **Touba** Ivory Coast
85 C2 **Toubkal, Jbel** *mt* Morocco
20 H7 **Touches,les** France
100 G3 **Touchet** Washington U.S.A.
119 N7 **Touchwood Hills** Saskatchewan Canada
18 H5 **Toucy** France
65 G3 **Toudao Jiang** *R* China
65 D3 **Toufendi** China
85 D6 **Tougan** Burkina
85 B6 **Tougé** Guinea
85 F2 **Touggourt** Algeria
85 C3 **Touila** Mauritania
19 J4 **Toul** France
85 C7 **Toulépleu** Ivory Coast
20 A5 **Toulinguet,Pte,du** France
122 E3 **Toulnustouc R** Quebec Canada
19 P18 **Toulon** France
99 R8 **Toulon** Illinois U.S.A.
102 F1 **Toulon** Nevada U.S.A.
19 O17 **Touloubre** *R* France
18 F9 **Toulouse** France
84 E5 **Toumma** Niger
85 C7 **Toumodi** Ivory Coast
68 C3 **Toungoo** Burma
21 L3 **Touques** France
21 L3 **Touques** *R* France
22 B2 **Touquet-Paris Plage, le** France
68 F3 **Tourakom** Laos
Tourane *see* **Da Nang**
20 C5 **Tourch** France
22 E2 **Tourcoing** France
21 L7 **Touriane** *reg* France
16 A1 **Touriñan, C** Spain
85 B4 **Tourine** Mauritania
20 G2 **Tourlaville** France
18 F10 **Tourmalet, Col du** France
22 E2 **Tournai** Belgium
128 D5 **Tournavista** Peru
18 F9 **Tournay** France
19 N14 **Tournon** France
21 M8 **Tournon-St.Martin** Indre-et-Loire France
40 A4 **Tournus** France
21 O3 **Tourny** France
130 J8 **Touros** Brazil
21 M4 **Tourouvre** France
21 M7 **Tours** France
21 L7 **Tour-St. Gélin, la** France
40 E5 **Tour Sallière** *mt* Switzerland
22 H4 **Tourteron** France
19 P18 **Tourves** France
21 N3 **Tourville-la-Rivière** France
21 L2 **Tourville-les-Ifs** France
21 O5 **Toury** France
86 C1 **Toussidé Pic** *mt* Chad
21 P1 **Toutencourt** France
119 S7 **Toutes Aides** Manitoba Canada
100 C3 **Toutle** Washington U.S.A.
20 G8 **Touvois** France
89 B9 **Touwsrivier** S Africa
37 O3 **Toužim** Czech Rep
127 J10 **Tovar** Venezuela
54 K3 **Tovarkovskiy** Russian Federation
27 C13 **Tovdal** Norway
27 C13 **Tovdalselv** *R* Norway
9 F3 **Tove, R** England
61 O5 **Towada-Hachimantai Nat. Park** Japan
61 O5 **Towada ko** *L* Japan
145 E1 **Towai** New Zealand
128 G2 **Towakaima** Guyana
139 J6 **Towamba** New South Wales Australia
110 H1 **Towanda** Illinois U.S.A.
107 O4 **Towanda** Kansas U.S.A.
95 L5 **Towanda** Pennsylvania U.S.A.
70 G7 **Towari** Sulawesi
9 F3 **Towcester** England
99 O2 **Tower** Minnesota U.S.A.
98 J3 **Tower City** North Dakota U.S.A.
95 L6 **Tower City** Pennsylvania U.S.A.
101 P5 **Tower Falls** Wyoming U.S.A.
110 H2 **Tower Hill** Illinois U.S.A.
144 A6 **Towing Head** New Zealand
106 H3 **Towner** Colorado U.S.A.
98 F1 **Towner** North Dakota U.S.A.
102 G5 **Townes Pass** California U.S.A.
111 J8 **Townley** Alabama U.S.A.
95 M7 **Townsend** Delaware U.S.A.
112 F6 **Townsend** Georgia U.S.A.
101 O3 **Townsend** Montana U.S.A.
112 D2 **Townsend** Tennessee U.S.A.
99 S4 **Townsend** Wisconsin U.S.A.
139 J6 **Townsend, Mt** Victoria Australia
141 K5 **Townshend I** Queensland Australia
141 H4 **Townsville** Queensland Australia
94 H5 **Townville** Pennsylvania U.S.A.
70 G6 **Towori, Teluk** *B* Sulawesi
86 F4 **Towot** Sudan
95 L7 **Towson** Maryland U.S.A.
70 G6 **Towuti** *L* Sulawesi
8 C3 **Towy, R** Wales
112 D2 **Toxaway, L** North Carolina U.S.A.
66 B3 **Toxkan He** *R* China
108 D4 **Toyah L** Texas U.S.A.
60 O3 **Tōya-ko** *L* Japan
61 L9 **Toyama** Japan
61 L8 **Toyama wan** *B* Japan
116 A3 **Toygunen** Russian Federation
61 L10 **Toyo** Japan
61 L10 **Toyoake** Japan
60 G11 **Toyohama** Japan
61 L11 **Toyohashi** Japan
61 L11 **Toyokawa** Japan
60 R3 **Toyokoro** Japan
61 J11 **Toyonaka** Japan
60 H10 **Toyooka** Japan
61 N8 **Toyosaka** Japan
61 L10 **Toyota** Japan
29 K9 **Töysä** Finland
57 E4 **Toytepa** Uzbekistan
85 F2 **Tozeur** Tunisia
116 M4 **Tozitna** *R* Alaska U.S.A.
36 C4 **Traben-Trarbach** Germany
79 F4 **Trâblous** Lebanon
78 G1 **Trabzon** Turkey
122 H6 **Tracadie** New Brunswick Canada
123 L8 **Tracadie** Nova Scotia Canada
122 F8 **Tracey** New Brunswick Canada
69 H8 **Tra Cu** Vietnam
102 C4 **Tracy** California U.S.A.
99 O8 **Tracy** Iowa U.S.A.
99 L5 **Tracy** Minnesota U.S.A.
110 L6 **Tracy City** Tennessee U.S.A.
22 E5 **Tracy-le-Mont** France
41 J6 **Tradate** Italy
119 O3 **Trade L** Saskatchewan Canada
110 J4 **Tradewater** *R* Kentucky U.S.A.
Tradom *see* **Zhongba**
99 O7 **Traer** Iowa U.S.A.
98 F10 **Traer** Kansas U.S.A.
16 C8 **Trafalgar, C** Spain
111 K8 **Trafford** Alabama U.S.A.
113 F11 **Trafford, L** Florida U.S.A.
131 B8 **Traful** *R* Argentina
131 B8 **Traful, L** Argentina
38 L5 **Tragwein** Austria
48 L5 **Traian** Romania
130 J9 **Traição, B. de** Brazil
133 C5 **Traiguén** Chile
133 C7 **Traiguén, I** Chile
100 H1 **Trail** British Columbia Canada
100 C7 **Trail** Oregon U.S.A.
98 F4 **Trail City** South Dakota U.S.A.
115 R3 **Traill Ø** *isld* Greenland
143 D6 **Trainor Hills** W Australia Australia
117 N5 **Trainor L** Northwest Territories Canada
21 P6 **Traînou** France
130 H10 **Traipu** Brazil
130 J9 **Trairi** *R* Brazil
38 N5 **Traismauer** Austria
21 M3 **Trait,le** France
52 H3 **Trakt** Russian Federation
111 F8 **Tralake** Mississippi U.S.A.
14 B4 **Tralee** Ireland
68 J6 **Tram Bo** Vietnam
40 F3 **Tramelan** Switzerland
68 G7 **Tram Kak** Cambodia
68 G7 **Tram Khnan** Cambodia
14 D4 **Tramore** Ireland
118 J6 **Tramping** Saskatchewan Canada
27 H13 **Tranås** Sweden
28 E4 **Tranbjerg** Denmark
133 D3 **Trancas** Argentina
124 G3 **Trancas** Mexico
18 E6 **Tranche, la** France
130 H5 **Trancoso** Brazil
16 C4 **Trancoso** Portugal
27 F14 **Tranemo** Sweden
13 F2 **Tranent** Scotland
69 D9 **Trang** Thailand
139 J4 **Trangie** New South Wales Australia
27 G11 **Trängslet** Sweden
69 H8 **Tranh De, Cua** *R* Vietnam
43 G7 **Trani** Italy
26 J2 **Tranöy** Norway
102 D5 **Tranquillity** California U.S.A.
19 Q18 **Trans** France
20 G4 **Trans** France
20 G5 **Trans** Ille-et-Vilaine France
146 C12 **Transantarctic Mts** Antarctica
118 C1 **Transcona** Manitoba Canada
Transkei *see* **Eastern Cape**
27 F11 **Transtrand** Sweden
Transvaal *see* **Eastern Transvaal, Northern Transvaal, North West, Pretoria-Witwatersrand-Vereeniging**
48 J4 **Transylvania** *reg* Romania

Transylvanian Alps *see* **Carpaţii Meridionali** *mts*
68 G8 **Tra On** Vietnam
41 L5 **Traona** Italy
43 E10 **Trapani** Sicily
101 L4 **Trapper Pk** Montana U.S.A.
21 P4 **Trappes** France
131 H3 **Trapua** *R* Brazil
13 E2 **Traquair** Scotland
139 H7 **Traralgon** Victoria Australia
17 F9 **Traras, Mt.des** Algeria
27 G15 **Traryd** Sweden
85 A5 **Trarza** *reg* Mauritania
45 P6 **Trasacco** Italy
42 E5 **Trasimeno, L** Italy
26 L6 **Träskholm** Sweden
109 P1 **Traskwood** Arkansas U.S.A.
16 C3 **Tras os Montes e Alto Douro** *prov* Portugal
16 B1 **Trasparga** Spain
36 B4 **Trassem** Germany
45 H3 **Trassilico** Italy
68 F6 **Trat** Thailand
38 K5 **Traun** Austria
99 U3 **Traunik** Michigan U.S.A.
38 J6 **Traunsee** *L* Austria
38 J6 **Traunstein** *mt* Austria
38 G6 **Traunstein** Germany
33 M5 **Trave** *R* Germany
138 F5 **Travellers L** New South Wales Australia
112 E3 **Travellers Rest** South Carolina U.S.A.
33 N5 **Travemünde** Germany
33 M5 **Travenberg** Germany
118 E8 **Travers** Alberta Canada
131 H7 **Traversay Islds** S Sandwich Is
94 B1 **Traverse B.Grand** Michigan U.S.A.
94 B1 **Traverse B.Little** Michigan U.S.A.
94 B2 **Traverse City** Michigan U.S.A.
98 K4 **Traverse, L** South Dakota U.S.A.
116 H4 **Traverse Pk** Alaska U.S.A.
45 H2 **Traversetolo** Italy
122 B5 **Travers, L** Quebec Canada
144 D5 **Travers, Mt** New Zealand
131 C5 **Travesia Puntana** *reg* Argentina
131 C4 **Travesia Tunuyán** *reg* Argentina
68 H8 **Tra Vinh** Vietnam
109 J5 **Travis, L** Texas U.S.A.
42 H4 **Travnik** Bosnia-Herzegovina
55 G4 **Travnoye** Russian Federation
44 F2 **Travo** Italy
70 P10 **Trawangan** Indonesia
14 D1 **Trawbreaga B** Ireland
109 N4 **Trawick** Texas U.S.A.
8 C2 **Trawsfynydd** Wales
143 C9 **Trayning** W Australia
42 G2 **Trbovlje** Slovenia
8 B1 **Tre-Arddur B** Wales
127 J3 **Treasure Beach** Jamaica
116 J3 **Treat I** Alaska U.S.A.
44 F2 **Trebbecco, L. di** Italy
44 F2 **Trebbia** *R* Italy
33 S8 **Trebbin** Germany
33 R4 **Trebel** *R* Germany
33 O7 **Trebel** Germany
18 G9 **Trèbes** France
20 C4 **Trébeurden** France
31 J6 **Třebíč** Czech Rep
42 J6 **Trebinje** Bosnia-Herzegovina
42 J6 **Trebišnica** *R* Bosnia-Herzegovina
48 G2 **Trebišov** Slovakia
42 H5 **Trebižat** *R* Bosnia-Herzegovina
Trebizond *see* **Trabzon**
144 A7 **Treble Mt** New Zealand
42 G3 **Trebnje** Slovenia
31 H6 **Třeboň** Czech Rep
20 B5 **Tréboul** France
20 D5 **Trébrivan** France
33 R10 **Trebsen** Germany
36 E4 **Trebur** Germany
8 C4 **Trecastle** Wales
44 E1 **Trecate** Italy
45 K1 **Trecenta** Italy
106 B7 **Trechado** New Mexico U.S.A.
8 C4 **Tredegar** Wales
41 N6 **Tredici Comuni** *reg* Italy
9 E3 **Tredington** England
20 E6 **Trédion** France
45 L3 **Tredozio** Italy
20 C4 **Trédrez** France
73 L6 **Tree I** Lakshadweep Indian Oc
101 R1 **Treelon** Saskatchewan Canada
20 G6 **Treffieux** France
40 B5 **Treffort** France
8 C1 **Trefnant** Wales
8 C1 **Trefriw** Wales
8 C3 **Tregaron** Wales
119 N8 **Tregarva** Saskatchewan Canada
20 C4 **Trégastel** France
101 L1 **Trego** Montana U.S.A.
102 E1 **Trego** Nevada U.S.A.
99 P4 **Trego** Wisconsin U.S.A.
8 B7 **Tregony** England
20 D4 **Trégorrois** *reg* France
141 K4 **Tregosse Islets & Reefs** Gt Barrier Reef Aust
20 D4 **Treguier** France
20 C6 **Trégunc** France
119 T9 **Treherne** Manitoba Canada
68 G8 **Tre, Hon** *isld* Vietnam
26 K8 **Trehörningsjö** Sweden
20 B5 **Tréhou, le** France
15 D4 **Treig, L** Scotland
18 G7 **Treignac** France
20 G7 **Treillières** France
131 G4 **Treinta y Tres** Uruguay
36 C3 **Treis-Karden** Germany
140 E5 **Trekelano** Queensland Australia
127 J2 **Trelawney** *parish* Jamaica
89 G1 **Trelawney** Zimbabwe
21 K7 **Trélazé** France
32 L6 **Trelde** Germany
28 D5 **Trelde Næs** *C* Denmark
133 D6 **Trelew** Argentina
27 F16 **Trelleborg** Sweden
8 D4 **Trelleck** Wales
22 G3 **Trélon** France
8 B2 **Tremadoc** Wales
8 B2 **Tremadoc B** Wales
18 E7 **Tremblade, la** France
20 H5 **Tremblay** France
21 N4 **Tremblay-les-Villages** France
117 L8 **Trembleur L** British Columbia Canada
106 F6 **Trementina** New Mexico U.S.A.
21 J7 **Trémentines** France
37 K3 **Tremersdorf** Germany
42 G6 **Tremiti, I.di** Italy
110 G1 **Tremont** Illinois U.S.A.
111 H7 **Tremont** Mississippi U.S.A.
95 L6 **Tremont** Pennsylvania U.S.A.
101 N8 **Tremonton** Utah U.S.A.
20 F5 **Trémorel** France
37 P4 **Třemošná** Czech Rep
17 H2 **Tremp** Spain
99 P5 **Trempealeau** Wisconsin U.S.A.
33 M5 **Tremsbüttel** Germany
69 G8 **Trem Trem** *R* Vietnam
99 U3 **Trenary** Michigan U.S.A.
121 S5 **Trenche** *R* Quebec Canada
48 E2 **Trenčin** Slovakia
28 C3 **Trend Å** *R* Denmark
32 K9 **Trendelburg** Germany
133 E5 **Trenel** Argentina
27 A11 **Trengereid** Norway
70 N9 **Trenggalek** Java
131 E5 **Trenque Lauquen** Argentina
Trent *see* **Trento**
112 K2 **Trent** *R* North Carolina U.S.A.
108 G3 **Trent** Texas U.S.A.
121 L8 **Trent Canal** Ontario Canada
41 N5 **Trentino-Alto Adige** *reg* Italy
41 O5 **Trento** Italy
45 Q8 **Tréntola** Italy
122 K8 **Trenton** Nova Scotia Canada
121 N8 **Trenton** Ontario Canada
113 E8 **Trenton** Florida U.S.A.
94 D4 **Trenton** Michigan U.S.A.
110 C1 **Trenton** Missouri U.S.A.
98 E9 **Trenton** Nebraska U.S.A.
95 N6 **Trenton** New Jersey U.S.A.
95 M3 **Trenton** New York U.S.A.
98 C1 **Trenton** North Dakota U.S.A.
110 M2 **Trenton** Ohio U.S.A.
112 F4 **Trenton** South Carolina U.S.A.
110 H6 **Trenton** Tennessee U.S.A.
13 H6 **Trent, R** England
21 N4 **Tréon** France
46 D2 **Trepča** Serbia Yugoslavia
21 N1 **Tréport, le** France
38 H8 **Treppo Carnico** Italy
120 C3 **Treptow L** Ontario Canada
133 F4 **Tres Arboles** Uruguay
131 E7 **Tres Arroyos** Argentina
20 G6 **Tresboeuf** France
128 F5 **Três Casas** Brazil
19 P16 **Trescléoux** France
9 F7 **Tresco** *isld* Isles of Scilly England
130 F7 **Três Corações** Brazil
33 N9 **Treseburg** Germany
15 B4 **Treshnish I** Scotland
46 E3 **Treska** *R* Macedonia
48 E7 **Treskavica** *mt* Bosnia-Herzegovina
130 D7 **Três Lagoas** Brazil
130 F6 **Três Marias, Barragem** *dam* Brazil
133 B7 **Tres Montes, Pen** Chile
16 E2 **Trespaderne** Spain
130 D10 **Tres Passos** Brazil
131 E7 **Tres Picos, Cerro** *pk* Argentina
106 E5 **Tres Piedras** New Mexico U.S.A.
102 C5 **Tres Pinos** California U.S.A.
130 F7 **Três Pontas** Brazil
133 C3 **Tres Puentes** Chile
130 G8 **Três Rios** Brazil
21 M6 **Tresson** France
31 J6 **Třešt'** Czech Rep
15 G2 **Tresta** Shetland Scotland
125 M8 **Tres Zapotes** Mexico
8 C4 **Tretower** Wales
19 P18 **Trets** France
27 D10 **Trettin** Norway
37 K6 **Treuchtlingen** Germany
33 N2 **Treuen** Germany
33 R8 **Treuenbrietzen** Germany
140 B5 **Treuer Ra** N Terr Australia
27 C12 **Treungen** Norway
20 E5 **Trévé** France
Treves *see* **Trier**
20 C5 **Trévézal,Roc** *mt* France
21 J3 **Trévières** France
41 L6 **Treviglio** Italy
17 F2 **Treviño** Spain
42 E3 **Treviso** Italy
8 A6 **Trevose Head** England
40 A6 **Trévoux** France
36 G2 **Treysa** Germany
31 H7 **Trhové Sviny** Czech Rep
27 H14 **Triabo** Sweden
139 J8 **Triabunna** Tasmania Australia
20 C4 **Triagoz, les** France
140 D2 **Trial B** N Terr Australia
47 V17 **Tríanda** Rhodes Greece
117 P8 **Triangle** Alberta Canada
100 J7 **Triangle** Idaho U.S.A.
89 G3 **Triangle** Zimbabwe
47 H8 **Tría Nisiá** *isld* Greece
48 E2 **Tribeč** *R* Slovakia
20 H3 **Tribehou** France
40 H1 **Triberg** Germany
33 R4 **Tribsees** Germany
141 H3 **Tribulation, C** Queensland Australia
119 O9 **Tribune** Saskatchewan Canada
107 J3 **Tribune** Kansas U.S.A.
43 G8 **Tricarico** Italy
43 J9 **Tricase** Italy
76 C5 **Trichur** India
9 E6 **Trickett's Cross** England
22 D4 **Tricot** France
139 H5 **Trida** New South Wales Australia
100 G8 **Trident Pk** Nevada U.S.A.
38 K7 **Trieben** Austria
37 N2 **Triebes** Germany
21 O3 **Trie-Château** France
37 P6 **Triefenried** Germany
21 P4 **Triel-sur-Seine** France
131 G4 **Trienta-y-Tres** Uruguay
36 B4 **Trier** Germany
37 K5 **Triesdorf** Germany
42 F3 **Trieste** Italy
42 E3 **Trieste, G.di** Italy
20 D4 **Trieux** *R* France
22 K5 **Trieux** France
37 P7 **Triftern** Germany
42 F2 **Triglav** *mt* Slovenia
20 F7 **Trignac** France
42 F7 **Trigno** *R* Italy
16 C7 **Triguerós** Spain
46 F5 **Tríkeri** Greece
46 E6 **Trikhonís, L** Greece
46 E5 **Tríkkala** Greece
46 E6 **Tríklinos** Greece
79 D3 **Trikomo** Cyprus
113 E9 **Trilby** Florida U.S.A.
17 F4 **Trillo** Spain
120 G2 **Trilsbeck L** Ontario Canada
14 E3 **Trim** Ireland
13 G4 **Trimdon** England
9 H4 **Trimley** England
99 M6 **Trimont** Minnesota U.S.A.
142 B5 **Trimouille I** W Australia Australia
18 F6 **Trimouille, la** France
124 D2 **Trincheras** Mexico
106 F4 **Trinchere** Colorado U.S.A.
83 L9 **Trincomalee** Sri Lanka
90 G11 **Trindade** *isld* Atlantic Oc
9 F4 **Tring** England
46 E5 **Tringía** *mt* Greece
121 T6 **Tring Junction** Quebec Canada
128 F6 **Trinidad** Bolivia
128 D2 **Trinidad** Colombia
126 D4 **Trinidad** Cuba
130 C10 **Trinidad** Paraguay
71 G4 **Trinidad** Philippines
131 G4 **Trinidad** Uruguay
100 A8 **Trinidad** California U.S.A.
106 F4 **Trinidad** Colorado U.S.A.
100 E2 **Trinidad** Washington U.S.A.
127 O2 **Trinidad** *isld* W Indies
127 O9 **Trinidad and Tobago** *rep* W Indies
133 B7 **Trinidad, Canal** Chile
131 E7 **Trinidad, I** Argentina
21 M4 **Trinité-de-Réville, la** France
20 E5 **Trinité-Porhoët, la** France
20 D6 **Trinité-sur-Mer, la** France
123 T5 **Trinity** Newfoundland Canada
109 L3 **Trinity** *R* Texas U.S.A.
109 M5 **Trinity** Texas U.S.A.
141 H3 **Trinity B** Queensland Australia
100 C8 **Trinity Center** California U.S.A.
127 P3 **Trinity Hills** Trinidad
146 C4 **Trinity I** *isld* Antarctica
116 K8 **Trinity Is** Alaska U.S.A.
146 D4 **Trinity Peninsula** *pen* Antarctica
102 F1 **Trinity Ra** Nevada U.S.A.
100 C9 **Trinity Res** California U.S.A.
69 A8 **Trinkat I** Nicobar Is
44 D1 **Trino** Italy
Trinquet, Fort *see* **Bir Mogreïn**
83 L12 **Triolet** Mauritius
112 B3 **Trion** Georgia U.S.A.
43 H9 **Trionto, C** Italy
69 C10 **Tripa** *R* Sumatra
Tripoli *see* **Trâblous** Lebanon
Tripoli *see* **Tarābulus** Libya
99 O7 **Tripoli** Iowa U.S.A.
46 E7 **Trípolis** Greece
84 E3 **Tripolitania** *reg* Libya
98 H6 **Tripp** South Dakota U.S.A.
36 D5 **Trippstadt** Germany
37 M2 **Triptis** Germany
75 O7 **Tripura** *prov* India
123 N3 **Triquet, L** Quebec Canada
32 J4 **Trischen** *isld* Germany
37 O4 **Tři Sekery** Czech Rep
90 H12 **Tristan da Cunha** Atlantic Oc
68 G7 **Tri Ton** Vietnam
33 M5 **Trittau** Germany
130 H9 **Triunfo** Brazil
76 C6 **Trivandrum** India
48 D2 **Trnava** Slovakia
21 K3 **Troarn** France
36 G7 **Trochtelfingen** Germany
26 F5 **Troena** *isld* Norway
28 F6 **Troense** Denmark
38 M7 **Trofaiach** Austria
147 Q9 **Trofimovsk** Russian Federation
42 G5 **Trogir** Croatia
42 H5 **Troglav** *mt* Croatia/Yugoslavia
36 C2 **Troisdorf** Germany
36 C6 **Troisfontaines** France
85 D1 **Trois Fourches, Cap des** Morocco
21 L7 **Trois Moutiers, les** France
122 C5 **Trois Pistoles** Quebec Canada
22 K3 **Trois Ponts** Belgium
121 S6 **Trois Rivières** Quebec Canada
127 N5 **Trois Rivières** Guadeloupe W Indies
83 M14 **Trois Swains, Les** *islds* Kerguelen Indian Oc
22 K3 **Trois Vierges** Luxembourg
54 M2 **Troitsa** Russian Federation
55 E1 **Troitsa** Tyumenskaya obl Russian Federation
55 D4 **Troitsk** Russian Federation
56 F4 **Troitsk** Russian Federation
54 J1 **Troitsk** Moskovskaya obl Russian Federation
55 D3 **Troitskiy** Russian Federation
52 J3 **Troitsko-Pechorsk** Russian Federation
55 F4 **Troitskoye** Russian Federation
55 C4 **Troitskoye** Bashkirskaya Respublika Russian Federation
127 L2 **Troja** Jamaica
28 B5 **Troldhede** Denmark
27 F13 **Trollhättan** Sweden
26 D9 **Trollheimen** *mt* Norway
26 C9 **Trolltindane** *mt* Norway
129 G4 **Trombetas** *R* Brazil
83 H6 **Tromelin I** Indian Oc
133 C5 **Tromen** *mt* Argentina
131 B6 **Tromen, V** Argentina
41 M6 **Trompia, V** Italy
26 K2 **Tromsö** Norway
26 K2 **Tromsöysund** Norway
55 F1 **Trom'yegan** *R* Russian Federation
102 G6 **Trona** California U.S.A.
131 B8 **Tronador** *pk* Arg/Chile
20 G4 **Tronchet, le** France
124 G6 **Troncón** Mexico
26 J3 **Trondenes** Norway
26 D8 **Trondheim** Norway
26 D8 **Trondheimsfjord** *inlet* Norway
26 E9 **Tronfjell** *mt* Norway
27 J10 **Trönödal** Sweden
42 F6 **Tronto** *R* Italy
21 M6 **Trôo** France
79 C4 **Troödos, Mt** Cyprus
12 D3 **Trool, L** Scotland
12 D2 **Troon** Scotland
43 G10 **Tropea** Italy
130 G4 **Tropeiros, Sa.dos** *mts* Brazil
103 M4 **Tropic** Utah U.S.A.
46 D2 **Tropojë** Albania
27 J13 **Trosa** Sweden
52 J2 **Trosh** Russian Federation
98 K6 **Trosky** Minnesota U.S.A.
119 N9 **Trossachs** Saskatchewan Canada
12 D1 **Trossachs** Scotland
14 E1 **Trostan** *mt* N Ireland
28 E6 **Trøstrup Korup** Denmark
48 M2 **Trostyanets** Ukraine
33 P9 **Trotha** Germany
98 C2 **Trotters** North Dakota U.S.A.
48 K4 **Trotuş** *R* Romania
101 T9 **Troublesome** Colorado U.S.A.
142 F2 **Troughton I** W Australia Australia
68 G6 **Troun** Cambodia
109 M3 **Troup** Texas U.S.A.
107 L4 **Trousdale** Kansas U.S.A.
122 F6 **Trousers, L** New Brunswick Canada
117 L6 **Trout** *R* British Columbia Canada
111 D10 **Trout** Louisiana U.S.A.
13 F5 **Troutbeck** England
103 L6 **Trout Cr** Arizona U.S.A.
100 E5 **Trout Cr** Oregon U.S.A.
121 L7 **Trout Creek** Ontario Canada
99 R3 **Trout Creek** Michigan U.S.A.
100 K2 **Trout Creek** Montana U.S.A.
103 L2 **Trout Creek** Utah U.S.A.
117 P10 **Trout L** British Columbia Canada
99 R3 **Trout L** Wisconsin U.S.A.
117 N5 **Trout Lake** Northwest Territories Canada
101 Q5 **Trout Pk** Wyoming U.S.A.
118 C2 **Trout R** Alberta Canada
123 O4 **Trout River** Newfoundland Canada
95 K5 **Trout Run** Pennsylvania U.S.A.
94 J5 **Troutville** Pennsylvania U.S.A.
94 H9 **Troutville** Virginia U.S.A.
21 L3 **Trouville** France
8 D5 **Trowbridge** England
139 H8 **Trowutta** Tasmania Australia
127 J2 **Troy** Jamaica
47 H5 **Troy** Turkey
111 L10 **Troy** Alabama U.S.A.
100 J3 **Troy** Idaho U.S.A.
110 K3 **Troy** Indiana U.S.A.
110 F3 **Troy** Missouri U.S.A.
100 K1 **Troy** Montana U.S.A.
95 P4 **Troy** New Hampshire U.S.A.
95 O4 **Troy** New York U.S.A.
112 H2 **Troy** North Carolina U.S.A.
110 M1 **Troy** Ohio U.S.A.
100 H4 **Troy** Oregon U.S.A.
95 L5 **Troy** Pennsylvania U.S.A.
109 K4 **Troy** Texas U.S.A.
94 G7 **Troy** West Virginia U.S.A.
46 G2 **Troyan** Bulgaria
55 E4 **Troyebratskiy** Kazakhstan
18 H4 **Troyes** France
95 P2 **Troy, N** Vermont U.S.A.
103 J3 **Troy Pk** Nevada U.S.A.
37 N3 **Tršnice** Czech Rep
48 F1 **Trstená** Slovakia
46 D1 **Trstenik** Serbia Yugoslavia
140 D1 **Truant I** N Terr Australia
119 N9 **Truax** Saskatchewan Canada
54 E4 **Trubchevsk** Russian Federation
54 C6 **Trubezh** *R* Ukraine
124 G5 **Truchas** Mexico
106 E5 **Truchas** New Mexico U.S.A.
36 D6 **Truchtersheim** France
Trucial States *see* **United Arab Emirates**
102 D2 **Truckee** California U.S.A.
102 E2 **Truckee** *R* Nevada U.S.A.
59 K3 **Trudovoye** Russian Federation
15 D4 **Truim** *R* Scotland
121 M5 **Truite, L. la** Quebec Canada
125 L2 **Trujillo** Honduras
128 C5 **Trujillo** Peru
16 D5 **Trujillo** Spain
106 F6 **Trujillo** New Mexico U.S.A.
127 J10 **Trujillo** Venezuela
Truk Is *see* **Chuuk**
99 M6 **Truman** Minnesota U.S.A.
110 F6 **Trumann** Arkansas U.S.A.
95 L4 **Trumansburg** New York U.S.A.
98 H9 **Trumbull** Nebraska U.S.A.
103 L5 **Trumbull, Mt** Arizona U.S.A.
69 C11 **Trumon** Sumatra
9 G3 **Trumpington** England
21 L4 **Trun** France
139 J5 **Trundle** New South Wales Australia
67 B5 **Trung Khanh Phu** Vietnam
69 G8 **Trung Lon,Hon** *isld* Vietnam
69 G8 **Trung Nho,Hon** *isld* Vietnam
138 E5 **Truro** South Australia Australia
122 J8 **Truro** Nova Scotia Canada
8 A7 **Truro** England
99 N8 **Truro** Iowa U.S.A.
95 R4 **Truro** Massachusetts U.S.A.
70 D2 **Trusan** Sarawak
108 H2 **Truscott** Texas U.S.A.
48 K3 **Truşeşti** Romania
37 J2 **Trusetal** Germany
48 H1 **Truskavets** Ukraine
14 C2 **Truskmore** *mt* Ireland
70 E2 **Trus Madi, G** *mt* Sabah
52 H2 **Trusovo** Russian Federation
111 K8 **Trussville** Alabama U.S.A.
46 G1 **Trŭstenik** Bulgaria
28 F4 **Trustrup** Denmark
117 M7 **Trutch** British Columbia Canada
106 C8 **Truth or Consequences** New Mexico U.S.A.
31 J5 **Trutnov** Czech Rep
21 J4 **Truttemer-le-Petit** France
95 L4 **Truxton** New York U.S.A.
18 G8 **Truyère** *R* France
46 G2 **Tryavna** Bulgaria
98 F8 **Tryon** Nebraska U.S.A.
145 E2 **Tryphena** New Zealand
27 F10 **Trysil** Norway
27 E10 **Trysilelv** *R* Norway
52 B6 **Tryškiai** Lithuania
31 J2 **Trzcianka** Poland
31 H2 **Trzebiez** Poland
31 K4 **Trzebnica** Poland
31 K3 **Trzemeszno** Poland
42 F2 **Tržič** Slovenia
53 G10 **Tsagan Aman** Russian Federation
Tsaidam *basin* *see* **Qaidam Pendi**
46 D5 **Tsamandás** Greece
Tsamkong *see* **Zhanjiang**
Tsangpo *R* *see* **Yarlung Zangbo Jiang** *R*
Tsaochwang *see* **Zaozhuang**
87 H11 **Tsaratanana** Madagascar
87 H10 **Tsaratanana, Massif du** *mt* Madagascar
87 D10 **Tsau** Botswana
88 G3 **Tsavo** Kenya
88 G3 **Tsavo East Nat. Park** Kenya
88 G3 **Tsavo West National Park** Kenya
89 A6 **Tsawisis** Namibia
41 M4 **Tschlin** Switzerland
55 D4 **Tselinnoye** Russian Federation
55 D5 **Tselinnyy** Russian Federation
55 F5 **Tselinograd** Kazakhstan
54 F3 **Tsementnyy** Russian Federation
52 G3 **Tsenogora** Russian Federation
56 C3 **Tsentral'nyy** Russian Federation
87 C11 **Tses** Namibia
58 D2 **Tsetserleg** Mongolia
85 E7 **Tsevié** Togo
87 D11 **Tshabong** Botswana
87 D7 **Tshabuta** Zaire
87 D10 **Tshane** Botswana
87 E8 **Tshangalele, L** Zaire
86 B7 **Tshela** Zaire
87 D7 **Tshibala** Zaire
86 B6 **Tshibobo, Pte** Gabon
86 D7 **Tshikapa** Zaire
87 D7 **Tshimbalanga** Zaire
87 E8 **Tshinsenda** Zaire
86 E7 **Tshofa** Zaire
89 E2 **Tsholotsho** Zimbabwe
Tšhqurghān *see* **Kholm**
86 D6 **Tshuapa** *R* Zaire
87 D10 **Tshwanne** Botswana
52 G2 **Tsil'ma** *R* Russian Federation
53 F10 **Tsimlyansk** Russian Federation
65 D6 **Tsinan** China
87 D11 **Tsineng** S Africa
46 G3 **Tsínga** *mt* Greece
Tsingtao *see* **Qingdao**
68 F1 **Tsinh Ho** Vietnam
Tsining *see* **Jining** Nei Monggol Zizhiqu
Tsin Ling *mt ra* *see* **Qin Ling** *mt ra*
87 H13 **Tsiombe** Madagascar
46 E5 **Tsiótion** Greece
58 G1 **Tsipa** *R* Russian Federation
87 H11 **Tsiroanomandidy** Madagascar
Tsitsihar *see* **Qiqihar**
89 C9 **Tsitsikammaberge** *mts* S Africa
89 C10 **Tsitsikammaberge Forest and Coastal National Park** S Africa
52 G6 **Tsivilsk** Russian Federation
87 H12 **Tsivory** Madagascar
52 D6 **Tsna** *R* Russian Federation
65 A1 **Tsomog** Mongolia
87 D10 **Tsootsha** Botswana
61 K11 **Tsu** Japan
61 M8 **Tsubame** Japan
61 K9 **Tsubata** Japan
61 O9 **Tsuchiura** Japan
60 O4 **Tsugaru-kaikyō** *str* Japan
61 N8 **Tsugawa** Japan
61 P13 **Tsuha** Okinawa
61 L10 **Tsukechi** Japan
61 P13 **Tsuken-jima** *isld* Okinawa
60 P2 **Tsukigata** Japan
61 J12 **Tsukiji** Japan
60 E12 **Tsukumi** Japan
87 C9 **Tsumeb** Namibia
87 C10 **Tsumis** Namibia
61 M10 **Tsuru** Japan
61 K10 **Tsuruga** Japan
61 K10 **Tsuruga-wan** *B* Japan
61 K9 **Tsurugi** Japan
60 H12 **Tsurugi-san** *mt* Japan
61 N7 **Tsuruoka** Japan
59 L4 **Tsururga** Japan
60 E12 **Tsurusaki** Japan
59 J5 **Tsushima** *isld* Japan
61 K10 **Tsushima** Japan
60 C11 **Tsushima-kaikyō** *str* Japan
60 C11 **Tsutsu** Japan
60 E11 **Tsuwano** Japan
60 H10 **Tsuyama** Japan
60 D12 **Tsuyazaki** Japan
48 M1 **Tsybulev** Ukraine
55 E1 **Tsyngaly** Russian Federation
52 D1 **Tsyp Navolok** Russian Federation
54 K1 **Tsyurupi, Im** Russian Federation
16 C3 **Tua** *R* Portugal
145 G3 **Tuahine Pt.** New Zealand
145 F3 **Tuai** New Zealand
145 E2 **Tuakau** New Zealand
14 C3 **Tuam** Ireland
145 D4 **Tuamarina** New Zealand
135 N10 **Tuamotu** *arch* Pacific Oc
135 M10 **Tuamotu Ridge** Pacific Oc
68 F2 **Tuan Giao** Vietnam
69 C11 **Tuangku** *isld* Sumatra
67 B3 **Tuanxi** China
144 B7 **Tuapeka Mouth** New Zealand
125 N2 **Tuapi** Nicaragua
53 E11 **Tuapse** Russian Federation
70 E1 **Tuaran** Sabah
144 A7 **Tuatapere** New Zealand
70 K8 **Tua, Tg** *C* Sumatra
56 D4 **Tuba** *R* Russian Federation
103 N10 **Tubac** Arizona U.S.A.
103 N5 **Tuba City** Arizona U.S.A.
71 B3 **Tubalai** *isld* Indonesia
78 H5 **Tubal, Wadi** Iraq
70 O9 **Tuban** Java
133 H3 **Tubarão** Brazil
80 E4 **Tubas** Jordan
70 C3 **Tubau** Sarawak
71 D6 **Tubbataha Reefs** Sulu Sea
118 J8 **Tuberose** Saskatchewan Canada
71 E7 **Tubigan** *isld* Philippines
71 E8 **Tubig Puti** Philippines
71 E4 **Tubile Pt** Philippines
36 G7 **Tübingen** Germany
55 C4 **Tubinskiy** Russian Federation
22 G2 **Tubize** Belgium
71 F6 **Tubod** Mindanao Philippines
142 A5 **Tubridgi Pt** W Australia Australia
84 G3 **Tubruq** Libya
70 E3 **Tubu** *R* Kalimantan
135 M10 **Tubuai Is** Pacific Oc
124 D2 **Tubutama** Mexico
127 K9 **Tucacas** Venezuela
100 H3 **Tucannon** *R* Washington U.S.A.
129 L6 **Tucano** Brazil
128 G7 **Tucavaca** Bolivia
18 G10 **Tuchan** France
67 A3 **Tucheng** China
117 J5 **Tuchitua** Yukon Territory Canada
117 L6 **Tuchodi** *R* British Columbia Canada
31 K2 **Tuchola** Poland
48 G1 **Tuchów** Poland
143 C7 **Tuckanarra** W Australia Australia
146 C12 **Tucker Glacier** *glacier* Antarctica
103 O9 **Tucson** Arizona U.S.A.
103 N9 **Tucson Aqueduct** Arizona U.S.A.
103 N9 **Tucson Mts** Arizona U.S.A.
133 D3 **Tucumán** *prov* Argentina
106 G6 **Tucumcari** New Mexico U.S.A.
129 G5 **Tucunaré** Brazil
127 M10 **Tucupido** Venezuela
127 N10 **Tucupita** Venezuela
129 J4 **Tucurui** Brazil
31 J2 **Tuczno** Poland
25 E6 **Tüddern** Germany
28 G6 **Tudeå** *R* Denmark
17 F2 **Tudela** Spain
16 D3 **Tudela de Duero** Spain
120 J3 **Tudhope** Ontario Canada
102 C2 **Tudor** California U.S.A.
85 F6 **Tudun Wade** Nigeria
16 C3 **Tuela** *R* Portugal
28 H5 **Tuelsø** Denmark
129 H4 **Tueré** *R* Brazil
21 M5 **Tuffe** France
136 K3 **Tufi** Papua New Guinea
8 B4 **Tufton** Wales
112 D3 **Tugaloo L** South Carolina U.S.A.
118 L8 **Tugaske** Saskatchewan Canada
89 G7 **Tugela** *R* S Africa
94 E9 **Tug Fork** *R* Kentucky U.S.A.
139 K5 **Tuggerah L** New South Wales Australia
116 K8 **Tugidak I** Alaska U.S.A.
71 G5 **Tugnug Pt** Samar Philippines
55 D1 **Tugrovskiy** Russian Federation
70 F4 **Tuguan Maputi** *isld* Indonesia
71 G7 **Tugubun Pt** Philippines
71 E2 **Tuguegarao** Philippines
55 D3 **Tugulym** Russian Federation
59 L1 **Tugur** Russian Federation
69 C12 **Tuhemberua** Indonesia
145 D4 **Tui** New Zealand
125 P10 **Tuila** Guatemala
65 A4 **Tui Lamin Sum** China
56 C4 **Tuim** Russian Federation
Tujiabu *see* **Yongxiu**
70 E3 **Tujung** Kalimantan
55 C4 **Tukan** Russian Federation
79 B8 **Tûkh** Egypt
145 F3 **Tukituki R** New Zealand
68 F6 **Tuk Luy** Cambodia
114 F4 **Tuktoyaktuk** Northwest Territories Canada
52 B6 **Tukums** Latvia
70 B5 **Tukung, Bt** *mt* Kalimantan
87 F7 **Tukuyu** Tanzania
125 K6 **Tula** Mexico
54 J2 **Tula** Russian Federation
119 O4 **Tulabi Lake** Saskatchewan Canada
58 C4 **Tulai Shan** China
117 N11 **Tulameen** British Columbia Canada
125 K7 **Tulancingo** Mexico
70 K8 **Tulangbawang** *R* Sumatra
102 E5 **Tulare** California U.S.A.
98 H5 **Tulare** South Dakota U.S.A.
102 E5 **Tulare Lake Bed** California U.S.A.
108 A2 **Tularosa** New Mexico U.S.A.
106 B8 **Tularosa Mts** New Mexico U.S.A.
106 D9 **Tularosa V** New Mexico U.S.A.
89 B8 **Tulbagh** *mt* S Africa
128 C3 **Tulcán** Ecuador
48 M5 **Tulcea** Romania
48 M2 **Tul'chin** Ukraine
102 E5 **Tule** *R* California U.S.A.
127 H9 **Tulé** Venezuela
Tuléar *see* **Toliara**
108 F1 **Tule Cr** Texas U.S.A.
100 D8 **Tule L** California U.S.A.
100 E8 **Tule L.Res** California U.S.A.
19 N16 **Tulette** France
89 F3 **Tuli** Zimbabwe
31 L3 **Tuliszków** Poland
52 D3 **Tulivaara** Finland
80 D4 **Tulkarm** Jordan
14 C4 **Tulla** Ireland
110 K6 **Tullahoma** Tennessee U.S.A.
139 J5 **Tullamore** New South Wales Australia
14 D3 **Tullamore** Ireland
18 G7 **Tulle** France
28 F7 **Tullebølle** Denmark
139 H5 **Tullibigeal** New South Wales Australia
40 B7 **Tullins** France
48 C2 **Tulln** Austria
38 N5 **Tullnerfeld** *reg* Austria
102 D4 **Tulloch Lake** *res* California U.S.A.
111 D10 **Tullos** Louisiana U.S.A.
14 E4 **Tullow** Ireland
141 H4 **Tully** Queensland Australia
95 L4 **Tully** New York U.S.A.
141 H4 **Tully Falls** Queensland Australia
140 E3 **Tully Inlet** Queensland Australia
52 D1 **Tuloma** *R* Russian Federation
65 H1 **Tulongshan** China
29 P8 **Tulos, Oz** *L* Russian Federation
52 D3 **Tulos, Oz** *L* Russian Federation
47 H2 **Tulovo** Bulgaria
52 J4 **Tulpan** Russian Federation
107 P5 **Tulsa** Oklahoma U.S.A.
117 G6 **Tulsequah** British Columbia Canada
14 C3 **Tulsk** Ireland
53 E7 **Tul'skaya Oblast'** *prov* Russian Federation
28 D4 **Tulstrup** Denmark
128 C3 **Tuluá** Colombia
125 Q7 **Tulum** Mexico
131 C4 **Tulumaya** *R* Argentina
55 C2 **Tulumbasy** Russian Federation
131 C3 **Tulum, V.de** Argentina
56 F4 **Tulun** Russian Federation
70 N10 **Tulungagung** Java
71 D5 **Tuluran** Philippines
71 H4 **Tulutu** Indonesia
55 C3 **Tulva** *R* Russian Federation
54 M1 **Tuma** Russian Federation
103 N10 **Tumacacori Nat.Mon** Arizona U.S.A.
128 C3 **Tumaco** Colombia
71 G7 **Tumadgo Pt** Mindanao Philippines
100 D5 **Tumalo** Oregon U.S.A.
70 C5 **Tumangmiri** Kalimantan
52 D6 **Tumanovo** Russian Federation
55 E2 **Tuman, Oz** *L* Russian Federation
51 P2 **Tumany** Russian Federation
56 E5 **Tumat-Tayga, Khrebet** *mts* Russian Federation
128 G2 **Tumatumari** Guyana
86 D6 **Tumba** Zaire
70 C5 **Tumbangmasuki** Kalimantan
70 C5 **Tumbangsamba** Kalimantan
70 C5 **Tumbangsenamang** Kalimantan
70 B5 **Tumbangtiti** Kalimantan
71 G7 **Tumbao** Philippines
139 J6 **Tumbarumba** New South Wales Australia
128 B4 **Tumbes** Peru
124 H8 **Tumbiscatio** Mexico
95 R1 **Tumbledown Mt** Maine U.S.A.
130 B9 **Tumburús** Argentina
9 F1 **Tumby** England
138 D5 **Tumby Bay** South Australia Australia
29 O4 **Tumcha** *R* Finland/Rus Fed
52 D2 **Tumchaozero, Ozero** *L* Russian Federation
65 B4 **Tumd Youqi** China
65 B4 **Tumd Zuoqi** China
80 G4 **Tumeira** Jordan
65 H3 **Tumen** China
59 J3 **Tumen** *R* China/Korea
128 F2 **Tumeremo** Venezuela
70 F2 **Tumindao** *isld* Philippines
130 H6 **Tumiritinga** Brazil
76 C4 **Tumkur** India
15 D4 **Tummel** *R* Scotland
59 M2 **Tumnin** *R* Russian Federation
77 H6 **Tump** Pakistan
70 D5 **Tumpah** Kalimantan
69 F9 **Tumpat** Malaysia
71 H5 **Tumputiga, Gunung** *mt* Sulawesi Indonesia
74 H8 **Tumsar** India
85 D6 **Tumu** Ghana
129 G3 **Tumucamaque, Sa** *mts* Brazil
139 J6 **Tumut** New South Wales Australia
52 H6 **Tumutuk** Russian Federation
27 F13 **Tun** Sweden
26 J9 **Tuna** Sweden
71 G7 **Tuna Bay** Mindanao Philippines
127 O2 **Tunapuna** Trinidad
128 E7 **Tunari** *mt* Bolivia
126 E4 **Tunas de Zaza** Cuba
131 E5 **Tunas, L** Argentina
77 D6 **Ţunb aş Sughrá** *isld* Iran
77 D6 **Ţunb Kubrá** *isld* Iran
78 G2 **Tunceli** Turkey
67 C7 **Tunchang** China
139 L4 **Tuncurry** New South Wales Australia
52 F3 **Tundra** Russian Federation
87 F7 **Tunduma** Zambia
88 F7 **Tunduru** Tanzania
47 H2 **Tundzha** *R* Bulgaria
28 J5 **Tune** Denmark
70 F2 **Tungku** Sabah
29 P6 **Tungozero** Russian Federation
67 G5 **Tung Shan** Taiwan
117 J5 **Tungsten** Northwest Territories Canada
102 F1 **Tungsten** Nevada U.S.A.
Tungting Lake *see* **Dongting Hu**
70 C4 **Tungun, Bt** *mt* Kalimantan
56 F1 **Tunguska** *R* Russian Federation
58 E2 **Tünhel** Mongolia
27 C11 **Tunhovdfjord** *L* Norway
76 F2 **Tuni** India
110 F7 **Tunica** Mississippi U.S.A.
43 C12 **Tunis** Tunisia
43 D11 **Tunis, G. de** Tunisia
84 D3 **Tunisia** *rep* N Africa
128 D2 **Tunja** Colombia
56 F5 **Tunkinskiye Gol'tsy** *mts* Russian Federation
65 B6 **Tunliu** China
26 E9 **Tunna** *R* Norway
120 G6 **Tunnel Dam** Ontario Canada
19 O18 **Tunnel du Rove** France
94 H7 **Tunnelton** West Virginia U.S.A.
26 F7 **Tunnsjö** *L* Norway
28 E5 **Tunø** Denmark
8 D1 **Tunstall** England
9 H3 **Tunstall** England
115 N6 **Tunungayualok I** Labrador, Nfld Canada
131 C4 **Tunuyán, R** Argentina
131 C4 **Tunuyán, Sa. de** *mts* Argentina
67 A1 **Tuo Jiang** *R* China
67 D4 **Tuojiang** China
65 E5 **Tuoji Dao** *isld* China
68 G6 **Tuol Khpos** Cambodia
102 D4 **Tuolumne** California U.S.A.
102 E4 **Tuolumne Meadows** California U.S.A.
29 L7 **Tuomioja** Finland
130 E7 **Tupã** Brazil
130 E6 **Tupaciguara** Brazil
128 F4 **Tupanaóca** Brazil
145 G2 **Tuparoa** New Zealand
111 H7 **Tupelo** Mississippi U.S.A.
109 L1 **Tupelo** Oklahoma U.S.A.
111 H7 **Tupelo Nat Battlefield** Mississippi U.S.A.
128 G4 **Tupinambaranas, I** Brazil
130 E4 **Tupiraçaba** Brazil
133 D2 **Tupiza** Bolivia
102 E6 **Tupman** California U.S.A.
29 L7 **Tupos** Finland
117 N8 **Tupper** British Columbia Canada
95 N2 **Tupper Lake** New York U.S.A.
133 D4 **Tupungato** *mt* Arg/Chile
65 E2 **Tuquan** China
128 C3 **Tuquerres** Colombia
67 D7 **Tuqu Wan** *B* China
66 D4 **Tura** China
75 O6 **Tura** India
55 D2 **Tura** *R* Russian Federation
145 E4 **Turakina** New Zealand
145 E4 **Turakirae Head** New Zealand
57 J5 **Turakurgan** Uzbekistan
56 D5 **Turan** Russian Federation
59 K1 **Turana, Khrebet** *mt* Russian Federation
145 E3 **Turangi** New Zealand
42 E6 **Turano** *R* Italy
45 N5 **Turano, L.di** Italy
126 G9 **Turbaco** Colombia
20 E7 **Turballe, la** France
77 H7 **Turbat** Pakistan
41 J3 **Turbenthal** Switzerland
126 F10 **Turbo** Colombia
17 H2 **Turbón** *mt* Spain
48 M1 **Turbov** Ukraine
48 H6 **Turburea** Romania
52 E3 **Turchasovo** Russian Federation
48 H4 **Turda** Romania
143 C6 **Turee Cr** W Australia Australia
16 E3 **Turégano** Spain
31 L3 **Turek** Poland
79 D10 **Tûr, El** Egypt
127 K10 **Turen** Venezuela
66 D3 **Turfan Depression** China
57 B1 **Turgay** *R* Kazakhstan
57 C1 **Turgay** Kazakhstan
55 D5 **Turgayskaya Stolovaya Strana** *dist* Kazakhstan/Rus Fed
121 L3 **Turgeon** *R* Quebec Canada
47 H1 **Tŭrgovishte** Bulgaria
55 D3 **Turgoyak** Russian Federation
47 J6 **Turgutlu** Turkey
78 F1 **Turhal** Turkey
52 C5 **Türi** Estonia
17 G5 **Turia** *R* Spain
129 J4 **Turiaçu** Brazil
127 L9 **Turiamo** Venezuela
31 L7 **Turiec** *R* Slovakia
126 E3 **Turiguano, I** Cuba
Turin *see* **Torino**
118 E9 **Turin** Alberta Canada
95 M3 **Turin** New York U.S.A.
55 D2 **Turinsk** Russian Federation
55 D3 **Turinskaya-Sloboda** Russian Federation
59 K2 **Turiy Rog** Russian Federation
48 D3 **Türje** Hungary
56 G4 **Turka** *R* Russian Federation
48 H1 **Turka** Ukraine
86 G5 **Turkana, L** Kenya
47 J4 **Türkeli** *isld* Turkey
41 O1 **Turkenfeld** Germany
57 E3 **Turkestan** Kazakhstan
57 E5 **Turkestanskiy Khrebet** *mts* Tajikistan/Uzbekistan etc
48 F3 **Túrkeve** Hungary
99 P7 **Turkey** *R* Iowa U.S.A.
108 G1 **Turkey** Texas U.S.A.
78 D2 **Turkey** *rep* W Asia
142 G3 **Turkey Creek** W Australia Australia
106 F6 **Turkey Mts** New Mexico U.S.A.
41 N1 **Türkheim** Germany
36 C4 **Türkismühle** Germany
47 L5 **Türkmendağı** *mt* Turkey
50 E4 **Turkmenistan** *rep* C Asia
57 B5 **Turkmen-Kala** Turkmenistan
57 B6 **Turkmenkarakul'** Turkmenistan
79 G1 **Türkoğlu** Turkey
127 H4 **Turks and Caicos Is** *isld group* W Indies
127 J4 **Turks Is** W Indies
29 J11 **Turku** Finland
27 M10 **Turku Pori** *reg* Finland
86 G5 **Turkwel** *R* Kenya
16 E5 **Turleque** Spain
102 D4 **Turlock** California U.S.A.
130 G5 **Turmalina** Brazil
117 J6 **Turnagain** *R* British Columbia Canada
145 F4 **Turnagain, C** New Zealand
38 M6 **Turnau** Austria
119 Q5 **Turnberry** Manitoba Canada
15 D5 **Turnberry** Scotland
119 S4 **Turnbull** Manitoba Canada
140 B5 **Turnbull, Mt** N Terr Australia
125 P9 **Turneffe Is** Belize
95 R2 **Turner** Maine U.S.A.
94 D2 **Turner** Michigan U.S.A.
101 R1 **Turner** Montana U.S.A.
100 C5 **Turner** Oregon U.S.A.
100 H3 **Turner** Washington U.S.A.
101 U6 **Turnercrest** Wyoming U.S.A.
142 B6 **Turner, Mt** W Australia Australia
142 G4 **Turner River** W Australia Australia
95 P4 **Turners Falls** Massachusetts U.S.A.
118 C8 **Turner Valley** Alberta Canada
101 P7 **Turnerville** Wyoming U.S.A.
22 H1 **Turnhout** Belgium
38 M6 **Turnitz** Austria
31 J5 **Turnov** Czech Rep
46 G1 **Turnu Măgurele** Romania
48 J5 **Turnu Roşu** Romania
57 H1 **Turobay** Kazakhstan
31 O5 **Turobin** Poland
139 J5 **Turon** *R* New South Wales Australia
107 M4 **Turon** Kansas U.S.A.
139 J5 **Tuross** *R* New South Wales Australia
66 D3 **Turpan** China
108 D7 **Turpin** Oklahoma U.S.A.
126 F4 **Turquino, Pico** *pk* Cuba
106 D9 **Turquoise** New Mexico U.S.A.
116 K6 **Turquoise L** Alaska U.S.A.
38 J8 **Turrach** Austria
110 F6 **Turrell** Arkansas U.S.A.
125 N5 **Turrialba** Costa Rica
19 Q16 **Turriers** France
15 F3 **Turriff** Scotland
55 D1 **Tursuntskiy Tuman, Oz** *L* Russian Federation
57 E5 **Tursunzade** Tajikistan
56 F5 **Turt** Mongolia
55 E2 **Turtas** *R* Russian Federation
57 B4 **Turtkul'** Uzbekistan
99 O1 **Turtle** *R* Ontario Canada
122 H8 **Turtle Cr** New Brunswick Canada
118 J5 **Turtleford** Saskatchewan Canada
141 G1 **Turtlehead I** Queensland Australia
141 K3 **Turtle I** Gt Barrier Reef Aust
142 C5 **Turtle I** W Australia Australia
70 F1 **Turtle Is** Philippines
85 B7 **Turtle Is** Sierra Leone
118 J5 **Turtle L** Saskatchewan Canada
98 F2 **Turtle L** North Dakota U.S.A.
99 O4 **Turtle L** Wisconsin U.S.A.
98 F1 **Turtle Mts** Manitoba/N Dakota Canada/U.S.A.
29 K5 **Turtola** Finland
98 H4 **Turton** South Dakota U.S.A.
145 E2 **Turua** New Zealand
66 B3 **Turugart** *pass* Kazakhstan
51 H2 **Turukhansk** Russian Federation
55 E1 **Turumeyevo** Russian Federation
129 G3 **Turuna** *R* Brazil
28 D6 **Turup** Denmark
9 F3 **Turvey** England
130 D10 **Turvo** *R* Brazil
53 B8 **Tur'ya** *R* Ukraine
31 L6 **Turzovka** Slovakia
111 J8 **Tuscaloosa** Alabama U.S.A.
111 J8 **Tuscaloosa, L** Alabama U.S.A.
42 D6 **Tuscania** Italy
94 F6 **Tuscarawas** *R* Ohio U.S.A.
100 J8 **Tuscarora** Nevada U.S.A.
94 K6 **Tuscarora Mt** Pennsylvania U.S.A.
110 H2 **Tuscola** Illinois U.S.A.
100 K2 **Tuscor** Montana U.S.A.

110 J7 **Tuscumbia** Alabama U.S.A.
110 D3 **Tuscumbia** Missouri U.S.A.
28 H5 **Tuse** Denmark
57 A2 **Tushchibas, Zaliv** *G* Kazakhstan
14 E4 **Tuskar Rock** Ireland
111 L9 **Tuskegee** Alabama U.S.A.
122 G10 **Tusket** Nova Scotia Canada
54 H5 **Tuskor'** *R* Russian Federation
115 O3 **Tussaaq** Greenland
102 G8 **Tustin** California U.S.A.
94 B2 **Tustin** Michigan U.S.A.
26 C8 **Tustna** *isld* Norway
116 M6 **Tustumena L** Alaska U.S.A.
31 M4 **Tuszyn** Poland
78 J2 **Tutak** Turkey
145 D1 **Tutamoe Range** New Zealand
52 E5 **Tutayev** Russian Federation
9 E2 **Tutbury** England
Tutera *see* **Tudela**
98 E6 **Tuthill** South Dakota U.S.A.
76 D6 **Tuticorin** India
46 D1 **Tutin** Serbia Yugoslavia
145 F3 **Tutira L** New Zealand
29 O5 **Tutiyarvi** Russian Federation
70 D3 **Tutoh** *R* Sarawak
129 K4 **Tutóia** Brazil
70 D2 **Tutong** Brunei
48 L4 **Tutova** *R* Romania
33 S5 **Tutow** Germany
47 H1 **Tutrakan** Bulgaria
48 K6 **Tutraken** Romania
117 F5 **Tutshi L** Yukon Territory Canada
101 L7 **Tuttle** Idaho U.S.A.
98 F2 **Tuttle** North Dakota U.S.A.
107 N6 **Tuttle** Oklahoma U.S.A.
37 K2 **Tüttleben** Germany
107 O2 **Tuttle Cr. Lake** Kansas U.S.A.
99 M6 **Tuttle L** Minnesota U.S.A.
41 J2 **Tuttlingen** Germany
Tuttut Nunaat *see* **Renland**
71 N9 **Tutuala** Timor
134 D1 **Tutuila** *isld* Amer Samoa
125 L9 **Tututepec** Mexico
71 O8 **Tutuwawang** Indonesia
111 F7 **Tutwiler** Mississippi U.S.A.
41 O2 **Tutzing** Germany
58 D2 **Tuul Gol** *R* Mongolia
29 L10 **Tuulos** Finland
29 P9 **Tuupovarra** Finland
29 O9 **Tuusniemi** Finland
137 Q3 **Tuvalu** *islds state* Pacific Oc
137 R6 **Tuvana-i-Colo** *isld* Pacific Oc
137 R6 **Tuvana-i-ra** *isld* Pacific Oc
56 E5 **Tuvinskaya Respublika** Russian Federation
70 E4 **Tuwau** *R* Kalimantan
103 L5 **Tuweep** Arizona U.S.A.
65 A5 **Tuwei He** *R* China
116 L6 **Tuxedni B** Alaska U.S.A.
118 A1 **Tuxedo** Manitoba Canada
112 E2 **Tuxedo** North Carolina U.S.A.
41 P3 **Tuxer Gebirge** *mt* Austria
119 M8 **Tuxford** Saskatchewan Canada
9 F1 **Tuxford** England
67 C1 **Tuxiang** China
125 L7 **Tuxpan** Mexico
124 H8 **Tuxpan** Jalisco Mexico
124 G7 **Tuxpan** Nayarit Mexico
125 N9 **Tuxtla Gutiérrez** Mexico
55 F2 **Tuy** *R* Russian Federation
16 B2 **Tuy** Spain
117 H6 **Tuya L** British Columbia Canada
68 J6 **Tuy An** Vietnam
67 B6 **Tuyen Quang** Vietnam
68 J6 **Tuy Hoa** Vietnam
52 H6 **Tuymazy** Russian Federation
77 A2 **Tūysarkān** Iran
78 D2 **Tuz Gölü** *L* Turkey
103 N7 **Tuzigoot Nat.Mon** Arizona U.S.A.
78 K4 **Tuz Khurmātū** Iraq
48 E6 **Tuzla** Bosnia-Herzegovina
78 H2 **Tuzla** *R* Turkey
48 N5 **Tuzly** Ukraine
27 F14 **Tvååker** Sweden
26 L7 **Tvärålund** Sweden
26 M6 **Tvärån** Sweden
28 E4 **Tved** Århus Denmark
28 F6 **Tved** Fyn Denmark
28 E3 **Tvede** Denmark
27 C13 **Tvedestrand** Norway
52 E6 **Tver'** Russian Federation
52 D6 **Tverskaya Oblast'** *prov* Russian Federation
28 E1 **Tversted** Denmark
52 E6 **Tvertsa** *R* Russian Federation
27 H15 **Tving** Sweden
28 D5 **Tvingstrup** Denmark
28 B4 **Tvis** Denmark
6 F1 **Tvøroyri** Faeroes
47 H2 **Tvŭrditsa** Bulgaria
68 B4 **Twante** Burma
31 K4 **Twardogóra** Poland
85 F4 **Twaret** Niger
121 N8 **Tweed** Ontario Canada
139 L3 **Tweed Heads** New South Wales Australia
118 F4 **Tweedie** Alberta Canada
13 E3 **Tweed, R** Scotland
13 E3 **Tweedsmuir** Scotland
117 K9 **Tweedsmuir Prov.Park** British Columbia Canada
87 D11 **Twee Rivieren** S Africa
118 L9 **Twelvemile L** Saskatchewan Canada
116 P4 **Twelvemile Summit** Alaska U.S.A.
14 B3 **Twelve Pins** *mt* Ireland
103 H7 **Twentynine Palms** California U.S.A.
143 F9 **Twilight Cove** W Australia Australia
123 S4 **Twillingate** Newfoundland Canada
38 L8 **Twimberg** Austria
100 B1 **Twin** Washington U.S.A.
101 N4 **Twin Bridges** Montana U.S.A.
98 K4 **Twin Brooks** South Dakota U.S.A.
108 G4 **Twin Buttes Res** Texas U.S.A.
119 O2 **Twin City** Ontario Canada
115 N7 **Twin Falls** Labrador, Nfld Canada
101 L7 **Twin Falls** Idaho U.S.A.
142 F5 **Twin Heads** *mt* W Australia Australia
94 C2 **Twin L** Michigan U.S.A.
99 U6 **Twin Lake** Michigan U.S.A.
117 P7 **Twin Lakes** Alberta Canada
116 K6 **Twin Lakes** Alaska U.S.A.
106 D2 **Twin Lakes** Colorado U.S.A.
101 L6 **Twin Lakes Res** Idaho U.S.A.
123 Q4 **Twin L.,N** Newfoundland Canada
123 R4 **Twin L.,S** Newfoundland Canada
95 Q2 **Twin Mountain** New Hampshire U.S.A.
102 D2 **Twin Peaks** California U.S.A.
101 L5 **Twin Peaks** Idaho U.S.A.
143 C10 **Twin Pks** W Australia Australia
143 D10 **Twin Rocks** W Australia Australia
138 E3 **Twins Cr** South Australia Australia
138 D4 **Twins, The** South Australia Australia
145 D4 **Twins, The** *mt* New Zealand
98 K2 **Twin Valley** Minnesota U.S.A.
100 E1 **Twisp** Washington U.S.A.
32 J7 **Twistringen** Germany
108 D8 **Twitty** Texas U.S.A.
117 J4 **Twitya** *R* Northwest Territories Canada
144 C6 **Twizel** New Zealand
106 H4 **Two Buttes** Colorado U.S.A.
106 H4 **Two Buttes Creek** Colorado U.S.A.
119 R8 **Two Creeks** Manitoba Canada
99 T5 **Two Creeks** Wisconsin U.S.A.
101 P3 **Twodot** Montana U.S.A.
139 K6 **Twofold B** New South Wales Australia
99 P2 **Two Harbors** Minnesota U.S.A.
116 L8 **Two Headed I** Alaska U.S.A.
118 F5 **Two Hills** Alberta Canada
101 P5 **Two Ocean Pass** Wyoming U.S.A.
99 T5 **Two Rivers** Wisconsin U.S.A.
9 E2 **Twycross** England
9 E5 **Twyford** England
9 F5 **Twyford** England
12 D4 **Twynholm** Scotland
48 H2 **Tyachev** Ukraine
28 H6 **Tybjerg** Denmark
28 D6 **Tybrind Vig** *B* Denmark
56 E1 **Tychany** *R* Russian Federation
55 G3 **Tychkino** Russian Federation
31 J2 **Tychowo** Poland
31 L5 **Tychy** Poland
26 E8 **Tydal** Norway
117 F7 **Tyee** Alaska U.S.A.
100 A1 **Tyee** Washington U.S.A.
94 J9 **Tye River** Virginia U.S.A.
94 H8 **Tygart V** West Virginia U.S.A.
59 J1 **Tygda** Russian Federation
101 N7 **Tyhee** Idaho U.S.A.
27 C10 **Tyin** *L* Norway
31 O2 **Tykocin** Poland
98 K5 **Tyler** Minnesota U.S.A.
94 J5 **Tyler** Pennsylvania U.S.A.
109 M3 **Tyler** Texas U.S.A.
100 H2 **Tyler** Washington U.S.A.
111 A9 **Tyler, L** Texas U.S.A.
111 F10 **Tylertown** Mississippi U.S.A.
28 D2 **Tylstrup** Denmark
56 C1 **Tym** *R* Russian Federation
48 F1 **Tymbark** Poland
59 M1 **Tymovskoye** Russian Federation
55 F2 **Tynay** Russian Federation
59 H1 **Tynda** Russian Federation
118 E1 **Tyndall** Manitoba Canada
98 J6 **Tyndall** South Dakota U.S.A.
144 C5 **Tyndall, Mt** New Zealand
26 J9 **Tynderö** Sweden
13 G4 **Tyne and Wear** *co* England
13 G3 **Tynemouth** England
118 J7 **Tyner** Saskatchewan Canada
122 J7 **Tyne Valley** Prince Edward I Canada
27 G11 **Tyngsjö** Sweden
31 H6 **Týn nad Vltava** Czech Rep
26 E9 **Tynset** Norway
8 C2 **Tyn-y-Groes** Wales
116 O5 **Tyone** *R* Alaska U.S.A.
Tyre *see* **Soûr**
27 D11 **Tyrifjorden** *L* Norway
27 G15 **Tyringe** Sweden
59 K1 **Tyrma** Russian Federation
48 L2 **Tyrnovo** Moldova
112 E2 **Tyron** North Carolina U.S.A.
14 D2 **Tyrone** *co* N Ireland
106 B9 **Tyrone** New Mexico U.S.A.
94 J6 **Tyrone** Pennsylvania U.S.A.
139 G6 **Tyrrell** *R* Victoria Australia
43 D8 **Tyrrhenian Sea** S Europe
28 D5 **Tyrsted** Denmark
26 H3 **Tysfjord** Norway
27 A12 **Tysnesöy** *isld* Norway
27 B11 **Tyssedal** Norway
27 J13 **Tystberga** Sweden
28 H6 **Tystrup** Denmark
31 O5 **Tyszowce** Poland
55 F3 **Tyukalinsk** Russian Federation
57 H4 **Tyulek** Kirghizia
53 G11 **Tyulen'i, Ostrova** *islds* Russian Federation
55 C4 **Tyul'gan** Russian Federation
55 E1 **Tyuli** Russian Federation
52 J5 **Tyul'kino** Russian Federation
55 E3 **Tyumen'** Russian Federation
50 F2 **Tyumenskaya Oblast'** *prov* Russian Federation
55 E4 **Tyuntyugur** Kazakhstan
57 C2 **Tyuratam** Kazakhstan
52 D1 **Tyuva Guba** Russian Federation
119 O8 **Tyvan** Saskatchewan Canada
48 M1 **Tyvrov** Ukraine
8 B2 **Tywyn** Wales
25 C3 **t'Zand** Netherlands
87 F10 **Tzaneen** S Africa
Tzepo *see* **Zibo**
46 E5 **Tzoumérka** *mt* Greece
67 G4 **Tz'u-kao Shan** *pk* Taiwan
25 E2 **Tzummarum** Netherlands

U

85 B3 **Uad el Jat** *watercourse* Western Sahara
116 H7 **Ualik, L** Alaska U.S.A.
142 B6 **Uaroo** W Australia Australia
128 G4 **Uatumá** *R* Brazil
129 L5 **Uaua** Brazil
130 G10 **Uauá** Brazil
128 E4 **Uaupés** Brazil
145 G3 **Uawa R** New Zealand
125 P9 **Uaxactún** Guatemala
130 G7 **Ubá** Brazil
56 B5 **Uba** *R* Kazakhstan
22 L2 **Ubach o. Worms** Netherlands
55 E4 **Ubagan** *R* Kazakhstan
130 G5 **Ubaí** Brazil
129 L6 **Ubaitaba** Brazil
86 C5 **Ubangi** *R* Cent Afr Republic/Zaire
Ubari *see* **Awbārī**
78 H6 **Ubayyid, Wadi al** Saudi Arabia
28 G5 **Ubby** Denmark
60 E12 **Ube** Japan
16 E6 **Ubeda** Spain
115 O3 **Ubekendt Ejland** *isld* Greenland
133 H1 **Uberaba** Brazil
130 B5 **Uberaba** *L* Brazil/Bolivia
36 B5 **Überherrn** Germany
130 E6 **Uberlândia** Brazil
41 K2 **Überlingen** Switzerland
85 F7 **Ubiaja** Nigeria
33 S9 **Ubigau** Germany
133 D2 **Ubina** *mt* Bolivia
94 E3 **Ubly** Michigan U.S.A.
68 F4 **Ubolratana** *res* Thailand
87 F11 **Ubombo** S Africa
68 G5 **Ubon Ratchathani** Thailand
36 F5 **Ubstadt-Weiher** Germany
79 C2 **Uçarı** Turkey
128 D5 **Ucayali** *R* Peru
128 D6 **Ucayali** *dept* Peru
47 N11 **Uçburun Yarımada** *pen* Turkey
22 G2 **Uccle** Belgium
16 E3 **Ucero** *R* Spain
47 N11 **Uçgaziler** Turkey
55 C4 **Uchaly** Russian Federation
57 K2 **Ucharal** Kazakhstan
61 O8 **Uchigō** Japan
60 F12 **Uchiko** Japan
115 K7 **Uchi Lake** Ontario Canada
60 O3 **Uchiura wan** *B* Japan
40 A4 **Uchizy** France
57 C4 **Uch Kuduk** Uzbekistan
57 C4 **Uchkuduk** Uzbekistan
57 K5 **Uchkurgan** Uzbekistan
32 J7 **Uchte** Germany
33 P7 **Uchte** *R* Germany
51 N3 **Uchur** *R* Russian Federation
22 L5 **Uckange** France
30 H2 **Ücker** *R* Germany
36 C2 **Uckerath** Germany
33 U4 **Uckeritz** Germany
9 G6 **Uckfield** England
33 T9 **Uckro** Germany
117 L11 **Ucluelet** British Columbia Canada
101 O6 **Ucon** Idaho U.S.A.
101 T5 **Ucross** Wyoming U.S.A.
56 G5 **Uda** *R* Russian Federation
76 C5 **Udagamandalam** India
74 E6 **Udaipur** India
75 M5 **Udaipur Garhi** Nepal
54 D6 **Uday** *R* Ukraine
76 D3 **Udayagiri** India
77 B7 **Udayd, Khawr al'** *inlet* Qatar/Saudi Arabia
42 G4 **Udbina** Croatia
28 H5 **Udby** Denmark
28 E3 **Udby** Århus Denmark
28 D6 **Udby** Fyn Denmark
28 E3 **Udbyhø** Denmark
28 E3 **Udbyneder** Denmark
27 E13 **Uddevalla** Sweden
12 D2 **Uddingston** Scotland
26 J6 **Uddjaur** *L* Sweden
25 E5 **Uden** Netherlands
32 M10 **Uder** Germany
76 C1 **Udgir** India
74 F2 **Udhampur** Kashmir
142 E4 **Udialla** W Australia Australia
42 E2 **Udine** Italy
56 E4 **Udinskiy Khrebet** *mts*
76 B4 **Udipi** India
37 P3 **Udlice** Czech Rep
55 B3 **Udmurtskaya Respublika** Russian Federation
52 E5 **Udomlya** Russian Federation
61 N11 **Udone-jima** *isld* Japan
68 F4 **Udon Thani** Thailand
140 B6 **Udor, Mt** N Terr Australia
59 L1 **Udskaya Guba** *B* Russian Federation
76 C5 **Udumalaippettai** India
47 H2 **Udvoy** *mt* Bulgaria
59 L1 **Udyl, Oz** *L* Russian Federation
51 L1 **Udzha** Russian Federation
70 G5 **Uëbonti** Sulawesi
33 U5 **Uecker** *R* Germany
33 T6 **Ueckermark** *reg* Germany
33 U5 **Ueckermünde** Germany
61 M9 **Ueda** Japan
25 F5 **Uedem** Germany
32 G8 **Üeffeln** Germany
98 K8 **Uehling** Nebraska U.S.A.
60 D13 **Ueki** Japan
70 G5 **Uekuli** Sulawesi
86 E5 **Uele** *R* Zaire
32 E7 **Uelsen** Germany
33 N7 **Uelzen** Germany
61 K11 **Ueno** Japan
61 N10 **Uenohara** Japan
86 E5 **Uere** *R* Zaire
36 B3 **Uess** *R* Germany
32 L5 **Uetersen** Germany
55 C4 **Ufa** Russian Federation
37 J4 **Uffenheim** Germany
55 C3 **Ufimskiy** Russian Federation
87 C10 **Ugab** *R* Namibia
116 J8 **Ugaiushak I** Alaska U.S.A.
116 L8 **Ugak I** Alaska U.S.A.
88 C4 **Ugalla** *R* Tanzania
116 E9 **Ugamak I** Aleutian Is
86 F5 **Uganda** *rep* Africa
116 L8 **Uganik I** Alaska U.S.A.
116 J8 **Ugashik B** Alaska U.S.A.
116 J8 **Ugashik Lakes** Alaska U.S.A.
28 C7 **Uge** Denmark
43 J9 **Ugento** Italy
28 H5 **Ugerløse** Denmark
28 E4 **Uggelhuse** Denmark
28 E1 **Uggerby** Denmark
28 E5 **Uggerslev** Denmark
16 E8 **Ugijar** Spain
28 E2 **Ugilt** Denmark
19 Q13 **Ugine** France
59 M2 **Uglegorsk** Russian Federation
55 C2 **Ugleural'skiy** Russian Federation
52 E6 **Uglich** Russian Federation
42 G4 **Ugljan** *isld* Croatia
42 H5 **Ugljane** Croatia
48 E6 **Ugljevik** Bosnia-Herzegovina
52 D5 **Uglovka** Russian Federation
Ugoi *see* **Ujiji**
54 G2 **Ugra** *R* Russian Federation
46 G1 **Ugŭrchin** Bulgaria
55 F1 **Ugut** Russian Federation
83 L10 **Uhana** Sri Lanka
31 K6 **Uherské Hradiště** Czech Rep
36 H6 **Uhingen** Germany
87 C10 **Uhlenhorst** Namibia
37 K4 **Uhlfeld** Germany
119 T2 **Uhlman L** Manitoba Canada
37 L2 **Uhlstädt** Germany
28 C5 **Uhre** Denmark
94 F6 **Uhrichsville** Ohio U.S.A.
29 N3 **Uhro Kekkosen Nat. Park** Finland
31 O4 **Uhrusk** Poland
15 B3 **Uig** Skye Scotland
87 C7 **Uíge** Angola
65 F4 **Ŭiju** N Korea
55 B6 **Uil** Kazakhstan
55 C6 **Uil** *R* Kazakhstan
128 E7 **Uiñamarco, L** Peru/Bolivia
103 L5 **Uinkaret Plat** Arizona U.S.A.
55 C3 **Uinskoye** Russian Federation
101 P9 **Uinta Mts** Utah U.S.A.
89 D9 **Uitenhage** S Africa
25 C3 **Uitgeest** Netherlands
25 C4 **Uithoorn** Netherlands
25 G2 **Uithuizen** Netherlands
25 G2 **Uithuizerwad** Netherlands
79 G10 **Ujayyijät, Abu** *well* Saudi Arabia
31 L5 **Ujazd** Poland
48 G3 **Újfehértó** Hungary
61 J11 **Uji** Japan
74 F7 **Ujiain** India
61 N9 **Ujiie** Japan
88 B4 **Ujiji** Tanzania
70 D4 **Ujohbilang** Kalimantan
48 E3 **Újpest** Hungary
31 K2 **Ujście** Poland
69 E12 **Ujungbatu** Sumatra
70 F7 **Ujung Pandang** Sulawesi
61 Q12 **Uka** Okinawa
61 L8 **Ukawa** Japan
88 D3 **Ukerewe** *isld* Tanzania
75 Q6 **Ukhrul** India
52 E4 **Ukhtoma** Russian Federation
89 B4 **Ukhwi Pan** Botswana
100 G4 **Ukiah** Oregon U.S.A.
61 P13 **Ukibaru-jima** *isld* Okinawa
116 D4 **Ukivok** Alaska U.S.A.
Ukkel *see* **Uccle**
115 O3 **Ukkusissat** Greenland
52 B6 **Ukmerge** Lithuania
27 H13 **Ukna** Sweden
54 G7 **Ukraine** *rep* E Europe
55 G3 **Ukrainka** Russian Federation
55 F4 **Ukrainka** Omskaya obl Russian Federation
42 H4 **Ukrina** *R* Bosnia-Herzegovina
55 D3 **Uksyanskoye** Russian Federation
31 N2 **Ukta** Poland
52 G3 **Uktym** Russian Federation
87 B8 **Uku** Angola
87 C8 **Ukuma** Angola
60 B12 **Uku-shima** *isld* Japan
6 M5 **Ula** *oil rig* North Sea
47 J7 **Ula** Turkey
58 E2 **Ulaanbaatar** Mongolia
65 A1 **Ulaan-Ereg** Mongolia
58 B2 **Ulaangom** Mongolia
139 J4 **Ulan** New South Wales Australia
58 C4 **Ulan** China
Ulan Bator *see* **Ulaanbaatar**
65 C2 **Ulan Hobor** China
Ulan Hot *see* **Horqin Youyi Qianqi**
65 E2 **Ulan Hua** China
53 G10 **Ulan-Khol** Russian Federation
48 L1 **Ulanov** Ukraine
65 A4 **Ulansuhai Nur** *L* China
56 G5 **Ulan-Ude** Russian Federation
131 C3 **Ulapes, Sa** *mts* Argentina
141 H7 **Ularunda** Queensland Australia
56 B5 **Ul'ba** Kazakhstan
51 N3 **Ul'banskiy Zaliv** *B* Russian Federation
28 C3 **Ulbjerg** Denmark
9 G1 **Ulceby Cross** England
42 J7 **Ulcinj** Montenegro Yugoslavia
13 E4 **Uldale** England
28 D5 **Uldum** Denmark
58 F2 **Uldz** *R* Mongolia
Uleåborg *see* **Oulu**
69 B10 **Uleelheue** Sumatra
27 D12 **Ulefoss** Norway
98 K2 **Ulen** Minnesota U.S.A.
52 C6 **Ulena** Lithuania
138 F3 **Ulenia, L** New South Wales Australia
58 F1 **Ulety** Russian Federation
28 A4 **Ulfborg** Denmark
28 A4 **Ulfborg Kirke** Denmark
37 J1 **Ulfen** Germany
65 D2 **Ulgai** China
65 D2 **Ulgain Gol** *R* China
13 G3 **Ulgham** England
76 A1 **Ulhasnagar** India
Uliastai *see* **Dong Ujimqin Qi**
58 C2 **Uliastay** Mongolia
86 E6 **Ulindi** *R* Zaire
48 G5 **Uljma** Serbia Yugoslavia
56 G3 **Ul'kan** Russian Federation
57 C1 **Ul'kayak** *R* Kazakhstan
28 D7 **Ulkebøl** Denmark
28 C5 **Ulkind** Denmark
56 G3 **Ul'kon** *R* Russian Federation
139 K6 **Ulladulla** New South Wales Australia
137 L8 **Ulladulla Trough** Pacific Oc
26 K9 **Ullånger** Sweden
27 F14 **Ullared** Sweden
26 M4 **Ullatti** Sweden
29 K8 **Ullava** Finland
17 H4 **Ulldecona** Spain
27 B11 **Ullensvang** Norway
28 F6 **Ullerslev** Denmark
28 D7 **Ullerup** Denmark
110 G4 **Ullin** Illinois U.S.A.
28 C3 **Ullits** Denmark
26 L2 **Ullsfjord** Norway
13 F4 **Ullswater** *L* England
59 K4 **Ullung Do** *isld* S Korea
36 H7 **Ulm** Germany
111 E7 **Ulm** Arkansas U.S.A.
101 T5 **Ulm** Wyoming U.S.A.
139 L3 **Ulmarra** New South Wales Australia
36 B3 **Ulmen** Germany
48 K5 **Ulmeni** Romania
38 L5 **Ulmerfeld** Austria
125 M2 **Ulmukhuas** Nicaragua
70 G7 **Uloe** Sulawesi
48 E7 **Ulog** Bosnia-Herzegovina
88 E9 **Ulongue** Mozambique
138 E2 **Uloowaranie, L** South Australia Australia
13 E5 **Ulpha** England
56 H1 **Ulqkhan Botuobuya** *R* Russian Federation
27 F14 **Ulricehamn** Sweden
143 E7 **Ulrich Ra** W Australia Australia
36 G2 **Ulrichstein** Germany
26 H8 **Ulriksfors** Sweden
25 F2 **Ulrum** Netherlands
59 J4 **Ulsan** S Korea
28 D7 **Ulsby** Germany
15 G1 **Ulsta** Shetland Scotland
28 E2 **Ulsted** Denmark
26 A9 **Ulstein** Norway
14 D2 **Ulster** *prov* N Ireland
95 L5 **Ulster** Pennsylvania U.S.A.
14 D2 **Ulster Canal** N Ireland
28 F5 **Ulstrup** Denmark
26 K4 **Ultevis** *mt* Sweden
139 G6 **Ultima** Victoria Australia
140 D6 **Ultim, Mt** N Terr Australia
41 O4 **Ultimo.V.d'** Italy
51 M2 **Ulu** Russian Federation
47 N10 **Ulu** *R* Turkey
125 P10 **Ulua** *R* Honduras
47 K4 **Ulubat Gölü** *L* Turkey
47 K6 **Ulubey** Turkey
Uluçınar *see* **Arsuz**
47 K4 **Ulu Dağ** *mt* Turkey
71 D5 **Ulugan B** Philippines
88 F5 **Uluguru** *mts* Tanzania
78 E3 **Ulukışla** Turkey
70 C4 **Ululselua, Bt** *mt* Kalimantan
66 D2 **Ulungur He** *R* China
66 D2 **Ulungur Hu** *L* China
Ulun Hua *see* **Siziwang Qi**
58 F1 **Ulunkhan** Russian Federation
Uluru *see* **Ayers Rock**
140 B7 **Uluru Nat Park** N Terr Australia
47 J5 **Ulus Dağı** *mt* Turkey
56 C2 **Uluyuya** *R* Russian Federation
15 B4 **Ulva** *isld* Scotland
13 E5 **Ulverston** England
139 H8 **Ulverstone** Tasmania Australia
27 B11 **Ulvik** Norway
27 M10 **Ulvila** Finland
26 K8 **Ulvön** *isld* Sweden
29 K6 **Ulvshale** *pen* Denmark
28 J7 **Ulv Sund** *chan* Denmark
52 G6 **Ul'yankovo** Russian Federation
53 G7 **Ul'yanovsk** Russian Federation
55 F5 **Ul'yanovskiy** Kazakhstan
101 L4 **Ulysses** Idaho U.S.A.
107 J4 **Ulysses** Kansas U.S.A.
98 J8 **Ulysses** Nebraska U.S.A.
57 D1 **Ulytau** Kazakhstan
57 D2 **Ulytau, Gory** *mts* Kazakhstan
57 C1 **Uly-Zhylanshyk** *R* Kazakhstan
Ulzburg *see* **Henstedt-Ulzburg**
48 N2 **Uman'** Ukraine
131 C2 **Umango, Cerro** *pk* Argentina
71 M9 **Umarese** Timor Indonesia
74 J7 **Umaria** India
74 C6 **Umarkot** Pakistan
138 E2 **Umaroona, L** South Australia Australia
113 F9 **Umatilla** Florida U.S.A.
100 F4 **Umatilla** Oregon U.S.A.
71 G6 **Umayan** *R* Philippines
95 Q2 **Umbagog L** New Hampshire U.S.A.
140 D2 **Umbakumba** Northern Territory Australia
108 E1 **Umbarger** Texas U.S.A.
140 C7 **Umbeara** N Terr Australia
42 E5 **Umbertide** Italy
136 K3 **Umboi** *isld* Papua New Guinea
52 D1 **Umbozero, Oz** *L* Russian Federation
144 B6 **Umbrella Mts** New Zealand
127 J1 **Umbrella Pt** Jamaica
42 E6 **Umbria** *prov* Italy
26 G5 **Umbukta** Norway
130 J9 **Umbuzeiro** Brazil
26 L8 **Umeå** Sweden
26 K7 **Ume älv** *R* Sweden
80 G5 **Um ed Dananir** Jordan
80 G6 **Um el 'Amad** Jordan
80 G7 **Um el Malid** Jordan
80 G4 **Um el Manabi** Jordan
71 B3 **Umera** Indonesia
80 G7 **Um er Risas** Jordan
26 H6 **Umfors** Sweden
118 L1 **Umfreville** Ontario Canada
88 B10 **Umfuli** *R* Zimbabwe
89 G7 **Umgeni** *R* S Africa
26 K7 **Umgransele** Sweden
41 N3 **Umhausen** Austria
88 B10 **Umi** *R* Zimbabwe
116 L2 **Umiat** Alaska U.S.A.
147 G1 **Umingmakkok** U.S.A.
89 G8 **Umkomaas** *R* S Africa
84 F4 **Umm al Aḩrār** Libya
79 H4 **Umm al'Amad** Syria
84 E4 **Umm al Arānib** Libya
77 D7 **Umm al Qaiwain** U.A.E.
86 E3 **Umm Bel** Sudan
79 D10 **Umm Bugma** Egypt
37 K3 **Ummerstadt** Germany
86 E3 **Umm Keddada** Sudan
86 E2 **Umm Lahai** Sudan
77 A4 **Umm Qasr** Iran
86 F3 **Umm Ruwaba** Sudan
Umm Sai'd *see* **Musay'īd**
86 F3 **Umm Saiyala** Sudan
77 C7 **Umm Shaif** *oil well* Persian Gulf
79 D10 **Umm Shomar, G** *mt* Egypt
79 C10 **Umm Tinâşşib,G** *mt* Egypt
26 H6 **Umnäs** Sweden
37 L2 **Umpferstedt** Germany
100 B6 **Umpqua** *R* Oregon U.S.A.
87 C8 **Umpulo** Angola
80 G4 **Um Qantara** Jordan
80 F3 **Um Qeis** Jordan
80 G8 **Um Quleib** Jordan
80 G6 **Um Quseir** Jordan
74 H8 **Umred** India
80 G7 **Um Rummana** Jordan
80 G7 **Um Shujeira el Gharbiya** Jordan
89 G2 **Umsweswe** *R* Zimbabwe
Umtali *see* **Mutare**
89 F8 **Umtata** S Africa
86 A4 **Umuahia** Nigeria
47 H4 **Umurbey** Turkey
89 G8 **Umzimkulu** *R* S Africa
89 F3 **Umzingwane** *R* Zimbabwe
42 G4 **Una** *R* Bosnia-Herzegovina/Croatia
130 H4 **Una** Brazil
130 J10 **Una** *R* Brazil
60 S2 **Unabetsu-dake** *mt* Japan
128 F6 **Unacurizal** Brazil
112 D5 **Unadilla** Georgia U.S.A.
95 M4 **Unadilla** New York U.S.A.
130 F5 **Unaí** Brazil
116 G5 **Unalakleet** Alaska U.S.A.
116 D10 **Unalaska I** Aleutian Is
144 D5 **Una, Mt** New Zealand
29 T9 **Unaós** Iceland
15 C2 **Unapool** Scotland
128 E2 **Unare** *R* Venezuela
29 M4 **Unari** Finland
70 G5 **Unauna** *isld* Sulawesi
17 G2 **Uncastillo** Spain
133 D1 **Uncia** Bolivia
106 C3 **Uncompahgre Pk** Colorado U.S.A.
106 B3 **Uncompahgre Plateau** Colorado U.S.A.
27 G13 **Unden** *L* Sweden
27 G13 **Undenäs** Sweden
138 F6 **Underbool** Victoria Australia
28 E2 **Understed** Denmark
27 K11 **Understen** *lighthouse* Sweden
27 H10 **Undersvik** Sweden
28 D5 **Underup** Denmark
99 L8 **Underwood** Iowa U.S.A.
98 E2 **Underwood** North Dakota U.S.A.
28 H5 **Undløse** Denmark
71 K10 **Undu,Tg** *C* Sumba Indonesia
54 D4 **Unecha** Russian Federation
128 E4 **Uneiuxi** *R* Brazil
79 F8 **Uneiza** Jordan
37 P4 **Uněšov** Czech Rep
52 E3 **Unezhma** Russian Federation
116 G9 **Unga I** Alaska U.S.A.
116 G4 **Ungalik** Alaska U.S.A.
139 H5 **Ungarie** New South Wales Australia
138 D5 **Ungarra** South Australia Australia
115 N6 **Ungava B** Quebec Canada
115 M5 **Ungava, Pen. d'** Quebec Canada
48 L3 **Ungeny** Moldova
41 M1 **Ungerhausen** Germany
59 K3 **Unggi** N Korea
128 D5 **União** Brazil
130 D10 **União da Vitória** Brazil
128 F4 **União do Marmará** Brazil
130 J10 **União dos Palmares** Brazil
112 E1 **Unicoi** Tennessee U.S.A.
48 D1 **Uničov** Czech Rep
31 L4 **Uniejów** Poland
42 F4 **Unije** *isld* Croatia
116 E9 **Unimak** Aleutian Is
116 E9 **Unimak I** Aleutian Is
85 C8 **Uni,Mt** Liberia
128 F4 **Unini** *R* Brazil
133 D5 **Unión** Argentina
127 O8 **Union** *isld* Lesser Antilles
130 C9 **Unión** Paraguay
98 C9 **Union** Colorado U.S.A.
99 N7 **Union** Iowa U.S.A.
111 F11 **Union** Louisiana U.S.A.
95 S2 **Union** Maine U.S.A.
111 G9 **Union** Mississippi U.S.A.
110 E3 **Union** Missouri U.S.A.
99 L9 **Union** Nebraska U.S.A.
107 N6 **Union** Oklahoma U.S.A.
100 H4 **Union** Oregon U.S.A.
112 F3 **Union** South Carolina U.S.A.
94 G9 **Union** West Virginia U.S.A.
131 E7 **Unión, B** Argentina
95 K7 **Union Bridge** Maryland U.S.A.
111 F10 **Union Church** Mississippi U.S.A.
110 M1 **Union City** Indiana U.S.A.
94 B4 **Union City** Michigan U.S.A.
94 C6 **Union City** Ohio/Indiana U.S.A.
94 H5 **Union City** Pennsylvania U.S.A.
110 G5 **Union City** Tennessee U.S.A.
100 C7 **Union Creek** Oregon U.S.A.
95 M5 **Uniondale** Pennsylvania U.S.A.
126 D3 **Unión de Reyes** Cuba
100 H3 **Union Flat Cr** Washington U.S.A.
100 E3 **Union Gap** Washington U.S.A.
17 G7 **Unión,La** Spain
112 F2 **Union Mills** North Carolina U.S.A.
103 M7 **Union,Mt** Arizona U.S.A.
Union of Soviet Socialist Republics *see* **Armenia, Azerbaijan, Belorussia, Estonia, Georgia, Kazakhstan, Kirghizia, Latvia, Lithuania, Moldova, Russian Federation, Tajikistan, Turkemenistan, Ukraine and Uzbekistan**
101 Q6 **Union Pass** Wyoming U.S.A.
112 D4 **Union Point** Georgia U.S.A.
118 D1 **Union Pt** Manitoba Canada
111 L9 **Union Springs** Alabama U.S.A.
95 L4 **Union Springs** New York U.S.A.
99 M10 **Union Star** Missouri U.S.A.
109 M9 **Union Stock Yards** Texas U.S.A.
111 J9 **Uniontown** Alabama U.S.A.
110 J4 **Uniontown** Kentucky U.S.A.
94 H7 **Uniontown** Pennsylvania U.S.A.
99 O9 **Unionville** Iowa U.S.A.
94 D3 **Unionville** Michigan U.S.A.
99 N9 **Unionville** Missouri U.S.A.
102 F1 **Unionville** Nevada U.S.A.
94 K8 **Unionville** Virginia U.S.A.
31 L2 **Unisław** Poland
77 C7 **United Arab Emirates (UAE)** Persian Gulf
6 **United Kingdom of Gt.Britain & N.Ireland (UK)** W Europe
92 **United States of America (USA)** N America
52 D3 **Unitsa** Russian Federation
118 H6 **Unity** Saskatchewan Canada
95 S2 **Unity** Maine U.S.A.
100 G5 **Unity** Oregon U.S.A.
17 G4 **Universales** *mt* Spain
17 F4 **Universales, Mts** Spain
111 G7 **University** Mississippi U.S.A.
111 K13 **University City** St Louis
110 F3 **University City** Missouri U.S.A.
109 O9 **University Park** Texas U.S.A.
36 C2 **Unkel** Germany
38 G6 **Unken** Austria
55 C3 **Unkurda** Russian Federation
32 G9 **Unna** Germany
74 J5 **Unnao** India
27 G14 **Unnaryd** Sweden
60 F12 **Unomachi** Japan
37 L6 **Unsernherrn** Germany
52 E2 **Unskaya Guba** *B* Russian Federation
15 G1 **Unst** Shetland Scotland
33 O10 **Unstrut** *R* Germany
61 P12 **Unten** Okinawa
38 N6 **Unter Berg** *mt* Austria
39 C2 **Unterbrunn** Germany
Unter Deufstetten *see* **Fichtenau**
41 M4 **Unter Engadin** *dist* Switzerland
36 H4 **Unterfranken** *dist* Germany
38 H8 **Untergailtal** *V* Austria
36 F5 **Unter Grombach** Germany
36 H6 **Untergröningen** Germany
37 M7 **Unterhaching** Germany
38 E7 **Unter inn-tal** *V* Austria
33 M7 **Unterlüss** Germany
37 K3 **Untermerzbach** Germany
36 H5 **Untermünkheim** Germany
37 K5 **Untern-Bibert** Germany
36 F5 **Unter Schwarzach** Germany
Untersteinbach *see* **Rauhenebrach**
38 J7 **Untertal** *R* Austria
38 J7 **Unter Tavern** Austria
41 H4 **Unterwalden** *canton* Switzerland
36 E2 **Unterwilden** Germany
37 M7 **Unter Zolling** Germany
55 E1 **Untor, Oz** *L* Russian Federation
27 G10 **Untorp** Sweden
128 E3 **Unturán, Sa. de** *mts* Venezuela
117 H7 **Unuk** *R* Alaska U.S.A.
21 N5 **Unverre** France
118 H6 **Unwin** Saskatchewan Canada
78 F1 **Ünye** Turkey
60 D13 **Unzen-Amakusa Nat. Park** Japan
60 D13 **Unzen dake** *mt* Japan
52 F5 **Unzha** Russian Federation
38 K7 **Unzmarkt** Austria
61 L9 **Uozu** Japan
54 H3 **Upa** *R* Russian Federation
101 P9 **Upalco** Utah U.S.A.
127 N10 **Upata** Venezuela
9 E5 **Upavon** England
87 E7 **Upemba, L** Zaire
115 O3 **Upernavik** Greenland
Upernavik Kujallek *see* **Søndre Upernavik**
12 E2 **Uphall** Scotland
98 F1 **Upham** North Dakota U.S.A.
89 B7 **Upington** S Africa
94 B6 **Upland** Indiana U.S.A.
98 H9 **Upland** Nebraska U.S.A.
9 G4 **Upminster** England
116 H6 **Upnuk L** Alaska U.S.A.
52 D1 **Upolaksha** Russian Federation
134 C2 **Upolu** *isld* Western Samoa
135 U4 **Upolu Pt** Hawaiian Is
117 P10 **Upper Arrow L** British Columbia Canada
122 G7 **Upper Blackville** New Brunswick Canada
9 F2 **Upper Broughton** England
8 C3 **Upper Chapel** Wales
123 P4 **Upper Humber R** Newfoundland Canada
145 E4 **Upper Hutt** New Zealand
99 P6 **Upper Iowa** *R* Iowa U.S.A.
122 E7 **Upper Kent** New Brunswick Canada
100 D7 **Upper Klamath L** Oregon U.S.A.
14 B5 **Upper L** Ireland
102 B2 **Upper L** California U.S.A.
117 F5 **Upper Laberge** Yukon Territory Canada
117 J5 **Upper Liard** Yukon Territory Canada
118 J1 **Upper Manitou L** Ontario Canada
127 P2 **Upper Manzanilla** Trinidad
95 L8 **Upper Marlboro** Maryland U.S.A.
145 D4 **Upper Moutere** New Zealand
122 K8 **Upper Musquodoboit** Nova Scotia Canada
99 M1 **Upper Red L** Minnesota U.S.A.
101 O5 **Upper Red Rock L** Montana U.S.A.
94 D6 **Upper Sandusky** Ohio U.S.A.
95 N2 **Upper Saranac L** New York U.S.A.
122 J8 **Upper Stewiacke** Nova Scotia Canada
94 H8 **Upper Tract** West Virginia U.S.A.
94 K7 **Upperville** Virginia U.S.A.
Upper Volta *see* **Burkina**
139 H7 **Upper Yarra Res** Victoria Australia
9 F2 **Uppingham** England
27 J12 **Upplands Väsby** Sweden
27 J12 **Uppsala** *county* Sweden
27 K12 **Uppsala** Sweden
116 C6 **Upright,C** St Matthew I, Alaska U.S.A.
119 N1 **Upsala** Ontario Canada
99 M4 **Upsala** Minnesota U.S.A.
122 F6 **Upsalquitch** New Brunswick Canada
74 G2 **Upshi** Kashmir
99 Q3 **Upson** Wisconsin U.S.A.
141 J4 **Upstart, C** Queensland Australia
9 H5 **Upstreet** England
8 D3 **Upton** England
94 B9 **Upton** Kentucky U.S.A.
98 B5 **Upton** Wyoming U.S.A.
84 F3 **Uqaylah,Al** Libya
79 H3 **Uquayribāt** Syria
126 F10 **Urabá,G.de** Colombia
36 G7 **Urach** Germany
128 F2 **Uracoa** Venezuela
58 E3 **Urad Zhongqi** China
61 N10 **Uraga** Japan
83 K11 **Uragasmanhandiya** Sri Lanka
60 Q3 **Urakawa** Japan
139 H5 **Ural** *mt* New South Wales Australia
55 C4 **Ural** *R* Kazakhstan/Rus Fed
100 K1 **Ural** Montana U.S.A.
139 K4 **Uralla** New South Wales Australia
5 R3 **Ural Mts** Russian Federation
50 E3 **Uralskiy Khrebet** *mts* Russian Federation
88 D4 **Urambo** Tanzania
139 H6 **Urana** New South Wales Australia
140 E5 **Urandangie** Queensland Australia
130 G4 **Urandi** Brazil
141 L7 **Urangan** Queensland Australia
111 D10 **Urania** Louisiana U.S.A.
114 J6 **Uranium City** Saskatchewan Canada
83 L10 **Uraniya** Sri Lanka
140 C2 **Urapunga** N Terr Australia
128 F3 **Uraricoera** Brazil
143 E9 **Uraryie Rock** *rock* W Australia Australia
61 P13 **Urasoe** Okinawa
57 E5 **Ura-Tyube** Tajikistan
60 P2 **Urausu** Japan
61 N10 **Urawa** Japan
55 D1 **Uray** Russian Federation
55 C4 **Urazmetova** Russian Federation
52 G6 **Urazovka** Russian Federation
54 K6 **Urazovo** Russian Federation
99 S9 **Urbana** Illinois U.S.A.
94 B6 **Urbana** Indiana U.S.A.
99 P7 **Urbana** Iowa U.S.A.
110 C4 **Urbana** Missouri U.S.A.
94 D6 **Urbana** Ohio U.S.A.
45 N4 **Urbania** Italy
95 L9 **Urbanna** Virginia U.S.A.
129 K4 **Urbano Santos** Brazil
16 E2 **Urbel** *R* Spain
45 N4 **Urbino** Italy
17 F2 **Urbión, Sa. de** *mts* Spain
22 F5 **Urcel** France
128 D6 **Urcos** Peru
18 E10 **Urdos** France
52 H2 **Urdyuzhskoye Oz** *L* Russian Federation
57 K2 **Urdzhar** Kazakhstan
52 G5 **Uren** Russian Federation
50 G2 **Urengoy** Russian Federation
145 E3 **Urenui** New Zealand
137 O4 **Uréparapara** *isld* Vanuatu
13 G5 **Ure,R** England
124 D3 **Ures** Mexico
145 F3 **Urewera Country** New Zealand
55 G3 **Urez** Russian Federation
Urfa *see* **Şanlıurfa**
38 K5 **Urfahr** Austria
41 O2 **Urfeld** Germany
52 G6 **Urga** *R* Russian Federation
59 K1 **Urgal** Russian Federation
17 H2 **Urgel, Seo de** Spain
57 B4 **Urgench** Uzbekistan
41 J4 **Uri** *canton* Switzerland
19 P14 **Uriage** France
111 J10 **Uriah** Alabama U.S.A.
144 C5 **Uriah, Mt** New Zealand
128 D3 **Uribe** Colombia
127 H9 **Uribia** Colombia
110 B3 **Urich** Missouri U.S.A.
101 P8 **Urie** Wyoming U.S.A.
128 F2 **Urimán** Venezuela
124 F4 **Urique** Mexico
41 H4 **Uri Rothstock** *mt* Switzerland
139 G3 **Urisino** New South Wales Australia
55 E4 **Uritskiy** Kazakhstan
29 K10 **Urjala** Finland
25 E3 **Urk** Netherlands
47 H6 **Urla** Turkey
48 K6 **Urlaţi** Romania
28 D5 **Urlev** Denmark
55 C4 **Urman** Russian Federation
79 G6 **'Urmān** Syria
55 E1 **Urmannyy** Russian Federation
52 G6 **Urmary** Russian Federation
59 K2 **Urmi** *R* Russian Federation
Urmia,L *see* **Orūmīyeh, Daryācheh-ye** *L*
55 F2 **Urninskoye Boloto** Russian Federation
52 J5 **Urolka** *R* Russian Federation
46 E2 **Uroševac** Serbia Yugoslavia
131 D7 **Urre Lauquen, L** Argentina
12 E3 **Urr,L** Scotland
99 P9 **Ursa** Illinois U.S.A.
37 J7 **Ursberg** Germany
25 C3 **Ursem** Netherlands
37 M5 **Ursensollen** Germany
52 F6 **Urshelskiy** Russian Federation
56 C4 **Ursk** Russian Federation
36 H6 **Urspring** Germany
26 M7 **Ursviken** Sweden
55 C4 **Urtazym** Russian Federation
58 B4 **Urt Moron** China
124 E4 **Uruáchic** Mexico
130 E4 **Uruaçu** Brazil
130 E4 **Uruana** Brazil
124 H8 **Uruapan del Progreso** Mexico
128 D6 **Urubamba** Peru
128 G4 **Urubu** *R* Brazil
129 G4 **Urucará** Brazil
127 N10 **Urucoa** Venezuela
128 F4 **Urucu** *R* Brazil
129 K5 **Uruçuí** Brazil
130 F5 **Urucuia** Brazil
130 B6 **Urucum** Brazil
129 G4 **Urucurituba** Brazil
131 F2 **Uruguaiana** Brazil
130 D10 **Uruguai,R** Brazil
131 G4 **Uruguay** *rep* S America
131 F4 **Uruguay, R** Argentina
79 G2 **Urūmaş Şughrá** Syria
Urumchi *see* **Ürümqi**
66 D3 **Ürümqi** China
69 C11 **Urung** Indonesia
139 L4 **Urunga** New South Wales Australia
128 F6 **Urupa** *R* Brazil
52 H6 **Urussu** Russian Federation
130 F4 **Urutágua** Brazil
130 E5 **Urutaí** Brazil
145 E3 **Uruti** New Zealand
77 J3 **Urūzgān** *reg* Afghanistan
146 D3 **Urville I, d'** Antarctica
20 G2 **Urville-Nacqueville** France
136 H2 **Urville, Tg. D'** *C* W Irian
89 B4 **Urwi** Botswana
60 P2 **Uryū** Japan
60 Q2 **Uryū** *R* Japan
60 Q1 **Uryū-ko** *L* Japan
58 G1 **Uryum** *R* Russian Federation
56 C3 **Uryup** *R* Russian Federation
53 F8 **Uryupinsk** Russian Federation
52 G6 **Urzhum** Russian Federation
48 K6 **Urziceni** Romania
36 B4 **Urzig** Germany
21 O3 **Us** France
60 E12 **Usa** Japan
71 E7 **Usada** *isld* Philippines
47 K6 **Uşak** Turkey
87 C10 **Usakos** Namibia
80 E5 **Ūsarīn** Jordan
146 C13 **Usarp Mts** *mts* Antarctica
133 F8 **Usborne** *hill* Falkland Is
33 T5 **Usedom** Germany
143 A7 **Useless Loop** W Australia Australia
80 D2 **Usha** Israel
116 L7 **Ushagat I** Alaska U.S.A.
50 G1 **Ushakova, Ostrova** *islds* Russian Federation
55 E3 **Ushakovo** Russian Federation
Ushant *see* **Ouessant, I. d'**
56 E5 **Ush-Bel'dir** Russian Federation
60 D13 **Ushibuka** Japan
48 L2 **Ushitsa** *R* Ukraine
61 L8 **Ushitsu** Japan
60 D12 **Ushizu** Japan

57 J2 Ushtobe Kazakhstan
133 D8 Ushuaia airport Argentina
129 H5 Usina Brazil
36 F3 Usingen Germany
8 D4 Usk Wales
27 A12 Uskedal Norway
8 C4 Usk,R Wales
Üskub see Skopje
47 N10 Üsküdar Turkey
47 J3 Üsküp Turkey
32 L9 Uslar Germany
54 L4 Usman Russian Federation
100 F3 U.S. Mil. Res. Yakima Firing Range Washington U.S.A.
56 D3 Usolka R Russian Federation
52 J5 Usol'ye Russian Federation
55 G4 Uspenka Kazakhstan
57 G1 Uspenskiy Kazakhstan
40 F7 Usseglio Italy
18 G7 Ussel France
13 H6 Usselby England
32 J10 Usseln Germany
29 K5 Usserød Denmark
18 F6 Usson du Poitou France
59 K2 Ussuri R Russian Federation
59 K3 Ussuriysk Russian Federation
21 K4 Ussy France
52 G6 Usta R Russian Federation
56 D5 Ust'-Abakan Russian Federation
52 G4 Ust' Alekseyevo Russian Federation
27 C11 Ustaoset Norway
53 G7 Ust'-Aza Russian Federation
55 D3 Ust-Bagaryak Russian Federation
56 B3 Ust'-Bakchar Russian Federation
52 H4 Ust' Chernaya Russian Federation
48 H2 Ust-'Chorna Ukraine
52 J5 Ust' Dolgaya Russian Federation
41 J3 Uster Switzerland
43 E10 Ustica, I. di Italy
30 H5 Ustií nad Labem Czech Rep
56 F2 Ust'Ilimsk Russian Federation
56 F3 Ust'-Ilimskoye Vodokhranilishche res Russian Federation
52 J3 Ust'-Ilych Russian Federation
Ustinov see Izhevsk
55 F2 Ust'-Ishim Russian Federation
55 G3 Ust'Izes Russian Federation
31 K1 Ustka Poland
56 B6 Ust'-Kamenogorsk Kazakhstan
58 G1 Ust'Karenga Russian Federation
55 C4 Ust'Katav Russian Federation
58 E1 Ust'-Kiran Russian Federation
55 C3 Ust Kishert Russian Federation
52 H3 Ust'Koin Russian Federation
52 H4 Ust'Kulom Russian Federation
56 G3 Ust'-Kut Russian Federation
55 D2 Ust' Loz'va Russian Federation
52 C5 Ust' Luga Russian Federation
52 J2 Ust' Lyzha Russian Federation
51 N2 Ust'Maya Russian Federation
51 L3 Ust-Muya Russian Federation
52 H4 Ust'Nem Russian Federation
59 K1 Ust'Niman Russian Federation
56 F4 Ust'-Ordynskiy Russian Federation
56 F4 Ust'-Ordynskiy Buryatskiy Avtonomnyy Okrug dist Russian Federation
46 G3 Ustovo Bulgaria
52 F4 Ust' Paden'ga Russian Federation
52 F3 Ust' Pinega Russian Federation
50 H2 Ust'-Port Russian Federation
52 F4 Ust' Puya Russian Federation
52 G4 Ust' Reka Russian Federation
31 O6 Ustrzyki Dolne Poland
52 D4 Ust'Sara Russian Federation
52 J3 Ust'-Shchugor Russian Federation
55 D1 Ust'-Tapsuy Russian Federation
55 F3 Ust'Tara Russian Federation
55 G3 Ust'Tarka Russian Federation
55 F3 Ust' Tava Russian Federation
52 H2 Ust' Tsil'ma Russian Federation
59 K1 Ust'Tyrma Russian Federation
56 F4 Ust'-Uda Russian Federation
52 J4 Ust' Un'ya Russian Federation
52 F3 Ust'ura Russian Federation
59 H1 Ust'urov Russian Federation
56 D5 Ust' Us Russian Federation
52 J2 Ust' Usa Russian Federation
55 D4 Ust'-Uyskoye Russian Federation
52 J3 Ust'-Voya Russian Federation
52 G3 Ust' Vyyskaya Russian Federation
52 F4 Ust'ya R Russian Federation
52 E5 Ust'ye Russian Federation
52 E6 Ust'ye R Russian Federation
50 E4 Ustyurt,Plato Kazakhstan/Uzbekistan
52 E5 Ustyuzhna Russian Federation
66 C3 Usu China
71 L10 Usu isld Indonesia
60 E12 Usuki Japan
125 P11 Usulután El Salvador
125 O9 Usumacinta R Mexico
70 D3 Usun Apau Plateau Sarawak
89 G6 Usutu R Swaziland
52 D6 Usvyaty Russian Federation
71 B2 Uta isld Indonesia
103 M2 Utah state U.S.A.
103 N1 Utah L Utah U.S.A.
29 M7 Utajärvi Finland
71 H9 Utan Indonesia
60 Q2 Utashinai Japan
79 G5 Utaybah, Buḩayrat al L Syria
99 L7 Ute Iowa U.S.A.
17 G3 Utebo Spain
106 G6 Ute Cr New Mexico U.S.A.
88 G6 Utenge,L Tanzania
106 E5 Ute Park New Mexico U.S.A.
37 P4 Uterý Czech Rep
55 G4 Utes Kazakhstan
88 G6 Utete Tanzania
68 D5 U Thai Thani Thailand
77 K7 Uthal Pakistan
32 J6 Uthlede Germany
79 H4 'Uthmānīyah Syria
68 G5 Uthumphon Phisai Thailand
129 G6 Utiariti Brazil
107 K3 Utica Kansas U.S.A.
94 D4 Utica Michigan U.S.A.
99 P6 Utica Minnesota U.S.A.
111 F9 Utica Mississippi U.S.A.
110 C2 Utica Missouri U.S.A.
101 P3 Utica Montana U.S.A.
98 J9 Utica Nebraska U.S.A.
95 M3 Utica New York U.S.A.
94 E6 Utica Ohio U.S.A.
17 G5 Utiel Spain
26 K7 Utifällan Sweden
119 W3 Utik L Manitoba Canada
145 E3 Utiku New Zealand
118 B3 Utikuma L Alberta Canada
27 H16 Utklippan isld Sweden
27 C10 Utla R Norway
27 H15 Utlängan isld Sweden
109 K5 Utley Texas U.S.A.
106 G4 Utleyville Colorado U.S.A.
74 D1 Utmanzai Pakistan
27 M12 Utö lighthouse Finland
27 K13 Utö Sweden
140 C5 Utopia N Terr Australia
109 H6 Utopia Texas U.S.A.
75 K5 Utraula India
25 D4 Utrecht Netherlands
89 G6 Utrecht S Africa
16 D7 Utrera Spain
27 A12 Utsira lighthouse Norway
29 N2 Utsjoki Finland
61 N9 Utsunomiya Japan
53 G10 Utta Russian Federation
68 E4 Uttaradit Thailand
74 H4 Uttar Pradesh prov India
27 H12 Uttersberg Sweden
28 G7 Utterslev Denmark
36 H4 Üttingen Germany
9 E2 Uttoxeter England
116 G2 Utukok R Alaska U.S.A.
137 O4 Utupua isld Santa Cruz Is
55 B5 Utva R Kazakhstan
37 O3 Útvina Czech Rep
52 H6 Utyashkino Russian Federation
32 M8 Utze Germany
33 S5 Utzedel Germany
29 O10 Uukuniem Finland
Uummannaq see Dundas
115 O3 Uummannaq Greenland
Uummannarsuaq Greenland see Farvel,Kap
29 L9 Uurainen Finland
56 D5 Üüreg Nuur L Mongolia
Uusikaarlepyy see Nykarleby
29 J11 Uusikaupunki Finland
29 L11 Uusimaa prov Finland
52 H6 Uva Russian Federation
48 F7 Uvac R Serbia Yugoslavia
103 K2 Uvada Nevada U.S.A.
128 D3 Uva, L Colombia
112 E5 Uvalda Georgia U.S.A.
108 H6 Uvalde Texas U.S.A.
54 B4 Uvarovichi Belarus
52 E6 Uvarovka Russian Federation
55 E2 Uvat Russian Federation
137 O6 Uvéa isld Îles Loyauté Pacific Oc
137 R4 Uvea isld Îles Wallis Pacific Oc
55 D4 Uvel'skiy Russian Federation
55 D3 Uvil'dy, Oz L Russian Federation
88 C4 Uvinza Tanzania
88 B3 Uvira Zaire
60 E13 Uwae Japan
60 F12 Uwajima Japan
84 H5 Uweinat,Jebel mt Sudan
135 V5 Uwekahuna Hawaiian Is
69 H12 Uwi isld Indonesia
121 L8 Uxbridge Ontario Canada
9 F4 Uxbridge England
65 A5 Uxin Ju China
125 P7 Uxmal Mexico
55 D4 Uy R Kazakhstan/Rus Fed
116 K8 Uyak B Alaska U.S.A.
51 O2 Uyandina R Russian Federation
56 D3 Uyar Russian Federation
15 G1 Uyea isld Scotland
15 G1 Uyeasound Scotland
50 H1 Uyedineniya,Ostrov isld Russian Federation
52 H2 Uyeg Russian Federation
47 K8 Uyluk Tepe mt Turkey
85 F7 Uyo Nigeria
47 K6 Uysal Dağı mt Turkey
55 D4 Uyskoye Russian Federation
57 F3 Uyuk Kazakhstan
133 D2 Uyuni Bolivia
48 G2 Uz R Slovakia
57 B3 Uzbekistan rep C Asia
48 F5 Uzdin Serbia Yugoslavia
20 E5 Uzel France
53 G8 Uzen', Malyy R Kazakhstan/Rus Fed
57 G4 Uzgen Kirghizia
48 G2 Uzh R Ukraine
48 G2 Uzhgorod Ukraine
56 C3 Uzhur Russian Federation
48 F7 Užice Serbia Yugoslavia
41 J3 Uznach Switzerland
52 F6 Uzola R Russian Federation
47 N10 Üzümce Turkey
47 K8 Üzümlü Turkey
47 H6 Uzun isld Turkey
88 E6 Uzungwa Tanzania
47 H3 Uzunköprü Turkey
57 B3 Uzynkair Kazakhstan

V

29 M9 Vaajakoski Finland
89 E6 Vaal R S Africa
29 M7 Vaala Finland
89 F6 Vaal Dam S Africa
29 N11 Vaalimaa Finland
87 E10 Vaalwater S Africa
29 M8 Vaaraslahti Finland
21 L6 Vaas France
29 J8 Vaasa Finland
25 E4 Vaassen Netherlands
29 L4 Vaattojärvi Finland
28 H7 Våbensted Denmark
57 C5 Vabkent Uzbekistan
130 C7 Vacaria,R Brazil
130 C7 Vacaria,Sa mts Brazil
131 B4 Vacas,Pta De Argentina
102 B3 Vacaville California U.S.A.
19 N17 Vaccarès, Etang de L France
52 F6 Vacha Russian Federation
126 H5 Vache, Île-à- Haiti
40 E5 Vacheresse France
19 N16 Vacqueyras France
52 F6 Vad Russian Federation
100 C3 Vader Washington U.S.A.
27 A10 Vadheim Norway
76 A3 Vādi India
42 G5 Vadice Croatia
106 E5 Vadito New Mexico U.S.A.
27 B12 Vadla Norway
44 D3 Vado Italy
44 D3 Vado, C. di Italy
74 E7 Vadodara India
124 F2 Vado de Santa María Mexico
52 D1 Vadozero, Oz L Russian Federation
26 R1 Vadsö Norway
27 G13 Vadstenna Sweden
48 M6 Vadu Romania
28 D2 Vadum Denmark
41 L3 Vaduz Liechtenstein
26 K3 Vadvetjåkko Nat. Park Sweden
28 H7 Væggerløse Denmark
29 K5 Værløse Denmark
26 F4 Vaeröy Norway
28 G5 Værslev Denmark
52 F4 Vaga R Russian Federation
26 J9 Vaga Sweden
26 D10 Vågåmo Norway
26 G3 Vagan Norway
42 G4 Vaganski mt Croatia
6 F1 Vágar isld Faeroes
55 E2 Vagay Russian Federation
Vağda see Erdemh
29 O2 Vaggetem Russian Federation
26 R2 Vaggetem-javrre L Norway
45 K4 Vaglia Italy
27 J13 Vagnahärad Sweden
16 B4 Vagos Portugal
27 F11 Vägsjöfors Sweden
26 A10 Vågsöy isld Norway
31 L6 Váh R Slovakia
29 J8 Vähäkyrö Finland
79 F8 Vahal Israel
111 G8 Vaiden Mississippi U.S.A.
21 K5 Vaiges France
36 F6 Vaihingen Germany
76 B1 Vaijapur India
52 C5 Väike-Maarja Estonia
26 L5 Vaikijaur Sweden
103 O9 Vail Arizona U.S.A.
106 D2 Vail Colorado U.S.A.
15 G2 Vaila isld Scotland
22 F5 Vailly-sur-Aisne France
134 B1 Vailoa Western Samoa
29 N11 Vainikkala Finland
45 Q7 Vairano Patenora Italy
20 G8 Vairé France
137 Q3 Vaitupu isld Tuvalu
46 F2 Vakarel Bulgaria
27 G11 Vakern Sweden
56 B1 Vakh R Russian Federation
57 F6 Vakhanskiy Khrebet mts Tajikistan
57 E5 Vakhsh Tajikistan
57 E5 Vakhsh R Tajikistan
57 E5 Vakhshstroy Tajikistan
52 G5 Vakhtan Russian Federation
52 D3 Vaknavolok Russian Federation
27 A11 Vaksdal Norway
83 L10 Valachchenai Sri Lanka
26 F8 Vålådalen Sweden
40 F5 Valais canton Switzerland
52 H5 Valamaz Russian Federation
46 F3 Valandovo Macedonia
20 E4 Val André, le France
21 J7 Valanjou France
27 G12 Valåsen Sweden
95 O4 Valatie New York U.S.A.
46 G6 Valáxa isld Greece
38 E8 Val Badia Italy
121 P6 Val Barrette Quebec Canada
26 G3 Valberg Norway
19 P15 Valbonnais France
122 E5 Val Brilliant Quebec Canada
25 E5 Valburg Netherlands
133 D6 Valcheta Argentina
121 S7 Valcourt Quebec Canada
41 O6 Valdagno Italy
16 D2 Valdavia R Spain
52 D5 Valday Russian Federation
52 D6 Valdayskaya Vozvyshennost' uplands Russian Federation
17 G4 Valde Algorfa Spain
16 D5 Valdecañas, Embalse de res Spain
17 F5 Valdeganga Spain
21 P4 Val-de-Marne dept France
52 B6 Valdemārpils Latvia
27 J13 Valdemarsvik Sweden
16 E4 Valdemoro Spain
17 F4 Valdemoro-Sierra Spain
16 C2 Valdeorras, El Barco de Spain
16 E6 Valdepeñas Spain
16 D3 Valderaduey R Spain
17 H4 Valderrobres Spain
99 T5 Valders Wisconsin U.S.A.
121 P7 Val des Bois Quebec Canada
112 F2 Valdese North Carolina U.S.A.
133 E6 Valdés, Pen Argentina
116 O6 Valdez Alaska U.S.A.
106 F4 Valdez Colorado U.S.A.
41 M5 Valdidentro Italy
131 A7 Valdivia Chile
131 A8 Valdivia prov Chile
20 H5 Val-d'Izé France
21 O3 Val-d'Oise dept France
121 N4 Val-d'Or Quebec Canada
113 D7 Valdosta Georgia U.S.A.
27 D11 Valdres plateau Norway
19 P16 Valdrome France
20 E3 Vale Channel Is
100 H6 Vale Oregon U.S.A.
98 C5 Vale South Dakota U.S.A.
48 G5 Valea Bistrei Romania
48 G3 Valea Lui Mihai Romania
48 J3 Valea Vişeului Romania
37 P3 Valeč Czech Rep
45 J1 Valéggio Italy
129 L6 Valença Brazil
21 O7 Valençay France
19 N15 Valence France
18 F8 Valence d'Agen France
18 F9 Valence-sur-Baïse France
17 G5 Valencia prov Spain
17 G5 Valencia Spain
127 K9 Valencia Venezuela
16 C5 Valência de Alcantara Spain
16 D2 Valencia de Don Juan Spain
16 B3 Valença do Minho Portugal
17 H5 Valencia,G de Spain
14 A5 Valencia I Ireland
127 L9 Valencia,L.de Venezuela
22 F3 Valenciennes France
19 P17 Valensole France
59 K3 Valentin Russian Federation
103 L6 Valentine Arizona U.S.A.
111 F12 Valentine Louisiana U.S.A.
101 R2 Valentine Montana U.S.A.
98 F7 Valentine Nebraska U.S.A.
108 C5 Valentine Texas U.S.A.
44 E1 Valenza Italy
27 E11 Våler Norway
109 H4 Valera Texas U.S.A.
127 J10 Valera Venezuela
27 A12 Valestrand Norway
130 H5 Vale Verde Brazil
41 M4 Valfurva R Italy
52 C5 Valga Estonia
120 K4 Val Gagné Ontario Canada
43 F11 Valguarnera Caropepe Sicily
6 N6 Valhall oil rig North Sea
7 M9 Valiant gas field North Sea
101 N1 Valier Montana U.S.A.
29 K4 Välinge Sweden
48 F6 Valjevo Serbia Yugoslavia
26 P2 Valjok Norway
19 Q15 Valjouffrey France
29 L10 Valkeakoski Finland
29 M11 Valkeala Finland
29 L5 Valkeavaara mt Finland
25 E7 Valkenburg Netherlands
25 D6 Valkenswaard Netherlands
54 G7 Valki Ukraine
Valkö see Valkom
29 M11 Valkom Finland
146 G8 Valkyrjedomen ice dome Antarctica
19 N17 Vallabrègues France
16 D3 Valladolid prov Spain
16 D3 Valladolid Spain
121 N4 Val Laflamme Quebec Canada
41 P4 Vallarga Italy
41 O6 Vallarsa R Italy
27 C12 Valle Norway
103 M6 Valle Arizona U.S.A.
38 E7 Valle Aurina Italy
106 C4 Vallecito Res Colorado U.S.A.
106 D5 Vallecitos New Mexico U.S.A.
45 O7 Vallecorsa Italy
131 B2 Valle Cura,Rio Del Argentina
40 G6 Valle d'Aosta aut reg Italy
42 A3 Valle d'Aosta Italy
124 G7 Valle de Banderas Mexico
16 E1 Valle de Cabuérniga Spain
127 M10 Valle de la Pascua Venezuela
128 C3 Valle del Cauca div Colombia
124 F4 Valle de Olivos Mexico
124 F4 Valle de Rosario Mexico
124 G4 Valle de Zaragoza Mexico
126 H9 Valledupar Colombia
85 E5 Vallée de Zgarat Mali
122 B7 Vallée Jonction Quebec Canada
85 E5 Vallée L'Azawak Mali/Niger
131 C3 Valle Fértil, Sa. de mts Argentina
128 F7 Valle Grande Bolivia
40 C5 Valleiry France
102 B3 Vallejo California U.S.A.
45 P7 Vallemaio Italy
40 H6 Valle Mosso Italy
26 M7 Vallen Västerbotten Sweden
26 J8 Vallen Väster Norrland Sweden
131 B2 Vallenar Chile
36 D3 Vallendar Germany
28 H6 Vallensved Denmark
27 K12 Vallentuna Sweden
45 O6 Vallepretra Italy
133 E2 Valle,R.del Argentina
20 H7 Vallet France
43 F13 Valletta Malta
122 J8 Valley Nova Scotia Canada
111 F9 Valley Mississippi U.S.A.
98 K8 Valley Nebraska U.S.A.
100 H1 Valley Washington U.S.A.
101 Q5 Valley Wyoming U.S.A.
8 B1 Valley Wales
107 N4 Valley Center Kansas U.S.A.
118 K7 Valley Centre Saskatchewan Canada
98 J3 Valley City North Dakota U.S.A.
107 P2 Valley Falls Kansas U.S.A.
100 E7 Valley Falls Oregon U.S.A.
121 Q7 Valleyfield Quebec Canada
111 L7 Valley Head Alabama U.S.A.
94 G8 Valley Head West Virginia U.S.A.
109 K4 Valley Mills Texas U.S.A.
116 K7 Valley of Ten Thousand Smokes Alaska U.S.A.
110 F3 Valley Park Missouri U.S.A.
101 L8 Valley Pass Nevada U.S.A.
94 B8 Valley Sta Kentucky U.S.A.
117 P8 Valleyview Alberta Canada
109 K2 Valley View Texas U.S.A.
Vallgrund, isld see Raippaluoto
109 M2 Valliant Oklahoma U.S.A.
45 M2 Valli di Comacchio reg Italy
18 F10 Vallier, Mt France
121 P6 Val Limoges Quebec Canada
21 M2 Valliquerville France
28 J6 Valløby Denmark
43 G8 Vallo di Diano Italy
43 G8 Vallo di Lucania Italy
45 L4 Vallombrosa Italy
94 A8 Vallonia Indiana U.S.A.
21 K6 Vallon-sur-Gée France
40 D4 Vallorbe Switzerland
27 D12 Vallöy Norway
17 H3 Valls Spain
27 H10 Vallsta Sweden
41 M3 Valluga mt Austria
27 J10 Vallvik Sweden
118 K9 Val Marie Saskatchewan Canada
16 E1 Valmaseda Spain
31 K6 Val. Meziříčí Czech Rep
52 C5 Valmiera Latvia
21 P3 Valmondois France
21 M2 Valmont France
106 E9 Valmont New Mexico U.S.A.
45 N6 Valmontone Italy
100 H9 Valmy Nevada U.S.A.
16 E1 Valnera mt Spain
20 H2 Valognes France
Valona see Vlorë
16 D3 Valoria la Buena Spain
16 C3 Valpaços Portugal
76 C5 Valparai India
119 N6 Valparaiso Saskatchewan Canada
131 B4 Valparaíso prov Chile
131 B4 Valparaíso Chile
124 H6 Valparaíso Mexico
111 K11 Valparaiso Florida U.S.A.
99 T8 Valparaiso Indiana U.S.A.
98 K8 Valparaiso Nebraska U.S.A.
40 F6 Valpelline V Italy
48 E5 Valpovo Croatia
40 G7 Valprato Soana Italy
122 A8 Val-Racine Quebec Canada
19 N16 Valréas France
89 E6 Vals R S Africa
74 E8 Valsād India
28 H7 Vålse Denmark
100 B5 Valsetz Oregon U.S.A.
28 D3 Valsgård Denmark
26 G7 Valsjö Sweden
27 H12 Valskog Sweden
29 J8 Valsörarna lighthouse Finland
41 L5 Valtellina V Italy
29 T9 Valthjofsstadhur Iceland
45 M4 Val Tiberina Italy
29 O8 Valtimo Finland
83 M12 Valton Mauritius
54 K6 Valuyki Russian Federation
85 A3 Valverde Canary Is
127 J5 Valverde Dominican Rep
17 F5 Valverde de Júcar Spain
16 C7 Valverde del Camino Spain
26 M5 Valvträsk Sweden
48 K3 Vama Romania
28 C6 Vamdrup Denmark
27 G10 Våmhus Sweden
88 H7 Vamizi isld Mozambique
27 E12 Vamma Norway
29 K10 Vammala Finland
46 G9 Vámos Crete Greece
48 G3 Vámospéros Hungary
78 J2 Van Turkey
109 M3 Van Texas U.S.A.
29 L10 Vanajanselka L Finland
109 L2 Van Alstyne Texas U.S.A.
101 S3 Vananda Montana U.S.A.
56 F1 Vanavara Russian Federation
68 G1 Van-Ban Vietnam
121 S5 Van Bruyssel Quebec Canada
110 B6 Van Buren Arkansas U.S.A.
94 B6 Van Buren Indiana U.S.A.
95 T6 Van Buren Maine U.S.A.
110 F5 Van Buren Missouri U.S.A.
68 J6 Van Canh Vietnam
22 K4 Vance Belgium
21 M6 Vancé France
112 K2 Vanceboro North Carolina U.S.A.
94 D8 Vanceburg Kentucky U.S.A.
68 G2 Van Chan Vietnam
57 F5 Vanchskiy Khrebet mts Tajikistan/Afghanistan
117 G11 Vancouver British Columbia Canada
100 C4 Vancouver Washington U.S.A.
143 C10 Vancouver,C W Australia Australia
116 E6 Vancouver, C Alaska U.S.A.
117 K10 Vancouver I British Columbia Canada
117 D5 Vancouver, Mt Alaska/Yukon Terr U.S.A./Canada
110 G3 Vandalia Illinois U.S.A.
110 E2 Vandalia Missouri U.S.A.
41 L3 Vandans Austria
28 A3 Vandborg Denmark
119 Q1 Vandekerckhove Saskatchewan Canada
28 C5 Vandel Denmark
112 L2 Vandemere North Carolina U.S.A.
89 E6 Vanderbijl Pk S Africa
94 C1 Vanderbilt Michigan U.S.A.
109 L7 Vanderbilt Texas U.S.A.
94 H6 Vandergrift Pennsylvania U.S.A.
117 M8 Vanderhoof British Columbia Canada
140 D3 Vanderlin I N Terr Australia
109 N1 Vandervoort Arkansas U.S.A.
106 B6 Vanderwagen New Mexico U.S.A.
28 B2 Vandet Sø L Denmark
140 B1 Van Dieman, C N Terr Australia
140 E3 Van Diemen,C Queensland Australia
140 B1 Van Diemen G N Terr Australia
55 E1 Vandmtor, Oz L Russian Federation
121 R5 Vandry Quebec Canada
110 G5 Vanduser Missouri U.S.A.
100 A9 Van Duzen R California U.S.A.
27 F13 Vänern L Sweden
27 F13 Vänersborg Sweden
95 L4 Van Etten New York U.S.A.
27 C10 Vang Norway
88 G4 Vanga Tanzania
87 H12 Vangaindrano Madagascar
27 F13 Vanga,N Sweden
78 J2 Van Gölü L Turkey
27 C10 Vangsmjösa Norway
118 K9 Vanguard Saskatchewan Canada
70 A1 Vanguard Bank S China Sea
137 M3 Vangunu isld Solomon Is
68 F3 Vang Vieng Laos
98 D2 Van Hook North Dakota U.S.A.
108 C4 Van Horn Texas U.S.A.
106 F5 Van Houten New Mexico U.S.A.
137 O4 Vanikoro Is Santa Cruz Is
26 K7 Vänjaurbäck Sweden
26 K7 Vänjaurträsk Sweden
51 S2 Vankarem Russian Federation
121 Q7 Vankleek Hill Ontario Canada
98 F5 Van Metre South Dakota U.S.A.
26 L1 Vanna isld Norway
26 L8 Vännäs Sweden
83 J9 Vannativillu Sri Lanka
20 E6 Vannes France
21 P6 Vannes-sur-Cosson France
68 J6 Van Ninh Vietnam
57 F4 Vannovka Kazakhstan
107 O7 Vanoss Oklahoma U.S.A.
87 C12 Vanrhynsdorp S Africa
141 F3 Vanrook Queensland Australia
74 E8 Vānsada India
94 E9 Vansant Virginia U.S.A.
27 G11 Vansbro Sweden
118 L6 Vanscoy Saskatchewan Canada
142 F2 Vansittart B W Australia Australia
115 L4 Vansittart I Northwest Territories Canada
18 H8 Vans, les France
29 L11 Vantaa R Finland
29 L11 Vantaa Finland
118 L9 Vantage Saskatchewan Canada
100 F3 Vantage Washington U.S.A.
98 B7 Van Tassell Wyoming U.S.A.
137 O3 Vanua Lava isld Vanuatu
137 Q5 Vanua Levu isld Fiji
137 O5 Vanuatu islds Pacific Oc
99 N9 Van Wert Iowa U.S.A.
94 C6 Van Wert Ohio U.S.A.
87 D12 Vanwyksvlei S Africa
67 A6 Van Yen Vietnam
26 A9 Vanylven Norway
26 A9 Vanylvsgapet B Norway
110 D5 Vanzant Missouri U.S.A.
48 M2 Vapnyarka Ukraine
19 Q18 Var dept France
44 B4 Var R France
44 G3 Vara R Italy
27 F13 Vara Sweden
126 D3 Varadero Cuba
21 H7 Varades France
19 P17 Varages France
44 B2 Varaita R Italy
41 H6 Varallo Italy
42 B3 Varallo Italy
77 B2 Varamin Iran
75 K6 Varanasi India
26 R1 Varangerfjorden inlet Norway
26 R1 Varangerhalvöya mt Norway
42 G7 Varano, L. di Italy
131 A8 Varas,Pto Chile
16 D6 Varas,R Spain
21 K3 Varaville France
44 E3 Varazze Italy
27 F14 Varberg Sweden
77 L2 Vardak prov Afghanistan
111 G8 Vardaman Mississippi U.S.A.
46 E3 Vardar R Macedonia
46 E6 Vardhoúsia Óri mt Greece
27 L11 Vårdö Finland
26 S1 Vardö Norway
52 E5 Varegovo Russian Federation
32 H6 Varel Germany
21 M2 Varengeville France
20 G3 Varenguebec France
21 J4 Varenne R France
19 J3 Varennes en Argonne France
40 B5 Varennes St.Sauveur France
21 O7 Varennes-sur-Fouzon France
48 E6 Vareš Bosnia-Herzegovina
41 J6 Varese Italy
40 A7 Vareze R France
27 F13 Vårgårda Sweden
55 E3 Vargashi Russian Federation
130 G10 Vargem R Brazil
130 F7 Varginha Brazil
18 G9 Varilhes France
112 J2 Varina North Carolina U.S.A.
27 G13 Väring Sweden
21 O5 Varize France
26 K5 Varjisträsk Sweden
29 N9 Varkaus Finland
143 C10 Varley,L W Australia Australia
27 F12 Varmland reg Sweden
27 F12 Värmlands-näs pen Sweden
47 J1 Varna Bulgaria
55 D4 Varna Russian Federation
111 G11 Varnado Louisiana U.S.A.
28 D6 Varnæs Denmark
27 G14 Vårnamo Sweden
27 F11 Värnäs Sweden
52 F5 Varnavino Russian Federation
108 B1 Varney New Mexico U.S.A.
31 H5 Varnsdorf Czech Rep
27 F14 Varnum Sweden
112 F5 Varnville South Carolina U.S.A.
79 D3 Varosha Cyprus
48 D3 Városlöd Hungary
48 E3 Várpalota Hungary
52 G2 Varsh, Oz L Russian Federation
28 E3 Vårst Denmark
78 H2 Varto Turkey
27 G13 Vartofta Sweden
83 K9 Varuniya Sri Lanka
46 E7 Varvára mt Greece
46 E1 Varvarin Serbia Yugoslavia
54 C10 Varvarovka Ukraine
130 G9 Várzea Alegre Brazil
130 G5 Várzea da Palma Brazil
129 G7 Várzea Grande Brazil
130 E9 Várzea,R Brazil
52 E1 Varzino Russian Federation
52 E2 Varzuga R Russian Federation
52 E2 Varzuga Russian Federation
18 H5 Varzy France
48 D3 Vas co Hungary
130 H11 Vasa Barris,R Brazil
76 A1 Vasai India
52 B5 Vasalemma Estonia
48 G2 Vásárosnamény Hungary
29 K4 Väsby Sweden
16 B7 Vascão R Portugal
48 G4 Vaşcău Romania
21 N3 Vascœuil France
52 G3 Vashka R Russian Federation
48 K2 Vashkovtsy Ukraine
100 C2 Vashon I Washington U.S.A.
98 G2 Vashti North Dakota U.S.A.
109 J2 Vashti Texas U.S.A.
54 H8 Vasil'kovka Ukraine
52 G3 Vasil'yevo Russian Federation
52 G6 Vasil'yevo Russian Federation
55 F2 Vasis Russian Federation
29 P11 Vaskelovo Russian Federation
52 C5 Vasknarva Estonia
29 M3 Vaskojoki R Finland
48 E4 Vaskút Hungary
21 K8 Vasles France
48 L4 Vaslui Romania
112 H2 Vass North Carolina U.S.A.
118 F1 Vassar Manitoba Canada
94 D3 Vassar Michigan U.S.A.
27 B12 Vassdalseggja mt Norway
26 K3 Vassijuare Sweden
21 J4 Vassy Calvados France
26 J4 Vastenjaure L Sweden
27 J12 Västerås Sweden
26 H7 Västerbotten reg Sweden
27 F11 Vasterdalälven R Sweden
26 J5 Västerfjäll Sweden
27 K12 Västerhaninge Sweden
27 H12 Västermo Sweden
26 J7 Vastermyrriset Sweden
26 J8 Väster Norr Land Sweden
27 J14 Västervik Sweden
27 J11 Västland Sweden
27 H12 Västmanland reg Sweden
42 F6 Vasto Italy
33 N6 Vastorf Germany
26 L8 Vastra Kvarken chan Sweden
48 D3 Vasvár Hungary
55 G2 Vasyugan R Russian Federation
21 O7 Vatan France
Vaté isld see Éfaté isld
33 P8 Väthen Germany
47 H7 Vathí Greece
46 E8 Váthia Greece
Vatican City see Vaticano, Citta del
45 M6 Vaticano, Citta del Italy
28 S9 Vatnajökull ice cap Iceland
26 B9 Vatne Norway
28 R9 Vatneyri Iceland
27 K12 Vätö Sweden
137 R5 Vatoa isld Fiji
87 H11 Vatomandry Madagascar
48 J3 Vatra Dornei Romania
27 G13 Vättern L Sweden
27 J11 Vattholma Sweden
41 K4 Vättis Switzerland
26 J10 Vattrång Sweden
40 C5 Vauche Marlioz,Mt.De France
19 O17 Vaucluse dept France
112 F4 Vaucluse South Carolina U.S.A.
40 C2 Vauconcourt France
21 L2 Vaucottes France
19 J4 Vaucouleurs France
36 B6 Vaucourt France
40 D4 Vaud canton Switzerland
21 N3 Vaudreuil, le France
122 H9 Vaughan Nova Scotia Canada
140 B5 Vaughan Springs N Terr Australia
101 O2 Vaughn Montana U.S.A.
108 B1 Vaughn New Mexico U.S.A.
128 D3 Vaupés div Colombia
21 K8 Vausseroux France
18 H9 Vauvert France
20 G2 Vauville France
40 D2 Vauvillers France
118 E8 Vauxhall Alberta Canada
87 J11 Vavatenina Madagascar
137 S5 Vava'u Group islds Tonga
52 H6 Vavozh Russian Federation
83 K9 Vavuniya Sri Lanka
118 J5 Vawn Saskatchewan Canada
27 K12 Vaxholm Sweden
27 G15 Växjö Sweden
20 G6 Vay France
76 D4 Vāyalpād India
50 F1 Vaygach, Ostrov isld Russian Federation
52 F3 Vaymuga R Russian Federation
129 L5 Vaza R Brazil
130 F5 Vazante Brazil
52 G3 Vazhgort Russian Federation
54 F1 Vazuzskoye Vodokhranilishche res Russian Federation
129 J6 Veadeiras Brazil
68 F7 Veal Renh Cambodia
28 D3 Vebbestrup Denmark
27 F16 Veberöd Sweden
98 J4 Veblen South Dakota U.S.A.
26 M7 Vebomark Sweden
33 M8 Vechelde Germany
25 F3 Vecht R Netherlands
32 H7 Vechta R Germany
32 H7 Vechta Germany
32 L10 Veckerhagen Germany
29 K5 Vedbæk Denmark
27 F14 Veddige Sweden
28 E3 Veddum Denmark
48 J6 Vedea Romania
28 A4 Vedersø Denmark
27 H12 Vedevåg Sweden
133 E4 Vedia Argentina
17 H6 Vedra isld Balearic Is
22 H3 Vedrin Belgium
28 E5 Vedslet Denmark
28 C6 Vedsted Denmark
28 G6 Ved Stranden Denmark
27 F13 Vedum Sweden
110 J1 Veedersburg Indiana U.S.A.
25 G2 Veendam Netherlands
25 E4 Veenendaal Netherlands
25 F2 Veenhuizen Netherlands
25 E2 Veenwouden Netherlands
25 A5 Veere Netherlands
25 A5 Veerse Meer Netherlands
33 N7 Veerssen Germany
28 E6 Veflinge Denmark
26 E6 Vega isld Norway
16 C2 Vega de Tera Spain
27 D13 Vegårs Vatn L Norway
29 K4 Vegeån R Sweden
32 J6 Vegesack Germany
28 D3 Veggerby Denmark
27 D11 Veggli Norway
46 E4 Vegorrítis, L Greece
118 F5 Vegreville Alberta Canada
108 A1 Veguita New Mexico U.S.A.
33 Q6 Vehlow Germany
27 M11 Vehmaa Finland
26 P1 Veidnes Norway
27 F15 Veinge Sweden
120 D3 Vein L Ontario Canada
133 D5 Veinticinco de Mayo Argentina
45 M5 Veio Italy
36 H4 Veitshöchheim Germany
28 J4 Vejby Denmark
28 C6 Vejen Denmark
28 A5 Vejers Denmark
28 D4 Vejerslev Denmark
28 E2 Vejgård Denmark
28 E4 Vejlby Århus Denmark
28 D5 Vejlby Vejle Denmark
28 C5 Vejle co Denmark
28 D5 Vejle Denmark
28 D5 Vejle Fjord inlet Denmark
28 H6 Vejlø Denmark
28 E7 Vejnæs Nokke C Denmark
37 P3 Vejprty Czech Rep
28 G5 Vejrhøj hill Denmark
28 F5 Vejrø isld Århus Denmark
28 G6 Vejrø isld Storstrøm Denmark
28 B5 Vejrup Denmark
28 F6 Vejstrup Denmark
28 J5 Veksø Denmark
52 F4 Vel R Russian Federation
127 H8 Vela, C. de la Colombia
22 E2 Velaines Belgium
46 E5 Velaóra Greece
106 E5 Velarde New Mexico U.S.A.
124 H5 Velardeña Mexico
18 H7 Velay, Mts du France
32 F10 Velbert Germany
37 M5 Velburg Germany
37 M4 Velden Germany
25 D6 Veldhoven Netherlands
47 J2 Veleka R Bulgaria
32 E9 Velen Germany
48 E3 Velencei Tó L Hungary
42 G2 Velenje Slovenia
46 E3 Veles Macedonia
46 F5 Velestinon Greece
17 F7 Vélez Blanco Spain
16 E8 Vélez Málaga Spain
17 F7 Vélez Rubio Spain
26 F6 Velfjord Norway
33 R4 Velgast Germany
130 G6 Velhas,R Brazil
42 H3 Velika Croatia
42 G3 Velika Gorica Croatia
48 G6 Velika Gradište Serbia Yugoslavia
42 F3 Velika Kapela dist Croatia
48 G6 Velika Plana Serbia Yugoslavia
52 G2 Velikaya Russian Federation
52 G5 Velikaya R Russian Federation
52 C6 Velikaya R Russian Federation
52 E4 Velikaya Guba Russian Federation
48 K1 Veliki Borki Ukraine
48 K1 Veliki Glubochek Ukraine
48 G2 Velikiy Bereznyy Ukraine
52 D6 Velikiye-Luki Russian Federation
52 G4 Velikiy Ustyug Russian Federation
54 M1 Velikodvorskiy Russian Federation
54 J6 Velikomikhaylovka Russian Federation
47 H1 Veliko Turnovo Bulgaria
52 H2 Velikovisochnoye Russian Federation
52 F5 Velikovo Russian Federation
54 M1 Velikoye, Oz L Russian Federation
85 B6 Velingara Senegal
46 F2 Velingrad Bulgaria
42 E6 Velino R Italy
42 E6 Velino, M mt Italy
54 C1 Velizh Russian Federation
48 E2 Velká Fatra mt Slovakia
48 G2 Vel'ké Kapušány Slovakia
31 L6 Velké Karlovice Czech Rep
48 D3 Velký Žitný Ostrov' reg Slovakia
38 L8 Vellach Austria
33 N6 Vellahn Germany
137 M3 Vella Lavella isld Solomon Is
45 J4 Vellano Italy
36 H5 Vellberg Germany
21 O8 Velles France
45 N6 Velletri Italy
28 D4 Vellev Denmark
28 A4 Velling Denmark
27 F16 Vellinge Sweden
45 O5 Vellino, M mt Italy
76 D4 Vellore India
56 D1 Vel'minskiye Porogi falls Russian Federation
56 D1 Vel'mo R Russian Federation
22 J5 Velosnes France
25 E4 Velp Netherlands
25 C4 Velsen Netherlands
52 F4 Vel'sk Russian Federation
52 H1 Vel't Russian Federation
33 S7 Velten Germany
22 D3 Vélu France
25 E4 Veluwe Netherlands
25 E4 Veluwemeer Netherlands
98 F1 Velva North Dakota U.S.A.
52 J3 Vel'yu R Russian Federation
90 E7 Vema Fracture Atlantic Oc
28 A4 Vemb Denmark
26 G9 Vemdalen Sweden
28 G6 Vemmelev Denmark
28 F7 Vemmenæs Denmark
29 K5 Ven isld Sweden
27 H14 Vena Sweden
27 D10 Venabygd Norway
12 D1 Venachar,L Scotland
131 E4 Venado Tuerto Argentina
45 Q7 Venafro Italy
128 F2 Venamo,Cerro mt Venezuela/Guyana
98 E9 Venango Nebraska U.S.A.
44 C1 Venaria Italy
100 G6 Venator Oregon U.S.A.
44 B1 Venàus Italy
130 E8 Venceslau Bráz Brazil
Venda see Vantaa
Venda see Northern Transvaal
45 L1 Venda mt Italy
16 B6 Vendas Novas Portugal
18 E6 Vendée dept France
52 G3 Vendenga Russian Federation
36 D6 Vendenheim France
22 D3 Vendin-le-Viel France
21 N6 Vendôme France
21 N8 Vendœuvres France
17 H3 Vendrell Spain
22 H4 Vendresse France
28 D2 Vendsyssel reg Denmark
45 M1 Veneta, Laguna Italy
116 P3 Venetie Landing Alaska U.S.A.
45 K1 Veneto reg Italy
52 F6 Venets Russian Federation
54 K2 Venev Russian Federation
45 M1 Venezia Italy
42 D3 Venezia-Euganea prov Italy
42 E3 Venezia,G.di Italy
128 E2 Venezuela rep S America
127 J9 Venezuela,G.de Venezuela
28 D4 Veng Denmark
55 G3 Vengerovo Russian Federation
76 A3 Vengurla India
16 D3 Venialbo Spain
116 H8 Veniaminof Vol Alaska U.S.A.
118 E4 Venice Alberta Canada
Venice Italy see Venezia
111 M12 Venice St Louis
113 E10 Venice Florida U.S.A.
111 G12 Venice Louisiana U.S.A.
19 N13 Vénissieux France
27 G11 Venjan Sweden
76 D4 Venkataguri India
76 E1 Venkatapuram India
25 F6 Venlo Netherlands
98 J3 Venlo North Dakota U.S.A.
119 M7 Venn Saskatchewan Canada
28 D2 Vennebjerg Denmark
32 E7 Vennebrügge Germany
27 C13 Vennesla Norway
28 B3 Venø Denmark
28 B3 Venø Bugt B Denmark
19 Q15 Venosc France
121 O7 Venosta Quebec Canada
41 N4 Venosta, Val Italy
41 N4 Venostie, Alpi Italy
25 E5 Venray Netherlands
27 M14 Venta R Latvia
124 E5 Ventana,Pta de la C Mexico
133 E5 Ventana,Sa ra Argentina
16 E8 Ventas de Zafarraya Spain
19 P16 Ventavon France
28 H5 Vented Denmark
44 C4 Ventimiglia Italy
9 E6 Ventnor England
43 E8 Ventotene, I Italy
19 O16 Ventoux, Mt France
33 P5 Ventschow Germany
27 M14 Ventspils Latvia
128 E3 Ventuari R Venezuela
102 E7 Ventura California U.S.A.
98 G3 Venturia North Dakota U.S.A.

113 F10 **Venus** Florida U.S.A.
109 K3 **Venus** Texas U.S.A.
138 C5 **Venus B** South Australia Australia
138 C5 **Venus Bay** South Australia Australia
124 H8 **Venustiano Carranza** Mexico
52 D4 **Vepsovskaya Vozvyshennost'** *uplands* Russian Federation
133 E3 **Vera** Argentina
17 F7 **Vera** Spain
109 H2 **Vera** Texas U.S.A.
133 D6 **Vera, B** Argentina
130 E8 **Vera Cruz** Brazil
125 L8 **Veracruz** Mexico
74 D8 **Veraval** India
42 B3 **Verbania** Italy
111 K9 **Verbena** Alabama U.S.A.
22 D5 **Verberie** France
52 E6 **Verbilki** Russian Federation
41 H7 **Vercelli** Italy
33 R5 **Verchen** Germany
21 K7 **Verchers,les** France
19 O15 **Vercors** *reg* France
19 Q16 **Verdaches** France
26 E8 **Verdal** Norway
26 E8 **Verdalsöra** Norway
133 D6 **Verde** *R* Argentina
130 E4 **Verde** *R* Brazil
133 F2 **Verde** *R* Paraguay
71 E4 **Verde** *isld* Philippines
103 N7 **Verde** *R* Arizona U.S.A.
85 A6 **Verde, C** Senegal
126 G3 **Verde, Cay** *isld* Bahamas
130 G4 **Verde Grande** *R* Brazil
98 H7 **Verdel** Nebraska U.S.A.
32 K7 **Verden** Germany
109 J1 **Verden** Oklahoma U.S.A.
131 E7 **Verde,Pen** Argentina
130 G4 **Verde Pequeno, R** Brazil
130 D7 **Verde,R** Brazil
21 N6 **Verdes** France
98 H7 **Verdigre** Nebraska U.S.A.
107 O3 **Verdigris** *R* Okla/Kansas U.S.A.
118 F9 **Verdigris L** Alberta Canada
130 D5 **Verdinho,Sa.do** *mts* Brazil
19 Q17 **Verdon** *R* France
99 L9 **Verdon** Nebraska U.S.A.
18 E7 **Verdon-sur-Mer, le** France
19 J3 **Verdun** France
18 F9 **Verdun-sur-Garonne** France
19 J6 **Verdun-sur-le-Doubs** France
124 E5 **Verdura** Mexico
52 D6 **Verech'ye** Russian Federation
89 E6 **Vereeniging** S Africa
119 P7 **Veregin** Saskatchewan Canada
121 N5 **Vérendrye, Réserve Faunique la** Quebec Canada
52 H5 **Vereshchagino** Russian Federation
52 E5 **Verestovo, Oz** *L* Russian Federation
54 H1 **Vereya** Russian Federation
85 B6 **Verga,C** Guinea
17 F1 **Vergara** Spain
133 G4 **Vergara** Uruguay
45 K3 **Vergato** Italy
36 B6 **Vergaville** France
141 G6 **Vergemont** *R* Queensland Australia
141 G6 **Vergemont** Queensland Australia
95 O2 **Vergennes** Vermont U.S.A.
45 L4 **Verghereto** Italy
45 R8 **Vérgine, M** *mt* Italy
16 C3 **Verín** Spain
41 K1 **Veringenstadt** Germany
56 H3 **Verkh Angara** *R* Russian Federation
55 C3 **Verkhiye Kigi** Russian Federation
52 J5 **Verkhnaya Yarva** Russian Federation
56 H3 **Verkhneangarskiy Khrebet** *mts* Russian Federation
55 C4 **Verkhnearshinskiy** Russian Federation
55 C4 **Verkhne-Avzyan** Russian Federation
54 F8 **Verkhnedneprovsk** Ukraine
54 E2 **Verkhnedneprovskiy** Russian Federation
50 H2 **Verkhneimbatsk** Russian Federation
54 M7 **Verkhnemakeyevka** Russian Federation
29 Q3 **Verkhnetulomskiy** Russian Federation
52 D1 **Verkhnetulomskoye, Vodokhranilishche** *L* Russian Federation
55 C4 **Verkhneural'sk** Russian Federation
52 H6 **Verkhne Yarkeyevo** Russian Federation
54 K8 **Verkhneye** Ukraine
55 G3 **Verkhneye Krasnoyarka** Russian Federation
52 D2 **Verkhneye Kuyto, Oz** *L* Russian Federation
55 C3 **Verkhniye Tatyshly** Russian Federation
55 D3 **Verkhniy Neyvinskiy** Russian Federation
52 H1 **Verkhniy Shar** Russian Federation
55 C3 **Verkhniy Tagil** Russian Federation
55 C1 **Verkhniy Vizhay** Russian Federation
55 D1 **Verkhniy Vizhay** Russian Federation
55 D3 **Verkhnyaya Pyshma** Russian Federation
55 D2 **Verkhnyaya Salda** Russian Federation
55 D4 **Verkhnyaya Sanarka** Russian Federation
55 G3 **Verkhnyaya Tarka** Russian Federation
52 G4 **Verkhnyaya Toyma** Russian Federation
52 G4 **Verkhnyaya Toz'ma** Russian Federation
55 C2 **Verkhnyaya Tura** Russian Federation
52 G5 **Verkhoshizhemye** Russian Federation
55 D2 **Verkhotur'ye** Russian Federation
52 F4 **Verkhovazh'ye** Russian Federation
48 J2 **Verkhovina** Ukraine
54 F8 **Verkhovtsevo** Ukraine
51 M2 **Verkhoyanskiy Khrebet** *mts* Russian Federation
55 D2 **Verkhyaya Sinyachikha** Russian Federation
54 F8 **Verkne Dneprovsk** Ukraine
55 D3 **Verkniy Ufaley** Russian Federation
52 G3 **Verkola** Russian Federation
118 J8 **Verlo** Saskatchewan Canada
26 C9 **Verma** Norway
22 E4 **Vermand** France
130 D4 **Vermelho,R** Brazil
18 H5 **Vermenton** France
118 G5 **Vermilion** Alberta Canada
99 T10 **Vermilion** Illinois U.S.A.
111 D11 **Vermilion** *R* Louisiana U.S.A.
94 E5 **Vermilion** Ohio U.S.A.
111 D12 **Vermilion B** Louisiana U.S.A.
118 J1 **Vermilion Bay** Ontario Canada
117 Q6 **Vermilion Chutes** Alberta Canada
103 M4 **Vermilion Cliffs** Utah U.S.A.
118 K1 **Vermilion L** Ontario Canada
99 O2 **Vermilion L** Minnesota U.S.A.
118 F5 **Vermilion Prov. Park** Alberta Canada
99 O2 **Vermilion Ra** Minnesota U.S.A.
107 O2 **Vermillion** Kansas U.S.A.
98 K7 **Vermillion** South Dakota U.S.A.
103 M5 **Vermillion Cliffs** *ra* Arizona U.S.A.
121 R5 **Vermillon** *R* Quebec Canada
46 E4 **Vérmion** *mt* Greece
95 P2 **Vermont** *state* U.S.A.
99 Q9 **Vermont** Illinois U.S.A.
21 J6 **Vern** France
41 N4 **Vernago, Lago di** Italy
101 Q9 **Vernal** Utah U.S.A.
102 C4 **Vernalis** California U.S.A.
21 L7 **Vernantes** France
44 G3 **Vernazza** Italy
101 P8 **Verne** Wyoming U.S.A.
87 D11 **Verneakpan** *L* S Africa
120 K6 **Verner** Ontario Canada
21 M4 **Verneuil** Eure France
18 G4 **Verneuil l'Etang** France
21 N7 **Verneuil sur-Indre** France
89 B7 **Verneuk Pan** S Africa
28 E6 **Verninge** Denmark
45 K3 **Vernio** Italy
21 L7 **Vernoil** France
117 O10 **Vernon** British Columbia Canada
122 K7 **Vernon** Prince Edward I Canada
21 N3 **Vernon** Eure France
46 E4 **Vérnon** *mt* Greece
111 H8 **Vernon** Alabama U.S.A.
103 P7 **Vernon** Arizona U.S.A.
98 D10 **Vernon** Colorado U.S.A.
111 L11 **Vernon** Florida U.S.A.
94 B8 **Vernon** Indiana U.S.A.
95 M3 **Vernon** New York U.S.A.
109 H1 **Vernon** Texas U.S.A.
101 N9 **Vernon** Utah U.S.A.
95 P4 **Vernon** Vermont U.S.A.
100 B4 **Vernonia** Oregon U.S.A.
140 B1 **Vernon Is** N Terr Australia
143 C6 **Vernon,Mt** W Australia Australia
21 M7 **Vernou** France
127 N4 **Vernou** Guadeloupe
21 O7 **Vernou-en-Sologne** France
20 G5 **Vern-sur-Seiche** France
113 G10 **Vero Beach** Florida U.S.A.
46 E4 **Véroia** Greece
44 H1 **Verolanuova** Italy
45 O6 **Veroli** Italy
121 O8 **Verona** Ontario Canada
45 J1 **Verona** Italy
110 C5 **Verona** Missouri U.S.A.
98 H3 **Verona** North Dakota U.S.A.
99 R7 **Verona** Wisconsin U.S.A.
101 T5 **Verona** Wyoming U.S.A.
19 O13 **Verpillière** France
138 D5 **Verran** South Australia Australia
111 E12 **Verret, L** Louisiana U.S.A.
127 H5 **Verrettes** Haiti
21 J8 **Verrie,la** France
19 N17 **Vers** France
21 P4 **Versailles** France
110 L2 **Versailles** Indiana U.S.A.
110 M3 **Versailles** Kentucky U.S.A.
110 D3 **Versailles** Missouri U.S.A.
94 C6 **Versailles** Ohio U.S.A.
55 D1 **Vershina** Russian Federation
58 G1 **Vershino-Darasunskiy** Russian Federation
32 H8 **Versmold** Germany
21 K3 **Verson** France
28 C5 **Verst** Denmark
21 K3 **Ver-sur-Mer** France
41 N4 **Vertana,Cima** *mt* Italy
122 C5 **Verte,I** Quebec Canada
20 C6 **Verte,I** France
18 F7 **Verteillac** France
129 H6 **Vertentes** *R* Brazil
130 J9 **Vertentes** Brazil
48 E3 **Vérteshegység** *mt* Hungary
126 E4 **Vertientes** Cuba
54 C5 **Vertiyevka** Ukraine
123 N2 **Verton,L** Quebec Canada
20 H7 **Vertou** France
22 H2 **Vertrijk** Belgium
18 H4 **Vertus** France
45 M4 **Verucchio** Italy
89 G7 **Verulam** S Africa
22 K2 **Verviers** Belgium
22 F4 **Vervins** France
119 M9 **Verwood** Saskatchewan Canada
8 B7 **Veryan B** England
41 J5 **Verzasca,Val** Switzerland
38 O8 **Veržej** Slovenia
29 M9 **Vesanto** Finland
22 L2 **Vesdre** *R* Belgium
21 O4 **Vesegre** *R* France
31 K7 **Veselí** Jihomoravský Czech Rep
55 C2 **Vesëlovka** Russian Federation
55 G4 **Veselovskoye** Russian Federation
55 E4 **Veselyy Podol** Kazakhstan
26 F6 **Vesfna** *R* Norway
21 K6 **Vesgre** *R* France
52 F3 **Veshkoma** Russian Federation
18 H3 **Vesle** *R* France
28 B2 **Vesløs** Denmark
20 H3 **Vesly** France
52 H3 **Veslyana** Russian Federation
52 H4 **Veslyana** *R* Russian Federation
40 D2 **Vesoul** France
107 M2 **Vesper** Kansas U.S.A.
99 R5 **Vesper** Wisconsin U.S.A.
27 F15 **Vessige** Sweden
99 L5 **Vesta** Minnesota U.S.A.
27 B13 **Vest Agder** *reg* Norway
95 L4 **Vestal Center** New York U.S.A.
26 H3 **Vestbygd** Norway
28 G7 **Vestenskov** Denmark
28 E6 **Vester Aby** Denmark
26 G3 **Vesterålen** *isld* Norway
147 G14 **Vesterålen** Norway
28 B3 **Vester Assels** Denmark
28 G7 **Vesterborg** Denmark
28 H6 **Vester Egede** Denmark
28 H6 **Vester Egesborg** Denmark
28 E2 **Vester Hassing** Denmark
28 D2 **Vester Hjermitslev** Denmark
29 K4 **Vester Karup** Sweden
28 C5 **Vesterlund** Denmark
28 C5 **Vester Nebel** Denmark
28 B5 **Vester Nykirke** Denmark
28 F2 **Vesterøhavn** Denmark
28 E6 **Vester Skerninge** Denmark
28 D7 **Vester Sottrup** Denmark
28 D3 **Vester Tørslev** Denmark
28 A3 **Vestervig** Denmark
27 C12 **Vestfj-Dal** Norway
146 G6 **Vestfjella** *mts* Antarctica
26 F4 **Vestfjorden** *inlet* Norway
27 D12 **Vestfold** *reg* Norway
146 J12 **Vestfold Hills** Antarctica
130 D7 **Véstia** Brazil
6 F1 **Vestmanna** Faeroes
28 S10 **Vestmannaeyjar** *islds* Iceland
26 B9 **Vestnes** Norway
29 T9 **Vestrahorn** *C* Iceland
28 G5 **Vestsjælland** *co* Denmark
26 G3 **Vestvågöy** Norway
45 Q8 **Vesuvio** *mt* Italy
52 E5 **Ves'yegonsk** Russian Federation
48 D3 **Veszprém** *co* Hungary
48 D3 **Veszprém** Hungary
48 D3 **Veszprémvarsány** Hungary
48 G4 **Vésztö** Hungary
89 E7 **Vet** *R* S Africa
98 E6 **Vetal** South Dakota U.S.A.
118 F6 **Veteran** Alberta Canada
98 B8 **Veteran** Wyoming U.S.A.
21 O3 **Vétheuil** France
54 C4 **Vetka** Belarus
27 H14 **Vetlanda** Sweden
52 G5 **Vetluga** Russian Federation
52 G5 **Vetluzhskiy** Russian Federation
52 G6 **Vetluzhskiy** Russian Federation
47 H1 **Vetovo** Bulgaria
52 C6 **Vetrino** Belarus
28 H6 **Vetterslev** Denmark
45 H3 **Vetto** Italy
26 M4 **Vetträsjärvi** Sweden
36 B2 **Vettweiss** Germany
21 L8 **Veude** *R* France
21 M2 **Veules** France
21 M2 **Veulettes** France
27 C12 **Veum** Norway
68 H6 **Veun Kham** Cambodia
22 D1 **Veurne** Belgium
94 B8 **Vevay** Indiana U.S.A.
26 F6 **Vevelstad** Norway
40 E5 **Vevey** Switzerland
46 E4 **Vévi** Greece
19 P15 **Veynes** France
103 L4 **Veyo** Utah U.S.A.
19 K4 **Vézelise** France
18 G7 **Vezère** *R* France
46 G2 **Vezhen** *mt* Bulgaria
52 H3 **Vezh'yudor** Russian Federation
22 K5 **Vezin** France
21 J7 **Vezins** Maine-et-Loire France
78 E1 **Vezirköprü** Turkey
36 B6 **Vezouse** *R* France
44 G3 **Vezzano Ligure** Italy
21 O5 **Viabon** France
45 J2 **Viadana** Italy
44 B1 **Via di Ciamarella** *mt* Italy
107 Q6 **Vian** Oklahoma U.S.A.
130 H7 **Viana** Espírito Santo Brazil
129 J4 **Viana** Maranhão Brazil
16 C2 **Viana del Bollo** Spain
16 B6 **Viana do Alentejo** Portugal
16 B3 **Viana do Castelo** Portugal
22 L4 **Vianden** Luxembourg
25 D5 **Vianen** Netherlands
68 F3 **Viangchan** Laos
45 J2 **Viano** Italy
130 E5 **Vianópolis** Brazil
29 L6 **Viantie** Finland
16 D7 **Viar** *R* Spain
44 H4 **Viareggio** Italy
18 G8 **Viaur** *R* France
119 O8 **Vibank** Saskatchewan Canada
28 B3 **Viborg** *co* Denmark
28 C4 **Viborg** Denmark
98 J6 **Viborg** South Dakota U.S.A.
43 G10 **Vibo Valentia** Italy
21 M5 **Vibraye** France
28 E4 **Viby** Århus Denmark
28 J5 **Viby** Roskilde Denmark
Vic *see* **Vich**
45 K4 **Vicchio** Italy
146 D4 **Vicecomodoro Marambio** *Argentina Base* Antarctica
18 E9 **Vic en Bigorre** France
130 F8 **Vicente S** Brazil
16 D4 **Vicente,S** *mt* Spain
45 L1 **Vicenza** Italy
119 M9 **Viceroy** Saskatchewan Canada
18 F9 **Vic-Fezensac** France
17 J3 **Vich** Spain
128 E3 **Vichada** *div* Colombia
131 G3 **Vichadero** Uruguay
52 F6 **Vichuga** Russian Federation
133 C4 **Vichuquén** Chile
18 H6 **Vichy** France
107 L5 **Vici** Oklahoma U.S.A.
109 O9 **Vickery** Texas U.S.A.
103 L8 **Vicksburg** Arizona U.S.A.
94 B4 **Vicksburg** Michigan U.S.A.
111 F9 **Vicksburg** Mississippi U.S.A.
45 Q8 **Vico Equense** Italy
42 E6 **Vico, L. di** Italy
45 J4 **Vicopisano** Italy
17 G3 **Vicort, Sierra de** *mts* Spain
130 H10 **Viçosa** Alagoas Brazil
130 G7 **Viçosa** Minas Gerais Brazil
41 L5 **Vicosoprano** Switzerland
45 N5 **Vicovaro** Italy
48 K3 **Vicovu de Sus** Romania
21 P8 **Vicq Exemplet** France
21 M8 **Vicq-sur-Gartempe** France
22 E5 **Vic-sur-Aisne** France
18 G8 **Vic-sur-Cère** France
7 M9 **Victor** *oil rig* North Sea
106 E3 **Victor** Colorado U.S.A.
101 O6 **Victor** Idaho U.S.A.
99 O8 **Victor** Iowa U.S.A.
101 L3 **Victor** Montana U.S.A.
94 K4 **Victor** New York U.S.A.
138 E6 **Victor Harbour** South Australia Australia
131 E4 **Victoria** *R* Argentina
131 E4 **Victoria** Argentina
138 F6 **Victoria** *state* Australia
140 B3 **Victoria** *R* N Terr Australia
139 G6 **Victoria** Victoria Australia
123 T6 **Victoria** Newfoundland Canada
100 B1 **Victoria** Vancouver I, Br Col Canada
131 A7 **Victoria** Chile
127 P5 **Victoria** Grenada
83 K12 **Victoria** Mahé I Indian Oc
43 F12 **Victoria** Malta
71 E3 **Victoria** Luzon Philippines
70 D2 **Victoria** Sabah
127 O3 **Victoria** *co* Trinidad
107 L3 **Victoria** Kansas U.S.A.
109 K7 **Victoria** Texas U.S.A.
94 J10 **Victoria** Virginia U.S.A.
119 V8 **Victoria Beach** Manitoba Canada
89 D1 **Victoria Falls** Zambezi R Zimbabwe
121 L8 **Victoria Harb** Ontario Canada
126 G2 **Victoria Hill** San Salvador Bahamas
114 H3 **Victoria I** Northwest Territories Canada
139 G5 **Victoria L** New South Wales Australia
123 P5 **Victoria L** *res* Newfoundland Canada
121 N5 **Victoria, L** Quebec Canada
88 D2 **Victoria, L** E Africa
146 C12 **Victoria Land** Antarctica
73 P4 **Victoria Mt** Burma
145 D4 **Victoria, Mt** New Zealand
136 K3 **Victoria, Mt** Papua New Guinea
86 F5 **Victoria Nile** *R* Uganda
142 B2 **Victoria Park** *dist* Perth, W Aust Australia
139 K5 **Victoria Pass** New South Wales Australia
140 B3 **Victoria R** N Terr Australia
123 P5 **Victoria R** Newfoundland Canada
144 D5 **Victoria Range** New Zealand
140 B3 **Victoria River Downs** N Terr Australia
114 J4 **Victoria Str** Northwest Territories Canada
145 D1 **Victoria Valley** New Zealand
121 T6 **Victoriaville** Quebec Canada
89 C8 **Victoria West** S Africa
123 L3 **Victor L** Quebec Canada
146 J8 **Victor, Mt** *mt* Antarctica
102 G7 **Victorville** California U.S.A.
140 C7 **Victory Downs** N Terr Australia
133 E4 **Vicuña** Argentina
133 C4 **Vicuña** Chile
28 B7 **Vidå** *R* Denmark
98 A2 **Vida** Montana U.S.A.
100 C5 **Vida** Oregon U.S.A.
103 K7 **Vidal** California U.S.A.
112 E5 **Vidalia** Georgia U.S.A.
111 E10 **Vidalia** Louisiana U.S.A.
83 K8 **Vidattaltivu** Sri Lanka
19 Q18 **Vidauban** France
109 K7 **Vidauri** Texas U.S.A.
28 B4 **Videbæk** Denmark
130 D10 **Videira** Brazil
48 K6 **Videle** Romania
47 O12 **Vídho** *isld* Greece
16 B6 **Vidigueira** Portugal
56 F3 **Vidim** Russian Federation
46 F1 **Vidin** Bulgaria
16 C1 **Vidio, C** Spain
74 G7 **Vidisha** India
52 D4 **Vidlitsa** Russian Federation
46 E1 **Vidojevica** *mt* Serbia Yugoslavia
31 O3 **Vidomlya** Belarus
109 N5 **Vidor** Texas U.S.A.
111 B11 **Vidor** Texas U.S.A.
118 H9 **Vidora** Saskatchewan Canada
18 H9 **Vidourle** France
6 F1 **Viðoy** *isld* Faeroes
48 K6 **Vidra** Romania
26 L6 **Vidsel** Sweden
28 D2 **Vidstrup** Denmark
42 J6 **Viduša** *mt* Bosnia-Herzegovina
52 C6 **Vidzy** Belarus
52 H4 **Vidz'yuyar** Russian Federation
21 L3 **Vie** *R* Calvados France
20 G8 **Vie** *R* Vendée France
37 O5 **Viechtach** Germany
131 D8 **Viedma** Argentina
133 C7 **Viedma, L** Argentina
20 H8 **Vieillevigne** France
108 C5 **Vieja, Sa** *mts* Texas U.S.A.
128 C6 **Viejas, Islas de las** Peru
Vielha *see* **Viella**
17 H2 **Viella** Spain
21 M4 **Vielle-Lyre, la** France
22 K3 **Vielsalm** Belgium
28 J6 **Viemose** Denmark
33 N9 **Vienenburg** Germany
68 E2 **Vieng Pou Kha** Laos
Vienna Austria *see* **Wien** Austria
110 H4 **Vienna** Illinois U.S.A.
95 M8 **Vienna** Maryland U.S.A.
98 J5 **Vienna** South Dakota U.S.A.
94 F7 **Vienna** West Virginia U.S.A.
18 F6 **Vienne** *dept* France
19 N13 **Vienne** France
21 L7 **Vienne** *R* France
131 B3 **Vientes, P. del** *pk* Arg/Chile
Vientiane *see* **Viangchan**
131 B6 **Viento, Cord. del** *ra* Argentina
127 M5 **Vieques** *isld* Puerto Rico
29 N8 **Vieremä** Finland
32 M6 **Vierlande** *reg* Germany
25 E5 **Vierlingsbeek** Netherlands
36 F4 **Viernheim** Germany
25 F6 **Viersen** Germany
21 J3 **Vierville-sur-Mer** France
41 H3 **Vierwaldstätter See** *L* Switzerland
21 P7 **Vierzon** France
124 H5 **Viesca** Mexico
33 Q6 **Viesecke** Germany
37 L1 **Vieselbach** Germany
52 C6 **Viesite Nereta** Latvia
21 J4 **Viessoix** France
42 G7 **Vieste** Italy
68 G3 **Vietnam** *rep* S E Asia
33 R7 **Vietnitz** Germany
68 G2 **Vietri** Vietnam
45 R8 **Vietri S. Mare** Italy
127 O8 **Vieux Fort** St Lucia
127 N5 **Vieux Fort,Pte.du** Guadeloupe W Indies
108 H3 **View** Texas U.S.A.
28 H5 **Vig** Denmark
52 F5 **Viga** *R* Russian Federation
71 E2 **Vigan** Luzon Philippines
18 H8 **Vigan, le** France
45 L2 **Vigarano Mainarda** Italy
45 J1 **Vigásio** Italy
18 F7 **Vigeois** France
44 E1 **Vigevano** Italy
43 G8 **Viggiano** Italy
129 J4 **Vigia** Brazil
16 B7 **Vigia** *mt* Portugal
133 D7 **Vigía, C** Argentina
71 E3 **Vigia Pt** Luzon Philippines
21 P6 **Viglain** France
45 O6 **Viglio** *mt* Italy
21 P1 **Vignacourt** France
44 D1 **Vignale Mon Ferrato** Italy
18 E10 **Vignemale** *mt* France/Spain
22 G4 **Vigneux Hocquet** France
45 K3 **Vignola** Italy
16 B2 **Vigo** Spain
45 L1 **Vigonza** Italy
142 C5 **Vigors,Mt** W Australia Australia
26 A9 **Vigra** *isld* Norway
27 A13 **Vigrestad** Norway
28 B2 **Vigsø** Denmark
29 L7 **Vihanti** Finland
21 J7 **Vihiers** France
48 G2 **Vihorlát** *mt* Slovakia
29 L11 **Vihti** Finland
29 K10 **Viiala** Finland
29 O9 **Viinijärvi** *L* Finland
29 M5 **Viiri** Finland
29 M8 **Viitasaari** Finland
76 A2 **Vijayadurg** India
76 E2 **Vijayawada** India
46 D4 **Vijosë** *R* Albania
28 S10 **Vik** Iceland
26 F6 **Vik** Norway
27 G11 **Vika** Sweden
29 M5 **Vikajärvi** Finland
27 H11 **Vikarbyn** Sweden
27 A12 **Vikedal** Norway
71 N9 **Vikeke** Timor
29 K4 **Viken** Sweden
27 G12 **Vikersvik** Sweden
27 D12 **Vikesund** Norway
46 F3 **Vikhren** *mt* Bulgaria
118 F5 **Viking** Alberta Canada
7 M9 **Viking** *oil rig* North Sea
6 M2 **Viking Bank** North Sea
7 M9 **Viking N** *oil rig* North Sea
7 M9 **Viking S** *oil rig* North Sea
27 H11 **Vikmanshyttan** Sweden
26 E7 **Vikna** *isld* Norway
26 E7 **Vikna** Norway
26 J9 **Viksjö** Sweden
55 F3 **Vikulovo** Russian Federation
71 M9 **Vila Armindo Monteiro** Timor
Vila Cabral *see* **Lichinga**
131 E4 **Vila Constitución** Argentina
88 G10 **Vila da Maganje** Mozambique
16 B7 **Vila do Bispo** Portugal
16 B3 **Vila do Conde** Portugal
87 F8 **Vila Gamito** Mozambique
20 H5 **Vilaine** *R* Ille-et-Vilaine France
20 F6 **Vilaine** *R* Morbihan France
17 H2 **Vilaller** Spain
87 F9 **Vila Machado** Mozambique
128 E6 **Vila Murtinho** Brazil
87 G11 **Vilanandro, Tanjona** *C* Madagascar
87 G10 **Vilanculos** Mozambique
52 C6 **Vilāni** Latvia
16 B5 **Vila Nova da Barquinha** Portugal
16 B3 **Vila Nova de Famalicão** Portugal
16 C3 **Vila Nova de Fozcoa** Portugal
16 B3 **Vila Nova de Gaia** Portugal
71 N9 **Vila Nova de Malaca** Timor
16 B7 **Vila Nova de Mil Fontes** Portugal
16 B4 **Vila Nova de Paiva** Portugal
16 B3 **Vila Pouca de Aguiar** Portugal
16 B3 **Vila Real** Portugal
16 C7 **Vila Real de Santo António** Portugal
16 C4 **Vilar Formoso** Portugal
106 H4 **Vilas** Colorado U.S.A.
111 M11 **Vilas** Florida U.S.A.
98 J5 **Vilas** South Dakota U.S.A.
71 N9 **Vila Salazar** Timor
87 F8 **Vila Vasco da Gama** Mozambique
129 H3 **Vila Velha** Amapá Brazil
130 H7 **Vila Velha** Espírito Santo Brazil
16 B5 **Vila Velha de Ródão** Portugal
16 B3 **Vila Verde** Portugal
128 D6 **Vilcabamba, Cord** *mts* Peru
48 H5 **Vîlcanului Muntii** *mt* Romania
48 J5 **Vîlcea** *reg* Romania
28 B4 **Vildbjerg** Denmark
28 B3 **Vile** Denmark
52 G4 **Viled'** *R* Russian Federation
37 P3 **Vilémov** Czech Rep
53 C7 **Vileyskoye Vodokhranilishche** *res* Belarus
52 H4 **Vil'gort** Komi Respublika Russian Federation
52 J4 **Vil'gort** Permskaya obl Russian Federation
26 J7 **Vilhelmina** Sweden
128 F6 **Vilhena** Brazil
53 C7 **Viliya** *R* Belarus
52 C5 **Viljandi** Estonia
31 O1 **Vilkaviškis** Lithuania
51 J1 **Vil'kitskogo, Proliv** *str* Russian Federation
48 M5 **Vilkovo** Ukraine
128 E8 **Villa Abecia** Bolivia
45 N6 **Villa Adriana** Italy
108 A5 **Villa Ahumada** Mexico
127 J5 **Villa Altagracia** Dominican Rep
133 E3 **Villa Angela** Argentina
131 C5 **Villa Atuel** Argentina
45 K1 **Villa Bartolomea** Italy
38 F8 **Villabassa** Italy
128 E6 **Villa Bella** Bolivia
Villa Bens *see* **Tarfaya**
128 E4 **Villa Bittencourt** Brazil
16 C2 **Villablino** Spain
16 E5 **Villacañas** Spain
16 E1 **Villacarriedo** Spain
16 E6 **Villa Carrillo** Spain
16 E4 **Villacastin** Spain
38 J8 **Villach** Austria
16 C2 **Villachica, L. de** Spain
43 B9 **Villacidro** Sardinia
Villa Cisneros *see* **Dakhla, Ad**
133 D4 **Villa Colón** Argentina
133 E4 **Villa Concepción del Tio** Argentina
133 E4 **Villa Constitucion** Argentina
124 G4 **Villa Coronado** Mexico
16 D2 **Villada** Spain
127 L9 **Villa de Cura** Venezuela
133 E4 **Villa del Rosario** Argentina
16 E2 **Villadiego** Spain
131 D3 **Villa Dolores** Argentina
41 H5 **Villadossola** Italy
45 L1 **Villa Estense** Italy
17 G4 **Villafamés** Spain
130 B10 **Villa Franca** Paraguay
16 C2 **Villafranca del Bierzo** Spain
17 G4 **Villafranca del Cid** Spain
16 C6 **Villafranca de los Barros** Spain
17 J3 **Villafranca del Penedés** Spain
45 J1 **Villafranca di Verona** Italy
45 L1 **Villafranca P** Italy
45 L1 **Villaga** Italy
16 B2 **Villagarcía de Arosa** Spain
109 N5 **Village Cr** Texas U.S.A.
109 N5 **Village Mills** Texas U.S.A.
131 G6 **Villa Gesell** Argentina
99 S10 **Villa Grove** Illinois U.S.A.
131 F3 **Villaguay** Argentina
133 F3 **Villa Guillermina** Argentina
133 F3 **Villa Hayes** Paraguay
125 N9 **Villahermosa** Mexico
133 E4 **Villa Huidobro** Argentina
21 K5 **Villaines-la-Jubel** France
21 M7 **Villaines-les-Rochers** France
21 K6 **Villaines-sous-Malicorne** France
128 F8 **Villa Ingavi** Bolivia
133 E5 **Villa Iris** Argentina
127 J5 **Villa Isabel** Dominican Rep
16 B1 **Villalba** Lugo Spain
16 E4 **Villalba** Madrid Spain
45 Q7 **Villa Literno** Italy
16 D2 **Villalón de Campos** Spain
133 E5 **Villalonga** Argentina
16 D3 **Villalpando** Spain
17 F6 **Villamanriqué** Spain
43 B9 **Villamar** Sardinia
131 D4 **Villa Maria** Argentina
133 D2 **Villa Martín** Bolivia
16 D8 **Villamartín** Spain
124 G4 **Villa Matamoros** Mexico
17 F5 **Villamayor de Santiago** Spain
21 O5 **Villamblain** France
133 D4 **Villa Mercedes** Argentina
133 E3 **Villa Minetti** Argentina
45 H3 **Villaminozzo** Italy
133 E2 **Villa Montes** Bolivia
16 B3 **Villa Nova da Cerveira** Portugal
45 L2 **Villanova March** Italy
127 H9 **Villanueva** Colombia
124 H6 **Villanueva** Mexico
106 E6 **Villanueva** New Mexico U.S.A.
16 D6 **Villanueva de Córdoba** Spain
17 F6 **Villanueva del Arzobispo** Spain
16 D6 **Villanueva de la Serena** Spain
16 D3 **Villanueva del Campo** Spain
16 E6 **Villanueva de los Infantes** Spain
17 J3 **Villanueva y Geltrú** Spain
48 E5 **Villány** Hungary
124 G4 **Villa Ocampo** Durango Mexico
16 C1 **Villaodrid** Spain
124 G4 **Villa Orestes Pereyra** Mexico
124 E3 **Villa Pesqueira** Mexico
43 C9 **Villaputzu** Sardinia
16 E2 **Villarcayo** Spain
19 P14 **Villard** France
19 P14 **Villard de Lans** France
17 G5 **Villar del Arzobispo** Spain
16 C5 **Villar del Rey** Spain
133 D5 **Villa Regina** Argentina
142 D4 **Villaret, C** W Australia Australia
130 B9 **Villa Rey** Paraguay
111 M8 **Villa Rica** Georgia U.S.A.
17 G4 **Villarluengo** Spain
43 F11 **Villarosa** Sicily
17 G5 **Villarreal** Spain
131 A7 **Villarrica** Chile
130 C9 **Villarrica** Paraguay
131 B7 **Villarrica, Vol** Chile
17 F5 **Villarrobledo** Spain
17 F3 **Villarroya de la Sierra** Spain
16 E5 **Villarubia de los Ojos** Spain
95 N7 **Villas** New Jersey U.S.A.
131 D2 **Villa Sanagasta** Argentina
131 D2 **Villa San Martín** Argentina
38 G9 **Villa Santina** Italy
17 F3 **Villasayas** Spain
133 D3 **Villa Unión** Argentina
108 G7 **Villa Union** Mexico
124 G6 **Villa Unión** Durango Mexico
124 F6 **Villa Unión** Sinaloa Mexico
128 D3 **Villavicencio** Colombia
16 D1 **Villaviciosa** Spain
16 D6 **Villaviciosa de Córdoba** Spain
128 C3 **Villavieja** Colombia
133 D2 **Villazón** Bolivia
36 C7 **Villé** France
21 N6 **Ville-aux-Clèrcs, la** France
21 H4 **Villebaudon** France
40 B6 **Villebois** France
18 F7 **Villebois Lavalette** France
19 Q17 **Villecroze** France
21 H7 **Villedieu-la-Blouère** Maine-et-Loire France
20 H4 **Villedieu-les-Poêtes** France
21 O8 **Villedieu-sur-Indre** France
21 M2 **Villedomer** France
21 M6 **Villedomer** France
18 H8 **Villefort** France
44 B4 **Villefranche** France
19 N13 **Villefranche** Rhône France
18 G9 **Villefranche de Lauragais** France
18 G8 **Villefranche-de-Rouergue** France
18 F8 **Villefranche-du-Perigord** France
21 O7 **Villefranche-sur-Cher** France
17 G4 **Villel** Spain
121 L5 **Ville-Marie** Quebec Canada
21 N4 **Villemeux-sur-Eure** France
121 M4 **Villemontel** Quebec Canada
18 G9 **Villemur sur le Tarn** France
17 G6 **Villena** Spain
19 N12 **Villeneuve** France
40 F6 **Villeneuve** Italy
18 G8 **Villeneuve d'Allier** France
22 E2 **Villeneuve d'Ascq** France
19 N15 **Villeneuve de Berg** France
18 E9 **Villeneuve de Marc** France
18 H4 **Villeneuve l'Archevêque** France
19 N17 **Villeneuve-lès-Avignon** France
21 P3 **Villeneuve-les-Sablons** France
18 G4 **Villeneuve-St Georges** France
18 F8 **Villeneuve-sur-Lot** France
18 H4 **Villeneuve-sur-Yonne** France
21 N7 **Villentrois** France
111 D11 **Ville Platte** Louisiana U.S.A.
21 M2 **Villequier** France
21 N6 **Villeromain** France
121 T6 **Villeroy** Quebec Canada
21 J3 **Villers-Bocage** Calvados France
21 P2 **Villers-Bocage** Somme France
21 P3 **Villers-Bretonneux** France
22 D4 **Villers-Carbonnel** France
22 E5 **Villers Cotterets** France
22 J4 **Villers Devant-Orval** Belgium
21 L4 **Villers-en-Ouche** France
22 J2 **Villers-le-Bouillet** Belgium
22 H3 **Villers-le-Gambon** Belgium
22 E3 **Villers-Outreaux** France
22 K5 **Villerupt-la-Montagne** *mt* France
21 L3 **Villerville** France
19 N13 **Villeurbanne** France
131 C3 **Villicun, Sa** *ra* Argentina
21 N8 **Villiers** France
21 J6 **Villiers-Charlemagne** France
41 J1 **Villingen-Schwenningen** Germany
99 M9 **Villisca** Iowa U.S.A.
36 E3 **Villmar** Germany
Vilna *see* **Vilnius**
118 F4 **Vilna** Alberta Canada
53 C7 **Vilnius** Lithuania
29 L9 **Vilppula** Finland
41 N2 **Vils** Austria
28 B3 **Vils** Denmark
27 M13 **Vilsandi Saar** *isld* Estonia
37 N7 **Vilsbiburg** Germany
37 M4 **Vilseck** Germany
37 P6 **Vilshofen** Germany
27 G15 **Vilshult** Sweden
28 B6 **Vilslev** Denmark
28 C3 **Vilsted** Denmark
28 B3 **Vilsund** Denmark
76 D5 **Viluppuram** India
42 J6 **Vilusi** Montenegro Yugoslavia
52 J5 **Vil'va** Russian Federation
22 G2 **Vilvoorde** Belgium
51 L2 **Vilyuy** *R* Russian Federation
51 M2 **Vilyuysk** Russian Federation
56 H1 **Vilyuyskoye Vodokhranilishche** *res* Russian Federation
16 C3 **Vimioso** Portugal
27 H14 **Vimmerby** Sweden
27 G11 **Vimo** Sweden
21 L4 **Vimoutiers** France
29 K8 **Vimpeli** Finland
30 H6 **Vimperk** Czech Rep
22 D3 **Vimy** France
111 H7 **Vina** Alabama U.S.A.
102 B2 **Vina** California U.S.A.
131 B4 **Viña de Mar** Chile
17 G6 **Vinalapó** *R* Spain
95 T2 **Vinalhaven** Maine U.S.A.
17 H4 **Vinaroz** Spain
40 B7 **Vinay** France
110 J3 **Vincennes** Indiana U.S.A.
146 G14 **Vincennes Bay** Antarctica
111 K8 **Vincent** Alabama U.S.A.
94 F7 **Vincent** Ohio U.S.A.
16 B7 **Vincente, C. de S** Portugal
128 C4 **Vinces** Ecuador
45 R7 **Vinchiaturo** Italy
133 D3 **Vinchina** Argentina
45 J4 **Vinci** Italy
28 B4 **Vind** Denmark
28 C3 **Vindblæs** Denmark
28 G7 **Vindeby** Denmark
26 H5 **Vindelälven** *R* Sweden
26 K6 **Vindelgransele** Sweden
26 L7 **Vindeln** Sweden
143 B7 **Vinden, Mt** W Australia Australia
28 C4 **Vinderslev** Denmark
28 B4 **Vinderup** Denmark
74 F7 **Vindhya Range** India
28 B4 **Vinding** Ringkøbing Denmark
28 D4 **Vinding** Vejle Denmark
28 D5 **Vinding** Vejle Denmark
28 F6 **Vindinge** Denmark
21 O8 **Vineuil** Indre France
21 N6 **Vineuil** Loir-et-Cher France
95 R5 **Vineyard Haven** Massachusetts U.S.A.
48 G4 **Vinga** Romania
27 H12 **Vingåker, V** Sweden
40 B2 **Vingeanne** *R* France
21 L4 **Vingt Hanaps** France
68 G3 **Vinh** Vietnam
16 C3 **Vinhais** Portugal
68 J7 **Vinh Cam Ranh** *B* Vietnam
68 J6 **Vinh Giat** Vietnam
Vinh Linh *see* **Ho Xa**
69 G8 **Vinh Loi** Vietnam
68 G7 **Vinh Long** Vietnam
68 H3 **Vinh Son** *B* Vietnam
67 B6 **Vinh Yen** Vietnam
46 E3 **Vinica** Macedonia
99 L3 **Vining** Minnesota U.S.A.
107 P5 **Vinita** Oklahoma U.S.A.
27 C12 **Vinje** Norway
26 C8 **Vinjeora** Norway
48 H6 **Vînju Mare** Romania
28 D4 **Vinkel** Denmark
48 E5 **Vinkovci** Croatia
26 M2 **Vinnelys** Norway
48 M1 **Vinnitsa** Ukraine
48 H2 **Vinogradov** Ukraine
19 P17 **Vinon** France
107 L7 **Vinson** Oklahoma U.S.A.
146 C7 **Vinson Massif** *mts* Antarctica
27 D10 **Vinstra** *R* Norway
71 E1 **Vintar** Luzon Philippines
99 O7 **Vinton** Iowa U.S.A.
111 C11 **Vinton** Louisiana U.S.A.
94 E8 **Vinton** Ohio U.S.A.
94 H9 **Vinton** Virginia U.S.A.
27 G12 **Vintrosa** Sweden
133 E6 **Vintter** Argentina
48 H4 **Vințu de Jos** Romania
76 D2 **Vinukonda** India
33 P7 **Vinzelberg** Germany
55 E3 **Vinzili** Russian Federation
102 C1 **Viola** California U.S.A.
100 H3 **Viola** Idaho U.S.A.
99 Q8 **Viola** Illinois U.S.A.
107 N4 **Viola** Kansas U.S.A.
99 Q6 **Viola** Wisconsin U.S.A.
101 P7 **Viola** Wyoming U.S.A.
118 B5 **Violet Grove** Alberta Canada
87 C11 **Vioolsdrif** Namibia
20 H6 **Vioreau, Grand Res. de** France
41 O4 **Vipiteno** Italy
33 R6 **Vipperow** Germany
42 F4 **Vir** *isld* Croatia
27 H13 **Virå** Sweden
71 G4 **Virac** Philippines
47 K5 **Virancık** Turkey
52 E3 **Virandozero** Russian Federation
48 G6 **Virciorova** Romania
119 R9 **Virden** Manitoba Canada
99 R10 **Virden** Illinois U.S.A.
29 J3 **Virdni** *mt* Finland
20 H3 **Vire** *R* France
21 J4 **Vire** France
27 G14 **Vireda** Sweden
142 B5 **Virehow, Mt** W Australia Australia
87 B9 **Virei** Angola
22 G3 **Virelles** Belgium
22 H3 **Vireux** Belgium
48 H4 **Vîrfurile** Romania
101 P1 **Virgelle** Montana U.S.A.
130 G5 **Virgem da Lapa** Brazil
17 F3 **Virgen,Sa.de la** *mts* Spain
107 P4 **Virgil** Kansas U.S.A.
98 H5 **Virgil** South Dakota U.S.A.
102 C1 **Virgilia** California U.S.A.
94 J10 **Virgilina** Virginia U.S.A.
45 J1 **Virgilio** Italy
103 L5 **Virgin** *R* Arizona U.S.A.
113 L7 **Virgin Gorda** *isld* Virgin Is
14 D3 **Virginia** Ireland
89 E7 **Virginia** S Africa
94 H9 **Virginia** *state* U.S.A.
101 N7 **Virginia** Idaho U.S.A.
99 Q10 **Virginia** Illinois U.S.A.
99 O2 **Virginia** Minnesota U.S.A.
98 K9 **Virginia** Nebraska U.S.A.
95 M10 **Virginia Beach** Virginia U.S.A.
101 O4 **Virginia City** Montana U.S.A.
102 E2 **Virginia City** Nevada U.S.A.
117 L5 **Virginia Falls** Northwest Territories Canada
121 L4 **Virginiatown** Ontario Canada
113 L7 **Virgin Is** W Indies
103 K5 **Virgin Mts** Nev/Ariz U.S.A.
130 G6 **Virginópolis** Brazil
19 P13 **Virignin** France
26 J4 **Virihaure** Sweden
19 O14 **Viriville** France
133 D8 **Vírjenes, C** Argentina
28 D4 **Virklund** Denmark
29 N9 **Virmasvesi** *L* Finland
29 N11 **Virolahti** Finland
99 Q6 **Viroqua** Wisconsin U.S.A.
42 H3 **Virovitica** Croatia
42 J6 **Virpazar** Montenegro Yugoslavia
29 K9 **Virrat** Finland
27 H12 **Virsbo** Sweden
27 H14 **Virserum** Sweden
29 N9 **Virtasalmi** Finland
48 J6 **Vîrtoapele** Romania
46 G1 **Vîrtoapele de Sus** Romania
22 K4 **Virton** Belgium
128 C5 **Virú** Peru
76 C6 **Virudunagar** India
52 C5 **Viru-Jaagup** Estonia
42 G5 **Vis** *isld* Croatia
27 H14 **Vi, S** Sweden
102 E5 **Visalia** California U.S.A.
19 N16 **Visan** France
45 J1 **Visano** Italy
71 F5 **Visayan Sea** Philippines
28 E3 **Visborg** Denmark
28 B6 **Visby** Sønderjylland Denmark
28 A3 **Visby** Viborg Denmark
27 K14 **Visby** Sweden
130 G7 **Visconde do Rio Branco** Brazil
119 M7 **Viscount** Saskatchewan Canada
114 J3 **Viscount Melville Sd** Northwest Territories Canada
22 K2 **Visé** Belgium
48 E7 **Višegard** Bosnia-Herzegovina
45 M3 **Viserba** Italy
16 B4 **Viseu** Portugal
48 J3 **Vişeu** *R* Romania
48 J3 **Vişeu de Sus** Romania
76 F2 **Vishakhapatam** India
52 H4 **Vishera** *R* Russian Federation
52 G5 **Vishkil'** Russian Federation
48 K1 **Vishnevets** Ukraine
55 F5 **Vishnevka** Kazakhstan
55 D3 **Vishnevogorsk** Russian Federation
55 D1 **Visim** *R* Russian Federation
55 C2 **Visim** Russian Federation
55 C2 **Visimo-Utkinsk** Russian Federation
46 G1 **Vişina Veche** Romania
27 G13 **Visingsö** Sweden
27 F14 **Viskafors** Sweden
27 F14 **Viskan** *R* Sweden
52 C6 **Viški** Latvia
28 G5 **Viskinge** Denmark
27 G15 **Vislanda** Sweden
124 D3 **Visnaga** Mexico
74 E7 **Visnagar** India
44 B2 **Viso** *mt* Italy
16 E6 **Viso del Marqués** Spain
48 E7 **Visoko** Bosnia-Herzegovina
46 E3 **Visoko** *mt* Macedonia
146 G2 **Visokoi I** S Sandwich Is S Atlantic Oc
40 G5 **Visp** Switzerland
27 H15 **Vissefjärda** Sweden
32 L7 **Visselhövede** Germany
28 E6 **Vissenbjerg** Denmark
40 G5 **Vissoie** Switzerland
102 G8 **Vista** California U.S.A.
128 F3 **Vista Alegre** Brazil
101 K8 **Vista Res** Nevada U.S.A.
28 F4 **Vistoft** Denmark
46 G3 **Vistonís, L** Greece
Vistula *R* *see* **Wisła** *R*
46 G1 **Vit** *R* Bulgaria
119 V9 **Vita** Manitoba Canada
76 B2 **Vita** India
54 B1 **Vitebsk** Belarus
42 E6 **Viterbo** Italy
16 C3 **Vitigudino** Spain
56 H4 **Vitim** *R* Russian Federation
58 F1 **Vitimskoye Ploskogor'ye** Russian Federation
42 H5 **Vitina** Bosnia-Herzegovina
46 E7 **Vitína** Greece
130 H7 **Vitória** Brazil
17 F2 **Vitoria** Spain
130 H4 **Vitória da Conquista** Brazil
130 J10 **Vitoria de Sta Antão** Brazil
42 H4 **Vitorog** *mts* Bosnia-Herzegovina
21 N5 **Vitray-en-Beauce** France
20 H5 **Vitré** France
123 N2 **Vitré,L** Quebec Canada
40 C2 **Vitrey** France
19 O18 **Vitrolles** France
21 P6 **Vitry-aux-Loges** France
22 D3 **Vitry-en-Artois** France
27 F11 **Vitsand** Sweden
Vitsi *mt* *see* **Vérnon** *mt*
26 M4 **Vittangi** *R* Sweden
28 A5 **Vittarp** Denmark
40 C1 **Vittel** France
28 D4 **Vitten** Denmark
27 J12 **Vittinge** Sweden
120 K10 **Vittoria** Ontario Canada
43 F12 **Vittoria** Sicily
43 F13 **Vittoriosa** Malta
42 E3 **Vittorio Ven** Italy
27 G15 **Vittsjö** Sweden
45 R7 **Vitulano** Italy
26 N5 **Vitvattnet** Sweden

40 F7 Viu Italy
28 C5 Viuf Denmark
18 H7 Vivarais, Mts du France
28 E3 Vive Denmark
17 G5 Viver Spain
16 B1 Vivero Spain
44 D1 Viverone, L. di Italy
51 J2 Vivi Russian Federation
109 O3 Vivian Louisiana U.S.A.
98 F6 Vivian South Dakota U.S.A.
19 N16 Viviers France
20 G4 Vivier-sur-Mer, Le France
28 E4 Vivild Denmark
21 L5 Vivoin France
138 D6 Vivonne South Australia Australia
18 F6 Vivonne France
133 F5 Vivorata Argentina
26 M4 Vivunki Sweden
124 C4 Vizcaíno,Des.de Mexico
124 B4 Vizcaíno,Sa *mts* Mexico
17 F1 Vizcaya *prov* Spain
47 J3 Vize Turkey
50 G1 Vize,Ostrova *islds* Russian Federation
52 G2 Vizhas Russian Federation
76 F1 Vizianagaram India
45 P1 Vižinada Croatia
52 H4 Vizinga Russian Federation
48 L6 Viziru Romania
31 K6 Vizovice Czech Rep
43 F11 Vizzini Sicily
25 B5 Vlaardingen Netherlands
48 L3 Vlădeni Romania
46 E2 Vladičin Han Serbia Yugoslavia
53 F11 Vladikavkaz Russian Federation
52 F6 Vladimir Russian Federation
48 F6 Vladimirci Serbia Yugoslavia
55 D4 Vladimirovka Kazakhstan
52 E6 Vladimirskaya Oblast' *prov* Russian Federation
54 E1 Vladimirskiy Tupik Russian Federation
53 B8 Vladimir Volynskiy Ukraine
59 K3 Vladivostok Russian Federation
52 E5 Vladychnoye Russian Federation
48 K4 Vlăhiţa Romania
46 E2 Vlajna *mt* Serbia Yugoslavia
142 A5 Vlaming Hd W Australia Australia
48 E6 Vlasenica Bosnia-Herzegovina
48 F6 Vlašić *mt* Serbia Yugoslavia
46 E2 Vlasotince Serbia Yugoslavia
31 K7 Vlčany Slovakia
25 C2 Vlieland *isld* Netherlands
25 D2 Vliestroom Netherlands
25 A6 Vlissingen Netherlands
25 F6 Vlodrop Netherlands
46 C4 Vlorë Albania
32 J8 Vlotho Germany
31 H7 Vltava *R* Czech Rep
52 E6 Vnukovo *airport* Russian Federation
45 L1 Vo Italy
109 H5 Voca Texas U.S.A.
38 J6 Vöcklabruck Austria
107 K2 Voda Kansas U.S.A.
68 H7 Vo Dat Vietnam
28 B6 Vodder Denmark
47 H1 Voditsa Bulgaria
52 E4 Vodla *R* Russian Federation
52 E4 Vodlozero, Oz *L* Russian Federation
30 H6 Vodňany Czech Rep
42 F4 Vodnjan Croatia
52 H3 Vodnyy Russian Federation
28 E2 Vodskov Denmark
15 G2 Voe Shetland Scotland
28 D4 Voel Denmark
28 E3 Voer Denmark
32 E9 Voerde Germany
32 F10 Voerde Germany
28 D4 Voerladegard Denmark
28 F2 Voerså Denmark
85 C7 Vofnjama Liberia
86 B4 Vogel *mt* Nigeria
41 O3 Vogelkar Sp *mt* Austria
36 G2 Vogelsberg *mt* Germany
44 F2 Voghera Italy
45 L2 Voghiera Italy
28 C3 Vognsild Denmark
41 H5 Vogogna Italy
Vohemar *see* Iharaña
37 N4 Vohenstrauss Germany
Vohibinany *see* Ampasimanolotra
87 H13 Vohimena, Tanjona *C* Madagascar
36 F1 Vöhl Germany
52 C5 Võhma Estonia
37 J7 Vöhringen Germany
32 F10 Vohwinkel Germany
88 G3 Voi Kenya
33 S4 Voigdehgn Germany
12 D1 Voil,L Scotland
48 L3 Voineşti Romania
40 C7 Voiron France
38 M7 Voitsberg Austria
46 F5 Voïviïs *L* Greece
28 C6 Vojens Denmark
26 H6 Vojmsjön *L* Sweden
37 N3 Vojtanov Czech Rep
48 E5 Vojvodina *aut rep* Serbia Yugoslavia
52 G5 Vokhma *R* Russian Federation
29 P7 Voknavolok Russian Federation
30 H6 Vokyně Czech Rep
52 H3 Vol' *R* Russian Federation
30 H7 Volary Czech Rep
98 A4 Volborg Montana U.S.A.
131 B3 Volcan,Cerro del *pk* Chile
106 D2 Volcano Colorado U.S.A.
Volcano B *see* Uchiura wan B
135 U5 Volcanoes Nat. Park Hawaiian Is
131 F6 Volcán, Sa. del *ra* Argentina
55 D2 Volchansk Russian Federation
55 H4 Volchikha Russian Federation
52 E5 Volchina *R* Russian Federation
54 H8 Volch'ya *R* Ukraine
28 D4 Voldby Denmark
28 F4 Voldby Denmark
28 E4 Voldum Denmark
25 D4 Volendam Netherlands
45 J1 Volfa Mantovana Italy
52 E5 Volga Russian Federation
52 E6 Volga *R* Russian Federation
99 P7 Volga *R* Iowa U.S.A.
98 K5 Volga South Dakota U.S.A.
52 E4 Volgo-Balt *canal* Russian Federation
53 F9 Volgograd Russian Federation
53 F9 Volgogradskaya Oblast' *prov* Russian Federation
52 D6 Volgo, Oz *L* Russian Federation
26 J7 Volgsele Sweden
98 J7 Volin South Dakota U.S.A.
47 H6 Volissós Greece
37 J4 Volkach Germany
25 B5 Volkerak Netherlands
38 L8 Völkermarkt Austria
37 J3 Völkershausen Germany
52 D5 Volkhov Russian Federation
36 B5 Völklingen Germany
32 K10 Volkmarsen Germany
48 L1 Volkovintsy Ukraine
31 P2 Volkovysk Belarus
32 L8 Völksen Germany
89 F6 Volksrust S Africa
25 E3 Vollenhove Netherlands
22 G2 Vollezele Belgium
32 J9 Völmerstod *mt* Germany
36 C5 Volmunster France
21 L6 Volnay Sarthe France
99 U6 Volney Michigan U.S.A.
44 F3 Vol Noci, L. di Italy
54 F8 Vol'nogorsk Ukraine
55 F4 Vol'noye Russian Federation
54 G9 Vol'nyansk Ukraine
51 J1 Volochanka Russian Federation
48 K1 Volochisk Ukraine
52 F6 Volodarsk Russian Federation
55 E4 Volodarskoye Kazakhstan
52 F4 Volodskaya Russian Federation
52 E5 Vologda Russian Federation
36 B7 Vologne *R* France
52 E4 Vologodskaya Oblast' *prov* Russian Federation
52 D6 Volok Russian Federation
52 E6 Volokolamsk Russian Federation
52 G2 Volokovaya Russian Federation
52 G2 Volonga Russian Federation
19 Q16 Volonne France
46 F5 Vólos Greece
52 E4 Voloshka Russian Federation
52 C5 Volosovo Russian Federation
48 H2 Volosyanka Ukraine
52 D5 Volot Russian Federation
48 H2 Volovets Ukraine
33 O8 Völpke Germany
33 S5 Völschow Germany
53 G8 Vol'sk Russian Federation
28 E2 Volstrup Denmark
130 H10 Volta Brazil
85 E7 Volta *R* Ghana
41 N7 Volta Italy
85 D6 Volta Blanche *R* Burkina/Ghana
98 F1 Voltaire North Dakota U.S.A.
142 F2 Voltaire, C W Australia Australia
85 D7 Volta,L Ghana
85 D6 Volta Noire *R* Burkina
130 G8 Volta Redonda Brazil
85 D6 Volta Rouge *R* Burkina/Ghana
42 D5 Volterra Italy
52 F3 Volteva Russian Federation
44 E3 Voltri Italy
45 R8 Volturara Irpina Italy
45 Q7 Volturno *R* Italy
46 F4 Vólvi, L Greece
19 P17 Volx France
52 G6 Volzhsk Russian Federation
53 F9 Volzhskiy Russian Federation
42 F6 Vomano *R* Italy
106 H2 Vona Colorado U.S.A.
118 L6 Vonda Saskatchewan Canada
87 H12 Vondrozo Madagascar
22 J3 Vonêche Belgium
116 K5 Von Frank Mt Alaska U.S.A.
52 F3 Vonga Russian Federation
28 C5 Vonge Denmark
40 B3 Vonges France
46 D6 Vónitsa Greece
129 H5 Von Martius,Cachoeira *rapids* Brazil
28 D6 Vonsbæk Denmark
28 C6 Vonsild Denmark
143 E7 Von Truer Tableland W Australia Australia
25 B4 Voorburg Netherlands
25 B5 Voorne Netherlands
25 B4 Voorschoten Netherlands
25 F4 Voorst Netherlands
25 E4 Voorthuizen Netherlands
29 T9 Vopnafjördhur *inlet* Iceland
29 T9 Vopnafjördhur Iceland
25 F6 Vopst Germany
29 J8 Vörå Finland
41 K4 Vorab *mt* Switzerland
41 L3 Vorarlberg *prov* Austria
38 N7 Vorau Austria
28 C5 Vorbasse Denmark
32 H8 Vörden Germany
25 F4 Vorden Netherlands
38 L7 Vordernberg Austria
41 J4 Vorder Rhein *R* Switzerland
28 H6 Vordingborg Denmark
46 G5 Vóreion Aiyaíon *admin region* Greece
19 P14 Voreppe France
54 D3 Vorga Russian Federation
28 B4 Vorgod Denmark
46 G5 Voríai Sporádhes *islds* Greece
50 F2 Vorkuta Russian Federation
27 E11 Vorma *R* Norway
28 D3 Vorning Denmark
55 G3 Vorob'yevo Russian Federation
53 F8 Vorona *R* Russian Federation
54 C3 Voronevo Belarus
54 L4 Voronezh *R* Russian Federation
54 L5 Voronezh Voronezhskaya obl Russian Federation
54 E5 Voronezh Ukraine
53 E8 Voronezhskaya Oblast' *prov* Russian Federation
48 M1 Voronovitsa Ukraine
52 F2 Voronov, Mys *C* Russian Federation
55 D2 Vorontsovka Russian Federation
50 H1 Vorontsovo Russian Federation
52 C6 Vorontsovo Russian Federation
52 E1 Voron'ya *R* Russian Federation
52 F5 Voron'ye Russian Federation
Voroshilovgrad *see* Lugansk
52 G5 Voroshno Russian Federation
54 N1 Vorovskogo, im Russian Federation
54 F5 Vorozhba Ukraine
33 S5 Vorpommern *reg* Germany
33 N8 Vorsfelde Germany
54 G6 Vorskala *R* Rus Fed/Ukraine
52 F6 Vorsma Russian Federation
52 C5 Võrtsjärv Estonia
52 C5 Võru Estonia
28 E4 Vorup Denmark
55 D1 Vor'ya *R* Russian Federation
55 D1 Vor'yapaul' Russian Federation
52 H3 Vorykva *R* Russian Federation
36 B7 Vosges *dept* France
40 E2 Vosges *mt* France
55 C4 Voskresenskoye Bashkirskaya Respublika Russian Federation
52 G6 Voskresenskoye Nizhegorodskaya obl Russian Federation
52 E5 Voskresenskoye Vologodskaya obl Russian Federation
89 C3 Vosloosrus S Africa
55 F4 Vosnesenka Kazakhstan
27 B11 Voss Norway
54 D9 Vossiyatskoye Ukraine
56 B6 Vost Kazakhstanskaya Oblast' *prov* Kazakhstan
52 E1 Vostochnaya Litsa Russian Federation
57 H2 Vostochno-Kounradskiy Kazakhstan
56 E4 Vostochnyy Sayan *mts* Russian Federation
146 F11 Vostok *Rus Fed Base* Antarctica
135 M9 Vostok I Pacific Oc
55 E1 Vostykhoy Russian Federation
109 N5 Votaw Texas U.S.A.
109 N5 Voth Texas U.S.A.
31 H6 Votice Czech Rep
52 H6 Votkinsk Russian Federation
137 O4 Vot Tandé *isld* Vanuatu
130 E7 Votuporanga Brazil
16 B4 Vouga *R* Portugal
21 L8 Vouillé Vienne France
46 E5 Voulgára *mt* Greece
46 E5 Voulgarélion Greece
19 N15 Voulte, la France
68 H6 Vœune Cambodia
21 M8 Vouneuil-sur-Vienne France
46 E4 Voúrinos *mt* Greece
21 K5 Voutré France
21 J8 Vouvant France
21 M7 Vouvray France
21 P7 Vouzeron France
22 G5 Vouziers France
21 P6 Vouzon France
21 O5 Voves France
27 H10 Voxna Sweden
27 H10 Voxnan Sweden
27 G14 Voxtorp Sweden
52 H5 Voya *R* Russian Federation
99 O1 Voyageurs Nat. Park Minnesota U.S.A.
51 P3 Voyampolka Russian Federation
48 J1 Voynilov Ukraine
52 D2 Voynitsa Russian Federation
Vöyri *see* Vörå
52 H3 Voy Vozh Russian Federation
52 J3 Voyvozh Russian Federation
52 G3 Vozhayel' Russian Federation
52 F4 Vozhega Russian Federation
52 E4 Vozhe, Oz *L* Russian Federation
52 H5 Vozhgaly Russian Federation
52 G3 Vozhgora Russian Federation
54 C9 Voznesensk Ukraine
52 E4 Voznesenye Russian Federation
55 F4 Vozvyshenka Kazakhstan
28 D2 Vrå Denmark
48 E2 Vráble Slovakia
27 C12 Vrådalsv *L* Norway
53 D10 Vradiyevka Ukraine
28 C4 Vrads Denmark
46 E6 Vrakhnéïka Greece
42 H5 Vran *mt* Bosnia-Herzegovina
48 K5 Vrancea *reg* Romania
48 K5 Vrancei, Muntii *mts* Romania
47 O13 Vranganiótika Greece
65 J3 Vrangel' Russian Federation
147 P3 Vrangelya, Os *isld* Russian Federation
42 H5 Vranica *mt* Bosnia-Herzegovina
46 E2 Vranje Serbia Yugoslavia
48 G2 Vranov Slovakia
22 G1 Vrasene Belgium
46 F1 Vratsa Bulgaria
55 E1 Vray *L* Russian Federation
42 H4 Vrbas *R* Bosnia-Herzegovina
31 K5 Vrbno Czech Rep
31 J5 Vrchlabí Czech Rep
48 F5 Vrdnik Serbia Yugoslavia
89 F6 Vrede S Africa
32 E8 Vreden Germany
32 G7 Vrees Germany
28 D2 Vrensted Denmark
28 F6 Vresen *isld* Denmark
22 H4 Vress France
20 G3 Vrétot, le France
27 G12 Vretstorp Sweden
42 H5 Vrgorac Croatia
76 D5 Vriddhachalam India
28 C4 Vridsted Denmark
25 G2 Vries Netherlands
25 G4 Vriezenveen Netherlands
27 G14 Vrigstad Sweden
41 K4 Vrin Switzerland
22 H4 Vringe-aux-Bois France
28 A3 Vrist Denmark
22 F3 Vrith-St.Léger France
22 H5 Vrizy France
28 A5 Vrøgum Denmark
22 B3 Vron France
47 H6 Vrondádhes Greece
46 F8 Vrondamás Greece
25 G4 Vroomshoop Netherlands
28 C4 Vroue Denmark
48 G5 Vršac Serbia Yugoslavia
45 P1 Vrsar Croatia
48 E1 Vrútky Slovakia
89 D6 Vryburg S Africa
89 G6 Vryheid S Africa
37 P4 Všeruby Czech Rep
37 O5 Všeruby Czech Rep
31 K6 Vsetín Czech Rep
55 C1 Vsevolodo Blagodatskoye Russian Federation
48 E2 Vtáčnik *mt* Slovakia
19 P12 Vuache, Mt de France
68 G2 Vu Ban Vietnam
46 G3 Vŭcha *R* Bulgaria
46 D2 Vučitrn Serbia Yugoslavia
20 G7 Vue France
25 D5 Vught Netherlands
48 E5 Vuka *R* Croatia
48 E5 Vukovar Croatia
118 D8 Vulcan Alberta Canada
7 M9 Vulcan *gas field* North Sea
48 H5 Vulcan Romania
43 G10 Vulcano, I Italy
46 F1 Vŭlchedrŭm Bulgaria
47 J1 Vŭlchidol Bulgaria
67 B7 Vu Liet Vietnam
48 L5 Vulkaneshty Moldova
43 G8 Vulture, Monte Italy
103 M8 Vulture Mts Arizona U.S.A.
68 J4 Vung Da Nang *B* Vietnam
68 J7 Vung Phan Thiet *B* Vietnam
68 H7 Vung Tau Vietnam
89 F2 Vungu *R* Zimbabwe
26 M5 Vuodas Sweden
29 N7 Vuokatti Finland
29 O11 Vuoksa *L* Russian Federation
29 O10 Vuoksenniska Finland
29 N7 Vuolijoki Finland
26 L5 Vuollerim Sweden
29 N5 Vuostimo Finland
29 N3 Vuotso Finland
26 N2 Vuovdasoaivve *mt* Norway
47 H2 Vŭrbitsa Bulgaria
52 G6 Vurnary Russian Federation
46 F1 Vŭrshets Bulgaria
28 C2 Vust Denmark
48 L4 Vutcani Romania
55 D4 Vvedenka Kazakhstan
100 F8 Vya Nevada U.S.A.
52 E2 Vyalozero, Oz *L* Russian Federation
52 F5 Vyaltsevo Russian Federation
29 P9 Vyartsilya Russian Federation
52 G5 Vyatka *R* Russian Federation
52 H6 Vyatskiye Polyany Russian Federation
59 K2 Vyazemskiy Russian Federation
54 E1 Vyazma *R* Russian Federation
54 F1 Vyaz'ma Russian Federation
52 F6 Vyazniki Russian Federation
52 C6 Vybor Russian Federation
29 O11 Vyborg Russian Federation
29 N11 Vyborgskiy Zaliv *G* Russian Federation
52 H4 Vychegda *R* Russian Federation
31 J5 Vychodočeský *reg* Czech Rep
56 F5 Vydrino Russian Federation
52 E3 Vyg *R* Russian Federation
48 N4 Vygoda Ukraine
54 F3 Vygonichi Russian Federation
52 D3 Vygozero, Oz *L* Russian Federation
52 F6 Vyksa Russian Federation
52 H3 Vym' *R* Russian Federation
52 G4 Vymsk Russian Federation
52 C5 Vyra Russian Federation
52 D5 Vyritsa Russian Federation
8 C2 Vyrnwy, L Wales
8 C2 Vyrnwy R Wales
54 B6 Vyshgorod Ukraine
31 K6 Vyškov Czech Rep
31 L6 Vysoká *mt* Czech Rep
52 G6 Vysokaya Gora Russian Federation
52 J4 Vysokaya Parma *plateau* Russian Federation
31 J6 Vysoké Mýto Czech Rep
59 L1 Vysokogornyy Russian Federation
52 E6 Vysokovsk Russian Federation
31 O3 Vysokoye Belarus
29 O11 Vysotsk Russian Federation
38 K4 Vyšší Brod Czech Rep
52 E4 Vytegra Russian Federation
52 G3 Vyya *R* Russian Federation
59 M2 Vzmor'ye Russian Federation

W

85 D6 Wa Ghana
86 H5 Waajid Somalia
25 D5 Waal *R* Netherlands
25 B5 Waalhaven Netherlands
25 D5 Waalwijk Netherlands
80 H2 Waamo lidow Kenya
25 D2 Waardgronden Netherlands
22 F1 Waarschoot Belgium
120 D2 Wababimiga L Ontario Canada
118 C5 Wabamun Alberta Canada
123 U6 Wabana Newfoundland Canada
117 Q7 Wabasca *R* Alberta Canada
118 D3 Wabasca Alberta Canada
110 J3 Wabash *R* U.S.A.
111 F7 Wabash Arkansas U.S.A.
94 B6 Wabash Indiana U.S.A.
99 O5 Wabasha Minnesota U.S.A.
113 G10 Wabasso Florida U.S.A.
99 L5 Wabasso Minnesota U.S.A.
120 F4 Wabatongushi L Ontario Canada
99 S4 Wabeno Wisconsin U.S.A.
Wabern *see* Egling
118 K1 Wabigoon Ontario Canada
121 R4 Wabino *R* Quebec Canada
120 A2 Wabinosh L Ontario Canada
120 C2 Waboose Dam Ontario Canada
120 F6 Wabos Ontario Canada
119 T4 Wabowden Manitoba Canada
31 L2 Wąbrzezno Poland
58 G5 Wabu Hu *L* China
115 N7 Wabush Labrador, Nfld Canada
102 E2 Wabuska Nevada U.S.A.
112 H4 Waccamaw *R* South Carolina U.S.A.
112 J3 Waccamaw, L North Carolina U.S.A.
113 D8 Waccasassa B Florida U.S.A.
95 M9 Wachapreague Virginia U.S.A.
36 H5 Wachbach Germany
36 E5 Wachenheim Germany
37 K4 Wachenroth Germany
33 R7 Wachow Germany
22 F1 Wachtbeke Belgium
25 F6 Wachtendonk Germany
36 G3 Wächtersbach Germany
32 G7 Wachtum Germany
95 Q4 Wachusett Res Massachusetts U.S.A.
135 M11 Wachusett Shoal Pacific Oc
71 H7 Waci Indonesia
32 K4 Wacken Germany
122 G2 Waco Quebec Canada
98 J9 Waco Nebraska U.S.A.
109 K4 Waco Texas U.S.A.
99 N5 Waconia Minnesota U.S.A.
122 G2 Wacouno R Quebec Canada
77 K6 Wad Pakistan
142 D6 Wadara Ra W Australia Australia
60 H10 Wadayama Japan
86 E3 Wad Banda Sudan
139 H8 Waddamana Tasmania Australia
84 F4 Waddān Libya
25 D2 Waddenzee Netherlands
9 F4 Waddesdon England
9 F1 Waddington England
95 M2 Waddington New York U.S.A.
117 L10 Waddington, Mt British Columbia Canada
94 B8 Waddy Kentucky U.S.A.
141 L7 Waddy Pt Queensland Australia
112 J2 Wade North Carolina U.S.A.
8 B7 Wadebridge England
119 O7 Wadena Saskatchewan Canada
99 L3 Wadena Minnesota U.S.A.
36 B4 Wadern Germany
32 H9 Wadersloh Germany
112 G3 Wadesboro North Carolina U.S.A.
123 T4 Wadham Is Newfoundland Canada
117 K10 Wadhams British Columbia Canada
9 G5 Wadhurst England
80 G6 Wadi es Sir Jordan
84 K5 Wâdi Gimâl I Egypt
86 F1 Wadi Halfa Sudan
79 F8 Wādi Mūsā Jordan
111 L8 Wadley Alabama U.S.A.
112 E5 Wadley Georgia U.S.A.
86 F3 Wad Medani Sudan
31 L6 Wadowice Poland
102 E2 Wadsworth Nevada U.S.A.
94 F5 Wadsworth Ohio U.S.A.
13 G6 Wadworth England
65 G7 Waegwan S Korea
109 K6 Waelder Texas U.S.A.
68 F4 Waeng Thailand
65 E2 Wafang China
Wafangdian *see* Fu Xian
77 A5 Wafra Iran
61 O6 Waga-gawa *R* Japan
120 B2 Wagaming Ontario Canada
111 H10 Wagarville Alabama U.S.A.
32 J7 Wagenfeld Germany
25 E5 Wageningen Netherlands
139 H6 Wagga Wagga New South Wales Australia
74 E8 Waghai India
36 F5 Waghäusel Germany
143 B10 Wagin W Australia Australia
101 R1 Wagner Montana U.S.A.
98 H6 Wagner South Dakota U.S.A.
107 P6 Wagoner Oklahoma U.S.A.
106 F5 Wagon Mound New Mexico U.S.A.
100 F6 Wagontire Oregon U.S.A.
106 D4 Wagon Wheel Gap Colorado U.S.A.
112 H3 Wagram North Carolina U.S.A.
31 K3 Wągrowiec Poland
100 J3 Waha Idaho U.S.A.
83 K9 Wahalkada Tank Sri Lanka
145 E2 Waharoa New Zealand
102 R12 Wahiawa Hawaiian Is
145 E2 Wahi,L New Zealand
36 F4 Wahlen Germany
36 C2 Wahn Germany
32 K7 Wahnebergen Germany
98 K8 Wahoo Nebraska U.S.A.
98 K3 Wahpeton North Dakota U.S.A.
33 S9 Wahrenbrück Germany
33 N7 Wahrenholz Germany
103 L3 Wah Wah Mts Utah U.S.A.
76 A2 Wai India
135 U6 Waiahukini Hawaiian Is
135 T3 Waiakoa Hawaiian Is
135 O1 Waialeale *pk* Hawaiian Is
102 R11 Waialee Hawaiian Is
102 R11 Waialua Hawaiian Is
102 R12 Waianae Hawaiian Is
102 R12 Waianae Ra Hawaiian Is
144 C6 Waianakarua New Zealand
144 B7 Waianiwa New Zealand
145 G2 Waiapu *R* New Zealand
144 B6 Waiatoto R New Zealand
144 D5 Waiau New Zealand
144 A6 Waiau *R* New Zealand
145 F3 Waiau R New Zealand
36 G6 Waiblingen Germany
37 N4 Waidhaus Germany
31 J7 Waidhofen Austria
38 L6 Waidhofen an der Ybbs Austria
71 B3 Waigama Indonesia
143 G8 Waigen Lakes W Australia Australia
71 C3 Waigeo W Irian
71 C3 Waigeo *isld* W Irian
37 J4 Waigolshausen Germany
144 C6 Waihao Forks New Zealand
145 D1 Waiharara New Zealand
145 E2 Waiheke I New Zealand
145 E2 Waihi New Zealand
144 A7 Waihoaka New Zealand
144 C7 Waihola New Zealand
145 D4 Waihopai *R* New Zealand
145 D1 Waihopo New Zealand
144 C5 Waiho R New Zealand
145 E2 Waihou New Zealand
145 E2 Waihou R New Zealand
145 F3 Waihua New Zealand
71 J9 Waikabubak Sumba Indonesia
144 B6 Waikaia New Zealand
144 B6 Waikaka New Zealand
145 E4 Waikanae New Zealand
102 S12 Waikane Hawaiian Is
145 F3 Waikareiti, L New Zealand
145 E2 Waikare, L New Zealand
145 F3 Waikaremoana, L New Zealand
145 E2 Waikaretu New Zealand
144 D5 Waikari New Zealand
145 E2 Waikato *admin region* New Zealand
145 E3 Waikato New Zealand
144 B7 Waikawa New Zealand
145 E4 Waikawa New Zealand
71 J9 Waikelo Teluk *B* Sumba Indonesia
138 E5 Waikerie South Australia Australia
135 U5 Waikii Hawaiian Is
142 A4 Waikiki W Australia Australia
102 S12 Waikiki Beach Hawaiian Is
71 L9 Waiklibang Indonesia
145 F3 Waikohu New Zealand
145 F3 Waikokopu New Zealand
144 B7 Waikotkoi New Zealand
144 C6 Waikouaiti New Zealand
144 A7 Waikouro New Zealand
102 V13 Wailuku Hawaiian Is
144 B7 Waimahaka New Zealand
144 A4 Waimakariri R New Zealand
145 D1 Waimamaka New Zealand
145 F3 Waimana New Zealand
102 S12 Waimanalo Hawaiian Is
144 C4 Waimangaroa New Zealand
71 J9 Waimanguar Indonesia
145 F3 Waimarama New Zealand
144 C4 Waimarie New Zealand
144 C6 Waimate New Zealand
145 E2 Waimauku New Zealand
135 Q2 Waimea Hawaiian Is
135 U4 Waimea Hawaiian Is
102 R11 Waimea B Hawaiian Is
70 G6 Waimenda Sulawesi
22 L3 Waimes Belgium
145 E3 Waimiha New Zealand
9 G1 Wainfleet England
71 K9 Waingapu Sumba Indonesia
145 E4 Waingawa New Zealand
135 O1 Wainiha Hawaiian Is
144 C5 Wainihinihi New Zealand
99 S3 Wainola Michigan U.S.A.
144 C6 Wainono Lagoon New Zealand
118 G6 Wainwright Alberta Canada
116 G1 Wainwright Alaska U.S.A.
145 F3 Waioeka R New Zealand
135 U6 Waiohinu Hawaiian Is
145 E1 Waiolira New Zealand
145 F3 Waiotapu New Zealand
145 E3 Waiouru New Zealand
144 B7 Waipahi New Zealand
102 R12 Waipahu Hawaiian Is
145 F3 Waipaoa New Zealand
145 D1 Waipapakauri New Zealand
145 E2 Waipa R New Zealand
144 D5 Waipara New Zealand
145 F3 Waipawa New Zealand
144 C6 Waipiata New Zealand
135 U4 Waipio Hawaiian Is
145 G3 Waipiro New Zealand
144 C6 Waipori, L New Zealand
145 E1 Waipu New Zealand
145 F3 Waipukurau New Zealand
145 F3 Wairakei New Zealand
145 E4 Wairarapa *admin region* New Zealand
145 E4 Wairarapa, L New Zealand
145 D4 Wairau Valley New Zealand
144 B7 Wairio New Zealand
145 F3 Wairoa New Zealand
145 E2 Wairoa R New Zealand
145 E1 Wairua *R* New Zealand
144 B7 Wairuna New Zealand
71 L9 Wairunu Flores Indonesia
37 L4 Waischenfeld Germany
145 F3 Waitahanui New Zealand
144 C5 Waitaha R New Zealand
144 B6 Waitahuna New Zealand
145 E2 Waitakaruru New Zealand
144 C6 Waitaki, L New Zealand
145 E1 Waitangi New Zealand
145 E3 Waitara New Zealand
145 E4 Waitarere New Zealand
144 D6 Waitati New Zealand
140 B5 Waite *R* N Terr Australia
145 F1 Waitemata Harb New Zealand
143 D8 Waite, Mt W Australia Australia
145 E2 Waitoa New Zealand
145 E3 Waitomo New Zealand
145 E3 Waitotara *R* New Zealand
145 E3 Waitotara New Zealand
100 G3 Waitsburg Washington U.S.A.
119 M6 Waitville Saskatchewan Canada
145 E2 Waiuku New Zealand
144 C5 Waiuta New Zealand
145 E2 Waiwera New Zealand
144 B7 Waiwera South New Zealand
71 B1 Wajabula Halmahera Indonesia
71 C2 Wajag *isld* Indonesia
71 B2 Wajamli Indonesia
61 K8 Wajima Japan
86 H5 Wajir Kenya
86 D5 Waka Zaire
60 D12 Wakamatsu Japan
60 B12 Wakamatsu-jima *isld* Japan
120 H5 Wakami L Ontario Canada
144 C5 Wakanui New Zealand
145 F3 Wakarara Range New Zealand
94 A5 Wakarusa Indiana U.S.A.
61 J10 Wakasa-wan *B* Japan
144 B6 Wakatipu, L New Zealand
119 M6 Wakaw Saskatchewan Canada
60 J11 Wakayama Japan
60 J12 Wakayama *prefect* Japan
61 P7 Wakayanagi Japan
107 L2 Wa Keeney Kansas U.S.A.
121 P7 Wakefield Quebec Canada
13 G6 Wakefield England
127 J2 Wakefield Jamaica
145 D4 Wakefield New Zealand
107 O2 Wakefield Kansas U.S.A.
99 R3 Wakefield Michigan U.S.A.
98 K7 Wakefield Nebraska U.S.A.
95 Q5 Wakefield Rhode I U.S.A.
95 K10 Wakefield Virginia U.S.A.
112 J2 Wake Forest North Carolina U.S.A.
134 H6 Wake I Pacific Oc
68 B4 Wakema Burma
122 H5 Wakenam Quebec Canada
94 A5 Wakerton Indiana U.S.A.
74 E1 Wakhan *reg* Afghanistan
60 H11 Waki Japan
60 O4 Wakinosawa Japan
107 N5 Wakita Oklahoma U.S.A.
60 P1 Wakkanai Japan
87 F11 Wakkerstroom S Africa
Wako *see* Watcomb
120 G6 Wakomata L Ontario Canada
139 G6 Wakool New South Wales Australia
119 S9 Wakopa Manitoba Canada
71 H7 Wakoru Indonesia
98 F4 Wakpala South Dakota U.S.A.
71 C3 Wakre W Irian
71 K9 Waku Indonesia
87 C8 Waku Kungo Angola
113 C7 Wakulla Florida U.S.A.
120 K2 Wakwayowkastic *R* Ontario Canada
103 L6 Walapai Arizona U.S.A.
83 K11 Walawe Ganga *R* Sri Lanka
33 O8 Walbeck Germany
36 D6 Walbourg France
94 D5 Walbridge Ohio U.S.A.
31 J5 Wałbrzych Poland
36 H1 Walburg Germany
139 K4 Walcha New South Wales Australia
38 G7 Walchen Austria
41 O2 Walchensee *L* Germany
25 A5 Walcheren Netherlands
38 F6 Walchsee Austria
117 K8 Walcott British Columbia Canada
98 K3 Walcott North Dakota U.S.A.
101 T8 Walcott Wyoming U.S.A.
142 E3 Walcott Inlet W Australia
101 M7 Walcott, L., Res Idaho U.S.A.
22 G3 Walcourt Belgium
31 J2 Wałcz Poland
38 L5 Wald Aist *R* Austria
36 F5 Waldangeloch Germany
36 D4 Waldböckelheim Germany
36 C2 Waldbreitbach Germany
36 D2 Waldbröl Germany
36 G5 Waldbrunn Baden-Württemberg Germany
36 G5 Waldbrunn Hessen Germany
143 B6 Waldburg Ra W Australia
33 T9 Walddrehna Germany
118 K8 Waldeck Saskatchewan Canada
36 G1 Waldeck Germany
101 T9 Walden Colorado U.S.A.
95 N5 Walden New York U.S.A.
37 O2 Waldenberg Germany
36 G6 Waldenbuch Germany
36 H5 Waldenburg Germany
110 F6 Waldenburg Arkansas U.S.A.
37 N4 Waldershof Germany
36 D5 Waldfischbach Germany
118 L6 Waldheim Saskatchewan Canada
37 P1 Waldheim Germany
36 H1 Waldkappel Germany
40 G1 Waldkirch Germany
30 H7 Waldkirchen Germany
36 F4 Waldmichelbach Germany
37 O5 Waldmünchen Germany
37 N4 Wald Naab *R* Germany
25 F6 Waldniel Germany
118 B9 Waldo British Columbia Canada
109 O2 Waldo Arkansas U.S.A.
113 E8 Waldo Florida U.S.A.
107 M2 Waldo Kansas U.S.A.
94 D6 Waldo Ohio U.S.A.
99 T6 Waldo Wisconsin U.S.A.
100 C6 Waldo L Oregon U.S.A.
95 L8 Waldorf Maryland U.S.A.
99 N6 Waldorf Minnesota U.S.A.
100 A5 Waldport Oregon U.S.A.
119 P8 Waldron Saskatchewan Canada
109 N1 Waldron Arkansas U.S.A.
146 G14 Waldron, C Antarctica
37 N3 Waldsassen Germany
41 H2 Waldshut Germany
37 J7 Waldstetten Germany
37 N4 Waldthurn Germany
36 B5 Waldwisse France
71 H5 Waleabahi *isld* Sulawesi
71 H5 Waleakodi *isld* Sulawesi
71 H5 Walea,Selat *str* Sulawesi
70 N9 Waleri Java
8 C3 Wales *princ* U.K.
116 C4 Wales Alaska U.S.A.
99 P2 Wales Minnesota U.S.A.
98 H1 Wales North Dakota U.S.A.
103 N2 Wales Utah U.S.A.
115 L4 Wales I Northwest Territories Canada
85 D6 Walewale Ghana
33 O5 Walfisch Germany
139 J4 Walgett New South Wales Australia
146 B7 Walgreen Coast Antarctica
37 N5 Walhalla *mt* Germany
98 J1 Walhalla North Dakota U.S.A.
112 D3 Walhalla South Carolina U.S.A.
70 N9 Walikukun Java
143 A8 Walkaway W Australia Australia
33 R5 Walkendorf Germany
33 N9 Walkenried Germany
140 B6 Walker *R* N Terr Australia
141 F3 Walker *R* Queensland Australia
100 C8 Walker California U.S.A.
99 P7 Walker Iowa U.S.A.
107 L3 Walker Kansas U.S.A.
111 F11 Walker Louisiana U.S.A.
99 M2 Walker Minnesota U.S.A.
110 B4 Walker Missouri U.S.A.
102 E2 Walker *R* Nevada U.S.A.
98 E4 Walker South Dakota U.S.A.
89 A10 Walker B S Africa
13 E2 Walkerburn Scotland
113 J10 Walker Cay *isld* Bahamas
119 V4 Walker L Manitoba Canada
122 E3 Walker L Quebec Canada
116 K3 Walker L Alaska U.S.A.
102 F3 Walker L Nevada U.S.A.
146 B7 Walker Mts Antarctica
102 G6 Walker Pk California U.S.A.
140 D2 Walker R N Terr Australia
70 D2 Walker Ra Sabah
141 J5 Walkerston Queensland Australia
94 G8 Walkersville West Virginia U.S.A.
120 J8 Walkerton Ontario Canada
112 G1 Walkertown North Carolina U.S.A.
99 U6 Walkerville Michigan U.S.A.
101 N3 Walkerville Montana U.S.A.
98 D5 Wall South Dakota U.S.A.
143 A8 Wallabi Group *islds* W Australia Australia
140 E3 Wallaby I Queensland Australia
141 F3 Wallaby I Queensland Australia
138 C4 Wallaby,Mt South Australia Australia
122 J8 Wallace Nova Scotia Canada
121 M7 Wallace Ontario Canada
100 K2 Wallace Idaho U.S.A.
107 J3 Wallace Kansas U.S.A.
99 T4 Wallace Michigan U.S.A.
98 E9 Wallace Nebraska U.S.A.
112 J3 Wallace North Carolina U.S.A.
98 J4 Wallace South Dakota U.S.A.
94 G7 Wallace West Virginia U.S.A.
120 H10 Wallaceburg Ontario Canada
109 O3 Wallace L Louisiana U.S.A.
118 B3 Wallace Mt Alberta Canada
120 J10 Wallacetown Ontario Canada
144 B7 Wallacetown New Zealand
142 D4 Wallal Downs W Australia Australia
143 C9 Wallambin, L W Australia Australia
141 K8 Wallangarra Queensland Australia
142 D5 Wallani Well W Australia Australia
141 H8 Wallan, R Queensland Australia
140 B6 Wallara Ranch N Terr Australia
138 D5 Wallaroo South Australia Australia
8 C1 Wallasey England
140 B3 Wallaston, Mt N Terr Australia
36 E2 Wallau Germany
139 H6 Walla Walla New South Wales Australia
100 G4 Walla Walla *R* Oregon U.S.A.
100 G3 Walla Walla Washington U.S.A.
138 C2 Wall Cr N Terr Australia
140 C7 Wall Creek N Terr Australia
36 F5 Walldorf Germany
37 J2 Walldorf Germany
37 L2 Wallendorf Germany
37 L3 Wallenfels Germany
32 H8 Wallenhorst Germany
95 M5 Wallenpaupack, L Pennsylvania U.S.A.
41 K3 Wallen See *L* Switzerland
32 L8 Wallensen Germany
139 K5 Wallerawang New South Wales Australia
37 O6 Wallersdorf Germany
36 F1 Wallershöhe *mt* Germany
37 J6 Wallerstein Germany
33 O10 Wallhausen Germany
142 B3 Walliabup W Australia Australia
9 E4 Wallingford England
145 F4 Wallingford New Zealand
95 P5 Wallingford Connecticut U.S.A.
95 P3 Wallingford Vermont U.S.A.
109 L6 Wallis Texas U.S.A.
137 R4 Wallis, Îles Pacific Oc
139 L4 Wallis L New South Wales Australia
99 L7 Wall L Iowa U.S.A.
36 D3 Wallmerod Germany
142 B6 Wall, Mt W Australia Australia
141 K6 Walloon Queensland Australia
94 C1 Walloon L Michigan U.S.A.
95 M9 Wallops I Virginia U.S.A.
100 H4 Wallowa Oregon U.S.A.
100 H4 Wallowa Mts Oregon U.S.A.
15 G2 Walls Scotland
28 C7 Wallsbüll Germany
139 K5 Wallsend New South Wales Australia
33 O7 Wallstawe Germany
32 J8 Wallucke Germany
100 G3 Wallula Washington U.S.A.
141 J7 Wallumbilla Queensland Australia
33 Q9 Wallwitzhafen Germany
9 H5 Walmer England
13 E5 Walney I England
99 R8 Walnut Illinois U.S.A.
107 K3 Walnut *R* Kansas U.S.A.
107 P4 Walnut Kansas U.S.A.
110 H7 Walnut Mississippi U.S.A.
103 N6 Walnut Canyon Nat.Mon Arizona U.S.A.
112 G1 Walnut Cove North Carolina U.S.A.
111 G9 Walnut Grove Mississippi U.S.A.
110 C4 Walnut Grove Missouri U.S.A.
109 O9 Walnut Hills Texas U.S.A.
110 F5 Walnut Ridge Arkansas U.S.A.
109 K3 Walnut Springs Texas U.S.A.
125 M2 Walpatanta Honduras
138 F6 Walpeup Victoria Australia
143 B10 Walpole W Australia Australia
137 O6 Walpole *isld* Pacific Oc
95 P3 Walpole New Hampshire U.S.A.
116 D8 Walrus I Pribilof Is Bering Sea
116 G7 Walrus Is Alaska U.S.A.
9 E2 Walsall England
37 K1 Walschleben Germany
36 E3 Walsdorf Germany
106 F4 Walsenburg Colorado U.S.A.
141 G3 Walsh *R* Queensland Australia
118 G9 Walsh Alberta Canada
106 H4 Walsh Colorado U.S.A.
117 D5 Walsh, Mt Yukon Territory Canada
22 J2 Walshoutem Belgium
25 B6 Walsoorden Netherlands
32 L7 Walsrode Germany
32 E9 Walsum Germany
112 G5 Walterboro South Carolina U.S.A.
111 L10 Walter F. George Res Alabama/Georgia
109 J1 Walters Oklahoma U.S.A.
37 K2 Waltershausen Germany
141 G8 Walter's Ra Queensland Australia
111 G8 Walthall Mississippi U.S.A.
121 O7 Waltham Quebec Canada
9 F2 Waltham England
101 P2 Waltham Montana U.S.A.
9 G4 Waltham Abbey England
9 F4 Waltham Cross England
98 K7 Walthill Nebraska U.S.A.
101 S6 Waltman Wyoming U.S.A.
122 J8 Walton Nova Scotia Canada
120 J9 Walton Ontario Canada
9 F5 Walton England
145 E2 Walton New Zealand
94 A6 Walton Indiana U.S.A.
94 C8 Walton Kentucky U.S.A.
95 M4 Walton New York U.S.A.
94 F8 Walton West Virginia U.S.A.
126 E6 Walton Bank Caribbean
94 B2 Walton Junc Michigan U.S.A.
9 H4 Walton-on-the-Naze England
110 G3 Waltonville Illinois U.S.A.
32 F9 Waltrop Germany
87 B10 Walvis Bay Namibia
90 J12 Walvis Ridge Atlantic Oc
99 S7 Walworth Wisconsin U.S.A.
143 C9 Walyahmoing *hill* W Australia
36 F5 Walzbuchtal Germany
87 C8 Wama Angola
86 A4 Wamba Nigeria
86 E5 Wamba Zaire
87 C7 Wamba *R* Zaire
139 H5 Wamboyne New South Wales Australia
107 O2 Wamego Kansas U.S.A.
25 D5 Wamel Netherlands
100 D4 Wamic Oregon U.S.A.
94 G6 Wampum Pennsylvania U.S.A.
101 R8 Wamsutter Wyoming U.S.A.

77 L3 **Wana** Pakistan
139 G3 **Wanaaring** New South Wales Australia
144 B6 **Wanaka** New Zealand
67 E3 **Wan'an** China
126 A2 **Wanapa** Bonaire Neth Antilles
120 K6 **Wanapitei L** Ontario Canada
95 N5 **Wanaque Res** New Jersey U.S.A.
99 U8 **Wanatah** Indiana U.S.A.
138 F5 **Wanbi** South Australia Australia
98 E6 **Wanblee** South Dakota U.S.A.
112 M2 **Wanchese** North Carolina U.S.A.
138 E3 **Wancoocha, L** South Australia Australia
130 C10 **Wanda** Argentina
59 K2 **Wanda Shan** *mt ra* China
118 E3 **Wandering River** Alberta Canada
37 K2 **Wandersleben** Germany
28 C7 **Wanderup** Germany
33 S7 **Wandlitz** Germany
141 J7 **Wandoan** Queensland Australia
141 G4 **Wando Vale** Queensland Australia
22 K2 **Wandre** Belgium
109 K1 **Wanette** Oklahoma U.S.A.
65 E4 **Wanfu** China
65 C7 **Wanfu He** *R* China
145 E3 **Wanganui** New Zealand
145 E4 **Wanganui** *admin region* New Zealand
144 C5 **Wanganui R** New Zealand
139 G6 **Wangaratta** Victoria Australia
138 D5 **Wangary** South Australia Australia
67 B2 **Wangcaoba** China
65 B5 **Wangcun** China
67 C2 **Wangcun** China
67 B4 **Wangdian** China
65 C5 **Wangdu** China
33 N4 **Wangels** Germany
41 L2 **Wangen** Germany
32 G5 **Wangerland** *reg* Germany
32 G5 **Wangerooge** Germany
9 H3 **Wangford** England
71 K10 **Wanggamet, Gunung** *mt* Sumba Indonesia
67 D4 **Wanggao** China
Wanggezhuang *see* **Jiaonan**
71 H7 **Wangiwangi** *isld* Indonesia
67 D2 **Wangjiachang** China
67 E1 **Wangjiadian** China
67 E1 **Wangjiang** China
68 D5 **Wangka** Thailand
65 G1 **Wangkui** China
Wang Mai Khon *see* **Sawankhalok**
67 C5 **Wangmao** China
67 B4 **Wangmo** China
65 H3 **Wangqing** China
68 D2 **Wan hsa-la** Burma
74 H8 **Wani** India
71 H7 **Wani** *mt* Indonesia
86 E5 **Wanie-Rukula** Zaire
111 F10 **Wanilla** Mississippi U.S.A.
65 E5 **Wanjialing** China
74 D7 **Wankaner** India
32 M4 **Wankendorf** Germany
Wankie *see* **Hwange**
86 H5 **Wanlaweyn** Somalia
119 Q4 **Wanless** Manitoba Canada
12 E3 **Wanlockhead** Scotland
143 G8 **Wanna Lakes** W Australia Australia
32 F9 **Wanne-Eickel** Germany
143 B9 **Wanneroo** W Australia Australia
67 F2 **Wannian** China
68 K3 **Wanning** China
33 S8 **Wannsee** Germany
76 D2 **Wanparti** India
65 C4 **Wanquan** China
125 M2 **Wanquibila** Honduras
65 A7 **Wanrong** China
13 G3 **Wansbeck, R** England
9 F2 **Wansford** England
67 C3 **Wanshan** China
67 D6 **Wanshan Qundao** *islds* China
145 F4 **Wanstead** New Zealand
9 E4 **Wantage** England
36 D6 **Wantzenau** France
120 K6 **Wanup** Ontario Canada
67 C1 **Wan Xian** China
67 C1 **Wanxian** China
65 C7 **Wanyang Hu** *L* China
58 E5 **Wanyuan** China
67 E2 **Wanzai** China
Wanzhi *see* **Wuhu**
33 O8 **Wanzleben** Germany
145 E3 **Waotu** New Zealand
94 C6 **Wapakoneta** Ohio U.S.A.
109 L1 **Wapanucka** Oklahoma U.S.A.
100 E3 **Wapato** Washington U.S.A.
119 N4 **Wapawekka Hills** Saskatchewan Canada
119 Q8 **Wapella** Saskatchewan Canada
101 N6 **Wapello** Idaho U.S.A.
99 P8 **Wapello** Iowa U.S.A.
119 S3 **Wapisu L** Manitoba Canada
117 O8 **Wapiti** *R* Alberta Canada
101 Q5 **Wapiti Ra** Wyoming U.S.A.
110 F4 **Wappapello Res** Missouri U.S.A.
95 O5 **Wappingers Falls** New York U.S.A.
99 O7 **Wapsipinicon** *R* Iowa U.S.A.
119 P2 **Wapus L** Saskatchewan Canada
123 N2 **Wapustagamau L** Quebec Canada
94 F9 **War** West Virginia U.S.A.
140 D1 **Waraga** N Terr Australia
86 H4 **Warandab** Ethiopia
76 D1 **Warangal** India
139 H6 **Waranga Res** Victoria Australia
139 H8 **Waratah** Tasmania Australia
139 H7 **Waratah B** Victoria Australia
99 N2 **Warba** Minnesota U.S.A.
9 F3 **Warboys** England
141 G6 **Warbreccan** Queensland Australia
118 C5 **Warburg** Alberta Canada
32 K10 **Warburg** Germany
138 E2 **Warburton** *R* South Australia Australia
139 H7 **Warburton** Victoria Australia
143 F7 **Warburton Mission** W Australia Australia
143 F7 **Warburton Ra** W Australia Australia
141 H7 **Ward** *R* Queensland Australia
145 E4 **Ward** New Zealand
111 H9 **Ward** Alabama U.S.A.
138 D5 **Wardang I** South Australia Australia
87 E11 **Warden** S Africa
100 F3 **Warden** Washington U.S.A.
32 H6 **Wardenburg** Germany
118 E6 **Warden Junc** Alberta Canada
94 J7 **Wardensville** West Virginia U.S.A.
74 H8 **Wardha** India
115 M1 **Ward Hunt I** Northwest Territories Canada
118 F8 **Wardlow** Alberta Canada
144 B5 **Ward, Mt** New Zealand
144 A6 **Ward, Mt** New Zealand
118 B9 **Wardner** British Columbia Canada
13 F5 **Wards Stone** *mt* England
117 L7 **Ware** British Columbia Canada
9 F4 **Ware** England
95 P4 **Ware** Massachusetts U.S.A.
145 D3 **Warea** New Zealand
22 E2 **Waregem** Belgium
8 D6 **Wareham** England
22 J2 **Waremme** Belgium
33 R5 **Waren** Germany
140 F6 **Warenda** Queensland Australia
32 G9 **Warendorf** Germany
144 B7 **Warepa** New Zealand
140 B4 **Ware Ra** N Terr Australia
112 E6 **Waresboro** Georgia U.S.A.
112 E3 **Ware Shoals** South Carolina U.S.A.
95 N7 **Waretown** New Jersey U.S.A.
25 G2 **Warffum** Netherlands
86 A2 **War Galoh** Somalia
9 F5 **Wargrave** England
139 K3 **Warialda** New South Wales Australia
33 P5 **Warin** Germany
68 G5 **Warin Chamrap** Thailand
109 J6 **Waring** Texas U.S.A.
116 H3 **Waring Mts** Alaska U.S.A.
13 F2 **Wark** England
31 N4 **Warka** Poland
121 N8 **Warkworth** Ontario Canada
13 G3 **Warkworth** England
145 E2 **Warkworth** New Zealand
8 D3 **Warley** England
9 F5 **Warlingham** England
21 P1 **Warloy-Baillon** France
89 A7 **Warmbad** Namibia
117 G6 **Warm Bay Hotsprings** British Columbia Canada
37 M4 **Warmensteinach** Germany
22 G5 **Warmeriville** France
9 E3 **Warmington** England
8 D5 **Warminster** England
25 C4 **Warmond** Netherlands
32 J8 **Warmsen** Germany
112 C5 **Warm Springs** Georgia U.S.A.
101 N3 **Warmsprings** Montana U.S.A.
102 H3 **Warm Springs** Nevada U.S.A.
100 D5 **Warm Springs** Oregon U.S.A.
94 H8 **Warm Springs** Virginia U.S.A.
100 G6 **Warm Springs Res** Oregon U.S.A.
89 B9 **Warmwaters Berg** *mt* S Africa
8 D6 **Warmwell** England
22 J2 **Warnant-Dreye** Belgium
120 B3 **Warneford** Ontario Canada
33 Q4 **Warnemünde** Germany
101 N1 **Warner** Alberta Canada
95 Q3 **Warner** New Hampshire U.S.A.
107 P6 **Warner** Oklahoma U.S.A.
98 H4 **Warner** South Dakota U.S.A.
100 F7 **Warner Lakes** Oregon U.S.A.
100 E8 **Warner Mts** California U.S.A.
112 D5 **Warner Robins** Georgia U.S.A.
102 H8 **Warner Springs** California U.S.A.
22 D2 **Warneton** Belgium
139 L3 **Warning,Mt** New South Wales Australia
33 Q5 **Warnow** *R* Germany
143 B10 **Waroona** W Australia Australia
74 H8 **Warora** India
141 K7 **Warra** Queensland Australia
138 F6 **Warracknabeal** Victoria Australia
139 H7 **Warragul** Victoria Australia
138 E3 **Warrakalanna,L** South Australia Australia
138 D5 **Warramboo** South Australia Australia
143 C8 **Warramboo** *mt* W Australia Australia
139 J3 **Warrambool** *R* New South Wales Australia
80 G4 **Warran** *R* Jordan
138 E2 **Warrandininna,L** South Australia Australia
142 D5 **Warrawagine** W Australia Australia
141 H7 **Warrego** *R* Queensland Australia
141 H6 **Warrego Ra** Queensland Australia
139 J4 **Warren** New South Wales Australia
120 K6 **Warren** Ontario Canada
111 D8 **Warren** Arkansas U.S.A.
100 K4 **Warren** Idaho U.S.A.
99 R7 **Warren** Illinois U.S.A.
94 B6 **Warren** Indiana U.S.A.
94 D4 **Warren** Michigan U.S.A.
98 K1 **Warren** Minnesota U.S.A.
101 R4 **Warren** Montana U.S.A.
95 Q3 **Warren** New Hampshire U.S.A.
94 G5 **Warren** Ohio U.S.A.
94 H5 **Warren** Pennsylvania U.S.A.
95 Q5 **Warren** Rhode I U.S.A.
109 N5 **Warren** Texas U.S.A.
94 J9 **Warren** Virginia U.S.A.
115 L3 **Warrender,C** Northwest Territories Canada
119 U5 **Warren Landing** Manitoba Canada
143 E8 **Warren, Mt** W Australia Australia
14 E2 **Warrenpoint** N Ireland
99 Q5 **Warrens** Wisconsin U.S.A.
99 R10 **Warrensburg** Illinois U.S.A.
110 C3 **Warrensburg** Missouri U.S.A.
95 O3 **Warrensburg** New York U.S.A.
89 D7 **Warrenton** S Africa
112 E4 **Warrenton** Georgia U.S.A.
110 E3 **Warrenton** Missouri U.S.A.
112 J1 **Warrenton** North Carolina U.S.A.
100 B3 **Warrenton** Oregon U.S.A.
94 K8 **Warrenton** Virginia U.S.A.
101 Q1 **Warrick** Montana U.S.A.
143 B8 **Warriedar Hill** W Australia Australia
138 D3 **Warrina** South Australia Australia
138 D3 **Warriners Cr** South Australia Australia
13 F6 **Warrington** England
144 D6 **Warrington** New Zealand
111 J11 **Warrington** Florida U.S.A.
111 K8 **Warrior** Alabama U.S.A.
138 E4 **Warriota Creek** South Australia Australia
138 F3 **Warri Warri** New South Wales Australia
138 F7 **Warrnambool** Victoria Australia
99 L1 **Warroad** Minnesota U.S.A.
141 J7 **Warrong** Queensland Australia
138 D5 **Warrow** South Australia Australia
139 J4 **Warrumbungle Ra** New South Wales Australia
141 F8 **Warry Warry** *R* Queensland Australia
Warsaw *see* **Warszawa**
99 P9 **Warsaw** Illinois U.S.A.
94 B5 **Warsaw** Indiana U.S.A.
94 C8 **Warsaw** Kentucky U.S.A.
110 C3 **Warsaw** Missouri U.S.A.
94 J4 **Warsaw** New York U.S.A.
112 J2 **Warsaw** North Carolina U.S.A.
95 L9 **Warsaw** Virginia U.S.A.
38 K6 **Warscheneck** *mt* Austria
86 A3 **Warshiikh** Somalia
118 E4 **Warspite** Alberta Canada
32 H10 **Warstein** Germany
31 M3 **Warszawa** Poland
31 H2 **Warszów** Poland
31 J3 **Warta** *R* Poland
31 L4 **Warta** Poland
38 N6 **Wartberg** Austria
37 J2 **Wartburg** Germany
37 M7 **Wartenberg** Germany
13 H6 **Warter** England
41 M3 **Warth** Austria
118 J7 **Wartime** Saskatchewan Canada
13 F6 **Warton** England
142 F3 **Warton Ra** W Australia Australia
110 K6 **Wartrace** Tennessee U.S.A.
70 E5 **Waru** Kalimantan
141 K8 **Warwick** Queensland Australia
121 T7 **Warwick** Quebec Canada
9 E3 **Warwick** England
13 F4 **Warwick** Cumbria England
112 D6 **Warwick** Georgia U.S.A.
95 N5 **Warwick** New York U.S.A.
98 H2 **Warwick** North Dakota U.S.A.
95 Q5 **Warwick** Rhode I U.S.A.
140 D2 **Warwick Chan** N Terr Australia
9 E3 **Warwickshire** *co* England
117 Q11 **Wasa** British Columbia Canada
120 K8 **Wasaga Beach** Ontario Canada
85 F6 **Wasagu** Nigeria
103 N2 **Wasatch Ra** Utah U.S.A.
102 E6 **Wasco** California U.S.A.
100 E4 **Wasco** Oregon U.S.A.
99 P3 **Wascott** Wisconsin U.S.A.
118 H5 **Waseca** Saskatchewan Canada
99 N5 **Waseca** Minnesota U.S.A.
121 L8 **Washago** Ontario Canada
101 Q6 **Washakie Needles** *mts* Wyoming U.S.A.
9 H3 **Washbrook** England
99 R9 **Washburn** Illinois U.S.A.
95 S7 **Washburn** Maine U.S.A.
98 E2 **Washburn** North Dakota U.S.A.
108 C8 **Washburn** Texas U.S.A.
114 J3 **Washburn L** Northwest Territories Canada
101 P5 **Washburn,Mt** Wyoming U.S.A.
144 C6 **Washdyke** New Zealand
8 C5 **Washford** England
60 H12 **Washiki** Japan
123 M3 **Washikuti** Quebec Canada
74 G8 **Wāshīm** India
121 S3 **Washimeska** *R* Quebec Canada
97 **Washington** *conurbation* District of Columbia
13 G4 **Washington** England
100 F2 **Washington** *state* U.S.A.
109 O2 **Washington** Arkansas U.S.A.
112 E4 **Washington** Georgia U.S.A.
99 R9 **Washington** Illinois U.S.A.
110 J3 **Washington** Indiana U.S.A.
99 P8 **Washington** Iowa U.S.A.
107 N2 **Washington** Kansas U.S.A.
111 D11 **Washington** Louisiana U.S.A.
110 E3 **Washington** Missouri U.S.A.
95 P3 **Washington** New Hampshire U.S.A.
95 N6 **Washington** New Jersey U.S.A.
112 K2 **Washington** North Carolina U.S.A.
94 G6 **Washington** Pennsylvania U.S.A.
109 L5 **Washington** Texas U.S.A.
103 L4 **Washington** Utah U.S.A.
94 J8 **Washington** Virginia U.S.A.
146 C12 **Washington, Cape** Antarctica
94 D7 **Washington Court Ho** Ohio U.S.A.
99 U4 **Washington I** Wisconsin U.S.A.
113 G9 **Washington,L** Florida U.S.A.
115 N1 **Washington Land** Greenland
95 Q2 **Washington, Mt** New Hampshire U.S.A.
109 J1 **Washita** *R* Oklahoma U.S.A.
101 Q4 **Washoe** Montana U.S.A.
100 C4 **Washougal** Washington U.S.A.
119 V7 **Washow B** Manitoba Canada
9 G2 **Wash, The** *G* England
100 G3 **Washtucna** Washington U.S.A.
22 G4 **Wasigny** France
31 O2 **Wasilków** Poland
71 N8 **Wasiri** Indonesia
79 E9 **Wasit** Egypt
78 K5 **Wāsit** *prov* Iraq
98 F1 **Waskada** Manitoba Canada
119 V2 **Waskaiowaka L** Manitoba Canada
118 L5 **Waskesiu L** Saskatchewan Canada
118 L5 **Waskesiu Lake** Saskatchewan Canada
118 E4 **Wasketenau** Alberta Canada
99 M1 **Waskish** Minnesota U.S.A.
109 N3 **Waskom** Texas U.S.A.
22 F3 **Wasmes** Belgium
31 K4 **Wąsosz** Poland
60 Q1 **Wassamu** Japan
112 F6 **Wassaw Sd** Georgia U.S.A.
36 C6 **Wasselonne** France
25 F6 **Wassenberg** Germany
37 J6 **Wasseralfingen** Germany
22 L4 **Wasserbillig** Luxembourg
37 K5 **Wassermungenau** Germany
37 K5 **Wassertrüdingen** Germany
22 F3 **Wassigny** France
102 F3 **Wassuk Ra** Nevada U.S.A.
19 J4 **Wassy** France
98 D5 **Wasta** South Dakota U.S.A.
79 B9 **Wasta,El** Egypt
13 E5 **Wast Water** *L* England
37 J2 **Wasungen** Germany
121 O3 **Waswanipi** Quebec Canada
120 K4 **Watabeag L** Ontario Canada
99 Q8 **Wataga** Illinois U.S.A.
83 L11 **Watagoda** *mt* Sri Lanka
70 G7 **Watampone** Sulawesi
71 L9 **Watanga, Teluk** *B* Flores Indonesia
70 F7 **Watansoppeng** Sulawesi
98 E4 **Watauga** South Dakota U.S.A.
109 M9 **Watauga** Texas U.S.A.
8 C5 **Watchet** England
118 L1 **Watcomb** Ontario Canada
9 G3 **Waterbeach** England
87 C10 **Waterberg Plateau Park** *nat park* Namibia
95 R3 **Waterboro** Maine U.S.A.
95 O5 **Waterbury** Connecticut U.S.A.
95 P2 **Waterbury** Vermont U.S.A.
126 F3 **Water Cays** *islds* Bahamas
112 G3 **Wateree L** South Carolina U.S.A.
120 K10 **Waterford** Ontario Canada
14 D4 **Waterford** *co* Ireland
14 D4 **Waterford** Ireland
102 D4 **Waterford** California U.S.A.
94 H5 **Waterford** Pennsylvania U.S.A.
14 E4 **Waterford Hbr** Ireland
8 A7 **Watergate B** England
119 S6 **Waterhan L** Manitoba Canada
118 J4 **Waterhen L** Saskatchewan Canada
140 C2 **Waterhouse** *R* N Terr Australia
140 C6 **Waterhouse Ra** N Terr Australia
140 A3 **Waterloo** N Terr Australia
22 G2 **Waterloo** Belgium
121 S7 **Waterloo** Quebec Canada
127 O2 **Waterloo** Trinidad
110 H7 **Waterloo** Alabama U.S.A.
109 O2 **Waterloo** Arkansas U.S.A.
110 F3 **Waterloo** Illinois U.S.A.
94 B5 **Waterloo** Indiana U.S.A.
99 O7 **Waterloo** Iowa U.S.A.
101 N4 **Waterloo** Montana U.S.A.
95 L4 **Waterloo** New York U.S.A.
8 C6 **Waterloo Cross** England
99 S8 **Waterman** Illinois U.S.A.
111 E10 **Waterproof** Louisiana U.S.A.
94 C2 **Waters** Michigan U.S.A.
99 R3 **Watersmeet** Michigan U.S.A.
118 D9 **Waterton Pk** Alberta Canada
99 N5 **Watertown** Minnesota U.S.A.
95 M3 **Watertown** New York U.S.A.
98 J5 **Watertown** South Dakota U.S.A.
110 K5 **Watertown** Tennessee U.S.A.
99 S6 **Watertown** Wisconsin U.S.A.
138 E5 **Watervale** South Australia Australia
111 G7 **Water Valley** Mississippi U.S.A.
108 G4 **Water Valley** Texas U.S.A.
95 O4 **Watervhet** New York U.S.A.
122 H8 **Waterville** Nova Scotia Canada
121 T7 **Waterville** Quebec Canada
95 S2 **Waterville** Maine U.S.A.
99 N5 **Waterville** Minnesota U.S.A.
95 M4 **Waterville** New York U.S.A.
100 E2 **Waterville** Washington U.S.A.
118 F2 **Waterways** Alberta Canada
70 N9 **Wates** Java
120 J10 **Watford** Ontario Canada
9 F4 **Watford** England
98 C2 **Watford City** North Dakota U.S.A.
107 P2 **Wathena** Kansas U.S.A.
143 B9 **Watheroo** W Australia Australia
117 P8 **Watino** Alberta Canada
106 F2 **Watkins** Colorado U.S.A.
99 M4 **Watkins** Minnesota U.S.A.
115 R4 **Watkins Bjerge** *mts* Greenland
95 L4 **Watkins Glen** New York U.S.A.
112 D4 **Watkinsville** Georgia U.S.A.
107 M6 **Watonga** Oklahoma U.S.A.
70 K9 **Waton,Tg** *C* Java
22 D2 **Watou** Belgium
71 B2 **Watowato,Bk** *mt* Halmahera Indonesia
119 M7 **Watrous** Saskatchewan Canada
106 F6 **Watrous** New Mexico U.S.A.
86 E5 **Watsa** Zaire
99 T9 **Watseka** Illinois U.S.A.
86 D6 **Watsi-Kengo** Zaire
141 F2 **Watson** *R* Queensland Australia
119 N6 **Watson** Saskatchewan Canada
111 E8 **Watson** Arkansas U.S.A.
99 L4 **Watson** Minnesota U.S.A.
99 L9 **Watson** Missouri U.S.A.
101 Q10 **Watson** Utah U.S.A.
117 J5 **Watson Lake** Yukon Territory Canada
95 L5 **Watsontown** Pennsylvania U.S.A.
83 J10 **Wattala** Sri Lanka
22 C2 **Watten** France
15 E2 **Watten** Scotland
32 F10 **Wattenscheid** Germany
138 D3 **Wattiwarriganna** *R* South Australia Australia
139 G3 **Wattle Vale** New South Wales Australia
143 F7 **Watt, Mt** W Australia Australia
117 P6 **Watt,Mt** Alberta Canada
9 G2 **Watton** England
9 F4 **Watton** England
107 Q5 **Watts** Oklahoma U.S.A.
112 C2 **Watts Bar Lake** Tennessee U.S.A.
94 H4 **Wattsburg** Pennsylvania U.S.A.
71 L9 **Watumanuk, Tanjong** *C* Indonesia
70 G6 **Watuwila,Bk** *mt* Sulawesi
38 G6 **Watzmann** *mt* Germany
136 K3 **Wau** Papua New Guinea
86 E4 **Wau** Sudan
120 K7 **Waubamick** Ontario Canada
121 L8 **Waubaushene** Ontario Canada
98 J4 **Waubay** South Dakota U.S.A.
98 J4 **Waubay L** South Dakota U.S.A.
139 L4 **Wauchope** New South Wales Australia
140 C5 **Wauchope** N Terr Australia
119 Q9 **Wauchope** Saskatchewan Canada
113 F10 **Wauchula** Florida U.S.A.
99 O6 **Waucoma** Iowa U.S.A.
100 G1 **Wauconda** Washington U.S.A.
118 F1 **Waugh** Manitoba Canada
142 D5 **Waukarlycarly, L** W Australia Australia
70 F5 **Waukata, G** *mt* Sulawesi
99 N8 **Waukee** Iowa U.S.A.
99 T7 **Waukegan** Illinois U.S.A.
99 S6 **Waukesha** Wisconsin U.S.A.
107 N5 **Waukomis** Oklahoma U.S.A.
99 P6 **Waukon** Iowa U.S.A.
98 E9 **Wauneta** Nebraska U.S.A.
99 R5 **Waupaca** Wisconsin U.S.A.
99 S6 **Waupun** Wisconsin U.S.A.
109 K1 **Waurika** Oklahoma U.S.A.
98 J7 **Wausa** Nebraska U.S.A.
99 R5 **Wausau** Wisconsin U.S.A.
99 T4 **Wausaukee** Wisconsin U.S.A.
94 C5 **Wauseon** Ohio U.S.A.
81 G8 **W Australian Ridge** Indian Oc
99 R5 **Wautoma** Wisconsin U.S.A.
99 S6 **Wauwatosa** Wisconsin U.S.A.
140 B3 **Wave Hill Police Station** N Terr Australia
110 J2 **Waveland** Indiana U.S.A.
141 K1 **Wavell Heights** *dist* Brisbane, Qnsld Australia
9 H3 **Waveney,R** England
122 J9 **Waverley** Nova Scotia Canada
145 E3 **Waverley** New Zealand
100 H2 **Waverley** Washington U.S.A.
112 F6 **Waverly** Georgia U.S.A.
110 G2 **Waverly** Illinois U.S.A.
99 O7 **Waverly** Iowa U.S.A.
107 P3 **Waverly** Kansas U.S.A.
110 C2 **Waverly** Missouri U.S.A.
98 K9 **Waverly** Nebraska U.S.A.
95 L4 **Waverly** New York U.S.A.
98 K4 **Waverly** South Dakota U.S.A.
110 J5 **Waverly** Tennessee U.S.A.
95 K9 **Waverly** Virginia U.S.A.
111 M9 **Waverly Hall** Georgia U.S.A.
141 F7 **Waverney** Queensland Australia
22 C2 **Wavrans-sur-l'Aa** France
22 H2 **Wavre** Belgium
22 D2 **Wavrin** France
118 E6 **Wavy L** Alberta Canada
68 C4 **Waw** Burma
120 F4 **Wawa** Ontario Canada
121 M3 **Wawagosic** *R* Quebec Canada
120 J4 **Wawaitin Falls** Ontario Canada
70 G6 **Wawalalindu** Sulawesi
119 S9 **Wawanesa** Manitoba Canada
84 F5 **Waw an Nāmūs** Libya
94 B5 **Wawasee,L** Indiana U.S.A.
70 G6 **Wawo** Sulawesi
102 E4 **Wawona** California U.S.A.
119 Q9 **Wawota** Saskatchewan Canada
70 G6 **Wawotebi** Sulawesi
109 L3 **Waxahachie** Texas U.S.A.
112 G3 **Waxhaw** North Carolina U.S.A.
111 F9 **Way** Mississippi U.S.A.
71 A3 **Wayakuba** Indonesia
101 O7 **Wayan** Idaho U.S.A.
Wayaobu *see* **Zichang**
112 E6 **Waycross** Georgia U.S.A.
68 F8 **Way,Ko** *isld* G of Thailand
143 D7 **Way, L** W Australia Australia
99 P8 **Wayland** Iowa U.S.A.
94 E9 **Wayland** Kentucky U.S.A.
94 B4 **Wayland** Michigan U.S.A.
99 P9 **Wayland** Missouri U.S.A.
94 K4 **Wayland** New York U.S.A.
118 E7 **Wayne** Alberta Canada
95 R2 **Wayne** Maine U.S.A.
94 D4 **Wayne** Michigan U.S.A.
110 C5 **Wayne** Missouri U.S.A.
98 J7 **Wayne** Nebraska U.S.A.
107 N7 **Wayne** Oklahoma U.S.A.
94 E8 **Wayne** West Virginia U.S.A.
110 H3 **Wayne City** Illinois U.S.A.
112 F4 **Waynesboro** Georgia U.S.A.
111 H10 **Waynesboro** Mississippi U.S.A.
94 K7 **Waynesboro** Pennsylvania U.S.A.
110 J6 **Waynesboro** Tennessee U.S.A.
94 J8 **Waynesboro** Virginia U.S.A.
94 F6 **Waynesburg** Ohio U.S.A.
94 G7 **Waynesburg** Pennsylvania U.S.A.
99 R9 **Waynesville** Illinois U.S.A.
110 D4 **Waynesville** Missouri U.S.A.
112 E2 **Waynesville** North Carolina U.S.A.
94 C7 **Waynesville** Ohio U.S.A.
107 M5 **Waynoka** Oklahoma U.S.A.
98 C7 **Wayside** Nebraska U.S.A.
108 F1 **Wayside** Texas U.S.A.
77 L3 **Wazi Khwa** Afghanistan
77 K1 **Wazirabad** Afghanistan
74 F2 **Wazirabad** Pakistan
31 L2 **Wda** *R* Poland
7 L11 **Weald, The** *reg* England
13 F4 **Wearhead** England
140 D3 **Wearyan** *R* N Terr Australia
141 H3 **Weary B** Queensland Australia
99 M10 **Weatherby** Missouri U.S.A.
107 M6 **Weatherford** Oklahoma U.S.A.
109 K3 **Weatherford** Texas U.S.A.
95 M6 **Weatherly** Pennsylvania U.S.A.
110 C4 **Weaubleau** Missouri U.S.A.
111 L8 **Weaver** Alabama U.S.A.
8 D1 **Weaverham** England
119 V6 **Weaver L** Manitoba Canada
100 C9 **Weaverville** California U.S.A.
118 J8 **Webb** Saskatchewan Canada
111 L10 **Webb** Alabama U.S.A.
111 F8 **Webb** Mississippi U.S.A.
109 H8 **Webb** Texas U.S.A.
110 B4 **Webb City** Missouri U.S.A.
107 P6 **Webbers Falls Res.** Oklahoma U.S.A.
142 G6 **Webb, Mt** W Australia Australia
145 F4 **Weber** New Zealand
106 G7 **Weber City** New Mexico U.S.A.
106 E2 **Webster** Colorado U.S.A.
113 E9 **Webster** Florida U.S.A.
99 O8 **Webster** Iowa U.S.A.
107 L2 **Webster** Kansas U.S.A.
95 Q4 **Webster** Massachusetts U.S.A.
95 K3 **Webster** New York U.S.A.
98 H1 **Webster** North Dakota U.S.A.
98 J4 **Webster** South Dakota U.S.A.
99 O4 **Webster** Wisconsin U.S.A.
99 N7 **Webster City** Iowa U.S.A.
110 F3 **Webster Groves** Missouri U.S.A.
22 H1 **Wechelderzande** Belgium
109 M4 **Weches** Texas U.S.A.
37 O2 **Wechselburg** Germany
71 A2 **Weda** Halmahera Indonesia
83 L11 **Wedagama** Sri Lanka
71 B2 **Weda,Teluk** *B* Halmahera Indonesia
133 E8 **Weddell I** Falkland Is
146 E4 **Weddell Sea** Antarctica
32 L7 **Weddemark** Germany
144 C6 **Wedderburn** New Zealand
100 A7 **Wedderburn** Oregon U.S.A.
32 K4 **Weddinghusen** Germany
32 K4 **Weddingstedt** Germany
32 L5 **Wedel** Germany
140 B6 **Wedge, Central Mt** N Terr Australia
112 G4 **Wedgefield** South Carolina U.S.A.
117 M10 **Wedge Mt** British Columbia Canada
122 G10 **Wedgeport** Nova Scotia Canada
8 D5 **Wedmore** England
9 D3 **Wednesbury** England
111 L8 **Wedowee** Alabama U.S.A.
100 C8 **Weed** California U.S.A.
121 T7 **Weedon** Quebec Canada
9 E3 **Weedon** England
95 L3 **Weedsport** New York U.S.A.
94 J5 **Weedville** Pennsylvania U.S.A.
71 C3 **Weeim** *isld* W Irian
119 P6 **Weekes** Saskatchewan Canada
111 E12 **Weeks** Louisiana U.S.A.
94 E9 **Weeksbury** Kentucky U.S.A.
Weeks I *see* **Puketutu I**
112 L1 **Weeksville** North Carolina U.S.A.
9 H4 **Weeley** England
142 B6 **Weeli Wolli Ck** W Australia Australia
139 J3 **Weemelah** New South Wales Australia
32 F6 **Weener** Germany
98 K9 **Weeping Water** Nebraska U.S.A.
25 E6 **Weert** Netherlands
109 K7 **Weesatche** Texas U.S.A.
28 C7 **Weesby** Germany
41 K3 **Weesen** Switzerland
25 D4 **Weesp** Netherlands
25 G1 **Weestereems** Netherlands
139 H5 **Weethalle** New South Wales Australia
9 G3 **Weeting** England
32 L8 **Weetzen** Germany
139 J4 **Wee Waa** New South Wales Australia
25 F5 **Weeze** Germany
33 O8 **Wefensleben** Germany
33 O8 **Weferlingen** Germany
33 O9 **Wegeleben** Germany
33 O8 **Wegenstedt** Germany
41 H3 **Weggis** Switzerland
32 J8 **Wegholm** Germany
31 J4 **Węgliniec** Poland
31 N1 **Wegorapa** *R* Poland
31 N1 **Węgorzewo** Poland
31 J2 **Węgorzyno** Poland
31 N3 **Węgrów** Poland
38 M6 **Wegscheid** Austria
38 J4 **Wegscheid** Germany
25 F2 **Wehe** Netherlands
40 G2 **Wehr** Germany
32 K9 **Wehrden** Germany
36 F3 **Wehrheim** Germany
65 D4 **Weichang** China
37 L6 **Weichering** Germany
38 M6 **Weichselboden** Austria
65 C7 **Weichuan** China
37 N2 **Weida** Germany
37 N4 **Weiden** Germany
36 E2 **Weidenau** Germany
37 M4 **Weidenberg** Germany
36 H6 **Weidenstetten** Germany
37 L3 **Weidhausen** Germany
94 C3 **Weidman** Michigan U.S.A.
65 D6 **Weifang** China
65 E6 **Weihai** China
58 E5 **Wei He** *R* China
65 G2 **Weihe** China
37 N6 **Weihmichl** Germany
36 E3 **Weilburg** Germany
36 F6 **Weil-der-Stadt** Germany
36 B2 **Weilerswist** Germany
36 H6 **Weilheim** Germany
36 E3 **Weilmünster** Germany
36 E3 **Weilnau** Germany
37 J5 **Weiltingen** Germany
65 B4 **Weilu** China
37 L2 **Weimar** Germany
109 L6 **Weimar** Texas U.S.A.
58 E5 **Weinan** China
110 F6 **Weiner** Arkansas U.S.A.
41 K2 **Weinfelden** Switzerland
36 E5 **Weingarten** Germany
36 F5 **Weingarten** Germany
36 F4 **Weinheim** Germany
67 A3 **Weining** China
36 G5 **Weinsberg** Germany
36 G6 **Weinstadt** Germany
141 F2 **Weipa** Queensland Australia
100 K3 **Weippe** Idaho U.S.A.
141 J8 **Weir** *R* Queensland Australia
121 Q7 **Weir** Quebec Canada
110 B4 **Weir** Kansas U.S.A.
111 G8 **Weir** Mississippi U.S.A.
109 K5 **Weir** Texas U.S.A.
143 B7 **Weiragoo Ra** W Australia Australia
107 Q4 **Weir City** Kansas U.S.A.
119 M5 **Weirdale** Saskatchewan Canada
95 Q3 **Weirs Beach** New Hampshire U.S.A.
113 F9 **Weirsdale** Florida U.S.A.
94 G6 **Weirton** West Virginia U.S.A.
37 N3 **Weischlitz** Germany
100 J5 **Weiser** Idaho U.S.A.
65 D7 **Weishan** China
65 C7 **Weishan Hu** *L* China
65 C7 **Weishi** China
Weishui *see* **Jingxing**
36 B4 **Weiskirchen** Germany
37 L3 **Weismain** Germany
36 F6 **Weissach** Germany
37 K5 **Weissenburg** Germany
37 M1 **Weissenfels** Germany
37 J7 **Weissenhorn** Germany
33 T7 **Weissensee** Berlin Germany
37 L1 **Weissensee** Thüringen Germany
37 M3 **Weissenstadt** Germany
36 H6 **Weissenstein** Germany
37 M3 **Weisser Main** *R* Germany
37 O5 **Weisser Regen** *R* Germany
40 G5 **Weisshorn** *mt* Switzerland
38 L7 **Weisskirchen** Austria
41 N4 **Weisskugel** *mt* Austria
112 B3 **Weiss Lake** Alabama U.S.A.
89 A5 **Weissrand Mts** Namibia
41 K3 **Weisstannen** Switzerland
33 S4 **Weitenhagen** Germany
41 M2 **Weitnau** Germany
67 F4 **Weitou** China
31 H7 **Weitra** Austria
38 N8 **Weixelbaum** Austria
38 K8 **Weixelsdorf** Austria
65 C6 **Wei Xian** China
65 D6 **Wei Xian** China
67 A3 **Weixin** China
67 A2 **Weiyuan** China
38 N7 **Weiz** Austria
41 H2 **Weizen** Germany
Weizhou *see* **Wenchuan**
68 J2 **Weizhou Dao** *isld* China
31 L1 **Wejherowo** Poland
119 S4 **Wekusko** Manitoba Canada
113 F8 **Welaka** Florida U.S.A.
138 C2 **Welbourn Hill** South Australia Australia
94 F9 **Welch** West Virginia U.S.A.
99 M6 **Welcome** Minnesota U.S.A.
89 A8 **Welcome Kop** *mt* S Africa
37 K7 **Welden** Germany
86 G3 **Weldiya** Ethiopia
143 D8 **Weld, Mt** W Australia Australia
119 M6 **Weldon** Saskatchewan Canada
102 F6 **Weldon** California U.S.A.
99 S9 **Weldon** Illinois U.S.A.
99 N9 **Weldon** Iowa U.S.A.
99 N9 **Weldon** *R* Missouri U.S.A.
112 L1 **Weldon** North Carolina U.S.A.
109 M4 **Weldon** Texas U.S.A.
106 G1 **Weldona** Colorado U.S.A.
13 G3 **Weldon Br** England
143 B7 **Weld Ra** W Australia Australia
107 O6 **Weleetka** Oklahoma U.S.A.
141 G7 **Welford** Queensland Australia
141 G7 **Welford Downs** Queensland Australia
83 K12 **Weligama** Sri Lanka
83 L11 **Weliwewa** Sri Lanka
22 K2 **Welkenraedt** Belgium
89 E6 **Welkom** S Africa
121 L10 **Welland Canal** Ontario Canada
9 F2 **Welland, R** England
142 A4 **Wellard** *dist* Perth, W Aust Australia
83 L11 **Wellawaya** Sri Lanka
113 E7 **Wellborn** Florida U.S.A.
36 H1 **Wellerode Wald** Germany
9 E3 **Wellesbourne** England
140 E3 **Wellesley Is** Queensland Australia
117 D4 **Wellesley L** Yukon Territory Canada
98 F9 **Wellfleet** Nebraska U.S.A.
37 L6 **Wellheim** Germany
22 J3 **Wellin** Belgium
9 F3 **Wellingborough** England
139 J4 **Wellington** New South Wales Australia
138 E6 **Wellington** South Australia Australia
123 S5 **Wellington** Newfoundland Canada
122 J9 **Wellington** Nova Scotia Canada
121 N9 **Wellington** Ontario Canada
122 H7 **Wellington** Prince Edward I Canada
8 D2 **Wellington** England
8 C6 **Wellington** England
145 E4 **Wellington** *admin region* New Zealand
145 F4 **Wellington** New Zealand
89 A9 **Wellington** S Africa
111 L8 **Wellington** Alabama U.S.A.
106 E1 **Wellington** Colorado U.S.A.
99 T9 **Wellington** Illinois U.S.A.
107 N4 **Wellington** Kansas U.S.A.
102 E3 **Wellington** Nevada U.S.A.
94 E5 **Wellington** Ohio U.S.A.
108 G1 **Wellington** Texas U.S.A.
103 O2 **Wellington** Utah U.S.A.
115 K2 **Wellington Chan** Northwest Territories Canada
133 C7 **Wellington, I** Chile
139 H7 **Wellington, L** Victoria Australia
143 D7 **Wellington Ra** W Australia Australia
108 E2 **Wellman** Texas U.S.A.
9 F1 **Wellow** England
8 D5 **Wells** England
107 N2 **Wells** Kansas U.S.A.
99 N6 **Wells** Minnesota U.S.A.
101 L8 **Wells** Nevada U.S.A.
95 N3 **Wells** New York U.S.A.
109 N4 **Wells** Texas U.S.A.
95 K5 **Wellsboro** Pennsylvania U.S.A.
99 O7 **Wellsburg** Iowa U.S.A.
95 L4 **Wellsburg** New York U.S.A.
94 G6 **Wellsburg** West Virginia U.S.A.
145 E2 **Wellsford** New Zealand
117 N9 **Wells Gray Prov. Park** British Columbia Canada
143 E7 **Wells, L** W Australia Australia
119 R1 **Wells L** Manitoba Canada
142 F3 **Wells, Mt** W Australia Australia
9 G2 **Wells-next-the-sea** England
95 P2 **Wells River** Vermont U.S.A.
94 E7 **Wellston** Ohio U.S.A.
110 E2 **Wellsville** Missouri U.S.A.
94 K4 **Wellsville** New York U.S.A.
101 O8 **Wellsville** Utah U.S.A.
103 K9 **Wellton** Arizona U.S.A.
119 S8 **Wellwood** Manitoba Canada
38 K5 **Wels** Austria
25 D6 **Welschap** Netherlands
36 B4 **Welschbillig** Germany
36 E1 **Welschenennest** Germany
122 F8 **Welsford** New Brunswick Canada
109 P5 **Welsh** Louisiana U.S.A.
8 D2 **Welshampton** England
142 B2 **Welshpool** *dist* Perth, W Aust Australia
122 F9 **Welshpool** New Brunswick Canada
8 C2 **Welshpool** Wales
13 H6 **Welton** England
32 G9 **Welver** Germany
119 Q8 **Welwyn** Saskatchewan Canada
9 F4 **Welwyn Garden City** England
36 H6 **Welzheim** Germany
8 D2 **Wem** England
86 D6 **Wema** Zaire
142 A1 **Wembley** *dist* Perth, W Aust Australia
117 O8 **Wembley** Alberta Canada
142 A1 **Wembley Downs** *dist* Perth, W Aust Australia
8 B7 **Wembury** England
37 K6 **Wemding** Germany
25 A5 **Wemeldinge** Netherlands
12 D2 **Wemyss B** Scotland
126 F2 **Wemyss Bight** Eleuthera Bahamas
65 C5 **Wen'an** China
100 E2 **Wenatchee** Washington U.S.A.
67 C7 **Wenchang** China
67 G3 **Wencheng** China
85 D7 **Wenchi** Ghana
67 A1 **Wenchuan** China
102 D1 **Wendel** California U.S.A.
101 L7 **Wendell** Idaho U.S.A.
98 K3 **Wendell** Minnesota U.S.A.
112 J2 **Wendell** North Carolina U.S.A.
36 D4 **Wendelsheim** Germany
37 L5 **Wendelstein** Germany
9 G3 **Wenden** England
36 D2 **Wenden** Germany
103 L8 **Wenden** Arizona U.S.A.
65 E6 **Wendeng** China
33 Q6 **Wendisch Priborn** Germany
33 O7 **Wendland** *reg* Germany
9 G2 **Wendling** England
100 C5 **Wendling** Oregon U.S.A.
86 G4 **Wendo** Ethiopia
33 O5 **Wendorf** Germany
9 F4 **Wendover** England
101 M9 **Wendover** Utah U.S.A.
98 B7 **Wendover** Wyoming U.S.A.
98 F5 **Wendte** South Dakota U.S.A.
22 E1 **Wenduine** Belgium
120 G5 **Wenebegon L** Ontario Canada
67 B3 **Weng'an** China
36 B4 **Wengerohr** Germany
67 D2 **Wengjiang** China
67 E4 **Wengyuan** China
65 D7 **Wen He** *R* China
36 G3 **Wenings** Germany
67 A1 **Wenjiang** China
68 K1 **Wenli** China
67 G2 **Wenling** China
141 F1 **Wenlock** *R* Queensland Australia
141 G2 **Wenlock** Queensland Australia
128 A7 **Wenman** *isld* Galapagos Is
32 L8 **Wennigsen** Germany
41 N3 **Wenns** Austria
99 R8 **Wenona** Illinois U.S.A.
67 C1 **Wenquan** China
67 A5 **Wenshan** China
65 C7 **Wenshang** China
65 B6 **Wenshui** China
67 B2 **Wenshui** China
57 K4 **Wensu** China
13 G6 **Wentbridge** England
138 F5 **Wentworth** New South Wales Australia
13 G6 **Wentworth** England
95 Q3 **Wentworth** New Hampshire U.S.A.
98 K6 **Wentworth** South Dakota U.S.A.
122 J8 **Wentworth Centre** Nova Scotia Canada
110 F3 **Wentzville** Missouri U.S.A.
65 B7 **Wenxi** China
65 B7 **Wen Xian** China
37 N5 **Wenzenbach** Germany
67 G3 **Wenzhou** China
113 F10 **Weohyakapka L** Florida U.S.A.
100 B9 **Weott** California U.S.A.
89 E7 **Wepener** S Africa
22 H3 **Wepion** Belgium
69 B10 **We, Pulau** *isld* Sumatra
33 T7 **Werbellin** Germany
33 T7 **Werbellinsee** *L* Germany
33 P7 **Werben** Germany
33 S9 **Werbig** Germany
22 K3 **Werbomont** Belgium
87 D11 **Werda** Botswana
37 N2 **Werdau** Germany
86 J4 **Werdēr** Ethiopia
33 R8 **Werder** Germany
32 G10 **Werdohl** Germany
80 E6 **Wered Yeriho** Jordan
32 G9 **Werl** Germany
32 G7 **Werlte** Germany
36 C1 **Wermelskirchen** Germany
33 R10 **Wermsdorf** Germany
36 H4 **Wern** *R* Germany
37 N4 **Wernberg** Germany
32 G9 **Werne** Germany
37 J4 **Werneck** Germany
117 F3 **Wernecke Mts** Yukon Territory Canada
98 D2 **Werner** North Dakota U.S.A.
33 T7 **Werneuchen** Germany
36 H3 **Wernfeld** Germany
119 U2 **Wernham L** Manitoba Canada
25 C6 **Wernhout** Netherlands
33 N9 **Wernigerode** Germany
37 J1 **Werra** *R* Germany
139 G7 **Werribee** Victoria Australia
138 F5 **Werrimull** Victoria Australia
139 K4 **Werris Cr** New South Wales Australia
32 G9 **Werse** *R* Germany
37 K7 **Wertach** *R* Germany
36 H4 **Wertheim** Germany
37 K6 **Wertingen** Germany
71 M9 **Werula** Indonesia
25 D3 **Wervershoof** Netherlands
32 E9 **Wesel** Germany
36 D5 **Weselberg** Germany
33 R6 **Wesenberg** Germany
32 H5 **Weser** *est* Germany
32 L9 **Weser** *R* Germany
107 J3 **Weskan** Kansas U.S.A.
86 G4 **Weska Weka** Ethiopia
109 K9 **Weslaco** Texas U.S.A.
121 N8 **Weslemkoon L** Ontario Canada
95 U2 **Wesley** Maine U.S.A.
123 T4 **Wesleyville** Newfoundland Canada
94 G4 **Wesleyville** Pennsylvania U.S.A.
32 F5 **Wesse** Germany
32 J4 **Wesselburen** Germany
36 B2 **Wesseling** Germany
140 D1 **Wessel Is** N Terr Australia
98 H5 **Wessington** South Dakota U.S.A.

98 H5 **Wessington Springs** South Dakota U.S.A.
111 D8 **Wesson** Arkansas U.S.A.
111 F10 **Wesson** Mississippi U.S.A.
139 G6 **West** Victoria Australia
32 G8 **West** Germany
111 G8 **West** Mississippi U.S.A.
109 K4 **West** Texas U.S.A.
94 C7 **West Alexandria** Ohio U.S.A.
140 B1 **West Alligator** *R* N Terr Australia
99 S7 **West Allis** Wisconsin U.S.A.
138 C5 **Westall,Pt** South Australia Australia
146 B8 **West Antarctica** Antarctica
13 G4 **West Auckland** England
113 B7 **West B** Florida U.S.A.
111 G12 **West B** Louisiana U.S.A.
109 N6 **West B** Texas U.S.A.
140 A3 **West Baines** *R* N Terr Australia
8 D6 **West Bay** England
111 L11 **Westbay** Florida U.S.A.
119 O7 **West Bend** Saskatchewan Canada
99 M7 **West Bend** Iowa U.S.A.
99 S6 **West Bend** Wisconsin U.S.A.
75 M7 **West Bengal** *prov* India
111 J8 **West Blockton** Alabama U.S.A.
99 L9 **Westboro** Missouri U.S.A.
99 Q4 **Westboro** Wisconsin U.S.A.
119 T8 **Westbourne** Manitoba Canada
99 P8 **West Branch** Iowa U.S.A.
94 C2 **West Branch** Michigan U.S.A.
13 G6 **West Bretton** England
117 O11 **Westbridge** British Columbia Canada
9 E2 **West Bridgford** England
9 E2 **West Bromwich** England
95 R3 **Westbrook** Maine U.S.A.
99 L5 **Westbrook** Minnesota U.S.A.
108 F3 **Westbrook** Texas U.S.A.
95 Q2 **West Burke** Vermont U.S.A.
15 G2 **West Burra** Shetland Scotland
139 H8 **Westbury** Tasmania Australia
8 D5 **Westbury** England
101 O1 **West Butte** *mt* Montana U.S.A.
139 H6 **Westby** New South Wales Australia
98 C1 **Westby** North Dakota U.S.A.
99 Q6 **Westby** Wisconsin U.S.A.
144 A6 **West C** New Zealand
127 H4 **West Caicos** *isld* Turks & Caicos Is
12 E2 **West Calder** Scotland
143 C11 **West Cape Howe** W Australia Australia
99 S8 **West Chicago** Illinois U.S.A.
106 E3 **Westcliffe** Colorado U.S.A.
144 B5 **West Coast** *admin region* New Zealand
109 M6 **West Columbia** Texas U.S.A.
99 O5 **West Concord** Minnesota U.S.A.
102 G7 **West Covina** California U.S.A.
9 G6 **Westdean** England
99 N8 **West Des Moines** Iowa U.S.A.
122 J9 **West Dover** Nova Scotia Canada
141 K2 **West End** *dist* Brisbane, Qnsld Australia
126 E1 **West End** Grand Bahama I
102 G6 **Westend** California U.S.A.
112 H2 **West End** North Carolina U.S.A.
22 D1 **Westende** Belgium
113 H11 **West End Pt** Bahamas
113 J11 **West End Settlement** Grand Bahama I
32 L4 **Westensee** *L* Germany
25 G3 **Westerbork** Netherlands
144 C5 **Westerfield** New Zealand
9 G5 **Westerham** England
22 H1 **Westerlo** Belgium
98 J9 **Western** Nebraska U.S.A.
89 B9 **Western Cape** *prov* S Africa
86 E4 **Western Equatoria** *prov* Sudan
76 A1 **Western Ghats** *mts* India
122 H10 **Western Hd** Nova Scotia Canada
120 K7 **Western Is** Ontario Canada
15 A3 **Western Isles** *reg* Scotland
139 H7 **Western Port** Victoria Australia
94 H7 **Westernport** Maryland U.S.A.
141 G5 **Western R** Queensland Australia
85 B4 **Western Sahara** *reg* Africa
134 A2 **Western Samoa** *islds* Pacific Oc
32 M9 **Westerode** Germany
25 A6 **Westerschelde** *chan* Netherlands
32 G6 **Westerstede** Germany
36 D2 **Westerwald** *reg* Germany
107 M3 **Westfall** Kansas U.S.A.
100 H6 **Westfall** Oregon U.S.A.
8 D2 **West Felton** England
142 B3 **Westfield** *dist* Perth, W Aust Australia
99 T10 **Westfield** Illinois U.S.A.
95 P4 **Westfield** Massachusetts U.S.A.
94 H4 **Westfield** New York U.S.A.
94 K5 **Westfield** Pennsylvania U.S.A.
99 R6 **Westfield** Wisconsin U.S.A.
122 F8 **Westfield Beach** New Brunswick Canada
110 B6 **West Fork** Arkansas U.S.A.
99 M6 **West Fork** *R* Minnesota U.S.A.
98 A1 **West Fork** *R* Montana U.S.A.
110 H4 **West Frankfort** Illinois U.S.A.
141 H7 **Westgate** Queensland Australia
9 H5 **Westgate** England
West Germany *see* **Germany**
8 C4 **West Glamorgan** *co* Wales
95 U1 **West Grand L** Maine U.S.A.
112 E6 **West Green** Georgia U.S.A.
9 F6 **West Grinstead** England
141 J7 **Westgrove** Queensland Australia
9 E3 **West Haddon** England
9 G5 **West Ham** England
94 E8 **West Hamlin** West Virginia U.S.A.
95 P6 **Westhampton Beach** Long I, New York U.S.A.
37 K7 **Westheim** Germany
36 E4 **West Hofen** Germany
109 K6 **Westhoff** Texas U.S.A.
36 C6 **Westhoffen** France
100 B1 **Westholme** British Columbia Canada
98 E1 **Westhope** North Dakota U.S.A.
68 A6 **West I** Andaman Is
83 M8 **West I** Cocos Is Indian Oc
146 J12 **West Ice Shelf** Antarctica
32 G10 **Westig** Germany
127 **West Indies** *arch* Caribbean
94 F10 **West Jefferson** North Carolina U.S.A.
94 D7 **West Jefferson** Ohio U.S.A.
22 E1 **Westkapelle** Belgium
25 A6 **Westkapelle** Netherlands
15 D5 **West Kilbride** Scotland
100 F8 **West L** Nevada U.S.A.
110 J1 **West Lafayette** Indiana U.S.A.
94 F6 **West Lafayette** Ohio U.S.A.
100 A6 **Westlake** Oregon U.S.A.
141 G6 **Westland** Queensland Australia
9 H3 **Westleton** England
99 P8 **West Liberty** Iowa U.S.A.
94 D9 **West Liberty** Kentucky U.S.A.
94 D6 **West Liberty** Ohio U.S.A.
13 E2 **West Linton** Scotland
118 D4 **Westlock** Alberta Canada
120 J10 **West Lorne** Ontario Canada
122 H2 **West Magpie R** Quebec Canada
9 G5 **West Malling** England
94 C7 **West Manchester** Ohio U.S.A.
141 J8 **Westmar** Queensland Australia
121 O7 **Westmeath** Ontario Canada
14 D3 **Westmeath** *co* Ireland
110 F6 **West Memphis** Arkansas U.S.A.
9 G4 **West Mersea** England
94 G5 **West Middlesex** Pennsylvania U.S.A.
9 E2 **West Midlands** *co* England
94 C7 **West Milton** Ohio U.S.A.
106 E2 **Westminster** Colorado U.S.A.
95 L7 **Westminster** Maryland U.S.A.
112 D3 **Westminster** South Carolina U.S.A.
95 P3 **Westminster** Vermont U.S.A.
140 E3 **Westmoreland** Queensland Australia
107 O2 **Westmoreland** Kansas U.S.A.
95 P4 **Westmoreland** New Hampshire U.S.A.
110 K5 **Westmoreland** Tennessee U.S.A.
127 H2 **Westmorland** *parish* Jamaica
103 J8 **Westmorland** California U.S.A.
87 E10 **West Nicholson** Zimbabwe
108 G6 **West Nueces** *R* Texas U.S.A.
8 D2 **Weston** England
144 C6 **Weston** New Zealand
70 D2 **Weston** Sabah
101 O7 **Weston** Idaho U.S.A.
94 C5 **Weston** Michigan U.S.A.
110 B2 **Weston** Missouri U.S.A.
98 K8 **Weston** Nebraska U.S.A.
94 D5 **Weston** Ohio U.S.A.
100 G4 **Weston** Oregon U.S.A.
94 G7 **Weston** West Virginia U.S.A.
98 A5 **Weston** Wyoming U.S.A.
89 E6 **Westonaria** S Africa
8 D5 **Weston-super-Mare** England
109 H2 **Westover** Texas U.S.A.
32 F6 **Westoverledingen** Germany
113 G11 **West Palm Beach** Florida U.S.A.
95 R2 **West Paris** Maine U.S.A.
110 J3 **Westphalia** Indiana U.S.A.
107 P3 **Westphalia** Kansas U.S.A.
94 K5 **West Pike** Pennsylvania U.S.A.
110 E5 **West Plains** Missouri U.S.A.
139 G8 **West Point** Tasmania Australia
122 H4 **West Point** Quebec Canada
116 P4 **West Point** *mt* Alaska U.S.A.
102 D3 **West Point** California U.S.A.
112 B5 **West Point** Georgia U.S.A.
110 J1 **Westpoint** Indiana U.S.A.
99 P9 **West Point** Iowa U.S.A.
94 B9 **West Point** Kentucky U.S.A.
111 H8 **West Point** Mississippi U.S.A.
95 N5 **West Point** New York U.S.A.
95 L9 **West Point** Virginia U.S.A.
111 L8 **West Point L** Alabama/ Georgia
West Polder *see* **Markermeer**
123 Q4 **Westport** Newfoundland Canada
14 B3 **Westport** Ireland
144 C4 **Westport** New Zealand
102 A2 **Westport** California U.S.A.
94 B7 **Westport** Indiana U.S.A.
95 O2 **Westport** New York U.S.A.
100 B3 **Westport** Oregon U.S.A.
98 H4 **Westport** South Dakota U.S.A.
110 H6 **Westport** Tennessee U.S.A.
100 A3 **Westport** Washington U.S.A.
118 A3 **West Prairie R** Alberta Canada
123 M10 **West Pt** Nova Scotia Canada
122 H7 **West Pt** Prince Edward I Canada
98 K8 **West Pt** Nebraska U.S.A.
122 G10 **West Pubnico** Nova Scotia Canada
126 A1 **Westpunt** Curaçao Neth Antilles
13 G4 **West Rainton** England
119 Q5 **Westray** Manitoba Canada
15 F1 **Westray Firth** Orkney Scotland
120 J5 **Westree** Ontario Canada
36 C5 **Westrich** *reg* Germany
117 L9 **West Road R** British Columbia Canada
13 F2 **Westruther** Scotland
123 P2 **West St. Modiste** Quebec Canada
110 H3 **West Salem** Illinois U.S.A.
94 E6 **West Salem** Ohio U.S.A.
99 P6 **West Salem** Wisconsin U.S.A.
145 F3 **Westshore** New Zealand
99 L7 **Westside** Iowa U.S.A.
100 E7 **West Side** Oregon U.S.A.
139 J7 **West Sister I** Tasmania Australia
7 L9 **West Sole** *oil rig* North Sea
95 Q2 **West Stewartstown** New Hampshire U.S.A.
9 F6 **West Sussex** *co* England
13 G5 **West Tanfield** England
25 D2 **West Terschelling** Netherlands
110 J2 **West Union** Illinois U.S.A.
99 P7 **West Union** Iowa U.S.A.
94 D8 **West Union** Ohio U.S.A.
94 G7 **West Union** West Virginia U.S.A.
94 C5 **West Unity** Ohio U.S.A.
117 L11 **Westview** British Columbia Canada
122 K8 **Westville** Nova Scotia Canada
111 L11 **Westville** Florida U.S.A.
99 T9 **Westville** Illinois U.S.A.
99 U8 **Westville** Indiana U.S.A.
107 Q6 **Westville** Oklahoma U.S.A.
94 G8 **West Virginia** *state* U.S.A.
22 D1 **West Vlaanderen** Belgium
8 B5 **Westward Ho** England
103 P2 **Westwater** Utah U.S.A.
111 F12 **Westwego** Louisiana U.S.A.
95 M4 **West Winfield** New York U.S.A.
141 K6 **Westwood** Queensland Australia
102 D1 **Westwood** California U.S.A.
109 L9 **Westworth** Texas U.S.A.
139 H5 **West Wyalong** New South Wales Australia
101 O5 **West Yellowstone** Montana U.S.A.
13 G6 **West Yorkshire** *co* England
71 O8 **Wetan** *isld* Indonesia
71 N8 **Wetar** *isld* Indonesia
71 N9 **Wetar, Selat** *str* Indonesia
118 D6 **Wetaskiwin** Alberta Canada
88 G4 **Wete** Tanzania
121 O3 **Wetetnagami** *R* Quebec Canada
37 M1 **Wethau** Germany
13 G6 **Wetherby** England
68 B1 **Wetlet** Burma
106 E3 **Wetmore** Colorado U.S.A.
109 J6 **Wetmore** Texas U.S.A.
106 E3 **Wet Mts** Colorado U.S.A.
98 H4 **Wetonka** South Dakota U.S.A.
32 F10 **Wetter** Germany
36 F2 **Wetter** Germany
36 F3 **Wetter** *R* Germany
36 F3 **Wetterau** *reg* Germany
22 F1 **Wetteren** Belgium
41 M3 **Wetter Spitze** *mt* Austria
41 O3 **Wetterstein Geb** *mt* Austria
33 P9 **Wettin** Germany
32 F8 **Wettringen** Germany
107 O6 **Wetumka** Oklahoma U.S.A.
111 K9 **Wetumpka** Alabama U.S.A.
68 C1 **Wetwun** Burma
36 F2 **Wetzlar** Germany
37 L3 **Wetzstein** *mt* Germany
36 B1 **Wevelinghoven** Germany
110 E1 **Wever** Iowa U.S.A.
113 B7 **Wewahitchka** Florida U.S.A.
136 J2 **Wewak** Papua New Guinea
107 O6 **Wewoka** Oklahoma U.S.A.
14 E4 **Wexford** *co* Ireland
14 E4 **Wexford** Ireland
14 E4 **Wexford B** Ireland
14 E4 **Wexford Harb** Ireland
118 L4 **Weyakwin L** Saskatchewan Canada
99 S5 **Weyauwega** Wisconsin U.S.A.
9 H2 **Weybourne** England
9 F5 **Weybridge** England
119 O9 **Weyburn** Saskatchewan Canada
38 L6 **Weyer** Austria
36 D2 **Weyerbusch** Germany
99 P4 **Weyerhauser** Wisconsin U.S.A.
36 D6 **Weyersheim** France
33 M7 **Weyhausen** Germany
9 E5 **Weyhill** England
122 G9 **Weymouth** Nova Scotia Canada
8 D6 **Weymouth** England
95 R4 **Weymouth** Massachusetts U.S.A.
141 G1 **Weymouth B** Queensland Australia
141 G2 **Weymouth,C** Queensland Australia
9 F5 **Wey, R** England
25 F4 **Wezep** Netherlands
145 E3 **Whakahora** New Zealand
145 E3 **Whakamaru** New Zealand
145 E3 **Whakapapa** New Zealand
145 E1 **Whakapara** New Zealand
145 F3 **Whakapunake** New Zealand
145 F4 **Whakataki** New Zealand
145 F2 **Whakatane** New Zealand
145 F3 **Whakatane** *R* New Zealand
68 D7 **Whale B** Burma
116 D10 **Whalebone C** Aleutian Is
113 K12 **Whale Cay** *isld* Bahamas
Whale I *see* **Motuhora I**
123 P2 **Whale I** Quebec Canada
9 E1 **Whaley Bridge** England
95 L10 **Whaleyville** Virginia U.S.A.
139 J3 **Whallan** *R* New South Wales Australia
13 F6 **Whalley** England
15 G2 **Whalsay** *isld* Shetland Scotland
13 G3 **Whalton** England
145 E4 **Whangaehu** New Zealand
145 E2 **Whangamata** New Zealand
145 E3 **Whangamomona** New Zealand
145 D4 **Whanganui Inlet** New Zealand
145 E3 **Whanganui National Park** New Zealand
145 G2 **Whangaparaoa** New Zealand
145 E2 **Whangaparaoa Pen** New Zealand
145 D1 **Whangape** New Zealand
145 E2 **Whangape, L** New Zealand
145 E1 **Whangarei** New Zealand
145 D1 **Whangaroa** New Zealand
145 E1 **Whangaruru Harbour** New Zealand
145 E4 **Wharanui** New Zealand
145 F4 **Whareama** New Zealand
13 G6 **Wharfe, R** England
95 N6 **Wharton** New Jersey U.S.A.
94 J5 **Wharton** Pennsylvania U.S.A.
109 L6 **Wharton** Texas U.S.A.
144 C5 **Whataroa** New Zealand
145 F3 **Whatatutu** New Zealand
145 E2 **Whatawhata** New Zealand
99 O8 **What Cheer** Iowa U.S.A.
100 C1 **Whatcom, L** Washington U.S.A.
111 J10 **Whatley** Alabama U.S.A.
68 F6 **Whatthana Nakhon** Thailand
102 C2 **Wheatland** California U.S.A.
98 B7 **Wheatland** Wyoming U.S.A.
98 A8 **Wheatland Res** Wyoming U.S.A.
120 H10 **Wheatley** Ontario Canada
9 E4 **Wheatley** England
110 E7 **Wheatley** Arkansas U.S.A.
99 S8 **Wheaton** Illinois U.S.A.
107 O2 **Wheaton** Kansas U.S.A.
98 K4 **Wheaton** Minnesota U.S.A.
110 B5 **Wheaton** Missouri U.S.A.
8 C5 **Wheddon Cross** England
107 J2 **Wheeler** Kansas U.S.A.
100 B4 **Wheeler** Oregon U.S.A.
108 D8 **Wheeler** Texas U.S.A.
117 Q4 **Wheeler L** Northwest Territories Canada
110 J7 **Wheeler L** Alabama U.S.A.
103 K3 **Wheeler Pk** Nevada U.S.A.
106 E5 **Wheeler Pk** New Mexico U.S.A.
102 F6 **Wheeler Ridge** California U.S.A.
94 E8 **Wheelersburg** Ohio U.S.A.
102 E7 **Wheeler Springs** California U.S.A.
94 G6 **Wheeling** West Virginia U.S.A.
98 C1 **Wheelock** North Dakota U.S.A.
94 E9 **Wheelwright** Kentucky U.S.A.
140 E6 **Whelan,Mt** Queensland Australia
13 F5 **Whernside** *mt* England
9 E5 **Wherwell** England
138 C5 **Whidbey I** South Australia Australia
100 C1 **Whidbey I** Washington U.S.A.
111 M11 **Whigham** Georgia U.S.A.
142 C5 **Whim Creek** W Australia Australia
138 B2 **Whinham, Mt** South Australia Australia
99 M2 **Whipholt** Minnesota U.S.A.
122 F9 **Whipple Pt** Nova Scotia Canada
9 F4 **Whipsnade** England
101 N1 **Whiskey Gap** Alberta Canada
119 T4 **Whiskey Jack Landing** Manitoba Canada
100 C9 **Whiskeytown** California U.S.A.
100 C9 **Whiskeytown-Shasta-Trinity Nat. Rec. Area** California U.S.A.
140 D5 **Whistleduck Creek** N Terr Australia
111 H11 **Whistler** Alabama U.S.A.
9 E2 **Whitacre** England
112 K1 **Whitakers** North Carolina U.S.A.
13 E5 **Whitbeck** England
123 T6 **Whitbourne** Newfoundland Canada
13 G4 **Whitburn** England
12 E2 **Whitburn** Scotland
121 M9 **Whitby** Ontario Canada
13 H5 **Whitby** England
8 D2 **Whitchurch** England
9 F4 **Whitchurch** England
9 E5 **Whitchurch** England
8 C4 **Whitchurch** Wales
111 E7 **White** *R* Arkansas U.S.A.
101 S10 **White** *R* Colorado U.S.A.
99 U6 **White** *R* Michigan U.S.A.
103 J3 **White** *R* Nevada U.S.A.
98 K5 **White** South Dakota U.S.A.
98 F6 **White** *R* South Dakota U.S.A.
108 F2 **White** *R* Texas U.S.A.
103 P2 **White** *R* Utah U.S.A.
100 D2 **White** *R* Washington U.S.A.
99 Q3 **White** *R* Wisconsin U.S.A.
123 Q3 **White B** Newfoundland Canada
118 J8 **White Bear** Saskatchewan Canada
123 P5 **White Bear L** *res* Newfoundland Canada
99 O4 **White Bear L** Minnesota U.S.A.
123 P6 **White Bear R** Newfoundland Canada
100 J4 **White Bird** Idaho U.S.A.
110 J5 **White Bluff** Tennessee U.S.A.
100 F3 **White Bluffs** Washington U.S.A.
122 E6 **White Brook** New Brunswick Canada
98 D4 **White Butte** South Dakota U.S.A.
119 W2 **Whitecap L** Manitoba Canada
111 E11 **White Castle** Louisiana U.S.A.
113 G10 **White City** Florida U.S.A.
107 O3 **White City** Kansas U.S.A.
106 F9 **White City** New Mexico U.S.A.
139 G4 **White Cliffs** New South Wales Australia
99 L10 **White Cloud** Kansas U.S.A.
94 B3 **White Cloud** Michigan U.S.A.
118 B4 **White Court** Alberta Canada
98 D1 **White Earth** North Dakota U.S.A.
108 E2 **Whiteface** Texas U.S.A.
95 O2 **Whiteface Mt** New York U.S.A.
120 J6 **Whitefish** Ontario Canada
117 Q11 **Whitefish** Idaho U.S.A.
99 U4 **Whitefish** *R* Michigan U.S.A.
101 L1 **Whitefish** Montana U.S.A.
99 T6 **Whitefish Bay** Wisconsin U.S.A.
118 E4 **Whitefish L** Alberta Canada
119 O2 **Whitefish L** Ontario Canada
116 K6 **Whitefish L** Alaska U.S.A.
99 V3 **Whitefish L** Michigan U.S.A.
99 M3 **Whitefish L** Minnesota U.S.A.
101 L1 **Whitefish L** Montana U.S.A.
119 N5 **White Fox** Saskatchewan Canada
115 N6 **Whitegull L** Quebec Canada
110 F2 **White Hall** Illinois U.S.A.
99 U6 **Whitehall** Michigan U.S.A.
101 N4 **Whitehall** Montana U.S.A.
99 P5 **Whitehall** Wisconsin U.S.A.
12 E5 **Whitehaven** England
95 M5 **White Haven** Pennsylvania U.S.A.
14 F2 **Whitehead** N Ireland
12 D4 **Whitehill** Scotland
116 N2 **White Hills** Alaska U.S.A.
103 K6 **White Hills** Arizona U.S.A.
117 F5 **Whitehorse** Yukon Territory Canada
100 D8 **White Horse** California U.S.A.
101 L9 **White Horse Pass** Nevada U.S.A.
127 M3 **White Horses** Jamaica
White I *see* **Kvitøya**
146 K9 **White I** Antarctica
115 L4 **White I** Northwest Territories Canada
145 F2 **White I** New Zealand
13 F1 **Whitekirk** Scotland
140 A5 **White L** N Terr/W Aust Australia
142 G5 **White, L** W Australia Australia
111 D12 **White L** Louisiana U.S.A.
99 U6 **White L** Michigan U.S.A.
98 H6 **White L** South Dakota U.S.A.
99 S4 **White Lake** Wisconsin U.S.A.
94 A7 **Whiteland** Indiana U.S.A.
139 J8 **Whitemark** Tasmania Australia
116 F4 **White Mountain** Alaska U.S.A.
14 E4 **White Mt** Ireland
116 O4 **White Mts** Alaska U.S.A.
102 F4 **White Mts** California U.S.A.
95 Q2 **White Mts** New Hampshire U.S.A.
117 P7 **Whitemud** *R* Alberta Canada
86 F3 **White Nile** *R* Sudan
86 F3 **White Nile** *prov* Sudan
86 F2 **White Nile Dam** Sudan
89 A4 **White Nossob** *R* Namibia
112 K3 **White Oak** North Carolina U.S.A.
109 M2 **White Oak Cr** Texas U.S.A.
109 O2 **White Oak L** Arkansas U.S.A.
118 K1 **White Otter L** Ontario Canada
98 D5 **White Owl** South Dakota U.S.A.
9 E5 **Whiteparish** England
100 D3 **White Pass** Washington U.S.A.
94 B5 **White Pigeon** Michigan U.S.A.
99 R3 **White Pine** Michigan U.S.A.
100 K2 **Whitepine** Montana U.S.A.
112 D1 **White Pine** Tennessee U.S.A.
103 J2 **White Pine Ra** Nevada U.S.A.
95 N5 **White Plains** New York U.S.A.
112 G1 **White Plains** North Carolina U.S.A.
123 R2 **White Pt** Belle Isle, Nfld
118 B8 **White R** British Columbia Canada
127 L2 **White R** Jamaica
94 B8 **White R** Indiana U.S.A.
98 F6 **White R** South Dakota U.S.A.
120 E4 **White River** Ontario Canada
95 P3 **White River Junc** Vermont U.S.A.
103 J3 **White River Valley** Nevada U.S.A.
100 J8 **White Rock** Nevada U.S.A.
109 O9 **White Rock** Texas U.S.A.
107 M2 **White Rock Cr** Kansas U.S.A.
103 K3 **White Rock Peak** Nevada U.S.A.
White Russia *see* **Belarus**
117 K9 **Whitesail L** British Columbia Canada
100 D4 **White Salmon** Washington U.S.A.
117 P6 **Whitesand** *R* Alberta Canada
8 B7 **Whitesand B** England
119 P7 **Whitesand R** Saskatchewan Canada
108 A3 **White Sands Missile Ra** New Mexico U.S.A.
108 A3 **White Sands Nat. Mon** New Mexico U.S.A.
95 M3 **Whitesboro** New York U.S.A.
109 L2 **Whitesboro** Texas U.S.A.
112 C4 **Whitesburg** Georgia U.S.A.
94 E9 **Whitesburg** Kentucky U.S.A.
White Sea *see* **Beloye More**
109 L9 **White Settlement** Texas U.S.A.
118 F1 **Whiteshell** Manitoba Canada
100 B4 **Whiteson** Oregon U.S.A.
119 U2 **Whitestone L** Manitoba Canada
101 P3 **White Sulphur Springs** Montana U.S.A.
110 K4 **Whitesville** Kentucky U.S.A.
94 K4 **Whitesville** New York U.S.A.
94 F9 **Whitesville** West Virginia U.S.A.
100 E3 **White Swan** Washington U.S.A.
119 M4 **Whiteswan L** Saskatchewan Canada
98 A1 **Whitetail** Montana U.S.A.
112 J3 **Whiteville** North Carolina U.S.A.
110 G6 **Whiteville** Tennessee U.S.A.
85 D7 **White Volta** *R* Ghana
94 B7 **Whitewater** *R* Indiana U.S.A.
101 S1 **Whitewater** Montana U.S.A.
106 B9 **Whitewater** New Mexico U.S.A.
99 S7 **Whitewater** Wisconsin U.S.A.
113 F12 **Whitewater B** Florida U.S.A.
120 A2 **Whitewater L** Ontario Canada
138 B4 **White Well** South Australia Australia
141 G5 **Whitewood** Queensland Australia
119 P8 **Whitewood** Saskatchewan Canada
98 C5 **Whitewood** South Dakota U.S.A.
98 J5 **Whitewood, L** South Dakota U.S.A.
109 L2 **Whitewright** Texas U.S.A.
139 H6 **Whitfield** Victoria Australia
13 F4 **Whitfield Hall** England
127 H2 **Whithorn** Jamaica
12 D4 **Whithorn** Scotland
145 E2 **Whitianga** New Zealand
117 G6 **Whiting** *R* Br Col/Alaska Canada/U.S.A.
107 P2 **Whiting** Kansas U.S.A.
95 N7 **Whiting** New Jersey U.S.A.
12 C3 **Whiting B** Scotland
95 P4 **Whitingham Res** Vermont U.S.A.
118 K6 **Whitkow** Saskatchewan Canada
118 F9 **Whitla** Alberta Canada
8 B4 **Whitland** Wales
101 O1 **Whitlash** Montana U.S.A.
13 G3 **Whitley Bay** England
94 C10 **Whitley City** Kentucky U.S.A.
98 F4 **Whitlocks Crossing** South Dakota U.S.A.
95 R4 **Whitman** Massachusetts U.S.A.
98 E7 **Whitman** Nebraska U.S.A.
98 H1 **Whitman** North Dakota U.S.A.
100 G3 **Whitman Mission Nat. Hist. Site** Washington U.S.A.
112 F3 **Whitmire** South Carolina U.S.A.
146 C8 **Whitmore Mts** *mts* Antarctica
121 M7 **Whitney** Ontario Canada
8 C3 **Whitney** England
98 C7 **Whitney** Nebraska U.S.A.
103 J5 **Whitney** Nevada U.S.A.
100 G5 **Whitney** Oregon U.S.A.
109 K4 **Whitney, L** Texas U.S.A.
102 F5 **Whitney, Mt** California U.S.A.
109 J7 **Whitsett** Texas U.S.A.
9 H5 **Whitstable** England
141 J5 **Whitsunday I** Queensland Australia
109 J3 **Whitt** Texas U.S.A.
94 G7 **Whittaker** West Virginia U.S.A.
99 M6 **Whittemore** Iowa U.S.A.
94 D2 **Whittemore** Michigan U.S.A.
116 N6 **Whittier** Alaska U.S.A.
102 F8 **Whittier** California U.S.A.
13 G3 **Whittingham** England
139 H7 **Whittlesea** Victoria Australia
9 F2 **Whittlesey** England
139 H5 **Whitton** New South Wales Australia
8 C3 **Whitton** Wales
13 G4 **Whittonstall** England
141 F7 **Whitula** *R* Queensland Australia
9 E1 **Whitwell** England
112 B2 **Whitwell** Tennessee U.S.A.
114 J5 **Wholdaia L** Northwest Territories Canada
138 D5 **Whyalla** South Australia Australia
123 L8 **Whycocomagh** Nova Scotia Canada
139 G3 **Whyjonta** New South Wales Australia
68 D3 **Wiang Pa Pao** Thailand
68 D2 **Wiang Phrao** Thailand
120 J8 **Wiarton** Ontario Canada
31 K5 **Wiązów** Poland
98 B2 **Wibaux** Montana U.S.A.
13 G6 **Wibsey** England
107 N4 **Wichita** Kansas U.S.A.
109 J1 **Wichita** *R* Texas U.S.A.
109 J2 **Wichita Falls** Texas U.S.A.
109 J1 **Wichita Mts** Oklahoma U.S.A.
15 E2 **Wick** Scotland
32 G10 **Wickede** Germany
103 M8 **Wickenburg** Arizona U.S.A.
122 J4 **Wickenden L** Quebec Canada
143 C10 **Wickepin** W Australia Australia
100 C1 **Wickersham** Washington U.S.A.
108 D4 **Wickett** Texas U.S.A.
9 G4 **Wickford** England
95 Q5 **Wickford** Rhode I U.S.A.
142 B5 **Wickham** W Australia Australia
9 E6 **Wickham** England
139 G7 **Wickham, C** Tasmania Australia
140 A3 **Wickham Mt** N Terr Australia
121 S7 **Wickham West** Quebec Canada
100 D6 **Wickiup Res** Oregon U.S.A.
110 G5 **Wickliffe** Kentucky U.S.A.
14 E4 **Wicklow** *co* Ireland
14 E4 **Wicklow** Ireland
8 D4 **Wickwar** England
31 L4 **Widawka** *R* Poland
36 G5 **Widdern** Germany
121 L6 **Widdifield** Ontario Canada
90 A11 **Wideawake** Ascension I
141 L7 **Wide B** Queensland Australia
116 J8 **Wide B** Alaska U.S.A.
8 C6 **Widecombe-in-the-Moor** England
138 B2 **Wide Gum** *R* South Australia Australia
94 G8 **Widen** West Virginia U.S.A.
141 H8 **Widgeegoara** *R* Queensland Australia
143 D9 **Widgiemooltha** W Australia Australia
71 B3 **Widi, Pulau Pulau** *islds* Indonesia
36 F4 **Wiebelsbach** Germany
36 C5 **Wiebelskirchen** Germany
31 K2 **Więcbork** Poland
36 C2 **Wied** Germany
Wiedenbrück *see* **Rheda-Wiedenbrück**
32 H6 **Wiefelstede** Germany
33 O10 **Wiehe** Germany
32 J8 **Wiehengebirge** *hills* Germany
36 D2 **Wiehl** Germany
31 M2 **Wielbark** Poland
31 J3 **Wieleń** Poland
31 M6 **Wieliczka** Poland
31 L4 **Wieluń** Poland
38 O5 **Wien** Austria
38 O6 **Wiener Neustadt** Austria
32 M7 **Wienhausen** Germany
116 M4 **Wien L** Alaska U.S.A.
33 O7 **Wiepke** Germany
31 O5 **Wieprz** *R* Poland
33 N7 **Wieren** Germany
109 O4 **Wiergate** Texas U.S.A.
25 D3 **Wieringen** Netherlands
25 C3 **Wieringermeer** Netherlands
31 L4 **Wieruszów** Poland
Wierzbnik *see* **Starachowice**
31 L2 **Wierzchucin** Poland
31 L2 **Wierzyca** *R* Poland
38 M8 **Wies** Austria
37 N4 **Wiesau** Germany
36 E3 **Wiesbaden** Germany
40 G2 **Wiese** *R* Germany
33 Q8 **Wiesenburg** Germany
36 H6 **Wiesensteig** Germany
37 L4 **Wiesent** *R* Germany
37 J4 **Wiesentherd** Germany
37 L4 **Wiesenttal** Germany
36 F5 **Wiesloch** Germany
32 G6 **Wiesmoor** Germany
32 F7 **Wietmarschen** Germany
32 L7 **Wietz** Germany
32 K7 **Wietzen** Germany
32 L7 **Wietzendorf** Germany
13 F6 **Wigan** England
98 B9 **Wiggins** Colorado U.S.A.
111 G11 **Wiggins** Mississippi U.S.A.
9 E6 **Wight, I. of** England
8 D3 **Wigmore** England
31 O2 **Wigry, Jezioro** *L* Poland
9 E2 **Wigston** England
13 E4 **Wigton** England
12 D4 **Wigtown** Scotland
25 F4 **Wijhe** Netherlands
25 E7 **Wijk** Netherlands
25 C4 **Wijk aan Zee** Netherlands
103 L7 **Wikieup** Arizona U.S.A.
120 J7 **Wikwemikong** Ontario Canada
41 K3 **Wil** Switzerland
83 L11 **Wila Oya** *R* Sri Lanka
98 K9 **Wilber** Nebraska U.S.A.
121 M7 **Wilberforce** Ontario Canada
140 D1 **Wilberforce,C** N Terr Australia
144 C5 **Wilberforce R** New Zealand
101 N3 **Wilborn** Montana U.S.A.
100 B6 **Wilbur** Oregon U.S.A.
100 G2 **Wilbur** Washington U.S.A.
94 E10 **Wilbur Dam** Tennessee U.S.A.
110 A7 **Wilburton** Oklahoma U.S.A.
9 F3 **Wilby** England
139 G4 **Wilcannia** New South Wales Australia
119 N8 **Wilcox** Saskatchewan Canada
99 M9 **Wilcox** Missouri U.S.A.
98 G9 **Wilcox** Nebraska U.S.A.
94 J5 **Wilcox** Pennsylvania U.S.A.
33 T8 **Wildau** Germany
36 F6 **Wildbad** Germany
33 R7 **Wildberg** Germany
36 F6 **Wildberg** Germany
123 Q4 **Wild Bight** Newfoundland Canada
102 H2 **Wildcat Pk** Nevada U.S.A.
119 V3 **Wilde** Manitoba Canada
37 J2 **Wildeck** Germany
37 O2 **Wildenfels** Germany
94 B10 **Wilder** Tennessee U.S.A.
41 O4 **Wilder Freiger** *mt* Austria
117 O9 **Wilderness Prov. Park** Alberta Canada
110 H6 **Wildersville** Tennessee U.S.A.
25 G2 **Wildervank** Netherlands
32 H7 **Wildeshausen** Germany
36 H3 **Wildflecken** Germany
120 A4 **Wild Goose** Ontario Canada
40 F5 **Wildhorn** *mt* Switzerland
101 P1 **Wild Horse** Alberta Canada
100 K8 **Wildhorse Res** Nevada U.S.A.
119 P4 **Wildnest L** Saskatchewan Canada
108 B8 **Wildorado** Texas U.S.A.
33 R8 **Wildpark** Germany
98 K2 **Wild Rice** *R* Minnesota U.S.A.
98 K3 **Wild Rice** *R* North Dakota U.S.A.
98 C1 **Wildrose** North Dakota U.S.A.
99 R5 **Wild Rose** Wisconsin U.S.A.
40 G5 **Wildstrubel** *mt* Switzerland
118 B5 **Wildwood** Alberta Canada
113 E9 **Wildwood** Florida U.S.A.
95 N8 **Wildwood** New Jersey U.S.A.
118 B1 **Wildwood Pk** Manitoba Canada
106 H3 **Wiley** Colorado U.S.A.
36 F6 **Wilferdingen** Germany
120 E2 **Wilgar** Ontario Canada
89 F6 **Wilge** *R* S Africa
138 C4 **Wilgena** South Australia Australia
146 H12 **Wilhelm II Land** Antarctica
129 G3 **Wilhelmina Geb** *mts* Suriname
25 D5 **Wilhelmina Kanal** Netherlands
136 J3 **Wilhelm, Mt** Papua New Guinea
Wilhelm Pieck Stadt *see* **Guben**
32 H5 **Wilhelmshaven** Germany
36 F2 **Wilhelmshütte** Germany
33 O5 **Wiligrad** Germany
70 N9 **Wilis** *mt* Java
95 M5 **Wilkes-Barre** Pennsylvania U.S.A.
112 F1 **Wilkesboro** North Carolina U.S.A.
146 E14 **Wilkes Coast** Antarctica
146 E13 **Wilkes Land** Antarctica
37 N2 **Wilkhau Hasslau** Germany
118 J6 **Wilkie** Saskatchewan Canada
146 D5 **Wilkins Coast** Antarctica
146 C5 **Wilkins Ice Shelf** Antarctica
138 C3 **Wilkinson L** South Australia Australia
112 D6 **Willacoochee** Georgia U.S.A.
103 M6 **Willaha** Arizona U.S.A.
100 B4 **Willamette** *R* Oregon U.S.A.
139 G5 **Willandra Billabong** *R* New South Wales Australia
100 B3 **Willapa** *R* Washington U.S.A.
139 G3 **Willara** New South Wales Australia
138 E2 **Willara, L** South Australia Australia
124 D3 **Willard** Mexico
98 C9 **Willard** Colorado U.S.A.
98 B3 **Willard** Montana U.S.A.
106 D7 **Willard** New Mexico U.S.A.
94 E5 **Willard** Ohio U.S.A.
101 N8 **Willard** Utah U.S.A.
95 M8 **Willards** Maryland U.S.A.
142 E4 **Willare Bridge Roadhouse** W Australia Australia
103 P9 **Willcox** Arizona U.S.A.
32 K9 **Willebadessen** Germany
22 G1 **Willebroek** Belgium
22 E2 **Willems** France
25 C5 **Willemsdorp** Netherlands
126 B1 **Willemstad** Curaçao Neth Antilles
25 B5 **Willemstad** Netherlands
140 B3 **Willeroo** N Terr Australia
8 D3 **Willersley** England
22 H4 **Willerzie** Belgium
9 F4 **Willesden** England
118 C6 **Willesden Green** Alberta Canada
120 B2 **Willet** Ontario Canada
143 B6 **Williambury** W Australia Australia
138 D3 **William Creek** South Australia Australia
119 S5 **William L** Manitoba Canada
138 F6 **William, Mt** Victoria Australia
143 B10 **William,Mt** W Australia Australia
140 F5 **Williams** *R* Queensland Australia
143 B10 **Williams** W Australia Australia
103 M6 **Williams** Arizona U.S.A.
102 B2 **Williams** California U.S.A.
110 K3 **Williams** Indiana U.S.A.
99 N7 **Williams** Iowa U.S.A.
99 L1 **Williams** Minnesota U.S.A.
99 S7 **Williams Bay** Wisconsin U.S.A.
99 O8 **Williamsburg** Iowa U.S.A.
94 C10 **Williamsburg** Kentucky U.S.A.
95 P4 **Williamsburg** Massachusetts U.S.A.
94 C7 **Williamsburg** Ohio U.S.A.
94 J6 **Williamsburg** Pennsylvania U.S.A.
95 L9 **Williamsburg** Virginia U.S.A.
127 K2 **Williamsfield** Jamaica
120 K8 **Williamsford** Ontario Canada
126 E2 **Williams I** Bahamas
117 M9 **Williams Lake** British Columbia Canada
99 N8 **Williamson** Iowa U.S.A.
95 K3 **Williamson** New York U.S.A.
94 E9 **Williamson** West Virginia U.S.A.
123 Q3 **Williamsport** Newfoundland Canada
99 T9 **Williamsport** Indiana U.S.A.
94 K7 **Williamsport** Maryland U.S.A.
95 K5 **Williamsport** Pennsylvania U.S.A.
94 C4 **Williamston** Michigan U.S.A.
112 K2 **Williamston** North Carolina U.S.A.
112 E3 **Williamston** South Carolina U.S.A.
94 C8 **Williamstown** Kentucky U.S.A.
95 O4 **Williamstown** Massachusetts U.S.A.
95 P2 **Williamstown** Vermont U.S.A.
94 F7 **Williamstown** West Virginia U.S.A.
110 F5 **Williamsville** Missouri U.S.A.
141 G8 **Willie's Ra** Queensland Australia
127 P4 **Willikie's** Antigua W Indies
95 P5 **Willimantic** Connecticut U.S.A.
118 E5 **Willingdon** Alberta Canada
117 P10 **Willingdon, Mt** Alberta Canada
32 J10 **Willingen** Germany
9 G3 **Willingham** England
13 G4 **Willington** England
109 M5 **Willis** Texas U.S.A.
94 G10 **Willis** Virginia U.S.A.
40 G3 **Willisau** Switzerland
141 K3 **Willis Grp** *islds* Gt Barrier Reef Aust
87 D12 **Williston** S Africa
113 E8 **Williston** Florida U.S.A.
98 C1 **Williston** North Dakota U.S.A.
112 F4 **Williston** South Carolina U.S.A.
117 M8 **Williston L** British Columbia Canada
110 G4 **Willisville** Illinois U.S.A.
8 C5 **Williton** England
102 A2 **Willits** California U.S.A.
119 P9 **Willmar** Saskatchewan Canada
99 L4 **Willmar** Minnesota U.S.A.
94 F5 **Willoughby** Ohio U.S.A.
138 E6 **Willoughby, C** South Australia Australia
117 M9 **Willow** *R* British Columbia Canada
116 M6 **Willow** Alaska U.S.A.
108 E8 **Willow** Oklahoma U.S.A.
119 P7 **Willowbrook** Saskatchewan Canada
119 M9 **Willow Bunch L** Saskatchewan Canada
98 F1 **Willow City** North Dakota U.S.A.
100 E9 **Willow Cr** California U.S.A.
100 H5 **Willow Cr** Oregon U.S.A.
118 D8 **Willow Cr. Prov. Park** Alberta Canada
117 O4 **Willow L** Northwest Territories Canada
98 J5 **Willow L** South Dakota U.S.A.
117 N4 **Willowlake** *R* Northwest Territories Canada
89 C9 **Willowmore** S Africa
140 C5 **Willowra** N Terr Australia
100 E8 **Willow Ranch** California U.S.A.
99 R4 **Willow Res** Wisconsin U.S.A.
99 O3 **Willow River** Minnesota U.S.A.
94 D4 **Willow Run** Michigan U.S.A.
119 M9 **Willows** Saskatchewan Canada
102 B2 **Willows** California U.S.A.
110 E5 **Willow Springs** Missouri U.S.A.
139 K4 **Willow Tree** New South Wales Australia
95 O2 **Willsboro** New York U.S.A.
142 G5 **Wills,L** W Australia Australia
109 L3 **Wills Point** Texas U.S.A.
138 E6 **Willunga** South Australia Australia
111 H11 **Wilmer** Alabama U.S.A.
33 T6 **Wilmersdorf** Germany
99 T7 **Wilmette** Illinois U.S.A.
138 E4 **Wilmington** South Australia Australia
95 M7 **Wilmington** Delaware U.S.A.
99 S8 **Wilmington** Illinois U.S.A.
112 K3 **Wilmington** North Carolina U.S.A.
94 D7 **Wilmington** Ohio U.S.A.
95 O4 **Wilmington** Vermont U.S.A.
99 L6 **Wilmont** Minnesota U.S.A.
107 L4 **Wilmore** Kansas U.S.A.
94 C9 **Wilmore** Kentucky U.S.A.
111 E8 **Wilmot** Arkansas U.S.A.
94 F6 **Wilmot** Ohio U.S.A.
144 B6 **Wilmot, L** New Zealand
144 A6 **Wilmot Pass** New Zealand
25 C4 **Wilnis** Netherlands
121 N7 **Wilno** Ontario Canada
36 E2 **Wilnsdorf** Germany
83 J9 **Wilpattu Nat.Park** Sri Lanka
138 E4 **Wilpena** *R* South Australia Australia
138 E4 **Wilpena** South Australia Australia
22 G1 **Wilrijk** Belgium
101 P3 **Wilsall** Montana U.S.A.
37 Q1 **Wilsdruff** Germany
32 L6 **Wilseder Berg** *hill* Germany
141 G7 **Wilson** *R* Queensland Australia
110 F6 **Wilson** Arkansas U.S.A.
107 M3 **Wilson** Kansas U.S.A.
111 E11 **Wilson** Louisiana U.S.A.
94 J3 **Wilson** New York U.S.A.
112 K2 **Wilson** North Carolina U.S.A.
109 K1 **Wilson** Oklahoma U.S.A.
108 F2 **Wilson** Texas U.S.A.
101 P6 **Wilson** Wyoming U.S.A.
138 A4 **Wilson Bluff** South Australia Australia
115 L4 **Wilson, C** Northwest Territories Canada
142 F5 **Wilson Cliffs** *hill* W Australia Australia
100 F2 **Wilson Creek** Washington U.S.A.
103 K3 **Wilson Cr. Ra** Nevada U.S.A.
146 C13 **Wilson Hills** Antarctica
106 H3 **Wilson Junc** Colorado U.S.A.
138 A2 **Wilson, L** South Australia Australia
110 J7 **Wilson L** Alabama U.S.A.

142 G5 **Wilson,Mt** W Australia Australia
102 G7 **Wilson, Mt** California U.S.A.
106 C4 **Wilson, Mt** Colorado U.S.A.
103 K3 **Wilson, Mt** Nevada U.S.A.
107 M3 **Wilson Res** Kansas U.S.A.
110 C4 **Wilson's Creek Battlefield Nat. Park** Missouri U.S.A.
139 H7 **Wilson's Promontory** Victoria Australia
12 E2 **Wilsontown** Scotland
98 F9 **Wilsonville** Nebraska U.S.A.
32 K6 **Wilstedt** Germany
32 K5 **Wilster** Germany
140 C2 **Wilton** *R* N Terr Australia
9 E5 **Wilton** England
109 N2 **Wilton** Arkansas U.S.A.
99 P8 **Wilton** Iowa U.S.A.
95 Q4 **Wilton** New Hampshire U.S.A.
98 F2 **Wilton** North Dakota U.S.A.
99 Q6 **Wilton** Wisconsin U.S.A.
9 E5 **Wiltshire** *co* England
22 K4 **Wiltz** Luxembourg
143 D7 **Wiluna** W Australia Australia
22 L4 **Wilwerwiltz** Luxembourg
119 S3 **Wimapedi L** Manitoba Canada
113 E10 **Wimauma** Florida U.S.A.
9 F5 **Wimbledon** England
145 F4 **Wimbledon** New Zealand
98 H2 **Wimbledon** North Dakota U.S.A.
118 D7 **Wimborne** Alberta Canada
9 E6 **Wimborne** England
22 B2 **Wimereux** France
113 B8 **Wimico, L** Florida U.S.A.
22 B2 **Wimille** France
38 K8 **Wimitz** *R* Austria
36 C6 **Wimmenau** France
138 F6 **Wimmera** *R* Victoria Australia
118 A3 **Winagami L** Alberta Canada
94 A5 **Winamac** Indiana U.S.A.
88 E2 **Winam Gulf** Kenya
139 G4 **Winbar** New South Wales Australia
87 E11 **Winburg** S Africa
8 D5 **Wincanton** England
12 E2 **Winchburgh** Scotland
9 E4 **Winchcomb** England
109 H4 **Winchell** Texas U.S.A.
9 G6 **Winchelsea** England
95 P4 **Winchendon** Massachusetts U.S.A.
121 P7 **Winchester** Ontario Canada
9 E5 **Winchester** England
144 C6 **Winchester** New Zealand
100 J3 **Winchester** Idaho U.S.A.
99 Q10 **Winchester** Illinois U.S.A.
94 C6 **Winchester** Indiana U.S.A.
94 C9 **Winchester** Kentucky U.S.A.
95 P4 **Winchester** New Hampshire U.S.A.
94 D8 **Winchester** Ohio U.S.A.
110 K6 **Winchester** Tennessee U.S.A.
109 K5 **Winchester** Texas U.S.A.
101 R6 **Winchester** Wyoming U.S.A.
100 A6 **Winchester Bay** Oregon U.S.A.
101 R6 **Wind** *R* Wyoming U.S.A.
138 D4 **Windabout, L** South Australia Australia
101 P2 **Windam** Montana U.S.A.
143 C9 **Windarling Pk** W Australia Australia
Windau *see* **Ventspils**
94 J6 **Windber** Pennsylvania U.S.A.
98 C6 **Wind Cave Nat. Park** South Dakota U.S.A.
36 F3 **Windecken** Germany
36 E5 **Winden** Germany
112 D4 **Winder** Georgia U.S.A.
141 K7 **Windera** Queensland Australia
13 F5 **Windermere** England
120 G5 **Windermere L** Ontario Canada
94 B6 **Windfall** Indiana U.S.A.
95 M6 **Wind Gap** Pennsylvania U.S.A.
95 R3 **Windham, S** Maine U.S.A.
32 K8 **Windheim** Germany
87 C10 **Windhoek** Namibia
143 D7 **Windich Springs** W Australia Australia
121 R5 **Windigo** Quebec Canada
107 P7 **Winding Stair Mts** Oklahoma U.S.A.
37 N4 **Windischeschenbach** Germany
38 K6 **Windischgarsten** Austria
95 M9 **Windmill Pt** Virginia U.S.A.
107 N3 **Windom** Kansas U.S.A.
99 L6 **Windom** Minnesota U.S.A.
106 C4 **Windom Pk** Colorado U.S.A.
141 G7 **Windorah** Queensland Australia
37 P6 **Windorf** Germany
99 T7 **Wind Point** Wisconsin U.S.A.
101 Q7 **Wind R. Ra** Wyoming U.S.A.
37 K5 **Windsbach** Germany
141 K1 **Windsor** *dist* Brisbane, Qnsld Australia
139 K5 **Windsor** New South Wales Australia
123 R5 **Windsor** Newfoundland Canada
122 H9 **Windsor** Nova Scotia Canada
120 H10 **Windsor** Ontario Canada
121 T7 **Windsor** Quebec Canada
9 F5 **Windsor** England
144 C6 **Windsor** New Zealand
106 F1 **Windsor** Colorado U.S.A.
95 P5 **Windsor** Connecticut U.S.A.
99 S10 **Windsor** Illinois U.S.A.
95 P4 **Windsor** Massachusetts U.S.A.
110 C3 **Windsor** Missouri U.S.A.
95 M4 **Windsor** New York U.S.A.
112 L2 **Windsor** North Carolina U.S.A.
112 F4 **Windsor** South Carolina U.S.A.
95 L10 **Windsor** Virginia U.S.A.
94 G6 **Windsor Heights** West Virginia U.S.A.
126 H4 **Windsor L.** Great Inagua I Bahamas
95 P5 **Windsor Locks** Connecticut U.S.A.
109 J2 **Windthorst** Texas U.S.A.
141 F7 **Windula** *R* Queensland Australia
127 O7 **Windward Is** W Indies
126 H5 **Windward Passage** Cuba/Haiti
116 N5 **Windy** Alaska U.S.A.
116 K5 **Windy Fork** *R* Alaska U.S.A.
119 P4 **Windy L** Saskatchewan Canada
117 Q5 **Windy Pt** Northwest Territories Canada
118 G3 **Winefred L** Alberta Canada
99 R3 **Winegar** Wisconsin U.S.A.
94 C3 **Winegars** Michigan U.S.A.
100 E2 **Winesap** Washington U.S.A.
118 C6 **Winfield** Alberta Canada
111 J8 **Winfield** Alabama U.S.A.
107 O4 **Winfield** Kansas U.S.A.
109 M2 **Winfield** Texas U.S.A.
8 D6 **Winfrith** England
98 F2 **Wing** North Dakota U.S.A.
110 J1 **Wingate** Indiana U.S.A.
106 B6 **Wingate** New Mexico U.S.A.
140 B2 **Wingate Mts** N Terr Australia
139 K4 **Wingen** New South Wales Australia
22 E1 **Wingene** Belgium
36 C6 **Wingen-sur-Moder** France
139 L4 **Wingham** New South Wales Australia
120 J9 **Wingham** Ontario Canada
9 H5 **Wingham** England
110 H5 **Wingo** Kentucky U.S.A.
32 K5 **Wingst** Germany
71 M9 **Wini** Timor Indonesia
101 Q2 **Winifred** Montana U.S.A.
98 J6 **Winifred** South Dakota U.S.A.
142 E5 **Winifred,L** W Australia Australia
115 L6 **Winisk** Ontario Canada
68 D5 **Winkana** Burma
25 C3 **Winkei** Netherlands
103 O9 **Winkelman** Arizona U.S.A.
9 F5 **Winkfield** England
37 O5 **Winklarn** Germany
8 C6 **Winkleigh** England
119 U9 **Winkler** Manitoba Canada
38 G8 **Winklern** Austria
100 C3 **Winlock** Washington U.S.A.
95 T1 **Winn** Maine U.S.A.
94 C3 **Winn** Michigan U.S.A.
140 B6 **Winnalls Ridge** N Terr Australia
85 D7 **Winneba** Ghana
99 M6 **Winnebago** Minnesota U.S.A.
98 K7 **Winnebago** Nebraska U.S.A.
99 S5 **Winnebago, L** Wisconsin U.S.A.
142 G6 **Winnecke Hills** N Terr/W Aust Australia
140 B4 **Winnecke,Mt** N Terr Australia
142 E6 **Winnecke Rock** *hill* W Australia Australia
99 S5 **Winneconne** Wisconsin U.S.A.
100 H9 **Winnemucca** Nevada U.S.A.
102 E1 **Winnemucca L** Nevada U.S.A.
36 G6 **Winnenden** Germany
98 G6 **Winner** South Dakota U.S.A.
99 T7 **Winnetka** Illinois U.S.A.
98 H7 **Winnetoon** Nebraska U.S.A.
101 R2 **Winnett** Montana U.S.A.
109 P4 **Winnfield** Louisiana U.S.A.
99 M2 **Winnibigoshish L** Minnesota U.S.A.
109 N6 **Winnie** Texas U.S.A.
118 F9 **Winnifred** Alberta Canada
33 O9 **Winnigen** Germany
142 A6 **Winning** W Australia Australia
36 D3 **Winningen** Germany
118 A1 **Winnipeg** Manitoba Canada
119 V8 **Winnipeg Beach** Manitoba Canada
119 T5 **Winnipeg, L** Manitoba Canada
119 S7 **Winnipegosis** Manitoba Canada
119 R6 **Winnipegosis, L** Manitoba Canada
95 Q3 **Winnipesaukee, L** New Hampshire U.S.A.
111 E9 **Winnsboro** Louisiana U.S.A.
112 F3 **Winnsboro** South Carolina U.S.A.
109 M3 **Winnsboro** Texas U.S.A.
112 E6 **Winokur** Georgia U.S.A.
103 N6 **Winona** Arizona U.S.A.
107 J2 **Winona** Kansas U.S.A.
99 S3 **Winona** Michigan U.S.A.
99 P5 **Winona** Minnesota U.S.A.
110 E4 **Winona** Missouri U.S.A.
109 M3 **Winona** Texas U.S.A.
100 H3 **Winona** Washington U.S.A.
109 P1 **Winona, L** Arkansas U.S.A.
95 O2 **Winooski** Vermont U.S.A.
95 P2 **Winooski** *R* Vermont U.S.A.
25 H2 **Winschoten** Netherlands
32 M6 **Winsen** Germany
32 L7 **Winsen** Germany
8 D1 **Winsford** England
98 J7 **Winside** Nebraska U.S.A.
9 F4 **Winslow** England
103 O6 **Winslow** Arizona U.S.A.
110 B6 **Winslow** Arkansas U.S.A.
110 J3 **Winslow** Indiana U.S.A.
95 S2 **Winslow** Maine U.S.A.
100 C2 **Winslow** Washington U.S.A.
137 R2 **Winslow Reef** Phoenix Is Pacific Oc
101 N5 **Winsper** Idaho U.S.A.
95 O5 **Winsted** Connecticut U.S.A.
9 E1 **Winster** England
13 G4 **Winston** England
101 O3 **Winston** Montana U.S.A.
106 C8 **Winston** New Mexico U.S.A.
112 G1 **Winston Salem** North Carolina U.S.A.
25 G2 **Winsum** Netherlands
118 H6 **Winter** Saskatchewan Canada
38 M6 **Winterbach** Austria
36 F1 **Winterberg** Germany
36 D4 **Winterberg** Germany
8 D6 **Winterbourne Abbas** England
9 E5 **Winterbourne Stoke** England
33 O7 **Winterfeld** Germany
113 F9 **Winter Garden** Florida U.S.A.
114 J3 **Winter Harb** Northwest Territories Canada
103 K9 **Winterhaven** California U.S.A.
113 F9 **Winter Haven** Florida U.S.A.
119 U3 **Wintering L** Manitoba Canada
36 G7 **Winterlingen** Germany
106 E2 **Winter Park** Colorado U.S.A.
113 F9 **Winter Park** Florida U.S.A.
95 T2 **Winterport** Maine U.S.A.
102 C3 **Winters** California U.S.A.
108 H4 **Winters** Texas U.S.A.
103 M8 **Wintersburg** Arizona U.S.A.
99 M8 **Winterset** Iowa U.S.A.
22 K2 **Winterslag** Belgium
25 G5 **Winterswijk** Netherlands
41 J3 **Winterthur** Switzerland
123 T6 **Winterton** Newfoundland Canada
13 H6 **Winterton** England
95 S7 **Winterville** Maine U.S.A.
95 R4 **Winthrop** Massachusetts U.S.A.
99 M5 **Winthrop** Minnesota U.S.A.
95 N2 **Winthrop** New York U.S.A.
100 E1 **Winthrop** Washington U.S.A.
99 T7 **Winthrop Harbor** Illinois U.S.A.
138 C2 **Wintinna** South Australia Australia
141 G5 **Winton** Queensland Australia
113 M9 **Winton** New Providence I Bahamas
144 B7 **Winton** New Zealand
99 P2 **Winton** Minnesota U.S.A.
112 K1 **Winton** North Carolina U.S.A.
95 M5 **Winton** Pennsylvania U.S.A.
100 E2 **Winton** Washington U.S.A.
101 Q8 **Winton** Wyoming U.S.A.
40 F1 **Wintzenheim** France
112 H4 **Winyah B** South Carolina U.S.A.
37 P6 **Winzer** Germany
99 M8 **Wiota** Iowa U.S.A.
33 N10 **Wipper** *R* Germany
36 C1 **Wipperfürth** Germany
33 O9 **Wippra** Germany
41 O3 **Wipp Tal** Austria
83 K11 **Wiraketiya** Sri Lanka
69 G14 **Wiralaga** Sumatra
32 F6 **Wirdum** Germany
25 E2 **Wirdum** Netherlands
9 E1 **Wirksworth** England
145 F2 **Wiroa I** New Zealand
138 E5 **Wirrabara** South Australia Australia
138 D4 **Wirraminna** South Australia Australia
138 F6 **Wirrega** South Australia Australia
138 C3 **Wirrida, L** South Australia Australia
138 C4 **Wirrulla** South Australia Australia
99 N2 **Wirt** Minnesota U.S.A.
22 B2 **Wirwignes** France
9 G2 **Wisbech** England
9 F5 **Wisborough Green** England
95 S2 **Wiscasset** Maine U.S.A.
32 K5 **Wischhafen** Germany
99 R5 **Wisconsin** *state* U.S.A.
99 R4 **Wisconsin** *R* Wisconsin U.S.A.
99 R6 **Wisconsin Dells** Wisconsin U.S.A.
99 R6 **Wisconsin, L** Wisconsin U.S.A.
99 R5 **Wisconsin Rapids** Wisconsin U.S.A.
101 M4 **Wisdom** Montana U.S.A.
94 E9 **Wise** Virginia U.S.A.
116 M3 **Wiseman** Alaska U.S.A.
101 N4 **Wise River** Montana U.S.A.
118 K7 **Wiseton** Saskatchewan Canada
119 O7 **Wishart** Saskatchewan Canada
12 E2 **Wishaw** Scotland
98 G3 **Wishek** North Dakota U.S.A.
100 E4 **Wishram** Washington U.S.A.
86 A2 **Wisil Dabarow** Somalia
31 L2 **Wisła** *R* Poland
48 E1 **Wisla** Poland
31 N6 **Wisłok** *R* Poland
33 O5 **Wismar** Germany
33 O5 **Wismarbucht** Germany
111 E10 **Wisner** Louisiana U.S.A.
98 K8 **Wisner** Nebraska U.S.A.
22 B2 **Wissant** France
36 D5 **Wissembourg** France
36 D2 **Wissen** Germany
9 G2 **Wissey, R** England
32 H8 **Wissingen** Germany
99 P5 **Wissota L** Wisconsin U.S.A.
31 N4 **Wista** *R* Poland
117 K9 **Wistaria** British Columbia Canada
109 N1 **Wister** Oklahoma U.S.A.
107 Q7 **Wister L** Oklahoma U.S.A.
89 F5 **Witbank** S Africa
89 E8 **Witberge** *mts* S Africa
89 A5 **Witbooisvlei** Namibia
119 U3 **Witchai L** Manitoba Canada
143 B10 **Witchcliffe** W Australia Australia
118 K5 **Witchekan L** Saskatchewan Canada
87 D11 **Witdrail** S Africa
9 G4 **Witham** England
9 F1 **Witham, R** England
8 C6 **Witheridge** England
9 G1 **Withern** England
13 J6 **Withernsea** England
106 C8 **Withington, Mt** New Mexico U.S.A.
113 E9 **Withlacoochee** *R* Florida U.S.A.
100 F2 **Withrow** Washington U.S.A.
31 K3 **Witkowo** Poland
123 U6 **Witless B** Newfoundland Canada
9 E4 **Witney** England
89 G5 **Witrivier** S Africa
22 K4 **Witry** Belgium
22 G5 **Witry-les-Reims** France
22 D2 **Witschate** Belgium
110 G2 **Witt** Illinois U.S.A.
28 A7 **Wittdün** Germany
37 L7 **Wittelsbach** Germany
32 F10 **Witten** Germany
98 F6 **Witten** South Dakota U.S.A.
33 S7 **Wittenau** Germany
33 R9 **Wittenberg** Germany
99 R5 **Wittenberg** Wisconsin U.S.A.
33 P7 **Wittenberge** Germany
33 O5 **Wittenburg** Germany
40 F2 **Wittenheim** France
142 C5 **Wittenoom** W Australia Australia
142 G4 **Wittenoom,Mt** W Australia Australia
37 O2 **Wittgensdorf** Germany
125 N2 **Witties, The** *islds* Nicaragua
36 H4 **Wittighausen** Germany
33 N7 **Wittingen** Germany
70 E2 **Witti Ra** Sabah
32 H8 **Wittlage** Germany
36 B4 **Wittlich** Germany
32 K7 **Wittlohe** Germany
103 M8 **Wittmann** Arizona U.S.A.
32 G5 **Wittmund** Germany
13 G4 **Witton Gilbert** England
13 G4 **Witton-le-Wear** England
30 G1 **Wittow** *pen* Germany
33 Q6 **Wittstock** Germany
87 C10 **Witvlei** Namibia
89 E5 **Witwatersberg** *ridge* S Africa
89 C2 **Witwatersrand** S Africa
32 L10 **Witzenhausen** Germany
8 C5 **Wiveliscombe** England
119 W2 **Wivenhoe** Manitoba Canada
139 L2 **Wivenhoe, Lake** *res* Australia
118 L8 **Wives** Saskatchewan Canada
9 H4 **Wix** England
31 O1 **Wizajny** Poland
22 C2 **Wizernes** France
31 M3 **Wkra** *R* Poland
31 L1 **Władysławowo** Poland
31 J4 **Wleń** Poland
31 L3 **Włocławek** Poland
31 O4 **Włodawa** Poland
31 M5 **Włoszczowa** Poland
33 O6 **Wöbbelin** Germany
9 F4 **Woburn** England
142 C5 **Wodgina** W Australia Australia
139 H6 **Wodonga** Victoria Australia
31 L5 **Wodzisław** Poland
25 B6 **Woensdrecht** Netherlands
25 C4 **Woerden** Netherlands
94 C10 **Wofford** Kentucky U.S.A.
25 D3 **Wognum** Netherlands
41 H3 **Wohlen** Switzerland
33 O5 **Wohlenberg** Germany
40 F4 **Wohlen See** *L* Switzerland
146 H7 **Wohlthat Massivet** *mts* Antarctica
36 F2 **Wohratal** Germany
32 J4 **Wöhrden** Germany
121 N7 **Woito** Ontario Canada
143 A8 **Wokarina** W Australia Australia
65 H1 **Woken** China
65 H1 **Woken He** *R* China
117 O8 **Woking** Alberta Canada
9 F5 **Woking** England
141 G5 **Wokingham** *R* Queensland Australia
9 F5 **Wokingham** England
33 S6 **Wokuhl** Germany
31 L4 **Wola** Poland
98 H8 **Wolbach** Nebraska U.S.A.
32 G9 **Wolbeck** Germany
101 T10 **Wolcott** Colorado U.S.A.
95 L3 **Wolcott** New York U.S.A.
32 E2 **Woldbrunn** Germany
33 T6 **Woldegk** Germany
141 J7 **Woleebee** Queensland Australia
117 G5 **Wolf** *R* Yukon Territory Canada
111 G11 **Wolf** *R* Mississippi U.S.A.
110 G6 **Wolf** *R* Tennessee U.S.A.
99 S4 **Wolf** *R* Wisconsin U.S.A.
36 E7 **Wolfach** Germany
37 P6 **Wolfachau** Germany
123 M3 **Wolf Bay** Quebec Canada
108 D7 **Wolf Cr** Texas/Okla U.S.A.
94 B10 **Wolf Cr. Dam** Kentucky U.S.A.
101 N2 **Wolf Creek** Montana U.S.A.
100 B7 **Wolf Creek** Oregon U.S.A.
106 D4 **Wolf Cr. Pass** Colorado U.S.A.
118 J6 **Wolfe** Saskatchewan Canada
95 Q3 **Wolfeboro** New Hampshire U.S.A.
109 L2 **Wolfe City** Texas U.S.A.
121 O8 **Wolfe Island** Ontario Canada
118 G4 **Wolfe L** Alberta Canada
33 Q9 **Wolfen** Germany
33 N8 **Wolfenbüttel** Germany
9 G2 **Wolferton** England
32 K10 **Wolfhagen** Germany
103 L5 **Wolf Hole** Arizona U.S.A.
123 L6 **Wolf I** Madeleine Is, Quebec Canada
117 H5 **Wolf L** Yukon Territory Canada
101 S4 **Wolf Mts** Wyo/Mont U.S.A.
98 G1 **Wolford** North Dakota U.S.A.
98 A1 **Wolf Pt** Montana U.S.A.
37 K5 **Wolframs-Eschenbach** Germany
41 O2 **Wolfratshausen** Germany
7 G13 **Wolf Rock** English Chan
38 L8 **Wolfsberg** Austria
33 N8 **Wolfsburg** Germany
37 N2 **Wolfsgefärth** Germany
36 E4 **Wolfskehlen** Germany
36 D4 **Wolfstein** Germany
122 H8 **Wolfville** Nova Scotia Canada
33 T4 **Wolgast** Germany
33 T4 **Wolgaster Fähre** Germany
31 H2 **Wolin** Poland
37 L3 **Wölkendorf** Germany
37 P2 **Wolkenstein** Germany
33 N10 **Wolkramsh** Germany
114 H3 **Wollaston, C** Northwest Territories Canada
133 D9 **Wollaston, Is** Chile
114 J6 **Wollaston L** Saskatchewan Canada
114 J6 **Wollaston Lake** Saskatchewan Canada
114 H4 **Wollaston Pen** Northwest Territories Canada
36 B2 **Wollersheim** Germany
140 E3 **Wollogorang** N Terr Australia
139 K5 **Wollongong** New South Wales Australia
36 D4 **Wöllstein** Germany
87 E11 **Wolmaransstad** S Africa
33 O9 **Wolmirsleben** Germany
33 P8 **Wolmirstedt** Germany
37 M6 **Wolnzach** Germany
31 N3 **Wołomin** Poland
31 K4 **Wołow** Poland
71 K9 **Wolowaru** Flores Indonesia
138 F6 **Wolseley** South Australia Australia
119 O8 **Wolseley** Saskatchewan Canada
98 H5 **Wolsey** South Dakota U.S.A.
36 B4 **Wolsfeld** Germany
13 G4 **Wolsingham** England
115 M5 **Wolstenholme, C** Quebec Canada
31 J3 **Wolsztyn** Poland
32 L7 **Wolthausen** Germany
33 M8 **Woltorf** Germany
25 F3 **Wolvega** Netherlands
8 D2 **Wolverhampton** England
94 C1 **Wolverine** Michigan U.S.A.
22 G2 **Wolvertem** Belgium
9 E5 **Wolverton** England
98 K3 **Wolverton** Minnesota U.S.A.
9 E3 **Wolvey** England
69 C10 **Wolya** *R* Sumatra
120 H5 **Woman River** Ontario Canada
13 G6 **Wombwell** England
95 L6 **Womelsdorf** Pennsylvania U.S.A.
138 F3 **Wompah** New South Wales Australia
140 D4 **Wonarah** N Terr Australia
143 E10 **Wonberna Rock** *rock* W Australia Australia
141 K7 **Wondai** Queensland Australia
22 F1 **Wondelgem** Belgium
100 B7 **Wonder** Oregon U.S.A.
116 M5 **Wonder L** Alaska U.S.A.
140 E6 **Wonditti,L** Queensland Australia
140 F4 **Wondoola** Queensland Australia
139 G4 **Wongalarroo L** New South Wales Australia
141 G5 **Wongalee** Queensland Australia
143 B9 **Wongan Hills** W Australia Australia
70 G4 **Wonggarasi** Sulawesi
59 J4 **Wŏnju** S Korea
70 N9 **Wonogiri** Java
70 N10 **Wonojoyo** Java
70 O9 **Wonokromo** Java
138 F4 **Wonominta** *R* New South Wales Australia
70 N9 **Wonosari** Java
70 M9 **Wonosobo** Java
71 N9 **Wonreli** Indonesia
59 J4 **Wŏnsan** N Korea
139 H7 **Wonthaggi** Victoria Australia
143 C6 **Wonyulgunna,Mt** W Australia Australia
138 D4 **Woocalla** South Australia Australia
116 O4 **Wood** *R* Alaska U.S.A.
94 J6 **Wood** Pennsylvania U.S.A.
98 F6 **Wood** South Dakota U.S.A.
140 D2 **Woodah I** N Terr Australia
113 F7 **Woodbine** Georgia U.S.A.
99 L8 **Woodbine** Iowa U.S.A.
107 N3 **Woodbine** Kansas U.S.A.
94 C10 **Woodbine** Kentucky U.S.A.
95 N7 **Woodbine** New Jersey U.S.A.
121 L9 **Woodbridge** Ontario Canada
9 H3 **Woodbridge** England
95 K8 **Woodbridge** Virginia U.S.A.
117 R6 **Wood Buffalo Nat. Park** Alberta Canada
139 L3 **Woodburn** New South Wales Australia
99 N8 **Woodburn** Iowa U.S.A.
110 K5 **Woodburn** Kentucky U.S.A.
100 C4 **Woodburn** Oregon U.S.A.
112 C5 **Woodbury** Georgia U.S.A.
95 M7 **Woodbury** New Jersey U.S.A.
110 K6 **Woodbury** Tennessee U.S.A.
112 F5 **Woodcliff** Georgia U.S.A.
140 C4 **Woodcock,Mt** N Terr Australia
139 L3 **Woodenbong** New South Wales Australia
144 B7 **Woodend** New Zealand
117 M11 **Woodfibre** British Columbia Canada
9 G4 **Woodford** England
127 P5 **Woodford** Grenada
14 C3 **Woodford** Ireland
140 C5 **Woodforde** *R* N Terr Australia
102 E3 **Woodfords** California U.S.A.
140 C5 **Woodgreen** N Terr Australia
9 F4 **Wood Green** England
9 F1 **Woodhall Spa** England
13 G6 **Woodhead** England
99 Q8 **Woodhull** Illinois U.S.A.
95 K4 **Woodhull** New York U.S.A.
142 D5 **Woodie Woodie** W Australia Australia
100 C2 **Woodinville** Washington U.S.A.
122 K8 **Wood Is** Prince Edward I Canada
119 U1 **Wood L** Manitoba Canada
119 O3 **Wood L** Saskatchewan Canada
98 F7 **Wood L** Nebraska U.S.A.
102 E5 **Woodlake** California U.S.A.
102 C3 **Woodland** California U.S.A.
110 J1 **Woodland** Illinois U.S.A.
94 J6 **Woodland** Pennsylvania U.S.A.
100 C4 **Woodland** Washington U.S.A.
109 N10 **Woodland Hills** Texas U.S.A.
106 E3 **Woodland Park** Colorado U.S.A.
119 U8 **Woodlands** Manitoba Canada
137 L3 **Woodlark** *isld* Papua New Guinea
110 G3 **Woodlawn** Illinois U.S.A.
142 A3 **Woodman Pt** W Australia Australia
118 L9 **Wood Mt** Saskatchewan Canada
117 C5 **Wood, Mt** Yukon Territory Canada
101 Q4 **Wood, Mt** Montana U.S.A.
138 D2 **Woodmurra Creek** South Australia Australia
117 M9 **Woodpecker** British Columbia Canada
118 E1 **Woodridge** Manitoba Canada
110 F3 **Wood River** Illinois U.S.A.
98 H9 **Wood River** Nebraska U.S.A.
140 E5 **Woodroffe** *R* N Terr/ Queensland Australia
138 B2 **Woodroffe, Mt** South Australia Australia
118 L9 **Woodrow** Saskatchewan Canada
106 G2 **Woodrow** Colorado U.S.A.
103 O7 **Woodruff** Arizona U.S.A.
107 L2 **Woodruff** Kansas U.S.A.
101 O8 **Woodruff** Utah U.S.A.
101 Q4 **Woods** *mt* Montana U.S.A.
109 K7 **Woodsboro** Texas U.S.A.
94 F7 **Woodsfield** Ohio U.S.A.
122 G10 **Woods Harbour** Nova Scotia Canada
139 H7 **Woodside** Victoria Australia
145 E4 **Woodside** New Zealand
103 O2 **Woodside** Utah U.S.A.
140 C4 **Woods,L** N Terr Australia
118 H1 **Woods, Lake of the** Minnesota/Ontario U.S.A./ Canada
111 D7 **Woodson** Arkansas U.S.A.
99 Q10 **Woodson** Illinois U.S.A.
109 H2 **Woodson** Texas U.S.A.
139 H7 **Woods Pt** Victoria Australia
141 H4 **Woodstock** Queensland Australia
122 E7 **Woodstock** New Brunswick Canada
9 E4 **Woodstock** England
99 S7 **Woodstock** Illinois U.S.A.
95 P3 **Woodstock** Vermont U.S.A.
95 Q2 **Woodstock, N** New Hampshire U.S.A.
107 M2 **Woodston** Kansas U.S.A.
95 M7 **Woodstown** New Jersey U.S.A.
95 Q2 **Woodsville** New Hampshire U.S.A.
138 E6 **Woodswell** South Australia Australia
121 M8 **Woodville** Ontario Canada
145 E4 **Woodville** New Zealand
110 K7 **Woodville** Alabama U.S.A.
111 M11 **Woodville** Florida U.S.A.
111 E10 **Woodville** Mississippi U.S.A.
94 D5 **Woodville** Ohio U.S.A.
109 N5 **Woodville** Texas U.S.A.
107 L5 **Woodward** Oklahoma U.S.A.
102 D4 **Woodward Res** California U.S.A.
122 F9 **Woodwards Cove** New Brunswick Canada
109 P4 **Woodworth** Louisiana U.S.A.
98 G2 **Woodworth** North Dakota U.S.A.
8 C5 **Woody B** England
139 L3 **Woody Head** New South Wales Australia
116 L8 **Woody Island** Alaska U.S.A.
123 P4 **Woody Point** Newfoundland Canada
119 Q6 **Woody R** Manitoba Canada
8 D3 **Woofferton** England
71 A3 **Wooi** Indonesia
8 D6 **Wool** England
8 B5 **Woolacombe** England
110 D3 **Wooldridge** Missouri U.S.A.
139 K5 **Woolemi Nat Park** New South Wales Australia
13 F3 **Wooler** England
118 D9 **Woolford Prov. Park** Alberta Canada
143 D9 **Woolgangie** W Australia Australia
141 G4 **Woolgar** Queensland Australia
143 C6 **Woolgathara** W Australia Australia
139 L4 **Woolgoolga** New South Wales Australia
143 D9 **Woolibar** W Australia Australia
140 C5 **Woolla Downs** N Terr Australia
9 G3 **Woolpit** England
102 F1 **Woolsey** Nevada U.S.A.
138 E4 **Wooltana** South Australia Australia
8 D5 **Woolverton** England
9 G5 **Woolwich** England
138 D4 **Woomera** South Australia Australia
138 B3 **Woomera Prohibited Area** South Australia Australia
95 Q5 **Woonsocket** Rhode I U.S.A.
98 H5 **Woonsocket** South Dakota U.S.A.
13 G3 **Wooperton** England
141 J6 **Woorabinda** Queensland Australia
143 A7 **Wooramel R** W Australia Australia
8 D2 **Woore** England
138 C3 **Woorong, L** South Australia Australia
94 F6 **Wooster** Ohio U.S.A.
9 E4 **Wootton Bassett** England
38 O6 **Wopfing** Austria
117 O7 **Wor** Alberta Canada
71 B2 **Wor** *isld* Halmahera Indonesia
33 M10 **Worbis** Germany
141 F2 **Worbody Pt** Queensland Australia
8 D3 **Worcester** England
89 A9 **Worcester** S Africa
95 Q4 **Worcester** Massachusetts U.S.A.
95 N4 **Worcester** New York U.S.A.
110 G3 **Worden** Illinois U.S.A.
101 R4 **Worden** Montana U.S.A.
100 D7 **Worden** Oregon U.S.A.
119 P9 **Wordsworth** Saskatchewan Canada
38 F7 **Wörgl** Austria
12 E4 **Workington** England
9 E1 **Worksop** England
25 D3 **Workum** Netherlands
101 S5 **Worland** Wyoming U.S.A.
8 D5 **Worle** England
33 Q9 **Wörlitz** Germany
8 D4 **Wormbridge** England
25 C4 **Wormerveer** Netherlands
22 C2 **Wormhoudt** France
13 F1 **Wormit** Scotland
33 P10 **Wormlitz** Germany
36 E4 **Worms** Germany
8 B4 **Worms Head** Wales
37 K6 **Wörnitz** *R* Germany
32 J6 **Worpswede** Germany
36 B1 **Worringen** Germany
36 E4 **Wörrstadt** Germany
143 E7 **Worsnop,Mt** W Australia
38 G7 **Wörth** Austria
38 O7 **Wörth** Austria
36 D6 **Wœrth** France
37 N6 **Wörth** Bayern Germany
36 E5 **Wörth** Rheinland-Pfalz Germany
99 M9 **Worth** Missouri U.S.A.
109 L4 **Wortham** Texas U.S.A.
8 C2 **Worthen** England
38 K8 **Wörther See** *L* Austria
127 P6 **Worthing** Barbados
9 F6 **Worthing** England
110 K2 **Worthington** Indiana U.S.A.
99 L6 **Worthington** Minnesota U.S.A.
99 O9 **Worthington** Missouri U.S.A.
94 D6 **Worthington** Ohio U.S.A.
109 L9 **Worth, L** Texas U.S.A.
94 B8 **Worthville** Kentucky U.S.A.
13 G6 **Wortley** England
71 A3 **Wosi** Halmahera Indonesia
118 E5 **Wostok** Alberta Canada
70 G6 **Wosu** Sulawesi
31 L4 **Wotczyn** Poland
121 T7 **Wotton** Quebec Canada
8 D4 **Wotton under Edge** England
70 G6 **Wotu** Sulawesi
25 D4 **Woudenberg** Netherlands
25 C5 **Woudrichem** Netherlands
98 D6 **Wounded Knee** South Dakota U.S.A.
25 B5 **Wouw** Netherlands
22 J5 **Wœvre, Forêt de** France
141 K6 **Wowan** Queensland Australia
71 H7 **Wowoni** *isld* Indonesia
31 L5 **Woźniki** Poland
9 F1 **Wragby** England
Wrangel I *see* **Vrangelya, Os**
117 G7 **Wrangell** Alaska U.S.A.
116 Q6 **Wrangell Mts** Alaska/Yukon Terr U.S.A./Canada
116 P5 **Wrangell-St. Elias Nat Park and Preserve** Alaska U.S.A.
9 G1 **Wrangle** England
106 H1 **Wray** Colorado U.S.A.
9 F2 **Wreak, R** England
141 G1 **Wreck B** Gt Barrier Reef Aust
32 H5 **Wremen** Germany
100 B5 **Wren** Oregon U.S.A.
112 E4 **Wrens** Georgia U.S.A.
118 E9 **Wrentham** Alberta Canada
9 H3 **Wrentham** England
95 Q4 **Wrentham** Massachusetts U.S.A.
8 D1 **Wrexham** Wales
30 H3 **Wriezen** Germany
121 O6 **Wright** Quebec Canada
71 G5 **Wright** Samar Philippines
107 L4 **Wright** Kansas U.S.A.
112 M1 **Wright Bros. Nat. Mem** North Carolina U.S.A.
107 P7 **Wright City** Oklahoma U.S.A.
138 A3 **Wright, L** South Australia Australia
138 F4 **Wright, Mt** New South Wales Australia
68 A7 **Wrightmyo** Andaman Is
109 N2 **Wright Patman L** Texas U.S.A.
103 O10 **Wrightson, Mt** Arizona U.S.A.
112 E5 **Wrightsville** Georgia U.S.A.
95 L6 **Wrightsville** Pennsylvania U.S.A.
112 K3 **Wrightsville Beach** North Carolina U.S.A.
102 G7 **Wrightwood** California U.S.A.
117 M4 **Wrigley** Northwest Territories Canada
32 L5 **Wrist** Germany
118 F9 **Writing-on-Stone Prov. Park** Alberta Canada
31 K4 **Wrocław** Poland
119 V6 **Wrong L** Manitoba Canada
31 J3 **Wronki** Poland
9 G5 **Wrotham** England
8 D2 **Wroxeter** England
9 H2 **Wroxham** England
119 Q7 **Wroxton** Saskatchewan Canada
9 E3 **Wroxton** England
31 J4 **Wschowa** Poland
31 L3 **Wtoctawskie, Jezioro** *res* Poland
65 C6 **Wu'an** China
143 B9 **Wubin** W Australia Australia
65 A6 **Wubu** China
65 E1 **Wuchagou** China
65 G2 **Wuchang** China
67 E1 **Wuchang** China
65 B6 **Wucheng** China
65 C6 **Wucheng** China
Wuchow *see* **Wuzhou**
65 B4 **Wuchuan** China
67 C2 **Wuchuan** China
67 B5 **Wucun** China
58 E4 **Wuda** China
65 E5 **Wudao** China
65 F3 **Wudaogou** China
66 E4 **Wudaoliang** China
67 C2 **Wudaoshui** China
65 D6 **Wudi** China
65 A6 **Wuding He** *R* China
138 D5 **Wudinna** South Australia Australia
58 D5 **Wudu** China
67 A1 **Wudu** China
67 C1 **Wufeng** China
67 C3 **Wugang** China
58 E4 **Wuhai** China
67 E1 **Wuhan** China
58 G5 **Wuhe** China
32 J6 **Wuhrden** *reg* Germany
67 F1 **Wuhu** China
65 C5 **Wuji** China
65 G2 **Wujia** China
67 C6 **Wujia** China
67 G1 **Wujiang** China
67 C2 **Wu Jiang** *R* China
65 F2 **Wujiazhan** China
67 F1 **Wukang** China
85 F7 **Wukari** Nigeria
65 G2 **Wulajie** China
32 F9 **Wulfen** Germany
33 P9 **Wulfen** Germany
33 Q6 **Wulfersdorf** Germany
32 F10 **Wülfrath** Germany
32 M6 **Wulfsen** Germany
32 M9 **Wulften** Germany
68 J1 **Wuli** China
65 D7 **Wulian** China
67 B1 **Wulian** China
67 A3 **Wulian Feng** *mts* China
65 B8 **Wulichuan** China
67 C5 **Wuli Jiang** *R* China
116 F3 **Wulik** *R* Alaska U.S.A.
65 H2 **Wulin** China
67 C2 **Wuling Shan** *mts* China
67 C1 **Wulingzhen** China
67 B2 **Wulong** China
71 O8 **Wulur** Indonesia
37 K5 **Wülzburg** Germany
85 G7 **Wum** Cameroon
139 H5 **Wumbulgel** New South Wales Australia
67 A3 **Wumeng Shan** *mts* China
67 C5 **Wuming** China
32 K6 **Wümme** *R* Germany
142 C3 **Wungang R** W Australia Australia
88 D6 **Wungu** Tanzania
67 E2 **Wuning** China
138 F5 **Wunkar** South Australia Australia
32 J9 **Wünnenberg** Germany
33 S8 **Wünsdorf** Germany
37 N3 **Wunsiedel** Germany
32 K8 **Wunstorf** Germany
75 Q7 **Wuntho** Burma
103 N6 **Wupatki Nat. Mon** Arizona U.S.A.
67 E4 **Wuping** China
32 F10 **Wuppertal** Germany
66 B4 **Wuqia** China
65 C5 **Wuqiang** China
65 C6 **Wuqiao** China
65 D5 **Wuqing** China
143 B8 **Wurarga** W Australia Australia
37 O7 **Wurmannsquick** Germany
85 F6 **Wurno** Nigeria
25 F7 **Würselen** Germany
95 N5 **Wurtsboro** New York U.S.A.
37 M3 **Wurzbach** Germany
36 H4 **Würzburg** Germany
33 R10 **Wurzen** Germany
67 C1 **Wu Shan** *mts* China
67 C1 **Wushan** China
67 D1 **Wushan** China
67 B1 **Wusheng** China
67 F2 **Wusheng** China
67 D1 **Wusheng Guan** *pass* China
57 J4 **Wushi** China
68 J2 **Wushi** China
67 C3 **Wu Shui** *R* China
67 G1 **Wusong** China
36 H3 **Wüstensachsen** Germany
33 Q7 **Wusterhausen** Germany
33 R7 **Wustermark** Germany
32 H6 **Wüsting** Germany
33 R7 **Wustrau** Germany
33 P4 **Wustrow** Germany
33 O7 **Wustrow** Germany
59 K2 **Wusuli Jiang** *R* China
41 H2 **Wutach** *R* Germany
65 B5 **Wutai** China
58 F4 **Wutai Shan** *mt ra* China
65 D3 **Wu-tan** China
67 C4 **Wutong** China
67 A2 **Wutongqiao** China
22 H1 **Wuustwezel** Belgium
58 D4 **Wuwei** China
67 F1 **Wuwei** China
67 C1 **Wuxi** China
67 G1 **Wuxi** China
65 B6 **Wuxiang** China
Wuxing *see* **Huzhou**
67 C5 **Wuxuan** China
Wuxue *see* **Guangji**
Wuyang *see* **Zhenyuan**
65 B6 **Wuyang** China
65 C6 **Wuyi** China
67 F1 **Wuyi** China
67 F2 **Wuyi** China
59 J2 **Wuyiling** China
67 E4 **Wuyi Shan** *mts* China
58 E3 **Wuyuan** China
67 F2 **Wuyuan** China
65 B5 **Wuzhai** China
65 G2 **Wuzhan** China
65 A6 **Wuzhen** China
67 D1 **Wuzhen** China
65 B7 **Wuzhi** China
67 C7 **Wuzhi Shan** *pk* China
58 E4 **Wuzhong** China
67 D5 **Wuzhou** China
141 F3 **Wyaaba Cr** Queensland Australia
99 P9 **Wyaconda** *R* Missouri U.S.A.
143 B9 **Wyalkatchem** W Australia Australia
139 H5 **Wyalong** New South Wales Australia
94 D4 **Wyandotte** Michigan U.S.A.
141 H7 **Wyandra** Queensland Australia
139 J5 **Wyangala Res** New South Wales Australia
141 G8 **Wyara** *L* Queensland Australia
101 T5 **Wyarno** Wyoming U.S.A.
110 G5 **Wyatt** Missouri U.S.A.
9 G5 **Wych Cross** England
139 G6 **Wycheproof** Victoria Australia
9 G5 **Wye** England
143 C8 **Wyemandoo** *mt* W Australia
8 D4 **Wye, R** Wales/England
99 Q5 **Wyeville** Wisconsin U.S.A.
109 L2 **Wylie** Texas U.S.A.
142 B6 **Wyloo** W Australia Australia
8 D5 **Wylye, R** England
95 S1 **Wyman Dam** Maine U.S.A.
118 K8 **Wymark** Saskatchewan Canada
100 E3 **Wymer** Washington U.S.A.
9 H2 **Wymondham** England
98 K9 **Wymore** Nebraska U.S.A.
142 G3 **Wyndham** W Australia Australia
144 B7 **Wyndham** New Zealand
142 E3 **Wyndham Ra** W Australia Australia
98 J3 **Wyndmere** North Dakota U.S.A.
110 F6 **Wynne** Arkansas U.S.A.
142 E4 **Wynne,Mt** W Australia Australia
107 N7 **Wynnewood** Oklahoma U.S.A.
114 H3 **Wynniatt B** Northwest Territories Canada
141 L7 **Wynnum** Queensland Australia
107 O5 **Wynona** Oklahoma U.S.A.
98 J7 **Wynot** Nebraska U.S.A.
139 H8 **Wynyard** Tasmania Australia
119 N7 **Wynyard** Saskatchewan Canada
99 R6 **Wyocena** Wisconsin U.S.A.
98 A5 **Wyodak** Wyoming U.S.A.
101 S4 **Wyola** Montana U.S.A.
138 B3 **Wyola, L** South Australia Australia
120 H10 **Wyoming** Ontario Canada
101 R6 **Wyoming** *state* U.S.A.
95 M7 **Wyoming** Delaware U.S.A.
99 R8 **Wyoming** Illinois U.S.A.
94 B4 **Wyoming** Michigan U.S.A.
99 N4 **Wyoming** Minnesota U.S.A.
94 J4 **Wyoming** New York U.S.A.
95 Q5 **Wyoming** Rhode I U.S.A.
101 P7 **Wyoming Pk** Wyoming U.S.A.
101 P7 **Wyoming Ra** Wyoming U.S.A.
139 K5 **Wyong** New South Wales Australia
138 F6 **Wyperfeld Nat Park** Victoria Australia
13 F6 **Wyre, R** England
31 K2 **Wyrzysk** Poland
31 O5 **Wysokie** Poland
31 N3 **Wysokie Mazowieckie** Poland
31 N3 **Wyszków** Poland
31 M3 **Wyszogrod** Poland
13 E5 **Wythburn** England
94 F10 **Wytheville** Virginia U.S.A.
83 M14 **Wyville-Thomson** *mt* Kerguelen Indian Oc

X

86 B1 **Xaafuun** Somalia
86 B1 **Xaafuun, Raas** *C* Somalia
86 A1 **Xadeed, Bannaanka** *plain* Somalia
66 B4 **Xaidulla** China
68 E3 **Xaignabouri** Laos
66 D5 **Xainza** China
87 F11 **Xai-Xai** Mozambique
125 P7 **Xal, Cerro de** *mt* Mexico
86 A2 **Xalin** Somalia
Xamba *see* **Hanggin Houqi**
129 J5 **Xambioa** Brazil
68 F2 **Xam Nua** Laos
65 A3 **Xangdin Hural** China
Xangdoring *see* **Xungba**
87 B9 **Xangongo** Angola
25 F5 **Xanten** Germany
46 G3 **Xánthi** Greece
130 D10 **Xanxerê** Brazil
128 E6 **Xapuri** Brazil
86 A3 **Xarardheere** Somalia
65 C2 **Xar Hudag** China
65 B3 **Xar Moron** China
59 G3 **Xar Moron He** *R* China
65 B3 **Xar Moron Sum** China
87 D10 **Xau, L** Botswana
129 J6 **Xavantes, Sa. dos** *mts* Brazil
57 L4 **Xayar** China
Xêgar *see* **Tingri**
110 H3 **Xenia** Illinois U.S.A.
94 D7 **Xenia** Ohio U.S.A.
128 F4 **Xeriuini** *R* Brazil
46 D5 **Xerovoúni** *R* Greece
67 F3 **Xiabaishi** China
Xiabancheng *see* **Chengde**
65 D4 **Xiabancheng** China
65 H2 **Xiachengzi** China
65 B7 **Xiachuan** China
67 D6 **Xiachuan Dao** *isld* China
Xiacun *see* **Rushan**
65 C4 **Xiahuayuan** China

67 E3 **Xiajiang** China
67 C4 **Xiajiang** China
65 C6 **Xiajin** China
66 F3 **Xiamaya** China
67 F4 **Xiamen** China
58 E5 **Xi'an** China
67 C2 **Xianfeng** China
58 C6 **Xiangcheng** China
65 B8 **Xiangcheng** China
67 D3 **Xiangdong** China
67 B5 **Xiangdu** China
58 F5 **Xiangfan** China
65 B7 **Xiangfen** China
65 D5 **Xianghe** China
65 B3 **Xianghuang Qi** China
67 D3 **Xiang Jiang** *R* China
65 H1 **Xianglan** China
65 A7 **Xiangning** China
66 B5 **Xiangquan He** *R* China
67 G2 **Xiangshan** China
67 G2 **Xiangshan Gang** *B* China
65 D7 **Xiangshui** China
67 D3 **Xiangtan** China
67 D3 **Xiangxiang** China
65 G2 **Xiangyang** China
67 D2 **Xiangyin** China
65 B6 **Xiangyuan** China
67 C5 **Xiangzhou** China
67 G2 **Xianju** China
58 F6 **Xianning** China
Xiannumiao *see* **Jiangdu**
Xiantaozhen *see* **Mianyang**
67 F3 **Xianxia Ling** *mt ra* China
58 E5 **Xianyang** China
67 F4 **Xianyou** China
65 G1 **Xiaobai** China
65 G2 **Xiaocheng** China
65 D3 **Xiaochengzi** China
65 D4 **Xiaochengzi** China
68 J1 **Xiaodong** China
Xiaofan *see* **Wuqiang**
67 D1 **Xiaogan** China
66 C2 **Xiaoguai** China
67 E1 **Xiaohexi** China
59 J1 **Xiao Hinggan Ling** *mt ra* China
Xiaojiang *see* **Pubei**
65 E3 **Xiaojieji** China
66 F4 **Xiao Qaidam** China
65 A7 **Xiao Shan** *ra* China
67 G1 **Xiaoshan** China
65 F4 **Xiaoshi** China
67 D4 **Xiao Shui** *R* China
65 A6 **Xiaosuan** China
65 C5 **Xiaowutai Shan** *mt* China
67 F2 **Xiao Xi** *R* China
65 D7 **Xiao Xian** China
Xiaoxita *see* **Yichang**
Xiaoyi *see* **Gong Xian**
65 B6 **Xiaoyi** China
67 F3 **Xiapu** China
Xiashi *see* **Haining**
65 B7 **Xia Xian** China
65 C7 **Xiayi** China
Xiayingpan *see* **Luzhi**
58 D6 **Xichang** China
67 C6 **Xichang** China
67 C2 **Xiche** China
Xicheng *see* **Yangyuan**
67 B1 **Xichong** China
67 A5 **Xichou** China
65 E2 **Xi Dorolj** China
67 D3 **Xidu** China
Xiedian *see* **Wanrong**
Xiejiaji *see* **Qingyun**
67 D1 **Xiemahe** China
68 F3 **Xieng Khoang** Laos
65 A7 **Xiexian** China
67 C6 **Xieyang Dao** *isld* China
65 F3 **Xifeng** China
67 B3 **Xifeng** China
65 D4 **Xifenqkou** China
66 D6 **Xigazê** China
65 E4 **Xi He** *R* China
65 G1 **Xiji** China
67 D5 **Xi Jiang** *R* China
65 E1 **Xikou** China
67 C2 **Xikou** China
65 B3 **Xil** China
66 E4 **Xiliangzi** China
67 B4 **Xilin** China
65 C2 **Xilin Gol** *R* China
65 H2 **Xilinhe** China
65 C3 **Xilin Hot** China
65 B2 **Xilin Qagan Obo** China
46 F6 **Xilókastron** Greece
65 D3 **Xiluga He** *R* China
67 B3 **Ximahe** China
65 E5 **Ximayi** *isld* China
58 C3 **Ximiao** China
65 E4 **Ximucheng** China
65 B7 **Xin'an** China
67 F2 **Xin'anjiang Shuiku** *res* China
Xin'anzhen *see* **Xinyi**
65 F2 **Xin'anzhen** China
59 H3 **Xinbin** China
Xin Bulag *see* **Xianghuang Qi**
58 G5 **Xincai** China
67 D2 **Xinchang** China
59 H6 **Xinchang** Zhejiang China
65 H1 **Xincheng** China
65 C5 **Xincheng** China
67 C4 **Xincheng** China
65 F3 **Xinchengzi** China
67 C7 **Xincun** China
Xindeng *see* **Chengyang**
65 G2 **Xindian** China
67 C1 **Xindianzi** China
67 A1 **Xindu** China
67 D4 **Xindu** China
67 E3 **Xinfeng** China
67 E4 **Xinfeng** China
67 E3 **Xingan** China
67 C4 **Xing'an** China
65 E4 **Xingcheng** China
65 C5 **Xingchi** China
67 E3 **Xingguo** China
65 B4 **Xinghe** China
65 G1 **Xinghua** China
67 F4 **Xinghua Wan** *B* China
65 J2 **Xingkai Hu** *L* China
65 D4 **Xinglong** China
65 G1 **Xinglongzhen** China
67 E4 **Xingning** China
67 B3 **Xingren** China
67 B4 **Xingren** China
65 F1 **Xingshan** China
67 C1 **Xingshan** China
58 F4 **Xingtai** China
65 C5 **Xingtang** China
67 F3 **Xingtian** China
129 H4 **Xingú** *R* Brazil
67 A2 **Xingwen** China
65 B5 **Xing Xian** China
66 E3 **Xingxingxia** China
65 B7 **Xingyang** China
67 E2 **Xingzi** China
57 L4 **Xinhe** China
65 C6 **Xinhe** China
Xin Hot *see* **Abag Qi**
67 D3 **Xinhua** China
67 C3 **Xinhuang** China
Xinhui *see* **Aohan Qi**
67 D5 **Xinhui** China
46 E5 **Xiniás, L** Greece
58 D4 **Xining** China
Xinji *see* **Shulu**
67 E2 **Xinjian** China
67 E2 **Xin Jiang** *R* China
65 B7 **Xinjiang** Shanxi China
Xinjiangkou *see* **Songzi**
66 C3 **Xinjiang Uygur Zizhiqu** China
65 E5 **Xinjin** China
67 A1 **Xinjin** China
65 E3 **Xinkai He** *R* China
65 C5 **Xinle** China
65 G2 **Xinli** China
65 D3 **Xinlin** China
65 E3 **Xinlitun** China
65 A5 **Xinminzhen** China
67 C3 **Xinning** China
Xinpu *see* **Lianyungang**
67 D2 **Xinqiang** China
67 D3 **Xinshao** China
65 D7 **Xintai** China
67 D1 **Xintankou** China
67 D4 **Xintian** China
65 D7 **Xinwen** China
67 E1 **Xin Xian** China
65 B7 **Xinxiang** China
67 D5 **Xinxing** China
68 J3 **Xinxing** China
67 E1 **Xinyang** China
65 D7 **Xinyi** China
67 C5 **Xinyi** China
65 D7 **Xinyi He** *R* China
67 C7 **Xinying** China
67 E3 **Xinyu** China
66 C3 **Xinyuan** China
65 D6 **Xinzhai** China
65 F2 **Xinzhan** China
65 G3 **Xinzhan** China
65 B7 **Xinzheng** China
65 B5 **Xinzhou** China
67 E1 **Xinzhou** China
58 F5 **Xiong'er Shan** *mt ra* China
65 C5 **Xiong Xian** China
65 E4 **Xiongyuecheng** China
65 B4 **Xiping** China
58 D4 **Xiqing Shan** *mt ra* China
129 K6 **Xique-Xique** Brazil
Xishuanghe *see* **Kenli**
67 B2 **Xishui** Guizhou China
67 E1 **Xishui** Hubei China
65 D2 **Xi Ujimqin Qi** China
67 F2 **Xiuning** China
67 C2 **Xiushan** China
67 E2 **Xiu Shui** *R* China
67 E2 **Xiushui** China
65 B7 **Xiuwu** China
65 F4 **Xiuyan** China
Xiwanzi *see* **Chongli**
66 D6 **Xixabangma Feng** *mt* China
65 A6 **Xi Xian** China
65 B6 **Xiyang** China
67 F3 **Xiyang** China
67 G3 **Xiyang Dao** *isld* China
67 B5 **Xiyang Jiang** *R* China
67 B5 **Xiyangjie** China
75 K1 **Xizang Gaoyuan** *plateau* China
66 C5 **Xizang Zizhiqu** *aut reg* China
65 E5 **Xizhong Dao** *isld* China
125 K8 **Xochimilco** Mexico
58 G5 **Xuancheng** China
67 C1 **Xuan'en** China
67 B1 **Xuanhan** China
58 F3 **Xuanhua** China
68 H7 **Xuan Loc** Vietnam
67 A3 **Xuanwei** China
58 F5 **Xuchang** China
86 H5 **Xuddur** Somalia
67 G2 **Xuedou Shan** *mt* China
67 C3 **Xuefeng Shan** *mts* China
65 A7 **Xuejiaying** China
Xugezhuang *see* **Fengnan**
Xuguit Qi *see* **Yakeshi**
67 E3 **Xu Jiang** *R* China
65 E4 **Xujiatun** China
Xulun Hobot Qagan *see* **Zhengxiangbai Qi**
Xulun Hoh *see* **Zhenglan Qi**
58 C5 **Xümatang** China
67 A4 **Xundian** China
66 C5 **Xungba** China
58 E5 **Xun He** *R* China
59 J2 **Xunke** China
67 E4 **Xunwu** China
65 C7 **Xun Xian** China
67 C3 **Xupu** China
66 D5 **Xuro Co** *L* China
65 C5 **Xushui** China
67 E3 **Xuwan** China
67 C6 **Xuwen** China
68 H7 **Xuyen Moc** Vietnam
58 E6 **Xuyong** China
58 G5 **Xuzhou** China

Y

100 K1 **Yaak** Montana U.S.A.
141 K6 **Yaamba** Queensland Australia
67 A2 **Ya'an** China
138 F6 **Yaapeet** Victoria Australia
71 A3 **Yaba** Indonesia
86 B5 **Yabassi** Cameroon
86 G5 **Yabēlo** Ethiopia
80 F4 **Yabis** *R* Jordan
46 G1 **Yablanitsa** Bulgaria
125 N2 **Yablis** Nicaragua
48 J2 **Yablonitse, Pereval** *pass* Ukraine
48 J2 **Yablonov** Ukraine
54 D6 **Yablonovka** Ukraine
58 E1 **Yablonovyy Khrebet** *mts* Russian Federation
79 G5 **Yabrūd** Syria
Yacacik *see* **Payas**
141 H5 **Yacamunda** Queensland Australia
Yacha *see* **Baisha**
100 A5 **Yachats** Oregon U.S.A.
67 C7 **Yacheng** China
60 D14 **Yachi** Japan
67 B3 **Yachi He** *R* China
130 C10 **Yaciretá** *isld* Paraguay
139 H6 **Yackandandah** Victoria Australia
100 C4 **Yacolt** Washington U.S.A.
133 E2 **Yacuiba** Bolivia
128 E6 **Yacuma** *R* Bolivia
128 E3 **Yacurai** Venezuela
80 D4 **Yad Hanna** Israel
112 F1 **Yadkin** *R* North Carolina U.S.A.
112 G1 **Yadkinville** North Carolina U.S.A.
80 B7 **Yad Mordekhay** Israel
80 C6 **Yad Rambam** Israel
68 H6 **Ya Drang** *R* Cambodia
52 G6 **Yadrin** Russian Federation
80 C5 **Yafo** Israel
84 E3 **Yafran** Libya
61 Q12 **Yagaji-jima** *isld* Okinawa
60 C13 **Yagami** Japan
47 J5 **Yağcılar** Turkey
60 P1 **Yagishiri-tō** *isld* Japan
124 G7 **Yago** Mexico
55 E2 **Yagodnyy** Russian Federation
52 G4 **Yagrysh** Russian Federation
126 E3 **Yaguajay** Cuba
131 G3 **Yaguari** *R* Uruguay
128 D4 **Yaguas** *R* Peru
124 E4 **Yagui** Mexico
80 D3 **Yagur** Israel
69 E9 **Yaha** Thailand
61 L10 **Yahagi-gawa** *R* Japan
100 J1 **Yahk** British Columbia Canada
124 H7 **Yahualica** Mexico
86 D5 **Yahuma** Zaire
78 E2 **Yahyali** Turkey
68 D6 **Yai, Khao** *mt* Burma/Thailand
61 N9 **Yaita** Japan
61 M11 **Yaizu** Japan
80 G5 **Yajuz** Jordan
116 Q6 **Yakataga** Alaska U.S.A.
59 H2 **Yakeshi** China
80 B8 **Yakhini** Israel
54 J1 **Yakhroma** Russian Federation
55 E2 **Yakhtur, Oz** *L* Russian Federation
100 E3 **Yakima** Washington U.S.A.
74 C8 **Yakmach** Pakistan
85 D6 **Yako** Burkina
117 E6 **Yakobi I** Alaska U.S.A.
86 D5 **Yakoma** Zaire
46 F2 **Yakoruda** Bulgaria
86 D4 **Yakossi** Cent Afr Republic
57 K4 **Yakrik** China
52 J4 **Yaksha** Russian Federation
52 G5 **Yakshanga** Russian Federation
52 H6 **Yakshur-Bod'ya** Russian Federation
101 L1 **Yakt** Montana U.S.A.
60 O3 **Yakumo** Japan
59 J5 **Yaku-shima** *isld* Japan
117 D6 **Yakutat** Alaska U.S.A.
117 C6 **Yakutat B** Alaska U.S.A.
51 M2 **Yakutsk** Russian Federation
56 H1 **Yakutskaya Respublika** Russian Federation
69 E9 **Yala** Thailand
47 K4 **Yalakdere** Turkey
83 L11 **Yala Nat. Park** Sri Lanka
138 B4 **Yalatta** South Australia Australia
144 D5 **Yaldhurst** New Zealand
117 N11 **Yale** British Columbia Canada
110 H2 **Yale** Illinois U.S.A.
99 M8 **Yale** Iowa U.S.A.
94 E3 **Yale** Michigan U.S.A.
107 O5 **Yale** Oklahoma U.S.A.
98 H5 **Yale** South Dakota U.S.A.
86 D5 **Yaleko** Zaire
100 C4 **Yale L** Washington U.S.A.
143 B8 **Yalgoo** W Australia Australia
86 D4 **Yalinga** Cent Afr Republic
127 L2 **Yallahs** *R* Jamaica
127 L3 **Yallahs** Jamaica
141 H6 **Yalleroi** Queensland Australia
143 B10 **Yallingup** W Australia Australia
139 H7 **Yallourn** Victoria Australia
111 F8 **Yalobusha** *R* Mississippi U.S.A.
86 C4 **Yaloké** Cent Afr Republic
66 F5 **Yalong Jiang** *R* China
47 K4 **Yalova** Turkey
48 M4 **Yalpug** *R* Moldova/Ukraine
48 M5 **Yalpug, Ozero** *L* Ukraine
138 F3 **Yalpunga** New South Wales Australia
48 L1 **Yaltushkov** Ukraine
65 E1 **Yalu He** *R* China
65 G4 **Yalu River** China/Korea
55 E4 **Yalym** Russian Federation
60 Q2 **Yamabe Karikachi Pass** Japan
61 Q6 **Yamada wan** *B* Japan
60 D12 **Yamaga** Japan
61 N7 **Yamagata** *prefect* Japan
61 O7 **Yamagata** Japan
60 D14 **Yamagawa** Japan
60 E11 **Yamaguchi** Japan
59 K1 **Yam-Alin', Khrebet** *mt* Russian Federation
50 F1 **Yamal, Poluostrov** *pen* Russian Federation
61 M10 **Yamanaka ko** *L* Japan
61 M10 **Yamanashi** *prefect* Japan
47 J6 **Yamanlar Dağı** *mt* Turkey
58 F1 **Yamarovka** Russian Federation
60 H10 **Yamasaki** Japan
121 S6 **Yamaska** Quebec Canada
113 G11 **Yamato** Florida U.S.A.
139 L3 **Yamba** New South Wales Australia
138 F5 **Yamba** South Australia Australia
139 G7 **Yambacoona** Tasmania Australia
85 B6 **Yambéring** Guinea
128 D3 **Yambi, Mesa de** Colombia
86 E5 **Yambio** Sudan
47 H2 **Yambol** Bulgaria
136 G3 **Yamdena** *isld* Moluccas Indonesia
Yamdrok Tso *L see* **Yamzho Yumco** *L*
68 C2 **Yamethin** Burma
80 E8 **Yam Hamelah** Israel
52 D6 **Yami** Russian Federation
61 O9 **Yamizo-san** *mt* Japan
80 F2 **Yam Kinneret** Israel
52 C5 **Yamm** Russian Federation
141 F7 **Yamma Yamma,L** Queensland Australia
79 E7 **Yammit** Israel
85 D7 **Yamoussoukro** Ivory Coast
101 R9 **Yampa** *R* Colorado U.S.A.
101 T9 **Yampa** Colorado U.S.A.
142 E3 **Yampi Sound** W Australia Australia
48 K1 **Yampol'** Ukraine
48 L2 **Yampol'** Ukraine
100 D7 **Yamsay Mt** Oregon U.S.A.
52 G4 **Yamskoye** Russian Federation
74 G5 **Yamuna** *R* India
74 G3 **Yamunanagar** India
55 G4 **Yamyshevo** Kazakhstan
66 E6 **Yamzho Yumco** *L* China
51 N2 **Yana** *R* Russian Federation
138 F6 **Yanac** Victoria Australia
60 D12 **Yanagawa** Japan
61 O8 **Yanagawa** Japan
61 P12 **Yanaha-jima** *isld* Okinawa
76 F2 **Yanam** India
65 A6 **Yan'an** China
128 D6 **Yanaoca** Peru
56 D2 **Yanashimskiy Polkan** *pk* Russian Federation
139 G4 **Yancannia** New South Wales Australia
109 H6 **Yancey** Texas U.S.A.
112 H1 **Yanceyville** North Carolina U.S.A.
65 A6 **Yanchang** China
77 B3 **Yanchashmeh** Iran
Yancheng *see* **Qihe**
59 H5 **Yancheng** China
67 F1 **Yancheng** China
143 B9 **Yanchep** W Australia Australia
65 A6 **Yanchuan** China
139 H5 **Yanco** New South Wales Australia
139 H6 **Yanco** *R* New South Wales Australia
143 D8 **Yandal** W Australia Australia
138 F3 **Yandama** *R* South Australia Australia
65 A4 **Yandian** China
143 C7 **Yandil** W Australia Australia
141 L7 **Yandina** Queensland Australia
68 B4 **Yandoon** Burma
85 C6 **Yanfolila** Mali
86 D5 **Yangambi** Zaire
66 E5 **Yangbajain** China
65 B7 **Yangcheng** China
Yangchuan *see* **Suiyang**
67 D5 **Yangchun** China
Yangcun *see* **Wuqing**
67 E5 **Yangcun** China
65 F3 **Yangdachengzi** China
142 A3 **Yangebup L** W Australia Australia
65 J2 **Yanggang** China
58 F3 **Yanggao** China
65 C6 **Yanggu** China
57 F4 **Yangibazar** Kirghizia
77 B2 **Yangi Emām** Iran
57 D5 **Yangi-Nishan** Uzbekistan
67 D6 **Yangjiang** China
65 E4 **Yangjiazhangzi** China
67 F3 **Yangkou** China
67 A4 **Yanglin** China
67 D2 **Yangloudong** China
65 C7 **Yangmiao** China
67 D3 **Yangming Shan** *mt* China
68 C4 **Yangon** Burma
52 E3 **Yangory** Russian Federation
67 D7 **Yangpu Gang** *inlet* China
65 B6 **Yangquan** China
67 D3 **Yangquan** China
65 C7 **Yangshan** China
67 D4 **Yangshan** China
Yangshe *see* **Shazhou**
67 C4 **Yangshuo** China
67 F1 **Yangtan** China
Yangtze Gorges *see* **Qutang Xia Wu Xia**
Yangtze Kiang *R see* **Chang Jiang** *R*
55 E2 **Yangutumskiye** Russian Federation
68 D6 **Yangwa** Burma
Yangwu *see* **Yuanyang**
67 E2 **Yangxin** China
65 B4 **Yangyuan** China
67 F1 **Yangzhong** China
67 F1 **Yangzhou** China
65 A6 **Yan He** *R* China
67 C2 **Yanhe** China
138 D5 **Yaninee, L** South Australia Australia
52 D4 **Yanis'yarvi, Oz** *L* Russian Federation
65 H3 **Yanji** China
65 C7 **Yanjin** China
67 A2 **Yanjin** China
67 B2 **Yanjing** China
138 F4 **Yanko Glen** New South Wales Australia
98 J7 **Yankton** South Dakota U.S.A.
65 C7 **Yanling** China
142 B6 **Yannarie** *R* W Australia Australia
Yannina *see* **Ioánnina**
54 B1 **Yanovichi** Belarus
52 G6 **Yanovo** Russian Federation
83 K9 **Yan Oya** *R* Sri Lanka
66 D3 **Yanqi** China
65 C4 **Yanqing** China
142 A5 **Yanrey** W Australia Australia
65 D4 **Yan Shan** *mts* China
65 D5 **Yanshan** China
67 F2 **Yanshan** China
67 A5 **Yanshan** China
65 B7 **Yanshi** China
67 F4 **Yanshi** China
59 J2 **Yanshou** China
51 N1 **Yanskiy Zaliv** *B* Russian Federation
139 H3 **Yantabulla** New South Wales Australia
59 H4 **Yantai** China
138 F3 **Yantara, L** New South Wales Australia
67 B1 **Yanting** China
65 G3 **Yantongshan** China
67 G2 **Yantou** China
47 H1 **Yantra** *R* Bulgaria
80 D2 **Yanūh** Israel
57 D3 **Yany Kurgan** Kazakhstan
65 C7 **Yanzhou** China
67 B3 **Yanzikou** China
86 C3 **Yao** Chad
61 J11 **Yao** Japan
Yaodu *see* **Dongzhi**
65 A6 **Yaotou** China
86 B5 **Yaoundé** Cameroon
65 D7 **Yaowan** China
65 A7 **Yao Xian** China
69 D9 **Yao Yai, Ko** *isld* Thailand
136 H2 **Yapen** *isld* W Irian
141 F4 **Yappar** *R* Queensland Australia
Yaqian *see* **Yuexi**
80 D8 **Yaqin** Jordan
127 J5 **Yaque del Sur** *R* Dominican Rep
124 E3 **Yaqui** *R* Mexico
100 A5 **Yaquina Head** Oregon U.S.A.
80 C5 **Yaqum** Israel
52 H5 **Yar** Russian Federation
126 F4 **Yara** Cuba
128 E1 **Yaracuy** *state* Venezuela
141 G6 **Yaraka** Queensland Australia
52 G6 **Yaransk** Russian Federation
47 K7 **Yaraşlı Gölü** *L* Turkey
47 K6 **Yarbasan** Turkey
8 C6 **Yarcombe** England
138 D4 **Yardea** South Australia Australia
80 F3 **Yardena** Israel
47 L8 **Yardımcı Burun** *C* Turkey
52 H3 **Yarega** Russian Federation
48 J2 **Yaremcha** Ukraine
137 O2 **Yaren** Nauru
52 G3 **Yarenga** Russian Federation
52 G4 **Yarensk** Russian Federation
9 H2 **Yare, R** England
128 D3 **Yari** *R* Colombia
61 L9 **Yariga-take** *mt* Japan
47 L5 **Yarimca** Turkey
47 N11 **Yarimca** Turkey
80 D1 **Yârîne** Lebanon
140 E5 **Yaringa** *R* Queensland Australia
128 E1 **Yaritagua** Venezuela
Yarkand *R see* **Yarkant He**
Yarkant *see* **Shache**
66 B4 **Yarkant He** *R* China
55 E3 **Yarkovo** Russian Federation
138 B4 **Yarle Lakes** South Australia Australia
66 D6 **Yarlung Zangbo Jiang** *R* China
13 G5 **Yarm** England
48 K1 **Yarmolintsy** Ukraine
122 F10 **Yarmouth** Nova Scotia Canada
9 E6 **Yarmouth** England
95 R3 **Yarmouth** Maine U.S.A.
95 R5 **Yarmouth** Massachusetts U.S.A.
80 F3 **Yarmuk** *R* Syria
103 M7 **Yarnell** Arizona U.S.A.
52 E5 **Yaroslavl'** Russian Federation
52 E5 **Yaroslavskaya Oblast'** *prov* Russian Federation
80 E1 **Yâroûn** Lebanon
54 J7 **Yarovaya** Ukraine
80 C5 **Yarqon** Israel
139 H7 **Yarra** *R* Victoria Australia
141 G2 **Yarraden** Queensland Australia
142 B5 **Yarraloola** W Australia Australia
139 H7 **Yarram** Victoria Australia
141 K7 **Yarraman** Queensland Australia
140 D4 **Yarran Ra** N Terr Australia
139 H6 **Yarrawonga** Victoria Australia
141 J5 **Yarrawonga Pt** Queensland Australia
143 B8 **Yarra Yarra Ls** W Australia Australia
142 D5 **Yarrie** W Australia Australia
141 H7 **Yarronvale** Queensland Australia
15 E5 **Yarrow** *R* Scotland
141 H5 **Yarrowmere** Queensland Australia
55 F1 **Yarsomovy** Russian Federation
54 D1 **Yartsevo** Russian Federation
128 C2 **Yarumal** Colombia
48 L2 **Yaryshev** Ukraine
86 D5 **Yasanyama** Zaire
137 Q5 **Yasawa Grp** *islds* Fiji
85 F6 **Yashi** Nigeria
85 E7 **Yashikera** Nigeria
60 F12 **Ya-shima** Japan
61 O6 **Yashima** Japan
60 F12 **Yashiro-jima** Japan
55 B4 **Yashkino** Russian Federation
54 J8 **Yasinovataya** Ukraine
48 J2 **Yasinya** Ukraine
54 J2 **Yasnogorsk** Russian Federation
68 G5 **Yasothon** Thailand
139 J5 **Yass** New South Wales Australia
47 M11 **Yassi** *isld* Turkey
60 G12 **Yasuda** Japan
60 G10 **Yasugi** Japan
77 B4 **Yāsūj** Iran
128 E6 **Yata** Bolivia
47 J7 **Yatağan** Turkey
85 E6 **Yatakala** Niger
106 G5 **Yates** New Mexico U.S.A.
94 H6 **Yatesboro** Pennsylvania U.S.A.
107 P4 **Yates Center** Kansas U.S.A.
115 K5 **Yathkyed L** Northwest Territories Canada
80 D5 **Yatma** Jordan
86 D5 **Yatolema** Zaire
Yatou *see* **Rongcheng**
61 M10 **Yatsuga take** *mt* Japan
61 L9 **Yatsuo** Japan
60 D13 **Yatsushiro** Japan
80 D8 **Yatta** Jordan
8 D5 **Yatton** England
128 E3 **Yatua** *R* Venezuela
128 D7 **Yauca** Peru
127 L5 **Yauco** Puerto Rico
112 H4 **Yauhannah** South Carolina U.S.A.
128 C6 **Yauyos** Peru
103 M7 **Yava** Arizona U.S.A.
57 E5 **Yavan** Tajikistan
124 E4 **Yavaros** Mexico
74 H8 **Yavatmāl** India
128 D6 **Yavero** *R* Peru
128 E8 **Yavi** Argentina
128 E2 **Yavi, Co** *mt* Venezuela
128 E3 **Yavita** Venezuela
55 E4 **Yavlenka** Kazakhstan
80 B6 **Yavne** Israel
80 F3 **Yavnee** Israel
31 O6 **Yavorov** Ukraine
29 O3 **Yavr** *R* Finland/Rus Fed
79 H1 **Yavuzeli** Turkey
68 B2 **Yaw** *R* Burma
60 F12 **Yawatahama** Japan
68 C2 **Yawng-hwe** Burma
67 B3 **Yaxi** China
Yaxian *see* **Sanya**
56 C3 **Yaya** Russian Federation
52 J5 **Yayva** *R* Russian Federation
77 C3 **Yazd** Iran
77 C4 **Yazd-e Khvāst** Iran
57 F5 **Yazgulemskiy Khrebet** *mts* Tajikistan
55 C4 **Yazikovo** Russian Federation
111 F9 **Yazoo City** Mississippi U.S.A.
52 J4 **Yaz'va** *R* Russian Federation
38 M5 **Ybbs** Austria
38 L6 **Ybbsitz** Austria
130 C9 **Ybycúi** Paraguay
28 A3 **Ydby** Denmark
28 D5 **Yding Skovhøj** *hill* Denmark
52 J3 **Ydzhid Parma** Russian Federation
52 J3 **Ydzhyd Patok** *R* Russian Federation
68 C5 **Ye** Burma
139 H6 **Yea** Victoria Australia
8 B7 **Yealmpton** England
Yebaishou *see* **Jianping**
86 C1 **Yebbi bou** Chad
21 M2 **Yébleron** France
68 D5 **Yebyu** Burma
66 B4 **Yecheng** China
17 G6 **Yecla** Spain
124 E3 **Yécora** Mexico
68 C3 **Yedashe** Burma
47 K8 **Yedi Burun** *C* Turkey
48 L2 **Yedintsy** Moldova
52 F3 **Yedoma** Arkhangel'skaya obl Russian Federation
52 H2 **Yedoma** Komi Respublika Russian Federation
84 F5 **Yédri** Chad
142 E4 **Yeeda River** W Australia Australia
138 D5 **Yeelanna** South Australia Australia
143 D7 **Yeelirrie** W Australia Australia
52 D5 **Yefimovskiy** Russian Federation
54 K3 **Yefremov** Russian Federation
55 G6 **Yegindybulak** Kazakhstan
55 E5 **Yegindykol'** Kazakhstan
56 F3 **Yegirma** *R* Russian Federation
53 F10 **Yegorlyk** *R* Russian Federation
54 L1 **Yegor'yevsk** Russian Federation
130 C10 **Yegros** Paraguay
109 K5 **Yegua Cr** Texas U.S.A.
16 D7 **Yeguas, Sa. de** *mts* Spain
131 B5 **Yeguas, Vol** Chile
86 F5 **Yei** Sudan
67 E1 **Yeji** China
85 D7 **Yeji** Ghana
55 D3 **Yekaterinburg** Russian Federation
55 D1 **Yekaterininka** Russian Federation
55 F3 **Yekaterininskoye** Russian Federation
59 J1 **Yekaterinoslavka** Russian Federation
54 K4 **Yekaterinovka** Russian Federation
68 A3 **Ye Kyun** *isld* Burma
52 H6 **Yelabuga** Russian Federation
53 F8 **Yelan'** *R* Russian Federation
55 D2 **Yelan'** Russian Federation
54 N5 **Yelan'-Koleno** Russian Federation
141 K8 **Yelarbon** Queensland Australia
58 F1 **Yeleninskiy** Russian Federation
54 J9 **Yelenovka** Ukraine
54 G3 **Yelenskiy** Russian Federation
54 K4 **Yelets** Russian Federation
55 E1 **Yelizarovo** Russian Federation
55 C5 **Yelizavetinka** Russian Federation
59 M1 **Yelizavety, Mys** *C* Russian Federation
15 G1 **Yell** *isld* Scotland
76 E2 **Yellandu** India
111 K10 **Yellow** *R* Alabama U.S.A.
99 Q5 **Yellow** *R* Wisconsin U.S.A.
119 M6 **Yellow Creek** Saskatchewan Canada
143 C9 **Yellowdine** W Australia Australia
119 N9 **Yellow Grass** Saskatchewan Canada
117 O9 **Yellowhead Pass** Alberta Canada
114 H5 **Yellowknife** Northwest Territories Canada
117 Q4 **Yellowknife** Northwest Territories Canada
99 L5 **Yellow Medicine** *R* Minnesota U.S.A.
139 H4 **Yellow Mt** New South Wales Australia
100 K5 **Yellow Pine** Idaho U.S.A.
Yellow R *see* **Huang He** *R*
59 H4 **Yellow Sea** China/Korea
110 N2 **Yellow Springs** Ohio U.S.A.
98 B2 **Yellowstone** *R* Montana U.S.A.
101 P5 **Yellowstone L** Wyoming U.S.A.
101 P5 **Yellowstone Nat. Park** Wyoming U.S.A.
15 G1 **Yell Sound** Scotland
110 D5 **Yellville** Arkansas U.S.A.
54 E2 **Yel'nya** Russian Federation
56 C1 **Yeloguy** *R* Russian Federation
55 E3 **Yeloshnoye** Russian Federation
55 C3 **Yelovo Barda** Russian Federation
16 C4 **Yeltes** *R* Spain
52 D6 **Yel'tsy** Russian Federation
125 M2 **Yelucá** *mt* Nicaragua
52 H3 **Yelva** *R* Russian Federation
8 B7 **Yelverton** England
115 L1 **Yelverton B** Northwest Territories Canada
85 E6 **Yelwa** Nigeria
55 D4 **Yemanzhelinsk** Russian Federation
112 G5 **Yemassee** South Carolina U.S.A.
72 E6 **Yemen** *rep* S W Asia
55 E3 **Yemets** *R* Russian Federation
52 F3 **Yemetsk** Russian Federation
52 F3 **Yemtsa** Russian Federation
52 D1 **Yena** Russian Federation
54 K8 **Yenakiyevo** Ukraine
68 B2 **Yenangyat** Burma
68 B2 **Yenangyaung** Burma
68 B3 **Yenanma** Burma
67 A6 **Yen Bai** Vietnam
67 A6 **Yen Chau** Vietnam
139 H5 **Yenda** New South Wales Australia
85 E7 **Yendi** Ghana
58 F1 **Yendondin** Russian Federation
55 E1 **Yendra** Russian Federation
55 E1 **Yendyr'** Russian Federation
68 C2 **Yengan** Burma
66 B4 **Yengisar** China
47 J5 **Yenice** Turkey
47 K5 **Yenice** Turkey
47 H6 **Yenifoça** Turkey
78 A3 **Yenihisar** Turkey
47 J5 **Yeniköy** Turkey
47 N10 **Yeniköy** Turkey
31 M1 **Yenino** Russian Federation
47 J7 **Yenipazar** Aydin Turkey
47 L4 **Yenipazar** Bilecik Turkey
47 K4 **Yenişehir** Turkey
56 D2 **Yenisey** *R* Russian Federation
56 D2 **Yeniseysk** Russian Federation
50 H1 **Yeniseyskiy Zaliv** *G* Russian Federation
56 D5 **Yenisey, Verkhn-e** *R* Russian Federation
68 G2 **Yen Lap** Vietnam
68 G1 **Yen Minh** Vietnam
47 Q14 **Yennádhi** Rhodes Greece
19 P13 **Yenne** France
52 E1 **Yenozero, Oz** *L* Russian Federation
68 G3 **Yen Thanh** Vietnam
116 M5 **Yentna** *R* Alaska U.S.A.
143 E8 **Yeo L** W Australia Australia
74 F8 **Yeola** India
Yeóryios *isld see* **Áyios** *isld*
139 J5 **Yeoval** New South Wales Australia
8 D6 **Yeovil** England
124 E3 **Yepachic** Mexico
54 K3 **Yepifan** Russian Federation
141 K6 **Yeppoon** Queensland Australia
46 F7 **Yeráki** Greece
124 J6 **Yerbabuena** Mexico
56 G1 **Yerbogachen** Russian Federation
21 N2 **Yère** *R* Seine-Inférieure France
55 F5 **Yerementau** *mt* Kazakhstan
47 J7 **Yeresik** Turkey
78 K1 **Yerevan** Armenia
53 F9 **Yergeni** *hills* Russian Federation
143 D8 **Yerilla** W Australia Australia
57 C3 **Yerimbet** Kazakhstan
102 E3 **Yerington** Nevada U.S.A.
78 E2 **Yerköy** Turkey
55 G5 **Yermak** Kazakhstan
55 F1 **Yermakovo** Russian Federation
56 D4 **Yermakovskoye** Russian Federation
55 F5 **Yermentau** Kazakhstan
52 H2 **Yermitsa** Russian Federation
124 G4 **Yermo** Mexico
102 H7 **Yermo** California U.S.A.
55 C4 **Yermolayevo** Russian Federation
54 H1 **Yermolino** Russian Federation
59 H1 **Yerofey Pavlovich** Russian Federation
79 E8 **Yeroham** Israel
141 K2 **Yeronga** *dist* Brisbane, Qnsld Australia
52 H2 **Yersa** *R* Russian Federation
25 B6 **Yerseke** Netherlands
52 G3 **Yertom** Russian Federation
52 F4 **Yertsevo** Russian Federation
128 C6 **Yerupaja** *mt* Peru
80 D6 **Yerushalayim** Israel
21 M2 **Yerville** France
68 B2 **Yesagyo** Burma
67 C1 **Yesanguan** China
52 D6 **Yesenovichi** Russian Federation
79 D1 **Yeşidere** Turkey
55 E5 **Yesil'** Kazakhstan
47 K5 **Yesil Dağı** *mt* Turkey
78 F1 **Yeşilırmak** *R* Turkey
Yeşilkent *see* **Erzin**
47 M11 **Yeşilköy** Turkey
47 K7 **Yeşilova** Turkey
79 D1 **Yeşiltepe** Turkey
108 C1 **Yeso** New Mexico U.S.A.
80 C6 **Yesodot** Israel
51 K2 **Yessey** Russian Federation
17 F6 **Yeste** Spain
80 F1 **Yesud Ha Ma'ala** Israel
13 F3 **Yetholm** Scotland
139 K3 **Yetman** New South Wales Australia
85 C3 **Yetti** *tribe* Mauritania
68 B1 **Yeu** Burma
20 F8 **Yeu, I.d'** France
55 F3 **Yevgashchino** Russian Federation
78 L1 **Yevlakh** Azerbaijan
21 P7 **Yèvre** *R* France
59 K2 **Yevreyskaya Avtonomnyy Oblast** *reg* Russian Federation
65 D6 **Ye Xian** China
53 E10 **Yeysk** Russian Federation
52 D6 **Yezerishche** Russian Federation
52 G5 **Yezhikha** Russian Federation
52 G3 **Yezhuga** *R* Russian Federation
20 E5 **Yffiniac** France
130 C9 **Yguazu, R** Paraguay
130 C9 **Yhú** Paraguay
47 J8 **Yialí** *isld* Greece
84 J3 **Yi' Allaq, Gebel** Egypt
79 E3 **Yialousa** Cyprus
47 H9 **Yianisádhes** *isld* Crete Greece
47 O12 **Yiannádhes** Greece
46 E4 **Yiannitsá** Greece
68 E1 **Yibang** China
Yibei *see* **Minglun**
67 A2 **Yibin** China
80 B6 **Yibna** Israel
67 D1 **Yichang** China
65 B7 **Yicheng** China
65 D7 **Yicheng** China
67 D1 **Yicheng** China
65 A6 **Yichuan** China
65 B7 **Yichuan** China
59 J2 **Yichun** China
67 E3 **Yichun** China
58 F5 **Yidu** China
65 D6 **Yidu** China
67 E2 **Yifeng** China
80 F1 **Yiftaḥ** Israel
65 B7 **Yi He** *R* China
65 D7 **Yi He** *R* China
67 E3 **Yihuang** China
65 A7 **Yijun** China
65 H1 **Yilan** China
47 J3 **Yıldız Dağları** *mts* Turkey
78 F2 **Yildizeli** Turkey
67 A3 **Yiliang** China
67 A4 **Yiliang** China
66 E4 **Yiliping** China
143 B10 **Yilliminning** W Australia Australia
67 B1 **Yilong** China
65 G2 **Yimianpo** China
68 B2 **Yin** *R* Burma
65 D7 **Yinan** China
68 C4 **Yinbaing** Burma
65 B7 **Yincheng** China
58 E4 **Yinchuan** China
143 D9 **Yindarlgooda, L** W Australia Australia
67 D1 **Yindian** China
67 D1 **Yingcheng** China
67 F3 **Yingchuan** China
65 J1 **Yingchun** China
67 D4 **Yingde** China
65 F4 **Ying'ebu** China
Yinggen *see* **Qiongzhong**
65 B7 **Ying He** *R* China
65 E4 **Yingkou** China
67 B1 **Yingshan** China
67 D1 **Yingshan** China
67 E2 **Yingtan** China
65 B5 **Ying Xian** China
65 D3 **Yin He** *R* China
66 C3 **Yining** China
67 C2 **Yinjiang** China
138 F5 **Yinkame** South Australia Australia
68 B1 **Yinmabin** Burma
65 F2 **Yinma He** *R* China
68 C4 **Yinnyein** Burma
65 A4 **Yin Shan** *mts* China
Yinxian *see* **Ningbo**
46 G5 **Yioúra** *isld* Greece
Yiquan *see* **Meitan**
131 G4 **Yi, R** Uruguay
86 G4 **Yirga Alem** Ethiopia
80 D2 **Yirka** Israel
86 F4 **Yirol** Sudan
80 E1 **Yir'on** Israel
140 D1 **Yirrkala** N Terr Australia
59 G2 **Yirshi** China
52 G3 **Yirva** *R* Russian Federation
65 D6 **Yi Shan** *mts* China
67 C4 **Yishan** China
65 D7 **Yishui** China
80 E6 **Yitav** Jordan
46 F8 **Yíthion** Greece
65 F3 **Yitong** China
65 F2 **Yitong He** *R* China
66 E3 **Yiwu** China
67 G2 **Yiwu** China
68 E2 **Yiwu** China
Yixian *see* **Yicheng**
65 E4 **Yi Xian** China
65 C5 **Yi Xian** China
67 F2 **Yi Xian** China
67 F1 **Yixing** China
65 D4 **Yixun He** *R* China
65 B7 **Yiyang** China
67 D2 **Yiyang** Hunan China
67 F2 **Yiyang** Jiangxi China
65 D6 **Yiyuan** China
67 D4 **Yizhang** China
67 F1 **Yizheng** China
29 N11 **Ylämaa** Finland
29 J11 **Yläne** Finland
29 K8 **Ylihärmä** Finland
29 M6 **Ylikiiminki** Finland
52 C2 **Ylikitka** *L* Finland
29 M6 **Yli-li** Finland
29 K9 **Ylistaro** Finland
29 K5 **Ylitornio** Finland
29 L7 **Ylivieska** Finland
29 L4 **Yllästunturi** *mt* Finland
29 K10 **Ylöjärvi** Finland
115 R3 **Ymers Ø** *isld* Greenland
21 O5 **Ymonville** France
52 J4 **Yndin** Russian Federation
27 J13 **Yngaren** *L* Sweden
86 B3 **Yo** Nigeria
109 K6 **Yoakum** Texas U.S.A.
60 O2 **Yobetsu** Japan
60 O2 **Yobetsu-dake** *mt* Japan
60 C12 **Yobuko** Japan
128 E7 **Yocalla** Bolivia
107 L3 **Yocemento** Kansas U.S.A.
111 G7 **Yocono** *R* Mississippi U.S.A.
106 F3 **Yoder** Colorado U.S.A.
98 B8 **Yoder** Wyoming U.S.A.
60 J11 **Yodo** Japan
60 G10 **Yodoe** Japan
80 D5 **Yo'ezer** Jordan
133 D8 **Yogan** *mt* Chile
47 J3 **Yoğuntaş** Turkey
70 N9 **Yogyakarta** Java
117 P10 **Yoho Nat. Park** British Columbia Canada
60 O2 **Yoichi** Japan
60 O2 **Yoichi dake** *mt* Japan
125 L2 **Yojoa, L. de** Honduras
60 H10 **Yōka** Japan
86 C5 **Yokadouma** Cameroon
61 K10 **Yōkaichi** Japan
61 O10 **Yōkaichiba** Japan
111 F9 **Yokena** Mississippi U.S.A.
61 K11 **Yokkaichi** Japan
86 B4 **Yoko** Cameroon
60 F12 **Yokogawara** Japan
62 **Yokohama** *conurbation* Japan
61 N10 **Yokosuka** Japan
61 O6 **Yokote** Japan
60 O4 **Yokotsu-dake** *mt* Japan
86 B4 **Yola** Nigeria
125 M4 **Yolaina, Cord. de** Nicaragua
57 B5 **Yolbarsli** Turkmenistan
65 E2 **Yolin Mod** China
86 D6 **Yolombo** Zaire
61 P13 **Yomitan Airport** Okinawa
61 Q12 **Yona** Okinawa
61 P13 **Yonabaru** Okinawa
60 G10 **Yonago** Japan
67 G4 **Yonagunijima** Japan
61 Q12 **Yonaha-dake** *mt* Okinawa
100 B6 **Yoncalla** Oregon U.S.A.
61 O5 **Yoneshiro-gawa** *R* Japan
61 O8 **Yonezawa** Japan
67 F4 **Yong'an** China
67 D2 **Yong'anshi** China
67 B2 **Yongchuan** China
67 F4 **Yongchun** China
67 C3 **Yongcong** China
67 E4 **Yongding** China
65 C5 **Yongding He** *R* China
59 J4 **Yongdŭngpo** S Korea
67 E3 **Yongfeng** China
67 C4 **Yongfu** China
65 A6 **Yonghe** China
59 J4 **Yonghŭng** N Korea
65 G5 **Yŏnghŭng-man** *B* N Korea
58 F5 **Yongji** China
65 G3 **Yongji** China
67 G2 **Yongjia** China
Yongjing *see* **Xifeng**
67 G2 **Yongkang** China
65 C6 **Yongnian** China
Yongning *see* **Xuyong**
58 D6 **Yongning** China
67 C5 **Yongning** China
65 C5 **Yongqing** China
67 A2 **Yongshan** China
67 C2 **Yongshun** China
67 E3 **Yongtai** China
67 F4 **Yongtai** China
67 E3 **Yongxin** China
67 D3 **Yongxing** China
67 E2 **Yongxiu** China
Yongyang *see* **Weng'an**
118 H6 **Yonker** Saskatchewan Canada
95 O6 **Yonkers** New York U.S.A.
107 P5 **Yonkers** Oklahoma U.S.A.
18 H5 **Yonne** *dept* France
18 H5 **Yonne** *R* France
68 B2 **Yonzingyi** Burma
128 D2 **Yopal** Colombia
57 H5 **Yopurga** China
143 B9 **York** W Australia Australia
13 G6 **York** England
111 H9 **York** Alabama U.S.A.
101 O3 **York** Montana U.S.A.
98 J9 **York** Nebraska U.S.A.
98 G1 **York** North Dakota U.S.A.
95 L7 **York** Pennsylvania U.S.A.
112 F3 **York** South Carolina U.S.A.
141 G1 **York, C** Queensland Australia
141 F2 **York Downs** Queensland Australia

138 D5 **Yorke Pen** South Australia Australia
138 D6 **Yorketown** South Australia Australia
115 K6 **York Factory** Manitoba Canada
123 O4 **York Harb** Newfoundland Canada
115 N2 **York, Kap** *C* Greenland
116 D4 **York Mts** Alaska U.S.A.
123 R2 **York Pt** Labrador, Nfld Canada
122 G5 **York R** Quebec Canada
142 F2 **York Sd** W Australia Australia
142 F2 **York Sound** W Australia Australia
119 P7 **Yorkton** Saskatchewan Canada
109 K7 **Yorktown** Texas U.S.A.
95 L9 **Yorktown** Virginia U.S.A.
95 R3 **York Village** Maine U.S.A.
99 S8 **Yorkville** Illinois U.S.A.
95 M3 **Yorkville** New York U.S.A.
125 L2 **Yoro** Honduras
71 B3 **Yoronga** *isld* Indonesia
102 D4 **Yosemite L** California U.S.A.
102 E4 **Yosemite Lodge** California U.S.A.
102 E3 **Yosemite National Park** California U.S.A.
61 M8 **Yoshida** Japan
61 P6 **Yoshihama-wan** *B* Japan
60 H11 **Yoshino** *R* Japan
60 F12 **Yoshino** Japan
61 K11 **Yoshino-Kumano Nat. Park** Japan
52 G6 **Yoshkar-Ola** Russian Federation
60 D12 **Yoshu** Japan
Yösönbulag *see* **Altay** Mongolia
101 M8 **Yost** Utah U.S.A.
61 O8 **Yotsukura** Japan
79 F9 **Yotvata** Israel
117 L11 **Youbou** British Columbia Canada
14 D5 **Youghal** Ireland
67 B5 **You Jiang** *R* China
85 B6 **Youkounkoun** Guinea
9 E1 **Youlgreave** England
139 J5 **Young** New South Wales Australia
119 M7 **Young** Saskatchewan Canada
103 O7 **Young** Arizona U.S.A.
138 D4 **Younghusband, L** South Australia Australia
138 E6 **Younghusband Pen** South Australia Australia
146 C14 **Young I** Antarctica
140 D3 **Young, Mt** N Terr Australia
144 B6 **Young Range** New Zealand
88 E7 **Youngs B** Malawi
118 F7 **Youngstown** Alberta Canada
111 L11 **Youngstown** Florida U.S.A.
94 J3 **Youngstown** New York U.S.A.
94 G5 **Youngstown** Ohio U.S.A.
111 D11 **Youngsville** Louisiana U.S.A.
106 D5 **Youngsville** New Mexico U.S.A.
112 J1 **Youngsville** North Carolina U.S.A.
94 H5 **Youngsville** Pennsylvania U.S.A.
101 Q6 **Younts Pk** Wyoming U.S.A.
102 B3 **Yountville** California U.S.A.
67 C2 **You Shui** *R* China
67 F3 **Youxi** China
67 D3 **You Xian** China
67 C2 **Youyang** China
65 H1 **Youyi** China
65 B4 **Youyu** China
141 G8 **Yowah** *R* Queensland Australia
143 C7 **Yowereena Hill** W Australia Australia
78 E2 **Yozgat** Turkey
130 B9 **Ypacarai, L** Paraguay
29 K11 **Ypäjä** Finland
130 C8 **Ypané, R** Paraguay
130 C8 **Ypé-jhú** Paraguay
130 B9 **Ypoá** *L* Paraguay
21 L2 **Yport** France
29 L7 **Yppäri** Finland
Ypres *see* **Ieper**
94 D4 **Ypsilanti** Michigan U.S.A.
100 C8 **Yreka** California U.S.A.
8 C3 **Yrfon** *R* Wales
8 C3 **Yspytty Ystwyth** Wales
18 H7 **Yssingeaux** France
57 G3 **Yssyk-Ata** Kirghizia
27 G16 **Ystad** Sweden
8 C4 **Ystalyfera** Wales
8 B3 **Ystrad Aeron** Wales
8 C3 **Ystrad-ffin** Wales
8 C3 **Ystwyth, R** Wales
15 F3 **Ythan, R** Scotland
26 G9 **Ytterhogdal** Sweden
27 J12 **Ytterjärna** Sweden
26 J8 **Ytterlännäs** Sweden
26 E8 **Ytteröy** Norway
26 L7 **Yttersjön** Sweden
67 D1 **Yuan'an** China
67 C4 **Yuanbao Shan** *mt* China
67 E1 **Yüan Hu** China
67 C2 **Yuan Jiang** *R* China
67 D2 **Yuanjiang** China
68 F1 **Yuan Jiang** *R* China
67 C2 **Yuanling** China
65 B5 **Yuanping** China
65 B7 **Yuanqu** China
65 C6 **Yuanshi** China
67 E3 **Yuan Shui** *R* China
65 B7 **Yuanyang** China
67 D3 **Yuanyue** China
60 J11 **Yuasa** Japan
102 C2 **Yuba** *R* California U.S.A.
102 C2 **Yuba City** California U.S.A.
60 P2 **Yūbari** Japan
60 Q2 **Yūbari dake** *mt* Japan
86 G4 **Yubdo** Ethiopia
60 R1 **Yūbetsu** Japan
60 S2 **Yūbetsu** Japan
61 M9 **Yubiso** Japan
80 G3 **Yubla** Jordan
128 D7 **Yucamani** *mt* Peru
125 P7 **Yucatan** *state* Mexico
90 A6 **Yucatan Basin** Atlantic Oc
126 A3 **Yucatan Chan** Caribbean
103 K7 **Yucca** Arizona U.S.A.
103 H4 **Yucca Flat** Nevada U.S.A.
106 B4 **Yucca House Nat. Mon** Colorado U.S.A.
65 C6 **Yucheng** China
65 C7 **Yucheng** China
65 B6 **Yuci** China
65 C3 **Yudaokou** China
51 N3 **Yudoma** *R* Russian Federation
67 E4 **Yudu** China
67 B1 **Yuechi** China
67 D1 **Yuekou** China
Yuelai *see* **Huachuan**
67 C1 **Yuelai** China
65 F2 **Yueliang Pao** *L* China
67 G2 **Yueqing** China
67 G2 **Yueqing Wan** *B* China
67 E1 **Yuexi** China
58 D6 **Yuexi He** *R* China
67 A2 **Yuexi He** *R* China
Yueyang *see* **Gu Xian**
67 D2 **Yueyang** China
60 E12 **Yufu-dake** *mt* Japan
52 G5 **Yug** *R* Russian Federation
52 G4 **Yuga** *R* Russian Federation
67 E2 **Yugan** China
55 F1 **Yugan** Russian Federation
42 H4 **Yugoslavia** *rep* S Europe
67 G1 **Yuhang** China
65 B4 **Yu He** *R* China
65 A5 **Yuhebu** China
67 B4 **Yuhong** China
67 G2 **Yuhuan** China
143 B8 **Yuin** W Australia Australia
67 C2 **Yu Jiang** *R* China
67 E2 **Yujiang** China
67 C5 **Yu Jiang** *R* China
52 H5 **Yukamenskoye** Russian Federation
47 J5 **Yukarıbey** Turkey
54 G2 **Yukhnov** Russian Federation
61 N9 **Yūki** Japan
116 J4 **Yuki** *R* Alaska U.S.A.
113 F7 **Yukon** Florida U.S.A.
107 N6 **Yukon** Oklahoma U.S.A.
116 Q4 **Yukon-Charley Rivers Nat Preserve** Alaska U.S.A.
117 E4 **Yukon Crossing** Yukon Territory Canada
55 E1 **Yukonda** *R* Russian Federation
116 E5 **Yukon Delta** Alaska U.S.A.
116 N3 **Yukon Flats Nat Mon** Alaska U.S.A.
116 M4 **Yukon R** Alaska/Yukon Terr U.S.A./Canada
114 F5 **Yukon Territory** Canada
60 E12 **Yukuhashi** Japan
66 B4 **Yukuriawat** China
52 F3 **Yula** *R* Russian Federation
55 C4 **Yuldybayevo** Russian Federation
146 C13 **Yule B** Antarctica
141 J7 **Yuleba** Queensland Australia
142 B2 **Yule Brook** Perth, W Aust Australia
113 F7 **Yulee** Florida U.S.A.
142 C5 **Yule R** W Australia Australia
65 A5 **Yulin** China
67 C5 **Yulin** China
67 C7 **Yulin** China
52 D2 **Yuma** Russian Federation
103 K9 **Yuma** Arizona U.S.A.
98 D9 **Yuma** Colorado U.S.A.
127 K5 **Yuma, B. de** Dominican Rep
103 K9 **Yuma Desert** Arizona U.S.A.
55 C4 **Yumaguzino** Russian Federation
138 C4 **Yumbarra Conservation Park** South Australia Australia
86 E6 **Yumbi** Zaire
58 C3 **Yumen** China
58 C3 **Yü-men-chen** China
58 C3 **Yumenzhen** China
58 F1 **Yumurchen** Russian Federation
143 A8 **Yuna** W Australia Australia
127 K5 **Yuna** *R* Dominican Rep
78 C2 **Yunak** Turkey
67 D5 **Yunan** China
67 C1 **Yun'anzhen** China
65 B7 **Yuncheng** China
65 C7 **Yuncheng** China
143 D8 **Yundamindera** W Australia Australia
67 D5 **Yunfu** China
128 E7 **Yungas, Las** *mts* Bolivia
139 G5 **Yungera** Victoria Australia
Yunhe *see* **Pei Xian**
67 F2 **Yunhe** China
67 C5 **Yunkai Dashan** *mts* China
67 D1 **Yunmeng** China
67 A4 **Yunnan** *prov* China
60 O4 **Yunokawa** Japan
60 D13 **Yunomae** Japan
60 F10 **Yunotsu** Japan
16 E4 **Yunquera de H** Spain
67 A4 **Yunshang** China
138 E4 **Yunta** South Australia Australia
58 F5 **Yun Xian** China
67 F5 **Yunxiao** China
67 C1 **Yunyang** China
65 B5 **Yunzhong Shan** *mts* China
67 C3 **Yuping** China
65 D4 **Yuqiao Shuiku** *res* China
67 B3 **Yuqing** China
Yuqingsi *see* **Aoxi**
60 O3 **Yūrappu-dake** *mt* Japan
124 H7 **Yurécharo** Mexico
56 B3 **Yurga** Russian Federation
55 D3 **Yurgamysh** Russian Federation
55 E3 **Yurginskiy** Russian Federation
128 C5 **Yurimaguas** Peru
52 G6 **Yurino** Russian Federation
52 H5 **Yurla** Russian Federation
55 C3 **Yurma** *mt* Russian Federation
52 G2 **Yuroma** Russian Federation
55 E2 **Yurovsk** Russian Federation
66 B4 **Yurungkax He** *R* China
60 T2 **Yururi-tō** *isld* Japan
52 G5 **Yur'ya** Russian Federation
52 J2 **Yur'yakha** *R* Russian Federation
52 F6 **Yur'yevets** Russian Federation
52 E6 **Yur'yev Pol'skiy** Russian Federation
55 C3 **Yuryuzan' Katav-Ivanovsk** Russian Federation
125 L3 **Yuscarán** Honduras
67 F2 **Yushan** China
67 C2 **Yushanzhen** China
65 B6 **Yushe** China
52 H1 **Yushino** Russian Federation
52 D3 **Yushkozero** Russian Federation
59 J3 **Yushu** China
66 F5 **Yushu** China
65 G2 **Yushugou** China
Yushuwan *see* **Huaihua**
78 H1 **Yusufeli** Turkey
60 F12 **Yusuhara** Japan
52 H5 **Yus'va** Russian Federation
65 C7 **Yutai** China
98 K8 **Yutan** Nebraska U.S.A.
52 H6 **Yutaza** Russian Federation
128 F7 **Yuti** Bolivia
65 D5 **Yutian** Hebei China
66 C4 **Yutian** Xinjiang Uygur Zizhiqu China
130 C10 **Yuty** Paraguay
67 F5 **Yü-weng Tao** Taiwan
Yuxi *see* **Daozhen**
65 B5 **Yu Xian** China
65 C5 **Yu Xian** China
65 B7 **Yu Xian** China
67 G1 **Yuyao** China
60 D11 **Yuya-wan** *B* Japan
52 F5 **Yuza** *R* Russian Federation
61 M9 **Yuzawa** Japan
52 F6 **Yuzha** Russian Federation
57 G5 **Yuzh Alichurskiy, Khrebet** *mts* Tajikistan
55 D4 **Yuzhnoural'skiy** Russian Federation
55 D4 **Yuzhnyy** Russian Federation
56 B4 **Yuzhnyy** Russian Federation
56 C6 **Yuzhnyy Altay, Khrebet** *mts* Kazakhstan
48 M2 **Yuzhnyy Bug** *R* Ukraine
55 C4 **Yuzhnyy Ural** *reg* Russian Federation
Yuzhou *see* **Chongqing**
55 G4 **Yuzno Podol'sk** Russian Federation
21 O4 **Yvelines** *dept* France
40 E4 **Yverdon** Switzerland
21 M2 **Yvetot** France
20 D4 **Yvias** France
20 F5 **Yvignac** France
22 H3 **Yvoir Anhee** Belgium
40 E4 **Yvonand** Switzerland
21 O6 **Yvoy-le-Marron** France
21 L5 **Yvre-l'Evèque** France
68 B2 **Ywamun** Burma
68 C3 **Ywathit** Burma
27 H13 **Yxviken** Sweden
21 J7 **Yzernay** France
21 M8 **Yzeures-sur-Creuse** France

Z

25 C4 **Zaandam** Netherlands
25 C4 **Zaandijk** Netherlands
42 H6 **Zāba** *mt* Bosnia-Herzegovina
80 E4 **Zababida** Jordan
48 F5 **Žabalj** Serbia Yugoslavia
48 G6 **Žabari** Serbia Yugoslavia
58 G2 **Zabaykal'sk** Russian Federation
80 F3 **Zabda** Jordan
56 F4 **Zabituy** Russian Federation
31 K5 **Ząbkowice** Poland
31 O3 **Zabłudów** Poland
77 K4 **Zābol** *prov* Afghanistan
77 G4 **Zabol** Iran
77 G6 **Zāboli** Iran
48 J2 **Zabolotov** Ukraine
31 K6 **Zábřeh** Czech Rep
31 L5 **Zabrze** Poland
125 P9 **Zacatal** Guatemala
125 N8 **Zacatali** Mexico
124 H6 **Zacatecas** *state* Mexico
124 H6 **Zacatecas** Mexico
125 P11 **Zacatecoluca** El Salvador
125 L9 **Zacatepec** Mexico
111 E11 **Zachary** Louisiana U.S.A.
33 O6 **Zachun** Germany
125 L2 **Zacualpa** Honduras
42 G4 **Zadar** Croatia
68 C7 **Zadetkale Kyun** *isld* Burma
68 C8 **Zadetkyi** Burma
68 C5 **Zadi** Burma
54 K4 **Zadonsk** Russian Federation
80 C5 **Zafriyya** Israel
31 J4 **Zagań** Poland
52 B6 **Zagare** Lithuania
45 N6 **Zagarolo** Italy
79 B8 **Zagazig** Egypt
43 C12 **Zaghouan** Tunisia
46 F5 **Zagorá** Greece
85 C2 **Zagora** Morocco
Zagorsk *see* **Sergiyev Posad**
42 G3 **Zagreb** Croatia
77 A3 **Zāgros Mountains** Iran
48 G6 **Zagubica** Serbia Yugoslavia
Zagunao *see* **Li Xian** Sichuan
77 G5 **Zāhedān** Iran
98 C1 **Zahl** North Dakota U.S.A.
79 F5 **Zahle** Lebanon
33 R9 **Zahna** Germany
77 B6 **Zahrān, Az** Saudi Arabia
57 H3 **Zailiyskiv Alatau, Khr** *mts* Kazakhstan
36 H7 **Zainingen** Germany
86 D6 **Zaire** *rep* Africa
86 D5 **Zaïre** *R* W Africa
86 B7 **Zaïre Central** Zaire
80 D5 **Zaita** Jordan
46 E1 **Zaječar** Serbia Yugoslavia
56 F5 **Zakamensk** Russian Federation
78 L1 **Zakataly** Azerbaijan
78 J3 **Zakho** Iraq
46 D7 **Zákinthos** *isld* Greece
31 N5 **Zaklików** Poland
48 F1 **Zakopane** Poland
31 M3 **Zakroczym** Poland
47 H9 **Zákros** Crete Greece
48 D4 **Zala** *R* Hungary
48 D4 **Zalaegerszeg** Hungary
16 C7 **Zalamea la Real** Spain
59 H2 **Zalantun** China
48 D4 **Zalaövo** Hungary
48 H3 **Zalău** Romania
48 K2 **Zaleshchiki** Ukraine
94 E7 **Zaleski** Ohio U.S.A.
31 N1 **Zales'ye** Russian Federation
31 M2 **Zalewo** Poland
31 H2 **Zalew Szczeciński** *lagoon* Germany/Poland
86 D3 **Zalingei** Sudan
50 E4 **Zaliv Kara Bogaz Gol** *B* Turkmenistan
59 K3 **Zaliv Petra Velikogo** *B* Russian Federation
84 E4 **Zallāf, Ramlat az** *sands* Libya
110 F4 **Zalma** Missouri U.S.A.
37 O3 **Zalmanov** Czech Rep
25 D5 **Zaltbommel** Netherlands
84 F4 **Zalṭen** Libya
52 D5 **Zaluch'ye** Russian Federation
68 B4 **Zalun** Burma
68 D6 **Zalut** Burma
56 G4 **Zama** Russian Federation
117 O6 **Zama L** Alberta Canada
71 E3 **Zambales Mts** Luzon Philippines
31 J5 **Žamberk** Czech Rep
87 G9 **Zambeze** *R* E Africa
87 D8 **Zambezi** Zambia
88 F10 **Zambézia** Mozambique
88 C7 **Zambia** *rep* Cent Africa
71 F7 **Zamboanga** Mindanao Philippines
71 F6 **Zamboanguita** Negros Philippines
126 G10 **Zambrano** Colombia
31 N3 **Zambrów** Poland
85 F6 **Zamfara** *R* Nigeria
128 C4 **Zamora** Ecuador
124 H8 **Zamora** Mexico
16 C3 **Zamora** *prov* Spain
16 D3 **Zamora** Spain
102 C3 **Zamora** California U.S.A.
125 L3 **Zamorano** Honduras
31 O5 **Zamość** Poland
61 P13 **Zampa-misaki** *C* Okinawa
128 F3 **Zamuro, Sa. del** *mts* Venezuela
84 E3 **Zamzam** Libya
86 B6 **Zanaga** Congo
17 F5 **Záncara** *R* Spain
25 H3 **Zandberg** Netherlands
22 G1 **Zandvliet** Belgium
25 C4 **Zandvoort** Netherlands
116 J3 **Zane Hills** Alaska U.S.A.
94 E7 **Zanesville** Ohio U.S.A.
74 G2 **Zangla** Kashmir
65 C6 **Zanhuang** China
41 L6 **Zanica** Italy
77 A1 **Zanjān** Iran
131 C3 **Zanjón, R** Argentina
43 E8 **Zannone, I** Italy
Zante *see* **Zákinthos**
143 E9 **Zanthus** W Australia Australia
88 G5 **Zanzibar** Tanzania
88 G5 **Zanzibar Chan** Tanzania
88 G5 **Zanzibar, I** Tanzania
54 J2 **Zaokskiy** Russian Federation
67 E3 **Zaolin** China
65 C6 **Zaoqiang** China
17 F4 **Zaorejas** Spain
85 F3 **Zaouatallaz** Algeria
67 F1 **Zaoxi** China
67 D1 **Zaoyang** China
67 D1 **Zaoyang Zhan** China
61 O7 **Zaō-zan** *vol* Japan
56 D3 **Zaozernyy** Russian Federation
65 D7 **Zaozhuang** China
98 E2 **Zap** North Dakota U.S.A.
46 D1 **Zapadna Morava** *R* Serbia Yugoslavia
54 A1 **Zapadnaya Dvina** *R* Belarus/Rus Fed
53 D6 **Zapadnaya Dvina** *R* Russian Federation
29 Q2 **Zapadnaya Litza** *R* Russian Federation
59 M1 **Zapadno Sakhalinskiy Khrebet** *mt* Russian Federation
56 B2 **Zapadnosibirskaya Ravnina** *lowland* Russian Federation
56 C5 **Zapadnyy Sayan** Russian Federation
37 O4 **Zapadočeský** *reg* Czech Rep
133 C5 **Zapala** Argentina
109 H9 **Zapata** Texas U.S.A.
126 D3 **Zapata, Pen. de** Cuba
125 M4 **Zapatera, I** Nicaragua
128 D2 **Zapatosa** Colombia
126 H10 **Zapatoza, Ciénaga de** Colombia
37 K3 **Zapfendorf** Germany
29 P2 **Zapolyarnyy** Russian Federation
54 G9 **Zaporozh'ye** Ukraine
124 H8 **Zapotiltic** Mexico
124 G7 **Zapotlán** Mexico
84 F4 **Zaqqūt** Libya
Zara *see* **Zadar**
78 F2 **Zara** Turkey
57 C4 **Zarafshan** Uzbekistan
108 A4 **Zaragoza** Chihuahua Mexico
108 G7 **Zaragoza** Coahuila Mexico
71 D2 **Zaragoza** Luzon Philippines
17 G3 **Zaragoza** *prov* Spain
17 G3 **Zaragoza** Spain
124 H4 **Zaragoza, Tiahualilo de** Mexico
88 G5 **Zaramu** Tanzania
77 E4 **Zarand** Kerman Iran
77 B2 **Zarand** Ostan-e Markazi Iran
48 G4 **Zărandului, Muntii** *mts* Romania
77 G4 **Zaranj** Afghanistan
52 C6 **Zarasai** Lithuania
131 F5 **Zárate** Argentina
54 K2 **Zaraysk** Russian Federation
127 M10 **Zaraza** Venezuela
57 F5 **Zardaly** Kirghizia
77 B3 **Zard Kuh** *mt* Iran
29 P3 **Zarechensk** Russian Federation
52 D2 **Zarechensk** Russian Federation
117 G7 **Zarembo I** Alaska U.S.A.
85 F6 **Zaria** Nigeria
56 C4 **Zarinsk** Russian Federation
46 E5 **Zárkon** Greece
85 D5 **Zarma** *reg* Mali
48 J5 **Zarneşti** Romania
31 M4 **Żarnów** Poland
33 T5 **Zarow** *R* Germany
80 F7 **Zarqa** *R* Jordan
77 C5 **Zarqān** Iran
33 N5 **Zarrentin** Germany
128 C4 **Zaruma** Ecuador
31 J4 **Żary** Poland
85 F3 **Zarzaïtine** Algeria
85 G2 **Zarzis** Tunisia
37 P1 **Zaschwitz** Germany
52 D2 **Zasheyek** Russian Federation
31 H4 **Zasieki** Poland
48 K2 **Zastavna** Ukraine
89 E8 **Zastron** S Africa
54 E6 **Zasul'ye** Ukraine
79 H7 **Zatab ash Shāmah** Saudi Arabia
37 Q3 **Žatec** Czech Rep
48 N4 **Zatoka** Ukraine
Zatoka Gdańsk *see* **Danzig, G. of**
31 L6 **Zator** Poland
33 R8 **Zauche** *reg* Germany
57 A4 **Zaunguzskiye Karakumy** Turkmenistan
109 N4 **Zavalla** Texas U.S.A.
Zavelstein *see* **Bad Teinach-Zavelstein**
22 G2 **Zaventem** Belgium
47 H1 **Zavet** Bulgaria
48 E6 **Zavidovići** Bosnia-Herzegovina
59 J1 **Zavitinsk** Russian Federation
146 G2 **Zavodovski** *vol* S Sandwich Is S Atlantic Oc
146 G2 **Zavodovski I** S Sandwich Is S Atlantic Oc
56 B4 **Zavodskoye** Russian Federation
68 C2 **Zawgyi** *R* Burma
31 L5 **Zawiercie** Poland
80 D5 **Zawiya** Jordan
84 E3 **Zāwiyah, Az** Libya
79 G3 **Zāwīyah, Jebel az** *mts* Syria
84 G3 **Zawīyat Masūs** Libya
56 F3 **Zayarsk** Russian Federation
79 G6 **Zaydī, Wādī az** *watercourse* Syria
56 B6 **Zaysan, Oz** *res* Kazakhstan
57 L1 **Zaysan, Ozero** *L* Kazakhstan
48 K1 **Zbarazh** Ukraine
31 J3 **Zbaszyń** Poland
48 J1 **Zborov** Ukraine
48 K1 **Zbruch** *R* Ukraine
48 G2 **Zdaňa** Slovakia
48 D1 **Ždanice** Czech Rep
30 H6 **Zdice** Czech Rep
31 L4 **Zduńska** Poland
Zealand *isld* *see* **Sjælland**
118 K7 **Zealandia** Saskatchewan Canada
99 N7 **Zearing** Iowa U.S.A.
57 F6 **Zēbāk** Afghanistan
117 K11 **Zeballos** British Columbia Canada
112 J2 **Zebulon** North Carolina U.S.A.
33 R6 **Zechlin** Germany
41 H5 **Zeda, Monte** Italy
22 E1 **Zedelgem** Belgium
22 E1 **Zeebrugge** Belgium
139 H8 **Zeehan** Tasmania Australia
25 A6 **Zeeland** Netherlands
94 A4 **Zeeland** Michigan U.S.A.
98 G4 **Zeeland** North Dakota U.S.A.
79 E7 **Zeelim** Israel
80 E8 **Ze'elim, N** *R* Israel
89 E5 **Zeerust** S Africa
25 E4 **Zeewolde** Netherlands
80 E2 **Zefat** Israel
85 C3 **Zegdou** Algeria
85 E5 **Zeggeren** *watercourse* Mali
31 N3 **Zegrzyńskie, Jezioro** *res* Poland
33 S7 **Zehdenick** Germany
33 S8 **Zehlendorf** Berlin
33 Q5 **Zehna** Germany
37 P1 **Zehren** Germany
110 G4 **Zeigler** Illinois U.S.A.
37 K3 **Zeil** Germany
25 D4 **Zeist** Netherlands
33 S10 **Zeithain** Germany
37 O7 **Zeitlarn** Germany
37 N1 **Zeitz** Germany
80 G3 **Zeizun** Syria
22 G1 **Zele** Belgium
31 N4 **Zelechów** Poland
37 P5 **Zelená Lhota** Czech Rep
52 D2 **Zelenborskiy** Russian Federation
55 D1 **Zelenoborsk** Russian Federation
54 E9 **Zelenodol'sk** Ukraine
29 O11 **Zelenogorsk** Russian Federation
54 J1 **Zelenograd** Russian Federation
31 M1 **Zelenogradsk** Russian Federation
54 E9 **Zelenoye** Ukraine
53 F11 **Zelenshuk** *R* Russian Federation
94 G6 **Zelienople** Pennsylvania U.S.A.
48 E2 **Želiezovce** Slovakia
42 G3 **Zelina** Croatia
46 D1 **Željin** *mt* Serbia Yugoslavia
36 E7 **Zell** Baden-Württemberg Germany
36 H4 **Zell** Bayern Germany
36 C3 **Zell** Rheinland-Pfalz Germany
98 H5 **Zell** South Dakota U.S.A.
37 K2 **Zella-Mehlis** Germany
38 H6 **Zell-a-moos** Austria
38 G7 **Zell-am-see** Austria
38 E7 **Zell-am-Ziller** Austria
38 L5 **Zell-bei-zellhof** Austria
33 S9 **Zellendorf** Germany
36 H4 **Zellingen** Germany
119 M7 **Zelma** Saskatchewan Canada
31 L4 **Zelów** Poland
36 C4 **Zeltingen-Rachtig** Germany
22 F1 **Zelzate** Belgium
43 D11 **Zembra, Ile** Tunisia
46 F2 **Zemen** Bulgaria
51 O1 **Zemlya Bunge** Russian Federation
50 D1 **Zemlya Frantsa-Iosifa** Russian Federation
50 D1 **Zemlya Georga** *isld* Franz Josef Land Russian Federation
50 F1 **Zemlya Vil'cheka** Franz Josef Land Russian Federation
38 E7 **Zemm** *R* Austria
48 G2 **Zempléni-Hory** *mt* Hungary
48 F6 **Zemun** Serbia Yugoslavia
107 M4 **Zenda** Kansas U.S.A.
67 D5 **Zengcheng** China
100 B9 **Zenia** California U.S.A.
42 H4 **Zenica** Bosnia-Herzegovina
54 F6 **Zen'kov** Ukraine
56 C4 **Zen'kovo** Russian Federation
37 K5 **Zenn** *R* Germany
22 G1 **Zenne** *R* Belgium
119 O5 **Zenon Park** Saskatchewan Canada
60 G11 **Zentsūji** Japan
125 L9 **Zenzontepec** Mexico
98 D4 **Zeona** South Dakota U.S.A.
109 J4 **Zephyr** Texas U.S.A.
113 E9 **Zephyrhills** Florida U.S.A.
143 D8 **Zephyr,Mt** W Australia Australia
57 E5 **Zerav'shanskiy Khrebet** *mts* Tajikistan/Uzbekistan
33 Q9 **Zerbst** Germany
36 B4 **Zerf** Germany
31 K3 **Zerków** Poland
40 G5 **Zermatt** Switzerland
101 U3 **Zero** Montana U.S.A.
46 D3 **Zerqan** Albania
33 U6 **Zerrenthin** Germany
80 C3 **Zerufa** Israel
66 E6 **Zêtang** China
32 G6 **Zetel** Germany
65 E6 **Zetouji** China
37 M2 **Zeulenroda** Germany
33 T8 **Zeuthen** Germany
32 K6 **Zeven** Germany
25 C5 **Zevenbergen** Netherlands
25 C5 **Zevenbergse Hoek** Netherlands
45 K1 **Zevio** Italy
59 J1 **Zeya** Russian Federation
25 F5 **Zeyenaar** Netherlands
59 J1 **Zeysko Bureinskaya Ravnina** *plain* Russian Federation
59 J1 **Zeyskoye Vodokhranilishche** *res* Russian Federation
47 J6 **Zeytindağ** Turkey
16 B4 **Zêzere** *R* Portugal
79 F4 **Zgharta** Lebanon
31 L4 **Zgierz** Poland
38 N8 **Zgornja Kungota** Slovenia
31 J4 **Zgorzelec** Poland
48 L2 **Zguritsa** Moldova
66 F5 **Zhag'yab** China
67 F3 **Zhaili** China
67 C5 **Zhaixu** China
55 E5 **Zhaksy** Kazakhstan
57 E1 **Zhaksykon** *R* Kazakhstan
57 G2 **Zhaksylyk** Kazakhstan
57 J3 **Zhalanash** Kazakhstan
55 E5 **Zhaltyr** Kazakhstan
57 C1 **Zhamanakkol', Ozero** *L* Kazakhstan
57 E1 **Zhanabas** Kazakhstan
57 B2 **Zhanakentkala** Kazakhstan
57 B2 **Zhanakurylys** Kazakhstan
57 C3 **Zhanatalap** Kazakhstan
57 E3 **Zhanatas** Kazakhstan
65 C4 **Zhangbei** China
Zhangde *see* **Anyang**
Zhangdian *see* **Zibo**
65 G3 **Zhangguangcai Ling** *mt ra* China
65 E3 **Zhanggutai** China
65 C6 **Zhang He** *R* China
67 C6 **Zhanghuang** China
65 C4 **Zhangjiakou** China
67 E1 **Zhangjiapang** China
67 E2 **Zhangjiashan** China
65 D7 **Zhanglou** China
67 C5 **Zhangmu** China
67 F4 **Zhangping** China
67 F4 **Zhangpu** China
65 D6 **Zhangqiu** China
65 D4 **Zhangsanying** China
67 E4 **Zhang Shui** *R* China
Zhangshuzhen *see* **Qingjiang**
59 H3 **Zhangwu** China
58 D4 **Zhangye** China
67 F4 **Zhangzhou** Fujian China
65 B6 **Zhangzi** China
65 E5 **Zhangzi Dao** *isld* China
65 D6 **Zhanhua** China
67 C6 **Zhanjiang** China
67 C6 **Zhanjiang Gang** *B* China
57 C3 **Zhankala** Kazakhstan
51 P1 **Zhannetty, Ostrov** *isld* Russian Federation
57 E1 **Zhanteli** Kazakhstan
67 A4 **Zhanyi** China
65 E2 **Zhanyu** China
67 F5 **Zhao'an** China
65 B6 **Zhaocheng** China
65 F1 **Zhaodong** China
Zhaoge *see* **Qi Xian**
67 C4 **Zhaoping** China
67 D5 **Zhaoqing** China
66 C3 **Zhaosu** China
67 A3 **Zhaotong** China
65 C6 **Zhao Xian** China
65 F2 **Zhaoyuan** China
65 E6 **Zhaoyuan** China
Zhaozhen *see* **Jintang**
59 J2 **Zhaozhou** China
67 G1 **Zhapu** China
52 D6 **Zhari** Russian Federation
54 D1 **Zharkovskiy** Russian Federation
57 K1 **Zharma** Kazakhstan
57 G1 **Zharyk** Kazakhstan
48 N1 **Zhashkov** Ukraine
51 M2 **Zhatay** Russian Federation
Zhaxi *see* **Weixin**
66 B5 **Zhaxigang** China
Zhdanov *see* **Mariupol'**
65 C7 **Zhecheng** China
67 F2 **Zhejiang** *prov* China
50 G1 **Zhelaniya, Mys** *C* Russian Federation
57 E1 **Zhel'dyadyr** *hills* Kazakhstan
31 N1 **Zheleznodorozhnyy** Russian Federation
56 F3 **Zheleznodorozhnyy** Irkutskaya obl Russian Federation
54 G4 **Zheleznogorsk** Russian Federation
56 F3 **Zheleznogorsk-Ilimsky** Russian Federation
Zhelou *see* **Ceheng**
54 E8 **Zheltyye Vody** Ukraine
67 B4 **Zhenfeng** China
67 B2 **Zheng'an** China
58 F4 **Zhengding** China
67 F3 **Zhenghe** China
67 D2 **Zhengjiayi** China
65 C3 **Zhenglan Qi** China
65 C3 **Zhengxiangbai Qi** China
65 B7 **Zhengzhou** China
67 G2 **Zhenhai** China
67 F4 **Zhenhai** China
67 F1 **Zhenjiang** China
65 F2 **Zhenlai** China
67 C5 **Zhenlong** China
67 B3 **Zhenning** China
67 C1 **Zhenping** China
Zhenwudong *see* **Ansai**
65 F1 **Zhenxiang** China
67 A3 **Zhenxiong** China
67 C3 **Zhenyuan** China
67 C1 **Zhenziling** China
67 F3 **Zherong** China
67 A4 **Zhetai** China
55 D5 **Zhetikol'** *L* Russian Federation
67 D1 **Zhicheng** China
67 A5 **Zhicun** China
48 J1 **Zhidachov** Ukraine
Zhifang *see* **Wuchang**
58 B3 **Zhifang** China
56 G4 **Zhigalovo** Russian Federation
51 M2 **Zhigansk** Russian Federation
57 E1 **Zhigerli** Kazakhstan
67 D1 **Zhijiang** China
67 C3 **Zhijiang** China
67 B3 **Zhijin** China
54 H7 **Zhikhar'** Ukraine
67 B6 **Zhilang** China
58 C5 **Zhi Qu** China
67 F2 **Zhitan** China
53 C8 **Zhitomir** Ukraine
54 G2 **Zhizdra** *R* Russian Federation
54 F3 **Zhizdra** Russian Federation
54 B4 **Zhlobin** Belarus
48 L1 **Zhmerinka** Ukraine
74 C3 **Zhob** Pakistan
77 L4 **Zhob** *R* Pakistan
51 P1 **Zhokhova, Ostrov** *isld* Russian Federation
57 C5 **Zhondor** Uzbekistan
Zhongba *see* **Jiangyou**
66 C6 **Zhongba** China
67 B5 **Zhongdong** China
67 C4 **Zhongdu** China
65 F1 **Zhonghe** China
67 A1 **Zhongjiang** China
65 B7 **Zhongmou** China
146 J11 **Zhongshan** *China Base* Antarctica
67 D4 **Zhongshan** China
67 D5 **Zhongshan** China
Zhongshu *see* **Renhuai**
65 B7 **Zhongtiao Shan** *ra* China
67 B1 **Zhong Xian** China
58 F5 **Zhongxiang** China
67 E4 **Zhongxin** China
65 B6 **Zhongyang** China
68 K3 **Zhongyuan** China
67 D2 **Zhoujiadian** China
58 F5 **Zhoukou** China
67 F3 **Zhouning** China
67 G1 **Zhoushan Dao** *isld* China
59 H5 **Zhoushan Qundao** China
48 J1 **Zhovten'** Ukraine
48 N3 **Zhovten'** Ukraine
59 H4 **Zhuanghe** China
67 B3 **Zhucang** China
65 D6 **Zhucheng** China
Zhuji *see* **Shangqiu**
67 G2 **Zhuji** China
67 G2 **Zhujia Jian** *isld* China
67 D6 **Zhujiang Kou** *B* China
Zhujing *see* **Jinshan**
54 E3 **Zhukovka** Russian Federation
54 H1 **Zhukovo** Russian Federation
65 C5 **Zhulong He** *R* China
65 D4 **Zhuluke** China
58 F5 **Zhumadian** China
58 G3 **Zhuolu** China
58 G4 **Zhuo Xian** China
65 B4 **Zhuozi** China
65 E6 **Zhuqiao** China
55 C6 **Zhuryn** Kazakhstan
57 G3 **Zhusandala, Step'** Kazakhstan
67 C1 **Zhushan** China
67 D3 **Zhuting** China
58 E5 **Zhuxi** China
65 A7 **Zhuyangzhen** China
67 A4 **Zhuyuan** China
57 J2 **Zhuzagashskiy** Kazakhstan
67 D3 **Zhuzhou** China
57 D4 **Ziadin** Uzbekistan
78 J3 **Zibar** Iraq
65 D6 **Zibo** China
65 A6 **Zichang** China
22 H2 **Zichem** Belgium
31 J9 **Zidani-Most** Slovenia
42 G2 **Zidani Most** Yugoslavia
47 J2 **Zidarovo** Bulgaria
33 R5 **Ziddorf** Germany
54 H7 **Zid'ki** Ukraine
31 K5 **Ziębice** Poland
33 P6 **Ziegendorf** Germany
36 G2 **Ziegenhain** Germany
37 M2 **Ziegenrück** Germany
140 B6 **Ziel,Mt** N Terr Australia
31 J4 **Zielona Góra** Poland
32 K10 **Zierenberg** Germany
25 A5 **Zierikzee** Netherlands
38 N4 **Ziersdorf** Austria
33 Q8 **Ziesar** Germany
31 P1 **Žiežmariai** Lithuania
79 B8 **Zifta** Egypt
68 A2 **Zigaing** Burma
55 C4 **Zigaza** Russian Federation
84 G4 **Zighan** Libya
68 B3 **Zigon** Burma
67 A2 **Zigong** China
58 F5 **Zigui** China
85 A6 **Ziguinchor** Senegal
52 C6 **Zigure** Latvia
65 D6 **Zi He** *R* China
37 P3 **Žihle** Czech Rep
65 C5 **Zijingguan** China
80 C3 **Zikhron Ya'aqov** Israel
78 E1 **Zile** Turkey
48 E1 **Žilina** Slovakia
84 F4 **Zillah** Libya
38 E7 **Zillertal** *R* Austria
38 E7 **Zillertaler Alpen** *mts* Austria
141 K1 **Zillmere** *dist* Brisbane, Qnsld Australia
52 C6 **Zilupe** Latvia
56 F4 **Zima** Russian Federation
125 K7 **Zimapán** Mexico
125 L9 **Zimatlán de Alvarez** Mexico
87 E9 **Zimba** Zambia
87 E9 **Zimbabwe** *rep* Africa
89 G3 **Zimbabwe** *ruins* Zimbabwe
87 F9 **Zimbue** Mozambique
99 N4 **Zimmerman** Minnesota U.S.A.
36 G1 **Zimmersrode** Germany
47 H2 **Zimnitsa** Bulgaria
46 G1 **Zimricea** Romania
87 F10 **Zinave Nat. Park** Mozambique
77 G2 **Zindajan** Afghanistan
85 F6 **Zinder** Niger
30 G1 **Zingst** *pen* Germany
38 L7 **Zinken** *mt* Austria
37 Q5 **Žinkovy** Czech Rep
33 T4 **Zinnowitz** Germany
99 T7 **Zion** Illinois U.S.A.
127 P4 **Zion** Nevis W Indies
103 M4 **Zion Can** Utah U.S.A.
103 M4 **Zion Nat. Park** Utah U.S.A.
94 A7 **Zionsville** Indiana U.S.A.
33 O5 **Zippendorf** Germany
80 D2 **Ẓippori** *R* Israel
80 E3 **Ẓippori** Israel
80 F3 **Ziqlab** *R* Jordan
128 D2 **Ziraquirá** Colombia
38 L7 **Zirbitz Kogel** *mt* Austria
42 G5 **Žirje** *isld* Croatia
101 T9 **Zirkel, Mt** Colorado U.S.A.
37 K5 **Zirndorf** Germany
46 D3 **Žirovnica** Macedonia
67 D2 **Zi Shui** *R* China
125 J8 **Zitácuaro** Mexico
67 B1 **Zitong** China
46 D5 **Zítsa** Greece
31 H5 **Zittau** Germany
41 L3 **Zitterklapfen** *mt* Austria
116 M4 **Zitziana** *R* Alaska U.S.A.
88 C2 **Ziwa Magharibi** *reg* Tanzania
86 G4 **Ziway Häyk'** *L* Ethiopia
67 F3 **Zixi** China
67 D4 **Zixing** China
65 C5 **Ziya He** *R* China
67 A1 **Ziyang** China
67 C3 **Ziyuan** China
67 B4 **Ziyun** China
67 F4 **Ziyundong Shan** *mt* China
41 L4 **Zizers** Switzerland
58 D6 **Zizhong** China
65 A6 **Zizhou** China
47 H1 **Zlataritsa** Bulgaria
31 L7 **Zlaté Moravce** Slovakia
46 D1 **Zlatibor** *mt* Serbia Yugoslavia
48 H4 **Zlatna** Romania
46 G3 **Zlatograd** Bulgaria
55 C3 **Zlatoust** Russian Federation
46 E3 **Zletovo** Macedonia
31 K6 **Zlín** Czech Rep
84 E3 **Zlitan** Libya
31 J2 **Złocieniec** Poland
31 L4 **Złoczew** Poland
30 H5 **Zloniee** Czech Rep
48 G6 **Zlot** Serbia Yugoslavia
31 J4 **Złotoryja** Poland
31 K2 **Złotów** Poland
37 P3 **Žlutice** Czech Rep
54 C4 **Zlynka** Russian Federation
56 B5 **Zmeinogorsk** Russian Federation
53 D10 **Zmeinyy, Ostrov** *isld* Ukraine
31 K4 **Żmigród** Poland
54 H7 **Zmiyev** Ukraine
56 C4 **Znamenityy** Russian Federation
54 D8 **Znamenka** Ukraine
54 D8 **Znamenka Vtoraya** Ukraine
31 K3 **Znin** Poland
31 J7 **Znojmo** Czech Rep
37 P2 **Zöblitz** Germany
45 J3 **Zocca** Italy
25 B4 **Zoetermeer** Netherlands
40 G3 **Zofingen** Switzerland
80 C5 **Ẓofit** Israel
41 L6 **Zogno** Italy
31 K7 **Zohor** Slovakia
77 B4 **Zohreh** Iran
68 A1 **Zokua** Burma
22 J1 **Zolder** Belgium
113 F10 **Zolfo Springs** Florida U.S.A.
36 E3 **Zollhaus** Germany
48 J1 **Zolochev** Ukraine
59 J1 **Zolotaya Goro** Russian Federation
54 N1 **Zolotkovo** Russian Federation
56 C4 **Zolotogorskiy** Russian Federation
54 D7 **Zolotonosha** Ukraine
88 E9 **Zomba** Malawi
Zongga *see* **Gyirong**
66 F4 **Zongjiafangzi** China
86 C5 **Zongo** Zaire
78 C1 **Zonguldak** Turkey
67 F1 **Zongyang** China
22 J2 **Zonhoven** Belgium
33 P10 **Zorbau** Germany
33 Q9 **Zörbig** Germany
80 F5 **Zōr el Hanāhina** Jordan
33 N9 **Zorge** Germany
33 N10 **Zörge** *R* Germany
16 D5 **Zorita** Spain
48 L4 **Zorleni** Romania
36 D6 **Zorn** *R* France
101 R2 **Zortman** Montana U.S.A.
31 L5 **Zory** Poland
85 C7 **Zorzor** Liberia
33 Q10 **Zöschen** Germany
33 S8 **Zossen** Germany
22 F2 **Zottegem** Belgium
86 C1 **Zouar** Chad
85 B4 **Zouerate** Mauritania
16 D10 **Zoumi** Morocco
65 D6 **Zouping** China
58 F4 **Zouquan** China
25 F2 **Zoutkamp** Netherlands
22 J2 **Zoutleeuw** Belgium
65 D7 **Zou Xian** China
67 C5 **Zouxu** China
48 F5 **Zrenjanin** Serbia Yugoslavia
42 G4 **Zrmanja** *R* Croatia
31 J6 **Zruč** Czech Rep
48 G3 **Zsáka** Hungary
33 R10 **Zschepplin** Germany
37 O1 **Zschopau** *R* Germany
37 P2 **Zschopau** Germany
37 O2 **Zschorlau** Germany
127 M10 **Zuata** Venezuela
128 E2 **Zuata** *R* Venezuela
113 E8 **Zuber** Florida U.S.A.
16 E7 **Zubia** Spain
54 F1 **Zubtsov** Russian Federation
80 D3 **Zububa** Israel
37 L6 **Zuchering** Germany
41 O4 **Zucherkütl** *mt* Austria
133 E1 **Zudañez** Bolivia
33 S4 **Zudar** Germany
85 C7 **Zuénoula** Ivory Coast
72 G5 **Ẓufār** *prov* Oman
41 H3 **Zug** *canton* Switzerland
58 F1 **Zugdeli** Russian Federation
41 H3 **Zuger See** *L* Switzerland
41 O3 **Zugspitze** *mt* Germany
25 B5 **Zuid Beijerland** Netherlands
25 G2 **Zuidbroek** Netherlands
25 D4 **Zuidelijk-Flevoland** Netherlands
Zuider Zee *see* **IJsselmeer**
25 C4 **Zuid Holland** *prov* Netherlands
25 F2 **Zuidhorn** Netherlands
25 G2 **Zuidlaarder Meer** Netherlands
25 B5 **Zuidland** Netherlands
25 G2 **Zuidlaren** Netherlands
25 F3 **Zuidwolde** Netherlands
16 D6 **Zújar** *R* Spain
17 F7 **Zújar** Spain
16 D6 **Zújar, Embalse de** *res* Spain
86 G2 **Zula** Eritrea
128 D2 **Zulia** *state* Venezuela
36 B2 **Zülpich** Germany
77 A5 **Ẓulūf, Aẓ** *oil well* Persian Gulf
42 G3 **Žumberačka gora** *mts* Yugoslavia
87 F9 **Zumbo** Mozambique
99 O5 **Zumbro** *R* Minnesota U.S.A.
99 O5 **Zumbro Falls** Minnesota U.S.A.
99 O5 **Zumbro R** Minnesota U.S.A.
125 K8 **Zumpango** Mexico
100 J4 **Zumwalt** Oregon U.S.A.
25 C6 **Zundert** Netherlands
85 F7 **Zungeru** Nigeria
58 G3 **Zunhua** China
106 B6 **Zuni** New Mexico U.S.A.
56 F5 **Zun-Morino** Russian Federation
67 B3 **Zunyi** China
67 B5 **Zuo Jiang** *R* China
65 B6 **Zuoquan** China
65 B4 **Zuoyun** China
67 B5 **Zuozhou** China
86 H3 **Zuqur, Az** *isld* Red Sea
41 J3 **Zürich** Switzerland
41 J3 **Zürich See** *L* Switzerland
42 G5 **Zut** *isld* Croatia
25 F4 **Zutphen** Netherlands
84 F4 **Zuwaylah** Libya
143 A7 **Zuytdorp Cliffs** W Australia Australia
56 G3 **Zvezdnyy** Russian Federation
89 G3 **Zvishavane** Zimbabwe
85 C7 **Zwedru** Liberia
36 C5 **Zweibrücken** Germany
37 N2 **Zwickau** Germany
25 F3 **Zwolle** Netherlands
56 B6 **Zyryanovsk** Kazakhstan

ACKNOWLEDGEMENTS

PICTURE CREDITS

The sources for the photographs and illustrations appearing on pages 34–65 are listed below. Credits read from top to bottom and left to right on each page.

PAGES

34-47 **Physical Earth maps**
by Duncan Mackay, copyright © Times Books, London.

48-49 **Star Charts**
Copyright © Bartholomew, Edinburgh

50-51 **Universe**
Virgo cluster Hale Observatories; *Fornax cluster* copyright © 1979 Royal Observatory, Edinburgh; *Large Magellanic Cloud* copyright © Royal Observatory, Edinburgh; *Pleiades* NOA/Science Photo Library; *Space telescope* Science Institute/ NASA/Science Photo Library; *Lagoon Nebula, Veil Nebula* and *Trifid Nebula* Hale Observations; *Space Telescope* NASA/Science Photo Library.

52-53 **Solar System**
The Sun NASA; *1 Deimos, 2 Ganymede, 3 Callisto* NSSDC/ NASA; *4 Io* U.S. Geological Survey, Flagstaff, Arizona, *5 Titan, 6 Enceladus, 7 Mimas, 8 Miranda, 9Ariel, 10 Titania* Jet Propulsion Laboratory/NASA; *Jupiter* NSSDC/NASA; *Saturn* NASA; *Uranus* Jet Propulsion Laboratory/NASA; *Neptune* NASA/Science Photo Library; *Mercury* NSSDC/NASA; *Mars (Mariner 9 images), Mars (Viking orbiter photo), Venus* NASA/Science Photo Library; *Moon* NASA/Science Photo Library.

54-55 **Space flight**
Space Telescope NASA/Science Photo Library; *launch vehicle* Roger Ressmeyer, Starlight/Science Photo Library; *Mir spacestation* Novosti Press Agency/Science Photo Library; *Meteosat image* ESA/PLI/Science Photo Library; *Java* NASA; *Milton Keynes, Faro, Craters of the Moon* Dr D.A. Rothery, Dept. of Earth Sciences, The Open University; *Galileo* NASA/Science Photo.

56-57 **Earth Structure**
Magnetosphere Encyclopaedia Universalis.

58-59 **Dynamic Earth**
Rock and hydrological cycles Encyclopaedia Universalis.

60-61 **Climate**
Waterspout J.E. Golden/Science Photo Library.

62-63 **Vegetation and Minerals**
Manganese nodules Robert Hessler/Seaphot Planet Earth Pictures.

64-65 **Energy**
Data from BP Statistical review of world energy June 1993.

The publishers would like to extend their grateful thanks to the following

Academy of Sciences and the National Atlas Committe, Moscow, Russian Federation

American Geographical Society, New York, U.S.A.

Professor D. H. K. Amiran, The Hebrew University, Jerusalem, Israel

Antarctic Place-Names Committee, London and G. Hattersley-Smith

Automobile Association of South Africa, Johannesburg, Republic of South Africa

Mr John C. Bartholomew, Edinburgh

The British Petroleum Company Ltd., London

Professor H. A. Brück, lately Astronomer Royal for Scotland, Edinburgh

Bureau of Coast and Geodetic Survey, Manila, Republic of the Philippines

Mrs J. E. Candy, Geographical Research Associates, Maidenhead

Centro de Geografia do Ultramar, Lisbon, Portugal

Ceskoslovenské Akademie Ved, Prague, Czech Republic

Columbia University Press, New York, U.S.A.

Commission de toponymie du Québec, Québec, Canada

Defense Mapping Agency, Aerospace Center, St Louis, Missouri, U.S.A.

Defense Mapping Agency Hydrographic Topographic Center, Washington, D.C., U.S.A.

Department of Lands and Survey, Wellington, New Zealand

Department of National Development, Director of National Mapping, Canberra, Australia

Mr John C. Dewdney, University of Durham

Embassy of the Republic of Indonesia, London

Esselte Map Service, Stockholm, Sweden

Dr M. W. Feast, Director, South African Astronomical Observatory, Cape Town, Republic of South Africa

Professor C. A. Fisher, School of Oriental & African Studies, University of London

Food & Agriculture Organisation of the United Nations, Rome, Italy

Foreign and Commonwealth Office, London

French Railways, London

Freytag-Berndt und Artaria, Vienna, Austria

Mr P.J.M. Geelan, London

General Directorate of Highways, Ankara, Turkey

General Drafting Company Inc., Convent Station, New Jersey, U.S.A.

Global Seismology Unit, Institute of Geological Sciences, Edinburgh

Office of the Geographer, Department of State, Washington, D.C., U.S.A.

Dr R. Habel, VEB Hermann Haack, Geographisch-Kartographische Anstalt, Gotha, Germany

Mr E. Hausman, Carta, The Israel Map and Publishing Company Ltd., Jerusalem, Israel

Mr Michael Hendrie, Astronomy Correspondent, *The Times*, London

H. M. Stationery Office, London

The High Commission of India, London

Office of the High Commission for Pakistan, London

Hunting Surveys Limited, Borehamwood, Hertfordshire

Hydrographic Office, Ministry of Defence, Taunton

Institute of Geological Sciences, Herstmonceux, Sussex

Institut Géographique Militaire, Brussels, Belgium

Institut Géographique National, Paris, France

Instituto Brasileiro de Geografia, Rio de Janeiro, Brazil

Instituto Geografico e Cadastral, Lisbon, Portugal

Instituto Geografico Militar, Lima, Peru

Instituto Geografico y Cadastral, Madrid, Spain

International Atomic Energy Agency, Vienna, Austria

International Hydrographic Bureau, Monaco

International Road Federation, London

Kongelig Dansk Geodætisk Institut, Copenhagen, Denmark

Mr P. Laffitte, École des Mines, Paris, France

Dr R. I. Lawless, Centre for Middle Eastern & Islamic Studies, University of Durham

Mr H.A.G. Lewis OBE Geographical Consultant, *The Times*, London

Dr S. Lippard, Department of Earth Sciences, The Open University, Milton Keynes

Professor P. McL. D. Duff, University of Strathclyde

Dr D. N. McMaster, University of Edinburgh

Professor R. E. H. Mellor, University of Aberdeen

Dr W. H. Menard, Jr., Scripps Institution of Oceanography, La Jolla, California, U.S.A.

The Meteorological Office, Bracknell, Berkshire

National Aeronautical and Space Administration (NASA), Washington, D.C., U.S.A.

National Geographic Society, Washington, D.C., U.S.A.

National Library of Scotland, Edinburgh

Nigerian Land and Survey Department, Lagos, Nigeria

Norges Geografiske Oppmåling, Oslo, Norway

Nuclear Engineering International, London

Ordnance Survey, Director General, Southampton

Permanent Committee of Geographical Names, London: Mr P. Woodman and Miss E. Shipley

Petroleum Information Bureau, London

Petroleum Press Service, London

Petroleum Publishing Co., Tulsa, Oklahoma, U.S.A.

Rand McNally & Co., Chicago, U.S.A.

Dr D. A. Rothery, Department of Earth Sciences, The Open University, Milton Keynes

Mr P. Rouveyrol, Bureau de Recherches Géologiques et Minières, Paris, France

Royal Geographical Society, London

Royal Observatory, Schmidt Unit, Edinburgh

Royal Scottish Geographical Society, Edinburgh

Mr John Sallnow, School of Environmental Sciences, Plymouth

Scientifc American, New York, U.S.A.

Scottish Development Department, Edinburgh

Soviet Geography: Theodore Shabad, Editor

State of Israel Department of Surveys, Tel Aviv, Israel

The Statesman's Year Book, London: Editors Dr John Paxton und Dr. Brian Hunter

Dr H. J. Störig, Lexikon-Redaktion, Munich, Germany

Survey Department, Singapore

Survey, Lands and Mines Department, Entebbe, Uganda

Survey of India, Dehra Dun, Uttar Pradesh, India

Survey of Kenya, Nairobi, Kenya

Surveyor General, Harare, Zimbabwe

Surveyor General, Ministry of Lands and Natural Resources, Lusaka, Zambia

Surveys and Mapping Branch, Department of Energy, Mines and Resources, Ottawa, Canada

Surveys & Mapping Division, Dar-es-Salaam, Tanzania

Touring Club Italiano und Dr S. Toniolo, Mailand, Italy

The Trigonometrical Survey Office, Pretoria, Republic of South Africa

The United States Board on Geographic Names, Washington, D.C., U.S.A.

The United States Geological Survey, Washington, D.C., U.S.A.

Mr P. E. Victor, Expéditions Polaires Françaises, Paris

Dr D. Whitehouse, Mullard Space Science Laboratory, Dorking, Surrey

North America
Key to map plates